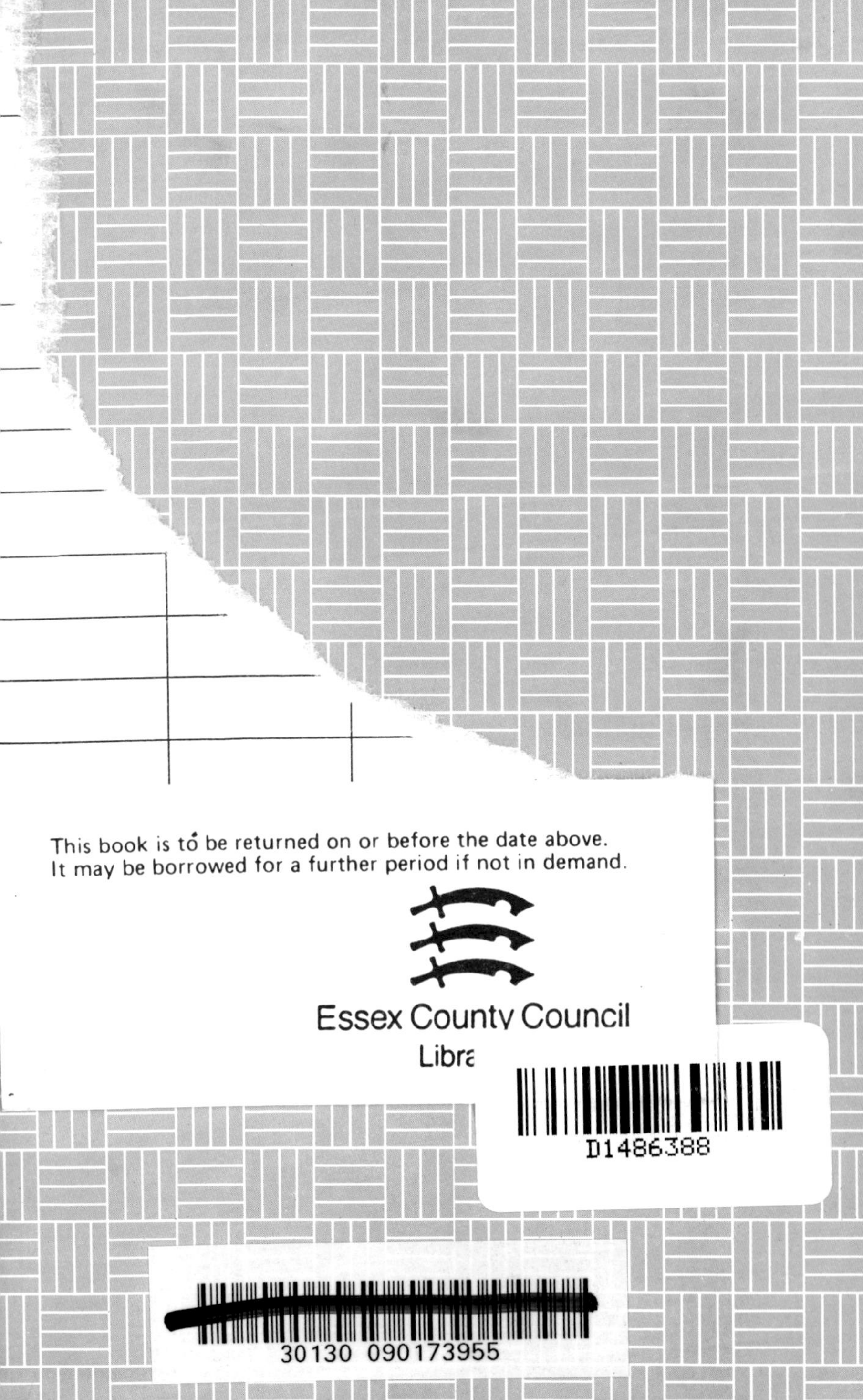

WALKER'S

RHYMING DICTIONARY

THE

RHYMING DICTIONARY

OF

THE ENGLISH LANGUAGE

IN WHICH THE WHOLE LANGUAGE IS ARRANGED ACCORDING TO ITS TERMINATIONS

WITH AN INDEX OF ALLOWABLE RHYMES

By J. WALKER

Author of "The Critical Pronouncing Dictionary"

Revised and Enlarged

By LAWRENCE H. DAWSON

Supplement compiled by
MICHAEL FREEMAN

London and New York

Reprinted in 1990 and 1991
by Routledge
11 New Fetter Lane, London EC4P 4EE

Simultaneously published in the USA and Canada
by Routledge
a division of Routledge, Chapman and Hall, Inc.
29 West 35th Street, New York, NY 10001

This edition with Supplement first published in 1983

Printed in Great Britain by
Redwood Press Limited, Melksham, Wiltshire

British Library Cataloguing in Publication Data

Walker, J.

The rhyming dictionary of the English language,
Rev. and enlarged ed.
1. English language – Rhyme – Dictionaries
I. Title II. Dawson, Lawrence H.
423,.1 PE1519

ISBN 0–415–05924–0

PREFACE

WALKER'S *Rhyming Dictionary*, though it never was in the true sense of the term a dictionary of rhymes, has been for over a hundred and fifty years a standard work of reference and has been a friend in need to generations of poets and rhymesters from Byron downwards. When John Walker, the ex-schoolmaster and the author of *The Critical Pronouncing Dictionary*, first published it in 1775 he half apologized for its title; he looked upon the use to which the rhymer might put it as something quite "insignificant" and as the "least advantage" of the Dictionary, and claimed that his object in compiling it was to "facilitate the orthography and pronunciation of the English language." What effect the *Rhyming Dictionary* has had towards the furtherance of this praiseworthy aim we have small means of ascertaining; but we have little hesitation in saying that its lasting popularity has been due more to the assistance that it affords the poet than to the help and suggestions it gives to the schoolmaster or orthoepist. It may be true, as Watts-Dunton said*, that "the moment a born-rhymer has chosen a word for the end of a line all the feasible rhymes in the language leap into his brain like sparks from a rocket"; but born-rhymers are few and far between and, as will be seen, it is not only to the rhymer that this Dictionary is of service.

In the present entirely new edition it has not been thought advisable to depart from the arrangement that has met with so much approval in the past, and consequently the words are grouped, not phonetically, but strictly alphabetically in accordance with the *reversed spelling* of the word; i.e. it is not the words *beginning* with A, B, C, etc., that will be found under those letters but those *ending* with them. Just as the ordinary dictionary starts with words commencing with *aa* and goes on with those in *aba-*, *abb-*, *abd-*, etc., so here the first entries are those ending in *-aa*, followed by those in *-ba*, *-ca*, *-da*, and so on, to the end of the vocabulary, where we find *buzz*, *fuzz*, and *muzz*. Therefore, in looking for a word the last letter is to be sought first, the last but one next, and so on; and the directing letters at the head of each page are to be looked for in the same way, that is from right to left. The word *Alphabet*, for instance, is wanted: keep the last letter in mind, and turn to that part of the Dictionary where the words ending in *t* are classed, which is, of course, near the end; *at* is the first word in this class, but *e* is the letter next wanted so the eye is run rapidly to the end of the *at's* till it comes to *bet*, *abet*, and so to *alphabet*.

The arrangement is perfectly simple, and after two or three trials the reader will be able to find his way about this "reverse-order" dictionary as rapidly

* *Poetry and the Renascence of Wonder* (1916), ch. ii.

and conveniently as he can over those constructed on the usual principles; but from the point of view of the consulter who is looking for *all* the rhymes to a given word it has certain disadvantages; for we find in juxtaposition such words as *baize* and *judaize*, *maritime* and *centime*—which do not rhyme at all—while many perfect rhymes, such as *yea* and *survey*, *doe* and *blow*, are separated by hundreds of pages. To remove any inconvenience that this might occasion an Index of monosyllabic rhymes has been prepared and will be found in the Appendix; and poet and rhymer are advised that they will save themselves a considerable amount of trouble and, perhaps, add to their poetic vocabulary if they spend an hour or two in making themselves thoroughly acquainted with the contents of this section. To many it may come as a surprise that the "ō" sound, for instance, can be represented terminally by no fewer than twenty-three different combinations of letters as well as by the single *o* of *go*, and that the terminal "s" sound may take any one of five forms.

Though we are obliged to abandon the claim of our eighteenth-century progenitor that "the principal object of this Dictionary is to throw light on the structure, orthography, and pronunciation of our language" it has interest and use for others than contributors to the "Poets' Corners" or the writer of humorous verse. To the phonetician and to the enthusiast for some new system of Simplified Spelling, the Index as well as the body of the work will give many ideas and will possibly provide many "horrid examples"; those who rack their brains in solving the Acrostics in our Sunday papers will, perchance, be saved many a rack and many a failure by our reverse alphabetical arrangement; and to others the grouping together of all the words in *-aster*, *-derm*, *-esse*, *-graphy*, *-ism*, *-itis*, *-latry*, *-mancy*, *-ology*, *-pathy*, and countless other suffixes and terminations will be a distinct advantage.

The vocabulary of the present edition is considerably larger than that of the last, containing as it does over 20,000 more words than its 34,000; but its increased usefulness is not to be estimated by the mere "counting of heads." A very large number of words that have for long ceased in any real sense to form part of the language and that appeared in earlier editions have been quietly dropped; spellings have been modernized and have, in nearly every case, been given in accordance with the Oxford English Dictionary; and the meanings of the words have been amplified and rewritten throughout. No Dictionary that has yet been published has included every word in the language, and we, naturally, would make no such absurd pretension; but we think we can claim that no word has been omitted that could be of any use to the poet, while a very large number that he would never use—except for humorous purposes—have been included. For a professedly *Rhyming* Dictionary our catholicity may seem surprising; but in its compilation we have borne in mind the requirements of others than songsters and, also, we may say in extenuation, that once a process of exclusion is allowed to start it is next to impossible to keep it within such bounds as will satisfy every class of consulter. We have, however, been able to save space by directing the reader to the main-word from adverbs in *-ly*, nouns in *ness*, adjectives in *-able*, and so forth, instead of giving the meanings in the places where these words occur, and also by abbreviating, or even omitting (except for a cross-reference), certain classes of words having a suffix.

There are many large groups of scientific and semi-scientific terms, each of which have corresponding adjectives, adverbs, and so on, formed by substitution or addition of suffixes. Words in *-ology*, for instance, form the basis of many others; we have from *Geology*, to take one example, geolo*gist*, geolo*gize*, geolo-*gizer*, geolo*gizing*, geolo*gic*, geolo*gical*, geolo*gically*, and even geolo*gian*. In some of such cases we have given all the derivatives, but in others we have stayed our hand and have directed the reader to the columns containing the main-words both for the meaning of the derivatives and for further rhymes. Similarly in the case of the negative and certain other prefixes; readers can be expected to remember when *un-*, *dis-*, *non-*, *mis-*, *post-*, *anti-*, *vice-*, *re-*, and so on, may be prefixed to words; and so, though the more important will be found here in their proper places, we have prevented an already large book from assuming unwieldy proportions by excluding them as a class.

It was not part of Walker's original scheme to include Proper Nouns, and neither is it ours; a few, however, are given in the main body of the Dictionary, and in the Index we have found room for a number the pronunciation of which are not self-evident.

L. H. D.

PREFACE TO THE SUPPLEMENT

In preparing the Supplement to *Walker's Rhyming Dictionary* I have attempted to use the discrimination of my predecessors in the selection of words. Nevertheless, from the very start I became aware of a perhaps obvious fact – that the world and its language have subtly increased. There is, in short, a vast choice of material for inclusion, and although I have tried to select those words that will be most useful in a general sense I am also aware that such a choice must needs be subjective. For example, I have included a reasonable amount of slang, knowing that that which we so term today is often tomorrow's accepted speech. Even so, decency forbids the inclusion of all the taboo words despite the frequency and casualness of their use in modern times. Also it may be that I have been lured into the preference of those words which have unusual endings, although not I trust to the exclusion of anything more important.

It will be observed that I have adhered as nearly as possible to the original format – definitions are not intended to be complete, but to provide a guide – and the Supplement is intended for use with the existing body of words. I would like to think that my predecessors would have approved my choice.

Michael B. Freeman

ABBREVIATIONS

a.	adjective
adv.	adverb
anc.	anciently
aux.	auxiliary
avoir.	avoirdupois
B.A.	Bachelor of Arts
c	about
C.	Centigrade, Central
C.G.S.	Centimetre-gram second
ch.	chapter
colloq.	colloquially
cond.	conditional
conj.	conjunction
contr.	contraction
contr. phr.	contracted phrase
cp.	compare
d.	died, pence
E.	East
esp.	especially
feud.	feudal
ft.	feet
gal., galls.	gallons
geol.	geology
gr.	gram.
grs.	grains
i.	intransitive
in., ins.	inches
ind.	indicative
imp., imper., imperat.	imperative
impers.	impersonal
int.	interjection
interrog.	interrogative
lb., lbs.	pound, pounds
mod.	modern
M.S.	Manuscript
M.S.S.	Manuscripts
mus.	musical
N.	North
neg.	negative
neut.	neuter
Nov.	November
obj.	objective
obs.	obsolete
p., part(s)	participle(s)
past	past tense
pers.	person, personal
pert.	pertaining
pl.	plural
p.m.	post-meridian
poss.	possessive
pref.	prefix
prep.	preposition
pres.	present
pret(s).	preterite(s)
pron.	pronoun
R.C., Rom. Cath.	Roman Catholic
refl.	reflexive
rel.	relative
s.	shillings, substantive
S.	South
S.I.	Système Internationale d'Unités
sing.	singular
sq.	square
suff.	suffix
temp.	time of
t., trans.	transitive
usu.	usually
v.	verb
W.	West

RHYMING DICTIONARY

A Indefinite article.
Baa int. Bleat of a sheep.
Caa-ba s. Sacred building at Mecca.
Inda'ba s. A conference of Zulu chiefs.
Dra'ba s. A genus of herbs including the whitlow-grasses.
Ab'ba s. Father, episcopal title.
Amœ'ba s. A microscopic animalcule.
Pe'ba s. A small S. American armadillo.
Zare'ba s. A pallisaded enclosure: a stockade.
Copai'ba s. An aromatic, resinous, pungent juice used in medicine.
Gam'ba s. A 'cello-like organ stop.
Trom'ba s. A trumpet.
Calum'ba s. A medicinal root.
Da'goba s. A Buddhist shrine.
Bona-ro'ba s. A showy wanton.
Yer'ba s. Maté; Paraguay tea.
Suc'cuba s. A female succubus.
Ju'ba s. A mane; mane-like growth on grasses, etc.
Tu'ba s. A brass wind-instrument like a saxhorn.
Saxtu'ba s. A large brass musical instrument.
Cataw'ba s. An American grape-vine; wine made from this.
Cloa'ca s. A sewer; the excrementory cavity of birds and lower animals.
Pac'a s. A large S. American rodent.
Alpac'a s. A Peruvian sheep; cloth made of its hair.
Ra'ca a. Beggarly; dissolute.
Malac'ca s. A cane walking-stick.
Polac'ca s. A three-masted Mediterranean vessel.
Yac'ca s. An Indian evergreen of the yew family; its timber.
Mec'ca s. The holy city of the Moslems; object of one's aims.
Feluc'ca s. A small vessel used in the Mediterranean.
Yuc'ca s. A Central and S. American plant of the lily family.
The'ca s. A sheath, spore-case.
Bibliothe'ca s. A library.
Glyptothe'ca s. A building for a collection of sculptures.
Ar'eca s. The betel-nut tree.
Chi'ca s. A red colouring-matter; an old Spanish dance.
Angel'ica s. Genus of umbelliferous plants.
Sil'ica s. A hard crystalline oxide of silicon.
Majol'ica s. Richly coloured or enamelled pottery.
Pli'ca s. A disease in which the hair becomes matted.
Rep'lica s. A copy, facsimile, duplicate.
Mi'ca s. A mineral easily split into shining, elastic plates.
Vom'ica s. An encysted mass of pus.
Nux vom'ica s. The seed of an E. Indian tree yielding the poison strychnine.
Harmon'ica s. A musical instrument played by striking or rubbing rods, plates, glasses, etc.
Japon'ica s. A common garden shrub; the camellia.
Veron'ica s. Genus of plants, including the figworts and speedwells; the cloth miraculously imprinted with Christ's visage.
Santon'ica s. Buds of a species of wormwood, used medicinally.
Ar'nica s. A plant yielding a drug used in medicine.
Pi'ca s. A size of type; morbid craving for unnatural foods; the genus of birds containing the magpie.
Spi'ca s. A spike (of a flower, etc.); a kind of spiral bandage.
Eri'ca s. A genus of shrubs; the heaths.
Lori'ca s. The carapace of a crustacean.
Ves'ica s. A bladder, cyst.
Sciat'ica s. Neuralgia of the hip or of the sciatic nerve.
Hepat'ica s. A ranunculaceous plant with white or purple flowers.
In'ca s. Title of the ancient kings of Peru.
Co'ca s. A Peruvian plant the leaves of which are chewed as a narcotic.
Tapio'ca s. A farinaceous food prepared from cassava.
Sambu'ca s. An ancient stringed musical instrument.
Noctilu'ca s. A genus of phosphorescent marine protozoans.
Verr'uca s. A wart; wart-like excrescence.
Cica'da s. A genus of stridulating insects.
Dad'a s. (*Childish*) Father.
Pana'da s. Bread boiled in water and sweetened.
Posa'da s. An inn in Spain.
Lamb'da s. The Greek letter Λ; a moth marked thus.
Ed'da s. One of two old Icelandic literary collections.
Androm'eda s. A Greek mythological heroine; a northern constellation.
Rese'da s. A pale greyish-green colour.
Ve'da (vā'-) s. The sacred writings of the Hindus.
Rig-Ve'da (-vā'da) s. The oldest of the four portions of the Vedic hymns.
Annel'ida s. The class of animals comprising the segmented worms, leeches etc.
Olla podri'da s. A stew of finely chopped meat and vegetables; an incongruous mixture.
Coloquin'tida s. Colocynth.
Bretwal'da s. A supreme king among the Anglo-Saxons.
Propagan'da s. Organized effort to make proselytes; a committee of cardinals.
Pan'da s. A racoon-like carnivorous mammal of the Himalayas.
Veran'da s. A light open portico or outer gallery.
Memoran'da s. Notes to serve as a reminder.
Observan'da s. Things to be observed.
Puden'da s. The genitals.
Agen'da s. Business to be transacted.
Corrigen'da s. Errors needing correction.
Hacien'da s. A S. American stock-raising estate
Delen'da s. Things to be deleted.

Golcon'da s. Inexhaustible wealth.
Osmun'da s. The flowering fern, or king fern.
Rotun'da s. A circular building.
Co'da s. Concluding passage of a musical composition.
Pago'da s. A Chinese or E. Indian temple; an obsolete Hindu coin.
Decap'oda s. A section of cephalopods and an order of crustaceans having ten tentacles or limbs.
Amphip'oda s. (*Amphipod*).
Pterop'oda s. Group of gastropod molluscs with membranous wing-like paddles.
Arthrop'oda s. Animals with jointed feet.
Rhizop'oda s. The lowest division of the protozoa.
So'da s. Carbonate or bi-carbonate of sodium, an alkali used in washing, etc.; water aerated with carbonic acid.
Gon'da s. A kind of Dutch cheese.
Spirae'a s. A genus of rosaceous plants.
Tra'bea s. The striped toga of ancient Roman consuls.
Panace'a s. A remedy for all diseases.
Ceta'cea s. An order of marine mammals.
Testa'cea s. An order of shell-bearing protozoa.
Crusta'cea s. Articulated animals having a shelly crust; crabs, shrimps, etc.
Ide'a s. An image conceived by the mind; a notion, abstract principle.
Crinoi'dea s. An order of echinoderms.
Hydran'gea s. A genus of flowering garden shrubs.
Trache'a s. The windpipe.
Bohea' s. An inferior kind of black tea.
Rhe'a s. A genus of S. American birds of the ostrich family; the ramie plant or its fibre.
She'a s. A tropical African tree.
Ke'a s. A mountain parrot of New Zealand that attacks sheep.
Lea s. A meadow; open country; fallow land.
Ga'lea s. A helmet-shaped organ or part.
Aza'lea s. A genus of shrubs with showy flowers.
Flea s. A small, agile, blood-sucking insect.
Coch'lea s. A spiral cavity in the ear.
Troch'lea s. A pulley-like cartilage.
Plea s. An excuse, apology, earnest entreaty; a lawsuit; defendant's answer.
Miscella'nea s. A collection of miscellaneous articles, especially literary.
Collecta'nea s. Collected excerpts from various authors; a commonplace book.
Casta'nea s. A genus of trees, including the chestnut.
Tin'ea s. A clothes-moth; ringworm.
Guin'ea s. An obsolete Eng. gold coin = 21s.
Corne'a s. The horny transparent membrane in front of the eyeball.
Diarrhœ'a s. A great looseness of the bowels.
Leucorrhœ'a s. A mucous discharge in females.
Sialorrhœ'a s. Excessive discharge of saliva.
Gonorrhœ'a s. An inflammatory disease affecting the urethra.
Spermatorrhœ'a s. Involuntary discharge of semen.
Hepatorrhœ'a s. A morbid flow of bile.
Galactorrhœ'a s. An excessive secretion of milk.
Otorrhœ'a s. Discharge from the ear.
Pyorrhœ'a s. A discharge of pus.
Apnœ'a s. Cessation of respiration.
Dyspnœ'a s. Difficulty of breathing.
Pea s. A leguminous flowering plant; one of its edible seeds.
Oc'rea s. The tubular sheath round the base of a petiole.
Chore'a s. St. Vitus's dance.
Ure'a s. A crystalline compound found in urine.
Sea s. The ocean; a portion of it; a flood.
O'versea a. Foreign; from beyond the sea.
Nau'sea s. Disposition to vomit; sickness.
Tea s. The dried leaves of a Far-Eastern shrub; decoction prepared from this; the plant; a light afternoon repast.
Galate'a s. A fine striped cotton fabric.
Fo'vea s. A small depression in the body.
Uve'a s. The posterior coloured layer of the iris.
Yea adv. Yes; truly. s. An affirmative; one voting thus.
Ze'a s. A genus of cereal grasses; maize.
Fa s. The fourth note in the tonic sol-fa notation.
Tere'fa a. Unclean (applied to those foods not allowed to Jews).
Sol-fa' v.i. To sing the notes of the gamut.
Tonic sol-fa' s. A system of scale arrangement used in teaching singing
So'fa s. A long padded seat with arms and back.
Tu'fa s. A soft calcareous rock.
Stu'fa s. Jet of steam from earth-fissure.
Ru'tabaga s. A variety of turnip.
Mal'aga s. A Spanish white wine.
Sa'ga s. An heroic romance of early Scandinavia.
Bode'ga s. A wine-shop.
Tele'ga (-lā'-) s. A four-wheeled Russian cart.
O'mega s. The last letter of the Greek alphabet; the end.
Quag'ga s. An equine animal of S. Africa.
Sai'ga (sā'-, sī-) s. An antelope of Asiatic Russia.
Quad'riga s. A two-wheeled chariot drawn by four horses abreast.
Stri'ga s. A short, stiff bristle, etc.; a fluting on a column.
Al'ga s. A seaweed.
Vedang'a (vā-) s. A supplement to the Veda.
Batang'a s. The outrigger on native boats in the Philippines.
Serin'ga s. A Brazilian rubber-tree.
Churing'a s. A totemistic amulet.
Syring'a s. A bushy, white-flowered shrub.
Don'ga s. A steep-sided watercourse in S. Africa.
Tong'a s. A light two-wheeled Indian cart.
To'ga s. The loose robe of the anc. Romans.
Yo'ga s. A Hindu system of asceticism.
Belu'ga s. The great sturgeon; the white whale.
Ru'ga s. A wrinkle, especially in membrane.
Ha int. Exclamation of surprise, etc.
Aha' int.
Ha'-ha s. A sunk hedge or fence.
Visca'cha s. A large S. Amer. burrowing rodent.
Chi'cha s. A fermented drink made from maize in the W. Indies.
Con'cha s. The largest concavity of the external ear; dome of an apse.
Mo'cha s. A high grade of coffee; a variety of chalcedony; an Abyssinian weight (1 gr. Troy).
Lor'cha s. A light Chinese coasting vessel.
Cachu'cha s. A Spanish dance.
Bud'dha s. Title of Gautama, the founder of Buddhism.
Gurk'ha s. One of a short, dark race of Nepal.
Ipecacuan'ha s. The dried root of a Brazilian plant used in medicine.
Pseudepig'rapha s. Spurious or uncanonical writings.
Synale'pha s. Suppression of a vowel-ending when next word begins with a vowel.

Al'pha s. First letter of the Greek alphabet.
Nym'pha s. A pupa, chrysalis.
Ty'pha s. A genus of marsh plants.
Pa'sha s. A Turkish and Egyptian title of rank.
Gei'sha s. A Japanese dancing-girl.
Jinrick'sha s. A light two-wheeled carriage drawn by a man.
Marana'tha s. A word used in anathematizing.
Naph'tha s. A highly inflammable hydrocarbon.
Goth'a s. Name given to a powerful German bomb-carrying aeroplane.
Gol'gotha s. "The place of skulls," a shambles.
Quo'tha int. Forsooth ! indeed !
Ber'tha s. Facetious name of a German long-range gun.
-ia suff. Forming abstract nouns, names of countries, diseases, botanical genera, etc.
Del'la Rob'bia a. Denoting a kind of terra-cotta ware
Amphib'ia s. Animals which can live either on land or in water.
Tib'ia s. The shinbone ; an ancient kind of flute.
-phobia suff. Fear, hatred, morbid dislike.
Toxipho'bia s. Unreasonable dread of being poisoned.
Bibliopho'bia s. Dread or hatred of books.
Anglopho'bia s. Unreasonable dislike of England.
Gallopho'bia s. Hatred or fear of the French and all things French.
Germano-pho'bia s. Unreasoning hatred or fear of Germany and the Germans.
Hydropho'bia s. Morbid dread of water, a symptom of rabies ; rabies.
Negropho'bia s. Hatred or dislike of the negroes.
Claustropho'bia s. Morbid dread of being confined in a narrow space.
Nosopho'bia s. Morbid dread of disease.
Sitopho'bia s. Refusal to take nourishment ; aversion to food.
Photopho'bia s. Morbid shrinking from light.
Euphor'bia s. The spurges, a genus of plants.
Fa'cia s. Tablet on a shop-front for name,etc.
Osteomala'cia s. Softening of the bones.
Brec'cia s. A conglomerate rock.
Estan'cia s. A S. American cattle ranch.
Fas'cia s. A belt, fillet, sash ; something shaped like this ; a facia.
Cyclopæ'dia, encyclopæ'dia s. A dictionary of arts and sciences.
Me'dia s. The median membrane of an artery, etc. ; a voiced mute ; means, agency.
Thanatophid'ia s. The venomous serpents.
Gonid'ia s. (*Gonidium*).
Epopœia s. Epopee.
Prosopopœ'ia s. Rhetorical figure representing things or abstractions as persons ; personification.
Onomatopœ'ia s. Use of a word whose sound resembles the thing signified.
Pharmacopei'a (-pē'a) s. A collection of formulæ for the preparation of medicines, drugs collectively as used in medicine.
Peripetei'a s. A reversal of circumstances, sudden change of fortune.
Mafi'a s. Active hostility to law (esp. in Sicily) ; persons taking part in this.
Taf'ia s. A kind of rum.
Ratafi'a (-fē'a) s. An almond flavouring ; a liqueur with this.
Raff'ia s. A species of palm from Madagascar ; fibre from this.
Dyspha'gia s. Difficulty in swallowing.
Polypha'gia s. Ability to eat, or morbid craving for all kinds of foods.
Paraple'gia s. Paralysis of both lower limbs.
Hemiple'gia s. Paralysis of one side of the body.
Pample'gia s. General paralysis.
Monopleg'ia s. Paralysis of a single part.
Log'gia s. An open corridor, arcade, or balcony.
Æsophagal'gia s. Pain or neuralgia in the gullet.
Cardial'gia s. An affection of the heart; heartburn.
Rachial'gia s. Pain in the spine.
Ischial'gia s. Pain in the hip ; sciatica.
Cephalal'gia s. Headache.
Dermal'gia s. Neuralgia of the skin.
Splenal'gia s. Pain in the spleen.
Rhinal'gia s. Nasal neuralgia.
Gonal'gia s. Pain in the knee.
Sternal'gia s. Pain in the chest.
Synal'gia s. Sympathetic pain.
Hypal'gia s. Freedom from pain.
Nephral'gia s. Pain in the kidneys.
Gastral'gia s. Neuralgia in the stomach.
Neural'gia s. Acute pain following a nerve, especially of the head or face.
Glossal'gia s. Pain in the tongue.
Dermatal'gia s. Neuralgia of the skin.
Odontal'gia s. Toothache.
Otal'gia s. Ear-ache.
Notal'gia s. Pain in the back.
Nostal'gia s. Home-sickness.
Coxal'gia s. Pain in the hip.
Myal'gia s. Cramp.
Lo'gia s. Traditional sayings, especially of Christ.
Steatopyg'ia s. Large accumulation of fat about the buttocks.
Bronch'ia s. The main divisions of the windpipe.
Didel'phia s. The family of marsupials including the opossums.
Mor'phia s. The narcotic principle of opium.
Lith'ia s. Oxide of lithium.
Stichomyth'ia (stik-) s. Dialogue in alternate metrical lines.
Lataki'a s. A strong kind of tobacco.
Luperca'lia s. An ancient Roman festival.
Rega'lia s. The ensigns of royalty ; emblems of nobility, etc. ; decorations, insignia.
Thali'a s. The muse of comedy and bucolic poetry.
Mamma'lia s. The class of animals comprising the mammals.
Bacchana'lia s. Drunken orgies ; originally a festival in honour of Bacchus.
Margina'lia s. Notes given in the margin of a book.
Termina'lia s. An ancient Roman festival.
Paraphernа'lia s. Appendages, trappings.
Saturna'lia s. An ancient Roman festival ; a period or occasion of general debauchery.
Genera'lia s. General principles.
Penetra'lia s. Inner parts of a building ; hidden things.
Digita'lia s. Digitalin.
Lobe'lia s. A genus of campanulaceous plants.
Aphe'lia s. Points in an orbit most distant from the sun.
Anthe'lia s. Mock suns.
Sca'glia (ska'lia) s. An Italian limestone.
Gang'lia s. (*Ganglion*).
Neurog'lia s. The tissue supporting the nerve-cells and nerve-fibres, especially in the brain and spinal cord.
Dah'lia s. A genus of composite plants from Mexico.
Memorabil'ia s. Things worth remembering.
Notabil'ia s. Notable things.
Cil'ia s. The eyelashes ; hairs resembling this on plants, etc.
Sedil'ia s. Series of stone canopied seats in a chancel.

Hæmophil'ia s. Constitutional tendency to hæmorrhage.
Lacertil'ia s. The reptilian order containing the lizards, iguanas, etc.
Camel'lia s. An evergreen shrub.
Melancho'lia s. Morbid or insane melancholy; great depression.
Scho'lia s. Marginal notes by early writers on classic authors.
Magno'lia s. A genus of N. American flowering shrubs.
Cryptoga'mia s. An order of plants not bearing true flowers, as ferns, lichens, seaweeds, etc.
La'mia s. A serpentine spirit of fable; a sorceress.
Adyna'mia s. Nervous debility.
Septicæ'mia s. Blood-poisoning through introduction of septic matter.
Glucohæ'mia s. Glucosuria.
Leucocythæ'mia s. A form of anæmia.
Cholæm'ia s. Morbid accumulation of bile.
Anæ'mia s. Want of, or poorness of, blood.
Spanæ'mia s. Poverty of blood.
Hydræ'mia s. An abnormally watery state of the blood.
Sapræ'mia s. Septic poisoning.
Uræ'mia s. A certain toxic condition of the blood.
Toxæ'mia s. Blood-poisoning.
Pyæ'mia s. Blood-poisoning.
Buli'mia s. Morbid craving for food.
Sim'ia s. The genus of anthropoid apes containing the orang-outangs.
Ophthal'mia s. Inflammation of the membranes of the eye.
Lagophthal'mia s. Morbid condition in which the eyes stand wide open, even in sleep.
Xerophthal'mia s. A red soreness of the eyes without discharge.
Kal'mia s. A N. American evergreen shrub.
Anos'mia s. Lack of the sense of smell.
Ocea'nia s. The island region of the S. Pacific.
Rapha'nia s. A form of ergotism.
Ma'nia s. Insanity; violent excitement or frenzy; a craze.
-ma'nia suff. Denoting special kinds of derangement, infatuation, etc.
Narcoma'nia s. Overpowering craving for narcotics
Theoma'nia s. Delusion that one is God.
Logoma'nia s. Form of insanity characterized by uncontrollable loquacity.
Potichoma'nia s. Craze for decorating the inside of transparent vessels.
Nymphoma'nia s. Erotic insanity in women.
Methoma'nia s. Dipsomania
Biblioma'nia s. A rage for accumulating rare books
Megaloma'nia s. Insanity characterized by self-exaltation; a craze for exaggeration, etc.
Meloma'nia s. An inordinate craving for music.
Angloma'nia s. Excessive fondness or respect for English things.
Galloma'nia s. A rage for French fashions, literature, etc.
Phylloma'nia s. Abnormal production of leaves.
Morphinoma'nia s. Irresistible craving for morphia.
Monoma'nia s. A mental derangement with regard to one particular subject.
Demonoma'nia s. Mania in which the patient believes he is possessed by demons.
Tulipoma'nia s. A craze for cultivating tulips.
Hydroma'nia s. Morbid craving for water.
Eleutheroma'nia s. An excessive or diseased love of freedom.
Metroma'nia s. A mania for versifying.
Pyroma'nia s. Insane craving to set things on fire.
Dipsoma'nia s. A craving for stimulants; alcoholism.
Sitoma'nia s. Morbid repugnance to food.
Erotoma'nia s. Morbid love; abnormal sexual passion.
Kleptoma'nia s. A morbid impulse to steal.
Cran'ia s. (*Cranium*).
Hemicra'nia s. Headache affecting only one side of the head.
Ura'nia s. The muse of astronomy.
Vesa'nia s. Insanity.
Tita'nia s. The queen of the fairies.
Avani'a s. A Turkish tax on Christians.
Encæ'nia s. A dedication festival, a commemoration of founders and benefactors.
Tæ'nia s. A fillet; the genus of tapeworms.
Garde'nia s. A genus of tropical plants with large fragrant flowers.
Neurasthe'nia s. General weakness of the nervous system; nervous prostration.
Catame'nia s. The menses.
Insig'nia s. Badges of office or rank.
Robin'ia s. The locust-tree or false acacia.
Scotodin'ia s. Dizziness, vertigo.
Actin'ia s. A genus of zoophytes.
Quin'ia s. Quinine.
Equin'ia s. A contagious disease among horses.
Gloxin'ia s. A genus of bright-flowered tropical plants.
Insom'nia s. Sleeplessness.
Zin'nia s. A plant of the aster family.
Zirco'nia s. An oxide of zirconium.
Bego'nia s. A genus of ornamental plants.
Cincho'nia s. An alkaloid in Peruvian bark.
Apho'nia s. Loss of voice.
Ischnophon'ia s. Weakness of voice.
Dyspho'nia s. Difficulty in speaking due to malformation of the organs.
Typhon'ia s. Stupor characteristic of typhus.
Chelo'nia s. The tortoises and turtles.
Vallo'nia s. A dried acorn-cup used in tanning, etc.
Ammo'nia s. A pungent gas composed of nitrogen and hydrogen.
Pneumo'nia s. Inflammation of the lungs.
Bigno'nia s. A genus of flowering plants.
Wellingto'nia s. A sequoia.
Her'nia s. Rupture; protrusion of the intestines or an organ.
Petu'nia s. A plant of the tobacco family with purple or variegated flowers.
Gastrodyn'ia s. Gastralgia.
Pleurodyn'ia s. Pain due to rheumatism of the chest-walls.
Paranoi'a s. Mental disease characterized by delusions.
Sequoi'a s. A genus of gigantic Californian conifers.
Sep'ia s. A dark brown pigment prepared from an excretion of the cuttle-fish.
Princip'ia s. First principles; elements.
Cornuco'pia s. The horn of plenty, an emblem of abundance.
Hemeralo'pia s. The abnormal condition in which one sees better by night or artificial light than by daylight.
Nyctalo'pia s. Day-blindness; vision that is better in dusk than in daylight.
Diplo'pia s. An eye-disease causing objects to appear double.
To'pia s. Mural decorations in ancient Roman houses.
Uto'pia s. An ideal social and political system.
Presbyo'pia s. Long-sightedness, "old age" sight.
Amblyo'pia s. Dimness of vision.
Polyo'pia s. Multiple vision.
Myo'pia s. Short-sightedness.

Oxyo'pia s. Excessive acuteness of sight.
A'ria s. A song for one voice.
Persicar'ia s. The peachwort, a common weed.
Araucar'ia s. A genus of coniferous plants.
Cochlear'ia s. A genus of plants including the horse-radish.
Fragar'ia s. The genus of Rosaceæ containing the strawberry.
Filiar'ia s. A genus of thread-like parasitic worms.
Malar'ia s. Noxious exhalations from swamps; an intermittent or remittent fever.
Talar'ia s. The winged sandals of Hermes.
Convallar'ia s. The lily-of-the-valley.
Turbellar'ia s. A genus of flat-worms.
Sigillar'ia s. A genus of fossil cryptogams.
Calceolar'ia s. A genus of herbaceous plants.
Radiolar'ia s. A division of marine protozoa.
Scrophular'ia s. Genus of plants containing the fig-wort.
A've Maria s. " Hail, Mary " ; the ave-bell.
Black Mar'ia s. (*Slang*) A prison van.
Arenar'ia s. A genus of very small herbs.
Cinerar'ia s. A genus of composite plants.
Balistrar'ia s. A cruciform aperture in a castle wall.
Datar'ia s. The papal chancery at Rome.
Serpentar'ia s. The Virginian snake-root.
Wistar'ia s. A climbing plant with lilac flowers.
Hypochon'dria s. Mental disorder characterized by exaggerated anxiety, especially concerning one's own health.
Hy'dria s. An ancient Greek water-jar.
Diphther'ia s. A dangerous and infectious throat disease.
Gaulther'ia s. A genus of evergreen aromatic shrubs.
Bacter'ia s. A genus of microscopic fungi.
Criter'ia s. (*Criterion*).
Aster'ia s. A precious stone.
Hyster'ia s. A nervous affection occurring in paroxysms.
Scor'ia s. Slag ; volcanic cinders.
Phantas-magor'ia s. An exhibition of dissolving views and illusions ; nightmare visions.
Thor'ia s. Oxide of thorium.
Pelor'ia s. Symmetry in flowers that are usually irregular.
Glor'ia s. A doxology.
Nor'ia s. A waterwheel that discharges water into a trough as it revolves.
Infusor'ia s. A class of parasitic and aquatic protozoa.
Victor'ia s. A four-wheeled carriage with movable hood.
Lat'ria s. The highest kind of worship ; that paid to God.
Vera'tria s. Veratrine.
Stri'a s. A superficial ridge or furrow.
Nu'tria s. Fur of the coypu, a S. American rodent.
Cu'ria s. The ancient Roman Senate-house ; the Roman See in its temporal capacity ; a mediæval court of justice.
Albuminur'ia s. A morbid condition causing excess of albumen.
Glucosur'ia s. A form of diabetes.
Hæmatur'ia s. Presence of blood in the urine.
Apha'sia s. Inability to speak, write, etc., due to mental lesion.
Phegma'sia s. Inflammation attended by fever.
Paronoma'sia s. A play upon words ; punning.
Antonoma'sia s. The substitution of an epithet for a proper name.
Euthana'sia s. Easy, painless death.
Dyscra'sia s. Morbid condition of the blood.
Xera'sia s. Disease of the hair by which it becomes dried up and dusty.
Fanta'sia s. A musical composition ; an improvisation.
Hæmosta'sia s. Congestion of blood.
Free'sia s. A genus of bulbous plants of the iris family.
Parrhe'sia s. Freedom of speech.
Pseudæsthe'sia s. Imaginary sensation after removal of a limb, etc.
Anæsthe'sia s. Loss of feeling.
Paræsthe'sia s. Hallucination.
Eccle'sia s. A church, congregation.
Sile'sia s. A thin, coarse, linen cloth.
Magnes'ia s. Oxide of magnesium used as an antacid.
Amne'sia s. Loss of memory.
Polyne'sia s. The islands of the S. Pacific.
Frambœ'sia s. Yaws, a tropical contagious disease.
Fu'chsia s. A genus of plants with drooping funnel-shaped flowers.
Artemis'ia s. A genus of composite plants.
Bank'sia s. An Australian flowering shrub.
Sympo'sia s. Convivial meetings.
Dyspep'sia s. Chronic indigestion.
Eupep'sia s. A good digestion.
Polydip'sia s. Insatiable thirst.
Photop'sia s. An affection of the eye in which coruscations, flashes, etc., are seen.
Tar'sia s. Wood mosaic or inlay.
Cas'sia s. The scented bark of the Chinese cinnamon.
Quas'sia s. A bitter wood and bark from tropical America.
Rus'sia s. A soft leather.
Intelligent'sia s. The intellectual or educated classes of a country.
Symphys'ia s. A deformity due to the growing together of parts.
Alsa'tia s. A refuge for rogues, a haunt of criminals.
Galac'tia s. A morbid flow of milk.
Gode'tia s. A genus of annual flowering plants.
Montbre'tia s. A genus of iridaceous flowering plants.
Mili'tia s. A body of citizen soldiers enrolled for emergencies.
Comi'tia s. An ancient Roman assembly for election of magistrates, etc.
En'tia s. (*Ens*) Entities.
Amen'tia s. Idiocy.
Demen'tia s. Idiocy, infatuation.
Differen'tia s. An essential attribute, specific difference.
Stron'tia s. An oxide of strontium.
Sco'tia s. A concave moulding.
Iner'tia s. Inactivity ; property by which matter tends to maintain its state.
Poinset'tia s. A showy S. American plant.
Hu'ia s. A New Zealand bird allied to the starlings.
Allelu'ia int.
Vi'a adv. By way of ; through.
Sal'via s. A genus of shrubby herbs including the sage.
Synov'ia s. The lubricating fluid in the joints.
Allu'via s. Matter washed away or deposited by rivers, floods, etc.
Atarax'ia s. Impassiveness.
Heterotax'ia s. Heterotaxy.
Cachex'ia s. General ill health.
Dysorex'ia s. Want of appetite.
Pyrex'ia s. Fever ; feverishness.
Ix'ia s. A S. African bulbous plant.
Panmix'ia s. Promiscuous cross - breeding ; chance mingling of hereditary characters.
Asphyx'ia s. Suffocation ; stoppage of the pulse.
Eschschol'tzia s. A genus of flowering herbs allied to the poppy.

Deut'zia s. A genus of shrubs of the saxifrage family.
Raz'zia s. A plundering foray, especially of Arabs for slaves.
Na'ja s. A venomous Indian snake; the cobra.
Sifak'a s. A lemur of Madagascar.
Ka'ka s. A New Zealand parrot.
Kana'ka s. A South Sea islander.
Vod'ka s. A Russian spirituous liquor.
Eure'ka int. Exultation over a discovery.
Balalai'ka s. A Russian stringed instrument.
Roma'ika s. The national dance of mod. Greece.
Troi'ka s. A three-horsed Russian carriage.
Swas'tika s. The fylfot, an ancient symbol.
Puk'ka a. (*Slang*) Genuine; superior.
Il'ka a. (*Scot.*) Each, every.
Pol'ka s. A lively Hungarian dance.
Poo'ka s. An Irish horse-like goblin.
Mazur'ka s. A lively Polish dance; music for this
Kibit'ka s. A Tartar tent; a Russian leather-covered vehicle.
Brit'zka s. An open carriage.
La int. Look! see! s. The sixth tone of the tonic sol-fa scale.
Cab'bala s. An exposition of the Pentateuch attributed to Moses.
Ga'la s. A show, fête; festivity.
Ciga'la s. The cicada.
Ar'gala s. A gigantic stork.
Har'mala s. Wild rue.
Koa'la s. A small Australian marsupial.
Marsa'la s. A white wine.
Mya'la s. A S. African antelope.
Che'la s. A claw of a crustacean.
Philome'la s. The nightingale.
Cedre'la s. A genus of tropical trees.
Te'la s. A web-like membrane, etc.
Muste'la s. The genus containing the weasels.
Seque'la s. An inference; the consequent of a disease.
Strobi'la s. Chain of segments forming a tape-worm.
Manil'a s. A cheroot. a. Applied to hemp from manila; a paper made from it.
Valhal'la s. The ancient Norseman's hall for the spirits of those slain in battle; a pantheon.
Clarabel'la s. A flute-like organ-stop.
Rubel'la s. German measles.
Cel'la s. The central part of a sanctuary.
Varicel'la s. Chicken-pox.
Predel'la s. An ornamented shelf, sculpture, etc., at back of an altar.
Lamel'la s. A thin plate or scale.
Columel'la s. The axis of fruit; stem in mosses; central pillar in corals, etc.
Canel'la s. A genus of West Indian plants.
Soldanel'la s. An Alpine plant of the primrose family.
Gentianel'la s. A dwarf species of gentian.
Fustanel'la s. The kilt worn in modern Greece, Albania, etc.
Fraxinel'la s. A species of rue or dittany.
Prunel'la s. A smooth, dark woollen fabric; a throat disorder, quinsy; a genus of plants; self-heal.
Umbrel'la s. A portable folding screen from rain or sun.
Cinderel'la s. A girl whose beauties or qualities are unappreciated.
Toccatel'la s. A short or light toccata.
Patel'la s. The cap of the knee; a limpet.
Tarantel'la s. A rapid Neapolitan dance.
Fenestel'la s. A niche at the south side of the altar for the piscina.
Scutel'la s. Scales or small plates on the bodies of animals.
Scil'la s. A squill.
Granadil'la s. A variety of passion-flower; its fruit
Seradil'la s. A species of clover.
Cedil'la s. The mark [̧] under c to show that it is pronounced s.
Seguidill'a (-dil'ya) s. A lively Spanish dance.
Redondil'la (-dē'lya) s. A Spanish stanza-form.
Codil'la s. The coarsest part of flax, etc.
Sapodil'la s. A W. Indian tree; its edible fruit.
Fringil'la s. A genus of birds containing the finches
Chinchil'la s. A small S. American rodent; its fur.
Mammil'la s. A nipple, nipple-shaped part.
Armil'la s. A bracelet; an obsolete astronomical instrument.
Manil'la a. Applied to cheroots from Manilla, to tough paper made from Manilla hemp, etc.
Vanil'la s. A climbing orchidaceous plant; its fragrant seed-pod; a flavouring extract from this.
Papil'la s. A minute elevation or protuberance on the skin, tongue, etc., or on plants.
Baril'la s. A seaside plant.
Camaril'la s. A secret body of intriguers.
Sarsaparil'la s. A plant of the smilax family; its root, used in medicine.
Fibril'la s. A little fibre.
Banderil'la s. A little dart used by bull-fighters.
Gueril'la s. Irregular or petty warfare; one taking part in such. a. Pertaining to this.
Goril'la s. A large and ferocious W. African anthropoid ape.
Pulsatil'la s. The pasque-flower.
Mantil'la s. A woman's light cape or veil.
Potentil'la s. A small brightly flowered plant for rock-gardens.
Scintil'la s. A spark, twinkle; an atom.
Flotil'la s. A small fleet; fleet of small boats.
Torti'lla (-tē'lya) s. The flat maize cake of the Mexicans.
Coquil'la s. A Brazilian nut used in turnery.
Vil'la s. A country seat, suburban house.
Fovil'la s. The substance in pollen which causes fertilization.
Maxil'la s. A jaw-bone.
Osteocol'la s. A kind of glue obtained from bones.
Chrysocol'la s. A lustrous opaline silicate of copper.
Hol'la s. and v.i. Hallo.
Corol'la s. The inner part of a flower.
Bull'a s. A round pendant.
Medul'la s. Marrow; the spinal cord.
Scyl'la s. One of two alternative dangers.
Parab'ola s. A curve; one of the conic sections.
Tom'bola s. A form of lottery.
Hyper'bola s. One of the conic sections.
Co'la s. A tropical African tree; its nut.
Gon'dola s. A long, narrow Venetian boat.
Rose'ola s. An eruption of rosy patches.
Fove'ola s. A very small pit, depression, or fovea
Ango'la s. A goat with long silky hair; fabric made from this.
Per'gola s. An arched or roofed trellis-work on a garden path.
Scaglio'la (skalyō'la) s. Plaster imitation of marble.
Vari'ola s. Smallpox.
Vi'ola (or vē-, viō'-) s. Instrument like a large violin; a plant of the pansy family.
Piano'la s. A mechanical piano-player.

Cu'pola s. A spherical vault on top of a building; the round top of a furnace; a furnace with this.
So'la s. Pith of an Indian plant used for sun-helmets, etc.
To'la s. An Indian weight (about 180 grs. troy).
Gorgonzo'la s. A kind of cheese.
Hex'apla s. An edition of the Scriptures in six versions in parallel columns.
Incunab'ula s. Books printed earlier than 1500.
Neb'ula s. A luminous stellar patch in the heavens.
Fib'ula s. The outer and smaller bone of the leg.
Fac'ula s. A luminous spot on the sun.
Mac'ula s. A freckle; a spot on the sun.
Trabec'ula s. A small bundle of connective fibres or tissue.
Fec'ula s. Lees; the nutritious part of wheat.
Vallec'ula s. A groove, channel.
Curric'ula s. (*Curriculum*).
Auric'ula s. A garden flower.
Animal'cula s. A general term for microscopic organisms.
Ced'ula s. A signed certificate; a S. American bond.
Scrof'ula s. A constitutional tuberculous disease.
Teg'ula s. A small scale-like appendage in some insects.
Lig'ula s. A tongue-like organ or part; a membranous appendage.
Ling'ula s. A genus of fossil brachiopods.
Ung'ula s. A hoof, claw, talon; a hooked surgical instrument.
Prim'ula s. A genus of herbaceous plants including the primrose.
For'mula s. A prescribed form; an expression for resolving certain mathematical problems; an expression of chemical composition.
Campan'ula s. A genus of plants with bell-shaped flowers.
Ran'ula s. A cystic tumour under the tongue.
Can'nula s. A small tube used by surgeons.
Lu'nula s. A crescent-shaped mark or part.
Scap'ula s. The shoulder-blade.
Cop'ula s. That which couples; word uniting the subject and predicate of a proposition.
Scop'ula s. The brush-like tuft on bees' legs.
Tor'ula s. Spherical bacteria in chain formation; a genus of parasitic fungi.
Gas'trula s. A cup-like stage of an embryo.
Penin'sula s. Piece of land almost surrounded by water.
Spat'ula s. Broad blade for spreading plasters, paint, etc.
Terebrat'ula s. A genus of deep-sea bivalve molluscs.
Taran'tula s. A large venomous spider of S. Europe.
Rot'ula s. The knee-cap.
Blas'tula s. The vesicular stage of an embryo.
Fis'tula s. A deep chronic abscess; an abnormal opening from one organ into another.
U'vula s. The fleshy body hanging from the back of the palate.
Pter'yla s. A tract or patch of feathers on a bird's skin.
Ma s. Child's word for "mother."
Ka'ma s. The Hindu god of love.
La'ma s. A Buddhist priest of Tibet or Mongolia.
Lla'ma s. A domesticated S. American camel-like quadruped; its wool.
Panama' s. A hat made from the leaves of a S. American screw-pine.
Dra'ma s. A play; dramatic literature.
Mel'odrama s. A play with startling and exaggerated incidents and sentiments.
Mon'odrama s. A dramatic piece for one performer.
Diora'ma s. A scenic exhibition producing natural effects and optical illusions.
Myriora'ma s. An exhibition of views in quick succession.
Cyclora'ma s. A cylindrical panorama viewed from inside.
Cosmora'ma s. An exhibition through lenses, etc., of views of the world.
Panora'ma s. A picture exhibited by being unrolled and passed before the spectator.
Polyora'ma s. A panorama.
Squa'ma s. A scale or scale-like part.
Ya'ma s. The Hindu god of the dead.
Chac'ma s. A S. African baboon.
Be'ma s. The chancel of a church.
Œde'ma s. A localized form of dropsy.
Myxœde'ma s. A cretinous disease of the thyroid gland.
Sche'ma s. A figure, outline, diagram, especially in logic, rhetoric, etc.
Erythe'ma s. A superficial skin-disease.
Serie'ma s. A red-legged, crested S. American bird.
U'lema (oo'-) s. The body of Moslem legal interpreters and administrators.
En'ema s. An injection; instrument with which this is made.
Cin'ema s. A place for cinematograph performances, a "picture palace."
Epichire'ma s. A syllogism in which the proof of the premises is within them.
Emphyse'ma s. Distention of cellular tissues caused by pressure of air.
Blaste'ma s. Protoplasm.
Empye'ma s. A collection of pus in the pleura.
Ec'zema s. A skin disease.
Mag'ma s. The molten rock of the earth's interior; gangue; a thick residuum.
Smeg'ma s. Secretion from these baceous glands.
Breg'ma s. The meeting-place of the coronal and sagittal sutures of the skull.
Enig'ma s. An obscure or ambiguous sentence, etc.; a riddle, an inexplicable thing.
Sterig'ma s. A stalk, a leaf-like expansion.
Sig'ma s. The Greek letter Σ, σ or ς.
Stig'ma s. A brand, mark of infamy; part of pistil of a plant.
Dog'ma s. A settled opinion or belief; a principle, maxim.
Zeug'ma s. Grammatical figure by which a word is made to apply to two nouns when it is only applicable to one of them.
Drach'ma s. A silver coin of ancient and modern Greece; a drachm.
Asth'ma s. A respiratory disease.
Min'ima s. (*Minimum*).
Quadrage'sima s. The first Sunday in Lent.
Quinquage'sima s. The Sunday next before Lent.
Septuages'ima s. The third Sunday before Lent.
Sexages'ima s. The second Sunday before Lent.
Penul'tima s. A penult.
Hal'ma s. A game played on a board of 256 squares.
Gam'ma s. The third letter of the Greek alphabet.
Digam'ma s. A letter of the oldest Greek alphabet.

Mamma' s. Child's name for "mother."
Mam'ma s. A milk-secreting organ.
Gem'ma s. A leaf-bud; a minute cellular body in the fructification of certain mosses; a bud-like outgrowth in polyps, etc.
Lem'ma s. A subsidiary proposition in mathematics; the husk of a fruit.
Dilem'ma s. A perplexing situation.
Trilem'ma s. A syllogism involving three alternatives.
Neurilem'ma s. The membranous sheath of a nerve.
Marem'ma s. A marshy plain near the sea in Italy
Stem'ma s. A pedigree, family tree; the simple eye of an insect; a facet of a compound eye.
Com'ma s. A grammatical mark [,] denoting a short pause; a bacillus of this shape
Mom'ma s. Affected Americanism for "mamma."
Gum'ma s. A kind of tumour.
Co'ma s. A state of trance; lethargy.
Sarco'ma s. A fleshy tumour; a form of cancer.
Glauco'ma s. A disease of the eye causing opacity.
Leuco'ma s. A white spot in the cornea due to a wound, etc.
Zygo'ma s. The arch joining the malar and temporal bones in the head.
Tracho'ma s. A disease of the eye.
Tricho'ma s. Plica, a disease of the hair.
Xantho'ma s. A skin disease characterized by yellowish tubercles.
Epithelio'ma s. A form of cancer attacking the epithelium.
Glio'ma s. A tumour of the brain, spinal cord, or retina.
Diplo'ma s. A document conferring privilege, power, or honour; a certificate.
Carcino'ma s. Cancer.
Pyono'ma s. A suppurating sore.
Lipo'ma s. A fatty tumour.
Fibro'ma s. A fibrous tumour.
Theobro'ma s. A tropical tree yielding cocoa.
Sclero'ma s. Morbid hardening of the skin; an indurated tumour.
Plero'ma s. Fullness, abundance.
Stro'ma s. Tissue forming framework of an organ.
Neuro'ma s. A nerve tumour.
Tyro'ma s. A fungoid disease of the hair.
So'ma s. An intoxicating liquor used in Hindu religious rites.
Microso'ma s. A minute granule in protoplasmic cells.
Steato'ma s. A fatty encysted tumour.
Myceto'ma s. A fungoid disease of the hands and feet.
Scoto'ma s. Scotomy.
Sto'ma s. A pore, especially in the surface skin of a leaf.
Lagos'toma s. Hare-lip.
Rhizo'ma s. (*Rhizome*).
Kar'ma s. Buddhist term for fate, destiny, or cumulative consequences of one's acts.
Scleroder'ma s. Morbid hardening of the skin.
Xeroder'ma s. A scaly affection of the skin.
Her'ma s. A bust of Hermes set on a pillar, anc. used as a boundary post.
Ter'ma s. A thin layer of grey matter in the brain.
Phas'ma s. A genus of orthopterous insects; a "walking leaf."
Mias'ma s. Poisonous exhalation, noxious affluvia; malaria.
Melas'ma s. Skin disease characterized by excess of black pigment.
Plas'ma s. Protoplasm; fluid part of the blood; a greenish, translucent variety of quartz.
Phantas'ma s. An imaginary existence, an optical illusion, a phantom.
Mahat'ma s. An adept in esoteric Buddhism.
Trau'ma s. An external wound; condition produced by such.
Cur'cuma s. A genus of plants of the ginger family.
Du'ma s. The parliament of the late Russian Empire.
Pneu'ma s. Spirit, soul.
Empyreu'ma s. The unpleasant taste and smell of animal or vegetable substances burned in close vessels.
Pu'ma s. The American panther or cougar.
Stru'ma s. Scrofula; a swelling on a petiole, etc.
Satsu'ma s. The hard, glazed pottery of Japan.
Cy'ma s. A wave-like moulding of a cornice.
Epen'dyma s. The lining membranes of the ventricles of the brain.
Collen'chyma s. The elastic protoplasmic cell tissue of plants.
Cinen'chyma s. Lactiferous tissue.
Paren'chyma s. The essential tissues of cell formation.
Scleren'chyma (sklĕr-) s. The woody tissue of plants.
Pleuren'chyma s. The woody tissue of plants.
Prosen'chyma s. Part of the cellular tissue of plants.
Try'ma s. A drupe-like fruit, as the walnut.
Na adv. (*Scot.*) No.
Caba'na s. A choice cigar.
Jac'ana s. A S. American wading bird.
Peca'na s. A variety of hickory from N. America.
Arca'na s. Mysteries.
Bandan'a s. A coloured handkerchief with spots
Befa'na s. A fay of Italian folklore.
Naga'na s. Tsetse-fly disease.
Fa'ta Morga'na s. A mirage observed in the Mediterranean.
Dian'a s. A huntress, sportswoman.
Lia'na s. A woody creeper of tropical forests.
Gymka'na s. A meeting for athletic or military sports.
La'na s. A close-grained S. American timber.
Pozzola'na s. A volcanic lava used in cement-making.
Ma'na s. Spiritual power claimed by spiritualists.
Quadru'mana s. The order of mammals comprising the monkeys, apes, baboons, etc.
Bana'na s. A tropical tree; its fruit.
Zena'na s. The women's apartments in Hindu houses.
Ra'na s. The genus of frogs and toads.
Gita'na s. A female gipsy.
Sulta'na s. Wife of a sultan; a dried yellow grape.
Tramonta'na s. A N. wind in the Mediterranean.
Curta'na s. The Sword of Mercy in the British regalia.
Gua'na s. A large Australasian lizard.
Igua'na s. A large American lizard.
Havan'a s. A cigar made in Cuba of native tobacco.
Nirva'na s. The Buddhist state of blessedness following extinction of self.
Echid'na s. A genus of Australasian mammals which lay eggs.
Muræ'na s. A large edible marine eel.
Verbe'na s. A cultivated S. American plant; vervain.
Sce'na s. A scene or elaborated solo in an opera.

Mod'ena s. A deep purple colour.
Saphe'na s. One of the leg veins.
Gale'na s. Lead ore; native sulphide of lead.
Cantile'na s. A ballad.
Prolegom'ena s. An introduction; preliminary observations.
Paralipom'ena s. Things omitted in a work.
Subpœ'na s. A writ commanding attendance. v.t. To serve with this.
Philope'na s. A forfeit-paying game played with double-kernelled almonds; the forfeit.
Are'na s. The area in an amphitheatre; a space for a contest, etc.
Cate'na s. A connected series.
Hye'na s. A carnivorous quadruped allied to the dog.
Maize'na s. Fine meal or farina prepared from maize.
Vicu'gna s. (*Vicuna*).
Mish'na s. The second century collection of Hebrew traditions, etc., forming the text of the Talmud.
-ina suff. Forming feminines, proper names, and names of groups of animals.
Jain'a s. An adherent of Jainism.
Pisci'na (-sē'na) s. Small stone basin in which the Eucharistic vessels are washed.
Gluci'na s. Oxide of glucinum.
Contadi'na s. An Italian peasant woman.
Vagi'na s. A sheath-like organ; the genital passage of females.
Angi'na s. Quinsy.
Chi'na s. Porcelain; ware of this. a. Made of porcelain; of or from China.
Trichi'na s. A nematode parasitic worm.
Skuptschi'na (-shē'-) s. The Parliament of Yugo-Slavia.
Seraphi'na (-fē'na) s. A form of harmonium.
Sali'na s. A salt marsh; a salt works.
Plastili'na s. A kind of modelling clay.
Semoli'na s. The grains of wheat-flour left after the finer grains have been sifted.
Santoli'na s. A genus of plants allied to the camomile.
Mi'na s. An anc. Greek weight (about 1 lb. avoir.); a coin worth 100 drachmæ; the mynah.
Lam'ina s. A thin plate or scale.
Foram'ina s. (*Foramen*).
Stam'ina s. Strength; power of endurance.
Grava'mina s. (*Gravamen*).
Alu'mina s. Oxide of aluminium.
Pi'na (pē'nya) s. A fine cloth made from pine-apple leaf fibres.
Cari'na s. A ridge-like structure.
Ocarin'a (-rēn-) s. An earthenware egg-shaped musical wind-instrument.
Fari'na s. Flour, meal.
Tsari'na (-rē'-) s. The wife of a tsar; a Russian empress.
Balleri'na s. A ballet girl.
Signori'na s. The Italian title of address corresponding to "Miss."
Orchestri'na s. A mechanical musical instrument for producing orchestral effects.
Toccati'na (-tē'-) s. A short or easy toccata.
Scarlati'na (-tē'na) s. Scarlet fever.
Sonati'na (-tē'-) s. A short or simple sonata.
Pati'na s. The green incrustation formed on bronze exposed to the air.
Cavati'na s. A musical air of one movement.
Ret'ina s. The nerve fibres and cells behind the eye-ball which receive sight impressions.
Skupshti'na s. The Serbian Parliament.
Concerti'na s. A musical instrument like the accordion.
Sesti'na (-tē'na) s. A complicated six-line stanza form.
Fluti'na s. A kind of accordion.
Harlequin'a s. A female harlequin or buffoon.
Quinqui'na (-kwē'-) s. Peruvian bark.
Ul'na s. The larger bone of the forearm.
An'na s. The sixteenth part of the Indian rupee.
Can'na s. A genus of ornamental plants.
Bandan'na s. A brightly coloured handkerchief.
Man'na s. Food miraculously supplied to the Israelites in the wilderness; saccharine exudation from species of ash.
Hosan'na s. A Jewish shout of praise to God.
Savan'na s. An extensive treeless plain of tropical America.
Hen'na s. Egyptian privet; orange-coloured dye from this.
Gehen'na s. Hell; a place of torment.
Sien'na s. A brownish-yellow earthy pigment.
Sen'na s. A leguminous plant; its dried leaves used as a purgative.
Transen'na s. A lattice enclosing a shrine.
Anten'na s. A sensory organ of insects and crustaceans.
Duen'na s. An elderly female companion; a chaperon, governess.
Pin'na s. The flap of the external ear; a marine bivalved mollusc; a fin.
Don'na s. Italian female title of courtesy; "Madam."
Belladon'na s. Deadly nightshade; a drug prepared from this.
Madon'na s. The Virgin Mary; a picture or statue representing the Virgin.
Pri'ma don'na s. Chief female singer in an opera.
Sun'na s. The traditional part of Mohammedan law.
Do'na s. A Spanish female title of courtesy; "Madam"; (*slang*) a donah.
Cincho'na s. Peruvian bark, the source of quinine.
Bello'na s. The Roman goddess of war.
Cremo'na s. A violin made at Cremona.
Pomo'na s. The Roman goddess of fruit-trees.
Coro'na s. The projecting face of a cornice; a halo round the sun or moon; the circumference of a compound radiated flower; the flat top of a tooth.
Zo'na s. Shingles, a form of herpes.
Nor'na s. One of the Norse fates.
Faun'a s. The animals peculiar to a region or epoch.
Avifau'na s. The birds of a district considered collectively.
Lacu'na s. A gap, opening, hiatus.
Vicu'ña (-koo'nya) s. A S. American ruminant allied to the llama; its wool; cloth made from this.
Indu'na s. A Zulu military chief.
Callu'na s. The ling.
Tu'na s. The great tunny.
Tsarev'na s. The daughter of a tsar.
Jerbo'a s. A long-legged mouse-like Egyptian rodent.
Co'coa s. A tropical palm-tree (*Cocos nucifera*) bearing the cocoa-nut; a preparation and drink made from the seeds of *Theobroma cacao*.
Who'a int. Call to stop horses, etc.
Ko'a s. An ornamental wood from the Sandwich Islands.
Hol'loa s. and v.i. Hallo.

Mo'a s. An extinct wingless, gigantic bird of New Zealand.
Quino'a s. A farinaceous S. American plant.
Po'a s. A genus of grasses.
Leipo'a s. The mound-bird of Australia.
Pro'a s. A long sailing canoe of E. Indian seas.
Sto'a s. A portico.
Actinozo'a s. Radiated animals.
Microzo'a s. Microscopic animals.
Hydrozo'a s. A group of aquatic animals including the jelly-fish.
Hæmatozo'a s. Parasites found in the blood.
Mycetozo'a s. A class of minute organisms, the slime-moulds.
Entozo'a s. (*Entozoon*).
Protozo'a s. The lowest division of the animal kingdom.
Polyzo'a s. A lowly organized division of invertebrates, mostly marine.
Pa s. Childish for "father."
Papa' s. Childish for "father."
Ta'pa s. Cloth made in Polynesia from the paper-mulberry.
Kal'pa s. A Brahman period of 4,320,000 years.
Tal'pa s. A wen; the genus containing the moles.
Catal'pa s. An American and Asiatic tree.
Spa s. A mineral spring, or place where one is.
Pu'pa s. A chrysalis.
Bar'bara s. A mnemonic used in logic.
Capybar'a s. A S. American rodent.
Caraca'ra s. The American vulture-hawk.
Bac'cara s. A gambling card-game.
Casca'ra s. A Californian bark from which an aperient is prepared.
Viha'ra s. An ancient Dravidian rock-hewn monastery.
Cith'ara s. A lyre-like musical instrument.
Tiar'a s. An ornamental head-dress; the Pope's crown.
Dulcamar'a s. The herb bittersweet.
Sam'ara s. A dry seed with wing-like expansions.
Tam'ara s. An Italian condiment.
Gema'ra s. A Hebrew commentary on the Mishna.
Nullip'ara s. A woman who has borne no child.
Plurip'ara s. A woman who has had more than one child.
Multip'ara s. A woman who has borne more than one child.
Ferra'ra s. An old name for a broadsword.
Solfata'ra s. A volcanic vent whence vapour issues.
Tanta'ra s. Quick notes on a trumpet, etc.
Taratan'tara s. The sound of a bugle, etc.
Candelab'ra s. A branched candlestick.
Dola'bra s. An ancient Roman pickaxe.
Al'gebra s. A method of computation in which quantities are denoted by signs.
Ster'nebra s. A serial segment of the vertebra.
Ter'ebra s. A boring ovipositor.
Ver'tebra s. A joint or segment of the spinal column.
Ze'bra s. An African striped quadruped allied to the horse.
Li'bra s. The Balance, the seventh sign of the zodiac.
Alham'bra s. The Moorish palace at Granada.
Um'bra s. A shadow, especially that from a planet or the moon by which the sun's light is cut off.
Penum'bra s. A shadow cast by an eclipse where light is partly cut off; point in a picture where light and shade blend.
Man'bra s. A Hindu charm; a Vedic hymn.
Co'bra s. A hooded venomous snake.
Delu'bra s. The innermost or most sacred parts of a temple.
Quad'ra s. A fillet of an Ionic base.
Cathe'dra s. The bishop's throne in a cathedral.
Ex'edra s. A portico, porch; a bishop's throne; a recess.
Cassan'dra s. A misleading prophetess of woe.
Tun'dra s. Treeless, marshy plain of N. Russia.
Hy'dra s. A fabulous, many-headed water-serpent; an evil to be overcome only by repeated effort.
Clep'sydra s. A contrivance to measure time by flow of water.
Er'a s. An epoch; a period or date from which time is reckoned.
Hetær'a s. A courtesan, esp. of ancient Greece.
Vis'cera s. Internal organs; the intestines.
Hed'era s. A genus of climbing plants, containing the ivy.
Foraminif'era s. (*Foraminifer*).
Rotif'era s. The aquatic wheel-animalcules.
He'ra s. The greatest of the Greek goddesses.
Ctenoph'era s. A class of jelly-fish having fringed locomotive organs.
Scler'a (sklĕr-) s. The sclerotic coat of the eye.
Cordiller'a s. A chain of mountains, especially in S. America.
Chol'era s. A disease accompanied by vomiting and violent purging.
Cam'era s. An apparatus for taking photographs.
Ephem'era s. A fly that lives only a day, the May-fly; a fever of one day's duration.
Chimer'a s. A fabulous fire-eating monster of hideous aspect; a foolish or incongruous fancy.
Gen'era s. (*Genus*).
Tem'pera s. Painting in distemper.
Op'era s. A musical drama; house where such are performed.
Caravan'sera s. An Oriental inn.
Dros'era s. The genus of plants including the sundew.
Tes'sera s. A small cube used in mosaic work.
Pat'era s. A saucer-like vessel anciently used for libations.
Etcet'era contr. phr. And other things, and so on.
Dip'tera s. An order of insects having two wings only.
Hemip'tera s. An order of winged insects feeding by means of sucking-tubes (lice, bed-bugs, aphides, etc.).
Lepidop'tera s. The order of insects comprising butterflies and moths.
Coleop'tera s. The order of insects including the beetles and weevils.
Orthop'tera s. An order of insects with two pairs of wings.
Homop'tera s. A class of insects having uniform wings.
Hymenop'tera s. An order of insects having four membranous wings.
Heterop'tera s. A subdivision of the Hemiptera including the bugs.
Chirop'tera s. The order of flying mammals, the bats.
Neurop'tera s. An order of insects having four membranous transparent wings.
Phyllox'era s. A hemipterous insect destructive to grape-vines; disease to vines caused by this.
Podag'ra s. Gout.
Pellag'ra s. An endemic skin-disease causing mania and nervous disorders.

Gonag'ra s. Gout in the knee.
Chirag'ra s. Gout in the fingers.
Ure'thra s. Duct by which urine is discharged.
Mith'ra s. The Persian sun-god.
Madeir'a s. A white wine.
Heg'ira s. The flight of Mohammed (A.D. 622) from which the Moslem era commences.
Lir'a s. An Italian silver coin (about 10d.).
O'kra s. A culinary herb.
Kok'ra s. An E. Indian wood used for flutes.
Bo'ra s. A keen N.E. wind in the Adriatic.
Pec'ora s. The group of ruminants including the oxen, sheep, deer, etc.
Dor'a s. The Defence of the Realm Act of 1914.
Pando'ra s. The first created woman according to Greek mythology.
Ag'ora s. The public square of an ancient Greek city.
Mandrag'ora s. Mandrake, narcotic.
Angor'a s. A goat with long silky hair; fabric made from this.
Anaph'ora s. The Eucharistic service in the Greek Church; repetition of words at the beginning of successive clauses.
Pleth'ora s. Overfulness, especially of blood; state of being too full or abundant; repletion.
Flor'a s. The plants belonging to a region; the Roman goddess of flowers.
Pas'siflora s. The passion-flower.
Mor'a s. The game of guessing how many fingers are held up; a S. American timber-tree.
Fe'mora s. The thigh-bones.
Rem'ora s. The sucking-fish.
Señor'a (-nyor'a) s. The Spanish equivalent of "Mrs."
Signor'a (Sēnyor'a) s. Italian equivalent for "Mrs." or "Madam."
Auror'a s. Illumination of the night sky in polar regions; the dawn.
Sor'a s. A N. American marsh-bird esteemed as food.
Psor'a s. Itch, scabies.
Herbiv'ora s. Animals that feed on vegetation.
Carniv'ora s. The order of mammals feeding on raw flesh.
Insectiv'ora s. An order of insect-eating mammals (moles, hedgehogs, etc.).
Cop'ra s. The dried kernel of the coco-nut from which the oil is extracted.
Sier'ra s. A saw-like ridge of mountains.
Ser'ra s. A saw-fish; a saw-like organ.
Ter'ra s. Earth.
Camor'ra s. A secret society in the old kingdom of Naples.
Sabur'ra s. Gritty matter accumulating through indigestion.
Dur'ra s. Indian millet.
Hurra' int. (*Hurrah*).
Ul'tra a. Extreme, extravagant, uncompromising. s. An ultraist.
Man'tra s. A Vedic hymn of praise.
Tan'tra s. One of the Sanskrit religious writings.
Con'tra prep. Against, opposite. s. The opposite (credit) side of an account; argument against.
Calyp'tra s. A cap covering the capsule of mosses.
Palæ'stra s. A wrestling-school or gymnasium in ancient Greece.
Or'chestra s. A body of musicians; the place for them in a theatre, etc.
Aspidis'tra s. A genus of plants from China and Japan.
Su'tra s. One of the Brahminical books of doctrine.
Ex'tra a. Over and above, additional. s. Something in addition.
Ely'tra s. (*Elytron*).
Au'ra s. An emanation; a premonitory symptom.
Lau'ra s. A collection of monastic cells, especially in the desert.
Pleu'ra s. The membrane on the interior of the thorax and investing the lungs.
Endopleur'a s. The internal integument of a seed.
Gour'a s. A genus of tropical pigeons.
Purpur'a s. A purple eruption symptomatic of various diseases; a genus of gasteropods.
Sur'a s. Any one of the chapters of the Koran.
Datur'a s. A genus of plants yielding narcotic poisons.
Villeggiatur'a s. A stay in the country.
Appoggiatu'ra s. A grace-note.
Cælatur'a s. Engraved metal-work.
Fioritur'a s. A flourish (in music).
Veltur'a s. An Italian four-wheeled carriage.
Angostu'ra s. A tonic bitters prepared from a S. American shrub.
Bravu'ra s. A showy, florid passage in music.
Lyr'a s. A northern constellation.
Me'sa s. A tableland with steeply sloping sides.
Impres'a s. An heraldic device or motto.
Vi'sa (vē'-) s. Endorsement on a passport.
Mimo'sa s. A genus of leguminous shrubs.
Vi'ce ver'sa adv. With the order or position changed reciprocally.
Bur'sa s. A synovial sac.
Dogaress'a s. The wife of a doge.
Abscis'sa s. One of the elements of reference by which a point is referred to a system of fixed rectilineal coordinate axes.
Vibris'sa s. A bristly hair or organ; a bristle-like feather.
Mantis'sa s. The decimal part of a logarithm.
Fos'sa s. A shallow depression (especially anatomically).
Babirous'sa s. A genus of wild swine found in the Celebes.
Medu'sa s. A jelly-fish.
Ta int. (*Childish*) Thank you!
Alba'ta s. German silver.
Tocca'ta s. A composition for the harpsichord.
Da'ta s. (*Datum*).
Rea'ta (-a'-) s. A lariat.
Bal'ata s. The dried gum of a S. American tree.
Ungula'ta s. The group of mammals having hoofs.
Anathe'mata s. Curses of excommunication.
Monotre'mata s. The lowest class of mammals.
Stig'mata s. Small red spots on the skin; miraculous impressions of Christ's wounds.
Carcino'mata s. Cancerous growths.
Sto'mata s. (*Stoma*).
Cyclostom'ata s. The class of fishes including the lampreys.
Autom'ata s. Mechanical figures imitating the actions of living beings.
Serena'ta s. A simple form of symphony.
Sona'ta s. A musical composition in related movements.
Ra'ta s. A New Zealand tree yielding hard red timber.
Vertebra'ta s. Group including all animals with a backbone.

Invertebra'ta s. Old collective name for animals with no backbone.
Inamora'ta s. A female lover.
Erra'ta s. A list of corrections.
Stra'ta s. (*Stratum*).
Ta-ta int. Good-bye!
Bata'ta s. The sweet potato of America.
Edenta'ta s. Order of mammals including the sloths, ant-eaters, etc., that lack fore teeth and canines.
Deject'a s. Excrements.
Analec'ta s. Collected literary fragments.
Notonec'ta s. A species of water-beetle.
Dic'ta s. (*Dictum*)
Be'ta s. Second letter of the Greek alphabet.
Taf'feta s. A smooth silky fabric.
The'ta s. The eighth letter of the Greek alphabet.
Pie'ta s. A representation of the Virgin and the dead Christ.
Excre'ta s Matter discharged from the body.
Se'ta s. A small spine or bristle on animals or plants.
Pese'ta (-sā'ta) s. Spanish silver monetary unit (about 9d.).
Ze'ta s. The room over a church porch.
Soft'a s. A student of Moslem theology and law.
Coai'ta s. The Brazilian spider-monkey.
Incog'nita s. A woman going in disguise or under an assumed name.
Amri'ta s. The ambrosia of Hindu myth.
Señori'ta (-nyorē'ta) s. Spanish equivalent of " Miss."
Del'ta s. The fourth letter of the Greek alphabet; space between diverging mouths of a river.
Shel'ta s. A jargon used by Irish vagrants.
Pel'ta s. The light shield of the ancient Greeks and Romans.
Lavol'ta s. An old dance for two.
Vedan'ta (vā-) s. A philosophical system founded on the Veda.
Infan'ta s. A Spanish or Portuguese princess.
Placen'ta s. The afterbirth.
Magen'ta s. A brilliant crimson aniline dye.
Polen'ta s. A porridge of maize, chestnut-meal, etc.
Amen'ta s. Catkins.
Rejectamen'ta s. Refuse.
Impedimen'ta s. Baggage.
Quin'ta s. A Spanish country house.
Jun'ta s. A legislative or administrative body in Spain, etc.
Io'ta s. A jot; very small quantity.
Pelo'ta s. A ball-game played by the Basques.
Ro'ta s. A list of persons taking duty in turn.
Quo'ta s. A proportional share; part assigned.
Lacer'ta s. The lizards.
Por'ta s. The aperture where a vein, etc., enters an organ.
Podes'ta s. A mayor in Italian towns.
Eges'ta s. Waste matter thrown out.
Inges'ta s. Food; any aliment taken into the body.
Sies'ta s. A short midday sleep.
Tes'ta s. Outer covering of a seed.
Ves'ta s. A wax match.
Zend-Aves'ta s. The scriptures of the ancient Persian religion.
Ballis'ta s. An ancient military engine.
Genis'ta s. A genus of shrubs with yellow flowers; the broom.
Aris'ta s. The beard of grasses and grain.
Vis'ta s. A long and narrow or extended view.
Cos'ta s. A rib or rib-like process.
Bat'ta s. Extra allowance to British officers in India.
Regat'ta s. A meeting for rowing and sailing matches.
Paramat'ta s. A light, twilled dress-fabric.
Anat'ta s. An orange-red dye used for colouring cheese.
Vendet'ta s. A blood feud; communal vengeance.
Codet'ta s. A short coda.
Mofet'ta s. A volcanic vent for noxious gases.
Comediet'ta s. A little comedy.
Ariet'ta s. A short lively tune or song.
Burlet'ta s. A musical farce.
Operet'ta s. A short, light opera.
Biret'ta s. A square cap worn by certain clergy.
Mozet'ta s. Cape worn by cardinals, abbots, etc.
Sag'itta s. The versed sine of an arc; a genus of marine worms.
Vit'ta s. A garland, especially as worn at ancient Roman sacrifices.
Terra-cot'ta s. A hard, reddish, unglazed pottery.
Gut'ta s. A drop; a sculptured drop-shaped ornament.
Ady'ta s. The innermost sanctuaries of ancient temples.
Bary'ta s. Oxide of barium.
Prætex'ta s. A purple-bordered Roman toga.
Taman'dua s. A species of American ant-eaters.
Pirag'ua s. A pirogue.
Sku'a s. A sea-bird allied to the gulls.
Qua adv. In the quality or capacity of; in so far as.
Sil'iqua s. An elongated pod or seed-vessel.
Man'tua s. A woman's loose gown.
A'va s. An intoxicating drink of the Sandwich Islanders.
Ka'va s. A Polynesian intoxicating beverage
La'va s. Molten rock, etc., discharged by volcanoes.
Cassa'va s. The farinaceous root of the manioc.
Gua'va s. A tropical fruit; the tree bearing this.
Gene'va s. A spirit distilled from grain and flavoured with juniper; gin. a. Pertaining to Geneva, or to the Calvinists.
Copai'va s. (*Copaiba*).
Di'va s. A prima donna.
Khediv'a s. Wife of a Khedive.
Sali'va s. Fluid secreted in the mouth.
Si'va (sē'-) s. The Destroyer and Reproducer of Life in the Hindu trinity.
Conjuncti'va s. The mucous membrane covering the inner surface of the eyelid and front of eyeball.
Vi'va (vē'-) int. Long live!
Vul'va s. External opening of the female genitals.
O'va s. (*Ovum*).
No'va s. A new star that suddenly appears and shortly fades away.
Lar'va s. An insect in the grub state.
Confer'va s. A genus of seaweeds.
U'va s. A pulpy indehiscent fruit, such as the grape.
Pesh'wa s. The chief of the Mahratta confederation.
Fet'wa s. Written opinion of a Mohammedan lawyer.
Cox'a s. The hip-joint; the first joint of insects.
Mox'a s. A vegetable down burnt on the skin as a counter-irritant.
Catt'leya s. A genus of orchids.
Kshat'riya s. The second of the four Hindu castes; the warriors.
Hoy'a s. A genus of tropical climbing shrubs.
Moy'a s. Mud thrown from volcanoes.

Guer'eza s. An Abyssinian monkey.
Col'za s. A variety of cabbage.
Extravagan'za s. A musical composition remarkable for wildness and incoherence.
Bonan'za s. A successful venture, especially in mining.
Stan'za s. A group of metrical lines; a verse.
Caden'za s. A closing flourish in music.
Influen'za s. Violent form of febrile catarrh.
Mir'za s. Persian title of honour.
Tsarit'za s. A tsarina.
Cory'za s. Cold in the head
Piaz'za s. A portico, veranda; an open market-place or square.
Taz'za (tăts'-) s. A flat cup on a foot.
Morbidez'za s. Delicacy of representation of flesh in paintings.
Huzza' int. A shout of joy; hurrah! v.i. and t. To make or greet with this cry.
Ba'obab s. A very large tree of tropical Africa.
Cab s. A hackney carriage; the shelter on a locomotive.
Scab s. An incrustation over a sore; a contagious disease of sheep, etc., also of plants; a blackleg in a strike; a dirty fellow. v.i. To form a scab.
Dab v.t. To touch gently, to moisten. s. A gentle blow, a small mass of something moist; a small flat-fish; an expert.
Confab' s. (*Slang*) A confabulation.
Gab s. The mouth; idle prate; loquacity.
Jab s. A sharp poke. v.t. To poke roughly; to stab.
Lab s. (*Slang*) A laboratory.
Blab v.t.; v.i. To talk or tell indiscreetly. s. One who does this.
Slab s. A thin piece of anything having a plane surface. v.t. To cover with slabs, saw slabs from.
Mab s. The queen of the fairies.
Nab v.t. (*Slang*) To catch or seize suddenly.
Do'ab s. A tongue of land between two confluent rivers (India).
Ar'ab s. A native of, or horse from, Arabia; a gamin. a. Arabian.
Scar'ab s. The sacred beetle of ancient Egypt; an amulet, etc., resembling this.
Crab s. A ten-legged crustacean; a zodiacal constellation; a small crane, windlass, portable capstan; a wild apple; a morose person. v.t. To claw, scratch; to criticize savagely. a. Sour, rough, austere.
Drab a. Dull brown or dim colour; commonplace, monotonous. s. This colour; a slut; a thick woollen cloth.
Grab v.t. To seize suddenly and with violence; to snatch. s. A sudden snatch; implement for seizing objects; rapacious acquisition.
Mihrab' s. Niche in a mosque indicating the direction of Mecca.
Tab s. Small flap or tag of linen, leather, etc.
Can'tab s. (*Slang*) A Cambridge undergraduate.
Stab v.t. and i. To pierce or kill with a pointed weapon; to give a wound; to injure secretly. s. A thrust or wound with a pointed weapon; a wound; a malicious injury.
Squab a. Thick; plump; unfledged. s. A short, fat person; an unfledged pigeon; a large, stuffed cushion.
Nawab' s. A native Indian viceroy.
Swab (swob) s. Mop for cleaning floors, etc. v.t. To rub or clean with this.
Abb s. Yarn for the warp of a woollen fabric.
Ebb s. Reflux of tide towards sea. v.i. To flow back, decline, decay.
Cu'beb s. The dried berry of a species of pepper.
Bleb s. A small vesicle on the skin.
Neb s. A beak, snout, nib, tip of anything.
Web s. Thing woven, textile fabric; large roll of paper; cobweb; membrane uniting toes of water-fowl; a film. v.t. To connect, envelop, etc., with a web.
Cob'web s. A spider's net; anything flimsy. a. Light, thin.
Bib s. A cloth worn by children on the breast. v.t. and i. To tipple.
Fib s. An untruth, harmless lie.
Gib s. A male cat or castrated cat.
Sa'hib s. Title used by Eastern natives in addressing Europeans.
Mem'-sahib s. A European mistress of a house in India.
Jib s. The triangular foremost sail of a ship; the arm of a crane. v.t. To shift (a sail, boom, etc.) from one side to the other. v.i. To stop suddenly or swerve (of a horse).
Glib a. Smooth, slippery; voluble.
Nib s. Point of a pen; a neb.
Snib s. A catch, bolt. v.t. To fasten with this.
Rib s. One of the curved bones attached to the spine; something resembling this; a vein in a leaf, ridge in cloth, etc. v.t. To furnish or enclose with ribs.
Car'ib s. One of an aboriginal W. Indian race
Crib s. A child's bed; a rack, framework, stall for oxen; a hut; a bin; a berth, situation; cribbage, hand at this; a translation, a plagiarism. v.t. To shut up in a crib; to pilfer; to copy illicitly from another, to use a translation. v.i. To crowd or be crowded together.
Drib s. A trifle, negligible amount.
Mid'rib s. The main rib of a leaf.
Sib a. Related to, belonging to.
Squib s. A skit, lampoon; a small fire work.
Alb s. An ecclesiastical vestment.
Bulb s. A bud, usually underground, producing a stem above and roots below.
I'amb s. An iambus.
Chol'iamb s. A verse with an iamb in the fifth foot and spondee in the sixth.
Chor'iamb s. A metrical foot of four syllables, first and last long, others short.
Jamb s. Side-post of a door, window, etc.
Lamb s. The young of the sheep; an innocent or gentle person. v.i. To bring forth lambs.
Dith'yramb s. An ancient Greek hymn in honour of Bacchus; a wild, impetuous song
Chimb s. The edge of a cask.
Limb s. A leg or arm; branch of a tree; edge of disc or sun, moon, etc.; graduated arc of sextant, etc.; (*slang*) a mischievous imp. v.t. To dismember.

Climb v.i. and t. To creep up step by step; to ascend, rise.
Bomb s. A hollow metal contrivance filled with high explosives. v.t. To attack with these.
Comb s. A toothed implement for separating hair, wool, etc.; the crest of a cock or of a wave; wax structure in which bees store honey. v.t. To separate and adjust with a comb. v.i. To roll over, as the crest of a wave.
Cat'acomb s. A subterranean burying passage.
Cock's-comb s. The comb of a cock; a fool's cap; various plants.
Cox'comb s. The comb worn in jesters' caps; the cap itself; a fop, a vain pretender.
Hon'eycomb s. The waxy structure made by bees for honey; similar formation of cells
Rhomb s. An equilateral parallelogram with oblique angles.
Aplomb' s. Assurance; self-possession.
Coulomb' s. Unit of quantity in measuring electricity.
Coomb s. A measure for corn (four bushels); a combe.
Stromb s. A gasteropod of tropic seas.
Tomb s. A grave, sepulchral monument. v.t. To bury.
Hec'atomb s. A great sacrifice (especially of 100 oxen).
Entomb' v.t. To put in a tomb; to bury.
Disentomb' v.t. To exhume, disinter.
Womb s. Organ of females in which the young is developed; any cavity.
Succumb' v.i. To give way, submit; to die.
Dumb a. Unable to speak, mute; speechless, taciturn.
Rhumb s. Any point of the compass; a line cutting all the meridians at the same angle.
Thumb s. The short thick finger. v.t. To soil with the fingers, handle awkwardly.
Plumb s. A plummet. a. Perpendicular; true, level. v.t. To adjust by the plummet; to examine by tests, to ascertain the depth or capacity of.
Numb a. Torpid; deprived of sensation and motion. v.t. To benumb.
Benumb' v.t. To render incapable of feeling, etc., especially by cold.
Crumb s. The soft part of bread; a fragment. v.t. To break into or cover with crumbs.
Bread'crumb s. A crumb of bread.
Cor'ymb s. An inflorescence, the top of which forms an even surface.
Bob s. Anything that plays loosely, or with jerks; (*slang*) a shilling v.t. To move in a short jerking manner. v.i. To have a jerking motion.
Cabob' s. A small piece of meat roasted with spices.
Na'bob s. A prince in the old Mogul Empire, a very rich man.
Cob s. A round lump; top or head of anything; a stout horse; a spider; a nut; composition of straw and clay for building; a male swan. v.t. To flog on the breech.
Kin'cob s. A rich East Indian textile fabric.
Fob s. A watch-pocket, especially in breeches' waistband. v.t. To put in one's pocket; to cheat, impose upon.
Gob s. The mouth, a mouthful, saliva.
Hob s. Part of grate on which things are put to be kept warm, a peg; a hobnail.
Job s. A piece of work; lucrative business; a piece of jobbery; a stab, prod. v.t. To let out or engage for hire; to stab or prod. v.i. To work at chance jobs or as a jobber; to let out horses.
Lob s. A lout; a slow underhand ball at cricket.
Blob s. A rounded drop, blot, or patch.
Mob s. A crowd, disorderly assembly. v.t. To attack in a mob.
Demob' v.t. (*Slang*) To demobilize.
Nob s. (*Slang*) The head; a swell; a point at cribbage.
Hob'nob v.i. To drink with, be intimate with.
Knob s. A rounded protuberance; a hard bunch.
Snob s. A vulgar person aping gentility; an upstart.
Rob v.t. To deprive of by force or unlawfully; to steal from.
Car'ob s. The Mediterranean locust-tree its fruit.
Throb v.i. To heave, vibrate, beat rapidly. s. A palpitation.
Sob v.i. To heave audibly in sorrow, etc. s. A convulsive sigh, sorrowful sound.
Stob s. A stump, stake.
Swob s. (*Swab*).
Barb s. A beard; the point that stands backward in a fish-hook, etc.; a high-mettled horse. v.t. To furnish with barbs.
Rhu'barb s. A plant of several species, some used in cooking and medicine.
Garb s. Dress, clothes; fashion of dress; an heraldic sheaf of corn. v.t. To attire.
Acerb' a. Sour.
Herb s. A soft-stemmed plant that dies to the root every year.
Pot'herb s. Any herb cooked for food.
Kerb s. Edging to a pavement.
Superb' a. Grand; magnificent; pompous.
Serb s. A native of Serbia; their language. a. Pertaining to Serbia, its people or language.
Verb s. Part of speech which affirms.
Ad'verb s. A modifying word.
Prov'erb s. An old, pithy saying; an adage, saw, byword.
Orb s. A circular or spherical body; a globe. v.t. To form into a circle; to surround.
Corb s. A basket, especially as used in collieries.
Sorb s. The service-tree; its fruit.
Absorb' v.t. To drink in or suck up.
Reabsorb' v.t. To absorb again.
Resorb' v.t. To absorb again.
Sang'uisorb s. A rosaceous plant formerly used as a styptic.
Sub'urb s. Outlying part of a city.
Curb s. Check, restraint, part of a bridle; a kerb-stone. v.t. To control, check, put a curb on.
Perturb' v.t. To agitate, disturb, confuse; to disquiet.
Disturb' v.t. To disquiet, perplex, trouble; to disorder.
Daub v.t. To smear, cover with a soft substance, paint coarsely. s. A smear; coarse painting.
Bedaub' v.t. To daub over, besmear.
Bub s. (*Slang*) Intoxicating drink.

Sill'abub s. A curdled mixture of wine or cider with milk.
Hub'bub s. Confused noise of voices; a tumult.
Beel'zebub s. The prince of evil spirits.
Cub s. The young of certain quadrupeds; a whelp; a mannerless lad. v.i. To bring forth cubs.
Dub v.t. To confer knighthood or a dignity upon, to tap with the sword; to speak of as, nickname; to trim; to smear with grease. v.i. To make the sound of a drum.
Rub-a-dub s. The sound of a drum.
Fub s. and v. Fob.
Hub s. The central cylindrical part of a wheel; (*slang*) a husband.
Chub s. A coarse river-fish.
Blub v.i. (*Slang*) To weep noisily.
Club s. A heavy staff; a stick of various forms used to strike the ball at golf, hockey, etc.; a suit at cards; an association for some common object, its meeting-place. v.t. To beat with a club. v.i. To join for some common purpose.
Slub s. A roll of wool slightly twisted. v.t. To draw out and twist (wool).
Nub s. A small lump, as of coal; a tangle.
Snub v.t. To slight offensively, check with sarcasm. s. A rebuff, check; a short or flat nose.
Pub s. (*Slang*) A public-house, tavern.
Rub v.t. To wipe, scour, polish; to smear with a substance. v.i. To move along with pressure or difficulty; to chafe. s. Friction; act of rubbing; an obstruction, difficulty; a rubber (in games).
Scrub v.t. To rub with a brush or something rough for cleaning. v.i. To use a brush, etc. s. A hard rub or wash; a worn-out brush; close, low bushes; a parsimonious fellow. a. Mean.
Drub v.t. To beat heartily, to cudgel.
Cher'ub s. A celestial spirit; a beautiful child.
Grub s. A caterpillar, maggot; (*slang*) food; a grimy person. v.t. To dig or root up.
Shrub s. A woody plant, a dwarf tree; a sweet, Oriental drink.
Sub s. (*Slang*) A subaltern, sub-editor, subscription, etc. v.i. To act as a substitute, etc.; to receive portion of pay in advance.
Tub s. An open wooden vessel for water, butter, etc.; a clumsy boat; a bath. v.t. To place in a tub; to bathe.
Stub s. A stump, remaining part. v.t. To grub up by the roots.
Waac s. A member of the *W*omen's *A*uxiliary *A*rmy *C*orps.
Tom'bac s. An alloy of copper and zinc.
Ipecac' s. Ipecacuanha.
Tacamahac' s. The N. American balsam poplar; an aromatic yellowish resin.
Gai'ac s. The tonka-bean of French Guiana.
Guai'ac s. Wood or resin from the guaiacum.
Zo'diac s. An imaginary celestial zone extending about 8 degrees each side of the ecliptic.
Car'diac a. Relating to the heart or to the upper orifice of the stomach. s. A stimulant for the heart or digestive organs.
Endocar'diac a. Pertaining to the endocardium.
Elegi'ac a. Pertaining to or like elegies; suited to elegy, sorrowful.
Cœ'liac a. Pertaining to the belly.
Geneth'liac a. Pertaining to astrological nativities. s. One skilled in casting horoscopes.
Il'iac a. Pertaining to the smaller intestines or to the hip-bone.
Doch'miac a. Pertaining to or consisting of dochmii. s. A line composed of these.
Ma'niac s. A madman. a. Raving mad.
Megaloma'niac s. One afflicted with megalomania; a very self-important person.
Angloma'niac s. One who has an excessive liking for English institutions, etc.
Monoma'niac s. One afflicted with monomania. a. Pertaining to this.
Dipsoma'niac s. One with a morbid craving for alcohol.
Kleptoma'niac s. One having an irresistible propensity to thievishness.
Demo'niac a. Pertaining to or possessed by demons; frantic. s. One possessed by a demon.
Simo'niac s. One guilty of simony.
Ammo'niac a. Of or belonging to ammonia.
Clun'iac s. A member of a reformed branch of the Benedictines. a. Pertaining to this order.
Paranoi'ac a. and s. Suffering from or one afflicted with paranoia.
Hypochon'driac a. Pertaining to or affected with hypochondria. s. A person so affected.
Ther'iac s. An antidote against poisonous bites.
Celer'iac s. A variety of celery.
Hyster'iac s. One subject to hysteria.
Syr'iac s. The language of the ancient Syrians. a. Pertaining to this or to Syria.
Antaphrodis'iac s. A drug which decreases sexual desire.
Sympo'siac a. Pertaining to a symposium. s. A meeting; table-talk at such.
Dionys'iac s. Pertaining to Bacchus or his worship.
Munt'jac s. A small deer of S.E. Asia.
Lac s. A red, resinous substance; 100,000 (of rupees).
Li'lac s. A sweet-scented shrub; the pale purple colour of its flower.
Shellac' s. Lac melted into thin plates.
Tar'mac s. A tar mixture for road-making.
Su'mac s. A shrub whose leaves are used in tanning, etc.
Alm'anac s. A calendar; a year-book.
Co'gnac s. A pure brandy from the grape.
Cal'pac s. An Oriental cap.
Cham'pac s. (*Champak*).
Bric-a-brac s. Petty antiquarian or artistic curiosities.
Se'rac' s. Pointed mass of ice in a broken glacier.
Tric'-trac s. An old form of backgammon.
Sac s. A membranous bag or small natural cavity in animal or vegetable tissue.
Cul-de-sac s. A street, vessel, etc., closed at one end.
Cor'sac s. The Tartar fox.
Biv'ouac s. A temporary encampment.
An'zac a. Pertaining to the *A*ustralian and *N*ew *Z*ealand *A*rmy *C*orps. s. The forces composing this.
Re'bec s. A rebeck.
Xe'bec (zē'-) s. A small three-masted Mediterranean vessel.
Lim'bec s. An alembic.

Hypoth'ec s. Legal security over property remaining in debtor's possession.
Fen'nec s. An African fox-like animal.
Spec s. (*Slang*) A speculation, chance.
Var'ec s. An impure carbonate of soda.
Tan'rec s. A small insectivorous mammal of Madagascar.
Sec s. Dry, especially of wine.
'Tec s. (*Slang*) A detective.
Tol'tec s. One of an early or legendary Mexican race.
Az'tec s. The leading tribe of ancient Mexico; its language. a. Pertaining to this or to Mexican antiquities
-ic suff. Forming adjectives denoting like or pertaining to, and names of sciences, arts, etc.
Alca'ic a. Of Alcæus, the Greek lyric poet. s. Verse in his metre.
Sponda'ic a. Pertaining to or consisting of spondees.
Farda'ic a. Inductive (of electric currents).
Juda'ic a. Pertaining to the Jews.
Trocha'ic a. Pertaining to or consisting of trochees. s. A trochaic verse.
Archa'ic a. Primitive; belonging to a former stage of civilization.
La'ic a. Secular; not clerical. s. A layman.
Arama'ic a. Belonging to Aram, or to the N. branch of the Semitic group of languages.
Ptolema'ic a. Pertaining to Ptolemy or to his obsolete astronomical system.
Roma'ic a. Pertaining to modern Greek. s. The vernacular of modern Greece.
Cyrena'ic a. Belonging to Cyrene, or to the ancient school of philosophy founded there.
Mesara'ic a. Mesenteric.
Hebra'ic a. Pertaining to the Hebrews or their language.
Cholera'ic a. (*Cholera*).
Mithra'ic a. Pertaining to Mithra or Mithraism.
Sa'ic s. A Levantine sailing-vessel.
Pharasa'ic a. Hypocritically sanctimonious; like the Pharisees.
Pharisa'ic a. Pertaining to or like the Pharisees; making a show of religion; hypocritical.
Mosa'ic s. Inlaid work of coloured glass, stone, etc. a. Pertaining to or composed of this; pertaining to Moses or the law given by him.
Prosa'ic a. Pertaining to or resembling prose; uninteresting.
Ta'ic s. The language of the Siamese, Shans, etc.
Alta'ic a. Pertaining to the Turanian peoples of the Altai Mountains, or to their languages.
Delta'ic a. Pertaining to a delta.
Volta'ic a. Pertaining to electricity chemically produced.
Stanza'ic a. Pertaining to stanzas; in verse formation.
Syllab'ic a. Pertaining to or consisting of a syllable or syllables.
Decasyllab'ic a. Having ten syllables. s. A line of ten syllables.
Hendeca-syllab'ic a. Containing eleven syllables. s. Such a line.
Disyllab'ic a. Consisting of two syllables or disyllables.
Parisyllab'ic a. Having the same number of syllables.
Quadrisyllab'ic a. Consisting of four syllables.
Trisyllab'ic a. (*Trisyllable*).
Multisyllab'ic a. Having many syllables.
Monosyllab'ic a. Pertaining to or consisting of monosyllables.
Octosyllab'ic a. Having eight syllables.
Polysyllab'ic a. Many-syllabled; characterized by long words.
Rab'ic a. Pertaining to rabies.
‖Tab'ic a. Tabetic.
Cubeb'ic a. Like or flavoured with cubeb.
Tereb'ic a. Pertaining to an acid obtained from oil of turpentine.
Iam'bic a. Pertaining to or composed of iambuses. s. A foot or verse composed of these.
Gal'liambic s. A rapidly moving metrical metre.
Choliam'bic a. (*Choliamb*).
Choriam'bic a. and s. (*Choriamb*).
Dithyram'bic a. Pertaining to a dithyramb; wild, boisterous. s. A dithyramb.
Alem'bic s. An obsolete chemical vessel.
Lim'bic a. Pertaining to or forming a limbus; marginal.
Rhom'bic a. Having the form of a rhomb.
Hydropho'bic a. Pertaining to or affected by hydrophobia.
Nio'bic a. Pertaining to or containing niobium.
Micro'bic a. Microbial.
Ytter'bic a. Containing or derived from ytterbium.
Sorb'ic a. Derived from rowan-berries.
Cu'bic a. Having the properties or form of a cube.
Pu'bic a. Pertaining to the pubes or pubis.
Cheru'bic a. (*Cherub*).
Sebac'ic a. Pertaining to the oily matter of animal glands.
Borac'ic a. Of or belonging to borax.
Thorac'ic a. Pertaining to the thorax.
Lac'cic a. Resembling lac or lacquer.
Gynæ'cic a. Pertaining to diseases peculiar to women.
Sili'cic a. Pertaining to or obtained from silica.
Masti'cic a. Pertaining to mastic.
Cal'cic a. Derived from or containing calcium.
Zin'cic (-sik) a. Containing or resembling zinc.
Glu'cic a. Derived from or pertaining to glucose.
Lactu'cic a. Pertaining to or derived from lettuces.
Decad'ic a. (*Decade*).
Rhœad'ic a. Derived from the red poppy.
Haggad'ic a. Pertaining to the Haggadah.
Triad'ic a. Pertaining to a triad; trivalent.
Nomad'ic a. Pertaining to nomads or a wander ing life.
Vanad'ic a. Pertaining to or obtained from vanadium.
Monad'ic a. Pertaining to or like a monad.
Farad'ic a. Applied to certain induced currents of electricity.
Sporad'ic a. Occurring singly or irregularly; separate.
Tetrad'ic a. Pertaining to a tetrad.
Sotad'ic a. Pertaining to the scurrilous style of versification of the ancient Greek poet Sotades.
Molyb'dic a. Pertaining to or containing molybdenum.
Orthopæ'dic a. Pertaining to orthopædy.
Encyclopæ'dic a. Pertaining to an encyclopædia; containing all knowledge; very learned.
Ve'dic (vā'-) a. Pertaining to the Veda.
Spheroid'ic a. Spheroidal.
Druid'ic a. Pertaining to the Druids, their rites, worship, etc.

Scal'dic a. Pertaining to the ancient Scandinavian scalds.
Heral'dic a. Pertaining to heralds or heraldry.
Iceland'ic a. and s. Pertaining to or a native of Iceland.
Wend'ic a. Pertaining to the Wends.
In'dic a. Of India ; Indian.
Syn'dic s. A magistrate ; an officer of Cambridge University.
Od'ic a. Pertaining to od, the force of mesmerism, etc.
O'dic a. Pertaining to or resembling an ode.
Sarco'dic a. Sarcodal.
Geod'ic a. Pertaining to geodes.
Cathod'ic a. (*Cathode*).
Method'ic a. Characterized by method ; systematic.
I'odic a. Pertaining to or containing iodine.
Period'ic a. Pertaining to a period or periods ; performed in a regular revolution ; happening at fixed intervals.
Melod'ic a. Pertaining to, containing, or of the nature of melody.
Plasmod'ic a. Pertaining to plasmodium.
Spasmod'ic a. Consisting in or relating to spasm ; convulsive.
Threnod'ic a. Pertaining to a threnody ; mournful.
Synod'ic a. Synodical.
Episod'ic a. Pertaining to or contained in an episode.
Rhapsod'ic a. Pertaining to or consisting of rhapsody ; unconnected.
Bar'dic a. Pertaining to the bards or to their poetic style.
Sephar'dic a. Pertaining to the Spanish or Portuguese Jews.
Goliar'dic a. Denoting certain mediæval satirical and ribald Latin poems.
Palu'dic a. Paludal.
Talmud'ic a. Pertaining to or contained in the Talmud.
Pu'dic a. Pertaining to the pudenda.
Caffe'ic a. Derived from coffee.
Rhe'ic a. Pertaining to or derived from rhubarb.
The'ic s. An excessive tea-drinker.
Ole'ic a. Pertaining to or derived from oil.
Diarrhœ'ic a. Pertaining to diarrhœa.
Mythopœ'ic a. Producing or giving rise to myths.
Dogmatopœ'ic a. Creating dogmas.
Onomatopœ'ic a. Pertaining to or characterized by onomatopœia.
Chore'ic a. (*Choree*).
Case'ic a. Obtained from cheese.
-fic suff. Forming adjectives from nouns, verbs, etc.
Malef'ic a. Mischief-making ; hateful.
Traf'fic s. Commerce, interchange of commodities, dealings ; persons, goods, etc., carried by railways, etc. ; persons passing to and fro. v.i. and t. To trade, barter.
Rabif'ic a. Causing rabies.
Morbif'ic a. Causing or tending to produce disease.
Pacif'ic a. Peaceable ; conciliatory ; suited to make peace.
Specif'ic a. Clearly distinguished ; precise ; pertaining to or constituting a species. s. An efficacious remedy, etc.
Lucif'ic a. Producing light.
Mucif'ic a. Muciferous.
Deif'ic a. Making divine.
Mellif'ic a. Melliferous.
Prolif'ic a. Bearing offspring, especially abundantly ; fruitful.
Chylif'ic a. (*Chyle*).
Magnif'ic a. Magnificent, grand.
Somnif'ic a. Inducing sleep.
Cornif'ic a. Producing horns or horny substance.
Tenebrif'ic a. Causing darkness.
Sudorif'ic a. Causing sweat. s. A medicine that induces sweating.
Calorif'ic a. Able to produce heat.
Colorif'ic a. Able to impart colour ; highly coloured.
Honorif'ic a. Expressing respect ; granting honour or dignity.
Sonorif'ic a. Producing sound.
Vaporif'ic a. Producing or tending to pass into vapour.
Soporif'ic a. Causing or tending to cause sleep. s. A drug, etc., effecting this.
Torporif'ic a. Producing torpor.
Terrif'ic a. Causing terror ; terrifying.
Horrif'ic a. Striking with horror ; very horrible.
Petrif'ic a. Able to convert into stone.
Aurif'ic a. Able to change other substances into gold.
Sensif'ic a. Producing sensation.
Ossif'ic a. Having power to ossify.
Beatif'ic a. Imparting or completing blissful enjoyment.
Lactif'ic a. Producing milk.
Scientif'ic a. Pertaining to, used in, or depending on the rules of science ; exact ; expert.
Pontif'ic a. Pertaining to the Pope ; relating to priests.
Vivif'ic a. Giving life ; reviving.
Su'fic a. Pertaining to sufism.
-phagic suff. Denoting eating or devouring.
Omophag'ic a. Omophagous.
Hæmorrhag'ic a. Pertaining to or affected with hæmorrhage.
Pelag'ic a. Pertaining to the deep or open sea.
Diallag'ic a. Pertaining to diallage.
Ellag'ic a. Pertaining to gall-nuts or to gallic acid.
Mag'ic s. Sorcery, witchcraft ; power producing astonishing effects. a. Pertaining to, produced by, or using this.
Chorag'ic a. (*Choragus*).
Trag'ic a. Pertaining to or of the nature of tragedy ; calamitous.
Hemipleg'ic a. Pertaining to or afflicted with hemiplegia.
Strateg'ic a. Pertaining to or effected by strategy.
Cardial'gic a. Pertaining to affections of the heart.
Cephalal'gic a. Pertaining to headache. s. A medicine for this.
Splenal'gic a. Pertaining or due to splenalgia.
Hypal'gic a. Characterized by hypalgia.
Gastral'gic a. Pertaining to gastralgia. s. A medicine for this.
Neural'gic a. Pertaining to a diseased condition of the nerves.
Odontal'gic a. and s. Pertaining to or a remedy for toothache.
Notal'gic a. Pertaining to or characterized by notalgia.
Nostal'gic a. Pertaining to or affected with homesickness.
Myal'gic a. Pertaining to or afflicted with cramp.
Diphthong'ic a. Pertaining to diphthongs.
Fun'gic a. Obtained from fungi.
Laryn'gic a. Pertaining to the larynx.
Pedagog'ic a. Suitable for or pertaining to a pedagogue ; pedantic.

Demagog'ic a. Applied to specious or artful methods of political oratory.
Isagog'ic a. Introductory.
Mystagog'ic a. Applied to the interpretation of, or initiation into, divine mysteries.
Log'ic s. The correct inter-connexion of ideas; art of reasoning; mode of arguing.
Dialog'ic a. Of the nature of a dialogue.
Mineralog'ic a. Pertaining to mineralogy.
Archæolog'ic a. Pertaining to archæology.
Geolog'ic a. Pertaining to or forming part of geology.
Theolog'ic a. (*Theological*).
Psycholog'ic a. Pertaining to psychology.
Patholog'ic a. Pathological.
Mytholog'ic a. Pertaining to mythology.
Biolog'ic a. Pertaining to biology.
Sociolog'ic a. Pertaining to social science.
Physiolog'ic a. Physiological.
Philolog'ic a. Pertaining to philology.
Entomolog'ic a. Pertaining to entomology.
Ethnolog'ic a. Pertaining to ethnology.
Chronolog'ic a. Pertaining to chronology.
Meteorolog'ic a. Pertaining to meteorology.
Astrolog'ic a. Pertaining to astrology.
Tautolog'ic a. Consisting of tautology.
Lethar'gic a. Pertaining to or affected with lethargy; drowsy; apathetic.
Geor'gic s. A poem on husbandry. a. Pert. to or treating of rural matters.
Theur'gic a. Supernatural; pertaining to theurgy.
Demiur'gic a. (*Demiurge*).
Metallur'gic a. Pertaining to metallurgy.
Panur'gic a. Able to do all kinds of work.
Dramatur'gic a. Pertaining to the art of dramatic poetry.
Thaumatur'gic a. Pertaining to magic or magicians.
Litur'gic a. Pertaining to public worship or to a liturgy.
Hic s. A sound like a hiccup.
Chic s. Style, smartness. a. Stylish, smart.
Stomach'ic (-măk'-) a. Pertaining to the stomach; aiding digestion. s. A medicine to excite the action of the stomach.
Noa'chic a. Pertaining to Noah or his times.
Tribrach'ic a. Composed of tribrachs.
Bac'chic a. Connected with Bacchus or with revels in his honour.
Stich'ic (stik'-) a. Pertaining to metrical lines.
Elench'ic a. (*Elenctic*).
Oligarch'ic a. Pertaining to an oligarch or oligarchy.
Patriarch'ic a. Of or pertaining to a patriarch or to patriarchy.
Anarch'ic a. Pertaining to anarchy.
Monarch'ic a. Pertaining to monarchy or a monarch; vested in a single ruler.
Hierar'chic a. Pertaining to a hierarch or hierarchy.
Psy'chic a. Pertaining to the mind or soul; spiritual, supernatural. s. One subject to psychical influence.
Seraph'ic a. Pertaining to or befitting a seraph; angelic.
Graph'ic a. Pertaining to the art of writing; pictorial; vivid; indicating by diagrams.
-graph'ic suff. Forming adjectives from words in *-graph* and *-graphy;* and many other adjectives formed from nouns in *-graph.*
Paragraph'ic a. Consisting of or broken in paragraphs.
Telegraph'ic a. Of or belonging to telegraphy; abbreviated.
Digraph'ic a. (*Digraph*).
Calligraph'ic a. Pertaining to beautiful penmanship.
Lexicograph'ic a. Pertaining to lexicography.
Chalcograph'ic a. (*Chalcography*).
Palæograph'ic a. Pertaining to palæography.
Ideograph'ic a. Applied to a symbol that suggests an idea without expressing its name.
Geograph'ic a. Pertaining to geography.
Choreograph'ic a. (*Choreography*).
Lithograph'ic a. Pertaining to lithography.
Chromo-lithograph'ic a. (*Chromolithograph*).
Biograph'ic a. Pertaining to or consisting of biography.
Auto-biograph'ic a. Of the nature of autobiography.
Idiograph'ic a. Pertaining to a signature or trade-mark.
Bibliograph'ic a. Connected with bibliography.
Crystal-lograph'ic a. (*Crystollography*).
Bolograph'ic a. Pertaining to a record of temperature variations.
Holograph'ic a. Written entirely by the hand of the author.
Stylograph'ic a. Applied to a fountain-pen having a point instead of a nib.
Demograph'ic a. (*Demography*).
Anemograph'ic a. Pertaining to the measurement of wind pressure.
Cosmograph'ic a. (*Cosmography*).
Ethnograph'ic a. Pertaining to ethnography.
Phonograph'ic a. Pertaining to or based upon phonography.
Chrono-graph'ic a. (*Chronography*).
Pornograph'ic a. Obscene, indecent.
Topograph'ic a. Pertaining to topography.
Cerograph'ic a. (*Cerography*).
Chirograph'ic a. Pertaining to handwriting.
Chorograph'ic a. (*Chorography*).
Photograph'ic a. Pertaining to photography.
Cryptograph'ic a. Pertaining to ciphers or secret writing.
Cartograph'ic a. (*Cartography*).
Epitaph'ic a. Pertaining to or of the nature of an epitaph.
Del'phic a. Pertaining to Delphi, or the oracle of Apollo there; ambiguous.
Didel'phic a. Pertaining to the didelphia.
Guelph'ic a. Pertaining to the Guelphs.
Troph'ic a. Pertaining to nutrition.
Stroph'ic a. Pertaining to, consisting of, or resembling strophes.
Catastroph'ic a. Of the nature of a catastrophe; disastrous.
Antistroph'ic a. Pertaining to an antistrophe.
Monostroph'ic a. Having one form of strophe only.
Apostroph'ic a. Pertaining to an apostrophe.
Theosoph'ic a. Pertaining to theosophy.
Philosoph'ic a. Pertaining to, according to, or given to philosophy; calm; unimpassioned.
Sapph'ic a. Pertaining to or in the manner of the Greek poetess, Sappho, especially of a metre used by her. s. This metre.
Or'phic a. Pertaining to Orpheus; mysterious; oracular.
Mor'phic a. Morphological.
Metamor'phic a. Subject to or pertaining to metamorphosis; transforming or transformed.
Dimor'phic a. Having two forms.
Trimor'phic a. Pertaining to or characterized by trimorphism.
Endomor'phic a. Pertaining to minerals found as endomorphs.

Pseudomor'phic a. Pseudomorphous.
Theomor'phic a. Having the semblance of God.
Idiomor'phic a. Having a distinct form of its own, especially in crystallography.
Ophiomor'phic a. Having the form of a snake.
Theriomor'phic a. Pertaining to theriomorphism.
Monomor'phic a. Having the same form through successive stages.
Zoomor'phic a. Pertaining to animal forms or to the deification of animals.
Anthropo-mor'phic a. Of or belonging to anthropomorphism.
Hetero-mor'phic a. Differing from type; having dissimilar forms.
Isomor'phic a. Crystallizing in the same geometrical form.
Pantomor'phic a. Assuming all shapes.
Automor'phic a. Ascribing one's own characteristics to another.
Polymor'phic a. Having many forms; capable of wide variation.
Glyph'ic a. Carved, sculptured.
Diaglyph'ic a. (*Diaglyph*).
Triglyph'ic a. Pertaining to or consisting of triglyphs.
Hieroglyph'ic s. A hieroglyph. a. Written in or covered with hieroglyphs.
Pyr'rhic s. A metrical foot of two short syllables; an ancient military dance. a. Pertaining to either of these or to Pyrrhus; denoting a costly victory.
Telepath'ic a. Pertaining to or effected by telepathy.
Philomath'ic a. Having a love of learning or letters.
Chrestomath'ic a. Pertaining to the study of good and useful things.
Gnath'ic a. Pertaining to the jaw.
Prognath'ic a. Having a projecting jaw.
Antipath'ic a. Of contrary character or disposition.
Homœopath'ic a. Belonging to homœopathy; infinitesimally small.
Osteopath'ic a. Pertaining to or affected by osteopathy.
Psychopath'ic a. Pertaining to or afflicted with mental disease.
Idiopath'ic a. Pertaining to a disease that is not occasioned by another.
Allopath'ic a. Pertaining to or practicising allopathy.
Hydropath'ic a. Pertaining to the treatment of disease by the application of water. s. An establishment where this treatment can be obtained.
Heteropath'ic a. Allopathic.
Electropath'ic a. (*Electropathy*).
Neuropath'ic a. Suffering from, or related to, a nervous disease.
Exopath'ic a. Originating externally (of diseases).
Spath'ic a. Resembling spar.
Feldspath'ic a. Pertaining to or containing feldspar.
Eth'ic a. Pertaining to morals; containing principles of morality.
Lith'ic a. Pertaining to stone in the bladder or to lithium.
Megalith'ic a. Applied to prehistoric monuments of colossal stones.
Trilith'ic a. Pertaining to or consisting of triliths.
Eolith'ic a. Describing stone implements of earlier than Palæolithic times.
Palæolith'ic a. Pertaining to the earlier Stone Age.
Neolith'ic a. Pertaining to the later Stone Age.
Monolith'ic a. Consisting of or pertaining to monoliths.
Ornith'ic a. Pertaining to birds.

Xan'thic a. Of a yellowish colour; denoting an oily acid prepared from xanthate of potassium.
Helmin'thic a. Pertaining to intestinal worms.
Labyrinth'ic a. Like a labyrinth.
Absin'thic a. Derived from or pertaining to wormwood; bitter.
Goth'ic a. Pertaining to the Goths or their language; rude, barbarous; applied to a pointed style of architecture and to black-letter type. s. The language of the Goths; Gothic architecture or type.
So'thic a. Denoting the ancient Egyptian method of reckoning the year by the heliacal rising of Sirius.
Myth'ic a. Pertaining to or described in myths; fabulous.
Vocal'ic a. Consisting of vowel sounds, or of the voice.
Vandal'ic a. Pertaining to or resembling the Vandals; barbarous, ferocious, rude.
Cephal'ic a. Pertaining to the head. s. A medicine for pain in the head.
Megacephal'ic a. Large-headed.
Encephal'ic a. Pertaining to the brain or to the contents of the skull.
Mesencephal'ic a. Pertaining to the mesencephalon.
Dolicho-cephal'ic a. Long-headed.
Macrocephal'ic a. Large-headed.
Microcephal'ic a. Having a very small skull.
Procephal'ic a. Pertaining to the anterior part of the brain.
Mesocephal'ic a. Denoting a skull midway between dolicho- and brachycephalic.
Leptocephal'ic a. Having a long and narrow skull.
Brachyce-phal'ic a. Having a skull the breadth of which is not less than four-fifths the length.
Platycephal'ic a. Applied to skulls that are flat and broad in proportion to length.
Omphal'ic a. Pertaining to the navel.
Pa'shalic s. The jurisdiction of a pasha.
Phthal'ic (thal'-) a. Pertaining to or derived from naphthalene.
Naphthal'ic a. Pertaining to or derived from naphthaline.
Ma'lic a. Derived from fruit.
Sal'ic a. Pertaining to or derived from an ancient Frankish Tribe of the lower Rhine.
Salic' a. Applied to a mediæval law regulating succession to a throne.
Ital'ic a. Applied to sloping type; pertaining to ancient Italy or its peoples apart from Rome.
Oxal'ic a. Obtained from, or pertaining to, sorrel (Lat. *oxalis*).
Philobib'lic a. Fond of books or literature.
Pub'lic a. Pertaining to the people; common; generally known. s. The people at large; (*slang*) a public-house.
Repub'lic s. A commonwealth.
Cyc'lic a. Pertaining to or recurring in a cycle; arranged in whorls; connected with a series of legends.
Hemicy'clic s. Arranged in spirals (of parts of an inflorescence, etc.).
Encyc'lic a. Sent to many persons or places.
Geocy'clic a. Pertaining to the revolutions of the earth.
Gael'ic a. Pertaining to the Gaels or their language. s. The language of the Gaels or Celts.
Goidel'ic a. Pertaining to the Goidels.
Angel'ic a. Of the nature or character of an angel.

Nickel'ic a. Pertaining to or containing nickel.
Rel'ic s. A fragment remaining; a memorial, especially of a saint, etc.
Tel'ic a. Expressing purpose (of words).
Philatel'ic a. Pertaining to stamp collecting.
Exil'ic a. Pertaining to exile, especially to that of the Jews in Babylon.
Pre-exil'ic a. Before the Exile (of the Jews to Babylon).
Medal'lic a. Pertaining to medals.
Gal'lic a. Pertaining to Gaul or France; of or obtained from galls on plants.
Pyrogal'lic a. Produced from gallic acid by heat.
Phal'lic a. Pertaining to the phallus, or to phallism, a primitive form of worship.
Thal'lic a. Applied to compounds of thallium.
Metal'lic a. Like or pertaining to metal.
Bimetal'lic a. Pertaining to a currency of two metals in a fixed ratio.
Non-metal'lic a. (*Negative*).
Monometal'lic a. Pertaining to monometallism.
Interval'lic a. Pertaining to an interval.
Fel'lic a. Pertaining to gall.
Vanil'lic a. Pertaining to or obtained from vanilla.
Cyril'lic a. Applied to the alphabet of the Slavs belonging to the Greek Church.
Idyl'lic a. Pertaining to or fitted for an idyll; picturesquely simple.
Podophyll'ic a. Pertaining to the may-apple or its products
Diabol'ic a. Pertaining to the devil; devilish; wickedly cruel or savage.
Parabol'ic a. Expressed by a parable; generated by the revolution of a parabola, having the form of a parabola.
Metabol'ic a. Of or characterized by change.
Holometabol'ic a. Applied to insects which undergo complete metamorphosis.
Ecbol'ic a. Producing abortion.
Embol'ic a. Pertaining to an embolus or to embolism.
Symbol'ic a. In the nature of or pertaining to a symbol; representative.
Carbol'ic a. Derived from coal or coal-tar. s. An antiseptic and disinfectant acid.
Hyperbol'ic a. Of the nature of an hyperbola; containing or relating to hyperbole.
Col'ic s. Pain in the intestines or bowels.
Æo'lic a. Of or belonging to Æolia, a part of ancient Greece.
Chol'ic a. Pertaining to bile.
Melanchol'ic a. Disordered by melancholy; gloomy.
Alcohol'ic a. Pertaining to or containing alcohol.
Cath'olic a. Universal; general; liberal; impartial; belonging to the whole body of Christians, or to the Latin Church as distinct from the Protestants. s. A member of the Catholic, or, especially, of the Roman Catholic, Church.
Variol'ic a. Pertaining or due to smallpox.
Vitriol'ic a. Pertaining to or having the qualities of vitriol; very caustic, malignant.
Frol'ic v.i. To gambol, play pranks. s. A merry prank; a sense of mirth. a. Joyous, frisky.
Petro'lic a. Pertaining to petroleum or petrol.
Diastol'ic a. Pertaining to diastole.
Epistol'ic a. Like a letter; consisting of epistles
Apostol'ic a. Of or belonging to the Apostles or their spiritual successors.
Systol'ic a. Pertaining to systole.
Gar'lic s. A bulbous plant with strong onion-like qualities.
Aulic' a. Of or belonging to the Council of the Holy Roman Empire.
Hydraul'ic a. Pertaining to hydraulics or to fluids in motion.
Salicyl'ic a. Pertaining to or derived from the willow, or from salicin or salicyl.
Odyl'ic a. Odic.
Bey'lic s. The district under a bey.
Hy'lic a. Relating to matter, material.
Methyl'ic a. Pertaining to or containing methyl.
Dactyl'ic a. Consisting of or pertaining to dactyls.
Am'ic a. Derived from or pertaining to ammonia.
Adam'ic a. Pertaining to or resembling Adam; naked.
Pre-Adam'ic a. Pre-Adamite.
Gam'ic a. Pertaining to sex (of plants).
Agam'ic a. Characterized by the absence of sexual action.
Monogam'ic a. Pertaining to or involving monogamy.
Phanerogam'ic a. Pertaining to or like a phanerogam.
Cryptogam'ic a. Pertaining to the Cryptogamia.
Cleistogam'ic a. Applied to plants that have non-opening and self-fertilizing flowers.
Exogam'ic a. Pertaining to exogamy.
Polygam'ic a. Polygamous.
Abraham'ic a. Pertaining to Abraham, or to his patriarchal dispensation.
Thalam'ic a. Pertaining to or resembling a thalamus.
Islam'ic a. Pertaining to Islam; Mohammedan.
Dynam'ic a. Pertaining to forces not in equilibrium, or to strength or force; energetic.
Adynam'ic a. Weak; without force.
Cera'mic a. Pertaining to pottery.
Dioram'ic a. Pertaining to diorama.
Cycloram'ic a. (*Cyclorama*).
Cosmoram'ic a. (*Cosmorama*).
Panoram'ic a. Pertaining to or like a panorama; widely extended (of a view); comprehensive.
Balsam'ic a. Containing or having the properties of balm or balsam.
Potam'ic a. Pertaining to rivers.
Senticæ'mic a. Pertaining to or due to septicæmia.
Anæ'mic a. Characterized by lack or poorness of blood.
Spanæ'mic a. Affected with spanæmia.
Uræ'mic a. Pertaining to or affected by uræmia.
Pyæ'mic a. Pertaining to or caused by pyæmia.
Racem'ic a Pertaining to or obtained from grape-juice.
Academ'ic a. Of, belonging to, or in the way of an academy or academician; scholarly, precise.
Ec'demic a. Coming from abroad (especially of diseases).
Epidem'ic a. Prevalent, affecting the whole community. s. A disease affecting many persons at once.
Pandem'ic a. Incident to the whole population (of diseases).
Endem'ic a. Peculiar to a locality or people. s. An endemic disease.
Chem'ic a. Pertaining to chemistry or drugs.

Alchem'ic a. Pertaining to alchemy.
Polem'ic s. A controversialist or controversy. a. Polemical.
Theorem'ic a. Theorematic.
Totem'ic a. Pertaining to totems or totemism.
System'ic a. Pertaining to the bodily system as a whole.
Sphyg'mic a. Pertaining to the pulse.
Ohm'ic a. Pertaining to ohms.
Logarith'mic a. Pertaining to or consisting of logarithms.
Rhyth'mic a. Pertaining to rhythm.
Mim'ic a. Imitative; imitating, sham. s. One who mimics. v.t. To imitate, especially in ridicule; to ape.
Pantomim'ic a. Pertaining to pantomime; representing characters, etc., in dumb-show.
Ophthal'mic a. Pertaining to or in the region of the eye.
Parallelo-gram'mic a. Having the properties of a parallelogram.
Com'ic a. Pertaining to comedy; funny, laughable.
Heroicom'ic a. Partaking of the heroic and the ludicrous.
Nom'ic a. In accord with routine; customary (especially of spelling); pertaining to a nome.
Gnom'ic a. Dealing in maxims; sententious.
Physiognom'ic (-ŏnom'-) a. Pertaining to physiognomy.
Pyrogno'mic a. Becoming incandescent when heated.
Econom'ic a. Pertaining to economy or economics; frugal.
Physiognom'ic a. Pertaining to physignomy.
Zoonom'ic a. Pertaining to zoonomy.
Deuteronom'ic a. Pertaining to the laws contained in Deuteronomy, or to the book itself.
Agronom'ic a. Pertaining to agricultural economics.
Metronom'ic a. Pertaining to the metronome or the marking of musical time.
Gastronom'ic a. Pertaining to the art of good feeding.
Autonom'ic a. Self-governing; independent.
Plutonom'ic s. Pertaining to plutonomy or economics.
Bro'mic a. Containing or pertaining to bromine.
Theobro'mic a. Pertaining to cocoa or chocolate.
Orthodrom'ic a. Pertaining to orthodromics.
Prodrom'ic a. Prodromal.
Loxodrom'ic a. Pertaining to oblique sailing.
Chro'mic a. Pertaining to chromium.
Dichro'mic a. Having or perceiving only two colours.
Atom'ic a. Pertaining to atoms or to the theory of atoms.
Diatom'ic a. Containing only two atoms.
Triatom'ic a. Having three atoms to the molecule.
Anatom'ic a. Pertaining to anatomy.
Phantom'ic a. Of the nature of a phantom.
Entom'ic a. Relating to insects.
Dichotom'ic a. (*Dichotomy*).
Microtom'ic a. Pertaining to the microtome or to microtomy.
Alexiphar'mic a. Pertaining to antidotes against poison. s. An antidote.
Ptar'mic a. Exciting sneezing.
Derm'ic a. Pertaining to the skin.
Taxider'mic a. Pertaining to taxidermy.
Ender'mic a. Acting through or applied to the skin.
Hypoder'mic a. Pertaining to parts under the skin, or to subcutaneous injections.

Ther'mic a. Pertaining to or due to heat.
Diather'mic a. Diathermanous.
Geother'mic a. (*Geothermal*).
Endosper'mic a. (*Endosperm*).
For'mic a. Pertaining to or produced by ants.
Mias'mic a. Miasmatous.
Plas'mic a. Pertaining to protoplasm or plasma.
Protoplas'mic a. Pertaining to or of the nature of protoplasm.
Maras'mic a. Pertaining to or affected with marasmus.
Phantas'mic a. Phatasmal; illusive; unreal.
Strabis'mic a. Strabismal.
Seis'mic (sīz'-) a. Pertaining to or produced by an earthquake.
Aphoris'mic a. Characterized by the use of aphorisms.
Os'mic a. Of or pertaining to osmium.
Cos'mic a. Pertaining to the universe; rising or setting with the sun.
Macrocos'mic a. Pertaining to the macrocosm.
Microcos'mic a. Pertaining to or resembling a microcosm.
Endos'mic a. Pertaining to endosmosis.
Cataclys'mic a. (*Cataclysm*).
Hu'mic a. Pertaining to mould.
Homonym'ic a. Homonymous.
Synonym'ic a. Of or pertaining to synonyms.
Eponym'ic a. Pertaining to eponyms.
Patronym'ic s. A name derived from an ancestor.
Metronym'ic a. Derived from the name of a mother or maternal ancestor. s. A name thus derived.
Metonym'ic a. Pertaining to or characterized by metonymy.
Zy'mic a. Pertaining to fermentation.
Enzym'ic a. Pertaining to enzmes.
Volcan'ic a. Pertaining to or produced by volcanoes.
Ocean'ic a. Pertaining to, occurring in, or like the ocean.
Interocean'ic a. Between or connecting two oceans.
Mangan'ic a. Pertaining to, containing, or resembling manganese.
Permangan'ic a. Containing manganese in its highest valency.
Organ'ic a. Pertaining to, consisting of, containing, or produced by an organ or the organs; pert. to the animal and vegetable worlds; organized.
Inorgan'ic a. Not being or derived from an organized structure; not having organs; pertaining to all elements and their compounds except those of carbon.
Mechan'ic a. Mechanical. s. An artisan, skilled workman, especially with or on machinery.
Theophan'ic a. Pertaining to theophany.
Aristophan'ic a. In the manner of Aristophanes.
Messian'ic a. Pertaining to Christ as the Messiah.
Melan'ic a. Dark-complexioned; negroid.
Porcellan'ic a. Of the nature of porcelain.
Roman'ic a. Derived from the Latin; pertaining to Rome, its people, or their descendants.
Alderman'ic a. Characteristic of or pertaining to an alderman.
German'ic a. Pertaining to Germany, its peoples or language. s. The primitive Teutonic language.
Talisman'ic a. Of the nature of a talisman; magical.
Pan'ic s. Sudden fright or fear, especially when groundless; public alarm; a commercial or financial crisis. a. Pertaining to this.

Tympan'ic a. Like a drum; pertaining to the tympanum.
Hispan'ic a. Pertaining to Spain or its people.
Koran'ic a. Pertaining to or derived from the Koran.
Uran'ic a. Pertaining to or containing uranium.
Charlatan'ic a. (*Charlatan.*)
Satan'ic a. Pertaining to, resembling, or emanating from Satan; devilish.
Tetan'ic a. Characteristic of tetanus. s. A medicine acting through the spinal cord.
Puritan'ic a. Pertaining to the Puritans, their doctrines, etc.; precise in religious observance; rigid.
Titan'ic a. Enormous, or superhuman strength or endowments; derived from titanium.
Sultan'ic a. Characteristic of a sultan.
Galvan'ic a. Applied to electricity produced by chemical action; voltaic.
Cyan'ic a. Derived from cyanogen.
Pic'nic s. A pleasure excursion with outdoor meal. v.i. To go on a picnic.
Saracen'ic a. Pertaining to the Saracens, their art, etc.
Scen'ic a. Pertaining to the stage; theatrical.
Metagen'ic a. Pertaining to metagenesis.
Glycogen'ic a. Pertaining to glycogen.
Pathogen'ic a. Pertaining to the origin and development of disease.
Pythogen'ic a. Produced by putrescence or filth.
Diogen'ic a. Cynical.
Crystallogen'ic a. (*Crystallogeny*).
Thermogen'ic a. Thermogenetic.
Monogen'ic a. Pertaining to monogenesis or monogenism; reproducing in one way only.
Hysterogen'ic a. Producing hysteria; hysterogenetic.
Phosphorogen'ic a. Causing phosphorescence.
Saprogen'ic a. Producing or pertaining to decay; decomposing.
Nitrogen'ic a. Nitrogenous.
Somatogen'ic a. Originating within the body.
Photogen'ic a. Producing or produced by the action of light; phosphorescent.
Protogen'ic a. Primitive; of earliest origin.
Eugen'ic a. Pertaining to healthy and sound breeding.
Polygen'ic a. Forming more than one compound with hydrogen.
Oxygen'ic a. Pertaining to, containing, or resembling oxygen.
Lichen'ic a. Pertaining to or obtained from lichens.
Sphen'ic a. Wedge-shaped.
Sthen'ic a. Having excessive vital or vigorous action.
Asthe'nic a. Characterized by debility.
Neurasthe'nic a. Pertaining to, resembling, or afflicted with neurasthenia.
Callisthen'ic a. Pertaining to light gymnastic exercises.
Demosthen'ic a. In the manner of Demosthenes.
Hygien'ic a. Pertaining to sanitary science and the laws of health.
Galen'ic a. According to the system of Galen, the ancient Greek physician; pertaining to or containing galena.
Selen'ic a. Derived from or containing selenium.
Hellen'ic a. Pertaining to or characteristic of ancient Greece.
Splen'ic a. Pertaining to or affecting the spleen.

Œcumen'ic a. Œcumenical.
Phren'ic a. Pertaining to the diaphragm.
Arsen'ic s. An element the oxide of which is highly poisonous.
Pyrolig'nic a. Pyroligneous, derived from wood by heat.
Tech'nic a. Technical. s. Technics.
Pyrotech'nic a. Pertaining to fireworks.
Polytech'nic a. Pertaining to the various industrial arts and sciences, or to an institution giving instruction in these. s. A technical college.
Splanch'nic a. Pertaining to the intestines or bowels.
Strych'nic a. Pertaining to or produced by strychnine.
Eth'nic a. Pertaining to races not Jewish or Christian; based on distinctions of race.
Rabbin'ic a. Pertaining to the Jewish rabbis or their learning. s. The later Hebrew language.
Jacobin'ic a. Pertaining to the Jacobites or their principles.
Vaccin'ic a. Pertaining to vaccine or vaccinia.
Succin'ic a. Pertaining to or derived from amber.
Kin'nikinic' s. Willow or sumac leaves prepared for smoking.
Clin'ic s. Hospital teaching with practical examples from patients; a class so taught.
Aclin'ic a. Without inclination or magnetic dip.
Policlin'ic s. A dispensary, out-patients' department.
Triclin'ic a. Having the three axes unequal and oblique (of crystals).
Isoclin'ic a. Having the same dip or magnetic inclination.
Polyclin'ic s. A general hospital.
Fellin'ic a. Pertaining to gall.
Kaolin'ic a. Pertaining to or resembling kaolin.
Brahmin'ic a. Pertaining to the Brahmins or Brahminism.
Fulmin'ic a. Pertaining to or capable of detonation.
Encrin'ic a. Encrinal.
Sin'ic a. Chinese.
Platin'ic a. Pertaining to or containing platinum.
Actin'ic a. Pertaining to actinism.
Diactin'ic a. Capable of transmitting actinic rays.
Turpentin'ic a. Containing or resembling turpentine.
Quin'ic a. Pertaining to quinine; obtained from cinchona bark.
Vin'ic a. Pertaining to or derived from wine.
Hym'nic a. Relating to hymns.
Tyran'nic a. Tyrannical.
Tan'nic a. Derived from or pertaining to tan or tannin.
Britan'nic a. British; pertaining to Great Britain or to the British Empire.
Stan'nic a. Pertaining to tin.
Fin'nic a. Belonging to the Finns or their language.
Hun'nic a. Pertaining to the ancient Huns or their language.
Pharaon'ic a. Pertaining to the ancient Egyptian Pharaohs or their age.
Carbon'ic a. Derived from or pertaining to carbon.
Bubon'ic a. Applied to an epidemic disease characterized by buboes.
Con'ic a. Pertaining to a cone; cone-shaped.
Lacon'ic a. Sententious; pithy

Dracon'ic a. Excessively severe.
Mecon'ic a. Contained in or obtained from the poppy.
Icon'ic a. Pertaining to or consisting of pictures; of conventional type.
Zircon'ic a. Pertaining to or derived from zirconium.
Glycon'ic s. A classical metre of three trochees and a dactyl.
Adon'ic a. Pertaining to Adonis, or to a metre composed of a dactyl and a spondee.
Chalcedon'ic a. (*Chalcedony*).
Hedon'ic a. Pertaining to pleasure.
Chelidon'ic a. Pertaining to the celandine
Sardon'ic a. Bitter, mocking, heartless.
Chameleon'ic a. (*Chameleon*).
Napoleon'ic a. Pertaining to Napoleon I, his family, or times.
Agon'ic a. Making no angle.
Trigon'ic a. (*Trigon*).
Geogon'ic a. Pertaining to geogony.
Theogon'ic a. Pertaining to or in the manner of a theogony.
Cosmogon'ic a. Pertaining to cosmogony or a cosmogony.
Phon'ic a. Phonetic.
Cataphon'ic a. Pertaining to cataphonics.
Telephon'ic a. Pertaining to the telephone.
Siphon'ic a. Siphonal.
Symphon'ic a. Pertaining to or resembling a symphony.
Cacophon'ic a. Strident, discordant.
Homophon'ic a. In unison; having the same pitch.
Microphon'ic a. Pertaining to the microphone.
Euphon'ic a. Agreeable in sound; pertaining to euphony.
Polyphon'ic a. Having many sounds or a combination of melodic structure; contrapuntal.
Typhon'ic a. Pertaining to or like a typhoon.
Pyrrhon'ic a. Pyrrhonean; sceptical.
Gnathon'ic a. Parasitical, sycophantic.
Chthon'ic a. Pertaining to the underworld.
Autochthon'ic a. Sprung from the soil, native.
Python'ic a. Oracular; prophetic.
Brython'ic a. Belonging to the Celtic races of Britain.
Ion'ic a. Denoting an order of architecture having capitals with volutes; pertaining to ions. s. The Greek dialect of Ionia.
Talion'ic a. Pertaining to or consisting in retaliation.
Ganglion'ic a. Pertaining to a ganglion.
Histrion'ic a. Pertaining to actors; theatrical; stagy.
Clon'ic a. (*Clonus*).
Cyclon'ic a. Pertaining to a cyclone.
Anticyclon'ic a. Pertaining to an anticyclone.
Cinnamon'ic a. (*Cinnamon*).
Demon'ic a. Of the nature of or inspired by demons.
Eudemon'ic a. Pertaining to eudemonism.
Hegemon'ic a. Predominant, controlling.
Mnemon'ic a. Pertaining to or aiding the memory.
Antimon'ic a. Pertaining to antimony.
Pulmon'ic a. Pulmonary. s. One having lung-disease; a medicine for this.
Scammon'ic a. Derived from scammony.
Solomon'ic a. Pertaining to Solomon; very wise.
Gnomon'ic a. Pertaining to the art of dialling.
Patho-gnomon'ic a. Characteristic of a disease.
Harmon'ic a. Pertaining to harmony; harmonious. s. An harmonic tone.
Philharmon'ic a. Loving music.
Anharmon'ic a. Not harmonic.
Enharmon'ic a. Having intervals less than a semitone.
Inharmonic' a. Not harmonic.
Sermon'ic a. Pertaining to sermons; in the style of a sermon.
Pneumon'ic a. Pertaining to the lungs. s. A medicine for lung affections.
Canon'ic a. Pertaining to a canon or to canon law; authoritative.
Zoon'ic a. Derived from or contained in animal substances.
Japon'ic a. Japanese.
Geopon'ic a. Pertaining to agriculture.
Aaron'ic a. Pertaining to Aaron or to the Jewish priesthood.
Macaron'ic a. Applied to comic verse in which words of different languages are used together.
Peristeron'ic a. Pertaining to pigeons.
Chron'ic a. Relating to time, of long duration; recurring; (*slang*) severe.
Iron'ic a. Expressing one thing and meaning the opposite.
Electron'ic a. Pertaining to electrons or the theory concerning them.
Byron'ic a. Moody, theatrical; like Byron's poetry.
Mason'ic a. Pertaining to freemasonry.
Opson'ic a. Pertaining to or affected by opsonin.
Parson'ic a. Pertaining to or characteristic of a parson.
Ton'ic a. Pertaining to tones or sounds; increasing the strength. s. The key-tone of the scale; a strengthening medicine.
Aton'ic a. Unaccented; wanting in bodily health.
Diaton'ic a. Of the regular musical scale without chromatic alterations.
Platon'ic a. Pertaining to the Greek philosopher Plato, his school, opinions, or philosophy.
Pentaton'ic a. Consisting of five musical tones.
Sub-ton'ic s. The note next below the tonic; a vocal consonant.
Tecton'ic a. Pertaining to construction; constructive.
Architecton'ic a. Belonging to construction; systematic.
Meton'ic a. Applied to the lunar cycle of nineteen years.
Epiton'ic a. Overstrained.
Milton'ic a. Pertaining to or resembling Milton's style; sonorous; sublime.
Enton'ic a. Exhibiting abnormal tension (of muscles, etc.).
Synton'ic a. Having syntony.
Orthoton'ic a. Having its own accent.
Neuroton'ic s. A medicine to strengthen the nervous system.
Teuton'ic a. Pertaining to the Germanic races. s. Their ancient language.
Pluton'ic a. Pertaining to Pluto; pertaining to igneous rocks.
Slavon'ic a. Of Slav race. s. The Slavonic language; a Slav.
Embryon'ic a. Pertaining to an embryo; undeveloped, immature.
Amphictyon'ic a. Applied to an ancient Greek council of states.
Ozon'ic a. Pertaining to, like, or containing ozone.
Car'nic a. Pertaining to the Tyrolese and Carinthian Alps and the inhabitants.
Satur'nic a. Affected with lead-poisoning.

Cerau'nic a. Due or pertaining to thunder and lightning.
Pu'nic a. Pertaining to the Carthaginians; treacherous.
Ru'nic a. Pertaining to or cut in runes; pertaining to the ancient Scandinavians. s. A style of type.
Tu'nic s. A short outer coat; a covering membrane.
Cyn'ic s. A Greek philosopher who professed contempt for riches, etc.; a misanthrope, a morose person.
Misogyn'ic a. Woman-hating.
Polygyn'ic a. Applied to plants having flowers with many pistils.
Epiplo'ic a. Pertaining to the epiploon.
Dyspno'ic a. Pertaining to dyspnœa.
Hero'ic a. Pertaining to or becoming a hero; intrepid, noble; relating to the deeds of heroes; epic.
Dichro'ic a. Exhibiting different colours when viewed from different directions.
Xanthochro'ic a. Denoting the fair-complexioned races.
Melanochro'ic a. Describing the races with dark hair and pale complexion.
Capro'ic a. Pertaining to a goat.
Tro'ic a. Trojan.
Sto'ic s. A disciple of Zeno, the Greek philosopher (fourth century B.C.). a. Stoical.
Zo'ic a. Pertaining to life; fossiliferous.
Benzo'ic a. Pertaining to or derived from benzoin.
Malacozo'ic a. Pertaining to the molluscs.
Archæozo'ic a. Pertaining to the dawn of life on earth.
Palæozo'ic a. Applied to the lowest fossil-bearing strata and the earliest forms of life.
Neozo'ic a. Belonging to the later Palæozoic period.
Heliozo'ic a. Heliozoan.
Hylozo'ic a. Pertaining to hylozoism.
Cainozo'ic a. Belonging to the third geological period.
Hypozo'ic a. Beneath the strata containing organic remains.
Microzo'ic a. Pertaining to the microzoa.
Mesozo'ic a. Pertaining to the secondary geological period or strata.
Entozo'ic a. Pertaining to the entozoa.
Protozo'ic a. Pertaining to or caused by protozoa.
Polyzo'ic a. Polyzoal.
Priap'ic a. Priapean.
Sinap'ic a. Pertaining to the mustard family of plants.
Ep'ic a. Composed in a lofty narrative poetical form; heroic. s. A poem in an elevated style, usually describing the deeds of heroes.
Orthoep'ic a. Pertaining to correct speech and pronunciation.
Olym'pic a. Pertaining to Olympia or to the games anciently held there.
Syncop'ic a. Syncopal.
-scop'ic suff. Pertaining to an instrument of observation.
Telescop'ic a. Pertaining to the telescope; collapsible lengthways.
Periscop'ic a. Viewed all round; pertaining to the periscope; denoting optical instruments with concavo-convex lenses.
Kaleidoscop'ic a. Pertaining to the kaleidoscope or its effects.
Orthoscop'ic a. Having correct vision.
Macroscop'ic a. Visible to the naked eye.
Microscop'ic a. Pertaining to the microscope; two small to be visible to unaided sight.
Hygroscop'ic a. Pertaining to or indicated by the hygroscope.
Electroscop'ic a. Pertaining to electroscopy.
Spectroscop'ic a. Pertaining to investigation by means of the spectroscope.
Ethiop'ic a. Belonging or pertaining to Ethiopia.
Canop'ic a. Applied to the jars for the reception of the entrails, etc., of corpses to be mummified, in ancient Egypt.
Sinop'ic a. Resembling or containing sinople.
Hydrop'ic a. Dropsical; resembling dropsy.
Lycanthrop'ic a. Pertaining to lycanthropy.
Theanthrop'ic a. Having both divine and human characters.
Therian-throp'ic a. Pertaining to deities half man and half beast.
Philanthrop'ic a. Characterized by love of and benevolence towards one's fellows.
Psilanthrop'ic a. Pertaining to or embodying psilanthropy.
Misanthrop'ic a Hating mankind; pertaining to a misanthrope.
Trop'ic s. Either of the two parallels of latitude 23½ degrees from the equator which the sun reaches at its greatest declination N. or S. a. Pertaining to the tropics; tropical.
Nyctitrop'ic a. Changing direction at night (of plants).
Orthotrop'ic a. Growing vertically or with a straight stem.
Heliotrop'ic a. Pertaining to or exhibiting heliotropism.
Apheliotrop'ic a. Turning away from the sun.
Allotrop'ic a. Of identical substance but different form.
Isotrop'ic a. Having the same properties in all directions.
Top'ic s. Subject of discourse or present interest.
Metop'ic a. Frontal; pert. to the forehead.
Heterotop'ic a. Pertaining to or characterized by heterotopy.
Presbyo'pic a. Having abnormally long sight.
Myop'ic a. Pertaining to or having short sight.
Lap'pic a. Pertaining to Lapland or its inhabitants.
Hip'pic a. Pertaining to horses or horse-racing.
Philip'pic s. An acrimonious declamation.
Monocar'pic a. Monocarpous.
As'pic s. A jelly used in cookery.
Typ'ic (tip'-) a. Typical.
Stereotyp'ic a. Pertaining to printing from stereotypes.
Daguerreo-typ'ic a. Pertaining to daguerreotype.
Monotyp'ic a. Characterized by a single type or example.
Electrotyp'ic a. Pertaining to electrotypography.
Bar'ic a. Relating to weight; derived from or containing barium.
Centrobar'ic a. Pertaining to the centre of gravity.
Isobar'ic a. Pertaining to isobars; of equal barometric pressure.
Rhabarbar'ic a. Pertaining to rhubard.
Dar'ic s. An ancient Persian gold coin.
Pindar'ic a. After the style of the Greek lyric poet, Pindar. s. An irregular ode.
Stear'ic a. Pertaining to, obtained from, or like stearin or tallow.
Ag'aric a. Pertaining to edible mushrooms.
Margar'ic a. Pertaining to pearl; pearly.

Sacchar'ic a. Pertaining to or obtained from sugar.
Amhar'ic s. The language used at the Abyssinian court.
Gemar'ic a. Pertaining to the Gemara.
Tartar'ic a. Derived from or containing tartar; pertaining to Tartarus or the infernal regions.
Fab'ric s. Frame of anything; a structure, building; cloth, texture.
Cer'ebric a. Cerebral.
Cam'bric s. A fine linen fabric.
Cim'bric a. Pertaining to the Cimbri, an ancient Jutish tribe. s. The language of the Cimbri.
Ru'bric s. The liturgical directions in a prayer-book; a heading, title.
Pic'ric a. Intensely bitter; especially of an acid used in high explosives, etc.
Polyhe'dric a. Having many sides.
Bal'dric s. A shoulder-belt for supporting a bugle, sword, etc.
Thean'dric a. Pertaining to the union of divine and human in Christ.
Cylin'dric a. (*Cylindrical*).
Hy'dric a. Pertaining to or containing hydrogen in chemical combination.
Suber'ic a. Pertaining to, of the nature of or extracted from cork.
Spher'ic a. In the form of a sphere.
Hemispher'ic a. Pertaining to or containing a hemisphere.
Atmospher'ic a. Pertaining to the atmosphere.
Sciather'ic a. Pertaining to sundials.
Diphther'ic a. Pertaining to diphtheria.
Val'eric a. Pertaining to or obtained from valerian.
Cler'ic s. A member of the clergy. a. Clerical.
Choler'ic a. Irascible, irritable.
Metamer'ic a. Pertaining to a metamere or to segmentation; having the same composition and molecular weight but different chemical properties.
Ephemer'ic a. Ephemeral.
Homer'ic a. Pertaining to or like Homer or his poetry.
Isomer'ic a. Having identical elements, molecular weight, etc., but different in physical characteristics and chemical properties.
Anisomer'ic a. Not isomeric.
Tur'meric s. An E. Indian ginger-like plant.
Numer'ic s. The numerical part of a mathematical expression.
Polymer'ic a. Polymerous.
Gener'ic a. Relating to a genus or kind; comprehensive.
Congener'ic a. (*Congenar*).
Phylac'teric a. Pertaining to phylacteries.
Climac'teric s. A critical period in human life. a. Pertaining to such, critical; occurring late in life.
Icter'ic a. Affected with or efficacious against jaundice. s. A remedy for this.
Sphincter'ic a. Sphincteral.
Enter'ic a. Pertaining to the intestines. s. Typhoid fever.
Lienter'ic a. Pertaining to lientery.
Mesenter'ic a. Pertaining to the mesentery.
Dysenter'ic a. Pertaining to, afflicted with dysentery.
Neoter'ic a. Recent in origin, modern.
Esoter'ic a. For the initiated only; private; select.
Exoter'ic a. Public, not secret; easy of comprehension.
Cholester'ic a. (*Cholesterine*).
Hyster'ic a. Hysterical.
Podag'ric a. Pertaining to or afflicted with gout.
Vampir'ic a. Pertaining to or resembling a vampire.
Empir'ic s. A quack, one without training who relies on experience or observation solely. a. Founded or acting on observation; pertaining to quackery.
Satir'ic a. Of the nature of, or conveying, satire; bitter, sarcastic.
Chiv'alric a. (*Chivalry*).
Cym'ric a. Pertaining to the Welsh. s. The Welsh language.
Bor'ic a. Of or containing borax.
Dor'ic a. Dorian (especially of dialect); rustic; denoting the severest style of Greek architecture.
Theor'ic a. Pertaining to public spectacles (in ancient Greece).
Meteor'ic a. Like, consisting of, or pertaining to meteors; brilliant but rapidly fading.
Phantasmagor'ic a. Pertaining to or of the nature of the illusions of phantasmagoria.
Allegor'ic a. Pertaining to or resembling allegory.
Paregor'ic s. An anodyne. a. Assuaging, mitigating.
Chor'ic a. Pertaining to or like a chorus.
Enchor'ic a. Enchorial.
Semaphor'ic a. Pertaining to semaphores.
Metaphor'ic a. Pertaining to metaphor; figurative.
Camphor'ic a. Pertaining to camphor.
Pyrophor'ic a. Pyrophorous.
Phosphor'ic a. Pertaining to phosphorus; phosphorescent.
Plethor'ic a. Characterized by plethora.
Calor'ic s. The fluid formerly supposed to be the cause of heat.
Chlor'ic a. Pertaining to chlorine.
Pylor'ic a. Pertaining to the pylorus.
Armor'ic a. Pertaining to Brittany, the ancient Armorica. s. The Breton language.
Ror'ic a. Pertaining to or like dew.
Psor'ic a. Causing itch or mange.
Rhet'oric s. Art of oratory or of effective or elegant speaking or writing; artificial eloquence; power of persuasion; declamation.
Histor'ic a. Celebrated in history; exhibited in or deduced from historical events.
Prehistor'ic a. Pertaining to the period prior to that known to history.
Fluor'ic a. Containing fluorine.
Cap'ric a. Pertaining to a goat or its odour.
Cu'pric s. Containing copper.
Fer'ric a. Pertaining to or extracted from iron, containing iron in its highest combining power.
Iat'ric a. Relating to medicine or physicians.
Psychiat'ric a. Treating or curing mental disease.
Elec'tric a. Containing, conveying, or produced by electricity; full of spirit and able to communicate it.
Dielec'tric a. Insulating, non-conducting. s. A substance which cannot transmit electricity.
Met'ric a. Metrical; pertaining to the decimal system of weights and measures, etc. s. Science of prosody.
Diamet'ric a. Directly adverse.
Hexamet'ric a. Pertaining to or of the nature of hexameters.
Calorimet'ric a. Pertaining to calorimetry.
Symmet'ric a. Proportional in its parts; having corresponding parts.

Geomet'ric a. Geometrical.
Dynamomet'ric a. Pertaining to a dynamometer or the measure of force.
Anemomet'ric a. Pertaining to wind measurement.
Thermomet'ric a. Pertaining to or made by means of a thermometer.
Clinomet'ric a. (*Clinometer*).
Trigonomet'ric a. Pertaining to trigonometry.
Chronomet'ric a. (*Chronometer*).
Baromet'ric a. Indicated by or pertaining to the barometer.
Isobaromet'ric a. Isobaric.
Hydromet'ric a. (*Hydrometry*).
Chloromet'ric a. (*Cholorometer*).
Isomet'ric a. Pertaining to or characterized by equality of measure.
Anisomet'ric a. Not isometric.
Bathymet'ric a. Pertaining to deep soundings or to life in the ocean depths.
Obstet'ric a. Pertaining to midwifery.
Cit'ric a. Derived from citron.
Ni'tric a. Pertaining to or containing nitrogen.
Vit'ric a. Like glass; pertaining to vitrics.
Tan'tric a. Pertaining to the Tantras.
Cen'tric a. Central.
Acent'ric a. Not having a centre, not about a centre.
Paracen'tric a. Deviating from circularity; changing the distance from a centre.
Eccen'tric a. Deviating from the centre or from the usual practice; not having the axis in the centre, not having the same centre; whimsical; anomalous. s. A mechanical contrivance for converting circular into reciprocal rectilinear motion; an odd, whimsical person.
Concen'tric a. Having a common centre; concentrated.
Geocen'tric a. Applied to astronomical distance relatively to the earth.
Egocen'tric a. Self-centred.
Heliocen'tric a. With reference to the sun as a centre.
Homocen'tric a. Having the same centre.
Anthropocent'ric a. Regarding mankind as the central fact of the universe.
Diop'tric a. Assisting vision by means of refraction of light; pertaining to dioptrics. s. The unit of refractive power.
Catadiop'tric a. Involving both reflection and refraction.
Catop'tric a. Pertaining to reflected light or to mirrors.
Gas'tric a. Pertaining to the stomach.
Agas'tric a. Without any definite alimentary canal.
Digas'tric a. Having a double belly.
Epigas'tric a. Pertaining to the upper and anterior part of the abdomen.
Perigas'tric a. Surrounding the alimentary canal.
Hypogas'tric a. Pertaining to, or situated in the lower middle of the abdomen.
Hepatogas'tric a. Relating to the liver and stomach.
Polygas'tric a. Having many stomachs.
Yt'tric a. Containing or derived from yttrium.
Ur'ic a. Pertaining to or derived from urine.
Aur'ic a. Pertaining to gold.
Mercur'ic a. Containing mercury.
Neur'ic a. Pertaining to or provided with nerves.
Sulphur'ic a. Derived from or containing sulphur.
Tellur'ic a. Pertaining to the earth, or to tellurium.
Purpur'ic a. Pertaining to purpura, or to purple.
Glucosur'ic a. Pertaining to glucosuria.
Panegyr'ic s. An encomium, eulogy.
Lyr'ic a. Pertaining to or suited for the lyre. s. A short poem, esp. for singing.
Satyr'ic a. Pertaining to or containing satyrs, especially of ancient Greek drama.
Butyr'ic a. Derived from butter.
Sic adv. Thus, exactly as here given.
Ba'sic a. Essential, fundamental; pertaining to a base.
Diaba'sic a. Pertaining to or consisting of diabase.
Diba'sic a. Having two atoms of hydrogen replaced by bases.
Triba'sic a. Having three hydrogen atoms replaceable by a base.
Monoba'sic a. Applied to acids having one hydrogen atom replaceable by a radical.
Polyba'sic a. Having more than one atom of hydrogen replaceable by a base.
Diastas'ic a. Pertaining to diastase.
Geode'sic a. Pertaining to extensive surveys of the earth's surface.
Mangane'sic a. Manganic.
Paradis'ic a. Pertaining to Paradise.
Foren'sic a. Pertaining to courts of law or to public debate.
Intrin'sic a. Inward; real; true; genuine.
Extrin'sic a. External; unessential.
Gluco'sic a. Glucic.
Lias'sic a. Belonging to the lowest strata of the Jurassic system.
Trias'sic a. Belonging to the strata between the Carboniferous and Jurassic systems.
Thalas'sic a. Pertaining to the sea.
Clas'sic s. A work of author of acknowledged excellence; one learned in Greek or Latin. a. Of the first rank (in literature, etc.); pertaining to the best Greek and Latin authors; refined, pure.
Juras'sic a. Belonging to the second period of the Mesozoic era.
Potas'sic a. Pertaining to, derived from, or containing potassium.
Quas'sic a. Derived from quassia.
Gneis'sic a. Gneissoid.
Prus'sic a. Derived from prussian blue.
Banau'sic a. Belonging to things mechanical.
Mu'sic s. Melody; science of harmonious sounds; the score of a composition.
Phys'ic s. Theory or practice of medicine; medicines in general. v.t. To treat with physic; to purge; to cure.
Tic s. Convulsive twitching of the facial muscles.
Adiabat'ic a. Impervious, especially to heat.
Metabat'ic a. (*Metabasis*).
Sabbat'ic a. Pertaining to the Sabbath.
Ecbat'ic a. Pertaining to ecbasis.
Acrobat'ic a. Pertaining to acrobats or their performances.
Mithridat'ic a. Pertaining to or of the nature of a mithridate or mithridatism.
Hydat'ic a. Pertaining to, resembling, or due to a hydatid.
Eleat'ic a. Denoting a Greek school of philosophy founded by Xenophanes.
Cuneat'ic a. Wedge-shaped, cuneiform.
Pancreat'ic a. Pertaining to the pancreas.
Hanseat'ic a. Pertaining to the Hanse, a mediæval N. German trading guild.
Sulphat'ic a. Pertaining to or derived from a sulphate.

Emphat'ic a. Bearing emphasis; accentuated, forcible; earnest.
Lymphat'ic a. Pertaining to or secreting lymph; phlegmatic, sluggish.
Phosphat'ic a. Containing phosphate or phosphoric acid.
Sciat'ic a. Pertaining to the hip; affecting the sciatic nerve.
Ischiat'ic a. Pertaining to the hip or to sciatica.
Adriat'ic s. The sea to the east of Italy.
Psoriat'ic a. Causing or resembling psoriasis.
Muriat'ic a. Pertaining to or obtained from sea-salt; hydrochloric.
Asiat'ic s. An inhabitant or native of Asia. a. Pertaining to Asia.
Fluviat'ic a. Fluvial.
Prelat'ic a. Pertaining to prelates or prelacy.
Dramat'ic a. Pertaining to the drama, theatrical; full of action and incident; impressive.
Melodramat'ic a. Of the nature of melodrama; overstrained
Hæmat'ic a. Pertaining to, containing, or acting on the blood; blood-coloured.
Œdemat'ic a. Œdematous.
Schemat'ic a. Arranged in a scheme or schema.
Rhemat'ic a. Pertaining to the formation of words or sentences.
Themat'ic a. Pertaining to a theme.
Emblemat'ic a. Pertaining to, comprising, or using emblems.
Problemat'ic a. Of the nature of a problem; questionable, disputable.
Enthymemat'ic a. (*Enthymeme*).
Kinemat'ic a. Pertaining to movement or to kinematics.
Theoremat'ic a. Pertaining to or comprised in a theorem.
Categoremat'ic a. (*Categorem*).
Semat'ic a. Pertaining to colouration of animals for purpose of warning, attracting, etc.
Systemat'ic a. Methodical; done according to system.
Synallagmat'ic a. Imposing reciprocal obligations.
Diaphrag'matic a. Pertaining to a diaphragm.
Pragmat'ic a. Pertaining to business or affairs of state; material; meddlesome; pertaining to pragmatism. s. A busybody; a sovereign decree.
Judgmat'ic a. Judicious; showing good judgment.
Apothegmat'ic a. Sententious; pertaining to or using apothegms.
Phlegmat'ic a. Abounding in phlegm; stolid, cold, indifferent.
Smegmat'ic a. Soapy, detersive. s. A detergent.
Paradigmat'ic a. Pertaining to or of the nature of a paradigm.
Enigmat'ic a. Pertaining to, containing, or like an enigma; obscure.
Stigmat'ic a. Marked with a stigma; impressing infamy; pertaining to stigmas.
Dogmat'ic a. Pertaining to dogma or a dogma; asserting authoritatively or arrogantly; positive.
Antasthmat'ic s. A medicine relieving asthma. a. Tending to relieve asthma.
Climat'ic a. Pertaining to or limited by a climate.
Dalmat'ic s. An ecclesiastical and royal vestment.
Grammat'ic a. Grammatical; pertaining to grammar; according to the rules of grammar.
Diagrammat'ic a. Like or pertaining to a diagram.
Anagrammat'ic a. Of the nature of an anagram.
Parallelo-grammat'ic a. (*Parallelogramm'ic*).
Monogram-mat'ic a. Of the nature of a monogram.
Chrono-grammat'ic a. (*Chronogram*).
Dilemmat'ic a. Pertaining to dilemmas.
Commat'ic a. In short clauses; concise.
Zygomat'ic a. Pertaining to the zygoma.
Idiomat'ic a. Peculiar to or characteristic of a language; vernacular.
Axiomat'ic a. Of the nature of an axiom; self-evident.
Diplomat'ic a. Pertaining to diplomacy or ambassadors; tactful, adroit; pertaining to diplomatics.
Aromat'ic a. Having a fragrant odour.
Chromat'ic a. Relating to colour; proceeding by semitones instead of by the regular intervals of the diatonic scale.
Dichromat'ic a. Having or producing two colours.
Panchromat'ic a. Uniformly sensitive to all colours (of photographic plates).
Monochro-mat'ic a. Presenting rays of light of one colour only.
Isochromat'ic a. Having the same colour.
Photo-chromat'ic a. Pertaining to the chromatic action of light.
Polychromat'ic a. Having many colours; iridescent.
Stromat'ic a. Pertaining to or resembling a stroma.
Somat'ic a. Pertaining to the body; material.
Phantomat'ic a. Phantasmal.
Symptomat'ic a. Pertaining to or according to symptoms; indicative.
Stomat'ic a. Pertaining to or resembling stomata.
Automat'ic a. Self-acting, working unconsciously.
Dermat'ic a. Pertaining to the skin.
Spermat'ic a. Pertaining to, conveying, or consisting of sperm; pertaining to the spermary.
Termat'ic a. Pertaining to the terma.
Miasmat'ic a. Resembling or pertaining to miasma.
Plasmat'ic a. Pertaining to plasma or protoplasm.
Aseismat'ic a. Not proof against earthquake shocks.
Schismat'ic a. Pertaining to, implying, of the nature of, or tending to schism. s. One who promotes schism; a heretic.
Numismat'ic a. Relating to coins or medals.
Porismat'ic a. Pertaining to a porism.
Prismat'ic a. Pertaining to or resembling, or separated or formed by, a prism; containing prisms.
Traumat'ic a. Pertaining to or adapted to the cure of wounds. s. A medicine for wounds.
Rheumat'ic a. Affected with, liable to, or characteristic of rheumatism.
Pneumat'ic a. Pertaining to, consisting of, or resembling air; inflated with, fitted to contain, or moved or played by means of air.
Empyreumat'ic a. (*Empyreuma*).
Synonymat'ic a. Pertaining to synonymy.
Fanat'ic a. Excessivelyenthusiastic, especially on religion. s. One unreasonably zealous, bigoted, or wildly extravagant in opinion.
Morganat'ic a. Applied to legal marriages the offspring of which do not inherit the father's rank or possessions.
Aplanat'ic a. Free from spherical aberration.
Agnat'ic a. Pertaining to descent on the father's side.
Lu'natic s. An idiot; a senseless fool. a. Insane; crazy.

Hepat'ic a. Pertaining to the liver; liver-coloured.
Pancrat'ic a. Pertaining to the pancratium.
Idiosyncrat'ic a. Of one's own individual temperament, etc.
Gynæcocrat'ic a. Pertaining to female government.
Theocrat'ic a. Pertaining to the direct rule of God.
Physiocrat'ic a. Pertaining to the physiocrats or their theories.
Ochlocrat'ic a. Pertaining to an ochlocracy.
Democrat'ic a. Pertaining to democracy; favouring popular rights.
Arithmocrat'ic a. Pertaining to government by majorities.
Timocrat'ic a. Pertaining to a timocracy or this form of government.
Socrat'ic a. In the manner of or pertaining to Socrates.
Pantisocrat'ic a. Pertaining to the pantisocracy; visionary.
Aristocrat'ic a. Pertaining to the privileged orders; stylish.
Autocrat'ic a. Pertaining to absolute government, exercising uncontrolled power.
Plutocrat'ic a. Relating to government by the wealthy or to the wealthy classes.
Bureaucrat'ic a. Consisting of, pertaining to, or tending towards government by State departments.
Quadrat'ic a. Pertaining to or like a square; involving the square of an unknown quantity.
Hierat'ic a. Consecrated to sacred uses; priestly.
Operat'ic a. Pertaining or appropriate to opera.
Pirat'ic a. Pertaining to pirates or piracy.
Errat'ic a. Eccentric; roving about; wandering, straying.
Protat'ic a. Pertaining to protasis.
Stat'ic a. Pertaining to bodies at rest.
Astat'ic a. Not taking a definite position or direction.
Anastat'ic a. Belonging to zincography.
Metastat'ic a. Relating to metastasis.
Ecstat'ic a. Pertaining to or producing ecstasy; entrancing; entranced.
Hypostat'ic a. Pertaining to substance as distinct from attributes; elemental, personal.
Hydrostat'ic a. Pertaining to or in accordance with the principle of the equilibrium of fluids.
Prostat'ic a. Pertaining to the prostate gland.
Aquat'ic a. Pertaining to water; living or growing in water.
Caryat'ic a. (*Caryatid*).
Didac'tic a. Giving or adapted to give instruction; doctrinal.
Lac'tic a. Pertaining to milk; derived from sour milk.
Galac'tic a. Pertaining to milk or its secretion; pertaining to the galaxy.
Stalac'tic a. Resembling or pertaining to a stalactite.
Parallac'tic a. Pertaining to the parallax of a heavenly body.
Catallac'tic a. Pertaining to exchange.
Prophylac'tic a. Preventing disease. s. A medicine for this.
Climac'tic a. Pertaining to a climax.
Emphrac'tic a. Able to close the pores of the skin; s. A medicine to effect this.
Prac'tic a. Practical, practised; cunning. s. Practice; a deed; a trick.
Syntac'tic a. Pertaining to or according to the rules of syntax.
Hec'tic a. Habitual; consumptive; (*slang*) highly exciting. s. A hectic fever or patient; a morbid flush.
Dialec'tic a. Pertaining to logic; logical; argumentative. s. One skilled in reasoning.
Catalec'tic a. Wanting a syllable at the end.
Acatalec'tic a. Not defective at the end (of a verse).
Eclec'tic a. Selecting, choosing at will, especially from doctrines, teachings, etc. s. A philosopher who does this.
Apoplec'tic a. Characteristic of or liable to apoplexy.
Synec'tic a. Connecting things of different nature.
Pec'tic a. Derived from or containing pectin.
Orec'tic a. Pertaining to the desires; impelling to gratification.
Deic'tic a. Proving directly; demonstrative.
Epideic'tic a. Showing off; demonstrative.
Apodeic'tic a. Evident beyond contradiction, necessarily true.
Elenc'tic a. Pertaining to elenchus, of or given to refutation or cross-examination.
Subarc'tic a. Pertaining to the regions bordering the Arctic.
Palæarc'tic a. Pertaining to the northern parts of the Old World.
Nearc'tic a. Pertaining to Northern North America.
Alphabet'ic a. Arranged in the order of the letters of the alphabet.
Diabe'tic a. Pertaining to or suitable for use in diabetes. s. One suffering from this.
Tabet'ic a. Pertaining to or affected with tabes; wasting away.
Hebet'ic a. Pertaining to youth.
Ace'tic a. Akin to or pertaining to vinegar; sour.
Geodet'ic a. Geodesic.
Exeget'ic a. Expository.
Ganget'ic a. Pertaining to the River Ganges.
Apologet'ic a. Excusatory, defensive.
Energet'ic a. Forcible, exhibiting energy; potent, effective.
Synerget'ic a. Working together.
Catechet'ic a. Consisting of questions and answers, pertaining to catechism.
Aphet'ic a. Characterized by aphesis.
Japhet'ic a. Pertaining to Japhet or his supposed descendants; Aryan.
Prophet'ic a. Containing or pertaining to prophecy.
Bathet'ic a. Characterized by bathos.
Mathet'ic a. Pertaining to mathesis.
Pathet'ic a. Affecting; exciting the feelings; sentimental.
Apathet'ic a. Characterized by apathy.
Antipathet'ic a. Having an antipathy for, opposed to.
Sympathet'ic a. Having a feeling in common with another.
Epithet'ic a. Abounding in or pertaining to epithets.
Antithet'ic a. Containing or pertaining to an antithesis.
Epenthet'ic a. Pertaining to epenthesis.
Parenthet'ic a. Pertaining to, expressed in, or contained in parentheses.
Synthet'ic a. Pertaining to or effected by synthesis.
Polysynthet'ic a. Combining or built up of several words; compounded of many ingredients.
Cosmothet'ic a. Believing in the existence of matter and affirming impossibility of knowing anything about it.

Hypothet'ic a. Founded on hypothesis; conjectural.
Prothet'ic a. Pertaining to prothesis.
Anæsthet'ic s. A substance which produces temporary insensibility.
Prosthet'ic a. Pertaining to or effected by prosthesis.
Rabiet'ic a. Pertaining or due to rabies.
Homilet'ic a. Pertaining to homilies or preaching.
Phylet'ic a. Racial.
Polyphylet'ic a. Having or belonging to many races; polygenetic.
Emet'ic a. Inducing vomiting. s. A preparation which produces vomiting.
Mimet'ic a. Apt to imitate; given to or characterized by mimicry.
Comet'ic a. Cometary.
Baphomet'ic a. (*Baphomet*).
Hermet'ic a. Pertaining to alchemy; perfectly air-tight.
Cosmet'ic s. An application to improve the complexion. a. Beautifying.
Epithymet'ic a. Pertaining to the desire.
Genet'ic a. Relating to the origin or birth of things.
Metagenet'ic a. Pertaining to metagenesis.
Congenet'ic a. Having the same origin or place and time of origin.
Psychogenet'ic a. Pertaining to psychogenesis.
Morphogenet'ic a. Pertaining to morphogeny.
Pathogenet'ic a. Pertaining to the development of or causing disease.
Abiogenet'ic a. Pertaining to spontaneous generation.
Gamogenet'ic a. Pertaining to gamogenesis.
Homogenet'ic a. Pertaining to or characterized by homogenesis; similar in structural relations.
Thermogenet'ic a. Pertaining to thermogenesis.
Parthenogenet'ic a. Pertaining to asexual generation.
Monogenet'ic a. Pertaining to or involving monogenesis; resulting from one process of formation.
Oogenet'ic a. Pertaining to oogeny or oogenesis.
Heterogenet'ic a. Pertaining to heterogenesis.
Hysterogenet'ic a. Of later botanical formation or development.
Pyrogenet'ic a. Producing heat, or feverishness; pyrogenous.
Ontogenet'ic a. Pertaining to ontogeny.
Protogenet'ic a. Protogenic.
Histogenet'ic a. Pertaining to the origin of tissues or to histogenesis.
Polygenet'ic a. Pertaining to the doctrine of polygenesis.
Splenet'ic a. Affected with spleen; morose, peevish. s. A medicine for diseases of the spleen.
Phrenet'ic a. Mentally disordered; frantic. s. A frantic person.
Threnet'ic a. Mournful; pertaining to a threnody.
Magnet'ic a. Pertaining to the magnet or to magnetism; exercising attraction.
Diamagnet'ic a. Pertaining to diamagnetism. s. A substance exhibiting this.
Kinet'ic a. Pertaining to or due to movement.
Telekinet'ic a. Pertaining to telekinesis.
Mitokinet'ic a. Productive of mitosis.
Phonet'ic a. Pertaining to the voice; representing voice-sounds.
Goet'ic a. Pertaining to necromancy or the black art.
Aloet'ic a. Pertaining to aloes.
Noet'ic a. Pertaining to, performed by, or originated in the intellect.
Poet'ic a. Pertaining to, suitable to, or expressed in poetry; having the beauties of poetry.
Mythopoet'ic a. Mythopœic.
Onomatopoet'ic a. Onomatopœic.
Zoet'ic a. Pertaining to life; vital.
Herpet'ic a. Pertaining to or afflicted with herpes.
Paret'ic a. and s. Suffering or a sufferer from paresis.
Cre'tic s. A metrical foot of a short syllable between two long, an amphimacer.
Syncret'ic a. Pertaining to the reconciliation of schools or systems against a common opponent.
Her'etic s. One holding unorthodox religious opinions.
Hysteret'ic a. Pertaining to hysteresis.
Theoret'ic a. Pertaining to, founded on, or confined to theory; speculative.
Anchoret'ic a. (*Anchoret*).
Diaphoret'ic a. Having power to increase perspiration. s. A medicine effecting this.
Plethoret'ic a. Plethoric.
Masoret'ic a. Relating to the Hebrew Masora, its authors, or its MSS.
Diuret'ic a. Exciting the secretion of urine. s. A medicine effecting this.
Pyret'ic a. Pertaining to or producing fever.
Apyret'ic a. Without fever.
Antipyret'ic a. Preventing or allaying fever. s. A medicine for this purpose.
Peripatet'ic a. Walking about, itinerant; pertaining to Aristotle's philosophy. s. An adherent of this; one who must walk because he cannot afford to ride.
Dietet'ic a. Pertaining to the rules of diet.
Zetet'ic a. Proceeding by inquiry. s. One who investigates.
Luet'ic a. Pertaining to infection or plague.
Helvet'ic a. Swiss; pertaining to the ancient Helvetii.
Cenobit'ic a. Pertaining to monasteries or monachism.
Calcit'ic a. (*Calcite*).
Hermaphrodit'ic a. Possessing the characteristics or organs of both sexes.
Osteit'ic a. Pertaining to or having osteitis.
Pharyngit'ic a. Pertaining to or affected by pharyngitis.
Laryngit'ic a. Pertaining to or affected with laryngitis.
Rachit'ic a. Pertaining to or affected with rickets.
Graphit'ic a. Pertaining to, consisting of, or resembling graphite.
Mephit'ic a. Offensive to the smell; pestilential.
Ophit'ic a. Pertaining to or resembling serpentine.
Enclit'ic a. Applied to a word or particle closely united to the preceding word.
Heteroclit'ic a. Heteroclite.
Israelit'ic a. Pertaining to Israel; Jewish; Hebrew.
Myelit'ic a. Pertaining to or affected with myelitis.
Typhlit'ic a. Pertaining or due to typhlitis.
Toxophilit'ic a. Pertaining to archery.
Syphilit'ic a. Pertaining to or affected with syphilis.
Corallit'ic a. (*Corallite*).
Tonsillit'ic a. Pertaining to or affected with tonsillitis.
Zeolit'ic a. Containing or consisting of zeolite.
Tremolit'ic a. Containing, like, or consisting of tremolite.

Oolit'ic a. Belonging to oolite, or the Oolite series.
Polit'ic a. Pertaining to or promoting a policy; well-devised; sagacious; subtle.
Impolit'ic a. Injudicious, inexpedient.
Coprolit'ic a. (*Coprolite*).
Graptolit'ic a. Resembling or containing graptolites.
Ichthyolit'ic a. Pertaining to ichthyolites.
Poplit'ic a. Popliteal.
Marlit'ic a. Pertaining to or resembling marlite.
Nummulit'ic a. Abounding in or resembling nummulites.
Granulit'ic a. Pertaining to or resembling granulite.
Spherulit'ic a. Containing or resembling spherulites.
Tachylit'ic a. Consisting of or containing tachylite.
Adamit'ic a. Pertaining to the first man or to the Adamites.
Pre-Adamit'ic a. Pre-Adamite.
Hamit'ic a. Pertaining to the dark races of N.E. Africa fabled to be descended from Ham.
Islamit'ic a. Pertaining to Islam.
Eremit'ic a. Pertaining to or like an eremite.
Semit'ic a. Pertaining to the fabled descendants of Shem (Hebrews, Phœnicians, Assyrians, Arabs, etc.), or their languages. s. One of these descendants.
Stalagmit'ic a. Pertaining to or resembling a stalagmite.
Ophthalmit'ic a. Pertaining to or having ophthalmitis.
Palmit'ic a. Derived from palm-oil.
Somit'ic a. Pertaining to or resembling a somite.
Tympanit'ic a. Pertaining to tympanites or to tympanitis.
Granit'ic a. Pertaining to, consisting of, or like granite.
Uranit'ic a. Pertaining to or resembling uranium.
Syenit'ic a. Like, containing, or composed of syenite.
Lignit'ic a. Containing or resembling lignite.
Aconit'ic a. Of or resembling aconite.
Ebionit'ic a. Pertaining to the Ebionites.
Dichroit'ic a. Dichroic.
Sybarit'ic a. Effeminate; luxurious; wanton.
Crit'ic s. A judge of literary or artistic merit; a reviewer; a severe judge.
Diacrit'ic a. Separating, distinguishing. s. A mark over or under a letter.
Oneir'ocritic a. Oneirocritical. s. An interpreter of dreams.
Hypercrit'ic s. A captious censor.
Dendrit'ic a. Resembling or marked like a tree; arborescent.
Diphtherit'ic a. Caused by or related to diphtheria.
Laterit'ic a. Pertaining to or resembling laterite.
Nephrit'ic a. Pertaining to the kidneys or to nephritis; affected with kidney disease. s. A medicine for such disease.
Tephrit'ic a. Pertaining to, consisting of, or containing tephrite.
Antarthrit'ic a. Tending to prevent or relieve gout. s. A medicine effecting this.
Pleurit'ic a. Pertaining to or affected with pleurisy.
Porphyrit'ic a. Pertaining to, consisting of, or like porphyry.
Pyrit'ic a. Pertaining to, consisting of, or resembling pyrites.
Parasit'ic a. Pertaining to or of the nature of a parasite; living on or deriving nourishment from another.
Endoparasit'ic a. (*Endoparasite*).
Felsit'ic a. Containing or resembling felsite.
Steatit'ic a. Derived from or resembling steatite.
Hæmatit'ic a. Pertaining to or containing hæmatite.
Jesuit'ic a. Pertaining to the Jesuits or their principles; sly, casuistical.
Quartzit'ic a. Resembling or containing quartzite.
Bal'tic s. The sea bordered by Sweden, Finland, Russia, and N. Germany.
Asphal'tic a. Of the nature of asphalt.
Basal'tic a. Composed of or resembling basalt.
Diastal'tic a. Denoting reflex action or a nerve governing this.
Peristal'tic a. Contracting in successive circles.
Systal'tic a. Pulsating (of the heart).
Cel'tic a. Pertaining to the Celts. s. Their language.
An'tic a. Odd; ridiculously wild. s. A buffoon.
Corybant'ic a. Pertaining to a corybant; madly excited.
Pedan'tic a. Characteristic of, suiting, or resembling a pedant.
Vedan'tic a. Pertaining to the Vedanta.
Gigan'tic a. Immense, extraordinary; resembling a giant.
Sycophan'tic a. Servilely obsequious or flattering.
Hierophan'tic a. Pertaining to a hierophant or to religious teaching.
Transatlan'tic a. Across the Atlantic; relating to the United States.
Man'tic a. Pertaining to prophecy or divination.
Geoman'tic a. Pertaining to geomancy.
Onoman'tic a. Pertaining to or done by onomancy.
Roman'tic a. Pertaining to or involving romance; fictitious; characterized by strangeness or variety; sentimental; extravagant.
Necroman'tic a. Connected with or performed by the "black art" or enchantment.
Pyroman'tic a. Pertaining to pyromancy.
Fran'tic a. Raving, furious; outrageous.
Quan'tic s. An integral function of variables.
Iden'tic a. Identical.
Odon'tic a. Dental.
Anacreon'tic a. Relating to the Greek poet, Anacreon. s. Verse written in his style.
Pon'tic a. Pertaining to the Black Sea.
Geron'tic a. Senile; pertaining to old age.
Acheron'tic a. (*Acheron*).
O'tic a. Pertaining to the ear.
-otic suff. Forming adjectives from nouns in *-osis*.
Chaot'ic a. Resembling chaos; confused.
Thrombot'ic a. Pertaining or due to thrombosis.
Helcot'ic a. Pertaining to ulcers or ulceration.
Narcot'ic a. Producing coma, stupor, sleep, or death; relieving pain. s. A substance that does this.
Mycot'ic a. Pertaining to or due to mycosis.
Anecdot'ic a. Composed of or pertaining to anecdotes.
Lago'tic a. Having ears like a hare's.
Indigot'ic a. Pertaining to indigo; indigo-coloured.
Argot'ic a. (*Argot*).
Morphot'ic a. Pertaining to morphosis.
Biot'ic a. Pertaining to life.

Symbiot'ic a. Pertaining to symbiosis.
Idiot'ic a. Relating to or like an idiot; absurd.
Semeiot'ic a. Pertaining to symptoms.
Periot'ic a. Surrounding the inner ear.
Patriot'ic a. Characterized by active love of one's country.
Nilot'ic a. Pertaining to the Nile, Egypt, or the Egyptians, etc.
Tylot'ic a. Pertaining to or affected with tylosis.
Demot'ic a. Pertaining to the people, vulgar (especially of an ancient Egyptian alphabet).
Anastomot'ic a. (*Anastomosis*).
Thermot'ic a. Pertaining to or resulting from heat.
Seismot'ic (sizmot'-) a. Seismic.
Osmot'ic a. Pertaining to or characterized by osmosis.
Endosmot'ic a. Pertaining to endosmosis.
Exosmot'ic a. Pertaining to or characterized by exosmosis.
Zymot'ic a. Pertaining to or due to fermentation.
Enzymot'ic a. Pertaining to enzymes.
Melanot'ic a. Pertaining to or resembling melanosis.
Kenot'ic a. Pertaining to kenosis.
Hypnot'ic a. Causing sleep; characterized by unnatural sleep; pertaining to hypnotism.
Epizoot'ic a. Pertaining to epidemics among animals; containing fossils. s. An epidemic among cattle.
Enzo'otic a. Corresponding in animals to "endemic" in man.
Nepot'ic a. Addicted to or pertaining to nepotism.
Despot'ic a. Uncontrolled; arbitrary, tyrannical.
Escharot'ic a. Tending or serving to form a scab; caustic.
Parot'ic a. Pertaining to a parotid gland, etc.
Necrot'ic a. Pertaining to necrosis.
Diocrot'ic a. Doubly pulsating.
Hidrot'ic a. Causing perspiration. s. A sudorific.
Erot'ic a. Pertaining to or prompted by love; amatory. s. A love-poem.
Rhinocerot'ic a. Pertaining to or like the rhinocerous.
Sclerot'ic a. Hardening; indurated; affected with sclerosis. s. The white of the eye.
Chlorot'ic a. (*Chlorosis*).
Amaurot'ic a. (*Amaurosis*).
Neurot'ic a. Pertaining to, situated in, or acting on the nerves; affected by neurosis. s. One suffering from neurosis; a nervously excitable person.
Mitot'ic a. Pertaining to mitosis.
Aptot'ic a. Without grammatical inflexion.
Anaptot'ic a. Becoming uninflected again.
Asymptot'ic a. (*Asymptote*).
Exot'ic a. Foreign; not produced at home. s. Anything of foreign origin, especially a plant.
Quixot'ic a. Extravagantly chivalrous; aiming at visionary ends.
Ichthyot'ic a. Characterized by ichthyosis.
Scep'tic s. A doubter, an incredulous person; agnostic.
Catalep'tic a. (*Catalepsy*).
Acatalep'tic a. Incomprehensible.
Epilep'tic a. Pertaining to epilepy. s. One affected with this.
Syllep'tic a. Pertaining to or containing syllepsis.
Nympholep'tic a. (*Nympholepsy*).
Prolep'tic a. Pertaining to prolepsis or anticipation; previous; antecedent.
Pep'tic a. Promoting or pertaining to the digestion; having good digestive powers. s. A medicine that aids digestion.
Dyspep'tic a. Pertaining to or suffering from dyspepsia. s. One subject to this.
Eupep'tic a. Pertaining to, characteristic of, or having a good digestion.
Bradypep'tic a. Of slow digestion.
Sep'tic a. Promoting putrefaction; producing blood-poisoning. s. A substance which produces sepsis.
Asep'tic a. Not liable to blood-poisoning or putrefaction.
Antisep'tic a. Preventing the growth of or destroying septic germs. s. A substance that effects this.
Eclip'tic s. Apparent path of sun round earth. a. Pertaining to this, or to an eclipse.
Ellip'tic a. Pertaining to an ellipse or ellipsis; having a part omitted.
Lithontrip'tic s. A medicine for dispersing stone in the bladder.
Op'tic s. An organ of sight. a. Pertaining to vision or the science of sight.
Cop'tic a. Pertaining to the Copts or the old Egyptian Christians. s. The language of the Copts.
Syncop'tic a. Syncopal.
Orthop'tic a. Pertaining to or characterized by normal binocular vision. s. The perforated backsight of a firearm.
Sciop'tic a. Pertaining to the camera obscura.
Synop'tic a. Affording a general view of the whole.
Autop'tic a. (*Autopsy*).
Apocalyp'tic a. Belonging to the Apocalypse; revealing hidden mysteries.
Glyp'tic a. Relating to the engraving of gems.
Anaglyp'tic a. Wrought in low relief.
Cryp'tic a. Occult; secret.
Styp'tic s. A medicament that arrests bleeding.
Cathar'tic a. Cleansing, purgative.
Aor'tic a. (*Aorta*).
Syr'tic a. Pertaining to or consisting of quicksands.
Bombas'tic a. Turgid, high sounding but empty.
Sarcas'tic a. Bitterly satirical; containing sarcasm.
Schedias'tic a. Extempore; done off-hand.
Autoschedias'tic a. Hastily improvised.
Orgias'tic a. Pertaining to or characterized by orgies; pertaining to the worship of Bacchus.
Chilias'tic a. (*Chiliast*).
Scholias'tic a. Pertaining to a scholiast or his work.
Encomias'tic a. Bestowing praise; flattering.
Ecclesias'tic s. A clergyman. a. Ecclesiastical.
Enthusias'tic a. Filled with enthusiasm, ardent; visionary.
Clas'tic a. Fragmentary (of rocks).
Cataclas'tic a. Belonging to a granular rock-formation.
Synclas'tic a. Having uniform curvature.
Plagioclas'tic a. Petaining to or resembling plagioclase; having the cleavage oblique.
Iconoclas'tic a. Given to destroying idols or accepted beliefs.

Elas'tic a. Having power to recover its former size after distortion, etc.; springing back. s. An elastic body, strip, etc.
Gelas'tic a. Pertaining to or causing laughter.
Inelas'tic a. Wanting elasticity.
Scholas'tic a. Pertaining to schools and education, or to the mediæval schoolmen; academic, pedantic. s. A schoolman; one given to subtleties; a mere scholar.
Plas'tic a. Having power to form a mass of matter; capable of being moulded; pertaining to modelling.
Esemplas'tic a. Moulding into one; unifying.
Neoplas'tic a. Pertaining to or due to neoplasty.
Organoplas'tic a. Producing organs.
Rhinoplas'tic a. Forming a nose.
Ceroplas'tic a. Pertaining to the art of wax-modelling.
Heteroplas'tic a. Pertaining to or characterized by heteroplasm or heteroplasty.
Polyplas'tic a. Assuming many forms; polymorphic.
Mas'tic s. A resin used for varnish; a kind of mortar.
Onomas'tic a. Pertaining to a name.
Paronomas'tic a. Pertaining to or consisting of punning.
Antonomas'tic a. (*Antonomasia*).
Gymnas'tic a. Pertaining to exercises for bodily development.
Pleonas'tic a. Using unnecessary words, redundant in expression.
Monas'tic a. Pertaining to a monastery or monks; retired, secluded. s. A monk.
Dynas'tic a. Pertaining to a dynasty.
Spas'tic a. Spasmodic.
Epispas'tic a. Blistering; drawing the skin. s. A preparation for effecting this.
Hudibras'tic a. In the style of Butler's "Hudibras"; mock-heroic; doggerel.
Dras'tic a. Powerful, active, vigorous.
Paraphras'tic a. Explaining in simpler, or another, language; not literal; diffuse.
Metaphras'tic a. Close or literal in translation.
Periphras'tic a. Expressed in more words than are necessary; circumlocutory.
Antiphras'tic a. (*Antiphrasis*).
Fantas'tic a. Fanciful, capricious; odd; uncertain; irrational. s. An absurd or whimsical person; a fop.
Asbes'tic a. (*Asbestos*).
Orches'tic a. Pertaining to dancing.
Majes'tic a. Having or exhibiting majesty; august; stately.
Domes'tic a. Pertaining to the house, one's family, or one's nation; staying much at home; tame. s. A household servant.
Anapes'tic a. Pertaining to anapests.
Agres'tic a. Rustic, uncouth.
Catachres'tic a. (*Catachresis*).
Tung'stic a. Pertaining to or derived from tungsten.
Archais'tic a. (*Archaism*).
Hebrais'tic a. Relating to the language, mode of thought, etc., of the ancient Hebrews.
Solecis'tic a. Pertaining to or involving solecism.
Haggadis'tic a. Pertaining to the Haggadah.
Methodis'tic a. Pertaining to or resembling Methodism.
Talmudis'tic a. Pertaining to or resembling the Talmud.
Deis'tic a. Pertaining to belief in God without acceptance of divine revelation.
Theis'tic a. Pertaining to or according to the doctrines of theism.
Atheis'tic a. (*Atheism*).
Ditheist'ic a. Pertaining to ditheism.
Tritheis'tic a. Pertaining to tritheism.
Pantheis'tic a. Pertaining to or founded on pantheism.
Henotheis'tic a. Pertaining to or adhering to henotheism.
Monotheis'tic a. Pertaining to monotheism.
Polytheis'tic a. Pertaining to or adhering to polytheism.
Fis'tic a. Pertaining to boxing; pugilistic.
Sufis'tic a. Pertaining to sufism.
Logis'tic a. Pertaining to proportion, or to logistics.
Dialogis'tic a. Dialogic.
Phlogis'tic a. Like or pertaining to phlogiston; inflammatory.
Antiphlogis'tic a. Allaying inflammation, cooling. s. A medicine to effect this.
Syllogis'tic a. Pertaining to or consisting of syllogisms.
Neologis'tic a. Given to or pertaining to the use of new words.
Dyslogis'tic a. Disparaging, censuring.
Eulogis'tic a. Pertaining to or characterized by eulogy.
His'tic a. Pertaining to tissue.
Catechis'tic a. Pertaining to a catechist or catechism.
Buddhis'tic a. (*Buddhism*).
Elohis'tic a. Pertaining to those parts of the Hexateuch (or the writers thereof) in which the word *Elohim* is used in place of *Yahveh* (*Jehovah*).
Sophis'tic a. Embodying sophistry, specious but fallacious; pertaining to a sophist.
Fetishis'tic a. Pertaining to fetishism or fetish-worship.
Cabbalis'tic a. (*Cabbala*).
Cannibalis'tic a. (*Cannibalism*).
Feudalis'tic a. (*Feudalist*).
Idealis'tic a. Given to forming or searching for ideals; moulding one's actions on ideals.
Realis'tic a. Pertaining to or characteristic of realism or realists.
Specialis'tic a. Pertaining to or befitting a specialist.
Socialis'tic a. Pertaining to or of the nature of socialism.
Imperialis'tic a. Pertaining to or advocating imperialism.
Materialis'tic a. Characterized by regard for secular to the neglect of spiritual interests.
Anomalis'tic a. Abnormal, irregular.
Formalis'tic a. Pertaining to or addicted to formalism.
Phenomenalis'tic a. Pertaining to phenomenalism.
Nominalis'tic a. Pertaining to or derived from the nominalists.
Annalis'tic a. (*Annalist*).
Rationalis'tic a. Pertaining to or conforming with rationalism or rationalists.
Traditionalis'tic a. Pertaining to or founded on traditionalism.
Paternalis'tic a. Pertaining to or resembling paternalism.
Journalis'tic a. In the manner of a journalist or of journalism.
Communalis'tic a. (*Communalism*).
Liberalis'tic a. (*Liberalist*).
Moralis'tic a. Suitable for or pertaining to moralists.
Humoralis'tic a. Pertaining to humoralism.

Pluralis'tic a. (*Pluralist*).

Naturalis'tic a. In accordance with nature ; pert. to natural history ; realistic.

Super-naturalis'tic a. Pertaining to or imbued with supernaturalism.

Fatalis'tic a. Pertaining to the doctrine that all that happens is the work of fate.

Capitalis'tic a. (*Capitalism*).

Vitalis'tic a. Vitalist.

Dualis'tic a. Consisting of two ; pertaining to dualism.

Individualis'tic a. Characterized by conduct centred in self, or by some personal peculiarity.

Sensualis'tic a. Sensual.

Ritualis'tic a. Pertaining to exaggerated observance of ritual.

Spiritualis'tic a. Pertaining to spiritualism or spiritualists.

Revivalis'tic a. Pertaining to or of the nature of a religious revival.

Royalis'tic a. Pertaining to or characteristic of royalists.

Evangelis'tic a. Pertaining to the four Evangelists, to their Gospels, or to Evangelism.

Novelis'tic a. Characteristic of or pertaining to novels.

Pugilis'tic a. Pertaining to boxing or pugilists.

Nihilis'tic a. Pertaining to nihilism or nihilists ; aiming at destruction of existing institutions.

Catabolis'tic a. (*Catabolism*).

Symbolis'tic a. Pertaining to symbolism or to the symbolists.

Monopolis'tic a. Pertaining to or characteristic of a monopoly or monopolist.

Somnam-bulis'tic a. Pertaining to sleep-walking or -walkers.

Oculis'tic a. Pertaining to oculists or their work.

Formulis'tic a. Pertaining to or imbued with formulism.

Stylis'tic a. Pertaining to or characteristic of a stylist.

Mis'tic s. A small Mediterranean coasting-vessel.

Euphemis'tic a. Pertaining to or given to the use of softened or pleasing terms.

Totemis'tic a. Pertaining to or like totemism.

Animis'tic a. (*Animism*).

Pessimis'tic a. Inclined to take a gloomy and despondent view of things.

Optimis'tic a. Characterized by optimism ; sanguine.

Thomis'tic (tō-) a. Pertaining to Thomism.

Nomis'tic a. Based upon law.

Mediumis'tic a. Pertaining to a spiritualistic medium.

Melanis'tic a. Affected with or of the nature of melanism.

Shamanis'tic a. Pertaining to Shamanism.

Romanis'tic a. (*Romanist*).

Humanis'tic a. Pertaining to humanism or the humanists.

Hellenis'tic a. Pertaining to the language, customs, etc., of the ancient Greeks, especially of the Greek Jews of early Christian times.

Jansenis'tic a. Pertaining to or resembling the tenets of the Jansenists.

Determinis'tic a. (*Determinism*).

Calvinis'tic a. Holding the tenets and acting on the principles of the reformer, Calvin.

Chauvinis'tic a. Prone to exhibiting exaggerated and aggressive patriotism.

Hedonis'tic a. Given to or pertaining to hedonism or pleasure.

Agonis'tic a. Pertaining to athletic contests.

Antagonis'tic a. Opposed to, contending with.

Impressionis'tic a. Pertaining to, produced by, or resembling impressionism.

Evolutionis'tic a. Pertaining to the theory of evolution.

Monis'tic a. Pertaining to or resembling monism.

Eudemonis'tic a. Pertaining to or founded on eudemonism.

Harmonis'tic a. Pertaining to harmonizing.

Canonis'tic a. (*Canonist*).

Anachronis'tic a. Pertaining to or involving an anachronism.

Synchronis'tic a. Synchronous ; simultaneous.

Communis'tic a. Holding the doctrines of the Communists ; believing in community of property.

Taois'tic (tou-) a. Pertaining to Taoism.

Egois'tic a. Acting on the theory that man's chief good is the complete development and happiness of self.

Hylozois'tic a. Hylozoic.

Papis'tic a. Applied opprobriously to Roman Catholic doctrines, practices, etc.

Eucharis'tic a. Pertaining to the Eucharist.

Diaris'tic a. Pertaining to diaries or to diary-writing.

Eris'tic a. Controversial. s. Disputation ; a controversialist.

Hetæris'tic a. Pertaining to hetærism.

Euhemeris'tic a. Pertaining to the theory that interprets myths as being founded on the doings of actual men.

Manneris'tic a. Affected with or characterized by mannerism.

Characteris'tic a. Constituting a character, distinguishing. s. A peculiarity, distinguishing feature.

Aphoris'tic a. (*Aphorism*).

Folkloris'tic a. Pertaining to folklore.

Humoris'tic a. Pertaining to or resembling a humorist.

Poris'tic a. Pertaining to or of the nature of a porism.

Terroris'tic a. Pertaining to terrorists ; characterized by terrorism.

Patris'tic a. Pertaining to the Early Church Fathers and their writings.

Heuris'tic a. Tending or serving to find out ; helping investigation.

Juris'tic a. Pertaining to jurisprudence, a jurist, or law.

Colouris'tic a. (*Colourist*).

Puris'tic a. Characteristic of purists.

Chrematis'tic a. Pertaining to gain or money-making.

Pragmatis'tic a. Pertaining to pragmatism.

Statis'tic a. Pertaining to statistics or to political economy.

Pietis'tic a. Pertaining to the Pietists ; characterized by piety.

Quietis'tic a. Pertaining to the Quietists or Quietism.

Syncretis'tic a. Pertaining to or characterized by syncretism.

Egotis'tic a. Given to over-frequent mention of oneself.

Artis'tic a. Pertaining to or characterized by art ; made in the manner of an artist.

Inartis'tic a. Not artistic ; devoid of taste.

Absolutis'tic a. Characterized by adherence to the theory of absolutism or despotism.

Linguis'tic a. Pertaining to language.

Euphuis'tic a. Pedantically affected in speech or writing ; pertaining to euphuism.

Altruis'tic a. Acting on principles of perfect unselfishness.

Casuis'tic a. Quibbling, sophistical.

Atavis'tic a. (*Atavism*).

Jehovis'tic a. Pertaining to the parts of the Pentateuch in which the name "Jehovah" is used for "God."
Gnos'tic a. Relating to knowledge; intellectual, pertaining to the Gnostics. s. An adherent of Gnosticism.
Agnos'tic s. One who neither affirms nor denies the existence of a God. a. Pertaining to this doctrine or standpoint.
Diagnos'tic a. Serving to distinguish, characteristic. s. A symptom, characteristic.
Geognos'tic a. Pertaining to geognosy.
Prognos'tic a. Foreshowing. s. An omen, prediction of some future event.
Acros'tic s. A word puzzle.
Araphoros'tic a. Seamless, not sewn.
Caus'tic a. Burning; corrosive; severe, satirical. s. A substance that burns or corrodes.
Diacaus'tic a. Formed by refracted rays.
Catacaus'tic a. Formed by reflected rays.
Encaus'tic a. Burnt in; pertaining to art of burning in colours. s. Method of painting in heated wax, etc.
Apolaus'tic a. Devoted to pleasure.
Fus'tic s. A W. Indian wood used in dyeing yellow.
Acous'tic a. Pertaining to the ear or hearing.
Diacous'tic a. Pertaining to the science of refracted sounds.
Rus'tic a. Pertaining to the country; rude; plain; artless; awkward. s. An unpolished inhabitant of the country, a clown.
Cys'tic a. Pertaining to or enclosed in a cyst.
Hepatocys'tic a. Relating to the liver and gall-bladder.
Mys'tic a. Remote from comprehension, obscure; mysterious; pertaining to mysticism.
At'tic a. Pertaining to Athens, a city in Attica. s. A story in the upper part of a house.
Let'tic a. and s. Lettish.
Glot'tic a. Pertaining to the glottis; glottal.
Epiglot'tic a. Pertaining to the epiglottis.
Polyglot'tic a. Polyglot.
Argonau'tic a. Pertaining to the Argonauts or to a voyage of discovery.
Aeronau'tic a. Pertaining to aerial navigation.
Scorbu'tic a. Pertaining to or affected with scurvy.
Propædu'tic a. Of the nature of preparatory instruction.
Pharmaceut'ic a. Pharmaceutical.
Maieu'tic a. Helping to evolve; pertaining to instruction by questions.
Halieu'tic a. Pertaining to fishing.
Hermeneu'tic a. Explanatory, interpreting.
Therapeu'tic a. Curative; pertaining to the art of healing.
Agreu'tic a. Skilful in or subsisting by the chase.
Toreu'tic a. Highly finished (of metal-work). s. Art of embossing and chasing metal.
Phagocy'tic a. Phagocytal.
Troglodyt'ic a. Pertaining to cave-dwellers or troglodytes.
Trachyt'ic a. Containing or resembling trachyte.
Neophyt'ic a. (*Neophyte*).
Thallophyt'ic a. Pertaining to or like the thallophytes.
Zoophyt'ic (fit'-) a. Pertaining to or resembling the zoophytes.
Microphyt'ic a. Microphytal.
Saprophyt'ic a. Pertaining to or resembling saprophytes.
Dialyt'ic a. Pertaining to dialysis.
Psychoanalyt'ic a. Pertaining to psychoanalysis.
Paralyt'ic a. Affected with or inclined to paralysis. s. A person so affected.
Catalyt'ic a. Relating to or effected by catalysis.
Chemolyt'ic a. (*Chemolysis*).
Plasmolyt'ic a. Due to or pertaining to plasmolysis.
Electrolyt'ic a. Pertain ng to electrolysis or electrolytes.
Histolyt'ic a. Pertaining to or due to histolysis.
Tol'uic a. Pertaining to or derived from toluene.
Slav'ic a. Slavonic. s. The Slavonic language.
Civ'ic a. Pertaining to a city or citizens; urban, municipal.
Pel'vic a. Pertaining to the pelvis.
Syl'vic a. Derived from wood.
Atax'ic a. Pertaining to ataxy; irregular.
Tox'ic a. Poisonous; pertaining to poison.
Antitox'ic a. Preventing the action of poisons.
Autotox'ic a. Self-poisoning.
Ich'thyic a. Pertaining to fishes.
Rhiz'ic a. Pertaining to the root of an equation.
Talc s. A foliated, magnesian mineral.
Banc s. The Bench.
Char'abanc s. A large car with transverse benches.
Franc s. A French silver coin (nominally about 9½d.).
Zinc s. A bluish-white metallic element. v.t. To coat with this.
Quid'nunc s. A busybody, a curious pryer.
Me'doc' s. A red wine.
Opodel'doc s. Soap-liniment.
Man'ioc s. The cassava; meal made therefrom.
Roc s. A gigantic fabulous bird of Arab legend.
Soc s. The right, in Anglo-Saxon times, of holding a local court; the district under such court.
Nos'toc s. A genus of blue-green freshwater algæ; star-jelly.
Hav'oc s. Widespread destruction; devastation.
Arc s. Part of the circumference of a circle or curve.
Marc s. Refuse matter after pressure of grapes.
En'dosarc s. Endoplasm.
Circ s. A prehistoric stone circle.
Orc s. The grampus; a fabulous sea-monster.
Fu'thorc s. The Runic alphabet.
Disc s. (*Disk*).
Fisc s. The state treasury, the public purse.
Sub'fusc a. Sad-coloured, dusky.
Mol'lusc s. One of a division of soft-bodied hard-shelled invertebrates including the snails.
Caou'tchouc s. Rubber.
Bad a. Not good; vicious.
Forbad' past. (*Forbid*).
Cad s. A low, badly behaved fellow.
Scad s. The horse-mackerel; salmon fry.
Cyc'ad s. One of an order of plants allied to the conifers.
Dad s. (*Childish*) Father.
Bedad' int. An Irish exclamation of surprise, etc.
Al'idad s. The moving indicator of an astrolabe.
Dead a. Deprived of life; dull; inanimate; utter; unerring.

Ide'a'd a. Having an idea or ideas.
-head suff. Denoting state or quality.
Head s. Uppermost part of man, or foremost part of animal, containing the brain, etc.; intellect; a chief; top; crisis; division of discourse. a. Chief, principal, first, highest. v.t. To form a head to; to lead, direct, oppose. v.i. To form a head; to be directed.
Ahead' adv.; a. Farther onward, in advance.
Dead'head s. One who has a free pass.
Round'head s. A Puritan of the Commonwealth period.
God'head s. The divine nature or essence; a deity.
Behead' v.t. To remove the head of.
Fore'head s. The upper part of the face.
Fig'ure-head s. A nominal leader having no real power.
Beast'lihead s. The condition or nature of a beast.
Drear'ihead s. Dreariness.
Boun'tihead s. Bounteousness; virtue.
Block'head s. A stupid fellow, a dolt.
Bulk'head s. A partition between decks on board ship.
Bill'-head s. A ruled form with name, address, etc., of tradesman printed thereon.
Maid'enhead s. State of being a maid; virginity, the hymen.
Dun'derhead s. A blockhead, dunce.
Blun'derhead s. A dolt, a fool.
Overhead' adv. Aloft; above.
Hogs'head s. 52½ imp. gall.; a butt, large cask.
Hot'head s. An impetuous, passionate person.
Lead (led) s. A soft, heavy, bluish-grey metallic element; thin plate separating lines of type; a plummet; plumbago for pencils. a. Made of or produced by lead. v.t. To cover or fit with lead.
Lead (lēd) v.t. To guide, conduct; to direct and govern; to precede; to influence; to begin. v.i. To go before and show the way; to be chief; to have a tendency. s. Guidance; precedence; example; cord for a dog; first play at cards, etc.
Blacklead' s. Graphite, plumbago. v.t. To polish with this.
Plead v.i. To argue in support of or against; to urge; to supplicate earnestly; v.t. To discuss and defend; to offer in excuse, to allege in defence.
Interplead' v.i. To try an incidental issue before the main cause can be heard.
Mislead' (-lēd') v.t. To lead astray, deceive, delude; to cause to mistake.
Mead s. A fermented drink made from honey; a meadow.
Knead v.t. To work and press into a mass, especially for bread.
Snead s. The handle of a scythe.
Read (rēd) v.t. To peruse, to utter aloud from print, MS., etc.; to see through; to explain. v.i. To peruse, study; to make sense. s. Act of reading.
Read (red) a. Versed in books; knowing by reading; learned.
Bread s. Food made of flour.
Sweet'bread s. The pancreas of a calf or sheep as food.
Short'bread s. A sweet, brittle cake.
Sow'bread (sou'-) s. One of the cyclamens.
Dread s. Habitual fear, terror. v.t. and i. To fear greatly. a. Exciting fear; terrible; venerable.
Adread' a. Afraid, terrified.
Thread s. A slender cord of cotton, silk, etc.; a line, link, vein. v.t. To pass a thread through the eye of; to string on a thread; to pass through with difficulty.
Or'ead s. A mountain-nymph.
Spread v.t. To extend in all directions; to expand; to disseminate. v.i. To stretch out, be diffused. s. Act of spreading; extent, compass; diffusion; (*slang*) a good meal.
Bespread' v.t. To spread over, to adorn.
Overspread' v.t. To spread, cover, or scatter over.
Outspread' a. Extended; expanded.
Mis-read' a. Read in a way that gives a wrong impression.
Tread v.i. and t. To set the foot on the ground; to walk, go, step, trample; copulate (of fowls). s. Act, manner, or sound of stepping; flat part of a stair; part of tire, etc., that touches the ground.
Stead s. Place another had or might have had.
Road'stead s. Place where ships ride at anchor off shore.
Bed'stead s. The frame for supporting a bed.
Bestead' v.t. To help. v.i. To avail. a. Situated, circumstanced.
Home'stead s. A farm with its buildings.
Farm'stead s. The dwelling, outbuildings, yards, etc., on a farm.
Instead' adv. In the place of; equivalent to.
Fad s. A whim, passing fancy, favourite theory.
Gad s. A spike, iron punch, wedge, etc. v.i. To wander idly about; to ramble; to spend time enjoying oneself.
Egad' int. A mild oath.
Begad' int. Mild expletive.
Had past and past part. (*Have*).
Jihad' s. A Mohammedan holy war.
Lym'phad s. An ancient one-masted galley.
Shad s. A food-fish of the herring family.
Upa'nishad s. One of the philosophical divisions of the Vedas.
Na'iad s. A water-nymph, river-goddess.
Plei'ad s. A brilliant group, especially a 16th century group of French poets.
Il'iad s. Homer's epic on the Trojan War; a long tragic story.
Chil'iad s. A thousand, 1000 years.
Jeremi'ad s. A lamentation; a tale of woe.
Decen'niad s. A period of ten years.
Quinquen'niad s. A period of five years.
Gwyn'iad s. A Welsh lake-fish of the salmon family.
Ascle'piad s. A verse invented by the Greek poet Asclepiades.
Olym'piad s. A period of four years in ancient Greek reckoning.
Hy'driad s. A water-nymph.
Tri'ad s. A collection or union of three; a common chord.
Myr'iad s. 10,000; an indefinitely great number. a. Innumerable.
Lad s. A youth, stripling.
Sal'ad s. Raw herbs, dressed with vinegar, etc.
Clad past part. (*Clothe*).
I'ronclad s. An armoured warship. a. Armour-plated.
Glad a. Cheerful, gay; elevated with joy.
Bal'lad s. A song, a light poem.
Mad a. Distracted; insane; crazy; furious. v.i. and t. To be, go, or make mad.

Heb'domad s. A week; a group of seven.
No'mad s. One who leads a wandering life. a. Wandering.
Mæ'nad s. A bacchante; a frenzied woman.
Ul'nad adv. Towards the ulna.
Gon'ad s. A sperm-gland from which an ovary develops.
Mon'ad s. A primary constituent of matter.
Goad s. A pointed stick for driving beasts; anything that rouses to action. v.t. To drive with a goad; to instigate.
Load s. A burden; freight; lading; weight. v.t. To freight; to charge, as a gun.
Reload' v.t. and i. To load again.
Overload' v.t. To load with too heavy a burden, etc.
Road s. A highway, public passage; a roadstead.
Broad a. Wide; indelicate.
Abroad' adv. In foreign countries, at large.
Rail'road s. A railway.
In'road s. A hostile incursion, an encroachment.
By-'road s. A private or obscure path.
Toad s. A tailless frog-like amphibian; an objectionable person.
Quo'ad prep. As regards; so far as.
Woad (wōd) s. A cruciferous plant, the leaves of which yield a blue dye.
Pad s. A footpath; an easy-paced horse; a highwayman; anything flattened; a soft saddle, cushion, pack of blotting-paper. v.i. To travel leisurely; to rob on foot. v.t. To stuff with padding.
Lam'pad s. A torch.
Foot'pad s. A highwayman working on foot.
Far'ad s. The standard unit of electrical capacity.
Brad s. A small headless nail.
Undergrad' s. (*Slang*) An undergraduate.
Tet'rad s. The number 4; a collection of four things.
Strad s. A Stradivarius.
Sad a. Sorrowful; melancholy; calamitous.
Oc'tad s. A group of eight.
Pen'tad s. A group of five; an element or radical with combining power of five.
Hep'tad s. A group of seven; an atom whose equivalence is seven atoms of hydrogen.
Du'ad s. Dyad.
Quad s. A quadrangle; a quadrat.
Squad s. A small number of soldiers or others.
Wad (wod) s. Soft mass of tow, etc., for packing; stopper for charge of a cartridge, etc.; an earthy oxide of manganese. v.t. To stop up with or press into a wad.
Hex'ad s. A group of six; an atom which can be combined with, substituted for, or replaced by six atoms of hydrogen.
Dy'ad s. A couple, pair; an atom whose equivalence is two.
Dry'ad s. A wood-nymph.
Ham'adryad s. A wood-nymph fabled to live and die with an individual tree; a venomous snake.
Add v.t. To join or unite as one sum to another; to annex, subjoin.
Superadd' v.t. To add over and over.
Odd a. Not paired; not exactly divisible by two; belonging to a broken set; casual; strange, eccentric.

Rudd s. A freshwater fish allied to the roach.
Sudd s. Massed vegetation floating in the Nile.
-ed suff. Forming past and past parts. of regular verbs (many of which are used as adjectives).
Unide'a'ed a. Stupid, having no ideas.
Bed s. A couch; a river channel; a layer; a plot for flowers. v.t. To put or plant in a bed.
Abed' adv. In bed.
Scab'bed a. Abounding or diseased with scabs.
Crab'bed a. Peevish, morose; perplexing; undecipherable.
Crib'bed a. Confined in a narrow space.
Demobbed' a. (*Slang*) Demobilized.
Club'bed a. Beaten with a club; club-shaped, butt ended.
Rub'bed a. Worn with use.
Inscri'bed a. Having an inscription thereon.
Embed' v.t. To lay as in a bed; to bed.
Hon'eycombed a. Full of cells or holes.
Lobed a. Having lobes.
Garb'ed a. Clothed, dressed.
Absorb'ed a. Sucked up, incorporated.
Hot'bed s. A flower-bed heated with manure; a place favouring rapid growth.
Bold'faced a. Impudent, shameless.
Shame'faced a. Bashful, modest, shy.
Bare'faced a. Shameless, bold, brazen.
Disgra'ced a. Put to shame, shown up.
Fleeced a. Furnished with a fleece.
Jaun'diced a. Affected with jaundice; prejudiced; jealous.
Unvoiced' a. Not spoken; not sonant.
Lat'ticed a. Having a lattice or lattices.
Discal'ced a. Barefooted, discalceate.
Affi'anced a. Betrothed.
Cir'cumstanced a. Situated.
Advanced' a. Far on; before one's age.
Exper'ienced a. Taught by trial; skilled through observation or use.
Inexper'ienced a. Not having experience; unskilled.
Floun'ced a. Furnished with flounces.
Denoun'ced a. Informed against, stigmatized.
Pronounced' a. Strongly marked; decided.
Forced a. Constrained, overstrained, unnatural.
Enforced' a. Not voluntary.
Barriea'ded a. Defended by barricades.
Bead'ed a. Furnished with beads.
Head'ed a. Having a head.
Pig-head'ed a. Obstinate, sullen.
Bull-head'ed a. With a massive head; obstinate; stupid.
Hot-head'ed a. Passionate, impetuous.
Lead'ed a. Fitted with or separated by leads.
Sha'ded a. Placed in the shade, obscured.
Jad'ed a. Tired out; overdone; worn.
Blocka'ded a. Subjected to a blockade.
Serena'ded a. Complimented with nocturnal music.
Woad'ed a. Stained with woad.
Degrad'ed a. Reduced in rank, etc.; mean base.
Embed'ded a. Sunk in another substance.
Wed'ded a. Married, pertaining to marriage intimately associated.
Stud'ded a. Set thickly or bestrewn with.
Unheed'ed a. Disregarded, ignored.
Speed'ed past and past part. (*Speed*).
Braid'ed a. Having the hair in plaits.
Decid'ed a. Settled; evident; resolute.
Undecid'ed a. Hesitating; irresolute.
One-sid'ed a. Partial, unfair.
Lop-si'ded a. Ill-balanced; not symmetrical.
Misguid'ed a. Foolish, led astray.

Provid'ed conj. On condition; with the understanding.
Disband'ed a. Dispersed, broken up as a body.
Hand'ed a. Having hands.
High-hand'ed a. Overbearing, domineering.
Back-han'ded a. With the back of the hand; indirect, unexpected.
Open-hand'ed a. Generous.
Underhand'ed a. Sly, unfair; secret.
Land'ed a. Having or consisting of real estate.
Brand'ed a. Marked, especially marked as infamous.
Strand'ed a. Left high and dry, left without resources.
Sand'ed a. Covered with sand; speckled.
Descend'ed a. Sprung from; tracing ancestry to.
Offend'ed a. Annoyed, displeased.
Unfriend'ed a. Not having friends.
Commend'ed a. Praised.
Inten'ded s. A fiancé or fiancée.
Mind'ed a. Disposed; inclined.
Wind'ed a. Rendered scant of breath.
Bond'ed a. Bound by a bond; put in bond.
Fund'ed a. Invested in public funds; forming part of the national debt.
Unfund'ed a. Floating (of a public debt).
Unbound'ed a. Having no limit; unrestrained.
Dumfound'ed a. Struck with bewilderment.
Confound'ed a. Perplexed; (*slang*) great; annoying; abominable.
Unfound'ed a. Void of foundation.
Round'ed a. Made round, completed.
Unground'ed a. Groundless; having no foundation.
Astound'ed a. Astonished, amazed.
Explo'ded a. Refuted, discredited (of theories, etc.).
Hood'ed a. Furnished with a hood; blinded.
Blue-blood'ed a. Of high descent.
Wood'ed a. Supplied with growing trees.
Bear'ded a. Having a beard or awn; barbed.
Disregard'ed a. Neglected, ignored.
Guard'ed a. Circumspect, cautious; defended.
Herd'ed a. Crowded together.
Belord'ed a. Constantly addressed as "My Lord."
Word'ed a. Set forth or phrased (thus) in words.
Sword'ed a. Furnished with a sword.
Includ'ed a. Contained, comprised.
Succeed' v.t. To come after, be successor to. v.i. To follow in order, ensue; to become heir; to be successful, to prosper.
Proceed' v.i. To pass or go forward or on; to make progress; to come forth; to take a degree, carry on a legal action.
Exceed' v.t. To pass or go beyond; to surpass. v.i. To go too far; to be more or larger.
Deed s. An action, exploit, performance, achievement; a written instrument.
Indeed' adv. In reality. int. Expressing irony, surprise, etc.
Misdeed' s. A wicked action, crime.
Feed v.t. To give food to; to supply with nourishment of anything of which there is constant need. v.i. To take food, eat. s. Fodder; (*slang*) meal; a pipe for feeding an engine, etc. a. Receiving a fee.
Overfeed' v.i. To feed to excess.
Heed v.t. and i. To attend to, mind, regard. s. Care, attention.
Bleed v.i. To lose blood. v.t. To cause another to lose blood.
Gleed s. An ember, a burning coal.
Meed s. Reward, recompense, gift.
Need s. Exigency; necessity; want. v.t. To have necessity for; to lack, require. v.i. To be necessary or wanted.
Kneed a. Having the specified kind of knee.
Speed s. Quickness, haste, dispatch v.i. To make haste, to prosper v.t. To dispatch hurriedly; to hasten or bring to a result.
God-speed' s. Success, prosperity.
Reed s. The straight stem of certain aquatic plants; musical pipe made of this; thin piece of wood or metal used in some wind-instruments and organ-pipes.
Breed v.t. To give birth to, to procreate. v.i. To produce offspring, to arise, to spread. s. A line of descendants, race.
Interbreed' v.t. and i. To breed from two different species.
Creed s. A summary or a solemn profession of religious belief.
Decreed' a. Decided or ordained authoritatively.
Screed s. A strip of cloth; a lengthy statement.
Jereed' s. A javelin used in the East.
Greed s. Avarice, rapacity, covetousness.
Fil'igreed a. Ornamented with filigree.
Treed a. Trapped up a tree.
Seed s. Product of a plant that may produce a similar plant; semen; progeny; first principle. v.i. To produce or shed seed. v.t. To sow; to run to seed.
An'iseed s. The seed of the anise, used in medicine.
Lin'seed s. The seed of flax.
Guaranteed' a. Warranted.
Steed s. A horse, war-horse.
Weed s. Any useless or noxious plant, anything useless; (*slang*) a cigar, tobacco. v.t. and i. To rid of or pull up weeds.
Sea'weed s. Any plant growing in the sea.
Bind'weed s. A convolvulus.
Cud'weed s. A common weed.
Poke'weed s. A poisonous N. American herb.
Catch'weed s. Cleavers.
Chick'weed s. A creeping weed.
Knap'weed s. A purple-flowered plant.
Tweed s. A light twilled woollen stuff.
Joint'weed s. Equisetum, mare's-tail.
Fed past and past part. (*Feed*).
Ruffed (ruft) a. Furnished with a ruff.
Hoofed a. Furnished with hoofs.
A'ged a. So many years old; of great age.
Engaged' a. Affianced; pledged; attached to a wall (of columns).
Disengaged' a. Separated; free; at leisure.
Fledged a. Feathered; able to fly.
Selv'edged a. Having a selvedge.
Jag'ged a. Having notches; cleft; uneven.
Snag'ged a. Snaggy.
Rag'ged a. Rent, battered; shaggy; rough; shabby.
Crag'ged a. Craggy, rugged.
Leg'ged a. Having a specified kind of leg.
Bow-legged' a. Having the legs bent outwards.
Dog'ged a. Determined; obstinate.
Wa'terlogged a. Flooded so as to lie nearly submerged.
Rug'ged a. Rough, full of projections; harsh, surly; robust; tempestuous.
Fang'ed a. Furnished with fangs.
Deranged' a. Slightly insane.

Loz'enged a. Diamond- or rhomb-shaped; arranged in lozenges.
Hinged a. Provided with a hinge or hinges.
Unhinged' a. Deranged; disordered.
Stringed a. Having strings.
Detached' a. Separated; free from prejudice; disinterested.
Attached' a. Connected; joined in feeling or affection.
Caboched' a. Borne full-faced (of heraldic animals).
Starched a. Stiff, precise, formal.
Bepatched' a. Mended with or wearing patches.
Wretch'ed a. Miserable, sunk in affliction; paltry, mean; worthless.
Blotched' a. Marked with blotches.
Shed s. A hut, pent-house; a ridge, watershed. v.t. To throw or give off, to emit; to pour out, spill, scatter. v.i. To cast off seed, etc.
Blood'shed s. Slaughter; murder.
Accom'plished a. Consummate; having graces and attainments.
Distin'guished a. Having distinction; eminent, illustrious; conspicuous.
Caboshed' a. (*Caboched*).
Wa'tershed s. High ridge between two river systems.
Unscathed' a. Uninjured.
Toothed a. Having teeth, jags, or projections.
Betroth'ed a. Engaged to be married. s. One in this position.
Ru'bied a. Adorned with or coloured like rubies.
Can'died a. Preserved in sugar; glistening.
Able-bod'ied a. Powerful; skilled (of seamen).
La'dified a. Affecting the airs of a fine lady.
Dan'dified a. Foppish.
Qual'ified a. Fitted by ability; modified.
Dig'nified a. Invested with dignity; stately.
Coun'trified a. Rustic in appearance or manners.
Diver'sified a. Distinguished by various forms, etc.; variegated.
Cit'ified a. Townish.
Cock'neyfied a. Having the ways, speech, etc., of a Londoner; townish.
Lied (lēd) s. A German ballad.
Lil'ied a. Covered with or resembling lilies.
Volks'lied (-lēt) s. A folk-song.
Bel'lied a. Corpulent.
Coll'ied a. Dark, gloomy.
Implied' a. Contained in substance but not expressed.
Pan'oplied a. In full armour.
Applied' a. Put to practical use.
Cran'nied a. Having crannies.
Hon'ied a. Honeyed.
Aston'ied a. Dumfounded.
Pied a. Variegated with spots or blotches.
Can'opied a. Covered by a canopy.
Pop'pied a. Covered with poppies; soporifically affected.
Sal'aried a. In receipt of a salary.
Var'ied past and past part. (*Vary*).
Liv'eried a. Having or entitled to a livery.
Fried past and past part. (*Fry*).
Stor'ied a. Celebrated in or adorned with scenes from story; having storeys.
Mar'ried a. United in or pertaining to marriage; conjugal.
Ser'ried a. In close, compact order.
Hur'ried a. Characterized by hurry; evidencing or done in a hurry.
Dais'ied a. Adorned with daisies.
Pal'sied a. Affected with palsy.
Quin'sied a. Affected with quinsy.
Drop'sied a. Afflicted with dropsy.
Cit'ied a. Containing cities.
Prop'ertied a. Possessing property.
Du'tied a. Charged with a duty.
En'nuied a. Affected with ennui.
I'vied a. Covered with ivy.
Scur'vied a. Affected with scurvy.
Fren'zied a. Affected with or proceeding from frenzy.
Beaked a. Having a beak.
Peaked a. Pointed; sharp.
Freaked a. Variegated, streaked.
Na'ked a. Being unclothed; bare; unarmed, unassisted.
Backed a. Furnished with a back or backing; seconded.
Cracked a. Half-witted.
Decked a. Adorned; furnished with a deck or decks.
Hen'pecked a. Governed or nagged at by one's wife.
Wick'ed a. Sinful; wilfully transgressing; abandoned.
Land'locked a. Enclosed by land.
Brocked a. (*Scot.*) Speckled black and white.
Balked a. Frustrated, baffled.
Stalked a. Having a stalk.
Booked a. Entered in a book; engaged.
Hooked a. Bent; furnished with hooks.
Crook'ed a. Bent, wry, not straight; dishonest.
Marked a. Pre-eminent; remarkable.
Corked a. Stopped with a cork; tasting of the cork; blackened with burnt cork.
Forked a. Branching, bifurcated, cleft.
Hawked a. Curved like a hawk's bill; streaked.
Led past and past part. (*Lead*).
Bled a. Divested of blood, or of money.
Fa'bled a. Legendary; celebrated in fable.
Bedrab'bled a. Dirty with mire and rain.
Spec'tacled a. Wearing spectacles.
Fas'cicled a. Clustered together.
Ar'ticled a. Bound by articles of apprenticeship.
Addled' a. Putrid, rotten.
Unbridled' a. Unrestrained.
Brindled' a. Streaked, tabby.
Unpar'alleled a. Unequalled; matchless.
Fled past and past part. (*Flee*).
Unruffled' a. Calm; not disturbed or agitated.
Newfan'gled a. New-fashioned; fond of novelties.
Hob'nailed a. Set with hobnails; rough and uneven.
Bob'-tailed a. Having the tail cut short.
De'tailed a. Related in detail; complete.
Unri'valled a. Having no rival; peerless.
Tram'melled a. Hampered, confined.
Bar'relled a. Packed in barrels; having a barrel or barrels.
Laur'elled a. Crowned with laurel.
Unhous'elled a. Not having received the sacrament.
Trav'elled a. Experienced in travelling.
Dishev'elled a. Hanging in disorder (of the hair).
Swelled past part. (*Swell*).
Skilled a. Skilful.
Frilled a. Furnished with a frill or frills.
Polled a. Lopped; wanting horns.
Steepled' a. Having a steeple or steeples.
Prin'cipled a. Having principles.
Crumpled' a. Wrinkled, curled.
Gnarled a. Knotty; full of knots; rugged.
Sled s. A vehicle on runners. v.t. and i. To convey in or travel by this.
Measled' a. Affected with measles; measly.
Bob'-sled s. Two sleighs coupled together.
Mis'led a. Led astray, deluded.
Disgrun'tled a. Disappointed, offended.
Bat'tled a. Drawn up in line of battle; furnished with embattlements.

Mettled' a. Mettlesome.
Unsettled' a. Not settled, decided, etc.; changeable; unpaid.
Inti'tuled a. Having a specified title.
Famed a. Celebrated, renowned.
Ashamed' a. Abashed; confounded.
Fore'named a. Mentioned previously.
Calmed a. Made calm or peaceful; becalmed.
Helmed a. Wearing a helm or helmet.
Domed a. Furnished with or shaped like a dome.
Cus'tomed a. Usual.
Accus'tomed a. Usual, wonted, familiar.
Bot'tomed a. Based, well-grounded.
Armed a. Furnished with arms; prepared for conflict.
Deformed' a. Misshapen, ugly.
Reformed' a. Corrected; purged of errors and abuses.
Informed' a. Enlightened; having information.
Assumed' a. Put on, pretended; taken for granted.
Or'phaned a. Bereft of a parent or parents.
Hard'ened a. Obstinate; callous; confirmed.
Li'chened a. Covered with lichen.
Chas'tened a. Subdued by suffering, etc.; restrained.
Wiz'ened a. Thin, shrunk, dried up.
Designed' a. Intentional.
Resigned' a. Submissive, patiently enduring.
Hare-'brained a. Rash, flighty.
Constrained' a. Acting under compulsion; forced.
Blood'stained a. Soiled with blood.
Refined' (-find') a. Freed from impurity or inelegance; highly cultured.
Confined' a. In childbed.
Bus'kined a. Wearing buskins; tragic, sublime.
Disinclined' a. Indisposed, averse to.
Deter'mined a. Resolute; limited.
Indeter'mined a. Not determined, not definite.
Groined a. Formed of intersecting arches.
Spined a. Having a spine.
Spav'ined a. Affected with spavin.
Damned a. Condemned; abominable, execrable. adv. Confoundedly, infernally.
Canned a. Put up in a tin.
Boned a. Furnished with or divested of bones.
Aban'doned a. Forsaken; profligate.
Impas'sioned a. Agitated or actuated by passion; excited.
Commis'sioned a. Holding a commission.
Non-commis'sioned a. Applied to military officers below rank of lieutenant.
Condi'tioned a. Circumstanced; determined by something else.
Zoned a. Having zones or concentric bands.
Learned past and past part. (*Learn*).
Learn'ed a. Erudite, scholarly; characterized by great learning.
Concerned' a. Interested, involved; solicitous.
Unconcerned' a. Not anxious; easy in mind.
Corned a. Cured by salting.
Adorned' a. Decked out.
Horned a. Furnished with horns; having horn-like extremities.
Gowned a. Clothed in or invested with a gown.
Renowned' a. Celebrated, famous; remarkable.
Crowned a. Invested with a crown; surmounted.
Intoed' a. With toes turned in.
Grot'toed a. Furnished with grottos.
Beneaped' a. Left aground by a neap tide.
Bi'ped s. A two-footed animal.
Tal'iped a. Club-footed.
Chel'iped s. Certain crustaceans.
Maxil'liped s. A foot-jaw in crustacea.
Sol'iped s. An animal whose hoofs are not cloven. a. Solid, ungulate.
Pal'niped a. Web-footed. s. A swimming bird.
Pin'niped a. Having feet like fins. s. A marine carnivore with flippers, as the seal, walrus, etc.
U'niped a. Having only one foot. s. Such an animal.
Parallelep'iped s. A solid bounded by six parallelograms, the opposite ones being parallel and equal to each other.
Ser'riped a. Having serrated feet.
Cir'riped s. A marine crustacean of the barnacle family.
Mul'tiped s. An insect having many feet. a. Many-footed.
Oc'toped s. An animal or insect with 8 feet.
Hipped a. Having the hip dislocated; having hips; affected with melancholia.
Sped past and past part. (*Speed*).
Quad'ruped s. A four-footed animal. a. Quadrupedal.
Red a. Of a colour resembling arterial blood. s. This colour; a pigment, dye; revolutionary.
Eared a. Having ears.
Feared a. Regarded with fear.
Seared a. Callous, hardened.
Dog's-eared a. Having the corners turned down (of leaves of books).
Ash'lared a. Covered with ashlar.
Home'bred a. Native; plain; artless.
Thor'oughbred (thŭr'-) a. Of pure, unmixed breed. s. Such an animal, especially a horse.
Ill-bred a. Rude; badly brought up.
In'bred a. Innate; natural.
Sa'cred a. Set apart for holy purpose; consecrated; divine.
Kin'dred s. Relationship, affinity, blood-relatives. a. Related; congenial; cognate.
Hun'dred s. Sum of 10 times 10; 100; a division of an English county. a. 10 times 10.
Blood-red' a. Red as blood.
Cham'bered a. Divided into compartments; enclosed.
Tim'bered a. Wooded.
Glan'dered a. Affected with glanders.
Ahung'ered a. Hungry.
Feath'ered a. Covered with feathers; having feathery appendages.
Weath'ered a. Hardened, disintegrated, or otherwise affected by the weather; made sloping (of roofs, etc.).
Cank'ered a. Corrupted by canker; peevish.
Man'nered a. Having manners or mannerism.
Cor'nered a. Having corners; placed in a difficult position.
Distem'pered a. Diseased in body; disordered in mind.
Trous'ered a. Wearing trousers.
Chart'ered a. Invested with privileges.
Clois'tered a. Secluded; immured.
Let'tered a. Marked with letters; erudite; belonging to learning.
Unlett'ered a. Unlearned; ignorant.
Liv'ered a. Having the specified kind of liver.
Dow'ered a. Provided with a dower.
Flow'ered a. Embellished with or bearing flowers.
Tow'ered (tou'-) a. Adorned or defended with towers.
Shred s. Piece torn off; a fragment. v.t. To cut or tear into small strips.
Haired a. Having hair.

Inspired' a. Inhaled; actuated or produced by supernatural agency.
Retired' a. Secluded, private; having given up business.
Acquired' a. Not inherent, gained by one's own efforts.
Barred a. Excluded, prohibited.
Furred a. Lined, coated, or ornamented with fur.
Ha'tred s. Great dislike, aversion, loathing; abhorrence; ill-will.
Mi'tred a. Wearing a mitre.
Scep'tred a. Wielding the sceptre; having royal power.
Fig'ured a. Adorned with, represented by, or accompanied by figures.
Per'jured a. Guilty of perjury; forsworn.
Col'oured a. Tinged; exaggerated; specious; of negro descent.
Ar'moured a. Protected by armour.
Fla'voured a. Having a distinct or a specified flavour.
Meas'ured a. Deliberate, well considered; moderate; stately.
Leis'ured a. Having leisure.
Assured' a. Safe, confident, full of assurance. s. An insured person.
Cul'tured a. Well-mannered, in a state of intellectual development.
Deben'tured a. Secured by debenture.
Deceased' a. Dead. s. One recently dead.
Diseased' a. Affected with disease; morbid, unhealthy.
Bi'ased a. Prejudiced.
Ar'rased a. Hung with arras.
Ir'ised a. Coloured like the rainbow.
Prac'tised a. Skilled, expert.
Advised' a. Deliberate, well considered.
Composed' a. Free from agitation, calm.
Disposed' a. Inclined, minded.
Indisposed' a. Disinclined; slightly ill.
Versed a. Familiar, skilled; reversed (of sines).
Unhors'ed a. Thrown or violently removed from horseback.
Cur'sed a. Deserving or under a curse; execrable, detestable.
Accur'sed a. Execrable, wicked, hateful.
Professed' (-fest') s. Avowed; acknowledged; pretending to be qualified.
Bless'ed a. Consecrated by religious rites, happy, beatified. s. The saints in heaven.
Depressed' a. Dejected, dispirited.
Cabossed' a. (*Caboched*).
Ted v.t. To turn and expose to the sun (of hay).
Lo'bated a. Lobate.
Glo'bated a. Spherical, spheroidal.
Sil'icated a. Combined, impregnated, or coated with silica.
Pli'cated a. Plicate.
Var'icated a. Having varices (of shells).
Fim'bricated a. (*Fimbriated*).
Cor'ticated a. (*Corticate*).
Unsophis'ticated a. Artless, ingenuous, simple.
Fal'cated a. Sickle-shaped.
Por'cated a. Formed in ridges.
Bi'furcated a. Divided into two branches.
Cus'pidated a. (*Cuspidate*).
Tra'beated a. (*Trabeate*).
Discal'ceated a. Barefooted, discalceate.
Gal'eated a. Shaped like a helmet.
Acu'leated a. Prickly; having a sting.
Seat'ed a. Sitting.
Fa'ted a. Decreed by fate; doomed.
Cor'rugated a. Wrinkled; having prominent ridges and furrows.
Brec'ciated a. Formed into breccia.
Fas'ciated a. Flattened through irregular growth (of plants).
Inta'gliated a. Engraved on a hard surface.
Cil'iated a. (*Cilia*).
Trifo'liated a. Bearing three leaves.
Lacin'iated a. Laciniate; jagged, much indented.
Ammo'niated a. Combined with ammonia.
Fim'briated a. Fringed.
Flor'iated a. Floriate.
Histor'iated a. Adorned with carved figures.
Mur'iated a. Treated with muriatic acid; put in brine.
A'lated a. Having wings.
Bela'ted a. Benighted; made late.
Relat'ed a. Connected by blood or marriage.
Inflat'ed a. Puffed up; bombastic; unduly raised in price.
Can'cellated a. Cross-barred.
Ocel'lated a. Ocellate.
Lam'ellated a. Lamellar.
Tes'sellated a. Formed in mosaic; inlaid; checquered.
Cas'tellated a. Turreted; battlemented.
Fi'brillated a. Fibrillar.
Cor'ollated a. Corollate.
Cu'cullated a. Cucullate.
Nucle'olated a. Having a nucleolus.
Trabec'ulated a. (*Trabecular*).
Acic'ulated a. Having sharp bristles, or fine irregular streaks.
Fascic'ulated a. (*Fasciculate*).
Canalic'ulated a. Minutely grooved.
Apic'ulated a. Ending abruptly in a point.
Dentic'ulated a. Finely toothed; formed into dentils.
Artic'ulated a. Jointed.
Cal'culated a. Prearranged; cold-blooded.
Acid'ulated a. Made slightly acid; soured.
Nod'ulated a. Covered with or characterized by nodules.
Teg'ulated a. Furnished with tegulæ or with tiles.
Lig'ulated a. Strap-shaped; having a ligula.
Cell'ulated a. Cellulate.
Num'mulated a. Coin-shaped.
Cren'ulated a. Finely notched or scalloped.
Annula'ted a. Wearing, marked with, or composed of rings.
Scap'ulated a. Having conspicuous scapular feathers.
Meth'ylated a. Mixed with methyl alcohol.
An'imated a. Lively, vivacious.
Pal'mated a. Palmate.
Crena'ted a. Notched, indented.
Echi'nated a. Echinate; spiny.
Foram'inated a. (*Foraminate*).
Acu'minated a. Brought to a point; stinging.
Car'inated a. Carinate.
Pat'inated a. Covered with patina.
Pec'tinated a. (*Pectinate*).
Pen'nated a. Pennate; winged.
Pin'nated a. Pinnate.
Opin'ionated a. Obstinate in opinion; dogmatic.
Cor'onated a. (*Coronate*).
Bloat'ed a. Swollen, puffed-up, pampered.
Dis'sipated a. Given to dissipation.
Cel'ebrated a. Famous, renowned.
Ver'tebrated a. Having a backbone.
A'erated a. Charged with air or carbonic acid gas; effervescent.
Cera'ted a. Covered with wax.
Accel'erated a. Having the velocity increased.
Dec'orated a. Ornamented; of the style of Gothic between Early English and Perpendicular.
Cam'phorated a. Treated with camphor.
Au'rated a. Gilded; containing or resembling gold.

Sa'ted a. Surfeited; satiated.
Ir'isated a. Showing prismatic colours.
Incras'sated a. Thickened; inspissated.
Decus'sated a. Crossed, intersected.
A'cetated a. Treated with acetic acid.
Dig'itated a. (*Digitate*).
Cap'itated a. Having a head, or a cluster in head form.
Pel'tated a. Peltate.
Denta'ted a. Toothed, indented.
Arc'uated a. Arched, bow-shaped.
Atten'uated a. Become thin or diluted.
Corn'uated a. Cornuate.
An'tiquated a. Old-fashioned, out of date.
Torqua'ted a. Having a coloured ring round the neck.
Infat'uated a. Besotted.
Sit'uated a. Situate; circumstanced.
Indebt'ed a. Being in debt; obliged to.
Redoubt'ed a. Dreaded.
Compact'ed a. Consolidated, firmly joined together.
Refrac'ted a. Deflected from a direct course.
Retrofrac'ted a. Bent back and appearing as if broken.
Cat'aphracted a. Covered with plates (of certain fishes).
Contrac'ted a. Limited, narrow, mean; betrothed.
Abstrac'ted a. Absentminded; purloined.
Distract'ed a. Confounded; mentally perturbed; crazed.
Affec'ted a. Given to false show.
Disaffect'ed a. Indisposed to favour; unfriendly.
Retroflec'ted a. Turned or carved backward.
Collect'ed a. Cool, self-possessed.
Connect'ed a. United; coherent; closely related.
Disconnect'ed a. Separated; incoherent.
Addic'ted a. Devoted to, prone to.
Afflic'ted a. Troubled; affected with mental or bodily pain.
Constrict'ed a. Drawn together, cramped; compressed in parts.
Ring'leted a. Having ringlets.
Hel'meted a. Wearing a helmet.
Lap'peted a. Having a lappet or lappets.
Tur'reted a. Having a turret or turrets.
Gift'ed a. Talented; well endowed intellectually.
Tuft'ed a. Adorned with or growing in a tuft.
Light'ed past and past part. (*Light*).
Blight'ed a. Mildewed; frustrated.
Delight'ed a. Experiencing great pleasure; charmed.
Benight'ed a. Overtaken by night; ignorant, uncivilized.
Sight'ed a. Having sight, not blind.
Hab'ited a. Dressed; wearing a habit.
Ined'ited a. Not revised; not published.
Accred'ited a. Officially recognized.
Conceit'ed a. Vain, egotistical.
Lim'ited a. Narrow; confined; restricted.
Spir'ited a. Animated, lively, courageous.
Detri'ted a. Worn away, disintegrated.
Attri'ted a. Worn away by friction.
Bel'ted a. Furnished with a belt, especially as a mark of rank.
Hilt'ed a. Furnished with a hilt.
Kilt'ed a. Wearing a kilt.
Stilt'ed a. Bombastic, pompous; applied to a certain kind of arch.
Vault'ed a. Arched; concave.
Scent'ed a. Having a scent.
Pre'cedented a. Having a precedent.
Indent'ed a. Notched, serrated; bound by indenture.
Tal'ented a. Furnished with talent or ability.
Lament'ed a. Mourned for; late.
Dement'ed a. Mad; infatuated.
Gar'mented a. Clothed; habited.
Content'ed a. Satisfied, content, happy.
Discontent'ed a. Dissatisfied, ill at ease; given to grumbling.
Unfrequent'ed a. Rarely visited; solitary.
Saint'ed a. Holy, consecrated; gone to heaven.
Joint'ed a. Having joints.
Anoint'ed a. Consecrated; smeared with oil. s. A consecrated person.
Point'ed a. Sharp; distinct; keen; severe; direct.
Wont'ed a. Customary; usual.
Undaunt'ed a. Fearless; intrepid.
Haunt'ed a. Troubled by spectral visitants.
Stunt'ed a. Dwarfed.
Big'oted a. Moved by bigotry.
No'ted a. Eminent; remarkable.
Boot'ed a. Furnished with boots; (*slang*) discharged ignominiously.
Devo'ted a. Vowed, consecrated; zealous, ardently attached.
Coadap'ted a. Mutually adapted or suited.
Adop'ted a. Taken as one's own.
Interrup'ted a. Having interruptions; broken.
Heart'ed a. Having a heart.
Depart'ed a. Past, bygone. s. The dead.
Concert'ed a. Mutually planned; arranged in parts (of music).
Exser'ted a. Standing out, projecting.
Shirt'ed a. Wearing a shirt.
Blast'ed a. Blighted; accursed.
Mast'ed a. Having masts or a mast.
Indigest'ed a. Not digested; not properly arranged; crude.
Conges'ted a. Closely crowded; unduly distended (with blood).
Crest'ed a. Having a crest.
In'terested a. Having an interest, concerned in; liable to be affected; biased.
Disin'terested a. Free from self-interest; unbiased; indifferent.
Vest'ed a. Not subject to contingency; robed.
Frost'ed a. Covered with frost or something resembling it; injured by frost.
Wors'ted s. Woollen yarn for knitting, etc.
(woos'-) a. Made of this.
Fus'ted a. Mouldy, fusty.
Crust'ed a. Antiquated, hoary.
Epaulet'ted a. Wearing epaulets.
Fret'ted a. Ornamented with fretwork or with interlaced patterns.
Carburet'ted a. Combined with carbon.
Sulphuret'ted a. Combined or saturated with sulphur.
Phos'phuretted a. Combined or impregnated with phosphorus.
Fit'ted a. Adapted, suitable.
Dot'ted a. Marked with dots; speckled.
Knot'ted a. Full of knots; gnarled.
Besot'ted a. Infatuated, stupefied.
Flu'ted a. Channelled; furrowed.
Volu'ted a. Having volutes.
Involu'ted a. Involute; folded.
Con'voluted a. Convolute.
Cornu'ted a. Horned, horn-shaped; cuckolded.
Out'ed a. Expelled, ejected.
Reput'ed a. Generally regarded though doubtful.
A'gued a. Afflicted with ague.
Hued a. Having a particular hue.
Torqued (torkd) a. Twisted; wreathed.
Bereav'ed a. Reft of a loved one by death.
Well-behaved' a. Having good manners.
Sleeved a. Having sleeves.
Peeved a. (*Slang*). Vexed, annoyed.
Aggrieved' v.t. (past). Grieved, pained, hurt.

Beloved' a. Much loved, dear. s. A loved one.
Approved' a. Regarded with approval; tested.
Reserved' a. Retained for particular use; cautious, reticent, shy.
Curved a. Bent without angles.
Wed v.t. and i. To take as a spouse, to marry.
Lan'tern-jawed a. Having a thin, long face.
Thewed a. Having thews; sinewy.
Flewed a. Furnished with flews.
Sin'ewed (-ūd) a. Having sinews; strong, vigorous.
Screwed a. (*Slang*) Drunk.
Strewed past. (*Strew*).
Bowed a. Bent, crooked.
Will'owed a. Abounding in willows.
Beetle-browed a. Having a prominent brow.
Bor'rowed a. Obtained as a loan; not genuine.
Avowed' a. Acknowledged.
Inflexed' a. Bent, curved inwards.
Ret'roflexed a. Retroflected.
Vexed a. Worried; filled with vexation; much debated.
Fixed a. Settled; unalterable; deprived of volatility.
Mixed a. Consisting of several constituents; not select; bewildered.
Foxed a. Stained with brown spots (of paper).
Rayed a. Having rays.
Ea'gle-eyed a. Sharp-sighted.
Keyed a. Having or to be used with a key.
Hon'eyed a. Sweet, sweetened.
Mon'eyed a. Having or consisting of money.
Blear'-eyed a. Having swollen or misty eyes.
Boss'-eyed a. Squinting; with only one eye.
Sam'oyed s. One of a Mongolian race of Siberia; their language.
Zed s. The letter z.
Crazed a. Decrepit; mentally deranged.
Crys'tallized a. Made crystalline; covered with crystals.
Gal'vanized a. Treated galvanically.
Au'thorized a. Vouched for; established by authority; legally warranted.
Bronzed a. Tanned, brown-coloured.
Blowzed' a. Red-faced, slatternly.
Smaragd' s. The emerald.
-id suff. Forming adjectives denoting quality, or members of a botanical order or zoological family.
Aid v.t. To help, assist. s. Support, assistance.
Thebaid' s. The territory of ancient Egyptian Thebes.
Laid past part. (*Lay*).
Inlaid' past and past part. (*Inlay*).
Plaid s. A striped or tartan wrap worn by Highlanders.
Maid s. A virgin; a female servant.
Hand'maid s. A female servant.
Bond'maid s. A female slave.
House'maid s. A female domestic servant.
Milk'maid s. A woman employed about a dairy.
Mer'maid s. A fabulous half-woman half-fish.
Brides'maid s. A girl attendant on a bride.
Paid past and past part. (*Pay*).
Prepaid' a. Paid in advance.
Unpaid' a. Not yet paid; not in receipt of pay.
Raid s. A foray, hostile incursion; a sudden police visit. v.t. To make a raid upon.
Braid s. A narrow kind of tape. v.t. To intertwine or plait.
Upbraid' v.t. To reproach, censure, taunt.
Afraid' a. Struck with fear, terrified.
Said (sed) a. The before-mentioned. past and past part. (*Say*).
Afore'said a. Named or recited before.
Gainsaid' past and past part. (*Gainsay*).
Unsaid' (-sed') a. Not spoken.
Staid a. Sober, sedate.
Bid v.t. To offer, to order, to invite. s. An offer of a price.
Rab'id a. Mad, raging; pertaining to hydrophobia.
Tab'id a. Tabetic.
Overbid' v.t. To bid more than.
Forbid' v.t. To prohibit, interdict, obstruct.
Mor'bid a. Unhealthy; diseased; pathological.
Tur'bid a. Muddy, not clear; disordered.
Outbid' v.t. To go beyond in offer.
Cid s. A Spanish commander or champion.
A'cid a. Sharp to the taste, sour. s. A sharp and sour substance.
Subac'id a. Moderately sour or acid.
Pla'cid a. Serene, tranquil; contented.
Hyrac'id a. Pertaining to the hyrax or cony.
Antac'id a. Counteracting acidity. s. A substance effecting this.
Flac'cid a. Lacking firmness; limp; flagging.
Ran'cid a. Having a rank smell; sour; musty.
Vis'cid a. Glutinous, sticky, tenacious.
Lu'cid a. Radiant, clear; transparent; perspicuous.
Pellu'cid a. Translucent, transparent; clear.
Mu'cid a. Mouldy, mushy; mucous.
Did past. (*Do*).
Can'did a. Impartial, frank, sincere; bright.
Splen'did a. Magnificent; illustrious; brilliant; famous.
Sor'did a. Mean, ignoble, base; niggardly.
Ka'tydid s. A N. American grasshopper living in trees.
Æneid' s. Virgil's epic on Æneas.
Ner'eid s. A sea-nymph; a marine centipede.
Pro'teid s. Protein.
Fid A bar to support the topmast; a tapering pin used on board ship.
Quad'rifid a. Cleft into four parts.
Tri'fid a. With three clefts.
Palmat'ifid a. Palmately cleft or divided.
Mul'tifid a. Divided into several parts (of leaves, etc.).
Oc'tofid a. In eight segments.
Sex'fid, sexifid a. Cleft into six parts.
Gid s. A disease in sheep.
Rig'id a. Not easily bent; stiff; unpliant.
Fri'gid a. Cold; dull; lifeless; formal.
Al'gid a. Cold.
Ful'gid a. Shining, glittering.
Tur'gid a. Inflated; bloated; pompous.
Hid past and past part. (*Hide*).
Or'chid s. A perennial plant with brilliant and curiously shaped flowers.
Kid s. A young goat; leather made from its skin; a small tub; a faggot; (*slang*) a child; deception. v.t. and i. To bring forth kids; (*slang*) to hoax.
Skid s. Chain or slipper for preventing rotation of a wheel; a side-slip (of bicycle, etc.). v.t. To check with a skid. v.i. To slip sideways.
Lid s. A cover for a box, etc.; an eyelid.
Cal'id a. Warm, tepid.
Chrys'alid s. A chrysalis.
Squal'id a. Mean; poverty-stricken.
Val'id a. Cogent, sound, conclusive.
Inval'id a. Of no legal force; void.
In'valid (-leed) a. Infirm through ill health, disabled, weak. s. An infirm or sick person
Invalid' (-leed') v.t. To disable; to register as unfit through sickness.

Fe'lid s. A member of the cat tribe.
Gel'id a. Extremely cold; frozen.
An'nelid s. An earth-worm or other invertebrate with segmented body.
Eye'lid s. The cover of the eye.
Cich'lid s. A tropical freshwater fish of the perch family.
Pal'lid a. Pale, wan.
Ol'id a. Fetid; stinking.
Sol'id a. Not liquid or gaseous; substantial; compact; not hollow; unanimous. s. A body naturally retaining a fixed form.
Sursol'id s. The fifth power of a number.
Stol'id a. Dull, phlegmatic, firm.
Slid past and past part. (*Slide*).
Mid a. Middle. prep. Amid.
Amid' prep. In the midst, among.
Py'ramid s. A solid figure standing on a three-, four-, or many-sided base terminating in a point.
Tim'id a. Wanting courage; easily frightened.
Des'mid s. A microscopic freshwater alga.
Hu'mid a. Moist, damp, watery.
Tu'mid a. Swollen; distended; bombastic.
Pyc'nid s. A pycnidium.
Arach'nid s. A spider, scorpion, or mite.
Cyp'rinid s. A fish of the carp family.
Le'onid s. One of a swarm of meteors appearing in November.
Pycnog'onid s. A marine spider.
-oid suff. Denoting resemblance.
Rhom'boid s. A parallelogram the angles of which are oblique and the adjacent sides unequal. a. Of this shape.
Strom'boid a. Resembling or shaped like the shell of a stromb.
Glob'oid a. Like a globe.
Ces'boid a. Ribbon-like. s. A tapeworm.
Cub'oid a. Resembling a cube. s. A solid with the sides not all equal; a bone on the outer side of the foot.
Mal'acoid a. Soft-bodied; mucilaginous.
Plac'oid a. Plate-shaped.
Li'macoid a. Resembling a slug. s. A slug.
Pin'acoid s. With two parallel faces (of crystals).
Cor'acoid s. A beak-shaped process on the shoulder-blade. a. Hook-shaped; like a crow's beak.
Hel'icoid a. Spirally curved. s. A screw-shaped surface.
Fil'icoid a. Like a fern. s. A fern-like plant.
Cri'coid a. Ring-like.
Tal'coid a. Talcose.
Hel'coid a. Resembling an ulcer.
Scin'coid a. Pertaining to the skinks.
Zinc'oid a. Resembling zinc.
Sar'coid a. Resembling flesh.
Dis'coid a. Like a disc or quoit.
Mollus'coid a. and s. Molluscan.
Mus'coid s. A moss-like plant. a. Resembling moss.
Fu'coid a. Resembling fucus or seaweed. s. A fossil plant.
Ga'doid s. and a. One of the, or belonging to the, cod-fish family.
Lamb'doid a. Formed like the Greek lambda (λ).
Pyram'idoid s. A solid resembling a pyramid.
Scarabæ'oid a. Pertaining to or resembling a scarab.
Clu'peoid a. Herring-like. s. A fish of the herring family.
Os'teoid a. Bony; like bone.
Pter'igoid a. Wing-like. s. A wing-shaped bone.
Al'goid a. (*Algæ*).
Trin'goid a. Pertaining to or resembling the sandpipers.
Spon'goid (spun'-) a. Sponge-like.
Fun'goid a. Like or of the nature of fungi.
Bat'rachoid a. (*Batrachia*).
Conchoid' s. A shell-like curve.
Sca'phoid a. Boat-shaped, especially of a bone of the carpus.
Acal'ephoid a. (*Acalaphæ*).
Xiph'oid (zif'-) a. Sword-shaped; ensiform.
Didel'phoid a. Resembling didelphia.
Rham'phoid a. Beak-shaped.
Lymph'oid a. Resembling lymph.
Ty'phoid a. Pertaining to or resembling typhus. s. Enteric fever.
Lith'oid a. Resembling stone.
Or'nithoid a. Bird-like.
Amian'thoid a. Resembling amianthus.
Hel'minthoid a. Resembling a parasitic worm; helminthic.
Conid'ioid a. (*Conidium*).
Gonid'ioid a. Pertaining to or resembling gonidia.
Car'dioid s. A heart-shaped curve.
Sim'ioid a. Pertaining to the Simia, a genus of anthropoid apes.
Tæ'nioid a. Resembling or pertaining to the tapeworms.
His'tioid a. Resembling tissue.
Amyg'daloid a. Almond-shaped.
Hal'oid a. Resembling salt. s. A salt of a halogen and a metal.
Ceph'aloid a. Head-shaped.
Enceph'aloid a. Pertaining to or like the brain. s. A variety of cancer.
Om'phaloid a. Resembling a navel.
Al'kaloid s. A nitrogenous base having an alkaline reaction. a. Resembling or with the properties of an alkali.
Sep'aloid a. Having sepals.
Pet'aloid a. Of the form of a petal.
Squa'loid a. Resembling a shark.
Hy'aloid a. Glassy. s. A transparent membrane in the eye.
Tab'loid s. A small medicinal tablet of certain make. a. Compressed, concentrated.
Cy'cloid s. Curve traced by any point of a circle rolling on a straight line.
Epicy'cloid s. A curve generated by the revolution of a point in the circumference of a circle rolling along the exterior of another circle.
Rep'tiloid a. Like a reptile.
Thal'loid a. Pertaining to or resembling a thallus.
Cor'alloid a. Formed of or branching like coral. s. An organism resembling coral.
Met'alloid a. Resembling a metal. s. An element like a metal in some particular way.
Crys'talloid a. Like a crystal. s. A crystal-like body.
Varicel'loid a. Pertaining to or resembling chicken-pox.
My'tilloid a. Pertaining to the mussels; resembling a mussel.
Col'loid a. Glue-like. s. An uncrystallizable, semi-solid substance.
Phyl'loid a. Like a leaf.
Parab'oloid s. The solid generated by the revolution of a parabola about its axis.
Mongoloid' a. Resembling a Mongol or Mongolian.
Var'ioloid a. Resembling smallpox. s. A modified form o ithis.

Sloid s. (*Sloyd*).
Tentac'uloid a. Of the nature of a tentacle.
Tuber'culoid a. Resembling or affected with tuberculosis.
Cell'uloid s. An ivory-like substance prepared from cellulose. a. Resembling cells.
An'nuloid a. Ring-shaped.
Con'dyloid a. Shaped like a condyle.
Am'yloid a. Starchy. s. A non-nitrogenous starchy food.
Cot'yloid a. Cup-shaped.
Styl'oid a. Style-like. s. A style-shaped process on the temporal bone.
Xy'loid a. Woody; ligneous.
Ses'amoid a. Nodular (especially of small bones in tendons).
Squa'moid a. Scale-like.
Sig'moid a. Curved like a sigma or S.
Eth'moid a. Resembling a sieve.
En'tomoid a. Resembling an insect. s. An insect-like creature or thing.
Des'moid s. Morbid fibrous tissue.
Pris'moid s. A prism-like body.
Cy'moid a. Resembling a cyme.
Gan'oid a. Applied to an order of fishes with hard shiny scales (sturgeons).
Tet'anoid a. Like tetanus.
Ad'enoid a. Like a gland, glandular; s. spongy growths between the back of the nose and throat.
Sphen'oid a. Wedge-shaped.
Glen'oid a. Socket-like.
Sole'noid s. An electro-magnet consisting of a cylindrical coil.
Hy'menoid a. Of membranous structure or nature.
Cten'oid a. Having comb-shaped scales (of certain fish).
Arach'noid a. Resembling a spider's web or a spider.
Tur'binoid a. Top-shaped; turbinate.
Cartilag'inoid a. (*Cartilage*).
Echi'noid a. Resembling or pertaining to the echinus or its family.
Del'phinoid a. Resembling the dolphins. s. An animal of the dolphin family.
Albu'minoid a. (*Albumen*).
Spi'noid a. Like a spine.
Crin'oid a. Lily-shaped. s. One of the Crinoidea.
Gelat'inoid a. Resembling gelatine. s. A gelatinous substance.
Plat'inoid s. An alloy resembling platinum; a. like platinum.
Co'noid a. Resembling a cone. s. A body shaped thus.
alm'onoid (sam'-) a. Resembling or allied to the salmon.
Cor'onoid a. Hooked, resembling a crow's beak.
Sturn'oid a. Like or pertaining to the starlings.
Zo'oid s. An individual organic cell. a. Having the nature of an animal.
Microzo'oid a. and s. Resembling or one of the microzoa.
Polyzo'oid a. Polyzoal. s. A polyzoon.
An'thropoid a. Resembling man.
Pithecan'thropoid a. Resembling or pertaining to Pithecanthropus.
Trap'poid a. Trappean.
Lu'poid a. Resembling lupus.
Pol'ypoid a. Like a polyp or polypus.
Scar'oid a. Pertaining to the family of parrot-fishes. s. A member of this.
Sac'charoid a. Having a granular structure.
Fi'broid a. Like a fibre.
Can'croid a. Resembling a cancer, or a crab.
Chan'croid a. (*Chancre*).
Salaman'droid s. and a. (*Salamandrian*).
Den'droid a. Resembling a tree; arborescent.
Cyl'indroid s. A body like a cylinder but with elliptical bases.
Chon'droid a. Like cartilage.
Hy'droid a. Hydra-like. s. One of the Hydrazoa.
Rhinoc'eroid a. Like or pertaining to the rhinocerous family.
Cong'eroid a. (*Conger*).
Spher'oid s. A nearly spherical body.
Hemispher'oid s. Half a spheroid.
Ther'oid a. Having animal characteristics.
Diph'theroid a. Resembling or akin to diphtheria.
An'theroid a. Of the nature or appearance of an anther.
An'eroid s. A form of barometer.
Bac'teroid a. (*Bacteria*).
As'teroid s. A small planet.
Hys'teroid a. Resembling hysteria.
Sangfroid' (-frwa) s. Coolness; presence of mind.
Ne'groid a. Resembling or pertaining to the negroes.
Cong'roid a. (*Conger*).
O'chroid a. Ochreous.
Me'teoroid s. A particle of "star-dust" becoming a luminous meteor on entering the earth's atmosphere.
Chor'oid a. Resembling the chorion, especially of the second coat of the eye.
Cu'proid a. Resembling copper. s. A twelve-angled crystal.
Viv'erroid a. Viverrine.
Saur'oid a. Saurian.
Neur'oid a. Like a nerve.
Sci'uroid a. Pertaining to or resembling the squirrels.
Lem'uroid a. Like or pertaining to the lemurs.
Thy'roid a. Shield-shaped, especially of a gland near the larynx.
Ellip'soid s. A solid, all plane sections of which are ellipses or circles.
Cis'soid a. Contained within two intersecting curves.
Gneis'soid a. Having characteristics of gneiss.
Medu'soid a. and s. Medusan.
Hy'datoid s. A membrane in the eye; the aqueous humour enclosed by this.
Hæ'matoid a. Resembling blood in appearance.
Nem'atoid s. and a. Nematode.
Derm'atoid a. Skin-like.
Pris'matoid s. A solid having polygonal bases and triangular faces.
Rheum'atoid a. Resembling rheumatism.
Than'atoid a. Resembling death.
Ker'atoid a. Pertaining to keratin; horny.
Ter'atoid a. Resembling a monster; abnormal.
Plan'etoid s. A planet-like body, an asteroid.
Her'petoid a. Serpent form.
Gran'itoid a. Resembling granite.
Negritoid' a. Resembling or pertaining to the Negritos.
Del'toid a. Trianglar. s. The shoulder-muscle which moves the arm.
Len'toid a. Lens-shaped.
Odon'toid a. Tooth-like.
Lacer'toid a. Pertaining to or resembling the lizards.
Mas'toid a. Resembling a breast or nipple.
Asbes'toid a. Fibrous; like asbestos. s. Byssolite.
Void a. Empty; ineffectual; null. s. An empty space. v.t. To make void; to nullify; to evacuate.
Avoid' v.t. To shun, escape, elude.
Næ'void a. Resembling a nævus.
Devoid' a. Destitute of, free from.
O'void a. Egg-shaped; oval. s. An oval figure.

Obo'void a. Obovate.
Hy'oid a. Having the form of the Greek upsilon (υ); denoting the bone between the root of the tongue and the larynx.
Ich'thyoid a. Fish-like.
Trap'ezoid a. Trapeziform. s. A quadrilateral figure in which two sides are parallel.
Rhiz'oid a. Root-like.
Spermatozo'id s. The male sexual fertilizing cell of certain plants.
Rap'id a. Very quick; swift; moving fast; hurried. s. A swift, broken current in a river.
Sap'id a. Savoury; not uninteresting.
Vap'id a. Insipid, flat, spiritless.
Intrep'id a. Fearless, undaunted.
Tep'id a. Lukewarm.
Insip'id a. Tasteless; dull; vapid.
Lim'pid a. Clear, transparent; perspicuous.
Tor'pid a. Numb, motionless, dull.
His'pid a. Rough with bristles.
Cus'pid s. A canine tooth.
Tricus'pid a. Having three cusps or points.
Cu'pid s. The Roman god of love; a beautiful boy.
Stup'id a. Dull and heavy; foolish; nonsensical.
Rid v.t. To clear, disencumber. a. Free, clear.
Ar'id a. Dry, parched.
Hy'brid a. Of different species, mongrel. s. A mongrel; an offspring of two different species.
Ac'rid a. Bitter, pungent.
As'terid s. A star-fish.
Grid s. A grating; a gridiron.
Thrid v.t. To pass through, thread.
Vir'id a. Green.
Flor'id a. Flowery; red; highly decorated.
Hor'rid a. Causing or able to cause horror; frightful.
Tor'rid a. Parched, dried with heat; scorching.
Strid past part. (*Stride*).
Pu'trid a. Rotten, decomposed; tainted.
Lur'id a. Ghastly pale; gloomy; dismal; sensational.
Sat'yrid s. One of a certain family of butterflies.
Hy'datid s. A watery cyst, usually due to a tapeworm.
Caryat'id s. A figure of a draped woman as support to entablature, etc.
Fe'tid a. Smelling offensively; malodorous.
Carot'id a. Applied to the two arteries conveying blood to the head.
Parot'id a. Situated near the ear. s. A salivary gland near the ear.
Pu'tid a. mean; worthless.
Lan'guid a. Faint; feeble; listless; lacking energy.
Pin'guid a. Fat, greasy, unctuous.
Flu'id s. A liquid; anything that flows readily. a. Capable of flowing; liquid, gaseous.
Quid s. Piece of tobacco for chewing; (*slang*) a sovereign.
Liq'uid a. Fluid; not solid; smooth, soft. s. A fluid; a letter with a smooth sound.
Squid s. A small variety of cuttle-fish.
Dru'id s. A priest of ancient Britain and Gaul; an official at the Welsh Eisteddfod.
Noc'tuid a. Pertaining to the largest family of Lepidoptera, certain moths.
Av'id a. Greedy, strongly desirous.
Pav'id a. Timid, fearful.
Impav'id a. Fearless.
Grav'id a. Pregnant.
Liv'id a. Discoloured; black-and-blue.
Viv'id a. Bright, lively; forcible; realistic.
Fer'vid a. Burning, fervent, impassioned.
Perfer'vid a. Very fervid.
Yid s. (*Slang*) A German or other Jew.
Bald a. Wanting hair; unadorned.
Pie'bald a. Of various colours; blotched variegated.
Rib'ald s. A coarse fellow; an abusive jester. a. Irreverent, scurrilous, licentious.
Skew'bald a. Piebald with blotches of colour other than black.
Scald v.t. To burn with hot liquid or steam. s. An injury caused thus; an ancient Scandinavian bard. a. Affected with scurf; scurvy.
Weald s. Tract of open forest land; a wold.
Her'ald s. An officer of arms; a precursor, messenger. v.t. To proclaim, introduce.
Em'erald s. A precious stone of a green colour; this colour; a small size of type.
Tyne'wald s. Legislative assembly of Isle of Man.
Eld s. Old age; old people.
Geld v.t. To castrate, emasculate; to expurgate.
Held past and past part. (*Hold*).
Behold' v.t., pret. and past part. (*Behold*).
Withheld' past and past part. (*Withhold*).
Bield s. (*Scot.*) Shelter, protection. a. Cosy.
Field s. Land enclosed by hedges, etc.; place where battle is fought; sphere of activity; open space; surface of an heraldic shield; all the competitors in a race, etc. v.t. and i. To watch and catch the ball in cricket, etc.
Afield' adv. In the open, out of doors, away.
Ches'terfield s. A sofa with two upright ends; an overcoat.
Chield s. (*Scot.*) A man, lad.
Shield s. A broad piece of defensive armour; a protection; an heraldic escutcheon. v.t. To defend, protect.
Wield v.t. To sway, use with full command.
Yield v.t. To produce; to afford, impart, give up. v.i. To submit, comply. s. That which is yielded; return, product.
Weld v.t. To hammer into union; to unite closely. s. A junction by welding; a species of mignonette yielding a yellow dye.
Yeld a. (*Scot.*) Not yielding milk.
Gild v.t. To overlay with thin gold; to adorn, illuminate.
Wer'gild s. Fine paid in Anglo-Saxon times to family of murdered or injured person by the aggressor.
Child s. A son or daughter; a young person.
Mild a. timid; tender; gentle; indulgent.
Build v.t. To raise, construct, strengthen. s. Form or mode of construction.
Rebuild' v.t. To build again, reconstruct.
Guild s. An association of merchants, craftsmen, or others for mutual advancement and protection.
Wild a. Not tame; undomesticated; rash; furious; frolicsome; stormy. s. An uninhabited and uncultivated region.
Old a. Not new; advanced in age; antiquated; of some particular age.

Bold a. Daring, fearless; impudent; steep.
Ko'bold s. An underground elf of German folklore.
Cold a. Not warm, chill; indifferent, stoical; unaffecting. s. Absence of heat; sensation produced by lack of warmth; inflammation resulting from chill.
Acold' a. Chilly, cold.
Scold v.t. and i. To chide angrily, to rail at; to find fault noisily. s. A nagging woman; a scolder.
-fold suff. Forming adjectives and adverbs of multiplication.
Fold s. A doubling of a flexible substance; that which is folded or enfolds; embrace; a pen for sheep. v.t. To double; to enclose within folds or a fold; to lay the arms together.
Hun'dredfold s. A hundred times as much.
Blind'fold a. Having the eyes covered. v.t. To bandage the eyes, to prevent seeing.
Nine'fold a. Nine times repeated.
Five'fold a. Five times as much or as great.
Scaf'fold s. Temporary timber structure for builders; platform for executions. v.t. To furnish with a scaffold.
Man'ifold a. Of different kinds; numerous and various. v.t. To multiply copies of.
Mul'tifold a. Many times doubled.
Twi-fold a. and adv. Twofold.
Enfold' v.t. To wrap up, to embrace; to shape in folds.
Ten'fold a. and adv. (*Ten*).
Sev'enfold a. Repeated or increased by seven times.
Pin'fold s. A pound, place for confining beasts.
Unfold' v.t. and i. To expand; to reveal, display.
Two'fold a. and adv. Double; doubly.
Four'fold a. and adv. Quadruple. s. Four times as much.
Eight'fold a. Eight times the number or quantity.
Six'fold a. Six times as much or as many.
Gold s. A bright yellow precious metal; money, wealth; anything very precious; gilding; gold colour. a. Made of, coloured like, or consisting of gold.
Mar'igold s. A bright yellow-flowered plant.
Hold v.t. To grasp; to maintain; to consider. v.i. To keep its parts together; to endure. s. Seizure; support; cavity in vessel for stowing cargo. int. Stop! forbear!
Behold' v.t. To view, to look at. int. Lo! observe!
Free'hold s. An estate in land not less than an estate for life, i.e. in fee-simple.
Lease'hold s. Tenure held by lease; property held thus. a. Held by lease.
House'hold s. A family or body of persons living together in a house. a. Domestic.
Strong'hold s. A fortress, refuge.
Withhold' v.t. To keep from action, obstruct, refuse to grant.
Uphold' v.t. To sustain, maintain, give moral support to.
Thresh'old s. A door-sill; a doorway, entrance.
Foot'hold s. Support for or at the foot; a position of security.
Cop'yhold s. An old form of legal tenure of land; land held thus.
Cuck'old s. A man whose wife is unfaithful. v.t. To make a cuckold of.
Mold s. Mould.
Sold past and past part. (*Sell*).
Told past and past part. (*Tell*).
Untold' a. Not revealed; not counted, innumerable.
Wold s. Open country, downland.
World s. The earth; the whole creation or universal system; sphere of existence; mankind; public life.
Un'derworld s. The infernal regions; the antipodes; the lowest classes.
Auld a. (*Scot.*) Old.
Could v. aux. (*Can*).
Could pret. (*Can*). Was able.
Should past (*Shall*).
Mould s. Fine, soft earth; shape in which a thing is cast; model, shape; mustiness, mildew. v.t. To form into a particular shape; to fashion.
Remould' v.t. To mould or fashion afresh.
Would (wud) past and cond. (*Will*).
And conj.
Band s. A bandage, a tie, a company of musicians. v.i. To unite together, associate.
Sar'aband s. A stately Spanish dance.
Con'traband a. Prohibited; smuggled. s. Smuggling, illegal traffic, smuggled goods.
Rib'band s. A spar temporarily holding a ship's ribs in position.
Rib'and s. A ribbon.
Disband' v.t. To dismiss from military service; to disperse a regiment, etc.
Hus'band s. A man who has a wife; a good manager. v.t. To manage with frugality, use economically.
Plat'band s. A border of flowers, etc.; a flat, rectangular architectural moulding; a square lintel.
Wrist'band s. Part of sleeve covering the wrist; a cuff.
Multiplicand' s. The number to be multiplied by another.
Deodand' s. A thing causing a person's death and forfeited therefor.
Brig'and s. A freebooter.
Ar'gand s. A lamp or gas-burner admitting air.
Hand s. The palm with fingers; measure of 4 in.; an employee; cards held at a game; a shoulder of pork. v.t. To give with the or guide by hand.
Behind'hand a., adv. In arrears, backward.
Fore'hand s. The upper hand, advantage. a. Foremost; not backhanded.
Before'hand adv. Previously.
Unhand' v.t. To set free from a grasp; to loose hold of.
Underhand' adv. Clandestinely; unfairly, by fraud. a. Secret, sly, unfair.
O'verhand a. and adv. Of delivery or service of a ball with the arm above the shoulder.
Short'hand s. A system of contracted writing.
Vi'and s. An article of food.
Land s. The solid portion of the earth; ground; real estate; nation or people. v.t. and i. To disembark, set or go ashore.
Bland a. Mild, gentle.
Head'land s. A promontory, cape.
Mid'land a. Situated in the interior of a country. s. The interior.
Newfound'land s. A large, shaggy breed of dog.
Wood'land s. Wooded country. a. Sylvan.
E'land s. A large S. African antelope.
Fore'land s. A promontory, headland, cape.

Gland s. An organ of secretion; an acorn.
High'land a. Pertaining to the Scottish Highlands.
North'land s. Countries in the North.
Hol'land s. An unbleached linen fabric.
Dream'land s. The region of fancy.
In'land a. Interior, confined to a country; not foreign. adv. In or towards the interior. s. The interior part of a country.
Main'land s. The continent; principal land as opposed to islands.
Up'land s. Elevated land. a. High in situation; pertaining to uplands.
Gar'land s. A wreath of flowers, etc.; a chaplet; the prize.
Won'derland s. Fairyland; a land of marvels, astonishing beauty or fertility, etc.
Bor'derland s. Land on the frontiers, debatable land.
Fa'therland s. One's native country.
Moth'erland s. One's native country.
Hin'terland s. Land lying behind a coast, frontier, etc.
O'verland a. Made or performed on or across the land.
Moor'land s. A moor; a waste, barren district.
Isl'and s. Land surrounded by water; anything isolated.
Out'land s. A foreign land. a. Foreign; outlying.
Low'land s. Low-lying country. a. Pertaining to this.
Demand' v.t. To claim as of right; to require; to question peremptorily or insistently. s. An authoritative claim; the thing claimed; desire to purchase.
Remand' v.t. To send back for further investigation. s. Act of remanding.
Rep'rimand v.t. To reprove or censure sharply. s. Severe reproof.
Command' v.t. To order, govern, have at one's disposal. v.i. To have chief power. s. Control, order; power of defending.
Countermand' v.t. To revoke, cancel, annul. s. An order revoking a previous order.
Gour'mand s. An epicure; one who demands delicate fare.
Expand' v.t. and i. To spread out, distend, dilate.
Rand s. A thin inner sole.
Brand s. A burning stick, a stigma. v.t. To mark with a hot iron, to stigmatize.
Grand a. Majestic, illustrious; magnificent, eminent.
In'tegrand s. An expression to be integrated.
Er'rand s. A message; business to be done by a messenger; purpose in going.
Strand s. A shore, beach; twist of a rope. v.t. and i. To run or force aground; to bring to a standstill.
Sand s. Powdered or finely broken rock; grit, pluck. v.t. To sprinkle or mix with sand.
Wea'sand(we'-) s. The windpipe.
Quick'sand s. A shifting sandbank; anything seemingly stable but treacherous.
Am'persand s. The sign "&."
Thou'sand a. and s. Ten hundred; a great many.
Stand v.i. To be erect; to pause, adhere; to offer oneself as candidate. v.t. To endure, resist; to pay for. s. Post, station; a stop, halt.
Withstand' v.t. To oppose, resist.
Understand' v.t. and i. To comprehend, perceive the meaning of, suppose to mean, to learn.
Misunderstand' v.t. To take in a wrong sense. Fail to understand.
Wand (wond) s. A thin staff; baton for musician, conjurer, etc.
End s. Extremity; conclusion; final state; limit; death; design, drift, aim. v.t. To terminate, conclude, destroy. v.i. To close, cease.
Bend v.t. To make crooked. v.i. To incline, bow. s. A deflection from the straight, a curve.
Preb'end s. Stipend of a canon; a prebendary, or his office.
Ascend' v.t. To mount, go up.
Reascend' v.t. and i. To climb or ascend again.
Descend' v.i. To come down; to be derived from, to pass to an heir. v.t. To move down, along, etc.
Condescend' v.i. To deign; to stoop, to yield.
Transcend' v.t. To surpass, excel.
Div'idend s. Number which is to be divided; share of profit, of debt owing, etc.; interest on stock.
Fend v.t. To ward off, shut out; to provide for. v.i. To get a living; to strive.
Defend' v.t. To protect; to fortify; to vindicate. v.i. to make defence; to contest a suit.
Offend' v.t. To make angry; to pain, annoy; to cause to neglect duty or to sin. v.i. To sin; to cause annoyance; to take offence.
Forfend' v.t. To avert, ward off.
Leg'end s. A marvellous traditional story; a non-historical tale; an inscription.
Sub'trahend s. Sum or number to be subtracted from another.
Reprehend' v.t. To accuse, reprove, censure.
Comprehend' v.t. To include, to understand, conceive.
Apprehend' v.t. To arrest, seize for trial. v.i. To understand, imagine.
Misapprehend' v.t. To fail to understand.
Fiend s. A devil; a diabolical or cruel person.
Friend s. A companion, confidant, ally; a Quaker.
Befriend' v.t. To favour, be kind to.
Lend v.t. To grant on condition of return.
Blend v.t. To mingle; to mix harmoniously. s. A mixture.
Mend v.t. To repair; to correct; to improve. v.i. To grow better, amend.
Amend' v.t. To correct, make better, rectify; v.i. To reform, grow better.
Emend' v.t. To correct, improve.
Commend' v.t. To commit to the care of, entrust; to praise.
Recommend' v.t. To commend to another; to advise; to make acceptable.
Discommend' v.t. To censure, express disapprobation of.
Pend v.i. To impend, await a settlement.
Depend' v.i. To rely on; to hang from, be contingent upon.
Vil'ipend v.t. To disparage, slight.
Sti'pend s. Remuneration, especially of a clergyman.
Impend' v.i. To be imminent, to threaten.
Compend' s. A compendium.
Append' v.t. To add to something.
Perpend' v.t. and i. To consider carefully, take thought. s. A large stone appearing on both sides of a wall.

Spend v.t. To lay out (money, etc.); to squander; to exhaust; to wear out. v.i. To expend money; to be consumed.
Misspend' v.t. To spend unwisely; to waste.
Suspend' v.t. To hang up, cause to depend; to cause to cease temporarily; to hinder.
Expend' v.t. To lay out, spend; to dissipate.
Rend v.t. To tear asunder or away. v.i. To split, be or become torn.
Rev'erend a. Worthy of reverence; title given to clergymen.
Trend v.i. To stretch, tend in a particular direction. s. General tendency.
Send v.t. To cause to go; to dispatch.
God'send s. An unexpected gain or acquisition.
Tend v.t. To watch, guard; to attend. v.i. To move in or have a certain direction.
Subtend' v.t. To extend under; to be opposite to.
Repetend' s. That part of a repeating decimal which recurs.
Pretend' v.t. To feign; to simulate; to represent falsely; to allege claim to; v.i. To lay claim; to assume a false character; to make believe.
Intend' v.t. To purpose, mean; to design; to prepare for.
Superintend' v.t. To exercise the oversight of, take charge of authoritatively.
Contend' v.i. To strive, vie, wrangle.
Obvertend' s. A certain proposition in logic.
In'vertend s. A proposition from which another is derived by inversion.
Convertend' s. A proposition in logic submitted to the process of conversion.
Portend' v.t. To foreshow, presage, threaten.
Distend' v.t. To stretch out, expand. v.i. To become expanded or inflated.
Attend' v.t. To wait on, to accompany. v.i. To heed, pay attention to.
Butt-end' s. The blunt end of anything.
Extend' v.t. To spread out, amplify, diffuse. v.i. To stretch, reach.
Coextend' v.t. To extend through the same space as another.
Min'uend s. Quantity from which another is to be subtracted.
Vend v.t. To sell, offer for sale.
Solvend' s. Substance to be dissolved.
Wend v.i. and t. To go, betake oneself. s. One of a Slav race of Prussia and Saxony.
Zend s. The ancient Iranian language, allied to Sanskrit.
Bind v.t. To confine, restrain, strengthen. v.i. To grow hard or stiff; to be obligatory.
Bear'bind s. Bindweed.
Abscind' v.t. To cut off, sever.
Rescind' v.t. To abrogate, revoke, repeal.
Prescind' v.t. To cut off; to consider independently.
Exscind' v.t. To cut off or out, to excise.
Teind (tend) s. (*Scot.*). A tithe.
Find v.t. To light upon, discover; to supply; to declare by verdict. s. A discovery; thing found.
Hind s. Female of the red deer; a farm servant. a. Pertaining to or at the back.
Behind' prep., adv. At the back of, inferior to.
Kind a. Benevolent; mild; indulgent; gentle. s. Race; genus; sort; classification.
Mankind' s. The race of men; men collectively.
Womankind' s. Womenfolk.
Humankind' s. Mankind.
Blind a. Destitute of sight. v.t. To reduce one to this state. s. A contrivance for excluding light.
Pur'blind a. Near-sighted; seeing dimly.
Mind s. The intellectual faculty in man; opinion; recollection; intention; inclination. v.t. To heed; to attend; to object to; to look after. v.i. To take care.
Remind' v.t. To put in mind, recall to memory.
Rind s. Husk; peel; outer coating.
Tam'arind s. A leguminous tree of the tropics; its pulpy fruit.
Grind v.t. To sharpen or polish by rubbing; to reduce to particles; to oppress. v.i. To turn a mill; to be pulverized; to study hard. s. Act or process of grinding; laborious work.
Wind s. A current of air; power of respiration; flatulence; empty talk. v.t. To let recover wind; to deprive of wind; to follow by scent.
Wind (wind) v.t. To bend, twist, coil; to blow, as a horn. v.i. To twine or twist; to meander. s. Wind (in poetry).
Whirl'wind s. A violent, progressing wind, moving spirally round an axis.
Interwind' v.t. To wind together.
Bond s. A written obligation; a chain, cord. v.t. To fasten together; to place in bond.
Vag'abond a. Wandering to and fro; pertaining to a vagrant. s. A vagrant, rascal, ne'er-do-well.
Sec'ond a. Next after first; repeated; inferior. s. One coming after; supporter of another; sixtieth of a minute or of a degree; a lower part in music. v.t. To follow, to support; to join with in assisting.
Se'cond v.t. To retire (an officer) temporarily or place on special service.
Abscond' v.i. To absent oneself, disappear, make off.
Fond a. Partial to, having affection for; foolish.
Plafond' s. An elaborate ceiling.
Blond a. Of fair complexion, flaxen. s. A person of fair complexion.
Di'amond s. The most valuable and hardest of gems; a rhombus; a card of a suit marked with these in red; a very small printing type. a. Resembling a diamond; set with diamonds; rhombus-shaped.
Alm'ond s. The stone of the fruit of the almond-tree.
Drom'ond s. A swift mediæval ship.
Pond s. A body of standing water, a small lake.
Despond' v.i. To be cast down, to despair.
Respond' v.i. To answer, reply; to suit. s. A versicle sung in response.
Correspond' v.i. To be congruous; to answer one to another; to communicate by letters.
Frond s. The leaf of a fern or palm.
Ayond' prep. (*Scot.*) Beyond.
Beyond' prep. On the farther side of. adv. At a distance.
Maund s. A basket; an Indian weight (about 83 lbs. avoir.).
Mor'ibund a. In a dying state.

Fu'ribund a. Raging, furious.
Cum'merbund s. A sash or waistband worn in India.
Ir'acund a. Passionate.
Fe'cund a. Prolific, fruitful.
Infec'und a. Unfruitful; barren.
Ver'ecund a. Bashful, modest.
Sec'und a. Of leaves arranged on one side of stalk only.
Ru'bicund a. Ruddy.
Joc'und a. Merry, blithe, gay.
Fund s. A supply of money; capital. v.t. To consolidate into stock, etc.; to place in a fund.
Refund' v.t. To pay back, reimburse. s. Money repaid.
Dachs'hund s. A long-bodied, short-legged dog.
Os'mund s. The flowering fern or king fern.
Bound s. A leap, a jump; a boundary. v.t. To fix limits to, enclose, restrain. a. Destined, intending to go.
Abound' v.i. To be in great plenty.
Superabound' v.i. To be very abundant.
O'verabound v.i. To abound more than enough.
Hide'-bound a. Having the hide or bark abnormally tight; narrow-minded.
Rebound' v.i. To spring back; to be reverberated. v.t. To drive back. s. Act of flying back after collision; resistance.
Re'bound a. Having a second binding (of books).
Redound' v.i. To come back as a consequence to have effect; to conduce.
Found v.t. To lay the basis of; to fix firmly, institute; to form with molten and moulded metal, to cast. past and past part. (*Find*).
Dumbfound' v.t. To confuse, perplex, strike dumb.
Confound' v.t. To blend indistinguishably; to abash; to throw into confusion.
Profound' a. Deep, deeply felt; very low; intense; learned; bending low; humble. s. The deep; the abyss.
Hound s. A hunting dog; a contemptible man. v.t. To hunt with hounds; to track down; to urge on.
Mahound' s. Mohammed; a false god, devil.
Blood'hound s. A large hound that tracks by scent.
Hore'hound s. A bitter, labiate herb used as a tonic, etc.
Gaze'hound s. A hound that hunts by sight.
Buck'hound s. A small variety of staghound.
Grey'hound s. A swift coursing dog.
Mound s. An artificial earthbank; a rampart; the globe of the regalia. v.t. To fortify with a mound.
Pound s. A weight (16 oz. avoir.); 20 shillings sterling; an enclosure for strayed beasts. v.t. To pulverize by beating; to confine in a pound.
Impound' v.t. To confine in a pound; to confiscate.
Compound' v.t. and i. To put together, mix; to adjust; to discharge a debt by paying part.
Com'pound s. A substance composed of two or more ingredients; an enclosure surrounding houses. a. Composed of two or more parts, ingredients, or words.
Decompound' a. Decomposite. v.t. To compound with compound substances.
Recompound' v.t. To mix over again.
Propound' v.t. To offer, propose; to produce a will for proof.
Expound' v.t. To explain, clear of obscurity, interpret.
Round a. Circular; cylindrical; spherical; large; roughly accurate; complete. s. That which is round; a circuit, series; a circular course, dance; a part-song; rung of a ladder; cut of beef. v.t. and i. To make or become round; to encircle, go round, make a circuit. adv. In a circle. prep. About, around.
Around' adv. In a circle, on every side. prep. About, near to.
Ground s. Soil; the surface of land; basis, foundation, reason; predominating tint. v.t. To fix firmly; to base; to found; to instruct in first principles. v.i. To run ashore (of a ship). past part. (*Grind*).
Aground' adv. Stranded, run ashore.
Fore'ground s. The nearest part; the part of a picture that seems to be nearest the eye.
Back'ground s. Position to the rear, a place of obscurity; the part of a picture subordinate to the foreground.
Un'derground a. Being below the surface. s. A subterranean railway.
Surround' v.t. To environ, encompass, invest.
Sound a. Whole; healthy; orthodox. s. A narrow arm of the sea; air-bladder of a fish; a probe; anything audible. v.t. To cause to emit sound; to measure the depth of; to examine medically, try to discover the opinion of, etc.; to pronounce. v.i. To give out a sound; to convey some impression by sound; to be spread or published.
Resound' v.i. To sound loudly, be filled with sound, re-echo. v.t. To sound again or repeatedly; to spread the fame of.
Unsound' a. Decayed; not orthodox.
Astound' v.t. To strike with wonder.
Wound past and past part. (*Wind*).
Wound(woond) s. An injury caused by violence; a cut, stab, etc.; damage; pain to the feelings. v.t. To injure, damage, pain, wound.
Ger'und s. A kind of verbal noun.
Obtund' v.t. To blunt, deaden.
Rotund' a. Rounded; spherical; complete.
Or'otund a. Sonorous; pompous, rhetorical.
Wynd s. (*Scot.*) An alley.
Od s. The force supposed to produce the phenomena of mesmerism, etc.
Cod s. A large marine food-fish; a husk, pod; small bag; the scrotum; (*slang*) a fellow, a hoax. v.t. (*Slang*) To hoax, play tricks on.
Peas'cod s. The legume or pericarp of the pea.
Hod'mandod s. A snail.
Eisteddfod s. A national congress of bards, etc., in Wales.
God s. The Supreme Being; a divinity, a deity.
Dem'igod s. A fabulous, half-divine hero.
Hod s. Trough in which labourer carries mortar, brick, etc.
Eph'od s. A vestment worn by the Jewish high-priest.
Shod a. Wearing boots or shoes.
Slip'shod a. Careless, slovenly.
Meth'od s. Mode of procedure; a regular order; system.
Per'iod s. Stated and recurring portion of time; cycle; series of events; end; a complete sentence; stop (.) at end of this.

Clod s. A lump of earth; a stupid fellow; (*slang*) coin. v.i. To clot.
Plod v.i. To travel laboriously; to drudge, toil. v.t. To tread with heavy steps.
Nod v.i. To make a slight bow, indicate a favourable reply; to be drowsy. v.a. To incline, signify by a nod. s. A quick motion of the head.
Syn'od (sin'-) s. A council; an ecclesiastical assembly.
Food s. Whatever feeds or augments; nourishment, provisions.
Good a. Opposite of bad; moral; useful; pious; virtuous. s. Benefit; advantage; prosperity. int. Well! right!
-hood suff. (*-head*).
-hood suff. Denoting state or quality.
Hood s. A loose covering for the head; an appendage to an academical gown; movable top to a motor-car, etc.; a cowl. v.t. To put a hood on; to cover, blind.
Maid'hood s. Maidenhead.
Child'hood s. State of being a child; period of youth.
Wife-hood s. State of being a wife.
False'hood s. A lie; treachery; quality of being false.
Brute'hood s. The condition of brutes.
King'hood s. State or condition of being a king.
Har'dihood s. Boldness; effrontery.
Foolhar'dihood s. Foolhardiness.
Like'lihood s. Probability; appearance of reality.
Live'lihood s. Support of life; maintenance.
Girl'hood s. State or time of being a girl.
Man'hood s. State of being a man; humanity; virility; manliness.
Wom'anhood s. State, character, or qualities of a woman.
Queen'hood s. Rank, character, or quality of a queen.
Fa'therhood s. State of being a father; authority or character of a father.
Moth'erhood s. State of being a mother.
Broth'erhood s. An association, fraternity.
Sis'terhood s. State of being a sister; a community of women.
Spin'sterhood s. Condition of being unmarried (of women); spinsters in general.
Neigh'bourhood (nā'-) s. State of being neighbours; the vicinity; nearness; neighbours collectively.
Monk's'-hood s. The aconite.
Cat'hood s. (*Cat*).
Knight'hood s. Dignity or condition of a knight; the body of knights.
Par'enthood s. State of being a parent.
Saint'hood s. Saintship.
Priest'hood s. Office or character of a priest; priests collectively.
Wid'owhood s. State of being a widow.
Ba'byhood s. The period when one is a baby; condition of being a baby.
Boy'hood s. Period when one is a boy.
Blood s. The red fluid circulating through the body; descent; a dandy; a dissipated character. v.t. To cause blood to flow from.
'Sblood int.
Flood s. A great flow of water, an inundation, deluge. v.t. and i. To overflow.
Mood s. Temper of mind; form of verb expressing manner in which the act, etc., is conceived; a form of syllogism.

Snood s. A ribbon for the hair.
Pood s. A Russian measure of weight (36 lb. avoir.).
Rood s. A crucifix; measure of 40 sq. rods (¼ acre).
Brood s. Offspring; the number hatched at once. v.i. To continue anxious.
Stood past and past part. (*Stand*).
Withstood' past and past part. (*Withstand*).
Understood' past and past part. (*Understand*).
Misunderstood' past and past part. (*Misunderstand*).
Wood (wud) s. A large collection of growing trees; substance of trees; timber. a. Mad; furious.
Red'wood s. A gigantic Californian tree; its timber.
Rose'wood s. A close-grained, dark red wood.
Wedg'wood s. A variety of pottery.
Dog'wood s. A genus of large shrubs; the cornel.
Log'wood s. A deep red wood used in dyeing.
Brush'wood s. Undergrowth; small twigs.
Cam'wood s. A hard red wood from W. Africa.
Worm'wood (werm'-) s. A perennial herb with bitter and tonic properties; gall.
Green'wood s. A wood in summer.
Un'derwood s. Small trees among larger.
Pod s. Seed vessel of leguminous plants. v.t. To remove peas, etc., from the pod. v.i. To fill out (of pods).
Ap'od s. A footless creature.
Dec'apod s. An animal having ten legs, arms, feelers, etc.; a ten-wheeled locomotive.
Meg'apod s. An Australasian mound-bird.
Myr'iapod s. A vermiform articulate animal, centipede. a. Having numerous feet.
Tet'rapod a. Having four limbs. s. A four-footed animal.
Hex'apod s. An insect having six legs.
Am'phipod s. One of the Amphipoda, a group of Crustaceans with legs for swimming and others for walking.
Tri'pod s. A three-legged stool, stand, etc.
Mel'ampod s. Black hellebore.
Ly'copod s. A club-moss.
Py'gopod s. One of the aquatic birds comprising the auks, loons, etc.
Gnath'opod s. The foot-jaw of crustaceans.
Brach'iopod s. A headless bivalve mollusc.
Branch'iopod s. A molluscoid animal with gills on the feet.
Cephal'opod s. A marine mollusc with tentacles grouped around the head.
Chil'opod s. A centipede.
Phyll'opod s. A crustacean with leaf-like feet.
Ty'lopod a. Having feet like those of the camel. s. A camel, llama, etc.
Steg'anopod s. One of an order of birds with all the toes webbed.
Chen'opod s. A genus of herbs, goosefoot.
Mac'ropod s. A long-footed crustacean; the spider-crab.
Pter'opod s. One of the pteropoda.
Gas'teropod s. One of a large class of univalve molluscs.
Ar'thropod s. An animal with jointed feet.
I'sopod s. A crustacean having seven pairs of legs of equal length.
Phys'opod s. A mollusc having suckers on the feet.
Oc'topod a. Having eight feet. s. An octoped.
Chæt'opod s. A group of bristly marine worms.
Rhiz'opod s. One of a class of protozoa.
Pol'ypod a. Having many feet. s. A millepede
Rod s. A straight, slender stick; a bundle of such for punishment; measure of 5½ yards.

Ram'rod s. Rod for using with a muzzle-loader.
Nim'rod s. A great hunter.
Prod s. A pointed instrument; a dig, stab. v.t. To thrust with a goad, etc.; to poke, nudge.
Down'trod a. Downtrodden.
Sod s. A green turf; clod of grass. v.t. To cover with this. past and past part. (*Seethe*).
Tod s. A thick ivy-bush; an old wool measure (28 lbs.); a bunch; a fox.
Quod s. (*Slang*) Prison; confinement.
Bard s. A Celtic minstrel, a poet.
Tab'ard s. A herald's sleeveless coat.
Scab'bard s. Sheath, especially for blade of sword.
Bombard' v.t. To attack with artillery or bombs; to assail with arguments or invective.
Card s. A rectangular piece of pasteboard. v.t. To comb or disentangle wool, etc.
Plac'ard s. A notice, etc., posted up; a poster. v.t. To post in a public place.
Bran'card s. A horse-litter.
Discard' v.t. and i. To throw aside as useless; to cast off, reject.
Stand'ard s. A distinctive flag or emblem; a rule, criterion, test; an upright support; a grade in some schools. a. Serving as a standard or criterion; standing by itself (of certain trees, etc.); permanent in quality.
Beard s. Hair growing on cheeks and chin; the awn of barley, etc. v.t. seize by the beard; to defy.
Grey'beard s. An aged man.
Afeard' a. Frightened, afraid.
Heard past and past part. (*Hear*).
Fard s. Face-paint. v.t. To rouge or paint the face; to cover the blemishes of.
Regard' v.t. To esteem, respect; to heed, observe; to consider. v.i. To look, pay attention. s. Gaze; respect; notice; deference.
Disregard' v.t. To neglect, slight. s. Omission to notice; state of being neglected.
Hag'gard a. Wild-looking; lean, pale, gaunt. s. An untrained hawk.
Lag'gard a. Slow; backward; wanting in energy. s. A loiterer.
Stag'gard s. A four-year-old stag.
Nig'gard s. A sordid, parsimonious fellow. a. Miserly, mean.
Bog'gard s. A bogey, a ghost.
Slug'gard s. An habitually lazy person.
Hard a. Impenetrable; firm; arduous, difficult; unfeeling; oppressive. adv. Close, diligently, with difficulty.
Chard s. Blanched stems of artichokes, etc.; a white beet.
Pil'chard s. A small, oily sea-fish.
Po'chard s. The sea-duck.
Or'chard s. An enclosure or assemblage of fruit-trees.
Shard s. A potsherd; a beetle's hard wing-case.
Gal'liard s. An obsolete lively dance; a merry person. a. Jaunty, gay.
Mil'liard s. 1000 millions.
Span'iard s. A native of Spain.
Pon'iard s. A small dagger. v.t. To stab or pierce with this.
Tank'ard s. A large drinking vessel.
Blink'ard s. A semi-blind person, a dodderer.
Drunk'ard s. One habitually or frequently drunk.
Lard s. The fat of hogs melted. v.t. To apply lard to; to interlard; to fatten; to stuff with bacon.
Mal'lard s. The wild duck.
Bol'lard s. A post on a wharf, etc., for securing ropes.
Lol'lard s. A follower of Wyclif.
Pol'lard s. A lopped tree; a mixture of bran and meal. v.t. To lop trees. a. Lopped.
Dul'lard s. A blockhead, dunce.
Interlard' v.t. To mix in; to interpose; to diversify by mixture.
Foulard' s. A thin fabric of silk or silk and cotton.
Pom'mard s. A red Burgundy wine.
Nard s. Spikenard; an unguent prepared from this.
Canard' s. A hoax, an absurd yarn.
Spike'nard s. A herb allied to valerian; an aromatic ointment prepared from this.
Ren'ard s. A fox.
Gur'nard s. A sea-fish of the genus *Trigla*.
Communard' s. A communalist.
Board s. A piece of sawn timber; a council; regular meals. v.t. To enter a ship; to enclose with boards; to supply regularly with meals. v.i. To take one's meals at another's house for payment.
Aboard' adv. Within a ship, on board.
Sea'board s. The seashore. a. Bordering on the sea.
Card'board s. Stiff thick paper or pasteboard.
Paste'board s. Stiff cardboard.
Black'board s. A board used by teachers for writing on with chalk.
Buck'board s. The projecting ledge over cart-wheels.
Duck'board s. A plank for crossing muddy places.
Mill'board s. Thick pasteboard.
In'board a. and adv. Placed towards centre of or within sides of a vessel.
Cup'board s. An enclosure or enclosed recess with shelves.
Gar'board s. The first plank on either side of the keel.
Lar'board s. Left-hand or port side of a vessel.
Star'board s. Right side on ship looking forwards.
O'verboard adv. Over the side of a ship.
Hoard s. A hidden store, an accumulation. v.t. and i. To amass, store up.
Pard s. A leopard; (*slang*) a mate, partner.
Leop'ard s. A large, spotted, feline animal.
Camel'opard s. The giraffe.
Sard s. A hard variety of chalcedony.
Vis'ard s. A visor.
Han'sard s. The official British Parliamentary reports.
Bras'sard s. A badge worn on the arm.
Petard' s. An exploding machine for bursting gates, etc.
Retard' v.t. To prevent from progress; to hinder, impede.
Dynamitard' s. A criminal employing dynamite.
Do'tard s. One who dotes; one in his dotage.
Bas'tard s. An illegitimate child; anything spurious. a. Illegitimate, counterfeit.
Das'tard s. A coward, poltroon. a. Cowardly.
Cos'tard s. A large round apple.
Bus'tard s. A large bird allied to the plovers.
Cus'tard s. A sweetened dish of milk and eggs baked or boiled.

Mus'tard s. An annual plant; condiment made from its seeds.
Guard v.t. To protect, defend, shield. v.i. To watch. s. Defence; a sentinel, escort, one in charge; caution.
Safe'guard s. One who or that which protects; a warrant of security. v.t. To protect.
Bla'ckguard s. A scurrilous person of low character. v.t. To revile in scurrilous language.
Van'guard s. Advance guard of an army; the first line.
Rear'guard s. Protecting troops at an army's rear.
Bod'y-guard s. A guard for the person; retinue, following.
Bou'levard s. A wide road planted with trees.
Ward (wŏrd) s. Watch, guard; room in a hospital; guardianship; a minor under a guardian; a defence in fencing; division of a city, etc.; part of a lock. v.t. To parry; to watch over, defend.
-ward suff. Expressing direction.
Award' v.t. To adjudge, determine, assign. s. The judgment of an arbitrator, sentence.
Sea'ward a. and adv. Situated toward or toward the sea.
Bed'ward adv. To or towards bed or bedtime.
Wind'ward s. Direction from which the wind blows. adv. and a. In or directed towards this.
Leew'ard a. and adv. Pertaining to or towards the lee side. s. The side of a vessel, etc., sheltered from the wind.
Home'ward adv. Towards home. a. Going in the direction of home.
Reward' v.t. To requite, recompense. s. A requital, recompense; what is given in return.
Stew'ard s. One managing affairs for another; official at clubs, etc.,. storekeeper or waiter on board ship.
Earth'ward adv. Toward the earth.
North'ward a. and adv. Toward the north.
South'ward a. and adv. Toward the south.
Back'ward adv. In a direction to the rear. a. Unwilling, sluggish; not advanced.
Awk'ward a. Inelegant, clumsy.
Heav'enward a. and adv. (*Heaven*).
In'ward a. and adv. Placed within; internal; in or towards the interior.
On'ward adv. Forward; on; in advance.
Cow'ard s. One lacking courage; a dastard, poltroon. a. Timid; base; expressive of cowardice.
Fro'ward a. Perverse, wayward.
Toward' prep. In the direction of; for, about. adv. At hand.
To'ward (too'-) a. Docile; apt.
Unto'ward a. Perverse; awkward, vexatious.
Up'ward a. Ascending; directed to a higher place. adv. Upwards.
Bear'ward s. A bear-keeper.
Rear'ward s. The latter part, end; the rear-guard. a. Situated in the rear. adv. Towards the rear.
Hith'erward adv. In this direction.
For'ward adv. Onward; progressively. a. Towards the front; in advance of; ready; pert; eager. v.t. To help or send onward; to transmit; to hasten.
Hencefor'ward adv. From this time forward.
Straight-for'ward a. Honest, open, frank.

Sward s. A grassy surface; turf.
Green'sward s. Turf green with grass.
Left'ward a. and adv. Pertaining to or towards the left.
East'ward a. and adv. Toward the east.
West'ward a. and adv. In or towards the west.
Out'ward a. External; exterior; visible, apparent; adventitious; corporeal. adv. To the outer parts; to a foreign country.
Way'ward a. Perverse; wilful; obstinate.
Yard s. Standard measure of 3 ft.; spar for extending a sail; piece of enclosed ground.
Kale'yard s. A kitchen-garden.
Vine'yard (vin'-) s. Enclosure for or plantation of vines.
Fore'yard s. The lowest of the foremast yards.
Church'yard s. The land surrounding a church; a burial-ground.
Dock'yard s. Enclosed area of wharves and docks; a naval repository and repairing place.
Hal'yard s. Rope for hoisting sails, etc.
Steel'yard s. A balance for weights.
Lan'yard s. A short rope for fastening tackle, etc.
Whin'yard s. A short sword, whingar.
Barn'yard s. Space adjoining a barn.
Boyard' s. A member of the old Russian nobility.
Savoy'ard s. A native of Savoy.
Haz'ard s. Chance, venture, accident; a game of dice. v.t. To risk, place in danger.
Haphaz'ard s. Mere chance, accident.
Maz'ard s. A small variety of black cherry.
Iz'ard s. The wild goat of the Pyrenees.
Liz'ard s. A small four-footed reptile.
Wiz'ard s. A sorcerer, magician. a. Enchanted; enchanting.
Iz'zard s. The letter "Z."
Diz'zard s. A blockhead, dolt.
Giz'zard s. The muscular stomach of a fowl.
Bliz'zard s. A violent storm of wind.
Buz'zard s. A species of falcon; a cockchafer.
Hal'berd s. A combination of battle-axe and spear.
Herd s. A number of beasts feeding or driven in company; a crowd, rabble; a keeper of a herd. v.i. To associate, go in herds; to act as a herd. v.t. To bring into a herd.
Goose'herd s. One who tends geese.
Shep'herd s. One who tends or keeps sheep; a pastor. v.t. To tend as a shepherd; to gather together.
Sherd s. A piece broken off, shard.
Pot'sherd s. A fragment of a broken pot.
Goat'herd s. One who tends goats.
Caird s. (*Scot.*) A travelling tinker.
Laird s. A Scots landowner or house-proprietor.
Bird s. A feathered, two-legged animal, usually winged.
Hang'bird s. The Baltimore oriole.
Black'bird s. A British song-bird.
Call'-bird s. A bird that decoys others.
Weird (Wērd) a. Unearthly; uncanny. s. Fate, destiny.
Gird v.t. To bind round, enclose, encircle. v.i. To gibe; to sneer. s. A sarcasm, sneer; a stroke with a whip.
Third a. Next after the second, being one of 3 equal parts. s. One of 3 equal parts; sixtieth part of a second of time; interval of tone and a semitone.

Cord s. A thick string; corded or ribbed material; a pile of wood (8 ft. by 4 ft. by 4 ft.); a sinew or other animal structure resembling a cord. v.t. To fasten with a cord.

Accord' v.t. To make agree, adjust, grant. v.i. To agree. s. Assent, correspondence of opinion, etc.; voluntary action.

Disaccord' v.i. To disagree. s. Disagreement.

Record' v.t. To register, make a note of.

Rec'ord s. A register, authentic memorial; known facts of a life, etc.; best performance of its kind; plate from which gramophone, etc., reproduces sounds.

Mis'ericord s. Part of a choir-stall used for resting against when standing.

Con'cord s. State of agreement; harmony, union; a consonant chord.

Dis'cord s. Want of agreement or concord; dissension; jarring union of musical sounds.

Ford s. A shallow part of a stream where it may be crossed by wading. v.t. and i. To cross by wading.

Afford' v.t. To be able to give or buy.

Chord s. String of a musical instrument; simultaneous and harmonious union of different sounds.

Dec'achord s. A ten-stringed musical instrument.

Oc'tachord s. An eight-stringed musical instrument; a system of eight sounds.

Pen'tachord s. A five-stringed instrument; a scale of five notes.

Hep'tachord s. A series of seven notes; a lyre with seven strings.

Hex'achord s. An interval of four tones and a semitone; a scale of six notes.

Tri'chord s. A three-stringed musical instrument.

Harp'sichord s. An obsolete forerunner of the pianoforte.

Mon'ochord s. A one-stringed instrument.

No'tochord s. The rudimentary backbone of embryonic and certain lower vertebrates.

Fiord' s. A narrow, precipitous inlet of the sea, especially in Norway.

Lord s. Superior, master, governor; a nobleman; the Supreme Being. v.i. To rule despotically; to domineer.

Land'lord s. A house-proprietor; master of an inn, etc.

Word s. A sound or combination of letters expressing an idea; a term, vocable; information; promise; a saying. v.t. To express in words.

Fore'word s. A preface.

Catch'word s. A popular saying; a cue; a displayed word in type.

Watch'word s. A password; a slogan.

Sword s. A cutting or thrusting weapon.

Broad'sword s. A large sword for cutting.

Pass'word s. A countersign, word by which friends can be distinguished from strangers.

By'word s. A saying, a taunt, a proverb.

Curd s. The coagulated part of milk. v.t. and i. To curdle, congeal.

Kurd s. A native of Kurdistan.

Gourd s. A plant with bottle-shaped fruit; the fruit; a utensil made of this.

Surd s. A quantity that cannot be expressed in rational numbers; a consonant uttered only with the breath. a. Incapable of being expressed in finite terms.

Absurd' a. Contrary to reason, ridiculous.

Fyrd s. The Anglo-Saxon array of all able to bear arms.

***Gaud** s. A trinket, piece of finery.

Laud s. Praise, commendation. v.t. To praise, extol.

Belaud' v.t. To praise excessively.

Applaud' v.t. To extol, praise highly.

Maraud' v.i. To plunder, rove in quest of booty.

Fraud s. Deceit; artifice to the injury of another; subtlety; a cheat.

Defraud' v.t. To deprive by fraud, to cheat.

Bud s. The first shoot of a plant; a germ. v.i. To put forth buds. v.t. To graft by inserting a bud.

Cud s. Food brought by ruminants from the first stomach to be rechewed.

Scud v.i. To fly with haste, run fast before the wind. v.t. To pass swiftly over. s. Act or spell of scudding; vapoury, wind-driven clouds.

Dud s. A useless or inefficient person or thing. a. Ineffective, sham.

Feud s. Deadly hostility, quarrel; fief, fee; tenure.

Thud s. A dull sound; blow causing this. v.t. To fall with or make a thud.

Mud s. Earth wet, soft, and adhesive; mire. v.t. To make turbid; to muddy.

Tal'mud s. The body of Hebrew laws and traditions not contained in the Pentateuch.

Loud a. Having a great sound; noisy; showy. adv. Loudly.

Aloud' adv. With audible voice or considerable noise.

Cloud s. Visible vapour suspended in air; anything that threatens or obscures; a great mass. v.t. To obscure, sully. v.i. To grow cloudy.

Becloud' v.t. To dim, obscure.

Overcloud' v.t. and i. To overspread with clouds.

Shroud s. A winding-sheet; anything which conceals. v.t. To dress for the grave; to hide, veil.

Enshroud' v.t. To cover with a shroud; to conceal.

Proud a. Feeling, showing, or having occasion for pride; haughty; vain.

Pud s. A hand, fore-paw.

Spud s. A short spade-like garden tool; (*slang*) a potato.

Stud s. Ornamental button, especially for collar; large-headed nail; set of breeding horses. v.t. To adorn with studs; to bestrew.

Bawd s. A procuress.

Lewd a. Lascivious; unchaste; indecent.

Shrewd a. Astute, discriminating.

Crowd s. A number of persons or things; a multitude, throng; the populace; an ancient form of fiddle. v.t. To fill to excess or by pressing together. v.i. To throng.

Hy'dromyd s. An Australian water-rat or beaver-rat.

Sloyd s. A system of manual training for the young.

Or'muzd s. The good principle in the Zoroastrian philosophy.

Par'cæ s. The Fates of Roman mythology.

Stri'gidæ s. The family of birds containing the owls.

Ves'pidæ s. The family of wasps.

Gramin'eæ s. The botanical order containing the grasses.

Al'gæ s. Seaweed.
Nu'gæ s. Literary trifles.
Branch'iæ s. Gills of fishes and amphibia.
Stri'æ s. (*Stria*).
Face'tiæ s. Humorous sayings; witticisms.
Minu'tiæ s. Precise or trivial details.
Reliq'uiæ s. Remnants; fossil remains.
Exu'viæ s. The cast skin, shells, etc., of animals; fossil animal remains.
Gral'læ s. The order of wading birds.
Fac'ulæ s. Luminous spots on the sun.
Ther'mæ s. Public baths in ancient Rome; hot springs.
Anten'næ s. The horn-like feelers of insects, etc.
Brae s. (*Scot.*) A slope bounding a river valley.
Ten'ebræ s. A Roman Catholic office for the Wednesday, Thursday and Friday of Holy Week.
Crucif'eræ s. A natural order of plants, the four petals of the flowers of which are disposed crosswise.
Aq'ua-vi'tæ s. Brandy.
Lig'num vi'tæ s. A very hard and heavy wood.
An'tæ s. Square pilasters.
Ballis'tæ s. Ancient military engines for hurling stones, etc.
Be v. aux.
Babe s. A baby; a guileless, innocent person.
As'trolabe s. An instrument for taking altitudes.
Ab'bé s. A priest without a cure.
He'be s. The goddess of youth, and wine-bearer to the Olympians; a waitress.
Ephebe' s. A free-born youth in ancient Greece not arrived at citizenship.
Glebe s. Land belonging to an ecclesiastical benefice.
Grebe s. A diving-bird.
Im'bibe v.t. To drink in, absorb.
Gibe v.t. and i. To mock, taunt, sneer at. s. A sneer, scoff.
Kibe s. An ulcerated chilblain.
Bribe s. Something given to corrupt or influence illegally. v.t. To influence, corrupt, or obtain by such means.
Scribe s. A writer, copyist; a Jewish doctor of law.
Ascribe' v.t. To attribute to, to impute.
Subscribe' v.t. and i. To sign; to assent; to donate money.
Describe' v.t. To delineate, relate, recount.
Redescribe' v.t. To describe afresh.
Prescribe' v.t. To order, appoint, to direct to be used medically. v.i. To dictate, give directions; to claim by prescription.
Cir'cumscribe v.t. To enclose within limits; to restrain, restrict.
Transcribe' v.t. To copy, write over again.
Inscribe' v.t. To write on, in, or down; to dedicate.
Conscribe' v.t. To enlist compulsorily.
Proscribe' v.t. To interdict, outlaw; to prohibit.
Su'perscribe v.t. To write above, on top, or on the outside of.
Tribe s. A family, race, class of people, animals, or plants.
Di'atribe s. A disputation; a lengthy invective.
Combe s. A valley, especially one running up from the sea.
Bunc'ombe s. Humbug, "eye-wash," political clap-trap.
Ado'be s. Dried brick.
-phobe suff. Fearing, disliking.
Fran'cophobe s. One having an unreasoning hatred for or fear of the French.
An'glophobe s. One who hates England and English things and people.
Gal'lophobe s. One who detests the French and everything French.
Slav'ophobe a. and s. Fearing, hating, or one who fears or hates the slaves.
Lobe s. A round projecting part; the lower part of the external ear.
Globe s. A sphere, ball; the world. v.t. To gather into a round mass.
Conglobe' v.t. To gather into a ball.
Robe s. An outer garment; gown of office, etc.; an elegant dress. v.t. To invest with a robe. v.i. To dress.
Mi'crobe s. Any minute organism; a bacterium.
Ward'robe (wŏrd'-) s. A cupboard for clothes.
Enrobe' v.t. To attire.
Probe s. Instrument for examining a wound, etc. v.t. To examine thoroughly; to apply a probe to.
Disrobe' v.t. and i. To divest of a robe; to undress.
Gerbe s. A wheat-sheaf, especially in heraldry.
Cube s. A regular solid body with six equal square sides; product from multiplying a number twice by itself. v.t. To raise to the third power.
Ju'be s. Rood-loft dividing choir from nave.
Ju'jube s. A spiny shrub and its fruit; a sweetmeat made with gum-arabic.
Tube s. A long cylinder for conveyance of fluids, etc.; a pipe; a deep-level electric railway. v.t. To furnish with a tube.
May'be adv. Perhaps; possibly.
Gybe v.t. and i. To shift from one side of a vessel to the other. s. Act or process of gybing.
Ace s. A single point on cards or dice.
Dace s. A small river-fish.
Ven'dace s. A small freshwater fish.
Peace s. State of quiet; tranquillity; respite from war; concord.
Face s. The front part of anything, esp. of the human (or an animal's) head; visage; effrontery; dial. v.t. To meet in front; to oppose; to finish with a thin covering; to turn up with facings. v.i. To turn the face, to look towards.
Deface' v.t. To disfigure, destroy.
Reface' v.t. To put a new face or surface on.
Pref'ace s. An introduction, prelude, foreword. v.t. To introduce by preliminary remarks.
Volte face (volt fahs) s. An entire change of front.
Efface' v.t. To rub out, cancel, obliterate.
Bon'iface s. An innkeeper.
Sur'face s. Exterior; superficies; external appearance. v.t. To polish, put a surface on.
Outface' v.t. To stare out of countenance; to brave.
Lace s. A cord for fastening; a delicate fabric of interlacing threads. v.t. To fasten with a lace; to adorn with lace; to interlace.
Pal'ace s. Official residence of a sovereign, bishop, etc.; a magnificent house.
Gla'cé a. Iced; glossy.
Neck'lace s. A string of gems, etc., for the neck.
Bull'ace s. A wild plum.
Enlace' v.t. To encircle, entwine.

Sol'ace v.t. To comfort, console. s. Consolation; relief; recreation.
Place s. A locality, position, open space in a town; quarters, rank, calling; residence; ground or occasion; stead. v.t. To set, locate, establish.
Replace' v.t. To put back in place; to put in place of another; to take the place of.
Birth'place s. The place where one was born.
Com'monplace a. Ordinary, trite, unoriginal. s. A usual topic or idea; a trite remark.
Displace' v.t. To remove, put out of place, discharge; to take the place of.
Misplace' v.t. To put in a wrong place; to devote to an undeserving object.
Interlace' v.t. To weave together. v.i. To be interwoven.
Pop'ulace s. The common people, the multitude.
Mace s. A heavy-headed staff; an emblem of authority; a spice.
Grimace' s. A distortion of the face. v.i. To make grimaces; to assume affected airs.
Pom'ace s. Crushed apples used in cider-making.
Men'ace v.t. To threaten. s. A threat.
Ten'ace s. (*Whist*) Best and third best in a suit in one hand.
Pin'nace s. A. small sailing vessel; an eight-oared boat.
Fur'nace s. An enclosed fireplace for producing intense heat.
Pace s. A step; space between feet in walking; gait. v.i. To walk, especially slowly. v.t. To measure by steps.
Pa'ce prep. By leave of.
Apace' adv. Quickly, hastily.
Car'apace s. Hard shell of a tortoise, crab, etc.
Space s. Extension; area; period or quantity of time; a while. v.t. To place at proper intervals; to arrange the spaces in.
In'terspace s. An intervening space.
Race s. Descendants of a common ancestor; tribe, stock; characteristic flavour, quality, or disposition; a contest in running, speed, etc.; a rapid course, swift progress, a career; a rapid channel; a root (especially of ginger). v.i. To run swiftly, contend in running. v.t. To cause to run thus.
Brace v.t. To draw tight, strengthen. s. That which holds tight.
Vam'brace s. Armour for the fore-arm.
Embrace' v.t. To clasp, hug, to include, comprise. s. A close encircling, a hug.
Grace s. Favour bestowed; divine favour; beauty, elegance of manner and bearing; kindness; one of three ancient goddesses renowned for beauty; an embellishment. v.t. To adorn, dignify, embellish.
Scape'grace s. A graceless, hare-brained fellow.
Disgrace' s. Dishonour, reproach, disrepute. v.t. To deprive of favour, degrade.
Ter'race s. A raised bank or flat area; a row of houses; a flat-topped roof. v.t. To form into terraces.
Trace s. Mark left by anything; a vestige; track; strap by which a vehicle is drawn. v.t. To follow by marks left; to track out; to delineate or copy with lines or marks.
Retrace' v.t. To trace back to the source or along the same path; to go over in reverse direction.
Ambs'ace s. The lowest throw at dice; ill luck.
Ro'sace s. A rose-window, rose-shaped ornament.
Ta'ce int. Be silent!
Viva'ce (vēva'chā) adv. In a lively way (*mus. direction*).
Fleece s. The wool shorn from a sheep; a sheep's coat. v.t. To strip of or cover with a fleece; to plunder, rob heartlessly.
Niece s. Daughter of one's brother or sister.
Piece s. A part of a whole; a short writing or composition; a coin; a single gun; a picture. v.t. To patch, join. v.i. To unite or join on.
Apiece' adv. To each one a share.
Time'piece s. A clock or watch.
Man'telpiece s. A mantel with shelf.
Mas'terpiece s. A chief work; anything done with superior skill.
Front'ispiece s. Illustration facing title-page; a façade.
Ice s. Frozen water; frozen cream, etc., flavoured; sugar coating for cakes. v.t. To convert into, cool with, or cover with ice.
-ice suff. Forming nouns.
Plaice s. A broad flat-fish.
Bice s. A blue or greenish pigment.
Dice s. Small cubes marked with spots used in gaming, casting lots, etc. v.i. and t. To play at or gamble with dice.
Cad'dice s. (*Caddis*).
Jaun'dice s. A liver-disease marked by yellowness of the skin, etc.
Bod'ice s. The part of a dress covering the bust; a corset.
Cow'ardice s. Want of courage.
Prej'udice s. Prepossession; an unwarranted predilection; bias; injury. v.t. To prepossess without due knowledge of facts; to damage, impair.
Ben'efice s. An ecclesiastical preferment.
Of'fice s. A public employment; function; place of business; persons transacting business in such place, a formulary of devotion.
Suffice' v.i. To be sufficient. v.t. To satisfy content.
Ed'ifice s. A large building.
Sac'rifice s. Act of offering anything, especially to God; thing offered; surrender for sake of something else. v.t. To make a sacrifice or offering to.
Or'ifice s. An opening, aperture, vent.
Ar'tifice s. Trick, fraud; cunning, duplicity.
Lice s. (*Louse*).
Chal'ice s. A cup, especially used in the Eucharist.
Mal'ice s. Disposition to harm others; deliberate spite.
For'talice s. A small fort.
An'glice adv. In the English manner.
Cil'ice s. A hair-shirt; hair cloth.
Gal'lice adv. In French.
Police' (-lēs') s. The civil force of a district; internal government of a community. v.t. To guard or regulate by police.
Accom'plice s. An associate, especially in crime.
Sur'plice s. A white, ecclesiastical vestment.
Splice v.t. To unite by interweaving (of rope) or overlapping (of timber, etc.); to scarf; (*slang*) to marry. s. Union by splicing; scarfing.

Slice s. A thin, broad piece cut off; broad knife for fish; a share. v.t. To cut into slices or parts; to divide.
Mice s. (*Mouse*).
Am'ice s. An ecclesiastical vestment.
Pum'ice s. A porous volcanic stone.
Nice a. Fastidious, dainty; discriminating; agreeable, delightful; accurate.
Cor'nice s. A moulded projection finishing a part, wall, etc.
Choice s. Option, selection, preference; best part. a. Select, precious, rare.
Rejoice' v.i. To be glad, to exult. v.t. To gladden.
Voice s. Articulate utterance; speech; expression; opinion; vote; a form of a verb. v.t. To give utterance or sonancy to.
In'voice s. List of goods dispatched giving various particulars. v.t. To make an invoice of; to enter on an invoice.
Pice s. A small Indian copper coin.
Pre'cipice s. An abrupt declivity, steep descent.
Cop'pice s. A small wood of undergrowth, etc.
Spice s. A fragrant or pungent substance used as flavouring; a trace, smack. v.t. To flavour.
All'spice s. The dried berry of pimento.
Hos'pice s. A convent in the Alps; place of rest for travellers.
Rice s. A cereal plant of tropical and sub-tropical countries; its small, pearly grain.
Av'arice s. Inordinate desire of gain, cupidity.
Den'tifrice s. Material for cleansing the teeth.
Grice s. A sucking-pig; an heraldic wild boar.
Thrice adv. Three times.
Liq'uorice s. A plant of the bean family; a drug or sweetmeat prepared from this.
Price s. Amount at which a thing is valued; cost, charge. v.t. To set a price on; to ascertain the price of.
Caprice' s. A whim, fancy.
Trice v.t. To haul, tie up. s. An instant.
Cic'atrice s. A cicatrix.
Cock'atrice s. A fabulous monster whose glance was fatal.
Improvisatri'ce s. A female improvisatore.
Cantatrice' s. A female singer.
Sice s. The six on dice.
Prac'tice s. A doing; customary use; performance as opposed to theory; dexterity; training; exercise of a profession; professional connexion.
Malprac'tice s. An evil practice; professional misconduct.
Poul'tice s. A soft composition applied to sores, etc. v.t. To cover or dress with this.
Entice' v.t. To allure, persuade, decoy, inveigle.
Appren'tice s. One bound by indenture. v.t. To bind one thus.
Scot'ice (-i-si) adv. In the Scottish manner.
No'tice s. An intimation, instruction, warning; act of noting; regard, attention. v.t. To note, heed, pay respect to; to give notice to.
Ar'mistice s. A cessation of hostilities prior to a treaty being made.
Sol'stice s. N. and S. points at which the sun is furthest from the equator; time of this (21 June and 22 December).
Inter'stice s. A small intervening space.
Jus'tice s. Equity; retribution; a judge.
Injus'tice s. Want of justice; iniquity.
Lat'tice s. A framework of crossing laths. a. Furnished with such. v.t. To form with cross-bars.
Brat'tice s. A partition, a timber lining.
Juice s. Sap of fruits and vegetables; fluid from meat; succulence.
Ver'juice s. Sour juice of crab-apples, etc.; sourness of temper, etc.
Sluice s. A vent for water, floodgate; opening through which anything flows, a stream; a rinsing. v.t. To wet abundantly, wash thoroughly.
Vice s. A fault; depravity; a gripping instrument.
Vi'ce adv. In place of.
Advice' s. Counsel, instruction.
Device' s. A contrivance, scheme, stratagem; an emblem.
Crev'ice s. A crack, fissure.
Nov'ice s. A beginner, tyro; an inexperienced person.
Ser'vice s. Act of serving; employment; state of being a servant; a kind office; willingness to act; use; formal publication; set of dishes; liturgy; a tree with small pear-like fruit.
Disser'vice s. Injury; mischief.
Twice adv. Two times; doubly.
Disturb'ance s. Commotion; excitement; derangement of the usual order.
Signif'icance s. Quality of being significant; expressiveness; import.
Insignif'icance s. Quality or state of being insignificant; triviality.
Dance v.i. To move with measured, rhythmical steps; to caper, frisk. v.t. To cause to dance, to dandle. s. A rhythmical stepping; performance of this; music to which it is set; a ball.
Forbid'dance s. Act of forbidding.
Rid'dance s. Act of ridding; state of being free; deliverance.
Abi'dance s. Continuance.
Void'ance s. Act of ejecting from a benefice; state of being void; vacancy.
Avoi'dance s. Act of shunning, avoiding, or annulling.
Guid'ance s. Act of guiding; a leading; government.
Misguid'ance s. Wrong direction or guidance.
Atten'dance s. Act of attending; persons attending; service.
Non-atten'dance s. (*Negative*).
Abun'dance' s. Great plenty, exuberance.
Super-abun'dance s. More than enough.
Redun'dance s. Quality of being redundant; superfluity.
Accor'dance s. Agreement, harmony.
Concord'ance s. State of being concordant; agreement; a verbal alphabetical index to a work.
Discor'dance s. State or quality of being discordant; inconsistency.
Ven'geance s. Retribution; unrestrained revenge.
Per'meance s. Permeation.
Sé'ance (sā'-) s. A session; meeting for spiritualistic manifestations.
Extrav'agance s. Excess, waste, prodigality.
El'egance s. Quality or state of being elegant; refinement.
Inel'egance s. Condition of being inelegant.

Ar'rogance s. Undue assumption of importance; haughtiness.
Chance s. Luck, course of events; hazard; opportunity; likelihood; fortuity v.i. To come to pass. v.t. (*slang*) To risk, hazard a. Fortuitous, casual.
Bechance' v.t. To befall, happen. adv. Accidentally, by chance.
Mumchance' s. An old game of hazard; a stupid person.
Perchance' adv. By chance, perhaps.
Mischance' s. Misfortune; ill-luck.
Enhance' v.t. To raise to a higher pitch; to raise in esteem, increase in price.
Insou'ciance s. Indifference; heedlessness.
Ra'diance s. Quality of being radiant; lustre; glitter.
Irra'diance s. Lustre, brightness.
Fian'cé s. A betrothed man.
Defi'ance s. A challenge; contempt of danger; open disobedience.
Affi'ance v.t. To betroth, pledge in marriage. s. Betrothal.
Alle'giance s. Obedience due, especially to a sovereign.
Reli'ance s. Act of relying; ground of confidence.
Alli'ance s. A league; relation by marriage.
Dal'liance s. Trifling; exchange of caresses.
Mésalliance' s. Marriage with an inferior.
Misalli'ance s. An improper association, especially marriage.
Bril'liance s. (*Brilliant*).
Compli'ance s. Consent; submission.
Incompli'ance s. Refusal or failure to comply.
Non-compli'ance s. (*Negative*).
Appli'ance s. Act of applying; aid; instrument.
Sup'pliance s. Entreaty; humble beseeching.
Var'iance s. Variation; state of varying; dissension.
Luxur'iance s. State of being luxuriant; rank growth; exuberance.
Askance' adv. Sideways, obliquely.
Lance s. A long spear; a lancer. v.t. To pierce with a lance; to open with a lancet.
Bal'ance v. To make or be of the same weight, to make equal. s. A pair of scales; equipoise; overplus.
Counter-bal'ance v.t. To oppose with an equal weight, act against equally, countervail. s. An equal opposing weight; equivalent.
Overbal'ance v.t. To exceed in weight, etc. v.i. To topple over.
Outbal'ance v.t. To exceed in weight or effect.
Val'ance s. Drapery hanging round a bed.
Sem'blance s. Seeming, similarity; image, appearance.
Resem'blance s. Likeness, similarity; that which is similar.
Vraisemblance' s. Appearance of truth; probability.
Fer-de-lance s. A S. American poisonous snake.
Glance s. A quick view, a glimpse; a sudden shoot of light, etc. v.i. To gleam; to dart aside; to move quickly; to look suddenly or obliquely.
Sib'ilance s. Sibilancy.
Ju'bilance s. Jubilation.
Vig'ilance s. Watchfulness.
Surveil'lance (-vâl'-) s. Watch; inspection.
Par'lance s. Form or manner of speech.
Am'bulance s. A conveyance for sick or wounded.
Sim'ulance s. Simulation.
Pet'ulance s. State of being petulant; pettishness.
Romance' s. A mediæval tale; a work of fiction; tendency to the wonderful or mysterious. a. Denoting the languages sprung from Latin. v.i. To deal in extravagant stories; to exaggerate, fabricate.
Affirm'ance s. Confirmation, ratification.
Conform'ance s. (*Conform*).
Perform'ance s. Act of performing; deed, achievement; an entertainment, exhibition.
Non-perform'ance s. (*Negative*).
Ord'nance s. Heavy guns; artillery.
Pen'ance s. Voluntary suffering for, or ecclesiastical punishment imposed for, sin.
Main'tenance s. Act of maintaining; means of support; continuance.
Count'enance s. Appearance, facial expression; aspect; the face, features; favour, encouragement. v.t. To favour, encourage, vindicate.
Dis-coun'tenance v.t. To put to shame; to refuse to recognize, to discourage. s. Unfriendly treatment, disapprobation.
Appur'tenance s. An adjunct, accessory.
Sus'tenance s. Act of sustaining; support; food.
Prev'enance s. Anticipation of the wishes of others.
Convenance' s. Conventional usages.
Prov'enance s Source, origin of.
Repug'nance s. Opposition or incompatibility of mind; antipathy.
Or'dinance s. An authoritative order, decree, rite, ceremony, etc.
Preor'dinance s. Antecedent decree or determination.
Finance' s. Science or management of public revenue and money matters; public funds; income. v.t. To provide funds for.
Dom'inance s. Ascendancy, authority.
Predom'inance s. Prevalence; ascendancy.
So'nance s. Quality or state of being sonant.
Res'onance s. Act of resounding; state or quality of being resonant.
Unis'onance s. Accordance of sounds.
Con'sonance s. Accord, especially in sound; agreement, consistency.
Incon'sonance s. (*Inconsonant*).
As'sonance s. A jingle or imperfect rhyme.
Dis'sonance s. A mingling of discordant sounds; want of agreement; inconsistency.
Gov'ernance s. Act, manner, etc., of governing; control.
Rance s. A variegated marble; a bar, prop.
Forbear'ance s. Act of forbearing; patience, mildness.
Clear'ance s. Act of clearing, state of being cleared; net profit.
Appear'ance s. Aspect of anything; act of appearing.
Reappear'ance s. Another appearance.
Non-appear'ance s. (*Negative*).
Disappear'ance s. Act of vanishing; removal from sight.
Remem'brance s. Act of remembering; anything remembered; a memorial; memory.
Encum'brance s. That which encumbers, burden, hindrance; liability.
Hin'drance s. Act of hindering; an impediment.
Protu'berance s. A bulge, projection.
Exu'berance s. Overflowing plenty; superfluity.

Pon'derance s. Weight, gravity.
Prepon'derance s. Superiority of power, influence, etc.; state or quality of preponderating.
Equipon'derance s. Equality of weight.
Sun'derance s. Act of sundering.
Suf'ferance s. Passive consent; allowance.
Vocif'erance s. Vociferation.
Fur'therance s. Assistance, a helping forward.
Tol'erance s. Quality of being tolerant; toleration.
Intol'erance s. Quality of being intolerant; want of toleration.
Tem'perance s. Moderation; self-restraint; sobriety.
Intem'perance s. Want of self-restraint, especially with reference to indulgence in alcohol.
Ut'terance s. Act of uttering; vocal expression; words uttered.
Sev'erance s. Act of severing; dividing.
Persever'ance s. Act of persevering; steadfastness; continued diligence.
Dissev'erance s. Act of dividing, state of being parted.
Deliv'erance s. Act of delivering; release, rescue.
Fra'grance s. A pleasant odour; sweetness of smell; quality of being fragrant.
Ig'norance s. State of being uneducated or uninformed; lack of knowledge.
Prance v.i. To spring and bound; to strut about. s. A leap, caper.
Trance s. State of insensibility; coma; an ecstasy.
Pen'etrance s. Quality of being penetrating; penetrativeness.
Recal'citrance s. Opposition; refractoriness.
En'trance s. Act of entering or of taking possession, office, etc.; power to enter; place where one enters; commencement.
Entrance' v.t. To put into a trance; to enchant.
Re-en'trance s. Act of entering again.
Mon'strance s. (*Rom. Cath.*) Transparent box in which the Host is carried.
Remon'strance s. Act of remonstrating; expostulation.
Procur'ance s. Procurement.
Dur'ance s. Imprisonment.
Endur'ance s. Act of bearing pain, etc., with fortitude; patience, resignation; continuance.
Insurance' s. Act of insuring against loss, etc.; this system.
Assur'ance s. Confidence, want of modesty.
Reassur'ance s. Assurance or confirmation repeated.
Defea'sance s. Act of annuling any contract.
Malfea'sance s. Evil or illegal conduct; an illegal deed.
Misfea'sance s. A wrong done; improper performance of a lawful act.
Pleas'ance s. Pleasure, gaiety; a pleasure-ground.
Complai'sance s. (*Complaisant*).
Obei'sance (-bā'-) s. A bow, curtsy.
Nui'sance s. That which is offensive, annoys, or produces inconvenience.
Renais'sance (-nās-) s. A renewal; the revival of letters in the fifteenth century; style of art developed by this.
Recon'naissance s. Exploration or survey for military purposes; force of troops or ships engaged in this.
Puis'sance s. Power, strength, might.
Impu'issance s. Powerlessness.
Us'ance (ūz'-) s. Period allowed for paying a foreign bill of exchange.
Rec'usance s. Recusancy.
Expect'ance s. Act or state of expecting; hope; expectation.
Reluc'tance s. Unwillingness; repugnance.
Hab'itance s. A habitation.
Exor'bitance s. Enormity; extravagance.
Concom'itance s. State of being concomitant.
Precip'itance s. Quality of being precipitant or precipitate; headlong hurry.
Inher'itance s. Act of inheriting; that which is inherited.
Disinher'itance s. State of being disinherited.
Hes'itance s. Hesitancy.
Repen'tance s. Act of repenting; state of being penitent; contrition.
Acquain'tance s. Knowledge of; a friend.
Non-acquain'tance s. Lack of acquaintance with.
Accep'tance s. Act of accepting; reception; written promise to pay.
Non-accept'ance s. (*Negative*).
Impart'ance s. Impartation.
Import'ance s. Quality of being important; weight, moment; rank.
Comport'ance s. Behaviour.
Sort'ance s. Suitableness.
Stance s. Golf-player's position when striking.
Sub'stance s. Matter, material; a body; essence; estate.
Dis'tance s. Space between two things; reserve. v.t. To leave behind in a race.
Outdis'tance v.t. To get ahead of, pass.
Desist'ance s. Act or state of desisting.
Resis'tance s. Act of resisting; quality of not yielding; opposition; check.
Non-resis'tance s. (*Negative*).
Assis'tance s. Help, succour.
Cir'cumstance s. An incident; condition of things surrounding an event. v.t. To place relatively or in a particular situation.
In'stance s. An example; solicitation; importunity; suggestion. v.t. To mention as an example.
Admit'tance s. Act or price of admission; entrance given.
Remit'tance s. Act of remitting money, etc.; sum remitted.
Permit'tance s. Act of permitting; permission.
Pit'tance s. A small allowance, quantity, or charity; a trifle.
Quit'tance s. Discharge from a debt, etc.; repayment; recompense.
Acquit'tance s. A judicial discharge.
Nuance' s. A slight difference of meaning, colour, style, etc.
Contin'uance s. Permanence, continuation, duration.
Discontin'uance s. Want of continuity; breaking off, termination.
Pursu'ance s. Act of pursuing or prosecuting; consequence.
Iss'uance s. Act of issuing.
Perpet'uance s. Perpetuation.
Advance' v. To bring or go forward; to lend. s. A going forward; a rise in price; a giving beforehand.
Griev'ance s. Wrong suffered; injury; hardship.
Rel'evance s. State of being relevant; pertinence.
Irrel'evance s. State or quality of being irrelevant.
Conni'vance s. Voluntary oversight, collusion; tacit consent.
Contri'vance s. Act of contriving; invention, device, apparatus; scheme, plot.

Observ'ance s. Act of observing; ceremonial reverence; rule of practice.
Inobser'vance s. Want of observance.
Non-obser'vance s. (*Negative*).
Allow'ance s. Sanction; salary; abatement. v.t. To put upon an allowance.
Disallow'ance s. Refusal to allow; rejection, prohibition.
Abey'ance s. A suspension of right, title, etc.
Convey'ance s. Act or means of conveying; a vehicle; act of transferring property, document by which this is effected.
Purvey'ance s. Act or process of purveying; procurement; provisions.
Joy'ance s. Gaiety; joy.
Annoy'ance s. That which annoys; act of annoying or state of being annoyed.
Clairvoy'ance s. Power of seeing things not present; second-sight.
Cog'nizance s. Knowledge, notice, recognition; judicial jurisdiction; an heraldic badge.
Recog'nizance s. An obligation; acknowledgment.
Incog'nizance s. State of being incognizant.
-ence suff. Forming abstract nouns.
Decum'bence s. Act, posture, or state of being decumbent.
Recum'bence s. State of being recumbent; act of resting.
Resorb'ence s. Resorption.
Compla'cence s. A feeling of inward satisfaction; a cause of pleasure; civility.
Malef'icence s. Evil-doing; noxiousness.
Benef'icence s. Active goodness, kindness.
Magnif'icence s. Grandeur of appearance; splendour; pomp.
Munif'icence s. Great liberality; generosity; bounty.
Li'cence s. Authority, leave, certificate giving permission; excess of liberty; licentiousness.
Ret'icence s. State of being reserved or reticent; taciturnity.
Frank'incense s. A fragrant resin used in perfumery and as incense.
In'nocence s. Quality or state of being innocent; freedom from guilt; simplicity.
Renas'cence s. Rebirth, renewal; the Renaissance.
-escence suff. Forming abstract nouns from inceptive verbs.
Tabes'cence s. Condition of wasting away.
Contabes'cence s. An atrophied condition in plants; a wasting away by disease.
Albes'cence s. Act of growing white.
Pubes'cence s. Puberty, or state of this; the down of plants.
Erubes'cence s. State of blushing, a blush.
Aces'cence s. Sourness.
Marces'cence s. State or quality of being marcescent.
Glauces'cence s. State of being glaucous.
Lapides'cence s. State or quality of being lapidescent; petrification.
Irides'cence s. The changeable, rainbow-like colouring of bubbles, etc.
Vivides'cence s. Greenness, especially of vegetation.
Candes'cence s. The glow of white-heat.
Incandes'cence s. State of being incandescent; white heat.
Frondes'cence s. Act or time of bursting into leaf.
Recrudes'cence s. A fresh breaking out; a relapse.
Rufes'cence s. A reddish or bronzy tinge.
Turges'cence s. Act of swelling; state of being swelled; bombast.
Quies'cence s. State or quality of being quiescent; repose; silence.
Acquies'cence s. Agreement, silent consent.
Cales'cence s. Increasing warmth.
Alkales'cence s. (*Alkali*).
Coales'cence s. Act of coalescing; union.
Opales'cence s. Iridescent light or reflection, as in the opal.
Convales'cence s. State of a convalescent; gradually recovering health.
Hyales'cence s. Process of becoming transparent.
Adoles'cence s. Period between childhood and youth.
Obsoles'cence s. State of becoming obsole.
Fremes'cence s. Tumult, uproar.
Spumes'cence s. Spuminess.
Tumes'cence s. (*Tumescent*).
Intumes'cence s. A swelling up through heat; tumidity; inflation.
Canes'cence s. Whiteness, hoariness.
Evanes'cence s. State of being liable to disappear.
Senes'cence s. State of growing old.
Juvenes'cence s. State of being youthful; a growing young.
Rejuvenes'cence s. Rejuvenation.
Lumines'cence s. Light unaccompained by incandescence.
Spines'cence s. State or quality of being spiny; a spiny growth.
Pruines'cence s. State of being covered with bloom.
Torpes'cence s. State of becoming torpid.
Accres'cence s. Continued growth, increase.
Concres'cence s. Act of growing together, coalescence.
Excres'cence s. That which grows unnaturally from something else; a superfluity.
Nigres'cence s. Process of becoming black; darkness of complexion.
Vires'cence s. Greenness; state of being virescent.
Arbores'cence s. A tree-like growth or characteristic.
Phosphores'cence s. State or quality of being phosphorescent.
Calores'cence s. The change of non-luminous to luminous heat-rays.
Flores'cence s. Season of flowering; flowering.
Reflores'cence s. A second florescence.
Efflores'cence s. Time, act, or process of flowering; eruption as in rash, etc.; formation of crust on efflorescing bodies; crust formed.
Inflores'cence s. Flowering; mode of flowering; collective flowers of a plant.
Sonores'cence s. Quality or state of being sonorescent.
Fluores'cence s. Property of certain bodies of emitting coloured light under certain conditions.
Vitres'cence s. State or quality of being vitreous or vitrescent.
Putres'cence s. State of putridness or becoming rotten.
Lates'cence s. State or quality of being latescent.
Lactes'cence s. Milkiness; milk-like appearance, etc.; becoming milky.
Delites'cence s. State of being concealed; period during which diseases, poisons, etc., lie dormant in the system.
Obmutes'cence s. Loss of speech; taciturnity.
Frutes'cence s. Quality or state of being shrubby.
Liques'cence s. State or quality of being liquescent.
Deliques'cence s. Act or state of being diliquescent.
Deferves'cence s. An abatement of feverish symptoms.
Efferves'cence s. Act of effervescing; visible excitement.
Dehis'cence s. Splitting open, as of seed-pods.

Indehis'cence s. Property of being indehiscent.
Reminis'cence s. Something remembered; recollection; power of recalling to mind.
Resipis'cence s. Wisdom after the event.
Concu'piscence s. Excessive or unlawful lust.
Oblivis'cence s. Forgetfulness.
Translu'cence s. Quality of being translucent; clearness.
Ca'dence s. A rhythmical modulation of the voice; the close of a musical phrase.
Deca'dence s. Decay; state of falling or declining.
Prece'dence s. Act or state of preceding; priority.
Antece'dence s. Act or state of preceding; priority.
Cre'dence s. Belief, credit; confidence; a table at the S. side of the altar.
Supersed'ence s. Supersedure.
Ac'cidence s. The part of grammar dealing with the changes in the form of words.
In'cidence s. An occurring; direction in which a body, ray of light, etc., falls.
Coin'cidence s. Agreement or concurrence, especially of events at the same time.
Dif'fidence s. Distrust of oneself, bashfulness.
Con'fidence s. Trust, firm belief; assurance; self-reliance; boldness; a secret.
Sub'sidence (*also* **-si'dence**) s. Act or process of subsiding.
Res'idence s. Act of residing; domicile; home; sojourn.
Dis'sidence s. Disagreement, dissent.
Ev'idence s. Testimony, certainty, proof.
Prov'idence s. Foresight; economy, prudence; care of God for his creatures; a providential circumstance.
Improv'idence s. Want of foresight; wastefulness.
Condescen'-dence s. Condescension.
Transcen'dence s. State of being transcendent; supereminence.
Resplend'ence s. State or quality of being resplendent.
Depend'ence s. State of being dependent; connexion and support; reliance, trust.
Indepen'dence s. Quality of being independent; self-reliance; a sufficient income.
Interdepen'-dence s. Mutual dependence.
Impen'dence s. State of impending; menacing attitude.
Superinten'-dence s. Oversight, control, guidance.
Abscon'dence s. Act of absconding; concealment.
Correspon'-dence s. Congruity; mutual adaptation; fitness; letters, intercourse by letters.
Im'pudence s. Quality of being impudent; effrontery; cheek.
Pru'dence s. Quality of being prudent; discretion.
Impru'dence s. Indiscretion; a rash or thoughtless act.
Jurispru'dence s. The science of law; the legal system of a country.
Fence s. An enclosing wall or boundary; that which defends; fencing, skill in this; a receiver of stolen goods. v.t. To secure by an enclosure; to defend; to ward off by argument. v.i. To practise fencing; to parry arguments; to prevaricate.
Defence' s. Protection; vindication; justification.
Offence' s. Act of offending; violation of law; an injury, affront; displeasure.
E'gence s. State of being needy.
In'digence s. Poverty, destitution.
Neg'ligence s. Neglect, carelessness; quality of being negligent.
Dil'igence s. Assiduity; steady application; a stage-coach.
Intel'ligence s. Exercise of the understanding, capacity for higher functions of the intellect; information.
Ex'igence s. Urgent or exacting want; distress; emergency.
Indul'gence s. Act or practice of indulging; a favour; gratification; intemperance; remission of penance.
Reful'gence s. Splendour; brilliancy.
Efful'gence s. A flood of light, great brilliancy; state of being effulgent.
Divul'gence s. A making known, revealing.
Contin'gence s. Contingency.
Submer'gence s. Act of submerging; state of being submerged.
Emer'gence s. Act of emerging.
Diver'gence s. A receding from each other in radiating lines.
Conver'gence s. Tendency towards one point.
Resur'gence s. Act of rising again.
Insur'gence s. Rebellion; insurgency.
Hence adv. From this time, place, cause, etc. int. Begone!
Thence adv. From that place or time.
Whence adv. From what or which place.
Faience' s. Glazed earthenware.
Defic'ience s. (*Deficiency*).
Profi'cience s. Proficiency.
Sci'ence s. Systematized knowledge, or a department of it, that which is known; skill.
Nes'cience s. Ignorance; want of knowledge.
Pre'science s. Foreknowledge; foresight.
Omnis'cience s. Infinite knowledge.
Con'science s. Faculty which judges between right and wrong; moral sense.
Obe'dience s. State of being obedient; act of obeying; submission to authority.
Non-obe'dience s. (*Negative*).
Disobe'dience s. Neglect or refusal to obey.
Expe'dience s. State or quality of being expedient; propriety; advisability.
Inexpe'dience s. Quality or state of being inexpedient.
Au'dience s. An assemblage of hearers; act of hearing; a formal interview.
Preau'dience s. Right of being heard before another.
Sa'lience s. State of being salient; a projection.
Resil'ience s. Act or capacity of springing back or rebounding.
Transil'ience s. A leap across; an abrupt transition.
Consil'ience s. Concurrence, agreement.
Dissil'ience s. Act of leaping or starting asunder.
Ebul'lience s. A boiling over; great enthusiasm.
Le'nience s. Leniency.
Preve'nience s. Act of going before; anticipation.
Conven'ience s. State or quality of being convenient; ease; suitable opportunity; a useful appliance or utensil.
Inconve'nience s. Quality of being inconvenient; annoyance; cause of difficulty.
Sa'pience s. Wisdom; affected learning or knowingness.
Incip'ience s. Inception.
Percip'ience s. Act or power of perceiving.
Desip'ience s. Foolishness, trifling.
Exper'ience s. Knowledge gained by trial; continued observation; that which is experienced, suffering. v.t. To try, know by trial, undergo.

Inexper'ience s. Absence or want of experience.
Prur'ience s. Lasciviousness; itching desire.
Esur'ience s. Greed.
Tran'sience s. State or quality of being transient; evanescent.
Pa'tience s. Quality of being patient; endurance; composure; perseverance; a game at cards for one.
Impa'tience s. Condition of being impatient.
Sen'tience s. Consciousness; mental life.
Subser'vience s. State of being subservient.
Non'chalance s. Indifference, coolness.
Va'lence s. Combining power of an element or radical.
Prev'alence s State or quality of being prevalent; superior influence, etc.
Univ'alence s. A combining power of one.
Triva'lence s. A valence of three.
Equiv'alence s. State of being equivalent; equality of value, etc.
Si'lence s. Absence of sound; forbearance of speech; calmness; secrecy; oblivion. v.t. To put to silence, to quiet.
Pes'tilence s. A plague, deadly epidemic; that which breeds vice, etc.
Ex'cellence s. State or quality of being excellent; superiority; a valuable quality; a title of honour.
Superex'cellence s. (*Superexcellent*).
Repell'ence s. Quality of being repellent.
Prepol'lence s. Superiority of power.
Equipol'lence s. Equality of power or force.
Red'olence s. Quality of being redolent.
In'dolence s. Sloth, laziness; love of this.
Condo'lence s. Expression or act of sympathy.
Vi'olence s. Quality of being violent; vehemence; outrage.
Som'nolence s. Drowsiness; inclination to sleep.
In'solence s. State or quality of being insolent; impudence.
Malev'olence s. Ill-will, evil disposition, personal hatred.
Benev'olence s. Charitable feeling, goodwill.
Tur'bulence s. (*Turbulent*).
Floc'culence s. State of being flocculent.
Suc'culence s. State of being succulent; juiciness.
Fec'ulence s. Quality of being feculent; that which is feculent.
Truc'ulence s. Terribleness of aspect; ferociousness.
Fraud'ulence s. Quality of being fraudulent.
Tem'ulence s. Drunkenness.
Crap'ulence s. Illness through immoderate drinking.
Op'ulence s. Wealth, riches, affluence.
Cor'pulence s. Excessive fatness.
Pulver'ulence s. Dustiness.
Vir'ulence a. Quality of being virulent; extreme malignity.
Pur'ulence s. State of being purulent; pus.
Flat'ulence s. State or condition of being flatulent.
Ve'hemence s. Impetuous force; impetuosity.
Commence' v.i. To start, begin. v.t. To enter upon, originate.
Recommence' v.t. To begin over again.
Im'manence s. Condition of being immanent; an indwelling.
Per'manence s. Condition or quality of being permanent or fixed; duration.
Imper'manence s. State of being temporary.
Em'inence s. Loftiness, a height; high rank, superiority; title given to cardinals.
Pre-em'inence s. State or quality of being pre-eminent.
Superem'inence s. Distinguished eminence.
Im'minence s. State of being or that which is imminent.
Prom'inence s. Projection; protuberance; eminence.
Con'tinence s. Restraint of the desires; chastity, temperance.
Incon'tinence s. Unchastity; inability to restrain evacuations.
Per'tinence s. State of being pertinent; suitability.
Imper'tinence s. Quality of being impertinent; rudeness.
Ab'stinence s. Act or practice of abstaining; continence.
Pence s. (*Penny*).
Twop'ence (tŭp') s. Sum of two pennies.
Spence s. A buttery, larder.
Six'pence s. English silver coin value six pennies.
Clar'ence s. A close four-wheeled carriage.
Transpar'ence s. State or quality of being transparent.
Def'erence s. Compliance, respect; courteous submissiveness.
Ref'erence s. Act of referring; allusion; respect; intimation; one referred to for a character; a testimonial.
Pref'erence s. Act of preferring; state of being, or thing, preferred; choice.
Dif'ference s. State of being different; dissimilarity; that which distinguishes; quarrel; remainder after subtraction. v.t. To distinguish between; to make different.
Indif'ference s. Quality or state of being indifferent; neutrality; unconcern; mediocrity; insignificance.
Circum'ference s. The line bounding a circle; circuit.
In'ference s. Conclusion drawn from premises; deduction.
Con'ference s. Act of conferring; meeting for consultation, etc.
Interfer'ence s. Act of interfering; clashing.
Non-interfer'ence s. (*Negative*).
Trans'ference s. Act of transferring; transfer.
Bellig'erence s. State of being at war.
Adher'ence s. Firm attachment.
Inher'ence s. State of inhering; existence in something.
Coher'ence s. A sticking together, congruity; state of being coherent.
Incoher'ence s. Want of connection or agreement.
Rev'erence s. Profound respect and esteem; act indicating this; disposition to venerate; one entitled to be revered. v.t. To revere.
Irrev'erence s. Absence of reverence; irreverent conduct.
Deter'rence s. Determent.
Abhor'rence s. Loathing; extreme aversion.
Occur'rence s. An event, incident.
Decur'rence s. State of being decurrent.
Recur'rence s. Act of recurring; return; resort.
Concur'rence s. A coming together; union; joint rights.
Non-concur'rence s. (*Negative*).
Ab'sence s. State of being absent; inattention.
Pres'ence s. State of being present; nearness; mien, personal appearance; company; a great personage.
Omnipre'sence s. State or quality of being omnipresent.
Es'sence s. Nature or being of anything; predominant qualities; perfume; volatile matter.

Quintes'sence s. Pure or concentrated essence.
La'tence s. Latency.
Com'petence s. State of being competent; sufficiency; qualification.
Incom'petence s. State or quality of being incompetent.
Ap'petence s. Instinctive desire; natural propensity.
Inap'petence s. Want of appetence or desire for food.
Pretence' s. Act of pretending; simulation; false show; assumption.
Pen'itence s. Condition of being penitent; remorse.
Impen'itence s. Obduracy; hardness of heart.
Ren'itence s. Resistance; reluctance.
Sen'tence s. Group of words expressing a complete thought; a judgment, opinion. v.t. To pass judgment upon; doom.
Po'tence s. An heraldic cross-ended cross.
Prepo'tence s. Prepotency.
Plenip'otence s. State of being invested with full powers.
Omnip'otence s. State or quality of being all-powerful; an almighty force.
Im'potence s. State or condition of being impotent; powerlessness.
Adver'tence s. Attention, regard.
Inadver'tence s. Quality of being inadvertent; fault, etc., through negligence or heedlessness.
Subsis'tence s. Real being; that which maintains existence.
Insis'tence s. Quality of being insistent.
Consis'tence s. State of being consistent; degree of density; firmness, coherence; harmony.
Persis'tence s. State or quality of being persistent; continuance of an effect after its cause is removed.
Exist'ence s. State of existing or being; anything that exists; life; continuation.
Pre-exist'ence s. Previous existence.
Inexis'tence s. State of not having existence or of being inherent.
Coexis'tence s. (*Coexist*).
Ref'luence s. A flowing back.
Af'fluence s. Abundance, wealth.
Ef'fluence s Act or state of flowing out; that which flows out.
Mellif'luence s. A sweet, smooth flow; quality or state of flowing thus.
Circum'fluence s. (*Circumfluent*).
In'fluence s. Agency or power which affects, modifies, or sways; authority; acknowledged ascendency. v.t. To sway, to bias.
Con'fluence s. A flowing together; meeting place of two or more streams; a concourse, assembly.
Fre'quence s. Frequency.
Se'quence s. State or quality of being sequent; succession; series.
Sub'sequence s. State of being subsequent.
Con'sequence s. A result, effect, inference; importance.
Incon'sequence s. Condition of being inconsequent; lack of logical sequence.
El'oquence s. Persuasive speech; oratory, fluency.
Blandilo'quence s. Flattering or ingratiating talk.
Grandil'oquence s. High, lofty language; bombastic.
Magnil'oquence s. Elevated language; pompous style.
Somnil'oquence s. Somniloquism.
Multil'oquence s. Loquacity.
Con'gruence' s. Accordance, consistency.
Conni'vence s. (*Connivance*).
Mince v.t. and i. To chop small; to speak affectedly; to gloss over. s. Meat, etc., minced.
Prince s. Son of a king or emperor; ruler of a principality; a sovereign; a chief.
Since adv. In the time past; ago; from then. prep. From the time of; after. conj. From the time when; because that.
Quince s. A tree allied to the pear; its fruit.
Evince' v.t. To show clearly; to demonstrate.
Convince' v.t. To persuade by argument, satisfy the mind of.
Prov'ince s. A region at a distance from the capital or dependent on a distant authority; large political division; sphere of action, business.
Wince v.i. To start back, recoil. s. A start as from pain.
Once adv. At one time, on one occasion; formerly. s. A single time. conj. As soon as.
Bonce s. A large marble, a game played with these.
Sconce s. A fixed projecting candle-stick; a candle-socket; a small fort; (*slang*) the head.
Ensconce' v.t. To cover as with a sconce; to protect, hide.
Nonce s. The present purpose or occasion.
Launce s. A sand-eel.
Bunce s. (*Slang*) Something to the good, unexpected profit.
Dunce s. An ignoramus; one slow in learning.
Ounce s. $\frac{1}{12}$ lb. troy; $\frac{1}{16}$ lb. avoir.; the lynx, the snow-leopard.
Bounce v.i. To spring suddenly; to boast. v.t. To cause to bound. s. A bound; boastfulness.
Flounce s. Frill or ruffle sewn to a gown, etc. v.t. To attach flounces to. v.i. To throw oneself about; to plunge, flounder.
Enounce' v.t. To enunciate.
Denounce' v.t. To threaten, accuse publicly; to give notice of termination of a treaty.
Renounce' v.t. To declare against, disclaim; to forsake. v.i. To fail to follow suit.
Announce' v.t. To proclaim, publish, declare.
Pronounce' v.t. and i. To articulate, speak distinctly or rhetorically; to utter formally; to declare.
Mispronounce' v.t. and i. To pronounce erroneously.
Pounce v.i. To fall on suddenly, to seize with the claws. v.t. To perforate, punch; to sprinkle or rub with pounce. s. A fine powder formerly used to prevent ink spreading on paper; the talon of a bird of prey.
Rounce s. A handle on a printing-press.
Trounce v.t. To beat severely.
Vi'va vo'ce (vē'-) adv. Orally. a. Oral.
Scarce a. Not plentiful or copious; rare.
Farce s. A low or very absurd comedy; force-meat stuffing. v.t. To stuff with force-meat.
Fierce a. Savage, ferocious, easily enraged.
Pierce v.t. To perforate or transfix with a pointed instrument; to force a way into; to reach. v.i. To enter, penetrate.

Transpierce' v.t. To pierce through, penetrate.
Tierce s. A cask of 42 gals.; sequence of three cards; a position in fencing.
Amerce' v.t. To punish by fining.
Com'merce s. Interchange of commodities; trade; intercourse. v.i. To trade.
Coerce' v.t. To restrain by force, to compel.
Ses'terce s. An ancient Roman coin (about 2d.)
Cir'ce s. An enchantress of Greek story; a seductive woman, a witch.
Force s. Strength, power, might; coercion; cogency; efficacy; a waterfall. v.t. To compel, to take by violence; to ripen prematurely; to stuff.
Deforce' v.t. To withold from possession of the rightful owner.
Enforce' v.t. To urge, compel, to constrain.
Reinforce' v.t. To add new strength to, strengthen by new assistance. s. A strengthening part.
Perforce' adv. Of necessity, by force.
Divorce' s. Legal dissolution of marriage division of things closely united. v.t. To dissolve the marriage between; to separate.
Source s. That from which anything proceeds; origin, first cause, spring.
Resource' s. Source of aid or support; expedience; skill; readiness.
-esce suff. Forming inceptive verbs.
Incandesce' v.i. and t. To glow or cause to glow with heat.
Recrudesce' v.i. To become sore or raw again.
Quiesce' v.i. To be silent (of letters).
Acquiesce' v.i. To agree, to be satisfied with.
Opalesce' v.i. To give forth a play of colours like the opal.
Coalesce' v.i. To grow into one, to unite.
Convalesce' v.i. To recover health.
Intumesce' v.i. To enlarge with heat; to swell.
Evanesce' v.t. To disappear, vanish.
Rejuvenesce' v.i. To grow young again. v.t. To give fresh vitality to.
Luminesce' v.i. To exhibit luminescence.
Effloresce' v.i. To blossom, crumble to powder, form crystals on the surface.
Phosporesce' v.i. To shine, as phosphorus, without combustion or sensible heat.
Fluoresce' v.i. To produce or exhibit fluorescence.
Deliquesce' v.i. To liquify, melt slowly in the air.
Effervesce' v.i. To froth, bubble, ferment; become excited.
Dehisce' v.i. To burst open (of anthers, etc.).
Sauce s. A liquid condiment; anything adding piquancy; impudence. v.t. To give flavour or interest to; to be pert to.
Traduce' v.t. To defame, calumniate.
Abduce' v.t. To draw away with an abductor; to lead away.
Adduce' v.t. To bring forward, allege.
Educe' v.t. To bring or draw out; to develop; to infer.
Deduce' v.t. To obtain by reasoning, to infer, to trace.
Reduce' v.t. To bring down, diminish, degrade; to bring into a certain state, arrangement, etc.; to restore to its proper place or condition.
Seduce' v.t. To lead astray, decoy; to corrupt.
Induce' v.t. To influence; to actuate; to produce or cause.
Superinduce' v.t. To bring in as an addition.
Conduce' v.i. To promote or answer an end; to contribute

Produce' v.t. To bring forth, exhibit; to yield, afford; to cause; to extend (a line).
Prod'uce s. What is produced; yield; agricultural products.
Reproduce' v.t. To produce again, copy.
Introduce' v.t. To make known; to present; to insert.
Deuce s. The two in cards and dice; the devil; mischief, confusion.
Luce s. A full-grown pike.
Douce a. Sober, sedate.
Puce a. Brownish purple.
Pre'puce s. The foreskin.
Spruce a. Neat, smart, trim; s. A variety of pine-tree. v.t. To smarten.
Truce s. Temporary cessation of hostilities; agreement for this.
Let'tuce s. An annual plant used in salads.
Syce s. A native Hindu groom.
Bade v.t. past (*Bid*).
Gambade' s. A leap of a horse, a caper.
Forbade' past (*Forbid*).
Aubade' s. Musical announcement of daybreak.
Cade s. A barrel of herrings or sprats.
Façade' s. The face or front view of a build ing.
Saccade' s. Sudden check of a horse with the reins; pressure of a violin bow on the strings.
Dec'ade s. Period of ten years; a group of ten.
Barricade' s. A hastily made fortification; a bar. v.t. To protect thus.
Alcade' s. The governor of a Moorish fortress.
Cavalcade' s. A procession of horsemen.
Brocade' s. A flowered silken stuff. v.t. To weave or work with raised patterns.
Arcade' s. A covered walk.
Cascade' s. A waterfall.
Ambuscade' s. A snare laid for the enemy. v. To lie or place in ambush.
Al'idade s. (*Alidad*).
Fade v.i. To wither, lose colour, lustre, or distinctness.
Ren'egade s. One faithless to principle, etc.; an apostate; a vagabond.
Brigade' s. A subdivision of an army. v.t. To form or combine into a brigade or brigades.
Hade s. Inclination of a fault or vein from the vertical. v.i. To slope away.
Shade s. Obscurity caused by interception of light; shelter; a shadow; a spirit; a screen; gradation of light; a scarcely perceptible difference. v.t. To screen from light, etc.; to obscure, darken. v.i. To pass off by degrees.
Sun'shade s. A parasol; an awning.
Night'shade s. A poisonous weed.
Jade s. A broken-down horse; a huzzy, woman (*in contempt*); an ornamental green stone. v.t. and i. To weary or become weary or fagged out.
Cockade' s. A knot of ribbon or a rosette worn in the hat.
Blockade' s. The investment of a place, especially by a hostile fleet. v.t. To invest a place thus.
Stockade' s. An enclosure of posts. v.t. To fortify with such.
Lade v.t. To put a load on or cargo in; to throw out with a ladle.
Escalade' s. An attack in which ladders are used. v.t. To scale; to mount and enter.

Mar'malade s. A jam made from oranges.
Salade' s. A sallet, a rounded helmet.
Blade s. Cutting part of a knife, sword, etc.; flat part of an oar; spire of grass; a gay young fellow.
Tway'blade s. A variety of orchid.
Glade s. A clear, open space in a wood.
Ev'erglade s. Low-lying marshland covered with high grass (U.S.A.).
Enfilade' v.t. To rake the length of a line of troops, etc., with shot. s. A raking fire.
Ballade' s. A conventional verse-form.
Fusil'lade s. Continuous discharge of firearms.
Accolade' s. Ceremonious shoulder-tap in the conferring of knighthood.
Overlade' v.t. To load with too great a cargo, etc.
Roulade' s. A quick run of notes or sounds.
Made past and past part. (*Make*).
Chamade' s. Call by drum or trumpet to a parley.
Pomade' s. Pomatum. v.t. To apply this.
Fumade' s. A smoked pilchard.
Esplanade' s. An open space between a citadel and the houses; a promenade.
Promenade' s. A walk for pleasure; place for this. v.i. To walk for amusement or show.
Serenade' s. Open-air music at night, especially by a lover; a nocturne. v.t. To sing or play a serenade to.
Grenade' s. A bomb thrown by hand.
Marinade' s. Fish, etc., pickled with wine and spices. v.t. To pickle thus.
Harliquinade' s. The part of a pantomime containing the pranks of the harlequin; an extravaganza.
Pasquinade' s. A lampoon, satirical writing. v.t. To lampoon.
Flanconnade' s. A thrust in fencing.
Dragonnade' s. A military persecution. v.t. To harass civilians with troops.
Colonnade' s. A range of columns at regular intervals.
Gasconade' s. A boast, boasting; bravado. v.i. To brag, boast.
Gabionade' s. A fortification formed of gabions.
Lem'onade s. A sweet drink flavoured with lemon.
Cannonade' v.t. To batter with cannon. s. A continued attack with guns.
Fanfaronade' s. Ostentation; bluster.
Carronade' s. A short cannon with large bore.
Cass'onade s. Unrefined sugar.
Escapade' s. A wild prank, mischievous adventure.
Gallopade' s. A sideways sort of gallop; a brisk dance.
Spade s. A digging implement; a suit at cards. v.t. To dig with a spade, use a spade on.
Charade' s. A species of riddle; an acted riddle.
Cam'arade s. Friend, comrade. int. A cry for quarter.
Parade' s. Pompous exhibition; assembly of troops for inspection, etc.; military display; ground for this; a spectacle; a promenade. v.i. To assemble in military order; to go about for show. v.t. To show off.
Abrade' v.t. To rub off, wear away.
Gingerade' s. An effervescent drink flavoured with ginger.
Masquerade' s. A masked ball; pretence; a disguise. v.i. To wear a mask; to pass oneself off as.

Grade s. Degree or rank in order, dignity, etc.; gradient. v.t. To place in order of rank; to bring to a desired slope.
Degrade' v.t. To lower, to disgrace, to humble; to wear away, disintegrate. v.i. To degenerate.
Tar'digrade a. Slow-moving. s. One of the sloth family.
Ver'migrade a. Moving like a worm.
Pin'nigrade a. Walking by means of flippers. s. A pinniped.
Rec'tigrade a. Walking in a straight line (of certain spiders).
Dig'itigrade a. Walking on the toes. s. An animal doing this, as the cats, dogs, weasels, etc.
Sal'tigrade a. Having legs formed for leaping, especially of spiders.
Plan'tigrade a. Walking on the sole.
Cen'tigrade a. Of one hundred degrees; graduated into one hundred equal parts.
Pro'nograde a. Habitually carrying the body horizontally.
Ret'rograde a. Going or bending backward; going to the worse; appearing to move from west to east. v.i. To go or move backward.
Ira'de s. A written decree of the Porte.
Tirade' s. A strain of invective, violent declamation.
Com'rade s. A companion, intimate associate; style of address among Socialists.
Trade s. Act or business of buying and selling; commerce, traffic; those engaged in such. v.i. and t. To barter, buy and sell, exchange.
Estrade' s. A low platform.
Balustrade' s. A row of posts carrying a handrail.
Palisade' s. A strong stake sharpened at both ends; a fence of these. v.t. To fortify or surround with these.
Torsade' s. An ornamental twisted ribbon, etc.
Passade' s. A push or thrust.
Crusade' s. An expedition for the recovery of the Holy Land; a romantic or enthusiastic enterprise. v.i. To engage in a crusade.
Rodomontade' s. Empty bluster; vaunting. v.i. To boast, rant.
Persuade' v.t. To influence by argument; to counsel, induce.
Dissuade' v.t. To advise against, deter.
Evade' v.t. To slip away from, elude, escape, baffle.
Invade' v.t. To enter with a hostile army; to encroach on, violate.
Pervade' v.t. To permeate, extend through, be diffused in.
Couvade' s. The custom among primitive peoples of the father of a new-born child lying in, etc.
Wade v.i. To walk through water or semi-fluid substance. v.t. To ford.
Cede v.t. To surrender, give up.
Accede' v.i. To comply with, agree to.
Recede' v.i. To retreat, withdraw; to slope backwards or away. v.t. To cede again.
Precede' v.t. To go before in place, time, or rank.
Secede' v.i. To withdraw from association.
Ep'icede s. A dirge, funeral ode.
Concede' v.t. To grant, admit, surrender. v.i. To yield, make concession.
Retrocede' v.t. To cede back. v.i. To go back, to recede.
Intercede v.i. To act between parties; to plead for others; to mediate

Glede s. The common kite.
Mill'epede s. A segmented myriapod.
Veloc'ipede s. An early form of bicycle.
Cir'ripede s. (*Cirriped*).
Cen'tipede s. A many-jointed articulate with numerous feet.
Stampede' s. Sudden rush due to panic. v.t. To disperse by causing sudden fright, etc. v.i. To take part in a stampede.
Impede' v.t. To hinder, obstruct.
Rede s. Counsel, advice; a story. v.t. To advise; to interpret.
Supersede' v.t. To come in the room of, replace; to overrule.
Suède (swād) s. Fine, soft kid-leather.
Swede s. A native of Sweden; a kind of turnip.
Ide s. A fish of the carp family.
-ide suff. Denoting certain chemical compounds.
Bide v.t. To wait for, endure, abide.
Abide' v.i. To dwell, wait, continue.
Car'bide s. A compound of carbon and another element.
Decide' v.t. To determine, adjudge, conclude. v.i. To come to a decision.
Bar'mecide s. One who gives illusory benefits.
De'icide s. The slaying of a god; the putting of Christ to death; one concerned in this.
Reg'icide s. The killing of a king; one who takes part in this.
Fun'gicide s. Anything that destroys fungi.
Fel'icide s. The slaying of a cat.
Pro'licide s. Crime of killing one's child before or immediately after birth.
Hom'icide s. Act of killing a human being; man-slayer.
Germ'icide s. A substance that destroys germs.
Verm'icide s. A medicine for destroying intestinal or other worms.
Tyran'nicide s. Act of slaying or one who slays a tyrant.
Lap'icide s. A stone-cutter.
Vul'picide s. The killing of a fox other than by hunting; a fox-killer.
Soror'icide s. The murder or a murderer of a sister.
Uxor'icide s. The murder or a murderer of one's wife.
Par'ricide s. The murder or a murderer of a father or mother.
Ma'tricide s. The murder of a mother; one who murders his mother.
Pat'ricide s. Parricide.
Fra'tricide s. The murder or murderer of a brother.
Vat'icide s. The murder or a murderer of a prophet.
Insec'ticide s. Substance for killing insects.
Fœ'ticide s. The destruction of a fœtus.
Parasit'icide s. Something that destroys parasites.
Vit'icide s. An insect, etc. injurious to vines.
Infan'ticide s. Murder or a murderer of an infant (especially new-born).
Gigan'ticide s. The slaying or a slayer of a giant.
Parent'icide s. The murder or a murderer of a parent.
Liber'ticide s. Destruction of or one who destroys, liberty.
Su'icide s. Self-murder; one guilty of this.
Lar'vicide s. A preparation for killing larvæ.
Coincide' v.i. To agree in position, happen at the same time, concur.
Nemat'ocide s. A substance that destroys nematodes.
Excide' v.t. To cut out, extirpate.
I'odide s. A compound of iodine and a metal.
Oph'icleide s. A large brass wind-instrument; the tuba stop of an organ.
Bo'na fi'de adv. In good faith. a. Genuine.
Confide' v.i. To put faith, believe. v.t. To entrust, give in charge of.
Hide v.t. To secrete, screen, withold from knowledge. v.i. To be or remain concealed. s. A skin; an old measure of land.
Chide v.t. To reprove, rebuke, blame. v.i. To scold, make a clamorous noise. s. A reproof, bickering.
Sul'phide s. A compound of sulphur with a element or radical.
Phos'phide s. A combination of phosphorous with another element or radical.
Elide' v.t. To strike out, to cut off (esp. a syllable).
Glide v.i. To flow or move gently and silently; to slide.
Collide' v.i. To come violently against.
Bo'lide s. A large meteor.
Slide v.i. To move along a surface by slipping; to glide. v.t. To thrust along, to pass imperceptibly. s. A smooth passage; sliding part of an apparatus; place for sliding; glass carrying picture or object for magic-lantern, microscope, etc.
Land'slide s. A landslip; a political debacle.
Backslide' v.i. To fall from right, apostatize.
Am'ide s. A compound derived from ammonia.
Bro'mide s. A combination of bromine with a metal or radical.
Nide s. A nest, a brood, especially of pheasants.
Cy'anide s. A compound of cyanogen and a metal.
Sel'enide s. A compound of selenium.
Snide a. (*Slang*) Sham.
Or'oide s. An alloy used in cheap jewellery.
Ride v.i. To be borne on the back of an animal, on a cycle, in a vehicle, etc.; to be a good horseman; to be at anchor. v.t. To sit on so as to be carried; to cause to ride; to carry; to domineer over. s. A riding excursion; path for riding on.
Bride s. A newly married woman.
Hy'dride s. A compound of hydrogen with another element or radical.
Deride' v.t. To laugh or scoff at. v.i. To jeer.
Gride v.t. To jar; to grate. s. A grating sound.
Chlor'ide s. Compound of chlorine with another element.
Lep'oride s. A supposed hybrid between hare and rabbit.
Flu'oride s. A compound of fluorine with an element or radical.
Pride s. Self-esteem—noble or inordinate; arrogance; dignity; that of which one is proud. v.t. To indulge in pride or elation.
Override' v.t. To supersede, set at naught, annul.
Ni'tride s. A compound of nitrogen with any other element or radical.
Stride v.i. To walk with long steps. v.i. To pass over with a step. s. A long step or gait.
Astride' adv. With legs apart.
Bestride' v.t. To sit on with legs astride.
Outride' v.t. To ride faster than.
Tell'uride s. A compound containing tellurium

Side s. Edge; one half of the body; rib part of animals; part between top and bottom; an opposed party or interest; (*slang*) bumptiousness. a. Lateral, oblique, indirect, broad. v.i. To embrace the opinions of one party.
Aside' adv. To one side. s. Something said under one's breath.
Sea'side s. Place or district on the coast; a holiday resort.
Subside' v.i. To sink to the bottom; to settle down, abate.
Broad'side s. Simultaneous firing of all the guns on one side of a ship.
Bed'side s. Place or companionship by a bed. a. Pertaining to the sick-room.
Beside' prep. At the side of, over and above. adv. Moreover, except.
Reside' v.i. To have one's home at; to be inherent in.
Fire'side s. The hearth; home; domestic life.
Preside' v.i. To exercise superintendence, act as chairman.
Offside' s. Space between ball and opponent's goal at football.
Along'side adv. By the side of.
Slick'enside s. A variety of galena.
Inside' prep. and adv. In the interior; contained within. a. Being within; internal. s. Interior portion; one or anything enclosed or within.
Glu'coside s. A vegetable substance yielding glucose on decomposition.
Diop'side s. Transparent pyroxene.
Wa'terside s. Margin of a river, the sea, etc.
Outside' s. The exterior, external surface; part or place beyond an enclosure, etc.; the utmost. a. Exterior; superficial. prep. On the outside of.
Way'side s. The side of a road. a. Situated at or growing by the side of a road.
Coun'tryside s. A rural district; dwellers in this.
Tide s. Ebb and flow of sea; flow; time, season. v.i. and t. To drive with the tide.
Betide' v. To happen (to), to come to pass.
Shrove'tide s. The two or three days before Ash Wednesday.
Hock'tide s. An old English festival on the second Monday and Tuesday after Easter.
E'ventide s. Evening.
Noon'tide s. and a. Noonday.
Whit'suntide s. Whit-Sunday (seventh Sunday after Easter) and the following day or two.
Guide v.t. To direct, lead, influence, regulate. s. One who or that which guides; a leader, conductor, adviser.
Misguide' v.t. To guide wrongly, lead astray.
Vi'de v. imper. See (directing attention).
Divide' v.t. and i. To separate, disunite; to distribute, apportion; to set at variance, be of different opinions. s. A dividing line, a watershed.
Subdivide' v.t. and i. To divide again or into more parts.
Provide' v.t. To supply, procure beforehand. v.i. To procure supplies; to afford; to stipulate previously.
Wide a. Extended far each way, broad; vast; remote; large; comprehensive; deviating considerably; (*slang*) knowing. s. A wide ball at cricket.
Ox'ide s. A compound of oxygen with another element or radical.
Perox'ide s. The oxide of a given base which contains the greatest quantity of oxygen.
Childe s. A scion of a noble family.
Til'de s. The diacritical sign ~.
Lande s. A heathy moor, especially in S.W. France.
Blende s. A native sulphide of lead.
Pitch'blende s. Oxide of uranium, a radium-bearing mineral.
Horn'blende s. A dark mineral consisting of silica with lime, magnesia, or iron.
Blonde a. Of fair hair and complexion. s. A fair woman.
Monde s. The fashionable world; society.
Dem'i-monde s. Persons of doubtful reputation.
Beau-monde' s. The world of fashion.
Ode s. A lyric poem of certain form.
-ode suff. Denoting something resembling or of the nature of.
Bode v.t., v.i. To portend, foreshadow.
Abode' s. Habitation, residence, stay. past (*Abide*).
Forebode' v.i. To foretell, prognosticate.
Code s. A systemmatic arrangement or digest of laws; a body of rules; a system of signals, secret words, etc.
Decode' v.t. To translate from code.
Zin'code s. Positive pole of a battery.
Sar'code s. Animal protoplasm.
Man'ucode s. A bright blue Papuan bird.
Ge'ode s. A hollow mineral nodule, usually lined with crystals.
Cath'ode s. The negative pole of an electric battery.
Lode s. A mineral vein; an open ditch.
Phyll'ode s. A leaf-like petiole.
Explode' v.i. To burst forth with violence; to burst into activity or passion. v.t. To cause to burst forth thus; to drive out of use or belief.
Mode s. Manner of being; form; method; variety; custom; fashion.
Commode' s. A chest of drawers; an eighteenth century head-dress; a night-stool.
Incommode' v.t. To inconvenience, disquiet.
Discommode' v.t. To inconvenience, annoy.
Node s. A knob, protuberance; a swelling on a bone; point of intersection of the great celestial circles.
An'ode s. The positive pole of an electric battery.
Thre'node s. A threnody, dirge.
Pal'inode s. A recantation.
Spi'node s. A cusp.
Plat'inode s. The negative pole of a voltaic cell.
Meg'apode s. (*Megapod*).
Ep'ode s. The third and last part of an ode.
An'tipode s. One living at the opposite side of the globe.
Spode a. Denoting a certain make of porcelain.
Rode past (*Ride*).
Erode' v.t. To eat into, wear away, corrode.
Corrode' v.t. To eat or wear away by degrees; to blight, canker, rust. v.i. To waste away gradually.
Elec'trode s. One of the poles of a galvanic battery.
Catelec'trode s. The negative pole of an electric battery.
Strode past (*Stride*).
Ep'isode s. A digression, incident; a separate story in another.
Rhap'sode s. An ancient Greek reciter.
Nem'atode s. A parasitic thread-worm or round-worm. a. Thread-like.

Trem'atode s. A liver-fluke, fluke-worm.
Voi'vode s. A Slavonic leader or governor; a Montenegrin general.
Ex'ode s. The catastrophe of an ancient Greek play, or the comic afterpiece of a Roman one.
Horde s. A nomadic tribe; a gang, rabble.
Dude s. A dandy, exquisite, fop.
Occlude' v.t. To close up, block; to keep in by absorption.
Preclude' v.t. To prevent, hinder, obviate.
Seclude' v.t. To shut up from others; to withdraw into solitude.
Include' v.t. To enclose, comprise, contain.
Conclude' v.t. To finish, determine, settle, infer. v.i. To make an end, come to a decision, draw an inference.
Exclude' v.t. To debar, prohibit, expel.
Elude' v.t. To escape by stratagem; to evade, baffle.
Delude' v.t. To deceive, beguile.
Prel'ude s. Something preparatory; an introductory performance. v.t. and i. To introduce with or play a prelude; to serve as introduction.
Allude' v.i. To hint at, insinuate.
Illude' v.t. To deceive, to mock.
Collude' v.i. To act in concert, especially fraudulently.
In'terlude s. Short play between the acts, etc.; short connecting piece of music.
Nude a. Bare, naked, undraped; void in law. s. An unclothed figure.
Denude' v.t. To strip, divest, lay bare.
Rude a. Rough, uneven; lacking delicacy, unrefined; untaught, barbarian; surly; boisterous; severe; shapeless.
Crude a. Raw, undigested, immature.
Prude s. A woman of affected modesty.
Obtrude' v.t. To intrude; to offer with unreasonable importunity. v.i. To enter without right.
Detrude' v.t. To thrust or push down.
Intrude' v.i. To thrust oneself in; to encroach. v.t. To thrust in.
Protrude' v.t. and i. To thrust forward, project.
Extrude' v.t. To thrust out; to drive out or off.
Transude' v.t. To ooze through the pores.
-tude suff. Forming abstract nouns.
Heb'etude s. Stupidity, obtuseness.
Qui'etude s. Repose, tranquillity; quiet.
Inqui'etude s. Restlessness; uneasiness.
Disqui'etude s. Want of tranquillity, anxiety.
Des'uetude s. Disuse; discontinuance of habit.
Man'suetude s. Gentleness, mildness.
Con'suetude s. Custom, usage.
Hab'itude s. Familiarity; long custom; habit.
Tab'itude s. A tabetic or wasting condition.
Solic'itude s. State of being solicitous; concern, anxiety.
Lon'gitude s. Distance east or west from a given place.
Simil'itude s. Likeness; resemblance; metaphor.
Verisimil'itude s. Appearance of truth; probability.
Dissimil'itude s. Want of similitude; unlikeness.
Sol'itude s. State of being alone; a lonely place; seclusion.
Am'plitude s. Largeness, copiousness.
Plen'itude s. State of being full or complete; plenty.
Mag'nitude s. Greatness; comparative size; importance.
Infin'itude s. Quality of being infinite; boundless extent or number.
Indefin'itude s. Indefiniteness.
Decrep'itude s. Feebleness through old age; senile decay.

Tur'pitude s. Moral baseness; vileness.
Nig'ritude s. Blackness; state of being black.
Pul'chritude s. Comeliness; beauty.
Lass'itude s. Fatigue, languor; lack of energy.
Crass'itude s. Stupidity, denseness.
Vicis'situde s. Regular change; one of the "ups and downs" of life.
Spiss'itude s. Denseness or compactness of soft substances.
Beat'itude s. Blessedness, heavenly bliss.
Lat'itude s. Breadth; scope; laxity; distance N. or S. from the equator, or of a star N. or S. of the ecliptic.
Plat'itude s. A commonplace or trite remark; a truism; insipidity.
Grat'itude s. A due sense of benefits; thankfulness.
Ingrat'itude s. Want of gratitude.
Exac'titude s. Exactness.
Inexact'itude s. Want of precision or correctness; an inexact statement, etc.
Rec'titude s. Uprightness; integrity; honesty.
Sanc'titude s. Holiness, saintliness.
Al'titude s. Loftiness, elevation, highest point.
Mul'titude s. Numerousness; a great number; a large crowd; the common herd.
Lent'itude s. Slowness.
Ap'titude s. Fitness, tendency, readiness.
Inap'titude s. Want of aptitude; unfitness.
Inep'titude s. Quality of being inept; a foolish action or utterance.
Promp'titude s. Quality of being prompt; quickness of decision.
Cer'titude s. Certainty.
Incer'titude s. Uncertainty; doubtfulness.
For'titude s. Patience under suffering; firmness; endurance.
At'titude s. Posture, position.
Pin'guitude s. Fatness; obesity.
Ser'vitude s. State of subjection; slavery.
Exude' v.t. To discharge through pores, etc. v.i. To flow from the body through the pores.
Formal'dehyde s. A colourless gas with antiseptic and disinfectant properties prepared from methyl alcohol.
-ee suff. Denoting a recipient, or the direct or indirect object.
Bee s. An hymenopterous social insect.
Bumble'-bee s. A large bee.
Bribee' s. One who accepts a bribe.
Baubee' s. An old Scots halfpenny.
Cee s. Shaped like C.
Fian'cée s. A betrothed woman.
Divorcee' s. A divorced person.
Sad'ducee s. One of a Jewish sect which denied the future state, existence of angels, etc.
Sycee' s. Silver in ingots used in China as money.
Dee s. A D-shaped buckle, etc.
Chickadee' s. A small N. American song-bird.
Fiddlededee' int. Nonsense! rubbish!
Chaldee' a. and s. (*Chaldean*).
Kill'dee s. A N. American plover.
Culdee' s. An ancient Scotch or Irish monk.
Grandee' s. A Spanish or Portuguese nobleman; a man of high rank.
Ven'dee s. One to whom a thing is vended.
Spon'dee s. A metrical foot of two longs.
Fee s. Reward for service; charge for professional services; a tenure; a fief. v.t. To pay a fee to; to engage by feeing.
Coff'ee s. A tropical tree; its berries; a beverage prepared from its seeds
Feof'fee s. One to whom a feoffment is made.
Toff'ee s. Sweet made of boiled sugar and butter.

Gee v.t. To turn to the right (of horses). int. Go on ! move faster !
Coccagee′ s. A cider-apple.
Mortgagee′ s. One to whom a mortgage is given.
Pledgee′ s. One to whom anything is pledged.
Gee-gee s. A horse.
Squeegee′ s. An implement for cleaning wet pavements, decks, etc.; a rubber roller.
Thuggee′ s. System of assassination practised by the thugs.
Obligee′ s. One to whom a bond is given.
Negligée′ s. A lady's loose gown.
Per′igee s. Point in the moon's orbit nearest the earth.
Pongee′ s. A fine, unbleached silken fabric.
Ogee′ s. A moulding with section like S.
Ap′ogee s. The point in a planet's orbit most distant from the earth.
Bargee′ s. A worker on a barge.
Burgee′ s. A small flag or pennant.
Refugee′ s. One who flees for protection; especially abroad.
Spa′hee s. (*Spahi*).
Coachee′ s. A coachman.
Manichee′ s. A Manichæan.
Tro′chee s. Metrical foot of two syllables, a long and a short.
Debauchee′ s. A profligate.
Vouchee′ s. Person summoned in a writ of right.
Tehee′ v.i. To laugh scornfully. s. A titter.
Ghee s. Butter from milk of the Indian ox.
Whanghee′ s. A knotted Chinese bamboo.
Fering′hee s. Native Indian name for a European.
Biographee′ s. The subject of a biography.
Coryphee′ s. A ballet-girl.
Garnishee′ s. One who has received legal notice to withhold payment of a debt.
Buck′shee s. (*Slang*) A tip; something for nothing.
Ban′shee s. A supernatural being that wails round a house at time of death.
Thee pron. Objective case of "thou."
Pri′thee int. I pray thee; please.
Hack′ee s. The N. American ground-squirrel.
Yankee′ s. A citizen of New England, inhabitant of the U.S.A.
Jokee′ s. One on whom a joke is played.
Lee s. Quarter towards which the wind blows; the sheltered side. a. Pertaining to this side.
Alee′ adv. On the lee side.
Bengalee′ s. A native or the language of Bengal. a. Pertaining to Bengal, its race, or language.
Mêl′ée s. A hand-to-hand or confused fight.
Flee v.i. and t. To run away; to escape; to shun.
Glee s. Joy, merriment; a part-song.
Bailee′ s. A receiver of goods in trust.
Ju′bilee s. A fiftieth year or anniversary; a season of festivity.
Mal′lee s. A dwarf species of eucalyptus.
Libell′ee s. One who is libelled.
Coul′ee s. A solidified lava-flow; a ravine.
Confirmee′ s. One who has received confirmation.
Smee s. The widgeon.
Mousmee′ s. A Japanese tea-house girl.
Née (nā) a. Denoting the maiden-name of a married woman.
Loanee′ s. One who accepts a loan.
Jampanee′ s. A bearer of a jampan.
Alienee′ s. One to whom property is transferred.
Consignee′ s. Person to whom goods are consigned; an agent.
Bargainee′ s. A purchaser.
Distrainee′ s. One on whom a distraint is made.
Ordinee′ s. One newly ordained.
Chinee′ a. and s. (*Slang*) Chinese.
Examinee′ s. One who undergoes examination.
Nominee′ s. One nominated, proposed for election or office, etc.
Illuminee′ s. One of the Illuminati.
Mat′inée (-nā) s. An afternoon performance.
Knee s. The principal joint in the leg; similarly shaped joint or piece.
Jinnee′ s. A demon of Mohammedan myth.
Donee′ s. One to whom a gift is made.
Abandonee′ s. One to whom something is abandoned.
Internee′ s. One who is interned.
Snickersnee′ s. A bowie-knife.
Pawnee′ s. One with whom a pawn is deposited.
Townee′ s. A non-University inhabitant of a University town.
Coo′ee s. An Australian call.
Escapee′ s. An escaped convict.
É′pée s. A duelling sword.
Cal′ipee s. The edible part of a turtle next the lower shell.
Rappee′ s. A pungent kind of snuff.
Toupee′ s. A small wig.
Rupee′ s. An Indian silver coin (worth about 1s. 4d.).
Ree s. The female ruff.
Pug′garee s. An Indian turban, or scarf for the hat.
Sangaree′ s. Diluted wine sweetened and spiced.
Stingaree′ s. A tropical stinging fish.
Dung′aree s. A coarse kind of calico.
Chickaree′ s. The American red squirrel.
Shika′ree s. A sportsman's native attendant in India.
Bummaree′ s. A Billingsgate middleman.
Rapparee′ s. An eighteenth-century Irish freebooter.
Decree′ s. An edict, law, judicial decision. v.t. To ordain, determine judicially. v.i. To make an edict resolve, determine.
Scree s. A steep mountain slope strewn with loose fragments.
Dree v.t. To suffer, endure.
Surrenderee′ s. One to whom property is surrendered.
Referee′ s. An umpire, arbitrator. v.i. To act as umpire.
Transferee′ s. One to whom a transfer is made.
Kedg′eree s. A dish of stewed fish, rice, and egg.
Free a. Unrestrained; being at liberty; not despotic; open; generous; gratuitous; licentious. adv. Freely. v.t. To set at liberty; to extricate, disentangle; to exempt.
Gree s. Goodwill, favour.
Agree′ v.i. To be in concord, to concur, grant.
Disagree′ v.i. To fail to accord; to be at variance, differ; to have ill effect on.
Degree′ s. A step; rank; title in a university; 360th part of a circle; sixty geographical miles.
Ped′igree s. Line of ancestors; genealogy, lineage.
Fil′igree s. Delicate gold or silver wire-work; ornamental tracery. a. Pertaining to, composed of, or resembling this.
Three a. and s. Consisting of one more than two; 3, iii; sum of 1 and 2.
Soirée (swa′rā) s. An evening party.

Jamboree' s. A spree; a merry-making.
Corroboree' s. A native Australian war-dance or festival.
Choree' s. A trochee.
Spree s. A frolic, carousal.
Tree s. Large perennial plant with trunk and branches; a gibbet; a crucifix; a boot-last. v.t. To cause to ascend a tree.
Whip'pletree s. Bar to which traces of harness are attached.
En'trée s. Entry; right or permission to enter; a made dish at dinner.
Boot'-tree s. A shaped block for putting in a boot.
Pu'rée (-rā) s. A clear soup.
See v.t. To perceive by the eye or the understanding; to notice, view, observe. v.i. To have the power of sight or intellectual perception; to pay regard. s. Diocese or jurisdiction of a bishop.
Releasee' s. One to whom property is released.
Foresee' v.t. To see or know beforehand, have prescience of.
Promisee' s. One to whom a promise is made.
Phar'isee s. A Jewish sect ostentatiously observant of ceremony; a hypocrite.
Devisee' s. One to whom anything is bequeathed.
Licensee' s. One to whom a licence is granted.
Parsee' s. An adherent of the Zoroastrian religion in India; a fire-worshipper.
Oversee' v.t. To look over, inspect, superintend.
Endorsee' s. One to whom a bill is assigned by endorsement.
Fricassee' s. A dish of fowl, rabbit, etc., cut small and stewed, v.t. To cook thus.
Lessee' s. One to whom a lease is granted.
Addressee' s. The person addressed.
Fusee' s. The cone round which the chain is wound in a clock, etc.; a match for smokers; a fuse.
Tee s. Small heap from which ball is struck at golf; a mark for quoits, etc.; the letter T.
Hiccatee' s. A freshwater tortoise of C.America
Dedicatee' s. One to whom a thing is dedicated.
Legatee' s. One to whom a legacy is bequeathed.
Manatee' s. An aquatic herbivorous mammal.
Coatee' s. A short coat.
Goatee' s. A small pointed beard on the chin.
Invitee' s. One invited.
Consultee' s. A person consulted.
Guarantee' s. One who binds himself to see that stipulations of another are carried out; an undertaking given with this object. v.t. To warrant, pledge oneself for.
Grantee' s. One to whom a grant or conveyance is made.
Warrantee' s. One to whom something is warranted.
Absentee' s. One who absents himself.
Presentee' s. One presented to a benefice.
Patentee' s. One to whom a patent is granted.
Appointee' s. One who receives an appointment.
Picotee' s. A kind of carnation.
Bootee' s. A kind of ladies' boot; a woollen boot for infants.
Devotee' s. A votary; a bigot, enthusiast.
Repartee' s. A witty retort.
Deportee' s. One who is banished.
Mestee' s. Offspring of a white and a quadroon.
Mus'tee s. Offspring of a white and a quadroon.
Trustee' s. One holding property for the use or benefit of another.
Settee' s. A sofa or seat with a back.
Remittee' s. One in receipt of a remittance.
Commit'tee s. A body of persons deputed to examine and report on or to manage some business.
Boycottee' s. One who is boycotted.
Allottee' s. One to whom something is allotted.
Put'tee s. Strip of cloth wound round the leg as a gaiter.
Suttee' s. Hindu custom of sacrificing a widow on her husband's funeral pyre; a widow thus burnt.
Marquee' s. A large tent.
Lev'ee s. A ceremonious reception, especially by a sovereign; a river embankment.
Corvee' s. Forced, unpaid labour.
Wee a. Very small; tiny.
Drawee' s. Person on whom a bill of exchange, etc., is drawn.
Advowee' s. The owner of an advowson.
Payee' s. One to whom money is to be paid.
Employee' s. One employed for wages.
Razee' s. A vessel the number of whose decks has been reduced.
Disseizee' s. One unlawfully put out of possession.
Cognizee' s. One to whom a fine of land is acknowledged.
Recognizee' s. One to whom a recognizance is made.
Mesmerizee' s. One who is mesmerized.
Chimpanzee' s. An African anthropoid ape.
Café s. A restaurant.
Auto-da-fé' s. A sentence of the Inquisition; its execution; the burning of a heretic.
Chafe v.t. To cause warmth or soreness by friction; to irritate, fret. v.i. To be heated or irritated.
Carafe' s. A glass water-bottle.
Strafe (strahf) v.t. To punish or injure severely. s. A violent assault.
Safe a. Secure; free from harm or risk; no longer dangerous. s. Fire-proof chest, strong-room; refrigerator.
Vouchsafe' v.t. and i. To deign, condescend, concede.
Agraffe' s. A hook; a builders' cramp.
Giraffe' s. An African ruminant with a very long neck.
Griffe s. The offspring of a mulatto woman and a negro; a claw in stone-work.
Réchauf'fé (rāshō'fā) s. A dish warmed up again; a medley of old materials.
Ruffe s. A freshwater fish allied to the perch.
Fife s. A small instrument like a flute. v.i. and t. To play on a fife.
Life s. Vitality; animation; present state of existence; mode of living; vivacity; a biography.
Knife s. A sharp-edged cutting instrument or part. v.t. To stab with a knife.
Rife a. Abounding, prevalent.
Strife s. Contention; dissension.
Loose'strife s. A tall flowering water-side plant.
Wife s. Lawful consort of a man.
Mid'wife s. Woman who assists at childbirth.
Good'wife s. The mistress of a house.
House'wife s. The mistress of a household.
Housewife (hus'zif) s. A case for holding needles, thread, etc.

Age s. Time of life; advanced years; a very long period.
Cab'bage s. A culinary vegetable; shreds of cloth. v.t. To purloin bits of cloth.
Crib'bage s. A card-game.
Gar'bage s. Animal refuse; entrails, etc.; offensive matter.
Herb'age s. Herbs collectively; pasture.
Cu'bage s. Process of determining cubic contents of a body.
Cage s. An enclosure for animals. v.t. To enclose in or as in a cage.
Encage' v.t. To shut up in a cage.
Soc'age s. An ancient feudal tenure.
Bos'cage s. Woodland, thick foliage.
Ad'age s. A proverb, maxim.
Hi'dage s. An ancient royal tax on every hide of land.
Guid'age s. Guidance; payment for safe conduct.
Fold'age s. The right of folding sheep.
Ban'dage s. A strip of material for binding wounds, etc., strengthening, or supporting. v.t. To fasten or tie up with a bandage; to apply a bandage.
Brig'andage s. Highway robbery.
Appen'dage s. A thing subordinate or additional to something else.
Wind'age s. Difference of diameter of bore and of bullet fired through it.
Bond'age s. Slavery, imprisonment.
Vag'abondage s. State of a vagabond; habit of idly wandering.
Pond'age s. Capacity of a pond; storage of water.
Fron'dage s. Fronds collectively.
Pound'age s. Percentage at so much in the pound; charge for pounding cattle, etc.
Impound'age s. Act of impounding.
Ground'age s. Fees paid for a ship when in a dock or port.
Cor'dage s. Cords collectively, rigging.
Mile'age s. Distance travelled; travelling allowance at so much per mile.
Lin'eage s. Direct descendants; progeny; ancestry.
Acre'age s. Area in acres; acres collectively or in the abstract.
Leaf'age s. Leaves collectively; foliage.
Roof'age s. Material for roofing.
Wharf'age s. Charge for using a wharf; wharves in general.
Gage s. A pledge, a pawn; a challenge. v.t. To pledge, to bind by security; to engage.
Déga'gé a. Easy, unembarrassed.
Bag'gage s. Luggage; a hussy.
Lug'gage s. Anything cumbersome; a traveller's packages.
Engage' v.t. To bind by contract, to pledge (especially in marriage); to employ. v.i. To bind oneself, to begin to fight.
Greengage' s. A green variety of plum.
Pre-engage' v.t. To engage by previous contract or influence.
Disengage' v.t. To extricate, liberate, uncouple. v.i. To release oneself, become detached.
Bur'gage s. An ancient tenure opposed to feudal tenure.
Mor'tgage s. Charge over property as security for debt. v.t. To grant or assign on mortgage.
Hæm'orrhage s. Discharge of blood; bleeding.
Ver'biage s. Over-profusion of words; wordiness.
Fo'liage s. Leaves collectively; carved representation of leaves.
Car'riage s. Act of carrying or transporting; charge for this; a wheeled vehicle; moving part of machinery; demeanour.
Miscar'riage s. An unfortunate event, a failure; abortion.
Mar'riage s. Matrimony; act or ceremony of marrying.
Remar'riage s. A second marriage.
Intermar'riage s. Marriage between tribes, families, etc.
Fer'riage s. Payment for transport by ferry.
Leak'age s. A leak; quantity escaping or entering; allowance for leaking of casks.
Break'age s. A breaking; allowance for things broken.
Soak'age s. Act of soaking; state of being soaked.
Pack'age s. A bundle, packet; charge for packing; act or manner of packing.
Track'age s. Railway tracks; right to use these; towage.
Sack'age s. Act of taking by storm.
Wreck'age s. Material, pieces, etc., from a wreck.
Dock'age s. Charge for use of a dock.
Lock'age s. Works of, or toll for passing through a lock on a canal, etc.
Truck'age s. Charge for conveyance in a truck; practice of bartering.
Tank'age s. Storage in or capacity of tanks; charge for this.
Link'age s. A system of links.
Shrink'age s. Reduction in bulk; diminution in value.
Cork'age s. Corking or uncorking of bottles; charge at hotels for wine consumed but not obtained on the premises.
Vas'salage s. State or condition of a vassal; dependence; slavery.
Assem'blage s. A concourse of persons.
Pu'celage s. State of virginity.
Pel'age s. The fur of an animal.
Fu'selage s. Framework of an aeroplane's body.
Chente'lage s. (*Chentage*).
Tu'telage s. Guardianship; protection.
Persiflage' s. Banter; frivolous treatment of a subject.
Cam'ouflage s. Disguise, concealment; deceptive painting, covering, talk, etc. v.t. To disguise or deceive thus.
Mu'cilage s. A gummy vegetable substance; a viscous lubricating animal secretion; gum.
En'silage s. Process of preserving fodder green in a silo; fodder after such storage. v.t. To preserve by this process.
Car'tilage s. The connective tissue in vertebrates; gristle.
Cur'tilage s. Ground adjoining and belonging to a dwelling.
Di'allage s. A dark green laminate mineral.
Dial'lage s. Consideration of an argument from all sides.
Small'age s. Wild celery.
Enal'lage s. Susbtitution of one number, case, mood, etc., of a word for another.
Hypal'lage s. Interchange of relations between terms in a sentence.
Tal'lage s. An ancient tax in England.
Stall'age s. Right of erecting a stall in a fair; rent for this.

Treil'lage (trāl'-) s. Trellis-work.
Pill'age s. Act of plundering; rapine; booty. v.t. To plunder, spoil.
Pu'pillage s. State of being a pupil.
Grill'age s. The cross-barred foundation of a pier, etc.
Till'age s. Operation or art of tilling; cultivated land.
Still'age s. Frame for placing things on for draining, etc.
Vill'age s. A small assemblage of houses.
Toll'age s. Payment or exaction of toll.
Ul'lage s. What a cask wants of being full.
Haul'age s. Charge for hauling; distance hauled.
Mage s. A magician, wonder-worker.
Dam'age s. An injury, hurt; detriment to any person or thing; loss incurred. v.t. To impair, cause damage to.
Ram'age a. Untamed (especially of hawks).
Ohm'age s. Resistance of an electrical conductor expressed in ohms.
Im'age s. A mental picture; a drawn, sculptured, or otherwise made similitude. v.t. To form an image, represent by an image.
Ar'chimage s. A chief magician, a wizard.
Pil'grimage s. The journey of a pilgrim.
Pri'mage s. Charge in addition to freightage; amount of water carried over from boiler to cylinder.
Scrim'mage s. A tussle, brawl, confused contest.
Rum'mage v.t. To search and examine roughly; to ransack. v.i. To search a place narrowly. s. A careful searching; odds and ends.
Scrum'mage s. A struggle between forwards in Rugby football.
Hom'age s. Fealty, respect, duty; obeisance. v.t. To pay homage to.
Plu'mage s. The feathers of a bird.
Or'phanage s. An institution for orphans; state of being an orphan.
Than'age s. Land held by a thane; tenure of this.
Man'age v.t. To conduct, administer; to have under control; to treat wisely. v.i. To direct affairs.
Misman'age v.t. To administer improperly. v.i. To behave or manage ill.
Ap'panage s. Lands set apart for the maintenance of younger children of sovereigns.
Cran'age s. Right of using a mechanical crane; price paid for this.
Careen'age s. Act of, place for, or charge for careening.
Ménage' s. A household; housekeeping.
Coz'enage s. Trickery, fraud.
Vill'ainage s. State of a feudal villain; serfdom.
Drain'age s. Act or art of draining; a system of drains; mode in which water in an area goes to the rivers.
Concu'binage s. Act or state of living with one of the opposite sex without being married.
Vic'inage s. Neighbourhood; state of being neighbours.
Bad'inage s. Banter, chaff.
Li'nage s. Printed matter reckoned by lines.
Coin'age s. Art or act of coining; coined money; monetary system; fabrication.
Lib'ertinage s. Conduct of a libertine.
Pan'nage s. Right or practice of feeding swine in a forest; payment for this; food eaten by swine.
Tan'nage s. Act, process, or result of tanning.
Ton'nage (tun'-) s. Duty paid on goods, ships, etc.; number of tons carried by a ship; ships, or freight carried by them, collectively.
Car'tonnage s. The material of which Egyptian mummy cases are made.
Dun'nage s. Faggots, etc., laid in a hold to raise the cargo or to prevent the cargo from shifting.
Pun'nage s. Punning.
Bea'conage s. Money paid to maintain a beacon
Pe'onage s. System of employing peons.
Wag'onage s. Charge for conveyance by wagon wagons collectively.
Si'phonage s. Action of a siphon.
Es'pionage s. The employment of spies; spying.
Com'monage s. Right of pasturing on a common or using anything in common; common land.
No'nage s. Minority; state of being under age.
Bar'onage s. Barons collectively; a book or printed list of these.
Chap'eronage s. Duties or position of a chaperon.
Envi'ronage s. Environment.
Ma'tronage s. Matrons collectively; matronly care.
Pat'ronage s. Special support or countenance; guardianship; power of appointing to office, a benefice, etc.; act of patronizing.
Par'sonage s. The benefice of a parish; a parson's residence.
Per'sonage s. One distinguished by rank, reputation, etc.; a fictional character; external appearance; an imposing air.
Car'nage s. Slaughter, massacre.
Page s. A youth attendant on a knight, bride, etc.; a boy in livery; one side of a leaf or sheet of paper. v.t. To paginate.
Eq'uipage s. Furniture; equipment; a state carriage with its attendants.
Rampage' v.i. To storm, rage. s. Violent behaviour; a frolic.
Dump'age s. Right of shooting rubbish, etc., on a place; charge for this.
Pump'age s. That which is raised or work done by pumping.
Wrap'page s. Act of wrapping; a wrap, wrapper.
Stop'page s. Act of stopping; state of being stopped.
Rage s. Violent anger or excitement; fury; rapture; craze. v.i. To be violently tumultuous; to act furiously, storm; to ravage.
Vic'arage s. Residence or benefice of a vicar.
Clear'age s. Clearance.
Arrear'age s. Backwardness; arrears.
Gar'age s. A building for housing motor vehicles.
Cell'arage s. Cellars collectively; space, or charge for storing, in a cellar.
Dispar'age v.t. To undervalue, decry, reproach
Um'brage s. Jealousy, offence, resentment; that which gives shade.
Peer'age s. Rank or dignity of a peer; peers collectively, a register of peers with their lineage, families, etc.
Steer'age s. Part of a ship allotted to lowest class of passengers; the steering of a ship.
Pil'ferage s. Act of pilfering; that which is pilfered.
Tel'pherage s. System of electrically driven carriers.
A'cierage s. Process of electroplating a metal with steel or iron.

Brok'erage s. A broker's business or commission.
Coop'erage s. Work or workshop of a cooper; price paid for cooper's work.
Light'erage s. Act of conveying by a lighter; charge for this.
Por'terage s. Business of a porter; carriage; charge for this.
Fos'terage s. Act or custom of fostering; state of being a foster-child.
Av'erage s. A mean proportion, medium. v.t. To fix a mean, make proportionate. a. Ordinary, medium.
Bev'erage s. Liquor to be drunk.
Le'verage s. Action of a lever; power gained by its use.
Sew'erage (sū'-) s. System of draining by sewers.
Flow'erage s. State of being in flower; flowers collectively.
Suf'frage s. A vote at an election; right of voting.
Os'sifrage s. The osprey.
Sax'ifrage s. A genus of rock plants.
Lair'age s. Act of putting cattle in sheds.
Mirage' s. An atmospheric optical illusion.
Um'pirage s. Right or authority to decide; arbitrament.
Enrage' v.t. To fill with rage, exasperate.
Bor'age s. An annual garden plant.
For'age s. Food for horses and cattle; act of foraging. v.i. and t. To search for supplies, rummage about; to ravage, plunder; to supply with forage.
An'chorage s. Ground for anchoring on.
Moor'age s. Place or charge for mooring.
Fac'torage s. Commission earned by a factor.
Proc'torage s. Management by a proctor.
Stor'age s. Act of storing; charge or space for this.
Tu'torage s. Guardianship; office or occupation of a tutor.
Bar'rage s. A dam in a river; the shells from a protecting artillery bombardment.
Demur'rage s. Delay, or compensation for the delay of a vessel, railway-truck, etc.; discount in exchanging notes or coin into bullion.
Ar'bitrage s. Calculation of financial differences with reference to rates of exchange.
Out'rage v.t. To injure by rough treatment; to abuse; to commit a rape upon. s. Gross injury; excessive violence or abuse.
Seign'eurage (sēn'-) s. Something taken by virtue of sovereign prerogative.
Har'bourage s. Shelter; refuge.
Cour'age s. Intrepidity; dauntlessness; hardihood.
Encour'age v.t. To give courage or confidence to; to urge; to foster.
Discour'age v.t. To deter one from, dishearten, depress.
Entourage' s. Retinue; environment.
Pas'turage s. Business of grazing cattle, etc.; grazing ground; grass for feed.
Sage a. Sapient, grave, judicious. s. A wise man, a venerable philosopher; a shrubby plant used in cooking.
Pres'age s. An omen, prognostic, presentiment.
Presage' v.t. To forbode, predict, to have a presentiment of.
Vis'age s. The countenance.
Envis'age v.t. To look directly at, to confront; to perceive intuitively.
Dos'age s. Process or method of dosing.
Cor'sage s. The body of a woman's dress.
Massage' s. Medical rubbing and kneading of the muscles. v.t. To treat thus.
Pas'sage s. A passing, going over, motion from point to point, journey; way through, or by which one passes; incident; part of a book, etc., referred to; an encounter.
Bras'sage s. Fee for coining money at a mint.
Mess'age s. A communication; an errand, mission.
Express'age s. Charge for conveyance of goods by express.
Repoussage' s. Art or process of hammering out metals into repoussé work.
Us'age (ūz'-) s. Manner of using, treatment; customary practice.
Saus'age s. Chopped pork, etc., stuffed in a prepared intestine.
Sur'plusage s. Surplus; excess.
Disu'sage s. Gradual cessation of use, etc.
Misus'age s. Ill-usage; abuse.
Boat'age s. Charge for carriage by boat.
Float'age s. Anything found floating, flotsam; buoyancy.
Me'tage s. Official measurement of coal; charge for this.
Bar'onetage s. Baronets collectively; a book or printed list of these.
Waft'age s. Conveyance through a buoyant medium; carriage.
Drift'age s. Drifting or drifted matter; distance a ship is driven in bearing up against wind and currents.
Freight'age s. Act of freighting; money paid for freight.
Knight'age s. A list or the body of knights.
Her'mitage s. The cell of a hermit; a retreat.
Exploit'age s. Exploitation.
Her'itage s. Estate devolved by succession; inheritance.
Fruit'age s. Fruit collectively; a fruit crop.
Vol'tage s. Electromotive force in volts.
Chant'age s. Blackmail.
Plant'age s. Vegetation; herbage.
Van'tage s. Advantage; state or place that affords this.
Advan'tage s. Superiority, benefit, profit. v.t. To give a better chance to, to benefit.
Disadvan'tage s. Want of advantage; unfavourable state, quality, circumstance, etc.; loss, detriment.
Percent'age s. Rate of interest, allowance, etc., on a hundred.
Cli'entage s. Clientele; system of patron and client; condition of a client.
Par'entage s. Lineage, extraction.
Mint'age s. That which is coined; duty paid for coining.
Vin'tage s. Time of grape-gathering; wine produced in one season.
Front'age s. The front part of a building, etc., extent of this.
Sab'otage s. Act of damaging employers' property during a strike.
Do'tage s. Senility; foolish old age; excessive fondness.
Anecdo'tage s. Anecdotes collectively; facetious term for garrulous old age.
Sacerdo'tage s. Sacerdotalism.
Ag'iotage s. Money-changing; stock-jobbing.
Pi'lotage s. The pay or guidance of a pilot.
Root'age s. A taking root; extirpation.
Potage' (-tazh') s. Soup.
Car'tage s. Act of carting; charge for this.
Short'age s. A deficiency; amount of this.
Port'age s. Act of or charge for carrying; freight.
Report'age s. Gossip.

Colportage′ s. Business of a colporteur.
Stage s. A raised platform, especially for theatrical performances; a scene of action; a stopping-place or distance between two such; degree of advancement, point reached. v.t. To exhibit on the stage.
Last′age s. A cargo; ballast; tonnage.
Wast′age s. Loss by use, decay, etc.
For′estage s. The rights of foresters.
Hos′tage s. A person left as surety.
Post′age s. Charge for conveying letters, etc., by post.
Cot′tage s. A small house, a cot.
Pot′tage s. Lentil or other porridge, stew of meat and vegetables.
Scu′tage s. (*Feud. law*) Payment in place of service.
Mut′age s. The checking of fermentation in must.
Lan′guage s. Human speech; speech peculiar to a nation; manner of expression.
Assuage′ v.t. To mitigate, allay, appease.
Mess′uage s. Dwelling-house with land, etc.
Cleav′age s. Act of splitting; way in which a mineral may be naturally split, or in which a party splits up.
Rav′age v.t. To lay waste, despoil, sack. s. Devastation; pillage.
Sav′age a. Wild; uncivilized; ferocious. s. A barbarian; a wild, uncultured, or brutal person. v.t. To bite and trample (of horses).
Sal′vage s. Compensation for saving; property saved.
Sel′vage s. Selvedge.
Lov′age s. An umbelliferous herb.
Wage s. Recompense. v.t. To engage in, carry on.
Brew′age s. The process or result of brewing.
Sew′age (sū′-) s. Matter carried off in sewers; filth.
Flow′age s. An overflowing; that which overflows.
Tow′age (tō′-) s. Act of or charge for towing.
Stow′age s. Act of, room for, or charge for stowing.
Swage s. A tool used for shaping wrought-iron. v.t. The shape with this.
Dray′age s. The use of a dray or charge for this.
Métayage′ s. System of land-holding by a métayer.
Quay′age (kē′-) s. Quay dues; room on quays; quays collectively.
Buoy′age s. A system of buoys; provision of buoys.
Voy′age s. A journey by sea. v.i. and t. To pass or travel over by water.
Badge s. A cognizance, mark of distinction. v.t. To furnish with this.
Cadge v.t. To get by wheedling or begging.
Madge s. The barn-owl, or magpie.
Edge s. Brink, margin; sharp part of a blade. v.t. To sharpen; make a border to. v.i. To move sideways bit by bit.
Hedge s. A fence of shrubs, etc.; a barrier. v.t. To surround with a hedge. v.i. To skulk; to act evasively; to bet on both sides.
Kedge s. A small anchor. v.t. To warp or move a ship by means of this.
Ledge s. A shelf-like projection, a ridge; stratum.
Fledge v.t. To furnish with feathers.
Pledge s. Anything deposited as security; the drinking of another's health. v.t. To put in pawn; to promise; to drink a health to.
Sledge s. A blacksmith's heavy hammer; a vehicle on runners; a toboggan. v.t. and i. To convey in or travel by this.
Kent′ledge s. Iron ballast on a ship's floor.
Knowl′edge s. Learning; clear perception; acquaintance.
Acknowl′edge v.t. To avow, confess, admit; to notice.
Foreknowl′edge s. Prescience.
Dredge s. An instrument for dragging; machine for removing mud, etc., from a river-bed, harbour, etc. v.t. To take with a dredge, use a dredge; to sprinkle flour on meat while roasting, sugar on pastry, etc.
Sedge s. A coarse, grass-like marsh-plant.
Vedge s. (*Slang*) A vegetable.
Selv′edge s. Edge of cloth woven to prevent unravelling.
Wedge s. A solid, tapering body. v.t. To split with a wedge; to drive, force, fix, fasten, etc., in the manner of a wedge.
Midge s. A gnat.
Ridge s. Top of any elongated elevation, a raised strip. v.t. To form a ridge of; to wrinkle.
Bridge s. A pathway over a river, ravine, railway, etc.; the upper part of the nose; a card game. v.t. To build a bridge over.
Abridge′ v.t. To shorten, condense.
Por′ridge s. Oatmeal boiled in water till thickened.
Car′tridge s. A case containing explosive charge and shot.
Part′ridge s. A well-known game-bird of the grouse family.
Bodge v.t. To mend or put together clumsily.
Dodge v.i. To start suddenly aside; to quibble. v.t. To evade; to pursue craftily. s. An evasion; a mean subterfuge; a trick.
Hodge s. A rustic labourer.
Lodge s. Small country-house; body of Freemasons, etc. v.t. To deposit for keeping; to accommodate temporarily. v.i. To have a temporary abode.
Splodge s. A daub, splash, smear.
Dislodge′ v.t. To drive from a place, to remove.
Podge s. A stout person.
Hodge′-podge s. A medley.
Stodge v.t. and i. To cram full, stuff. s. Stodgy food.
Budge v.i. To stir, move off. s. Lamb fur worn with the wool outwards.
Fudge s. Stuff, nonsense; exclamation of contempt; a soft sweetmeat. v.t. To patch up temporarily, to make shift, fake.
Judge s. A civil officer who hears and determines causes; one skilled to decide on anything, an expert. v.i. To act as judge, to form an opinion. v.t. To try; to esteem.
Adjudge′ v.t. To decree, sentence.
Rejudge′ v.t. To judge again, re-examine.
Prejudge′ v.t. To judge or condemn without hearing.

Misjudge' v.t. and i. To mistake in judging, err in judgment, form unjustifiable opinions.
Sludge s. Mire, ooze, slush.
Smudge s. A blot, smear; a stifling smoke. v.t. and i. To blot, stain, make dirty.
Nudge v.t. To touch gently, as with the elbow. s. A slight or significant push thus.
Pudge s. A short, squat person.
Drudge s. One employed in menial or in uncongenial, ill-paid work; a hack. v.i. To work hard with small profit, to slave.
Grudge v.t. To give reluctantly; to feel discontent at. v.i. To be envious. s. Reluctance in giving; ill-will; secret enmity.
Begrudge' v.t. To envy the possession of.
Trudge v.t. and i. To travel on foot, esp. weariedly. s. Such a walk.
Liege a. Bound by or pertaining to feudal tenure. s. A vassal, a subject; a lord, sovereign.
Siege (sēj) s. A set attack on a fortified place; continued attempt to gain possession.
Besiege' v.t. To lay siege to, to invest.
Sac'rilege s. Violation of sacred things.
Sort'ilege s. Divination by drawing lots.
Priv'ilege s. A personal or peculiar advantage; an immunity, exemption. v.t. To confer a privilege upon; to exempt, authorize.
Allege' v.t. To affirm, declare, maintain.
Col'lege s. An association having certain powers and engaged in some common pursuit; a seminary for higher education; building occupied by such.
Manège' s. Horsemanship; school for teaching this or for training horses.
Barège' s. A light gauzy dress fabric.
Prot'égé (-āzhā) s. One under another's protection.
Cortège' s. A train of attendants; a procession.
Beige s. An unbleached woollen dress material.
Oblige' v.t. To please, gratify; to compel. v.i. To be obliging.
Disoblige' v.t. To be unaccommodating to, to offend by incivility.
Négli'gé s. State of undress; free and easy attire.
Tige (tēzh) s. Shaft of a column; a stalk.
Prestige' s. Influence or fame due to past successes, character, etc.
Ves'tige s. Mark made in passing; a trace; a footprint.
Bilge s. The broadest part of a ship's bottom; foul water that collects here.
Bulge s. The broadest part of a cask, etc.; a protuberance. v.i. To swell out.
Indulge' v.t. To favour, gratify, humour. v.i. To gratify oneself.
Effulge' v.i. To shine forth; to become famous.
Divulge' v.t. To make public, to impart.
Gange v.t. To bind a fish-hook or line with wire.
Change s. Alteration, variation, substitution, vicissitude; small coin. v.i. and t. To alter, substitute, exchange; to undergo variation.
Interchange' v.t. To exchange, reciprocate; to cause to alternate. v.i. To change reciprocally; to alternate. s. Alternate succession; barter, commerce.
Counterchange' v.t. To exchange, reciprocate.
Coun'terchange s. Exchange, reciprocation.
Exchange' v.t. To give and take reciprocally. v.i. To be changed or received in exchange for. s. Interchange; barter; the balance of money.
Mélange' s. A mixture, medley.
Flange s. A projecting edge or rim.
Mange s. A skin disease of dogs and cattle.
Blancmange' s. A confection of sweetened cornflour, etc., with milk, and jellied.
Range v.t. To place in order, set in rows; to wander through. v.i. To rank; to rove about. s. A row; extent; distance traversed by projectile; place for gun practice; a kitchen grate.
Derange' v.t. To put out of order, disorganize, confuse.
Grange s. A farm with outbuildings, etc.; a barn.
Or'ange s. A well-known round, yellow fruit; the evergreen tree bearing it. a. Reddish-yellow; pertaining to an orange; pertaining to the Protestants of Ireland, and especially of Ulster.
Sporange' s. A spore-case.
Arrange' v.t. To put in order, adjust.
Rearrange' v.t. To arrange in another order.
Prearrange' v.t. To arrange beforehand.
Disarrange' v.t. To put out of order; to confuse.
Strange a. Odd, singular; unfamiliar; unacquainted.
Estrange' v.t. To keep at a distance, to alienate.
Chal'lenge s. An invitation to contest, answer, etc.; demand; exception taken. v.t. To defy, summon to a contest, demand as a right, object to as not qualified.
Avenge' v.i. and t. To revenge, punish.
Scav'enge v.t. and i. To clear or clean streets, act as a scavenger.
Revenge' v.t. To take vengeance for; to avenge. s. Infliction of injury in return for injury; retaliation; vindictive feeling.
Loz'enge s. A four-sided equilateral figure with two acute and two obtuse angles; a woman's heraldic shield; a medicated sweetmeat.
Hinge s. The joint on which a door, lid, etc., turns; that on which anything depends. v.i. To turn on a hinge; to depend on.
Impinge' v.i. To fall or strike against; to clash.
Cringe v.i. To crouch or bend with servility, to fawn. s. A servile action, flattering obsequiousness.
Fringe s. An ornamental trimming or border; the front hair cut short and straight. v.t. To border with a fringe.
Infringe' v.t. To break, violate. v.i. To encroach.
Springe s. A snare, noose.
Astringe' v.t. To bind together, constrict.
Syr'inge s. Tubular instrument for injecting liquids. v.t. To inject, spray, or cleanse with this.
Singe v.t. To burn slightly. s. A burning of the surface.

Tinge v.t. To colour slightly; to modify the character of. s. A tint; a flavour.
Swinge v.t. To thrash. s. A heavy blow; sweep of anything in motion.
Twinge s. A short, sharp pain; a pang. v.t. To affect with such.
Con'gé s. Leave to depart; leave-taking; a bow.
Longe s. Long rope used in training horses.
Sponge (spŭnj) s. A marine protozoan; its soft, fibrous, elastic framework, especially when prepared and used as an absorbent, etc.; a sponger. v.t. To cleanse, obliterate, absorb, etc., with a sponge. v.i. To live parasitically or as a sponger.
Lunge s. A sudden thrust with a sword, etc.; a longe. v.i. To make a lunge; to strike at or rush forward suddenly.
Blunge v.t. To mix clay, etc., in pottery making.
Plunge v.t. To immerse, especially in a fluid; to thrust into. v.i. To dive, rush in; to throw oneself headlong or about; to gamble recklessly. s. Act of thrusting into water, etc.; act of pitching like an unruly horse.
Lounge v.i. To idle, loll about, live lazily. s. An idle stroll; place for reclining at ease.
Scrounge v.t. and i. (*Slang*) To pilfer, cadge. s. A cadger.
Expunge' v.t. To rub out, efface, cancel.
Gamboge' s. A reddish-yellow resin used as a pigment and in medicine.
Doge s. The chief magistrate in the old republics of Venice and Genoa.
Anago'ge s. A mystical interpretation of the Scriptures.
Epago'ge s. The use of particular examples to prove universal conclusions.
Parago'ge s. The addition of a syllable to the end of a word.
Eloge' s. A funeral oration, a panegyric.
Hor'ologe s. A time-piece.
Barge s. A large flat-bottomed boat used for transport. v.i. (*Slang*) To lurch into or rush against.
Charge s. Care; injunction; expense; person or thing committed to care; load of a cartridge, battery, machine, etc.; an onset; an heraldic bearing. v.t. To impose as a load, task, trust, etc; to command, accuse, place to the account of; to rush upon, fall on. v.i. To make a sudden attack.
Recharge' v.t. To load a fire-arm a second time; to attack again. s. A second or fresh charge.
Coun'tercharge s. An accusation brought in answer to another; a counterclaim. v.t. To make a charge against in return or in opposition.
Overcharge' v.t. To make too high a charge; to charge too fully or heavily; to cloy, oppress,
O'vercharge s. An excessive charge, burden, etc.
Surcharge' v.t. To overload; to lay upon as a special charge. s. An excessive load; an extra or over-charge.
Discharge' v.t. To dismiss; to pay a debt, unload, perform. v.i. To empty or unload itself; to explode. s. Act of discharging; unloading; firing off; dismissal; release from obligation, debt, etc.; performance; absolution; ransom.
Litharge' s. Protoxide of lead.
Large a. Big; of great bulk or extent; great in number.
Enlarge' v.t. To make larger, dilate; to set free. v.i. To grow larger; to discuss a matter fully.
Marge s. A margin, shore; (*slang*) margarine.
Targe s. A small shield.
Cierge s. A wax candle used in R. C. rites.
Concierge' s. A hall-porter, door-keeper.
Merge v.i. To be swallowed or lost. v.t. To cause to be incorporated.
Submerge' v.t. To put under or cover with water; to overwhelm. v.i. To sink.
Emerge' v.i. To rise out of; to come into view, appear.
Asperge' v.t. To sprinkle with holy water.
Serge s. A strong, twilled, woollen stuff.
Deterge' v.t. To cleanse, purge away.
Absterge' v.t. To cleanse, purge.
Verge s. Extreme edge, brink; a rod of office, mace; compass; a spindle. v.i. To approach; to slope; to border on.
Diverge' v.i. To tend from a point in different directions; to deviate, vary.
Converge' v.i. To tend to the same point, to approach.
Dirge s. A mournful ditty or tune; a funeral song.
Forge s. A smithy, furnace. v.t. To beat into shape, to fashion; to form by heating and hammering; to counterfeit. v.i. To commit forgery; to go on slowly and laboriously.
Gorge s. The throat, gullet; a narrow passage between mountains. v.t. and i. To satiate, glut.
Regorge' v.t. To swallow again or eagerly; to vomit.
Engorge' v.t. To swallow greedily. v.i. To feed voraciously.
Disgorge' v.t. To vomit; to discharge violently; to give up.
Porge v.t. To render carcases clean for Jewish consumption.
Urge v.t. To push, drive; to incite.
Dem'iurge s. God as creator; a mysterious agent in the creation of the world.
Scourge v.t. To whip severely; to chastise, harass. s. A lash, whip; punishment with this; an affliction; one who harasses.
Purge v.t. To cleanse, purify, to clear from accusation. v.i. To become pure. s. Act of purging, that which purges; a cathartic.
Spurge s. A plant with an acrid, milky juice.
Surge s. A large wave. v.i. To swell, rise high.
Resurge' v.i. To rise again.
Dram'aturge s. A dramatist.
Thau'maturge s. A wonder-worker, magician.
Gauge v.t. To ascertain the capacity or measurement of; to appraise. s. A measure, measuring rod, etc.; calibre; size; standard; distance between railway metals.
-fuge suff. Expressing a driving out, getting rid of.
Ref'uge s. Protection; an asylum, retreat; an expedient.
Ver'mifuge s. A drug for expelling worms.
Feb'rifuge s. Medicine for dispelling or allaying fever.
Cen'trifuge s. A machine for separating cream from milk.

Insec'tifuge s. Substance for keeping insects away.
Sub'terfuge s. An evasion, shift.
Huge a. Enormous, vast, immense.
Del'uge s. A general inundation; a heavy downpour; a torrent. v.t. To flood.
Gouge s. A scooping chisel with round edge; (*slang*) a swindle. v.t. To force or scoop out with or as with a gouge.
Rouge s. A cosmetic for giving a red colour; a polishing powder for metals. v.i. and t. To colour or tinge with rouge.
He pron. The man or male previously alluded to.
Ache s. A continued pain. v.i. To be in continued pain.
Cache s. Hidden stores; the place where they are hidden. v.t. To conceal in a place of safety.
Head'ache s. Persistent pain in the head.
Tooth'ache s. Pain in the teeth.
Pap'ier-mâ'ché s. A hard material made from paper, etc., pulped with glue or size.
Panache' (-ash') s. A cluster of feathers on a helmet, etc.; display; swagger.
Apache' s. A Parisian hooligan.
Ear'ache s. Pain in the ear.
Or'ache s. Orach, the mountain-spinach.
Tache s. A freckle, blemish.
Sab'retache s. A leather case hung from sword-belt of cavalry officers.
Heart'ache s. Mental anguish.
Moustache' s. The hair of the upper lip.
Attach'é s. One attached to the suite of an ambassador.
Soutache' s. A narrow braid or trimming.
Gou'ache s. A method of painting in opaque water-colour.
Flèche s. A slender pointed spire.
Crèche s. A public nursery.
Cli'ché s. A stereotype; a hackneyed phrase.
Miche v.i. To play truant, skulk.
Niche s. A hollow or recess in a wall.
Pastiche' (-tēsh') s. A pasticcio.
Av'alanche s. A vast body of snow, ice, etc., sliding down a mountain.
Carte-blanche s. Unlimited authority.
Cynanch'e s. A disease of the throat, tonsils, etc.
Synec'doche s. Figure of speech by which whole is put for part or part for whole.
Brioche' s. A light cake.
Cloche s. A bell-shaped glass for forcing plants.
Guilloche' s. An interlaced ornamentation.
Tro'che s. A medicinal lozenge.
Démarche' s. A change in diplomatic action.
Récher'ché (-shar'shā) a. Choice, elegant; much sought after.
Schottische' (shotēsh') s. A lively variety of polka.
Gauche a. Awkward, tactless.
Douche s. A jet directed on to some part of the body; instrument for effecting this. v.t. and i. To apply or take a douche.
Gobe'mouche s. A credulous simpleton.
Barouche' s. A four-wheeled carriage with movable top.
Farouche' a. Savage, shy, uncouth.
Polatouche' s. A Siberian flying-squirrel.
Cartouche' s. A cartridge, an architectural scroll; an Egyptian device enclosing a signature.
Capuche' s. A hood.
Ruche' s. A ruffled strip of lace, gauze, etc.
Psy'che s. The soul, spirit, mind.
Lim'itrophe a. On the border.
Stroph'e s. Division of Greek choral ode.
Anas'trophe s. Inversion of the natural order of words.
Catas'trophe s. A final event, disaster, or calamity; a cataclysm.
Epis'trophe s. A figure in which successive clauses end with the same word.
Antis'trophe s. A choral response; a retort.
Apos'trophe s. The sign of the possessive; an aside to an imaginary audience.
Phil'osophe s. A pretender to philosophy.
She pron. The woman or female referred to.
The a. and adv.
Bathe v.t. To wash the body, to immerse in water. s. A swim.
Scathe s. Damage, harm, injury. v.t. To hurt; to destroy.
Sheathe v.t. To put into a sheath; to protect by a casing.
Breathe v.i. To draw air into the lungs and expel it.
Wreathe v.t. To form into a wreath; to entwine; to encircle. v.i. To be interwoven, curled round, etc.
Lathe s. A machine for turning wood, etc.; an administrative division of Kent.
Loathe v.t. To feel disgust at; to abominate. v.i. To feel nausea or abhorrence.
Spathe s. Leaf-shaped bract around a spadix.
Rathe a. Coming before the usual time. adv. Early, soon.
Swathe v.t. To bind in a bandage or wrappings. s. A bandage, etc.
Seethe v.t. To steep in hot liquid; to boil. v.i. To be boiling; to be agitated.
Teethe v.i. To cut the teeth.
Leth'e s. A river of Hades which induced forgetfulness in those who drank of it; oblivion.
Lithe a. Flexible, pliant, limber.
Blithe a. Cheerful, gay.
Writhe v.i. To be distorted or to squirm with pain. v.t. To twist, distort. s. Act of writhing.
Tithe s. A tenth part, especially as allotted for ecclesiastical use. v.t. To tax to the amount of a tenth.
Withe s. A flexible, slender branch; an osier band.
Nepen'the s. A draught or drug supposed to induce forgetfulness of sorrow; an anodyne.
Ab'sinthe s. A liqueur flavoured with wormwood.
Clothe v.t. To put clothes on, cover or spread over.
Reclothe' v.t. To provide with or put new clothes on.
Soothe v.t. To calm, tranquillize; to soften; to flatter, gratify.
Scythe s. Instrument for mowing grass, etc. v.t. To cut with this.
Cor'bie s. The raven, or crow.
Spe'cie (-shē) s. Bullion; metallic money.
Die v.i. To cease from living, expire, perish. s. A small cube for gaming with (*see* DICE); the cubical part of a pedestal; stamp for impressing coin, etc.; machine for cutting out or stamping.
Cad'die s. A lad attending on a golfer.
Had'die s. (*Scot.*) A haddock.
Lad'die s. A small lad.

Medji'die s. A Turkish order of merit; a Turkish silver coin.
Or'gandie s. A light, transparent muslin.
Hood'ie s. The hooded crow.
Bird'ie s. Little bird.
Geor'die s. (*Slang*) A coal-miner.
Fie' int. Expressing contempt, disgust, etc.
Ré'gie (rā'zhē) s. A State monopoly in certain countries.
Dog'gie s. A little dog, pet dog.
Bo'gie s. A spook; an imaginary hindrance.
Lo'gie s. Imitation jewellery for the stage.
Bou'gie s. A wax candle; a surgeon's instrument.
Hie v.i. To hasten, hurry.
Mash'ie s. An iron golf-club.
Both'ie s. A hut, hovel.
Buck'ie s. A whelk.
Cock-a-leek'ie s. Scots broth of fowl and leeks.
Book'ie s. (*Slang*) A bookmaker.
Cook'ie s. A bun, small cake.
Rook'ie s. (*Slang*) A recruit.
Birk'ie s. (*Scot.*) A fellow, a man. a. Gay, sprightly.
Hawk'ie s. A cow with a white face.
Lie v.i. To utter falsehood with intent to deceive; to recline, rest on anything at full length; to remain, to depend; to be sustainable in law. s. A falsehood.
Meal'ie s. S. African maize.
Coal'ie s. (*Slang*) A coal-miner.
Belie' v.t. To give the lie to, to counterfeit.
Bail'ie s. A Scottish municipal magistrate.
Gil'lie s. A Highland gamekeeper or attendant on sportsmen.
Col'lie s. A Scottish sheep-dog.
Cool'ie s. A native labourer in India and the Far East.
Doo'lie s. A Hindu litter or stretcher.
Overlie' v.t. To lie over or upon something.
Girl'ie s. Pet name for a girl.
Ram'ie s. An Asiatic plant; fibre or fabric made from this.
Bonhomie' s. Geniality, good nature.
Sty'mie s. Position in golf when a ball on the green is directly between striker's and the hole. v.t. To hinder thus.
Ge'nie s. A spirit or demon of Mohammedan myth.
Dom'inie s. A schoolmaster.
Hor'nie s. (*Scot.*) The Devil.
Brown'ie s. A kind of sprite.
Pie s. A crust baked with meat or fruit under it; the magpie; disordered type.
Cap'-à-pie adv. From head to foot.
Mag'pie s. A chattering, black and white bird of the crow family; circle next the bull's-eye.
Kel'pie s. A horse-like water-demon.
Char'pie s. Lint for dressing wounds.
Dear'ie s. A beloved one.
Fa'erie s. Fairyland. a. Visionary, unsubstantial.
Camara'derie s. Good fellowship, comradeship.
Minau'derie (-nō-) s. Affectation; coquettishness.
Eer'ie a. Awe-inspiring, weird.
Menag'erie s. Collection of wild animals.
Lin'gerie s. Linen articles of clothing, etc.
Gauch'erie s. Awkwardness; a clumsy or tactless blunder.
Dia'blerie s. Devilry; diabolism; wild mischief.
Espiè'glerie s. Impishness, roguishness.
Gendarm'erie s. The armed police of France.
Flan'erie s. The practice of idling.
Bizar'rerie s. Grotesqueness, eccentricity.
Lama'serie s. A Tibetan monastery.
Bras'serie s. A brew-house.
Patis'serie s. Pastry.
Causerie' s. A chatty essay.
Passe'menterie s. Ornamental embroidery with metallic threads, etc.
Co'terie s. An exclusive circle or society; a clique.
Jacquerie' s. A revolt of peasants, especially that in France in 1357.
Grotes'querie s. Grotesque quality or objects.
Brus'querie s. Unceremoniousness, bluntness.
Rev'erie s. A waking dream; deep musing; brown study.
Clamjam'phrie s. Rubbish; a contemptible lot.
Prair'ie s. An extensive, grassy tract.
Cal'orie s. The unit of heat.
Knob'kerrie s. A Kaffir bludgeon.
Cor'rie s. A circular, steep-sided mountain hollow.
Dhur'rie s. A coarse cotton fabric made in India.
Eyr'ie s. Nest or breeding-place of bird of prey.
Val'kyrie s. One of the twelve divine maidens of Odin who chose those to be slain in battle.
Bourgeoisie' s. The shop-keeping class.
Prim'sie a. Demure, prim.
Lass'ie s. A little girl.
Jal'ousie s. A Venetian blind; a louvre, blind.
Tie v.t. To bind, fasten with a knot; to constrain. v.i. To score equally with. s. That which binds; a fastening; ribbon for neck; bond; equality in numbers.
Nigh'tie s. (*Slang*) A night-gown.
Capernoi'tie s. (*Scot.*) The head, the noddle.
Shel'tie s. A Shetland pony.
Lin'tie s. (*Scot.*) A linnet.
Auntie' s. Aunt.
Cloot'ie s. The Devil.
Sor'tie s. A sally, especially from a besieged place.
Tot'tie s. A little child, a darling.
Vie v.i. To strive for superiority, contend.
Ca'vie s. (*Scot.*) A hen-house.
Eau-de-vie s. Brandy.
Gar'vie s. A sprat.
Outvie' v.t. To exceed, surpass.
Bow'ie s. A long double-edged knife.
Dix'ie s. A field-service kettle.
Nix'ie s. A water-sprite.
Capercail'zie s. The wood-grouse.
Assoil'zie v.t. (*Scot.*) To acquit by judicial sentence.
Gaberlun'zie s. A strolling beggar.
Sobran'je (-bra'nye) s. The Bulgarian Parliament.
Kop'je s. A small hill in S. Africa.
Bake v.t. To harden by heat, to cook in an oven.
Cake s. A sweetened mass of flour, etc., baked. v.t. and i. To form into a cake or mass.
Pan'cake s. A thin batter cake fried.
Short'cake s. A sweet, brittle cake.
Fake s. A single coil of rope; (*slang*) a dodge, swindle, deception. v.t. To coil, tuck up; (*slang*) to cover up defects; to fabricate, falsify, cheat.
Hake s. A sea-fish of the cod family.
Shake v.t. To cause to tremble, shiver, vibrate rapidly, move forcibly to and fro; to agitate; to trill. v.i. To tremble, shiver, quake. s. A vacillating motion, rapid movement to and fro, tremor; a trill agitation; a crack in timber.

Lake s. Large body of water surrounded by land; a red pigment.
Flake s. A layer, scale; a feathery particle. v.t. To form into flakes. v.i. To brake off in flakes.
Slake v.t. To quench; to cool; to mix, as lime with water. v.i. To become extinct or slaked.
Make v.t. To create, form, produce, effect. s. Form, structure; shape; texture; one's like, match, or mate.
Remake' v.t. To make over again; to recast.
Snake s. A serpent; a treacherous, cold-blooded person.
Spake past (*Speak*).
Rake' (-kĕ') s. An aromatic liquor of the near East.
Rake s. Implement used for collecting hay, in gardening, etc.; a debauchee; projection of upper parts of ship; slope. v.t. To collect, smooth, scrape together, etc., with a rake; to ransack; to enfilade. v.i. To use a rake.
Brake s. A contrivance to retard or arrest moving wheels. v.t. To apply this; to crush flax or hemp.
Crake s. The landrail; its grating cry.
Corn'crake s. The landrail.
Drake s. The male of the duck; the Mayfly.
Shel'drake s. A large, handsome wild-duck.
Man'drake s. A narcotic plant with forked root.
Strake s. Continuous range of planks from stem to stern of a vessel; iron band on a wheel.
Garboard-strake' s. The row of planks next the keel.
Sake s. Cause, end, reason; regard for a person, etc.
Sak'é (-ā) s. A Japanese intoxicating drink.
Name'sake s. One having the same name as another, especially in compliment.
Keep'sake s. A small gift, a memento.
Forsake' v.t. To abandon, renounce.
Take v.t. To lay hold of, accept; to choose, understand; to swallow. v.i. To catch; to have effect; to please. s. Fish caught at one haul; takings.
Retake' v.t. To take again, recapture.
Wap'entake (wŏp'-) s. Old division of certain English counties.
Up'take s. Shaft for upward passage of air in a mine; (*Scot.*) intelligence.
Partake' v.i. To share; to have or take part in; to participate.
Undertake' v.t. To take upon oneself; to engage in; to guarantee. v.i. To promise, stand bound.
Overtake' v.t. To come up with, come upon, take by surprise.
Stake s. A post; anything wagered; hazard. v.t. To mark, support, etc., with stakes; to wager.
Mistake' v.t. To take wrongly, misunderstand. v.i. To err in judgment, opinion, etc. s. A blunder; an error in judgment or opinion.
Sweep'stake s. A prize made up of several stakes.
Quake v.i. To tremble; to shake with fear, cold, etc. s. A quiver; a tremulous agitation; a shaking.
Earth'quake s. A volcanic shaking or moving of part of the earth's surface.
Wake v.i. To awake, be roused from sleep. v.t. To arouse. s. A vigil; watching of a corpse by night; track of ship, etc.
Awake' a. Not asleep, vigilant. v.i. To cease from sleep. v.t. To arouse from sleep.
Wide'awake a. Alert; knowing. s. A soft, broad-brimmed hat.
Reawake' v.i. To awake again.
Kit'tiwake s. A common seagull.
Wack'e s. A softish, basalt-like rock.
Grey'wacke s. Conglomerate of grit rock and pebbles.
Eke v.t. To increase, prolong; to supply what is scanty. adv. Also, likewise.
Bike s. (*Slang*) A bicycle.
Dike s. A ditch; an embankment; a vein of igneous rock. v.t. To drain or surround with dikes; to secure by a bank.
Like a. Resembling; similar; feeling disposed. adv. and prep. Similarly, in the same manner. v.t. To be pleased with; to approve. v.i. To be pleased; to choose. s. A liking, fancy; a counterpart.
-like suff. Forming adjectives and adverbs.
Alike' adv. With resemblance, similar.
God'like a. Resembling God; divine.
Belike' adv. Probably, likely.
Life'like a. Like a living person; true to the original.
Wife'like a. Wifely; pertaining to a wife.
King'like a. Like a king.
Death'like a. Resembling death.
Work'manlike a. Like a good workman; skilful.
War'like a. Fit, disposed for, or pertaining to war; soldierly.
Dislike' v.t. To have an aversion to. s. Antipathy, aversion.
Mislike' v.t. and i. To dislike, have aversion to. s. Dislike, disapprobation.
La'dylike a. With manners befitting a lady.
Pike s. A long lance, a spear; a voracious freshwater fish; a toll-bar, a turnpike road.
Ram'pike s. A withered tree, a stump.
Turn'pike s. A toll-gate on a road; road with these.
Spike s. A long nail, pointed rod; an ear of corn; a variety of inflorescence. v.t. To fasten, set, or close with a spike; to impale.
Shrike s. The butcher-bird.
Trike s. (*Slang*) A tricycle.
Strike v.i. To hit; to turn aside rapidly, to light upon; to be stranded; to stop work to get better terms. v.t. To smite, thrust in; to mint; to sound (of clocks); to lower (flag, etc.); to occur to. s. Act of employees who leave work to enforce certain conditions; a strickle.
Al'sike s. A species of clover.
Tike s. A cur; a low fellow.
Coke s. Coal from which gas has been extracted. v.t. To turn into coke.
Choke v.t. To stifle, suffocate, check. v.i. To have the windpipe blocked, to stifle. s. Action or noise of choking; constriction in a gun-barrel.
Ar'tichoke s. An esculent plant like the thistle.
Joke s. A jest; raillery; anything witty or not in earnest. v.i. To make jokes, to sport.
Bloke s. (*Slang*) A chap, fellow.
Cloke s. and v.t. (*Cloak*).
Moke s. (*Slang*) A donkey.

Smoke s. Exhalation from burning matter; vapour; idle talk; use of tobacco. v.i. To emit smoke; to use tobacco opium, etc. v.t. To dry or preserve by smoke; to fumigate; to burn or use in smoking.
Poke v.t. To push against with something pointed; to feel for, grope; to stir. s. A thrust, jog, nudge; a bag, pocket; projecting front to a bonnet.
Mo'poke s. The Australian night-jar.
Spoke s. A radial arm of a wheel; rung of a ladder. v.t. To furnish with spokes. past (*Speak*).
Bespoke' v.t., past Ordered beforehand.
Broke v.t., past part. (*Break*). v.i. To act as a go-between.
Stroke s. A blow; a sudden effect; affliction. v.t. To rub gently in one direction.
Soke s. Soc.
Stoke v.t. To supply fuel to a furnace. v.i. To act as stoker.
Evoke' v.t. To call up, summon forth.
Revoke' v.t. To annul, repeal, reverse. v.t. To fail to follow suit (at cards) when one can do so. s. Act of revoking (at cards).
Invoke' v.t. To address in prayer; to call upon earnestly for assistance, etc.
Convoke' v.t. To call together, summon to meet.
Provoke' v.t. To arouse to anger, incense; to stimulate to action.
Yoke s. Bond of connexion, especially between two beasts of draught side by side; a pair draught animals; shoulder-piece of a garment; a burden; servitude. v.t. To join or couple; to enslave, confine.
Schip'perke (skip'erki) s. A small breed of tailless lap-dog.
Burke v.t. To suppress, dispose of quietly.
Rebuke' v.t. To chide, reprehend sharply. s. A reprimand, severe reproof.
Duke s. One of the highest order of nobility; ruler of a duchy.
Archduke' s. A prince of the former Austrian or Russian imperial family.
Mam'eluke s. One of the former Egyptian cavalry.
Fluke s. The arm of an anchor; a parasitic worm in sheep, etc.; a flat-fish; an accidental success. v.i. To score by luck.
Puke v.t. and i. To vomit. s. A vomit; an emetic.
Peruke' s. A small wig.
Dyke s. (*Dike*).
Vandyke' s. A deep-pointed lace collar.
Fyke s. A bag-net for trapping fish.
Ale s. A fermented malt liquor.
Bale s. A bundle; mischief, sorrow. v.t. To pack in bundles.
Timbale' (-bahl') s. A shaped dish of fish, etc., with cream and white of egg.
Locale' s. Scene or locality of an event, etc.
Percale' s. A fine, closely woven cotton fabric.
Scale s. A weighing instrument; a thin flake, membranous part, layer; an incrustation; a ladder; a graduated series or thing; gradation; the gamut. v.t. To strip or take off in scales; to climb by or as by a ladder; to graduate. v.i. To come off in thin layers.
Dale s. A low place between hills, a vale
Gale s. A strong storm of wind; a smal shrub growing in bogs; periodical payment of rent.
Regale' v.t. To entertain sumptuously; to gratify. v.i. To feast.
Yaff'ingale s. The green woodpecker.
Far'thingale s. A hooped frame for extending the gown; a hoop-petticoat.
Gal'ingale s. An aromatic root tasting like ginger formerly used in medicine.
Night'ingale s. A small migratory singing-bird; an invalid's bed-jacket.
Mar'tingale s. Strap to prevent a horse raising his head; a system of doubling stakes after losses.
Hale a. Sound, hearty, robust.
Inhale' v.t. To draw into the lungs.
Shale s. A soft, laminated, argillaceous rock.
Whale s. An air-breathing, warm-blooded marine mammal. v.i. To engage in whale-fishing.
Exhale' v.t. To evaporate; to emit.
Kale s. A plant allied to the cabbage.
Male s. One of the begetting sex; a he-animal; a plant having stamens only. a. Pertaining to this sex; masculine.
Fe'male s. One of the sex that brings forth young; a woman. a. Belonging to this sex; feminine.
Fina'le s. The end of a piece of music; close.
Rationa'le s. A series of reasons, statement of principles.
Pale a. Wan, white of look; pallid; dim. s. A pointed stake; a fence; an enclosure; a broad perpendicular stripe on a heraldic shield. v.i. To turn pale, lose colour. v.t. To make pale; to enclose with pales.
Impale' v.t. To transfix; to put to death thus; to enclose with palings; to unite coats-of-arms vertically on the shield.
Râle s. A rattling sound in breathing.
Gen'érale s. The morning drum-call to infantry.
Ora'le s. A veil worn by the Pope.
Chorale' s. A plain tune or chant sung in unison.
Morale' s. Mental condition, especially of troops.
Pastora'le s. A musical composition on a rural theme; a rustic dance.
Sale s. Act of selling; thing or amount sold; an auction; a disposal of goods at reduced prices.
Whole'sale s. Sale of goods in large quantities or to retailers. a. Dealing thus; done in the mass; indiscriminate. adv. In large quantities, on a large scale.
Tale s. A story, narrative; number reckoned.
Stale a. Not new; vapid; trite; worn-out. s. Urine (of horses, etc.). v.i. To make water (of beasts).
Vale s. A valley.
Va'le int. Farewell.
In'tervale s. A low tract between hills or along a river.
Wale s. A weal.
Gun'wale s. The upper edge of a ship's side.
Able a. Having ability, or sufficient power, skill, etc., to do something; efficient.
Club'bable a. Sociable, fitted for membership of a club.
Bri'bable a. (*Bribe*).

Ascri'bable a. (*Ascribe*).
Subscrib'able a. That may be subscribed.
Describ'able a. (*Describe*).
Indescrib'able a. Incapable of being described.
Circum-scri'bable a. (*Circumscribe*).
Inscrib'able a. That may be inscribed.
Climb'able a. (*Climb*).
Prob'able a. More likely than not; credible.
Improb'able a. Not likely to be true or to happen.
Absorb'able a. (*Absorb*).
Impertur'bable a. Not readily disturbed or excited; calm.
Cable s. A stout rope; a chain for an anchor; a submarine telegraph wire, or a message by it. v.i. and t. To send by cable.
Pla'cable a. Appeasable; capable of being pacified; forgiving.
Implac'able a. Not to be appeased or pacified; inexorable.
Displac'able a. (*Displace*).
Pec'cable a. Liable to sin.
Impec'cable a. Not liable to sin; faultless.
Erad'icable a. That may be rooted out or destroyed.
Inerad'icable a. That cannot be eradicated.
Med'icable a. That may be healed or cured.
Pred'icable a. Capable of being affirmed of something. s. A general attribute or abstract notion.
Vin'dicable a. Capable of vindication.
Multiplic'able a. Multipliable.
Ap'plicable a. Suitable, fit; capable of being applied.
Inap'plicable a. Not applicable; irrelevant.
Ex'plicable a. Capable of explanation.
Inex'plicable a. Not to be explained or interpreted; unaccountable.
Am'icable a. Friendly, kind, obliging.
Commun'icable a. Capable of being imparted or transmitted.
Incommu'-nicable a. That cannot be communicated or shared.
Excommu'-nicable a. Liable or deserving to be excommunicated.
Des'picable a. Base, mean, contemptible.
Ex'tricable a. That may be extricated.
Inex'tricable a. Not to be disentangled or solved; inescapable.
Prac'ticable a. That may be effected or performed; feasible.
Imprac'ticable a. Not practicable; unmanageable; stubborn.
Mas'ticable a. That can be masticated.
Prognos'ticable a. That can be foreshadowed or presaged.
Vo'cable s. A word, especially considered phonologically.
Revoc'able a. Capable of being revoked or recalled.
Irrev'ocable a. Incapable of being revoked or recalled; unalterable.
Cas'cable s. Knob at end of a cannon.
Con'fiscable a. Confiscatable.
Ed'ucable a. Capable of being educated.
Man'ducable a. That can be chewed.
Lead'able a. That may be led.
Knead'able a. That may be kneaded.
Read'able a. Capable of being or fit to be read; worth reading; legible.
Persuad'able a. That may be persuaded.
Eva'dable a. (*Evade*).
Wad'able a. That may be waded.
Bid'dable a. Obedient, willing.
Decid'able a. Capable of being decided.
For'midable a. Terrible; powerful; exciting fear.
Void'able a. That may be annulled or voided.
Avoi'dable a. (*Avoid*).
Guid'able a. That may be guided.
Wield'able a. That may be wielded.
Yield'able a. That may be yielded.
Weld'able a. Capable of being welded.
Mould'able a. That may be moulded.
Demand'able a. (*Demand*).
Understand'-able a. That may be comprehended.
Ascen'dable a. (*Ascend*).
Defend'able a. (*Defend*).
Lend'able a. That may be lent.
Mend'able a. That may be mended.
Amen'dable a. (*Amend*).
Emen'dable a. (*Emend*).
Commend'able a. Worthy of commendation.
Recommend'-able a. Worthy of recommendation.
Depend'able a. That may be relied upon.
Find'able a. That may be found.
Fund'able a. That may be funded.
Compound'able a. Capable of being combined or compounded.
Decompound'-able a. (*Decompound*).
Wound'able (woond'-) a. That may be wounded.
Guard'able a. In a state to be guarded.
Reward'able a. Capable of being rewarded.
Ford'able a. That may be forded.
Laud'able a. Praiseworthy; healthful.
Delud'able a. (*Delude*).
Peace'able a. Free from war or disturbance pacific; calm.
Deface'able a. (*Deface*).
Efface'able a. That may be obliterated or cancelled.
Ineffac'eable a. Incapable of being effaced.
Replace'able a. That may be replaced.
Irreplace'able a. Having nothing to take its place.
Trace'able a. Capable of being traced.
No'ticeable a. That may be noticed; noteworthy.
Ser'viceable a. Able or willing to render service of use; durable.
Disser'viceable a. Harmful, injurious.
Bal'anceable a. (*Balance*).
Pronounce'able a. Capable of being pronounced.
Pierce'able a. That may be pierced.
Enforce'able a. (*Enforce*).
Divorce'able a. Capable of being divorced.
Agree'able a. Pleasant; suitable to, accordant.
Disagree'able a. Unpleasant; offensive; contrary.
Car'riageable a. Practicable for vehicles.
Mar'riageable a. Fit or of suitable age for marriage.
Dam'ageable a. Causing damage; susceptible of damage.
Man'ageable a. That can be managed; tractable.
Pledge'able a. That may be pledged.
Knowl'edgeable a. Sharp, intelligent.
Acknowl'-edgeable a. (*Acknowledge*).
Chan'geable a. Liable to change; variable; fickle.
Interchange'-able a. Admitting of exchange.
Exchange'able a. (*Exchange*).
Chal'lengeable a. (*Challenge*).
Charge'able a. (*Charge*).
Forge'able a. Capable of being forged.
Gauge'able a. That may be gauged or measured.
Sale'able a. Capable of being sold; finding a ready sale.
Mal'leable a. That may be rolled, beaten, or drawn out; pliant.
Immall'eable a. Not malleable.
Blame'able a. (*Blame*).
Name'able a. That may be named.
Per'meable a. Penetrable; capable of being permeated.

Imper'meable a. Not permitting passage, as of a fluid; impervious.
Shape'able a. Capable of being shaped.
Hire'able a. That may be hired.
Liv'eable a. Worth living; fit to live with or in.
Fable s. An apologue, story enforcing a precept; a fiction.
Af'fable a. Courteous, of easy manners.
Ineff'able a. Unspeakable; beyond expression.
Gable s. The pointed end or triangular part of the end of a house.
Prop'agable a. That may be propagated.
Refrag'able a. Refutable.
Irrefrag'able a. Unanswerable; undeniable.
Seg'regable a. Capable of being set apart.
Ob'ligable a. Acknowledging or complying with obligation.
Ir'rigable a. That may be irrigated.
Indefat'igable a. Unwearied; persevering.
Lit'igable a. Such as can be litigated.
Mit'igable a. Capable of being alleviated.
Immit'igable a. Incapable of being softened down.
Nav'igable a. That can be navigated.
Innav'igable a. Not navigable.
Lev'igable a. That may be pulverized.
Sing'able a. Capable of being sung.
Prolong'able a. That may be prolonged.
Inter'rogable a. Capable of being interrogated.
Sub'jugable a. That may be subjugated.
Impeach'able a. Deserving impeachment, capable of being impeached.
Preach'able a. That may be preached.
Teach'able a. That may be taught; capable of being taught; docile.
Reproach'able a. Deserving reproach.
Irreproach'able a. Blameless; entirely upright.
Approach'able a. (*Approach*).
Inapproach'able a. Not approachable; inaccessible.
Detach'able a. (*Detach*).
Attach'able a. (*Attach*).
Quench'able a. That may be extinguished.
Pinch'able a. (*Slang*) That may be pinched or stolen.
Search'able a. Capable of being investigated or examined.
Catch'able a. (*Catch*).
Match'able a. That can be matched or equalled.
Snatch'able a. That may be snatched.
Sketch'able a. That may be sketched.
Debauch'able a. (*Debauch*).
Touch'able a. That may be touched; tangible.
Avouch'able a. (*Avouch*).
Weigh'able (wā'-) a. That may be weighed.
Laugh'able a. That excites laughter; ridiculous, comical.
Plough'able a. Arable.
Wash'able a. Capable of being washed.
Fish'able a. Capable of being fished.
Pub'lishable a. That may be published.
Abol'ishable a. (*Abolish*).
Polish'able a. Capable of being polished.
Accom'plishable a. (*Accomplish*).
Dimin'ishable a. (*Diminish*).
Tar'nishable a. (*Tarnish*).
Pun'ishable a. Liable to or worthy of punishment.
Per'ishable a. Liable to decay, subject to destruction. s. Anything liable to deterioration or decay.
Imper'ishable a. Not liable to perish; everlasting.
Disting'uishable a. Able to be distinguished.
Indisting'uishable a. Incapable of being distinguished.
Exting'uishable a. Capable of being extinguished.
Inexting'uishable a. Not capable of being extinguished; unquenchable.
Van'quishable a. Capable of being defeated.
Breath'able a. (*Breathe*).
Bequeath'able a. (*Bequeath*).
Tith'able a. That may be tithed.
Appre'ciable a. (*Appreciate*).
Inappre'ciable a. So small as almost to escape notice; insignificant.
Justi'ciable a. Liable to be tried in a court of justice.
Enun'ciable a. That may be enunciated.
So'ciable a. Adapted for or fond of society; companionable, friendly. s. An open carriage with facing seats; tricycle with two seats side by side.
Amer'ciable a. Liable to amercement.
Reme'diable a. That may be remedied.
Irreme'diable a. Not to be remedied; irreparable.
Repu'diable a. Admitting of repudiation.
Rarefi'able a. Capable of being rarefied.
Liquefi'able a. That may be liquefied.
Specifi'able a. That may be specified.
Acidifi'able a. Capable of being converted into acid.
Solidifi'able a. That may be solidified.
Modifi'able a. That may be modified.
Alkalifi'able a. Capable of being converted into an alkali.
Salifi'able a. Capable of being formed into or of forming a salt.
Qualifi'able a. That may be qualified.
Mollifi'able a. That may be mollified.
Verifi'able a. Capable of being verified.
Vitrifi'able a. Capable of being vitrified.
Gasifi'able a. That may be turned into gas.
Falsifi'able a. That may be falsified.
Rectifi'able a. That may be rectified.
Quantifi'able a. That may be quantified.
Identifi'able a. Capable of being identified.
Notifi'able a. That must be reported.
Certifi'able a. (*Certify*).
Fortifi'able a. That may be fortified.
Justifi'able a. That can be justified.
Satisfi'able a. Capable of being satisfied.
Cler'giable a. Admitting to benefit of clergy.
Li'able a. Answerable; bound.
Reli'able a. Trustworthy.
Affil'iable a. Capable of being affiliated or assigned to.
Pli'able a. Easy to be bent; readily yielding; flexible.
Multipli'able a. Capable of being multiplied.
Compli'able a. Compliant; inclined to comply.
A'miable a. Charming; worthy of being loved.
Deni'able a. That may be denied.
Undeni'able a. Incontestable, indisputable.
Ex'piable a. Capable of being expiated.
Inex'piable a. That cannot be atoned for; implacable.
Var'iable a. Changeable; fickle; inconstant. s. That which is variable.
Invar'iable a. Not liable to change; uniform; fixed.
Fri'able a. Readily crumbled.
Tri'able a. Able to be tried; that may be tested.
Sa'tiable a. That may be satiated or glutted.
Insa'tiable a. That cannot be satisfied; greedy.
Pit'iable a. Deserving or worthy of pity or compassion; lamentable.
Propi'tiable a. That may be appeased or reconciled.
Nego'tiable a. That may be negotiated, or transferred by endorsement, etc.

Du'tiable a. Liable to imposition of a duty or customs.
Vi'able a. Born alive and capable of living.
Lev'iable a. That may be levied.
En'viable a. Exciting or capable of exciting envy.
Speak'able a. Capable of being spoken.
Break'able a. (*Break*).
Shak'able a. That may be shaken.
Mistak'able a. Liable to be mistaken or misunderstood.
Awak'able a. (*Awake*).
Attack'able a. (*Attack*).
Mock'able a. That may be mocked.
Bank'able a. Capable of being banked.
Think'able a. Capable of being imagined.
Unthink'able a. Incapable of being conceived; highly improbable.
Drink'able a. Fit for drinking. s. A beverage.
Shrink'able a. Capable of being shrunk.
Sink'able a. That may be sunk.
Smok'able a. Fit or adapted to be smoked.
Remark'able a. Noticeable; extraordinary; eminent.
Work'able a. Capable of being worked; worth working; practicable.
Scal'able a. Capable of being scaled.
Conceal'able a. (*Conceal*).
Congeal'able a. (*Congeal*).
Heal'able a. That may be healed.
Repeal'able a. Capable of being or liable to be repealed.
Irrepeal'able a. Not repealable; irrevocable.
Appeal'able a. That may be appealed against or appealed to.
Exhal'able a. That may be exhaled or can exhale.
Bail'able a. (*Bail*).
Mail'able a. That may be posted.
Sail'able a. Navigable.
Assail'able a. (*Assail*).
Avail'able a. Able to effect the object or to be used with advantage; valid; profitable.
Reconcil'able a. Capable of being reconciled.
Irreconcil'able a. That cannot be reconciled; totally inconsistent or incompatible.
Assim'ilable a. (*Assimilate*).
Foil'able a. That may be frustrated or defeated.
Call'able a. (*Call*).
Smell'able a. That may be smelt.
Compel'lable a. (*Compel*).
Inappell'able a. Not to be appealed against; final.
Expel'lable a. That may be expelled.
Tell'able a. That may be told.
Till'able a. That may be tilled.
Distil'lable a. Able to be distilled.
Control'lable a. (*Control*).
Incontroll'able a. Not controllable.
Toll'able a. Capable of being levied for toll.
Syl'lable s. Word or part of word capable of separate articulation. v.t. To syllabize.
Decasyl'lable s. A word or line of ten syllables.
Hendeca-syl'lable s. A line or verse of eleven syllables.
Disyl'lable s. A word of two syllables.
Quadri-syl'lable s. A word of four syllables.
Trisyl'lable s. A word of three syllables.
Multisyl'lable s. A polysyllable.
Monosyl'lable s. A word of one syllable.
Octosyl'lable s. A word of eight syllables.
Polysyl'lable s. A word of many syllables.
Vi'olable a. That may be violated.
Invi'olable a. Not to be violated, profaned, or injured; sacred.

Consol'able a. (*Console*).
Inconsol'able a. Not to be consoled.
Cal'culable a. (*Calculate*).
Incal'culable a. Not to be estimated in advance; not to be reckoned upon; uncertain.
Inoc'ulable a. That can be inoculated.
Cir'culable a. (*Circulate*).
Coag'ulable a. Able to coagulate or be coagulated.
Reg'ulable a. Capable of being regulated.
Rul'able a. Conformable to rule; capable of being ruled.
Fram'able a. That may be framed.
Tam'able a. Capable of being tamed.
Redeem'able a. That may be redeemed.
Irredeem'able a. Not redeemable; not subject to be paid at its nominal value.
Claim'able a. (*Claim*).
Reclaim'able a. Capable of being reclaimed.
Irreclaim'able a. Incapable of being reclaimed; inveterate.
Es'timable a. Capable or worthy of being esteemed.
Ines'timable a. That cannot be estimated; priceless.
Inflam'mable a. Readily set on fire or excited; easily inflamed.
Swim'mable a. That may be traversed by swimming.
Fath'omable a. Capable of being sounded or comprehended.
Ran'somable a. That may be ransomed.
Cus'tomable a. Customary; liable to duty.
Farm'able a. Capable of being cultivated or farmed.
Affirm'able a. (*Affirm*).
Confirm'able a. (*Confirm*).
Reform'able a. That may be reformed or amended.
Irreform'able a. Incapable of being reformed.
Conform'able a. Having the same form; corresponding; compliant.
Perform'able a. Practicable.
Transform'able a. That may be transformed.
Resum'able a. That may be resumed.
Presum'able a. Such as may be taken for granted.
Consum'able a. (*Consume*).
Inconsu'mable a. Not consumable; not intended for consumption.
Clean'able a. (*Clean*).
Loan'able a. That may be lent.
Ena'ble v.t. To make able, authorize, empower.
Re-enable' v.t. To enable again.
A'lienable a. That may be alienated.
Ina'lienable a. Incapable of being alienated or transferred.
Ame'nable a. Liable to be brought to account; submissive; responsible.
O'penable a. That may be opened.
Disena'ble v.t. To deprive of power, disqualify.
Ten'able a. Capable of being held or maintained.
Conven'able a. That may be assembled.
Preg'nable a. Capable of being taken by force.
Impreg'nable a. That cannot be taken; invincible.
Sign'able (sīn'-) a. Capable of being signed.
Design'able a. Capable of being marked out.
Consign'able a. (*Consign*).
Assign'able a. (*Assign*).
Impugn'able a. That may be impugned or gainsaid.
Expugn'able a. Capable of being conquered.
Inexpug'nable a. Incapable of being forcibly subdued; impregnable.
Ordain'able a. That may be ordained.
Gain'able a. That may be gained.
Explain'able a. That may be explained.
Drain'able a. Capable of being drained.

Train'able a. Capable of being trained.
Restrain'able a. Capable of being restrained.
Distrain'able a. Able to be distrained upon.
Constrain'able a. (*Constrain*).
Obtain'able a. That can be obtained.
Maintain'able a. That may be maintained.
Contain'able a. (*Contain*).
Ascertain'able a. (*Ascertain*).
Stain'able a. Capable of receiving stain.
Sustain'able a. Capable of being sustained.
Attain'able a. (*Attain*).
Medic'inable a. Having the power of healing.
Fin'able a. Liable to be fined.
Defin'able a. That may be defined.
Indefin'able a. That cannot be defined.
Confin'able a. (*Confine*).
Imag'inable a. That can be imagined.
Invag'inable a. Capable of being invaginated.
Declin'able a. That may be declined.
Indeclin'able a. Having no inflexions.
Incli'nable a. Having a tendency; inclined.
Dis'ciplinable a. Capable of being or liable to be disciplined.
Indis'ciplinable a. Not to be subjected to discipline.
Lam'inable a. Capable of being split into laminæ.
Contam'inable a. (*Contaminate*).
Exam'inable a. That may be examined.
Elim'inable a. Capable or worthy of being eliminated.
Abom'inable a. Detestable, hateful; unclean.
Ger'minable a. Capable of germinating.
Term'inable a. Capable of being terminated; having a given period.
Deter'minable a. That may be determined.
Predeterm'inable a. (*Predetermine*).
Indeterm'inable a. Impossible to be determined, ascertained, or fixed.
Inter'minable a. Unending; boundless; wearisomely protracted.
Conter'minable a. Capable of being regarded as conterminate.
Illu'minable a. That may be illuminated.
Dam'nable a. Worthy of damnation; odious.
Condem'nable a. (*Condemn*).
Tan'nable a. That may be tanned.
Run'nable a. Applied to a stag fit for the chase.
Par'donable a. Admitting of pardon; venial.
Con'scionable a. Governed by conscience; reasonable, just.
Uncon'scionable a. Unreasonable; inordinate; vast.
Fash'ionable a. According to the prevailing mode; genteel; stylish; observant of fashion.
Compan'ionable a. Sociable.
Pen'sionable a. In position to be granted a pension.
Impas'sionable a. Capable of being stirred to passion.
Impres'sionable a. Easily impressed; susceptible of impression.
Ac'tionable a. Furnishing ground for an action at law.
Objec'tionable a. Liable to objections; unpleasant.
Sanc'tionable a. That may be sanctioned.
Men'tionable a. That may be mentioned.
Excep'tionable a. Liable to exception; objectionable.
Unexcep'tionable a. Free from objection; excellent.
Propor'tionable a. Capable of being proportioned or made proportional.
Dispropor'tionable a. (*Disproportion*).
Ques'tionable a. That may be questioned; suspicious.
Com'monable a. Held in common; that may be pastured on.
Reas'onable a. Influenced by or agreeable to reason; fair; within due limits.
Trea'sonable a. Involving treason.
Sea'sonable a. Suitable to the time or occasion; opportune.
Unsea'sonable a. Untimely; ill-timed.
Poi'sonable a. That may be poisoned.
Per'sonable a. Of good appearance; handsome.
Aton'able a. Able to be expiated.
Gov'ernable a. That may be governed or controlled.
Burn'able a. (*Burn*, v.).
Return'able a. Capable of being or required to be returned.
Tun'able a. Capable of being tuned; harmonious.
Ca'pable a. Able, fitted, or qualified for; competent.
Inca'pable a. Not capable; not having sufficient power; unqualified.
Inesca'pable a. Unavoidable; inevitable.
Pal'pable a. Perceptible by the touch; evident, plain.
Impal'pable a. Not perceptible by touch; intangible.
Cul'pable a. Guilty, criminal, immoral.
Excul'pable a. Capable or deserving of exculpation.
Jump'able a. That may be jumped over.
Devel'opable a. (*Develop*).
Tapp'able a. That may be tapped.
Extirp'able a. That may be extirpated.
Grasp'able a. That may be grasped or understood.
Dup'able a. Gullible, easily to be deceived.
Ar'able a. Fit for tillage or ploughing.
Bear'able a. Capable of being borne, tolerable.
Hear'able a. That may be heard.
Wear'able a. That may be worn.
Par'able a. An allegorical fable with a moral.
Rep'arable a. Capable of being repaired or put right.
Irrep'arable a. Not capable of being repaired; irremediable.
Sep'arable a. Capable of being separated.
Insep'arable a. Not to be parted; indivisible; indissoluble.
Com'parable a. Worthy or capable of being compared.
Incom'parable a. Admitting of no comparison; matchless.
Spar'able s. Small nail used by shoemakers.
Ex'ecrable a. Deserving execration; detestable.
Quad'rable a. Capable of quadrature or of being squared.
Remem'berable a. Worth remembering.
Lac'erable a. That may be lacerated.
Ul'cerable a. Capable of becoming ulcerated.
Consid'erable a. Worthy of consideration, possessing consequence; of importance, size, or value.
Inconsid'erable a. Unimportant; insignificant.
Ren'derable a. Capable of being rendered.
Pon'derable a. Capable of being weighed; having weight.
Impon'derable a. Without weight.
Steer'able a. That may be steered.
Ref'erable a. Assignable; imputable.
Pref'erable a. More desirable.
Of'ferable a. That may be offered.
Suf'ferable a. That may be tolerated, endured, or permitted.
Insuf'ferable a. Not to be endured; intolerable.
Infer'able a. That may be inferred; deducible.
Transfer'able a. Capable of being transferred.
Deci'pherable a. (*Decipher*).
Indeci'pherable a. Illegible.

Smoth'erable a. That may be smothered.

Tol'erable a. Endurable; fairly good.

Intol'erable a. Unendurable; not to be borne.

Nu'merable a. Capable of being numbered.

Innu'merable a. Countless; extremely numerous.

Gen'erable a. Capable of being generated.

Ven'erable a. Worthy of veneration; deserving respect from age.

Vul'nerable a. Liable to injury; assailable.

Invul'nerable a. Incapable of receiving harm; unassailable.

Tem'perable a. Capable of being tempered.

Su'perable a. Conquerable.

Insu'perable a. That cannot be overcome or surmounted.

Mis'erable a. Very unhappy; wretched; causing misery; worthless, abject.

Al'terable a. (*Alter*).

Inal'terable a. Unalterable.

En'terable a. That may be entered or entered upon.

Ut'terable a. That may be uttered.

Con'querable a. (*Conquer*).

Sev'erable a. That may be severed.

Insev'erable a. That cannot be severed.

Deliv'erable a. (*Deliver*).

Pul'verable a. Capable of being pulverized.

Recov'erable a. Capable of being recovered or restored.

Irrecov'erable a. That cannot be recovered; irreparable.

Discov'erable a. (*Discover*).

Indiscov'erable a. Not discoverable.

An'swerable a. Liable to be called to account; capable of being answered.

In'tegrable a. Capable of being integrated.

Repair'able a. Reparable.

Ad'mirable a. Worthy of admiration, very satisfactory.

Respir'able a. Capable of being or fit to be breathed.

Irres'pirable a. Unfit for respiration.

Transpir'able a. Capable of being transpired.

Inspir'able a. That may be inspired.

Perspir'able a. Capable of being perspired.

Desir'able a. Worthy of desire, agreeable.

Undesir'able a. Unpleasant; unconvenient. s. Such a person; a good-for-nothing.

Acquir'able a. (*Acquire*).

Ador'able a. (*Adore*).

Imper'forable a. That cannot be perforated.

Deplor'able a. Lamentable, grievous, pitiable.

Mem'orable a. Worthy to be remembered; remarkable.

Commem'-orable a. (*Commemorate*).

Va'porable a. Capable of being vaporized.

Evap'orable a. That may be evaporated.

Stor'able a. That may be stored.

Restor'able a. Capable of being restored.

Inex'orable a. Not to be moved by entreaty; unyielding.

Confer'rable a. (*Confer*).

Inerr'able a. Infallible; free from error.

Aver'rable a. (*Aver*).

Demur'rable a. Liable to exception or objection.

Pen'etrable a. Capable of being penetrated; susceptible of moral impression.

Impen'etrable a. That cannot be penetrated; impervious; hard.

Seques'trable a. Capable of being sequestered.

Reg'istrable a. Capable of being or liable to be registered.

Admin'istrable a. (*Administer*).

Demon'strable a. Capable of certain proof.

Indemon'-strable a. Not susceptible of proof.

Cur'able a. That may be cured.

Secur'able a. That may be secured.

Incur'able a. That cannot be cured; irre mediable. s. A person disease beyond cure.

Procur'able a. That may be procured.

Dur'able a. Lasting; permanent; firm.

Endur'able a. Able to be borne.

Per'durable a. Very lasting; permanent.

Col'ourable a. Able to be coloured; speciou plausible.

Hon'ourable a. Worthy of honour; illustrious honest, fair.

Dishon'ourable a. Bringing or deserving dishonour shameful.

Fa'vourable a. kind; propitious; auspicious.

Pleas'urable a. Pleasing, giving pleasure.

Meas'urable a. That may be measured or est mated.

Immeas'urable a. Immense; incapable of bein measured.

Cen'surable a. Worthy of censure.

Men'surable a. Measurable; having rhythm.

Immen'surable a. Not to be measured.

Commen'-surable a. Having a common measure.

Incommen'-surable a. Having no common measure c standard of comparison.

Insur'able a. Capable of being insured c insured against.

Sat'urable a. That may be saturated.

Conjec'turable a. That may be conjectured.

Trit'urable a. That may be ground down fine c masticated.

Rup'turable a. That may be ruptured.

Tor'turable a. That may be tortured.

Sable s. A small Arctic carnivore allied t the weasel; its fur; a brush mad of this; black (especially i heraldry); a mourning garmen a. Black; gloomy. v.t. To rende black or dismal.

Leas'able a. That may be leased or held b lease.

Appeas'able a. (*Appease*).

Inappeas'able a. Not to be appeased.

Increas'able a. That may be increased.

Pur'chasable a. Capable of being bought; corrup

Eras'able a. That may be erased or oblite ated.

Prais'able a. That may be praised.

Apprais'able a. (*Appraise*).

Exercis'able a. (*Exercise*).

Disa'ble v.t. To render incapable; to impai

Seis'able a. Capable of being put in possessio of.

Demis'able a. Bequeathable.

Surmis'able a. That may be conjectured.

Compri'sable a. (*Comprise*).

Chastis'able a. (*Chastise*).

Advi'sable a. (*Advise*).

Devis'able a. Capable of being devised or be queathed.

Revis'able a. Capable of being or liable to b revised.

Excis'able a. Liable or subject to excise.

Cleans'able a. (*Cleanse*).

Li'censable a. That may be licensed.

Condens'able a. (*Condense*).

Incondens'able a. Incapable of condensation.

Dispens'able a. Capable of being dispensed c dispensed with.

Indispen'sable a. That cannot be dispensed with necessary.

Depos'able a. (*Depose*).

Impos'able a. That may be imposed.

Decompos'able a. (*Decompose*).

Oppos'able a. That may be opposed or resisted

Suppos'able a. That may be supposed.

Superpos'able a. That may be superposed.

Dispos'able a. Subject to disposal ; liable to be made use of.
Transpos'able a. Capable of being transposed.
Lap'sable a. That can be lapsed.
Trav'ersable a. Capable of being traversed.
Convers'able a. Disposed to converse, sociable.
Pass'able a. Capable of being passed, navigated etc. ; tolerable, mediocre.
Impass'able a. That cannot be passed.
Com'passable a. Capable of being accomplished.
Surpass'able a. Capable of being surpassed.
Wit'nessable a. Capable of being witnessed.
Redress'able a. Capable of being redressed.
Assess'able a. (*Assess*).
Guess'able a. That may be guessed.
Kiss'able a. Able or desirable to be kissed.
Us'able (ūz'-) a. That may be used.
Abu'sable a. (*Abuse*).
Accu'sable a. (*Accuse*).
Excus'able a. Admitting of excuse or justification ; pardonable.
Inexcu'sable a. Unjustifiable ; indefensible.
Analy'sable a. (*Analyse*).
Table s. Piece of furniture for putting things on ; a meal ; a schedule. v.t. To lay on or form into a table.
Abat'able a. (*Abate*).
Debat'able a. Capable of being discussed ; open to question.
Confiscat'able a. (*Confiscate*).
Eat'able a. Fit to be eaten. s. Anything fit for food.
Comeat'able a. Easy to get at, accessible.
Repeat'able a. That may be repeated.
Treat'able a. That may be treated.
Hat'able a. Worthy of hatred ; detestable.
Pal'atable a. Agreeable to the taste ; savoury.
Relat'able a. That may be related.
Inflat'able a. That may be inflated.
Dilat'able a. Capable of being expanded ; elastic.
Translat'able a. Capable of being translated.
Boat'able a. Navigable.
Float'able a. Able to float ; navigable.
Rat'able a. Capable of being set at a certain value ; liable to taxation.
Get-at'-able a. That can be reached, attained, or influenced.
Stat'able a. That may be stated.
Doubt'able a. Questionable.
Redoubt'able a. Formidable ; valiant.
Ac'table a. Capable of being performed on the stage ; practically possible.
Tract'able a. Docile ; manageable.
Retract'able a. That may be retracted.
Intrac'table a. Not easily governed ; unmanageable.
Attrac'table a. (*Attract*).
Extract'able a. That may be extracted.
Reject'able a. That may be rejected.
Delect'able a. Delightful, highly pleasing.
Collect'able a. (*Collect*).
Respect'able a. Worthy of respect, reputable ; moderately good.
Suspect'able a. Capable of being suspected.
Expect'able a. That may be expected.
Detect'able a. (*Detect*).
Contradict'able a. (*Contradict*).
Predict'able a. That may be foretold.
Indict'able (-dīt'-) a. Liable to be indicted ; forming a ground of indictment.
Inflict'able a. (*Inflict*).
Ineluc'table a. Not to be escaped or avoided.
Veg'etable s. A plant, especially a culinary one. a. Pertaining to or like plants.
Pock'etable a. That can be put in a pocket.
Mar'ketable a. Saleable.
Retable' s. Small shelf at the back of an altar.
Inter'pretable a. That may be interpreted.
Cov'etable a. (*Covet*).
Shift'able a. That may be shifted or moved.
Right'able a. That may be righted.
Hab'itable a. Fit to be dwelt in.
Inhab'itable a. Fit for habitation.
Du'bitable a. Liable to be doubted.
Indu'bitable a. Unquestionable, not admitting of doubt.
Ci'table a. Capable of being cited.
Excit'able a. Capable of being excited or roused into activity.
Inexcit'able a. Not susceptible of excitement.
Extradi'table a. Subject to or rendering one liable to extradition.
Cred'itable a. Bringing credit or honour ; estimable.
Discred'itable a. Disgraceful, disreputable.
Hered'itable a. That may be inherited.
For'feitable a. Liable to be forfeited.
Prof'itable a. Bringing profit ; lucrative ; advantageous.
Cog'itable a. Capable of being thought about or over.
Incog'itable a. Not thinkable.
Im'itable a. That may be imitated.
Lim'itable a. That may be limited.
Illim'itable a. Boundless ; vast ; infinite.
Inim'itable a. That cannot be imitated ; unsurpassed.
Indom'itable a. Untameable ; indefatigable.
Exploit'able a. That may be exploited.
Decap'itable a. Capable of being beheaded.
Precip'itable a. Capable of being precipitated.
Hos'pitable a. Kind to strangers or guests.
Inhos'pitable a. Not inclined to hospitality desolate.
Char'itable a. Full of, pertaining to, or supported by charity ; liberal, kind.
Her'itable a. Capable of being inherited.
Inherit'able a. Capable of inheriting or being inherited.
Ver'itable a. Genuine ; actual ; true.
Ir'ritable a. Easily provoked ; fretful.
Vis'itable a. Liable to be visited or inspected.
Eq'uitable a. Distributing equal justice ; impartial ; upright.
Ineq'uitable a. Not equitable ; not just.
Suit'able a. Fitting ; proper ; becoming.
Inev'itable a. Incapable of being avoided prevented, or resisted.
Assaul'table a. (*Assault*).
Insult'able a. Capable of being insulted.
Consult'able a. (*Consult*).
Plant'able a. That may be planted or settled.
Transplant'able a. That may be transplanted.
Ten'antable a. Fit for occupation.
Grant'able a. Capable of being granted.
War'rantable a. Justifiable ; old enough for the chase (of deer).
Lam'entable a. To be lamented ; doleful ; deplorable.
Ferment'able a. That may be fermented.
Rent'able a. That may be rented or leased.
Present'able a. Fit to be presented, introduced, or seen.
Represent'able a. That may be represented.
Pa'tentable a. That may be patented.
Prevent'able a. That may be prevented.
Print'able a. Capable or allowable of being printed.
Count'able a. That may be numbered ; accountable.
Accoun'table a. Liable to be called on for an account ; responsible.
Mount'able a. That may be mounted.
Surmoun'table a. Capable of being surmounted.
Insurmount'able a. Incapable of being overcome.
Her'iotable a. Subject to heriot.

Not'able a. Worthy of note; remarkable. s. A person of distinction.
Denot'able a. Capable of being denoted.
Shoot'able a. That may be shot, shot at, or shot over.
Po'table a. Drinkable.
Quot'able a. That may be quoted; suitable for quotation.
Vot'able a. That may be voted or voted on.
Adap'table a. (*Adapt*).
Inadap'table a. Not adaptable.
Accep'table a. (*Accept*).
Tempt'able a. That may be tempted.
Attemp'table a. (*Attempt*).
Assert'able a. (*Assert*).
Com'fortable a. At ease; free from want, trouble, pain, etc.; quietly happy.
Port'able a. Capable of being carried or easily conveyed.
Import'able a. That may be imported.
Compor'table a. Suitable, consistent.
Support'able a. That may be supported or endured.
Insupport'able a. Insufferable; intolerable.
Transport'able a. That may be transported; involving transportation.
Export'able a. That may be exported.
Sort'able a. That may be sorted.
Stable s. A building for horses or beasts. v.t. and i. To put or dwell in this. a. Firm; steady; constant.
Tast'able a. That may be tasted.
Test'able a. That may be tested; capable of being bequeathed or given in evidence.
Detest'able a. Worthy of detestation; execrable.
Contest'able a. (*Contest*).
Incontest'able a. Undeniable; indisputable.
Twist'able a. That may be twisted.
Con'stable s. An officer of the peace; a policeman.
Adjust'able a. (*Adjust*).
Trust'able a. Fit to be trusted.
Get'table a. That can be got or obtained.
Regrett'able a. Admitting of or deserving regret.
Admit'table a. (*Admit*).
Commit'table a. (*Commit*).
Rebutt'able a. That may be rebutted.
Contrib'utable a. Liable to be contributed; subject to contribution.
Distrib'utable a. Capable of being distributed.
Attrib'utable a. (*Attribute*).
Prosecut'able a. That may be prosecuted.
Exec'utable a. That may be executed.
Ref'utable a. That may be refuted; capable of disproof.
Irref'utable a. That cannot be refuted; unanswerable.
Confut'able a. That may be confuted.
Mut'able a. Liable to change; fickle; variable.
Immut'able a. Unchangeable, invariable.
Commut'able a. That may be exchanged, or converted into money.
Incommu'table a. That cannot be commuted, changed, or exchanged.
Permut'able a. Interchangeable.
Transmut'able a. That may be transmuted.
Rep'utable a. Creditable; respectable.
Disrep'utable a. Low, shameful, discreditable.
Imput'able a. That may be imputed to a person; chargeable.
Comput'able a. (*Compute*).
Incompu'table a. Incapable of being computed.
Dis'putable a. Capable of being disputed.
Indis'putable a. Not admitting of question.
Inscrut'able a. Hidden; that cannot be understood.
Stat'utable a. In conformity to or made by statute.
Res'cuable a. Capable of being rescued.
Subdu'able a. That may be subdued.
Ar'guable a. Capable of being argued, open to argument.
Val'uable a. Having great value, precious. s. A thing of value.
Inval'uable a. Very precious; priceless.
Contin'uable a. Capable of being continued.
Eq'uable a. Uniform; proportionate; even.
Une'quable a. Changeful; fitful.
Su'able a. Capable of being sued.
Pursu'able a. Capable of being or fit to be pursued.
Iss'uable a. That may be issued.
Perpet'uable a. That may be made perpetual.
Cleav'able a. Capable of being split asunder.
Weav'able a. That may be woven.
Sav'able a. Capable of being saved.
Achiev'able a. (*Achieve*).
Believ'able a. Credible.
Reliev'able a. Capable of being relieved.
Retriev'able a. Capable of being retrieved or made good.
Irretriev'able a. Not retrievable; irreparable.
Deceiv'able a. Capable of being deceived.
Receiv'able a. That may be received.
Conceiv'able a. Capable of being conceived in the mind.
Inconceiv'able a. Incapable of being conceived by the mind; unthinkable, incredible.
Perceiv'able a. Capable of being perceived.
Imperceiv'able a. Imperceptible.
Forgiv'able a. That may be forgiven.
Deriv'able a. That may be derived; deducible.
Depriv'able a. (*Deprive*).
Contri'vable a. (*Contrive*).
Reviv'able a. That may be revived.
Salv'able a. That may be saved.
Solv'able a. That may be solved.
Irresol'vable a. Incapable of being resolved.
Insol'vable a. That cannot be solved or explained.
Dissolv'able a. Capable of being dissolved or broken up.
Lov'able a. Worthy of love; amiable.
Mov'able a. Capable of being moved. s. Anything that can be moved.
Remov'able a. Able or liable to be moved.
Irremov'able a. Not removable; permanent.
Unmov'able a. Firm, stedfast, unalterable.
Prov'able a. That may be proved.
Reprov'able a. Deserving reproof.
Improv'able a. Susceptible of improvement; capable of being used to advantage.
Approv'able a. (*Approve*).
Disprov'able a. Capable of being disproved.
Observ'able a. That may be observed; remarkable.
Preserv'able a. Capable of being preserved.
View'able a. That may be viewed.
Renew'able a. That may be renewed.
Screw'able a. That may be screwed.
Allow'able a. (*Allow*).
Disallow'able a. (*Disallow*).
Swal'lowable a. Capable of being swallowed.
Know'able a. That may be known.
Grow'able a. That can be grown.
Avow'able a. (*Avow*).
Tax'able a. That may be taxed.
Fix'able a. That may be fixed.
Mix'able a. That may be mixed.
Pay'able a. Capable of being paid; justly due.
Repay'able a. That may be repaid.
Prepay'able a. That must be paid in advance.
Impay'able a. Priceless; beyond description.
Defray'able a. (*Defray*).
Convey'able a. (*Convey*).
Survey'able (-vā'-) a. Capable of being surveyed.

Enjoy'able a. Capable of being enjoyed.
Employ'able a. Capable of being employed or used.
Buy'able a. (*Buy*).
Squeez'able a. Capable of being squeezed.
Criticiz'able a. That may be or is worthy of being criticized.
Oxidiz'able a. That may be oxidized.
Realiz'able a. Capable of being realized.
Generaliz'able a. That may be generalized.
Mobiliz'able a. That may be mobilized.
Fertili'zable a. That may be fertilized.
Utiliz'able a. That may be turned to account.
Civili'zable a. (*Civilize*).
Crystalli'zable a. (*Crystallize*).
Vitrioliz'able a. That may be vitriolized.
Organi'zable a. Capable of being organized.
Cogn'izable a. Capable of being known or made the subject of judicial investigation.
Recogniz'able a. Capable of being recognized.
Incog'nizable a. Not capable of being apprehended.
Polari'zable a. Capable of being polarized.
Vaporiz'able a. (*Vaporize*).
Siz'able a. Of considerable or reasonable size.
Volatiz'able a. (*Volatize*).
Quiz'zable a. That may be quizzed.
Babble v.i. To prattle like a child, to talk idly.
Dabble v.t. To keep on dabbing, to sprinkle. v.i. To play about in water; to do anything superficially.
Bedabble' v.t. To sprinkle, splash.
Gabble v.i. To talk noisily or rapidly; to jabber, chatter. s. Loud or rapid empty talk; cackle.
Rabble s. A tumultuous crowd; the vulgar; a rake used in puddling metal.
Scrabble v.i. To scrape, paw with the hands; to scrawl. s. Act of scrabbling; a scramble.
Drabble v.t. To draggle, bemire.
Grabble v.i. To grope about, to grovel.
Prabble s. A squabble. v.i. To chatter.
Squabble v.i. To wrangle, contend noisily or pettily. s. A petty quarrel.
Wabble v.i. and s. (*Wobble*).
Pebble s. A small roundish stone; rock-crystal.
Dibble s. A pointed tool for making holes in the ground for seed. v.t. and i. To plant or make holes with a dibble.
Kibble s. A strong bucket for raising ore at a mine.
Nibble v.t. and i. To bite little by little; to bite cautiously at; to cavil. s. A little bite.
Cribble s. A coarse sieve.
Scribble v.t. and i. To write carelessly or hastily; to card (wool) roughly.
Dribble v.i. To fall in drops, to slaver, trickle. v.t. To throw down or let fall in drops; to take a football on by a succession of slight kicks.
Fribble v.i. To trifle, act frivolously. a. Trifling, silly. s. A silly fellow, a coxcomb.
Quibble s. An evasion, cavil; a pun. v.i. To prevaricate, evade by artifice.
Cobble v.t. To mend roughly, to botch; to pave with cobbles. s. A roundish stone or lump of coal.
Gobble v.t. To swallow hastily or in large pieces. v.i. To swallow food noisily; to make the sound of a turkey.
Hobble v.i. To walk lamely, move unevenly. s. A halting gait; a shackle; a perplexity.
Nobble v.t. (*Slang*) To catch, get hold of, win over by underhand means.
Wobble v.i. To move unsteadily, stagger; to vacillate. s. A swerve, wobbling movement.
Bubble s. A vesicle of liquid filled with air or gas; a cavity in glass, ice, etc.; a fraudulent scheme, anything unreal. v.t. To rise in bubbles, to make a sound like bubbling water.
Hubble-bubble s. A hookah; an uproar, babel.
Nubble s. A nub, small lump.
Rubble s. Fragments of stone, etc., used in masonry.
Stubble s. Stumps of corn-stalks left after reaping; bristly hair.
Feeble a. Weak; debilitated; deficient in vigour, etc.
Enfeeble' v.t. To make weak or feeble.
Treble a. Triple; soprano. s. A soprano voice or singer. v.t. and i. To make or become threefold.
-ible suff. Able.
Bible s. The Christian scriptures.
Fen'cible s. A soldier enlisted for home service only.
Vin'cible a. Conquerable.
Invin'cible a. Not to be conquered.
Convinc'ible a. Capable of convicting or refutation.
Unconvin'cible a. Incapable of being convinced.
Coer'cible a. Capable of coercion; deserving to be coerced.
For'cible a. Strong, mighty; cogent, efficacious; done by force.
Iras'cible a. Prone to anger; irritable.
Vitres'cible a. Capable of being vitrified.
Putres'cible a. Liable to become putrid.
Fermentes'cible a. Able to cause or capable of fermentation.
Mis'cible a. That may be mixed with.
Immis'cible a. Incapable of being mixed.
Cognos'cible a. Capable of being known; liable to judicial cognizance.
Incognos'cible a. Beyond cognition.
Tradu'cible a. That may be traduced.
Addu'cible a. (*Adduce*).
Educ'ible a. That may be elicited; deducible.
Deduc'ible a. (*Deduce*).
Redu'cible a. Capable of being reduced; convertible.
Irredu'cible a. Not to be reduced or lessened.
Seduc'ible a. Capable of being seduced.
Condu'cible a. Able to further or promote an end.
Produ'cible a. Capable of being produced.
Cru'cible s. A chemist's melting-pot.
Ad'dible a. That may be added.
Ed'ible a. Eatable, fit for eating. s. Anything fit for food.
Ined'ible a. Not eatable.
Cred'ible a. Worthy of belief or credit.
Incred'ible a. Impossible to be believed; not to be credited.
Man'dible s. The under jaw in vertebrates, and the pair in birds, insects, etc.
Descend'ible a. That may be passed down or transmitted.
Extend'ible a. Capable of being extended.
Ven'dible a. Saleable.
Corrod'ible a. That may be corroded.
Au'dible a. That may be heard.
Inau'dible a. Not audible; that cannot be heard.
Leg'ible a. Easy to be read; apparent.
Illeg'ible a. Not readable.
El'igible a. Fit to be chosen; desirable.
Inel'igible a. Not capable of being elected.
Neg'ligible a. Not to be regarded; of no importance.

Intel'ligible a. Capable of being understood.
Dir'igible a. That may be directed or steered. s. An airship as distinct from an aeroplane.
Cor'rigible a. Deserving punishment; capable of being corrected.
Incor'rigible a. Incapable of being amended or improved; irreclaimable. s. One in this state.
Ex'igible a. That may be exacted.
Fran'gible a. That may be easily broken.
Refrang'ible a. Capable of being refracted.
Irrefrang'ible a. Inviolable; not susceptible of refraction.
Infrang'ible a. That cannot be broken, or violated.
Tan'gible a. Perceptible by touch; capable of realization.
Intan'gible a. Impalpable; not to be grasped by the mind; unfounded.
Ting'ible a. That may be tinged.
Fun'gible a. That can be replaced by another. s. A thing that can be replaced by an equivalent.
Indel'ible a. Not to be effaced, lost, or forgotten.
Fal'lible a. Liable to error or to be mistaken.
Infal'lible a. Exempt from liability to error or failure.
Gull'ible a. Easily duped.
Expon'ible a. Capable of or requiring explanation.
Discern'ible a. Capable of being discerned; visible, evident.
Indiscern'ible a. Not distinguishable or visible.
Foi'ble s. A moral weakness, a frailty.
Ter'rible a. Causing terror; frightful, shocking.
Hor'rible a. Exciting horror; hideous; awful.
Thur'ible s. Kind of censer for incense.
Feas'ible a. That may be done; practicable.
Defea'sible a. That may be annulled or forfeited.
Indefeas'ible a. Not to be defeated; incapable of being made void.
Infeas'ible a. Not practicable.
Persuas'ible a. Capable of being persuaded.
Ris'ible a. Exciting laughter; inclined to laugh; ludicrous.
Vis'ible a. Perceptible by the eye; conspicuous; not concealed.
Divis'ible a. Capable of being divided, especially without remainder.
Indivis'ible a. Not divisible; not exactly divisible. s. Anything not divisible.
Invis'ible a. That cannot be seen; imperceptible.
Expans'ible a. Capable of being expanded.
Inexpans'ible a. Incapable of being expanded.
Defens'ible a. That may be vindicated, maintained, or justified.
Indefen'sible a. Incapable of being defended.
Prehen'sible a. Admitting of being seized.
Reprehen'sible a. Culpable, consurable.
Comprehen'sible a. That may be comprehended; intelligible.
Incomprehen'sible a. Incapable of being understood; inconceivable.
Apprehen'sible a. (*Apprehend*).
Inapprehen'sible a. Not apprehensible; unintelligible.
Suspens'ible a. That may be suspended.
Sens'ible a. Perceptible by the senses or the mind; easily affected; reasonable; intelligent.
Insen'sible a. Not perceived or perceptible by the senses; inappreciable; unconscious; heedless; callous.
Tens'ible a. Capable of being extended.
Disten'sible a. Capable of being distended.

Ostens'ible a. Put forth for show; apparent, not real.
Extens'ible a. Capable of being extended.
Responsi'ble a. Liable, answerable, accountable; involving responsibility; trustworthy.
Irrespon'sible a. Not responsible or reliable; not to be trusted.
Collap'sible a. Liable to collapse; made so as to collapse for easy packing.
Submers'ible a. Capable of being submerged. s. A submarine.
Revers'ible a. That may be reversed.
Irrevers'ible a. Not reversible; not to be annulled.
Introvers'ible a. Capable of introversion.
Pas'sible a. Susceptible of feeling or suffering.
Impass'ible a. Incapable of suffering or passion; unfeeling.
Acces'sible a. Approachable, attainable; capable of being reached.
Inaccess'ible a. Not accessible; not affable.
Depress'ible a. (*Depress*).
Repress'ible a. Capable of being repressed.
Irrepress'ible a. Not to be repressed.
Impress'ible a. Capable of being impressed; susceptible.
Compress'ible a. Capable of being compressed.
Incompress'ible a. Not compressible.
Suppress'ible a. That may be suppressed.
Insuppress'ible a. That cannot be suppressed.
Express'ible a. Capable of being expressed.
Inexpress'ible a. Not capable of being expressed or described; unspeakable.
Admis'sible a. Qualified for holding office, etc.; allowable as evidence.
Inadmis'sible a. That cannot be admitted or allowed.
Remiss'ible a. That may be remitted.
Irremis'sible a. Unpardonable.
Omiss'ible a. That may be omitted.
Permis'sible a. Allowable.
Transmis'sible a. That may be transmitted.
Intrans-mis'sible a. Not capable of being transmitted.
Pos'sible a. Liable to happen; that may exist or be done; likely.
Impos'sible a. Not possible, impracticable.
Compos'sible a. Capable of coexisting.
Discuss'ible a. Capable of being discussed.
Plau'sible a. Apparently right; superficially pleasing; specious.
Fus'ible a. Capable of being fused.
Diffu'sible a. Capable of being diffused.
Infus'ible a. Incapable of being fused.
Protru'sible a. Capable of protrusion.
Compat'ible a. Consistent, not incongruous, suitable.
Incompat'ible a. Not consistent with; irreconcilably different.
Contrac'tible a. Capable of being drawn together.
Indefect'ible a. Not subject to decay, failure, etc.
Affec'tible a. Capable of being affected or influenced.
Effec'tible a. Practicable, feasible.
Perfec'tible a. Capable of becoming or being made perfect.
Imperfec'tible a. Incapable of being perfected.
Reflect'ible a. That may be reflected.
Connect'ible a. (*Connect*).
Dissect'ible a. Capable of being dissected.
Conduct'ible a. Able to be led or conducted.
Destruct'ible a. Capable of being or liable to be destroyed.
Indestruc'tible a. Not capable of being destroyed or decomposed.
Ignit'ible a. Capable of being ignited.
Decep'tible a. Liable to be deceived.
Recep'tible a. Admitting reception.

Percept'ible a. Capable of being perceived.
Impercep'tible a. Not perceptible; not readily apprehended; impalpable.
Suscep'tible a. Impressible; sensitive; easily influenced.
Insuscep'tible a. Not capable of being affected.
Prescrip'tible a. Depending on or derived from prescription.
Imprescrip'tible a. Not capable of being impaired by claims founded on prescription; not dependent on external authority.
Circum-scrip'tible a. Capable of being circumscribed.
Contemp'tible a. Worthy of contempt, despicable.
Discerp'tible a. Separable.
Indiscerp'tible a. Not to be destroyed by dissolution.
Excerp'tible a. That may be excerpted or extracted.
Corrupt'ible a. Liable to corruption.
Incorrup'tible a. Incapable of corruption, decay, or dissolution; inflexibly just; unbribable.
Impart'ible a. Not capable of partition.
Aver'tible a. (*Avert*).
Subvert'ible a. Capable of being subverted.
Revert'ible a. Capable of being reverted.
Divert'ible a. Capable of being diverted.
Invert'ible a. That may be inverted.
Convert'ible a. Capable of being converted, changed, or exchanged.
Inconver'tible a. Not capable of being changed into something else.
Controver'tible a. Capable of being controverted.
Incontro-ver'tible a. That cannot be controverted; indisputable.
Perver'tible a. Capable of being perverted.
Suggest'ible a. That may be suggested.
Digest'ible a. Capable of being digested; wholesome.
Indigest'ible a. Not easily digested; not to be received or patiently endured.
Comes'tible s. An eatable.
Resis'tible a. Capable of resisting or being resisted.
Irresist'ible a. Incapable of being resisted or successfully opposed.
Exist'ible a. That may exist.
Exhaust'ible a. Capable of being exhausted.
Inexhaust'ible a. That cannot be exhausted; unfailing.
Combus'tible a. Capable of taking fire, inflammable.
Incombus'tible a. That cannot be burned.
Flex'ible a. Easily bent; pliant, manageable.
Reflex'ible a. Reflectible.
Inflex'ible a. Incapable of being bent; unyielding; firm of purpose.
Amble v.i. To move between a walk and a trot. s. This motion, especially of a horse.
Pre'amble s. An introductory statement.
Gamble v.i. To play for money. s. A speculation.
Shamble v.i. To shuffle along, walk awkwardly. s. An awkward gait.
Ramble v.i. To rove about without object; to talk incoherently; to straggle. s. A roaming excursion.
Bramble s. Blackberry bush.
Scramble v.i. To go on all-fours, to clamber; to push roughly, struggle. v.t. To mix up and cook. s. Act of scrambling or jostling; eager contest; a rough-and-tumble.
Wamble (wom-) v.i. To rumble, be affected with nausea. s. A heaving.
Tremble v.i. To shiver, quake, shake involuntarily. s. A tremor, shivering; fear.
Resemble' v.t. To be like.
Ensem'ble s. The whole; all the parts taken together.
Assem'ble v.t. and i. To meet, call, or gather together.
Reassemble' v.t. and i. To assemble again.
Dissem'ble v.i. To play the hypocrite. v.t. To mask, disguise, make a pretence of.
Thimble s. Finger-cap used in sewing.
Nimble a. Lithe and active; agile; prompt.
Wimble s. A boring-tool, gimlet. v.t. To bore with this.
Bumble s. A jack-in-office. v.i. To boom or buzz.
Scumble v.t. To cover (a painting) lightly with semi-opaque colours.
Fumble v.i. To grope about, to act uncertainly or clumsily.
Humble a. Lowly, submissive, unpretending. v.t. To abase, lower.
Jumble v.t. To mix confusedly together. s. A confused mass; disorder.
Mumble v.i. and t. To speak or utter indistinctly; to chew with the mouth closed. s. A mutter.
Rumble v.i. To make a low, heavy, continued sound; (*slang*) to comprehend, grasp. v.t. (*Slang*) to understand, get to the bottom of. s. A rumbling sound; back seat above the boot of a carriage.
Crumble v.t. and i. To break or part into small pieces; to pulverze, decay.
Grumble v.i. To complain, find fault; to growl. s. Act of grumbling; a complaint.
Tumble v.i. and t. To roll about, fall suddenly; to rumple, overturn. s. A fall, somersault.
Stumble v.i. To trip in walking; to light on. s. An act of stumbling.
Coble s. A square-sterned fishing-boat.
Noble a. Illustrious; of lofty lineage; magnanimous; stately. s. A peer; an old English gold coin.
Ig'noble a. Of low birth; not honourable; base, degraded.
Ennoble' v.t. To make noble, bestow a peerage on, dignify.
Garble v.t. To select such parts as are wanted; to corrupt, falsify by omissions.
Marble s. A calcareous compact stone; this sculptured or inscribed; small, hard ball used in games. a. Made of or like marble. v.t. To stain like marble.
Warble (worble) v.t. and i. To sing in a quavering way, to trill, carol. s. A quavering modulation of the voice; a song; a hard tumour on a horse's back.
Burble v.i. To gurgle, bubble, simmer.
Sol'uble a. Capable of being solved or dissolved.
Resol'uble a. Capable of being dissolved again.
Res'oluble a. Resolvable.
Insol'uble a. Incapable of being dissolved or solved; inexplicable.
Dissol'uble a. Dissolvable; capable of being broken up.
Indis'soluble a. Not to be dissolved or disintegrated; stable.
Vol'uble a. Talkative, garrulous; volubilate.
Double a. Twofold, two of a sort; of extra size, strength, etc.; deceitful. s. Twice as much, a sharp run; a duplicate. v.t. and i. To make or increase twofold; to fold in two; to sail round a cape; to run; to use wiles or trickery.

Redouble' v.t. To double again; augment greatly. v.i. To become greatly or repeatedly increased.
Rouble s. The Russian monetary unit (silver, nominally worth 2s. 1d.).
Trouble v.t. To agitate, disturb, give distress to; to molest, vex. s. That which annoys or disturbs; state of being troubled.
Chas'uble s. An ecclesiastical vestment.
Deba'cle s. Sudden breaking up of river ice; an overthrow, confusion.
Treacle s. A brown syrup from sugar.
Macle s. A twin crystal; a mascle.
Man'acle s. A handcuff. v.t. To secure with these, to fetter.
Bin'nacle s. The compass-box of a ship.
Pin'nacle s. A high, slender spire or turret; a rocky peak; a summit.
Bar'nacle s. A marine cirriped; a parasite, hanger-on.
Tab'ernacle s. A place of worship, especially the tent used as such by the ancient Jews.
Mir'acle s. A deviation from nature; a marvel; a mediæval religious drama.
Spir'acle s. A blow-hole (in whales), an air-passage in insects, etc.
Or'acle s. Revelation by a deity; place where or medium through which such revelation was given; a wise or authoritative person or utterance.
Cor'acle s. A light boat made of wicker-work covered with leather, etc.
Spec'tacle s. A show, sight, pageant.
Pen'tacle s. A five-pointed star-like figure.
Ten'tacle s. Feeler of an insect or animal.
Recep'tacle s. A container, holder, reservoir; vessel or place of deposit; apex of a flower-stalk.
Concep'tacle s. That in which anything is contained.
Ob'stacle s. An impediment, hindrance.
-icle suff. Denoting a diminutive.
Cu'bicle s. Portion of a bedroom partitioned off.
I'cicle s. A hanging point of ice.
Fas'cicle s. A small bundle; a close cluster of leaves, flowers, etc.; a separate division of a book issued in parts.
Rad'icle s. The rudimentary or embryonic root of a plant.
Appen'dicle s. A small appendage.
Cau'dicle s. Part of the stigma of orchids.
Ve'hicle s. A conveyance, carriage; a medium.
Cal'icle s. A small cup-shaped organ.
Sil'icle s. A seed-vessel shorter than a siliqua.
Pell'icle s. A thin skin or crust.
Vitel'licle s. A yolk-sac.
Fol'licle s. A small sac or gland; a seed-vessel.
Caul'icle s. A rudimentary stem; the leafy top of a Corinthian column.
Pan'icle s. A branching form of inflorescence.
San'icle s. Black snake-root, a small plant.
Admin'icle s. An aid; auxiliary evidence.
Chron'icle s. A history, record; pl., annals. v.t. To record, register.
Fu'nicle s. A funiculus.
Tu'nicle s. An ecclesiastical vestment.
Cur'ricle s. A two-wheeled chaise for two horses.
Cicat'ricle s. The germinating point in the yolk of an egg.
Ven'tricle s. A cavity of the body.
U'tricle s. An air-cell, sac-like cavity.
Au'ricle s. The external ear.
Ves'icle s. A small bladder, sac, blister, bubble, etc.
Ver'sicle s. A short verse, especially in divine service.
Os'sicle s. A small bone; an osselet; a calcareous substance in various animals.
Ret'icle s. A fine-lined network, especially across telescope-lens.
Can'ticle s. A pious song, a division of a poem.
Den'ticle s. A small tooth; a projecting point.
Convent'icle s. A secret meeting; a meeting-place of dissenters.
Mon'ticle s. A mound; a small volcanic cone.
Ar'ticle s. A particular commodity, a part of speech, a stipulation. v.t. To bind in apprenticeship.
Par'ticle s. A minute portion, an atom, jot; a word that is never inflected.
Tes'ticle s. One of two glands secreting seminal fluid in males.
Cu'ticle s. Outer skin, epidermis.
Clav'icle s. The collar-bone.
Ancle s. (*Ankle*).
Uncle s. Brother of one's parent; husband of one's aunt; (*slang*) a pawn-broker.
Car'buncle s. A precious stone; a hard inflamed tumour.
Peduncle' s. Stem supporting flower and fruit of a plant; a stalk-like process in certain animals.
Si'phuncle s. A suctorial tube in insects, etc.
Ho'muncle s. A dwarf, homunculus.
Car'uncle s. A small fleshy excrescence.
Fu'runcle s. A boil, a superficial tumour.
Bin'ocle s. A pair of field- or opera-glasses.
Mon'ocle s. A single eyeglass.
Socle s. A low, rectangular pedestal, plinth, or base.
Tu'bercle s. A small projection or tuber; small mass of morbid matter within the substance of an organ.
Circle s. A ring, round body, enclosure. v.t. To revolve round, enclose. v.i. To move circularly.
Sem'icircle s. A half circle.
Encir'cle v.t. To surround, to environ.
Mascle s. A perforated heraldic lozenge.
Muscle s. A fleshy, highly contractile fibrous organ; physical strength.
Cor'puscle s. A minute particle; a minute animal or protoplasmic cell.
Cycle s. An orbit in the heavens; a recurring circle of years; a bicycle or tricycle. v.i. To ride a bicycle, etc.; to recur or revolve in a cycle.
Bi'cycle s. A two-wheeled vehicle driven by pedals or a motor. v.i. To ride this.
Hem'icycle s. A semicircle; a semicircular space.
Ep'icycle s. A circle whose centre moves round in the circumference of a greater circle.
Tri'cycle s. A cycle with three wheels. v.i. To ride this.
Mul'ticycle s. A velocipede with four or more wheels.
Mon'ocycle s. A velocipede with a single wheel.
Cal'ycle s. A small calyx.
Beadle s. A petty officer.
Treadle s. A lever worked by the foot. v.i. To use this.
Ladle s. A large, deep spoon. v.t. To serve with this.

Cradle s. A rocking bed for infants; place where anything is nurtured; light framework. v.t. To lay in a cradle; to nurture.
Addle a. Barren, unfruitful.
Skedaddle' v.i. To run off precipitately. s. A hasty flight.
Fiddle-faddle s. Trifling talk, nonsense; a trifle.
Paddle v.i. To dabble, play about with water, wade barefooted; to use a paddle. v.t. To propel with a paddle. s. A short, broad-bladed oar; the blade of an oar, board of a waterwheel, foot of a turtle, etc.
Raddle v.t. To paint the face coarsely; to twist together. s. Red ochre; a hedge of interwoven branches; a stick used by hedgers.
Straddle v.i. To stand or walk with legs wide apart. v.t. To sit astride, to stride across. s. This act; a certain stake at poker and contract on the Stock Exchange.
Saddle s. Seat for a rider on an animal's back, bicycle, etc.; something resembling or used as such. v.t. To put a saddle on; to encumber.
Staddle s. A stack-stand; a small tree.
Waddle (wodl) v.i. To walk with a rolling gait like a duck. s. Such a gait.
Swaddle (swodl) v.t. To swathe in wraps, bind tight.
Twaddle s. Foolish talk; prattle. v.i. To talk sillily; to prate.
Heddle s. One of certain wires or cords in a loom.
Meddle v.i. To intervene officiously.
Intermeddle' v.i. To intrude officiously.
Peddle v.i. To fuss over trifles; to work as a pedlar. v.t. To sell goods from door to door, to hawk.
Reddle s. Ruddle.
Diddle v.t. (*Slang*) To cheat, swindle. v.i. To waste time, trifle.
Tarradiddle' s. A fib.
Fiddle s. A violin; a rack to prevent plates, etc., slipping off the table at sea. v.t. and i. To play on a fiddle; to trifle.
Kiddle s. A weir, etc., in a river for trapping fish.
Middle a. Equally distant from the extremes; mean; intervening. s. The middle point, central portion.
Piddle v.i. To act in a trifling way; to potter around.
Riddle s. A coarse sieve; an enigma. v.t. To sieve with a riddle; to perforate with shot, argument, etc. v.i. To speak enigmatically or ambiguously.
Griddle s. An iron plate for baking cakes on; a wire sieve or screen. v.t. To sieve with a griddle.
Twiddle v.t. and i. To play with the fingers, twirl. s. A twist, twirl.
Coddle v.t. To treat tenderly, pamper. s. One that does this—to himself or others.
Mol'lycoddle s. A milksop. v.t. To pamper.
Noddle s. (*Slang*) The head.
Toddle v.i. and t. To walk unsteadily or carelessly. s. A saunter, stroll; a toddling walk.
Buddle s. A vat in which ore is washed in mines.
Cuddle v.i.and t. To embrace, lie snugly together, hug. s. An embrace.
Fuddle v.i. To drink to excess. v.t. To intoxicate; to make stupid. s. State of being muddled, especially with drink.
Huddle v.i. To press together confusedly. v.t. To throw together promiscuously. s. A confused mass; disorder.
Muddle v.t. To confuse, bewilder; to make a mess of; to fuddle with drink. v.i. To act in a confused manner. s. A confused state; a mess; bewilderment.
Puddle s. A small muddy pool. v.t. To make muddy; to make watertight with clay; to convert cast to wrought iron.
Ruddle s. Red ochre for marking sheep. v.t. To colour with this.
Wheedle v.t. To coax, persuade by flattery.
Needle s. Small-eyed and pointed instrument used for sewing; the pointer of a compass.
Tweedle s. Sound of a stringed instrument.
Idle a. Lazy; sluggish; unemployed. v.i. and t. To spend time in inaction, to waste idly.
Bridle s. The head-reins of a horse; restraint. v.t. To put a bridle on, to curb, check.
Sidle v.i. To move sideways or to one side.
Candle s. A wick surrounded by tallow or wax.
Dandle v.t. To fondle, trifle with, dance up and down on the knee.
Handle s. That by which anything is held; means for effecting a purpose. v.t. To touch, manage; to discourse on.
Rehandle' v.t. To deal with a second time.
Mishandle' v.t. To ill-treat.
Kindle v.t. To set on fire; to excite to action. v.i. To take fire; to be roused; to bring forth young.
Rekindle' v.t. To kindle, inflame, or excite again.
Enkindle' v.t. To set on fire; to rouse to action.
Spindle s. The pin used in spinning; a small axis; a slender stalk. v.i. To grow spindle-shaped.
Brindle a. Tawny, streaked.
Dwindle v.i. To shrink, diminish. s. A shrinking, decline.
Swindle v.t. and i. To cheat, defraud. s. Act of swindling; a fraudulent trick or scheme; a deception.
Fondle v.t. To caress, treat fondly.
Bundle s. A package made up loosely, a roll. v.t. To tie in a bundle.
Trundle s. A little wheel, low vehicle on such, a truck. v.t. and i. To roll.
Bodle s. An old Scots copper coin of small value.
Boodle s. (*Slang*) Money, capital; the whole lot; bribery.
Caboodle' s. (*Slang*) The crowd, the lot.
Doodle s. A noodle, simpleton. v.t. To cheat, diddle.
Flap'doodle s. Nonsense; swank.
Noodle s. A fool, a simpleton.
Canoodle' v.i. (*Slang*) To bill and coo.
Poodle s. A small, long-haired dog.
Girdle s. A waist-belt; an iron plate for baking cakes on. v.t. To bind or adorn with a girdle, sash, etc.; to encircle.
Engirdle' v.t. To surround with a girdle; to encompass.

Curdle v.t. and i. To change into curds, to coagulate, congeal.
Hurdle s. A frame of interlaced sticks. v.t. To close or cover with hurdles.
Caudle s. A warm drink of spiced gruel and wine.
Dawdle v.i. To idle about, waste time. s. A dawdler; act of dawdling.
Abele' s. The white poplar.
-cele Combining suffix denoting a tumour.
Varicocele' (-sēl) s. Varicose enlargement of the veins of the spermatic cord.
Vesicocele' s. Hernia of the bladder.
Tracheocele' s. A tumour in the trachea.
Enceph'alocele s. Hernia of the brain.
Neph'rocele s. Hernia of the kidneys.
Glossocele' s. A morbid protrusion of the tongue.
Ste'atocele s. A fatty tumour of the scrotum.
Spermatocele' s. Morbid distension of the spermatic vessels.
Hep'atocele s. Hernia of the liver.
Cys'tocele s. Hernia through protrusion of the bladder.
De'le v.t. Direction to printers to delete marked matter.
Anele' v.t. To anoint with oil.
Cli'entele s. One's clients collectively; patients; customers; adherents.
Ste'le s. An upright pillar, usually inscribed for sepulchral purposes.
Baffle v.t. To elude, frustrate.
Snaffle s. A bridle having a hinged, curbless bit. v.t. (*Slang*) To filch.
Raffle s. A kind of lottery. v.t. and i. To dispose of by means of or to engage in this.
Waffle (wofl) s. A thin, hard kind of cake.
Yaffle s. The green woodpecker.
Whiffle v.i. To prevaricate, equivocate.
Piffle s. (*Slang*) Twaddle, nonsense. v.i. To behave in a trifling way.
Coffle s. A gang of slaves travelling to market.
Scuffle s. A confused fight, a rough-and-tumble. v.i. To struggle thus; to shuffle.
Shuffle v.t. To shove one way and the other; to move the feet by pushing them along; to change position of cards in a pack. v.i. To shift ground, move in a slovenly manner; to quibble. s. Act of shuffling, mixing, etc; prevarication.
Muffle v.t. To wrap up, conceal; to deaden the sound of. s. A vessel used in assaying; the naked portion round nose of ruminants and rodents; a large mitten, boxing-glove.
Snuffle v.i. To breathe noisily, speak through the nose; to snivel. v.t. To utter in a nasal or canting way. s. Act or sound of snuffling; cant.
Souffle s. A soft murmur detected in an organ by the stethoscope.
Sou'fflé (soo'flā) s. A light dish of white of egg, cream, etc.
Ruffle v.t. To disorder, disturb, agitate; to surprise; to make into a ruff. v.t. To play the bully; to swagger. s. A ruff, frill; state of agitation; a low beat of a drum.
Truffle s. A fleshy fungus used for seasoning.
Rifle v.t. To plunder, pillage; to furnish the interior of with spiral grooves. s. A hand fire-arm the inside of the barrel of which is spirally grooved.
Trifle s. A thing of slightest value; a sweet dish. v.i. To act, etc., with levity. v.t. To dissipate, waste.
Stifle v.t. and i. To smother, suppress. s. The joint of a horse's hind-leg; a horse's patella; a disease affecting either of these.
Purfle v.t. To embroider, decorate richly.
Eagle s. A large bird of prey; the Roman standard; a gold coin of the U.S.A. (about £2).
Beagle s. A small hunting-hound.
Por'beagle s. A voracious species of shark.
Espiè'gle a. Roguish, full of pranks.
Daggle v.t. To trail through the mud, to bemire.
Gaggle v.i. To cackle, make a noise like a goose.
Haggle v.i. To bargain insistently, chaffer. s. A wrangle over terms.
Draggle v.t. To drag along in mud; to bemire or soil thus. v.i. To straggle, lag behind.
Bedraggle' v.t. To soil in the mire.
Straggle v.i. To ramble, be dispersed, occur at intervals.
Waggle v.i. and t. To sway, wag quickly and frequently.
Giggle v.t. To laugh foolishly, to titter. s. A puerile laugh, a snigger.
Higgle v.i. To chaffer; to fuss over trifles.
Jiggle v.t. To jerk to and fro.
Niggle v.i. To trifle, worry over petty details.
Sniggle v.i. and t. To fish for or catch eels in a certain way.
Wriggle v.i. To move to and fro with writhing; to squirm. v.t. To put into a quick reciprocating motion. s. A wriggling motion.
Wiggle v.t. and i. To wriggle, squirm.
Boggle v.i. To stammer, start, hesitate.
Goggle v.i. To strain or roll the eyes. s. A strained rolling of the eyes; a squint. a. Prominent, staring.
Joggle v.t. and i. To shake slightly; to totter. s. A joint in masonry or woodwork.
Toggle s. A short wooden pin serving as a button, fastening, etc.
Guggle v.i. To gurgle.
Juggle v.i. and t. To play tricks by sleight-of-hand; to deceive, obtain, etc., by trickery. s. A trick, imposture.
Smuggle v.t. To import or export illegally; to convey clandestinely.
Snuggle v.t. and i. To lie or draw close to for warmth.
Struggle v.i. To strive, contend; to labour. s. A forcible or violent effort; a contest.
Paigle s. The cowslip, buttercup.
Inveigle' (-vēgl) v.t. To persuade, wheedle, or entrap into evil.
Angle s. A point where two lines meet. v.t. To confine in an angle. v.i. To fish with rod and line.
Bangle s. An Oriental bracelet.
Dangle v.i. To hang loosely; to follow officiously. v.t. To swing, to carry loosely suspended.
Fandangle' s. A gewgaw; a nonsensical idea.
Tri'angle s. A figure having three sides and angles.
Jangle v.i. To sound harshly or discordantly; to bicker. v.t. To cause to sound harshly. s. A discordant sound; contention.

Mangle v.t. To mutilate, hack; to smooth or polish linen, etc. s. A rolling press for smoothing linen.
Spangle s. A small glittering metallic ornament. v.t. To set or sprinkle with these.
Brangle s. A quarrel. v.i. To wrangle, dispute.
Quad'rangle s. A plane, four-sided figure; an inner square of a building.
Strangle v.t. To throttle, choke; to suppress.
Wrangle v.i. To dispute, argue, quarrel. s. An altercation, angry dispute.
Tangle s. A knot of things interwoven; an edible seaweed. v.t. To knot together confusedly; to entangle. v.i. To become intertwined.
Rec'tangle s. A four-sided figure having only right angles.
Entangle' v.t. To interweave so that separation is difficult; to confuse; to entrap.
Disentangle' v.t. To unravel, clear, extricate from perplexity, etc.
Sep'tangle s. Figure with seven sides and seven angles.
Wangle v.t. (*Slang*) To fabricate, manipulate, use in an unscrupulous way; to dodge.
Twangle v.i. and t. To twang.
Sex'angle s. A hexagon.
Ingle s. A fire on the hearth; a chimney-corner.
Cingle s. A belt, girth.
Sur'cingle s. A girth for a horse; a girdle.
Dingle s. A dell.
Shingle s. Loose pebbles or gravel; thin wooden slat for roofing. v.t. To roof with these.
Jingle v.i. and t. To sound with a metallic tinkling; to rhyme. s. Such a sound; a correspondence or repetition of sounds; doggerel.
Mingle v.t. To mix up together; to blend with. v.i. To be mixed, to join.
Commingle' v.i. To mix together, blend.
Intermingle' v.t. and i. To mingle together, intermix, be incorporated.
Cringle s. An iron ring for the bolt-rope of a sail; a withe for fastening a gate.
Tringle s. A curtain-rod, especially for a bed; a small square Doric ornament.
Single a. Not more than one; individual; unmarried; sincere. s. One run, game, opponent, etc. v.t. To select individually.
Tingle v.i. To feel a thrilling sensation. v.t. To make give a ringing sound.
Swingle s. The thrashing part of a flail; wooden implement for beating flax. v.t. To clean (flax) with this.
Bungle v.t. To botch, do clumsily. s. A clumsy performance.
Jungle s. Land covered with brushwood, reeds, and thick vegetation, especially in India.
Ogle v.t. and i. To look at amorously; to cast amorous glances.
Gargle v.t. To rinse the mouth and throat with antiseptic liquid. s. A liquid for this.
Burgle v.t. and i. To break in and rob.
Gurgle v.i. To make or flow with a bubbling, purling sound. s. This sound.
Bugle s. A hunting-horn or military trumpet. v.i. To sound this.
-ile suff. Capable of being, pertaining to, etc.
Bile s. The bitter fluid secreted by the liver; anger.
Hab'ile a. Handy, adroit.
La'bile a. Liable to chemical or other change.
Canta'bile a. In an easy, flowing style (of music).
Mo'bile a. Movable; easily moved; changeable.
Immo'bile a. Wanting motion, not moving easily; immovable.
Locomo'bile s. A locomotive for the roads. a. Able to change place.
Automo'bile s. A motor-car.
Stro'bile s. A multiple fruit, as the pine-cone.
Vol'ubile a. Volubilate.
Nu'bile a. Marriageable (especially of women, or of age).
Fac'ile a. Easy to be done; easy of access; flexible; pliant.
Grac'ile a. Slender, thin.
Im'becile s. A weak-minded, idiotic person. a. Half-witted, fatuous.
Dif'ficile a. Difficult to deal with; impractible.
Dom'icile s. A home, permanent residence. v.t. To establish in a fixed residence. v.i. To dwell.
Rec'oncile v.t. To make friendly again; to conciliate; to harmonize.
Do'cile a. Teachable, tractable; pliant.
Indo'cile a. Not capable of being taught.
Ædile' s. A magistrate in ancient Rome.
Croc'odile s. A large amphibious lizard-like reptile.
File s. A wire, case, or other device on or in which papers are kept in order; a list; set of periodicals; row of soldiers, etc., ranged one behind the other; instrument for rasping. v.t. To arrange in a file; to bring before a court by present papers; to rasp. v.i. To march one after another.
Defile' v.t. To make foul, pollute; to violate; to march off in a line. s. A narrow pass in which troops can march only in file.
Pro'file s. An outline, especially of the face seen sideways; contour. v.t. To draw in or shape to a profile.
Ag'ile a. Nimble, active.
Frag'ile a. Brittle; easily broken; delicate.
Nar'ghile (-lā) s. A hookah.
-phile suff. Denoting a friend or devotee of, loving.
Fran'cophile s. A lover or admirer of France and the French.
Bib'liophile s. A book-lover.
Gas'trophile s. A lover of his stomach or of good feeding; a glutton.
While s. Space of time. conj. During the time that; as long as. v.t. To pass (time) pleasantly.
Awhile' adv. For a short time.
Erewhile' adv. Formerly; some time ago.
Meanwhile' adv. In the time intervening. s. Intervening time.
Mile s. A measure of length, 1760 yards.
Sim'ile (-i-li) s. Word or phrase by which one thing is likened to another.
Facsim'ile s. An exact copy.
Cam'omile s. An odoriferous, medicinal herb.
Smile v.i. To show laughter, pleasure, joy, etc., by the features only; to appear propitious. v.t. To express by a smile, effect by smiling. s. Act of smiling; facial expression of mirth, joy, scorn, etc.
An'ile a. Feeble-minded, old-womanish.
Campani'le s. A bell-tower.
Se'nile a. Pertaining to or proceeding from old age.

Ju'venile a. Young; pertaining or suited to youth. s. A young person.
Pile s. A stake or beam driven into the ground as a support; a mass, heap; nap on cloth, hair; a galvanic battery. v.t. To heap, amass; to support with or drive piles into.
Compile' v.t. To gather and compose from various sources.
Ther'mopile s. A thermo-electric battery.
Spile s. A small peg or spigot; a stake.
Rile v.t. To make angry, annoy.
Fe'brile a. Pertaining to, indicating, or derived from fever.
Ster'ile a. Unfruitful; destitute of ideas, etc.
Pu'erile a. Trifling; childish.
Vir'ile a. Manly; masculine; procreative.
Scur'rile a. Scurrilous.
Sile v.t. To strain (of milk). s. A strainer.
Resile' v.i. To spring back; to resume its original shape.
Expan'sile a. Capable of expanding.
Ensile' v.t. To put (fodder) into a silo, ensilage.
Prehen'sile a. Adapted to seize or grasp; grasping.
Pen'sile a. Hanging; pendent; pendulous.
Extens'ile a. Capable of being stretched out or protruded.
Ses'sile a. Stalkless; attached by the base.
Scis'sile a. Capable of being cut.
Fis'sile a. Capable of being cleft in the direction of the grain.
Mis'sile a. Capable of being thrown, hurled, etc. s. A projectile, weapon.
Protru'sile a. Capable of protrusion.
Tile s. A broad thin brick used for roofing; (*slang*) a hat. v.t. To cover with tiles; to guard against intrusion.
Rep'licatile a. Capable of being folded back.
Flu'viatile a. Fluvial.
Vol'atile a. Lively; flight; readily diffusible.
Vi'bratile a. Able to vibrate.
Pul'satile a. Capable of being struck or beaten.
Ver'satile a. Readily turning; changeable; having many accomplishments.
Sax'atile a. Pertaining to or inhabiting rocks.
Sub'tile (*also* sŭtl) a. Thin, very fine; subtle.
Frac'tile a. Liable to cleave or break.
Trac'tile a. Capable of being drawn out.
Retract'ile a. Capable of being drawn back.
Contrac'tile a. Able to draw together or shrink; having power to shorten itself.
Protrac'tile a. Capable of extension.
Tac'tile a. Pertaining to or perceived by touch; capable of being touched.
Projec'tile s. A body projected through the air, especially from a fire-arm. a. Impelling or impelled forward; given by impulse.
Erect'ile a. Capable of being erected.
Sec'tile a. Capable of being sliced.
Insec'tile a. Of the nature of insects.
Fic'tile a. Moulded into form.
Duc'tile a. Capable of being drawn into threads; tractable, pliable, flexible.
Induc'tile a. Not ductile.
Produc'tile a. Extensible; ductile.
Mer'cantile a. Pertaining to trade or commerce.
In'fantile a. Pertaining to infants or infancy; childish.
Pan'tile s. A tile with a curved surface.
Gen'tile a. Heathen; not Jewish. s. One who is not a Jew; a pagan.
Quin'tile s. Aspect of planets when separated by 72°.
Mo'tile a. Having powers of self-motion.
Rep'tile s. A crawling animal; a snake; a grovelling person. a. Creeping; grovelling; servile.
Rup'tile a. Breaking open (of buds, etc.)
Quar'tile s. Aspect of planets when distant from each other 90°.
Fer'tile a. Fruitful; able to produce abundantly; plenteous.
Infer'tile a. Unproductive; barren.
Exser'tile a. Capable of standing out or projecting.
Tor'tile a. Twisted, wreathed.
Stile s. Set of steps over a fence, etc.; pin of a dial.
Turn'stile s. Revolving barrier that allows only one to enter at a time.
Hos'tile a. Pertaining to an enemy; antagonistic; repugnant.
Fu'tile a. Trifling, worthless; ineffectual; frivolous.
Inu'tile a. Useless.
Ru'tile s. A reddish-brown dioxide of titanium.
Sex'tile s. Aspect of two planets when separated by 60°.
Bissex'tile s. Leap year.
Tex'tile a. Pertaining to or suitable for weaving. s. A woven fabric.
Guile s. Craft, cunning, deceit.
Beguile' v.t. To impose upon, deceive.
Vile a. Sordid, despicable; morally base.
Revile' v.t. To vilify, abuse.
Ser'vile a. Befitting or pertaining to a slave; slavish, mean; cringing.
Wile s. A trick, stratagem. v.t. To entice.
Ax'ile a. Situated in an axis.
Ex'ile s. Banishment, a person banished. v.t. To banish, transport, drive away.
Flex'ile a. Flexible; supple.
Cackle s. The noise of a hen; idle chatter. v.i. To make the noise of a goose or hen; to gossip.
Hackle s. A fly for angling; a long, pointed feather; raw silk; light, flimsy substance; a comb for dressing flax. v.t. To comb flax or hemp; to hack, mangle.
Shackle s. A fetter, handcuff; anything hindering free action; a coupling link. v.t. To put in fetters, to confine; to join with a link.
Ram'shackle a. Falling to pieces.
Mackle s. A blur in printing.
Crackle v.i. To make short snapping noises. s. A rapid succession of such; a kind of glass, porcelain, etc., apparently covered with cracks.
Grackle s. Any bird allied to the starlings.
Tackle s. Apparatus; a ship's rigging. v.t. To seize, lay hold of, set to work on.
Deckle s. A frame used in paper-making.
Heckle v.t. To hackle, dress flax; to cross-question, put vexatious questions to.
Speckle s. A small speck or stain. v.t. To mark or variegate with such.
Freckle s. A brownish spot; a blemish. v.t. and i. To mark or become marked with these.
Fickle a. Liable to change; wavering; inconstant.
Mickle a. Much; great. s. A large amount.
Pickle s. A solution of salt and water; brine; vegetables, fish, etc., preserved in vinegar; state of worry; a troublesome child. v.t. To preserve in or season with pickle.

Brickle a. Fragile; troublesome.
Prickle s. A little prick; a small sharp projection. v.t. To prick slightly, to tingle.
Trickle v.i. To fall in drops. s. A small stream.
Strickle s. Instrument for levelling grain in a measure; straight-edge for whetting scythes.
Sickle s. A reaping-rhook.
Tickle v.t. To affect by touching lightly; to please, flatter. s. Act or sensation of tickling.
Stickle v.i. To contend pertinaciously for something.
Cockle s. A bivalve edible mollusc; darnel or some other weed; a crease, pucker. v.i. To pucker up. v.t. To curl, crease.
Hockle v.t. To hamstring.
Buckle s. A contrivance for fastening straps, etc. v.t. To fasten with this.
Par'buckle s. A purchase made by passing the two ends of a rope through a bight, used in hoisting or lowering bulky objects.
Huckle s. The hip, haunch.
Chuckle s. A short, suppressed laugh. v.i. To laugh thus; to exult quietly.
Muckle a. and s. (*Scot.*) Mickle.
Knuckle s. Joint of a finger; a beast's knee-joint. v.i. To yield. v.t. To strike with the knuckles.
Ruckle v.t. and i. To crease, wrinkle.
Bruckle a. Brittle, precarious.
Truckle v.i. To yield obsequiously, to cringe. s. A small wheel or castor.
Suckle v.t. To give suck to, nurse at the breast.
Hon'eysuckle s. The woodbine, a climbing fragrant plant.
Ankle s. The joint connecting foot and leg.
Rankle v.i. To fester; to continue to irritate.
Crankle v.t. To bend, twist. s. A bend or twist.
Inkle s. A broad linen tape.
Kinkle s. A slight twist.
Crinkle v.i. To bend in short turns, to wrinkle. v.t. To form with wrinkles. s. A winding, turn, wrinkle.
Sprinkle v.t. and i. To scatter in small drops. s. A small quantity scattered; a light shower; a sprinkler.
Wrinkle s. A small ridge, furrow, or crease; a tip, dodge. v.t. and i. To contract or fold into furrows.
Tinkle s. A succession of small bell-like sounds. v.i. and t. To make or cause to make such.
Winkle s. An edible sea-snail, periwinkle.
Per'iwinkle s. A trailing plant with blue or white flower; an edible, gastropod, marine mollusc.
Twinkle v.i. To sparkle, shine intermittently. s. A scintillation; a rapid, tremulous movement.
Sparkle v.i. To glitter, emit sparks; to be animated. s. A scintillation; brilliance.
Dalle s. A flat paving slab.
Salle s. A spacious hall, large room.
Belle s. A beautiful young woman.
Gabelle' s. A pre-Revolution French tax, especially on salt.
Nacelle' s. The basket of a balloon, framework below an airship.
Sarcelle' s. A variety of wild-duck.
Sardelle' s. A small fish allied to the sardine.
Villanelle' s. A short poem of intricate construction.
Fontanelle' s. Space between the bones of an infant's skull.
Crenelle' s. An opening in a battlemented parapet.
Quenelle' s. A savoury meat-or fish-cake.
Jargonelle' s. A variety of early pear.
Prunelle' s. A superior variety of prune.
Aquarelle' s. A kind of painting in thin colours.
Chanterelle' s. An edible fungus.
Pip'istrelle s. The common British bat.
Demoiselle' s. A damsel; the Numidian crane.
Mademoiselle' s. Title given to unmarried ladies Miss.
Fil'oselle s. Coarse floss silk.
Moselle' s. A white wine.
Bagatelle' s. A game played with balls and a cue; a trifle.
Immortelle' s. An unfading or everlasting flower; a wreath made of these.
Gazelle' s. A species of antelope.
Tenaille' s. (*Tenail*).
Braille s. Printing for the blind.
Grisaille' s. Monochrone painting in tones of grey.
Deshabille' s. Undress; being carelessly attired.
Dishabille' s. Deshabille.
Spadille' (-dil') s. Ace of spades in ombre and quadrille.
Réveille' (-vel'i) s. Morning signal for soldiers to rise.
Chenille' s. A tufted cord used in dress trimming.
Rille s. A narrow valley on the moon.
Quadrille' s. A square dance for sets of four couples; music for this; an old card-game.
Grille s. An open grating, lattice-work screen, etc.
Bastille' s. A state prison.
Pastille' s. A conical medicated or aromatic lozenge.
Ai'guille s. A slender peak of rock.
Vaude'ville (vōd'vil) s. A dramatic piece with light songs.
Cheville' s. A peg of a violin, etc.
Tulle s. Fine silk open-work.
Bole s. The stem of a tree; an unctuous clay containing iron.
Roc'ambole s. A species of garlic.
Car'ambole s. A cannon at billiards.
Hypob'ole s. A method of reasoning.
Hyper'bole s. Exaggeration.
Cole s. A plant of the cabbage family.
Car'acole s. A wheeling movement made by a horse. v.i. To make this movement.
Bore'cole s. A curled variety of cabbage.
Prat'incole s. A bird allied to the plovers.
Dole s. Lamentation; a cause of grief; a portion; alms; gratuity; unemployment pay. v.t. To distribute.
Gir'andole s. A branching chandelier or bracket for lights.
Condole' v.i. To grieve with another; to sympathize.
Ar'eole s. An areola.
Cre'ole s. A European born in the W. Indies or Spanish America.
Au'reole s. A gold disk round the head of a saint, etc., a nimbus.
Brac'teole s. A small bract.
Hole s. A hollow place in a solid; an aperture, crevice; a burrow; a mean hovel; a subterfuge. v.t. To make a hole in; to drive into a hole.
Dhole s. The Indian wild dog.

Bore'hole s. A recess made with a boring tool.
Bung'hole s. The aperture in which a bung fits.
But'tonhole s. A slit for a button; a nosegay. v.t. To detain in conversation.
Loop'hole s. A small opening for shooting through, etc.; a means of evasion.
Top-hole' a. (*Slang*) Excellent; ripping.
Thole s. A fulcrum for an oar. v.t. To endure, suffer.
Port'hole s. Aperture for light and air in a ship's side.
Whole a. Containing the total; complete, entire; sound, healthy. s. A complete thing, system, combination, etc.; entirety.
Blow'-hole s. An air-hole; a spiracle of a cetacean.
Heart'-whole a. Not in love; of good courage.
Spong'iole (spŭnj'-) s. The spongy extremity of a radicle.
Fo'liole s. One of the parts of a compound leaf.
Var'iole s. A pock-mark, small depression.
Or'iole s. A bird with bright yellow and black plumage.
Glor'iole s. A halo, nimbus.
Cap'riole s. A leap made by a horse without advancing.
Car'riole s. A small open carriage.
Pet'iole s. The foot-stalk of a leaf.
Os'tiole s. A small pore in fungi, sponges, etc.
Cajole' v.t. To delude by flattery.
Mole s. A dark, raised spot on the skin; a pier, breakwater; a small burrowing mammal.
Carmagnole' s. A song and dance of the French Revolution; one of the Revolutionaries.
Pole s. A long, tapering, rounded piece of wood; measure of 5½ yards or 30¼ square yards; either extremity of axis of earth or celestial sphere; the pole-star; one of the two points of a magnet or battery at which force is at maximum intensity; a native of Poland. v.t. To push with a pole.
Tad'pole s. Larva of a frog or toad.
Red'pole s. A variety of finch.
Catch'pole s. (*Catchpoll*).
Ran'tipole s. A harum-scarum person.
Bib'liopole s. A bookseller.
May'pole s. A decorated pole to dance round on May-day.
Rôle s. Part taken by an actor; any conspicuous performance or function.
Bar'carole s. A boat-song of Venetian gondoliers.
Rig'marole s. A long confused statement; nonsense.
Fum'arole s. A smoke-vent on a volcano.
Parole' s. Word of honour, promise; military countersign. v.t. To put or release on parole.
Fu'sarole s. A moulding on Doric and other capitals.
Az'arole s. The Neapolitan medlar.
Ban'derole s. A long narrow flag with forked ends.
Cas'serole s. A covered earthenware pot for cooking.
Sole s. Bottom of foot, shoe, etc.; a marine flat-fish. a. Single, individual; alone. v.t. To furnish (shoe, etc.) with a sole.
Gir'asole s. A variety of opal.
Cam'isole s. A petticoat-bodice.
Console' v.t. To cheer in distress, to soothe.
Con'sole s. A supporting bracket or corbel.
Turn'sole s. The heliotrope or other plant supposed to turn with the sun.
Ris'sole s. A fried ball of minced meat, etc.
Cit'ole s. A mediæval stringed instrument like the dulcimer.
Stole s. Narrow band worn on the shoulders by priests; a fur necklet. past. (*Steal*).
Dias'tole s. Period of relaxation of heart's muscle.
Pistole' s. An obsolete Spanish gold coin.
Sys'tole s. The contraction of the heart.
Vac'uole s. A minute cavity in an organ, etc.
Vole s. A mouse like rodent; winning all the tricks in a deal.
Ben'zole s. Benzene.
Maple s. A tree of the sycamore family; its wood.
Staple s. A mart; a chief commodity or constituent; raw material; small pointed metal loop. a. Chief; commercially established. v.t. To sort (wool) according to staple.
Steeple s. A tapering tower on a church, etc.; a spire.
Par'ticiple s. A word having the properties of both an adjective and a verb.
Man'ciple s. A steward, purveyor, especially to a college.
Prin'ciple s. A source or origin; a fundamental truth; right rule of conduct; maxim; motive.
Disci'ple s. A pupil, scholar, adherent; one of the first twelve followers of Christ.
Man'iple s. Part of the eucharistic vestment; a division of the ancient Roman legion.
Triple a. Threefold. v.t. To treble.
Mul'tiple a. Manifold; several times. s. Quantity containing another a certain number of times without remainder.
Equimul'tiple a. Multiplied by the same quantity. s. Any number multiplied by the same as another.
Ample a. Great in bulk, liberal, diffusive.
Trample v.t. To tread heavily under foot; to treat with insolence. s. Act or sound of trampling.
Sample s. A piece as specimen; an example. v.t. To test; to have an experience of.
Ensample' s. A pattern, model. v.t. To exemplify.
Exam'ple s. A copy, pattern; a precedent; a warning.
Temple s. A place of worship, sanctuary; flat part between forehead and ear.
Stemple s. A cross-bar in the shaft of a mine.
Dimple s. A small hollow in the cheek or other part. v.t. and i. To mark with or form dimples.
Pimple s. A small inflamed pustule; a blotch.
Rimple s. A wrinkle, fold. v.t. and i. To wrinkle or become puckered.
Simple a. Not complicated, complex, compound, or involved; artless, silly, sincere; mere. s. A medicinal herb; something not compounded.
Wimple s. A covering for the neck and shoulders, especially as worn by nuns. v.t. To fold or lay in plaits; to cover as with a veil.
Rumple v.t. To make uneven, crease, disorder. s. A crease.

Crumple v.t. To draw or press into wrinkles. v. To shrivel.
People s. A community, nation; persons in general, folk; one's near relations. v.t. To populate.
Repeople' v.t. To furnish afresh with inhabitants.
Dispeople' v.t. To depopulate.
Sin'ople s. Red ferruginous quartz; (*in heraldry*) green.
Apple s. A fruit.
Dapple s. A blotch, spot. v.t. To variegate with spots and streaks. a. Blotched, variegated.
Pine'-apple s. A tropical plant; its fruit.
Grapple v.t. To lay hold of, seize. v.i. To contend in close fight.
Thrapple s. Thropple.
Nipple s. Teat of a woman or female animal; something resembling this; a nozzle.
Ripple s. The dimpling of the surface of water; an undulation; a comb for cleaning flax. v.i. To become fretted or dimpled; to make a sound as of breaking ripples. v.t. To cover with small ripples; to clean flax from seeds, etc.
Cripple s. A lame person. v.t. To lame, disable.
Tipple v.t. and i. To drink alcoholic liquors repeatedly. s. Strong drink.
Stipple v.t. and i. To engrave by means of dots. s. This mode of engraving; work done thus.
Hopple v.t. To fetter by tying the feet together. s. A shackle.
Thropple s. The wind-pipe, gullet.
Topple v.i. To fall forward, tumble over. v.t. To overturn.
Stopple s. A bung, plug. v.t. To close with this.
Supple a. Flexible; yielding; fawning. v.t. and i. To make or become pliant, etc.
Purple s. Red mixed with blue; a purple robe; regal power. a. Of this colour; dyed with blood. v.t. To make purple.
Dec'uple a. Tenfold. v.t. and i, To increase tenfold.
Duple a. Double, twofold.
Couple s. A pair, brace; man and wife; a leash. v.t. and i. To join or come together; to unite.
Scruple s. A very small quantity; twenty grains; hesitation; doubt. v.i. To hesitate, doubt.
Quad'ruple a. Fourfold. v.t. and i. To multiply or be multiplied by four.
Oc'tuple a. Eightfold. v.t. To multiply by eight.
Cen'tuple a. Hundredfold. v.t. To multiply by a hundred.
Quin'tuple a. Multiplied by five. v.t. To make fivefold.
Sep'tuple a. Sevenfold. v.t. and i. To multiply by seven.
Sex'tuple a. Sixfold. v.t. and i. To multiply by six.
Carle s. (*Carl*).
Merle s. The blackbird.
Orle s. An heraldic bearing like a fillet.
Toasle s. (*Teasel*).
Fo'c'sle s. Forecastle.
Isle s. A small island.
Aisle s. The wings or side of a church.
Birsle v.t. (*Scot.*). To scorch, toast.
Tussle s. A struggle, contest. v. To scuffle.
Tousle v.t. To dishevel, rumple.
Subtle (sŭtl) a. Tenuous; sly, cunning, shrewd.
Beetle s. A coleopterous insect; a heavy mallet. v.i. To jut out, hang over.
Title s. A name, inscription; an appellation of honour or dignity; claim of or document proving a right. v.t. To name, call by a title.
Betitle' v.t. To entitle, dignify with a title.
Entitle' v.t. To give a title or right to; to style; to characterize.
Disentitle' v.t. To deprive of title or right to.
Mistitle' v.t. To call by a wrong title.
Cantle s. A fragment. v.t. To cut into pieces.
Scantle v.t. To partition. s. A small slate.
Mantle s. A cloak, covering; cone for incandescent gas-light. v.t. To cover, disguise. v.i. To cream; to show changes of hue.
Dismantle' v.t. To strip of adornments, appurtenances, dress, etc.; to break up.
Gentle a. Well-born; refined; meek, peaceable, placid; kindly; soothing. s. A person of good birth; a maggot used by anglers as bait.
Pintle s. A pin for a hinge, etc.
Gruntle s. (*Scot.*) A pig's snout.
Disgruntle' v.t. To disappoint, disconcert.
Footle v.i. (*Slang*) To potter about, trifle. s. Rubbish, twaddle.
Rootle v.i. To grub, root as a pig.
Tootle v.t. and i. To toot gently or continuously.
Dartle v.t. and i. To keep on shooting forth.
Startle v.t. To fright, surprise, shock.
Kirtle s. An upper garment; a petticoat.
Chortle v.t. and i. To chuckle loudly.
Hurtle v.i. To clash violently, meet in shock; to whirl. s. A crashing noise, a collision.
Turtle s. A sea-tortoise; the common wild dove.
Myrtle s. A fragrant evergreen shrub anciently sacred to Venus.
Castle s. A large fortified building; a piece in chess.
Fore'castle s. The forward part of a ship.
Nestle v.i. To lie close and snug; to settle oneself. v.t. To cuddle, cherish.
Pestle s. Implement for pounding in a mortar.
Trestle s. A supporting frame.
Wrestle v.i. To contend in grappling; to strive vehemently. s. A wrestling bout.
Ist'le s. Species of agave from Mexico.
Thistle s. A plant with prickly stems, leaves, and involucres.
Whistle v.i. To utter a clear shrill sound through the lips or some instrument; to sound shrilly. v.t. To utter or signal thus. s. Such a sound; instrument for producing it; (*slang*) the throat.
Mistle s. The missle-thrush.
Epistle' s. A written communication; a letter.
Bristle s. The stiff hair of swine, etc. v.t. To stand erect as bristles.
Gristle s. Cartilage, especially in meat.
Jostle v.t. and i. To push against, elbow; to hustle. s. A hustling, crowding.
Apostle' s. One sent to preach the Gospel.
Throstle s. The song-thrush; a machine for spinning.
Bustle v.i. To hurry about and be busy. s. Hurry, tumult; a pad worn by women at the back.

Hustle v.t. and i. To shake together in confusion; to jostle; to act energetically or pushfully. s. Hurry, hustling.
Justle v.t. To jostle.
Rustle v.i. To make a noise like that of dry leaves agitated. s. Such sound, a rustling.
Battle s. A fight between armed parties, a combat. v.i. To contend in fight.
Embattle' v.t. To arrange in order of battle, arm for battle; to furnish with battlements.
Cattle s. Domesticated bovine animals; (*slang*) horses, objectionable persons.
Rattle v.i. To make a sharp, rapidly repeated noise; to jabber, bustle. v.t. To cause to make such a noise; to scold; to annoy. s. A toy or instrument producing a clattering sound; such a sound; a jabberer.
Brattle s. A rattling noise, a scamper. v.i. To make such a noise or to scamper.
Prattle v.i. To talk childishly or idly. s. Trifling chatter.
Tattle v.i. To gossip, tell tales. s. Idle or trifling talk; gossip.
Wattle (wotl) s. A thin branch; a hurdle of these interlaced; rod supporting thatch; fleshy excrescence under throat of cock, etc.; the Australian acacia. v.t. To bind or interweave with twigs; to construct by plaiting.
Fettle v.t. To put in right order; to work with zeal. v.i. To be busy. s. Good condition.
Kettle s. A metal vessel with spout and handle for boiling water.
Mettle s. Quality of temperament, etc.; ardour; spirit.
Nettle s. A common stinging plant. v.t. To sting, provoke, irritate.
Settle v.t. To establish; to quiet; to determine; to adjust, pay; to colonize. v.i. To subside; to become fixed, calm, etc.; to adjust differences. s. A long high-backed bench.
Resettle' v.t. and i. To settle or install again.
Whittle v.t. To shave or slice with a knife; to thin down, pare away. s. A long knife.
Kittle v.i. To kitten.
Skittle s. One of the pins in ninepins.
Little a. Not big; of short duration; paltry; mean. s. A small quantity, space, time, etc. adv. In a small degree, etc.
Belittle' v.t. To make little, depreciate.
Spittle s. Ejected saliva.
Lick'spittle s. An abject flatterer.
Brittle a. Fragile, apt to break.
Tittle s. A particle, jot.
Bottle s. A glass receptacle for liquors. v.t. To put into bottles.
Blue'bottle s. A fly with a large bluish belly.
Dottle s. Plug of tobacco left in a pipe after smoking.
Mottle v.t. To variegate, dapple. s. A blotch, spot.
Pottle s. A tankard; measure of four pints; a punnet.
Throttle s. The windpipe, gullet. v.t. To choke, strangle.
Cuttle s. A marine molluscan Cephalopod; an octopus, squid.
Scuttle s. A shallow basket; household vessel for coal; hatch or lid for this in a wall, roof, deck, etc.; a short run, quick pace. v.t. To sink by making holes in (a ship). v.i. To hurry, bustle.
Guttle v.t. and i. To eat voraciously, to guzzle.
Shuttle s. Boat-shaped carrier of thread in weaving- and sewing-machines, etc.
-ule suff. Having a diminutive force.
Lob'ule s. A small lobe.
Glob'ule s. A little globe; a globe-shaped particle.
Bar'bule s. A hooked filament from the barb of a feather.
Tu'bule s. A little tube, small pipe.
-cule suff. Expressing diminutiveness.
Mac'ule s. A spot, stain; a macula.
Sac'cule s. A small sac, a cyst.
Floc'cule s. A small or loose tuft.
Mo'lecule s. A particle into which all matter can be divided.
Cu'bicule s. A cubicle.
Fas'cicule s. (*Fascicle*).
Rid'icule s. Derision, banter; sarcasm. v.t. To laugh at, deride, mock.
Caul'icule s. (*Caulicle*).
Ver'micule s. A minute worm.
Spic'ule s. A minute needle-shaped part; a small spica.
Cicat'ricule s. A cicatricle.
Poet'icule s. A poetaster.
Ret'icule s. A small lady's hand-bag.
Mon'ticule s. A monticle, volcanic cone.
Animal'cule s. A very minute animal.
Mon'ocule s. A monoculus.
Bas'cule s. An apparatus worked by weights at one end.
Flos'cule s. A floret.
Majus'cule s. A capital letter.
Minus'cule a. Small, miniature. s. A small letter; anything very small.
Opus'cule s. A minor literary or musical composition.
Corpus'cule s. A corpuscle.
Nu'cule s. A small nut-like seed.
Sched'ule (shed'-) s. An annexed list, inventory, or document.
Quer'quedule s. A pin-tail duck.
Gland'ule s. A small gland.
Mod'ule s. Size of a part taken as a unit of proportion for the whole.
Nod'ule s. A small node, lump, or tumour.
Trag'ule s. The chevrotain.
Lig'ule s. A ligula.
Vir'gule s. A twig, small rod.
Thu'le s. The northernmost piece of land known to the ancients.
Pil'ule s. A small pill or pellet.
Cell'ule s. A little cell.
Pet'iolule s. A small petiole.
Mule s. Offspring of a male ass and a mare; any hybrid animal; an obstinate person; a machine for cotton-spinning.
Rac'emule s. A small raceme.
Gem'mule s. A small bud or gemma.
Gran'ule s. A particle, a small grain.
Gal'linule s. The moor-hen.
Spi'nule s. A diminutive spine.
Pin'nule s. A smaller division of a pinnate leaf; a small fin, barb of a feather, etc.
Zon'ule s. A small zone or girdle.
Lu'nule s. Crescent at base of finger-nail; a lunula.
Joule s. The unit of electrical energy.

Pule v.i. To whine plaintively, to whimper.
Stip'ule s. A small leaf-like appendage.
Cup'ule s. A little cup, as that of the acorn; a cup-like organ.
Rule s. Instrument for drawing straight lines; a guiding principle or law; authority, government. v.t. To mark with straight lines; to govern. v.i. To have power, exercise authority.
Fer'ule s. A cane or rod for punishment. v.t. To punish with this.
Spher'ule s. A small sphere.
Glom'erule s. A compact flower-cluster forming a head.
Spor'ule s. A small or secondary spore.
Fer'rule s. Ring round end of a cane, tool-handle, etc., to prevent splitting.
Overrule' v.t. To influence or control; to disallow, rule against.
Misrule' s. Disorder, confusion; bad government.
Cu'rule a. Applied to the chair and office of the highest ancient Roman magistrate.
Cap'sule s. The seed vessel of a plant; an envelope for drugs.
Spat'ule s. A broad, spatula-like part.
Punc'tule s. A minute point or speck.
Noc'tule s. The great European bat.
Fruc'tule s. A drupel; part of a compound fruit.
Pus'tule s. A pimple containing pus; a blister.
Frus'tule s. The shell of a diatom.
Mu'tule s. A projecting block under the corona of the Doric cornice.
Val'vule s. A small valve.
O'vule s. A rudimentary seed; ovum before fertilization.
Ner'vule s. A small nerve of nervure.
Yule s. Christmas-time.
Axle s. The bar on or with which a wheel revolves.
Av'entayle s. The movable front of a helmet.
Con'dyle s. A rounded projection at end of a bone.
Spon'dyle s. A vertebra.
Od'yle s. Od, odic force.
Chyle s. The milky fluid extracted from food in the intestines and passed into the blood.
Gar'goyle s. A grotesque waterspout.
Cot'yle s. An ancient Greek measure of capacity; the hollowed bone of a knuckle or joint.
Style s. Manner of writing; characteristic mode in art, etc.; pin of a dial; a burin; title; part of a pistil. v.t. To term, designate.
Dec'astyle s. A portico having ten columns.
Dodec'astyle s. A portico having twelve columns.
Di'astyle s. An arrangement of columns in which three diameters of these are allowed for each inter-columniation.
Tet'rastyle s. A portico with four columns.
Oc'tastyle s. A building with eight columns in front.
Pen'tastyle s. A building with five columns in front.
Hex'astyle a. Having six columns.
Di'style s. A portico having two columns.
Ep'istyle s. An architrave.
Per'istyle s. A range of columns round a building, etc.
Py'gostyle s. The vomer or ploughshare bone in birds.
Or'thostyle s. An arrangement of architectural columns in a straight row.
Cy'clostyle s. An apparatus for producing copies of written or typewritten documents.
Mon'ostyle a. In the same style throughout; consisting of a single shaft or column.
Hy'postyle s. A covered colonade, a pillared hall.
Pro'style s. A portico entirely in front of a building.
Pol'ystyle a. Having or supported on many columns.
Sys'tyle s. Arrangement of columns two diameters apart.
Bamboozle' v.t. To hoax, swindle, mystify.
Foozle v.t. To make a mess of, to bungle. s. A bungling stroke or effort; a fogy.
Dazzle v.t. To overpower with light, splendour, conglomeration of colour, etc. v.i. To be intensely bright, to be overpowered by glitter, etc. s. Anything which dazzles; a method of painting ships, etc., so as to disguise their true outline.
Bedazzle' v.t. To confuse by dazzling.
Razzle-dazzle s. A rowdy spree.
Frazzle v.t. and i. To fray, tatter, unravel. s. A frayed end, shred; state of being badly used.
Embezzle' v.t. To appropriate by breach of trust.
Fizzle v.i. To fizz; to bungle, fail badly. s. Sound of fizzing; a fiasco, ignominious failure.
Mizzle v.i. To drizzle; (*slang*) to decamp. s. A very fine rain.
Drizzle s. Small or fine rain, wet mist. v.i. and t. To rain or shed in small drops.
Frizzle v.t. To curl, crisp; to fry bacon v.i. To hiss while frying. s. Frizzed hair.
Grizzle s. A grey colour; a grey-haired person, grey hair; whimpering; a sniveller. v.i. To whimper, whine.
Sizzle v.i. To make a hissing sound. s. Such a sound.
Swizzle v.t. and i. To tipple, bib. s. (*Slang*) A swindle.
Twizzle v.i. To spin round and round.
Nozzle s. A projecting spout; a mouth-piece.
Fuzzle v.t. To fuddle, intoxicate.
Guzzle v.i. and t. To eat or drink greedily or frequently. s. A debauch.
Muzzle s. The projecting nose and mouth an animal; cover for this to prevent biting; mouth of a gun, etc. v.t. To put a muzzle on; to gag.
Nuzzle v.t. To rub the nose against; to root up with the nose. v.i. To nestle, hide the head, burrow with the snout.
Puzzle v.t. To involve in perplexity; to nonplus. s. Something which perplexes; a problem; state of bewilderment.
Me pers. pron. The person speaking.
Came v.i. (past part.) (*Come*).
Became' v. (past) (*Become*).
Dame s. A lady; a schoolmistress, matron title of honour for women.
Bel'dame s. An old woman, a hag.
Fame s. Public report; renown, celebrity; honour. v.t. To make famous.

Defame' v.t. To censure falsely, caluminate, slander.
Game s. Sport; jest; exercise for amusement, etc.; scheme; animals hunted. v.i. To play at any sport; to gamble. a. Plucky; ready, willing; crippled, lame.
Hame s. One of the curved metals round a horse's collar.
Shame s. Consciousness of guilt, feeling occasioned by this; disgrace, ignominy; reproach. v.t. To make ashamed, cover with reproach.
Lame a. Crippled; hobbling; imperfect.
Blame v.t. To censure. s. Reproach.
Réclame' s. Notoriety; self-advertisement.
Flame s. A blaze; ardour of temper; a sweetheart. v.i. To burn with fire; to break out violently.
Aflame' adv.; a. Flaming.
Inflame' v.t. To set on fire; to excite, incense; to make morbidly red and swollen. v.i. To grow red and swollen; to become excited.
Name s. Appellation, title; reputation, character, renown; authority, behalf. v.t. To mention by name; to specify; to designate.
Rename' v.t. To name afresh, give a new name to.
Fore'name s. A first or Christian name.
Nick'name s. A name given in derision or familiarity. v.t. To give a nickname to.
Sur'name s. The family name. v.t. To give a surname to.
Misname' v.t. To call by a wrong name.
Macra'mé s. Knotted work; a fringe of this.
Frame v.t. To make, construct, fabricate; to contrive, plan; to place in a frame. s. A structure; something composed of parts fitted together; framework; mood, disposition.
Same a. Not different; identical; being of like kind; just mentioned.
Ses'ame (-a-mi) s. An E. Indian herb, oil from which is used as a laxative.
Tame a. Domesticated, not wild; gentle; spiritless. v.t. To make docile, to subdue.
Ac'me s. The culmination.
Raceme' s. An inflorescence in which flowers with pedicels of unequal length stand on one stem.
Deme s. A township in ancient Greece; a modern Greek commune.
Ac'ademe s. An academy.
Scheme s. A combination of things adjusted by design; a system, plot, project; a diagram. v.t. To plan, plot, contrive.
Blaspheme' v.i. and t. To speak impiously of God; to use profanity.
Theme s. The subject of a discourse; short dissertation; a basic melody.
En'thymeme s. An argument consisting only of an antecedent and a consequent deduced from it; a syllogism with one premise suppressed.
Quin'quereme s. A galley with five benches of oars.
Bi'reme s. A Roman galley with two banks of oars.
Quad'rireme s. A galley with four benches of rowers.
Tri'reme s. An ancient war-galley with three benches of oars.
Supreme' a. Highest in authority, importance, etc.; utmost, final.
Mon'otreme s. One of the Monotremata.
Extreme' a. Outermost, furthermost, final, conclusive. s. The utmost point, highest degree, end, extremity; great necessity.
Dime s. Ten-cent silver coin of U.S.A.
Régime' (-zhēm') s. Mode of management or government; prevailing system.
Chime s. A consonance of sounds of many instruments or of bells in harmony; a set of bells; the edge of a cask. v.i. To sound or be in harmony, to correspond; to jingle. v.t. To cause to sound in harmony.
Lime s. Calcareous earth; quicklime; a lemon-like fruit; the linden-tree. v.a. To manure with lime; to smear with birdlime.
Sublime' a. High in excellence; lofty, grand. v.t. To render sublime; to sublimate. v.i. To be susceptible of sublimation.
Clime s. A region, district; climate.
Bird'lime s. A glutinous substance to ensnare birds.
Quick'lime s. Lime burned but not slaked.
Brook'lime s. A variety of speedwell.
Slime s. Viscous mud, mucous, etc. v.t. To smear with this.
Mime s. A farce characterized by mimicry and gesture; a mimic, clown.
Pan'tomime s. A representation in dumb-show; an amusing, spectacular, and burlesque theatrical entertainment.
An'imé s. Resine for varnish.
Rime s. Hoar-frost; rhyme. v.t. and i. To cover with or congeal into rime.
Crime s. A breach of law; any great wickedness.
Grime s. Foul matter, engrained dirt. v.t. To sully, to soil deeply.
Begrime' v.t. To soil with dirt.
Prime a. First; original; first-rate, excellent; principal; divisible only by itself and 1. s. The earliest stage; the best part. v.t. To make ready or instruct beforehand; to supply with gunpowder; to apply the first colour in painting. v.i. To carry over water to the cylinder.
Time s. Measurement of or particular point of duration; epoch; opportunity; leisure; present life; rhythm. v.t. To adapt to the time; to measure as to time.
Bed'time s. Time to go to bed.
Life'time s. The duration of one's life.
Some'time adv. Once, formerly. a. Former.
Afore'time adv. Previously. s. Time past.
Before'time adv. Formerly.
Spring'time s. The season of spring.
Mar'itime a. Pertaining to or bordering on the sea; nautical.
Meantime' adv. In the time intervening. s. Intervening time.
Cen'time s. A French coin, 100th of a franc.
Op'time (-ti-me) s. One standing next after the wranglers in the mathematical tripos at Cambridge.
Pas'time s. An entertainment; sport, amusement, diversion.
Mistime' v.t. To time wrongly. v.i. To neglect the proper time.
Day'time s. Day as opposite to night.
Play'time s. Time for play.

Prox'ime adv. Nearest.
Or'iflamme s. The ancient royal banner of France.
Gramme s. The metric standard unit of weight (15.43 grs. troy).
Dec'agramme s. A weight of ten grammes (about ⅓ oz.).
Dec'igramme s. One-tenth of a gramme.
Mill'igramme s. 1000th part of a gramme.
Kil'ogramme s. A French measure of weight, about 2⅕lb. avoir.
Pro'gramme s. Plan of performance, things to be done, etc.
Consommé' s. A strong meat soup.
Come v.i. To draw nigh, move hitherward, arrive; to happen, appear, result.
Become' v.i. To come to be, to change to. v.t. To suit, be worthy of.
Misbecome' v.t. To suit ill; not to befit.
Wel'come a. Received with gladness; grateful; pleasing. s. Kind reception of a newcomer. v.t. To salute with kindness, receive hospitality.
In'come s. Revenue; annual receipts.
Overcome' v.t. To get the better of; to subdue, vanquish. v.i. To gain the superiority.
Out'come s. That which follows from something else; issue.
Dome s. Hemispherical cupola; an arched roof.
Lith'odome s. A small mollusc living in rocks.
Ster'eome s. A strengthening tissue in certain plants.
Home s. Abode of oneself or one's family; one's own country; a place, institution, etc., affording home comforts; a goal. a. Domestic; personal, close. adv. Pointedly, intimately. v.i. and t. To go home, dwell, provide with a home.
Tri'chome s. A prickle, outgrowth (on plants).
Glome s. A roundish head of flowers.
Phyll'ome s. A leaf or analagous organ.
Mome s. A numskull, dolt.
Nome s. A province, especially of modern Greece or Egypt.
Gnome s. An imaginary being dwelling underground; a maxim, aphorism.
Met'ronome s. Instrument for measuring musical time.
Gas'tronome s. An epicure; a connoisseur of food.
Pome s. A fleshy fruit, as of the apple, pear, quince, etc.
Per'ispome s. A perispomenon.
Pal'indrome s. A word or sentence that reads the same backwards as forwards.
Hip'podrome s. A circus for equestrianism; a race-course.
A'erodrome s. An area for the alighting, racing, etc., of aeroplanes.
Prod'rome s. A preliminary symptom of disease.
Chrome s. Chromium; a yellow pigment.
En'dochrome s. A colouring matter in plants.
He'liochrome s. A photograph in natural colours.
Hæm'ochrome s. The colouring matter of blood.
Sten'ochrome s. A form of colour-printing.
Mon'ochrome s. A painting in a single colour.
Pho'tochrome s. A coloured photograph.
Pol'ychrome a. Painted or printed in several colours. s. A statue, etc., executed thus.
Some a. A certain; a little; indefinite; about. pron. An indefinite quantity, etc.; certain individuals.
-some suff. Forming adjectives denoting full of.
Frol'icsome a. Full of frolics, given to gambolling or pranks.
Glad'some a. Pleased, pleasing, joyful; causing joy.
Hand'some a. Finely featured, well formed; ample; liberal.
Glee'some a. Merry, gay.
Three'some s. A game of golf for three; a party of three.
Lithe'some a. Lissom; nimble.
Blithe'some a. Gay, light-hearted.
Joke'some a. Given to joking.
Gam'blesome a. Given to gambling.
Trouble'some a. Giving trouble, vexatious irksome.
Meddle'some a. Given to meddling.
Cud'dlesome a. Fit to be cuddled.
Gig'glesome a. Given to giggling.
Tangle'some a. Tangly; entangled.
Dole'some a. Doleful, sorrowful.
Whole'some a. Tending to promote health; salubrious; not morbid; beneficial.
Met'tlesome a. High-spirited; ardent.
Game'some a. Merry; inclined to sport.
Lone'some a. Secluded from society; unfrequented; dismal.
Tire'some a. Wearisome, fatiguing; tedious.
Ven'turesome a. Inclined to venture; daring risky.
Adven'turesome a. Adventurous.
Grue'some a. Horrible, frightful, repulsive.
Awe'some a. Full of or inspiring awe.
Loath'some a. Exciting disgust or abhorrence; odious; nauseous.
Tooth'some a. Pleasing to the taste.
Froth'some a. Characterized by froth; frothy.
Noi'some a. Offensive, disgusting; noxious.
Drear'isome a. Dreary.
We'arisome a. Tedious; producing weariness.
Freak'some a. Freakish; full of freaks.
Pick'some a. Fastidious, over-particular.
Trick'some a. Tricky.
Dark'some a. Gloomy, dark.
Irk'some a. Tedious, wearisome.
Quirk'some a. Quirkish.
Murk'some a. Murky.
Heal'some a. (*Scot.*) Wholesome.
Quar'relsome a. Apt to quarrel; irascible.
Toil'some a. Laborious; attended with fatigue and pain.
Ful'some a. Nauseous, gross, offensive.
Bur'densome a. Oppressive, hard to bear.
Win'some a. Charming, attractive, lovely.
Chro'mosome s. A segment of a cell.
Tryp'anosome s. A minute, whip-like, parasitic protozoan causing sleeping-sickness, etc.
Mi'crosome s. (*Microsoma*).
Ur'osome s. The terminal somatome of a vertebrate.
Pyr'osome s. A phosphorescent ascidian of tropical seas.
Two'some a. and s. Denoting something done or performed by two.
Fear'some a. Fearful; terrible.
Cum'bersome a. Unweildly, unmanageable, burdensome.
Both'ersome a. Annoying, troublesome.
Four'some a. Done by four persons. s. A game between two pairs.
Hu'moursome a. Led by caprice; petulant; humorous.
Fla'voursome a. Pleasing to taste or smell.
Light'some a. Gay, cheering; airy.
Delight'some a. Affording delight; delicious.
Gay'some a. Merry; full of gaiety.
Toy'some a. Disposed to trifle; wanton.
Tome s. A ponderous volume.
So'matone s. A somite.

Rach'itome (răk'-) s. Surgeon's knife for use on the vertebræ.
Epit'ome s. A summary, abridgment; a compendium.
Sar'cotome s. A surgeon's knife.
Pharyng'otome s. An instrument for making incisions in the throat.
Lith'otome s. An instrument used in lithotomy.
Mi'crotome s. Apparatus for cutting sections for microscopic examination.
Scler'otome s. The knife used in sclerotomy.
Pla'giostome s. A shark or ray.
Cy'clostome s. A cyclostomatous fish, a lamprey.
Rhiz'ome s. A creeping stem growing beneath the surface.
Gendarme' s. An armed policeman, especially in France.
Forme s. A body of type, set, and locked up in a chase.
Heaume s. A large, heavy helmet.
Neume s. A group of notes sung to one syllable in plain-song.
Fume s. Smoke, vapour; rage; idle conceit. v.i. To smoke, to vapour; to be in a rage.
Per'fume s. A pleasant odour; scent; fragrance.
Perfume' v.t. To impregnate with a pleasant odour; to scent.
Leg'ume s. A two-valved pod.
Inhume' v.t. To bury, inter.
Exhume' v.t. To disinter, unbury.
Relume' v.t. To light or kindle again.
Flume s. Channel for water driving a mill; an artificial channel for gold-washing, etc.
Glume s. The husk or chaff of grain.
Illume' v.t. To lighten, enlighten.
Reillume' v.t. To light up again.
Vol'ume s. A book, especially a large one; space occupied, bulk; quantity or strength.
Plume s. A bird's feather; a bunch or tuft of these; a token of honour, etc. v.t. To adjust the feathers of; to pride, value.
Deplume' v.t. To deprive of plumage, honour, etc.
Spume s. Froth, foam, scum. v.i. To froth.
Brume s. Mist, fog.
Grume s. Viscous fluid; a clot as of blood.
Subsume' v.t. To include under a general heading.
Résu'mé (-mā) s. A summing up, recapitulation.
Resume' v.t. and i. To begin or take up again; to recapitulate; to recommence.
Presume' v.t. To suppose to be true, take for granted; to make bold. v.i. To infer; to take liberties.
Consume' v.t. To use up or destroy by fire, waste, decomposition, etc.; to use up articles of food. v.i. To waste away, be burned up.
Assume' v.t. To take upon oneself, arrogate. v.i. To be arrogant.
Bitume' v.t. To smear with bitumen.
Costume' s. Dress, attire; established mode of dress, dress of a period or people.
Impos'tume s. A collection of pus, an abscess.
Cyme s. A flat-topped or convex flower-cluster.
Chyme s. Pulp of partially digested food from which the chyle is to be extracted.
Rhyme s. Correspondence of sound in final word or syllable of verse; a word rhyming with another. v.i. To accord in sound; to make verses. v.t. To put into rhyme.
Berhyme' v.t. To celebrate or ridicule in rhyme.
Thyme (tīm) s. A small aromatic shrub.
Zyme s. A ferment.
Az'yme s. The Passover cake of unleavened bread.
Enzyme' s. A chemical or unorganized ferment.
Bane s. That which causes ruin; woe, mischief.
Flea'bane s. A composite plant supposed to drive away fleas.
Hen'bane s. A perennial plant; a poison extracted from this.
Urbane' a. Courteous, civil, polite.
Wolf'sbane s. A species of aconite.
Rats'bane s. Poison for rats.
Cane s. A reed, a walking-stick. v.t. To beat with a cane.
Chicane' s. Sharp practice, tricks; score awarded to hand destitute of trumps in bridge, etc. v.t. To cheat, swindle.
Hur'ricane s. A violent storm of wind.
Dane s. A native of Denmark; a large, short-haired dog.
Cis'padane a. On the south of the River Po.
Mun'dane a. Worldly; pertaining to the world.
Ultramun'dane a. Being external to the world or the solar system; pertaining to the supernatural.
Antemun'dane a. Existing before the creation of the world.
Supermun'dane a. Superior to things of this world.
Intermun'dane a. Being between worlds.
Fane s. A temple, church.
Profane' a. Not sacred, temporal; irreverent, blasphemous. v.t. To desecrate, treat with irreverence.
Sal'angane s. The Chinese swift that builds edible nests.
Tri'phane s. A silicate of aluminuim and lithium.
Lith'ophane s. A transparent porcelain.
Cy'mophane s. A variety of chrysoberyl.
Hy'drophane s. A variety of opal.
Pyr'ophane s. A variety of opal.
Thane s. A class of lower nobility among the Anglo-Saxons.
Meth'ane s. A colourless, inflammable, hydrocarbon gas.
Liane' s. Liana.
Lane s. A passage between hedges; a narrow street or way.
Plane a. Flat, even; lying or constituting a plane. s. A flat or even surface; a carpenter's smoothing tool; a supporting surface of a flying-machine; a large-leaved tree. v.t. To make smooth; to use a carpenter's plane. v.i. To travel in an aeroplane.
Bi'plane s. An aeroplane with two planes, one above the other.
Tri'plane s. Aeroplane with three supporting planes.
Mul'tiplane s. An aeroplane with more than two supporting planes.
Vol'plane v.i. To glide down with engine shut off (of aeroplane). s. Such a descent.
Mon'oplane s. An aeroplane with one supporting plane.
Hy'droplane s. A swift, skimming motor-boat.
Aer'oplane s. A flying-machine heavier than air.
Purs'lane s. A succulent pot-herb.
Mane s. Hair on neck of horse, lion, etc.
Bi'mane s. A two-handed animal.

Germane′ a. Relevant, pertinent.
Humane′ a. Merciful; kind; benevolent.
Quad′rumane s. A four-handed animal; a monkey.
Inane′ a. Empty; void of sense; useless. s. Infinite empty space.
Pane s. A square of glass; piece of cloth, etc., let in for ornament.
March′pane s. Marzipan.
Fran′gipane s. A kind of pastry containing cream and almonds.
Elecampane′ s. Starwort; a sweetmeat.
Coun′terpane s. A coverlet for a bed.
Ra′ne s. A Hindu queen; consort of a rajah.
Mem′brane s. A thin extended skin.
Crane s. A migratory wading-bird; a machine for raising heavy weights; a bent pipe for draining liquor from a cask. v.i. To stretch out one's neck.
En′docrane s. The inner surface of the cranium.
Sane a. Sound and healthy, especially in mind.
Insane′ a. Mentally deranged, mad; exceedingly rash; intended for insane persons.
Bel′tane s. Old May-day (Scotland).
Pen′tane s. A hydrocarbon contained in petroleum, etc.
Mon′tane a. Pertaining to mountainous regions.
Tramon′tane a. Lying, being, or coming from beyond the Alps; barbarous.
Ultramon′tane a. Being beyond the mountains, especially the Alps; Italian; papal. s. A dweller S. of the Alps; a supporter of ultramontanism.
Intermon′tane a. Between or among mountains.
Cismon′tane a. On the north side of the Alps opposite to ultramontane.
Transmon′tane a. Situated beyond the mountains.
Tar′tane s. A one-masted Mediterranean vessel.
Soutane′ s. A priest's cassock.
Douane′ s. A continental custom-house.
Vane s. A weathercock; broad part of a feather; blade of a windmill.
Pavane′ s. A slow, stately dance.
Wane v.t. To grow less; to diminish, as the moon; to fail. s. Act or process of waning.
Ac′ne s. A pimple; an eruption of these.
-ene suff. Denoting a hydrocarbon.
Ter′ebene s. A liquid hydrocarbon obtained from oil of turpentine and used in medicine.
Nicene′ a. Pertaining to Nicæa, or to the Ecclesiastical Councils held there.
Ep′icene a. Having the characters of both sexes; sexless; neutral.
E′ocene a. Belonging to the earliest Tertiary period.
Pli′ocene a. Denoting the last of the Tertiary periods, the geological epoch preceding the pleistocene.
Mi′ocene a. Denoting the middle division of the Tertiary period or strata.
Pleis′tocene a. Pertaining to the geological epoch following the last of the Tertiary periods. s. The Glacial epoch.
Scene s. A stage, a device on this; distinct part of a play, a spectacle, view; an exhibition of feeling, a row.
Damascene′ v.t. To inlay metal with another metal; to give a streaked or watered appearance to steel. s. A native of Damascus; a damson.
Obscene′ a. Immodest, indecent; offensive to chastity and delicacy.

Dene s. A sandy down, a dune.
Du′odene s. Group of twelve musical notes used as a unit of construction.
Sagene′ s. A fishing-net.
In′digene s. An indigenous plant or animal.
Gaz′ogene s. Apparatus for making aerated water.
Selt′zogene s. Apparatus for aerating water.
Achene′ s. A small carpel with a single seed.
Sphene (sfeen) s. Titanite.
Phos′phene s. An image produced by pressure on the eye-ball.
Ruthene′ s. A member of a Russian race on the borders of Poland and Czecho-Slovakia.
Hy′giene s. Science of preserving health, especially of communities.
Skene s. A skean.
Scalene′ a. Having the three sides unequal (of triangles).
Glene s. The pupil of the eye; a cavity in a bone.
Hellene′ s. A Greek, ancient or modern.
Gas′olene s. A volatile and inflammable mixture extracted from petroleum used for heating and lighting.
Am′ylene s. An anæsthetic.
Acet′ylene s. A colourless gas used for lighting.
For′mene s. Methane.
Cu′mene s. An aromatic hydrocarbon from cumin oil.
Ter′pene s. A hydrocarbon obtained chiefly from conifers.
Nazarene′ s. A native of Nazareth; early term of contempt for a Christian.
Hip′pocrene s. A spring on Mount Helicon sacred to the Muses.
Serene′ a. Calm, clear; unruffled. s. Clear expanse of sky.
Gang′rene s. First stage of mortification. v.i. and t. To mortify or cause mortification in.
Threne (thrēn) s. A lamentation, threnody.
Terrene′ (-rēn′) a. Pertaining to the earth; terrestrial.
Pyr′ene s. The stone of a drupe; a hydrocarbon obtained from coal.
Arrasene′ s. A thread of wool and silk.
Ker′osene s. An illuminating oil.
Tol′uene s. A liquid derived from coal-tar.
Trinitrotol′uene s. A high explosive; T.N.T.
Contravene′ v.t. To transgress, oppose, obstruct.
Subvene′ (-ven′) v.i. To happen.
Convene′ v.t. To call together, convoke. v.i. To assemble.
Slovene′ s. Member of a Slav race of Carinthia.
Supervene′ v.i. To come extraneously; to happen.
Intervene′ v.i. To come or be between; to interpose, interfere.
Ben′zene s. A hydrocarbon used as an illuminant and for removing grease spots, etc.
Champagne′ s. A sparkling white wine.
Cockaigne′ s. A fabled land of luxury.
Frankalmoigne′ s. A tenure by which religious corporations held lands in perpetuity.
Eau-de-Cologne′ s. A perfumed spirit.
Epergne′ s. An ornamental stand for a table.
Daph′ne s. A genus of small evergreen shrubs allied to the laurel.
-ine suff. Forming adjectives indicating, pertaining to or of the nature of; also feminine nouns and names of alkaloids and bases.
The′baine s. A poisonous alkaloid from opium.
Cocaine′ s. An alkaloid from coca leaves, used as a local anæsthetic.

Demi-mondaine' s. A woman of doubtful reputation.
Delaine' s. A fabric of wool and cotton.
Mousseline-de-laine' s. An untwilled woollen dress fabric.
Châtelaine s. The mistress of a castle or château a set of chains attached to a lady's belt for keys, trinkets, etc.
Pto'maine s. A highly poisonous alkaloid present in decaying animal and vegetable matter.
Mi'graine s. Megrum ; a bilious headache.
Moraine' s. Line of debris carried by a glacier.
Quin'zaine s. A five-versed poem or stanza.
Bine s. A flexible shoot or stem.
Can'nabine a. Pertaining to hemp.
Car'abine s. (*Carbine*).
Sab'ine s. One of an ancient Italian race.
Wood'bine s. The wild honeysuckle.
Combine' v.i. To come into union, coalesce, league together. v.t. To cause to unite, to join. s. A union of interests for trade purposes.
Col'umbine s. A perennial plant with brightly coloured flowers; Harlequin's dancing partner in pantomime.
To'bine s. A stout twilled silk fabric.
Car'bine s. A short rifle.
Tur'bine s. Machine rotating on a shaft.
Con'cubine s. A kept woman, mistress.
Thy'lacine s. A Tasmanian wolf-like marsupial.
Psit'tacine a. Of or pertaining to the parrot family.
Vac'cine s. The virus of cowpox. a. Pertaining to or obtained from cows; pertaining to vaccination.
Interne'cine a. Deadly; mutually destructive.
Med'icine s. A remedy taken internally; a drug; science of curing diseases. v.t. To treat with medicine.
Quin'icine s. An alkaloid compound obtained from quinine.
Sor'icine a. Pertaining to the shrews; shrew-like.
Cap'sicine s. The essential principle of capsicum.
Plas'ticine s. A modelling substance resembling clay.
Cal'cine v.t. To reduce to quicklime or powder; to burn to ashes. v.i. To undergo calcination.
Pho'cine a. Pertaining to the seal family.
Hir'cine a. Like a goat, especially in smell.
Por'cine a. Resembling or pertaining to pigs.
Fas'cine s. Bundle of faggots used in fortification, for filling ditches, etc.
Pis'cine a. Pertaining to fishes.
Glau'cine a. Having a bluish-hoary appearance.
Cal'ycine a. Like a calyx.
Acal'ycine a. Devoid of calyx.
Dine v.i. To eat dinner. v.t. To give a dinner to.
Mus'cadine s. A musky variety of grape.
Gren'adine s. A gauzy silk or woollen fabric; a dish of dressed veal or chicken.
Incar'nadine v.t. To make red, to tinge blood colour.
Gradine' s. A sculptor's toothed chisel.
Smarag'dine a. Pertaining to, consisting of, or resembling emerald.
Quin'idine s. An alkaloid obtained from some cinchona barks.
Al'dine a. Pertaining to the Venetian printer, Aldus.
Brig'andine s. Plate-armour for the body.
Cel'andine s. A genus of plants of the poppy family.
Al'mandine s. Precious garnet.
Nan'dine s. A ring-tailed paradoxure of W. Africa.
Un'dine (-dēn) s. A female water-spirit.
Hirun'dine a. Like a swallow.
I'odine s. A non-metallic element used in medicine.
Mus'cardine s. A fatal disease among silkworms.
Ber'nardine s. A Cistercian monk.
Sar'dine s. A small fish cured and preserved in oil; a scriptural precious stone.
Gab'erdine s. A long, coarse frock worn by mediæval Jews, pilgrims, etc.
Hab'erdine s. A dried salted cod.
Sor'dine s. A mute or damper for a musical instrument.
Tur'dine a. Pertaining to or resembling birds of the thrush family.
Palu'dine a. Paludal.
Nar'ceine s. A bitter alkaloid contained in opium.
Caf'feine s. A vegetable alkaloid.
The'ine s. The bitter principle of tea and coffee.
Vice'reine s. The wife of a viceroy.
Seine (sān) s. A large fishing-net with floats and weights. v.t. and i. To catch fish or to fish with this.
Fine a. Pure, subtle, delicate; showy; refined, elegant. s. A mulct, penalty, forfeit. v.t. To purify, refine; to mulct.
Define' v.t. To fix the limits of; to explain, describe.
O'lefine s. One of a series of hydrocarbons forming oily compounds with bromine and chlorine.
Refine' v.t. To purify, clear from dross. v.i. To become pure; to improve in accuracy, delicacy, etc.; to affect nicely.
Confine' v.t. To shut up, imprison, restrain.
Con'fine s. Boundary; borderland; confinement.
Su'perfine a. Very fine; of extra quality.
Imag'ine v.t. To picture to oneself, conceive, fancy. v.i. To have a notion.
En'gine s. Means, device; mechanical (or other) contrivance; machine for converting energy into mechanical power.
Trin'gine a. Pertaining to or resembling the sandpipers.
Pro'togine s. A variety of granite found in the Alps.
Aubergine' s. The egg-plant or its fruit.
Chine s. An animal's spine; piece adjoining this for cooking; the chimb of a cask; a ravine. v.t. To sever the backbone of.
Machine' s. Any contrivance used to transmit force and motion; political party organization.
Ser'aphine (-fēn) s. A form of harmonium.
Trephine' s. An improved form of trepan.
Sylph'ine a. Resembling or in the manner of a sylph.
Cam'phine s. An illuminant prepared from turpentine.
Mor'phine s. Morphia, the principle alkaloid of opium.
Phos'phine s. Phosphuretted hydrogen.
Catarrh'ine a. (*Catarrh*).
Mur'rhine a. Denoting a delicate kind of fluor-spar ware.
Plat'yrrhine a. Having a broad, thick nose.
Shine vi.. To emit rays, glisten; to be animated, gay, or brilliant; to be glossy. v.t. To polish, cause to shine. s. Fair-weather; lustre, polish (*slang*) a shindy.

Moon'shine s. Moonlight; show without substance; unreality.
Sun'shine s. The light of the sun; warmth; favourable influence.
Outshine' v.t. To excel in lustre or excellence.
Thine pron. and a. Thy.
Amaran'thine a. Like the amaranth; unfading.
Xan'thine s. Xanthin.
Terebin'thine a. Pertaining to or resembling terebinth or turpentine.
Hyacin'thine a. Made of or like hyacinths; of violet or dark auburn colour; curling (of hair).
Labyrin'thine a. Like or pertaining to a labyrinth, intricate.
Whine v.i. To utter a plaintive cry; to complain. v.t. To utter in a peevish way. s. A peevish cry, unmanly complaint.
Kine s. Cows.
Line s. Longitudinal extension; thread; 1/12 inch; regular infantry; trench, rampart. v.t. To cover on the inside; to mark with lines.
Aline' v.t. To range in line.
Percaline' (-lēn') s. A glassy cotton cloth.
Naph'thaline s. A colourless, crystalline, solid hydrocarbon.
Al'kaline s. With the properties of an alkali.
Antal'kaline s. A substance that counteracts an alkali.
Tour'maline s. A coloured, translucent gem-stone with electrical properties.
Sep'aline a. Having sepals.
O'paline a. Pertaining to or like opal. s. A translucent kind of glass.
Sa'line a. Impregnated with salt. s. A salt-marsh, -pan, -spring, etc.
Veg'etaline s. Imitation ivory, etc., prepared from wood fibre.
Hy'aline a. Transparant; crystalline. s. The glassy surface of the sea; the clear sky.
Decline' v.i. To bend downwards; to fail; not to comply. v.t. To bend downward; to refuse; to change the termination of a noun. s. A falling off, deterioration; consumption.
Recline' v.t. and i. To lean back; to rest or repose.
Incline' v.t. To slope; to be favourably disposed; to have some desire. v.t. To cause to slope or bend; to dispose.
In'cline s. A slope, gradient; an inclination.
Mon'ocline s. A monoclinal fold.
Ghib'beline s. One of a faction which arose in the tenth century in favour of the Emperor.
Bee'-line s. The shortest route between two places.
Fe'line a. Pertaining to cats or the cat tribe; cat-like; stealthy.
Nick'eline s. Niccolite.
Cam'eline s. Camlet.
Vas'eline s. Yellowish petroleum jelly used as an ointment.
Mousseline' s. Fine French muslin.
Mus'teline a. Pertaining to the weasel amily. s. A member of this.
Ha'zeline s. An astringent drug prepared from the wych-hazel.
Strob'iline a. Strobilaceous.
An'iline s. A chemical base used in dyeing.
Rosan'iline s. A compound and salt derived from aniline.
Aq'uiline a. Eagle-like; hooked.
In'quiline s. An animal living in the abode of another.
Cab'alline a. Pertaining to horses.
Ral'line a. Pertaining to the rails (birds).
Cor'alline a. Consisting of, like, or containing coral. s. A submarine calcareous seaweed; an artificial red colouring matter.
Met'alline a. Resembling metal; impregnated with metallic salts.
Crys'talline a Consisting of or like crystal; clear, pellucid.
Sabel'line a. Pertaining to or coloured like sable.
Isabel'line a. Of a greyish-yellow colour.
Vitel'line a. Like or pertaining to the yolk of egg.
Su'illine a. Hog-like.
Cor'olline a. Pertaining to a corolla.
Sib'ylline a. Prophetic; oracular; cryptic.
Beryl'line a. Resembling a beryl.
Saxic'oline a. Living or growing among rocks.
Leu'coline s. An organic compound distilled from coal-tar.
Ban'doline s. An ointment for the hair.
Noctil'ioline a. Belonging to a certain genus of S. American bats.
Moline' a. Describing a variety of heraldic cross. s. This cross.
Crinoline' s. A hooped petticoat; a fabric of horse-hair and linen.
Quin'oline s. A compound forming the basis of many medicines, dyes, etc.
Capit'oline a. Pertaining to the Roman Capitol.
Ben'zoline s. Impure benzene.
Grap'line s. A grapnel.
Dis'cipline s. Training; method of government; military regulation; subjection to laws; correction.
Com'pline s. (*Complin*).
Car'line s. A hag, witch; a genus of thistles.
Mar'line s. A small two-stranded line used on ships.
Underline' v.t. To mark with a line beneath.
Interline' v.t. To write between lines.
Rat'line (-lin) s. Small rope traversing the shrouds of a ship, making rungs.
Bunt'line s. A rope to prevent a sail bellying.
Out'line s. The line by which a figure is defined; contour; general plan. v.t. To sketch, draw the exterior line of.
Caul'ine a. Pertaining to a stem.
Acau'line a. Without a stem.
Paul'ine a. Pertaining to St. Paul or his writings.
Bac'uline a. Pertaining to flogging.
Mas'culine a. Male; manly; unwomanly.
In'duline a. A bluish, greyish, or violet dye-stuff.
Fig'uline a. Fictile; made of clay.
Prim'uline s. A yellow dye-stuff.
Ur'suline s. and a. One of, or belonging to, a certain order of nuns.
Vit'uline a. Pertaining to calves, of calving.
Bow'line s. A rope for making a sail stand close to the wind.
Mine a. Belonging to me. s. A deep pit whence minerals, etc., are taken; underground passage for explosives or bomb, etc., used in such. v.t. To dig into, obtain by digging; to sap. v.i. To burrow; to practise secret methods of inquiry.
Am'ine s. A compound derived from ammonia.
Syc'amine s. The black mulberry-tree.
Car'damine s. A genus of cruciferous plants.

Fam'ine s. Distressing scarcity, especially of food; starvation.
Cal'amine s. A zinc ore.
Vit'amine s. A constituent of many foods, absence of which induces rickets, beri-beri, etc.
Exam'ine v.t. To inspect or inquire into carefully; to interrogate; to scrutinize.
Re-exam'ine v.t. To examine again.
Crim'ine int. (*Criminy*).
Bro'mine s. A non-metallic element.
Theobro'mine s. The bitter alkaloid in cocoa seeds.
Car'mine s. A red or crimson pigment.
Er'mine s. An animal allied to the weasel, valued for its white fur; the fur.
Undermine' v.t. To sap; to injure by underhand methods.
Deter'mine v.t. To terminate, conclude; to adjust; to ascertain exactly. v.i. To end; to resolve.
Predeter'mine v.t. To determine beforehand, predoom.
Coun'termine s. An underground passage from which to destroy the mines of an enemy; a frustrating stratagem. v.t. and i. To oppose by or place countermines.
Jas'mine s. A sweet-scented climbing plant.
Des'mine s. Stilbite, a mineral crystallizing in silken tufts.
Illu'mine v.t. To illuminate; to enlighten.
Nine a. and s. One more than eight.
Can'ine a. Pertaining to dogs.
Sol'anine s. A poisonous alkaloid found in solanaceous plants.
Ra'nine a. Pertaining to the under-side of the tongue-tip.
Saf'franine s. A yellow colouring matter obtained from saffron.
Plat'anine a. Plataneous.
Cy'anine s. A blue dye.
Mez'zanine s. A low story between higher ones; the floor below the stage in a theatre.
Strych'nine s. A poisonous alkaloid.
Del'phinine s. A vegetable alkaloid.
Fem'inine a. Pertaining or relating to females; womanly; effeminate.
As'inine a. Like a donkey.
Quinine'(-nēn') s. A medicinal alkaloid obtained from cinchona bark.
Johan'nine a. Pertaining to the apostle John or his writings.
Fes'cennine a. Applied to early Latin poetry of a coarse kind.
Co'nine s. A poisonous alkaloid extracted from hemlock.
Le'onine a. Lion-like; majestic; pertaining to a lion or to one of the Popes Leo.
Cin'chonine s. Cinchonia.
Pav'onine a. Pertaining to or resembling the peacock. s. A lustre on certain ores.
Ebur'nine a. Made of or resembling ivory.
Sat'urnine a. Gloomy; morose.
Macedoine' s. A jelly enclosing pieces of fruit.
Her'oine s. A female hero; a principal female character.
Pine s. A genus of coniferous trees; the timber of one of these; a pineapple. v.i. To languish, droop, wither; to yearn for.
Sin'apine s. The organic base of mustard.
Rap'ine s. Act of plundering; pillage; violence.
Repine' v.i. To fret oneself; to murmur.
Pitch'pine s. A variety of pine rich in resin.
Al'pine a. Pertaining to the Alps
Subal'pine a. Pertaining to a high region not above timber-line.
Cisal'pine a. South of the Alps.
Transal'pine a. Lying or being on the N. or W. of the Alps.
Vul'pine a. Pertaining to or resembling the fox; cunning.
Opine' v.i. and t. To think, suppose, express an opinion.
Chopine' s. A high-heeled patten.
At'ropine s. A poison obtained from deadly nightshade.
Or'pine s. A plant of the stone-crop family.
Spine s. The backbone; a large thorn, prickle.
Ves'pine a. Pertaining to or like a wasp.
Por'cupine s. A large rodent with sharp, erectile spines.
Lu'pine s. A showy leguminous plant. a. Pertaining to or like the wolf.
Supine' a. Lying face upward; negligent, listless.
Su'pine s. A verbal noun in Latin.
Mar'garine s. Artificial butter.
Sac'charine s. An extremely sweet substance obtained from coal-tar. a. Pertaining to or having the qualities of sugar.
Marine' (-ēn') a. Pertaining to, produced by, or used at sea; maritime. s. The shipping of a country; a soldier employed on a warship.
Ultramarine' (-rēn') s. A deep blue pigment. a. Situated beyond the sea.
Aquamarine' s. A variety of beryl.
Submarine' (-rēn') a. Being, growing, or acting beneath the sea's surface. s. A vessel (especially for war) that may be submerged.
Transmarine' (-rēn') a. Lying or being beyond the sea.
Nec'tarine s. A smooth-skinned variety of peach.
Mazarine' a. and s. A deep rich blue.
Brine s. Water impregnated with salt.
Pe'brine (pā'brēn) s. A parasitic disease of silkworms.
Col'ubrine a. Pertaining to snakes, especially the colubers.
Vol'ucrine a. Pertaining to birds.
Ce'drine a. Pertaining to or made of cedar.
Mean'drine s. A tropical coral.
Salaman'drine a. Pertaining to the salamanders able to endure extreme heat.
Alexan'drine n. A verse of twelve syllables.
Chon'drine s. Gelatine from cartilage.
Glyc'erine s. A colourless, sweet liquid extracted from fats.
Fer'ine a. Wild, untamed; brutish.
Tangerine' s. A native of Tangiers; a small variety of orange. a. Pertaining to Tangiers.
Ath'erine s. A sand-smelt.
Pel'erine s. A lady's long cape.
Chol'erine s. A mild form of cholera.
Vi'perine a. Pertaining to or like the vipers.
An'serine a. Goose-like.
Pas'serine a. Belonging to the Passeres, or perchers, the largest order of birds.
Adul'terine a. Born of or relating to adultery.
Choles'terine s. A fatty substance found in the bile.
Butterine' s. An artificial butter.
U'terine a. Pertaining to the womb; born of the same mother only.
Riv'erine a. Pertaining to or resembling a river; riparian.
Wol'verine (wul'-) s. A N. American carnivore allied to the sable.

Per'egrine s. A species of falcon.
Nig'rine s. A ferruginous variety of rutile.
Ti'grine a. Like or pertaining to a tiger.
Shrine s. A casket for relics; a tomb of a saint; a hallowed place.
Enshrine' v.t. To enclose in a shrine; to cherish.
Sapph'irine a. Resembling or made of sapphire. s. A pale blue mineral.
Chlor'ine s. A yellowish-green, non-metallic gaseous element.
Lep'orine a. Pertaining to or having the nature of a hare.
Vic'torine s. A small fur tippet; a variety of peach.
Flu'orine s. A non-metallic gaseous element.
Cap'rine a. Like a goat.
Cyp'rine a. Belonging to the carp family.
Terrine' s. An earthenware jar for delicacies.
Viv'errine a. Pertaining to or like animals of the civet kind.
Trine a. Triple. s. A triad; the Trinity; aspect of planets distant 120° from each other.
La'trine s. A privy, especially in camp or barracks.
Ver'atrine s. A highly poisonous vegetable alkaloid.
Doc'trine s. A principle in any science; dogma, tenet, precept.
Pet'rine a. Pertaining to or derived from the apostle, Peter.
Cit'rine a. Like a citron; greenish-yellow.
Accip'itrine a. Belonging to or resembling the hawks; sharp-sighted, predatory.
Vit'rine s. A glass case.
Lacus'trine a. Pertaining to or living in or on a lake.
Lus'trine s. A glossy silk fabric.
Dex'trine s. Dextrin.
Ur'ine s. The fluid secreted by the kidneys.
Taur'ine a. Bull-like; pertaining to Taurus.
Neur'ine s. The essential substance of nerves; a poisonous ptomaine.
Figurine' s. A statuette.
Sci'urine a. Pertaining to or resembling the squirrels.
Mur'ine a. Relating to mice, rats, etc.
Tambourine' s. A shallow, one-sided drum with loose jingles.
Datur'ine s. An alkaloid obtained from the thorn-apple.
Vul'turine a. Vulturous.
Aven'turine s. A gold-spangled glass.
Az'urine s. The blue roach.
Bu'tyrine s. An oil obtained from the action of butyric acid on glycerine.
Papyr'ine a. Resembling papyrus or papyri.
Sine s. A perpendicular drawn from one end of an arc to the diameter through the other end.
Fuch'sine s. A deep red colouring matter.
Cuisine' s. Cookery; style of cooking.
Cosine' s. The sine of the complement of an arc or angle.
E'osine s. Eosin.
Sep'sine s. A poisonous ptomaine found in certain decaying substances.
Ur'sine a. Pertaining to or having the qualities of a bear.
Brank'ursine s. The acanthus.
Lim'ousine s. A motor-car with closed body.
Tine s. A prong of a deer's horn; tooth of a harrow, spike of a fork, etc.
Cre'atine s. An organic substance in flesh.
Leg'atine a. Pertaining to a legate or his power.
Latin'e adv. In or as in Latin.

Pal'atine a. Pertaining to a palace; possessing royal privileges; pertaining to the palate. s. One invested with royal privileges and rights; one of the two bones forming the hard palate.
Gel'atine s. A translucent animal substance of the consistence of jelly.
Benedic'tine s. One of an order of monks; a liqueur.
Di'etine s. A local convention or subordinate diet.
Acon'itine s. An alkaloid derived from aconite.
Corybant'ine a. Corybantic.
In'fantine a. Infantile.
Brig'antine s. A two-masted vessel.
Elephan'tine a. Huge, clumsy, unwieldy.
Chrysele-phant'ine a. Made of ivory and gold.
Bril'liantine s. An ointment for the hair.
Galantine' s. A dish of white meat spiced and jellied.
Eg'lantine s. The sweetbrier.
Adaman'tine a. Incapable of being broken, extremely hard.
Diaman'tine a. Having the qualities of the diamond.
Amaran'tine a. (*Amaranthine*).
Quar'antine s. Prescribed time of non-intercourse for a ship, etc., suspected of infection. v.t. To prohibit from intercourse.
Levan'tine a. Pertaining to the Levant. s. A native of or trader in the Levant a stout silk fabric.
Observ'antine s. One of a strict branch of Franciscans.
Byzan'tine a. Of the style of architecture, painting, etc., characteristic of the Eastern Empire.
Den'tine s. The ivory foundation of a tooth.
Triden'tine a. Pertaining to the Council of Trent, or to Trent.
Ar'gentine a. Of or containing silver. s. A small silvery fish.
Val'entine s. A sweetheart chosen on 14th February (St. Valentine's Day); an amatory or satirical picture or letter sent on this day.
Ser'pentine a. Pertaining to or resembling a serpent; coiling, sinuous; subtle s. A rock with a mottled, snake-skin appearance when polished.
Tur'pentine s. A resinous substance from conifers; oil or spirit from this.
Bar'quentine s. A three-masted vessel.
Cispon'tine a. North of the Thames in London.
Transpon'tine a. Beyond or across the bridge melodramatic.
Tontine' (-tēn') s. A form of cumulative annuity.
Nic'otine s. A poisonous, oily alkaloid contained in tobacco.
Nar'cotine s. A tasteless, crystalline compound found in opium.
Er'gotine s. The bitter principle in ergot of rye.
Guil'lotine s. A machine for beheading, or for cutting paper, tonsils, etc.; curtailment of parliamentary debate. v.t. To execute or cut with a guillotine.
Ser'otine s. A common European bat.
Lib'ertine s. A debauchee, rake. a. Licentious.
Lacer'tine a. Pertaining to the lizards; resembling a lizard.
Nemer'tine s. A marine worm.
Ves'pertine a. Pertaining to or done n the evening.
Trav'ertine s. A porous rock used for building.
Asbes'tine a. Like or made of asbestos.
Des'tine v.t. To appoint, fix, doom.

Predes'tine v.t. To decree beforehand, foreordain.
Clandes'tine a. Secret, sly, underhand.
Celes'tine s. A monastic order; a member of this; native sulphate of strontium.
Laur'estine s. Laurustinus.
Intes'tine a. Internal; not foreign; civil. s. The membranous canal from stomach to anus.
Phil'istine s. One of an ancient Palestinian race; a person deficient in culture or of narrow views.
Trap'pistine s. A nun of the Trappist order; a liqueur made by Trappists.
Pris'tine a. Belonging to the earliest time; primitive.
Sis'tine a. Pertaining to one of the popes, Sixtus.
Amethys'tine a. Composed of or resembling amethyst.
Bottine' s. A small boot.
Routine' (-tēn') s. Any regular course of action.
Mat'utine a. Pertaining to the morning; early.
Calix'tine s. A member of a Hussite sect.
Beguine' s. A member of a Dutch sisterhood.
An'guine a. Snaky.
Sang'uine a. Having the colour of blood; ardent; hopeful. s. Blood-colour; a drawing in red chalk.
Ensang'uine v.t. To stain with blood.
Consan'guine a. Consanguineous.
Exsang'uine a. Bloodless; having poor blood.
Gen'uine a. Free from adulteration; real; true.
Eq'uine a. Pertaining to the horse or the horse family.
Vine s. Climbing plant that bears grapes.
Ravine' (-vēn') s. A narrow gorge, a deep pass.
Land'gravine s. The wife of a landgrave.
Mar'gravine s. The wife of a margrave.
Pals'gravine s. The consort of a palsgrave.
Aberdevine' s. The siskin.
Divine' a. Pertaining to God; holy, sacred; of highest excellence. v.t. To foretell, presage; to conjecture. s. One versed in divinity; a clergyman.
Ol'ivine s. A variety of chrysoprase.
Al'vine a. Pertaining to the belly.
Mil'vine a. Pertaining to the kites. s. A bird of this family.
O'vine a. Pertaining to or like sheep.
Bo'vine a. Resembling or pertaining to oxen.
Cer'vine a. Belonging to the deer family.
Ner'vine a. Affecting the nerves. s. A nerve-tonic.
Cor'vine a. Pertaining to crows.
Wine s. Fermented juice of the grape.
Swine s. A pig; hogs collectively; a beastly or debased person.
Twine v.t. To twist together, form by twisting; to embrace. v.i. To unite closely; to bend, meander. s. A convolution; act of winding; strong thread.
Entwine' v.t. To twist together.
Intertwine' v.t. and i. To twist together.
Lau'wine s. An avalanche.
Pyrox'ine s. Augite, a silicate of lime, magnesium, or manganese.
Bux'ine s. An alkaloid from the box-tree.
Thy'ine a. Denoting a precious wood (*Bible*).
Bombazine' s. A twilled fabric of silk and worsted.
Magazine' s. A storehouse; a repository for ammunition, etc.; a periodical publication.
Or'ganzine s. Very fine silk twisted in strands; a fabric made of this.
Ben'zine s. (*Benzene*).
Tragedienne' s. A tragic actress.
Comedienne' s. A comedy actress.
Sicilienne' s. A fine ribbed silk.
Tyrolienne' s. A Tyrolese dance and song.
Julienne' s. A clear soup.
Equestrienne' s. A female equestrian.
Parisienne' s. A female inhabitant or native of Paris.
Varsovienne' s. A Polish dance.
Cayenne' s. A hot, red pepper prepared from capsicum.
Chaconne' s. An old Spanish dance.
Cloisonné' a. Partitioned; applied to certain enamel-work.
Cret'onne s. A patterned cotton fabric.
One a. Single, individual, any. s. The first of the simple units; its symbol (I). pron. Any person; a thing.
Bone s. The hard substance supporting the fabric of an animal body. v.t. To take out the bones; (*slang*) to steal.
Whale'bone s. Elastic horny substance found in palate of certain whales.
Huckle-bone s. The hip-bone or ankle-bone.
Back'bone s. The spine; strength, pluck.
Trombone' s. A deep-tone brass slide trumpet.
Cone s. A solid, tapering body having a circle for its base; the fruit of firs, pine-trees, etc.
Scone (skon) s. A soft, baked barley or wheaten cake.
Done (dun) past part. (*Do*); (*slang*) cheated, baffled. int. Agreed, accepted.
Condone' v.t. To pardon, forgive.
Undone' (-dun') a. Annulled; ruined; unfastened; not done.
Bombardo'ne s. A brass musical instrument; an organ-stop.
Fordone' a. Ruined, worn-out, exhausted.
Some'one s. Somebody.
Gone past part. (*Go*). a. Beyond hope; ruined.
Begone' v. (*imperat.*) Get off! Clear out!
Woe'begone a. Overwhelmed with woe.
Foregone' a. Past; determined before.
Forgone' a. Renounced, relinquished.
By'gone a. Past. s. A past event.
Hone s. A stone used for sharpening instruments. v.t. To sharpen on this. v.i. To moan, whine.
Ohone' int. An Irish cry of lamentation.
Phone v.t. and i. To telephone, use the telephone. s. A voice-sound.
-phone suff. Denoting an instrument that makes, conveys, records, etc., sound or voice.
Meg'aphone s. Speaking trumpet for calling to distances.
Dic'taphone s. An apparatus for recording and afterwards reproducing sounds from dictation.
Tel'ephone s. Electrical instrument for transmitting sounds to a distance. v.t. and i. To use this.
Au'diphone s. An instrument for conveying sound to deaf-mutes.
Aur'iphone s. An ear-trumpet.
Kalei'dophone s. Instrument for exhibiting the character of sound-waves.
Ra'diophone s. Instrument for production of sound through radiant energy.
Xy'lophone s. A musical instrument in which wooden bars are struck.
Gram'ophone s. An instrument for recording and reproducing sounds.
Hom'ophone s. A word of the same sound as another but different meaning.

Mi'crophone s. Instrument for intensifying feeble sounds.
Hy'drophone s. An instrument for detecting sound through water.
Sax'ophone s. A brass wind-instrument with reed mouthpiece.
Pol'yphone s. A symbol standing for a number of sounds.
Shone (shon) past and past part. (*Shine*).
Conversazio'ne s. A social meeting for some literary, artistic, or scientific object.
Lone a. Without company; unfrequented.
Alone' a. Single, solitary.
Cy'clone s. An extensive rotatory storm; state of the atmosphere in which the lowest pressure is central.
Anticy'clone s. The outward flow of air from a region of high barometric pressure.
Anem'one s. The wind-flower; a marine actinia.
Agapem'one s. An abode of love.
None a. and pron. No one; not any one. adv. In no respect; not at all.
Quinone' s. A compound obtained from quinic acid or the benzene hydrocarbons.
Pone s. A loaf of maize-meal; the player on the dealer's right at cards.
Depone' v.t. To assert under oath; to depose. v.i. To testify under oath, make an assertion.
Repone' v.t. To replace, rehabilitate.
Postpone' v.t. To defer to a later time; to put off, adjourn.
Lazzaro'ne s. A Neapolitan beggar.
Crone s. An old ewe; an old woman.
Drone s. The male of the bee; an idler; a low, humming sound; a lower pipe of a bagpipe. v.i. To live in idleness, to dream; to give a low dull sound, hum.
Ladrone' s. A highwayman, pirate, vagabond.
Padro'ne s. An innkeeper, master of a Mediterranean sailing-vessel.
Cicero'ne s. A guide.
Throne s. A royal seat, chair of state. v.t. To place on a throne; to exalt.
Dethrone' v.t. To depose from a throne, drive from position.
Enthrone' v.t. To place on a throne, invest with sovereignty or as a bishop.
Prone a. Flat on the face; headlong; sloping; apt, inclined to.
Tone s. Sound in relation to its pitch, etc., or as expressive of sentiment, etc.; timbre; mood; prevailing character; hue; healthy condition. v.t. and i. To give tone to, receive tone; to harmonize.
Atone' v.i. To make satisfaction, to expiate.
A'cetone s. A liquid used in the manufacture of chloroform and as a solvent.
Ke'tone s. An organic compound formed by distillation of an organic acid.
Sem'itone s. Half a tone in music.
Bar'itone s. A male voice between bass and tenor; a singer with this.
Ses'quitone s. A minor third (*music*).
Intone' v.i. and t. To recite or chant in monotone; to speak in a level tone.
Mon'otone s. A single key or musical sound; unvaried pitch of the voice.
Elec'trotone s. Electrotonus.
Pep'tone s. The substance into which food is disintegrated and transformed by the gastric juice.
Stone s. A broken piece of rock; a pebble; calculus; a gem; nut of a fruit; 14 lbs. avoir. a. Made of or like stone. v.t. To pelt or kill with stones; to free from or furnish with stones.
Tomb'stone s. Memorial stone over a tomb.
Kerb'stone s. Large stone of a kerb.
Rub'stone s. A whetstone.
Head'stone s. Stone at the head of a grave.
Glad'stone s. A light portmanteau.
Load'stone s. Magnetic oxide of iron.
Toad'stone s. An igneous, non-metalliferous trap-rock.
Sand'stone s. A rock formed of consolidated sand, etc.
Grind'stone s. A circular revolving stone on which tools are sharpened.
Free'stone s. A stone which can be cut in any direction; a kind of peach.
Mile'stone s. A stone marking the miles on a road.
Tile'stone s. An argillaceous stone.
Lime'stone s. A rock of which the basis is carbonate of lime.
White'stone s. A fine kind of granite.
Cling'stone s. A kind of peach.
Hearth'stone s. The stone floor of a hearth; soft whitening stone; fireside.
Fel'stone s. Felsite.
Hail'stone s. A frozen drop of rain.
Mill'stone s. One of the circular grinding stones of a mill.
Brim'stone s. Sulphur.
Rot'tenstone s. A friable stone used for polishing.
Whin'stone s. A hard, basalt-like rock.
Tin'stone s. Native oxide of tin.
Moon'stone s. An opalescent variety of feldspar.
Corn'stone s. An earthy concretionary limestone.
Horn'stone s. Chert.
Turn'stone s. A bird allied to the plover.
Soap'stone s. Steatite.
Drip'stone s. The projecting moulding over a doorway, window, etc.
Hoar'stone s. A landmark.
Moor'stone s. A variety of granite.
Whet'stone s. Piece of stone used for sharpening.
Grit'stone s. A hard sandstone.
Key'stone s. Central stone of an arch; fundamental principle, etc.
Grey'stone s. A volcanic rock composed of feldspar and augite.
Ho'lystone s. Soft sandstone used for scrubbing decks. v.t. To scrub with this.
Parox'ytone s. A Greek word having the acute accent on the penultimate.
Proparox'ytone a. Having an acute on the antepenultimate.
Ev'eryone s. Every person.
Zone s. A girdle; one of the five great divisions of the earth bounded by circles parallel to the equator. v.t. To encircle with a zone.
Canzo'ne s. A Provençal song.
Ozone' s. A condensed, allotropic form of oxygen; (*slang*) sea air.
Lucarne' s. A dormer window.
Erne s. The golden eagle; the sea-eagle.
Lucerne' s. The fodder-plant purple medick.
Lierne' s. A short rib in Gothic vaulting.
Caserne' s. (*Casern*).
Terne s. Inferior tinplate.
Sauterne' (sōtern') s. A white wine from Bordeaux.
Borne v.t. (past part.) (*Bear*).
Sea'-borne a. Carried by sea.
Forborne' past part. (*Forbear*).

Cromorne' s. One of the reed stops of an organ.
Bourne s. A bound, limit.
Noc'turne s. A representation of a night-scene; a serenade.
Mesne (mēn) s. Middle; intermediate.
Demesne' s. Estate attached to a mansion.
Puisne (pū'ni) a. Younger or inferior in rank.
Beaune s. A red wine.
Posau'ne (-zou'-) s. A powerful reed-stop on the organ.
Trib'une s. An elected magistrate among the ancient Romans; a platform, rostrum, bishop's throne.
Dune s. A hill or ridge of sand; a down.
Tri'une a. Three in one.
June s. The sixth month.
Jejune' a. Scanty; wanting in substance or interest.
Lune s. A figure enclosed by two intersecting arcs; anything crescent-shaped.
Dem'ilune s. A crescent, especially in fortification.
Plen'ilune s. The full moon; time of this.
Immune' a. Enjoying immunity; free from attack.
Commune' v.i. To converse together familiarly, to confer.
Com'mune s. A territorial district in France and Belgium; municipal self-government; a municipality; the Parisian socialistic party of 1871, their rule; intimate converse, communion.
Rune s. A letter of the ancient Norse alphabet; poetry in runes.
Prune v.t. To trim, lop off, rid of superfluity. v.i. To dress, prink. s. A dried plum.
Tune s. A short melody; harmony; correct intonation; mood. v.t. To put into tune; to adapt.
Nep'tune s. The Roman god of the sea; the planet furthest from the sun.
For'tune s. Chance, luck; destiny; means of living; great wealth. v.i. To befall, happen.
Misfor'tune s. Ill-luck; mischance; calamity.
Im'portune v.t. To solicit pertinaciously; to request with urgency; to tease. a. Untimely; importunate.
Op'portune a. Seasonable, well-timed; suitable.
Inop'portune a. Not seasonable; inconvenient.
Attune' v.t. To make musical, put in tune.
Picayune' s. A small coin of Span. N. America.
Dyne s. The unit for measuring force.
An'odyne s. A medicine which relieves pain.
Chlor'odyne s. An anodyne containing chloroform, opium, etc.
Eyne s. Eyes (*obs.*).
An'drogyne s. An effeminate man.
Groyne s. Structure running out at right angles from shore to prevent encroachment of sea.
Syne adv. (*Scot.*) Long ago.
Langsyne' adv. (*Scot.*) Long ago. s. Time long past.
O'boe (-boy) s. A treble, wood-wind instrument with a double reed.
Doe s. The female of the buck.
Foe s. An enemy, opponent; a persecutor.
Chig'oe s. The jigger, a W. Indian and S. American flea.
Hoe s. A tool for cutting weeds, breaking clods, etc. v.i. and t. To use or break with this.
Tuck'ahoe s. A N. American underground fungus.
Shoe (shoo) s. An outer foot-covering not extending to the ankle; an iron plate nailed to a horse's hoof, runner of a sled, etc. v.t. To furnish with shoes; to cover at the end or bottom.
Pek'oe s. A fine kind of tea.
Al'oe s. A plant yielding a medicinal gum.
Floe s. A large mass of floating ice.
Fel'loe s. The rim, or a curved segment, of a wheel.
Dip'loe s. Spongy tissue in the skull.
Sloe s. A shrub of the plum family; its fruit.
Canoe' s. A light boat propelled by paddles.
Hoop'oe s. A crested bird with fine plumage.
Roe s. A small species of deer; female of the hart; the spawn of fish.
Throe s. Anguish; a pang.
Toe s. One of the five members at the extremity of the foot. v.t. To touch or reach with this; to kick; to mend the toe of a boot, etc.
Mis'tletoe s. A parasitic plant with white, glutinous berries.
Tip'toe adv. On the tip of the toes. v.i. To walk or stand thus.
Woe s. Grief, sorrow, misery; calamity.
Ape s. A kind of monkey, a mimic, a foolish fellow. v.t. To mimic, to form oneself on.
Cape s. A headland; a cloak for the shoulders.
Scape s. The shaft of a column; a peduncle rising directly from a root.
Sea'scape s. A marine painting.
Land'scape s. An extensive view; a picture of country scenery.
Escape' v.t. To flee from, avoid, shun; to pass without harm. v.i. To be free, regain one's liberty. s. Flight; evasion of restraint or custody; means of flight; a leakage.
Sky'scape s. A view of clouds or sky.
Gape v.i. To yawn, stare open-mouthed with wonder. s. This act; a yawn; width of opening of mouth or beak.
Ag'ape s. A love-feast.
Agape' adv. Staring with eagerness or surprise.
Chape s. The catch of a buckle, etc.
Shape v.t. To form, fashion; to adjust; to image. v.i. To suit. s. External structure, character, or appearance of a thing; form, make; a model.
Ship'shape s. In good order; properly arranged.
Jape s. A jest, joke. v.i. To play tricks; to joke.
Nape s. The back of the neck.
Rape s. Violent seizure, especially of a woman; violation; a plant allied to the turnip; a division of Sussex. v.t. To violate, ravish.
Sara'pe (-pā) s. S. American horseman's blanket-cloak.
Crape s. A thin, crisp, transparent stuff, usually black and used for mourning.
Scrape v.t. To rub with something rough, to clean thus, to erase; to collect or save with difficulty. v.i. To abrade; to rub with a rasping sound; to make an awkward bow; to pass or get through narrowly. s. Act, effect, or sound of scraping; an awkward bow; a narrow escape.

Drape v.t. To clothe or decorate with cloth; to arrange drapery.
Grape s. The fruit of the vine; grape-shot.
Tape s. Narrow fillet of woven cotton, etc. v.t. To furnish, bind, etc., with tapes.
Swape s. A long oar; a pump-handle.
Crêpe s. Any crape other than black.
Crê'pé a. Frizzled.
Re'cipe s. A prescription, formula, for making medicines, dishes, etc.
Hipe s. A certain throw in wrestling. v.t To throw an opponent by means of this.
Kipe s. Basket for catching fish.
Snipe s. A game-bird with a long bill; simpleton. v.i. To shoot snipe; to pick off single enemies from cover.
Gut'tersnipe s. A street-arab.
Pipe s. A long tube; a wind musical instrument; a tube with a bowl for smoking; a wine-cask of about 105 galls.; a bird's call. v.i. To whistle, play on a pipe, etc., to have a shrill sound. v.t. To play on a wind-instrument; to utter shrilly.
Wind'pipe s. The trachea, breathing passage.
Bag'pipe s. An instrument consisting of reed-pipes and a wind-bag for producing musical sounds.
Pitch'pipe s. A small pipe for ensuring accuracy of musical pitch.
Horn'pipe s. A lively sailor's dance; music for this.
Blow'pipe s. A tube used for blowing through.
Ripe a. Mature; finished; perfect.
Gripe v.t. and i. To hold hard, pinch, squeeze; to give pain to the bowels. s. Grasp, grip; that which grasps.
Tripe s. Stomach of ruminant as food.
Stripe s. A long narrow marking; a streak; stroke with a lash or mark made by this. v.t. To variegate with lines.
Stipe s. A stalk; stem-like support.
Wipe v.t. To cleanse by rubbing; to efface. s. Act of wiping; a hard blow.
Swipe v.i. and t. To hit with great force; to gulp down. s. A hard blow.
Poulpe s. The octopus.
Ope a. Open. v.t. and i. To open.
Cope s. An ecclesiastical vestment; the sky, anything spread overhead; the top part of a foundry mould. v.t. To cover with a cope or coping; to barter. v.i. To form an overhang; to encounter, contend successfully with; to make a bargain, to deal.
Peric'ope s. A citation, quotation, especially in public worship.
Syn'cope s. Interior omission of one or more letters from a word; a fainting fit.
Apoc'ope s. A cutting off of the last letter or syllable.
Scope s. Outlook, sphere; amplitude of range; sweep, extent.
-scope suff. Denoting an instrument for observation.
Tel'escope s. Optical instrument for viewing distant objects. v.t. and i. To close the different parts of, shut up.
Kon'iscope s. Instrument for showing amount of dust in the air.
Spinthar'iscope s. Instrument for exhibiting rays emitted by radium.
Polar'iscope s. Instrument for examination of polarization of light.
Per'iscope s. An arrangement of mirrors enabling one in a trench, submarine, etc., to view objects outside.
Ir'iscope s. Instrument for exhibiting prismatic colours.
Au'riscope s. An instrument for examining the ear.
Al'tiscope s. A periscope.
Strob'oscope s. Instrument for observing periodic motion.
Kaleid'oscope s. An optical toy exhibiting a variety of coloured symmetrical forms.
Dipleid'oscope s. An instrument for determining the moment of transit of a star, etc., over the meridian.
En'doscope s. An instrument for examining internal organs or cavities.
Phonen'doscope s. A variety of stethoscope.
Pseud'oscope s. A stereoscopic instrument for reversing images.
Rhe'oscope s. A galvanoscope.
Ster'eoscope s. A binocular optical instrument for giving to plane pictures the appearance of solids.
Pharyn'goscope s. Instrument for inspecting the throat.
Laryn'goscope s. Instrument for examining the larynx.
Steth'oscope s. Instrument used to distinguish sounds in the chest.
Bi'oscope s. Moving pictures; a cinematographic exhibition.
Hag'ioscope s. An oblique opening in a church wall to allow sight of the altar.
He'lioscope s. A reflecting telescope for examining the sun.
Myr'ioscope s. A kind of kaleidoscope.
Polem'oscope s. An optical instrument for viewing objects obliquely.
Ophthal'moscope s. Instrument for examining the interior of the eye.
Ther'moscope s. Instrument for indicating changes of temperature.
Seis'moscope (siz'-) s. A kind of seismograph.
Cy'moscope s. Instrument for detecting electrical waves.
Galvan'oscope s. An instrument for detecting the presence and ascertaining the direction, etc., of electric currents.
Lych'noscope s. A low window in a church, "a leper-window."
Tei'noscope s. Optical instrument correcting the chromatic aberration of light.
Rhi'noscope s. Mirror for examining the nasal passages.
Prax'inoscope s. A form of zoetrope.
Phon'oscope s. Instrument for making sound vibrations visible.
Chron'oscope s. An instrument for measuring velocity of projectiles.
Bar'oscope s. A weather-glass.
Mi'croscope s. An optical magnifying instrument.
Hy'droscope s. A clepsydra; a hygroscope.
Si'deroscope s. Instrument for detecting magnetism.
Hy'groscope s. Instrument for showing relative degree of atmospheric moisture.
Ure'throscope s. Instrument for examining the urethra.
Spir'oscope s. A spirometer.
Hor'oscope s. Scheme of the heavens from which astrologers cast nativities or make predictions.

Fluor'oscope s. An apparatus for observing the effect of R ntgen rays.
Elec'troscope s. Instrument for detecting presence, etc., of electricity in a body.
Spec'troscope s. Optical instrument for analyzing spectra.
Staur'oscope s. Instrument for examining optical properties of crystals.
Gyr'oscope s. An instrument to illustrate the principles of circular motion.
Pyr'oscope s. Instrument for measuring intensity of radiant heat.
Chromat'oscope s. A form of reflecting telescope.
Stat'oscope s. A form of aneroid for detecting minute variations.
Rec'toscope s. Instrument for examining the rectum.
O'toscope s. An instrument for examining the ear.
Phenakis'to-scope s. A scientific toy like a zoetrope.
Cys'toscope s. An instrument for examination of the bladder.
Mu'toscope s. An early form of cinematograph.
Dope s. A viscous liquid; a drug, a stupefying drink, powder, etc.; (*slang*) cocaine. v.t. and i. To administer or take dope or drugs.
Hope s. Anticipation; trust; confidence. v.i. To entertain hope; to trust. v.t. To desire with expectation.
Stan'hope s. A light two- or four-wheeled carriage; a certain printing-press.
Wan'hope (wŏn'-) s. Despair.
Lope v.i. To move with long strides. s. This motion.
Elope' v.i. To go off clandestinely; to run away (especially with a lover).
An'telope s. A ruminant akin to the deer.
En'velope s. A wrapper, especially of a letter; that which envelops.
In'terlope v.i. To traffic without proper licence; to interfere.
Slope s. An inclined surface, an oblique direction. a. Inclined, inclining. v.t. and i. To direct obliquely, to incline, be inclined.
Aslope' a. Sloping. adv. Obliquely, with a slant.
Gant'lope s. The punishment of the gauntlet.
Mope v.i. To be dull and spiritless. s. A dispirited person.
Pope s. The Bishop of Rome; head of the Roman Catholic Church.
Ep'ope s. An epic poem; epic poetry.
Rope s. A thick cord; cable; halter; string of things. v.t. To pull by or fasten or enclose with a rope. v.i. To become thready.
Phal'arope s. A snipe-like wading bird.
Grope v.i. To feel about as in the dark; to seek blindly.
Ly'canthrope s. One afflicted with lycanthropy; a wer-wolf.
Phil'anthrope s. A philanthropist.
Mis'anthrope s. A hater of mankind.
Trope s. A word used figuratively; a figure of speech.
Chrom'atrope s. A rotating magic lantern.
Thau'matrope s. An optical toy in which painted figures appear to move.
Zo'etrope s. The wheel of life, an optical toy.
He'liotrope s. A genus of plants of the borage family; a purple tint; bloodstone.
Pyr'ope s. A deep red variety of garnet.
Tope s. A mango-grove; a Buddhist monument; a small shark. v.i. To tipple habitually.
Met'ope (-ŏpi) s. Space between the triglyphs in a Doric frieze.
Met'ope (-ŏp) s. Middle frontal portion of a crab.
Pres'byope s. A long-sighted person.
My'ope s. A short-sighted person.
Genappe' s. A smooth worsted yarn for braids etc.
Frap'pé a. Iced.
Steppe s. A vast, treeless plain, especially in Russia.
Grippe s. Influenza.
Euter'pe s. The Muse of music.
Dupe s. One easily deceived. v.t. To impose upon, cheat.
Jupe s. A woman's skirt.
Coupé' s. A small, four-wheeled closed carriage; a railway compartment with seat on one side only.
Troupe s. Company of performers.
Drupe s. A stone fruit.
Stupe s. A warm fomentation; (*slang*) a fool.
Slype s. Narrow covered passage from transept to chapter-house.
Type s. An emblem; ideal representative; model; printing letters. v.t. and i. To write with a typewriter.
Ec'type s. A copy from an original; a cast in relief.
Ar'chetype s. The primitive type or model.
Chem'itype s. A process of printing from an impression chemically produced in relief.
An'titype s. That which is represented by the symbol.
Zinc'otype s. A zincograph
Ster'eotype s. A metal plate presenting a facsimile of set type. v.t. To take a stereotype of; to establish in fixed form.
Daguer'reotype s. A process of photographing on metal plates; a photo so produced.
Log'otype s. A single piece of type comprising two or more letters.
Graph'otype s. A process for obtaining printing-blocks without engraving.
He'liotype s. A surface-printed picture direct from a photograph.
Col'lotype s. A method of reproduction from a gelatine film; a print thus produced.
Li'notype s. A machine for setting and casting type in lines.
Plat'inotype s. A method of printing photographs.
Phon'otype s. A character used in phonetic printing.
Mon'otype s. A single representative of its kind; a machine that casts and sets single types.
Cer'otype s. A process of copper-plate engraving.
Fer'rotype s. A photo taken on an iron plate by a collodion process.
Elec'trotype s. The facsimile of type, an engraving, medal, etc., produced by electrical deposition of copper on a mould from the original; process of obtaining such. v.t. To copy by this process.
Papyr'otype s. A kind of photo-lithography.
Pho'totype s. A printing-plate or print produced by photo-engraving.
Pro'totype s. An earliest example; a model, archetype.
Au'totype s. A facsimile.

Re prep. In the matter of.
Re (rā) s. The second tone of the diatonic scale.
Are v. aux.
Bare a. Unclothed, not covered. v.t. To strip.
Thread'bare a. Almost worn-out; hackneyed.
Care s. Caution; heed; charge, with responsibility; object of attention, trouble. v.i. To be anxious; to be inclined.
Scare v.t. To alarm, terrify suddenly. s. Panic; unreasoning fear.
Dare v.i. To have courage, to venture. v.t. To defy, challenge.
Outdare' v.t. To surpass in daring.
Fare s. Price of conveyance; person carried; food. v.i. To happen; to subsist; to feed.
Field'fare s. A species of thrush.
Thor'oughfare (thŭr'-) s. Passage through; a frequented street.
Wel'fare s. Prosperity; health; success.
Fan'fare s. A flourish of trumpets.
War'fare s. War; hostilities; military service.
Hare s. A swift, timid rodent with long ears, long hind legs, and split upper lip.
Chare s. A job, turn of work, chore. v.t. To do odd jobs.
Phare s. A lighthouse, pharos.
Share s. A part, allotment, portion bestowed; lot; a ploughshare. v.t. To portion among two or more; to participate in. v.i. To receive a portion.
Plough'share s. The part of a plough that cuts the ground.
Cav'iare s. The roe of sturgeon prepared as a relish; something unappreciated by the crowd.
Blare v.i. To bellow, roar.
Declare' v.t. To make known publicly; to reveal. v.i. To avow.
Flare v.i. To burn or glitter unsteadily; to give out a dazzling light. s. A broad, unsteady light.
Glare s. A dazzling light; a piercing look. v.i. To flare, shine with great lustre; to look fiercely.
Mare s. The female of the horse.
Night'mare s. A terrifying dream due to oppression.
Snare s. A noose-trap for small animals; a wile, artifice. v.t. To catch in a snare; to ensnare, inveigle.
Ensnare' v.t. To entrap; to defeat treacherously.
Pare v.t. To shave or trim off; to cut away bit by bit.
Prepare' v.t. To make ready; to fit, adapt, adjust, make, provide. v.i. To get ready.
Compare' v.t. To examine the relations and likenesses between; to liken one to another; to inflect in degrees of comparison. v.i. To bear comparison. s. Comparison.
Spare a. Meagre, scanty; parsimonious; held in reserve. v.t. To use frugally or tenderly; to omit, withhold from. v.i. To be frugal or forbearing.
Rare a. Uncommon, scarce; thinly scattered; of loose texture; not dense; not frequent; underdone (of meat).
Cu'rare s. A vegetable poison used by Indians on arrows and as an anæsthetic.
Tare s. The common vetch, darnel; allowance for weight of container; weight of a vehicle without its load.
Hectare' s. A French measure of nearly 2½ acres.
Lætar'e s. The 4th Sunday in Lent.
Stare v.i. To look steadily, to gaze. v.t. To affect by staring. A fixed look; the starling.
Outstare' v.t. To face down; to browbeat.
Square a. Having four equal sides and four right angles; forming a right angle; honest, upright; suitable. s. A figure or area with four equal sides and right angles; instrument with one edge at right angles to another; relation of harmony; equality; product of a number multiplied by itself. v.t. To make square; to adjust, fit; to settle (accounts); to multiply a number by itself. v.i. To suit, agree; to adopt a fighting attitude.
Ware s. Goods; manufactured articles; pottery. a. Conscious; wary. v. imp. Beware.
Aware' a. Informed of, conscious; vigilant.
Unaware' a. Inattentive; not conscious.
Hard'ware s. Ironmongery.
Beware' v.i. To take care, regard with caution.
Earth'enware s. Ware made of baked clay; pottery.
Tin'ware s. Vessels of tin-plate.
I'ronware s. Goods made of iron.
Sil'verware s. Table utensils of silver.
Sware past (*Swear*).
Macabre' a. Gruesome.
Sa'bre s. A cavalry sword. v.t. To strike or kill with this.
Gue'bre s. A Parsee, fire-worshipper.
Fi'bre s. A thread-like portion or rootlet of a plant; something resembling this.
Cal'ibre s. The bore of a gun, etc.; capacity, standing.
Tim'bre (tanbr) s. Quality of a sound.
Om'bre s. An old card-game.
Som'bre a. Dull, gloomy.
Acre' s. A land-measure, 4840 square yards.
Wise'acre s. A pretender to wisdom.
Fia'cre s. A French hackney-cab.
Pola'cre (-ker) s. A polacca.
Na'cre s. Mother-of-pearl.
Mas'sacre s. Butchery, carnage, slaughter. v.t. To slay wholesale, kill indiscriminately.
Chan'cre s. A venereal ulcer.
Me'diocre a. Of moderate quality; commonplace.
Lu'cre s. Gain in money, etc.; emolument; pelf.
Involu'cre s. Collection of bracts round a cluster of flowers.
Ca'dre s. The permanent establishment of a military unit.
Double-entendre' s. An ambiguous expression, one meaning of which is indelicate.
Ere adv. Before, sooner than. prep. Before (in time).
Quær'e s. A query. v.t. To question, inquire.
Cere v.t. To cover or coat with wax. s. The wax-like skin on a bird's beak.
Sincere' a. Honest; real; not feigned.
Insincere' a. Deceitful; hypocritical.
Adipocere' s. The substance into which bodies buried in damp places is converted.
Bayadère' s. A Hindu dancing-girl.
Belvedere' s. A pavilion on top of a building.

Fere s. A mate, companion (*obs.*).
Interfere' v.i. To clash; to interpose; to meddle with the affairs of others.
Here adv. In this place; in the present state or life.
Adhere' v.i. To stick or cling to.
Inhere' v.i. To be fixed in something else; to belong to a subject.
Cohere' v.i. To stick together, follow regularly, be consistent.
Sphere s. An orb, globe; a star, etc.; apparent surface of the heavens; range, province, compass of influence. v.t. To enclose or place in a sphere; to make spherical.
Hem'isphere s. One half of a sphere, especially the terrestrial or celestial.
Plan'isphere s. Representation of a sphere (especially the celestial) on a plane.
Ensphere' v.t. To place in or form into a sphere.
Neph'elosphere s. The cloud-atmosphere of a planet, etc.
Chro'mosphere s. The gaseous envelope of the sun seen at a total eclipse.
At'mosphere s. The air surrounding the earth.
Hy'drosphere s. The mass of water forming our oceans and seas.
Pho'tosphere s. The luminous envelope of the sun or a star.
There adv., s., and int.
Where (hwair) adv., interrog., pron.
Some'where adv. In some unspecified place.
Elsewhere' adv. In or to some other place.
No'where adv. Not in any place, state, etc.
Ev'erywhere adv. In every place.
Glacière' s. An ice-cave.
Vivandière' (-air') s. A female sutler.
Bersaglier'e s. An Italian sharpshooter.
Première' s. First performance of a play, etc.
Jardinière' s. An ornamental vase for plants.
Portière' s. Curtain across a door or doorway.
Condottier'e s. An Italian mercenary soldier; a leader of these.
Rivière' s. A necklace of gems.
Mere a. That or this only; absolute. s. A lake, pool.
Par'amere s. One of a set of symmetrical segments of an organism.
Met'amere s. A sonite, a body-segment.
Cash'mere s. A fabric made from goat's wool.
Chimere' s. The silk robe of a bishop.
Cass'imere s. A fine twilled cloth.
Ker'seymere s. Cassimere.
Ampère' s. The unit in measuring the strength of an electric current.
Miserer'e s. The 51st Psalm; a cry for mercy; a misericord.
Con'frère s. A fellow-member of one's profession, etc.
Sere s. The pawl of a fire-arm's lock. a. Sear.
Misère' s. (*Cards*) The call of taking no tricks.
Ptere (tēr) s. A wing-like organ.
Hec'tostere s. A French solid measure (about 3531 cubic feet).
Austere' a. Severe, stern, harsh.
Revere' v.t. To venerate, regard with awe and respect.
Severe' a. Serious; rigid; austere; rigorous.
Persevere' v.i. To pursue any design steadily; to be constant, to continue.
Trouvère' (-vair) s. A mediæval poet of N. France.
Were past (*Be*).
Gru'yère s. A milk cheese full of cavities.
Tuyère' s. The blast-pipe of a furnace.
Zaff're (zăf'er) s. (*Zaffer*).
Ea'gre s. A tidal wave in an estuary.
Mea'gre a. Lean, emaciated; scanty.
Mai'gre a. Suitable for fast-days. s. A large Mediterranean fish.
Chig're s. (*Chigoe*).
Em'igré s. An emigrant.
O'gre s. A cruel, imaginary monster.
Mau'gre adv. In spite of.
Sep'ulchre s. A tomb, especially in rock.
O'chre (-ker) s. A variety of clay containing iron; a yellow pigment.
Eu'chre s. A card game. v.t. (*Slang*) To defeat, outwit.
Ire s. Anger; passion.
Lais'sez-faire s. The principle of non-interference.
Doctrinaire' s. An impractical political theorizer; an ideologist. a. Visionary, impractical.
Questionnaire' s. A series of questions on some subject.
Millionaire' s. One having 1,000,000 pounds, dollars, etc.; a very rich man.
Concessionaire' s. One holding a concession, especially from the Government.
Commission-aire' s. One of a body of time-expired service men employed as messengers, etc.
Proletaire' s. A proletarian.
Secretaire' s. A bureau, writing-desk.
Solitaire' s. A single gem in a setting; a large stud; game for one person; a recluse; an extinct bird allied to the dodo.
Dire a. Dreadful, terrible; mournful.
Fire s. Heat and light; combustion; flame; a conflagration; discharge of fire-arms; ardour, spirit. v.t. To set on fire; to irritate; to animate; to bake; to cause to explode. v.i. To take fire; to discharge fire-arms.
Afire' adv., a. On fire, burning.
Bon'fire s. An outdoor fire at rejoicings, etc.
Misfire' s. Failure to explode or go off. v.i. To fail thus.
Spit'fire s. A pugnacious, irascible person.
Hire s. Recompense for temporary use; pay, allowance. v.t. To procure by payment for temporary use; to let; lease; to bribe.
Sam'phire s. An aromatic herb growing on sea-cliffs.
Sapph'ire s. A very hard, blue, precious stone.
Shire s. A county, territorial division.
Mire s. Mud; swampy ground. vt. To plunge in or soil with mire. v.i. To sink in mire.
Admire' v.t. To regard with delight or love; to esteem.
Bemire' v.t. To soil with mire.
Quag'mire s. A quaking bog; a marsh.
Pis'mire s. An ant.
Præmuni're s. Offence of introducing papal authority into England; writ against one charged with this or with giving allegiance to the Pope.
Pour'boire s. A tip, gratuity.
Moire s. Watered silk; a watered appearance.
Moir'é a. Watered (of silk); clouded (of metals).
Armoire' s. A cupboard.
Ba'ignoire s. A box level with the stage or stalls.
Conser'vatoire s. An institution for instruction in music, elocution, etc.
Escritoire' s. A writing-desk.
Rep'ertoire (-twar) s. Stock of plays, pieces, etc., ready for performance.
Vam'pire s. A blood-sucking spectre; an extortioner; a kind of bat.

Em'pire s. Supreme power in governing; body of principalities, states, dominions, etc., under central rule; sway.
Um'pire s. An arbitrator, referee, judge. v.t and i. To act as umpire.
Spire s. A tapering structure; a steeple; a blade of grass, sprout, etc.; a coil, a twist.
Aspire' v.i. To desire with eagerness; to rise.
Respire' v.i. and t. To breathe, take breath again, breathe in and out.
Transpire' v.t. To emit, exhale, send off in vapour. v.i. To pass off as vapour.
Inspire' v.t. To take into the lungs; to breathe into; to infuse ideas, poetic spirit, etc., into; to animate v.i. To draw in breath.
Reinspire' v.t. To inspire again.
Conspire' v.i. To combine secretly for an illegal purpose; to plot; to concur.
Perspire' v.i. and t. To sweat, emit by the pores.
Suspire' v.i. To breathe deep, to sigh.
Expire' v.i. To emit breath; to die, come to an end. v.t. To breathe out, to exhale.
Sire s. A progenitor; title of address to a king, etc.; male parent of a horse, etc.
Grand'sire s. A grandfather; a male ancestor.
Desire' v.t. To long for, covet; to beseech. v.i. To have desire. s. Aspiration; eagerness to have and enjoy; lust.
Tire v.t. and i. To exhaust the strength of; to weary or become weary. s. A band on the rim of a wheel; a head-dress.
Sat'ire s. A writing ridiculing folly, etc., sarcasm, irony.
Retire' v.i. To draw or go back, keep aloof; to retreat, withdraw, recede; to go to bed. v.t. To cause to retire; to pay when due. s. A signal to retire.
Sal'tire s. A St. Andrew's cross (X).
Entire' a. Whole, complete in all parts; unshared; sincere.
Attire' v.t. To dress, array. s. Clothes; head-dress.
Quire s. twenty-four sheets of paper; a choir.
Acquire' v.t. To gain by one's labour, to become possessed of.
Require' v.t. To insist upon having; to claim by right or as indispensable.
Inquire' v.i. To ask questions, make search. v.t. To ask about, seek by asking.
Squire s. A country landowner or gentleman; a beau. v.t. To escort (a woman).
Esquire' s. An attendant on a knight; a title of courtesy.
Wire s. Metal drawn into slender thread; the telegraph. v.t. and i. To bind with wire, put a wire on; to send or communicate by telegraph.
Gen're s. Kind, class; painting which depicts scenes of ordinary life.
Ore s. Mineral from which metal is extracted.
Bore v.t. To pierce; to vex or weary. s. A hole made by boring; the tube of a fire-arm; an advancing tidal wave in a river; a worrying, annoying person.
Hell'ebore s. A ranunculaceous plant; the Christmas rose.
Forbore' past (*Forbear*).
Core s. The heart, or inner part of anything; the central part of an apple, pear, etc. v.t. To remove the core from.
Albacore' s. A large species of tunny.
Hal'icore s. The genus to which the dugong belongs.
Man'ticore s. A fabulous, human-headed monster.
Encore' adv. int. Again, once more; call for a repetition. v.t. and i. To make such a call.
Score s. A notch, a long scratch; an account, debt; 20; points made in a game; draught of a musical composition; motive. v.t. To notch, make scratches on; to record; to make points in games; to orchestrate. v.i. To keep a score; to win points.
Fourscore' a. and n. Four times twenty; eighty.
Adore' v.t. and i. To reverence, worship; to love intensely.
Dum'bledore s. The humble bee, the cockchafer.
Bat'tledore s. A bat for use with a shuttlecock.
Ste'vedore s. One who loads and unloads ships.
Moidore' s. An obsolete Portuguese gold coin (about 27s.).
Ban'dore s. An old stringed musical instrument.
Pan'dore s. A lute-like musical instrument.
Com'modore s. A naval officer above a captain; president of a yacht-club; a captain of pilots.
Fore a. Anterior, not behind; before. adv. In the part that precedes. int. (*Golf*) Beware.
Afore' prep. Before, nearer in place or time. adv. In time past, in front.
Pin'afore s. A small apron.
Before' prep. In front of, farther onward, superior to. adv. Sooner than; in times past, hitherto.
There'fore adv. For that cause.
Where'fore adv. For what reason? on which account. s. Reason why.
Heretofore' adv. Formerly.
Gore s. Clotted blood, a triangular piece of cloth. v.t. To pierce with a horn.
Chore s. A spell of work, chare.
-phore suff. Denoting a bearer.
Sem'aphore s. Apparatus for visible signalling at a distance.
Sperm'ophore s. The placenta in plants.
Gon'ophore s. A long stalk holding the pistils and stamens in certain plants.
Car'pophore s. The central axis in many flowers.
Spir'ophore s. Instrument for restoring suspended respiration.
Elec'trophore s. An electrophorus.
Chromat'ophore s. A pigmented cell in fishes' scales feathers, etc.
Pneumat'ophore s. A gas-mask used in mines.
Shore s. Land bordering the sea or a large body of water; prop as temporary support to a building, etc. v.t. To support with these. past (*Shear*).
Ashore' adv. On the land; stranded.
Sea'shore s. The coast; ground between high and low water mark.
Fore'shore s. The shore between high and low watermark.
Inshore' adv. Near or towards the shore.

Whore s. A prostitute. v.i. To fornicate; to worship strange gods.
Lore s. Collected traditions on a subject; counsel; part between eye and beak of birds.
Galore' adv. In plenty; abundantly.
Folk'-lore s. Popular traditions, superstitions, etc.
Deplore' v.t. To lament over, regret, bewail.
Implore' v.t. To beseech, crave, solicit. v.i. To supplicate.
Explore' v.t. To search into, scrutinize; to travel for discovery.
More a. Greater in amount, quantity, number, etc. adv. In a greater degree, etc.; in addition. s. A greater quantity, etc.; something further.
Syc'amore s. A tree allied to the maple and plane.
Sag'amore s. Head of a N. American Indian tribe.
Syc'omore s. The Syrian fig-tree.
Soph'omore s. A second-year student in certain American Universities.
Farthermore' adv. Moreover; besides.
Furthermore' adv. Moreover, besides.
Evermore' adv. Always, continually.
Nevermore' adv. At no future time.
Clay'more s. The two-edged Highland sword.
Tenor'e (-ā) s. A tenor singer.
Ignore' v.t. To pass without notice; to declare ignorance of.
Snore v.i. To breathe hoarsely through the nose in sleep. s. Sound or act of this.
Pore s. A minute orifice in the skin. v.i. To examine steadily.
Mill'epore s. A species of coral.
Mad'repore s. A variety of coral; animal producing it.
Re'tepore s. A variety of zoophyte.
Extem'pore adv. Without preparation or meditation. a. Extemporaneous.
Spore s. The reproductive body in a cryptogam; a unicellular reproductive body in protozoa, etc.
En'dospore s. The inner layer of the wall of a spore.
Zy'gospore s. A spore produced by junction of two similar gametes.
Zo'ospore s. A spore having power of independent motion.
Crore s. A hundred lacs of rupees.
Frore a. Frozen; frosty. adv. Keenly, frostily.
Furore' s. Great enthusiasm; a rage.
Sore s. Place where skin and flesh are ruptured; a wound, ulcer. a. Tender, painful; distressing, severe. adv. Severely, grievously.
Bed'sore s. A sore occasioned by long lying in bed.
Eye'sore s. Something offensive to the sight.
Tus'sore s. A coarse strong kind of silk.
Foot'sore a. Having the feet tender.
Tore past (*Tear*).
Tore s. A torus.
Improvisator'e s. One who improvises; an extempore versifier.
Store s. Plenty; a warehouse, large shop; a hoard. v.t. To accumulate for future use; to supply; to deposit in a store.
Restore' v.t. To bring back from a state of decay, etc.; to repair; to cure; to give back.
-vore suff. Denoting an animal feeding on the substance indicated.
Her'bivore s. One of the herbivora.
Car'nivore s. A flesh-eating animal or plant.
Insec'tivore s. An insect-eating mammal.
Wore past (*Wear*).
Swore past (*Swear*).
Forswore' past (*Forswear*).
Yore adv. Long since; in old time.
Bizarre' a. Fantastic, extravagant.
Parterre' s. An ornamental flower garden; the seats behind the orchestra in a theatre.
The'atre s. Place for exhibition of dramatic performances, etc., also for surgical operations; a place of action.
Amphithe'atre s. A theatre of elliptical shape.
Spec'tre s. An apparition, ghost.
Me'tre s. Measure applied to versification; rhythm, verse; French measure of length (39.37 in.).
Me'tre s. One who or that which measures; a measuring instrument; metre. (*See* METER.)
Dec'ametre s. A measure of ten metres.
Dec'imetre s. One-tenth of a metre.
Mill'imetre s. 1000th part of a metre.
Cen'timetre s. The 100th of a metre.
Kil'ometre s. French measure of distance, ·621 m le.
Hec'tometre s. A French measure of length (328 feet).
Saltpe'tre s. Nitre; potassium nitrate.
Li'tre (lē'ter) s. Unit of capacity in metric system (about 1¾ pints).
Dec'alitre s. A liquid measure of ten litres (about 2¼ gallons).
Dec'ilitre s. One-tenth of a litre.
Mill'ilitre s. 1000th part of a litre.
Cen'tilitre s. The 100th of a litre.
Kil'olitre s. A French liquid measure, about 220 gallons.
Hec'tolitre s. A French measure for liquids (about 26¼ gallons).
Mi'tre s. The episcopal head-dress; a junction of two boards at an angle. v.t. To confer a mitre upon; to join or shape with a mitre.
Ni'tre s. Saltpetre; potassium nitrate.
Goi'tre s. Morbid enlargement of the thyroid gland.
Reconnoi'tre v.t. To make a preliminary survey, especially for military purpose. v.i. To take part in a reconnaissance.
Phil'tre s. A love-charm. v.t. To excite with a love-potion; to charm to love.
An'tre s. A cavern.
Cen'tre s. The exact middle point of anything; an axis, pivot, nucleus, point of concentration.
Ep'icentre s. (*Epicentrum*).
Pericen'tre s. Point in any body's orbit nearest to the centre.
Rencontre' s. and v.i. Rencounter.
Scep'tre (sep'ter) s. The royal staff, the symbol of authority.
Dar'tre s. A skin disease.
Cadas'tre s. A register of property as a basis of taxation.
Pias'tre s. A small Turkish and Egyptian silver coin.
Bis'tre s. A brown pigment.
Lus'tre s. Sheen, glitter; a cut-glass chandelier; a glossy fabric.
Ou'tré (oo'trā) a. Extravagant; fantastic; bizarre.
Accout're v.t. To equip, furnish with arms, etc.
-ure suff. Forming abstract nouns.
Roque'laure (rōk'-) s. A short cloak for men.

Cure s. Act of healing; a remedy; state of being cured; spiritual charge of souls; (*slang*) a wag, eccentric person. v.t. To heal, make well; to pickle. v.i. To effect a cure.
Cu'ré s. A parish priest.
Si'necure s. A paid office without duties.
Secure' a. Free from care, risk, etc.; impregnable; safe; over-confident. v.t. To make certain or safe; to protect; to enclose, to get possession of.
Insecure' a. Not safe; apprehensive of danger.
Ped'icure s. A chiropodist; treatment of the feet.
Man'icure v.t. To tend the finger-nails, etc. s. The dressing and care of the hands and nails.
Ep'icure s. One given to luxury; a voluptuary.
Procure' v.t. To obtain, acquire, get. v.i. To act as procurer.
Obscure' a. Dark; dim; doubtful; indistinct. v.t. To make dark, less intelligible, or less visible; to dim, to conceal.
Proce'dure s. Act or manner of proceeding; step taken; progress; conduct.
Superse'dure s. Act of superseding.
Endure' v.t. To bear, sustain, undergo.
Ron'dure s. A circle; something spherical.
Ver'dure s. Greenness of vegetation; foliage.
Or'dure s. Dung; excrement.
Bordure' s. An heraldic border.
Coiffure' s. Method of hairdressing; a head-dress.
Fig'ure s. Shape, semblance, image; a statue; a diagram; a character representing a number; price; a metaphor, type. v.t. To make a likeness of; to image in the mind. v.i. To make a figure, be distinguished.
Prefig'ure v.t. To foreshow; to suggest by similitudes.
Config'ure v.t. To give shape or form to.
Disfig'ure v.t. To mar the appearance of; to deface.
Trans'figure v.t. To change or idealize the figure of.
Lig'ure s. Ligurite; a jacinth-like stone.
Hachure' s. Shading by short lines in maps, engravings, etc.
Brochure' s. A pamphlet.
Debouchure' s. The mouth of a river.
Embouchure' s. Mouth of a river; mouthpiece or blow-hole of a wind instrument.
Graph'iure s. A S. African rodent like a dormouse.
Abjure' v.t. To renounce upon oath.
Adjure' v.t. To charge solemnly, enjoin.
In'jure v.t. To do wrong to; to damage, wound.
Con'jure v.t. To raise up by enchantment, to effect by jugglery. v.i. To practise the arts of a conjurer.
Conjure' v.t. To appeal to by a sacred name; bind by an oath.
Per'jure v.t. To swear falsely, forswear.
Lure s. A bait, enticement. v.t. and i. To entice, attract.
Velure' s. A kind of velvet.
Fail'ure s. Cessation of supply; non-performance; insolvency; an unsuccessful person or thing.
Allure' v.t. To attract, entice; to wheedle.
Colure' s. Either of two great circles intersecting at right angles in the poles of the equator.
Mure v.t. To shut up, wall in.
Demure' a. Staid, grave, sober; prim.
Immure' v.t. To enclose, confine.
Manure' s. Dung, compost, or other fertilizer. v.t. To treat with this.
Ten'ure s. Manner in which lands, etc., are held; period of holding.
Inure' v.t. To habituate, accustom, harden to. v.i. To come into operation, take effect.
Tournure' s. Contour, figure; a woman's bustle.
Pure a. Unadulterated; clean, clear; real, sincere; absolute; chaste.
Guipure' s. Imitation antique lace; a kind of gimp.
Impure' a. Adulterated; defiled, unclean; not grammatically correct.
Pur'pure s. Heraldic purple.
Parure' s. A set of jewels.
Sure a. Certain; unfailing; safe.
Pleas'ure s. Agreeable sensations or emotions; what the will prefers; that which pleases; frivolous enjoyment. v.t. To give pleasure to, to gratify.
Displeas'ure s. Dissatisfaction; slight anger or irritation.
Meas'ure s. Magnitude of a thing; a standard, measuring line; amount allotted; course of action; metre; a dance. v.t. To ascertain size, etc., of; to estimate; to pass over; to allot. v.i. To have a certain extent.
Admeas'ure v.t. To apportion.
Treas'ure (trĕzh'-) s. Accumulated wealth; anything highly valued; great abundance. v.t. To prize greatly; to hoard.
Ra'sure s. Act of erasing.
Embra'sure s. Opening in a parapet, etc., for cannon.
Eras'ure s. Act of erasing; obliteration.
Leis'ure s. Freedom from business or hurry. a. Not spent in work.
Cocksure' a. Perfectly certain; self-confident, arrogant.
Ensure' v.t. To make safe or sure.
Cen'sure s. Disapproval; reprimand. v.t. To blame, find fault with.
Insure' v.t. To make secure, especially against loss; to contract for a sum to be paid at death, in certain events, etc.
Reinsure' v.t. To insure again, especially in favour of one who already has insured it.
Ton'sure s. Act of shaving, especially crown of head; state of being so shorn; mark of admission to Roman Catholic priesthood.
Clo'sure s. Act of shutting, state of being shut; power of bringing a debate to an end. v.t. To stop a debate thus.
Enclo'sure s. Act of enclosing (especially common land); anything enclosed.
Foreclos'ure s. Act of foreclosing.
Disclo'sure s. Act of disclosing; thing revealed.
Cyn'osure s. The constellation the Little Bear, which contains the North Star; any centre of attraction.
Compo'sure s. Calmness, tranquillity.
Discompo'sure s. State of being discomposed; agitation, disquiet.
Expo'sure s. Act of exposing; state of being exposed; situation; danger.
Assure' v.t. To make sure, give confidence: to insure.
Reassure' v.t. To assure anew; to free from fear, etc.

Pres'sure s. Act of pressing; constraining force; straits, difficulty; action of a force against some obstruction.
Fis'sure s. A cleft; a narrow chasm or opening. v.t. and i. To cleave or become cleft.
Com'missure s. A joint, seam; line or point of junction.
Chaussure' s. Boots, shoes, etc.
Cu'bature s. Cubage.
Ju'dicature s. Power to dispense justice; a court of justice or its jurisdiction.
Trip'licature s. A triplication.
Caricature' s. Exaggeration of some characteristic, a ridiculing likeness or description. v.t. To make a caricature of.
Can'didature s. The state or fact of being a candidate.
Fea'ture s. Form or appearance of a person or thing; good appearance; lineament; a marked peculiarity. v.t. To portray; to present on the cinema screen.
Defea'ture v.t. To disfigure; to disguise.
Crea'ture s. A created being, a human; something imagined; one who owes advancement to another; a mere tool. a. Pertaining to the body.
Lig'ature s. Anything that binds; a cord for tying blood-vessels.
Nun'ciature s. Office or state of a nuncio.
Min'iature s. A small portrait on ivory, etc.; art of painting on a small scale. a. Represented very small.
Stri'ature s. Striation.
Tab'lature s. A painting, especially on a wall or ceiling; an ancient system of musical notation.
Entab'lature s. An architrave, frieze, and cornice.
No'menclature s. A system of terminology, or of technical names in some branch of science.
Fil'ature s. Reeling of silk from cocoons; apparatus or establishment for this.
Leg'islature s. A body invested with power to make laws.
Mature' a. Ripe; perfected by time; ready; having become payable. v.t. and i. To make or become ripe or perfect; to become payable.
Prem'ature a. Too early; not prepared; untimely.
Lim'ature s. Act of filing; filings.
Cli'mature s. Climate.
Immature' a. Not ripe, not fully developed.
Ar'mature s. Weapons; a piece of soft metal for increasing magnetic or electric power.
Na'ture s. The creation, universe, world of matter; essential qualities, natural character, animal force; natural condition of man, undomesticated state of animals, etc.; sort, kind.
Dena'ture v.t. To divest of essential character.
Cren'ature s. A scallop; small rounded tooth on a leaf-edge.
Sig'nature s. Person's name written with his own hand; printers' mark at foot of first page of sheet.
Declin'ature s. Refusal to acknowledge legal jurisdiction.
Quad'rature s. Act of squaring; a square; relative position of heavenly bodies distant from each other 90°.
Tem'perature s. Degree of sensible heat.
Lit'erature s. Literary knowledge, learning, or productions; collective writings of a country, period, etc.
Col'orature s. The use of musical variations, etc., in harmony.
Ser'rature s. Serration.
Mag'istrature s. Magistracy.
Dicta'ture s. Dictatorate.
Stat'ure s. The natural height.
Cur'vature s. Deflexion from a straight line.
Fix'ature s. A hair-gum.
Manufac'ture s. Process of making anything by labour; anything made from raw materials. v.t. To make by labour; to fabricate without real grounds. v.i. To be occupied in manufacture.
Compact'ure s. Compact structure.
Frac'ture s. A breach, rupture; breaking of a bone. v.t. To break across. v.i. To break.
Refrac'ture v.t. To fracture again.
Pre'fecture s. Office, jurisdiction or dignity of a prefect.
Conjec'ture s. Surmise; opinion without proof. v.t. To judge by guess. v.i. To form conjectures.
Projec'ture s. A jutting beyond the surface.
Lec'ture s. A formal discourse; a reprimand. v.i. To deliver lectures. v.t. To reprove.
Ar'chitecture s. The art or science of building.
Pic'ture s. A painting, illustration, likeness. v.t. To represent pictorially; to describe vividly.
Depic'ture v.t. To depict, represent.
Stric'ture s. Censure; contraction of a duct.
Cinc'ture s. A belt, enclosure. v.t. To gird, enclose.
Tinc'ture s. An extract or solution of the active principles of some substance; a tint, tinge. v.t. To flavour, tinge.
Junc'ture s. A junction, union; a crisis.
Conjunc'ture s. A combination of important events; a crisis.
Punc'ture s. A small hole made by a point; act of pricking. v.t. To pierce.
Struc'ture s. A building, manner of building; form, make.
Substruc'ture s. A foundation, under-structure.
Superstruc'ture s. Anything built on something else; superstruction.
Por'traiture s. Art of making portraits or describing vividly; a portrait.
Expen'diture s. Act of expending, a laying out; expense; money spent.
For'feiture s. Act of forfeiting; loss of some right, etc., or a misdeed or omission; that which is forfeited.
Discom'fiture s. Defeat, rout; frustration.
Primogen'iture s. Seniority by birth among children; eldest child's exclusive right to inheritance of real property on intestacy.
Ultimogen'iture s. Inheritance by the youngest son.
Progen'iture s. Begetting; offspring.
Porphyrogen'iture s. Succession of an heir during the reign of the father.
Gar'niture s. Furniture, trimmings, embellishment.
Fur'niture s. Equipment; movable household articles; chattels.
Nour'iture s. Nourishment; nurture.
Ves'titure s. Animals' covering, as hair, scales, etc.
Dives'titure s. Divestment; state of being stripped.
Inves'titure s. Act of investing or installing in any office. benefice, etc.; that with which one is invested.

Cul'ture s. Cultivation; refinement of mind and manners; rearing of bacteria, etc.; crop of such.
Pis'ciculture s. Artificial breeding and preserving of fish.
Ostreicul'ture s. Artificial cultivation of oysters.
Pom'iculture s. Fruit-growing.
Vin'iculture s. Cultivation of vines for wine.
A'piculture s. Bee-keeping.
Stirp'iculture s. Eugenics; breeding of special stocks.
Ol'ericulture s. Cultivation of pot-herbs.
Ser'iculture s. The breeding of silkworms.
Ag'riculture s. The science of cultivating the soil.
Ar'boriculture s. The culture of trees and shrubs.
Flor'iculture s. The cultivation of flowers.
Vit'iculture s. Grape- or wine-growing.
Hor'ticulture s. Art of cultivating gardens.
A'viculture s. The rearing of birds.
Syl'viculture s. Forestry.
Bov'iculture s. Cattle-raising.
Mul'ture s. Toll paid for grinding grain or pulverizing ore.
Sep'ulture s. Interment; burial.
Vivisep'ulture s. Burial alive.
Vul'ture s. A rapacious, carrion-eating bird.
Deben'ture s. A writing acknowledging a debt.
Inden'ture s. A written contract, deed under seal between parties.
Cal'enture s. A fever with delirium.
Gar'menture s. Dress, clothing.
Ven'ture s. A hazard, speculation, chance, stake. v.i. and t. To make a venture, dare; to risk.
Adven'ture s. An enterprise, a hazard. v.t. To risk. v.i. To venture, dare.
Peradven'ture adv. Perhaps; by chance.
Misadven'ture s. An unfortunate accident; ill-luck; mishap.
Attain'ture s. Attainder; dishonour.
Join'ture s. Estate settled on wife to be enjoyed after husband's decease. v.t. To settle a jointure upon.
Cap'ture v.t. To seize, arrest, take by force. s. That which is seized or made prisoner.
Recap'ture v.t. To retake. s. Act of retaking, especially a lost prize.
Rap'ture s. Ecstasy, transport.
Enrap'ture v.t. To transport with pleasure.
Scrip'ture s. A sacred writing, especially (pl.) the Bible.
Sculp'ture s. Art of carving in stone, etc.; a carved figure; carved work. v.t. To carve; to form, as images in stone, etc.
Rup'ture s. Act of breaking; a breach; open hostility; hernia.
Disrup'ture v.t. To disrupt. s. Disruption.
Depart'ure s. Act of departing, withdrawal, abandonment.
Ap'erture s. A small opening, a passage.
O'verture s. Opening of negotiations, proposal, offer; a musical prelude or introduction.
Cov'erture s. Shelter, secrecy; the legal state of a married woman.
Discov'erture s. State of an unmarried woman or a widow.
Tor'ture s. Anguish; extreme pain; infliction of this. v.t. To cause to suffer in excess; to torment; to distort.
Nur'ture v.t. To nourish, train, cherish. s. Upbringing; education; nourishment.
Pas'ture s. Grass or grass-land for cattle, horses, etc. v.t. To feed on growing grass. v.i. To graze.
Depas'ture v.t. To graze upon, to put to graze.
Ges'ture s. Motion to express sentiment passion, etc.; gesticulation.
Purpres'ture s. Illegal encroachment on public property.
Ves'ture s. Clothing; apparel.
Moist'ure s. That which makes damp; dampness.
Pos'ture s. Attitude, carriage; state or condition. v.t. and i. To place in or assume an attitude.
Impos'ture s. Act or conduct of an impostor; fraud, delusion.
Fu'ture s. That which is to come or happen hereafter; time to come; prospective state, etc. a. That will be; pertaining to time to come.
Su'ture s. Line along which two parts are sewn or joined by their margins; act of sewing. v.t. To unite thus.
Tex'ture s. A thing woven; manner or construction of weaving.
Contex'ture s. Interweaving of parts into a whole; disposition of parts.
Fix'ture s. A permanent appendage or adjunct; anything fixed or permanently attached.
Mix'ture s. Act of mixing; state of being mixed; a compound.
Admix'ture s. Act of mixing; a foreign element.
Immix'ture s. State of being involved or mixed up.
Commix'ture s. (*Commix*).
Intermix'ture s. A mass formed by mixture.
Pyrogravure' s. Pyrography; design, etc., produced by poker-work.
Photogravure' s. A process of pictorial reproduction.
Autogravure' s. A process of photo-engraving.
Ner'vure s. A rib or vein in an insect's wing or leaf.
Flex'ure s. Act, process, or manner of bending; part bent.
Deflex'ure s. A bending or turning aside.
Paradox'ure s. A civet-like mammal of S. Asia.
Das'yure s. A small Australasian marsupial.
Az'ure a. Blue like the sky.
Seiz'ure s. Act of seizing; sudden attack (of disease, etc.).
Reseiz'ure s. A second seizure.
Chef-d'œuvre s. A masterpiece.
Hors d'œuvre s. A relish or dish before the meal proper.
Manœu'vre s. Management; dexterous movement, especially of troops, etc.; stratagem. v.i. To perform manœuvres, employ stratagem, manage with address. v.t. To move by or cause to perform manœuvres.
Byre s. A cow-house.
Eyre s. A journey, circuit; a court of itinerant justices.
Gyre s. A revolution; circular motion. v.t. and i. To whirl.
Mel'aphyre s. A dark variety of porphyry.
Lyre s. A harp-like stringed instrument.
Pyre s. A funeral or other pile to be burnt.
Mel'ampyre s. Cow-wheat.
Tyre s. (*Tire*).
Base a. Mean; of little value; illegitimate; deep. s. The lower part of anything; pedestal; foundation; substance which neutralizes an acid; position from which army conducts operations. v.t. To place on a basis, to found.
Abase' v.t. To bring low.
Di'abase s. An igneous rock, a form of dolerite.

Debase' v.t. To degrade, make mean.
Sur'base s. Cornice at top of a pedestal or base.
Case s. An instance; state; an inflection of nouns; statement, box, covering, frame. v.t. To enclose in a case.
Encase' v.t. To put in a case.
Car'case s. A dead body, a framework.
Stair'case s. A flight of stairs with the balustrade, etc.
Ease s. Quiet; freedom from pain; facility.
Cease v.i. To leave off, to stop. v.t. To discontinue.
Decease' s. Death.
Predecease' v.t. To die before another. s. A death thus.
Surcease' s. Cessation. v.i. To cease.
Lease v.t. To grant or hold lands, etc., on lease. s. A letting of lands, etc., for rent for a period; contract for this.
Release' v.t. To set at liberty, to acquit. s. Liberation; discharge.
Please v.t. To excite agreeable emotions in; to delight, gratify, humour. v.i. To give pleasure; to comply; to think fit.
Displease' v.t. To offend, dissatisfy, provoke. v.i. To disgust.
Pease s. Peas collectively, or used as food.
Appease' v.t. To calm, satisfy, reconcile.
Crease s. Mark made by folding; lines near the wickets in cricket. v.t. and i. To make creases in, to become wrinkled.
Decrease' v.i. To become less; to wane. v.t. To make less.
De'crease s. Lessening; waning.
Increase' v.i. and t. To become or make greater; to augment, advance in numbers, size, quality, etc.; to add to.
In'crease s. Augmentation, addition, increment; a growing large in size, quality, etc.; offspring.
Grease s. Animal fat in a soft state; oily matter. v.t. To smear with or lubricate with grease; (*slang*) to bribe.
Disease' s. A malady; illness, sickness.
Hearts'ease s. The wild pansy; peace of mind.
Tease v.t. To separate the fibres of; to annoy, torment, pester.
Chase v.t. To pursue; to persecute; to engrave, emboss. s. Hunting, thing hunted, hunting-ground; forward part of a gun; frame to surround set type; a groove.
Steeple'chase s. A horse-race across country.
Enchase' v.t. To set in gold; to adorn, emboss; to enshrine.
Pur'chase v.t. To buy, obtain by outlay, etc. s. Act of buying; thing bought; power (of lever, etc.).
Repur'chase v.t. To buy back. s. That which is so bought.
Phase s. Appearance or state of a phenomenon that undergoes change; an aspect; a particular change of the moon, etc.
Pol'yphase s. Having two or more phases (of electric currents).
Ukase' s. A Russian imperial edict.
Bla'sé a. Worn-out through over-indulgence dulled in emotion.
Per'iclase s. Native magnesia.
Ol'igoclase s. A soda-lime feldspar.
Or'thoclase s. Potash feldspar.
Pla'gioclase s. A class of rock-forming minerals or feldspars.
Eu'clase s. A transparent silicate of aluminium and glucinum.
Erase' v.t. To rub out, efface, obliterate.
Phrase s. Mode of speech; idiom; pithy expression; part of a sentence.
Par'aphrase s. A free restatement or translation. v.t. To make a paraphrase of; to explain or translate freely.
Met'aphrase s. A literal translation.
Per'iphrase s. Periphrasis. v.t. and i. To express by or use circumlocution.
Prase s. A leek-green variety of quartz.
Chrys'oprase s. An apple-green variety of chalcedony.
Diop'tase s. A green ore of copper.
Invert'ase s. An enzyme that inverts sugar-cane.
Di'astase s. A ferment or enzyme which is an agent in plant and animal digestion.
Vase s. An ornamental vessel for domestic, and formerly sacrificial, use.
-ese suff. Belonging to (a country, etc.); in the style of (a writer, etc.).
Obese' a. Fat, corpulent.
Di'ocese s. The see of a bishop, a bishopric.
Archdi'ocese s. The see of an archbishop.
Fel'o-de-se s. Suicide; a suicide.
Geese s. (*Goose*).
Cheese s. The curd of milk solidified and ripened; a mass of ground apples pressed together; (*slang*) the correct thing. v.t. (*Slang*) To stop, cease.
Creese s. A Malayan dagger.
These pl. (*This*).
Cingalese' s. A native or the language of Ceylon. a. Pertaining to Ceylon or its people, etc.
Journalese' s. Mediocre journalistic style.
Novelese' s. Style or language suitable for novels.
Tyrolese' a. and s. Pertaining to or a native of Tyrol.
Carlylese' s. The literary style of Thomas Carlyle.
Siamese' (-mēz') a. Pertaining to Siam. s. A native or the language of Siam.
Burmese' (-mēz') a. Pertaining to Burma. s. A native, the natives, or the language of Burma.
Man'ganese s. A hard, greyish, metallic element; its oxide.
Japanese' a. Pertaining to Japan or its people. s. A native or the language of Japan.
Javanese' a. Pertaining to Java. s. A native or the language of Java.
Sienese' (sēenēz') a. Pertaining to Siena. s. A native or artist of this Italian town.
Bolognese' a. Of Bologna. s. An inhabitant of Bologna.
Chi'nese a. Of or pertaining to China. s. A native of China.
Pekinese' a. Pertaining to Pekin. s. An inhabitant of Pekin; a small Chinese spaniel.
Ruskinese' s. Ruskin's literary style.
Johnsonese' s. The pompous, inflated style of Dr. Johnson.
Chersonese' s. A peninsula.
Genoese' s. A native or inhabitant of Genoa. a. Pertaining to Genoa.
Maltese' a. Pertaining to Malta or its people. s. A native, the people, or the language of Malta; a variety of spaniel.

Portuguese' a. and s. Pertaining to, a native of, or language of Portugal.
Genevese' s. An inhabitant or native of Geneva. a. Genevan.
Cockneyese' s. Idiom or twang peculiar to Londoners.
-ise suff. Forming abstract nouns.
Chaise s. A light carriage.
Malaise' s. A premonitory feeling of uneasiness.
Marseillaise' s. The French national hymn.
Mayonnaise' s. A kind of salad or salad-dressing.
Polonaise' s. A dance in slow time; a dress for women.
Raise v.t. To lift, set upright, heighten; to excite; to construct, levy, originate; to inflate; to cause (a siege) to be abandoned.
Braise v.t. A method of stewing meat, etc.
Fraise s. A sloping palisade of stakes; tool for enlarging a hole.
Praise s. Commendation, eulogy; homage to God. v.t. To express approbation of; to extol, glorify.
Bepraise' v.t. To overwhelm with praises.
Appraise' v.t. To set a price upon, to value.
Dispraise' v.t. To censure, blame. s. Reproach, censure.
Upraise' v.t. To raise or lift up.
Bise s. A dry north wind prevalent in Switzerland.
Precise' a. Definite, exact; strictly correct; punctilious.
Cir'cumcise v.t. To remove the foreskin.
Incise' v.t. To cut into; to engrave.
Concise' a. Brief, abridged, terse.
Ex'ercise s. Labour; practice; physical exertion. v.t. To set in action; to employ, to train, to practise; to give anxiety to. v.i. To take exercise.
Excise' s. Tax on commodities of home consumption and production, or for licences to deal in such. v.t. To cut out, delete, remove from.
Par'adise s. The Garden of Eden; heaven; a place of bliss.
Mer'chandise s. Objects of commerce; wares; trade.
Gal'liardise s. Merriment, mirth.
Seise (sēz) v.t. To put in possession of
Fran'chise s. Freedom; privilege; a right, immunity; right of voting for a M.P.; citizenship.
Affran'chise v.t. To set at liberty physically or morally.
Enfran'chise v.t. To set free; to make free of; to grant the right to vote to.
Disfran'chise v.t. To deprive of a franchise; to dispossess of the rights of a citizen.
Valise' (-lēs') s. A small portmanteau.
Mise (mēz) s. A treaty, settlement by arbitration.
Demise' s. Death, especially of a sovereign. v.t. To bequeath.
Chemise' s. A woman's under-garment.
Remise' v.t. To release a claim to, to surrender. s. A release of property.
Premise' v.t. To set forth beforehand. v.i. To make or state antecedent propositions.
Prem'ise (-is) s. Proposition antecedently supposed or proved; each of first two propositions of syllogism in logic, from which inference is drawn.
Prom'ise s. A verbal or written engagement; a binding declaration; hope. v.t. To engage to do, refrain from doing, etc.; to assure. v.i. To give assurance, afford hopes.
Com'promise s. Arrangement for amicable settlement; mutual concession. v.t. To settle thus; to involve; to endanger the interests of.
Surmise' v.t. and i. To guess, suspect. s. A supposition, conjecture.
An'ise s. A species of parsley.
Noise s. Any kind of sound, outcry; clamour, din; scandal. v.t. To spread by report.
Poise s. Balance; equilibrium; carriage. v.t. and i. To make of equal weight, place in equilibrium; to be balanced.
Eq'uipoise s. Equality of weight or force; equilibrium.
Coun'terpoise s. A weight sufficient to balance another; equilibrium; equal powers in opposition; their mutual relations. v.t. To counterbalance.
Por'poise s. A gregarious delphinine cetacean.
Toise s. An old French measure (about 77 ins.).
Tor'toise s. A land or freshwater turtle.
Tur'quoise s. A greenish-blue opaque precious stone.
Pi'sé (pē'zā) s. Rammed clay for building walls, etc.
Despise' v.t. To disdain, look down upon, regard with contempt.
Rise v.i. To get up; to ascend, mount; to slope upwards; to come into existence or into sight; to rebel. s. Act of rising; elevation; origin; appearance above horizon; increase, advance.
Arise' v.i. To ascend, mount upward.
Rearise' v.i. To arise again.
Cerise' a. Cherry-coloured.
Sun'rise s. First appearance of sun above horizon; hour of this.
Prise v.t. To force open with a lever. s. Leverage.
Emprise' s. An undertaking, enterprise.
Comprise' v.t. To embrace, enclose, contain.
Apprise' v.t. To inform, give notice of.
En'terprise s. That which is undertaken; an adventure; willingness or ardour to engage in such. v.t. To undertake, venture upon.
Surprise' v.t. To fall upon or take unexpectedly; to astonish. s. Act of coming upon, etc., unawares; state of being surprised; amazement.
Treat'ise s. A composition or dissertation on some subject.
Prac'tise v.t. To do frequently or habitually; to put in practice, teach by practice, exercise a profession; to commit. v.i. To perform certain acts frequently; to exercise an employment; to try stratagems.
Ad'vertise v.t. To announce, publish notice of.
Mor'tise s. A hole in timber, etc., to admit a tenon. v.t. To cut a mortise in; to join thus.
Chastise' v.t. To punish or correct by beating.
Guise s. Mien, habit, appearance. v.i. and t. To dress up, play at mumming.
Disguise' v.t. To change the appearance of, counterfeit, dissemble. s. Something put on to conceal; a pretence.
Marquise' (-kēz') s. A marchioness; a ring with oval cluster of gems.
Bruise v.t. To hurt with blows. s. A hurt with something blunt and heavy.

Cruise s. A sailing to and fro for pleasure or in search of the enemy. v.i. To sail hither and thither.
Vi'sé (vē'zā) s. Endorsement on a passport. v.t. To put a visé on.
Advise' v.t. To counsel.
Preadvise' v.t. To advise beforehand.
Devise' v.t. To contrive, plot; to assign by will. s. Act of bequeathing; a will or clause bequeathing real estate.
Revise' v.t. To re-examine for correction; to review; to amend. s. A second proof-sheet.
Previse' v.t. To know beforehand; to forewarn.
Im'provise v.t. To speak, sing, play, etc., extempore; to extemporize.
Supervise' v.t. To oversee and direct; to superintend.
Wise a. Having wisdom, sagacious; making use of knowledge, skilled; containing wisdom. s. Manner; mode.
-wise suff. Forming adverbs of manner.
Broad'wise adv. Across; by way of the breadth.
End'wise adv. Endways.
Side'wise adv. Toward or on one side; laterally.
Edge'wise adv. Edgeways; sideways.
Like'wise adv. and conj. In like manner; moreover.
Long'wise adv. (*Lengthwise*).
Breadth'wise adv. By way of the breadth.
Length'wise adv. and a. In the direction of the length; longitudinally.
Con'trariwise adv. On the other hand; conversely.
Clock'wise adv. From left to right like the hands of a clock.
No'wise adv. In no way.
Oth'erwise adv. In a different manner; in other respects.
Cor'nerwise adv. Diagonally; with the corner in front.
Cross'wise adv. Across; in the form of a cross.
Flat'wise adv. With the flat side undermost.
Slant'wise adv. Slantly.
Coast'wise adv. By way of or along the coast.
A'nywise adv. In any manner or degree.
False a. Not true; dishonest; treacherous; counterfeit.
Valse s. A waltz.
Else pron. and a. Other; one besides.
Grilse s. A young salmon.
Dulse s. A reddish edible seaweed.
Pulse s. The beating of the heart or an artery; vibration; leguminous seeds.
Repulse' v.t. To repel, beat back; to rebuff. s. Act of repulsing; refusal; snub.
Im'pulse s. Application or effect of force; influence on the mind; sudden resolve; motive.
Convulse' v.t. To agitate violently, affect with convulsions, excite laughter in.
Temse s. A sieve.
Cleanse v.t. To render or become clean.
Hanse s. A trading corporation, especially a N. German guild of the thirteenth century.
Manse s. Residence of a Presbyterian minister.
Expanse' s. That which is expanded; wide smooth extension.
Cense v.t. To perfume with incense.
Li'cense v.t. To permit; to grant a licence to.
In'cense s. Perfume burnt in religious rites. v.t. To perfume with this.
Incense' v.t. To enflame, provoke, exasperate.
Dense a. Thick, compact; obtuse.
Condense' v.t. To compress, concentrate, reduce from a gas to a liquid or solid. v.i. To become dense, grow thick.
Flense v.t. To flench (a whale, etc.).
Immense' a. Huge, vast, unbounded.
Prepense' a. Premeditated; afterthought.
Rec'ompense s. An equivalent for anything; amends, reward, requital. v.t. To compensate, make up for, requite, reward.
Propense' a. Naturally inclined; prone.
Dispense' v.t. To deal out; to administer, apply; to grant dispensation for; to prepare or give out medicine.
Suspense' s. State of uncertainty; indecision; temporary cessation.
Expense' s. Act of expending; disbursement; cost, charge.
Sense s. Feeling; perception; discernment; a faculty of perception; meaning; good judgment.
Non'sense s. Unmeaning language; folly; absurdity.
Tense a. Stretched tight; rigid; not lax. s. One of forms verbs take to indicate time.
Subtense' s. That which subtends.
Intense' a. Strained; strict; extreme in degree; severe.
Rinse v.t. To cleanse by washing.
Response' s. An answer; act of responding; a responsory.
-ose suff. Denoting abundance or fullness; also carbohydrates and certain compounds.
Gib'bose a. Gibbous.
Bulbose' a. Bulb-shaped; pertaining to a bulb.
Corym'bose a. (*Corymbiform*).
Globose' a. Spherical, like a globe.
Herbose' a. Herby.
Verbose' a. Abounding in words; prolix.
Morbose' a. Morbid, diseased.
Floc'cose a. Covered with woolly tufts.
Suc'cose a. Juicy; full of sap.
Bel'licose a. Warlike, inclined to war.
Var'icose a. Morbidly dilated (of veins).
Cicat'ricose a. (*Cicatrix*).
Ven'tricose a. Having a protruding belly; distended.
Cor'ticose a. Resembling or made of bark.
Fru'ticose a. Shrubby, shrub-like; pertaining to shrubs.
Tal'cose a. Consisting of, containing, or like talc.
Jocose' a. Humorous; full of jokes.
Glu'cose s. Dextrose, grape-sugar.
Ver'rucose a. Warty; wart-like.
Dose s. Amount of medicine given at one time; something to be swallowed. v.t. To give in doses, give medicine to.
Lap'idose a. Stony; growing among stones.
Frondose' a. Bearing or like fronds; leafy.
Nodose' a. Knotty; having nodes.
Stri'gose a. Having or resembling strigæ or bristles.
Ru'gose a. Wrinkled, corrugated.
Hose s. Stockings, etc.; a long flexible tube.
Chose past (*Choose*).
Metamor'phose v.t. To change into a different form.
Those pl. (*That*).
Spa'those a. Spathaceous.
Feldspath'ose a. Feldspathic.
Whose (hooz) pron. Possessive case of "who."
Gran'diose a. High-sounding; imposing; bombastic.

Relig'iose a. Morbidly religious.
Spong'iose (spŭnj'-) a. Spongious.
Fo'liose a. Leafy; abounding in leaves.
E'briose a. Drunk; characterized by drunkenness.
O'tiose a. Indolent; useless; not necessary.
Lose v.t. To mislay, fail to keep, forfeit; not to gain; to miss; to bewilder. v.i. To suffer loss.
Close (-ōz) v.t. To shut, bring together the parts of; to stop, finish; to confine. v.i. To come together, coalesce; to end; to agree to; to grapple with. s. End; junction; union of parts; cadence; grapple in wrestling.
Close (-ōs) s. An enclosed space; a passage from a street to a court or house; precinct of a cathedral. a. Shut fast; pent up, confined; stuffy, stagnant; secret, secretive; niggardly; compact, dense; strict; intimate; accurate. adv. In a close manner or state.
Foreclose' v.t. To shut out, bar; to take away right of redemption of a mortgage.
Enclose' v.t. To surround, to encompass; to shut up in.
Par'close s. A screen or railing round a shrine, etc.
Disclose' v.t. To uncover, reveal, make known.
Fi'lose a. Ending in a thread-like process.
Pi'lose a. Hairy.
Lamel'lose a. Lamellar.
Trem'ellose a. Gelatinous.
Cap'illose a. Hairy.
Pap'illose a. Papillary.
Fi'brillose a. Furnished with fibrils.
Medul'lose a. Medullary.
Dolose' a. With criminal intent.
Acau'lose a. Stemless.
Tu'bulose a. Tubulous.
Floc'culose a. Woolly; minutely floccose.
Radic'ulose a. Having radicles.
Silic'ulose a. Bearing or resembling silicules.
Vermic'ulose a. Worm-shaped; full of worms worm-eaten.
Febric'ulose a. Slightly feverish.
Retic'ulose a. Reticulated.
Frutic'ulose a. Resembling a small shrub.
Loc'ulose a. Locular.
Vas'culose a. Vascular. s. A constituent of vegetable tissue.
Gland'ulose a. Glandular.
Nod'ulose a. Nodulated.
Ru'gulose a. Finely wrinkled.
Cell'ulose s. The basis of vegetable tissue. a. Consisting of cells.
Ham'ulose a. Like a little hook.
Ram'ulose a. Having many small branches.
Stim'ulose a. Having stinging hairs.
Spi'nulose a. Covered with small spines.
An'nulose a. Ringed.
Tor'ulose a. Having alternate swellings and contractions.
Fis'tulose a. Fistular.
Læv'ulose s. Fruit-sugar.
Riv'ulose a. Furrowed (of leaves).
Ner'vulose a. Minutely nerved.
An'chylose v.i. To become stiff, grow together.
Ha'mose a. Curved like a hook; having hooks.
Ramose' a. Branching; full of branches.
Squa'mose a. Scale-like; squamous.
Vamose' v.i. (*Slang*) To decamp, clear out.
Rac'emose a. Bearing racemes, as the currant.
Ri'mose a. Full of cracks (of tree-bark).
Co'mose a. Hairy, filamentous.
Mar'mose s. A pouchless opossum of S. America.
Os'mose s. Osmosis.
Endos'mose s. Endosmosis.
Ex'osmose s. Exosmosis.
Fumose' a. Producing fumes; smoke-coloured.
Glumose' a. Having glumes.
Plu'mose a. Having or resembling plumes; feathery.
Stru'mose a. Strumous.
Cymose' a. Bearing or pertaining to cymes.
Lach'rymose a. Tearful; ready to weep; glum.
Nose s. The organ of smell; power of smelling; scent; sagacity; a nozzle. v.t. and i. To smell, scent; to track; to pry officiously into.
Ar'enose a. Full of sand; gritty.
Ve'nose a. Venous; consisting of veins.
Di'agnose v.t. To distinguish; to ascertain the nature, etc., of a disease from the symptoms.
Lig'nose s. A powerful explosive found in lignin.
Ulig'inose a. Growing in swamps; uliginous.
Lam'inose a. Laminate; plate-like.
Acu'minose a. Terminating gradually in a flat, narrow end.
Spin'ose a. Full of or armed with spines.
Far'inose a. Producing farina; covered with flour-like dust; meally.
Pru'inose a. Covered with bloom.
Pannose' a. Having a texture like that of cloth (of leaves).
Car'nose s. (*Carneous*).
Lacu'nose a. Pertaining to or containing lacunæ.
Caboose' s. A cook's galley.
Calaboose' s. A prison.
Goose s. A web-footed bird larger than a duck; a tailor's smoothing-iron; a silly person.
Mongoose' s. A small carnivorous Indian mammal that preys on snakes.
Wayz'goose s. Annual festivity for printers.
Choose v.t. To make choice of, prefer. v.i. To make a selection, have the power of choice.
Loose a. Not attached; unbound; not compact; vague; wanton; lax. v.t. To untie, detach, set free. s. Vent; relaxation.
Moose s. A N. American deer allied to the elk.
Vamoose' v.i. (*Slang*) To decamp.
Noose s. A running knot; a snare. v.t. To catch in a noose; to entrap.
Papoose' s. A child (among the N. American Indians).
Pose s. An assumed attitude; an artistic posture. v.t. To place in an attitude for sake of effect; to puzzle, embarrass by questioning. v.i. To strike an attitude, behave affectedly.
Juxtapose' v.t. To place near or next.
Depose' v.t. To dethrone, remove from office. v.i. To bear witness, give testimony in writing.
Repose' v.t. To rest, place at rest; to put confidence in. v.i. To rest, lie at rest; to rely. s. Tranquillity; composure; a resting.
Ad'ipose a. Fat; oily.
Impose' v.t. To lay or place on; to inflict to palm off upon; to deceive.
Reimpose' v.t. To impose again.

Superimpose' v.t. To impose or lay on something else.
Compose' v.t. To form by uniting, to constitute; to write; to set type; to calm.
Decompose' v.t. To resolve into original elements, to analyse; to cause to rot. v.i. To putrefy.
Recompose' v t. To compose again; to tranquillize.
Discompose' v.t. To diconcert, interfere with, throw into disorder.
Propose' v.t. To offer for consideration, acceptance, etc.; to intend. v.i. To lay schemes; to offer oneself.
Pappose' a. Downy.
Oppose' v.t. To place over or act against; to hinder, resist. v.i. To make objections, act obstructively.
Suppose' v.t. To assume without proof; to imagine, conceive.
Presuppose' v.t. To assume beforehand, take for granted.
Superpose' v.t. To lay over or on something.
Interpose' v.t. To place between; to offer an objection, etc. v.i. To meddle, interfere, mediate; to put in a remark.
Pur'pose s. Intention; aim or object to be accomplished or reached. v.t. and i. To intend, design, resolve, mean.
Dispose' v.t. To place, arrange, bestow; to incline the mind of.
Predispose' v.t. To include beforehand, adapt previously.
Indispose' v.t. To make disinclined; to render unfit or slightly ill.
Transpose' v.t. To change place or order of; to substitute one for the other.
Expose' v.t. To lay open, to explain; to deprive of concealment, divulge.
Expo'sé s. A formal declaration of facts; an exposure.
Pol'ypose a. Polypous.
Rose s. A plant of many species; its flower; a reddish colour; a rosette, a perforated nozzle. a. Coloured like the rose. v. Past (*Rise*).
Arose' v.i. (pret.) (*Arise*).
Sac'charose s. A sugar turning polarized light to the right.
Brose s. (*Scot.*) Porridge.
La'brose a. Having thick lips.
Crib'rose a. Cribriform.
Su'crose s. Cane-sugar.
Erose' a. Irregularly indented (of leaves).
Tu'berose s. A bulbous plant with fragrant white flowers. a. Tuberous.
Op'erose a. Wrought with labour; wearisome.
Lit'erose a. Markedly or affectedly literary.
Vir'ose a. Virous.
Prim'rose s. An early flowering perennial plant; its pale yellow flower; the colour of this.
Morose' a. Sour of temper, sullen; churlish.
Porose' a. Porous.
Sop'orose a. Causing sleep; sleepy.
Prose s. All language not in verse; tedious talk, etc. v.t. To write prose, talk tediously. a. Pertaining to or composed of prose; prosaic.
Squar'rose a. Full of projections; jagged.
Brier-rose' s. The wild rose.
Cir'rose a. (*Cirrus*).
Cic'atrose a. Covered with scars.
Dex'trose s. Sugar obtained from starch and dried fruits; grape-sugar.
Neur'ose a. Well supplied with nervures; neurotic.
Gyrose' a. Marked with wavy lines.
Stig'matose a. Stigmatic.
Com'atose a. Drowsy, lethargic.
Tricho'matose a. Affected with trichoma.
Ker'atose s. The horny substance in sponges. a. Horny; made of horn.
Lactose' s. Milk-sugar.
Galac'tose s. A glucose obtained from milk-sugar.
Pec'tose s. An insoluble compound found in unripe fruits.
Fruc'tose s. Fruit-sugar.
A'cetose a. Sour, like vinegar; causing acetification.
Setose' a. Having the surface set with bristles.
Mal'tose s. A sugar obtained by the action of malt on starch.
Filamen'tose a. Filamentary; bearing filaments.
Tomen'tose a. Covered with long matted hairs.
Sarmen'tose a. Bearing runners (of plants); like a runner.
Ven'tose a. Windy; flatulent.
Schist'ose a. Admitting of cleavage into slabs.
Cystose' a. Containing cysts.
Sil'iquose a. Siliquous.
Anfrac'tuose a. Sinuous, tortuous.
Tor'tuose a. Twisted (of stems).
Flex'uose a. Winding, serpentine, crooked.
Næ'vose a. Spotted, freckled.
Rivose' a. Sinuously furrowed.
Ner'vose a. Nerved (of leaves); having nervures (of butterflies, etc.).
Quartz'ose a. Containing, consisting of, or resembling quartz.
Apse s. A vaulted recess in a church.
Lapse s. A gradual falling; unnoticed passing; a slip; a failing in duty, etc. v.i. To glide slowly; to fall by degrees; to fail in duty. v.t. To allow to slip away, fall from membership, etc.
Elapse' v.i. To glide or pass away.
Relapse' v.t. To slip, slide, or fall back. s. A falling back.
Illapse' s. A sliding in; a sudden attack.
Collapse' v.i. To fall in or together suddenly to break down; to shrink. s. A falling in; breakdown; sudden and complete failure.
Prolapse' v.i. To slip or fall out of place. s. A prolapsus.
Traipse v.i. To gad about in a sluttish way. s. A slattern.
Eclipse' s. Temporary obscuration, especially of a heavenly body by another. v.t. To darken a luminary, to extinguish; to outshine, excel.
Ellipse' s. A regular oval; an oblique section of a cone; an ellipsis.
Glimpse s. A transient view; a faint resemblance or tinge. v.i. To appear by glimpses. v.t. To catch a glimpse of.
Copse s. A coppice, thicket.
Corpse s. A dead body, especially of a human being.
Apoc'alypse s. Revelation, disclosure.
Carse s. (*Scot.*) Low fertile land near a river.
Hearse s. A carriage for conveying the dead.
Rehearse' v.t. To repeat; to relate; to recite for experiment and improvement.
Coarse a. Large in bulk; gross; common; not refined; indelicate.
Hoarse a. Harsh; having a rough, deep voice.

Parse v.t. To analyse a sentence, word, etc., and describe it grammatically.
Sparse a. Thinly scattered; not dense.
Erse s. The Gaelic dialect of the Scottish Highlands.
Herse s. A harrow-like portcullis.
Submerse′ v.t. To submerge. a. Growing under water.
Immerse′ v.t. To plunge into a fluid, etc.; to engage deeply.
Asperse′ v.t. To vilify, slander.
Disperse′ v.t. and i. To scatter here and there; to dispel, dissipate.
Intersperse′ v.t. To scatter here and there among.
Terse a. Concise; pithy; curt.
Verse s. A line of poetry; a stanza; metre, poetry; short division of a chapter.
Averse′ a. Disinclined to, unwilling.
Trav′erse v.t. To cross, thwart; to contradict. a. Transverse. s. Something that is transverse.
Obverse′ a. Set in opposition or as counterpart to. s. Side of coin with head on it.
Ad′verse a. Calamitous, contrary.
Reverse′ v.t. To turn or cause to turn back; to invert, transpose, revoke. s. That which is contrary; a complete change; the under side; misfortune; defeat. a. Turned backward; with a contrary direction.
Diverse′ a. Unlike, dissimilar; various.
U′niverse s. The whole creation.
Inverse′ a. Opposite in order or relation; inverted.
Converse′ v.i. To talk familiarly, discourse easily.
Con′verse s. Conversation, close connexion; something forming a counterpart, a complement. a. Opposite, reciprocal.
Perverse′ a. Stubborn, intractable; petulant.
Transverse′ a. Lying across or crosswise. s. The longer axis of an ellipse.
Birse s. A bristle.
Corse s. A corpse.
Endorse′ v.t. To write one's name on the back of; to assign thus; to ratify, approve.
Gorse s. A prickly shrub with yellow flowers; furze.
Horse s. A hoofed quadruped used for draught and burden; cavalry; various things resembling or analagous to a horse. v.t. To supply with a horse; to bestride.
Unhorse′ v.t. To throw from a horse.
Morse s. The walrus; the clasp of a cope. a. Denoting the dot-and-dash system of telegraphy.
Remorse′ s. Reproach of conscience; regret.
Premorse′ a. Terminating abruptly (of roots, etc.).
Norse a. Pertaining to Norway or its people. s. The Norwegian language.
Retrorse′ a. Bent backward, reverted.
Introrse′ a. Turned towards the axis.
Sin′istrorse a. Sinistrorsal.
Extrorse′ a. Turned outwards.
Dextrorse′ a. Rising spirally from left to right.
Torse s. An heraldic wreath.
Worse (wers) a. More bad; more unwell; more badly off; inferior. adv. More badly, etc.; less. s. A worse state, etc.; defeat; loss.
Reimburse′ v.t. To repay, refund.
Disburse′ v.t. To pay out, expend.
Curse v.t. To invoke evil against; to blight, injure, torment. v.i. To swear, blaspheme. s. An imprecation; invocation of divine vengeance upon; execration, torment.
Nurse s. A caretaker of infants or the sick; one who suckles a child. v.t. To act as nurse to; to rear; to foment, foster, to tend the sick.
Bourse s. A Stock Exchange.
Course s. Act of moving from one place to another; route; orderly progress or succession; methodical action; conduct; career; series of lectures, etc.; a layer of stones in masonry; part of a meal served at one time. v.t. To hunt, chase after, especially hares; to run through or over. v.i. To run with speed.
Recourse′ s. Resorting to for help; a source of help.
Con′course s. A moving together; an assembly, crowd.
Wa′tercourse s. A stream; channel for water.
In′tercourse s. Connexion by reciprocal dealings; fellowship; familiarity.
Discourse′ s. Conversation; a sermon, speech. v.i. To talk of or treat of formally. v.t. To utter, give forth.
Purse s. Small bag for money; a treasury; money. v.t. To put in a purse; to contract in wrinkles.
Cut′purse s. A thief, highwayman.
Fougasse′ s. A small mine used against enemy trenches.
Chasse s. A liqueur after coffee.
Chas′sé s. A gliding step in dancing. v.i. To perform this.
Pal′liasse s. A mattress stuffed with straw.
Déclas′sé a. Degraded from one's social position.
Filasse′ s. Prepared fibre.
Mas′sé s. A stroke at billiards with the cue held nearly vertically.
Pas′sé a. Faded; beyond the first beauty.
Impasse′ s. A blind alley, inextricable position.
Rasse s. A small civet of the Far East.
Tirasse′ s. The pedal-coupler of an organ.
Wrasse s. A prickly spined sea-fish.
Crevasse′ s. A deep fissure in a glacier.
Princesse′ a. Applied to a woman's skirt and bodice cut in one piece.
Fesse s. A broad horizontal band across the centre of an heraldic shield.
Noblesse′ s. Foreign nobility.
Finesse′ s. Artifice, stratagem. vi.. To use artifice to gain an end. v.t. To manage by trickery.
Bouilabaisse′ s. A rich fish-stew.
Pelisse′ s. A coat for ladies or children.
Coulisse′ s. A groove in which a sluice-gate, theatrical scene, etc., slides.
Cuisse s. Armour for the thighs.
Fosse s. A ditch, moat, trench.
Pos′se s. A force, as of constables.
Crosse s. The racket-like stick used in lacrosse.
Lacrosse′ s. A ball-game somewhat like hockey.
Repous′sé s. Ornamental metalwork formed in relief by hammering.
Retrous′sé a. Turned up (of the nose).
Tset′se s. A S. African blood-sucking fly.
Petunt′se s. A white earth of feldspar and kaolin.
Use (ūs) s. Utility; benefit; habit; custom;

Use (ūz) v.t. and i. To employ, make use of; to be wont or accustomed.
Cause s. That which produces a result or occasions an action; a legal process. v.t. To effect, produce, by the occasion of.
Because' conj. For the reason that.
Clause s. A paragraph; a self-contained portion of a sentence.
Applause' s. Loud praise, encomium.
Pause s. A short cessation; hesitation; a stop in music. v.i. To make a short stop; to deliberate, hesitate.
Men'opause s. The change of life in women.
Abuse' (-z) v.t. To make an ill use of, to vilify, to defile.
Abuse' (-s) s. Ill use, rude reproach, unjust censure.
Disabuse' v.t. To undeceive.
Accuse' v.t. To charge with fault; to blame.
Reaccuse' v.t. To accuse again.
Excuse' (-z) v.t. To free from imputation, clear from blame, absolve, pardon; to overlook; to free from an impending duty, etc.; to ask pardon for.
Excuse' (-s) s. Act of excusing; a plea in extenuation; apology; that which excuses.
Farceuse' s. A female farceur.
Accoucheuse' s. A midwife.
Mitrailleuse' s. A machine-gun with a number of barrels.
Petroleuse' s. A female petroleur.
Meuse s. Gap in fence used by a hare; a loophole.
Chartreuse' s. A pale green or yellow liqueur.
Danseuse' s. A female professional dancer.
Masseuse' s. A woman who gives massage.
Fuse v.t. To melt, to liquefy by heat. v.i. To melt. s. A tube of combustible matter used in blasting, etc.; a safety device to break electric circuit.
Refuse' v.t. To deny (a request, etc.); to decline, reject. v.i. To decline to accept something offered.
Ref'use a. Rejected; worthless. s. Waste matter; dregs; trash.
Effuse' (-z-) v.t. To pour out, emit, shed abroad.
Effuse' (-s-) a. Spreading loosely (of a flower).
Diffuse' (-z) v.t. and i. To pour forth, circulate, dissipate.
Diffuse' (-s) a. Scattered, spread out; not concise.
Suffuse' v.t. To overspread as from within.
Circumfuse' v.t. To pour round; to bathe in or with.
Infuse' v.t. To pour in; to steep; to instil, inspire.
Confuse' v.t. To jumble together, disorder; to abash, perplex.
Profuse' a. Copious; superabundant; lavish.
Perfuse' v.t. To sprinkle, spread, or pour over or through
Interfuse' v.t. and i. To permeate, pervade; to mix together.
Transfuse' v.t. To make pass from one vessel to another; to transfer (blood) from one animal to another.
Enthuse' v.i. To be enthusiastic about.
Recluse' a. Shut up; sequestered. s. One who lives secluded; a hermit.
Muse s. One of the nine goddesses of classic myth presiding over the arts; poetic inspiration; a fit of abstraction. v.i. To ponder, meditate engage in reverie.
Amuse' v.t. To divert, beguile, gratify.
Bemuse' v.t. To make confused or fuddled.
Hypot'enuse s. Side of right-angled triangle opposite the right angle.
Lob'scouse s. Hashed meat and vegetables for sailors.
Douse v.t. and i. To plunge into water; to put out (a light).
House s. An abode, habitation; a family; a commercial establishment; a legislative body.
House (howz) v.t. To place in a house; to lodge, shelter.
Chouse v.t. To defraud, bamboozle. s. One easily cheated; a tool; a trick.
Mad'house s. A lunatic asylum.
Bake'house s. A bakery.
Rehouse' v.t. To house anew.
Ware'house s. Building for storage of goods; a large shop. v.t. To deposit in a warehouse.
Wash'house s. A laundry; a scullery.
Block'-house s. A detached fort.
Work'house s. Public establishment for paupers.
Beer'house s. A house licensed to sell beer but not spirits.
Poor'house s. The workhouse.
Boat'-house s. A house by the water in which boats are kept.
Light'house s. A tower with a light to direct mariners.
Pent'house s. A lean-to shed or roof.
Out'house s. A structure separated from the main building.
Louse s. A wingless, blood-sucking, parasitic insect.
Louse (louz) v.t. and i. To clean from lice.
Blouse s. A loose outer garment.
Mouse s. A small rodent infesting houses, fields, etc.
Mouse (mouz) v.i. To hunt for or catch mice.
Zamouse' (-moos') s. The short-horned buffalo of W. Africa.
Cole'mouse s. A small dusky bird.
Rear'mouse s. A bat.
Flit'termouse s. A bat.
Dor'mouse s. A small hibernating rodent.
Tit'mouse s. A small insectivorous bird.
Spouse s. A husband or wife.
Espouse' v.t. To give or take in marriage; to adopt; to defend.
Rouse v.t. To awaken; to stir up, provoke. v.i. To awake, arise. s. Reveille: a bumper, carouse.
Arouse' v.t. To wake from sleep.
Carouse' v.i. To drink abundantly, to drink a toast. s. A carousal.
Grouse s. A gallinaceous game-bird, especially the red or black moor-fowl. v.i. (*Slang*) To grumble.
Souse v.t. and i. To plunge into water, steep in pickle; to fall suddenly. s. Anything pickled; a plunging into water.
Ruse s. A stratagem, trick, fraud.
Cruse s. A small pot, cup, bottle.
Druse s. A crystal-studded cavity in a rock.
Cer'use s. White lead.
Peruse' v.t. To read, especially attentively; to consider.
Abstruse' a. Difficult of comprehension.
Disuse' s. Cessation of use, custom, etc.; desuetude.
Disuse' (-z) v.t. To cease to use or practise; to disaccustom.
Misuse' (-ūz') v.t. To use improperly, maltreat, misapply.
Misuse' (-ūs') s. Improper use; abuse.
Obtuse' a. Not pointed; dull; stupid.
Retuse' a. Having a rounded, indented end.

Contuse' v.t. To bruise without breaking the skin.
Hawse s. Situation of cables before a vessel's stern, when moored with two anchors; part of the bow in which holes for the anchor cables are made.
Tawse s. (*Taws*).
Dowse v.t. To use the divining-rod for discovering of water, metals, etc.
Browse v.t. To pasture or feed upon. v.i. To crop and eat food; to read desultorily.
Drowse v.i. To doze, to be or become sleepy. v.t. To make heavy with sleep; to spend time idly.
Di'alyse v.t. To separate by chemical dialysis.
An'alyse v.t. To disect into its elements, to resolve into first principles.
Par'alyse v.t. To affect with paralysis; to render powerless.
Elec'trolyse v.t. To effect chemical change in by electrolysis.
Ate past. (*Eat*).
Bate v.t. To abate, remit, bar. v.i. To diminish.
Abate' v.t. To lessen; to lower in price.
Debate' v.t. To dispute, argue, discuss. v.i. To deliberate. s. An argument, a wordy contest.
Rebate' v.t. To diminish; to make a discount from. s. An abatement, discount, allowance.
Se'bate s. A salt of sebacic acid.
Cel'ibate s. An unmarried person. a. Vowed to a single life.
Lim'bate a. Having a different coloured border.
Ster'eobate s. A basis of solid masonry.
Nio'bate s. A salt of niobic acid.
Lo'bate a. In the form of or characterized by lobes.
Glo'bate a. Spherical globe-shaped.
Conglo'bate v.t. To form into a ball. a. Gathered into a ball.
Quadrilo'bate a. Having four lobes.
Tri'lobate a. Having three lobes.
Multilo'bate a. Having many lobes.
Styl'obate s. Base supporting a row of columns.
Pro'bate s. Official proof, especially of a will; act of proving wills.
Rep'robate v.t. To disapprove strongly; to condemn, reprehend. a. Abandoned to vice or punishment. s. One morally lost; a depraved person.
Ap'probate v.t. To express approval of.
Exac'erbate v.t. To exasperate, render more violent.
Sorb'ate s. A salt of sorbic acid.
In'cubate v.t. To sit on eggs to hatch; to hatch by artificial means.
Ju'bate a. Fringed with long hairs; having a mane.
Placate' v.t. To appease, pacify, conciliate.
Vacate' v.t. To make vacant; to annul; to leave unoccupied.
Bac'cate a. Berried, berry-like.
Sac'cate a. Forming or contained in a sac.
Des'iccate v.t. To exhaust of moisture, to dry up. a. Dried up.
Exsic'cate v.t. To exhaust the moisture from.
De'fecate v.t. To purify, clarify, rid of impurities. v.i. To void excrement.
The'cate a. Having a theca.
Hypoth'ecate v.t. To pledge, mortgage.
Dep'recate v.t. To avert by prayer; to regret.
Im'precate v.t. To invoke evil; to curse.
Syllab'icate v.t. To pronounce by syllables.
Rad'icate a. Having a root, rooted.
Erad'icate v.t. To root out, extirpate.
Irrad'icate v.t. To fix firmly, enroot.
Ab'dicate v.i. To renounce one's rights, to resign.
Ded'icate v.t. To consecrate, devote; to inscribe to. a. Dedicated.
Med'icate v.t. To impregnate with anything medicinal.
Pred'icate v.t. and i. To affirm one thing of another; to assert. s. That which is affirmed of the subject; word or words in a proposition expressing this.
In'dicate v.t. To show, point out.
Vin'dicate v.t. To justify, defend, maintain.
Syn'dicate s. A body of syndics; a financial association. v.t. To combine in or manage through a syndicate.
Adju'dicate v.t. To adjudge by law.
Preju'dicate v.t. To prejudge; to prejudice. a Judged beforehand.
Pacif'icate v.t. To pacify.
Nidif'icate v.i. To build a nest or nests.
Pontif'icate s. State, dignity, or term of office of a high-priest or pope. v.i. To officiate as a pontiff or pope.
Certif'icate s. A written testimony, a legal declaration. v.t. To verify by or furnish with a certificate.
Vivif'icate v.t. To vivify.
For'ficate a. Deeply forked, as tail of certain birds.
Del'icate a. Pleasing to the senses; dainty; soft; effeminate; not strong.
Indel'icate a. Coarse, unrefined; indecent.
Spif'licate v.t. (*Slang*) To damage, do for.
Sil'icate s. A salt of silicic acid.
Vell'icate v.t. and i. To twitch, move spasmodically.
Pli'cate a. Plaited, folded like a fan.
Rep'licate a. Folded back (as a leaf). v.t. To fold back on itself; to make a replica of.
Trip'licate a. Trebled, threefold. s. A third copy. v.t. To treble.
Mul'tiplicate a. Consisting of many; multiple.
Im'plicate v.t. To involve, entangle, connect with.
Com'plicate v.t. To make complex; to entangle, involve.
Sup'plicate v.t. To beg for earnestly and humbly, to importune. v.i. To implore.
Du'plicate a. Double, twofold; an exact copy. v.t. To double; to make a replica of.
Redu'plicate v.t. To redouble, multiply, repeat.
Quadru'plicate a. Fourfold. v.t. To quadruple.
Centu'plicate s. and v.t. (*Centuple*).
Quintu'plicate a. Consisting of five parts, etc. s. A set of five; one of five similar things. v.t. To make fivefold.
Ex'plicate v.t. To unfold the meaning of, explain. a. Evolved, unfolded.
For'micate a. Resembling an ant.
For'nicate v.i. To commit fornication.
Commun'icate v.t. To impart, reveal, bestow, give a share of. v.i. To confer; to open into; to share; to partake of the Holy Communion.
Intercom-mu'nicate v.i. To enjoy mutual communication; to have free passage to and from.
Excom-mu'nicate v.t. To eject from the communion of, especially of the Church. a. Excommunicated. s. One who is excommunicated.
Tu'nicate s. One of a large class of Metazoa. a. Having a tunic.
Spi'cate a. Having spices or spikes.
Prevar'icate v.i. To quibble, speak evasively.

Divar'icate v.t. and i. To break or divide into two branches; to fork. a. Widely divergent.
Fab'ricate v.t. To construct, frame; to invent, to devise falsely.
Im'bricate v.t. To lap one over the other. v.i. To be arranged thus. a. Arranged thus (of scales, leaves, etc.).
Fim'bricate a. (*Fimbriate*).
Lu'bricate v.t. To make slippery with oil, etc.; to cause to work easily.
Ru'bricate v.t. To mark or distinguish with red; to furnish with or arrange in a rubric.
Ser'icate a. Made of silk; silky, downy.
Lor'icate a. Covered with defensive scales.
In'tricate a. Complicated; obscure; involved.
Ex'tricate v.t. To disentangle, disembarrass, rescue.
Mur'icate a. Furnished with prickles (of plants).
Sur'icate s. A small S. African mammal allied to the weasel.
Ves'icate v.t. To raise blisters on.
Authen'ticate v.t. To make or prove genuine or authoritative.
Cor'ticate a. Having or resembling a cortex.
Decor'ticate v.t. To strip the bark or husk from.
Ur'ticate v.t. To sting like or whip with nettles.
Mas'ticate v.t. To grind and crush with the teeth.
Domes'ticate v.t. To accustom to home-life and household management; to tame.
Phlogis'ticate v.t. To combine phlogiston with.
Dephlogis'ticate v.t. To deprive of the supposed principle of inflammability.
Sophis'ticate v.t. To obscure with sophistry; to garble, vitiate, debase; to make artificial. v.i. To be sophistical.
Prognos'ticate v.t. To foretell from signs; to presage, betoken.
Rus'ticate v.i. To dwell in the country. v.t. To banish temporarily from a University.
Intox'icate v.t. To make drunk; to excite greatly with joy, etc.
Fal'cate a. Hooked like a sickle.
De'falcate v.t. To take away fraudulently; to misappropriate.
In'culcate v.t. To impress by frequent admonitions; to instil.
Sul'cate a. Longitudinally furrowed.
Trisul'cate a. Having three furrows, forks, or prongs.
Trun'cate v.t. To cut short, maim. a. Cut short; terminating abruptly.
Detrun'cate v.t. To cut down, lop, shorten.
Suf'focate v.t. To choke; to kill by smothering; to extinguish. v.i. To become choked or smothered.
Locate' v.t. To place, settle; to determine the site of.
Al'locate v.t. To distribute, allot.
Col'locate v.t. To place side by side or in order; to arrange.
Dis'locate v.t. To displace; to put out of joint. a. Dislocated.
Em'brocate v.t. To rub a diseased part with oil, etc.
Recip'rocate v.i. To act interchangeably. v.t. To give and return mutually; to requite.
Ad'vocate v.t. To plead the cause of, to support. s. A counsel or counsellor.
Equiv'ocate v.t. To speak with a view to mislead; to prevaricate, shuffle.
De'marcate v.t. To fix the limits of.
Al'tercate v.i. To wrangle, dispute.
Por'cate a. Formed in ridges.
Fur'cate a. Forked.
Furcate' v.i. To fork; to split into branches.
Bi'furcate v.i. To divide into two branches.
Con'fiscate v.t. To appropriate, seize as forfeited. a. Confiscated.
Lemnis'cate s. A curve like the figure 8 sideways.
Ob'fuscate v.t. To darken, cloud, bewilder.
Cor'uscate v.i. To gleam, sparkle.
Ed'ucate v.t. To instruct youth; to train and develop the faculties.
Man'ducate v.t. To chew, masticate.
Car'ucate s. An old measure of land, about 120 acres.
Date s. Time or day when anything happened; era; age; the fruit of a tropical palm. v.t. To note the time of. v.i. To reckon time; to have origin.
Van'adate s. A salt of vanadic acid.
Gradate' v.t. To arrange by gradual steps. v.i. To pass gradually from one tint to another.
Molyb'date s. A salt of molybdic acid.
Dep'redate v.t. To subject to plunder and pillage.
Sedate' a. Calm, tranquil, serene; serious.
An'tedate v.t. To date before the true time. s. Prior date.
Elu'cidate v.t. To explain, make clear, throw light on.
Can'didate s. One who seeks a place or appointment.
Val'idate v.t. To make valid; to ratify.
Inval'idate v.t. To weaken the validity of; to render not valid; to overthrow.
Consol'idate v.t. To make solid, compress, condense, unite. v.i. To become solid, united, etc. a. Consolidated, solidified.
Intim'idate v.t. To overawe, deter with threats.
Lap'idate v.t. To kill by stoning.
Dilap'idate v.i. To go to ruin, fall by decay. v.t. To damage.
Cus'pidate a. Tapering to a sharp, stiff point; having small eminences.
Mith'ridate s. An antidote against poison.
Chlor'idate v.t. (*Chloridize*).
Liq'uidate v.t. To pay off; to wind up (a business); to adjust the affairs of (a bankrupt, etc.).
Man'date s. An authoritative command, order, or commission; a Papal rescript.
Fe'cundate v.t. To impregnate, make fruitful.
In'undate v.t. To flood; to submerge, deluge.
Accom'modate v.t. To adapt; to reconcile.
Cor'date a. Heart-shaped.
Misdate' v.t. To date incorrectly. s. A wrong date.
Cau'date a. Having a tail.
Ecau'date a. Tailless, stemless, spikeless.
Longicau'date a. Long-tailed.
Curvicau'date a. Having the tail curved.
Denu'date v.t. To denude. a. Stripped, made bare.
Tra'beate a. Not arched; having an entablature.
Chalyb'eate a. Impregnated with iron. s. A spring or water so impregnated.
Discal'ceate a. Barefoot (esp. of certain monks).
Cro'ceate a. Croceous.
Ide'ate v.t. and i. To form ideas, to imagine. s. The actual existence corresponding to an idea.
Tra'cheate a. Having tracheæ.
Gal'eate a. Helmet-shaped.
Nu'cleate v.i. and t. To form or form into a nucleus. a. Having a nucleus.
Enu'cleate v.t. To make manifest, elucidate, solve.
Coch'leate a. Circular, spiral

Pi'leate a. Having a pileus or cap.
O'leate s. A salt of oleic acid.
Acu'leate a. Furnished with a sting; prickly.
Per'meate v.i. To pass through the pores or interstices of; to sink in.
Lin'eate a. Marked with lines.
Delin'eate v.t. To depict, describe, design.
Cu'neate a. Wedge-shaped.
Clyp'eate a. Shaped like a round shield.
Create' v.t. To originate; cause to exist, produce, constitute, appoint.
Rec'reate v.t. To refresh after toil; to amuse. v.i. To take recreation.
Recreate' v.t. To create anew. a. Recreated.
Oc'reate a. Having ocreæ; booted.
Pro'create v.t. To generate, beget.
Au'reate a. Golden; splendid.
Laur'eate a. Crowned with laurel; eminent as a poet or scholar. s. One crowned with laurel; a Poet Laureate.
Baccalau'reate s. The degree of Bachelor (of Arts, etc.).
Ros'eate a. Rose-coloured; optimistic.
Nau'seate v.i. and t. To feel or cause to feel nausea or loathing.
Brac'teate a. Formed of thin metal plates; furnished with bracts.
Ebrac'teate a. Without bracts.
Fo'veate a. Pitted; having foveæ.
Fate s. Destiny; inevitable necessity; doom; lot.
Gate s. A swinging door; a large entrance, the frame closing this; a way, avenue; admission money.
Ag'ate s. An ornamental stone.
Run'agate s. A fugitive; a vagabond; an apostate.
Prop'agate v.t. To multiply by generation; to diffuse. v.i. To have issue.
Extrav'agate v.i. To wander at will; to go beyond proper bounds.
Di'vagate v.i. To wander from the point; to digress.
Var'iegate v.t. To mark or diversify with different colours.
Leg'ate s. An ambassador from the Pope.
Legate' v.t. To bequeath.
Del'egate s. A representative, deputy. v.t. To commission or depute as agent with full powers.
Rel'egate v.t. To dispatch, consign; to banish.
Negate' v.t. To nullify; to deny.
Ab'negate v.t. To deny wholly, to repudiate.
Seg'regate v.t. To set apart. a. Set apart; solitary.
Ag'gregate v.t. and i. To collect together, to accumulate. s. The result of parts collected. a. Formed by collection of parts.
Con'gregate v.t. To collect together. v.i. To assemble, come together.
Lich'gate s. A churchyard gate with a roof.
Li'gate v.t. To tie with a ligature.
Ob'ligate v.t. To bring under obligation; to bind oneself.
Prof'ligate a. Abandoned to vice. s. An utterly dissolute person.
Col'ligate v.t. To connect, bring together.
Fum'igate v.t. To perfume; to disinfect by smoke.
Frig'ate s. A warship with one covered gun-deck; a cruiser.
Ir'rigate v.t. To cause water to flow over land; to moisten; to wash (a wound).
Lit'igate v.t. To contest in law. v.i. To carry on a lawsuit.
Mit'igate v.t. To render less severe; to alleviate, moderate. v.i. To become assuaged.

Cas'tigate v.t. To correct, chastise.
Inves'tigate v.t. To search out, inquire into.
In'stigate v.i. To incite, urge on, impel.
Fus'tigate v.t. To cudgel.
Nav'igate v.t. and i. To manage or sail in a ship.
Circum-nav'igate v.t. To sail round the globe.
Lev'igate v.t. To make smooth, grind to powder. a. Smooth, polished.
Prom'ulgate v.t. To announce, declare, proclaim.
Vul'gate s. St. Jerome's Latin translation of the Bible.
E'longate v.t. To lengthen, draw out. a. Extended; slender in proportion to length.
Do'gate s. Office or dignity of a doge.
Homol'ogate v.t. To admit, approve.
Ab'rogate v.t. To repeal, to annul.
Der'ogate v.i. To withdraw a part from; to degenerate. v.t. To detract from; to disparage.
Supererer'ogate v.i. To do more than duty requires.
Ar'rogate v.t. To assume, boast; to claim proudly.
Inter'rogate v.t. To question; to examine thus.
Sur'rogate s. A deputy, especially of a bishop.
Vir'gate a. Erect; rod-like. s. An old division of land.
Ob'jurgate v.t. To chide, reprove.
Ex'purgate v.t. To purge of anything offensive, noxious, erroneous, etc.; to render pure.
Bil'lingsgate s. Foul language.
Ju'gate a. Having leaflets in pairs.
Sub'jugate v.t. To subdue, enslave, compel to submit.
Quadriju'gate a. Quadrijugous.
Triju'gate a. Having three pairs of leaflets.
Con'jugate v.t. To join together; to inflect (a verb) through its several forms. a. Joined in pairs, coupled; kindred in origin and meaning. s. A word having the same derivation as another.
Ru'gate a. Wrinkled, ridged.
Cor'rugate v.t. To wrinkle, contract into furrows. a. Wrinkled.
Hate v.t. To detest, abhor, abominate. s. Extreme dislike; loathing.
Sar'dachate s. A variety of agate.
Matriar'chate s. A matriarchal state.
Patriarch'ate s. The office, dignity, or jurisdiction of a patriarch.
Tet'rarchate s. Office, jurisdiction, or district of a tetrarch.
Ex'archate s. Jurisdiction, rank, or status of an exarch.
Mos'chate a. Having a musky smell.
Cal'iphate s. The office, dignity, or dominion of a caliph; a caliph's term of office.
Sul'phate s. A salt of sulphuric acid.
Phos'phate s. A salt of phosphoric acid; a fertilizer containing these.
Xan'thate s. A salt of xanthic acid.
La'biate a. Having lips or lip-like parts.
Corym'biate a. Having blossoms in the form of corymbs.
Gla'ciate v.t. To polish or scratch by means of ice; to cover with sheets of ice. v.i. To be turned to ice.
Ema'ciate v.t. To make lean or thin; to waste.
Depre'ciate v.t. To lessen in price; to undervalue, to disparage. v.i. To fall in value.
Appre'ciate v.t. To estimate justly, to esteem highly. v.i. To rise in value.
Offi'ciate v.i. To perform a duty; to act as an official.

Patri'ciate s. The dignity of a patrician; nobility; the aristocracy.
Enun'ciate v.t. and i. To announce; to utter distinctly, pronounce.
Denun'ciate v.t. To denounce.
Annun'ciate v.t. To announce, to bring tidings.
Conso'ciate v.t. To associate. v.i. To form an association. s. An associate, accomplice.
Asso'ciate v.t. To join in company with. v.t. To keep company with. s. A companion.
Disso'ciate v.t. To separate, disunite.
Cru'ciate a. Having petals arranged crosswise.
Excru'ciate v.t. To torture, torment.
Glad'iate a. Sword-shaped,
Ra'diate a. Arranged radially. v.t. and i. To emit rays; to shine; to spread abroad; to enlighten.
Era'diate v.t. and i. To shoot forth or emit, as rays of light.
Unira'diate a. Uniradial.
Multira'diate a. Having many rays.
Irra'diate v.t. To dart rays upon; to brighten.
Me'diate v.i. To negotiate between parties, to intercede. a. Middle, intervening; acting indirectly.
Imme'diate a. With nothing intervening; direct; with no interval of time.
Interme'diate a. Being in the middle; between two extremes; intervening, interjacent. v.i. To act as intermediary.
Glochid'iate a. Barbed (of hairs on plants).
Dimid'iate v.t. To halve. a. Divided into halves.
Repu'diate v.t. To disown, disavow, refuse to recognize; to divorce.
Colle'giate a. Belonging to or instituted as a college.
Non-colle'giate a. Not belonging to a college; not having colleges.
Fastig'iate a. Tapering to a point (of plants).
Bra'chiate a. Having branches in pairs.
Branch'iate a. Furnished with gills.
Dibranch'iate s. A cephalopod having only two gills. a. Having only two gills.
Retal'iate v.t. and i. To return like for like, especially evil for evil; to make reprisals.
Cil'iate a. (*Cilia*).
Domicil'iate v.t. and i. To domicile.
Concil'iate v.t. To win the regard of, bring to friendliness; to reconcile.
Affil'iate v.t. To establish the paternity of; to receive into fellowship.
Humil'iate v.t. To humble, depress, mortify.
Pal'liate v.t. To extenuate, mitigate, gloss.
Fo'liate v.i. and t. To split or beat into thin plates; to decorate with leafy ornamentation.
Quinquefol'iate a. Having five leaflets.
Unifol'iate a. Having but one leaf.
Quadrifo'liate a. Having four leaflets.
Trifo'liate a. Three-leaved.
Latifo'liate a. Broad-leaved.
Perfo'liate a. Surrounding the stem at the base (of leaves).
Exfo'liate v.i. To come away in scales; to become converted into scales.
Spo'liate v.t. To plunder, spoil.
Am'pliate v.t. To enlarge, amplify.
Lacin'iate a. Cut into deep fringes, notched, fringed.
Min'iate v.t. To illuminate; to paint with vermilion.
Calum'niate v.t. and i. To accuse falsely.
U'niate s. (*Uniat*).
O'piate s. A medicine containing opium a narcotic
Marsu'piate a. Furnished with a pouch.
Ex'piate v.t. To atone for a crime; to appease.
Vicar'iate a. Having delegated power. s. Delegated office, etc.
Proletar'iate s. (*Proletariat*).
Secretar'iate s. A body of secretaries.
Var'iate v.t. and i. To alter, make or become different; to diversify.
E'briate v.t. To intoxicate.
Ine'briate v.t. To intoxicate. a. Drunk. s. An habitual drunkard.
Fim'briate a. Bordered with hairs; fringed.
Ser'iate a. Arranged in a series. v.t. To arrange thus.
Excor'iate v.t. To strip off the skin or bark.
Flor'iate a. Florally adorned; ornamented floridly.
Professor'iate s. Body of professors at a University, etc.
Impro'priate v.t. To convert to private use (of church property). a. Vested in a layman.
Appro'priate v.t. To take as one's own, to set apart. a. Adapted to, suitable for.
Inappro'priate a. Not appropriate; unsuitable.
Misappro'priate v.t. To take for one's own use wrongly.
Expro'priate v.t. To deprive of, take for public use.
Repa'triate v.t. and i. To restore or return to one's country.
Expa'triate v.t. To banish, exile; to renounce one's citizenship.
Stri'ate a. Finely channelled; marked with striæ.
Striate' v.t. To mark with striæ.
Infur'iate v.t. To provoke to fury, to madden. a. Enraged.
Mur'iate s. Commercial chloride.
Luxur'iate v.i. To grow or live luxuriantly; to indulge without restraint.
Prus'siate s. One of various compound cyanides.
Expa'tiate v.t. To extend, diffuse. v.i. To take a wide circuit or view; to descant.
Ingra'tiate v.t. To get into another's favour; to insinuate oneself.
Sa'tiate v.t. To satisfy the desire of; to cloy, glut. a. Glutted.
Insa'tiate a. Never satisfied.
Ini'tiate v.t. To originate; to instruct in the rudiments; to introduce into a society, etc.
Propi'tiate v.t. To appease; to make propitious.
Vit'iate (vish'-) v.t. To make faulty, invalid, or ineffectual; to contaminate.
Novi'tiate s. State of being, or the probation of, a novice.
Substan'tiate v.t. To make real; to prove, establish.
Transub-stan'tiate v.t. To change the substance of.
Consub-stan'tiate v.t. and i. To unite in or join into one substance.
Circum-stan'tiate v.t. To make circumstantial, establish.
Licen'tiate s. One licensed to exercise a profession, practise an art, etc.
Differen'tiate v.t. To make different; to distinguish by a difference. v.i. To become different.
Nego'tiate v.i. To transact business; to treat. v.t. To arrange for; to sell, pass; to convert a bill, etc., into cash; to overcome a difficulty, etc.
Ter'tiate v.t. To perform for the third time; to examine the thickness of ordnance.
A'viate v.i. To fly a flying-machine.
Landgra'viate s. Territory, office, or jurisdiction of a landgrave.

Margra'viate s. Margravate.
Ob'viate v.t. To get over, remove; to prevent by interception.
De'viate v.i. To wander, go astray, swerve.
Alle'viate v.t. To make light, to allay, to ease.
Abbre'viate v.t. To make short or shorter; to abridge.
Lixiv'iate v.t. To leach, to subject to lixiviation. a. Pertaining to lye.
Exu'viate v.i. and t. To cast off, cast the skin, shell, etc. (of animals).
Asphyx'iate v.t. To suffocate.
Skate s. A metal shoe for sliding on ice; a flat-fish. v.i. To slide on skates.
Bleth'erskate s. One who talks arrant nonsense.
Late a. Coming after the usual time; tardy; recent; modern; deceased. adv. After the usual or proper time; recently.
A'late a. Having wings, or parts like wings.
Inter'calate v.t. To insert between others, esp. of days.
Car'dinalate s. The office or dignity of a cardinal.
Pal'ate s. The roof of the mouth; taste; relish.
Ox'alate s. A salt of oxalic acid.
Oblate' a. Flattened at the poles.
Ob'late s. One dedicated to service in a religious order.
Sublate' v.t. To deny (in logic).
Elate' v.t. To elevate, puff up, exalt. a. Lifted up, puffed up, exultant.
Sphac'elate v.i. and t. To mortify, become gangrenous, affect with gangrene.
Delate' v.t. To accuse, inform against.
Regelate' v.i. To freeze together again.
Chel'ate a. Furnished with chelæ.
Relate' v.i. To stand in some relation, to pertain. v.t. To narrate; to ally by kindred.
Prel'ate s. An ecclesiastical dignitary; a bishop, cardinal, etc.
Cor'relate v.t. To place in mutual relation. v.i. To be reciprocally related. s. A correlative. a. Mutually related.
Deflate' v.t. To let air or gas out of; to let down.
In'sufflate v.t. To breathe or blow air into or upon.
Inflate' v.t. To distend with wind or breath; to raise above normal value.
Sib'ilate v.t. and i. To utter with or make a hissing sound.
Ju'bilate v.i. To exult, express joy.
Jubila'te s. The 100th Psalm; a shout of exultation.
Volu'bilate a. Climbing by winding (of plants); rotating readily.
Dilate' v.t. and i. To widen, expand; to tell diffusely, expatiate.
Invig'ilate v.i. To act as an invigilator.
Anni'hilate v.t. To destroy, bring to nothingness.
Assim'ilate v.t. and i. To render or become similar.
Dep'ilate v.t. To strip of hair.
Horrip'ilate v.t. and i. To produce or experience horripilation.
Op'pilate v.t. To block up, obstruct.
Ven'tilate v.t. To supply with fresh air, expose to the air; to let be openly discussed.
Mut'ilate v.t. To main, mangle, injure by excision.
Circumval'late v.t. To surround with a rampart.
Flabel'late a. Fan-shaped.
Um'bellate a. Pertaining to or like an umbel; umbelliferous.
Pedicel'late a. Having pedicels
Can'cellate a. Cross-barred.
Ocel'late a. Resembling an eye; having ocelli.
Flag'ellate v.t. To whip, scourge. a. Having whip-like processes.
Lamel'late a. Lamellar.
Cren'ellate v.t. To fortify a building with battlements.
Appel'late a. Pertaining to appeals.
Interpel'late v.t. To question, interrupt with a question.
Patel'late a. Patellar.
Stel'late a. Resembling a star; radiating.
Rostel'late a. Furnished with a rostellum.
Scutel'late a. Covered with scales; like a scutellum.
Vac'illate v.i. To fluctuate, sway to and fro, waver.
Penic'illate a. Pencil-shaped; having tufts.
Vertic'illate a. Arranged in a whorl, or round a stem or pedicel.
Os'cillate v.i. To swing, as a pendulum; to vibrate, fluctuate.
Sig'illate a. Marked with seal-like impressions.
Mam'millate a. Having nipples or similar protuberances.
Vanil'late s. A salt of vanillic acid.
Papil'late a. Papillary.
Pu'pillate a. Having a central spot.
Fi'brillate a. Fibrillar.
Tit'illate v.t. To excite pleasurably.
Can'tillate v.t. To chant, intone.
Scin'tillate v.i. To emit sparks; to sparkle.
Distil'late s. The product of distillation.
Vexil'late a. Vexillar.
Collate' v.t. To compare critically; to arrange in order; to appoint to or institute in a benefice.
Decol'late v.t. To behead. a. Cut off short.
Cor'ollate a. Like or having corollas.
Cu'cullate a. Hooded, like a hood.
Machic'olate v.t. To furnish with machicolations.
Choc'olate s. A paste, or beverage made from this, prepared from the seeds of the cacao or cocoa tree; a dark brown colour.
Per'colate v.i. and t. To pass or cause to pass through small interstices, as liquid; to filter.
Lan'ceolate a. Tapering at each end.
Ur'ceolate a. Shaped like a pitcher.
Lin'eolate a. Marked with minute lines.
Are'olate a. Marked by intersecting lines.
Fave'olate a. Cellular; honeycombed.
Al'veolate a. Vaulted like a beehive; honeycombed.
Trifo'liolate a. Bearing three leaflets.
Vit'riolate v.t. To convert into a sulphate.
E'tiolate v.t. and i. To blanch by excluding the sunlight; to become pale.
Pet'iolate a. Having a petiole.
Vi'olate v.t. To transgress; to injure, to ravish.
Invi'olate a. Not profaned; unbroken.
Im'molate v.t. To sacrifice, offer in sacrifice.
Inter'polate v.t. To foist in; to add a spurious passage, etc., to.
Pro'late a. Extended in direction of the longer axis.
Des'olate a. Uninhabited, solitary, comfortless. v.t. To depopulate, lay waste.
I'solate v.t. To place by itself; to detach.
In'solate v.t. To expose to or dry in the sun; to ripen or prepare thus.
Discon'solate a. Deeply dejected; sad, melancholy, sorrowful.
Apost'olate s. The office of an apostle; leadership.
Vac'uolate a. Containing vacuoles.

Plate s. A flattened piece of metal; a shallow vessel of earthenware, etc., for food at table; silver and gold utensils; engraved metal or page of stereotype for printing; a full-page illustration. v.t. To coat thinly with metal.
Book'plate s. A label showing the ownership of a book.
Tem'plate s. (*Templet*).
Con'template v.t. To meditate on, study; to have in view; to purpose, plan.
O'moplate s. The scapula, shoulder-blade.
Electroplate' v.t. To cover a metal object with a deposit of another metal by means of electricity. s. Articles plated thus.
Slate s. A dark grey laminated rock; a slab of this. v.t. To cover with slates; to abuse, berate.
Leg'islate v.i. To make or enact a law or laws.
Translate' v.t. To render into another or express in clearer language; to transfer.
Mistranslate' v.t. To translate wrongly.
Confab'ulate v.i. To talk familiarly together; to gossip.
Tab'ulate v.t. To arrange in tabular form, reduce to synopses. a. Broad and flat; arranged in laminæ.
Mandib'ulate a. Mandibular.
Infundib'ulate a. Funnel-shaped.
Infib'ulate v.t. To fasten with a clasp, padlock, etc.
Vestib'ulate a. Vestibular.
Am'bulate v.i. To walk about.
Pream'bulate v.i. To make a preamble.
Circum-am'bulate v.i. To walk round about.
Somnam'bulate v.i. To walk in one's sleep.
Peram'bulate v.t. To walk through, go round or about.
Sub'ulate a. Awl-shaped.
Tu'bulate a. Tubular; tubulous.
Ejac'ulate v.t. To throw out, as an exclamation. v.i. To utter ejaculations.
Interjac'ulate v.t. To interject.
Mac'ulate v.t. To spot, stain. a. Spotted; impure.
Immac'ulate a. Spotless; perfect.
Vernac'ulate v.t. and i. To express in or use the vernacular.
Tentac'ulate a. Having or resembling tentacles.
Sac'culate a. Furnish with a sac or sacs.
Trabec'ulate a. (*Trabecular*).
Pec'ulate v.i. To embezzle.
Spec'ulate v.i. To form conjectures, meditate; to risk, venture.
Orbic'ulate a. In the form of an orb.
Acic'ulate a. Needle-shaped.
Fascic'ulate a. Collected in small bundles or bunches.
Pedic'ulate a. Having pedicels.
Canalic'ulate a. Minutely grooved.
Vermic'ulate v.t. To decorate with wavy or worm-like lines. a. Marked thus; worm-eaten; vermicular.
Panic'ulate a. Arranged like or branching in panicles.
Genic'ulate a. Bent abruptly like the knee.
Apic'ulate a. Terminating abruptly in a little point.
Spic'ulate a. Spicular.
Turric'ulate a. Having a long spire (of shells).
Matric'ulate v.t. To admit to membership of a university, etc., by enrolling the name. v.i. To be admitted thus. s. One who has matriculated.
Auric'ulate a. Having ears, or protuberances like ears.
Vesic'ulate a. Bladdery; vesicular.
Stratic'ulate a. Arranged in thin strata.
Retic'ulate v.t. To divide into network, mark with intersecting lines. v.i. To be arranged in a network. a. Formed of or resembling this.
Dentic'ulate a. Finely toothed.
Artic'ulate a. Having joints. v.i. To form words, to utter distinctly.
Inartic'ulate a. Not uttered distinctly; dumb; not jointed.
Partic'ulate a. Pertaining to or existing as particles.
Multartic'ulate a. Many-jointed.
Gestic'ulate v.i. To make gestures in speaking or in place of speaking.
Testic'ulate a. Shaped like a testicle.
Unguic'ulate a. Unguicular.
Cal'culate v.t. To compute, reckon.
Miscal'culate v.t. To calculate erroneously.
Carunc'ulate a. (*Caruncle*).
Oc'ulate a. Having eye-like markings.
Unioc'ulate a. Unilocular.
Multiloc'ulate a. Divided into many chambers.
Inoc'ulate v.t. To introduce germs into the body with object of conferring immunity; to imbue or infect with.
Oper'culate a. Having an operculum or lid.
Cir'culate v.i. To move in a circle, pass round. v.t. To cause to pass round.
Emas'culate v.t. To castrate; to weaken, make effeminate; to expurgate to excess.
Os'culate v.i. and t. To kiss; to connect through intermediate links (of zoological species), to touch (of curves, etc.).
Inos'culate v.i. To unite, as two vessels at their extremities; to anastomose. v.t. To unite by apposition or contact.
Ad'ulate v.t. To flatter servilely.
Acid'ulate v.t. To tinge with acid.
Strid'ulate v.i. To make a creaking noise, as grasshoppers, etc.
Pen'dulate v.i. To swing as a pendulum; to hesitate.
Un'dulate v.i. To roll, have a wavy motion. a. Wavy.
Mod'ulate v.t. To proportion, adjust; to inflect in a natural or musical manner. v.i. To pass from one key (*music*) into another.
Coag'ulate v.t. To cause to curdle or become curd-like. v.i. To curdle.
Reg'ulate v.t. To adjust by rule, put in order.
Lig'ulate a. Strap-shaped.
An'gulate a. Angular. v.t. To make angular.
Triang'ulate v.t. To survey by means of a series of triangles; to make triangular. a. Marked with triangles.
Stran'gulate v.t. To strangle.
Ling'ulate a. Tongue-shaped.
Ung'ulate a. Hoofed; hoof-shaped; belonging to the Ungulata. s. A hoofed animal.
Subun'gulate a. Having both hoofs and digits.
Solidun'gulate s. A mammal having a solid hoof on each foot. a. Solidungulous.
Cell'ulate a. Formed of cells.
Stel'lulate a. Stellular.
Pul'lulate v.i. To bud, sprout, develop.
U'lulate v.i. To howl, hoot.
Em'ulate v.t. To strive to equal or excel; to rival.
Sim'ulate v.t. To assume the appearance of, to feign, mimic.
Dissim'ulate v.i. To dissemble, feign.

Stim'ulate v.t. To rouse to greater exertion; to incite.
For'mulate v.t. To express in a formula; to state concisely and systematically.
Cu'mulate v.t. and i. To accumulate. a. Heaped up.
Accu'mulate v.t. and i. To pile up, amass.
Campan'ulate a. Bell-shaped.
Gran'ulate v.t. and i. To break or form into grains; to become rough on the surface.
Cren'ulate a. Finely notched or scalloped.
Annulate' a. Ringed; composed of rings or segments.
Lu'nulate a. Crescent-shaped.
Manip'ulate v.t. To work or treat with the hands; to work on so as to disguise.
Stip'ulate v.i. To contract, make an agreement. a. Furnished with stipules.
Cop'ulate v.t. To couple together. v.i. To have sexual intercourse. a. Joined, connected.
Pop'ulate v.t. To furnish with inhabitants. v.i. To propagate.
Depop'ulate v.t. To clear of inhabitants, reduce the population of.
Repop'ulate v.t. To repeople.
Cup'ulate a. Like a cupule.
Spher'ulate a. Spherular.
Ser'rulate a. Having minute notches.
In'sulate v.t. To make into an island; to place by itself; to prevent transfer of electricity, etc., by interposition of non-conductors.
Con'sulate s. The official residence, jurisdiction, or term of office of a consul.
Procon'sulate s. Office or term of office of a proconsul.
Spat'ulate a. Shaped like a spatula.
Congrat'ulate v.t. To felicitate, wish joy to on some happy occasion.
Absquat'ulate v.i. To clear out, decamp.
Punc'tulate a. Marked with small spots.
Capit'ulate v.i. and t. To surrender on terms.
Recapit'ulate v.t. To relate in brief; to repeat. v.i. To give a summary of that previously said, etc.
Fis'tulate v.i. To become a pipe or hollow. v.t. To make hollow like a pipe.
Pos'tulate s. An assumed position or condition. v.t. To assume without proof, take for granted.
Expos'tulate v.t. To remonstrate, reason earnestly with.
Us'tulate a. Scorched; having a scorched appearance.
Pus'tulate v.t. and i. To form into pustules. a. Covered with excrescences.
O'vulate v.i. To produce eggs or ovules from the ovary.
Salic'ylate s. A salt of salicylic acid.
Meth'ylate v.t. To mix or saturate with methyl alcohol.
Mate s. A comrade; an equal; one of a pair; a ship's officer; the final move in chess. v.t. To match, couple; to vie with; to checkmate, confound. v.i. To pair.
Mat'é (-ā) s. An infusion of the leaves of Paraguay tea.
Amal'gamate v.i. To combine, blend, merge into one.
Ha'mate a. Hooked.
Des'quamate v.t. and i. To scale off, peel.
Stalemate' s Position in chess when neither the king nor any piece on his side can move. v.t. To bring to a standstill.
Cremate' v.t. To burn, especially to dispose of the dead thus.
Case'mate s. An armoured enclosure for guns, a bomb-proof shelter.
Sig'mate a. S or sigma-shaped.
Dec'imate v.t. To take the tenth part of, kill every tenth man of; to destroy a large proportion of.
Sub'limate v.t. To convert by heat into vapour and return to solidity by cooling; to purify. s. A product of sublimation. a. Being treated thus.
Cli'mate s. Condition of a place in relation to temperature and weather; a region with reference to this.
Col'limate v.t. To adjust to the proper line of sight; make parallel.
An'imate v.t. To quicken, give life to. a. Possessing life.
Rean'imate v.t. To animate anew, to encourage.
Inan'imate a. Not endowed with life, inactive; spiritless.
Exan'imate a. Destitute of life; spiritless.
Pri'mate s. An archbishop; an ecclesiastical chief.
Legit'imate a. Lawful; genuine; allowable; born in wedlock. v.t. To make lawful; to legitimize.
Illegit'imate a. Born out of wedlock; illogical; not authorized.
Ul'timate a. Last, final, utmost.
Penul'timate a. Last but one. s. A penult.
Ante-penul'timate s. Last syllable but two of a word.
In'timate a. Familiar; close in friendship. v.t. To hint, point out indirectly. s. A close friend.
Op'timate s. A nobleman; a chief man of a city.
Es'timate v.t. To form an opinion of; to rate, compute. s. An approximate judgment as to value, etc.
Prox'imate a. Next; immediate; close.
Approx'imate v.t. and i. To bring or come near, to approach. a. Near, approaching.
Checkmate' s. The position of the king at chess when it cannot evade check; a defeat; v.i. To give checkmate; to defeat, frustrate.
Pal'mate a. Like a hand with outspread fingers; web-footed.
Gem'mate a. Having buds; produced by gemmation.
Consum'mate a. Complete, perfect.
Con'summate v.t. To bring to completion; to perfect.
In'mate s. One dwelling in the same house as another.
Co'mate a. Bushy, hairy.
Dip'lomate s. One who has received a diploma.
Bro'mate s. A salt of bromic acid.
Chro'mate s. A salt of chromic acid.
Ship'mate s. A fellow-sailor.
Help'mate s. A companion, partner; a spouse.
For'mate s. A salt of formic acid.
Conform'ate s. Having the same form.
Mess'mate s. An associate; one eating at the same table.
Impos'tumate v.t. and i. To affect with or form an abscess.
Play'mate s. A companion in games.
Ging'lymate v.i. To form a hinge.
Man'ganate s. A salt of manganic acid.
Perman'ganate s. A salt of permanganic acid.
Khan'ate s. Dominion or jurisdiction of a khan.
La'nate a. Woolly; resembling wool.
Ex'planate a. Spread out flat.
Em'anate v.i. To issue or flow from; to arise.
Al'dermanate s. The office, dignity, or term of office of an alderman.

Impa'nate a. Embodied in (the eucharistic) bread.
Pome'granate (pom'-) s. A tropical Asiatic tree; its globular, many-seeded, edible fruit.
Metro-pol'itanate s. See or office of an archbishop.
Ti'tanate s. A salt of titanic acid.
Sul'tanate s. Office, rule, or territory of a sultan.
Cy'anate s. A salt of cyanic acid.
Hydrog'enate v.t. To charge with or cause to combine with hydrogen.
Ox'ygenate v.t. To treat or impregnate with oxygen.
Deox'ygenate v.t. To deoxidize.
Hy'phenate v.t. To join with a hyphen.
A'lienate v.t. To estrange, to transfer property.
Sel'enate s. A salt of selenic acid.
Ven'enate a. Infected with poison.
Cre'nate a. Notched.
Sen'ate s. A body of councillors; upper branch of legislature in certain countries.
Cat'enate v.t. To link together.
Concat'enate v.t. To link together, unite in a series.
Sep'tenate a. Growing in sevens or in seven parts (of leaves).
Reju'venate v.t. and i. To make or become young again.
Ag'nate s. A relative on the father's side. a. Related on the father's side, akin.
Mag'nate s. A person of distinction.
Stag'nate v.i. To cease to flow; to become or remain inactive.
Impreg'nate v.t. To make pregnant; to saturate.
Des'ignate v.t. To indicate, distinguish; to appoint, select.
Cog'nate a. Allied by blood or origin; kindred. s. A kinsman; anything allied to another.
Tur'binate a. Top-shaped; spiral.
Derac'inate v.t. To pluck up by the roots extirpate.
Vac'cinate v.t. To inoculate with vaccine.
Vatic'inate v.t. and i. To prophesy.
Lan'cinate v.t. To rend, lacerate.
Un'cinate a. Hooked at the end; having a hook.
Run'cinate a. Toothed, serrated.
Ratioc'inate v.i. To reason deductively.
Fas'cinate v.t. To bewitch, enchant; to captivate.
Hallu'cinate v.t. To produce false impressions.
Or'dinate a. Arranged in rows; regular. s. A certain mathematical line or distance.
Subor'dinate a. Inferior in rank, etc. s. One in a lower position. v.t. To make or treat as subordinate or as of secondary importance.
Insubor'dinate a. Not submissive; mutinous.
Inor'dinate a. Irregular; immoderate; excessive.
Co-or'dinate v.t. To bring into orderly relation; to harmonize; to make equal in rank. a. Equal in rank, authority, etc.; not subordinate. s. Lines used as elements of reference to determine the position of a point.
Inco-or'dinate a. Without co-ordination.
Testu'dinate a. Arched like a tortoise.
Pag'inate v.t. To number or mark the pages of.
Vag'inate a. Pertaining to or resembling the vagina.
Evag'inate v.t. To turn inside out (of tubes).
Invag'inate v.t. To put into a sheath; to introvert upon itself.
Orig'inate v.t. To be the origin or cause of; to bring into existence. v.i. To rise, begin.
Mar'ginate a. Having a margin; edged. v.t To furnish with a margin.
Immar'ginate s. Not having a rim (of flowers, leaves, etc.).
Mach'inate v.i. To contrive, plot.
Echi'nate a. Furnished with spines, like the hedgehog, or with prickles, as certain plants.
Decli'nate a. Bent down in a curve.
Rec'linate a. Bent downwards (of leaves).
Pol'linate v.t. To fecundate with pollen.
Lam'inate v.t. and i. To form or split into thin layers. a. Consisting of layers one over the other.
Foram'inate a. Perforated; having foramina.
Contam'inate v.t. To soil, corrupt, defile. a. Having defilement, corrupt, polluted.
Stam'inate a. Having stamens.
Effem'inate a. Womanish, unmanly; voluptuous.
Gem'inate a. Arranged in pairs. v.t. and i. To double, to occur in pairs.
Quadrigem'-inate a. Fourfold.
Ingem'inate v.t. To double, repeat.
Tergem'inate a. Tergeminous.
Insem'inate v.t. To sow; to plant in the mind.
Dissem'inate v.t. To sow; to diffuse, circulate.
Elim'inate v.t. To cast out, expel, get rid of.
Crim'inate v.t. To accuse or prove guilty of a crime; to condemn.
Recrim'inate v.i. To retort a charge. v.t. To accuse in return.
Incrim'inate v.t. To charge with a crime; to involve in a charge.
Discrim'inate v.t. To select, distinguish; to mark as different. v.i. To make a difference. a. Distinctive.
Indiscrim'inate a. Without discrimination; promiscuous.
Cul'minate v.i. To come or be in the meridian, to reach the highest point.
Ful'minate v.i. To thunder, to explode. v.t. To cause to detonate, to denounce.
Com'minate v.t. To threaten, denounce.
Abom'inate v.t. To detest, loathe.
Dom'inate v.t. To govern, prevail over. v.i. To predominate.
Predom'inate v.t. To surpass in strength, influence, etc.; to prevail, rule.
Nom'inate v.t. To name, designate, propose by name.
Denom'inate v.t. To give a name to; to designate.
Prenom'inate v.t. To name beforehand.
Innom'inate a. Not named; nameless.
Ger'minate v.i. To sprout, shoot, put forth.
Ter'minate v.t. and i. To bound, put an end to, come to an end. a. Bounded, limitable.
Deter'minate a. Limited; distinct; resolute. v.t. To determine.
Pre-deter'minate a. Determined beforehand.
Indeter'minate a. Not precise; indefinite.
Inter'minate a. Unbounded; endless.
Conter'minate a. Having the same bounds; contiguous.
Exter'minate v.t. To root out, abolish, extirpate.
Ver'minate v.t. To breed vermin.
Acu'minate a. Tapering to a point. v.t. To give keenness to.
Illu'minate v.t. To light up, enlighten; to adorn with lights, coloured pictures, decorative letters, etc.
Ru'minate v.i. To chew the cud; to meditate, ponder. v.t. To chew over again; to muse on.
Su'pinate v.t. To turn (the hand) upward.

Resu'pinate a. Turned upside down; apparently inverted.
Car'inate a. Keel-shaped.
Man'darinate s. Office or jurisdiction of a mandarin.
Glyc'erinate v.t. To mix with glycerine.
Per'egrinate v.i. To travel from place to place; to live abroad.
Indoc'trinate v.t. To imbue with any doctrine; to instruct.
Ur'inate v.i. To pass urine.
Assas'sinate v.t. To murder by surprise.
Palat'inate s. The province or seigniory of a palatine.
Gelat'inate v.t. and i. To convert or be converted into jelly or a jelly-like substance.
Pec'tinate a. Resembling the teeth of a comb.
Procras'tinate v.i. and t. To be dilatory, put off action; to defer.
Ob'stinate a. Stubborn; headstrong, refractory.
Predes'tinate v.t. To predetermine, foredoom. a. Foreordained.
Deglu'tinate v.t. To loosen by dissolving the glue.
Agglu'tinate v.t. To turn into glue, to cause to adhere; to compound. a. Glued or combined together.
Conglu'tinate v.t. and i. To glue together; to heal by uniting.
Exsang'uinate v.t. To drain off blood.
Qui'nate a. Having five parts or petioles.
Pul'vinate a. Cushion-like.
Tan'nate s. A salt of tannic acid.
Stan'nate s. A salt of stannic acid.
Pen'nate a. Winged; plume-shaped.
Latipen'nate a. Having broad wings.
Impen'nate a. Wingless; having only rudimentary wings. s. A wingless bird; the penguins, etc.
Innate' a. Inborn; not acquired.
Cir'cinnate a. Rolled up (of fern-leaves, etc.).
Cach'innate v.i. To laugh immoderately.
Pin'nate a. Shaped like a feather; finned.
Connate' a. Innate, congenital; united at the base.
Car'bonate s. A salt of carbonic acid.
Diac'onate s. Office, title, dignity of a deacon.
Donate' v.t. To bestow as a gift.
Pho'nate v.t. and i. To make a vocal sound, utter vocally.
Pas'sionate a. Easily moved to or by passion; vehement; hasty.
Compas'sionate a. Merciful, sympathic. v.t. To feel compassion for.
Dispas'sionate a. Free from passion; cool; moderate.
Frac'tionate v.t. To separate mixtures by distillation, etc.
Affec'tionate a. Tender, full of affection.
Func'tionate v.i. To function, operate.
Propor'tionate a. Proportional. v.t. To make proportional.
Dispro-por'tionate a. Unsuitable; inadequate.
Extor'tionate a. Pertaining to, characterized by, or implying extortion.
Sto'lonate a. Bearing stolons.
Pul'monate a. Having lungs, s. A mollusc with lungs.
Mu'cronate a. Terminating abruptly in a point.
Cor'onate a. Having or arranged like a crown.
Res'onate v.i. To resound, reverberate.
Per'sonate v.t. To assume the character or appearance of.
Imper'sonate v.t. To personify, assume the character of.
De'tonate v.t. and i. To explode with a loud noise.
In'tonate v.i. To sound the notes of the scale. v.t. To intone.

Zon'ate a. Marked with concentric coloured bands.
Incar'nate a. Clothed or embodied in flesh.
In'carnate v.t. To clothe with or embody in flesh; to endue with life.
Hi'bernate v.i. To pass the winter in seclusion, or in lethargic sleep.
Ter'nate a. Arranged in threes.
Al'ternate v.t. and i. To succeed by turns, to perform alternately.
Alter'nate a. Interchangeable, reciprocal.
Subalter'nate a. Succeeding by turns; inferior.
Con'sternate v.t. To affright, dismay.
Ornate' a. Highly ornamented, richly embellished; florid.
Inornate' a. Not ornate.
Coad'unate a. Joined together; adnate.
Sho'gunate s. Office or term of office of a shogun.
Lu'nate a. Crescent-shaped.
For'tunate a. Successful; prosperous; lucky.
Impor'tunate a. Urgent in demand; persistent, troublesome.
In'choate a. Begun but not finished; undeveloped. v.t. To originate.
Pate s. The head, especially its top.
Pâ'té s. A pie, patty.
Antic'ipate v.t. To enjoy or possess in anticipation.
Partic'ipate v.i. To partake, share, have a share n.
Eman'cipate v.t. To liberate.
Prin'cipate s. The form of government of the early Roman emperors; a principality.
For'cipate a. Formed like a forceps.
Dis'sipate v.t. To scatter; to squander. v.i. To separate and disappear; to be extravagant or dissolute.
Con'stipate v.t. To block; to render costive.
Pal'pate v.t. To examine by touch.
In'culpate v.t. To show to be in fault; to incriminate.
Ex'culpate v.t. To clear from imputation of fault or guilt; to absolve.
Syn'copate v.t. To contract (a word) by interior omission; to commence (a tone) on an unaccented and continue on an accented beat.
Sco'pate a. Brush-shaped; scopiform.
Epis'copate s. A bishopric; the body of bishops.
Ex'tirpate v.t. To eradicate, destroy.
Spate s. A heavy flood, especially in mountain streams.
Cris'pate a. Curled or wrinkled at the edges.
Nun'cupate v.t. To dedicate by declaration, declare orally.
Rate s. Comparative value; proportion; degree; tax; assessment. v.t. To fix the value, etc., of; to estimate; to scold angrily, to reprove. v.i. To have rank; to make an estimate.
Stear'ate s. A salt of stearic acid.
Mar'garate s. A salt of margaric acid.
Sac'charate s. A salt of saccharic acid.
Exhil'arate v.t. To make cheerful, to enliven.
Sep'arate v.t. To part, sever, disjoin. v.i. To become disunited. a. Distinct; disconnected; individual.
Insep'arate a. Not disjoined; inseparable.
Dis'parate a. Unequal, unlike.
Gla'brate a. Becoming smooth from age.
Cel'ebrate v.t. To extol; to honour by solemn rites; to commemorate. v.i. To officiate at the Eucharist.
Spinicer'ebrate a. Having a brain and spinal cord.
Ter'ebrate v.t. To bore.
Ver'tebrate s. An animal having a backbone. a. Having a backbone.

Inver'tebrate a. Destitute of backbone; lacking firmness. s. An animal without a backbone.
Li'brate v.t. To balance. v.i. To be in equipoise; to oscillate.
Cal'ibrate v.t. To try or ascertain the calibre of; to graduate (a gauge, etc.).
Equili'brate v.t. To balance, to keep in equipoise.
Crib'rate a. Cribriform, perforated.
Vi'brate v.i. To move to and fro, oscillate, quiver. v.t. To cause to do this.
Ad'umbrate v.t. To shadow out faintly.
Lu'cubrate v.i. To study by lamplight, work laboriously.
Crate s. A large wicker case for crockery, etc.; an open framework of wood for packing cycles, etc.
Des'ecrate v.t. To profane, dishonour.
Con'secrate v.t. To set apart as sacred, to dedicate to God. a. Sacred, consecrated.
Ex'ecrate v.t. To denounce evil against; to abhor, abominate.
Pic'rate s. A salt of picric acid.
Ful'crate a. Having a fulcrum.
Quad'rate a. Having four sides; square. s. A square. v.i. To agree, match.
Hy'drate s. A chemical compound of water and some other substance.
Dehy'drate v.t. To deprive of water.
A'erate v.t. To impregnate with carbonic acid.
Berate' v.t. To chide vehemently.
Lib'erate v.t. To set at large, to free.
Delib'erate v.i. To consider, hesitate. v.t. To balance well in the mind. a. Cautious, cool, not hurried.
Rever'berate v.i. To resound; to be reflected (of sound, etc.); to echo. v.t. To return (sound); to repel from side to side.
Protu'berate v.i. To bulge out.
Exu'berate v.t. To abound; to indulge freely in.
Cer'ate s. A thick ointment.
Lac'erate v.t. To tear, rend; to harrow. a. Torn; mangled.
Mac'erate v.t. To soften by steeping in water; to cause to waste away.
Ul'cerate v.t. and i. To affect with or form an ulcer.
Incar'cerate v.t. To imprison, confine.
Vis'cerate v.t. To disembowel.
Evis'cerate v.t. To disembowel, to gut.
Fed'erate v.t. and i. To federalize. a. United by league; confederate.
Confed'erate a. United in a league allied by treaty. s. An ally. v.t. and i. To unite in a league.
Desid'erate v.t. To feel the loss of; to miss.
Consid'erate a. Mindful of others; given to consideration.
Inconsid'erate a. Lacking in consideration, especially for others; thoughtless; injudicious.
Prepon'derate v.t. and i. To outweigh; to exceed in power or influence.
Equipon'derate v.t. To be equal in weight. v.i. To counterbalance.
Mod'erate a. Not going to extremes; temperate; reasonable. s. A person of moderate views. v.t. To pacify; to restrain; to mitigate. v.i. To become less violent; to preside as a moderator.
Immod'erate a. Excessive, unreasonable.
Vocif'erate v.i. To cry out vehemently, to clamour. v.t. To utter, bawl, etc., loudly.
Prolif'erate v.i. To grow or reproduce itself by proliferation.
Exag'gerate v.t. To increase beyond due limits; to depict extravagantly. v.i. To speak hyperbolically.
Refrig'erate v.t. To cool; to preserve food in cold storage.
A'cierate v.t. To turn into steel.
Vizier'ate s. Office or jurisdiction of a vizier.
Val'erate s. A salt of valeric acid.
Accel'erate v.t. To hasten, to quicken.
Tol'erate v.t. To put up with, permit; to suffer to be.
Glom'erate v.t. To gather into a ball. v.i. To come together into a mass. a. Compactly clustered.
Agglom'erate v.t. To heap or collect into a mass. v.i. To gather in a mass. a. Heaped up.
Conglom'erate a. Gathered into a round body. s. A natural rock composed of pebbles cemented together. v.t. and i. To gather into a ball, to collect in a mass.
Enu'merate v.t. To reckon up, count; to recapitulate.
Gen'erate v.t. To produce, procreate, form, cause to be.
Degen'erate v.i. To grow worse, to deteriorate. s. One who has sunk below the normal type. a. Fallen from a better to a worse state.
Regen'erate v.t. To produce anew; to bring into a better state. a. Born anew, changed to a spiritual state.
Ven'erate v.t. To regard with respect; to revere.
Incin'erate v.t. To burn to ashes.
Itin'erate v.i. To travel from place to place.
Exon'erate v.t. To exculpate, acquit.
Remu'nerate v.t. To pay for services.
Tem'perate a. Self-restrained; abstemious; mild (of climate).
Intem'perate a. Not temperate; given to excessive use of alcohol.
Op'erate v.i. To exert power, strength, or moral influence; to perform a surgical operation. v.t. To cause, occasion, put in or keep in operation.
Co-op'erate v.i. To act with another, to contribute to an effect.
Exas'perate v.t. To irritate greatly, to provoke; to embitter.
Des'perate a. Hopeless; fearless; rash; extremely dangerous; irretrievable.
Depau'perate v.t. To impoverish, deprive of vigour. a. Imperfectly developed.
Recu'perate v.t. and i. To restore or be restored to health, etc.; to gain back losses, recover position.
Vitu'perate v.t. To reproach, rate, censure.
Commis'erate v.t. To pity, condole with.
Invet'erate a. Firmly established; obstinate.
It'erate v.t. To repeat constantly; to do, make, etc., over and over again.
Reit'erate v.t. To repeat again and again.
Lit'erate a. Educated; learned. s. One able to read and write.
Oblit'erate v.t. To erase, rub out, efface.
Illit'erate a. Unlettered; untaught; rude. s. An uneducated person.
Translit'erate v.t. To represent by means of other alphabetic characters.
Adul'terate v.t. To corrupt by some foreign mixture. a. Adulterous; spurious.
Cœlen'terate s. An individual of the sponge or medusa families. a. Belonging to either of these.

Presbyt'erate s. Office or term of office of a presbyter.
Assev'erate v.t. To affirm with great solemnity.
Pul'verate v.t. To pulverize.
Fra'te s. A friar.
Grate s. A framework of bars, especially over a window or for holding coals. v.t. To furnish with a grate or grating ; to wear away by rubbing ; to offend. v.i. To rub roughly on ; to have a harsh sound or an annoying effect.
De'flagrate v.t. and i. To consume or be consumed by rapid combustion.
Regrate' v.t. To trade so as to raise prices.
In'tegrate v.t. To make into a whole ; to give the sum or total ; to find the integral of. a. Made up of integrant parts ; entire.
Redin'tegrate v.t. To restore, make whole again.
Migrate' v.i. To pass to another country.
Em'igrate v.i. To leave one's own country and settle in another.
Remi'grate v.i. To migrate again, return.
Im'migrate v.i. To enter a country with object of setting.
Trans'migrate v.i. To pass from one body, place, jurisdiction, etc., to another.
De'nigrate v.t. To blacken, defame.
Ingrate' s. An ungrateful person. a. Ungrateful, unpleasant.
Irate' a. Angry ; enraged.
Pir'ate s. A robber on the high seas ; a ship engaged in piracy ; one who appropriates the writings of others for profit.
As'pirate v.t. To pronounce with full breath. s. A rough breathing ; or mark to denote this.
E'virate v.t. To emasculate.
Le'virate s. Tribal custom of marriage by a brother-in-law of his brother's widow.
Decem'virate s. A governing body of ten ; office or term of office of the decemvirs.
Trium'virate s. Office of a triumvir ; group of triumvirs ; set of three men.
Centum'virate s. Office or jurisdiction of a centumvir.
Duum'virate s. Union of two men in one office ; dignity, rule, etc., of a duumvir.
Orate' v.i. (*Slang*) To speechify, harangue.
Elab'orate a. Carefully wrought, highly finished. v.t. To produce with labour, perfect with painstaking.
Collab'orate v.i. To work in association with (especially of literary, artistic, or scientific work).
Corrob'orate v.t. To confirm, bear additional witness to.
Dec'orate v.t. To ornament, adorn, beautify.
Redec'orate v.t. To decorate anew.
Edul'corate v.t. To sweeten ; to purify.
Per'forate v.t. To bore through, penetrate.
Imper'forate a. Not perforated ; having no orifice.
Invig'orate v.t. To strengthen, animate, encourage.
Reinvig'orate v.t. To give fresh animation to.
Phos'phorate v.t. To combine or impregnate with phosphorus.
Me'liorate v.t. and i. To make or grow better ; to improve.
Ame'liorate v.t. and i. To render or become easier, to improve.
Deter'iorate v.i. and t. To grow or make worse ; to reduce in value ; to degenerate.
Pri'orate s. Government by a prior.
Ma'jorate s. Rank or office of a major.
Pe'jorate v.t. To disparage, depreciate.
Lor'ate a. Strap-shaped.
Chlo rate s. A salt of chloric acid.
Decol'orate v.t. To decolour.
Commem'orate v.t. To celebrate the memory of ; to be a memorial of.
Oppig'norate v.t. To pawn.
Evap'orate v.i. To pass off in vapour ; to be wasted. v.t. To dissipate in fumes or vapour. a. Dispersed in vapour.
Cor'porate a. United in a legal body and empowered to act as an individual.
Tricor'porate a. Having three bodies.
Incor'porate v.t. To form into one body ; to blend ; to form into a corporation. v.i. To unite, coalesce. a. United in one body.
Per'orate v.i. To deliver an oration, speechify.
Dicta'torate s. Office or term of office of a dictator.
Elec'torate s. Body of electors ; dignity or territory of an elector.
Collec'torate s. Collectorship.
Inspec'torate s. Office of, residence of, or district under an inspector.
Expec'torate v.t. and i. To spit, spit out, eject from the lungs.
Rec'torate s. Rectorship.
Direc'torate s. A body of directors ; position of a director.
Protec'torate s. Government, or district governed, by a protector ; authority of a superior over an inferior.
Doc'torate s. The degree of a doctor.
Pas'torate s. Office, rank, or district of a pastor.
Flu'orate s. A salt of fluoric acid.
Prate v.i. To be loquacious, talk to little purpose. v.t. To utter foolishly. s. Trifling talk.
Narrate' v.t. To tell, relate, to give an account of.
Underrate' v.t. To rate too low.
Ser'rate v.t. To notch, give a saw-like edge to. a. Notched.
Overrate' v.t. To rate at too much, value too highly.
Cir'rate a. (*Cirrus*).
Pen'etrate v.t. To pierce, perforate, bore ; to cause to feel ; to comprehend. v.i. To pass ; to affect the feelings.
Im'petrate v.t. To obtain by petition or prayer.
Per'petrate v.t. To commit, be guilty of ; to do.
Ar'bitrate v.t. To hear and judge, to settle.
Cit'rate s. A salt of citric acid.
Recal'citrate v.i. To express repugnance, refuse compliance.
Ni'trate s. A salt of nitric acid.
Ti'trate v.t. To subject a solution to titration.
Fil'trate s. A liquid that has been filtered. v.t. and i. To filter.
Infil'trate v.i. and t. To enter or cause to enter by penetrating the pores ; to percolate.
Cul'trate a. Shaped like a knife ; sharp-edged.
Con'centrate v.t. To bring to a common centre, combine, condense.
Tar'trate s. A salt of tartaric acid.
Castrate' v.t. To geld, emasculate.
Or'chestrate v.t. To score or compose music for an orchestra.
Fen'estrate a. Perforated, as if with windows.
Se'questrate v.t. To sequester.
Mag'istrate s. A civil officer who tries minor offences ; a Justice of the Peace.
Dem'onstrate v.t. To prove with certainty, make evident ; to exhibit. v.i. To take part in a demonstration.
Rem'onstrate v.i. To give strong reasons against ; to expostulate.
Ros'trate a. Having a beak or beak-like process.

Nudiros'trate a. Having a bare beak.
Latiros'trate a. Latirostral.
Pros'trate a. Lying at full length, or at mercy. v.t. To overthrow, lay flat; to abase humbly.
Lus'trate v.t. To purify.
Ill'ustrate v.t. To make plain, elucidate; to exemplify by means of figures, etc.; to explain or adorn by means of pictures.
Frus'trate v.t. To bring to nought, make void; to balk, foil. a. Vain, ineffectual, useless.
Ur'ate s. A salt of uric acid.
Cur'ate s. A clerical assistant of an incumbent; a clergyman not endowed with tithes.
Ac'curate a. Free from error, correct.
Inac'curate a. Not accurate.
Ob'durate a. Impenitent; stubborn.
In'durate v.i. To grow hard, harden. v.t. To make hard; to render obdurate. a. Hardened; unfeeling.
Ful'gurate v.i. To flash like lightning; to suffer shooting pains.
Inau'gurate v.t. To institute, induct, consecrate.
Sul'phurate v.t. To treat or impregnate with sulphur.
Tell'urate s. A salt of telluric acid.
Dep'urate v.t. To purify, cleanse. v.i. To become pure.
Sup'purate v.i. To generate pus.
Pur'purate s. A salt of purpuric acid.
Immen'surate a. Unmeasured.
Commen'surate a. Proportional having equal measure.
Incommen'surate a. Incommensurable; inadequate.
Mat'urate v.t. and i. To ripen; to suppurate.
Sat'urate v.t. To soak, impregnate.
Supersat'urate v.t. To add to beyond saturation.
Mic'turate v.i. To urinate.
Trit'urate v.t. To grind to a fine powder; to masticate.
Gyrate' v.i. To revolve round a centre, to move spirally.
Gyr'ate a. Circular, convoluted.
Circumgy'rate v.i. To turn or spin round.
Lyr'ate a. Shaped like a lyre.
Sate v.t. To surfeit, cloy, satiate. past (*Sit*).
Extrav'asate v.t. To let out of the proper vessels, as blood.
Mar'quisate s. Dignity or lordship of a marquis.
Improv'isate v.t. To improvise, extemporize.
Pul'sate v.i. To beat, throb.
Com'pensate v.t. To requite, make amends for, make equal return to. v.i. To make amends.
Insen'sate a. Destitute of sense; stupid; besotted.
Ter'giversate v.i. To practise evasion. s. A subterfuge, shift.
Incras'sate v.t. and i. To make or become thick or thicker.
Inspis'sate v.t. To thicken by boiling or evaporation. a. Thickened.
Decus'sate v.t. and i. To intersect at acute angles. a. Crossed acutely; arranged in this manner.
Lac'tate s. A salt of lactic acid.
Ablac'tate v.t. To wean from the breast.
Tract'ate s. A treatise, tract.
Humec'tate v.t. To moisten.
Dictate' v.t. and i. To command; to give instructions what to write.
Dic'tate s. An order, injunction; precept.
Nic'tate v.i. To wink, nictitate.
Punc'tate a. Pointed; ending in points.
Coarc'tate a. Pressed together.
Eruc'tate v.t. To belch up; to discharge from the stomach, as wind.
Heb'etate v.t. To make blunt; to stupefy. a. Blunt, obtuse.
A'cetate s. A salt formed with acetic acid and a base.
Veg'etate v.i. To grow as a plant; to lead an idle or monotonous life.
Capac'itate v.t. To qualify, to enable.
Incapac'itate v.t. To render incapable; to disqualify.
Felic'itate v.t. To congratulate.
Os'citate v.i. To yawn, gape.
Resus'citate v.t. and i. To restore from seeming death; to revive, revivify.
Med'itate v.i. To ponder, cogitate. v.t. To plan, think on.
Premed'itate v.t. and i. To revolve in the mind or consider beforehand.
Ag'itate v.t. To shake, to discuss, to stir.
Flag'itate v.t. To demand importunately.
Dig'itate a. Having finger-like processes or leaflets arranged like fingers.
Tridig'itate a. Having three digits.
Cog'itate v.i. To ponder, reflect, meditate.
Precog'itate v.t. To consider or contrive beforehand.
Excog'itate v.t. To think out, discover by thinking.
Regur'gitate v.t. and i. To throw or be thrown back in great quantity.
Ingur'gitate v.t. and i. To swallow down or eat greedily.
Habil'itate v.t. To furnish with means. v.i. To become qualified for.
Rehabil'itate v.t. To reinstate, restore to former position.
Debil'itate v.t. To weaken, enfeeble, impair.
Facil'itate v.t. To make easy or less difficult.
Imbecil'itate v.t. To render feeble or fatuous.
Mil'itate v.i. To operate or tell against; to have influence.
Im'itate v.t. To copy, mimic, counterfeit.
Delim'itate v.t. To delimit.
San'itate v.t. and i. To improve the condition of, or to carry out sanitary measures.
Cap'itate a. Having a head.
Decap'itate v.t. To behead.
Crep'itate v.i. To crackle.
Decrep'itate v.t. To calcine so as to cause a continual crackling. v.i. To crackle.
Precip'itate v.t. To hurl headlong; to hasten excessively; to cause to fall to the bottom. a. Headlong, overhasty. s. A substance deposited from a solution.
Pal'pitate v.i. To beat or pulsate rapidly and excitedly; to tremble.
Ir'ritate v.t. To inflame; to rouse to anger to fret, exasperate.
Hes'itate v.i. To pause, to be doubtful.
Necess'itate v.t. To make necessary or unavoidable; to compel.
Nic'titate v.i. To wink, blink.
Grav'itate v.i. To tend to centre of attraction; to be affected by gravitation.
Lev'itate v.i. To make lighter. v.i. To rise and float in the air without natural support.
Pel'tate a. Shield-shaped (of leaves).
Den'tate a. Toothed, indented.
Eden'tate a. Having no incisor teeth.
Triden'tate a. Tridental.
Latiden'tate a. Having broad teeth.
Multiden'tate a. Armed with many teeth.

Or'ientate v.t. To cause to be from east to west; to place or turn toward the east; to find the bearings of. v.i. To move or turn toward the east.
Segmen'tate a. Segmented.
Po'tentate s. A monarch; one possessing great power.
Front'ate a. (*Botanical*) Increasing in breadth.
No'tate a. Marked with spots (of leaves, etc.).
An'notate v.t. To note down; to add notes to.
Rotate' v.i. and t. To revolve or cause to revolve round an axis.
Ro'tate a. Wheel-shaped (of corollas, etc.).
Sep'tate a. Partitioned; divided by a septum.
State s. Condition, position, rank, degree; the civil power; body politic; whole body of people. a. National; governmental. v.t. To assert, narrate.
Has'tate a. Spear-shaped.
Dev'astate v.t. To ravage, destroy.
Estate' s. Fortune; possessions; landed property; rank, condition, quality.
Restate' v.t. To state again, express differently.
Tes'tate a. Having left a will.
Intes'tate a. Dying without having made a valid will; not bequeathed. s. A deceased person who has left no valid will.
Tungs'tate s. A salt of tungstic acid.
Aris'tate a. Awned, bearded.
Cris'tate a. Having a crest, tufted.
Instate' v.t. To establish, install.
Reinstate' v.t. To replace in a former state; to repair.
Cos'tate a. Costal.
Ecos'tate a. Having no central rib (of certain leaves).
Unicos'tate a. Having one principal nerve, rib, or ridge.
Tricos'tate a. Three-ribbed.
Laticos'tate a. Having broad ribs.
Curvicos'tate a. Having bent ribs (of leaves, etc.).
Apos'tate s. One who has renounced his faith, a renegade.
Pros'tate a. Situated in front. s. The prostate gland.
Understate' v.t. To represent as less than the truth.
In'terstate a. Pertaining to relations between states.
Overstate' v.t. To state too strongly; to exaggerate.
Misstate' v.t. To state wrongly.
Sag'ittate a. Shaped like an arrow-head.
Gut'tate s. Speckled, besprinkled (of plants).
Mutate' v.i. and t. To change, modify, be transmuted.
Nu'tate v.i. To droop (especially of plants).
Circumnu'tate v.i. To turn successively in all directions (of plants).
Am'putate v.t. To cut off.
Evac'uate v.t. To make empty or void; to remove; to withdraw from.
Arc'uate a. Bow-shaped, arched.
Grad'uate v.t. To divide into or mark with degrees. v.i. To take a University degree; to change gradually. s. One who has received a University degree.
Undergrad'uate s. University student who has not taken his first degree.
Postgrad'uate a. Carried on after graduation.
Individ'uate v.t. To distinguish from others of the species; to discriminate.
Eval'uate v.t. To value carefully, ascertain the amount of.
Tol'uate s. A salt of toluic acid.
Atten'uate v.t. To make thin. v.i. To become thin or weak. a. Slender, tapering.
Exten'uate v.t. To lessen; to impair; to palliate.
Sin'uate a. Bending; winding in and out.
Insin'uate v.t. To hint artfully, suggest by allusion. v.i. To creep or wind in; to ingratiate oneself.
Contin'uate a. Continuous; uninterrupted.
Superan'nuate v.t. To disqualify or retire through old age.
Corn'uate a. Cornuted.
Equate' v.t. To make equal; to reduce to an equation or to an average.
Ad'equate a. Equal to, sufficient.
Inad'equate a. Insufficient, disproportionate.
Liquate' v.t. To melt, liquefy.
An'tiquate v.t. To make obsolete or old-fashioned.
Propin'quate v.i. To approach.
Appropin'quate v.i. To draw near to, to approach.
Œs'truate v.i. To rut (of animals).
Men'struate v.i. To discharge the menses.
Infat'uate v.t. To make foolish; to inspire with an extravagant passion.
Ac'tuate v.t. To influence, put in action.
Effec'tuate v.t. To bring to pass, to effect.
Punc'tuate v.t. To separate into sentences, etc., by points.
Fluc'tuate v.i. To move as a wave; to vacillate, waver.
Fruc'tuate v.i. To come to fruit.
Perpetu'ate v.t. To make perpetual; to preserve from extinction or oblivion.
Habit'uate v.t. To accustom, to make familiar by use.
Sit'uate a. Permanently fixed; having a position.
Accen'tuate v.t. To stress; to pronounce or mark with an accent.
Event'uate v.i. To issue as a consequence; to terminate.
Ex'cavate v.t. To hollow out, form by hollowing, make a cavity in.
Cla'vate a. Club-shaped.
Ag'gravate v.t. To make worse, to exasperate.
Mar'gravate s. Office, jurisdiction, or territory of a margrave.
Savate' s. (*French*) Boxing in which kicking is allowed.
El'evate v.t. To raise aloft; to exalt, improve, animate; to make higher or louder.
Khediv'ate s. Dominion, jurisdiction, or term of office of a Khedive.
Sal'ivate v.t. and i. To excite or discharge saliva in excess.
Insal'ivate v.t. To mix with saliva, as food in eating.
Pri'vate a. Personal; separate from others; secret, not public. s. A common soldier.
Tit'ivate v.t. and i. To adorn, make smart.
Cul'tivate v.t. To till, prepare for crops; to refine, foster, improve; to civilize.
Mo'tivate v.t. To motive, instigate.
Cap'tivate v.t. To subdue; to fascinate.
Æs'tivate v.i. To fall into a summer torpor.
Val'vate a. Having or resembling a valve.
Syl'vate s. A salt of sylvic acid.
O'vate a. Egg-shaped.
Obo'vate a. Ovate with the narrow end downwards
Ren'ovate v.t. To make new again, revive.
In'novate v.i. To introduce novelties or changes.
Lar'vate a. Wearing a mask.

Coacer'vate a. Accumulated, clustered.
Ner'vate a. Having ribs (of leaves, etc.).
En'ervate v.t. To weaken, to render effeminate.
Ener'vate a. Weakened; wanting in vigour.
Inner'vate v.t. To give nervous energy to; to invigorate.
Cur'vate a. Curved, bent.
Recur'vate a. Bent backward or outward.
Incur'vate v.t. To cause to bend, especially inwards. a. Curved inward.
Lux'ate v.t. To dislocate.
Sol'mizate v.i. To use the sol-fa system.
Entr'acte s. Interval or performance between the acts of a play.
Pol'ychæte s. A marine worm.
Fête s. A festival, entertainment. v.t. To feast.
Effete' a. Worn-out, exhausted; sterile.
Suffete' (-fēt') s. A principal magistrate in ancient Carthage.
Ex'egete s. One skilled in exegesis.
Mache'te s. The long, heavy cutlass used in S. America.
Æs'thete s. One who worships the beautiful.
Par'aclete s. One called to aid; the holy Ghost, the Comforter.
Delete' v.t. To erase, efface.
Ath'lete s. One trained in athletics.
Décol'leté a. Low-necked (of dresses).
Ob'solete a. No longer used; antiquated; not fully developed or atrophied (of organs, etc.).
Deplete' v.t. To empty; to exhaust the strength, resources, etc., of.
Replete' a. Completely full; thoroughly imbued.
Complete' a. Finished; entire; perfect. v.t. To fulfil, achieve, bring to a perfect state.
Incomplete' a. Not complete; imperfect.
Mete v.t. To measure, allot. s. A boundary.
Gamete' s. A germ-cell capable of uniting with another for reproduction.
Compete' v.i. To contend as rivals, strive emulously.
Re'te s. A network, especially of nerves, etc.; a plexus.
Accrete' v.i. To increase by natural growth.
Secrete' v.t. To deposit in a place of hiding; to separate from the blood (in animals) or sap (in plants).
Con'crete a. Formed by particles united in one mass; congealed; existing in a subject; not abstract. s. A mass formed by concretion; a hard, solid, artificial building stone.
Concrete' v.i. To unite in a mass; to become solid.
Discrete' a. Separate, distinct; not concrete or continued.
Indiscrete' a. Not separated.
Excrete' v.t. To discharge as useless; to eject.
Terete' (-rēt') a. Cylindrical and smooth.
Tête-à-tête' (-tāt') a. Face to face; confidential. s. A private talk. adv. In private.
Asyn'artete a. Disconnected, not rhythmical.
Man'suete a. Tame, gentle.
-ite suff. Implying a follower of or belonging to it; also denoting fossils, minerals, explosives, etc.
Bite v.t. To sever with the teeth, to hold fast. s. Act of biting; piece bitten off.
Flea'bite s. The bite of a flea; a trivial wound; a trifle.
Rech'abite s. A total abstainer.
Back'bite v.t. and i. To slander, censure, speak ill of.
Stil'bite s. A hydrous silicate of aluminium, calcium, and sodium.
Jac'obite s. An adherent of James II after his abdication, or of his descendants. a. Pertaining to these.
Tri'lobite s. A fossil arachnid.
Cœ'nobite s. A monk living in community.
Cite v.t. To summon; to quote; to call or name in confirmation of.
Om'phacite s. A grass-green pyroxene.
An'thracite s. A hard mineral coal.
Os'tracite s. A fossil oyster-shell.
Accite' v.t. To summon, to cite.
Recite' v.t. To rehearse, repeat, enumerate.
Benedi'cite s. The invocation of a blessing. int. Bless you!
Fili'cite s. A fossil fern.
Ser'icite s. A scaly variety of muscovite.
Cal'cite s. Crystallized carbonate of lime.
Tal'cite s. A massive variety of talc.
Incite' v.t. To stir up, animate, provoke.
Zinc'ite s. A native oxide of zinc.
Ple'biscite (plā'-) s. A direct vote of the people.
Leu'cite s. A glassy silicate of aluminium and potassium.
Excite' v.t. To rouse, animate, stir up.
Ex'tradite v.t. To deliver under a treaty of extradition.
Lyd'dite s. A powerful explosive.
Ex'pedite v.t. To facilitate, hasten. a. Free from impediment; expeditious.
Smarag'dite s. A green variety of hornblende.
Indite' v.t. To compose, dictate, write.
Rec'ondite a. Abstruse, profound; hidden.
Incon'dite a. Ill-composed; crude.
Hermaph'rodite s. An animal in which the two sexes are united. a. Hermaphroditic.
Cor'dite s. A smokeless explosive.
Er'udite a. Learned; conversant with books.
Turf'ite s. One devoted to horse-racing.
Ec'logite s. A variety of metamorphic rock.
Ter'gite s The upper plate of a segment in certain animals.
Mal'achite s. Green carbonate of copper, an ornamental stone.
Halot'richite s. Iron alum.
En'trochite s. A segment of an encrinite.
Graph'ite s. Blacklead, plumbago.
Sulphite' s. A salt of sulphurous acid.
Oph'ite s. Serpentine. a. Pertaining to or like a snake.
Phos'phite s. A salt of phosphorous acid.
Hel'minthite s. A fossilized worm-track.
White a. Having the colour of snow; pale; pure, unsullied. s. The colour of snow; centre of a target; one of the white race of men.
Lint'white s. (*Scot.*) A linnet.
Shi'ite s. One of a great Mohammedan sect.
Kite s. A bird of prey; a light paper-covered frame for flying.
Skite s. (*Slang*) A contemptible fellow.
Blath'erskite s. (*Bletherskate*).
-lite suff. Forming names of minerals, etc.
So'dalite s. A vitreous silicate of sodium and aluminium.
Ret'inalite s. A variety of serpentine.
Phy'salite s. A coarse variety of topaz.
Pyrophys'alite s. A coarse, opaque variety of topaz.
Hy'alite s. A variety of opal.
Het'eroclite a. Deviating from the usual; abnormal, irregular. s. An anomalously formed or declined word.
Élite' s. The best, the pick.
Pre-Raph'aelite a. Pertaining to artistic style before time of Raphael, or to a nineteenth-century school of painters. s. A member of this school.

Ish'maelite s. An outcast; one at war with society.
Is'raelite s. A Jew.
Nick'elite s. Niccolite.
Car'melite s. A White Friar, a mendicant monk.
Flite v.i. To brawl, scold. s. A scolding; wordy strife.
Gastroph'ilite s. A glutton, gastrophite.
Toxoph'ilite s. An archer. a. Pertaining to archery.
My'tilite s. A fossil mussel.
Cor'allite s. A coral-shaped fossil or piece of marble.
Crystal'lite s. A definitely formed particle present in rapidly cooled volcanic rocks.
Pat'ellite s. A fossil limpet.
Sat'ellite s. A small planet revolving round another; an obsequious follower.
Lac'colite s. An intrusive mass of lava.
Nic'colite s. A copper-red arsenide of nickle.
Crocid'olite s. A blue silicate of iron and sodium resembling asbestos.
Theod'olite s. A surveying instrument.
Ze'olite s. A hydrous silicate found in cavities of igneous rocks.
Graph'olite s. Slate for writing on.
I'olite s. A blue hydrous silicate of magnesium, aluminium, and ferrous iron.
Var'iolite s. A variety of basalt.
Trem'olite s. A white variety of hornblende.
Cim'olite s. A friable clay resembling Fuller's earth.
Entom'olite s. A fossil insect.
Mar'molite s. A pearly-green variety of serpentine.
Ich'nolite s. A fossil footprint.
Phon'olite s. Clinkston, a volcanic rock.
O'olite s. A species of limestone.
Zo'olite a. Fossilized animal substance.
Polite' a. Refined, courteous, well-behaved, urbane.
Scap'olite s. A mineral composed of calcium, aluminium, etc.
Impolite' a. Ill-mannered, rude.
Cosmop'olite s. A citizen of the world; one free from national feeling or prejudices.
Car'polite s. A fossil fruit.
Typ'olite s. A stone impressed with the figure of a plant or animal.
Den'drolite s. A fossil plant; fossilized wood.
A'erolite s. A meteoric stone.
Si'derolite s. A meteorite containing iron.
En'terolite s. A stony calculus.
Me'teorolite s. A meteorite, aerolite.
Cop'rolite s. Fossil dung.
Staur'olite s. A reddish-brown, crystalline, ferrous-silicate of aluminium.
Bys'solite s. Asbestoid.
Grap'tolite s. A fossil pencil-shaped zoophyte.
Ix'olite s. A reddish mineral resin found in bituminous coal.
Rhy'olite s. An igneous rock.
Ich'thyolite s. A fossil fish.
Cry'olite s. A fluoride of aluminium and sodium from Greenland.
Chry'olite s. A translucent variety of olivine; peridot.
Topaz'olite s. A yellow or green variety of garnet.
Hop'lite s. A heavily armed soldier of ancient Greece.
Marl'ite s. A hardening variety of marl.
Perl'ite s. A vitreous volcanic rock.
Zur'lite s. A volcanic rock from Vesuvius.
Novac'ulite s. A fine slate; a hone.
Ventric'ulite s. One of the fossil sponges.
Num'mulite s. A coin-shaped fossil foraminifer.
Gran'ulite s. A fine-grained metamorphic rock.
Spher'ulite s. A rounded mass of radiating fibrous structure occurring in various rocks.
O'vulite s. A fossil egg.
Laz'ulite s. An azure-blue mineral.
Tach'ylite s. A variety of basalt.
Styl'ite s. A mediæval ascetic living on top of a pillar.
Mite s. A very small coin; a minute amount; a tiny child; a minute arachnid, esp. infesting cheese.
Ad'amite s. A descendant of Adam; one of a sect the objects of which were a return to the primitive state of nature.
Pre-Ad'amite s. One existing, or holding that people existed, before Adam. a. Existing before Adam; pertaining to the pre-Adamites.
Ham'ite s. A descendant of Ham; one of a group of N. E. African peoples.
Goth'amite s. A foolish person; a New Yorker.
Cal'amite s. A fossil plant from coal measures.
Bed'lamite s. A lunatic.
Is'lamite s. A Mohammedan.
Dy'namite s. A highly explosive compound of nitro-glycerine with a silicious earth. v.t. To destroy with this.
Wolf'ramite s. Wolfram, a tungsten ore.
Sam'ite s. A rich mediæval silk fabric.
Er'emite s. A hermit.
Se'mite s. One reputed to be descended from Shem (a Jew, Phœnician, Arab, Abyssinian, etc.). a. Semitic.
Stal'agmite s. Deposit of stalactic matter on floor of a cave, etc.
Psam'mite s. Sandstone.
Dol'omite s. A magnesian carbonate of lime.
Chro'mite s. A mineral containing chromium.
So'mite s. A segment of certain animals.
Diat'omite s. A deposit composed of or containing diatoms.
Mid'shipmite s. A small or young midshipman.
Ther'mite s. A mixture containing aluminium capable of producing intense heat.
Ter'mite s. The white ant.
Smite v.t. and i. To strike, afflict, blast; to kill by a blow; to collide.
Proz'ymite s. One who used leavened bread in the Eucharist.
Vul'canite s. Vulcanized rubber.
Man'ganite s. Grey manganese ore.
Stron'tianite s. A carbonate of strontium.
Vesu'vianite s. A volcanic vitreous silicate.
Mel'anite s. A black variety of garnet.
Por'cellanite s. A semi-vitrified clay.
Gran'ite s. A hard rock composed of quartz, feldspar, and mica.
Bas'anite s. A black variety of quartz; touchstone.
Ti'tanite s. Sphene, titano-silicate of calcium.
Syl'vanite s. A tellurid of gold and silver.
Cy'anite s. A hard, bluish, translucent mineral.
Pyc'nite s. A variety of topaz.
Molyb'denite s. A sulphide of molybdenum.
Sel'enite s. A salt of selenium; crystalline sulphate of lime; an inhabitant of the moon.
Sy'enite s. A crystalline rock containing hornblende and feldspar.
Ignite' v.t. and i. To set on fire, catch fire; to kindle.
Reignite' v.t. To set fire to again.
Lig'nite s. A brown, woody kind of coal.
Gel'ignite s. A high explosive.
Kain'ite s. A natural compound of sulphate used as a fertilizer.

Suc'cinite s. Amber; a yellow variety of garnet.
Vanad'inite s. A mineral consisting of lead vanadate and lead chloride.
Fi'nite a. Having limits, terminated, bounded.
Def'inite a. Certain, limited, precise.
Indef'inite a. Not definite, precise, or limited; uncertain; vague.
In'finite a. Boundless, unlimited in space, time, amount, etc.; not circumscribed in any way. s. Infinity; time or space that is infinite; God.
Kal'inite s. Native potash alum.
Mel'inite s. A high explosive.
Gad'olinite s. A crystalline silicate of yttrium.
Tur'pinite s. A violent explosive.
Cri'nite a. Hairy; like a tuft.
En'crinite s. The stone-lily, a fossil crinoid.
Er'inite s. A native green arseniate of copper.
Bel'emnite s. The fossilized internal bone of a cephalopod.
Sun'nite s. An orthodox Moslem who accept the Sunna.
Eb'onite s. Vulcanite.
Ac'onite s. Monk's hood or wolf's-bane.
Glau'conite s. A hydrous silicate of iron, potassium, etc.
Eb'ionite s. A Christian sect of the first and second centuries.
Xy'lonite s. A form of celluloid.
Lim'onite s. Hydrous sesquioxide of iron.
Am'monite s. A fossil spiral shell.
Mar'onite s. One of a Christian sect on Mount Lebanon.
Gab'bronite s. A bluish variety of scapolite.
Nec'ronite s. A fetid variety of orthoclase.
Jeff'ersonite s. A dark green pyroxene.
To'nite s. A powerful blasting explosive.
Unite' v.t. To bring together, associate, combine. v.i. To become one, to combine; to coalesce.
Reunite' v.t. and i. To unite or be united again.
Disunite' v.t. To destroy the union or break the concord of; to divide, sever. v.i. To become separate, to part.
Spite s. Ill-will, malice; a grudge. v.t. To treat or thwart maliciously; to vex.
Despite' s. Malice, malignity, hatred; contumely. prep. In spite of.
Res'pite s. Postponement; temporary intermission; reprieve. v.t. To grant a respite to.
Pol'ypite s. A single polyp.
Rite s. A religious ceremony or usage; form, observance.
Syb'arite s. A voluptuous or effeminate person;
Mar'garite s. Pearl mica.
Sac'charite s. A granular variety of feldspar.
Laz'arite s. A Lazarist.
Naz'arite s. A Hebrew under certain vows of abstinence.
Na'crite s. A pearly variety of mica.
Pic'rite s. A blackish-green rock containing magnesia.
Hyp'ocrite s. A pretender to virtue, etc., that is not possessed, a dissembler.
Lac'tocrite s. Apparatus for determining amount of fat in milk.
Archiman'drite s. The superior of a monastery in the Greek Church.
Den'drite s. A mineral or stone showing tree-like markings.
Glau'berite s. A mineral composed of the sulphates of soda and lime.
Cer'ite s. A hydrous silicate of cerium.
Ozoc'erite s. A bituminous fossil resin used in candle-making, etc.
Ab'derite s. Democritus; a stupid person.
Si'derite s. Spathic iron; chalybite.
Ker'ite s. Artificial rubber used in insulating.
Dol'erite s. A variety of trap-rock.
Jas'perite s. A red variety of jasper.
Lat'erite s. A red, porous rock.
Elat'erite s. Elastic bitumen.
Pret'erite s. The past tense. a. Past.
Cassit'erite s. The ore of tin.
Guerite' s. A loop-holed tower on a bastion.
Marguerite' (-ēt') s. The ox-eye daisy.
Neph'rite s. Jade, kidney-stone.
Teph'rite s. A volcanic basaltic rock.
Er'ythrite s. A variety of feldspar.
Lab'radorite s. An iridescent variety of feldspar.
Me'teorite s. A meteoric stone, fallen star.
An'chorite s. A hermit.
Phos'phorite s. A phosphate rock.
Thor'ite s. A rare, blackish silicate of thorium found in Norway.
Di'orite s. A granite-like rock.
Chlor'ite s. A salt of chlorous acid; a soapy mineral.
Mi'norite s. A Franciscan friar.
Mill'eporite s. A fossil millepore.
Mad'reporite s. A fossil coral.
Flu'orite s. Fluor.
Az'orite s. A variety of zirconium.
Sprite s. A spirit, apparition, elf.
Cu'prite s. Red oxide of copper.
Trite a. Commonplace; hackneyed.
Con'trite a. Very repentant; penitent, humble, sorrowful.
Attrite' a. Rubbed down, penitent through fear of consequences.
Ro'burite s. A powerful flameless explosive.
Sec'urite s. A high explosive used for blasting.
Lig'urite s. An apple-green variety of titanite.
Ful'gurite s. A vitrified sand-tube or rock whose surface has been fused by lightning.
Fa'vourite s. Person or thing regarded with special affection; one unduly favoured. a. Beloved; preferred before others.
Tell'urite s. A salt of tellurous acid; an oxide of tellurium.
Az'urite s. Blue carbonate of copper.
Write v.t. To set down in words or letters; to form with a pen, etc.; to compose; to send in writing. v.i. To form letters, etc., on paper; to have writing as one's occupation; to be an author.
Type'write v.t. and i. To write with a typewriter.
Underwrite' v.t. To become answerable for. v.i. To practise marine insurance.
Cerar'gyrite s. An ore of silver.
Pyrar'gyrite s. A native sulphide of silver and antimony.
Por'phyrite a. Porphyry.
Chalcopyr'ite s. Copper pyrites.
Site s. Situation; place where anything is fixed; locality.
Par'gasite s. A bluish-green variety of hornblende.
Thau'masite s. A compound of calcium.
Par'asite s. A hanger-on, a sycophant; an animal or plant living upon or in another.
Endopar'asite s. An internal or intestinal parasite.
En'toparasite s. An internal parasite.
Dyoph'isite s. One who held that the divine and human natures were combined in Christ.
Req'uisite a. Necessary, essential, indispensable. s. That which is necessary, etc.

Prereq'uisite a. Previously required for the effecting of some end. s. That which is necessary.
Per'quisite s. Something allowed, expected, or taken beyond wages.
Ex'quisite a. Choice, select, of great excellence; keen; not easily satisfied, discriminating; refined. s. A fop.
Carte-de-visite' s. A small photograph.
Fel'site s. An igneous rock composed of feldspar and quartz.
Com'posite a. Made up of different parts; belonging to a rich order of architecture; noting plants whose flowers are in dense heads s. A compound; a composite substance or term.
Decompos'ite a. Compounded of compounds or more than once. s. Something compounded of compound parts.
Incom'posite a. Uncompounded; simple.
Ap'posite a. Proper, well adapted, suitable.
Inap'posite a. Not apposite, not fit or suitable.
Op'posite a. Placed in front; contrary; adverse; s. An adversary; a contrary thing, term, etc.
Huss'ite s. A follower of the Reformer, John Huss.
Pyrolu'site s. Native marganese dioxide.
Cer'usite s. A native carbonate of lead.
Monophy'site s. One of an Eastern heretical sect of the fifth century.
Ste'atite s. Soapstone, a variety of talc.
Hæm'atite s. Red or brown iron-ore; ferric oxide.
Peg'matite s. A coarse crystalline rock occurring in granites.
Hep'atite s. Liverstone, a variety of barytes.
Rat'ite a. Pertaining to the family of birds, including the ostriches, emus, etc.
Za'ratite s. A hydrous carbonate of nickel.
Stal'actite s. Pendent mass of calcareous matter from roof fo a cave, etc.
Mi'metite s. Native arsenate of lead.
Mag'netite s. Magnetic oxide of iron.
Ap'petite s. Natural desire; relish for food.
Vol'tite s. An insulating material.
Pic'otite s. A variety of spinel.
Perido'tite s. A crystalline rock consisting largely of olivine.
Par'tite a. Almost entirely divided (of leaves).
Bipar'tite a. In two corresponding parts.
Unipar'tite a. Formed of a single part.
Quadripar'tite a. Divided into, consisting of, or shared by four.
Tripar'tite a. Divided into three parts; having three copies; made between three parties.
Multipar'tite a. Divided into many parts.
Sexpar'tite a. Divided into six.
Celes'tite s. The mineral, celestine.
Bal'istite s. A powerful explosive.
Pit'tite s. One who patronizes the pit at a theatre.
Quite adv. Completely, entirely; very.
Requite' v.t. To repay, recompense; to retaliate on.
Mesquite' (-kēt) s. (*Mesquit*).
Suite (swēt) s. A retinue; set (of rooms, furniture, etc.); a connected series.
Le'vite s. One of the tribe of Levi; a priest.
Invite' v.t. To ask to a place or to do something; to attract. v.i. To give invitation; to allure.
Mus'covite s. A native of Moscow, a Russian; mica.
Twite s. The mountain linnet.
Baux'ite s. A clay from which aluminium is obtained.
Zeux'ite s. A variety of tourmaline.

Pu'seyite s. A Tractarian.
Quart'zite s. A hard sandstone containing quartz.
As'phalte s. Bituminous pitch, or an artificial substitute. v.t. To cover with this.
Svelte a. Slender, graceful.
Confidante' s. A female confidant.
Andan'te adv. Moderately slow (of music).
Infan'te s. A Spanish or Portuguese prince other than the heir-apparent.
Intrigante' s. A female intriguer.
Bacchan'te s. A priestess of Bacchus; a frenzied woman.
Pococuran'te (-tā) a. Indifferent. s. An apathetic person, a trifler.
Figuran'te s. A female figurant.
Dilletan'te s. A lover of the fine arts; a dabbling amateur. a. Art-loving; amateurish.
Debutante' s. A woman making a first appearance in public.
Clairvoy'ante s. A woman possessing the power of second-sight.
Cognoscent'e s. A connoisseur.
Enceinte' s. Space with ramparts, enclosing lines. a. Pregnant.
Tardamen'te (-tā) adv. (*Musical direction*) Slowly.
Subitamen'te (-tā) adv. (*Musical direction*) Suddenly.
Détente' s. Relief from strained relations between two states.
Entente' s. A friendly understanding between nations.
Quinte s. The fifth thrust or parry in fencing.
Mon'te s. A Spanish gambling card-game.
Cote s. A sheep-fold; a hut, cot.
Dote v.i. To have the intellect impaired, especially by age; to regard over-fondly.
An'ecdote s. A passage in private life; a short relation of such.
Ep'idote s. A silicate of alumina, calcium, and iron.
An'tidote s. A medicine that counteracts poison.
Red'ingote s. A long-skirted, double-breasted coat.
Table d'hôte s. The common table for guests at an inn, etc.
Tel'ephote s. Apparatus for reproducing pictures at a distance.
Pap'illote s. A curl-paper.
Mote s. A speck, a small particle.
Wit'enagemote (-mōt) s. The Anglo-Saxon parliament.
Remote' a. Distant in place or time; alien, abstracted, slight.
Promote' v.t. To forward, advance, contribute to the increase or power of; to elevate; to form (a company).
Smote past (*Smite*).
Note s. A mark, symbol, visible sign; a single sound in music, mark representing this; short remark, comment, letter, etc.; a bill; piece of paper money; notice; reputation; distinction. v.t. To observe carefully; to distinguish, mark; to enter in a book.
Denote' v.t. To mark, betoken, signify.
Connote' v.t. To imply, signify, involve.
Foot'note s. A note at the bottom of a page.
Ba'bacoote s. A short-tailed lemur.
Capote' s. A woman's long cloak with a hood.
Com'pote s. Stewed fruit.
Rote s. Mere repetition or effort of memory an obsolete stringed instrument.

Wrote past (*Write*).
Cre'osote s. A strong antiseptic oily liquid obtained from tar, wood, etc. v.t. To saturate with this.
Tote v.t. To carry, bear, haul.
Ap'tote s. An indeclinable noun.
Tet'raptote s. A Greek noun having only four cases.
Pent'aptote s. A noun having five cases.
Trip'tote s. A Greek noun having only three cases.
As'ymptote s. A line that continually approaches but never reaches a curve.
Quote v.t. To cite (a literary passage, fact, etc.); to adduce, repeat; to name the price of.
Misquote' v.t. To quote erroneously.
Vote s. Formal expression of wish, opinion, etc.; suffrage; thing conferred by or result of voting. v.t. and i. To choose by or to give a vote.
Devote' v.t. To dedicate, appropriate by vow, doom.
Outvote' v.t. To exceed in number of votes given.
Coyote' s. The Mexican prairie wolf.
Carte' s. A thrust in fencing; a bill of fare.
Écar'té s. A game of cards for two.
Ex-par'te a. One-sided.
Forte s. That in which one excels, one's strong point.
For'te adv. Direction to sing or play with force.
Pianofor'te s. A keyed and stringed musical instrument.
Porte s. The Turkish government.
Baste v.t. To drip gravy, etc., on meat while roasting; to sew slightly; to beat soundly.
Caste s. A division of society, especially in India.
Haste s. Rapidity, hurry, precipitance. v.i. To move quickly, be speedy. v.t. To drive or hurry on.
Chaste a. Pure, virtuous, innocent, modest.
Paste s. A semi-fluid mass; a mixture of flour, etc., used in cookery or as an adhesive; prepared clay for porcelain, etc.; fine glass used in imitation jewellery. v.t. To fasten or treat with paste.
Impaste' v.t. To make into paste; to lay on colours thickly.
Taste v.t. To perceive by the palate; to partake of; to experience. s. Flavour; perception; faculty of enjoying the beautiful, etc.; an inclination.
Fore'taste s. An anticipation of.
Distaste' s. Aversion, disrelish, disgust. v.t. Not to have relish for; to loathe.
Waste v.t. To ravage; to wear away gradually, employ prodigally, squander. v.i. To decrease gradually. s. Act of wasting; that which is wasted; refuse; gradual decrease; a desert. a. Valueless; desolate, bare; dismal.
Modiste' (-dēst) s. A dressmaker, milliner.
Batiste' s. A kind of cambric.
Artiste' s. A public performer.
Riposte' s. A quick return thrust in fencing; a retort.
Barbette' s. A mound on which guns are mounted; a platform for guns in a warship.
Facette' s. A little face; a small surface.
Dancette' s. The zigzag moulding in Norman architecture.
Dancet'té a. Indented (of heraldic charges).
Pincette' s. A pair of tweezers.
Vedette' s. A mounted sentry on outpost.
Estafette' s. A military courier.
Mofette' s. (*Mofetta*).
Suffragette' s. A militant female supporter of "woman's rights."
Sergette' s. A thin kind of serge.
Planchette' s. A small board on castors used for obtaining automatic writing.
Manchette' s. An ornamental cuff.
Fourchette' s. A small fork or fork-shaped object.
Oubliette' s. An underground dungeon.
Storiette' s. A short, pithy story.
Serviette' s. A table-napkin.
Galette' s. A flat, round cake.
Pal'ette s. A thin, oval tablet on which a painter mixes his pigments.
Tablette' s. A projecting coping-stone.
Om'elette s. (*Omelet*).
Flannelette' s. A cotton imitation of flannel.
Novelette' s. A short, sentimental novel.
Espagnolette' s. A kind of bolt for fastening casements.
Cassolette' s. A perforated perfume-box.
Landaulette' s. A motor-car with movable hood.
Epaulette' s. (*Epaulet*).
Roulette' s. A game of chance; an engraver's tool.
Palmette' s. An architectural palm-leaf shaped ornament.
Fumette' s. The smell of "high" game.
Pianette' s. A small piano.
Woollenette' s. An imitation or inferior woollen cloth.
Linenette' s. A cotton imitation of linen.
Vignette' (vinyet') s. Floral ornamentation in printing; cut with no defined border; head-and-shoulders portrait.
Lorgnette' s. Long-handled eye-glasses.
Bassinette' s. A hooded cradle or perambulator.
Cassinette' s. A mixed cloth of cotton and wool.
Wagonette' s. A light four-wheeled carriage with facing longitudinal seats.
Marionette' s. A puppet worked by strings.
Mignonette' s. A fragrant, greenish-flowered plant.
Maisonette' s. A small house; a house structurally divided into two dwellings.
Chansonette' s. A short song.
Lunette' s. Aperture in a concave ceiling; a flattish watch-glass; a detached bastion; blinker for a horse.
Brunette' s. A dark woman. a. Brown haired, of dark complexion.
Pipette' s. A thin, small, glass tube.
Cigarette' s. Tobacco rolled in paper for smoking.
Charette' s. A chariot.
Umbrette' s. A grallatorial African bird.
Soubrette' s. A pert waiting-maid in comedy.
Poudrette' s. A fertilizing manure.
Leaderette' s. A short editorial article.
Leatherette' s. Imitation leather.
Cashmerette' s. Imitation cashmere.
Ban'nerette s. A small banner.
Aigrette' s. A tuft of feathers or spray of gems worn on the head.
Vinaigrette' s. A smelling-bottle.
Lorette' s. A Parisian courtesan.
Pierrette' s. A female pierrot.
Burette' s. A small graduated glass tube.
Curette' s. A surgical instrument for removing growths, etc. v.t. To operate on with this.
Amourette' s. A trifling lover affair.
Chevrette' s. Thin goatskin leather.
Chemisette' s. A woman's under-bodice, a camisole.

Anisette' s. A liqueur from aniseed.
Noisette' s. A hardy variety of rose.
Grisette' s. A young French working-class woman.
Rosette' s. A rose-shaped ornament; a knot of ribbons.
Fos'sette s. A dimple.
Musette' s. A small French bagpipe; a reed-stop on the organ.
Pousette' s. To swing partners in a country dance.
Silhouette' s. A solid black profile likeness.
Pirouette' s. A whirling round on the toes. v.i. To whirl thus.
Plaquette' s. A small plaque.
Briquette' s. A block of compressed coal-dust.
Et'iquette s. Established rules of precedence, ceremonial, etc.; conventional rules of behaviour.
Banquette' s. A raised platform in a trench.
Coquette' s. A female flirt. v.i. To flirt, to trifle in love; to take up a task lightly with no intention of completing it.
Moquette' s. A carpet fabric of wool and hemp.
Croquette' s. A fried ball of forcemeat.
Statuette' s. A small statue.
Corvette' s. A war-sloop with flush deck and one tier of guns.
Cuvette' s. A clay crucible; a small scoop.
Eprouvette' s. A spoon used in assaying, etc.
Layette' s. The outfit for a new-born infant.
Sayette' s. A fabric of silk with wool or cotton.
Gazette' s. A newspaper, especially an official one. v.t. To insert or announce in a gazette; to publish officially.
Cocotte' s. A demi-mondaine.
Wy'andotte s. A breed of domestic fowl.
Calotte' s. A small skull-cap.
Char'lotte s. A kind of apple-pudding.
Sans-culotte' a. Republican; revolutionary.
Garrotte' s. A method of execution by strangling or by severing the spinal cord; strangulation. v.t. To execute or render insensible by this means.
Gavotte' s. A dance resembling the minuet.
Sau'te (sō'tā) s. Lightly fried.
Trib'ute s. Sum paid by one nation to another; a contribution, offering.
Contrib'ute v.t. To give in common with others or as one's share. v.i. To give a part; to conduce.
Distrib'ute v.t. To divide among several, deal out, apportion.
Redistrib'ute v.t. To distribute again.
Attrib'ute v.t. To set down, to ascribe.
At'tribute s. A thing attributed to anyone.
Cute a. Clever, sharp, cunning.
Acute' a. Sharp; keen-witted.
Pros'ecute v.t. and i. To pursue a purpose, persist in, carry on; to indict, sue.
Per'secute v.t. To pursue with malignity; to harass, especially on religious grounds.
Ex'ecute v.t. To carry into effect, achieve; to make valid; to put to death. v.i. To perform a duty, etc.; to play on an instrument.
Elec'trocute v.t. To execute by electricity.
Émeute' s. A seditious mob, a riot.
Refute' v.t. To prove to be false; to repel.
Confute' v.t. To prove to be false.
Argute' a. Shrill, sharp; shrewd.
Chute s. A rapid descent in a river; a funnel, hopper; a slide for toboggans, etc.
Parachute' s. An umbrella-like contrivance by which safe descent can be made from a balloon, etc.
Jute s. A hemp-like fibre.
Lute s. A guitar-like stringed instrument; a composition for sealing joints, protecting retorts from fire, etc. v.i. To play the lute. v.t. To close or cover with lute.
Salute' v.t. To greet, kiss, show civility. v.i. To perform a salutation; s. Act of saluting; a bow, kiss; a discharge of guns.
Flute s. A wooden musical wind-instrument; a longitudinal channel along a column, etc. v.i. To play, on a flute. v.t. To form flutes in.
Dilute' v.t. To make thin, weaken. a. Diluted, colourless.
Pollute' v.t. To make foul or unclean; to contaminate, defile.
Ab'solute a. Positive, unconditional, complete.
Res'olute a. Having a fixed purpose; firm; steadfast.
Irres'olute a. Undecided; wavering.
Dis'solute a. Wanton, licentious, vicious.
Volute' s. A spiral scroll in architectural capitals.
Ob'volute a. Arranged so as to overlap alternately (of leaves).
Ev'olute s. A special kind of curve on which another is formed.
De'volute v.t. To transfer power; to depute.
Rev'olute a. Rolled back from the edge (of leaves).
In'volute a. Rolled up; folded. s. A curve traced by the end of a string wound upon another curve.
Con'volute a. Rolled on itself; having convolutions.
Mute a. Silent, dumb, not pronounced, or having its sound checked. s. A dumb person; a funeral attendant; a mute consonant; a pad for muffling sound. v.t. To apply a mute to strings of instruments. v.i. To dung (of birds only).
Commute' v.t. To exchange, put one thing for another; to reduce the severity of.
Permute' v.t. To change thoroughly; to subject to permutation.
Transmute' v.t. To transform, change.
Minute' a. Very small; trifling; precise.
Min'ute s. A sixtieth part of an hour or degree; a short sketch, a note. v.t. To write a note of.
Comminute' v.t. To make small, to pulverize.
Route s. Course travelled or planned out; a march.
Depute' v.t. To appoint as a substitute; to send with authority.
Repute' v.t. To account, reckon. s. Reputation; character attributed; estimate.
Disrepute' s. Loss or lack of reputation; disgrace.
Impute' v.t. To charge upon, to ascribe.
Compute' v.t. To reckon, estimate, number.
Dispute' v.t. and i. To argue for and against; to contend for in argument; to wrangle. s. A controversy, altercation, debate.
Brute s. An animal; a beast-like person. a. Senseless, savage, bestial.
Imbrute' v.t. and i. To brutalize or become brutalized.
Hir'sute a. Hairy, unshorn.
Stat'ute s. A law, enactment, fundamental rule.
Sub'stitute s. Person or thing in place of another. v.t. To exchange, put one in place of another.

Des'titute a. Forsaken, friendless ; in want.
In'stitute v.t. To found, fix, establish. s. That which is instituted ; an institution, established law, principle.
Con'stitute v.t. To establish, enact, give form to, compose ; to appoint or depute.
Recon'stitute v.t. To put together or set up again ; to give a new constitution to.
Pros'titute s. A harlot ; a base hireling. v.t. To put to base uses ; to offer for lewd purposes for hire.
Astute' a. Cunning, shrewd, acute.
Sixte s. One of the parries in fencing.
-cyte suff. (*In Biology*) Denoting a cell.
Leu'cocyte s. A colourless corpuscle in the blood, tissue, etc.
Phag'ocyte s. A leucocyte that digests and destroys microbes.
Hæmat'ocyte s. A blood-corpuscle.
Trog'lodyte s. A cave-dweller.
Trach'yte s. A feldspathic volcanic rock.
-phyte suff. Denoting a plant or vegetable organism.
Ep'iphyte s. A plant growing upon another but not drawing nourishment therefrom.
Pter'idophyte s. A fern.
Ne'ophyte s. A proselyte, novice, tyro. a. Newly entered.
Zy'gophyte s. A plant reproduced by means of zygospores.
Lith'ophyte s. A calcareous polyp, a coral.
Thal'lophyte s. A thallogen.
Derm'ophyte s. A fungus parasitic on the skin.
Zo'ophyte s. An animal resembling a plant ; a sponge, coral, etc.
Car'pophyte s. A red seaweed.
Mi'crophyte s. A microscopic vegetable organism.
Hy'drophyte s. An aquatic plant.
A'erophyte s. A plant growing entirely in the air.
Sap'rophyte s. A plant that lives on decaying matter.
En'trophyte s. A plant parasitic internally.
Pro'tophyte s. A microscopic plant of the lowest organization.
Pros'elyte s. A convert.
Ac'olyte s. An attendant in the Roman Church.
Elec'trolyte s. A compound that can be decomposed by electrolysis.
Imbue' v.t. To saturate with, dye with, cause to drink in ; to inspire.
Cue s. A hint ; closing words of a speech ; part one is to play in his turn ; humour ; the straight rod used in billiards.
Bar'becue s. A large gridiron ; an animal roasted whole. v.t. To broil or roast whole.
Curl'icue s. A fantastic curl, a flourish.
Fes'cue s. A twig ; a wand for pointing ; a genus of grasses.
Res'cue v.t. To free from danger, liberate. s. Deliverance from restraint, danger, etc.
Miscue' v.i. (*Billiards*) To fail to strike the ball properly. s. This failure.
Due a. Owing, owed ; proper ; fit ; without deviation ; expected. adv. Directly. s. That which belongs to one ; that which it is necessary to pay ; right, just title.
Subdue' v.t. To overpower, vanquish ; to tone down.
Res'idue s. The remainder ; residuum.
Endue' v.t. To invest with ; to endow.
Ven'due s. An auction.
Overdue' a. Past the time of payment ; more than due.

Queue (kū) s. A pig-tail ; line of persons, etc., waiting admission or attention. v.i. To form into a queue.
A'gue s. A malarial fever.
League s. An alliance ; a compact ; three miles or knots. v.i. and t. To confederate, combine together with.
Col'league s. An associate in office, partner.
Teague (tēg) s. (*Slang*) An Irishman.
Blague s. Humbug.
Plague s. A calamity ; anything that vexes ; a pestilence. v.t. To trouble, torment ; to afflict with disease or calamity.
Vague (vāg) a. Indistinct ; ill-defined ; ambiguous.
Sarigue' (-rēg') s. A S. American opossum.
Intrigue' v.i. To plot ; to engage in an intrigue. v.t. To perplex, interest. s. An underhanded plot ; a liaison ; secret love.
Fatigue' s. Weariness, lassitude ; toil ; non-military work of soldiers. v.t. To tire with labour, to weary.
Cangue s. A Chinese instrument of torture.
Gangue s. The matrix in which ores are bedded.
Harangue' s. A declamation, tirade, pompous oration. v.i. To make an harangue. v.t. To address an harangue to.
Den'gue s. An infectious fever of tropical climes.
Meringue' (-răng) s. A sweetened confection of white of egg, etc.
Disting'ué a. Distinguished in appearance, etc.
Tongue (tung) s. The organ of taste and speech ; speech, language ; a strip ; pin of buckle. v.t. and i. To use the tongue.
Hart's'-tongue s. A fern with tongue-shaped leaves.
Embogue' v.i. To discharge (as a river into the sea).
Disembogue' v.t. To discharge at the mouth (as a river).
Ped'agogue s. A schoolmaster ; a pedantic, formal person.
Helmin'-thagogue s. A medicine for expelling worms.
Chol'agogue s. A drug promoting secretion of bile.
Pty'lagogue (-gog) s. Substance inducing flow of saliva.
Dem'agogue s. A factious orator or agitator.
Emmen'agogue s. A medicine that promotes menstruation.
Syn'agogue s. A congregation of Jews for worship ; the meeting-place.
Hy'dragogue s. A purgative causing copious secretion of fluid.
Mys'tagogue s. One who interprets mysteries ; a custodian of church relics.
Si'alogogue (-gog) s. Medicine promoting flow of saliva.
Galac'togogue s. An agent which increases the flow of milk.
-logue suff. Representing Greek *logos*, word, speech, and forming nouns.
Dec'alogue s. The Ten Commandments.
Di'alogue s. Discourse between two or more.
An'alogue s. An analogous word ; a parallel.
Cat'alogue s. A methodical list of names, etc. v.t. To make a list of.
Ec'logue s. A pastoral poem.
Ep'ilogue s. A short speech or poem addressed by an actor to the spectators at the end of a play.
Collogue' v.i. To talk confidentially ; to intrigue.

Ide'ologue s. A theorist, visionary.
The'ologue (-lōg) s. A theologist.
Hom'ologue s. Something homologous; a corresponding part or organ.
Sin'ologue (-lōg) s. One versed in the Chinese language, etc.
Mon'ologue s. A soliloquy; a poem, etc., for a single speaker.
Ap'ologue s. A moral tale, a fable.
Pro'logue (-log) s. Spoken introduction to a dramatic piece; preface.
Du'ologue s. A dialogue or dramatic composition for two.
Rogue (rōg) s. A vagrant; a cheat; a wag, a sly fellow; a solitary, ferocious elephant.
Brogue s. The Irish accent; a coarse heavy shoe.
Pirogue' (-rōg') s. A canoe made of a hollowed trunk.
Prorogue'(-rōg) v.t. and i. To adjourn.
Togue (tōg) s. The great lake trout of N. America.
Vogue (vōg) s. Current fashion, popular mode.
Ar'gue v.i. To reason, debate, dispute.
Redar'gue v.t. To refute, disprove.
Rear'gue v.t. and i. To argue a matter over again.
Exergue' s. Space beneath base line on a coin, etc.; inscription therein.
Morgue s. A public mortuary.
Fugue s. A musical composition in which the different parts follow and repeat each other.
Hue s. Colour, tint; a clamour, shouting.
Val'ue s. Worth; estimation; price; equivalent. v.t. To appraise; to prize.
Underval'ue v.t. To rate below the true worth, to esteem lightly.
Outval'ue v.t. To exceed in value.
Blue s. One of the primary colours. a. Of this colour, sky-coloured.
Clue s. A ball of thread, especially as used as a guide; a direction or hint to the solution of a problem.
Flue s. An air-passage, especially for conveying smoke and flame from a fire, gaseous products from a tubular boiler, etc.; light down, fluff. v.i. and t. To splay or cause of spray.
Glue s. An impure gelatine used as a cement. v.t. To join with this; to unite.
Slue v.t. and i. To turn or swing on a pivot. s. Such a motion.
Ingénue' s. An ingenuous girl.
Ven'ue s. Place where an action, trial, etc., is laid; a thrust.
Av'enue s. An alley of trees, a broad walk.
Rev'enue s. Annual income, especially of a State.
Det'inue s. Unlawful detention.
Ret'inue s. Train of attendants; suite.
Contin'ue v.t. To carry on uninterruptedly; to prolong; to persevere in. v.i. To remain, stay, last; to persevere.
Discontin'ue v.t. and i. To intermit, interrupt the continuity of, lose cohesion or continuity.
Rou'é (ru'ā) s. A rake, debauchee.
Spue v. and s. Spew.
Conspue' v.t. To spit upon, abuse.
Claque s. A body of hired applauders.
Plaque (plăk) s. An ornamental disk or plate; a badge.
Opaque' (-pāk') a Impervious to rays of light; not transparent; obscure.
Saque s. A loose-fitting gown or coat.
Cosaque' s. A Cossack dance.
Cheque s. An order or draft on a bank.
Caique' s. A vessel used in the Levant.
Cacique' s. A ruler in ancient Mexico, the W. Indies, etc.
Sal'ique a. Salic.
Oblique' (-lēk') a. Neither direct, parallel, nor perpendicular; slanting.
Clique s. A coterie, an exclusive group.
Silique' (-lēk') s. A siliqua.
Appli'qué s. Ornament laid on some other material.
Technique' (-nēk') s. Method or performance; execution.
Clinique' s. A clinic.
Unique' (-nēk') a. Single in kind or excellence; without an equal.
Pi'qué (pē'kā) s. A figured cotton fabric.
Pique (pēk) s. Feeling of annoyance or resentment; ill-will; a grudge. v.t. To affect with envy, to irritate; to pride or value (*reflexively*).
Repique' (-pēk') s. A score of thirty points at piquet.
Perique' s. A strong kind of tobacco.
Physique' (-zēk') s. Physical organisation; natural constitution.
Pratique'(-tēk') s. Licence to a ship to trade, etc., after quarantine.
Critique' s. A written criticism.
Antique' a. Ancient, of old fashion. s. A relic of past times.
Bezique' s. A card game.
Cat'afalque s. A temporary canopy used at funerals; a hearse.
Pul'que (-kā) s. A drink made from the Mexican agave.
Cinque s. Five, especially on dice or cards.
Breloque' s. A pendant on a watch-chain.
Baroque' a. Grotesque, odd.
Toque (tōk) s. A small, round, brimless bonnet.
Eq'uivoque s. An ambiguous term or speech; equivocation.
Barque s. A vessel with three masts and no mizzen topsail.
Marque s. Used of a letter licensing a private vessel to attack enemy shipping.
Cirque s. A circular space.
Torque (tork) s. An ancient Gaulish collar of twisted gold.
Basque s. A lady's jacket cut with a skirt; a member of a non-Aryan race of the Pyrenees.
Casque s. A helmet.
Masque s. A common form of dramatic entertainment in the seventeenth century.
-esque suff. Like; in the style or manner of.
Alhambresque' a. In the Moorish style of decoration.
Arabesque' s. An Arabian style of decoration.
Raphaelesque' (-lesk) a. After the manner of the Italian painter Raphael (d. 1520)
Burlesque' v.t. To lampoon, to turn to ridicule. s. A lampoon, a farce.
Romanesque' (-nesk') a. Denoting a style of architecture preceding Gothic.
Germanesque' a. In German style.
Gardenesque' a. In garden style.
Harlequinesque' a. Like harlequin or a harlequinade.
Gorgonesque' a. In the manner of or resembling a Gorgon.
Lionesque' a. In the manner of or like a lion.
Barbaresque' a. In a barbarous style.
Picaresque' a. Pertaining to rogues and adventurers, or to romances in which such are the heroes.
Moresque' a. In Moorish style. s. Moorish decoration.
Humoresque' s. A capricious or humorous musical composition.

Picturesque' (-resk') a. Pleasing to the eye; like a picture.
Sculpturesque' (-resk') a. Like a statue; sculptural.
Dantesque' a. In the style of Dante.
Gigantesque' a. Gigantic.
Grotesque' a. Odd, fantastic, bizarre. s. Whimsical ornamentation; a fantastic figure.
Blottesque' a. Having masses of colour heavily laid on.
Statuesque' (-esk') a. Resembling or partaking of the character of a statue.
Bisque s. Unglazed white porcelain.
O'dalisque s. A female slave or concubine in Turkey.
Ris'qué a. Indelicate; bordering on the indecent.
Mosque s. A Mohammedan place of worship.
Brusque a. Rough mannered, unpolished.
Chibouque' s. (*Chibouk*).
Rue v.t. To lament, grieve for. s. A bitter plant with a fetid odour.
Imbrue' v.t. To steep, soak, saturate.
Accrue' v.i. To be added; to arise (as profits).
Sprue s. Hole by which molten metal is poured into a mould; metal left in this.
True a. Conformable to fact; real; genuine; exact; right; loyal.
Con'strue v.t. To combine syntactically; to arrange words so as to show the meaning; to translate.
Misconstrue' v.t. To mistake the meaning of, interpret erroneously.
Sue v.t. To follow up; to prosecute; especially judicially; to seek in marriage. v.i. To petition; to woo; to prosecute a suit at law.
Ensue' v.t. To follow, pursue. v.i. To succeed, come after.
Per'sue s. The track of a wounded deer.
Pursue' v.t. To follow with view to overtake; to chase, to prosecute; to imitate. v.i. To go on, proceed.
Iss'ue s. Act of passing out; delivery; exit; consequence; offspring; ulcer artificially produced. v.i. To pass or flow out; to accrue; to terminate. v.t. To send out, put into circulation.
Reis'sue v.t. To issue a second time. s. A second issue.
Tis'sue s. A gauzy woven fabric; a primary layer of organic substance; a fabrication. v.t. To form into tissue; to variegate.
Stat'ue s. Sculptured or cast representation of a person, etc.
Habit'ué s. A regular frequenter.
Vir'tue s. Moral goodness; chastity; efficacy.
Battue' s. The driving of game from cover.
Revue' s. A spectacular theatrical medley burlesquing topical events, etc.
Ave' int. Hail! welcome! farewell! s. An Ave Maria.
Cave s. An underground hollow with an opening; a den, grotto; a seceding group from a party. v.t. To hollow out v.i. To give way, fall in.
Ca've int. Beware!
Con'cave a. Hollow and curved, as the inside of a sphere. s. A hollow, an arch. v.t. To make hollow.
Deave v.t. To deafen.
Heave v.t. To lift, raise, cause to swell; to force (a groan) from the breast; to throw. v.i. To rise; to pant, retch. s. An effort upwards, a pant, sighing; a throw.
Upheave' v.t. To lift up from beneath.
Sheave s. Wheel in a block, etc., over which a rope works. v.t. To gather into sheaves.
Leave s. Permission; liberty granted; licence; a farewell. v.t. To let remain; to quit, abandon; to have remaining at death; to bequeath. v.i. To depart; to cease; to come into leaf.
Cleave v.i. To adhere, be attached closely, be faithful to; to split, part asunder. v.t. To divide forcibly, cut through.
Interleave' v.t. To insert blank leaves between other leaves.
Sleave s. The knotted part of silk; floss or refuse silk. v.t. To separate (threads)
Reave v.t. and i. To deprive of by force, bereave, pillage.
Bereave' v.t. To make destitute, to take away from.
Weave (wēv) v.t. To form into a web; to insert; to contrive. v.i. To practise weaving.
Inweave' v.t. To weave together, intertwine by weaving.
Interweave' v.t. To weave together, intermix, connect closely.
Gave past (*Give*).
Aga've s. The aloe.
Forgave' past (*Forgive*).
Have v.t. To possess, to hold, to contain; to procure, to bring forth.
Behave' v.i. To conduct oneself; to demean.
Misbehave' v.i. To conduct oneself improperly.
Shave v.t. To make smooth by cutting the surface closely; to remove hair from the skin with a razor; to cut thin slices from; to skim along. v.i. To cut off the beard with a razor. s. A cutting of the beard thus; a thin slice; a narrow escape.
Spoke'shave s. A small two-handled plane for dressing curved woodwork.
Lave v.t. To bathe, wash the side of, flow past.
Clave past (*Cleave*).
Lat'iclave s. A broad purple stripe worn by ancient Roman senators.
Enclave' s. A state completely surrounded by a foreign country. a. *Heraldry*) Dovetailed.
Con'clave s. The body of cardinals; their assembly to elect a pope; (a private meeting.
Slave s. One held in bondage or subject to another's will; a drudge. v.i. To labour as a slave.
Enslave' v.t. To reduce to slavery.
Nave s. Body of a church; central block of a wheel.
Knave s. A rascal; the jack at cards.
Pave v.t. To floor with brick or stone, cover with paving; to prepare the way for.
Rave v.i. To be delirious, talk frantically or irrationally; to dote. v.t. To say wildly.
Brave a. Courageous, bold, valiant. s. A fearless warrior. v.t. To set at defiance.

Crave v.t. To beg, ask earnestly, to desire strongly.
Grave a. Solemn, sedate; important; thoughtful. v.t. To carve or engrave; to impress deeply; to clean a ship's bottom. s. A tomb.
Wald'grave s. Old German title of nobility.
Wild'grave s. German title of nobility.
Land'grave s. An old German title of nobility.
Engrave' v.t. To cut figures, etc., in metal, wood, etc.; to impress deeply.
Mar'grave s. A German title of nobility.
Bur'grave s. The commandant of a German fortified town
Pals'grave s. Former title of a German Count Palatine.
Deprave' v.t. To make bad, to vitiate.
Ar'chitrave s. A moulding round a door or window.
Save v.t. To make safe; to preserve from injury; to rescue; to lay up, spare. v.i. To avoid waste. prep. Except. conj. Unless. s. Something saved.
Oc'tave s. The eighth day after or the week immediately following a church festival; the musical scale, or its eighth tone; any group of eight.
Stave s. Curved strip for a cask; a stanza; the musical staff. v.t. To burst a hole in; to put off, delay.
Zouave' (zoo-ahv) s. A short, round-fronted, sleeveless jacket; an Oriental soldier in the French army.
Suave (swāv) a. Bland, agreeable, gracious.
Wave s. A ridge of moving water; an undulation; signal made by waving. v.t. and i. To undulate; to sway or play loosely; to brandish; to beckon.
Eve s. Evening; day before a church festival; a preceding period.
Sleeve s. Part of garment for the arm, anything resembling this.
Reeve s. Formerly a chief magistrate of a town, etc.; the female ruff. v.t. To pass (a rope) through a hole in a block, a ring, etc.
Screeve v.t. and i. (*Slang*) To write or draw, especially with coloured chalks on pavements.
Port'reeve s. Former title of a chief magistrate.
Steeve v.i. To be at a certain angle (of a bowsprit). v.t. To stow cargo with a steeve. s. Apparatus for stowing cargo.
Achieve' v.t. To perform, finish, obtain.
Thieve v.i. and t. To practise or take by theft.
Believe' v.t. To put confidence in. v.i. To trust.
Make'believe s. A pretence, sham. a. Unreal, counterfeit.
Disbelieve' v.t. Not to believe; to refuse credit to.
Relieve' v.t. To alleviate, mitigate, ease, succour; to release from duty; to give variety to; to cause to appear to project.
Grieve v.i. To mourn, to feel grief. v.t. To cause pain or sorrow to; to lament over. s. An overseer.
Reprieve' v.t. To remit or suspend the punishment of; to relieve temporarily. s. Suspension of execution; respite.
Retrieve' v.t. To find again; to restore, repair.
Sieve (siv) s. Utensil for separating smaller particles of a loose substance.
Cleve s. The steep side of a hill (in Devon).
Champleve' s. A process of enamelling by insertion of colouring matter in grooves cut in the metal surface to be treated.
Név'é (-ā) s. Snow at head of glacier not yet compressed into ice.
Breve s. A note equal to two semibreves; the diacritic marking a short vowel.
Sem'ibreve s. A long note in music.
-ive suff. Serving, tending, or disposed to.
Glaive s. A broadsword, falchion.
Naive' a. Ingenuous, artless; unaffected.
Waive v.t. To forgo, relinquish; to defer.
Coer'cive a. Compulsory; able to compel.
Divorc'ive a. Having power to divorce.
Cres'cive a. Increasing, augmenting.
Deduc'ive a. Performing the act of deduction.
Condu'cive a. Tending to promote or forward.
Dive v.i. To plunge into water head first; to go deep. s. A plunge head first; a low-class drinking-bar.
Khedive' s. Title of the former Viceroys of Egypt.
En'dive s. A salad-plant of the chicory family.
Gerun'dive s. A verbal adjective; the future passive participle.
Deceive' v.t. To mislead, impose upon. v.i. To act deceitfully.
Receive (-sēv') v.t. To accept; to entertain; to admit; to take stolen goods. v.i. To hold a reception.
Conceive' v.t. To form in the womb; to picture in the mind or to the imagination; to understand, believe. v.i. To become pregnant; to form an idea.
Preconceive' v.t. To form a previous notion or idea of.
Misconceive' v.t. To have a wrong idea of; to interpret wrongly; misjudge.
Perceive' v.t. To obtain knowledge of through the senses; to see to be true, discern, comprehend.
Five a. and s. Four and one more; half of ten.
Give v.t. To bestow; to confer without reward. v.i. To relent, to soften; to yield to pressure. s. State of yielding; elasticity.
O'give s. The diagonal rib of a groined vault; a pointed arch.
Ar'give s. A native of Argos, a Greek. a. Of Argos, Greek.
Forgive' v.t. To pardon, absolve, remit.
Misgive' v.t. To fill with doubt, deprive of confidence; to fail.
Hive s. A receptacle for honey-bees; the bees inhabiting this; a place full of industry. v.t. and i. To put in or live in a hive; to swarm together.
Chive s. A small onion-like herb.
Ar'chive s. A repository for ancient records.
Bee'hive s. A case for keeping and rearing bees.
Shive s. A thin slice, a splinter.
Skive v.t. To split into thin layers, to pare (of leather).
Live (liv) v.i. To have life, exist; to dwell; to subsist; to acquire a livelihood.
Live a. Having life; not dead; ignited, active, effective, full of energy.
Alive' a. Having life; cheerful.
Relive' v.t. and i. To live over again or afresh

Ol'ive s. An evergreen tree; its fruit; a yellowish-green or -brown colour; beef, etc., cut in slice, rolled up, and flavoured.
Outlive' v.t. To survive, live beyond.
Connive' v.i. To forbear to see, wink at.
Rive v t. To tear, cleave, or split asunder. v.i. To be rent asunder.
Drive v.t. To push forward, impel, hurry on; to guide or convey in a carriage. v.t. To be impelled onwards; to aim at; to strike with force. s. A journey in a carriage, car, etc.; a road for driving on; a sweeping stroke or blow; a driving of game, cattle, the enemy, etc.
Derive' v.t. To deduce, trace, draw from. v.i. To proceed, to originate.
Shrive v.t. and i. To receive the confession of and absolve; to confess (oneself).
Thrive v.i. To prosper, be successful.
Deprive' v.t. To take from, dispossess, bereave of.
Arrive' v.i. To come to a place, to reach; to happen.
Contrive' v.t. To devise, invent, effect. v.i. To form designs, to plot.
Strive v.i. To make an effort; to struggle.
Abra'sive s. A polishing substance; a. Wearing.
Sua'sive a. Able to persuade or influence.
Dissua'sive a. Tending to dissuade. s. An argument or advice against a measure.
Persua'sive a. Tending or able to persuade.
Assua'sive a. Assuaging, soothing.
Eva'sive a. Tending to evade; marked by evasion.
Inva'sive a. Making invasion; aggressive.
Perva'sive a. Tending or able to pervade.
Adhe'sive a. Sticking, tenacious.
Cohe'sive a. Having power of cohering.
Incohe'sive a. Incoherent.
Deci'sive a. Conclusive; positive; convincing.
Indeci'sive a. Not final or conclusive; vacillating.
Inci'sive a. Cutting deeply; sharply expressive; trenchant.
Deris'ive a. Mocking, ridiculing, deriding.
Divis'ive a. Forming division or distribution; creating discord.
Emul'sive a. Softening; milk-like; yielding oil by expression.
Repul'sive a. Arousing or exhibiting repulsion.
Impul'sive a. Able to impel; urging forward; actuated or governed by impulse.
Compul'sive a. Having power to compel.
Propul'sive a. Driving forward.
Expul'sive a. Driving away; expelling.
Revul'sive a. Tending to cause revulsion. s. A counter-irritant.
Divul'sive a. Tending to rend asunder.
Convul'sive a. Spasmodic; producing or attended by convulsions.
Expan'sive a. Serving, tending, or having capacity to expand; comprehensive; effusive.
Inexpan'sive a. Not able to expand or dilate.
Incen'sive a. Tending to excite; inflammatory.
Descen'sive a. Tending downwards.
Defen'sive a. Serving to defend; resisting aggression. s. An attitude or condition of defence.
Offen'sive a. Causing displeasure, anger, evil, or injury; pertaining to or used in attack; annoying; disgusting. s. State, method, or posture of one who attacks.
Inoffen'sive a. Unobjectionable harmless
Reprehen'sive a. Containing reproof.
Compre-hen'sive a. Extending widely; comprising much; able to understand.
Incompre-hen'sive a. Not comprehensive, limited.
Apprehen'sive a. Fearful, nervous.
Inappre-hen'sive a. Not apprehensive; regardless.
Pen'sive a. Thoughtful; sad, sober.
Rec'ompensive a. That recompenses.
Suspen'sive a. Having power to suspend; uncertain.
Expen'sive a. Occasioning expense; costly; lavish.
Inexpen'sive a. Cheap.
Inten'sive a. Admitting of intension; concentrated; serving to give emphasis. s. A word, exclamation, etc., giving emphasis.
Osten'sive a. Exhibiting; ostensible.
Exten'sive a. Having wide extent; large; comprehensive.
Coexten'sive a. (*Coextend*).
Respon'sive a. Able, ready, or inclined to respond; correspondent.
Irrespon'sive a. Not responsive.
Correspon'sive a. Answering, adapted.
Explo'sive a. Tending or liable to explode or to explosion; violent. s. A substance which will explode; a mute, discontinuous consonant.
Pur'posive a. With intent.
Corro'sive a. Tending to corrode; vexing; acrimonious. s. That which corrodes.
Asper'sive a. Slanderous, calumnious.
Disper'sive a. Tending to disperse; causing dispersion.
Deter'sive s. A cleansing agent. a. Having power to cleanse.
Abster'sive a. Having cleansing properties.
Subver'sive a. Tending to subvert.
Inver'sive a. Marked by inversion.
Introver'sive a. Turning or tending to turn inwards.
Perver'sive a. Tending to pervert or corrupt.
Extor'sive a. Serving to extort.
Cur'sive a. Flowing; written in a running hand.
Decur'sive a. Running down; decurrent.
Precur'sive a. Introductory, leading up to; forerunning.
Incur'sive a. Making a raid or an attack.
Discur'sive a. Rambling, desultory; argumentative.
Excur'sive a. Rambling; deviating.
Mas'sive a. Bulky; ponderous; substantial.
Pas'sive a. Not active but acted on; suffering; unresisting; inert; applied to a verb expressing the effect, etc., of an action, etc.
Impas'sive a. Not susceptible of pain, suffering, or excitement; unmoved.
Succes'sive a. Following in order; consecutive.
Reces'sive a. Tending to go back; receding.
Conces'sive a. (*Concession*).
Exces'sive a. Marked by excess; extreme, vehement.
Redres'sive a. Tending to redress; affording relief.
Regres'sive a. Passing back; returning.
Aggres'sive a. Quarrelsome, taking the first step against.
Digres'sive a. Pertaining to or consisting in digression.
Ingres'sive a Pertaining to entrance; entering.
Progres'sive a. Moving forward, advancing; advocating progress.
Retrogres'sive a. Going or moving backward.

Transgres'sive a. Characterized by transgression; tending to transgress.
Depress'ive a. Able or tending to depress.
Repres'sive a. Able or tending to repress.
Impres'sive a. Producing an impression on the mind; solemn.
Compres'sive a. (*Compress*).
Oppres'sive a. Burdensome; unjustly severe; tyrannical.
Suppres'sive a. Tending to suppress.
Expres'sive a. Serving to express; indicative; emphatic; full of expression.
Inexpres'sive a. Inexpressible; without expression or meaning; dull.
Posses'sive a. Pertaining to, having, or denoting possession.
Mis'sive s. A message, letter. a. Intended to be sent; missile.
Submis'sive a. Ready to submit; yielding, compliant.
Nonsubmis'sive a. (*Negative*).
Admis'sive a. Tending to admit, implying admission.
Emis'sive a. Sending out; emitting.
Remis'sive a. Remitting; abating; forgiving.
Permis'sive a. Granting leave; allowing; suffered without hindrance.
Intermis'sive a. Recurring after intervals; intermittent.
Dismis'sive a. Giving leave to depart.
Transmis'sive a. Capable of being transmitted.
Succus'sive a. Characterized by a shaking movement.
Concus'sive a. (*Concussion*).
Percus'sive a. Acting by percussion; striking against.
Repercus'sive a. Causing to reverberate; driven back.
Jus'sive a. Expressing command.
Applau'sive a. Approbative.
Abu'sive a. Practising abuse, offensive.
Effu'sive a. Pouring out; showing overflowing feeling or kindness; gushing.
Diffu'sive a. Tending to diffuse; spreading, circulating, widely distributed.
Infu'sive a. Able to infuse.
Perfu'sive a. Sprinkling; adapted to sprinkle or perfuse.
Transfu'sive a. Tending to transfuse.
Preclu'sive a. Shutting out; tending to preclude.
Seclu'sive a. Tending to seclude.
Inclu'sive a. Enclosing, containing, comprehending.
Conclu'sive a. Final; convincing.
Inconclu'sive a. Not conclusive; indecisive.
Exclu'sive a. Able to exclude, not taking into account. s. One of a coterie; a contribution to a single paper.
Elu'sive a. Practising elusion; fallacious; evasive.
Delu'sive a. Tending to mislead, unreal, deceptive.
Prelu'sive a. Previous; introductory.
Allu'sive a. Making allusion to, hinting at.
Illu'sive a. Delusive, deceptive.
Collu'sive a. Fraudulently concerted.
Amus'ive a. Tending to amuse.
Obtru'sive a. Disposed to obtrude.
Intru'sive a. Tending or apt to intrude; entering without right or welcome.
Protru'sive a. Thrusting or impelling forward.
Extru'sive a. Thrusting or tending to thrust outwards.
Com'bative a. Fighting; pugnacious.
Pro'bative a. Serving for trial or proof.
Rep'robative a. Pertaining to or expressing reprobation.
Sic'cative a. Drying, causing dryness. s. A siccative substance.
Desic'cative a. Tending to dry; drying. s. A desiccant.
Ex'siccative a. Tending or able to dry.
Prec'ative a. Precatory.
Dep'recative a. That serves to deprecate; having the form of a prayer; containing protest or entreaty.
Erad'icative a. Tending or serving to eradicate.
Ded'icative a. Pertaining to dedication; dedicatory.
Med'icative a. Tending to cure or heal.
Indic'ative a. Showing, informing; applied to the mood of a verb that declares or interrogates.
Vin'dicative a. Tending or intended to vindicate.
Ju'dicative a. Having power to judge.
Qual'ificative a. Qualifying.
Signif'icative a. Expressive of something; signifying.
Jus'tificative a. Justificatory.
Viv'ificative a. Able to animate or renew life in.
Vell'icative a. Given to or causing twitching.
Replic'ative a. Pertaining to replication.
Multiplica'tive a. Tending or having the power to multiply.
Im'plicative a. Tending to implicate or imply.
Du'plicative a. Having the quality of doubling.
Redu'plicative a. Pertaining to or formed by reduplication.
Ex'plicative a. Serving to explain or interpret.
Commun'icative a. Not reserved, inclined to impart news, etc.
Incommun'icative a. Not inclined to impart information.
Excommu'nicative a. Pertaining to or conveying excommunication.
Fric'ative s. A consonant produced by friction of the breath through a narrow opening (*F*, *sh*, *th*).
Prognos'ticative a. Foretelling; serving to foretell.
Suf'focative a. Tending or able to suffocate.
Loc'ative a. Denoting a place. s. The grammatical case doing this.
Coll'ocative a. (*Collocate*).
Voc'ative a. Pertaining to or used in addressing. s. Case of a noun used in addressing.
Evoc'ative a. Tending or serving to call forth.
Provoc'ative a. Serving or tending to provoke. s. A stimulant.
Ed'ucative a. Of use in education; instructive.
Da'tive s. Grammatical case that follows verbs expressing giving, etc.; that which may be disposed of at pleasure.
Quid'dative a. Constituting or containing the essence.
Sed'ative a. Tending to calm; allaying irritability. s. A medicine effecting this.
Elu'cidative a. Tending to elucidate; explanatory.
Consol'idative a. Tending to consolidate; healing.
Accom'modative a. (*Accommodate*).
Retard'ative a. Tending to retard; causing delay.
Lau'dative a. Laudatory.
Crea'tive a. Having power to create; creating.
Rec'reative a. Reinvigorating; pertaining to recreation.
Pro'creative a. Having power to beget.
Prop'agative a. Propagating; tending to propagate.

Neg'ative a. Opposite of positive; denying; implying negation or absence. s. A word which denies; a proposition by which something is denied; a photographic picture in which lights and shadows are reversed. v.t. To veto.
Abnega'tive a. (*Abnegate*).
Seg'regative a. Tending to segregate; characterized by segregation.
Ag'gregative a. (*Aggregate*).
Irr'igative a. Serving to irrigate.
Mit'igative a. Tending to mitigate.
Inves'tigative a. Addicted to or marked by investigation.
Ab'rogative a. (*Abrogate*).
Prerog'ative s. An exclusive privilege, peculiar or hereditary right.
Interrog'ative a. Denoting or expressed as a question. s. A word used in questioning.
Pur'gative a. Having power to purge. s. A cathartic.
Depre'ciative a. Depreciatory.
Appre'ciative a. Expressing appreciation, esteeming favourably.
Enun'ciative a. Pertaining to enunciation or utterance.
Denun'ciative a. Denunciatory.
Renun'ciative a. Renouncing.
Pronun'ciative a. Pertaining to pronunciation.
Asso'ciative a. (*Associate*).
Disso'ciative a. Causing or tending to cause disunion.
Radia'tive a. Pertaining to or exhibiting radiation.
Irra'diative a. Tending to irradiate.
Me'diative a. Mediating, used in mediation.
Retal'iative a. Retaliatory.
Concil'iative a. (*Conciliate*).
Pal'liative a. Serving to palliate or extenuate. s. Anything that mitigates.
Var'iative a. Pertaining to or showing variation.
Appro'priative a. Involving propriation; tending to appropriate.
Ini'tiative a. Serving to initiate. s. A first step; power of leading.
Alle'viative a. (*Alleviate*).
Talk'ative a. Given to talking.
Ab'lative s. A Latin noun-case implying direction, separation from, etc.
No'menclative a. Pertaining to naming or nomenclature.
Rel'ative a. Having relation; respecting; relevant; not absolute; indicating relation. s. Something considered in its relation to something else; a kinsman; a word relating to another.
Irrel'ative a. Without mutual relations; unconnected.
Correl'ative a. Having a mutual relation; corresponding to each other. s. One who or that which stands in reciprocal relation.
Revela'tive a. Revealing.
Assim'ilative a. (*Assimilate*).
Op'pilative a. Obstructive; constipating.
Ven'tilative a. Pertaining to or adapted for ventilation.
Compel'lative s. Name by which one is addressed.
Appel'lative s. An appellation; a common noun.
Ill'ative a. Relating to illation; expressing or of the nature of an inference.
Os'cillative a. Oscillatory.
Vi'olative a. Violating; tending to violate.
Prola'tive a. Extending, especially of words filling out a predicate.
Contemp'lative a. Given to contemplation; thoughtful.
Super'lative a. Most eminent, supreme. s. That which is most eminent; the highest degree of comparison, a word in this degree.
Leg'islative a. Pertaining to or capable of the enacting of laws. s. The legislature; the legislative function.
Ejac'ulative a. (*Ejaculate*).
Spec'ulative a. Given to, involving, or concerning speculation; theoretical; hazardous.
Gestic'ulative a. Pertaining to or represented by gesticulation.
Cal'culative a. (*Calculate*).
Inoc'ulative a. Pertaining to or characterized by inoculation.
Cir'culative a. Tending to circulate, promoting circulation.
Emas'culative a. (*Emasculate*).
Mod'ulative a. Serving to modulate.
Coag'ulative a. Causing coagulation.
Reg'ulative a. Regulating; tending to regulate.
Em'ulative a. Emulous.
Sim'ulative a. Simulated; feigned.
Stim'ulative a. Tending to stimulate. s. A stimulant.
Cu'mulative a. Tending to accumulate; increasing by successive additions.
Accu'mulative a. (*Accumulate*).
Manip'ulative a. Pertaining to or performed by manipulation.
Cop'ulative a. Serving to unite; uniting the sense as well as the words. s. A copulative conjunction.
Congrat'ulative a. (*Congratulate*).
Recapit'ulative a. Recapitulatory.
Expos'tulative a. Expostulatory.
Am'ative a. Disposed to loving.
Amal'gamative a. (*Amalgamate*).
Exclam'ative a. (*Exclamatory*).
Desquam'ative a. Pertaining to desquamation, liable to peel off.
An'imative a. Able to impart life or spirit.
Es'timative a. Inclined or able to estimate.
Approx'imative a. (*Approximate*).
Calm'ative a. Tending to soothe. s. A cooling medicine.
Gem'mative a. Pertaining to gemmation.
Con'summative a. (*Consummate*).
Affirm'ative s. That affirms, positive.
Confirm'ative a. Having power to confirm.
Form'ative a. Giving form; plastic. s. A word formed according to some analogy.
Reform'ative a. Tending to produce reformation.
Inform'ative a. Conveying information or instruction.
Trans-form'ative a. Tending or having power to transform.
Na'tive a. Pertaining to a place by birth; indigenous; inborn; produced by nature. s. One born in or a product of a place or country.
Em'anative a. Issuing; producing by emanation.
San'ative a. Healing; curative.
Des'ignative a. Serving to indicate.
Com'binative a. (*Combine*).
Ratioc'inative a. Pertaining or addicted to ratiocination.
Subor'dinative a. Expressing subordination.
Co-or'dinative a. (*Co-ordinate*).
Imag'inative a. Endowed with imagination; due to or characterized by this.
Orig'inative a. Originating; tending or able to originate.
Contam'inative a. (*Contaminate*).
Gem'inative a. Characterized by gemination.
Dissem'inative a. Tending to disseminate.

Crim'inative a. Relating to or invoking accusation.
Recrim'inative a. Retorting accusations.
Discrim'inative a. Serving to distinguish; discriminating.
Dom'inative a. Ruling, imperious.
Nom'inative a. Naming, designating. s. The simple form of a noun, the subject of the verb.
Denom'inative a. Conferring or constituting a distinctive name.
Car'minative a. Expelling flatulence. s. A medicine effecting this.
Ger'minative a. Germinal; able to grow.
Ter'minative a. Tending or serving to terminate; definitive; absolute.
Deter'minative a. Limiting, defining; decisive. s. That which decides or specifies; a demonstrative pronoun.
Illu'minative a. Tending to illuminate; throwing light upon.
Ru'minative a. Given to rumination; fully meditated.
Ur'inative a. Provoking the flow of urine.
Procras'tinative a. Given to procrastination.
Agglu'tinative a. (*Agglutinate*).
Conglu'tinative a. Having power to stick together.
Con'ative a. Pert. to conation; endeavouring.
Do'native s. A gift, gratuity; a benefice given directly by a patron. a. Vested or vesting by this form of presentation.
Opin'ionative a. Opinionated.
Alter'native a. Offering a choice between two. s. Either of two courses, etc., open to one.
Incho'ative a. Expressing or indicating beginning.
Antic'ipative a. (*Anticipate*).
Partic'ipative a. Capable of participating.
Nun'cupative a. Oral, not written.
Declar'ative a. Explanatory.
Exhil'arative a. Serving or tending to exhilarate.
Repar'ative a. Tending to repair or make good.
Prepar'ative a. Tending or serving to prepare; preparatory. s. That which tends or serves to prepare; an act of preparation.
Compar'ative a. Estimated by comparison; not positive. s. The grammatical inflection expressing this.
Vi'brative a. Vibratory.
Adum'brative a. (*Adumbrate*).
Ex'ecrative a. Serving to execrate; execratory.
Lu'crative a. Profitable; bringing money.
Delib'erative a. Pertaining to deliberation; having the right to deliberate.
Lac'erative a. Tending to lacerate.
Fed'erative a. Uniting; joining in a league.
Confed'erative a. (*Confederation*).
Desid'erative a. Expressing desire. s. A desideratum; a verb expressing desire.
Prolif'erative a. Proliferating; tending to proliferate.
Exag'gerative a. Containing or tending towards exaggeration.
Refrig'erative a. Cooling. s. A cooling medicine.
Accel'erative a. (*Accelerate*).
Enu'merative a. Counting or reckoning up one by one.
Gen'erative a. Having power to generate; pertaining to generation.
Degen'erative a. Tending to degenerate.
Regen'erative a. Caused by or pertaining to regeneration.
Ven'erative a. Pertaining to veneration; reverent.
Exon'erative a. Freeing from an obligation; exonerating.
Remu'nerative a. Fitted to remunerate; yielding proper reward.
Tem'perative a. Able to temper.
Imper'ative a. Obligatory, authoritative, peremptory; expressive of command. s. The mood of a verb expressing command, etc.
Op'erative a. Active; efficacious; effective; practical. s. An artisan.
Inop'erative a. Producing no effect.
Co-op'erative a. Working with others for a common end.
Recu'perative a. Pertaining to recuperation; restorative; able to recuperate.
Vitu'perative a. Consisting of vituperation; abusing, railing.
Commis'erative a. Having or showing pity.
It'erative a. Repeating; denoting repetition.
Reit'erative a. Expressing reiteration.
Allit'erative a. Pertaining to alliteration.
Al'terative s. A medicine that gradually restores to health. a. Promoting alteration.
In'tegrative a. Tending to integrate.
Perspir'ative a. Performing the act of perspiration.
Elab'orative a. Serving or tending to elaborate.
Corrob'orative a. Corroborating. s. A corroborant.
Dec'orative a. Suited to adorn or embellish.
Per'forative a. Having power to perforate.
Invig'orative a. Invigorating.
Ame'liorative a. (*Ameliorate*).
Deter'iorative a. Tending to deteriorate.
Pe'jorative a. Disparaging.
Explor'ative a. Exploratory.
Commem'orative a. (*Commemorate*).
Pig'norative a. Pledging, pawning.
Evap'orative a. Pertaining to or producing evaporation.
Cor'porative a. Pertaining to a corporation.
Incor'porative a. Incorporating or tending to incorporate.
Expect'orative a. Expectorant.
Restor'ative a. Having power to restore health, etc. s. Medicine, treatment, etc., effecting this.
Nar'rative a. In the form of a or pertaining to narration. s. A tale, story, recital of events.
Pen'etrative a. Tending to penetrate; piercing.
Concen'trative a. (*Concentrate*).
Min'istrative a. Serving to aid; pertaining to ministration.
Admin'istrative a. Pertaining to administration, executive.
Demon'strative a. Serving to demonstrate, express, or indicate; manifesting the feelings strongly.
Remon'strative a. Remonstrating; of the nature of remonstrance.
Illus'trative a. Serving to illustrate or elucidate.
Cur'ative a. Tending to cure. s. A healing medicine.
In'durative a. Pertaining to or producing induration.
Fig'urative a. Representing something else; emblematic; metaphorical.
Prefig'urative a. Showing by previous types, etc.; prefiguring.
Depur'ative a. Tending or able to cleanse.
Sup'purative a. Tending to suppurate; promoting suppuration.
Mat'urative a. Ripening; conducing to suppuration.
Pul'sative a. Pulsatory.
Condens'ative a. Tending to or able to condense.
Compen'sative a. Compensating. s. An equivalent.
Dispen'sative a. Granting dispensation.

Inten'sative a. and s. Intensive.
Adver'sative a. Denoting antithesis.
Conver'sative s. Relating to social intercourse; social.
Incras'sative a. Having the power of thickening.
Caus'ative a. Expressing a reason, causal; causing.
Accus'ative a. and s. Objective; the case of a noun which signifies that it is the object of a verb.
Recu'sative a. Rejective.
Expect'ative a. Pertaining or giving rise to expectation.
Cunc'tative a. Causing delay; tardy.
Veg'etative a. Growing, having power to grow; pertaining to growth; vegetating.
Inter'pretative a. Serving to interpret; containing explanation.
Inhab'itative a. Pertaining to inhabitation.
Du'bitative a. Tending to or expressive of doubt.
Recitative (-tēv') s. A kind of musical recitation; the recitation itself.
Resus'citative a. Tending to resuscitate; reviving.
Excit'ative a. Tending to excite; containing excitement.
Med'itative a. Given to or expressing meditation.
Cog'itative a. Contemplative; given to thought.
Qual'itative a. Pertaining to or estimable according to quality.
Im'itative a. Given to, aiming at, or done in imitation.
Lim'itative a. Tending to limit; restrictive.
Author'itative a. Having authority, dictatorial.
Ir'ritative a. Irritating; serving or tending to irritate.
Hes'itative a. Showing or characterized by hesitation.
Quan'titative a. Relating to or having regard to quantity.
En'titative a. Pertaining to an entity.
Eq'uitative a. Pertaining to equitation.
Vi'tative s. The faculty of self-preservation.
Grav'itative a. Causing to gravitate; tending to a centre.
Fac'ultative a. Empowering; permissive; optional.
Consul'tative a. (*Consult*).
Augmen'tative a. Having the power or quality of increasing.
Alimen'tative a. Pertaining to nutrition.
Experimen'tative a. Experimental.
Fermen'tative a. Causing, produced by or consisting in fermentation.
Argumen'tative a. Consisting of or delighting in argument; controversial.
Presen'tative a. Pertaining to or having the right of presentation; capable of being apprehended or of apprehending.
Represen'tative a. Representing; fitted or serving to represent; typical. s. One who or that which represents.
Misrepresen'tative a. Tending to convey a false impression. s. An unfaithful representative.
Ten'tative a. Experimental, essaying. s. A trial, conjecture.
Frequen'tative a. and s. Denoting a word that expresses frequent repetition.
Preven'tative a. Preventive.
Flo'tative a. Capable of floating; tending to float.
Denot'ative a. Signifying; designating without implying attributes.
Conno'tative a. Implying something additional or attributive.
Ro'tative a. Turning as a wheel.
Op'tative a. Expressive of desire. s. A verbal form expressing this.
Co-opta'tive a. Electing by co-optation.
Hor'tative a. Giving or containing advice; encouraging.
Dehort'ative a. Tending to dissuade.
Exhort'ative a. Containing or serving for exhortation.
Por'tative a. Pertaining to or capable of carrying.
Manifes'tative a. Serving to make public or obvious.
Gust'ative a. Pertaining to gustation.
Ref'utative a. Tending to refute; pertaining to refutation.
Mu'tative a. Pertaining to or characterized by mutation.
Commut'ative a. Relative to exchange; interchangeable.
Transmut'ative a. Pertaining to or involving transmutation.
Sternu'tative a. Causing sneezing. s. A substance effecting this.
Pu'tative a. Reputed; commonly regarded as.
Impu'tative a. Imputable; coming by inputation.
Compu'tative a. (*Compute*).
Dispu'tative a. Apt to cavil or controvert; disputatious.
Evac'uative a. Serving or tending to evacuate; cathartic.
Insin'uative a. Stealing on the affections, etc.; using insinuations; giving hints.
Contin'uative s. Statement expressing permanence or duration; a conjunction.
Punc'tuative a. Pertaining to punctuation.
Deriv'ative a. Derived, secondary. s. That which is derived; a word taking its origin in another.
Pri'vative a. Causing or expressing privation; not positive. s. That of which the essence is the absence of something; an added particle giving a negative meaning to a word.
In'novative a. Pertaining to or introducing innovations.
Preserv'ative a. Preservatory. s. That which preserves; a preventive of decay, etc.
Conser'vative a. Preservative; maintaining exist ing institutions. s. A Tory; one opposed to radical changes.
Cur'vative a. Having slightly bent edges (of petals, etc.).
Lax'ative a. Loosening the bowels. s. A medicine that effects this.
Relax'ative a. Having the quality of relaxing.
Fix'ative a. Serving to fix. s. A substance bringing stability to a thing.
Ac'tive a. Agile; busy; expressing action or transition of action from an agent to an object.
Reac'tive a. Having power or tending to react.
Stupefac'tive a. Stupefying.
Rarefac'tive a. Producing or marked by rarefaction.
Putrefac'tive a. Pertaining to or causing putrefaction.
Liquefac'tive a. Pertaining to or causing liquefaction.
Petrifac'tive a. Able to convert organic substances into stone; pertaining to petrifaction.
Olfac'tive a. Olfactory.
Enac'tive a. Having power to enact.
Inac'tive a. Not active.
Coac'tive a. Serving to compel or constrain; acting in concurrence.
Retroac'tive a. Designed to retroact; retro spective.
Counterac'tive a. (*Counteract*).
Refrac'tive a. Having power to refract; pertaining to refraction.

Diffrac'tive a. Producing diffraction.
Trac'tive a. Serving to draw; attracting.
Subtrac'tive a. Tending or able to subtract.
Detrac'tive a. Tending to detract; slanderous.
Retrac'tive a. Able or willing to retract.
Contrac'tive a. Tending or serving to contract.
Protrac'tive a. Prolonging; continuing.
Abstrac'tive a. Able to abstract, tending to abstraction.
Distrac'tive a. Causing distraction or perplexity.
Attrac'tive a. Able to attract, enticing.
Extrac'tive a. Capable of being extracted; serving or tending to extract.
Defec'tive a. Imperfect; faulty; deficient.
Refec'tive a. Refreshing. s. That which refreshes.
Affec'tive a. Pertaining to the affections; emotional.
Effec'tive a. Producing its proper or a striking effect; efficacious; fit for service; real. s. One who is efficient.
Ineffec'tive a. Not effective; useless.
Non-effec'tive a. Not fit for active service.
Infec'tive a. Infectious.
Perfec'tive a. Calculated or tending to perfect.
Imperfec'tive a. Expressing action as incomplete, continuing, or reiterated.
Objec'tive a. Pertaining to an, contained in the, resembling the, or in the position of the, object; external; extrinsic. s. Point of direction; lens of optical instrument nearest the object.
Subjec'tive a. Pertaining to a subject or to one's own consciousness; exhibiting personality.
Ad'jective s. A word qualifying a noun. a. Added to, dependent.
Ejec'tive a. Tending to eject.
Projec'tive a. Pertaining to or derived by projection.
Elec'tive a. Bestowed by election; exerting power of choice.
Selec'tive a. Pertaining to or capable of selection; choosing.
Reflec'tive a. Throwing back rays or images; meditating.
Inflec'tive a. Capable of bending; inflexional.
Intellec'tive a. Pertaining to or produced by the intellect.
Collec'tive a. Formed by gathering; gathered; joint.
Recollec'tive a. Pertaining to recollection.
Humec'tive a. Tending to make moist. s. Humectant.
Connec'tive a. Having the power of connecting; tending to connect. s. A Conjunction.
Respec'tive a. Relating severally to each; relative.
Irrespec'tive a. Regardless of; without reference to.
Circumspec'tive a. Careful of consequences.
Prospec'tive a. Looking forward; pertaining to the future. s. Prospect.
Retrospec'tive a. Tending or fitted to look back; affecting or referring to what is past.
Introspec'tive a. Capable of, exercising, or pertaining to introspection.
Perspec'tive a. Representation on plane surface of objects as they appear to the eye; vista.
Erec'tive a. Setting upright; raising.
Direc'tive a. Able to direct; capable of receiving direction.
Correc'tive a. Tending or having power to correct. s. That which tends to correct, rectify, or counteract.
Detec'tive s. A police officer or private agent employed in investigating crime, etc. a. Suitable for or used for detecting.
Ar'chitective a. Pertaining to architecture.
Protec'tive a. Affording protection; sheltering.
Invec'tive s. Violent censure, abuse, or reproach; vituperation. a. Abusive.
Contradic'tive a. Contradictory.
Predic'tive a. Foretelling; prophetic.
Indic'tive a. Declared publicly.
Vindic'tive a. Revengeful; malignant.
Interdic'tive a. Tending to interdict; interdictory.
Jurisdic'tive a. Exercising jurisdiction.
Fic'tive a. Imaginative; imaginary; fictitious.
Afflic'tive a. Causing affliction, distressing.
Inflic'tive a. Tending or able to inflict.
Conflic'tive a. Tending to conflict.
Depic'tive a. (*Depict*).
Astric'tive a. and s. Astringent.
Restric'tive a. Tending or able to restrict.
Constric'tive a. Serving to bind, contract, or compress.
Convic'tive a. (*Convict*).
Distinc'tive a. Marking or expressing distinction.
Indistinc'tive a. Not distinctive.
Instinc'tive a. Prompted by instinct; spontaneous.
Extinc'tive a. (*Extinct*).
Subjunc'tive a. Denoting form of verb expressing condition, contingency, etc.
Adjunc'tive a. (*Adjunct*).
Conjunc'tive a. Serving to unite; copulative; connective.
Disjunc'tive a. Separating, disjoining. s. A disjunctive conjunction or proposition.
Concoc'tive a. (*Concoct*).
Traduc'tive a. Pertaining to or consisting of traduction.
Adduc'tive a. Tending to lead or draw together.
Deduc'tive a. Deduced, or capable of being duced, from premises.
Reduc'tive a. Having the power of reducing.
Seduc'tive a. Alluring; tending to lead astray.
Induc'tive a. Relating to or proceeding by induction; derived by inference.
Conduc'tive a. Conducting.
Produc'tive a. Able to produce; producing; efficient; yielding results.
Reproduc'tive a. Pertaining to or employed in reproduction.
Introduc'tive a. Introductory.
Obstruc'tive a. Hindering; tending or intended to hinder. s. One who hinders the transaction of business.
Destruc'tive a. Causing destruction; mischievous, pernicious; negative.
Instruc'tive a. Conveying instruction.
Construc'tive a. Having power or ability to construct; derived by interpretation; inferred.
Reconstruc'tive a. Pertaining to or characterized by reconstruction.
Reple'tive a. Tending to make replete; filling.
Comple'tive a. Making complete.
Ex'pletive a. Filling up, superfluous. s. A superfluous word, etc.; an exclamation; an oath.
Decre'tive a. Having the force of a decree.
Secre'tive a. Given to secrecy; uncommunicative; promoting or causing secretion.
Concre'tive a. Promoting concretion.
Discre'tive a. Disjunctive, separating.
Excre'tive a. Able to excrete; promoting excretion.

Prohib'itive a. Tending to prohibit; implying prohibition.
Exhib'itive a. Serving for exhibition.
Exci'tive a. Excitative.
Trad'itive a. Traditional.
Ad'ditive a. That may be or is to be added.
Red'ditive a. Corresponding; correlative.
Imped'itive a. Tending to impede.
Au'ditive a. Pertaining to hearing.
Fugitive' a. Unstable, volatile, short-lived. s. A deserter, one who flees; a refugee.
Prim'itive a. Ancient; pertaining to the origin or the earliest times; primary. s. That which is original; an early worker in the arts, etc.; an underived word.
Vom'itive a. Vomitory.
Dor'mitive a. Promoting sleep, narcotic. s. A soporific.
Gen'itive s. A case in declension of nouns and pronouns; the possessive.
Primogen'itive a. Pertaining to primogeniture.
Philo-progen'itive a. Characterized by love of offspring; prolific.
Len'itive a. Mitigating, assuasive, softening. s. Medicine or application for easing pain.
Splen'itive a. Passionate, impetuous.
Cog'nitive a. (*Cognition*).
Defin'itive a. Decisive; positive; express. s. A word used to limit the application of a noun.
Infin'itive s. Applied to the mood of a verb that expresses action without limitation of person or number.
Mon'itive a. Admonitory.
Admon'itive a. Implying admonition.
U'nitive a. Causing or tending to unite.
Pu'nitive a. Pertaining to, involving, or awarding punishment.
Aper'itive s. A laxative medicine.
Preter'itive a. Pertaining to the preterite or the past.
Nu'tritive a. Pertaining to nutrition; nutritious. s. A nourishing food.
Innu'tritive a. Not nourishing.
Acquis'itive a. Capable of making or desirous to make acquisitions.
Inquis'itive a. Curious, prying.
Tran'sitive a. Denoting a verb which may be followed by an object.
Intran'sitive a. Expressing an action or state limited to the agent.
Sen'sitive a. Having feeling, or acute sensibility; easily affected.
Insen'sitive a. Not sensitive to.
Pos'itive a. Actual, explicit, absolute; not admitting of doubt, etc., confident; indisputable, decisive; affirmative; opposite to negative. s. Reality; that which is positive; the positive degree.
Prepos'itive a. Prefixed. s. A word or particle prefixed.
Compos'itive s. (*Composite*).
Suppos'itive a. Implying supposition.
Transpos'itive a. Made by or consisting in transposition.
Expos'itive a. Serving to explain; expository.
Fac'titive a. Effecting; causative.
Repet'itive a. Repetitious.
Compet'itive a. Pertaining to or carried out by competition.
Appet'itive a. Having or characterized by appetite.
Vet'itive a. Able to veto; prohibiting.
To'titive s. Any number as small as a given number, the two being relatively prime.

Par'titive a. Denoting a part. s. A word denoting partition.
Fru'itive a. Pertaining to fruition.
Intu'itive a. Perceived mentally without reasoning; based on intuition self-evident.
Consul'tive a. (*Consult*).
Sub'stantive s. A noun. a. Betokening or expressing existence; pertaining to the essence of anything.
Incen'tive s. That which incites or provokes. a. Inciting; encouraging.
Penden'tive s. A triangular support of a dome or circular structure.
Presen'tive a. Presenting a conception, etc., directly to the mind, not symbolic; presentative.
Reten'tive a. Retaining; holding back; not forgetful.
Atten'tive a. Paying attention, heedful.
Inatten'tive a. Not attentive; heedless; remiss.
Preven'tive a. Tending or serving to prevent. s. That which prevents; an antidote previously taken.
Circumven'tive a. Deceiving by trick.
Inven'tive a. Quick at contrivance; able to invent; ingenious; imaginative.
Plain'tive a. Containing a plaint, indicating grief; sad.
Mo'tive s. That which incites to motion; purpose; musical theme. a. Causing motion; having power to move. v.t. To prompt, to supply with a motive.
Emo'tive a. Exciting emotion.
Locomo'tive s. A railway engine. a. Pertaining to locomotion or to travel; moving or able to move from place to place.
Promo'tive a. Tending to promote.
Vo'tive a. Pertaining to or dedicated by a vow.
Cap'tive s. A prisoner. a. Taken prisoner; fascinated.
Adap'tive a. (*Adapt*).
Decep'tive a. Tending or apt to deceive, liable to mislead.
Recep'tive a. Able or inclined to take in and contain.
Precep'tive a. Giving precepts; didactic.
Incep'tive a. Beginning; expressing or indicating this.
Concep'tive a. (*Conception*).
Percep'tive a. Having the faculty of perceiving; pertaining to or used in perception.
Impercep'tive a. Unperceiving; wanting in perception.
Suscep'tive a. Readily receiving impressions.
Intussus-cep'tive a. Pertaining to or characterized by intussusception.
Excep'tive a. Including; making or being an exception.
Descrip'tive a. Containing or given to description; able to describe.
Prescrip'tive a. Consisting in or acquired by long use and enjoyment; giving precise directions.
Circum-scrip'tive a. Defining the external form.
Transcrip'tive a. Done as from a copy.
Inscrip'tive a. Pertaining to or of the nature of an inscription.
Proscrip'tive a. Pertaining to or consisting in proscription.
Redemp'tive a. Serving or tending to redeem.
Subsump'tive a. Pertaining to or containing a subsumption.
Resump'tive a. Resuming; taking up again.
Presump'tive a. Grounded on probability.

Consump'tive a. Destructive; affected with or inclined to consumption.
Assump'tive a. (*Assume*).
Adop'tive a. Due to adoption; fitted to adopt.
Absorp'tive a. (*Absorb*).
Resorp'tive a. Tending to resorb.
Rup'tive a. Rupturing; tending to rupture.
Erup'tive a. Breaking forth; attended with or producing eruption.
Interrup'tive a. Tending to interrupt; interrupting.
Irrup'tive a. Rushing in; tending to irruption.
Corrup'tive a. Having the quality of corrupting or vitiating.
Disrup'tive a. Causing or accompanied by disruption.
Asser'tive a. Dogmatical.
Rever'tive a. Tending to revert; changing.
Diver'tive a. Tending to divert; amusing.
Abor'tive a. Immature, untimely, unsuccessful.
Spor'tive a. Gay, frolicsome; provocative of sport.
Tor'tive a. Wreathed, coiled.
Contor'tive a. Expressing contortion.
Distor'tive a. Causing or having distortion.
Extor'tive a. (*Extorsive*).
Fur'tive a. Stealthy; surreptitious; got by theft.
Ges'tive a. Befitting a festival; joyous, gay.
Sugges'tive a. Containing suggestion; hinting at what is not apparent.
Diges'tive a. Promoting or causing digestion in the stomach. s. Anything which aids digestion.
Indiges'tive a. Tending to or suffering indigestion; dyspeptic.
Inges'tive a. Pertaining to or having the function of ingesting.
Conges'tive a. Inducing or caused by congestion.
Res'tive a. Unwilling to go forward; stubborn; impatient.
Arres'tive a. (*Arrest*).
Resis'tive a. Tending or disposed to resist.
Cos'tive a. Constipated.
Exhaus'tive a. Serving or tending to exhaust; thorough.
Inexhaus'tive a. Not exhaustive.
Combus'tive a. (*Combustible*).
Retrib'utive a. Retributory.
Contrib'utive a. Contributing, assisting, promoting.
Distrib'utive a. Distributing; pertaining to distribution; expressing or indicating distribution.
Attrib'utive a. (*Attribute*).
Consec'utive a. Following in a train or logically.
Inconsec'utive a. Not in regular order.
Exec'utive a. Designed or fitted for; carrying laws into effect or superintending their enforcement. s. The administrative branch, especially of the government.
Res'olutive a. Able to resolve, dissolve, or relax.
Evolu'tive a. Evolutionary; promoting evolution.
Involu'tive a. Involute; folded.
Dimin'utive a. Very small, tiny. s. A derivative suggesting something smaller.
Sub'stitutive a. Tending to provide a substitute; making or capable of substitution.
Con'stitutive a. That constitutes; having power to establish, enact, etc.
Revive' v.i. To return to life; to become reanimated; to emerge from neglect, etc. v.t. To bring again to life; to refresh.
Convive' s. A guest at a banquet; a boon companion.
Survive' v.t. To outlive, outlast. v.i. To live longer than another and at the same time; to be still in existence.
Wive v.t. and i. To provide with or take a wife.
Reflex'ive a. Denoting action upon the agent or by the subject upon itself; referring back to the grammatical subject; reflective.
Influx'ive a. Exerting or giving influence.
Calve v.i. To bring forth a calf.
Halve v.t. To divide into two equal parts.
Salve s. A healing ointment; palliative action; treatment, etc. v.t. To apply salve to; to soothe, heal; to save from a wreck, a fire, etc.
Sal've s. (*Roman Catholic Church*) An antiphon addressed to the Virgin.
Lip'salve s. Ointment for the lips; flattery.
Valve s. A leaf of a folding door; lid in a pipe, etc., allowing passage only one way; one division of a shell.
Bi'valve s. A mollusc with two shells that open and shut; an oyster.
U'nivalve s. A mollusc whose shell is in one piece. a. Having but one valve.
Mul'tivalve s. A shell having more than two valves.
Delve v.t. To dig; to fathom, get to the bottom of. v.i. To work with the spade, to search assiduously.
Helve s. The handle of a tool.
Shelve v.i. To incline, be sloping. v.t. To put on a shelf, fit with shelves; to defer indefinitely.
Twelve a. and s. Consisting of or the sum of 10 and 2; 12, xii.
Solve v.t. To clear up, make clear, explain.
Absolve' v.t. To pardon, remit, free from.
Resolve' v.t. and i. To separate the component parts of; to solve; to determine, decide; to melt. s. Resolution; fixed purpose.
Dissolve' v.t. To liquefy; to separate into component parts; to disconnect, break up, put an end to; to cause to vanish. v.i. To be melted, to become soft or languid; to break up.
Evolve' v.t. To unroll, unfold, disentangle. v.i. To open or disclose itself.
Devolve' v.t. To pass from one to another. v.i. To be delegated; to descend in succession.
Revolve' v.i. To turn or roll round on an axis. v.t. To rotate; to consider repeatedly.
Involve' v.t. To roll up, envelop; to imply, include; to complicate; to raise a quantity to any given power.
Convolve' v.t. To roll or wind together or on itself.
Intervolve' v.t. To involve one within another.
Above' prep., adv. Higher than, more than, overhead.
Cove s. A small creek or inlet; a sheltered recess; a concave moulding; a fellow, chap. v.t. To arch over.
Al'cove s. A recess in a room, etc.
Dove s. A bird of the pigeon family; the emblem of innocence, also of the Holy Ghost.
Hove past (*Heave*).
Shove (shŭv) v.t. and i. To push against, jostle, propel; to make one's way thus. s. A strong, hard push.
Jove s. The chief of the Roman gods, Jupiter.

Love v.t. To regard with affection; to like, delight in. v.i. To be in love. s. Warm affection; the passion between the sexes; a sweetheart.
Clove s. An aromatic spice; a small bulb on a larger one. v. past Split; cloven.
Glove s. A covering for the hand.
Fox'glove s. A common plant (*Digitalis*) whose leaves have sedative properties.
Move v.t. To put in motion; to rouse, prevail on; to propose. v.i. To change position, residence, etc.; to stir; to make a proposal. s. Act of moving; a movement; action taken.
Remove' v.t. To move from its place, take away, displace. v.i. To go away, change residence. s. A removal, departure; degree of difference; course at a meal.
Hoove s. A disease of cattle.
Behoove' v.t. To befit, to suit. v.i. To be needful or due to.
Groove s. A long, hollow cut; a furrow. v.t. To make furrows or grooves in.
Rove v.i. To wander, ramble. v.t. To wander over; to ravel out, to card (wool) into flakes. past (*Reave*). s. Act of roving; a stroll; wool, cotton, etc., slightly twisted.
Drove s. A herd of cattle, flock of sheep, etc.; a crowd, moving mass of people. v.i. To drive cattle, etc., in droves.
Grove s. A tree-shaded walk; a small wood.
Man'grove s. A tree growing in tropical swamps.
Throve past (*Thrive*).
Prove v.t. To try or ascertain by experiment; to verify, demonstrate; to show by testimony. v.i. To make trial; to be found by experience.
Reprove' v.t. To rebuke, censure, especially orally.
Improve' v.t. and i. To make or grow better; to use to good purpose; to rise in value.
Approve' v.t. To commend; to like.
Disapprove' v.t. To pass unfavourable judgment upon; to censure, reject.
Disprove' v.t. To prove to be false or erroneous; to confute.
Strove past (*Strive*).
Stove s. A closed-in fireplace; a hot-house. v.t. To heat or dry in a stove. past (*Stave*).
Wove past and past part. (*Weave*).
Carve v.t. To cut, sculpture, serve meat at table.
Starve v.i. To suffer extremely or perish with hunger or cold; to be very indigent. v.t. To distress or kill with hunger, etc.; to make inefficient by want.
Nerve s. An organ of sensation and notion in animals; energy; courage; fortitude; (*slang*) audacity.
Innerve' v.t. To innervate.
Unnerve' v.t. To deprive of strength, composure, etc.
Serve v.t. To work for, act as servant to; be subordinate to; to render worship to; to deliver or transmit to. v.i. To wait, attend; to be a servant; to suffice, suit.
Observe' v.t. To regard attentively; to utter casually, to obey. v.i. To attend; to comment.
Subserve' v.t. and i. To serve, be instrumental to.
Deserve' v.t. To be worthy of, to merit; to earn.
Reserve' v.t. To keep in store, withhold. s. Act of reserving; that which is retained; restraint of the feelings; tract of land set apart for some purpose; troops kept for emergency.
Preserve' v.t. To protect, keep from injury, etc.; to save from decay; to maintain; to keep free from trespass, etc., so as to breed game. s. Anything preserved, as fruit, vegetables, etc.; place for preservation of game.
Conserve' v.t. To save, preserve; to candy, pickle. s. Anything conserved, especially fruit.
Disserve' v.t. To injure, harm.
Verve s. Spirit, fervour, enthusiasm.
Swerve v.i. To turn aside, deviate. s. Act of swerving; sudden deflection.
Curve s. A bending without angles; thing bent. v.i. and t. To bend or cause to bend without angles.
Recurve' v.t. To bend backwards.
Incurve' v.t. To cause to curve inwards.
Mauve s. A purple or lilac colour.
Gyve s. A fetter, shackle. v.t. To fetter, chain.
We pers. pron. Plural of "I."
Awe s. Reverential fear, dread. v.t. To affect with reverence or fear.
Overawe' v.t. To restrain by awe, to intimidate.
Ewe s. A female sheep.
Owe v.t. and i. To be indebted in or to; to be bound to pay; to be obliged for.
Howe s. A valley, hollow.
Axe s. An iron instrument for hewing and chopping.
An'nexe s. An addition to a building.
Ye pron. Second person plural.
Aye int. Yes. s. An affirmative vote. adv. Always.
Aye-aye s. A small Madagascan lemur.
Bye s. Something incidental or secondary; an extra.
Good-bye' int. and s. Farewell.
Bye'-bye int. Good night, good-bye. s. Bed, bedtime.
Dye s. A colouring liquid; a tinge, stain v.t. To give a new and permanent colour to, to stain. v.i. To take a colour; to work as a dyer.
Redye' v.t. To dye over again.
Eye s. The organ of vision; power of perception; sight; hole of a needle, etc.; a loop or ring; a bud of a plant. v.t. To watch, spy.
Dead'eye s. A wooden block to receive the lanyard.
Bull's'eye s. The centre of a target; a hemispherical lens; a sweetmeat.
Kye s. (*Cow*).
Lye s. An alkaline solution used in soap-making, etc.
Employ'é s. An employee.
Rye s. A cereal plant and its seed.
Gram'arye s. Witchcraft, magic, necromancy.
Stye s. Swelling on eyelid.
Wye s. A Y-shaped part or thing.
Bumbaze' v.t. (*Scot.*) To bamboozle.
Daze v.t. To stupefy, stun, confuse.
Gaze v.i. To look intently; to stare, gape. s. A fixed look; look of eagerness, etc.

Haze s. A slight fog; mist. v.t. To make hazy; to play practical jokes on, to harass with overwork.
Autoschediaze' v.t. To improvise.
Laze v.i. and t. To be idle, waste time in idleness. s. A spell of idleness.
Blaze s. A flame; a white spot; brilliance. v.i. To flame, to emit a bright light. v.t. To proclaim, noise abroad.
Ablaze' adv., a. On fire; brilliant.
Emblaze' v.t. To emblazon.
Glaze v.t. To furnish with windows or glass; to encrust with some vitreous substance; to make glossy. v.i. To become glassy. s. A vitreous or transparent coating.
Maze s. A labyrinth; state of bewilderment. v.t. To perplex.
Amaze' v.t. To astonish, perplex, surprise.
Naze s. A promontory.
Raze v.t. To demolish, dismantle; to efface.
Braze v.t. To solder with brass.
Craze v.t. To impair the intellect of; to make cracks in china. s. An inordinate desire, passing enthusiasm or mania for.
Graze v.i. To eat grass; to supply grass to; to rub lightly in passing. v.t. To touch or injure slightly in passing; to feed with growing grass. s. A slight touch, an abrasion.
Adze s. A kind of axe.
Wheeze v.i. To breathe noisily or hard. s. Such a sound; (*slang*) a joke, gag.
Sneeze v.i. To emit air violently, noisily, and involuntarily through the nose. s. An act of sneezing.
Breeze s. A gentle gale; a disturbance.
Freeze v.i. To be congealed or hardened into ice by cold; to shiver with cold; to stagnate. v.t. To congeal; to chill.
Squeeze v.t. To press closely, hug; to harass by extortion. v.i. To pass by pressing. s. Application of pressure; compression; a hug; a crowd.
Frieze s. A coarse woollen cloth; the middle division of an entablature; a horizontal strip on a wall.
Trapeze' (-pēz') s. Swinging cross-bar for gymnastics; a trapezium.
-ize suff. Forming verbs.
Baize s. A coarse woollen stuff.
Ju'daize v.i. To conform to Jewish rites, etc.; to reason and interpret like a Jew. v.t. To convert to Judaism.
Ar'chaize v.i. To affect ancient manners, style, etc. v.t. To make archaic.
Maize s. Indian corn.
He'braize v.t. To make Hebrew or Hebraistic. v.i. To become Hebrew, act in Hebrew fashion.
Syl'labize v.t. To separate into or pronounce by syllables.
Os'tracize v.t. To banish or cut off from society.
Gre'cize v.t. To render Grecian, to translate into Greek.
La'icize v.t. To render secular.
Eth'icize v.t. To make ethical or treat ethically.
Goth'icize v.t. To make Gothic or barbarous.
Ital'icize v.t. To print in italics; to emphasize.
An'glicize v.t. To make or turn into English, to give an English form to.
Gal'licise v.t. and i. To make or become French.
Cathol'icize v.t. and i. To make or become Catholic.
Sin'icize v.t. and i. To make or become Chinese.
Clas'sicize v.t. To make classic. v.i. To effect the classic style.
Grammat'icize v.t. To render grammatical.
Fanat'icize v.t. and i. To render or become fanatical.
Polit'icize v.t. and i. To make political, play the politician.
Crit'icize v.t. To judge or examine critically; to pick out faults, animadvert upon.
Monas'ticize v.i. To live as a monk.
Scot'ticize v.t. and i. To make or become Scotch.
Ex'orcize v.t. To expel by prayers or ceremonies; to cast out evil spirits.
Nom'adize v.t. and i. To make or become nomadic.
Hy'bridize v.t. To produce by interbreeding or cross-fertilization.
Chlor'idize v.t. To treat with a chloride.
Sub'sidize v.t. To furnish with a subsidy.
Liq'uidize v.t. To liquefy.
Ox'idize v.t. and i. To combine with oxygen, convert into an oxide; to make rusty; to rust.
Deox'idize v.t. To deprive of oxygen or reduce from state of an oxide.
Meth'odize v.t. To arrange systematically.
I'odize v.t. To treat with or subject to iodine.
Mel'odize v.t. To make melodious. v.i. To compose melodies.
Psalm'odize v.i. To write or sing psalms.
Rhap'sodize v.t. and i. To utter rhapsodies; to speak in a highly exaggerated way.
Gor'mandize v.i. To eat greedily or to excess.
Ag'grandize v.t. To enlarge; to exalt.
Fe'cundize v.t. To fecundate, make fruitful.
Stand'ardize v.t. To reduce to a proper or fixed standard.
Jeop'ardize v.t. To put in jeopardy; to imperil.
Bas'tardize v.t. (*Bastard*).
Seize v.t. To take hold of by force; to grasp; to attack. v.i. To take hold or possession.
Reseize' v.t. To seize again; to take possession of (lands, etc.) which have been disseized.
Disseize' v.t. To deprive of possession; to dispossess illegally.
El'egize v.t. and i. To compose an elegy upon to write plaintively.
Diph'thongize v.t. To make into a diphthong.
Geneal'ogize v.i. To trace or investigate pedigrees.
Dial'ogize v.i. To discourse in dialogue.
Anal'ogize v.t. (*Analogy*).
Epil'ogize v.t. and i. To compose or deliver an epilogue.
Syl'logize v.i. To reason by syllogisms.
Ideol'ogize v.t. To indulge in visionary speculations about.
Geol'ogize v.i. To make geological investigations.
Theol'ogize v.i. To frame a theological system. v.t. To render theological.
Neol'ogize v.i. To practise neologism or neology.
Anthol'ogize v.i. (*Anthology*).
Mythol'ogize v.t. To relate or explain myths or the fables of a nation.
Homol'ogize v.i. and t. To be or make homologous.
Etymol'ogize v.t. To give the etymology of. v.i. To search into the origin of words.
Apol'ogize v.i. (*Apology*).
Pro'logize v.i. To deliver a prologue.
Tautol'ogize v.i. To repeat in different words.

Eu'logize v.t. To praise, extol.
En'ergize v.i. To act with vigour. v.t. To give strength to.
Mon'achize v.t. and i. To make monks of; to become or live as a monk.
Cat'echize v.t. To instruct or elicit information by means of questions.
Mon'archize v.i. To play the sovereign.
Eu'nuchize v.t. To convert into a eunuch.
Apos'trophize v.t. To address in or with apostrophe.
Theos'ophize v.i. To be addicted to theosophy.
Philos'ophize v.i. To reason like a or act the philosopher; to reason, moralize.
Anthropomor'phize v.t. (*Anthropomorphism*).
Sym'pathize v.i. To have a common feeling, feel in consequence of what another feels.
Dock'ize v.t. To turn a water-way into a series of docks.
Verb'alize v.t. To convert into a verb. v.i. To be verbose.
Rad'icalize v.t. To make radical.
Cler'icalize v.t. (*Cleric*).
Fo'calize v.t. To focus.
Lo'calize v.t. To make local; to ascertain the place of; to identify with or restrict to a place.
Vo'calize v.t. To utter, make sonant. v.i. To practice singing on the vowel-sounds.
Devo'calize v.t. To make voiceless or non-sonant.
Scan'dalize v.t. To give offence to, to shock.
Feu'dalize v.t. To reduce to feudal tenure.
Ide'alize v.i. To imagine, form ideals. v.t. To make ideal, embody in an ideal form.
Rea'lize v.t. To make real; to achieve; to acquire; to render effective; to convert into money. v.i. To receive value for property.
Le'galize v.t. To make lawful; to sanction.
Prod'igalize v.t. To spend lavishly.
Naph'thalize v.t. To impregnate with naphtha.
Spec'ialize v.t. To differentiate; to assign a specific use, etc., to. v.i. To become differentiated; to employ oneself as or train for a specialist.
Artifi'cialize v.t. (*Artificial*).
Provin'cialize v.t. To make provincial.
So'cialize v.t. To render social; to regulate by socialistic principles.
Commer'cialize v.t. (*Commercial*).
Ra'dialize v.t. To cause to radiate as from a centre.
Cor'dialize v.t. and i. To render or become cordial.
Testi-mo'nialize v.t. To present a testimonial to.
Particip'ialize v.t. To put in the form of a participle.
Ether'ialize v.t. To render ethereal; to convert into or saturate with ether.
Imper'ialize v.t. To render imperial.
Mater'ialize v.t. To make or regard as material. v.i. To become actual fact.
Immater'ialize v.t. To make immaterial.
Arter'ialize v.t. To pass the blood through the lungs.
Memor'ialize v.t. To present a memorial to; to petition thus.
Mercur'ialize v.t. To affect with or expose to the action of mercury.
Substant'ialize v.t. and i. To make or become substantial.
Poten'tialize v.t. To render potential.
Mar'tialize v.t. To make martial or military.
Al'kalize v.t. (*Alkali*).
Dec'imalize v.t. To reduce or adapt to the decimal system.

Form'alize v.t. To render formal; to formulate
Nor'malize v.t. To make normal.
Can'alize v.t. To convert to a canal; to make a canal through.
Phenom'enalize v.t. To treat or conceive as phenomenal.
Pe'nalize v.t. To inflict a penalty on; to handicap.
Sig'nalize v.t. To make remarkable or noteworthy.
Profes'sionalize v.t. To make professional.
Na'tionalize v.t. To make national, change from private into state ownership; to naturalize.
Dena'tionalize v.t. To deprive of national rights.
Denomi-na'tionalize v.t. To make denominational.
Inter-na'tionalize v.t. To bring under the control of different nations.
Ra'tionalize v.t. To make rational, explain by rationalism.
Irra'tionalize v.t. To make irrational.
Sec'tionalize v.t. To divide, arrange, or represent in sections.
Conven'-tionalize v.t. (*Conventional*).
Institu'-tionalize v.t. To convert into or treat as an institution.
Constitu'-tionalize v.t. To render constitutional.
Per'sonalize v.t. To make personal; to personify.
Car'nalize v.t. To sensualize, materialize.
Exter'nalize v.t. To give external shape to; to treat as consisting of externals.
Journ'alize v.t. To enter in a journal. v.i. To keep a journal; to work as a journalist.
Pa'palize v.t. and i. To make papal, conform to the papacy.
Munic'ipalize v.t. To form into a municipality.
O'palize v.t. To convert into opal-like substance.
Lib'eralize v.t. To render liberal, free from narrow views.
Fed'eralize v.t. and i. To form into or combine in a political confederacy.
Gen'eralize v.t. To extend from particulars to universals. v.i. To form general ideas.
Min'eralize v.t. To give mineral qualities to; to impregnate with mineral matter.
Lit'eralize v.t. To interpret or put in practice in a literal sense.
Mor'alize v.t. To interpret or apply in a moral sense. v.i. To make moral reflections on.
Demor'alize v.t. To corrupt, deprave.
Cen'tralize v.t. and i. To bring to a centre, to concentrate; to group under one authority.
Decen'tralize v.t. To reverse the state of centralization in government.
Neu'tralize v.t. To render neutral, inoperative, or ineffectual; to counteract.
Plur'alize v.t. To make grammatically plural.
Rur'alize v.t. and i. To make or become rural.
Nat'uralize v.t. To make natural; to confer rights of a native on; to acclimatize.
Denat'uralize v.t. To render unnatural; to deprive of rights of citizenship.
Gut'turalize v.t. To form in the throat.
Na'salize v.t. and i, To pronounce nasally, speak through the nose.
Univer'salize v.t. To make universal.
Capit'alize v.t. To convert into capital.
Vi'talize v.t. To animate, give life to.
Devi'talize v.t. To deprive of vitality, render lifeless.

Tan'talize v.t. To torment with unrealizable prospects.
Den'talize v.t. To pronounce as a dental.
Occiden'talize v.t. To render Occidental, imbue with Occidentalism.
Transcenden'talize v.t. To make transcendental.
Orien'talize v.t. and i. To make or become Eastern in character, etc.
Experimen'talize v.t. To make experiments.
Sentimen'talize v.i. To affect sensibility or sentiment.
Departmen'talize v.t. To form into departments.
To'talize v.t. and i. To total, gather into a total.
Immor'talize v.t. To perpetuate the memory of.
Brut'alize v.t. (*Brutal*).
Du'alize v.t. To make dual or twofold.
Individ'ualize v.t. To single out; to connect with one particular individual.
Lin'gualize v.t. To change into a lingual.
E'qualize v.t. To make equal.
Vis'ualize v.t. To give a visible form to; to make visible.
Sen'sualize v.t. To make sensual.
Ac'tualize v.t. To render actual, to describe realistically.
Intellec'tualize v.t. To make intellectual, treat intellectually.
Rit'ualize v.t. and i. To make or become ritualistic.
Spir'itualize v.t. To make spiritual; to refine, imbue with spirituality.
Mu'tualize v.t. and i. To make or become mutual.
Sex'ualize v.t. To give or assign sex to.
Roy'alize v.t. To make royal.
Ob'elize v.t. To mark with an obelisk.
Evan'gelize v.i. and t. To preach the gospel, to convert to belief in the gospel.
Nick'elize v.t. To nickel.
Nov'elize v.t. To make into a novel.
Sta'bilize v.t. To make stable.
Mo'bilize v.t. To make mobile, put in a state of readiness, especially for active service.
Demo'bilize v.t. To disband troops.
Immo'bilize v.t. To render immobile or incapable of mobilization.
Sim'ilize v.t. and i. To make or become similar.
Ster'ilize v.t. To make sterile, deprive of productive power.
Fos'silize v.t. and i. To convert or become converted into a fossil; to become old-fashioned.
Volat'ilize v.t. and i. To evaporate.
Subt'ilize (sŭt'-) v.t. and i. To make or become subtle or subtile.
Fer'tilize v.t. To make productive; to make rich (of soil); to fecundate.
U'tilize v.t. To make use of, turn to account.
Civ'ilize v.t. To reclaim from savagery; to refine.
Met'allize v.t. To give metallic properties or appearance to.
Crys'tallize v.t. To cause to form crystals. v.i. To take a crystalline form.
Bos'wellize v.i. To write biography.
Tran'quillize v.t. To render tranquil, pacify, appease.
Diab'olize v.t. To make devilish, turn into a devil.
Parab'olize v.t. To convert into a parable.
Metab'olize v.t. To perform the function of metabolism.

Sym'bolize v.t. To typify; to represent by symbols, treat as symbolical.
Car'bolize v.t. To impregnate with carbolic acid.
I'dolize v.t. To make an idol of, worship idolatrously.
Vit'riolize v.t. To convert into a sulphate.
Monop'olize v.t. To obtain a monopoly of; to engross entirely.
Fab'ulize v.i. To invent or recount fables.
For'mulize v.t. To formulate.
Macad'amize v.t. To repair or make a road with stone broken small.
In'famize v.t. To make infamous; to defame.
Al'chemize v.t. (*Alchemy*).
Eu'phemize v.t. and i. To make use of or express in euphemism.
Pol'emize v.i. To argue disputatiously.
I'temize v.t. To set forth in detail.
Sys'temize v.t. To reduce to system.
Min'imize v.t. To reduce to a minimum; to represent as of trifling importance, etc.
Pil'grimize v.i. To go on pilgrimage.
Vic'timize v.t. To make a victim of; to dupe
Legit'imize v.t. To render legitimate or lawful.
Op'timize v.i. and t. To be optimistic, treat optimistically.
Max'imize v.t. To raise to a maximum.
Econ'omize v.i. To manage with prudence or frugality. v.t. To turn to the best account, use sparingly.
Auton'omize v.t. To make self-governing.
At'omize v.t. To reduce to fine particles.
Anat'omize v.t. To dissect.
Epit'omize v.t. To abridge, summarize.
Phlebot'omize v.i. To let blood (from a vein).
Dichot'omize v.t. and i. To cut or divide into two parts, halves, or pairs; to show as a semicircle (of the moon).
Synon'ymize v.t. To express by synonyms.
Repub'licanize v.t. To convert to republican principles.
Amer'icanize v.t., v.i. (*American*).
Vul'canize v.t. To change the properties of rubber by vulcanization.
Moham'medanize v.t. To convert to or make conformable to Mohammedanism.
Pa'ganize v.t. To render pagan or heathenish. v.i. To behave like pagans.
Or'ganize v.t. To arrange; to give an organic structure to; to establish, order, and systematize. v.i. To unite into an organic whole.
Reor'ganize v.t. To bring again to an organized state.
Disor'ganize v.t. To destroy the organic system or connected structure of; to throw into disorder.
Mech'anize v.t. To make mechanical.
In'dianize v.t. To make Indian.
Bohe'mianize v.i. To live in an unconventional way.
Antiquar'ianize v.i. (*Antiquarian*).
Pedes'trianize v.i. To practise walking.
Rus'sianize v.t. To make Russian, bring in accord with Russian thought, customs, etc.
Chris'tianize v.t. and i. To convert or be converted to Christianity.
Ro'manize v.t. To convert to Roman Catholicism. v.i. To use Latin idiom, etc.; to conform to Roman Catholicism.
Ger'manize v.t. and i. To conform or make conform to German ideas, customs, etc.
Hu'manize v.t. and i. To render or become human or humane.

Dehu'manize v.t. To brutalize, divest of human character.
Tet'anize v.t. To cause tetanus in.
Cosmopol'itanize v.t. To render cosmopolitan.
Pur'itanize v.t. and i. To make or become Puritan.
Bot'anize v.i. To collect or study plants.
Gal'vanize v.t. To apply galvanism to, to stimulate thus; to rouse to action.
Ky'anize v.t. To render (wood) proof against decay.
Hydrog'enize v.t. (*Hydrogenate*).
Dehy'drogenize v.t. To deprive of hydrogen.
Nitrog'enize v.t. To imbue with nitrogen.
Ox'ygenize v.t. To oxidize.
Deox'ygenize v.t. To deoxidize.
Heath'enize v.t. To render heathen.
Hell'enize v.t. and i. To make Greek, permeate with Greek culture, adopt or follow Greek methods, etc.
Phenom'enize v.t. To make phenomenal; to phenomenalize.
Albu'menize v.t. (*Albumen*).
Reju'venize v.t. and i. To rejuvenate.
Cog'nize v.t. To perceive, know, recognize.
Rec'ognize v.t. To know again, to avow knowledge of, indicate appreciation of.
Cocain'ize v.t. To treat with cocaine.
Platitu'dinize v.i. To talk in or utter platitudes.
Attitu'dinize v.i. To posture, assume affected attitudes.
Ka'olinize v.t. To convert into kaolin.
Fem'inize v.t. and i. To make or become feminine or womanish.
Effem'inize v.t To render effeminate.
Bitu'minize v.t. (*Bitumen*).
Lat'inize v.t. To give a Latin form to; to translate into Latin. v.i. To use Latin idioms, etc.
Gelat'inize v.t. and i. To gelatinate.
Plat'inize v.t. To coat or treat with platinum.
Kerat'inize v.i. To become converted into keratin.
Glu'tinize v.t. To render viscous or gluey.
Scru'tinize v.t. To search closely, examine into critically.
Div'inize v.t. To treat as divine; to deify.
Sol'emnize v.t. To celebrate with solemn ceremonies; to make solemn.
Hauss'mannize v.t. To rebuild a town on an expensive scale.
Tyr'annize v.t. and i. To act the tyrant, rule despotically.
Eb'onize v.t. To make black or like ebony.
Car'bonize v.t. (*Carbon*).
Ag'onize v.t. To torture. v.i. To suffer agony.
Antag'onize v.t. To compete with. v.i. To act in opposition.
Gor'gonize v.t. To gaze at so as to paralyse; to stare out of countenance.
Cin'chonize v.t. To treat with quinine.
Sym'phonize v.t. and i. To harmonize.
Eu'phonize v.t. and i. To make euphonious sounds, speak euphoniously.
I'onize v.t. To convert into ions.
Collo'dionize v.t. To treat will collodion.
Relig'ionize v.t. To make religious. v.i. To profess religion.
Li'onize v.t. To treat or show off as an object of interest.
U'nionize v.t. To form into a union, to unify.
Frac'tionize v.t. To break up into fractions.
Revolu'tionize v.t. To change completely.
Disill'usionize v.t. To free from illusions.
Col'onize v.t. To found a colony in; to settle colonists in.
De'monize v.t. To make devilish, bring under influence of demons.
Har'monize v.t. To bring into accord; to set accompanying parts to. v.i. To be in harmony or in friendship; to agree, blend.
Ser'monize v.i. To compose, write, or deliver sermons.
Can'onize v.t. To enrol in the list of saints; to sanction as canonical.
Ca'ponize v.t. To castrate.
Syn'chronize v.i. To agree in time, be simultaneous. v.t. To make to agree in time.
Enthron'ize v.t. To enthrone, induct.
Pat'ronize v.t. To act as patron toward, to support; to assume the air of a superior toward.
Pla'tonize v.i. To adopt the opinions of Plato or the Platonists. v.t. To explain by or accommodate to these.
Skel'etonize v.t. To reduce to a skeleton or outline.
Syn'tonize v.t. To make syntonic, to harmonize.
Electrot'onize v.t. To affect nerves, muscles, etc., by galvanism.
Pep'tonize v.t. To treat food with pepsin.
Glut'tonize v.i. To gorge, stuff oneself.
O'zonize v.t. To charge with ozone.
Mod'ernize v.t. and i. To make or become modern.
Frat'ernize v.i. To associate with on brotherly terms.
Eter'nize v.t. To make eternal, to immortalize.
West'ernize v.t. To make Western, imbue with Occidental thought, etc.
Im'munize v.t. To render immune.
Syn'copize v.t. To syncopate.
Philan'thropize v.t. To practise philanthropy on, treat philanthropically.
Misan'thropize v.t. and i. To make or be misanthropic.
Bar'barize v.t. To convert to barbarism.
Mac'arize v.t. To bless; to congratulate.
Vul'garize v.t. To make vulgar.
Gar'garize v.t. To gargle.
Di'arize v.t. and i. To keep or enter in a diary.
Pla'giarize v.t. To purloin from the writings, inventions, etc., of another.
Famil'iarize v.t. To make familiar, to accustom, habituate.
Pecu'liarize v.t. To appropriate. make peculiar.
Po'larize v.t. To communicate polarity to; to change a ray so that it exhibits polarization.
Depol'arize v.t. To deprive of polarity, free from polarization
Vernac'ularize v.t. To make vernacular; to vernaculate.
Sec'ularize v.t. To convert from spiritual or monastic to secular or wordly use.
Partic'ularize v.t. To enumerate in detail. v.i. To be attentive to particulars.
Tuber'cularize v.t. To infect with tuberculosis.
Cir'cularize v.t. To send circulars to.
Vas'cularize v.t. To render vascular.
Reg'ularize v.t. To make regular.
Sing'ularize v.t. To make singular; to particularize.
For'mularize v.t. To formulate.
Pop'ularize v.t. To make popular; to spread among the people.
Sum'marize v.t. To reduce to a summary.
Mar'marize v.t. To convert into marble by metamorphism.
Mil'itarize v.t. To imbue with militarism.
Tar'tarize v.t. To impregnate with tartar.
Brize s. A gadfly.
Mer'cerize v.t. To give a gloss to cotton fabrics by chemical means.

Gran'gerize v.t. To extra-illustrate with inserted prints, etc.
E'therize v.t. To put under the influence of ether.
Bow'dlerize v.t. To expurgate.
Euhe'merize v.t. To explain myths rationalistically.
Mes'merize v.t. To bring into an hypnotic state or trance.
Pau'perize v.t. To reduce to pauperism.
Depau'perize v.t. To change from a state of pauperism; to get rid of paupers.
Char'acterize v.t. To designate; to describe or mark the qualities or character of.
Cau'terize v.t. To sear with a hot iron or caustic.
Pul'verize v.t. To reduce to powder. v.i. To fall to dust.
Sat'irize v.t. To make the object of satire.
Her'borize v.i. To botanize, search for plants.
O'dorize v.t. To make odorous; to perfume.
Deo'dorize v.t. To deprive of odour, disinfect.
The'orize v.i. To form theories; to speculate.
Al'legorize v. (*Allegory*).
Aph'orize v.i. To write or utter aphorisms.
Au'thorize v.t. To justify; to make legal.
Decol'orize v.t. To decolour.
Mem'orize v.t. To commit to memory; to cause to be remembered.
Va'porize v.t. and i. To convert or become converted into vapour.
Tem'porize v.i. To procrastinate; to comply with the time or occasion.
Extem'porize v.i. To speak extempore, to make an off-hand speech. v.t. To do in an unpremeditated manner.
Ter'rorize v.t. To rule by intimidation.
Proc'torize v.t. To catch and punish an undergraduate (of proctors).
Prize s. Anything captured or seized by force; anything worth striving for; a reward. v.t. To value highly; to rate; to prise.
Main'prize s. Writ commanding sheriff to allow prisoner to be at large on bail; deliverance of a prisoner on security.
Apprize' v.t. To inform, give notice of.
Misprize' v.t. To slight, undervalue.
Cic'atrize v.t. and i. To heal or induce formation of a cicatrix.
Elec'trize v.t. To electrify.
Sym'metrize v.t. To reduce to symmetry.
Geom'etrize v.i. To work by geometrical methods.
Pas'teurize v.t. To sterilize milk by exposing it to a high temperature.
Sul'phurize v.t. To sulphurate.
Desul'phurize v.t. To deprive of sulphur.
Pan'egyrize v.t. To extol, praise highly.
Mar'tyrize v.t. To martyr, make a martyr of.
Size s. Magnitude, bigness, bulk; a relative measure; a kind of glue. v.t. To arrange according to size, take the size of; to cover with size.
Em'phasize v.t. To utter with emphasis; to lay stress on, make impressive.
Paren'thesize v.t. To insert as a parenthesis; to enclose within parentheses.
Syn'thesize v.t. To combine or produce by synthesis.
Hypoth'esize v.t. and i. To assume, to form hypotheses.
Apotheo'size v.t. To deify, glorify.
Capsize' v. To upset, overturn. s. An overturn.
Assize' s. A session or sitting; a periodical court of law.
Mithrid'atize v.t. To render poison-proof by taking gradually increasing doses of it.
Me'diatize v.t. To render dependent.
Prel'atize v.i. and t. To support or bring under the influence of prelacy.
-matize suff. Many verbs formed from nouns in *-am*.
Dram'atize v.t. To convert a novel, etc., into a play; to describe dramatically.
Schem'atize v.t. To arrange in a schema, to formulate.
Anath'ematize v. (*Anathema*).
Em'blematize v.t. To symbolize; to illustrate by an emblem.
Sys'tematize v.t. To reduce to system.
Prag'matize v.t. To represent or regard as real to rationalize.
Enig'matize v.i. To deal in riddles.
Stig'matize v.t. To mark with a brand of infamy, characterize by a term of reproach; to mark with the stigmata.
Dog'matize v.i. To assert positively, lay down with arrogance or undue confidence.
Accli'matize v.t. To inure or adapt to a climate.
Legit'imatize v.t. To legitimize.
Illegit'imatize v.t. To render or declare illegitimate.
Diagram'-matize v.t. To make a diagram, present in digrammatic form.
Anagram'-matize v.t. (*Anagram*).
Diplo'matize v.i. To act as a diplomatist, or diplomatically.
Aro'matize v.t. To give an aroma to.
Achro'matize v.t. To deprive of colour.
Democ'ratize v.t. and i. To make or become democratic.
Apos'tatize v.i. To abandon one's creed or party.
Al'phabetize v.t. To arrange in alphabetical order.
Anæs'thetize v.t. To render temporarily insensible.
Mag'netize v.t. To communicate magnetic properties to; to attract, influence, etc., as by a magnet; to mesmerize. v.i. To become magnetic.
Diamag'netize v.t. To affect with diamagnetism.
Demag'netize v.t. To deprive of magnetic polarity; to rouse from a mesmeric state.
Mon'etize v.t. To convert into or adopt as money; to give a standard value to.
Demon'etize v.t. To deprive coinage of its standard value, or to withdraw it from use.
Po'etize v.i. To write as a poet, compose verse.
Sem'itize v.t. To make Semitic.
Sen'sitize v.t. To render sensitive, especially of photographic paper.
Jes'uitize v.t. and i. To convert or become converted to Jesuitism.
Sycophan'tize v.i. To play the sycophant.
Prot'estantize v.t. To make Protestant.
Nar'cotize v.t. To imbue with a narcotic; to put into a state of narcosis.
Eg'otize v.i. To indulge in egotism.
Hel'otize v.t. To reduce to serfdom.
Hyp'notize v.t. To affect with hypnotism; to entrance.
Nec'rotize v.i. and t. To undergo or affect with necrosis.
Baptize' v.t. To christen.
Amor'tize v.t. To deaden, extinguish, destroy.
Dep'utize v.i. To act as a deputy. v.t. To depute.
Pros'elytize v.i. To make converts.
Solil'oquize v.i. To utter a soliloquy.
Ventril'oquize v.i. To practise ventriloquism.
Quinze s. A game at cards.
Winze s. Shaft sunk in mine from one level to another.
Bonze s. A Buddhist priest.

Bronze s. An alloy, chiefly of copper and tin. a. Made of or resembling bronze. v.t. To make brown.
Doze v.i. To sleep lightly. s. A nap.
Gloze v.t. To palliate, extenuate. v.i. To comment. s. Flattery; specious talk.
Ooze s. Soft mud; slime, especially on the ocean bed; an exudation. v.i. To issue gently; to percolate.
Booze (*Slang*) s. Intoxicating liquor. v.i. To drink to excess.
Snooze s. A nap, short sleep. v.i. To doze.
Froze past (*Freeze*).
Toze v.t. To unravel.
Furze s. A prickly shrub, gorse.
Gauze s. A thin, light, transparent fabric.
Fuze s. A fuse.
Blowze s. A ruddy, fat-faced woman.
Deaf a. Incapable or dull of hearing; unwilling to hear.
Sheaf s. A bundle, especially of unthreshed stalks of grain. v.t. To sheave.
Leaf s. A thin, expanded organ of plants; sheet of two pages in a book, etc.; one side of a double door; hinged or removable part of table, shutter, etc. v.i. To shoot out leaves, produce foliage.
In'terleaf s. A blank leaf inserted.
Overleaf' adv. On the next page.
Oaf s. A changeling; a lout, dolt.
Loaf s. A shaped mass of bread; a conical lump of sugar; an idle time. v.i. To lounge, idle about.
Graf s. A German count.
Beef s. The flesh of oxen.
Reef s. Portion of sail which can be rolled up; ridge of rock, etc., near sea's surface; vein of gold- or diamond-bearing rock. v.t. To take in a reef (of a sail); to shorten (a mast, etc.).
Chef s. A professional cook.
Fief s. An estate held by military service; feudal tenure
Chief a. Highest; most important, eminent, influential, etc. s. Head, leader; chieftain; the upper third of an heraldic shield.
Ker'chief s. A linen head-dress.
Neck'erchief s. A wrap for the neck.
Hand'kerchief s. A piece of linen or silk for wiping the nose, etc.; a neck-cloth.
Mis'chief s. Harm; trivial evil or vexation; cause of this; annoying conduct.
Thief s. One who steals.
Kief s. The drowsy trance produced by smoking bhang.
Lief adv. Willingly; gladly.
Belief' s. Act of believing; faith; religion, creed.
Disbelief' s. Refusal of credence; system of error.
Misbelief' s. Erroneous belief; false religion.
Relief' s. Alleviation of pain, etc.; that which alleviates; succour, redress; one who relieves another of duty; prominence; relievo.
Bas'-relief s. Sculpture in which the figures do not project far from the background.
Brief a. Short, concise. s. An abstract of a client's case. v.t. To engage counsel.
Grief s. Sorrow; affliction; regret.
Clef s. A character prefixed to the staff in music to determine the pitch.
Gaff s. A stick with a large metal hook used by fishermen; a spar; a low-class entertainment; (*slang*) outcry. v.t. To seize with a gaff. v.i. (*Slang*) To gamble, toss.
Shan'dygaff s. A mixture of beer and ginger-beer.
Chaff s. Husks of grain; fine cut hay, etc.; light ridicule, banter. v.t. To make fun of, banter.
Chiff'chaff s. The willow-wren.
Pilaff' s. A dish of boiled rice, meat, and spices.
Raff s. Refuse; dregs; the mob.
Draff s. Refuse; anything worthless.
Riff'raff s. The rabble, the lower orders.
Staff s. A stick, pole, baton; a prop, support; a directing body of officers, personnel of a business, etc.; five parallel lines on which music is written.
Pike'staff s. The shaft of a pike.
Dis'taff s. The staff from which flax is spun.
Tip'staff s. A sheriff's officer.
Quaff v.t. and i. To drain to the bottom, drink copiously.
Whiff s. Sudden expulsion of smoke, etc.; a puff; a light sculling boat; a small cigar; a variety of flat-fish. v.t. and i. To blow or puff lightly; to fish by towing the bait from a boat.
Skiff s. A small light sculling boat.
Cliff s. A high, steep rock; precipice.
Bail'iff s. A sheriff's officer.
Bumbail'iff s. An under bailiff.
Miff s. A petty quarrel.
Sniff v.i. To draw air audibly through the nose. v.t. To smell. s. Act of sniffing; anything taken thus.
Tar'iff s. A table of duties; customs on imports and exports; a price list. v.t. To draw up a list of duties; to price.
Mid'riff s. The diaphragm.
Sher'iff s. Chief Crown officer of a shire.
Hip'pogriff s. A fabulous winged horse.
Tiff s. Slight quarrel, peevishness.
Cait'iff s. A knave, a scallawag.
Plain'tiff s. One who begins a lawsuit.
Pon'tiff s. The Pope; a high-priest.
Stiff a. Rigid, inflexible; stubborn; formal. s. (*Slang*) A bully, swindler; a horse certain to lose; a corpse.
Mas'tiff s. A large, strong dog.
Off adv., prep., a., s.
Scoff v.i. To jeer, mock. v.t. To treat with derision. s. Expression of scorn.
Doff v.t. To put off (dress); to defer.
Feoff v.t. To invest with a fee or feud. s. A fief.
Enfeoff' v.t. To give a fief to, invest with a fee.
Koff s. A two-masted Dutch vessel.
Toff s. (*Slang*) A dude; a person of consequence.
Buff s. Leather prepared from buffalo hide. a. Light yellow.
Rebuff' v.t. To check or repel discourteously. s. A sudden check; unexpected repulse.
Cuff s. A blow, slap; end of a sleeve. v.t. To strike with the hand or fist.
Hand'cuff s. A manacle. v.t. To secure with these.

Duff s. (*Slang*) Boiled flour pudding. v.t. (*Slang*) To fake, alter brands, cheat.
Huff s. Swell of sudden anger; disappointment; act of huffing at draughts. v.t. To remove one's opponent's piece from the draught-board when he omits to capture with it.
Luff v.i. To keep close to the wind. s. The weather-edge of a fore-and-aft sail.
Bluff a. Big, surly, unpolished, blustering. s. A high steep bank or shore; pretence of strength with intent to gain by deception. v.t. To outwit or hoax an opponent.
Fluff s. Down, nap; flocculent matter.
Muff s. A cover for both hands; a blunderer, simpleton. v.t. and i. To bungle, fail in.
Snuff s. Pulverized tobacco or medicament for taking in the nose; a drawing up into the nose; charred wick. v.t. To draw in through the nose, to sniff. v.i. To take snuff; to trim (a wick, etc.).
Puff v.i. To breathe hard. v.t. To inflate, drive with a blast; to praise extravagantly. s. Sudden emission of breath, a short blast; light pastry; exaggerated praise.
Ruff s. A fluted collar; ring of fur or feathers round neck of certain animals and birds; a bird allied to the sandpiper; an old card-game; act of trumping in. v.t. To trump; to heckle (flax). v.i. To trump.
Scruff s. The nape of the neck.
Wood'ruff s. A sweet-scented woodland plant.
Gruff a. Sour of aspect; harsh in voice, manners, etc.
Dan'druff s. Scurf from the head.
Tuff s. An earthy deposit of volcanic materials.
Stuff s. Material of which anything is made; goods; texture of any kind. v.t. To pack, fill, thrust in. v.i. To feed greedily
Bread'stuff s. Flour, the grain of cereals.
If conj. Supposing that, etc.
Na'if a. Naïve.
Waif s. A stray or ownerless person, animal, etc.; a homeless child.
Redif' s. A soldier of the Turkish reserve; this reserve.
Ca'lif s. A Mohammedan title of honour; a ruler.
Coif s. A head-dress; a cap formerly worn by sergeants-at-law.
Quoif s. A cap or hood.
Sherif' (-rēf') s. A descendant of Mohammed's daughter, Fatima.
Ser'if s. Fine cross-line of a letter.
Mas'sif s. The central mass of a mountain range.
Hus'sif s. A case for pins, needles, etc., a housewife.
Mé'tif s. Offspring of a white and a quadroon.
Motif' (-têf') s. The dominant principle in a work of art, etc.
Calf s. The young of the cow; the thick part of the lower leg.
Half s. One of two equal parts. a. Consisting of half. adv. In an equal degree or part.
Behalf' s. Favour, interest, sake.
Elf s. A fairy, goblin; a mischievous person.
Delf s. A kind of porcelain; earthenware.
Shelf s. Horizontal board for holding things; a ledge; a reef.
Pelf s. Money, riches.
Self s. One's own person; the individual; personal interest.
Oneself' pron. The reflexive form of "one."
Himself' pron. Reflexive or emphatic form of "he."
Herself' pron. Reflexive form of "she."
Ourself' pron. Used by kings, etc., in place of *myself*.
Yourself' pron. *You*; you alone or in particular, etc.
Itself' pron. "It" used emphatically or reflexively.
Thyself' pron. Emphatic form after or in place of "thou."
Myself' pron. I, me (*used for emphasis*).
Guelf s. Guelph.
Golf s. A Scottish game played with clubs and small hard balls over commons, etc. v.i. To play golf.
Wolf (wulf) s. A ferocious carnivore allied to the dog; a cunning or rapacious person. v.t. To devour ravenously.
Wer'wolf s. A man turned wolf, or possessing power to do so.
Gulf s. A deep bay or inlet; a chasm; abyss.
Engulf' v.t. To swallow up; to plunge into.
Of prep.
Hereof' adv. Of, concerning, or from this.
Thereof' adv.
Whereof' adv.
Oof s. (*Slang*) Money; lucre.
Shadoof' s. An irrigating apparatus used on the Nile, etc.
Hoof s. Horny part of a horse's foot. v.t. (*Slang*) To kick.
Behoof' s. Profit, advantage, benefit.
Loof s. The palm of the hand.
Aloof' adv. Apart.
Kloof s. A ravine in S. Africa.
Roof s. The cover of a house, barn, vehicle, etc.; top of the mouth. v.t. To cover with a roof; to house.
Proof s. Evidence; something serving to convince or test; trial; firmness; standard of strength in spirit; trial impression in printing, photography, engraving, etc. a. Impenetrable, successful in resisting. v.t. To make a substance proof.
Reproof' s. Censure; blame.
Wa'terproof' a. Impervious to water. s. Cloth, a garment, etc., made waterproof. v.t. To render thus.
Disproof' s. Proof of error; refutation.
Woof s. The threads that cross the warp; the weft; texture.
Scarf s. A narrow shawl for the shoulders; a joint in timber, a groove. v.t. To cut a scarf in.
Wharf (hworf) s. A quay, landing-place. v.t. To moor at or deposit goods on a wharf.
Dwarf s. A person, animal, plant, etc., much below normal size. a. Below natural size; stunted. v.t. To stunt, to check the development of.
Zarf s. An ornamental holder for a coffee-cup.
Kerf s. The slit made by a saw, etc.; spot where something has been cut off; a cutting, lopping; cut straw, etc., for thatching.

Serf s. A feudal labourer; a slave, drudge.
Corf s. A basket used in mines; a perforated receptacle for keeping fish alive in water.
Scurf s. Dry scales from the skin; especially of the head; dandruff.
Surf s. The breaking sea; foam from this.
Turf s. Surface of grass-land; a race-course, horse-racing.
Pouf s. A large cushion for the floor.
Bag s. A sack or pouch; a small receptacle of cloth, leather, etc.
Hand'bag s. A small bag for carrying.
Dag s. An obsolete pistol; a dagger.
Rigs'dag s. The Danish Parliament.
Riks'dag s. The Swedish Parliament.
Fag v.i. To drudge, to become weary. v.t. To use as a drudge, tire by labour. s. A drudge; a small schoolboy performing tasks for a senior; (*slang*) a cigarette.
Gag v.t. To stuff the mouth, especially to prevent speaking; to silence. v.i. To introduce unauthorized words, etc., into a part (of actors). s. Something thrust into the mouth to prevent speaking, hold it open, etc.; the closure (parliament); interpolations in an actor's part.
Hag s. An ugly old woman; a witch; an eel-like, parasitic fish.
Shag s. Coarse hair, nap cloth, etc.; a strong shredded tobacco; the crested cormorant.
Jag s. A notch; a ragged piece, etc.; (*slang*) a spree, "beano." v.t. To cut or tear raggedly or into notches.
Lag v.i. To loiter, hang about, stay behind. v.t. (*Slang*) To arrest. a. Coming behind; sluggish. s. Retardation of movement; the last-comer, fag-end; (*slang*) a convict.
Flag s. A cloth with device, banner, ensign; a paving-stone; a water-plant. v.i. To grow spiritless, to droop; to hang loose. v.t. To deck with flags, lay with flagstones.
Slag s. Fused refuse, dross of a metal; vitrified cinders; scoria. v.i. and t. To form or convert into slag.
Mag s. The magpie; (*slang*) a gossiping, chat; a halfpenny. v.i. To chatter.
Nag s. A small riding-horse, a pony. v.t. To tease, scold, or annoy continually and pertinaciously. v.i. To be continually finding fault.
Tu'tenag s. An alloy of copper, zinc, and nickel; a kind of spelter.
Knag s. A knot in wood; a peg; shoot of an antler.
Snag s. A short sharp branch or stump, especially when in a river-bottom. v.t. To damage (a vessel) on a snag.
Rag s. A fragment of cloth; a tatter; hard, rough stone; (*slang*) a spree, disorderly conduct; a flag. v.t. To irritate, play rough jokes on; to reprimand.
Brag v.i. To boast, swagger. s. A card-game; boasting, bluff.
Crag s. A steep, rugged rock or cliff; pliocene shelly deposits.
Scrag s. Something dry and lean, with roughness; a neck piece of meat; a bony person. v.t. To grasp round the neck; to throttle.
Drag v.t. To pull along by force; to haul; to explore with a drag. s. A net or an instrument with hooks drawn along the bottom of the water, a dredging machine or implement; a skid, clog; a heavy harrow; a coach; a hunt with artificial scent.
Bully'rag v.t. To abuse scurrilously; to torment with low practical jokes.
Sag v.i. To bend, sink in the middle. v.t. To cause to give way. s. Act or state of sagging.
Tag s. Any slight appendage; a catch-word, hackneyed quotation. v.t. To fit with a point; to append.
Land'tag s. The German legislative body.
Rag'tag s. The rabble.
Stag s. Male of the red deer; a hart.
Reichs'tag s. The German parliament.
Quag s. A bog, marsh.
Wag v.t. and i. To swing, sway; to nod. s. A wit, humorist; act of wagging.
Scal'lawag s. An undersized animal; a mean person, a ne'er-do-well.
Wig-wag v.t. and i. To wag or move to and from; to signal thus.
Swag s. Booty; proceeds of a burglary. v.i. To sag.
Zig'zag a. Having short, sharp turns. s. Something that has such. v.t. and i. To form or move with short turns.
Beg v.i. To ask alms, to live upon alms. v.t. To entreat; to take for granted.
Fil'ibeg s. A kilt.
Keg s. A small cask.
Leg s. Supporting limit of an animal, especially from knee to foot; anything functioning as or resembling this.
Cleg s. A horse-fly.
Fore'leg s. A front leg of a quadruped.
Black'leg s. One who works during a strike of his fellows; a swindling gambler.
Pro'leg s. A foot-like organ in caterpillars.
Nut'meg s. The spicy seed of an Indian tree.
Peg s. A wooden pin for fastening, hanging things from, marking, etc.; a drink of spirits. v.t. To fasten, restrict, score, etc., with pegs.
Egg s. The ovum of birds, reptiles, fishes, etc.; spawn. v.t. To urge on, to instigate.
Big a. Great in bulk, pregnant.
Dig v.t. To open and turn up with a spade; to delve, hollow out. v.i. To work with a spade. s. A thrust, poke.
Fig s. A tree of the mulberry family; its fruit; a mere trifle; (*slang*) attire, outfit. v.t. To dress, deck.
Gig s. A light one-horse carriage; a ship's boat; a romp, jig; a fish-spear.
Fish'gig s. A pronged spear for taking fish.
Whirl'igig s. A rotating toy; a roundabout; a water-beetle; a rotation.
Fiz'gig s. A flighty or flirting girl.
Whig s. Member of a seventeenth-century political party; forerunners of the Liberals.
Jig s. A lively dance or tune; a piece of mechanism for various uses. v.i. To dance a jig, to skip about. v.t. To jerk, jolt; to sieve.
Thing'umajig s. A thing.

Pfen'nig s. A German copper coin, one-hundredth of a mark.
Pig s. The domestic swine; oblong mass of unforged metal. v.t. and i. To bring forth or act like pigs.
Rig v.t. To dress, clothe; to furnish with gear, etc.; to manipulate prices. s. Dress; style of the masts, etc., of a ship; manipulation of prices, a swindle, a sportive trick.
Brig s. A small square-rigged, two-masted vessel.
Thimble'rig s. A cheating sleight-of-hand trick. v.i. To practise this.
Grig s. A cricket, grasshopper; a sand-eel; a merry soul.
Prig s. A conceited, self-opinionated fellow. v.t. To steal.
Sprig s. A small shoot or twig; a lad; a small nail.
Trig v.t. To check or skid (a wheel). s. A skid; a dandy. a. Neat, spruce.
Wig s. False hair covering for the head. v.t. To scold, rate.
Big'-wig s. An important or highly placed personage.
Per'iwig s. A small wig, peruke.
Ear'wig s. A garden insect.
Swig v.t. and i. To drink copiously. s. A deep draught.
Twig s. A small shoot or branch. v.t. (*Slang*) To understand.
Bang v.t. To beat, to thump. v.i. To go off with a loud sudden noise. s. A heavy blow; a loud sharp noise.
Go'bang s. A Japanese game played with counters.
Pro'bang s. Surgeon's instrument for introduction into throat.
Fang s. A tusk, a long pointed tooth; a serpent's poison-tooth; a talon.
Gang s. A company, squad, herd; a set of tools worked together; a gangue. v.i. (*Scot.*) To go.
Hang v.t. To suspend; to put to death by suspending by the neck; to furnish with hangings; to cause to droop. v.i. To be suspended; to dangle, linger, droop; to be executed; to be steep. s. General tendency, drift.
Bhang s. An intoxicant or narcotic prepared from hemp.
Rehang' v.t. To hang over again.
Overhang' v.t. and i. To impend, jut, project, or hang over.
Whang v.t. To beat, as a drum. s. Sound of this; a blow, bang.
Liang s. A Chinese weight (about 1¼ oz. avoir.).
Lang a. (*Scot.*) Long.
Clang v.t. To strike together with a metallic sound. v.i. To produce or emit such a sound. s. A ringing sound.
Slang s. Words or phrases of a colloquial, vulgar, or canting nature; jargon. v.t. To address coarsely or with vituperation. v.i. To use slang.
Ylang'-ylang s. A Malayan tree; a perfume distilled from its flowers.
Siamang' s. An E. Indian gibbon.
Pang s. A sharp, momentary pain; short mental distress; agony.
Trepang' s. The sea-slug.
Rang past (*Ring*).
Boom'erang s. An Australian missile weapon of wood.
Serang' s. A Lascar boatswain.
Sprang past (*Spring*).
Sang past (*Sing*).
Par'asang s. An ancient Persian measure (nearly four miles).
Lin'sang s. An E. Indian animal resembling the civet-cat.
Tang s. A strong taste, a distinctive quality; a projecting piece; a twanging noise. v.i. To make a ringing sound.
Mus'tang s. The wild horse of American prairies.
Orang'-utang s. (*Orang-utan*).
Vang s. One of a pair of guy-ropes steadying a gaff.
Twang s. A nasal modulation of the voice; sound as that of a stretched string suddenly let go. v.i. and t. To make this sound or cause to sound thus.
Gin'seng s. An aromatic herb valued in China as a drug.
-ing suff. Forming verbal nouns, participial adjectives, diminutives, patronymics, etc.; denoting occupations, results, materials used, etc.
Bing s. A pile, a heap (especially of ore).
Web'bing s. Strong fabric used for straps, suspenders, etc.
Bib'bing s. Constant indulgence in strong liquors.
Rib'bing s. A system of ribs, as in a roof.
Cub'bing s. Cub-hunting.
Dub'bing s. Grease for leather, boots, etc.
Club'bing s. A disease in cabbages and similar plants.
Drub'bing s. A good beating, a cudgelling.
Plumb'ing s. Art of casting and working in lead, mending cisterns, etc., pipes, etc., for conveying water.
Daub'ing s. Coarse painting.
Tub'ing s. Series of or material for tubes; a piece of tube.
Fac'ing s. A surface covering; a coloured collar, etc.
Lac'ing s. A lace for fastening; a fastening with this.
Men'acing a. Threatening.
Bra'cing a. Strengthening, invigorating.
Tra'cing s. Act of following a trace, or of copying a drawing by following the lines through transparent paper, etc.; copy so traced.
Ic'ing s. Sugar coating for cakes.
Rejoic'ing s. Joyfulness; merrymaking.
Entic'ing a. Alluring; seductive.
Lat'ticing s. Lattice-work, lattice.
Entranc'ing a. Ravishing, delightful.
Convey'ancing s. Profession of a conveyancer.
Fenc'ing s. Swordsmanship; act of making or material used in making fences; guard round machinery.
Minc'ing a. Affectedly elegant.
Convinc'ing a. Leaving no reason for doubt, compelling assent.
Bounc'ing a. Plump and healthy, lusty; large.
Pronounc'ing a. Teaching or indicating pronunciation.
Trounc'ing s. A thrashing, defeat.
Pierc'ing a. Penetrating; keen; severe.
Ding v.t. To strike, beat violently. v.i. To ring, tinkle.
Bead'ing s. An ornamental moulding.
Head'ing s. Inscription at the head, title of a section; gallery in a mine.
Shead'ing (shĕd'-) s. One of the six divisions of the Isle of Man.
Lead'ing a. Conducting; alluring; principal. s. Influence, guidance.

Plead'ing s. Making a plea or supplication; written statement in a litigant's suit.
Read'ing a. Studious. s. Act, practice, or art of reading; scholarship; form or rendering of a passage; public entertainment at which passages are read; introduction of a Bill to Parliament.
Lad'ing s. Freight; burden; cargo.
Load'ing s. A burden, cargo.
Degrad'ing a. Lowering the level or character.
Pad'ding s. Act of stuffing, or material used; literary matter merely increasing bulk.
Wad'ding (wod'-) s. Material for making wads; cotton-wool.
Bed'ding s. The materials of a bed.
Shed'ding s. Sheds; material for these.
Wed'ding s. Marriage; nuptial ceremony.
Bid'ding s. A command.
Forbid'ding a. Disagreeable, repulsive.
Pud'ding s. A dish, hard or soft, boiled or baked, and variously compounded; a sausage.
Preced'ing a. Going before.
Proceed'ing s. Progress; transaction; step.
Exceed'ing a. Great in extent, duration, etc. adv. Exceedingly.
Feed'ing s. Act of giving or taking food; food.
Bleed'ing s. A running or a letting of blood; hæmorrhage.
Reed'ing s. A reed-like moulding.
Breed'ing s. Formation of manners; behaviour, deportment.
Bi'ding s. Stay.
Abi'ding a. Permanent, stable.
Hi'ding s. Concealment, state of being hidden; (*slang*) a thrashing.
Backsli'ding s. (*Backslide*).
Ri'ding s. Act of one who rides; path for riding on; one of the three divisions of Yorkshire.
Si'ding s. A side track for shunting.
Geld'ing s. Act of castrating; a castrated animal, especially horse.
Bield'ing s. (*Scot.*) Protection.
Yield'ing a. Compliant; flexible; accommodating.
Build'ing s. Anything built, as a house.
Wild'ing s. A wild fruit-tree.
Scold'ing s. A noisy reprimand, railing.
Scaf'folding s. A scaffold; materials for this.
Hold'ing s. A grasp; that which is held; tenure, occupation.
Mould'ing s. Anything formed in a mould; grooved ornamental part of woodwork, cornice, etc.
Land'ing s. Act of going or putting ashore; level space at top of stairs; a pier.
Command'ing a. Exercising command; impressive; overlooking.
Stand'ing a. Erect; established, permanent; stagnant. s. Station; relative place; repute.
Notwith-stand'ing prep. and conj. Although; nevertheless.
Understand'ing s. Comprehension; discernment; intellect; anything agreed upon. a. Intelligent.
Misunder-stand'ing s. Misconception; error; slight quarrel.
Outstand'ing a. Projecting outward; prominent; not yet paid or dealt with.
End'ing s. A conclusion, termination.
Condescend'ing a. Patronizing.
Pend'ing a. Remaining in suspense, undecided. prep. During.
Bind'ing a. Obligatory. s. The cover of a book; anything that fastens or binds.
Find'ing s. Discovery; that which is found; verdict.
Correspond'ing a. Agreeing, answering, suiting.
Abound'ing a. (*Abound*).
Ground'ing s. Elementary instruction.
Sounding' a. Sonorous, resonant. s. Act of measuring depths.
Astound'ing a. (*Astound*).
Bo'ding s. An omen, prediction. a. Presageful, ominous.
Forebo'ding s. Presage, anticipation (especially of evil).
Flood'ing s. Act of inundating; an inundation.
Regard'ing prep. Concerning, respecting.
Board'ing s. A casing made of boards.
Hoard'ings. A temporary screen of boards during building, for advertisement purposes, etc.
Gird'ing s. That which girds; sneering, taunting.
Accord'ing part. a. Agreeing with, suitable. prep. Just as; consistent with.
Record'ing a. Registering.
Lord'ing s. Equivalent of "lord" (*obs.*).
Word'ing s. Mode of verbal expression; form of stating.
Be'ing s. Existence, anything existing. conj. Seeing that.
See'ing conj. In view of the fact that, inasmuch as.
Foresee'ing a. Exercising foresight; provident.
Swinge'ing a. Huge; very large.
Off'ing s. Part of the sea nearer the horizon than the shore.
Duff'ing a. Counterfeit; faked.
Stuff'ing s. Filling; seasoning.
Roof'ing s. Material for a roof; a roof; act of putting this on.
Wa'terproofing s. Waterproof cloth, etc.
Engag'ing a. Winning, pleasing.
Man'aging a. Having the control; careful; economical.
Pag'ing s. The marking of the pages in a book.
Encour'aging a. Furnish ground for hope; favouring.
Discour'aging a. Dispiriting, deterring, disheartening.
Sta'ging s. A scaffolding.
Edg'ing s. A border, fringe; narrow lace.
Lodg'ing s. A temporary residence.
Bag'ging s. Material for bags.
Flag'ging s. Act of paving with flags; a flagstone pavement.
Leg'ging s. A gaiter.
Rig'ging s. The cordage or ropes of a ship.
Wig'ging s. A scolding, reprimand.
Pet'tifogging a. Quibbling; paltry, mean.
Hog'ging s. Partition of scantlings filled with bricks.
Flog'ging s. A punishment by whipping.
Rug'ging s. Material for making rugs.
Obli'ging a. Disposed to oblige; courteous, kind, complaisant.
Disobli'ging s. Unaccommodating, not civil or compliant.
Hang'ing s. Act of suspending; execution on the gallows.
Ring'ing a. Sounding like a bell; sonorous. s. The sound of a bell.
Up'bringing s. Training, breeding.
Long'ing s. An eager desire, craving.
Belong'ing s. That which pertains to one.
Diver'ging a. Divergent, going farther asunder.
For'ging s. A piece of forged metal-work.

Teach'ing s. Act of one who teaches; that which is taught.
Planch'ing s. The laying of floors; a flooring.
Search'ing a. Penetrating, thorough. s. Minute inquiry.
Birching' s. A flogging.
Hatch'ing s. Cross-line shading in engravings, etc.
Thatch'ing s. The work of a thatcher.
Etch'ing s. An impression from an etched plate; the art of an etcher.
Fetch'ing a. Charming, taking, attractive.
Witch'ing a. Suited to enchantment or sorcery.
Bewitch'ing a. Fascinating.
Touch'ing a. Affecting; pathetic.
Laugh'ing a. Fit to be treated or accompanied with laughter. s. Laughter.
Dash'ing a. Daring; showy.
Lash'ing s. A rope for securing; a flogging.
Thrash'ing s. A flogging, drubbing, heavy defeat.
Wash'ing s. Act of cleansing with water, etc.; clothes, etc., sent to the wash.
Sneesh'ing s. Snuff.
Refresh'ing a. Reanimating; enlivening.
Fish'ing s. The sport of angling; a fishery.
Fam'ishing a. Extremely hungry.
Aston'ishing a. (*Astonish*).
Gar'nishing s. Act of ornamenting, especially dishes; ornamentation.
Flourish'ing a. Thriving; making a show.
Nour'ishing a. Helping to nourish; nutritious.
Disting'uishing a. Constituting a distinction; peculiar.
Rav'ishing a. Enchanting, enrapturing.
Gush'ing a. Issuing suddenly and violently (of fluids); demonstratively affectionate.
Blush'ing a. Modest; blooming; rosy.
Push'ing a. Energetic; enterprising.
Crush'ing a. Overwhelming.
Thing s. Any lifeless object or material; whatever exists separately; a matter, event; a Scandinavian legislative body.
Scath'ing a. Withering; bitingly severe.
Sheath'ing s. That which sheathes; metal covering of a ship's bottom.
Breath'ing s. Respiration; aspiration; utterance; exercise.
Loath'ing s. Disgust, aversion. a. Abhorring.
Teeth'ing s. Process, period, or act of cutting the teeth.
Some'thing s. Some indeterminate thing. adv. In some degree.
Tith'ing s. The levying of tithes; that which is taken as tithe; a set of ten householders bound as sureties for each other.
Clo'thing s. Clothes, dress.
Noth'ing s. Not anything; naught; nonentity. adv. In no degree.
Tooth'ing s. Projecting bricks left in the end of a wall.
Far'thing s. The fourth part of a penny.
Nor'thing s. Distance or progress toward the north.
Stor'thing s. The parliament of Norway.
Lands'thing s. The Upper House of the Danish parliament.
South'ing s. Act of going south or crossing the meridian.
Play'thing s. A toy.
Ev'erything s. All things; something of very great importance.
King s. A male sovereign; a playing-card; the chief piece at chess.
Ba'king s. Quantity baked at once; a baker's business. a. Very hot.
Sneak'ing a. Mean, servile; shamefaced.
Speak'ing s. Act of uttering words; discourse. a. Animated; live-like.
Ma'king s. Act of forming, causing, etc.; possibility or opportunity of success, etc.; essential quality.
Watch'making s. Occupation of a watchmaker.
Dress'making s. Art or business of a dressmaker.
Cloaking' s. Material for cloaks.
Soak'ing a. Such as to soak. s. A drenching.
Tak'ing a. Pleasing, attractive. s. Capture; state of excitement.
Undertak'ing s. Any business, etc., one engages in; an attempt, enterprise.
Pains'taking a. Carefully laborious; sparing no pains. s. Conscientious labour.
Back'ing s. Anything forming a back or support.
Whack'ing s. A thrashing. a. (*Slang*) Large; extraordinary.
Black'ing s. A preparation for polishing black leather.
Rack'ing a. Tormenting; excruciating.
Sack'ing s. Coarse stuff for sacks.
Neck'ing s. Hollow part of column between capital and shaft.
Maf'ficking s. A riotous celebration or rejoicing.
Rol'licking a. Frolicsome; jolly; boisterous.
Prick'ing s. Sensation of sharp pain; trace left by a hare's foot.
Tick'ing s. Material for mattress covers.
Cock'ing s. Cock-fighting.
Shock'ing a. Seeking to shock; disgusting; offensive.
Smock'ing s. Honeycomb work for smock-frocks.
Frock'ing s. Material for smock-frocks.
Stock'ing s. A close-fitting covering for foot and leg.
Blue'stocking s. A literary or learned woman.
Duck'ing s. A thorough wetting; immersion.
Suck'ing a. Not yet weaned; inexperienced.
Reek'ing a. Soiled with steam or smoke; stinking.
Lik'ing s. State of being pleased; inclination; preference.
Strik'ing a. Surprising, notable, impressive.
Vi'king s. An early Scandinavian pirate.
Talk'ing a. Able to talk.
Erl'king s. A goblin of Scandinavian legend.
Hulk'ing a. Unwieldly, awkward.
Plank'ing s. Planks collectively, flooring.
Spank'ing s. A slight thrashing. a. (*Slang*) Dashing, brisk, stunning.
Think'ing a. Having the faculty of thought; cogitative. s. Imagination; judgment.
Bro'king s. The business of a broker.
Provok'ing a. Annoying; exasperating.
Cark'ing a. Burdensome, oppressive.
Mark'ing s. Marks; colouring. a. Producing a mark.
Work'ing a. Engaged in work, especially manually; laborious. s. Act of labouring; operation; portion of mine which has been or is being worked.
As'king s. A request.
-ling suff. Forming nouns having diminutive force, and adverbs.
Ling s. The common heather; a slender, edible sea-fish.
Deal'ing s. Conduct, behaviour; intercourse, traffic.
Heal'ing a. Tending to heal; mild, soothing s. Act or process of curing.
Appeal'ing a. Suppliant.
Seal'ing s. Catching and trading in seals.
Steal'ing s. Theft; larceny.

Whal'ing s. Trade or occupation of whale-fishing.
Pa'ling s. A fence formed with pales.
Stabl'ing s. Accommodation in a stable.
Am'bling a. Going at the most easy pace of a horse.
Ram'bling a. Wandering about; disconnected; incoherent.
Bram'bling s. The mountain finch.
Trembl'ing s. A tremor; act or state of quaking.
Rum'bling s. A low, continued sound.
Tumbl'ing s. Acrobatic performance.
Snob'ling s. A petty snob, a whipper-snapper.
Mar'bling s. Imitation of marble; veined colouring.
Cling v.i. To adhere closely, especially by winding round. v.t. To cause to adhere to.
Ped'dling a. Trifling, insignificant.
Fid'dling a. Trifling; petty, futile.
Mid'dling a. Of middle quality, rank, etc.; second-rate.
Tiddl'ing s. Fishing for sticklebacks.
Pud'dling s. Process of converting cast into wrought iron.
Reed'ling s. A titmouse.
Seed'ling s. A plant reared from the seed.
Kid'ling s. A small kid; a little child.
World'ling s. A worldly person.
Hand'ling s. Action of touching or feeling; art or style of drawing, composing, or manipulating.
Brand'ling s. A small worm used by anglers as bait.
Kind'ling s. Act of setting light to; shavings, etc., for lighting fires.
Fon'dling s. Person or thing fondled.
Found'ling s. A deserted child.
Ground'ling s. A person of low artistic taste, one of the vulgar; a fish that keeps at the bottom.
Cod'ling s. A young cod; a codlin.
Bard'ling s. A minor poet.
Lord'ling s. A young lord; a petty lord.
Prince'ling s. A petty or little prince.
Feel'ing s. Sense of touch; sensibility: capacity for or condition of emotion; opinion; agitation. a. Sensitive; possessing or indicating great sensibility.
Cage'ling s. A small cage-bird; a young prisoner.
Change'ling s. A child left or taken in place of another; a fickle person.
Cringe'ling s. A cringer.
Ath'eling s. An Anglo-Saxon title of nobility.
Shiel'ing s. (*Scot.*) A hut for sportsmen, shepherds, etc.
Hire'ling s. One who serves for hire. a. Mercenary.
Squire'ling s. A petty squire.
Wise'ling s. A wiseacre.
Shave'ling s. A man shaved, especially a monk.
Starve'ling s. A starved person, animal, etc. a. Lean, hungry.
Fling v.t. To cast, dart, throw, hurl. v.i. To flounce; to plunge about; to rush off angrily. s. A cast or throw; a gibe; unrestrained enjoyment; a lively dance; a plunge, flounce.
Baf'fling a. Bewildering; checking; eluding.
Maf'fling s. A simpleton.
Shuffl'ing a. Evasive.
Trifl'ing a. Trivial, worthless.
Half'ling s. A stripling. a. Half grown.
Pur'fling s. Ornamental bordering.
Fledg'ling s. A bird just fledged; an inexperienced person.
Nig'gling a. Petty, finicky; over-elaborated.
Smug'gling s. The importing or exporting of goods without paying the duty thereon.
An'gling s. The sport of fishing with rod and line.
Wrangl'ing s. A noisy quarrel.
King'ling s. A petty king.
Bungl'ing a. (*Bungle*).
Young'ling s. A young person or animal.
Vetch'ling s. A plant allied to the vetches.
Flesh'ling s. One devoted to carnal pleasures.
Ail'ing a. Sickly.
Fail'ing s. Act of one who fails; imperfection; fault; foible.
Unfail'ing a. Certain; not missing.
Rail'ing s. A fence; connected series of posts; rails collectively.
Sail'ing s. Act of one who or that which sails; art of navigation.
Tail'ing s. Part of a brick in the wall.
Prevail'ing a. Having more influence; superior in force; prevalent.
Ceil'ing s. The upper interior surface of a room.
Veil'ing (vāl'-) s. Material for veils.
Boil'ing s. Ebullition; act of subjecting to heat. a. Very hot.
Foil'ing s. An ornamentation in architectural tracery; a deer's track on grass.
Til'ing s. Tiles collectively; act of laying these.
Weak'ling s. A feeble person.
Oak'ling s. A young oak.
Crack'ling s. Small abrupt reports; rind of roast pork.
Tackl'ing s. Tackle, appurtenances.
Chick'ling s. The cultivated vetch.
Duck'ling s. A young duck.
Suck'ling s. Child or animal not yet weaned.
Ink'ling s. A hint, intimation, suspicion.
Twinkl'ing s. A twinkle, scintillation; an instant.
Dark'ling adv. In the dark. a. Gloomy, obscure.
Call'ing s. Summons; vocation, profession.
Gall'ing a. Vexing, irritating.
Di'alling s. Art of measuring with or constructing dials.
Appal'ling a. Terrifying, frightful.
Enthral'ling a. Fascinating, captivating.
Met'alling s. Broken stones, etc., for roads.
Compel'ling a. Forcing, obligatory.
Spell'ing s. Manner of forming words of letters; act of one who spells.
Tell'ing a. Having great effect.
Fu'elling s. Firing, fuel.
Gru'elling s. (*Slang*) A defeat; severe punishment.
Rev'elling s. Revelry.
Grov'elling a. Abject, mean, base.
Dwel'ling s. Abode, place of residence.
Tow'elling (tou-') s. Material for towels; (*slang*) a thrashing.
Swell'ing s. Act of expanding; state of being swollen; a tumour, etc.
Fill'ing a. Satisfying. s. A making full, materials for this; woof of a fabric.
Chil'ling a. Distant in manner; making cold.
Shil'ling s. An English silver coin, $\frac{1}{20}$ of £1.
Kill'ing a. (*Slang*) Fascinating; extraordinarily funny.
Mil'ling s. Serrated edge of a coin.
Frill'ing s. Light material for making frills.
Thrill'ing a. Enthralling, intensely exciting.
Trill'ing s. One child of a triplet.
Still'ing s. Stand for a cask.

Quil'ling s. A narrow pleated border on lace, etc.
Will'ing a. Consenting; ready; spontaneous; prompt.
Ean'ling s. A new-born lamb.
Wean'ling s. A newly weaned child or animal.
Yean'ling s. A lamb, kid.
Twin'ling s. A twin lamb.
Fool'ing s. Buffoonery.
School'ing s. Instruction in school; reprimand.
Tool'ing s. Ornamental work done with a tool.
Sap'ling s. A young tree.
Strip'ling s. A youth.
Dump'ling s. A small boiled or baked pudding.
Fop'ling s. A petty fop.
Coup'ling s. Act of bringing or coming together; connexion; that which couples or unites things.
Dar'ling s. One dearly loved, a pet. a. Dearly beloved.
Shear'ling s. A sheep that has been but once sheared.
Pearl'ing s. Process of husking barley.
Year'ling s. An animal between one and two years old.
Spar'ling s. The smelt.
Star'ling s. A small, blackish, gregarious bird.
Sand'erling s. A small wading bird.
Un'derling s. An inferior assistant; a mean fellow.
Steer'ling s. A young or small steer.
Fin'gerling s. The young of salmon or trout.
Ster'ling a. Of standard value; genuine.
East'erling s. A native of eastern Germany or the Baltic.
Fos'terling s. A foster-child.
Curl'ing s. A game on ice in which smooth stones are slid at a mark.
Hurl'ing s. A game like football, formerly played in Cornwall.
Sling s. A stone-throwing appliance; a throw, stroke; a hanging bandage, rope with hooks, etc.; gin-toddy. v.t. To hurl, cast; to suspend by a sling.
Gos'ling s. A young goose.
Nurs'ling s. An infant.
Cat'ling s. A little cat; thin catgut.
Rat'ling s. A ratline.
Bee'tling a. Overhanging.
Gift'ling s. A trivial gift.
Wit'ling s. One with small wit.
Bant'ling s. A bastard.
Scant'ling s. Small piece of cut timber; sectional measurement of timber or stone; a small portion; a rough draft; trestle for a cask.
Mant'ling s. Material for mantles; heraldic scroll-work.
Grunt'ling s. A young pig.
Foo'tling a. (*Slang*) Piffling, pettifogging.
Startl'ing a. Alarming, surprising.
Priest'ling s. (*In contempt*) A priest.
Nest'ling s. A bird not old enough to leave the nest.
Wrestl'ing s. Act of one who wrestles.
Bris'tling s. A small sardine-like fish.
First'ling s. The earliest born; the first offspring (of animals, or of the season).
Rat'tling a. (*Slang*) Splendid, first-rate.
Tattl'ing s. Tattle. a. Chattering, gossiping.
Nettl'ing s. A process of joining two ropes end to end.
Rul'ing s. An authoritative decision. a. Predominant; controlling.
Brawl'ing a. (*Brawl*).
Bowl'ing s. Act of delivering the ball at cricket or of the bowl at bowls; a form of skittles.
Fowl'ing s. The sport of shooting or catching wild-fowl.
Howl'ing a. That howls; dreary; (*slang*) glaring.
Gray'ling s. A freshwater fish of the salmon family.
Daz'zling a. Excessively bright, glittering, confusing, etc.
Scream'ing a. Crying out with a scream; causing uproarious laughter.
Flam'ing a. Blazing; intensely hot or bright; vehement; florid.
Gloam'ing s. Evening twilight.
Fram'ing s. Framework, a frame; setting.
Reem'ing s. The opening of seams for caulking.
Seem'ing a. Apparent but not real; specious. s. Appearance; semblance.
Beseem'ing a. Becoming.
Schem'ing a. Plotting; given to intrigue.
Flem'ing s. A native of Flanders.
Pri'ming s. Powder used to ignite a charge; first colour laid on.
Lem'ming s. A rodent allied to the rat.
Brim'ming a. Overflowing.
Trim'ming s. Act of one who trims; that with which anything is trimmed; appendages.
Hum'ming a. That hums; strong (of ale, blows, etc.).
Drum'ming s. Act of beating a drum, tapping repeatedly with the fingers, etc.; sound made by the grouse and other birds.
Com'ing a. Future; approaching. s. Approach, arrival.
Becom'ing a. Suitable, befitting, appropriate.
Forthcom'ing a. Ready to appear; making appearance. s. A coming forth.
Incoming' a. Entering on possession. s. Entrance, arrival; income.
Short'coming s. Failure of performance of duty; a failing.
Blooming' a. Flowering, thriving in health, beauty and vigour; (*slang*) exceeding, very.
Farm'ing s. The business of cultivating land.
Charm'ing a. Bewitching, pleasurable.
Alar'ming a. Causing apprehension or fear.
Warm'ing s. (*Slang*) A thrashing.
Presum'ing a. Presumptuous.
Assu'ming a. (*Assume*).
Unassum'ing a. Retiring; modest.
Can'ing s. Castigation with a cave.
Mean'ing s. That which is meant; signification; purport. a. Significant.
Costean'ing s. A process by which miners seek lodes.
Car'avaning s. Living or travelling in a caravan.
Gar'dening s. Work in a garden; horticulture.
Green'ing s. Act of becoming green; a green variety of apple.
Queen'ing s. A variety of apple.
Overween'ing a. Arrogant; presumptuous. s. Excessive conceit.
Stiff'ening s. Anything used to give stiffness to.
Awak'ening s. An arising from sleep or indifference. a. Rousing.
Thick'ening s. That which thickens (especially liquids).
Op'ening a. Beginning. s. A place which is open, a gap; a beginning, prelude; act of making open; an opportunity.
Threat'ening a. Indicating a menace or impending evil; imminent.

Sweet'ening s. That which makes sweet or sweeter.
Whit'ening s. Act of making or state of becoming white; material for making white.
Fast'ening s. Act of making fast or secure; that with which anything is fastened.
Christ'ening s. Act of baptizing.
Leav'ening s. Leaven.
Rav'ening s. Eagerness for plunder.
E'vening s. The close of the day; the latter part, decline of life.
Design'ing a. Crafty, insidious, treacherous. s. The art of sketching out designs.
Complain'ing a. Querulous, grumbling.
Grain'ing s. Painting in imitation of wood; milling on a coin.
Train'ing s. Diet, exercises, etc.; for athletics; practice, exercise.
Entertain'ing a. Affording entertainment; diverting, amusing.
Fin'ing s. Process of refining, or of clarifying; material used to fine liquors.
Imag'ining s. A mere idea, a fantasy.
Lin'ing s. An inside covering; contents.
Adjoin'ing a. Next to, touching.
Groin'ing s. The intersecting of arches.
Pin'ing s. Wasting, languishing.
Damn'ing s. Involving damnation; cursing.
Win'ning a. Attractive, charming.
Cun'ning a. Skilful; knowing; astute, artful, crafty. s. Skill; artfulness, subtlety.
Gun'ning s. Game-shooting.
Run'ning s. Act of one who or that which runs; power or chance of winning a race, etc.; discharge from a sore. a. Kept for racing; discharging; following in succession.
Stun'ning a. (*Slang*) Splendid; ripping.
Reck'oning s. Act of one who reckons; calculation; adjustment of accounts.
Balloo'ning s. Aeronautics.
Reas'oning s. Act or process of exercising the faculty of reason; argumentation.
Sea'soning s. A relish; something added to give piquancy.
Learn'ing s. Act of learning; education; erudition.
Yearn'ing s. A longing desire for, tenderness towards. a. Longing.
Warn'ing s. Caution against danger, etc.; act of giving this; previous notice.
Concern'ing prep. With reference to.
Discern'ing a. Discriminating; acute. s. Discernment.
Horn'ing s. The appearance of the crescent moon.
Morn'ing s. The first part of the day; early part of a period, etc. a. Pertaining to or suitable for this.
Burn'ing a. Ardent; exciting; flagrant.
Heart'burning a. Causing jealousy, enmity, etc. s. Discontent, secret enmity.
Churn'ing s. Butter made at one operation.
Mourn'ing s. Lamentation; dress worn by mourners. a. Sorrowing; expressive of grief.
Turn'ing s. A turn, bend; a diverging road, place where it diverges; art or operation of working with a lathe.
Light'ning s. The electric flash that attends thunder.
Aw'ning s. A movable canvas shelter from sun or rain.
Dawn'ing s. Time of dawn, beginning.
Fawn'ing a. Courting servilely, cringing.
Yawn'ing a. Sleepy; slumbering, to gape.
Crown'ing a. Perfecting; final, highest.
Do'ing pres. p. (*Do*).
Misdo'ing s. A wrong done, fault, offence.
Go'ing s. Act of moving; departure; way; state of roads. a. In operation; existing, to be had.
Fore'going a. Preceding, previously mentioned.
In'going a. Entering. s. An entrance.
Out'going s. Departure; outlay, expenditure. a. Leaving.
Ping s. A short ringing sound.
Scrap'ing s. Something scraped off; (pl.) savings.
Deep'ing s. A fathom strip of twine netting for fishing-nets.
Keep'ing s. Action of guarding, preserving, etc.; care, custody; accord, congruity. a. That can be kept.
House'keeping s. Management of a household; domestic economy.
Sweep'ing a. Comprehensive.
Pi'ping a. Shrill, whistling, feeble. s. A whistling; covered cord for trimming, etc.; cord-like decoration; a system of pipes.
Gri'ping a. Grasping; extortionate; pinching the bowels.
Help'ing s. Portion of food served at table.
Pim'ping a. Small, puny, feeble.
Dump'ing s. Practice of exporting below cost-price.
Thump'ing a. Extraordinarily big, etc.; remarkable.
Lump'ing a. Large; plentiful.
Co'ping s. The highest course of a wall, parapet, etc., usually projecting.
Wal'loping (wol'-) s. A drubbing. a. (*Slang*) Whopping.
Strap'ping a. Big, strong, muscular.
Wrap'ping s. A wrapper; a wrap, shawl, etc.
Chip'ping s. A fragment chipped off.
Ship'ping s. Ships collectively, especially those of a port, country, etc.; tonnage.
Whip'ping s. A flogging; flagellation.
Clip'ping s. A piece clipped off. a. (*Slang*) Showy, first-rate.
Snip'ping s. A small bit; a fragment.
Rip'ping a. (*Slang*) Fine; first-rate.
Drip'ping s. A falling in drops; melted fat that falls from roasting meat.
Trip'ping s. Act of one who trips; a light dance.
Shop'ping s. Act of visiting shops for making purchases.
Whop'ping a. (*Slang*) Big; monstrous.
Top'ping a. (*Slang*) Excellent; first-rate.
Cup'ping s. Act of bleeding with a cupping-glass.
Carp'ing a. (*Carp*).
Rasp'ing a. Harsh, especially in sound.
Grasp'ing s. Avaricious; greedy of gain.
Lar'ruping s. (*Slang*) A thrashing.
Ring s. A circle, especially of gold for the finger; area for games, etc.; a group of persons; a metallic sound as of a bell. v.t. To cause to sound by striking; to encircle; to repeat loudly or earnestly. v.i. To sound, as a bell; to resound; to cause to be filled with report.
Dar'ing a. Courageous, fearless. s. Boldness; presumption; a method of catching birds.
Ear'ing s. A small line for fastening the sail to a yard, etc.
Bear'ing s. Deportment; situation with respect to something else; tendency; a charge on a shield; the part of an axle resting on supports.

Overbear'ing a. Imperious; domineering; dogmatical.
Forbear'ing a. Patient; long-suffering.
Endear'ing a. Making dear; exciting affection.
Gear'ing s. Working parts; tackle; train of toothed wheels, etc., for transmitting motion.
Hear'ing s. Faculty or act of perceiving sound; judicial trial; audience; reach of the ear.
Clear'ing s. Act or process of making clear; land cleared for cultivation.
Tear'ing a. (*Slang*) Furious, violent.
Sea'faring a. Following the business of a seaman.
Way'faring s. A journey, especially on foot. a. Travelling, passing.
Flar'ing a. Dazzling; gaudy.
Glar'ing a. Shining dazzlingly; staring; too conspicuous; notorious.
Roar'ing s. A loud, continuous sound. a. Shouting, boisterous; brisk, thriving.
Par'ing s. A piece pared off; rind.
Spar'ing a. Scarce, scanty; niggardly, chary.
Bring v.t. To convey or carry to, to fetch from.
Sa'cring s. Consecration.
Yeld'ring s. The yellow-hammer.
Consid'ering prep. Taking into account; making allowance for.
Bewil'dering a. Perplexing, confusing.
Ren'dering s. A return; translation; interpretation.
Thun'dering a. Emitting thunder or denunciations; (*slang*) remarkable. adv. Tremendously, remarkably.
Blun'dering a. (*Blunder*).
Or'dering s. Arrangement; disposition.
Bor'dering s. Border, edging.
Cheer'ing a. Bringing gladness.
Mountaineer'ing s. The sport of climbing mountains.
Engineer'ing s. Science of directing natural sources of power for use of man in construction of roads, etc., and in management of all prime movers.
Domineer'ing a. Tyrannizing, hectoring.
Privateer'ing s. Warlike proceedings, etc., of a privateer.
Of'fering s. That which is offered; an oblation.
Suf'fering s. The bearing of pain, etc.; pain endured; distress.
Fin'gering s. Act of touching with the fingers; manner of playing a keyed instrument; loose worsted.
Ling'ering a. Given to linger; protracted.
Gath'ering s. Act of assembling; an assemblage; a boil, abscess.
Ingath'ering s. Act or result of collecting or gathering.
Lath'ering s. (*Slang*) A flogging.
With'ering a. Such as to wither or blast.
Hank'ering s. Ardent or wistful desire; longing.
Bick'ering s. Quarrelling, petulant argument.
Glim'mering s. A glimmer, twinkle; an inkling.
Sum'mering s. An early variety of apple.
Trous'ering s. Material for trousers.
Cen'tering s. The frame on which an arch is constructed.
Quar'tering s. Assignment of tents or lodging for soldiers; the division of an heraldic shield.
Plas'tering s. Plaster-work; a covering of plaster.
West'ering a. Passing to the west (of the sun).
Rois'tering a. Blustering, turbulent.
Blus'tering a. (*Bluster*).
Bat'tering a. A violent assault.
Flat'tering a. Bestowing flattery; gratifying.
Smat'tering s. A slight superficial knowledge.
Let'tering s. Act of impressing or forming letters; letters formed; a title.
Persever'ing a. Given to persevere; constant in purpose.
Cov'ering s. That which covers; an envelope; protection.
Flow'ering a. That flowers; flowery.
Overpow'ering a. Excessive in degree or amount; irresistible.
Tow'ering (tou'-) a. Very high; extreme; violent.
Air'ing s. Exposure to air; an outdoor excursion.
Fair'ing s. A present purchased at a fair.
Despair'ing a. Hopeless, desperate.
Fir'ing s. Act of discharging fire-arms; fuel; act of treating with fire.
Tir'ing a. Wearying; exhausting the strength or patience.
Retir'ing a. Reserved, unobtrusive.
Bull'ring s. An arena for bull-baiting or bull-fighting.
Enring' v.t. To encircle; to adorn with a ring.
Bor'ing s. That which is bored; a trial shaft for a mine.
Shor'ing s. Timbers used as shores for a building, etc.
Floor'ing s. Material for floors; a platform.
Moor'ing s. The place at which a ship is made fast.
Doc'toring a. Medical treatment; adulteration, falsification.
Spring v.i. To leap, bound, dart; to warp; to arise, originate. v.t. To arouse; to crack; to propose suddenly. s. A leap; an elastic body; elasticity; a fountain, source; season when plants begin to grow; starting of a seam, etc.
Head'spring s. Source; origin.
Off'spring s. Progeny; descendants.
Main'spring s. Chief spring of a watch; main cause of any action.
Day'spring s. Dawn.
Ear'ring s. An ornamental pendant worn in the ear.
Her'ring s. A clupeoid marine food-fish.
Stir'ring a. Exciting, stimulating.
Recur'ring a. Being repeated.
String s. A small cord; a series; chord of a musical instrument. v.t. To furnish with or put on a string; to strip the strings from; to make tense.
Ham'string s. One of the tendons of the thigh. v.t. To lame by cutting this.
Lus'tring s. Lustrine.
Bow'string s. The string which bends the bow. v.t. To strangle with this.
Dur'ing prep. For the continuance of.
Endur'ing a. Bearing; lasting, permanent.
Non-jur'ing a. Not swearing allegiance.
Allur'ing a. (*Allure*).
Neigh'bouring (nā'-) a. Situated or living near.
Col'ouring s. Style of using colour colour applied; false show.
Fa'vouring a. Countenancing, supporting; resembling.
Fla'vouring s. Seasoning; that which flavours.
Devour'ing a. That devours; consuming, wasting.
Reassur'ing a. Restoring confidence.
Wring v.t. To twist, wrench, squeeze; to pervert; to strain out of position; to extort. s. A squeeze.

Banx'ring s. A Javanese tree-shrew.
Sing v.i. and t. To utter with musical modulations; to celebrate in song.
Ca'sing s. Outside covering.
Leas'ing s. Deceit, lying; a lie.
Pleas'ing a. Giving pleasure; gratifying; acceptable.
Chas'ing s. Engraved or embossed work on metal.
Prom'ising a. Giving grounds for good hopes; favourable.
Ris'ing s. An ascending; a revolt; a knoll.
En'terprising a. Bold to undertake; venturesome.
Surpris'ing a. Exciting surprise; extraordinary.
Upris'ing s. Act of rising up; a rebellion.
Los'ing a. Bringing or causing loss.
No'sing s. The prominent edge of a step, etc.; prying.
Impos'ing a. Impressive; majestic.
Cours'ing s. Act or sport of hunting hares with greyhounds.
Pass'ing a. Departing, going by; transient. adv. Exceedingly.
Surpass'ing a. Very excellent.
Embar'rassing a. Causing difficulties; perplexing, worrying.
Bless'ing s. A means of happiness; that which promotes welfare; a benediction.
Dress'ing s. Act of one who dresses; application to a wound, etc.; condiment, seasoning; the finish of linen, silk, etc.; manure.
Press'ing a. Important; urgent, importunate.
Depress'ing a. Dispiriting, disheartening.
Distress'ing a. Inflicting, indicating, or arising from distress.
Prepossess'ing a. Biasing; attractive, charming.
Mis'sing a. Lost, wanting, absent.
Embos'sing a. Act of making figures in relief.
Gloss'ing s. Preparation of silk thread so as to make it glossy.
Cross'ing s. Act of one who or that which crosses; place where passengers may cross; act of interbreeding.
Mus'ing s. Meditation.
Amus'ing a. Causing mirth or diversion.
Hous'ing s. Action of the verb "to house"; a cloth for covering horses.
Rous'ing a. Having power to excite; astonishing.
Ting s. A sharp sound as of a bell. v.i. To make this.
Ba'ting prep. With the exception of.
Intox'icating a. Tending to intoxicate; causing intoxication.
Accom'modating a. Obliging; adaptable.
Beat'ing s. A castigation.
Heat'ing a. Promoting warmth; exciting.
Nau'seating a. Causing nausea.
Excru'ciating a. Extremely painful.
Humil'iating a. Tending to humiliate; mortifying.
Des'olating a. Ruining, ravaging.
Plat'ing s. Act of coating with silver or gold, etc.; a thin coating of metal.
Slat'ing s. Act of tiling with slates; a scolding.
Cir'culating a. Recurring, current.
Lan'cinating a. Cutting, darting (of pain).
Fas'cinating a. Irresistibly charming; bewitching.
Discrim'inating a. Distinctive; discerning.
Ful'minating a. Thundering, explosive.
Al'ternating a. Changing successively or in turns.
Coat'ing s. A covering, layer; material for coats.
Float'ing a. Resting on the surface of a fluid; unattached; not invested; fluctuating.
Rat'ing s. Act of fixing a rate; rate fixed; class or grade of a seaman, or those in one of these.
Grat'ing a. Harsh, irritating. s. A frame work or lattice of parallel or crossed bars.
Pene'trating a. Sharp, piercing; discerning.
Insin'uating a. Given to or characterized by insinuation; insinuative.
Fluc'tuating a. Wavering; unsteady.
Ag'gravating a. Exasperating, annoying.
Cap'tivating a. Enticing, seductive.
Ac'ting a. Doing the duties of another. s. Art of performing on the stage.
Attrac'ting a. (*Attract*).
Exac'ting a. Severe in demand; urgently requiring.
Affec'ting a. Pathetic, moving.
Respect'ing prep. In regard to; in respect of.
Non-conduct'ing a. Not conducting heat or electricity.
Sheet'ing s. Cloth for sheets.
Fleet'ing a. Passing quickly, transient.
Meet'ing s. A coming together, assembly; persons assembled.
Greet'ing s. Act of welcoming; a salutation.
Sweet'ing s. A sweet apple; a darling.
Jack'eting s. (*Slang*) A thrashing.
Blank'eting s. Material for blankets; blankets collectively.
Junk'eting s. Festivity, revelry.
Car'peting s. Stuff of which carpets are made; carpets in general; (*colloquial*) a slating.
Rus'seting s. A russet apple.
Vel'veting s. The nap of velvet; velvet goods.
Shaft'ing s. System of shafts, pulleys, etc., for transmission of power.
Shop'lifting s. Larceny committed in a shop.
Yacht'ing (yot'-) s. Sailing or racing for pleasure in a yacht.
Slight'ing a. Casting scorn or a slight on.
Bi'ting a. Sharp, sarcastic.
Exci'ting a. Calling or rousing into action; producing excitement.
Whit'ing s. Fine chalk prepared for whitening. etc.; a marine food-fish.
Writ'ing s. Anything written; an inscription, literary composition, legal document.
Invit'ing a. Seductive; attractive.
Salt'ing s. Application of salt for preservation.
Bel'ting s. Material for belts for machinery.
Quilt'ing s. Act of making a quilt; material for quilts.
Revolt'ing a. Disgusting; horrible.
Insult'ing a. Containing or conveying insult.
Consul'ting a. Giving advice; used for consultations.
Cant'ing a. Whining, hypocritical. s. Cant.
Enchant'ing a. Charming, ravishing.
Want'ing (wŏnt'-) a. Absent, deficient; remiss. prep. Without.
Paint'ing s. Act, art or practice of representing objects by means of colours. Vivid description in words; thing painted; a picture.
Point'ing s. The filling of joints in brickwork, etc.
Print'ing s. Act, art, or practice of impressing letters, etc., on paper, etc.; typography.
Haunt'ing a. Persistent; recurring in an irritating way.
Bunt'ing s. A finch-like bird; material for making flags; flags collectively.
Hunt'ing s. The chase. a. Pertaining to or given to this.

Mount'ing s. That in which anything is mounted or set off; trimming, setting.
Wains'coting s. Wainscot; material for this.
Free'booting a. Pertaining to freebooters or freebootery.
Foot'ing s. Place for standing; firm foundation; established place; tread; basis.
Shoot'ing s. Act of discharging fire-arms, etc.; a sporting estate or right to shoot game on this.
Excep'ting prep. With rejection of; excluding.
Part'ing s. Act of dividing; a division; thing divided; dividing line; a separation.
Divert'ing a. Entertaining, amusing.
Shirt'ing s. Material for shirts.
Skirt'ing s. Board running round bottom of wall of a room, etc.
Sting v.t. To wound with a sting; to cause acute pain to. s. A sharp-pointed, poison-bearing organ; the thrust of this, pain caused by or as by this.
Cas'ting s. A metal cast, anything formed by founding.
East'ing s. Distance travelled at sea in an easterly direction.
Fast'ing s. Religious abstinence from food.
Hast'ing a. Hurrying; maturing early. s. An early kind of pea.
Last'ing a. Permanent; durable. s. A woollen stuff used for making shoes.
Bal'lasting s. Ballast.
Everlast'ing a. Eternal, immortal; continuing indefinitely. s. Eternity; a flower which retains its colour for long after plucking.
Coasting' a. Applied to vessels that ply along the coast, to trade between ports in the same country, etc.
In'teresting a. Arousing or engaging the attention or curiosity.
Vest'ing s. Material for vests.
West'ing s. Distance travelled or deviation westward.
Hos'ting s. A foray, military expedition.
Frost'ing s. A composition resembling hoar-frost for covering cakes.
Exhaust'ing a. Tending to exhaust or completely tire out.
Disgust'ing a. Provoking disgust, nasty, nauseous.
Bat'ting s. Action of the verb "to bat"; cotton or wool in sheets.
Plat'ting s. Slips of plaited straw, etc., for hat-making.
Mat'ting a. Material for mats; mats collectively.
Tat'ting s. A kind of knotted lace-work.
Par'getting s. Decorative plaster-work.
Net'ting s. Netted fabric.
Jen'netting s. An early variety of apple.
Ret'ting s. Act or process of steeping flax to loosen the fibre.
Set'ting s. Action of the verb "to set"; that in which something is set; music set for certain words.
Beset'ting a. Habitually or constantly tempting, attacking, etc.
Wet'ting s. A drenching, soaking.
Fit'ting a. Appropriate, right, proper. s. Act of making fit.
Befit'ting a. Suitable, becoming.
Knit'ting s. Formation of fabric by knitting; fabric formed.
Sit'ting s. A session; period of this; an allotted seat; set of eggs for incubation.
Witt'ing a. Knowing; with knowledge.
Unwit'ting a. Not knowing; unconscious.
Twit'ting s. An upraiding, taunt.
Jot'ting s. A memorandum.
Cut'ting a. Serving to cut; sharp-edged; sarcastic, bitter. s. A piece cut off or out; an incision, excavation; a twig.
Flut'ing s. A furrow; fluted work; sound like that of a flute.
Out'ing s. An excursion, trip.
Grout'ing s. Mortar used in the joints of masonry, etc.; act or process of filling with this.
Embogu'ing s. A river-mouth.
Ensu'ing a. Coming next after.
Shav'ing s. A thin slice.
Pa'ving s. Pavement.
Rav'ing a. Mad, furious. s. Wild talk, gesticulation, etc.
Crav'ing s. A longing or strong desire for.
Engrav'ing s. Act or art of cutting figures, etc., on wood, stone, or metal; that which is engraved; an impression or print from this.
Sav'ing a. Economical, frugal; expressing reservation. s. What is saved. prep. Excepting; with due respect to.
Forgiv'ing a. Merciful; disposed to forgive.
Misgiv'ing s. A failure of confidence; doubt.
Thanks'giving s. Act of returning thanks; words expressing this; a thank-offering.
Liv'ing a. Having life; in use or action. s. Means or manner of subsistence; a benefice.
Lov'ing a. Fond, affectionate; expressing love.
Glov'ing s. Occupation of making gloves.
Mov'ing a. Causing or in motion; persuading; pathetic.
Shrov'ing s. The festivities just before Lent.
Observ'ing a. Giving particular attention; attentive.
Deserv'ing a. Merited, meritorious. s. Act or state of meriting.
Wing s. Limb of a bird or insect by which it flies; side of a building; side division of an army, etc. v.t. To furnish with wings; to wound in the wing; to traverse by flying. v.i. To fly.
Draw'ing s. Action of "to draw"; a sketch or delineation in pencil, crayon, etc.; distribution of prizes in a lottery, etc.
Red'wing s. A bird of the thrush family.
Sew'ing (sō'-) s. That which is sewed; stitches made.
Ow'ing a. Due as a debt; ascribable; on account of.
Low'ing s. The mooing of a cow.
Flow'ing a. Moving as a stream; copious; fluent; waving.
Follow'ing s. A body of adherents. a. Coming next after.
Know'ing a. Experienced; cunning, wide-awake; smart.
Lap'wing s. A bird of the plover family.
Swing v.t. and i. To sway, oscillate, move when suspended; to be hanged. s. Act of swinging; oscillation; apparatus for swinging; free course.
Bees'wing s. The second crust formed in long-kept wine.
Wax'wing s. A bird having horny appendages like red sealing-wax on the secondaries of the wings.

Relax'ing a. Not bracing (of climate).
Box'ing s. Art and practice of fighting with the fists.
May'ing s. Gathering of may, etc., on May-day.
Fray'ing s. The velvet on a deer's horns.
Say'ing s. That which is said; an expression, proverb.
Sooth'saying s. The foretelling of events.
Gainsay'ing s. Contradiction, opposition.
Dy'ing a. About to die, perishing; mortal, perishable; associated with death. s. Death; act of fading away.
Undy'ing a. Immortal; unceasing; imperishable.
Survey'ing s. Branch of mathematics by which measurement of areas and their delineation is effected.
Grat'ifying a. Pleasing; affording satisfaction.
Ly'ing pres. part. (*Lie*). s. Habit of telling lies; falsification; being recumbent. a. Telling lies; false.
Out'lying a. At a distance from the main body; remote.
Annoy'ing a. (*Annoy*).
Cry'ing a. Clamant; calling for vengeance or notice.
Wor'rying (wŭr'-) a. Causing worry or anxiety.
Haz'ing s. Practical jokes, especially of a disagreeable kind.
Blaz'ing a. Radiant, lustrous; very evident.
Glaz'ing s. Act or art of a glazer; glaze; enamel.
Ama'zing a. Extraordinary, astonishing, unexpected.
Freez'ing a. Very cold; distant, stand-offish.
Gor'mandizing s. Gluttony.
Demor'alizing a. Tending to destroy the morals of.
Tan'talizing a. Teasing, provoking.
Siz'ing s. Act of sorting or arranging by size; a weak kind of glue.
Ding'dong s. The sound of a bell; a jingle; a monotonous sound.
Quan'dong s. A small Australian tree; its edible fruit.
Gong s. A one-ended metallic drum.
Du'gong s. An herbivorous, aquatic mammal of Indian seas.
Hong s. A foreign warehouse in China.
Souchong' s. A black tea from China.
Thong s. A strap or string of leather. v.t. To furnish, fasten, or thrash with this.
Diph'thong s. A union of two vowels in one sound; a digraph.
Triph'thong s. Combination of three vowels to form one sound; a trigraph.
Mon'ophthong s. A single uncompounded vowel sound; two vowels pronounced as one.
Long a. Not short; reaching to a great distance or extent; protracted; prolix; late. s. Something that is long. adv. To a great extent, to a distant point. v.i. To desire earnestly.
-long suff. Forming adverbs.
Along' adv. In a line with, lengthwise; onward; together. prep. Through the length.
Kalong' s. The Malayan flying-fox.
Ob'long a. Longer than broad. s. An oblong figure or thing.
Head'long adv. Head-first; rashly, violently. a. Steep; precipitate; thoughtless.
End'long adv. Lengthwise; straight along.
Belong' v.i. To be the property of; appertain to.
Side'long a. Oblique. adv. Laterally, obliquely.
Live'long a. Lasting through life; tedious.
Flong s. Paper used as a mould in stereo typing.
Cach'olong s. A variety of opal.
Prolong' v.t. To lengthen, especially in time; to protract, delay.
Fur'long s. An eighth of a mile; 220 yards.
Among' prep. Mingled or associated with.
Scup'pernong s. An American variety of muscadine.
Ping'-pong s. Table-tennis.
Throng s. A crowd.
Prong s. A pointed projection; a spike of a fork.
Strong a. Having power; firm; robust; vigorous; effectual; forcible.
Head'strong a. Unrestrained, stubborn, obstinate.
Wrong a. Not right, fit, according to rule, etc.; incorrect. s. Anything that is not right; an injury, injustice. adv. Amiss; erroneously. v.t. To treat with injustice; to injure.
Song s. That which is sung; vocal music; poetry; a trifle.
Sing'song s. An impromptu concert; monotonous rhythm. a. Done in monotone or monotonously.
E'vensong s. Evening worship; the time for this.
Bil'tong s. Strips of sun-dried buffalo meat.
Bung s. A stopper for a barrel. v.t. To stop up a vent.
Dung s. The excrement of animals; manure. v.t. To manure. v.i. To void excrement.
Fung s. A fabulous Chinese bird; a phœnix.
Hung past (*Hang*).
Un'derhung a. Projecting (of the lower jaw).
Lung s. One of the pair of respiratory organs.
Clung past and p.p. (*Cling*).
Flung past and past part. (*Fling*).
Slung past and past part. (*Sling*).
Young (yŭng) a. Being in the early stage of life; youthful; pertaining to youth; inexperienced. s. The offspring of an animal.
Pung s. A toboggan, sled.
Rung s. A step of a ladder, cross-bar of a chair. past and past part. (*Ring*).
Sprung a. (*Slang*) Slightly intoxicated. past part. (*Spring*).
Strung past and past part. (*String*).
Overstrung' a. Strained too much; too highly strung.
Wrung past and past part. (*Wring*).
Sung past part. (*Sing*).
Swung past (*Swing*).
Bog s. A morass, quagmire. v.t. To whelm in mud and mire.
Embog' v.t. To plunge into or encumber in a bog.
Cog v.i. To wheedle, deceive. v.t. To deceive anybody; to furnish with cogs. s. A tooth on a wheel for transmitting motion.
Incog' a. and adv. Incognito.
Dog s. A member of a carnivorous family of quadrupeds, the greater part of which is domesticated; a gay young spark; a mean fellow. v.t. To follow closely; to worry with importunity.
Bull'dog s. A strong, thick-set English dog.
Ban'dog s. A fierce watch-dog.

Fog s. A thick mist, dense vapour; after-grass. v.t. To becloud; to bewilder. v.i. To become foggy.
Befog' v.t. To involve in obscurity, to confuse.
Pet'tifog v.i. To do small or mean business as a lawyer; to use chicanery.
Agog' adv. In a state of desire or expectancy.
Hog s. A castrated boar; a glutton; a dirty fellow. v.t. To cut short, especially a horse's tail or mane. v.i. To bend, as a ship's bottom.
Hedge'hog s. A small insectivorous mammal covered with spines.
Jog v.t. To push lightly; to give notice thus. v.i. To trot or travel slowly. s. A push, shake.
Log s. A bulky piece of timber; contrivance for ascertaining rate of ship's progress; record of this.
Clog s. An impediment, hindrance; a shoe with a wooden sole. v.t. To encumber, obstruct, hamper. v.i. To become loaded, impeded, or stopped up.
Flog v.t. To beat with a rod, whip, etc.; to lash.
Slog v.t. and i. To hit hard and at random. s. Such a stroke.
Put'log s. Short piece of timber for supporting floor of a scaffold.
Nog s. A wooden pin or brick; a strong ale; a noggin.
Cran'nog s. A prehistoric lake-dwelling.
Dan'nebrog s. The national flag of Denmark.
Frog s. A small amphibious animal; a spindle-shaped button; the loop of a scabbard; a tender substance in a horse's sole.
Grog s. Rum or other spirit with water.
Prog s. (*Slang*) Food, especially for a journey; a University proctor. v.t. To proctorize.
Tog v.t. To dress up.
Tautog' s. The American blackfish.
Gol'liwog s. A grotesque doll with black face and frizzy hair.
Pol'liwog s. A tadpole.
Her'zog s. German title corresponding to "Duke."
Py'garg s. The osprey.
Erg s. The unit of energy or work.
Ice'berg s. A large, floating mass of ice.
Burg s. A township, a fortress.
Simurg' s. An enormous bird of Persian legend.
Bourg s. A town built round a castle.
Fau'bourg s. A suburb.
Quahaug (quaw'hog) s. A large N. American clam.
Bug s. An evil-smelling insect.
Hum'bug s. An imposition, hoax; a deceiver. int. Nonsense! v.t. To impose upon, hoax; to cajole.
Dug s. The teat of a breast; past and past part. (*Dig*).
Fug s. Stuffiness, frowsiness.
Hug v.t. To embrace closely; to sail near the coast. s. A close embrace; a grip in wrestling.
Thug s. One of a sect of Indian robbers and assassins; a cut-throat.
Bun'ny-hug s. A dance in which the partners embrace.
Jug s. A small vessel with a handle for holding liquors; (*slang*) a prison. v.t. To stew or put in a jug.
Lug v.t. To haul, drag. s. A tug; the ear; a projecting part; a large marine worm.
Plug s. Anything used to stop a hole; a bung; a quid of tobacco. v.t. To stop with a plug; (*slang*) to work hard at.
Slug s. A shell-less snail destructive to plants; a roughly shaped bullet, strip of type-metal.
Mug s. A cylindrical cup with no foot; (*slang*) the face; a fool, one easily duped. v.i. and t. (*slang*) to study hard, to get up a subject.
Smug a. Neat, spruce; affectedly nice; pedantic. s. A precise, pedantic, self-satisfied person; one who refuses to join in sport.
Snug a. Cosy, warm; compact.
Pug s. A small variety of dog; a monkey; clay for bricks.
Rug s. A heavy, woollen coverlet, mat, etc.
Drug s. A medicine, or ingredient of medicines; anything for which the sale is small. v.t. To season with drugs; to introduce a narcotic into; to dose to excess with drugs.
Shrug v.i. and t. To draw up or contract the shoulders to express dislike, etc. s. This gesture.
Trug s. A wooden basket, milkpail, etc.; a hod.
Tug v.t. and i. To pull with effort, to haul along, struggle. s. A violent pull; a steam-boat for towing.
Ah int.
Bah int.
Mas'tabah s. An early form of Egyptian tomb.
Hagga'dah s. The legendary, homiletic part of the Talmud.
Whid'ah s. A small W. African weaver-bird.
Veran'dah s. (*Veranda*).
Pur'dah s. Curtain of women's apartments in the East.
How'dah s. A canopied seat carried by an elephant.
O'beah s. Witchcraft practised in W. Africa and the W. Indies.
Loo'fah s. Brush, etc., made from a fibrous sponge-gourd.
Halak'hah s. The Rabbinical commentary on the Mosaic law.
E'phah s. A Hebrew measure (about 1½ bushels).
Shah s. The king of Persia.
Pad'ishah s. Official title of the Shah of Persia and other Eastern potentates.
Shi'ah (shē'-) s. A Shüte.
Par'iah s. One belonging to the lowest caste in S. India; an outcast.
Messi'ah s. Christ; the Anointed One.
Jah s. One of the Hebrew names of God.
Ra'jah s. A native Indian prince; a Hindu of high rank.
Mahara'jah s. An Indian native prince.
Hallelu'jah s. A Hebrew ascription of praise to God.
Be'kah s. A Hebrew weight (¼ oz.).
Lun'kah s. A strong Indian cheroot.
Pun'kah s. A large fan suspended from above.
Hook'ah s. A tobacco-pipe in which the smoke passes through water.
Se'lah s. A word of doubtful meaning occurring in the Psalms.
Deli'lah s. A seductive woman.
Al'lah s. The Mohammedan title of the Deity.
Wal'lah (wol'la) s. Anyone employed on business specified; a fellow (esp. in India).

Fel'lah s. An Egyptian peasant.
Bismil'lah int. In the name of Allah !
Mul'lah s. A Mohammedan title for persons learned in the Koran, etc.
Nul'lah s. A ravine or gully in India.
Koo'lah s. A small Australian marsupial.
Al'mah s. An Egyptian dancing-girl.
Sheki'nah s. The visible presence of Jehovah in the Jewish Temple.
Do'nah s. (*Slang*) A sweetheart, fancy-woman.
My'nah s. A starling of S.E. Asia.
Pah int. Expressing disgust.
O'pah s. A brilliantly coloured variety of mackerel.
Massor'ah s. A body of mediæval Rabbinical dissertations on the text of the Scriptures.
Tor'ah s. The will of God as revealed to Moses.
Ar'rah int.
Jar'rah s. The W. Australian mahogany gum-tree.
Sir'rah s. Reproachful or contemptuous form of address to men.
Hurrah' int. Exclamation of joy or applause.
Sur'ah s. A chapter of the Koran; a soft silk fabric.
Chee'tah s. The Indian hunting-leopard.
Shit'tah s. Hebrew name of a tree, probably the acacia.
Jeho'vah s. The most sacred of the Hebrew names for God.
Yah int. Exclamation of contempt or derision.
Ay'ah s. A Hindu nursemaid.
Ray'ah (rī'a) s. A non-Moslem subject of Turkey.
Dahabee'yah s. A travelling house-boat on the Nile.
Gun'yah s. A native Australian hut.
Each a. and pron. Every one considered separately.
Beach s. The sea-shore, the coast. v.t. To run upon a beach.
Leach v.t. To wash by letting liquid slowly pass through. v.i. To part with soluble constituents by percolation. s. A tub or chamber for leaching ashes, bark, etc.; solution obtained by leaching.
Bleach v.t. To whiten by removing the original colour.
Pleach v.t. To lace branches together, to entwine.
Peach s. A well-known tree of the almond family, and its fruit. v.i. (*Slang*) To inform against, turn informer.
Impeach' v.t. To censure, charge, arraign.
Reach v.t. To extend, arrive; to attain, penetrate to. v.i. To stretch out the hand to touch; to make efforts to attain. s. Act or power of extending to ; scope; straight stretch of river.
Breach s. An opening, rent, gap; a breaking of a law, etc.; a quarrel. v.t. To break the walls of.
Preach v.i. To deliver a sermon, give earnest advice. v.t. To deliver in public.
Overreach' v.t. To reach or extend beyond; to outwit.
Outreach' v.t. To reach or extend beyond.
Teach v.t. To impart the knowledge of; to instruct, educate, counsel.
Wal'lach (wol'ak) s. A Wallachian.
Stom'ach (stŭm'ak) s. A membranous sac, the organ of digestion. v.t. To put up with, resent.
Sas'senach s. An Englishman.
Spin'ach s. A succulent annual herb cooked for food.
Can'nach s. (*Scot.*) The cotton-grass.
Cor'onach s. A Highland or Irish dirge, a lament.
Coach s. A large, closed four-wheeled passenger vehicle; a railway carriage; a tutor, athletic trainer. v.t. To convey by coach; to prepare for an examination, race, etc.
Slow'coach s. A dull, dilatory or inactive person.
Loach s. A fish of the carp family.
Poach v.t. To boil eggs divested of shell; to take game illegally; to trample. v.i. To trespass, especially for purpose of stealing game; to plunder; to intrude unfairly; to become swampy.
Roach s. A small freshwater fish; upward curve in foot of a square sail.
Broach v.t. To pierce, to start a subject.
Abroach' adv. Pierced; allowing liquor to run out freely.
Encroach' v.i. To advance by stealth, to infringe.
Cock'roach s. The black-beetle.
Reproach' v.t. To upbraid, rebuke. s. Censure; source of blame; disgrace.
Approach' v.t. To draw near, to approximate. s. An avenue, path; act of drawing near.
Rach (rătch) s. A hunting-dog.
San'darach s. A whitish variety of resin.
Lar'ach s. The site of an ancient Gaelic village.
Brach s. A female hound.
Am'phibrach s. A foot of three syllables, one long between shorts.
Tri'brach s. Metrical foot of three shorts.
Cet'erach s. A genus of ferns.
Or'ach s. The mountain-spinach.
Cur'rach s. A coracle, a light skiff.
Detach' v.t. To disconnect, sever, separate.
Attach' v.t. To bind, fasten; to arrest, lay hold of. v.i. To adhere.
Beech s. A nut-bearing forest tree.
Leech s. A suctorial aquatic annelid; a doctor; an extortioner; the perpendicular or after edge of a sail. v.t. and i. To apply leeches to.
Speech s. Faculty of speaking; that which is spoken; talk; a saying; an oration.
Breech s. Lower part of body; club end of a gun. v.t. To put into breeches.
Screech v.i. To scream out or utter shrilly; to shriek. s. A harsh, shrill cry.
Beseech' v.t. To implore, entreat.
Crom'lech s. A prehistoric stone monument.
Czech s. The Bohemian language. a. Bohemian.
Quaich s. (*Scot.*) A metal-bound wooden cup.
Chich s. A dwarf pea.
Which pron. and a., interrog. and rel.
Lich s. A corpse.
Rich a. Wealthy; valuable; fertile; mellow; highly flavoured.
Enrich' v.t. To make rich, to adorn; to fertilize.
Os'trich s. A large African bird with valuable feathers.
Stich (stik) s. A metrical line; a line from the Bible.
Tet'rastich s. A stanza, epigram, etc., of four lines.

Oc'tastich s. A stanza of eight lines.
Pent'astich s. A verse composition of five lines.
Hep'tastich s. A poem of seven verses.
Hex'astich s. A poem or extract of six lines or verses.
Dis'tich s. A couplet of verse.
Hem'istich s. An uncompleted verse; half a verse.
Tris'tich (-tik) s. A set of three metrical lines.
Mon'ostich s. A single metrical line complete in itself.
Cesar'evich s. The eldest son of a tzar.
Tsar'evich s. A son of a tsar.
Sand'wich s. Two slices of bread with meat, etc., between them.
Belch v.i. To eject wind from the stomach.
Squelch v.t. To crush, extinguish. s. A heavy blow.
Welch (*see* WELSH).
Filch v.t. To steal, pilfer.
Milch a. Giving milk; kept for milking.
Pilch s. A wrapper for an infant.
Gulch s. A deep ravine or water-course.
Mulch s. Rotting straw, etc., strewn over plants for protection. v.t. To cover with this.
Ganch v.t. To execute by impaling.
Blanch v.t. and i. To change to white, to whiten.
Planch s. A slab, flat piece of stone. v.t. To cover with planks, to floor.
Ranch s. A cattle- or horse-raising farm in America. v.i. To farm or work on a ranch.
Branch s. A limb; bough of a tree; a part diverging. v.i. To spread or divide in branches or subdivisions.
Lamel'libranch s. A mollusc having two pairs of gills.
Elas'mobranch s. One of a class of fishes having plate-like gills (sharks, rays, etc.).
Scranch v.t. To grind with the teeth.
Stanch v.t. To stop the flow of (blood). a. Staunch.
Bench s. A table for working at; a long seat; the body of judges.
Disbench' v.t. To deprive a bencher of his status.
Blench v.i. To shrink, to start back.
Clench v.t. To rivet; to grasp or fix firmly.
Elench' s. An elenchus.
Flench v.t. To skin or strip the blubber from (a whale, etc.).
Drench v.t. To wet thoroughly, soak; to purge violently; to give a horse a draught. s. A soaking; medicine for horses or cattle.
French a. Pertaining to France or its people. s. The inhabitants of France; their language.
Trench s. A long narrow ditch or military excavation. v.t. To cut a trench or trenches in. v.i. To encroach.
Retrench' v.t. To cut down, curtail, abridge; to furnish with a retrenchment. v.i. To live at less expense.
Entrench' v.t. To surround with or defend with trenches; to encroach upon.
Wrench v.t. To twist or force by violence; to strain. s. A violent twisting pull; a sprain; implement for turning bolts, etc.
Tench s. A fish of the carp family.
Stench s. A malodorous or fetid smell.
Quench v.t. To extinguish; to put an end to; to stifle.
Wench s. A young woman (especially depreciatively).
Inch s. One-twelfth of a foot; (*Scot.*) an island.
Cinch s. A broad saddle-girth; (*slang*) a sure hold, a certainty.
Finch s. A small singing bird.
Gold'finch s. A song-bird with bright yellow on the wings.
Chaf'finch s. A small English song-bird.
Bull'finch s. A small British bird.
Green'finch s. A common singing-bird.
Haw'finch s. The common grosbeak.
Chinch s. A bed-bug.
Linch s. A ledge, ridge; unploughed strip between fields.
Clinch v.t. To clench a nail, drive home a statement, etc., fasten a rope. s. Act of clinching; a grip; a pun.
Flinch v.i. To shrink, withdraw; to flench (a whale).
Pinch v.t. To squeeze, especially between the fingers, to nip; to afflict, distress; (*slang*) to steal. v.i. To press painfully; to bear hard; to be covetous. s. A nip, close compression with the fingers; as much as can be taken between finger and thumb; distress, difficulty, straits.
Squinch s. An arch across an angle to support a superimposed structure.
Winch s. A windlass; crank for turning an axle.
Conch (konk) s. A marine shell; a trumpet resembling such in shape.
Haunch s. The thigh, hip, flank; shoulder of an arch.
Launch v.t. To throw, hurl forth; to set going; to cause to slide into water. v.i. To glide; to enter a new sphere of activity, etc.; to expatiate. s. Act or process of launching a ship; a warship's largest boat; a pleasure-boat.
Paunch s. The belly, abdomen; the first stomach of a ruminant.
Staunch a. Firm; steadfast; constant and zealous.
Bunch s. A collection, cluster, or tuft, as of flowers, etc. v.t. To form or gather in a bunch. v.i. To grow in a bunch.
Hunch s. A hump, lump; a jerk. v.t. To arch, as the back; to shove, especially with the elbow.
Lunch s. Light meal between breakfast and dinner. v.i. To eat lunch.
Clunch s. A lump; hard chalky stone.
Munch v.t. and i. To chew audibly or with much jaw-movement.
Punch s. A buffoon; a fat, short-legged man or horse; a spirituous liquor; a blow; instrument for making holes. v.t. To perforate; to hit with the fist.
Crunch v.t. To grind with the teeth, crush with the foot.
Lynch v.t. To judge and execute by mob-law.
Loch s. (*Scot.*) A lake; a land-locked arm of the sea
Gral'loch v.t. To disembowel a deer. s. The offal of a deer.
E'poch s. A fixed point of time; a period; a date.
Pi'broch (pē'-) s. A form of bagpipe music.
Arch s. Part of a circle or ellipse, an arc. a. Chief; lively, waggish. v.t. To form or shape as an arch.

Search v.t. To look for; to examine, investigate. v.i. To inquire.
Research' s. Diligent inquiry or examination; original study. v.t. To search and examine diligently or again.
Ol'igarch s. One of those constituting an oligarchy.
Chil'iarch s. A commander of a thousand men.
Ma'triarch s. A female head of a primitive tribe.
Pa'triarch s. The head of a race, tribe, or family; a dignitary of the Orthodox Church superior to an archbishop; a venerable old man.
Eccle'siarch s. A ruler of the church.
Her'esiarch s. A leading heretic.
Sympo'siarch s. The leader of a feast; toast-master.
Larch s. A coniferous tree.
Phy'larch s. The chief of a clan, especially in ancient Greece.
March s. Military or stately walk; distance traversed; musical composition for marching to; a frontier; third month of the year. v.i. To move in order or in a stately manner; to border on.
Pol'emarch (-mark) s. An ancient Athenian magistrate.
Nom'arch s. A ruler of a nome or nomarchy.
Countermarch' v.i. To march back or in reverse order. s. Action of counter-marching; change in position of the wings or face of a battalion.
Outmarch' v.t. To march faster than, leave behind.
An'arch s. A leader of revolt.
Inarch' v.t. To graft by inserting a scion without separating it from its parent tree.
Mon'arch s. A sole ruler; a sovereign; a chief of its class.
Parch v.t. and i. To scorch or be scorched; to shrivel with heat.
Ep'arch s. Governor of an eparchy; a Russian bishop.
Top'arch s. A petty king in ancient Greece.
Hi'erarch s. A chief priest, prelate, etc.
Tri'erarch s. Captain of an Athenian trireme.
Overarch' v.t. and i. To cover with or hang over like an arch.
Tet'rarch s. An ancient Roman governor of the fourth part of a province.
Starch s. A white, granular, vegetable substance forming glucose, etc., and used for stiffening linen, etc. a. Stiff, prim. v.t. To stiffen with starch.
Ex'arch s. A governor, viceroy; a superior bishop.
Perch s. A spiny, freshwater fish; a pole, rod, roost for fowls; 5½ yards. v.i. and t. To light (of birds) or place on a perch, branch, etc.
Birch s. A tree; a switch made from its twigs. v.t. To castigate with a birch.
Smirch v.t. To stain, besmear, defile.
Besmirch' v.t. To sully, soil.
Scorch v.t. To parch, shrivel, burn superficially. v.i. To be hot enough to burn a surface; to be very hot or dried up; (*slang*) to cycle, etc., at excessive speed. s. Mark made by scorching.
Porch s. A covered approach or entrance.
Torch s. A light for carrying; a flambeau.
Curch s. A kerchief.
Church s. A building consecrated for Christian worship; the collective body or a particular body of Christians; the clergy; ecclesiastical authority. v.t. To return thanks publicly in church.
Lurch s. Losing position in certain card-games; a sideways roll, stagger. v.i. To roll suddenly to one side.
Pasch s. The Passover, Easter.
Romansch' s. The language of the Grisons.
Stellenbosch' v.t. To relieve one of his command by giving him an appointment of less responsibility.
Kirsch s. Kirschwasser.
Batch s. The bread made at one baking the whole lot.
Catch v.t. To seize, entangle, overtake. v.i. To be entangled; to spread by infection. s. Act of seizing; that which catches or is caught; gain; a singing-round.
Hatch v.t. To produce young from eggs; to plot; to shade by crosslines. s. A brood; act of coming from the egg; opening in a deck, or frame over this; a trap-door.
Thatch s. A roof-covering of straw, etc. v.t. To cover with this.
Nut'hatch s. A small bird of the wood-pecker family.
Latch s. A catch or fastening of a door. v.t. To fasten with this.
Slatch s. The slack of a rope.
Match s. A person or thing equal to or like another; a pairing for or one eligible for marriage; a contest; slip tipped with combustible material for igniting. v.t. To equal, set against as equal; to suit. v.i. To agree, tally.
Overmatch' v.t. To be more than a match for.
Natch s. The rump of an ox.
Snatch v.t. To seize hastily or without warning. v.i. To make a grasp, try to seize. s. A hasty seizing or attempt; a short period of action; a small portion.
Patch s. A piece fastened on to repair a hole, etc.; a small plot of ground; a lout. v.t. To mend or adorn with a patch; to botch, compose carelessly.
Dispatch' v.t. To send off in haste or specially; to perform quickly; to conclude; to put to death. s. Act of dispatching; speedy performance, due diligence; communication on public business.
Ratch s. A ratchet or ratchet-wheel.
Cratch s. A manger, hay-rack.
Scratch v.t. and i. To mark or wound slightly with something sharp; to tear with the nails; to withdraw from a competition, etc. s. A slight wound, score; line from which runners, etc., start; competitor most heavily handicapped. a. Miscellaneous, hastily collected.
Watch (woch) s. Act of watching; vigil; guard; a sentry, time or place of his duty; pocket timepiece. v.i. To keep awake, act as guard, wait. v.t. To look with close attention to.
Etch v.t. To make designs on copper, glass, etc., by lines eaten in by acid. v.i. To practise etching.

Fetch v.t. To go and bring; to heave (a sigh); to obtain as its price. v.i. To bring oneself, move, arrive. s. A stratagem, artifice; a wraith.
Ketch s. A two-masted vessel.
Sketch s. A rough draft, an outline. v.t. To draw or construct the outline or rough draft of; to design, depict, paint.
Letch s. A craving; ardent desire.
Retch v.i. To make an effort to vomit.
Stretch v.t. To draw out tight; to lengthen, spread out, strain. v.i. To extend; to have elasticity. s. Act of stretching; state of being stretched; extent, scope; a spell.
Wretch s. A miserable, unfortunate or despicable person; a scoundrel.
Vetch s. A fodder-plant allied to the bean.
Itch s. Irritation of the skin; a contagious disease. v.i. To feel an itch; to desire eagerly.
Aitch s. The letter "H."
Bitch s. A female dog.
Ditch s. A trench for water; a moat. v.t. and i. To dig a ditch.
Fitch s. The polecat; its fur.
Hitch v.i. To move by jerks; to be entangled. v.t. To fasten, hook, raise by jerks. s. A catch or catching; a temporary delay or obstruction; a knot.
Flitch s. The side of a hog salted and cured.
Snitch v.i. (*Slang*) To inform. s. The nose.
Pitch s. A thick, black, resinous substance; degree of elevation; highest rise; descent; space between wickets (at cricket). v.t. To smear with pitch; to set the keynote of; to set in array; to toss; to thrust; to fix, set. v.i. To settle; to fall headlong; to rise and fall; to fix choice.
El'dritch a. Weird, uncanny.
Car'ritch s. (*Scot.*) The Catechism.
Stitch v.t. and i. To sew or unite by means of stitches. s. A single pass of a needle in sewing, complete link in knitting, etc.; a sharp pain in the side.
Quitch s. Couch-grass.
Witch s. A woman practising sorcery; an old and ugly or a fascinating woman. v.t. To enchant.
Bewitch' v.t. To charm, fascinate, cast a spell upon.
Switch s. A flexible twig; a movable rail or connexion. v.t. To beat with or transfer by a switch.
Twitch v.t. To pull with a sudden jerk. v.i. To move spasmodically. s. A short, sudden pull or contraction; appliance to control a refractory horse; quitch-grass.
Botch v.t. To patch clumsily. s. A clumsy patch.
Scotch v.t. To incise or wound slightly. s. A slight cut, shallow incision.
Scotch a. Pertaining to Scotland, its people, dialect, etc. s. The people or dialect of Scotland; Scotch whisky.
Hop'scotch s. A child's street-game.
Blotch s. A spot on the skin, a pustule.
Splotch s. A splodge, smear.
Notch s. A nick, V-shaped cut; an indentation. v.t. To cut a notch in; to indent.
Hotch'potch s. A jumble; a hash of meat, vegetables, etc.
Crotch s. A forking, parting of two branches.
Nautch s. An exhibition by Indian dancing girls.
Cutch s. Catechu.
Scutch v.t. To dress (flax, raw cotton, etc.) by beating.
Dutch a. Pertaining to Holland or its people. s. The people of Holland; their language; (*slang*) a costermonger's wife.
Hutch s. A coop or cage for small animals; a chest; a hovel.
Clutch s. A grip, seizure, grasp; (pl.) the hands, rapacity; a device for connecting and disconnecting moving parts of machinery; a sitting of eggs. v.t. To seize, clasp, clinch. v.i. To catch, snatch.
Mutch s. (*Scot.*) A woman's cap.
Crutch s. A support used by cripples.
Debauch' v.t. To corrupt, vitiate. v.i. To riot. s. Excess, especially in drinking; lewdness.
Pen'tateuch s. The first five books of the Old Testament.
Hep'tateuch s. The first seven Books of the Old Testament.
Hex'ateuch s. The first six Books of the Old Testament.
Much a. Great in quantity or amount; long in time. s. A great quantity; abundance. adv. In a great quantity; by far.
Insomuch' adv. To such a degree.
Overmuch' adv. In too great a degree. s. More than sufficient.
Inasmuch' adv. Seeing that.
Eu'nuch s. A castrated male, especially one employed in a harem.
Ouch s. The setting of a gem or seal; a carcanet.
Debouch' v.i. To march or issue from a confined space.
Couch v.t. To lay down; to compose to rest; to state in words; to operate for cataract. v.i. To lie down for repose, concealment, etc.; to stoop, bend. s. A lounge, sofa, bed; first coat of paint; layer of barley for malting.
Slouch v.i. To walk with a stoop or in a slovenly manner. v.t. To bend or cause to hang down. s. An ungainly gait or position; an awkward fellow, piece of work, etc.; a downward bend.
Mouch v.i. To play truant, loaf about; to slouch.
Scar'amouch s. A boastful poltroon.
Pouch s. A small bag; a pocket. v.t. To pocket, put in a pouch.
Crouch v.i. To bend low, stoop, lie down; to cringe, fawn. s. Action of crouching.
Grouch v.i. To grumble, s. A grumble; discontent.
Touch v.t. To perceive by feeling; to come in contact with; to refer to. v.i. To be in contact; to take effect; to call (as a ship at port). s. Sense of feeling, act of touching, contact; a little; distinctive handling.
Retouch' v.t. To improve by new touches.
Vouch v.t. To affirm, answer for. v.i. To bear witness.
Avouch' v.t. To affirm, maintain, justify.
Such a. and pron.

None'such s. A paragon; a variety of apple.
Dip'tych s. An altar-piece, writing-tablet, etc., of two-hinged leaves.
Trip'tych (-tik) s. Three-hinged panels carved or painted.
Eh int. Expressing surprise, question, etc.
Sak'ieh s. An Egyptian water-raising apparatus.
Zap'tieh (-ā) s. A Turkish policeman.
Shille'lagh (-lē'la) s. A cudgel (in Ireland).
Heigh int. Calling attention, etc.
Sleigh (slā) s. A vehicle on runners for use over snow.
Bob'sleigh s. A double-runner sleigh for tobogganing.
Neigh (nā) s. The cry or whinny of a horse. v.i. To utter this cry.
Inveigh' v.i. To rail against, utter invectives, express reproach.
Weigh (wā) v.t. To examine by the balance, ascertain the weight of; to consider; to raise (anchor). v.i. To have a specified weight; to bear heavily.
Outweigh' v.t. To exceed in weight, importance, influence, etc.
High a. Lofty, elevated; dignified, noble; great; strong; far advanced; tending to putrefaction. adv. In a high manner; to a great degree.
Thigh s. Part of leg between knee and trunk.
Nigh adv. Near, almost. a. Near; closely allied. prep. Close to.
Sigh (sī) v.i. To make a deep single respiration. v.t. To utter sighs or laments over. s. A deep, long breath.
Burgh s. A Scottish town with a charter.
Rox'burgh s. A style of bookbinding with leather back.
Ugh (oo) int. Exclamation of horror, disgust, etc.
Us'quebaugh (-baw) s. A kind of whisky; an Irish cordial.
Faugh int. Expressing disgust.
Haugh s. Low-lying tract near a river.
Laugh v.i. To express merriment by involuntary noise, to be convulsed by merriment; to treat with contempt. v.t. To express, affect, or effect by laughter.
Bough s. A branch or limb of a tree.
Cough s. A violent and noisy effort of the lungs to throw off irritating matter. v.i. To make such an effort, to expel air or offensive matter from the lungs. v.t. To expectorate, eject by a cough.
Hic'cough s. (*Hiccup*).
Dough s. An unbaked mass of flour moistened and kneaded.
Hough (hok) s. Joint between knee and fetlock of a horse, etc. v.t. To hamstring.
Chough s. A bird of the crow family.
Though (thō) conj.
Although' conj. Though, be it so, notwithstanding.
Lough s. A lake, loch, arm of the sea.
Clough s. A narrow valley.
Plough (plow) s. An implement for preparing the soil for sowing; agriculture, tillage; a grooving machine; a failure in an examination. v.t. To turn up with a plough; to run through in sailing; to reject an examination entrant. v.i. To labour with a plough; to advance through obstacles.
Fur'lough s. Military leave of absence.
Slough (*as "plough"*) s. A place of deep mud; a morass.
Slough (*as "enough"*) s. The cast skin of a snake; dead tissue. v.t. and i. To cast the skin; to mortify and come off.
Enough' a. Sufficient, adequate. adv. sufficiently, fully, quite. s. A sufficiency.
Rough (ruff) a. Not smooth; rugged; uncivil, rude; harsh, cruel, austere. v.t. To rough-hew; to roughen. s. State of being rough; a hooligan.
Through (throo) prep., adv., and a.
Bor'ough s. A corporate town.
Yar'borough s. A hand at whist, etc., with nine high.
Thor'ough (thŭr'-) a. Complete; perfect.
Trough (trof) s. A long hollow vessel; depression between waves.
Sough (sŭf) s. The murmuring sound of light wind. v.i. To make this sound.
Tough (tŭf) a. Flexible without being brittle; tenacious; durable; firm; stubborn. s. (*Slang*) A hooligan.
Lakh s. 100.000 (of rupees).
Sheikh s. Chief of an Arab tribe; a Mohammedan dignitary.
Sikh (sēk) s. Member of a Hindu religious community.
Oh int. Expressing surprise, pain, etc.; and used in entreaty, invocation, etc.
Boh int.
Pooh int. Expressive of contempt.
Pooh-pooh' v.t. To make light of, dismiss with derision.
Par'aph s. The flourish under one's signature.
Ser'aph s. An angel of the highest order.
Graph s. A diagram, curve, etc., displaying statistics.
-graph suff. Denoting a writing, something written, or a writer.
Sci'agraph s. A vertical section of a building; a photograph by X-rays.
Di'agraph s. An instrument for assistance in drawing diagrams, enlargements, etc.
Par'agraph s. A distinct section of a writing, discourse, etc.; a brief notice; the printer's mark (¶).
Tel'egraph s. Apparatus (especially electrical) for sending messages to a distance. v.t. and i. To send a message by this, to use a telegraph.
Di'graph s. A combination of two letters to express one sound.
Plan'igraph s. Instrument for reproducing drawings on some other scale.
Ep'igraph s. An inscription, especially on a building, statue, etc.
Per'igraph s. An inaccurate delineation.
Tri'graph s. Group of three letters representing one sound.
Hel'icograph s. Apparatus for describing spirals.
Zin'cograph s. A zinc plate on which a design is etched; impression from this.
On'cograph s. An instrument that records changes detected by an oncometer.
Ei'dograph s. Instrument for copying drawings in a different scale.
Pseud'ograph s. A literary forgery.
Ide'ograph s. A symbolical representation of an object or idea.
O'leograph s. A lithographic picture in oils.

Mim'eograph s. A duplicating apparatus or writing, etc.
Chor'eograph s. A choreographer.
Log'ograph s. A logotype ; a logogram.
Psy'chograph s. Instrument for producing supernatural writing.
Glyph'ograph s. A plate prepared by glyphography.
Lith'ograph v.t. To draw or engrave on stone for printing. s. An impression from a drawing on stone.
Chromo-lith'ograph s. A colour-print from engraving on stone.
Bi'ograph s. A cinematograph.
Ra'diograph s. Instrument for measuring radiation; a negative or photograph produced by Röntgen rays. v.t. To obtain a negative thus.
Id'iograph s. A private mark, trademark.
Car'diograph s. An apparatus for recording heart-beats.
He'liograph s. Apparatus for signalling by flashes of reflected sunlight ; instrument for photographing the sun ; engraving obtained by photogravure.
Hyal'ograph s. Apparatus for etching on glass.
Cy'clograph s. Instrument for describing large arcs.
Al'lograph s. A signature written by one person for another.
Oscil'lograph s. Instrument for recording the variations of an electric current.
Sill'ograph s. A writer of satires.
Coll'ograph s. A gelatine copying-machine.
Bo'lograph s. An automatic record of temperature variations.
Hol'ograph s. A document whole in the writing of he from whom it proceeds. a. Wholly written thus.
Styl'ograph s. A kind of fountain-pen.
Xy'lograph s. An engraving on wood ; impression from this.
Dy'namograph s. A recording dynamometer.
Anem'ograph s. An instrument for recording wind-pressure.
Sphyg'-mograph s. Instrument for recording pulse-beats.
Udom'ograph s. A registering rain-gauge.
Ho'mograph s. A word having more than one origin and meaning.
Chro'mograph s. An apparatus for reproducing writing, drawings, etc.
Ther'mograph s. An automatic temperature recorder.
Seis'mograph (siz'-) s. Instrument for recording shocks, tremors, etc., due to earth-movements.
Os'mograph s. An instrument for registering osmotic pressure.
Ky'mograph s. Apparatus for recording pulse-waves, respiratory movements, etc.
Phren'ograph s. Instrument for registering the respiratory movements of the diaphragm.
Sten'ograph s. A character used in shorthand.
Ich'nograph s. A ground-plan.
Incli'nograph s. Instrument for recording the declination of the compass.
Actin'ograph s. An instrument for recording the chemical action of solar rays.
Phon'ograph s. An instrument for the registration and reproduction of sounds ; a phonogram.
Mon'ograph s. A treatise on a single thing or class.
Chro'nograph s. A chronometer, a stop-watch.
Try'pograph s. A kind of stencil.
Bar'ograph s. A self-recording barometer.

Mi'crograph s. A pantograph for very minute work ; a minute picture.
Hi'erograph s. A hierogram.
Chir'ograph s. A formally written and signed document.
Spir'ograph s. Instrument for recording respiratory movements.
Me'teorograph s. Instrument for recording meteorological phenomena.
Elec'trograph s. The record of an electrometer.
Spec'trograph s. Apparatus for reproducing spectra.
Papyr'ograph s. A machine for producing facsimiles from MSS.
Ellip'sograph s. Instrument for describing ellipses.
Cinemat'-ograph s. An apparatus for exhibiting moving pictures.
Hec'tograph s. Machine for multiplying copies of drawings, etc.
Perspec'to-graph s. Instrument for drawing objects in perspective mechanically.
Pic'tograph s. A pictorial word-symbol.
Noc'tograph s. A kind of writing-frame for the blind.
Magnet'ograph s. Instrument for recording terrestrial magnetic variations.
Hyet'ograph s. A chart giving the rainfall in various regions.
Pan'tograph s. An instrument for copying a drawing, etc., on the same or a different scale.
Scot'ograph s. An instrument for writing in the dark.
Pho'tograph s. A picture obtained by photography. v.t. To take a picture thus.
Comp'tograph s. A recording calculating machine.
Cryp'tograph s. Secret writing ; a system of this.
Au'tograph s. A person's own handwriting ; a MS. in the author's handwriting.
Telau'tograph s. Telegraphic instrument for reproducing writing at a distance.
Phonaut'o-graph s. A precursor of the phonograph.
Mu'tograph s. Apparatus for taking a rapid succession of photographs.
Pol'ygraph s. An apparatus for multiplying copies of writing, etc.
Ep'itaph s. An inscription on a tomb ; a composition in honour of the dead.
Cen'otaph s. A sepulchral monument to a person or persons buried elsewhere.
Ac'aleph s. A jelly-fish.
Ca'liph s. A Mohammedan ruler.
Guelph s. One of a mediæval Italian faction aiming at independence.
Sylph s. An imaginary being inhabiting air ; a graceful girl.
Humph int. Expressing doubt, deliberation, disapproval, etc.
Tri'umph s. Victory ; achievement ; joy for success. v.i. To succeed ; to celebrate victory with pomp ; to exult.
Galumph' v.i. To exult.
Lymph s. Any transparent fluid ; coagulable fluid in animals ; matter containing the virus used in vaccination.
En'dolymph s. A clear fluid contained in the ear.
Nymph s. A goddess of the mountains, groves, waters, etc. ; a lovely young girl ; a nympha.
Par'anymph s. A "best man" at ancient Greek weddings.
Soph s. (*Slang*) A sophister, or sophomore.
The'osoph s. A theosophist.
Per'imorph s. A mineral enclosing another.
En'domorph s. A mineral enclosed in another.
Pseud'omorph s. A mineral whose crystals have the form of another.

Glyph s. A fluting, usually vertical; a hieroglyph.
Di'aglyph s. An intaglio.
An'aglyph s. A figure in low relief.
Tri'glyph s. An ornament on a Doric frieze with three perpendicular grooves.
Lith'oglyph s. A carving on stone or on a gem.
Dactyl'ioglyph s. An engraver of gems; engraver's mark on rings, gems, etc.
Hi'eroglyph s. A sacred character or sign, especially the picture-writing of the ancient Egyptian priests.
Pet'roglyph s. A rock-carving.
Log'ogryph s. A word-puzzle.
Catarrh' s. Inflammation of the mucous membrane, especially of the respiratory organs.
Myrrh s. A transparent, aromatic gum-resin; an umbelliferous plant, sweet cicely.
Ash s. A well-known forest timber-tree; residue from combustion.
Bash v.t. To strike hard or violently. s. A violent blow.
Abash' v.t. To make ashamed, to confuse.
Cal'abash s. A gourd.
Cash s. Money, ready money. v.t. To turn into money.
Encash' v.t. To convert into cash; to realize.
Dash v.t. To throw, cast, sprinkle; to cause to strike suddenly; to sketch out; to frustrate, abash. v.i. To rush with violence. s. A violent rushing, or striking of two bodies; a slight admixture; vigour, go, bluster; a printer's mark (—).
Slap'dash adv. At random, in a careless manner; all at once.
Bald'erdash s. A worthless mixture; jargon, nonsense.
Spat'terdash s. A gaiter, legging.
Leash s. Leather thong to hold dogs; a lash; v.t. To hold or fasten by a leash.
Fash v.t. To annoy, bother. v.i. To be vexed; to take pains. s. Trouble, pains; vexation.
Gash s. A deep cut; a gaping wound. v.t. To make such a cut or wound in; to slash.
Hash s. Minced meat; medley; mess. v.t. To mince and mix; to hack.
Rehash' v.t. To hash up again; to remodel. s. Anything served up again or in a new form.
Lash s. The thong of a whip, a scourge; an eyelash. v.t. To strike with a lash; to satirize; to tie with a cord. v.i. To ply the whip.
Calash' s. A light pleasure carriage; a large head-dress formerly worn by women.
Clash v.t. To strike noisily against. v.i. To dash noisily together; to conflict, interfere. s. Collision; noise produced by this; opposition, conflict.
Flash s. A sudden blaze, transitory burst of light; an instant. a. Vulgarly showy; sham. v.i. To emit sudden light; to exhibit ready wit. v.t. To send out in flashes.
Plash v.t. To splash, dash with water; to lop off or to intertwine branches, to pleach. s. A puddle, small pool, splash; branch partly cut and bound to others.
Splash v.t. and i. To bespatter with liquid; to dash water about. s. Liquid matter thrown upon anything; stain or damage from or noise of this; (*slang*) a commotion, sensation.
Pearl'ash a. Carbonate of potassium.
Slash v.t. To cut by striking violently and at random. v.i. To strike thus. s. A long cut; a cut made at random.
Mash v.t. To mix or beat into a mass; (*slang*) to pay court to. s. A blended mass; mixture of malt, etc., and hot water to form wort; (*slang*) A sweetheart.
Mish'mash s. A hotchpotch.
Smash v.t. To break violently to pieces. v.i. To go to pieces; to become bankrupt. s. A breaking to pieces; utter destruction; ruin.
Gnash v.i. To grind the teeth.
Cal'ipash s. The green edible part of a turtle next the upper shell.
Rash a. Hasty, overbold, foolhardy. s. An eruption on the skin.
Brash s. Loose rock or rubble; a slight affection of the alimentary canal.
Crash v.t. To break to pieces or dash together violently. v.i. To make a loud clattering noise. s. A noise as of many things broken at once; a sudden failure, commercial collapse; coarse linen cloth.
Mid'rash s. Ancient Jewish commentaries on the Scriptures.
Thrash v.t. To thresh; to beat soundly, flog; to overcome.
Trash s. Anything worthless; dross, dregs; bruised sugar-canes.
Sash s. An ornamental belt or scarf; the frame of a window. v.t. To furnish with sashes or frames.
Pot'ash s. Crude potassium carbonate, a powerful alkali.
Quash v.t. To beat down or in pieces; to crush; to annul.
Squash v.t. To crush, press flat. s. Something crushed or easy to crush; fall of a soft body; pulp; a thong; a ball-game played with rackets; a pumpkin-like fruit of N. America.
Mus'quash s. A N. American aquatic rodent, the musk-rat.
Wash (wosh) v.t. To cleanse with water, etc.; to flow along; to tint lightly. v.t. To stand washing, to stand a test. s. Act of washing; clothes, etc., washed together; flow of or sound made by water; a thin coat of colour; a lotion.
Awash' adv. On a level with the water; helpless.
White'wash s. Mixture of lime and water, etc., for whitening walls; false colouring to restore confidence. v.t. To cover with whitewash; to clear from aspersions, etc.
Eye'wash s. (*Slang*) Humbug, deception, blarney.
Wish'wash s. Weak liquor; feeble talk.
Swash v.i. To make the noise of splashing; to bluster. v.t. To strike noisily. s. A narrow channel within a sandbank; a dashing of water.
Bak'sheesh s. A tip, gratuity.
Flesh s. The muscular part of an animal; the body; carnality; mankind; kindred; animals used for food; meat. v.t. To feed with or initiate to the taste of flesh.

Horse'flesh s. Horses collectively; horse as food.
Mesh s. Interstice of a net; network.
Enmesh' v.t. To net, entangle.
Nesh a. Tender, friable; poor-spirited.
Fresh a. Cool; vigorous; full of health; brisk; not faded or stale, in good condition, not salt; clearly remembered; unused.
Afresh' adv. Anew, again.
Refresh' v.t. To make fresh again, restore strength, etc., to; to revive; to renovate. v.i. To take refreshment.
Thresh v.t. To beat out, separate the grain from (corn).
-ish suff. Forming adjectives denoting of the nature of, or somewhat.
Bob'bish a. (*Slang*) In good health; brisk.
Hob'bish a. Elvish; rustic.
Snob'bish a. Pertaining to, resembling, or with the manners of a snob.
Cub'bish a. Like a cub.
Club'bish a. Disposed to associate.
Rub'bish s. Waste matter; anything worthless; nonsense.
Tub'bish a. Tubby, corpulent.
Fur'bish v.t. To rub till bright, burnish; to renovate.
Refur'bish v.t. To furbish up afresh.
Ni'cish a. Somewhat nice.
Dish s. A large plate for serving meat in, etc.; food served. v.t. To put in or make like a dish; (*slang*) to frustrate.
Jad'ish a. In the manner of a jade.
Rad'ish s. A cultivated cruciferous plant; its edible root.
Bad'dish a. (*Bad*).
Fad'dish a. Faddy.
Gad'dish a. Inclined to gad about.
Sad'dish a. Somewhat sad.
Ed'dish s. Second crop of grass; aftermath.
Red'dish a. Somewhat red.
Yid'dish s. The Hebraized German dialect used by German Jews. a. Consisting of or pertaining to this.
Odd'ish a. Somewhat odd.
Clod'dish a. Loutish, clumsy.
Swed'ish a. Pertaining to the inhabitants or language of Sweden. s. The language of the Swedes.
Wid'ish a. Somewhat wide.
Child'ish a. Befitting a child; puerile.
Wild'ish a. Rather wild, inclined to be wild.
Old'ish a. Somewhat old.
Cold'ish a. (*Cold*).
Blan'dish v.t. To soothe, flatter; to soften.
Outlan'dish a. Strange, rude, barbarous.
Brand'ish v.t. To flourish, as a weapon, to wave.
Stand'ish s. A stand for pens and ink.
Fiend'ish a. Like a fiend; diabolic.
Cav'endish s. A cake tobacco.
Wend'ish a. and s. Pertaining to or the language of the Wends.
Hound'ish a. Like a hound; contemptible.
Round'ish a. Somewhat round.
Tun'dish s. A funnel.
Mod'ish a. Fashionable.
Good'ish a. Fairly good, not so bad.
Bar'dish a. (*Bard*).
Hard'ish a. Somewhat hard.
Du'dish a. Like or characteristic of a dude.
Loud'ish a. Somewhat loud; on the showy side.
Proudish' a. Somewhat proud.
Rud'ish a. Somewhat rude.
Pru'dish a. Like a prude; very precise; affectedly scrupulous.
Blue'ish a. (*Blue*).
Fish s. An equatic animal breathing with gills only. v.i. To angle; to try to obtain by artifice.
Oaf'ish a. In the manner of an oaf.
Gold'fish s. A golden red carp.
White'fish s. A N. American salmonoid fish; any fish with white flesh.
Raff'ish a. Disreputable; dissipated.
Draff'ish a. Like draff; worthless.
Stiff'ish a. Rather stiff.
Off'ish a. Distant, stiff in manner.
Huff'ish a. Petulant, peevish.
Gruf'fish a. Somewhat gruff.
Stock'fish s. Split cod, etc., dried in the sun.
Calf'ish a. (*Calf*).
El'fish a. Like an elf; mischievous.
Self'ish a. Caring chiefly or only for one's own interests; influenced by personal advantage.
Wolf'ish a. Like a wolf; ravenous.
Sun'fish s. A large globe-shaped fish.
Oof'ish a. (*Slang*) Having some money.
Dwarf'ish a. Like a dwarf, very small.
Craw'fish s. A crayfish.
Cray'fish s. The freshwater lobster.
Hag'gish a. Like a hag.
Wag'gish a. Like a wag; roguish; sportive.
Dreg'gish a. Foul with dregs; feculent.
Whig'gish a. Pertaining to or resembling the Whigs or their theories.
Pig'gish a. Like pigs; filthy, greedy; obstinate.
Prig'gish a. Conceited; affectedly precise.
Dog'gish a. Churlish, snappy.
Hog'gish a. Having the qualities or manners of a hog; gluttonous; filthy; selfish.
Slug'gish a. Habitually lazy or inactive; inert; dull.
Long'ish a. Somewhat long.
Ob'longish a. Somewhat oblong.
Strong'ish a. Somewhat strong.
Young'ish a. Somewhat young; youthful.
Larg'ish a. Somewhat large.
Rough'ish a. Somewhat rough.
Tough'ish (tŭf'-) a. Rather tough.
Nym'phish a. In the manner of nymphs.
Hash'ish s. Bhang; Indian hemp used as a narcotic.
Bak'shish s. (*Baksheesh*).
Whish int. Silence! s. A whistling sound.
Bleak'ish a. (*Bleak*).
Freak'ish a. Whimsical, capricious; abnormal.
Weak'ish a. Somewhat weak.
Snak'ish a. Like a snake.
Rak'ish a. Wild, dissolute; having a great slope (of masts).
Black'ish a. (*Black*).
Knack'ish a. Knacky.
Brack'ish a. Salty.
Quack'ish a. Like a quack; boastful.
Peck'ish a. (*Slang*) Hungry.
Thick'ish a. Somewhat thick.
Trick'ish a. Given to tricks, tricky.
Sick'ish a. Somewhat sick.
Cock'ish a. Cocky.
Pea'cockish a. Like a peacock; vainglorious, strutting.
Stock'ish a. Dull, loutish.
Buck'ish a. Foppish.
Puck'ish a. Merrily mischievous.
Greek'ish a. Greek.
Dank'ish a. Somewhat dank.
Frank'ish a. Pertaining to the Franks.
Prank'ish a. Full of pranks.
Pink'ish a. Somewhat pink.
Monk'ish a. Pertaining to monks; monastic.

Book'ish a. Studious; full of book-learning.
Spook'ish a. Ghost-like.
Dark'ish a. Somewhat dark.
Lark'ish a. Given to sprees; frolicsome.
Park'ish a. Of the nature of a park.
Spark'ish a. Gay, showy; well-dressed.
Quirk'ish a. Addicted to subterfuge or using quirks.
Turk'ish a. Pertaining to Turkey or the Turks. s. The language of the Turks.
Dusk'ish a. Dusky.
Gawk'ish a. Gawky.
Mawk'ish a. Apt to cause loathing; insipid.
Pa'lish a. Somewhat pale.
Estab'lish v.t. To settle, ratify; to enact by authority; to found, institute.
Re-estab'lish v.t. To set up or establish again.
Disestab'lish v.t. To break up what has been established; to sever the connexion between Church and State.
Fee'blish a. Somewhat feeble.
Pub'lish v.t. To make public, to promulgate; to issue books, etc.
Repub'lish v.t. To publish again.
Genteel'ish a. Genteel; somewhat genteel.
Cam'elish a. (*Camel*).
Rel'ish v.t. To enjoy the taste of, give a pleasing flavour to. v.i. To have a pleasing flavour, give pleasure. s. A pleasing taste; enjoyable quality; condiment.
Disrel'ish s. Distaste; bad taste; aversion. v.t. To feel disgust at; to make nauseous.
Nov'elish a. In the manner of a novel; somewhat new or strange.
Eng'lish a. Pertaining to England, its people or language. s. This people or language. v.t. To translate into English.
Frail'ish a. Somewhat frail.
Dev'ilish a. Wicked in the extreme, infernal, befitting a devil; (*slang*) awful, awfully.
Tickl'ish a. Easily affected by tickling; puzzling; precarious.
Small'ish a. Rather small.
Embel'lish v.t. To decorate, adorn.
Hell'ish a. Pertaining to hell; infernal; detestable.
Swell'ish a. Dandified.
Doll'ish a. Like a doll.
Dull'ish a. Rather dull.
Full'ish a. Somewhat full.
Gull'ish a. Somewhat easy to dupe.
Abol'ish v.t. To do away with, annul, make void.
Demol'ish v.t. To throw down, raze, destroy.
Cool'ish a. Somewhat cool.
Fool'ish a. Acting without discretion; silly, unwise; deficient in understanding.
Pol'ish v.t. To make smooth and glossy, or elegant and polite. v.i. To become smooth, etc. s. Smooth, glossy surface produced by friction; refinement; elegance of manners.
Po'lish a. Pertaining to Poland or its people. s. The language or people of Poland.
Accom'plish v.t. To complete, effect, fulfil.
Purpl'ish s. Somewhat purple.
Girl'ish a. Like or befitting a girl; pertaining to a woman's youth.
Churl'ish a. Surly; like a churl.
Gaul'ish a. Pertaining to Gaul or ancient France. s. The language of Gaul.
Mul'ish a. Obstinate; stubborn.
Ghoul'ish a. In the manner of a ghoul; fiendish.
Owl'ish a. Like an owl.
Styl'ish a. Fashionable; smart.
Squeam'ish a. Easily nauseated; fastidious, over-scrupulous.
Fam'ish v.i. To suffer extreme hunger. v.t. To starve.
La'mish a. Somewhat lame.
Rhem'ish a. Pertaining to Rheims, especially an English translation of the New Testament (1582).
Blem'ish s. A mark of deformity, a stain. v.t. To mar; to tarnish, defame.
Flem'ish a. Pertaining to Flanders. s. Its language.
Qualm'ish a. Inclined to vomit.
Ram'mish a. Ram-like; strong-scented.
Dim'mish a. Somewhat dim.
Slim'mish a. Somewhat slim.
Hom'ish a. Homelike, like a home.
Gnom'ish a. Like a gnome; elvish.
Rom'ish a. Applied derogatorily to Roman Catholic doctrines, opinions, practices, etc.
Skir'mish s. An irregular fight, desultory contest. v.i. To fight in a slight or preliminary way.
Fum'ish a. Passionate; smoky.
Ban'ish v.t. To exile, drive away.
Dan'ish a. Pertaining to Denmark or the Danes. s. The language of the Danes.
Plan'ish v.t. To smooth or level (metals) by light blows.
Ro'manish a. Pertaining to or characteristic of the Church of Rome.
Wom'anish a. Like a woman; effeminate.
Span'ish a. Pertaining to Spain. s. Its language or people.
Charlatan'ish a. (*Charlatan*).
Van'ish v.i. To disappear suddenly, be lost to view.
Maid'enish a. Like a maiden.
Hoy'denish a. With the manners of a hoyden.
Spleen'ish a. Splenetic, morose.
Green'ish a. Somewhat green.
Rhen'ish a. Pertaining to the Rhine. s. Rhine wine.
Heath'enish a. Pertaining to pagans; idolatrous barbarous.
Deplen'ish v.t. To empty of contents.
Replen'ish v.t. To fill up again, stock abundantly.
Kit'tenish a. Playful; like a kitten.
Vix'enish a. Shrewish; vixenly.
Fi'nish a. Somewhat fine.
Fin'ish v.t. To complete, put an end to, perfect. v.i. To come to an end. s. Completion, the last touch; high polish.
Griff'inish a. Like a griffin.
Dimin'ish v.t. and i. To make or grow less; to impair; to taper.
Swin'ish a. Befitting or like swine; brutish.
Clan'nish a. Closely united; pertaining to a clan.
Man'nish a. Masculine; characteristic of a man.
Wan'nish (wŏn'-) a. Somewhat wan or sickly.
Fin'nish a. Pertaining to the Finns, their country, or language. s. Their language.
Thin'nish a. Somewhat thin.
Hun'nish a. Hunnic; savage, bloodthirsty, barbarian.
Nun'nish a. In the manner of nuns.
Drag'onish a. Resembling a dragon; fierce.

Babylon'ish a. Of or pertaining to Babylon, its inhabitants, or their customs, etc.
Admon'ish v.t. To reprove gently, to advise.
Preadmon'ish v.t. To admonish beforehand.
Premon'ish v.t. To forewarn.
Com'monish a. Rather common, ordinary.
Dro'nish a. Idle, sluggish.
To'nish a. (*Slang*) Smart, fashionable.
Aston'ish v.t. To amaze, surprise greatly.
Glut'tonish a. Like a glutton.
Gar'nish v.t. To embellish; to warn, give notice to. s. An adornment, decoration.
Tar'nish v.t. and i. To sully, to lose lustre. s. State of being soiled; a blemish.
Var'nish s. A solution of gum, etc., for coating surfaces; gloss. v.t. To coat with this; to gloss over.
Corn'ish a. Pertaining to Cornwall. s. The ancient language of Cornwall.
Horn'ish a. Resembling horn.
Bur'nish v.t. To polish, give a gloss to. s. A lustre; gloss, brightness.
Fur'nish v.t. To provide, equip; to afford, offer for use.
Refur'nish v.t. To supply with new furniture.
Pun'ish v.t. To chastise, chasten; to hurt.
Clown'ish a. Awkward, boorish; like a buffoon.
Brown'ish a. (*Brown*).
Town'ish a. Characteristic of town life.
Pish int. Expressing contempt.
A'pish a. (*Ape*).
Cheap'ish a. (*Cheap*).
Sheep'ish a. Like a sheep; bashful.
Scamp'ish a. Like a scamp.
Damp'ish a. Somewhat damp.
Imp'ish a. Having the qualities of an imp; mischievous.
Romp'ish a. Given to romping; inclined to romp.
Dump'ish a. Sad, melancholy, dejected.
Lumpish' a. Like a lump; inert; stupid.
Mump'ish a. Sulky; dull; sour.
Frump'ish a. Dowdy, prim, old-fashioned.
Grump'ish a. Inclined to be grumpy.
Mo'pish a. Given to moping.
Po'pish a. Pertaining to or taught by the Roman Catholic Church (*used offensively*).
Lap'pish a. Pertaining to Lapland or the Lapps. s. The language of the Lapps.
Snap'pish a. Sharp in reply; churlish, irascible.
Hip'pish a. Melancholy, depressed.
Fop'pish a. Fop-like, affected; vain of dress.
Up'pish a. Arrogant, pert, conceited.
Wasp'ish a. Like a wasp; irritable, bitter.
Bar'ish a. (*Bare*).
Bear'ish a. Bear-like; rough, uncouth.
Gar'ish a. Gaudy, showy.
Mar'ish s. A marsh.
Night'marish a. Like a nightmare.
Par'ish s. An ecclesiastical district; a civil division of a county.
Squar'ish a. Nearly square.
Gib'berish s. Rapid, inarticulate talk; nonsense. a. Unmeaning.
Queer'ish a. Rather queer, questionable.
Ti'gerish a. Fierce; like a tiger.
Cher'ish v.t. To hold dear, treat tenderly, support.
Quak'erish a. Like a Quaker; prim; precise.
Lick'erish a. Dainty; greedy; lecherous.
Per'ish v.i. To be ruined or destroyed; to decay, die.
Vi'perish a. Having the qualities of the viper; viperous.
Wa'terish a. Resembling water; thin, diluted.
Bit'terish a. (*Bitter*).
Fe'verish a. Affected with, indicating, or resembling fever; agitated; inconstant.
Clev'erish a. (*Clever*).
Liv'erish a. Having a disordered liver; out of sorts.
Quiv'erish' a. Quivering; given to this.
Impov'erish v.t. To make poor; to exhaust.
Ir'ish a. Pertaining to Ireland or its people; produced in Ireland; like an Irishman. s. The people of Ireland collectively; their language.
Whor'ish a. Characteristic of a whore; unchaste.
Boor'ish a. (*Boor.*)
Moor'ish a. Pertaining to Morocco or the Moors; arabesque; pertaining to or of the nature of a moor.
Liq'uorish a. Fond of strong drink; lickerish.
Cur'rish a. Like a cur; surly.
Am'ateurish a. (*Amateur*).
Flour'ish v.i. To thrive, prosper; to be alive or at work; to boast; to make flourishes. s. Prosperity; an ostentatious or rhetorical embellishment; display.
Reflour'ish v.i. To flourish again.
Nour'ish v.t. To supply with nutriment; to sustain, encourage, foster.
Va'pourish a. Splenetic, hypochondriacal.
Sour'ish a. Rather sour.
Vul'turish a. Vulturous.
Loos'ish a. Somewhat loose.
Miss'ish a. Like a young girl, prim.
Lat'ish a. Somewhat late, not very recent.
Goa'tish a. Goat-like; lecherous.
Pic'tish a. Pertaining to or resembling the Picts.
Sweet'ish a. Somewhat sweet.
Fe'tish s. An object or animal made the subject of worship; any object of unreasonable devotion.
Soft'ish a. Rather soft; effeminate.
Light'ish a. Somewhat light.
Slight'ish a. Somewhat slight.
Whit'ish a. Somewhat white.
Israeli'tish a. Israelitic.
Brit'ish a. Pertaining to the early or present inhabitants of Great Britain, or to Great Britain or the British Empire.
Salt'ish a. Somewhat salt.
Colt'ish a. Frisky, unruly, inexperienced.
Dolt'ish a. Dolt-like, stupid.
Syc'ophantish a. Characterized by sycophancy.
Dilletan'tish a. (*Dilletante*).
De'centish a. Moderately good.
Kent'ish a. Belonging to Kent.
Faint'ish a. Somewhat faint.
Blunt'ish a. (*Blunt*).
Runt'ish a. Like a runt; dwarfish.
Smart'ish a. Rather smart.
Tart'ish a. Somewhat tart; acid.
Start'ish a. Skittish (of horses).
Flirt'ish a. In the manner of a flirt.
Short'ish a. Somewhat short.
Cat'tish a. (*Cat*).
Fat'tish a. Somewhat fat.
Flat'tish a. Somewhat flat.
Let'tish a. Pertaining to the Letts. s. Their language.
Martinet'tish s. Like a martinet.
Pet'tish a. Peevish; fretful.
Coquet'tish a. Befitting or in the manner of a coquette.
Wet'tish a. Somewhat wet.

Skit'tish a. Easily frightened; capricious; coquettish.
Scot'tish a. Pertaining to Scotland or its people; produced in Scotland.
Sot'tish a. Habitually fuddled with drink; doltish; besotted.
Slut'tish a. Like a slut; careless, untidy.
Rut'tish a. Lewd, lustful.
Lout'ish a. Like a lout; awkward.
Stout'ish a. Inclined to be corpulent.
Brut'ish a. (*Brute*),
Beau'ish a. (*Beau*).
A'guish a. (*Ague*).
An'guish s. Acute mental suffering; agony.
Lan'guish v.i. To be or become feeble; to pine away; to look with tenderness. s. Languishment.
Disting'uish v.t. To separate; to recognize by characteristics; to discriminate; to make eminent, to honour. v.i. To exercise discrimination.
Exting'uish v.t. To smother, quench; to put an end to.
Ro'guish a. Resembling or proper for a rogue; slightly mischievous.
Cliqu'ish a. Pertaining to or like a clique.
Van'quish v.t. To overcome, conquer; to confute.
Relin'quish v.t. To renounce, forsake, give up.
Lav'ish a. Prodigal, wasteful, extravagant. v.t. To expend with profusion, squander.
Slav'ish a. Pertaining to or befitting slaves; servile, cringing.
Knav'ish a. Like a knave; deceitful.
Rav'ish v.t. To seize and carry off by force to violate; to enrapture.
Enrav'ish v.t. To enchant, enrapture.
Peev'ish a. Fretful, easily vexed, petulant,
Thiev'ish a. Given to stealing.
El'vish a. Elfish, mischievous.
Der'vish s. A Moslem mendicant friar.
Wish v.t. and i. To have a desire, to long for, hanker after; to imprecate. s. A desire, longing, request.
Raw'ish a. Somewhat raw.
Jew'ish a. Pertaining to the Jews; like a Jew.
New'ish a. Somewhat new.
Shrew'ish a. Bad-tempered, vixenish (of women).
Cow'ish a. Like a cow.
Low'ish a. Somewhat low.
Tal'lowish a. Resembling tallow.
Yell'owish a. Somewhat yellow.
Swish v.i. and t. To make a noise as of a stick through air; to cane. s. A whistling sound; a stroke with the birch.
Mon'dayish a. Disinclined to work (especially of clergy).
Clay'ish a. (*Clay*).
Ba'byish a. (*Baby*).
Boo'byish a. (*Booby*).
Toad'yish a. In the manner of a toady; parasitical.
Dan'dyish a. (*Dandy*).
San'dyish a. Somewhat sandy.
Grun'dyish a. Inclined to be prudish.
Good'yish a. Affectedly pious.
Dow'dyish a. Like a dowdy.
Whey'ish (hwā'-) a. Resembling or containing whey.
Monk'eyish a. Like a monkey.
Flun'keyish a. In the manner of a flunkey.
Grey'ish a. Somewhat grey.
Sky'ish a. Skyey; ethereal.
Boy'ish a. (*Boy*).
Coy'ish a. Somewhat coy.
Hobble-dehoy'ish a. (*Hobbledehoy*).

Toy'ish a. Toy-like.
Pup'pyish a. Like a puppy.
Dry'ish a. Rather dry.
Dirt'yish a. Rather dirty.
Pret'tyish a. Somewhat pretty.
Heav'yish s. Somewhat weighty or dejected.
Welsh s. The people or language of Wales. a. Pertaining to these. v.t. and i. To swindle at horse-races.
Bosh s. Empty talk, folly. int. Nonsense!
Gosh int. A mild oath.
Galosh' s. An overshoe; a part of a boot.
Slosh v. and s. Slush.
Tarboosh' s. A brimless, conical fez.
Papoosh' s. A loose, heel-less Eastern slipper.
Posh a. (*Slang*) Smart, swagger, well-dressed.
Tosh s. and int. (*Slang*) Rubbish, nonsense.
Mac'kintosh s. A rubbered waterproof material; garment made of this.
Harsh a. Rough; austere; morose; severe.
Marsh s. A watery tract of land; a bog, swamp.
Bush s. A thick shrub or shrubbery; the uncultivated parts of Australia; the metal lining in the bearings of a machine.
Am'bush s. The concealment of troops for surprising the enemy; the place of concealment; the troops hidden. v.t. and i. To lie hidden, to trap.
Gush v.i. To flow or rush out with violence; to be effusively sentimental. s. A sudden issue of fluid; fluid thus issuing; effusiveness.
Hush v.t. and i. To make or be silent. s. Silence; stillness. int. Silence! be still! whist!
Lush a. Luxuriant in growth; juicy, succulent. s. (*Slang*) Strong drink.
Blush v.i. To betray shame or confusion by involuntary reddening of the face. s. A red colour suffusing the face, a rosy tint.
Ablush' adv. Blushing, ruddy.
Flush v.t. To colour, redden; to cause to take wing; to cleanse by flooding. v.i. To blush; to take wing; to flow swiftly, become filled suddenly. s. A flow of blood to the face; a cleansing with a rush of water; vigour, bloom; a hand of one suit at cards. a. Fresh; even or level with.
Plush s. A fabric with a velvet nap on one side.
Slush s. Soft mud, sludge; piffle. v.t. To bemire with slush; to wash thoroughly.
Mush s. A soft pulp; mash; (*slang*) an umbrella.
Push v.t. To press against with force, to shove; to urge. v.i. To make an effort; to force one's way. s. Pressure applied; a thrust, effort; an emergency; an attack; (*slang*) a crowd, group.
Rush v.i. To drive forward impetuously; to enter with undue eagerness. v.t. To push, urge, etc., with violence; to hurry; to take by sudden assault; (*slang*) to swindle, overcharge. s. Act of rushing; a sudden onslaught, movement of people, etc.; sudden stress of work; a long thin-stemmed plant; its stem; anything worthless.

Brush s. An instrument for sweeping, removing dust, painting, etc.; a fox's tail. v.t. To use or clean with a brush.
Crush v.t. To press together, squeeze, bruise, overpower. v.i. To be pressed to force one's way. s. A violent squeezing; a crowd.
Frush s. The frog of a horse's foot; a disease in this; an onset, encounter. v.t. To batter, smash down. a. Brittle.
Thrush s. A common song-bird; an infantile mouth-disease; a foot-disease in horses.
Bul'rush s. A variety of reed or papyrus.
On'rush s. An onset, attack.
Tush s. A horse's canine tooth. int. Expressing contempt.
Bath s. A place or receptacle for bathing or swimming; ablution.
Sab'bath s. Rest; a day in each week kept holy and observed by rest from all secular employments, the Jewish Sabbath falls on the seventh day of the week, but the Christian Sabbath on the first.
Death s. Extinction of life; cause of this; mortality.
Heath s. A small flowering shrub; place overgrown with this; a wild tract.
Sheath s. Case for a sword, etc., a scabbard; insect's wing-case.
Beneath' prep. Under, below in rank; unworthy of.
Underneath' adv. and prep. Beneath, below.
Breath s. Air drawn in and expelled from the lungs.
Wreath s. A garland; anything curled or twisted.
Bequeath' v.t. To leave by will to another.
Hath v. Third person singular of "to have."
Lath s. A thin strip of wood for supporting plaster, tiles, etc. v.t. To cover or line with laths.
Phil'omath s. A lover of learning; a scholar.
After'math s. The second crop of grass in the same year.
Pol'ymath s. A great scholar.
Snath s. The handle of a scythe.
Oath s. A solemn affirmation or promise; an imprecation.
Loath a. Unwilling, averse.
Path s. A footway, track; course of action, conduct, etc.
Hom'œopath s. A homœopathist.
Os'teopath s. A practitioner of osteopathy.
Psy'chopath s. One suffering from mental disease.
Hy'dropath s. A hydropathist.
Neur'opath s. A person liable to or suffering from a nervous disorder.
War'path s. N. American Indian expedition for war.
By'path s. A subsidiary or little-frequented path.
Rath s. A prehistoric Irish earthwork. a. Rathe.
Strath s. A wide valley with a river running through it.
Wrath s. Deep anger; indignation, exasperation.
Swath (swawth) s. Ridge of cut corn, etc., left lying; space left by this; the sweep of a scythe.
Breadth s. Measure from side to side, extent.
Hair'breadth s. A minute distance.
Hun'dredth a. The ordinal of 100; s. One of a hundred equal parts.
Width s. Extent from side to side; wideness, breadth.
Thou'sandth a. and s. (*Thousand*).
Teeth s. (*Tooth*).
Nine'tieth a. The ordinal of 90. s. One of ninety equal parts.
Fif'tieth a. The ordinal of 50. s. One of fifty equal parts.
Eight'ieth a. and s. (*Eighty*).
Sev'entieth a. and s. (*Seventy*).
Twen'tieth a. and s. (*Twenty*).
Thir'tieth a. and s. (*Thirty*).
For'tieth a. The ordinal of 40; s. one of forty equal parts.
Six'tieth a. Next after the fifty-ninth. s. One of sixty equal parts.
Shib'boleth s. A word or other thing that distinguishes one party from another; a discredited theory.
Tur'peth s. The purgative root of an E. Indian plant.
Fifth a. The ordinal of 5. s. One of five equal parts.
Twelfth s. One of twelve equal parts. a. Next after the eleventh.
Length s. Horizontal extension; quality of being long.
Strength s. Muscular force; potency; numbers of an army, etc.
Eighth a. Coming next after the seventh. s. One of eight equal parts.
Faith s. Belief; fidelity; probity; sincerity.
Wraith s. Phantom of a living person; a spectre.
Saith (seth) 3rd sing. pres. (*Say*).
Had'ith s. Body of traditional sayings, etc., of Mohammed.
Kith s. Kindred.
Lith s. A joint; a division.
-lith suff. Forming nouns designating stones, etc.
Meg'alith s. A great stone monument; a cromlech.
Tri'lith s. A prehistoric monument consisting of two upright stones with a third resting on them.
Tal'lith s. The Jewish praying-scarf.
Lac'colith s. An intrusive mass of lava.
E'olith s. A very primitive form of stone implement.
Pal'æolith s. A stone implement from the earlier Stone Age.
Ne'olith s. An implement, etc., of the later Stone Age.
Mon'olith s. A monument, etc., consisting of a single stone.
Ac'rolith s. A statue with only the head and limbs of stone.
A'erolith s. A meteorite.
Nemathel'minth s. A nematode.
Smith s. One who works in metals.
White'smith s. A tin-smith.
Black'smith s. A smith who works in iron.
Lock'smith s. Maker or repairer of locks.
Gun'smith s. A maker or repairer of small-arms.
Zen'ith s. The point directly overhead; the highest point, culmination.
Pith s. The soft, spongy "marrow" of plants; the spinal cord; the quintessence; vigour; cogency.
Crith s. The unit of weight for gases.
Mi'crocrith s. The weight of an atom of hydrogen.
Frith s. A firth.
Sith conj. Since; seeing that.
With prep.
Herewith' adv. With this.
Therewith' adv.
Wherewith' adv.

Forthwith' adv. Immediately; without delay.
Health s. Freedom from disease; sound bodily and mental state; a toast of well-wishing.
Stealth s. Furtiveness; secret procedure.
Wealth (welth) s. Riches; opulence; affluence.
Com'monwealth s. The body politic, whole body of citizens; a republic; a federation.
Filth s. Dirt; corruption; pollution.
Spilth s. That which is split; overplus.
Tilth s. Cultivation; depth of soil tilled.
Warmth s. State or quality of being warm; gentle heat; enthusiasm.
Trag'acanth s. A gum used in medicine; the leguminous shrub yielding this.
Pyr'acanth s. An evergreen thorn with red berries.
Per'ianth s. The calyx enveloping a single flower.
Am'aranth s. An unfading plant, the symbol of immortality.
Rhiz'anth s. A plant flowering from the root.
Greenth s. Greenness; verdure.
Nineteenth' a. The ordinal of 19. s. A nineteenth part.
Fifteenth' a. The ordinal of 15. s. One of fifteen equal parts.
Eighteenth' a. Coming next after the seventeenth. s. One of eighteen equal parts.
Seventeenth' a. and s. (*Seventeen*).
Thirteenth' a. and s. (*Thirteen*).
Fourteenth' a. The ordinal of fourteen. s. One of fourteen equal parts.
Sixteenth' a. and s. (*Sixteen*).
Tenth a. and s. (*Ten*).
Elev'enth a. and s. Next after the tenth; one of eleven equal parts.
Sev'enth a. Coming next after the sixth. s. The next after the sixth; a seventh part.
Ter'ebinth s. The turpentine tree; its resin.
Jac'inth s. A variety of zircon, a gem.
Hy'acinth s. A bulbous flowering plant; jacinth, a red variety of zircon.
Plinth s. The lowest division of the base of a column, pedestal, etc.
Hel'minth s. A parasitic intestinal worm.
Ninth a. Next after the eighth. s. One of nine equal parts.
Lab'yrinth s. A maze; anything inexplicable; part of the internal ear.
Decil'lionth a. and s. (*Decillion*).
Mil'lionth s. One of a million equal parts. a. Coming last of a million.
Tril'lionth a. (*Trillion*).
Month s. One of the twelve divisions of the year; period of the moon's revolution.
Twelve'month s. A year.
Col'ocynth s. The bitter-apple or its fruit; a purgative extract from this.
Sab'aoth s. (*Hebrew*) Hosts, armies.
Both a., pron. The one and the other, the two. conj. As well.
Goth s. An ancient Teuton; a barbarian.
Loth a. Loath.
Cloth s. A woven fabric of wool, cotton, etc.; drop-scene in a theatre; the clerical profession; covering for a meal-table.
Broad'cloth s. A fine kind of woollen cloth.
Cere'cloth s. A waxed cloth used in embalming.
Box'-cloth s. A tough, closely woven cloth.
Sloth s. Laziness, sluggishness; a S. American mammal.
Moth s. A lepidopterous insect allied to the butterfly; that which imperceptibly consumes or destroys anything.
Be'hemoth s. The hippopotamus (?).
Mam'moth s. A huge extinct elephant. a. gigantic, huge.
Booth s. A stall or tent in a fair; a polling-station.
Tol'booth s. (*Scot.*) A town jail.
Smooth a. Having an even surface; not rough, ruffled, or obstructed; level, flat; bland, flattering. v.t. To make smooth, easy, or flowing.
Sooth s. Truth; reality.
Forsooth' adv. In truth; certainly; very well.
Tooth s. Bony growth in the jaws used in masticating food; a toothlike projection, cog, etc.; palate. v.t. To furnish with teeth; to indent.
Broth s. Liquor in which flesh has been boiled.
Froth s. Spume, foam; unsubstantial talk or matter.
Troth s. Fidelity; truth.
Betroth' v.t. To affiance in marriage.
Wroth a. Angry; incensed.
Quoth v.t. Said, spoke.
Depth s. Deepness; a deep place; the deepest or middle part; sagacity; abstruseness.
Earth s. The world we inhabit; mould; dry land; the hole of a fox. v.t. To cover with earth. v.i. To burrow.
Dearth s. Scarcity; privation.
Hearth s. A fireplace, fireside; the home.
Unearth' v.t. To bring from the earth; to bring to light.
Garth s. A close, yard, small enclosed place.
Berth s. A sleeping-place on board ship; a ship's station.
Birth s. Coming into life; extraction; family.
Firth s. A narrow arm of the sea.
Girth s. Circumference; that which girds; broad belt for saddle.
Mirth s. Merriment, festivity, joviality.
Forth adv. Forward; abroad; out of doors.
Henceforth' adv. From this time forward.
North s. The point opposite the south. a. Situated in or towards, or pertaining to the North. adv. Towards or in the north. v.i. To veer towards the north.
Ha'p'orth a. Halfpennyworth, a trivial amount.
Worth (werth) s. Price; desert; value; excellence. a. Equal in value to; deserving of; having. v.i. To betide,
Pen'nyworth s. As much as can be bought for 1d.; a bit; a good bargain.
Fourth a. The ordinal of 4. s. One of four equal parts.
Sleuth (slooth) s. Track of man or beast as known by scent.
Az'imuth s. The direction of an object in reference to the cardinal points.
Altaz'imuth s. An instrument for taking the altitude and azimuth of stars.
Ver'muth s. A spirituous, aromatic liqueur.
Bis'muth s. A brittle, reddish-white metal.
Uncouth' (-kooth') a. Having awkward manners; strange; odd.
Mouth s. The aperture between and cavity within the lips through which food is taken; an opening, orifice; outlet of a river. v.i. To speak pompously, to vociferate. v.t. To utter with an affectedly big voice.
Drouth s. Drought.

South s. Point of compass opposite to the north; region in which the sun is at midday; a southern part. a. Lying or being toward the south; pertaining to or from the south. adv. Toward the south. v.t. To move in this direction.
Youth (ūth) s. State of being young; period of freshness, inexperience, etc.; a young man; young persons generally.
Ruth s. Tenderness; compassion.
Truth s. That which is true; conformity to fact; veracity; integrity.
Growth s. Act or process of growing; advancement; vegetation.
Un'dergrowth s. Shrubs, etc., growing among larger ones.
Out'growth s. That which has grown out of anything.
Sixth a. Next after the fifth. s. One of six equal parts; an upper form at schools; the interval of four tones and a semitone.
Myth s. A tradition embodying beliefs of a people as to their gods, origin, etc.; a parable; an invented story.
I pron. Denoting oneself. s. The ego.
-i suff. Denoting plural of certain Latin and Italian nouns.
A'i s. The S. American three-toed sloth.
As'sagai s. The Zulu javelin or hurling spear.
Nil'gai s. The nylghau.
Shanghai' (hī') v.t. To drug a man then ship him as a sailor.
Serai' s. Caravanserai.
Caravan'serai s. An Oriental inn; a halting-place for caravans.
Sam'urai (-rī) s. One of the old Japanese military caste.
Dzig'getai s. A species of wild ass.
Banzai' int. A Japanese cry of triumph.
Waha'bi (-bē) s. One of a strict Moslem sect.
Rab'i s. The Hindu grain crop reaped in the spring.
Kohlra'bi s. A turnip-shaped cabbage.
Rab'bi s. A Jewish doctor of law.
Al'ibi s. Elsewhere; in another place.
O'bi s. A Japanese coloured sash.
Dho'bi s. A Hindu washerman.
Ca'di s. A Turkish judge.
Wa'di s. Bed of a stream that is usually dry.
Marave'di s. An obsolete Spanish coin of small value.
Mah'di s. The Messiah of Mohammedans.
Garibal'di s. A loose kind of blouse.
Jaboran'di s. A S. American plant used in medicine.
Effen'di s. Turkish title of a state official, lawyer, etc.
Hindi' s. The Aryan language of N. India.
Salmagun'di s. A dish of chopped meat, fish, vinegar, etc.; a medley.
Sephar'di s. A Spanish or Portuguese Jew.
Su'fi s. A Mohammedan mystic.
Ma'gi s. The three Wise Men of the East.
Bostan'gi s. A guard of the Sultan's seraglio.
Yo'gi s. A Hindu ascetic; a devotee of yoga.
Hi int. Calling attention, etc.
Spa'hi s. An Algerian cavalryman in the French army.
Ka'michi s. The horned screamer of S. America.
Leiot'richi s. The smooth-haired races of mankind.
Ulot'richi s. The woolly-haired races.
Bronch'i s. The main divisions of the windpipe.
Litchi (lēchē) s. A Chinese fruit, or its tree.
Rish'i s. A Hindu saint, sage, or poet.
Mun'shi s. A native secretary or teacher of languages in India.
Doch'mii s. (*Dochmius*).
To'rii (-ri-ē) s. The gateless gateway of Japanese temples.
Hadj'i s. A Mohammedan who has made the pilgrimage to Mecca.
Kha'ki a. Dull grey, dust-coloured. s. Cloth, etc., of this colour; uniform made of this.
Sa'ki s. A S. American monkey.
Ski (shē) s. A long narrow runner strapped to the foot for use on snow-fields.
Li s. Chinese measure of length (about 660 yards), and weight (about ⅓ grain).
Bengali' a. Of Bengal, its inhabitants, or language. s. A native or the anguage of Bengal.
Ar'gali s. An Asiatic mountain sheep.
Ka'li s. The salt-wort.
Al'kali s. A base of caustic properties which combines with an acid to form a salt.
Antal'kali s. Something that neutralizes an alkali.
Pa'li s. The sacred language of Buddhists; a dialect of Sanskrit.
Ses'eli s. A genus of umbelliferous plants, including meadow-saxifrage.
Swahi'li (-hē'-) s. A Bantu people of Zanzibar and district; their language.
Teocal'li s. An ancient Mexican pyramidal temple.
Vermicel'li s. A kind of slender macaroni.
Cancel'li s. Lattice-work between the choir and body of a church.
Baccill'i s. (*Baccillus*).
Chill'i s. The dried pod of the red pepper or capsicum.
Piccalil'li s. A pungent vegetable pickle.
Lapil'li s. Volcanic ashes.
Bouilli' s. Stewed meat.
Vill'i s. (*Villus*)
Osman'li a. and s. Ottoman.
Broc'coli s. A species of cabbage.
Trip'oli s. Rottenstone.
Patchou'li s. An Indian plant; a perfume prepared therefrom.
Lap'is laz'uli s. A rich blue stone: its colour.
Mi s. The third note of the diatonic scale.
Ag'ami s. A S. American bird of the crane family.
Go'rami s. A Japanese nest-building food-fish.
Dem'i a. Prefix meaning half.
El'emi s. An oily resin from the pitch-tree of Manilla.
Sal'mi s. Salmis.
Deca'ni a. Pertaining to the S. side of a cathedral choir.
Frangipa'ni s. Frangipane.
Mahara'ni s. A native Indian sovereign princess.
Hindusta'ni s. The Indian vernacular, a mixture of western Hindi with Arabic, Persian, etc.
Dewa'ni s. The office of a dewan.
Fantocci'ni s. Puppets, marionettes.
Mei'ni (mā'-) s. A household, retinue.
Gem'ini s. The constellation, the Twins, the third sign of the Zodiac.
Anno Dom'ini s. (*Facetious*) Old age.
Alum'ni s. Pupils in relation to their place of education.
Sun'ni s. A Sunnite.
Macaro'ni s. A tube-shaped food of dried wheaten paste; a medley; a fop.
Lazzaro'ni s. Neapolitan beggars.

Polloi' s. The mob, rabble.
Xanthoc'roi s. The fair whites or blonds.
Melanoch'roi s. Denoting the races with dark hair and pale complexions.
Oc'troi s. An import duty levied at the gates of some continental cities.
Bor'zoi s. A Russian wolf-hound.
Pi s. Confused or unsorted type. a. (*Slang*) Pious.
Oka'pi s. A giraffe-like ruminant.
Kép'i s. The French military hat.
Pi'pi s. A tropical American plant; its pod, used in tanning.
Im'pi s. A regiment of Zulu warriors.
Certiorar'i s. A writ calling for records or removing a case to a higher court.
Cu'rari s. Curare.
Chariva'ri s. A mock serenade; a hubbub.
Col'ibri s. A variety of humming-bird.
In'dri s. A Madagascan lemur, the babacoote.
Ber'iberi s. A disease characterized by paralysis and dropsy.
Bersaglier'i s. Italian sharpshooters.
Per'i s. A female descendant of the fallen angels excluded from the Mohammedan paradise.
Har'a-ki'ri s. Japanese method of suicide when in disgrace, etc.
Kuk'ri s. The curved knife of the Ghurkas.
Maor'i (mour'i) s. A Polynesian native of New Zealand; their language.
Caneph'ori s. Sculptured figures carrying baskets on the head.
A posterior'i adv. From effects to causes; inductively.
A prior'i adv. From cause to effect, deductively.
A fortior'i adv. Much more so, still more conclusively.
Kau'ri s. A New Zealand resin-bearing tree.
Amphig'ouri s. A meaningless metrical rigmarole.
Hour'i s. A nymph of the Mohammedan paradise.
Pot-pouri' (pō-poorē') s. Dried rose-petals mixed with spices as a perfume; a medley.
Si (sē) s. The seventh note of the diatonic scale.
Qua'si conj. and pref. As if; seeming; not real.
Pachi'si s. An Indian game played on a board marked in a cross of squares.
Ni'si conj. Unless; if not.
Rever'si s. A game with two-coloured counters.
Illumina'ti s. Persons of special enlightenment; applied to members of certain philosophical sects.
Coa'ti s. A small American carnivorous mammal.
Jupati' s. A Brazilian palm yielding fibre.
Litera'ti s. The learned.
Spermacet'i s. A semi-transparent fatty matter obtained from the sperm-whale.
Tap'eti s. A hare-like rodent of S. America.
Muf'ti s. An official expounder of Mohammedan law; civilian dress.
Wap'iti (wŏp'-) s. The large deer of N. America.
Chian'ti s. A red Italian wine.
Démen'ti s. An official contradiction of a rumour.
Confet'ti s. Small sweetmeats; small coloured paper discs thrown at festivals, etc.
Spaghet'ti s. A variety of macaroni.
Bandit'ti s. A band of outlaws; freebooters.
Tut'ti-frut'ti s. A dish of various fruits with cream, etc.
Tut'ti adv. Direction for all to perform together (*in music*).
Agou'ti s. A S. American rodent.
En'nui s. Boredom, listlessness, tedium.
Char'qui s. Sun-dried beef.
Etui' s. A case of needles, work-box.
Pecca'vi int. Expressing acknowledgment of error, or contrition.
Div'i-div'i s. A tropical plant used in tanning and dyeing.
Ki'wi s. The apteryx of New Zealand.
Tax'i s. A public motor vehicle fitted with a taximeter.
Samaj' s. A Hindu association for religious purposes.
Raj s. Rule, sovereignty (in India).
Taj s. A Persian crown or head-dress.
Hadj s. A pilgrimage to Mecca.
Dak s. In India, transport by relays of horses.
Ko'dak s. A portable camera.
Beak s. The bill of a bird; a point (*slang*) a magistrate.
Gros'beak s. A finch with a thick bill.
Leak s. A hole letting water, air, etc., in or out. v.i. To let water, etc., thus.
Bleak a. Cold and desolate; exposed to the winds.
Sneak v.i. To creep slyly, behave meanly, tell tales. v.t. (*Slang*) To steal. s. One who sneaks; a mean fellow; a tale-bearer.
Peak s. A point, summit; the top of a hill. v.t. To raise (a sail) perpendicularly. v.i. To look sickly.
Apeak' adv. Pointed upwards.
Fore'peak s. The furthest end of a ship's forecastle.
Speak v.i. To talk, deliver a speech; to argue; to be expressive. v.t. To utter, pronounce, express.
Bespeak' v.t. To order in advance; to forebode.
Break v.t. To part by violence; to tame; to dismiss. s. A disruption; an opening, a pause, a failure; a sequence of scoring strokes at billiards.
Out'break s. A bursting forth, violent manifestation; a revolt.
Day'break s. First appearance of daylight.
Bar'ley-break s. An obsolete rustic game.
Creak v.i. To make a harsh grating sound. s. Such a sound.
Freak s. A caprice, whim; a prank; a monstrosity; an eccentric person.
Streak s. An irregular line; a narrow stripe of colour. v.t. To form streaks in.
Wreak v.t. To carry out in passion, etc., inflict. s. Vengeance; fury.
Teak s. An E. Indian tree; its very hard and heavy timber.
Steak s. Slice of beef, etc., cut for broiling.
Beef-steak' s. A slice of beef broiled, or for broiling.
Squeak v.i. To utter a sharp, shrill cry, make a sharp noise. s. Such a sound; a narrow escape.
Weak a. Feeble; infirm; vacillating; pliant; ineffective; denoting verb inflected by addition of letter or syllable.
Tweak v.t. To twitch; to squeeze between the fingers. s. A pinch, nip, sharp jerk.
Oo'miak s. An Eskimo skin-covered boat.
U'miak (oo'-) s. Fishing-boat of Eskimo women.

San'jak s. An administrative division of a Turkish vilayet.
Munt'jak s. A small deer of S.E. Asia.
Yash'mak s. Face-veil of Moslem women.
Oak s. A forest tree; its timber; outer door to chambers.
Cloak s. A loose outer garment; a disguise, pretext. v.t. To cover with a cloak; to hide, conceal. v.i. To put on one's cloak.
Croak s. The cry of a frog or raven; a murmur. v.i. To make a low, hoarse noise; to murmur.
Soak v.t. To steep in liquid; to drench. v.i. To lie steeped; to drink to excess. s. A drenching; a drinking bout.
Cham'pak s. An E. Indian tree.
Oo'pak s. A kind of black tea.
Slovak' s. and a. Member of or pertaining to a Slav race of N. Hungary.
Yak s. The long-haired wild-ox of Tibet.
Kay'ak s. The sealskin canoe used by the Eskimos.
Dy'ak s. One of the aboriginal race of Borneo.
Nabk s. The nebbuk, a thorny shrub.
Back s. The hinder part of a thing; the spine. adv. To the place whence one came. v.t. To mount; to second, support; to bet on.
Aback' adv. Backwards.
Huck'aback s. A coarse linen cloth; towelling.
Hold'back s. Hindrance; detention; obstacle.
Zwie'back (tswē'-) s. A kind of rusk.
Stickle'back s. A small, spiny-backed, freshwater fish.
Bare'back a. adv. Without a saddle.
Horse'back s. The back of a horse.
Hog'back s. A long ridged hill.
Hunch'back s. A humpback.
Thorn'back s. The British skate.
Hump'back s. A crooked back; a person with this.
Hack v.t. To cut, hew, chop; to let out for hire. s. A notch, rough cut; a kick; a horse let out for hire; a literary drudge.
Shack s. Liberty of winter pasturage; fallen acorns, etc.; a rough shanty, hut.
Whack s. A heavy or resounding blow; (*slang*) a share. v.t. and i. To strike resoundingly.
Jack s. Contrivance for various purposes; knave at cards; male of certain animals; a young pike; defensive coat of leather; leather drinking vessel; small flag; the Union flag; the mark at bowls. v.t. To hoist or move with a jack.
Black'jack s. A zinc ore, an old leather drinking vessel.
Flap'jack s. A broad pancake.
Slap'jack s. A flat cake baked on a griddle.
Skip'jack s. A leaping coleopterous insect.
Nat'terjack s. A species of toad with yellow-striped back.
Boot'jack s. A wooden crotch for use in taking off a top-boot.
Lack s. Deficiency; that which is needed; failure. v.t. To be in need of, to want. v.i. To be wanting.
Alack' int. Alas!
Black a. Destitute of light, very dark, gloomy; dismal, foul. s. The darkest colour; a negro; mourning.
Clack v.i. To make a sharp, sudden noise; to chatter. v.t. To cause to make a sudden noise. s. A sharp repeated sound; prattle; a chatter-box; a contrivance in the hopper of a corn-mill.
Pol'lack s. A sea-fish of the cod family.
Slack a. Loose, limp; careless, remiss, dull. adv. In a slack manner. s. Part of rope, etc., hanging loose; small coal. v.t. and i. To slacken; to be listless.
Smack v.i. To make a noise with the lips; to taste, savour. v.t. To make a sharp noise with; to slap. s. A sharp noise, loud kiss, slap; a slight taste, smattering; a small sailing vessel.
Alm'anack s. (*Almanac*).
Knack s. Facility of performance; dexterity.
Knick'-knack s. An ornamental trifle, gewgaw.
Snack s. A light repast; a share.
Pack s. A bundle, bale; set of playing-cards, or of dogs; a gang; area of floating ice. v.t. To make up into a bundle; to fill with contents; to manipulate fraudulently; to dismiss hastily. v.i. To make up bundles; to clear off.
Repack' v.t. To pack again.
Cal'pack s. An Oriental triangular cap.
Rack s. Instrument of torture; anything used for stretching; anguish; a frame for fodder; bar with teeth on one edge for a cog-wheel; thin flying clouds; wreck, ruin. v.t. To stretch, distort, torture; to harass; to draw off from the lees.
Tam'arack s. The black larch of N. America.
Shab'rack s. A cavalryman's saddle-cloth.
Crack s. A fissure, sudden sharp sound, sounding blow, partial separation of parts. v.t. To break partially, to fissure; to cause to sound abruptly; to snap; to say smartly; to extol. v.i. To be fractured; to utter a sharp sound; to brag; to chat. a. Of superior excellence.
Gim'crack s. A trivial device or mechanism. a. Trivial, worthless.
Ar'rack s. Native distilled spirits in the East.
Bar'rack s. A building for housing troops. v.i. (*Slang*) To cheer ironically.
Carrack' s. A large merchant-ship.
Track s. A trace, footprint, wheel-rut; course. v.t. To follow by a trace; to tow (a vessel).
Wrack s. Seaweed thrown on the shore; thin, flying cloud; ruin.
Sack s. A rough canvas bag; an old white wine; the looting of a place; plunder; (*slang*) dismissal. v.t. To pillage, ransack.
Ruck'sack (rook'-) s. A knapsack.
Wool'sack s. Lord Chancellor's seat in House of Lords.
Ran'sack v.t. To plunder; to search narrowly.
Knap'sack s. A bag carried at the back for necessaries.
Grip'sack s. A hand-bag.
Hav'ersack s. A bag for a soldier to carry provisions, etc.
Cos'sack s. One of a mixed Turkish race in S. Russia.
Tack s. A small nail; a ship's rope; course of a ship, etc. v.t. To

fasten slightly, to append. v.i. To sail by successive changes of course.

Hack'matack s. The American black larch.

Stack s. Large pile of straw, hay, etc.; group of chimneys; tall, single chimney; detached tower of rock. v.t. To pile in stacks.

Hay'stack s. A thatched pile of hay in the open.

Attack' v.t. To assault, assail, fall on. s. An assault.

Quack v.i. To cry like the duck; to brag, play the quack. s. A boastful pretender; a charlatan, mountebank. a. Pertaining to quackery or quacks.

Thwack v.t. To whack.

Beck s. A bow, a nod; a rivulet. v.i. and t. To make a mute signal; to call by such.

Re'beck s. An obsolete three-stringed musical instrument.

Pinch'beck s. An alloy resembling gold. a. Imitation, sham.

Pur'beck a. Applied to a fine variety of building-stone.

Deck v.t. To cover, dress, array, adorn. s. The floor on a ship.

Bedeck' v.t. To adorn.

Heck s. A grating; a rack for fodder.

Check s. A restraint, hindrance; a token; exposure of the king at chess to attack; a cross-lined pattern or fabric. v.t. To repress, curb, rebuke; to mark off, compare with a counterpart; to attack the king at chess. v.i. To pause.

Countercheck' v.t. To oppose, check. s. Check, stop, rebuke.

Keck v.i. To heave, make a retching sound.

Fleck s. A spot, freckle, speck; a patch of light or colour. v.t. To dapple, to variegate.

Neck s. Part of body connecting the head with the trunk; narrow tract of land; any slender part.

Break'neck a. Heedless of consequences; hazardous.

Wry'neck s. A distorted or stiff neck; a bird allied to the woodpecker.

Peck s. One-fourth of a bushel; eight quarts; a great deal; a sharp stroke or mark made with the beak; (*slang*) a mouthful, a hasty meal. v.t. To strike or pick up with the beak or a sharp instrument. v.i. To make strokes thus.

Co'peck s. A Russian copper coin.

Speck s. A spot, stain; a flaw; a minute particle. v.t. To spot.

Reck v.i. To take heed, care.

Wreck s. Overthrow; vessel disabled or destroyed at sea; such destruction; a disabled or infirm person; a ruin. v.t. To bring to ruin, cause to become a wreck.

Ship'wreck s. The destruction or loss of a ship at sea; ship so destroyed; ruin. v.t. To ruin, wreck. v.i. To be ruined.

Med'ick s. A plant allied to the clover.

Ben'edick s. A newly married man.

Maf'fick v.i. To hold a wild, riotous celebration.

Chick s. A young bird, a chicken; a little child.

Pea'chick s. The young of the peafowl.

Dab'chick s. The little grebe.

Thick a. Dense; turbid; foggy; crowded; dull; intimate. s. The thickest part. adv. Close together; indistinctly.

Kick v.t. To strike with the foot, or in recoiling. v.i. To perform this action; to show opposition. s. A blow with the foot; recoil of a firearm.

Lick v.t. To draw the tongue over; to lap, take in by the tongue; (*slang*) to flog. s. Act of licking; a smear (of paint); a blow; a great pace.

Nib'lick s. Golf-club with small, heavy iron head.

Click v.i. To make a small, sharp noise, to tick. s. A slight sharp sound; the articulation of certain S. African natives; a catch for a lock, bolt, or ratchet-wheel.

Flick s. A sharp stroke as with a whip. v.t. To strike with such a stroke.

Kill'ick s. A small anchor.

Rol'lick v.i. To behave jovially or boisterously. s. A spree, jollity.

Slick a. Smooth, sleek; easily done. adv. Immediately; deftly.

Cow'lick s. A tuft of hair turned up.

Nick s. Exact point of time; a notch, dent; a score. v.t. To hit on exactly, touch luckily; to notch, to suit.

Snick v.t. To cut, snip. s. A slight notch, cut, or hit.

Pick v.t. To pluck, cull; to peck at; to separate; to cleanse by removing; to open a lock. v.i. To nibble; to pilfer. s. A sharp-pointed tool; choice, selection.

Rick s. A stack of hay, etc., in the open; a sprain. v.t. To pile into ricks; to wrench or sprain.

Brick s. Burnt clay shaped in a mould; a small loaf; (*slang*) a good fellow, a "sport." v.t. To lay with bricks.

Crick s. Spasmodic stiffness of the neck.

Lim'erick s. A five-lined nonsense verse.

Prick s. A slender pointed instrument; a puncture with such; a thorn; a sting, torment. v.t. To puncture with a prick; to spur, goad, sting; to erect (the ears). v.i. To be pricked or punctured; to spur onward.

Der'rick s. Apparatus for raising heavy weights.

Trick s. A sly fraud, dexterous artifice, prank; all the cards played in one round. v.t. To deceive, cheat; to dress, adorn fantastically. v.i. To live by fraud.

Strick s. A strickle.

Wrick v.t. To sprain, twist (the back, neck, etc.). s. A wrench, sprain.

Hay'rick s. A haystack.

Sick a. Ill; inclined to vomit; disgusted.

Sea'-sick a. Suffering from sea-sickness.

Home'sick a. Depressed through absence from home.

Love'sick a. Languishing with love.

Brain'sick a. Flighty; daft.

Fos'sick v.i. (*Slang*) To rummage about.

Tick s. A parasite infesting sheep, etc; case for mattresses, material for this; credit; sound made by a clock, etc.; a tiny mark. v.i. and t. To give credit; to make the sound of a watch etc. to mark

Stick s. A staff, rod; an awkward person. v.t. To pierce; to fasten thus or by gluing, etc.; to fix. v.i. To adhere; to be brought to a stop; to scruple.
Knob'stick s. (*Slang*) A workman who refuses to join in a strike.
Candle'stick s. A holder for a candle.
Maul'stick s. Padded stick used by artists to steady the hand in working.
Broom'stick s. The handle of a broom.
Quick a. Swift, nimble; sprightly; alive; sensitive; pregnant. s. A growing plant for hedges; the living flesh; sensitiveness.
Wick s. The fibrous string or band supplying grease or oil to the flame in candles and lamps; a village; an oblique hit in curling.
Bail'iwick s. The district under a bailie or bailiff.
Bock s. A large beer-glass; a kind of lager beer.
Cock s. The male of the domestic fowl and other birds; a vane; a leader; a tap; hammer of a gun; small heap of hay. v.t. To set erect; to set jauntily on one side (of hats); to look knowing; to set a trigger.
Acock' adv. Cocked; defiantly.
Pea'cock s. A gallinaceous bird with rich plumage and beautiful tail-feathers.
Wood'cock s. A game-bird allied to the snipe.
Shuttle'cock s. A cork stuck with feathers used in certain games.
Spatch'cock s. A fowl cooked as soon as killed. v.t. To interpolate (words) hurriedly.
Spitch'cock s. An eel split and broiled.
Black'cock s. The male of the black grouse.
Turn'cock s. One in charge of a water-main.
Weather'cock s. Revolving vane to show direction of wind; a fickle person.
Bil'lycock s. A round, hard felt hat.
Dock s. A common weed; part of a tail left after clipping; an enclosure to receive vessels; place for accused person in court. v.t. To curtail, clip; to deduct from; to bar; to place in a dock.
Had'dock s. A sea-fish allied to the cod.
Shad'dock s. A large, orange-like fruit of the E. and W. Indies.
Pad'dock s. A small stable-field under pasture; an enclosure at a race-course; a frog.
Pid'dock s. A bivalve mollusc.
Rud'dock s. The redbreast.
Can'dock s. The yellow water-lily.
Bur'dock s. A plant with prickly burs.
Hock s. A light wine; a hough.
Chock s. A block or wedge of wood. v.t. To wedge or support with this; to fill up. adv. Tightly, fully.
Mo'hock s. An aristocratic ruffian of eighteenth-century London.
Shock s. A violent collision, blow, onset, etc.; sudden emotion or derangement of the nervous system; a pile of sheaves; a thick mass of hair. v.t. To strike against suddenly, or with surprise, disgust, horror, etc.; to offend; to collect (sheaves) into shocks. a. Shaggy.
Hol'lyhock s. A tall, bright-flowered garden plant.
Bubbl'y-jock s. A turkey.
Lock s. Fastening apparatus for doors, etc.; part of a gun; tuft of hair; enclosure in river, etc; a fastening together. v.t. To fasten with lock and key; to confine; to join firmly, embrace closely. v.i. To become fast or united.
Block s. An obstruction; a solid mass of stone, etc.; a shaped mould; a pulley. v.t. To stop, obstruct.
Clock s. A mechanical time-piece not adapted for the pocket; embroidery on the side of a stocking; the dung-beetle.
Dead'lock s. A complete standstill.
Pad'lock s. A movable lock with a semicircular link for use with a staple. v.t. To fasten or provide with such.
Wed'lock s. Matrimony; state of marriage.
Fore'lock s. A lock of hair on the forehead.
Hav'elock s. A sun-guard for the back of the neck.
Flock s. A company of sheep, birds, etc.; a congregation; a lock of wool or hair; refuse of cotton, wool, etc. v.i. To gather in a crowd.
Pick'lock s. An implement (other than a key) for opening a lock; a thief.
Hill'ock s. A little hill or mound.
Bull'ock s. An ox or castrated bull.
Mul'lock s. Rock containing no gold; refuse; rubbish.
Hem'lock s. An umbelliferous plant yielding a poison used in medicine.
Car'lock s. Isinglass.
Char'lock s. The wild mustard.
War'lock s. A wizard, magician.
Interlock' v.i. To unite, embrace. v.t. To unite by overlapping or by a series of connexions.
Fet'lock s. Tuft behind a horse's pastern; a shackle to prevent a horse running off.
Row'lock (rul'ok) s. A crotch or notch as fulcrum for an oar.
Shy'lock s. A usurious Jew or money-lender.
Mock v.t. To deride, delude, mimic, defy contemptuously. v.i. To express derision, etc. a. Sham, assumed. s. Derision; a sneer.
Bemock' v.t. To flout, deride.
Cam'mock s. The rest-harrow.
Ham'mock s. A suspended bed.
Mam'mock s. A shapeless lump.
Dram'mock s. Oatmeal and water ready for cooking.
Hum'mock s. A mound; a rounded ridge of ice.
Smock s. A blouse; a chemise.
Nock s. A notch, especially of a bow or arrow.
Knock v.t. and i. To strike with something heavy; to strike against, clash, rap.
Ban'nock s. A flat round cake.
Jan'nock a. and adv. Straightforward, thorough.
Dun'nock s. The hedge-sparrow.
Pock s. A pustule, especially in smallpox.
Rock s. A large stone or mass of stony material; a hard sweetmeat; a distaff used in spinning. v.t. To move backward and forward as on a pivot, to swing. v.i. To reel, totter.
Rack'arock s. An explosive used in blasting.
Brock s. A badger.
Crock s. An earthen vessel; soot on a pot; a broken-down machine, horse, etc.; a fool, an invalid. v.i. To collapse, break down

Bed'rock s. The lowest stratum; bottom; fundamental principles.
Lav'erock s. The lark.
Frock s. A dress coat, outer garment.
Unfrock' v.t. To deprive of priestly status.
Disfrock' v.t. To unfrock.
Sham'rock s. A species of trefoil, the emblem of Ireland.
Tar'rock s. A tern or other gull.
Sock s. Short woven covering for foot; shoe worn by ancient comic actor; comedy; (*slang*) a hard blow. v.t. (*Slang*) To hit with a blow or missile.
Cas'sock s. The long outer robe worn by clergy, vergers, etc.
Has'sock s. Tuft of grass; cushion for kneeling on.
Tus'sock s. A tuft or clump of grass.
Stock s. A post, trunk of tree, wooden piece of rifle, etc.; lineage; capital sum, funded money; cattle; liquid foundation of soup, etc.; a garden plant. v.t. To provide with a stock; to have in store. a. Kept in stock; permanent.
Pen'stock s. A wooden trough or conduit.
Al'penstock s. A mountaineers' iron-shod stick.
Lin'stock s. A forked staff to hold a match, anciently used in firing cannon.
Mat'tock s. A kind of pickaxe.
Bit'tock s. A little bit, a short distance.
But'tock s. The rump; a throw in wrestling.
Fut'tock s. One of the timbers in the compound rib of a vessel.
Put'tock s. A species of kite.
Gar'vock s. A sprat.
Buck s. The male of various animals; a fop. v.i. To jump viciously with the head down; (*slang*) to swagger.
Roe'buck s. The male roe.
Prong'buck s. A N. American ruminant.
Duck s. A web-footed water-fowl; an untwilled cotton fabric; a quick plunge; a bob of the head; a term of endearment, a score of o at cricket. v.i. To plunge under water; to bob the head, to cringe. v.t. To throw or dip into water, to wet thoroughly.
Chuck v.i. To cluck like a hen. v.t. To tap under the chin; to fling, throw. s. The call of a hen to her chickens; a tap; a throw, toss; the part of a lathe that holds the wood to be turned; a fowl, chick; an old term of endearment.
Wood'chuck s. A N. American rodent of the marmot family.
Shuck s. A husk, pod. v.t. To remove the shell, etc., from.
Luck s. Fortune (good or bad); chance, hap; success.
Cluck s. The call of a hen to her chickens. v.t. and i. To make the noise of a brooding hen, to call thus.
Pluck v.t. To snatch, pull sharply, strip by plucking; to reject in an examination. s. The heart, liver, and lungs of a beast; courage, indomitableness.
Muck s. Dung, filth; anything vile or filthy. v.t. To make dirty; to make a mess of.
Amuck' adv. Indiscriminately, headlong.
Kal'muck s. One of a Mongolian race of W.C. Asia; a kind of shaggy cloth.
Chip'muck s. A N. American squirrel-like rodent.
Canuck' s. (*Slang*) A Canadian.
Puck s. A mischievous sprite; a disk used as a ball in ice-hockey.
Ruck s. A heap, rick; a multitude; the common herd; a wrinkle, crease. v.t. and i. To crease, be drawn into wrinkles.
Truck s. Low carriage for heavy weights, a barrow; cap at top of flagstaff or mast; barter, exchange of commodities; part payment in goods. v.t. and i. To barter.
Awe'struck a. Filled with awe.
Suck v.t. and i. To draw in with the mouth; to imbibe, absorb; to draw the breast. s. An act or spell of sucking; milk drawn from the breast; (*slang*) a hoax.
Tuck s. Horizontal fold in a garment; afterpart of ship; small net; beat of drum; a tucket; (*slang*) sweets, pastry, etc. v.t. To press in or together; to fold under, make a tuck in.
Cheek s. The side of the face; assurance, impudence. v.t. and i. To be impudent, to be saucy to.
Leek s. A vegetable allied to the onion.
Cleek s. An iron-headed golf-club.
House'leek s. A plant with thick, fleshy leaves growing on walls.
Gleek s. An obsolete card-game.
Sleek a. Smooth; glossy. v.t. To make smooth and even.
Meek a. Mild, gentle, submissive.
Peek v.i. To peep, look slily through.
Reek s. Smoke, vapour; stench. v.i. To emit smoke, etc.; to stink.
Creek s. A small inlet on the coast; a backwater; a brook.
Greek s. A native or the language of Greece; (*slang*) a cheat. a. Pertaining to Greece or its people.
Fen'ugreek s. A plant whose seeds are used by farriers.
Seek v.t. and i. To search for, solicit; to have recourse to.
Week s. Period of seven days, especially from Sunday to Saturday inclusive.
Shriek v.i. To scream, cry out shrilly. v.t. To utter thus. s. A sharp, shrill outcry, a yell.
Ter'ek s. An Asiatic species of sandpiper.
Trek v.i. To travel, especially by ox-wagon; to migrate. s. Travel by wagon; distance covered.
Haik s. An Arab's upper garment.
Hy'grodeik (-dīk) s. A kind of hygrometer.
Mou'jik s. A Russian peasant.
Selam'lik s. The part of a Moslem house for men.
Raskol'nik s. A Russian dissenter from the Orthodox Church.
Bol'shevik a. and s. Bolshevist.
Balk s. A ridge left unploughed; timber; an obstacle, a disappointment. v.t. To avoid, frustrate, hinder, dispute contentiously. v.i. To swerve, refuse to leap.
Calk s. A point on a horse-shoe to prevent slipping. v.t. To rough-shoe a horse with these.
Chalk s. A soft, white impure carbonate of lime; a crayon. v.t. To mark with chalk.

Talk v.i. To utter words, converse, prate. s. Conversation, chat; rumour.
Stalk s. Stem of a plant, fruit, wine-glass, etc.; a pompous gait. v.i. To walk pompously. v.t. To track and follow stealthily.
Walk (wawk) v.i. To move by steps without running. v.t. To pass through or over by walking; to lead about. s. Act of spell of walking; gait; a promenade; sphere; tract of grazing-ground.
Cake'-walk s. A negro dance or procession.
Outwalk' v.t. To walk faster than.
Elk s. The largest species of deer; the moose.
Whelk s. An edible, marine, spiral-shelled gasteropod.
Yelk s. Yolk.
Ilk a. The same.
Bilk v.t. To defraud by non-fulfilment of an engagement. s. Such a deception.
Milk s. A whitish fluid secreted by females as nourishment for their young; similar liquid as in certain plants, cocoanuts, etc. v.t. To draw milk from; to relieve of the contents, especially surreptitiously.
Silk s. Thread spun by *Bombyx mori*, the silkworm; fabric woven from this; a K. C.'s gown or office. a. Made of silk.
Folk s. People in general, one's own people.
Gen'tlefolk s. Persons of good breeding.
Wom'enfolk s. Women collectively; those of one's own household.
Nor'folk s. A loose kind of jacket.
Kins'folk s. Relations, family.
Polk v.i. To dance the polka.
Yolk (yōk) s. Yellow part of egg.
Baulk s., v.t. and i. (*Balk*).
Caulk v.t. To plug the seams of a ship with oakum.
Bulk s. Magnitude; the mass; a bench. v.i. To appear great or of importance.
Hulk s. The body of an old ship; an unwieldy ship or person.
Skulk v.i. To sneak out of the way; to lurk. s. A skulker.
Sulk v.i. To be sullen or ill-humoured. s. A fit of this.
Bank s. A ridge, heap, or sloping piece of ground; a shoal; a tier of seats, etc.; an establishment for conducting financial business. v.i. and t. To deposit or have money deposited in a bank; to heap up in a bank.
Moun'tebank s. An itinerant quack doctor; a charlatan.
Embank' v.t. To bank up, to protect or enclose with a bank.
Dank a. Damp, moist; cold through wetness.
Hank s. A skein of thread, etc.; a coil.
Shank s. The middle joint or bone of the leg; the shin.
Red'shank s. The red-legged sandpiper.
Thank v.t. To express gratitude for.
Lank a. Lean; long and thin; lax.
Blank a. Lacking something, empty; pale. s. A void space; paper, tickets, etc., unwritten or unprinted upon; the bull's-eye of a target.
Clank v.t. and i. To make a sound as of solid metallic bodies striking together. s. Such a sound.
Flank s. The fleshy part of the side; the side of an army, a building, etc.; extreme right or left. v.t. To be situated at the side, pass on the side, place troops at the side.
Outflank' v.t. To get round the side of.
Plank s. A wide, thick board; a statement of political aim. v.t. To cover with planks; to lay down as on a plank; to exhibit cash.
Spank v.t. To strike with the open hand. v.i. To go at a lively pace. s. A sounding blow.
Rank s. A row, line; dignity; class. v.i. To have a certain order, belong to a class. a. High-growing; luxuriant; rancid.
Brank s. Buckwheat.
Crank s. A bent axis for changing circular into reciprocating motion, or the reverse; a bend, turn; a whim, fit of temper; a faddy or deranged person. a. Out of gear, loose, shaky.
Drank past (*Drink*).
Frank s. A member of the German peoples who overran France in the Dark Ages.
Frank a. Open, ingenuous, sincere; liberal. v.t. To free from expense of postage; to liberate. s. An authorization to send a letter, etc., free; letter or package so sent.
Shrank past (*Shrink*).
Prank v.t. and i. To adorn showily, dress up, have a showy appearance. s. A frolic, merry trick.
Sank past (*Sink*).
Tank s. A large cistern; a heavily armoured and armed enclosed motor-car for offensive operations.
Stank past (*Stink*).
Swank v.i. (*Slang*) To put on side, swagger. s. Bluster, side.
Yank v.t. To twitch, pull sharply. s. A sharp jerk; (*slang*) a Yankee.
Ink s. Liquid writing or viscous printing material. v.t. To daub with this.
Chink s. A small fissure, a gap; a sharp metallic sound; (*slang*) ready money; a Chinaman. v.t. To clink, cause to jingle. v.i. To crack; to emit a sound of jingling.
Think v.i. To cogitate, have the mind occupied; to fancy, intend. v.t. To imagine, consider.
Bethink' v. refl. To consider, call to mind.
Kink s. An abrupt twist in a wire, etc.; a crotchet, whim. v.i. and t. To run into kinks or cause to kink.
Skink s. A small burrowing lizard.
Link s. A single ring of a chain; anything connecting; 7.92 in.; a torch v.t. To connect or attach, to unite. v.i. To be connected.
Blink v.i. To wink; to glimmer. v.t. To shut out of sight, evade. s. A glimpse, glance; the brilliant reflection from ice-fields at sea.
Ice'blink s. Luminous reflection from ice-fields.
Clink s. A sharp, tinkling, metallic sound; (*slang*) prison. v.i. and t. To make or cause to make a sharp, metallic sound.
Bob'olink s. An American song-bird.
Interlink' v.t. To connect by links.
Slink v.i. To sneak off, steal away; to miscarry (of animals). s. A premature calf.

Mink s. A stoat-like animal; its fur.
Pink s. A garden flower, a carnation; a light rose colour; a huntsman's scarlet coat; something supremely excellent. v.t. To prick, stab; to pierce with small holes, cut in scallops.
Spink s. The chaffinch.
Rink s. Patch of ice for curling; prepared floor for skating or roller-skating. v.i. To skate on a rink.
Brink s. Edge, brim.
Drink s. Liquor for consumption; potion; any beverage, alcoholic liquor. v.i. To swallow liquor; to take alcoholic liquor in excess. v.t. To imbibe, absorb, suck in.
Shrink v.i. To grow smaller; shrivel; to recoil. v.t. To cause to contract.
Prink v.t. and i. To dress for show; to strut.
Sink v.i. To fall gradually, decline, droop. v.t. To cause to sink; to dig in; to suppress. s. A drain for dirty water.
Counter'sink v.t. To chamfer a hole for a screw-head, etc. s. A chamfered hole, a tool for making this.
Stink v.i. To emit an offensive smell. s. A strong, disgusting smell.
Wink v.i. and t. To shut and open the eye quickly; to signal or intimate thus; to twinkle. s. Act of winking; a private hint.
Hood'wink v.t. To deceive, impose on.
Swink v.i. and t. To toil, to exhaust with labour. s. Drudgery.
Conk s. (*Slang*) The nose.
Honk s. The hoot of a motor-horn, etc.
Monk s. One of a religious community bound to celibacy.
Bunk s. A seaman's berth; (*slang*) a hurried flight. v.i. To decamp, run off.
Funk s. Fear, terror; a coward. v.t. and i. To be in a state of terror, be afraid, shrink, shirk.
Hunk s. A lump, hunch.
Chunk s. A short thick lump or piece.
Junk s. A Chinese flat-bottomed vessel; pieces of old rope, salt beef; a chunk.
Skunk s. A N. American carnivorous mammal; its fur.
Slunk past and past part. (*Slink*).
Punk s. Touchwood; amadon.
Spunk s. Touchwood; pluck, spirit; (*Scot.*) a match.
Drunk a. Intoxicated, tipsy.
Shrunk past part. (*Shrink*).
Trunk s. Main stem of a tree; body of an animal; main body; proboscis of elephant, etc.; chest for clothes, etc.; long wooden tube.
Ree'bok s. A small S. African antelope.
Spring'bok s. A S. African gazelle.
Sjam'bok s. A rhinoceros hide whip.
Steen'bok s. A S. African antelope.
Gems'bok s. A large S. African antelope.
Grys'bok s. A S. African antelope.
Amok' adv. (*Amuck*).
Book s. A bound volume; a division of a literary work. v.t. To register in a book; to take tickets; to engage.
Hand'book s. A small treatise, a manual.
Cook v.t. To prepare food for the table by fire; to concoct, garble, falsify. v.i. To undergo the process of cooking. s. One who prepares food for the table.
Hook s. Anything bent so as to catch hold or catch hold of; a sickle. v.t. To catch with a hook; to entrap. v.i. To curve.
Bill'hook s. A heavy knife with hooked end for pruning hedges, etc.
Shook s. A set of staves for a hogshead, boards for a case, etc. v. past (*Shake*).
Boat'hook s. A long pole furnished with an iron point and hook.
Look v.i. To direct the eyes so as to see; to gaze; to expect; to appear. s. Act of looking; glance; mien, air, appearance.
Overlook' v.t. To oversee, superintend; to view from a higher place; to pass over indulgently.
Out'look s. Act of looking out; watch; place for this; prospect.
Nook s. A corner; a cozy recess.
Snook s. The placing of the thumb to the nose in derision.
Spook s. A ghost, hobgoblin.
Rook s. A gregarious bird of the crow family; a cheat, sharper; a castle in chess. v.t. To swindle; to charge extortionately.
Brook s. A rivulet. v.t. To put up with, endure.
Crook s. A bend, or bent thing; a shepherd's staff, pastoral staff; (*slang*) a swindler. v.t. and i. To bend, make a hook on.
Nain'sook s. A thick jaconet muslin.
Forsook' past (*Forsake*).
Took past (*Take*).
Stook s. A small collection of standing sheaves. v.t. To set up in stooks.
Ka'pok s. A fine tropical fibre.
Ark s. A chest or close vessel; a large raft.
Bark s. A dog's cry; the rind of a tree. v.i. To make the noise of dogs, to clamour; to strip the bark from a tree.
Debark' v.t. To disembark.
Shag'bark s. A species of hickory; its nut.
Embark' v.i. To go on board; to engage in, start on.
Re-embark' v.t. and i. To embark again.
Dis'embark v.t. and i. To send or go on land from a ship.
Cark s. Care, anxiety.
Dark a. Destitute of light; obscure; gloomy; disheartening; secret; ignorant. s. Darkness; state of obscurity, ignorance, etc. v.t. To obscure, darken.
Hark v.i. To listen. int. Listen! attend!
Shark s. A large, voracious sea-fish; an unscrupulous sharper. v.t. To pick up hastily or slyly. v.i. To swindle; to live by one's wits.
Stink'ard s. A stinking person; a mean fellow; a carnivore allied to the skunk.
Lark s. A small singing-bird; (*slang*) a frolic, spree. v.i. (*Slang*) To sport.
Wood'lark s. A small variety of lark.
Tit'lark s. A small migratory song-bird.
Sky'lark s. The common lark. v.i. (*Slang*) To frolic, play practical jokes.
Mark s. An impression, stamp, distinguishing sign; a characteristic; pre-eminence; object aimed at; extreme estimate; a German coin.

v.t. To make marks on; to denote; to observe, heed. v.i. To note; to remark.

Land'mark s. A fixed object serving as guide; a boundary-mark.

Remark' v.t. To note, observe, express; to call attention to. v.i. To say or observe. s. Notice; observation in words; comment.

Re-mark' v.t. To mark again.

Birth'mark s. A mark or blemish borne from birth.

Ear'mark v.t. To mark for identification; to allocate, set aside.

Wa'termark s. Height to which water has risen; device wrought into paper. v.t. To mark with such.

Coun'termark s. An additional mark for identification, etc. v.t. To affix such a mark.

Post'mark s. Mark stamped by postal authorities on letters, etc. v.t. To stamp with this.

Park s. Large tract of ground kept for pleasure, game, etc.; space occupied by or group of wagons, artillery, animals, etc. v.t. To enclose in or assemble together in a park.

Impark' v.t. To enclose for a park; to shut up in a park.

Spark s. A detached incandescent particle; a transient light; a feeble germ; a gay man. v.i. To emit sparks; to play the lover.

Dispark' v.t. To cause to be no longer a park; to throw open.

Sark s. (*Scot.*) A shirt.

Bare'sark s. and a. (*Berserk*).

Stark a. Stiff; downright; mere. adv. Absolutely.

Aard'vark s. African ground-hog.

Bul'wark s. A fortification; a security.

Hau'berk s. A coat of mail.

Jerk v.t. To give a sudden pull, thrust, etc., to; to throw with a quick motion. v.i. To move suddenly. s. A sudden thrust, twist, spring, etc.; a spasmodic movement.

Clerk s. A writing assistant in an office, a book-keeper; a clergyman; a lay parish officer; a scholar.

Perk v.t. To make oneself smart. v.i. To be jaunty, impudent, etc. a. Pert, perky.

Ber'serk s. A fierce Norse warrior, a brave. a. Frenzied.

Irk v.t. To weary, bore. v.i. To become tired.

Birk s. (*Scot.*) The birch tree.

Dirk s. A dagger, poinard.

Shirk v.t. and i. To seek to avoid duty; to get out of meanly. s. A shirker.

Kirk s. (*Scot.*) A church; the Established Church of Scotland.

Steen'kirk s. A lace cravat worn by men in the eighteenth century.

Smirk s. A silly or affected smile, a simper. v.i. To look affectedly kind, to smile conceitedly.

Quirk s. An artful evasion or distinction; a quibble; a sharp retort.

Cork s. A species of oak; its bark; a stopper or bung made from this. v.t. To stop or furnish with a cork.

Fork s. An implement with prongs; a prong; a branch; point of division. v.i. To divide into two, to branch. v.t. To pitch or raise with a fork.

Pitch'fork s. A pronged implement for lifting sheaves, etc. v.t. To lift with this; to thrust unsuitably or suddenly.

Pork s. Swine-flesh as food.

More'pork s. The Australian night-jar.

Stork s. A large migratory wading bird.

Work (werk) v.i. To labour, put forth effort; to take effect, to ferment. v.t. To bring about, labour upon, accomplished; to fashion. s. Labour, effort; achievement; a task; result of force acting; result of artistic or other effort.

Bead'work s. Ornamental work in beads.

Wood'work s. Things, parts, etc., made of wood.

Frame'work s. The frame of a structure; a supporting fabric; arrangement; skeleton.

Fire'work s. A preparation of combustible materials for making pyrotechnic displays, signals, etc.

Patch'work s. Work composed of irregularly shaped coloured pieces; anything of incongruous parts.

Brush'work s. Manipulation of a paint-brush; style of this.

Earth'work s. A mound for defence; an embankment.

Hand'iwork s. Produce of manual labour; deed.

Brick'work s. Builder's work in brick; bricklaying.

Clock'work s. The movements of or train of wheels in a clock.

Horn'work s. An outwork of two demi-bastions and a curtain.

Overwork' v.t. and i. To work beyond the strength.

Net'work s. An open-work fabric; a system of intersecting lines.

Fret'work s. Ornamental perforated woodwork.

Out'work s. Part of a fortress beyond the principal wall.

Wax'work s. A wax model; modelling in wax.

York v.t. To bowl a player with a yorker.

Lurk v.i. To lie hid or in wait; to skulk.

Murk s. Darkness, gloom.

Turk s. A Moslem inhabitant or subject of Turkey; a troublesome person.

Ask v.t. and i. To request; to inquire, petition, demand, interrogate.

Bask v.t. and i. To lie in the sun, warmth, or favour.

Cask s. A hollow wooden vessel; a barrel. v.t. To put in a cask.

Flask s. A bottle, especially for the pocket; a powder-horn.

Mask s. A cover for the face; a disguise; a pretence; a masque. v.t. To disguise, conceal.

Dam'ask s. A fabric with raised figures woven in the pattern; steel made with a wavy pattern. a. Having the colour of the damask rose.

Ber'gamask s. A rustic dance.

Unmask' v.t. To strip of disguise; to expose.

Task s. Duty imposed; labour. v.t. To impose a task upon; to oppress.

Overtask' v.t. To impose too heavy a task upon.

Desk s. A table or inclined slope for writing on; a box for writing-paper, etc.; a reading-stand.

Bisk s. A rich soup.

Disk s. A flat circular plate; the face of the sun, moon, etc.; central part of a composite flower.

Whisk v.t. To move or agitate with a quick, sweeping motion. v.i. To move

nimbly. s. A rapid sweeping motion; a light brush; implement for frothing cream, etc.
Ob'elisk s. A tall, tapering, monolithic column; a reference-mark (†).
Bas'ilisk s. A fabulous serpent that could slay by a glance.
Risk s. Hazard; jeopardy; chance of harm. v.t. To hazard; to venture.
Tam'arisk s. An evergreen shrub with feathery white or pink flowers.
Brisk a. Lively, alert; full of spirit.
As'terisk s. A reference mark (*).
Frisk v.i. To dance about gaily, to frolic. s. A frolic, gambol.
Len'tisk s. The mastic tree.
Bosk s. A thicket.
Kiosk' s. An open summerhouse; a light, street building or stall.
Norsk a. Norse.
Torsk s. A fish allied to the cod.
Busk s. A thin strip of metal, etc., in corsets. v.t. and i. To prepare, make ready.
Dusk s. Twilight, tendency to darkness. a. Darkish; shadowy. v.i. To grow or appear dark.
Husk s. Integument of certain fruits or seeds; a disease in cattle. v.t. To divest of husk.
Musk s. An odoriferous, resinous substance obtained from the male musk deer; the odour; a similarly perfumed plant.
Rusk s. A light, brittle biscuit.
Tusk s. A long, pointed, protruding tooth.
Auk s. A northern sea-fowl.
Neb'buk s. A thorny Oriental shrub (traditionally said to have furnished Christ's crown of thorns).
Tom'buk s. An alloy used for cheap jewellery.
Chabouk' s. A horse-whip.
Chibouk' s. A long Turkish tobacco-pipe.
Bash'i-bazouk' s. A lawless and brutal Turkish irregular soldier.
Vol'apük s. An artificial universal language.
Cawk s. A variety of baryta.
Dawk s. (*Dak*).
Gawk s. A booby; an awkward, tactless person.
Hawk s. A falconoid bird of prey; a rapacious person; effort to cough up phlegm. v.i. To hunt with hawks, practise falconry; to clear the throat noisily. v.t. To carry about for sale.
Tom'ahawk s. Battle-axe of the N. American Indians. v.t. To strike or kill with this.
Mohawk' s. One of a tribe of N. American Indians.
Gos'hawk s. A large short-winged hawk.
Squawk v.i. To utter a harsh, shrill scream. s. Such a sound.
Gowk s. An awkward simpleton; the cuckoo.
Ba'al s. The god of the Phœnicians.
Graal s. The mystic vessel said to have been used by Christ at the Last Supper; the Holy Grail.
Kraal s. A S. African native village or hut.
Kur'saal s. A public hall for gaming, dances, etc.
Taal s. S. African Dutch.
Cabal' s. A faction, a party engaged in intrigue. v.i. To plot.
At'abal s. A kettle-drum.
Can'nibal s. One who eats human flesh.
Scrib'al a. Pertaining to a scribe or his duties.
Tri'bal a. Pertaining or belonging to a tribe.
Intertri'bal a. Carried on between tribes.
Gim'bal s. A combination of rings for suspending anything in a constant position.
Tim'bal s. A kettle-drum.
Cym'bal s. A disk of brass used in pairs as a musical instrument.
Herb'al a. Pertaining to herbs; a treatise on plants.
Verb'al a. Pertaining to words; literal; oral; derived directly from a verb.
Dandi'acal a. Pertaining to or like a dandy or the ways of a dandy.
Prosodi'acal a. Prosodical.
Zodi'acal a. Pertaining to or within the zodiac.
Heli'acal a. Rising just before the sun; pertaining to the sun.
Mani'acal a. Raving mad.
Dipsomani'acal a. (*Dipsomania*).
Demoni'acal a. Devilish; pertaining to possession by a demon.
Simoni'acal a. Guilty of or obtained by simony.
Theri'acal a. Pertaining to a theriac.
Paradisi'acal a. Like or pertaining to paradise.
Car'acal s. The Persian lynx.
Buc'cal a. Pertaining to the cheek.
Cæ'cal a. Of or like the cæcum.
Fæ'cal a. Pertaining to excrement.
The'cal a. Pertaining to or resembling a theca.
Bibliothe'cal a. Pertaining to a library.
-ical suff. Forming adjectives from adjectives and nouns in *-ic*.
La'ical a. Laic; secular.
Algebra'ical a. (*Algebra*).
Pharisa'ical a. Pharisaic.
Cu'bical a. Cubic.
Cheru'bical a. (*Cherub*).
Far'cical a. Pertaining to or appropriate to farce; ludicrous.
Monad'ical a. Monadic.
Rad'ical a. Pertaining to or proceeding from the root; fundamental; original; underived; politically reforming. s. A primitive word; a base of a compound; a political reformer; a root of another quantity.
Sporad'ical a. (*Sporadic*).
Med'ical a. Pertaining to medicine; healing, curative.
Spheroid'ical a. Spheroidal.
Verid'ical a. Truthful.
Jurid'ical a. Pertaining to the dispensation of justice.
Causid'ical a. Pertaining to advocacy.
Druid'ical a. (*Druidic*).
Method'ical a. Pertaining to or characterized by method; systematic.
Period'ical a. Periodic. s. A publication appearing at regular intervals.
Spasmod'ical a. Spasmodic.
No'dical a. Pertaining to the celestial nodes.
Synod'ical a. Pertaining to a synod or to the conjunction of heavenly bodies.
Episod'ical a. (*Episodic*).
Prosod'ical a. Pertaining to or according to the rules of prosody.
Rhapsod'ical a. (*Rhapsodic*).
Talmud'ical a. (*Talmudic*).
Magnif'ical a. Magnificent, sublime.
Pontif'ical a. Pertaining to or befitting a high-priest or pope; papal. s. A book containing various ecclesiastical offices.
Vivif'ical a. Vivific.
Mag'ical a. Magic.

Trag'ical a. (*Tragic*).
Strateg'ical a. (*Strategic*).
Pedagog'ical a. (*Pedagogic*).
Anagog'ical a. (*Anagoge*).
Synagog'ical a. Pertaining to a synagogue.
Log'ical a. Pertaining to, skilled in, or according to the rules of logic; reasonable.
-logical suff. Forming adjectives from nouns in *-logy*.
Analog'ical a. (*Analogy*).
Illog'ical a. Ignorant or careless of the rules of logic; contrary to these rules.
Amphibo-log'ical a. (*Amphibology*).
Symbolog'ical a. (*Symbology*).
Archæolog'ical a. (*Archæology*).
Geolog'ical a. Pertaining to geology.
Theolog'ical a. Pertaining to theology.
Neolog'ical a. Employing new words; pertaining to neology.
Concholog'ical a. (*Conchology*).
Psycholog'ical a. Pertaining or relating to psychology.
Patholog'ical a. Pertaining to pathology or to disease.
Etholog'ical a. Treating of or pertaining to ethology.
Antholog'ical a. (*Anthology*).
Mytholog'ical a. Pertaining to mythology or myths; fabulous.
Biolog'ical a. (*Biology*).
Amphibio-log'ical a. (*Amphibiology*).
Bibliolog'ical a. (*Bibliology*).
Craniolog'ical a. (*Craniology*).
Bacteriolog'ical a. (*Bacteriology*).
Assyriolog'ical a. (*Assyriology*).
Ecclesiolog'ical a. (*Ecclesiology*).
Physiolog'ical a. Pertaining to physiology or to the bodily organs.
Ætiolog'ical a. (*Ætiology*).
Homolog'ical a. Characterized by homology.
Entomolog'ical a. Pertaining to entomology or to insects.
Cosmolog'ical a. (*Cosmology*).
Etymolog'ical a. Pertaining to etymology.
Campano-log'ical a. (*Campanology*).
Ethnolog'ical a. Ethnologic.
Carcinolog'ical a. (*Carcinology*).
Terminolog'ical a. (*Terminology*).
Chronolog'ical a. (*Chronology*).
Anthropo-log'ical a. (*Anthropology*).
Tropolog'ical a. Characterized or varied by tropes.
Necrolog'ical a. (*Necrology*).
Chorolog'ical a. (*Chorology*).
Astrolog'ical a. (*Astrology*).
Climatolog'ical a. (*Climatology*).
Egyptolog'ical a. (*Egyptology*).
Christolog'ical a. (*Christology*).
Tautolog'ical a. Having the same signification.
Doxolog'ical a. Pertaining to a doxology.
Embryolog'ical a. (*Embryology*).
Lethar'gical a. Lethargic.
Theur'gical a. (*Theurgic*).
Metallur'gical a. Metallurgic.
Sur'gical a. Pertaining to surgeons or surgery.
Thaumatur'-gical a. (*Thaumaturgic*).
Litur'gical a. Pertaining to a liturgy.
Synecdoch'ical a. Pertaining to or containing synecdoche.
Squirear'chical a. Pertaining to the squirearchy.
Oligarch'ical a. Oligarchic.
Anar'chical a. (*Anarchy*).
Monarch'ical a. Monarchic.
Hierar'chical a. Hierarchic.
Tetrarch'ical a. Pertaining to a tetrarch or tetrarchate.
Gerontar'chical a. Pertaining to government by aged men.
Psy'chical a. Psychic; non-natural; occult; spiritualistic.
Seraph'ical a. (*Seraphic*).
Graph'ical a. Graphic.
-graph'ical suff. Forming adjectives from words in *-graph* and *-graphy*.
Pseudepi-graph'ical a. Pertaining to pseudepigrapha.
Geograph'ical a. Pertaining to geography.
Biograph'ical a. (*Biography*).
Autobio-graph'ical a. (*Autobiography*).
Biblio-graph'ical a. (*Bibliography*).
Cosmo-graph'ical a. (*Cosmography*).
Anthropo-graph'ical a. (*Anthropography*).
Cerograph'ical a. (*Cerography*).
Chiro-graph'ical a. (*Chirographic*).
Choro-graph'ical a. (*Chorography*).
Cinemato-graph'ical a. (*Cinematograph*).
Photo-graph'ical a. (*Photographic*).
Autograph'ical a. (*Autography*).
Theosoph'ical a. Pertaining to theosophy.
Philosoph'ical a. Philosophic.
Hieroglyph'ical a. Hieroglyphic.
Philomath'ical a. Philomathic.
Idiopath'ical a. Idiopathic.
Eth'ical a. Ethic.
Myth'ical a. Mythic.
Bib'lical a. Of or pertaining to the Bible.
Cy'clical a. (*Cyclic*).
Encyc'lical a. Sent to many persons or places. s. A circular letter, especially from the Pope to the Bishops.
Angel'ical a. (*Angel*).
Evangel'ical a. Contained in or pertaining to the Gospel; earnest for pure Gospel truth; applied to the Low Church party.
Hel'ical a. Spiral; like a helix.
Umbil'ical a. Pertaining to the navel.
Fil'ical a. Pertaining to the ferns.
Basil'ical a. (*Basilica*).
Diabol'ical a. Diabolic.
Parabol'ical a. Parabolic.
Symbol'ical a. (*Symbolic*).
Hyperbol'ical a. (*Hyperbolic*).
Apostol'ical a. (*Apostle*).
Dynam'ical a. Dynamic; pertaining to dynamism.
Academ'ical a. (*Academy*). s. Cap and gown.
Epidem'ical a. Pertaining to or caused by an epidemic.
Chem'ical a. Pertaining to chemistry. s. A substance produced by or used in chemical processes.
Alchem'ical a. (*Alchemy*).
Polem'ical a. Pertaining to or given to controversy; disputatious.
Rhyth'mical a. Pertaining to rhythm.
Inim'ical a. Hostile, hurtful; repugnant; unfavourable to.
Com'ical a. Ludicrous; exciting mirth; comic.
Econom'ical a. Frugal, careful, thrifty.
Ineconom'ical a. Not economical.
Deutero-nom'ical a. (*Deuteronomic*).
Astronom'ical a. (*Astronomy*)

Taxonom'ical a. Pertaining to taxonomy.
Atom'ical a. (*Atom*).
Anatom'ical a. (*Anatomy*).
Phantom'ical a. Of the nature of a phantom.
Zootom'ical a. Pertaining to zootomy.
Microtom'ical a. Microtomic.
Cos'mical a. Cosmic.
Micro-cos'mical a. Microcosmic.
Patronym'ical a. Pertaining to or of the nature of a patronymic.
Metonym'ical a. Metonymic.
Mechan'ical a. Pertaining to mechanics, mechanism, machinery, or material forces; done by force of habit.
Talisman'ical a. Talismanic.
Charlatan'ical a. (*Charlatan*).
Satan'ical a. Satanic.
Puritan'ical a. Puritanic.
Botan'ical a. (*Botany*).
Scen'ical a. Scenic.
Hygien'ical a. (*Hygienic*).
Galen'ical a. Pertaining to or containing galena.
Œcumen'ical a. Belonging to or representative of the whole Christian world; universal, general.
Arsen'ical a. (*Arsenic*).
Tech'nical a. Pertaining to the mechanical arts, or to any science, business, etc.
Pyrotech'nical a. Pertaining to fireworks.
Eth'nical a. Ethnic.
Rabbin'ical a. Pertaining to the rabbis, or to their opinions, teaching, learning, etc.
Fin'ical a. Over-nice; fastidious.
Clin'ical a. Pertaining to a patient in bed, or to instruction at a clinic.
Brahmin'ical a. Pertaining to the Brahmins or Brahminism.
Domin'ical a. Pertaining to or indicating Sunday.
Sin'ical a. Pertaining to sines.
Tyran'nical a. Pertaining to or characteristic of a tyrant; unjustly severe; despotic.
Con'ical a. Having the form of a cone; pertaining to a cone.
Cosmogon'ical a. (*Cosmogonic*).
Tautophon'ical a. Repeating the same sound.
Histrion'ical a. Histrionic.
Mnemon'ical a. Mnemonic.
Gnomon'ical a. Gnomonic.
Harmon'ical a. Harmonic.
Inharmon'ical a. Not harmonical.
Canon'ical a. In accordance with canon law; in the canon of Scripture; authoritative. s. Ecclesiastical vestments.
Aaron'ical a. Priestly; of the Jewish priesthood.
Iron'ical a. Containing or given to irony; subtly sarcastic.
Thrason'ical a. Boastful; bragging.
Architec-ton'ical a. (*Architectonic*).
Cyn'ical a. Misanthropic, sarcastic.
Hero'ical a. Heroic.
Sto'ical a. Having the passions subdued; bearing pain or pleasure with indifference; unfeeling.
A'pical a. (*Apex*).
Ep'ical a. Pertaining to or resembling an epic.
Orthœ'pical a. Pertaining to orthœpy.
Spectro-scop'ical a. (*Spectroscopic*).
Thean-throp'ical a. (*Theanthropic*).
Philan-throp'ical a. Philanthropic.
Misanthrop'ical a. Misanthropic.
Trop'ical a. Pertaining to or characteristic of the tropics; of the nature of a trope, figurative.
Heliotrop'ical a. Heliotropic.
Top'ical a. Pertaining to or in the nature of a topic; local.
Typ'ical (tip'-) a. Pertaining to or of the nature of a type; emblematic, representative, figurative.
Daguerreo-typ'ical a. (*Daguerreotypic*).
Lum'brical a. Pertaining to or like a worm.
Ru'brical a. Pertaining to or placed in the rubric; marked with red.
Cylin'drical a. Having the shape of a cylinder.
Spher'ical a. Sphere-shaped; relating to spheres.
Hemispher'ical a. Hemispheric.
Atmospher'ical a. (*Atmosphere*).
Cler'ical a. Relating to the clergy or to a clerk.
Chimer'ical a. Fantastic, purely imaginary.
Numer'ical a. Pertaining to number; consisting of numbers.
Gener'ical a. Generic.
Climacter'ical a. Climacteric.
Esoter'ical a. Esoteric.
Exoter'ical a. Exoteric.
Hyster'ical a. Pertaining to, affected with or troubled with hysteria.
Chirag'rical a. (*Chiragra*).
Empir'ical a. Empiric.
Satir'ical a. Satiric; ironical, bitter, censorious.
Allegor'ical a. (*Allegory*).
Categor'ical a. Belonging to a class or category; unconditional, absolute.
Metaphor'ical a. Metaphoric.
Orator'ical a. Pertaining to or becoming an orator; eloquent, flowery, florid.
Rhetor'ical a. Pertaining to or involving rhetoric; oratorical.
Histor'ical a. Pertaining to history as distinct from legend or fiction; famous, historic.
Theat'rical a. Pertaining to the theatre or to acting; stagy, artificial.
Iat'rical a. Iatric.
Psychiat'rical a. Psychiatric.
Elec'trical a. Electric.
Met'rical a. Pertaining to or composed in metre; pertaining to measurement.
Diamet'rical a. Pertaining to a diameter; direct directly opposed.
Dynamet'rical a. Pertaining to a dynameter.
Hexamet'rical a. Hexametric.
Isoperi-met'rical a. Having equal perimeters.
Symmet'rical a. Symmetric.
Asymmet'rical a. (*Asymmetry*).
Geomet'rical a. Pertaining to, done, or prescribed by geometry.
Biomet'rical a. (*Biometry*).
Craniomet'rical a. (*Craniometry*).
Thermo-met'rical a. (*Thermometric*).
Clinomet'rical a. (*Clinometer*).
Trigono-met'rical a. (*Trigonometric*).
Chrono-met'rical a. (*Chronometer*).
Anthropo-met'rical a. (*Anthropometry*).
Baromet'rical a. (*Barometer*).
Hydromet'rical a. (*Hydrometry*).
Electro-met'rical a. Pertaining to an electrometer or to the measurement of electrical force.

Isomet'rical a. Isometric.

Obstet'rical a. Pertaining to midwifery.

Cen'trical a. (*Centric*).

Geocen'trical a. Geocentric.

Catadiop'trical a. (*Catadioptric*).

Panegyr'ical a. Containing eulogy; encomiastic.

Lyr'ical a. Lyric; appropriate for song.

Ves'ical a. Pertaining to a bladder (especially the urinary).

Lackadais'ical a. Affectedly sentimental or careless.

Phthis'ical (thiz'-) a. Having or pertaining to phthisis.

Whim'sical a. Full of whims; capricious; slyly humorous.

Nonsen'sical a. Unmeaning; foolish; absurd.

Drop'sical a. Pertaining to or afflicted with dropsy.

Clas'sical a. Classic; pertaining to the classics.

Mu'sical a. Pertaining to, fond of, or skilled in music; melodious.

Phys'ical a. Pertaining to nature or natural productions; bodily; material; pertaining to physics.

Cataphys'ical a. Opposed to the laws of nature.

Metaphys'ical a. Pertaining to metaphysics; transcendental; abstuse.

Sabbat'ical a. Denoting, among the Jews, every seventh year.

Emphat'ical a. (*Emphatic*).

Prelat'ical a. Prelatic.

Dramat'ical a. (*Dramatic*).

Mathemat'ical a. Pertaining to mathematics; rigidly accurate.

Emblemat'ical a. (*Emblematic*).

Problemat'ical a. Problematic.

Kinemat'ical a. Kinematic.

Theoremat'ical a. (*Theorematic*).

Pragmat'ical a. Pragmatic; meddling; impertinent.

Judgmat'ical a. Judgmatic.

Enigmat'ical a. (*Enigmatic*).

Dogmat'ical a. Dogmatic.

Asthmat'ical a. (*Asthmatic*).

Grammat'ical a. Pertaining to or according to the rules of grammar.

Anagram-mat'ical a. (*Anagram*).

Idiomat'ical a. (*Idiomatic*).

Axiomat'ical a. (*Axiom*).

Somat'ical a. Somatic.

Symptomat'ical a. (*Symptomatic*).

Automat'ical a. (*Automatic*).

Miasmat'ical a. Miasmatic.

Schismat'ical a. Schismatic.

Prismat'ical a. Prismatic.

Empyreu-mat'ical a. (*Empyreuma*).

Fanat'ical a. Fanatic.

Idiosyncrat'ical a. (*Idiosyncratic*).

Theocrat'ical a. (*Theocratic*).

Ochlocrat'ical a. (*Ochlocratic*).

Socrat'ical a. Socratic.

Aristocrat'ical a. (*Aristocratic*).

Autocrat'ical a. (*Autocratic*).

Pirat'ical a. Pertaining to piracy; having the character of a pirate.

Stat'ical a. Static.

Ecstat'ical a. *Ecstatic*).

Apostat'ical a. (*Apostate*).

Hypostat'ical a. (*Hypostatic*).

Hydrostat'ical a. (*Hydrostatic*).

Prac'tical a. Pertaining to practice or use; not merely theoretical; derived from practice; evincing skill.

Tac'tical a. Pertaining to tactics.

Syntac'tical a. (*Syntactic*).

Epideic'tical a. Epideictic.

Alphabet'ical a. (*Alphabetic*).

Ascet'ical a. (*Ascetic*).

Exeget'ical a. Pertaining to exegesis; explanatory.

Apologet'ical a. (*Apologetic*).

Epexeget'ical a. Pertaining to epexegesis

Catechet'ical a. (*Catechetic*).

Prophet'ical a. Prophetic.

Antipathet'ical a. (*Antipathetic*).

Metathet'ical a. Taking place by metathesis.

Antithet'ical a. (*Antithetic*).

Parenthet'ical a. Parenthetic.

Synthet'ical a. (*Synthetic*).

Nomothet'ical a. Legislative; arising from law.

Cosmothet'ical a. (*Cosmothetic*).

Æsthet'ical a. (*Æsthetic*).

Arithmet'ical a. (*Arithmetic*).

Genet'ical a. (*Genetic*).

Homogenet'ical a. Homogenetic.

Threnet'ical a. (*Threnetic*).

Noet'ical a. Noetic.

Poet'ical a. Poetic.

Heret'ical a. Containing or pertaining to heresy.

Theoret'ical a. (*Theoretic*).

Anchoret'ical a. (*Anchoret*).

Dietet'ical a. Dietetic.

Cœnobit'ical a. (*Cœnobite*).

Mephit'ical a. Mephitic.

Heteroclit'ical a. Heteroclite.

Polit'ical a. Pertaining to politics or public policy; public; derived from governmental office.

Cosmopolit'ical a. Relating to world-wide polity.

Metropolit'ical a. Pertaining to a metropolis, or to a metropolitan or his see.

Adamit'ical a. (*Adamite*).

Eremit'ical a. Eremitic.

Hermit'ical a. Pertaining to or suited for a hermit.

Granit'ical a. Granitic.

Sybarit'ical a. Sybaritic; voluptuous.

Crit'ical a. Pertaining to criticism; fastidious; inclined to find fault; relating to a crisis, momentous.

Diacrit'ical a. Diacritic.

Hypocrit'ical a. Insincere; pertaining to or characterized by hypocrisy.

Oneir'ocritical a. Pertaining to the interpretation of dreams.

Hypercrit'ical a. Over-critical, excessively exact.

Dendrit'ical a. (*Dendritic*).

Parasit'ical a. Parasitic.

Jesuit'ical a. Pertaining to the Jesuits; crafty; casuistical.

Levit'ical a. Pertaining to the Levites or to Leviticus; priestly.

Pedan'tical a. Pedantic.

Iden'tical a. The very same.

Authen'tical a. (*Authentic*).

Anecdot'ical a. (*Anecodote*).

Idiot'ical a. Idiotic.

Thermot'ical a. (*Thermotic*).

Despot'ical a. Despotic, tyrannical.

Scep'tical a. Pertaining to or being a sceptic; doubting.

Syllep'tical a. (*Sylleptic*).

Prolep'tical a. (*Proleptic*).

Ellip'tical a. Elliptic.

Op'tical a. Optic.

Synop'tical a. (*Synoptic*).

Autop'tical a. (*Autopsy*).

Apocalyp'tical a. (*Apocalypse*).

Carthar'tical a. (*Cathartic*).

Vert'ical a. Pertaining to the apex or zenith; perpendicular to the horizon.

Cor'tical a. Pertaining to, consisting of, or resembling bark; external.

Vor'tical a. Pertaining to or resembling a vortex.

Orgias'tical a. Orgiastic.

Encomias'tical a. (*Encomiastic*).

Ecclesias'tical a. Pertaining to the Church or its organization; not lay or secular.
Monas'tical a. Monastic.
Fantas'tical a. Fantastic.
Majes'tical a. Majestic.
Catachres'tical a. (*Catachresis*).
Methodis'tical a. Methodistic.
Deis'tical a. (*Deistic*).
Theis'tical a. (*Theistic*).
Atheis'tical a. (*Atheistic*).
Pantheis'tical a. Pantheistic.
Catechis'tical a. (*Catechist*).
Buddhis'tical a. (*Buddhist*).
Sophis'tical a. Sophistic.
Theo-sophis'tical a. Pertaining to or addicted to theosophy.
Rationalis'tical a. Rationalistic.
Agonist'ical a. (*Agonistic*).
Canonis'tical a. (*Canonical*).
Egois'tical a. (*Egoist*).
Papis'tical a. Pertaining to Roman Catholics or their doctrine.
Eucharis'tical a. Eucharistic.
Manneris'tical a. Manneristic.
Character-is'tical a. (*Characteristic*).
Juris'tical a. (*Juristic*).
Statis'tical a. Statistic.
Egotis'tical a. (*Egotistic*).
Artis'tical a. (*Artistic*).
Casuist'ical a. (*Casuistic*).
Geognos'tical a. Pertaining to geognosy.
Acros'tical a. (*Acrostic*).
Rumbus'tical a. Rough, boisterous.
Acou'stical a. (*Acoustic*).
Mys'tical a. (*Mystic*).
Nau'tical a. Pertaining to ships, sailors, and navigation.
Aeronau'tical a. (*Aeronautics*).
Pharma-ceut'ical a. Pertaining to the knowledge or art of pharmacy.
Hermeneu'tical a. Pertaining to hermeneutics or interpretation.
Therapeu'tical a. Pertaining to therapeutics or to healing.
Analyt'ical a. (*Analytic*).
Cer'vical a. Pertaining to the neck.
Index'ical a. Pertaining to or like an index.
Lex'ical a. Pertaining to the words of a language, or to a lexicon.
Pyrex'ical a. Pertaining to pyrexia; feverish.
Paradox'ical a. Of the nature of paradox; inclined to be perverse.
Quiz'zical a. Comical.
Proven'çal a. Pertaining to Provence, its people, or language. s. The Romance tongue of the Middle Ages.
Tin'cal s. Crude borax.
Junc'al a. Juncaceous.
Trunc'al a. Pertaining to the trunk or body.
Fo'cal a. Pertaining to or situated at a focus.
Pho'cal a. Pertaining to the seal family.
Lo'cal a. Pertaining or limited to a place. s. An inhabitant of a place; a suburban train.
Recip'rocal a. Alternate; mutual; done by each to other. s. That which is reciprocal to another.
Irrecip'rocal a. Not reciprocal.
Vo'cal a. Pertaining to the voice or to utterance; having a vowel character, sonant. s. A vowel.
Univ'ocal a. Having one meaning only; having unison of sounds. s. A word with only one meaning.
Multiv'ocal a. Ambiguous. s. An ambiguous word.
Equiv'ocal a. Having different significations; uncertain; ambiguous.
Unequiv'ocal a. Clear, evident, not doubtful.
Homocer'cal a. Having the tail equally lobed (of fish).
Nover'cal a. Pertaining to, suitable to, or in the manner of a step-mother.
Ras'cal s. A tricky rogue, a scamp.
Mes'cal s. A Mexican intoxicating drink.
Fis'cal a. Pertaining to the public revenue; financial; a public prosecutor.
Obelis'cal a. Pertaining to or resembling an obelisk.
Menis'cal a. Like a meniscus.
Fau'cal a. Pertaining to the fauces; guttural.
Du'cal a. Pertaining to a duke or dukedom.
Archdu'cal a. Pertaining to an archduke.
Noctilu'cal a. Phosphorescent.
Decad'al a. (*Decade*).
Hebdom'adal a. Consisting of seven days; occurring every week.
Dæ'dal a. Mazy; ingenious; formed with art.
Med'al s. A small metal memorial for wearing.
Ped'al s. A lever, as of a machine, bicycle, organ, etc., worked by the foot. v.t. To work a pedal with the foot.
Pe'dal a. Pertaining to a foot or similar organ of locomotion; pertaining to a pedal.
Sesquipe'dal a. Sesquipedalian.
Quadru'pedal a. Having four legs.
Barmeci'dal a. (*Barmecide*).
Regici'dal a. Pertaining to regicide or regicides.
Prolici'dal a. Pertaining to prolicide.
Homici'dal a. Pertaining to homicide; murderous.
Germici'dal a. Destroying germs; pertaining to germicides.
Vermici'dal a. Pertaining to killing worms or to vermicides.
Tyrannici'dal a. (*Tyrannicide*).
Sororici'dal a. (*Sororicide*).
Parrici'dal a. Pertaining to or committing parricide.
Matrici'dal a. Pertaining to matricide.
Fratrici'dal a. Pertaining to fratricide.
Insectici'dal a. Pertaining to the killing of insects.
Infantici'dal a. Pertaining to infanticide.
Septici'dal a. Dividing the partitions (of the dehiscence of pods).
Suici'dal a. In the nature of suicide; ruinous.
Pyram'idal a. Tapering to a point; pertaining or to like a pyramid.
Rhomboid'al a. Of the shape of a rhomboid.
Cuboid'al a. (*Cuboid*).
Helicoid'al a. (*Helicoid*).
Discoi'dal a. Disc-like; flat and circular.
Fucoid'al a. Pertaining to or like fucus.
Lambdoid'al a. Lambdoid.
Conchoid'al a. (*Conchoid*).
Typhoid'al a. Pertaining to or resembling typhus or enteric fever.
Lithoid'al a. Lithoid.
Cycloid'al a. Pertaining to a cycloid; resembling a circle.
Epicycloid'al a. Pertaining to or like an epicycloid.
Metalloi'dal a. (*Metalloid*).
Colloi'dal a. Gelatinous, gluey.
Sigmoi'dal a. Sigmoid.
Ethmoid'al a. Resembling a sieve.
Prismoid'al a. Pertaining to or like a prismoid.
Sphenoid'al a. Wedge-shaped.
Crinoid'al a. Pertaining to or containing crinoids.
Conoid'al a. Conoid.
Spheroid'al a. Pertaining to or resembling a spheroid.

Hemispheroid'al a. Pertaining to or containing a hemispheroid.
Asteroid'al a. Like an asteroid.
Negroid'al a. Negroid.
Meteoroid'al a. Pertaining to meteoroids.
Toroi'dal a. Pertaining to or like a torus.
Gyroid'al a. Arranged or moving in spirals.
Ellipsoid'al a. Pertaining to or like an ellipsoid.
Prismatoid'al a. Of the nature of a prismatoid.
Planetoid'al a. Resembling a planet.
Ovoid'al a. Ovoid, egg-shaped.
Cus'pidal a. Ending in a point.
Bri'dal s. A wedding or wedding feast.
Ap'sidal a. Pertaining to or resembling an apse.
Ti'dal a. Pertaining to the tides; ebbing and flowing.
Scan'dal s. Reproachful aspersion; disgrace; shame; slander.
San'dal s. A kind of light shoe; denoting the fragrant wood of an E. Indian tree.
Van'dal s. One of an ancient barbarian race of Teutons; a wilful destroyer of works of art, etc.
Preben'dal a. Pertaining to a prebend or prebendary.
Puden'dal a. Pertaining to the pudenda.
Sen'dal s. A light silken fabric.
Od'al s. A form of freehold tenure obtaining in Orkney and Shetland.
Sarco'dal a. Pertaining to or resembling sarcode.
I'odal s. An oily liquid prepared from iodine and alcohol.
Mo'dal a. Pertaining to form or mood, not to the essence.
No'dal a. Pertaining to or resembling a node.
Trin'odal a. Having three joints.
Interno'dal a. Situated between the nodes.
Syn'odal a. Synodical.
Po'dal a. Pertaining to the feet.
Ap'odal a. Footless.
Decap'odal a. Pertaining to the Decapoda.
Hexap'odal a. Hexapod.
Trip'odal a. Having three legs; like a tripod.
Antip'odal a. Pertaining to the antipodes.
Arthrop'odal a. (*Arthropoda*).
Cau'dal a. Pertaining to the tail.
Subcau'dal a. Situated under the tail.
Longicau'dal a. Long-tailed.
Feud'al a. Pertaining to, founded on, or consisting of tenure by service, custom, etc.; pertaining to feuds.
Palu'dal a. Pertaining to marshes; malarial.
Conceal' v.t. To hide, to disguise, dissemble.
Deal s. A part, degree; distribution of cards at games; fir or pine timber; a plank. v.t. To distribute, allot. v.i. To make distribution; to traffic, carry on business, manage.
Ide'al a. Mental, imaginary; perfect. s. An imaginary idea of perfection.
Beau-ide'al s. A conception of ideal beauty or perfection.
Or'deal s. An ancient trial to determine guilt or innocence; test, severe trial.
Misdeal' v.i. To deal wrongly (*cards*). s. A wrong deal.
Œsophage'al a. Pertaining to the œsophagus.
Perige'al a. Pertaining to the perigee.
Menin'geal a. Pertaining to the meninges.
Syrin'geal a. Pertaining to the syrinx.
Congeal' v.t. To freeze; to stiffen by cold or terror. v.i. To grow hard or stiff.
Pharyn'geal a. Pertaining to or connected with the pharynx.
Laryn'geal a. Pertaining to the larynx.
Coc'cygeal a. (*Coccyx*).
Heal v.t. and i. To make or become whole; to cure, restore to health; to reconcile.
Trache'al a. Pertaining to the trachea
Wheal s. A Cornish tin mine.
Leal a. (*Scot.*) Loyal, true.
Nu'cleal a. Nuclear.
Meal s. A repast; ground corn.
Piece'meal adv. In fragments; by little and little. a. Made of parts or pieces; separate.
Inch'meal adv. By inches.
Homoge'neal a. Homogeneous.
Heteroge'neal a. Heterogeneous.
Hymene'al a. Pertaining to marriage. s. A nuptial song.
Cochine'al s. A scarlet dye stuff obtained from the Mexican insect, *Coccus cacti*.
Lin'eal a. In a direct line from an ancestor hereditary; linear.
Patrilin'eal a. By male descent.
Rectilin'eal a. Rectilinear.
Multilin'eal a. Having many lines.
Curvilin'eal a. Curvilinear.
Centrolin'eal a. Converging to a centre.
Interlin'eal a. Interlinear.
Pine'al a. Shaped like a pine-cone, especially of a gland in front of the cerebellum.
Anneal' v.t. To temper glass or metals by heat.
Perone'al a. Pertaining to the fibula.
Peritone'al a. Pertaining to or affecting the peritoneum.
Diarrhœ'al a. Pertaining to diarrhœa.
Peal s. A succession of sounds, as from bells or thunder; a set of bells, a chime; a young salmon. v.i. To give out a peal. v.t. To cause to ring or sound.
Repeal' v.t. To revoke, abrogate, annul. s. Abrocation; revocation.
Pharmacopœi'al a. Pertaining to or contained in a pharmacopeia.
Appeal' v.i. and t. To refer to a superior; to call upon for assistance, charity, etc.; to implore; to challenge. s. The taking of a case to a higher tribunal; an earnest request.
Clyp'eal a. (*Clypeate*).
Real a. Not fictitious; genuine, actual; pertaining to fixtures.
Re'al (rā'-) s. A Spanish silver coin (about 2½d.).
Cer'eal s. Edible farinaceous seeds or grain. a. Pertaining to wheat and other grain.
Sider'eal a. Pertaining or according to the stars; starry.
Ether'eal a. Pertaining to or like the ether or upper sky; heavenly; intangible.
Vener'eal a. Pertaining or due to sexual intercourse.
Funer'eal a. Pertaining to funerals, dismal, gloomy.
Bor'eal a. Pertaining to the north or the north wind.
Arbor'eal a. Belonging to, growing on, or frequenting trees.
Marmor'eal a. Like or made of marble.
Corpor'eal a. Having a body; material (opposed to spiritual).
Incorpor'eal a. Immaterial; unsubstantial; spiritual.
Ure'al a. Pertaining to or containing urea.
Purpur'eal a. Purple.
Empyr'eal a. Formed of pure fire or light trebly refined.

Seal s. Impression in wax, etc., stamp for making this; that which makes fast, stable, authentic, etc.; a marine mammal. v.t. To set a seal to or on; to ratify, confirm; to shut, keep close.
Dei'seal s. Motion towards the right; clockwise.
Ros'eal a. Resembling or suggesting a rose.
Symphys'eal a. Characterized by symphysis.
Teal s. A small freshwater duck.
Lac'teal a. Pertaining to milk; milky; conveying chyle. s. A duct for conveying chyle from the alimentary canal.
Brac'teal a. Resembling a bract.
Poplit'eal a. Pertaining to the ham or the hollow behind the knee.
Steal v.i. To take by theft; to gain by address or imperceptibly. v.i. To practise theft; to slip away, in, etc., unperceived.
Os'teal a. Osseous; bony.
Perios'teal a. Pertaining to or like the periosteum.
Glute'al a. Pertaining to the buttocks.
Pu'teal a. Raised stonework round a well.
Squeal v.i. To cry with a shrill, prolonged sound. s. Such a cry.
Veal s. Calf-flesh as food.
Reveal' v.t. To make known, especially by divine means.
Fo'veal a. Pertaining to a fovea.
Uve'al a. Pertaining to the uvea.
Weal s. A wale, mark of a stripe; welfare, prosperity. v.t. To mark with weals.
Com'monweal s. The state; its welfare.
Zeal s. Passionate ardour; warmth; enthusiasm.
Off'al s. Refuse; parts of carcass unfit for food.
Gal s. (*Slang*) Girl.
Sarcoph'agal a. Feeding on flesh.
Pla'gal a. Having the principal tones lying between the fifth of the key and its octave.
As'tragal s. The ankle-joint.
Le'gal a. Pertaining to, authorized by, or according to law; lawful; judicial.
Ille'gal a. Contrary to law, unlawful.
Re'gal a. Pertaining to a king; kingly.
Vicere'gal a. Pertaining to a viceroy or viceroyalty.
Prod'igal a. Expending to excess or without necessity; extravagant. s. A spendthrift.
Mad'rigal a. A short amorous or pastoral poem; a part-song.
War'rigal (wŏr'-) s. The Australian dingo; a scamp, outlaw.
Al'gal a. Pertaining to seaweed.
Gin'gal s. An obsolete E. Indian breech-loading fire-arm.
Spring'al s. A lad, youth.
Diphthong'al a. Pertaining to diphthongs.
Triphthong'al a. Pertaining to or consisting of a triphthong.
Mono-phthong'al a. Consisting of or pertaining to monophthongs.
Fun'gal a. Pertaining to or resembling a fungus. s. A fungus.
Pharyn'gal a. Pharyngeal.
Syn'agogal a. (*Synagogical*).
Ar'gal adv. Therefore.
Ter'gal a. Pertaining to the back.
Fu'gal a. Pertaining to or like a fugue.
Vermifu'gal a. Pertaining to a vermifuge or to the expulsion of worms.
Febrif'ugal a. Pertaining to febrifuges.
Centrif'ugal a. Tending to fly from the centre.
Ju'gal a. Pertaining to the cheek-bone.
Con'jugal a. Pertaining to marriage or married life.
Fru'gal a. Thrifty, sparing; economical.
Py'gal a. Pertaining to or near the rump.
Zy'gal a. H-shaped.
Stom'achal (stŭm'-) a. Pertaining to the stomach.
Mon'achal a. Pertaining to monks; monastic.
Hem'istichal a. Pertaining to or written in hemistichs.
Ep'ochal a. Pertaining to an epoch; remarkable.
Tro'chal a. Wheel-shaped.
Matriar'chal a. Pertaining to a matriarch or matriarchy.
Patriarch'al a. Pertaining to or subject to a patriarch; venerable.
Monarch'al a. Pertaining to or suiting a monarch, regal.
Pas'chal a. Pertaining to the Passover or to Easter.
Sen'eschal s. A steward, bailiff.
Pentateuch'al a. Pertaining to the Pentateuch.
Nu'chal a. Pertaining to the back of the neck or thorax.
Eu'nuchal a. Pertaining to eunuchs.
Bur'ghal a. (*Burgh*).
Triumph'al a. Pertaining to a triumph.
Nym'phal a. Nymphean.
Apoc'ryphal a. (*Apocrypha*).
Catarrh'al a. (*Catarrh*).
Mar'shal s. One who orders processions, state ceremonies, etc.; a military or air officer of the highest rank. v.t. To array, dispose in order. v.i. To assemble.
Gnath'al a. Pertaining to the jaw.
Le'thal a. Deadly; causing oblivion.
Zen'ithal a. Pertaining to the zenith.
Withal' (-awl') adv. With the rest; moreover.
Wherewithal' (awl) adv. Wherewith. s. Necessary means.
Ben'thal a. Pertaining to the depths of the ocean.
Betroth'al s. Act of betrothing.
Azimu'thal a. (*Azimuth*).
Nar'whal s. An Arctic cetacean with a long tusk.
-ial suff. Forming adjectives.
La'bial a. Pertaining to the lips. s. A letter sounded with the lips.
Tib'ial a. Pertaining to the tibia.
Stib'ial a. Having the qualities of antimony.
Micro'bial a. Pertaining to or resembling microbes.
Adver'bial a. (*Adverb*).
Proverb'ial a. Pertaining to or like a proverb commonly known.
Connu'bial a. Relating to marriage or the married state.
Fac'ial a. Pertaining to the face.
Trifa'cial a. Pertaining to a pair of cranial nerves.
Gla'cial a. Consisting of ice; pertaining to glaciers; icy, frozen.
Ra'cial a. Pertaining to a race or nation.
Spec'ial a. Particular; appropriate; not general. s. Person or thing intended for a particular purpose.
Espec'ial a. Distinguished among others of the same kind; chief; particular.
Judi'cial a. Relating to a proceeding from a judge or court; showing judgment; discerning; impartial.

Prejudi'cial a. Causing prejudice; injurious; mischievous.
Injudi'cial a. Not judicial.
Benefi'cial a. Useful, profitable, advantageous.
Offi'cial a. Pertaining to an office or public duty; acting by virtue of office. s. One holding a public office.
Sacrifi'cial a. Pertaining to or consisting in sacrifice.
Artifi'cial a. Done or made by art, not nature.
Inartifi'cial a. Not artificial; not according to the rules of art; characterized by simplicity.
Superfi'cial (-fish'al) a. Pertaining to or being on the surface; shallow.
Cicatric'ial a. (*Cicatrix*).
Finan'cial a. Pertaining to finance or revenue; monetary.
Provin'cial a. Pertaining to, forming, or characteristic of a province; countrified, unpolished.
Un'cial a. Denoting the kind of capital letters used in ancient Greek and Latin MSS. s. One of these letters; a MS. in them.
Quincun'cial a. Pertaining to or resembling the quincunx.
Pronun'cial a. Pertaining to pronunciation.
Internun'cial a. Pertaining to an internuncio; communicating between different parts (of nerves).
So'cial a. Pertaining to society, community, or union; familiar; sociable.
Disso'cial a. Unfriendly to society.
Commer'cial a. Pertaining to or connected with trade; s. A commercial traveller.
Fidu'cial a. Confident, undoubting; fiduciary.
Cru'cial a. Decisive, searching; relating to or in the form of a cross.
Di'al s. A plate for showing the hour by the sun's shadow; the face of a clock, indicator, etc.; (*slang*) the face.
Ra'dial a. Pertaining to rays or radii; radiating; pertaining to the radius bone of the arm, or to radium.
Unira'dial a. Having but one arm, ray, or radius.
Multira'dial a. Having many radii.
Me'dial a. Middle, mean; pertaining to an average.
Reme'dial a. Affording or intended for remedy.
Pre'dial a. Consisting of or attached to lands or farms.
Rachid'ial a. Vertebral, spinal.
Conid'ial a. (*Conidium*).
Gonid'ial a. Pertaining to gonidia.
Presid'ial a. Pertaining to a fortified place or presidio.
Pran'dial a. Relating to dinner.
Antepran'dial a. Pertaining to the time just before dinner.
Postpran'dial a. After dinner.
Gerun'dial a. Pertaining to a gerund.
Allo'dial a. Held independently; not feudal.
Threno'dial a. (*Threnodic*).
Po'dial a. Pertaining to or resembling a podium.
Proso'dial a. Prosodical.
Custo'dial a. Pertaining to custody or guardianship.
Car'dial a. Relating to the heart or its diseases.
Cor'dial a. Proceeding from the heart; sincere, affectionate; cheering; tending to stimulate the heart. s. A stimulating, warming medicine or drink.
Primor'dial a. First in order; original. s. First principle or element.
Exor'dial a. Pertaining to an exordium; introductory.
Colle'gial a. Pertaining to a college.
Vestig'ial a. Pertaining to or of the nature of a vestige.
Sporan'gial a. Pertaining to or like a spore-case.
Conju'gial a. Pertaining to spiritual marriage.
Bra'chial a. Of or resembling an arm.
Pete'chial a. Having livid spots.
Branch'ial a. Of or of the nature of gills.
Abranch'ial a. Destitute of gills.
Bronch'ial a. (*Bronchi*).
Paro'chial a. Pertaining to a parish; pettifogging, narrow.
Monarch'ial a. Monarchal.
Phi'al s. A small glass bottle.
Epitaph'ial a. Epitaphic.
Be'lial s. The devil; one of the fallen angels.
Myce'lial a. Pertaining to or like fungus-spawn.
Epithe'lial a. Pertaining to the epithelium; consisting of cell-tissues.
Fil'ial a. Pertaining to or befitting a son or daughter.
Proe'mial a. Introductory; prefatory.
Gre'mial a. Resident in the University. s. An ecclesiastical vestment.
Bino'mial s. A mathematical expression consisting of two terms united by + or −.
Quadrino'mial a. Consisting of four algebraic terms.
Trino'mial a. Consisting of three terms. s. Such a quantity connected by the sign + or −.
Mono'mial s. An expression consisting of a single term.
Polynom'ial s. An algebraical expression consisting of two or more terms. a. Containing many names or terms.
Deni'al s. Act of denying or refusing; a negation.
Ge'nial a. Cheery, kindly, cordial; pertaining to the chin.
Conge'nial a. Of like taste or disposition; kindly; pleasant.
Primoge'nial a. First-born; primary; pertaining to primogeniture.
Achen'ial a. (*Achene*).
Sple'nial a. Pertaining to the splenius; splint-like.
Me'nial s. A domestic servant. a. Servile, low, mean.
Catame'nial a. (*Catamenia*).
Ve'nial a. Pardonable; not heinous.
Xe'nial a. Pertaining to hospitality.
Fin'ial a. A terminal architectural ornament.
Decen'nial a. Lasting ten years; happening once in ten years.
Tricen'nial a. Pertaining to or consisting of thirty years.
Vicen'nial a. Lasting or occurring every twenty years.
Bien'nial a. Occurring every two years; lasting two years.
Trien'nial a. Continuing three years; happening, etc., once in three years.
Millenn'ial a. Pertaining to the millennium. s. A thousandth anniversary.
Quadren'nial a. Comprising or occurring once in four years.
Peren'nial a. Lasting through the year; continuing without stop; never-failing. s. A plant that lives more than two years.
Octen'nial a. Recurring every eighth year lasting eight years.

Centen'nial a. Pertaining to a centenary; happening once a century. s. A celebration of a centenary.
Bicenten'nial a.; s. (*Bicentenary*).
Quadri-centen'nial s. A 400th anniversary. a. Pertaining to a period of 400 years.
Octocenten'nial a. Pertaining to an 800th anniversary.
Septen'nial a. Continuing or happening once in seven years.
Quinquen'nial a. Occurring once in or lasting five years.
Noven'nial a. Occurring every ninth year.
Sexen'nial a. Lasting six years; occurring once every six years.
Colo'nial a. Pertaining to a colony. s. An inhabitant of a colony.
Mo'nial s. A mullion.
Ceremo'nial a. Pertaining to ceremony. s. An established system of ceremony.
Matrimo'nial a. Pertaining to matrimony; connubial.
Patrimo'nial a. Pertaining to a patrimony; inherited.
Antimo'nial a. (*Antimony*).
Testimo'nial s. A certificate of character; a present by subscription. a. Pertaining to or containing testimony.
Baro'nial a. (*Baron*).
Her'nial a. Pertaining to hernia.
Particip'ial a. Having the nature of or formed from a participle.
Troop'ial s. An American bird resembling the starling.
Espi'al s. Act of espying; observation.
Marsu'pial s. An animal the female of which carries its young in a pouch. a. Pertaining to or resembling a pouch, or pertaining to these animals.
Vicar'ial a. Pertaining to a vicar; vicarious.
Diar'ial a. Pertaining to a diary or diarist.
Malar'ial a. Producing or pert. to malaria.
Bursar'ial a. (*Bursar*).
Commissar'ial a. (*Commissary*).
Glossar'ial a. Pertaining to glossaries.
Nectar'ial a. Of the nature of a nectary.
Sectar'ial a. Pertaining to or denoting a sect.
Secretar'ial a. Pertaining to the duties of a secretary.
Notar'ial a. Pertaining to a notary, his duties, etc.
Actuar'ial a. (*Actuary*).
Fune'brial a. Pertaining to funerals, funerary.
Decri'al s. Censure, condemnation by this.
Aer'ial a. Relating to, resembling, or inhabiting the air; immaterial. s. Part of the receiving apparatus in wireless telegraphy.
Fer'ial a. Pertaining to days other than feast or fast days, or to holidays.
Manager'ial a. Pertaining to or characteristic of a manager.
Diphther'ial a. Pertaining to diphtheria.
Vizier'ial a. Pertaining to a vizier.
Imper'ial a. Pertaining to or befitting an empire or an emperor; supreme, superior. s. A small beard on the chin; a size of paper (30 = 22 in.).
Ser'ial a. Pertaining to or consisting of a series. s. A work appearing in successive parts or numbers.
Mater'ial a. Pertaining to or consisting of matter; corporeal, not spiritual; essential. s. Substance of which anything is made.
Immater'ial a. Not consisting of matter; spiritual; irrelevant.
Bacter'ial a. (*Bacteria*).
Sphincter'ial a. Sphincteral.
Acroter'ial a. Pertaining to a pedestal for a statue.
Arter'ial a. (*Artery*).
Monaster'ial a. Pertaining to a monastery.
Magister'ial a. Authoritative; dictatorial; oracular.
Minister'ial a. Pertaining to ministers or to a ministry.
Presbyter'ial a. Pertaining to a presbyter.
Ambassador'ial a. (*Ambassador*).
Phantas-magor'ial a. Phantasmagoric.
Enchor'ial a. Common to or used in a country native, popular.
Author'ial a. Pertaining to an author or authorship.
Memor'ial s. Anything to preserve memory; a record; an address. a. Pertaining to memory; serving to commemorate.
Immemor'ial a. Beyond memory or tradition; out of mind.
Armor'ial a. Pertaining to heraldry or to armour.
Manor'ial a. Pertaining to a manor.
Rasor'ial a. Pertaining to the order of birds including the domestic fowl.
Risor'ial a. Pertaining to or causing laughter.
Scansor'ial a. Climbing, adapted for climbing; pertaining to the climbing-birds.
Censor'ial a. (*Censor*).
Suspensor'ial a. Suspensory.
Sensor'ial a. Pertaining to the sensorium.
Sponsor'ial a. Pertaining to a sponsor.
Tonsor'ial a. Pertaining to a barber or to shaving.
Cursor'ial a. Pertaining to the cursores.
Professor'ial a. Pertaining to or characteristic of professors.
Gressor'ial a. Adapted for walking.
Fossor'ial a. Adapted for or relating to digging.
Infusor'ial a. Pertaining to or composed of infusoria.
Piscator'ial a. Relating to fish or fishing.
Prefator'ial a. Prefatory.
Purgator'ial a. Pertaining to purgatory.
Expurgator'ial a. Expurgatory.
Gladiator'ial a. Pertaining to gladiators or their exhibitions.
Mediator'ial a. Pertaining to a mediator or to intercession.
Grallator'ial a. Pertaining to the wading birds.
Legislator'ial a. Pertaining to a legislator or to the legislature.
Amator'ial a. Pertaining to love or courtship.
Senator'ial a. Pertaining to or befitting a senate or senator.
Gubernator'ial a. Pertaining to government or to a governor.
Orator'ial a. Pertaining to an orator or to oratory.
Laborator'ial a. Pertaining to the laboratory.
Curator'ial a. Pertaining to a curator or his work.
Improvisa-tor'ial a. Pertaining to improvisation.
Accusator'ial a. (*Accusatory*).
Natator'ial a. Pertaining to swimming or to the swimming birds.
Spectator'ial a. Pertaining to a spectator.
Dictator'ial a. Pertaining to or befitting a dictator; imperious, overbearing.
Visitator'ial a. Pertaining to a judicial visitor.
Saltator'ial a. Pertaining to or characterized by saltation; leaping.
Gestator'ial a. For carrying.
Equator'ial a. Pertaining to the equator; an astronomical telescope.
Observator'ial a. Pertaining to an observatory or work done there.

Factor'ial a. Pertaining to a factor, or to a series of mathematical factors.
Prefector'ial a. Prefectural.
Inspector'ial a. Inspectoral.
Rector'ial a. Pertaining to a rector.
Director'ial a. Pertaining to a director, directorate, or directory.
Sector'ial a. Adapted for cutting like scissors.
Tector'ial a. Forming a covering.
Vector'ial a. Pertaining to a vector.
Pictor'ial a. Pertaining to, illustrated by, or forming pictures.
Tinctor'ial a. Pertaining to colouring or dyeing.
Doctor'ial a. Doctoral.
Proctor'ial a. Pertaining to a proctor.
Auctor'ial a. (*Authorial*).
Suctor'ial a. Adapted for or adhering by sucking.
Prætor'ial a. Prætorian.
Proprietor'ial a. Pertaining to ownership; proprietary.
Editor'ial a. Pertaining to an editor or his work. s. A leading article.
Auditor'ial a. (*Auditor*).
Janitor'ial a. Pertaining to a door-keeper's duties.
Progenitor'ial a. Pertaining to or of the nature of a progenitor.
Monitor'ial a. Pertaining to or conducted by monitors; admonitory.
Territor'ial a. Pertaining to a territory or district. s. A member of a territorial force.
Exterritor'ial a. Outside the jurisdiction of the country in question.
Inquisitor'ial a. Pertaining to or like the Inquisition; prying.
Cantor'ial a. Pertaining to a precentor, or to the north side of the choir.
Inventor'ial a. Pertaining to an inventory.
Raptor'ial a. Rapacious; pertaining to or like birds of prey.
Preceptor'ial a. Pertaining to a preceptor or to teaching.
Scriptor'ial a. Pertaining to script or writing.
Sartor'ial a. Pertaining to a tailor or tailoring.
Reportor'ial a. Pertaining to a reporter or his profession.
Quæstor'ial a. Pertaining to a quæstor.
Consistor'ial a. Pertaining to a consistory.
Executor'ial a. Pertaining to the office or duties of an executor.
Sutor'ial a. Pertaining to a cobbler or his work.
Tutor'ial a. Pertaining to or exercised by a tutor.
Textor'ial a. Pertaining to weaving.
Uxor'ial a. Pertaining to a wife; uxorious.
Tri'al s. Act of trying; a judicial examination; a test, experiment.
Retri'al s. A second trial.
Pedes'trial a. Pertaining to or employing the feet.
Trimes'trial a. Happening, etc., every three months.
Terres'trial a. Pertaining to or existing on the earth; pertaining to land as distinct from water; earthly, mundane.
Mistri'al a. An inconclusive trial.
Indust'rial a. Pertaining to industry or its products.
Bur'ial s. Act of burying; a funeral.
Cu'rial a. Pertaining to the Papal curia.
Mercur'ial a. Flighty, fickle; pertaining to or containing mercury.
Seigneur'ial (sānūr'-) a. Pertaining to a lord of the Manor.
Centur'ial a. (*Century*).
Gymna'sial a. Pertaining to a gymnasium.
Cra'sial a. Crasis.
Trophe'sial a. Pertaining or due to trophesy.
Me'sial a. Pertaining to or situated in the middle, especially of the body; median.
Paradis'ial a. Like or pertaining to paradise; heavenly; blissful.
Sympo'sial a. Pertaining to a drinking-party or merry-making.
Controver'sial a. Disputatious; pertaining to controversy.
Abba'tial a. Pertaining to an abbey or abbot.
Prima'tial a. Pertaining to the office of primate.
Spa'tial a. Relating or belonging to space.
Interspa'tial a. Pertaining to an interspace.
Trinoc'tial a. Lasting three nights.
Equinoc'tial a. Pertaining to or occurring at the equinox. s. The celestial equator.
Ini'tial a. Beginning; pertaining to this; incipient. s. First letter of a word or name. v.t. To append one's initials to.
Preteri'tial a. Having ceased from activity.
Recrementi'tial a. Recremental.
Solsti'tial a. Pertaining to or happening at a solstice.
Intersti'tial a. Pertaining to, occupying, or forming interstices.
Substan'tial a. Having substance; real; solid; moderately wealthy.
Insubstan'tial a. Unreal, unsubstantial; flimsy.
Consubstan'tial a. Having the same substance or essence.
Circumstan'tial a. Pertaining to circumstances; particular; minute. s. An incidental.
Reminiscen'tial a. Reminiscent.
Creden'tial a. Giving a title to credit. s. That which gives such title; a testimonial, certificate authorizing or accrediting.
Confiden'tial a. Communicated in or enjoying confidence.
Residen'tial a. Suitable for or pertaining to residences.
Presiden'tial a. Presiding; pertaining to a president.
Eviden'tial a. Relating to or furnishing evidence; clearly proving.
Providen'tial a. Effected by or referable to Divine Providence.
Roden'tial a. Pertaining to or resembling the rodents.
Pruden'tial a. Dictated by, exercising, or proceeding from prudence.
Jurispruden'tial a. Understanding law.
Intelligen'tial a. Pertaining to, having, or exercising intelligence.
Tangen'tial a. Pertaining to or consisting of a tangent.
Scien'tial a. Pertaining to science.
Sapien'tial a. Pertaining to or conveying wisdom.
Experien'tial a. Pertaining to or derived from experience.
Pestilen'tial a. Producing or tending to produce plague; noxious, pernicious; destructive.
Exponen'tial a. Pertaining to exponents.
Deferen'tial a. Expressing or implying deference; respectful.
Referen'tial a. Intended for or containing a reference.
Preferen'tial a. Giving, indicating, or having a preference.
Differen'tial a. Creating a difference; discriminating; noting an infinitely small quantity.
Inferen'tial a. Pertaining to or by way of inference.

Conferen'tial a. (*Conference*).
Transferen'tial a. Involving or pertaining to transfer.
Reveren'tial a. Proceeding from or expressing reverence.
Irreveren'tial a. Not reverential.
Torren'tial a. In torrents; pouring.
Essen'tial a. Pertaining to the essence; indispensable; very important.
Inessen'tial a. Not indispensable.
Non-essen'tial a. and s. (*Negative*).
Coessen'tial a. Partaking of the same essence.
Quintessen'tial a. Like or consisting of quintessence.
Peniten'tial a. Proceeding from expressing, or pertaining to penitence.
Poten'tial a. Existing in possibility, not in fact; possible, latent.
Equipoten'tial a. Having the same or constant potential.
Existen'tial a. Pertaining to existence.
Influen'tial a. Having or exerting influence; powerful.
Sequen'tial a. Following in order or as a result.
Consequen'tial a. Following as an effect; pompous.
Incon-sequen'tial a. Inconsequent; of no consequence.
Nup'tial a. Pertaining to marriage; done at or constituting a wedding.
Antenup'tial a. Preceding marriage.
Post-nup'tial a. Subsequent to marriage.
Mar'tial a. Pertaining to or suited for war; warlike.
Par'tial a. Affecting a part only; not indifferent; biased; fond.
Impar'tial a. Equitable, just, fair.
Ter'tial a. and s. Pertaining to or one of the tertiary feathers.
Bes'tial a. Resembling or of the nature of a beast; beastly.
Celes'tial a. Pertaining to heaven or the heavens. s. An inhabitant of heaven; a Chinaman.
Obse'quial a. Pertaining to funeral rites.
Exe'quial a. Pertaining to exequies.
Ventrilo'quial a. Pertaining to, resembling, or using ventriloquism.
Collo'quial a. Pertaining to or used in ordinary conversation; not literary.
Vi'al s. A small vessel for holding liquids. v.t. To put in a vial.
Ga'vial s. The crocodile of the Ganges.
Quadriv'ial a. Pertaining to the quadrivium; having four ways meeting.
Triv'ial a. Trifling, unimportant.
Conviv'ial a. Pertaining to an entertainment; festal, jolly.
Lixiv'ial a. Obtained by lixiviation.
Jo'vial a. Mirthful, jolly, gay.
Syno'vial a. Pertaining to synovia.
Flu'vial a. Pertaining to, caused by, or living in rivers.
Dilu'vial a. Relating to the Deluge; produced by a flood; pertaining to the glacial drift.
Postdilu'vial a. Postdiluvian.
Allu'vial a. Deposited by flowing water.
Plu'vial a. Pertaining to or abounding in rain; rainy.
Exu'vial a. Pertaining to exuviæ.
Ax'ial a. (*Axis*).
Biax'ial a. Having two axes.
Uniax'ial a. Having a single axis.
Periax'ial a. Surrounding an axis.
Coax'ial a. Having a common axis.
Pyrex'ial a. Pertaining to pyrexia; feverish.
Trape'zial a. Pertaining to or resembling a trapeze or trapezium.
Jack'al s. A wild animal allied to the dog.
Sal'al s. A Californian shrub bearing edible berries.
Fal'-lal s. A gewgaw, trinket.
Ra'mal a. Pertaining to a branch.
Hæm'al a. Pertaining to blood, or to the side of the body containing the heart.
Hi'emal a. Wintry; pertaining to winter.
Dec'imal a. Numbered by tens; tenth. s. A tenth.
Duodec'imal a. Proceeding in computation by twelves.
An'imal s. A living creature having sensation and power of voluntary motion. a. Relating to animals; pertaining merely to the sentient parts of a creature.
Min'imal a. Pertaining to or like a minim or minimum.
Pri'mal a. Primeval; primitive; first.
Nonages'imal a. Pertaining to ninety, or to a nonagesimal. s. The point of the ecliptic highest above the horizon at any given moment.
Quadrages'imal a. Pertaining to or used in Lent.
Sexages'imal a. Sixtieth; pertaining to sixty.
Viges'imal a. Twentieth; consisting of twenties.
Milles'imal a. Consisting of thousandths; pertaining to thousandth.
Infinites'imal a. Infinitely small; negligible. An infinitely small quantity.
Centes'imal a. Hundredth; by the hundred. s. A hundredth part.
Sep'timal a. Relating to or based on the number 7.
Prox'imal a. Placed near the axis.
Mam'mal s. An animal that suckles its young.
Gim'mal s. A set of interlocking rings; a gimbal; a gemel.
Bro'mal s. An oily liquid produced by the action of bromine on alcohol.
Homod'romal a. Turning or moving in the same direction.
Prodro'mal a. Pertaining to preliminary symptoms.
Derm'al a. Pertaining to or consisting of skin.
Taxider'mal a. Pertaining to taxidermy.
Hypoder'mal a. Hypodermic.
Ther'mal a. Pertaining to heat.
Geother'mal a. Pertaining to the internal heat of the earth.
Isother'mal a. Pertaining to isotherms; illustrating distribution of temperature.
Form'al a. In set form; relating to outward form; precise; ceremonious.
Inform'al a. Not official; without formality.
Nor'mal a. According to rule; conformed to type; ordinary. s. The usual state, etc.; the mean value, temperature, etc.; a perpendicular.
Abnor'mal a. Not conforming to type.
Supernor'mal a. Beyond what is normal.
Transnor'mal a. Beyond what is normal.
Mias'mal a. Miasmatic.
Phantas'mal a. Pertaining to or like a phantasm; spectral, illusive.
Strabis'mal a. Pertaining to or affected with squinting.
Dis'mal a. Gloomy, dark, dreary; sorrowful, dire.
Seis'mal (siz'-) a. Pertaining or due to an earthquake.
Catechis'mal a. (*Catechism*).
Embolis'mal a. Pertaining to embolism.
Chris'mal a. Pertaining to chrism.
Pris'mal a. Prismatic.
Sabbatis'mal a. (*Sabbatism*).
Rheumatis'mal a. Pertaining to rheumatism.
Baptis'mal a. (*Baptism*).
Abys'mal a. Like an abyss; unfathomable.

Cataclys'mal a. (*Cataclysm*).
Paroxys'mal a. Pertaining to or characterized by paroxysms.
Bru'mal a. Pertaining to winter.
Parenchy'mal a. Pertaining to or consisting of parenchyma.
Lach'rymal a. Generating or pertaining to tears. s. A lachrymatory.
A'nal a. (*Anus*).
Ba'nal a. Trivial, commonplace.
Canal' s. An artificial watercourse; a duct in the body.
Dec'anal a. Pertaining to a dean or deanery, or to the S. side of a cathedral choir.
Rurideca'nal a. Pertaining to a rural dean.
Bac'chanal a. Pertaining to Bacchus or his revels; drunken. s. A devotee of Bacchus; a drunken reveller.
Duode'nal a. Pertaining to the duodenum.
Phenom'enal a. Pertaining to a phenomenon; very extraordinary.
Nou'menal a. Pertaining to or of the nature of noumena.
Pe'nal a. Pertaining to, inflicting, threatening, or incurring punishment; that punishes; vindictive.
Re'nal a. Pertaining to the kidneys.
Ar'senal s. A storehouse for or factory of guns, arms, ammunition, etc.
Ven'al a. Mercenary, base, sordid; pertaining to a vein.
Reg'nal a. Pertaining to a reign.
Sig'nal s. A sign for communication, especially at a distance; an indication. v.i. and t. To communicate by signals. a. Remarkable, worthy of note.
Domain'al a. Pertaining to a domain.
Tur'binal a. Top-shaped; turbinate.
Vac'cinal a. Vaccinic.
Medic'inal a. Pertaining to medicine; containing healing ingredients.
Offi'cinal a. Used in, kept in, or pertaining to a shop, especially an apothecary's; authorized by the pharmacopœia.
Vatic'inal a. Pertaining to or containing prophecy.
Vic'inal a. Near; neighbouring.
Un'cinal a. Hooked at the end.
Calyc'inal a. Like or pertaining to a calyx.
Nun'dinal a. Pertaining to a fair or market-day.
Car'dinal a. Principal, chief, fundamental. s. A high dignitary of the Roman Catholic Church.
Or'dinal a. Denoting order or succession. s. A number denoting this; a book containing rubrics, an ordination service, etc.
Palu'dinal a. Paludal.
Longitu'dinal a. Pertaining to longitude; running lengthwise.
Latitu'dinal a. Pertaining to or in the direction of latitude.
Testu'dinal a. Pertaining to or like the tortoise.
Fi'nal a. Ultimate; conclusive; decisive; mortal.
Imag'inal a. Pertaining to an imago.
Pag'inal a. Consisting of pages.
Vagi'nal a. Pertaining to the vagina.
Orig'inal a. Pertaining to the origin; first, primitive; not copied; having power to originate. s. Origin, source; archetype; that from which anything is copied or translated; one of marked peculiarity.
Aborig'inal a. Primitive, pristine.
Mar'ginal a. Pertaining to, at, or written on a margin; near the limit.
Vir'ginal a. Pertaining to or befitting a virgin; maidenly; pure.
Rhi'nal a. Pertaining to the nose.
Pericli'nal a. Sloping from a common centre (of strata).
Syncli'nal a. Sloping down towards a common point.
Monocli'nal a. Having one oblique inclination (of strata).
Isocli'nal a. Having the same inclination or dip.
Dis'ciplinal a. Disciplinary.
Lam'inal a. Laminar.
Stam'inal a. Pertaining to stamens.
Sem'inal a. Pertaining to seed; germinal; propagative; rudimentary.
Teg'minal a. Pertaining to a tegmen.
Lim'inal a. Liminary.
Sublim'inal a. Pertaining to subconsciousness; hardly perceived.
Crim'inal a. Relating to crime; wicked, guilty. s. One guilty or convicted of crime.
Vim'inal a. Pertaining to, consisting of, or producing twigs.
Abdom'inal a. Pertaining to the abdomen.
Nom'inal a. Pertaining to a name; not actual, existing in name only.
Adnom'inal a. Adjectival.
Cognom'inal a. Pertaining to a surname.
Pronom'inal a. Pertaining to or like a pronoun.
Ger'minal a. Pertaining to a germ; beginning to develop.
Term'inal s. An end piece; a clamping screw on a battery. a. Pertaining to or forming the end.
Conter'minal a. Bordering contiguous.
Volu'minal a. Pertaining to volume.
Spi'nal a. Pertaining to the backbone.
Dorsispi'nal a. Pertaining to the back and spine.
Cari'nal a. (*Carina*).
Cri'nal a. Pertaining to the hair.
En'crinal a. Pertaining to or containing encrinites.
Tri'nal a. Trine, threefold.
Doctri'nal a. Pertaining to or containing doctrine.
Ur'inal s. A vessel for urine; place for urinating.
Mat'inal a. Pertaining to matins or the morning.
Triac'tinal a. Having three rays.
Pec'tinal a. Pertaining to or resembling a comb or the scallops.
Ret'inal a. Pertaining to the retina.
Intes'tinal a. Pertaining to the intestines.
Matu'tinal a. Pertaining to the morning; early.
Ing'uinal a. Pertaining to the groin.
Hym'nal s. A collection of hymns.
Diac'onal a. Pertaining to a deacon.
Archidiac'onal a. Pertaining to the office of archdeacon.
Cotyle'donal a. Resembling a cotyledon.
Diag'onal s. A line from an angle of a four- (or more) sided figure to a non-adjacent angle. a. Extending thus; oblique.
Tetrag'onal a. Pertaining to a tetragon; having four sides or angles.
Octag'onal a. Having eight sides and eight angles.
Pentag'onal a. Having five corners or angles.
Heptag'onal a. Having seven angles or sides.
Hexag'onal a. Having six sides and six angles.
Trig'onal a. Having three angles; triangular.
Orthog'onal a. Rectangular; right-angled; at right angles.
Polyg'onal a. Having many angles.
Si'phonal a. Pertaining to or effected by a siphon.

Antiph'onal a. (*Antiphony*).
Sul'phonal s. A crystalline sulphur compound used as a sedative.
Autoch'thonal a. (*Autochthon*).
Sali'cional s. The salicet stop of an organ.
Merid'ional a. Pertaining to the meridian; pertaining to or situated in the south. s. An inhabitant of S. France.
Obsid'ional a. Pertaining to a siege.
Re'gional a. Pertaining to a region.
Tri'onal s. A hypnotic drug.
Septen'trional a. Pertaining to the north; northern.
Occa'sional a. Incidental; casual; occurring at times.
Vi'sional a. Pertaining to or like a vision.
Revis'ional a. Pertaining to revision.
Previs'ional a. Characterized by foresight.
Divis'ional a. Pertaining to a division.
Provis'ional a. For the occasion; temporary.
Descen'sional a. Pertaining to descent.
Dimen'sional a. (*Dimension*).
Ten'sional a. Pertaining to tension; resulting from stretching.
Ver'sional a. Pertaining to a version.
Rever'sional a. Reversionary.
Tor'sional a. Pertaining to or resembling torsion.
Excur'sional a. Pertaining to an excursion.
Pas'sional s. A book containing narratives of the sufferings, etc., of martyrs.
Succes'sional a. Pertaining to or involving succession; consecutive.
Reces'sional a. Pertaining to the return of the choir to the vestry. s. A hymn sung during this.
Preces'sional a. Pertaining to a precession.
Proces'sional s. Pertaining to or used in processions. s. A Roman Catholic service-book.
Confes'sional s. The place where a confessor receives confessions.
Profes'sional a. Pertaining to or engaged in a profession. s. A member of a profession; a non-amateur in sport, games, athletics, etc.
Non-profes'sional a. Amateur; not skilled.
Digres'sional a. Digressive.
Congres'sional a. Pertaining to a congress.
Progres'sional a. Tending to progress; pertaining to progression.
Expres'sional a. Pertaining to or having the power of expression.
Ses'sional a. Pertaining to a session or the sessions.
Commis'sional a. (*Commission*).
Delu'sional a. Delusive.
Proba'tional a. Serving for trial.
Voca'tional a. Pertaining to a calling or vocation.
Convoca'tional a. (*Convocation*).
Educa'tional a. Pertaining to education.
Grada'tional a. Pertaining to gradation; by regular steps.
Idea'tional a. Pertaining to or brought about by ideation.
Recrea'tional a. Recreative.
Congrega'tional a. Pertaining to a congregation or to the Congregationalists; independent.
Interroga'tional a. Pertaining to or of the nature of an interrogation.
Conjuga'tional a. (*Conjugation*).
Associa'tional a. (*Association*).
Varia'tional a. Pertaining or due to variation.
Revela'tional a. Pertaining to revelation.
Obla'tional a. Pertaining to or of the nature of an oblation.
Rela'tional a. Having or indicating some relation.
Transla'tional a. Pertaining to or involving translation.
Reforma'tional a. Pertaining to reformation or the Reformation.
Informa'tional a. Pertaining to or of the nature of information.
Na'tional a. Pertaining to a nation; general, public.
Vena'tional a. Pertaining to venation.
Declina'tional a. (*Declination*).
Inclina'tional a. Pertaining to inclination.
Denomina'-tional a. Pertaining to a denomination.
Termina'tional a. Pertaining to a termination.
Cona'tional a. (*Conation*).
Interna'tional a. Relating to, affecting, or regulating the intercourse between two or more nations.
Ra'tional a. Endowed with or agreeable to reason; sane; judicious.
Vibra'tional a. Pertaining to vibration.
Inspira'tional a. Pertaining to or of the nature of inspiration.
Irra'tional a. Contrary to reason; absurd.
Gyra'tional a. Pertaining to gyration.
Com-pensa'tional a. (*Compensation*).
Sensa'tional a. Pertaining to sensations; exciting great interest; startling.
Conversa'tional a. Pertaining to conversation familiar.
Gravita'tional a. Pertaining to gravitation.
Presenta'tional a. Pertaining to a presentation.
Repre-senta'tional a. Pertaining to representation.
Rota'tional a. Pertaining to or characterized by rotation.
Disserta'tional a. (*Dissertation*).
Sta'tional a. Pertaining to a station or position
Saluta'tional a. Pertaining to salutation.
Deputa'tional a. Pertaining to deputations.
Observa'tional a. Pertaining to observation or an observation.
Fac'tional a. Pertaining to a faction.
Frac'tional a. Pertaining to or constituting a fraction; insignificant.
Refrac'tional a. Refractive.
Trac'tional a. Pertaining to traction.
Affec'tional a. Pertaining to the or having affections.
Interjec'tional a. Thrown in; parenthetical; pertaining to or of the nature of an interjection.
Reflec'tional a. Pertaining to or caused by reflection.
Correc'tional a. Correction.
Insurrec'tional a. Pertaining to or of the nature of insurrection.
Sec'tional a. Pertaining to a section; partial.
Vivisec'tional a. Pertaining to or effected by vivisection.
Intersec'tional a. Pertaining to intersections.
Benedic'tional s. (*Benediction*).
Jurisdic'tional a. Pertaining to jurisdiction.
Fic'tional a. Pertaining to, consisting of, or founded on fiction.
Fric'tional a. Pertaining to or caused by friction.
Func'tional a. Pertaining to an office or function affecting the action, not the structure, of an organ.
Conjunc'tional a. Pertaining to conjunction.
Induc'tional a. Inductive.
Instruc'tional a. Pertaining to teaching or education.
Construc'tional a. Pertaining to construction; structural.
Secre'tional a. Pertaining or due to secretion.
Concre'tional a. (*Concretion*).

Discre'tional a. Left to discretion.
Tradi'tional a. Pertaining to or derived from tradition.
Addi'tional a. (*Addition*).
Condi'tional a. Containing or depending on conditions; not absolute; limited.
Voli'tional a. Pertaining to the exercise of the will.
Cogni'tional a. (*Cognition*).
Appari'tional a. (*Apparition*).
Inquisi'tional a. Relating to inquiry or inquisition; inquisitorial.
Transi'tional a. Involving or denoting transition.
Posi'tional a. Pertaining to or fixed by position.
Preposi'tional a. Pertaining to or having the nature of a preposition.
Proposi'tional a. Pertaining to or like a proposition.
Opposi'tional a. Pertaining to or constituting opposition.
Supposi'tional a. Hypothetical.
Transposi'tional a. Containing or involving transposition.
Repeti'tional a. Pertaining to or containing repetition.
Tui'tional a. Pertaining to tuition.
Intui'tional a. Pertaining to, characterized, or derived from intuition.
Inten'tional a. Done purposely.
Conven'tional a. Agreed upon; founded on use or tradition; slavishly observant of social customs.
Mo'tional a. Pertaining to or produced by motion.
Emo'tional a. Pertaining to emotion; easily affected by emotion.
No'tional a. Pertaining to or given to notions; abstract; fanciful.
Devo'tional a. Pertaining to religious devotion.
Concep'tional a. (*Conception*).
Excep'tional a. Forming an exception; of marked excellence; unusual.
Transcrip'tional a. Pertaining to or effected by transcribing.
Inscrip'tional a. Pertaining to an inscription.
Op'tional a. Depending on or left to one's own choice.
Adop'tional a. (*Adoption*).
Propor'tional a. Relating to or having a due proportion. s. A number or quantity in a proportion.
Dispropor'tional a. Showing disproportion; inadequate.
Distor'tional a. (*Distortion*).
Precau'tional a. Precautionary.
Circumlocu'tional a. (*Circumlocution*).
Evolu'tional a. Pertaining to evolution.
Substitu'tional a. Pertaining to substitution; substituted.
Institu'tional a. Pertaining to institution; of the nature of, having, or managed by an institution; elementary.
Constitu'tional a. Inherent in the constitution; consistent with the civil constitution; legal. s. A walk for health's sake.
Flex'ional a. Pertaining to or caused by flexion.
Inflex'ional a. Pertaining to or having grammatical inflexions.
Connex'ional a. (*Connexion*).
Flux'ional a. Pertaining to fluxions.
Ver'onal s. A hypnotic and opiate drug.
Syn'chronal a. Synchronous.
Thron'al a. Pertaining to the throne or regal state.
Cor'onal a. Pertaining to the crown of the head, a corona, or a crown. s. A crown, garland.
Ma'tronal a. Pertaining or suitable to a matron; motherly.
Pa'tronal a. Performing the functions of a patron; favouring.
Sea'sonal a. Pertaining to a season or period.
Unis'onal a. Being in unison.
Per'sonal a. Pertaining to or belonging to a person or individual; private; denoting the grammatical person.
Uniper'sonal a. Existing as one person (of God); denoting verbs having only a third person.
Triper'sonal a. Consisting of three persons.
Imper'sonal a. Not personal; not having personal existence or personality; denoting a verb used only in the third sing. (e.g. *it snows*).
Ton'al a. Pertaining to tone or tonality.
Can'tonal a. (*Canton*).
Zon'al a. Pertaining to a zone.
Polyzo'nal a. Composed of many annular segments.
Car'nal a. Fleshly, sensual, worldly.
Hiber'nal a. Pertaining to winter.
Lucer'nal a. Pertaining to a lamp.
Infer'nal a. Relating to the lower regions; diabolical.
Parapher'nal a. Pertaining to paraphernalia.
Hodier'nal a. Pertaining to the present day.
Super'nal a. Relating to things above; heavenly.
Ter'nal a. Consisting of threes. s. A ternary.
Mater'nal a. Motherly; befitting a mother.
Pater'nal a. Pertaining to or derived from a father; fatherly; hereditary.
Frater'nal a. Brotherly, friendly; pertaining to brethren.
Eter'nal a. Always existing, without beginning or end; unchangeable.
Coeter'nal a. Equally eternal.
Sempiter'nal a. Everlasting; endless.
Inter'nal a. Inward; not external; dependent on or derived from itself; domestic, as opposed to foreign.
Ster'nal a. Pertaining to the sternum.
Hester'nal a. Of yesterday.
Exter'nal a. Outward, exterior; visible, not being within; accidental, irrelevant; foreign.
Ver'nal a. Pertaining to the spring; blooming.
Diur'nal a. Pertaining to the day; daily. s. A service-book used in the Roman Catholic Church.
Jour'nal s. Account of daily doings; book containing such; diary; newspaper, periodical; the part of an axle that moves in bearings.
Noctur'nal a. Relating to or done by night.
Diutur'nal a. Of long continuance.
Faun'al a. Pertaining to a fauna.
Tribun'al s. A judgment-seat; a board of arbitrators.
Lacu'nal a. Pertaining to or containing lacunæ.
Comm'unal a. Pertaining to a commune, a community, or communalism.
Coal s. Fossilized timber, etc., used as fuel; a burning substance; charcoal. v.t. and i. To supply with or take in coal.
Recoal' v.t. and i. To furnish with or take in a fresh supply of coal.
Char'coal s. Black, porous, impure carbon obtained by burning wood or bone, etc.
Foal s. The young of a horse, ass, etc. v.i. and t. To bring forth a foal.

Goal s. The limit in a race; a mark, spot, etc., to be attained, success in reaching this; aim, purpose.
Shoal s. A throng, multitude; a shallow, sand-bank. v.i. To form a shoal (especially of fish); to become shallower.
Microzo'al a. Pertaining to the microzoa.
Entozo'al a. Pertaining to the entozoa.
Polyzo'al a. Pertaining to or resembling the polyzoa.
Pal s. (*Slang*) A mate, comrade, close friend.
Pa'pal a. Pertaining to the Pope, or to the papacy.
Se'pal s. A leaf or division of a calyx.
Munic'ipal a. Pertaining to local self-government, or to a corporation or city.
Prin'cipal a. First, chief; most important; essential. s. A president, head; one primarily engaged; capital sum.
Pal'pal a. Pertaining to a palp.
O'pal s. An iridescent, vitreous form of hydrous silica.
Co'pal s. A resin from a Mexican tree; varnish made from this.
Syn'copal a. Pertaining to or characterized by syncope.
Epis'copal a. Governed by, pertaining to, or vested in bishops.
Archiepis'copal a. Pertaining to an archbishop or his office.
Non-epis'copal a. (*Negative*).
No'pal s. A Central American species of cactus.
Perit'ropal a. Rotatory.
Orthot'ropal a. Growing straight.
Appal' v.t. To frighten, daunt, terrify.
Carp'al a. Pertaining to the carpus.
Metacar'pal a. Pertaining to the metacarpus.
Pu'pal a. Pertaining to a chrysalis.
Archety'pal a. (*Archetype*).
Pal'pebral a. Pertaining to the eyebrow or eyelid.
Cer'ebral a. Pertaining to the brain.
Ver'tebral a. Pertaining to vertebræ or the spine.
Inver'tebral a. Invertebrate.
Um'bral a. Pertaining to an umbra.
Sa'cral a. Pertaining to the sacrum.
Decahe'dral a. Having ten sides.
Tetrahe'dral a. Having or composed of four sides.
Octahe'dral a. Pertaining to or resembling an octahedron.
Pentahe'dral a. Having five equal sides.
Hexahe'dral a. Having six sides.
Dihe'dral a. Having two plane faces.
Hemihe'dral a. Having only half the faces necessary to complete symmetry (of crystals).
Trihe'dral a. Having three equal sides.
Cathe'dral s. The principal church of a diocese. a. Pertaining to a cathedral or to a bishop's throne; authoritative.
Polyhe'dral a. Having many sides.
Lib'eral a. Generous; bountiful; open-handed. s. An advocate of liberal principles.
Illib'eral a. Not liberal; sordid; uncharitable.
Pu'beral a. Pertaining to puberty.
Vis'ceral a. Pertaining to the viscera.
Fed'eral a. Pertaining to a league; composed of states united but retaining internal independence. s. A federalist.
Hed'eral a. Composed of or pertaining to ivy.
Si'deral a. Sidereal.
Fal'deral s. A trifle, gewgaw.
Pon'deral a. Pertaining to or fixed by weight.
Fer'al a. Wild, not domesticated; escaped from captivity; fierce.
Foraminif'eral a. Pertaining to the foraminifera.
Porif'eral a. Pertaining to the sponges; like a sponge.
Periph'eral a. Pertaining to or constituting a periphery; external.
Spher'al a. Spherical; pertaining to the celestial sphere.
An'theral a. (*Anther*).
Bicam'eral a. Having two chambers.
Unicam'eral a. Having a single chamber.
Tetram'eral a. Consisting of four parts.
Ephem'eral a. Beginning and ending in a day; transient.
Hu'meral a. Pertaining to the shoulder.
Nu'meral a. Pertaining to or denoting number. s. A symbol or group of figures expressing a number.
Gen'eral a. Not special or restricted, usual; generic; common, public, extensive; taken as a whole. s. Military officer next below field-marshal; the whole, a comprehensive notion.
Outgen'eral v.t. To exceed in generalship.
Min'eral s. An inorganic body found in the earth. a. Pertaining to, consisting of, or impregnated with minerals.
Fu'neral s. A burial, interment; obsequies.
Puer'peral a. Happening after child-birth.
Tes'seral a. Composed of tesseræ.
Lat'eral a. Pertaining to, on, or proceeding from the side.
Quinquelat'eral a. Having five sides.
Bilat'eral a. Two-sided.
Unilat'eral a. One-sided; arranged on or turned towards one side only.
Quadrilat'eral a. Having four sides and angles. s. A plane figure having these.
Trilat'eral a. Having three sides.
Multilat'eral a. Having many sides.
Septilat'eral a. Seven-sided.
Equilat'eral a. Having all the sides equal.
Collat'eral a. Side by side, parallel; descending from the same stock but not one from the other. s. A kinsman; additional security to a bond, etc.
Octolat'eral a. Eight-sided.
Sphinc'teral a. Pertaining to or of the nature of sphincter.
Lit'eral a. According to the verbal meaning; not figurative; expressed by letters.
Quinquelit'eral a. Consisting of five letters.
Unilit'eral a. Consisting of only one letter.
Trilit'eral a. Consisting of three letters. s. A three-lettered word or root.
Ap'teral a. Wingless; without side columns.
Dip'teral a. Being surrounded by a double row of columns.
Hemip'teral a. Pertaining to the Hemiptera.
Perip'teral a. Having columns all round (of temples).
Lepidop'teral a. Pertaining to the Lepidoptera.
Orthop'teral a. Belonging to the Orthoptera.
Hymenop'teral a. Pertaining or relating to the Hymenoptera.
Monop'teral s. A monopteros. a. Pertaining to this.
Gas'teral a. Pertaining to the stomach.
Presbyt'eral a. Pertaining to a presbyter.
Sev'eral a. Separate, distinct; various; more than two, but not many.
Podag'ral a. Gouty; pertaining to gout.
In'tegral a. Whole; forming essential part. s. A whole.

Sepul'chral a. Suggestive of the grave; pertaining to burial.
Hypæth'ral a. Open to the sky.
Ure'thral a. Pertaining to the urethra.
Cleith'ral a. Having a roof (of ancient temples).
Enthral' v.t. To enslave, captivate.
Ad'miral s. A naval officer of the highest rank.
Spir'al s. A curve winding like a screw. a. Winding thus; pertaining to a spire.
Decem'viral a. Pertaining to a decemvir.
Centum'viral a. (*Centumvir*).
Or'al a. Delivered verbally, not written; pertaining to the mouth.
Cor'al s. The calcareous secretion of certain marine zoophytes; a piece of this; an infant's toy made from it; the ovary of the lobster. a. Made of or resembling coral; red, pink.
Ster'coral a. Pertaining to dung.
Go'ral s. A Himalayan antelope allied to the chamois.
Hor'al a. Relating to an hour or to the time; occurring every hour.
Chor'al a. Pertaining to a choir or chorus; chanted.
Thor'al a. Pertaining to the marriage-bed.
Lor'al a. Pertaining to a bird's lore.
Flor'al a. Pertaining to flowers or to floras.
Triflor'al a. Bearing three flowers.
Chlor'al s. A narcotic liquid.
Mor'al a. Relating to morality; ethical; virtuous; probable. s. Practical application of a story, etc.; morale; morality.
Fe'moral a. Belonging to the thigh.
Balmor'al s. A Scotch cap; a kind of laced boot.
Immor'al a. Not moral; vicious; dishonest.
Non-mor'al a. Neither moral nor immoral; not ethical.
Circumor'al a. Surrounding the mouth.
Hu'moral a. Of or proceeding from the bodily humours.
Por'al a. Pertaining to the pores.
Cap'oral s. A coarse kind of tobacco.
Tem'poral a. Belonging to this world, secular; pertaining to the temples of the head.
Extem'poral a. Extemporaneous.
Cor'poral s. The lowest grade of army N.C.O.; a linen cloth to cover the elements in the Eucharist. a. Pertaining to the body; material.
Bicor'poral a. Having two bodies.
Tricor'poral a. Having three bodies.
Ror'al a. Pertaining to or like dew.
Soror'al a. Pertaining to or characteristic of a sister.
Auror'al a. (*Aurora*).
Prefec'toral a. Prefectural.
Elec'toral a. Pertaining to or consisting of electors.
Pec'toral a. Pertaining to the breast or to diseases of the chest. s. A breastplate, especially of the Jewish high priest; a medicine for chest complaints.
Inspec'toral a. Pertaining to inspection or an inspector.
Sec'toral a. Pertaining to a sector.
Protec'toral a. Pertaining to a protector or protectorate.
Doc'toral a. Pertaining to the degree of practice of a doctor.
Pas'toral a. Pertaining to shepherds, to rural life, or to ministers and the care of souls. s. A poem of rural life; a letter from a bishop to his clergy.
Lit'toral a. Pertaining to the shore. s. Tract along the coast.
Mayor'al a. Pertaining to a mayor.
Chaparral' s. A thicket.
Corral' s. A yard for cattle, etc. v.t. To pen in a corral.
Sabur'ral a. Pertaining to saburra.
Spec'tral a. Ghost-like; pertaining to the spectrum.
Diamet'ral a. Pertaining to a diameter.
Sym'metral a. Symmetric.
Ar'bitral a. Pertaining to arbitration.
Mi'tral a. Like a mitre.
Accip'itral a. Hawk-like.
Cen'tral a. Of, containing, situated in or near the centre; chief, dominant.
Paracen'tral a. Situated near the centre.
Ven'tral a. Abdominal; pertaining to the surface opposite the back.
Dorsiven'tral a. Having both back and under-surface shaped alike.
As'tral a. Pertaining to the stars; also to matters spiritualistic.
Subas'tral a. Beneath the stars; terrestrial.
Cadas'tral a. (*Cadastre*).
Plas'tral a. Pertaining to or resembling a plastron.
Ances'tral a. Pertaining to or derived from ancestors.
Orches'tral a. Pertaining to or suitable for an orchestra.
Fenes'tral a. Pertaining to windows.
Campes'tral a. Pertaining to fields.
Rupes'tral a. Inhabiting rocks.
Seques'tral a. Pertaining to sequestrum.
Magis'tral a. Suiting a magistrate; authoritative; specially prescribed.
Mis'tral s. A cold, dry N.W. wind of S. France
Sinis'tral a. Turning to the left (of a spiral shell).
Clois'tral a. Pertaining to a cloister or a monastic establishment.
Ros'tral a. Pertaining to or resembling a rostrum.
Longiros'tral a. Having a long slender bill.
Lamelliros'tral a. Having a lamellose bill (of ducks, etc.).
Coniros'tral a. Having a thick conical beak.
Cultriros'tral a. Having a beak shaped like a coulter or knife.
Latiros'tral a. Having a broad or wide beak.
Curviros'tral a. Having a curved beak.
Aus'tral a. Pertaining to or situated in the south.
Claus'tral a. Pertaining to a or the cloister; refined.
Plau'stral a. Pertaining to wagons.
Lus'tral a. Pertaining to or used in purification; pertaining to a lustrum.
Neu'tral a. Not of either party, indifferent; neither acid nor alkaline, positive nor negative; having neither stamens nor pistils; asexual. s. A person or nation siding with neither party.
Dex'tral a. With the whorls (of a shell) turning towards the right.
Au'ral a. Pertaining to the ear; or to an aura.
Procur'al s. Procurement.
Pleur'al a. Pertaining to the pleura.
Neur'al a. Pertaining to the nerves or the nervous system.
Au'gural a. Pertaining to augurs or augury.
Inau'gural a. Pertaining to or done at an inauguration.
Jur'al a. Pertaining to law or jurisprudence.
Tellur'al a. Pertaining to the earth.

Plur'al a. Containing more than one. s. The number of the noun, verb, etc. signifying more than one.
Mur'al a. Pertaining to or like a wall.
Intramur'al a. Between or within the walls or boundaries.
Intermur'al a. Situated between walls.
Hypu'ral a. Situated beneath the tail (of fishes).
Rur'al a. Pertaining to the country, farming, etc.; rustic.
Crur'al a. Pertaining to or shaped like a leg.
Sur'al a. Pertaining to the calf of the leg.
Cæsur'al a. (*Cæsura*).
Commissur'al a. (*Commissure*).
Divis'ural a. Divisional.
Men'sural a. Pertaining to measure.
Caricatur'al a. (*Caricature*).
Nomencla'tural a. Pertaining to nomenclature.
Nat'ural a. Pertaining to, produced, or constituted by nature; not artificial; not revealed; unaffected. s. An idiot; a sign in music.
Non-nat'ural a. (*Negative*).
Supernat'ural a. Beyond natural laws; miraculous.
Preternat'ural a. Out of the regular course of things.
Prefec'tural a. Pertaining to a perfect, his duties, etc.
Conjec'tural a. Depending on conjecture.
Interjec'tural a. Interjectional.
Architec'tural a. (*Architecture*).
Struc'tural a. Pertaining to a structure or building.
Substruc'tural a. Of the nature of or pertaining to a substructure.
Cul'tural a. (*Culture*).
Agricul'tural a. (*Agriculture*).
Arboricul'tural a. (*Arboriculture*).
Floricul'tural a. Pertaining to floriculture.
Horticul'tural a. Pertaining to horticulture.
Scrip'tural a. Pertaining to, contained in, or according to the Scriptures.
Sculp'tural a. Pertaining to sculpture.
Ges'tural a. Pertaining to gesture.
Pos'tural a. Pertaining to posture.
Gut'tural a. Pronounced in or by the throat. s. A letter or sound thus pronounced.
Su'tural a. Pertaining to a suture or seam.
Tex'tural a. Pertaining to texture.
Gyr'al a. Moving in a circle; whirling.
Papyr'al a. Pertaining to papyrus or papyri.
Sal s. Chemical name for salt.
Bas'al s. (*Base*).
Na'sal a. Pertaining to or affected by the nose. s. A sound uttered partly through the nose.
Va'sal a. Pertaining to a vas or duct.
Apprais'al s. (*Appraise*).
Repri'sal a. Act of retaliation.
Surpri'sal s. Act of surprising suddenly; state of being surprised.
Sis'al a. Applied to the fibre of an American aloe used for cordage.
Revis'al s. Revision; act of revising.
Men'sal a. Monthly; pertaining to or used at the table.
Bimen'sal a. Occurring every two months; lasting two months.
Commen'sal a. Eating at the same table. s. An animal living on or in another without being parasitic.
Spon'sal a. Pertaining to marriage or a spouse.
Respon'sal s. A response, responsory.
Depo'sal a. Act of deposing.
Repo'sal s. Act of reposing.
Propo'sal s. That which is proposed; an offer.
Suppo'sal s. Act of supposing; supposition.
Presuppo'sal s. Presupposition.
Interpos'al a. That which is interposed; act of interposing.
Dispos'al s. Act or power of disposing; distribution.
Transpos'al s. Transposition.
Rehears'al a. Act of rehearsing; trial performance.
Tar'sal a. Pertaining to the tarsus.
Metatar'sal a. Pertaining to the metatarsus.
Dispers'al s. Dispersion.
Quaquaver'sal a. Turning in all directions, especially of strata.
Revers'al s. A change, overthrow; act of reversing.
Univer'sal a. Pertaining to or comprising all; whole, total. s. A general notion or idea.
Transver'sal a. Transverse. s. A straight line cutting across others.
Dor'sal a. Pertaining to, shaped like, or situated on the back. s. A dorsal fin.
Sinistror'sal a. Directed towards or turning to the left.
Succur'sal a. Serving as a chapel of ease.
Vas'sal s. A retainer, feudal tenant; a slave.
Mis'sal s. The Roman Catholic mass-book.
Dismiss'al s. Act of dismissing; leave to go; a setting aside.
Dos'sal s. An ornament hanging at the back of an altar.
Gloss'al a. Pertaining to the tongue.
Colos'sal a. Huge, gigantic.
Abys'sal a. (*Abysmal*).
Caus'al a. Relating to, expressing, or due to a cause.
Medu'sal a. Of or belonging to the jelly-fishes.
Spous'al a. Pertaining to a spouse or to marriage. s. Marriage.
Espous'al a. Act of espousing; betrothal; the adopting of a cause.
Carous'al s. A jovial feast, a spree.
Peru'sal a. Act of perusing or reading.
Fa'tal a. Appointed by fate; destructive; deadly.
Pal'atal a. Pertaining to or uttered by aid of the palate. s. A letter pronounced with the aid of the palate.
Na'tal a. Pertaining to or dating from birth; pertaining to the buttocks.
Prena'tal a. Anterior to birth.
Post-na'tal a. Subsequent to birth.
Ra'tal s. Ratable value of property.
Stra'tal a. Like strata; stratiform.
Cac'tal a. Allied to the cactuses.
Dialec'tal a. Pertaining to or resembling a dialect or dialects.
Rec'tal a. Pertaining to the rectum.
Edic'tal a. Pertaining to an edict.
Veg'etal a. Pertaining to or of the nature of plants; common to plants and animals.
Pari'etal a. Pertaining to a wall, especially those of the cavities of the body.
Vari'etal a. Pertaining to a variety.
Skel'etal a. Pertaining to a skeleton or framework.
Met'al s. An elementary substance having high specific gravity, lustre, and opacity, and usu. fusible by heat and malleable; broken stone for roads.
Fœ'tal a. Pertaining to a fœtus.
Pet'al s. One of the leaves of a corolla.
Centrip'etal a. Tending to move toward the centre.
Decre'tal a. Pertaining to a decree. s. A papal decree.
Hy'etal a. Pertaining to rain or rainfall.

Or'bital a. Pertaining to or resembling an orbit.
Cu'bital a. Pertaining to the forearm.
Ci'tal s. Impeachment; summons.
Recit'al s. Act of reciting; narration; musical performance.
Dig'ital a. Pertaining to a digit.
Gen'ital a. Pertaining to generation or procreation.
Unigen'ital a. Only-begotten.
Congen'ital a. Pertaining to an individual from birth, constitutional.
Primogen'ital a. Primogenitary.
Urinogen'ital a. Pertaining to the urinary and reproductive organs.
Encrini'tal a. Encrinal.
Cap'ital a. Chief, good, punishable by death. s. The upper part of a column; a chief city; the stock of a bank, etc.; a large letter.
Occip'ital a. Pertaining to the occiput.
Bicip'ital a. Two-headed; pertaining to the biceps.
Ancip'ital a. Having two sharp edges.
Sincip'ital a. Pertaining to the sinciput.
Spit'al s. A hospital.
Hos'pital s. An institution for the treatment of the sick; a refuge for the infirm, etc.
Mar'ital a. Pertaining to a husband or to married life.
Detri'tal a. Pertaining to or consisting of detritus.
Requit'al s. Act of requiting; retribution.
Recruit'al a. Recruitment.
Vi'tal a. Pertaining or necessary to life; essential.
Consonan'tal a. Of the nature of a consonant.
Quadran'tal a. Pertaining to a quadrant.
San'tal s. Sandal-wood.
Sextan'tal a. Pertaining to the sextant.
Cen'tal s. A weight of 100 lbs.
Placen'tal a. Pertaining to or having a placenta.
Den'tal a. Pertaining to the teeth or to dentistry. s. A letter formed by the aid of the teeth.
Eden'tal a. Edentate. s. An edentate animal.
Biden'tal s. A place struck by lightning.
Acciden'tal a. and s. (*Accident*).
Occiden'tal a. Western; setting after the sun.
Inciden'tal a. Casual, accidental. s. Something that is incidental.
Coinciden'tal a. (*Coincident*).
Triden'tal a. Having three teeth or prongs.
Transcenden'tal a. Supereminent; abstrusely speculative; pertaining to that which can be determined a priori.
Labioden'tal a. Formed or pronounced by aid of lips and teeth.
Linguden'tal a. Uttered by joint action of tongue and teeth.
Orien'tal a. Eastern, easterly; pertaining to, situated in, or derived from the East. s. A native of the East.
Men'tal a. Pertaining to the mind; intellectual; pertaining to the chin.
Medicamen'tal a. Pertaining to or resembling medicaments.
Predicamen'tal a. (*Predicament*).
Nidamen'tal a. Pertaining to eggs or a nest.
Fundamen'tal a. Essential, important; pertaining to or serving as a basis.
Ligamen'tal a. Ligamentous.
Firmamen'tal a. Pertaining to the firmament; celestial.
Ornamen'tal a. Serving or pertaining to ornament.
Sacramen'tal a. Pertaining to or constituting sacrament.
Temperamen'tal a. Pertaining to one's temperament.
Atramen'tal a. Black, inky.
Testamen'tal a. Testamentary.
Elemen'tal a. Pertaining to the four ancient elements or to first principles; uncompounded, rude, initial. s. A spirit formerly supposed to inhabit one of the four elements.
Implemen'tal a. Pertaining to or of the nature of an implement; instrumental.
Complemen'tal a. Complementary.
Supplemen'tal a. Added to supply what is wanted; additional.
Tenemen'tal a. Pertaining to a tenement; held by tenants.
Recremen'tal a. Consisting of superfluous matter.
Incremen'tal a. Pertaining to increment.
Excremen'tal a. Pertaining to or of the nature of excrement.
Fragmen'tal a. Pertaining to or consisting of fragments; disconnected.
Segmen'tal a. Pertaining to or of the nature of a segment.
Pigmen'tal a. Pigmentary.
Pedimen'tal a. Pertaining to a pediment.
Impedimen'tal a. Pertaining to or of the nature of an impediment.
Condimen'tal a. (*Condiment*).
Rudimen'tal a. Rudimentary.
Regimen'tal a. Pertaining to or concerning a regiment.
Alimen'tal a. (*Aliment*).
Complimen'tal a. (*Compliment*).
Experimen'tal a. Pertaining to, skilled in, given to, derived from or affording experiment.
Detrimen'tal a. Causing detriment or injury.
Nutrimen'tal a. Nutritious; nutrient.
Sentimen'tal a. Abounding with sentiment; artificially tender.
Governmen'tal a. Pertaining to or sanctioned by a government.
Developmen'tal a. Pertaining to development; evolutionary.
Departmen'tal a. Pertaining to a department.
Documen'tal a. Pertaining to, consisting of, or derived from documents.
Tegumen'tal a. Pertaining to or resembling a tegument.
Monumen'tal a. Pertaining to, suitable for, or serving as a monument; of great importance.
Instrumen'tal a. Serving as means; due to the instrument used; pertaining to or produced by instruments.
Continen'tal a. Pertaining to a continent; European.
Componen'tal a. (*Component*).
Ren'tal s. Total income from rents; rent-roll.
Paren'tal a. Pertaining to or befitting parents; tender.
Tren'tal s. Series of thirty masses for the dead.
Quin'tal s. A metric weight of about 220½ lbs. avoir.; a hundredweight.
Fon'tal a. Pertaining to a font or to baptism.
Fron'tal a. Pertaining to or situated at the front. s. A front piece; a small pediment; ornamental hanging for an altar.
Horizon'tal a. Parallel to or pertaining to the horizon; level. s. A horizontal line, bar, etc.
Recoun'tal s. A recounting, recital.
Contrapun'tal a. Pertaining to or according to the rules of counterpoint.
Do'tal a. Pertaining to a dowry.
Extrado'tal a. Not belonging to dower.
Anecdo'tal a. (*Anecdote*).

Antido'tal a. (*Antidote*).
Sacerdo'tal a. Pertaining to priests or the priesthood.
Nep'otal a. Pertaining to or like a nephew.
Ro'tal a. Pertaining or according to a rota.
Scro'tal a. Pertaining to or resembling the scrotum.
To'tal a. Complete; pertaining to the whole. s. The whole, the aggregrate. v.t. and i. To ascertain the total of, to amount to.
Teeto'tal a. Pertaining or pledged to total abstinence from intoxicants.
Piv'otal a. Pertaining to or constituting a pivot.
Sep'tal a. Pertaining to a septum, or to a sept.
Mor'tal a. Subject to death; human; deadly. s. A human being.
Immor'tal a. Not subject to death; endless, eternal. s. One who is immortal.
Port'al s. A door, gateway. a. Applied to a vein connected with the liver.
Cur'tal s. A horse with a docked tail. a. Cropped; niggardly.
Coast'al a. Pertaining to or bordering on the coast.
Ped'estal s. Base of a column, statue, etc.
Fes'tal a. Pertaining to a feast or holiday; joyous, gay.
Ves'tal a. Pertaining to the ancient Roman goddess, Vesta; virginal, chaste. s. A virgin consecrated to Vesta; a virgin; a nun.
Dis'tal a. Denoting the extremity of a bone, etc., farthest from point of attachment.
Cos'tal a. Pertaining to the ribs.
Supracos'tal a. Situated above or outside the ribs.
Pentecos'tal a. Pertaining to Pentecost.
Intercos'tal a. Placed or lying between the ribs.
Post'al a. Pertaining to the post or mail service.
Crys'tal s. A regular solid mineral body; pure transparent quartz; a kind of glass. a. Consisting of or like crystal; clear.
Sag'ittal a. Pertaining to or like an arrow.
Remit'tal s. A giving up; remission.
Commit'tal s. (*Commitment*).
Recommit'tal s. Renewed reference to a committee; a second commitment.
Non-commit'tal s. State of not being committed to any course. a. Impartial.
Quit'tal a. Quittance; requital.
Acquit'tal s. (*Acquit*).
Glot'tal a. Pertaining to or produced in the Glottis.
Polyglot'tal a. Polyglot.
Rebut'tal s. Giving of evidence annulling that previously heard.
Refu'tal a. Refutation.
Bru'tal a. Resembling a brute; savage; coarse; sensual.
Phagocy'tal a. Pertaining to or of the nature of phagocytes.
Microphy'tal a. Pertaining to microphytes.
Du'al a. Expressing or consisting of two; twofold, double.
Grad'ual a. Proceeding by degrees or step by step.
Subdu'al s. Act of subduing.
Resid'ual a. Remaining after a part is taken. s. A remainder.
Vid'ual a. Pertaining to widowhood; viduous.
Individ'ual a. Subsisting singly as a whole; pertaining to one only; particular. s. A single being, person, or thing.
Lin'gual a. Pertaining to or formed by the tongue. s. A letter formed by the tongue.
Quadrilin'gual a. Speaking or written in four languages.
Trilin'gual a. Pertaining to or expressed in three languages.
Coling'ual a. Having the same language.
Ung'ual a. Pertaining to or having a nail, hoof, or claw.
Man'ual a. Pertaining to or done with the hands. s. A small book; keyboard of an organ.
Gen'ual a. Pertaining to the knee.
Contin'ual a. Without interruption, very frequent, incessant.
An'nual a. Returning or happening every year; lasting or performed in a year. s. A thing happening or work published once a year; a plant lasting only one season.
Bian'nual a. (*Biennial*).
Corn'ual a. Pertaining to a horn or a horn-shaped process.
E'qual a. Having the same bulk, extent, value, degree, rank, rights, etc. s. One not inferior or superior to another. v.t. To make, be, or become equal to.
Sube'qual a. Nearly equal.
Coe'qual a. Equal with another. s. One equal with another.
Ror'qual s. A whale with dorsal fins.
Œs'trual a. Pertaining to sexual desire (of animals).
Mens'trual a. Monthly; pertaining to the menses.
Cas'ual a. Happening by chance, accidental. s. A tramp.
Vis'ual a. Pertaining to or used in sight.
Trimen'sual a. Happening, etc., every three months.
Sen'sual a. Pertaining to or affecting the senses; devoted to the gratification of the appetite; carnal; lewd.
Us'ual (ūz'-) a. Habitual; frequent; ordinary.
Ac'tual a. Existing in act, real.
Fac'tual a. Relating to or containing facts.
Contrac'tual a. Implying or relating to a contract.
Tac'tual a. Pertaining to the sense or organs of touch.
Contac'tual a. (*Contact*).
Effec'tual a. Producing the desired effect; efficacious, adequate.
Ineffec'tual a. Inefficient; fruitless; impotent.
Lec'tual a. Confining to bed.
Intellec'tual a. Possessing intellect; relating or appealing to the intellect.
Vict'ual v.t. To supply with provisions for sustenance; provide with food.
Revict'ual v.t. To resupply, reprovision.
Punc'tual a. Done at exact time; observant of nice points; exact.
Perpet'ual a. Never ceasing; uninterrupted; everlasting.
Habit'ual a. Formed or acquired by use; customary.
Obit'ual a. Of or pertaining to obits. s. An obituary.
Rit'ual a. Pertaining to consisting of or involving rites; ceremonious. s. Manner of performing divine service; a book of rites.
Spir'itual a. Pertaining to spirit; incorporeal; intellectual; divine; ecclesiastical.
Accent'ual a. Relating to accent.

Event'ual a. Happening as a result; pertaining to a final issue; ultimate.
Conven'tual a. and s. Belonging to or a member of a convent.
Precep'tual a. Preceptive.
Concep'tual a. Pertaining to conception.
Vir'tual a. Equivalent so far as effect is concerned.
Mu'tual a. Reciprocal; interchanged; shared by or common to two or more.
Tex'tual a. Pertaining to or contained in the text.
Contex'tual a. Pertaining to the context.
Sex'ual a. Pertaining to sex, the sexes, or their relationships.
Asex'ual a. Without sex or sexual functions.
Bisex'ual a. Comprising both sexes.
Unisex'ual a. Of one sex only; not hermaphrodite.
Upheav'al s. Act of upheaving; a violent disturbance.
Na'val a. Maritime; pertaining to a navy or to ships.
Mediæ'val a. Pertaining to or characteristic of the Middle Ages.
Longe'val a. Long-lived.
Retriev'al s. Act of retrieving.
Prime'val a. Belonging to the first ages; pristine.
Coe'val a. Of equal age, of contemporary duration. s. A contemporary.
Roun'cival s. The marrowfat pea.
Khediv'al a. Pertaining to a khedive or his rule.
Gerundi'val a. Pertaining to a gerundive
Gingi'val a. Pertaining to the gums.
Ogi'val a. Pertaining to or resembling an ogive.
Ni'val a. Niveous; growing in snow.
Car'nival s. The three days' festival before Lent; revelry.
Ri'val s. A competitor, antagonist. a. Emulous; having the same claims v.t. To vie with, emulate.
Depriv'al s. Deprivation.
Arri'val s. (*Arrive*).
Corri'val s. A competitor, rival. a. Emulous.
Outri'val v.t. To surpass as a rival.
Dati'val a. Pertaining to the dative.
Nominati'val a. Pertaining to the nominative case.
Imperati'val a. Pertaining to the imperative mood.
Accusati'val a. (*Accusative*).
Adjecti'val a. (*Adjective*).
Geniti'val a. Pertaining to the genitive case.
Infiniti'val a. Pertaining to the infinitive mood.
Substanti'val a. Pertaining to or resembling a substantive.
Æs'tival, Es'tival a. Belonging to or produced in the summer.
Fes'tival s. A day of civil or religious joy; a feasting. a. Festive, joyous.
Diminuti'val a. Expressing diminution.
Reviv'al s. Act of reviving; recovery of life, vigour, etc.; a religious awakening.
Survi'val s. Act of surviving; person, thing, habit, etc., still existing.
Val'val a. Pertaining to or like a valve.
O'val a. Egg-shaped; elliptical.
Subo'val a. Nearly oval.
Remov'al s. Act of removing; change of place; dismissal.
Reprov'al s. Act of reproving; reproof.
Approv'al s. (*Approve*).
Disapprov'al s. Dislike; act of disapproving.
Disprov'al s. Act of disproving.
Lar'val a. Pertaining to or in the stage of a larva.
Ser'val s. The African tiger-cat.
In'terval s. Space or amount of separation between things; interstice; time elapsed; difference between sounds.
Withdraw'al s. Act of withdrawing; a recalling.
Review'al s. Act of reviewing; a review; revision.
Renew'al s. Act of renewing; that renewed.
Bestow'al s. (*Bestow*).
Avow'al s. (*Avow*).
Disavow'al s. A repudiation, disclaimer.
Coax'al a. (*Coaxial*).
Plex'al a. Pertaining to a plexus.
Cox'al a. Pertaining to the hip.
Gay'al s. The domesticated ox of India.
Defray'al s. Act of defraying.
Betray'al s. (*Betray*).
Portray'al s. Act of portraying; representation.
Loy'al a. Faithful, true, devoted, especially to the sovereign or government.
Disloy'al a. False to allegiance; treacherous.
Roy'al a. Pertaining to the crown; pertaining to or befitting a king; under the patronage of royalty; noble, illustrious. s. A size of paper (20 × 25 ins.); a small sail above the topgallant; a stag with twelve or more points.
Viceroy'al a. Viceregal.
Pennyroy'al s. A kind of mint formerly used in medicine.
Gha'zal s. An Oriental lyric in couplets all of the same rhyme.
Capsi'zal s. (*Capsize*).
Quet'zal s. A brilliant Central American bird.
-el suff. Forming diminutives, frequentatives, and nouns denoting instrument or agent.
Gael s. A Celt.
Tael s. A Chinese silver coin (about 5s.) and weight ($1\frac{1}{3}$ oz.).
Ba'bel s. A confused noise of talking; disorder.
La'bel s. A slip for writing on and attaching to something; a codicil; an heraldic charge. v.t. To affix a label to; to describe as.
Rela'bel v.t. To attach a fresh label to.
Is'abel a. and s. Light yellow; buff colour.
Reb'el s. One who forcibly opposes, resists, or renounces allegiance to the government. a. Rebellious; acting in revolt.
Rebel' v.i. To oppose lawful authority; to revolt.
Cerebel' s. The cerebellum.
Jez'ebel s. An impudent or wanton woman.
Li'bel s. A defamatory writing; malicious publication. v.t. To lampoon, issue a libel against.
Um'bel s. An umbrella-like inflorescence.
Bar'bel s. A coarse river fish.
Cor'bel s. A projecting bracket for supporting a cornice, parapet, etc. v.t. To furnish with or support by means of corbels.
Tes'tacel s. A carnivorous slug.
Ru'bicel s. A yellowish variety of spinel ruby.
Rad'icel s. A subsidiary root.
Ped'icel s. A short stalk supporting one flower only.
Len'ticel s. A lens-shaped mass of cells in bark.
Vor'ticel s. A bell-animalcule.
Can'cel v.t. To erase, cross out, or revoke a writing. s. Matter deleted.
Chan'cel s. The eastern end of a church.
Li'oncel s. A small heraldic lion.

Par'cel s. A small bundle, package; a part, portion. a. and adv. Part, half, in part. v.t. To divide and distribute by portions.
Tier'cel s. A male falcon.
Excel' v.t. and i. To surpass, especially in good qualities.
Muscadel' s. Rich wine from muscadine grapes, or the grape; a variety of pear.
Cit'adel s. A fort in a city; a stronghold.
Bedel s. A ceremonial officer at some Universities.
In'fidel a. Unbelieving; sceptical. s. One who disbelieves, especially in the Christian religion.
Goi'del s. A member of the Gadhelic branch of Celts.
Ron'del s. A form of rondeau.
Round'el s. A round disk; a circular heraldic charge; a rondel.
As'phodel s. An undying flower of Greek myth.
Model s. A pattern, standard, or miniature in three dimensions; something to be copied; a copy, a mould. v.t. To form after a pattern; to form in model. v.i. To make a model.
Remodel' v.t. To model anew, refashion.
Yodel v.t. and i. To sing or cry with sudden change from chest-voice to falsetto. s. Such a cry; a yodelling contest.
Far'del s. A bundle, pack.
Eel s. A snake-like fish; a slippery person.
Feel v.t. To perceive by touch, examine by touching, experience, be affected by. v.i. To have perception, to have the sensibilities touched. s. Perception; sensation.
Heel s. The hind part of the foot; a cant. v.i. To cant over. v.t. To add a heel to (a boot, etc.).
Wheel s. A circular frame turning on an axis; old instrument of torture; a rotation, compass; a cycle. v.i. and t. To turn round or cause to do so; to revolve, roll forward; to cycle.
Keel s. Principal timber in a ship, extending from head to stern; corresponding part in iron vessels; a ship. v.i. To capsize.
Vakeel' s. A Hindu deputy, attorney, etc.
Manchineel' s. A W. Indian tree with poisonous sap.
Kneel v.i. To incline, fall on, or support the body on the knees.
Peel v.t. To strip off the skin or bark; to pillage, plunder. v.i. To come off, to strip. s. The thin rind of anything; a bakers' wooden shovel; a square fortified tower.
Reel s. A bobbin for thread; revolving frame on which yarn, etc., is wound; a lively Scots dance; a stagger; v.i. To wind on a reel; to stagger, sway; to dance a reel.
Creel s. A wicker basket, especially for anglers.
Seel v.t. To sew the eyelids (of a hawk) together.
Genteel a. Polite, well-bred, decorous.
Steel s. Hardened and refined iron; a sword; a knife-sharpener; hardness, rigour. v.t. To furnish with or treat with steel; to harden.
Weel s. An osier fish-trap.
Aweel' adv. (*Scot.*) Well then.
Duff'el s. A coarse woollen cloth with thick nap.
Cud'gel s. A short, thick club. v.t. To beat with this.
An'gel s. A messenger between God and man; a guardian spirit; an obsolete English gold coin.
Arch'angel s. An angel of the highest order.
Evan'gel s. The four Gospels; a gospel.
Hy'drogel s. Protoplasmic jelly.
Satch'el s. A small sack or bag.
Bush'el s. A dry measure of four pecks; a large quantity.
Beth'el s. A chapel.
Broth'el s. A house of prostitution.
Sa'miel s. The simoom.
Span'iel s. A small, silky-haired, long-eared variety of dog.
Stan'iel s. A kestrel.
Krieg'spiel s. The war-game.
Glock'enspiel s. A set of metal bars tuned to produce music when struck by hammers.
Bon'spiel s. A curling match.
Matériel' s. Stock-in trade; available means.
Or'iel s. A projecting polygonal window.
Nick'el s. A hard, whitish, malleable metal a small U.S.A. coin. v.t. To coat with nickel.
Pum'pernickel s. A German rye bread.
Shek'el s. An ancient Hebrew weight and coin.
Yo'kel s. A rustic, ploughboy, bumpkin.
Hallel' s. A Hebrew hymn of praise.
Par'allel s. A line equally distant throughout from another line; this state or condition; conformity; likeness, resemblance; comparison. a. Extended in the same direction and in all parts equally distant, equidistant; like, similar. v.t. To cause to be parallel; to be equal to; to resemble in all essentials.
Cam'el s. A large ruminant quadruped.
Béch'amel s. A white sauce with cream.
Enam'el s. A semi-transparent or opaque glossy substance used for coating; a glossy surface; the smooth substance on a tooth. v.t. To lay enamel on, paint in enamel, adorn with colours.
Car'amel s. The last boiling of sugar; a sweetmeat.
Gem'el s. A ring formed of intertwined rings. a. Paired; in couples.
Tram'mel s. A long net; shackles for horses; anything to impede movement.
Entram'mel v.t. To entangle, hamper.
Stam'mel s. A dull red woollen cloth; this colour.
Pom'mel (pum'-) s. A knob, especially on a sword-hilt or saddle-bow. v.t. To beat or strike with the fists.
Trom'mel s. A revolving drum for separating ore.
Hum'mel a. Having no horns (of cattle).
Küm'mel s. A caraway-flavoured liqueur.
Cal'omel s. Medicinal chloride of mercury.
Phil'omel s. The nightingale.
Œ'nomel s. The mead of the ancient Greeks.
Hy'dromel s. A liquor consisting of honey diluted in water.
Grom'el s. Gromwell.
Pan'el s. Compartment of wainscotting, doors, etc.; one of the faces of a hewn stone; a thin board for painting a picture on; a list as of

jurors or insurance doctors; a jury. v.t. To form or furnish with panels.

Empan'el v.t. To enrol, to enter on the list of jurors.

Fontanel' s. Space between the bones of an infant's skull.

Spig'nel s. An aromatic umbelliferous plant.

Spin'el s. A variously coloured crystalline alumniate of magnesium.

Sen'tinel s. One keeping watch; a sentry.

Crack'nel s. A hard brittle biscuit.

Sim'nel s. A rich cake eaten at mid-Lent.

Can'nel s. A hard, bituminous coal.

Chan'nel s. The bed of a stream; a narrow sea; a furrow; a way of passage. v.t. To groove.

Flan'nel s. A soft, nappy, woollen cloth.

Scran'nel a. Thin; feeble; reedy.

Fen'nel s. An umbelliferous plant with yellow flowers.

Ken'nel s. A hutch or house for dogs; a pack of hounds; the hole of a fox, etc.; a gutter, puddle. v.i. and t. To lodge or keep in a kennel.

Peronnel' s. Body of persons employed in some service, especially public.

Fun'nel s. A conical receptacle for conducting liquids, etc., into vessels with small openings; the upper part of a chimney.

Gun'nel s. The butter-fish, a common British blenny; a gunwale.

Runnel s. A rivulet; a gutter.

Trunnel s. A treenail.

Tunnel s. An underground passage. v.t. and i. To form such.

Man'gonel s. A mediæval military battering-engine.

Colonel (ker'nel) s. The commander of a regiment.

Petronel' s. A large pistol used by horsemen in the seventeenth century.

Chevronel' s. A half-width chevron.

Grap'nel s. An anchor or grappling tool with several claws.

Shrap'nel s. Shell filled with bullets which scatter when it explodes.

Dar'nel s. A weed growing among corn.

Char'nel a. Containing corpses. s. A charnel-house where bones are deposited.

Ker'nel s. The substance in a nut or fruit-stone; the gist, essence.

Pim'pernel s. A small plant with blue, scarlet, or white flowers.

Cor'nel s. A shrub and its fruit; dogwood.

Ko'el s. An E. Indian cuckoo.

Noel' s. A Christmas carol.

Chap'el s. A place of worship, especially for dissenters or semi-private bodies; a portion of a large church containing an altar; a body of compositors.

Whitechap'el s. Unsportsmanlike play at cards, etc.

Lap'el s. The fold on a coat below the collar.

Repel' v.t. To drive back, check the advance of, repulse. v.i. To cause repugnance.

Sti'pel s. A secondary stipule.

Scal'pel s. A dissecting knife.

Impel' v.t. To drive forward; to instigate, incite.

Compel' v.t. To force, constrain, necessitate.

Propel' v.t. To drive forward, urge on.

Estop'pel s. An impediment; result of estopping.

Car'pel s. A simple pistil, or part of a compound one.

Dispel' v.t. To drive away; to dissipate.

Gos'pel s. God's word; divinity; theology. a. Relating to or accordant with the gospel.

Cu'pel s. A vessel used in assaying. v.t. To assay in this.

Dru'pel s. A pulpy fruit having many small stony seeds, as the raspberry.

Expel' v.t. To drive or force out; to eject, exile.

Appar'el s. Dress, outer clothing.

Gam'brel s. The hind leg of a horse; a piece of bent wood used for suspending carcases.

Whim'brel s. The curlew.

Tim'brel s. Obsolete tambourine-like instrument.

Tum'brel s. A rough, two-wheeled cart.

Quad'rel s. A square block.

Man'drel s. The revolving shank of a lathe, spindle of a circular saw, etc.

Span'drel s. Triangular space between curve of an arch and rectangle enclosing it.

Scoun'drel s. A worthless, unprincipled fellow; a rogue, villain. a. Base, mean.

Taf'ferel s. Upper part of ship's stern.

Dog'gerel s. Loose, irregular versification; wretched jingle.

Hog'gerel s. A sheep in its second year.

Mack'erel s. A marine food-fish.

Pick'erel s. A small or young pike.

Cock'erel s. A young cock; a quarrelsome young fellow.

Dot'terel s. A small migratory plover.

Hav'erel s. A bletherer.

Chev'erel s. and a. (*Cheveril*).

Gang'rel s. A vagrant.

Mon'grel a. Of mixed breed. s. A cross-bred dog; a hybrid.

For'el s. Parchment used for bookbindings.

Morel' s. An edible fungus; the black nightshade; a morello.

Bar'rel s. A cask; a measure (36 gallons) of beer.

Quar'rel s. An angry dispute, a brawl; cause of contention; a square-headed arrow or bolt; a lozenge-shaped pane; a glazier's diamond. v.i. To dispute violently, to squabble.

Squir'rel s. A small, bushy-tailed, arboreal rodent.

Bor'rel s. Unlearned, rude.

Sor'rel s. A herb allied to the dock; a yellowish or reddish-brown colour. a. Of this colour.

Pet'rel s. A long-winged, web-footed sea-bird.

Wast'rel s. Waste; a waif; a good-for-nothing; a prodigal.

Kes'trel s. A small species of hawk.

Min'strel s. A bard, singer, musician.

Laur'el s. A glossy-leaved evergreen shrub; its foliage as a wreath of honour, for victors, etc.

Eas'el s. A frame for supporting a picture, etc.

Teasel s. A plant having large flower-heads covered with stiff hooked awns. v.t. To dress (cloth) with these.

Weas'el s. A small British carnivore allied to the ferret.

Hand'sel s. A gift for luck; earnest money. v.t. To give this to; to use for the first time.

Ground'sel s. An annual, low-growing plant; a groundsill.

Chis'el s. A sharp, bevelled cutting-tool. v.t. To cut with a chisel; (*slang*) to swindle.

Dam'sel s. A young unmarried woman; a girl.
Tin'sel s. Glittering, metallic cloth, etc.; anything showy and of little value. a. Consisting of tinsel; showy. v.t. To adorn with tinsel.
Coun'sel s. Advice; deliberation, consultation; a barrister. v.t. To advise, admonish, recommend.
Lo'sel s. A scamp, ne'er-do-well. a. Lazy, worthless.
Mor'sel s. A mouthful; a small piece.
Tor'sel s. A scroll-like ornament; supporting projection for a beam.
Tass'el s. A pendent ornament. v.t. To adorn with such.
Ches'sel s. A cheese-mould.
Ves'sel s. Receptacle for fluids, etc.; a ship; tube for blood, etc.
Scis'sel s. Metal clippings.
Mis'sel s. A species of large thrush.
Mus'sel s. A bivalve mollusc.
Rus'sel s. A twilled fabric like rep.
Fu'sel s. A poisonous, oily, alcoholic product.
Hous'el s. The Eucharist. v.t. To administer the sacrament to.
Muscatel' s. Muscadel.
Moschatel' a. A small greenish-flowered musky herb.
Ra'tel s. A nocturnal mammal allied to the badger.
Be'tel s. A shrub with evergreen leaves having narcotic properties.
Man'tel s. Ornamental facing round fireplace.
O'vermantel s. A set of shelves, etc., over a mantelpiece.
Lin'tel s. Horizontal beam over door, etc,
Hotel' s. A superior inn; a French town-mansion.
Car'tel s. An agreement between belligerents; a written challenge to a duel; a combination to control prices, etc.
Pas'tel s. A coloured crayon; a drawing made with, or the art of drawing with, this.
Lis'tel s. A small architectural fillet.
Hos'tel s. An inn; extra-collegiate hall at a University.
Bat'tel v.i. To get one's provisions at the college buttery.
Chat'tel s. Movable property.
Du'el s. A set fight between two persons; single combat; contest.
Fu'el s. Substance for feeding a fire; that which increases heat, excitement, etc.
Se'quel s. That which follows; a continuation.
Cru'el a. Hard-hearted, void of pity, brutal.
Gru'el s. Oatmeal boiled in water.
Gavel s. Partition of land among the tribe at death of holder; a chairman's mallet; a small heap of grain not tied up.
Mach'iavel s. An unscrupulous intriguer.
Na'vel s. The cicatrix of the umbilical cord.
Ravel v.t. To entangle, confuse, involve. v.i. To become tangled or unwoven.
Car'avel s. A carvel.
Gravel s. Hard sand, small pebbles; a disease of the kidneys. v.t. To cover with or cause to stick in gravel; to perplex, baffle.
Unrav'el v.t. To disentangle; to extricate.
Trav'el v.i. To make a journey. v.t. To journey over. s. Act or account of travelling; range of a piston, etc.
Bevel a. Oblique, slanting. s. A slant at an angle other than a right angle; an instrument for measuring angles. v.t. and i. To cut or slant to an angle.
Dishev'el v.t. To disarrange, disorder.
Kev'el s. A belaying-cleat.
Level a. Horizontal; even; having no superiority. s. Instrument for finding the horizontal; surface without inequalities.
Rev'el v.i. To carouse, make merry, esp. riotously. s. A carousal, riotous feast.
Sniv'el v.i. To whine, cry; to run at the nose. s. Mucus running from the nose; affected weeping; cant.
Drivel v.i. To slaver; to be weak or silly; to dote; to talk rubbish. s. Slaver; nonsensical talk, twaddle.
Shrivel v.i. To wither, become wrinkled. v.t. To cause to shrink or contract.
Swivel s. A ring turning on a pin; small pivoted cannon. v.i. and t. To turn on a pivot.
Hovel s. An open-sided shed; a miserable shanty.
Shovel (shŭv-) s. A shallow-bladed scoop with a handle. v.t. To take up and throw with this.
Nov'el a. New; of recent origin or introduction; strange. s. A work of fiction.
Grovel v.i. To lie prone; to be mean or sycophantic.
Car'vel s. A Turkish frigate or various other ships.
Mar'vel v.i. To wonder, be astonished. s. Something very astonishing.
Jew'el s. A precious stone, a gem; a treasure. v.t. To adorn or fit with jewels.
New'el s. The central structure supporting the steps of a winding staircase; column at top or bottom of a stair.
Crew'el s. Fine worsted; embroidery worked with this.
Tew'el s. A chimney, tuyère.
Bow'el s. One of the intestines; an entrail; the interior part of anything; the seat of pity; compassion. v.t. To take out the bowels of; to eviscerate.
Embow'el v.t. To eviscerate; to hide away, bury, secrete.
Disembowel' v.t. To gut, eviscerate.
Dow'el s. A pin used for joining two pieces; a thin wooden curtain-rod. v.t. To fasten together with dowels.
Row'el (rou'-) s. The sharp wheel of a spur.
Trow'el s. A mason's flat-bladed or gardener's scoop-shaped tool.
Tow'el (tou'-) s. A cloth used for wiping. v.t. To wipe; (*slang*) to thrash.
Vow'el s. A sound which can be uttered without a consonant.
Ha'zel s. A tree bearing a light brown nut. a. Reddish brown.
Bez'el s. A sloping edge, as of a cutting tool or the side of a gem.
Man'gel-wur'zel s. A variety of beet.
Pret'zel s. A brittle salted biscuit.
Ouz'el (ooz'-) s. The blackbird.
Kohl s. Powdered antimony for staining the eyelids.
Buhl s. Ornamental inlaid work with brass, tortoiseshell, dead gold, etc.

-il suff. Capable of being, pertaining to, etc.
Ail v.i. To be unwell or in pain, to suffer sickness.
Bail s. Temporary setting free of an accused person on security; the outer wall of a castle; a piece of wood placed transversely on cricket stumps. v.t. To stand as surety; to empty water from a boat.
Fail v.i. To be wanting, fall short; to be affected by want; to decline; to become insolvent; to perish.
Ab'igail s. A waiting-woman.
Hail s. Frozen drops of rain; a call, salutation. v.i. To pour down as hail; to belong to (a place). v.t. To salute, call.
Jail s. A prison, lock-up, gaol.
Kail s. Kale.
Flail s. Implement for threshing grain by hand.
Mail s. Chain-armour; letter bag, carrier, or conveyance; letters, post. v.t. To post, send by mail; to arm with mail.
Blackmail' s. Money paid to avoid exposure. v.t. To extort money by means of threats.
Nail s. Horny substance at end of fingers and toes; a metal spike, 2¼ ins. v.t. To fasten or stud with nails; to make secure.
Hob'nail s. A heavy, round-headed nail.
Tree'nail s. A pin or nail of hard wood.
Tenail' s. A parapet between two bastions in a fort.
Ag'nail s. A whitlow, a sore at the root of a nail.
Snail s. A slimy, shelled, air-breathing mollusc; a sluggard.
Pail s. An open vessel for carrying water, etc.
Rail s. A bar of wood or metal; a railway; one of the lines of this; the corncrake, water-rail. v.t. To enclose or furnish with rails. v.i. To scold, use abusive language.
Brail s. A short cord for trussing up or furling a sail; the bottom flap of a bell-tent. v.t. To fasten or haul up by brails.
Hand'rail s. A protecting rail on stairs, etc.
Land'rail s. The corncrake.
Derail' v.t. and i. To throw or run off the rails.
Frail a. Weak; decaying; easily led astray. s. A rush basket for figs, etc.
Taff'rail s. Rail round a ship's stern.
Grail s. The holy vessel said to have been used by Christ at the Last Supper and brought to England by Joseph of Arimathea.
Engrail' v.t. To variegate; to notch; to spot.
Mon'orail s. A railway consisting of a single rail.
Trail s. Scent left by hunted animal; track followed; something dragged behind. v.t. To drag along behind; to follow by the trail, v.i. To be dragged along, to hang loosely.
Sail s. A sheet of canvas for catching the wind; a sailing-ship; a passage or excursion by sea. v.i. To be carried on the surface of the water; to glide. v.t. To navigate.
Me'sail s. The visor of a helmet.
Fore'sail s. The chief sail on the foremast.
Lug'sail s. A square sail hanging obliquely.
Assail' v.t. To fall upon, to attack hostilely.
Was'sail s. A carouse, a festive season; spiced ale. v.i. To hold a festivity.
Sprit'sail s. The sail extended by a sprit.
Outsail' v.t. To sail faster than.
Stay'sail s. Any sail extended on a stay.
Sky'sail s. A light sail above the royal.
Try'sail s. A small fore-and-aft sail on a gaff.
Tail s. Hinder or lower part; long flexible appendage; limitation.
Bob'-tail s. A tail cut short; the rabble.
Detail' v.t. To particularize; to appoint for a particular service.
De'tail s. An item; a minute account; a narrative, recital.
Drab'ble-tail s. A slattern.
Draggle'tail s. A slut.
Retail' v.t. To sell in small quantities; to give details of, tell in detail.
Re'tail s. Sale of commodities in small quantities.
Horse'tail s. A cryptogamous plant; the Turkish standard.
Mouse'tail s. A ranunculaceous plant.
White'tail s. The wheatear.
Dove'tail s. A shaped tenon for fastening boards together. v.t. and i. To unite by dovetails; to fit exactly or ingeniously.
Wag'tail s. A small bird of several species.
Pig'tail s. Tail of a pig; long twist of hair worn at back of head.
Cock'tail s. A horse with docked tail: a beetle; a mixed drink of flavoured spirits.
Fan'tail s. A variety of domestic pigeon.
Entail' v.t. To settle inalienably on a person or thing; to enforce on; to make necessary. s. That which is entailed; an estate limited in descent to particular heirs.
Disentail' v.t. To free from or break the entail.
Pin'tail s. A duck or grouse with pointed tail.
Curtail' v.t. To shorten, reduce, abridge.
Quail v.i. To shrink, lose spirit, be dejected. s. A small migratory bird.
Squail s. A counter used in squails.
Vail v.t. To lower in token of submission, etc. v.i. To yield. s. A tip, gratuity.
Avail' v.i. To be of use, to answer.
Trav'ail s. Painful toil; pangs of childbirth. v.i. To labour.
Prevail' v.i. To overcome; to be in force; to gain influence.
Countervail' v.t. To act against with equal power, to counterbalance; to thwart; to compensate. s. Equal weight or value; compensation.
Wail v.t. and i. To lament, bewail, weep. s. A mournful cry.
Bewail' v.t. To lament, mourn for, bemoan.
Bul'bil s. A small, secondary bulb.
Cod'icil s. An addendum to a will.
Pen'icil s. A small tuft of hairs; a pledget.
Ver'ticil s. Arrangement of plant parts round a stem.
Pen'cil s. Implement of blacklead, etc., for writing and drawing; a small brush for painting; art of painting or drawing; a collection of rays of light. v.t. To mark with a pencil; to draw or paint.
Sten'cil s. Thin plate with pattern cut through it. v.t. To mark with or form by this

Coun'cil s. An assembly for consultation or advice; local administrative body; a congress, convocation.
Bob'adil s. A braggart.
Pic'cadil s. A high ruff worn in the seventeenth century.
Daff'odil s. A bulbous plant of the genus Narcissus.
Cor'beil s. A sculptured basket.
Ceil v.t. To line the roof of.
Deil s. (*Scot.*) The devil.
Ver'meil (-mil) s. Vermilion; silver or bronze gilt.
Non'pareil s. Something of unequalled excellence, a variety of apple; a small-sized type. a. Unique, unrivalled.
Teil (tēl) s. The linden.
Veil (vāl) s. Thin or transparent cover for the face; screen; disguise. v.t. To cover with a veil; to conceal,
Fulfil' v.t. To accomplish, effect, complete.
Strig'il s. A skin-scraper used by ancient Greek athletes.
Sig'il s. A seal, signet.
Vig'il s. Keeping watch; sleeplessness; evening before a feast-day.
Ar'gil s. Potter's clay.
Gar'gil s. A disease affecting swine, cattle, etc.
Troch'il s. The trochilus.
Ar'chil s. A purple dyestuff.
Or'chil s. A colouring-matter obtained from some lichens; a lichen yielding this.
Ni'hil s. Nothing; an irrelevance.
Gal'lophil s. One devoted to French ways, etc.
Ne'grophil s. A friend of the negro race.
Slav'ophil a. and s. Loving or a lover of the Slavs.
Vakil' s. (*Vakeel*).
Mil s. 1000th part of an inch.
Tam'il s. The language of S. India and Ceylon.
Nil s. Nothing.
An'il s. A species of indigo.
Oil s. An unctuous, inflammable, animal, vegetable, or mineral liquid; a pigment made with oil. v.i. To smear or lubricate with oil.
Boil v.i. To be hot, to have a bubbling motion through heat. v.t. To cook by boiling; to heat to boiling point. s. An inflamed tumour.
Aboil' adv. On the boil.
Par'boil v.t. To cook partially by boiling.
Coil v.t. To wind in rings. s. Rings formed by winding; noise, uproar.
Bel'accoil s. Hearty welcome.
Recoil' v.i. To rebound; to shrink; to fall back. s. A starting or falling back.
Foil v.t. To defeat, frustrate; to dull. s. Frustration; a fencing-sword; a thin plate of metal or leaf-like object; anything serving to set something off to advantage.
Tre'foil s. A plant with three-lobed leaves; a three-cusped ornament.
Quat'refoil s. An ornamental figure in four segments of circles.
Cinque'foil s. Plants of the genus *Potentilla*; an architectural foliation in five compartments.
Mul'tifoil s. An architectural leaf-ornament of more than five divisions.
Mil'foil s. The yarrow.
Tin'foil s. Tin alloy beaten into sheets.
Coun'terfoil s. A portion of a document retained as a check.
Sex'foil s. A six-leaved flower or ornament.
Moil v.i. To boil, drudge. v.t. To weary.
Tur'moil s. Commotion, disturbance, confusion.
Spoil v.t. To damage, mar; to plunder. v.i. To decay, become corrupted. s. Plunder, booty; corruption or cause of this (especially in politics).
Despoil' v.t. To plunder, deprive.
Roil v.t. To make turbid; to irritate.
Broil v.t. To cook meat over a fire. s. A tumult, uproar.
Embroil' v.t. To throw into confusion or contention; to disturb, trouble.
Disembroil' v.t. To free from confusion.
Soil v.t. To tarnish, make dirty; to feed with green fodder. s. A dirty spot; taint; filth; the top layer of the earth's surface; land.
Sub'soil s. Stratum immediately beneath the surface.
Assoil' v.t. To pardon; to atone for; to dispel.
Toil s. Labour, drudgery; a snare. v.i. To labour with fatigue, progress painfully.
Entoil' v.t. To entrap.
Pu'pil s. The opening in the iris through which light passes; a young scholar; a minor.
Ar'il s. Additional covering of a seed.
Fi'bril s. A little fibre.
Nom'bril s. Point midway between fesse-point and base-point of an escutcheon.
Tum'bril s. (*Tumbrel*).
Ten'dril s. Twining part of a plant.
Per'il s. Impending danger; risk, hazard to expose to danger, to risk.
Imper'il v.t. To bring into danger.
Chev'eril s. Soft kid-leather. a. Yielding, pliant.
A'pril s. The fourth month of the year.
Nos'tril s. One of the air-passages of the nose.
Bas'il s. A fragrant herb; sheepskin for bookbinding.
Dea'sil s. Deiseal.
Uten'sil s. Implement for domestic use.
Ton'sil s. One of two glands on each side of the throat.
Dos'sil s. A plug for stanching a wound.
Fos'sil a. Found underground; petrified and preserved in rock. s. A petrified organic body found in rock; an antiquated person.
Mofus'sil s. An Indian rural as distinct from urban district.
Fus'il s. An obsolete musket; an heraldic lozenge-shaped bearing.
Den'til s. One of a series of rectangular projections in a cornice.
Len'til s. A small leguminous plant; its seed.
Tor'mentil s. A weed with small yellow flowers.
Ven'til s. Air-regulating shutter in organ-pipes.
Pon'til s. An iron rod used in glass-making.
Until' conj. and prep. Till.
Dis'til v.t. To cause to fall in drops; to obtain by distillation. v.i. To fall in drops, to trickle.
Pis'til s. The female organ in flowering plants.
Instil' v.t. To pour in, as by drops; to infuse slowly; to insinuate imperceptibly.
Pos'til s. A marginal note.
Apos'til s. A marginal note.
Fauteuil' s. An arm-chair; a seat in the stalls (theatre).
Tran'quil a. Peaceful, serene, undisturbed.
Jon'quil s. The rush-leaved narcissus.

Cav'il v.i. To object captiously. s. A frivolous objection.
E'vil a. Having bad qualities; wicked, sinful. s. That which is not good; wrong; malady. adv. Not well, ill.
Devil s. Satan; an evil spirit; a very wicked or cruel person; a printer's errand-boy; the dasyure. v.t. To grill with pepper. v.i. To prepare a case for a barrister, work for an author, etc.
Bedevil' v.t. To throw into utter confusion.
Weev'il s. A small beetle, the larvæ of which are most distructive to grain, etc.
Civ'il a. Pertaining to a city or citizenship; lay as opposed to ecclesiastical, naval, or military; polite.
An'vil s. The iron block on which smiths hammer.
Cher'vil s. A herb used in salads.
Ax'il s. Angle formed by union of leaf and stem.
Vex'il s. The vexillum of a flower.
Brazil' s. A red dye-wood; a triangular nut.
Alguazil' s. A Spanish constable.
All a. The whole of; every part of. adv. Quite, completely.
Ball s. A round body, a globe, bullet; a dancing entertainment.
Base'ball s. An American ball-game akin to rounders.
Eye'ball s. The pupil of the eye.
High'ball s. A whisky and soda.
Black'ball v.t. To reject by negative votes.
Foot'ball s. An inflated bladder cased in leather; game played with this.
Snow'ball s. A round mass of snow pressed together. v.t. and i. To pelt with or throw these.
Call v.t. To summon, name, invoke. v.i. To make a short visit. s. A cry, shout; an invitation, summons; a formal visit; a blowing of a bugle.
Recall' v.t. To call or bring back; to recollect; to revoke. s. A calling back; revocation.
Scall s. Scabbiness; scab; scurf on the head.
Miscall' v.t. To call by a wrong name, to abuse.
Hold'all s. A wrap for carrying clothes, umbrellas, etc.
Be'-all s. The consummation.
Fall v.i. To drop down; to decline, decrease; to ebb, empty; to happen; to utter carelessly. s. Downfall; tumble; ruin, death; cadence; a cascade; declivity; that which falls; a veil; a lapse; autumn.
Befall' v.t. To betide, happen, come about.
Rain'fall s. Amount of rain in a given district; a shower.
On'fall s. An attack, onset.
Down'fall s. A falling downward; sudden loss of rank, fortune, etc., ruin.
Wa'terfall s. A cascade, cataract.
Night'fall s. Dusk, the coming of night.
Pit'fall s. A covered pit for catching wild beasts; a snare.
Foot'fall s. The sound of a footstep.
Out'fall s. An outlet.
Gall s. The bile; rancour, malignity; an excrescence on oaks and other plants; a sore caused by chafing; soreness, irritation. v.t. To chafe, to make sore by rubbing; to annoy.
Spur'gall s. A sore caused by the spur.
Hall s. A large room or entrance; a manor house; a college.
Shall v. aux. Expressing futurity, conditionality, command, intention, etc.
Mall s. A shaded public walk; a heavy mallet. v.t. To beat with this.
Pall'mall s. An old game resembling croquet; the mallet used; place where it was played.
Small a. Not large; little, petty, diminutive.
Pall s. A mantle; an ecclesiastical vestment; the cloth covering of a coffin at a funeral. v.t. To cloak, invest, or cover with a pall; to depress, dispirit; to cloy, to make insipid. v.i. To become vapid; to lose spirit, taste, etc.
Spall v.t. and i. To splinter, chip; to break up ore. s. A splinter, flake.
Thrall s. A slave; bondman; slavery. v.t. To enslave, enthral. a. In servitude.
Enthrall' v.t. (*Enthral*).
Disenthrall' v.t. To set free, to emancipate.
Tall a. High in stature, lofty; (*slang*) exaggerated.
Stall s. A stable, a compartment of this; a booth; a seat in a church choir, or in a theatre. v.t. To put in a stall. v.i. To stick fast, as in mud.
Head'stall s. A bridle without the bit.
Forestall' v.t. To anticipate.
Install' v.t. To set in a seat; to invest with office.
Bor'stall s. A hillside track.
Lay'stall s. A dung-heap; place where milch-cows are kept.
Squall v.i. To scream violently. s. A loud harsh cry; sudden gust, especially with rain, snow, etc.
Wall s. Fence of brick or stone, etc.; side of a building; protection. v.t. To enclose with or defend by a wall.
Gad'wall s. A large freshwater duck.
Set'wall s. Valerian.
Wit'wall s. The green woodpecker (and applied to other birds).
My'all s. An Australian acacia.
Ell s. A measure of length (English 45 ins.).
Bell s. A hollow, metal, sonorous body. v.i. To bellow (of a stag, etc.). v.t. To attach a bell to.
Blue'bell s. A bulbous flowering plant.
Cell s. A small, close room; a cavity, cave; the unit of structure of living things; a division of an electric battery.
Ensor'cell v.t. To bewitch.
Dell s. A narrow little valley.
Fell past. (*Fall*).
Fell a. Cruel, savage, inhuman. s. The hide of a beast, fleece; a rocky or barren hill. v.t. To hew or knock down; to sew a seam. past part. Having fallen.
Hell s. Abode of the devil, place and state of punishment of souls of the wicked.
Rake'hell s. A dissolute fellow, a debauchee.
Shell s. A hard outer covering, especially of molluscs, certain other animals, seeds, etc.; a slight hollow structure; a coffin; bomb

bursting projectile. v.t. To strip of shell, take out of the shell; to bombard. v.i. To cast the shell.

Bomb'shell s. A shell thrown from a gun; an exceptionally surprising or alarming occurrence.

Hard'shell a. Uncompromising, unyielding.

Nut'shell s. The hard shell of a nut.

Pell-mell' adv. In utter confusion, in great disorder.

Smell s. Faculty by which odours are perceived; scent. v.t. To perceive by the nose; to detect. v.i. To give out an odour; to exercise the sense of smell.

Knell s. Sound of a bell rung at a funeral. v.i. To toll.

Snell s. Short length of gut for fish-hooks.

Pell s. A skin, hide; a roll of parchment.

Spell s. A charm; fascination; a turn of work, etc. v.t. and i. To form words of letters; to read; to import.

Respell' v.t. To spell again.

Misspell' v.t. To spell wrongly.

Sell v.t. To transfer to another for an equivalent, especially in money; to betray. v.i. To practise selling; to be sold. s. A trick, hoax.

Resell' v.t. To sell over again.

Undersell' v.t. To sell at a lower price than.

Tell v.t. To relate, explain, inform; to number. v.i. To give an account; to take effect.

Retell' v.t. To tell again.

Foretell' v.t. To predict, foreshadow.

Quell v.t. To subdue, put down, quiet.

Well s. A spring; pit sunk for water; a source; space in building for stairs or lift. v.i. To bubble up, issue forth. adv. In a proper manner; skilfully; considerably. a. In sound health; prosperous; comfortable; convenient; advantageous.

Dwell v.i. To sojourn, reside in a place; to hang upon with care.

Speed'well s. A blue-flowered variety of veronica.

Indwell' v.t. and i. To dwell in, abide within.

Bride'well s. A mad-house.

Farewell' s. and int. A parting salutation; adieu.

Grom'well s. A genus of herbs of the Borage family.

Ne'er-do-well s. A good-for-nothing.

Swell v.i. and t. To expand, dilate, increase in bulk; to bulge out; to puff up. s. Act of swelling; gradual increase; a surge; appliance for regulating intensity of sound in an organ; a dandy, person of importance.

Yell v.i. and t. To cry out sharply, scream; to utter thus. s. A loud scream; cry of horror, etc.; outcry.

Ill a. Bad; evil; sick; not in health; unfavourable; ugly. s. Evil; calamity; disease, pain. adv. Badly; with pain.

Bill s. A bird's beak; an account of money due; a presentment to a grand jury. v.i. To caress, as doves.

Hand'bill s. A loose printed sheet.

Twi'bill s. A two-headed battle-axe, mattock,

Horn'bill s. A genus of birds with bone-crested bills.

Brown'-bill s. A halberd formerly used by soldiers.

Crane's'bill s. The wild geranium.

Wax'bill s. A small bird with a bill resembling red sealing-wax.

Play'bill s. A printed advertisement of a play.

Wry'bill s. A variety of plover.

Dill s. An annual herb having carminative seeds.

Fill v.t. To make full; to satisfy, glut. v.i. To grow full. s. As much as satisfies, a full supply.

Refill' v.t. To fill again,

Re'fill s. A fresh fill.

Gill s. The breathing organ in fish; the under surface of fungi; a woody glen, ghyll; one-fourth of a pint; ground ivy; a wanton or sportive girl.

Hill s. An eminence less than a mountain; a heap.

Chill a. Cold; formal, distant; dispirited. s. A shivering sensation of coldness; discouragement; a mould in which to cast iron. v.t. To affect with cold; to discourage.

Dung'hill s. A heap of dung; a mean abode, vile situation.

Uphill' a. Leading or rising up; difficult, laborious.

Thill s. Shaft of a cart, etc.

Kill v.t. To deprive of life; to slaughter for food; to deaden. s. Thing killed or act of killing.

Skill s. Understanding with dexterity aptitude.

Mill s. Machine for grinding corn, etc.; (*slang*) a fight. v.t. To grind; to indent the edge of a coin; to full cloth; (*slang*) to fight.

Tread'mill s. A wheel revolved by persons treading on steps in its periphery.

Wind'mill s. Mill driven by action of the wind on sails.

Pill s. Dose of medicine in pellet form; anything unpleasant to be accepted; (*slang*) a ball. v.t. To dose with or form into pills; to plunder; to exclude by blackballing.

Spill v.t. To cause to flow over; to shed. v.i. To run or fall out; to perish, be lost. s. A tumble, fall; slip of paper, etc., for lighting.

Rill s. A small brook, streamlet.

Brill s. An edible sea-fish.

Drill v.t. To pierce with a drill; to train soldiers; to teach by repeated exercise; to sow in rows; to furrow. v.i. To take a course of military exercises. s. A boring tool; military exercise or training; a furrow; machine for sowing seed in rows a heavy twilled cotton cloth; a kind of baboon.

Man'drill s. A fierce W. African baboon.

Frill s. An edging or ruffle on a dress, etc. v.t. To decorate with frills.

Grill v.t. To broil on a gridiron; to harass. s. A gridiron; grilled food.

Shrill a. Sharp, piercing (of sounds). v.t. and i. To utter an acute or piercing sound.

Thrill v.i. To throb with excitement. v.t. To affect with pleasurable emotions. s. A wave of emotion, moment of excitement; a throb.
Trill s. A quaver, shake. v.t. To utter tremulously. v.i. To shake or quaver.
Sill s. Lowest piece in windows or door; threshold.
Ygg'drasill s. The world-tree of Scandinavian mythology.
Ground'sill s. The timber in a building next the ground.
Whin'sill s. A hard, basalt-like rock.
Till v.t. To cultivate. prep and conj. Up to the time of or when. s. A money-drawer in a shop.
Still a. Silent; motionless; calm. v.t. To make quiet, to calm, appease, check; to distil. adv. To this time; habitually; always; nevertheless. s. Apparatus for distilling; a distillery: stillness, quiet.
Stand'still s. A cessation, stoppage.
Quill s. A strong feather, especially of a goose; this made into a pen; spine of a porcupine, etc.; a weaver's reed. v.t. To plait, to wind on a quill.
Squill s. A liliaceous plant whose bulb is used in medicine.
Crow'quill s. A very fine pen (originally of a crow's quill).
Vill s. A hamlet, parish.
Will v. aux. Expressing futurity, willingness, or determination. v.t. and i. To wish, determine by choice; to bequeath. s. Wish; determination; inclination; volition; legal declaration concerning disposal of property after death.
Goodwill' s. Kindly feeling; acquiescence established custom of a business.
Whip'-poor-will s. An American bird allied to the nightjar.
Swill v.t. and i. To rinse; to drink greedily or to excess. s. A washing; liquid food.
Twill s. A ribbed textile fabric. v.t. To weave this.
Boll s. A rounded seed-vessel; a Scottish measure for grain.
Gly'cocoll s. A crystalline compound occurring in bile.
Doll s. A child's puppet; an empty-headed woman.
Loll v.i. To lean idle or carelessly; to hang loose (as a dog's tongue).
Moll s. (*Slang*) A wench, hussy.
Noll s. The head.
Hob'binoll s. A rustic.
Knoll s. A small round hill. v.t. and i. To toll, ring, knell.
Poll s. The back of the head; register of persons; act of voting; an election. v.t. To lop, shear, remove the head of; to enrol; to receive or give as votes.
Poll s. A parrot; a student at Cambridge who does not try for honour honours; a pass degree.
Catch'poll s. A bailiff's assistant.
Roll v.t. To cause to revolve, to move by turning on an axis; to wrap round on itself; to level with a roller. v.i. To revolve on an axis, turn over and over; to move circularly; to run on wheels; to emit a sound like a drum rapidly beaten; act of rolling, state of being rolled; that which rolls or is rolled; a scroll; a small loaf.
Scroll s. Roll of paper or parchment; an ornamental volute; a flourish.
Droll a. Odd, facetious, ludicrous. s. A jester, a farce.
Bead'-roll s. A list of persons to be prayed for.
Enroll' v.t. (*Enrol*).
Troll v.t. To sing a catch; to pass round. v.i. To fish for pike by trolling. s. A going round; a part-song; a reel on a fishing-rod; a dwarf of Scandinavian folklore.
Stroll v.i. To roam, saunter. s. A leisurely walk, a ramble.
Plim'soll s. A cloth shoe with rubber sole; a sand-shoe.
Toll s. Tax on travellers or vehicles; excise; stroke of a bell. v.i. To pay or receive toll; to sound (a bell) slowly and uniformly. v.t. To cause (a bell) to sound thus.
Atoll' s. A coral island with central lagoon.
Bull s. The male ox; a papal edict; a humorous blunder. v.t. To buy stock for a rise.
Cull v.t. To pick, select.
Scull s. A light oar; one using a pair of these. v.t. To propel by sculls.
Dull a. Stupid, slow, heavy; obtuse; blunt; not bright; overcast; dispirited; uninteresting. v.t. and i. To make or become dull, stupid, blunt, etc.; to sully.
Full a. Having no space empty, saturated. adv. Without abatement; exactly. v.t. To cleanse cloth from its oil.
Gull s. A sea-bird; a dupe. v.t. To trick, impose upon.
Hull s. A husk, pod, shell; the body of a ship. v.t. To divest of husk, etc.; to pierce the hull with a cannon-ball.
Skull s. Bony case that encloses brain.
Num'skull s. A blockhead, dullard.
Lull v.t. To soothe to sleep; to quiet. v.i. To subside. s. A temporary calm.
Mull v.t. To heat, spice, and sweeten (ale, etc.); to fail at a catch, etc. s. A failure, muddle; a horn snuff-box; a thin muslin.
Null a. Having no legal force; useless.
Pull v.t. To haul towards one; to drag; to pluck. v.i. To draw, tug. s. Act of pulling, a twitch, tug; a struggle; a drink.
Trull s. A trollop, strumpet.
I'dyll s. A short pastoral poem; a scene of rustic life.
-phyll suff. Denoting a leaf.
Cat'aphyll s. A rudimentary leaf.
Xan'thophyll s. The yellow colouring matter of autumnal leaves.
Chlor'ophyll s. The green colouring matter of plants.
Mes'ophyll s. The inner cellular tissue of plants.
-ol suff. Denoting an alcohol or an oil.
Gaol s. Jail.
Gam'bol v.i. To frisk about, to frolic. s. A skipping or frisking about.
Sym'bol s. A type, emblem, representation.
Ob'ol s. An obolus.
Col s. A mountain-pass.
Guai'acol s. A constituent of guiacum resin and wood tar.
Car'acol s. and v. (*Caracole*).

Sar'cocol s. An Eastern gum-resin.
Pro'tocol s. Original copy or rough draft of a treaty, etc.
Gly'col s. A class of compounds between ethyl alcohol and glycerine.
I'dol s. An image, especially one worshipped; anything on which the affections are strongly set.
She'ol s. The Hebrew abode of the dead.
Mon'gol s. One of an Asiatic race inhabiting Mongolia. a. Pertaining to these.
Ar'gol s. Impure tartar deposited in wine-vats by fermentation.
Alcohol' s. Highly rectified or pure spirit.
Men'thol s. A waxy, crystalline, medicinal substance.
Vit'riol s. Sulphuric acid or one of its salts.
Vi'ol s. An early form of violin.
Thy'mol s. An antisceptic prepared from oil of thyme.
Phe'nol s. A hydrocarbon used as a disinfectant, antiseptic, dye-base, etc.; carbolic acid.
Cool a. Not very warm; dispassionate, self-possessed; impudent. s. A moderate degree of cold. v.t. To make cool, to calm, moderate. v.i. To lose heat, ardour, enthusiasm, etc.
Fool s. One deficient in understanding; a silly person; a buffoon; a dish made of stewed fruit and cream. v.i. To play the fool. v.t. To deceive, make a fool of. a. Foolish.
Befool' v.t. To make a fool of, to dupe.
School s. A place for instruction; a body of pupils or followers; a sect; branch of study at a University; a shoal of fish. v.t. To tutor, train, discipline.
Pool s. A small pond; a deep place in a shallow river; the stakes, or receptacle for them, in some games; a commercial venture in which a number share; a game on the billiard-table. v.t. and i. To contribute to a common venture.
Whirl'pool s. A circular eddy; a vortex.
Spool s. Small cylinder for winding thread, etc., on; a reel. v.t. To wind on a spool.
Drool v.i. To slaver, drivel.
Tool s. An implement; a hireling. v.t. To shape or mark with a tool; to drive (a coach, etc.).
Stool s. A low, backless seat or bench; an evacuation from the bowels.
Toad'stool s. A poisonous fungus.
Fald'stool s. A portable folding stool used in churches.
Wool (wul) s. Soft, hair-like growth on sheep; short, thick hair; woollen yarn, worsted.
Car'ol s. A song, especially of Christmas; warbling of birds. v.i. and t. To sing carols, celebrate in carols.
Glyc'erol s. Glycerine.
Ban'derol s. (*Banderole*).
Ban'nerol s. A small square banner used at funerals.
Enrol' v.t. To write in a roll or register, to enlist.
Patrol' s. A military guard; march round of this at night. v.i. and t. To go the rounds in a camp, garrison, etc.; to pass round, as a guard.
Pet'rol s. Refined petroleum spirit.
Control' v.t. To restrain, govern, regulate. s. That which serves to check or restrain; superintendence, authority.
Fur'furol s. An oil produced in the dry distillation of sugar, wood, or other carbohydrate.
Sol s. The sun; gold (*in heraldry*); fifth tone in the diatonic scale.
Parasol' s. A small umbrella for keeping off the sun's rays.
En'tresol s. A low story between two higher ones.
Cap'itol s. The national temple in ancient Rome; a senate-house.
Pis'tol s. A small fire-arm for use with one hand. v.t. To shoot with this.
Wit'tol s. One who consents to his wife's infidelity.
Extol' v.t. To eulogize, laud, commend.
Friv'ol v.i. To trifle, behave frivolously.
Ben'zol s. Benzene.
Carl s. A rude rustic; a kind of hemp.
Earl s. Title of nobility next below marquis.
Pearl s. A lustrous, iridescent, roundish substance found in the oyster and used as a gem; something very precious; a small size of type.
Impearl' v.t. To form into or decorate with or as with pearls.
Harl s. Fibre of flax or hemp, barb of a feather; an artificial fly.
Jarl s. A Norse or Dutch chieftain.
Marl s. A calcareous clay used for fertilizing.
Gnarl s. A knot or protuberance in a tree.
Snarl v.i. To growl, as an angry dog; to speak churlishly; to become entangled. v.t. To emboss (metalware); to entangle.
Quarl s. A species of jelly-fish.
Birl v.i. To spin or twirl noisily.
Girl s. A female child; a young unmarried woman.
Thirl s. A hole, aperture.
Whirl v.t. and i. To turn round rapidly, move quickly. s. A rapid turning, whirling motion.
Skirl s. The shrill sound of the bagpipes. v.i. To make this sound.
Swirl s. A whirling motion; an eddy. v.i. To form eddies.
Twirl v.t. and i. To turn round rapidly, to spin. s. A rapid circular motion.
Ceorl s. An Anglo-Saxon freeman.
Schorl s. Black tourmaline.
Whorl s. Arrangement of more leaves than two round a common centre; one turn of a spiral.
Burl s. A knot in cloth.
Curl s. A ringlet of hair, wave, flexure. v.t. To form into ringlets. v.i. To take a coiled form; to play at curling.
Furl v.t. To roll or wrap up and fasten.
Hurl v.t. To throw with violence; to utter vehemently. s. Act of throwing thus.
Churl s. A rustic; an ill-bred, surly fellow; a miser.
Knurl s. A knot, excrescence.
Purl s. A fringe; inversion of stitches in knitting; a gentle murmur (as of a brook), a ripple; a malt liquor. v.t. To ornament with a fringe, etc. v.i. To make a murmuring sound; to eddy, ripple.

Axolotl' s. A Mexican water-lizard.
Caul s. A close-fitting cap; the amnion, or a portion of it.
Gaul s. A native of ancient France.
Haul v.t. To pull, draw, drag by force. s. A pull; fish taken by one draw of net; amount taken at once.
Keel'haul v.t. To punish by hauling under the keel.
Down'haul s. Rope by which a sail is hauled down.
Overhaul' v.t. To examine thoroughly; to overtake in chase.
Miaul' v.i. To cry like a cat.
Maul s. A heavy wooden hammer. v.t. To beat, bruise, handle roughly.
Waul v.i. To cry as a cat, to squall.
Cat'erwaul v.i. To make the cry of a fighting cat. s. This scream.
Bul'bul s. An Eastern singing-bird.
Pic'ul s. A Chinese weight (133⅓ lb.).
-ful suff. Full of, abounding in; quantity required to fill.
Dread'ful a. Terrible, awe-inspiring; shocking, horrid.
Deed'ful a. Always doing something.
Heed'ful a. Circumspect; attentive; giving heed.
Need'ful a. Full of need; requisite. s. (*Slang*) money.
Hand'ful s. A much as the hand can hold; a small quantity; a troublesome person or job.
Mind'ful a. Attentive; regarding with care.
Regard'ful a. Taking notice; heedful; attentive.
Disregard'ful a. Negligent, heedless.
Peace'ful a. Possessing peace; calm; not disturbed.
Grace'ful a. Beautiful with dignity; full of elegance, etc.
Disgrace'ful a. Bringing disgrace or dishonour; shameful.
Voice'ful a. Vocal; sonorous.
Force'ful a. Forcible; possessing energy, acting with power.
Resource'ful a. Full of resource.
Spade'ful s. As much as a spade will hold.
Pride'ful a. Full of pride, over-proud.
Bode'ful a. Ominous.
Glee'ful a. Merry, joyous.
Presage'ful a. Ominous; foreboding.
Change'ful a. Full of change, mutable.
Venge'ful a. Vindictive.
Revenge'ful a. Full of revenge; vindictive.
Scathe'ful a. Injurious, harmful.
Wake'ful a. Unable to sleep; restless; vigilant.
Bale'ful a. Pernicious, deadly; full of evil.
Thimble'ful s. A very small quantity of liquid.
Needle'ful s. As much cotton, etc., as is put into a needle at once.
Guile'ful a. Deceitful, fraudulent, cunning.
Dole'ful a. Sorrowful, sad; lamentable; gloomy.
Game'ful a. Sportive, full of mirth.
Shame'ful a. Bringing disgrace; disgraceful; degrading.
Blame'ful a. (*Blame*).
Time'ful a. Early; seasonable.
Bane'ful a. Noxious, harmful.
Tune'ful a. Melodious, musical.
Woe'ful a. Distressed with woe, unhappy; bringing calamity; paltry.
Hope'ful a. Full of or giving rise to hope; sanguine.
Care'ful a. Full of care; anxious; attentive.
Ire'ful a. Angry, wrathful.
Dire'ful a. Dreadful, terrible.
Ease'ful a. Promoting ease; comfortable lazy.
Praise'ful a. Commendable.
Sense'ful a. Significant.
Repose'ful a. Restful; tranquil.
Pur'poseful a. Having a purpose; intentional.
Remorse'ful a. Full of remorse; compassionate.
Use'ful a. Of use; advantageous; beneficial.
Fate'ful a. Fraught with fate; decisive; fatal.
Hate'ful a. Causing hate; feeling hatred; odious.
Plate'ful s. As much as will fill a plate.
Grate'ful a. Thankful; expressing gratitude; pleasing, welcome.
Spiteful' a. Malignant; malicious.
Despite'ful a. Malicious, malignant.
Taste'ful a. Characterized by good taste.
Distaste'ful a. Unpleasant to the taste; nauseous; offensive.
Waste'ful a. Extravagant, lavish; characterized by waste.
Rue'ful a. Sorrowful; expressing sorrow.
Bag'ful s. (*Bag*.)
Wrong'ful a. Injurious; unfair; wrong.
Reproach'ful a. Containing or expressing reproach.
Watch'ful a. Vigilant, cautious, wary.
Bash'ful a. Modest, embarrassed.
Fish'ful a. Abounding in fish.
Wish'ful a. Having or showing desire.
Blush'ful a. Excessively meek or modest.
Push'ful a. Energetic; self-assertive.
Death'ful a. Fraught with death; deadly.
Breath'ful a. Full of breath, lively; odorous.
Loath'ful a. Full of loathing; disgusting.
Wrath'ful a. Very angry; greatly incensed.
Faith'ful a. Loyal, trusty; sincere; full of faith.
Health'ful a. Promoting health; salubrious.
Slothful' a. Addicted to sloth; inactive.
Mirth'ful a. Merry, gay, amusing.
Mouth'ful s. As much as the mouth will contain; a small quantity.
Youth'ful a. Young; juvenile.
Truth'ful a. Habitually veracious; closely adhering to truth.
Fan'ciful a. Dictated by or arising from fancy; baseless; fantastical; whimsical.
Merc'iful a. Full of mercy; compassionate.
We'ariful a. Wearied, tired out.
Pit'iful a. Full of pity; compassionate; paltry. contemptible.
Plen'tiful a. Containing or yielding an abundant supply.
Boun'tiful a. Generous; abundant, plenteous.
Beaut'iful a. Very handsome; fair, elegant.
Du'tiful a. Careful in executing duties; obedient; reverential.
Sack'ful s. As much as a sack will hold.
Thank'ful a. Grateful; acknowledging gratitude.
Prank'ful a. Full of pranks or tricks.
Book'ful a. Full of book-learning.
Risk'ful a. Risky; venturesome.
Bush'elful s. (*Bushel*).
Shov'elful (shŭv'-) s. As much as a shovel will hold.
Pail'ful s. Quantity that a pail will hold.
Wail'ful a. Given to wailing; distressful.
Skil'ful a. Having skill; expert; dexterous.
Toil'ful a. Toilsome.
Wil'ful a. Deliberate; stubborn, obstinate.
Soul'ful a. Rich in or expressing the higher qualities; emotional.
Dream'ful a. Full of dreams, visionary.
Brim'ful a. Full to the brim.
Arm'ful s. (*Arm*).
Harm'ful a. Injurious, hurtful.

Charm'ful a. Abounding in charm.
Can'ful s. (*Can*).
Man'ful a. Brave; manly.
Moan'ful a. Expressing sorrow; moaning.
Pan'ful s. As much as a pan will hold.
Spleen'ful a. Affected with spleen; morose.
Disdain'ful a. Full of or expressing disdain.
Gain'ful a. Profitable, advantageous, lucrative; devoted to gain.
Pain'ful a. Occasioning pain, distress, or uneasiness; difficult, requiring toil; distressing.
Sin'ful a. Full of sin; wicked, unholy.
Ba'sinful s. (*Basin*).
Spoon'ful s. As much as a spoon will hold.
Scorn'ful a. Full of contempt; disdainful.
Horn'ful s. The contents of a drinking-horn.
Mourn'ful a. Sad, calamitous; expressing grief.
Cap'ful s. (*Cap*).
Sap'ful a. Abounding with sap.
Wor'shipful a. Deserving of worship.
Help'ful a. Furnishing help; useful; beneficial.
Cup'ful s. The contents or capacity of a cup.
Car'ful s. (*Car*).
Fear'ful a. Inspiring fear; dreadful; timorous; apprehensive.
Tear'ful a. Shedding tears; weeping.
Won'derful a. Astonishing, marvellous; admirable.
Cheer'ful a. Happy; lively, animated.
Mas'terful a. Domineering, imperious.
Pow'erful a. Mighty, strong; intense.
Prayer'ful a. Given to prayer, devotional.
Despair'ful a. Hopeless, utterly despondent.
Glass'ful s. What a glass will hold.
Success'ful a. Resulting in success; prosperous, fortunate.
Distress'ful a. Painful; attended by distress.
Threat'ful a. Of menacing ways or appearance.
Hat'ful s. As much as a hat will hold.
Boat'ful s. (*Boat*).
Doubt'ful a. Not settled in opinion; hesitating; full of doubts; precarious; suspicious; risky.
Tact'ful a. Having tact.
Neglect'ful a. Showing neglect; heedless.
Respect'ful a. Marked by respect; courteous deferential.
Disrespect'ful a. Wanting in respect; uncivil.
Forget'ful a. Apt to forget; neglectful; oblivious.
Pock'etful s. As much as a pocket will hold.
Buck'etful s. (*Bucket*).
Fret'ful a. Peevish, irritable, captious.
Regret'ful a. Full of regret.
Delight'ful a. Affording great pleasure; lovely.
Right'ful a. Consonant to justice; having a or being by just claim; true; equitable.
Fright'ful a. Terrible, awful, shocking.
Spright'ful a. Sprightly; vivacious.
Thought'ful a. Given to thinking; considerate.
Deceit'ful a. Given to deceit; fraudulent, delusive.
Fit'ful a. Spasmodic, capricious; inconstant.
Fruit'ful a. Fertile; prolific.
Resent'ful a. Inclined to resent; easily provoked.
Event'ful a. Distinguished by events.
Pot'ful s. As much as a pot will hold.
Art'ful a. Cunning; full of guile.
Sport'ful a. Merry, frolicsome; done in jest.
Hurt'ful a. Causing hurt; detrimental, injurious.
Boast'ful a. Bragging.
Rest'ful a. Soothing, inducing rest; at rest.
Quest'ful a. Searching; curious; prying.
Mist'ful a. Abounding in mists.
Wist'ful a. Engrossed; sadly longing; pensive.
Lust'ful a. Lewd; libidinous.
Trust'ful a. Trusting; confiding.
Distrust'ful a. Apt to distrust; suspicious diffident.
Mistrust'ful a. Suspicious, wanting confidence.
Aw'ful a. That strikes with awe; venerable; exceeding.
Law'ful a. Agreeable to, allowed by, or constituted by law; competent; legal; legitimate.
Bar'rowful s. (*Barrow*).
Sor'rowful a. Expressing or producing sorrow; sad; disconsolate; dreary.
Box'ful s. (*Box*).
Play'ful a. Sportive; given to levity.
Bel'lyful s. (*Belly*).
Joy'ful a. Full of joy; very glad.
Mogul' s. A Mongolian.
Ma'nul s. A wild cat of Tibet and Siberia.
Annul' v.t. To make void, abolish; to repeal.
Disannul' v.t. To annul, render void.
Foul a. Not clean or clear; filthy; impure; obscene; tempestuous; entangled. v.i. To become dirty, clogged, etc.; to come into collision. s. An unfair piece of play; a colliding.
Befoul' v.t. To make foul or dirty.
Ghoul s. A demon fabled to devour corpses.
Soul s. The immortal spirit of man; a person; essence; fervour.
Con'sul s. One of the two chief magistrates of the Roman Republic; a government official who protects in a foreign country the commercial interests of his own.
Procon'sul s. An ancient Roman magistrate or governor; a colonial governor.
Awl s. A boring tool.
Bawl v.i. To cry loudly or vehemently. v.t. To proclaim by outcry. s. A loud prolonged cry.
Brad'awl s. A small boring tool.
Shawl s. A large wrap for the shoulders.
Pawl s. A catch or ratchet.
Brawl v.i. To quarrel noisily, to squabble. s. A noisy quarrel; scurrility; uproar.
Crawl v.i. To creep, advance slowly, slyly, or weakly. s. Act of crawling; an enclosure in shallow water for keeping fish alive.
Scrawl v.t. and i. To write or draw awkwardly or carelessly, to scribble. s. Unskilful writing; a piece of bad or hasty writing.
Drawl v.t. and i. To utter in or speak with a slow, prolonged, or affected tone. s. This manner of speaking.
Sprawl v.i. To lie stretched out, to spread irregularly.
Trawl s. A net for dragging the sea-bottom. v.i. To fish with this.
Yawl s. A small sailing-boat or ship's boat; a yell. v.i. To yell, howl.
Mewl v.i. To whine, whimper; to mew.
Owl s. A nocturnal, carnivorous bird.
Bowl s. A hollow shallow vessel, a drinking vessel; a ball made with a bias. v.t. and i. To roll or deliver a ball or bowl at various games; to play at bowls.
Cowl s. A monk's hooded garment; a chimney cover turning with the wind; a water-vessel carried on a pole.

Scowl v.i. To frown; to look angry or sullen. s. A frown; gloom.
Fowl s. Birds collectively, a bird, especially a domestic bird.
Pea'fowl s. A peacock or peahen.
Gare'-fowl s. The great auk.
Wa'terfowl s. Birds that frequent water.
Howl v.i. To cry as a wolf or dog, to roar. s. A loud protracted wail.
Jowl s. The cheek.
Job'bernowl s. A blockhead.
Growl v.i. To snarl like a dog; to grumble. s. The angry sound of a dog; a murmuring, grumble.
Prowl v.i. and t. To rove stealthily, esp. for prey; to roam over. s. Act of one who prowls.
Yowl v.i. To howl, yell; yawl. s. A mournful howl.
Sib'yl s. A prophetess; woman fortune-teller.
Sal'icyl s. The radical of salicylic acid.
Spon'dyl s. A vertebra.
Cac'odyl s. A stinking compound of arsenic and methyl.
Lith'ophyl s. A fossil leaf or impression.
Eth'yl s. A colourless gas consisting of hydrogen and carbon.
Meth'yl s. The hypothetical radical of wood-spirit and other organic compounds.
For'myl s. The radical of formic acid.
Pho'nyl s. The radical of which phenol is a hydrate.
Ber'yl s. A silicious pale green mineral.
Chrysober'yl s. A yellowish or greenish gem-stone.
Dac'tyl s. A metrical foot of one long syllable followed by two short.
Tridac'tyl a. Tridactyllous.
Artiodac'tyl s. An ungulate with an even number of toes.
Pterodac'tyl s. An extinct flying reptile.
Perissodac'tyl s. An ungulate quadruped in which all the feet are odd-toed.
Am v. aux. (*Be*).
Salaam' (-lahm') s. An Oriental form of salutation. v.t. and i. To salute, make obeisance to.
Ma'am s. Short for "madam."
Praam s. A flat-bottomed barge.
Cam s. An eccentric portion of a wheel or shaft.
Dam s. A female parent (of beasts); a bank to keep back water; the water kept back; a causeway. v.t. To erect or confine by a dam; to obstruct.
Ad'am s. The first man; the unregenerate state of man.
Macad'am s. Broken stone for road-mending. v.t. To macadamize.
Mad'am s. Complimentary title given to ladies.
Cod'dam s. A public-house guessing game.
Schiedam' s. Hollands gin.
Bel'dam s. A hideous old woman, a hag.
Gran'dam s. An old woman, a grandmother.
Commen'dam a. Holding a benefice temporarily.
Quon'dam a. Having been formerly.
Beam s. A main, horizontal timber in a building, etc.; a part of a balance; a ray of light. v.i. To emit rays, to shoot forth.
Abeam' adv. At right angles to the keel.
White'beam s. A shrubby tree with silvery undersides to the leaves.
Quick'beam s. The quicken, rowan.
Moon'beam s. Ray of light from the moon.
Horn'beam s. A small, tough-timbered tree.
Sun'beam s. A ray of sunlight.
Fleam s. A lancet, especially for bleeding cattle, etc.
Gleam v.i. To glimmer; to flash or dart as rays of light. s. A small stream of light; brightness.
Ream s. Twenty quires of paper (480 sheets). v.t. To enlarge a hole, especially in metal.
Bream s. A freshwater fish. v.t. To burn seaweed, etc., off a ship's bottom.
Cream s. The richer part of milk, a dish prepared from this; the best part or essence of anything. v.t. To skim cream from. v.i. To froth, mantle.
Scream v.i. To utter a sharp, sudden cry; to shriek. s. A sharp shrill cry; a shriek.
Dream s. Thoughts during sleep; an idle fancy. v.i. To have visions; to imagine, conceive as possible. v.t. To see in or as in a dream; to spend idly.
Stream s. A brook, current; drift; a regular series. v.t. and i. To move in a stream; to float in the air; to pour out abundantly.
Seam s. The joining of two edges of cloth; juncture; scar; vein of coal, metal, etc. v.t. To form a seam upon, join by sewing; to scar.
Team s. Horses, etc., harnessed together; persons associated for a game, etc. v.t. To join together in or haul with a team.
Steam s. Vapour of boiling water. v.i. To give this off; to rise as vapour; to sail by steam. v.t. To expose to steam.
Gam s. A herd of whales.
Amal'gam s. A combination of mercury with some other metal.
Phan'erogam s. A seeding or flowering plant.
Crypt'ogam s. A plant not bearing true flowers, as the mosses.
Ham s. Hind part of thigh; a leg of pork cured.
Cham s. A ruler of Tartary; an autocrat.
Ging'ham s. A striped linen or cotton fabric; (*slang*) a cheap umbrella.
Og'ham s. The writing of the ancient Irish; a character of or inscription in this.
Brough'am s. A closed four-wheeled carriage.
Sham a. False, counterfeit. s. That which appears other than it is; an imposture, fraud. v.t. To feign. v.i. To pretend.
Pe'tersham s. A heavy woollen cloth; clothes made of this.
Whim'wham s. A whim; a plaything.
Jam s. A conserve of fruit; a crush, squeeze; stoppage due to this; title of certain Indian princes. v.t. To squeeze, compress; to block up. v.i. To become unworkable through jamming.
Kai'makam s. A Turkish governor or military officer.
Lam v.t. (*Slang*) To thrash.
Malaya'lam s. The language of Malabar.
Clam s. A bivalve edible shellfish; a clamp, vice.
Bed'lam s. A mad-house.
Flam s. Imposture; humbug.
Flim'flam s. Nonsense, bosh; deception.
Slam v.t. To shut noisily; to bang; to defeat completely. s. A violent shutting of a door; the winning of every trick at bridge, etc.

Is'lam s. Mohammedanism; Mohammedans collectively.
Imam' s. A Mohammedan priest.
Hammam' s. A Turkish bath.
Jerobo'am s. A very large drinking-vessel or wine-bottle.
Foam s. Bubbles on surface of a liquid; froth, spume. v.i. To froth; to rage.
Loam s. Rich vegetable mould; marl. v.t. To cover with this.
Cloam s. Clay pottery.
Gloam v.i. To begin to grow dark.
Roam v.i. To wander without definite purpose; to rove.
Pam s. The knave of clubs (at loo).
Ram s. A male sheep; a battering implement, machine, or engine; steel beak of a warship; a sign of the Zodiac. v.t. To strike or batter with a ram; to cram.
Cram v.t. To crowd, stuff, fill with food; to coach for an exam. v.i. To stuff, gorge; to prepare hastily for an exam. s. System of cramming for exams; a crush, crowd; (*slang*) a lie.
Dram s. One-eighth of an ounce troy ($\frac{1}{16}$ oz. avoir.); a small quantity; a tot of spirits.
Wolf'ram s. An ore of tungsten.
Gram s. The chick-pea; a gramme.
-gram suff. Indicating something drawn or written.
Di'agram s. An illustrative outline; a geometrical figure or scheme.
An'agram s. An inversion of the letters of a word or sentence.
Tet'ragram s. A word of four letters.
Pen'tagram s. A pentacle.
Cable'gram s. A message by cable.
Tel'egram s. Message sent by telegraph.
Mill'igram s. (*Milligramme*).
Marco'nigram s. Message sent by wireless telegraphy.
Ep'igram s. A concise and witty poem; a pointed or antithetical saying.
Tri'gram s. A trigraph.
Cen'tigram s. The 100th of a gramme.
Ide'ogram s. An ideograph.
Ster'eogram s. A stereographic drawing.
Log'ogram s. A character representing a word.
Psy'chogram s. Supernatural writing.
He'liogram s. Message sent by heliograph.
Parallel'ogram s. A right-lined quadrilateral figure whose opposite sides are parallel and equal.
Kil'ogram s. (*Kilogramme*).
Sphyg'mogram s. A tracing of the beat of the pulse.
Therm'ogram s. A record from the thermograph.
Seis'mogram (sīz'-) s. A record from a seismograph.
Spen'ogram s. A wedge-shaped character.
Phon'ogram s. A character representing a voice-sound; a phonographic record.
Mon'ogram s. A character composed of two or more letters interwoven.
Chro'nogram s. A date in Roman numerals concealed in words.
Lip'ogram s. A writing in which a certain letter is not used.
Bar'ogram s. The record produced by a barograph.
Aer'ogram s. Message sent by wireless telegraphy.
Hi'erogram s. A sacred writing or symbol.
Grog'ram s. A coarse fabric of silk and mohair or silk and wool.
Hec'togram s. A French weight of about 3½ oz. avoir.
Cryp'togram s. A cipher, cipher-writing.
Telau'togram s. A message sent by telautograph.
Bairam' s. A Mohammedan festival.
Buck'ram s. Strong stiffened linen-cloth. a. Made of buckram; stiff, precise.
Mar'joram s. A herb of the mint family.
Pram s. A perambulator; a praam.
Tram s. Rail or track of a tramway; a car running on this; a kind of silk thread.
Bal'sam s. An unctuous, aromatic, healing substance.
Opobal'sam s. Balm of Gilead.
Jet'sam s. Goods thrown overboard to lighten a ship.
Flot'sam s. Goods which float after shipwreck.
Tam-tam s. A tom-tom.
Ban'tam s. A small gamecock with feathered shanks.
Wig'wam (-wom) s. A N. American Indian hut.
Swam past (*Swim*).
Yam s. A large esculent tuber of the tropics.
Ly'am s. A leash for hounds.
Nizam' s. A Turkish regular soldier; title of sovereign of Hyderabad.
Em s. The letter *m*; the unit of measure in typography.
'Em pron. Them.
Di'adem s. A fillet, tiara, crown; emblem of royalty.
An'adem s. A garland.
I'dem s. The same (as above, etc.).
Tan'dem adv. One after another (especially of horses). s. A vehicle with two horses harnessed thus; bicycle for two seated thus.
Deem v.t. To suppose, judge, estimate. v.i. To come to a decision.
Redeem' v.t. To buy back, ransom, atone for, rescue, recover; to perform (a promise).
Misdeem' v.t. To judge erroneously.
Hakeem' s. A Moslem physician.
Seem v.i. To present an appearance, to look or feel as if.
Beseem' v.t. and i. To be fit, suitable, or proper for; to be seemly.
Teem v.t. To bring forth; to be prolific to pour out, empty.
Esteem' v.t. To value; to respect, prize. s. High value; great regard.
Disesteem' s. Low regard, disfavour. v.t. To regard with disapproval.
Gem s. A precious stone; a jewel, treasure. v.t. To adorn with gems.
Brum'magem a. Sham, spurious; cheap and tawdry.
Strat'agem s. An artifice, trick; a piece of generalship.
Begem' v.t. To adorn with gems.
Hem s. Edge of a garment, etc., sewn down; border; a short warning cough. v.t. To form a hem on; to shut in, surround; to give a warning cough.
Ahem' int.
Sa'chem s. A N. American Indian chief.
Dir'hem s. A Moslem measure of weight; a small Moroccan silver coin (about 4d.).
Them pron. Obj. case of "they."
An'them s. A sacred song, usually in parts.
Re'quiem s. A mass sung for the dead.
Em'blem s. A figure, symbol, device. v.t. To symbolize; to illustrate by an emblem.

Prob'lem s. Question to be solved; a matter difficult of settlement.
Mos'lem s. A Mohammedan. a. Pertaining to to the Mohammedans.
Xy'lem (zī'-) s. The woody tissue of a plant.
Phlo'em s. The cells, fibres, etc., forming the softer portions of bark; bast.
Po'em s. A metrical composition, piece of poetry.
Pro'em s. Preface; introduction.
Har'em s. The women's quarters in Oriental houses.
The'orem s. A proposition to be proved; a speculative truth.
Cat'egorem s. A word capable of being employed by itself as a logical term.
I'tem s. A separate particular; a piece of news. adv. Also.
To'tem s. A natural object used as a clan symbol among primitive races.
Post-mor'tem adv. and a. After death. s. An examination of a dead body.
Stem s. Main stalk of a plant; peduncle of a flower; a slender part; prow of a ship. v.t. To remove the stems of; to make way against; to check.
Mer'istem s. Growing vegetable tissue or cells.
Sys'tem s. A method; regular order; whole connected scheme.
Ap'ozem s. A decoction.
Di'aphragm s. A dividing membrane; the muscle between the chest and abdomen; midriff.
Ep'iphragm s. The disk closing the shell of a mollusc.
Ap'ophthegm s. A terse, pointed saying; a maxim.
Phlegm (flem) s. Mucus from the throat; stolidity.
Par'adigm (-dīm) s. An example, especially of a word with its inflections.
Drachm s. One-eighth of an ounce troy.
Ohm s. The unit of electrical resistance.
Mi'crohm s. One-millionth of an ohm.
Log'arithm s. The exponent of the power to which a given invariable number must be raised in order to produce another given number.
Rhythm s. Metre, verse; periodical emphasis in this or in music; harmonious flow.
Aim v.t. To direct or point at an object. v.i. To point with a weapon; to direct the purpose. s. The object aimed at; direction of pointing; purpose.
Claim v.t. To challenge or demand as a right. v.i. To be entitled to anything. s. A demand, right to demand, thing demanded; land staked off in mine-field.
Acclaim' v.t. To greet or salute with applause.
Declaim' v.i. To harangue, speak rhetorically. v.t. To utter thus.
Reclaim' v.t. To reform; to recover by discipline, cultivation, etc.; to tame.
Proclaim' v.t. To promulgate, announce publicly; to outlaw.
Coun'terclaim s. An opposing or answering claim; a claim made by a defendant. v.t. and i. To make or bring such a claim.
Disclaim' v.t. To disown, renounce.
Exclaim' v.i. To cry out abruptly, to shout. v.t. To declare with loud vociferation.
Maim v.t. To cripple, mutilate. s. A disabling injury.
Cher'ubim s. Cherubs.
Dim a. Not clearly seen; dark; obscure. v.t. and i. To render or become dim.
Bedim' v.t. To make dim, to obscure.
Blen'heim s. A variety of spaniel; a species of apple.
Him pron. Obj. case of "he."
Elo'him s. One of the Hebrew names of God.
Ter'aphim s. Household oracular deities of the ancient Jews.
Whim s. A caprice, fancy, sudden idea.
Ha'kim s. A Moslem judge or governor.
Skim v.t. To clear cream, scum, etc., from the surface of; to pass near or lightly touching the surface of. v.i. To glide along near the surface; to glance through superficially.
Malaya'lim s. The Malabar Dravidians.
Glim s. (*Slang*) A light.
Slim a. Slight; slender; unsubstantial; crafty.
Mus'lim s. and a. Moslem.
Den'im s. A course twilled cotton fabric.
Min'im s. A note equal to two crotchets; a drop, one-sixtieth of a dram; a dwarf.
Pay'nim s. A pagan, heathen.
Rim s. An outer edge, border, margin. v.t. To furnish with or serve as a rim.
Brim s. The edge of anything, the top. v.i. To be full to the brim.
Scrim s. Strong cloth used in upholstery.
In'terim s. The meantime. a. Provisional.
Grim a. Severe, relentless; horrible, ghastly.
Me'grim s. A neuralgic pain in the head; a whim.
Pil'grim s. A traveller, especially to a holy place.
Prim a. Formal, precise; affectedly nice. v.t. To arrange very precisely.
Trim a. Neat, in good order; dapper, smart. v.t. To put in good order, to embellish. v.i. To hold a middle course. s. Order, condition.
Ur'im s. A sacred object among the ancient Jews.
Pur'im s. A Jewish festival.
Spar'sim adv. Here and there; sparsely.
Pas'sim adv. Here and there; everywhere.
Verba'tim adv. Word for word, in the same words.
Grada'tim adv. Gradually; by degrees.
Seria'tim adv. In regular order.
Litera'tim adv. Literally; letter for letter.
Vic'tim s. A living being sacrificed; a person or thing destroyed; a dupe.
Shit'tim s. The wood of the shittah-tree.
Vim s. (*Slang*) Vigour, energy.
Swim v.i. To float or move progressively in water; to be borne along by a current; to glide; to be flooded; to reel, be dizzy. v.t. To traverse by swimming; to cause to swim or float. s. Act of swimming; place frequented by fish; the main current.
Max'im s. A general principle, an adage; a quick-firing machine-gun.
Balm s. Balsam; anything that mitigates pain.
Embalm' v.t. To preserve (especially a corpse) from putrefaction; to imbue with scents.

Calm a. Quiet, undisturbed, tranquil. s. Serenity, quiet, repose. v.t. To pacify, make still.
Becalm' v.t. To render still; to tranquillize.
Realm s. A kingdom; domain, sphere.
Malm s. A soft, friable kind of limestone.
Palm s. Inner part of hand; a measure of three or four inches; the broad part of an antler; one of a large family of endogenous trees; a leaf of this, especially as a symbol of triumph or rejoicing; reward, a token of success. v.t. To conceal in the palm; to pass off fraudulently; to bribe.
Psalm s. A sacred song, especially a hymn attributed to David.
Qualm s. Nausea; faintness; conscientious scruple.
Elm s. A large forest-tree; its timber.
Helm s. A ship's rudder; a helmet.
Whelm v.t. To engulf, cover completely, overburden.
Overwhelm' v.t. To immerse and bear down, crush, utterly subdue.
Film s. A pellicle or thin skin; a strip of prepared celluloid for taking photographic or cinematographic pictures. v.t. To record on such a film; to cover with a film. v.i. To become covered with a film.
Holm s. Low-lying land liable to flooding; the ilex.
Haulm s. The stalk of grain, beans, etc.
Culm s. Stems of corn and grasses; stone-coal, anthracite.
Houyhnhnm (whinm) s. A fictitious race of horses endowed with reason and superior to man (*Gulliver's Travels*).
-dom suff. Denoting state, rank, rule, dignity, office, etc.
Dom s. Title of certain members of the Benedictine and Carthusian orders.
Club'dom s. Clubs generally; club life.
Prince'dom s. Rank, jurisdiction or territory of a prince.
Free'dom s. Liberty; state of being free; independence; franchise.
Wage'dom s. Wage-earners collectively.
Duke'dom s. Territory, rank, or quality of a duke.
Bumble'dom s. Parochial officialism; parish officers collectively.
Bea'dledom s. Beadles collectively.
Puzzle'dom s. Puzzlement.
Pope'dom s. Office, dignity, or jurisdiction of the Pope.
Bore'dom s. A state of ennui; the domain of bores; bores collectively.
Whore'dom s. Practise of fornication; lewdness.
Chief'dom s. (*Chief*).
Serf'dom s. State or condition of serfs.
King'dom s. Territory ruled by a king, realm; a primary division of natural objects; place where anything holds sway.
Hal'idom s. Holiness; word of honour.
Clerk'dom s. The office of clerk; clerks collectively.
Offi'cialdom s. Body of officials; officialism.
Thral'dom s. Servitude; condition of a thrall.
Sel'dom adv. Rarely; not often.
Dev'ildom s. Devilry; pandemonium.
Earl'dom s. Rank, title, or position of an earl.
Ran'dom s. Course without definite object; chance. a. Haphazard; left to chance.
Heath'endom s. Pagans collectively; that part of the world where they predominate.
Chris'tendom s. Christians generally; the portion of the world in which Christianity prevails.
Junk'erdom s. Junkers collectively; their principles, etc.
Mas'terdom s. Dominion, command; masterful quality.
Heir'dom s. Condition of an heir; that which is inherited.
Bach'elordom s. The state of a bachelor; bachelors collectively.
Mar'tyrdom s. Doom or death of a martyr.
Wis'dom s. Quality or state of being wise; wiseness, sagacity, prudence, common sense.
Cau'cusdom s. (*Caucus*).
Flun'keydom s. Flunkeys collectively.
Cock'neydom s. Londoners collectively.
Top'sy-tur'vydom s. Condition of being disordered or confused.
Fath'om s. A measure of length, six feet. v.t. To ascertain the depth or import of; to comprehend.
Whom (hoom) pron. Obj. case of "who."
Id'iom s. A peculiarity of phrase; dialect.
Ax'iom s. A self-evident or agreed truth; a maxim.
Whil'om adv. Formerly. a. Quondam.
Car'damom s. The aromatic capsule of various species of amomum.
Ven'om s. Poison injected by serpents, etc.; spite, malice.
Enven'om v.t. To impregnate with poison; to taint with malice, etc.
Gran'nom s. A four-winged fly.
Boom s. A bar across a harbour; a spar for extending the bottom of sails; a sudden increase in business, price, demand, etc.; a hollow roar. v.t. To stir up popular demand. v.i. To increase in favour, price, etc.; to make a low, hollow sound.
Coom s. Refuse matter, drippings from journal boxes, etc.
Doom v.t. To pronounce judgment on; to ordain as a penalty; to fine, assess a tax on; to destine. s. Judicial sentence; penalty; unhappy fate.
Foredoom' v.t. To determine beforehand, to predestinate.
Loom s. A frame or machine for weaving cloth; the handle of an oar; the guillemot. v.i. To appear large and indistinct.
Bloom s. A blossom. v.i. To produce blossoms, to flower.
Abloom' adv. Blooming.
Gloom s. Darkness, obscurity; sadness. v.i. To shine obscurely, to be clouded, dark, sullen.
Heir'loom s. A chattel which descends with the freehold.
Simoom' s. A hot, dry wind of Arabia and Africa.
Spoom v.i. To scud, sail rapidly.
Room s. Space, stead; apartment; scope.
Broom s. A shrub with bright yellow flowers; a besom or sweeping implement.
Bed'room s. A sleeping apartment.
Groom s. A servant in charge of horses; a stableman; a bridegroom. v.t. To tend, as a groom does horses.
Bride'groom s. A man newly, or about to be, married.
Mush'room s. A rapid-growing edible fungus; an upstart. a. Ephemeral. v.i. To expand (of bullets).
Ball'room s. A hall for large dancing-parties.
Zoom v.i. To turn upwards suddenly when in flight (of aeroplanes).

Pom s. A Pomeranian dog.
Pom'pom s. A quick-firing gun for one-pounders.
Rom s. A male gipsy.
Car'om s. A cannon in French and American billiards.
From prep. Away.
Therefrom' adv.
Wherefrom' adv.
Pogrom' s. Systematic massacre, especially of Jews in Russia.
Mael'strom s. A violent whirlpool; a turmoil.
Be'som s. A broom made of twigs.
Chris'om a. Anointed with chrism. s. A white cloth so treated put on a child at baptism or at death within a month after.
Han'som s. A two-wheeled cab with high back-seat for driver.
Ran'som v.t. To redeem from captivity. s. Release; price paid for this.
Tran'som s. Horizontal bar across a window; a cross-beam.
Bos'om s. The breast of a woman. a. Confidential, intimate.
Embos'om v.t. To cherish; to hide, half conceal.
Unbos'om v.t. To reveal in confidence.
Lis'som a. Lithe; supple; nimble.
Blos'som s. The flower of a plant, a bloom. v.i. To break into flower.
Tom s. A male cat.
At'om s. An indivisible particle of matter; a very minute portion.
Di'atom s. A minute unicellular alga.
Tom-tom s. A native drum or gong in the East.
Phan'tom s. An apparition, spectre, ghost.
Symp'tom s. An indication, sign, token.
Cus'tom s. Habit; established practice; habitual buying of goods; long-established usage; a tax on goods.
Accus'tom v.t. To habituate, inure to.
Bot'tom s. The lowest part fo anything. v.t. To found; to furnish with a seat or bottom; to fathom.
Bux'om s. Plump; lively.
Arm s. The limb between hand and shoulder; an inlet from the sea; a branch of the military service; a weapon of war. v.t. To furnish with weapons or with means of attack or defence. v.i. To take arms; to be provided with means of resistance.
Barm s. Yeast; the froth of fermented liquors.
Rearm' v.t. To arm afresh.
Forearm' v.t. To prepare beforehand, arm in advance.
Farm s. A tract of cultivated land; ground let for tillage, pasturage, etc.; the house, outbuildings, stock, etc., of a farmer. v.t. To let out to tenants; to cultivate; to lease. v.i. To cultivate the soil.
Harm s. Injury; mischief; misfortune. v.t. To hurt, damage.
Charm s. Enchantment; a spell, amulet, trinket. v.t. To subdue or control by occult influence or by fascination; to captivate, enchant. v.i. To please greatly.
Alarm' s. Sudden terror; a cry of warning. v.t. To terrify, to disturb, to call to arms.
Disarm' v.t. To deprive of means of attack or defence; to reduce the armed forces.
Warm (wŏrm) a. Not cold; zealous; earnest; flushed. v.t. and i. To make or become warm, animated, etc.
Luke'warm a. Tepid; cool; half-hearted.
Swarm s. A cluster of bees, etc.; a crowd. v.i. To leave a hive *en masse*; to crowd; to climb by clasping.
Berm s. A narrow path behind the parapet of a fort.
Derm s. The true skin.
Mal'acoderm s. A soft-skinned animal; a sea-anemone.
Sar'coderm s. A fleshy layer in certain seeds.
En'doderm s. An inner layer, especially of the wall of a cell, a blastoderm, etc.
Phel'loderm s. A layer of cellular tissue in trees, etc.
Echi'noderm s. One of a class of animals which includes the sea-urchin. a. Prickly, having a bristly skin.
Scler'oderm s. A horny integument; the skeletal tissue of corals.
Mes'oderm s. The central germ layer of the embryonic cell.
Ec'toderm s. The outer layer of a cellular tissue.
Ex'oderm s. The epidermis.
Pach'yderm s. A hoofed, non-ruminant, thick-skinned animal.
Germ s. That which develops into an embryo; a micro-organism, microbe; source, origin.
Herm s. A herma.
Therm s. Amount of heat required to raise 1 gr. of water 1° C.
Isoge'otherm s. A line connecting points having the same mean temperature beneath the surface.
I'sotherm s. Chart line connecting points having the same mean annual temperature.
Isobath'ytherm s. A line connecting points where the temperature is the same at given depths.
Sperm s. Semen; the cachalot whale; spermaceti yielded by this.
Ep'isperm s. The outer skin of a seed.
Per'isperm s. The albumen of a seed.
En'dosperm s. The albumen of a seed.
An'giosperm s. A plant whose seeds are contained in a closed ovary.
Gym'nosperm s. A plant having naked seeds (*e.g.* the pine).
Lep'tosperm s. A myrtaceous Australian plant.
Term s. A limit; period of session, etc.; day on which rent, etc., is due; a word, expression; a condition; v.t. To name, call.
Firm a. Strong; hard, compact, solid; steady. v.t. To make firm, fix firmly. s. A commercial house; the partners or members.
Affirm' v.t. and i. To declare positively; to confirm.
Reaffirm' v.t. To affirm again.
Disaffirm' v.t. To deny, annul.
Infirm' a. Enfeebled, sickly; irresolute.
Confirm' v.t. To make firm, add strength to, render valid; to administer the rite of confirmation to.
Squirm v.i. To writhe about, wriggle. s. Such a movement.
Corm s. A bulb-like stem of certain plants.
Form s. Shape; style; a long seat; the bed of a hare. v.t. To give shape, style, or fashion to; to mould; to create.
Deform' v.t. To deface, disfigure, dishonour.
Reform' v.t. and i. To change from worse to better; to amend, restore, be corrected. s. Act of reforming; improvement, amendment.

Re-form' v.t. To form again or anew.
Bi'form a. Partaking of two forms.
Bul'biform a. Shaped like a bulb.
Rhom'biform a. Rhomb-shaped.
Cym'biform a. Boat-shaped, navicular.
Corym'biform a. Shaped like a corymb.
Sco'biform a. Resembling shavings or sawdust.
Cu'biform a. Cube shaped.
Limac'iform a. Shaped like or resembling a slug.
Bac'ciform a. Berry-shaped.
Sac'ciform a. In the shape of a sac.
Cæc'iform a. Shaped like the cæcum.
The'ciform a. In the shape of a theca.
Radic'iform a. Root-like.
Filic'iform a. Fern-shaped.
Culic'iform a. Shaped like a mosquito.
Spi'ciform a. In the shape of a spica.
Lumbric'iform a. Resembling a worm.
Cortic'iform a. Resembling bark or rind.
Fal'ciform a. Sickle-shaped.
Un'ciform a. Having a curved or hooked form.
Pis'ciform a. Shaped like a fish.
Lu'ciform a. Resembling light.
Nu'ciform a. Nut-shaped.
Cru'ciform a. Cross-shaped.
Verru'ciform a. Wart-like.
Calyc'iform a. Shaped like a calyx.
Proboscid'-iform a. Of the nature of a proboscis.
Gland'iform a. Acorn-shaped; resembling a gland.
Cor'diform a. Heart-shaped.
De'iform a. God-like; conformable to the will of God.
Horde'iform s. Like barley.
Nu'cleiform a. Resembling a nucleus.
Arane'iform a. Shaped like a spider.
Cune'iform a. Wedge-shaped, especially of the letters of writing of ancient Babylonia, etc.
Clu'peiform a. Of the shape of a herring.
Clyp'eiform a. (*Clypeate*).
Prote'iform a. Changing or changeable in shape.
Spong'iform (spŭnj'-) a. Resembling a sponge.
Fun'giform a. Having a fungus-shaped head.
Branch'iform a. Shaped like gills.
Spath'iform a. Resembling spar.
Cyath'iform a. Cup-shaped.
A'liform a. Wing-shaped.
Petal'iform a. Petalous; petaloid.
Squa'liform a. Of the shape of a shark.
Chel'iform a. Claw-shaped.
Gang'liform a. Of ganglion shape.
Umbil'iform a. Of the shape of a navel.
Strobil'iform a. In the form of a strobile.
Cil'iform a. (*Cilia*).
Monil'iform a. Shaped like a string of beads.
Funil'iform a. Formed of fibres.
Pi'liform a. Hair-shaped.
Reptil'iform s. Serpent-shaped.
Cor'alliform a. Like coral; branching.
Metal'liform a. Like a metal.
Cell'iform a. Cell-shaped.
Flagel'liform a. Whip-shaped.
Lamel'liform a. Thin and flat; scale-like.
Sell'iform a. Saddle-shaped.
Patel'liform a. Patellar.
Stel'liform a. Star-shaped; radiated.
Scutel'liform a. Shield-shaped.
Morbil'liform a. Pertaining to or resembling measles.
Mammil'liform a. Nipple-shaped.
Papil'liform a. Shaped like a papilla.
Spiril'liform a. Spiral-shaped (of bacteria).
Still'iform a. Drop-shaped.
Vill'iform a. Like villi.
Cucul'liform a. Cucullate, hood-shaped.
Parabol'iform a. Resembling a parabola.
Hyperbol'iform a. Having the form of a hyperbola.
Caul'iform a. Stalk-shaped.
Strombu'liform a. Twisted spirally screw-wise.
Subu'liform a. Awl-shaped.
Tubu'liform a. Having the form of a small tube.
Spiracu'liform a. Resembling a spiracle.
Tentac'uliform a. Shaped like a tentacle.
Spic'uliform a. Dart-like; spicule-shaped.
Vesic'uliform a. Like a bladder in shape.
Oc'uliform a. In the form of an eye.
Pocu'liform a. Cup-shaped.
Oper'culiform a. Shaped like a lid or operculum.
Vas'culiform a. Shaped like a flowerpot.
Ligu'liform a. Tongue-shaped.
Granu'liform a. Shaped like a granule.
Toru'liform a. In the shape of torula.
Spat'uliform a. Spatulate.
Rotu'liform a. Shaped like the knee-cap.
Fistu'liform a. Tubular; like a fistula in shape.
Cobyl'iform a. Cup-shaped.
Styl'iform a. Shaped like a style.
Ha'miform a. Hook-shaped.
Squa'miform a. Scale-like.
Rem'iform a. Oar-shaped.
Mam'miform a. Shaped like a breast or nipple.
Mum'miform a. Of the shape, etc., of a mummy.
Po'miform a. Shaped like a pome or apple.
Ver'miform a. Worm-shaped; vermicular.
Cucu'miform a. Shaped like a cucumber.
Ra'niform a. Frog-shaped.
Gran'iform a. Grain-shaped.
Re'niform a. Kidney-shaped.
Acin'iform a. Clustered in berries.
Pampin'iform a. Curling like a vine-tendril.
Resin'iform a. Like resin.
Pectin'iform a. Pectinate.
Colum'niform a. (*Column*).
Pen'niform a. Shaped like a feather.
Anten'niform a. Shaped like antennæ.
Co'niform a. Of the shape of a fir- of pine-cone.
Corn'iform a. Horn-shaped.
U'niform a. Unvaried in form; invariable; consistent. s. Regimental dress of a soldier, etc.
Lu'niform a. Crescent-shaped.
Scap'iform a. Shaped like a scape.
Na'piform a. Turnip-shaped.
Scop'iform a. Brush-like; furnished with brush-like hairs.
Ves'piform a. Resembling a wasp.
Scalar'iform a. Ladder-shaped; marked as with rungs.
Var'iform a. Varying in form.
Dolab'riform a. Hatchet-shaped.
Fi'briform a. Shaped like a fibre.
Crib'riform a. Resembling a sieve, perforated.
Colu'briform a. Like the colubers.
Cancri'form a. Like a crab, like a cancer.
Den'driform a. Dendroid, arborescent.
Cylin'driform a. Cylindrical.
Aer'iform a. Of the nature of air.
Tuber'iform a. Shaped like a tuber.
Spher'iform a. Sphere-shaped; globular.
Viper'iform a. Shaped like a viper.
Crater'iform a. Shaped like a crater or a cup.
Scor'iform a. In the form of scoria or dross.
Flor'iform a. Flower-shaped.
Vapor'iform a. Gaseous.
Cap'riform a. Goat-like in shape.
Scal'priform a. Chisel-shaped.
Ser'riform a. Notched; saw-like.
Viver'riform a. Shaped like a weasel.
Cir'riform a. Fringe-shaped.
Tri'form a. Having a triple form.
Vit'riform a. Resembling glass.
Cul'triform a. Knife-shaped.
Calyp'triform a. Hood-shaped.
Elyt'riform a. Shaped like an elytron.
Au'riform a. Shaped like an ear.

Taur'iform a. Bull-like.
Secur'iform a. Axe-shaped.
Pandur'iform a. Fiddle-shaped.
Mur'iform a. Arranged like bricks in a wall.
Pur'iform a. In the form of or like pus.
Pyr'iform a. Pear-shaped.
Gas'iform a. Of the nature or form of gas.
Na'siform a. Nose-shaped.
Vas'iform a. Having the form of a vas or duct.
Pis'iform a. Shaped like a pea.
En'siform a. Sword-shaped.
Vers'iform a. Varying in form.
Diver'siform a. Of different or various forms.
Urs'iform a. Like a bear.
Bur'siform a. Pouch-shaped.
Fos'siform a. Shaped like a pit or cavity.
Medu'siform a. Like a jelly-fish.
Fus'iform a. Tapering at both ends.
Stigmat'iform a. Of the shape of a stigma.
Strat'iform a. In strata-like formation.
Stalac'tiform a. Having the shape of a stalactite.
Punc'tiform a. Like a dot; punctate.
Fruc'tiform a. Formed in the manner of fruit.
Re'tiform a. Net-like; reticulated.
Set'iform a. Bristle-like.
Digit'iform a. Finger-shaped.
Granit'iform a. Like granite in formation.
Mul'tiform a. Having many forms or appearances.
Den'tiform a. Shaped like a tooth or set of teeth.
Len'tiform a. Lens-shaped.
Serpent'iform a. Serpentine.
Ro'tiform a. Wheel-shaped.
Sep'tiform a. Sevenfold.
Res'tiform a. Cord-like.
Cys'tiform a. Shaped like a cyst.
Gut'tiform a. Drop-shaped.
Lin'guiform a. Tongue-shaped.
Ung'uiform a. Shaped like a nail or claw.
A'quiform a. Liquid.
Siliq'uiform a. Elongated like a siliqua.
Clav'iform a. Club-shaped.
Val'viform a. Shaped like a valve.
O'viform a. Egg-shaped.
Lar'viform a. Of the shape of a larva.
Cur'viform a. Of a curved shape.
Plex'iform a. Intricate; in the form of network.
Trape'ziform a. Shaped as a trapezium.
Riz'iform a. Shaped like rice-seeds.
Inform' v.t. To give form or life to; to acquaint, instruct. v.i. To give information, bring a charge against. a. Shapeless.
Misinform' v.t. To give erroneous information to.
Conform' v.t. To shape alike, bring into harmony with, adapt. v.i. To comply, act in accordance.
Io'doform s. An antiseptic iodine compound.
Chlor'oform s. A volatile liquid used as an anæsthetic and bleaching agent.
Perform' v.t. To carry through, accomplish, effect. v.i. To act a part, play on a musical instrument, etc.
Misform' v.t. To put into an ill shape.
Transform' v.t. To change the appearance or disposition, etc., of.
Plat'form s. A raised floor, part of a railway station, stage, rostrum, etc.; a party programme; oratory.
Ging'lyform a. Fashioned like a ginglymus or elbow.
Cairn'gorm s. A golden-brown variety of quartz
Norm s. A rule, standard; a type.
Storm s. A violent disturbance of the atmosphere; civil or domestic commotion; adversity; an assault in force. v.i. To blow, rain, snow, etc., with violence; to rage. v.t. To attack, take by assault.
Worm (werm) s. A soft-bodied, invertebrate, creeping animal; an intestinal parasite; a debased or servile person; a spiral part or thing. v.i. To wriggle; to work secretly. v.t. To effect or extract stealthily; to insinuate oneself.
Lob'worm s. A large worm used by anglers.
Blind'worm s. A small, snake-like lizard.
Blood'worm s. A small red earth-worm used by anglers.
Tape'worm s. A parasitic worm in man and other vertebrates.
Wire'worm s. The larva of the click-beetle.
Ring'worm s. A vesicular contagious skin-disease.
Book'worm s. A studious person; a larva that eats holes in books.
Maw'worm s. An intestinal worm.
Land'sturm s. The old general levy in Germany; the last reserves.
Sar'casm s. Irony; a satirical remark.
Or'gasm s. Excitement and turgescence of an organ.
Chasm s. A deep gorge; a gap, hiatas.
Sched'iasm s. Something done off-hand.
Autosched'iasm s. Something hastily improvised.
Chiasm' s. The crossing of the optic nerves.
Chil'iasm s. The doctrine of Christ's personal reign during the millennium.
Enthu'siasm s. Ardent zeal; fervour of soul; sanguineness.
Icon'oclasm s. The breaking of idols; disregard of accepted beliefs, etc.
Plasm s. Plasma.
Cat'aplasm s. A poultice.
Met'aplasm s. The formative material of protoplasm; change in a word by alteration of a letter, etc.
En'doplasm s. The semi-fluid inner layer of protoplasm.
Ne'oplasm s. A morbid growth of new tissue.
Id'ioplasm s. The portion of a protoplasmic cell supposed to give rise to inherited characteristics.
Het'eroplasm s. A morbid formation of tissue.
Pro'plasm s. A matrix, mould.
Ec'toplasm s. Outer layer of protoplasm; a material emanation held by spiritualists to proceed from mediums in certain circumstances.
Pro'toplasm s. A glutinous, insoluble, contractile substance forming the physical basis of life; germinal matter.
Deut'oplasm s. The matter in an egg that nourishes the embryo.
Ple'onasm s. Use of more words than are necessary.
Spasm s. An involuntary muscular contraction; a convulsive effort, movement, etc.
Phan'tasm s. A phantom; a figment, delusion, optical illusion.
Ism s. A doctrine or theory (*contemptuously*).
-ism suff. Forming abstract nouns denoting doctrine, theory, system, etc.
Sa'baism s. The worship of the heavenly host.
Ju'daism s. Doctrine, rites, etc., of the Jews; conformity to these.
Ar'chaism s. Use of past styles of language, art, custom, etc.
La'maism s. The Buddhism of Tibet and Mongolia.
He'braism s. A Hebrew idiom, etc.; Hebraic character; servile allegiance to conscience.
Mith'raism s. Worship (in ancient Persia) of the sun-god, Mithra.

Ul'traism s. Principles of those advocating extreme measures.
Phar'isaism s. Doctrines, conduct, etc., of the Pharisees; hypocrisy in religion.
Mo'saism s. The laws, etc., attributed to Moses; attachment to his system or doctrines.
Pro'saism s. That which is in or is characteristic of prose.
Vol'taism s. Electricity produced by chemical action; galvanism.
Ba'bism s. The tenets of a mystical, pathe-istic, modern Persian sect.
Snob'bism s. Snobbery.
Cam'bism s. (*Cambist*).
Plumb'ism s. Lead-poisoning.
Lamb'dacism s. Lallation.
Os'tracism s. Act of ostracizing; expulsion.
Rhot'acism s. Exaggerated or wrong pronunciation of *r*.
Io'tacism s. Excessive use, or the pronunciation of, the *iota* in Greek.
Sol'ecism s. Impropriety or barbarism in language; a breach of good manners.
Gre'cism s. A Greek idiom; a Hellenism.
Goth'icism s. A Gothic idiom, etc.; barbarism.
Bib'licism s. Strict adherence to the literal meaning of the Bible.
An'glicism s. An idiom or custom peculiar to the English.
Gal'licism s. A French idiom or peculiarity.
Phal'licism s. Worship or veneration of the phallus.
Cathol'icism s. The faith, doctrines, rites, etc., of the whole Catholic Church, or of the Roman Catholics.
Academ'icism s. Academical or professorial mannerism.
Hispan'icism s. A Spanish idiom.
Sin'icism s. A Chinese idiom or expression.
Lacon'icism s. A concise, pithy saying; sententious style.
Histrion'icism s. Stage representation, histrionics.
Hiber'nicism s. An Hibernianism.
Cyn'icism s. Morose contempt for the pleasures and arts of life.
Sto'icism s. Indifference to pain or pleasure; the tenets, etc., of the Stoics.
Empir'icism s. Method or practice of an empiric; the doctrine that all knowledge is founded on experience.
Dor'icism s. A peculiarity of Doric dialect.
Geocen'tricism s. The theory that the earth is the centre of the planetary system.
Clas'sicism s. Classical idiom, style, or expression.
Grammat'icism s. A point in grammar.
Fanat'icism s. Excessive zeal, wild notions of religion; frenzy.
Eclec'ticism s. Practice of selecting and using views, etc., from several different systems; a composite school of philosophy, art, etc.
Ascet'icism s. The principles, habits, etc., of ascetics.
Æsthet'icism s. The system or principles of æsthetes; æsthetics.
Athlet'icism s. Devotion to athletics; the practices of athletes.
Phonet'icism s. Phonetic writing or representation.
Peripatet'icism s. Philosophical system of Aristotle.
Brit'icism s. (*Britishism*).
Crit'icism s. Act or art of judging, especially literary or artistic work; exhibition of the merits of these, a critical essay; censure.
Oneir'ocriticism s. The interpretation of dreams.
Cel'ticism s. A peculiarity, idiom, etc., of Celts.
Roman'ticism s. State or quality of being romantic; the literary cult or trend opposed to classicism.
Narcot'icism s. Narcotism.
Kenot'icism s. The doctrine of kenosis.
Erot'icism s. Amatory sentiment; melancholia caused by love.
Exot'icism s. A foreign phrase, plant, etc.; state of being exotic.
Scep'ticism s. Doubt, uncertainty, incredulity.
Ecclesias'ticism s. Principles, spirit, etc., of ecclesiastics; devotion to ecclesiastical method, doctrine, etc.
Scholas'ticism s. The methods, subtleties, etc., of the mediæval schoolmen.
Monas'ticism s. The monastic life, system, etc.
Gnos'ticism s. The religious system of an early sect which combined Oriental theology and Greek philosophy with Christianity.
Agnos'ticism s. (*Agnostic*).
Mys'ticism s. Doctrine of those maintaining that they have direct intercourse with the divine Spirit, obscurity of doctrine.
At'ticism s. Idiom characteristic of Attic Greek; concise and elegant expression.
Witt'icism s. A witty saying, a jest.
Scot'ticism s. A Scottish idiom or expression.
Civ'icism s. Citizenship; patriotism.
Ex'orcism s. Act of exorcizing; prayer, incantation, etc., for this.
Turc'ism s. Manners, characteristics, etc., of the Turks.
Leu'cism s. Leucosis.
Nom'adism s. State of being a nomad.
Mon'adism s. Theory that the universe is composed of monads.
Far'adism s. Medical treatment by electricity.
Fad'dism s. Addiction to fads.
Encyclopæ'dism s. Compilation of an encyclopædia; very extensive knowledge.
Mah'dism s. Rule of or state of allegiance to the Mahdi.
In'validism s. State of being an invalid.
Hy'bridism s. Act or process of interbreeding.
Dru'idism s. The religious system, etc., of the Druids.
Propagan'dism s. Art or practice of propagating tenets, etc.
Vag'abondism s. Vagabondage.
Stund'ism s. Tenets, etc., of the Stundists.
Meth'odism s. Doctrines, worship, etc., of the Methodists.
I'odism s. The morbid effects of overdoses of iodine.
Bar'dism s. The system, etc., of the bards.
Lol'lardism s. The tenets of the Lollards.
Bla'ckguardism s. (*Blackguard*).
Land'lordism s. Proceedings of landlords with regard to their tenants; system under which land is rented.
De'ism s. Belief in the existence of a God without accepting divine revelation.
Sad'duceeism s. Doctrines, etc., of the Sadducees.
Yank'eeism s. American idiom, characteristics, etc.
Parsee'ism s. The religion, customs, etc., of Parsees.
Absentee'ism s. (*Absentee*).
Suttee'ism s. The practice of suttee.
Or'angeism s. The political doctrines, etc., of the Irish Protestants.
The'ism s. Belief in the existence of a supreme God; morbid condition due to excessive tea-drinking.

A'theism s. Denial of or disbelief in the existence of a God.
Trithe'ism s. Doctrine that the three persons of the Trinity are distinct Gods.
Pan'theism s. Doctrine that nature as a whole and " God " are synonymous.
Sciothe'ism s. Ancestor-worship.
Hylothe'ism s. Doctrine or belief that matter is God ; pantheism.
Hen'otheism s. Belief in one supreme god among many.
Mon'otheism s. Doctrine or belief that there is but one God.
Polythe'ism s. Doctrine or worship of a plurality of gods.
Monroe'ism s. Policy that interference on American continent by European Powers shall not be tolerated, with declaration of U.S. disinterestedness in European politics.
Pac'ifism s. Doctrine of non-resistance ; opposition to militarism.
Su'fism s. The doctrines of the Sufis.
Geoph'agism s. Geophagy.
Suf'fragism s. The principles and propaganda of suffragists.
Whig'gism s. Principles, practices, etc., of the Whigs.
Thug'gism s. Thuggee.
Noth'ingism s. Nihilism.
Ped'agogism s. Work, character, or manners of a pedagogue.
Demagog'ism s. Demagogy.
Paral'ogism s. A reasoning false in point of form ; a fallacy ; an unwarranted conclusion.
Syl'logism s. Form of argument in three propositions.
Prosyl'logism s. A syllogism preliminary or essential to another.
Neol'ogism s. Introduction of new words or doctrines ; a new word, expression, or doctrine.
Yo'gism s. The Hindu ascetic system of yoga.
Syn'ergism s. Doctrine that salvation is effected through union of human energy and divine grace.
Mon'achism s. Monasticism ; monkishness.
Cat'echism s. A form of instruction by questions and answers ; an elementary treatise on religious doctrine.
Mas'ochism s. Delight in suffering through one of the opposite sex.
Pa'triarchism s. A patriarchal system of government.
An'archism s. (*Anarchy*).
Mon'archism s. Monarchic principles, etc. ; advocacy of them.
Hi'erarchism s. Hierarchical principles, etc.
Church'ism s. Adherence to the principles of an established Church.
Schism (sizm) s. Division, especially among those of the same faith.
Eu'nuchism s. State of being a eunuch.
Bud'dhism s. The religious system founded in India by Gautama (fifth century B.C.).
Catas'trophism s. Theory that changes in the earth's surface are due to cataclysms.
Soph'ism s. A specious but fallacious argument.
Theos'ophism s. Belief in theosophy ; pretension to direct divine illumination.
Philos'ophism s. Affectation to philosophy ; sophistry.
Amor'phism s. The absence of regular crystalline structure.
Metamor'phism s. State or process of metamorphosis.
Dimor'phism s. Power of crystallizing into, or property of having, two distinct forms.
Trimor'phism s. Existence in certain plants and animals of three distinct forms.
Therio-mor'phism s. Belief in gods in animal form.
Mono-mor'phism s. State or quality of being monomorphic.
Anthropo-mor'phism s. The representation of God or gods as man-like ; attribution to animals, etc., of human qualities.
Hetero-mor'phism s. Heteromorphy.
Isomor'phism s. Quality of being isomorphic.
Automor'phism s. Attribution of one's own characteristics, etc., to another.
Polymor'phism s. State of being polymorphous.
Eng'lishism s. An idiom or peculiarity of the English.
Ir'ishism s. Idiom or mode of speech peculiar to the Irish.
Fet'ishism s. Idolatry of primitive races worship of fetishes.
Brit'ishism s. An idiom or custom peculiar to Great Britain.
Gnath'ism s. The relation of the jaw formation to the facial angle.
Prog'nathism s. Projection of the lower jaw.
Er'ethism s. Irritation ; excitement of a tissue, etc.
Di'theism s. Doctrine of existence of two gods (good and evil) ; dualism.
Cab'balism s. (*Cabbala*).
Can'nibalism s. (*Cannibal*).
Tri'balism s. Social organization, etc., of tribes.
Verb'alism s. A verbal expression ; an empty form of words ; wordiness.
Rad'icalism s. The theories, system, etc., of political radicals.
Syn'dicalism s. System advocated by certain extremists of obtaining demands by means of a general strike.
Evan-gel'icalism s. Evangelical principles.
Cler'icalism s. Undue influence by the clergy.
Theat'ricalism s. A stage habit, trick, etc.
Clas'sicalism s. (*Classical*).
Lo'calism s. State of being local ; word, phrase, etc., peculiar to a place.
Vo'calism s. Exercise of the vocal organs ; a vocal sound.
Van'dalism s. Spirit or conduct of Vandals ; hostility to the arts, etc.
Mo'dalism s. Doctrine that the Three Persons of the Trinity are merely different modes of being.
Feu'dalism s. System by which land was held in return for military service.
Ide'alism s. Practice of forming ideals ; theory which denies the existence of matter.
Re'alism s. Doctrine of the realists ; fidelity to life in art, etc.
Le'galism s. Strict adherence to legal form.
Re'galism s. Doctrine of royal supremacy over the Church.
Dolico-ceph'alism s. Condition of being long-headed.
Neph'alism s. Teetotalism.
Stib'ialism s. Antimonial poisoning.
Proverb'ialism s. A proverbial phrase or locution.
Ra'cialism s. National principles, system, sentiment, etc.
Spec'ialism s. Devotion to a particular branch of study, etc.
Offi'cialism s. Excessive official routine.
Provin'cialism s. A peculiarity of provincials ; narrow outlook.

Soc'ialism s. Co-operation under state ownership.
Com-mer'cialism s. Trading or huckstering spirit; commercial practices.
Primor'dialism s. Primordiality.
Paro'chialism s. Quality of being parochial; pettiness of interests, etc.
Colo'nialism s. An idiom or peculiarity of colonials.
Ceremo'nialism s. Adherence to ceremony.
Imper'ialism s. Government by an emperor; imperial power, spirit, state, or policy.
Mater'ialism s. Denial of a spiritual principle in man; theory that there is nothing in the universe but matter.
Immater'ialism s. Doctrine that matter is only existent in the mind; theory that spiritual beings exist or are possible.
Tri'alism s. A threefold union; doctrine of such.
Indus'trialism s. System of social organization based on industrial occupations.
Cu'rialism s. (*Curial*).
Mercur'ialism s. Chronic poisoning by mercury.
Contro-ver'sialism s. (*Controversial*).
Experi-en'tialism s. The doctrine that all ideas and knowledge are gained by individual experience.
Prefer-en'tialism s. The system of perferential treatment in commerce.
Mar'tialism s. Militarism.
Collo'quialism s. A common form of speech.
An'imalism s. Brutishness.
Form'alism s. Quality of being formal; ceremonial religion.
Phenom'enal-ism s. Theory that knowledge is concerned only with phenomena.
Nom'inalism s. The principles of nominalists.
Re'gionalism s. Regional sectionalism.
Confes'sional-ism s. Principle of making confession, or of formulating the beliefs of a Church and exacting adherence to them.
Profes'sional-ism s. Stamp spirit, etc., of a profession or of professionals in sport.
Congre-ga'tionalism s. A self-governing system of Church government; independency.
Na'tionalism s. Devotion to the nation; policy of national independence; patriotic sentiment, etc.
Denomina'-tionalism s. Class spirit; system of religious sects, especially in matters of education.
Inter-na'tionalism s. Promotion of community of interests between nations.
Ra'tionalism s. System of opinions deduced from reason.
Sensa'tionalism s. Theory that all knowledge is derived from sensation; employment of sensational methods.
Sec'tionalism s. Sectional feeling; provincialism.
Tradi'tionalism s. Adherence to or the system of tradition.
Intui'tionalism s. Doctrine that the perception of truth is intuitive.
Conven'tional-ism s. Arbitrary custom; a conventional phrase, etc.
Institu'tional-ism s. The upholding of the authority, etc., of established institutions (especially ecclesiastical)
Constitu'tional-ism s. Theory of constitutional rule; adherence to a constitution.
Triper'sonalism s. The doctrine of the Trinity.
Car'nalism s. Sensualism.
Pater'nalism s. State or principles of government similar to that of a father over his children.
Exter'nalism s. The metaphysical doctrine dealing only with externals.
Journ'alism s. Occupation of writing for or conducting a newspaper, etc.
Commun'alism s. Social system based on ownership of means of subsistence; anarchical communism.
Pa'palism s. The system of the papacy.
Munic'ipalism s. Municipal government; a system of this.
Cer'ebralism s. The theory that mental activity arises in the brain.
Lib'eralism s. Liberal principles; the practices of liberals.
Fed'eralism s. The principles of federal government.
Gen'eralism s. A general statement, opinion, etc.
Lit'eralism s. Practice of following literal sense; tendency to adopt literal interpretations.
Chlor'alism s. Morbid effects of taking chloral.
Mor'alism s. Morality as distinct from religion.
Hu'moralism s. Theory that disease arises from affections of the humours.
Cen'tralism s. A policy of centralization.
Plur'alism s. The holding of more than one benefice or office at the same time; the philosophical doctrine opposed to monism.
Rur'alism s. The rural life; rural quality; a rustic idiom.
Nat'uralism s. Mere state of nature; doctrine that there is no action by any supernatural power in the universe realism.
Super-nat'uralism s. Belief in the supernatural.
Preter-nat'uralism s. Preternatural state, belief, or doctrine; a preternatural occurrence, etc.
Gut'turalism s. Guttural quality; throatiness.
Commen'salism s. (*Commensal*).
Univer'salism s. Doctrine that all men will finally be saved.
Fa'talism s. The doctrine of fate or inevitable necessity.
Capit'alism s. The economic system under which Capital, not Labour, plays the leading part.
Hos'pitalism s. The hospital system.
Vi'talism s. Doctrine that the principles of life are distinct from those of the inorganic world.
Tan'talism s. A teasing with vain hopes.
Acciden'talism s. (*Accidental*).
Occiden'talism s. The character, culture, etc., of Western peoples.
Trans-cenden'talism s. State of being transcendental; a transcendental philosophy.
Orien'talism s. An idiom, custom, etc., peculiar to Orientals; knowledge of Eastern languages, etc.
Elemen'talism s. The theory that the ancient deities represented the forces of nature.
Experi-men'talism s. Theory or practice of relying on experiment; empiricism.
Senti-men'talism s. Character or behaviour of a sentimentalist.
Sacer-do'talism s. System, character, etc., of a priesthood; devotion to this.
Teeto'talism s. Principles of teetotallers.
Brut'alism s. (*Brutal*).
Du'alism s. Duality; a system based on a double principle, as on good and evil, divine and human, mind and matter.
Individ'ualism s. Quality of being individual; system under which each works for his own ends; self-interest.

Sen'sualism s. Sensuality; doctrine of sensationalism.
Intellec'tualism s. Cultivation of the intellect; doctrine that knowledge is derived from pure reason.
Rit'ualism s. Prescribed forms of religious observance; extreme adherence to rites.
Spir'itualism s. Belief in communicability with the departed through agency of a "medium"; practise of this; the philosophical doctrine opposed to materialism.
Concep'tualism s. Theory that the mind can form for itself general conceptions of individual objects.
Mu'tualism s. Doctrine that welfare is based on mutual dependence.
Mediæ'valism s. Devotion to the institutions, etc., of the Middle Ages; mediæval belief or practice.
Loy'alism s. Principles, etc., of loyalists.
Roy'alism s. Principles or conduct of royalists; characteristics of monarchy.
Pty'alism s. Morbid and copious secretion of saliva.
Men'delism s. A theory of heredity.
Evan'gelism s. Preaching or promulgation of the Gospel.
Par'allelism s. State of being parallel; resemblance.
Scoun'drelism s. Baseness; rascality; turpitude.
Pantagru'elism s. Coarse buffoonery, especially with an ostensible serious purpose.
Prob'abilism s. Doctrine of probabilists.
Automo'bilism s. (*Automobile*).
Pu'gilism s. Art or practice of fighting with the fists.
Ni'hilism s. Any doctrine of negation; a former Russian form of anarchism.
Biblioph'ilism s. (*Bibliophile*).
Negroph'ilism s. Friendship for the negro race.
Gastroph'ilism s. Gluttony.
Zo'ilism s. Carping or malignant criticism.
Mer'cantilism s. System of society based on commerce.
Gen'tilism s. Heathenism, paganism.
Dev'ilism s. Devil-worship; devilry.
Phal'lism s. Phallicism.
Bimet'allism s. The system by which gold and silver could be used as legal tender with a fixed ratio between the two.
Monomet'allism s. A one-metal standard for coinage.
Psel'lism s. Lisping, stammering; a vocal defect.
Machiavel'lism s. Machiavellianism.
Bos'wellism s. Boswell's style of biography.
Vanil'lism s. A skin-disease due to prolonged handling of vanilla.
Diab'olism s. Devil-worship; sorcery, black magic; devilry.
Catab'olism s. Change from compound to simple substances.
Katab'olism s. The degeneration of complex organic compounds into simpler compounds.
Metab'olism s. Process of chemical change in living bodies which builds up or breaks down protoplasm.
Em'bolism s. Insertion of days or years to produce regularity of time; action of an embolus in causing apoplexy, etc.
Sym'bolism s. System of symbols; anti-realism or anti-classicism.
Hyper'bolism s. Use of hyperbole; a hyperbolic expression.
Al'coholism s. Condition due to chronic or excessive absorption of intoxicants.
Sci'olism s. Superficial knowledge.
Som'nolism s. Drowsy condition due to hypnotism.
Monop'olism s. System, practices, etc., of monopolists.
Somnam'bulism s. Act of walking, etc., in sleep; this state.
Noctam'bulism s. Somnambulism.
Animal'culism s. (*Animalcule*).
For'mulism s. Strict observance of formulas.
Bot'ulism s. Poisoning caused by a ptomaine found in decomposing sausages, etc.
Sali'cylism s. State produced by overdosing with salicylates.
Ben'thamism s. The Utilitarian philosophy.
Is'lamism s. The Mohammedan religion.
Dy'namism s. Theory explaining phenomena as the ultimate result of immanent force.
Acad'emism s. Platonism.
Chem'ism s. Chemical attraction; affinity.
Heterophe'mism s. Heterophemy.
Eu'phemism s. Use of a delicate word or expression in place of an offensive one; word, etc., so used.
Mos'lemism s. Mohammedanism.
Extrem'ism s. Extreme doctrines or practices.
To'temism s. Belief in or system based on totems.
An'imism s. The primitive belief that all things, living or not, possess soul.
Pess'imism s. Doctrine that evil and pain are supreme, or that the trend of things is towards evil; tendency to take gloomy views; fatalism.
Legit'imism s. Doctrine of monarchical heredity and divine right.
Op'timism s. Doctrine that everything in nature is ordered for the best; disposition to take hopeful views.
Tho'mism (tō'-) s. The theological and philosophical system of St. Thomas Aquinas.
Bro'mism s. Condition produced by long use of bromide of potassium.
Dichro'mism s. Colour-blindness in which only two colours can be distinguished.
At'omism s. The atomic theory of the ancients.
O'piumism s. Habitual use of opium; morbid condition caused by this.
Repub'licanism s. Republican form of government; attachment to this.
An'glicanism s. The theory or principle, or a peculiarity of the Church of England.
Amer'icanism s. An idiom or custom peculiar to citizens of the United States.
Vat'icanism s. Doctrine of papal supremacy adhesion to papal authority.
Vol'canism s. Principles of volcanic action.
Moham'medanism s. The Moslem religion contained in the Koran.
-eanism (See words ending in *-ean*).
Manichæ'anism s. The heresy of Manes and his followers.
Pythagore'anism s. Pythagorism.
Pa'ganism s. Heathenism.
Hoo'liganism s. Rowdiness; manners of hooligans.
Or'ganism s. An organized body; organic structure; a living animal or plant.
Mech'anism s. Construction of a machine; parts of a machine taken collectively.

Plebei'anism (-bē'-) s. Quality or state of being plebeian; vulgarity.
Tradu'cianism s. Doctrine held by Traducianists.
Confu'cianism s. The doctrine and ethical system of Confucius.
Rosi-cru'cianism s. The tenets, etc., of the Rosicrucians.
Arca'dianism s. (*Arcadian*).
Solifid'ianism s. The tenets of Solifidians.
Ruf'fianism s. Act or conduct of a ruffian.
Pela'gianism s. The doctrines of Pelagius, an heretical monk of the fourth century.
Ma'gianism s. The religious system, etc., of the Magi; Zoroastrianism.
Sweden-bor'gianism s. The doctrines of the Swedenborgians.
Aris-tote'lianism s. (*Aristotelian*).
Machiavel'-lianism s. Duplicity (especially political); crafty intrigue.
Bohe'mianism s. (*Bohemian*).
Anti-nom'ianism s. (*Antinomian*).
Socin'ianism s. Tenets, etc., of Socinus (sixteenth century) and his followers; a form of Unitarianism.
Armin'ianism s. (*Arminian*).
Hiber'nianism s. A phrase, manner, etc., peculiar to Irishmen.
Uto'pianism a. Quality of being socially and politically ideal; a chimerical scheme.
Ar'ianism s. (*Arian*).
Nothing-ar'ianism s. The principles, etc., of one who cares for no particular religious or political creed.
Millen-ar'ianism s. Doctrine of the Millenarians.
Valetudin-ar'ianism s. Condition, ways, etc., of valetudinarians; infirmity.
Latitudinar'-ianism s. Latitudinarian doctrines or attitude; a latitudinarian condition or system.
Doctrin-ar'ianism s. Doctrinairism.
Agrar'ianism s. (*Agrarian*).
Infra-lapsar'ianism s. The doctrine of the Infralapsarians.
Supra-lapsar'ianism s. The doctrines of the Supralapsarians.
Tractar'ianism s. The principles of High Church reform advocated by the Oxford Movement.
Sectar'ianism s. Quality or character of a sectarian; devotion to party interests.
Vegetar'ianism s. Theory and practice of vegetarians.
Prole-tar'ianism s. Condition or political position of the proletariat.
Utilitar'ianism s. Doctrine of the greatest happiness of the greatest number.
Humani-tar'ianism s. The principles of Humanitarians.
Unitar'ianism s. The doctrines of the Unitarians.
Necessi-tar'ianism s. Doctrines, etc., of Necessitarians.
Ubiqui-tar'ianism s. The doctrine that Christ's body is omnipresent at the Eucharist.
Trinitar'ianism s. Doctrine of Trinitarians.
Anti-quar'ianism s. (*Antiquarian*).
Spencer'ianism s. The teachings, philosophy, method, etc., of Herbert Spencer.
Presby-ter'ianism s. The form of Church government by presbyters; doctrines of those adhering to this.
Pedes'trianism s. Art or practice of walking.
Eques'trianism s. Horsemanship.
Cartes'ianism s. The philosophy of Descartes (d. 1650).
Rabelais'ianism (-lāz'-) s. A coarsely satirical expression.
Precis'ianism s. Absurdly excessive exactness.
Concre'tianism s. The doctrine that soul and body are generated and progress together.
Eras'tianism s. The principles and tenets of the Erastians; state control of religion.
Mel'anism s. Dark coloration of the skin, etc.
Sha'manism s. A superstitious religion among certain N. Asiatic and N. American tribes.
Ro'manism s The tenets, etc., of the Church of Rome.
Ger'manism s. A German idiom or peculiarity.
Nor'manism s. An idiom, etc., peculiar to Normans.
Hu'manism s. System of philosophy primarily concerned with man in his relations to the world; devotion to humanity.
Nan'ism s. Dwarfishness.
Lu'theranism s. The doctrines taught by Luther.
Charl'atanism s. (*Charlatan*).
Sa'tanism s. Diabolic disposition or wickedness; devil-worship.
Cosmo-pol'itanism s. Condition or character of a cosmopolite.
Pur'itanism s. Doctrines, practices, etc., of Puritans.
Ultra-mon'tanism s. Principles of those holding extreme views in favour of papal supremacy, infallibility, etc.
Gal'vanism s. Electricity produced by chemical action; application of this.
Wes'leyanism s. Tenets, etc., of the Wesleyans.
Gombeen'ism s. System of petty usury, especially in Ireland.
Monog'enism s. Monogeny.
Heath'enism s. Paganism; idolatry.
A'lienism s. State of an alien; treatment and study of mental disorders.
Hell'enism s. A Greek idiom, etc.; Greek culture, nationalism, etc.; cultivation of Greek ideas, style, etc.
Ple'nism s. Theory that all space is full of matter.
Jan'senism s. The tenets of the Jansenists.
For'eignism s. A foreign idiom, custom, etc.
Tech'nism s. Technicality.
Cocain'ism s. State produced by excessive use of cocaine.
Jain'ism s. An Indian non-Brahminical religion.
Rab'binism s. A rabbinic expression or phraseology.
Al'binism s. State of being an albino.
Jac'obinism s. The principles, etc., of the Jacobins.
Multitu'dinism s. Doctrine that the many are of more importance than the individual.
Mor'phinism s. Morbid condition due to habitual use of morphine.
Lar'rikinism s. Hooliganism.
Fem'inism s. The woman's movement in politics, etc.; womanly characteristics.
Brah'minism s. The religious system of the Hindus.
Ter'minism s. Doctrine that each man has a limited period for repentence.
Deter'minism s. Doctrine that conduct and action is determined by conditions outside the actor's free-will.
Indeterm'inism s. Theory that the will is not determined by external causes.

Illu'minism s. Principles of the Illuminati.
Strych'ninism s. Strychnine poisoning.
Vul'pinism s. Foxiness; craft.
Lat'inism s. A Latin idiom or mode of expression.
Ac'tinism s. The property in light rays to which their chemical action is due.
Cre'tinism s. A kind of idiocy peculiar to certain parts of the Alps.
Byzan'tinism s. (*Byzantine*).
Nic'otinism s. Condition arising from excessive use of tobacco.
Lib'ertinism s. Conduct of a libertine.
Des'tinism s. Fatalism.
Phil'istinism s. Mode of thinking, etc., of Philistines; lack of taste.
Cal'vinism s. The theology, doctrine, and tenets of the Reformer, John Calvin.
Chau'vinism s. Exaggerated and bellicose patriotism.
Dar'winism s. The doctrine of the origin of species by natural selection.
Lac'onism s. Laconicism.
Gas'conism s. A bragging; a boast; bravado.
He'donism s. Doctrine that pleasure is the chief good.
Antag'onism s. Opposition, active disagreement; an opposing principle.
Cin'chonism s. Bodily condition due to overdoses of quinine.
Eu'phonism s. An agreeable sound or combination of sounds.
Polyph'onism s. State of being polyphonic; polyphony.
Pyr'rhonism s. Scepticism; universal doubt.
Autoch'thonism s. (*Autochthon*).
Py'thonism s. Art of ambiguous prediction.
Relig'ionism s. Practice or affectation of religion.
Li'onism s. Practice of lionizing.
U'nionism s. The principle of combining; policy of a Unionist.
Seces'sionism s. The tenets, etc., of secessionists.
Progres'sionism s. Tenets and practices of progressionists.
Impres'sionism s. A school of painting whose aim is broad general effect as opposed to elaboration of detail.
Post-impres'sionism s. The theory and art of the post-impressionists.
Illu'sionism s. Theory that regards all external things as mere illusions.
Crea'tionism s. Doctrine that the individual soul is immediately created by God.
Associa'tionism s. The theory that mental and moral phenomena are due to association of ideas.
Annihila'tionism s. (*Annihilation*).
Trans-migra'tionism s. Doctrine of metempsychosis.
Inspira'tionism s. Doctrine that the Bible is divinely inspired throughout.
Restora'tionism s. Doctrine of the ultimate restoration of all to happiness.
Presenta'tionism s. Doctrine that the ultimate elements of all mental processes depend on immediate cognition.
Salva'tionism s. Doctrine, methods, etc., of the Salvation Army.
Obstruc'tionism s. The hindering of progress.
Aboli'tionism s. Principle or system of abolition.
Intui'tionism s. Intuitionalism.
Evolu'tionism s. The theory of evolution.
Zi'onism s. Aims and principles of the Zionists.
Mon'ism s. System or theory that matter and mind are one.
De'monism s. Belief in demons.
Eude'monism s. Philosophical system founding moral obligation upon its relation to happiness.
Mor'monism s. The doctrine, etc., of the Mormons.
Anach'ronism s. A mis-dating of events, etc.
Prach'ronism s. The error of fixing a date later that it should be.
Metach'ronism s. Error of placing an event after its real time.
Syn'chronism s. Simultaneousness; a tabular arrangement of contemporary events.
Pro'chronism s. Error of dating an event too early.
Isoch'ronism s. State or quality of being isochronous.
Byr'onism s. (*Byronic*).
Pla'tonism s. The doctrines of Plato and his followers.
Dal'tonism s. Colour-blindness.
Syn'tonism s. Syntony.
Plu'tonism s. The theory held by the Plutonists.
Sax'onism s. An idiom of the Saxon language.
Mod'ernism s. Modern practice, mode of expression, etc.; tendency towards freedom of thought, especially in the Roman Catholic Church.
Sat'urnism s. Lead-poisoning.
Com'munism s. Doctrine of community of property; a state of society in which this is attained.
Op'portunism s. Formation of policy to meet varying circumstances; time-serving; trimming.
Taoism (tou'-) s. A Chinese religious system.
Eg'oism s. System in which the good of the individual is the chief standard of moral action; selfishness.
Jin'goism s. Bellicose patriotism; Chauvinism.
Ech'oism s. Onomatopœia.
Hy'loism s. Hylotheism.
Baboo'ism s. A phrase, custom, etc., characteristic of a baboo.
Voodoo'ism s. A superstitious system of magic, witchcraft, snake-worship, etc., practised by negroes in the W. Indies, etc.
Her'oism s. Qualities or character of a hero fortitude.
Ne'groism s. An idiom, etc., peculiar to negroes.
Dichro'ism s. Property of exhibiting different colours when viewed in different directions.
Shin'toism s. Shinto.
Hylozo'ism s. Doctrine that matter is the origin of all life.
Sin'apism s. A mustard plaster.
Thean'thropism s. State of being God and man; ascription of human attributes to God.
Psilan'thropism s. Doctrine that Christ was solely human.
Mal'apropism s. A ridiculous misuse of words.
Nyctit'ropism s. Quality of being nyctitropic.
Geot'ropism s. Tendency to grow towards the earth's centre.
Orthot'ropism s. State of being orthotropic.
Heliot'ropism s. Movement of flowers or leaves towards the sun.
Apheliot'ropism s. A turning away from the sun.
Allot'ropism s. (*Allotropy*).
Hydrot'ropism s. Tendency in plants to turn towards or away from water.
Isot'ropism s. Isotropy.
Met'opism s. Persistence of the frontal suture.
Heterot'opism s. Heterotopy.
Bar'barism s. An uncivilized condition, want of refinement; an impropriety of speech.
Mac'arism s. A blessing.

Vul'garism s. Act, speech, etc., characteristic of the vulgar; vulgarity.
Gar'garism s. A gargle.
Incen'diarism s. Arson; practices of incendiaries.
Pla'giarism s. Act of plagiarizing; literary or other original matter stolen.
So'larism s. Theory that fathers mythology on solar myths.
Vernac'ularism s. An idiom peculiar to one's native tongue.
Sec'ularism s. State of being secular; an ethical system opposed to ecclesiasticalism.
Cæs'arism s. Imperialism; autocratic rule.
Mil'itarism s. Military spirit, domination, or aggression, warlike policy.
Hetær'ism s. A primitive form of communal marriage; recognised concubinage.
Spen'cerism s. Spencerianism.
Gran'gerism s. Extra-illustration; practice of inserting additional prints, etc.
E'therism s. Effects produced by administration of ether.
Wer'therism s. Mawkish, romantic sentimentality.
Shak'erism s. Principles, etc., of the Shakers.
Quak'erism s. A peculiarity, or the doctrine, characteristics, etc., of the Quakers.
Junk'erism s. The principles, methods, etc., of Junkers.
Metam'erism s. Segmentation; state of being metameric.
Euhe'merism s. Reference of myths to historical tradition.
Isom'erism s. Identity of elements and atomic proportions, with difference in amount combined in the compound molecule, and of its essential qualities.
Mes'merism s. Art of inducing an hypnotic state in which the inducer controls the mind and actions of the patient; this state.
Polym'erism s. State of being polymerous; a form of chemical isomerism.
Man'nerism s. Peculiarity of manner.
Spoon'erism s. Accidental and ludicrous transposition of initials.
Pau'perism s. State of being a pauper; destitution.
Asphet'erism s. Communism.
Neot'erism s. A neologism, introduction of new expressions, etc.
As'terism s. A small cluster of stars; a reference mark (⁂).
Chrism s. Consecrated oil used in Christian rites.
Doctrinair'ism s. The theories or principles of doctrinaires.
Proletair'ism s. Proletarianism.
Vam'pirism s. Belief in vampires; blood-sucking.
Em'pirism s. A conclusion derived empirically.
Pythag'orism s. Philosophical theories, etc., of Pythagoras.
Rig'orism s. Strict adherence, especially to theological dogma.
Al'gorism s. The Arabic system of notation.
Aph'orism s. A maxim, adage.
Adiaph'orism s. Attitude of regarding certain theological questions as non-essential.
Phos'phorism s. Phosphorus necrosis.
Me'liorism s. Doctrine that society may be improved by effort.
Probabil'iorism s. Doctrine that when several courses are open that that seems most probably right should be taken.
Bach'elorism s. (*Bachelor*).
Hu'morism s. Humorousness; humoralism.
Por'ism s. A proposition concerned with the indeterminateness of certain problems.
Ter'rorism s. System of government by intimidation.
Prism s. A solid figure having parallelograms for sides, and similar, equal and parallel plane figures for ends.
An'eurism s. A pulsating arterial tumour.
Am'ateurism s. (*Amateur*).
Pas'teurism s. A method of treating diseases by inoculation with the virus of the same disease.
Pur'ism s. Fastidious niceness, especially in choice of words.
Na'turism s. Nature-worship.
Sol'ipsism s. Doctrine that the only knowledge possible is that of oneself.
Sab'batism s. Intermission of labour, as on the Sabbath.
Ac'robatism s. (*Acrobat*).
Mith'ridatism s. Immunity against a poison through gradually becoming used to it.
Schem'atism s. The Kantian process of understanding.
Prag'matism s. Pragmatic behaviour; philosophical system that stresses the practical as opposed to the abstract side of thought.
Sig'matism s. Defective pronunciation of the letter *s*.
Astig'matism s. Defect of a lens, especially of the eye.
Dog'matism s. Arrogance or positiveness in opinion.
Anagram'matism s. (*Anagram*).
Chro'matism s. Abnormal colouration of plants, etc.
Achro'matism s. Quality of being achromatic.
Parachro'matism s. Colour-blindness.
Autom'atism s. (*Automaton*).
Sperm'atism s. Emission of semen.
Trau'matism s. Morbid condition due to trauma.
Rheu'matism s. An inflammatory disease affecting the muscles and joints.
Than'atism s. Belief in annihilation at death.
Don'atism s. The principles of the Donatists.
Sep'aratism s. Disposition to withdraw, especially from a Church, etc.; this practice.
Democ'ratism s. Democratic principles, aims, etc.
Bureau'cratism s. The system of bureaucratic government.
Mod'eratism s. Opinions, policy, etc., of a moderate party.
Ter'atism s. Monstrosity; anomaly.
Conser'vatism s. (*Conservative*).
Doc'etism s. Doctrine that Christ had only a phantasmal body.
Sympathet'ism s. Morbid tendency to be sympathetic.
Polysyn'thetism s. Formation of polysynthetic words.
Pi'etism s. A reform movement in the Lutheran Church in the seventeenth century; exaggerated or spurious religious sentiment.
Qui'etism s. The system, doctrine, etc., of the Quietists.
Ob'soletism s. A disused word, phrase, etc.
Mag'netism s. Force whereby certain bodies naturally attract or repel each other, gives rise to polarity, etc.; science treating of magnetic phenomena; power of attraction.
Diamag'netism s. The force which causes certain magnetized bodies to point E. and W. instead of N. and S.

Syn'cretism s. Attempted reconciliation of various systems of thought.
Jac'obitism s. The principles, etc., of the Jacobites.
Cœnobit'ism s. Monachism.
Hermaph'-roditism s. Union of sexes in one individual.
Meph'itism s. Mephitic poisoning.
Cosmop'olitism s. (*Cosmopolitanism*).
Sem'itism s. Semitic character, qualities, or idiom.
Porphyro-gen'itism s. (*Porphyrogeniture*).
Eb'ionitism s. The tenets of the Ebionites.
U'nitism s. Monism.
Syb'aritism s. Voluptuousness.
Naz'aritism s. The doctrines, practices, etc., of Nazarites.
Spir'itism s. Spiritualism.
Fa'vouritism s. Disposition to favour one or some to the neglect of others.
Par'asitism s. State, manners, etc., of a parasite.
Dyoph'isitism s. The doctrine of the dyophisites.
Jes'uitism s. The doctrines, principles, etc., of the Jesuits.
Fortu'itism s. The doctrine that natural causes arise from chance, not design.
Oc'cultism s. Occult theory or practice; belief in mysterious powers.
Comt'ism s. Positivism; the philosophy of Comte.
Gi'gantism s. Giantism.
Syc'ophantism s. Habits or characteristics of sycophants.
Gi'antism s. Abnormal development.
Tar'antism s. An obscure nervous disease.
Ig'norantism s. Obscurantism.
Pococuran'tism s. State of indifference.
Obscur'antism s. System or principles of an obscurant.
Dilletan'tism s. The qualities or practices of dilletantes.
Prot'estantism s. The Protestant faith.
Irreden'tism s. The policy of the irredentists.
Sci'entism s. Methods, etc., characteristic of scientists.
Adif'ferentism s. State of indifference.
Nar'cotism s. State caused by continual use of narcotics; narcosis.
Eg'otism s. Habit of too frequently using the word *I*; self-praise; vanity.
Er'gotism s. Poisoning due to eating diseased grain; arguing, wrangling.
Id'iotism s. An idiom; idiocy.
Pat'riotism s. The qualities of a patriot; active love of one's country.
Zeal'otism (zĕl'-) s. Zealotry.
Hel'otism s. Condition of a helot; slavery.
Pi'lotism s. Pilotry.
Hu'guenotism s. The religion of the Huguenots.
Hyp'notism s. A sleep-like condition or trance caused artificially; mode of producing this.
Ne'potism s. Favouritism towards relations.
Des'potism s. Absolute authority; tyranny.
Par'rotism s. Mechanical repetition of words, sentiments, etc.; inoriginality of idea.
Quix'otism s. Absurdly chivalrous notions, acts, etc.
Bap'tism s. Act of baptizing.
Pedobap'tism s. The baptism of infants.
Chart'ism s. The principles of certain English political reformers (1837-48).
Boy'cottism s. (*Boycott*).
Pol'yglottism s. Power of speaking in several languages.
Sans-culott'ism s. Revolutionary principles or methods.
Ab'solutism s. State of being obsolute; system of unlimited despotism.
Mut'ism s. Dumbness; inability to hear.
Ne'ophytism s. (*Neophyte*).
Pros'elytism s. Act or process of proselytizing.
Babu'ism s. (*Babooism*).
Hindu'ism s. The social regulations, polytheistic religion, etc., of the Hindus.
Eu'phuism s. Pedantic affectation of high-flown language.
Cliqu'ism s. (*Clique*).
Somnil'oquism s. Act or habit of talking in one's sleep.
Ventril'oquism s. Act or art of speaking so that the voice seems to come from elsewhere.
Tru'ism s. An undoubted truth, a platitude.
Al'truism s. Unselfishness; regard for others.
At'avism s. Reappearance of a characteristic of an ancestor more remote than a parent.
Civ'ism s. (*Civicism*).
In'civism s. Want of patriotism or good citizenship.
Recid'ivism s. Persistent relapsing into crime; state of being an habitual criminal.
Progres'sivism s. Principles, etc., of a reformer.
Neg'ativism s. Doctrine of a negationist.
Objec'tivism s. Philosophical system treating the world as reality and as source of knowledge.
Subjec'tivism s. Doctrine that all knowledge is purely subjective.
Collec'tivism s. A form of socialism; theory of collective ownership.
Pos'itivism s. The philosophical system of Comte, which limits itself to human experience.
Intu'itivism s. Doctrine that ideas of right and wrong are intuitive.
Toad'yism s. Arts or practices of sycophants.
Dan'dyism s. Foppishness; ways of dandies.
Grun'dyism s. Prudishness.
Dow'dyism s. Dowdiness; characteristics of dowdies.
Row'dyism s. Practices of roughs; hooliganism.
Jock'eyism s. The practices of jockeys.
Monk'eyism s. Conduct of a monkey; resemblance to a monkey's ways.
Flunk'eyism s. Character or quality of a flunkey.
Cock'neyism s. An idiom or pronunciation peculiar to Londoners.
Fo'gyism s. Principles or habits of fogies.
Za'nyism s. State or character of a zany.
Fun'nyism s. A funny expression, manner, speech, etc.
Pup'pyism s. Youthful conceit or affectation.
Vol'untaryism s. Principle that education, or the Church, etc., should be maintained voluntarily and not by the State.
Tor'yism s. The principles, etc., of Tories.
Mac'rocosm s. The great world, the universe; the whole.
Mi'crocosm s. A little world; miniature society; man as epitomizing the universe.
Abysm' s. A fathomless pit; hell; an abyss.
Cat'aclysm s. A deluge; a great natural convulsion.
Par'oxysm s. A convulsion, fit; any sudden and violent pain, action, etc.
Gaum v.t. To smear, bedaub.
Meer'schaum s. A soft magnesian clay; tobacco pipe of this.
Imaum' s. An imam, Mohammedan priest.
Se'bum s. Fatty matter secreted by the sebaceous glands.

Al'bum s. A blank book for writing in, insertion of portraits, etc.
Guai'acum s. A genus of S. American and W. Indian trees; a resin, or drug prepared therefrom, obtained from one of these.
Tarax'acum s. Genus of plants including the dandelion; a drug prepared from its root.
Cæ'cum s. The blind gut or intestine.
Va'de-me'cum s. A small guide-book, book of reference, etc.
Mod'icum s. A small quantity.
Col'chicum s. A genus of plants yielding a medicinal drug.
Basil'icum s. An ointment.
Cap'sicum s. A tropical plant from which cayenne pepper and chillies are made.
Viat'icum s. Provisions for a journey; Eucharist given to the dying.
Scum s. Impurities rising to surface of liquors; dross. v.t. To remove scum from.
Tu'cum s. A S. American palm.
Smed'dum s. Fine powder; ore in minute particles.
Se'dum s. Genus of plants including the stonecrop.
Dum'dum s. A soft-nosed expanding bullet.
Memoran'dum s. A note to help memory.
Avizan'dum s. Consideration.
Haben'dum s. Part of a legal conveyance of an estate.
Adden'dum s. An addition, appendix.
Puden'dum s. The genital organs.
Corrigen'dum s. An error needing correction.
Tenen'dum s. Clause in a deed defining the tenure.
Referen'dum s. Submission of a political question to the direct vote of the electorate.
Secun'dum prep. According to; following.
Corun'dum s. A very hard mineral, native crystalline alumina.
Urodæ'um s. Part of the cloaca in birds and reptiles.
Propylæ'um s. A large gateway, especially to a temple.
Athenæ'um s. A literary or scientific association.
Gynæ'ceum s. The women's quarters in an ancient Roman or Greek house; the female organs of a flower.
Lyce'um s. The Athenian garden where Aristotle taught; his philosophy; an institution for literary instruction, etc.
Ode'um s. A theatre of ancient Greece; a concert-hall.
Ge'um s. A genus of rosaceous plants; herb-bennet, avens.
Hypoge'um s. The part of a building below ground-level.
Rheum s. Thin, serous discharge from mucous membrane; tears.
I'leum s. Part of the small intestine.
Pi'leum s. The top of the head (of birds).
Lino'leum s. A floor-cloth hardened with oxidized linseed-oil, etc.
Petro'leum s. Rock-oil; an inflammable, bituminous liquid found in the earth.
Nitro'leum s. Nitro-glycerine.
Mausole'um s. A magnificent tomb or monument.
Calca'neum s. The bone of the heel.
Succeda'neum s. A substitute.
Prytane'um s. A public hall in ancient Greece.
Peritone'um s. The membrane investing the internal surface of the abdomen, etc.
Castor'eum s. An oil substance secreted by beavers.
Colosse'um s. An amphitheatre, especially the Flavian in ancient Rome.
Muse'um s. A collection of objects illustrating natural science, antiquities, etc.; building for this.
Perios'teum s. The fibrous membrane investing the bones.
Fum s. A fabulous Chinese bird.
Gum s. A viscid resinous substance used for sticking things together; a tree exuding this; the fleshy sockets of the teeth. v.t. To fasten or stiffen with gum.
Be'gum s. A female ruler in India.
Al'gum s. A biblical tree (? sandal-wood).
Tar'gum s. An Aramaic paraphrase of a portion of the Old Testament.
Ter'gum s. A tergite.
Hum v.i. To make the noise of bees, to sing inarticulately. s. Act of humming; a droning or murmuring sound. int. Implying doubt or deliberation.
Chum s. An intimate friend, a "pal." v.i. To make friends with, share rooms with.
Sor'ghum s. A tall cereal fodder-plant.
Zy'thum s. A malt beverage of ancient Egypt.
-ium suff. Denoting metallic elements, etc.
La'bium s. A lip or lip-like part.
Stib'ium s. Antimony.
Cam'bium s. The soft cell-tissue of trees which forms new wood.
Colum'bium s. Niobium, a metallic element.
Nio'bium s. A metallic element resembling tantalum.
Er'bium s. A rare metallic earth.
Ter'bium s. A rare metallic element
Ytter'bium s. A rare metallic element.
Euphor'bium s. A poisonous, inflammable resin obtained from some African euphorbia.
Apothe'cium s. The spore-case in lichens.
Sili'cium s. Silicon.
Cal'cium s. A metallic element resembling zinc.
Cala'dium s. A genus of plants of the Arum family.
Palla'dium s. An ancient miraculous statue of Pallas at Troy; a safeguard; a steel-grey metallic element of the platinum group.
Vana'dium s. A rare metallic element.
Ra'dium s. A metallic element emitting invisible rays that penetrate bodies opaque to light.
Sta'dium s. An ancient Greek measure (about 202 yards); an arena for races, games, etc.; a stage in a disease.
Epice'dium s. A funeral ode, a dirge.
Me'dium s. A mean; middle position; an agent. a. Middle; middling.
Interme'dium s. Intermediate space; an intervening agent.
Cypripe'dium s. A genus of orchids; lady's-slipper.
Sore'dium s. A reproductive bud in lichens.
Te'dium s. Irksomeness; wearisomeness.
Rubid'ium s. A silvery-white metallic element.
Pycnid'ium s. A receptacle in certain fungi.
Conid'ium s. An asexual spore of certain fungi.
Gonid'ium s. An asexual reproductive spore present in algæ, fungi, and lichens.
Spærid'ium s. One of the protuberances on a sea-urchin.
Perid'ium s. The outer envelope of certain fungi.
Irid'ium s. A heavy metallic element of the platinum group.

Scan'dium s. A rare metallic element.
Antepen'dium s. The cloth covering the front of an altar.
Compen'dium s. An abridgment, epitome.
In'dium s. A rare, silver-white, malleable metallic element.
O'dium s. Offensiveness; dislike; quality that provokes hatred.
Rho'dium s. A metallic element of the platinum group; the Jamaica rosewood.
Allo'dium s. Land the absolute property of the owner.
Plasmo'dium s. A mass of mobile protoplasm; a genus of protozoa present in the blood in malaria.
Po'dium s. The pedestal of a column; a low wall; a foot-like organ.
Sympo'dium s. (*Botany*) An axis made up of successive secondary axes.
Lycopo'dium s. The genus comprising the club-mosses; an inflammable powder obtained from these.
Pseudopo'dium s. A contractile mass of protoplasm in certain protozoa.
So'dium s. A soft, silver-white metallic element.
Pericar'dium s. The membranous sac enclosing the heart.
Endocar'dium s. The membrane lining the cavities of the heart.
Myocar'dium s. The muscular substance of the heart.
Exor'dium s. Beginning of anything, especially of a discourse.
Pla'gium s. The crime of kidnapping.
Pata'gium s. The fold of skin used in flying by bats, flying squirrels, etc.
Florile'gium s. An anthology.
Colle'gium s. An ecclesiastical body not controlled by the state.
Sporan'gium s. A spore-case.
Uropyg'ium s. The rump in birds.
Pteryg'ium s. Mass of hypertrophied conjunctiva.
Xenodoch'ium s. A guest-room, especially in a monastery.
Gal'ium s. A genus of herbaceous plants.
Gnaphal'ium s. A genus of woolly plants including the cudweed.
Myce'lium s. The spawn of fungi.
He'lium s. An inert gaseous element present in the atmosphere.
Epithe'lium s. The cell-tissues lining the alimentary canal and other surfaces.
Endothe'lium s. The membrane lining blood-vessels, etc.
Il'ium s. The upper part of the hip-bone.
Gal'lium s. A highly fusible, grey, metallic element.
Thal'lium s. A rare metallic element.
Prothal'lium s. The thalloid organ of ferns.
Pal'lium s. The ecclesiastical pall; the mantle of a mollusc.
Bdell'ium s. An Oriental resin.
Subsel'lium s. A projection under a seat in a choir-stall.
Beryl'lium s. Glucinum, a metallic element.
Taurobo'lium s. Ritual sacrifice of a bull and baptism in its blood.
Scho'lium s. A marginal annotation, especially of one of the classics.
Nebu'lium s. An element known only by a green line in the nebular spectrum.
Thala'mium s. A spore-case in algæ.
Epithala'mium s. A nuptial hymn.
Prothala'mium s. A marriage-song.
Cad'mium s. A malleable white metallic element.
Pre'mium s. A reward, bounty, prize to be won; a bonus, allowance.
Gelsem'ium s. A genus of climbing plants including the yellow jasmine.
Enco'mium s. Formal praise; eulogy, panegyric.
Chro'mium s. A steel-grey metallic element.
Os'mium s. A greyish metallic element.
Didym'ium s. A compound metal occurring in cerite.
Germa'nium s. A greyish metallic element.
Cra'nium s. The skull, brain-pan.
Pericra'nium s. The fibrous membrane investing the skull.
Gera'nium s. A widely distributed genus of plants including the crane's-bill.
Ura'nium s. A malleable radioactive metallic element.
Tita'nium s. A metallic element.
Prosce'nium s. Part of stage in front of drop-scene.
Ruthen'ium s. A spongy metallic element.
Selen'ium s. A non-metallic element resembling tellurium.
Tirocin'ium s. Apprenticeship, pupilage.
Delphin'ium s. The genus of plants comprising the Larkspurs.
Triclin'ium s. A dining-couch of the ancient Romans.
Min'ium s. Red lead; a vermilion pigment.
Postlimin'ium s. Right of restoration to former status, ownership, and nationality of things or persons taken in war.
Condomin'ium s. Joint ownership or sovereignty.
Alumin'ium s. A very light, malleable, and ductile white metallic element.
Decen'nium s. A period of ten years.
Bien'nium s. A period of two years.
Millen'nium s. The anticipated thousand-year reign of Christ on earth.
Quadren'nium s. A period of four years.
Septen'nium s. A period of seven years.
Quinquen'nium s. A period of five years.
Co'nium s. The genus containing the hemlock; a drug prepared from this.
Meco'nium s. Inspissated poppy juice.
Zirco'nium s. An earthy metallic element.
Syco'nium s. A multiple fruit, as the fig.
Pelargo'nium s. A fragrant plant of the geranium family with large, bright flowers.
Eupho'nium s. A large brass wind-instrument.
Polo'nium s. A radioactive substance found in pitchblende.
Stramo'nium s. A drug used for asthma.
Pandemo'nium s. Hell; the abode of the evil spirits; uproar, confusion.
Ammo'nium s. The compound radical contained in the salts produced by the action of ammonia on acids.
Harmo'nium s. A keyed musical instrument like a small organ.
O'pium s. A narcotic prepared from juice of the white poppy.
Gossyp'ium s. The genus of shrubs including the cotton-plant.
Bar'ium s. An element, one of the alkaline earths.
Columbar'ium s. A pigeon-house; a chamber in a catacomb.
Herbar'ium s. A collection of dried plants scientifically arranged.
Ophidar'ium s. A place for keeping snakes.
Tepidar'ium s. The central warm room in ancient Roman baths.
Caldar'ium s. A Roman hot bath.
Sudar'ium s. A napkin; especially that miraculously impressed with the face of Christ.
Solar'ium s. Room built for catching the sun's rays.
Oar'ium s. An ovary.
Sacrar'ium s. Space between altar and altar-rails; a bird's sacrum.

Cinerar'ium s. A storage-place for cremated remains.
Honorar'ium s. Fee for professional services.
Rosar'ium s. A rose-garden.
Insectar'ium s. A cage for breeding insects.
Planetar'ium s. A contrivance representing the motions and orbits of the planets.
Termitar'ium s. A cage for white ants.
Septar'ium s. A nodule with radiating fissures filled with foreign matter.
Aquar'ium s. A receptacle or building for keeping and exhibiting live fish.
Vivar'ium (-vair'-) s. Place for keeping animals in something approaching the natural state.
Equilib'rium s. Equality of weight or force; a just balance; state of rest produced by this.
Oppro'brium s. Reproach, disgrace; scurrilous language.
Teu'crium s. The germander.
Scolopen'drium s. The group of ferns containing the hart's-tongue.
Hypo-chon'drium s. A part of the abdomen.
Cer'ium s. A rare metallic element.
Megather'ium s. A gigantic extinct sloth from S. America.
Dinother'ium s. A gigantic fossil pachyderm.
Notother'ium s. An extinct gigantic marsupial of Australia.
Imper'ium s. Absolute power; command; dominion.
Elater'ium s. A powerful vegetable purgative.
Bacter'ium s. A genus of minute fission fungi.
Sericter'ium s. The spinning-gland of silkworms.
Psalter'ium s. The third stomach of a ruminant.
Acroter'ium s. A pedestal on a pediment; a pinnacle.
Magister'ium s. The teaching authority of the Roman Catholic Church.
Delir'ium s. Mental aberration; strong excitement; frenzy.
Cibor'ium s. A canopy over an altar, etc.; a covered chalice; a pyx.
Cor'ium s. Body-armour of the ancient Romans; the innermost layer of the skin.
Trifor'ium s. Gallery in wall over the arches of nave or choir.
Thor'ium s. A rare metallic element.
Empor'ium s. A mart, commercial centre; a large shop.
Suspensor'ium s. A supporting ligament, bone, etc.
Sensor'ium s. The nervous system; an organ of sense.
Aspersor'ium s. A vessel for holy water.
Sudator'ium s. A hot-air bath.
Cremator'ium s. A place where corpses are cremated.
Fumator'ium s. Room or apparatus for fumigating.
Sanator'ium s. Establishment for treatment of the sick, especially consumptives; a convalescent hospital.
Inclinator'ium s. A dipping-compass.
Morator'ium s. Period during which payment of debts is legally deferred.
Prosector'ium s. A dissecting laboratory.
Prætor'ium s. A Roman general's quarters in camp.
Auditor'ium s. Space occupied by an audience.
Scriptor'ium s. Place for writing, especially in a monastery.
Haustor'ium s. A sucker of a parasitic plant.
A'trium s. The entrance hall of a Roman dwelling.
Epigas'trium s. The upper part of the abdomen.
Mesogas'trium s. A band of peritoneum in the embryonic stomach.
Yt'trium s. A rare metallic element of the cerium group.
Tellur'ium s. A rare non-metallic element.
Collyr'ium s. An eye-salve.
Marty'rium s. A chapel to the honour of a martyr.
Gymna'sium s. A place for athletic and gymnastic exercises; a German secondary school of the highest grade.
Wa'sium s. Thorium.
Cæs'ium s. A rare alkaline metallic element.
Magne'sium s. A white, malleable, metallic element.
Sympo'sium s. A convivial meeting; a discussion embracing various views on some subject.
Potas'sium s. A lustrous metallic element.
Elys'ium s. The mythical abode of dead heroes; any delightful place.
Sola'tium s. A compensation.
Cyma'tium s. A cyma.
Pancra'tium s. A contest combining boxing and wrestling in the ancient Greek games.
Stron'tium s. A metallic element resembling calcium.
Sester'tium s. An ancient Roman money of account (1000 sesterces).
Consort'ium s. A coalition, amalgamation.
Nastur'tium s. A trailing plant with strongly scented, showy flowers.
Os'tium s. The mouth or opening of an organ.
Deliq'uium s. Faintness; swoon; a maudlin mood.
Quadriv'ium s. The mediæval course of study comprising arithmetic, astronomy, and music.
Triv'ium s. The three arts of grammar, logic, and rhetoric.
Lixiv'ium s. Lye.
Efflu'vium s. Exhalation from putrefying matter; a noxious smell.
Dilu'vium s. A deposit of earth, etc., caused by a flood.
Allu'vium s. Deposit made by running water, floods, etc.
Implu'vium s. The square rain-water tank of an ancient Roman house.
Complu'vium s. An opening in a roof.
Trape'zium s. A plane quadrilateral figure having no parallel sides; a bone in the carpus.
Oak'um s. Loose hemp; old, untwisted rope.
Bunk'um s. Talk for effect; anything done merely for show; humbug.
Al'um s. A white, crystalline mineral salt with astringent properties.
Tan'talum s. A silvery-white metallic element.
Hood'lum s. An American hooligan.
Ve'lum s. A membrane; the soft palate.
Glum a. Sullen, moody, dejected.
Hi'lum s. The scar where a seed was attached to its base.
Pi'lum s. The heavy javelin of the ancient Romans.
Val'lum s. A rampart.
Label'lum s. Part of the corolla of an orchid.
Flabel'lum s. The great fan borne in papal processions; a fan-like appendage.
Cerebel'lum s. The smaller, posterior brain.
Flagel'lum s. A whip-like appendage; a trailing shoot.
Skel'lum s. A scoundrel; a rotter.
Clitel'lum s. The thick part of an earth-worm.
Rostel'lum s. A beak-like part or process.
Haustel'lum s. The sucking organ of certain insects, etc.
Scutel'lum s. A small plate or scale on an animal's body.
Vell'um s. A fine kind of parchment.

Aspergil'lum s. A brush for sprinkling holy water.
Spiril'lum s. A genus of spiral-shaped bacteria.
Vexil'lum s. The square military flag of the ancient Romans; a bishop's pennon, processional banner; large upper petal of certain flowers.
Plum s. A fleshy fruit with a kernel; tree bearing this; a raisin; (*slang*) a fortune, windfall, £100,000.
Pep'lum s. The outer gown worn by ancient Greek women.
Slum s. A mean and dirty back street. v.i. To visit such for charitable purposes.
Tintinab'ulum s. A small bell; a jingling of such.
Pab'ulum s. Means of nutriment; food.
Acetab'ulum s. A socket, especially the socket of the hip-joint.
Diac'ulum s. Diachylon, an adhesive plaster.
Tenac'ulum s. A surgical instrument.
Hibernac'ulum s. Winter quarters of a hibernating animal.
Supernac'ulum s. Wine of the choicest kind.
Vibrac'ulum s. A filamentous appendage on some protozoans.
Umbrac'ulum s. An umbrella-shaped appendage to a plant.
Tentac'ulum s. A tentacle or vibrissa.
Sustentac'ulum s. A supporting tissue, part, etc.
Spec'ulum s. Surgeon's instrument for dilating body-passages for inspection; a reflector.
Spic'ulum s. A needle-like organ, etc.
Curric'ulum s. A fixed course of studies.
Retic'ulum s. The second stomach of ruminants.
Vin'culum s. A bond; a tie, especially in algebra.
Oper'culum s. The gill-cover of a fish; a closing lid or valve of a plant or animal.
Vas'culum s. A botanist's collecting-case.
Opus'culum s. An opuscule.
Pen'dulum s. A suspended body that swings freely.
Coag'ulum s. A coagulated mass; a blood-clot.
Cing'ulum s. The girdle of an alb.
Ros'trulum s. The beak of a flea.
Sep'tulum s. A small septum.
Asy'lum s. A refuge, a sanctuary; an institution for mental patients.
Mum s. A strong German beer. a. Silent. int. Hush! v.i. To play as a mummer.
Chrysan'themum s. A genus of composite plants.
Mesembryan'themum s. A bright-flowered genus of plants with fleshy leaves.
Min'imum s. The smallest amount, degree, etc. a. Least possible.
Max'imum s. Greatest degree or quantity. a. Greatest.
Olib'anum s. An aromatic resin used for incense.
Gal'banum s. A bitter, musky gum-resin formerly used in medicine.
Arca'num s. A mystery; something revealed only to initiates.
Lad'anum s. A dark, odorous resin.
Lau'danum s. Tincture of opium.
Orig'anum s. Wild marjoram.
Or'ganum s. (*Organon*).
Lan'thanum s. A rare metallic element.
Tym'panum s. The middle ear; the ear-drum; triangular face of a pediment.
Fræ'num s. A connecting membrane, as beneath the tongue.
Molybde'num s. A rare metallic element.
Duode'num s. The first portion of the small intestine.
Scale'num s. A scalene triangle.
Ple'num s. Space; a condition of fullness.
Sphag'num s. A genus of cryptogams.
Mag'num s. A two-quart bottle.
Interreg'num s. Period of vacancy of a throne, between two governments, etc.
Lig'num s. Wood.
Gluci'num s. The metallic element beryllium.
Antirrhi'num s. A genus of plants, the snapdragons.
Plat'inum s. A valuable, very ductile and malleable metallic element.
Polygo'num s. A genus of plants including the knot-grass, etc.
Ster'num s. The breast-bone.
Epister'num s. The upper part of the breast-bone.
Labur'num s. A yellow-flowered tree.
Vibur'num s. Genus of plants containing the honeysuckle, laurustinus, etc.
Alburn'um s. The soft part of wood next the bark.
Jeju'num s. A portion of the small intestine.
Pantoum' (-toom') s. An intricate kind of verse-form.
Wam'pum (wom'-) s. Small beads made of shells used by N. American Indians as money and ornaments.
Rum s. A spirit distilled from molasses. a. Queer, odd.
Ar'um s. A genus of plants containing the wake-robin and cuckoo-pint.
Lab'arum s. The standard with Christian symbols adopted by Constantine the Great.
Har'um-scar'um a. Wild; hare-brained.
Alar'um s. An alarm; an alarm-clock.
La'brum s. A lip or lip-like part.
Candelab'rum s. A branched candlestick.
Cer'ebrum s. The chief part of the brain.
Simula'crum s. Likeness; faint representation; sham.
Sa'crum s. The triangular bone forming the dorsal part of the pelvis.
Ful'crum s. Support on which a lever rests, point about which it moves.
Scrum s. A Scrummage.
Drum s. A hollow, cylindrical musical instrument beaten with sticks; a cylinder; the tympanum of the ear. v.i. To beat on a drum, make a continual tapping; to throb; to tout for customers, recruits, etc. v.t. To play on a drum; to summon or expel by beat of drum.
Ket'tledrum s. A hemispherical drum of brass or copper.
Hum'drum a. Dull; commonplace, stupid. s. A dull fellow; tedious talk; monotony.
Panjan'drum s. A self-important or high and mighty person.
Conun'drum s. A riddle, puzzling question.
Ser'um s. The thin, transparent portion of blood; watery part of curdled milk; lymph.
Thrum v.t. To drum, tap; to cover with thrums. v.i. To strum. s. End of weavers' threads cut off; any coarse yarn.
Bar'athrum s. A bottomless pit; anything insatiable.
Hydrar'girum s. Quicksilver.
Decor'um s. Seemliness, decency; polite usage.
Indecor'um s. Want of propriety; an unseemly act.
For'um s. A tribunal; platform for an orator; jurisdiction.

Varior'um s. Denoting an edition containing notes by various hands.
Jor'um s. A large drinking-vessel or its contents.
Cockalor'um s. A game of leap-frog.
Cus'tos
Rotulor'um s. The chief civil officer of a county.
Quor'um s. Number or company sufficient for transaction of business.
Vera'trum s. The hellebore.
Elec'trum s. An alloy of copper, zinc, and nickel; anciently an alloy of gold and silver, argentiferous gold.
Plec'trum s. Instrument for plucking or striking strings of musical instruments.
Tan'trum s. A burst of passion or ill-humour.
Epicen'trum s. The point over the focus of an earthquake.
Strum v.t. and i. To play unskilfully or carelessly.
Œs'trum s. The gad-fly; a vehement desire; the sexual heat of animals.
Seques'trum s. Dead bone detached but remaining in place.
Sis'trum s. A simple musical instrument of ancient Egypt.
Nos'trum s. A quack or patent medicine.
Ros'trum s. Beak of a bird or of a ship; a platform, pulpit.
Lus'trum s. Period of five years among the ancient Romans.
Bay-rum' s. An aromatic spirit used as a hair dressing.
Sum s. Aggregate of two or more numbers, etc.; the whole; essence; completion; arithmetical problem. v.t. To bring into one whole; to comprise.
Oma'sum s. The third stomach of a ruminant.
Gyp'sum s. Hydrous sulphate of calcium.
Odontoglos'sum s. A genus of brightly coloured orchids.
Opos'sum s. An American marsupial quadruped.
Alys'sum s. A genus of Cruciferous plants.
Da'tum s. An ascertained or granted fact from which others can be deduced.
Ultima'tum s. A final proposition or condition.
Poma'tum s. An ointment for the hair. v.t. To apply this.
Desidera'tum s. That of which the lack is felt; a want generally acknowledged.
Erra'tum s. A mistake in printing or writing.
Stra'tum s. A layer spread out horizontally.
Substra'tum s. That which is spread under; an underlying layer.
Superstra'tum s. A stratum resting on another.
Rec'tum s. The lowest part of the large intestine.
Dic'tum s. A positive assertion; a proverb.
Sanc'tum s. A retreat for privacy.
Punc'tum s. A spot, point of colour; punctilio.
Salice'tum s. A garden of willows.
Querce'tum s. A collection of living oaks.
Arbore'tum s. An enclosure for growing rare trees.
Equise'tum s. The genus of Cryptgams containing the horsetails.
Adian'tum s. A genus of ferns (maidenhair, etc.).
Quan'tum s. Quantity; amount.
Amen'tum s. A catkin.
Ramen'tum s. Membranous scales formed on leaves, etc.
Omen'tum s. A membranous covering of part of the bowels; the caul.
Momen'tum s. Impetus; force possessed by matter in motion.
Tomen'tum s. Pubescence on leaves composed of matted hairs.
Sarmen'tum s. A prostrate shoot, a runner.
Tormen'tum s. An ancient war-engine.
Scro'tum s. The bag containing the testicles.
Facto'tum s. A man-of-all-work, a handy-man.
Teeto'tum s. A small top marked with numbers, used in games of chance.
Sep'tum s. A partition, especially in a cell, the heart, nose, etc.
Stum s. Unfermented grape-juice. v.t. To renew (wine) by mixing must with it.
Frus'tum s. The part of a cone, etc., remaining when the top is cut off by a plane parallel to the base.
Spu'tum s. Spittle; expectorated matter from the lungs.
Ady'tum s. A shrine; an inner chamber.
Vac'uum s. Space unoccupied by matter or from which the air has been exhausted; a void.
Resid'uum s. That which is left after any process of separation or purification.
Men'struum s. A solvent.
O'vum s. The female germ which develops into an embryo after fertilization; an ovule; an egg.
Swum past part. (*Swim*).
Shawm s. An obsolete clarinet-like wind instrument.
On'ym s. A technical term.
Pseud'onym s. An assumed name.
Hom'onym s. A word having the same sound (and usually spelling) as another but differing from it in meaning.
An'onym s. One who conceals his true name; a pseudonym.
Mon'onym s. A name consisting of a single word.
Syn'onym s. A word having the same meaning as another.
Ep'onym s. One whose name is given to a place, period, people, etc.
Typ'onym s. A name based on a type.
Par'onym s. A paronymous word.
Het'eronym s. A word having two or more pronunciations and meanings (*e.g.* *bow*).
An'tonym s. A word expressing the contrary of another.
Cryp'tonym s. A secret name.
Polyon'ym s. A synonym.
An a. The indefinite article before a vowel or mute h.
Ban s. A curse, excommunication, interdiction; a Croatian governor. v.t. To proclaim, outlaw, forbid.
The'ban a. and s. Pertaining to or a native of ancient Thebes.
Cor'ban s. A Jewish offering to God.
Ur'ban a. Pertaining to a town or city.
Subur'ban a. Pertaining to, of the nature of, or inhabiting a suburb. s. A dweller in a suburb.
Tur'ban s. An Oriental head-dress.
Ses'ban s. A tropical bean.
Can s. A metal vessel or cup for liquors. v.i. To be able.
Bar'acan s. A coarse kind of cloth.
Malacos'tracan a. and s. Belonging to or a member of the division of crustaceans containing the crabs and lobsters.
Pecan' s. A variety of hickory.
Bar'bican s. An advanced work defending the entrance to a fortress.
In'dican s. A constituent of the indigo-plant.
Pub'lican s. A tavern-keeper; formerly a collector of taxes.
Repub'lican a. Pertaining to, consisting of, or characteristic of a republic. s. An advocate of republican principles.

Pel'ican s. A large, web-footed bird with an enormous bill.
An'glican a. Pertaining to the established Church of England. s. A member of this, especially of the High Church School.
Basil'ican a. (*Basilica*).
Gal'lican a. Pertaining to the ancient Church of France; ultramontane.
Pem'mican s. Dried meat pounded and mixed with fat, etc.
Domin'ican s. One of an order of friars founded by St. Dominic (1216). a. Pertaining to this order.
Coper'nican a. Pertaining to the astronomical system of Copernicus.
Amer'ican a. Pertaining to America, or to the United States. s. A citizen of the U.S.A.
Armor'ican a. Pertaining to Brittany (formerly Armorica).
Vat'ican s. The palace of the Pope; papal authority.
Mex'ican a. Pertaining to Mexico. s. A native or inhabitant.
Can'can s. A wild kind of French dance.
Coon'-can s. A game of cards.
Scan v.t. To scrutinize; to mark or measure by metrical feet. v.i. To be metrically correct.
Francis'can s. A mendicant friar of the order of St. Francis. a. Pertaining to St. Francis or to his order of Grey Friars.
Pris'can a. Primitive, pristine.
Os'can s. One of an ancient Italian people; their language. a. Pertaining to this.
Mollus'can a. and s. Pertaining to or one of the molluscs; snail-like.
el'la Crus'can a. Artificial, affected (of literary style).
Etrus'can a. and n. Etrurian.
Tus'can a. and s. Pertaining to, or a native, or the language of Tuscany.
Antelu'can a. Of the time just before daybreak.
ou'can (too'-) s. A brilliant American bird with an enormous beak.
Bil'ly-can s. An Australian bushman's teapot.
Ramadan' s. The annual fast of the Mohammedans.
oham'medan s. A follower of or believer in Mohammed and his religion. a. Pertaining to Mohammed or Mohammedanism.
Redan' s. A projecting salient in a fort.
Sedan' s. A covered chair for carrying a single person.
Annel'idan s. An annelid. a. Pertaining to these.
Meru'lidan a. Pertaining to birds of the thrush family.
Arach'nidan a. Belonging to the spider family, s. A member of this.
Echin'idan s. A sea-urchin.
Op'pidan s. A boy at Eton not on the foundation.
Acar'idan a. Pertaining to the mites or ticks. s. One of these insects.
Har'ridan s. A decayed strumpet, an old vixen.
Sol'dan s. Mediæval Eastern ruler; sultan.
Ran'dan s. A pleasure-boat for three rowers; (*slang*) a spree.
Hexap'odan s. Hexapod.
Shan'drydan s. A light cart; a hooded chaise; a broken-down vehicle.
-ean suff. Belonging to; like.
Ean v.i. To bring forth lambs.
Manichæ'an s. A follower of the third-century Persian heretic, Manes. a. Pertaining to this heresy or its adherents.
Spelæ'an a. Pertaining to or inhabiting caves.
Aramæ'an a. Pertaining to Syria or its language. s. A Syrian; the Syrian language.
Linnæ'an a. Pertaining to Linnæus or his botanical classification.
Pæ'an s. A song of rejoicing or triumph.
Bean s. A kidney-shaped seed in a long pod.
Amœbe'an a. (*Amœba*).
Bog'bean s. The buckbean.
Buck'bean s. A water-plant with pinkish-white flowers.
Jacobe'an a. Of the reign or period of James I.
Phocace'an a. Phocine.
Solena'cean s. A mollusc of the Razor-fish family a. Pertaining to this family.
Ostra'cean s. A bivalve mollusc; one of the oyster family.
Rosa'cean s. A member of the Rose family.
Ceta'cean s. A member of the Cetacea, a whale, dolphin, etc. a. Belonging to this order.
Testa'cean s. A shell-fish, mollusc.
Crusta'cean s. One of the Crustacea. a. Belonging to this class.
Laodice'an a. Lukewarm, especially in matters of religion.
Lynce'an a. Pertaining to the lynx; sharp-sighted.
O'cean s. The sea as a whole; one of the great areas into which this is divided. a. Pertaining to this.
Cadu'cean a. (*Caduceus*).
Sadduce'an a. Pertaining to the Sadducees.
Dean s. An ecclesiastical, university, or collegiate dignitary.
Asclepiade'an a. Of or pertaining to the Asclepiad metre.
Sotade'an a. Sotadic.
Archimede'an a. Pertaining to the ancient Greek mathematician, Archimedes.
Proboscid'ean a. Having a proboscis. s. Such an animal.
Orchid'ean a. Belonging to the orchid family.
Euclid'ean a. Pertaining to or according to the axioms, etc., of Euclid.
Arachnid'ean a. (*Arachnidan*).
Clupeoi'dean a. Clupeoid.
Acaride'an a. (*Acaridan*).
Chalde'an a. Pertaining to Chaldea or its language. s. The language or a native of Chaldea.
Pande'an a. Pertaining to the god Pan.
Antipode'an a. (*Antipodes*).
Gean s. The wild cherry.
Perige'an a. Pertaining to the perigee.
Palæoge'an a. Pertaining to the early conditions of the earth's surface.
Apoge'an a. (*Apogee*).
Auge'an a. Filthy, almost beyond purifying.
Trache'an a. Pertaining to the trachea.
Nymphe'an a. Pertaining to, appropriate to, or inhabited by nymphs; pupal.
Orphe'an a. Pertaining to Orpheus; melodious.
Lethe'an a. Causing or pertaining to oblivion.
Prome'thean a. Inspiring; having a life-giving quality.
Jean s. A twilled cotton cloth.
Skean s. A Highlander's dagger.
Lean v.i. To rest against; to slope or slant; to tend towards. v.t. To cause to lean; to support. s. A leaning, slope; part of meat without fat. a. Thin, not plump; consisting of muscular tissue; meagre; sterile; unremunerative.

Clean a. Free from dirt; without stain or defect; pure, sinless; free from limitation; complete. adv. Quite, entirely, adroitly. v.t. To free from dirt, to purify.
Sophocle'an a. Pertaining to or characteristic of Sophocles.
Glean v.t. To gather what reapers leave behind; to pick up here and there.
Coch'lean a. (*Cochlear*).
Galile'an a. Pertaining to Galilee; pertaining to Galileo or to the telescope invented by him. s. A native of Galilee.
Zoil'ean a. Malignant, severe (of criticism).
Achille'an a. Heroic; invincible; like Achilles.
Hercu'lean a. Tremendously strong; exceedingly difficult.
Ceru'lean a. Sky-blue.
Mean v.t. To purpose; to signify. v.i. To have meaning. a. Low-minded, base; stingy; contemptible; middle; intermediate. s. Average rate or degree; middle state.
Cadme'an a. Applied to a victory that brings disaster to the victor.
Bemean' v.t. To debase.
Demean' v.t. To behave; to debase (oneself).
Misdemean' v.i. To behave ill.
Pygme'an a. Dwarfish; little.
Subterra'nean a. Under the earth.
Hymene'an a. Hymeneal.
Ebur'nean a. Made of ivory.
Etne'an a. Pertaining to Mount Etna.
Pean s. An heraldic fur.
Priape'an a. Pertaining to Priapus, the Roman god of procreation.
Cyclope'an a. Pertaining to the Cyclops; immense, gigantic.
Europe'an a. Pertaining to Europe or its inhabitants. s. A native of Europe.
Trappe'an a. Consisting of or resembling trap (rock).
Euter'pean a. Pertaining to Euterpe or to music.
Cæsar'ean a. (*Cæsarian*).
Nectar'ean a. Resembling or sweet as nectar.
Tartar'ean a. Pertaining to Tartarus; hellish.
Cythere'an a. Pertaining to Venus or to sexual love.
Vener'ean a. Lustful.
Hyperbor'ean s. A dweller in the most northerly regions. a. Very far north; Arctic; frigid.
Pythagore'an s. A follower of the ancient philosopher Pythagoras. a. Pertaining to him or his philosophy.
Terpischore'an a. Pertaining to dancing.
Marmor'ean a. Like or made of marble.
Epicure'an a. Belonging to the school of philosophy founded by Epicurus; devoted to pleasure, sensuous. s. A follower of Epicurus; a gourmand, sensualist.
Empyre'an s. The highest heaven, supposed by the ancients to be the only seat of pure fire. a. Empyreal; pertaining to the empyrean or to the upper sky.
Theocrite'an a. In the style of Theocritus; pastoral.
Dante'an a. Relating to or in the style of Dante; sombre.
Gigante'an a. Gigantic.
Atlante'an a. Huge, colossal.
Adamante'an a. Excessively hard; unbending.
Prote'an a. Readily changing form or appearance.
Nemer'tean s. A marine worm.
Costean' v.i. To sink shafts to the rock in search of a lode.
Teleos'tean a. Pertaining to the Teleostei, an order of osseous fishes. s. A fish of this order.
Procrus'tean a. Violently reducing to strict conformity.
Glute'an a. Pertaining to the buttocks.
Quean s. A wench, slut; a woman.
Wean v.t. To accustom to do without the breast; to detach, disengage from s. (*Scot.*) A child.
Yean v.t. and i. To give birth to (of sheep, etc.).
Fan s. An instrument to agitate the air or for winnowing grain; a wing. v.t. To cool with a fan; to winnow; to stimulate.
Phylloph'agan s. An animal feeding on leaves.
Xyloph'agan s. An insect that bores into wood.
Zooph'agan a. Feeding on animals. s. One who or that which does this.
Saproph'agan s. A beetle living on putrid matter.
Coproph'agan s. A beetle or other insect living on dung.
Rhizoph'agan a. Rhizophagous; an animal that subsists on roots.
Lag'an s. Wreckage lying at the bottom of the sea.
Pa'gan s. A heathen; one neither Christian, Jew, nor Mohammedan. a. Pertaining to the worship or worshippers of false gods; heathen.
Suf'fragan a. Assisting. s. An assistant bishop
Sa'gan s. Deputy of the Jewish High Priest
Began' v. (past) (*Begin*).
Balbrig'gan s. Knitted cotton hose, etc.
Tobog'gan s. A sled for sliding on snow. v.i. To use this.
Car'digan s. A knitted woollen waistcoat with sleeves.
Hoo'ligan s. A young ruffian, a street rowdy.
Ptar'migan s. A bird of the grouse family.
Or'igan s. Wild marjoram.
Wig'an s. A canvas-like cotton fabric.
Lo'gan s. A large naturally balanced stone.
Slo'gan s. A Highland war-cry; a watchword, motto.
Or'gan s. Instrument or means; part of a living being by which some function is performed; a large keyed, musical wind-instrument a newspaper.
Clach'an s. A Highland village.
Yat'aghan s. The long, double-curved Turkish dagger.
Khan s. A ruler or chief in Tartary Afghanistan, etc.; a caravansera
Astrakhan' s. Fine furry wool from Persia lambs.
Acaleph'an s. A jelly-fish. a. Belonging to th family.
Or'phan s. A child bereaved of one parent o both. a. Bereft thus.
Than conj.
Levi'athan s. An immense sea-monster; a ver large ship.
Pathan' (-tan') s. A turbulent, independent Afgha
Elizabeth'an a. Pertaining to the times of Quee Elizabeth, or to the architectur literature, etc., of those times. A writer of that period.
-ian suff. Forming nouns or adjectives.
Altai'an a. Of the peoples (or their language near the Altai mountains.
Fa'bian a. Delaying, dilatory; cautious.
Ara'bian a. Pertaining to Arabia or i language. s. A native or t language of Arabia.

Sa'bian s. One of an ancient Eastern religious sect.
Swa'bian a and s. Pertaining to or a native of Swabia.
Amphib'ian s., a. (*Amphibia*).
Micro'bian a. Microbial.
Serb'ian a. and s. Serb.
Les'bian a. and s. Pertaining to or a native of Lesbos.
Ru'bian s. The colouring principle of madder.
Gynæ'cian a. Relating to women.
Gre'cian a. Pertaining to Greece. s. A Greek; a Greek scholar.
Magic'ian s. One skilled in magic, a sorcerer; a conjurer.
Logic'ian s. One skilled in logic.
Academi'cian s. A member of an academy.
Mechanic'ian s. One skilled in mechanics; a machine maker or worker.
Rhetori'cian s. One versed in or who teaches the art of rhetoric; a bombastic or artificial orator.
Patri'cian a. Of noble birth; pertaining to or appropriate to a noble. s. One of high birth or noble family.
Electri'cian s. One skilled in the science and application of electricity.
Metri'cian s. A metrist.
Symmetri'cian s. A symmetrist.
Geometri'cian s. One skilled in geometry.
Obstetri'cian s. One skilled in obstetrics.
Musi'cian s. One skilled in the art of music.
Physi'cian s. A doctor, one skilled in medicine.
Metaphysi'cian s. One skilled in metaphysics.
Mathemati'cian s. One versed in mathematics.
Practi'cian s. A practitioner.
Tacti'cian s. One skilled in tactics.
Dialectic'ian s. A logician, one skilled in dialectics.
Arithmeti'cian s. One skilled in arithmetic.
Phoneti'cian s. One versed in phonetics.
Theoreti'cian s. A theorist.
Politi'cian s. One versed in the science of, or taking part in, government; one devoted to politics.
Opti'cian s. A maker of or dealer in optical instruments.
Statisti'cian s. One versed in the science of statistics.
Acousti'cian s. A student or professor of acoustics.
Cister'cian s. One of an order of Benedictine monks. a. Pertaining to this order.
Confu'cian a. and s. Pertaining to or a follower of Confucius.
Rosicru'cian s. A member of an occult secret society. a. Pertaining to this society.
Aca'dian a. Belonging to Nova Scotia. s. A native or inhabitant of this.
Accad'ian a. Pertaining to a Sumerian or pre-Semitic race in Babylonia, or to its language. s. A member or the language of this race.
Arca'dian a. Ideally pastoral. s. An ideal rustic.
Orca'dian a. and s. Pertaining to or a native of the Orkneys.
Palla'dian a. Of the architectural school of Palladio (d. 1580).
Cana'dian s. Pertaining to Canada. s. An inhabitant of Canada.
Ra'dian s. An arc equal in length to its radius; angle subtending such an arc.
Trage'dian s. An actor in or writer of tragedies.
Me'dian a. Situated in or passing through or along the middle; intermediate.
Come'dian s. An actor or writer of comedy.
Ascid'ian a. (*Ascidia*).
Nereid'ian a. Pertaining to the nereids. s. A nereid.
Nullifid'ian s. An infidel. a. Having no religion.
Solifid'ian s. One who maintains that faith alone is sufficient for justification.
Rachid'ian a. Vertebral; spinal.
Aphid'ian s. An aphis or plant-louse. a. Pertaining to these.
Ophid'ian a. Belonging to the Reptilian family of snakes. s. A snake.
Merid'ian s. An imaginary great circle on the earth's surface; midday; culmination.
Postmerid'ian a. Pertaining to or in the afternoon.
Obsid'ian s. A dark vitreous lava.
Quotid'ian a. Occurring daily. s. Anything returning daily, especially a fever.
Dravid'ian a. Pertaining to the aboriginal races of India or to their language.
Ovid'ian a. In the manner of Ovid (Roman poet).
In'dian a. Pertaining to India, the E. or W. Indies, or to the American aborigines. s. A native of India or the Indies; one of the aborigines of America.
Proso'dian s. A prosodist.
Custo'dian s. A keeper, superintendent.
Guard'ian s. A protector, keeper, warden. a. Protecting.
Gor'dian a. Complicated; hard to solve or unravel.
Lyd'ian a. Pertaining to Lydia (Asia Minor); effeminate. s. A native or the language of Lydia.
Plebei'an (-be'an) a. Pertaining to or consisting of the common people. s. One of the lower classes.
Hyge'ian a. Pertaining to health or hygiene.
Saf'fian s. A variety of leather tanned with sumac.
Ruf'fian s. A brutal man, a lawless desperado. a. Brutal.
Pela'gian s. A follower of the heretical fourth-century monk, Pelagius. a. Pertaining to the deep or open sea.
Archipela'gian a. and s. (*Archipelago*).
Ma'gian a. Pertaining to the Magi or to Magianism. s. A Magus.
Brodingna'gian a. Huge, enormous.
Colle'gian s. A member of a college.
Norwe'gian s. A native or the language of Norway. a. Pertaining to Norway or its people.
Glaswe'gian s. A native of Glasgow.
Cantabrig'ian a. Relating to Cambridge University. s. A member of this.
Bel'gian a. Pertaining to Belgium, its language, or inhabitants; a native of Belgium.
Spong'ian (spunj'-) a. Pertaining to the sponges.
Theolo'gian s. One versed in theology; a divine.
Neolo'gian s. A neologist. a. Neological.
Swedenbor'gian s. Member of a certain mystical sect. a. Pertaining to this sect or its doctrines.
Geor'gian a. Relating to a period of English history when a George was king; pertaining to Georgia. s. A native of Georgia.
Ogyg'ian a. Primæval; of remotest antiquity.
Malacop-teryg'ian a. Belonging to the group of soft-finned fishes.
Styg'ian a. Pertaining to the River Styx gloomy.
Sela'chian s. A fish of the shark family. Pertaining to this family.
Walla'chian s. A native or the language of Wallachia in Roumania. a. Pertaining to Wallachia or its people.

Noa'chian a. Noachic.

Batrach'ian a., s. (*Batrachia*).

Eusta'chian a. Pertaining to the Italian sixteenth-century physician, Eustachius.

Aristarch'ian a. Severely critical.

Pa'phian a. Pertaining to Venus or her worship. s. A courtesan.

Delph'ian a. (*Delphic*).

Christa-del'phian s. A sect, or member of a sect, claiming apostolic origin.

Didel'phian a. Pertaining to the didelphia.

Hyacin'thian a. Hyacinthine.

Corinth'ian a. Pertaining to Corinth; applied to an ornate order of architecture; licentious; elaborate. s. A gay man-about-town.

Labyrin'thian a. Winding; intricate.

Scyth'ian a. Pertaining to ancient Scythia or its people. s. One of this race; its language.

Pyth'ian a. Pertaining to the priestess of Apollo at Delphi, her oracles, or to the games held there every four years.

Pickwick'ian a. Denoting some sense other than the obvious one; merely technical.

Dæda'lian a. Labyrinthine, curiously wrought, dædal.

Sesqui-peda'lian a. Measuring a foot and a half; many-syllabled; given to using long words. s. A pedantic, many-syllabled word.

Mamma'lian a. Pertaining to the mammalia.

Bacchana'lian a. (*Bacchanal*).

Saturna'lian a. Pertaining to the Saturnalia, or to unrestrained licentiousness.

Episcopa'lian a. Pertaining to episcopacy or government by bishops. s. One belonging to an episcopal church.

Non-episcopa'lian a. and s. (*Negative*).

Austra'lian a. Pertaining to Australia. s. An inhabitant of this.

Sa'lian a. Pertaining to the ancient Roman priests of Mars; pertaining to an ancient Frankish tribe of the Lower Rhine.

Ital'ian a. Pertaining to Italy. s. A native or the language of Italy.

Placenta'lian s. A mammal having a placenta.

Casta'lian a. Pertaining to Castalia or to the Muses; poetical.

Liverpud'lian s. A native of Liverpool.

De'lian a. Pertaining to Delos.

Mende'lian a. Pertaining to Mendelism.

Mephisto-phe'lian a. Crafty; scoffing; sardonic.

Carne'lian, Corne'lian s. A red variety of chalcedony.

Corne'lian s. A variety of chalcedony; the wild cornel.

Opisthocœ'lian s. An animal whose vertebræ are hollow behind.

Aure'lian a. Golden. s. An Entomologist.

Aristote'lian a. (*Aristotelean*).

An'glian a. Pertaining to the Angles, early colonizers of Britain.

Zwing'lian a. and s. Pertaining to or a follower of the Swiss Reformer, Zwingli (d. 1531).

Perfectibil'ian s. A perfectionist.

Crocodil'ian a. Pertaining to a crocodile.

Virgil'ian a. Pertaining to or in the style of Virgil.

Reptil'ian a. Pertaining to or resembling a reptile. s. A reptile.

Lacertil'ian a. Belonging to the reptilian order Lacertilia.

Civil'ian s. One not belonging to the arme forces; one learned in Civil law

Exil'ian a. Exilic.

Pre-exil'ian a. Pre-exilic.

Machiavel'lian a. Crafty; addicted to intrigue politically cunning.

Boswel'lian a. In the style of James Boswel biographer of Dr. Johnson.

Tul'lian a. In the style of Cicero.

Æo'lian a. Pertaining to Æolia, or to Æolu god of the winds.

Mongo'lian a. Pertaining to Mongolia or i people. s. A Mongol; the la guage of these.

Capito'lian a. Pertaining to the Capitol ancient Rome.

Ju'lian a. Pertaining to or originated b Julius Cæsar.

Allophyl'ian a. Of non-Aryan and non-Semit race.

Polyga'mian a. State of bearing hermaphrodi and unisexual flowers on the sam plant.

Bohe'mian s. A native of or the language Bohemia; a gipsy; one living free, unconventional life. a. Fr and easy; unsettled; unr strained by the conventions society.

Is'thmian a. Pertaining to the Isthmus Corinth or to the games ancient celebrated there.

Sim'ian a. Ape-like. s. An anthropoid ape.

Podophthal'mian s. A stalk-eyed crustacean.

Antinom'ian a. Opposed to the moral law. s. On holding that this is not binding o Christians.

Per'mian a. Belonging to the uppermo Palæozoic strata or system.

Ver'mian a. Worm-like.

Ban'ian s. A Hindu merchant; the India fig-tree.

Ocea'nian a. and s. Pertaining to or an inhab tant of Oceania.

Zela'nian a. Pertaining to New Zealand.

Pomera'nian s. A small, long-haired breed of dog the spitz-dog; a native of Pom erania. a. Pert. to Pomerania.

Ira'nian a. Pertaining to Persia. s. Persian; the Persian group languages.

Tura'nian a. Altaic, Scythian.

Lithua'nian s. and a. A native of, the language o or pertaining to Lithuania.

Transylva'nian a. and s. Pertaining to or a native Transylvania.

Fe'nian s. A member of an Irish secre society which endeavoured to se up a separate republic.

Ruthe'nian a. Pertaining to the Ruthenes or the language. s. A Ruthene; the language.

Arme'nian s. A native or the language Armenia. a. Pertaining to A menia or its language.

Sire'nian s. A marine mammal allied to th whales. a. Pertaining to these.

Slove'nian a. Pertaining to the Slovenes; the language.

Socin'ian s. A follower of Socinus, a Unitaria a. Pertaining to this creed or i adherents.

Sardin'ian s. A native of Sardinia. a. Pert. the island or the former kingdom

Armin'ian s. One who maintains the doctrin of free-will. a. Pertaining to A minius, the Dutch theologian wh (c. 1600) advocated this.

Abyssin'ian a. Pertaining to Abyssinia or its inhabitants. s. A native of this country.
Eleusin'ian a. Pertaining to Eleusis, or to the secret rites there celebrated to Demeter; esoteric.
Augus'tinian a. Pertaining to St. Augustine, fifth-century Bishop of Hippo, to his doctrines, or to the order of friars named after him. s. One of these friars.
Darwin'ian a. Pertaining to Darwin or Darwinism. s. An adherent of Darwin's scientific theories.
Hun'nian a. Hunnic.
Ao'nian a. Pertaining to Aonia, or to the Muses.
Serbo'nian a. Denoting a difficulty from which there is no escape.
Baco'nian a. Pertaining to Francis Bacon, his philosophy, or the fancy that credits him with the authorship of the plays, etc., known as Shakespeare's. s. An upholder of this fancy.
Draco'nian a. Inflexible; extremely rigorous or cruel (of laws).
Helico'nian s. Pertaining to Helicon or the Muses.
Caledo'nian a. Pertaining to Scotland, the ancient Caledonia. s. A Scotsman.
Sardo'nian a. Being sardonic. s. A sardonic person.
Aberdo'nian s. A native of Aberdeen.
Gorgon'ian a. Pertaining to or like a Gorgon.
Pyrrho'nian a. Pertaining to or imbued with Pyrrhonism.
Chtho'nian a. (*Chthonic*).
Io'nian a. Pertaining to Ionia or its people. s. An ancient inhabitant of Ionia; the Greek dialect of Ionia.
Chelo'nian a. and s. (*Chelonia*).
Babylo'nian a. Pertaining to Babylon; magnificent, luxurious. s. An inhabitant of Babylon.
Demo'nian a. Demoniac.
Lappo'nian a. Lappish.
Cicero'nian a. Easy, flowing; in the style of Cicero.
Nero'nian a. Pertaining to or like Nero; tyrannical; debauched.
Johnson'ian a. Pertaining to Dr. Johnson or his style; pompous.
Eto'nian s. One educated at Eton.
Milton'ian a. Miltonic.
Pluto'nian a. Pertaining to Pluto, or to the interior of the earth; infernal.
Newton'ian a. Pertaining to Sir Isaac Newton or his theories; discovered or invented by him.
Favo'nian a. Pertaining to the west wind; mild; auspicious.
Slavo'nian a. and s. Slavonic.
Pavo'nian a. Pavonine; peacock-like.
Devo'nian a. Pertaining to Devon, or to the Old Red Sandstone. s. A native of Devon.
Oxo'nian s. A member of Oxford University. a. Pertaining to this or to Oxford.
Amazo'nian a. (*Amazon*).
Bezo'nian s. A beggar.
Hiber'nian a. Pertaining to Ireland. s. An Irishman.
Aver'nian a. Hellish; pertaining to Lake Avernus, near the entrance to Hades.
Eburn'ian a. Of or like ivory.
Satur'nian a. Pertaining to Saturn, or to the Golden Age.
Mancu'nian s. A native of Manchester.
Neptu'nian a. Pertaining to Neptune or the sea deposited by the sea (of rocks). s. A Neptunist.
Tetragyn'ian a. Having four pistils.
Pentagyn'ian a. Denoting a plant with five pistils.
Heptagyn'ian a. Having seven pistils.
Hexagyn'ian a. Hexagynous.
Æscula'pian a. Pertaining to Æsculapius, the Roman god of medicine, to doctors, or to the healing art.
Olym'pian a. Pertaining to Mount Olympus, the home of the Greek gods; celestial; godlike. s. One of the Greek gods.
Cornuco'pian a. Pertaining to the cornucopia or to abundance.
Salo'pian s. and a. A native of, or pertaining to, Shropshire.
Fallo'pian a. Denoting certain ducts in mammals discovered by Fallopius (sixteenth-century Italian anatomist).
Uto'pian a. Ideal; impracticable.
Thes'pian a. Pertaining to dramatic acting. s. An actor.
Ar'ian s. A follower of Arius. a. Pertaining to this fourth-century heretic, or to his doctrines.
Barbar'ian s. A brutal, savage, or uncultured person.
Araucar'ian a. (*Araucaria*).
Abecedar'ian a. Alphabetical. s. One who teaches or is learning the alphabet.
Trachear'ian s. One of a division of arachnids having tracheæ.
Shakespear'ian a. Pertaining to Shakespeare; resembling his style.
Vulgar'ian s. A vulgar, rich person. a. Vulgar.
Nothingar'ian a. Believing nothing. s. One belonging to no particular sect or party.
Hungar'ian a. Pertaining to Hungary. s. A native or the language of Hungary.
Diar'ian s. A diarist.
Apiar'ian a. Relating to bees. s. A bee-keeper.
Topiar'ian a. Pertaining to the topiary art.
Euskar'ian a. Basque. s. The language of the Basques; a Basque.
Malar'ian s. Malarial.
Turbellar'ian a. and s. Pertaining to or one of the Turbellaria.
Procellar'ian s. A bird of the petrel family. a. Belonging to this family.
Radiolar'ian a. Pertaining to the protozoa, Radialaria. s. One of these.
Hexaplar'ian a. Hexaplar.
Aular'ian a. Pertaining to a hall, especially as opposed to a college.
Tipular'ian a. and s. Pertaining to or one of the crane-flies.
Mar'ian a. and s. Pertaining to or an adherent of Queen Mary; pertaining to the Virgin Mary.
Grammar'ian s. One versed in grammar; a philologist.
Planar'ian s. A minute, flat, marine or fresh-water worm.
Nonagenar'ian s. One who is ninety years old, or in his nineties. a. Ninety years old.
Quinquagenar'ian s. A person fifty years old. a. Fifty years old.
Septuagenar'ian s. One between sixty-nine and eighty years old. a. Of such an age.
Sexagenar'ian s. One between fifty-nine and seventy years of age. a. Of such an age.
Octogenar'ian s. One of eighty years old, or between eighty and ninety. a. Octogenary.

Millenar'ian a. Consisting of one thousand years; pertaining to the millennium. s. One who believes in this.
Premillenar'ian s. One holding that the Second Advent will precede the millennium.
Catenar'ian a. Like a chain.
Centenar'ian s. A person one hundred years (or more) old.
Valetudinar'ian s. An invalid. a. Infirm; sickly.
Latitudinar'ian s. One who does not attach much importance to dogma; one not rigidly orthodox. a. Free from prejudice; lax in matters of religion.
Plati-tudinar'ian s. and a. One who indulges in, or indulging in, platitudes.
Disciplinar'ian s. One who enforces rigid discipline. a. Disciplinary.
Predestinar'ian s. One maintaining the doctrine of predestination. a. Pertaining to this.
Alcyonar'ian s. A zoophyte.
Lunar'ian s. An inhabitant of or investigator of the moon.
Par'ian a. Pertaining to Paros or its marble. s. A fine porcelain clay.
Ripar'ian a. Pertaining to the bank of a river. s. Owner of riverside property.
Librar'ian s. One in charge of a library.
Agrar'ian a. Pertaining to landed property or to fields; growing wild.
Cæsar'ian a. Pertaining to Julius Cæsar; imperial. s. A supporter of autocracy.
Rosar'ian s. A rose-fancier.
Infralapsar'ian s. A Calvinist who held that the elect were already fallen at the time of election. a. Holding this doctrine.
Supralapsar'ian s. A Calvinist who believed that election was decreed before the Fall. a. Pertaining to this doctrine.
Sublapsar'ian a. Infralapsarian.
Sabbatar'ian s. One regarding the seventh day of the week as the Sabbath; a strict observer of Sunday or the Sabbath. a. Pertaining to the Sabbath or the Sabbatarians.
Celibatar'ian s. A celibate.
Tractar'ian a. and s. Pertaining to or a supporter of Tractarianism.
Sectar'ian a. Pertaining, belonging, or peculiar to a sect. s. One of a sect; a schismatic.
Vegetar'ian s. One who abstains from animal food. a. Pertaining to such or to their principles, etc.
Proletar'ian a. Pertaining to the common people. s. One of the proletariat.
Utilitar'ian a. Pertaining to utility or to utilitarianism. s. An adherent of this.
Limitar'ian s. One believing in limited redemption. a. Tending to limit.
Humanitar'ian a. Humane. s. A philanthropist; one holding Christ to have been mere man; one believing in the unaided perfectibility of human nature.
Sanitar'ian s. One skilled in or an advocate of hygiene.
Trinitar'ian a. Pertaining to the doctrine of the Trinity. s. One holding this.
Unitar'ian s. A Christian not accepting the doctrine of the Trinity. a. Pertaining to Unitarians.
Necessitar'ian s. One holding that man's actions, etc., are predetermined.
Ubiquitar'ian s. One adhering to ubiquitarianism.
Fruitar'ian s. One who limits his diet to fruit.
Parlia-mentar'ian s. One experienced in parliamentary institutions, etc.; an adherent of Parliament, especially in the English Civil War.
Sacra-mentar'ian a. Pertaining to the sacraments or the Sacramentarians. s. One who lays stress on sacramental observance; one of a sixteenth-century Lutheran sect.
Establish-mentar'ian s. A supporter of an established Church.
Libertar'ian a. Pertaining to the doctrine of free-will. s. An advocate of this, or of liberty.
Antiquar'ian a. Pertaining to the study of antiquities. s. An antiquary.
Cantuar'ian a. Pertaining to Canterbury, or to the see.
Ovar'ian a. Pertaining to an ovary.
Cam'brian a. Welsh, of Wales (the ancient Cambria); applied to a system of palæozoic strata. s. A Welshman.
Cim'brian a. and s. (*Cimbric*).
Cum'brian a. Pertaining to Cumberland or Strathclyde. s. A native of these parts.
Northum'brian s. A native of Northumbria or of Northumberland; the dialect of ancient Northumbria. a. Pertaining to this district.
Colum'brian a. Pertaining to the U.S.A.
Decan'drian a. Having ten stamens.
Salaman'drian s. and a. One of the or pertaining to the salamanders.
Pentan'drian a. Denoting a plant with five stamens.
Heptan'drian a. Having seven stamens.
Hexan'drian a. Having six stamens.
Polyan'drian a. Having many stamens.
Iber'ian a. and n. Pertaining to, a native of, or the language of ancient Iberia (*i.e.* Spain and Portugal).
Siber'ian a. Pertaining to Siberia. s. A native of Siberia.
Spencer'ian a. Pertaining to the synthetic philosophy of Herbert Spencer.
Lucifer'ian a. Satanic; devilish.
Pier'ian a. Pertaining to the muses.
Valer'ian s. An herbaceous, medicinal plant with a nauseous smell.
Cimmer'ian a. Pertaining to the fabled Cimmerii, who lived in darkness; profoundly obscure, dark.
Hesper'ian a. Western; Occidental.
Spenser'ian a. Pertaining to Edmund Spenser or the stanza of his *Faerie Queene*. s. This stanza.
Presbyter'ian s. A member of a Presbyterian Church; an adherent of Presbyterianism. a. Governed by presbyters; pertaining to this form of Church government.
Oliver'ian a. and s. Pertaining to or an adherent of Oliver Cromwell.
Doctrinair'ian a. and n. (*Doctrinaire*).
Dor'ian a. Relating to Doris (part of ancient Greece) or its people. s. An inhabitant of Doris.
Gregor'ian a. Pertaining to or instituted by Pope Gregory I or XIII.
Infusor'ian a. and n. Pertaining to or one of the infusoria.
Orator'ian s. A member of a Roman Catholic congregation of the Oratory. Pertaining to this.
Saltator'ian a. Saltatorial.
Valedictor'ian s. One who delivers a valedictory.
Victor'ian a. Pertaining to Queen Victoria or her times. s. A person then flourishing.

Prætor'ian a. Pertaining to a prætor, or to the bodyguard of a Roman emperor. s. A member of such bodyguard.
Stentor'ian a. Very loud-voiced.
Nestor'ian s. An adherent of the fifth-century heretic, Nestorius, or his doctrines.
Histor'ian s. A writer or student of history.
Cyp'rian s. A Cyprist; a prostitute. a. Pertaining to Cyprus, to the worship of Venus, or to lewdness.
Zoroas'trian a. and s. Pertaining to or a follower of Zoroaster, founder of the ancient Persian religion.
Pedes'trian a. Going or performed on foot; dull, slow. s. One who journeys on foot.
Rupes'trian a. Composed of or inscribed on rocks.
Eques'trian a. Pertaining to horses or their management; riding on or performed by one on horseback. s. A horseman.
Lacus'trian s. A lake-dweller. a. Lacustrine.
Saur'ian s. A reptile with legs; a lizard, crocodile. a. Pertaining to or resembling such.
Dinosaur'ian a. Pertaining to the dinosaurs. s. A dinosaur.
Mercur'ian a. Mercurial.
Du'rian s. A Malayan fruit.
Holothur'ian s. One of a genus of Echinoderms comprising the sea-slugs.
Silur'ian a. Pertaining to the ancient Silures or the part of England and Wales inhabited by them. s. The lowest subdivision of the Palæozoic strata.
Tellur'ian s. An inhabitant of the earth.
Etrur'ian a. and n. Pertaining to or a native of Etruria.
Syr'ian s. An inhabitant or the language of Syria. a. Pertaining to this.
Assyr'ian a. Pertaining to Assyria or its language. s. A native or the language of Assyria.
Tyr'ian a. Pertaining to ancient Tyre or its people; purple.
A'sian a. Of or pertaining to Asia or its inhabitants.
Cauca'sian a. Belonging to the regions of the Caucasus, or to its peoples or their descendants. s. A member of a race from this region.
Australa'sian a. Pertaining to Australasia. s. An inhabitant or native of this.
Rabelai'sian a. Pertaining to Rabelais, the French humorist; coarsely and boisterously extravagant and satirical.
Athana'sian a. Pertaining to St. Athanasius, a third-century Bishop of Alexandria, or to the creed formerly attributed to him.
Eura'sian s. One of mixed European and Asiatic blood.
Mile'sian a. Irish. s. An Irishman.
Mangane'sian a. Manganic.
Magne'sian a. Pertaining to, containing, or resembling magnesia.
Indone'sian a. Of or belonging to the East Indies.
Polyne'sian a. and s. Pertaining to or a native of Polynesia.
Ete'sian a. Blowing at stated periods; periodical; yearly.
Arte'sian a. Of Artois, applied to a certain kind of well.
Cartes'ian a. (*Cartesianism*).
Precis'ian s. A rigid observer of rule, a formalist.
Paradis'ian a. Paradisial.
Aphrodis'ian a. (*Aphrodisiac*).

Paris'ian a. Of or belonging to Paris. s. Native or inhabitant of Paris.
Fris'ian a. Pertaining to Friesland or its inhabitants. s. The language.
Circen'sian a. Pertaining to the Roman circus.
Walden'sian a. and s. Pertaining to or one of the Waldenses.
Albigen'sian a. Pertaining to the Albigenses, a twelfth-century sect of Reformers.
Per'sian a. Pertaining to Persia, its people, or their language. s. A native or the language of Persia; a silky long-haired cat; a kind of thin silk.
Circas'sian a. and s. Pertaining to or an inhabitant of Circassia.
Parnas'sian a. Pertaining to Parnassus, or to the Muses; poetical.
Hes'sian a. Belonging to Hesse; denoting a high boot with tassels. s. A native of Hesse; a coarse cloth; a Hessian boot.
Rus'sian a. Pertaining to Russia. s. A native of Russia; its language.
Prus'sian a. Pertaining to Prussia or its inhabitants. s. A native of Prussia.
Malthu'sian a. Denoting or pertaining to the theory that population, if unchecked, increases too rapidly.
Carthu'sian s. A member of an order of monks founded at Chartreux (1084). a. Pertaining to this order, or to the Charterhouse School or Institution.
Homoiou'sian s. One who held that the Son was of like but not the same essence as the Father.
Homoou'sian s. One who held that the Son was of the same essence as the Father; a Trinitarian. a. Consubstantial.
Heteroou'sian a. and n. Holding or one holding that Christ was of a different substance from God the Father.
Elys'ian a. Pertaining to Elysium; blissful.
Dalma'tian a. Of Dalmatia. s. A large, black-spotted hound.
Hora'tian a. Pertaining to or resembling the poetry or style of Horace.
Alsa'tian a. Pertaining to Alsace, or to the district south of Fleet Street, London, where criminals and low characters used to congregate. s. A native of Alsace; a desperado, town bully, adventurer.
Nova'tian s. A follower of the third-century heretic, Novatius. a. Pertaining to him, his heresy, or his followers.
Vene'tian a. and s. Pertaining to or a native of Venice; a slatted blind.
Noe'tian a. Pertaining to the doctrines of Noetius, a second-century heretic. s. An adherent of this heresy.
Lute'tian a. Parisian.
Helve'tian a. Swiss. s. A Swiss.
Coryban'tian a. Corybantic.
Byzan'tian a. (*Byzantine*).
Gen'tian s. A bitter herb used medicinally.
Teren'tian a. In the style of Terence (Roman dramatic poet).
Stron'tian s. Strontia. a. Made of or resembling this.
Nico'tian a. Pertaining to tobacco.
Bœo'tian a. Dull, stupid. s. A native of Bœotia, part of ancient Greece, famous for its heavy-witted inhabitants.
Egyp'tian a. Pertaining to Egypt or its inhabitants. s. A native of Egypt.
Mar'tian a. and s. Pertaining to or an inhabitant of Mars.

Gilbert'ian a. Ludicrously topsy-turvy.
Lacer'tian a. Pertaining to the lizards.
Ter'tian a. Occurring or having paroxysms every third day (of fevers). s. Such a fever.
Eras'tian s. One maintaining that the Church should be dependent on the State.
Chris'tian s. A follower of Christ, believer in His teaching and religion. a. Pertaining to Christ or Christianity; Christlike; civilized.
Fus'tian s. A thick, twilled cotton fabric; bombast, clap-trap. a. Pompous, pretentious.
Lillipu'tian a. Pigmy, diminutive. s. A very small person.
A'vian a. Pertaining to birds.
Scandina'vian a. Pertaining to Scandinavia, its language, etc. s. A native of or the languages of Scandinavia.
Belgra'vian a. Pertaining to Belgravia, a fashionable part of London. s. A member of the Upper Ten.
Mora'vian s. One of a Protestant sect founded in Germany by emigrants from Moravia in the eighteenth century.
Bata'vian a. Dutch, pertaining to Holland (anciently Batavia).
Jo'vian a. Pertaining to the deity or planet, Jupiter.
Harro'vian a. Pertaining to Harrow School. s. One educated there.
Ser'vian a. and s. Serbian.
Dilu'vian a. Diluvial.
Antedilu'vian a. Pertaining to times before the Flood; very antiquated. s. One who lived before the Flood; an old-fashioned person.
Postdilu'vian a. Being or happening after the Flood. s. Person or animal living after the Flood.
Peru'vian a. Pertaining to or obtained from Peru. s. A native of Peru.
Hertz'ian a. Pertaining to the electro-magnetic vibrations discovered by Hertz.
Be'jan s. A freshman at some Scottish Universities.
Tro'jan a. Pertaining to Troy. s. An inhabitant or warrior of Troy; a hero.
Myrob'alan s. A dried, astringent, plum-like fruit.
Aceph'alan s. A mollusc.
Cat'alan s. A native of the language of Catalonia. a. Pertaining to Catalonia.
Clan s. A tribe; a group of families having a common ancestor; a sect.
Élan' s. Ardour, zeal, dash.
Rag'lan s. A loose overcoat.
Uh'lan (oo'-) s. A German light cavalryman.
Ku-klux-klan s. An American secret society.
Cas'tellan s. Governor of a castle.
Pol'lan s. An Irish lake fish allied to the salmon.
So'lan s. The gannet.
Or'tolan s. A small European bunting.
Plan s. A drawing, draft, sketch; a scheme, model, project. v.t. and i. To form a plan; to scheme.
Rataplan' s. The beat or sound of a drum.
Yu'lan s. A Chinese magnolia with large showy flowers.
Man s. An adult male human being; the human race; a piece used in playing chess or draughts. v.t. To guard, supply, or furnish with men; to fortify.
Sea'man s. A mariner, sailor; a person able to navigate a ship.
Sha'man s. A medicine-man or priest of the Shamanists.

Chi'naman s. A native of China.
Cab'man s. A driver of a cab.
Freed'man s. A slave who has been set at liberty
Hus'bandman s. A farmer, tiller of the ground.
Hod'man s. A bricklayer's labourer; a drudge.
Good'man s. The head of a family; a husband.
Hood'man s. The "blindman" in blindman's buff.
Wood'man s. A forester; a wood-cutter.
Rod'man s. An angler.
Place'man s. One holding office.
Police'man s. An ordinary member of a police force; a constable.
Glee'man s. A minstrel.
Free'man s. One not a slave; a citizen.
Liege'man s. A liege vassal.
Or'angeman s. A member of a society of Irish Protestants.
Barge'man s. A bargee.
Scythe'man s. One who uses a scythe.
Pike'man s. A soldier armed with a pike.
Le'man s. A sweetheart, mistress.
Noble'man s. A peer.
Middle'man s. An intermediary.
Fugle'man s. Leader of a file of soldiers.
Gen'tleman s. A man of good birth, position, or refinement.
Line'man s. Man working on a railway, telegraph line, etc.
Foe'man s. An enemy in war.
Hard'wareman s. One dealing in hardware.
Fire'man s. One who extinguishes fires; a stoker.
Fore'man s. A chief man; leader of a jury; workman supervising others.
Long'shoreman s. A landsman employed about wharves, etc.
Excise'man s. An officer charged with collecting excise.
Horse'man s. One skilled in riding or managing horses.
Norse'man s. An inhabitant of Norway; an ancient Scandinavian.
Rag'man s. One who deals in rags.
Hang'man s. A public executioner.
Coach'man s. One who drives a coach or carriage.
Hench'man s. A page, male attendant, faithful follower.
Church'man s. A cleric; an Episcopalian.
Watch'man s. A guard, sentinel, night-caretaker.
Switch'man s. One in charge of railway switches.
Scotch'man s. A native of Scotland.
Plough'man s. One who ploughs; a rustic.
Fresh'man s. A first-year student; a novice.
Bush'man s. One of a tribe of S. African aborigines; a dweller in the Australian bush.
North'man s. A Scandinavian.
Pack'man s. One who bears a pack; a pedlar.
Lock'man s. A sheriff in the Isle of Man.
Milk'man s. A man who sells milk.
Silk'man s. A dealer in or maker of silk.
Book'man s. A student or writer of books.
Work'man s. A manual worker.
Wheel'man s. A steersman; a cyclist.
Oil'man s. A dealer in oils, etc.
Bell'man s. A public crier; a bell-ringer.
Bill'man s. One armed with a bill or halberd.
Pull'man s. A railway saloon or sleeping-car.
Dol'man s. A loose Turkish cloak; a kind of mantle for women; a hussar's jacket.
School'man s. A mediæval philosopher or divine; an academical pedant.
Mus'sulman s. A Mohammedan.
Lan'damman s. The chief magistrate in some Swiss cantons.
Pen'man s. A good writer.

Unman′ v.t. To unnerve, deprive of courage.
Gun′man s. One who uses a gun; an armed desperado.
Yeo′man (yo′-) s. Small landed proprietor; gentleman-farmer; member of the yeomanry.
Drag′oman s. An interpreter or guide in the East.
Ro′man a. Pertaining to Rome or its people, or to Roman Catholicism; upright (of letters). s. A native, resident, or citizen of Rome.
Toman′ s. A Persian gold coin (about 7s.).
Ot′toman a. Pertaining to the Turks. s. A Turk; a sofa without back or arms.
Wom′an (wum′) s. An adult human female; the female sex.
Gen′tlewoman s. A woman of good birth and manners; a lady.
Fore′woman s. A workwoman supervising others.
Horse′woman s. A woman skilled in riding and managing horses.
Work′woman s. A female operative.
Wash′er-woman s. A laundress.
Beads′woman s. A woman appointed to pray for another; an almswoman.
Sales′woman s. A woman employed to sell goods.
Kins′woman s. A female relation.
Oars′woman s. A female rower.
Chap′man s. A pedlar.
Ship′man s. A sailor.
Mid′shipman s. A naval cadet.
Shop′man s. A small tradesman; one serving in a shop or working in a mechanic's workshop.
Car′man s. A carter; one in charge of a car.
Shear′man s. One who shears metal.
Spear′man s. One armed with a spear.
Lum′berman s. A lumberer.
Al′derman s. A member of a city corporation or County Council.
Ger′man a. Sprung from the same parents; closely connected; germane; pertaining to Germany. s. A native of Germany; its language.
Wash′erman s. A laundryman.
Fish′erman s. One whose occupation s to catch fish.
Mer′man s. The male of the mermaid.
Su′perman s. A hypothetical being superior to man.
Wa′terman s. A boatman, ferryman.
Slaugh′terman (slaw′-) s. One who kills beasts for market.
Air′man s. An aviator.
Chair′man s. The president of a meeting, etc.; one who draws Bath chairs.
Fir′man s. An Oriental decree, passport, licence, etc.
Nor′man s. A Northman; a native of Normandy. a. Pertaining to Normandy or the Normans.
Ur′man s. Swampy forest land in Siberia.
Beads′man s. A man appointed to pray for another; an almsman.
Heads′man s. An executioner.
Leads′man s. The sailor who heaves the lead.
Seeds′man s. One who deals in seeds; a sower.
Bands′man s. A player in a band of music.
Lands′man s. One unused to seafaring.
Bonds′man s. A slave.
Rounds′man s. A tradesman's carrier or messenger; a policeman who inspects patrols.
Back′woods-man s. A settler in remote places.
Guards′man s. An officer or man in the Guards.
Herds′man s. One who tends cattle.
Swords′man s. One skilled in use of the sword.
Trades′man s. A shopkeeper.
Brides′man s. A male attendant on a bride at her wedding.
Sides′man s. A churchwarden's assistant.
Brakes′man s. A railway guard.
Spokes′man s. One who speaks for others.
Dales′man s. A dweller in a dale.
Sales′man s. One employed to sell goods.
Tales′man s. One summoned to make good a deficiency on a jury.
Lines′man s. Soldier of a line regiment; an umpire watching the line at football, etc.
States′man s. One versed in the art of or taking a leading part in government.
Drags′man s. The driver of a coach or dray.
Gangs′man s. A ganger.
Tal′isman s. An amulet, charm, spell.
Cracks′man s. (*Slang*) A burglar.
Locks′man s. Keeper of a canal- or river-lock.
Banks′man s. A surface worker at a mine.
Marks′man s. One who shoots well.
Spoils′man s. A politician working for personal gain.
Alms′man s. One in regular receipt of charity.
Helms′man s. A steersman.
Grooms′man s. A bachelor friend attending a bridegroom.
Clans′man s. Member of a clan.
Kins′man s. A male relation.
Gowns′man s. One whose professiona habit is a gown, as a barrister, a University man, etc.
Towns′man s. Dweller in a town a fellow citizen.
Oars′man s. A rower.
Privateers′man s. A master of or sailor on a privateer; a privateer.
Steers′man s. One who steers a vessel.
Moors′man s. A dweller on a moor.
Press′man s. One attending to a printing-press; a journalist.
Bats′man s. A player who uses the bat at cricket, etc.
Crafts′man s. A skilled artisan.
Handicrafts′-man s. One employed in handicraft.
Drafts′man s. One who draws up documents; a draughtsman.
Yachts′man (yots′-) s. Owner of a yacht; one who yachts.
Draughts′man s. One who designs, plans, makes mechanical drawings, etc.; a draftsman; a piece used in draughts.
Points′man s. One in charge of railway switches; policeman on point-duty.
Hunts′man s. One who hunts; one in charge of the hounds.
Punts′man s. One good at managing a punt.
Scots′man s. A native of Scotland.
Sports′man s. One skilled in outdoor sport; a candid, fair-dealing, unafraid person.
Days′man s. An umpire.
Bat′man s. An officer's soldier-servant.
Boat′man s. One who looks after boats; an expert oarsman.
Select′man s. A municipal officer in New England towns.
Het′man s. A Cossack commander or leader.
Mer′chantman s. A merchant ship.
Foot′man s. A male liveried servant.
Post′man s. One who delivers posted letters.
Hu′man a. Pertaining to or having the qualities of man; not divine. s. A human being.

Inhu'man a. Barbarous; uncivilized; unfeeling.
Superhu'man a. Beyond what is human.
Preterhu'man a. More than human, superhuman.
Bow'man s. One armed with a bow; the rower nearest the bow.
Show'man s. Proprietor of a circus, etc.
Cay'man s. An American alligator.
Lay'man s. One of the people as distinct from the clergy; a non-professional.
Dray'man s. The driver of a dray.
High'wayman s. One who robs on the highway.
Hand'yman s. A man-of-all-work; one of the Royal Marines.
Jour'neyman s. A qualified artisan; a drudge.
Cler'gyman s. A man in holy orders, minister of the Gospel.
Fly'man s. Driver of a fly; worker of scenes, etc., from the flys at a theatre.
Tal'lyman s. One who keeps a tally, or sells on the instalment plan.
Toy'man s. A dealer in toys.
Nur'seryman s. One who rears plants in a nursery.
Liv'eryman s. A freeman of the City of London.
Fer'ryman s. One who keeps a ferry.
In'fantryman s. A foot-soldier.
Coun'tryman s. A dweller in the country; a rustic; a fellow national; an inhabitant or native of a region.
Ves'tryman s. A member of a vestry.
Jury'man s. A juror.
Fin'nan s. A smoke-dried haddock.
Eo'an a. Pertaining to the dawn; eastern.
Joan s. "Darby's" elderly and comfortable wife.
Loan s. Act of lending; money or anything lent. v.t. and i. To lend.
Moan v.t. To lament, deplore. v.i. To utter moans. s. A low, prolonged sound of suffering, etc.
Samo'an s. A native or the language of Samoa. a. Pertaining to Samoa.
Bemoan' v.t. and i. To deplore, lament, moan over.
Mino'an a. Pertaining to ancient Crete. s. The language or an inhabitant of this.
Roan a. Of a dark colour thickly spotted with light; a mixed red colour. s. A roan horse; a soft, sheepskin leather.
Groan v.i. To moan as in pain or sorrow. s. A moaning or sighing sound.
Heliozo'an a. Pertaining to the Heliozoa, or sun-animalcules.
Microzo'an a. and s. Pertaining to or one of the microzoa.
Hydrozo'an s. A member of the Hydrozoa. a. Pertaining to this class.
Protozo'an a. Pertaining to the protozoa. s. An animal of this division.
Polyzo'an a. and s. Pertaining to, resembling, or one of the polyzoa.
Pan s. A shallow, open dish; a pond for evaporating salt water; part of a gun-lock; the skull; the chief rural deity of the Greeks.
Japan' s. A very hard varnish. v.t. To cover with this.
Sapan' s. A Malayan tree yielding a red dyewood.
Sauce'pan s. A long-handled metal pot for boiling.
Trepan' s. Cylindrical saw for perforating the skull. v.t. To use this; to entrap, swindle.
Marzipan' s. A paste or cake of sweet almonds and sugar.
Jam'pan s. A sedan chair used in India.
Sam'pan s. A flat-bottomed Chinese riverboat.
Tym'pan s. A thin, tightly stretched membrane; a drum, tympanum.
Trag'opan s. The crimson or horned pheasant.
Span s. Extent, reach; space between extended thumb and little finger (9 ins.), stretch of an arch, etc.; any short duration; a yoke of beasts. v.t. To extend across; to measure with extended hand. past (*Spin*).
Inspan' v.t. and i. To yoke (especially oxen).
Ran past (*Run*).
Catam'aran s. A surf-boat, raft.
Bran s. The husk of wheat, etc.
Cran s. A measure of 37½ gallons for herrings.
Scran s. Broken victuals; refuse.
Lu'theran a. Pertaining to the Reformer, Luther, or his doctrines. s. A disciple or adherent of Lutheranism.
Cat'eran s. A Highland marauder.
Vet'eran a. Old in practice, especially in war. s. An old, experienced soldier or other person.
Dip'teran a. Pertaining to the Diptera.
Hemip'teran s. An individual of the Hemiptera.
Lepidop'teran a. and s. Pertaining to or a member of the order of Lepidoptera.
Orthop'teran a. and s. Belonging to or a member of the Orthoptera.
Hymenop'teran s. A member of the Hymenoptera. a. Hymenopteral.
Cheirop'teran s. A bat (animal).
Alcoran' s. The Koran, the sacred book of the Mohammedans.
Koran' s. The Mohammedan scriptures.
Tor'an s. Ceremonial gateway to a Buddhist temple.
Spor'ran s. The fur pouch worn in Highland dress.
Thysanur'an s. A spring-tail (wingless insect).
Sov'ran a. Sovereign.
Bas'an s. Prepared sheepskin for bookbinding.
Dioc'esan s. Pertaining to a bishop. s. A bishop or archbishop.
Parmesan' a. Pertaining to or from Parma (Italy),
Courtesan' s. A prostitute.
Ptis'an s. Barley-water.
Artisan' s. A manual worker.
Partisan' s. An adherent of a faction. a. Adhering thus.
Salvar'san s. An arsenical compound used as an injection in certain diseases.
Medu'san s. A jelly-fish. a. Pertaining to these.
Tan v.t. To convert skins into leather; to brown by exposure to sun; (*slang*) to thrash. s. A bark of trees; sunburn, a brown colour.
Plat'an s. The plane tree.
Charl'atan s. An empty pretender, a quack.
Tar'latan s. A thin transparent muslin.
Sa'tan s. The devil; the chief of the fiends.
Tibe'tan a. and s. Pertaining to or a native of Tibet.
Caftan' s. A vest worn in Turkey and the East.
Neapol'itan a. and s. Pertaining to, distinctive of, or an inhabitant of Naples.
Pentapol'itan a. Pertaining to a pentapolis.
Cosmopol'itan a. Common to all the world; free from local or national prejudices. s. A cosmopolite.

Metropol'itan a. Pertaining to or situated in the metropolis; pertaining to an archbishopric. s. An archbishop.
Capitan' s. A captain.
Samar'itan s. A native of Samaria; a charitable person.
Pur'itan s. An early dissenter from the Church of England; one very strict in religious matters. a. Pertaining to, resembling, or characterizing the Puritans.
Ti'tan s. An earth-giant of mythology; a person of superhuman strength.
Wit'an s. Members of a witenagemot.
Sul'tan s. A Mohammedan sovereign; a variety of poultry.
Fan'tan s. A Chinese gambling game.
Quin'tan a. Recurring once in five days. s. Such a fever.
Sep'tan a. Recurring on the seventh day (of fever, etc.).
Spar'tan a. Pertaining to Sparta or its people; hardy; undaunted. s. A native or one with the characteristics of a native of Sparta.
Tar'tan s. A checkered woollen stuff; a plaid of this.
Quart'an a. Pertaining to the fourth; occurring every fourth day. s. An intermitting ague.
Sac'ristan s. A sacrist; a sexton.
Cap'stan s. An apparatus for winding in cables on board ship.
August'an a. Pertaining to Augustus Cæsar or his times; classical; refined; dignified.
Harmat'tan s. A dry hot wind blowing from Central Africa to the Altantic, December to February.
Rattan' s. Stem of various palms, used for walking-canes.
Orang-utan' s. A large anthropoid ape of Borneo, etc.
Lapu'tan a. and s. Visionary.
Du'an s. A canto (especially in Gaelic poetry).
Guan s. A S. American bird allied to the curassou.
Gargan'tuan a. Gigantic; incredibly big.
Van s. A large covered vehicle; front part of an army, fleet, etc.; leaders; a winnowing or sifting appliance. v.t. To sift (ore).
Pav'an s. The pavane, a stately dance.
Car'avan s. A company travelling together by road; a conveyance one can live in.
Gene'van a. Pertaining to Geneva or to Calvinism. s. An inhabitant of Geneva; a Calvinist.
Divan' s. A Turkish court of justice; a council, council chamber; a cushioned seat against a wall.
Sivan' s. The third month of the Jewish ecclesiastical year.
El'van s. An igneous rock.
Syl'van a. Pertaining to or growing in woods; shady. s. A deity of the woods; a satyr.
Cordovan' s. Spanish leather.
Wan (won) a. Pale; languid; morose.
Dewan' s. A Hindu steward.
Gow'an s. The daisy.
Row'an s. The mountain-ash.
Swan (swon) s. A large, web-footed, aquatic bird.
Malay'an a. and s. Malay.
Wes'leyan a. and s. Pertaining to or a member of the Church founded by John Wesley.
Shin'tiyan s. The loose trousers of Mohammedan women.
Ban'yan s. (*Banian*).
Ar'yan a. Pertaining to the Eastern branch of the Indo-European group of races and languages. s. A member of this.
Baz'an s. (*Basan*).
Barbizan' s. A battlement; an overhanging turret on a tower.
Kist'vaen s. A prehistoric stone-slab tomb.
Ben s. A mountain peak; (*Scot.*) an inner room.
Sar'acen s. A mediæval Mussulman; an Arab.
Den s. Lair of a wild beast; a hovel; a sanctum.
Dead'en v.t. To make dull, insensible, etc.; to abate the force or vigour of.
Lead'en a. Made of or like lead; slow; burdensome; inert.
Menha'den s. A sea-fish of the herring family.
La'den past part. (*Lade*).
Broad'en v.i. and t. To make or become broad or broader.
Glad'den v.t. To make glad, to cheer.
Mad'den v.t. and i. To make or become mad.
Sad'den v.t. and i. To make or become sad.
Red'den v.t. and i. To make or become red; to blush.
Forbid'den a. Prohibited, interdicted.
Hid'den past part. (*Hide*). a. Concealed.
Mid'den s. A dung-hill.
Rid'den past part. (*Rid*).
Bed'ridden a. Unable to get up from bed.
Strid'den past part. (*Stride*).
Priest-rid'den a. Managed or governed by priests.
Hod'den s. Coarse woollen cloth. a. Plain; homely.
Down'trodden a. Oppressed; trampled upon.
Sod'den a. Soaked, saturated; badly cooked. v.t. and i. To saturate, become sodden.
Sud'den a. Happening without warning; hasty; instantaneous.
E'den s. The garden where Adam and Eve first lived; a delightful region, abode of bliss and innocence, state of perfect happiness.
Maid'en s. A girl, spinster, maid; an early form of guillotine. a. Pertaining to maidens; unused, unpolluted; first.
Mer'maiden s. A mermaid.
Wid'en v.t. and i. To make or become wide.
Weald'en a. Pertaining to the Weald of Kent. s. A series of freshwater deposits of the Lower Cretaceous system.
Mild'en v.t. and i. To make or become mild.
Old'en a. Old, ancient, bygone.
Embold'en v.t. To give boldness to, to encourage.
Gold'en a. Made of or like gold; splendid, rich; most valuable; auspicious.
Behold'en a. Under an obligation; indebted.
Gul'den s. An obsolete European coin.
Quar'enden s. A dark-red early apple.
Lin'den s. A soft-timbered tree with heart-shaped leaves; the lime.
Bound'en a. Obliged, bound.
Wood'en s. Made of wood; clumsy; awkward; spiritless.
Gar'den s. Ground set apart for flowers, etc.; a well-cultivated tract. v.i. To cultivate a garden. a. Pertaining to a garden; not wild.
Bear'-garden s. A scene of confusion, noise, and disorder.
Hard'en v.t. and i. To make or become hard, unfeeling, etc.; to confirm in wickedness; to become inured.

Ward'en (wŏrd'-) s. A guardian, keeper; head of a college, etc.; a variety of pear.
Bur'den s. A load; freight; a chorus. v.t. To load, oppress.
Overbur'den v.t. To load too heavily.
Disbur'den v.t. To lay off as oppressive; to unload; to ease the mind.
Loud'en v.i. To become gradually louder.
Hoy'den s. A rough or loutish girl. a. Rude, brazen.
E'en s. and adv. Even.
Been v. aux. (past) (*Be*).
Shebeen' s. A low or unlicensed drinking establishment.
Gombeen' s. Usury.
Dudeen' s. A short tobacco-pipe.
Car'rageen s. A gelatinous seaweed.
Fellaheen' s. Egyptian peasants.
Sheen s. Glitter, lustre, splendour.
Keen a. Sharp; eager; severe; piercing. s. Lamentation, wailing (at Irish funerals). v.t. and i. To raise or mourn with the keen.
Palankeen' s. A palanquin.
Nankeen' s. A yellowish cotton cloth.
Baleen' s. Whalebone.
Colleen' s. (*Irish*) A girl.
Spleen s. A glandular organ in the stomach; spite; melancholy.
Traneen' s. The crested dog's-tail grass.
Mavour'neen s. (*Irish*) My dear one.
Peen s. The wedge-shaped end of a hammer.
Spal'peen s. (*Irish*) A rogue, rascal.
Careen' v.t. To lay a vessel on its side for repairs. v.i. To incline to one side.
Screen s. A slight partition; barrier between chancel and nave; a coarse sieve. v.t. To conceal; shelter; to sieve.
Green a. Verdant; unripe; inexperienced. s. The colour of growing herbage; a grassy plot. v.t. and i. To make or grow green.
Sea'-green a. A faint bluish green.
Shagreen' s. A leather with granular surface; shark-skin.
Sen'green s. The house-leek.
Ev'ergreen a. Always green; always young or fresh. s. A plant having green leaves all the year round.
Squireen' s. One (especially in Ireland) half squire and half farmer.
Boreen' s. (*Irish*) A bridle-path, a lane.
Moreen' s. A stout fabric for curtains, etc.
Preen v.t. To trim (especially of birds their feathers).
Tureen' s. Deep vessel for holding soup.
Seen past part. (*See*).
Teen s. Grief; vexation. v.t. To vex.
Lateen' a. Denoting a triangular sail. s. A vessel with this.
Sateen' s. A glossy cotton fabric.
Nineteen' a. and s. Nine and ten.
Velveteen' s. A cotton imitation of velvet.
Fifteen' a. and n. Five and ten.
Eighteen' a. and s. Consisting of or the sum of 8 and 10.
Canteen' s. A store in camp or barracks where provisions, drink, etc., are sold; a soldier's water-bottle; a case of cultery.
Seventeen' s. Sum of 7 and 10; symbol representing this (17, xvii). a. Consisting of seven and ten.
Poteen' s. Irish whisky illicitly distilled.
Umpteen' a. (*Slang*) Numerous; any number of.
Thirteen' a. One more than twelve. s. Sum of 10 and 3 (13, xiii).
Fourteen' a. and n. Four and ten; 14.
Man'gosteen s. An E. Indian tree and its fruit.
Ratteen' s. A thick woollen stuff.
Sixteen' a. Consisting of six and ten. s. Sum of these; its symbol (16, xvi.).
Queen s. The consort of a king; a female sovereign; a reigning beauty; a piece at chess; a playing-card. v.i. To play the queen.
Ween v.i. To fancy, be of opinion.
Hallowe'en' s. 31st October; evening preceding All Hallows.
Between' prep. In the midst of.
Armozeen' s. Black silk used for clerical gowns, etc.
Fen s. A marsh, bog; marshy country.
Deaf'en v.t. To make deaf, to overpower with noise.
Stiff'en v.t. and i. To make or become stiff.
-gen suff. Expressing produced, producing, or growth.
Twig'gen a. Made of twigs.
Gly'cogen s. A starch-like compound occurring in animal tissues.
En'dogen s. A monocotylednous plant which grows by additions developed from inside, as the palms and canes.
Hal'ogen s. One of the elements whose sodium salts resemble sea-salt.
Thal'logen s. One of the lowest class of plants (fungi, lichens, etc.).
Phel'logen s. Cork-tissue.
Plas'mogen s. Formative protoplasm.
Zy'mogen s. A substance developing into a ferment.
Cyan'ogen s. A poisonous gas composed of carbon and nitrogen.
Fibrin'ogen s. A protein found in fibrin.
Ac'rogen s. A cryptogam.
Hy'drogen s. An inflammable, colourless, inodorous gaseous element of extreme lightness.
Scler'ogen s. The hard matter of vegetable cells.
Ni'trogen s. A tasteless, odourless, colourless, gaseous element forming ⅘ths of the atmosphere.
Pyr'ogen s. A substance inducing fever.
Pho'togen s. A light hydrocarbon used as an illuminant.
Pep'togen s. Anything promoting the formation of pepsin.
Ex'ogen s. A plant or tree which increases its diameter by addition of new wood on the outside.
Cry'ogen s. Freezing mixture.
Rhiz'ogen s. A plant parasitic on the roots of another.
Larg'en v.t. and i. To make or grow large.
Ox'ygen s. A colourless, gaseous element, present in air and water, and essential to life.
Hen s. The female of any bird, especially the domestic fowl.
Pea'hen s. The female peafowl.
Beech'en a. Made of beech.
Li'chen s. A cryptogamous parasitic fungus; a skin-eruption.
Birch'en a. Made of birch.
Grosch'en s. An obsolete German silver coin.
Kitch'en s. A room for cooking.
Rough'en v.t. and i. To make or become rough.
Tough'en (tŭf'-) v.t. and i. To make or become tough or tougher.
Hy'phen s. Mark (-) joining syllables or words.
Ash'en a. Pertaining to the ash-tree; made of ash; of the colour of ashes.

Nesh'en v.t. To make tender or succulent.
Fresh'en v.t. and i. To make or become fresh; to revive.
Then adv. and conj.
Hea'then s. A pagan, idolater; a barbarian. a. Pagan; barbarous.
Length'en v.t. and i. To make or become long or longer; to extend.
Strength'en v.t. and i. To make stronger, increase in strength.
Smooth'en v.t. and i. To smooth or become smooth.
Earth'en a. Made of earth, baked clay, etc.
Bur'then (*Burden*).
When adv., interrog. pron.
Lien (lē'en) s. Right of detention until satisfaction of a claim.
A'lien a. Of foreign extraction; repugnant to. s. A foreigner.
Mien s. Air; appearance; manner.
Ken v.t. To know, recognize, descry. s. Cognizance, view; (*slang*) a low tavern.
Weak'en v.t. and i. To make or become weak.
Oak'en a. Made or consisting of oak.
Kra'ken s. A fabulous sea-monster.
Forsak'en a. Abandoned; renounced; cast off.
Tak'en past part. (*Take*).
Mistak'en a. In error; incorrect; wrong.
Wak'en v.t. and i. To arouse from sleep; to wake, cease from sleeping.
Awak'en v.t. and i. To rouse or rise from sleep.
Black'en v.t. and i. To make or become black or blacker.
Slack'en v.t. and i. To become or cause to be slack; to slake (lime).
Brack'en s. A fern; a brake.
Chick'en s. The young of the domestic hen.
Thick'en v.t. and i. To make or become thick or thicker.
Brick'en a. Made of bricks.
Strick'en past part. (*Strike*).
Sick'en v.i. To become ill, sick, or disgusted. v.t. To disgust; to make sick or qualmish.
Quick'en v.t. and i. To make or become alive, lively, or reinvigorated; to stimulate; to move quickly or more quickly. s. The mountain-ash, rowan.
Wick'en s. The mountain-ash.
Li'ken v.t. To compare, represent as similar to.
Li'ken (lē-) s. A Chinese provincial tax.
Silk'en a. Made of, resembling, or pertaining to silk; soft; silky.
Drunk'en a. Intoxicated; given to, caused by, or characterized by drunkenness.
Shrunk'en a. Withered, shrivelled, contracted.
Spo'ken past part. (*Speak*).
Bespo'ken v.t. (past part.) (*Bespeak*).
Outspo'ken a. Speaking freely; candid, frank.
Bro'ken a. Separated into fragments.
To'ken s. A sign, indication; coin current but unauthorised; a souvenir, keepsake.
Beto'ken v.t. To signify, denote, foreshadow.
Foreto'ken v.t. To prognosticate, predict. s. A previous sign.
Dark'en v.t. and i. To make or become dark or darker; to obscure, to render gloomy, ignorant, etc.
Heark'en v.i. To listen attentively to.
Ab'len s. The bleak.
Mag'dalen s. A reclaimed prostitute; an asylum for such.
Glen s. A narrow valley.
Fal'len past part. (*Fall*).
Down'fallen a. Ruined.
Crest'fallen a. Dispirited, abashed.
Wool'len a. Made of or consisting of wool. s. Cloth made of wool.
Pol'len s. The fecundating dust of flowers.
Swol'len past part. (*Swell*).
Sul'len a. Gloomily angry and silent; dismal, baleful.
So'len s. The razor-fish.
Sto'len past part. (*Steal*).
Men s. (*Man*).
Amen' int. So be it. s. The end.
Cyc'lamen s. A genus of low-growing tuberous plants having beautiful flowers.
Vela'men s. A membrane; a velum.
Fora'men s. A little opening, perforation.
Dura'men s. Heart-wood of exogenous trees.
Sta'men s. Fertilizing organ of a flower.
Tuta'men s. A protecting part.
Grava'men s. Ground of complaint; grievance complained of.
Ya'men s. Official residence of a Chinese governor.
Se'men s. The male fertilizing fluid.
Teg'men s. Covering of an organ in animal or plant.
Spec'imen s. A representative part; a sample.
Reg'imen s. Systematic management, especially of meals, exercise, etc.
Li'men s. Stage at which stimulus to the nerves ceases to produce an impression.
Mo'limen s. Natural effort to perform some physical function.
Dol'men s. A cromlech.
Cul'men s. The ridge on top of a bird's beak.
O'men s. A sign, prognostic, augury. v.t. To predict, foretell.
Abdo'men s. The lower belly.
Præno'men s. A first name, Christian name.
Agno'men s. A surname; an epithet.
Cogno'men s. A surname.
Wom'en (wim'-) s. (*Woman*).
Ger'men s. The rudimentary seed-vessel of a plant.
Albu'men s. A substance present in the white of egg and in blood.
Acu'men s. Quickness of perception, sharpness.
Hegu'men s. Head of a Greek monastery.
Legu'men s. A legume, a two-valved pod.
Energu'men s. A demoniac; a fanatic.
Catechu'men s. A neophyte; one receiving doctrinal instruction before baptism.
Ru'men s. The first stomach of a ruminant.
Ceru'men s. Wax secreted by the ear.
Bit'umen s. Mineral pitch; natural asphalt.
Hy'men s. The Greek god of marriage; the virginal membrane.
Lin'en s. Cloth made of flax; sheets, underclothing, etc. a. Made of flax.
Pen s. A writing implement; a nib; a quill, writing; an enclosure for sheep, etc.; a coop. v.t. To write; to confine in a narrow space.
Cheap'en v.t. To beat down the price of.
Misshap'en a. Deformed; wrongly shaped.
Deep'en v.t. and i. To make or become deeper.
Steep'en v.t. and i. To make or become steep.
Rip'en v.t. and i. To grow or make ripe.
Damp'en v.t. and i. To damp or become damp; to dull, deject.
Hemp'en s. Made of or resembling hemp.
Impen' v.t. To enclose in a narrow space.

O'pen a. Not closed or obstructed; free of access; artless, frank. v.t. To unclose; to disclose; to begin. v.i. To come unclosed; to crack; to make a start.
Reo'pen v.t. and i. To open again.
Hap'pen v.i. To fall out, chance.
Shar'pen v.t. and i. To make or become sharp.
As'pen s. The trembling poplar. a. Made of its wood; trembling like the aspen.
Chil'dren s. Progeny; descendants; disciples.
Breth'ren s. (*Brother*).
Si'ren s. A fabulous sea-nymph; a dangerously fascinating woman; a foghorn; a sirenian. a. Bewitching.
Bar'ren a. Not fruitful; desert; unproductive.
War'ren (wŏr'-) s. Breeding-place of wild rabbits.
Wren s. A small passerine bird.
Sen s. A Japanese copper coin (about ¼d.)
Spie'geleisen (spē'-) s. A variety of cast-iron containing manganese.
Sam'isen s. A Japanese three-stringed musical instrument.
Ris'en past part. (*Rise*).
Aris'en v.i. (past and past part.) (*Arise*).
Chos'en past part. (*Choose*).
Loos'en v.t. and i. To make or become loose.
Coars'en v.t. and i. To make or grow coarse.
Hoars'en v.t. and i. To make or become hoarse.
Sar'sen s. A sandstone boulder, especially of Wilts.
Wors'en (wers'-) v.t. and i. To make or become worse.
Les'sen v.t. and i. To make or become less; to depreciate; to abate.
Ten s. One and nine, (10, x). a. One more than nine.
Eat'en past part. (*Eat*).
Beat'en v.t. (past part.); a. (*Beat*).
Wheat'en a. Made of wheat.
Threat'en v.t. and i. To use threats to; to menace.
Plat'en s. The flat part of a printing-press.
Oat'en a. Made of oat-meal; consisting of oat straw.
Pat'en s. The shallow dish on which the Eucharistic bread is placed.
Pec'ten s. A comb-like structure as in the eye of birds and reptiles; a marine bivalve mollusc, a scallop.
Sweet'en v.t. and i. To make or become sweet or sweeter.
Qui'eten v.t. and i. To quiet.
Often (ofn) adv. Frequently; many times.
Soften (sofn) v.t. and i. To make or become soft or softer; to mitigate.
Height'en v.t. To make higher, to raise; to enhance, intensify. v.i. To increase, augment.
Light'en v.i. To become brighter; to flash. v.t. To illuminate; to flash forth; to enlighten ; to make less heavy; to cheer, gladden.
Enlight'en v.t. To supply with light; to make clear, to instruct.
Bright'en v.t. and i. To make or become bright or brighter.
Fright'en v.t. To terrify, scare, alarm.
Tight'en v.t. and i. To make or become tight.
Strait'en v.t. To confine; to make narrow or tense; to press with necessity.
Whit'en v.t. and i. To make or become white.
Mol'ten a. Melted; made of melted metal. past part. (*Melt*).
Lent'en a. Pertaining to Lent; meagre.
Heart'en s. To animate, encourage, stir up.
Enheart'en v.t. To cheer, encourage.
Disheart'en v.t. To discourage, dispirit.
Kin'dergarten s. A school for infants.
Mar'ten s. A small carnivorous mammal of the weasel tribe.
Smart'en v.t. and i. To make or become smart.
Short'en v.t. To curtail, make short or shorter. v.i. To contract.
Foreshort'en v.t. To represent figures as they appear in perspective.
Fasten v.t. To make fast or firm, to cement, secure, fix. v.i. To become fast; to seize.
Hasten v.i. and t. To move with speed, cause to hurry.
Chasten v.t. To correct by punishment; to discipline, restrain.
Tung'sten s. A heavy metallic element.
Listen v.i. To hearken, attend to.
Glisten v.i. To glitter, sparkle. s. A gleam, sparkle.
Moisten v.t. and i. To make or become damp or moist.
Christen v.t. To baptize, to give a name to.
Bat'ten s. A narrow piece of board. v.t. and i. To fatten, to grow fat, live in luxury.
Fat'ten v.t. and i. To make or become fat; to feed for the table; to manure, fertilize.
Lat'ten s. A fine kind of brass.
Flat'ten v.t. To make flat, to level; to render less sharp; to make dull, to deject. v.i. To become flat; to pall.
Pat'ten s. A clog; a wooden shoe on an iron ring.
Rat'ten v.t. To molest or injure a workman or employer during a strike.
Bit'ten v. (past part.) (*Bite*).
Kit'ten s. A young cat. v.i. To bring forth young, as a cat.
Mit'ten s. A glove with a thumb-division but no fingers.
Smit'ten past part. (*Smite*).
Writ'ten past part. (*Write*).
Got'ten (*obs.*) past part. (*Get*).
Begot'ten v. (past part.) (*Beget*).
Misbegot'ten a. Bastard; hideous.
Forgot'ten past part. (*Forget*).
Misgot'ten a. Unjustly obtained.
Rot'ten a. Putrid, decayed, corrupt; (*slang*) contemptible, unpleasant.
Glu'ten s. A tenacious nitrogenous substance in flour.
Hen'equen s. Sisal-hemp.
Heav'en s. The sky; the abode of God and the blessed; bliss.
Leav'en s. A fermenting mixture; yeast. v.t. To ferment by or mix with a leaven; to imbue, taint.
Ha'ven s. A harbour, port; a refuge.
Ra'ven s. A large, black bird allied to the crows.
Rav'en v.t. To devour voraciously. v.i. To plunder, be greedy. s. Rapacity; prey.
Cra'ven s. One vanquished in fight; a coward, paltry fellow. a. Cowardly, faint-hearted.
Gra'ven a. Carved, inscribed.
E'ven s. Evening. a. Level, smooth; uniform; on an equality; just; parallel to; divisible by two without remainder. adv. Exactly; likewise, moreover; verily. v.t. To make level, to equalize, to balance.
Elev'en a. Ten and one. s. Sum of 10 and 1; a side at cricket or football.

Sev'en s. Sum of 1 and 6; symbol representing this (7, vii). a. Consisting of one more than six.
Li'ven v.t. and i. To make or become lively; to cheer up.
Enli'ven v.t. To give life, action, or spirit to; to invigorate.
Riv'en past part. (*Rive*).
Shriv'en a. Having confessed and received absolution.
Thriv'en past part. (*Thrive*).
Striv'en past part. (*Strive*).
Ov'en s. A closed place for baking, heating, or drying.
Clo'ven a. Cleft; divided into two.
Slov'en (sluv'-) s. A careless, negligent person or worker; a slattern.
Pro'ven past part. Proved.
Wo'ven past part. (*Weave*).
Wen s. An encysted tumour; an abnormal growth.
Flax'en a. Made of or like flax; pale yellow.
Wax'en a. Made of, consisting of, or resembling wax; waxy.
Mix'en s. A dunghill.
Vix'en s. A she-fox; an ill-tempered, shrewish woman.
Ox'en s. (*Ox*).
Yen s. The Japanese monetary unit (=about 2s. 1d.).
Doy'en s. The senior member of a body.
Bra'zen a. Impudent, defiant; made of or like brass; v.t. To face anything defiantly and with effrontery.
Diz'en v.t. To dress gaudily.
Bediz'en v.t. To deck out tawdrily.
Miz'en s. A fore-and-aft sail on the aftermost mast. a. Hindmost.
Den'izen s. An inhabitant, resident; a naturalized alien. v.t. To naturalize.
Cit'izen s. An inhabitant or freeman of a city or republic.
Wiz'en v.t. and i. To dry up, shrivel. a. Wizened.
Coz'en v.t. To cheat, defraud, beguile.
Fro'zen past part. (*Freeze*).
Thegn s. A thane.
Campaign' s. A series of operations in warfare; the period of this.
Champaign' s. Flat, open country.
Arraign' v.t. To accuse; to set forth.
Condign' a. Well deserved; suitable.
Deign v.i. and t. To condescend, vouchsafe.
Feign v.t. To pretend, make a show of, imagine.
Reign s. Royal supremacy; period of a sovereign's rule. v.i. To rule as sovereign; to prevail.
Sov'ereign s. A supreme ruler, monarch; English gold coin (=20s.). a. Supreme; royal; effectual.
For'eign a. Of another country or nation; alien; irrelevant.
Align' v.t. (*Aline*).
Malign' (-leen') a. Having a very evil disposition; malignant; pernicious. v.t. To traduce, defame.
Benign' a. Kind, gracious, courteous.
Coign s. A corner, point of observation.
Frankalmoign' s. (*Frankalmoigne*).
Sign (sīn) s. An indicating mark; a signal; a symptom; an omen. v.i. To make a sign, to signal. v.t. To affix one's signature to.
Design' v.t. To sketch out, draw the outline of; to purpose, intend. s. A sketch; a project, intention.
Resign' v.t. To surrender, relinquish, renounce; to submit. v.i. To give up office.
En'sign s. A distinguishing banner, a nautical flag; a badge, emblem; formerly the lowest commissioned infantry officer.
Consign' v.t. To give or transfer formally to entrust, assign, commit.
Undersign' v.t. To sign at the foot of.
Coun'tersign v.t. To sign additionally; to attest a signature. s. Such a signature; a military password.
Assign' v.t. To allot, make over to another. s. One to whom something is or is to be assigned.
Reassign' v.t. To assign again, transfer back.
Repugn' (-pūn') v.i. To oppose, resist. v.t. To combat.
Impugn' v.t. To call in question, contradict.
Propugn' (-pūn') v.t. To defend, vindicate.
Oppugn' (-pūn') v.t. To oppose, controvert.
Expugn' v.t. To conquer, take by assault.
Blue'john s. A variety of fluor-spar.
Dem'ijohn s. A large glass bottle enclosed in wickerwork.
In prep. and adv. Within, inside of, etc.; not out.
-in suff. Denoting certain neutral chemical compounds.
Ordain' v.t. To set in order, regulate; to appoint, decree; to invest with ecclesiastical functions.
Preordain' v.t. To appoint beforehand, predetermine.
Disdain' v.t. To regard with contempt; to scorn, despise. s. Feeling of contempt, scorn; arrogance.
Fain a. Glad; contented. adv. Gladly; readily.
Gain s. Profit, emolument, benefit. v.t. to acquire, obtain, procure, attain. v.i. To advance, get the advantage.
Again' adv. A second time, once more.
Regain' v.t. To recover possession of; to retrieve.
Bar'gain s. A verbal agreement for sale, a contract. v.t. To transfer for a consideration. v.i. To make a contract; to expect.
Chain s. A series of connected links or rings; a surveyor's measure (66 ft.). v.t. To fasten or connect with a chain; to enslave.
Enchain' v.t. To fasten with a chain, to bind.
Jain s. and a. An adherent of or pertaining to Jainism.
Lain past part. (*Lie*).
Blain s. A pustule, a sore.
Chil'blain s. An irritating inflammation on exposed parts due to cold.
Porce'lain s. A fine, translucent kind of earthenware; the best china.
Chât'elain s. A governor of a castle, castellan.
Vill'ain s. A knave, scoundrel, rogue; a feudal serf.
Plain a. Smooth, level; clear; evident; artless; simple; bare. s. A flat expanse, tract of level ground. adv. Distinctly.
Chap'lain s. The officiating clergyman attached to a private chapel, institution, ship, regiment, etc.
Complain' v.i. To express distress, dissatisfaction, or objection; to murmur; to ail.

Explain' v.t. To make clear; to elucidate. v.i. To give explanations.
Cham'berlain s. A high official in royal courts.
Slain past part. (*Slay*).
Main a. Chief, principal; mighty; directly applied. s. Strength; great effort; a chief gas- or water-pipe; the ocean; cock-fight; throw at dice.
Amain' adv. With vehemence, violently.
Legerdemain' s. Sleight of hand; jugglery.
Remain' v.i. To stay or be left behind; to continue, endure.
Domain' s. Dominion; estate; demesne.
Pear'main s. A variety of apple.
Mort'main s. Unalienable possession.
Pain s. Uneasiness or suffering of body or mind; a penalty; anguish. v.t. To cause pain to; to distress.
Rain s. Water that falls from the clouds. v.i. To fall in drops from the clouds. v.t. To shower down, supply abundantly.
Brain s. The nervous matter enclosed in the skull; the seat of sensation; understanding. v.t. To dash out the brains of.
Drain s. A sewer; a channel or trench for water, etc.; act of drawing off. v.t. To draw off gradually, to exhaust of; to carry off sewage, etc. v.i. To flow off gradually; to be emptied thus.
Riv'erain a. Pertaining to or living near a river. s. One living near or on a river.
Su'zerain s. A superior lord, lord paramount.
Refrain' v.t. To hold back, curb, restrain. v.i. To forbear, abstain. s. The burden of a song; musical repetition.
Grain s. A seed; corn collectively; the smallest particle; one-seven-thousandth of a lb. avoir.; granular texture; dye. v.t. To granulate; to paint in imitation of fibres.
Engrain' v.t. To dye in the grain; to imbue.
Ingrain' v.t. To dye in the grain or yarn; to infix deeply. a. Dyed thus; inherent.
Sprain v.t. To overstrain (a muscle, ligament, etc.). s. An excessive strain without dislocation.
Terrain' s. A region, stretch of ground.
Mur'rain s. An infectious and fatal cattle-disease.
Train s. Retinue; line of powder leading to mine, etc.; series of connected carriages on railway. v.t. To bring up, educate, form by exercise.
Quat'rain s. A four-lined stanza.
Detrain' v.t. and i. To alight or cause to alight from a train.
Entrain' v.t. and i. To put or get into a railway train.
Strain v.t. To stretch tight; to exert to the utmost; to sprain; to make forced or unnatural; to filter. v.i. To exert oneself. s. A violent effort; injurious tension of the muscles, etc.; theme; a tune; tendency; family blood.
Restrain' v.t. To hold back, check, hinder, restrict.
Distrain' v.t. To seize goods for debt.
Constrain' v.t. To urge or hold back by force; to compress; to necessitate.
Overstrain' v.i. To strain to excess; make too violent efforts.
Tain s. Tinfoil for mirrors.
Obtain' v.t. To gain. procure, earn. v.i. To be prevalent or in common use.
Detain' v.t. To keep back, withhold, hinder, hold in custody.
Retain' v.t. To continue to hold; to keep in pay; to detain, engage.
Chief'tain s. A leader; head of a clan, tribe, etc.
Brit'ain s. England, Wales, and Scotland.
Plan'tain s. A common weed; a tropical tree allied to the banana.
Maintain' v.t. To keep in some particular state; to support, uphold; to vindicate; to assert.
Quin'tain s. Game of tilting; object to be tilted at.
Contain' v.t. To comprise, enclose, comprehend, be able to hold.
Foun'tain s. A spring or source of water; an artificial jet; a first principle, source.
Moun'tain s. A very large hill; a great pile; anything huge. a. Pertaining to or found on mountains.
Catamoun'tain s. The puma, panther; wild-cat.
Chev'rotain s. A very small ungulate, the mouse-deer.
Cap'tain s. A leader; the commander of a company, troop, man-of-war, liner, side, team, etc. v.t. To lead, act as captain.
Cer'tain a. Sure, indubitable, unquestionable, not specifically named.
Uncer'tain a. Doubtful; inconstant.
Ascertain' v.t. To find out by inquiry or trial; to make certain.
Pertain' v.i. To be the property, right, or duty of; to belong, relate.
Appertain' v.i. To belong or relate to.
Entertain' v.t. To maintain; to show hospitality to; to divert; to take into consideration. v.i. To receive guests.
Cur'tain s. A hanging covering for door, window, etc.; a screen in a theatre; part of a rampart between two bastions; a cover, protection. v.t. To enclose, furnish, or protect with a curtain.
Stain v.t. To sully, tarnish, pollute; to dye. s. A discolouration; a colour; a taint, tarnish, pollution.
Abstain' v.i. To keep from; to forbear.
Blood'stain s. A smear of blood.
Sustain' v.t. To support, aid; to endure; to hold valid.
Attain' v.t. and i. To gain; reach, obtain.
Sex'tain s. A stanza of six lines.
Vain a. Unsubstantial, unreal; ineffectual; worthless; conceited, showy.
Ver'vain s. A small, purple-flowered weed of the verbena family.
Wain s. A farm-wagon.
Cord'wain s. A kind of leather, Cordovan.
Swain s. A rustic, a country lover.
Boat'swain s. A petty officer on board ship.
Cox'swain s. A steersman, especially of a light racing boat; a naval petty officer.
Twain a. Two. s. A pair, couple.
Quat'orzain s. A fourteen-lined verse or poem.
Bin s. A receptacle for storing (wine, corn, dust, etc.). v.t. To store in a bin.
Cab'in s. A hut; a compartment on board ship. v.t. To confine in a small space.
Can'nabin s. A narcotic obtained from hemp.

Ar'abin s. The soluble principle in gum arabic.
Rab'bin s. A rabbi.
Bob'bin s. A wooden pin to wind thread, etc., on; a round tape.
Dob'bin s. A draught-horse.
Cu'bebin s. A vegetable principle found in cubeb seeds.
Throm'bin s. Substance to which coagulation of blood is due.
Jac'obin s. One of a club of extremists during the French Revolution; a variety of pigeon.
Glo'bin s. A protein present in red blood-corpuscles.
Hæmoglo'bin s. The colouring matter of red blood-corpuscles.
Rob'in s. The redbreast, a small warbler.
Cher'ubin s. A cherub.
Tarax'acin s. The bitter principle of taraxacum.
Lac'cin s. The colouring principle in lac.
Clav'ecin s. An early form of harpsichord.
Sal'icin s. The bitter crystalline, medicinal substance obtained from willow-bark.
Ser'icin s. Gelatinous matter contained in silk.
Cor'ticin s. An alkaloid obtained from aspen bark.
Far'cin s. Farcy.
Or'cin s. A crystalline compound yielding colouring-matter, found in certain lichens.
Resor'cin s. A compound of resin with caustic potash, used in dyeing and medicine.
Pu'trescin s. A poison found in decaying animal matter.
Din s. A loud or continued noise. v.t. To stun or annoy thus.
Ladin' s. A dialect spoken in the Engadine.
Pal'adin s. One of the twelve peers of Charlemagne; a distinguished champion; a hero.
Am'idin s. Starch in solution, the soluble matter in starch.
Fluores'cein s. A dye-stuff obtained from coal-tar.
Geg'enschein s. A form of zodiacal light; the counter-glow.
Xan'thein (zăn'the-) s. Yellow colouring-matter of flowers that is soluble in water.
Skein (skān) s. A coil or quantity of yarn, wool, etc.
Nu'clein s. Any amorphous substance present in cell nuclei.
Mul'lein s. Aaron's rod, an herbaceous plant.
O'lein (-in) s. The liquid part of fat.
Terreplein' (tareplān') s. Platform for guns behind a parapet.
Fräu'lein s. A German spinster or young lady.
Rein (rān) s. Strap of bridle by which a horse is governed; restraint. v.t. To control, restrain.
Herein' adv. In this.
Therein' adv.
Wherein' adv.
Serein' (sā-) s. A fine evening rain in the tropics.
Zoll'verein s. The customs union of the former German Empire.
Ca'sein s. The basis of cheese.
Os'sein s. The gelatinous tissue of bone.
Pro'tein s. An amorphous organic substance, an essential constituent of animal and vegetable tissue; the essential principle of food.
Frank'enstein s. One overwhelmed by his own production; a monstrous creation.

Vein (vān) s. A blood vessel, especially one for impure blood; a rib (in plants); cleft in rock filled with some other substance, a seam; a streak; disposition. v.t. To fill or variegate with veins.
Fin s. One of the organs of motion and balance in a fish.
Graf'in s. A German countess.
Par'affin s. A waxy substance obtained from petroleum, etc.; an oil extracted from this.
Bif'fin s. A red cooking-apple.
Grif'fin s. A fabulous winged monster; a watchful guardian.
Tif'fin s. A light lunch.
Cof'fin s. The case in which a corpse is buried; the hollow part of a horse's hoof. v.t. To put into a coffin.
Muf'fin s. A light, spongy tea-cake.
Rag'amuffin s. A ragged, disreputable fellow.
Puf'fin s. A marine diving-bird.
Elf'in s. A little elf, an urchin. a. Elfish.
Gin s. Geneva, a distilled spirit; a snare; a machine for raising weights; another for cleaning cotton; an Australian female aboriginal. v.t. To entrap; to clean cotton with a gin; to begin.
Begin' v.t. and i. To start, commence, enter on something new or afresh.
Pig'gin s. A small wooden pail.
Nog'gin s. A small mug; a gill, ¼ pint.
Or'igin s. Beginning; cause; source; derivation.
Fun'gin s. The cellulose of fungi, etc.
Vir'gin s. A maid; a sign of the Zodiac. a. Chaste; unsullied; untaken.
Hin s. A Jewish liquid measure (about 1½ gallon).
Chin s. The front part of the lower jaw.
Bald'achin s. A canopy over a throne, altar, etc.
Ur'chin s. A pert or mischievous boy; an echinus; a hedgehog.
Cap'uchin s. A member of a branch of the Franciscan order.
Dol'phin s. A cetaceous mammal; the porpoise; the dorado; an aphis infesting beans; a mooring-post, an anchored spar.
Dauph'in s. The heir-apparent in the old French monarchy.
Shin s. Fore-part of leg between knee and ankle. v.t. To climb.
Thin a. Lean; slender; not thick; meagre; slight. v.t. and i. To make or become thin or thinner. adv. Thinly.
Lec'ithin s. A complex substance found in animals and plants.
Within' adv and prep.; s. The inside.
Xan'thin s. The yellow insoluble colouring matter of flowers.
Ab'sinthin s. The bitter principle in wormwood.
Colocyn'thin s. The bitter principle of colocynth.
Whin s. Furze, gorse; a hard, basalt-like rock.
-kin suff. Forming diminutives.
Kin s. Relationship; relatives. a. Of the same nature; related.
Akin' a. Related to, resembling.
Byrla'kin int. An obsolete oath.
Ta'kin s. A goat-like Tibetan ruminant.
Lamb'kin s. A small lamb.
Bod'kin s. An instrument to draw tape, etc., through a hem; a large hair-pin.
Prince'kin s. A petty or little prince.

Brod'ekin s. A high boot.
Ram'ekin s. A dish of cheese boiled with egg.
Mutch'kin s. (*Scot.*) About ¾ pint.
Spill'ikin s. A narrow slip of bone, etc., used in certain games.
Man'ikin s. A little man, a dwarf; an anatomical model.
Fin'ikin a. Finical.
Min'ikin s. A pet; a diminutive thing. a. Diminutive.
Can'nikin s. A small metal drinking vessel.
Pan'nikin s. A small metal pan or drinking vessel.
Lar'rikin s. An Australian hooligan.
Boot'ikin s. A small boot; a knitted gaiter.
Cu'tikin s. A long gaiter.
Cal'kin s. A turned edge or other contrivance on a horse's shoe to prevent slipping.
Malkin (Maw'kin) s. A kitchen wench; a scarecrow.
Grimal'kin s. An old she-cat; a spiteful old woman.
Wel'kin s. Vault of heaven; sky.
Bum'kin s. A small boom to extend the foresail, mainsail, or mizzen.
Rum'kin s. An old drinking-vessel.
Nap'kin s. A small linen cloth or towel.
Pip'kin s. A small earthen pot or jar.
Bump'kin s. A clumsy lout, an awkward rustic.
Pump'kin s. A gourd-like plant; its fruit.
Park'in s. A sweetmeat of oatmeal and treacle.
Kil'derkin s. A small barrel; about eighteen gallons.
Gher'kin s. A young or small variety of cucumber pickled.
Jer'kin s. A short coat, especially of leather.
Nip'perkin s. A small cup; its contents.
Fir'kin s. Nine gallons; 56 lbs. (of butter).
Skin s. Natural external covering of the body, a fruit, plant, etc.; hide; a thin outer covering. v.t. To flay, to strip off the skin. v.i. To become covered with skin.
Red'skin s. A N. American Indian.
Mole'skin s. The fur of the mole; a cloth resembling this.
Doe'skin s. The skin of a doe; a twilled woollen cloth.
Fore'skin s. The prepuce.
Gris'kin s. The lean part of a pig's loin.
Sis'kin s. Small migratory bird allied to the goldfinch.
Sheep'skin s. The skin of a sheep; parchment made therefrom.
Bear'skin s. The skin of a bear; the tall fur headdress of the British Guards.
Bus'kin s. A high boot; the tragic vein, tragedy.
Cat'kin s. The inflorescence of the willow, hazel, etc.
Amyg'dalin s. A crystalline substance extracted from bitter almonds.
Form'alin s. A strongly antiseptic solution of formaldehyde.
Dig'italin s. An alkaloid prepared from the foxglove.
San'talin s. The red colouring matter of sandal-wood.
Pty'alin s. A ferment contained in saliva.
Gob'lin s. An ugly, mischievous sprite.
Hobgob'lin s. An elf, especially one of forbidding appearance.
Cod'lin s. An apple for baking.
Maud'lin a. Fuddled; half drunk; mawkishly sentimental.
Go'belin a. Denoting a superior French tapestry.
Zep'pelin s. A large dirigible airship.
Jav'elin s. A light spear for throwing.
Rav'elin s. A detached work in fortification.
Metheg'lin s. Welsh mead.
Mech'lin s. A light kind of lace.
Crack'lin s. Crackle glass or porcelain.
Frank'lin s. A freeholder of feudal times not liable to feudal service.
Roccel'lin s. A dye obtained from orchil.
Vitel'lin s. The protein in the yolk of egg.
Podoph'illin s. A cathartic resin obtained from the root of the may-apple.
Medul'lin s. Cellulose from certain piths.
Krem'lin s. A Russian citadel, especially in Moscow.
Drum'lin s. A narrow hill or ridge.
Dun'lin s. The red-backed sandpiper.
Ka'olin s. A fine porcelain clay.
Fran'colin s. A brilliantly coloured bird allied to the partridge.
Man'dolin s. A guitar-like musical instrument.
Pang'olin s. The scaly ant-eater.
Violin' s. A four-stringed musical instrument played with a bow.
Vi'olin s. An emetic prepared from the violet.
Lan'olin s. An unctuous substance extracted from wool.
Cip'olin s. A green-veined marble.
Com'plin s. The last of the canonical hours in the breviary.
Pop'lin s. A ribbed fabric of silk and worsted.
Berlin' s. A four-wheeled carriage; fine worsted for fancy work.
Mer'lin s. A small variety of falcon.
Pur'lin s. A horizontal timber resting on principal rafters and supporting the boards of the roof.
Mas'lin s. A mixture of different kinds of grain. a. Made of this.
Mus'lin s. Fine, thin stuff made of cotton.
Rat'lin s. A ratline.
Tarpau'lin s. Waterproofed canvas.
Glob'ulin s. An albumenous protein obtained from animals and plants.
Tuber'culin s. A ptomaine due to the tubercle bacillus; a culture injected in cases of tuberculosis.
In'ulin s. A starchy powder obtained from the roots of elecampane.
Mou'lin s. A vertical shaft in a glacier.
Lu'pulin s. The bitter principle of hops.
Ceru'lin s. A blue colouring-matter.
Ky'lin s. A fabulous and decorative Chinese animal.
Hæmatox'ylin s. The colouring principle of logwood.
Gam'in s. A street arab.
Ben'jamin s. Benzoin.
Ver'min s. Noxious animals singly or collectively.
Plas'min s. A protein in the plasma of the blood.
Albu'min s. (*Albumen*).
Cum'in s. An umbelliferous plant; its aromatic seeds.
Legu'min s. A protein contained in many seeds.
Duralu'min s. An alloy of aluminium.
Nico'tianin s. A neutral substance extracted from tobacco.
Mel'anin s. A black pigment of the skin.
Ger'anin s. An astringent obtained from some species of geranium.
Lig'nin s. Xylogen; the essential substance of wood.
Tan'nin s. Astringent principle of oak-bark; tannic acid.
Op'sonin s. A constituent of blood serum.
San'tonin s. The bitter principle of santonica.

Coin s. A piece of stamped metal for use as money; money. v.t. To convert into money, to mint; to fabricate.
Sain'foin s. A clover-like fodder-plant.
Join v.t. To couple, unite, combine; to associate, to add. v.i. To be in contact or close; to unite with in marriage, etc. s. Place, act, etc., of joining.
Subjoin' v.t. To append, annex.
Adjoin' v.i. To be contiguous to.
Rejoin' v.t. To join again, reunite. v.i. To come together again; to retort, to answer a charge.
Surrejoin' v.i. To reply to defendant's rejoinder.
Enjoin' v.t. To prescribe; to prohibit; to put an injunction on.
Conjoin' v.i. To unite, associate. v.t. To cause to come together.
Disjoin' v.t. and i. To separate or become separated; to part.
Misjoin' v.t. To join unfitly or improperly.
Loin s. Part of animal between ribs and haunch.
Sir'loin s. The upper part of a loin of beef.
Purloin' v.t. To filch, pilfer; to plagiarize.
Tal'apoin s. A Buddhist monk; a W. African monkey.
Fi'broin s. The chief constituent of silk, etc.
Her'oin s. A morphine sedative preparation.
Groin s. The depressed part of the thigh; hollow intersection of vaults crossing each other.
Quoin s. An external angle, especially of a building; a wedge used for various purposes.
Ben'zoin s. A balsamous resin used in medicine and for incense.
Pin s. A small pointed implement or peg of metal, wood, etc.; a pointed and headed piece of wire. v.t. To fasten with this, to secure; to enclose.
Jal'apin s. An amorphous glucoside in jalap.
Ter'rapin s. An edible freshwater tortoise of N. America.
Inch'pin s. The sweetbread of a deer.
Linch'pin s. A pin holding a wheel to the axle.
Scul'pin s. A spiny marine fish.
Chop'in s. A Scotch wine-quart.
Pip'pin s. A variety of apple.
Ter'pin s. A derivative of oil of turpentine.
Spin v.t. To draw out and twist into threads; to whirl; to protract; to form (a web) of threads. v.i. To practise spinning; to rotate. s. A twirl (of a top, etc.); a run on a bicycle, etc.
Crisp'in s. A shoemaker.
Man'darin s. A Chinese official; dark yellow dye or colour.
Stear'in s. The harder part of animal fat.
Tam'arin s. A S. American marmoset.
Cou'marin s. The aromatic principle of the tonka-bean.
Aliz'arin s. A dyestuff originally obtained from madder.
Fi'brin s. The albuminoid constituent of blood which causes it to clot.
San'hedrin s. The ancient great council of the Jews.
Suber'in s. A cellulose present in cork.
Cer'in s. A crystalline substance obtained from cork.
Ser'in s. A small finch allied to the canary.
Cul'verin s. A long, slender, obsolete gun.
Grin v.i. To show the teeth in laughter, scorn, etc. s. This act; a forced or set smile.
Chagrin' s. Vexation, disappointment. v.t. To vex, put out of humour.
Fior'in s. White bent-grass.
Flor'in s. A two-shilling piece.
Quer'citrin s. The yellow colouring matter of quercitron.
Dex'trin s. A gummy substance obtained from starch.
Laur'in s. A crystalline substance obtained from laurels and bays.
Bu'rin s. An engraver's tool for metal.
Neur'in s. Nerve-energy.
Pur'purin s. A red dyestuff.
Sin s. Wickedness, iniquity; moral depravity; crime. v.i. To transgress, to violate divine law.
Ba'sin s. A hollow vessel; a small pond; a dock.
Moc'casin s. A soft leather shoe in one piece.
Cer'asin s. A gum from cherry- and plum-trees.
Sas'in s. An Indian antelope.
Toc'sin s. An alarm-bell.
Res'in s. A solid, inflammable, vegetable exudation.
Rai'sin s. A dried grape.
Seis'in (sēz'-) s. Possession of land under a freehold.
Kham'sin s. A hot southerly wind in Egypt.
E'osin s. A pink-coloured dyestuff used for staining microscopic specimens.
Ros'in s. Prepared resin for violin bows, etc. v.t. To treat with this.
Hæmato'sin s. Hæmatin.
Pep'sin s. A ferment contained in the gastric juice.
Sep'sin s. (*Sepsine*).
Tryp'sin s. A digestive ferment found in the pancreatic juice.
Spadas'sin s. A bravo; a duellist.
Assas'sin s. A murderer.
Quas'sin s. The bitter principle of quassia.
Cous'in s. Son or daughter of an uncle or aunt; a kinsman.
Tin s. A white, malleable, metallic element; a dish, container, etc., coated with this; (*slang*) money. v.t. To plate with tin, put in a tin.
Pan'creatin s. A proteid found in the pancreas.
Lat'in a. Pertaining to the people of ancient Latium in Italy; Roman. s. The language of the ancient Romans.
Mat'in a. Matinal.
Hæ'matin s. An amorphous constituent of blood.
Chro'matin s. A granular protoplasmic substance found in the nucleus of cells.
Ker'atin s. The chief constituent of hair, feathers, nails, etc.
Sat'in s. A glossy silk fabric.
I'satin s. A compound obtained by oxidizing indigo.
Galac'tin s. A nitrogenous constituent of milk.
Pec'tin s. An amorphous compound found in fruits, etc.
Phenac'etin s. An antipyretic drug obtained from phenol.
Bull'etin s. An official account of public news.
Cre'tin s. One afflicted with cretinism.
Chi'tin s. The horny basis of the shells of crustaceans, insects, etc.
Laman'tin s. The manatee.
Cathar'tin s. The active principle of senna.
Mar'tin s. A bird of the swallow family.
Free'martin s. A cow born as twin with a bull, and usually barren.
Aus'tin s., a. Augustinian.

Highfalu'tin a. Bombastic, affected.
Glu'tin s. Vegetable gelatine.
Ga'duin s. An essential constituent of cod-liver oil.
Pen'guin s. A web-footed marine bird.
Pin'guin s. A W. Indian fruit of the pine-apple family.
Bed'ouin s. A nomadic Arab. a. Pertaining to these ; wandering.
Quin s. A variety of scallop.
Bald'aquin s. (*Baldachin*).
Har'lequin s. A character in pantomime ; a buffoon.
Lam'brequin s. Covering for a knight's helmet.
Se'quin s. An ancient gold coin of Venice; a spangle.
Palanquin' s. A Hindu litter borne on men's shoulders.
Mar'oquin s. Morocco leather.
Ru'in s. That which destroys ; fall, overthrow ; anything in decay ; this state. v.t. To damage essentially, bring to ruin ; to dilapidate.
Bru'in s. The bear.
Bav'in s. Brushwood ; a bundle of this.
Fla'vin s. A yellow vegetable dyestuff.
Spav'in s. Swelling in joint of horse's hind-leg.
Rav'in s. Plunder ; prey.
Sav'in s. An evergreen bush, oil from berries of which is used in medicine.
Lev'in s. Lightning.
Replev'in s. An action for replevy ; writ for this.
Cov'in s. A collusive agreement between persons to the detriment of another.
Win v.t. To gain in competition ; to reach, attain ; to allure. v.i. To gain the victory. s. A success.
Twin s. One of two born at a birth ; one of a pair. a. Being thus ; very similar ; twofold. v.t. and i. To pair with, form pairs.
Tax'in s. A resinous substance from yews.
Tox'in s. A poisonous substance, especially a ptomaine.
Antitox'in s. A substance that neutralizes the action of a toxin.
Disseiz'in s. Unlawful dispossession of a land-holder.
Hoact'zin s. A S. American bird.
Muez'zin s. A Mohammedan crier of the hour of prayer.
Kiln s. A stove or furnace for drying or hardening. v.t. To dry or bake in this.
Damn v.t. To condemn, especially to death and eternal punishment ; to censure. v.i. To swear profanely. s. An oath ; a negligible amount. int. An oath.
Condemn' v.t. To pronounce to be wrong ; to blame ; to pass judicial sentence upon, pronounce unfit for use.
Sol'emn a. Grave ; serious ; reverential.
Contemn' v.t. To despise, scorn.
Limn v.t. To depict, portray.
Col'umn s. A solid pillar ; perpendicular section of a page or line of figures ; body of troops.
Au'tumn s. The season between summer and winter.
Hymn s. A song of adoration. v.t. and i. To worship with or sing hymns.
Inn s. A hotel, tavern ; a college of law.
Finn s. A native of Finland.
Jinn s. The demons of Mohammedan myth.
Linn s. A waterfall ; a pool ; a ravine.
Sally-lunn' s. A kind of tea-cake.
On prep and adv.
Gib'bon s. A long-armed anthropoid ape.
Rib'bon s. A narrow web of silk or satin ; a narrow strip ; a badge.
Eb'on s. Ebony. a. Like ebony ; very black.
Am'bon s. A pulpit, lectern.
Bon'-bon s. A sweetmeat, a sugar-plum.
Car'bon s. A non-metallic element native in diamond and graphite.
Con v.t. To peruse carefully, learn ; to direct the steering of a ship. s. Against.
Ba'con s. Flesh of a hog salted, cured, and dried.
Bea'con s. A signal fire ; a conspicuous mark v.t. To give light to as a beacon.
Dea'con s. One in the lowest degree of holy orders ; a lay assistant.
Archdea'con s. The principal assistant of a bishop.
Panphar'macon s. A panacea.
I'con s. A sacred image or portrait, especially in the Eastern Church.
Ru'bicon s. A final, decisive boundary ; a term in piquet, etc.
Etymolog'icon s. An etymological dictionary.
Sil'icon s. A dark-brown non-metallic element.
Basil'icon s. (*Basilicum*).
Cathol'icon s. A panacea ; a general medical treatise.
Kamptu'licon s. A floor-covering like linoleum.
Synonym'icon s. A dictionary of synonyms.
Eire'nicon s. A proposal for peace.
Pantech'nicon s. A storehouse for furniture ; van for removing furniture.
Euphon'icon s. A kind of pianoforte.
Harmon'icon s. An harmonica.
Stereop'ticon s. A kind of magic lantern.
Sciop'ticon s. A variety of magic lantern.
Onomas'ticon s. A dictionary, vocabulary.
Monas'ticon s. A book dealing with monasteries.
Lex'icon s. A dictionary.
Fal'con s. A small bird of prey ; a trained hawk.
Ger'falcon s. A large Arctic falcon.
Soup'çon s. The slightest trace or flavour of.
Gar'çon s. A waiter.
Zir'con s. A translucent silicate of zirconium
Gas'con s. A native of Gascony ; a braggart
Don s. Title of courtesy in Spain, "Sir," "Mr." ; a person of consequence ; a fellow, etc., at a University. v.t. To put on, invest oneself with.
Cel'adon s. A pale sea-green colour.
Abad'don s. Hell ; the angel of the bottomless pit.
Armaged'don s. The final battle of the nations ; a decisive or sanguinary battle.
Boustrophe'don a. Applied to a form of writing in which the lines read alternately from left to right and right to left.
Cotyle'don s. The seed-leaf of an embryo plant ; a genus of evergreens.
Acotyle'don s. A plant having no cotyledons ; the mosses, lichens, etc.
Dicotyle'don s. A plant with two cotyledons.
Monocotyle'don s. A plant with one cotyledon, as the grasses, palms, etc.
Pyram'idon s. A deep-toned organ stop.
Myr'midon s. One who ruthlessly executes orders.
Gui'don s. A small forked or pointed flag ; a standard-bearer.
Aban'don v.t. To desert, forsake, quit.
Abandon' s. Freedom from restraint, careless in manner.

Clar'endon s. A heavy-faced type.
Ten'don s. Ligature attaching muscle to bone.
Labyrin'thodon s. An extinct amphibian.
My'lodon s. An extinct sloth-like edentate mammal.
Iguan'odon s. A gigantic, extinct, herbivorous reptile.
Sphen'odon s. A lizard-like reptile of New Zealand.
Chæt'odon s. A genus of brilliantly coloured fishes.
Glyp'todon s. An extinct S. American quadruped allied to the armadillos.
Mas'todon s. An extinct animal allied to the elephant.
Bombar'don s. A large brass wind-instrument.
Lard'on s. Slice of bacon for larding.
Par'don v.t. To forgive; to absolve from penalty; to acquit. s. Forgiveness; remission of penalty.
Guer'don s. A reward, recompense.,
Cor'don s. An ornamental cord or ribbon; a line of men, ships, etc.; a projecting row of stones in a wall.
Bour'don s. The bass stop on an organ; the drone of a bagpipe.
Euroc'lydon s. A tempestuous easterly wind in the Mediterranean.
Æ'on s. An immensely long period, an age of the universe.
Ode'on s. An odeum.
Melo'deon s. A reed instrument like an accordion.
Widg'eon s. A small migratory wild duck.
Dudg'eon s. Anger, indignation; the hilt of a dagger.
Gudg'eon s. A small freshwater fish; (*slang*) a dupe; a bearing of a shaft, socket for rudder, etc.
Bludg'eon s. A blunt, heavy weapon. v.t. To beat or strike with this.
Curmudg'eon s. A niggardly person.
Trudg en s. A kind of hard-over-hand swimming.
Badi'geon s. Filling-up material for defects in stone, woodwork, etc.
Pig'eon s. A bird of the order Columbæ, a dove; a dupe, simpleton. v.t. To fleece, swindle.
Dun'geon s. A close, underground prison, a dark cell.
Hab'ergeon s. Armour for neck and breast.
Bour'geon v.t. To put forth buds.
Sur'geon s. A medical practitioner treating injuries,etc., by mechanical means.
Stur'geon s. A large anadromous food-fish.
Pan'cheon s. A large earthenware vessel.
Scun'cheon s. A splay in a window-opening, etc.; a rebate in masonry.
Lun'cheon s. Lunch.
Nun'cheon s. Luncheon.
Pun'cheon s. Tool for piercing, stamping, etc.; cask of 84 or 120 gallons.
Trun'cheon s. A policeman's baton; a short staff.
Escut'cheon s. A shield, especially an armorial shield; the name-plate on a coffin; a perforated plate for a key-hole.
Phe'on s. The heraldic broad arrow.
Le'theon s. Sulphuric ether, an anæsthetic.
Pan'theon s. A temple dedicated to all the gods; all the deities worshipped by a people.
Chame'leon s. An arboreal lizard which can slightly change its colour to suit its surroundings; a changeable person.
Gal'leon s. A large vessel of three or four decks used in the sixteenth and seventeenth centuries.
Napo'leon s. A French gold coin of twenty francs; a card-game.
Ne'on s. A gaseous element of the atmosphere.
Pe'on s. (*India*) A native constable or attendant; (*Spanish American*) a day-labourer, serf.
Hereon' adv. On this.
Thereon' adv.
Whereon' adv.
Chif'fon s. Light gauze used for trimming.
Grif'fon s. A griffin; a kind of vulture; a variety of terrier.
-gon suff. Angled; having angles.
Dec'agon s. A plane figure with ten sides and ten angles.
Hendec'agon s. A plane figure of eleven sides and eleven angles.
Quindec'agon s. A plane fifteen-sided figure.
Sarcoph'agon s. A flesh-eating insect, a flesh-fly.
Chil'iagon s. A figure with 1000 angles.
Flag'on s. A large wine-vessel with a narrow mouth.
Non'agon s. A plane figure having nine sides and nine angles.
Par'agon s. A perfect model, a pattern; a diamond of over 100 carats; a large size of type.
Drag'on s. A fabulous winged monster; a fierce person; a kind of lizard; a northern constellation.
Snap'dragon s. A plant of the Antirrhinum genus; game in which raisins are plucked from lighted brandy.
Tar'ragon s. A herb allied to wormwood.
Tet'ragon s. A plane figure with four angles.
I'sagon s. A figure whose angles are equal.
Oc'tagon s. A plane figure of eight sides and eight angles.
Pen'tagon s. A plane figure having five angles and five sides.
Pro'tagon s. A nitrogenous compound found in the brain, etc.
Hep'tagon s. A plane figure having seven sides and seven angles.
Mar'tagon s. The Turk's-cap lily.
Wag'on s. A strong, four-wheeled cart for heavy roads; open railway truck.
Hex'agon s. A plane figure of six sides and six angles.
Tri'gon s. A triangle; a triangular implement, harp, etc.; a trine.
Zi'gon s. A connecting bar; a small bone in the head.
Or'thogon s. A rectangular figure, or right-angled triangle.
Tro'gon s. A brilliantly coloured bird of tropical America.
Ar'gon s. An inert, colourless and odourless gaseous element.
Jar'gon s. Unintelligible talk; gabble; technical language; slang; a transparent variety of zircon.
Er'gon s. The unit of energy; an erg.
Parer'gon s. A subsidiary or accessory work.
Gor'gon s. A mythic woman of terrible aspect whose gaze turned beholders to stone; a terrible or repulsive woman.
De'mogorgon s. A mysterious and terrifying infernal divinity.
Pol'ygon s. A plane figure of many angles.
Try'gon s. A sting-ray.
Cab'ochon s. A gem cut and polished, but without facets.
Ar'chon s. A chief magistrate in ancient Greece.
Tor'chon (**-shun**) s. A coarse kind of lace; a dish-cloth; a hard, hand-made drawing-paper.

Si'phon s. Bent tube for drawing off liquids; bottle with spring-valve for aerated waters. v.t. and i. To convey or flow by a siphon.
An'tiphon s. A song or anthem for two parts.
Col'ophon s. An inscription on the last page of a book, paper, etc., giving printer's and publisher's name, etc.
Autoch'thon s. An original inhabitant; one sprung from the soil.
Tri'lithon s. A trilith.
Anacolu'thon s. Absence of grammatical construction.
Py'thon s. A genus of large snakes.
I'on s. In electrolysis, one of the opposite parts of the electrolyte; in electric conduction through gases, one of the electrified particles to which conductivity is due.
Ga'bion s. A wicker cylinder filled with earth for defences.
Al'bion s. Britain.
Sym'bion s. A symbiotic organism.
Suspi'cion s. Feeling of one who suspects; mistrust, jealousy.
Coer'cion s. Restraint, compulsion; act or process of being coerced.
Sci'on s. A shoot; a descendant.
Gamma'dion s. An ornament consisting of four gammas, the swastika.
Enchirid'ion s. A text-book, manual.
Collo'dion s. A solution of gun-cotton in ether forming a film.
Accor'dion s. A keyed musical wind-instrument with reeds and bellows.
Gorgonei'on s. A sculptured Gorgon's head.
Trisag'ion s. Hymn to God in which "Holy" is thrice repeated.
Conta'gion s. Transmission of disease by contact; pestilential influence; infection.
Le'gion s. Ancient Roman body of (some 6000) infantry; any great number; a military force.
Re'gion s. A tract of the globe; country; territory; sphere.
Relig'ion s. Recognition of God; system of belief and worship; piety.
Irrelig'ion s. Indifference to or contempt of religion; impiety.
Eucholo'gion s. A formulary of prayers in the Greek Church.
Fal'chion s. A short, broad sword.
Stanch'ion s. A prop, support, post.
Fash'ion s. Form of anything; style of dress; style; custom; high society. v.t. To give shape to; to form; to fit.
Refash'ion v.t. To fashion anew, remodel.
Cush'ion s. A stuffed bag or padded surface; air or steam acting as a buffer. v.t. To seat on or furnish with a cushion.
Li'on s. A large, carnivorous, feline mammal; an object of interest and curiosity; the fifth sign of the Zodiac.
Scal'ion s. A variety of onion.
Tatterdema'lion s. A ragged fellow.
Tal'ion s. The law of retaliation; retaliatory punishment.
Battal'ion s. A body of infantry companies forming an administrative unit.
Dan'delion s. A common composite plant with yellow flowers.
Perihe'lion s. Point in the orbit of a planet or comet nearest the sun.
Aphe'lion s. The point of an orbit most distant from the sun.
Parhe'lion s. A mock sun.
Anthe'lion s. A mock sun.
Triskel'ion s. Figure composed of three legs bent and joined at the thigh.
Gang'lion s. A nerve centre; a lymphatic gland; a tumour.
Vermil'ion s. A brilliant red pigment and colour.
Postil'ion s. One riding on one of the horses of a carriage and directing them.
Pavil'ion s. A tent, marquee; building on cricket-ground, etc., for players.
Rascal'lion s. A rascal.
Rapscal'lion s. A rascal, ne'er-do-well.
Medal'lion s. A large medal; a tablet.
Stal'lion s. An uncastrated horse.
Rebel'lion s. Resistance to lawful authority sedition; mutiny.
Stel'lion s. A lizard of the Levant.
Bil'lion s. A million millions; or, in U.S.A., a thousand millions.
Tourbil'lion s. A revolving firework.
Turbil'lion s. A vortex.
Decil'lion s. A million raised to the tenth power (1 followed by 60 o's).
Modil'lion s. The ornamental bracket below a Corinthian cornice.
Mil'lion s. A thousand thousand.
Nonil'lion s. One million raised to the nineth power (1 followed by 54 o's).
Pil'lion s. Cushion attached to rear of a saddle as a supplementary seat.
Quadril'lion s. Number produced by raising one million to its fourth power (1 followed by 24 o's); in U.S.A. and France the fifth power of one thousand (1 followed by 15 o's).
Tril'lion s. One million raised to the third power (1 followed by 18 o's).
Octil'lion s. One million raised to the eighth power (1 followed by 48 ciphers).
Centil'lion s. The hundredth power of a million.
Quintil'lion s. A million raised to the fifth power (1 followed by 30 o's); or, in France and U.S.A., the sixth power of one thousand (1 followed by 18 o's).
Cotil'lion s. A dance for four or eight persons music for this.
Septil'lion s. The seventh power of a million (1 followed by 42 o's).
Sextil'lion s. The sixth power of a million (1 followed by 36 o's).
Bul'lion s. Gold or silver in the lump.
Cul'lion s. A mean wretch, dastard.
Scul'lion s. A kitchen drudge, especially a boy.
Mul'lion s. Vertical bar separating compartments of a window.
Rul'lion s. (*Scot.*) A shoe of untanned leather.
Prothala'mion s. A prothalamium.
Compan'ion s. A comrade, associate; one living with another for pay; a member of some orders of knighthood; the frame on deck through which light passes below; a ship's stairway. a. Going with or matching something. v.t. and i. To accompany, consort with.
Fran'ion s. A crony; a loose woman.
Wan'ion (wŏn'-) s. Ill-luck; mischief.
Min'ion s. A favourite; a servile dependant; a small size of type.
Domin'ion s. Supreme authority; territory over which authority is exercised; a region.
Pin'ion s. A feather, quill, wing; a small cog-wheel; a fetter for the arm. v.t. To confine the wings or arms of; to cripple by cutting off the outermost joint of a wing.

Opin'ion s. A mental conviction; a judgment, belief, notion.
Am'nion s. A membrane enclosing the unborn fœtus.
Run'nion s. A mangy animal, scurvy person.
Trun'nion s. Supporting knob on each side of a cannon.
On'ion (un'-) s. A plant of the genus Allium; its pungent bulb.
Quater'nion s. A quaternary.
U'nion s. Act of joining; a confederacy; concord; agreement; a trade-union; a workhouse; a fabric of cotton, silk, etc.; the British flag ("Union Jack").
Reu'nion s. A union formed anew; a familiar assembly.
Commu'nion s. A mutual participation in anything; concord; celebration of the Lord's Supper; a religious community.
Inter-commu'nion s. Mutual communion.
Non-u'nion a. Not belonging to or pertaining to a trade union.
Interu'nion s. Reciprocal union.
Disu'nion s. Termination of a union; breach of concord; state of being disunited.
Cam'pion s. An annual plant.
Cham'pion s. One ready to contest with all comers; a zealous advocate; an undefeated athlete or player. v.t. To support a cause. a. (*Slang*) First-rate.
Lam'pion s. A coloured glass light-shade for illuminations.
Ram'pion s. A bell-flower.
Tam'pion s. A stopper.
Tom'pion s. Stopper of a cannon; a printers' inking-pad.
Scor'pion s. An arachnid with jointed, venomous tail; a scourge with metal points; Scorpio.
Du'pion s. A double cocoon formed by silkworms.
Clar'ion s. A shrill, narrow-tubed trumpet; the sound of this. a. Loud and clear.
Hippar'ion s. An extinct horse-like ainmal.
Ker'ion s. Inflammation of the hair-follicles.
Criter'ion s. A principle or standard by which a thing can be judged.
Acroter'ion s. (*Acroterium*).
Mezer'ion s. A small shrub with lilac-like flowers.
Ori'on s. A large constellation crossed by the equinoctial line.
Chor'ion s. The outer membrane enveloping the unborn fœtus; external membrane of seeds.
Mor'ion s. A helmet having no beaver or visor.
Car'rion s. Dead; putrefying flesh. a. Pertaining to or feeding on this.
Septen'trion s. The Great Bear; the northern regions.
Orches'trion s. An orchestrina.
His'trion s. A stage-player.
Decur'ion s. A Roman officer over ten men; a town councillor in modern Italy.
Centur'ion s. A Roman commander of one hundred soldiers.
-sion suff. Forming nouns.
Occa'sion s. Occurrence; opportunity; need. v.t. To cause incidentally; to produce.
Abra'sion s. Act or result of abrading; a scraping, a wound so caused.
Corra'sion s. The wearing down of rocks by natural agencies.
Sua'sion s. Act of persuading.
Persua'sion s. Act of persuading; settled conviction; a creed; a sect.
Dissua'sion s. Exhortation against a thing; a. dissuasive.
Eva'sion s. Act of evading; equivocation; subterfuge.
Inva'sion s. Act of invading; an incursion, violation.
Perva'sion s. Act of pervading.
Adhe'sion s. Act of sticking to, adhering.
Inhe'sion s. Inherence.
Cohe'sion s. Act of sticking together; attraction by which bodies are kept together; coherence.
Incohe'sion s. Incoherence.
Le'sion s. A hurt, wound, injury.
Decis'ion s. Act or result of deciding; judgment.
Indecis'ion s. Irresolution; hesitation.
Precis'ion s. Quality of being precise; exactness.
Circumcis'ion s. Act of circumcising; spiritual purification; the Jews.
Incis'ion s. Art of incising; a gash; trenchancy.
Concis'ion s. Mutilation, circumcision; conciseness.
Excis'ion s. Act of excising; extirpation; deletion.
Elis'ion s. Act of eliding; suppression of a final vowel or syllable.
Collis'ion s. Act of colliding; a violent clashing; conflict.
Deris'ion s. Act of deriding; ridicule, contempt, mockery.
Mispris'ion s. Neglect, oversight; an almost capital offence.
Vis'ion s. Act or faculty of seeing; that which is seen; a dream, fancy, apparition. v.t. To imagine; to present as a vision.
Revis'ion s. Act of revising; that which is revised.
Previs'ion s. Foresight; prescience.
Divis'ion s. Partition; disunion; a rule in arithmetic; section of an army under a general, or of a fleet under one command.
Subdivis'ion s. Act of subdividing; part obtained by this.
Provis'ion s. Act of providing, that which is provided; previous preparation; proviso; victuals. v.t. To store with provisions.
Supervis'ion s. Act of supervising; superintendence.
Emul'sion s. A soft, milk-like medicine.
Repul'sion s. Act, tendency, or process of repelling; dislike; aversion.
Impul'sion s. Act of impelling; impelling force; a driving against.
Compul'sion s. Act of compelling; state of being compelled; constraint.
Propul'sion s. Action of propelling; a force which drives forward; an impulse.
Expul'sion s. Act of expelling; ejection.
Avul'sion s. A plucking or rending from.
Evul'sion s. Act of pulling out or back.
Revul'sion s. Sudden and violent change of feeling, etc.; marked repugnance.
Divul'sion s. Act of plucking away or rending asunder.
Convul'sion s. A series of violent contractions and relaxations of the muscles; a violent disturbance or commotion.

Scan'sion s. Act of scanning verse.
Man'sion s. A large dwelling-house.
Expan'sion s. Act of expanding; state of being expanded; expanse; space.
Recen'sion s. A revision of a text, an edited version.
Incen'sion s. Act of setting or state of being on fire.
Ascen'sion s. Act of ascending.
Reascen'sion s. A second ascension.
Descen'sion s. Act of falling or moving downwards; degradation.
Condescen'sion s. Act of condescending; courtesy, complaisance.
Prehen'sion s. Act of seizing.
Reprehen'sion s. Reproof, censure.
Compre-hen'sion s. Act or power of comprehending; understanding.
Apprehen'sion s. Fear; arrest for trial.
Inappre-hen'sion s. Want of apprehension.
Misappre-hen'sion s. A mistaking, misconception, mistake.
Declen'sion s. Act or state of declining; refusal; variation of nouns to form cases.
Dimen'sion s. Bulk, extent, capacity.
Pen'sion s. An allowance for past services, disablement, etc.; a Continental boarding-house.
Suspen'sion s. Act of suspending, state of being suspended; abeyance; temporary delay, deprivation, etc.
Dissen'sion s. Disagreement; breach of friendship; strife.
Ten'sion s. Act of stretching; state of being stretched; tightness; elastic force.
Preten'sion s. Act of laying claim; an assumed right.
Inten'sion s. Act of straining, stretching, or intensifying; this state; intensity.
Disten'sion s. Act of distending; breadth, expansion.
Exten'sion s. Act of extending; state of being extended; enlargement; space.
Coexten'sion s. Equal extension.
Spon'sion s. Act of becoming surety for another.
Explo'sion s. Act of exploding; a sudden and loud discharge.
Ero'sion s. The wearing away of coast, etc., by action of sea or weather; act of eroding.
Corro'sion s. Act or process of corroding; a corroded state.
Submer'sion s. Act of submerging; state of being put under water, etc.
Emer'sion s. Action of emerging; a reappearance.
Immer'sion s. Act of immersing; state of being immersed or deeply engaged.
Asper'sion s. Calumny, vilification.
Disper'sion s. Act or result of being scattered; diffusion.
Intersper'sion s. Act or result of interspersing.
Deter'sion s. Act of cleansing or purging.
Abster'sion s. Act of cleansing.
Ver'sion s. A translation, rendering; act of translating; an account.
Aver'sion s. Repugnance, antipathy.
Contraver'sion s. Turning to the opposite side; antistrophe.
Obver'sion s. A method of logical inference.
Subver'sion s. Act of subverting; state of being subverted; utter ruin.
Anim-adver'sion s. Reproof, criticism.
Ever'sion s. Act of turning inside out.
Rever'sion s. A reverting; return to past state; succession to an office after present holder's term; return of an estate to grantor or his heirs.
Diver'sion s. Act of diverting; that which diverts; amusement; a feigned attack.
Inver'sion s. Act of inverting; change of order, time, or place.
Conver'sion s. Act of changing from one condition, party, belief, etc., to another; appropriation of property; interchange of terms in logic.
Retrover'sion s. Displacement in a reverse position.
Introver'sion s. Act of introverting; state of being introverted.
Perver'sion s. Act of perverting; change to something worse; misapplication.
Tor'sion s. Act of twisting; force with which this is resisted.
Incur'sion s. A raid, sudden invasion.
Discur'sion s. Desultory talk.
Excur'sion s. A journey, ramble, expedition; a digression.
Pas'sion s. Strong feeling or emotion, or its expression; a suffering or enduring.
Impas'sion v.t. To stir to ardour or passion.
Compas'sion s. Pity, sympathy.
Dispas'sion s. Freedom from passion.
Ces'sion s. Yielding, surrender.
Acces'sion s. Act of acceding; augmentation; the attaining of a throne.
Succes'sion s. A following in order; a series; act or right of inheriting or succeeding; lineage.
Reces'sion s. Act of receding; retirement; a receding part.
Reces'sion (rē-) s. Act of ceding back.
Preces'sion s. Act of going before; advance.
Seces'sion s. Act of seceding; withdrawal from fellowship.
Conces'sion s. Act of conceding; thing conceded; a grant.
Proces'sion s. Act of proceeding; a marching forward; an advancing train of persons, etc.
Retroces'sion s. Act of retroceding.
Introces'sion s. A depression, a shrinking of parts inwards.
Interces'sion s. Act of interceding; mediation.
Confes'sion s. Acknowledgment; act of confessing; thing confessed; a creed.
Profes'sion s. Act of professing; declaration; vocation; persons engaged in a calling.
Egres'sion s. Act of going out.
Regres'sion s. Act of returning; reversion to type.
Aggres'sion s. First act of hostility; attack.
Digres'sion s. A turning aside; departure, or act of departing, from the main subject.
Ingres'sion s. Act of entering.
Progres'sion s. Act of moving forward; regular advance; progress.
Retrogres'sion s. Act of retrogressing; deterioration.
Transgres'sion s. A sin, violation of law, etc.
Pres'sion s. Act of pressing; pressure.
Depres'sion s. Act of depressing; a sinking of a surface; abasement; dejection; low barometric pressure.
Repres'sion s. Act of repressing; check, restraint.
Impres'sion s. Act of impressing; that which is impressed; effect produced; vague idea; edition of a book.
Reimpres'sion s. A reprint.

Compres'sion s. Act of compressing; state of being compressed; condensation.
Oppres'sion s. Act of oppressing; cruelty, severity; dullness of spirits.
Suppres'sion s. Act of suppressing; state of being suppressed.
Expres'sion s. Act of expressing or of representing; utterance; vivid representation of sentiment, feeling, etc.; musical tone; representation of a quantity in algebra.
Ses'sion s. Sitting of a court, etc., for business; time or term of this.
Obses'sion s. State of being obsessed; fixed idea.
Superses'sion s. State of superseding or being superseded.
Posses'sion s. Act or state of possessing; occupancy; anything owned.
Preposses'sion s. Bias, bent, inclination; preoccupation.
Disposses'sion s. Deprivation of possession; this state.
Scis'sion s. Act of cutting; state of being cut.
Abscis'sion s. Act of cutting off.
Rescis'sion s. Act of rescinding or annulling.
Fis'sion s. A cleaving or breaking up into parts; subdivision as natural process of reproduction.
Mis'sion s. Act of sending; state of being sent; duty on which one is sent; persons sent; organization, etc., of missionaries.
Submis'sion s. Act of submitting; surrender; resignation.
Admis'sion s. Act of admitting; introduction.
Readmis'sion s. A further or second admission.
Preadmis'sion s. Previous admission.
Emis'sion s. Act of throwing or shooting out; thing sent out or put in circulation at one time.
Demis'sion s. Act of resigning; humiliation.
Remis'sion s. Act of remitting; discharge of a debt, etc.; pardon.
Commis'sion s. Trust; a body of men joined in an office, their appointment; warrant; document investing one with an office; the office; allowance to agent; perpetration. v.t. To appoint, depute.
Omis'sion s. Neglect of duty; something omitted; act of omitting.
Intromis'sion s. Act of intromitting.
Permis'sion s. Formal consent; leave, licence; act of permitting.
Intermis'sion s. Temporary cessation, pause; intervening period, interval.
Dismis'sion s. Dismissal.
Transmis'sion s. Act of transmitting; transference; passage through.
Manumis'sion s. Emancipation.
Succus'sion s. Act of shaking; a shaking of the thorax in diagnosis.
Concus'sion s. A violent shock; act of agitating.
Percus'sion s. Act of tapping or striking, especially the body in diagnosis; collision, impact; beating of musical instruments.
Repercus'sion s. Act of driving back; reverberation; recoil.
Discus'sion s. Examination by argument; debate; disputation.
Fu'sion s. Act or state of being melted or liquefied; blending, coalescence.
Affu'sion s. A pouring upon.
Effu'sion s. Act of pouring out; dispersion; shedding; outpouring of emotion or feeling, effusiveness.
Diffu'sion s. Act of diffusing; dispersion, spread, propagation.
Suffu'sion s. Act or process of suffusing; state of being or that which is suffused.
Circumfu'sion s. Act or state of being circumfused.
Infu'sion s. Act of infusing; instillation; act, process, or product of steeping; a tincture.
Confu'sion s. State of being confused; loss of self-possession; shame; defeat.
Profu'sion s. State or quality of being profuse; extravagance; rich abundance.
Perfu'sion s. Act of sprinkling or perfusing.
Interfu'sion s. Act or result of interfusing.
Transfu'sion s. Act of transfusing, or of passing blood from one to another.
Occlu'sion s. Act or result of shutting up; imperforation.
Reclu'sion s. State of retirement from the world.
Preclu'sion s. A shutting out, obviating.
Seclu'sion s. Separation from society, etc.; solitude, privacy.
Circumclu'sion s. Act of completely enclosing.
Inclu'sion s. Act of including.
Conclu'sion s. The finish; inference, consequence; act of concluding.
Interclu'sion s. Interception; a stopping.
Exclu'sion s. Act of excluding, state of being excluded; prohibition.
Elu'sion s. Act of eluding; evasion.
Delu'sion s. Act of deluding; an imposition, fallacy, error.
Allu'sion s. A reference; a hint, suggestion.
Illu'sion s. Hallucination; a false show, deception, fallacy.
Disillu'sion v.t. To disillusionize. s. Freedom from illusions.
Collu'sion s. Secret agreement for fraud; connivance.
Prolu'sion s. A preliminary trial, attempt, etc.; a prelude.
Obtru'sion s. Act of obtruding.
Intru'sion s. Act of intruding; entrance uninvited; encroachment; penetration of one rock, etc., through another.
Protru'sion s. Act of protruding; state of being protruded.
Extru'sion s. Act of extruding; expulsion.
Obtu'sion s. Act of making obtuse; state of being dulled or blunted.
Contu'sion s. A severe bruise, act of contusing.
Pertu'sion s. Act of piercing or punching holes in.
-tion suff. Forming nouns of action or condition.
Liba'tion s. Ceremonial act of pouring wine on the ground; a potation.
Limba'tion s. A limbus.
Joba'tion s. A long-winded or reproving lecture.
Loba'tion s. State of being lobed; formation of lobes.
Congloba'tion s. Act of conglobing; a round body.
Triloba'tion s. State of being trilobate.
Proba'tion s. Act of proving; trial; novitiate.
Reproba'tion s. Strong disapproval; condemnation.
Approba'tion s. Approval, a liking.
Disapproba'tion s. Disapproval.
Exacerba'tion s. Act of exacerbating, state of being exacerbated.
Perturba'tion s. Act of perturbing; cause of disquiet; irregularity in motion of heavenly body.
Incuba'tion s. Act of incubating; maturation of poison, etc., in the system.
Tituba'tion s. Nervous fidgetiness.
Ca'tion s. The positive element evolved at a cathode in electrolysis.

Vaca'tion s. Act of vacating; intermission; recess.
Desicca'tion s. Act or state of being desiccated or freed from moisture.
Exsicca'tion s. Act or operation of exsiccating; state of being dried up.
Defeca'tion s. Purification; act of separating from lees.
Hypotheca'tion s. Act or contract by which property is hypothecated.
Depreca'tion s. Prayer for removal of evil; entreaty for pardon.
Impreca'tion s. Act of imprecating; a curse.
Syllabica'tion s. Act or method of dividing words into syllables.
Radica'tion s. Process of taking root; state of having a root.
Eradica'tion s. Act of eradicating; total destruction.
Abdica'tion s. Relinquishment, especially of a throne.
Dedica'tion s. Act of dedicating; words in which a book, etc., is dedicated.
Medica'tion s. Act or process of medicating.
Predica'tion s. Act of predicating; assertion.
Indica'tion s. Act of indicating; a mark; token, symptom.
Vindica'tion s. Act of vindicating; defence, justification.
Syndica'tion s. Act or process of forming a syndicate.
Adjudica'tion s. (*Adjudicate*).
Prejudica'tion s. Act of prejudicating.
-fica'tion suff. Forming nouns from verbs in *-fy*.
Pacifica'tion s. Act of pacifying; reduction to a peaceful state.
Specifica'tion s. Act of specifying; designation of particulars; statement of details, etc.
Silicifica'tion s. Act or process of silicifying.
Calcifica'tion s. Impregnation with or deposition of lime salts; a stage or process of petrifaction.
Decalcifica'tion s. (*Decalcify*).
Dulcifica'tion s. Act or process of making sweet.
Edifica'tion s. Instruction, especially spiritual.
Acidifica'tion s. (*Acidify*).
Solidifica'tion s. Act of making solid.
Nidifica'tion s. Act, process, or result of nest-building.
Dandifica'tion s. (*Dandify*).
Codifica'tion s. (*Codify*).
Modifica'tion s. Act of modifying; state of being modified; change.
Deifica'tion s. Act of deifying.
Frenchifica'tion s. Act, process, or result of Frenchifying.
Salifica'tion s. Act or process of salifying.
Qualifica'tion s. Act of qualifying; state of being qualified; suitable quality or endowment; ability; modification, diminution.
Disqualifica'tion s. Act of disqualifying, state of being disqualified; a disability.
Vilifica'tion s. Act of defaming.
Mellifica'tion s. Production or making of honey.
Jollifica'tion s. A scene of festivity; merry-making.
Mollifica'tion s. Act of mollifying or appeasing.
Nullifica'tion s. Act of nullifying; a rendering void.
Prolifica'tion s. Production of buds from leaves, etc.; the generation of young.
Amplifica'tion s. (*Amplify*).
Exemplifica'tion s. That which exemplifies; a showing by example.
Simplifica'tion s. Act or process of simplifying.
Chylifica'tion s. (*Chylify*).
Ramifica'tion s. Process or result of branching set of branches; an offshoot.
Mummifica'tion s. Act of mummifying.
Humifica'tion s. A turning into mould.
Chymifica'tion s. (*Chymify*).
Panifica'tion s. Process of converting into bread.
Magnifica'tion s. A magnifying; apparent enlargement of an object; laudation.
Lignifica'tion s. Act or process of lignifying.
Significa'tion s. Act of signifying; that which is signified; meaning, sense.
Damnifica'tion s. (*Damnify*).
Indemnifica'tion s. Act of indemnifying; that which indemnifies; reimbursement.
Saponifica'tion s. Act or process of saponifying.
Personifica'tion s. Art of personifying, or endowing with personality; embodiment.
Carnifica'tion s. (*Carnify*).
Unifica'tion s. Act of unifying or uniting into one.
Typifica'tion s. (*Typify*).
Scarifica'tion s. Operation of scarifying.
Lubrifica'tion s. Act of lubricating or making smooth.
Chondrifica'tion s. (*Chondrify*).
Verifica'tion s. Act of verifying; confirmation.
Nigrifica'tion s. Action or process of blackening.
Transmogrifica'tion s. Act or result of transforming.
Scorifica'tion s. Act or process of scorifying.
Glorifica'tion s. Act of glorifying; state of being glorified.
Caprifica'tion s. An artificial method of fertilizing fig-trees.
Horrifica'tion s. Act of horrifying; state of being horrified.
Electrifica'tion s. Act or state of electrifying or being electrified.
Petrifica'tion s. Petrifaction; obduracy.
Nitrifica'tion s. Act or process of becoming nitrous.
Vitrifica'tion s. Vitrifaction.
Devitrifica'tion s. (*Devitrify*).
Thurifica'tion s. Act of burning incense.
Purifica'tion s. Act of purifying; a cleansing from guilt.
Gasifica'tion s. Conversion into gas.
Falsifica'tion s. Act of falsifying; wilful misrepresentation.
Emulsifica'tion s. (*Emulsify*).
Versifica'tion s. Art or practice of versifying; metrical composition.
Diversifica'tion s. Act of diversifying; variation; variegation.
Classifica'tion s. Systematic arrangement.
Ossifica'tion s. Process of changing into bone.
Beatifica'tion s. Act of beatifying; a preliminary step to canonization.
Ratifica'tion s. Act of ratifying.
Gratifica'tion s. Act of gratifying; that which gratifies; recompense.
Stratifica'tion s. Arrangement in strata or layers.
Lactifica'tion s. Production or secretion of milk.
Rectifica'tion s. Act or operation of rectifying or amending.
Sanctifica'tion s. Act of sanctifying; hallowing; consecration.
Fructifica'tion s. Act or process of fructifying; a plant's organs of reproduction.
Acetifica'tion s. (*Acetify*).
Granitifica'tion s. Formation into granite.
Stultifica'tion s. Act of stultifying.
Quantifica'tion s. Act or process of quantifying.
Identifica'tion s. Proof of identity; act of identifying.
Notifica'tion s. Act of notifying; intimation.
Certifica'tion s. Act of certifying.
Fortifica'tion s. Art of fortifying; defensive works; a fort; additional strength.

Mortifica'tion s. Act or result of mortifying; gangrene; subduing of the passions; chagrin.
Testifica'tion s. Act of testifying.
Justifica'tion s. Act of justifying, state of being justified; vindication; defence.
Mystifica'tion s. Act of perplexing; something designed to mystify.
Brutifica'tion s. The rendering brutal or like a brute.
Sanguifica'tion s. Conversion of food into blood.
Vivifica'tion s. Act of vivifying; revival.
Revivifica'tion s. Renewal or restoration of life.
Publica'tion s. Act of making public or publishing; that which is published.
Republica'tion s. Act of republishing; a reprint.
Spiflica'tion s. A crushing, suppression.
Vellica'tion s. Act of twitching or of causing to twitch; a convulsive motion.
Plica'tion s. Act of folding; a fold, plait.
Replica'tion s. A reply, rejoinder; an imitation.
Triplica'tion s. Act or result of trebling.
Multiplica'tion s. Act or process of multiplying; state of being multiplied; reproduction of animals.
Implica'tion s. Act of implicating; state of being implicated; inference; entanglement.
Complica'tion s. Intricate blending of parts; entanglement.
Applica'tion s. Act of applying; request; thing applied; close study.
Misapplica'tion s. Wrong use; misuse.
Supplica'tion s. Humble petition; solicitation.
Duplica'tion s. Act or result of doubling; multiplication by two.
Reduplica'tion s. Act of reduplicating; state of being doubled.
Quadruplica'tion s. Act or process of quadruplicating.
Centuplica'tion s. (*Centuple*).
Explica'tion s. Act of explicating; explanation, interpretation.
Formica'tion s. An irritation of the skin.
Fornica'tion s. Unlawful sexual intercourse.
Communica'tion s. Act of communicating, that which is communicated; message, news, intercourse.
Intercommunica'tion s. Reciprocal communication or intercourse.
Excommunica'tion s. Act or sentence of excommunication; deprivation of Church privileges.
Varica'tion s. Condition of having varices.
Prevarica'tion s. Act of quibbling; evasion of the truth; verbal misrepresentation.
Divarica'tion s. A parting, forking; equivocation.
Fabrica'tion s. Act of fabricating; a falsehood.
Imbrica'tion s. State of lapping one over the other; curve like that of roof-tiles.
Lubrica'tion s. Act or process of lubricating.
Rubrica'tion s. Act or process of rubricating; that which is rubricated.
Lorica'tion s. A covering of hard plates or scales.
Extrica'tion s. Act of extricating.
Vesica'tion s. Act or process of raising blisters.
Authentica'tion s. Act of authenticating.
Decortica'tion s. (*Decorticate*).
Excortica'tion s. Act of stripping off bark.
Urtica'tion s. Stinging, as though from nettles.
Mastica'tion s. Act of masticating.
Domestica'tion s. Act of domesticating, state of being domesticated.
Sophistica'tion s. Act of adulterating or debasing the purity of.
Prognostica'tion s. Act of prognosticating; presage.
Rustica'tion s. Act of rusticating; state of being rusticated.
Toxica'tion s. Poisoning.
Intoxica'tion s. State of being intoxicated; act of intoxicating; elation.
Defalca'tion s. A breach of trust; embezzlement.
Inculca'tion s. Act of inculcating.
Trunca'tion s. Act of lopping; state of being cut short.
Detrunca'tion s. Act or result of lopping.
Suffoca'tion s. Act of suffocating; state of being stifled.
Loca'tion s. Situation; district.
Alloca'tion s. Distribution, assignment.
Colloca'tion s. Arrangement, disposition.
Disloca'tion s. State of being dislocated, act of dislocating; displacement of a joint.
Embroca'tion s. Act of rubbing a diseased part; the lotion used.
Reciproca'tion s. Act of reciprocating; alternation.
Voca'tion s. A calling, trade, profession.
Avoca'tion s. Business, occupation, calling.
Evoca'tion s. Summons; calling forth.
Revoca'tion s. Act of calling back; repeal, reversal.
Univoca'tion s. Agreement of name and meaning.
Equivoca'tion s. Ambiguity of speech; quibbling.
Invoca'tion s. Act of invoking; supplication in prayer.
Convoca'tion s. Act of calling together; an assembly, especially of clergy or University graduates.
Provoca'tion s. Act of provoking; that which provokes.
Demarca'tion s. The fixing of a boundary; division.
Alterca'tion s. A quarrel, heated dispute.
Furca'tion s. A branching.
Bifurca'tion s. A division into two branches either of the branches.
Confisca'tion s. Act of confiscating.
Obfusca'tion s. Act or result of darkening or confusing.
Corusca'tion s. A glittering; intellectual brilliancy.
Educa'tion s. Process of educating; systematic course of instruction; result of this.
Manduca'tion s. Mastication, chewing.
Grada'tion s. An orderly arrangement; one step in a series; regular advance.
Degrada'tion s. Act of degrading; state of being degraded; disgrace.
Retrograda'tion s. Act of retrograding; state of being retrograded.
Exhereda'tion s. A disinheriting.
Depreda'tion s. Plundering, spoiling.
Elucida'tion s. Act of elucidating; explaining.
Hida'tion s. Ancient method of assessing by or reckoning in hides.
Valida'tion s. Act of validating; state of being validated.
Invalida'tion s. Act of invalidating; state of being invalidated.
Consolida'tion s. (*Consolidate*).
Intimida'tion s. Act of intimidating; threat.
Lapida'tion s. Act of or martyrdom by stoning.
Delapida'tion s. Decay or damage through disrepair.
Trepida'tion s. Trembling of the body; state of alarm.
Liquida'tion s. Act or process of liquidating.
Emenda'tion s. Correction; act of altering for the better.
Commenda'tion s. Praise; recommendation, compliments.
Recommenda'tion s. Act of recommending; favourable representation; that which procures favour.

Fecunda'tion s. Act or process of rendering fruitful.
Inunda'tion s. Act of inundating; a deluge.
Founda'tion s. The basis of a structure; act of founding; endowment; an endowed institution; first principles.
Accommoda'tion s. Adaptation; settlement; supply of something needful; lodgings; a loan.
Retarda'tion s. Act of retarding; delaying; diminution of speed.
Backwarda'tion s. Amount paid by seller to purchaser of stock for privilege of deferring delivery.
Lauda'tion s. Act of praising; praise.
Infeuda'tion s. Enfeoffment; act of putting one in possession of an estate in fee.
Denuda'tion s. Act of denuding; exposure of rocks by the action of water.
Suda'tion s. Sweating; sweat.
Desuda'tion s. A copious sweating.
Transuda'tion s. Act or process of transuding.
Exuda'tion s. Act of exuding; matter exuded.
Trabea'tion s. Unarched architectural construction.
Idea'tion s. Act of forming ideas.
Nuclea'tion s. Act or process of nucleating; formation of nuclei.
Enuclea'tion s. Act of making clear or solving.
Permea'tion s. Act of permeating.
Linea'tion s. Markings in lines.
Delinea'tion s. Act of depicting; portrait, draught, description.
Allinea'tion s. Alinement.
Interlinea'tion s. Act of interlining; matter inserted between lines.
Crea'tion s. Act of creating; aggregate of created things; the universe; act of appointing, investing, etc.; a production of art, etc.
Recrea'tion s. Refreshment after toil; amusement, diversion.
Re-crea'tion s. A new creation.
Procrea'tion s. Act of procreating.
Laurea'tion s. Act of crowning with laurel.
Nausea'tion s. Act of nauseating; state of being nauseated.
Inlaga'tion s. Restoration of an outlaw to civil rights.
Propaga'tion s. Act of propagating; spread of anything; generation.
Divaga'tion s. A digression.
Variega'tion s. Act of variegating; diversity of colour.
Lega'tion s. Act of sending a legate or diplomatic mission; an embassy; ambassador and suite.
Delega'tion s. Act of delegating; persons delegated; a commission.
Relega'tion s. Act of relegating; removal; banishment.
Allega'tion s. Affirmation, declaration.
Nega'tion s. Denial, act of denying; contradiction.
Abnega'tion s. Denial, renunciation, self-sacrifice.
Denega'tion s. Contradiction.
Segrega'tion s. Separation from others; act of segregating.
Aggrega'tion s. A collection; act of aggregating.
Congrega'tion s. Act of congregating; a collection, assemblage, religious body meeting for worship.
Liga'tion s. Act or process of binding; a ligature.
Obliga'tion s. That which obligates; the binding power of an oath, etc.; any act by which one becomes bound to do or forbear doing something; indebtedness for a favour, etc.
Deliga'tion s. A binding up.
Alliga'tion s. Act of tying or uniting together.
Colliga'tion s. Alliance; generalization.
Fumiga'tion s. Act of fumigating; vapour.
Irriga'tion s. Act or process of irrigating.
Litiga'tion s. Act or process of litigating; a lawsuit.
Mitiga'tion s. Act of mitigating; alleviation.
Castiga'tion s. Punishment, especially severe.
Investiga'tion s. Act or process of investigation; inquiry; scrutiny.
Instiga'tion s. Act of instigating; incitement.
Fustiga'tion s. A cudgelling, flogging.
Naviga'tion s. Act or art of navigation.
Circumnaviga'tion s. Act of circumnavigating.
Leviga'tion s. Act of making smooth or pulverizing.
Noctiviga'tion s. Act or habit of wandering by night.
Promulga'tion s. Act of promulgating; open declaration.
Elonga'tion s. Act of lengthening; continuation; apparent distance of a planet from the sun.
Prolonga'tion s. Act of prolonging; extension.
Homologa'tion s. Act of homologating; ratification.
Roga'tion s. A solemn supplication, litany.
Abroga'tion s. Act of abrogating; annulment.
Deroga'tion s. Act of derogating; diminution, detraction.
Supereroga'tion s. Performance of more than duty or necessity requires.
Proroga'tion s. Adjournment, especially of Parliament.
Arroga'tion s. Act of arrogating.
Interroga'tion s. Act of interrogating; a question; a question-mark (?).
Objurga'tion s. Reproof; reprehension; act of chiding.
Purga'tion s. Act of purifying or purging.
Compurga'tion s. Justifying one's veracity by the oath of others.
Expurga'tion s. Act of expurgating; purification.
Subjuga'tion s. Act of subjugating; subdual.
Conjuga'tion s. Act or process of conjugating; inflection of verbs; a class of verbs similarly conjugated.
Corruga'tion s. Act of corrugating; a wrinkle.
Glacia'tion s. Act or process of glaciating.
Emacia'tion s. State of being emaciated; extreme leanness.
Deprecia'tion s. Act of depreciating, fall in value; allowance for wear and tear.
Apprecia'tion s. Just or favourable valuation; rise in price.
Officia'tion s. Act of officiating.
Enuncia'tion s. Act or manner of enunciating; expression; declaration.
Denuncia'tion s. Act of denouncing; a public menace.
Renuncia'tion s. Act of renouncing; disavowal; self-denial.
Annuncia'tion s. Act of announcing, especially the Incarnation and the festival (25th March) in memory of this.
Pronuncia'tion s. Act or mode of pronouncing; utterance.
Mispronuncia'tion s. Wrong pronunciation.
Consocia'tion s. Intimate union; fellowship.
Associa'tion s. Union; an assembly of persons with similar aims, tastes, etc.
Dissocia'tion s. Act of dissociating; disunion; decomposition.
Deforcia'tion s. A withholding by force or fraud of rightful possession.
Fascia'tion s. Union of stems, etc., in ribbon-like form; binding up of injured parts.

Excrucia'tion s. Agony; torture.

Radia'tion s. Act of radiating; emission of rays.

Eradia'tion s. Emission of light or splendour.

Irradia'tion s. Act of irradiating; illumination; apparent enlargement due to this.

Media'tion s. Act of mediating; intercession.

Intermedia'tion s. Intervention.

Repudia'tion s. Act of repudiating; disavowal.

Retalia'tion s. Act of retaliating; reprisal, retribution.

Cilia'tion s. (*Cilia*).

Domicilia'tion s. A permanent residence.

Concilia'tion s. Act of gaining favour; reconciliation of disputes, etc.

Reconcilia'tion s. Act of reconciling; state of being reconciled; renewal of friendship; propitiation.

Filia'tion s. Relation of a child to its father; descent; affiliation.

Affilia'tion s. Adoption; act of affiliating.

Humilia'tion s. Act of humbling; state or cause of being humbled.

Pallia'tion s. Act of palliating; that which palliates; extenuating circumstances.

Folia'tion s. Act of forming into leaves or into laminæ, or of decorating with leaf-like designs; foliage.

Defolia'tion s. Falling of the leaf.

Exfolia'tion s. Scaling off.

Spolia'tion s. Robbery, pillage.

Despolia'tion s. Act of plundering; state of being plundered.

Calumnia'tion s. Act of caluminating; slander.

Columnia'tion s. Systematic arrangement of columns.

Inter-columnia'tion s. Clear space between columns.

Expia'tion s. Act of expiating; satisfaction; atonement.

Varia'tion s. Act or process of varying; change; mutation; deviation.

Inebria'tion s. Drunkenness, intoxication.

Seria'tion s. Formation or arrangement in sequence.

Excoria'tion s. Act of excoriating; an abrasion.

Floria'tion s. Floral ornamentation; a musical flourish.

Impropria'tion s. Act of putting a benefice into lay hands; a benefice, etc., impropriated.

Appropria'tion s. Act of appropriating; application to special use.

Dis-appropria'tion s. Wrongful taking, especially of money.

Expropria'tion s. Act of dispossessing or depriving of.

Repatria'tion s. Act of repatriating; state of being repatriated.

Expatria'tion s. State of being exiled; act of expatriating or of forsaking one's country.

Stria'tion s. A stria; state of being striated.

Expatia'tion s. Act of expatiating.

Satia'tion s. State of being satiated.

Initia'tion s. A beginning; formal introduction.

Propitia'tion s. Act of propitiating; atonement; that which appeases.

Vitia'tion (vish-) s. Act of vitiating; depravation.

Substantia'tion s. Act or result of substantiating.

Tran-substantia'tion s. Change into another substance, especially that of the bread and wine in the Eucharist.

Con-substantia'tion s. The doctrine of the presence of the actual body and blood of Christ in the sacramental elements.

Differentia'tion s. (*Differentiate*).

Negotia'tion s. A negotiating; diplomatic bargaining.

Avia'tion s. Science and art of travelling in the air.

Obvia'tion s. Act of obviating; state of being obviated.

Devia'tion s. Act of deviating; error; divergence.

Allevia'tion s. Mitigation.

Abbrevia'tion s. Act or result of shortening; a contraction.

Lixivia'tion s. Process of extracting soluble matter from insoluble by filtering or leaching, as alkali from ashes.

Exuvia'tion s. Process of casting the old skin, etc. (of animals).

Asphyxia'tion s. (*Asphyxiate*).

Debarka'tion s. Disembarkation.

Embarka'tion s. Act of going or putting on board.

Disembarka'tion s. Act of disembarking or landing.

Imparka'tion s. The converting of open land into a park.

Intercala'tion s. Insertion of anything between others, as of a day in the calendar.

Hala'tion s. Patch of light on a photographic place.

Inhala'tion s. Act of inhaling; that which is inhaled.

Exhala'tion s. Act or process of exhaling; evaporation; effluvium.

Abla'tion s. A taking away; wearing down of a rock.

Obla'tion s. An offering, sacrifice, especially in worship; act of offering.

Subla'tion s. Denial (in logic).

Ela'tion s. Elevation of mind or spirits; pleasurable pride.

Sphacela'tion s. Process of becoming or making gangrenous.

Dela'tion s. Accusation; act of informing.

Gela'tion s. Solidification through cold.

Regela'tion s. The fusing by freezing of ice particles after thawing.

Congela'tion s. Act or process of congealing; mass congealed.

Anhela'tion s. Difficult respiration, panting.

Rela'tion s. Act of relating or telling; narrative; state of being related; relative quality; consanguinity; person connected thus, kinsman.

Interrela'tion s. Relation between two or more parties, etc.

Correla'tion s. Reciprocal relation; act of bringing into correspondence.

Vela'tion s. The formation of a velum.

Revela'tion s. Act of revealing; thing revealed; the Apocalypse.

Defla'tion s. Act of deflating; state of being deflated.

Affla'tion s. Act of breathing or blowing upon.

Insuffla'tion s. Act of blowing or breathing into or upon.

Infla'tion s. Act of inflating; state of being distended, puffed up, or unduly raised in price.

Confla'tion s. A fusing or blending together.

Sibila'tion s. Sibilancy.

Jubila'tion s. A rejoicing; a feeling of triumph.

Floccila'tion s. Plucking of the bed-clothes in delirium.

Dila'tion s. (*Dilatation*).

Invigila'tion s. Act of an invigilator.

Annihila'tion s. Complete destruction.

Assimila'tion s. Act of assimilating; state of resemblance or identity.

Depila'tion s. The pulling out or stripping of hair.

Horripila'tion s. Creepy feeling through terror, disease, etc.
Compila'tion s. Act of compiling; a work which is compiled.
Oppila'tion s. An obstruction.
Ventila'tion s. Act of ventilating or of winnowing; free exposure to air; public exposure.
Mutila'tion s. Act of mutilating; state of being mutilated.
Lalla'tion s. Pronunciation of *r* as *l*.
Installa'tion s. Act of installing or instituting.
Valla'tion s. A rampart.
Contra-valla'tion s. A chain of forts raised by besiegers.
Circum-valla'tion s. An enclosing rampart.
Flabella'tion s. Cooling with a fan.
Cancella'tion s. Act of cancelling; mark of deletion.
Flagella'tion s. A scourging, flogging.
Crenella'tion s. (*Crenellate*).
Compella'tion s. Manner of address; ceremonious appellation.
Appella'tion s. A name, title.
Interpella'tion s. Act of interpellating; question put in a legislative assembly to a minister.
Cupella'tion s. Refining of gold, silver, etc., in a cupel.
Tessella'tion s. Mosaic work.
Castella'tion s. (*Castellated*).
Constella'tion s. A group of fixed stars; an assemblage of splendours.
Illa'tion s. A deduction, inference from premises.
Vacilla'tion s. A wavering, unsteadiness.
Oscilla'tion s. Act or state of oscillating, vibration.
Fibrilla'tion s. A fibrous structure; a fringe.
Titilla'tion s. Pleasurable excitement.
Cantilla'tion s. (*Cantillate*).
Scintilla'tion s. Act of scintillating; a twinkling.
Distilla'tion s. Act of distilling; process of vapourizing a substance and condensing the vapour to liquid; the product of this.
Instilla'tion s. Act or process of instilling.
Colla'tion s. Act of collating; a light repast.
Decolla'tion s. Act of beheading.
Machicola'tion s. Opening in castle tower for shooting or dropping missiles upon assailants; gallery, etc., with such openings.
Percola'tion s. Act of percolating; filtration.
Areola'tion s. A small space bounded by a different colour, texture, etc.
Variola'tion s. Inoculation with smallpox virus.
Vitriola'tion s. Act or process of vitriolating.
Etiola'tion s. Operation of blanching plants, etc.; paleness.
Viola'tion s. Act of violation; infringement; an injury.
Immola'tion s. A sacrifice; act of sacrificing.
Interpola'tion s. Act of interpolating; spurious passage, etc., inserted.
Desola'tion s. Act of desolating, state of being desolated; ruin; loneliness; affliction.
Isola'tion s. State of being isolated; insulation.
Insola'tion s. Act or process of exposing to the sun; sunstroke.
Consola'tion s. Act of comforting, state of being comforted; that which comforts or soothes.
Contempla'tion s. Act of contemplating; meditation.
Legisla'tion s. Act of making laws.
Transla'tion s. Act of translation; that which has been translated; a transference.
Mistransla'tion s. A wrong translation.
Confabula'tion s. A private or familiar talk.
Tintinabula'tion s. The jingling of bells.
Tabula'tion s. Act of tabulating; state of being tabulated.
Infibula'tion s. Act of confining with a clasp and padlock.
Tribula'tion s. Severe affliction; trouble.
Ambula'tion s. Act of walking, a walk.
Circumambula'tion s. (*Circumambulate*).
Funambula'tion s. Rope-dancing.
Perambula'tion s. Act of perambulating.
Noctambula'tion s. Sleep-walking.
Ejacula'tion s. A sudden exclamation; a short prayer.
Macula'tion s. Act of spotting; a blemish.
Pecula'tion s. Act of peculating; embezzlement.
Specula'tion s. Act or practice of speculating; contemplation; theory; a risky financial venture.
Fascicula'tion s. State of being clustered; a cluster, bunch.
Vermicula'tion s. Worm-like motion; state of being vermiculate, vermicular, or worm-eaten; vermiculated work.
Genicula'tion s. State or position of being bent abruptly.
Matricula'tion s. Act of matriculating.
Reticula'tion s. Network; state of being reticulated.
Denticula'tion s. State of being denticulate.
Articula'tion s. Junction of the bones of a skeleton, parts of a plant, etc.; a joint, the parts between a joint; utterance, speech.
Gesticula'tion s. Act of gesticulating; a gesture.
Calcula'tion s. Act or result of calculating; forethought; scheme.
Miscalcula'tion s. An erroneous calculation.
Inocula'tion s. Act or practice of inoculating.
Tubercula'tion s. Formation of or a system of tubercles; state of being tubercular.
Circula'tion s. Act of circulating; extent to which anything circulates.
Emascula'tion s. Act of emasculating; state of being emasculated.
Oscula'tion s. Kissing; contact of curves.
Inoscula'tion s. Junction of vessels, etc., so that their contents may pass from one to the other.
Adula'tion s. Gross flattery.
Stridula'tion s. A creaking noise, as that of crickets, etc.
Undula'tion s. A waving or vibratory motion; gentle slope.
Modula'tion s. Act of modulating or of inflecting the voice; change from one scale to another; melody.
Nodula'tion s. Process of becoming or state of being nodular.
Coagula'tion s. (*Coagulate*).
Regula'tion s. Act of regulating; a principle, law, order.
Angula'tion s. Making of angles; angular form.
Triangula'tion s. Operation of, or series of triangles in, triangulating.
Strangula'tion s. Act of strangling; suffocation.
Cellula'tion s. (*Cellule*).
Pullula'tion s. Budding; germination.
Ulula'tion s. A howl as of a wolf.
Emula'tion s. Act of emulating; competition, rivalry; strife.

Dissimula'tion s. Hypocrisy.
Stimula'tion s. Act of stimulating; state of being stimulated.
Nummula'tion s. Arrangement of blood-corpuscles in rouleaux.
Formula'tion s. Act of formulating; that which is formulated.
Accumula'tion s. A mass, heap; a collection made gradually.
Granula'tion s. Act of forming into grains; healing of wounds by formation of minute fleshy bodies; such a body.
Crenula'tion s. A series of fine notches.
Annula'tion s. Ring-like structure or markings.
Vapula'tion s. A flogging.
Manipula'tion s. Art, act, or mode of manipulating.
Stipula'tion s. Act of stipulating; a contract or item in it; arrangement, etc., of stipules.
Copula'tion s. Act of coupling; coition.
Popula'tion s. Act or operation of peopling; whole number of persons in a given area; the inhabitants.
Depopula'tion s. Act of depopulating; state of being depopulated.
Gastrula'tion s. The formation of a gastrula.
Insula'tion s. Act of insulating; state of being insulated.
Congratula'tion s. Act of congratulating.
Punctula'tion s. A point.
Capitula'tion s. (*Capitulate*).
Recapitula'tion s. Act of recapitulating; a summary.
Postula'tion s. Act of postulating; assumption.
Expostula'tion s. Act of expostulating; protest.
Ustula'tion s. Act of scorching, etc.; the burning of wine.
Pustula'tion s. State of being pustulated or pustulous.
Ovula'tion s. The formation of eggs in the ovary, or their discharge therefrom.
Defama'tion s. Act of defaming; slander.
Amalgama'tion s. Act, operation, or result of amalgamating.
Acclama'tion s. A shout of applause.
Declama'tion s. A passionate discourse.
Reclama'tion s. Demand for restoration; recovery.
Conclama'tion s. A general outcry.
Proclama'tion s. Act of publishing abroad; an official or public announcement.
Exclama'tion s. A loud outcry; a passionate sentence; an interjection.
Desquama'tion s. Separation of the skin in flakes or scales.
Racema'tion s. A bunch, as of grapes.
Crema'tion s. Act or custom of cremating.
Decima'tion s. Act of decimating; a tithing.
Himat'ion s. An ancient Greek's outer garment.
Lima'tion s. Act of filing or polishing.
Sublima'tion s. Act of sublimating; state of being sublimated; exaltation.
Acclima'tion s. Acclimalization by natural process.
Collima'tion s. (*Collimate*).
Anima'tion s. Life, vigour.
Reanima'tion s. Revival, state of being reanimated.
Legitima'tion s. Act of legitimizing.
Illegitima'tion s. Act of making or state of being illegitimate.
Intima'tion s. A hint; an announcement.
Estima'tion s. Act of estimating; opinion, especially favourable; esteem; honour.
Approxima'tion s. A coming near.
Gamma'tion s. The gammadion.
Inflamma'tion s. Act of inflaming; state of being inflamed; painful swelling and redness of a part; heat, passion.
Gemma'tion s. Asexual formation of a new individual by budding or protusion; act of budding; disposition of buds; vernation.
Summa'tion s. Addition; an aggregate.
Consumma'tion s. Act of consummating; end; perfection.
Affirma'tion s. Act of affirming; declaration.
Reaffirma'tion s. Another affirmation of the same.
Confirma'tion s. Act of confirming or establishing; an episcopal rite by which one is admitted to full Church privileges.
Forma'tion s. Act of forming; manner in which a thing is formed; arrangement.
Deforma'tion s. A disfiguring, defacing, distortion.
Reforma'tion s. Act of reforming; state of being reformed; amendment; the Protestant revolution of the sixteenth century.
Re-forma'tion s. A new formation or forming.
Malforma'tion s. An irregular or anomalous formation or structure of parts.
Informa'tion s. Act of informing; intelligence communicated; knowledge acquired; formal accusation before a magistrate.
Misinforma'tion s. Wrong information.
Conforma'tion s. Act of conforming; manner in which a thing is formed; structure.
Malconforma'tion s. Imperfect or disproportionate formation.
Transforma'tion s. Act of transforming; an entire change in form, character, etc.
Chrisma'tion s. Act of applying chrism.
Inhuma'tion s. Act of inhuming; interment.
Exhuma'tion s. Act of digging up from the grave.
Depluma'tion s. Act or result of depluming.
Lachryma'tion s. A weeping.
Na'tion s. Body of people under the same government or inhabiting the same country.
Profana'tion s. Act of profaning, violating, or treating with contempt or abuse.
Explana'tion s. Act of explaining; that which makes clear; interpretation.
Emana'tion s. Act of emanating; that which emanates from a source; efflux.
Remana'tion s. A reabsorption.
Trepana'tion s. Operation of trepanning.
Impana'tion s. Doctrine of the union of Christ's material body with the Eucharistic bread.
Miscegena'tion s. A mixture of races, especially white and black.
Hydrogena'tion s. Act of hydrogenating.
Oxygena'tion s. Act or process of oxygenating.
Deoxygena'tion s. Act or process of deoxygenating.
Hyphena'tion s. Act or result of hyphenating.
Aliena'tion s. Act of alienating.
Abaliena'tion s. Transference of the title of a property.
Crena'tion s. Notches on an edge.
Catena'tion s. (*Catenate*).
Concatena'tion s. A series of links or things dependent on each other.
Sustenta'tion s. Support; maintenance of life; preservation from falling.
Vena'tion s. System of veins in an insect's wing, a leaf, etc.
Rejuvena'tion s. State of being or growing young again; renewal of youth.
Agna'tion s. Relationship on the father's side.
Stagna'tion s. Condition of being stagnant, dull, lethargic, etc.; cessation of flow.
Impregna'tion s. Act of impregnating; fecundation; saturation.

Indigna'tion s. Mingled feeling or anger and disdain; displeasure at what is unworthy or base.
Designa'tion s. Act of designating; appointment; appellation, description.
Resigna'tion s. Act of resigning; state of being resigned; patience; submissiveness.
Consigna'tion s. Act of consigning.
Assigna'tion s. An appointment; assignment.
Cogna'tion s. Relation through a common ancestor; participation in the same nature.
Combina'tion s. Act of combining, state of being combined; union, alliance; (pl.) an under-garment for body and legs.
Turbina'tion s. Act of spinning or whirling.
Vaccina'tion s. Act, art, or practice of vaccinating.
Vaticina'tion s. Prophecy; prediction.
Calcina'tion s. Act or operation of calcining.
Lancina'tion s. Laceration; a piercing pain.
Ratiocina'tion s. Act or process of reasoning.
Fascina'tion s. Act of fascinating; enchantment; charm; spell.
Hallucina'tion s. A false sense-perception; delusion; an illusion.
Ordina'tion s. Act of ordaining; state of being ordained; conferring of holy orders.
Subordina'tion s. Act of subjecting; inferiority; place of rank among inferiors.
Insubordina'tion s. Disobedience to lawful authority.
Preordina'tion s. Act of foreordaining; previous determination.
Co-ordina'tion s. State of being co-ordinate; act of harmonizing parts, etc.
Inco-ordina'tion s. Want of co-ordination.
Imagina'tion s. Power by which the mind forms ideas, reproduces previously perceived objects, pictures future or recalls past experiences, etc.; fancy; a notion.
Pagina'tion s. Act of paginating; figures, etc., used to indicate position of pages in a book.
Evagina'tion s. Act of evaginating.
Invagina'tion s. Act or process of invaginating.
Origina'tion s. Act of originating; mode of production.
Margina'tion s. Peculiarity marking a margin.
Machina'tion s. A plot, artful scheme.
Declina'tion s. Act of declining; deviation from.
Reclina'tion s. Act of leaning or reclining.
Inclina'tion s. Act of inclining; deviation from the normal; disposition, proclivity; tendency; liking.
Disinclina'tion s. Lack of desire to; unwillingness.
Pollina'tion s. The fertilizing of a flower with pollen.
Lamina'tion s. State of being laminated; arrangement in layers.
Contamina'tion s. Act of contaminating; pollution, taint.
Examina'tion s. Act of examining; careful inquiry into facts, etc.; studious scrutiny.
Gemina'tion s. A doubling, duplication, repetition.
Ingemina'tion s. Act of doubling or reiterating.
Semina'tion s. The natural dispersal of seeds by plants.
Insemina'tion s. Act of inseminating.
Dissemina'tion s. Act of disseminating; propagation.
Elimina'tion s. Act of eliminating.
Crimina'tion s. Accusation.
Recrimina'tion s. Mutual charges or accusations.
Discrimina'tion s. Discernment, judgment; act of discriminating.
Culmina'tion s. Transit of a heavenly body over the meridian; the highest point, consummation.
Fulmina'tion s. Act of fulminating, that which is fulminated; anathema, denunciation.
Commina'tion s. A denunciation; recital of Divine threats.
Abomina'tion s. Hatred; object of hatred.
Domina'tion s. Act of dominating; government, rule, authority; the fourth order of angels.
Predomina'tion s. Act of predominating; predominance.
Nomina'tion s. Act or power of nominating; state of being nominated.
Denomina'tion s. Act of naming; title; class; religious sect.
Prenomina'tion s. Act of naming beforehand.
Germina'tion s. Process of germinating; the first act of growth.
Termina'tion s. Act of ending; end, conclusion, result.
Determina'tion s. Act of determining; conclusion; resolution; delimitation.
Predetermina'tion s. Act of predetermining; a purpose previously formed.
Indetermina'tion s. Vacillation.
Extermina'tion s. Act of exterminating; eradication, extirpation.
Vermina'tion s. Breeding of vermin.
Acumina'tion s. (*Acuminate*).
Illumina'tion s. Act of illuminating; that illuminated or which illuminates; bright decoration; splendour.
Rumina'tion s. Act or process of ruminating; meditation.
Supina'tion s. Act of lying or state of being laid face upward.
Fibrina'tion s. Excess of fibrin in the blood.
Peregrina'tion s. A wandering about; a sojourning abroad.
Chlorina'tion s. Extraction of gold from ore by treatment with chlorine.
Indoctrina'tion s. Instruction in the rudiments and principles of any science, etc.
Urina'tion s. Act or process of passing urine.
Assassina'tion s. Murder by surprise.
Gelatina'tion s. Act or process of gelatinating.
Patina'tion s. Patina.
Procrastina'tion s. Dilatoriness; habit of deferring action.
Destina'tion s. Act of destining; purpose, fate; place to which one is bound or thing is sent.
Predestina'tion s. Act of predestinating; doctrine that the fate of all persons and things is divinely foreordained from eternity.
Festina'tion s. Hurry, haste.
Agglutina'tion s. Loose combination of roots to form words.
Conglutina'tion s. (*Conglutinate*).
Ruina'tion s. Subversion; overthrow; demolition.
Divina'tion s. Act or art of foretelling the future; augury.
Damna'tion s. Condemnation, especially to eternal punishment; severe censure of a play, etc.; a profane oath.
Condemna'tion s. Act or state of being condemned; judgment; cause of blame.
Cachinna'tion s. A guffaw.
Cona'tion s. Faculty of voluntary agency.
Dona'tion s. Act of giving; a gift, present, offering.

Condona'tion s. Act of pardon, forgiveness.
Phona'tion s. Uttering of sounds by the voice.
Fractiona'tion s. Act or process of fractionating.
Corona'tion s. Solemn act of crowning a sovereign.
Persona'tion s. Act of personating, especially with intent to deceive at elections, etc.
Impersona'tion s. Act of impersonating; personification.
Detona'tion s. Act or process of detonating; a loud report; violent outburst.
Intona'tion s. Accent; modulation of the voice; utterance with a special tone.
Carna'tion s. A rosy-pink or flesh colour; the cultivated clove-pink.
Incarna'tion s. Act of taking on a human form and nature; a vivid personification.
Reincarna'tion s. Rebirth; metempsychosis.
Hiberna'tion s. Act of hibernating; winter torpor.
Guberna'tion s. Guiding control; government.
Alterna'tion s. Reciprocal succession; interchange.
Consterna'tion s. Terrified amazement, horror, dismay.
Verna'tion s. Arrangement of leaves within the bud.
Suborna'tion s. Act or crime of suborning.
Eburna'tion s. Diseased condition in which the bone becomes unnaturally dense.
Coaduna'tion s. (*Coadunate*).
Luna'tion s. A lunar month.
Inchoa'tion s. A beginning, inception.
Anticipa'tion s. Act of anticipating; foretaste.
Participa'tion s. Act or state of sharing with others or of taking part in something.
Mancipa'tion s. The legal method of transferring property in ancient Rome.
Emancipa'tion s. Liberation; freeing or freedom from slavery.
Dissipa'tion s. Act of dissipating; state of dispersion; dissolute course of life; trifling diversion.
Obstipa'tion s. Severe costiveness.
Constipa'tion s. Costiveness; imperfect evacuation.
Palpa'tion s. Act of touching or feeling.
Inculpa'tion s. Act of inculpating; state of being inculpated.
Exculpa'tion s. Act of exculpating.
Syncopa'tion s. Contraction of a word or performance of a musical passage by syncopating.
Extirpa'tion s. Eradication; total destruction.
Usurpa'tion s. Act of usurping; illegal seizu e.
Crispa'tion s. (*Crispate*).
Occupa'tion s. Act of occupying or of taking possession; business, calling.
Preoccupa'tion s. Preoccupancy; prior occupation.
Nuncupa'tion s. Oral declaration.
Ra'tion s. Allowance, especially of provisions. v.t. To supply with or put on fixed rations.
Declara'tion s. Act of declaring; that which is declared; legal specification.
Exhilara'tion s. Act of exhilarating; cheerfulness, liveliness.
Repara'tion s. Act of repairing or making amends; that done for this purpose; restoration; indemnification.
Prepara'tion s. Act of preparing; state of being or that which is prepared.
Separa'tion s. Act of separating; disunion; partial divorce.
Celebra'tion s. Honour bestowed; praise; solemnization.
Cerebra'tion s. The functioning of the brain.
Terebra'tion s. Act of boring.
Vertebra'tion s. Arrangement in vertebræ.
Libra'tion s. Act of librating; state of being balanced.
Antilibra'tion s. Weighing of one thing against another.
Equilibra'tion s. State of being equally balanced or in equipoise.
Vibra'tion s. Act of vibrating; oscillation; a swing.
Adumbra'tion s. A faint outline or resemblance.
Exprobra'tion s. Censure, upbraiding.
Lucubra'tion s. Night-study; a pedantic or learned composition.
Obsecra'tion s. Entreaty; act of imploring.
Desecra'tion s. Act of desecrating; profanation.
Consecra'tion s. Act of consecrating; dedication; ordination of a bishop.
Execra'tion s. Act of cursing; curse; that which is execrated.
Dehydra'tion s. Deprivation of water or its constituent elements.
Aera'tion s. Impregnation of a liquid with carbonic acid gas.
Libera'tion s. Act of liberating; state of being set free.
Delibera'tion s. Careful consideration, prudence; leisurely action.
Reverbera'tion s. Act of reverberating; an echo.
Lacera'tion s. Act of lacerating; tear or breach made.
Macera'tion s. Act or process of macerating.
Ulcera'tion s. Process of forming into an ulcer; state of being ulcerated.
Incarcera'tion s. Imprisonment; act of incarcerating.
Eviscera'tion s. Act or result of eviscerating.
Federa'tion s. Act of federating; a league, confederacy.
Confedera'tion s. Act of or compact for confederating; a union of states, a league, parties to a league.
Desidera'tion s. A want, a thing lacked.
Considera'tion s. Act of considering; careful thought; motive of action, equivalent; importance.
Reconsidera'tion s. Act of reconsidering; renewed consideration.
Inconsidera'tion s. Want of due consideration; inattention to consequences.
Pondera'tion s. Act of weighing or pondering.
Prepondera'tion s. Preponderance.
Modera'tion s. Act of moderating; state of being moderate; temperance.
Immodera'tion s. Excess.
Vocifera'tion s. Act of vociferating; bawling, violent outcry.
Prolifera'tion s. Reproduction by budding; prolification.
Exaggera'tion s. Representation beyond truth; hyperbole.
Refrigera'tion s. Act of cooling or refrigerating; state of being cooled.
Bothera'tion s. Bother, act of bothering. int. Confound it!
Smothera'tion s. A smother; state of being smothered.
Accelera'tion s. Act of hastening; increased speed.
Tolera'tion s. Act of tolerating; freedom from bigotry; allowance of that not fully approved.
Concamera'tion s. An internal division of a shell.
Glomera'tion s. Act of forming into a spherical body; thing so formed.
Agglomera'tion s. Act of agglomerating; a heap.
Conglomera'tion s. A miscellaneous collection, mixed mass; act of conglomerating.
Numera'tion s. Act, process, or art of numbering.
Enumera'tion s. Act of enumerating; a detailed account; a recapitulation.

Genera'tion s. Act of generating; single succession in descent; people living at the same time; period; breed.
Degenera'tion s. Act or process of degenerating; state of being degenerated; deterioration, decay.
Regenera'tion s. Act of regenerating; regeneracy; reproduction; replacement of lost parts, etc.
Venera'tion s. Reverence; respect mingled with awe.
Cinera'tion s. Reduction to ashes.
Incinera'tion s. Act of reducing to ashes.
Exonera'tion s. Act of exonerating; state of being exonerate.
Remunera'tion s. Act of remunerating; payment, recompense.
Opera'tion s. Act or process of operating; agency; method of working; effect; series of military movements; act performed with or without instruments on the body.
Co-opera'tion s. Act of co-operating; concurrent effort or labour; a form of partnership.
Exaspera'tion s. Irritation; rage; fury.
Despera'tion s. Act of despairing; state of despair or hopelessness.
Depaupera'tion s. Act of depauperating; state of being depauperated.
Recupera'tion s. Recovery.
Vitupera'tion s. Abuse; severe censure; scurrility.
Commisera'tion s. Act of commiserating; pity.
Itera'tion s. Act of repeating or iterating.
Reitera'tion s. Repeated repetition.
Oblitera'tion s. Act of obliterating; effacement.
Allitera'tion s. Commencement of words in close succession with identical sounds.
Translitera'tion s. Act or result of transliterating.
Altera'tion s. Partial change.
Adultera'tion s. Corruption or debasement by some foreign mixture.
Chattera'tion s. Loquacity.
Assevera'tion s. (*Asseverate*).
Deflagra'tion s. A sudden and violent combustion.
Conflagra'tion s. A great fire.
Integra'tion s. Act of making entire; a mathematical operation.
Redintegra'tion s. Restoration, renovation.
Migra'tion s. Act of migrating; removal from one place to another.
Emigra'tion s. Act of emigrating.
Remigra'tion s. Migration to the former place.
Immigra'tion s. Act of immigrating.
Transmigra'tion s. Act of transmigrating; metempsychosis.
Denigra'tion s. Defamation.
Delira'tion s. Delirium.
Admira'tion s. Wonder mingled with esteem.
Spira'tion s. The procession of the Holy Ghost.
Aspira'tion s. Strong wish or desire; pronunciation of a syllable with a marked breathing.
Respira'tion s. Act or process of breathing.
Transpira'tion s. Cutaneous exhalation.
Inspira'tion s. Act of drawing in of breath or of inspiring; Divine or other influence; state of being inspired; an idea, feeling, etc., prompted from without.
Suspira'tion s. Act of sighing; a sigh.
Expira'tion s. Act of breathing out; exhalation; death; end; matter expired.
Ora'tion s. A formal or eloquent speech.
Elabora'tion s. Act or process of producing with labour, state of being so produced.
Collabora'tion s. Co-operation in work (*collaborate*).
Corrobora'tion s. Act of corroborating, confirmation.
Decora'tion s. Act of decorating, that which adorns; a badge.
Edulcora'tion s. Act or process of edulcorating.
Adora'tion s. Act of adoring; worship, homage.
Perfora'tion s. Act or result of perforating; series of holes separating stamps, etc.
Imperfora'tion s. An imperforated state.
Invigora'tion s. Act of invigorating; state of being invigorated.
Meliora'tion s. Act or result of meliorating.
Ameliora'tion s. A making better, improvement.
Deteriora'tion s. State of growing worse; having become inferior.
Pejora'tion s. Disparagement.
Deflora'tion s. Act of deflowering; the shedding of pollen.
Colora'tion s. Act or state of being coloured; colouring, variegation.
Decolora'tion s. (*Decolour*).
Discolora'tion s. State of being discoloured; stain, blemish.
Implora'tion s. Supplication.
Explora'tion s. Act of exploring; careful examination.
Commemora'tion s. Act of commemorating; public celebration in memory of someone or something.
Pignora'tion s. Act of pledging or pawning.
Evapora'tion s. Act or process of evaporating; transformation into vapour.
Corpora'tion s. A corporate body; a municipal council; the stomach.
Incorpora'tion s. Act of incorporating; state of being incorporated; a corporate body.
Spora'tion s. The formation of spores.
Perora'tion s. The concluding part of a discourse.
Expectora'tion s. Act of expectorating; matter spat out.
Restora'tion s. Act of restoring; state of being restored; that which is restored; replacement; recovery.
Stupra'tion s. Rape.
Narra'tion s. Act of narrating; a narrative.
Aberra'tion s. A deviation from the natural direction; mental derangement.
Serra'tion s. An edge-notching, like a saw.
Susurra'tion s. A whispering, rustling.
Penetra'tion s. Act of penetrating; sagacity; discrimination.
Impetra'tion s. Act of obtaining by petition.
Perpetra'tion s. Act of perpetrating; an evil action.
Arbitra'tion s. Act of arbitrating.
Recalcitra'tion s. Opposition; repugnance.
Nitra'tion s. Act or process of nitrating.
Titra'tion s. A process of determining amount of some constituent in a solution.
Filtra'tion s. Act or process of filtering.
Infiltra'tion s. Act or process of infiltrating.
Concentra'tion s. Act of concentrating; state of being concentrated.
Castra'tion s. (*Castrate*).
Orchestra'tion s. Arrangement of music for an orchestra.
Fenestra'tion s. System of windows in a building.
Sequestra'tion s. Act of reserving a disputed possession until judgment is given; state of being set aside; retirement.
Registra'tion s. Act of registering; enrolment.
Ministra'tion s. Act of ministering; service.
Administra'tion s. Act of administering; the executive part of a government; period during which this holds office.
Maladministra'tion s. Bad management, especially by public officers.

Demonstra'tion s. Act or process of demonstrating; proof; a public exhibition, meeting for support, etc.; movement of troops to mislead the enemy.
Remonstra'tion s. Remonstrance, protest.
Prostra'tion s. Act of prostrating; condition of being prostrate; great depression.
Claustra'tion s. Act of confining in a cloister or monastery.
Lustra'tion s. Ceremonial purification.
Illustra'tion s. Act of illustrating; state of being illustrated; that which illustrates; an example; picture to elucidate the text.
Frustra'tion s. Act of frustrating; disappointment, defeat.
Instaura'tion s. Renewal, restoration.
Procura'tion s. Act of procuring; management of another's affairs; document authorizing this; a proxy.
Obscura'tion s. Act of obscuring; state of being obscured.
Dura'tion s. Continuance in time; permanency.
Indura'tion s. Insensibility.
Neura'tion s. Arrangement of nerves in insects' wings.
Figura'tion s. Act of giving determinate form; mixture of concords and discords.
Prefigura'tion s. Act of prefiguring, state of being prefigured.
Configura'tion s. External form; relative position of the planets.
Trans-figura'tion s. A change of appearance, especially that of Christ on the Mount; feast in commemoration of this.
Fulgura'tion s. Flashing of lightning; sudden brightening of gold and silver in the crucible.
Inaugura'tion s. Act of inaugurating; ceremonies connected with such act.
Sulphura'tion s. Action of sulphurating.
Abjura'tion s. Act of abjuring; oath taken.
Objura'tion s. A binding by oath.
Adjura'tion s. Solemn entreaty; charge.
Conjura'tion s. Act of conjuring or invoking; a solemn adjuration; a magic spell.
Depura'tion s. Act of cleansing; cleanliness.
Suppura'tion s. Process of forming pus; pus.
Mensura'tion s. The art, act, or practice of measuring.
Matura'tion s. Process of maturing; suppuration.
Satura'tion s. Complete impregnation; act of saturating.
Tritura'tion s. Act of triturating.
Sutura'tion s. Joining by suture.
Nervura'tion s. Arrangement of nervures.
Gyra'tion s. Act of whirling round a centre; circular or spiral motion.
Circum-gyra'tion s. Act of whirling round.
Extravasa'tion s. Effusion of blood from the proper vessels.
Ir'isation s. Iridescence; act or process of making iridescent.
Improvisa'tion s. Act of composing or rendering extemporaneously; an impromptu.
Pulsa'tion s. Act of beating or throbbing; a beat, throb.
Incensa'tion s. Act of offering incense in worship.
Condensa'tion s. Act of condensing; reduction to a denser form.
Compensa'tion s. Act of compensating; recompense, amends.
Dispensa'tion s. Act of dispensing; good or evil dealt out by Providence; indulgence granted by the Pope.
Sensa'tion s. Perception by senses; feeling; power of this; excitement.
Tergiversa'tion s. Shifting, evasion; fickleness.
Malversa'tion s. Corruption, etc., by one in an office of trust.
Conversa'tion s. Act of conversing, a familiar talk; intercourse.
Indorsa'tion s. Act or process of endorsing.
Cassa'tion s. Act of annulment.
Incrassa'tion s. Inspissation.
Cessa'tion s. Ceasing, stop.
Inspissa'tion s. Act or process of thickening or rendering denser.
Succussa'tion s. Succussion; a trotting.
Decussa'tion s. Act of crossing or state of being crossed at an acute angle; X-shaped intersection.
Causa'tion s. Act of causing; agency by which an effect is produced.
Accusa'tion s. A charge; blame; impeachment.
Dilata'tion s. Act of dilating; state of being dilated; diffuseness.
Acclimata'tion s. (*Acclimation*).
Nata'tion s. Act or art of swimming.
Jacta'tion s. Act of throwing; agitation of the body; jactitation.
Lacta'tion s. Suckling; act of giving milk.
Retracta'tion s. Withdrawal; recantation.
Affecta'tion s. False pretence, an artificial manner.
Delecta'tion s. Delight, enjoyment.
Humecta'tion s. A moistening.
Expecta'tion s. Act or state of expecting; prospect of good to come, of reaching a given age, etc.
Dicta'tion s. That which is dictated; authoritative command; act of dictating.
Nicta'tion s. Nictitation.
Cuncta'tion s. Delay, dilitatoriness.
Coarcta'tion s. (*Coarctate*).
Eructa'tion s. Act of belching; a bursting forth.
Vegeta'tion s. Act or process of vegetating; plants in general.
Fœta'tion s. The formation of a fœtus.
Superfœta'tion s. A second conception before the birth of the first.
Interpreta'tion s. Act of interpreting; explanation representation on the stage.
Misinterpre-ta'tion s. A wrong interpretation.
Habita'tion s. Act of inhabiting; place of abode; dwelling.
Inhabita'tion s. Act of inhabiting; a dwelling.
Cohabita'tion s. (*Cohabit*).
Dubita'tion s. Act of doubting; hesitation, uncertainty.
Cita'tion s. Official notice to appear; act of citing; thing cited; mention.
Incapacita'tion s. A disqualification; want of capacity.
Recita'tion s. Act of reciting; an elocutionary exhibition; piece for reciting.
Felicita'tion s. Congratulation.
Pollicita'tion s. A voluntary promise; an offer.
Solicita'tion s. Act of soliciting.
Incita'tion s. Act of inciting; an incitement.
Exercita'tion s. Exercise; practice; use.
Resuscita'tion s. Act of reviving or coming to life again.
Excita'tion s. Act of exciting or producing excitement; excitement produced.
Medita'tion s. Act of meditating; contemplation.
Premedita'tion s. Previous deliberation; design formed beforehand.
Agita'tion s. Excitement, discussion, disturbance.
Digita'tion s. Division into finger-like processes.

Presti-digita'tion s. Legerdemain, conjuring.
Cogita'tion s. Meditation; act of thinking.
Precogita'tion s. Previous consideration.
Excogita'tion s. Act of devising in the thoughts.
Gurgita'tion s. A bubbling, gurgling.
Regurgita'tion s. A surging back by the entrance.
Ingurgita'tion s. Act of gorging or drinking greedily.
Habilita'tion s. Qualification; capacitation.
Rehabilita'tion s. Act of rehabilitating; restoration to former rights, etc.
Facilita'tion s. Act of facilitating.
Imita'tion s. Act of imitating; a likeness, repetition.
Limita'tion s. Act of limiting; state of being limited; a shortcoming.
Delimita'tion s. Act of delimiting; a boundary.
Sanita'tion s. Hygiene; drainage; adoption of sanitary measures.
Exploita'tion s. Act of exploiting; employment of labour for merely personal ends.
Capita'tion s. A tax, grant, etc., per head.
Decapita'tion s. Act of beheading.
Crepita'tion s. A sharp crackling sound.
Decrepita'tion s. Act of decrepitating.
Precipita'tion s. Act of precipitating, state of being precipitated; tumultuous haste.
Palpita'tion s. Violent or irregular pulsation of the heart.
Irrita'tion s. Act of irritating; annoyance; exasperation.
Hesita'tion s. Act of hesitating.
Visita'tion s. Act of visiting; a formal visit; communication of Divine wrath or favour.
Necessita'tion s. A making or state of being made necessary.
Mussita'tion s. A mumbling, muttering.
Jactita'tion s. Malicious or wrongful pretension to marriage; restlessness; boasting.
Nictita'tion s. Act of winking or blinking.
Equita'tion s. Horsemanship.
Gravita'tion s. Tending to the centre; force through which all particles of matter tend towards each other.
Levita'tion s. A rising and floating of the body in air, as claimed by Spiritualists.
Invita'tion s. Act or words of inviting; attraction.
Salta'tion s. A leaping; beating, palpitation.
Exalta'tion s. State of being exalted; elevation in dignity, etc.
Occulta'tion s. The hiding of a heavenly body by intervention of another.
Ausculta'tion s. Act of listening, especially with a stethoscope.
Consulta'tion s. Act of consulting; a meeting for consulting or deliberation.
Exulta'tion s. Act of exulting, triumphing.
Decanta'tion s. Act of decanting.
Recanta'tion s. Act of recanting; retraction.
Incanta'tion s. Act of enchanting; enchantment; magical words or ceremonies; use of these.
Planta'tion s. Group of growing trees; place planted; act of planting; estate for cultivation of cotton, tobacco, tea, rubber, or other exports.
Transplanta'-tion s. Act of transplanting; state of being transplanted.
Denta'tion s. Form, formation, or arrangement of teeth.
Indenta'tion s. A notch; a cut or angular depression in a margin.
Orienta'tion s. Act of orientating; position east and west; a turning toward the east.
Menta'tion s. Mental action cerebration.

Lamenta'tion s. Act of lamenting; audible grie
Ornamenta'tion s. That which ornaments; act art of ornamenting; state of bei ornamented.
Castramenta'-tion s. Art of arranging camps.
Cementa'tion s. Act of cementing; conversion iron into steel.
Dementa'tion s. Madness.
Supplementa'-tion s. Supplement; act of supplemen ing.
Segmenta'tion s. Act or process of dividing in segments.
Pigmenta'tion s. The colouration by presence pigment-cells.
Augmenta'tion s. A thing added; an addition to coat of arms; act or state of bei augmented.
Sedimenta'tion s. Act or process of depositing se ment.
Regimenta'tion s. Organization into a regiment system.
Alimenta'tion s. Act or quality of affording nouris ment.
Experimenta'-tion s. Art or practice of making expe ments.
Commenta'tion s. Explanations of a commentator
Fomenta'tion s. Act of fomenting; lotion, e applied.
Fermenta'tion s. Conversion of an organic substar into new compounds by a ferme with evolution of heat, bubbli and chemical decompositio agitation, excitement.
Documenta'-tion s. The use of historical documents.
Argumenta'-tion s. Act or process of arguing.
Frumenta'tion s. A largess of corn among ancient Romans.
Instrumenta'-tion s. Means; agency; manner of pla ing upon or scoring for musi instruments.
Presenta'tion s. Act of presenting; a forn offering or bestowing; a setti forth; act or right of submittin person for a benefice.
Representa'-tion s. Act of representing; drama performance; an image; a monstrance.
Misrepresenta'-tion s. Act of giving a false represen tion; an incorrect account.
Assenta'tion s. Assent by way of flatte adulation.
Tenta'tion s. Trial; temptation.
Ostenta'tion s. Pretentious parade; pomp; boa ing.
Frequenta'tion s. Act or habit of frequenting.
Confronta'tion s. Act of confronting.
Flota'tion s. Act or state of floating; launch of a business, etc.
Nota'tion s. Act or manner of recording marks; the marks used.
Denota'tion s. Act of denoting; that which indicated; a sign, mark.
Annota'tion s. A marginal or other note or co mentary.
Connota'tion s. That which constitutes the me ing; the qualities implied.
Pota'tion s. Act of drinking; a draught; carouse.
Rota'tion s. Act of rotating; rotary motic succession in a series.
Quota'tion s. Act of quoting; passage quot the naming of a price, or the pr named.
Misquota'tion s. An erroneous quotation.
Capta'tion s. An attempt to get by playing another's feelings.

Adapta'tion s. Act or state of being adapted; the process or result of fitting, adapting, modifying, etc.
Preadapta'tion s. Previous adjustment to some end.
Inadapta'tion s. Want of adaptation.
Coadapta'tion s. (*Coadapted*).
Accepta'tion s. Act of accepting; the received meaning of a word or phrase.
Tempta'tion s. Act of tempting; state of being tempted; an allurement.
Co-opta'tion s. Election by co-opting.
Imparta'tion s. Act of imparting; communication.
Disserta'tion s. A formal discourse, elaborate disquisition.
Flirta'tion s. Coquetry; a playing at courtship.
Horta'tion s. Advice; encouragement.
Dehorta'tion s. Dissuasion.
Exhorta'tion s. Act or practice of exhorting; counsel.
Deporta'tion s. Act of transporting to a foreign land; state of being banished.
Importa'tion s. Act or practice of importing; quantity imported.
Transporta'tion s. Act of transporting or conveying; state of being transported; penal banishment.
Exporta'tion s. Act of exporting.
Sta'tion s. Post assigned; position; situation; a halt, especially on railways. v.t. To assign a position to.
Impasta'tion s. Process of combining materials into a paste, especially for porcelain; the resulting combination.
Devasta'tion s. Act or result of devastating.
Manifesta'tion s. Act of making public; exhibition, revelation.
Infesta'tion s. Act of infesting; molestation.
Gesta'tion s. Act of carrying young in the womb; period of this.
Molesta'tion s. Act of molesting, annoyance.
Afforesta'tion s. Act of making or tending a forest.
Testa'tion s. Act or power of bequeathing.
Obtesta'tion s. Act of supplicating or of protesting.
Detesta'tion s. Act of detesting; loathing, abhorrence.
Contesta'tion s. Act of contesting, a struggle, dispute.
Protesta'tion s. A solemn affirmation or protest; act of protesting.
Attesta'tion s. Testimony; the witnessing of a will, deed etc.
Aerosta'tion s. Aeronautics.
Gusta'tion s. Act or faculty of tasting.
Crusta'tion s. An incrustation.
Incrusta'tion s. Act or process of encrusting; a surface crust or coating.
Refuta'tion s. Act or process of refuting; proof of error, etc.
Confuta'tion s. Act or process of confuting; disproof.
Luta'tion s. Act of process of luting.
Saluta'tion s. Act of saluting or greeting, or that which is done.
Muta'tion s. Act or process of changing; modification; a species produced by variation.
Commuta'tion s. Act of commuting; exchange; payment made in commuting.
Permuta'tion s. Exchange of one for another; arrangement in all possible orders.
Transmuta'tion s. Act of transmuting; state of being transmuted.
Nuta'tion s. The vibratory motion of the earth's axis; a nodding or drooping.
Circumnuta'tion s. The irregular bending of a growing plant.
Sternuta'tion s. Act of sneezing.
Deputa'tion s. Act of deputing; persons commissioned to act for others.
Reputa'tion s. Estimation in which one is generally held; general credit; good name.
Amputa'tion s. A cutting off, especially of a limb.
Imputa'tion s. Act of imputing; that which is imputed; censure, reproach.
Computa'tion s. An estimate, calculation.
Disputa'tion s. Act of disputing; argumentation.
Evacua'tion s. Act of evacuating; that which is discharged.
Gradua'tion s. Regular progression; division into degrees; act of receiving or giving University degrees.
Individua'tion s. Act of separating into individuals or of endowing with individuality.
Valua'tion s. Act of appraising; estimation of worth.
Evalua'tion s. Act or result of evaluating.
Attenua'tion s. Act of making thin; less strong, etc.
Extenua'tion s. Act of extenuating; palliation; mitigation.
Insinua'tion s. Art or power of insinuating; hint; wheedling manner.
Continua'tion s. Act of continuing; succession, extension.
Discontinua'tion s. Breach of continuity; disruption.
Superannua'tion s. State of being superannuated; a retiring pension.
Equa'tion s. A making equal; equal division; a quantity to be taken in order to give a true result.
Liqua'tion s. Act or process of melting metals to purify them.
Eliqua'tion s. Liquefaction.
Appropinqua'tion s. Act of coming or bringing nearer.
Œstrua'tion s. Act of œstruating; state of rutting.
Menstrua'tion s. Act, process, or period of menstruating.
Infatua'tion s. Act of infatuating; state of being infatuated; besottedness.
Actua'tion s. Effectual operation.
Effectua'tion s. A bringing to pass, accomplishing.
Punctua'tion s. Act or art of punctuating a writing, etc.; system of stops.
Fluctua'tion s. Change, vicissitude; a rising and falling.
Fructua'tion s. Fruition; fruit-like decoration.
Perpetua'tion s. A making perpetual; permanent continuation.
Habitua'tion s. State of being habituated; act of habituating.
Situa'tion s. Location, site; relative position; circumstances; employment, office.
Accentua'tion s. Application of accent; mode of pronunciation.
Concava'tion s. Act of making concave.
Excava'tion s. Act of hollowing out; a cavity.
Lava'tion s. Act of washing.
Aggrava'tion s. Provocation, exasperation.
Deprava'tion s. Act of depraving; degeneracy.
Eleva'tion s. Act of elevating, state or position of being elevated; a hill; representation to scale of the side or end of a building, etc.; angle of gunfire.
Saliva'tion s. Excessive discharge of saliva.
Insaliva'tion s. Act or process of insalivating.
Deriva'tion s. Act of deriving; deduction; etymology of a word, process of tracing this.

Priva'tion s. Act of depriving; state of being deprived; degradation in rank; want, destitution.

Depriva'tion s. Act of depriving, state of being deprived; bereavement; want.

Cultiva'tion s. Art or practice of cultivating; tillage; refinement, advancement.

Motiva'tion s. Act of motivating; incitement.

Captiva'tion s. (*Captivate*).

Æstiva'tion s. Internal arrangement of a bud; act of being torpid during the summer.

Salva'tion s. Act of saving; deliverance from evil; that which saves.

Ova'tion s. A spontaneous expression of popular homage.

Nova'tion s. Substitution of a new legal obligation for an old one.

Renova'tion s. Act of making new; state of being renovated.

Innova'tion s. A novelty; act of innovating.

Starva'tion s. State of being starved; extreme hunger, famine.

Coacerva'tion s. (*Coacervate*).

Nerva'tion s. Arrangement of nerves, or of ribs in leaves, insects' wings, etc.

Enerva'tion s. Act of enervating; effeminacy.

Innerva'tion s. Act of innerving; nervous activity.

Observa'tion s. Act, power, or habit of observing; that which is noticed; a remark.

Reserva'tion s. Act of reserving; something withheld; a limitation or qualification.

Preserva'tion s. Act of preserving; state of being preserved; security.

Conserva'tion s. Act of conserving; preservation.

Cur'vation s. Act of curving; a curve.

Recurva'tion s. Act of recurving; a bending backward.

ncurva'tion s. Act of bending or bowing; curvature.

Laxa'tion s. Act of loosening; state of being slack.

Relaxa'tion s. Act of relaxing; remission of tension, rigour, etc.; recreation.

Taxa'tion s. Act of imposing taxes, or of assessing a bill of cost.

Annexa'tion s. Act of annexing; addition.

Vexa'tion s. Act of vexing, state of being vexed; annoyance; chagrin; irritation.

Fixa'tion s. Act or process of fixing; state of being fixed.

Luxa'tion s. Act of dislocating; state of being dislocated.

Fluxa'tion s. Act of fluxing.

Judaiza'tion s. Act or process of Judaizing.

Laiciza'tion s. Act of rendering secular.

Hybridiza'tion s. Act of hybridizing; hybridism.

Oxidiza'tion s. Act or process of oxidizing.

Deoxidiza'tion s. Act or process of deoxidizing.

Aggrandiza'tion s. (*Aggrandize*).

Standardiza'tion s. Act or process of standardizing.

Fardiza'tion s. Medical treatment by electricity.

Bastardiza'tion s. (*Bastardize*).

Syllogiza'tion s. Act or process of syllogizing.

Dockiza'tion s. Act or process of converting into docks.

Focaliza'tion s. Act of focussing; state of being focussed.

Localiza'tion s. Act of localizing; state of being localized.

Vocaliza'tion s. (*Vocalize*).

Devocaliza'tion s. (*Devocalize*).

Feudaliza'tion s. Act of feudalizing.

Idealiza'tion s. Act, process, or product of idealizing.

Realiza'tion s. Act of realizing; state of being realized.

Legaliza'tion s. Act of legalizing.

Socializa'tion s. (*Socialize*).

Radializa'tion s. Act or result of making radial.

Imperializa'tion s. Act of imperializing.

Materializa'tion s. Act of materializing; state of being materialized.

Arterializa'tion s. (*Arterialize*).

Alkaliza'tion s. Act of rendering alkaline.

Decimaliza'tion s. (*Decimalize*).

Formaliza'tion s. Act or result of rendering formal.

Normaliza'tion s. State of being made normal.

Canaliza'tion s. (*Canalize*).

Nationaliza'tion s. Act of changing from private to state ownership.

Denationaliza'tion s. (*Denationalize*).

Internationaliza'tion s. Act or result of internationalizing.

Liberaliza'tion s. Act or process of liberalizing.

Generaliza'tion s. Act or process of generalizing or making general; a general inference.

Moraliza'tion s. Act of moralizing; interpretation in a moral sense.

Demoraliza'tion s. Act of demoralizing.

Decentraliza'tion s. (*Decentralize*).

Neutraliza'tion s. Act or result of neutralizing.

Naturaliza'tion s. Act of naturalizing, especially an alien.

Denaturaliza'tion s. (*Denaturalize*).

Universaliza'tion s. (*Universalize*).

Capitaliza'tion s. (*Capitalize*).

Vitaliza'tion s. (*Vitalize*).

Devitaliza'tion s. Act of devitalizing; state of being devitalized.

Tantaliza'tion s. Act of tantalizing.

Totaliza'tion s. (*Totalize*).

Immortaliza'tion s. Act of immortalizing.

Brutaliza'tion s. (*Brutalize*).

Individualiza'tion s. Act, process, or result of individualizing.

Visualiza'tion s. (*Visualize*).

Intellectualiza'tion s. Act or process of intellectualizing.

Spiritualiza'tion s. Act or process of spiritualizing.

Stabiliza'tion s. Act or process of stabilizing.

Mobiliza'tion s. Act of mobilizing.

Demobiliza'tion s. (*Demobilize*).

Steriliza'tion s. Act or process of sterilizing.

Fossiliza'tion s. Act or process of fossilizing.

Fertiliza'tion s. Act or process of fertilizing.

Utiliza'tion s. (*Utilize*).

Civiliza'tion s. State of being civilized; opposed to barbarism.

Crystalliza'tion s. Process, act, or system of crystallizing.

Tranquilliza'tion s. Act of tranquillizing.

Symboliza'tion s. Act or process of symbolizing.

Formuliza'tion s. Act of formulizing; that which is formulized.

Minimiza'tion s. Act, process, or result of minimizing.

Victimiza'tion s. (*Victimize*).

Legitimiza'tion s. Act of legitimizing.

Solmiza'tion s. The sol-fa system of musical notation.

Economiza'tion s. Act or process of economizing.
Atomiza'tion s. (*Atomize*).
Americaniza'tion s. (*Americanize*).
Vulcaniza'tion s. Process of causing rubber to combine with sulphur.
Organiza'tion s. Act or process of organizing; state of being organized; an organized system, concern, etc.
Inorganiza'tion s. State of being without organization.
Disorganiza'tion s. Act or result of disorganizing.
Christianiza'tion s. (*Christianize*).
Humaniza'tion s. Act of humanizing.
Galvaniza'tion s. Action of galvanizing.
Helleniza'tion s. Act or process of hellenizing.
Cocainiza'tion s. (*Cocainize*).
Bituminiza'tion s. (*Bituminize*).
Diviniza'tion s. (*Divinize*).
Solemniza'tion s. Act of solemnizing; celebration.
Carboniza'tion s. (*Carbonize*).
Ioniza'tion s. Act of converting or conversion into ions.
Coloniza'tion s. Act of colonizing; state of being colonized.
Harmoniza'tion s. Act or state of harmonizing.
Canoniza'tion s. Enrolment of a deceased person in the list of saints; state of being canonized.
Synchroniza'tion s. Act or process of synchronizing.
Enthroniza'tion s. Enthronement, especially of a bishop.
Moderniza'tion s. Act of modernizing.
Fraterniza'tion s. Act or state of fraternizing.
Immuniza'tion s. Act of rendering immune.
Barbariza'tion s. (*Barbarize*).
Familiariza'tion s. Process or act of making familiar.
Polariza'tion s. Act of polarizing; state of being polarized, or of having polarity.
Depolariza'tion s. (*Depolarize*).
Vasculariza'tion s. (*Vascularize*).
Formulariza'tion s. Act or result of formularizing.
Populariza'tion s. Act or result of popularizing.
Militariza'tion s. Act of militarizing; state of militarism.
Merceriza'tion s. Process of mercerizing.
Grangeriza'tion s. Grangerism.
Bowdleriza'tion s. (*Bowdlerize*).
Mesmeriza'tion s. Art, act, or process of mesmerizing.
Pauperiza'tion s. Act of pauperizing.
Characteriza'tion s. (*Characterize*).
Cauteriza'tion s. (*Cauterize*).
Pulveriza'tion s. Act of reducing to dust.
Arboriza'tion s. Tree-like appearance or markings.
Deodoriza'tion s. Act or process of deodorizing.
Theoriza'tion s. Act, process, or result of theorizing.
Authoriza'tion s. (*Authorize*).
Decoloriza'tion s. (*Decolorize*).
Vaporiza'tion s. Act or process of vaporizing.
Temporiza'tion s. Act of temporizing.
Extemporiza'tion s. Act or result of extemporizing.
Cicatriza'tion s. (*Cicatrize*).
Electriza'tion s. Electrification.
Carburiza'tion s. (*Carburize*).
Pasteuriza'tion s. Sterilization of milk.
Sulphuriza'tion s. Act of sulphurizing.
Volatiza'tion s. (*Volatize*).
Dramatiza'tion s. The setting forth of a novel, etc., as a play.
Stigmatiza'tion s. Act of branding; state of being stigmatized.
Acclimatiza'tion s. Process or state of becoming or being acclimatized.
Aromatiza'tion s. (*Aromatize*).
Hepatiza'tion s. Conversion of the lungs into a liver-like substance.
Anæs'thetization s. (*Anæsthetize*).
Magnetiza'tion s. Act or process of magnetizing.
Monetiza'tion s. Act or result of monetizing.
Demonetiza'tion s. (*Demonetize*).
Sensitiza'tion s. Act or process of sensitizing.
Amortiza'tion s. Act or right of alienating lands.
Ac'tion s. Exertion of power or its effect; deed; demeanour; series of events in a play, etc.; a battle; a suit at law.
Redac'tion s. Act of editing or reducing to order; a digest.
Reac'tion s. A reacting, reciprocal action; exhaustion due to over-exertion; excitement following depression.
Fac'tion s. A party acting from selfish motives; a clique, junto; dissension.
-fac'tion suff. Denoting making, turning, or converting.
Labefac'tion s. Decay; ruin.
Tabefac'tion s. Emaciation through disease.
Rubefac'tion s. Act of causing redness; redness due to a counter irritant.
Calefac'tion s. Act of making or state of being warm.
Tumefac'tion s. Act of tumefying; a swelling.
Benefac'tion s. A benefit conferred; doing of a benefit.
Tepefac'tion s. Tepidity; act or process of tepefying.
Stupefac'tion s. Act of stupefying; insensibility.
Rarefac'tion s. Act or process of rarefying.
Torrefac'tion s. Operation of parching or roasting.
Putrefac'tion s. Act or process of putrefying; decomposition.
Liquefac'tion s. Act, operation, or state of being liquefied.
Lubrifac'tion s. Lubrification.
Petrifac'tion s. Process of changing into stone; a fossil.
Vitrifac'tion s. Act, process, or operation of vitrifying.
Olfac'tion s. The sense or process of smelling.
Satisfac'tion s. Act of satisfying; state of being satisfied; compensation.
Dissatisfac'tion s. State of being dissatisfied; displeasure; dislike.
Inac'tion s. Idleness; sluggishness.
Coac'tion s. Force, compulsion.
Retroac'tion s. Action returned or backward.
Pac'tion s. A pact.
Impac'tion s. Act of becoming or state of being impacted.
Interac'tion s. Reciprocal or intermediate action.
Counterac'tion s. Action in opposition; neutralization.
Frac'tion s. A fragment, small part; a part into which a number may be divided.
Refrac'tion s. Act of refracting; state of being refracted; change of direction in rays.
Diffrac'tion s. Decomposition of light causing fringes of alternating colours.
Infrac'tion s. Breach; violation (of promise, etc.).
Trac'tion s. Act or method of drawing a body along; state of being so drawn.

Subtrac'tion s. The taking of a number or quantity from a greater.
Detrac'tion s. Act of detracting; depreciation, slander.
Retrac'tion s. Act of retracting or withdrawing; withdrawal; recantation.
Contrac'tion s. Act of shrinking or contracting; shortening; abbreviation.
Protrac'tion s. Act of protracting; that which is protracted.
Abstrac'tion s. Taking away; state of being engrossed in thought; a mental conception.
Distrac'tion s. Confusion of attention; that which causes this; relaxation; state of disordered reason.
Attrac'tion s. Act of attracting; that which attracts; power or act of alluring.
Extrac'tion s. Act of extracting; thing extracted; lineage.
Transac'tion s. Affair; the doing of any business.
Exac'tion s. Authoritative or unjust demand; extortion.
Defec'tion s. Desertion; apostasy.
Refec'tion s. Refreshment; a light repast.
Affec'tion s. State of being affected; fondness.
Disaffec'tion s. Ill-will, disloyalty, hostility.
Effec'tion s. Creation, production.
Infec'tion s. Act or process of infecting; that which infects; contagion.
Disinfec'tion s. Act of disinfecting.
Confec'tion s. A sweetmeat; a drug made palatable; a ready-made dress.
Perfec'tion s. State of being perfect or complete; a quality, endowment, etc., of great excellence.
Imperfec'tion s. A fault, defect, deficiency.
Trajec'tion s. Act of trajecting.
Abjec'tion s. Act of casting away; abasement.
Objec'tion s. Act of objecting; that presented in opposition; scruple; doubt.
Subjec'tion s. Act of subjecting; state of being subjected.
Insubjec'tion s. Disobedience to government.
Ejec'tion s. Act of or state of being ejected.
Dejec'tion s. Act of casting down or dejecting; depression; melancholy.
Rejec'tion s. Act of rejecting; repulse.
Injec'tion s. Act of injecting; that which is injected; introduction of a liquid into the body.
Projec'tion s. Act of projecting; part jutting out; a scheme; a plan, delineation.
Interjec'tion s. Act of interjecting; an exclamation.
Lec'tion s. A reading; a difference in a text.
Elec'tion s. Act of choosing, especially by vote; voluntary preference; predestination.
Prelec'tion s. Reading of a discourse in public.
Selec'tion s. Act of selecting; choice; things selected.
Deflec'tion s. (*Deflexion*).
Reflec'tion s. Act of reflecting; that which is reflected; an image, heat, etc., thrown back; meditation; capacity for judging; reproach.
Circumflec'tion s. (*Circumflex*).
Predilec'tion s. A prepossession in favour.
Intellec'tion s. Act or process of understanding.
Collec'tion s. Act of collecting; things gathered; assemblage.
Recollec'tion s. Act or power of recollecting; a reminiscence; period of remembrance.
Bolec'tion s. A projecting moulding.
Connec'tion s. (*Connexion*).
Circumspec'tion s. Attention to details; cautiousness.
Inspec'tion s. Act of inspecting or overseeing; careful survey; examination.
Prospec'tion s. Act of looking forward.
Retrospec'tion s. Act or faculty of surveying things past.
Introspec'tion s. Act of examining one's own thoughts, etc.
Erec'tion s. Act of erecting, anything erected; a building.
Direc'tion s. Act of directing; course, guidance; address on a letter; command; body of directors.
Redirec'tion s. A new address (on a letter, etc.).
Misdirec'tion s. Act of directing wrongly.
Correc'tion s. Act of correction, state of being corrected; improvement; counteraction; criticism; punishment.
Resurrec'tion s. A rising again from the dead, especially that of Christ or that at the Last Day.
Insurrec'tion s. A seditious rising; rebellion.
Sec'tion s. Act of cutting; division; a part cut off or representation of this. v.t. To sectionalize.
Venesec'tion s. Act or operation of letting blood.
Bisec'tion s. Act of bisecting; division into two equal parts.
Trisec'tion s. Act or result of dividing into three.
Vivisec'tion s. Experimental cutting of a living animal.
Transec'tion s. Act or result of transecting.
Insec'tion s. A cutting in, incision.
Intersec'tion s. Act or state of intersecting; point at which lines, etc., cross each other.
Dissec'tion s. Act of dissecting or of cutting up and investigating anatomically.
Detec'tion s. Act of detecting; the discovery of traces, symptoms, crime, etc.
Protec'tion s. Act of protecting; a guard, defence; system of favouring home-produced against foreign goods.
Evec'tion s. An inequality in the moon's longitude.
Convec'tion s. Act of conveying; a process of transmission.
Dic'tion s. Style, language; mode of utterance.
Contradic'tion s. Assertion of the contrary, denial; inconsistency.
Addic'tion s. Act of addicting; propensity.
Maledic'tion s. A curse, imprecation.
Valedic'tion s. A bidding farewell; an adieu.
Benedic'tion s. A blessing, act of blessing; invocation.
Predic'tion s. Act of fortelling; thing foretold; augury.
Indic'tion s. An ancient cycle of fifteen years.
Interdic'tion s. Act of interdicting; prohibition.
Jurisdic'tion s. Legal authority; extent of power.
Fic'tion s. A feigned story; novels collectively; a falsehood.
Derelic'tion s. Abandonment; neglect (as of duty).
Afflic'tion s. State of being afflicted; distress.
Inflic'tion s. Act of inflicting; that which is inflicted; calamity, trouble.
Conflic'tion s. (*Conflict*).
Emic'tion s. The discharge of urine.
Depic'tion s. Portrayal, delineation, description.
Fric'tion s. Act of rubbing bodies together; resistance caused in this; disagreement.
Astric'tion s. Act of binding; restriction.
Obstric'tion s. State of being constrained; obligation.

Restric'tion s. Act of restricting; state of being restricted; limitation.
Constric'tion s. Contraction; state of being constricted.
Perstric'tion s. Stricture, censure.
Evic'tion s. Act of turning a tenant from his house, etc.
Convic'tion s. Act of convicting; state of being convicted or convinced; strong belief.
Sanc'tion s. Ratification; approbation; authority; countenance. v.t. To give validity to; to confirm, authorize.
Tinc'tion s. Colouring material; act or process of colouring.
Distinc'tion s. Division, discrimination; distinguishing quality; superiority, eminence.
Indistinc'tion s. Want of distinction.
Extinc'tion s. Act of extinguishing; destruction; extermination.
Unc'tion s. Act of anointing; an ointment; quality in language which excites emotion, etc.; religious fervour.
Func'tion s. Employment, office, faculty; a ceremonial; a quantity dependent upon another for corresponding changes. v.i. To operate.
Junc'tion s. Act, operation, or place of joining, state of being joined; union.
Injunc'tion s. Act of enjoining; a command; admonition.
Conjunc'tion s. Union, combination; a word connecting sentences or co-ordinating words in the same sentence.
Disjunc'tion s. Act of disjoining; disunion.
Inunc'tion s. Anointing; smearing with oil, etc.
Compunc'tion s. Remorse, regret, contriction.
Expunc'tion s. Act of erasing or cancelling.
Decoc'tion s. Act of boiling a substance in water to extract its virtues; preparation resulting.
Concoc'tion s. A mixture; plot; act of concocting.
Auc'tion s. A public sale of property to the highest bidder; a variety of the card-game bridge. v.t. and i. To sell by auction.
Traduc'tion s. Transference of conclusions from one order of reasoning to another; traducement.
Abduc'tion s. Act of taking away (especially a person) by fraud or force.
Adduc'tion s. Act of bringing towards.
Educ'tion s. Art of educing.
Deduc'tion s. Act of deducting; abatement; inference, consequence.
Reduc'tion s. Act of reducing; conversion to a given state; subjugation; diminution.
Seduc'tion s. Act of seducing, especially inducing a woman to surrender her chastity; an enticement; attractiveness.
Circumduc'tion s. A leading about, annulling.
Induc'tion s. Act of inducting; investiture of a clergyman; a prelude; inferential method of reasoning; conclusion arrived at; electrical transference without direct contact.
Conduc'tion s. Transmission (of heat, electricity, etc.) by means of a conductor.
Produc'tion s. Act or process of producing; product; prolongation; literary composition.
Reproduc'tion s. Act or process of reproducing; a copy.
Introduc'tion s. Act of introducing; presentation; preliminary discourse; elementary treatise.
Ruc'tion s. (*Slang*) A row, fuss, commotion.
Obstruc'tion s. Act of obstructing; an impediment; check.
Substruc'tion s. Under-building; foundation.
Destruc'tion s. Demolition, overthrow, ruin; that which destroys; death.
Instruc'tion s. Act of instructing, teaching, education.
Construc'tion s. Act of constructing, thing constructed, style of structure; arrangement of words, sense, interpretation.
Reconstruc'tion s. Reorganization, especially of a business.
Miscon-struc'tion s. Wrong interpretation.
Superstruc'tion s. Act of building upon; a superstructure.
Suc'tion s. Act or process of sucking.
Dele'tion s. Act of deleting; an erasure.
Deple'tion s. Act of depleting; blood-letting.
Reple'tion s. State of being full; surfeit; plethoric state.
Imple'tion s. Act of filling; state of being full.
Comple'tion s. Fulfilment, accomplishment; act or state of being complete.
Incomple'tion s. Incompleteness.
Accre'tion s. Increase by natural growth.
Secre'tion s. Act of secreting; matter secreted.
Concre'tion s. Act of concreting; state of being concreted; mass concreted; solid matter formed by congealing, coagulation, etc.
Discre'tion s. Quality of being discreet; prudence, judgment.
Indiscre'tion s. Imprudence; an indiscreet act.
Excre'tion s. Act or process of excreting; that which is excreted.
Imbibi'tion s. Drinking in; absorption.
Inhibi'tion s. Act of inhibiting; legal writ stopping further proceeding in a case.
Prohibi'tion s. Act of prohibiting, especially sale of intoxicants; interdict.
Exhibi'tion s. Act of exhibiting; a display, thing displayed, public show; an allowance for educational assistance.
Ambi'tion s. Desire of advance or power.
Tradi'tion s. Anything orally handed down; act of handing thus from father to son.
Extradi'tion s. The surrender, under treaty, of criminals by one government to another.
Addi'tion s. Act of adding; thing added; increase.
Superaddi'tion s. Act of adding something extraneous; that which is added.
Reddi'tion s. Restitution.
Edi'tion s. Form in which a work is published; the whole impression of a book.
Expedi'tion s. Quality of being expedite; haste, promptness; an important or warlike enterprise, excursion, etc.; persons making such.
Sedi'tion s. Minor disorder in a state; civic discord; revolt.
Rendi'tion s. Act of rendering; surrender, translation.
Vendi'tion s. Act of vending; sale.
Condi'tion s. State; quality; temper; external circumstances; stipulation.
Precondi'tion s. Prior condition.
Perdi'tion s. Entire loss or ruin; utter destruction; eternal death.

Audi'tion s. Action or faculty of hearing; a sound.
Subaudi'tion s. Act of understanding something not expressed.
Erudi'tion s. Learning; knowledge gained from books.
Coali'tion s. Union, combination; temporary conferation of parties having different interests.
Ebulli'tion s. A bubbling up, boiling over; effervescence; sudden outburst.
Aboli'tion s. Act of abolishing; state of being abolished.
Demoli'tion s. Act of demolishing; ruin.
Voli'tion s. Power of willing, choice.
Inani'tion s. Emptiness; exhaustion through hunger.
Igni'tion s. Act of igniting; state of being kindled.
Cogni'tion s. Act of knowing; thing known; consciousness, perception.
Recogni'tion s. Act of recognizing; acknowledgment; avowal.
Precogni'tion s. Antecedent knowledge or examination.
Defini'tion s. Act or result of defining; a concise explanation; distinctness.
Moni'tion s. Instruction; warning.
Admoni'tion s. Gentle censure; advice.
Preadmoni'tion s. Previous warning.
Premoni'tion s. Previous warning; presentiment.
Muni'tion s. Materials used in war; military stores.
Premuni'tion s. An anticipation of objections.
Ammuni'tion s. Military stores, especially materials for fire-arms.
Coi'tion s. Conjunction, copulation.
Appari'tion s. An appearance, a phantom.
Preteri'tion s. Act of passing over; state of being passed over.
Detri'tion s. A wearing away by natural agencies.
Contri'tion s. Heartfelt sorrow for sin; state of being contrite.
Attri'tion s. A rubbing down, wearing away; repentance.
Nutri'tion s. Function, act, or process of promoting growth or nourishing; nourishment.
Malnutri'tion s. Defective nutrition.
In'nutrition s. Want of nutrition.
Micturi'tion s. Morbid desire to urinate; act of passing water.
Vomituri'tion s. Retching.
Parturi'tion s. Act of being delivered of young.
Acquisi'tion s. Act of acquiring; that which is acquired; a gain.
Requisi'tion s. Act of requiring; demand; that required. v.t. To make formal or authoritative demand for.
Inquisi'tion s. A judicial inquiry; a Catholic anti-heretical tribunal.
Perquisi'tion s. An accurate or minute inquiry.
Disquisi'tion s. An argumentative inquiry; dissertation; rambling discourse.
Transi'tion s. Passage from one place, state, etc., to another; change from one key to another.
Posi'tion s. Place, situation; posture; rank; state of being placed; thesis.
Juxtaposi'tion s. Placing or being placed next or near to.
Deposi'tion s. Evidence on oath; dethronement; act of depositing.
Preposi'tion s. A word governing a noun, pronoun, or clause.
Imposi'tion s. Act of imposing; act of ordaining; a tax, duty, school punishment; an imposture.
Composi'tion s. Act of composing, especially a literary or musical work; thing or work composed; a compound, mixture; setting of type; agreement to pay part instead of whole; part paid.
Decomposi'tion s. Act or process of decomposing; decay.
Proposi'tion s. A proposal; a complete sentence; a mathematical statement.
Apposi'tion s. Act of placing opposite; relation of one noun to another.
Opposi'tion s. Act of opposing; hostile resistance; contradiction; inconsistency; opponents collectively.
Supposi'tion s. Act of supposing; that which is supposed; surmise.
Presupposi'tion s. Act of presupposing; previous surmise.
Superposi'tion s. State of being situated above or upon something.
Interposi'tion s. Interposal; intervention; mediation.
Disposi'tion s. Act, style, or manner of disposing; arrangement; physical or mental tendency arising from natural condition, acquired aptitude, etc.; moral character.
Predisposi'tion s. State of being predisposed; previous propensity, etc.
Indisposi'tion s. Disinclination, aversion; a slight illness.
Transposi'tion s. Act of transposing; state of being transposed.
Exposi'tion s. Act of exposing, or of expounding; interpretation; a work containing explanations; a public exhibition.
Peti'tion s. A request, supplication, prayer. v.t. To make a request to, to solicit.
Repeti'tion s. Act of repeating; that which is repeated; recital.
Competi'tion s. Contest for the same object; rivalry; struggle for existence or gain.
Denti'tion s. Teething; period of this; arrangement of the teeth.
Accrementi'tion s. Growth by budding.
Parti'tion s. Act of dividing; state of being divided; division; distinction; that which divides. v.t. To divide into shares or distinct parts.
Triparti'tion s. Division by threes or into three.
Forti'tion s. Trusting in or selecting by chance.
Supersti'tion s. Popular or groundless belief in the supernatural.
Degluti'tion s. Act or power of swallowing.
Frui'tion s. Attainment, fulfilment, enjoyment.
Tui'tion s. Guardianship; instruction.
Intui'tion s. Immediate perception; apprehension of the truth without reasoning.
Men'tion v.t. To signify in words; to name. s. A brief notice, remark.
Deten'tion s. Act of detaining; restraint; confinement.
Reten'tion s. Act of retaining; custody; memory.
Inten'tion s. Act of intending; design, purpose, drift.
Conten'tion s. Act of contending; strife, quarrel, dispute.
Absten'tion s. Act of abstaining.
Osten'tion s. The elevation of the Host for adoration.
Atten'tion s. Close application, regard, courtesy,

Inatten'tion s. Want of attention or consideration; neglect.
Contraven'tion s. Violation.
Subven'tion s. Act of supporting; aid; a subsidy.
Preven'tion s. Act of preventing; obstruction.
Circumven'tion s. Fraud, imposture.
Inven'tion s. Act, faculty, or power of inventing; ingenuity; a new contrivance or device.
Conven'tion s. An assembly; an agreement, treaty; a recognized custom or usage.
Superven'tion s. Act of supervening.
Interven'tion s. Act of intervening; interposition, interference.
Non-interven'tion s. (*Negative*).
Lo'tion s. A medicinal wash; a cosmetic.
Mo'tion s. Act, process, or power of moving; change of place; proposal made. v.t. To make a sign with the hand.
Emo'tion s. Mental excitement; passion.
Commo'tion s. Violent agitation, tumult, excitement.
Locomo'tion s. Movement or power of movement from place to place.
Promo'tion s. Act of promoting; condition of being promoted; elevation.
No'tion s. A mental conception; idea; sentiment; opinion.
Preno'tion s. A previous notion; foreknowledge.
Po'tion s. A draught, especially of medicine.
Devo'tion s. Act of devoting; piety; ardent love; eagerness.
Cap'tion s. Seizure; heading of a chapter, page, newspaper article, etc.
Recap'tion s. Recovery of goods, wife, etc., from unlawful withholding; a second writ for recovery on distraint.
Usucap'tion s. Acquisition of title to property by uninterrupted possession for a certain term.
Contrap'tion s. (*Slang*) A contrivance, apparatus.
Decep'tion s. A cheat, fraud; act of deceiving, state of being deceived.
Recep'tion s. Act of receiving; admission; entertainment; welcome.
Incep'tion s. Beginning, commencement.
Concep'tion s. Act of conceiving; state of being conceived; apprehension; image formed in the mind; mental faculty which originates ideas.
Preconcep'tion s. Act of preconceiving; opinion previously formed.
Misconcep'tion s. A mistake; false opinion.
Percep'tion s. Act or faculty of perceiving; cognizance; discernment; sensation.
Preperceр'tion s. A previous perception.
Appercep'tion s. Self-consciousness.
Intercep'tion s. Act of intercepting.
Introsuscep'tion s. Act of taking in or receiving within.
Intussuscep'tion s. Reception of one part within another.
Excep'tion s. Act of excepting; thing excepted, not included, or specified as distinct; an objection; cause of offence.
Subrep'tion s. Act of obtaining something by surprise or fraud.
Surrep'tion s. Act or process of getting surreptitiously.
Scrip'tion s. Handwriting; style of this.
Subscrip'tion s. Act of subscribing; that which is subscribed.
Descrip'tion s. Act of describing; relation, account; a definition.
Rescrip'tion s. The answering of a letter.
Prescrip'tion s. Act of prescribing; that which is prescribed; medical recipe; a claim by virtue of use, custom, etc.
Circumscrip'tion s. Exterior line of a body; limitation; bound.
Transcrip'tion s. Act of transcribing; a transcript.
Inscrip'tion s. Act of inscribing; words inscribed; address to a person; title of an illustration, etc.
Conscrip'tion s. Compulsory enrolment for nationa service.
Proscrip'tion s. Act of proscribing; outlawry denunciation.
Superscrip'tion s. That which is written above.
Emp'tion s. Act of purchasing.
Ademp'tion s. A taking away; revocation.
Redemp'tion s. Act of redeeming; state of being redeemed; repurchase; ransom; deliverance.
Pre-emp'tion s. Act or right of purchasing before others.
Coemp'tion s. Act of purchasing the whole of a commodity.
Exemp'tion s. Act of exempting; state of being exempted.
Gump'tion s. Understanding, common sense; a medium for mixing colours.
Sump'tion s. The major premise of a syllogism.
Subsump'tion s. Act of subsuming; state of being or that which is subsumed.
Resump'tion s. Act of resuming.
Presump'tion s. Act of or ground for presuming; supposition; forward or arrogant conduct, etc.
Consump'tion s. Act of consuming, use of commodities; destruction, waste; a wasting disease; phthisis.
Assump'tion s. Act of assuming; thing assumed.
Op'tion s. Choice, power of choosing.
Adop'tion s. Act of adopting; state of being adopted; acceptance.
Preop'tion s. Right of first choice.
Discerp'tion s. Severance; a severed portion.
Excerp'tion s. Act of excerpting; thing selected.
Absorp'tion s. Act or process of imbibing or absorbing; engrossment of the mind.
Reabsorp'tion s. Act of reabsorbing.
Resorp'tion s. Act of resorbing; state of being reabsorbed.
Erup'tion s. A breaking out; explosion, violent emission.
Interrup'tion s. Act of interrupting; a break, obstruction, stoppage; cause of this.
Irrup'tion s. A sudden invasion; incursion.
Corrup'tion s. Act or process of corrupting; pollution, taint; depravity; bribery; misrepresentation.
Incorrup'tion s. Freedom from corruption.
Disrup'tion s. Act of breaking asunder, state of being so broken.
Deser'tion s. Act of abandoning, state of being abandoned.
Inser'tion s. Act of inserting; anything inserted; place or mode of attachment of a part.
Asser'tion s. Act of asserting; a positive statement.
Exer'tion s. Act of exerting; effort.
Abor'tion s. A premature birth.
Por'tion s. A part; a share; a dowry; fate. v.t. To share, parcel; to endow.
Propor'tion s. Comparative relation, relative size, etc.; share; symmetry. v.t. To adjust; to form with symmetry.

Dispropor'tion s. Want of proportion or symmetry. v.t. To make unsuitable, mismatch.
Mispropor'tion v.t. To proportion wrongly.
Appor'tion v.t. To allot, portion out.
Retor'tion s. Bending, turning, or twisting back; retaliation.
Contor'tion s. Twisting of face, limbs, etc.; partial dislocation.
Distor'tion s. Act or result of distorting; visible deformity.
Extor'tion s. Act of extorting; thing extorted; illegal or oppressive exaction.
Bas'tion s. A strengthening work to a rampart; a salient angle of a fortress.
Sugges'tion s. Act of suggesting; a hint, tentative proposal.
Diges'tion s. Act or power of digesting; process which food undergoes in the stomach; operation of heating with a solvent; assimilation.
Indiges'tion s. Weakness of stomach; difficulty in digesting; dyspepsia.
Inges'tion s. Act or process of ingesting.
Conges'tion s. Abnormal accumulation, as of persons, traffic, blood in capillaries, etc.
Ques'tion s. Act of asking; an interrogation; inquiry; subject of debate. v.i. and t. To ask a question, to interrogate, to doubt.
Us'tion s. Act of burning; cauterization.
Exhaus'tion s. Act of exhausting; state of being exhausted or deprived of strength, spirits, etc.
Moxibus'tion s. Cauterization by means of moxa.
Combus'tion s. Act or process of taking fire and burning; chemical combination attended with heat and light.
Cau'tion s. Provident care, wariness, heed; (*slang*) a droll, something extraordinary. v.t. To warn.
Precau'tion s. Prudent foresight; a guarding measure taken beforehand.
Retribu'tion s. Act of repaying; requital; retaliation.
Contribu'tion s. Act of contributing; that which is contributed; article sent to a periodical, etc.
Distribu'tion s. Act of distributing; apportionment; dispersal.
Redistribu'tion s. Rearrangement, as of parliamentary constituencies.
Attribu'tion s. Act of attributing; quality, etc., attributed.
Consecu'tion s. State of being consecutive; a series; sequel.
Prosecu'tion s. Act or process of prosecuting; party instituting proceedings.
Persecu'tion s. Act of persecuting; state of being persecuted; continued annoyance.
Execu'tion s. Act of executing; performance; accomplishment; act of completing a legal instrument; act of putting to death as a legal penalty.
Locu'tion s. Style of speech; a phrase.
Elocu'tion s. Mode of speech, oral delivery; oratory, eloquence.
Ventrilocu'tion s. Ventriloquism.
Allocu'tion s. Act or way of speaking; a formal address.
Circumlocu'tion s. Roundabout way of speaking; periphrasis.
Interlocu'tion s. A dialogue, conference, intermediate discussion.
Electrocu'tion s. Execution by electricity.
Ablu'tion s. Act of cleansing; purification.
Dilu'tion s. Act or result of diluting.
Pollu'tion s. Act of polluting; defilement, contamination, taint.
Solu'tion s. A dissolving; liquid combination so produced; disentanglement of a problem, etc.; state of being solved; correct answer.
Absolu'tion s. Acquittal; remission of sins.
Resolu'tion s. Act or process of separating the component parts; state of being or that which is resolved or determined; determination; a formal decision.
Irresolu'tion s. Want of decision; vacillation.
Dissolu'tion s. Act of dissolving; decomposition; death; the breaking up of an assembly.
Volu'tion s. A spiral turn; whorl of a shell.
Obvolu'tion s. State of being obvolute.
Evolu'tion s. Act of unfolding; development; theory of generation; prescribed movement of troops.
Devolu'tion s. Delegation of authority; transference; descent by inheritance; lapse through desuetude.
Revolu'tion s. Act of revolving; circular motion; a circuit; a cycle of time; total change; political overthrow.
Circumvolu'tion s. Act of rolling round; a coil; revolution.
Involu'tion s. Act or result of involving, complication; envelope; the raising of a quantity to any power assigned.
Convolu'tion s. Act of rolling together; a winding, spiral.
Diminu'tion s. Act of diminishing; subtraction, amount subtracted.
Comminu'tion s. Act of comminuting; pulverization.
Substitu'tion s. Act of substituting; state of being substituted.
Destitu'tion s. Want; extreme poverty.
Restitu'tion s. Act of restoring; amends.
Institu'tion s. Act of instituting; that which is instituted; an association for the promotion of some object; building for this; an established law, custom, etc.
Constitu'tion s. Frame or character of body or mind; established form of government; system of fundamental rules and ordinances; a law.
Prostitu'tion s. Act or practice of prostituting; debasement.
Obliv'ion s. State of being forgotten; forgetfulness; an amnesty.
Allu'vion s. Formation of new land by the action of the sea.
Flex'ion s. Act or process of bending; a bend; part bent.
Deflex'ion s. Act of deflecting; departure from true course; deviation.
Reflex'ion s. (*Reflection*).
Inflex'ion s. Act of inflecting; state of being inflected; a fold; a voice-modulation; declensional or conjugational variation of noun or verb; diffraction.
Genuflex'ion s. Act of bending the knee, especially in worship.
Complex'ion s. Colour of the face; general appearance; temperament.
Connex'ion s. Act of connecting; state of being connected; relationship; acquaintanceship; a religious body; a body of customers, etc.
Disconnex'ion s. State of being separated or incoherent.
Crucifix'ion s. Act of crucifying; the death of Christ.

Transfix'ion s. Act of transfixing; a method of amputation.
Flux'ion s. Act of flowing; matter that flows; an infinitely small quantity.
Deflux'ion s. The downward flow of humours.
Efflux'ion s. Efflux.
Zi'on s. A hill in Jerusalem; residence of ancient Hebrew kings; a nonconformist chapel.
Don'jon s. The central keep of a mediæval castle.
Beck'on v.i. and t. To make a sign by nodding, a motion of the hand, etc.
Reck'on v.t. and i. To calculate, compute, estimate; to consider.
Gon'falon s. An ensign, standard.
Enceph'alon s. The brain.
Mesenceph'alon s. The mid-brain.
Epenceph'alon s. The hinder division of the brain.
Prosenceph'alon s. The anterior part of the brain.
Salon s. A reception-room; a reception of or circle of eminent persons in literature, art, etc.
Tal'on s. Claws of a bird of prey; an ogee moulding.
Fel'on s. One convicted of a felony; a whitlow. a. Cruel, malicious.
Ech'elon s. Arrangement of bodies of troops in a step-like formation. v.t. To place troops thus.
Mel'on s. A fleshy, edible gourd.
Mam'elon s. A small rounded hill.
My'elon s. The spiral cord.
Mou'flon s. The wild sheep of Corsica and Sardinia.
Gal'lon s. A measure of capacity; one-eighth of a bushel.
Bil'lon s. Alloy for coinage.
Car'illon s. A chime of bells; a tune played on this.
Bouillon' s. Broth, soup
Quil'lon s. Part of hand-guard of sword.
Co'lon s. A grammatical point (:) marking a pause; the large intestine.
Semico'lon s. A punctuation mark (;).
Ei'dolon s. An image, apparition.
Sto'lon s. A sucker, a trailing shoot that takes root.
Mer'lon s. Part between embrasures of battlemented parapet.
Diach'ylon s. An adhesive plaster.
Py'lon s. A monumental gateway; turning-point in an aerodrome.
Tel'amon s. Sculptured male figure acting as support.
Cin'namon s. The aromatic inner bark of a tree from Ceylon, used as a flavouring and in medicine.
De'mon s. An evil spirit; a devil.
Cacode'mon s. An evil spirit, a nightmare.
Lem'on s. A yellowish, oval, very acid fruit; its tree; its colour.
Pentste'mon s. A genus of plants with showy tubular flowers.
Phleg'mon s. A tumour of the cellular tissue.
Salm'on (săm-) s. A large food and sporting fish.
Gam'mon s. A smoked ham; nonsense, humbug; a defeat at backgammon. v.t. To salt and cure, to make into bacon; to hoax. v.i. To make pretences; to chaff.
Backgam'mon s. A game for two, played with dice and draughtsmen.
Mam'mon s. Worldly riches or gain.
Persim'mon s. A N. American tree with hard wood and astringent, plum-like fruit; the fruit.
Com'mon s. Belonging equally to many, general; usual; of no rank; of small value. s. An open public ground. v.i. To have a right in a common; to board together.
Intercom'mon v.i. To share with others, participate.
Discom'mon v.t. To deprive of rights of common or of a privilege.
Sum'mon v.t. To cite, notify to appear, call upon to surrender.
Resum'mon v.t. To summon or convene again.
Sol'omon s. A sage, wise man.
Gno'mon s. The style or pointer of a dial; a geometrical figure.
Ser'mon s. A religious discourse, homily.
Mor'mon s. A member of an American religious body formerly polygamous.
Ichneu'mon s. A N. African, carnivorous, weasel-like animal.
Et'ymon s. An original form. primitive word.
Anon' adv. Presently, soon.
Can'on s. Law; a formula; a rule of doctrine; the accepted body of the Holy Scriptures; a member of a cathedral chapter; list of saints.
Cañ'on s. (*Canyon*).
Fan'on s. A napkin used at the Eucharist.
Gon'fanon s. A gonfalon.
Or'ganon s. A logical system or method of thought.
Xo'anon (zō'-) s. A primitive wooden image said to have fallen from heaven.
Par'thenon s. The temple of Athene on the Acropolis at Athens.
Prolegom'enon s. An introductory treatise on a subject.
Phenom'enon s. An appearance, especially one whose cause is not immediately obvious; something extraordinary.
Perispo'menon s. A Greek word with a circumflex on the last syllable.
Properispo'menon s. A word with a circumflex on the penultimate.
Nou'menon s. A thing in itself apart from its characteristics or phenomena.
Ten'on s. End of a piece of wood fitted into a mortise.
Xe'non (zĕ'-) s. An inert gaseous element occurring in the atmosphere.
Chi'gnon s. A pad formerly worn by women in the hair.
Mign'on a. Small and delicate; dainty.
Champign'on s. An agaric.
Can'non s. A large piece of artillery; the striking of two balls successively by another. v.i. To make a cannon, as at billiards.
Pen'non s. A small pointed or swallow-tailed flag.
Boon s. A favour, gift. a. Jolly, companionable.
Baboon' s. A large kind of monkey.
Coon s. A racoon; (*American slang*) a sly fellow; a negro.
Cacoon' s. A large African bean.
Racoon' s. An arboreal, nocturnal, N. American mammal.
Barracoon' s. A fortified slave-market in Africa.
Cocoon' s. The silky case of a chrysalis.
Tycoon' s. Title used by the Shogun of Japan, 1854-68.
Rigadoon' s. A brisk dance for two.
Bridoon' s. A military snaffle and rein.
Cardoon' s. A plant of the artichoke family.
Buffoon' s. A low jester; a merryandrew.
Lagoon' s. A shallow lake, especially connected with the sea.

Dragoon' s. A cavalry soldier. v.t. To discipline; to enslave.
Typhoon' s. A violent hurricane of the China Seas.
Shoon s. Obsolete for "shoes."
Loon s. A worthless scamp, a fool; the guillemot or other gull.
Saloon' s. A large room, hall, cabin, railway carriage, etc.; a public room; a drinking-bar.
Pan'taloon s. A buffoon in pantomime.
Doubloon' s. A Spanish gold coin (about £1).
Balloon' s. A large bag, filled with gas, that will rise and float in the air.
Galloon' s. A narrow braid of cotton, silk, etc., with metallic thread interwoven.
Shalloon' s. A light worsted fragment.
Walloon' s. One of a mixed race of the French and Belgian frontier; their dialect. a. Pertaining to this.
Epiplo'on s. The omentum.
Moon s. A satellite, especially of the earth; a month. v.i. To stare vacantly, wander idly.
Hon'eymoon s. The first month after marriage.
Noon s. The middle of the day; twelve o'clock.
Fore'noon s. The early part of the day.
Afternoon' s. The time between midday and evening.
Lampoon' s. A personal or bitter satire. v.t. To calumniate, libel, satirize.
Harpoon' s. A barbed spear for throwing at whales. v.t. To strike, catch, or kill with this.
Spoon s. A small ladle for liquids; an object shaped somewhat thus; a mawkish lover. v.t. To take up with a spoon. v.i. To make love foolishly.
Macaroon' s. A sweet almond-flavoured cake.
Picaroon' s. A wrecker, pirate; a cheating rogue.
Maroon' a. Claret-coloured, brownish crimson. s. This colour; a detonating firework; a fugitive slave of the W. Indies or their descendants. v.t. To put and leave on a desolate island.
Gambroon' s. A twilled linen fabric.
Croon s. A low continued murmuring sound. v.i. To hum, sing in a low tone.
Gadroon' s. An ornamental row of convex fluted curves.
Quadroon' s. Offspring of a mulatto and a white.
Seroon' s. A leather package containing drugs, figs, etc.
Octoroon' s. The offspring of a quadroon and a white.
Poltroon' s. An arrant coward.
Quintroon' s. Offspring of a white and an octoroon.
Soon adv. Before long; shortly; early.
Monsoon' s. A trade-wind of the Indian Ocean.
Bassoon' s. A bass musical wind-instrument with a reed.
Cas'soon s. A square depression in a ceiling.
Gossoon' s. (*Irish*) A lad.
Toon s. A red timbered Indian tree.
Ducatoon' s. An old silver Venetian coin.
Frigatoon' s. An old Venetian sailing-vessel.
Platoon' s. A section or subsection of soldiers.
Ratoon' s. Sprout from root after sugar-cane has been cut.
Musketoon' s. An obsolete kind of musket.
Spitoon' s. A vessel to spit in.
Pontoon' s. A flat-bottomed boat; a lighter; a float; a card-game.
Spontoon' s. An obsolete military half-pike or halberd.
Cartoon' s. A large-scale drawing or design; a political caricature. v.t. To draw a cartoon.
Festoon' s. A garland of flowers, drapery, etc., hanging in a curve; carving representing this. v.t. To form into or adorn with festoons.
Swoon v.i. To faint. s. A fainting fit.
Zo'on s. The product of a fertilized ovum.
Epizo'on s. An animal parasitic upon the outside of another.
Spermatozo'on s. A male sexual sperm-cell of an animal.
Ectozo'on s. A parasite living on the outside of another animal.
Entozo'on s. An animal living within the body of another.
Protozo'on s. An individual of the protozoa.
Phytozo'on s. A zoophyte.
Bryozo'on s. One of the Polyzoa.
Polyzo'on s. One of the Polyzoa.
Ca'pon s. A castrated fowl.
Weap'on (wep'-) s. Implement of offence or defence.
Crep'on s. A crapy stuff of silk and wool.
Cram'pon s. A hooked iron bar, a grappling iron; spike in a mountaineer's boot.
Tam'pon s. A plug for stopping hæmorrhage.
Pom'pon s. An ornamental tuft, ball, etc., for hats; a small chrysanthemum.
Ship'pon s. A cattle-shed.
Tar'pon s. A large sporting fish of the herring family.
Upon' prep.
Hereupon' adv. On this; hereon.
Thereupon' adv.
Whereupon' adv. In consequence of, or immediately after, which.
Ju'pon s. A petticoat.
Cou'pon s. A detachable interest certificate attached to a transferable bond; a detachable ticket or certificate of other kinds.
Bar'on s. A peer of the lowest ran .
Fan'faron s. A bully, blusterer, empty boaster.
Char'on s. The fabled ferryman of Hades.
Diates'saron s. An interval of a fourth in music; the harmony of the Four Gospels.
Mac'ron s. Short line above a lettert o show it is pronounced long.
Squad'ron s. Main unit of a cavalry regiment; detachment of warships, yachts, etc.
Decahe'dron s. A ten-sided solid.
Chiliahe'dron s. A figure with one thousand sides.
Tetrahe'dron s. A solid figure enclosed by four triangles.
Ikosahe'dron s. A twenty-sided solid figure.
Octahe'dron s. A solid contained by eight equal and equilateral triangles.
Pentahe'dron s. A solid figure having five equal sides.
Triacontahe'-dron s. A solid figure having thirty sides.
Heptahe'dron s. A solid, seven-sided figure.
Hexahe'dron s. A six-sided solid; a cube.
Dihe'dron s. A figure with two sides or surfaces.
Trihe'dron s. Figure having three equal sides.
Rhombohe'-dron s. A solid bounded by six equal rhombs.
Polyhe'dron s. A solid contained by many sides.
Cal'dron s. A large kettle or boiler.
Chal'dron s. A measure for coals (36 bushels).
Caul'dron s. A deep vessel for boiling in.
Lepidoden'dron s. A fossil plant from the coal-measures.

Rhododen'dron s. A large evergreen shrub with handsome flowers.
Lirioden'dron s. The N. American tulip-tree.
Erig'eron s. A genus of aster-like plants.
Her'on s. A long-necked wading bird.
Ach'eron s. A river of Hades; the underworld.
Per'cheron s. A swift breed of horses from Perche, Normandy.
Ail'eron s. The movable edge of the plane of an aeroplane.
Hexae'meron s. Period of six days, especially the Creation period.
Chap'eron s. An elderly lady as escort to a young one.
Se'ron s. (*Seroon*).
Saf'fron s. A bulbous plant with deep yellow flower.
Cham'fron s. Armour for a horse's head.
Ne'ophron s. The white vulture of Egypt.
South'ron (sŭth'-) s. An inhabitant of the south, especially (*Scot.*) an Englishman. a. Pertaining to the south; English.
I'ron s. The commonest metallic element; an implement made of this; a fetter. v.t. To smooth with an iron.
Grid'iron s. A grate for broiling meat, etc., on; a framework of parallel beams.
And'iron s. A support for logs burnt at an open fire.
Envi'ron v.t. To surround, encompass; to involve.
Bor'on s. The element present in borax.
Oxymor'on s. A figure in which an epithet of totally contrary import is added to a word.
A'pron s. Cloth, leather, etc., worn in front as a protection to the clothes.
Gar'ron s. A small breed of horse.
Per'ron s. A platform in front of a building with steps.
Ma'tron s. An elderly married woman; a female superintendent.
Na'tron s. Native carbonate of soda.
Pa'tron s. One who supports or protects a person, institution, etc.; one who has the gift of a benefice, professorship, etc.
Elec'tron s. A particle charged with negative electricity forming a constituent part of an atom; electrum.
Cit'ron s. An evergreen tree bearing a large lemon-like fruit; the fruit. a. Yellow.
Quer'citron s. The bark of the black oak, used in tanning, etc.
Plas'tron s. A leather bodyguard for fencers; the under shell of a tortoise, etc.
Ely'tron s. The horny sheath covering an anterior wing of a beetle.
Aleur'on s. An albuminoid found in seeds.
Fleur'on s. A floral tail-piece, etc.
Neur'on s. A nerve-cell with its processes and ramifications.
Chev'ron s. An heraldic ordinary composed of two stripes meeting at an angle; the distinguishing badge of a N.C.O.
Gyr'on s. An heraldic triangular charge.
Xerom'yron s. A dry ointment.
Son (sŭn) s. A male child.
Ba'son s. (*Basin*).
Rea'son s. The rational faculty; a cause, motive, explanation; justice, equity. v.i. To argue rationally; to discuss. v.t. To examine or persuade by arguments.
Trea'son (trē'-) s. Offence of attempting to overthrow a sovereign, etc.; disloyalty, treachery.
Sea'son s. One of four divisions of year; a time, suitable time; seasoning. v.t. To acclimatize, inure; to add zest to; to qualify. v.i. To become habituated; to grow fit for use.
Ma'son s. A stone-worker; a freemason.
Free'mason s. A member of a secret society or fraternity.
Diapa'son s. A chord in music which includes all tones; harmony; a fundamental stop in an organ.
Gam'beson s. A thick wadded and quilted mediæval tunic.
Whore'son s. A bastard. a. Scurvy, mean.
Wave'son s. Goods floating from a wreck.
Liai'son s. Illicit intimacy between a man and woman; bond of union.
Malmai'son s. A variety of blush-rose, also of carnation.
Bi'son s. A large wild ox.
Mal'ison s. A curse, malediction.
Ben'ison s. A blessing, benediction.
Ven'ison (ven'zon) s. The flesh of deer as food.
U'nison s. Accordance; harmony; concord. a. Sounding together.
Poi'son s. A substance noxious to life; venom. v.t. To infect with poison, to taint.
Capar'ison s. A saddle covering, clothing. v.t. To cover with a cloth, to dress handsomely.
Compar'ison s. Act of comparing; state of being compared; relation; simile; grammatical inflection.
Gri'son s. A S. American carnivorous mammal; a variety of monkey.
Or'ison s. Prayer; supplication.
Pris'on s. Place of confinement and punishment, a jail. v.t. To confine.
Impris'on v.t. To confine in prison; to deprive of liberty.
Gar'rison s. Military body stationed in a fort or town. v.t. To place a garrison in.
Jet'tison s. The casting of goods overboard as jetsam. v.t. To effect this.
Kel'son s. An internal keel.
Tel'son s. The last segment of the abdomen of Crustacea.
Dam'son s. A small black plum; tree bearing this.
Ram'son s. The broad-leaved garlic; its bulbous root.
Sam'son s. A man of great strength.
Stem'son s. A curved timber supporting the scarfs of a vessel.
Crim'son s. A deep red colour. a. Of this colour. v.t. To dye crimson. v.i. To turn crimson, to blush.
Chan'son s. A song.
Ten'son s. A verse-contest between troubadours.
Spon'son s. Projecting gun-embrasure from a warship.
Ar'son s. Malicious burning of property.
Par'son s. A clergyman, vicar.
Squar'son s. A landed clergyman, squire and parson in one.
Per'son s. A living human; the body; outward appearance; each of the three Beings of the Trinity; each of the three relations of the subject or object of a verb.
Ur'son s. A N. American porcupine.

Less'on s. A task of exercise; precept; portion of Scripture for church reading. v.t. To teach; to admonish.
Cais'son s. An ammunition chest; a contrivance for laying foundations in deep water, raising sunken vessels, etc.
Bis'son a. Half-blind.
Bau'son s. The badger.
Advow'son s. Right of presentation to a Church benefice.
Hy'son s. A species of green tea.
Ton (tun) s. Weight of 2240 lbs.
Ton (ton) s. The fashion; high mode.
Bat'on s. A truncheon, a stuff. v.t. To hit with this.
Hyper'baton s. Change of the natural order of words and sentences.
Tetragram'-maton s. The sacred consonants (J.H.V.H.) symbolizing Jehovah.
Autom'aton s. A machine that simulates the action of living beings; one who acts mechanically.
Sher'aton a. Denoting an eighteenth-century style of furniture.
Ao'ton s. A quilted jacket worn as body-armour.
Pha'eton s. A light, four-wheeled open carriage.
Skel'eton s. The bones of an animal in natural position; outline, frame.
Endoskel'eton s. The internal bony structure of vertebrates.
Dermoskel'-eton s. The hard outer covering of tortoises, crabs, etc.
Exoskel'eton s. The bony exterior skeleton of certain invertebrates; hoofs, nails, etc., of vertebrates.
Single'ton s. A single card of a suit in a hand.
Feuille'ton s. Story or light article in a newspaper.
Simple'ton s. A feeble-minded or gullible person.
Se'ton s. A twist of silk, etc., placed in a wound, to cause suppuration.
Bed'lington s. A small variety of terrier.
Well'ington s. A high boot reaching to the knee.
Or'pington s. A variety of domestic fowl,
Chi'ton s. A loose robe or tunic; a genus of limpet-like molluscs.
Brit'on s. One of British race.
Tri'ton s. An ancient Greek sea-deity; a gasteropod mollusc; an aquatic salamander.
Plank'ton s. The minute organic matter floating or drifting in the sea.
Mel'ton s. A stout cloth without nap.
Stil'ton s. A rich kind of cheese.
Canton' v.t. To divide into parts; to billet.
Can'ton s. A division of a country; a small square in the corner of an heraldic shield.
San'ton s. A Mohammedan saint.
Wanton' (wŏnt'-) a. Unrestrained; licentious; lascivious. s. An unchaste person.
Bad'minton s. A game played with bats and shuttlecocks; a kind of claret-cup.
Front'on s. A pediment, frontal.
Cro'ton s. A genus of strong-smelling herbaceous plants.
Lep'ton s. A small ancient Greek coin, a mite.
Baralip'ton s. A mnemonic for the first figure of a syllogism.
Kryp'ton s. A gaseous element occurring in the air.
Bar'ton s. A farm-yard.
Car'ton s. A paste-board case; a white disc in a bull's-eye; a shot hitting this.
Rib'ston s. A variety of apple.
Phlogis'ton s. The hypothetical element to which fire and combustion was formerly supposed to be due.
Pis'ton s. Short piece of metal fitting exactly in a cylinder and working to and fro inside it.
Bos'ton s. A dance; a card-game resembling whist.
Cot'ton s. The soft downy substance in the pod of the cotton-plant used for making thread, etc.; thread or cloth made from this. v.i. To agree with, to become closely attached to.
But'ton s. A knob or stud for fastening the dress, etc. v.t. To fasten or furnish with buttons.
Glut'ton s. One who eats to excess; one greedy for anything; the wolverine.
Mut'ton s. Flesh of sheep used as food.
Teu'ton s. One of Germanic race.
Sex'ton s. A minor church officer acting as care-taker, usher, grave-digger, etc.
Phy'ton s. A plant-unit.
Won pret. and past part. of Win.
Sax'on s. A native of Saxony; an Anglo-Saxon, Englishman; language of of the Saxons. s. Pertaining to the people, their language, or country.
Ex'on s. An officer of the Yeomen of the Guard.
Yon a. and adv. Yonder.
Ray'on s. A radius.
Cray'on s. A pencil of coloured chalk; a drawing made with this. v.t. To sketch with crayons.
Hal'cyon s. The kingfisher. a. Peaceful, calm.
Apol'lyon s. A name of the Devil.
Can'yon s. A long and narrow mountain gorge.
Amphit'ryon s. A very hospitable host.
Bla'zon v.t. To display; to explain heraldically. s. A coat of arms or a description of such.
Embla'zon v.t. To adorn with heraldic figures; to sing the praises of.
Am'azon s. A masculine or pugnacious woman; a female warrior.
Hori'zon s. Apparent junction of earth and sky.
Barn s. A building for hay, grain, etc.
Darn v.t. To mend holes in cloth by sewing. s. A place so mended. int. A mild oath.
Ce'darn a. Made of cedar-wood.
Earn v.t. To gain by labour, acquire, obtain.
Learn v.i. To gain knowledge, receive instruction. v.t. To acquire knowledge of or skill in; to fix in the memory.
Yearn v.i. To feel tenderness; to long for.
Tarn s. A small mountain lake.
Warn (worn) v.t. To caution against; to advise.
Forewarn' v.t. To give previous notice of.
Yarn s. Spun thread or cotton; a story, tale. v.i. To tell a story.
Secern' v.t. To separate, distinguish.
Concern' s. Business, affair, care, solicitude. v.t. To relate to, to interest.
Unconcern' s. Absence from anxiety or solicitude.
Discern' v.t. To descry, make out; to judge, distinguish.
Mod'ern a. Pertaining to the present or to recent times; new, newish. s. A person of modern times.

Fern s. A cryptogam producing fronds.
Hern s. The heron.
Leath'ern a. Made of or consisting of leather.
Cith'ern s. A mediæval stringed instrument.
Nor'thern a. Being in the north; toward or proceeding from the north. s. A northerner.
South'ern (sŭth'-) a. Pertaining to, situated in or towards, or coming from the south. s. A Southerner.
Kern s. An ancient Irish foot-soldier; a boor; the projecting part of type; a quern.
Pern s. The honey-buzzard.
Lam'pern s. The river-lamprey.
Casern' s. Temporary lodgings for soldiers.
Tern s. A sea-bird; a set of three. a. Ternate.
Leo'tern s. A reading-desk, especially in churches.
Altern' a. Alternate. adv. Alternately.
Sub'altern a. Subordinate. s. Military officer below rank of captain.
Salt'ern s. Place where sea water is evaporated.
Lan'tern s. A transparent case for a light; part of a lighthouse containing the light; a small dome, etc., for giving light within.
Intern' v.t. To hold in custody; to disarm and confine.
Quar'tern s. The fourth part of a pint or peck; a loaf of about 4 lbs.
Stern a. Austere, rigid, harsh. s. The hind part of a ship; rump of an animal.
Astern' adv. In or at the hinder part of a ship.
East'ern a. Situated in, pertaining to, or blowing from the east. s. An Oriental.
Pas'tern s. The part of a horse's leg between the fetlock-joint and the hoof.
West'ern a., adv., s. (*West*).
Cis'tern s. A small reservoir.
Pos'tern s. A back door; a small or private entrance.
Slat'tern s. A negligent woman, a slut.
Pat'tern s. A model; a sample, instance; an ornamental design. v.t. To copy, make in imitation; to serve as an example.
Bit'tern s. A large bird of the heron family.
Cit'tern s. A cithern.
Git'tern s. An obsolete guitar-like instrument.
Pot'tern a. Pertaining to potters or pottery.
Extern' a. External. s. A student not residing in college.
Quern s. A hand-mill for grinding grain.
Cav'ern s. A cave. v.t. To hollow out; to enclose in a cavern.
Tav'ern s. An inn, public-house.
Gov'ern v.t. To manage, rule; to restrain, regulate; to steer. v.i. To exercise authority.
Misgov'ern v.t. To govern ill, administer unfaithfully.
Wy'vern s. A two-legged heraldic dragon.
Bairn s. A child.
Cairn s. A large heap of stones as a sepulchre, memorial, or landmark.
Born a. Brought forth, brought into the world.
Stub'born a. Obstinate; inflexible.
Base'-born a. Of low birth; illegitimate.
High'-born a. Of noble birth.
Inborn' a. Implanted by nature.
Suborn' v.t. To bribe, especially to commit perjury.
Corn s. Grain; seeds growing in ears and made into flour; a horny excrescence on a toe, etc. v.t. To preserve with salt in grains; to granulate.
A'corn s. The fruit of the oak.
Lon'gicorn s. A beetle having long antennæ.
Lamel'licorn s. One of a group of beetles.
U'nicorn s. A fabulous, one-horned, horse-like creature.
Quad'ricorn s. An animal having four horns or antennæ.
Cap'ricorn s. The tenth sign of the Zodiac.
Ser'ricorn a. Having serrated antennæ.
Tri'corn a. Three-horned. s. A three-cornered hat.
Cav'icorn a. Having hollow horns. s. A hollow-horned ruminant.
Clav'icorn s. A group of beetles.
Pop'corn s. Parched maize.
Pep'percorn s. The fruit of the pepper plant; anything quite insignificant.
Scorn s. Contempt; an object of this. v.t. To despise, hold in great contempt.
Bar'leycorn s. A grain of barley; a third of an inch.
Adorn' v.t. To embellish, deck with ornaments.
Readorn' v.t. To adorn again.
Horn s. A hard projection on head of certain animals; substance of this; a trumpet; drinking-cup; something resembling a or made of horn. v.t. To gore with horns.
Wald'horn s. A French horn without valves.
Leghorn' s. A kind of straw plait; a hat made from this; a breed of fowl.
Prong'horn s. Prongbuck, an antelope-like ruminant.
Krumm'horn s. A clarinet-like organ-stop.
Green'horn s. A novice; a simpleton.
Shorn past part. (*Shear*).
Harts'horn s. Impure carbonate of ammonia.
Thorn s. A prickly shrub; a spine; anything troublesome.
Bas'set-horn s. A tenor clarinet.
Black'thorn s. The sloe.
Buck'thorn s. A low shrubby tree with black bark and thorny branchlets.
Lan'thorn s. A lantern.
Haw'thorn s. The white-thorn, may.
Sax'horn s. A brass wind-instrument.
Lorn a. Abandoned; undone; lonely.
Love'lorn a. Forsaken by one's lover; pining away for love.
Forlorn' a. Deserted; in pitiful plight pitiable; abject; lost.
Morn s. Morning; the next day.
Norn s. One of the Norse Fates.
Torn past part. (*Tear*).
Worn past part. (*Wear*).
Overworn' a. Wearied; trite, commonplace.
Sworn past part. (*Swear*).
Man'sworn a. Perjured, forsworn.
Forsworn' past part. (*Forswear*).
Outworn' a. Worn-out; obsolete.
Urn s. A kind of vase; a container for ashes of the dead. v.t. To enclose in an urn.
Burn v.t. To consume with or harden by fire, to scorch. v.i. To be on fire, to rage, to be inflamed with desire. s. The result of burning; a streamlet.
Al'burn s. Alburnum.
Heart'burn s. A burning pain in the stomach.
Au'burn a. Reddish brown, chestnut.

Churn s. A vessel in which butter is made. v.t. To agitate cream for making butter; to shake violently.
Inurn' v.t. To place in a cinerary urn.
Bourn s. A stream; a limit, bourne.
Adjourn' v.t. To put off, postpone. v.i. To leave off for a future occasion.
Soj'ourn (suj'-) s. A temporary residing. v.i. To dwell for a time.
Mourn v.i. To grieve, be sorrowful; to wear mourning. v.t. To deplore.
Spurn v.t. To reject with disdain, treat contemptuously. v.i. To manifest disdain. s. Scornful rejection.
Turn v.i. To move round, shift position; to depend. v.t. To shape on a lathe; to divert; to employ. s. Movement; revolution; shock; opportunity; item in programme; musical embellishment.
Sat'urn s. An ancient Roman and Greek agricultural deity; one of the planets.
Noc'turn s. One of the divisions of matins.
Return' v.i. To go or come back; to come again; to reply. v.t. To bring or send back; to repay, recompense; to report officially; to elect. s. Act of returning; that returned; formal report; profit on labour, etc.
Tac'iturn a. Reserved; habitually silent.
Overturn' v.t. To subvert, ruin, destroy; to capsize.
Az'urn a. Azure.
Bos'n s. A boatswain.
'un pron. Colloquial for "one."
Faun s. A rural deity, half man, half goat, of the Romans.
Lep'rechaun s. A dwarfish sprite of Irish folklore.
Bun s. A small sweetened cake.
Dun a. Of a dull-brown colour; gloomy, dark. s. A persistent creditor; importunate demand for payment; a debt-collector. v.t. To press persistently for payment of a debt; to pester.
Fun s. Sport, merriment, frolic.
Gun s. Any fire-arm, especially a cannon or sporting rifle.
Begun' v. (past part.) (*Begin*).
Sho'gun s. The former hereditary military ruler of Japan.
Hun s. One of a barbarian race that overran Europe in the fourth and fifth centuries; a bloodthirsty savage.
Shun v.t. To avoid, keep clear of.
Thick'un s. (*Slang*) A sovereign.
Ya'mun s. (*Yamen*).
Nun s. A female devotee living in a convent; a variety of pigeon.
Noun s. A word used as the name of anything; a substantive.
Pro'noun s. A word used in place of a noun.
Pun s. A play upon words, a quibble. v.i. To make a pun, use the same word in different senses.
Spun past and past part. (*Spin*).
Home'spun a. Plain; coarse; inelegant. s. Cloth spun at home.
Run v.i. To move swiftly on foot; to flee, spread, flow, ply, continue in operation, be current; to have a certain direction or purport. v.t. To cause to run, flow, etc.; to melt; to pursue; to smuggle; to carry on. s. Act of running; course; tenor; a trip; general demand on a bank; place for animals to run in; generality.
Overrun' v.t. To spread over in excess; to ravage; to subdue. v.i. To extend beyond due length, etc.; to overflow.
Outrun' v.t. To exceed in running; to surpass.
Sun s. Central body of the solar system; sunshine. v.t. To expose to the sun.
Whit'sun s. Whitsuntide. a. Pertaining to this.
Tun s. A large cask; 252 gallons.
Stun v.t. To make senseless or dizzy with a blow; to overpower sense of hearing; to astonish.
Awn s. The beard of barley, grass, etc.
Bawn s. An enclosure for cattle.
Dawn s. The break of day; first appearance of light, beginning. v.i. To grow light; to begin.
Fawn s. A young deer; light brown colour; mean flattery. v.i. To cringe; to bring forth a fawn. a. Light brown.
Lawn s. A smooth grass-plot; a fine linen.
Pawn s. Anything deposited as security; state of being held as a pledge; a piece of the lowest rank in chess. v.t. To deposit in pledge or as security for money borrowed; to pledge; to wager.
Spawn s. Ejected ova of fish, frogs, etc.; matter from which fungi are produced. v.t. and i. To deposit, as spawn; to bring forth; to issue.
Brawn s. Muscle, strength; the flesh of a boar; pig's head spiced and potted.
Drawn a. Unsheathed; distorted; eviscerated; depicted; applied to a contest in which neither side wins.
Withdrawn' past part. (*Withdraw*).
Prawn s. A crustacean like a large shrimp.
Yawn v.i. To gape involuntarily. s. A gape, gaping; an opening wide.
Strewn past part. (*Strew*).
Own a. Belonging or proper to; individual v.t. To possess; to acknowledge as one's own; to admit. v.i. To confess to.
Down s. Fine hair, soft feathers, pubescence of plants; tract of bare, hilly country; a dune, hill. adv. In a descending direction; on the ground; into smaller compass; paid on the spot. prep. Along in descent; toward the mouth of; away from the town or centre. a. Depressed, downcast. v.t. (*Slang*) To put down, overthrow.
Adown' adv. Down; in a descending direction.
Shake'down s. A makeshift bed.
Break'down s. Collapse; total failure; a negro dance.
Sun'down s. Sunset.
Godown' s. An E. Indian warehouse.
Low'-down a. Abject, mean. adv. Contemptibly.
Gown s. A long, loose garment.
Shown (shōn) past and past part. (*Show*).
Overblown' a. Past the prime bloom (of flowers).
Fly'-blown a. Tainted by maggots; corrupted.
Clown s. A bumpkin, the buffoon in a circus, etc. v.i. To act the clown.
High'flown a. Bombastic; proud.
Renown' s. Celebrity; reputation.
Known past part. (*Know*).
Foreknown' a. Known beforehand.

Brown a. Dusky, inclining to red or yellow. s. This colour; (*slang*) a copper coin. v.t. To make brown. v.i. become brown, get sunburnt.
Crown s. An ornament for the head; the emblem of royalty; top of anything; completion, perfection; sovereignty, royalty; a silver coin (5s.). v.t. To invest with a crown or with royal dignity; to form the top of; to complete, perfect.
Dis'crown v.t. To deprive of a crown.
Drown v.t. To suffocate in water; to inundate, overwhelm. v.i. To be suffocated in water, etc.
Frown v.i. To look stern or displeased. s. A wrinkling of the brow, expression of displeasure, a scowl.
Grown past part. (*Grow*).
Thrown (thrōn) past part. (*Throw*).
Disown' v.t. To disavow, refuse to acknowledge.
Town s. Collection of houses larger than a village; inhabitants of such; a metropolis.
Hep'tagyn s. A plant with seven pistils.
Hex'agyn s. A plant having six styles.
Mon'ogyn s. A plant having flowers with one pistil.
O s. A O-shaped mark. int. Used in entreaty, surprise, solemn address, etc.
Caca'o s. A tropical tree yielding cocoa and chocolate.
Curacao' s. A liqueur.
Bo int.
Lava'bo s. Ceremonial ablution of a priest's hands during Mass; towel or basin used at this.
Gaze'bo s. A projecting balcony or windowed turret in a garden commanding a view.
Bil'bo s. A rapier; a swashbuckler.
Am'bo s. (*Ambon*).
Cram'bo s. A game of rhymes.
Sam'bo s. Nickname for a negro.
Bim'bo s. A brandy punch.
Akim'bo adv. With hands on hips and elbows turned out.
Lim'bo s. The uttermost limit of hell; purgatory; prison.
Um'bo s. The boss of a shield; a knob.
Bum'bo s. Rum punch.
Gum'bo s. A hairy, herbaceous plant; its unripe fruit used as seasoning.
Mum'bo-jum'bo s. Any object of stupid veneration.
Nelum'bo s. A large water-lily, the sacred lotus of India and China.
Ho'bo s. (*Slang*) A U.S. tramp or vagrant.
Theor'bo s. An old two-headed, stringed musical instrument.
Bu'bo s. A swelling or abscess in a gland.
Maca'co s. A variety of lemur.
Guana'co s. An Andean llama.
Toura'co s. A brilliant African bird.
Gua'co s. A tropical American plant.
Tobac'co s. A narcotic American plant; its leaves prepared for smoking.
Siroc'co s. An oppressive wind blowing N. from the Sahara.
Moroc'co s. A fancy leather made from goatskin.
Stuc'co s. Fine plaster for walls, etc.; work made of this. v.t. To overlay with this.
Med'ico s. A medical student, doctor.
Fi'co s. A snap of the fingers.
Beccafi'co s. A small migratory bird.
Magnif'ico s. A grandee, especially of Venice.
Cal'ico s. Cotton cloth.
Bar'rico s. A small cask.
Por'tico s. A covered colonnade; a porch.
Mis'tico s. A mistic.
Catafal'co s. (*Catafalque*).
Ban'co s. The Bench; a term applied to money of account.
Calaman'co s. A Flemish woollen stuff.
Zin'co s. A zincograph.
Bron'co s. An untamed horse.
Un'co' a. (*Scot.*) Remarkable, strange. adv. Very.
Jun'co s. A N. American finch.
Bo'co s. (*Slang*) The nose.
Co'co s. (*Cocoa*).
Roco'co s. A debased kind of ornamentation. a. In this style; grotesque, tasteless.
Lo'co s. A locomotive.
Po'co adv. Little (*mus. direction*).
To'co s. (*Slang*) Punishment.
Tur'co s. An Algerian in the French army.
Fias'co s. A failure, breakdown; an ignominious sequel.
Tedes'co a. German (of painting).
Fres'co s. Method of painting on freshly laid stucco walls. v.t. To decorate a wall thus.
Alfres'co adv. In the open air.
Moris'co s. A moor, especially of Spain; the Moorish language; a morris dance. a. Moorish.
Do (doo) v.t. or aux. To practise, perform, achieve, bring about, finish, cook, etc. v.t. To act; to fare in health; to succeed; to suffice, avail. s. (*Slang*) A swindle; a big affair.
Do s. The first syllable in the major diatonic scale (tonic sol-fa).
Gamba'do s. A gambade; a horseman's legging.
Barrica'do s. A barricade.
Avoca'do s. The alligator pear. a. W. Indian fruit.
Da'do s. Square base of a column; moulding round the lower part of a wall, etc.
Mika'do s. The Emperor of Japan.
Amon'tillado s. A kind of sherry.
Bastina'do s. Punishment by beating the soles of the feet. v.t. To beat thus.
Carbona'do s. Flesh scored across and grilled. v.t. To broil thus on coals.
Torna'do s. A violent tempest, a hurricane.
Strappa'do s. An old military punishment.
Spa'do s. A castrated person or animal.
Despera'do s. A desperate or reckless ruffian.
Sangra'do s. A quack doctor.
Dora'do s. A brilliantly coloured fish.
El Dora'do s. An imaginary land of gold; inexhaustible gold-mine or riches.
Passa'do s. A push or thrust.
Pinta'do s. A species of petrel; a guinea-fowl.
Brava'do s. Defiant behaviour.
Muscova'do s. Raw or unrefined sugar.
Tole'do s. A Spanish sword.
Torpe'do s. The electric ray, the cramp-fish; an explosive engine propelled under water. v.t. To attack, destroy, etc., with this.
Cre'do s. A creed, especially the Apostles' or Nicene.
Tere'do s. A worm-like marine boring mollusc.
Ure'do s. A rust-fungus; nettle-rash.
Der'ring-do s. Desperate courage; valour.
Sol'do s. Small Italian coin (=½d.).

Ritordan'do adv. Slower (*mus. direction*).
Calan'do a., adv. Gradually getting slower and softer (of music).
Tremolan'do adv. Tremulously (*mus. direction*).
Comman'do s. A body of civilians called up for military service; an expedition by such.
Rallentan'do adv. Gradually slower (*mus. direction*).
Scherzan'do adv. Playfully (*mus. direction*).
Sforzan'do adv. With sudden emphasis (*mus. direction*).
Crescen'do adv. With an increasing volume of sound (of music). s. A gradual increase of sound.
Inquiren'do s. Legal authority for an inquiry on behalf of the Crown.
Diminuen'do adv. Noting a gradual lowering of the voice.
Innuen'do s. An indirect allusion, insinuation.
Ron'do s. A musical composition in which a theme is repeated and varied.
Ton'do s. A decorative majolica plate with broad flat rim.
Undo' (-doo') v.t. To reverse what has been done, to annul; to take to pieces.
Basso-profun'do s. The lowest male voice.
Do'do s. A large extinct wingless bird of Mauritius.
Quasimo'do s. The first Sunday after Easter.
To-do' (-doo') s. A commotion.
Well-to-do' a. Well off, in easy circumstances.
Tar'do a. and adv. Slow, slowly (*mus. direction*).
Overdo' v.t. and i. To do or perform too much; to fatigue; to cook too long.
Fordo' v.t. To destroy, undo; to exhaust.
Misdo' v.t. To do wrongly. v.i. To commit a crime.
Outdo' v.t. To excel, surpass.
Scu'do s. Obsolete Italian silver coin (about 4s.).
Testu'do s. A shield-screen used by ancient Roman troops.
Cicisbe'o s. A gallant attendant upon a married woman.
Le'o s. The fifth sign of the Zodiac.
Cam'eo s. A stone with coloured layers cut in relief.
Ster'eo s. A stereotyped plate.
Buff'o a. Burlesque, comic.
Go v.i. To proceed, depart, move, walk, travel; to be about to do; to be sold; to fare, become, avail. s. The fashion, mode, craze.
Ago' a., adv. Gone by, past, since.
Lumba'go s. A rheumatic affection in the region of the loins.
Plumba'go s. Blacklead, graphite, a form of carbon.
Da'go s. A low-class southern European immigrant in the U.S.A.
Pichicia'go s. A small armadillo of S. America.
Ka'go s. A Japanese litter or palanquin.
Gala'go s. A long-tailed African lemur.
Archipel'ago s. A sea abounding in small islands.
Ima'go s. The fully developed insect.
Vira'go s. A turbulent woman, a loud-voiced shrew.
Farra'go s. A confused medley; a hotchpotch.
Sa'go s. A granulated starch used for puddings.
Eg'o s. A man's self; personality; individual consciousness.
Non-eg'o s. The external world or object as opposed to the ego.
Forego' v.t. To quit possession of, resign, lose.
Ru'bigo s. A kind of rust on plants.
In'digo s. A blue vegetable dye; the plant from which this is obtained.
Serpi'go s. A skin-disease.
Porri'go s. A disease of the scalp.
Intertri'go s. Inflammation of the skin caused by friction of parts.
Pruri'go s. A skin disease; intolerable itching.
Impeti'go s. A skin disease marked by small pustules.
Lenti'go s. A freckle, or eruption of these.
Ver'tigo s. Giddiness, dizziness.
Hidal'go s. A Spanish nobleman.
Fandan'go s. A lively dance for two.
Man'go s. An E. Indian tree and its fruit.
Tan'go s. A complicated dance for couples.
Contan'go s. Commission paid to a seller of stock for deferring time of payment.
Bing'o s. (*Slang*) Brandy.
Ding'o s. The Australian wild dog.
Jin'go int. A mild oath. s. A lout-mouthed patriot. a. Bellicosely patriotic.
Lin'go s. (*Slang*) A language, dialect; speech.
Flamin'go s. A long-necked, long-legged bird with bright red plumage.
Grin'go s. Mexican's slang name for an Englishman or American.
Sting'o s. Old beer; strong liquor.
Con'go s. (*Congou*).
Pon'go s. A large African anthropoid ape.
Mung'o s. A superior kind of shoddy.
Eryng'o s. A plant from which a sweetmeat was formerly prepared.
Embar'go s. Prohibition upon shipping not to leave a port; a hindrance. v.t. To lay an embargo on; to hinder.
Car'go s. Freight carried by a ship.
Supercar'go s. Officer on merchant ship superintending commercial transactions.
Lar'go adv. Slowly, with dignity (*mus. direction*).
Sar'go s. A sea-bream.
Botar'go s. A fish relish.
Er'go adv. Therefore; consequently.
Undergo' v.i. To bear, suffer, experience.
Vir'go s. A constellation; the sixth sign of the Zodiac.
Forgo' v.t. To renounce, give up, go without.
Outgo' v.t. To go beyond or faster than; to surpass; to overreach.
Out'go s. Outlay; expenditure.
Ho int. Exclamation to call attention, etc.
Ech'o s. The reverberation or reflection of a sound. v.i. To resound, be sounded back. v.t. To return sound; to repeat approvingly; to imitate closely.
Re-ech'o v.t. To echo back. v.i. To be reverberated; to resound.
Ranch'o s. A ranch.
Pon'cho s. A cloak or cape with a central slit for the head.
Gau'cho s. A half-bred Spanish and Indian inhabitant of the S. American pampas.
Heigh-ho' int. Expressing languor, disappointment, etc.
Oho' int. Expressing surprise, exultation, etc.
Soho' int. A huntsman's hallo.
Who (hoo) pron., interrog.
Tally-ho' s. and int. A huntsman's cry.
Capri'ccio s. A lively musical composition.
Nun'cio s. A papal ambassador to a foreign power.

Internun'cio s. Papal representative at republics and small courts; a messenger.
Braggado'cio s. A boaster, braggart.
Ra'dio v.t. and i. To transmit or signal by wireless telegraphy.
Presid'io s. A fortified post in Spanish S. America.
Stu'dio s. The working-room of an artist.
A'gio s. A premium paid for exchange from one currency into another.
Ada'gio adv. A musical direction indicating slow time. s. A slow movement.
Solfeg'gio (-fedg'ō) s. Sol-fa; a singing exercise in solmization.
Arpeg'gio s. Production of the tones of a chord in rapid succession.
Gor'gio s. Gipsy name for a non-gipsy.
Borach'io s. A drunkard.
Pista'chio s. A small tree of W. Asia; its nut; the flavour of this.
Pasticc'io (-tic'ō) s. A musical, literary, or artistic medley; a cento.
Cli'o s. The Muse of epic poetry and history.
Sera'glio (-ra'lyo) s. A harem.
Inta'glio s. An engraved gem.
Imbro'glio s. A complicated plot; a misunderstanding.
Punctil'io s. A nice point of exactness in conduct, etc.
Vespertil'io s. The genus comprising the bats.
O'lio s. A dish of stewed meat; a medley.
Fo'lio s. A sheet of paper once folded; a book made of such sheets; a leaf of paper; the number on a page.
Portfo'lio s. Case for loose papers, etc.; office and functions of a minister of state.
Curcu'lio s. The corn-weevil.
Dai'mio s. A feudal lord of old Japan.
Ba'gnio s. A bath-house; a brothel.
Scor'pio s. The eighth sign of the Zodiac, and a zodiacal constellation.
Lothar'io s. A libertine.
Scenar'io s. The outline of a play, etc.
Impresar'io s. Manager of an opera, etc.
Cheerio' int. Buck up! Good-bye!
Cimbor'io s. Dome over the intersection of nave and transepts.
Orator'io s. A musical composition of semi-dramatic and sacred character for voices and instruments.
Tri'o (trē'-) s. Composition for three voices or instruments; performers of such; any set of three.
Cur'io s. A curiosity, piece of bric-a-brac.
Pa'tio s. The open, inner court of a Spanish house.
Ra'tio s. Fixed relation; rate; quota.
Ban'jo s. A stringed musical instrument played by plucking with the fingers.
Shak'o s. A peaked military head-dress.
Geck'o s. A genus of small lizards.
Jock'o s. A chimpanzee.
Ging'ko s. A Japanese tree with fan-shaped leaves.
To'ko s. (*Slang*) Punishment.
Lo int. See! behold!
Cym'balo s. The dulcimer.
Buff'alo s. A species of large wild ox.
Ha'lo s. A luminous circle round the sun or moon, head of a saint, etc.; ideal glory. v.t. and i. To form into or surround with a halo.
Bum'malo s. A small Asiatic fish.
Pueb'lo s. A settlement in Spanish America.
Pom'elo s. The grape-fruit, shaddock.
Si'lo s. Air-tight trench or chamber for preserving green fodder.
Hallo' int. Exclamation of surprise, etc.; call to dogs. v.t. and i. To make this call; to call loudly, to cheer.
'cel'lo s. A violoncello.
Violoncel'lo (-chel'-) s. A large bass violin.
Niel'lo s. Ornamentation on metal by filling incisions with a black alloy; the alloy used.
Punchinel'lo s. A buffoon.
Ritornel'lo s. A musical prelude or interlude.
Stornel'lo s. An improvised folk-song.
Prunel'lo s. A superior kind of prune.
Cobra-de-capel'lo s. A cobra.
Saltarel'lo s. An old southern skipping dance.
Morel'lo s. An acid variety of cherry.
Martel'lo s. A circular, isolated coastal-defence tower.
Duel'lo s. A duel; practice of or code of laws for duelling.
Peccadil'lo s. A slight offence; a petty fault.
Armadil'lo s. A S. American quadruped with a hard, bony shell.
Negril'lo s. A negro dwarf; a negrito.
Diab'olo s. A game played with a double-coned top and a string on two sticks.
Pic'colo s. A small flute.
Trem'olo s. A tremulous effect in music.
Po'lo s. A ball-game resembling hockey, played on ponies.
So'lo s. An air or song by a single voice or instrument; a card-game, a declaration in this.
O'volo s. A convex architectural moulding.
Dy'namo s. Machine for converting mechanical into electrical energy.
Par'amo s. A treeless plain of S. America.
Twelve'mo s. Duodecimo.
Octodec'imo a. Formed of sheets folded to eighteen leaves. s. A book composed of such.
Sextodec'imo s. Booked formed of sheets folded into sixteen leaves.
Duodec'imo a. Formed of sheets folded in twelve leaves. s. A book made up of such sheets; the size of this.
Es'kimo s. An Indian of tribes inhabiting Arctic America and Greenland.
Pri'mo s. First part in a duet; a superior official of the Ancient Order of Buffaloes.
Larghiss'imo adv. Very slowly (*mus. direction*).
Generaliss'imo s. The commander-in-chief of an army drawn from allies.
Pianis'simo a. and adv. Very soft (*mus. direction*).
Altis'simo adv. In the second octave above the treble stave.
Fortis'simo adv. Very loud (*mus. direction*).
Prestis'simo adv. Very quickly (*mus. direction*).
Bravis'simo int. Very good indeed!
Ul'timo adv. Last month.
Prox'imo adv. In the month following this.
Ec'ce-ho'mo s. A picture representing Christ crowned with thorns.
Chro'mo s. A chromolithograph.
Duo'mo s. An Italian cathedral.
No adv. Expressing denial or refusal; not in any degree. a. Not any; none; not any one. s. A negative vote.
Hurrica'no s. A hurricane.
Volca'no s. A burning mountain emitting gases, lava, etc.
Bean'o s. (*Slang*) A spree, jollification.
Pia'no a. and adv. Soft (*mus. direction*).

Pian'o s. A pianoforte.
Lla'no s. A treeless plain in S. America.
Pam'pano s. A food-fish of the E. Atlantic.
Tim'pano s. A kettle-drum.
Pom'pano s. An edible fish of the N. Altantic.
Sopra'no s. The highest female voice; a singer with this.
Mez'zo-sopra'no s. Female voice between contralto and soprano; one having such voice.
Gita'no s. A gipsy.
Capita'no s. An Italian captain.
Gua'no s. Droppings of sea-fowl valuable as manure. v.t. To fertilize with this.
Le'no s. A thin cotton fabric.
Albi'no s. A person or animal with abnormally white skin and hair and pink eyes.
Bambi'no s. A baby; an image of the infant Christ in swaddling bands.
Ladin'o s. The old Castilian language; a half breed descendant of C. American Indians and whites.
Gradi'no s. A gradine.
Contadi'no s. An Italian peasant.
Baldachi'no s. (*Baldachin*).
Maraschi'no s. A liqueur distilled from black cherries.
Rhi'no s. (*Slang*) Money; a rhinoceros.
Ki'no s. An astringent gum obtained from various tropical trees used in dyeing and tanning.
Cippoli'no s. (*Cipolin*).
Dom'ino s. A masquerade dress, a half-mask; person wearing one of these; a piece in the game of dominoes.
Piani'no s. A small piano.
Meri'no s. A Spanish variety of long-haired sheep; cloth made of its wool.
Peperi'no (-rē'nō) s. A brown, porous, volcanic tufa.
Tenori'no (-rē'no) s. A falsetto tenor singer or voice.
Vetturi'no (-rē'-) s. Proprietor or driver of a vettura.
Casi'no s. A place of public entertainment, dancing, gambling, etc.
Cassi'no s. A four-handed card-game.
Andanti'no adv. Rather quicker than andante (*mus.*).
Festi'no s. A mnemonic word in logic.
Duetti'no s. A short duet.
Kakemo'no s. A Japanese picture on rollers.
Kimo'no s. A long, loose outer garment.
Infer'no s. Hell; place resembling this.
Contor'no s. Contour, outline.
Ju'no s. The principal Roman goddess, wife of Jupiter; a beautiful and stately woman.
Boo s. An expression of contempt or aversion. v.t. To groan at, to hoot.
Baboo' s. A native Hindu clerk; a semi-educated and Europeanized Bengali.
Bugaboo' s. A bogy.
Peekaboo' s. Bo-peep, a child's game; a transparent blouse.
Taboo' s. A traditional or religious prohibition. a. Interdicted. v.t. To forbid approach to, use or mention of, etc.
Bamboo' s. A large tropical reed.
Coo s. The note of the dove. v.i. To make this sound; to act in a loving manner.
Koo'doo s. A S. African antelope.
Voodoo' s. Voodooism; a votary of this. a. Pertaining to this. v.t. To put a spell on by this.
Goo'-goo a. (*Slang*) Amatory.
Burgoo' s. A sailors' name for porridge.
Yahoo' s. A degraded, bestial person.
Boo-hoo' v.i. To weep noisily; to hoot. s. The sound of this.
Shoo int. Begone! away! v.t. To drive away thus.
Tu-whoo' s. The cry of an owl.
Cuck'oo s. A migratory bird; its note; a silly fellow.
Loo s. A card-game played with a pool. v.t. To cause to pay into the pool.
Hullabaloo' s. A noisy uproar.
Ig'loo s. An Eskimo hut.
Moo s. The low of a cow. v.i. To make this sound.
Napoo' int. (*Slang*) No good! finished! nothing doing!
Shampoo' v.t. To rub and massage the body; to lather; to wash the head. s. Act of shampooing.
Kangaroo' s. A pouched ruminating marsupial of Australia.
Karoo' s. An elevated desert in S. Africa.
Wallaroo' s. A species of kangaroo.
Gillaroo' s. An Irish variety of trout.
Wanderoo' (wŏn'-) s. A langur-monkey; a macaque.
Too adv. As well; over; more than enough.
Cockatoo' s. A large crested parrot.
Tattoo' s. Drum-call to soldiers; a pattern on the skin produced by pricking in pigments. v.i. To beat a tattoo. v.t. To mark the skin as mentioned.
Woo v.t. To court, make love to.
Zoo s. A (or *the*) Zoological Gardens.
Ka'kapo s. The New Zealand ground-parrot.
Tem'po s. Rate of movement (*in music*).
Com'po s. Trade term for various compositions.
Ship'po s. Japanese cloisonné ware.
Trop'po adv. Too much (*in music*).
Far'o s. A gambling card-game.
Zing'aro s. A gipsy.
Gua'charo s. The S. American goatsucker.
Pifferar'o s. A bagpipe-player.
Tar'o s. A tropical edible plant of the arum family.
Gab'bro s. A rock consisting of feldspar and magnesian minerals.
Mu'cro s. A sharp process or organ.
Hy'dro s. A hydropathic hotel.
Piff'ero s. A pipe, bagpipe.
Her'o s. A valiant man; a principal character.
Rancher'o s. One employed on a ranch.
Estancier'o s. The proprietor of an estancia.
Caballer'o s. A Spanish dance; a stately Spanish grandee.
Boler'o s. A Spanish dance; a short jacket for women.
Primer'o s. An absolete card-game.
Llaner'o s. A dweller on a llano.
Campaner'o s. The Brazilian bell-bird.
Pamper'o s. A cold south-west wind of S. America.
Sombrer'o s. A soft, wide-brimmed hat.
Torer'o s. A bull-fighter on foot.
Monter'o s. A Spanish huntsman's cap.
Ter'u-ter'o s. The lapwing of Cayenne.
Vaquer'o s. A Mexican herdsman.
Zer'o s. The cipher, O, nil; point on a scale dividing positive and negative quantities.

Fro adv. From, backward.
Alle'gro adv. Briskly (*mus.*). **s.** A movement in this style.
Ne'gro s. One of the black, woolly-haired African race, a. Pertaining to this race; dark-skinned.
Genro' s. The confidential advisers of the Emperor of Japan.
Pro s. (*Slang*) A professional player, actor, etc.
Pro prefix, meaning for.
Sbir'ro s. An Italian policeman.
Elec'tro s. Electro-plate; an electrotype.
Maes'tro s. A great performer or teacher of music.
Chiaroscur'o s. Treatment of light and shade in painting, etc.; use of contrast in literary and other work.
Pyr'o s. Pyrogallic acid.
Tyro' s. A beginner, novice.
So adv., conj., and int.
Provi'so s. A conditional stipulation.
Al'so conj. As well, in addition.
Capriccio'so adv. Freely, fantastically (of music).
Serio'so adv. Solemnly (*mus. direction*).
Furio'so adv. With vehemence (*mus. direction*).
Pompo'so adv. In a dignified manner (*mus. direction*).
Vigoro'so adv. Energetically (*mus. direction*).
Timoro'so s. With hesitation (*mus. direction*).
Strepito'so adv. In an impetuous style (*mus. direction*).
Spirito'so adv. In a spirited manner (*mus. direction*).
Maesto'so adv. In a dignified manner (*mus. direction*).
Affetuo'so adv. Feelingly (of music).
Virtuo'so s. One devoted to or skilled in the fine arts.
Ver'so s. Left-hand page; the reverse of a coin, etc.
Rever'so s. The left-hand page of an open book.
Tor'so s. Trunk of a statue.
Bas'so s. Bass; a bass singer.
Sargas'so s. Floating weed of the N. Atlantic.
Las'so s. A leather rope with a running noose. v.t. To catch with this.
Ges'so s. Gypsum used for decorative work; stucco.
Hu'so s. The beluga or great sturgeon.
To (too) prep. and adv.
Stacca'to adv. With each note sharply distinct (*mus. direction*).
Pizzica'to a. Played by plucking the strings (of a violin, etc.).
Lega'to adv. In a smooth, even manner (*mus. direction*).
Obbliga'to s. An inseparable instrumental accompaniment to voices, etc.
Toma'to s. A tropical plant and its fruit.
Vibra'to (vēbrah'-) s. A pulsating effect in music.
Modera'to adv. In moderate time (*mus. direction*).
Litera'to s. A literary man.
Inamora'to s. A lover (*man*).
Castra'to s. An emasculated male.
Pota'to s. A plant of many species; its esculent tuber.
Sforza'to adv. With sudden emphasis (*mus. direction*).
Rec'to s. The right-hand page of an open book.
Sanbene'to s. Garment worn by condemned heretics of the Spanish Inquisition.
Magne'to s. Contrivance for igniting the explodent in the cylinder of an internal-combustion engine.
Hereto' adv. To this.
Thereto' (-too') adv.
Whereto (-too') adv.
Ve'to s. An authoritative prohibition; power or right of forbidding. **v.t.** To prohibit.
Sub'ito adv. Rapidly (*mus. direction*).
Graffi'to s. A scratched inscription, especially at Pompeii.
Peshi'to (-shē'tō) s. The fifth-century Syriac version of the Bible.
Incog'nito a. and adv. Private; under an assumed name. **s.** One unknown or under an assumed name.
Boni'to s. The striped tunny and similar fish.
Horni'to s. A small smoking mound on a volcano.
Negri'to s. One of a race of dwarfish negroes of Africa and Oceania.
Coqui'to s. A S. American nut-bearing palm.
Mosqui'to (-kē'to) s. A blood-sucking insect.
Al'to s. The highest male voice; a singer with this.
Contral'to s. The lowest female voice; singer or voice taking this part; the part taken.
Mol'to adv. Much, very (*mus. direction*).
Can'to s. A division of a long poem.
Esperan'to s. An artificial language intended for a means of communication between all peoples.
Coran'to s. An old dance.
Cen'to s. A composition formed of passages from various sources.
Cinquecen'to s. The sixteenth-century in Italy, especially in reference to its literary and artistic activity.
Quattrocen'to s. The fifteenth century, especially with reference to Italian art.
Len'to adv. Slowly (*mus. direction*).
Pronuncia-men'to s. A proclamation, manifesto.
Portamen'to s. A gliding passage from one note to another.
Memen'to s. A souvenir, memorial.
Rifacimen'to s. A remodelling, especially of a literary work.
Pimen'to s. A W. Indian tree; its aromatic berry, used as a spice; allspice.
In'to prep. In and to; noting entrance or direction from without.
Hereinto' adv. Into this.
Whereinto' adv.
Shin'to s. The non-Buddhist religious system of Japan.
Un'to (-too) prep. To.
Hereunto' adv. Unto this or this time.
Jun'to s. A faction, cabal.
Pho'to s. A photograph.
Telepho'to s. Lens for use in telephotography.
Ex-vo'to s. A thank-offering placed in a church.
Espar'to s. A coarse grass used for making mats, paper, etc.
Quar'to s. A book of quarter-sheet size. a. Of this form or size.
Concer'to s. A musical composition for a solo instrument with orchestral accompaniment.
Hitherto' adv. Up to this place, time, limit.
Impas'to s. A thick layer of colour; application of this.
Manifes'to s. A public declaration.
Pres'to adv. Quickly; in haste. **s.** A musical passage in quick time.
Gus'to s. Zest, relish, enjoyment.
Mulat'to s. Offspring of a white and a negro.
Annat'to s. An orange-red dyestuff.

Concet'to s. Affected wit.
Zuchet'to (-ket'-) s. The skull-cap of Roman Catholic priests.
Ghet'to s. The Jews' quarter of a town.
Larghet'to adv. Somewhat slowly (*mus. direction*).
Stilet'to s. A small dagger; a pointed instrument.
Palmet'to s. A species of dwarf palm.
Lazaret'to s. A hospital for contagious diseases.
Libret'to s. Book of words of an opera, etc.
Allegret'to adv. Somewhat briskly (*mus.*).
Falset'to s. An artificial voice; tones above the natural compass.
Terzet'to s. A short composition for three performers.
Dit'to s. The aforesaid, the same thing. adv. As before; also.
Ot'to s. Altar.
Ridot'to s. An entertainment; a masked ball.
Fagot'to s. The bassoon.
Lot'to s. A game of chance played on a 90-square board.
Mot'to s. Short phrase or single word expressing a maxim, rule of conduct, etc.
Pot'to s. A small tailless W. African lemur.
Grot'to s. A small ornamental cavern.
Risot'to s. An Italian dish of rice, onion, chicken, etc.
Plu'to s. The ancient Greek god of the infernal regions.
Tenu'to adv. Sustained (*mus. direction*).
Sostenu'to adv. In a sustained, prolonged manner (*mus. direction*).
Scru'to s. A trap-door in a stage.
Sex'to s. A book formed of sheets folded into six leaves.
Du'o s. A duet.
Trid'uo s. A three days' service (Roman Catholic Church).
Bra'vo s. A desperado, ruffian.
Bravo' int. Well done!
Octa'vo s. A book composed of sheets folded to eight leaves; the size of such book or paper. a. Of this size.
Relie'vo (-ā'vō) s. Raised or embossed work.
Al'to-relie'vo s. High relief.
Mez'zo-relie'vo s. Half-relief (*in sculpture*).
Sal'vo s. A volley; a burst of applause.
De no'vo adv. All over again; from the beginning.
Zemst'vo s. An elected local administrative body in Russia.
Wo int. Whoa! s. Woe.
Two a. and s. One more than one; the sum of this (2, ii).
Em'bryo s. The first rudiments of an unborn animal, etc.; first state of anything. a. Pertaining to the earliest stages.
Mesti'zo s. A half-breed of Spaniard with Creole or American Indian.
Coro'zo s. A S. American ivory-nut tree.
Scherz'o s. A lively musical piece or movement.
Mez'zo a. Middle, mean (*in music*). s. A mezzo-soprano voice or singer.
Intermez'zo s. A short, light musical piece; an interlude.
Cap s. A head-dress; a cover, top piece. v.t. To put a cap on, to complete, to excel; to salute by touching the cap.
Mad'cap a. Hare-brained, eccentric. s. An impulsive, eccentric person.
Red'cap s. The goldfinch.
White'cap s. A small bird of the warbler family.
Blue'cap s. The blue titmouse.
Han'dicap s. A race, etc., in which allowance is made for inferiors. v.t. To equalize by handicap.
Black'cap s. A British warbler.
Fools'cap s. A jester's cap with bells; a size of paper (17 × 14 in.).
Night'cap s. A cap worn in bed; a final drink.
Heap s. A pile; an accumulation; a crowd. v.t. To raise in a pile, to amass.
Cheap a. Of small cost or value.
Leap v.i. To jump, bound, spring. v.t. To cross by leaping. s. A jump, etc.; space crossed by jumping a sudden transition.
Neap a. Low or lowest (of tides).
Reap v.t. To harvest; to clear of a crop; to gather, gain. v.i. To perform the act of reaping; to receive the reward of labour, etc.
Gap s. An opening, breach, hiatus; a vacuity.
Stop'gap s. A temporary substitute.
Hap s. Chance, that which happens. v.i. To befall.
Chap s. A crack in the flesh; the jaw: a youth. v.t. and i. To split, crack come open in long slits.
Mishap' s. Accident, calamity, mischance.
Mayhap' adv. Perhaps.
Jap a. and s. (*Slang*) Japanese.
Lap s. The part of the clothes over the knees when sitting; part of a thing that covers another; a single round in races; a lick; sound of rippling water. v.t. To wrap, enfold, to lick up, wash gently against. v.i. To be turned over; to ripple.
Jal'ap s. The dried roots of a Mexican plant used as a cathartic.
Clap v.t. To strike noisily; to applaud by striking the hands together. v.i. To come together suddenly and noisily; to strike the hands together in applause. s. A loud or sharp noise made by collision; applause.
Flap s. Anything broad that hangs loose; a light stroke with such, a slap. v.t. To beat with a flap, to move thus. v.i. To ply the wings with noise.
Overlap' v.t. and i. To extend so as to lie or rest upon.
Bur'lap s. A coarse kind of canvas.
Slap v.t. To strike with the open hand or something broad. s. A blow given thus. adv. Instantly; quickly.
Dew'lap s. The fleshy folds hanging from the throats of oxen.
Map s. A flat delineation of part of the earth's surface. v.t. To make a map of, plan.
Nap s. Woolly substance on surface of some cloth, plants, etc.; Napoleon, a card-game; a short sleep. v.i. To doze; to be unwary.
Han'ap s. A goblet.
Kid'nap v.t. To steal or abduct a human being.
Knap s. A knob, protuberance; rising ground. v.t. To snap, strike with a snapping sound, chip off.
Snap v.t. To break short; to bite, seize suddenly. v.i. To bite at; to break without bending. s. A quick bite, sudden breaking, sharp noise; a spring catch; a snapshot; a card-game; a biscuit.

Snip'snap s. Lively dialogue. a. Quick, brisk.
Soap s. An alkaline substance used in washing. v.t. To wash with this.
Pap s. A teat, nipple; soft food for infants.
Gen'ipap s. A S. American fruit with a vinous taste.
Rap s. A quick, smart blow; any worthless thing. v.i. To knock, strike a quick, sharp blow. v.t. To strike with a quick blow.
Scrap s. A small bit, fragment; a cutting; (*slang*) a fight, scuffle. v.t. To make scrap of, discard as worn-out. v.i. (*slang*) To fight, spar.
Frap v.t. To undergird, to bind with rope.
Thrap v.t. To fasten round, bind.
Trap s. A snare, ambush; contrivance in drains for preventing return of effluvia; a two-wheeled vehicle; a door in a floor or roof; an igneous rock; (*slang*) a policeman. v.t. and i. To catch in or furnish with a trap; to be caught or impeded; to caparison.
Sat'rap s. A provincial governor in ancient Persia.
Entrap' v.t. To ensnare, to catch as in a trap.
Clap'trap s. Showy speeches, humbug.
Strap s. A long, narrow slip of leather, metal, etc., for fastening, etc. v.t. To fasten or beat with this.
Wrap v.t. To roll or fold together; to envelope, enfold. s. A shawl, rug, muffler.
Enwrap' v.t To wrap, enfold; to engross; to implicate.
Sap s. The juice of plants; a trench; (*slang*) hard study. v.t. To mine, undermine. v.i. To proceed by mining or secret work; (*slang*) to be studious.
Tap v.t. and i. To touch lightly, knock gently; to broach. s. A gentle touch; a pipe or hole for drawing liquor, a plug; a bar-room.
Swap (swop) v.t. To exchange. s. An exchange.
Yap v.i. To yelp, bark. s. Such a cry.
Deep a. Extending far down or far in; low in situation; hidden; solemn; grave in sound; designing; mysterious; heart-felt. s. The sea, an abyss.
Cheep s. The cry of a young bird. v.i. To make this sound.
Sheep s. (sing. and pl.) A ruminant, hollow-horned, gregarious animal, wild and domesticated, valued for its flesh and wool; a timorous or subservient person.
Keep v.t. To hold, guard, detain; to perform, observe, be true to; to support. v.i. To last, remain unimpaired. s. Care, guard; sustenance; a strong tower.
Up'keep s. Maintenance.
Sleep v.i. To slumber, to be dormant or inactive. s. A natural, temporary suspension of volition; slumber, repose, dormant state.
Asleep' adv.; a. In a state of sleep, not awake.
Oversleep' v.i. To sleep too long.
Peep v.i. To chirp, as a chick; to begin to appear; to look slily through or at. s. A chirp; first appearance or outlook; a sly look.
Bo-peep' s. A childish game.
Creep v.i. To crawl, move, or grow along the ground; to move stealthily; to steal in; to fawn, cling to, to shiver.
Steep a. Very sloping, precipitous. s. A cliff, precipice; process of or liquid for steeping. v.t. To soak or saturate in liquid.
Weep v.i. To shed tears, lament. v.t. To shed tears over; to exhaust with weeping.
Sweep v.i. To move along swiftly and continuously or with pomp. v.t. To clean with a broom; to carry along with a brushing stroke; to pass rapidly over with the eye. s. Reach of a stroke, etc.; a curve; a sweepstake; a chimney-sweeper.
Skep s. A wickerwork basket; a straw beehive.
Sal'ep s. A fattening meal made from roots of certain orchids.
Ju'lep s. A sweet drink.
Stoep (stoop) s. A veranda (S. Africa).
Rep s. A fabric with a finely corded surface.
Dem'i-rep s. A woman of doubtful chastity.
Step s. One move of foot, a pace; gait; a rise; something as means of ascent; gradation. v.i. To walk. v.t. To set the foot of, as of a mast.
In'step s. The arched, middle portion of the human foot.
Overstep' v.t. To step over or beyond; to exceed.
Misstep' s. A wrong or false step.
Foot'step s. Act of treading; tread; sound of this.
Dip v.t. To immerse, plunge in a liquid. v.i. To plunge into a liquid and emerge; to look cursorily, choose by chance; to incline. s. The inclination of the magnetic needle; a hasty bath or swim; a cheap candle; a liquid for washing sheep, a curtsy.
Hip s. The thigh-joint, haunch; the fruit of the briar; melancholia.
Chip s. A small thin slice; a fragment cut or broken off; a strip of fibre for making hats. v.t. To cut or break chips off. v.i. To break or fly into chips.
Ship s. Any large sea-going vessel. v.t. and i. To take, put, or go aboard; to transport in a ship; to hire or engage for service in a ship.
-ship suff. Denoting state, quality, office, tenure of office, skill, etc.
Head'ship s. Office of a principal; chief place; authority.
Mid'ship s. The middle part of a boat. a. Situated here.
Friend'ship s. State of being friends; intimacy and attachment arising from mutual esteem; an act of good-will.
God'ship s. Deity; rank of a god.
Hard'ship s. Severe labour or want; anything hard to bear.
Guard'ship s. A vessel for harbour defence.
Ward'ship s. Guardianship; tutelage.
Lord'ship s. State of being a lord; a lord's territory, jurisdiction, title, or dignity; sovereignty.
Appren'ticeship s. (*Apprentice*).
Just'iceship s. Office of a justice.

Acquain'tanceship s. (*Acquaintance*).
Com'radeship s. (*Comrade*).
Trustee'ship s. Office or functions of a trustee.
Judge'ship s. Office of a judge.
Bea'dleship s. (*Beadle*).
Disci'pleship s. State of being a disciple.
Apos'tleship s. (*Apostle*).
Um'pireship s. Office or authority of an umpire.
Lec'tureship s. Office, etc., of lecturer.
Ad'vocateship s. (*Advocate*).
Can'didateship s. (*Candidate*).
Laur'eateship s. The office of Poet Laureate.
Leg'ateship s. Office, etc., of a legate.
King'ship s. Office or dignity of a king.
Clerk'ship s. (*Clerk*).
Car'dinalship s. (*Cardinal*).
Gen'eralship s. Office, skill, or conduct of a general; tactful diplomacy or organization.
Ad'miralship s. (*Admiral*).
Con'sulship s. Office or term of office of a consul.
Procon'sulship s. Proconsulate.
Dean'ship s. Office or personality of a dean.
Guard'ianship s. Office of guardian; care, protection.
Librar'ianship s. Office or post of a librarian.
Clan'ship s. System of state of clans.
Sea'manship s. The skill of a seaman; art of navigation.
Horse'manship s. Skill in riding and managing horses.
Coach'manship s. (*Coachman*).
Church'manship s. (*Churchman*).
Work'manship s. Skill, art, style, etc., of a good workman; handicraft.
Pen'manship s. Art or style of writing.
Al'dermanship s. (*Alderman*).
Chair'manship s. (*Chairman*).
States'manship s. Qualifications or employments of a statesman.
Marks'manship s. The skill of a marksman.
Oars'manship s. The art of rowing.
Sports'manship s. Practices of sportsmen; skill in field sports.
Tranship' v.t. To transfer from one vessel, etc., to another.
Partisan'ship s. Adherence to a party.
Queen'ship s. Queenhood.
Cit'izenship s. State of being or rights of a citizen.
En'signship s. Rank or office of an ensign.
Chap'lainship s. (*Chaplain*).
Cham'berlainship s. Office of a chamberlain.
Chief'tainship s. (*Chieftain*).
Cap'tainship s. (*Captain*).
Kin'ship s. Relationship.
Ar'chonship s. (*Archon*).
Compan'ionship s. Fellowship, association; the compositors engaged on a job.
Cham'pionship s. State of being a champion; supremacy, leadership.
Rela'tionship s. State of being related.
Son'ship (sŭn) s. State of being a son.
Town'ship s. Territory of a town; division of some parishes.
Schol'arship s. Erudition; foundation for the support of a student.
Reg'istrarship s. Office of registrar.
War'ship s. Armed vessel for use in war.
Mem'bership s. State of being a member; the members of a body.
Lead'ership s. State or condition of a leader.
Read'ership s. Office of reader, especially at a University.
El'dership s. Office of elder.
Comman'dership s. (*Commander*).
Preach'ership s. Office of preacher.
Pre'miership s. Office of premier or prime minister.
Speak'ership s. Office of speaker.
Part'nership s. State of being a partner; an association of persons in business; joint interest or property.
Own'ership s. State of being an owner; just claim.
Keep'ership s. Office of keeper.
Inter'pretership s. Office of an interpreter.
Writ'ership s. Office of a writer, especially in Scotland.
Mas'tership s. Office of a master; rule, mastery.
Pres'bytership s. Presbyterate.
Air'ship s. A balloon, especially a dirigible balloon.
Heir'ship s. State, privileges, etc., of an heir right of inheriting.
Au'thorship s. (*Author*).
Pri'orship s. State or office of a prior.
Chan'cellorship s. Status, office, or rank of a chancellor.
Cen'sorship s. Office of censor.
Sen'atorship s. Office or dignity of a senator.
Arbitra'torship s. (*Arbitrator*).
Administra'torship s. (*Administrator*).
Procura'torship s. Office or dignity of a procurator.
Dicta'torship s. Office of dictator.
Collec'torship s. Office or jurisdiction of a collector.
Rec'torship s. Office or rank of a rector.
Protec'torship s. Office of protector or regent.
Proc'torship s. Office or dignity of a proctor.
Propri'etorship s. State of being a proprietor.
Au'ditorship s. (*Auditor*).
Mon'itorship s. Office of monitor.
Exec'utorship s. Office of an executor.
Coadju'torship s. (*Coadjutor*).
Tu'torship s. Office or occupation of a tutor.
Wor'ship (wer'-) v.t. To adore, revere, respect. v.i. To perform religious service. s. Act of adoring or paying honour, especially to God; religious service; dignity; deference; a title of respect.
Survey'orship (-vā'-) s. Office of surveyor.
Au'gurship s. (*Augur*).
Pre'fectship s. Prefecture.
Cadet'ship s. (*Cadet*).
Light'ship s. A moored vessel carrying a light for guidance.
Ser'geantship (sar'-) s. Office, rank, or status of sergeant.
Re'gentship s. Office of regent; vicarious authority.
Saint'ship s. Character or qualities of a saint.
Thwart'ship a. and adv. Across the vessel.
Court'ship s. Act of wooing or soliciting in marriage.
Fel'lowship s. State of being a fellow; dignity of a fellow; means of maintaining a fellow, companionship; joint interest.
La'dyship s. Rank or position of a lady; also as a title.
Demy'ship s. A scholarship at Magdalen, Oxon.
Vice'royship s. Viceroyalty.
Preb'endaryship s. Office of a prebendary.
Or'dinaryship s. Office or dignity of an ordinary.
Sec'retaryship s. Office of a secretary.
Whip s. A lash for driving; a driver; M.P. who has to summon his party; summons he sends out. v.t. To drive with lashes, flog; to

beat into a froth; to snatch suddenly. v.i. To move or start suddenly.

Horse'whip s. A whip for horses. v.t. To thrash.

Kip s. Hide of young cattle; (*slang*) a bed, common lodging-house.

Skip v.i. To bound, spring, leap. v.t. To pass over by leaping; to omit. s. A light spring or leap; captain of a side at bowls, etc.

Lip s. One of the fleshy exterior parts of the mouth; a part resembling this; edge; (*slang*) impudence.

Clip v.t. To shear, trim with scissors, cut short; to clasp, embrace, surround closely. v.i. To go swiftly. s. Act or product of sheep-shearing; a blow; an appliance for gripping.

Hare'lip s. Congenital fissure of the upper lip.

Fil'lip v.t. To strike with a jerk of the finger-nail; to flick. s. A sudden blow thus; an incentive.

Slip v.i. To slide, move along smoothly; to slink out; to err; to pass imperceptibly. v.t. To convey secretly; to cut slips from; to let loose; to disengage oneself from. s. Act of slipping; an unintentional error, etc.; a scion, cutting; a leash; an escape; a long narrow piece; a loose garment; inclined way in a dock.

Land'slip s. Sliding of a mass of land from a mountain; the mass that slides down.

Cow'slip s. A species of primrose.

Tu'lip s. A bulbous plant of the lily family; one of its flowers.

Ox'lip s. The great cowslip.

Nip s. A pinch, bite; a check to vegetation by frost, etc.; a small drink. v.t. To squeeze, pinch, pinch off; to blast, wither. v.i. To take a nip (of spirits, etc.).

Tur'nip s. A plant with a fleshy edible root; its root.

Snip v.t. To clip with scissors. s. A single cut with these; a bit cut off, a shred; (*slang*) a choice piece of information, etc.; a tailor.

Pars'nip s. An umbelliferous plant; its edible root.

Cat'nip s. Catmint.

Pip s. The seed of a fruit; a spot on cards; a disease in fowls; (*slang*) melancholia, the hump. v.t. To plough in an examination; to blackball.

Rip v.t. To separate by cutting or tearing; to tear off violently. v.i. To tear; to go at great speed. s. A rent made by ripping; a tear; (*slang*) a scamp.

Scrip s. A satchel, wallet; a certificate of stock; a schedule.

Drip v.i. To fall in drops, dribble. v.t. To let fall in drops. s. A falling in drops; a projecting moulding, eaves.

Grip v.t. and i. To clutch, grasp with the hand, hold fast. s. Act of grasping; a grasp; a hilt or handle; a hand-bag.

Trip v.i. To move lightly, skip; to stumble; to err. v.t. To cause to fall; to loose an anchor. s. A light step; a stumble; a mistake; a jaunt.

Can'trip s. (*Scot.*) A piece of mischief, an incantation.

Strip v.t. To make naked; to rob, plunder. v.i. To take off the clothes. s. A long narrow piece.

Outstrip' v.t. To advance beyond; leave behind.

Sip v.t. and i. To drink in small quantities. s. Small drink taken with the lips.

Gos'sip s. A tattler; tittle-tattle. v.i. To talk idly; to spread rumours; to chat.

Tip s. Point, end, extremity; a tap; a small money gift; private information; place for rubbish. v.t. To tap, touch; to cause to lean; to discharge thus; to give a gratuity to.

Quip s. A sarcastic jest, sharp retort. v.t. and i. To taunt, scoff, deride.

Equip' v.t. To fit out, furnish; to array.

Zip s. Sound of a flying or striking projectile.

Alp s. A high, snow-capped mountain.

Scalp s. The skin of the head, with the hair on it. v.t. To deprive of this.

Palp s. A jointed sense-organ in insects, etc.

Help v.t. To assist, relieve; to remedy; to avoid. v.t. To lend aid. s. Assistance; remedy; relief; a helper.

Whelp s. A cub, puppy. v.t. and i. To give birth to, bring forth pups (of bitches, etc.).

Kelp s. Calcined ashes of seaweed from which iodine is prepared; the seaweed used.

Yelp v.i. To bark shrilly, utter a sharp, quick cry. s. Such a cry.

Megilp' s. A medium used by oil-painters.

Gulp v.t. To swallow eagerly, to suck down. s. Act of taking a large swallow.

Pulp s. Any soft mass; soft part of fruit. v.t. To reduce to or deprive of pulp.

Camp s. An encampment; assemblage of inhabited tents; ground for this. v.i. To encamp, to pitch a camp.

Decamp' v.i. To depart quickly, take oneself off.

Aide-de-camp s. An officer attendant on a general or royalty.

Encamp' v.i. To make or to take up position in a camp. v.t. To form into or place in a camp.

Scamp s. A rogue, swindler. v.t. To do perfunctorily.

Damp a. Moist, humid. s. Moist air, fog; depression of spirits; discouragement. v.t. To moisten; to dispirit, restrain.

Gamp s. (*Slang*) A large, clumsy umbrella.

Champ v.i. To bite frequently. v.t. To bite into small pieces.

Lamp s. Contrivance for supplying light or heat, especially by agency of oil.

Clamp s. A strengthening piece of iron, etc.; a heavy footstep; a heap of bricks, coal, potatoes, etc. v.t. To make firm with a clamp; to store in a clamp v.i. To tread clumsily.

Ramp v.i. To spring, romp, frolic; to rear; to rage; to slope up. s. An inclined plane; a sloping part; a vulgar woman; a swindle.

Cramp s. A spasmodic contraction of a limb or muscle; restraint; S-shaped iron binding masonry, etc. v.t. To afflict with spasms; to restrain, hinder; to bind firmly together.

Tramp v.t. and i. To tread under or travel on foot; to stroll. s. Act or sound of tramping; a journey on foot; a trading vessel not following a regular course; a vagrant.

Tamp v.t. To fill up (a blast-hole); to ram in or down.

Stamp v.t. To impress; to strike downwards with the foot; to coin, form; to fix a postage stamp to. v.i. To strike the foot forcibly downward. s. Act of or instrument for stamping; mark impressed; postage stamp; character.

Restamp' v.t. To stamp again.

Vamp s. Upper leather of a boot; an added piece; improvised accompaniment. v.t. To provide with a vamp; to patch up. v.i. To improvise.

Swamp (swomp) s. A bog, morass. v.t. To fill and overset (as a boat); to sink in a swamp; to overwhelm.

Hemp s. An Indian herbaceous plant; rope fibre made from this; bhang.

Kemp s. The coarse or knotty hairs of wool.

Imp s. A sprite; a mischievous child. v.t. To graft, to insert a feather in a broken wing.

Gimp s. An edging of silk, woollen, or cotton braid; a wired fishing-line.

Jimp a. Neat, handsome; elegant in shape.

Skimp v.t. To do carelessly. v.i. To be niggardly.

Limp v.i. To walk lamely, to halt. s. Act of limping. a. Pliant; easily bent; flaccid.

Blimp s. A small airship.

Pimp s. A procurer, pander. v.i. To pander.

Crimp v.t. To curl, frill, corrugate, flute; to cause to become firm and crisp (as fish for cooking); to decoy for service at sea. s. One who decoys men, especially for service at sea.

Scrimp v.t. To make scant, limit. v.i. To be niggardly, to skimp. a. Scanty. adv. Barely.

Shrimp s. A small edible crustacean; a manikin.

Primp v.t. and i. To make prim, behave primly; to prink oneself.

Comp s. (*slang*) A compositor.

Pomp s. Ostentation, grandeur; show of magnificence; pride.

Romp v.i. To frolic roughly; to leap about; to move quickly. s. A boisterous child; rough play.

Tromp s. Blowing apparatus used in furnaces.

Bump s. A heavy blow; the noise made by or a lump produced by such. v.t. To strike heavily against. v.i. To collide.

But'terbump s. The bittern.

Dump s. A small thick object; a thud; a pile of refuse or place for shooting this; a melancholy tune, melancholy. v.t. To throw in a heap, put down carelessly; to export surplus goods with object of underselling.

Hump s. A protuberance, especially at the back; (*slang*) the blues.

Chump s. A short, thick end-piece; (*slang*) the head.

Thump v.t. To beat with dull, heavy blows. s. Such a blow; sound of this.

Jump v.i. To leap, spring; to tally, agree. v.t. To pass over hastily or by a leap. s. Act of jumping; a leap, bound.

Buck'-jump v.i. To jump with the feet drawn together and the back arched (of a horse). s. Such a jump.

Lump s. A small, shapeless mass; a cluster. v.t. To throw into a mass; to take in the gross; (*slang*) to put up with; a suctorial fish.

Clump s. A cluster; a shapeless mass; a thick piece of leather for boot-repairing; (*slang*) a heavy blow with the hand. v.t. To tread heavily; to form into a clump.

Flump s. Sound of a dull, heavy fall. v.t. To throw down heavily.

Plump a. Fat, chubby; unqualified, blunt. v.t. To swell, fatten; to cause to drop heavily. v.i. To be swelled; to fall suddenly; to give all one's votes to a single candidate. adv. At once, suddenly.

Slump v.i. To sink or fall suddenly, especially of prices, etc. s. A collapse, sudden fall in price; the gross amount.

Mump v.i. To beg whiningly; to sulk, mope; to mumble. v.t. To overreach; to munch.

Pump s. Machine for raising water, extracting or inflating with air, etc.; a light shoe. v.t. To work a pump; to elicit artfully.

Rump s. The end of the backbone; the buttocks.

Crump a. Crisp, brittle.

Frump s. A dowdy, dull, or old-fashioned woman.

Trump s. A privileged or winning card; a good fellow on whom one can depend; a trumpet; sound made by this or by an elephant, etc. v.i. and t. To play or take with a trump; to forge, fabricate.

Sump s. Pit in floor of a mine.

Tump s. A hillock. v.t. To form a hillock round (a plant, etc.).

Stump s. Part of a tree, limb, etc., left after some has been removed; a stub; a wicket in cricket. v.t. To tour making speeches; to put out in cricket in a certain way. v.i. To walk heavily or stiffly.

Mug'wump s. An independent voter; a consequential person.

Cop s. A hill; the top of some things; the conical roll of thread on a spindle; (*slang*) a policeman, a capture. v.t. (*Slang*) To seize, arrest, catch.

Fop s. A dandy, dude, coxcomb.

Hop s. A jump on one leg; a bitter plant, its flower; (*slang*) a dance. v.i. To dance, skip lightly, limp.

Chop v.t. To cut with a quick blow or blows, to mince; to barter, exchange. v.i. To dispute; to shift suddenly. s. Act of chopping; stroke; piece chopped off, especially of meat with portion of rib; quality, brand.

Shop s. Place where goods are sold retail or where mechanics work; one's trade, profession, etc.; talk or jargon concerning this. v.i. To visit shops as a purchaser. v.t. (*slang*) To arrest or imprison.
Bish'op s. Ecclesiastical head of a diocese; a man at chess; a drink. v.t. (*slang*) To fake a horse.
Archbish'op s. A chief bishop, a primate.
Work'shop s. Place in which a handicraft is carried on.
Beer'shop s. A low public-house; an "off-licence."
Whop v.t. To beat severely. s. A sudden fall.
Lop v.t. To cut off or shorten; to allow to hang down. v.i. To hang limply, droop. s. A lop-eared rabbit.
Gal'op s. A lively dance. v.i. To dance this.
Devel'op v.t. To disclose, make known, unfold gradually. v.i. To evolve to a more perfect state; to progress; to become visible gradually.
Redevel'op v.t. To develop again.
Envel'op v.t. To surround, to cover; to wrap up.
Flop v.i. To tumble about; to sway or fall heavily. v.t. To let fall noisily, to cause to strike with a heavy sound. s. Act, motion, or sound of flopping. adv. Suddenly.
Scal'lop s. An edible bivalve mollusc; one of its shells; a dish resembling this; an indented edging. v.t. To cook in a scallop; to indent an edge.
Gal'lop v.i. To run with leaps or very fast; to ride thus. s. A fast pace of a horse, especially by leaps.
Shal'lop s. A light open boat.
Wal'lop (wol'-) v.t. To beat soundly, to drub. v.i. To boil noisily and rapidly; to waddle.
Col'lop s. A slice of meat.
Trol'lop s. A slatternly woman, or one of bad character.
Plop s. The soft sound of a falling object; a fall. v.t. and i. To fall with or make this sound.
Or'lop s. The lowest deck of a ship having three or more.
Slop s. Spilled liquid; dirty water; a puddle; weak drink; ready-made clothes. v.t. and i. To overflow, spill; to soil thus.
Slip'slop a. Feeble; jejune.
Mop s. A cloth broom for cleaning floors, etc.; a thick head of hair; a servant's hiring-fair; a grimace. v.t. To wipe or clean with a mop. v.i. To make grimaces.
Knop s. A knob; an architectural ornament.
Coop s. A cage with one side barred or netted for poultry, etc. v.t. To confine in a narrow compass, to crowd.
Scoop s. A kind of large ladle or shovel; a gouge; act of scooping; (*slang*) early publication of sensational news. v.t. To take out or empty with a scoop; to excavate, hollow out.
Hoop s. A band to confine staves of casks; a ring; a crinoline. v.t. To fasten with hoops; to encircle.
Whoop s. A shout of pursuit; a halloo, hoot; cough of whooping-cough. v.i. and t. To utter or mock with such cries.
Loop s. A doubling or folding of a string, etc.; a ring; a circuit. v.t. To form into or fasten with a loop; to perform a circuit.
Saloop' s. An infusion of sassefras; salep.
Cloop s. The sound of drawing a cork.
Sloop s. A one-masted sailing vessel.
Poop s. The stern of a ship; the highest or aftmost deck.
Nin'compoop s. A silly fool; blockhead.
Scroop s. A harsh, grating noise. v.i. To make this.
Droop v.i. To hang down; to pine away, languish, be dejected. v.t. To let hang down or sink. s. A drooping position or state.
Troop s. Collection of persons; body of soldiers; unit of cavalry; signal on the drum. v.i. To collect in numbers; to march in a body. v.t. To form into troops.
Stoop v.i. To bend forward; to submit; to deign. s. A bend of the back or shoulders; a stoep.
Swoop v.t. and i. To fall on and seize; to catch on the wing. s. Downward flight of a bird of prey; a sudden snatching.
Pop s. A small, quick sound; ginger-beer. v.i. To make this sound; to jump forth or move about suddenly. v.t. To thrust or bring to notice suddenly; to heat to bursting; (*slang*) to pawn.
Lol'lipop s. A sweetmeat.
Crop s. Corn, etc., while growing; harvest; act of cutting, as hair; the crow of birds; a looped whip-stock; an outcrop. v.t. To cut off the ends of, to cut close; to browse; to gather before it falls; to cultivate.
Out'crop s. The part of an inclined stratum appearing at the surface. v.i. To appear thus.
Drop s. A globule of liquid, small quantity; an earring; part of a gallows; a fall; distance fallen or to fall. v.t. To pour in drops; to let fall; to let down; to utter casually to give up. v.i. To fall, or fall in drops; to cease; to come unexpectedly.
Bedrop' v.t. To wet or sprinkle with drops.
Rain'drop s. A particle of rain.
Eaves'drop s. Water dripping from eaves. v.i. To listen to private conversation.
Dew'drop s. A drop of dew.
Snow'drop s. An early, bulbous plant with white flower.
Prop s. A support, stay. v.t. To support, sustain.
Cal'trop s. A pointed implement to wound horse's feet.
Strop s. Strip of leather for sharpening razors. v.t. To sharpen with this
Sop s. Food steeped in liquid and softened; something given to pacify. v.t. To steep in liquor. v.i. To be soaked, wet through.
Milk'sop s. An effeminate person.
Hys'sop s. A blue-flowered labiate plant.
Top s. Highest part; a whirling toy. a. Highest, being on top. v.i. To rise above, be eminent. v.t. To surmount, cap.

Fore'top s. Platform at top of a foremast.
Overtop' v.t. To rise above; to transcend, surpass; to obscure.
Stop v.t. To stuff up, close; to put an end to. v.i. To come to an end; to stay, cease. s. Obstruction; pause; a punctuation mark; vent on a wind-instrument; series of organ pipes.
Estop' v.t. To bar, debar, especially by one's own act.
Swop v.t. (*Swap*).
Lapp s. A native of Lapland.
Repp s. Rep.
Carp v.i. To censure, find fault naggingly. s. A family of freshwater fishes.
Ep'icarp s. The rind or skin of fruits.
Mer'icarp s. One of two seed-bearing carpels into which certain fruits split.
Per'icarp s. The seed-vessel of a plant.
Syn'carp s. An aggregate fruit, as the raspberry.
Sar'cocarp s. The fleshy part of a fruit.
En'docarp s. The inner layer of the pericarp.
Pod'ocarp s. The foot-stalk of a fruit.
Pseud'ocarp s. A fruit not consisting entirely of the ovary.
Xy'locarp (zī'-) s. A hard, woody fruit; tree bearing such.
Mon'ocarp s. A monocarpous plant.
Schiz'ocarp s. A dry fruit which splits into one-seeded portions.
Scarp s. A very steep slope. v.t. To cut away nearly perpendicularly.
Escarp' s. A precipitous part of a fortification. v.t. To make into or furnish with a steep slope.
Coun'terscarp s. The exterior slope of the ditch protecting a fort.
Harp s. A triangular stringed instrument played by plucking. v.i. To play on a harp; to repeat tiresomely, to dwell on.
Sharp a. Keen-edged; not blurred; witty; acid; shrill; pointed. s. A note raised a semitone; sign denoting this (♯). v.t. To sharpen. adv. Sharply; exactly; punctually.
Warp (worp) s. Thread running the long way of a fabric; rope used in moving a ship. v.t. and i. To turn or twist out of shape; to pervert; to move (a ship) with a tight warp.
Mould'warp s. The mole.
Chirp v.i. To emit a sound as of crickets or birds. s. A short, sharp note.
Thorp s. A village, hamlet.
Usurp' v.t. To appropriate wrongfully.
Asp s. The aspen-tree; the Egyptian cobra; viper.
Gasp v.i. To pant or labour for breath. v.t. To emit with a gasp. s. Short, painful catching of the breath.
Hasp s. A clasp folding over a staple. v.t. To secure or shut with this.
Clasp s. A metal buckle, brooch, or other catch; a bar on a medal-ribbon. v.t. To shut or fasten with a clasp; to embrace.
Rasp s. A coarse file v.t. To rub with a rough implement; to grate. v.i. To rub or grate.
Grasp v.t. To lay hold of, grip, seize. v.i. To make a clutch. s. A grip; reach; power of comprehending.
Wasp (wosp) s. A stinging, bee-like insect.
Lisp v.i. To substitute *th* for *s* in speaking; to speak affectedly. v.t. To pronounce thus. s. Act or habit of lisping.
Crisp a. Brittle; easily broken; formed into stiff curls; effervescing. v.t. To curl, make wavy. v.i. To form little curls.
Wisp s. A small bunch of straw, hair, or the like.
Will-o'-the-wisp' s. The ignis-fatuus.
Cusp s. Point formed by meeting of two curves; tip of a crescent.
Up adv. Aloft; on high; not down. prep. From below to above; on or along.
Scaup s. A sea-duck; a bed of mussels.
Whaup s. (*Scot.*) The curlew.
Cup s. A small drinking vessel; anything cup-shaped; a vessel for drawing blood; liquor in a cup. v.t. To bleed with a cupping-glass.
Hic'cup s. A short, audible catching of the breath. v.i. and t. To make or utter with this sound.
But'tercup s. A common yellow field-flower.
Pick'-me-up s. A tonic, restorative.
Ketch'up s. A sauce made from mushrooms, etc.
Lock'up s. Place for temporary confinement of arrested persons.
Coup s. A stroke, blow; a quick, successful action.
Recoup' v.t. To compensate, indemnify.
Can'taloup s. A kind of melon.
Roup s. A disease in poultry; hoarseness; (*Scot.*) an auction. v.t. (*Scot.*) To sell by auction.
Croup s. The part of a horse behind the saddle; the buttocks; a disease of the windpipe in children.
Group s. An assemblage of objects or persons; a cluster; a class. v.t. To form into a group or groups.
Soup s. Liquid food made from meat and vegetables.
Stoup (stoop) s. Basin for holy water; a flagon.
Pup s. A puppy, whelp. v.i. To bring forth puppies.
Lar'rup v.t. (*Slang*) To thrash, flog.
Chir'rup v.i. To twitter, chirp. s. A twittering sound.
Stir'rup s. Loop for horseman's foot.
Syr'up s. Any sweet thick fluid.
Sup v.t. and i. To take into the mouth by the lips; to take supper, give supper to. s. A sip.
Tup s. A male sheep. v.t. and i. To butt.
Titt'up v.i. To move in a prancing, jaunty way. s. A prance, a lively step.
Gyp s. A male college servant at Cambridge.
Hyp s. Morbid depression of spirits melancholia.
Pol'yp s. An aquatic animal of low organization; a sea-anemone.
Bazaar' s. An Oriental market; a sale for charitable purposes.
Bar s. An obstacle, long strip of wood or metal; a bolt; a counter; tribunal; the body of barristers. v.t. To hinder, prohibit, secure.
Cal'abar s. The fur of a grey squirrel.
Cin'nabar s. Red mercuric sulphide. a. Vermilion.
Debar' v.t. To exclude, preclude, hinder.
Liquidam'bar s. A genus of tropical trees; resin from these.
Lum'bar a. Pertaining to the loins.

I'sobar s. Chart line connecting places at which mean height of barometer is the same.
Durbar' s. An Indian ruler's court; state reception in India.
Disbar' v.t. To deprive a barrister of his status.
Car s. A chariot, vehicle; a tramway or railway carriage.
Tri'car s. A small three-wheeled motor-car.
Vic'ar s. Holder of a benefice the tithes of which are impropriated.
Cal'car s. A spur at the base of a petal, on a bird's leg, etc.
Tram'car s. A street car running on rails.
Tro'car s. Surgical instrument for evacuating fluids.
Au'tocar s. A motor-car.
Scar s. Mark left by a wound; a cliff; bare place on a hill. v.t. To mark with a scar. v.i. To cicatrize.
Las'car s. An E. Indian sailor.
Jem'adar s. A native Indian subaltern.
Ched'dar s. A kind of cheese.
Ce'dar s. A large, evergreen timber-tree.
Subahdar' s. Principal native officer in a Hindu regiment.
Ressaldar s. A native Indian cavalry captain.
Hav'ildar s. A sergeant in a Sepoy regiment.
Cal'endar s. A register of the days of the year; a year-book.
Zem'indar s. A privileged native land-holder in Bengal.
Deodar' s. A large Himalayan cedar.
Hos'podar s. Title of governor of Moldavia or Wallachia.
Tab'erdar s. A scholar of Queen's, Oxford.
Sir'dar s. A commander; the Egyptian commander-in-chief.
Bor'dar s. A villein of the lowest rank under the feudal system.
Ear s. Organ of hearing; power of judging harmony; a spike of corn.
Bear s. A large plantigrade quadruped. v.t. and i. To carry, bring forth, tolerate.
Abear' v.t. To put up with.
Cud'bear s. A crimson vegetable dye.
Bug'bear s. A bogy; something that causes fear.
Overbear' v.t. To repress, overwhelm, subdue.
For'bear s. A forefather, ancestor.
Forbear' v.i. To pause, abstain from; to be patient.
Dear a. Beloved; precious; costly; scarce. s. A loved one. adv. At a high price.
Endear' v.t. To make dear or beloved.
Fear s. Apprehension of danger; solicitude; object of fear; reverence. v.t. To feel fear, to dread; to reverence. v.i. To be afraid.
Gear s. Goods; clothing; harness; working apparatus or adjustment; a train of toothed wheels. v.t. To put gear on; to harness.
Head'gear s. Covering or ornaments for the head; top works of a mine-shaft.
Hear v.t. To perceive by the ear; to attend; to listen to favourably; to try in court. v.i. To have the faculty of hearing; to be told.
Rehear' v.t. To try a second time, hear again.
Overhear' v.t. To hear by chance or stratagem.
Shear v.t. and i. To cut with shears; to clip (esp. wool) from; to fleece.
Blear a. Dimmed, sore. v.t. To dim or impair.
Clear a. Bright, shining; open, fair shrill; acute; free from debt, obstruction, guilt, etc.; exempt. adv. Quite, entirely, plainly. v.t. To free from obstructions or obscurity; to cleanse; to justify to leap over; to pay customs dues. v.i. To become clear or fair; (*slang*) to get out.
Nu'clear a. Pertaining to or constituting a nucleus.
Coch'lear a. Pertaining to the cochlea; spoon-shaped.
Troch'lear a. Pertaining to the trochlea.
Smear v.t. To spread with anything viscous; to bedaub, pollute. s. Blotch made with an unctuous or adhesive substance; a daub.
Besmear' v.t. To daub with something sticky; to defile.
Near adv. Almost; closely; sparingly. a. Nigh; intimate; parsimonious; on the left (of a horse). prep. Close to. v.t. and i. To approach, come near.
Lin'ear a. Pertaining to, composed of, or resembling a line or lines; slender.
Rectilin'ear a. Right-lined; consisting of or bounded by straight lines.
Curvilin'ear a. Consisting of or bounded by curved lines.
Collin'ear a. In the same straight line.
Interlin'ear a. Written between the lines.
Pear s. A well-known tree akin to the apple; its fruit.
Appear' v.i. To be or become visible; to seem.
Reappear' v.i. To appear again.
Disappear' v.i. To vanish from sight, be lost to view.
Spear s. A long, pointed weapon; a sharp, barbed instrument. v.t. To pierce or kill with a spear. v.i. To shoot into a long stem.
Rear s. The hind part, as of an army, etc.; background. a. Being behind; hindmost. v.t. To bring up from birth; to breed; to raise, build up. v.i. To rise on the hind legs.
Drear a. Dismal, gloomy, dreary.
Uprear' v.t. To rear up, raise.
Arrear' s. That which remains unpaid.
Sear v.t. To wither, dry up; to make callous. a. Dry, parched.
Dog's-ear s. The corner of a leaf of a book turned down. v.t. To turn down corners of leaves carelessly.
Tear (tare) v.t. To pull to pieces, rend, lacerate. v.i. To part on being pulled; to rush violently. s. A rent.
Tear (tēr) s. Drop of fluid moistening or flowing from the eye; a tear-shaped drop.
Wheat'ear s. A small migratory bird, the stone-chat.
Wear v.t. To put or have on; to waste by rubbing, etc., to destroy by degrees; to have an appearance of; to veer, bring on the other tack. v.i. To endure or bear the consequences of use, time, etc.; to be consumed slowly. s. Act of wearing, thing worn; style of dress; consumption by use.
Swear v.t. and i. To make a solemn declaration; to utter as an or make a promise upon oath; to cause to take an oath.
Forswear' v.t. To abjure, renounce upon oath to swear falsely.

Outswear' v.t. To bear down by swearing.
Outwear' v.t. To last longer.
Year s. Period of the earth's circuit of its orbit; twelve months; age, old age; time of life.
Far a. Remote, distant. adv. Very remotely; by many degrees; to a certain point.
Afar' adv. From, at, or to a distance.
Gar s. A fish with a long pointed snout.
A'gar-a'gar s. A gelatinous substance obtained from seaweed and used in soup.
Vin'egar s. Thin and impure acetic acid; anything sour.
Sag'gar s. A vessel used in kilning porcelain.
Beg'gar s. One who begs, a mendicant. v.t. To reduce to beggary, to exhaust.
Cigar' s. A tapering roll of tobacco-leaf for smoking.
Pol'igar s. A feudal chief in S. India.
Real'gar s. Disulphide of arsenic; red orpiment.
Vul'gar a. Pertaining to or characteristic of the common people; common; low; boorish. s. The common people.
Hang'ar s. A large shed, especially for aeroplanes.
Sang'ar s. A rough fortification against Indian tribesmen.
Whing'ar s. A short sword, dirk.
Khid'mutgar s. A Hindu butler.
Cou'gar s. The puma; the American panther.
Su'gar s. A sweet, granular substance obtained from the sugar-cane, beet, etc. v.t. To sprinkle, mix, season, etc., with this; to sweeten. a. Pertaining to or made of sugar.
Char s. A trout-like fish; (*slang*) a woman who goes out charing. v.t. and i. To burn slightly; blacken or become blackened by fire; to do housework and odd jobs by the day.
Es'char s. A dry slough or scab.
Nen'uphar s. The white water-lily.
Col'cothar s. A brown-red oxide of iron used as a polishing powder; jewellers' rouge.
Justi'ciar s. An early English chief officer of the Crown.
Li'ar s. One who tells falsehoods.
Gang'liar a. Pertaining to a ganglion.
Atrabil'iar a. Atrabilious.
Concil'iar a. Pertaining to a council.
Famil'iar a. Pertaining to a family, domestic; unceremonious, affable. s. An intimate; a personal evil spirit.
Fo'liar a. Pertaining to or of the nature of leaves.
Pecu'liar a. Pertaining to or characteristic of one thing or person; singular; appropriate; particular. s. Exclusive property; a church not under jurisdiction of a bishop.
Bri'ar s. (*Brier*).
Fri'ar s. A brother of a mendicant monastic order.
An'tiar s. The Upas-tree; its poison.
Jar s. A glass or earthen vessel; a rattling vibration; a harsh sound; a clash; contention. v.i. To strike together discordantly; to clash; to quarrel. v.t. To shake; to cause a tremulous motion in.
Ajar' adv. Partly open.
Hand'jar s. An Oriental broad-bladed dagger.
Night'jar s. The goatsucker.
Shikar' s. Big-game hunting in India.
Sir'kar s. The British government in India.
Es'kar s. A long mound of glacial drift.
Lar s. A tutelary Roman divinity; a Malayan gibbon.
A'lar a. Wing-shaped.
Sca'lar s. A pure number. a. Scalariform.
Ma'lar a. Pertaining to the cheek or cheek-bone. s. The cheek-bone.
Med'lar s. A rosaceous fruit-tree; its fruit.
Ped'lar s. An itinerant trader, a hawker.
Ste'lar a. Pertaining to or resembling a stele.
Tu'telar a. Tutelary.
Ve'lar a. Pertaining to or effected by means of the soft palate.
Bur'glar s. A robber of houses by night.
Ash'lar s. Squared stone for building.
Subnu'bilar a. Situated beneath the clouds.
Fi'lar a. Pertaining to or furnished with threads.
Hi'lar a. Pertaining to the hilum.
Sim'ilar a. Resembling, like; uniform.
Verisim'ilar a. Having the appearance of truth; likely.
Dissim'ilar a. Unlike.
Pi'lar a. Pertaining to the hair.
Cerebel'lar a. Pertaining to the cerebellum.
Um'bellar a. Pertaining to or having the form of an umbel.
Cel'lar s. An underground room for storing liquor, coal, etc.; a stock of wine; a table receptacle for salt.
Varicel'lar a. Pertaining or due to chicken-pox.
Lamel'lar a. Composed of or arranged in lamellæ.
Tes'sellar a. Formed of tessaræ, as a mosaic.
Patel'lar a. Like a patella; pan-shaped.
Clitel'lar a. (*Clitellum*).
Stel'lar a. Pertaining to the stars.
Rostel'lar a. Like or having a rostellum.
Interstel'lar a. Situated among the stars.
Scutel'lar a. (*Scutellate*).
Pill'ar s. A perpendicular support, a column; prop; stability. v.t. To support as by a pillar.
Cat'erpillar s. The larva of a lepidopterous insect.
Fi'brillar a. Pertaining to or resembling a fibril.
Ton'sillar a. Pertaining to the tonsils.
Pulvil'lar a. Pertaining to or having pulvilli.
Ax'illar a. Pertaining to the armpit.
Vexil'lar a. Having a vexillum (of flowers).
Col'lar s. Something worn round the neck; The upper edge of a coat, etc.; neck-band of a dog, horse, etc.; the astragal of a column. v.t. To seize roughly, get hold of.
Dol'lar s. A silver coin and monetary unit of U.S.A., Canada, etc. (value about 4s. 2d.); (*slang*) five shillings.
Sol'lar s. A raised floor in a mine.
Ur'ceolar a. Pitcher-shaped.
Nucle'olar a. Pertaining to or constituting a nucleolus.
Are'olar a. Consisting of areolæ.
Alve'olar a. Pertaining to the tooth-sockets.
Schol'ar s. A pupil, student; a man of letters; one holding a scholarship.
Modi'olar a. Pertaining to the modiolus.
Vari'olar a. Pertaining or due to smallpox.
Pet'iolar a. Pertaining to or supported on a petiole.
Osti'olar a. Pertaining to or like an ostiole.
Mo'lar a. Having power to grind; pertaining to, acted on, or exerted by a mass. s. A grinding tooth.

Po'lar a. Pertaining to, surrounding, or from the N. or S. Pole; pertaining to the magnetic, electric, or mathematical pole; opposite; having polarity.
Unipol'ar a. Having but one pole or kind of polarity.
Circumpol'ar a. About or near the pole; moving round the pole.
So'lar a. Pertaining to or proceeding from the sun.
Circumso'lar a. Revolving round or near the sun.
Vac'uolar a. Containing vacuoles.
Vo'lar a. Pertaining to the palm of the hand or sole of the foot.
Hex'aplar a. Sextuple; in or containing six columns.
Tem'plar s. One of a mediæval military religious order; a lawyer or law student.
Exem'plar s. A model, pattern, copy.
Pop'lar s. A tree of several varieties.
Tintinab'ular a. Relating to bells or their sound.
Incunab'ular a. Pertaining to incunabula.
Tab'ular a. Having a flat surface; formed in scales; classified in a table.
Neb'ular a. Pertaining to nebulæ.
Mandib'ular a. Pertaining to or like a mandible.
Infundib'ular a. Funnel-shaped.
Fib'ular a. Pertaining to the fibula.
Vestib'ular a. Pertaining to or like a vestibule.
Lob'ular a. Shaped like a lobule.
Glob'ular a. Shaped like a globe; spherical; composed of globules.
Multilob'ular a. Having many lobes.
Tu'bular a. Tube-shaped; consisting of or furnished with tubes.
Multitu'bular a. Having many tubes.
Piac'ular a. Expiatory; able to atone; atrociously bad.
Tabernac'ular a. Pertaining to a tabernacle, especially that of the ancient Jews.
Vernac'ular a. Indigenous. s. One's native tongue or dialect.
Spirac'ular a. Having or resembling spiracles.
Orac'ular a. Pertaining to or like an oracle; authoritative; sententious; ambiguous.
Spectac'ular a. Pertaining to or of the nature of a show.
Tentac'ular a. Pertaining to or resembling a tentacle.
Receptac'ular a. Pertaining to the receptacle of a plant.
Sac'cular a. Like a sac.
Trabec'ular a. Pertaining to a trabecula; having or consisting of trabeculæ.
Molec'ular a. Pertaining to or consisting of molecules.
Spec'ular a. Having a smooth, reflecting surface; denoting a crystalline variety of hæmatite.
Sec'ular a. Temporal; worldly; not spiritual. s. A layman; a church official not ordained.
Orbic'ular a. Resembling an orb; spherical.
Acic'ular a. Needle-shaped, slender.
Fascic'ular a. Growing in bunches or tufts.
Radic'ular a. Pertaining to or like a radicle.
Pedic'ular a. Lousy.
Appendic'ular a. (*Appendicle*).
Perpendic'ular a. Upright; at right angles to the horizon or to a given line. s. A vertical or upright line or direction.
Slantendic'ular a. (*Slang*) Slanting.
Vehic'ular a. Pertaining to or serving as a vehicle.
Calic'ular a. Cup-shaped.
Pellic'ular a. Resembling or consisting of a pellicle.
Follic'ular a. Pertaining to or resembling follicles.
Vermic'ular a. Pertaining to or resembling a worm; vermiculated.
Canic'ular a. Pertaining to the dog-days; very hot.
Funic'ular a. Consisting of or dependent on a cord or cable.
Apic'ular a. Like a small apex; situated at the top.
Spic'ular a. Pertaining to or resembling a spicule; dart-like.
Matric'ular a. Entered on a register; pertaining to the matrix.
Ventric'ular a. Pertaining to or resembling a ventricle.
Utric'ular a. Pertaining to a utricle.
Auric'ular a. Pertaining to the ear, confidential.
Vesic'ular a. Pertaining to or consisting of vesicles; having interstices; hollow.
Versic'ular a. Pertaining to verses.
Tussic'ular a. Pertaining to, due to, or resembling a cough.
Retic'ular a. Netted; formed with interstices.
Dentic'ular a. Pertaining to or resembling a denticle.
Lentic'ular a. Resembling a lentil or a doubly convex lens; pertaining to the lens of the eye.
Artic'ular a. Pertaining to joints.
Partic'ular a. Individual; pertaining to a single person or thing; fastidious; circumstantial. s. A single instance, point, or matter.
Vortic'ular a. Vortical.
Testic'ular a. Testiculate.
Cutic'ular a. Pertaining to the cuticle.
Unguic'ular a. Having nails or claws; shaped like these.
Clavic'ular a. Pertaining to the collar-bone.
Navic'ular a. Shaped like a boat, especially of a bone in the foot or hand.
Animal'cular a. (*Animalcule*).
Carbun'cular a. (*Carbuncle*).
Homun'cular a. Pertaining to a dwarf; diminutive.
Carun'cular a. (*Caruncle*).
Furun'cular a. Characterized by or affected with boils.
Avun'cular a. Pertaining to an uncle or that relationship.
Oc'ular a. Depending on or perceived by the eye; visual.
Joc'ular a. Given to jesting; merry; sportive.
Loc'ular a. Having or composed of cells.
Quinqueloc'ular a. Having five cells.
Biloc'ular a. Having two cells.
Uniloc'ular a. Consisting of a single cell.
Quadriloc'ular a. Having four cells.
Triloc'ular a. Three-celled.
Multiloc'ular a. Having many cells or compartments.
Senoc'ular a. Having six eyes (of some spiders).
Binoc'ular a. Having two eyes; using both at once. s. An optical instrument for use with both eyes at once.
Monoc'ular a. One-eyed; adapted for use with one eye at a time.
Multoc'ular a. Having more than two eyes.
Tuber'cular a. Having or affected with tubercles or tuberculosis.
Oper'cular a. Pertaining to or like an operculum. s. The gill-cover of a fish.
Cir'cular a. Round, ending in itself. s. A notice, etc., sent to a number of persons.

Semicir'cular a. In the shape of a half circle.
Tor'cular s. A kind of tourniquet.
Vas'cular a. Pertaining to, full of, consisting of, or operating by means of vasa or ducts.
Flos'cular a. Having little, or many, flowers or florets.
Crepus'cular a. Pertaining to the twilight; glimmering, obscure.
Corpus'cular a. Pertaining to corpuscles; atomic.
Mus'cular a. Pertaining to or having well-developed muscles; brawny.
Calyc'ular a. Pertaining to or having a calyx.
Gland'ular a. Having, consisting of, or of the nature of glands.
Nod'ular a. Pertaining to or characterized by nodules or nodes.
Gu'lar a. Pertaining to the throat.
Reg'ular a. Orderly, exact; conformed to a rule, etc.; methodical; thorough. s. A soldier of a permanent army; a monk who has taken the vows.
Irreg'ular a. Not according to precedent, established custom, etc.; disorderly; anomalous; variable.
Teg'ular a. Consisting of or resembling tiles.
Lig'ular a. Tongue-shaped.
An'gular a. Having an angle; stiff, formal.
Decan'gular a. Having ten angles.
Bian'gular a. Having two angles.
Trian'gular a. Three-sided.
Equian'gular a. Consisting of or having equal angles.
Quadran'gular a. Having four angles and sides.
Rectan'gular a. Right-angled; placed at right angles.
Octan'gular a. Having eight angles.
Multan'gular a. Having many angles.
Pentan'gular a. Having five angles.
Heptan'gular a. Having seven angles.
Septan'gular a. Having seven angles.
Quinquan'gular a. Having five angles.
Hexan'gular a. Having six angles.
Sexan'gular a. Having six angles; hexagonal.
Lin'gular a. Tongue-shaped.
Sin'gular a. Single, not plural; odd; peculiar. s. The singular number.
Un'gular a. Pertaining to or like a hoof.
Solidun'gular a. Solid-hoofed.
Ju'gular a. Pertaining to the neck or throat; s. A large vein in the neck.
Pil'ular a. Like a pilule.
Cell'ular a. Pertaining to or resembling cells.
Unicell'ular a. Composed of a single cell.
Multicell'ular a. Having many cells.
Stel'lular a. Set with or shaped like small stars.
Ham'ular a. Like a little hook.
Num'mular a. Nummary; resembling coins.
Tu'mular a. Heaped; pertaining to a tumulus.
Campan'ular a. Bell-shaped.
Ran'ular a. Pertaining to ranula.
Gran'ular a. Composed of or resembling granules.
An'nular a. Ring-shaped; pertaining to a ring.
Can'nular a. Like or furnished with a small tube.
Lu'nular a. Crescent-shaped.
Scap'ular a. Pertaining to the shoulder; an ecclesiastical vestment; a bandage for the shoulder; certain feathers of birds.
Suprascap'ular a. Situated above the shoulder-blade.
Interscap'ular a. Situated between the shoulder blades.
Manip'ular a. Pertaining to a maniple, or to manipulation.
Stip'ular a. Pertaining to, provided with, or resembling stipules.
Pop'ular a. Pertaining or suitable to the multitude; familiar; plain; prevalent; generally liked.
Cup'ular a. Like a cupule.
Spher'ular a. Pertaining to or resembling a spherule.
Spor'ular a. Pertaining to or like a sporule.
Gas'trular a. Pertaining to a gastrula, or to this stage.
In'sular a. Pertaining to or of the nature of an island or the inhabitants of an island; narrow-minded.
Penin'sular a. Pertaining to or like a peninsula.
Con'sular a. Pertaining to a consul.
Procon'sular a. Pertaining to or governed by a proconsul.
Pentacap'sular a. Having five capsules.
Tes'sular a. Isometric (of crystals).
Gross'ular a. Pertaining to the gooseberry. s. A variety of garnet.
Spat'ular a. Shaped like a spatula.
Capit'ular a. Pertaining to an ecclesiastical chapter; growing in small heads (of plants).
Tit'ular a. Existing in name only; nominal.
Vit'ular a. Pertaining to a calf or calving.
Fis'tular a. Hollow and cylindrical; of the nature of a fistula.
Pus'tular a. Like or affected with pustules.
Val'vular a. Pertaining to or resembling a valve.
Bival'vular a. Having two valves; double-shelled.
Unival'vular a. Having only one valve.
Multival'vular a. Having many valves.
O'vular a. Pertaining to or resembling an ovule.
Ner'vular a. Having or pertaining to nervules.
U'vular a. Pertaining to or resembling the uvula.
Con'dylar a. Condyloid.
Dac'tylar a. Pertaining to the fingers or toes.
Sty'lar a. Pertaining to a writing-style.
Asty'lar a. Without columns or pillars.
Monosty'lar a. Consisting of a single shaft or column.
Mar v.t. To injure, spoil, deface. s. A blemish.
Jac'amar s. A S. American insectivorous bird.
Pal'mar a. Pertaining to, or of the breadth of, the palm of the hand. s. A muscle or nerve of this.
Ful'mar s. A sea-bird allied to the petrels.
Dam'mar s. A kind of resin.
Gram'mar s. Art of or system of principles and rules for speaking or writing.
Cymar' s. A woman's light robe.
The'nar s. The palm or sole. a. Pertaining to either.
Di'nar s. A small silver coin of some Eastern countries.
Pol'linar a. Covered with pollen-like dust.
Minar' s. A beacon-tower.
Lam'inar a. Arranged in, consisting of, or having the form of laminæ.
Sem'inar s. A group of students taking an advanced course.
Pulvi'nar s. A cushion-like organ or part.
Knar s. A knot or protuberance in a tree.
Ul'nar a. Pertaining to the ulna.
Colum'nar a. Formed in or like columns.
Intercolum'nar a. Situated between columns.
Lacu'nar a. Lacunal. s. A ceiling having sunk panels.
Lu'nar a. Pertaining to, influenced by, or resembling the moon.
Sublu'nar a. Sublunary.
Semilu'nar a. Like a crescent or half-moon.
Nov'ilunar a. Pertaining to the new moon.

Interlu'nar a. Pertaining to the period of moon's invisibility.
Oar s. Long-bladed pole for rowing boats. v.i. and t. To row or impel by rowing.
Boar s. The male pig.
Hoar a. White or greyish-white, especially with age. s. Antiquity; rime, hoar-frost.
Roar v.i. To utter a deep cry, as a lion; to cry with a long, loud sound, make a confused din; to squall. v.t. To cry out aloud. s. The sound of roaring; a loud, continued sound.
Up'roar s. Disturbance; a noisy tumult, clamour.
Soar v.i. To mount on wings; to rise high. s. A towering flight.
Outsoar' v.t. To soar beyond or higher than.
Be'zoar s. A calculous concretion occurring in the stomach of certain ruminants.
Par s. State of equality; parity; equal value; (*slang*) a paragraph.
Spar s. A crystalline, non-metallic mineral; a long beam, mast; a boxing contest, a feigned blow. v.i. To box or pretend to; to wrangle.
Calc'spar s. Calcareous spar.
Feld'spar s. A crystalline mineral consisting of silica and alumina.
Reg'istrar s. One who registers; a keeper of records; a recorder.
Bur'sar s. The treasurer of a college; one in receipt of a bursary.
Macas'sar s. A hair-oil.
Antimacas'sar s. A removable covering for chair-backs, etc.
Hussar' s. A light cavalry soldier.
Tsar s. Title of the Russian Emperors.
Tar s. Liquid pitch; a sailor. v.t. To treat with tar.
Avatar' s. An incarnation of a Hindu deity; manifestation.
Nec'tar s. The drink of the gods; honey in flowers; any pleasant drink.
Or'bitar a. Orbital.
Scim'itar s. A short sword with curved blade.
Sitar' s. A guitar-like instrument of the Hindus.
Guitar' s. A six-stringed musical instrument played with the fingers.
Al'tar s. An elevated place for sacrifices; a communion-table.
Can'tar s. An Oriental weight (about 120 lbs.)
Plan'tar a. Pertaining to the sole of the foot.
Tar'tar s. A concretion deposited from wines; an incrustation on teeth; a native of Tartary, one of a Mongoloid race; an irritable or fiery person. a. Pertaining to Tartary or its peoples.
Mor'tar s. Vessel in which substances are pounded; short cannon for high-angle fire; bricklayer's cement.
Star s. A luminous celestial body; ornament, badge of honour, figure with radiating points; a brilliant person. v.t. To adorn or mark with stars; to distinguish. v.i. To shine as a star (of actors, etc.).
Lode'star s. The pole-star; an aim; guiding principle.
Day'star s. The morning star.
At'tar s. Essential oil.
Cot'tar s. A Scottish peasant paying rent by his labour.
Feu'ar s. A granter of land in feu; a holder of such land.
Jag'uar s. A carnivorous feline animal.
Bed'eguar s. A mossy growth on rose-trees.
Val'var a. Pertaining to or like a valve.
Vul'var a. Pertaining to or resembling the vulva.
In'var s. An alloy of nickel and steel.
Sam'ovar s. A copper tea-urn used in Russia.
War s. Open hostilities between nations, etc.; profession of arms; art of war; enmity. v.i. To make or carry on war; to compete.
Tul'war s. A curved Hindu cutlass.
Sowar' s. An Hindu trooper or mounted orderly.
Mag'yar s. One of the Mongolian race predominant in Hungary.
Boyar' s. A Russian noble or land-owner.
Laz'ar s. A leprous beggar.
Czar s. The Tsar.
Si'zar s. A student at Cambridge paying reduced fees.
Riz'zar s. A haddock dried in the sun.
-er suff. Denoting an agent or doer, an inhabitant of, one connected with, comparison or an action; also a termination of some frequentative verbs.
Ca'ber s. (*Scot.*) A heavy beam tossed as a sport.
Cal'aber s. (*Calabar*).
Dab'ber s. One who or that which dabs.
Jab'ber v.i. To chatter, talk indistinctly. v.t. To utter rapidly. s. Indistinct or nonsensical talk; gabble.
Blab'ber s. A tell-tale, tattler. v.i. To talk incoherently.
Slab'ber v.i. To slobber.
Grab'ber s. One who grabs.
Stab'ber s. One who stabs; a pointed implement.
Swab'ber (swob'-) s. One who uses a swab.
Bib'ber s. A tippler.
Dib'ber s. A dibble.
Fib'ber s. One who tells fibs.
Gib'ber v.i. To speak rapidly, incoherently, or excitedly. s. Gibberish.
Jib'ber s. A horse that jibs; (*slang*) a waverer.
Job'ber s. One who does small jobs; a dealer in stocks and shares; one who lets out horses and carriages; one who turns a public office, etc., to private advantage.
Blob'ber a. Thick and protruding (of lips).
Clob'ber s. (*Slang*) Clothes; impedimenta. v.t. To botch, patch up.
Slob'ber v.i. To let saliva run from the mouth; to be maudlin. v.t. To drivel over; to bungle. s. Drivel.
Rob'ber s. One who robs, a thief.
Lub'ber s. A heavy, clumsy fellow; a bad seaman.
Blub'ber s. The fat of whales and other marine mammals v.i. To weep noisily.
Slub'ber v.t. To do lazily or imperfectly; to daub.
Rub'ber s. One who or that which rubs; caoutchouc, a piece of this; a masseur; series of three games (or the best two out of three) at whist, etc.
Scrub'ber s. One who scrubs; a scrubbing implement or machine.
Drub'ber s. One who drubs another; a thick stick.
Grub'ber s. One who grubs; a tool for stirring the soil.

Imbi'ber s. One who imbibes; a drinker.
Gi'ber s. A scoffer, sneerer.
Zin'giber s. The genus of tropical plants including the ginger.
Li'ber s. The inner bark of exogens.
Bri'ber s. (*Bribe*).
Scri'ber s. A tool for marking lines.
Subscri'ber s. One who subscribes.
Descri'ber s. One good at description.
Prescri'ber s. One who prescribes.
Cir'cumscriber s. (*Circumscribe*).
Transcri'ber s. One who transcribes; a copyist.
Inscri'ber s. One who inscribes.
Proscri'ber s. One who proscribes.
Am'ber s. A pale yellow fossilized resin.
Cam'ber s. A convex bend in a surface.
Cham'ber s. An apartment; a closed space; a legislative assembly.
Clam'ber v.i. To climb with exertion.
Grisam'ber s. Ambergris.
Em'ber s. A live coal, smouldering remnant; a. Applied to certain days set aside by the Church for fasting.
Decem'ber s. The twelfth and last month of the year.
Mem'ber s. A limb or organ; one or part of an aggregate or body.
Remem'ber v.t. To recall to or bear in mind; to have in memory, think of; to tip.
Dismem'ber v.t. To divide limb from limb or part from part; to mutilate, sever.
Septem'ber s. The ninth month of the year.
Novem'ber s. The eleventh month of the year.
Lim'ber s. Detachable part of a gun-carriage; a gutter on board ship. a. Flexible; lissom. v.t. and i. To attach the limber to a gun-carriage.
Climb'er s. One who or that which climbs, especially a plant or bird.
Tim'ber s. Wood suitable for industrial use; trees. v.t. To furnish or make with timber.
Bomb'er s. Soldier, aeroplane, etc., that throws bombs.
Comb'er s. A long, curling wave.
Com'ber s. The wrasse.
Beach'comber s. A long, rolling wave; an Australasian vagrant.
Scom'ber s. The genus of fishes including the mackerel.
Um'ber s. A dark brown earthy pigment; a grayling; an umbrette.
Cum'ber v.t. To clog, hamper, impede; to distract. s. A hindrance.
Encum'ber v.t. To clog, load, impede.
Disencum'ber v.t. To free from hindrances.
Cu'cumber s. A trailing plant; its elongated fruit.
Lum'ber s. Things thrown aside as useless; refuse; sawn timber. v.t. To encumber, obstruct. v.i. To move cumbrously; to prepare timber for sale.
Clum'ber s. A variety of spaniel.
Plumb'er s. One who works in lead, repairs pipes, etc.
Slum'ber v.i. To doze, sleep lightly. s. Light sleep; repose.
Num'ber s. A unit or series of units; a numeral; a multitude; metrical arrangement of syllables; difference of verbal form expressing unity or plurality; part of a periodical. v.t. To count, put a number on, reach the number of.
Renum'ber v.t. To number again.
Outnum'ber v.t. To exceed in number.
So'ber a. Not intoxicated; habitually temperate; staid; dull. v.t. and i. To make or become sober or grave.
Octo'ber s. The tenth month of the year; beer brewed in October.
Bar'ber s. A hair-dresser. v.t. To shave, cut the hair, etc.
Ber'ber s. A native of N. Africa; the languages of these.
Absorb'er s. (*Absorb*).
Disturb'er s. One who disturbs; a brawler.
Daub'er s. (*Daub*).
Col'uber s. A genus of harmless snakes.
Tu'ber s. An underground fleshy stem; a knot or swelling.
Fa'cer s. One who faces; (*slang*) a disconcerting surprise.
Defa'cer s. One who defaces.
Pref'acer s. One who writes prefaces.
Sur'facer s. One who makes surfaces.
Pla'cer s. A gold-bearing deposit of sand or gravel.
Repla'cer s. One who or that which replaces.
Ma'cer s. A mace-bearer.
Amphim'acer s. A metrical foot of one short between two longs.
Grima'cer s. One who makes grimaces.
Men'acer s. One who threatens.
Pa'cer s. One who sets the pace in a race.
Spa'cer s. One who spaces.
Ra'cer s. Person, horse, machine, etc., that races.
Bra'cer s. A guard for the arm.
Embra'cer s. One who or that which embraces.
Tra'cer s. One who traces; a tracing tool.
Soc'cer s. (*Slang*) Association football.
Fleec'er s. One who fleeces, strips, or exacts.
Piec'er s. One who pieces; a patcher.
Di'cer s. A gambler with dice.
Of'ficer s. One holding an office; holder of a commission in the armed forces, etc. v.t. To furnish with officers.
Sac'rificer s. One who makes a sacrifice.
Chel'icer s. A claw-like antenna of spiders and scorpions.
Sli'cer s. One who or that which slices; a broad, flat knife.
Rejoi'cer s. One who rejoices.
Spi'cer s. One who seasons with or deals in spices.
Enti'cer s. One who entices.
Jus'ticer s. A jucticiary.
Ul'cer s. An open, suppurating sore, internal or external.
Can'cer s. A malignant tumour that eats away surrounding tissues.
Dan'cer s. One who dances, especially professionally.
Lan'cer s. A cavalryman armed with a lance.
Bal'ancer s. (*Balance*).
Geoman'cer s. One skilled in geomancy.
Roman'cer s. One who romances or writes romances.
Nec'romancer s. A wizard, magician.
Count'enancer s. One who countenances or favours something.
Remem'brancer s. A memento; the senior master of the Supreme Court.
Encum'brancer s. One who holds a charge on another's property.
Pran'cer s. An animal that prances.
Advan'cer s. (*Advance*); a money-lender.
Convey'ancer s. A lawyer who draws up conveyances.
Fen'cer s. One who practises or teaches fencing; a fence builder; a horse good at leaping.
Intel'ligencer s. A messenger; a spy.

Si'lencer s. One who or that which silences, especially an appliance on a motor-car, etc.
Spen'cer s. A short, sleeved jacket; a fore-and-aft sail.
Rev'erencer s. One who reverences.
Win'cer s. One who winces.
Boun'cer s. (*Bounce*).
Renoun'cer s. One who renounces.
Pronoun'cer s. One good at pronouncing; one who pronounces.
Gro'cer s. A dealer in tea, sugar, household articles, etc.
Green'grocer s. A seller of vegetables and fruit.
Pier'cer s. One who pierces; an implement for piercing.
Mer'cer s. A dealer in silks, linens, woollens, etc.
For'cer s. One who or that which forces or drives.
Defor'cer s. A deforciant.
Divor'cer s. One who procures a divorce.
Sau'cer s. A shallow dish for a cup.
Tradu'cer s. A calumniator.
Addu'cer s. (*Adduce*).
Sedu'cer s. One who seduces.
Produ'cer s. One who produces.
Introdu'cer s. One who introduces.
Head'er s. A dive head-foremost; a brick with its end outwards from the wall.
Lead'er s. One who leads; a chief; an editorial article.
Ring'leader s. A leader of persons engaged in wrongdoing.
Plead'er s. One who pleads, an advocate.
Interplead'er s. A suit to decide to which of two parties payment from a third is due.
Knead'er s. One who kneads; a machine for this.
Read'er s. One who reads, especially aloud and in church; a corrector of the press; a University lecturer; a reading-book.
Thread'er s. One who or that which threads.
Spread'er s. One who or that which spreads.
Tread'er s. (*Tread*).
Home'steader s. One in occupation of a homestead.
Promena'der s. One who promenades.
Serena'der s. One who serenades.
Gascona'der s. A braggart.
Load'er s. One who or that which loads.
Breech-load'er s. A gun loaded at the breech.
Masquerad'er s. One who masquerades; a pretender.
For'rader a. and adv. (*Slang*) Forward, in advance.
Tra'der s. Person or vessel engaged in trade; a tradesman.
Crusa'der s. One who engages in a crusade.
Persua'der s. One who or that which persuades.
Dissua'der s. One who advises against.
Inva'der s. One who invades; a hostile intruder.
Wa'der s. One who wades; a wading-bird; a high, waterproof boot.
Ad'der s. The common viper; an adding machine.
Gad'der s. One who rambles or spends time idly.
Lad'der s. A frame with rungs for climbing; means of rising.
Blad'der s. A membranous sac in animal bodies; a blister.
Mad'der s. A shrubby, climbing plant; dye obtained from this.
Bed'der s. A Cambridge charwoman; a plant for bedding out.
Shed'der s. One who sheds or causes to flow out.
Ted'der s. One who teds.
Bid'der s. (*Bid*).
Forbid'der s. One who forbids.
Kid'der s. (*Slang*) A humbug, hoaxer.
Dod'der s. A parasitic twining plant. v.i. To totter; to be infirm in body or mind.
Fod'der s. Dry food stored up for cattle. v.t. to supply with fodder.
Plod'der s. A laborious traveller or worker.
Nod'der s. One who nods.
Ud'der s. Milk-secreting organ of cows, etc.
Shud'der v.i. To tremble with fear, aversion, cold, etc. s. A sudden trembling or shiver.
Rud'der s. Instrument by which a vessel is steered.
Seced'er s. One who secedes.
Interced'er s. One who intercedes; a mediator.
Succeed'er s. A successor; one who succeeds.
Proceed'er s. One who proceeds.
Feed'er s. One who fattens cattle or supplies food; an eater; a bib; an affluent; an encourager or supplier.
Speed'er s. One who or that which speeds.
Breed'er s. (*Breed*).
Seed'er s. Instrument for planting seeds, removing seeds from fruit, etc.
Weed'er s. One who weeds; a weeding-tool.
Lieder (lēd'er) s. German ballads.
Raid'er s. One who raids.
Upbraid'er s. One who upbraids.
Abi'der s. (*Abide*).
Ci'der s. The fermented juice of apples.
Deci'der s. One who or that which decides.
Ei'der s. A duck of Arctic seas.
Hi'der s. One who hides.
Gli'der s. One who or that which glides; a flying machine without an engine.
Sli'der s. One who or that which slides.
Backsli'der s. (*Backslide*).
Sni'der s. An early form of breach-loading rifle.
Moi'der v.t. To confuse, muddle. v.i. To talk incoherently.
Embroi'der v.t. To adorn with figures, patterns, etc., in needlework; to add embellishments to a story, etc.
Voi'der s. One who or that which empties or annuls.
Spi'der s. A web-spinning, insect-like arachnid; a long-legged or spider-like object.
Ri'der s. One who rides; an addendum, a corollary; a problem for solving.
Deri'der s. One who derides or scoffs at anything.
Out'rider s. One on horseback attending a carriage.
Si'der s. One who takes sides.
Resi'der s. A dweller.
Presi'der s. One who presides.
Insi'der s. One within; one in the secret, etc.
Consid'er v.t. To fix the mind on; to have respect to; to regard to be. v.i. To think seriously, ponder.
Reconsid'er v.t. To review; to take up for renewed consideration.
Outsi'der s. One not belonging to the party, set, etc.
Divid'er s. One who or that which divides; a pair of compasses.
Provi'der s. One who provides.
Al'der s. A common English tree,

Scald'er s. One who or that which scalds.
Spal'der s. One who spalls or chips stone, etc.
El'der a. Older; prior. s. A senior, predecessor; a layman having certain ecclesiastical authority; a small shrub with white flowers and dark red berries.
Geld'er s. One who gelds.
Field'er s. One who fields at cricket, etc.
Wield'er s. One who wields.
Yield'er s. One who yields.
Weld'er s. One who welds; tool for welding.
Buil'der s. (*Build*).
Guil'der s. An obsolete Dutch coin.
Bewil'der v.t. To perplex, confuse, muddle.
Scold'er s. One who scolds.
Fold'er s. One who folds; an instrument for folding paper; a four-page handbill.
Scaf'folder s. One who erects scaffolds.
Hold'er s. One who or that which holds or contains; one who possesses; a tenant.
Behold'er s. (*Behold*).
Free'holder s. One who has a freehold.
Share'holder s. One owning a share in a joint-stock company.
Lease'holder s. One holding a lease.
House'holder s. The occupier of a house.
Withhold'er s. One who withholds.
Uphold'er s. A supporter, defender.
Stadt'holder s. A chief magistrate of the Netherland United Provinces.
Copy'holder s. One holding land by copyhold.
Pol'der s. Tract of reclaimed land below sea- or river-level.
Sol'der (*also* **saw'der, sod'der**). s. A fusible alloy for uniting metals. v.t. To unite with this.
Boul'der s. A large rounded stone.
Shoul'der s. Joint by which or part where the arm or fore-leg is joined to the body; a protuberance resembling this; a support. v.t. To push with or take upon the shoulder. v.i. To push forward.
Moul'der v.i. To crumble, turn to dust, waste away gradually. s. One who moulds.
Smoul'der (smōl'-) v.i. To burn in a smothered or flameless way; to exist in a suppressed state. s. A smouldering state.
African'der s. One born in S. Africa of white parents.
Dan'der v.i. To wander about aimlessly. s. (*Slang*) Temper, anger.
Olean'der s. An evergreen shrub bearing clusters of red or white flowers.
Mean'der v.i. To wind about, be intricate. s. A winding course.
Gan'der s. The male of the goose; a noodle.
Back-hand'er s. A blow with the back of the hand; an indirect attack.
Corian'der s. A plant having aromatic seeds.
Ice'lander s. A native of Iceland.
High'lander s. A native of the Scottish Highlands.
Philan'der v.i. To flirt.
Hol'lander s. A Dutchman.
In'lander s. One who lives inland.
Col'ander s. A strainer for vegetables.
Up'lander s. A dweller in the uplands.
Slan'der s. A malicious or false report; oral defamation. v.t. To injure thus, to calumniate, defame.
Isl'ander s. A dweller on an island.
Out'lander s. A foreigner, alien.
Low'lander s. A native of the Lowlands of Scotland.
Calaman'der s. A hard, beautifully marked Indian wood.
Salaman'der s. A lizard-like amphibian; a mythical animal or genie formerly supposed to live in fire.
Deman'der s. A demandant.
Comman'der s. One in authority; a general; member of certain knightly orders.
Poman'der s. A perfumed ball carried in a perforated box; the box itself.
German'der s. A plant formerly used in medicine; the speedwell.
Gerryman'der v.i. To divide a district into electoral divisions unfairly; to manipulate for selfish ends.
Pan'der v.i. To minister to the lust or passion of. s. One who does this.
Brand'er s. (*Brand*).
Goosan'der s. A swimming-bird, the merganser.
By'stander s. An onlooker.
Squan'der v.t. To spend wastefully; to dissipate.
Wand'er (wŏnd'-) v.i. To rove, deviate, go astray; to be delirious.
Hexan'der s. A plant having six stamens.
Ben'der s. (*Slang*) A sixpenny-piece.
Descend'er s. One who descends.
Fen'der s. A guard before a fire; a protection for the sides of a ship; that which defends.
Defend'er s. One who defends; a protector, vindicator.
Offend'er s. One who offends; a transgression; a trespasser.
Gen'der s. A sex; distinction of sex in words.
Engen'der v.t. To form in embryo; to beget, generate.
Reprehend'er s. One who reprehends, a chider.
Lend'er s. One who lends.
Cal'ender s. A machine for making cloth or paper glossy. v.t. To glaze with a calender.
Cull'ender s. A colander.
Slen'der a. Long and thin; slim; fragile.
Mend'er s. One who mends.
Recommend'er s. One who recommends.
Spend'er s. One who spends.
Suspend'er s. An attachment for holding up stockings, etc.
Ren'der v.t. To give in return, pay back, surrender; to present, afford; to translate; to clarify; to plaster roughly. s. A first coat of plaster; one who rends.
Surren'der v.t. To relinquish, deliver up or yield to another. v.i. To yield. s. Act of surrendering; a yielding.
Send'er s. One who sends.
Ten'der a. Sensitive; delicate; easily pained. v.t. To offer. s. One who tends; an offer; small vessel or vehicle attending another with supplies, etc.
Pretend'er s. One who pretends; one who makes false claim to.
Contend'er s. One who contends, an antagonist.
Lav'ender s. A sweet-scented plant; its colour, fragrance, or oil.
Prov'ender s. Dry food for beasts.
Remain'der s. That which remains, residue; a limited interest in an estate; unsold copies of a book jobbed off. a. Left over.
Detain'der s. A writ of detainer.
Attain'der s. Extinction of civil rights.
Bind'er s. One who or that which binds.
Cin'der s. A burnt coal, ember; slag.

Find'er s. One who finds; a sighting apparatus attached to a camera, microscope, etc.
Path'finder s. An explorer, pioneer.
Hind'er a. Pertaining to or at the back.
Hin'der v.t. To obstruct, impede, retard. v.i. To cause a hindrance.
Cyl'inder s. A circular body of uniform diameter; the chamber in which a piston works.
Remind'er s. That which or one who reminds.
Join'der s. The coupling of two defendants or things in one lawsuit.
Rejoin'der s. A reply, retort; answer of a defendant.
Surrejoin'der s. Plaintiff's reply to defendant's rejoinder.
Misjoin'der s. Improper writing of parties in an action, etc.
Grind'er s. One who grinds; a grinding-machine.
Tin'der s. A dry, inflammable substance used for kindling fire.
Wind'er s. One who winds; a winding-machine.
Sec'onder s. A supporter; one who seconds.
Abscon'der s. (*Abscond*).
Pon'der v.t. To weigh in the mind, consider. v.i. To deliberate.
Won'der (wun'-) s. A remarkable event, person, thing, etc.; feeling excited by such, astonishment. v.i. To marvel; to entertain doubt, curiosity, etc.
Yon'der a. Being at a distance; that or those there. adv. At a distance but within view.
Un'der prep. Subordinate to; less than; beneath. adv. In a lower condition. a. Subject; subordinate; lower.
Laun'der v.t. To wash and get up linen.
Maun'der v.i. To mutter, grumble indistinctly.
Dun'der s. The dregs of cane-juice (used in rum-distilling).
Thun'der s. Noise following lightning-flash. v.i. To emit this sound, make a loud noise. v.t. To utter with violence.
Blun'der s. A bad mistake. v.i. To err stupidly, to stumble. v.t. To confound.
Plun'der v.t. To pillage, rob, despoil. s. Robbery, pillage, spoil.
Boun'der s. An unmannered person.
Brass'bounder s. A ship's officer in the merchant service.
Foun'der s. One who casts metal; one who originates, institutes, or endows something. v.i. To fill with water and sink; to miscarry; to go lame (of horses).
Confoun'der s. (*Confound*).
Floun'der s. A flat-fish; a stumbling effort. v.i. To struggle or stumble violently or with difficulty; to blunder.
Pound'er s. One who pounds; implement for pounding; thing of specified number of pounds.
Compound'er s. One who compounds.
Propound'er s. One who propounds.
Expound'er s. One who expounds, an expositor.
Round'er s. One who or a tool that rounds; a run in rounders.
Sound'er s. One who or that which sounds.
Wound'er (woond'-) s. One who or that which wounds.
Sun'der v.t. To disunite, sever, divide.
Asun'der adv. Apart; in a divided state.
Forbo'der s. One who predicts (especially evil).
Explo'der s. One who or that which explodes.
Tab'arder s. One who wears a tabard.
Card'er s. One who cards wool; a species of thistle.
Regard'er s. One who regards.
Lar'der s. Room where provisions are kept.
Board'er s. One who boards in another's house; one who boards a ship in action.
Hoard'er s. One who hoards.
Retard'er s. One who or that which retards.
Guard'er s. One who guards or protects.
Ward'er (wŏrd'-) s. A jailer, guard.
Reward'er s. One who rewards.
For'warder s. One who helps or sends forward; a promoter. adv. Forward, in advance, "forrader."
Gird'er s. A beam supported at both ends for supporting a superstructure.
Or'der s. Method; rule; command; class; public tranquillity; a religious fraternity. v.t. To place in order, regulate, adjust; to command. v.i. To give orders.
Bor'der s. An outer edge; a boundary, limit. v.t. To provide with a border. v.i. To be contiguous, to approach near.
Accor'der s. (*Accord*).
Recor'der s. One who records; a judicial officer; a kind of flute; a registering apparatus.
Disor'der s. Want of order; disturbance of the peace; a malady. v.t. To disturb the order of, to throw into confusion; to derange.
Mur'der s. Homicide with malice aforethought. v.t. To slay a human being thus, to assassinate; to mangle, ruin.
Maraud'er s. A roving plunderer.
Defraud'er s. (*Defraud*).
Delu'der s. One who deludes.
Collu'der s. (*Collude*).
Obtrud'er s. One who or that which obtrudes.
Intrud'er s. One who intrudes.
Saw'der s. Blarney, flattery.
Chow'der s. A stew of fish, pork, biscuits, etc. v.t. To make into a chowder.
Pow'der s. A dry substance in particles; dust; gunpowder. v.t. To reduce to fine particles; to sprinkle or treat with powder. v.i. To fall to dust, to use powder.
Bepow'der v.t. To cover with powder.
Gun'powder s. An explosive mixture of saltpetre, sulphur, and carbon.
Crowd'er s. A player on the crowd.
-eer suff. Denoting an agent, person concerned, etc.
E'er adv. Ever.
Beer s. A fermented alcholic liquor made from malted grain and flavoured with hops, etc.
Deer s. A ruminant quadruped of the genus *Cervus*.
Kill'deer s. A N. American plover, the killdee.
Commandeer' v.t. To seize for military or official purposes.
Rein'deer (rān'-) s. A partly domesticated deer of N. latitudes.
Cheer s. Disposition; good fare; state of joy; applause; facial expression. v.t. To applaud, encourage. v.i. To grow cheerful, utter cheers.
Mynheer' s. A Dutchman.

Sheer a. Pure; unmingled; mere; perpendicular. adv. Outright; vertically. v.i. To deviate from a course; to go aside or away. s. Upward curvature of a vessel at stem or stern; a swerving course.
Tabasheer' s. A medicinal concretion found in bamboo joints.
Fetisheer' s. A sorcerer.
Jeer v.i. To scoff, flout. v.t. To make a mock of; to deride.
Leer s. A sidelong look of malice, triumph, or lust. v.i. To look with a leer.
Chant'icleer s. The domestic cock.
Cameleer' s. A camel-driver.
Fleer v.t. and i. To deride, mock, leer; to gibe or sneer at. s. Mockery, derision.
Bandoleer' s. (*Bandolier*).
Pistoleer' s. An expert with the pistol.
Ameer' s. (*Amir*).
Emeer' s. Emir.
Ne'er adv. Never.
Buccaneer' s. A pirate. v.i. To act as a pirate.
Caravaneer' s. One in charge of or attached to a caravan.
Whene'er' (-air') adv. Whenever.
Veneer' s. A thin facing of superior wood. v.t. To overlay with this; to put a gloss on.
Mountaineer' s. One who dwells among or who climbs mountains.
Carbineer' s. A soldier armed with a carbine.
Muffineer' s. A dish for hot muffins; a sugar-castor.
Engineer' s. One skilled in engineering; one in charge of an engine. v.t. To carry out engineering; to contrive; to manage.
Domineer' v.i. To rule arbitrarily or with insolence.
Mutineer' s. One who mutinies. v.i. To mutiny.
Scrutineer' s. An examiner of votes at an election.
Pioneer' s. One preparing the way for others. v.t. To go before and prepare the way.
Specksioneer' s. Chief harpooner on a whaler.
Electioneer' v.i. To work for a candidate at an election.
Auctioneer' s. The salesman at or manager of an auction.
Timoneer' s. A helmsman.
Cannoneer' s. An artilleryman.
Sneer v.i. To express contempt by a look; to scoff. s. A look of derision, disdain, etc.; a jibe.
Whoe'er' (hoo-air') pron. Whoever.
Whosoe'er' pron. Whosoever.
Peer s. An equal, associate; a nobleman. v.i. To look narrowly or curiously; to pry, peep.
Compeer' s. An equal, associate.
Career' s. A race; course of action; way of living, profession. v.i. To move rapidly.
Where'er (-air') adv. Wherever.
Seer s. One who sees or foresees; a prophet.
Mah'seer s. A large E. Indian river-fish.
O'verseer s. A superintendent, supervisor.
Whate'er' (-air') pron. Whatever.
Privateer' s. A private vessel licensed for acts of war. v.t. To cruise or war in a privateer.
Targeteer' s. A soldier armed with a target.
Crocheteer' s. A faddy person.
Musketeer' s. A soldier armed with a musket.
Pamphleteer' s. A writer of pamphlets; a hack.
Muleteer' s. A mule-driver.
Sonneteer' s. A writer of sonnets. v.i. To compose sonnets.
Garreteer' s. One who lives in a garret.
Profiteer' v.i. To make undue profits, especially in time of emergency. s. One who does this.
Pulpiteer' s. A preacher. v.i. To preachify (*derisive*).
Volunteer' s. One who serves by choice. a. Entering into service freely; composed of volunteers. v.t. To offer voluntarily. v.i. To enter into service without compulsion.
Charioteer' s. The driver of a chariot.
Steer v.t. and i. To guide and govern, as a vessel, aeroplane, etc.; to direct one's course. s. A bullock.
Gazetteer' s. A geographical dictionary; a writer in a gazette.
Queer a. Odd, droll; strange.
Veer v.i. To turn aside or about.
Cha'fer s. A beetle, cockchafer.
Cock'chafer s. A large brown beetle.
Loaf'er s. A lounger, idler.
Wa'fer s. A thin cake, disk, etc.; the Eucharistic bread (R.C.). v.t. To seal with a wafer.
Defer' v.t. To put off, postpone; to submit. v.i. To delay; to yield to the opinion of another.
Reef'er s. One who reefs; a symmetrical double knot; a double-breasted jacket.
Refer' v.t. To trace back, attribute; to assign to. v.i. To have recourse; to allude; to appeal; to apply.
Prefer' v.t. To choose rather; to exalt, esteem more than another.
Gaf'fer s. An aged man, an old rustic.
Chaf'fer v.i. To haggle.
Quaf'fer s. One who quaffs; a drinker.
Zaf'fer s. An impure oxide of cobalt.
Dif'fer v.i. To be at variance; to disagree, to quarrel.
Of'fer v.t. To present for acceptance or rejection; to attempt; to bid; tender. v.i. To present itself; to declare a willingness. s. Act of offering, bidding, etc.; sum bid; proposal.
Cof'fer s. A chest for valuables; a sunken panel.
Scof'fer s. One who scoffs.
Gof'fer v.t. To plait or flute; to crimp. s. A wavy edging; iron with which this is produced.
Prof'fer v.t. To offer for acceptance. s. Offer made.
Chauf'fer s. A portable stove.
Buf'fer s. A contrivance for deadening concussion.
Duf'fer s. A stupid or useless fellow; anything counterfeit.
Huf'fer s. A blusterer, braggart.
Bluf'fer s. (*Bluff*).
Snuf'fer s. A snuff-taker.
Puf'fer s. One who puffs; an intentionally exaggerating commender.
Suf'fer v.t. To undergo, endure with pain; to permit. v.i. To undergo pain, loss, punishment, etc.

Stuf'fer s. One who stuffs, especially skins of animals.
Lu'cifer s. The morning star; Satan; a match ignitible by striking.
Cru'cifer s. A cross-bearer; one of the Cruciferæ.
Heif'er s. A young cow that has not calved.
Fif'er s. One who plays a fife.
Lif'er s. (*Slang*) A sentence to imprisonment for life.
Chel'ifer s. A genus of spiders.
Umbel'lifer s. An umbelliferous plant.
Mam'mifer s. A mammal.
Vaccin'ifer s. Animal supplying vaccine.
Foramin'ifer s. One of a division of minute hard-shelled marine protozoa.
Con'ifer s. A cone-bearing tree.
Son'ifer s. An instrument for assisting the deaf to hear.
Secur'ifer s. A sand-fly.
Thur'ifer s. One who carries a thurible.
Ro'tifer s. A minute aquatic animalcule.
Pil'fer v.i. and t. To practise or acquire by petty theft.
Golf'er s. A golf-player.
Cham'fer s. A groove, slope, or bevel. v.t. To cut in a slope; to flute, groove.
Infer' v.t. To deduce, conclude, imply. v.i. To draw inferences.
Confer' v.t. To bestow, award. v.i. To consult together, discuss seriously.
Go'fer s. A kind of biscuit.
Roof'er s. One who repairs or puts on roofs.
Wa'terproofer s. One who makes cloth, etc., waterproof.
Trans'fer s. Act of transferring, thing transferred; conveyance of right, etc.
Transfer' v.t. To make over, to convey from one place or person to another.
Laa'ger s. A defensive encampment in S. Africa.
Soc'ager s. One who held land by socage.
Bond'ager s. (*Scot.*) A cotter rendering service for his cottage.
Ea'ger a. Ardent, earnest, keen; impetuous.
La'ger s. A light German beer.
Pill'ager s. A plunderer, ravager.
Vill'ager s. s. A dweller in a village.
Rum'mager s. One who rummages.
Scrum'mager s. A forward in Rugby football.
Hom'ager s. One who does homage or who holds a fee by this.
Man'ager s. One who manages or controls; a good economist.
Misman'ager s. One who manages ill.
Tan'ager s. A brilliant S. American finch.
On'ager s. The Asiatic wild ass.
Dispar'ager s. One who disparages.
For'ager s. One who forages.
Encour'ager s. One who encourages.
Vin'tager s. A grape-gatherer.
Front'ager s. The owner of a frontage.
Sta'ger s. One of long experience.
Cot'tager s. One who lives in a cottage.
Rav'ager s. One who despoils or ravages.
Wag'er s. Something staked or hazarded. v.t. and i. To stake, bet.
Dow'ager s. A widow in possession of a dower.
Voy'ager s. A traveller, especially by sea.
Badg'er s. A burrowing, nocturnal quadruped. v.t. To pester, worry.
Cadg'er s. (*Cadge*).
Hedg'er s. One who plants or trims hedges.
Ledg'er s. An account-book; a large, flat stone; a horizontal scaffold-pole; an anchored fishing-line.
Pledg'er s. One who pledges.
Dredg'er s. One who dredges; a dredging machine or vessel; a box with perforated lid for sprinkling.
Abridg'er s. (*Abridge*).
Bodg'er s. (*Bodge*).
Codg'er s. An odd or miserly old man.
Dodg'er s. One who dodges, a trickster.
Lodg'er s. One lodging in another's house.
Judg'er s. One who judges.
Drudg'er s. A drudge.
Grudg'er s. One who grudges.
Besieg'er s. (*Besiege*).
Col'leger s. A foundation scholar at Eton.
In'teger s. A whole number; the whole of anything.
Ag'ger s. The rampart of an ancient Roman camp.
Dag'ger s. A short stabbing weapon; a printer's reference mark (†).
Gag'ger s. An actor who gags.
Jag'ger s. One who or that which jags.
Lag'ger s. One who lags; a laggard.
Nag'ger s. One who nags.
Drag'ger s. One who or that which drags.
Tag'ger s. One who tags.
Stag'ger v.i. To reel, totter; to hesitate, waver. v.t. To cause to reel, etc.; to astonish. s. A staggering movement.
Swag'ger v.i. To behave in a self-confident, blustering, or defiant way. s. This kind of gait or behaviour. a. Smart, fashionable, tip-top.
Egg'er s. One who gathers eggs.
Dig'ger s. One who digs; a gold-miner; (*slang*) a spade at cards, etc.
Jig'ger s. One who jigs; a contrivance for separating ore, etc.; a sieve; a potter's wheel; an iron golf-club; a cue-rest at billiards; the chigoe.
Nig'ger s. A negro; any black native.
Snig'ger v.i. To laugh in a suppressed way. s. A silly or half-suppressed laugh.
Rig'ger s. One who rigs; a cylindrical pulley or drum.
Trig'ger s. Catch by which a gun is fired.
Out'rigger s. A projection at the side of a boat for a rowlock; a racing boat with these.
Dog'ger s. A Dutch fishing-vessel.
Pet'tifogger s. A mean, second-rate, or quibbling lawyer.
Whole-hog'ger s. A thorough-going person; one prepared to "go the whole hog."
Log'ger s. A lumber-man.
Slog'ger s. A hard hitter.
Hum'bugger s. A deceiver, hoaxer.
Lug'ger s. A small two- or three-masted vessel.
Mug'ger s. The Indian crocodile.
Hug'ger-mug'ger s. Privacy, secrecy. a. Clandestine; confused; mean. v.i. To muddle. v.t. To hush up.
Nug'ger s. A broad, flat-bottomed Nile boat.
Rug'ger s. (*Slang*) Rugby football.
Tug'ger s. (*Tug*).
Obli'ger s. One who obliges.
Disobli'ger s. One who disobliges.
Ar'miger s. One entitled to use heraldic arms.
Ti'ger s. A large carnivorous feline mammal; a page-boy.
Bul'ger s. (*Bulge*).
Indul'ger s. One who indulges in.
Divul'ger s. One who divulges.
Ang'er s. Wrath, resentment; passion excited by real or fancied injury. v.t. To irritate, make angry.
Bang'er s. (*Bang*).
Dan'ger s. Hazard, peril, exposure to injury.

Endan'ger v.t. To expose to danger, to risk.
Gang'er s. A labourers' overseer.
Dop'pel-ganger s. An apparition of a living person; a wraith.
Hang'er s. One who or that which hangs; a short broadsword; a double curve.
Chan'ger s. (*Change*).
Exchan'ger s. One who changes foreign monies.
Phalan'ger s. A small marsupial; a flying-squirrel.
Man'ger s. Food-trough for cattle, etc.
Ran'ger s. A rover; superintendent of a park.
Bush'ranger s. An Australian highwayman.
Stran'ger s. One unknown to another; a guest; a foreigner.
Chal'lenger s. (*Challenge*).
Pas'senger s. A traveller, especially by a public conveyance; a wayfarer.
Mess'enger s. Bearer of a message; an emissary.
Aven'ger s. (*Avenge*).
Scav'enger s. A street-cleaner; a creature that feeds on carrion.
Reven'ger s. One who revenges.
Har'binger s. A forerunner, precursor. v.t. To precede; to announce the approach of.
Fin'ger s. One of the five extremities of the hand. v.t. To handle, touch lightly; to pilfer. v.i. To play a keyed instrument well.
Fore'finger s. The finger next the thumb.
Wharf'inger s. Proprietor or overseer of a wharf.
Gin'ger s. A tropical root used in cookery and medicine; (*slang*) go, dash, spiciness. v.t. To flavour with ginger; (*slang*) to inspirit.
Whing'er s. A short sword, whingar.
Lin'ger v.i. To hesitate, loiter, saunter.
Malin'ger v.i. To feign illness.
Sling'er s. One who slings; a sling.
Ring'er s. One who rings, especially chimes.
Crin'ger s. One who cringes.
Infrin'ger s. One who infringes.
Spring'er s. One who or that which springs; a spaniel, etc., that rouses game; bottom stone of an arch.
Klip'springer s. A small African antelope.
Der'ringer s. A short-barrelled, large-bored pistol.
Por'ringer s. A small bowl for soup, etc.
String'er s. One who strings; timber receiving ends of stairs in staircase.
Wring'er s. One who wrings; a wringing-machine.
Sing'er s. One who sings, especially professionally.
Min'nesinger s. A mediæval German lyric poet.
Tin'ger s. One who or that which tinges.
Sting'er s. One who or that which stings.
Swing'er s. (*Swing*).
Cong'er s. A large species of sea-eel.
Prolong'er s. One who or that which prolongs.
Mon'ger (mŭng'-) s. (*As suff.*) A dealer in.
Scare'monger s. One who foments panic.
Whore'monger s. A fornicator.
Cheese'monger s. One who deals in cheese.
Fish'monger s. A dealer in fish.
I'ronmonger s. A dealer in hardware.
Cos'termonger s. A coster.
News'monger s. One who deals in or disseminates news.
Spong'er (spŭnj'-) s. A hanger-on, parasitical dependent.
Wrong'er s. One who wrongs another.
Hung'er s. Sensation due to lack of food; craving for food; eager desire. v.i. To crave, especially for food.
Plun'ger s. One who or that which plunges; the piston of a pump; a spendthrift.
Loun'ger s. One who lounges; an idler.
Scroun'ger s. (*Slang*) A cadger, petty thief.
-loger suff. Denoting one versed in or practising some science.
Campanol'oger s. (*Campanology*).
Chronol'oger s. A chronologist.
Horol'oger s. One skilled in horology; a maker of time-pieces.
Astrol'oger s. (*Astrology*).
Charg'er s. A war-horse; a large dish; one who charges.
Surcharg'er s. One who surcharges.
Discharg'er s. Apparatus for unloading an electric battery.
Mer'ger s. The merging of an estate, etc., in another.
Ver'ger s. Officer carrying a verge, mace-bearer; a church usher.
For'ger s. One guilty of forgery; one who forges.
Ur'ger s. One who urges.
Scour'ger s. One who scourges, afflicts, or harasses.
Pur'ger s. One who or that which purges.
Au'ger s. A large boring tool.
Gau'ger s. One who gauges, especially casks, etc., for Excise purposes.
Her pron. Poss. and obj. of "she."
Impeach'er s. One who impeaches.
Preach'er s. One who preaches.
Teach'er s. One who teaches; a schoolmaster or mistress.
Stom'acher (stŭm'-) s. Ornamental part of a woman's dress (eighteenth century).
Poach'er s. One who poaches or trespasses in search of game.
Encroach'er s. One who encroaches.
Reproach'er s. One who reproaches.
Screech'er s. One who or that which screeches.
Lech'er s. One given to lewdness.
Mich'er s. One who plays truant or hides away.
Bel'cher s. A blue and white spotted handkerchief.
Squelch'er s. A crushing retort; a squelch.
Fil'cher s. A pickpocket, petty thief.
Ranch'er s. One employed on or owning a ranch.
Stanch'er s. One who or that which stanches.
Bench'er s. A senior member of one of the Inns of Court.
Drench'er s. One who or that which drenches; a heavy downpour; an implement for assisting in dosing horses, etc.
Trench'er s. A large wooden platter; one who cuts trenches.
Quench'er s. That which quenches; (*slang*) a long drink.
Clinch'er s. One who or that which clinches; a decisive argument.
Flinch'er s. One who flinches.
Pinch'er s. One who or that which pinches.
Munch'er s. One who munches.
Punch'er s. One who or that which punches; an American cowboy.
Clo'cher s. A bell-tower.
Ar'cher s. One who uses a bow and arrow.
Search'er s. One who searches.
Research'er s. One who researches.
March'er s. One who marches; a warden or inhabitant of the marches.
Starch'er s. One who starches; a machine for this.
Perch'er s. One who or that which perches; a perching bird.

Scorch'er s. One who or that which scorches; (*slang*) a staggering yarn, etc.
Lurch'er s. A cross-bred hound.
Catch'er s. (*Catch*).
Thatch'er s. One who roofs houses with thatch.
Snatch'er s. One who snatches.
Patch'er s. One who patches.
Scratch'er s. One who or that which scratches, especially a bird.
Watch'er s. One who watches.
Etch'er s. One who etches.
Fetch'er s. One who fetches.
Sketch'er s. One who sketches.
Fletch'er s. A maker of bows and arrows.
Stretch'er s. One who or that which stretches; a litter for carrying a person.
Ditch'er s. One who digs ditches.
Snitch'er s. (*Slang*) A common informer.
Pitch'er s. One who pitches (especially the ball at baseball); a vessel with a spout; a cup-like portion of certain leaves.
Stitch'er s. One who sews.
Twitch'er s. (*Twitch*).
Botch'er s. (*Botch*).
Butch'er s. One who slaughters animals for food, a meat-seller; one delighting in bloody deeds. v.t. To slaughter for food or cruelly for the pleasure of it; to hack and mangle.
Debauch'er s. A corrupter, seducer.
Mouch'er (mooch'-) s. A loafer, skulker.
Touch'er s. One who or that which touches; a narrow shave.
Vouch'er s. One who vouches; a confirmatory document.
Inveigh'er s. A railer.
Weigh'er s. One who weighs; a weighing-machine.
Sigh'er (sī'-) s. One who sighs.
Drogh'er s. A slow-sailing coaster used in the W. Indies.
Bur'gher s. An inhabitant of a burgh or town.
Laugh'er s. One who laughs.
Plough'er s. A ploughman.
-grapher suff. Forming agent nouns corresponding to nouns in *-graph* and *-graphy*.
Teleg'rapher s. A telegraphist.
Callig'rapher s. (*Calligraphy*).
Lexicog'rapher s. The compiler of a dictionary.
Chalcog'rapher s. (*Chalcography*).
Choreog'rapher s. Composer or designer of a ballet; a dancing-master.
Logog'rapher s. An ancient Greek prose-writer.
Chromo-lithog'rapher s. (*Chromolithograph*).
Biog'rapher s. (*Biography*).
Auto-biog'rapher s. (*Autobiography*).
Bibliog'rapher s. (*Bibliography*).
Historio-g'rapher s. An official historian; writer of a history of a special period, etc.
Crystal-log'rapher s. (*Crystallography*).
Demog'rapher s. A student of or worker in demography.
Cosmog'rapher s. One versed in cosmography.
Ethnog'rapher s. One versed in ethnography.
Chronog'rapher s. A chronicler.
Chirog'rapher s. An expert in writing; a former legal officer who engrossed fines.
Chorog'rapher s. (*Chorography*).
Photog'rapher s. One who takes photographs.
Cryptog'rapher s. One skilled in cryptography.
Cartog'rapher s. A map-maker.
Ci'pher s. The figure o; nothing; any numeral; a nonentity; secret writing; a device. v.i. To use figures. v.t. To write in a secret code.
Deci'pher v.t. To discover the meaning of, unravel, explain.
Tel'pher s. An electrical or other automatic carrier for goods; this system or plant.
Tri'umpher s. A victor; one who exults.
Go'pher s. A burrowing animal; wood Noah's ark was made of.
Chron'opher s. An electrical instrument for sending time-signals.
Theos'opher s. A theosophist.
Philos'opher s. One versed in or devoted to philosophy; a lover of wisdom; a philosophic person.
Gastros'opher s. One skilled in the art of good eating.
Bash'er s. (*Bash*).
Dash'er s. One who or that which dashes; a float.
Hab'erdasher s. A dealer in tapes, thread, etc.
Lash'er s. One who flogs; the water rushing over or below a weir.
Splash'er s. One who or that which splashes; a splash-board or screen.
Slash'er s. One who slashes.
Mash'er s. (*Slang*) A dude; a lady-killer.
Smash'er s. One who or that which smashes; a heavy fall, smashing blow.
Rash'er s. A thin slice of bacon.
Thrash'er s. One who thrashes; implement for thrashing; the fox-shark.
Wash'er s. One who or that which washes; ring to secure tightness.
White'washer s. One who whitewashes.
Swash'er s. (*Swash*).
Flesh'er s. A butcher.
Fresh'er s. (*Slang*) A freshman.
Refresh'er s. That which refreshes, especially a drink; extra fee paid to counsel for adjournments, etc.
Thresh'er s. One who threshes; a threshing-machine.
Fur'bisher s. One who furbishes or renovates.
Yid'disher s. (*Slang*) A German or other Jew.
Fish'er s. A fisherman; a fishing boat; (*slang*) a Treasury note.
King'fisher s. A small fish-eating bird with brilliant plumage.
Pub'lisher s. One who publishes, especially books.
Abol'isher s. (*Abolish*).
Polish'er s. One who or that which polishes; a polishing agent.
Accom'plisher s. (*Accomplish*).
Skir'misher s. One who skirmishes or takes part in a skirmish.
Plan'isher s. One who or a tool which planishes.
Fin'isher s. Man or machine performing some final operation; a settling blow.
Dimin'isher s. One who or that which diminishes.
Admon'isher s. (*Admonish*).
Gar'nisher s. One who garnishes.
Var'nisher s. One who varnishes.
Bur'nisher s. (*Burnish*).
Fur'nisher s. One who furnishes or supplies furniture.
Pun'isher s. One who punishes.
Nour'isher s. One who or that which nourishes.
Brit'isher s. One of British race.
Lan'guisher s. One who languishes.
Exting'uisher s. A utensil for extinguishing a light; one who extinguishes.
Van'quisher s. A conqueror.
Relin'quisher s. One who relinquishes.
Lav'isher s. One who lavishes; an extravagant person.

Rav'isher s. One who ravishes or rapes.
Wish'er s. One who wishes.
Welsh'er s. A swindler, especially on race-courses.
Ko'sher s. Ceremonially pure or right, especially of Jewish food, etc.
Ush'er s. A door-keeper, especially at law-courts, etc.; an assistant teacher. v.t. To introduce, show, to forerun.
Gush'er s. One who or that which gushes.
Flush'er s. One who flushes drains.
Push'er s. One who pushes; an energetic, forceful person.
Rush'er s. One who rushes.
Ba'ther s. (*Bathe*).
Feath'er s. A plume of a bird; projection on a board to fit into a groove; birds collectively; kind. v.t. To turn an oar horizontally in rowing.
Heath'er s. Heath, ling, with small red or white flowers.
Leath'er s. Dressed hide of an animal. a. Leathern. v.t. To cover or furnish with leather; (*slang*) to flog.
Whit'leather s. A specially dressed tough and pliable leather.
Breath'er s. A breathing-space; one who or that which breathes.
Weath'er (wĕth'-) s. State of the atmosphere. a. Turned toward the wind; windward. v.t. and i. To affect by or stand the effects of the weather.
Aweath'er adv. To the weather side, towards the wind.
Fa'ther s. A male parent; an ancestor; the begetter of offspring; the oldest member of a society, etc.; an early leader of the Church; a title given to priests.
Fore'father s. An ancestor, progenitor.
Gath'er v.t. To collect, glean; to pucker; to infer. v.i. To come or draw together; to concentrate. s. A fold in cloth, etc.; a pucker.
Forgath'er v.i. To gather together, to meet.
Lath'er s. The froth of soap and water or of a horse's sweat. v.i. To form or become covered with lather. v.t. To cover with lather; (*slang*) to thrash.
Blath'er v.i. To talk nonsense or unceasingly. s. Voluble nonsense.
Loath'er s. One who loathes.
Ra'ther adv. More willingly, preferably; somewhat.
E'ther s. A hypothetical medium pervading all space; the clear upper air; a light, volatile, and inflammable fluid used as an anæsthetic.
Togeth'er adv. In company; without intermission.
Altogeth'er adv. Entirely, wholly; without exception.
Wheth'er pron. Which of the two. conj. Introducing an indirect question.
Bleth'er v.i., s. (*Blather*).
Neth'er s. Lower; being beneath.
Teth'er s. A rope to confine a horse, etc. v.t. To tie up with this.
Weth'er s. A castrated ram.
Cith'er s. A kind of guitar, a cithern.
Dith'er v.t. To quiver, tremble.
Ei'ther a. or pron. One or the other; each of two (also conj.).
Nei'ther a., pron., conj. Not either; not the one nor the other.
Hith'er adv. To this place or point. s. Situated on this side.
Thith'er adv. To that place, etc.
Whith'er adv., interrog. and rel.
Slith'er v.i. To slide unsteadily.
Tith'er s. One who collects or receives tithes.
With'er v.i. To fade, shrivel, droop. v.t. To cause to fade; to blight.
Zith'er s. A stringed musical instrument.
An'ther s. The part of a stamen containing pollen.
Pan'ther s. The leopard, puma, or jaguar.
Oth'er a. and pron. Not the same; not this; second of two.
Both'er v.t. To vex, annoy, worry. v.i. To trouble oneself. s. A trouble, vexation. int. Expressive of impatience.
Foth'er v.t. To stop a leak by letting down a sail over it. s. 19½ cwt. of lead; a heavy weight.
Moth'er s. One that has borne offspring; a female parent, head of a convent, etc.; source, origin; a slimy growth that gathers in vinegar, etc. a. Native, inborn; vernacular. v.t. To act as mother towards.
Smoth'er v.t. To stifle, suffocate, suppress. v.i. To be stifled, etc.; to smoulder. s. A stifling cloud of smoke, etc.; a smouldering.
Anoth'er pron. and a. Not the same, different; any other.
Smooth'er s. An implement for something.
Sooth'er s. One who or that which soothes.
Poth'er s. Bustle, tumult, commotion.
Broth'er s. A male born of the same parents; a fellow-creature.
Far'ther a. More remote. adv. At or to a greater distance; moreover, in addition.
Fur'ther adv. To a greater distance. a. More remote, more advanced. v.t. To forward, promote, assist.
Mouth'er s. One who mouths.
South'er s. A south wind.
-ier suff. Denoting occupation.
Bier s. The support of a coffin or the conveyance for taking a corpse to the grave.
Gam'bier s. A vegetable extract used as an astringent, in dyeing, etc.
Glac'ier s. A stream-like accumulation of ice and snow.
Fan'cier s. One who breeds and sells domestic pets; an amateur.
Finan'cier s. One skilled in financial operations; a capitalist.
Brigadier' s. An officer commanding a brigade.
Grenadier' s. A member of a British regiment of Foot-Guards; a tall infantryman; a S. African bird.
Sol'dier (-jer) s. One engaged in military service. v.i. To serve thus.
Embod'ier s. One who or that which embodies or incorporates.
Halberdier' s. One armed with a halberd.
Bombardier' s. An artillery N.C.O. below a sergeant.
Boulevardier' s. A "man about town," one who frequents the boulevards.
Defi'er s. One who defies.
Stu'pefier s. One who or that which stupefies.
Liq'uefier s. Apparatus for liquefying, especially gases.
Pac'ifier s. One who pacifies; a peacemaker.
Mod'ifier s. One who or that which modifies.
De'ifier s. One who deifies.
Speech'ifier s. One who speechifies.
Qual'ifier s. One who or that which qualifies.

Vil'ifier s. One who vilifies; a slanderer.
Nul'lifier s. One who or that which nullifies.
Mag'nifier s. One who or that which magnifies, an optical instrument.
U'nifier s. One who or that which unifies.
Typ'ifier s. One who or that which typifies.
Scar'ifier s. One who scarifies; a scarificator; implement for loosening soil.
Ver'ifier s. (*Verify*).
Scor'ifier s. One who or that which scorifies.
Pur'ifier s. One who or that which purifies.
Fal'sifier s. One who falsifies.
Inten'sifier s. An agent for rendering more intense or denser.
Vers'ifier s. One who makes verses; a poetaster.
Clas'sifier s. (*Classify*).
Rat'ifier s. One who ratifies.
Grat'ifier s. One who gratifies.
Rec'tifier s. One who or that which rectifies.
Sanc'tifier s. One who sanctifies; the Holy Spirit.
Stul'tifier s. One who stultifies.
Cer'tifier s. (*Certify*).
For'tifier s. One who or that which fortifies.
Mor'tifier s. One who or that which mortifies.
Tes'tifier s. One who testifies; a witness.
Jus'tifier s. One who justifies; one who absolves from guilt.
Beaut'ifier s. (*Beautify*).
Sang'uifi'er s. A producer of blood.
Sat'isfier s. One who or that which satisfies.
Ar'gufier s. (*Argufy*).
Cashier' s. Person in charge of cash, payments, etc. v.t. To dismiss, get rid of.
Clo'thier s. A maker or seller of clothes or cloth.
Seraskier' s. A Turkish commander-in-chief or war minister.
Espal'ier s. Lattice-work on which to train trees; a tree so trained.
Cavalier' s. A horseman; a squire; a lover; an adherent of Charles I. a. Gay, sprightly; off-hand, haughty. v.t. To escort a lady.
Chevalier' s. A horseman; member of certain knightly orders.
Chandelier' s. A branched hanging support for lights.
Cordelier' s. A Franciscan Observantist monk.
Gaselier' s. An ornamental pendant with branches for burning gas.
Atel'ier s. A studio.
Fusilier' s. An infantryman formerly armed with a fusil.
Ral'lier s. One who rallies.
Col'lier s. A worker in a coal-mine; a ship transporting coal.
Bandolier' s. A belt for carrying cartridges.
Gondolier' s. A Venetian boatman.
Electrolier' s. A bracket or chandelier for electric lights.
Repli'er s. One who replies.
Mul'tiplier s. Number by which another is multiplied; one who or that which multiplies.
Compli'er s. One who complies.
Suppli'er s. One who or that which supplies.
Out'lier s. One who resides away from his office or business; rock or stratum lying apart from the main mass.
Haul'ier s. One who hauls, especially a workman in a mine.
Pre'mier s. A prime minister. a. Chief, principal.
Costum'ier s. A maker of or dealer in costumes.
Douanier' s. A custom-house officer.
Deni'er s. One who denies.
Denier' s. A small obsolete French coin ($\frac{1}{12}$th of a sou).
Carabinier' s. (*Carbineer*).
Pan'nier s. A wicker basket, especially for strapping on a horse; a frame for a skirt; a full looped skirt.
Chiffonier' s. A small sideboard with cupboards.
Gonfalonier' s. A chief standard-bearer.
Ver'nier s. A small sliding scale for taking minute measurements.
Pier s. A projecting land-place; pillar between windows, etc.; stone-work supporting an arch, etc.
Ra'pier s. A light, narrow sword.
Cop'ier s. An imitator, plagiarist; a transcriber.
Oc'cupier s. One who occupies; an occupant.
Croup'ier s. A chairman; a superintendent at a gaming table.
Bri'er s. A prickly shrub; the white or tree heath.
Sweet'brier s. The wild-rose.
Cri'er s. One who cries or proclaims.
Decri'er s. One who decries.
Descri'er s. One who descries.
Dri'er s. One who or that which dries; anything that will exhaust moisture.
Pri'er s. One who pries.
Bar'rier s. A fence; obstruction.
Car'rier s. (*Carry*).
Far'rier s. One who shoes horses; a horse-doctor.
Har'rier s. A dog used for hare-hunting; a falconoid bird; one who harries.
Quar'rier s. One who works in or owns a quarry.
Ter'rier s. A small dog that will go into burrows; book giving ownership, boundaries, etc., of estates.
Wor'rier (wŭr'-) s. One who or that which worries.
Cur'rier s. A leather-dresser.
Fur'rier s. One who prepares furs; a dealer in furs.
Hur'rier s. One who hurries.
Spur'rier s. One who makes spurs.
Tri'er s. One who tries or tests.
Destrier' s. A war-horse.
Cour'ier s. An express messenger; a travelling attendant who makes the arrangements.
Proph'esier s. One who prophesies.
O'sier s. A species of willow.
Ho'sier s. One who deals in hosiery.
Hoo'sier s. A native or citizen of Indiana.
Cro'sier s. The pastoral staff of a bishop.
Tar'sier s. A small lemur of Malay.
Cuirassier' s. A soldier armed with a cuirass.
Dos'sier s. A portfolio, documents relating to a case, a person's antecedents, etc.
Harquebusier' s. One armed with a harquebus.
Ti'er s. One who or that which ties.
Tier (tēr) s. A row, rank.
Mé'tier s. One's particular business or line.
Ren'tier (-tyā) s. One whose income is from rentes.
Front'ier s. The extreme part or border of a country. a. Bordering, co-terminous.
Court'ier s. A frequenter of royal courts; one of polished manners; one who solicits favours.
Cot'tier s. A peasant living in a cot; an Irish cottar.
Put'tier s. A worker with putty.
Clav'ier s. The key-board of a piano, etc.
Pa'vier s. One who lays pavements; a ram for levelling paving-stones.
Brevier' s. A small printing type.
En'vier s. One who envies.
Gla'zier s. One who sets window-glass.

Bra'zier s. One who works in brass; a pan for holding a coal-fire.
Gra'zier s. One who rears and fattens cattle.
Vi'zier (-zēr') s. A high officer in Mohammedan countries.
Ba'ker s. A bread and cake maker or seller.
Bea'ker s. A large glass drinking-vessel.
Speak'er s. One who delivers a speech; the president of the House of Commons.
Break'er s. A large wave breaking on the beach.
Wreak'er s. One who wreaks vengeance, etc.
Squeak'er s. One who or that which squeaks; a young pigeon; an informer.
Fa'ker s. One who fakes furniture, etc.; a cheat, fabricator.
Sha'ker s. One who or that which shakes; apparatus for shaking things; member of an American sect.
La'ker s. One of the Lake Poets.
Ma'ker s. The Creator; one who makes.
Peace'maker s. One who makes peace or reconciles.
Watch'maker s. One who repairs or makes watches.
Book'maker s. A professional taker of bets.
Dress'maker s. One who makes ladies' dresses.
Spin'naker s. A large triangular sail.
Croak'er s. A grumbler.
Soak'er s. One who soaks; a hard drinker.
Ra'ker s. One who rakes.
Sa'ker s. A large falcon for hawking; an obsolete cannon.
Forsa'ker s. One who forsakes.
Ta'ker s. One who takes.
Parta'ker s. A participator.
Un'dertaker s. One who manages funerals; one who undertakes.
Mista'ker s. One who mistakes.
Pains'taker s. A laborious person.
Qua'ker s. One who quakes; a member of the Society of Friends.
Back'er s. One who backs, especially bills, etc.; a supporter.
Whack'er s. (*Slang*) A whopper; anything extraordinary.
Clack'er s. (*Clack*).
Slack'er s. A lazy person; a waster.
Smack'er s. A resounding blow; a noisy kiss.
Knack'er s. A horse-slaughterer, dealer in old horses, etc.
Pack'er s. One whose business it is to pack.
Rack'er s. One who racks or torments.
Crack'er s. One who or that which cracks; a small exploding firework; a biscuit.
Track'er s. One who or that which tracks; a connecting part in an organ.
Sack'er s. A looter, plunderer.
Ran'sacker s. One who ransacks.
Tack'er s. One who tacks.
Check'er s. (*Chequer*).
Fleck'er v.t. To fleck, variegate, stipple.
Peck'er s. One who or that which pecks, especially a bird; (*slang*) spirits; the appetite.
Wood'pecker s. A forest-bird that taps trees for insects.
Wreck'er s. One who brings about or plunders from wrecks.
Bick'er v.i. To squabble pettishly; to glisten, flicker. s. A noise as of bickering.
Dick'er s. Ten; especially ten hides. v.i. and t. To barter, haggle, exchange.
Maf'ficker s. One who takes part in a riotous celebration.
Traf'ficker s. One who traffics.
Kick'er s. One who or that which kicks.
Lick'er s. One who licks.
Click'er s. A foreman compositor; one who cuts leather for shoemakers.
Flick'er v.i. To flutter; to waver or fluctuate as an unsteady flame. s. A wavering gleam.
Mim'icker s. One who mimics.
Smick'er v.i. To smile affectedly, look amorously.
Nick'er s. One who nicks; (*slang*) a pilferer.
Pic'nicker s. One who goes on a picnic.
Snick'er v. and s. Snigger.
Pick'er s. One who or that which picks.
Prick'er s. One who or that which pricks; a prick.
Fos'sicker s. (*Slang*) One who rummages about.
Tick'er s. (*Slang*) A watch.
Stick'er s. One who or that which sticks; a butchers' knife.
Wick'er s. A small twig or osier; work made of this. a. Made of such.
Cock'er v.t. To pamper, coddle, indulge. s. A fighting-cock; a variety of spaniel.
Dock'er s. A dock-labourer.
Shock'er s. That which shocks; a sensational novel.
Lock'er s. A drawer, cupboard, etc., that can be locked.
Mock'er s. One who mocks.
Knock'er s. One who knocks; a hammer to a door.
Rock'er s. Curved piece on which a cradle, etc., rocks; trough for washing ore; one who rocks.
Sock'er s. (*Slang*) Association football.
Buck'er s. A buck-jumper.
Duck'er s. A duck farmer; a diving bird.
Pluck'er s. One who plucks; a machine used in wool-combing.
Puck'er v.t. and i. To gather in small folds; to wrinkle. s. A fold or collection of this; perplexity.
Suck'er s. One who or that which sucks; a sucking organ; piston of a pump; shoot of a plant; (*slang*) a sweet.
Tuck'er s. Ornamental frill round top of a woman's dress; one who tucks.
Seek'er s. One who seeks; an inquirer.
Young'ker s. (*Slang*) A youngster, youth.
Pi'ker s. (*Slang*) A tramp.
Stri'ker s. One who or that which strikes.
Trek'ker s. One who treks.
Talk'er s. One who talks; a boaster.
Stalk'er s. One who stalks.
Walk'er s. One who walks.
Milk'er s. One who or that which milks; an animal yielding milk.
Bulk'er s. One who ascertains freightage, etc., changeable for goods on board ship.
Skulk'er s. One who skulks; a shirker.
An'ker s. An old measure for wine (about 9 gallons).
Bank'er s. A proprietor of, partner in, or manager of a bank; a gambling game.
Cank'er s. A malignant ulcer; anything that corrodes; a disease in horse's feet, and in trees. v.t. and i. To corrode, corrupt.
Hank'er v.i. To desire eagerly, long for.
Flank'er s. One who or that which flanks.
Spank'er s. One who spanks or who moves briskly; the after-sail of a ship; something larger, etc., than ordinary.

Rank'er s. An officer promoted from the ranks.
Ink'er s. A roller for inking type.
Think'er s. One who thinks, especially in some specified way.
Blink'er s. One who blinks; a screen to prevent a horse seeing sideways.
Clink'er s. Vitrified slag; (*slang*) something exceptional, a thumping lie, etc.
Rink'er s. One who rinks.
Drink'er s. One who drinks; a drunkard.
Shrink'er s. One who shrinks.
Prink'er s. One who prinks; a coxcomb.
Sink'er s. One who or that which sinks; a well-digger.
Tink'er s. A mender of metal ware. v.i. and t. To mend pots, etc.
Stink'er s. A stinkard; anything that smells offensively.
Wink'er s. One who winks.
Bunk'er s. A large bin; a natural or artificial obstruction on a golf-course.
Moss'bunker s. The menhaden.
Junk'er s. A young German aristocrat.
Hunk'er s. One opposed to political progress; an old fogy.
Co'ker s. Cocoa (commercial form of the word).
Cho'ker s One who or that which chokes; a collar.
Jo'ker s. One who plays jokes, a merry fellow; an extra card used in some games.
Smo'ker s. One who cures by smoke; one who smokes tobacco, etc.; a smoking carriage or concert.
Cook'er s. A cooking-stove; one who falsifies or garbles.
Hook'er s. A two-masted Dutch vessel.
Look'er s. One who looks.
On'looker s. A spectator.
Snook'er s. A variety of pool played on the billiard table.
Po'ker s. One who pokes; implement for poking; a card-game.
Bro'ker s. An intermediary between buyer and seller.
Pawn'broker s. One who lends money on pawns.
Stro'ker s. One who strokes.
Sto'ker s. One who tends a furnace.
Bark'er s. One who or that which barks; (*slang*) a pistol.
Shark'er s. A swindler; a rapacious person.
Mark'er s. One who or that which marks or scores; a counter.
Remark'er s. One who remarks.
Jerk'er s. One who or that which jerks.
Ber'serker s., a. (*Berserk*).
Shirk'er s. One who shirks; one who lives by his wits.
Cork'er s. (*Slang*) A settler, poser.
Pork'er s. A young pig for eating.
York'er s. A ball pitching immediately in front of bat (at cricket).
Lurk'er s. One who lurks, a skulker.
Ask'er s. (*Ask*).
Mask'er s. One who wears a mask; a masquer.
Whisk'er s. Hair growing on the cheeks; bristles on lip of cat, etc.
Frisk'er s. One who frisks.
Dan'sker s. A Dane.
Tusk'er s. An elephant or wild boar with large tusks.
Hawk'er s. A pedlar, street-seller.
Conceal'er s. (*Conceal*).
Deal'er s. A trader; one who deals the cards.
Heal'er s. One who or that which heals.
Repeal'er s. One who repeals or advocates repeal.
Seal'er s. One who seals, especially a Chancery official; a person or vessel engaged in seal-fishing.
Steal'er s. One who steals.
Squeal'er s. One who squeals; (*slang*) an informer.
Inha'ler s. One who inhales; instrument for assisting inhaling.
Tha'ler (ta'-) s. An old German silver coin.
Wha'ler s. Ship or man employed in whaling.
Whole'saler s. A trader who deals wholesale.
Wa'ler s. An Australian horse used by cavalry in India.
Fa'bler s. A writer of fables.
Bab'bler s. (*Babble*).
Dab'bler s. One who dabbles; a trifler.
Gab'bler s. One who gabbles; a chatterer.
Squab'bler s. One who squabbles.
Dib'bler s. One who dibbles; a machine for dibbling.
Nib'bler s. One who nibbles; a carper.
Scrib'bler s. One who scribbles; a hack writer; a carding machine for wool, etc.
Drib'bler s. One who dribbles.
Quib'bler s. One who quibbles.
Cob'bler s. A mender of boots and shoes; a cooling drink of wine, etc.
Gob'bler s. A glutton; a turkey-cock.
Hob'bler s. One who hobbles; a casual dock labourer.
Nob'bler s. One who nobbles; a swindler.
Wob'bler s. One who wobbles; a vacillating person.
Bub'bler s. (*Bubble*).
Am'bler s. (*Amble*).
Gam'bler s. One who gambles.
Ram'bler s. One who rambles; a creeping or climbing plant.
Scram'bler s. One who scrambles.
Dissem'bler s. A hypocrite.
Fum'bler s. A groper; one who acts awkwardly.
Hum'bler s. One who humbles himself or abases others.
Jum'bler s. One who mixes things in confusion.
Mum'bler s. One who mumbles.
Rum'bler s. One who or that which rumbles.
Grum'bler s. One who grumbles; a discontented person.
Tum'bler s. One who or that which tumbles; an acrobat; a drinking-glass; part of a lock; variety of pigeon.
Stum'bler s. One who stumbles.
Gar'bler s. One who garbles.
War'bler (wor-) s. One who or bird which warbles; a small bird of several species.
Doub'ler s. One who or that which doubles.
Troub'ler s. One who or that which troubles.
Chron'icler s. A writer of annals.
Strad'dler s. One who straddles.
Sad'dler s. One who makes or sells saddles, etc.
Wad'dler (wod-) s. One who waddles.
Twad'dler s. A foolish talker.
Med'dler s. One who meddles or interferes.
Intermed'dler s. One who intermeddles; a busybody.
Ped'dler s. (*Pedlar*).
Did'dler s. (*Slang*) A swindler.
Fid'dler s. One who plays a fiddle or who fiddles.
Rid'dler s. One who speaks in riddles.
Tid'dler s. A stickleback; a feather tickler.
Tod'dler s. One who toddles; a tiny child.
Fud'dler s. A drunkard.

Mud'dler s. One who muddles or messes about.
Pud'dler s. One who puddles iron.
Whee'dler s. One who wheedles, a coaxer.
I'dler s. An idle person, a loafer.
Dan'dler s. One who dandles.
Chand'ler s. A dealer in or maker of candles; a retailer of oil, cord, paints, etc.
Kind'ler s. One who kindles or excites.
Swind'ler s. A trickster, one who defrauds.
Fon'dler s. One who fondles.
Gird'ler s. A girdle-maker.
Hurd'ler s. A hurdle-maker; one who runs hurdle-races.
Daw'dler s. One who dawdles.
Feel'er s. One who feels; an organ of touch; a proposal, etc., to ascertain views.
Heel'er s. One who heels boots, etc.
Wheel'er s. Horse next carriage in a tandem, etc.; a wheelwright; a cyclist.
Four-wheel'er s. A cab with four wheels.
Kneel'er s. One who kneels; cushion, etc., for kneeling on.
Peel'er s. One who peels; implement for peeling; (*slang*) a policeman.
Reel'er s. One who reels or winds on a reel.
Bat'teler s. (*Battel*).
Baf'fler s. (*Baffle*).
Whif'fler s. A shifty person; an equivocator.
Rif'fler s. A file with curved ends.
Shuf'fler s. One who shuffles or prevaricates.
Muf'fler s. A scarf for the throat; a pad for deadening sound; a bandage, padded glove, mitten.
Snuf'fler s. One who snuffles.
Ruf'fler s. A swaggerer; instrument for making ruffles.
Ri'fler s. A plunderer.
Tri'fler s. One who trifles.
Hag'gler s. One who haggles, a hard bargainer.
Strag'gler s. One who or that which straggles; a vagabond.
Gig'gler s. One who giggles.
Hig'gler s. One who higgles; a huckster.
Nig'gler s. A trifler, pettifogger.
Wrig'gler s. One who wriggles.
Jug'gler s. A performer by sleight-of-hand.
Smug'gler s. A person or vessel engaged in smuggling.
Strug'gler s. One who struggles.
Invei'gler (-vē-) s. One who inveigles; a seducer.
An'gler s. One who fishes with rod and line.
Dan'gler s. One who dangles about, especially after women.
Jan'gler s. A noisy, wrangling fellow.
Man'gler s. One who mangles.
Span'gler s. One who spangles.
Stran'gler s. One who strangles.
Wran'gler s. One who wrangles; (*Cambridge*) a first-class honours-man in mathematics.
Min'gler s. One who mingles.
Bun'gler s. (*Bungle*).
O'gler s. One who ogles; a coquette.
Bu'gler s. One who plays or a soldier who transmits signals on a bugle.
Bail'er s. (*Bail*).
Jail'er s. The keeper of a prison.
Blackmail'er s. (*Blackmail*).
Nail'er s. A nail-maker.
Rail'er s. One who makes or fits rails; one who scolds or scoffs.
Derail'er s. One who or that which derails.
Trail'er s. One who or that which trails; a vehicle drawn by another.
Sail'er s. A ship (with reference to sailing power).
Was'sailer s. A carouser.
Retail'er s. One who sells by retail or who retails.
Rec'onciler s. One who reconciles or harmonizes.
Smil'er s. One who smiles.
Oil'er s. One who or that which oils; a can for using lubricating oil.
Boil'er s. A vessel in which boiling takes place, or steam is generated.
Pot'boiler s. An inferior, quickly-turned-out picture, literary work, etc.
Recoil'er s. That which or one who recoils.
Spoil'er s. One who spoils; a pillager.
Despoil'er s. A plunderer, ravager.
Broil'er s. (*Broil*).
Toil'er s. One who toils; a worker.
Compil'er s. One who compiles.
Til'er s. A maker or layer of tiles; a door-keeper among freemasons.
Beguil'er s. (*Beguile*).
Revil'er s. One who reviles.
Cack'ler s. (*Cackle*).
Heck'ler s. One who heckles or puts puzzling questions.
Tick'ler s. One who or that which tickles; a puzzle.
Stick'ler s. An obstinate contender over trifles.
Buck'ler s. A small round shield. v.t. To shield, defend.
Swash'buckler s. A bully, bravo.
Truck'ler s. One who truckles, an obsequious person.
Sprink'ler s. An appliance or utensil for sprinkling.
Tink'ler s. One who or that which tinkles; a bell.
Spark'ler s. That which or one who sparkles.
Cabal'ler s. (*Cabal*).
Foot'baller s. One who plays football.
Call'er s. One who pays a call or visit.
Cal'ler a. Freshly caught (of fish); refreshing.
Mar'shaller s. One who disposes in due order.
Sig'naller s. One employed in signalling.
Hos'pitaller s. One of a mediæval religious order of knighthood.
Teeto'taller s. One pledged to entire abstinence from intoxicants.
Forestall'er s. One who buys up commodities so as to control the sale.
Squall'er s. One who squalls.
Vict'ualler s. A caterer, innkeeper.
Laissez-aller s. Freedom, especially from governmental interference.
Li'beller s. A lampooner, one who libels.
Mod'eller s. One who models; a worker in plastic art.
Yo'deller s. One who yodels, especially a Tyrolese mountaineer.
Fel'ler s. One who fells trees.
Enam'eller s. One who enamels.
Smell'er s. One who smells; (*slang*) the nose.
Repell'er s. One who or that which repels.
Impell'er s. One who impels.
Propell'er s. One who or that which propels screw for propelling steamships aeroplanes, etc.
Spell'er s. One who spells; a spelling-book.
Gos'peller s. An evangelist, missionary; the reader of the Gospel in the Communion service.
Quar'reller s. One who quarrels.
Sell'er s. One who sells.
Tell'er s. One appointed to count votes; bank official who receives and pays out money.
Quell'er s. One who or that which quells.
Trav'eller s. One who travels; a commercial agent going from place to place.

Lev'eller s. One who aims at destroying social inequalities.
Rev'eller s. One who revels.
Sniv'eller s. One who snivels; a whiner.
Driv'eller s. A slaverer; a dotard; one who talks nonsense.
Hov'eller s. An unlicensed boatman.
Shov'eller (shŭv'-) s. One who shovels; the spoon-bill duck.
Grov'eller s. One who grovels; an abject person.
Dwel'ler s. A resident, inhabitant.
Jew'eller s. A dealer or worker in jewels.
Sten'ciller s. One who stencils.
Fill'er s. One who or that which fills; a funnel.
Fulfill'er s. One who fulfils or accomplishes.
Thill'er s. The horse between the thills.
Mill'er s. One who keeps or works in a mill.
Spill'er s. One who spills; a trawl-line; a small seine.
Grill'er s. One who grills; a utensil for grilling.
Sill'er s. (*Scot.*) Money; silver.
Till'er s. Lever of a rudder; one who tills, tilling-machine; asucker, sapling. v.i. To put forth suckers.
Distill'er s. One who distils; a manufacturer of whisky, etc.; apparatus for distilling.
Instill'er s. One who instils.
Cav'iller s. (*Cavil*).
Will'er s. One who wills.
Swill'er s. One who swills; a heavy drinker.
Knoll'er s. One who tolls a bell.
Poll'er s. One who polls trees; a voter.
Roll'er s. One who or that which rolls; a cylinder for smoothing, etc.; a long, broad bandage; a heavy, swelling wave.
Car'oller s. (*Carol*).
Log'-roller s. A literary man who puffs a fellow-author's productions.
Enroll'er s. One who enrols.
Troll'er s. One who trolls.
Controll'er s. One who controls; a comptroller.
Comptroll'er s. An official examiner of public accounts.
Stroll'er s. One who strolls, a roamer.
Toll'er s. One who tolls; a bell for tolling.
Extoll'er s. One who extols.
Scull'er s. One who sculls; boat rowed with sculls.
Full'er s. One whose business is to full cloth; a groove-making tool.
Gull'er s. A trickster, impostor.
Mull'er s. A vessel for mulling ale, etc.; stone on which pigments are ground.
Pull'er s. One who or that which pulls.
Gaol'er s. The keeper of a prison; a jailer.
Condo'ler s. One who condoles.
Chol'er s. Anger, irritability.
Cajol'er s. (*Cajole*).
Cool'er s. A vessel in which liquors are cooled; anything that cools.
Tool'er s. One who or that which tools.
Consol'er s. One who consoles.
Sta'pler s. A dealer in staple commodities.
Tram'pler s. One who tramples.
Sam'pler s. Piece of embroidered work as exhibition of skill.
Sim'pler s. A herbalist.
Tip'pler s. An habitual drinker.
Stip'pler s. One who stipples.
Coup'ler s. One who or that which couples
Snarl'er s. One who snarls.
Pourpar'ler (-lā) s. Request for or preliminaries of conference.
Whirl'er s. One who or that which whirls.
Curl'er s. One who plays at curling.
Hurl'er s. One who hurls or plays hurling.
Purl'er s. (*Slang*) A heavy fall, a "cropper."
Ant'ler s. A branch of a stag's horn.
Start'ler s. One who or that which startles.
Turt'ler s. One who hunts for turtles.
Nes'tler s. One who nestles.
Wres'tler s. One who wrestles.
Whis'tler s. One who or that which whistles.
Os'tler s. A stableman at an inn, etc.
Bus'tler s. (*Bustle*).
Hus'tler s. One who hustles; a pushful person.
Prat'tler s. One who prattles; a babbler.
Tat'tler s. A gossip, scandal-monger.
Set'tler s. One who settles; a colonist; a conclusive statement, etc.
Gut'tler s. A glutton.
But'ler s. A male servant in charge of the cellars, wine, plate, etc.
Cut'ler s. One who makes or deals in knives, etc.
Sut'ler s. A camp-follower who sells provisions to troops.
Haul'er s. A haulier.
Miaul'er s. A cat.
Rid'iculer s. One who ridicules.
Rul'er s. Instrument with straight edges or sides for drawing lines; a governor, sovereign.
Brawl'er s. (*Brawl*).
Crawl'er s. One that crawls; a slow-moving cab.
Scrawl'er s. One who scrawls.
Sprawl'er s. One who or that which sprawls.
Trawl'er s. A vessel employed in trawling; one who trawls.
Bowl'er s. One who bowls or plays at bowls; a low, hard, round hat.
Fowl'er s. A sportsman who pursues wild-fowl.
Howl'er s. One who howls; a S. American monkey; (*slang*) a ridiculous error.
Jowl'er s. A thick-jawed dog.
Growl'er s. One that growls; a grumbler; (*slang*) a four-wheeled, horse-drawn cab.
Prowl'er s. One who or that which prowls.
Foo'zler s. A bungler; a fogy.
Embez'zler s. One who embezzles.
Guz'zler s. One who guzzles; a glutton.
Puz'zler s. One who or that which puzzles.
Ream'er s. An instrument or tool used in reaming.
Cream'er s. A separating machine or implement.
Scream'er s. One who or that which screams; a family of S. American birds.
Dream'er s. One who dreams; one who spends his time in vain projects; a visionary.
Stream'er s. A long narrow flag; a beam of light.
Steam'er s. A vessel propelled by steam; a cooking utensil.
Defam'er s. One who defames.
Nam'er s. One who gives a name.
Roam'er s. One who roams.
Fram'er s. One who frames; a schemer.
Gos'samer s. A cobwebby substance floating in the air in summer; a thin fabric.
Tam'er s. One who tames wild animals.
Bêche-de-mer s. The sea-slug.
Redeem'er s. One who redeems, especially Christ, the Saviour of the world.

Schem'er s. One who schemes; a contriver, plotter.
Aim'er s. (*Aim*).
Declaim'er s. (*Declaim*).
Proclaim'er s. One who proclaims.
Disclaim'er s. One who renounces; formal disavowal; a denial.
Exclaim'er s. One who exclaims.
Dul'cimer s. A wired musical instrument played on with sticks.
Rudesheim'er s. A white Rhine wine.
Chim'er s. (*Chimere*).
Sublim'er s. One who or that which sublimes.
Lor'imer s. A loriner.
Prim'er s. An elementary school-book; a size of type.
Pri'mer s. That which primes.
Embalm'er s. One who embalms corpses.
Palm'er s. A pilgrim who had been to the Holy Land; an itinerant monk; a hairy caterpillar; one good at palming, a cheat.
Gam'mer s. An old woman, a grandmother.
Ham'mer s. A tool for driving nails, beating metals, etc.; part of a gun-lock. v.t. and i. To work with, beat, or forge with a hammer; to labour.
Sham'mer s. One who shams or feigns.
Yellow-ham'mer s. One of the buntings with yellow and brown plumage.
Ram'mer s. Implement for ramming.
Cram'mer s. One who crams; a tutor who prepares pupils for special exams.
Stam'mer v.i. and t. To speak or utter haltingly; to stutter. s. This defective utterance.
Yam'mer v.i. To whine, whimper.
Hem'mer s. One who hems; a machine for hemming.
Shim'mer v.i. To glisten faintly or tremulously; to glimmer. s. A tremulous gleaming.
Kim'mer s. A cummer.
Skim'mer s. Utensil for skimming liquids; the shearwater, razor-bill.
Glim'mer v.i. To shine faintly and intermittently, to flicker. s. An unsteady light; a faint gleam.
Brim'mer s. A full glass, a bumper.
Trim'mer s. One who trims; one who fluctuates between opposing parties.
Sim'mer v.i. To boil gently. s. A state of simmering or suppressed ebullition.
Swim'mer s. One who swims.
Cum'mer s. A godmother, a gossipy woman.
Scum'mer s. Instrument for removing scum.
Hum'mer s. Anything that hums, as an insect.
Slum'mer s. One who visits slums philanthropically.
Mum'mer s. A masked player in dumb-show; an actor (*in contempt*).
Rum'mer s. A deep drinking-glass.
Drum'mer s. One who performs on the drum; a commercial traveller.
Sum'mer s. The warmest season of the year; a lintel, girder. a. Pertaining to summer. v.i. To pass the summer.
Mid'summer s. 21st June; the height of summer.
Bres'summer s. (*Breastsummer*).
Breastsum'mer s. A beam supporting the front of a building.
O'mer s. An ancient Hebrew measure (about 5 pints).
Com'er s. A visitor, one who arrives.
Wel'comer s. One who welcomes.
In'comer s. One who comes in, arrives, takes possession; an immigrant.
Hom'er s. A pigeon that will fly home; a Hebrew measure (liquid, 75 gallons.; dry, 11 bushels).
Astron'omer s. (*Astronomy*).
Gastron'omer s. A gastronome.
Misno'mer s. A wrong or inapplicable name, etc.; a misapplied term.
Boom'er s. (*Boomster*).
Bloom'er s. A plant that blooms; a blunder; a knickerbocker costume for women.
Ran'somer s. One who ransoms.
Cus'tomer s. One dealing regularly at a place; (*slang*) a fellow.
Vo'mer s. A thin bone in the nose.
Farm'er s. One who cultivates land, pastures, cattle, etc.; one who contracts to collect taxes, etc.
Charm'er s. One who charms; a magician.
Warm'er s. That which warms.
Term'er s. One holding an estate for a term.
Confirm'er s. One who confirms.
Or'mer s. An edible marine bivalve.
Dor'mer s. A vertical window in a sloping roof.
For'mer a. Preceding in time; mentioned before another; long past.
Deform'er s. (*Deform*).
Reform'er s. One who aims at or effects reformation.
Inform'er s. One who informs, especially concerning crime for pay.
Misinform'er s. One who gives wrong information.
Conform'er s. One who conforms; a conformist.
Perform'er s. One who performs; an actor, musician, etc.
Transform'er s. One who or that which transforms; apparatus for changing the potential of an electric current.
Perfum'er s. A maker of or dealer in perfumes; one who perfumes.
Presum'er s. One who presumes; an arrogant person.
Consum'er s. (*Consume*).
Costum'er s. A costumier.
Rhym'er s. One who rhymes; a versifier.
Clean'er s. (*Clean*).
Glean'er s. One who gleans.
Profan'er s. One who profanes; a blasphemer.
Tobog'ganer s. One who toboggans.
Plan'er s. One who uses a carpenter's plane; an airman.
Loan'er s. One who grants a loan.
Lar'cener s. One guilty of larceny.
Par'cener s. A co-heir.
Copar'cener s. A co-heir or co-heiress.
Gar'dener s. One who tends or keeps a garden.
Hard'ener s. One who or that which hardens.
Green'er s. (*Slang*) A novice; a blackleg.
Stiff'ener s. One who or that which stiffens.
Con'gener s. A thing of the same genus or origin.
Kitch'ener s. A close cooking-range.
Strength'ener s. That which strengthens.
Weak'ener s. One who or that which weakens.
Wa'kener s. One who wakens.
Slack'ener s. One who slackens.
Quick'ener s. One who or that which quickens
Cheap'ener s. (*Cheapen*).
O'pener s. One who or that which opens; an implement for opening tins, etc.
Sharp'ener s. One who or that which sharpens.
War'rener s. Keeper of a warren.
Loos'ener s. One who or that which loosens.
Threat'ener s. One who threatens.
Sweet'ener s. That which makes sweet or sweeter.
Soften'er s. One who or that which softens.
Enlight'ener s. One who or that which enlightens.
Tight'ener s. That which tightens.

Whit'ener s. One who or that which whitens.
Short'ener s. One who or that which shortens.
Fast'ener s. One who or that which fastens, makes firm, or secures.
Has'tener s. One who hastens.
Chas'tener s. (*Chasten*).
Lis'tener s. One who listens, a hearer.
Moist'ener s. That which moistens.
Rav'ener s. One who or that which ravens.
E'vener s. One who or that which makes even.
Enliv'ener s. One who or that which enlivens.
Scriv'ener s. A notary; a money-broker; a literary hack.
Conven'er s. One who calls an assembly together.
Interven'er s. One who intervenes.
Coz'ener s. A cheat.
Campaign'er s. One who serves on a campaign.
Feign'er s. One who feigns or makes an unreal show.
For'eigner s. An alien; an outsider.
Malign'er (-leen'er) s. One who maligns.
Sign'er (sīn'-) s. One who signs.
Design'er s. One who designs artistically; a contriver, plotter.
Resign'er s. One who resigns.
Impugn'er s. One who impugns.
Propugn'er (-pūn'er) s. A defender.
Oppugn'er (-pūn'-) s. One who oppugns, resists, or controverts.
Ordain'er s. One who ordains.
Gain'er s. One who gains advantage, profit, etc.
Bar'gainer s. (*Bargain*).
Explain'er s. One who explains.
Drain'er s. One who or that which drains; a drain-builder.
Grain'er s. One who paints in imitation of wood; his implement.
Train'er s. One who trains horses, etc., for races.
Strain'er s. One who or that which strains; a filter.
Restrain'er s. One who or that which restrains.
Obtain'er s. One who obtains.
Detain'er s. One who detains; detention of what is another's; a writ authorizing a gaoler to hold a prisoner on another charge.
Retain'er s. One who retains or is retained; an adherent, follower; fee to counsel.
Maintain'er s. One who or that which maintains.
Contain'er s. (*Contain*).
Entertain'er s. One who entertains or amuses.
Stain'er s. One who or that which stains.
Abstain'er s. (*Abstain*).
Non-abstain'er s. (*Negative*).
Sustain'er s. One who or that which sustains.
Cord'wainer s. A shoemaker.
Cal'ciner s. (*Calcine*).
Di'ner s. One who dines; a railway dining-car.
Sein'er (sān'-) s. One who fishes with a seine.
Nier'steiner s. A Rhenish white wine.
Refin'er s. One who refines, especially metals; apparatus for purifying gas.
Confin'er s. One who confines.
Imag'iner s. One who imagines; a visionary.
Shin'er s. One who or that which shines; (*slang*) a sovereign.
Whin'er s. One who whines.
Lin'er s. One who makes or fits linings; lining, as of a cylinder; a vessel belonging to a passenger line.
Reclin'er s. One who or that which reclines.
Inclin'er s. One who or that which inclines.
Mil'liner s. One who makes or sells women's hats.
Mi'ner s. One who works in a mine, or who lays mines.
Exam'iner s. One who examines.
Deter'miner s. One who determines.
Coin'er s. One who coins, especially one who makes counterfeit coin.
Join'er s. One who joins; a woodworker.
Purloin'er s. One who purloins.
Repin'er s. One who repines.
Mar'iner s. A seaman, sailor.
Lor'iner s. Maker of bits, bridles, spurs, etc.
Ru'iner s. One who or that which ruins.
Divin'er s. One who practises divination; a dowser.
Twin'er s. One who or that which twines.
Contem'ner s. (*Contemn*).
Lim'ner s. An artist, portrait-painter.
Ban'ner s. A large square flag; a standard, especially one bearing a national emblem.
Can'ner s. A tinner of fruit, meat, fish, etc.
Fan'ner s. One who or that which fans.
Lan'ner s. The female of the lanneret.
Plan'ner s. One who plans or schemes.
Man'ner s. Method, mode; bearing, conduct; habit; custom; sort.
Japan'ner s. One who varnishes with japan or deals in Japanned goods.
Span'ner s. One who or that which spans; a screw-key.
Tan'ner s. One who tans; (*slang*) a sixpence.
Van'ner s. A sifting appliance for testing ore.
Ten'ner s. (*Slang*) A £10-note.
In'ner a. Interior; farther inward; spiritual; hidden. s. Part of target next the bull's-eye.
Din'ner s. The principal meal of the day; a banquet.
Skin'ner s. One who skins; a furrier.
Pin'ner s. A pin-maker; a coif; a pinafore.
Spin'ner s. One who spins; a machine for spinning; a spider.
Sin'ner s. A transgressor of the Divine law; one persistently sinning.
Tin'ner s. A worker in or plater with tin.
Win'ner s. One who or that which wins.
Scun'ner s. (*Scot.*) Disgust, loathing.
Gun'ner s. An artilleryman; a naval warrant officer.
Pun'ner s. A tool for ramming earth, etc.
Run'ner s. One who runs; a racer; a messenger; an agent, tout; a smuggler; a detective; that on which anything runs; a stem running along and taking root; a twining or climbing plant; a cursorial bird.
Fore'runner s. A messenger sent in advance; a precursor; an ancestor.
Stun'ner s. One who or that which stuns; (*slang*) anything astonishing or excellent.
On'er (wun'er) s. (*Slang*) Something or someone extraordinary; a heavy blow; a hit for one run.
Lon'doner s. A native or citizen of London.
Par'doner s. One who pardons; a seller of papal indulgences.
Gon'er s. (*Slang*) One who is ruined or beyond hope.
Wag'oner s. A wagon-driver.
Parish'ioner s. One who belongs to a parish.
Occa'sioner s. One who or that which is the occasion of.
Pen'sioner s. One in receipt of a pension; a dependent.
Rever'sioner s. One who has a reversion.

Mis'sioner s. One in charge of a parochial mission.
Commis'sioner s. One commissioned to perform some office, one acting under a warrant.
Proba'tioner s. One undergoing probation; a novice.
Founda'tioner s. One supported from an endowment.
Sta'tioner s. One who sells writing materials, etc.
Confec'tioner s. One who makes or sells sweetmeats.
Exhibi'tioner s. A student in receipt of an exhibition.
Practi'tioner s. One engaged in the exercise of some profession; a doctor.
Peti'tioner s. One who makes or presents a petition.
Redemp'tioner s. One who redeems himself from debt, etc.
Por'tioner s. One who divides or apportions.
Extor'tioner s. One who practises extortion.
Ques'tioner s. An interrogator.
Execu'tioner s. One who executes, especially a sentence of death.
Reck'oner s. One who reckons; a book of tables.
Alm'oner s. A dispenser of alms; a hospital official.
Com'moner s. One below the rank of a peer; one having the right to pasturage on a common.
Sum'moner s. One who summons.
Schoon'er s. A sailing-vessel with two or more masts; a tall drinking-glass.
Balloon'er s. (*Balloonist*).
Lampoon'er s. One who lampoons; a satirist.
Harpoon'er s. A whaler who throws or shoots a harpoon.
Postpo'ner s. One who postpones.
I'roner s. One who uses a smoothing-iron; a machine for ironing.
Cor'oner s. An officer who holds an inquiry in cases of sudden death, treasure-trove, etc.
Rea'soner s. One who reasons.
Sea'soner s. A condiment, seasoning.
Poi'soner s. One who poisons.
Pris'oner s. One in prison or under arrest; a captive.
Embla'zoner s. One who emblazons.
Learn'er s. One who learns; a student, apprentice.
Gar'ner s. A granary, repository. v.t. To gather in, store up.
Discern'er s. One who can discern or make distinctions.
Nor'therner s. A native of the north.
South'erner (sŭth'-) s. A native of the south, especially the S. States of U.S.A.
West'erner s. A person living in the West; an Occidental.
Suborn'er s. One who suborns.
Cor'ner s. A projecting extremity, angle; a nook, retired place; an embarrassed position; a district; an artificial shortage brought about to raise prices. v.t. To drive into a corner; to buy up a commodity.
Scorn'er s. One who scorns.
Ador'ner s. (*Adorn*).
Horn'er s. One who deals in or works in horn; a horn-blower.
Burn'er s. (*Burn*).
Soj'ourner (suj'-) s. One who resides temporarily.
Mourn'er s. One who attends a funeral; one who mourns.
Spurn'er s. One who spurns.
Turn'er s. One who turns things in a lathe; a variety of pigeon.
Cent'ner s. A German and American weight (about 110 lbs.).
Vint'ner s. A wine-merchant.
Part'ner s. An associate, especially in business or in games; a spouse.
Copart'ner s. A joint partner, associate.
De'jeuner s. Breakfast, lunch.
Commun'er s. One who communes; member of a commune.
Ru'ner s. One who wrote in runes.
Prun'er s. One who prunes; a pruning-hook.
Tun'er s. One who tunes musical instruments.
Im'portuner s. One who importunes.
Pawn'er s. One who pawns or deposits a pledge.
Spawn'er s. The female fish.
Own'er s. A rightful possessor.
Sun'downer s. (*Slang*) A tramp (*Australian*).
Crown'er s. A coroner.
Drown'er s. One who is drowning.
O'er prep., adv., a. Over.
Bo'er s. A Dutch S. African.
Stuc'coer s. A worker in stucco.
Do'er s. One who does; an agent.
Wrong'doer (-doo-) s. One who does wrong.
Undo'er (-doo'-) s. One who reverses what has been done, or who ruins.
Misdo'er s. One who does wrongly, an offender.
Go'er s. One who goes; a speedy horse, etc.; a "fast" person.
Forego'er s. A predecessor; an ancestor.
Echo'er s. One who echoes.
Sho'er (shoo'-) s. One who shoes horses.
Woo'er s. One who woos; a lover.
Per prep. By means of; through; by.
Ca'per v.i. To prance about. s. A skip, spring; the bud of a plant pickled and used as a condiment.
Leap'er s. One who or that which leaps.
Reap'er s. One who or a machine which reaps.
Ga'per s. An animal, bird, etc., that gapes.
Sha'per s. One who or that which shapes.
Di'aper s. Cloth figured with a diamond pattern; a napkin, towel. v.t. To variegate, diversify, flower in embroidery.
Ja'per s. A joker; one who japes.
Han'aper s. A hamper; an office of the old Chancery Court.
Pa'per s. A thin, flexible, manufactured material for printing or writing on, etc.; a sheet of this; a document; a bill of exchange, bank-note; a newspaper. v.t. To cover with or wrap in paper.
News'paper s. A periodical print that circulates news and advertisements.
Scra'per s. One who scrapes; implement for scraping or scraping on; a miser.
Sky'scraper s. A very tall building; a triangular skysail.
Dra'per s. One who sells cloths, etc.
Ta'per s. A small candle, wick of a candle; gradual diminution of thickness. a. Regularly narrowed toward the point. v.t. and i. To become or cause to become taper.
Cheep'er s. A young game-bird.
Keep'er s. One in charge of another, of a place, etc.; a gamekeeper; a ring worn to guard another.
Time'keeper s. A watch which or person who records time.
House'keeper s. One in charge of a house; a principal female servant.

Book'keeper s. A clerk who keeps accounts.
Shop'keeper s. A retail tradesman.
Sleep'er s. One who sleeps; beam supporting railway rails; a railway-car for sleeping in.
Peep'er s. A chick just hatched; one who peeps; (*slang*) the eye.
Creep'er s. One who or that which creeps; a creeping plant, bird, etc.; a spike on a boot to prevent slipping; a four-clawed grapnel.
Steep'er s. Vat, etc., in which things are steeped.
Weep'er s. One who weeps; a black crape mourning scarf, veil, cuff, etc.
Sweep'er s. (*Sweep*).
Lep'er s. One infected with leprosy.
Sni'per s. A soldier detailed for sniping.
Jun'iper s. An evergreen shrub with bluish berries used to flavour gin.
Pi'per s. One who plays on a pipe or bag-pipe.
Gos'siper s. A gossip; one who spreads rumours about others.
Vi'per s. A venomous snake; the adder.
Wi'per s. One who wipes; (*slang*) a handkerchief.
Swi'per s. One who swipes.
Scalp'er s. One who scalps.
Help'er s. An assistant, auxiliary.
Pulp'er s. A pulping machine or implement.
Camp'er s. One who camps, especially for pleasure.
Scam'per v.i. To run hastily, clear off. s. A hurried run or tour.
Damp'er s. A valve in a flue to regulate the draught; any checking or deadening apparatus or influence.
Ham'per s. A large covered basket; cumbrous rigging, etc. v.t. To impede, embarrass, perplex.
Pam'per v.t. To gratify to the full; to spoil.
Ramp'er s. A swindler.
Tramp'er s. One who tramps; a tramp-steamer; a vagrant.
Tam'per v.i. To meddle, attempt to interfere with; to adulterate.
Stamp'er s. One who stamps.
Vamp'er s. One who vamps.
Tem'per s. Hardness of metals; due mixture; temperament, disposition; anger, irritation. v.t. To qualify; to form to a proper hardness.
Distem'per s. A morbid state of the body; bad constitution of the mind; a disease of young dogs; a pigment mixed with size; a painting with such. v.t. To disease, to derange, ruffle.
Attem'per v.t. To temper, modify; to accommodate.
Whim'per v.i. and t. To whine, utter in a whining voice. s. A whining or querulous cry.
Sim'per v.i. To smirk, smile affectedly. s. A silly or affected smile.
Bump'er s. One who or that which bumps; a glass filled to the brim. a. (*slang*) Extraordinary, whacking.
Dump'er s. One who dumps surplus goods on a country.
Thump'er s. One who or that which thumps; (*slang*) anything extraordinary.
Jump'er s. A person, insect, etc., that jumps; a tool that works by jumps; a knitted outer body-garment.
Buck'jumper s. A horse that attempts to unseat its rider by arching the back and jumping viciously.
Lump'er s. A labourer who unloads ships.
Plump'er s. One who plumps at an election; vote so given.
Pump'er s. One who pumps.
Stump'er s. One who stumps.
Co'per s. A dealer, especially in horses.
Do'per s. One addicted to drug-taking; one who dopes horses.
Lo'per s. One who strides along.
Devel'oper s. That which develops; a chemical used in photography.
Gal'loper s. One who or a horse that gallops; an aide-de-camp.
Wal'loper (wol'-) s. One who wallops; (*slang*) anything extraordinarily large, ect.
Pot-wall'oper s. A voter on a pre-1832 franchise.
In'terloper s. One who interferes officiously an intruder.
Mo'per s. One given to moping.
Coop'er s. One who makes barrels; a mixture of stout and porter. v.t. To make or repair casks.
Hoop'er s. One who hoops casks; the wild swan.
Whoop'er s. One who whoops.
Loop'er s. The larva of the geometer or other moth; instrument for looping.
Troop'er s. A calvary soldier; a transport for soldiers.
Prop'er a. One's own, individual; natural, correct; exact; just.
Improp'er a. Unsuitable; unqualified; unbecoming; erroneous.
To'per s. An habitual tippler.
Han'dicapper s. One who handicaps.
Dap'per a. Smart; nimble; little and active.
Did'apper s. A diving bird; the dabchick.
Lap'per s. One who or that which laps.
Clap'per s. One who or that which claps; the tongue of a bell.
Flap'per s. One who or that which flaps; a half-grown wild duck; a young girl.
Map'per s. A map-drawer.
Kid'napper s. One who forcibly abducts a person.
Knap'per s. One who breaks or shapes flints.
Snap'per s. One who or that which snaps.
Whip'per-snap'per s. An insignificant, presumptuous person.
Snip'per-snap'per s. An insignificant fellow.
Rap'per s. One who raps; a door-knocker.
Scrap'per s. (*Slang*) A boxer; one who spars.
Trap'per s. One who hunts animals for their fur.
Strap'per s. One who uses a strap; a groom; (*slang*) a tall, strong person.
Un'derstrapper s. An inferior, a petty fellow.
Wrap'per s. One who wraps; a wrap; loose indoor garment for women.
Sap'per s. One who saps; a member of the Royal Engineers.
Tap'per s. (*Tap*).
Pep'per s. A plant, and its aromatic pungent seed. v.t. To sprinkle with pepper; to pelt with shot.
Step'per s. One who or that which steps.
Dip'per s. One who or that which dips; a vessel for dipping liquids; a small diving-bird; the Great Bear.
Ship'per s. One who sends goods for transportation.
Wor'shipper s. One who worships.
Whip'per s. One who whips.
Kip'per s. Herring split and salted; male salmon at spawning season. v.t. To cure and smoke herrings, etc.
Skip'per s. One who skips; a skipping beetle, fish, etc.; a sea-captain.

Clip'per s. One who clips; a fast-sailing vessel; (*slang*) anything first-rate.
Flip'per s. The limb of a turtle, seal, etc.; (*slang*) the hand.
Slip'per s. One who or that which slips; a light shoe; iron shoe for wheel of wagon.
Nip'per s. One who or that which nips; the great claw of a crab, etc.
Snip'per s. One who or that which snips.
Rip'per s. One who or that which rips; (*slang*) a fine thing or person.
Frip'per s. A dealer in old clothes.
Grip'per s. One who or that which grips.
Trip'per s. One who trips; an excursionist.
Strip'per s. One who or that which strips.
Sip'per s. One who sips.
Tip'per s. One who tips.
Cop'per s. A reddish, metallic, ductile element; a coin, vessel, boiler, etc., made of this; (*slang*) a policeman. v.t. To cover, plate, or sheathe with copper. a. Made of or resembling copper.
Dop'per s. A member of the Dutch Reformed Church in S. Africa.
Hop'per s. One who hops; a hopping insect; a hop-gatherer; a funnel for passing grain, etc., into a mill; a barge for conveying dredgings.
Chop'per s. One who chops; a chopping implement.
Shop'per s. One who goes shopping.
Grass'hopper s. An orthopterous leaping insect.
Whop'per s. Anything extraordinarily large, etc.; a thumping lie.
Crop'per s. A pigeon with a large crop; a fall, especially from a horse.
Drop'per s. One who or that which drops.
Eaves'dropper s. A secret listener.
Top'per s. (*Slang*) A top-hat.
Stop'per s. One who or that which stops; a plug, stopple. v.t. To close with this.
Up'per a. Higher in place, rank, power, etc. s. Upper part of a shoe.
Cup'per s. One who bleeds with a cupping-glass.
Scup'per s. Channel for carrying off water from decks.
Crup'per s. The buttocks of a horse; strap to prevent saddle shifting forward.
Sup'per s. The last meal of the day.
Carp'er s. (*Carp*).
Harp'er s. A harp-player.
Sharp'er s. A sharpener; a tricky fellow, swindler.
Warp'er (worp'-) s. One who or that which warps.
Scorp'er s. A jewellers' gouging tool.
Usurp'er s. One who usurps.
Gasp'er s. (*Slang*) A cheap cigarette, a fag.
Jas'per s. A coloured variety of quartz.
Clasp'er s. Anything that clasps.
Rasp'er s. A rasp; (*slang*) an unpleasant or extraordinary person or thing.
Grasp'er s. One who grasps.
Ves'per s. Venus, the evening star; evening. a. Pertaining to this or to vespers.
Whis'per v.i. To speak softly, under the breath, or with suspicion. v.t. To utter in a low tone. s. A whispering tone or voice; anything whispered; a hint, insinuation.
Lis'per s. One who lisps.
Crisp'er s. An implement for crisping hair, nap, etc.
Pros'per v.t. To favour, to make to succeed. v.i. To succeed, thrive.
Scaup'er s. A wood-engraver's gouge.
Pau'per s. A poor person, especially one supported by poor-relief or by alms.
Group'er s. A tropical sea-fish.
Su'per s. A supernumerary, especially on the stage.
Ster'eotyper s. One who makes stereotypes.
Daguer'reotyper s. One who makes daguerreotypes.
Dar'er s. One who dares.
Bear'er s. One who bears, especially the coffin at a funeral; the bringer of a letter; a support.
Hear'er s. One of an audience.
Shear'er s. One who shears, especially sheep.
Clear'er s. One who clears.
Tear'er s. One who tears.
Wear'er s. One wearing anything.
Swear'er s. (*Swear*).
Forswear'er s. A perjurer.
Sea'farer s. A sailor, seaman.
Way'farer s. A pedestrian, traveller.
Shar'er s. One who shares or has a share.
Cell'arer s. One in charge of a cellar.
Snar'er s. One who snares.
Roar'er s. One who or that which roars; a riotous fellow; a broken-winded horse.
Par'er s. An implement for paring.
Prepar'er s. One who prepares.
Spar'er s. One who spares.
Star'er s. One who stares.
Squar'er s. One who squares.
Cal'endrer s. One who calenders.
Jab'berer s. One who jabbers; a voluble talker.
Lum'berer s. One who cuts and prepares timber.
Slum'berer s. One who slumbers.
Num'berer s. One who numbers; a numbering machine.
Sor'cerer s. A wizard, magician.
Fod'derer s. One who fodders cattle.
Embroid'erer s. One who embroiders.
Philan'derer s. A flirt.
Slan'derer s. One who slanders.
Squan'derer s. One who spends lavishly and wastefully.
Wand'erer (wŏnd'-) s. One who wanders; a traveller.
Surrend'erer s. One who surrenders.
Hin'derer s. One who hinders; an obstructer.
Pon'derer s. One who ponders.
Won'derer s. One who wonders.
Maun'derer s. A grumbler, murmurer.
Thun'derer s. A violent denouncer.
Blun'derer s. (*Blunder*).
Plun'derer s. One who plunders.
Ver'derer s. Officer in charge of the royal forests.
Or'derer s. One who orders.
Bor'derer s. One dwelling on or near a frontier.
Mur'derer s. One guilty of murder.
Jeer'er s. One who jeers, a mocker.
Sneer'er s. One who sneers; a scoffer.
Steer'er s. A steersman; one who steers.
Of'ferer s. One who offers.
Suf'ferer s. One who suffers.
Pil'ferer s. One who pilfers, a petty thief.
Interfer'er s. One who interferes; a meddler.
Wag'erer s. One who makes a wager or bet.
Stag'gerer s. One who staggers; that which causes staggering.
Swag'gerer s. One who swaggers.
Fin'gerer s. A pilferer; one who fingers.
Ling'erer s. One who lingers.
Malin'gerer s. One who feigns illness.
Coher'er s. An electrical conductor used in wireless.

Deci'pherer s. One who deciphers.
Gath'erer s. One who gathers.
Fur'therer s. One who advances or promotes a cause.
Ham'merer s. One who uses a hammer.
Stam'merer s. One who stammers.
Cor'nerer s. One who engineers a corner in a commodity.
Ca'perer s. (*Caper*).
Tam'perer s. (*Tamper*).
Tem'perer s. One who tempers.
Whim'perer s. One who or that which whimpers.
Sim'perer s. One who simpers.
Whis'perer s. One who whispers; a tale-teller.
Ca'terer s. One who caters.
Wa'terer s. (*Water*).
Slaugh'terer (slaw'-) s. One who slaughters; a slaughter-man.
Loi'terer s. An idler, loafer.
Frui'terer s. One who deals in fruit.
Pal'terer s. One who palters.
Shel'terer s. One taking shelter.
Adul'terer s. (*Adultery*).
Poul'terer s. One who deals in poultry.
Ren'terer s. One who renters.
Saun'terer s. One who saunters or strolls.
Encoun'terer s. An opponent.
Bar'terer s. (*Barter*).
Plas'terer s. One who plasters walls, etc.
Pes'terer s. One who pesters; an importunate worrier.
Roi'sterer s. A blustering, turbulent fellow; a reveller.
Uphol'sterer s. One who upholsters rooms, furniture, etc.
Fos'terer s. One who fosters; a nurse.
Blus'terer s. (*Bluster*).
Chat'terer s. (*Chatter*).
Flat'terer s. One who flatters; a wheedler.
Smat'terer s. One whose knowledge is superficial.
Tit'terer s. One who titters; a giggler.
Tot'terer s. One who totters.
Ut'terer s. One who utters something.
Splut'terer s. One who splutters.
Mut'terer s. One who mutters.
Sput'terer s. One who sputters.
Stut'terer s. One who stutters.
Pew'terer s. One who works in pewter.
Lac'querer s. A worker in lacquer.
Ha'verer s. One who havers, a bletherer.
Pala'verer s. One who palavers.
Slav'erer s. One who slavers.
Qua'verer s. One who quavers.
Wav'erer s. One who wavers.
Rever'er s. One who reveres.
Deliv'erer s. A saviour, preserver.
Discov'erer s. One who discovers; an explorer.
Flow'erer s. A plant that flowers.
An'swerer s. (*Answer*).
Repair'er s. One who repairs; a restorer.
Impair'er s. One who impairs or damages.
Despair'er s. One who despairs.
Hir'er s. One who hires or lets on hire.
Admir'er s. (*Admire*).
Inspir'er s. One who inspires.
Desir'er s. One who desires.
Requir'er s. One who requires.
Inquir'er s. One who inquires.
Wir'er s. One who fixes wires.
Bor'er s. (*Bore*).
Cor'er s. An implement to remove the core from fruit.
Scor'er s. One who scores.
Ador'er s. (*Adore*).
Implor'er s. A suppliant.
Explor'er s. One who explores.
Snor'er s. One who snores.
Floor'er s. That which floors; a knock-down blow or argument.
Por'er s. One who pores.
Hec'torer s. A bully; one who hectors.
Stor'er s. One who stores.
Restor'er s. One who or that which restores.
Spar'rer s. A boxer; one who spars.
Transfer'rer s. One who transfers something.
Stir'rer s. One who stirs; implement for stirring.
Demur'rer s. An objection, especially on ground of irrelevancy or legal insufficiency; one who demurs.
Spur'rer s. One who spurs.
Reconnoi'trer s. One who reconnoitres.
Cur'er s. One who heals; one who preserves food.
Procur'er s. One who procures, especially for immoral purposes.
Endur'er s. One who endures.
Abjur'er s. (*Abjure*).
In'jurer s. One who injures.
Mur'murer s. A grumbler, complainer.
La'bourer s. One who labours; one whose work needs little skill.
Har'bourer s. One who shelters another.
Suc'courer s. One who succours.
Scour'er s. One who or that which scours.
Ar'mourer s. A maker or repairer of arms or armour; a N.C.O. in charge of the arms.
Hon'ourer s. One who honours or confers an honour.
Dishon'ourer s. One who dishonours; a seducer.
Pour'er s. One who or that which pours.
Va'pourer s. A braggart, bully.
Meas'urer s. One who measures; appliance for measuring.
Treas'urer s. One in charge of a treasury, the funds of a company, etc.
Insur'er s. One who insures.
Assur'er s. (*Assure*).
U'surer s. One who lends money at exorbitant interest.
Manufac'turer s. One who manufactures or owns a manufactory.
Lec'turer s. One who lectures.
Ven'turer s. One who ventures.
Adven'turer s. (*Adventure*).
Cap'turer s. (*Capture*).
Tor'turer s. One who tortures.
Ves'turer s. One in charge of church vestments.
Pos'turer s. One who strikes attitudes; a contortionist.
Releas'er s. One who releases.
Pleas'er s. One who or that which pleases.
Greas'er s. One who or that which greases; (*slang*) a Mexican.
Teas'er s. One who or that which teases; a poser.
Chas'er s. One who chases or steeplechases; a gun on board ship for use in a chase.
Steeple'chaser s. A horse trained for steeplechases.
Pur'chaser s. One who purchases.
Eras'er s. Something with which writing can be erased.
Kais'er s. An emperor, especially of the former German Empire.
Rais'er s. One who or that which raises.
Prais'er s. One who praises.
Apprais'er s. (*Appraise*).
Ex'erciser s. One who exercises.
Fran'chiser s. One having a parliamentary vote.
Enfran'chiser s. One who enfranchises.
Mi'ser s. One who hoards money and lives meanly; a niggard.
Prom'iser s. One who promises.
Surmis'er s. One who surmises.

Despis'er s. One who despises.
Ris'er s. One who rises ; vertical part of a step.
Surpris'er s. One who or that which surprises.
Prac'tiser s. One who practises
Ad'vertiser s. (*Advertise*).
Chasti'ser s. (*Chastise*).
Guis'er s. A mummer, a person disguised.
Bruis'er s. A pugilist.
Cruis'er s. A person or ship (especially a warship) that cruises.
Advi'ser s. (*Advise*).
Devi'ser s. One who devises.
Revi'ser s. One who revises.
Repul'ser s. One who repulses.
Cleans'er s. One who or that which cleanses ; a detergent.
Mergan'ser s. The goosander.
Cen'ser s. A vessel for holding burning incense.
Li'censer s. One who grants licences.
Condens'er s. One who or that which condenses ; a lens for concentrating rays of light.
Rec'ompenser s. One who recompenses.
Dispens'er s. One who makes up medicines ; one who dispenses.
Rins'er s. A rinsing machine.
Clo'ser s. (*Close*).
Enclo'ser s. One who or that which encloses.
No'ser s. (*Slang*) A fall or hit on the nose.
Choos'er s. (*Choose*).
Pos'er s. One who puzzles with difficult questions ; a puzzling question or statement.
Depos'er s. One who deposes.
Repos'er s. One who reposes.
Impos'er s. One who imposes.
Compos'er s. One who composes, especially music.
Decompos'er s. (*Decompose*).
Propos'er s. One who proposes.
Oppos'er s. One who opposes.
Suppos'er s. One who supposes.
Interpos'er s. One who interposes.
Dispos'er s. One who disposes.
Expos'er s. One who exposes.
Pros'er s. A tedious speaker or writer.
Relaps'er s. One who relapses, especially into vice, etc.
Trav'erser s. One who or that which traverses.
Revers'er s. One who or that which reverses.
Endors'er s. One who endorses.
Disburs'er s. One who pays out.
Curs'er s. A blasphemer, one who curses.
Nurs'er s. One who nurses.
Cours'er s. A swift horse ; a dog used in coursing ; a fast-running bird.
Purs'er s. Ship's officer in charge of accounts, provisions, etc.
Pas'ser s. One who passes ; one one casually meets.
Tres'passer s. One who trespasses.
Har'asser s. One who harasses.
Grass'er s. (*Slang*) A jobbing printer.
Can'vasser s. One who solicits votes, custom, subscriptions, etc.
Kirsch'wasser s. An alcholic drink distilled from black cherries.
Cess'er s. A ceasing of liability.
Less'er a. Smaller ; inferior.
Har'nesser s. Maker of or dealer in harness.
Dress'er s. One who dresses another ; a surgeon's assistant ; a kitchen sideboard.
Address'er s. (*Address*).
Redress'er s. One who rights a wrong.
Guess'er s. One who guesses.
Kis'ser s. One who kisses; (*slang*) the mouth.
Doss'er s. (*Slang*) One who sleeps in a common lodging-house.
Jos'ser s. (*Slang*) A fellow, chap.
Glos'ser s. One who puts a gloss on ; an annotator.
Engros'ser s. One who engrosses documents.
Toss'er s. One who tosses.
Tus'ser s. Tussore.
Us'er (ūz'-) s. One who uses ; continued use of a thing.
Mau'ser (mou'-) s. A magazine rifle or pistol.
Abu'ser s. (*Abuse*).
Accu'ser s. (*Accuse*).
Cau'cuser s. (*Caucus*).
Excu'ser s. One who excuses.
Diffu'ser s. One who or that which diffuses.
Infu'ser s. One who infuses ; infusing agent.
Mu'ser s. One who muses ; an absent-minded person.
Mou'ser (-zer') s. A cat good at catching mice.
Espous'er s. One who espouses.
Rous'er s. One who or that which rouses ; anything that startles.
Carous'er s. (*Carouse*).
Grous'er s. (*Slang*) A grumbler, complainer.
Peru'ser s. One who reads with attention.
Haws'er s. A small cable.
Dow'ser s. One who uses the divining-rod.
Gey'ser s. An eruptive boiling spring, especially in Iceland ; apparatus for heating water rapidly.
Di'alyser s. Apparatus for performing dialysis.
An'alyser s. (*Analyse*).
Aba'ter s. (*Abate*).
Deba'ter s. One taking part in a debate.
Ca'ter v.i. To supply food, amusement, etc.
Eat'er s. One who eats.
Beat'er s. One who or that which beats ; one who rouses game from coverts.
Toad-eat'er s. A sycophant, hanger-on.
Beef'eater s. A Yeoman of the Guard ; a Tower of London warder.
Heat'er s. One who or that which heats ; metal for heating a smoothing-iron.
Cheat'er s. (*Cheat*).
The'ater s. (*Theatre*).
Repeat'er s. One who repeats ; a watch that strikes when required ; a quick-firing fire-arm ; an indeterminate decimal.
Treat'er s. One who treats.
Sweat'er s. One who or which sweats or causes sweating ; a jersey.
Ha'ter s. One who hates.
Psychi'ater s. A mental specialist.
Skat'er s. One who skates.
-later suff. Denoting a worshipper or devotee of.
El'ater s. The click-beetle or skip-jack.
Relat'er s. One who relates.
Idol'ater s. A worshipper of idols ; an excessive admirer.
Ophiol'ater s. A serpent worshipper.
Bibliol'ater s. One unreasonably devoted to books.
Heliol'ater s. A sun-worshipper.
Iconol'ater s. An image-worshipper.
Zool'ater s. An animal worshipper.
Pla'ter s. One who plates articles, fits plates in shipbuilding, etc. ; a second-rate racehorse.
Sla'ter s. One who slates buildings.
Ma'ter s. (*Slang*) Mother.
Du'ra ma'ter s. Membrane enveloping the brain.
Bloat'er s. A smoke-dried herring.
Pa'ter s. (*Slang*) Father

Cra'ter s. Mouth of a volcano; a circular cavity in the ground.
Gra'ter s. A rough-surfaced utensil for rubbing off small particles of a substance.
Regra'ter s. One who regrates.
Pra'ter s. One who prates or talks foolishly.
Bar'rater s. (*Barrator*).
Ta'ter s. (*Slang*) A potato.
Sta'ter s. A gold coin of ancient Greece.
Wa'ter (waw'-) s. Transparent fluid composed of oxygen and hydrogen; the sea; saliva; urine; lustre of a diamond. v.t. To wet, supply with water; to give a wavy appearance to. v.i. To take in water, run with water.
Fresh'water a. Pertaining to or living in fresh as opposed to salt water.
Break'water s. A wall to protect shipping against heavy seas.
Back'water s. Water fed by the back flow of a river; a creek, lagoon; the wash from a steamship.
Shear'water s. A sea-bird allied to the petrels.
Cut'water s. The fore part of a ship's prow.
Doubt'er s. One who doubts; a sceptic.
Char'acter s. A distinctive mark; manner of writing, etc.; reputation; qualities, good qualities; a testimonial; an odd person; a person in a book, etc.; description. v.t. To characterize.
Protract'er s. One who protracts.
Perfect'er s. One who makes perfect or complete.
Reject'er s. One who rejects.
Neglect'er s. One who neglects.
Connect'er s. One who or that which connects.
Respect'er s. One who has a regard for.
Expect'er s. One who expects, an expectant.
Indict'er (-dit'-) s. One who indicts.
Inflic'ter s. One who inflicts.
Depic'ter s. One who depicts.
Sphinc'ter s. A muscle that contracts or closes an orifice.
Obstruct'er s. One who obstructs.
Deter' v.t. To prevent or discourage by fear; to dissuade.
Skeet'er s. (*Slang*) A mosquito.
Cath'eter s. A tubular surgical instrument.
Qui'eter s. One who makes quiet.
Rack'eter s. A noisy reveller.
Crick'eter s. One who plays cricket.
Rock'eter s. A pheasant that flies high.
Junk'eter s. A feaster, reveller.
Mar'keter s. One who deals in a market.
Meter s. A measuring apparatus.
-meter suff. Denoting a measuring instrument.
Diam'eter s. A straight line passing through the centre of a circle and terminating at each end in the circumference; the length of this.
Viam'eter s. Instrument for ascertaining distance travelled.
Dynam'eter s. Instrument to determine magnifying power of telescopes.
Param'eter s. A constant quantity in an equation.
Tetram'eter s. A verse of four measures.
Litram'eter s. Instrument for ascertaining specific gravities of liquids.
Octam'eter s. A line of eight metrical feet.
Pentam'eter s. A verse of five feet.
Heptam'eter s. A verse of seven metrical feet.
Hexam'eter s. A verse of six feet, either dactyls or spondees.
Velocim'eter s. Apparatus for measuring velocity.
Dim'eter s. A verse of two measures.
Acidim'eter s. An apparatus for measuring the strength of acids.
Salim'eter s. Instrument for ascertaining the salinity of a solution.
Planim'eter s. Instrument for measuring area of plane surfaces.
Saccharim'eter s. Instrument for ascertaining quantity of sugar in any solution.
Polarim'eter s. Instrument for measuring amount of polarization of light.
Perim'eter s. The outer boundary of a figure.
Calorim'eter s. An apparatus for measuring heat.
Colorim'eter s. Instrument for measuring density of colour.
Vaporim'eter s. Instrument for measuring pressure of gases.
Trim'eter s. A verse of three measures each of two feet.
Tasim'eter s. Apparatus for measuring minute variations in pressure, etc.
Pulsim'eter s. Instrument for measuring beat of the pulse.
Densim'eter s. Instrument for measuring specific gravity.
Altim'eter s. Instrument for measuring angles of altitude.
Voltim'eter s. Instrument for measuring voltage.
Gravim'eter s. An instrument for ascertaining the specific gravity of bodies.
Taxim'eter s. Device for registering fare due in a cab.
Am'meter s. An instrument for measuring the strength of electric current.
Ohm'meter s. Instrument for indicating resistance in ohms.
Tribom'eter s. Apparatus for measuring sliding friction.
Oncom'eter s. Instrument to measure changes in size of internal organs.
Viscom'eter s. Instrument for determining viscosity of liquids.
Speedom'eter s. Apparatus for indicating speed of machinery, etc.
Pedom'eter s. Instrument for indicating distance walked.
Hodom'eter s. A distance-measurer for wheeled vehicles.
Floodom'eter s. Instrument for measuring the height of floods.
Udom'eter s. A rain-gauge.
Elæom'eter s. Instrument for ascertaining he specific gravity of oils.
Aræom'eter s. An hydrometer.
Geom'eter s. A geometrician; a kind of moth or its caterpillar.
Tacheom'eter s. (*Tachymeter*).
Rheom'eter s. Instrument for measuring force, etc., of the circulation of the blood.
Oleom'eter s. Instrument for determining purity, etc., of oils.
Stereom'eter s. Instrument for measuring the volume of solid bodies, or for determining specific gravity of liquids, etc.
Taseom'eter s. Instrument for measuring structural strains.
Logom'eter s. A scale for measuring chemica equivalents.
Ergom'eter s. An instrument for measuring quantity or power of ergs.
Tachom'eter s. Instrument for measuring speed.
Echom'eter s. Instrument for measuring duration of sounds.
Trechom'eter s. Appliance for measuring distance covered by a vehicle.
Graphom'eter s. A surveyor's instrument for taking angles.

Bathom'eter s. An instrument for measuring ocean-depths.
Stethom'eter s. Instrument for measuring the chest during respiration.
Glaciom'eter s. Apparatus for measuring rate of motion of glaciers.
Radiom'eter s. Instrument for measuring or showing the effects of radiant energy.
Stadiom'eter s. A form of theodolite.
Audiom'eter s. An instrument for testing hearing.
Eudiom'eter s. Instrument for ascertaining quantity of oxygen in air.
Heliom'eter s. A delicate astronomical measuring instrument.
Craniom'eter s. An instrument for measuring skulls.
Goniom'eter s. Instrument for measuring angles, especially of crystals.
Variom'eter s. Instrument for measuring variations of magnetic force.
Potentiom'eter s. Instrument for measuring potential difference of electric pressure.
Fluviom'eter s. Apparatus for measuring the rise and fall of a river.
Pluviom'eter s. A rain-gauge.
Cyclom'eter s. Instrument for measuring circles or for recording distance travelled by a cycle.
Nilom'eter s. Apparatus for measuring rise and fall of a river, especially the Nile.
Oscillom'eter s. Instrument for measuring the roll of a ship.
Sillom'eter s. Instrument for ascertaining speed of a ship.
Scintillom'eter s. Instrument for measuring stellar scintillation.
Bolom'eter s. An electrical instrument for very exact measurement of heat.
Alcoholom'eter s. An instrument for ascertaining the alcoholic content of a liquid.
Dynamom'eter s. Instrument for measuring energy exerted by living beings or machines.
Anemom'eter s. A wind gauge.
Arithmom'eter s. A calculating machine.
Pulmom'eter s. Instrument for measuring lung-capacity.
Thermom'eter s. Instrument for measuring temperature.
Seismom'eter (sizmom'-) s. A seismograph.
Osmom'eter s. Instrument for measuring acuteness of sense of smell.
Atmom'eter s. An instrument for ascertaining rate of exhalation of moisture.
Cymom'eter s. Instrument for measuring length and frequency of waves in wireless telegraphy.
Zymom'eter s. Instrument for ascertaining degree of fermentation.
Diaphanom'eter s. An instrument for measuring atmospheric transparency.
Planom'eter s. A gauge for plane surfaces.
Manom'eter s. Apparatus for measuring elastic force of gases.
Sphygmomanom'eter s. Instrument for ascertaining blood-pressure in an artery.
Galvanom'eter s. An apparatus for determining the intensity, etc., of electric currents.
Cyanom'eter s. An instrument for determining depth of atmospheric tint.
Pycnom'eter s. A flask used in measuring specific gravity of liquids.
Salinom'eter s. Instrument for determining amount of brine in marine engine boilers.
Clinom'eter s. An instrument for measuring angles of elevation, slope of strata, etc.
Declinom'eter s. Apparatus for measuring the declination of a magnetic needle.
Inclinom'eter s. Instrument for determining intensity of terrestrial magnetic force.
Urinom'eter s. Instrument for ascertaining specific gravity of urine.
Actinom'eter s. An instrument for measuring the heat of the sun's rays.
Vinom'eter s. Instrument for ascertaining alcoholic strength of wine.
Phonom'eter s. Instrument for recording sound-wave vibrations.
Chronom'eter s. An accurate watch or time-keeper.
Tronom'eter s. A delicate seismometer.
Sonom'eter s. Instrument for measuring or testing sounds.
Tonom'eter s. A tuning-fork.
Oom'eter s. An appliance for measuring birds' eggs.
Barom'eter s. An instrument for measuring the pressure of the atmosphere.
Vibrom'eter s. Instrument for measuring vibrations.
Ombrom'eter s. A rain-gauge.
Macrom'eter s. Instrument for measuring distant or inaccessible objects.
Microm'eter s. An instrument used with telescope or microscope for measuring minute distances.
Dendrom'eter s. An instrument for measuring trees.
Chondrom'eter s. A balance for weighing grain.
Hydrom'eter s. Instrument for determining specific gravities, or for measuring velocity or discharge of water.
Spherom'eter s. Instrument for measuring the radii and curvature of spheres.
Hygrom'eter s. Instrument for measuring atmospheric moisture.
Psychrom'eter s. Instrument for measuring atmospheric humidity.
Spirom'eter s. Instrument for measuring lung capacity.
Orom'eter s. An instrument for ascertaining the height of mountains.
Chlorom'eter s. Instrument for testing bleaching power of chloride of lime.
Electrom'eter s. Instrument for measuring electrical force.
Spectrom'eter s. Instrument for measuring deflection of rays by a prism.
Nitrom'eter s. Apparatus for determining amount of nitrogen in a substance.
Pyrom'eter s. Instrument for measuring high temperatures.
Gasom'eter s. A large reservoir for storage of gas at gas-works.
Opisom'eter s. An instrument for measuring curved lines.
Pulsom'eter s. Vacuum pump for raising water.
Drosom'eter s. An instrument for measuring fall of dew.
Hypsom'eter s. A thermometrical instrument for determining altitudes.
Pneumatom'eter s. Instrument to measure quantity of air taken in or given out at one breathing.
Lactom'eter s. Apparatus for determining the specific gravity of milk.
Stactom'eter s. A pipette for counting drops of a liquid.
Magnetom'eter s. Instrument for measuring magnetic forces.
Hyetom'eter s. A rain-gauge.

Sensitom'eter s. Instrument for ascertaining the sensitiveness of photographic plates.
Pantom'eter s. A measuring instrument for angles, elevations, distances, etc.
Tintom'eter s. Scale or apparatus for determining tints.
Photom'eter s. Instrument for measuring relative intensity of light.
Comptom'eter s. A calculating machine.
Optom'eter s. Instrument for ascertaining range of vision, etc.
Cyrtom'eter s. Instrument for measuring the curves of a chart.
Cryom'eter s. Instrument for measuring low temperatures.
Kryom'eter s. A thermometer for measuring low temperatures.
Piezom'eter s. Instrument for measuring pressure or compressibility of liquids.
Volu'meter s. Instrument for measuring volume of a gas.
Tachym'eter s. Instrument used in rapid surveying.
Dasym'eter s. An instrument for ascertaining the density of gases.
Pe'ter v.i. To give out, come to an end.
Trum'peter s. One who sounds or plays a trumpet; one who proclaims or denounces; a variety of pigeon.
Inter'preter s. One who interprets; one who translates spoken words.
Ure'ter s. Duct conveying urine from the kidneys.
Masse'ter s. The muscle of the lower jaw.
Phy'seter s. The genus including the sperm-whales.
Ban'queter s. (*Banquet*).
Af'ter adv., prep., a., conj.
Hereaf'ter adv. After this; in a future state. s. The future life.
Thereaf'ter adv.
Hereinaf'ter adv. In the following part of this.
Thereinaf'ter adv.
Raf'ter s. A roof-timber.
Draft'er s. One who makes a draft.
Graft'er s. One who grafts.
Waft'er s. One who or that which wafts.
Shift'er s. One who shifts; a shifty person.
Shop'lifter s. A pilferer from shops.
Sift'er s. One who sifts; a sieve; a castor.
Swift'er s. A rope used on board ship for fastening, etc.
Loft'er s. A special golf-club.
Croft'er s. A Scottish peasant-proprietor.
Freight'er s. One who loads or charters a ship; a cargo-boat; a carrier.
Fight'er s. One who fights, a warrior.
Light'er s. An instrument for lighting or igniting; one who lights; a large open boat. v.t. To carry in a lighter.
Blight'er s. (*Slang*) A person, especially an obnoxious one; a scamp.
Moon'lighter s. One of a gang of Irish ruffians who committed nocturnal outrages on behalf of the Land League.
Lamp'lighter s. One who lights street lamps.
Slight'er s. One who slights.
Right'er s. One who sets right.
Daugh'ter s. A female child or descendant.
Laugh'ter s. Act or sound of laughing.
Slaugh'ter (slaw'-) s. Extensive, unnecessary, or indiscriminate killing; massacre; killing of beasts for market. v.t. To slay thus; to butcher.
Gait'er s. A covering for the leg above the shoe.
Wait'er s. One who waits; one who serves at table; a salver.
Bi'ter s. (*Bite*).
Inhab'iter s. An inhabitant.
Prohib'iter s. One who or that which prohibits.
Back'biter s. An underhand slanderer.
Ar'biter s. An umpire, referee.
Reci'ter s. One who recites; book containing recitations.
Inci'ter s. One who incites; an agitator.
Exci'ter s. One who or that which excites.
Indi'ter s. One who indites.
Ver'diter s. An azure pigment.
Coun'terfeiter s. A forger; a coiner of base money.
For'feiter s. One who incurs a forfeit.
Sur'feiter s. One who surfeits.
Dy'namiter s. A criminal employing dynamite.
Lim'iter s. One who or that which limits.
Smi'ter s. One who smites.
Igni'ter s. One who sets on fire; a contrivance for igniting.
Uni'ter s. One who or that which unites.
Loi'ter v.i. To be idly slow in moving; to loaf about.
Chap'iter s. An architectural capital.
Ju'piter s. The chief god of the Romans; the largest planet.
Wri'ter s. A clerk, amanuensis; an author; (*Scot.*) a solicitor.
Type'writer s. Keyed instrument for writing by means of type.
Un'derwriter s. An insurer; one who underwrites the shares of a company.
Requit'er s. One who requites.
Recruit'er s. One who recruits.
Fruit'er s. A tree that bears fruit; a ship for carrying fruit.
Invi'ter s. One who invites.
Al'ter v.t. To make a change in. v.i. To change, vary.
Fal'ter v.i. To hesitate, waver; to fail.
Hal'ter s. A horse's headstall and rope; rope for hanging. v.t. To put a halter on.
Sesquial'ter a. In the proportion of 3 to 2.
Pal'ter v.i. To act insincerely; to trifle, haggle.
Sal'ter s. A salt worker, maker, or seller; one who salts (food).
Psal'ter (sawl'-) s. The Book of Psalms, especially as given in the Prayer Book.
Dry'salter s. A dealer in salted meats, pickles, etc., also in drugs, chemicals, dye-stuffs, etc.
Shel'ter s. An asylum, refuge; protection. v.i. To take shelter. v.t. To screen, protect.
Hel'ter-skel'ter a. Hurried and confused. s. Confusion, bustle.
Smel'ter s. One whose occupation is smelting.
Spel'ter s. Impure zinc.
Wel'ter v.i. To wallow, tumble about, roll (in). s. A turmoil. a. Heavy-weight (in sport).
Swel'ter v.i. To suffer from heat; to perspire profusely; to cause languor.
Fil'ter s. A strainer for liquids. v.t. To purify by passing through this. v.i. To percolate.
Infil'ter v.t. and i. To infiltrate.
Phil'ter s. A potion or charm intended to cause love. v.t. To charm to love.
Mil'ter s. A male fish in breeding time.
Tilt'er s. One who tilts.
Quilt'er s. One who quilts; machine for quilting.
Bolt'er s. A contrivance for separating flour from bran.
Revol'ter s. One who revolts; a rebel.

Default'er s. One who makes default; a delinquent.
Gaul'ter s. One who dresses land with gault.
Vault'er s. One good at vaulting.
Boul'ter s. A fishing-line with a number of hooks.
Coul'ter s. The sharp fore-iron of a plough.
Insul'ter s. One who insults.
Consul'ter s. One who consults.
Ban'ter v.t. To chaff, rally. s. Raillery, jocular teasing.
Can'ter s. A moderate gallop. v.i. To move with this.
Decan'ter s. An ornamental glass bottle; one who decants.
Chant'er s. One who chants; the drone of a bagpipe.
Enchant'er s. A magician, one who delights or fascinates.
Trochan'ter s. One of several bony processes on the thigh-bone.
Tam-o'-shan'ter s. A close-fitting Scotch cap.
Plant'er s. One who plants; owner of a plantation.
Supplant'er s. One who supplants.
Transplant'er s. One who transplants; tool for transplanting trees, etc.
Rant'er s. One who rants, especially a preacher.
Grant'er s. One who grants.
War'ranter s. One who warrants.
Trant'er s. A pedlar, huckster.
Instan'ter adv. At once; immediately.
Levant'er s. An inhabitant of or a wind from the Levant; an absconder.
Want'er (wŏnt'-) s. One who wants.
En'ter v.t. and i. To come or go into or in; to begin, engage in; to register; to take possession of; to be an ingredient of.
Re-en'ter v.t. and i. To enter again or anew.
Lament'er s. One who laments; a mourner.
Or'namenter s. One who ornaments; a decorator.
Exper'imenter s. One who experiments.
Foment'er s. An instigator, inciter.
Repent'er s. One who repents.
Car'penter s. A worker in timber. v.t. and i. To do such work or make by carpentry.
Rent'er s. A tenant; one holding by virtue of paying rent. v.t. To fine-draw.
Resent'er s. One who resents.
Present'er s. One who presents.
Represent'er s. One who or that which represents.
Misrepresent'er s. One who misrepresents.
Consent'er s. One who consents.
Dissent'er s. One who dissents; a nonconformist; a dissident.
Ten'ter s. A frame for stretching cloth.
Frequent'er s. One who frequents.
Ven'ter s. The abdomen, belly (especially of insects).
Prevent'er s. One who or that which prevents.
Inter' v.t. To bury; to place in a grave.
Paint'er s. One who paints; a decorator; an artist in colours; a rope to fasten a boat.
Hint'er s. One who hints.
Splint'er s. A thin strip broken off. v.t. To split, shiver, etc., into splinters.
Mint'er s. One who mints money.
Joint'er s. A long plane; a bricklayer's tool.
Point'er s. Anything that points; a sporting dog.
Print'er s. One employed in printing.
Sprint'er s. A quick short-distance runner.
Sin'ter s. A siliceous or calcareous mineral deposit.
Disinter' v.t. To take out of the grave; to bring to light.
Tint'er s. One who or that which tints; an engraver's tool.
Squint'er s. One who squints.
Win'ter s. Cold season of the year; a cheerless situation. v.i. To pass the winter. v.t. To keep during winter.
Twin'ter s. A two-year-old ox.
Confront'er s. (*Confront*).
Haunt'er s. One who or that which haunts.
Saunt'er v.i. To ramble about idly, to stroll. s. A leisurely walk.
Taunt'er s. One who upbraids bitterly.
Vaunt'er s. A braggart, boaster.
Bunt'er s. New Red Sandstone.
Hunt'er s. One who hunts, a huntsman; a horse used in the chase; a watch with hinged metal cover over the face.
Shunt'er s. A railway servant employed in shunting.
Count'er s. One who or that which counts; anything used to reckon; a calculator; coin-shaped piece of bone, metal, etc.; table on which money is counted, goods exposed for sale, etc.; a parry in fencing. adv. Contrary, in an opposite way or direction. a. Adverse; opposing. v.t. and i. To oppose, return blow for blow, etc.
Encount'er s. A meeting, conflict, duel. v.t. To meet face to face or hostilely; to attack and try to refute.
Rencount'er s. A meeting, especially in opposition; a sudden contest. v.i. To meet an enemy unexpectedly; to clash.
Mount'er s. One who mounts.
Surmount'er s. One who surmounts.
Punt'er s. One who punts; a gambler.
Grunt'er s. One who grunts; a hog.
Sco'ter s. A large sea-duck.
Ri'oter s. One who riots.
Promo'ter s. One who promotes, especially companies.
No'ter s. One who makes notes or takes note.
Free'booter s. A plunderer, pirate, buccaneer.
Scoot'er s. A child's toy like a long skate with a handle.
Foot'er s. (*Slang*) Football (the game).
Hoot'er s. A steam-whistle, siren; one who hoots.
Shoot'er s. One who or that which shoots; a revolver; ball delivered without bouncing.
Loot'er s. A pillager; one who loots.
Root'er s. One who roots up, an extirpator.
Toot'er s. (*Toot*).
Quot'er s. One who quotes.
Vot'er s. One who uses or has a vote.
Adap'ter s. (*Adapt*).
Chap'ter s. A division of a book; a body of canons, a meeting of this.
Accep'ter s. (*Accept*).
Intercep'ter s. One who intercepts.
Excep'ter s. (*Exceptor*).
Hemip'ter s. An individual of the Hemiptera.
Temp'ter s. One who tempts; the Devil.
Promp'ter s. One who prompts actors, etc.
Sump'ter s. A pack-horse, -mule, etc.; its driver.
Helicop'ter s. An aeroplane that will rise and descend vertically, and hover.
Adop'ter s. (*Adopt*).
Coleop'ter s. A beetle.

Diop'ter s. An ancient form of theodolite; the unit of refractive power.
Interrup'ter s. One who interrupts.
Corrup'ter s. One who corrupts.
Bar'ter v.i. To traffic by exchange. v.t. To exchange in commerce. s. Traffic by exchange.
Car'ter s. A driver of a cart; a carrier.
Dart'er s. One who darts; a long-necked swimming-bird.
Gar'ter s. Band for holding a stocking up; mark of the highest order of English knighthood.
Char'ter s. A written instrument conferring rights and privileges. v.t. To establish by charter; to hire or let by charter (of ships).
Impart'er s. One who imparts.
Start'er s. One who starts; a competitor in a race, etc.
Quar'ter s. The fourth part of anything; 28 lbs.; 8 bushels; three months; division of a shield; district; assigned position; lodging; mercy to a beaten foe. v.t. To divide into four equal parts; to cut to pieces; to furnish with lodging; to assign; to add to other arms on a shield.
Thwart'er s. One who thwarts.
Desert'er s. One who quits (especially the army or navy) without leave.
Subvert'er s. One who subverts.
Revert'er s. One who or that which reverts a reversion.
Divert'er s. One who or that which diverts.
Convert'er s. One who converts; a retort in which Bessemer steel is made.
Pervert'er s. One who perverts.
Squirt'er s. One who or that which squirts.
Com'forter s. Anyone or thing that comforts; a woollen scarf; the Holy Ghost.
Exhort'er s. One who exhorts.
Snort'er s. Person or animal that snorts; (*slang*) anything extraordinary.
Por'ter s. One who carries luggage, etc., for hire; a doorkeeper; a dark malt-liquor.
Report'er s. One who reports, especially public proceedings or for a newspaper.
Import'er s. One who imports goods.
Support'er s. One who or that which supports; an adherent; figure at side of heraldic shield.
Sport'er s. One who sports.
Transport'er s. (*Transport*).
Export'er s. One who exports.
Sort'er s. One who sorts.
Resort'er s. One who resorts.
Retort'er s. One who retorts.
Extort'er s. One who extorts; an extortioner.
Hurt'er s. One who hurts.
-ster suff. Denoting an agent, and sometimes a female.
As'ter s. A composite plant with star-like flowers.
Alabas'ter s. A soft, marble-like mineral.
Cast'er s. (*Castor*).
Medicas'ter s. A quack.
Grammaticas'ter s. A pettifogging grammarian.
Criticas'ter s. A mean little critic.
East'er s. Christian festival in commemoration of the Resurrection.
Feast'er s. A partaker of a feast; a reveller.
Northeast'er s. A north-east wind.
Oleas'ter s. The wild olive.
Fast'er s. One who abstains temporarily from food, especially from religious motives.
Chias'ter s. A species of sponge.
Pilast'er s. A square column projecting slightly from a wall, etc.
Plas'ter s. Composition of lime, etc.; calcined gypsum; an adhesive medicinal substance. v.t. To cover or treat with plaster; to lay on roughly.
Mas'ter s. An owner; employer; teacher in a school; commander of a vessel; one eminently skilled in some art. v.t. To excel in; to bring under control. a. Having control, chief.
Bur'gomaster s. The mayor of certain Dutch and Belgian towns.
Ship'master s. The captain or skipper of a ship.
Quar'termaster s. Military officer in charge of quarters, provisions, clothing, etc.; naval petty officer attending the helm, signals, etc.
Post'master s. Superintendent of a post-office.
Canas'ter s. A coarse tobacco.
Pinas'ter s. A species of pine.
Boast'er s. (*Boast*).
Coast'er s. A coasting vessel.
Roast'er s. One who or that which roasts; a contrivance, furnace, etc., for roasting.
Toast'er s. One who toasts; implement for toasting.
Disas'ter s. A sudden misfortune or calamity; grief.
Tast'er s. One who tastes, especially the quality of liquor or food.
Poetas'ter s. A versifier, a tenth-rate poet.
Wast'er s. One who wastes; a spendthrift; a wastrel.
Dab'ster s. An expert.
Gab'ster s. An idle talker, a prater.
Fib'ster s. One who tells fibs.
Lob'ster s. A common edible marine crustacean.
Road'ster s. A vessel riding at anchor; a horse, car, cycle, etc., intended for the road.
Old'ster s. An oldish person.
Rod'ster s. An angler.
Es'ter s. A compound ether derived from an oxygenated acid.
Fes'ter v.i. To suppurate; to rankle, become corrupt. s. A purulent tumour; act or state of festering.
Man'ifester s. One who or that which makes public.
Infest'er s. One who or that which infests.
Suggest'er s. One who or that which suggests.
Digest'er s. One who digests; that which aids digestion; apparatus for cooking food, dissolving bones, etc.
Jest'er s. A buffoon.
Joke'ster s. A joker.
Ar'balester s. One armed with an arbalest.
Moles'ter s. One who molests.
Game'ster s. A gambler.
Trimes'ter s. Period or term of three months.
Rhyme'ster s. A poor poet.
Pes'ter v.t. To worry, harass, perplex.
For'ester s. One in charge of or an inhabitant of a forest.
Arres'ter s. (*Arrest*).
Wrest'er s. One who wrests.
Test'er s. One who or that which tests; canopy over a pulpit, bed, etc.; (*slang*) a sixpence.
Protest'er s. One who protests.
Request'er s. One who requests.
Sequest'er v.t. To seclude, isolate; to appropriate. v.i. To renounce interest in estate of a late husband.

Har'vester s. A reaper, reaping machine; a harvest-bug.

Northwest'er s. A north-west wind.

Sou'west'er s. A wide-brimmed, waterproof, sailors' hat.

Yes'ter a. Pertaining to yesterday, the last, or the previous.

Song'ster s. One skilled in singing; a song-bird.

Young'ster s. A lad, youth.

Flog'ster s. One who flogs.

-ister suff. Denoting an agent.

Leis'ter s. A pronged fish-spear for salmon.

Reg'ister s. A roll, official record; accounts regularly kept; book for such entries; device for indicating work done, etc.; musical compass; an organ stop; air-passage in a furnace, etc. v.t. To record, enter in a register. v.i. To correspond in relative position (of print).

Soph'ister s. A second-year student at Cambridge.

Lis'ter s. One who makes out lists.

Blis'ter s. A pustule, a thin bladder on the skin; something that will cause this. v.i. To rise in blisters. v.t. To raise blisters on; to apply a blister to.

Glis'ter v.i. To glisten, be bright. s. Glitter, lustre.

Mis'ter s. Form of address (Mr.) prefixed to men's names.

Palm'ister s. A palmist.

Ban'ister s. A hand-rail with support on stairs.

Can'ister s. A metal case or box.

Gan'ister s. A hard variety of sandstone; a lining for furnaces.

Min'ister s. An officer of the State or Church. v.i. To perform service; to afford supplies, contribute.

Admin'ister v.t. To manage, dispense, distribute.

Sin'ister a. Uulucky, ominous, bad; on the left side (especially in heraldry).

Clois'ter s. An arcade round an open space; a monastery.

Rois'ter v.i. To behave uproariously, to riot.

Quir'ister s. A chorister.

Chor'ister s. A member of a choir.

Bar'rister s. A lawyer who has the right to plead; an advocate, counsel.

Sis'ter s. Female born of same parents; a female of the same society, kind, etc.; a hospital nurse.

Resis'ter s. One who resists.

Twist'er s. One who or that which twists; (*slang*) a shifty person, swindler.

Trick'ster s. One given to playing tricks.

Huck'ster s. A retailer of small wares; a hawker; a mean fellow. v.i. To deal in small wares; to higgle.

Bol'ster s. A long pillow; a pad. v.t. To prop with a bolster; to support, maintain.

Holst'er s. Leather saddle-case for a pistol.

Uphol'ster v.t. To supply with furniture, curtains, etc.; to stuff and cover chairs, cushions, etc.

Ul'ster s. A long loose overcoat.

Team'ster s. One in charge of a team.

Ham'ster s. A rat-like hibernating rodent.

Deem'ster s. A judge in the Isle of Man; an umpire.

Boom'ster s. One who tries to attain success, notoriety, etc., by advertising methods.

Min'ster s. The church of a monastery; a cathedral church.

Spin'ster s. An unmarried woman.

Mon'ster s. Something abnormal, misshapen or of great size; an imaginary creature; one unnaturally cruel or evil. a. Huge.

Pun'ster s. One addicted to punning.

Cos'ter s. A street seller of fruit, vegetables, etc.

Fos'ter v.t. To nurse, cherish; to pamper; to promote.

Pat'ernos'ter s. The Lord's Prayer, a rosary; a weighted fishing-line with hooks attached at intervals.

Boost'er s. A contrivance for intensifying an electric alternatic current; (*slang*) a pushful man.

Roost'er s. Male of the domestic fowl.

Post'er s. A large placard; one who posts this up.

Bill'-poster s. One who sticks up placards on hoardings, etc.

Four-post'er s. A bedstead with posts at the corners supporting a canopy.

Ros'ter s. List of names of persons for duty.

Tenuiros'ter s. One of a group of slender-billed birds.

Recurviros'ter s. A bird with the beak turned upward.

Zos'ter s. The ancient Greek girdle worn by men; shingles.

Tap'ster s. One who serves liquor in a bar.

Whip'ster s. A whipper-snapper.

Tip'ster s. One who supplies tips on racing.

Burst'er s. One who collapses or goes bankrupt.

Malt'ster s. A maker of malt.

Aus'ter s. The south wind.

Exhaust'er s. One who or that which exhausts.

Bus'ter s. (*Slang*) Something extraordinary; a dashing fellow; a spree.

Fil'ibuster s. A buccaneer, freebooter. v.i. To take part in a lawless military expedition.

Dust'er s. Cloth or brush for removing dust; a sieve.

Adjust'er s. (*Adjust*).

Bal'uster s. A small column in a balustrade.

Blus'ter v.i. To roar like the wind; to swagger ostentatiously. s. Swagger, brag, "bounce."

Clus'ter s. A bunch or collection of things, as plants, pillars, persons, stars; a group. v.i. To grow or gather in a mass. v.t. To collect into a close body.

Flus'ter v.t. To confound, muddle. s. Confusion, agitation.

Mus'ter v.t. To collect troops, etc.; to bring together. v.i. To meet in one place. s. An assembling of troops; array.

Thrust'er s. (*Thrust*).

Trust'er s. One who trusts.

Brew'ster s. A brewer.

Throw'ster s. One who throws silk.

Shys'ter s. (*Slang*) A tricky, dishonest person.

Clys'ter s. An enema, an injection per rectum.

Oys'ter s. An edible bivalve mollusc.

Xys'ter (zis'-) s. Surgeon's instrument for scraping bones.

Bat'ter v.t. To beat violently, to strike continuously. s. A mixture beaten together with a liquid.

Scat'ter v.t. To strew about, to sprinkle. v.i. To be dispersed, to straggle apart.

Hat'ter s. A maker or seller of hats.

Chat'ter v.i. To talk idly, rapidly, or carelessly; to utter inarticulate sounds, to jabber. s. Idle talk; sounds like an ape's or magpie's.

Shat'ter v.t. To break at once into many pieces; to disorder, overthrow. v.i. To be broken into fragments.

Lat'ter a. Later; modern; the last mentioned.

Clat'ter v.i. To make a rattling noise; to chatter. v.t. To strike with a rattling noise. s. Such a noise; empty talk.

Flat'ter v.t. To gratify the vanity, etc., of; to please by artful commendation or with false hopes.

Plat'ter s. A large, shallow dish.

Splat'ter v.t. and i. To make a continuous splashing; to splutter.

Mat'ter s. Substance, body; subject of thought or action; concern; pus. v.i. To be of moment, to signify.

Smat'ter v.t. To have a slight knowledge, to talk superficially. s. A smattering.

Nat'ter v.i. To be peevish or fault-finding.

Pat'ter v.i. and t. To make a noise like falling hail; to cause to strike in drops, to sprinkle; to repeat mutteringly; to talk glibly. s. A quick succession of light sounds; glib talk, prattle.

Spat'ter v.t. To sprinkle with liquid; to asperse.

Bespat'ter v.t. To spatter thoroughly.

Rat'ter s. A dog that hunts rats.

Sprat'ter s. One who fishes for sprats.

Tat'ter s. A rag; torn shred.

Squat'ter s. One who squats; one who appropriates land and settles thereon; an Australian stock-owner.

Bet'ter a. More good, improved. s. A superior; one who bets. v.t. To make better, to advance.

Abet'ter s. (*Abet*).

Fet'ter s. A chain for the feet; anything that confines or restrains. v.t. To put fetters on; to restrain, hamper.

Get'ter s. One who obtains.

Beget'ter s. (*Beget*).

Par'getter s. A plasterer.

Forget'ter s. One who forgets.

Whet'ter s. (*Whet*).

Let'ter s. An alphabetic character; an epistle; the literal meaning. v.t. To form letters on.

Set'ter s. One who sets (type, jewels, etc.); a sporting dog.

Reset'ter s. A receiver of stolen property.

Tet'ter s. An eruptive skin disease.

Bit'ter a. Sour, sharp tasting; grievous, calamitous.

Embit'ter v.t. To make bitter or more bitter; to exasperate.

Fit'ter s. One who fits; one who assembles pieces of machinery.

Out'fitter s. One who supplies outfits.

Chit'ter v.i. To shiver, chatter; to twitter.

Lit'ter s. A portable bed; straw, etc., for animals' beds; a birth of animals; scattered rubbish; disorder. v.t. To scatter about untidily. v.i. To give birth to a litter.

Flit'ter v.i. To flit about, flutter.

Glit'ter v.i. To sparkle; to be showy or specious. s. A bright, sparkling light; brilliancy; show.

Split'ter s. One who or that which splits.

Slit'ter s. One who or that which slits.

Submit'ter s. One who submits.

Remit'ter s. One who remits or makes remittance; remission.

Omit'ter s. One who omits.

Permit'ter s. One who permits.

Transmit'ter s. (*Transmit*).

Nit'ter s. The bot-fly.

Knit'ter s. One who knits; a knitting-machine.

Spit'ter s. One who spits.

Frit'ter s. A small pancake enclosing fruit; a shred, fragment. v.t. To cut or break small; to waste away.

Writ'ter s. (*Slang*) One who serves a writ.

Sit'ter s. One who sits; a bird incubating; a bird, etc., presenting an easy shot.

Tit'ter v.i. To laugh restrainedly. s. A giggle.

Quit'ter s. One who quits; a shirker; an ulcer on a horse's hoof.

Twit'ter v.i. To utter short, tremulous sounds, to chirp. s. A chirping; one who twits or taunts.

Ot'ter s. A web-footed, furred, aquatic mammal feeding on fish.

Cot'ter s. A key or bolt for fastening part of a structure.

Boy'cotter s. (*Boycott*).

Dot'ter s. Instrument for making dots.

Blot'ter s. A book or pad with leaves of blotting-paper.

Plot'ter s. One who plots; a conspirator.

Pot'ter s. A maker of or worker in earthenware; porcelain, etc. v.i. To trifle with work; to dawdle.

Spot'ter s. One who or that which spots.

Rot'ter s. (*Slang*) An undesirable, a waster.

Garrot'ter s. One who garottes, especially with intent to rob.

Tot'ter v.i. To reel, shake, be unsteady.

Ut'ter v.t. To speak, pronounce, declare. a. Complete, total; absolute.

But'ter s. The oily part of milk; churned cream.

Abut'ter s. (*Abut*).

Rebut'ter s. Answer of a defendant.

Surrebut'ter s. Plaintiff's reply to defendant's rebutter.

Cut'ter s. One who or that which cuts; a one-masted-vessel.

Gut'ter s. A channel in a street for water. v.t. To form gutters in. v.i. To burn wastefully and smokily (of candles).

Shut'ter s. One who or that which shuts; solid or slatted cover for window, etc.; device for opening camera lens.

Clut'ter s. A confused collection, noise, etc.; commotion, disorder. v.t. To crowd together in confusion. v.i. To make a fuss.

Flut'ter v.i. To flap the wings rapidly; to be in agitation. v.t. To throw into confusion; agitate. s. Quick, confused motion; hurry, disorder.

Splut'ter v.t. and i., s. Sputter.

Mut'ter v.t. To utter indistinctly. v.i. To speak in a low voice; to murmur, grumble. s. An indistinct utterance; a low rumbling; a murmur.

Put'ter s. A golf-club for putting; one who putts.

Sput'ter v.i. To spray out saliva, throw forth moisture; to utter words quickly and indistinctly. v.t. To emit with a spluttering noise. s. Saliva thrown out; confused incoherent speaking.

Strut'ter s. One who struts.
Stut'ter v.i. To hesitate in speech, to stammer. s. Broken utterance.
Cau'ter s. A branding-iron.
Neu'ter a. Of neither gender or party; neutral; sexless; intransitive (of verbs). s. The neuter gender; anything that is neuter; a sterile animal, insect, etc.
Refut'er s. One who refutes.
Herr'nhuter s. A Moravian.
Salut'er s. One who salutes.
Pollut'er s. One who pollutes.
Transmut'er s. (*Transmute*).
Out'er a. On the outside; external. s. The outer part of a target.
Dout'er s. An extinguisher.
Shout'er s. One who shouts.
Flout'er s. One who flouts; a scoffer.
Pout'er s. One who pouts; a variety of pigeon.
Spout'er s. One who or that which spouts.
Rout'er s. Plane used for groove-cutting.
Sou'ter (soo'-) s. (*Scot.*) A cobbler.
Tout'er s. One who touts; a tout.
Imput'er s. One who imputes.
Comput'er s. (*Compute*).
Disput'er s. One who disputes.
Few'ter s. A rest on a saddle for a lance.
Pew'ter s. A silvery-grey alloy of tin and lead; a vessel or utensil of this. a. Made of this.
Dex'ter a. Right as opposed to left.
Ambidex'ter s. One who uses both hands with equal facility. a. Possessing this power, ambidextron.
Ox'ter s. The armpit.
Pres'byter s. An elder, especially in the Presbyterian Church; a priest.
Res'cuer s. One who rescues; a deliverer.
Subdu'er s. One who subdues.
Lea'guer s. A siege, besieging army; a party to a league.
Belea'guer v.t. To surround with troops, blockade.
Pla'guer s. One who plagues; an annoying, importunate person.
Intri'guer s. One who intrigues.
Harang'uer s. One who harangues, a pompous speaker.
Cat'aloguer s. An expert in cataloguing.
Hu'er s. In Cornwall, one giving notice of the presence of shoals of fish.
Val'uer s. An appraiser.
Glu'er s. One who glues.
Contin'uer s. A continuator.
Lac'quer s. A yellowish varnish; wood or metal decorated with this. v.t. to cover with lacquer.
Cheq'uer s. A pattern of squares in alternating colours; a chess-board. v.t. To mark with this pattern; to variegate, diversify.
Excheq'uer s. The English court of record taking cognizance of revenue and rights of the Crown.
Con'quer v.t. To gain by force; to subjugate; to surmount. v.i. To overcome, gain the victory.
Recon'quer v.t. To conquer over again.
Mas'quer s. A player in a masque.
Pursu'er s. One who pursues; the plaintiff.
Iss'uer s. One who or that which issues.
Aver' v.t. To vouch, assert, declare positively.
Beav'er s. A small furred aquatic rodent; (*slang*) a bearded man, a beard.
Heav'er s. One who or that which heaves.
Cleav'er s. One who cleaves; a butcher's axe.
Reav'er s. A pillager, robber.
Weav'er s. One who weaves; one of various birds building nests by weaving.
Ha'ver v.i. To blether. s. Nonsense; foolish talk.
Shav'er s. A barber; a youngster; a wag.
La'ver s. A large basin; an edible seaweed.
Pala'ver s. Idle talk; a long conference; flattery. v.t. and i. To hold a palaver; to talk idly; to humbug, flatter.
Sla'ver s. A vessel or a person engaged in the slave-trade.
Slav'er (slăv-) s. Saliva dribbling from the mouth. v.i. To slabber, be besmeared with saliva. v.t. To smear with saliva.
Ensla'ver s. One who enslaves; a fascinating woman.
Pa'ver s. A pavier.
Gra'ver s. An engraver; an engraving tool.
Engra'ver s. One who engraves, especially pictorial illustrations.
Sa'ver s. One who or that which saves; a frugal person.
Qua'ver v.i. To tremble, shake, vibrate; to sing or speak tremulously. s. A rapid vibration, shake; a note equal to half a crotchet.
Sem'iquaver s. Half a quaver in music.
Dem'i-sem'i-qua'ver s. Half a semi-quaver.
Wav'er v.i. To be unsettled; to vacillate.
Ev'er adv. At any time; always.
Screev'er s. A pavement-artist.
Weev'er s. A spiny rayed marine fish.
Fe'ver s. Disease accompanied by increased heat, quick pulse, languor, and thirst; excitement. v.t. and i. To put in or be seized with fever.
Whichev'er a. and pron.
Achiev'er s. (*Achieve*).
Believ'er s. (*Believe*).
Disbeliev'er s. One who does not believe; a sceptic, atheist.
Misbeliev'er s. One who believes wrongly or in a false religion.
Reliev'er s. One who relieves.
Retriev'er s. A dog trained to bring in shot game.
Le'ver s. Bar for raising a weight, etc., by turning on a fulcrum; a kind of watch. v.t. and i. To move with or use a lever.
Clev'er a. Talented; quick, ingenious.
Can'tilever s. A projecting beam or girder for supporting a balcony, etc.
Nev'er adv. At no time; not at all; in no degree.
Whenev'er adv. At whatever time.
Whoev'er pron.
Soev'er adv.
Wheresoev'er adv.
Whichsoev'er a. and pron.
Whensoev'er adv. At what time soever.
Whosoev'er pron.
Whithersoev'er adv. To what place soever.
What'soever pron and a. (*Whatever*).
Howsoev'er adv. In whatsoever manner, etc.
Wherev'er adv. At, in, or to whatever place.
Forev'er adv. Eternally, at all times. s. Eternity.
Sev'er v.t. and i. To separate, part forcibly.
Dissev'er v.t. To part in two, divide.
Whatev'er pron. Anything; all that which. a. No matter what.
Howev'er adv. In whatever manner, etc.; notwithstanding.
Waiv'er s. Act of waiving.
Di'ver s. One who dives, especially to work under water; a diving-bird.

San'diver s. A whitish scum on glass in fusion.
Deceiver s. One who deceives; an impostor.
Receiv'er (-sēv'er) s. One who or that which receives; an official appointed to hold property in trust; one who buys stolen goods.
Perceiv'er s. One who perceives.
Fiv'er s. (*Slang*) A £5 note.
Giv'er s. One who gives.
Forgiv'er s. One who forgives.
Law'giver s. A legislator.
Hi'ver s. One who collects bees into a hive.
Shiv'er v.i. To quake, tremble, quiver from cold, etc.; to fly into splinters. v.t. To break into fragments or shivers. s. Act of shivering, a quaking; a shive, fragment.
Skiv'er s. A paring-tool for leather; thin leather split from sheepskin.
Liv'er s. A dark red organ secreting bile; one who lives; a dweller.
Cal'iver s. An obsolete musket.
Deliv'er v.t. To set free, release; to yield; to discharge, send forth, disburden of.
Ol'iver s. A small trip-hammer worked by the foot.
Sliv'er s. A splinter, slip cut off. v.t. To cut into long thin pieces.
Min'iver s. Fur of the Siberian squirrel.
Conni'ver s. One who connives.
Riv'er s. A large stream of water; a copious flow.
Dri'ver s. One who or that which drives; a wooden-headed golf-club; the after-sail in a ship; anything that communicates motion.
Shriv'er s. A confessor.
Thriv'er s. One who or that which thrives or flourishes.
Contri'ver s. (*Contrive*).
Striv'er s. One who strives.
Stiv'er s. An obsolete Dutch coin; any coin of small value.
Quiv'er s. A sheath for arrows. v.i. To shake tremulously; to shudder, shiver.
Reviv'er s. One who or that which revives.
Sal'ver s. A metal tray for servants handing things.
El'ver s. A young eel.
Del'ver s. One who delves.
Hel'ver s. A helve, tool-handle.
Sil'ver s. A lustrous, white, metallic element; coin, plate, etc., made of this; money, a. Made of or resembling silver. v.t. To cover with or cause to resemble silver; to coat with an amalgam of tin and quicksilver; to tinge with white.
Quick'silver s. Mercury.
Sol'ver s. One who or that which solves.
Absol'ver s. (*Absolve*).
Dissol'ver s. One who or that which dissolves.
Revol'ver s. One who or that which revolves; a pistol with a revolving breech for a number of cartridges.
Cul'ver s. A wood-pigeon.
O'ver prep. Above; denoting motive, occasion, superiority, etc.; across; throughout; upwards of. adv. From side to side; above the top; completely; too. a. Upper, covering. s. A series of six balls from the same bowler at cricket.
Cov'er v.t. To overspread, cloak, defend; to wrap up, secrete; to be sufficient for; to include. s. Anything spread over another; disguise; shelter; place at table for one.
Recov'er v.t. To win back; to repair the loss of; to make up for. v.i. To grow well, regain a former state; to succeed in a lawsuit.
Recov'er (rē-) v.t. To cover afresh.
Discov'er v.t. To disclose, bring to light, have the first sight or knowledge of.
Rediscov'er v.t. To discover afresh.
Moreo'ver adv. Further; likewise.
Hov'er v.i. To hang fluttering in air; to remain over; to loiter about.
Wind'hover s. The kestrel.
Lov'er s. A wooer, sweetheart; one in love or who loves.
Clo'ver s. A trefoil used for fodder.
Glov'er s. One who makes or sells gloves.
Plov'er s. A migratory grallatorial bird.
Mov'er s. One who or that which moves or gives motion; a proposer, instigator.
Remov'er s. One who removes, especially furniture.
Ro'ver s. A wanderer; a pirate; a fickle person; a chance mark in archery.
Drov'er s. One who drives cattle, etc., to market; a cattle-dealer.
Prov'er s. One who or that which proves or tests.
Reprov'er s. One who reproves.
Improv'er s. One who or that which improves an apprentice.
Approv'er s. (*Approve*).
Tro'ver s. Acquisition of goods; action to recover damages for wrongful conversion of property.
Pass'over s. A Jewish feast commemorating the deliverance from Egypt.
Sto'ver s. Fodder for cattle.
Car'ver s. One who carves; a tool for carving with.
Serv'er s. One who or that which serves.
Observ'er s. One who observes; a spectator.
Deserv'er s. One who merits reward (or punishment).
Preserv'er s. One who or that which preserves.
Conserv'er s. One who protects; one who conserves fruit.
Louv'er s. A roof-turret with openings for escape of smoke.
Gnaw'er s. One who or that which gnaws.
Draw'er s. One who draws; a sliding box in a case.
Wire'drawer s. One who draws metal into wires.
Withdraw'er s. One who withdraws.
Taw'er s. A leather-dresser.
Ew'er s. A pitcher with a wide spout.
Hew'er s. One (especially a miner) who hews.
Chew'er s. One who chews tobacco.
View'er s. One who views; an inspector.
Review'er s. One who reviews, especially publications.
In'terviewer s. One who interviews, especially on behalf of a newspaper.
Skew'er s. A pin of wood or metal for meat.
Renew'er s. One who renews.
Brew'er s. One who brews.
Screw'er s. One who screws; an implement for screwing.
Sew'er (sō'-) s. One who sews.
Sew'er (sū'er) s. An underground drain.
Bow'er s. An arbour, a shady recess; an anchor carried at the bow; a knave in euchre.
Embow'er v.i. and t. To lodge in or cover with a bower; to shelter with trees.
Cow'er v.i. To quail through fear; to shrink, couch.
Dow'er s. Property brought by a wife to her

husband on marriage; husbands property enjoyed by his widow; dowry.

Wid'ower s. A man whose wife is dead.

Show'er (shou'-) s. A short or light fall of rain, etc.; a copious supply. v.t. To water with a shower; to bestow liberally. v.i. To rain in showers.

Show'er (shō'-) s. One who shows.

Low'er v.t. To bring down in height, force, price, etc; to pull down. v.i. To become less or lower; to fall; to lour.

Blow'er s. One who or that which blows; an apparatus used for blowing or by means of which blowing is done.

Flow'er s. The blossom of a plant; youth; the prime; the best part; an ornamental expression. v.i. To blossom. v.t. To decorate with flowers.

Wind'flower s. The wood-anemone.

Deflow'er v.t. To cull the best parts of; to ravage, ravish.

Reflow'er v.i. To flower again.

Saf'flower s. An E. Indian plant yielding a bright red dye.

Caul'iflower s. A variety of cabbage.

Wall'flower s. A sweet-smelling garden-plant; lady without a partner at a dance.

Sun'flower s. A tall plant with large yellow-rayed flowers.

Gil'lyflower s. The clove-pink.

Glow'er v.i. To scowl, to stare sullenly. s. A fierce or sullen stare.

Tal'lower s. A worker with tallow.

Swal'lower s. One who swallows.

Fol'lower s. One who follows; an adherent, disciple, imitator; a dependant; an admirer.

Mo'wer s. One who mows; a mowing-machine.

Know'er s. One who knows.

Win'nower s. One who winnows; a winnowing machine.

Pow'er s. Ability to act; strength; influence; authority; a state, institution, or individual exercising control; armed force; mechanical advantage; product of self-multiplication.

Empow'er v.t. To give power, authority, or to force to; to enable.

Overpow'er v.t. To vanquish by force; to crush, subdue.

Row'er s. One who rows, an oarsman.

Grow'er s. One who or that which grows; a cultivator.

Throw'er s. One who or that which throws.

Sor'rower s. One who sorrows.

Sow'er (sō'er) s. One who sows seeds.

Tow'er (tou'-) s. A lofty building or part of a building; a fortress; a protection. v.i. To soar; to reach high, be lofty.

Stow'er (stō'-) s. One who stows.

An'swer s. A reply, a solution. v.i. To reply; to be accountable; to succeed. v.t. To reply to; to suit.

Coax'er s. One who coaxes.

Hoax'er s. One who hoaxes or deceives in sport.

Tax'er s. One who taxes.

In'dexer s. One who makes indexes.

Vex'er s. One who annoys or irritates.

Fix'er s. One who or that which fixes.

Mix'er s. One who or that which mixes.

Six'er s. Anything equal to or containing six.

Box'er s. A pugilist; a member of a Chinese secret society.

-yer suff. Denoting an agent.

Lay'er s. One who or that which lays; a stratum; coat (of paint, etc.); a shoot laid underground for propagation.

Flay'er s. One who flays.

Brick'layer s. One who lays bricks for building.

Play'er s. One who plays; an actor; a performer on a musical instrument; a professional cricketer.

Slay'er s. One who slays; a murderer.

Way'layer s. A highwayman.

May'er s. One who goes maying.

Pay'er s. One who pays; one on whom a bill of exchange is drawn.

Bray'er s. A wooden ink-muller used by printers; a donkey.

Defray'er s. (*Defray*).

Pray'er s. A supplicant; one who prays.

Prayer s. A supplication, entreaty; act of or form of words used in praying.

Spray'er s. One who sprays; an appliance for spraying.

Betray'er s. (*Betray*).

Portray'er s. One who portrays.

Stray'er s. One who strays.

Sooth'sayer s. A prophet, prognosticator.

Gainsay'er s. One who controverts; a contradicter.

Assay'er s. (*Assay*).

Méta'yer s. A tenant receiving seed, stock, etc., from the landlord and paying him part of the produce.

Stay'er s. One who or that which stays.

Dy'er s. One whose occupation is dyeing.

Obey'er (-bā'-) s. One who obeys.

Lam'mergeyer s. The great bearded vulture.

Mon'eyer s. A banker; an authorized coiner.

Prey'er s. One who or that which preys.

Convey'er s. One who or that which transports anything from place to place.

Shy'er s. One who or a horse, etc., which shies.

Fly'er s. One who flies or flees; a flying jump, etc.; a fly-wheel.

Oy'er s. A hearing or trial of causes in law.

Foyer' s. The entrance-hall of a theatre.

Cal'oyer s. A Greek monk.

Employ'er s. One who employs workpeople.

Destroy'er s. One who destroys; a vessel for combatting torpedo-boats.

Toy'er s. One who toys.

Dry'er s. (*Drier*).

Fry'er s. A vessel for frying fish.

Buy'er s. One who buys, especially or a retailer.

Law'yer s. One who practises or is versed in law.

Bow'yer s. A bow-maker.

Twyer s. A tuyère.

Gaz'er s. One who gazes.

Blaz'er s. A bright-coloured flannel sports jacket; (*slang*) a lie.

Glaz'er s. One who glazes earthenware; apparatus for glazing.

Ma'zer s. A large wooden drinking-bowl.

Gra'zer s. An animal that grazes.

Gee'zer s. (*Slang*) An old woman.

Sneez'er s. One who sneezes.

Freez'er s. A refrigerator.

Squeez'er s. One who or that which squeezes; playing-card with value marked in corner.

Tweez'er v.t. To pluck out with or use tweezers.

Ebene'zer s. A dissenting chapel.

Ju'daizer s. One who Judiazes.

Crit'icizer s. A critic, fault-finder.
Gor'mandizer s. A glutton.
Meth'odizer s. One who methodizes.
Seiz'er s. One who seizes.
Syl'logizer s. One who syllogizes.
Cat'echizer s. (*Catechize*).
Sym'pathizer s. (*Sympathize*).
Gen'eralizer s. One who generalizes.
Mor'alizer s. One who moralizes.
Neu'tralizer s. One who or that which neutralizes.
To'talizer s. A betting machine; system of this.
Spir'itualizer s. One who or that which spiritualizes.
Ster'ilizer s. Apparatus for sterilizing.
Fer'tilizer s. A fertilizing substance; a manure.
Civ'ilizer s. (*Civilize*).
Tran'quillizer s. One who calms or tranquillizes.
Sym'bolizer s. (*Symbolize*).
I'dolizer s. One who idolizes; an idolater.
Monop'olizer s. One that monopolizes.
Vic'timizer s. One who victimizes; a swindler.
At'omizer s. A contrivance for spraying liquids.
Or'ganizer s. One charged with organizing anything; a systematic manager.
Rec'ognizer s. One who recognizes.
Scru'tinizer s. One who scrutinizes.
Sol'emnizer s. One who solemnizes.
Li'onizer s. One who lionizes.
Col'onizer s. (*Colonize*).
Har'monizer s. One who or that which harmonizes.
Ser'monizer s. One who preaches.
Syn'chronizer s. (*Synchronize*).
Pat'ronizer s. One who patronizes.
Mod'ernizer s. One who modernizes.
Frat'ernizer s. One who fraternizes.
Po'larizer s. That which polarizes.
Depo'larizer s. (*Depolarize*).
Gran'gerizer s. One who grangerizes.
Mes'merizer s. A mesmerist.
Pul'verizer s. Machine for reducing liquid to fine spray.
Deo'dorizer s. A deodorizing agent.
The'orizer s. One who theorizes; a theorist.
Decol'orizer s. A decolorant.
Va'porizer s. Appliance for vaporizing liquids.
Tem'porizer s. One who temporizes.
Extem'porizer s. One who extemporizes.
Electri'zer s. One who or that which can or does electrify.
Siz'er s. A perforated plate for sorting small objects by size; one who sizes.
Mag'netizer s. One who magnetizes.
Ap'petizer s. A drink or condiment intended to promote appetite.
Sen'sitizer s. A sensitizing agent.
Gloz'er s. A flatterer.
Snooz'er s. One who snoozes.
How'itzer s. A short piece of ordnance for high-angle fire.
Swit'zer s. A Swiss.
Waltz'er s. One who waltzes.
Selt'zer s. An aerated mineral water.
Kreuz'er s. An obsolete German farthing.
Elec'trolyzer s. An agent used in electrolysis.
Quiz'zer s. One who quizzes.
Buz'zer s. A buzzing insect; an apparatus for making a humming noise.
Land'wehr s. The old German reserve of time-expired men.
Mohr s. A W. African gazelle.
Air s. The fluid we breathe; a light breeze; a tune; mien, bearing, affectation. v.t. To expose to the air; to dry or ventilate thus.
Fair a. Beautiful; light-complexioned; not cloudy; favourable, reasonable; just; legible; moderately good. adv. Openly; on good terms. s. The female sex, a beautiful woman; a free market; a show, bazaar.
Affair' s. Business; anything done or to be transacted.
Hair s. Dry, elastic filaments rising from the skin; anything similar; a minute distance or difference.
Chair s. A movable, backed seat for one; an iron support for securing railway lines. v.t. To carry in triumph.
Maid'enhair s. A fern with delicate fronds.
Mo'hair s. The hair of the Angora goat; fabric made from it.
Lair s. The couch or den of a wild beast; a cattle-shed.
Éclair' s. A small iced cake.
Flair s. Discernment, instinct for right appreciation.
Glair s. The white of an egg; any viscous matter.
Debonair' a. Elegant, gracious, courteous.
Pair s. Two things of a kind suited to each other or used together; a thing in two similar parts; a brace, couple; two opponents agreeing not to vote. v.i. To join in couples; to suit, fit, to agree with an opponent that neither votes. v.t. To form a pair of; to unite in a pair.
Repair' v.t. To restore, mend; to retrieve. v.i. To go, betake oneself. s. Restoration to sound state; good condition; a frequented place.
Disrepair' s. Want of repair; dilapidation.
Impair' v.i. To diminish in quantity, excellence, strength, etc.; to injure.
Despair' v.i. To be without or to give up hope. s. Hopelessness, despondency.
Cor'sair s. A pirate or his vessel; a privateer.
Stair s. A step or flight of steps.
Vair s. An heraldic fur.
Na'dir s. Point of heavens opposed to the zenith; the lowest point.
Mudir' s. A local governor in Turkey or Egypt.
Heir s. One who lawfully inherits, an inheritor.
Coheir' s. A joint heir.
Their pron. Poss. case of "they."
Weir (wēr) s. Dam for raising height of a stream; fence for catching fish.
Fir s. An evergreen conifer.
Kaf'fir s. One of a large African Bantu race; their language.
Men'hir s. An upright prehistoric stone monument.
Whir v.i. To whirl round or fly with a buzzing sound. s. Such a sound; a whizzing.
Fakir' s. A Mohammedan or Hindu mendicant monk.
Amir' s. A ruler in some Eastern countries.
Emir' s. An Arab or Saracen prince, commander, etc.
Sou'venir (soo'venēr) s. A keepsake memento.
Coir s. Cocoa-nut fibre for matting, etc.
Bou'doir s. A lady's retiring room.
Choir s. A company of singers; space allotted to them; the chancel. v.t. and i. To sing a hymn, sing together.
Re'trochoir s. Extension of a church behind the altar.
Loir s. A large variety of dormouse.
Couloir' s. A long, narrow mountain gorge.

Mem'oir s. A biographical notice; a short essay.
Peignoir (pānwar') s. A dressing-gown.
Rouge-et-noir' (-nwar) s. A gambling game.
Voussoir' (vooswar') s. A wedge-shaped stone in an arch.
Ab'attoir s. A slaughter-house.
Trot'toir s. A side-walk.
Dev'oir s. A service, duty.
Res'ervoir (vwar) s. Place where anything, especially water, is stored.
Ta'pir s. A hoofed, swine-like mammal of S. America.
Sir s. Term of formal address to a man; prefix to name of a baronet and knight.
Santir' (-tēr) s. A kind of dulcimer played in the East.
Stir v.t. To rouse, agitate, provoke, disturb. v.i. To move oneself; to be out of bed. s. Motion, bustle, agitation.
Astir' adv., a. Active, stirring.
Bestir' v.t. To stir up, put into action.
Le'vir s. One obliged by tribal custom to marry his deceased brother's widow.
El'zevir a. Belonging or relating to the Dutch publishers of this name (1592-1681). s. A book published or type used by them.
Decem'vir s. One of ten magistrates in ancient Rome; the body of these ten.
Trium'vir s. One of three united in office, especially in ancient Rome.
Centum'vir s. A judge among the ancient Romans.
Duum'vir s. One of two magistrates in ancient Rome.
Elix'ir s. A magic liquor of the alchemists; quintessence; a cordial.
Or conj. Introducing an alternative. adv. Ere; sooner than. s. Gold (*in heraldry*).
-or suff. Denoting agent or agency, or forming nouns of condition.
Ta'bor s. A small drum.
Ar'bor s. A spindle.
Dor s. A loud-humming beetle; the cockchafer.
Picador' s. A horseman in a bull-fight.
Toreador' s. A mounted bull-fighter.
Mirador' s. A belvedere turret.
Comprador' s. A native intermediary between European merchants and other natives in the Far East.
Ambas'sador s. An accredited representative of one state to another.
Mat'ador s. The man who kills the bull in a bull-fight; a card at ombre, etc.; a domino game.
Corregidor' s. A Spanish magistrate.
Ni'dor s. The smell of roast meat.
Cus'pidor s. A spittoon.
Cor'ridor s. A communicating passage or gallery.
Stri'dor s. A creaking noise, as of grasshoppers.
Ven'dor s. One who vends; the seller.
Con'dor s. The S. American vulture.
Louis d'or' s. An obsolete French gold coin.
Tu'dor a. Pertaining to the English dynasty from Henry VII to Elizabeth, or to this period.
Me'teor s. A luminous celestial body; a shooting star.
Feof'for s. One who grants a feoff.
Mortgagor' s. One who gives a mortgage.
Na'gor s. A small Senegalese antelope.
Pledg'or s. One who pledges.
Ob'ligor s. One bound by a bond.
Ri'gor s. A convulsive shuddering with sudden coldness.
Ful'gor s. Dazzling brightness; splendour.
Clan'gor s. A sharp, ringing sound; a series of clangs.
Abhor' v.t. To detest, loathe.
I'chor s. The ethereal substitute for blood in the veins of the Greek gods; watery discharge from a wound, etc.
An'chor s. An instrument for holding a ship at rest when floating. v.t. and i. To hold fast by or to cast an anchor.
Vouch'or s. One acting as security for another.
Mark'hor s. A mountain goat of Central Asia.
Met'aphor s. A figure of speech; similitude.
Eph'or s. A chief magistrate in ancient Sparta.
Cam'phor s. A white crystalline substance with strong aromatic smell obtained by distillation from certain plants.
Phos'phor s. Lucifer, the morning star.
Thor s. The ancient Scandinavian god of war.
Au'thor s. An originator; a writer of original books.
-ior suff. Forming comparatives of adjectives, and nouns expressing agent, thing that acts, etc.
Se'nior a. Elder; more advanced in age or rank. s. One in this position; one older than another.
Ju'nior a. Younger; later in office; lower in rank. s. One younger or beneath another.
Infer'ior a. Lower in place, excellence, etc.; subordinate. s. A person lower in rank, power, etc.
Super'ior a. Higher in quality, place, etc. s. One more advanced or elevated than another; chief of a monastery, etc.
Ulter'ior a. Being beyond or on the further side; remote; not pertinent; unavowed.
Anter'ior a. Going before, prior.
Inter'ior s. The inside; the internal or inland parts. a. Being within; internal, inner, inland.
Poster'ior a. Later; behind in position.
Exter'ior a. External, on the outside or outer side; foreign. s. Outward surface of a thing; that which is external or non-essential.
Pri'or a. Preceding; antecedent; pre-eminent. adv. Previously. s. The monastic head next below an abbot.
War'rior (wŏr'-) s. A fighting-man, soldier.
Excel'sior a. More lofty; higher.
Ma'jor a. Greater in quantity, size, etc.; more important. s. A person of full age; army officer next above captain.
Squal'or s. Squalidity; meanness, filthiness.
Bach'elor s. An unmarried man.
Bailor' s. One who entrusts another with goods for some specific purpose.
Sail'or s. A seaman, mariner; a seafarer.
Tail'or s. Maker of men's clothes. v.i. To work as a tailor.
Sim'ilor s. Alloy used for imitation gold jewelry

Pal'lor s. Paleness.
Chan'cellor s. A high judicial officer; president of a court, university, etc.
Coun'sellor s. One who is consulted and gives advice, especially on legal matters.
Coun'cillor s. A member of a council.
Set'tlor s. One who makes a settlement of property.
Clam'or s. Clamour.
Trem'or s. An involuntary shivering; trembling.
Term'or s. A termer.
Nor conj. And not.
Man'or s. Large landed estate; a lordship.
Señor' (-nyor') s. The Spanish equivalent of "Mr."
Ten'or s. Drift, a settled course; a high male voice.
Si'gnor (sē'nyor) s. Italian equivalent for "Mr." or "sir."
Consignor' s. One who consigns goods to another.
Monsignor' (-sēnyor) s. Title of prelates and other dignitaries of the Roman Catholic Church.
Assignor' s. One who transfers a right or property.
Bar'gainor s. A seller of real property.
Distrain'or s. One who distrains or levies a distress.
Mi'nor a. Smaller, inferior, subordinate; less than a semitone. s. One under full age; a minor key, etc.
Do'nor s. A giver, benefactor.
Gov'ernor s. One who governs; one holding supreme power; a tutor; a piece of mechanism for maintaining uniform velocity; (*slang*) one's father or employer.
Boor s. A rude, uncultured person; a rustic.
Door s. The entrance of a house, apartment, etc.; means of access; a hinged leaf for closing an entrance.
In'door a. Being within doors.
Out'door a. Being or living outside.
Floor s. The lower surface of a room, vessel, etc.; a story of a building. v.t. To cover with a floor; to knock down; to answer completely.
Moor s. An open heath; a native of Morocco and adjoining parts. v.t. To secure a ship by anchors. v.i. To anchor, lie at anchor.
Black'amoor s. A negro.
Koh'-i-noor s. A famous diamond in the British regalia; anything priceless.
Poor a. Needy; badly supplied; unsatisfactory; meagre; unproductive; mean; paltry; devoid of value or merit; weak; worthy of pity. s. The needy or indigent.
Spoor s. The track of a wild animal. v.t. To track game.
Sa'por s. Distinctive flavour.
Tor'por s. Torpidity.
Stu'por s. A dazed condition; torpor.
Em'peror s. The ruler of an empire.
Con'queror s. A victor.
Recov'eror s. Person obtaining a judgment at law.
Er'ror s. Deviation from the right course; inaccuracy; blunder, fault; violation of law or duty.
Ter'ror s. Great fear; alarm; consternation.
Mir'ror s. A looking-glass; a pattern. v.t. To reflect.
Hor'ror s. Strong feeling of fear and detestation; a shuddering; that which excites terror or repulsion.
Jur'or s. One serving on a jury.
Con'juror s. A juggler, one who practises sleight-of-hand.
Conjur'or s. One bound with others by an oath.
Non-jur'or s. One who refused to take the oath of allegiance after the English revolution of 1688.
Assur'or s. An underwriter.
Releasor' s. One releasing property, etc., to another.
Inci'sor s. Fore-tooth that cuts the food.
Sei'sor (sē'-) s. One who takes possession.
Prom'isor s. One who engages or undertakes.
Vis'or s. Perforated part of helmet for seeing through.
Devis'or s. One who bequeaths by will.
Divis'or s. Number by which the dividend is divided.
Provis'or s. The purveyor to or steward of a religious house.
Su'pervisor s. A superintendent, overseer.
Cen'sor s. An official examiner of plays, books, etc., and other writings intended for publication; a severe critic. v.t. To control publication thus; to expurgate.
Accen'sor s. One who looks after the candles in Roman Catholic churches.
Recen'sor s. One who makes recensions.
Suspen'sor s. A suspensorium.
Ten'sor s. A muscle that stretches part to which it is fixed.
Exten'sor s. A muscle which extends any part of the body.
Spon'sor s. A godparent; a guarantor.
Precur'sor s. A forerunner; a sign, omen.
Succes'sor s. One who follows; one who takes the place left by another.
Pre'decessor s. One who precedes another; an ancestor.
Anteces'sor s. A previous owner.
Interces'sor s. A mediator; a bishop temporarily administering a see during a vacancy.
Confes'sor s. One who confesses or who hears confession; a martyr, saint.
Profes'sor s. One making formal or open profession; a University teacher of the highest rank.
Lessor' s. One who grants a lease.
Aggres'sor s. One who commences a quarrel or hostilities.
Transgres'sor s. One who transgresses, a sinner.
Depres'sor s. One who or that which depresses (as a muscle).
Compres'sor s. One who or that which compresses.
Oppres'sor s. One who oppresses; a tyrant.
Suppres'sor s. One who suppresses.
Asses'sor s. One who makes an assessment; an adviser of a judge on technical matters.
Posses'sor s. One who possesses; the owner.
Scis'sor v.t. To cut with scissors.
Occlu'sor s. An organ that occludes or closes.
Tor s. A bleak, rocky hill.
Proba'tor s. An examiner, approver.
In'cubator s. Apparatus for hatching eggs by artificial heat, or for rearing prematurely born children.
Des'iccator s. An apparatus for drying substances.
Ex'siccator s. An apparatus for extracting the moisture from substances.
De'fecator s. One who or that which purifies.
Hypoth'ecator s. One who hypothecates; a mortgagor.

Dep'recator s. One who deprecates.
Ab'dicator s. (*Abdicate*).
Ded'icator s. One who dedicates anything.
In'dicator s. One who or that which indicates; a recording apparatus.
Vin'dicator s. One who vindicates or justifies.
Adju'dicator s. (*Adjudicate*).
Pac'ificator s. A peacemaker.
Signif'icator s. One who or that which signifies.
Vinif'icator s. Apparatus for condensing alcoholic vapours in wine-making.
Scar'ificator s. An instrument used in cupping.
Sac'rificator s. One who offers a sacrifice.
Multiplica'tor s. A multiplier.
Du'plicator s. A machine for making copies.
Explica'tor s. An interpreter, expositor.
For'nicator s. One guilty of fornication.
Commu'nicator s. One who informs; apparatus or means by which one can communicate with another.
Excom-mu'nicator s. One who excommunicates.
Prevar'icator s. A quibbler.
Fab'ricator s. One who fabricates.
Lu'bricator s. Apparatus for lubricating machinery.
Ru'bricator s. One who rubricates.
Decor'ticator s. Machine for stripping husks from grain.
Mas'ticator s. One who or a machine which masticates.
Sophis'ticator s. One who sophisticates or adulterates.
Prognos'ticator s. One who divines the future from present signs.
De'falcator s. (*Defalcate*).
In'culcator s. One who inculcates.
Recip'rocator s. One who or that which reciprocates.
Ev'ocator s. One who or that which evokes.
Equiv'ocator s. One who equivocates.
Con'fiscator s. One who confiscates.
Ed'ucator s. One who educates or instructs.
Dep'redator s. One who plunders.
Elu'cidator s. One who explains; an expositor.
Inval'idator s. One who or that which invalidates.
Intim'idator s. One who intimidates or threatens.
Delap'idator s. A person or agent causing delapidation.
Liq'uidator s. One who winds up the affairs of a company, etc.
Manda'tor s. One who gives a mandate.
E'mendator s. One who removes faults.
Com'mendator s. One who holds a benefice temporarily.
Lauda'tor s. One who praises or eulogizes.
Delin'eator s. One who delineates.
Crea'tor s. The Being that creates; a maker, producer.
Pro'creator s. One who begets; a sire.
Cav'eator s. One who enters a caveat.
Prop'agator s. One who propagates.
Lega'tor s. A testator.
Al'ligator s. A large saurian from America and China.
Fum'igator s. One who or that which fumigates.
Ir'rigator s. One who irrigates.
Mit'igator s. One who or that which mitigates.
Cas'tigator s. (*Castigate*).
Inves'tigator s. One who investigates; an inquirer.
In'stigator s. One who instigates or incites another.
Nav'igator s. One skilled in navigation; an explorer by sea.
Circum-nav'igator s. (*Circumnavigate*).
Prom'ulgator s. One who promulgates decrees, etc.
Inter'rogator s. One who interrogates.
Compurga'tor s. One who testifies to the innocence of another.
Ex'purgator s. One who expurgates.
Sub'jugator s. One who subjugates; a conquerer.
Cor'rugator s. A muscle that contracts the brows.
Appre'ciator s. (*Appreciate*).
Enun'ciator s. One who enunciates, a good pronouncer.
Denun'ciator s. One who denounces or makes denunciations.
Annun'ciator s. A person, instrument, or indicator that announces.
Glad'iator s. One who fought publicly for entertainment in ancient Rome; a prize-fighter.
Ra'diator s. A body or apparatus that radiates.
Me'diator s. One who mediates; an intercessor.
Repu'diator s. One who repudiates.
Concil'iator s. One who conciliates.
Spo'liator s. A plunderer.
Calum'niator s. One who calumniates.
Ex'piator s. One who makes expiation.
Var'iator s. (*Variate*).
Impro'priator s. A layman to whom church property is impropriated.
Appro'priator s. (*Appropriate*); a religious corporation owning a benefice.
Expa'tiator s. One who expatiates.
Ini'tiator s. One who initiates.
Propi'tiator s. One who propitiates or atones.
Vit'iator (vish'-) s. One who vitiates or corrupts.
Nego'tiator s. One who negotiates.
Via'tor s. A traveller, wayfarer.
A'viator s. One who flies an aeroplane, airship, etc; an aeronaut.
De'viator s. One who or that which deviates.
Alle'viator s. (*Alleviate*).
Abbre'viator s. One who abridges; a Papal official who condenses petitions, etc.
Asphyx'iator s. (*Asphyxiate*).
Es'calator s. A moving stairway.
No'menclator s. One who gives names to things; a dictionary compiler.
Dela'tor s. A paid informer.
Rela'tor s. A relater; a prosecutor.
In'sufflator s. Instrument used for insufflation.
Dila'tor s. A muscle, instrument, etc., for dilating.
Invig'ilator s. One who watches students during an examination.
Anni'hilator s. (*Annihilate*).
Assim'ilator s. (*Assimilate*).
Dep'ilator s. An instrument or application for removing hair.
Ven'tilator s. Contrivance for ventilating.
Mu'tilator s. One who mutilates.
Flag'ellator s. One who scourges himself or others, especially fanatically.
Interpel'lator s. An interpellant.
Os'cillator s. That which oscillates; a pendulum.
In'stillator s. One who instils.
Colla'tor s. One who collates sheets for binding; one who collates to a benefice.
Per'colator s. A filtering machine.
Vi'olator s. One who violates; a ravisher.
Im'molator s. One who offers a sacrifice.
Des'olator s. One who lays waste; a ravager.
I'solator s. One who or that which isolates.
Con'templator s. One who contemplates.
Leg'islator s. One who makes laws; member of a legislature.
Transla'tor s. One who translates.
Tab'ulator s. One who or that which tabulates.

Peram'bulator s. A child's carriage pushed from behind; instrument for measuring distance travelled.
Pec'ulator s. One who peculates; an embezzler.
Spec'ulator s. One who speculates, especially financially.
Artic'ulator s. One who pronounces carefully; one who articulates skeletons.
Gestic'ulator s. One who gesticulates.
Cal'culator s. A person or machine that calculates.
Inoc'ulator s. One who inoculates.
Cir'culator s. (*Circulate*).
Ad'ulator s. A flatterer.
Strid'ulator s. Anything that stridulates.
Mod'ulator s. One who or that which modulates.
Coag'ulator s. (*Coagulate*).
Reg'ulator s. One who or that which regulates.
Em'ulator s. A rival, competitor.
Sim'ulator s. One who or that which simulates.
Dissim'ulator s. One who dissimulates, a dissembler.
Stim'ulator s. One who stimulates; a stimulant.
Accu'mulator s. An apparatus for the storage of electrical energy.
Gran'ulator s. An appliance for granulating.
Manip'ulator s. One who manipulates.
Stip'ulator s. One who makes a stipulation.
Depop'ulator s. One who or that which depopulates.
In'sulator s. A non-conductor of heat or electricity.
Congrat'ulator s. One who congratulates.
Pos'tulator s. One who postulates.
Expos'tulator s. One who expostulates.
Crema'tor s. A furnace for cremating corpses.
Dec'imator s. (*Decimate*).
Col'limator s. An optical apparatus for determining error of or effecting collimation.
Es'timator s. One who estimates.
Con'summator s. (*Consummate*).
Conform'ator s. A device for ascertaining shape of a thing to be fitted.
A'lienator s. (*Alienate*).
Sen'ator s. A member of a senate.
Reju'venator s. One who or that which makes young again.
Propugna'tor s. A defender, champion.
Vac'cinator s. One who vaccinates.
Buc'cinator s. The muscle in the cheek.
Vatic'inator s. A prophet.
Fas'cinator s. One who or that which fascinates.
Orig'inator s. One who or that which originates.
Mach'inator s. An intriguer, plotter.
Dec'linator s. An instrument for taking the declination and inclination of a plane.
Dissem'inator s. One who disseminates.
Recrim'inator s. One who recriminates.
Dom'inator s. A ruler, ruling power; predominant influence.
Nom'inator s. One who nominates.
Denom'inator s. One who or that which denominates; the number below the line in vulgar fractions.
Ter'minator s. One who or that which terminates.
Deter'minator s. One who or that which determines.
Exter'minator s. One who or that which exterminates.
Illu'minator s. One who or that which illuminates; a decorator of MSS., etc.
Ru'minator s. One who or that which ruminates.
Su'pinator s. A muscle in the hand.
Per'egrinator s. One who peregrinates; a wanderer.
Assas'sinator s. An assassin.
Procras'tinator s. One who procrastinates.
Predes'tinator s. One who predestinates; a predestinarian.
Dona'tor s. A giver, donor.
Res'onator s. That which resonates or detects resonance; a sounding board.
Per'sonator s. One who personates another.
Imper'sonator s. One who impersonates.
De'tonator s. One who or that which detonates a fog-signal.
Al'ternator s. A dynamo for generating an alternating current.
Antic'ipator s. (*Anticipate*).
Partic'ipator s. A participant.
Eman'cipator s. (*Emancipate*).
Ex'tirpator s. One who or that which extirpates.
Sep'arator s. A divider; apparatus for separating cream from milk.
Cel'ebrator s. (*Celebrate*).
Vibra'tor s. A vibrating part; that which vibrates.
Des'ecrator s. One who desecrates.
Con'secrator s. (*Consecrate*).
Lib'erator s. One who liberates.
Mod'erator s. The President of a meeting, especially of a Presbyterian synod.
Vocif'erator s. One who vociferates.
Exag'gerator s. One who exaggerates.
Refrig'erator s. A cold store; apparatus for rapid cooling.
Accel'erator s. A device for changing or increasing the speed of some operation.
Tol'erator s. (*Tolerate*).
Nu'merator s. One who numbers; part of a vulgar fraction above the line.
Enu'merator s. One who enumerates.
Gen'erator s. One who or that which produces or begets.
Regen'erator s. One who or that which regenerates; a device in furnaces, etc., by means of which waste heat is utilized.
Ven'erator s. One who venerates.
Incin'erator s. Furnace for destruction of refuse, etc., or for cremation.
Im'perator s. An emperor; a victorious general of ancient Rome.
Op'erator s. One who or that which operates.
Co-op'erator s. One who co-operates; a member of a co-operative society.
Vitu'perator s. An abusive, railing person.
Lit'erator s. A pretender to learning.
Translit'erator s. (*Transliterate*).
Adul'terator s. One who adulterates food, drink, etc.
De'flagrator s. A battery or other agent for producing rapid combustion.
In'tegrator s. An apparatus for determining the value of an integral.
Migra'tor s. A migrant.
Trans'migrator s. A transmigrant.
De'nigrator s. A calumniator, one who denigrates.
As'pirator s. A contrivance for drawing in air or gas.
Res'pirator s. Appliance for breathing through.
In'spirator s. Apparatus for drawing in air.
Conspir'ator s. One who conspires.
Or'ator s. An eloquent public speaker.
Elab'orator s. One who elaborates.
Collab'orator s. (*Collaborate*).
Corrob'orator s. (*Corroborate*).
Dec'orator s. One who embellishes; a house-painter.
Edul'corator s. One who or that which sweetens or removes acidity.
Per'forator s. A perforating instrument or machine.
Invig'orator s. One who or that which invigorates.
Ame'liorator s. (*Ameliorate*).

Cor'porator s. A member of a corporation.
Incor'porator s. One who incorporates.
Bar'rator s. One who stirs up litigation out of malice or for some ulterior end.
Narra'tor s. One who narrates a story, etc.
Per'petrator s. One who perpetrates, the guilty one.
Ar'bitrator s. An arbiter.
Con'centrator s. An apparatus for separating dry pulverized ore.
Se'questrator s. One who sequestrates.
Admin'istrator s. (*Administrate*).
Dem'onstrator s. One who demonstrates or teaches by means of exhibition and experiment.
Rem'onstrator s. One who remonstrates.
Ill'ustrator s. One who illustrates, especially books.
Cura'tor s. One in charge of a museum, library, etc.
Proc'urator s. One who manages another's affairs; an ancient Roman provincial fiscal officer.
Inau'gurator s. One who inaugurates or performs an inauguration ceremony.
Sul'phurator s. Apparatus used in sulphurating.
Dep'urator s. One who or that which cleanses.
Ob'turator s. A membrane, muscle, etc., closing a cavity or orifice.
Trit'urator s. Apparatus for reducing to fine powder.
Improv'isator s. An improvisatore.
Pulsa'tor s. A jigging-machine; a pulsometer.
Com'pensator s. (*Compensate*).
Ter'giversator s. One who practises shifts and evasions.
Glossa'tor s. An annotator.
Specta'tor s. A looker-on, observer.
Dicta'tor s. One who dictates; one invested with absolute power.
Puncta'tor s. One who marks with points, especially Hebrew texts.
Resus'citator s. One who brings to life again.
Med'itator s. One who meditates.
Ag'itator s. A professional exciter of political agitation.
Prestidig'itator s. A conjurer, juggler.
Habil'itator s. One who supplies means.
Im'itator s. One who mimics.
Precip'itator s. One who or that which precipitates.
Aus'cultator s. (*Auscultation*).
Or'ientator s. A surveyors' instrument.
Com'mentator s. An expositor, annotator.
An'notator s. (*Annotate*).
Rota'tor s. That which imparts circular motion.
Dev'astator s. One who devastates.
Testa'tor s. One who leaves a will.
Com'mutator s. An apparatus for changing the course of an electric current; a commutor.
Am'putator s. (*Amputate*).
Scruta'tor s. A close inquirer.
Evac'uator s. One who evacuates.
Val'uator s. An appraiser.
Exten'uator s. One who extenuates.
Insin'uator s. One who insinuates.
Contin'uator s. One who continues unfinished work.
Equa'tor s. The great circle which divides the earth into the N. and S. hemispheres; the circle in the heavens coinciding with the plane of this.
Exequa'tor s. The written credentials of a consul, etc.; official authorization for papal bulls.
Ex'cavator s. One who or a machine which excavates.
Leva'tor s. A muscle that raises some part.
El'evator s. One who or that which elevates; a lift, hoist.
Cul'tivator s. One who cultivates; a kind of harrow.
Ren'ovator s. One who renovates or repairs.
In'novator s. One who introduces changes or novelties.
Conser'vator s. A preserver, guardian, member of a conservancy.
Totaliza'tor s. A totalizer.
Debt'or s. One indebted.
Ac'tor s. One who acts, especially a professional performer on the stage.
Fac'tor s. An agent, deputy; one of the quantities which, when multiplied together, form a product.
Calefac'tor s. A small cooking-stove.
Mal'efactor s. An evil-doer, a felon.
Ben'efactor s. One who confers a benefit.
Refrac'tor s. That which refracts; a refracting telescope.
Trac'tor s. One who or that which draws or pulls.
Detrac'tor s. One who detracts; a slanderer; a muscle drawing one part from another.
Retrac'tor s. Anything, especially a muscle, used for drawing back.
Contrac'tor s. One who contracts, especially to perform work on specified terms.
Protrac'tor s. Instrument for laying down or measuring angles; that which protracts, as a muscle, etc.
Attrac'tor s. (*Attract*).
Extrac'tor s. One who extracts; an implement for extracting.
Transac'tor s. One who transacts anything.
Exac'tor s. One who exacts; an extortioner.
Effec'tor s. One who effects; a maker, doer.
Hec'tor s. A bully. v.t. and i. To bully, play the bully, bluster.
Objec'tor s. One who objects.
Ejec'tor s. One who or that which ejects.
Injec'tor s. One who or that which injects; apparatus for performing injections.
Projec'tor s. One who forms a scheme, especially of a wild nature.
Lec'tor s. A public reader, especially in churches.
Elec'tor s. One who does or may elect; a voter; one of the German princes formerly entitled to elect the Emperor.
Prelec'tor s. One who reads a discourse in public.
Selec'tor s. One who selects.
Deflec'tor s. One who or that which deflects.
Reflec'tor s. One who reflects; a surface for reflecting images or rays; a mirror.
Neglec'tor s. One who neglects.
Collec'tor s. (*Collect*).
Connec'tor s. (*Connecter*).
Prospec'tor s. One who prospects or explores for ore.
Inspec'tor s. One who inspects, an overseer.
Rec'tor s. An incumbent whose tithes are not impropriated; head of some colleges, etc.
Erec'tor s. That which erects; an erecting muscle.

Direc'tor s. One who directs, instructs, etc.; one who transacts the affairs of a trading company, bank, etc.; device for controlling electric current, etc.
Correc'tor s. One who or that which corrects; a censor.
Sec'tor s. Part of a circle between two radii and an arc; a mathematical instrument.
Bisec'tor s. A bisecting line.
Viv'isector s. A vivisectionist.
Prosec'tor s. A dissector.
Dissec'tor s. One who dissects.
Detec'tor s. One who or that which detects.
Protec'tor s. One who or that which protects; a guardian, supporter.
Vec'tor s. A certain mathematical line or quantity.
Contradic'tor s. One who contradicts.
Predic'tor s. A prophet, foreteller.
Lic'tor s. An ancient Roman civil officer.
Constric'tor s. That which constricts, as a muscle; a serpent which crushes its prey.
Vic'tor s. A conqueror, winner.
Evic'tor s. One who evicts.
Concoc'tor s. One who concocts.
Doc'tor s. One licensed to practise medicine, a physician; one who has received the highest degree at a University. v.t. To treat as a doctor; to alter for the better; to adulterate, falsify.
Proc'tor s. A University official who keeps order; an advocate, a law-officer.
Abduc'tor s. (*Abduct*).
Adduc'tor s. A muscle bringing one part towards another.
Educ'tor s. One who or that which educes.
Induc'tor s. One who inducts a clergyman; an electrical appliance.
Conduc'tor s. One who or that which conducts; a leader, director; a medium for transmission of heat, electricity, etc.
Non-conduc'tor s. A substance that does not permit (or permits only with difficulty) transmission of heat or electricity.
Transduc'tor s. A muscle of the great toe.
Destruc'tor s. A kiln for burning refuse.
Instruc'tor s. One who instructs; a teacher.
Construc'tor s. (*Construct*).
Præ'tor s. An ancient Roman magistrate.
Propræ'tor s. An ancient Roman governor or magistrate.
Fe'tor s. A stench.
Rhe'tor s. A mere orator.
Propri'etor s. An owner, rightful possessor.
Secre'tor s. One who or that which secretes.
Trai'tor s. One guilty of treachery. a. Traitorous.
Inhib'itor s. One who inhibits.
Prohib'itor s. One who prohibits.
Exhib'itor s. One who exhibits.
Solic'itor s. A legal practitioner advising clients and instructing counsel; an attorney.
Exci'tor s. A nerve in the spinal group.
Ed'itor s. One who prepares literary work for publication; one who conducts a newspaper or periodical.
Cred'itor s. One to whom a debt is due.
Au'ditor s. One appointed to check accounts; a hearer.
Jan'itor s. A door-keeper.
Primogen'itor s. The first father or forefather.
Progen'itor s. A direct ancestor.
Mon'itor s. One who warns or admonishes; a senior pupil having certain authority over juniors; a kind of ironclad; a large lizard.
Admon'itor s. One who admonishes.
Premon'itor s. One who or that which gives previous warning.
Appar'itor s. An usher or petty officer in a court.
Her'itor s. One who inherits.
Inher'itor s. One who inherits.
Coher'itor s. A coheir.
Inquis'itor s. One who makes inquisition; a functionary of the Inquisition.
Vis'itor s. One who makes a call; an inspector.
Depos'itor s. One who makes a deposit.
Prepos'itor s. A school monitor, præpostor.
Ovipos'itor s. The tubular organ with which insects deposit their eggs.
Compos'itor s. One who sets type for printing.
Expos'itor s. One who explains; an interpreter, commentator.
Compet'itor s. A rival; one who competes.
Suit'or s. A petitioner; a wooer.
Absol'vitor s. An acquittal.
Ser'vitor s. An attendant, servant.
Consultor' s. A member of a consultative body.
Can'tor s. A precentor.
Guarantor' s. One who guarantees.
Grantor' s. One who makes a grant or conveyance.
War'rantor s. One who gives legal warrant.
Accen'tor s. The hedge-sparrow.
Succen'tor s. A deputy precentor.
Precen'tor s. Leader of a cathedral choir; a member of a chapter; a minor canon.
Len'tor s. Sluggishness of temperament, etc.; viscidity of blood.
Men'tor s. A wise and faithful counsellor.
Tormen'tor s. One who or that which torments.
Circum-feren'tor s. A surveyor's instrument.
Assen'tor s. A signatory to a nomination in support of the proposer and seconder.
Sten'tor s. One with a loud voice; a howling monkey.
Inven'tor s. One who invents; a contriver.
Mo'tor s. That which moves or causes motion; generation of mechanical power; internal combustion engine; an automobile. a. Causing or imparting motion. v.i. and t. To drive, ride, or convey in a motor-car.
Locomo'tor a. Pertaining to locomotion, s. That which is capable of locomotion.
Cap'tor s. One who makes a capture.
Accep'tor s. One who accepts a bill of exchange.
Precep'tor s. An instructor; head of a school.
Suscep'tor s. One who undertakes anything; a sponsor.
Excep'tor s. One who makes exceptions; a caviller.
Sculp'tor s. One who sculptures.
Emp'tor s. A purchaser.
Excerp'tor s. One who makes excerptions.
Cham'pertor s. One who through purchase carries on a lawsuit so as to obtain a share of the gain.
Asser'tor s. (*Assert*).
Cas'tor s. A closed vessel with perforated top; small swivelled wheel for chair, etc.; the beaver.
Pas'tor s. One in charge of a flock; a minister.
Quæs'tor s. A civil and military official of ancient Rome.
An'cestor s. A forefather, progenitor.

Nes'tor s. A wise old counsellor.
Attes'tor s. One who attests.
Inves'tor s. One who invests, especially money.
Polyhis'tor s. A very learned person.
Resis'tor s. An electrical resisting device.
Assis'tor s. An assistant.
Præpos'tor s. A school monitor.
Impos'tor s. A cheat; a deceiver under a false character.
Abet'tor s. (*Abet*).
Car'burettor s. An apparatus by means of which air is impregnated with the gas of carbon compounds.
Contrib'utor s. One who contributes; a writer for periodicals, etc.
Distrib'utor s. One who or that which distributes.
Pros'ecutor s. One who prosecutes, especially in a criminal suit.
Per'secutor s. One who persecutes.
Exec'utor s. One who executes or performs; one appointed by a testator to execute his will.
Locu'tor s. A spokesman.
Colloc'utor s. One who takes part in a discussion, conference, etc.
Proloc'utor s. A speaker, chairman.
Interloc'utor s. One taking part in a conversation.
Coadju'tor s. An assistant; a colleague.
Commu'tor s. One who or that which commutes; a commutator.
Su'tor s. A cobbler.
Tu'tor s. A guardian; a teacher, especially private. v.t. To train, instruct, discipline.
In'stitutor s. One who institutes.
Con'stitutor s. (*Constitute*).
Pros'titutor s. One who prostitutes.
Lan'guor s. Lassitude, inertness; debility.
Flu'or s. Fluoride of calcium, a brittle, transparent mineral.
Liq'uor s. A fluid; the liquid part of anything; a spirituous drink.
Cru'or s. Gore, coagulated blood.
Survi'vor s. One who survives; the longer living.
Sal'vor s. One who or a ship which salves.
Flex'or s. A muscle causing a limb or part to bend.
Mayor s. The chief magistrate of a borough.
Convey'or s. (*Conveyer*).
Purvey'or s. One who sells provisions; a caterer.
Survey'or (-vā'-) s. One who surveys; a land-measurer, estate-agent, inspector.
Ra'zor s. Sharp knife for shaving with. v.t. To shave.
Disseizor' s. One who unlawfully dispossesses another of an estate.
Cognizor' s. One who acknowledges the right of the cognizee in a fine of land.
Recognizor s. One who enters into a recognizance.
Carr s. Reclaimed marshland.
Charr s. A fish of the trout family.
Parr s. A young salmon before the smolt stage.
Err v.i. To wander, stray from rectitude; to mistake.
Herr s. German title corresponding to "Mr."
Chirr v.i. To make the monotonous sound of the grasshopper. s. This sound.
Shirr s. Elastic thread inserted in cloth. v.t. To gather by means of this.
Skirr v.t. and i. To pass over or move rapidly; to scour, scud.
Dorr s. A dor; kind of beetle.
Burr s. A rough edge left on metal after cutting, etc.; rough sounding of "r"; a whirring noise; a clinker; a bur. v.t. and i. To pronounce one's "r's" roughly, to grate.
Churr s. The cry of the night-jar.
Purr s. The low murmur of a cat. v.t. To make this sound, or a low sound of content.
Scaur s. A bare place on a mountain.
Gaur s. A large Indian wild ox.
Meg'alosaur s. A gigantic extinct carnivorous lizard.
Di'nosaur s. A gigantic mesozoic reptile.
Had'rosaur s. A gigantic fossil saurian.
Pter'osaur s. An extinct flying reptile.
Cen'taur s. A mythological monster half man and half horse.
Bucen'taur s. The state barge of the Venetian doges.
Mi'notaur s. A mythological bull-headed monster.
Bur s. A prickly fruit or calyx; an excrescence on a tree; (*slang*) a sponger, parasite.
Sam'bur s. An Asiatic deer, the Indian elk.
Cur s. A mongrel; a surly fellow.
Occur' v.i. To happen; to come to the mind.
Recur' v.i. To come back; to occur again; to have recourse.
Incur' v.t. To expose oneself to, become liable or subject to.
Concur' v.i. To agree, consent, act in conjunction with.
Baha'dur s. A title given by Hindus to English officers.
Farceur' s. One who plays jokes; an actor in or writer of farces.
Douceur' s. A gift, tip, bribe.
Gran'deur s. Quality of being grand; splendour, magnificence, impressiveness.
Coiffeur' s. A hairdresser.
Chauffeur' s. A motor-car driver.
Voltigeur' s. A French rifleman.
Accoucheur' s. A man-midwife.
Cise'leur s. Chased or engraved work.
Siffleur' s. A professional whistler; the mountain marmot.
Persifleur' s. A banterer; one who indulges in persiflage.
Jong'leur s. A mediæval itinerant French minstrel.
Tirailleur' s. A French sharpshooter.
Mitrailleur' s. One firing a mitrailleuse.
Petroleur' s. An incendiary.
Flaneur' s. A lounger, loafer.
Entrepreneur' s. A contractor, organizer.
Seign'eur (sān'yer) s. A feudal lord; a lord of the manor.
Monseign'eur (-sānyeur) s. Title of honour of cardinals and other dignitaries.
Sabreur' s. A cavalryman.
Franc-tireur' s. An irregular foot-soldier (esp. French).
Écraseur' s. A surgical instrument for performing cutting operations without hæmorrhage.
Friseur' s. A hairdresser.
Poseur' s. One who poses, especially mentally; an affected person.
Chasseur' s. A huntsman; a light-armed French soldier.
Masseur' s. A man who gives massage.
Connoisseur' s. A critical judge of any fine art.
Am'ateur s. A non-professional, especially in sport.
Litterateur' s. A man of letters.
Restaurateur' s. Keeper of a restaurant.
Redacteur' s. A book-editor.
Raconteur' s. A good story-teller.

Colporteur' s. An itinerant seller of Bibles, tracts, etc.
Hauteur' s. Haughtiness, arrogance.
Claqueur' s. A hired applauder.
Liqueur' s. A flavoured alcoholic cordial.
Fur s. Fine hair on certain animals; a coating resembling fur; furred animals. a. Pertaining to or made of fur. v.t. To coat or line with fur.
Fur'fur s. Scurf, dandruff.
Lan'gur s. An Asiatic long-tailed monkey.
Au'gur s. A soothsayer, diviner.
Mo'hur s. A British Indian gold coin (15 rupees).
Sul'phur s. A yellow, non-metallic element; brimstone. a. Pale-yellow.
Blur s. A smear, stain. v.t. To obscure, blot, render indistinct.
Slur v.t. To pass lightly over, pronounce indistinctly, speak slightingly of. s. A slight reproach or disgrace; a a blur; a slurring in singing, etc., curve denoting this.
Testa'mur s. Certificate granted on passing an examination.
Demur' v.i. To hesitate, doubt, object. s. Pause; scruple, objection.
Fe'mur s. The thigh-bone.
Le'mur s. A nocturnal animal allied to the monkeys.
Mur'mur v.i. To make a low continued sound; to complain, grumble. s. A low, confused sound; a grumble; subdued speech.
Reaumur' (râ-ō-) a. Applied to a thermometer in which the boiling point is 80° and the freezing point 0°.
Knur s. A knot in timber; a hard lump.
Our a. Pertaining to or belonging to us.
-our suff. Forming nouns denoting an act or agent.
Giaour s. Turkish name for a Christian or other non-Mohammedan.
La'bour s. Physical or mental exertion; pains; toil; work; travail. v.i. To use exertion, toil; to be in travail. v.t. To fabricate, elaborate.
Bela'bour v.t. To thump severely.
Overla'bour v.t. To work on too much, elaborate excessively.
Neigh'bour (nā'-) s. One who lives near to another. v.t. To be near to; to adjoin.
Tam'bour s. A small bass drum; an embroidery frame, a kind of embroidery; part of an architectural column. v.t. and i. To embroider on a tambour.
Calembour' s. A pun.
Ar'bour s. A bower formed by interlacing tree-stems, etc.; a shady retreat.
Har'bour s. A station for ships, haven; an asylum. v.t. To entertain, shelter. v.i. To take shelter.
Suc'cour v.t. To relieve, aid, cherish. s. Aid; assistance in distress.
Ran'cour s. Deep malignity; inveterate hatred.
Scour v.t. To rub hard for cleaning; to move rapidly over. v.i. To cleanse; to range, rove; to search about.
Dour a. Stern, gloomy.
Trou'badour (troo'-) s. An early Provençal poet.
Can'dour s. Sincerity, openness.
Splen'dour s. Brilliant lustre; great show of richness, etc.; eminence; pomp.
O'dour s. Any scent, good or bad; fragrance.
Ar'dour s. Warmth of passion or affection; enthusiasm.
Four a. and s. Twice two; 4.
Rig'our s. Stiffness; austereness; severity, especially of climate.
Vig'our s. Active force; energy; strength.
Hour s. Space of sixty minutes; particular time; appointed time.
-iour suff. Forming nouns expressing an agent, thing that acts, etc.
Beha'viour s. Conduct, deportment.
Misbeha'viour s. Improper or rude behaviour; ill-conduct.
Pa'viour s. A pavier.
Sa'viour s. One who rescues or preserves, especially Christ.
Abatjour' s. A skylight.
Lour v.i. To appear dark, stormy, or gloomy; to scowl. s. Gloominess; sullenness; a scowl.
Val'our s. Courage; bravery; prowess in war.
Flour s. The finer and edible part of ground corn; fine soft powder. v.t. To sprinkle with this.
Col'our s. Tint, a pigment, paint; complexion; pretext; a flag. v.t. To give tint to, to paint; to give a specious appearance to. v.i. To show colour, to blush.
Decol'our v.t. To deprive of colour.
Recol'our v.t. To paint over again or with new colours.
Tri'colour s. A flag of three colours, especially that of France.
Versicol'our (-kul'-) a. Having various colours; changeable in colour.
Discol'our v.t. and i. To alter the colour of; to change colour, fade; to stain.
Miscol'our v.t. To misrepresent.
Dol'our s. Grief, distress, anguish.
Par'lour s. A sitting-room, reception-room.
Amour' s. A love-affair.
Clam'our s. Vociferation; uproar; outcry.
Bel'amour s. A sweetheart.
Glam'our s. Magic influence; witchery; charm.
Enam'our v.t. To inflame with love.
Par'amour s. A lover (of either sex); a concubine.
Ar'mour s. Defensive covering or arms
Hu'mour s. Jocularity, a form of the comic, fun; mood, caprice, whim; a bodily fluid. v.t. To indulge, give way to, suit.
Ru'mour s. Popular report, a current story. v.t. To spread abroad.
Tu'mour s. A morbid swelling, infective growth.
Demean'our s. Conduct, behaviour, carriage.
Misdemean'our s. Ill-behaviour; an offence inferior to felony.
Hon'our s. Dignity; high rank; fame. v.t. To respect, revere; to accept or pay.
Dishon'our s. Want of honour; ignominy, reproach. v.t. To bring shame on; to debauch, ravish; to refuse to accept or pay a bill, etc.
Pour v.t. and i. To cause to flow, to flow; to emit, issue forth in a stream.
Va'pour s. A gaseous substance; steam, a fume, an exhalation. v.i. To boast; to give off vapour.
Down'pour s. A heavy fall of rain.
Outpour' v.t. To send forth in a stream; to effuse.
Out'pour s. An overflow; a pouring out.

Sour a. Not sweet; acid, bitter; pungent; morose, peevish. v.t. and i. To make or become sour.
Vav'asour s. A vassal who had vassals under him.
Tour s. A circuit; an excursion. v.i. To make a tour.
Detour' s. A roundabout way, a digression.
Lim'itour s. A mendicant friar limited to a district.
Con'tour s. Boundary line, outline.
Endeav'our v.i. To attempt, try, essay, aim. s. An attempt, effort, exertion.
Fa'vour s. Good-will; a kind act; leave; a knot of ribbons; advantage. v.t. To regard with kindness, to befriend, take the part of; to facilitate; to resemble.
Disfa'vour s. State of not being in favour; a disobliging act. v.t. To treat or regard with disesteem.
Fla'vour s. Relish; savour; taste; scent. v.t. To give flavour to.
Sa'vour s. Flavour, relish, odour. v.i. To have a particular taste or scent; to betoken. v.t. To give a flavour to.
Devour' v.t. To eat up greedily; to appropriate or destroy wantonly; to waste, consume.
Fer'vour s. Warmth; intensity of feeling or expression; zeal.
Your a. Pertaining or belonging to you.
Spur s. Small goad worn on a horseman's heel; a sharp outgrowth; anything projecting; a stimulus. v.t. To prick with spurs; to urge, incite. v.i. To ride hard.
Tus'sur s. Tussore.
Imprima'tur s. License to print; official sanction.
Zeph'yr s. The west wind; a gentle breeze; a gauzy material.
Sat'yr (-er) s. A lascivious sylvan deity of myth, half man and half goat.
Mar'tyr s. One who suffers or dies for any great cause. v.t. To persecute, torture, or put to death for adherence to belief.
Protomar'tyr s. The first martyr, St. Stephen; the first to suffer in a cause.
As adv., conj., rel. pron.
Fracas' s. A disturbance, row, brawl.
Dor'cas s. A sewing-meeting.
En-tout-cas s. A light umbrella; a parasol.
Mi'das s. A fabulously wealthy man.
Ju'das s. A traitor.
Superse'deas s. A suspensory writ.
Pan'creas s. An abdominal gland the secretion from which aids digestion; the sweetbread.
Whereas' conj.
Bor'eas s. The north wind.
Overseas' adv. Abroad.
Gas s. An elastic aeriform fluid, especially coal-gas for illuminating and heating purposes. v.t. To attack, kill, or injure by means of gas. v.i. (*Slang*) To talk at large, to boast.
Has 3rd sing. (***Have***).
Bi'as s. Weight on one side; inclination, mental bent. v.t. To incline to one side, to prejudice.
Li'as s. A bluish, clayey limestone; series of strata characterized by this.
A'lias adv. Otherwise (named). s. An assumed name.
Paterfamil'ias s. The father of a family, head of a household.
Anani'as s. A liar.
Tri'as s. Strata between the Carboniferous and Jurassic.
Galima'tias s. Nonsense, a farrago.
Alas' int. Expressive of grief, regret, pity, etc.
Bal'as s. A variety of ruby.
Erysip'elas s. An acute inflammatory disease of the skin.
Chas'selas s. A sort of grape.
Bo'las s. A missile weapon used by S. American Indians.
Pho'las s. A stone-boring bivalve.
At'las s. A volume of maps.
Dow'las s. Coarse linen cloth.
Pyja'mas s. A sleeping suit of loose coat and trousers.
Candle'mas s. The Feast of the Purification (2nd Feb.).
Mich'aelmas s. Feast of St. Michael (29th Sept.); autumn.
Lam'mas s. 1st August.
Mar'tinmas s. The feast of St. Martin (11th Nov.).
Chris'tmas s. The festival of the nativity, Dec. 25th; this season.
Hal'lowmas s. All Hallows, 1st November.
Ana'nas s. The pine-apple plant; its fruit.
Mæce'nas s. A liberal patron of art or letters.
Whenas' adv. When; while.
Pso'as s. One of the two hip muscles.
Pas (pa) s. A step in dancing; precedence.
Lam'pas s. Swelling in roof of a horse's mouth.
Pam'pas s. The vast plains of southern S. America.
U'pas s. A Javanese tree of the fig family with poisonous sap.
Hip'pocras s. An old medicinal wine.
Dinoc'eras s. An extinct genus of gigantic herbivorous horned and tusked mammals.
Cop'peras s. A green sulphate of iron; green vitriol.
Sas'safras s. A bush of the laurel family; its aromatic bark, used in medicine.
Mith'ras s. Mithra.
Ar'ras s. Tapestry.
Vas s. A duct, vessel.
Can'vas s. Rough, unbleached cloth; a painting on this; sails. a. Made of canvas.
Was (woz) 3rd sing. past (*Be*).
Abrax'as s. A mystical word; a gem or amulet with it engraved thereon.
Ey'as s. A young unfledged hawk.
Nibs s. Crushed cocoa-seeds.
Scobs s. Shavings; raspings of ivory, metal, etc.
Mull'igrubs s. Colic; the blues.
Elegi'acs s. Verse consisting of alternate hexameters and pentameters.
-ics suff. Forming names of sciences, arts, philosophies, etc.
Orthopæ'dics s. Orthopædy.
Strateg'ics s. Strategy.
Pedagog'ics s. Art or science of teaching.
Isagog'ics s. Introductory investigations regarding the Bible.
Litur'gics s. The study or doctrine of liturgies.
Hieroglyph'ics s. Hieroglyphic writing.
Eth'ics s. Moral science; body of rules drawn from this.
Ital'ics s. Sloping letters or type.
Symbol'ics s. Study of ancient Christian symbols.
Hydraul'ics s. The science that treats of fluids, especially water, in motion; application of water-power.

Dynam'ics s. Science of moving forces; moving force of any kind, or laws which relate to them.
Hydro-dynam'ics s. The science that treats of the dynamics of liquids.
Ceram'ics s. The art of pottery.
Polem'ics s. Controversy, esp. theological.
Physiog-nom'ics s. Physiognomy.
Econom'ics s. Study and science of wealth and its application; political economy.
Pyronom'ics s. The science of heat.
Orthodrom'ics s. The art of sailing in a direct course, or on the arc of a great circle.
Loxodrom'ics s. The art of oblique sailing by the rhumb-line.
Synonym'ics s. Synonymy.
Mechan'ics s. Branch of physics treating of motion and force; science of machinery.
Eugen'ics s. Science relating to the development and improvement of offspring.
Callisthen'ics s. Exercises to promote bodily health and beauty.
Tech'nics s. The doctrine of arts; technical terms, etc.
Pyrotech'nics s. Art of making or exhibiting fireworks.
Con'ics s. That part of geometry which treats of a cone and its curves.
Hedon'ics s. Branch of ethics dealing with pleasure.
Cataphon'ics s. The science of reflected sounds.
Histrion'ics s. Art of acting; theatricals; humbug.
Eudemon'ics s. Eudemonism.
Mnemon'ics s. The art of or rules for assisting the memory.
Gnomon'ics s. The art or science of dialling.
Harmon'ics s. Science of musical sounds.
Geopon'ics s. The science of agriculture.
Tecton'ics s. Art of constructing buildings, etc.
Architecton'ics s. The science of architecture; systematization, especially of knowledge.
Ceraun'ics s. Science of heat and electricity.
Hero'ics s. High-flown, bombastic language.
Trop'ics s. Region between the Tropics of Cancer and of Capricorn.
Spher'ics s. Spherical geometry and trigonometry.
Hyster'ics s. A fit of hysteria.
Met'rics s. The science of prosody.
Obstet'rics s. Midwifery.
Vit'rics s. Science dealing with glass; glassy materials.
Diop'trics s. The science of refracted light.
Catop'trics s. The science of reflected light.
Phys'ics s. Science of properties and changes of matter, especially motion and energy; natural philosophy.
Metaphys'ics s. The philosophy of mind; science of principles and causes.
Hæmat'ics s. The science of the blood.
Mathemat'ics s. The science which treats of quantity, magnitude, and numbers.
Kinemat'ics s. The science of pure motion.
Systemat'ics s. Systematology.
Dogmat'ics s. The science of Christian doctrine; doctrinal theology.
Diplomat'ics s. Art of ascertaining the authenticity, date, etc., of ancient documents.
Chromat'ics s. Science of colours.
Litho-chromat'ics s. Art of taking impressions from oil-paintings on stone.
Somat'ics s. Somatology.
Numismat'ics s. Scientific study of coins and medals.
Pneumat'ics s. Science of the mechanical properties of air and other elastic fluids.
Stat'ics s. Branch of dynamics treating of relations between forces in equilibrium.
Hydrostat'ics s. The science that treats of the pressure and equilibrium of liquids at rest.
A'erostatics s. The science treating of the equilibrium and pressure of gases; aeronautics.
Didac'tics s. The art or science of teaching.
Catallac'tics s. Political economy.
Tac'tics s. Art of disposing forces for battle; manœuvering.
Dialec'tics s. Logic; the art of reasoning; the analytical investigation of truth.
Exeget'ics s. Science of interpretation; exegesis.
Apologet'ics s. Defensive argument.
Energet'ics s. Physical dynamics.
Catechet'ics s. The branch of theology dealing with oral instruction.
Athlet'ics s. The practice of physical exercises.
Homilet'ics s. The art of preaching.
Hermet'ics s. Alchemy; chemistry.
Magnet'ics s. Science or principles of magnetism.
Kinet'ics s. That branch of mechanics which deals with motion as affected by force.
Phonet'ics s. Science of articulate sounds.
Poet'ics s. Theory or principles of poetry.
Theoret'ics s. The speculative parts of a science.
Dietet'ics s. The science of food or diet.
Pol'itics s. Science of government; political affairs, contests, management, etc.
Seman'tics s. Science of the development of the meanings of words.
Semeiot'ics s. Semeiology.
Op'tics s. The science of light and vision.
Glyp'tics s. The art of engraving on gems.
Ceroplas'tics s. Art of wax-modelling.
Gymnas'tics s. The art of performing athletic exercises; course of instruction, discipline, etc., in these.
Orches'tics s. The art of dancing.
Sphragis'tics s. The science or study of engraved seals.
Logis'tics s. Art of arithmetical calculation; system in which logarithms of sexagesimal numbers are employed.
Ballis'tics s. The science of projectiles in motion.
Patris'tics s. The doctrines of the early Christian Fathers; the study of these.
Chrematis'tics s. Political economy with relation to wealth-production.
Statis'tics s. Classification and tabulation of facts; science of subjects as elucidated by facts.
Linguis'tics s. The science of languages.
Acous'tics s. The science of sound and hearing.
Diacous'tics s. Science of refracted sounds.
Catacous'tics s. The science of reflected sounds or echoes.
Pharma-ceu'tics s. The science of preparing drugs; pharmacy.
Pædeu'tics s. The science of education.
Propædeu'tics s. Preliminary education or instruction.
Halieu'tics s. The art of fishing.
Hermeneu'tics s. Science of interpretation (especially of the Bible).
Therapeu'tics s. Medical science dealing with the treatment of disease.
Psycho-therapeu'tics s. Treatment of disease by hypnotic means.

Toreu'tics s. (*Toreutic*).
Civ'ics s. Science of municipal government; duties of a citizen.
Leads (ledz) s. Flat roof covered with lead.
Hy'ads s. The Hyades.
Odds s. Inequality; advantage; chances in favour of one; an allowance to an inferior; ratio between two sides of a bet; strife.
Pro'ceeds s. Yield, issue, product.
Needs adv. Of necessity, indispensably.
Weeds s. A widow's mourning dress.
Hæm'orrhoids s. Piles.
Ad'enoids s. Spongy formations at the back of the nose.
High'lands s. A mountainous region, especially in Scotland.
Hol'lands s. A kind of gin.
Cal'ends s. The first day of the old Roman month.
Amends' s. Compensation, recompense.
Sec'onds s. A coarse kind of flour.
Funds s. Finances, money.
Grounds s. Dregs, sediment; park-land, gardens.
Zounds int. Expressing anger, annoyance, etc.
Back'woods s. Remote, uncultivated parts.
Em'erods s. Hæmorrhoids.
Regards' s. Good wishes; compliments.
Hards s. The refuse of flax or wool.
Bil'liards s. A game played with cues and three balls on a cloth-covered table having cushioned sides.
-wards suff. Expressing direction.
Back'wards adv. With the back forwards; towards the back or the past.
In'wards adv. (*Inward*). s. The entrails.
Down'wards adv. From higher to lower; in a descending course; from a remote time.
Towards' prep. (*Toward*).
Up'wards adv. To a higher place; more.
Af'terwards adv. In subsequent time.
For'wards adv. Forward.
West'wards adv. Towards the west.
Duds s. (*Slang*) Clothes; rags.
Shrouds s. Ropes from the mast-heads steadying the masts.
Suds s. Very soapy water; lather.
Ta'bes s. Emaciation; a wasting disease.
Pu'bes s. The hypogastric region; the hair of this.
Bra'ces s. Suspenders for the trousers.
Fæ'ces s. Excrement; sediment.
Appen'dices s. (*Appendix*).
In'dices s. Pl. of "index" in mathematical use.
Co'dices s. (*Codex*).
Ca'lices s. (*Calix*).
A'pices s. (*Apex*).
Aus'pices s. Omens, favourable appearances.
Rec'trices s. The quill-feathers of a bird's tail.
Tec'trices s. The covert feathers of a bird.
Cor'tices s. (*Cortex*).
Cal'ces s. (*Calx*).
Fas'ces s. The insignia of the ancient Roman lictors; a bundle of rods.
Pis'ces s. The twelfth sign of the Zodiac, the Fishes.
Fau'ces s. The hinder part of the mouth.
Ca'lyces s. (*Calyx*).
Succades' (-kādz') s. Candied fruits.
Ha'des s. The lower world, place of departed spirits.
Plei'ades s. A cluster of small stars in Taurus.
Hy'ades s. A cluster of stars in the constellation Taurus.
Dry'ades s. (*Dryad*).
Ides s. Certain days in the ancient Roman calendar.
Bo'na fi'des s. Good faith, guarantees.
Aph'ides s. (*Aphis*).
Eumen'ides s. The Furies of Greek myth.
Leon'ides s. The swarm of meteors appearing in the constellation Leo in November.
Ascar'ides s. Intestinal worms.
Canthar'ides s. Dried Spanish flies used medicinally.
Besides' prep. In addition to. adv. Moreover.
Ap'sides s. (*Apse, apsis*).
Antip'odes s. The opposite side of the globe; those who live on opposite sides.
Em'ydes s. (*Emys*).
Lees s. Dregs, sediment.
Amba'ges s. Equivocation.
Dam'ages s. Value of injury done; monetary reparation; (*slang*) cost, charge.
Wa'ges s. Payment for work done, etc.; recompense.
Phalan'ges s. The small bones of the fingers and toes.
Menin'ges s. The three membranes enveloping the brain and spinal cord.
Syrin'ges s. (*Syrinx*).
Boaner'ges s. A vociferous or ranting preacher.
Asper'ges s. The sprinkling of a congregation with holy water.
Lach'es s. Negligence; inexcusable delay.
Breech'es s. A garment worn by men on the legs.
Rich'es s. Abundant wealth; opulence.
Ash'es s. Remains of anything burnt, especially of a cremated corpse.
Fresh'es s. The mingling of fresh and salt water in rivers.
Cacoe'thes s. An almost irresistible propensity.
Nepen'thes s. (*Nepenthe*).
Clothes s. Garments, raiment; blankets, etc., for a bed.
Sca'bies s. The itch.
Ra'bies s. Hydrophobia.
Dar'bies s. (*Slang*) Handcuffs.
Spe'cies (-shēz) s. A class; a group of similar organisms; sort, variety.
Superfi'cies (-fish'iēz) s. A surface; its area.
Hur'dies s. The buttocks.
Man'yplies (men'-) s. The third stomach of a ruminant.
Sa'nies (-ni-ēz) s. A thin discharge from wounds, etc.
Ar'ies s. The first of the zodiacal constellations, the Ram.
Car'ies s. An ulceration of bone.
Sun'dries s. Miscellaneous or trivial articles or items.
Con'geries s. A collection or heap of particles or bodies.
Ser'ies (sēr'ez) s. A connected succession; a course.
Hostil'ities s. Acts of war.
Human'ities s. Polite literature or learning; the classics.
Ob'sequies s. Funeral rites.
Ex'equies s. Funeral ceremonies, obsequies.
Mov'ies (moov'-) s. (*Slang*) A cinema show, "the pictures."
Collu'vies s. Filth; refuse matter.
Ta'les s. Writ summoning one to fill a vacancy on a jury.
Eat'ables s. Food; the solid parts of a meal.
Mov'ables s. Furniture, goods.
Col'ly-wobbles s. (*Slang*) Stomach-ache.
Shambles s. A slaughter-house; scene or place of carnage.
Umbles s. The entrails of a deer.

Numbles s. The entrails of deer.
Bar'nacles s. A twitch with which the nose of a restive horse is seized when it is to be shod; an instrument of torture; (*slang*) spectacles.
Spec'tacles s. Glasses worn to assist vision.
Isos'celes a. Having only two sides equal (of triangles).
Mephis-toph'eles s. A tempter; a devil.
Snuffles s. Cold in the head.
Goggles s. Large spectacles; shields for a horse's eyes; the staggers (in sheep).
Strangles s. A swelling in a horse's throat.
Shingles s. A skin-disease, herpes.
Whiles adv. (*Scot.*) Sometimes.
Piles s. Hæmorrhoids; small tumours about the anus.
Arles s. Earnest-money.
Measles s. A contagious febrile disease.
Skittles s. The game of ninepins.
Gules a. and s. Red (in heraldry).
Bouts-ri'més s. A game of capping verses.
Betimes' adv. Early, in good time.
Some'times adv. At indefinite times.
Ker'mes s. Dried bodies of an insect used in dyeing carmine.
Ter'mes s. The white ant.
Ver'mes s. Former group-name of the earthworms, leeches, etc.
Ma'nes s. Spirits of the dead, especially among the ancient Romans.
Ro'manes s. The gipsy language.
Fines s. Fine or powdery ores.
Ima'gines s. (*Imago*).
Aborig'ines s. The indigenous inhabitants of a country.
Impetig'ines s. (*Impetigo*).
Intes'tines s. The entrails, bowels, guts.
Valenciennes' (-ĕn') s. A rich kind of lace.
Persiennes' (-si-en') s. Slatted window-blinds or shutters.
Saw'bones s. (*Slang*) A surgeon.
La'zybones s. An idle fellow.
Hor'mones s. Secretions from internal glands.
Nones s. The ninth day before the ides in the the ancient Roman calendar; the Roman Catholic office for 3 p.m. (ninth hour after sunrise).
Bil'boes s. Shackles for the feet.
Does 3rd pres. ind. (*Do*).
Dom'inoes s. A game played with twenty-eight variously dotted pieces of ivory.
Pet'itoes s. A pig's trotters.
Dit'toes s. (*Slang*) A suit of the same cloth throughout.
Jack'anapes s. A coxcomb, whippersnapper.
Grapes s. A cluster of tumours on the fetlock of horses.
Trapes s. and v. (*Traipse*).
Tal'ipes s. Club-foot.
Bag'pipes s. (*Bagpipe*).
Gripes s. Pinching pains in the abdomen.
Sti'pes s. A stalk, stipe.
Swipes s. Weak or inferior beer.
Her'pes s. A skin-disease, cutaneous eruption.
Lar'es s. Tutelary Roman divinities.
Unawares' adv. Unexpectedly; inadvertently.
Scansor'es s. The climbing-birds.
Cursor'es s. An order of birds with very strong legs and rudimentary wings; ostriches, emus, etc.
Grallator'es s. The order of wading birds.
Raptor'es s. The order containing the birds of prey.
Belles-lettres s. The humanities, pure literature.
Lem'ures s. The spirits of the dead among the ancient Romans.
Prem'ises s. A building and its adjuncts.
Repris'es s. Yearly payments made out of manors and lands.
Walden'ses s. A French dissenting sect founded in the twelfth century.
Men'ses s. The monthly discharges of females.
Amanuen'ses s. (*Amanuensis*).
Glas'ses s. Spectacles.
Molas'ses s. Uncrystallizable syrup drained from sugar.
Cates s. Provisions; dainties.
Acha'tes s. A trusty friend.
Prima'tes s. The highest order of mammals, including the lemus, monkeys, apes, etc., and man.
Na'tes s. The buttocks.
Pena'tes s. The household gods of the ancient Romans.
An'nates s. The first year's profits of a benefice.
Dispar'ates s. Things so unlike that they admit of no comparison.
Diabe'tes s. A urinary disease.
Myxomyce'tes s. The slime-moulds.
-i'tes suff. Denoting minerals, etc.
Tympani'tes s. Swelling caused by air in the intestines.
Sori'tes s. An abridged form of stating a series of syllogisms in which the result is an absurdity; a sophistical argument on such lines.
Pyri'tes s. Sulphur combined with iron or other metal.
Eq'uites s. An ancient Roman order of nobility; knights.
Atlan'tes s. Colossal statues supporting masonry.
Rentes s. French Government annuities.
Chorizon'tes s. Ancient critics who held that the Homeric poems were not the work of a single author.
Xero'tes s. A dry habit of body.
Li'totes s. Figure of speech in which the meaning is softened; an understatement.
Cer'tes adv. Assuredly.
Cor'tes s. The legislative bodies of Spain and Portugal.
Sor'tes s. Divination by chance selection of a passage from an author.
Ceras'tes s. The horned viper.
Herpes'tes s. The genus of mammals containing the mongoose, etc.
Pantalettes' s. Detachable leg-frills formerly worn by children.
Bary'tes s. Native sulphate of barium.
Lu'es s. Plague; infection.
Eaves s. The projecting lower edges of a roof.
Heaves s. A disease of horses.
Leaves s. (*Leaf*).
Greaves s. Armour for the legs; scraps of fat, etc.
Loaves s. (*Loaf*).
Beeves s. Oxen.
Di'ves s. A very rich man.
Fives s. A game resembling tennis played against a wall; a disease in horses.
Hives s. An eruptive disease allied to chicken-pox.
Lives s. (*Life*).
Knives s. (*Knife*).
Vives s. A diseased condition of horses' ears.
Wives s. (*Wife*).
Calves s. (*Calf*).
Halves s. (*Half*).
Elves s. (*Elf*).

Themselves' (-selvz) pron. Emphatic form of "them."
Ourselves' pron., pl. We (*often emphatic*); not others.
Ax'es s. (*Axis*).
Yes adv. Expressing affirmation or consent. s. An affirmative.
Fis'ticuffs s. Combat with the fists.
Dad'dy-long-legs s. The crane-fly.
Dregs s. Sediment, lees; the vilest part.
Ti'dings s. News; a report.
Surround'ings s. Environment; circumstances.
Sound'ings s. Part of the sea depth of which can be sounded; measurements taken thus.
Dig'gings s. A gold-mine, gold-field; (*slang*) lodgings.
Hang'ings s. Fabrics hung up as draperies.
Lash'ings s. (*Slang*) Abundance.
Flesh'ings s. Flesh-coloured tights worn by acrobats, etc.
Tak'ings s. Receipts.
Pick'ings s. Odds and ends, gleanings.
Mid'dlings s. The coarser part of flour.
Tail'ings s. Refuse, esp. of grain or ore.
Fil'ings s. Fragments rubbed off with a file.
Swill'ings s. Hog-wash; liquid food.
Chit'terlings s. The smaller intestines of swine, etc., as food.
Mos'lings s. Thin shreds of leather.
Settl'ings s. Lees, sediment, dregs.
Coam'ings s. The raised border round hatches on a ship.
Skim'mings s. Material removed by skimming.
Hap'penings s. Chance occurrences.
Gain'ings s. Earnings, profits.
In'nings s. Batsman's turn of play at cricket; period of this, or of office; play of one side when batting.
Win'nings s. Amount won.
Earn'ings s. That which is earned; wages.
Do'ings s. Things done; events; goings on; behaviour.
Sweep'ings s. Things collected by sweeping; litter.
Trap'pings s. Ornamental harness; finery.
Strip'pings s. The last milk drawn from a cow.
Drop'pings s. Anything that has fallen in drops; dung of birds or beasts.
Moor'ings s. Place where a ship is moored; anchors, cables, etc., used in mooring.
Salt'ings s. A salt-marsh; salt-lands.
Beest'ings s. The first milk of a cow that has calved.
Hus'tings s. A place of election.
Get'tings s. Profits, gains.
Fit'tings s. Fixtures; apparatus; things fixed on.
Leav'ings s. Residue; refuse, remnants.
Fix'ings s. Trimmings, outfit; adjuncts of any kind.
Jongs s. The old Scots pillory.
Tongs s. A two-pronged implement for handling coals, heated metals, etc.
Togs s. (*Slang*) Clothes.
Au'rochs s. An extinct wild ox.
Is 3rd sing. pres. ind. (*To be*).
Da'is s. Raised floor (or table thereon) at upper end of a dining-hall; a canopied seat.
Beaujolais' s. A red wine.
Bis adv. Twice; again.
Can'nabis s. A genus of plants containing Indian hemp.
Ar'abis s. A genus of cruciferous plants.
I'bis s. A bird allied to the stork.
Pu'bis s. A bone of the pelvis.
Gla'cis s. The outer slope of a fortification.
Pré'cis (prā'sē) s. An abstract, summary.
Probos'cis s. A long snout; elephant's trunk; insect's sucking-tube.
Charyb'dis s. One of a pair of alternative risks (the other being called "Scylla").
Cad'dis s. The larva of the May-fly; a worsted yarn.
Reis (rās) s. A former Portuguese and Brazilian money of account.
Mil'reis (-rās) s. A Portuguese silver coin (about 4s. 5d.).
Æ'gis s. A shield; protection.
Hag'gis s. A Scotch dish of sheep's maw, liver, lights, heart, etc.
Walpur'gis s. Applied to the night before May 1st; the witches' Sabbath.
His a. Belonging to him.
Rach'is (răk-) s. The axial stem of a plant or inflorescence; the shaft of a feather.
Or'chis s. The typical genus of the orchid family; an orchid.
Aph'is s. A plant-louse, green-fly.
This a. and pron.
Œnan'this a. Having the odour of wine.
Lis s. An ancient Irish earthwork.
Transversa'lis s. A muscle lying across other parts.
Chrys'alis s. A pupa, the last stage before a lepidopterous insect becomes perfect.
Digita'lis s. A genus of plants containing the foxglove; a drug prepared from this.
Ox'alis s. The genus of plants including the wood-sorrel.
Chab'lis s. A white wine.
Fleur-de-lis' s. The iris; the ancient heraldic emblem of France.
Syph'ilis s. An infectious venereal disease.
Chal'lis s. A fine twilled woollen fabric.
Trel'lis s. Frame of wooden lattice work. v.t. To furnish with a trellis.
Torticol'lis s. Stiff-neck.
Portcul'lis s. A vertically sliding defence to a fortress gateway.
Amaryl'lis s. Lily-asphodel.
Pentap'olis s. A confederacy of five towns.
Acrop'olis s. The citadel of a city, especially ancient Athens.
Necrop'olis s. A cemetery.
Prop'olis s. A resinous substance used by bees in hives.
Metrop'olis s. A mother-city; chief city or capital of a country.
Tam'is s. A cloth sieve.
Impri'mis adv. First in order.
Sal'mis (-mē) s. A rich dish of stewed game.
Epider'mis s. The scarf-skin of the body; the outer skin of animals and plants.
Pe'nis s. The male organ of generation.
Lych'nis s. The genus of plants including the campion.
Fi'nis s. The end, conclusion.
Ten'nis s. Game in which a ball is struck to and fro across a net.
Ado'nis s. A beautiful young man; a dandy; the pheasant's eye.
Dinor'nis s. A gigantic New Zealand bird long extinct.
Notor'nis s. An extinct gigantic coot of New Zealand.
Æpyor'nis s. A gigantic fossil bird.
Fu'nis s. The umbilical cord.
Vaudois (vōdwa') a. Pertaining to the Waldenses, or to the Swiss canton of Vaud. s. A Waldensian; an inhabitant or the dialect of Vaud.

Bour'geois a. Pertaining to the middle classes; commonplace, humdrum; s. A small printing type.
Cham'ois s. A horned goat-like ruminant; a soft kind of leather.
Av'oirdupois s. A system of weight; (*colloq.*) plumpness, weight.
Pat'ois (-wa) s. Provincial form of speech; dialect.
Sina'pis s. The genus of crucifers including the mustard plant.
Ta'pis (-pē) s. Carpeting; tapestry.
Euchar'is s. A bulbous S. American plant.
Can'tharis s. The Spanish fly.
Deb'ris s. Broken fragments; rubbish.
Ephem'eris s. A journal; an astronomical or astrological almanac.
Cystop'teris s. A genus of ferns.
Ver'digris s. Green rust of brass or copper.
Mis'tigris s. The joker in certain card-games.
Am'bergris s. A fragrant, opaque, ash-coloured substance secreted by the sperm-whale.
Ir'is s. The rainbow; appearance resembling this; the coloured circle round the pupil of the eye; the flag-flower.
Lor'is s. An Asiatic lemur.
Ar'ris s. The edge formed by two surfaces meeting.
Or'ris s. A species of iris, the root of which is used in perfumery.
Mor'ris s. A rustic dance.
Ba'sis s. Foundation, groundwork; a base.
Anab'asis s. A march up-country; a military expedition.
Parab'asis s. A choral part in ancient Greek comedy.
Metab'asis s. Transition from one subject, remedy, etc., to another.
Ec'basis s. An argument dealing with probabilities.
Pha'sis s. An astronomical phase.
Em'phasis s. Stress in utterance, force; importance.
Proph'asis s. Prognosis.
i'asis suff. Denoting a disease.
Trichi'asis s. Inversion of the eyelashes; a disease of the kidneys, also of the breasts.
Gomphi'asis s. Looseness of the teeth.
Lithi'asis s. Formation of stone in the bladder.
Trypanoso-mi'asis s. Sleeping-sickness due to infection of the blood by a trypanosome.
Trichini'asis s. Disease produced by trichinæ.
Hypo-chondri'asis s. Hypochondria.
Scleri'asis s. Induration of tissues.
Phthiria'sis s. Pediculosis.
Siri'asis s. Sunstroke.
Psori'asis s. An itching skin disease.
Satyri'asis s. Maniacal lewdness in males.
Pityri'asis s. A parasitic skin-disease.
Elephanti'asis s. A disease in which the skin becomes greatly thickened.
Odonti'asis s. Cutting of the teeth.
Osteocla'sis s. Operation of breaking a bone to make good some defect.
Oa'sis s. Fertile spot in a desert.
Cra'sis s. The contraction of vowels into one long vowel; the mixture of bodily constituents.
Metaph'rasis s. A literal translation.
Periph'rasis s. Circumlocution; roundabout speaking.
Antiph'rasis s. Use of words in an opposite sense; irony.
Epit'asis s. The portion of a play in which the plot is developed.
En'tasis s. The convex curvature given to a column.
Prot'asis s. A proposition, maxim.
Sta'sis s. Stagnation of the blood.
Catas'tasis s. The part of a drama leading up to the catastrophe.
Metas'tasis s. Metabolism; removal of a disease from one part to another.
Iconos'tasis s. The screen in a Greek church on which icons are placed.
Hypos'tasis s. Substance; each of the three divisions of the Godhead.
Exege'sis s. Interpretation; exposition.
Epexege'sis s. Additional explanation; further statement.
Lache'sis s. One of the Fates; a genus of S. American rattlesnakes.
Orche'sis s. The art of dancing.
Aph'esis s. Loss of a vowel at the beginning of a word.
The'sis s. A proposition, theme.
Thes'is s. The unaccented part of a metrical foot.
Diath'esis s. Predisposing bodily condition.
Mathe'sis s. Learning; mathematical knowledge.
Metath'esis s. Transposition, especially of the letters in a word.
Antith'esis s. An opposition of words, etc., in the same sentence; contrast.
Epen'thesis s. Insertion of a letter or syllable in a word.
Paren'thesis s. An explanatory word or sentence; the sign of the ( ).
Syn'thesis s. A putting together, building up from parts.
Hypoth'esis s. An assumed proposition, a supposition.
Proth'esis s. The getting ready of the elements for use in the Eucharist; part of church where this takes place.
Prosthe'sis s. Addition of an artificial part to the body.
Ochle'sis s. Unhealthy state due to overcrowding.
Em'esis s. The action of vomiting.
Nem'esis s. Just retribution or punishment.
Hæmatem'esis s. Vomiting of blood.
Mime'sis s. Mimicry.
Tme'sis s. Insertion of a word between the parts of a compound word.
Gen'esis s. Creation, orgination; act or mode of producing or begetting.
Paragen'esis s. A kind of hybridism.
Metagen'esis s. Alternation of sexual and asexual generations.
Epigen'esis s. The theory that the germ is newly created, not merely evolved.
Pangen'esis s. Reproduction from every unit of the organism.
Palingen'esis s. A rebirth, renewal; a great geological change; metempsychosis.
Glycogen'esis s. Formation of sugar from glycogen, as in the liver.
Osteogen'esis s. Formation or growth of bone.
Psychogen'esis s. The development of the mind or soul.
Morpho-gen'esis s. Morphogeny.
Pathogen'esis s. The generation and development of a disease.
Mythogen'esis s. The creation of myths.
Pythogen'esis s. Generation through filth.
Biogen'esis s. The theory that every living organism has proceeded from a living organism.
Abiogen'esis s. Production of life from non-living matter.

Hylogen'esis s. The origin of matter.
Phylogen'esis s. Phylogeny.
Gamogen'esis s. Sexual reproduction.
Homogen'esis s. Natural descent in which successive generations are alike.
Thermogen'esis s. Production of animal heat.
Organogen'esis s. The development of organs n animals and plants.
Partheno-gen'esis s. Generation without sexual union; virgin birth.
Xenogen'esis s. Heterogenesis.
Monogen'esis s. Unity of origin; asexual reproduction.
Oogen'esis s. Formation of the ovum prior to fertilization and development into the embryo.
Lipogen'esis s. The formation of fat
Heterogen'esis s. Spontaneous generation; production of offspring differing from the parent; alternation of generations.
Spermato-gen'esis s. The development of spermatozoa.
Ontogen'esis s. Ontogeny.
Histogen'esis s. Science of the origin of tissues.
Phytogen'esis s. Phytogeny.
Symphyo-gen'esis s. Formation of organ, etc., by growing together of separate parts.
Pyogen'esis s. The formation of pus.
Embryo-gen'esis s. Embryogeny.
Schizogen'esis s. Reproduction by fission.
Polygen'esis s. Doctrine that the human race sprang from more than one pair.
Telekine'sis s. Production of motion in a body without apparent cause.
Anamne'sis s. Recollection, remembrance.
Noe'sis s. Operation of intelligence only.
Onomato-pœ'sis s. Onomatopœia.
Aposiope'sis s. Abrupt breaking off of a sentence.
Par'esis s. Incomplete paralysis.
Aphær'esis s. Taking of a letter or syllable from the beginning of a word.
Diær'esis s. A mark (¨) placed over one of two vowels to show that they are to be pronounced separately.
Synær'esis s. Contraction of two syllables or vowels into one.
Hystere'sis s. A retardation or lagging effect, especially in magnetism.
Catachre'sis s. A forced or wrong use of words.
Phthi'sis (thī'-) s. Pulmonary consumption.
Cri'sis s. A decisive stage; turning-point, especially in the course of a disease; a conjuncture.
Peristal'sis s. The automatic motion of the alimentary canal, etc., by which the contents are moved along.
Xeran'sis s. State of being dried up.
Amanuen'sis s. One who takes down from dictation; a secretary.
-osis suff. Denoting morbid condition.
Thrombo'sis s. Local coagulation of the blood.
Toxico'sis s. Morbid state due to poisoning.
Helco'sis s. Ulceration.
Narco'sis s. State induced by narcotics; stupor.
Sarco'sis s. A fleshy tumour.
Glauco'sis s. Glaucoma.
Leuco'sis s. Pallor; the morbid condition of albinism.
Myco'sis s. Any disease caused by parasitic fungi.
Syco'sis s. Barber's itch.
Apod'osis s. The consequent clause in a conditional sentence expressing the result.
Lordo'sis s. Curvature of the spine forward.
Apotheo'sis s. Deification, glorification.
Tricho'sis s. Any disease of the hair.
Psycho'sis s. Mental derangement, especially functional; a momentary mental state.
Metem-psycho'sis s. Transmigration of souls.
Gompho'sis s. The form of articulation by which the teeth fit into their sockets.
Morpho'sis s. Mode of development of an organism.
Anamor-pho'sis s. An image, etc., so distorted that when properly viewed or reflected it will appear in its true proportions.
Meta-morpho'sis s. Transformation; result of this.
Hetero-morpho'sis s. Abnormal structure, etc.; deformity.
Grypho'sis s. Abnormal in-growing of the nails.
Cirrho'sis s. A disease of the liver.
Xantho'sis s. Yellow discoloration of the skin.
Symbio'sis s. Parasitism, especially in plants for mutual advantage or necessity.
Necrobio'sis s. Senile decay of living tissue.
Meio'sis s. Depreciative hyperbole.
Helio'sis s. Blotches caused on leaves by concentrated sun-rays through glass; sunstroke.
Scolio'sis s. Lateral curvature of the spine.
Pediculo'sis s. Lousiness.
Tuberculo'sis s. An infectious disease due to presence of tubercles in the tissues; consumption.
Strongylo'sis s. A disease in cattle caused by a parasitic worm.
Anchylo'sis s. Stiffness of a joint; consolidation of bones.
Ankylo'sis s. The growing together of two bones.
Pterylo'sis s. Arrangement of feathers on a bird's skin.
Tylo'sis s. A thickening inflammation of the eyelids.
Anastomo'sis s. The uniting of veins, arteries, etc., by connecting branches.
Osmo'sis s. The gradual mingling of fluids separated by a porous membrane.
Endosmo'sis s. The percolation of a fluid through a porous membrane.
Exosmo'sis s. Outward passage of gases and liquids through pores.
Ecchymo'sis s. Bruise, or discolouration caused by subcutaneous effusion of blood.
Zymo'sis s. Fermentation; any zymotic disease.
Melano'sis s. Morbid deposit of black pigment in tissues.
Cyano'sis s. A disease in which the skin becomes lead-coloured.
Keno'sis s. Christ's renunciation of Godhead through the Incarnation.
Diagno'sis s. Art of distinguishing diseases.
Stegno'sis s. Constriction of the pores or bowels, etc.
Progno'sis s. A forecast as to the probable course of a disease.
Carcino'sis s. Cancerous disease.
Trichino'sis s. Trichiniasis.
Hypno'sis s. A deep sleep produced artificially.
Madaro'sis s. Loss of hair, especially eyebrows.
Marmaro'sis s. Process of marmarizing.
Fibro'sis s. Fibrous degeneration of an organ.
Necro'sis s. Mortification, especially of bone.
Synchon-dro'sis s. Firm articulation of bones by means of cartilage.
Sclero'sis s. Morbid thickening of a tissue.
Metachro'sis s. Change of colour (as in some lizards).

Arthro'sis s. Articulation.
Diarthro'sis s. Free articulation of the bones.
Enarthro'sis s. A ball-and-socket joint.
Synarthro'sis s. Union of bones disallowing motion.
Chloro'sis s. A form of anæmia ; loss of colour in a plant.
Soro'sis s. A clustered fruit, as the mulberry, etc.
Amauro'sis s. Decay or loss of sight due to nerve affection.
Neuro'sis s. Any functional nervous disease ; any nervous activity that originates or accompanies mental activity.
Pyro'sis s. Heartburn.
Dipso'sis s. Morbid craving for drink.
Hæmato'sis s. The formation of blood ; conversion of venous into arterial blood.
Stigmato'sis s. A spotty form of inflammation.
Terato'sis s. Pathological monstrosity.
Mito'sis s. The usual process of biological cell-division.
Pto'sis s. Paralysis of the eyelid.
Phagocyto'sis s. The destruction of micro-organisms by phagocytes.
Ichthyo'sis s. A disease in which the skin acquires a scaly appearance.
Ap'sis s. One of the two points in an elliptical orbit the greatest of the least distance from the central body.
Syllep'sis s. Simultaneous use of a word literally and metaphorically.
Prolep'sis s. Rhetorical figure by which objections are anticipated ; error of dating an event too early.
Sep'sis s. Putrefaction ; blood-poisoning.
Asep'sis s. Freedom from blood-poisoning, etc.
Paraleip'sis (-lip'-) s. A pretended or apparent omission.
Thlip'sis s. External constriction of blood-vessels.
Ellip'sis s. A rhetorical figure by which words are omitted ; omission.
Synop'sis s. A general view, epitome.
Thanatop'sis s. A meditation on death.
Ar'sis s. In prosody, the stressed part of a foot.
Cathar'sis s. Purgation, purification.
Cassis' (-sēs') s. A black-currant cordial.
Chas'sis s. The base-frame of a gun, motor-car, etc.
Mis'sis s. One in charge of a house ; mistress.
Salpiglos'sis s. A genus of flowering plants from S. America.
Tus'sis s. A cough.
Anacru'sis s. An upward beat at the beginning of a verse.
Ec'dysis s. Shedding of a first skin ; exuviation.
Synchy'sis s. An eye-disease.
Diaph'ysis s. The shaft of a bone.
Ly'sis s. A gradual cooling down in fever.
Dial'ysis s. A process for separating colloid from crystalline substances ; omission of connecting words.
Anal'ysis s. A resolution of anything into its elements.
Psycho-anal'ysis s. Mental analysis applied therapeutically.
Paral'ysis s. Loss or weakening of voluntary motion and often of sensation ; powerlessness, incapacity.
Catal'ysis s. Chemical action by contact in which the agent undergoes no change.
Chemol'ysis s. Chemical decomposition.
Plasmol'ysis s. The contraction of protoplasm or of cell-walls.
Atmol'ysis s. Separation of a mixture of gases.
Hydrol'ysis s. Decomposition by the action of the constituents of water.
Electrol'ysis s. The decomposition of a chemical compound by means of an electric current.
Histol'ysis s. Decay and dissolution of the organic tissues.
Hæmop'tysis s. A spitting of blood from the lungs.
Clem'atis s. A genus of ranunculaceous plants.
Gra'tis a. and adv. For nothing, without charge.
Mé'tis s. Offspring of a white and an American-Indian.
-i'tis suff. Denoting inflammation.
Phlebi'tis s. Inflammation of a vein.
Appendici'tis s. Inflammation of the vermiform appendix.
Cardi'tis s. Inflammation of the heart.
Pericardi'tis s. Inflammation of the pericardium.
Endocardi'tis s. Inflammation of the endocardium.
Myocardi'tis s. Inflammation of the cardium.
Ostei'tis s. Inflammation of bone.
Œsophagi'tis s. Inflammation of the œsophagus.
Meningi'tis s. Inflammation of the meninges.
Myelomeningi'tis s. Spinal meningitis.
Salpingi'tis s. Inflammation of the salpinx.
Pharyngi'tis s. Inflammation of the pharynx.
Laryngi'tis s. Inflammation of the larynx.
Rachi'tis s. Rickets.
Trachi'tis s. Inflammation of the trachea.
Bron'chitis s. Inflammation of the bronchial tubes.
Mephi'tis s. A noxious exhalation.
Gnathi'tis s. Inflammation of the upper jaw.
Cephali'tis s. Inflammation of the brain.
Encephali'tis s. Inflammation of the brain.
Hyali'tis s. Inflammation in the eye.
Myeli'tis s. Inflammation of the spinal cord.
Poliomyeli'tis s. Inflammation of the gray matter of the spinal cord ; paralysis due to this.
Typhli'tis s. Inflammation of the cæcum.
Perityphli'tis s. Inflammation of the tissue surrounding the cæcum.
Tonsilli'tis s. Inflammation of the tonsils.
Coli'tis s. Inflammation of the colon.
Uli'tis s. Inflammation of the gums.
Spondyli'tis s. Inflammation of the vertebræ.
Ophthalmi'tis s. Ophthalmia of all the structures of the eye.
Tympani'tis s. Inflammation of the ear-drum.
Adeni'tis s. Inflammation of the lymphatic glands.
Duodeni'tis s. Inflammation of the duodenum.
Spleni'tis s. Inflammation of the spleen.
Phreni'tis s. Inflammation of the brain ; madness.
Vagini'tis s. Inflammation of the vagina.
Rhini'tis s. Inflammation of the nose.
Lamini'tis s. Inflammation in a horse's foot.
Retini'tis s. Inflammation of the retina.
Peritoni'tis s. Inflammation of the peritoneum or of the bowels.
Blephari'tis s. Inflammation of the eyelid.
Ovari'tis s. Inflammation of the ovaries.
Cerebri'tis s. Inflammation of the brain.
Chondri'tis s. Inflammation of the cartilage.
Ureteri'tis s. Inflammation of the ureter.
Enteri'tis s. Inflammation of the bowels.
Mesenteri'tis s. Inflammation of the mesentery.
Hysteri'tis s. Inflammation of the uterus.
Uteri'tis s. Inflammation of the womb.
Nephri'tis s. Inflammation of the kidneys.
Urethri'tis s. Inflammation of the urethra.
Arthri'tis s. Inflammation of the joints as in gout.
Iri'tis s. Inflammation of the iris.

Gastri'tis s. Inflammation of the stomach.
Pleuri'tis s. Pleurisy.
Neuri'tis s. Inflammation of a nerve.
Myosi'tis s. Inflammation of a muscle.
Glossi'tis s. Inflammation of the tongue.
Pancreati'tis s. Inflammation of the pancreas.
Diaphragmati'tis s. Inflammation of the diaphragm.
Stomati'tis s. Inflammation of the mouth.
Dermati'tis s. Inflammation of the skin.
Hepati'tis s. Congestion or inflammation of the liver.
Kerati'tis s. Inflammation of the cornea.
Prostati'tis s. Inflammation of the prostate gland.
Recti'tis s. Inflammation of the rectum.
Oti'tis s. Inflammation of the ear.
Paroti'tis s. Mumps; inflammation of the parotid gland.
Scroti'tis s. Inflammation of the scrotum.
Scleroti'tis s. Inflammation of the sclerotic.
Masti'tis s. Inflammation of the breast (in women).
Periosti'tis s. Inflammation of the periosteum.
Cysti'tis s. Inflammation of the bladder.
Encysti'tis s. An encysted tumour.
Conjunctivi'tis s. Inflammation of the conjunctiva.
Vulvi'tis s. Inflammation of the vulva.
Synovi'tis s. Inflammation of a synovial membrane.
Coxi'tis s. Inflammation of the hip-joint.
Man'tis s. An insectivorous, orthopterous insect.
Stephano'tis s. A fragrant tropical climbing plant.
Myoso'tis s. Genus of plants including the forget-me-not.
A'qua-for'tis s. Impure nitric acid.
Syr'tis s. A quicksand.
Tes'tis s. A testicle.
Abat'tis s. Felled trees used as a fortification or barrier.
Glot'tis s. The upper opening of the windpipe.
Epiglot'tis s. A valve of cartilage at the base of the tongue.
Periglot'tis s. The skin of the tongue.
Cu'tis s. The true skin below the cuticle.
Ten'uis s. A hard or surd mute in Greek.
Lou'is s. An old French gold coin.
Mar'quis s. A peer ranking next below a duke.
Vis s. Force, energy.
Cla'vis s. A translation, crib.
Ma'vis s. The throstle, song-thrush.
Vis-a-vis' (-vē') adv. Face to face. s. One who or that which is opposite to another.
Clev'is s. An iron hook or ring at the end of a beam, shaft, etc.
Pel'vis s. The bony enclosure of the lower part of the abdominal cavity.
Par'vis s. The open space in front of a cathedral, etc.
Wis v.t. To know, be aware.
Lew'is s. Contrivance for lifting heavy stones by means of a split wedge.
Brew'is s. Broth.
Iwis' adv. Certainly.
Ywis' adv. Certainly.
Ax'is s. The real or imaginary line on which a body revolves.
Prophylax'is s. Art of preserving from or preventing diseases.
Prax'is s. Practice; exercise or discipline for a specific purpose.
Tax'is s. Order; classification; manual treatment in surgery.
Phyllotax'is s. Systematic arrangement of leaves on an axis.
Hypotax'is a. Subordinate grammatical construction.
Heterotax'is s. Heterotaxy.
Epistax'is s. Bleeding at the nose.
Orex'is s. Desire; appetite.
Epizeux'is s. A figure in which a word is repeated with vehemence.
Bar'racks s. Buildings for housing troops.
Hoicks int. A shout to urge on hounds.
Yoicks int. Cry to urge on fox-hounds.
Fid'dlesticks int. Nonsense! rubbish!
Gold'locks s. The buttercup, or other yellow flowers.
Stocks s. An instrument of punishment for detention; framework supporting ship while building; shares, the funds.
Shucks int. Expressing contempt.
Breeks s. (*Scot.*) Breeches.
Long'shanks s. A long-legged person; the stilt (bird).
Thanks s. Expression of gratitude.
Branks s. A gag for punishing scolds.
Fenks s. Refuse of whale-blubber.
Methinks' v. impers. It seems to me.
Jinks s. Frolics, jollification.
Links s. Undulating, sandy ground near the sea; a golf-course.
Tiddl'ywinks s. A game played by snapping counters.
Hunks s. A sordid wretch; a miser.
Zooks int. Expressing surprise, incredulity, etc.
Works s. A factory, industrial establishment; mechanism, building operations, etc.
Wa'terworks s. Place for the collection and distribution of water.
Lawks int. A vulgar exclamation.
Pontif'icals s. Ecclesiastical vestments and insignia, especially of a bishop or pope.
Canon'icals s. Ecclesiastical robes and vestments.
Theat'ricals s. Amateur dramatic performances.
Nup'tials s. A wedding.
An'nals s. Historical records.
Inter'nals s. Intrinsic qualities; the entrails.
Exter'nals s. Outward parts; forms, ceremonies; non-essentials.
Mor'als s. Doctrine or practice of the duties of life, conduct, etc.; ethics.
Gen'itals s. The external organs of generation.
Vi'tals s. Parts essential to life.
Regimen'tals s. Military dress.
Victuals (vitlz) s. Food; provisions. v.t. and i. To supply with or lay in provisions.
Flan'nels s. Trousers or underclothing made of flannel.
Bat'tels s. Provisions provided by the authorities for members of a college.
Wels (vĕltz) s. The sheat-fish.
Bow'els s. The intestines; the seat of pity.
En'trails s. The bowels, intestines; internal parts.
Squails s. A game played with counters on a marked board.
Noils s. Tangles in wool.
O'veralls s. Loose trousers worn over others to protect them.
Consols' s. British Government consolidated securities.
Meseems' v. impers. It seems to me.
Alms s. A charitable gift.
Cus'toms s. Duties on merchandise imported or exported.
Dol'drums s. The dumps, part of the ocean near the equator where calms prevail.
Or'leans s. A cloth of mixed cotton and wool.
Means s. Measures adopted; agency; income, resources.
Sans prep. Without.

Ens s. Entity; existence; being.
Smithereens' s. Tiny fragments.
Greens s. Leaves and stem of young cabbages, etc., used for cooking.
Teens s. Years of age from thirteen to nineteen.
Gens s. A clan or family among the ancient Romans.
Dick'ens s. (*Slang*) The deuce, the devil.
Lens s. A magnifying or diminishing glass; the crystalline, focussing part of the eye.
Delir'ium tre'mens s. Mental disease caused by chronic alcoholism.
Lo'cum-te'nens s. A substitute, especially for a clergyman or doctor.
Av'ens s. Herb bennet, and other plants.
Remains' s. That which is left; remainder; literary works published after author's death; a corpse.
Pains s. Care, toil, trouble; the throes of childbirth.
Brains s. The seat of intellect; intellectual power.
Reins (rānz) s. The kidneys, loins.
Jug'gins s. (*Slang*) A fool, fat-head.
Mug'gins s. A children's card-game; a simpleton.
With'ershins adv. In the contrary direction; to the left.
Thumb'ikins s. The thumbscrew, an old instrument of torture.
Galligas'kins s. Loose breeches; gaiters for sportsmen.
Ai'blins adv. (*Scot.*) Possibly, perhaps.
Nine'pins s. The game of bowling at nine skittles.
Mat'ins s. Morning worship or songs, etc.; time of this.
Banns s. Notice given in church of an intended marriage.
Respon'sions s. The preliminary examination for the Oxford B.A.
Transac'tions s. Reports of proceedings of learned societies.
Instruc'tions s. Directions; orders.
Muni'tions s. Military stores; material for any enterprise.
Flux'ions s. The analysis of infinitely small variable quantities.
Com'mons s. Untitled people; the lower House of Parliament; fare.
Sum'mons s. Command to appear, especially in a law-court.
Pan'taloons s. Trousers; under-drawers for men.
Eftsoons' adv. Shortly afterwards.
Pons s. A connecting band of fibres.
Envi'rons s. The surrounding neighbourhood of a place.
But'tons s. A page-boy.
Cha'os s. An empty, infinite space; a disordered mass; confusion.
Prona'os s. The vestibule of an ancient temple.
Cos s. A variety of lettuce.
Par'ados s. A parapet protecting defenders against fire from the rear.
Intra'dos s. The under surface of an arch.
Extra'dos s. The exterior curve of an arch.
Rer'edos s. Ornamental screen behind the altar.
Ku'dos s. Fame, renown, credit.
Lo'gos s. The Divine Word, the Second Person of the Trinity.
Ba'thos s. A ludicrous descent from the elevated to the mean.
Pa'thos s. That which excites tender emotions; expression of deep feeling; sentiment.
E'thos s. Moral character; custom.
Theot'okos s. A title of the Virgin Mary.
Om'phalos s. The boss of a shield; the hub.
De'mos s. The mob; democracy.
Ther'mos s. A vacuum flask.
Cos'mos s. The universe as a whole; an ordered system; order.
Tem'enos s. Sacred enclosure attached to an ancient Greek temple.
Ep'os s. The early poetry of Greece; an epic.
Tri'pos s. Examination for honours at Cambridge.
Apropos' adv.; a. To the purpose; opportunely.
Malapropos' (-pō') adv. Unseasonably; unsuitably.
Phar'os s. A lighthouse, beacon.
Rhinoc'eros s. A large pachydermatous ungulate mammal with one or two horns on the nose.
Monoc'eros s. A one-horned animal.
Monop'teros s. A circular building composed of columns supporting a roof.
Asbes'tos s. An incombustible fibrous mineral.
Cus'tos s. A keeper, custodian.
Pet'tichaps s. One of the warblers.
Perhaps' adv. By chance; it may be; possibly.
Traps s. One's personal baggage.
Bi'ceps s. A muscle of the arm and thigh. a. Two-headed.
Quad'riceps s. An extensor muscle in the leg.
Tri'ceps s. A muscle having three heads.
Prin'ceps s. A chief or head man; an original.
For'ceps s. A surgeon's tongs, pincers, etc.; a grasping organ.
Creeps s. A feeling of shrinking horror.
Seps s. A venomous snake; a serpent-like lizard.
Hips s. Fruit of the dog-rose.
Amid'ships adv. In or towards the middle of a ship.
Thrips s. A minute insect injurious to grain.
Con'tretemps s. A mishap, an untoward incident.
Dumps s. Sadness, depression.
Mumps s. An infectious inflammation of the parotid glands; the sulks.
Scops s. A genus of owls.
Cy'clops s. A one-eyed giant of Greek myth.
Troops s. Soldiers.
Props' s. (*Slang*) Stage requisites.
Schnapps s. Hollands gin.
Corps' s. A division of the army; a disciplined body of men, etc.
Turps s. Oil or spirit of turpentine.
Shears s. A two-bladed cutting instrument like large scissors or with a spring; sheers.
Mars s. The Roman god of war; one of the planets.
Lan'cers s. A kind of quadrille.
Pin'cers s. A two-jawed pivoted implement for gripping, extracting, etc.
Malan'ders s. A skin-disease of horses.
Glan'ders s. A contagious disease in horses.
Sal'lenders s. A dry inflammation on a horse's hind-leg.
Flin'ders s. Fragments, splinters.
Round'ers s. A ball-game.
Sheers s. A hoisting apparatus consisting of spars and tackle.
Snuff'ers s. Kind of scissors for trimming wicks.
Stag'gers s. A disease causing horses, etc., to reel; vertigo.
Hers pron. Her (possessive) when used without a noun.
Blu'chers s. A strong leather half-boot.

With'ers s. Ridge between horse's shoulder-blades.
Pli'ers s. A pair of pincers with flat parallel jaws.
Knack'ers s. Castanets.
Check'ers s. Draughts (the game).
Knick'ers s. Knickerbockers.
Knick'er-bockers s. Loose breeches.
Bloom'ers s. Cloth knickerbockers for women.
Man'ners s. Studied civility; morals.
Cal'lipers s. Compasses for measuring convex bodies, or calibres.
Nip'pers s. Small pincers; pair of pince-nez.
Ves'pers s. Evening service, or time of this in the Roman Catholic Church.
Trous'ers s. Two-legged garment from waist to ankles.
Headquar'ters s. The centre of authority.
Cleav'ers s. Goose-grass.
Revers' (-vair') s. Lapel of a coat, etc.
Di'vers a. Several, sundry.
Cliv'ers s. Goose-grass, cleavers.
Esto'vers s. Tenant's right to wood for repairs, fuel, etc.
Draw'ers s. Light under-breeches.
Tweez'ers s. Small pincers.
Stairs s. A flight of steps.
Backstairs' s. Private stairs. a. Indirect, underhand.
Downstairs' a. and adv. Down the stairs, on or to a lower floor.
Upstairs' a. and adv. Ascending the stairs; pertaining to the upper parts of the house.
Theirs pron. Possessive case of "they."
Dev'oirs s. Politeness, courtesy.
Poster'iors s. The hinder part or an animal's body, the rump.
Indoors' adv. Within a house, etc.
Outdoors' adv. In the open air.
Scis'sors s. A cutting instrument with two pivoted blades.
Ours a. Belonging to us.
All-fours' s. A card-game.
Col'ours s. A banner; a flag.
Yours a. and pron. Belonging to you; that or those pertaining or belonging to you.
Ass s. A donkey; a dolt.
Bass s. A fish of the perch family; fibre of the lime-tree, a basket made of this; the lowest male voice, a low-pitched instrument. a. Deep, low in sound.
Car'cass s. A dead body.
Gal'leass s. An obsolete vessel larger than a galley and smaller than a galleon.
Megass' s. Residue of sugar-cane after crushing.
Jack'ass s. A male ass; a fool.
Lass s. A girl; a sweetheart.
Class s. A rank or order; a division, group, grade. v.t. To rank together, form into a class or classes, classify.
Outclass' v.t. To excel.
Wind'lass s. Revolving cylinder for raising weights.
Glass s. A transparent, brittle substance; a vessel, utensil, mirror, lens, etc., made of this; quantity a glass vessel holds. a. Made of glass. v.t. To glaze; to mirror.
I'singlass s. Gelatine prepared from air-bladders of certain fish.
Gal'loglass s. An armed retainer of the ancient Irish chiefs.
Cut'lass s. A broad curved sword.
Mass s. A lump; magnitude; an assemblage; the generality; the Roman Catholic Communion Service. v.t. and i. To form into a mass; to assemble in crowds.
Amass' v.t. To form into a mass; to accumulate.
Pass v.i. To move, to go by or past; to change, die, vanish; to be current; to thrust (in fencing, etc.); to succeed in an examination. v.t. To go past; to cross; to live through; to undergo successfully; to ignore; to enact; to void. s. A narrow passage, a defile; a permit; manipulation; extremity.
Repass' v.t. and i. To pass again.
Com'pass s. A circuit; limit, extent, range; instrument for ascertaining direction; instrument for describing circles. v.t. To pass round; besiege, invest; to obtain, contrive.
Encom'pass v.t. To enclose, encircle; to pass or sail round.
Overpass' v.t. To pass over; to omit, neglect.
Surpass' v.t. To go beyond in anything; to excel.
Tres'pass v.i. To enter illegally, to intrude. s. A sin, wrongful act.
Har'ass v.t. To weary with importunity; to vex.
Brass s. A yellow alloy of copper and zinc; something made of this; impudence. a. Made of brass. v.t. To coat with brass.
Crass a. Thick, coarse, obtuse, stupid.
Frass s. Wood-refuse left by a boring insect.
Grass s. Common green herbage; a grain-yielding or pasture plant. v.t. To cover with grass.
Cuirass' s. A breast-plate and back-plate; armour on a warship.
Morass' s. Soft, wet ground; a bog.
Embar'rass v.t. To involve in difficulties; to distress.
Disembar'rass v.t. To free from embarrassment.
Mat'rass s. A long-necked oval vessel used in distilling.
Strass s. Paste for artificial gems.
Tass s. A goblet; a small draught.
Tarantass' s. A four-wheeled Russian carriage.
Quass s. A thin, sour, Russian beer.
Kavass' s. A Turkish armed constable.
Kvass s. Russian beer made from rye.
Can'vass v.t. and i. To examine thoroughly, discuss; to solicit votes, orders, etc., from. s. Close examination; soliciting.
Ess s. An "S"; an object shaped like this.
Ab'bess s. The female superior of a convent, etc.
Cess s. A local tax.
Ac'cess s. Approach, or means of this; admission.
Success' s. Act of succeeding; something that succeeds; favourable result; prosperity.
Recess' s. An alcove, niche; a withdrawing period of suspension of business.
Princess' s. A female of the rank of a prince a prince's consort.
Pro'cess s. Act of proceeding; progress course; series of actions; progressive act; regular manner of activity; method or practice of reproducing pictures; a projecting part.

Ab'scess s. A gathering of purulent matter.
Excess' s. That which exceeds; superfluity; intemperance.
God'dess s. A female deity; a woman worthy of worship.
Druidess' s. A female druid.
Leop'ardess s. A female leopard.
Stewardess' s. A female steward.
Shep'herdess s. A female shepherd.
Confess' v.t. To acknowledge, own, admit as true; to hear a confession. v.i. To make confession.
Profess' v.t. To declare openly, avow; to pretend to knowledge of. v.i. To confess.
Largess' s. A reward; generous bounty; liberality.
Bur'gess s. A citizen, a freeman.
Chess s. A game for two played with 32 pieces on a board of 64 squares.
Duch'ess s. The wife or widow of a duke; a female holder of a duchy.
Archduch'ess s. The wife or widow of an archduke.
Jess s. A short strap for a hawk's leg.
Less a. Smaller; not so great, numerous, important, etc. adv. In a smaller or lower degree. s. A smaller part, quantity, etc.; the inferior.
-less suff. Destitute of; free from.
Ide'aless a. Void of ideas, empty-headed.
Bless v.t. To invoke a blessing upon; to praise or glorify for benefits; to make happy.
Cab'less a. (*Cab*).
Limb'less a. Destitute of limbs.
Tomb'less a. Destitute of a tomb.
Traff'icless a. Destitute of traffic.
Head'less a. Without a head; having no leader
Bread'less a. Without food.
Dread'less a. Free from fear; intrepid.
Deed'less a. Inactive.
Heed'less a. Careless; thoughtless; negligent.
Meed'less a. Without reward.
Need'less a. Unnecessary; not required; superfluous.
Seed'less a. Having no seeds.
Lid'less a. Having no lid; uncovered; vigilant.
Child'less a. Without offspring.
Hand'less a. Not having hands.
Land'less a. Having no real estate.
Gland'less a. Destitute of glands.
End'less a. Having no end; interminable, eternal; perpetually recurring.
Friend'less a. Destitute of friends.
Wind'less a. Calm; out of breath.
Bound'less a. Without bounds, limitless.
Ground'less a. Unfounded; false; without warrant.
Sound'less a. Silent, noiseless; unfathomable.
God'less a. Acknowledging no God; irreligious, wicked.
Blood'less a. Anæmic; without bloodshed; spiritless.
Wood'less a. Having no woods or wood.
Beard'less a. (*Beard*).
Regard'less a. Careless, negligent, indifferent.
Guard'less a. Having no guard or defence; reckless.
Reward'less a. Without reward.
Lord'less a. Having no lord or master.
Word'less a. Without words; silent, speechless.
Sword'less a. Having no sword.
Bud'less a. (*Bud*).
Cloud'less a. Clear, unclouded.
Shroud'less a. Having no shrouds.
Bribe'less a. Unbribable.
Lobe'less a. Devoid of lobes.
Face'less a. Destitute of a face.
Grace'less a. Void of grace, wicked, abandoned.
Voice'less a. Having no voice; dumb.
Price'less a. Of inestimable worth.
Fence'less a. Unenclosed; undefended.
Defence'less a. Without defence; unprotected; weak.
Con'scienceless a. (*Conscience*).
Force'less a. Devoid of strength, energy, or initiative; feeble.
Resource'less a. Without resource.
Fade'less a. Not fading; undying.
Shade'less a. Destitute of shade or shadow.
Pride'less a. Being destitute of pride.
Guide'less a. Having no guide or guidance.
Tree'less a. Destitute of trees.
Life'less a. Destitute of life; inactive; dull, spiritless.
Wife'less a. Having no wife; widowed.
Age'less a. Never ending; immemorial.
Bridge'less a. (*Bridge*).
Liege'less a. Not bound to a superior; disloyal.
Change'less a. Unchanging.
Scathe'less a. Without damage, unharmed.
Nevertheless' conj. But for all that; notwithstanding.
Brake'less a. (*Brake*).
Smoke'less a. Emitting no smoke.
Scale'less a. Having no scales.
Smile'less a. Without a smile.
Guile'less a. Artless, honest, sincere.
Fame'less a. Without renown.
Shame'less a. Wanting modesty; brazen-faced
Blame'less a. Innocent.
Flame'less a. Destitute of flame or ardour.
Name'less a. Without a name; not known, not famous; inexpressible; unfit to be named.
Frame'less a. Destitute of a frame.
Tame'less a. Not capable of being tamed.
Crime'less a. Innocent.
Time'less a. Without end; untimely.
Home'less a. Without a home.
Rhyme'less a. Without rhyme.
Mane'less a. Destitute of a mane.
Spine'less a. Being without a spine; feeble.
Bone'less a. (*Bone*).
Tone'less a. Having no tone; unmusical.
Stone'less a. Having no stone (of fruit).
Tune'less a. Not harmonious, not in tune silent.
Shoe'less a. Having or wearing no shoes.
Toe'less a. Having no toes.
Shape'less a. Having no regular form.
Hope'less a. Destitute of hope; despairing; desperate.
Care'less a. Negligent, heedless; free from anxiety.
Hire'less a. Gratuitous, unpaid.
Desire'less a. Having no desire; unambitious.
Tire'less a. Unwearied; having no tires.
Wire'less a. Without a wire. s. Wireless telegraphy. v.t. and i. To send a message or communicate by this.
Core'less a. Not having a core.
Shore'less a. Having no shore; of infinite extent.
Cen'treless a. Without centre.
Lus'treless a. Having no sheen or lustre.
Cure'less a. Without remedy.
Meas'ureless a. Vast, boundless; inestimable.
Fea'tureless a. Having no distinct features.
Fu'tureless a. With no future or prospects.
Base'less a. Unfounded; groundless.
Ease'less a. Without ease; uncomfortable.
Cease'less a. Without cessation, incessant.
Noise'less a. Making no sound, silent.
Expense'less a. Of no expense or cost; bearing no expense.

Sense'less a. Destitute of sense; contrary to reason; incapable of feeling.
Nose'less a. Having no nose.
Remorse'less a. Without remorse; pitiless; cruel.
Use'less a. Worthless; of no service; unavailing.
Cause'less a. Without a cause or reason.
Spouse'less a. Having no spouse; unmarried.
Note'less a. Unmusical; not worthy of notice.
Vote'less a. Being without a vote.
Taste'less a. Without flavour or taste; vapid.
Tongue'less a. Speechless; mute.
Hue'less a. Colourless.
Val'ueless a. Of no value; worthless.
Iss'ueless a. Having no issue or progeny.
Vir'tueless a. Having no virtue or virtues.
Grave'less a. Without a tomb; unburied.
Wave'less a. Free from waves; unagitated.
Sleeve'less a. Without sleeves; wanting a pretext.
Mo'tiveless a. Purposeless, having no motive.
Love'less a. Not loving, or loved; void of love.
Glove'less a. Destitute of gloves.
Move'less a. Immovable.
Nerve'less a. Destitute of energy, vigour, etc.; flabby.
Awe'less a. (*Awe*).
Eye'less a. Destitute of eyes; blind.
Breeze'less a. (*Breeze*).
Leaf'less a. Destitute of leaves; bare.
Brief'less a. Without briefs; having no clients.
Grief'less a. Having no sorrow or regrets.
Self'less a. Unselfish; with no regard for self.
Roof'less a. Having no roof, home, or shelter.
Proof'less a. Wanting sufficient evidence.
Leg'less a. Without legs.
Twig'less a. Having no twigs.
Fang'less a. Destitute of fangs.
King'less a. Being without a king.
Mean'ingless a. Destitute of meaning.
Spring'less a. Having no spring.
String'less a. Destitute of strings.
Sting'less a. Having no sting.
Wing'less a. Having no wings.
Speech'less a. Dumb; silent, especially through emotion.
Branch'less a. (*Branch*).
Stanch'less a. Incapable of being stanched.
Quench'less a. Inextinguishable; irrepressible.
Search'less a. Inscrutable.
Match'less a. Having no equal; unrivalled.
Cash'less a. Moneyless.
Flesh'less a. Lean, scraggy.
Blush'less a. (*Blush*).
Death'less a. Immortal, imperishable.
Breath'less a. Out of breath; dead; calm and still; panting; eager.
Nathless' adv. Nevertheless.
Path'less a. Destitute of paths; unexplored.
Faith'less a. False, disloyal; unreliable, perfidious; unbelieving.
Pith'less a. Wanting strength, cogency, or force.
Tooth'less a. Having no teeth.
Mirth'less a. Without mirth; sad, joyless.
Worth'less a. Valueless; contemptible.
Ruth'less a. Pitiless, cruel; barbarous.
Truth'less a. False; unreliable.
Mer'ciless a. Void of mercy; pitiless, cruel.
Rem'ediless a. Incurable.
Bod'iless a. (*Body*).
Pen'niless a. Destitute of money; very poor.
We'ariless a. Incapable of being wearied; tireless.
Wor'riless (wŭr'-) a. Having no worries.
Pit'iless a. Hard-hearted, cruel, merciless; exciting no pity.
Track'less a. Pathless; untravelled; leaving no track.
Feck'less a. Feeble, weak; inefficient.
Fleck'less a. Spotless; blameless.
Speck'less a. Not specked; unspotted.
Reck'less a. Heedless; rashly negligent.
Luck'less a. Unfortunate; ill-fated.
Stalk'less a. Not having a stalk.
Bank'less a. (*Bank*).
Thank'less a. Ungrateful; not deserving thanks.
Trunk'less a. Destitute of a trunk.
Work'less a. Having no work; unemployed.
Wheel'less a. Having no wheels.
Sail'less a. Destitute of sails.
Tail'less a. Having no tail.
Soul'less a. Without magnanimity; mean; spiritless.
Beam'less a. (*Beam*).
Dream'less a. Free from dreams.
Stream'less a. Having no streams.
Seam'less a. Without a seam.
Stem'less a. Having no stem.
Aim'less a. (*Aim*).
Rim'less a. Having no rim.
Helm'less a. Rudderless; without a helm or helmet.
Fath'omless a. Not to be fathomed; bottomless.
Bloom'less a. (*Bloom*).
Blos'somless a. (*Blossom*).
Bot'tomless a. Unfathomed, unfathomable; without a seat.
Arm'less a. (*Arm*).
Harm'less a. Not injurious; unharmed.
Term'less a. Unlimited.
Form'less a. Without definite form; shapeless.
Sum'less a. Countless.
Or'ganless a. Having no organ or organs.
Gain'less a. Unprofitable; not producing gain.
Chain'less a. Without a chain; unrestrained.
Pain'less a. Free or relieved from pain or anxiety.
Rain'less a. Without rain; dry.
Brain'less a. Idiotic, silly; destitute of brains.
Stain'less a. Free from stain; unblemished.
Fin'less a. Destitute of fins.
Sin'less a. Free from sin; innocent, pure.
Suspi'cionless a. Without suspicion; trustful.
Fash'ionless a. Without shape or fashion.
Pas'sionless a. Void of passion; calm-tempered.
Expres'sionless a. Deficient in expression.
Founda'tionless a. Baseless; without foundation.
Mo'tionless a. Wanting motion; being at rest.
Por'tionless a. Having no portion or dowry.
Ques'tionless a. Beyond a question; certain.
Weap'onless a. Having no weapons; unarmed.
But'tonless a. (*Button*).
Horn'less a. Destitute of horns or horn.
Unless' conj. If it be not that; except.
Gun'less a. Destitute of guns.
Sun'less a. Dark; gloomy.
Renown'less a. Inglorious.
Town'less a. Destitute of a town.
Hap'less a. Unfortunate, luckless.
Nap'less a. Not having a nap.
Sap'less a. Destitute of sap; withered.
Sleep'less a. Without sleep; wakeful, vigilant; having no rest.
Ship'less a. Having no ships.
Help'less a. Unable to help oneself; affording no help; irremediable.
Lamp'less a. Having no lamps or light.
Top'less a. Having no top; supereminent.
Ear'less a. Without ears; deaf; unwilling to hear.
Fear'less a. Bold; undaunted.
Gear'less a. Without gear or gearing.
Tear'less a. Shedding no tears.

Oar'less a. Having no oars.
Star'less a. With no stars visible; very dark.
Cum'berless a. Free from encumbrance.
Slum'berless a. Sleepless; vigilant.
Num'berless a. Innumerable, countless.
Lead'erless a. Without a guide or leader.
Ud'derless a. Having no udders.
Rud'derless a. Having no rudder; out of control.
Rid'erless a. Without a rider.
Or'derless a. Disorderly; out of order or rule.
Bor'derless a. (*Border*).
Cheer'less a. Gloomy, dispiriting.
Peer'less a. Having no equal; superexcellent.
Feath'erless a. Destitute of feathers; unfledged.
Fa'therless a. Not having a father living; with author unknown.
Moth'erless a. Having lost a mother.
Ham'merless a. Not having a hammer.
Man'nerless a. Devoid of manners or good breeding.
Own'erless a. Having no owner.
Sup'perless a. Without supper.
Wa'terless a. Destitute of water.
Char'acterless a. Without character; commonplace.
Mas'terless a. Without a master; uncontrolled.
Sis'terless a. Having no sister.
Lov'erless a. Not having a suitor.
Flow'erless a. Destitute of flowers.
Pow'erless a. Weak; impotent.
Air'less a. Close, musty; calm.
Hair'less a. Destitute of hair.
Heir'less a. Having no successor.
Har'bourless a. Having no harbour.
O'dourless a. Having no scent.
Col'ourless a. Wanting in colour, pale; devoid of emotion, passion, etc.; dull.
Hu'mourless a. Devoid of humour.
Sa'vourless a. Insipid.
Spur'less a. Not wearing spurs.
Grass'less a. Void of grass.
Stress'less a. Without stress.
Sweat'less a. Destitute of sweat.
Hat'less a. Without a hat.
Doubt'less adv. Without doubt; unquestionably.
Bract'less a. (*Bract*).
Tact'less a. Having no tact.
Effect'less a. Producing no effect, ineffectual.
Ob'jectless a. Having no object; purposeless.
Duct'less a. Destitute of ducts.
Pock'etless a. Having no pockets.
Shift'less a. Failing through negligence or incapacity.
Rift'less a. Without a rift.
Drift'less a. Aimless; without definite object or meaning.
Thrift'less a. Not thrifty or thriving; wasteful.
Weight'less a. Having no weight; light; unimportant.
Sight'less a. Wanting sight; unsightly.
Thought'less a. Careless; without thought or thinking.
Prof'itless a. Void of profit; useless.
Lim'itless a. Boundless; having no limits.
Spir'itless a. Dejected, depressed; listless.
Fruit'less a. Not bearing fruit; unprofitable.
Wit'less a. Destitute of wit; indiscreet; idiotic.
Salt'less a. Devoid of salt.
Guilt'less a. Innocent; free from guilt.
Fault'less a. Perfect; without fault or blemish.
Result'less a. Fruitless; without result.
Scent'less a. Destitute of odour.
Relent'less a. Implacable, pitiless.
Taint'less a. Pure; unblemished.
Point'less a. Having no point; dull, stupid.
Stint'less a. Abundant, without restriction.
Daunt'less a. Fearless, intrepid.
Count'less a. Innumerable, beyond computation.
Boot'less a. Without boots; profitless, unavailing.
Foot'less a. Destitute of feet.
Root'less a. Having no root.
Spot'less a. Without a spot; unblemished.
Corrupt'less a. Not liable to be corrupted.
Art'less a. Natural; guileless; unskilful.
Heart'less a. Without feeling or affection; pitiless; faint-hearted.
Chart'less a. Without a chart.
Desert'less a. Without merit.
Shirt'less a. Wearing or having no shirt.
Com'fortless a. Cheerless; lacking comfort.
Support'less a. Without support.
Hurt'less a. Doing no injury; without harm; unhurt.
Rest'less a. Never still; agitated; unsettled; sleepless.
List'less a. Inattentive; careless; indifferent; languid.
Christ'less a. Without faith in Christ.
Resist'less a. Incapable of resisting or being resisted.
Exhaust'less a. That cannot be exhausted; tireless.
Trust'less a. Unworthy of trust; faithless.
Spout'less a. Destitute of a spout.
Law'less a. Contrary to or unauthorized by law; unrestrained, licentious; anomalous.
Claw'less a. (*Claw*).
Flaw'less a. Without a flaw or defect.
Dew'less a. Without dew; unbedewed.
Thew'less a. Destitute of strength or vigour.
View'less a. Invisible.
Sin'ewless a. Destitute of strength or vigour.
Shad'owless a. Having no shadow.
Sex'less a. Having no sexual characteristics.
Ray'less a. Destitute of light; having no rays.
Stay'less a. Wearing no stays.
Hob'byless a. Being without a hobby.
Key'less a. Wound without a detachable key.
Hon'eyless a. Destitute of honey.
Mo'neyless a. Destitute of money.
Joy'less a. Destitute of joy; unenjoyable.
Mess s. A dish, meal; number of persons feeding together; muddle, confusion. v.i. To take meals together. v.t. To jumble, muddle.
Ness s. A cape, promontory.
-ness suff. Forming nouns denoting state, condition, or quality.
Ti'taness s. A female Titan; a giantess.
Sultaness' s. A sultana.
Drab'ness s. Commonplaceness, dullness.
Glib'ness s. Quality of being glib.
Dumb'ness s. (*Dumb*).
Numb'ness s. (*Numb*).
Superb'ness s. (*Superb*).
Specif'icness s. Specificity.
Prolif'icness s. State of being prolific.
Bad'ness s. (*Bad*).
Dead'ness s. Inertness, indifference.
Glad'ness s. State or quality of being glad; pleasure.
Mad'ness s. Lunacy; frenzy; extreme folly.
Broad'ness s. Breadth.
Sad'ness s. (*Sad*).
Odd'ness s. State or quality of being odd.
Crab'bedness s. (*Crabbed*).
Bare'facedness s. Impudence, shamelessness.
Pig-head'edness s. (*Pig-headed*).
Jad'edness s. State of being jaded or worn-out.
Guard'edness s. Caution, circumspection.
Jag'gedness s. State of being jagged.

Rag'gedness s. (*Ragged*).
Crag'gedness s. (*Cragged*).
Dog'gedness s. Pertinacity, determination.
Rug'gedness s. (*Rugged*).
Detach'edness s. Disinterestedness.
Starch'edness s. (*Starched*).
Wretch'edness s. (*Wretched*).
Pied'ness s. State of being parti-coloured.
Hur'riedness s. (*Hurried*).
Na'kedness s. (*Naked*).
Wick'edness s. (*Wicked*).
Hook'edness s. State of being hooked.
Crook'edness s. (*Crooked*).
Mark'edness s. (*Marked*).
Learn'edness s. Erudition; scholarship.
Cramp'edness s. (*Cramp*).
Red'ness s. (*Red*).
Seared'ness s. State of being seared; callousness.
Prepar'edness s. State of being ready.
Sa'credness s. (*Sacred*).
Tired'ness s. Weariness; exhaustion.
Retired'ness s. State of retirement; solitude; privacy.
Assur'edness s. (*Assured*).
Compo'sed-ness s. (*Composed*).
Cur'sedness s. (*Cursed*).
Bless'edness s. State of being blessed; felicity; heavenly joys.
Cus'sedness s. (*Slang*) Perverseness, obstinacy.
Diffu'sedness s. State of being diffused, spread abroad, or scattered.
Bloat'edness s. Quality of being bloated.
Indebt'edness s. State of being under an obligation.
Compact'ed-ness s. (*Compacted*).
Affect'edness s. (*Affected*).
Collect'edness s. (*Collected*).
Disconnect'ed-ness s. (*Disconnected*).
Conceit'edness s. (*Conceited*).
Dement'edness s. (*Demented*).
Content'edness s. (*Contented*).
Malcon-tent'edness s. State of being malcontented.
Discon-tent'edness s. (*Discontented*).
Point'edness s. (*Pointed*).
Devo'tedness s. (*Devoted*).
Disin'terested-ness s. (*Disinterested*).
Cur'vedness s. State of being curved.
Fix'edness s. Steadfastness; immobility.
Staid'ness s. (*Staid*).
Rab'idness s. (*Rabid*).
Mor'bidness s. (*Morbid*).
Tur'bidness s. Turbidity, muddiness.
A'cidness s. (*Acid*).
Pla'cidness s. (*Placid*).
Flac'cidness s. Flaccidity.
Ran'cidness s. (*Rancid*).
Pellu'cidness s. Quality of being pellucid; transparency.
Can'didness s. Candour.
Sor'didness s. (*Sordid*).
Rig'idness s. Rigidity.
Fri'gidness s. Frigidity.
Tur'gidness s. Turgidity.
Squal'idness s. (*Squalid*).
Val'idness s. Validity.
Pal'lidness s. (*Pallid*).
Sol'idness s. Solidity.
Stol'idness s. Stolidity.
Tim'idness s. (*Timid*).
Tu'midness s. (*Tumid*).
Void'ness s. State or quality of being void; inefficacy, nullity.
Rap'idness s. (*Rapid*).
Sap'idness s. Sapidity.
Vap'idness s. Vapidity, dullness.
Tep'idness s. (*Tepid*).
Insip'idness s. Insipidity.
Lim'pidness s. Limpidity.
Tor'pidness s. Torpidity.
Stup'idness s. Stupidity.
Ar'idness s. (*Arid*).
Ac'ridness s. (*Acrid*).
Flor'idness s. Floridity.
Hor'ridness s. (*Horrid*).
Tor'ridness s. Torridity.
Pu'tridness s. Putridity; corruption.
Lur'idness s. (*Lurid*).
Fe'tidness s. State of being malodorous; stench.
Pu'tidness s. Foulness; worthlessness.
Lan'guidness s. (*Languid*).
Liq'uidness s. Liquidity.
Viv'idness s. (*Vivid*).
Fer'vidness s. Quality of being fervid; fervour
Bald'ness s. (*Bald*).
Mild'ness s. (*Mild*).
Wild'ness s. (*Wild*).
Old'ness s. (*Old*).
Bold'ness s. Courage; audacity; effrontery.
Cold'ness s. (*Cold*).
Bland'ness s. (*Bland*).
Grand'ness s. State or quality of being grand; grandeur.
Kind'ness s. Quality of being kind; a kind act
Blind'ness s. (*Blind*).
Pur'blindness s. State of being purblind.
Fond'ness s. Affection, partiality.
Profound'ness s. (*Profound*).
Round'ness s. (*Round*).
Sound'ness s. Quality of being sound, healthy, or unimpaired.
Good'ness s. Desirable qualities; kindness favour; generosity.
Hag'gardness s. State or condition of being haggard.
Back'wardness s. (*Backward*).
Awk'wardness s. (*Awkward*).
In'wardness s. Inner quality or essence.
Fro'wardness s. Disobedience; perverseness.
For'wardness s. Quality or state of being forward; pertness; lack of reserve.
Straight-for'wardness s. (*Straightforward*).
Way'wardness s. (*Wayward*).
Haphaz'ard-ness s. State of being haphazard.
Weird'ness s. (*Weird*).
Absurd'ness s. (*Absurd*).
Loud'ness s. (*Loud*).
Lewd'ness s. (*Lewd*).
Shrewd'ness s. (*Shrewd*).
Com'mon-placeness s. (*Commonplace*).
Nice'ness s. (*Nice*).
Choice'ness s. (*Choice*).
Scarce'ness s. Lack of plenty; dearth.
Fierce'ness s. Quality of being fierce.
Douce'ness s. Sedateness.
Spruce'ness s. (*Spruce*).
Nude'ness s. Nudity.
Rude'ness s. (*Rude*).
Crude'ness s. (*Crude*).
Free'ness s. State or quality of being free; candour; liberality.
Safe'ness s. (*Safe*).
Rife'ness s. (*Rife*).
Sage'ness s. (*Sage*).
Sav'ageness s. (*Savage*).
Strange'ness s. (*Strange*).
Large'ness s. (*Large*).
Huge'ness s. (*Huge*).
Lithe'ness s. (*Lithe*).

Blithe'ness s. (*Blithe*).
Wideawake'ness s. (*Wideawake*).
Like'ness s. Similarity; a portrait, image; guise.
Pale'ness s. (*Pale*).
Stale'ness s. (*Stale*).
Impertur'bableness s. (*Imperturbable*).
Pla'cableness s. Placability.
Am'icableness s. (*Amicable*).
ommun'icableness s. (*Communicable*).
?rac'ticableness s. (*Practicable*).
mprac'ticableness s. (*Impracticable*).
For'midableness s. Quality of being formidable.
ommend'ableness s. (*Commendable*).
)epend'ableness s. (*Dependable*).
Peace'ableness s. (*Peaceable*).
Trace'ableness s. (*Traceable*).
'er'viceableness s. (*Serviceable*).
Agree'ableness s. (*Agreeable*).
isagree'ableness s. (*Disagreeable*).
Ian'ageableness s. (*Manageable*).
han'geableness s. (*Changeable*).
nterchange'ableness s. State of being interchangeable.
'harge'ableness s. (*Chargeable*).
lame'ableness s. State or quality of being blameworthy.
Ineff'ableness s. (*Ineffable*).
ndefat'igableness s. Indefatigability.
rreproach'ableness s. Blamelessness.
augh'ableness s. (*Laughable*).
er'ishableness s. Perishability.
mper'ishableness s. Imperishability.
So'ciableness s. Sociability.
reme'diableness s. Incurability.
ustifi'ableness s. Justifiability.
Reli'ableness s. Trustworthiness.
Pli'ableness s. State of being pliable or easily influenced; pliancy.
Var'iableness s. Variability.
nvar'iableness s. Invariability.
Fri'ableness s. Friability.
nsa'tiableness s. Insatiability.
Pit'iableness s. (*Pitiable*).
rink'ableness s. (*Drinkable*).
emark'ableness s. (*Remarkable*).
vail'ableness s. (*Available*).
reconcil'ableness s. Irreconcilability.
redeem'ableness s. Irredeemability.
flam'mableness s. Inflammability.
Ten'ableness s. (*Tenable*).
tain'ableness s. (*Attainable*).
om'inableness s. (*Abominable*).
erm'inableness s. (*Terminable*).

Inter'minableness s. State of being interminable.
Par'donableness s. (*Pardonable*).
Con'scionableness s. (*Conscionable*).
Fash'ionableness s. State or quality of being fashionable.
Compan'ionableness s. (*Companionable*).
Reas'onableness s. (*Reasonable*).
Trea'sonableness s. (*Treasonable*).
Sea'sonableness s. (*Seasonable*).
Tun'ableness s. (*Tunable*).
Pal'pableness s. (*Palpable*).
Cul'pableness s. (*Culpable*).
Irrep'arableness s. (*Irreparable*).
Sep'arableness s. (*Separable*).
Insep'arableness s. (*Inseparable*).
Incom'parableness s. (*Incomparable*).
Num'berableness s. (*Numberable*).
Consid'erableness s. (*Considerable*).
Inconsid'erableness s. (*Inconsiderable*).
Pon'derableness s. (*Ponderable*).
Impon'derableness s. (*Imponderable*).
Pref'erableness s. (*Preferable*).
Suf'ferableness s. (*Sufferable*).
Tol'erableness s. (*Tolerable*).
Intol'erableness s. State of being intolerable.
Ven'erableness s. (*Venerable*).
Vul'nerableness s. Vulnerability.
Su'perableness s. (*Superable*).
Insu'perableness s. (*Insuperable*).
Irrecov'erableness s. (*Irrecoverable*).
Ad'mirableness s. (*Admirable*).
Desir'ableness s. Desirability.
Ador'ableness s. (*Adorable*).
Deplor'ableness s. (*Deplorable*).
Impen'etrableness s. (*Impenetrable*).
Incur'ableness s. (*Incurable*).
Dur'ableness s. Lastingness, permanence.
Endur'ableness s. (*Endurable*).
Dishon'ourableness s. (*Dishonourable*).
Fa'vourableness s. Quality or state of being favourable.
Immeas'urableness s. (*Immeasurable*).
Cen'surableness s. (*Censurable*).
Commen'surableness s. (*Commensurable*).
Advi'sableness s. (*Advisable*).
Indispen'sableness s. (*Indispensable*).
Convers'ableness s. (*Conversable*).
Impass'ableness s. (*Impassable*).
Excus'ableness s. (*Excusable*).
Inexcus'ableness s. (*Inexcusable*).
Tract'ableness s. (*Tractable*).
Intract'ableness s. Intractability.

Delect'ableness s. (*Delectable*).
Respect'ableness s. Respectability.
Mar'ketableness s. (*Marketable*).
Indu'bitableness s. (*Indubitable*).
Cred'itableness s. (*Creditable*).
Prof'itableness s. (*Profitable*).
Illim'itableness s. State or quality of being boundless.
Inim'itableness s. (*Inimitable*).
Hos'pitableness s. (*Hospitable*).
Inhos'pitableness s. (*Inhospitable*).
Char'itableness s. (*Charitable*).
Suit'ableness s. Suitability.
Inev'itableness s. Inevitability.
War'rantableness s. (*Warrantable*).
Account'ableness s. (*Accountable*).
Insurmount'ableness s. (*Insurmountable*).
Po'tableness s. (*Potable*).
Accep'tableness s. (*Acceptable*).
Com'fortableness s. (*Comfortable*).
Port'ableness s. (*Portable*).
Stable'ness s. Stability.
Detest'ableness s. (*Detestable*).
Permut'ableness s. (*Permutable*).
Disrep'utableness s. (*Disreputable*).
Indis'putableness s. (*Indisputable*).
Inscrut'ableness s. Inscrutability.
Val'uableness s. (*Valuable*).
Conceiv'ableness s. (*Conceivable*).
Inconceiv'ableness s. (*Inconceivable*).
Lov'ableness s. (*Lovable*).
Mov'ableness s. Movability.
Immov'ableness s. (*Immovable*).
Allow'ableness s. (*Allowable*).
Know'ableness s. State of being knowable.
Tax'ableness s. (*Taxable*).
Enjoy'ableness s. (*Enjoyable*).
Fee'bleness s. Quality or condition of being feeble.
Vin'cibleness s. Vincibility.
Invinc'ibleness s. Invincibility.
Coer'cibleness s. (*Coercible*).
For'cibleness s. State or quality of being forcible.
Irras'cibleness s. Irrascibility.
Irredu'cibleness s. Irreducibility.
Produ'cibleness s. (*Productible*).
Au'dibleness s. (*Audible*).
Fran'gibleness s. Frangibility.
Tan'gibleness s. (*Tangible*).
Indiscern'ibleness s. (*Indiscernible*).
Ter'ribleness s. (*Terrible*).
Hor'ribleness s. (*Horrible*).
Vis'ibleness s. Visibility.
Invis'ibleness s. Invisibility.
Reprehen'sibleness s. (*Reprehensible*).
Incomprehen'sibleness s. (*Incomprehensible*).
Sen'sibleness s. Susceptibility; reasonableness; intelligence.
Respon'sibleness s. Responsibility.
Impass'ibleness s. (*Impassible*).
Plau'sibleness s. (*Plausible*).
Impercep'tibleness s. (*Imperceptible*).
Suscep'tibleness s. Susceptibility.
Contemp'tibleness s. (*Contemptible*).
Incontro-ver'tibleness s. (*Incontrovertible*).
Irresist'ibleness s. (*Irresistible*).
Inexhaust'ibleness s. (*Inexhaustible*).
Combust'ibleness s. (*Combustible*).
Nimble'ness s. (*Nimble*).
Hum'bleness s. (*Humble*).
Noble'ness s. Quality of being noble; greatness; magnanimity.
Ignoble'ness s. (*Ignoble*).
Insol'ubleness s. (*Insoluble*).
Double'ness s. State of being double; duplicity.
I'dleness s. (*Idle*).
Single'ness s. (*Single*).
Ju'venileness s. Juvenility.
Vile'ness s. (*Vile*).
Fickle'ness s. Changeability, instability.
Whole'ness s. (*Whole*).
Ample'ness s. (*Ample*).
Simple'ness s. Simplicity.
Supple'ness s. (*Supple*).
Gentle'ness s. Quality of being gentle; tenderness.
Brittle'ness s. (*Brittle*).
Game'ness s. Quality of being game or plucky.
Lame'ness s. (*Lame*).
Same'ness s. State of being similar or identical; dullness.
Tame'ness s. (*Tame*).
Extreme'ness s. (*Extreme*).
Sublime'ness s. State or quality of being sublime.
Prime'ness s. State of being first; excellence.
Wel'comeness s. (*Welcome*).
Frol'icsomeness s. State or quality of being frolicsome.
Hand'someness s. Quality of being handsome; generousness.
Lithe'someness s. (*Lithesome*).
Trouble'someness s. (*Troublesome*).
Meddle'someness s. (*Meddlesome*).
Dole'someness s. (*Dolesome*).
Whole'someness s. (*Wholesome*).
Mettle'someness s. (*Mettlesome*).
Lone'someness s. (*Lonesome*).
Tire'someness s. (*Tiresome*).
Ven'turesomeness s. (*Venturesome*).
Adven'turesomeness s. (*Adventuresome*).
Grue'someness s. Quality of being gruesome.
Awe'someness s. (*Awesome*).
Loath'someness s. (*Loathsome*).
Noi'someness s. (*Noisome*).
We'arisomeness s. (*Wearisome*).
Irk'someness s. (*Irksome*).
Quar'relsomeness s. (*Quarrelsome*).
Toil'someness s. (*Toilsome*).
Ful'someness s. State or quality of being fulsome.
Win'someness s. (*Winsome*).
Fear'someness s. Quality or state of being fearsome.
Cum'bersomeness s. (*Cumbersome*).
Hu'moursomeness s. (*Humoursome*).

ight'someness s. (*Lightsome*).
elight'someness s. (*Delightsome*).
Mun'daneness s. Worldliness; quality of being of this world.
Profane'ness s. Profanity.
Humane'ness s. (*Humane*).
Sane'ness s. Sanity.
Insane'ness s. Insanity.
Serene'ness s. (*Serene*).
Fine'ness s. Quality or state of being fine; purity of metals.
Superfine'ness s. (*Superfine*).
Ias'culineness s. Masculinity.
Fem'inineness s. Quality of being feminine.
Supine'ness s. (*Supine*).
andes'tineness s. (*Clandestine*).
ang'uineness s. (*Sanguine*).
Gen'uineness s. State or quality of being genuine.
Divine'ness s. State of being divine.
One'ness s. Singleness; uniqueness, unity; sameness.
Prone'ness s. (*Prone*).
Jejune'ness s. (*Jejune*).
p'portuneness s. (*Opportune*).
op'portuneness s. (*Inopportune*).
Ripe'ness s. (*Ripe*).
read'bareness s. (*Threadbare*).
Spare'ness s. (*Spare*).
Rare'ness s. (*Rare*).
Square'ness s. (*Square*).
Aware'ness s. (*Aware*).
Som'breness s. (*Sombre*).
Sincere'ness s. (*Sincere*).
Austere'ness s. (*Austere*).
Severe'ness s. Severity.
Mea'greness s. (*Meagre*).
Entire'ness s. Entirety.
Sore'ness s. (*Sore*).
Secure'ness s. Security.
Demure'ness s. (*Demure*).
Pure'ness s. (*Pure*).
Sure'ness s. (*Sure*).
Mature'ness s. Maturity.
mature'ness s. Quality of being premature; too great haste.
Base'ness s. State or quality of being low, mean, or unworthy.
Obese'ness s. Corpulence.
Precise'ness s. (*Precise*).
Concise'ness s. (*Concise*).
False'ness s. Quality of being false.
Dense'ness s. (*Dense*).
ropense'ness s. Propensity.
Tense'ness s. (*Tense*).
Intense'ness s. Intensity.
Verbose'ness s. Verbosity, prolixity.
Jocose'ness s. Jocosity.
O'tioseness s. (*Otiose*).
Close'ness s. (*Close*).
Loose'ness s. State or quality of being loose; laxity.
Operose'ness s. (*Operose*).
Morose'ness s. *Morose*).
Coarse'ness s. (*Coarse*).
Hoarse'ness s. (*Hoarse*).
Sparse'ness s. (*Sparse*).
Terse'ness s. (*Terse*).
Averse'ness s. (*Averse*).
Ad'verseness s. (*Adverse*).
Diverse'ness s. Diversity.
'erverse'ness s. (*Perverse*).
Diffuse'ness s. Quality of being diffuse; lack of conciseness; verbosity.
Profuse'ness s. (*Profuse*).
bstruse'ness s. (*Abstruse*).

Del'icateness s. (*Delicate*).
Com'plicateness s. (*Complicate*).
Sedate'ness s. (*Sedate*).
Prof'ligateness s. Profligacy.
Me'diateness s. Mediacy.
Imme'diateness s. (*Immediate*).
Appro'priateness s. (*Appropriate*).
Inappro'priateness s. (*Inappropriate*).
Late'ness s. State or quality of being late.
Oblate'ness s. (*Oblate*).
Invi'olateness s. Inviolacy.
Pro'lateness s. (*Prolate*).
Des'olateness s. Desolation.
Discon'solateness s. (*Disconsolate*).
Immac'ulateness s. Immaculacy.
Artic'ulateness s. (*Articulate*).
Inartic'ulateness s. State or quality of being inarticulate.
Inan'imateness s. (*Inanimate*).
Legit'imateness s. (*Legitimate*).
Ul'timateness s. (*Ultimate*).
Cognate'ness s. (*Cognate*).
Subor'dinateness s. (*Subordinate*).
Inor'dinateness s. (*Inordinate*).
Discrim'inateness s. Quality of discriminating.
Deter'minateness s. (*Determinate*).
Indeter'minateness s. (*Indeterminate*).
Ob'stinateness s. (*Obstinate*).
Innate'ness s. (*Innate*).
Pas'sionateness s. (*Passionate*).
Compas'sionateness s. (*Compassion*).
Affec'tionateness s. (*Affectionate*).
Ornate'ness s. (*Ornate*).
In'choateness s. State or quality of being inchoate.
Sep'arateness s. (*Separate*).
Delib'erateness s. Deliberation.
Consid'erateness s. (*Considerate*).
Inconsid'erateness s. Inconsideration.
Mod'erateness s. (*Moderate*).
Degen'erateness s. Degeneration.
Regen'erateness s. Regeneracy.
Tem'perateness s. (*Temperate*).
Des'perateness s. Desperation.
Invet'erateness s. Long-standing obstinacy.
Illit'erateness s. Illiteracy.
Elab'orateness s. (*Elaborate*).
Ac'curateness s. (*Accurate*).
Commen'surateness s. (*Commensurate*).
Incommen'surateness s. (*Incommensurate*).
Precip'itateness s. Precipitance.
Ad'equateness s. (*Adequate*).
Inad'equateness s. (*Inadequacy*).
Pri'vateness s. Privacy.
Effete'ness s. State of being effete.
Ob'soleteness s. (*Obsolete*).
Complete'ness s. (*Complete*).
Incomplete'ness s. State of being unfinished or defective.
Concrete'ness s. (*Concrete*).
Rec'onditeness s. (*Recondite*).

White'ness s. (*White*).
Polite'ness s. (*Polite*).
Impolite'ness s. (*Impolite*).
Def'initeness s. (*Definite*).
Indef'initeness s. (*Indefinite*).
In'finiteness s. (*Infinite*).
Pret'eriteness s. State of being past.
Trite'ness s. (*Trite*).
Con'triteness s. Contrition.
Req'uisiteness s. (*Requisite*).
Ex'quisiteness s. (*Exquisite*).
Com'positeness s. (*Composite*).
Ap'positeness s. (*Apposite*).
Op'positeness s. (*Opposite*).
Remote'ness s. (*Remote*).
Chaste'ness s. Chastity.
Cute'ness s. (*Cute*).
Acute'ness s. (*Acute*).
Ab'soluteness s. (*Absolute*).
Res'oluteness s. (*Resolute*).
Irres'oluteness s. Irresolution.
Dis'soluteness s. (*Dissolute*).
Mute'ness s. (*Mute*).
Minute'ness s. Tininess; extreme precision.
Hir'suteness s. State of being bristly or unshorn.
Astute'ness s. (*Astute*).
Due'ness s. (*Due*)
Vague'ness (văg'-) s. (*Vague*).
Opaque'ness s. Opacity.
Oblique'ness (-lēk'-) s. (*Oblique*).
Unique'ness (-nēk'-) s. (*Unique*).
Picturesque'ness s. (*Picturesque*).
Grotesque'ness s. State of being grotesque.
Statuesque'ness s. (*Statuesque*).
Brusque'ness s. (*Brusque*).
True'ness s. (*True*).
Condu'civeness s. (*Conducive*).
Forgive'ness s. Act of forgiving, pardon; disposition to pardon.
Persua'siveness s. (*Persuasive*).
Eva'siveness s. (*Evasive*).
Adhe'siveness s. (*Adhesive*).
Cohe'siveness s. (*Cohesive*).
Deci'siveness s. (*Decisive*).
Indeci'siveness s. Indecision.
Inci'siveness s. (*Incisive*).
Divi'siveness s. (*Devisive*).
Repul'siveness s. (*Repulsive*).
Impul'siveness s. (*Impulsive*).
Compul'siveness s. (*Compulsive*).
Expan'siveness s. (*Expansive*).
Offen'siveness s. (*Offensive*).
Inoffen'siveness s. (*Inoffensive*).
Comprehen'siveness s. (*Comprehensive*).
Incomprehen'siveness s. (*Incomprehensive*).
Apprehen'siveness s. (*Apprehensive*).
Inapprehen'siveness s. Quality of being inapprehensive.
Pen'siveness s. (*Pensive*).
Expen'siveness s. (*Expensive*).
Inexpen'siveness s. Cheapness.
Exten'siveness s. (*Extensive*).
Respon'siveness s. (*Responsive*).
Explo'siveness s. (*Explosive*).
Pur'posiveness s. (*Purposive*).
Corro'siveness s. (*Corrosive*).
Disper'siveness s. (*Dispersive*).
Discur'siveness s. (*Discursive*).
Excur'siveness s. (*Excursive*).
Mas'siveness s. (*Massive*).
Pas'siveness s. Passivity.
Impas'siveness s. Impassivity.
Succes'siveness s. (*Successive*).
Regres'siveness s. (*Regressive*).
Aggres'siveness s. (*Aggressive*).
Digres'siveness s. (*Digressive*).
Progres'siveness s. (*Progressive*).
Impres'siveness s. (*Impressive*).
Oppres'siveness s. (*Oppressive*).
Expres'siveness s. (*Expressive*).
Inexpres'siveness s. (*Inexpressive*).
Posses'siveness s. (*Possessive*).
Submis'siveness s. (*Submissive*).
Permis'siveness s. (*Permissive*).
Abu'siveness s. (*Abusive*).
Effu'siveness s. (*Effusive*).
Diffu'siveness s. (*Diffusive*).
Conclu'siveness s. (*Conclusive*).
Inconclu'siveness s. (*Inconclusive*).
Exclu'siveness s. (*Exclusive*).
Elu'siveness s. (*Elusive*).
Delu'siveness s. (*Delusive*).
Allu'siveness s. (*Allusive*).
Illu'siveness s. (*Illusive*).
Collu'siveness s. (*Collusive*).
Obtru'siveness s. (*Obtrusive*).
Intru'siveness s. (*Intrusive*).
Com'bativeness s. (*Combative*).
Signif'icativeness s. (*Significative*).
Commu'nicativeness s. (*Communicative*).
Incommu'nicativeness s. (*Incommunicative*).
Accommoda'tiveness s. (*Accommodative*).
Creative'ness s. (*Creative*).
Neg'ativeness s. (*Negative*).
Talk'ativeness s. (*Talkative*).
Rel'ativeness s. Relativity.
Contemp'lativeness s. (*Contemplative*).
Super'lativeness s. (*Superlative*).
Spec'ulativeness s. State or quality of being speculative.
Cu'mulativeness s. (*Cumulative*).
Am'ativeness s. (*Amative*).
Na'tiveness s. State or quality of being native.
Imag'inativeness s. (*Imaginative*).
Opin'ionativeness s. (*Opinionative*).
Remu'nerativeness s. (*Remunerative*).
Imper'ativeness s. (*Imperative*).
Dec'orativeness s. (*Decorative*).
Pen'etrativeness s. (*Penetrative*).
Concen'trativeness s. Faculty of fixing the thoughts and attention on anything.
Demon'strativeness s. (*Demonstrative*).
Fig'urativeness s. State or quality of being figurative.
Inhabita'tiveness s. Propensity to permanent residence; love of home.
Med'itativeness s. (*Meditative*).
Veg'itativeness s. (*Vegitative*).
Cogita'tiveness s. (*Cogitative*).
Im'itativeness s. (*Imitative*).
Author'itativeness s. (*Authoritative*).

rgumen'ta-tiveness s. (*Argumentative*).
epresen'ta-tiveness s. (*Representative*).
ttrac'tiveness s. (*Attractive*).
Defec'tiveness s. (*Defective*).
Effec'tiveness s. (*Effective*).
neffec'tiveness s. (*Ineffective*).
Infec'tiveness s. Infectivity.
Objec'tiveness s. State or quality of being objective.
ubjec'tiveness s. State of being subjective.
Reflec'tiveness s. (*Reflective*).
rospec'tive-ness s. (*Prospective*).
ntrospec'tive-ness s. (*Introspective*).
ontradic'tive-ness s. (*Contradictive*).
Vindic'tiveness s. (*Vindictive*).
Seduc'tiveness s. (*Seductive*).
roduc'tiveness s. (*Productive*).
estruc'tive-ness s. Quality of destroying.
nstruc'tiveness s. (*Instructive*).
onstruc'tive-ness s. (*Constructive*).
Secre'tiveness s. (*Secretive*).
rohib'itive-ness s. (*Prohibitive*).
Fu'gitiveness s. State of being fugitive.
Prim'itiveness s. (*Primitive*).
hiloprogen'i-tiveness s. Love of offspring.
Nu'tritiveness s. (*Nutritive*).
cquis'itive-ness s. (*Acquisitive*).
nquis'itiveness s. (*Inquisitive*).
ran'sitiveness s. (*Transitive*).
Sen'sitiveness s. (*Sensitive*).
nsen'sitiveness s. (*Insensitive*).
Pos'itiveness s. Actualness; undoubting assurance; certainty.
Intu'itiveness s. (*Intuitive*).
Reten'tiveness s. (*Retentive*).
Atten'tiveness s. (*Attentive*).
natten'tive-ness s. (*Inattentive*).
Inven'tiveness s. (*Inventive*).
Plain'tiveness s. (*Plaintive*).
Decep'tiveness s. (*Deceptive*).
Recep'tiveness s. Receptivity.
ercep'tiveness s. (*Perceptive*).
uscep'tiveness s. (*Susceptive*).
onsump'tive-ness s. (*Consumptive*).
Asser'tiveness s. (*Assertive*).
Abor'tiveness s. (*Abortive*).
Spor'tiveness s. (*Sportive*).
ugges'tiveness s. (*Suggestive*).
Res'tiveness s. (*Restive*).
Cos'tiveness s. Constipation.
xhaus'tive-ness s. (*Exhaustive*).
onsec'utive-ness s. (*Consecutive*).
nconsec'utive-ness s. (*Inconsecutive*).
imin'utive-ness s. (*Diminutive*).
Reflex'iveness s. (*Reflexive*).
Deaf'ness s. (*Deaf*).
Brief'ness s. (*Brief*).
Stiff'ness s. (*Stiff*).
Bluff'ness s. (*Bluff*).
Gruff'ness s. Harshness, asperity.
Aloof'ness s. (*Aloof*).
Big'ness s. (*Big*).
Trig'ness s. Spruceness, smartness.
Pierc'ingness s. (*Piercing*).
Yield'ingness s. (*Yielding*).
Bind'ingness s. (*Binding*).
Obli'gingness s. (*Obliging*).
Disobli'ging-ness s. (*Disobliging*).
Noth'ingness s. Non-existence; utter insignificance.
Tak'ingness s. (*Taking*).
Shock'ingness s. (*Shocking*).
Strik'ingness s. (*Striking*).
Thrill'ingness s. (*Thrilling*).
Will'ingness s. (*Willing*).
Seem'ingness s. (*Seeming*).
Becom'ingness s. (*Becoming*).
Charm'ingness s. (*Charming*).
Spar'ingness s. (*Sparing*).
Impos'ingness s. (*Imposing*).
Last'ingness s. Durability; permanence.
Everlast'ing-ness s. State or quality of being everlasting.
Sav'ingness s. Parsimony; frugality.
Lov'ingness s. (*Loving*).
Know'ingness s. (*Knowing*).
Ob'longness s. State of being longer than broad.
Wrong'ness s. (*Wrong*).
Smug'ness s. (*Smug*).
Snug'ness s. (*Snug*).
Rich'ness s. (*Rich*).
Staunch'ness s. (*Staunch*).
Arch'ness s. Waggish mischief or mirthfulness.
Starch'ness s. Primness; formality.
Much'ness s. (*Much*).
High'ness s. Elevation; title of princes.
Rough'ness s. (*Rough*).
Thor'oughness (thŭr'-) s. (*Thorough*).
Tough'ness (tŭf'-) s. (*Tough*).
Rash'ness s. Foolhardiness; over-boldness.
Nesh'ness s. (*Nesh*).
Fresh'ness s. State of quality of being fresh.
Snob'bishness s. Snobbery.
Cad'dishness s. The manners and habits of cads.
Fad'dishness s. (*Faddish*).
Red'dishness s. (*Reddish*).
Clod'dishness s. (*Cloddish*).
Child'ishness s. (*Childish*).
Outland'ishness s. (*Outlandish*).
Fiend'ishness s. The qualities or cruelty of a fiend.
Mo'dishness s. (*Modish*).
Pru'dishness s. (*Prudish*).
Raff'ishness s. (*Raffish*).
Off'ishness s. (*Offish*).
Huff'ishness s. (*Huffish*).
Self'ishness s. (*Selfish*).
Wolf'ishness s. (*Wolfish*).
Dwarf'ishness s. (*Dwarfish*).
Wag'gishness s. Waggery; joking.
Whig'gishness s. (*Whiggish*).
Pig'gishness s. (*Piggish*).
Prig'gishness s. (*Priggish*).
Dog'gishness s. (*Doggish*).
Hog'gishness s. (*Hoggish*).
Slug'gishness s. (*Sluggish*).
Freak'ishness s. State of being freakish; abnormality.
Ra'kishness s. Debauchery.
Brack'ishness s. (*Brackish*).
Trick'ishness s. (*Trickish*).
Sick'ishness s. (*Sickish*).
Block'ishness s. (*Blockish*).
Prank'ishness s. (*Prankish*).
Book'ishness s. (*Bookish*).
Maw'kishness s. (*Mawkish*).
Dev'ilishness s. (*Devilish*).
Tickl'ishness s. (*Ticklish*).
Hell'ishness s. (*Hellish*).
Doll'ishness s. (*Dollish*).
Fool'ishness s. Folly; quality of being foolish.

Girl'ishness s. State of being girlish.
Churl'ishness s. (*Churlish*).
Mul'ishness s. (*Mulish*).
Ghoul'ishness s. The practices of ghouls.
Styl'ishness s. (*Stylish*).
Squeam'ishness s. (*Squeamish*).
Ram'mishness s. (*Rammish*).
Wom'anishness s. (*Womanish*).
Green'ishness s. Quality of being somewhat green.
Heath'enish-ness s. (*Heathenish*).
Swi'nishness s. (*Swinish*).
Clan'nishness s. (*Clannish*).
Man'nishness s. (*Mannish*).
Hun'nishness s. (*Hunnish*).
To'nishness s. (*Tonish*).
Clown'ishness s. (*Clownish*).
A'pishness s. Mimicry; ways of apes.
Sheep'ishness s. (*Sheepish*).
Romp'ishness s. (*Rompish*).
Lump'ishness s. (*Lumpish*).
Mo'pishness s. (*Mopish*).
Snap'pishness s. (*Snappish*).
Fop'pishness s. Foppery; quality or habits of a fop.
Up'pishness s. (*Uppish*).
Wasp'ishness s. (*Waspish*).
Gar'ishness s. State or quality of being garish.
Lick'erishness s. (*Lickerish*).
Wa'terishness s. (*Waterish*).
Fe'verishness s. (*Feverish*).
Whor'ishness s. (*Whorish*).
Boor'ishness s. Unmannerly or uncouth ways and habits.
Cur'rishness s. (*Currish*).
Am'ateurish-ness s. Quality of being amateurish or non-professional.
Va'pourishness s. (*Vapourish*).
Sweet'ishness s. (*Sweetish*).
Whi'tishness s. (*Whitish*).
Pet'tishness s. (*Pettish*).
Skit'tishness s. (*Skittish*).
Sot'tishness s. (*Sottish*).
Slut'tishness s. (*Sluttish*).
Lout'ishness s. (*Loutish*).
Bru'tishness s. Brutality, the ways of brutes.
Ro'guishness s. (*Roguish*).
Blu'ishness s. An approximation to blue.
Cliqu'ishness s. (*Cliquish*).
Lav'ishness s. (*Lavish*).
Sla'vishness s. (*Slavish*).
Kna'vishness s. (*Knavish*).
Peev'ishness s. (*Peevish*).
Thiev'ishness s. Thievery.
Jew'ishness s. (*Jewish*).
Shrew'ishness s. (*Shrewish*).
Ba'byishness s. A characteristic of babies.
Boy'ishness s. Youthfulness; the ways of boys.
Harsh'ness s. State or quality of being harsh.
Lush'ness s. State of being lush or succulent.
Flush'ness s. Fulness; abundance.
Loath'ness s. Unwillingness; reluctance.
Smooth'ness s. (*Smooth*).
Uncouth'ness s. (*Uncouth*).
Scab'biness s. (*Scabby*).
Shab'biness s. (*Shabby*).
Flab'biness s. State of being flabby or feeble.
Knob'biness s. (*Knobby*).
Fub'biness s. Plumpness, squatness.
Chub'biness s. (*Chubby*).
Scrub'biness s. (*Scrubby*).
Grub'biness s. Griminess.
Shrub'biness s. (*Shrubby*).
Stub'biness s. (*Stubby*).
Ra'ciness s. (*Racy*).
I'ciness s. (*Icy*).
Spi'ciness s. (*Spicy*).
Juic'iness s. Condition of being juicy.
Sauc'iness s. (*Saucy*).

Head'iness s. State or quality of being heady.
Read'iness (red'-) s. Promptness; state of being ready; handiness; willingness.
Thread'iness s. (*Thready*).
Stead'iness s. (*Steady*).
Sha'diness s. (*Shady*).
Fad'diness s. (*Faddy*).
Gid'diness s. Sensation or condition of being giddy; flightiness.
Mud'diness s. (*Muddy*).
Rud'diness s. (*Ruddy*).
Heed'iness s. Heedfulness.
Need'iness s. (*Needy*).
Speed'iness s. (*Speedy*).
Reed'iness s. (*Reedy*).
Greed'iness s. Avarice; gluttony; insatiable covetousness; state of being greedy.
Seed'iness s. (*Seedy*).
Ti'diness s. (*Tidy*).
Mould'iness s. (*Mouldy*).
Handi'ness s. Quality of being handy.
Randi'ness s. (*Randy*).
Sand'iness s. (*Sandy*).
Wind'iness s. (*Windy*).
Good'iness s. Affected piety.
Blood'iness s. (*Bloody*).
Mood'iness s. (*Moody*).
Brood'iness s. (*Broody*).
Wood'iness s. (*Woody*).
Hard'iness s. Quality of being hardy.
Foolhard'iness s. Recklessness; state of being foolhardy.
Tar'diness s. (*Tardy*).
Word'iness s. (*Wordy*).
Sturd'iness s. (*Sturdy*).
Gaud'iness s. State or quality of being gaudy.
Bawd'iness s. (*Bawdy*).
Dowd'iness s. Shabbiness, untidiness.
Rowd'iness s. (*Rowdy*).
Leaf'iness s. State of being leafy.
Beef'iness s. Fleshiness; stolidity.
Huff'iness s. (*Huffy*).
Fluff'iness s. Quality or state of being fluffy.
Snuff'iness s. (*Snuffy*).
Puff'iness s. (*Puffy*).
Stuff'iness s. (*Stuffy*).
Scurf'iness s. (*Scurfy*).
Turf'iness s. (*Turfy*).
Sta'giness s. (*Stagy*).
Dodg'iness s. (*Dodgy*).
Stodg'iness s. (*Stodgy*).
Bag'giness s. (*Baggy*).
Shag'giness s. (*Shaggy*).
Crag'giness s. (*Craggy*).
Scrag'giness s. (*Scraggy*).
Leg'giness s. (*Leggy*).
Dreg'giness s. (*Dreggy*).
Fog'giness s. State of being foggy.
Clog'giness s. (*Cloggy*).
Grog'giness s. State of being groggy; tipsiness.
Sog'giness s. (*Soggy*).
Fug'giness s. State of being fuggy or stuffy.
Mug'giness s. (*Muggy*).
Bul'giness s. (*Bulgy*).
Slang'iness s. (*Slangy*).
Mang'iness s. (*Mangy*).
Spring'iness s. (*Springy*).
String'iness s. (*Stringy*).
Sting'iness s. (*Stingy*).
Spong'iness (spŭnj-) s. (*Spongy*).
Preach'iness s. Preachy.
Poach'iness s. (*Poachy*).
Starch'iness s. (*Starchy*).
Church'iness s. (*Churchy*).
Patch'iness s. (*Patchy*).
Scratch'iness s. (*Scratchy*).
Sketch'iness s. (*Sketchy*).

Stretch'iness s. (*Stretchy*).
Tetch'iness s. (*Tetchy*).
Pitch'iness s. (*Pitchy*).
Slouch'iness s. (*Slouchy*).
Touch'iness s. (*Touchy*).
Dough'iness s. (*Doughy*).
Dauphiness' s. The wife af a dauphin.
Flash'iness s. Quality of being flashy; showiness.
Trash'iness s. (*Trashy*).
Wash'iness s. (*Washy*).
Flesh'iness s. State or quality of being fleshy.
Fish'iness s. Quality of being fishy.
Marsh'iness s. (*Marshy*).
Bush'iness s. (*Bushy*).
Breath'iness s. (*Breathy*).
Length'iness s. (*Lengthy*).
Pith'iness s. (*Pithy*).
Health'iness s. (*Healthy*).
Stealth'iness (stelth'-) s. (*Stealthy*).
Wealth'iness s. (*Wealthy*).
Filth'iness s. State or quality of being filthy; filth.
Froth'iness s. State of being frothy.
Earth'iness s. (*Earthy*).
Swarth'iness s. (*Swarthy*).
Wor'thiness s. (*Worthy*).
Sea'worthiness s. (*Seaworthy*).
Blame'worthiness s. (*Blameworthy*).
Praise'worthiness s. (*Praiseworthy*).
Trust'worthiness s. (*Trustworthy*).
Leak'iness s. (*Leaky*).
Streak'iness s. (*Streaky*).
Shak'iness s. (*Shaky*).
Flak'iness s. Quality of being flaky.
Quak'iness s. (*Quaky*).
Knack'iness s. (*Knacky*).
Tack'iness s. (*Tacky*).
Trick'iness s. (*Tricky*).
Stick'iness s. (*Sticky*).
Cock'iness s. (*Cocky*).
Pock'iness s. State of being pock-marked or pocky.
Rock'iness s. (*Rocky*).
Stock'iness s. (*Stocky*).
Luck'iness s. Luck.
Pluck'iness s. (*Plucky*).
Muck'iness s. (*Mucky*).
Cheek'iness s. (*Cheeky*).
Chalk'iness s. (*Chalky*).
Milk'iness s. (*Milky*).
Silk'iness s. (*Silky*).
Bulk'iness s. (*Bulky*).
Sulk'iness s. (*Sulky*).
Ink'iness s. (*Inky*).
Pink'iness s. Quality or condition of being pink.
Smok'iness s. (*Smoky*).
Jerk'iness s. (*Jerky*).
Perk'iness s. (*Perky*).
Quirk'iness s. (*Quirky*).
Murk'iness s. (*Murky*).
Frisk'iness s. State or quality of being frisky.
Bosk'iness s. (*Bosky*).
Dusk'iness s. (*Dusky*).
Husk'iness s. (*Husky*).
Musk'iness s. (*Musky*).
Flu'kiness s. Quality of making lucky shots.
Gawk'iness s. State or quality of being gawky.
Pawk'iness s. (*Pawky*).
Scal'iness s. (*Scaly*).
Meal'iness s. (*Mealy*).
Shoal'iness s. (*Shoaly*).
Dead'liness s. (*Deadly*).
World'liness s. (*Worldly*).
Friend'liness s. Friendly disposition.
Kind'liness s. State of being kindly; a kindly deed.
God'liness s. Quality of being godly; reverence for God.
Good'liness s. State or quality of being goodly.
Nig'gardliness s. Quality of being niggardly; stinginess.
Das'tardliness s. (*Dastardly*).
Cow'ardliness s. (*Cowardly*).
Lord'liness s. Magnificence; haughtiness; arrogance.
Prince'liness s. (*Princely*).
Steel'iness s. (*Steely*).
Like'liness s. State or quality of being likely.
Time'liness s. (*Timely*).
Come'liness s. (*Comely*).
Home'liness s. (*Homely*).
Lone'liness s. State of being lonely.
Shape'liness s. (*Shapely*).
Leis'ureliness s. (*Leisurely*).
State'liness s. (*Stately*).
Live'liness s. (*Lively*).
Love'liness s. (*Lovely*).
King'liness s. (*Kingly*).
Ug'liness s. (*Ugly*).
Flesh'liness s. (*Fleshly*).
Loath'liness s. (*Loathly*).
Earth'liness s. (*Earthly*).
Oil'iness s. (*Oily*).
Wi'liness s. (*Wily*).
Prick'liness s. (*Prickly*).
Sick'liness s. (*Sickly*).
Hil'liness s. (*Hilly*).
Chil'liness s. (*Chilly*).
Sil'liness s. (*Silly*).
Jol'liness s. Jollity.
Wool'liness s. (*Woolly*).
Seem'liness s. (*Seemly*).
Clean'liness s. (*Cleanly*).
Man'liness s. (*Manly*).
Gen'tlemanliness s. Quality of being gentlemanly.
Wom'anliness s. (*Womanly*).
Maid'enliness s. (*Maidenly*).
Queen'liness s. (*Queenly*).
Heav'enliness s. (*Heavenly*).
Slov'enliness (sluv'-) s. (*Slovenly*).
Ma'tronliness s. (*Matronly*).
Slat'ternliness s. (*Slatternly*).
Ho'liness s. Sanctity; state of being or that which is consecrated; title of the Pope.
Ear'liness s. (*Early*).
Pearl'iness s. (*Pearly*).
Beg'garliness s. (*Beggarly*).
Lub'berliness s. (*Lubberly*).
Or'derliness s. (*Orderly*).
Disor'derliness s. (*Disorderly*).
Weath'erliness s. (*Weatherly*).
Fa'therliness s. Quality of being fatherly.
Moth'erliness s. (*Motherly*).
Broth'erliness s. (*Brotherly*).
Nor'therliness s. (*Northerly*).
South'erliness (sŭth-) s. (*Southerly*).
Man'nerliness s. (*Mannerly*).
Mi'serliness s. (*Miserly*).
Mas'terliness s. (*Masterly*).
Sis'terliness s. (*Sisterly*).
Poor'liness s. (*Poorly*).
Bur'liness s. (*Burly*).
Curl'iness s. (*Curly*).
Neigh'bourliness (nā'-) s. (*Neighbourly*).
Sur'liness s. (*Surly*).
Knight'liness s. (*Knightly*).
Spright'liness s. (*Sprightly*).

Sight'liness s. (*Sightly*).
Saint'liness s. (*Saintly*).
Court'liness s. (*Courtly*).
Beast'liness s. (*Beastly*).
Ghast'liness s. State or quality of being ghastly.
Priest'liness s. Priestly manner or appearance.
Brist'liness s. (*Bristly*).
Cost'liness s. (*Costly*).
Ghost'liness s. Quality of being ghostly.
Low'liness s. (*Lowly*).
Cream'iness s. (*Creamy*).
Dream'iness s. (*Dreamy*).
Steam'iness s. (*Steamy*).
Ga'miness s. State of being high (of meat, etc.).
Loam'iness s. (*Loamy*).
Li'miness s. (*Limy*).
Sli'miness s. (*Slimy*).
Gri'miness s. Condition of being grimy; foulness.
Balm'iness s. (*Balmy*).
Film'iness s. Condition of being filmy.
Clam'miness s. (*Clammy*).
Gum'miness s. State or quality of being gummy.
Rum'miness s. (*Rummy*).
Gloom'iness s. Quality or state of being gloomy.
Room'iness s. (*Roomy*).
Storm'iness s. (*Stormy*).
Worm'iness s. (*Wormy*).
Spum'iness s. (*Spumy*).
Rain'iness s. (*Rainy*).
Shin'iness s. (*Shiny*).
Lin'iness s. (*Liny*).
Spin'iness s. (*Spiny*).
Can'niness s. Caution, shrewdness; frugality.
Uncan'niness s. (*Uncanny*).
Skin'niness s. (*Skinny*).
Bon'niness s. (*Bonny*).
Fun'niness s. Quality of being funny; humourousness.
Sun'niness s. (*Sunny*).
Bon'iness s. (*Bony*).
Moon'iness s. (*Moony*).
Spoon'iness s. (*Spoony*).
Ston'iness s. (*Stony*).
Horn'iness s. (*Horny*).
Pu'niness s. (*Puny*).
Brawn'iness s. (*Brawny*).
Soap'iness s. (*Soapy*).
Sleep'iness s. (*Sleepy*).
Creep'iness s. (*Creepy*).
Stri'piness s. (*Stripy*).
Scrimp'iness s. (*Scrimp*).
Dump'iness s. (*Dumpy*).
Jump'iness s. (*Jumpy*).
Lump'iness s. (*Lumpy*).
Grump'iness s. Surliness, ill-temper.
Rop'iness s. (*Ropy*).
Hap'piness s. State of being happy; joy; good luck.
Snap'piness s. (*Snappy*).
Scrap'piness s. (*Scrappy*).
Trap'piness s. (*Trappy*).
Sap'piness s. (*Sappy*).
Chip'piness s. (*Chippy*).
Slip'piness s. (*Slippy*).
Flop'piness s. Quality of being floppy or flaccid; slovenliness.
Slop'piness s. (*Sloppy*).
Sop'piness s. (*Soppy*).
Sec'ondariness s. (*Secondary*).
Smear'iness s. (*Smeary*).
Drear'iness s. State or quality of being dreary.
We'ariness s. (*Weary*).
Su'gariness s. (*Sugary*).
Char'iness s. (*Chary*).
Exem'plariness s. (*Exemplary*).
Pri'mariness s. (*Primary*).
Cus'tomariness s. (*Customary*).
Mer'cenariness s. (*Mercenary*).
Ple'nariness s. (*Plenary*).
Or'dinariness s. (*Ordinary*).
Sang'uinariness s. (*Sanguinary*).
Vi'sionariness s. (*Visionary*).
Sta'tionariness s. (*Stationary*).
Hoar'iness s. (*Hoary*).
Tem'porariness s. (*Temporary*).
Contem'porariness s. (*Contemporary*).
Ar'bitrariness s. (*Arbitrary*).
Con'trariness s. State or quality of being contrary.
Hered'itariness s. (*Hereditary*).
Sol'itariness s. (*Solitary*).
San'itariness s. (*Sanitary*).
Sed'entariness s. (*Sedentary*).
Elemen'tariness s. (*Elementary*).
Frag'mentariness s. State of being fragmentary.
Rudimen'tariness s. (*Rudimentary*).
Mo'mentariness s. (*Momentary*).
Vol'untariness s. (*Voluntary*).
Invol'untariness s. (*Involuntary*).
Sal'utariness s. (*Salutary*).
War'iness s. (*Wary*).
Taw'driness s. (*Tawdry*).
Slob'beriness s. (*Slobbery*).
Pow'deriness s. (*Powdery*).
Beer'iness s. (*Beery*).
Cheer'iness s. (*Cheery*).
Feath'eriness s. Quality or state of being feathery.
Smoth'eriness s. (*Smothery*).
Fi'eriness s. Quality of being fiery.
Pa'periness s. (*Papery*).
Slip'periness s. (*Slippery*).
Wa'teriness s. (*Watery*).
But'teriness s. The qualities or appearance of butter.
Sil'veriness s. (*Silvery*).
Show'eriness (shou'-) s. (*Showery*).
Hung'riness s. (*Hungry*).
Air'iness s. (*Airy*).
Hair'iness s. State or quality of being hairy.
Mir'iness s. (*Miry*).
Wir'iness s. (*Wiry*).
Gor'iness s. State of being gory or blood-stained.
Cur'soriness s. (*Cursory*).
Elu'soriness s. (*Elusory*).
Illu'soriness s. (*Illusory*).
Concil'iatoriness s. (*Conciliatory*).
Dil'atoriness s. (*Dilatory*).
Satisfac'toriness s. (*Satisfactory*).
Refrac'toriness s. Perverse or sullen obstinacy.
Contradic'toriness s. (*Contradictory*).
Perfunc'toriness s. (*Perfunctory*).
Tran'sitoriness s. (*Transitory*).
Des'ultoriness s. (*Desultory*).
Peremp'toriness s. (*Peremptory*).
Star'riness s. (*Starry*).
Mer'riness s. Merriment.
Sor'riness s. (*Sorry*).
Pal'triness s. (*Paltry*).
Sul'triness s. (*Sultry*).
Win'triness s. (*Wintry*).
Sa'vouriness s. (*Savoury*).
Eas'iness s. (*Easy*).
Greas'iness s. State of being greasy.
Queas'iness s. (*Queasy*).
Fub'siness s. Squatness, dumpiness.

Chees'iness s. (*Cheesy*).
Nois'iness s. (*Noisy*).
Flim'siness s. Unsubstantiality; quality of being flimsy.
Clum'siness s. (*Clumsy*).
Co'siness s. (*Cosy*).
Ro'siness s. (*Rosy*).
Pro'siness s. (*Prosy*).
Tip'siness s. (*Tipsy*).
Hors'iness s. (*Horsy*).
Purs'iness s. (*Pursy*).
Gas'siness s. State or quality of being gassy.
Glass'iness s. Quality of being glassy.
Mass'iness s. (*Massy*).
Brass'iness s. (*Brassy*).
Grass'iness s. State of being grassy.
Mess'iness s. (*Messy*).
Dress'iness s. (*Dressy*).
Gloss'iness s. Quality or condition of being glossy.
Moss'iness s. (*Mossy*).
Dross'iness s. (*Drossy*).
Fuss'iness s. State or quality of being fussy.
Muss'iness s. (*Mussy*).
Bus'iness s. Occupation, trade; concern; work; bargaining; a shop, etc.
Lou'siness s. (*Lousy*).
Mous'iness s. (*Mousy*).
News'iness s. (*Newsy*).
Drows'iness s. (*Drowsy*).
Meat'iness s. (*Meaty*).
Peat'iness s. (*Peaty*).
Sweat'iness s. (*Sweaty*).
Slat'iness s. (*Slaty*).
Throat'iness s. (*Throaty*).
Sleet'iness s. (*Sleety*).
Fidg'etiness s. Restlessness.
Croch'etiness s. (*Crotchety*).
Craft'iness s. (*Crafty*).
Shift'iness s. (*Shifty*).
Thrift'iness s. (*Thrifty*).
Loft'iness s. (*Lofty*).
Weight'iness s. (*Weighty*).
Flight'iness s. Quality or state of being flighty.
Haught'iness s. Disdainful pride; arrogance.
Naught'iness s. (*Naughty*).
Draught'iness s. (*Draughty*).
Dought'iness s. (*Doughty*).
Drought'iness s. State of being parched for want of rain; thirstiness.
Fruit'iness s. State of being fruity.
Salt'iness s. (*Salty*).
Guilt'iness s. Guilt, criminality.
Fault'iness s. Quality of being faulty.
Cant'iness s. (*Scot.*) (*Canty*).
Scant'iness s. (*Scanty*).
Daint'iness s. (*Dainty*).
Flint'iness s. Quality of being flinty; hard-heartedness.
Jaunt'iness s. (*Jaunty*).
Mag'gotiness s. (*Maggoty*).
Soot'iness s. (*Sooty*).
Emp'tiness s. State of being empty; exhaustion; void space; want of knowledge, sense, solidity, etc.
Heart'iness s. (*Hearty*).
Dirt'iness s. (*Dirty*).
Yeast'iness s. (*Yeasty*).
Has'tiness s. Quality of being hasty.
Nas'tiness s. (*Nasty*).
Tes'tiness s. (*Testy*).
Mis'tiness s. (*Misty*).
Frost'iness s. Condition or quality of being frosty.
Thirst'iness s. (*Thirsty*).
Blood'thirstiness s. (*Bloodthirsty*).
Dust'iness s. (*Dusty*).
Fust'iness s. Mouldiness, mustiness.
Lust'iness s. State or quality of being lusty.
Must'iness s. (*Musty*).
Rust'iness s. (*Rusty*).
Crust'iness s. (*Crusty*).
Trust'iness s. (*Trusty*).
Chat'tiness s. (*Chatty*).
Nat'tiness s. (*Natty*).
Pet'tiness s. Small-mindedness; triviality.
Pret'tiness s. Quality of being pretty; petty adornment; finicalness.
Wit'tiness s. (*Witty*).
Knot'tiness s. (*Knotty*).
Snot'tiness s. (*Snotty*).
Spot'tiness s. (*Spotty*).
Smut'tiness s. (*Smutty*).
Gout'iness s. State of being gouty.
Heav'iness s. (*Heavy*).
Wav'iness s. (*Wavy*).
Groov'iness s. State of having grooves.
Scurv'iness s. Baseness; meanness.
Dew'iness s. (*Dewy*).
Sin'ewiness s. (*Sinewy*).
Shad'owiness s. (*Shadowy*).
Show'iness s. (*Showy*).
Snow'iness s. (*Snowy*).
Wax'iness s. (*Waxy*).
Fox'iness s. State or condition of being foxy.
Sleaz'iness s. (*Sleazy*).
Ha'ziness s. Quality of being hazy.
La'ziness s. (*Lazy*).
Ma'ziness s. (*Mazy*).
Cra'ziness s. (*Crazy*).
Wheez'iness s. (*Wheezy*).
Breez'iness s. (*Breezy*).
Siz'iness s. (*Sizy*).
Do'ziness s. (*Dozy*).
Ooz'iness s. (*Oozy*).
Gauz'iness s. Quality of being gauzy.
Frow'ziness s. State of being dirty, slovenly, or frowzy.
Diz'ziness s. (*Dizzy*).
Fuz'ziness s. State or quality of being fuzzy; fuzz.
Muz'ziness s. (*Muzzy*).
Bleak'ness s. (*Bleak*).
Weak'ness s. Quality or state of being weak; irresolution; a failing.
Black'ness s. (*Black*).
Slack'ness s. (*Slack*).
Thick'ness s. State of being thick; measure through; thick part.
Sick'ness s. Illness; nausea; a disease.
Sea'-sickness s. Nausea and vomiting brought on by the motion of a ship.
Home'sickness s. Depression of spirits due to absence from home.
Quick'ness s. (*Quick*).
Sleek'ness s. (*Sleek*).
Meek'ness s. (*Meek*).
Lank'ness s. (*Lank*).
Blank'ness s. (*Blank*).
Rank'ness s. (*Rank*).
Frank'ness s. Sincerity, candour, openness.
Dark'ness s. State or quality of being dark; wickedness, ignorance.
Brisk'ness s. (*Brisk*).
Pharisa'icalness s. (*Pharisaic*).
Cu'bicalness s. (*Cubic*).
Sporad'icalness s. (*Sporadic*).
Trag'icalness s. Tragicality.
Log'icalness s. Logicality.
Symbol'icalness s. (*Symbolic*).
Com'icalness s. (*Comical*).
Tech'nicalness s. (*Technical*).
Fin'icalness s. Quality of being finical.
Tyran'nicalness s. (*Tyrannical*).
Con'icalness s. (*Conical*).
Cyn'icalness s. (*Cynical*).

Sto'icalness s. Stoicism.
Typ'icalness s. (*Typical*).
Spher'icalness s. Roundness; sphericity.
Symmet'ricalness s. (*Symmetrical*).
Lackadais'icalness s. (*Lackadaisical*).
Whim'sicalness s. (*Whimsical*).
Nonsen'sicalness s. (*Nonsensical*).
Mu'sicalness s. Musicality.
Pragmat'icalness s. (*Pragmatical*).
Prac'ticalness s. (*Practical*).
Crit'icalness s. (*Critical*).
Iden'ticalness s. (*Identical*).
Authen'ticalness s. (*Authentical*).
Ver'ticalness s. Verticality.
Vo'calness s. Vocality.
Artifi'cialness s. (*Artificial*).
Superfi'cialness s. Superficiality.
Conge'nialness s. (*Congenial*).
Ve'nialness s. Veniality.
Confiden'tialness s. (*Confidential*).
Triv'ialness s. Triviality.
Jo'vialness s. Joviality.
Lit'eralness s. Literality.
Tem'poralness s. (*Temporal*).
Cen'tralness s. (*Central*).
Rur'alness s. (*Rural*).
Nat'uralness s. (*Natural*).
Supernat'uralness s. (*Supernatural*).
Preternat'uralness s. (*Preternatural*).
Acciden'talness s. (*Accidental*).
Grad'ualness s. State of being gradual.
Cas'ualness s. (*Casual*).
Us'ualness s. (*Usual*).
Effec'tualness s. (*Effectual*).
Ineffec'tualness s. Ineffectuality.
Spir'itualness s. Spirituality.
O'valness s. (*Oval*).
Lev'elness s. (*Level*).
Frail'ness s. State or quality of being frail.
Tran'quilness s. Tranquillity.
Small'ness s. (*Small*).
Tall'ness s. (*Tall*).
Ill'ness s. State of being ill; sickness; disease.
Shrill'ness s. (*Shrill*).
Still'ness s. (*Still*).
Droll'ness s. (*Droll*).
Dull'ness s. (*Dull*).
Full'ness s. State or quality of being full; satiety; volume.
Cool'ness s. (*Cool*).
Dread'fulness s. (*Dreadful*).
Heed'fulness s. (*Heedful*).
Need'fulness s. (*Needful*).
Mind'fulness s. (*Mindful*).
Regard'fulness s. (*Regardful*).
Peace'fulness s. (*Peaceful*).
Grace'fulness s. State or quality of being graceful.
Disgrace'fulness s. (*Disgraceful*).
Force'fulness s. Power, state or quality of being forceful.
Resource'fulness s. (*Resourceful*).
Pride'fulness s. (*Prideful*).
Change'fulness s. (*Changeful*).
Venge'fulness s. (*Vengeful*).
Revenge'fulness s. (*Revengeful*).
Wake'fulness s. (*Wakeful*).
Bale'fulness s. (*Baleful*).
Guile'fulness s. Quality of being guileful; duplicity.
Dole'fulness s. (*Doleful*).
Shame'fulness s. (*Shameful*).
Blame'fulness s. (*Blameful*).
Bane'fulness s. (*Baneful*).
Tune'fulness s. (*Tuneful*).
Woe'fulness s. (*Woeful*).
Hope'fulness s. (*Hopeful*).
Care'fulness s. (*Careful*).
Dire'fulness s. (*Direful*).
Ease'fulness s. (*Easeful*).
Praise'fulness s. (*Praiseful*).
Repose'fulness s. (*Reposeful*).
Remorse'fulness s. (*Remorseful*).
Use'fulness s. (*Useful*).
Hate'fulness s. Quality of being hateful.
Grate'fulness s. Quality or condition of being grateful.
Spite'fulness s. (*Spiteful*).
Taste'fulness s. (*Tasteful*).
Distaste'fulness s. (*Distasteful*).
Waste'fulness s. (*Wasteful*).
Rue'fulness s. (*Rueful*).
Wrong'fulness s. (*Wrongful*).
Watch'fulness s. (*Watchful*).
Bash'fulness s. (*Bashful*).
Wish'fulness s. (*Wishful*).
Push'fulness s. (*Pushful*).
Death'fulness s. A resemblance to death.
Loath'fulness s. (*Loathful*).
Wrath'fulness s. (*Wrathful*).
Faith'fulness s. State or quality of being faithful.
Health'fulness s. (*Healthful*).
Sloth'fulness s. (*Slothful*).
Mirth'fulness s. (*Mirthful*).
Youth'fulness s. (*Youthful*).
Truth'fulness s. (*Truthful*).
Fan'cifulness s. (*Fanciful*).
Mer'cifulness s. (*Merciful*).
Pit'ifulness s. (*Pitiful*).
Plen'tifulness s. (*Plentiful*).
Beaut'ifulness s. (*Beautiful*).
Du'tifulness s. (*Dutiful*).
Thank'fulness s. (*Thankful*).
Skil'fulness s. (*Skilful*).
Wil'fulness s. (*Wilful*).
Soul'fulness s. (*Soulful*).
Harm'fulness s. Harm; injuriousness.
Man'fulness s. (*Manful*).
Pain'fulness s. (*Painful*).
Sin'fulness s. (*Sinful*).
Scorn'fulness s. (*Scornful*).
Mourn'fulness s. (*Mournful*).
Wor'shipfulness s. (*Worshipful*).
Help'fulness s. (*Helpful*).
Fear'fulness s. Quality or state of being fearful.
Tear'fulness s. (*Tearful*).
Won'derfulness s. (*Wonderful*).
Cheer'fulness s. (*Cheerful*).
Mas'terfulness s. (*Masterful*).
Pow'erfulness s. (*Powerful*).
Prayer'fulness s. (*Prayerful*).
Success'fulness s. (*Successful*).
Doubt'fulness s. (*Doubtful*).
Tact'fulness s. (*Tactful*).
Neglect'fulness s. (*Neglectful*).
Respect'fulness s. (*Respectful*).
Forget'fulness s. State or quality of being forgetful.
Fret'fulness s. Condition of being fretful or peevish.
Regret'fulness s. (*Regretful*).
Delight'fulness s. (*Delightful*).
Right'fulness s. (*Rightful*).
Fright'fulness s. Actions or methods that cause terror

Thought'fulness s. (*Thoughtful*).
Deceit'fulness s. (*Deceitful*).
Fit'fulness s. Quality of being fitful.
Art'fulness s. (*Artful*).
Sport'fulness s. (*Sportful*).
Hurt'fulness s. (*Hurtful*).
Boast'fulness s. (*Boastful*).
Rest'fulness s. (*Restful*).
Wist'fulness s. (*Wistful*).
Lust'fulness s. (*Lustful*).
Trust'fulness s. (*Trustful*).
Distrust'fulness s. (*Distrustful*).
Mistrust'fulness s. (*Mistrustful*).
Aw'fulness s. (*Awful*).
Law'fulness s. (*Lawful*).
Sor'rowfulness s. (*Sorrowful*).
Play'fulness s. (*Playful*).
Joy'fulness s. (*Joyful*).
Foul'ness s. State of being foul; filthiness.
Dim'ness s. (*Dim*).
Slim'ness s. (*Slim*).
Grim'ness s. Quality of being grim; relentlessness.
Prim'ness s. (*Prim*).
Trim'ness s. (*Trim*).
Calm'ness s. (*Calm*).
Lis'somness s. (*Lissom*).
Bux'omness s. (*Buxom*).
Warm'ness s. Warmth.
Luke'warmness s. (*Lukewarm*).
Firm'ness s. Quality of being firm.
Glum'ness s. Condition or quality of being glum.
Rum'ness s. (*Rum*).
Hum'drumness s. (*Humdrum*).
Lean'ness s. State of being lean; meagreness.
Clean'ness s. (*Clean*).
Mean'ness s. Inferiority; baseness; stinginess.
Human'ness s. (*Human*).
Wan'ness (wŏn'-) s. (*Wan*).
Hidden'ness s. State of being hidden.
Sod'denness s. (*Sodden*).
Sud'denness s. (*Sudden*).
Wood'enness s. (*Wooden*).
Keen'ness s. (*Keen*).
Green'ness s. Quality or condition of being green; inexperience.
Drunk'enness s. State of being drunk; inebriety.
Outspo'kenness s. (*Outspoken*).
Sul'lenness s. (*Sullen*).
O'penness s. (*Open*).
Bar'renness s. (*Barren*).
Rot'tenness s. (*Rotten*).
E'venness s. State of being even.
Braz'enness s. Impudence, effrontery.
For'eignness s. State or quality of being foreign.
Plain'ness s. (*Plain*).
Cer'tainness s. (*Certain*).
Vain'ness s. Vanity.
Thin'ness s. (*Thin*).
Sol'emnness s. (*Solemn*).
Com'monness s. (*Common*).
Wan'tonness s. (*Wanton*).
Mod'ernness s. (*Modern*).
Stern'ness s. (*Stern*).
Stub'bornness s. (*Stubborn*).
Forlorn'ness s. State or condition of being forlorn.
Brown'ness s. State or quality of being brown; sunburn.
Deaconess' s. A female deacon.
Py'thoness s. The priestess of Apollo at Delphi, who gave oracles.
Marchioness' s. Wife or widow of a marquess.
Li'oness s. A female lion.
Demoness' s. A female demon.
Can'oness s. A member of certain female religious communities.
Bar'oness s. The wife or widow of a baron; a female holding a barony in her own right.
Pa'troness s. A female patron.
Cheap'ness s. (*Cheap*).
Deep'ness s. Depth.
Steep'ness s. (*Steep*).
Damp'ness s. (*Damp*).
Limp'ness s. State of being limp or flaccid.
Sharp'ness s. (*Sharp*).
Crisp'ness s. (*Crisp*).
Dear'ness s. (*Dear*).
Clear'ness s. (*Clear*).
Near'ness s. (*Near*).
Drear'ness s. Dreariness.
Har'ness s. Equipment for horses. v.t. To put harness on.
Lim'berness s. Lissomness; flexibility.
So'berness s. Sobriety.
Wil'derness s. A wild, uncultivated region; a waste.
Slen'derness s. (*Slender*).
Ten'derness s. Gentleness, kindness, compassion.
Queer'ness s. (*Queer*).
Ea'gerness s. (*Eager*).
Prop'erness s. (*Proper*).
Bit'terness s. (*Bitter*).
Ut'terness s. State or quality of being extreme.
Clev'erness s. (*Clever*).
Inverness' s. A sleeveless cloak with a cape.
Gov'erness s. A female teacher.
Fair'ness s. State of being fair; freedom from impurity; candour.
Poor'ness s. (*Poor*).
Dour'ness s. Gloominess, moroseness.
Sour'ness s. (*Sour*).
Crass'ness s. Crassitude, stupidity.
Dread'lessness s. (*Dreadless*).
Heed'lessness s. (*Heedless*).
Need'lessness s. (*Needless*).
Child'lessness s. (*Childless*).
End'lessness s. (*Endless*).
Friend'lessness s. State of being friendless.
Bound'lessness s. (*Boundless*).
Ground'lessness s. State of being unfounded or baseless.
God'lessness s. Wickedness; atheism.
Beard'lessness s. (*Beardless*).
Regard'lessness s. Indifference, negligence.
Cloud'lessness s. (*Cloudless*).
Grace'lessness s. Depravity, profligacy.
Voice'lessness s. (*Voiceless*).
Price'lessness s. (*Priceless*).
Defence'lessness s. State of being undefended.
Life'lessness s. (*Lifeless*).
Shame'lessness s. (*Shameless*).
Blame'lessness s. Freedom from guilt; innocence.
Bone'lessness s. (*Boneless*).
Shape'lessness s. (*Shapeless*).
Hope'lessness s. (*Hopeless*).
Care'lessness s. (*Careless*).
Base'lessness s. (*Baseless*).
Cease'lessness s. (*Ceaseless*).
Noise'lessness s. (*Noiseless*).
Sense'lessness s. (*Senseless*).
Remorse'lessness s. (*Remorseless*).
Use'lessness s. (*Useless*).
Taste'lessness s. (*Tasteless*).
Val'uelessness s. (*Valueless*).
Love'lessness s. (*Loveless*).
Nerve'lessness s. (*Nerveless*).
Leaf'lessness s. (*Leafless*).
Brief'lessness s. (*Briefless*).
Self'lessness s. (*Selfless*).
Speech'lessness s. (*Speechless*).

Quench'less-ness s. (*Quenchless*).
Match'lessness s. (*Matchless*).
Death'lessness s. (*Deathless*).
Breath'lessness s. (*Breathless*).
Faith'lessness s. State or quality of being faithless.
Mirth'lessness s. (*Mirthless*).
Worth'lessness s. (*Worthless*).
Ruth'lessness s. (*Ruthless*).
Truth'lessness s. (*Truthless*).
Mer'cilessness s. (*Merciless*).
Pen'nilessness s. Extreme poverty.
Pit'ilessness s. (*Pitiless*).
Feck'lessness s. Quality of being feckless; inefficiency.
Reck'lessness s. (*Reckless*).
Thank'lessness s. (*Thankless*).
Soul'lessness s. (*Soulless*).
Form'lessness s. Quality or condition of being formless.
Stain'lessness s. (*Stainless*).
Sin'lessness s. (*Sinless*).
Pas'sionless-ness s. (*Passionless*).
Sun'lessness s. (*Sunless*).
Sleep'lessness s. (*Sleepless*).
Help'lessness s. (*Helpless*).
Fear'lessness s. Quality or state of being fearless.
Cheer'lessness s. (*Cheerless*).
Peer'lessness s. (*Peerless*).
Fa'therlessness s. State of being fatherless.
Pow'erlessness s. (*Powerless*).
Tact'lessness s. (*Tactless*).
Shift'lessness s. (*Shiftless*).
Thrift'lessness s. (*Thriftless*).
Sight'lessness s. (*Sightless*).
Thought'less-ness s. (*Thoughtless*).
Prof'itlessness s. (*Profitless*).
Spir'itlessness s. (*Spiritless*).
Fruit'lessness s. State or quality of being fruitless.
Wit'lessness s. (*Witless*).
Guilt'lessness s. Innocence.
Relent'lessness s. (*Relentless*).
Point'lessness s. (*Pointless*).
Daunt'lessness s. (*Dauntless*).
Boot'lessness s. (*Bootless*).
Spot'lessness s. (*Spotless*).
Art'lessness s. (*Artless*).
Heart'lessness s. (*Heartless*).
Hurt'lessness s. (*Hurtless*).
Rest'lessness s. (*Restless*).
List'lessness s. (*Listless*).
Law'lessness s. (*Lawless*).
Flaw'lessness s. State of being flawless or perfect.
Joy'lessness s. (*Joyless*).
Remiss'ness s. (*Remiss*).
Cross'ness s. Ill-humour, peevishness, vexation.
Gross'ness s. Coarseness; want of delicacy.
Vis'cousness s. Stickiness.
Rau'cousness s. (*Raucous*).
Tremen'dous-ness s. (*Tremendous*).
Stupen'dous-ness s. (*Stupendous*).
Hid'eousness s. (*Hideous*).
Rampa'geous-ness s. (*Rampageous*).
Umbra'geous-ness s. (*Umbrageous*).
Outra'geous-ness s. (*Outrageous*).
Coura'geous-ness s. (*Courageous*).
Advanta'geous-ness s. (*Advantageous*).
Disadvan-ta'geousness s. (*Disadvantageous*).
Gor'geousness s. State or quality of being gorgeous.

Miscella'neous-ness s. (*Miscellaneous*).
Contempora'ne-ousness s. (*Contemporaneous*).
Extempora'ne-ousness s. (*Extemporaneous*).
Simulta'ne-ousness s. State or quality of being simultaneous.
Instanta'ne-ousness s. Instantaneity.
Consentane-ousness s. (*Consentaneous*).
Sponta'neous-ness s. Spontaneity.
Homoge'neous-ness s. Homogeneity.
Heteroge'ne-ousness s. Heterogeneity.
Erro'neousness s. (*Erroneous*).
Co'piousness s. (*Copious*).
Calcar'eousness s. (*Calcareous*).
Vit'reousness s. Vitreosity; glassiness.
Sulphur'eous-ness s. (*Sulphureous*).
Nau'seousness s. (*Nauseous*).
Right'eousness s. (*Righteous*).
Pit'eousness s. (*Piteous*).
Plen'teousness s. (*Plenteous*).
Boun'teousness s. (*Bounteous*).
Court'eousness s. (*Courteous*).
Discourt'eous-ness s. Discourtesy.
Beaut'eousness s. (*Beauteous*).
Du'teousness s. (*Duteous*).
Amor'phous-ness s. (*Amorphous*).
Du'biousness s. Dubiety.
Effica'cious-ness s. (*Efficacious*).
Perspica'cious-ness s. Perspicacity.
Auda'ciousness s. (*Audacious*).
Sala'ciousness s. (*Salacious*).
Falla'ciousness s. Quality of being fallacious.
Contuma'ci-ousness s. Contumacy.
Tena'ciousness s. (*Tenacious*).
Pertina'cious-ness s. Pertinacity.
Capa'ciousness s. (*Capacious*).
Rapa'ciousness s. Rapacity.
Spa'ciousness s. (*Spacious*).
Gra'ciousness s. Quality of being gracious.
Vora'ciousness s. (*Voracious*).
Loqua'cious-ness s. Loquacity.
Viva'ciousness s. Vivacity.
Spe'ciousness s. (*Specious*).
Pre'ciousness s. Quality of being precious.
Judi'ciousness s. (*Judicious*).
Injudi'cious-ness s. (*Injudicious*).
Offi'ciousness s. (*Officious*).
Deli'ciousness s. (*Delicious*).
Perni'ciousness s. (*Pernicious*).
Auspi'ciousness s. (*Auspicious*).
Inauspi'cious-ness s. (*Inauspicious*).
Suspi'ciousness s. (*Suspicious*).
Capri'ciousness s. (*Capricious*).
Meretri'cious-ness s. (*Meretricious*).
Vi'ciousness s. (*Vicious*).
Preco'ciousness s. Precocity.
Fero'ciousness s. Ferocity.
Con'sciousness s. State of being conscious; facult[y] by which one realizes one's se[lf] etc.; sense of guilt or innocenc[e].
Lus'ciousness s. (*Luscious*).

Te'diousness s. (*Tedious*).
Perfid'iousness s. (*Perfidious*).
Insid'iousness s. (*Insidious*).
Fastid'iousness s. Squeamishness ; extreme delicacy.
Invid'iousness s. (*Invidious*).
Compen'diousness s. (*Compendious*).
O'diousness s. (*Odious*).
Melo'diousness s. (*Melodious*).
Commo'diousness s. (*Commodious*).
Incommo'diousness s. (*Incommodious*).
Stu'diousness s. (*Studious*).
Conta'giousness s. (*Contagious*).
Sacrileg'iousness s. (*Sacrilegious*).
Egre'giousness s. (*Egregious*).
Prodig'iousness s. (*Prodigious*).
Relig'iousness s. (*Religious*).
Irrelig'iousness s. (*Irreligious*).
Litig'iousness s. Litigiosity.
Contume'liousness s. (*Contumelious*).
Bil'iousness s. (*Bilious*).
Atrabil'iousness s. (*Atrabilious*).
Supercil'iousness s. (*Supercilious*).
Punctil'iousness s. (*Punctilious*).
Rebel'liousness s. (*Rebellious*).
Abste'miousness s. (*Abstemious*).
Inge'niousness s. Ingenuity.
Calum'niousness s. (*Calumnious*).
Acrimo'niousness s. (*Acrimonious*).
Querimo'niousness s. (*Querimonious*).
Parsimo'niousness s. (*Parsimonious*).
Sanctimo'niousness s. (*Sanctimonious*).
Im'piousness s. (*Impious*).
Precar'iousness s. (*Precarious*).
Nefar'iousness s. (*Nefarious*).
Multifar'iousness s. (*Multifarious*).
Gregar'iousness s. State or quality of being gregarious.
Hilar'iousness s. Hilarity.
Uproar'iousness s. (*Uproarious*).
Contrar'iousness s. (*Contrarious*).
Var'iousness s. (*Various*).
Oppro'briousness s. (*Opprobrious*).
Lugu'briousness s. (*Lugubrious*).
Imper'iousness s. (*Imperious*).
Ser'iousness s. (*Serious*).
Myster'iousness s. (*Mysterious*).
Labor'iousness s. (*Laborious*).
Inglor'iousness s. (*Inglorious*).
Vainglor'iousness s. (*Vainglorious*).
Victor'iousness s. (*Victorious*).
Meritor'iousness s. (*Meritorious*).
Notor'iousness s. Notoriety.
Uxor'iousness s. (*Uxorious*).
Indus'triousness s. (*Industrious*).
Illus'triousness s. (*Illustrious*).
Cur'iousness s. (*Curious*).
Fu'riousness s. State or quality of being furious.
Injur'iousness s. (*Injurious*).
Perjur'iousness s. (*Perjurious*).
Penur'iousness s. (*Penurious*).
Spur'iousness s. (*Spurious*).
Usur'iousness s. (*Usurious*).
Luxur'iousness s. (*Luxurious*).
Ostenta'tiousness s. (*Ostentatious*).
Vexa'tiousness s. (*Vexatious*).
Fac'tiousness s. State or quality of being factious.
Frac'tiousness s. State or quality of being fractious.
Infec'tiousness s. (*Infectious*).
Contradic'tiousness s. (*Contradictious*).
Face'tiousness s. Wit, good-humour, merriment.
Ambi'tiousness s. (*Ambitious*).
Expedi'tiousness s. (*Expeditious*).
Sedi'tiousness s. (*Seditious*).
Flagi'tiousness s. State of being flagitious ; atrociousness.
Propi'tiousness s. (*Propitious*).
Nutri'tiousness s. (*Nutritious*).
Facti'tiousness s. Quality of being factitious.
Ficti'tiousness s. Quality of being fictitious.
Suppositi'tiousness s. (*Supposititious*).
Adventi'tiousness s. (*Adventitious*).
Supersti'tiousness s. (*Superstitious*).
Licen'tiousness s. (*Licentious*).
Conscien'tiousness s. (*Conscientious*).
Preten'tiousness s. (*Pretentious*).
Senten'tiousness s. (*Sententious*).
Conten'tiousness s. (*Contentious*).
Cap'tiousness s. (*Captious*).
Excep'tiousness s. Peevishness.
Bump'tiousness s. (*Bumptious*).
Cau'tiousness s. (*Cautious*).
Incau'tiousness s. (*Incautious*).
Obse'quiousness s. (*Obsequious*).
Ob'viousness s. (*Obvious*).
De'viousness s. (*Devious*).
Pre'viousness s. (*Previous*).
Lasciv'iousness s. (*Lascivious*).
Obliv'iousness s. (*Oblivious*).
Per'viousness s. (*Pervious*).
Imper'viousness s. (*Impervious*).
Nox'iousness s. (*Noxious*).
Obnox'iousness s. (*Obnoxious*).
Innox'iousness s. (*Innoxious*).
Scan'dalousness s. (*Scandalous*).
Zeal'ousness (zĕl'-) s. (*Zealous*).
Anom'alousness s. (*Anomalous*).
Per'ilousness s. (*Perilous*).
Scur'rilousness s. Scurrility.
Cal'lousness s. (*Callous*).
Mar'vellousness s. (*Marvellous*).
Friv'olousness s. Frivolity.
Neb'ulousness s. (*Nebulous*).
Mirac'ulousness s. (*Miraculous*).
Ridic'ulousness s. (*Ridiculous*).
Metic'ulousness s. (*Meticulous*).
Cred'ulousness s. Credulity.
Sed'ulousness s. Sedulity ; unremitting industry.
Pen'dulousness s. (*Pendulous*).

Scrof'ulousness s. (*Scrofula*).
Em'ulousness s. (*Emulous*).
Trem'ulousness s. (*Tremulous*).
Pop'ulousness s. (*Populous*).
Scru'pulousness s. (*Scrupulous*).
Quer'ulousness s. (*Querulous*).
Gar'rulousness s. Garrulity.
Fa'mousness s. (*Famous*).
Pusillan'imousness s. Pusillanimity.
Unan'imousness s. Unanimity.
Ven'omousness s. (*Venomous*).
Enor'mousness s. (*Enormous*).
Gru'mousness s. State of being clotted or coagulated.
Stru'mousness s. (*Strumous*).
Anon'ymousness s. (*Anonymous*).
Rav'enousness s. (*Ravenous*).
Vill'ainousness s. (*Villainous*).
Moun'tainousness s. (*Mountainous*).
Libid'inousness s. (*Libidinous*).
Multitu'dinousness s. (*Multitudinous*).
Hein'ousness s. (*Heinous*).
Oleag'inousness s. (*Oleaginous*).
Vertig'inousness s. (*Vertiginous*).
Crim'inousness s. (*Criminous*).
Om'inousness s. (*Ominous*).
Lu'minousness s. Luminosity.
Volu'minousness s. (*Voluminous*).
Ru'inousness s. (*Ruinous*).
Poi'sonousness s. (*Poisonous*).
Monot'onousness s. Monotony.
Pul'pousness s. (*Pulpous*).
Pom'pousness s. (*Pompous*).
Bar'barousness s. (*Barbarous*).
Vivip'arousness s. Viviparity.
Sca'brousness s. (*Scabrous*).
Fi'brousness s. Quality of being fibrous.
Cum'brousness s. (*Cumbrous*).
Lu'dicrousness s. (*Ludicrous*).
Won'drousness s. (*Wondrous*).
Ul'cerousness s. (*Ulcerous*).
Slan'derousness s. (*Slanderous*).
Pon'derousness s. Ponderosity.
Vocif'erousness s. (*Vociferous*).
O'doriferousness s. (*Odoriferous*).
Soporif'erousness s. (*Soporiferous*).
Dan'gerousness s. (*Dangerous*).
Treach'erousness s. (*Treacherous*).
Lech'erousness s. Lechery.
Cantank'erousness s. (*Cantankerous*).
Nu'merousness s. (*Numerous*).
On'erousness s. (*Onerous*).
Obstrep'erousness s. (*Obstreperous*).
Pros'perousness s. Prosperity.
Bois'terousness s. (*Boisterous*).
Prepos'terousness s. (*Preposterous*).
Cadav'erousness s. (*Cadaverous*).
Decor'ousness s. (*Decorous*).
Indecor'ousness s. (*Indecorous*).
Odor'ousness s. (*Odorous*).
Rig'orousness s. (*Rigorous*).
Vig'orousness s. (*Vigorous*).
Lan'guorousness s. Languor.
Dol'orousness s. (*Dolorous*).
Am'orousness s. (*Amorous*).
Clam'orousness s. (*Clamorous*).
Tim'orousness s. (*Timorous*).
Hu'morousness s. (*Humorous*).
Sonor'ousness s. Sonority.
Por'ousness s. (*Porous*).
Va'porousness s. State of being vaporous.
Trai'torousness s. (*Traitorous*).
Ster'torousness s. (*Stertorous*).
Mon'strousness s. (*Monstrous*).
Ven'turousness s. (*Venturous*).
Adven'turousness s. (*Adventurous*).
Cov'etousness s. (*Covetous*).
Solic'itousness s. (*Solicitous*).
Calam'itousness s. (*Calamitous*).
Precip'itousness s. (*Precipitous*).
Circu'itousness s. (*Circuitous*).
Ubiq'uitousness s. (*Ubiquitous*).
Gratu'itousness s. Quality of being gratuitous.
Fortu'itousness s. Fortuity.
Momen'tousness s. (*Momentous*).
Ri'otousness s. (*Riotous*).
Vac'uousness s. (*Vacuous*).
Conspic'uousness s. (*Conspicuous*).
Inconspic'uousness s. (*Inconspicuous*).
Perspic'uousness s. (*Perspicuous*).
Innoc'uousness s. (*Innocuous*)
Promis'cuousness s. Promiscnity.
Decid'uousness s. (*Deciduous*).
Assid'uousness s. (*Assiduous*).
Ar'duousness s. (*Arduous*).
Contig'uousness s. Contiguity.
Super'fluousness s. State of being superfluous; superfluity.
Ingen'uousness s. (*Ingenuous*).
Disingen'uousness s. (*Disingenuous*).
Stren'uousness s. (*Strenuous*).
Incon'gruousness s. Incongruity.
Sen'suousness s. (*Sensuous*).
Fat'uousness s. Quality of being fatuous; fatuity.
Unc'tuousness s. State or quality of being unctuous; greeasinss.
Impet'uousness s. Impetuosity.
Spir'ituousness s. (*Spirituous*).
Tumul'tuousness s. (*Tumultuous*).
Contemp'tuousness s. (*Contemptuous*).
Sump'tuousness s. (*Sumptuous*).
Presump'tuousness s. (*Presumptuous*).
Volup'tuousness s. (*Voluptuous*).
Vir'tuousness s. (*Virtuous*).
Tor'tuousness s. (*Tortuous*).
Inces'tuousness s. Incest.
Tempes'tuousness s. (*Tempestuous*).
Mis'chievousness s. (*Mischievous*).
Ner'vousness s. (*Nervous*).
Joy'ousness s. (*Joyous*).
Neat'ness s. (*Neat*).

Great'ness s. Magnitude; grandeur; quality of being great.
Fat'ness s. Quality or state of being fat; fat; greasy matter; fertility.
Flat'ness s. State or quality of being flat.
Compact'ness s. (*Compact*).
Intact'ness s. State of being intact.
Exact'ness s. Quality of being exact.
Inexact'ness s. Inexactitude.
Per'fectness s. (*Perfect*).
Imper'fectness s. (*Imperfect*).
Ab'jectness s. (*Abject*).
Select'ness s. (*Select*).
Circumspect'-ness s. (*Circumspect*).
Direct'ness s. Quality or state of being direct.
Indirect'ness s. (*Indirect*).
Correct'ness s. (*Correct*).
Incorrect'ness s. (*Incorrect*).
Strict'ness s. (*Strict*).
Succinct'ness s. (*Succinct*).
Distinct'ness s. (*Distinct*).
Indistinct'ness s. (*Indistinct*).
Fleet'ness s. Swiftness of foot; speed.
Meet'ness s. Fitness; suitability.
Discreet'ness s. (*Discreet*).
Indiscreet'ness s. Indiscretion.
Sweet'ness s. (*Sweet*).
Qui'etness s. (*Quiet*).
Disqui'etness s. Want of peace, disturbance.
Se'cretness s. (*Secret*).
Wet'ness s. State or quality of being wet.
Deft'ness s. (*Deft*).
Swift'ness s. (*Swift*).
Soft'ness s. (*Soft*).
Straight'ness s. (*Straight*).
Light'ness s. State or quality of illumination; absence of duskiness; state of being not heavy; buoyancy; nimbleness; grace; wantonness.
Slight'ness s. (*Slight*).
Right'ness s. Rectitude; straightness.
Bright'ness s. (*Bright*).
Down'rightness s. Straightforwardness.
Up'rightness s. (*Upright*).
Tight'ness s. (*Tight*).
Strait'ness s. (*Strait*).
Implic'itness s. (*Implicit*).
Explic'itness s. (*Explicit*).
Inexplic'itness s. (*Inexplicit*).
Fit'ness s. State of being fit.
Adroit'ness s. (*Adroit*).
Maladroit'ness s. (*Maladroit*).
Wit'ness s. Attestation, testimony, evidence; one who or that which furnishes proof or evidence. v.i. To bear testimony. v.t. To attest; to see as a spectator.
Salt'ness s. (*Salt*).
Occult'ness s. (*Occult*).
Scant'ness s. (*Scant*).
Val'iantness s. (*Valiant*).
Pli'antness s. Pliancy.
Pleas'antness s. (*Pleasant*).
Re'centness s. Recency.
Strin'gentness s. Stringency.
Si'lentness s. (*Silent*).
Transpar'ent-ness s. Transparence.
Intent'ness s. (*Intent*).
Faint'ness s. State of being faint; loss of strength, colour, control, etc.
Quaint'ness s. (*Quaint*).
Gaunt'ness s. State of being gaunt.
Blunt'ness s. (*Blunt*).
Hot'ness s. (*Hot*).
Apt'ness s. (*Apt*).
Inapt'ness s. Inaptitude.
Inept'ness s. Ineptitude.
Prompt'ness s. (*Prompt*).
Abrupt'ness s. (*Abrupt*).
Corrupt'ness s. (*Corrupt*).
Incorrupt'ness s. (*Incorrupt*).
Smart'ness s. (*Smart*).
Tart'ness s. (*Tart*).
Stal'wartness s. (*Stalwart*).
Alert'ness s. (*Alert*).
Inert'ness s. (*Inert*).
Pert'ness s. (*Pert*).
Mal'apertness s. (*Malapert*).
Expert'ness s. (*Expert*),
Short'ness s. (*Short*).
Curt'ness s. (*Curt*).
Fast'ness s. Quality of being fast; a stronghold, fortress.
Stead'fastness s. (*Steadfast*).
Vast'ness s. (*Vast*).
Man'ifestness s. (*Manifest*).
Moist'ness s. (*Moist*).
August'ness s. (*August*).
Just'ness s. Quality of being just; equity; uprightness.
Taut'ness s. (*Taut*).
Stout'ness s. (*Stout*).
Devout'ness s. (*Devout*).
Raw'ness s. State of being raw.
Few'ness s. State of being few.
Skew'ness s. (*Skew*).
New'ness s. (*New*).
Low'ness s. State or quality of being low.
Cal'lowness s. (*Callow*).
Shal'lowness s. (*Shallow*).
Mel'lowness s. (*Mellow*).
Yel'lowness s. State or quality of being yellow.
Hol'lowness s. (*Hollow*).
Slow'ness s. (*Slow*).
Nar'rowness s. (*Narrow*).
Lax'ness s. Laxity.
Prolix'ness s. Prolixity.
Grey'ness s. State or quality of being grey; gloom.
Glu'eyness s. Quality or state of being gluey.
Shy'ness s. Timidity; state of being retiring.
Sly'ness s. (*Sly*).
Coy'ness s. (*Coy*).
Dry'ness s. (*Dry*).
Wry'ness s. (*Wry*).
Bus'yness s. State of being busy.
Lo'ess s. A loamy rock deposited in certain river-valleys.
Caress' v.t. To treat with affection; to fondle. s. An act of endearment.
Vo'taress s. A female votary or devotee.
Cress s. A cruciferous plant used in salads.
An'cress s. An anchoress.
Wa'tercress s. A creeping aquatic plant.
Dress v.t. To clothe; to cleanse a wound; to put in good order, make straight; to prepare food. v.i. To put on clothes, pay regard to dress; to range in a line. s. Clothes, attire; a woman's gown.
Ambas'sadress s. The wife of an ambassador; a woman acting as an ambassador.
Address' v.t. To direct; to apply to, speak to. s. An application; speech to a person, a discourse; tact; direction of a letter.
Readdress' v.t. To direct to another address.
Redress' v.t. To set right, adjust, rectify; to make amends. s. Reparation; relief; deliverance.
Redress' (rē-) v.t. and i. To dress again.
Undress' v.i. and t. To strip, divest of clothes.
Un'dress s. Ordinary attire; a loose dress.
Laun'dress s. A washerwoman.

Foun'dress s. A woman who originates or endows an institution, etc.
Ward'ress (wŏrd'-) s. A female jailer.
Sor'ceress s. A female sorcerer.
Mur'deress s. A woman guilty of murder.
Peer'ess s. The wife of a peer; a female peer.
Manageress' s. A female manager.
Ar'cheress s. A female archer.
Shakeress' s. A female Shaker.
Qua'keress s. A female member of the Society of Friends.
Jaileress' s. A female jailer.
Ca'teress s. A female caterer.
Adul'teress s. A female adulterer.
Huck'steress s. A female huckster.
E'gress s. Act or power of going out; end of transit of a satellite, etc.
Ne'gress s. A female negro.
Re'gress s. Return; regression.
Regress' v.i. To move back.
Digress' v.i. To turn aside, deviate.
Ti'gress s. A female tiger; a virago.
In'gress s. Entrance; act or power of entering.
Con'gress s. An assembly, synod, convention; meeting of diplomatic representatives; the legislature of the U.S.A.
O'gress s. A female ogre.
Pro'gress s. A moving forward, advance, development; journey of state.
Progress' v.i. To advance, go forward, improve.
Retrogress' v.i. To go backward; to degenerate.
Transgress' v.t. To violate, infringe. v.i. To sin.
Heir'ess s. A female heir.
Coheir'ess s. A joint heiress.
An'choress s. A female hermit.
Au'thoress s. A female author.
Super'ioress s. Female chief of a nunnery, etc.
Pri'oress s. The female superior of a convent.
Tail'oress s. A female tailor.
Tu'toress s. A female tutor.
Mayor'ess s. Wife of a mayor.
Press v.t. To squeeze, crush; to urge, enforce; to emphasize; to solicit importunately; to force into service. v.i. To bear heavily, push with force; to crowd. s. A crushing; a crowd; instrument for squeezing; a cupboard; machine for or art and business of printing; publications collectively; newspapers, periodicals.
Depress' v.t. To press down; to humble; to deject, dispirit.
Repress' v.t. To restrain, suppress, quell.
Em'press s. The consort of an emperor; the female ruler of an empire.
Impress' v.t. To stamp; to fix in the mind; to affect strongly; to seize for or compel to enter the public service.
Im'press s. Act of marking or mark made by pressure; an impression.
Reimpress' v.t. To impress again.
Compress' v.t. To press together, squeeze, condense.
Oppress' v.t. To overburden, harass; to crush, subdue.
Suppress' v.t. To put down, quell; to stifle.
Harp'ress s. A female harp-player.
Let'terpress s. Printed matter apart from illustrations.
Express' v.t. To press or squeeze out; to declare, make known, reveal; to send by express. a. Directly stated; explicit; closely resembling; dispatched specially. s. A train not stopping intermediately; a special messenger; a quick conveyance. adv. For a particular purpose; with urgency.
Cy'press s. A coniferous tree, used as an emblem of mourning; a kind of satin.
Tress s. A lock of hair.
Idol'atress s. A female idolater.
Or'atress s. A female orator.
Specta'tress s. A female spectator.
Dicta'tress s. A female dictator.
Im'itatress s. A female imitator.
Ac'tress s. A female actor.
Ben'efactress s. A female benefactor.
Detrac'tress s. A female detractor.
Elec'tress s. Wife or widow of a German Elector.
Inspec'tress s. A female inspector.
Rec'tress s. A female governor.
Direc'tress s. A female director.
Protec'tress s. A female protector.
Vic'tress s. A female victor.
Seduc'tress s. A woman seducer.
Conduc'tress s. A woman conductor.
Instruc'tress s. A female instructor.
Propri'etress s. A female proprietor.
Trai'tress s. A female traitor.
Wait'ress s. A female attendant at table.
Inhab'itress s. A female inhabitant.
Ar'bitress s. A female arbitrator or judge.
Ed'itress s. A woman editor.
Jan'itress s. A female door-keeper.
Progen'itress s. A progenitrix.
Mon'itress s. A female monitor at school.
Inher'itress s. A female inheritor.
Inquis'itress s. A female inquisitor.
Enchant'ress s. A female enchanter, a fascinating woman.
Invent'ress s. A female inventor.
Joint'ress s. A woman who has a jointure.
Hunt'ress s. A female hunter.
Cap'tress s. A female who makes a capture.
Precep'tress s. A female teacher.
Sculp'tress s. A female sculptor.
Temp'tress s. A female tempter.
For'tress s. A stronghold; a fortified place.
Por'tress s. A female porter or gate-keeper.
Stress s. Constraint; weight; violence; strain. v.t. To subject to stress or force.
An'cestress s. A female ancestor.
Song'stress s. A female singer.
Distress' s. Great suffering of body or mind; that which causes this; state of danger or destitution; act or right of distraining. v.t. To afflict with pain or anguish; to seize for debt.
Mis'tress s. A woman in authority or having control or mastery; a female teacher; head of a household; sweetheart; concubine.
Post'mistress s. A female postmaster.
Seams'tress s. A needle-woman.
Fos'tress s. A foster-mother.
Semp'stress s. A sewing-woman, seamstress.
Mat'tress s. A soft, quilted bed.
But'tress s. A projecting support for a wall. v.t. To prop, support.
Procur'ess s. A female procurer.
Du'ress s. Constraint, imprisonment.
Adven'turess s. A woman living by her wits and gaining position by false pretences.
Obsess' v.t. To beset, haunt, harass; to delude.
Assess' v.t. To rate, to fix a charge to be paid.
Reassess' v.t. To assess anew.
Possess' v.t. To own, to have and hold; to be master of; to seize.

Repossess' v.t. To possess again.
Prepossess' v.t. To preoccupy; to bias.
Dispossess' v.t. To deprive of possession.
Proph'etess s. A female prophet.
Po'etess s. A female poet.
Hermitess' s. A female hermit.
Gi'antess s. A female giant.
Coun'tess s. Wife or widow of a count or earl; lady holding this title in her own right.
Vis'countess (vī'-) s. Wife of a viscount; a peeress of this rank.
Priest'ess s. A female priest.
Host'ess s. A female host; landlady of an inn.
Guess v.i. To conjecture, surmise. s. An opinion, etc., based on insufficient evidence, a conjecture.
Mar'quess s. (*Marquis*).
Jew'ess s. A female Jew.
Prow'ess s. Bravery; courage; valour.
Gneiss s. A laminated rock containing quartz, feldspar, mica, etc.
Speiss s. A compound of arsenic with nickel, copper, etc.
Edel'weiss s. A small Alpine white-flowered plant.
Hiss v.i. To make a sound like the letter "s," especially in contempt; to whizz. v.t. To show disapprobation thus. s. This sound.
Kiss s. A salute by joining the lips; a slight touch. v.i. and t. To salute thus; to join lips.
Hotch'kiss s. A type of rapid-fire gun.
Miss s. A young woman; form of address to an unmarried woman; a failure to reach, hit, etc.; want. v.t. To fail to reach, find, etc.; to omit, overlook; to feel the want of. v.i. To be unsuccessful.
Amiss' a. In error, improper. adv. Improperly, faultily.
Remiss' a. Careless, lax, dilatory.
Prem'iss s. A premise in logic.
Dismiss' v.t. To send away, remove from office, etc.; discard.
Ku'miss s. Alcoholic liquor made by the Tartars from mare's milk.
Swiss s. A native or the people of Switzerland. a. Pertaining to Switzerland.
Boss s. A knob, a decorative projection; a master; a bad aim or attempt. v.t. To manage, control.
Emboss' v.t. To cover with bosses; to ornament in relief.
Doss s. (*Slang*) A bed, a night's rest. v.i. (*Slang*) To go to bed, to sleep.
Hoss s. (*Slang*) A horse.
Joss s. A Chinese idol.
Loss s. Act of losing; that which is lost; detriment; forfeiture.
Floss s. The downy substance of plants; the exterior of a silk-worm's cocoon.
Gloss s. Sheen, superficial lustre, specious appearance; a note, comment. v.t. To give lustre, etc., to; to render plausible; to annotate.
Bu'gloss s. A plant of the borage family.
Moss s. A morass; a low, cryptogamous plant. v.t. To cover with moss.
Kaross' s. A native S. African garment of skin.
Cross s. An upright stake with a transverse bar for crucifixion, the emblem of the Christian religion; the religion itself; misfortune, anything that thwarts; a hybrid. a. Athwart, transverse; peevish, fretful. v.t. To draw a line or lay a body across; to pass across; to cancel, mark with a cross; to perplex; to interbreed. v.i. To be athwart, to move across.
Across' adv., prep. From side to side.
Recross' v.t. and i. To cross or pass over again.
Dross s. The scum of melting metals; refuse.
Gross a. Great, bulky; whole, entire; unrefined; stupid; vulgar; impure; indelicate. s. The main body, mass; twelve dozen.
Engross' v.t. To copy in a large hand; to absorb; to monopolize.
Al'batross s. A large sea-bird.
Toss v.t. To pitch, throw with violence, agitate. v.i. To roll and tumble. s. A pitch, throw; state of being tossed.
Buss s. A kiss. v.t. To kiss.
Blun'derbuss s. A short gun with wide bore.
Cuss s. (*Slang*) A curse; a fellow. v.i. (*Slang*) To curse, swear.
Succuss' v.t. To shake suddenly, as in diagnosis.
Percuss' v.t. To tap on, especially in diagnosis.
Discuss' v.t. To examine by argument; to debate, reason upon.
Fuss s. Bustle, tumult; ado about trifles. v.i. To worry, bustle about.
Muss s. State of confusion; mess; a scramble. v.t. To disarrange.
Puss s. A cat; a hare.
Russ s. A Russian; the Russian language.
Truss s. Bundle of hay, etc.; belt or bandage used for hernia; an unyielding frame formed of girders, etc. v.t. To bind close; to skewer and fasten; to hang.
Abyss' s. A chasm, a deep pit.
Greats s. The final examination for the Oxford B.A.
Floats s. The footlights of a theatre.
Groats s. Oats with the hulls taken off; broken wheat.
Pan'dects s. The digested code of Roman civil law prepared by order of Justinian.
Effects' s. Goods; movables; personal estate.
An'alects s. Literary gleanings.
Rack'ets s. A game resembling tennis played against a wall.
Rick'ets s. Softening of the bone in children.
Gib'lets s. The internal eatable parts of a fowl, goose, etc.
Entremets' s. Extra dishes after the chief dishes at dinner.
As'sets s. Property available for paying liabilities.
Lights s. The lungs of animals.
Foot'lights s. The row of lights in front of a theatre stage.
Tights s. Clothes fitting closely to the body.
Draughts s. A game for two played on a chess-board; checkers.
Its pron. Possessive of "it."
Waits s. Band of street carol-singers at Christmas time.
Droits s. Legal perquisites.
Quoits s. The game of quoit-throwing.
Grits s. The coarse part of meal; wheat fragments smaller than groats.
Quits a. Even with.
Blew'its s. An edible mushroom.
Intersec'ants s. Intersecting lines.

Pants s. Men's under-drawers; trousers.
Odd'ments s. Remnants, odds and ends.
El'ements s. Rudiments or first principles of an art or science; data used in calculations; the Eucharistic bread and wine.
Cere'ments s. Grave-clothes.
Con'tents s. Things contained in a vessel, book, etc.; table of subjects.
Faints s. Impure spirit which comes over in distilling whisky.
Scots a. Scottish. s. The Scottish dialect.
Boots s. A male servant at a hotel.
Sly'boots s. An arch or artful person.
Hoots int. Expressing disgust, impatience, etc.
Orts s. Fragments, leavings, odds and ends.
Shorts s. The bran and coarse part of meal; knee-breeches.
Botts s. A disease in horses, sheep, etc., caused by worms.
Guts s. (*Vulgar*) The intestines; the belly; (*slang*) pluck.
Here'abouts adv. Somewhere near here.
There'abouts adv.
Where'abouts adv. Near which place. s. Approximate locality.
Grouts s. Dregs, grounds.
Us pl. pron. Objective case of "we."
San'ta Claus s. Father Christmas.
'Bus s. An omnibus.
Syl'labus s. A list, table of contents, programme; a compendium.
Cot'tabus s. The game of throwing wine at a mark played at ancient Greek banquets.
Ephe'bus s. (*Ephebe*).
Phœ'bus s. Apollo; the sun.
Re'bus s. A sort of riddle.
Er'ebus s. The lower world; region between earth and Hades.
Har'quebus s. An obsolete kind of musket.
Circum-ben'dibus s. A roundabout route; a circumlocution.
Gi'bus s. An opera-hat.
Om'nibus s. A large public vehicle. a. Embracing several items, etc.
Iam'bus s. Two-syllabled poetic foot, a short followed by a long.
Choriam'bus s. A choriamb.
Lim'bus s. A border differentiated in colour or structure.
Nim'bus s. A halo; a rain-cloud.
Rhom'bus s. A rhomb.
Throm'bus s. Clot of blood in a blood-vessel.
Jaco'bus s. An English gold coin, *temp.* James I.
Suc'cubus s. A demon of mediæval folklore.
In'cubus s. A demon; nightmare; an oppressive person or thing.
Ab'acus s. The square slab at the top of a column; a counting-frame.
Amar'acus s. An aromatic plant.
Coc'cus s. A genus of destructive hemipterous insects; a spherical bacterium; a spore in cryptogams.
Protococ'cus s. A genus of unicellular algæ.
Streptococ'cus s. A genus of bacteria many of which are virulently pathogenic.
Floc'cus s. Tuft at end of tail of some animals; down on fledglings.
Galeopithe'cus s. A genus of flying lemurs.
Umbil'icus s. The navel; a navel-like depression or scar.
Posti'cus s. Turned away from the axis (of leaves, etc.).
In'cus s. A small bone of the internal ear.
Fo'cus s. Point of convergence of rays; point of concentration. v.t. To bring to a focus.
Ho'cus v.t. To impose upon; to cheat; to drug, dope. s. An impostor; drugged liquor.
Lo'cus s. The exact place.
Ho'cus-po'cus s. A fraud, trick, incantation; a juggler. v.t. and i. To cheat; to juggle.
Cro'cus s. A small bulbous plant of the iris family.
Quer'cus s. The genus of trees including the oaks.
Cir'cus s. An arena for equestrian performances; a company of such performers; a circular space where roads meet.
Hibis'cus s. A genus of tropical mallows.
Dis'cus s. A quoit.
Menis'cus s. A lens having one side convex and the other concave.
Lentis'cus s. The mastic tree.
Cus'cus s. An Indian grass used in basket-work, etc.
Cau'cus s. A meeting for nomination of political candidates, laying down a policy. etc.; the managing committee of a political party. v.t. and i. To work through a close party organization.
Fu'cus s. A genus of common seaweeds.
Mu'cus s. A viscid fluid secreted by the mucous membrane; similar animal fluids.
Gra'dus s. A prosodical dictionary.
Smarag'dus s. The emerald.
Sol'idus s. An ancient Roman coin; a shilling; stroke (/) denoting this.
Ni'dus s. A nest, place of incubation, especially of insects; seat, site, central point.
Mo'dus s. A way, manner, mode.
No'dus s. A knotty point, a crux.
Ex'odus s. A departure, especially of a number of persons.
Coryphæ'us s. A chief, leader, especially of the ancient Greek chorus.
Uræ'us s. The snake symbol of sovereignty in ancient Egypt.
Cadu'ceus s. Mercury's rod.
Mor'pheus s. The Roman god of dreams.
Nu'cleus s. Central point about which matter, etc., gathers; central part of a cell; head of a comet.
Pi'leus s. The brimless cap of the ancients; the top of a mushroom.
Mal'leus s. A small hammer-shaped bone in the internal ear.
Sole'us s. A muscle of the calf of the leg.
Acu'leus s. A sting, a prickle.
Clyp'eus s. The shield-like part of an insect's head.
Chore'us s. A choree.
Glute'us s. A large muscle in the buttock.
Zeus (zūs) s. The supreme deity of the ancient Greeks.
Sarcoph'agus s. A stone coffin.
Œsoph'agus s. The gullet.
Ma'gus s. A priest among the Medes and Persians; a magician.
Areop'agus s. The supreme court of ancient Athens.
Aspar'agus s. A culinary vegetable.
Chora'gus s. Leader or principal of the ancient Greek chorus.
Tra'gus s. A small process in the ear

Va'gus a. Out of place. s. The pneumogastric nerve.
Ne'gus s. A drink of hot wine with sugar and spice; the sovereign of Abyssinia.
Strate'gus s. A military commander in ancient Greece.
Mundung'us s. A strong, ill-smelling tobacco.
Fun'gus s. A flowerless plant; a toadstool, etc.; a spongy excrescence.
Bo'gus a. Sham, counterfeit.
Ar'gus s. A watchful person.
Bac'chus s. The Roman god of wine; wine.
Elen'chus s. Argument in which the opponent is forced to be self-contradictory.
Ornithorhyn'chus s. The duck-billed platypus, an Australian egg-laying mammal.
Syn'ochus s. A continued fever.
Ty'phus s. A contagious fever.
Scir'rhus s. A hard cancerous growth.
Thus adv.
Can'thus s. The angle formed by the eyelids.
Acan'thus s. A prickly plant; a conventional sculptured representation of this.
Calycan'thus s. A N. American shrub.
Dian'thus s. A genus of plants including the pinks.
Amian'thus s. Mountain flax; a variety of asbestos.
Galan'thus s. The genus of bulbous plants that includes the snowdrop.
Polyan'thus s. A garden variety of primrose.
Schizan'thus s. A plant with fringed leaves and showy flowers.
Lec'ythus s. An ancient Greek vase.
My'thus s. A myth.
Bathyb'ius s. Slime from ocean beds.
Gla'dius s. The pen of a cuttle-fish.
Ra'dius s. A straight line from the centre to the circumference of a circle; a bone of the fore-arm.
Sar'dius s. A Scriptural precious stone.
Re'gius a. Appointed by the sovereign.
Bac'chius s. A metrical foot, two longs followed by one short.
Gastrocne'mius s. A large muscle in the calf of the leg.
Doch'mius s. A five-syllabled metrical foot (one short, two long, one short, one long).
Ge'nius s. Mental bent or inclination; great, intellectual, imaginative, inventive, etc., faculty; one endowed with this; individual character; a tutelary spirit.
Sple'nius s. A double muscle in the neck.
Arse nious a. Containing arsenic.
Antimo'nious a. Containing or composed of antimony.
Retiar'ius s. A gladiator armed with a net.
Denar'ius s. An ancient Roman silver coin; a penny.
Septenar'ius s. A verse of seven feet.
Sagittar'ius s. One of the signs of the Zodiac, the Archer.
Aquar'ius s. The eleventh sign of the Zodiac, the Water-bearer.
Stradivar'ius s. A violin made by Antonio Stradivari (d. 1737).
Sir'ius s. The dog-star.
Sartor'ius s. One of the thigh-muscles.
Sester'tius s. An ancient Roman coin (about 2d.).
Astrag'alus s. The ball of the ankle-joint; a genus of leguminous plants.
Cynoceph'alus s. A dog-headed man of ancient myth; a baboon.
Buceph'alus s. A riding-horse.
Ta'lus s. The ankle-bone; slope of a rampart; sloping heap of rock at base of a cliff.
Tan'talus s. A set of decanters locked in an open case; a genus of wading birds.
Sphac'elus s. Gangrene; necrosis.
An'gelus s. A prayer in memory of the Annunciation said in Roman Catholic churches; the bell that calls to this.
Troch'ilus s. The Egyptian plover; a small humming-bird.
Nau'tilus s. A genus of cephalopods; the argonaut.
Cal'lus s. A hardening of the skin; a formation of bone uniting a fracture.
Phal'lus s. The emblem of a generative power as an object of primitive worship.
Thal'lus s. A plant having no true root, stem, or leaves.
Ocel'lus s. A simple eye of an insect; one of the parts of a compound eye; an eye-like marking.
Vitel'lus s. Yolk of egg.
Entel'lus s. The sacred monkey of the Hindus.
Bacil'lus s. A genus of microscopic rod-shaped bacteria.
Aspergil'lus s. A genus of microscopic fungi.
Vil'lus s. A short hair-like process on membranes.
Pulvil'lus s. The pad of an insect's foot.
Bo'lus s. A large pill.
Em'bolus s. A clot in a blood-vessel.
Ob'olus s. A small silver coin of ancient Athens.
Discob'olus s. A quoit-thrower; statue of an athlete throwing the discus.
Ho'lus-bo'lus adv. At one gulp, all at once.
Urce'olus s. A pitcher-shaped part or organ.
Nucle'olus s. A nucleus within another.
Malle'olus s. One of the two projecting bones of the ankle.
Alve'olus s. A small cavity; tooth socket; cell of honeycomb.
Gladi'olus s. A genus of herbaceous bulbous plants.
Modi'olus s. The central axis of the cochlea of the ear.
Plus s. The sign (+) of addition. a. Above zero; positive; additional. prep. With the addition of.
Non'plus v.t. To bewilder, confound. s. State of perplexity; a quandary.
O'verplus s. Anything over; surplus.
Sur'plus s. Excess; balance.
Coc'culus s. A genus of Eastern climbing shrubs.
Floc'culus s. A small lock or flock; a lobe in the cerebellum.
Fascic'ulus s. A division of a book, a fascicle.
Pedic'ulus s. The body-louse.
Funic'ulus s. The umbilical cord; a fibre connecting the seed to a plant.
Fontic'ulus s. The depression above the breast-bone.
Cal'culus s. A stone in the bladder, etc.; a method of calculating.
Siphun'culus s. A siphuncle.
Homun'culus s. A dwarf, manikin.
Ranun'culus s. Genus of plants containing the buttercup, etc.
Loc'ulus s. A small cavity; a cell.
Monoc'ulus s. A small crustacean with a single median eye.
Sur'culus s. A shoot from a root; a sucker.
Calyc'ulus s. A little calyx.
Mod'ulus s. Quantity or coefficient expressing the measure of some specified force, etc.

Reg'ulus s. The purer ore that sinks during smelting; the crested wren.
Fam'ulus s. An attendant, especially one on a wizard.
Ham'ulus a. A little hook; a hooked bristle.
Ram'ulus s. A small branch.
Mim'ulus s. A genus of herbaceous plants including the monkey-flower.
Stim'ulus s. That which stimulates; an incitement; a sting.
Cu'mulus s. A cloud in the form of dense heaps.
Cirrocu'mulus s. A cloud-formation of small white masses.
Tu'mulus s. A sepulchral mound, barrow.
Vol'vulus s. A twisting of an intestine.
Convol'vulus s. A genus of twining plants including the bindweed.
Gon'gylus s. A spore of certain fungi, seaweeds, etc.
Styl'us s. A style, pointed writing implement.
Manda'mus s. Writ from a superior authority commanding performance of some specified duty.
Cal'amus s. The sweet flag; a genus of palm-trees, also of fishes.
Thal'amus s. Inner women's room in ancient Greek houses; a large ganglion in the brain; the receptacle of a plant.
Ra'mus s. A branched or forked part.
Ignora'mus s. An ignorant person, a dunce.
Hippopot'amus s. A large amphibious pachydermatous quadruped of African rivers.
Sphyg'mus s. A pulsation.
Is'thmus s. Neck of land connecting two larger portions.
An'imus s. Hostile spirit.
Pri'mus a. First, eldest. s. The presiding bishop in the Episcopal Church of Scotland.
Mit'timus s. A warrant of committal to prison.
Ul'mus s. Genus of trees including the elm.
Prod'romus s. (*Prodrome*).
Sapros'tomus s. Foulness of breath.
Bu'tomus s. The flowering rush.
Chias'mus s. Inversion of the order of words in the second of two parallel phrases.
Maras'mus s. Wasting away of the body.
Strabis'mus s. A squint; squinting.
Laryngis'mus s. A spasmodic affection of the glottis.
Tris'mus s. Lock-jaw.
Lit'mus s. A blue vegetable dye, turned red by acids and back to blue by alkalis.
Hu'mus s. Mould, especially from decayed leaves, etc.
Thy'mus s. A gland in lower part of neck.
Ging'lymus s. A joint admitting of motion in only one plane, as the elbow.
Euon'ymus s. A genus of evergreens including the spindle-tree.
A'nus s. The exterior orifice of the intestines.
Ja'nus s. The two-faced Roman god of gates and doors.
Ur'anus s. The most ancient of the Greek gods; the seventh of the major planets.
Tet'anus s. A spasmodic affection; lockjaw.
Ge'nus s. A class of objects divided into subordinate species.
Scale'nus s. A triangular muscle of the neck.
Sile'nus s. A drunken old roisterer.
Ve'nus s. The ancient Roman goddess of love and beauty; one of the planets.
A'cinus s. A fleshy fruit like the raspberry.
Echi'nus s. The sea-urchin; a rounded moulding in the capital of Doric and Ionian columns.
Mi'nus prep. or a. Less by; short of. s. The sign of subtraction (—).
Ter'minus s. A boundary; the end especially of a railway.
Si'nus s. A hollow, recess; a cavity in a bone; a fistula.
Laurusti'nus s. An ornamental evergreen shrub.
Frax'inus s. The genus of trees containing the ash.
Alum'nus s. A pupil, a graduate.
O'nus s. Burden; responsibility.
Bo'nus s. An extra dividend or payment; a premium.
Clo'nus s. An irregular spasmodic muscular contraction.
Electrot'onus s. The alteration of muscular activity under galvanic influence.
Photot'onus s. The sensibility of plants, etc., to light.
Cothur'nus s. The thick-soled buskin worn by actors in Greek and Roman tragedy.
-ous suff. Forming names of many chemical compounds, and adjectives denoting abounding in.
Gib'bous a. Humped; convex; protuberant.
Bul'bous a. Bulb-shaped.
Lim'bous a. With slightly overlapping borders.
Helioph'obous a. Turning away from sunlight.
Glo'bous a. Spherical, globular.
Her'bous a. Herby.
Lu'bricous a. Lubricious.
Cor'ticous a. (*Corticose*).
Tal'cous a. Talcose.
Zin'cous a. Zinky; pertaining to the electro-positive element of a battery.
Sar'cous a. Composed of flesh or muscle.
Dis'cous a. Disk-like; flat and circular.
Vis'cous a. Sticky, clammy, viscid.
Fus'cous a. Brown or greyish black; dingy.
Subfus'cous a. Sad-coloured, dull.
Mollus'cous a. Molluscan.
Cous'cous s. A N. African dish of stewed flour and mutton.
Glau'cous a. Sea-green; covered with down of this colour.
Rau'cous a. Hoarse, harsh.
Cadu'cous a. Falling prematurely (of leaves, etc.).
Mu'cous a. Pertaining to, like, covered with, or secreting mucus; slimy.
Ver'rucous a. Warty; wart-like.
Van'adous a. Pertaining to or containing vanadium.
Molyb'dous a. Pertaining to or containing molybdenum.
Mu'cidous a. Mouldy, mucid.
Multif'idous a. Multifid.
Nefan'dous a. Unmentionable; atrocious.
Tremen'dous a. Terrifying through overpowering violence or magnitude, etc.; enormous.
Stupen'dous a. Amazing; prodigious; of astonishing size.
Fron'dous a. Producing leaves and flowers in one organ.
Decap'odous a. Pertaining to the Decapoda.
Lagop'odous a. With feet thickly covered with hair or feathers.
Tylop'odous a. Tylopod.
Steganop'odous a. Having all the toes webbed.
Heterop'odous a. Having the foot modified into a swimming-organ.

Gasterop'odous a. Belonging to or characteristic of the gasteropods.
Isopo'dous a. Pertaining to an isopod or its class.
Haz'ardous a. Full of hazard; dangerous, risky.
Ligniper'dous a. Destructive of wood.
-eous suff. Forming adjectives.
Plum'beous a. Consisting of or resembling lead.
Faba'ceous a. Bean-like, leguminous.
Seba'ceous a. Tallowy; made of, conveying or containing fatty matter.
Bulba'ceous a. Bulbous; having a bulb or bulbs.
Herba'ceous a. Pertaining to or of the nature of herbs.
Mica'ceous a. Pertaining to, containing, or resembling mica.
Erica'ceous a. Belonging to or resembling the heath family of shrubs.
Urtica'ceous a. Like nettles.
Junca'ceous a. Pertaining to or resembling the rushes.
Cycada'ceous a. Belonging to or pertaining to the cycads.
Preda'ceous a. Predatory; living by prey.
Orchida'ceous a. Belonging to the orchid family.
Larda'ceous a. Like or consisting of lard.
Hordea'ceous a. Pertaining to or resembling barley.
Palea'ceous a. Chaffy; consisting of or resembling chaff.
Ocrea'ceous a. Pertaining to or resembling an ocrea.
Torfa'ceous a. Growing in bogs.
Tufa'ceous a. Consisting of, containing, or like tufa.
Saxifraga'ceous a. Pertaining to or resembling the saxifrages.
Funga'ceous a. Pertaining to or resembling fungi.
Spatha'ceous a. Having or resembling spathes.
Acantha'ceous a. Armed with spines, prickly.
Euphorbia'ceous a. Pertaining to the euphorbia.
Rubia'ceous a. Pertaining to or resembling the madder family of plants.
Lilia'ceous a. Pertaining to or like lilies.
Tilia'ceous a. Like or allied to the linden.
Allia'ceous a. Pertaining to or like onions or garlic.
Folia'ceous a. Pertaining to or like a leaf; leafy.
Polemoni-a'ceous a. Pertaining to the phlox family of plants.
Coria'ceous a. Made of leather; stiff, leathery.
Scoria'ceous a. Like scoria; pertaining to dross.
Strobila'ceous a. Pertaining to, resembling, or bearing strobiles.
Fila'ceous a. Consisting of threads.
Fringilla'ceous a. Pertaining to the finches.
Argilla'ceous a. Clayey, containing clay.
Corolla'ceous a. Having a corolla.
Ampulla'ceous a. Swelling, bottle-shaped.
Viola'ceous a. Violet-coloured; of the violet family.
Marla'ceous a. Resembling marl.
Perla'ceous a. Like pearl; nacreous.
Stipula'ceous a. Stipular.
Ferula'ceous a. Pertaining to canes or reeds.
Grossula'ceous a. Belonging to the order of plants containing the gooseberry.
Chyla'ceous a. (*Chyle*).
Amyla'ceous a. Pertaining to or resembling starch.
Lima'ceous a. Pertaining to the slug family.
Palma'ceous a. Pertaining to or resembling palms.
Ulma'ceous a. Pertaining to or of the nature of the elms.
Gemma'ceous a. Pertaining to or resembling leaf-buds.
Poma'ceous a. Of the nature of the fruit of the apple, pear, quince, etc.; like a pome.
Diatoma'ceous a. Consisting of or containing diatoms.
Gluma'ceous a. Consisting of or like glumes.
Solana'ceous a. Pertaining to the genus of plants containing the potato, nightshade, etc.
Membran-a'ceous a. (*Membranous*).
Verbena'ceous a. Belonging to the verbena family of plants.
Solena'ceous a. Pertaining to the family of razor-fishes; resembling these.
Arena'ceous a. Sandy.
Avena'ceous a. Pertaining to or resembling oats.
Arundina'ceous a. Resembling a reed.
Gallina'ceous a. Pertaining to the pheasants, partridges, turkeys, etc.
Gramina'ceous a. Pertaining to the grasses.
Spina'ceous a. Pertaining to or resembling spinach.
Farina'ceous a. Made of or yielding flour or farina; mealy.
Vina'ceous a. Pertaining to wine or grapes; wine-coloured.
Carbona'ceous a. Containing carbon; like coal or carbon.
Cinchona'ceous a. (*Cinchona*).
Papil'ion-aceous a. Resembling a butterfly; having a winged corolla.
Anona'ceous a. Pertaining to the pineapple.
Sapona'ceous a. Soapy.
Scolopa'ceous a. Pertaining to or resembling birds of the Scolopax family.
Drupa'ceous a. Bearing, pertaining to, or of the nature of drupes.
Cera'ceous a. Waxen, waxy.
Hedera'ceous a. Pertaining to or resembling ivy.
Olera'ceous a. Edible, succulent (of herbs).
Papavera'ceous a. Belonging to the poppy family.
Ochra'ceous a. Ochreous.
Arbora'ceous a. Woody; wooded; like a tree.
Stercora'ceous a. Pertaining to or like dung.
Marmora'ceous a. Pertaining to or like marble.
Porra'ceous a. Greenish; like leeks.
Ostra'ceous a. Pertaining to molluscs of the oyster family.
Fura'ceous a. Thievish.
Furfura'ceous a. Scurfy; producing or like scurf.
Papyra'ceous a. Made of or like papyrus; papery.
Butyra'ceous a. Like butter.
Rosa'ceous a. Pertaining to the rose family; rose-like.
Ceta'ceous a. (*Cetacea*).
Creta'ceous a. Of the nature of or abounding in chalk.
Seta'ceous a. Bristly; consisting of or resembling bristles.
Cucurbita'-ceous a. Of or like the gourds.
Pyrita'ceous a. Pertaining to or resembling pyrites.
Amenta'ceous a. Like or bearing catkins.
Lomenta'ceous a. Resembling or bearing loments.
Frumen-ta'ceous a. Made of or like grain.
Charta'ceous a. Resembling paper or parchment.
Myrta'ceous a. Pertaining to or resembling plants of the myrtle family.
Testa'ceous a. Consisting of or having a hard shell.
Crusta'ceous a. Having a shell; belonging to the Crustacea.
Psitta'ceous a. Belonging to the parrot family; parrot-like.
Trutta'ceous a. Pertaining to or resembling trout.
Oliva'ceous a. Of the colour of olives.
Malva'ceous a. Resembling or belonging to the mallow family.
Conferva'ceous a. (*Conferva*).

Spadi'ceous a. Bearing or resembling a spadix.
Sili'ceous a. Pertaining to, containing, or resembling silica.
Pumi'ceous a. Of the nature of pumice.
Puni'ceous a. Bright red or purple.
Pi'ceous a. Pertaining to or like pitch; black; inflammable.
Seri'ceous a. Silky, downy; made of or resembling silk.
Cro'ceous a. Like saffron, saffron-coloured.
Hid'eous a. Horrible, frightful, shocking.
Orchid'eous a. Belonging to the orchid family.
Tipulid'eous a. Resembling a crane-fly.
Rampa'geous a. Rowdy, boisterous.
Umbra'geous a. Shady; shaded.
Outra'geous a. Involving or characterized by outrage; atrocious; exorbitant.
Coura'geous a. Bold, fearless; full of courage.
Advanta'geous a. Profitable, beneficial.
Disadvan-ta'geous a. Attended with disadvantage; detrimental.
Gor'geous a. Magnificent; richly ornate; showy.
Ra'meous a. Pertaining to branches.
Time'ous a. (*Scot.*) Betimes; timely.
Gem'meous a. Gemmy.
Succeda'neous a. Pertaining to or acting as a substitute; substituted.
Porcella'neous a. Of the nature of porcelain.
Miscella'neous a. Mixed; consisting of several kinds.
Membra'neous a. (*Membranous*).
Contempor-a'neous a. Living or happening at the same time.
Extempor-a'neous a. Unpremeditated; off-hand; for the occasion.
Terra'neous a. Growing on land.
Subterra'neous a. Subterranean.
Extra'neous a. Not belonging to or dependent on; irrelevant.
Plata'neous a. Pertaining to or like the platan or plane-tree.
Coeta'neous a. Of the same age; coeval.
Simulta'neous a. Existing or happening at the same time.
Instanta'neous a. Done or happening in a moment.
Consenta'neous a. Accordant; consistent; suitable.
Dissenta'neous a. Disagreeing, contrary.
Sponta'neous a. Proceeding from natural feeling or internal impulse; voluntary.
Cuta'neous a. Pertaining to or affecting the skin.
Subcuta'neous a. Situated under or pertaining to what is under the skin.
Homoge'neous a. Of the same kind or nature.
Heteroge'neous a. Differing in kind; having dissimilar qualities.
Pergame'neous a. Like parchment.
Ig'neous a. Pertaining to, consisting of, resembling, or due to the action of fire.
Lig'neous a. Woody; wooden.
Pyrolig'neous a. Generated by the distillation of wood.
Uredin'eous a. Of the nature of or affected with uredo.
Arundin'eous a. Reedy.
Testudin'eous a. Like the shell of a tortoise.
Gramin'eous a. Pertaining to the grasses; resembling grass.
Stramin'eous a. Consisting of or like straw; chaffy.
Stamin'eous a. Pertaining to stamens.
Vimin'eous a. Made of or producing twigs.
Fulmin'eous a. Fulminating; pertaining to fulmination.
Sanguin'eous a. Pertaining to, coloured like, or abounding in blood; plethoric.
Consanguin'-eous a. Of the same blood; related by birth.
Erro'neous a. Mistaken; incorrect; containing error.
Car'neous a. Resembling flesh.
Cor'neous a. Horny, hard.
Calcar'eous a. Resembling lime or limestone.
Nectar'eous a. Resembling or sweet as nectar.
Tartar'eous a. Consisting of or resembling tartar.
Na'creous a. Like or consisting of mother-of-pearl.
Suber'eous a. Suberic.
Cer'eous a. Waxy.
Vener'eous a. Lecherous, lustful.
O'chreous a. Pertaining to, containing, or resembling ochre.
Glair'eous a. Like glair; viscous and transparent.
Arbor'eous a. Arboreal; wooded.
Cu'preous a. Like or composed of copper.
Vit'reous a. Consisting of, obtained from, or like glass.
Sulphur'eous a. Consisting of or having the qualities of sulphur.
Ca'seous a. Resembling cheese.
Ga'seous a. In the form of or like gas.
Gris'eous a. Bluish-grey.
Gyp'seous a. Resembling, containing, or consisting of gypsum.
Os'seous a. Composed of, resembling, or full of bones; bony; ossified.
Nau'seous a. Loathsome; disgusting.
Lac'teous a. Milky; lacteal.
Right'eous a. Upright; honest; virtuous; equitable.
Pit'eous a. Exciting, evincing, or deserving pity; sad; miserable; pitiful; paltry.
Despit'eous a. Despiteful.
Plen'teous a. Having plenty; abundant; fruitful.
Boun'teous a. Full of bounty, generously inclined.
Court'eous a. Polite, affable, complaisant.
Discourt'eous a. Uncivil, rude.
Beaut'eous a. Beautiful; endowed with beauty.
Du'teous a. Obedient, dutiful.
Lu'teous a. Brownish-yellow.
A'queous a. Watery; formed in or consisting of water.
Suba'queous a. Formed or being under water.
Terra'queous a. Consisting of land and water.
Niv'eous a. Snowy; resembling snow.
Uve'ous a. Resembling a grape; pertaining to the uvea.
Ru'fous a. Reddish; brownish-red.
-phagous suff. Denoting eating or devouring.
Poe'phagous a. Grass-eating; pertaining to the kangaroos.
Sarcoph'agous a. Feeding on flesh.
Mycoph'agous a. Given to eating fungi.
Creoph'agous a. Carnivorous.
Ostreoph'agous a. Feeding on oysters.
Lithoph'agous a. Eating or perforating stone (of molluscs).
Ophioph'agous a. Feeding on snakes.
Phylloph'agous a. Feeding on leaves.
Xyloph'agous a. Boring into wood (of insects).
Omoph'agous a. Eating raw flesh.
Ento-moph'agous a. Feeding on insects.
Zooph'agous a. Feeding on animals.
Anthropo-ph'agous a. Cannibal, man-eating.
Hippoph'agous a. Feeding on horse-flesh.
Carpoph'agous a. Fruit-eating.
Necroph'agous a. Feeding on carrion.
Androph'agous a. Cannibal.
Saproph'agous a. Living on decaying matter.
Coproph'agous a. Feeding on dung (as certain beetles).
Sauroph'agous a. Feeding on lizards, etc.

Scatoph'agous a. Feeding on dung.

Galacto-ph'agous a. Living on milk.

Phytoph'agous a. Subsisting on plants.

Ichthyo-ph'agous a. Subsisting on fish.

Rhizoph'agous a. Feeding on roots.

Polyph'agous a. Omnivorous; greedy; voracious.

Nucif'ragous a. Feeding on nuts.

Soliv'agous a. Wandering alone.

Noctiv'agous a. Wandering by night.

Stri'gous a. Covered with strigæ or bristles.

Al'gous a. Resembling or full of seaweed.

Wrong'ous a. (*Scot.*) Illegal.

Fun'gous a. Like fungi; spongy; unsubstantial; excrescent.

Anal'ogous a. Presenting some resemblance.

Homol'ogous a. Having the same relative position. proportion, import, structure, etc.

Heterol'ogous a. Consisting of different elements or non-corresponding parts.

Lucif'ugous a. Shunning the light.

Se'jugous a. Having six pairs of leaflets.

Quadriju'gous a. Having four pairs of leaflets.

Triju'gous a. Having three pairs of leaflets.

Ru'gous a. Corrugated, creased.

Steatop'ygous a. Having fat buttocks.

Az'ygous a. Not paired; occurring singly.

Dis'tichous a. Arranged in or having two rows (of leaves).

Monos'tichous a. Arranged in or consisting of a single layer.

Adel'phous a. Having the stamens in groups.

Diadel'phous a. Applied to flowers in which the stamens are united into two bundles.

Monadel'phous a. Having the filaments of the stamens united.

Pentadel'phous a. Having the stamens united in five sets.

Lymph'ous a. Resembling lymph.

Amor'phous a. Shapeless; unorganized; not conforming to rule.

Dimor'phous a. Having two forms.

Trimor'phous a. Characterized by trimorphism.

Pseudo-mor'phous a. Having a false form or shape.

Idiomor'phous a. Having its own proper shape, especially of crystals.

Ophio-mor'phous a. (*Ophiomorphic*).

Therio-mor'phous a. Having the form of an animal.

Mono-mor'phous a. (*Monomorphic*).

Anthropo-mor'phous a. Resembling man or mankind.

Hetero-mor'phous a. (*Heteromorphic*).

Pyromor'phous a. Crystallizing after fusion by heat.

Isomor'phous a. (*Isomorphic*).

Polymor'phous a. (*Polymorphic*).

Ty'phous a. Pertaining to or of the nature of typhus.

Catarrh'ous a. (*Catarrh*).

Scir'rhous a. Due to scirrhus; indurated.

Orthog'nathous a. Straight-jawed.

Hypog'nathous a. With the lower mandible longer than the upper.

Prog'nathous a. Having a projecting jaw.

Saurog'nathous a. Having a lizard-like palate (of birds).

Isogna'thous a. Having the jaws projecting equally.

Plectog'-nathous a. Having the cheek-bones united with the jaws (of certain fishes).

Monan'thous a. Bearing but one flower on each stalk.

Synan'thous a. Having flowers and leaves appearing together.

Helmin'thous a. Infested with intestinal worms.

-ious suff. Forming adjectives implying characterized by, full of, etc.

Sca'bious a. Affected with scabies; covered with scabs; a low plant with white, pink, or bluish flowers.

Amphib'ious a. Able to live both in water and on land; pertaining to land and water.

Du'bious a. Doubtful, not settled; wavering in opinion.

Biba'cious a. Given to tippling.

Effica'cious a. Effectual; producing the desired effect.

Ineffica'cious a. Producing no effect or result.

Perspica'cious a. Quick-sighted; keen.

Pervica'cious a. Very obstinate or perverse.

Proca'cious a. Pert, forward.

Eda'cious a. Greedy, ravenous.

Menda'cious a. Untruthful; false.

Morda'cious a. Biting; sarcastic; scathing.

Auda'cious a. Daring; impudent.

Saga'cious a. Discerning, shrewd, judicious.

Fuga'cious a. Fleeting, transitory.

Sala'cious a. Lewd, lustful.

Falla'cious a. Deceitful, misleading; sophistical.

Fuma'cious a. Addicted to smoking, or to tobacco.

Contuma'cious a. Opposing lawful authority; perverse, obstinate.

Tena'cious a. Unyielding; retentive; adhesive.

Pugna'cious a. Disposed to fight; quarrelsome.

Mina'cious a. Threatening.

Pertina'cious a. Obstinately adhering to any design, intent, etc.; stubborn.

Capa'cious a. Roomy, spacious.

Rapa'cious a. Greedy of plunder; subsisting on prey; voracious.

Spa'cious a. Roomy, capacious; extensive.

Fera'cious a. Fruitful, fertile.

Vera'cious a. Habitually truthful; characterized by truth.

Gra'cious a. Exhibiting grace; benignant, benevolent; bland.

Vora'cious a. Ready to devour; ravenous.

Sequa'cious a. Following; logically consistent; servile.

Loqua'cious a. Talkative; garrulous.

Viva'cious a. Lively, animated; tenacious of life.

Diœ'cious a. Having pistils and stamens on different plants, or the sexes in

Monœ'cious a. Having male and female organs on the same plant; hermaphrodite.

separate individuals.

Synœ'cious a. Having pistils and stamens in one flower.

Spe'cious a. Showy; apparently right; superficially fair; plausible.

Pre'cious a. Valuable; prized; over-refined.

Judi'cious a. Sagacious; prudent; discreet.

Injudi'cious a. Void of or done without judgment; unwise.

Offi'cious a. Meddling; intrusive; too forward in kindness.

Inoffi'cious a. Not attentive; inoperative; regardless of natural obligation.

Mali'cious a. Evil-disposed; spiteful; rancorous; full of malice.

Deli'cious a. Highly pleasing; charming.

Cili'cious a. Made of or consisting of hair.

Sili'cious a. (*Siliceous*).

Perni'cious a. Destroying or injuring; noxious; mischievous.

Auspi'cious a. Fortunate; propitious.

Inauspi'cious a. Unlucky, ill-starred; unfavourable.
Suspi'cious a. Inclined to suspect; raising suspicion; mistrustful.
Avari'cious a. Grasping, greedy; niggardly.
Lubri'cious a. Slippery; elusive; lascivious.
Capri'cious a. Governed by caprice; unsteady.
Meretri'cious a. Showily alluring; lewd.
Vi'cious a. Having vices; wicked; refractory.
Preco'cious a. Ripe before due time; prematurely forward.
Fero'cious a. Savage, rapacious, barbarous.
Atro'cious a. Extremely cruel or wicked; outrageous; flagrant.
Con'scious a. Knowing by sensation, perception, or in one's own mind; aware.
Subcon'scious a. Partially conscious.
Lus'cious a. Very sweet and delicious; cloying.
Vana'dious a. Vanadous.
Te'dious a. Wearisome; irksome; tardy.
Perfid'ious a. Treacherous; guilty of or involving perfidy; disloyal.
Ophid'ious a. Ophidian; snake-like.
Insid'ious a. Lying in wait; treacherous; sly.
Fastid'ious a. Squeamish, easily disgusted.
Invid'ious a. Tending to provoke envy or hatred; envious; offensive.
Compen'dious a. Concise but comprehensive; succinct.
O'dious a. Hateful; detestable; abominable.
Melo'dious a. Characterized by or producing melody; sweetly sounding.
Commo'dious a. Roomy; suitable.
Incom-mo'dious a. Not affording advantage; inconvenient; tending to incommode.
Stu'dious a. Given to study; diligent; careful.
Amba'gious a. Circumlocutory; ambiguous.
Conta'gious a. Communicable by contact; infectious, catching; pestilential.
Non-conta'gious a. (*Negative*).
Sacrileg'ious a. Violating sacred things.
Egre'gious a. Remarkable; eminently bad.
Prodig'ious a. Enormous; monstrous; portentous; extraordinary.
Relig'ious a. Pertaining to or imbued with religion; pious; bound by vows; used in worship. s. A monk or nun.
Irrelig'ious a. Not religious; impious; ungodly.
Litig'ious a. Inclined to litigation; quarrelsome; open to legal dispute.
Spong'ious (spŭnj'-) a. Spongy; having cavities like a sponge.
Acanthop-teryg'ious a. Pertaining to the perches and other spiny-finned fishes.
Stru'thious a. Pertaining or belonging to the ostrich family.
Contume'lious a. Insolent; abusive, contemptuous.
Bil'ious a. Affected by bile.
Atrabil'ious a. Affected by black bile; splenetic; melancholy.
Antibil'ious a. Counteracting biliousness.
Supercil'ious a. Disdainful, haughty, overbearing.
Punctil'ious a. Exact in forms of ceremony, etc.
Reptil'ious a. Resembling a reptile.
Rebel'lious a. Engaged in rebellion; mutinous; insubordinate.
Fo'lious a. Leafy; abounding in leaves.
Rotundi-fo'lious a. Having round leaves.
Nudifo'lious a. Having smooth leaves.
Latifo'lious a. Broad-leaved.
Centifo'lious a. Hundred-leaved.
Tenuifo'lious a. Having narrow leaves.
Abste'mious a. Temperate, sparing, especially in the use of drink.
Sim'ious a. Resembling the Simia, a genus of anthropoid apes.
Exim'ious a. Excellent, illustrious.
Sa'nious a. Resembling sanies.
Primoge'nious a. Primogenial.
Inge'nious a. Having ability or cleverness; apt in contriving; skilful.
Ruthe'nious a. Pertaining to or derived from ruthenium.
Sele'nious a. Of or containing selenium.
Ignomin'ious a. Shameful; infamous; dishonourable.
Calum'nious a. Containing or implying calumny.
Sympho'nious a. Agreeing in sound; harmonious.
Eupho'nious a. Agreeable in sound; euphonic.
Felo'nious a. Having the quality of a felony; villainous; malicious.
Ceremo'nious a. Consisting of or according to rites; precise, formal.
Acrimo'nious a. Bitter, severe, sarcastic.
Parsimo'nious a. Characterized by parsimony; niggardly; penurious.
Sanctimo'nious a. Making a show of piety.
Harmo'nious a. Musically concordant; with parts adapted; without dissension.
Inharmo'nious a. Unmusical.
Querimo'nious a. Complaining, querulous.
Impecu'nious a. Without money; hard up.
Pi'ous a. Filially dutiful; devout, reverent; holy.
Im'pious a. Irreverent, profane; destitute of piety.
Co'pious a. Large in quantity or amount, abundant, exuberant.
Car'ious a. Affected with caries.
Precar'ious a. Insecure; uncertain; dubious.
Vicar'ious a. Delegated; acting for or performed in place of another; pertaining to a substitute.
Calcar'ious a. (*Calcareous*).
Scar'ious a. Membranous and dry (of plants).
Nefar'ious a. Wicked in the extreme; infamous.
Quinque-far'ious a. Arranged in five parts or rows.
Omnifar'ious a. Of all varieties or forms.
Trifar'ious a. Arranged in three rows.
Multifar'ious a. Having great multiplicity or diversity; of various kinds.
Vagar'ious a. Wandering; whimsical, capricious.
Gregar'ious a. Living in herds or groups.
Malar'ious a. Producing or pertaining to or of the nature of malaria.
Burglar'ious a. Pertaining to burglars or burglary.
Hilar'ious a. Cheerful, merry.
Grossular'ious a. (*Grossulaceous*).
Quadri-genar'ious a. Consisting of four hundred.
Testudinar'ious a. Of the appearance of tortoise-shell.
Pollinar'ious a. Pollinar.
Uproar'ious a. Making an uproar; tumultuous.
Temerar'ious a. Reckless, headstrong.
Contrar'ious a. Inclined to oppose; perverse.
Acetar'ious a. Used in salads.
Var'ious a. Different, several; changeable.
E'brious a. Addicted to drink; drunk.
Oppro'brious a. Containing or consisting of opprobrium; abusive.
Lugu'brious a. Dismal; funereal.
Salu'brious a. Promoting health; healthy.
Insalu'brious a. Unhealthy.
Ciner'ious a. Ashen, ash-coloured.
Imper'ious a. Dictatorial, arrogant, tyrannical.
Ser'ious a. Sedate; earnest; important.

Deleter'ious a. Noxious, injurious.
Myster'ious a. Inexplicable, obscure, occult; fond of mystery.
Delir'ious a. Light-headed; raving; wildly excited.
Labor'ious a. Industrious; persevering in work; laboured; toilsome.
Glor'ious a. Full of glory; celebrated; grand, brilliant.
Inglor'ious a. Not bringing honour; disgraceful.
Vainglor'ious a. Boastful; characterized by vain-glory.
Censor'ious a. Expressing or given to censure.
Saltator'ious a. Saltatory; saltatorial.
Victor'ious a. Having conquered; triumphant; associated with victory.
Demeritor'ious a. (*Demerit*).
Meritor'ious a. Praiseworthy; having merit.
Inquisitor'-ious a. Inquisitorial.
Notor'ious a. Publicly known, conspicuous (especially in a bad sense).
Raptor'ious a. Raptorial.
Uxor'ious a. Foolishly fond of one's wife.
Indus'trious a. Diligent; characterized by industry.
Illus'trious a. Distinguished, famous; conferring glory.
Yt'trious a. Containing or derived from yttrium.
Cur'ious a. Inquisitive; addicted to research; strange, singular.
Incur'ious a. Not inquisitive; indifferent; commonplace.
Fur'ious a. Violent, impetuous; raging, vehement.
Strangur'ious a. Afflicted with or pertaining to strangury.
Injur'ious a. Harmful; causing injury; tending to injure.
Perjur'ious a. Guilty of perjury.
Penur'ious a. Showing penury or scarcity; avaricious; miserly; parsimonious.
Spur'ious a. Counterfeit; not legitimate.
Usur'ious a. Practising or pertaining to usury.
Luxur'ious a. Addicted to luxury; supplied with luxuries; voluptuous.
Cæs'ious a. Bluish or greenish grey.
Monoou'sious a. Having the same substance (of the Son and the Father).
Ostenta'tious a. Characterized by ostentation; showy.
Flirta'tious a. Characterized by flirting or coquetry.
Disputa'tious a. Inclined to dispute; disputative.
Vexa'tious a. Causing vexation; harassing.
Fac'tious a. Given to faction; promoting dissension; seditious.
Frac'tious a. Quarrelsome, peevish, cantankerous.
Infec'tious a. Capable of infecting; liable to be diffused.
Contradic'tious a. Cavilling, disputatious.
Compunc'tious a. Implying or feeling compunction.
Face'tious a. Witty, sportive, good-humoured.
Ambi'tious a. Aspiring.
Expedi'tious a. Prompt; alert; characterized by or possessed of expedition.
Sedi'tious a. Pertaining to, tending to excite, or resembling sedition; factious.
Flagi'tious a. Flagrant; highly criminal.
Gentili'tious a. Pertaining to a gens, tribe, or nation.
Propi'tious a. Favourable; ready to be merciful.
Nutri'tious a. Serving to nourish; efficient as food.
Innutri'tious a. Not nutritious or nourishing.
Facti'tious a. Artificial; unnatural; affected.
Ficti'tious a. Containing fiction; feigned; counterfeit.
Deleti'tious s. Such that it will stand erasures (of paper, etc.).
Repeti'tious a. Repeating; containing repetition.
Secreti'tious a. Produced by animal or vegetable secretion.
Adsciti'tious a. Taken as supplemental.
Subditi'tious a. Foisted in.
Suppositi'tious a. Substituted; spurious.
Accrementi'-tious a. Pertaining to growth by budding.
Recrementi'-tious a. Recremental.
Excrementi'-tious a. Pertaining to or containing excrement.
Adventi'tious a. Accidental; accessory.
Surrepti'tious a. Done, produced, or obtained by stealth; clandestine.
Ascripti'tious a. Additional; ascribed to.
Supersti'tious a. Pertaining to, evincing, or full of superstition.
Licen'tious a. Dissolute; wanton; profligate.
Conscien'tious a. Regulated by conscience; scrupulous.
Preten'tious a. Full of pretension; showy; making specious claims.
Senten'tious a. Axiomatic; short and energetic.
Conten'tious a. Quarrelsome; inclined to or characterized by contention.
Cap'tious a. Apt to cavil; fitted to perplex; petulant.
Decep'tious a. Deceitful.
Excep'tious a. Censorious; peevish.
Bump'tious a. Self-assertive; uppish.
Gump'tious a. Possessing common sense or shrewdness.
Scrump'tious a. Delicious; first-rate.
Golup'tious a. Delicious, lovely.
Tor'tious (-shus) a. Done wrongfully; injurious.
Rumbus'tious a. Turbulent, rampageous.
Cau'tious a. Heedful, wary.
Incau'tious a. Not cautious; indiscreet; unwary.
Obse'quious a. Submissively or servilely compliant; fawning.
Ob'vious a. Plain to the eye or understanding; evident.
De'vious a. Wandering; out of the way; erring.
Pre'vious a. Antecedent; prior.
Lasciv'ious a. Lewd; provoking lust.
Obliv'ious a. Forgetful; causing forgetfulness; abstracted.
Multiv'ious a. Having several ways; pointing in many directions.
En'vious a. Feeling, exhibiting, or dictated by envy.
Per'vious a. Allowing passage; permeable.
Imper'vious a. Impenetrable; not permitting passage.
Plu'vious a. Abounding in rain, pluvial.
An'xious a. Solicitous, concerned; mentally distressed.
Nox'ious a. Harmful; unwholesome; pernicious.
Obnox'ious a. Odious; offensive; unpopular.
Innox'ious a. Harmless, innocuous.
Scan'dalous a. Exciting reprobation; bringing shame; base; libellous.
Jeal'ous a. Suspicious of a rival; emulous.
Zeal'ous (zĕl'-) a. Full of zeal; fervent; eager.
Ceph'alous a. Having a head.
Aceph'alous a. Without a head, beginning, or superior.
Triceph'alous a. Three-headed.
Enceph'alous a. Having a distinct head (of certain molluscs).

Dolicoceph'alous a. Long-headed.
Ateleoceph'alous a. Having an imperfect skull.
Monoceph'alous a. Having a single head (especially of flowers).
Autoceph'alous a. Having an independent chief.
Anom'alous a. Deviating from the usual; not according to rule.
Sep'alous a. Having sepals.
Trisep'alous a. Having three sepals.
Monosep'alous a. Having only one sepal.
Pet'alous a. Having petals.
Apet'alous a. Having no petals.
Pentapet'alous a. Having five petals.
Dipet'alous a. Having two petals.
Planipet'alous a. Having flat petals.
Gamopet'alous a. Having the petals united.
Monopet'alous a. Having a single petal, or the corolla in one piece.
Polypet'alous a. Having separate or many petals.
Troubl'ous a. Full of trouble, agitated; troublesome.
Cau'telous a. Tricky, treacherous.
-philous suff. Having a fondness for; loving.
Helioph'ilous a. Attracted by sunlight.
Anemoph'ilous a. Applied to plants that are fertilized by wind-borne pollen.
Entomoph'ilous a. Attractive to insects.
Syph'ilous a. Syphilitic.
Pi'lous a. Abounding with or consisting of hair.
Per'ilous a. Full of or involving peril; dangerous.
Scur'rilous a. Using low, abusive, or indecent language; foul-mouthed.
Cal'lous a. Hard-hearted, obdurate.
Thal'lous a. Applied to compounds of thallium.
Cerebel'lous a. (*Cerebellar*).
Li'bellous a. Containing a libel; defamatory.
Can'cellous a. Reticulated, cross-barred.
Mar'vellous a. Exciting wonder or surprise.
Morbil'lous a. Pertaining to or resembling measles.
Vill'ous a. Furnished with villi; covered with silky hairs (of plants); downy.
Aphyl'lous a. Destitute of leaves.
Decaph'yllous a. Having ten leaves in the perianth.
Enneaph'yllous a. Having nine leaflets (of compound leaves).
Tetraphyl'lous a. Having four leaves.
Heptaph'yllous a. Having seven leaves or sepals.
Hexaphyl'lous a. Having six leaves or sepals.
Diphyl'lous a. Having two leaves or sepals.
Epiphyl'lous s. Growing upon a leaf, or on the perianth.
Quadriphyl'lous a. Having four leaves.
Triphyl'lous a. Three-leaved.
Endoph'yllous a. Denoting leaves evolved from a sheath.
Gamophyl'lous a. Having the leaves united.
Microphyl'lous a. Having small leaves.
Heterophyl'lous a. Having different leaves on the same plant.
Polyphyl'lous a. Having many leaves.
Tridac'tylous a. Having three fingers or toes.
Amphib'olous a. Doubtful; ambiguous.
Radicic'olous a. Infesting roots.
Spongic'olous (spŭnj'-) a. Inhabiting sponges.
Stagnic'olous a. Inhabiting stagnant water.
Terric'olous a. Living on or in the earth.
Saxic'olous a. Living or growing among rocks.
Lute'olous a. Slightly yellow.
Vari'olous a. Pertaining to, due to, or designating smallpox.
Friv'olous a. Of little worth; trivial; given to trifling, silly.
Par'lous a. Difficult, perilous; critical.
Fab'ulous a. Related to fable; fictitious; extravagant.
Sab'ulous a. Sandy, gritty.
Neb'ulous a. Cloudy; vague; indistinct; pertaining to or resembling nebulæ.
Bib'ulous a. Addicted to tippling.
Noctam'bulous a. Sleep-walking.
Tu'bulous a. Tubular, composed of tubuliform florets.
Mirac'ulous a. Wonderful; performed supernaturally.
Orac'ulous a. Oracular.
Floc'culous a. Flocculose.
Pedic'ulous a. Lousy; full of lice.
Ridic'ulous a. Fitted to excite ridicule; droll; ludicrous.
Follic'ulous a. Abounding in or producing follicles.
Vermic'ulous a. Vermiculose.
Ventric'ulous a Ventricular.
Metic'ulous a. Over-scrupulous; pedantically careful about details.
Cal'culous a. Affected with or resembling a calculus.
Loc'ulous a. Locular.
Monoc'ulous a. Monocular.
Tuber'culous a. Tubercular.
Flos'culous a. Floscular.
Cred'ulous a. Disposed to believe without much evidence, unsuspicious.
Incred'ulous a. Indisposed to believe; sceptical.
Sed'ulous a. Assiduous; steadily industrious.
Acid'ulous a. Slightly sour or acid.
Rigid'ulous a. Rather stiff (of plants).
Strid'ulous a. Making a small, grating noise, as crickets, etc.
Gland'ulous a. Glandular.
Pen'dulous a. Hanging, swinging; loosely pendent.
Un'dulous a. Undulating; undulatory.
Nod'ulous a. Nodulated.
Scrof'ulous a. Affected with or pertaining to scrofula.
Solidun'gulous a. Having hoofs that are not cloven.
Or'gulous a. Proud, haughty.
Cell'ulous a. Consisting of cells.
Ram'ulous a. Ramulose.
Em'ulous a. Ambitiously desirous of equalling or excelling another; envious; contentious.
Trem'ulous a. Shaking, quivering; irresolute.
Cu'mulous a. Pertaining to or resembling a cumulus.
Gran'ulous a. Granular.
Crap'ulous a. Crapulent.
Pop'ulous a. Containing many inhabitants in proportion to area.
Scru'pulous a. Cautious, punctilious; very conscientious.
Unscru'pulous a. Regardless of principle; having no scruples.
Scaber'ulous a. Somewhat scabrous (of plants).
Quer'ulous a. Habitually complaining; whining.
Tor'ulous a. Torulose.
Gar'rulous s. Loquacious; tiresomely talkative.
Pat'ulous a. Spreading; branching; expanded.
Eden'tulous a. Edentate.
Tor'tulous a. Bulging at intervals like knotted rope.
Fis'tulous a. Fistular.
Pus'tulous a. Full of or covered with pus.
Chyl'ous a. (*Chyle*).
Sym'phylous a. Of the same race (in entomology).

Didac'tylous a. Having only two fingers, toes, or claws.
Monodac'tylous a. Having but one finger or toe.
Sys'tylous a. Having the styles united (of plants).
Fa'mous a. Celebrated, renowned; remarkable, excellent.
In'famous a. Having an evil reputation; notoriously vile.
Big'amous a. Pertaining to bigamy.
Dig'amous a. Pertaining to a second marriage.
Trig'amous a. Married three times; having three spouses at once.
Endog'amous a. Marrying only within the tribe.
Dichog'amous a. Applied to flowers having pistils and stamens maturing at different times.
Homog'amous a. Having all the florets hermaphrodite, or the stamens and pistils ripe at the same time.
Monog'amous a. Monogamic.
Oog'amous a. Reproducing through union of male and female cells.
Phanerog'amous a. Phanerogamic.
Heterog'amous a. Having flowers or florets sexually different; alternating by generations in method of reproduction.
Isog'amous a. Characterized by isogamy.
Cryptog'amous a. (*Cryptogamia; cryptogamy*).
Cleistog'amous a. (*Cleistogamic*).
Exog'amous a. Pertaining to exogamy.
Polyg'amous a. Pertaining to polygamy; having a plurality of wives; polygamian.
Ha'mous a. Having hooks; hamose.
Didyn'amous a. Applied to plants having four stamens.
Bal'samous a. (*Balsam*).
Squa'mous a. Covered with scales; scale-like.
Blas'phemous a. Impiously irreverent; given to profanity.
Longan'imous a. Characterized by longanimity; patient.
Pusillan'imous a. Mean-spirited; cowardly; timid.
Magnan'imous a. Elevated in soul or sentiment; noble-minded; brave.
Unan'imous a. Being of one mind; agreeing; formed with or indicating unanimity.
Ri'mous a. Full of cracks (of tree-bark).
Si'mous a. Having a flat nose.
Gum'mous a. Like gum.
Floric'omous a. Having the head adorned with flowers.
Ven'omous a. Full of venom; poisonous; noxious, malignant.
Heteron'omous a. Subject to the rule of another; diverging from type.
Auton'omous a. Self-governing.
Anad'romous a. Applied to fishes that ascend rivers to spawn.
Catad'romous a. Returning to the sea to breed (of eels, etc.).
Homod'romous a. Turning or moving in the same direction.
Polychro'mous a. Polychromatic.
Diat'omous a. Having crystals with one diagonal cleavage.
Tetrachot'omous a. Separated into four branches, etc.
Dichot'omous a. Regularly dividing by pairs (*botany*).
Hylot'omous a. Wood-cutting (of insects).
As'tomous a. Having no mouth.
Diather'mous a. Diathermanous.
Asper'mous a. Seedless.
Tetrasper'mous a. Having four seeds.
Heptasper'mous a. Having seven seeds.
Trisper'mous a. Three-seeded.
Angiosper'mous a. Having the seeds enclosed in a pericarp.
Gymnosper'mous a. Pertaining to the gymnosperms.
Enor'mous a. Huge, immense; excessive; flagitious.
Mias'mous a. Miasmatic; miasmatous.
Fu'mous a. Producing or full of fumes; vaporous.
Hu'mous a. Pertaining to or containing humus.
Post'humous a. Born after death of the father; published after author's death; continuing after one's decease.
Glu'mous a. Having glumes.
Spu'mous a. Consisting of foam; frothy.
Bru'mous a. Wintry, foggy.
Gru'mous a. Clotted, thick, viscid.
Stru'mous a. Scrofulous; having strumæ or swellings.
Cy'mous a. Cymose.
Did'ymous a. Twin; growing in pairs.
Chym'ous a. (*Chyme*).
Paren'chymous a. (*Parenchymal*).
On'ymous a. Bearing a name; not anonymous.
Pseudon'ymous a. Bearing or using an assumed name.
Homon'ymous a. Having different significations or applications; ambiguous.
Anon'ymous a. Nameless; without the real name.
Synon'ymous a. Having the same meaning.
Epon'ymous a. Furnishing an eponym; named thus.
Paron'ymous a. Having the same derivation, or a similar sound but different spelling and meaning.
Heteron'ymous a. Characterized by heteronymy.
Polyon'ymous a. Having several names.
Az'ymous a. Unleavened.
Nous s. Mind, intellect; intelligence.
Diaph'anous a. Transparent; pellucid.
Hydroph'anous a. Becoming translucent or brighter when put under water.
Porell'anous a. Of the nature of porcelain.
Bim'anous a. Two-handed.
Pedim'anous a. Having feet shaped like hands (of lemurs, etc.).
Ather'manous a. Impervious to heat rays.
Diather'manous a. Having the property of transmitting radiant heat.
Quadru'manous a. Four-handed; of the monkey family.
Mem'branous a. Pertaining to, consisting of, or like membrane.
Ur'anous a. Pertaining to or containing uranium.
Ti'tanous a. Containing or resembling titanium.
Lar'cenous a. Like or committing larceny; thievish.
Molyb'denous a. Molybdous.
Syncotyle'denous a. Having the cotyledons united.
Monocotyle'denous a. Having a single cotyledon.
Polycotyle'denous a. A plant whose seeds have more than two cotyledons.
Bur'denous a. Burdensome.
-genous suff. Indicating born, bearing, or producing.
Viridig'enous a. Imparting greenness.
Indig'enous a. Native; not exotic.
Kalig'enous a. Forming alkalis.
Corallig'enous a. Producing coral.
Germig'enous a. Producing germs.
Omnig'enous a. Consisting of all kinds.
Epig'enous a. Growing upon the surface (of fungi, etc.).

Terrig'enous a. Produced by or derived from the earth.
Gelatig'enous a. Producing gelatine.
Endog'enous a. Developing or growing internally.
Trichog'enous a. Promoting the growth of the hair.
Pathog'enous a. (*Pathogenetic*).
Lithog'enous a. Stone producing; forming coral.
Halog'enous a. Pertaining to or consisting of halogens.
Thallog'enous a. Pertaining to or like a thallogen.
Homog'enous a. Homogenetic.
Monog'enous a. Pertaining to monogenesis.
Carpog'enous a. Producing fruit.
Acrog'enous a. (*Acrogen*).
Hydrog'enous a. Pertaining to or containing hydrogen.
Nitrog'enous a. Pertaining to or containing nitrogen.
Pyrog'enous a. Produced by fire; igneous.
Autog'enous a. Self-produced; independent.
Exog'enous a. Growing by successive additions beneath the bark (of trees).
Polyg'enous a. Having many varieties.
Oxyg'enous a. Oxygenic.
Li'chenous a. Pertaining to lichens.
Prole-gom'enous a. Introductory.
Gang'renous a. Pertaining to, affected by, or due to gangrene.
Ve'nous a. Pertaining to or contained in the veins.
Rav'enous a. Furiously rapacious; voracious; famished.
Spag'nous a. Pertaining to or resembling the peat-mosses.
Porcelain'ous a. Pertaining to or resembling porcelain.
Vill'ainous a. Suited to or like a villain; depraved; base; mean.
Moun'tainous a. Full of mountains; huge.
Hir'cinous a. Smelling like a goat.
Muce'dinous a. Mouldy; like mildew.
Libid'inous a. Having lustful desires; characterized by lewdness.
Ten'dinous s. Full of or pertaining to tendons.
Palu'dinous a. Pertaining to marshes; malarial.
Vicissi-tu'dinous a. Characterized by vicissitudes.
Latitu'dinous a. Having latitude, especially of thought, etc.
Platitu'dinous a. Given to talking in platitudes.
Multitu'dinous a. Very numerous; manifold.
Fortitu'dinous a. Marked by fortitude; courageous.
Hein'ous a. Atrocious, flagrant, abominable.
Lumba'ginous a. Pertaining to or affected with lumbago.
Plumbag'inous a. Containing, consisting of, or resembling plumbago.
Oleag'inous a. Oily, unctuous; fawning.
Mucilag'inous a. Pertaining to, resembling, or secreting mucilage.
Cartilag'inous a. Of or resembling cartilage.
Virag'inous a. Like or pertaining to a virago.
Farra'ginous a. Like or pertaining to a farrago; confused.
Rubig'inous a. Rusty in colour.
Ulig'inous a. Oozy, slimy.
Fulig'inous a. Sooty, smoky; gloomy.
Serpig'inous a. Like or pertaining to serpigo.
Porrig'inous a. Affected with porrigo.
Prurig'inous a. Pertaining or tending to prurigo.
Impetig'inous a. Pertaining to or affected by impetigo.
Lentig'inous a. Freckly; scurfy.
Vertig'inous a. Whirling; liable to or affected with giddiness.
Vortig'inous a. Vortical, whirling.
Aeru'ginous a. Resembling or pertaining to verdigris.
Ferru'ginous a. Containing particles of iron or iron-rust; resembling iron-rust.
Di'clinous a. With stamens and pistils on separate flowers.
Inquili'nous a. Denoting insects that live in the nests, etc., of others.
Foram'inous a. Having foramina; porous.
Tergem'inous a. Forking with three pairs of leaflets.
Crim'inous a. Guilty of a crime, criminal.
Om'inous a. Foreboding evil; inauspicious.
Abdom'inous a. (*Abdomen*).
Conter'minous a. Having the same limits; conterminate.
Ver'minous a. Tending to breed, infested by, or due to vermin.
Albu'minous a. (*Albumen*).
Legu'minous a. Producing legumes.
Lu'minous a. Emitting light; bright; lucid.
Volu'minous a. Being in many volumes; bulky; copious.
Ceru'minous a. (*Cerumen*).
Bitu'minous a. (*Bitumen*).
Spi'nous a. Spine-shaped, thorn-like; spinose.
Fi'brinous a. Composed of or like fibrin.
Cit'rinous a. Lemon-like in taste or colour.
Ur'inous a. Partaking of the qualities of urine.
Res'inous a. Resembling, obtained from, or pertaining to resin.
Gelat'inous a. Of the nature and consistence of gelatine; gelatinoid; viscous.
Plat'inous a. Pertaining to or containing platinum.
Cre'tinous a. Afflicted with cretinism.
Serot'inous a. Appearing late in season.
Velu'tinous a. Velvety.
Glu'tinous a. Viscous, tenacious; like glue.
Mu'tinous a. Disposed to mutiny; turbulent.
Exsang'uinous a. Destitute of or having only poor blood.
Ru'inous a. Bringing, tending to bring to, or characterized by ruin; composed of ruins; dilapidated; pernicious.
Vi'nous a. Pertaining to or like wine.
Cov'inous a. Fraudulent, collusive.
Tyr'annous a. Arbitrary, tyrannical, unjustly severe.
Stan'nous a. Pertaining to tin.
Concin'nous a. Harmonious, elegant.
Cotyle'donous a. Possessing or pertaining to cotyledons.
Acoty-le'donous a. (*Acotyledon*).
Dicoty-le'donous a. Having two cotyledons.
Trig'onous a. Trigonal, triangular.
Heterog'onous a. Characterized by heterogony.
Cacoph'onous a. Discordant, harsh sounding.
Homoph'onous a. Homophonic; of the same sound.
Polyph'onous a. Polyphonic.
Autoch'-thonous a. Belonging to the soil; native; aboriginal.
Syn'chronous a. Simultaneous; happening at the same time.
Asyn'chronous a. Without coincidence in time.
Isoch'ronous a. Taking equal time; moving or vibrating equally.
Unis'onous a. Being in unison.
Poi'sonous a. Having the qualities of poison; deadly; corrupting.
Horris'onous a. Having a terrifying sound.
Multis'onous a. Having many sounds.
Con'sonous a Agreeing in sound, harmonious.
Homot'onous a. Of the same tone; equable.
Monot'onous a. Uttered in an unvarying tone; wanting variety; tedious.
Glut'tonous a. Given to excessive eating or to gluttony.
Sempiter'nous a. Everlasting; endless.

Cav'ernous a. Huge and hollow; full of caverns.
Unicor'nous a. One-horned.
Quadricor'nous a. Having four horns or antennæ.
Burnous' s. An Arab cloak.
Albur'nous a. Pertaining to alburnum.
-gynous suff. Pertaining to women; having female organs (of plants).
Enneag'ynous a. Having nine pistils.
Pentag'ynous a. Denoting a plant with five pistils.
Heptag'ynous a. Having seven pistils.
Hexag'ynous a. Having six styles (of plants).
Epig'ynous a. Growing on the top of the ovary (of stamens, etc.).
Tri'gynous a. Having three pistils.
Philog'ynous a. Fond of women.
Monog'ynous a. Having but one pistil; mating with one female only.
Androg'ynous a. Hermaphrodite.
Proterog'ynous a. Having the pistil mature before the stamens.
Octog'ynous a. Having eight pistils.
Polyg'ynous a. Having many styles or stigmas.
Xanthoc'roous a. Xanthocroic.
Pul'pous a. Consisting of or resembling pulp.
Pom'pous a. Displaying pomp; affectedly dignified or serious.
Catawam'pous a. (*Catawampus*).
Orthot'ropous a. Growing straight.
Isot'ropous a. Isotropic.
Heterot'opous a. Characterized by heterotopy.
Pap'pous a. Downy.
Acar'pous a. Sterile; producing no fruit.
Syncar'pous a. Composed of several carpels consolidated into one.
Sychnocar'pous a. Perennial.
Monocar'pous a. Bearing fruit but once and then dying.
Apocar'pous a. Having the carpels distinct.
Autocar'pous a. Consisting of pericarp only.
Rhizocar'pous a. Having a perennial root but annual stem.
Lu'pous a. Pertaining to or affected with lupus.
Pol'ypous a. Like a polyp or polypus; affected with polypi.
Orthot'ypous a. Having a straight cleavage (of minerals).
Bar'barous a. Uncivilized, uncouth; rude; cruel.
Sac'charous a. Saccharine; pertaining to sugar.
-parous suff. Producing; bringing forth.
Mucip'arous a. Secreting mucus.
Nymphip'arous a. Producing chrysalises.
Primip'arous a. Producing young for the first time.
Gemmip'arous a. Producing buds; propagating by gemmation.
Omnip'arous a. Producing all things.
Unip'arous a. Normally producing one at a birth; having one stem or axis.
Plurip'arous a. Bringing forth more than one at a birth.
Dorsip'arous a. Dorsiferous.
Fissip'arous a. Reproducing by spontaneous fission.
Multip'arous a. Producing many at a birth.
Vivip'arous a. Producing young in a living state.
Ovovivip'arous a. Producing young by ova hatched within the body.
Ovip'arous a. Producing young by eggs hatched outside the body.
Larvip'arous a. Producing larvæ.
Nec'tarous a. Sweet as nectar.
Sca'brous a. Rough, rugged; awkward to handle.
Gla'brous a. Smooth; bald.
Ten'ebrous a. Dark; gloomy.
Fi'brous a. Having or consisting of fibres.
Som'brous a. Gloomy, sombre.
Cum'brous a. Vexatious; bulky, heavy; giving trouble.
Lu'dicrous a. Laughable; droll; ridiculous.
Chan'crous a. (*Chancre*).
Polyhe'drous a. Having many sides.
Decan'drous a. Having ten stamens.
Dian'drous a. Denoting plants the flowers of which have only two stamens.
Anan'drous a. Not having stamens.
Monan'drous a. Having only one stamen.
Gynan'drous a. Having the stamens and pistils united.
Proteran'drous a. Having the stamens mature before the pistil.
Tetran'drous a. Having four stamens.
Pentan'drous a. Pentandrian.
Heptan'drous a. Having seven stamens.
Hexan'drous a. Having six stamens.
Polyan'drous a. Practising or pertaining to polyandry.
Won'drous (wun'-) a. Marvellous; prodigious; admirable. adv. Wonderfully.
Hy'drous a. Containing water; watery.
Anhy'drous a. Destitute of water (especially of crystallization).
Slum'berous a. Inviting slumber; drowsy.
Tu'berous a. Having wart-like prominences; like, containing, or consisting of tubers.
Ul'cerous a. Like or affected with ulcers.
Can'cerous a. (*Cancer*).
Glan'derous a. Pertaining to or resembling glanders.
Slan'derous a. Containing or disposed to slander.
Pon'derous a. Very heavy; forcible; important.
Thun'derous a. Thundery.
Foun'derous a. Failing; liable to sink; puzzling.
Mur'derous a. Pertaining to, guilty of, or meditating murder; savage, bloodthirsty.
-ferous suff. Denoting bearing, producing, or having.
Bulbif'erous a. Bearing bulbs.
Limbif'erous a. Having a border or margin.
Corymbif'erous a. Bearing corymbs.
Herbif'erous a. Producing vegetation.
Morbif'erous a. Causing disease.
Nubif'erous a. Bringing clouds.
Baccif'erous a. Bearing berries.
Coc'ciferous a. Bearing berries.
Succif'erous a. Producing or conveying sap.
Thecif'erous (-sif'-) a. Having thecæ.
Silicif'erous a. Producing or containing silica.
Laticif'erous a. Conveying or producing latex.
Corticif'erous a. Bearing bark or rind.
Calcif'erous a. Producing lime.
Zincif'erous (-sif'-) a. Yielding zinc.
Uncif'erous a. Furnished with hooks (of leaves, etc.).
Vocif'erous a. Clamorous; making a loud outcry.
Furcif'erous a. Having forked appendages (as certain butterflies).
Lucif'erous a. Giving light; affording means of discovery.
Mucif'erous a. Secreting or promoting the secretion of mucous.
Nucif'erous a. Producing nuts.
Crucif'erous a. Bearing a cross; belonging to the order Cruciferæ.
Calycif'erous a. Bearing a calyx.
Soredif'erous a. Bearing or producing soredia.
Proboscidif'erous a. Having a proboscis.
Glandif'erous a. Bearing acorns or similar fruit.
Diamondif'erous a. Yielding diamonds.
Frondif'erous a. Producing fronds.

Geodif'erous a. Containing geodes.
Oleif'erous a. Oil-bearing.
Sporangif'erous a. Bearing sporangia.
Tergif'erous a. Bearing on the back (of ferns and seed).
Branchif'erous a. Furnished with gills.
Conchif'erous a. Shell-bearing.
Lethif'erous a. Deadly; bringing destruction.
Conidiif'erous a. Bearing conidia.
Mammalif'erous a. Containing fossilized remains of mammals.
Salif'erous a. Producing salt.
Chelif'erous a. (*Chelate*).
Nickelif'erous a. Containing nickel.
Umbilif'erous a. Having a navel.
Strobilif'erous a. Producing strobiles.
Pilif'erous a. Having hairs.
Fossilif'erous a. Containing fossils.
Reptilif'erous a. Containing fossil reptiles.
Corallif'erous a. Coral-bearing.
Metallif'erous a. Yielding or producing metals.
Umbellif'erous a. Producing or bearing umbels.
Cellif'erous a. Having cells.
Mellif'erous a. Yielding or producing honey.
Lamellif'erous a. Bearing or composed of lamellæ.
Clitellif'erous a. (*Clitellum*).
Stellif'erous a. Abounding with stars.
Argillif'erous a. Yielding clay.
Papillif'erous a. Bearing or producing papillæ.
Folif'erous a. Bearing leaves.
Prolif'erous a. Producing buds from leaves, etc., or new individuals from parts.
Petrolif'erous a. Yielding petrol.
Caulif'erous a. Having a stalk.
Tentaculif'erous a. Armed with or producing tentacles.
Spiculif'erous a. Bearing or producing spicules.
Vesiculif'erous a. Producing bladders.
Unguiculif'erous a. Having nails, claws, or hoofs.
Operculif'erous a. Operculate.
Cellulif'erous a. Having cells.
Ramulif'erous a. Bearing small branches.
Gemmulif'erous a. Producing or propagating by gemmæ.
Granulif'erous a. Bearing or full of granules.
Spinulif'erous a. Bearing spinules.
Cupulif'erous a. Bearing cupules.
Sporulif'erous a. Bearing or producing sporules.
Chylif'erous a. (*Chyle*).
Balsamif'erous a. Producing balsam.
Squamif'erous a. Having scales.
Cadmif'erous a. Producing cadmium.
Racemif'erous a. Bearing racemes.
Palmif'erous a. Bearing palms.
Culmif'erous a. Bearing culm; abounding in anthracite.
Mammif'erous a. Having breasts; mammalian.
Gemmif'erous a. Producing gems; producing or propagating by buds.
Gummif'erous a. Producing gum.
Pomif'erous a. Bearing fruit or apples.
Fumif'erous a. Producing fumes.
Glumif'erous a. Having glumes.
Lanif'erous a. Bearing wool.
Granif'erous a. Grain-producing.
Titanif'erous a. Yielding titanium.
Guanif'erous a. Producing guano.
Selenif'erous a. Containing selenium.
Ignif'erous a. Producing fire.
Lignif'erous a. Yielding or producing wood.
Pollinif'erous a. Producing or adapted for carrying pollen.
Laminif'erous a. Bearing or having laminæ.
Foraminif'erous a. Producing or containing foraminifera; having many holes or chambers.
Staminif'erous a. Bearing stamens.
Seminif'erous a. Producing seed; conveying semen.
Luminif'erous a. Yielding light.
Bituminif'erous a. Producing bitumen.
Spinif'erous a. Bearing or producing spines.
Urinif'erous a. Producing urine.
Resinif'erous a. Yielding resin.
Platinif'erous a. Producing or containing platinum.
Omnif'erous a. Producing all kinds.
Somnif'erous a. Inducing sleep; soporific.
Mannif'erous a. Yielding manna.
Tannif'erous a. Yielding tannic acid.
Stannif'erous a. Bearing or producing tin.
Pennif'erous a. Bearing or producing feathers.
Antennif'erous a. Furnished with antennæ.
Carbonif'erous a. Producing coal; applied to coal-bearing strata.
Conif'erous a. Bearing cones (of the pines, firs, etc.).
Stolonif'erous a. Putting forth stolons.
Sonif'erous a. Producing or carrying sound.
Ozonif'erous a. Producing ozone.
Cornif'erous a. Containing hornstone.
Prunif'erous a. Bearing plums.
Scapif'erous a. Having a scape (of plants).
Saccharif'erous a. Producing sugar.
Nectarif'erous a. Producing or yielding nectar.
Umbrif'erous a. Giving shade; shady.
Tuberif'erous a. Bearing tubers.
Cerif'erous a. Producing wax.
Hederif'erous a. Bearing ivy.
Antherif'erous a. Having anthers.
Odorif'erous a. Diffusing fragrance; odorant.
Sudorif'erous a. Secreting or producing perspiration.
Florif'erous a. Bearing flowers.
Porif'erous a. Having pores.
Vaporif'erous a. Producing or giving off vapour.
Soporif'erous a. Soporific; narcotic.
Cuprif'erous a. Copper-bearing.
Ferrif'erous a. Yielding iron.
Cirrif'erous a. Producing tendrils.
Nitrif'erous a. Containing or yielding nitre.
Rostrif'erous a. Having a beak; adorned with beaks.
Yttrif'erous a. Yielding yttrium.
Aurif'erous a. Gold-bearing.
Thurif'erous a. Producing frankincense.
Tellurif'erous a. Containing tellurium.
Gypsif'erous a. Producing gypsum.
Dorsif'erous a. Applied to ferns having the seeds at the back of the fronds.
Ossif'erous a. Yielding bones.
Byssif'erous a. Producing a byssus (of molluscs, fungi, etc.).
Stigmatif'erous a. Bearing stigmas.
Stomatif'erous a. Having stomata.
Lactif'erous a. Secreting or conveying milk.
Fructif'erous a. Bearing fruit.
Setif'erous a. Bearing or producing bristles.
Pyritif'erous a. Containing pyrites.
Gultif'erous a. Yielding resin or sap.
Diamantif'erous a. Yielding diamonds.
Argentif'erous a. Producing silver.
Septif'erous a. Bearing septa.
Pestif'erous a. Pestilential; noxious; infectious; vexatious.
Sanguif'erous a. Conveying blood.
Aquif'erous a. Conveying or yielding water.
Valvif'erous a. Having valves.
Ovif'erous a. Egg-bearing.
-gerous suff. Bearing, having.
Prolig'erous a. Producing young; proliferous.
Surculig'erous a. Producing suckers.
Squamig'erous a. Bearing scales.
Armig'erous a. Entitled to bear heraldic arms.
Lanig'erous a. Bearing wool.
Spinig'erous a. Spiniferous.

Pennig'erous a. Having feathers, feathered.
Cornig'erous a. Bearing horns.
Cirrig'erous a. Having tendrils or fringes.
Elytrig'erous a. Furnished with elytra.
Setig'erous a. Covered with bristles.
Lentig'erous a. Having a crystalline lens.
Clavig'erous a. Bearing a club.
Ovig'erous a. Carrying eggs.
Larvig'erous a. Producing larvæ.
Dan'gerous a. Attended with or causing danger.
Treach'erous a. Guilty of or involving treachery; traitorous, faithless; deceptive.
Lech'erous a. Lustful; addicted to lewdness.
Synan'therous a. Having the anthers growing together.
Cank'erous a. Of the nature of canker; corroding.
Cantank'erous a. Quarrelsome, captious, ill-natured.
Scle'rous a. Hardened; indurated.
Tetram'erous a. Consisting of four parts.
Pentam'erous a. Composed of five parts; having five joints.
Heptam'erous a. Having or consisting of seven parts.
Ephem'erous a. Ephemeral.
Dim'erous a. Having two parts; in pairs (of plants and insects).
Tri'merous a. Having three parts.
Heterom'erous a. Differing in composition or character of parts.
Nu'merous a. Consisting of many; rhythmical.
Polym'erous a. Consisting of many parts.
Gen'erous a. Liberal, munificent; magnanimous.
Multigen'erous a. Having many kinds.
Congen'erous a. Congeneric; concurring in the same action (as muscles).
On'erous a. Burdensome; oppressive.
Obstrep'erous a. Loud; noisy; turbulent.
Vi'perous a. Viperish; venomous, malignant.
Pros'perous a. Thriving, successful; flourishing.
Ser'ous a. Resembling or pertaining to serum, watery.
Slaugh'terous (slaw'-) a. Murderous; destructive.
Adul'terous a. Pertaining to or guilty of adultery.
Ap'terous a. Wingless.
Tetrap'terous a. Having four wings.
Dip'terous a. Two-winged; belonging to the Diptera.
Hemip'terous a. Pertaining to the Hemiptera.
Perip'terous a. Feathered on all sides.
Lepidop'terous a. Pertaining to the Lepidoptera.
Coleop'terous a. (*Coleoptera*).
Orthop'terous a. Belonging to the Orthoptera.
Hymenop'-terous a. Hymenopteral.
Monop'terous a. One-winged (of certain seeds).
Macrop'terous a. Long-winged.
Microp'terous a. Having small wings or feet.
Heterop'terous a. Having wings of dissimilar parts; pertaining to the Heteroptera.
Cheirop'terous a. (*Cheiroptera*).
Isop'terous a. Having the wings equal.
Bois'terous a. Stormy; tumultuous; intractable.
Prepos'terous a. Irrational, absurd, utterly foolish.
Blus'terous a. Blustering; boisterous.
Cadav'erous a. Corpse-like, pale and ghastly looking.
Papav'erous a. Resembling the poppy.
Pul'verous a. Powdery.
Podag'rous a. Gouty; pertaining to gout.
Vinai'grous (-nā'-) a. Sour, acid; crabbed.
O'chrous a. Ochreous.
Anarth'rous a. Without joints.
Desir'ous a. Wishful; eager; full of desire.
Vir'ous a. Poisonous; emitting a fetid odour.
Chiv'alrous a. Pertaining to chivalry; gallant, noble.
Ar'borous a. Pertaining to or formed by trees.
Decor'ous a. Seemly, decent, becoming; behaving with propriety.
Indecor'ous a. Unseemly; unbecoming.
Ran'corous a. Full of rancour; malevolent.
Ni'dorous a. Like the smell of roast meat.
O'dorous a. Having or emitting an odour; fragrant.
Ino'dorous a. Having no scent.
Rig'orous a. Severe; precise; relentless.
Vig'orous a. Possessing vigour; exhibiting strength; forceful.
Ful'gorous a. Dazzlingly bright.
Clan'gorous a. (*Clangor*).
I'chorous a. Composed of or like ichor.
-phorous suff. Denoting bearing.
Phylloph'orous a. Leaf-bearing.
Pyroph'orous a. Igniting spontaneously; light producing.
Galactoph'-orous a. Producing milk.
Phos'phorous a. Pertaining to, resembling, or derived from phosphorus.
Val'orous a. Brave; valiant.
Radiciflor'ous a. Flowering from the root.
Calyciflor'ous a. With the petals and stamens growing on the calyx.
Uniflor'ous a. Bearing only one flower.
Triflor'ous a. Bearing three flowers.
Noctiflor'ous a. Flowering at night.
Multiflor'ous a. Having many flowers.
Chlor'ous a. Pertaining to or combined with chlorine.
Dol'orous a. Full of or occasioning grief; painful; distressing.
Am'orous a. Inclined to or relating to love; besotted.
Clam'orous a. Noisy, turbulent.
Glam'orous a. Full of glamour.
Tim'orous a. Fearful; timid.
Hu'morous a. Full of humour, exciting laughter; jocose; whimsical.
Ru'morous a. Pertaining to or like a rumour.
Canor'ous a. Melodious, resonant.
Sonor'ous a. Resonant; impressive; sounding rich or full.
Por'ous a. Full of pores; spongy.
Va'porous a. Full of or proceeding from vapours; flatulent; unsubstantial.
Sop'orous a. Causing sleep; sleepy.
Gymnospor'ous a. Having naked spores.
Polypor'ous a. Having many pores.
Trai'torous a. Guilty of treason; treacherous, faithless.
Ster'torous a. Characterized by deep snoring; hoarsely breathing.
Lan'guorous a. Characterized by langour.
-vorous suff. Feeding on the substance indicated.
Fla'vorous a. Pleasing to taste or smell.
Herbiv'orous a. Feeding upon vegetation.
Bacciv'orous a. Living or berries.
Succiv'orous a. Subsisting on sap.
Radiciv'orous a. Subsisting on roots.
Pisciv'orous a. Subsisting on fish.
Fuciv'orous a. Feeding on seaweeds.
Muciv'orous a. Feeding on the juices of plants.
Nuciv'orous a. Feeding on nuts.
Fungiv'orous a. Feeding on fungi.
Frugiv'orous a. Feeding on fruit.
Reptiliv'orous a. Eating reptiles.
Melliv'orous a. Honey-eating.
Vermiv'orous a. Subsisting on worms.
Raniv'orous a. Subsisting on frogs.
Graniv'orous a. Feeding on grain.
Ligniv'orous a. Wood-eating.

Graminiv'orous a. Subsisting on grass, etc.
Omniv'orous a. Devouring everything indiscriminately.
Carniv'orous a. Flesh-eating; insectivorous.
Ossiv'orous a. Feeding on bones.
Insectiv'orous a. Subsisting on insects.
Sanguiv'orous a. Subsisting on blood.
Lep'rous a. Infected with leprosy.
Squar'rous a. Squarrose.
Fer'rous a. Pertaining to or containing iron in its lowest combining power.
Cir'rous a. (*Cirrus*).
Susur'rous a. Susurrant.
Idol'atrous a. Given to idolatry.
Ophiol'atrous a. Given to serpent-worship.
Bibliol'atrous a. Given to excessive admiration of books.
Heliol'atrous a. Addicted to sun-worship.
Zool'atrous a. Given to the worship of animals.
Pet'rous a. Hard as stone; stony.
Saltpet'rous a. Pertaining to or like saltpetre.
Ni'trous a. Obtained from or resembling nitre.
Goi'trous a. Affected with or pertaining to goitre.
Disas'trous a. Attended with disaster; calamitous, grievous.
Œs'trous a. Œstrual.
Sin'istrous a. Pertaining or inclined to the left; ill-omened.
Mon'strous a. Unnatural; huge; shocking; outrageous; incredible.
Impos'trous a. Pertaining to or characterized by imposture.
Latiros'trous a. Latirostral.
Lus'trous a. Full of lustre; shining.
Dex'trous a. Ready and skilful with the hands; quick mentally; done with dexterity.
Ambidex'trous a. Able to use both hands equally well.
Au'rous a. Pertaining to gold.
Mercur'ous a. Containing mercury.
Ver'durous a. Covered with verdure.
Fur'furous a. Producing or like scurf.
Sul'phurous a. Pertaining to sulphur; containing sulphur in its lowest valency.
Tell'urous a. Containing or resembling tellurium.
Mur'murous a. Attended with murmurs.
Anour'ous a. Tailless.
Vul'turous a. Like a vulture; rapacious.
Ven'turous a. Venturesome.
Adven'turous a. Prone to incur risk; daring; full of hazard.
Rap'turous a. Ecstatic; ravishing.
Tor'turous a. Pertaining to or involving torture.
Mos'chatous a. Musky.
Erysipel'atous a. Pertaining to or characteristic of erysipelas.
Œde'matous a. Characterized by or affected with œdema; swollen with fluid.
Myxœde'matous a. Characterized by or afflicted with myxœdema.
Erythe'matous a. Pertaining to erythema.
Monotre'matous a. Pertaining to or like the Monotremata.
Emphyse'matous a. (*Emphysema*).
Eczem'atous a. Characterized or caused by eczema.
Sarco'matous a. Pertaining to or resembling sarcoma.
Glauco'matous a. Pertaining to or affected with glaucoma.
Carcino'matous a. (*Carcinoma*).
Myceto'matous a. Afflicted with or like mycetoma.
Astom'atous a. Mouthless.
Cyclostom'atous a. Having a circular suctorial mouth (of the lampreys, etc.).
Polystom'atous a. Having many mouths.
Autom'atous a. Acting spontaneously.
Rhizo'matous a. Resembling a rhizome.
Echinoder'matous a. Echinoderm.
Scleroderm'atous a. Having a hard integument o skeletal tissue.
Pachyderm'atous a. Pertaining to a pachyderm thick-skinned.
Mias'matous a. Miasmal; malarious.
Collenchym'atous a. (*Collenchyma*).
Parenchy'matous a. Pertaining to or consisting c parenchyma.
Sclerenchy'matous a. Pertaining to or consisting o sclerenchyma.
A'cetous a. Like vinegar; causing acetifica tion.
Disqui'etous a. Causing uneasiness or anxiety.
Cov'etous a. Eagerly desirous; avaricious.
Felic'itous a. Happy; appropriate; well applied.
Infelic'itous a. Unfortunate; unhappy.
Solic'itous a. Eager to obtain; anxious t avoid; careful.
Hal'itous a. Like or produced by breath vaporous.
Calam'itous a. Disastrous; of the nature of calamity.
Precip'itous a. Very steep; headlong, sudden.
Spir'itous a. Like spirit; refined; ardent.
Pyr'itous a. Pyritic.
Necess'itous a. Destitute; being in want or need
Rat'itous a. Pertaining to the family of bird including the ostriches, emus, etc
Circu'itous a. Indirect.
Ubiq'uitous a. Existing everywhere or in a places.
Iniq'uitous a. Characterized by iniquity criminal.
Fatu'itous a. Characterized by fatuity.
Gratu'itous a. Voluntary; free; without mo tive; uncalled for.
Pitu'itous a. Consisting of or pertaining t mucus.
Fortu'itous a. Happening by chance; casual.
Accliv'itous a. Sloping steeply upwards.
Decliv'itous a. (*Declivity*).
Procliv'itous a. Steep, abrupt.
Co'baltous a. (*Cobalt*).
Ligamen'tous a. Pertaining to, forming, or forme of a ligament.
Velamen'tous a. Pertaining to or resembling velamen.
Filamen'tous a. Filamentary; bearing filaments.
Momen'tous a. Of weighty consequence.
Tomen'tous a. Tomentose.
Sarmen'tous a. Sarmentose.
Porten'tous a. Serving to presage; foreshadow ing ill.
Ri'otous a. Involving or engaging in riot seditious; wanton.
Cham'pertous a. (*Champerty*).
Tung'stous a. Pertaining to or resemblin tungsten.
Schist'ous a. Schistose.
Cys'tous a. Containing or resembling cysts.
Vac'uous a. Void; expressionless; inane.
Transpic'uous a. Transparent.
Conspic'uous a. Obvious to the eye, manifest illustrious.
Inconspic'uous a. Not readily discernible; un obtrusive.
Perspic'uous a. Clear to the understanding.
Noc'uous a. Hurtful, noxious.
Innoc'uous a. Harmless; safe.
Promis'cuous a. Indiscriminate; confused; miscellaneous.
Decid'uous a. Not evergreen; falling off; shed

Indecid'uous a. Evergreen.
Assid'uous a. Diligent.
Vid'uous a. Widowed; vidual.
Ar'duous a. Difficult, laborious.
Ambig'uous a. Susceptible of more than one meaning; equivocal, obscure.
Irrig'uous a. Well-watered; serving to irrigate.
Contig'uous a. In contact, near.
Exig'uous a. Small, scanty.
Mellif'luous a. Flowing sweetly or smoothly.
Sanguif'luous a. Running with blood.
Circum'fluous a. Circumfluent.
Super'fluous a. More than is necessary; redundant.
Ingen'uous a. Candid, frank, artless.
Disingen'uous a. Not noble, mean.
Stren'uous a. Energetic; ardent, earnest.
Ten'uous a. Thin; minute; rarefied.
Sin'uous a. Bending; crooked; curving in and out.
Contin'uous a. Joined together closely; without break; extended.
Discontin'uous a. Not continuous.
Sil'iquous a. Bearing, pertaining to, or resembling siliquas.
Somnil'oquous a. Apt to talk in sleep.
Ventril'oquous a. Speaking ventriloquially.
Con'gruous a. Suitable, appropriate; consistent.
Incon'gruous a. Inconsistent, inappropriate, not suitable.
Mens'truous a. Pertaining to the menses.
Sen'suous a. Pertaining to, addressing, or derived from the senses; readily affected.
Insen'suous a. Not sensuous.
Fat'uous a. Stupid, foolish, meaningless.
Anfrac'tuous a. Winding, tortuous.
Unc'tuous a. Oily, greasy; full of assumed fervour.
Fruc'tuous a. Fruitful, fertile.
Infruc'tuous a. Not fruitful; unprofitable.
Impet'uous a. Violent, passionate; rushing with great force.
Spir'ituous a. Consisting of or containing distilled spirit.
Tumul'tuous a. Full of tumult; disorderly.
Contemp'tuous a. Expressive of contempt; scornful.
Sump'tuous a. Involving great expense; magnificent.
Presump'tuous a. Full of or characterized by presumption; taking undue liberties.
Volup'tuous a. Full of pleasure; luxurious; ministering to, exciting, or addicted to, sensuality.
Vir'tuous a. Characterized by virtue; chaste.
Tor'tuous a. Twisting, crooked; not straightforward.
Inces'tuous a. Guilty of or involving incest.
Tempes'tuous a. Characterized by tempests; very stormy.
Flex'uous a. Full of turns or windings; bending; having alternating curves.
Saxica'vous a. Rock-boring.
Conca'vous a. (*Concave*).
Næ'vous a. Nævose.
Ren'dezvous (-voo) s. Place agreed upon for meeting; a resort. v.i. To meet or assemble at a set place.
Longe'vous a. Long-lived.
Mis'chievous a. Making mischief; hurtful; destructive; noxious.
Griev'ous a. Causing grief or pain; oppressive; atrocious.
Decli'vous a. Sloping downward.
Procli'vous a. Sloping forward (of teeth).
Ful'vous a. Tawny, fox-coloured.
Ner'vous a. Pertaining to or affecting the nerves; possessing nerves; sinewy, strong; having the nerves easily affected; timid.
Recur'vous a. Bent or curved backward.
Joy'ous a. Joyful; causing joy.
Noy'ous a. Vexatious, annoying.
Epirhi'zous a. Growing on a root.
Polyrhi'zous a. Having many roots.
Pus s. Matter produced by suppuration.
Pal'pus s. A palp.
Hippocam'pus s. The sea-horse; one of two convolutions in the brain.
Gram'pus s. A large marine mammal.
Rum'pus s. A disturbance, uproar.
Catawam'pus s. A very fierce beast; vermin.
O'pus s. A work; a musical composition.
Lago'pus s. The genus of birds including the ptarmigan.
Mo'pus s. (*Slang*) Any small coin.
Pter'opus s. Genus comprising the flying-foxes.
Pithecanthro'pus s. The supposed connecting-link between man and the apes.
Oc'topus s. An eight-armed cephalopod mollusc; the cuttle-fish.
Pap'pus s. The downy tuft of the dandelion and other plants; the first appearance of beard.
Protohip'pus s. An extinct, horse-like quadruped.
Car'pus s. The wrist.
Metacar'pus s. Part of hand between wrist and fingers.
Cor'pus s. A body or collection of anything, especially of writings by one author or on one subject.
Lu'pus s. A tuberculous skin-disease.
Gaw'pus s. A simpleton, ninny.
Pol'ypus s. A tumour in one of the mucous cavities; a polyp.
Plat'ypus s. The ornithorhynchus, an egg-laying mammal.
Ac'arus s. A genus of ticks and mites.
Scar'us s. The parrot-fish.
Tar'tarus s. The infernal regions of the ancient Greeks.
Var'us s. A variety of club-foot; knock-knee; acne.
Cer'berus s. The three-headed dog guarding the entrance to Hades; a fierce, vigilant guardian.
Hu'merus s. The long bone of the upper arm.
Hes'perus s. The evening star.
Ic'terus s. Jaundice; a genus of birds including the orioles.
U'terus s. The womb.
Vir'us s. Poisonous matter; the special contagion of a disease; extreme acrimony.
Wal'rus (wawl'-) s. A marine carnivorous mammal of the Arctic.
Chor'us s. A body of singers; a part-song; a refrain; the speaker of a prologue or epilogue. v.t. and i. To sing or utter simultaneously.
Caneph'orus s. (*sing.*) (*Canephori*).
Electroph'orus s. Instrument for transforming mechanical into electro-static energy by induction.
Pyroph'orus s. A substance taking fire on exposure to the air.
Phos'phorus s. A non-metallic, inflammable, poisonous element.
Pylor'us s. Orifice in stomach through which food passes to duodenum.
Sor'us s. A cluster, as of spore-cases; a patch on fern-fronds.
Tor'us s. Semicircular moulding at column base; receptacle of the axis of a flower; a rounded protuberance.
Cir'rus s. A tendril, filament, barbule; a wispy cloud.

Cit'rus s. A genus of trees containing the orange, lemon, etc.
Œs'trus s. Œstrum.
Ur'us s. The extinct wild ox.
Thesaur'us s. A lexicon, comprehensive volume.
Plesiosaur'us s. A large extinct marine reptile.
Megalosaur'us s. (*Megalosaur*).
Ichthyosaur'us s. An extinct gigantic marine reptile.
Tau'rus s. The second zodiacal constellation, and sign of the Zodiac.
Eu'rus s. The east wind.
Dolichur'us s. A verse having an extra foot.
Arctur'us s. The Dog-star.
Gyr'us s. A convolution of the brain.
Papyr'us s. An Egyptian reed from which was anciently made a material for writing upon; a MS. on this.
Peg'asus s. The winged horse of Bellerophon; poetic inspiration.
Aboma'sus s. The fourth stomach of a ruminant.
Pet'asus s. The winged hat of Mercury.
Rhe'sus s. A greyish-brown Indian macaque.
Crœ'sus s. A very rich man.
Ni'sus s. A striving; an effort.
Cen'sus s. An official enumeration of the people, and other statistical information, of a country.
Consen'sus s. Agreement, unanimity.
Prolap'sus s. A slipping out of place of an organ or part.
Tar'sus s. The bones of the foot; a bird's shank.
Metatar'sus s. Part of foot between ankle and toes.
Ver'sus prep. Against.
Excur'sus s. A dissertation by way of addendum.
Thyr'sus (ther'-) s. The ivy-wreathed wand of Bacchus.
Parnas'sus s. Mountain in Greece sacred to Apollo and the Muses; poetry, literature.
Narcis'sus s. A genus of bulbous flowering plants; the daffodil, jonquil, etc.
Mis'sus s. Missis; (*slang*) one's wife.
Colos'sus s. A gigantic statue, especially that of Apollo anciently at Rhodes; a dominating personality.
Moloss'us s. A metrical foot of three longs.
Bys'sus s. The tuft by which certain molluscs anchor themselves; a thread-like stipe on some fungi.
Mea'tus s. A duct or passage of the body.
Hia'tus s. An opening, gap, lacuna.
Fla'tus s. Wind in the stomach; flatulence.
Affla'tus s. Inspiration.
Infla'tus s. A breathing into; inspiration.
Sena'tus s. Governing body of a University.
Appara'tus s. Things provided as means to some end; device, appliance.
Salera'tus s. A baking-powder made from bicarbonate of potash or soda.
Stra'tus s. A horizontal layer of cloud.
Cu'mulo-stra'tus s. Cumulous clouds with a stratified appearance.
Cirrostra'tus s. A low, horizontal sheet of cloud in fleecy masses.
Sta'tus s. Rank, condition; relative standing; legal position.
Cac'tus s. A spiny plant.
Delec'tus s. A book of passages for translation, especially from Latin.
Conspec'tus s. A general survey; a synopsis.
Prospec'tus s. Plan, scheme; descriptive proposal.
Rec'tus s. Name of various muscles.
Ic'tus s. The rhythmical accent in metre; beat of the pulse.
Benedic'tus s. The Hymn of Zacharias used as a canticle.
Ric'tus s. Gape, expanse of mouth.
Sanc'tus s. The hymn, "Holy! Holy! Holy!"
Quie'tus s. Final acquittance; death.
Bole'tus s. A genus of fungi.
Pine'tus s. A plantation of pine-trees.
Fœ'tus s. The young of an animal in the womb or egg when distinctly formed.
Im'petus s. Force applied to anything motion.
Vagi'tus s. First cry of an infant.
Hal'itus s. An exhalation.
Frem'itus s. Vibration; pathological murmur.
Porphyro-gen'itus a. Born in the purple, especially of Byzantine princes.
Emer'itus a. Of a professor, etc., who has served his time of office.
Detri'tus s. Debris, gravel, deposits by attrition.
Pruri'tus s. Itching.
Sal'tus s. A sudden break in continuity.
Tin'tus s. Ringing in the ears.
Lo'tus s. The Egyptian water-lily; a plant whose fruit was fabled to cause forgetfulness.
Gymno'tus s. The S. American electric eel.
Eucalyp'tus s. A genus of Australian trees; an antiseptic oil prepared from these.
Ces'tus s. A girdle, marriage zone, the girdle of Venus; a weighted boxing-glove.
Cis'tus s. The rock-rose.
Trismegis'tus a. Thrice great.
Xys'tus s. A portico in ancient Greece; a garden-walk.
Arbu'tus s. An evergreen shrub.
Car'duus s. A thistle.
Ig'nis-fat'uus s. A flitting light on marshes; will-o'-the-wisp.
Fa'vus s. A disease of the scalp.
Nœ'vus s. A congenital blemish, birth-mark.
Cor'vus s. The genus of birds including the raven, rook, jackdaw and crow.
Plex'us s. Any network of nerves, vessels, etc.; an intricate combination.
Complex'us s. A muscle in the neck.
Nex'us s. A bond, link, close connexion.
Amphiox'us s. A small marine fish; the lancelet.
Haws s. Inflammatory disease in a horse's eyelid.
Taws s. (*Scot.*) A leather thong or thongs used for punishment.
Yaws s. Frambœsia, a contagious tropical disease.
Flews s. The drooping, hanging chaps of a large hound.
Mews s. A range of stables.
News s. Recent intelligence; tidings.
Trews s. (*Scot.*) Tartan trousers.
Gal'lows s. An erection for hanging criminals.
Bel'lows s. An instrument for supplying air or wind to fires, musical instruments, etc.
Now'adays adv. In these times. s. The present time.
Stays s. A corset.
Ways s. Timbers from which a ship is launched.
-ways suff. Forming adverbs of direction, manner, etc.
Broad'ways adv. In the direction of breadth.
End'ways adv. On end; end to end; end foremost.
Side'ways adv. Sidewise.
Edge'ways adv. With the edge turned up or forward.
Long'ways adv. By way of the length; lengthwise.

Length'ways adv. In the direction of the length.
Al'ways adv. Ever; at all times.
Slant'ways adv. Slantly.
Least'ways adv. At least; or rather.
Hendi'adys s. Figure by which one idea is presented by two words or phrases.
Ich'thys s. The early Christian fish-like symbol for Christ.
Flys s. Gallery over theatre proscenium where curtains, etc., are controlled.
Chlam'ys s. A Greek cloak; a plant's floral envelope.
Em'ys s. The freshwater tortoise.
Lag'omys s. A genus of small rodents allied to the hares.
Pter'omys s. Genus comprising the flying squirrels.
Erin'nys s. One of the three furies of ancient Greek myth.
Lam'boys s. Steel skirt of Tudor period armour.
At prep.
Bat s. A club, especially one used to strike a ball in certain games; a flying mammal; (*slang*) a good fast pace. v.i. To play or strike with a bat.
Brick'bat s. A piece of a brick.
Com'bat v.i. To fight, strive. v.t. To oppose, contend against. s. A fight, struggle, contest.
Wom'bat s. A small Australian marsupial.
Ac'robat s. A tumbler, rope-dancer, gymnastic performer.
Cat s. Any member of the species *Felis* (lion, tiger, etc.), especially the domestic cat; a flogging implement, cat-o'-nine-tails. v.i. (*Slang*) To vomit.
Pole'cat s. A carnivore allied to the weasel.
Magnif'icat s. The song of the Virgin (Luke i. 46–55).
Pull'icat s. A kind of silk handkerchief.
Hell'-cat s. A witch.
Scat s. A brisk shower.
Requies'cat s. A prayer for the repose of the dead.
Mus'cat s. Muscadel.
Kit'cat s. A size of portrait (28×36 in.); tip-cat.
Duc'at s. An old coin of Italy and Europe generally.
Concor'dat s. An agreement on ecclesiastical matters between the pope and a secular authority.
Eat v.t. To chew and swallow; to consume; to corrode. v.i. To take food; to corrode.
Beat v.t. To strike repeatedly; to overcome, crush, surpass. v.i. To throb; to sail against the wind. s. A stroke; a pulsation; the regular round of a policeman, etc.
Dead'-beat a. Thoroughly exhausted, worn-out.
Brow'beat v.t. To bully.
Feat s. An achievement, performance, exploit.
Defeat' v.t. To frustrate, foil, overthrow, conquer. s. An overthrow; loss of battle.
Or'geat s. A drink made from barley and sweet almonds.
Heat s. Warmth; hot weather; degree of temperature; ardour; course at a race. v.t. and i. To make or grow hot; to warm with passion, etc.
Cheat v.t. To deceive and defraud, to trick. s. A deception, imposture; one who cheats.
Escheat' v.i. To be forfeited by failure of heirs. s. Reversion of lands through extinction of heirs; lands reverting thus.
Reheat' v.t. To heat again.
Wheat s. An annual cereal plant; its grain.
Buck'wheat s. A plant the seeds of which are ground for meal.
Leat s. Artificial water-course for a mill.
Bleat v.i. To cry as a sheep; to whine. s. This cry.
Cleat s. A piece of wood or iron to fasten ropes upon; a wedge.
Pleat s. A crease; one of a series of folds. v.t. To fold in creases.
Meat s. The flesh of quadrupeds as food; food in general.
Force'meat s. Seasoning for stuffing.
Neat a. Trim, tidy; smart; without addition of water. s. Bovine cattle.
Peat s. A kind of turf used as fuel.
Repeat' v.t. To utter or do again; to recapitulate; to imitate. v.i. To recur, happen again; to be tasted a second time.
Hereat' adv. At or by reason of this.
Thereat' adv.
Whereat' adv.
Great a. Large in bulk or number; important; weighty; sublime.
Threat s. A menace; denunciation.
Treat v.t. To negotiate, handle, act towards; to discourse on, entertain. s. An entertainment, something affording pleasure.
Retreat' v.i. To withdraw, retire from an enemy, etc. s. Act of retiring; place to which one retires; seclusion; an asylum, refuge.
Maltreat' v.t. To ill-treat, abuse.
Entreat' v.t. and i. To beseech, pray, make entreaties.
Estreat' s. A duplicate of a document levying a fine. v.t. To levy under an estreat.
Seat s. Place or thing on which one sits, a chair, bench; a residence, site, station; a right to sit, a constituency; way of sitting. v.t. To place on a seat, to settle; to assign seats to; to fix; to repair with a new seat.
Unseat' v.t. To remove from or deprive of a seat (especially in an elected assembly).
Teat s. A nipple, pap, dug.
Cav'eat s. Legal process to stop proceedings.
Sweat v.i. To perspire; to toil. v.t. To exude; to employ at lowest possible wages. s. Perspiration; state of or moisture resembling this; toil, drudgery.
Ex'eat s. A written leave of absence.
Fat a. Full-fed; plump, flesh; coarse, gross; rich, fertile. s. The unctuous part of animal flesh; the best or richest part of anything. v.t. To make fat.
Gat s. A narrow passage between sandbanks, cliffs, etc.
Nou'gat (-ga) s. A sweet almond-flavoured confection.
Hat s. A covering for the head.
Chat v.i. To talk lightly and easily. s. Light, familiar talk; a bird of the warbler family; (*slang*) a louse.
Entrechat' s. A step in dancing.

Whin'chat s. A small bird allied to the wheatear.
Cush'at s. The wood-pigeon or ring-dove.
That a., pron., adv., and conj.
What (hwot) pron., interrog. and rel.; a., adv., interrog.
Some'what adv. Rather; to some extent. s. Something; more or less.
Fi'at s. A peremptory decree or order.
U'niat s. A member of an Oriental Church acknowledging the supremacy of the Pope.
Lar'iat s. A picketing rope; a lasso. v.t. To secure or catch with this.
Commissar'iat s. The department of an army that attends to provisioning, etc.
Proletar'iat s. The lowest class of the community; the wage-earners.
Skat s. A game like piquet.
Éclat' s. Conspicuous success, social distinction.
Flat a. Level; lying prostrate; below the true pitch (*mus.*); dull, insipid. s. An extended plain; a shallow; a flat note, the mark indicating lowering of pitch; a floor of a house; a dupe, fool. v.t. To flatten.
Tal'lat s. A hay-loft.
Plat s. A small plot of ground. v.t. To plait.
Slat s. A thin narrow strip for Venetian blinds, bedsteads, etc.; a sharp blow. v.t. To slap, beat.
Mat s. Article or fabric of interwoven rushes, etc.; a lustreless surface. v.i. To grow thickly together, to become entangled. v.t. To dull.
Dip'lomat s. One engaged in diplomacy; a tactful person.
For'mat s. External appearance and make-up of a book.
Gnat s. A small two-winged fly.
Assignat' s. Paper money of the French Revolution.
Oat s. A cereal plant; its grain used for food.
Boat s. A small open vessel, usually propelled by oars. v.i. To go in a boat.
Gun'boat s. A small, heavily armed warship.
Coat s. A man's upper outer sleeved garment; external covering of a beast; a layer over another; an armorial shield. v.t. To cover with a coat or layer.
Red'coat s. A British soldier.
Pet'ticoat s. A woman's under-skirt. a. Feminine, female.
Turn'coat s. A renegade, apostate.
O'vercoat s. A greatcoat.
Sur'coat s. A short outer coat.
Waist'coat (wes'kut) s. Short sleeveless garment worn under the coat.
Goat s. A long-haired ruminant quadruped with horns.
Scape'goat s. One bearing the blame of others.
Bloat v.t. and i. To grow or make coarse and turgid; to cure by salting and smoking.
Float v.i. and t. To rest or cause to rest on the surface of a fluid; to set afloat. s. Anything that floats; a raft, cork on a fishing-line; a ball-cock; a plasterer's trowel; a dray for heavy goods.
Afloat' adv., a. Floating; on the water.
Refloat' v.t. and i. To float again after submersion, etc.
Gloat v.i. To stare at with admiration, avarice, malignity, etc.
Moat s. Ditch round a castle, etc.
Groat s. A fourpenny piece.
Throat s. Fore part of neck; the gullet.
White'throat s. A small bird of the warbler family.
Troat s. Cry of a rutting buck.
Stoat s. The ermine; a weasel.
Pat v.t. To strike lightly, tap. s. A light, quick blow; a flat lump, especially of butter. a. Fit, convenient, exactly suitable. adv. seasonably, fitly.
Pit'apat adv. In a flutter, excitedly.
Spat s. Spawn of oysters and other shell-fish; a cloth gaiter for foot and ankle. v.t. and i. To spawn. past (*Spit*).
Rat s. A small rodent larger than the mouse; one who deserts his party; a blackleg. v.i. To hunt rats; to desert one's party; to work for less than trade-union rates.
Car'at s. A weight used for precious stones; applied to denote the fineness of gold.
Nac'arat s. A pale red colour.
Bac'carat s. A gambling game played with cards.
Brat s. (*Contemptuously*) A child.
-crat suff. Denoting a partisan, member, or supporter.
Gynæ'cocrat s. A female ruler.
The'ocrat s. One ruling in a theocracy.
Phys'iocrat s. A supporter of physiocracy.
Och'locrat s. A partisan of ochlocracy.
Dem'ocrat s. One in favour of democracy or republicanism.
Panti'socrat s. A member of and believer in the pantisocracy.
Ar'istocrat s. A patrician, a member of a privileged order; one favouring rule by an aristocracy.
Au'tocrat s. An absolute ruler.
Plu'tocrat s. One possessing power due to riches.
Bu'reaucrat s. A government official.
Drat int. Confound! bother!
Quad'rat s. Piece of type-metal for leaving blanks in printing.
Dan'diprat s. A little fellow, a whipper-snapper.
Sprat s. A small food-fish of the herring family.
Jur'at s. A person under oath.
Surat' s. A coarse cotton cloth.
Sat past and past part. (*Sit*).
Tat v.t. and i. To make by tatting.
Hab'itat s. Natural abode of locality of an animal or plant.
Ægro'tat s. Leave of absence for reasons of health.
Rhe'ostat s. Contrivance for regulating an electric current.
He'liostat s. A mirror moved by clockwork reflecting the sun's rays to a fixed point.
Ther'mostat s. Automatic apparatus for regulating temperature.
Hy'drostat s. Apparatus for detecting the presence of water, or for preventing explosion of boilers.
A'erostat s. A balloon, airship, flying-machine.
Si'derostat s. An astronomical instrument used with the telescope.
Lo'quat s. The Japanese plum.
Squat v.i. To sit upon one's heels; to settle on land without right. a. Short, dumpy.
Vat s. A large vessel for liquors. v.t. To place, make, or treat in a vat.
Cravat' s. A man's neckcloth.

Vi'vat (vē'-) int. Long live !
Debt s. That which is owed to another; obligation.
Doubt v.i. To be in uncertainty, to waver, hesitate; to fear. v.t. To hesitate to believe; to suspect, feel apprehensive. s. Uncertainty, suspicion; a wavering in opinion.
Redoubt' s. A detached, enclosed outwork in fortification.
Act v.i. To exert power, be in action, carry out duties, etc., produce an effect, behave. v.t. To perform, especially on the stage; to feign. s. Anything done or doing, process of this; a decree, law; a main division of a play.
Redact' v.t. To prepare for publication.
React' v.i. To act in return or reciprocally. v.t. To perform afresh.
Fact s. A thing done, deed; action; reality, truth.
Enact' v.t. To establish by law, decree.
Re-enact' v.t. To enact again.
Coact' v.t. To compel, control.
Retroact' v.i. To act backward, in return, or in opposition.
Pact s. An agreement, league, covenant.
E'pact s. The moon's age at the beginning of the year; excess of the solar beyond the lunar year.
Im'pact s. A forcible blow; collision.
Impact' v.t. To drive firmly or closely together.
Compact' a. Closely united; solid, dense; concise. v.t. To consolidate, unite firmly.
Com'pact s. An agreement, contract.
Cat'aract s. A waterfall, downpour; an opacity of the eye.
Bract s. A small leaf below a calyx; a thin scale of metal.
Interact' v.t. To act upon each other. s. An interlude.
Counteract' v.t. To act in opposition; to defeat, frustrate; to neutralize.
Overact' v.t. and i. To act to excess or more than is necessary.
Refract' v.t. To turn aside rays of light; to bend back sharply.
Diffract' v.t. To break into parts.
Cat'aphract s. The scaly armour of certain animals.
Tract s. An extent of land; a period; a pamphlet.
Subtract' v.t. To deduct, take away from.
Detract' v.t. To take something away from; to slander.
Retract' v.t. To draw back; to recall; to disown, recant. v.i. To take back what has been said.
Tet'ract a. Having four branches. s. A four-rayed sponge spicule.
Con'tract s. Agreement, bond; document containing such.
Contract' v.t. To cause to shrink, reduce to less compass; to be liable to, make a bargain; to betroth. v.i. To shrink up, to make a mutual agreement.
Precontract' v.t. To make a contract in advance.
Precon'tract s. A contract made beforehand.
Protract' v.t. To lengthen, draw out, continue.
Ab'stract s. A summary, abridgment. a. Not concrete, general; existing in the mind only.
Abstract' v.t. To take away; to steal; to separate and consider by itself; to make an epitome.
Distract' v.t. To perplex; to turn the attention from; to divert; to render insane or crazy.
Attract' v.t. To draw to; to allure, entice.
Extract' v.t. To draw out; to select; to copy out; to find the root of a number.
Ex'tract s. That which is drawn out or selected; a passage from a book, etc.; abstract; essence.
Transact' v.t. To do, perform, manage.
Tact s. Nice perception; adroitness.
Intact' a. Entire; unimpaired.
Con'tact a. A touching, close union of bodies.
Exact' a. Methodical, accurate, strict. v.t. To demand of right; to extort.
Inexact' a. Not precisely correct or true.
Pan'dect s. A treatise containing the whole of any science.
Defect' s. Imperfection; failure; blemish.
Refect' v.t. To refresh with food.
Pre'fect s. A governor in ancient Rome, modern France, etc.; a school monitor.
Affect' v.t. To act upon, move the feelings of; to pretend; to aim at.
Disaffect' v.t. To fill with discontent; to disorder.
Effect' s. That which is done; result; aim, purpose; efficacy; fulfilment; something intended to produce an impression; impression produced. v.t. To bring about, accomplish, produce as a result.
Infect' v.t. To taint with disease or bad qualities; to corrupt.
Disinfect' v.t. To cleanse or preserve from infection.
Per'fect a. Complete; having all that is requisite; faultless; expressing completed action (of verbs). v.t. To accomplish; to make perfect; to make skilful.
Imper'fect a. Not complete; defective. s. Tense expressing uncompleted action or state.
Pluper'fect a. Denoting that tense which expresses that the action was finished at the time mentioned.
Traject' v.t. To transmit.
Traj'ect s. A ferry.
Ab'ject a. Mean, despicable.
Object' v.t. and i. To urge against, oppose, offer as an objection.
Ob'ject s. Visible or tangible thing; motive; purpose; word or clause governed by a trans. verb or preposition.
Sub'ject s. One owing allegiance; theme; nominative of a verb; the thinking agent. a. Ruled by another.
Subject' v.t. To make subordinate; to make liable; to cause to undergo.
Eject' v.t. To throw out, expel, cast forth.
Deject' v.t. To cast down, depress, afflict.
Reject' v.t. To throw away, discard; to decline, repel.
Inject' v.t. To throw or put in or into.
Munject' s. An Indian vegetable dye used in place of madder.
Project' v.i. To shoot forward; to jut out. v.t. To cast forward; to scheme, devise; to delineate.
Proj'ect s. That projected or designed; a plan; an idle scheme.
Interject' v.t. To throw in between; to interpose.
Di'alect s. Language, speech; local idiom; patois.

Elect′ a. Chosen, picked out. v.t. To choose by vote; to select for office, etc. s. One or those chosen or set apart.
Re-elect′ v.t. To elect a second time.
Non-elect′ a. and s. (*Negative*).
Select′ a. Chosen; picked out; to choose, take from a number.
Deflect′ v.t. To turn aside, to deviate. v.i. To cause to turn or bend.
Reflect′ v.t. To bend or throw back, especially after striking a surface; to mirror. v.i. To throw back light, heat, etc.; to meditate; to bring reproach.
Inflect′ v.t. To bend; to vary a noun or verb; to modulate (the voice).
Gen′uflect v.i. To bend the knee as in worship.
Neglect′ v.t. To treat with no regard; to overlook. s. Omission; slight; negligence.
In′tellect s. Understanding; genius; talent.
Collect′ v.t. To bring together; get payment of; infer, deduce. v.i. To accumulate.
Col′lect s. A short prayer for a special day or occasion.
Re-collect′ v.t. To gather together again.
Recollect′ v.t. and i. To remember, recall to memory, succeed in remembering.
Connect′ v.t. To fasten together, establish association between. v.i. To become joint or coherent; to have a close relation.
Disconnect′ v.t. To dissolve the connexion of; to sever.
As′pect s. Appearance; situation.
Respect′ v.t. To notice specially; to esteem, honour, prize; to relate to. s. Act of respecting or holding in estimation; relation; reference.
Disrespect′ s. Incivility; irreverence. v.t. To show disrespect to.
Cir′cumspect a. Cautious, wary.
Inspect′ v.t. To view, examine.
Pros′pect s. A look-out, view, survey.
Prospect′ v.t. and i. To examine for or seek metals, precious stones, etc.
Ret′rospect s. View of things past; backward survey. v.t. To consider retrospectively.
Introspect′ v.t. To look into; to examine one's own mind.
Suspect′ v.t. To mistrust, think guilty. v.i. To imagine guilt, have a suspicion.
Sus′pect s. A suspected person. a. Suspected, doubtful.
Expect′ v.t. To wait for, await; to hope, anticipate.
Erect′ a. Upright, perpendicular; bold, undismayed. v.t. To set upright; to build; to exalt.
Direct′ a. Straight, progressive, straightforward; in line of father and son; express. v.t. To show the right course to; to adjust, regulate; to order; to instruct.
Redirect′ v.t. To direct again (as a letter).
Indirect′ a. Circuitous; not straightforward; not tending or resulting directly.
Misdirect′ v.t. To give a wrong direction to, direct wrongly.
Arrect′ a. Pointed upwards; alert.
Correct′ v.t. To set right; to counteract; to chastise. a. Right, accurate, exact.
Incorrect′ a. Inaccurate; erroneous.
Porrect′ v.t. To stretch out horizontally.
Resurrect′ v.t. To bring back to life or into use.
Sect s. A body of persons who have separated from others; a religious denomination.
Ven′esect v.t. and i. To let blood, phlebotomize.
Bisect′ v.t. To cut into two, especially into two equal parts.
Trisect′ v.t. To divide into three.
Viv′isect v.t. To experiment on a living animal by cutting.
Transect′ v.t. To cut across.
In′sect s. A small articulate animal with head, thorax, and abdomen plainly separated, three pairs of legs, and usually winged.
Intersect′ v.t. To cut in between, to divide. v.i. To cut into one another; to meet and cross.
Dissect′ v.t. To cut in pieces; to anatomize to examine minutely.
Detect′ v.t. To discover, bring to light.
Ar′chitect s. A designer of houses, etc.; one who builds up or constructs anything.
Protect′ v.t. To defend, shield; to guard against foreign competition.
Contradict′ v.t. and i. To assert to be the contrary; to oppose, deny the truth of a statement.
Addict′ v.t. To apply habitually; to accustom (oneself) to.
E′dict s. A public proclamation, a decree.
Ben′edict s. A newly married man.
Predict′ v.t. To foretell, prophesy; to bode.
Indict′ (-dit) v.t. Formally to charge with crime.
In′terdict v.t. To forbid, prohibit; to cut off from communion. s. A prohibition; papal deprivation of ecclesiastical rights and privileges.
Ver′dict s. Decision of a jury; judgment.
Delict′ s. An offence; commission of an offence.
Rel′ict s. A widow.
Der′elict a. Forsaken, abandoned; unfaithful. s. Anything left or abandoned.
Afflict′ v.t. To distress, grieve, harass.
Inflict′ v.t. To impose (as a punishment); to cause to suffer from.
Con′flict s. A fight; clashing of views, etc.
Conflict′ v.i. To meet in opposition, be antagonistic.
Pict s. One of an ancient race of N. E. Scotland.
Depict′ v.t. To paint, portray, describe.
Strict a. Exact, rigid; not loose or vague.
Astrict′ v.t. To bind up, compress, restrict.
Restrict′ v.t. To limit, confine, curb.
Dis′trict s. A limited territorial division; a region, circuit.
Constrict′ v.t. To draw together, contract.
Evict′ v.t. To dispossess by legal process; to turn out.
Convict′ v.t. To prove or find to be guilty.
Con′vict s. A criminal sentenced to penal servitude.
Mulct s. A fine. v.t. To fine; to deprive.
Sa′crosanct a. Sacred and inviolable by religious custom.
Succinct′ a. Concise, terse, brief.
Pre′cinct s. A bounding line; part near this; ground immediately surrounding.
Tinct s. A colour, tint. a. Tinctured. v.t. To tint, tincture.
Distinct′ a. Different, separate; clear, plain.
Indistinct′ a. Not distinct; faint.
In′stinct s. Natural or spontaneous impulse; intuitive feeling.
Instinct′ a. Animated from within; inspired.

Extinct' a. Extinguished; having died out.
Inextinct' a. Not extinct; not quenched.
Defunct' a. Dead, deceased. s. A dead person.
Ad'junct s. An appendage; an unnecessary addition.
Injunct' v.t. To restrain by legal injunction.
Conjunct' a. Conjoined, closely connected.
Disjunct' a. Disjointed, separated.
Decoct' v.t. To prepare by boiling; to digest by heat.
Concoct' v.t. To prepare by mixing; to plot, devise.
Duct s. A canal or tube, especially in animals and plants.
Vi'aduct s. A long bridge on many arches.
Abduct' v.t. To lead or entice away wrongly.
E'duct s. Thing brought to light by analysis, etc.; an inference.
Lymph'æduct s. Bodily vessel conveying lymph.
Deduct' v.t. To take away, subtract.
Aq'ueduct s. An artificial over-ground conduit for water.
Ven'tiduct s. A subterranean ventilating passage.
O'viduct s. Passage from which the ova pass from the ovary.
Circumduct' v.t. To lead astray; to contravene, nullify.
Conduct' v.t. To lead or guide; attend, manage. v.i. To behave.
Con'duct s. Act or method of leading; skilful guidance; convoy, guard; behaviour, deportment.
Miscon'duct s. Ill behaviour; mismanagement; misdemeanour.
Misconduct' v.t. To conduct amiss, mismanage.
Prod'uct s. That which is produced; result; number resulting from multiplication.
Reluct' v.i. To be disinclined, make resistance.
Eruct' v.t. To belch up, eject from the stomach.
U'sufruct s. Right to use of another's property.
Obstruct' v.t. To block up, bar, impede.
Instruct' v.t. To teach; to advise; to furnish with orders.
Construct' v.t. To build, put together, frame, devise.
Reconstruct' s. To construct over again, reorganize.
Nor'denfeldt s. A rapid-firing machine-gun.
Veldt s. Treeless grass county of S. Africa.
-et suff. Noting a diminutive.
Bet v.t. To wager. s. That which is staked; a wager.
Abet' v.t. To urge on; to assist in nefarious action.
Al'phabet s. The collection of letters of any language properly arranged.
Rab'bet s. Groove in edge of board to receive another board. v.t. To cut this.
Drab'bet s. Coarse linen used for smock-frocks.
Gib'bet s. A gallows; part of a crane. v.t. To hang on a gibbet; to expose to scorn or ridicule.
Flibb'ertigib'-bet s. A flighty, impetuous person; a gossip.
Gob'bet s. A mouthful, a lump.
Quod'libet s. A knotty point; a musical medley.
Tibet' s. A goat's hair-cloth.
Zib'et s. A small civet of India and Africa.
Bar'bet s. A tropical bird of the toucan family.
Sher'bet s. A cooling Eastern drink flavoured with fruit.
Sor'bet s. A fruit-flavoured ice; sherbet.
Fac'et s. A little face, a small surface.
Hic ja'cet s. An epitaph.
Lacet' s. Braided or crotcheted trimming.
Pla'cet s. An affirmative vote.
Sal'icet s. One of the stops on an organ.
Vide'licet adv. Namely; to wit; viz.
Sci'licet adv. To wit, namely.
Dul'cet a. Sweet to the ear or senses; melodious.
Lan'cet s. A small, sharp surgical knife. a. Denoting a long, narrow, pointed window.
Av'ocet s. A wading bird.
Ter'cet s. A triplet (in prosody, etc.).
Fau'cet s. A beer-tap.
Cadet' s. A younger brother, a student at a military or naval school.
Bidet' s. A vessel for bathing in astride.
Beet s. A vegetable with thick, fleshy root, yielding sugar.
Feet s. Plural of foot.
Sheet s. Broad, thin expanse of anything, especially of cloth for beds, paper for printing, etc., rolled metal, etc.; rope for lower corner of sail. v.t. To fold in, furnish with, or make into sheets.
Broad'sheet s. A large sheet printed on one side only.
Parakeet' s. A small long-tailed parrot.
Lorikeet' s. A genus of Malayan parrots.
Leet s. A manorial court or its jurisdiction; list of candidates for an office.
Fleet v.i. To fly swiftly; to be in a transient state. a. Swift of pace; quick, nimble. s. A squadron or body of ships; a navy.
Sleet s. Hail or snow falling with rain. v.i. To snow or hail thus.
Meet v.i. To encounter, come together, assemble. v.t. To come in contact with, light on; to receive, satisfy. a. Fit, seemly, suitable, qualified. s. An assembly of huntsmen.
Help'meet s. A helpmate.
Discreet' a. Prudent, cautious, circumspect.
Indiscreet' a. Incautious; injudicious; rash.
Afreet' s. An Oriental goblin; a malicious sprite.
Greet v.t. To salute, to accost. v.i. To weep. s. Lamentation, weeping.
Street s. A paved or city road.
Sweet a. Resembling sugar in taste; pleasing to the smell, sight, etc.; fragrant, restful, delightful, beloved. s. That which is sweet; a comfit; a darling.
Buff'et s. A cupboard for wine, glasses, etc.; a refreshment bar; a hard blow. v.t. To beat, beat about, contend against.
Get v.t. To procure, obtain; to seize, win; to reach; to beget. v.i. To arrive at by degrees; to become.
Gadg'et s. (*Slang*) An appliance, tool, handy contrivance.
Pledg'et s. A lint compress for a wound, etc.
Fidg'et v.i. To move about uneasily. s. Restlessness; one who fidgets.
Midg'et s. A dwarf; a tiny object.
Budg'et s. A bundle; the annual statement of a country's financial position. v.i. To make estimates to meet anticipated expenditure.
Beget' v.t. To engender, procreate, produce.
Brag'get s. Honey and ale fermented with spices.

Hog'get s. A yearling sheep.
Nug'get s. A lump of native metal.
Drug'get s. A coarse woollen stuff; an over-carpet.
Gar'get s. A distemper in cattle.
Par'get v.t. To cover with plaster. s. Plaster.
Tar'get s. A mark to be shot at; a small shield.
Forget' v.t. To lose the remembrance of; to overlook, neglect.
Gor'get s. Armour for the throat or neck; a ruffle; necklace.
Cach'et s. Distinguishing mark; stamp; characteristic.
Sach'et (săsh'ā) s. A small bag for perfume.
Planch'et s. A disk for stamping as coin.
Man'chet s. A small, fine wheaten loaf.
Linch'et s. A linch.
Ric'ochet (-shā) s. A skipping, as of a projectile. v.t. and i. To rebound thus; to hit after a ricochet.
Roch'et s. A vestment like a surplice worn by bishops; the red gurnard.
Crotch'et s. A note half the length of a minim; a whim, perverse conceit; a square bracket in printing.
Crochet' s. A sort of figured ornamental needlework. v.t. and i. To knit or make in crochet.
Hatch'et s. A small, short-handled axe.
Latch'et s. A lace for a sandal, etc.
Match'et s. A machete, cutlass.
Ratch'et s. A pivoted catch for teeth of a wheel or rack.
Treb'uchet s. A mediæval war-engine; a snare for birds; a delicate balance.
Proph'et s. One who foretells events; an interpreter.
To'phet s. Place near Jerusalem where corpses and refuse were burnt; hell.
Ash'et s. A large flat dish.
Fresh'et s. A sudden flood through heavy rains, etc.
Ep'ithet s. An adjective denoting any quality, good or bad; a title.
Whet v.t. To sharpen on a stone; to stimulate, excite. s. Act of whetting; an appetizer, dram.
Di'et s. Victuals; special course of feeding, regimen; a legislative assembly. v.t. To feed by medical rule. v.i. To eat sparingly or according to directions.
Qui'et a. Still; peaceable; calm; silent. s. Freedom from disturbance, noise, etc.; tranquillity. v.t. To calm, pacify.
Inqui'et a. Unquiet; restless.
Disqui'et s. Lack of tranquillity, anxiety. v.t. To make uneasy, disturb.
Sov'iet s. A popular assembly of soldiers or workmen for managing their affairs (especially in Russia).
Jet s. A dense black variety of lignite; a spouting; that which spouts forth; orifice for gas, etc. v.t. and i. To emit or issue in a jet; to spout forth.
Jack'et s. A short coat; covering of a steam-pipe, etc. v.t. To cover with a jacket; (*slang*) to thrash.
Blue'jacket s. A sailor in the Navy.
Plack'et s. Slit left in skirt, etc., for convenience in putting on.
Pack'et s. A small package; a vessel employed in carrying that has fixed times for sailing.
Rack'et s. A strung bat for tennis, etc.; a clamour, rumpus. v.i. To make a din, to frolic.
Brack'et s. A projection from a wall to act as a support; a mark enclosing words. v.t. To support by, place within, or connect by brackets.
Tack'et s. A clout-nail, tack.
Beck'et s. A contrivance for confining loose ropes, etc., on board ship.
Thick'et s. A close wood of small trees.
Pick'et s. A sharpened stake; a military guard, outpost; strikers who try to persuade those at work to strike. v.t. To fence with or fasten to a picket; to act as a picket during a strike.
Crick'et s. A chirping or creaking insect; a low stool; an open-air game played with a ball, bat, and wickets. v.i. To play cricket.
Prick'et s. A buck in his second year.
Tick'et s. A marked label of card or paper; certificate of right of admission, etc. v.t. To mark by or furnish with a ticket.
Wick'et s. A small door, especially in a larger one; a cricket-stump; pitch between sets of these.
Dock'et s. A summary, digest; direction on goods; formal record of judicial proceedings. v.t. To mark titles of papers on back; to make an abstract.
Lock'et s. A small ornamental case for wearing.
Pock'et s. A small bag, especially in a garment; a measure for hops, etc.; a sack; one of the six bags on a billiard table; a mass of rich ore in a working. v.t. To put or conceal in a pocket; to appropriate; to put up with.
Rock'et s. A cruciferous salad plant; a perennial garden plant; a projectile firework. v.i. To fly fast and high.
Brock'et s. A stag of the second year.
Crock'et s. A carved foliated architectural ornament.
Sprock'et s. A cog on a wheel engaging with a chain, etc.; a wheel set with these.
Sock'et s. Cavity into which anything fits.
Buck'et s. A vessel in which water is drawn or carried; a holder slung to a saddle for a rifle, etc. v.i. and t. To ride hard or recklessly; to hurry at the end of a stroke in rowing.
Tuck'et s. A fanfare.
Bank'et s. A gold-bearing stone in S. Africa.
Blank'et s. A woollen covering for a bed, horses, etc.
Trink'et s. A small ornament.
Junk'et s. Dish of milk curdled by rennet. v.t. To feast, make merry.
Mark'et s. Place for buying and selling; occasion of use of this; rate of purchase; demand of commodities. v.i. To deal in a market. v.t. To offer for sale.
New'market s. A card-game.
Bas'ket s. A case or container made of interwoven twigs.
Cas'ket s. A small chest for jewels, etc.; a coffin.
Gas'ket s. A cord on the yard to tie the sail to it; hemp or washer for packing pistons, etc.
Las'ket s. A loop of line at the foot of a sail.

Bris'ket s. The part of an animal next the ribs.
Fris'ket s. The frame holding a sheet of paper to be printed.
Bos'ket s. A thicket, a grove.
Mus'ket s. An obsolete fire-arm for infantry.
Let v.t. To allow, permit; to lease; to hinder, impede. v.i. To be leased. s. A hindrance; stoppage (at tennis, etc.); a letting (of a house, etc.).
-let suff. Diminutive.
Chal'et s. A small villa.
Val'et s. A gentleman's body-servant. v.t. To act as valet to.
Ab'let s. The bleak.
Ca'blet s. A small cable.
Ga'blet s. A small gable or ornamental canopy.
Tab'let s. A small flat, surface; a thin slip for writing on; a note-book; a lozenge.
Drib'let s. A negligible quantity.
Trib'let s. A goldsmith's tool; mandrel used in making tubes, etc.
Gob'let s. A drinking vessel with a stem and no handle.
Herb'let s. A little herb.
Orb'let s. A little orb.
Doub'let s. Two of a kind; one of a pair; a close-fitting body-garment; a counterfeit gem; one of two words of the same origin but different form.
Sublet' v.t. To lease as a lessee to another.
Circ'let s. A little circle, a small ring.
Pond'let s. A little pond.
Frond'let s. A small frond.
Round'let s. A little circle or circular thing.
Rod'let s. A little rod.
Lord'let s. A petty lord.
Bud'let s. A small bud.
Cloud'let s. A little cloud.
Lobe'let s. A small lobe.
Brace'let s. An ornamental band worn on the wrist.
Lance'let s. A small fish of the lowest class of vertebrates.
Prince'let s. A petty or little prince.
Ban'delet s. A small stripe; a flat moulding round a column.
Ron'delet s. A form of rondel.
Lake'let s. A small lake.
Pike'let s. A small tea-cake, a crumpet.
Spike'let s. A small spike (especially of flowers).
Joke'let s. A poor or trivial joke.
Flame'let s. A small flame.
Om'elet s. A kind of egg fritter flavoured or stuffed.
Drupe'let s. A drupel.
Verse'let s. A short or trifling verse.
Os'selet s. A hard, bony substance in a horse's knee; a cuttle-bone.
Note'let s. A little note.
Wave'let s. A ripple.
Valve'let s. A small valve.
Nerve'let s. A small nerve.
Eye'let s. A small hole to receive a lace.
Leaf'let s. A small leaf; a one-page handbill.
Ea'glet s. A young eagle.
Reg'let s. Strip used for separating type.
Gig'let s. A giggler; a giddy girl. a. Wanton; giddy.
King'let s. A petty king; the golden-crested wren.
Ring'let s. A small ring; a curl.
Spring'let s. A little spring or fountain.
Sing'let s. An under-vest.
Wing'let s. A small wing.
Gog'let s. An Indian earthenware water-vessel.
Bu'glet s. A small bugle.
Branch'let s. A little branch.
Pam'phlet s. A small unbound book; a tract.
Tooth'let s. A small tooth or projection.
Toi'let s. A dressing-table; cloth over this; act or mode of dressing; attire.
Oak'let s. A small oak.
Hack'let s. The kittiwake.
Neck'let s. A chain, fur, etc., worn round the neck.
Stalk'let s. A small stalk.
An'klet s. An ornamental ring worn on the ankle.
Book'let s. A small book, a pamphlet.
Brook'let s. A rivulet, little brook.
Spark'let s. A small spark; a contrivance for aerating water.
Bal'let s. A spectacular theatrical dance.
Mal'let s. A wooden hammer.
Pal'let s. A tool used by potters, gilders, etc.; a lever in a clock; a valve in an organ; a small rude bed.
Sal'let s. A bowl-shaped helmet of the fifteenth century.
Tal'let s. A hay-loft.
Wal'let (wol'-) s. A knapsack; a pocket-case.
Swal'let (swol'-) s. An opening in limestone into which a stream runs.
Um'bellet s. A small or partial umbel.
Pell'et s. A little, rounded lump; a small shot.
Bill'et s. A stick of wood; a small note civilian lodgings for soldiers; a situation, berth. v.t. To quarter soldiers on civilians.
Fill'et s. A little band, especially for the hair; a fleshy piece of meat; meat rolled together. v.t. To bind or adorn with a fillet; to deprive fish or meat of bone.
Skill'et s. A long-handled pan for boiling water.
Mill'et s. A grain-bearing grass.
Quill'et s. A quibble, subtlety.
Will'et s. A N. American sandpiper.
Coll'et s. The setting of a stone in a ring; a socket.
Bull'et s. A solid missile for a fire-arm.
Cull'et s. Broken glass for remelting.
Gull'et s. The throat, passage for food.
Mull'et s. A marine food-fish frequenting estuaries; an heraldic five-pointed star.
Surmull'et s. The red mullet.
Pull'et s. A young hen.
Cam'let s. A fabric made of silk, wool, and hair.
Stream'let s. A small stream, rill.
Ham'let s. A small village.
Sam'let s. A young salmon.
Stem'let s. A small stem.
Gim'let s. A small screwed boring tool.
Arm'let s. A band or armour worn on the arm.
In'let s. A means of entrance; a creek.
Run'let s. A small cask; a rivulet.
Town'let s. A little town.
Flageolet' s. A flute-like instrument blown from the end.
Cabriolet' s. A one-horse chaise.
Tri'olet (trē'-) s. An eight-lined verse with special rhyme-scheme.
Vi'olet s. Genus of plants including the pansy; a bluish-purple colour. a. Of this colour.
Ser'polet s. Wild thyme.
Pis'tolet s. A miniature pistol.

Vo'let (-lā) s. A wing of a triptych.
Chap'let s. A wreath, garland; a small moulding; one third of a rosary.
Trip'let s. A group of three; one of three born at a birth; three lines rhyming together.
Tem'plet s. A gauge, pattern, mould.
Drop'let s. A diminutive drop.
Coup'let s. Two lines that rhyme.
Quin'tuplet s. A set of five.
Scar'let s. A bright red colour; official dress of this. a. Of this colour.
Ear'let s. A little ear.
Star'let s. A very small star.
Var'let s. A menial; a rascal.
Feath'erlet s. A small feather.
Ster'let s. A small kind of sturgeon.
Cov'erlet s. An outer cover for a bed.
Has'let s. Part of a pig's entrails used as food.
Isl'et s. A small island.
Cors'let s. Body-armour; the thorax of insects.
Cross'let s. A small cross.
Bat'let s. A small bat.
Swift'let s. A bird of the swift family.
Fruit'let s. A drupel.
Cant'let s. A morsel.
Gant'let s. Gauntlet.
Plant'let s. A small plant.
Mant'let s. A bullet-proof shield; a short mantle.
Front'let s. A fillet for the forehead; a bird's forehead.
Gaunt'let s. An armoured glove; a stout glove covering the wrist; a punishment in which the culprit ran between two files of men who thrashed him as he passed.
Root'let s. A little root, a radicle.
Heart'let s. A little heart; a nucleus.
Mart'let s. An heraldic footless bird.
Part'let s. A neck-ruff formerly worn by women.
Tart'let s. A small tart.
Fort'let s. A small fort.
Cut'let s. A small slice of meat from loin or neck.
Nut'let s. A very small nut.
Out'let s. Place or means of exit; outfall; passage out.
Trout'let s. A small trout.
Landaulet' s. A small landau; a landaulette.
Epaulet' s. Ornament or badge worn on the shoulder.
Cu'let s. The bottom surface of a brilliant-cut diamond.
Am'ulet s. A charm against witchcraft, etc.; a talisman.
An'nulet s. A little ring; a small flat fillet below the capital of a column.
Lu'nulet s. A small lunula; coloured semicircular spot.
Rivu'let s. A small river, brook.
Owl'et s. A small or young owl.
Ar'rowlet s. A small arrow; a feathery seed.
Ray'let s. A small ray.
Styl'et s. A stilletto; a probe.
Met past and past part. (*Meet*).
Hel'met s. Armour for the head; head-dress worn by policemen, firemen, etc.; a part or object shaped like this.
Mam'met s. An idol, doll.
Em'met s. An ant.
Grom'met s. A ring made of rope.
Plum'met s. A weight attached to a line for sounding depths, determining a perpendicular, etc.; the weight and line.
Grum'met s. A rope ring used on board ship.
Com'et s. A luminous heavenly body revolving round the sun in a very eccentric orbit.
Baphom'et s. An idol said to have been worshipped by the Knight's Templars.
Ar'met s. A kind of helmet.
Gour'met s. A connoisseur in food and drink; an epicure.
Kis'met s. Fate; destiny.
Mau'met s. An idol, puppet, mammet.
Fu'met s. The dung of deer.
Cal'umet s. The American-Indian pipe of peace.
Net s. A meshed texture used to catch fish, birds, etc., and in certain ball-games. v.t. To make into or catch in a net; to make a clear gain of. a. Being clear of all deductions.
Car'canet s. A jewelled collar.
Al'kanet s. A red vegetable dye.
Plan'et s. A celestial body revolving round the sun.
Castanet' s. An instrument making a snapping noise.
Sar'cenet s. A fine, thin, silk fabric.
Gen'et s. A small animal of the civet family.
Te'net s. An opinion, etc., maintained.
Lans'quenet s. A German mercenary of the fifteenth and sixteenth centuries; a card-game.
Mag'net s. The loadstone; steel or iron bar to which the attracting properties of this have been imparted; that which powerfully attracts.
Sig'net s. A small seal.
Cyg'net s. A young swan.
Cab'inet s. A small room; a case for curiosities; the ministers of state.
Tab'inet s. A watered silk and wool fabric.
Bobbinet' s. A machine-made cotton net.
Robinet' s. A faucet on board ship.
Stockinet' s. A light knitted material.
Muslinet' s. A coarse kind of muslin.
Estam'inet s. A café, smoking saloon.
Spin'et s. An obsolete instrument of the harpischord type.
Clarinet' s. A keyed reed musical instrument.
Basinet' s. A light, round helmet.
Satinet' s. A thin kind of satin.
Martinet' s. A strict disciplinarian.
Gan'net s. A sea-bird; the solan goose.
Ben'net s. The herb *Geum urbanum*.
Jen'net s. A small Spanish horse.
Ren'net s. Membrane of calf's stomach prepared; a variety of apple.
Lin'net s. A common song-bird.
Bon'net s. A close-fitting head-dress; a dome-shaped casing, as over the engine in front of a motor-car.
Ballonnet' s. A small balloon, especially one in an airship's envelope.
Son'net s. A poem of fourteen lines with a definite rhyme-scheme.
Pun'net s. A small shallow basket for fruit.
Jac'onet s. A fine white cotton cloth.
Fal'conet s. A kind of shrike.
Drag'onet s. A small fish allied to the gobies.
Bur'gonet s. A light helmet.
Li'onet s. A young lion.
Bar'onet s. An hereditary titled order of commoners.
Cor'onet s. A little crown; an ornamental fillet; a surmounting band.
Ba'yonet s. A dagger-like weapon for fixing to a rifle. v.t. To stab with this.
Canzonet' s. A short song, especially in an opera.

Gar'net s. A deep-red transparent crystalline gem.
Cor'net s. A kind of trumpet; a cavalry officer who bore the standard; a conical paper bag.
Hor'net s. Stinging insect of the wasp kind.
Bur'net s. A brown-flowered plant.
Gur'net s. The gurnard, a sea-fish.
Bas'net s. (*Basinet*).
Po'et s. A writer of poems; an imaginative creator.
Pet s. A favourite, darling; a fit of peevishness. v.t. To fondle, treat indulgently.
Lim'pet s. A conical gasteropod adhering to rocks.
Crum'pet s. A thin sort of muffin; (*Slang*) the head.
Trum'pet s. A brass wind-instrument; sound of this. v.t. To proclaim, publish by sound of trumpet. v.i. To make a sound as of a trumpet (especially of elephants).
Strum'pet s. A prostitute.
Lap'pet s. A little lap or flap hanging loose.
Tap'pet s. A small lever in machinery.
Whip'pet s. A cross between greyhound and terrier.
Snip'pet s. A small bit, a fragment.
Sip'pet s. A small piece of toast for garnishing, etc.
Tip'pet s. Covering for neck and shoulders.
Mop'pet s. A pet; a rag doll.
Pop'pet s. A puppet, a darling; a framework or piece of mechanism for various purposes.
Pup'pet s. A doll; a figure moved by wires; one who is a mere tool.
Car'pet s. A heavy fabric for covering floors. v.t. To cover with a carpet; (*colloq.*) to censure an employee.
Toupet' (-pā') s. A small wig.
Ret v.t. To prepare (flax) by soaking, macerating, etc.
Cab'aret s. A French tavern; a theatrical performance.
Tab'aret s. A satin fabric used in upholstery.
Car'et s. A mark (Λ) indicating an omission.
Claret' s. A light, red wine; (*slang*) blood.
Cellaret' s. A small case or drawer for bottles.
Minaret' s. A slender turret, especially on a mosque.
Lazaret' s. A lazaretto.
Lab'ret s. A lip-ornament of the Alaskans, etc.
Se'cret a. Hidden, private; kept from general knowledge, etc. s. Something concealed; a mystery.
Swim'meret s. A swimming organ of a crustacean.
Ban'neret s. A former grade of knighthood.
Lan'neret s. A kind of long-tailed falcon.
Spin'neret s. The spinning organ of a spider, etc.
Lev'eret s. A hare in its first year.
Velveret' s. Inferior velvet.
Flow'eret s. A little flower.
Fret v.t. To chafe, corrode, wear away; to vex, irritate; to variegate. v.i. To be vexed or peevish; to rankle. s. Irritation, peevishness; pierced ornamental work.
E'gret s. A bird of the heron family.
Regret' v.t. To grieve over; to repent, bewail. s. Grief at something past; remorse; self-condemnation.
Tab'oret s. A small tabor.
An'choret s. A hermit.
Flor'et s. A small flower.
Am'oret s. A sweetheart; a love-knot.
Mpret s. The sovereign of Albania.
Inter'pret v.t. To explain, expound; to make intelligible; to translate.
Misinter'pret v.t. To interpret erroneously; to misunderstand.
Bar'ret s. A biretta.
Gar'ret s. A small upper room; a top story.
Fer'ret s. A partially domesticated weasel-like animal; narrow tape of wool, silk, etc. v.t. To hunt with a ferret; to pry into, rummage about.
Ter'ret s. A ring on harness.
Skir'ret s. A species of parsnip.
Tur'ret s. A small tower or spire.
Tret s. Allowance for damage to goods during transit.
Carburet' s. A compound of carbon with another element. v.t. To make such a compound.
Fleur'et a. A small flower-shaped ornament.
Tell'uret s. A telluride.
Tab'ouret s. A small seat without back or arms; an embroidery frame.
Set s. Complete suit or assortment; clique; descent of the sun, etc.; attitude, bent. v.t. To fix, place, dispose, appoint, estimate; to plant; to reduce a fracture. v.i. To solidify, become fixed; to sink below the horizon; to point out game; to tend. a. Regular; firm, fixed, placed, etc.; squared by rule; determined.
Beset' v.t. To surround, blockade, waylay; to press on all sides.
Reset' v.t. To set over again, furnish with a new setting. v.i. To receive stolen goods.
Thick'set a. Growing close together; stumpy. s. A close hedge.
Quick'set v.t. To plant with shrubs, etc., for a hedge. s. A hawthorn, etc., so planted. a. Made of this.
Inset' v.t. To fix in, insert.
In'set s. An insertion; a small map, etc., in a larger one; something let in.
On'set s. An assault, attack.
Sun'set s. Disappearance of sun below horizon; hour of this.
Clos'et s. A small private room; a large cupboard. v.t. To receive for a private consultation.
Marmoset' s. A small tropical American monkey.
Upset' v.t. To overturn, discompose. v.i. To be overturned.
Up'set s. Act of upsetting; state of being upset.
Som'erset (sŭm'-) s. and v.i. Somersault.
Vers'et s. A short composition for the organ.
Overset' v.t. To upset; to overthrow.
O'verset s. An upsetting; ruin.
Cor'set s. A stiffened body-garment worn by women.
Bas'set s. A short-legged hunting dog; an old card-game.
Cres'set s. A torch; an open lamp, beacon, etc., especially one carried on a pole.
Cos'set s. A pet lamb. v.t. To pet, mollycoddle.
Pos'set s. Hot milk curdled by wine, etc.
Gus'set s. A triangular piece of cloth sewn in a garment; an angle-iron or bracket.

Rus'set a. Of a reddish-brown colour; homespun; rustic. s. A variety of apple.
Out'set s. Beginning; start.
Octet' s. Musical composition for eight voices or instruments.
Quintet' s. Musical composition for five performers; the performers.
Motet' s. A vocal composition adapted to sacred words.
Septet' s. Musical composition for seven performers; a group of seven.
Quartet' s. Musical composition in four parts; the four performers of such.
Stet v.t. Let it stand (direction to compositor); to cancel a correction thus.
Ses'tet s. A sextet; last six lines of a sonnet.
Duet' s. Song or air in two parts, music for two performers.
Lan'guet s. A tongue-shaped part or organ.
Minuet' s. A stately, regular dance in triple time.
Tour'niquet s. Instrument for compressing an artery.
Piquet' (-ket') s. A card-game for two.
Briquet' s. A block of compressed coal-dust, etc.
So'briquet (-kā) s. An assumed name, nickname.
Ban'quet s. A feast; an entertainment. v.t. To treat with a feast. v.i. To feast.
Coquet' s. A male flirt. v.i. To coquette.
Ro'quet (-kā) v.t. To strike another ball with one's own (*croquet*). s. This stroke.
Cro'quet s. An open-air game played with mallets, balls, and hoops. v.i. and t. To play croquet or a certain stroke in the game.
Par'quet (-ki) s. A flooring of parquetry. v.t. To floor a room with this.
Bouquet' s. A bunch of flowers; the aroma of wine.
Cru'et s. A small vial for vinegar, oil, etc.
Su'et s. The hard fat from the lumbar region of oxen.
Vet s. (*Slang*) A veterinary surgeon.
Chevet' s. An apse.
Revet' v.t. To face (a wall, etc.) with masonry.
Brev'et s. A document conferring a rank, etc., especially one giving an officer a title above that he actually holds. v.t. To grant brevet rank.
Civ'et s. A musky substance obtained from the civet-cat used in perfumery.
Ol'ivet s. An artificial pearl.
Riv'et s. A fastening pin clinched at both ends. v.t. To join or fasten with such.
Griv'et s. An Abyssinian monkey.
Priv'et s. An evergreen shrub.
Triv'et s. A three-legged stand; support for kettle, etc., at the fire.
Vel'vet s. A rich silk stuff with soft nap. a. Made of or like this.
Cov'et v.t. To hanker after; to long for unlawfully. v.i. To have an inordinate desire.
Ver'vet s. A small African monkey.
Curvet' s. A leap of a horse, the fore-legs being off the ground. v.i. To make this leap, to frisk.
Du'vet (-vā) s. A down quilt.
Wet a. Soaked with, containing, or consisting of liquid; damp, moist; watery; rainy. s. Moistness; anything that wets; rain. v.t. To make wet.
Yet adv. Still, further; at the same time; hitherto. conj. Nevertheless.
Vilayet' s. A province of the Turkish Empire.
Aft a.; adv. Abaft; astern.
Abaft' adv. or prep. In or towards the hinder part of a ship.
Daft a. Idiotic, weak-minded, thoughtless.
Haft s. The handle of a weapon, tool, etc. v.t. To set in or fit with a haft.
Shaft s. Cylindrical, column-shaped part; stem of spear, etc.; an arrow, axle, carriage-pole; well-like entrance to a mine.
Raft s. Logs, planks, etc., fastened together for floating. v.t. and i. To transport or travel on such.
Craft s. Ability, skill; artifice; guile manual art; a vessel.
Wood'craft s. Skill in forestry, wood-working, etc., or in the chase.
Leech'craft s. The healing art.
Witch'craft s. Sorcery; magic.
Hand'icraft s. Manual occupation; skill in this.
Pen'craft s. Penmanship; authorship.
Priest'craft s. Fraud or imposition in religious matters; the stratagems of priests.
Draft s. An order for money; bill of exchange; detachment of men or things; a rough sketch. v.t. To draw out, call forth, select, sketch.
Redraft' v.t. To draw up again. s. A second draft.
Graft s. A shoot inserted into a growing tree; municipal or political corruption; illicit gains. v.t. To insert a graft on; to propagate thus.
Engraft' v.t. To graft upon; to incorporate; to instil.
Waft v.t. To bear through a fluid or buoyant medium; to carry gently along.
Eft s. The newt.
Deft a. Neat, dextrous, apt.
Heft s. Act of heaving; a lift, upward effort. v.t. To lift, try the weight of.
Theft s. Act of thieving; thing stolen.
Left a. Opposed to the right. s. The side opposite the right. past and past part. (*Leave*).
Cleft past and past part. (*Split*). s. A crack, crevice, fissure.
Reft past and past part. (*Reave*).
Bereft' v.t. (past) (*Bereave*).
Weft s. Threads passing through the warp; the woof; a web.
Gift s. A thing given; a present, donation. v.t. To endow with any faculty, power, etc.
Shift v.t. To change, alter, remove. v.i. To change place or direction, principles, occupation, etc.; to change one's clothes; to resort to expedients. s. A change of place, form, character, etc.; an expedient, trick, fraud; a relay of men; a spell of work; a chemise.
Make'shift s. A temporary expedient.
Lift v.t. To hoist, elevate; to exalt; to steal, appropriate. v.i. To raise, rise. s. Act of lifting; assistance; a rise in condition; an elevator; the sky.
Uplift' v.t. To raise aloft, elevate.
Up'lift s. An upheaval of strata, etc., an uplifting.
Smift s. Fuse for firing a blasting charge.
Rift s. A cleft, fissure. v.t. and i. To cleave, split.

Drift s. Tendency, aim, scope; anything driven by wind or water; current, speed or direction of this, distance vessel is driven by this; glacial deposit; a ford (S. Africa). v.t. To drive into heaps. v.i. To move along as driven; to gather in heaps; to float on or as on a current. a. Drifted by wind or water.
Adrift' adv. Floating at random; not under control.
Spin'drift s. Fine spray blown from waves; fleecy clouds.
Shrift s. Confession made to a priest; absolution.
Thrift s. Good husbandry; frugality; the sea-pink.
Spend'thrift s. A prodigal; one who wastes his money. a. Wasteful.
Un'thrift s. A prodigal, a thriftless person.
Sift v.t. To separate by a sieve; to divide the good from the bad; to scrutinize.
Swift a. Quick; fleet; ready, expeditious. s. A swallow-like bird.
Oft adv. Often.
Loft s. Space immediately under a roof; a raised gallery; a pigeon house. v.t. To cause to soar.
Aloft' adv. High up; in the sky.
Croft s. Piece of enclosed ground adjoining a house; small farm.
Soft a. Not hard; yielding; tender; effeminate; not harsh or strong; simple, spoony. adv. Softly. s. A weak-minded simpleton.
Toft s. A homestead.
Tuft s. A cluster, bunch of hair, feathers, etc. v.t. To separate into or adorn with tufts.
Can'dytuft s. An annual garden plant.
Yacht (yot) s. A light pleasure- or racing-vessel. v.i. To sail in a yacht.
Straight a. Direct; not crooked; upright; honest. s. A straight part or stretch of anything.
Bight s. A small bay; a loop in a rope, etc.
Dight a. Dressed, adorned.
Bedight' a. Decked out.
Eight a. and s. Twice four; 8.
Height s. Elevation; eminence; extent, degree; upward distance.
Sleight (slīt) s. Dexterity, especially in manual manipulation.
Freight s. The cargo of a ship; lading; charge for transportation; hire of a ship. v.t. To load; to hire for carrying.
Weight (wāt) s. Quality of being heavy; heaviness; amount of this; a heavy load, mass, etc.; pressure; importance, power.
Hun'dred-weight s. 112 lb. avoir.
O'verweight s. Weight beyond what is due; preponderance.
Pen'nyweight s. The twentieth of an ounce Troy, twenty-four grains.
Fight s. A combat, conflict, engagement. v.i. To strive for victory, contend. v.t. To battle against; to win by striving.
Hight v.i. Called, named.
Light s. That which renders objects visible; a window; knowledge; explanation; point of view. a. Bright; clear; not heavy; not arduous; slight; gay; giddy. adv. Lightly, cheaply. v.t. To give light to; to ignite. v.i. To brighten; to alight; to come by chance.
Alight' v.i. To get down, settle on. a. Lighted, kindled.
Blight s. That which withers anything; mildew; fungoid growths or parasites on plants. v.t. To affect with blight; to frustrate.
Delight' s. Pleasurable emotion; gratification. v.t. To please greatly, give high satisfaction to. v.i. To be highly pleased.
Candle'light s. The light of a candle; the gloaming.
Relight' v.t. To light again.
Flight s. Act, power, or mode of flying; space passed by flying; a flock of birds; series of steps; volley; an extravagant sally; a fleeing, hasty departure.
Twi'light s. The half-light between sunset and dark. a. Pertaining to this; obscure, dim.
Moon'light s. The light of the moon. a. Illuminated by this; occurring during moonlight.
Sun'light s. The light of the sun.
Plight s. A solemn promise; a predicament, risky position. v.t. To pledge (one's word), promise, engage.
Lamp'light s. Light from lamps.
Star'light s. The light of the stars.
Slight a. Unimportant; inadequate; weak; careless; slender; scorn, disdain. v.t. To disregard; to do carelessly.
Day'light s. Light of day; publicity.
Sky'light s. Window in a roof or ceiling.
Might s. Power; strength; force; ability. past. (*May*).
Night s. Time from sunset to sunrise; daily period of darkness; state of ignorance, etc.
Mid'night s. Twelve o'clock at night. a. Pertaining to this; very dark.
Knight s. A military attendant; one holding a non-hereditary dignity entitling him to the prefix "Sir"; a piece at chess.
Sen'night s. A week.
Overnight' s. The previous evening. adv. On or during this.
Fort'night s. A period of two weeks.
Right a. Straight; opposed to left; upright; correct; just; not wrong; perpendicular. adv. Correctly; very; to the right hand; directly. s. Justice; prerogative; authority; freedom from error; side opposite the left. v.t. To put right, set upright, do justice to. v.i. To come right, resume a vertical position.
Aright' adv. Right, properly, becomingly.
Bright a. Shining, clear, not dull; cheerful, witty.
Eye'bright s. The euphrasy.
Fright s. Sudden terror; alarm; consternation; an ugly or ridiculous-looking person. v.t. To frighten.
Affright' v.t. To terrify. s. Sudden fright; terror.
Forthright' adv. Straight forward; straightway.
Forth'right a. Straightforward; direct.

Down'right adv. Straight down; perpendicular; in plain terms. a. Unceremonious, blunt; absolute.
Up'right a. Erect; honest, just. s. A vertical piece.
Out'right adv. Immediately; completely.
Wright s. An artificer, workman.
Wheel'wright s. A wheel-maker.
Ship'wright s. One who builds ships.
Cart'wright s. A cart-builder.
Play'wright s. A dramatist.
Cop'yright s. Exclusive right to print or produce a literary, artistic, or musical work, etc. a. Relating to or protected by copyright. v.t. To secure by copyright.
Sight (sīt) s. Faculty of seeing; vision; view; spectacle; estimation; appliance for guiding the eye. v.t. To descry; to give the proper elevation and direction to.
Fore'sight s. Prescience, forethought; penetration.
Eye'sight s. Vision; observation.
In'sight s. Power of discernment; a thorough knowledge.
O'versight s. Watchful care, supervision; an omission, mistake.
Tight a. Not loose; tense; tenacious; close; taut; (*slang*) drunk.
Wight s. A person, being.
Aught s. Anything whatever. adv. In any respect.
Caught past and past part. (*Catch*).
On'slaught s. A furious assault or attack.
Naught s. A cipher; nothing; not anything. a. Worthless. adv. In no degree.
Fear'naught s. A heavy woollen fabric.
Draught s. Act of drawing, pulling, selecting troops, etc.; things, troops, etc., drawn; quantity of liquid drawn at once; current of air; a piece at draughts. v.t. To draft.
In'draught s. Current of air, etc., drawn in.
Fraught a. Laden, charged; filled, stored.
Distraught' a. Distracted, agitated.
Taught past and past part. (*Teach*).
Ought v. imp. It is fit, right, proper, or necessary; should. s. Naught; a cipher.
Bought v.t. (past part.) (*Buy*).
Fought past and past part. (*Fight*).
Thought s. Act or process of thinking; conception, sentiment, fancy. past and past part. (*Think*).
Methought' v. impers. It seemed to me.
Fore'thought s. Prescience; previous consideration.
Afore'thought a. Premeditated.
Mer'rythought s. The forked bone of a bird's breast.
Nought s., a., and adv. Naught.
Dread'nought s. A fearless person; a thick overcoat; a large and heavily armed battleship.
Brought v.t. (past and past part.) (*Bring*).
Drought s. Dryness; want of rain; thirst.
Wrought (rawt) past and past part. (*Work*).
Unwrought' a. Worked in among other things.
Overwrought' a. Exhausted with work or excitement.
Sought (sawt) past and past part. (*Seek*).
Besought' v.t. (past part.) (*Beseech*).
Klepht s. A Greek brigand.
It pron. third pers. neut.
Ait s. Small island in river.
Bait s. A lure for fish, etc.; refreshment for horses on a journey. v.t. To set traps for game, etc.; to feed horses when travelling; to harass bulls, badgers, etc., with dogs for sport. v.i. To halt on a journey for refreshment.
White'bait s. Fry of sprats, herrings, etc.
Gait s. Manner of walking, carriage, bearing.
Plait s. A fold; a braid as of hair. v.t. To fold, double in narrow folds; to braid; to involve.
Trait (trā) s. A feature, characteristic mark.
Por'trait s. That which is portrayed; a likeness; vivid description.
Strait a. Confined, restricted, strict. s. A narrow passage or stretch of water; distress, difficulty.
Distrait' a. Absent-minded; inattentive.
Wait v.i. To expect, to stay; to attend, to serve at table. v.t. To await. s. Act or period of waiting.
Await' v.t. and i. To wait for, expect; to be in store for.
Bit s. A morsel; the part of a bridle that goes in a horse's mouth; a boring tool. v.t. To put the bit in a horse's mouth.
Hab'it s. Custom; long usage; state of body natural or acquired; aptitude; dress. v.t. To clothe, array.
Inhab'it v.t. To live in, occupy. v.i. To dwell, abide.
Cohab'it v.i. To live together as husband and wife.
Rab'bit s. A small burrowing rodent.
Deb'it s. The debtor side of a ledger. v.t. To charge with debt.
Adhib'it v.t. To apply, append, employ.
Inhib'it v.t. To restrain, hinder, check.
Prohib'it v.t. To forbid, debar, hinder.
Exhib'it v.t. To offer to view, to display. s. That which is exhibited; a legal document or written statement.
Am'bit s. Bounds, scope.
Gam'bit s. A chess-opening in which a pawn or piece is sacrificed.
O'bit s. A person's death; notice of this; a funeral ceremony.
Post-o'bit s. A bond securing to a lender money on some person's death.
Or'bit s. The path of a heavenly body; the cavity of or surrounding parts of the eye; course of action.
Cu'curbit s. A gourd; a gourd-shaped vessel.
Tur'bit s. A variety of pigeon.
Tit'bit s. A dainty morsel.
Cu'bit s. Measure of length (18 to 22 ins.); the fore-arm.
Ou'bit s. A hairy caterpillar.
Cit s. A townsman.
Tac'it a. Implied but not expressed.
Def'icit s. Deficiency, especially in an account; amount of this.
Lic'it a. Lawful; allowed.
Elic'it v.t. To evoke, extract, draw out.
Illic'it a. Prohibited; unlawful.
Solic'it v.t. and i. To make petition to; to beg earnestly; to invite.
Implic'it a. Inferred; tacitly comprised.
Explic'it a. Distinctly stated; clear; positive.
Inexplic'it a. Not clearly defined or stated.
Ad'it s. An horizontal entrance to a mine.
Ed'it v.t. To prepare for publication; to alter, garble.
Re-ed'it v.t. To revise, edit again.
Cred'it s. Reliance on truth of something; belief; reputation derived from confidence; trust given or re-

ceived; expectation of future payment; side of an account on which receipts are entered. v.t. To trust, believe; to sell or lend to in confidence of future payment; to attribute.

Accred'it v.t. To vouch for, furnish with credentials.

Discred'it v.t. To disbelieve; to bring reproach on. s. Want of credit; disgrace, reproach.

Ban'dit s. A highway robber, especially as a member of a band.

Pun'dit s. One learned in Hindu law, literature, etc.; a pedant.

Au'dit s. An official examination of accounts. v.t. To make such examination.

Plau'dit s. A shout of praise; acclamation.

Albe'it conj. Be it so, although.

Howbe'it adv. Nevertheless.

Deceit' s. Fraud, deception, duplicity.

Conceit' s. An idea, thought; self-flattering opinion; a quaint fancy.

Coun'terfeit v.t. To imitate or copy, especially without right and intending to pass off as genuine; to simulate; to coin. a. Made in imitation, forged. s. An impostor; a forgery, base imitation.

For'feit s. A fine, mulct, penalty. v.t. To lose by some breach of condition.

Sur'feit v.t. and i. To feed to excess; to satiate, clog. s. Excess in eating or drinking; nausea caused by this.

Fah'renheit s. A thermometer with freezing point marked 32° and boiling point 212°.

Fit s. A paroxysm; commotion; disorder; sudden and brief activity; due adjustment of dress to body. a. Qualified; proper; apt; suitable; right. v.t. To suit, adapt; to qualify. v.i. To be proper or becoming; to be adapted.

Befit' v.t. To be suitable for; to be incumbent upon.

Ben'efit s. An act of kindness; advantage; favour conferred; a performance in aid of someone or something. v.t. To do a service to. v.i. To gain advantage.

Refit' v.t. To prepare or fit out a second time; to repair.

Sof'fit s. Under surface of a cornice, etc.

Com'fit s. A sweetmeat.

Discom'fit v.t. To vanquish, to scatter in battle, rout.

Prof'it s. Advantage, benefit, pecuniary or other gain. v.i. To derive profit, improve. v.t. To benefit.

Misfit' s. A bad fit or match; a badly fitting garment.

Out'fit s. A fitting out; equipment.

Bag'git s. A salmon that has just spawned.

Dig'it s. A finger; finger's breadth, ¾ in.; any one of the numerals; $\frac{1}{12}$th diameter of the sun or moon.

Hit v.t. To strike, reach, attain, suit. s. A blow; a lucky chance, fortuitous event.

Chit s. A child, young person; a note, a servant's reference.

Whit s. The least particle; a jot.

Tu-whit' s. The cry of an owl.

Kit s. Outfit of a soldier or sailor; the whole lot; a wooden tub; a chest; a small violin; a kitten.

Stick'it a. (*Scot.*) Stuck.

Bethank'it s. (*Scot.*) Grace after meat.

Skit s. A lampoon, slight satire.

Lit past and past part. (*Light*).

Flit v.i. To fly with rapid motion, to flutter; to remove house suddenly to avoid payment of rent.

Wagon-lit' (-lē') s. A railway sleeping-car.

Sun'lit a. Lit up by the sun.

Split v.t. To divide lengthwise; to cleave. v.i. To part asunder, burst; to break faith. s. A crack, rent; breach, schism.

Slit v.t. To cut lengthwise or into strips; to split, rend. s. A long cut, narrow opening.

Submit' v.t. To yield; to surrender to authority, etc.; to refer. v.i. To surrender, acquiesce; to suffer patiently.

Admit' v.t. To allow to enter; to concede.

Readmit' v.t. To admit again.

Emit' v.t. To send forth, to let fly, to exhale.

Demit' v.t. and i. To resign, lay down (office); to yield.

Remit' v.t. To send or put back; to relax, abate; to forgive. v.i. To slacken.

Lim'it s. Bound; border; utmost extent. v.t. To set a bound to, confine within bounds.

Delim'it v.t. To fix the limits of.

Sem'mit s. An under-vest.

Commit' v.t. To entrust, consign; to send to prison; to perpetrate; to pledge or compromise (oneself).

Recommit' v.t. To commit again, refer back.

Sum'mit s. The top; utmost elevation.

Omit' v.t. To leave out, pass by, neglect.

Intromit' v.t. To send in; to admit.

Vom'it v.t. and i. To throw up from the stomach; to spew. s. Matter ejected from the stomach through the mouth; an emetic.

Her'mit s. A religious solitary; a recluse, anchorite.

Permit' v.t. To allow, consent to, grant; to concede, tolerate.

Per'mit s. A written permission; warrant, leave.

Pretermit' v.t. To pass by, omit, disregard.

Intermit' v.t. To cause to cease temporarily; to suspend. v.i. To cease for a time.

Transmit' v.t. To convey, hand down, make over.

Manumit' v.t. To release from slavery.

Nit s. Egg of a louse or other parasitic insect.

Knit v.t. To make, unite, or weave by texture without a loom. v.i. To grow together.

U'nit s. One; a single thing, person, or group; a quantity assumed as a standard.

Dacoit' s. One of a gang of robbers and murderers in India or Burma.

Doit s. A Dutch coin of very small value a trifle, jot.

Ex'ploit s. A deed, act, feat, especially when heroic.

Exploit' v.t. To turn to account, utilize; to use or work for one's own profit or purpose.

Droit s. A legal right or due.

Adroit' a. Dexterous, skilful.

Maladroit' a. Clumsy; ungraceful.

Intro'it s. Antiphon sung or said as the priest goes to the altar at Mass.

Quoit s. A heavy, flat, iron ring thrown at a mark as a game. v.i. To throw or play at quoits.
Pit s. A deep hole; a well; the shaft of a mine; a cavity, depression; back part of theatre floor. v.t. To mark with small hollows; to set in antagonism to.
Decrep'it a. Infirm; worn-out by age.
Pip'it s. A bird of the lark family.
Cock'pit s. An area for cock-fighting; a temporary lower-deck hospital on a man-of-war in action.
Pul'pit s. A raised place for a preacher; preachers collectively; preaching.
Arm'pit s. The hollow under the shoulder.
Tap'pit a. (*Scot.*) Crested.
Spit s. Bar on which meat is roasted; point of low land running into the sea; spittle; spitting. v.t. and i. To transfix, put (meat) on a spit; to eject (saliva) from the mouth.
Turn'spit s. One who turns the spit, a menial; a variety of terrier.
Brit s. The young of the herring or sprat.
Inher'it v.t. To receive as an heir or by nature from a progenitor. v.i. To come into possession thus.
Disinher'it v.t. To cut off from inheritance.
Mer'it s. Desert, reward, worth. v.t. To deserve, earn; to be entitled to.
Demer'it s. That which detracts from merit or deserves censure.
Frit s. The materials of which glass is made. v.t. To calcine this.
Grit s. Sand; sharp particles; texture of stone; (*slang*) spirit, firmness. v.t. and i. To grate.
Spir'it s. The breath of life, the soul; a sprite; mood; courage; intent; distilled alcoholic liquor. v.t. To encourage; to convey away secretly.
Dispir'it v.t. To discourage, deject, depress.
Inspir'it v.t. To infuse life, animation, etc., into; to inspire.
Pra'krit s. Any one of the Hindu dialects based on Sanskrit.
San'skrit s. The ancient language of the Hindus.
Cul'prit s. One arraigned for or convicted of a crime; an offender.
Sprit s. A small spar crossing a sail diagonally.
Esprit' s. Spirit, soul, wit.
Bow'sprit s. A large spar projecting over the bow of a ship.
Wor'rit (wŭr'-) v. and s. (*Worry*).
Writ s. Anything written; especially a legal document commanding one to do something. past and past part. (*Write*).
Sit v.i. To rest on the lower part of the trunk; to incubate; to be placed, remain; to be engaged in public business. v.t. To keep one's seat upon.
Vis'it v.t. To go to, call on, attend; to afflict. v.i. To make calls. s. Act of visiting; a call.
Revis'it v.t. To visit again.
Tran'sit s. Act of passing; passage, especially of a heavenly body across disc of another.
Pos'it v.t. To postulate, assume, premise.
Juxtapos'it v.t. To place near, to juxtapose.
Depos'it v.t. To lay up, lay down; to place; to commit, entrust. s. Anything deposited; a pledge, security.
Repos'it v.t. To lay up for safety, etc.
Ovipos'it v.i. To deposit eggs.
Pro'sit int. Good health! good luck to you!
Assump'sit s. A promise founded on a consideration; an action to enforce such promise.
Tit s. A titmouse, tomtit, etc.; a morsel; a small horse; a slight blow; a teat.
Cir'cuit s. Space enclosed in a circle; visitation of judges, etc.
Bis'cuit s. A small plain cake baked hard and crisp.
Con'duit s. A channel or pipe for water.
Bruit s. Noise, tumult; report. v.t. To rumour.
Recruit' s. A newly enlisted soldier; one newly joined. v.t. To supply with new men; to repair by fresh supplies; to reinvigorate. v.i. To gain new supplies, health, etc.
Fruit s. The product of a tree; the seed or matured ovary; that which is produced; offspring; effect. v.i. To bear fruit.
Suit (sūt) s. Series; petition; pursuit; courtship; set of men's outer clothes. v.t. and i. To fit, answer, serve, agree.
Jes'uit s. A member of the Roman Catholic Society of Jesus; (*slang*) a crafty person, a prevaricator.
Non'suit s. The stoppage of a suit during trial. v.t. To subject to this.
Pursuit' s. Act of pursuing; quest; employment.
Law'suit s. An action in a court of law.
Quit v.t. To release from obligation, etc.; to discharge; to leave, give up. a. Discharged, absolved; free, clear.
Acquit' v.t. To absolve, set free from charge.
Mesquit' s. A leguminous shrub of Central America.
Dav'it s. One of a pair of arms having tackle to raise a boat by.
Affida'vit s. A written declaration on oath.
Wit s. Sense; intelligence, intellect; humour, irony; a bright and humorous person. v.i. To know, be aware.
God'wit s. A shore-bird resembling the curlew.
Pe'wit s. The lapwing; its cry.
Twit v.t. To taunt, reproach.
Outwit' v.t. To surpass in stratagem, frustrate by superior ingenuity.
Ex'it s. Departure, as of an actor from the stage; a going out; death; a way out.
Alt s. The higher register of sounds.
Co'balt s. A greyish metallic element; a blue pigment.
Dalt s. A foster-child.
Dealt past and past part. (*Deal*).
Halt v.i. To stop, especially in walking; to hestitate. v.t. To cause to stop. a. Limping, crippled. s. A limp; a stopping; lame people.
As'phalt s. A hard, bituminous substance used for paving.
Piss'asphalt s. Mineral tar.
Shalt v. aux., 2nd sing. (*Shall*).
Malt s. Barley steeped in water, made to germinate, and dried in a kiln. v.t. and i. To convert or be converted into malt.
Smalt s. Glass tinged deep blue with cobalt.

Salt s. Chloride of sodium; a substance for seasoning and preserving food; product of the combination of a base and an acid; wit; an old sailor. a. Impregnated with salt; pungent. v.t. To season or sprinkle with salt.
Bas'alt s. A dark volcanic rock.
Su'persalt s. An acid salt.
Dry'salt v.t. To cure by drying and salting.
Exalt' v.t. To elevate; to raise in power, rank, dignity, etc.; to extol.
Belt s. A girdle; flexible strap used in machinery; broad strip or zone of country. v.t. To encircle or invest with a belt; to thrash.
Celt s. A member or descendant of an ancient race of N.W. Europe; a prehistoric stone or bronze implement.
Felt s. A fabric made of wool, etc., without weaving. v.t. To make into or cover with this. v.i. To become matted together. past part. (*Feel*).
Heart'felt a. Deeply or sincerely felt.
Melt v.t. To make liquid, to soften; to overcome by emotion. v.i. To become liquid, dissolve, be softened; to pass by imperceptible degrees.
Smelt s. A small silvery fish of the salmon family. v.t. To melt (ore) to separate the metal. past and past part. (*Smell*).
Knelt past and past part. (*Kneel*).
Pelt s. A skin with the hair on; a blow, stroke from something thrown; great speed or impetus. v.i. To beat violently, as rain; to keep on throwing; to hurry. v.t. To strike or assail with missiles.
Spelt s. A S. European variety of wheat. past and past part. (*Spell*).
Welt s. Strip of leather between the upper and sole of a boot. v.t. To furnish with this; (*slang*) to flog.
Dwelt past and past part. (*Dwell*).
Gilt a. Gilded, adorned. s. Gilding.
Hilt s. Handle of a sword or dagger.
Jilt v.t. and i. To deceive in love, play the jilt. s. A woman who capriciously throws her lover over.
Kilt s. The kind of petticoat worn by Highlanders. v.t. To fold or pleat like a kilt.
Lilt v.i. To sing cheerfully; to dance in jerky fashion. s. A lively tune or rhythm.
Milt s. The spleen; soft roe of fishes.
Spilt v. (past and past part.) (*Spill*).
Silt s. Deposit of fine earth from water. v.t. To choke with mud. v.i. To percolate; to ooze.
Tilt s. A covering overhead, a small awning; inclination forward; thrust or charge with a lance, a tournament; a large, pivoted hammer. v.i. To heel over; to charge with a lance. v.t. To raise at one end, tip; to forge with a tilt; to cover with an awning.
Stilt s. Pole with step attached for raising foot in walking; a bird allied to the plover.
Built v. (past and past part.) (*Build*).
Guilt s. Sin, crime, criminality; offence.
Quilt s. Padded cover for a bed, etc. v.t. To stitch together with soft fabric between.
Wilt v.i. To wither, droop. v. aux. 2nd sing. (*Will*).
Bolt s. A sliding bar or fastener; stout metal pin with a head; a missile of a cross-bow; a thunderbolt; a sudden surprise; a sudden starting off, escape. v.t. To fasten with a bolt; to swallow hastily; to sieve, make trial of. v.i. To run or break away.
Thun'derbolt s. A missile supposed to be discharged by thunder; a fulmination, denunciation.
Colt s. A male foal; a foolish young fellow; a young professional cricketer.
Dolt s. A blockhead, dunce, simpleton.
Holt s. A grove, plantation; a burrow, covert.
Jolt v.t. and i. To shake or move along with sudden jerks. s. A sudden jerk or shock.
Smolt s. A young salmon.
Volt s. A standard electrical unit; circular tread of a horse; sudden leap in fencing.
Revolt' v.i. To renounce allegiance, to rebel; to be disgusted. v.t. To repel, shock, nauseate. s. Rebellion; sedition.
Ar'chivolt s. Inner contour of an arch.
Ult adv. Contraction of "ultimo."
Fault s. A blemish, defect, flaw; a dislocation of strata.
Default s. Omission of duty; crime; failure. v.i. To fail in fulfilling a contract, engagement, etc.
Gault s. A series of beds of clay and marl between the upper and lower green-sand.
Som'ersault (sŭm'-) s. A leap heels over head. v.i. To make this.
Assault' v.t. To assail, storm. s. A violent attack.
Vault s. An arched roof; a cellar, cave; a leap, especially with the hand on something. v.i. To leap thus, to bound. v.t. To arch; to leap over.
Cult s. Worship; system of or rites and ceremonies of a religion.
Occult' a. Hidden from the eye or understanding; mystical, supernatural, esoteric. v.t. To cut off from view.
Dif'ficult a. Arduous; not easy to be done; perplexing.
Adult' s. A person grown to maturity. a. Having arrived at maturity.
Indult' s. A licence from the Pope.
Tu'mult s. Commotion, a stir; uproar.
Penult' s. The last syllable but one of a word.
Antepenult' s. The last syllable but two.
Moult (mōlt) v.i. and t. To shed the feathers, shell, horns, etc., at certain periods. s. Act of moulting.
Poult s. A young chicken, partridge, etc.
Cat'apult s. An ancient military engine for hurling stones, etc.; a toy for discharging small shot. v.t. and i. To throw or shoot with this.
Result' v.i. To issue or proceed as a consequence; to ensue, end. s. Consequence; effect; outcome; inference.
Insult' v.t. To treat with insolence; to affront. v.i. To behave with insolent triumph.

In'sult s. An affront, outrage, indignity; an insulting speech, etc.
Consult' v.i. To take counsel, deliberate, seek advice. v.t. To ask advice of, decide or act in favour of.
Jurisconsult' s. One learned in law; a jurist.
Exult' v.i. To rejoice triumphantly; to glory.
Ant s. A social hymnopterous insect.
Cor'ybant s. A priest of Cybele; a wildly excited dancer.
Can't v. aux. (*Negative*) Can not.
Cant s. Hypocritical speech; whining; gargon, slang; a slope, bevel; a jerk. v.i. To speak insincerely or whiningly; to tilt over. v.t. To tip; give a bevel to; throw with a jerk. a. Lusty, lively, brisk.
Va'cant a. Empty; void; thoughtless.
Pec'cant a. Sinning; criminal; not healthy.
Impec'cant a. Impeccable, sinless.
Desic'cant a. Drying up.
Des'iccant s. An application for drying sores, etc.
Ex'siccant a. Drying. s. A drying medicine or preparation.
Decant v.t. To pour off gently, or from one vessel into another.
Recant' v.t. To retract, revoke, recall.
Sec'ant a. Cutting. s. A line that cuts another.
Cosec'ant s. The secant of the complement of an arc or angle.
Intersec'ant a. Interesting.
Rad'icant a. Producing roots from a stem.
Ab'dicant s. One who abdicates. a. Abdicating.
Pred'icant s. A preaching friar.
Men'dicant a. Begging; practising beggary. s. A beggar, begging monk.
In'dicant a. Pointing out.
Nidif'icant a. Nest-building.
Signif'icant a. Having a meaning; betokening; expressive.
Insignif'icant a. Unimportant; trivial; contemptible.
Ap'plicant s. One who applies.
For'micant a. Almost imperceptible (of the pulse).
Commun'icant s. One who partakes of Holy Communion; one who imparts information. a. Communicating; branching from or into.
Non-commu'nicant s. (*Negative*).
Fab'ricant s. A manufacturer.
Lu'bricant s. A substance for oiling or greasing. a. Oiling.
Ves'icant s. A blistering application. a. Raising blisters.
Tox'icant a. Poisonous. s. A poison.
Intox'icant s. An intoxicating liquor. a. Intoxicating.
Scant v.t. To limit, stint. v.i. To become less. a. Barely sufficient.
Des'cant s. A song, variation of an air; a comment.
Descant' v.i. To sing in parts; to comment at large upon, dilate on.
Corus'cant a. Flashing, sparkling.
Ped'ant s. A pretender to superior learning; a narrow-minded scholar.
Confidant' s. A confidential friend, one entrusted with secrets.
Consol'idant a. Serving to consolidate. s. A conglutinant.
Demand'ant s. One who demands; a plaintiff
Commandant' s. A military governor.
Descend'ant s. Offspring from an ancestor.
Ascendant' a. Rising, superior, predominant. s. Superiority.
Defend'ant s. Person prosecuted in a court.
Pen'dant s. Anything hanging, especially by way of ornament; an appendix, a counterpart; a pennant.
Depend'ant s. A subordinate, a retainer.
Inten'dant s. A manager.
Atten'dant s. One in attendance on another. a Accompanying.
Fon'dant s. A soft sweetmeat.
Abun'dant a. Plentiful.
Superabun'dant a. Abounding to excess.
Redun'dant a. Superfluous; superabundant; copious.
Regard'ant a. Observant; looking backward.
Guard'ant a. Full-faced (*in heraldry*).
Ver'dant a. Green; covered with growing vegetation; inexperienced.
Accor'dant a. Corresponding, consonant.
Concor'dant a. In agreement, harmonious, correspondent.
Discor'dant a. At variance, clashing; inharmonious.
Mor'dant a. Biting, sarcastic; serving to fix colours. s. A fixative used in dyeing, etc.
Pag'eant s. A brilliant display, parade, procession, etc.; something showy; pomp; a series of historical tableaux, etc.
Ser'geant (sar'-) s. A N.C.O. above corporal; a police officer.
Meant (ment) past and past part. (*Mean*).
Per'meant a. Passing through; permeating.
Fainé'ant a. Doing nothing; shiftless. s. A loafer, idler.
Rec'reant a. Cowardly, craven. s. A mean-spirited wretch.
Pro'creant a. Generating; fruitful; Pertaining to procreation.
Mis'creant s. A base fellow, an unprincipled scoundrel.
In'fant s. A baby; a young child; a person under twenty-one. a. Pertaining to infants.
Ter'magant s. A shrewish woman, a scold. a. Brawling, turbulent.
Extrav'agant a. Going beyond due bounds; excessive; unrestrained; profuse in expenditure.
Soliv'agant a. Wandering alone.
Noctiv'agant a. Wandering by night.
El'egant a. Beautiful, pleasing; neat; refined.
Inel'egant a. Wanting in grace, refinement, etc.
Con'gregant s. A member of a congregation.
Ob'ligant a. Obligating. s. One who binds himself or places himself under obligation.
Ir'rigant s. A ditch for irrigating. a. Irrigating.
Lit'igant a. Disposed to litigate; engaged in a lawsuit. s. One thus engaged.
Mit'igant a. Tending to mitigate; lenitive.
Ar'rogant a. Proud; haughty; self-conceited.
Cor'rugant a. Able to corrugate.
Chant v.t. and i. To sing, intone; to celebrate in song. s. Song; music for psalms, canticles, etc.
Bac'chant s. A bacchanal. a. Fond of wine.
Enchant' v.t. To influence by magic; to charm, fascinate.
Pen'chant (-shong) s. Inclination; liking.
Trench'ant a. Cutting, sharp, caustic.
Disenchant' v.t. To free from enchantment.
Mer'chant s. A wholesale trader; an importer. a. Pertaining to trade; commercial.

Couch'ant a. Lying in repose or hid; lying with the head raised (*in heraldry*).
El'ephant s. The largest existing quadruped, pachydermatous, with flexible probocis and long curved tusks; a size of paper (28 in. by 23 in.).
Triumph'ant a. Victorious; exultant.
Syc'ophant s. A fawning dissembler, a parasite.
Hi'erophant s. A religious teacher, a priest.
Offi'ciant s. One who officiates.
Renun'ciant a. Renouncing. s. One who renounces.
Defor'ciant s. One who illegally retains the property of another.
Insou'ciant a. Careless, unconcerned.
Ra'diant a. Radiating, giving out rays; beaming; joyful.
Irra'diant a. Emitting rays of light.
Me'diant s. The third note of a scale.
Subme'diant s. The sixth tone of the scale.
Defi'ant a. Challenging, hostile; openly disobedient.
Gi'ant s. A fabled or real person of excessive stature or powers; anything abnormally large. a. Like a giant; extraordinarily big.
Val'iant a. Brave, courageous, heroic.
Reli'ant a. Confident.
Humil'iant a. Humiliating.
Bril'liant a. Shining, sparkling; of outstanding talent. s. A fine diamond; a small printing type.
Pli'ant a. Capable of being bent; easily influenced; tractable.
Compli'ant a. Yielding, obliging, submissive.
Sup'pliant a. Entreating. s. A humble petitioner.
Contrar'iant a. Antagonistic, opposed.
Var'iant a. Varying; showing variation. s. A different form, type, version, etc.
Invar'iant a. Not varying or subject to variation.
Ine'briant a. Intoxicating. s. An intoxicant.
Delir'iant a. Tending to produce delirium. s. A drug effecting this.
Luxur'iant a. Exuberant in growth; abundant; ornate.
Nego'tiant s. A negotiator.
Se'jant a. Sitting (of heraldic beasts).
Pred'ikant s. A minister of the Dutch Reformed Church in S. Africa.
Askant' adv. Sideways, awry.
Non'chalant a. Indifferent, cool.
Inhal'ant a. Inhaling; used for this. s. That which is inhaled; an inhaler.
Exhal'ant a. Having the quality of exhaling.
Resem'blant a. Resembling.
Assail'ant s. One who assails.
Sib'ilant a. Making or uttered with a hissing sound.
Ju'bilant a. Rejoicing; shouting with joy; triumphant.
Vig'ilant a. Watchful; wary; circumspect.
Horrip'ilant a. Causing horripilation; creepy.
Ru'tilant a. Ruddy, reddish; glowing.
Cal'lant s. (*Scot.*) A lad.
Gal'lant a. Brave, high-spirited; courtly. s. A man of fashion, a beau.
Gallant' a. Specially attentive to women; pertaining to love. v.t. To attend as a cavalier; to pay court to.
Flagel'lant s. A fanatical scourger. a. Given to scourging.
Propel'lant s. That which propels; an explosive.
Appel'lant s. One who appeals.
Interpel'lant a. Interrogatory. s. A questioner; one who interpellates.
Scin'tillant a. Scintillating, twinkling.
Vo'lant a. Able to fly; flying; current; nimble.
Plant s. A vegetable organism; tools, fixtures, machinery, etc., necessary to a business; (*slang*) a prepared fraud or swindle; a decoy. v.t. To set in the ground for growth; to cultivate; to establish; to direct cannon. v.i. To sow seed.
Replant' v.t. To plant ground or plant in the ground again.
Implant' v.t. To plant, fix; to insert; to instil.
Supplant' v.t. To displace and take the place of, to oust.
Transplant' v.t. To plant in another place.
Slant a. Sloping; oblique. v.t. and i. To turn or be turned from a direct line; to lie obliquely, slope. s. A slanting direction or plane.
Aslant' adv., prep. Slantways, obliquely.
Am'bulant a. Walking, itinerant.
Somnam'bulant a. and s. Sleep-walking.
Noctam'bulant a. Night-walking.
Os'culant a. Kissing; just coming into contact.
Strid'ulant a. Harsh; stridulous.
Coag'ulant s. A substance which causes coagulation.
U'lulant a. Howling; given to howling.
Trem'ulant a. Tremulous. s. A tremolo.
Sim'ulant a. Simulating; feigning.
Stim'ulant a. Serving to stimulate. s. Anything that stimulates.
Congrat'ulant a. Congratulating.
Pet'ulant a. Peevish; captious; irritable.
Pos'tulant s. One who makes a request; a candidate.
Ad'amant s. Anything extremely hard or impenetrable.
Clam'ant a. Begging earnestly; beseeching; clamorous.
Claim'ant s. One who claims.
Dor'mant a. Sleeping, quiescent, not active; in abeyance.
Inform'ant s. One who gives intelligence.
Misdemean'ant s. One guilty of a misdemeanour.
Em'anant a. Emanating.
Ten'ant s. One who rents from another. v.t. To hold as a tenant.
Appur'tenant a. Belonging to as of right.
Lieuten'ant (lef-) s. Officer who takes the place of an absent superior; one next below captain (army) or commander (navy).
Rev'enant s. An apparition, spirit of one dead.
Cov'enant s. A contract, written agreement. v.t. To grant by covenant. v.i. To enter into a formal agreement; to stipulate.
Stag'nant a. Dull, motionless; impure from want of motion.
Reg'nant a. Exercising regal authority; predominant.
Preg'nant a. Being with young; significant.
Indig'nant a. Feeling wrath and contempt; annoyed.
Malig'nant a. Extremely malevolent; heinous; virulent; incurable. s. A malevolent person.
Benig'nant a. Gracious; favourable.
Poi'gnant a. Sharp to the taste; penetrating, keen, painful.
Repug'nant a. Contrary, hostile; inconsistent; offensive.
Oppug'nant a. Resisting; hostile.

Complain'ant s. One who complains; a plantiff.
Or'dinant a. Ordaining; regulating. s. One who confers orders.
Exam'inant s. An examiner.
Cul'minant a. On the meridian; at the highest point; supreme.
Ful'minant s. Something that explodes. a. Fulminating.
Dom'inant a. Presiding, prevailing. s. The fifth tone of the scale.
Subdom'inant s. The fourth tone above the tonic.
Predom'inant a. Prevalent; ruling; controlling.
Super-dom'inant s. The sixth tone of the scale.
Ger'minant a. Sprouting, developing.
Deter'minant s. That which terminates; sum of a series of products of several numbers, formed according to specified laws. a. Determinative, decisive.
Lu'minant a. Luminous.
Illu'minant s. An illuminating substance, etc. a. Illuminating.
Ru'minant a. Chewing the cud. s. An animal that does this.
Conglu'tinant a. Serving to unite or heal. s. A medicament that heals wounds by conglutination.
Rem'nant s. Portion remaining; fragment.
Pen'nant s. A long, narrow flag carried at the mast-head.
So'nant a. Sounding; sounded, voiced.
Res'onant a. Able to return sound; echoing; reverberating.
Unis'onant a. Being in unison.
Horris'onant a. Having a terrifying sound.
Multis'onant a. Having many sounds.
Con'sonant s. A letter that cannot be sounded by itself. a. Agreeing, according, congruous.
Incon'sonant a. Not consonant or concordant with.
As'sonant a. Resembling in sound; not consonant.
Dis'sonant a. Discordant; harsh.
Hi'bernant a. Hibernating.
Re'boant a. Re-echoing; loudly resounding.
Pant v i. To breathe heavily or in a laboured way, to gasp; to palpitate, throb. s. A quick or heavy breathing; a gasp, palpitation.
Discrep'ant a. At variance, disagreeing, inconsistent.
Antic'ipant s. One who anticipates.
Partic'ipant a. Sharing, taking part. s. One who participates, takes a part in, or shares.
Ramp'ant a. Rearing; springing; exuberant, frisky.
Flip'pant a. Nimble of speech, pert.
Trip'pant a. Walking (*in heraldry*).
Oc'cupant s. One who occupies; one in possession or residence.
Rant s. Bombast. v.i. To declaim violently, use bombastic language.
Declar'ant s. One who makes a declaration.
Exhil'arant a. Exciting joy. s. That which exhilarates.
Cel'ebrant s. The performer of a religious rite, especially the priest officiating at the Eucharist.
Ter'ebrant a. Boring. s. A boring insect, mollusc, etc.
Vi'brant a. Tremulous; resonant.
Quad'rant s. The quarter of a circle or its circumference; instrument for taking altitudes.
Hy'drant s. A discharge-pipe for water-mains, etc.
Rever'berant a. Resounding.
Protu'berant a. Swelling.
Exu'berant a. Characterized by abundance; superfluous.
Prepon'derant a. Outweighing; preponderating.
Equipon'derant a. Having the same weight.
Vocif'erant a. Vociferous. s. A bawler, one who vociferates.
Refrig'erant a. Cooling. s. That which cools.
Tol'erant a. Enduring; favouring toleration.
Intol'erant a. Not tolerant; bigoted.
Gen'erant a. Producing. s. A line, surface, or solid generated by the motion of a point, line, or surface.
Itin'erant a. Moving from place to place; not settled. s. A wanderer, travelling preacher, etc.
Co-op'erant a. Co-operating. s. One who or that which co-operates.
It'erant a. Repeating; iterating.
Adul'terant s. A substance used for adulteration.
Persever'ant a. Persevering.
Grant v.t. To bestow, give; to concede. s. A gift, bestowal, conveyance in writing.
Fla'grant a. Outrageous; notorious.
Fra'grant a. Sweet-smelling, odorous.
Infra'grant a. Malodorous.
Va'grant a. Wandering, roving, unsettled. s. A vagabond, tramp.
In'tegrant a. Making part of a whole; necessary for completion of a whole.
Mi'grant s. A person, bird, or animal that migrates. a. Migrating.
Em'igrant s. One who emigrates. a. Emigrating; pertaining to emigration.
Im'migrant s. One who settles in a strange country.
Transmi'grant s. One who or that which transmigrates. a. Characterized by transmigration.
Spir'ant s. A consonant uttered with perceptible emission of breath.
Aspir'ant s. One who aspires; a candidate.
Ro'borant a. Strengthening. s. A tonic.
Corrob'orant a. Strengthening. s. A tonic.
O'dorant a. Bearing odours; odoriferous.
Decol'orant s. A bleaching substance. a. Bleaching.
Cor'morant s. A voracious British sea-bird; a glutton.
Ig'norant a. Illiterate; unenlightened; without knowledge or learning.
Expect'orant a. Promoting discharges from the lungs. s. A medicine doing this.
Ar'rant a. Thorough.
War'rant (wor'-) s. Act or instrument giving authority or justifying some action; a voucher; guarantee, security. v.t. To guarantee, authorize, justify.
Er'rant a. Deviating, roving; wandering in search of adventure.
Aber'rant a. Deviating from the path or from normal.
Knight-er'rant s. A knight who travelled in search of adventures.
Cur'rant s. A small dried grape; a garden shrub; the red, white, or black fruit of this.
Demur'rant s. A demur, objection.
Susur'rant a. Rustling, whispering.
Pen'etrant a. Able to penetrate; sharp.
Recal'citrant a. Refractory; showing opposition.
En'trant s. One who enters.
In'trant s. One who enters on a duty or into a society, etc.
Subin'trant a. Characterized by rapidly succeeding paroxysms.

Reg'istrant s. One who registers anything.
Min'istrant a. Acting as a minister or attendant.
Admin'istrant a. Administering. s. One who administers.
Demon'strant s. One who demonstrates.
Remon'strant a. Remonstrating; containing remonstrance. s. One who remonstrates.
Res'taurant s. An eating-house, public dining-place.
Obscur'ant s. An opponent of enlightenment or reform.
Fig'urant s. A ballet-dancer; an actor who merely walks on.
Jur'ant s. One who takes an oath. a. Taking an oath.
Courant' s. An old dance. a. In a running attitude (*heraldry*).
Sat'urant s. A neutralizing substance. a. Saturating.
Tyr'ant (tīr'-) s. An absolute, despotic, or cruel ruler; an autocrat.
Pheas'ant s. A well-known game-bird.
Pleas'ant a. Fit to please; agreeable; gratifying; gay.
Peas'ant s. A rural labourer, a hind, ploughman.
Complai'sant a. Courteous, polite, urbane.
Soi-di'sant (swadē'zong) a. Self-styled; would-be.
Obei'sant (-bā'-) a. Submissive; showing readiness to obey.
Cor'posant s. The St. Elmo's fire seen at mast-heads, etc., during storms.
Ver'sant s. General slope of land; area sloping in one direction.
Con'versant a. Versed in, well acquainted with, closely connected.
Pas'sant a. Applied to heraldic animals depicted as walking.
Inces'sant a. Unceasing; unremitting; perpetual.
Confes'sant s. One who confesses to a priest.
Depres'sant a. Lowering, sedative. s. A sedative medicine.
Puis'sant a. Mighty, powerful.
Impu'issant a. Powerless, impotent.
Rec'usant a. Obstinate in refusal; refusing to conform. s. A nonconformist; one refusing to acknowledge state authority.
Com'batant a. Disposed to fight; fighting. s. A fighter; an armed man in war.
Non-com'batant s. A civilian attached to an army. a. (*Negative*).
Blat'ant a. Bellowing; clamorous.
Infla'tant s. That with which anything may be inflated.
Dila'tant s. A substance that can be dilated. a. Able to dilate.
Na'tant a. Swimming; floating.
Superna'tant a. Floating on the surface.
Disinfec'tant s. A substance for removing or warding off infection.
Humec'tant a. Moistening. s. A diluent.
Expec'tant a. Expecting, looking for, awaiting. s. One who waits in expectation.
Oc'tant s. The eighth part of a circle; position or aspect of a heavenly body when 45 degrees distant from another or from some given point.
Reluc'tant a. Unwilling, averse; granted unwillingly.
Heb'etant a. Blunt; obtuse.
Hab'itant s. A French native of Lower Canada.
Inhab'itant s. One residing permanently in a place.
Exor'bitant a. Exceeding due bounds; extravagant.
Solic'itant a. Soliciting. s. One who solicits.
Inci'tant a. Stimulating. s. A stimulant.
Os'citant a. Yawning, sleepy; negligent.
Resus'citant a. Resuscitating. s. One who comes to life again.
Excit'ant s. A stimulant.
Regur'gitant a. Regurgitating.
Mil'itant a. Combatant; warlike; engaged in war.
Vol'itant a. Volant; flying.
Concom'itant a. Accompanying; concurrent. s. One who or that which accompanies; an accompaniment.
Crep'itant a. Crackling.
Precip'itant a. Rushing headlong; urged violently. s. A precipitating agent.
Ir'ritant s. That which irritates; an application to set up irritation. a. Producing inflammation.
Counter-ir'ritant s. An irritant removing some other irritation. a. Acting thus.
Hes'itant a. Dubious, undecided.
Vis'itant s. A guest; a migratory bird.
Annu'itant s. One in receipt of an annuity.
Eq'uitant a. Riding on horseback; overlapping (of leaves).
Sal'tant a. Leaping (*heraldry*).
Resul'tant s. A force the joint effect of two or more forces. a. Resulting from a combination.
Consul'tant s. One who consults or is consulted.
Exul'tant a. Rejoicing; displaying exultation.
Repen'tant a. Repenting, feeling penitent.
Accoun'tant s. One skilled or employed in keeping or examining accounts.
Moun'tant s. Paste for mounting photographs, etc.
Flo'tant a. Floating, swimming (*Heraldic*).
Accep'tant s. One who accepts.
Accomp'tant s. An accountant.
Impor'tant a. Momentous; of consequence; grave.
Contes'tant s. One who contests.
Prot'estant s. An adherent of Luther at the Reformation; a member of a reformed or non-Roman Catholic Church. a. Pertaining to the faith and principles of those who protest against the Church of Rome.
Protes'tant a. Making a protest.
Dis'tant a. Remote in place, time, relationship, etc.; reserved, shy.
Equidis'tant a. At the same distance from the same point.
Resis'tant s. One who resists. a. Resisting.
Assis'tant s. A helper.
In'stant a. Pressing, urgent; immediate; present, current. s. A moment. adv. Quickly.
Con'stant a. Stedfast, permanent, perpetual; resolute; remaining unchanged. s. That which remains unchanged; a fixed quantity.
Incon'stant a. Changeable; fickle; unstable.
Debutant' s. A man making a first appearance in public.
Exec'utant s. One who performs, especially on a musical instrument.
Ad'jutant s. An officer assisting a commanding officer; a large stork.
Nu'tant a. Nodding; drooping.
Dis'putant s. One who disputes.
Extant' a. Still in existence, in being.
Sex'tant s. The sixth part of a circle; instrument for measuring angular distances, taking altitudes, etc.

Evac'uant a. Evacuative. s. A purgative.
Contin'uant a. Continuing, prolonged.
Quant s. A flanged punt-pole for muddy waters.
Pi'quant (pē'-) a. Pungent, sharp; pleasantly attractive.
Clin'quant a. Resplendent, gaudy. s. Tawdry finery.
Tru'ant s. One who shirks duty; a loiterer. a. Shirking, wilfully absenting oneself.
Men'struant a. Subject to monthly flowing.
Pursu'ant a. Consequent; conformable; according.
Iss'uant a. Emerging.
Sav'ant s. A man of learning.
Levant' s. The eastern part of the Mediterranean and adjoining countries; the wind from here. v.i. To abscond.
Rel'evant a. Pertinent, applicable.
Irrel'evant a. Not to the point; inapplicable.
Sal'ivant a. Exciting saliva. s. A medicine for this.
Gallivant' v.i. To gad about.
Pur'suivant s. An attendant on a herald.
Ser'vant s. One employed by another for wages; one who serves or does services.
Obser'vant a. Watchful; mindful; attentive. s. An Observantine.
Inobser'vant a. Not observant; heedless.
Conser'vant a. Preserving from destruction or decay.
Ad'juvant s. An assistant, auxiliary. a. Helping.
Want (wŏnt) s. Need; deficiency; poverty. v.t. To lack; to desire, need. v.i. To be in want, be deficient.
Relax'ant s. A relaxing medicine.
Flamboy'ant a. Characterized by florid tracery, etc.; elaborately ornate.
Chatoy'ant a. Lustrous, changing colour. s. A stone that changes colour like a cat's eye.
Buoy'ant a. Floating; light; cheerful.
Clairvoyant s. One having second-sight. a. Pertaining to or having the faculty of clairvoyance.
Bez'ant s. A Byzantine gold coin; an heraldic charge.
Cogn'izant a. Having knowledge of.
Recog'nizant a. Recognizing.
Incog'nizant a. Unaware, unconscious.
Wouldn't neg. (*Would not*).
-ent suff. Forming adjectives; and nouns denoting an agent.
Bent s. Inclination; mental bias; a wiry grass.
Lam'bent a. Playing about; flickering.
Succum'bent a. Submissive.
Decum'bent a. Lying down, prostrate.
Recum'bent a. Lying down; reclining; inactive.
Incum'bent a. Resting upon; imposed as a duty. s. One holding a benefice of which the tithes are impropriated.
Superincum'bent a. Resting on something else.
Procum'bent a. Lying face downward; prone; trailing.
Resorb'ent a. Swallowing; absorbing a second time.
Cent s. A hundred; an American coin (1ooth of a dollar); a trifle.
Ja'cent a. Lying at length.
Subja'cent a. Underlying; in a lower situation.
Adja'cent a. Near or next to, contiguous.
Circumja'cent a. Bordering; lying round.
Superja'cent a. Lying above something.
Interja'cent a. Lying or being between; intervening.
Compla'cent a. Gratified; displaying satisfaction.
Ac'cent s. Modulation, tone, or stress of voice; manner of speaking; mark indicating vocal stress.
Accent' v.t. To express or note the accent of.
De'cent a. Becoming, seemly, modest; passable.
Inde'cent a. Offensive to modesty; obscene.
Re'cent a. Late, fresh, modern.
Precent' v.i. To act as precentor.
Malef'icent a. Hurtful; causing evil to.
Benef'icent a. Doing good; munificent, bountiful.
Magnif'icent a. Grand; splendid; showy.
Munif'icent a. Generous, very liberal; bountiful.
Ret'icent a. Inclined to keep silent; taciturn.
Demul'cent a. Softening, mollifying. s. A medicine to soothe irritation.
In'nocent a. Free from guilt; simple-hearted; harmless. s. An idiot, simpleton.
Scent v.t. To perceive by smell; to imbue with odour. s. Odour, perfume; sense of smell; odour left by an animal; course of pursuit; a clue.
Ascent' s. A mounting upwards; means of ascending.
Nas'cent a. Beginning to exist; just appearing; not mature.
Adnas'cent a. (*Adnate*).
Renas'cent a. Rising into life or being again; able or likely to be reborn.
-escent suff. Forming adjectives from inceptive verbs.
Tabes'cent a. Wasting away.
Contabes'cent a. Wasting away.
Albes'cent a. Passing into white; whitish.
Herbes'cent a. Becoming herbaceous.
Pubes'cent a. Arriving at puberty; covered with down (of leaves).
Rubes'cent a. Reddish; tending to become red.
Erubes'cent a. Reddish, blushing.
Aces'cent a. Tending to sourness.
Marces'cent a. Withering without falling.
Glauces'cent a. Tending to become glaucous.
Descent' s. Act of descending; a downward slope; invasion; a passing to an heir; lineage.
Lapides'cent a. Petrifying; tending to petrify.
Irides'cent a. Exhibiting changing colours as position is altered.
Virides'cent a. Greenish; becoming green.
Candes'cent a. Glowing with a white heat.
Incandes'cent a. Glowing or intensely luminous with heat.
Recrudes'cent a. Breaking out afresh; growing painful again.
Rufes'cent a. Tinged with red.
Riges'cent a. Growing stiff or rigid.
Turges'cent a. Swelling; growing big.
Quies'cent a. Resting; dormant; tranquil; mute.
Acquies'cent a. Agreeing; resting satisfied
Alkales'cent a. Slightly alkaline.
Coales'cent a. (*Coalescence*).
Opales'cent a. Characterized by opalescence.
Convales'cent a. Recovering from illness. s. One who is recovering health.
Hyales'cent a. Tending to become glassy.
Adoles'cent a. Advancing to maturity.
Violes'cent a. Tending to a violet colour.
Obsoles'cent a. Going out of use.
Caules'cent a. Having a true stem.
Spinules'cent a. Having small spines; spiny.
Fremes'cent a. Noisy, riotous.
Spumes'cent a. Frothy.
Tumes'cent a. Tumid; slightly swollen.

Intumes'cent a. Swelling; becoming tumid.
Canes'cent a. Hoary, approaching whiteness.
Evanes'cent a. Vanishing, fleeting, passing away.
Gangrenes'cent a. Tending to gangrene.
Senes'cent a. Growing old.
Juvenes'cent a. Being or growing young.
Rejuvenes'cent a. Becoming or causing to become young again.
Ignes'cent a. Emitting sparks; scintillating.
Lignes'cent a. Becoming woody; somewhat woody.
Lumines'cent a. Emitting light unaccompanied by incandescence.
Spines'cent a. Tending to be spinous; thorny.
Torpes'cent a. Becoming torpid or numb.
Glabres'cent a. Slightly glabrous; tending to become smooth.
Cres'cent a. Increasing; shaped like the new moon. s. This shape; the increasing moon; the Turkish standard or power, Mohammedanism; a curved row of houses.
Accres'cent a. Increasing.
Decres'cent a. Waning; tapering from base to summit.
Excres'cent a. Growing out in a morbid or preternatural manner.
Nigres'cent a. Blackish; growing black.
Vires'cent a. Abnormally green; tending to become green.
Arbores'cent a. Having the characteristics of trees.
Phosphores'cent a. Luminous without sensible heat; shining with a faint light, like phosphorus.
Flores'cent a. Flowering; pertaining to florescence.
Efflores'cent a. Liable to effloresce; showing efflorescence.
Sonores'cent a. Emitting sound through agency of light or heat.
Fluores'cent a. Having the quality of fluorescence.
Vitres'cent a. Capable of being formed into or tending to become glass.
Putres'cent a. Growing putrid; pertaining to putrefaction.
Purpures'cent a. Purplish.
Lates'cent a. Becoming obscure or latent.
Lactes'cent a. Producing milk or a milk-like juice; turning to or resembling milk.
Delites'cent a. Concealed, dormant.
Obmutes'cent a. Characterized by obmutescence.
Frutes'cent a. Shrubby.
Liques'cent a. Tending to become liquid; melting.
Deliques'cent a. Liquefying in the air.
Flaves'cent a. Turning yellow.
Revives'cent a. Reviving; recovering energy.
Fulves'cent a. Inclined to be fulvous.
Deferves'cent a. (*Defervescence*).
Efferves'cent a. Bubbling through disengagement of gas.
Dehis'cent a. Opening, as the capsule of a plant.
Indehis'cent a. Not opening spontaneously (of pods, etc.).
Reminis'cent a. Capable of calling or inclined to call to mind.
Resipis'cent a. Restored to one's right mind; being wise after the event.
Concu'piscent a. (*Concupiscence*).
Abdu'cent a. Able to draw parts back or away (of muscles).
Addu'cent a. Drawing to a given point.
Redu'cent s. That which reduces.
Lu'cent a. Shining, bright, resplendent.
Noctilu'cent a. Shining by night.
Translu'cent a. Allowing light to pass through; clear.

Dent s. Mark made by a blow with a blunt instrument; tooth of a wheel, etc. v.t. To make a dent in.
Ca'dent a. Having rhythmical cadence going down (of heavenly bodies).
Deca'dent a. In a state of decay; deteriorating, falling off.
Prece'dent a. Going before; anterior.
Pre'cedent s. Something done or said serving as an example or authority.
Antece'dent a. Going before, prior. s. That which goes or has gone before; the noun to which a relative refers.
Interce'dent a. Mediating.
Cre'dent a. Believing, giving credit.
Bi'dent s. A two-pronged fork.
Ac'cident s. An unexpected happening; a mishap, casualty; a non-essential quality or attribute.
Oc'cident s. The West; the western quarter: Western culture, etc.
In'cident a. Casual, fortuitous, occasional. s. That which happens; an event; casualty.
Coin'cident a. Having coincidence; concurring.
Ei'dent a. Diligent, attentive.
Dif'fident a. Distrustful of one's self; suspicious.
Con'fident a. Full of or having confidence; trustful; assured; self-reliant.
Tri'dent s. A three-pronged sceptre or spear.
Stri'dent a. Harsh, grating, creaking.
Res'ident a. Dwelling in a place for some time; residing; inherent. s. One who dwells in a place; a public minister at a foreign court.
Non-res'ident a. and s. (*Negative*).
Pres'ident s. One who presides; a chairman; elected chief of a republic.
Dis'sident a. Not agreeing, dissenting. s. One who dissents; a dissenter.
Ev'ident a. Plain to the sight; obvious.
Prov'ident a. Foreseeing; prudent; frugal.
Improv'ident a. Wanting foresight; careless; thriftless.
Can'dent a. Glowing, white-hot.
Scan'dent a. Climbing by means of tendrils.
Ascen'dent a., s. (*Ascendant*).
Descen'dent a. Descending; proceeding from an original.
Transcen'dent a. Surpassing; supremely excellent; going beyond the bounds of human knowledge.
Splen'dent a. Shining, brilliant; very conspicuous.
Resplen'dent a. Shining with brilliant lustre; gloriously bright.
Pen'dent a. Hanging; projecting; pendulous.
Depen'dent a. Hanging down; subordinate; contingent.
Indepen'dent a. Free; bold; not subject to control. s. A Congregationalist.
Interdepen'dent a. Mutually dependent.
Impen'dent a. Impending; imminent.
Superinten'dent s. An overseer, manager, controller.
Indent' v.t. To notch; to mark with inequalities; to bind by indenture v.i. To be notched; to wind in and out. s. A notch, jag.
Despon'dent a. Despairing, depressed and inactive.
Co-respon'dent s. A joint respondent, especially in a divorce suit.
Correspon'dent a. Congruous with; suitable; answering. s. One with whom one interchanges letters; a newswriter

Obtun'dent s. A medicine for deadening pain; a demulcent.
Explo'dent s. An explosive consonant.
Ro'dent a. Gnawing. s. An animal that gnaws.
Corro'dent a. Having power to corrode. s. A substance that corrodes.
Ar'dent a. Burning; fervent, eager.
Mor'dent s. A melodic grace in music.
Im'pudent a. Wanting modesty; insolent; pert; saucy.
Pru'dent a. Careful; provident; discreet; judicious.
Impru'dent a. Injudicious, indiscreet; careless.
Jurispru'dent a. Understanding law. s. One who understands law.
Protru'dent a. Protruding.
Stu'dent s. One engaged in study; a pupil, scholar.
Fent s. A placket or opening in a garment.
Gent s. (*Slang*) A gentleman. a. High-born, graceful (*obs.*).
A'gent s. One who acts for another, a deputy; an active cause or power.
Rea'gent s. A substance used to detect presence of other bodies.
Coa'gent s. One who acts with; an associate. a. Acting with.
Re'gent a. Ruling; exercising vicarious authority. s. One governing in place of the sovereign.
In'digent a. Being in want; poor; destitute.
Neg'ligent a. Careless; neglectful.
Dil'igent a. Industrious, painstaking, persevering.
Intel'ligent a. Sagacious; well informed; clever.
Cor'rigent s. A corrective medicine. a. Corrective.
Intran'sigent a. Irreconcilable; uncompromising; intractable. s. An uncompromising adherent; an advanced Radical.
Ex'igent a. Pressing, requiring immediate attention, etc.
Indul'gent a. Indulging; disposed to indulge; forbearing; gentle.
Ful'gent a. Shining, dazzling, bright.
Reful'gent a. Shining brightly; splendid.
Efful'gent a. Shining brightly; diffusing radiance.
Emul'gent a. Milking or draining out, especially of veins and arteries. s. An emulgent vessel; a preparation to excite the flow of bile.
Plan'gent a. Resounding; beating, as a wave.
Tan'gent s. A straight line meeting without intersecting a curve. a. Meeting thus.
Cotan'gent s. The tangent of the complement of an arc or angle.
Rin'gent a. Irregular (of a corolla).
Refrin'gent a. Refractive.
Strin'gent a. Severe; rigid; binding.
Astrin'gent a. Contracting animal tissues; strengthening. s. A medicine that contracts and strengthens.
Constrin'gent a. Having the quality of contracting.
Contin'gent a. Incidental; dependent upon an uncertainty. s. A contingency; an apportionment; a quota, especially of troops.
Pun'gent a. Sharp; acrid; stinging.
Co'gent a. Convincing; pressing on the mind.
Ar'gent s. Silver (*in heraldry*). a. Silvery.
Mar'gent s. A margin, shore.
Emer'gent a. Emerging.
Deter'gent s. A cleansing medicine or application. a. Cleansing, purging.
Abster'gent a. Having cleansing qualities. s. Something that purges or cleanses.
Diver'gent a. Diverging; receding from each other.
Conver'gent a. Tending to one point or object; approaching.
Ur'gent a. Pressing, importunate; vehement.
Resur'gent a. Rising again, especially from the dead. s. One who rises from the dead.
Insur'gent a. Rising against the government; rebellious; surging in. s. A rebel.
Assur'gent a. Ascending; rising aggressively.
Con'trahent a. Contracting.
Pschent s. The double crown of ancient Egypt.
Am'bient a. Surrounding, investing.
Circum-am'bient a. Surrounding; going round.
-fa'cient suff. Giving sense of producing the action of the verb to which it is added.
Sorbefa'cient a. Sucking up; promoting absorption. s. An absorbing substance.
Rubefa'cient a. Making red. s. A counter-irritant producing redness of the skin.
Calefa'cient a. Causing or exciting warmth. s. A medicine that increases bodily heat.
Tumefa'cient a. Producing swelling.
Stupefa'cient a. Stupefying. s. Anything promoting stupefaction.
Liquefa'cient a. Serving to liquefy. s. That which liquefies.
Parturifa'cient a. Promoting parturition. s. A medicine used for producing premature delivery.
Defic'ient a. Wanting, defective.
Effic'ient a. Effective, efficacious; competent.
Ineffic'ient a. Wanting in ability or capacity.
Coeffic'ient a. Co-operating, acting in union. s. Anything co-operating; a multiplying quantity placed before another quantity or symbol.
Suffi'cient a. Enough, sufficing; adequate; fit, able.
Insuffi'cient a. Inadequate; wanting in power, ability, etc.; incommensurate.
Profi'cient a. Well skilled, competent, versed. s. An expert, adept.
Non-profi'cient a. (*Negative*).
An'cient a. Old, antique; that happened in past times.
Nes'cient a. Ignorant; agnostic.
Pre'scient a. Far-seeing; having foreknowledge.
Omnis'cient a. Having universal knowledge; all-knowing, all-seeing.
Incon'scient a. Unconscious.
Gra'dient s. Proportionate ascent or descent of several planes; slope.
Obe'dient a. Submissive to authority.
Disobe'dient a. Neglecting or refusing to obey.
Expe'dient a. Proper, fit, convenient. s. A means to an end; a shift.
Inexpe'dient a. Not advisable or judicious; disadvantageous.
Ingre'dient s. A component part.
Au'dient a. Listening.
Sa'lient a. Projecting, prominent; leaping (*heraldry*). s. A portion of defences projecting towards the enemy.
Cli'ent s. An employer of a lawyer; one under patronage.
Resil'ient a. Springing or inclined to spring back.
Transil'ient a. Extending across; spanning.
Consil'ient a. Concurring.
Dissil'ient a. Bursting open with elasticity starting asunder.

Emol'lient a. Softening, making supple. s. An application which allays irritation.
Ebul'lient a. Boiling over; very enthusiastic.
Le'nient a. Mild; merciful; clement.
Preve'nient a. Going before; preventive.
Conve'nient a. Suitable, handy, close by, opportune.
Inconve'nient a. Wanting due facilities; unsuitable; disadvantageous; inopportune.
Superve'nient a. Coming as something additional.
Interve'nient a. Coming or occurring between; intervening.
Sa'pient a. Wise; would-be wise; discerning.
Recip'ient s. One who receives. a. Receiving.
Incip'ient a. Arising; in the early stages.
Percip'ient a. Having the faculty of perception. s. One who perceives, especially telepathically.
Impercip'ient a. Imperceptive.
Intercip'ient a. Intercepting; seizing by the way.
Suscip'ient a. Receiving; admitting.
Desip'ient a. Foolish, nonsensical.
Aper'ient s. A purgative medicine. a. Laxative, purgative.
Or'ient s. The East; the eastern horizon. a. Rising, as the sun; eastern; shining; perfect (of pearls). v.t. To orientate.
Hir'rient a. Trilled.
Nu'trient a. Conveying nourishment; nutritious. s. Anything that nourishes.
Prur'ient a. Inclined to lewdness; lascivious.
Esur'ient a. Greedy; grasping.
Partur'ient a. Bringing forth or about to bring forth young.
Tran'sient a. Momentary, fleeting, passing quickly.
Pa'tient a. Without murmuring; persevering; not easily provoked; not hasty. s. A person under medical treatment.
Impa'tient a. Hasty; very uneasy; not enduring quietly.
Out'patient s. A non-resident hospital patient.
Sen'tient a. Having the faculty of perception. s. One who is sentient.
Presen'tient a. Perceiving beforehand.
Insen'tient a. Not sentient; inanimate.
Consen'tient a. Agreeing, accordant.
Assen'tient s. One who agrees. a. Assenting to.
Dissen'tient a. Disagreeing; declaring dissent.
To'tient s. Number of totitives in a given number.
Quo'tient s. Number resulting from division.
Abor'tient a. Barren, sterile.
Discu'tient a. Able to disperse morbid matter. s. A medicine effecting such dispersal.
Subser'vient a. Obsequious; useful as means.
Kent s. A punting-pole. v.i. To punt.
Lent s. The ecclesiastical forty days fast (Ash Wednesday to Easter); past and past part. (*Lend*).
-lent suff. Denoting full of.
Tal'ent s. An ancient weight and coin; intellectual ability; a special faculty or aptitude.
Prev'alent a. Gaining superiority or advantage; extensively existing, prevailing.
Div'alent a. Having power to combine with two univalent elements or radicals.
Univ'alent a. Having a combining power of one.
Quadriv'alent a. Having a combining power of four.
Triv'alent a. Having a valence of three.
Multiv'alent a. Having several degrees of valency.
Equiv'alent a. Equal in value, weight, worth, etc.; of the same import.
Blent a. Mingled.
Relent' v.i. To become less harsh, etc.; to yield.
Si'lent a. Not making any sound; absolutely quiet or still; speechless; taciturn; not pronounced.
Pes'tilent a. Pestilential; contaminating; troublesome.
Ex'cellent a. Surpassing others; worthy, choice, distinguished.
Superex'cellent a. Excellent beyond what is usual.
Repel'lent a. Repelling, or tending to repel; repulsive; deterring.
Impel'lent a. Having power to impel. s. Driving force.
Propel'lent a. Propelling; driving forward.
Expel'lent a. Expelling.
Prepol'lent a. Having superior influence; prevailing.
Equipol'lent a. Having equal power; equivalent.
O'lent a. Fragrant, odorous.
Do'lent a. Sorrowful, doleful.
Red'olent a. Diffusing odour; strong-scented; characterized by.
In'dolent a. Habitually lazy; causing no pain.
Vi'olent a. Furious; impetuous; passionate.
Sanguin'olent a. Bleeding.
Som'nolent a. Sleepy, drowsy.
Multip'olent a. Having manifold power.
In'solent a. Haughty; insulting; impudent.
Malev'olent a. Ill-disposed; spiteful; malicious.
Benev'olent a. Kind, charitable.
Tur'bulent a. Tumultuous, disorderly; riotous.
Floc'culent a. Tufted, woolly; pertaining to the down of fledglings.
Suc'culent a. Juicy; full of juice.
Fec'ulent a. Full of dregs; turbid.
Es'culent a. Good for food; edible. s. Anything eatable.
Lu'culent a. Lucid, clear, manifest.
Mu'culent a. Slimy; full of mucus.
Truc'ulent a. Ferocious, violent, fell.
Fraud'ulent a. Practising fraud; dishonest.
Tem'ulent a. Drunk; intoxicating.
Crap'ulent a. Sick from over-indulgence in liquor.
Op'ulent a. Rich; wealthy; affluent.
Cor'pulent a. Very fat or fleshy; stout.
Puber'ulent a. Downy (of plants).
Pulver'ulent a. Powdery, dusty.
Vir'ulent a. Extremely poisonous; bitterly malignant.
Pur'ulent a. Containing or resembling pus; putrid.
Flat'ulent a. Windy in the stomach and intestines; empty; vain.
-ment suff. Form nouns of result, state, action, etc.
Medic'ament s. A healing substance or application.
Predic'ament s. Condition; state; plight.
Fund'ament s. The lower part of the body; the buttocks.
Lin'eament a. Characteristic features; form, outline.
Lig'ament s. anything that binds; a substance binding one bone to another.
Par'liament s. A supreme legislative assembly, especially of Great Britain.
Lament' v.i. To mourn, grieve, regret. v.t. To bewail, deplore. s. A lamentation; a dirge.
Fil'ament s. A slender thread; a fibre.
Ar'mament s. War munitions and equipment; an armed force.
Disarm'ament s. Act of disarming; reduction of armed forces.
Firm'ament s. The sky or heavens.
Or'nament s. Decoration; anything that adorns; a church accessory, vestment, etc. v.t. To adorn, embellish.

Tour'nament s. A mock-fight; a contest of skill in which a number take part.
Sac'rament s. A solemn religious rite; the Eucharist.
Tem'perament s. Individual character; frame of mind.
Arbit'rament s. Award of an arbitrator, authoritative decision.
Addit'ament s. Something added.
Heredit'ament s. Inheritable property.
Tes'tament s. A will; one of the two divisions of the Bible.
Enjamb'ment s. The running of the sense of a verse beyond the limit of a couplet.
Entomb'ment s. Burial.
Withhold'ment s. Act of withholding; state of being withheld.
Disband'ment s. Act of disbanding.
Command'-ment s. An order; a Divine command.
Amend'ment s. A change for the better, reformation; a correction, alteration.
Intend'ment s. Legal intent or meaning.
Astound'ment s. Astonishment.
Bombard'ment s. An attack with artillery or bombs.
Cement' s. A substance for causing adhesion, especially of stones; a bond of union. v.t. To unite with cement, to unite firmly.
Deface'ment s. That which mars; injury to the appearance; obliteration.
Efface'ment s. Act or result of effacing.
Sol'acement s. Act of solacing; state of being solaced.
Replace'ment s. Act of replacing; a substitute.
Emplace'ment s. A platform for guns.
Displace'ment s. Act of displacing; quantity of water displaced by a floating body.
Misplace'ment s. Act of misplacing; state of being wrongly placed.
Embrace'ment s. A clasp, embrace.
Entice'ment s. Act or practice of enticing; an allurement, temptation.
Enhance'ment s. Act of enhancing; augmentation.
Entrance'ment s. State of being entranced, enchanted, or delighted.
Advance'ment s. Act of moving forward; improvement.
Commence'-ment s. Beginning, origin; day for conferring of degrees at certain Universities.
Convince'ment s. Conviction.
Enounce'ment s. A pronouncement.
Denounce'ment s. Denunciation.
Renounce'ment s. Act of disclaiming; renunciation.
Announce'-ment s. Act of announcing; declaration.
Amerce'ment s. A fine.
Deforce'ment s. The withholding of that which lawfully belongs to another.
Enforce'ment s. Act of enforcing; compulsion; that which enforces.
Reinforce'ment s. Act of reinforcing; additional troops, etc.
Divorce'ment s. A divorce.
Traduce'ment s. Act of traducing; misrepresentation.
Reduce'ment s. Act of reducing.
Seduce'ment s. Seduction; act of seducing.
Conduce'ment s. (*Conduce*).
Dement' v.t. To madden.
Bode'ment s. An omen.
Agree'ment s. Harmony, conformity, stipulation.
Disagree'ment s. Difference; unsuitableness; discrepancy; wrangle.
Engage'ment s. Act of engaging; an obligation; betrothal; business; a battle, conflict.
Pre-engage'-ment s. Prior engagement.
Disengage'-ment s. Act or state of being disengaged; liberty; leisure.
Man'agement s. Act of managing; superintendence; a managing body; ingenuity.
Misman'age-ment s. Bad management.
Dispar'age-ment s. Injurious comparison; derogation.
Encour'age-ment s. Act of encouraging; incentive.
Discour'age-ment s. Act of discouraging; state of being discouraged; that which discourages.
Assuage'ment s. Mitigation.
Lodge'ment s. Act of lodging; state of being lodged; a deposit.
Dislodge'ment s. Act of dislodging; state of being dislodged.
Derange'ment s. Act of deranging; disorder, especially mental.
Arrange'ment s. Orderly disposition, result of arranging.
Rearrange'-ment s. Act or result of rearranging.
Prearrange'-ment s. A previous arrangement.
Disarrange'-ment s. State of being disarranged; confusion.
Estrange'ment s. Alienation of affection.
Avenge'ment s. Revenge.
Impinge'ment s. Act or state of impinging.
Infringe'ment s. Act of violating; non-fulfilment.
Divulge'ment s. A making known, imparting.
Enlarge'ment s. Act of enlarging; state of being enlarged; expansion; release.
Engorge'ment s. Act of swallowing greedily; congestion.
Rapproche'-ment s. Reconciliation, especially between nations.
Accouche'ment s. Child-birth.
Ve'hement a. Ardent; fervent; impetuous.
Fake'ment s. (*Slang*) A deception, fraud, fake.
Regale'ment s. Entertainment, feasting; gratification.
Impale'ment s. Act of impaling; space enclosed by palings; vertical division of heraldic shield.
Disa'blement s. State or condition of being disabled.
Entable'ment s. An entablature.
Babble'ment s. Babble.
Rabble'ment s. A rabble.
Scribble'ment s. Anything scribbled; careless piece of writing.
Enfeeble'ment s. Enervation; act of weakening.
Em'blement s. Produce of land sown or planted; claim of outgoing tenant for growing crops.
Tremble'ment s. A trembling.
Ennoble'ment s. Act of ennobling; that which ennobles.
Clem'ent a. Mild; lenient; indulgent.
Inclem'ent a. Severe, rough, harsh; stormy.
El'ement s. A substance that cannot be separated by chemical process into other substances; anciently earth, air, fire, and water; a fundamental part or principle; proper sphere; an ingredient.
Inveigle'ment (-vēgl'-) s. Act of inveigling; seduction to evil.
Entangle'ment s. State of being entangled or involved; intricacy.
Reconcile'ment s. Reconciliation.
Defile'ment s. Act of defiling; state of being defiled; pollution.

Beguile'ment s. Act of beguiling; temptation.
Revile'ment s. Act or practice of reviling; abuse.
Cajole'ment s. Cajolery.
Im'plement s. A tool, instrument. v.t. To fulfil the conditions of, to carry into effect.
Com'plement s. That which completes or supplies a deficiency; full quantity; crew of a ship.
Sup'plement s. An addition, appendix.
Supplement' v.t. To make additions to, complete by addition.
Accouple'ment s. State of being coupled together; act of coupling; a brace.
Battle'ment s. A parapet with openings.
Settle'ment s. Act of settling; state of being settled; establishment, installation; colonization, a colony; arrangement, liquidation; jointure to a woman at marriage.
Resettle'ment s. Act of resettling; state of subsiding again.
Bamboo'zlement s. (*Bamboozle*).
Daz'zlement s. Dazzle; state of dazzle.
Embez'zlement s. Act of fraudulently appropriating property committed to one's trust.
Puzzle'ment s. A state of perplexity; bewilderment.
Ten'ement s. A dwelling-house.
Refine'ment s. Act or process of refining; elegance; culture; affected nicety.
Confine'ment s. Restraint, imprisonment; detention by sickness, especially by childbirth.
Aline'ment s. Act of ranging or being ranged in line; things so ranged.
Enshrine'ment s. State of being enshrined.
Entwine'ment s. State of being entwined.
Intertwine'ment s. An intertwining.
Postpone'ment s. Act of postponing; temporary delay.
Dethrone'ment s. Deposition.
Enthrone'ment s. Act of enthroning or inducting a bishop; state of being enthroned.
Atone'ment s. Act of atoning; reparation; reconciliation to God.
Escape'ment s. Device in a watch by which circular is converted into vibratory motion.
Elope'ment s. Act of eloping (especially with a lover).
Dec'rement s. Gradual decrease; diminution.
Rec'rement s. Superfluous or useless matter; refuse.
In'crement s. Process of increasing; matter added; profit; augmentation.
Ex'crement s. That which is excreted; dung.
Retire'ment s. Act of retiring; state of being withdrawn; place to which one retires; privacy.
Acquire'ment s. Anything acquired; an attainment; act of acquiring.
Require'ment s. Act of requiring; that required; an essential thing or condition.
Accou'trement s. Military dress and equipment.
Procure'ment s. Act of procuring; agency.
Prefig'urement s. Prefiguration.
Disfig'urement s. That which disfigures; a blemish.
Abjure'ment s. (*Abjure*).
Allure'ment s. A temptation, enticement.
Inure'ment s. Habit; practice.
Meas'urement s. Act of measuring; amount ascertained.
Admeas'urement s. Act of measuring; dimensions ascertained; apportionment.
Base'ment s. A storey below ground level.
Abase'ment s. State of being abased; degradation.
Debase'ment s. Act of debasing, state of being debased.
Case'ment s. A hinged window.
Ease'ment s. That which gives ease, accommodation; a right of way, right to light, etc.
Release'ment s. Act of releasing.
Appease'ment s. Act of appeasing or being appeased; satisfaction.
Erase'ment s. Act of erasing; obliteration.
Appraise'ment s. Valuation.
Affran'chisement s. Act of making free, emancipation.
Enfran'chisement s. Act of enfranchising, state of being enfranchised; release.
Disfran'chisement s. State of being disfranchised.
Adver'tisement s. Public notice; information.
Diver'tisement s. Source of amusement; a short entertainment.
Chas'tisement s. Punishment, especially by beating.
Endorse'ment s. Act of endorsing, assignment thus; signature; sanction, approval.
Reimburse'ment s. Repayment.
Disburse'ment s. Act of disbursing; money paid out.
Empresse'ment s. Cordiality; display of eagerness.
Éclair'cissement s. Explanation or clearing up of an obscurity, etc.
Amuse'ment s. Diversion, entertainment.
Abate'ment s. Act of abating; mitigation deduction.
Debate'ment s. (*Debate*).
State'ment s. Act of stating; that which is stated.
Reinstate'ment s. Condition of being reinstated.
Understate'ment s. A representation that is less than the truth.
Misstate'ment s. An incorrect statement.
Incite'ment s. An incentive, stimulus; incitation.
Excite'ment s. Act of exciting; state of being excited; stimulation.
Denote'ment s. A sign, indication.
Subdue'ment s. Act of subduing.
Dénoue'ment s. A winding up, catastrophe.
Bereave'ment s. State of being bereaved, especially by death.
Enslave'ment s. Act of enslaving; slavery.
Pave'ment s. A level covering of stones to a footway, floor, etc.
Involve'ment s. Act of involving; state of being financially embarrassed.
Move'ment s. Act or manner of moving; gesture; wheel-work; military evolution; efforts, etc., directed to some end; part of a musical composition.
Improve'ment s. Act of improving; state of being improved; progress; beneficial alteration, etc.
Approve'ment s. The improvement of commons by enclosure.
Gaze'ment s. A gazing, especially as in wonder.
Amaze'ment s. Feeling of surprise and wonder; perplexity.
Aggran'dizement s. Augmentation; act of aggrandizing.
Feoff'ment s. Grant of a fee with living of seizin; instrument or mode of such grant.
Enfeoff'ment s. Act of giving or deed conveying the fee-simple of an estate.
Frag'ment s. A part broken off from a whole; a small part.

Acknowl'-edgment s. Act of acknowledging; recognition; something in return for a favour.
Abridg'ment s. An epitome, summary.
Judg'ment s. Act of judging; discrimination or mental faculty for this; opinion; sentence.
Adjudg'ment s. Act of judging or adjudging; verdict.
Prejudg'ment s. Act of prejudging.
Misjudg'ment s. Wrong determination.
Seg'ment s. A part cut off or into which anything naturally divides. v.i. and t. To divide into segments.
Fig'ment s. An invention, imagination; a fiction.
Pig'ment s. Substance used to impart colour to bodies; paint, colouring matter.
Augment' v.t. To enlarge, make bigger. v.i. To grow larger, increase.
Aug'ment s. Enlargement by addition, increase.
Impeach'ment s. Act of impeaching; accusation; arraignment for treason, etc.
Preach'ment s. A sermon, tedious advice (*in derision*).
Encroach'ment s. Act of encroaching; inroad; that which is taken by encroaching.
Detach'ment s. Act of detaching; state of being detached; thing detached, especially body of troops or ships for special service.
Attach'ment s. Act of attaching; thing attached; connection; devotion, fidelity.
Enrich'ment s. Act of enriching; that which enriches.
Retrench'ment s. Act of retrenching; reduction of expenditure; a supporting trench or work.
Entrench'ment s. A trench or series of trenches.
Parch'ment s. Goat- or sheep-skin dressed for writing on, bookbindings, etc.; a document on this.
Catch'ment s. A surface on which water may be collected.
Hatch'ment s. A funeral escutcheon.
Bewitch'ment s. Charm, fascination.
Abash'ment s. Consternation, confusion through shame.
Enmesh'ment s. Entanglement.
Refresh'ment s. Act of refreshing; restoration of strength, vigour, etc.; that which refreshes, food and drink.
Blan'dishment s. (*Blandish*).
Estab'lishment s. A settlement; a permanent organization, business, or residence; confirmation; sanction.
Disestab'lish-ment s. Severance of the connexion between Church and State.
Pub'lishment s. Act of making publicly known.
Embel'lish-ment s. Ornament, adornment.
Abol'ishment s. Abolition.
Accom'plish-ment s. Fulfilment; embellishment, acquirement.
Blem'ishment s. A blemish.
Ban'ishment s. Act of banishing; exile.
Replen'ishment s. That which replenishes; supply.
Admon'ish-ment s. Admonition.
Aston'ishment s. Amazement; state of being astonished.
Gar'nishment s. An embellishment; a legal warning or notice.
Pun'ishment s. Act of punishing; penalty inflicted.
Impov'erish-ment s. Act of impoverishing; state of being impoverished.
Nour'ishment s. Act of nourishing; food; sustenance.
Lan'guishment s. State or act of languishing; lassitude; loss of vigour.
Exting'uish-ment s. Act of extinguishing; suppression, nullification.
Relin'quish-ment s. Act of leaving or quitting; a forsaking.
Lav'ishment s. State of being lavish; profuse expenditure.
Rav'ishment s. Abduction; state of being ravished; rape; ecstasy.
Betroth'ment s. Betrothal.
Rai'ment s. Clothes, apparel.
Ped'iment s. The triangular part over a portico, doorway, etc.
Imped'iment s. That which impedes; hindrance, obstruction.
Sed'iment s. That which settles in a liquid; dregs.
Embod'iment s. That which is embodied; a complete system.
Disembod'i-ment s. (*Disembody*).
Con'diment s. A relish; seasoning.
Ru'diment s. A first principle; anything undeveloped.
Reg'iment s. Body of troops under a colonel.
Al'iment s. Food, nourishment.
Habil'iment s. Dress, clothes.
Com'pliment s. Expression of approbation, praise, regard, etc. v.t. To express praise of, to flatter. v.i. To use compliments.
Accom'pani-ment s. That which accompanies; a subordinate part in music.
Lin'iment s. An embrocation, ointment.
Fun'niment s. Fun, drollery.
Mu'niment s. A title-deed, charter, record.
Dissep'iment s. A division in a part or organ.
Or'piment s. Trisulphide of arsenic used in dyeing yellow.
Drear'iment s. Dreariness.
Exper'iment s. A practical test; a trial, proof. v.i. To try, to search out by trial.
Dir'iment a. Nullifying, especially with respect to marriage.
Mer'riment s. Joyousness; mirth; hilarity.
Wor'riment (wŭr'-) s. State of being worried; anxiety.
Det'riment s. Loss; damage; injury.
Nu'triment s. Food; that which nourishes.
Sen'timent s. Sensibility; feeling.
Presen'timent s. Previous opinion, etc.; impression of something about to happen.
Embank'ment s. Act or process of embanking; a raised bank.
Conceal'ment s. Act or state of being concealed; suppression of truth; hiding-place.
Congeal'ment s. (*Congeal*).
Enthral'ment s. State of being enthralled.
Instal'ment s. A part paid, issued, etc., at regular intervals.
Propel'ment s. Propulsion; a propelling device.
Rav'elment s. An entanglement.
Bev'elment s. Process of bevelling.
Bail'ment s. Delivery of goods; bailing of an accused person.
Derail'ment s. Derailing of a train, tram-car, etc.
Engrail'ment s. Act or result of engrailing.
Entail'ment s. Act of entailing; condition of being entailed.
Curtail'ment s. A shortening, abridgment.
Bewail'ment s. Act of bewailing.
Fulfil'ment s. Accomplishment, performance, execution.
Nonfulfil'ment s. (*Negative*).
Recoil'ment s. Recoil.
Despoil'ment s. Despoliation.
Embroil'ment s. Disturbance; state of contention

Instil'ment s. Act of instilling; thing instilled.
Dev'ilment s. Mischief, roguery.
Bedev'ilment s. State of disorder; demoniacal possession.
Enrol'ment s. Act of enrolling; a register.
Control'ment s. Power or act of controlling; state of being controlled.
Epaule'ment s. A short parapet in fortification.
Annul'ment s. Act or result of annulling.
Embalm'ment s. (*Embalm*).
Com'ment s. A remark, criticism, interpretative note.
Comment' v.i. To make critical or explanatory notes or remarks on. v.t. To annotate.
Awak'enment s. An awakening.
Enlight'enment s. State of being enlightened; act of enlightening.
Bediz'enment s. Tawdry finery.
Arraign'ment s. Act of arraigning; accusation.
Eloign'ment s. Remoteness.
Consign'ment s. Act of consigning; thing consigned; writing by which a thing is consigned.
Assign'ment s. Thing assigned; writ assigning; act of assigning.
Impugn'ment s. Contradiction.
Ordain'ment s. Ordination.
Enchain'ment s. Act of enchaining; state of being enchained.
Distrain'ment s. Distraint.
Obtain'ment s. Act or process of obtaining; that which is obtained.
Detain'ment s. Act of detaining.
Ascertain'ment s. (*Ascertain*).
Entertain'ment s. Act of receiving as host, amusing, entertaining; that which entertains, a banquet, show; amusement.
Attain'ment s. Act of attaining, that which is attained; an acquirement.
Aban'donment s. State of being abandoned.
Disuill'sion-ment s. State of being free from illusions.
Propor'tion-ment s. A proportioning; state of being proportioned.
Appor'tion-ment s. Distribution of proper shares, act of apportioning.
Envi'ronment s. Act of environing; that which encompasses surrounding objects, circumstances, etc.; conditions under which one lives.
Impris'onment s. Act of imprisoning; state of being imprisoned.
Canton'ment s. Quarters for troops.
Bla'zonment s. Act of blazoning, or of diffusing abroad.
Embla'zon-ment s. Act or art of blazoning; blazonry.
Secern'ment s. Process or act of secreting.
Concern'ment s. That which interests; affair; importance.
Discern'ment s. Faculty of distinguishing; judgment; penetration.
Intern'ment s. Act of interning; state of being interned.
Gov'ernment s. Direction, rule; public administration; executive power; province.
Misgov'ern-ment s. Ill administration, irregularity.
Adorn'ment s. An ornament.
Adjourn'ment s. Act or interval of adjourning.
Soj'ournment (suj'-) s. Temporary residence.
Foment' v.t. To poultice, bathe with warm lotions; to abet, instigate.
Lo'ment s. A pod containing seeds in separate cells.
Mo'ment s. A second, a minute portion of time; momentum; importance.
Ship'ment s. Act of shipping; a consignment.
Tranship'ment s. Act of transhipping.
Equip'ment s. Act of equipping; state of being equipped; that with which one is equipped.
Decamp'ment s. Hurried departure.
Encamp'ment s. Act of encamping; a camp.
Devel'opment s. Act of developing; state of being developed; maturity, completion.
Envel'opment s. Act of enveloping; that which surrounds, wraps, or envelops.
Escarp'ment s. A steep declivity.
Recoup'ment s. Compensation.
Endear'ment s. That which endears; state of being endeared; a caress.
Gar'ment s. An article of clothing; apparel.
Dismem'ber-ment s. Act or result of dismembering; separation.
Bewil'derment s. State of being perplexed.
Won'derment s. Surprise; state of wonder.
Fer'ment s. That which causes fermentation; intestine commotion; tumult.
Ferment' v.t. To produce fermentation in; to agitate. v.i. To undergo fermentation; to be agitated.
Defer'ment s. Postponement, delay.
Prefer'ment s. Act of advancing in office, etc.; promotion; a superior office.
Deci'pherment s. (*Decipher*).
Attem'perment s. (*Attemper*).
Deter'ment s. Act of deterring; that which deters; a deterrent.
Inter'ment s. Act of burying; burial.
Disinter'ment s. Act of disinterring.
Bet'terment s. A making better; improvement, especially to an estate.
Embit'terment s. That which embitters; state of being embittered.
Belea'guer-ment s. Siege, blockade.
Aver'ment s. Affirmation, declaration.
Dissev'erment s. Disseverance.
Tor'ment s. Great pain, torture; that which causes pain.
Torment' v.t. To irritate, afflict, tease.
Har'assment s. Act of harassing; state of being harassed.
Embar'rass-ment s. Perplexity, uneasiness, entanglement, trouble.
Disembar'-rassment s. (*Disembarrass*).
Impress'ment s. Act of impressing men for the public service.
Assess'ment s. Act of assessing; valuation; sum charged.
Reassess'ment s. A new assessment.
Emboss'ment s. Work in relief, raised work.
Engross'ment s. Act of engrossing; thing engrossed.
Treat'ment s. Act or manner of treating; usage; remedial course.
Enact'ment s. Passing of a bill; a decree.
Re-enact'ment s. A second enactment of the same.
Eject'ment s. Expulsion, ejection.
Indict'ment (-dit'-) s. Act of indicting; a formal charge of crime.
Beset'ment s. State of being beset; a besetting sin.
Revet'ment s. A facing of stone, etc.; retaining wall.
Fit'ment s. A piece of furniture, a fitting.
Refit'ment s. A second fitting out.
Remit'ment s. Act of remitting; a remittance.
Commit'ment s. Act of committing; a sending for trial or to prison.
Recommit'-ment s. Recommittal.

Recruit'ment s. Act or business of recruiting.
Enchant'ment s. Act of enchanting; magic; fascination.
Disenchant'ment s. Freedom from enchantment or illusion.
Resent'ment s. Act of resenting; displeasure; indignation.
Present'ment s. Act of presenting; state of being presented; representation; report by a grand jury.
Represent'ment s. Representation.
Content'ment s. State of being contented, satisfaction, content.
Discontent'ment s. State of being discontented.
Oint'ment s. An unctuous salve or cosmetic.
Appoint'ment s. Act of or state of being appointed; agreement to meet; order; position, office.
Reappoint'ment s. A second appointment to the same office.
Disappoint'ment s. State of being disappointed; failure of expectation; that which disappoints.
Allot'ment s. Act of allotting, portion allotted; small piece of land for cultivating.
Apart'ment s. A room.
Depart'ment s. A separate part, office, or division.
Impart'ment s. Act of imparting.
Compart'ment s. One of the parts into which anything is divided.
Deport'ment s. Demeanour, behaviour, carriage.
Assort'ment s. Distribution into classes; things assorted.
Arrest'ment s. Act of arresting; seizure of property.
Vest'ment s. A garment; robe of office.
Divest'ment s. Act of divesting.
Invest'ment s. Act of besieging, or of laying out money; money laid out; that in which money is invested.
Enlist'ment s. Act of enlisting; state of being enlisted.
Re-enlist'ment s. Act of enlisting again.
Adjust'ment s. Act of adjusting; settlement; arrangement.
Abut'ment s. State of abutting; that which abuts.
Rebut'ment s. A statement or evidence that annuls that previously given.
Hut'ment s. A camp of huts; housing in huts.
Doc'ument s. A written paper containing proof, evidence, etc.; an authoritative writing. v.t. To furnish with or prove by means of documents.
Teg'ument s. A protective covering.
Integ'ument s. A natural covering; the skin.
Ar'gument s. A reason offered, a plea; subject of discourse or discussion; a synopsis.
Rear'gument s. A fresh arguing of a case, etc.
Emol'ument s. Profit, remuneration.
Mon'ument s. Structure erected as or anything serving as a memorial; a notable instance.
In'strument s. That by which anything is effected; a tool; a contrivance for producing music; a document; a subservient person.
Achieve'ment s. An exploit, thing done; act of achieving; an heraldic shield.
Withdraw'ment s. Act of withdrawing; state of being withdrawn.
Endow'ment s. Act of settling a dower or fund on one; property permanently appropriated to any object; natural capacity.
Disendow'ment s. Lawful taking away of endowments (especially of a church).
Bestow'ment s. Act of bestowing; donation.
Pay'ment s. Act of paying; that which is paid; reward; requital.
Repay'ment s. Act of repaying; sum or thing repaid.
Prepay'ment s. Payment in advance.
Defray'ment s. Act of defraying.
Enjoy'ment s. Condition or cause of enjoying; pleasure, satisfaction.
Deploy'ment s. Act or result of deploying.
Employ'ment s. Act of employing; regular occupation; function.
Anent' prep. About, with reference to.
Rem'anent s. A residue. a. Remaining.
Im'manent a. Inherent, indwelling; not transient.
Per'manent a. Continuing without change; durable, lasting; not decaying.
Imper'manent a. Not permanent.
Em'inent a. Exalted; distinguished, illustrious.
Pre-em'inent a. Surpassing all others.
Superem'inent a. Eminent in a superior degree.
Im'minent a. Impending; threatening; at hand.
Prom'inent a. Standing out; conspicuous; protuberant.
Con'tinent a. Temperate, chaste, exercising self-control. s. A large connected tract of land; the mainland of Europe.
Incon'tinent a. Not restraining the passions; unchaste.
Per'tinent a. Relating to the matter in hand; apposite.
Imper'tinent a. Irrelevant; officious; pert.
Ab'stinent a. Abstemious.
Po'nent a. Western.
Depo'nent s. A witness, one who makes an affidavit; a deponent verb. a. Having a passive form with an active meaning.
Compo'nent s. A constituent part, ingredient. a. Composing; helping to form a whole.
Propo'nent s. One who makes a proposal. a. Proposing.
Oppo'nent s. An antagonist, adversary. a. Opposing, adverse.
Predispo'nent a Disposing beforehand.
Expo'nent s. One who explains or displays anything; an executant, expositor; the index power in algebra.
Secern'ent a. Secretory. s. A secreting organ; a drug for promoting secretion.
Fornent' adv. and prep. Directly opposite to.
Pent a. Shut up, confined.
Repent' v.i. To feel regret for some action; to be sorry or penitent. v.t. To regret, feel contrition for.
Re'pent a. Creeping (of plants).
Ser'pent s. A snake, a footless reptile; an obsolete bass wind-instrument.
Spent past and past part. (*Spend*).
Forspent' a. Worn-out, exhausted with toil.
Misspent' past and past part. (*Misspend*).
Rent s. Sum paid periodically for use of something; a tear, split; schism. v.t. To let or hold on lease or for a consideration. v.i. To be let. past and past part. (*Rend*).
Celar'ent s. A mnemonic word in logic.
Par'ent s. A father or mother; source; cause.
Appar'ent a. Evident; seeming; that may be seen.
Transpar'ent a. Pervious to light; clear; frank.

Brent a. Steep; smooth, unwrinkled.
Def'erent a. Deferential; conveying fluids. s. That which carries; a vessel or duct conveying fluids.
Af'ferent a. Bringing or conducting inwards.
Ef'ferent a. Conveying outwards and discharging (of veins, etc.).
Dif'ferent a. Unlike, dissimilar; distinct.
Equidif'ferent a. Having equal differences; arithmetically proportional.
Indif'ferent a. Unbiased; unconcerned; apathetic; middling.
Ger'ent s. A manager, ruler.
Viceger'ent s. A deputy. a. Having or exercising delegated authority.
Bellig'erent a. Warlike; carrying on war. s. A nation or individual engaged in war.
Adher'ent a. Sticking to. s. A partisan, follower.
Inher'ent a. Innate; naturally pertaining.
Coher'ent a. Sticking together; connected; consistent.
Incoher'ent a. Loose, disconnected.
Rev'erent a. Expressing reverence; submissive.
Irrev'erent a. Lacking in reverence; disrespectful.
Sempervi'rent a. Evergreen.
Deter'rent a. Deterring; tending to deter. s. That which deters.
Hor'rent a. Bristling; on end.
Abhor'rent a. Exciting loathing; inconsistent with.
Tor'rent s. A violent rushing, a rapid stream.
Cur'rent a. Passing at or belonging to the present time or stated period; circulating; generally acknowledged. s. A flowing body of water, air, etc.; general tendency.
Decur'rent a. Extending downward, as the base of a leaf.
Recur'rent a. Returning from time to time; turning in the opposite direction (especially of veins, etc.).
Precur'rent a. Occurring beforehand.
Concur'rent a. Acting or happening in conjunction or at the same time; co-operating; concomitant.
Sent past and past part. (*Send*).
Absent' v. refl. To take oneself away from, withdraw from.
Ab'sent a. Not present, wanting.
Resent' v.t. To take ill, consider as an affront.
Pres'ent a. Being at hand; now existing; quick in emergency. s. Present time; a gift, donation.
Present' v.t. To bring before, introduce formally; to give, bestow; to nominate to; to aim, point.
Represent' v.t. To exhibit; to personate; to serve as a symbol of.
Misrepresent' v.t. To represent falsely or incorrectly.
Omnipre'sent a. Present in all places at the same time.
Consent' v.i. To agree, concur, assent. s. Agreement to a proposal; accord.
Assent' s. Act of agreeing, consent. v.i. To express agreement, to concede as true.
Dissent' v.i. To disagree; be of a contrary opinion or nature. s. Act of dissenting; disagreement; separation from the Established Church.
Tent s. Portable canvas shelter; roll of lint to keep a wound open; a red wine. v.i. and t. To lodge in or supply with tents; to keep open with a tent; (*Scot.*) to watch, tend.
La'tent a. Lying hid; not apparent or active; potential.
Pa'tent a. Open, manifest; protected by patent; lacquered (of leather). s. A document granting a privilege, as of nobility, or securing exclusive right for a period to an invention, etc. v.t. To secure this right for.
Annec'tent a. Connecting.
Detent' s. A pin, catch, etc., locking or unlocking a movement in clock-work.
Com'petent a. Qualified; having good right; suitable.
Incom'petent a. Not competent; incapable; wanting legal or other qualifications; inadmissible.
Ap'petent a. Eagerly desirous.
Inap'petent a. Characterized by inappetence.
Pen'itent a. Repentant; contrite. s. One who repents.
Impen'itent a. Not penitent; obdurate.
Ren'itent a. Reluctant, resisting.
Intent' a. Fixed, resolved on. s. Design, purpose, meaning.
Content' a. Satisfied, at rest, easy in mind. v.t. To satisfy the mind of, to gratify, please. s. Satisfaction, state of being contented.
Con'tent s. Capacity, power of containing; meaning.
Mal'content s. A discontented person, especially one dissatisfied with the government. a. Discontented.
Discontent' a. Want of content; dissatisfaction; cause of this. v.t. To make dissatisfied or uneasy.
Po'tent a. Strong; powerful; efficacious.
Prepo'tent a. Very powerful.
Armip'otent a. Mighty in arms.
Plenip'otent a. Possessing full power.
Omnip'otent a. All-powerful; possessing unlimited power.
Im'potent a. Powerless, feeble, wanting sexual power. s. One who is impotent.
Adver'tent a. Attentive.
Inadver'tent a. Negligent, heedless; not paying attention.
Por'tent s. That which foretokens, especially evil; an evil omen.
Distent' a. Spread out; expanded; swollen.
Subsis'tent a. Inherent; having real being.
Insis'tent a. Insisting; urgent.
Consis'tent a. Possessing firmness or permanence; congruous, harmonious.
Inconsis'tent a. Discordant; not suitable; incompatible with; not uniform; self-contradictory.
Persis'tent a. Tenacious, fixed; inclined or able to persist.
Exis'tent a. Having being.
Pre-exis'tent a. Existing beforehand.
Inexis'tent a. Not having being; not existing; inherent.
Non-exis'tent a. (*Negative*).
Coexis'tent a. (*Coexist*).
Ostent' s. Manner, air; a token, portent.
Remit'tent a. Alternately increasing and decreasing. s. Malaria alternating thus.
Intromit'tent a. Intromitting.
Intermit'tent a. Ceasing at intervals. s. A fever which intermits.
Extent' s. Space or degree to which a thing is extended; size, length.
Ung'uent s. An ointment.

Ab'luent a. Cleansing. s. A substance that cleanses or removes impurities.
Flu'ent a. Liquid; flowing; voluble, eloquent.
De'fluent a. Flowing down. s. That which flows down.
Ref'luent a. Flowing back; ebbing; returning.
Af'fluent a. Flowing to; wealthy, abundant. s. A river flowing into another.
Ef'fluent a. Flowing out; a stream flowing out of another or out of a lake; discharge from a sewage tank.
Mellif'luent a. Mellifluous.
Circum'fluent a. Flowing round.
In'fluent a. Flowing in. s. A tributary.
Con'fluent a. Running into each other, flowing together, united. s. A river that runs into another.
Inter'fluent a. Flowing between or into each other.
Dil'uent a. Diluting. s. That which dilutes.
Fre'quent a. Often occurring, repeated, doing a thing often.
Frequent' v.t. To go to habitually, visit often.
Infre'quent a. Uncommon; unusual.
Se'quent a. Following; succeeding.
Sub'sequent a. Following in time or order.
Con'sequent a. Following naturally or by inference. s. That which follows; effect, inference.
Incon'sequent a. Not following from the premises; illogical; irrelevant.
Delin'quent s. A culprit, offender. a. Failing, neglecting.
El'oquent a. Speaking fluently, persuasive.
Grandil'oquent a. Given to pompous language; bombastic.
Magnil'oquent a. Using lofty or bombastic language.
Multil'oquent a. Talkative, loquacious.
Con'gruent a. Suitable, agreeing, correspondent.
Incon'gruent a. Unsuitable; inconsistent.
Ob'struent a. Obstructing. s. Anything blocking a passage of the body.
Deob'struent a. Removing obstructions; aperient. s. A medicine effecting this.
Constit'uent a. Existing as a part, component; having power to elect or appoint. s. An essential or component part; one having a vote.
Vent s. An aperture; emission; escape. v.t. To let out, emit, pour forth. v.i. To come to the surface to breathe (of others, etc.).
Ad'vent s. A coming; approach, especially the season four weeks before Christmas.
Event' s. An occurrence, incident; the consequence of anything.
Prevent' v.t. To hinder, obstruct, impede; to thwart.
Conni'vent a. Forbearing to see; convergent.
Sol'vent a. Able to dissolve; able to pay all debts. s. A fluid that dissolves substances.
Resol'vent s. That which can resolve or cause solution.
Insol'vent a. Being unable to pay one's debts. s. One who cannot meet his creditors.
Dissol'vent a. Having power to dissolve or melt. s. A menstruum, solvent.
Obvol'vent a. Curved inward or downward.
Circumvent' v.t. To outwit, get the best of.
Invent' v.t. To devise something new; to concoct, fabricate; to find out.
Con'vent s. A community of monks or nuns; a monastery.
Fer'vent a. Ardent, glowing; zealous.
Vol-au-vent' (-vong) s. A raised meat-pie.
Went past (*Go*).
Aint contr. v. (*colloq.*) Are not.
Faint v.i. To become feeble; to sink motionless; to swoon. s. Act of fainting, a swoon. a. Weak, languid; timorous; lacking distinctness; feebly done.
Plaint s. Complaint; lament; a lawsuit; a sad song.
Complaint' s. Expression of grief, dissatisfaction, censure, etc.; a charge, accusation; ailment.
Paint s. A substance used in painting; a pigment; rouge. v.t. To colour, apply paint to; to portray, depict, describe vividly. v.i. To practise the art of painting.
Bepaint' v.t. To paint over.
Repaint' v.t. To paint again.
Restraint' s. Act of restraining; check; hindrance; repression; limitation.
Distraint' s. Action of distraining.
Constraint' s. Necessity, restraint, urgency.
Saint s. A holy person; one canonized. v.t. To make a saint of.
Taint s. A trace of decay, etc.; a corrupting influence; a blemish. v.t. and i. To infect, sully, corrupt.
Attaint' v.t. To stain, taint, disgrace. s. A stain; a writ to inquire whether a jury has given a false verdict.
Quaint a. Fantastic; odd and antique; whimsical.
Acquaint' v.t. To make to know or known; to inform, make familiar.
Dint s. A dent, a blow. v.t. and i. To mark with or make a dint.
Feint s. A false appearance; a mock assault. v.i. To make a pretended attack (on).
Sep'tuagint s. A Greek version (third to first centuries B.C.) of the Old Testament and Apocrypha.
Hint s. A slight allusion, a suggestion. v.t. To suggest, allude to, intimate.
Lint s. Downy linen for dressing wounds.
Flint s. A hard siliceous stone; anything very hard.
Skin'flint s. A miser.
Glint s. A glimpse, glance, gleam. v.t. To glance, peep forth.
Splint s. A thin rigid strip for helping a broken bone to set; a splinter. v.t. To support with splints.
Mint s. Place where money is coined; an aromatic plant. v.t. To coin; to invent.
Cal'amint s. A herb of the mint family.
Spear'mint s. The common garden mint.
Var'mint s. (*Slang*) An objectionable person or animal.
Pep'permint s. A plant of the mint family; an essential oil distilled from this; its aromatic flavour.
Cat'mint s. A labiate plant.
Joint s. A joining, junction, hinge; articulation of limbs; piece of meat. a. Shared; acting in concert; joined. v.t. To form with or divide into joints; to fit together.
Conjoint' a. United, associated, co-operating.
Disjoint' v.t. To put out of joint, dislocate. a. Out of order, disconnected.
Anoint' v.t. To smear with oil or ointment; to consecrate by unction.

Point s. A sharp end; a headland; a full stop, period; that which has neither length, breadth, nor thickness; exact spot; purpose; characteristic; punctilio; gist. v.i. To direct the finger, etc., at an object; to show distinctly. v.t. To aim, indicate, punctuate; to make pointed; to fill the joints of with mortar.
Repoint' v.t. To apply new pointing to brick-work, etc.; to supply a new point to.
Embonpoint' s. Plumpness, especially in women; fleshiness.
Appoint' v.t. To fix, allot; to nominate; to equip. v.i. To ordain, determine.
Reappoint' v.t. To appoint again to the same post.
Disappoint' v.t. To defeat of hope; to baulk, tantalize, deprive of.
Coun'terpoint s. Art of composing music in parts, the setting of a harmony of parts to a melody.
Pour'point s. A quilted doublet.
Aroint' int. Avaunt!
Pint s. Half a quart.
Print v.t. To stamp, impress, take an impression of; to mark by pressure, especially from type. v.i. To practise the art of typography; to publish. s. Mark made by pressure; state of being printed; a newspaper, an engraving, printed calico.
Reprint' v.t. To print again.
Re'print s. A new printing or impression.
Imprint' v.t. To impress, especially on the mind; to stamp.
Im'print s. A stamp; name of publisher with place and date of publication on title-page.
Sprint v.t. and i. To run at full speed. s. Such a run.
Misprint' v.t. To print incorrectly. s. A mistake in printing.
Foot'print s. The mark of a foot; evidence of a person's presence.
Tint s. A tinge, dye, hue. v.t. To tinge.
Aq'uatint s. A method of etching by aquafortis.
Mon'otint s. A picture in only one colour.
Mez'zotint s. A process or method of engraving. v.t. To engrave in mezzotint.
Stint v.t. To restrain within limits, to confine. s. Bound, restriction; allotted amount; a small sand-piper.
Quint s. A sequence of five cards of a suit.
Squint s. An oblique look; want of coincidence of the optic axes; (*slang*) a look. a. Looking obliquely, askance, or with suspicion. v.i. To look with the eyes differently directed or with eyes half shut. v.t. To cause to squint.
Su'int s. Natural grease of wool.
Vint v.t. To make wine.
Don't imperat. Do not.
Loph'odont s. An animal whose molars have ridges on the crowns.
Selen'odont s. An animal with crescent-shaped ridges on the molars.
Cyprin'odont s. A fish of the pike family.
Font s. A baptismal vessel; a set of printing type.
Front s. The fore-part of anything; the forehead; effrontery. v.t. To oppose directly or face to face. v.i. To face, look. a. Relating to the front or face.
Fore'front s. The extreme front, the foremost place.
Affront' s. Insult; open defiance. v.t. To insult, offend.
Confront' v.t. To face, set together for comparison, oppose.
Wont s. Custom, habit. a. Accustomed (to). v. aux. To be used (to).
Won't neg. (*Would not*).
Ayont' prep. (*Scot.*) Beyond.
Learnt past and past part. (*Learn*).
Burnt past and past part. (*Burn*).
Aunt s. A sister of one's parent.
Daunt v.t. To intimidate, discourage.
Gaunt a. Lean, emaciated, haggard.
Haunt v.t. To resort to; to frequent as a spirit. s. A place much frequented; a favourite spot.
Jaunt s. A ramble, trip, excursion. v.i. To rove about.
Flaunt v.i. To move ostentatiously, behave pertly. v.t. To parade, show off. s. Impudent parade; boasting; finery.
Romaunt' s. A tale of chivalry.
Taunt v.t. To reproach, revile, upbraid. s. A sarcastic reproach. a. Tall (of masts).
Vaunt v.i. To brag, exult. v.t. To boast of. s. A brag.
Avaunt' int. Hence! begone!
Bunt s. The swelling part of a sail or net; a fungoid disease of wheat. v.t. and i. To push, butt.
Ex'eunt v.i. Stage direction to performers to retire.
Hunt v.t. To chase, pursue; to manage hounds. v.i. To follow the chase. s. Pursuit to catch or kill wild animals; association of huntsmen; pack of hounds.
Shunt v.t. To turn off to the side (especially of railway trains); to put off upon one. v.i. To go aside. s. A turn aside leaving the principal line free; contrivance for switching electric current to another circuit.
Lunt s. Match-cord; a slow match; smoke.
Blunt a. Not sharp; dull, on the edge or in the understanding; unceremonious. v.t. To make blunt or dull. s. (*Slang*) Money, coin.
Count v.t. To enumerate, compute, consider, judge. v.i. To possess a certain value, be reckoned; to depend or rely upon. s. Reckoning, sum of; particular charge in an indictment, statement of plaintiff's case; continental title equal to English "earl."
Account' s. A reckoning; register of cash transactions; narration; importance; end; advantage. v.t. To reckon, consider, deem, value. v.i. To give or provide reasons; to explain.
Recount' v.t. To relate, to narrate in detail.
Recount' (rē-) v.t. To count afresh. s. A new count.
Dis'count s. Rebate or allowance made on an account, etc.; deduction for interest not incurred; act of discounting.
Discount' v.t. To deduct from the account. v.i. To make allowance for.
Miscount' v.t. and i. To count wrongly. s. An erroneous numbering.

Vis'count (vī'-) s. Peer next below an earl.
Fount s. A fountain, a well; a set of printing type.
Mount s. A high hill; a horse or other animal ridden; a horse-block; a frame, setting. v.i. To rise; to get on horseback, etc.; to amount. v.t. To raise aloft, to climb; to furnish with horses; to set in something.
Amount' s. Sum total; effect, result. v.i. To result in, mount up to.
Par'amount a. Superior, principal, chief. s. The highest in rank, etc.
Catamount' s. (*Catamountain*).
Tan'tamount a. Equivalent; equal.
Remount' v.t. and i. To mount or ascend again, make a fresh ascent; to supply with fresh horses.
Re'mount s. A fresh horse or mount.
Surmount' v.t. To overcome, subdue; to surpass.
Dismount' v.i. To come down, alight from a horse. v.t. To bring or throw down; to dismantle.
Punt s. A flat-bottomed boat; a certain kick at football. v.t. To propel or convey in a punt; to kick a football before it touches the ground. v.i. To bet, play against the bank; to go about in a punt.
Runt s. Any undersized animal; a dwarf; a boor.
Brunt s. Onset, shock; heat of battle.
Grunt s. The noise of a hog; a groan. v.i. To make a deep, guttural sound.
Stunt v.t. To check in growth. s. A stunted animal, etc.; a turn of work, a feat.
Aroynt' int. (*Aroint*).
Jabot' s. A lace frill, neck-ruffle.
Sab'ot (-ō) s. A wooden shoe.
Ab'bot s. The male superior of an abbey or monastery.
Tal'bot s. A large breed of hunting hound.
Bur'bot s. An eel-like freshwater fish.
Tur'bot s. A short, broad, flat-fish.
Cot s. A hut, shelter; a small bed, light bedstead.
Dove'cot s. A small house for domestic pigeons.
Pi'cot (-kō) s. A small ornamental loop.
Har'icot s. A stew or ragout; the French bean.
A'pricot s. A peach-like fruit; the tree bearing this.
Per'sicot (-kō) s. A cordial made from peaches, nectarines, etc.
Mas'sicot s. Yellow protoxide of lead.
Scot s. An assessment, tax, payment; a native of Scotland.
Mas'cot s. A talisman, amulet.
Wains'cot s. Timber lining to walls of a room.
Dot s. A small mark, speck, or spot; a dowry; (*slang*) the head. v.t. To make with a dot or dots; to speckle. v.t. To make dots.
Per'idot s. A translucent, apple-green variety of chrysolite.
Fyl'fot s. The swastika.
Got past and past part. (*Get*).
Ma'got s. A tailless Barbary ape.
Fag'got s. A bundle of twigs bound together; a kind of sausage; a shrivelled old woman.
Mag'got s. A grub, worm; a whimsy.
Big'ot s. One obstinately wedded to his own opinion.
Gig'ot s. A leg of mutton.
Spig'ot s. A peg for a cask; a faucet.
In'got s. A mass of cast or unwrought metal.
Ar'got s. Slang.
Er'got s. A fungoid disease of grain and grasses; a preparation from rye diseased thus, used in medicine.
Forgot' past (*Forget*).
Hot a. Of high temperature; fiery, burning; acrid; violent; lustful. adv. Ardently, angrily. v.t. To heat.
Shot s. Missile for a fire-arm; discharge of this; act of shooting; range; a marksman; stroke at various games; attempt; a reckoning, score. v.t. To load with shot. a. Chatoyant, iridescent.
Blood'shot a. Suffused with blood (of the eyes.)
Buck'shot s. A large shot used in cartridges for game.
Gun'shot s. The range of a gun.
Snap'shot s. An instantaneous photograph.
Up'shot s. The conclusion, final issue.
Ear'shot s. Hearing distance.
Un'dershot a. Moved by water passing underneath.
Bow'shot s. The distance an arrow can be shot.
Id'iot s. One of defective intellectual powers; a fool. a. Idiotic.
Gal'liot s. A small, swift galley.
Ri'ot s. Tumult, uproar; revelry. v.i. To engage in riot; to revel.
Char'iot s. A stately vehicle, especially one used in war, processions, etc.
Her'iot s. A fine paid to the lord of the manor at death of a landholder.
Lor'iot s. The golden oriole.
Cyp'riot s. A native of Cyprus.
Pa'triot s. One who loves his country and zealously supports it. a. Devoted to one's country.
Compat'riot s. A fellow-countryman.
Chev'iot s. Cloth for men's wear.
Jot s. The least quantity, an iota. v.t. To note in writing.
Lot s. Fortune, fate; one's share; a distinct portion; a considerable quantity. v.t. To allot, to portion.
Zeal'ot (zĕl'-) s. One full of zeal; an ardent partisan.
Cach'alot s. The sperm-whale.
Blot s. A stain, smudge; an obliteration. v.t. To spot or stain; to dry up; to cancel.
Clot s. A lump, especially of soft matter concreted; a coagulated mass. v.i. To become thick, to coagulate. v.t. To make into clots.
Bibe'lot (bib'lō) s. A knick-knack.
O'celot s. The Mexican tiger-cat or panther.
Hel'ot s. A bondsman in ancient Sparta; a slave.
Pen'taglot a. In five languages.
Hep'taglot s. A book in seven languages.
Gig'lot s. and a. (*Giglet*).
Pol'yglot a. Containing, pertaining to, or speaking several languages. s. A book set forth in, or a person speaking, many languages.
Mel'ilot s. A leguminous plant.
Pi'lot s. One who steers a ship, especially in difficult waters; a guide; a light locomotive. v.t. To direct the course of; to guide through dangers, etc.
Allot' v.t. To apportion; to give by lot.

Bal'lot s. A ball or paper used for secret voting; system of voting thus. v.i. To vote secretly.
Shallot' s. A plant of the onion family; its bulb.
Plot s. A small piece of land; a building site; a scheme, conspiracy, stratagem, intrigue; the plan of a novel, etc. v.t. To make a plan of; to devise, contrive, plan. v.i. To form a scheme against; to conspire.
Mar'plot s. One who frustrates a scheme by officious interference.
Coun'terplot s. A plot to defeat another plot. v.t. To oppose or frustrate thus.
Har'lot s. A prostitute.
Slot s. A narrow slit, oblong hole; the track of a deer.
Mot s. A note on a bugle.
Mot (mō) s. A short, witty saying.
Ber'gamot s. A species of orange and of pear; a fragrant oil from the orange, the aroma of this; a kind of mint.
Guil'lemot s. A sea-bird allied to the auks.
Bon mot' s. A witty saying.
Mar'mot s. An Alpine rodent.
Mot'mot s. A Central and S. American bird allied to the kingfisher.
Not adv. Expressing negation, denial, or refusal.
Forget'menot s. A small plant with bright blue flowers.
Hu'guenot s. A French Protestant of the sixteenth and seventeenth centuries.
Knot s. An entanglement of threads, hair, etc.; a tie; a joint of a plant; a group; a puzzling question; a nautical mile; a small snipe-like bird.
Can'not v. aux. (*neg.*) Unable or not allowed to.
Snot s. Mucus from the nose; a contemptible person.
Boot s. A covering for the foot and leg; an instrument of torture; a compartment on a coach for luggage; profit. v.t. To put boots on; (*slang*) to kick out; to profit, advantage.
Coot s. A small black water-fowl; a simpleton.
Ban'dicoot s. The large Indian rat; a small Australian marsupial.
Scoot v.i. (*Slang*) To run away, bolt.
Foot s. The lower extremity of the leg; a base; the infantry; 12 ins.; combination of syllables in a verse. v.i. To dance, skip, walk, etc. v.t. To tread; kick; to add a foot to (a stocking, etc.).
Afoot' adv. On foot, walking; in action.
Bare'foot a. Without shoes or stockings.
Fore'foot s. The anterior foot of a quadruped.
Ten'derfoot s. A novice.
Hoot v.i. To shout in contempt, cry as an owl. v.t. To drive out with noise and shouts. s. A cry in contempt.
Shoot v.t. To discharge a gun; to hit or kill with a projectile; to send forth or empty out suddenly; to push forward; to pass rapidly through or under; to score a goal. v.i. To perform the act of discharging; to be propelled, emitted, etc.; to germinate; to make progress; to move quickly; to overspread; to project; to aim at the goal. s. Discharge of a fire-arm, etc.; act of propelling; act of striking or trying to strike with a missile; a young branch; a shooting match or party.
Off'shoot s. A branch from the main stem; a side-issue.
Loot v.t. To plunder, pillage. s. Military or other plunder; illicit gains.
Galoot' s. (*Slang*) A rowdy or uncouth fellow.
Cloot s. A cloven hoof, or one half of it.
Moot v.t. To start a subject. s. An assembly of freemen of a township, etc.; a student's debate. a. Open to discussion; arguable.
Raj'poot s. A Hindu aristocrat.
Root s. Lower part of plant through which nourishment is obtained; origin; a radical; word from which others are formed. v.i. To be firmly fixed. v.t. To plant firmly, impress durably; to tear up, eradicate.
Cheroot' s. A cigar with thick, blunt ends.
Enroot' v.t. To implant firmly.
Uproot' v.t. To tear up by the roots.
Ar'rowroot s. A nutritious starch extracted from various tubers.
Soot s. Black powder deposited by smoke. v.t. To cover or foul with this.
Toot v.i. To make a noise like that of a horn. v.t. To sound (a horn, etc.). s. Blast of a horn.
Pot s. A round vessel of metal or earthenware for holding plants, containing liquids, cooking in, etc. v.t. To put, plant, or preserve in pots; to pocket a billiard-ball; to shoot.
Capot' s. The winning of all tricks at piquet by one player.
Dep'ôt s. A place of deposit; storehouse; regimental headquarters; a railway station.
Repot' v.t. To put into another pot (of plants).
En'trepôt s. A bonded warehouse; a commercial centre.
Chasse'pot s. An old French breech-loading needle-gun.
Hotch'pot s. A putting together of property for equal division; a hotchpotch.
Gal'ipot s. A yellowish resin or turpentine used in making Burgundy pitch.
Tal'ipot s. An E. Indian palm.
Gal'lipot s. A small glazed earthenware pot.
Spot s. A blot, stain, speck; a flaw, blemish; a locality. v.t. To make a spot on; to sully; to detect, notice.
Des'pot s. An absolute sovereign, a tyrant.
Toss'pot s. A tippler.
Rot v.i. To decay, putrefy. v.t. To make putrid or corrupt. s. Process of rotting; putrefaction; nonsense; a fatal disease in sheep.
Tar'ot (-ō) s. One of a pack of seventy-eight old Italian playing-cards.
Grot s. A grotto.
Car'rot s. A plant with reddish, edible root.
Gar'rot s. A surgeon's tourniquet; a sea-duck.
Par'rot s. A brightly feathered tropical bird that can imitate the human voice.
Pi'errot (pē'erō) s. A buffoon or singer in loose white and black garb and a whitened face.
Trot v.i. and t. To run or cause to run with small steps. s. The jolting high pace of a horse; a small child; an old woman.

Jog'trot a. Humdrum, monotonous.
Sot s. An habitual drunkard.
Besot' v.t. To make sottish or doting.
Tot s. Anything small, especially a child; a dram of spirits; a sum in addition. v.t. and i. To add or mount up.
Pal'etot (-tō) s. A loose cloak or overcoat.
Hott'entot s. One of the aboriginal race of Cape Colony; language of this race; a barbarous person.
Al'iquot a. Applied to a part of a number by which the whole is divisible without remainder.
Div'ot s. A turf for roofing; piece cut up by bad stroke at golf.
Piv'ot s. A fixed point, shaft, etc., on which anything turns or oscillates; a turning-point; that on which important results depend. v.t. To hinge upon.
Wot v.i. To know, be aware.
Swot s. Hard study; a plodding student. v.i. To study laboriously.
Ey'ot s. A little island, an ait.
Ry'ot s. A Hindu peasant or farmer.
Apt a. Suitable, liable, ready.
Adapt' v.t. To fit to; to adjust, suit.
Inapt' a. Not apt; not fit; unskilful.
Unapt' a. Unfit; dull.
Rapt a. Carried away in an ecstasy; absorbed.
Accept' v.t. To receive with consent; to admit, agree to, understand; to agree to an offer, acknowledge an obligation to pay.
Pre'cept s. Any order as an authoritative rule of action; an injunction; a maxim.
Con'cept s. An abstract general idea or notion; an object conceived by the mind.
Per'cept s. Object of perception.
Intercept' v.t. To stop or seize by the way; to interrupt communication; to include.
Intussuscept' v.t. To receive into some other thing or part.
Except' prep. Exclusively of; unless. v.t. To leave out specifically; to reject.
Adept' s. One well skilled in the given art. a. Completely versed, well up in.
Kept past and past part. (*Keep*).
Y-clept' a. Called; named.
Bib'lioklept s. One who is unable to refrain from stealing books.
Nym'pholept s. One stricken with nympholepsy.
Slept past and past part. (*Sleep*).
Inept' a. Unsuitable, improper; foolish, nonsensical.
Crept past and past part. (*Creep*).
Sept s. A family or clan, especially in Ireland.
Tran'sept s. Cross part of a church or cathedral.
Wept past and past part. (*Weep*).
Swept past and past part. (*Sweep*).
Receipt' (-sēt') s. Act of receiving; that which is received; written acknowledgment of this; a recipe. v.t. To give a receipt for.
Script s. Piece of writing; handwriting; type resembling this.
Sub'script a. Written underneath.
Non'descript a. Not hitherto or easily described; irregular. s. An odd person or thing.
Re'script s. An official decision; edict.
Pre'script s. A direction, command. a. Prescribed.
Tran'script s. A written copy.
Con'script a. Enrolled, enlisted by conscription. s. One compelled to serve in the armed forces.
Conscript' v.t. To conscribe.
Post'script s. Addition made to a letter after signature, or to a composition after its close.
Man'uscript s. Document, etc., written by hand. a. Hand-written.
Unkempt' a. Uncombed, shaggy; unpolished.
Tempt v.t. To entice; to allure, attract.
Contempt' s. Scorn, disdain; state of being despised; disregard of the rules, etc., of a court.
Attempt' v.t. To try to do, to make the effort. s. An essay, enterprise.
Reattempt' v.t. To attempt again. s. A new attempt.
Exempt' v.t. To grant immunity from; to excuse. a. Free by privilege.
Accompt' v., s. (*Account*).
Prompt a. Ready; alert; done without delay. v.t. To excite to action to suggest; to assist one who forgets his part.
Copt s. An ancient Egyptian; an Egyptian Christian.
Adopt' v.t. To take and treat as one's own; to embrace.
Co-opt' v.t. To elect into a body by the votes of the members.
Ex'cerpt s. An extract, a selected passage. v.t. To make extracts from; to select, to cite.
Abrupt' a. Broken off, sudden; unceremonious.
Erupt' v.i. To break out as a skin disease, volcano, etc.
Bank'rupt s. One who cannot discharge his liabilities. a. Unable to pay debts. v.t. To put one in this position.
Interrupt' v.t. To stop by breaking in. v.i. To make interruption.
Corrupt' a. Putrid; depraved; infected with errors. v.t. To render corrupt, make impure; to debauch, bribe; to falsify. v.i. To become corrupt.
Incorrupt' a. Not affected with decay; pure; untainted; unbribable.
Disrupt' v.t. To tear asunder. a. Rent asunder, broken.
Crypt s. A vault, especially beneath a church.
Art s. Practical skill, its application; cunning; trade; profession of painter.
Cart s. A horsed vehicle for carrying goods. v.t. To carry or convey by cart.
Dart s. A small lance, a sharp-pointed missile. v.t. To throw, shoot, emit. v.i. To let fly, shoot along rapidly.
Heart s. The central organ of the blood's motion; the seat of life, will, affections, etc., conscience; courage; earnestness; a suit of cards.
Green'heart s. A hard West Indian wood.
Sweet'heart s. A lover.
Brag'gart s. A boaster.
Bog'gart s. A hobgoblin.
Hart s. A stag; male of the red deer.
Chart s. A sea-map for use of sailors; a skeleton map; a tabular statement. v.t. To map, lay down on a chart.
Mart s. A market, auction-room.
Smart v.i. To feel a pungent pain; to rankle, feel wounded. s. Sharp,

lively pain; anguish. a. Stinging, keen, poignant, severe; spruce, fashionable; vivacious, witty; fresh, adv. Smartly.
Fou'mart s. The polecat.
Too'art s. An Australian tree yielding very hard timber.
Part s. A portion, piece, share; duty; business; character in a play. v.t. To divide, distribute; to disunite; to intervene. v.i. To become separated or broken; to depart.
Apart' adv. Separately; aside.
Depart v.t. To quit, leave, go away. v.i. To deviate, pass away; to die.
Ram'part s. A bulwark, defence. v.t. To fortify with these.
Impart' v.t. To give; to reveal, communicate the knowledge of.
Coun'terpart s. A corresponding part; a duplicate; one exactly like another; a musical part accompanying another.
Dispart' v.t. and i. To part asunder, divide. s. The difference in thickness of the mouth and breech of a cannon.
Tart a. Sour, acid; severe. s. A small fruit pie, etc.
Start v.i. To move suddenly, wince; to set out. v.t. To startle, rouse suddenly; to originate. s. A sudden movement, a twitch; outset; handicap.
Red'start s. A migratory song-bird.
Restart' v.t. and i. To start again.
Up'start s. A parvenu.
Quart (kwort) s. Two pints; vessel to contain this.
Quart (cart) s. A thrust in fencing.
Wart (wort) s. A hard excrescence on the skin.
Thwart a. Transverse, oblique. s. Seat in boat for rower. v.t. To frustrate.
Athwart' adv. Transversely. prep. From side to side.
Stal'wart a. Strong, sturdy, resolute. s. Such a person.
Swart a. Swarthy; dark-coloured.
Al'bert s. A short watch-chain.
Hal'bert s. A halberd.
Fil'bert s. The nut of the cultivated hazel.
Cam'embert s. A soft cheese from Normandy.
Cert s. (*Slang*) A certainty.
Concert' v.t. To plan, arrange mutually.
Con'cert s. Agreement in a design; harmony; performance of a number of singers, players, etc.
Preconcert' v.t. To settle by previous agreement.
Disconcert' v.t. To throw into disorder; to baffle, foil; to disquiet.
Chert s. Impure flinty rock.
Alert' a. Wideawake, vigilant, prompt.
Inert' a. Unable to move of itself or to resist force applied; lifeless; inactive.
Pert a. Forward; saucy; impudent.
Mal'apert a. Impudent, saucy, pert. s. Such a person.
Expert' a. Experienced, dextrous, skilful, adroit.
Ex'pert s. An expert person; a technical or scientific witness.
Inexpert' a. Unskilful.
Des'ert s. A waterless, treeless, uninhabited region; solitude. a. Uninhabited, desolate, waste.
Desert' v.t. To forsake, abandon. v.i. To quit without leave. s. What one deserves; merit or demerit.
Insert' v.t. To set or place in or among.
Reinsert' v.t. To insert again.
Assert' v.t. To state positively; to affirm, maintain.
Reassert' v.t. To assert again.
Dessert' s. The last course at dinner, fruit, sweets, etc.
Dissert' v.i. To discourse formally, write a dissertation.
Exsert' a. Standing out, projecting.
Vert s. Everything that grows and bears leaf in a forest; right to cut this; (*Heraldry*) green; a pervert or convert. v.i. To change one's religion.
Avert' v.t. To turn away from, to divert, ward off.
Obvert' v.t. To turn toward or downward.
Subvert' v.t. To overthrow; to corrupt.
Advert' v.i. To refer or allude to; to regard.
Animadvert' v.i. To criticize, censure.
Evert' v.t. To turn outwards or inside out.
Revert' v.t. To turn back (especially the eyes). v.i. To return to a former state, condition, etc.; to come back to a previous holder.
Divert' v.t. To turn aside, draw away from; to amuse.
Cul'vert s. An arched drain under a road, etc.
Invert' v.t. To turn upside down, reverse, change the position of.
In'vert s. An inverted arch.
Convert' v.t. To transmute; to cause to turn from one state, party, religion, etc., to another; to transpose the terms of.
Con'vert s. One who is converted, especially from another (or no) religion to Christianity.
O'vert a. Open, public, manifest.
Cov'ert a. Secret, private, insidious. s. A thicket.
Femme-cov'ert s. A married woman.
Discov'ert a. Unmarried; widowed.
Re'trovert v.t. To displace in a reverse position.
Introvert' v.t. To turn inwards or upon itself; to invert.
Controvert' v.t. To call in question, attempt to disprove.
Pervert' v.t. To turn from truth; to corrupt, misapply, misinterpret.
Per'vert s. One who has been perverted.
Wert 2nd sing. past (*Be*).
Exert' v.t. To put forth strongly; to perform.
Airt s. (*Scot.*) A point of the compass.
Dirt s. Anything filthy, foul, or soiled; soiling matter; mud, mire. v.t. To make dirty.
Girt past part. (*Gird*). v.i. To gird, surround. a. Girded, bound.
Sea'-girt a. Surrounded by the sea.
Shirt s. A loose, under body-garment worn by men; a woman's blouse.
Skirt s. Lower, loose part of a garment; a petticoat; extreme part; border. v.t. and i. To border or be on the border.
Out'skirt s. Border; suburb.
Flirt v.t. To fling suddenly; to move lightly to and fro. v.i. To play the coquette. s. A sudden jerk; a jeer; one who flirts.
Spirt s., v.i. and t. (*Spurt*).
Squirt v.t. To eject from a small orifice in a stream. v.i. To spurt out. s. A syringe, small jet; (*slang*) an insignificant person).
Bort s. Small chippings from diamonds.
Abort' v.i. To bring forth prematurely. v.t. To render abortive.

Es'cort s. An attendant; a guard; a protecting force.
Escort' v.t. To accompany as a safeguard or protection.
Fort s. A fortified place; a fortress, detached part of this.
Roque'fort (rōk'for) s. A goat's-milk cheese.
Ef'fort s. An exertion of power; attempt, endeavour.
Com'fort v.t. To console, make comfortable. s. Consolation, relief, quiet enjoyment.
Recom'fort v.t. To console again, give new strength to.
Discom'fort s. Lack of comfort; inquietude.
Dehort' v.t. To dissuade.
Co'hort s. The tenth part of a Roman legion; a body of warriors.
Short a. Not long, tall, or extended in time; inadequate; scanty; lacking less; limited; abrupt; crisp; concise; severe; unaccented. s. A short syllable or vowel; mark indicating this (˘). adv. Abruptly; suddenly; so as to be short. v.t. To shorten.
Exhort' v.t. To incite by counsel; to advise, caution.
Mort s. The bugle-call at the death of hunted deer; a salmon in the third year.
Amort' a. Lifeless.
Snort v.i. To force air noisily through the nose; to laugh contemptuously. s. Loud sound produced thus.
Port s. A harbour; a gate; opening in a ship's side, port-hole; left side of a ship; steam-passage in cylinder, etc.; mien, deportment; a red wine of Oporto. v.t. To turn the helm to the left; to hold a rifle slantingly across the body.
Sea'port s. A coastal town with a harbour.
Deport' v.t. To carry or send away; to exile; to conduct, behave (oneself).
Report' v.t. and i. To relate, give account of; to take down as spoken; to lay a charge against. s. That which is reported; a rumour; noise of explosion; official statement; reputation.
Import' v.t. To bring from abroad; to signify, imply; to be of moment to; to concern.
Im'port s. Anything brought in from abroad; signification; drift; importance.
Comport' v.t. To conduct, behave (oneself). v.i. To suit, agree.
Dav'enport s. A small writing-desk with drawers.
Rapport' s. Sympathetic relationship.
Support' v.t. To uphold, prop; to endure; to maintain, assist. s. Act of supporting; a prop; maintenance.
Pur'port s. Design; meaning; import.
Purport' v.t. To imply, signify; to intend.
Sport s. Pastime, that which diverts; outdoor recreation; horse-racing; a jest; a deviation from the normal or an example of this. v.i. To jest, divert oneself; to vary considerably from type. v.t. To display ostentatiously.
Disport' v.i. To play, gambol. v.t. To divert, amuse.
Trans'port s. Conveyance from one place to another; ship used for conveying soldiers; ecstasy.
Transport' v.t. To convey from one place to another; to enchant.
Pass'port s. A licence permitting a person to travel abroad.
Export' v.t. To carry or send (goods) abroad.
Ex'port s. Act of exporting; thing exported.
Sort s. A number, collection, or class of similar things, individuals, etc.; species; a set; manner, nature, character. v.t. To classify; to select from a number.
Resort' v.i. To betake oneself, have recourse, repair frequently. s. Recourse; concourse; a haunt.
Re-sort' v.t. To sort again.
Con'sort s. A partner, companion; wife or husband.
Consort' v.i. To associate; to accord.
Assort' v.t. To sort, arrange. v.i. To suit, agree.
Tort s. A private wrong; injury.
Retort' v.i. To return an argument, etc., make a severe reply. v.t. To bend or throw back; to return. s. A sharp rejoinder, repartee; vessel used in distilling, coal-gas production, etc.
Contort' v.t. To twist with violence, to wrench.
Bis'tort s. The snakeweed.
Distort' v.t. To twist out of natural shape; to pervert.
Extort' v.t. To wring or force from; to exact.
Cavort' v.i. To prance about, to frisk.
Wort (wert) s. Infusion of malt for fermenting into beer; a herb.
Mad'wort s. Alyssum; the catchweed.
Wound'wort s. A plant supposed to heal wounds.
Pile'wort s. The lesser celandine.
Mule'wort s. A fern.
Sneeze'wort s. The wild pellitory.
Rag'wort s. A yellow-flowered plant.
Mug'wort s. A plant related to wormwood.
Stitch'wort s. A common hedge plant with star-like flowers.
Spleen'wort s. A fern of the genus Asplenium.
Soap'wort s. A trailing herbaceous plant.
Spear'wort s. A species of ranunculus.
Ad'derwort s. Snakeweed.
Set'terwort s. Stinking hellebore.
Bit'terwort s. Yellow gentian.
But'terwort s. A small insectivorous plant.
Liv'erwort s. A cryptogamic plant.
Glass'wort s. A seashore plant.
Throat'wort s. The nettle-leaved bell-flower.
Lust'wort s. The sundew.
Saw'wort s. A plant with serrated leaves.
Curt a. Abrupt; somewhat rude; concise.
Hurt v.t. To harm, damage. v.i. To be painful. s. A wound; injury; harm.
Unhurt' a. Not harmed; safe and sound.
Blurt v.t. To utter unadvisedly, to divulge improperly.
Court s. An enclosed space; residence of a sovereign; a sovereign's retinue and family; judges assembled for deciding causes; a judicial body, place where it sits; a state reception; a piece of ground, or subdivision thereof, for certain games; attention paid to gain favour; flattery. v.t. To seek the favour or affections of, to woo. v.i. To make love.
Spurt v.i. To gush out in a jet; to make a sudden and violent effort. v.t. To

force out violently. s. A forcible jet of liquid; a sudden, vigorous effort.
Bast s. The inner bark of the lime; bass.
Bom'bast s. Inflated style; high-sounding language, fustian. a. Turgid, inflated, bombastic.
Cast v.t. To throw, scatter; to moult; to add up. s. A throw; anything formed from a mould.
Broad'cast a. Scattered by hand (of seed); widely disseminated. v.t. To scatter, to disseminate widely, especially by wireless telegraphy.
Recast' v.t. To throw, cast, or mould anew; to compute a second time.
Forecast' v.t. To calculate beforehand, predict.
Fore'cast s. A prediction; calculation of probable future events; foresight.
Down'cast a. Cast downward; dejected. s. The downward ventilating shaft in a mine.
Up'cast s. Ventilating shaft of a mine.
Sar'cast s. A sarcastic person.
Overcast' v.t. To cover with gloom; to cloud, darken; to sew an edge over and over. a. Clouded over, dull.
Out'cast s. A degraded person; an exile, vagabond.
East s. The part of the heavens where the sun rises; countries situated in the East. a. In or toward the East. adv. Eastwards.
Beast s. A quadruped; an ox; a brutal or highly objectionable man.
Feast s. A banquet; a festival; feasting. v.t. To entertain sumptuously, gratify luxuriously. v.i. To feed thus, to be highly delighted.
Least a. Smallest. adv. In the smallest or lowest degree. s. The smallest amount, etc.
Breast s. The front part of the body between neck and belly; a pap; the seat of the affections. v.t. To oppose, bear the breast against.
Abreast' adv. In a line, side by side.
Red'breast s. The robin.
Yeast s. Barm used for leavening bread; a substance produced in fermentation.
Fast a. Swift, moving rapidly; firm, closely adhering; durable, unfading; pleasure-seeking. adv. Swiftly; firmly; in a dissipated manner. v.i. To abstain from food. s. Abstinence from or deprivation of food; a day set apart for this.
Stead'fast a. Firm, constant, resolute.
Hold'fast s. That which holds fast; a catch; support.
Hand'fast v.t. To bind by contract, to pledge; to marry. s. A grasp; a contract; engagement to marry; restraint.
Shame'fast a. Shamefaced.
Sooth'fast a. Truthful; loyal; steadfast.
Break'fast s. The first meal of the day. v.i. To partake of this.
Flab'bergast v.t. To astonish, confound, amaze.
Hast 2nd sing. (*Have*).
Aghast' a. Amazed; in a stupefied state.
Chil'iast s. An adherent of chiliasm, a millenarian.
Scho'liast s. A commentator; a grammarian who annotated the classics.
Enco'miast s. A panegyrist, flatterer.
Enthu'siast s. One moved by enthusiasm; a fanatic, zealot.
Pancrat'iast s. A contestant in the pancratium.
Di'kast s. An ancient Athenian judge or juryman.
Last a. Hindmost; coming at or pertaining to the end; final; utmost; meanest; most recent. s. The last thing done, etc.; the end; death; a block on which shoes are made. adv. On or for the last time. v.i. To continue in existence or unimpaired; to hold out, endure.
Blast s. A violent gust of wind; loud sound from a trumpet; pernicious influence, blight. v.t. To blight, destroy, blow up with explosives.
Ep'iblast s. The outer layer of the blastoderm.
Hy'poblast s. The inner layer of a blastoderm.
Mer'oblast s. An ovum of which one portion is germinal and one nutritive.
Mes'oblast s. The mesoderm.
Coun'terblast s. A strong argument, etc., in opposition.
Icon'oclast s. An image-breaker; one who attacks accepted beliefs, customs, etc.
Bal'last s. Heavy material, especially for steadying a ship, regulating ascent of balloon, etc.; broken stone, etc., for use in road-making. v.t. To furnish or lay with ballast.
En'doplast s. The nucleus in some forms of protoplasm.
Pro'toplast s. An original, a copy to be imitated.
Outlast' v.t. To last longer than.
Mast s. Pole in a ship to support sails; fruit of the beech, oak, etc.
Fore'mast s. The first mast of a ship towards the head.
Beech'-mast s. The fruit of the beech-tree.
Main'mast s. The principal mast of a ship.
Dur'mast s. A variety of oak.
Dismast' v.t. To deprive of masts.
Gym'nast s. An expert in gymnastics.
Dy'nast s. A ruler; founder of a dynasty.
Oast s. Kiln for drying hops or malt.
Boast v.t. To brag of. v.i. To talk ostentatiously, to exalt oneself. s. A vaunting; a cause of boasting.
Coast s. The seashore; a toboggan slide; a ride downhill on a cycle, etc., without using pedals or motive power. v.t. To sail near to, keep close to. v.i. To sail from port to port of the same country; to slide downhill, descend on a cycle, etc., without using power.
Roast v.t. To cook by exposure to heat; to parch thus; (*slang*) to banter. v.i. To be roasted. s. Act of roasting; piece of meat so cooked.
Toast s. Slice of bread browned at the fire; sentiment proposed or person or thing honoured in drinking. v.t. To brown or scorch before the fire; to drink in honour of.
Past a. Not present or future; gone by; ended. s. Former time. prep. Beyond. adv. By; so as to pass.
Repast' s. A meal; act of taking this.
Par'aphrast s. One who paraphrases.
Met'aphrast s. One who makes literal translations, changes prose into verse, etc.
Contrast' v.t. To set in opposition, to compare. v.i. To stand in contrast to.
Con'trast s. Unlikeness or comparison of qualities or things.

Fan'tast s. A visionary; a fantastic person or writer.
Vast a. Enormous; great in importance, etc. s. Boundless space.
Avast' int. Stop! desist!
Wast (wost) 2nd sing., past (*Be*).
Didst past (*2nd sing.*) (*Do*).
Midst s. The middle. prep. In the middle.
Amidst' prep. In the middle or the thick of; enveloped with.
Wouldst (wudst) 2nd sing., past and cond. (*Will*).
-est suff. Forming the superlative degree of adjectives and adverbs.
An'apæst s. A metrical foot of three syllables, two short followed by one long.
Best a. Most good, advanced, correct, etc. s. That which is superlatively good, utmost. adv. In the highest degree; with most ease, propriety, etc. v.t. (*Slang*) To get the better of, to beat.
Incest s. Sexual relations between persons closely related.
Eld'est s. The oldest, especially of those surviving.
Would'est 2nd sing., past and cond. (*Will*).
Mod'est a. Humble, diffident; restrained, retiring; decorous; chaste.
Immod'est a. Forward; indelicate.
Wil'debeest s. The S. African gnu.
Har'tebeest s. A large S. African antelope.
Man'ifest a. Plain, evident, manifest. s. Invoice of ship's cargo. v.t. To make public.
Infest' v.t. To swarm over; to haunt; to harass, annoy.
Gest s. A deed, exploit (*obs.*).
Al'magest s. A work on astrology or alchemy.
Suggest' v.t. To hint, insinuate, intimate.
Digest' v.t. To assimilate through the stomach; to soften by a heated liquid; to arrange under proper heads; to think out.
Di'gest s. A system, compendium, abridgment; a collection of Roman laws.
Redigest' v.t. To digest again.
Ingest' v.t. To take into the stomach.
Congest' v.t. To gather into a mass; to overcharge (with blood). v.i. To accumulate to excess.
Hest s. A command, injunction.
Al'kahest s. The universal solvent of the alchemists.
Chest s. A box with lid, a case; the part of the body enclosed by ribs and breastbone.
Behest' s. Command, injunction.
Far'thest a. Most distant. adv. At or to the greatest distance.
Fur'thest a. Most remote. adv. At or to the greatest distance.
Priest s. A religious minister, officiating clergyman.
Jest v.t. To divert, make merriment; to sport. s. A joke, pleasantry; a laughing-stock.
Lest conj. For fear that; in case.
Ar'balest s. A steel crossbow.
Blest' a. Made or making happy or blessed, cheering; consecrated. s. The Saints in heaven.
Molest' v.t. To annoy, harass, vex, disturb.
Nest s. Retreat formed by a bird for egg-laying and hatching; place used by insects, etc., for similar purposes; collection of graduated boxes, etc.; a snug abode. v.i. To build or occupy a nest.
Hon'est a. Upright, sincere; chaste, just.
Dishon'est a. Lacking in honesty; fraudulent; perfidious.
Ear'nest a. Ardent, zealous; importunate. s. Seriousness; pledge of more to follow.
Pest s. Plague, pestilence; a nuisance; a mischievous person.
Tem'pest s. A violent storm.
Rin'derpest s. A malignant, contagious cattle disease.
Rest s. Cessation of labour; peace; repose; appliance for support; place where one may rest; pause; a check; remainder; the others. v.i. To cease from labour; to take repose; to be supported; to remain, be left. v.t. To lay at rest.
Crest s. A crowning tuft, plume, or other decoration (natural or artificial); a helmet; an heraldic badge or device; the top. v.t. To furnish with a crest, serve as a crest for.
In'terest v.t. To concern, engage the attention of. s. Concern, regard; advantage; profit from money lent or invested; influence with a person.
Unrest' s. Restlessness; disquiet; unhappiness.
For'est s. A tract of land densely covered with trees. a. Sylvan, pertaining to forests. v.t. To convert into a forest.
Defor'est v.t. To clear of forest.
Affor'est v.t. To convert into forest-land.
Reaffor'est v.t. To convert again into forest.
Disaffor'est v.t. To clear of timber; to free from forest laws.
Disfor'est v.t. To clear of forest.
Im'prest s. A public loan or advance.
Arrest' v.t. To hinder the motion or action of; to obstruct; to apprehend, seize. s. The taking of a person; seizure; hindrance; stoppage.
Wrest v.t. To turn, twist, especially with violence; to pervert, distort. s. A violent wrench; a turning implement.
Pal'impsest s. A parchment, etc., which has been rewritten on after earlier writing has been erased.
Test s. A standard, criterion; examination; means of trial; oath taken at initiation; a hard outer covering. v.t. To prove by experiment; to try severely; to attest, verify.
Obtest' v.t. To supplicate; to beg for. v.i. To protest.
Detest' v.t. To hate, abhor, abominate.
Contest' v.t. To call in question, strive for. v.i. To strive; to emulate.
Con'test s. Strife, debate, earnest dispute; combat, battle.
Protest' v.i. To affirm publicly or formally. v.t. To assert; to declare refusal of payment (of a bill).
Pro'test s. Formal declaration of dissent; declaration that acceptance or payment of a bill has been refused.
Attest' v.t. and i. To bear witness, call to witness, give proof of.
Guest s. A visitor, a temporary resident.
Quest s. Act of seeking; search, pursuit; object of search; official inquiry; a jury.
Bequest' s. Anything bequeathed.

Request' v.t. To ask, beg. s. Act of asking; solicitation; that asked for; state of being sought after.
In'quest s. A judicial inquiry, especially into cause of death; jury investigating.
Con'quest s. Act of conquering; that which is won; a gaining by struggle, victory.
Recon'quest s. A second conquest.
Vest s. An undergarment for the trunk; a waistcoat. v.t. To clothe with a garment; to endow, invest (with authority, etc.). v.i. To devolve, descend to; to take effect, as a title, etc.
Devest' v.t. To divest, alienate.
Divest' v.t. To strip off clothes, armour, etc.; to deprive.
Invest' v.t. To array; to clothe with office or authority; to besiege; to lay out money, make an investment.
Har'vest s. The season when corn is reaped; crop gathered; consequences; product of labour. v.t. To reap, gather.
West s. Cardinal point opposite the east; the region of sunset. adv. Towards or in the west. a. Being in or towards, or coming from the west.
Zest s. That which gives relish; keen enjoyment.
Amongst' prep. Among; throughout; of the number.
-ist suff. Denoting agent, follower, adherer, etc.
Ju'daist s. One who conforms to Judaism.
Ar'chaist s. An imitator of old styles; an antiquary.
La'maist s. A Tibetan or Mongolian Buddhist.
Al'gebraist s. (*Algebra*).
He'braist s. One versed in Hebrew language and learning.
Mith'raist s. A worshipper of Mithra.
Ul'traist s. One who advocates extreme measures.
Pro'saist s. A writer of prose.
Waist s. Narrow part of body above hips; middle part of ship, etc.
Ba'bist s. (*Babism*).
Ar'abist s. A student of Arabic.
Cam'bist s. A money-changer, bill-broker.
Iam'bist s. One who writes in iambuses.
Cu'bist s. One of a modern school of painters.
Cist s. A chest used in the Eleusinian mysteries; a Celtic tomb covered with a flat stone.
Phar'macist s. A pharmaceutist.
Sol'ecist s. One who commits a solecism.
Mosa'icist s. A writer in mosaic.
Myth'icist s. A student or interpreter of myths.
Bib'licist s. A biblical student.
Pub'licist s. A journalist, especially on international law or foreign politics.
Polem'icist s. A controversialist.
Tech'nicist s. One skilled in technics.
Empir'icist s. An empiric; one holding the theory of empiricism.
Clas'sicist s. A classical scholar.
Phys'icist s. One versed in the science of physics.
Kenot'icist s. One holding the doctrine of kenosis.
Roman'cist s. A romancer.
Ex'orcist s. One who exorcizes or pretends to cast out demons.
Hagga'dist s. One learned in the Haggadah.
Bal'ladist s. A ballad-writer.
Fad'dist s. One addicted to fads.
Or'thopæ'dist s. One who practises orthopædy.
Encyclopæ'dist s. A compiler or editor of an encyclopædia; one of very extensive knowledge.
Or'chidist s. One who cultivates or is a connoisseur of orchids.
Pyr'amidist s. A student of ancient pyramids, especially those of Egypt.
Lap'idist s. A lapidary.
Con'trabandist s. A smuggler.
Propagan'dist s. One who devotes himself to propaganda.
Leg'endist s. A teller or writer of legends.
Stun'dist s. Member of a Russian dissenting body.
Meth'odist s. A member of a dissenting evangelical sect.
Mo'dist s. A follower of fashion.
Psalm'odist s. A writer or singer of psalms.
Thren'odist s. The writer of a threnody.
Mon'odist s. One who writes monodies.
Chirop'odist s. One who practises chiropody.
Par'odist s. A writer of parodies.
Pros'odist s. One versed in prosody.
Rhap'sodist s. A rhapsode; a professional reciter; one who rhapsodizes.
Or'chardist s. One who tends orchards.
Concord'ist s. A compiler of a concordance.
Tal'mudist s. One versed in the Talmud.
De'ist s. An adherent of deism.
Pol'tergeist s. A supposed mischievous household sprite.
Zeit'geist s. The intellectual or spiritual tendency of a period.
The'ist s. One who believes in a personal God.
A'theist s. One who denies the existence of God.
Tri'theist s. A believer in the doctrine of tritheism.
Pan'theist s. An adherent of pantheism.
Mon'otheist s. A believer in monotheism.
Pol'ytheist s. A worshipper of many gods.
Canoe'ist s. One who manages a canoe.
Cue'ist s. A billiard-player.
Fist s. The clenched hand. v.t. To strike with this.
Pac'ifist s. A supporter of pacifism.
Gist s. The essence of a question.
Geoph'agist s. One who eats earth.
Creoph'agist s. A flesh-eater.
Omoph'agist s. One who eats raw flesh.
Hippoph'agist s. One who feeds on horse-flesh.
Galactoph'agist s. One who lives on milk.
Pantoph'agist s. A man or animal that will eat anything eatable.
Suf'fragist s. An advocate of the extension of the suffrage.
Mas'sagist s. One who gives massage.
Le'gist s. One learned in law.
El'egist s. A writer of elegies.
Sacrile'gist s. One who violates sacred things.
Strat'egist s. One skilled in strategy.
Drug'gist s. A dealer in drugs.
Al'gist s. An expert in or student of seaweeds.
-logist suff. Forming nouns denoting one skilled in some science.
Geneal'ogist s. One skilled in genealogy.
Dial'ogist s. Speaker in or writer of dialogues.
Anal'ogist s. One who busies himself with analogy.
Mineral'ogist s. One versed in the science of minerals.
Symbol'ogist s. (*Symbology*).
Pharmacol'ogist s. One skilled in pharmacy.
Archæol'ogist s. (*Archæology*).

Crustaceol'ogist s. (*Crustaceology*).
Geol'ogist s. One versed in geology.
Theol'ogist s. One versed in theology.
Neol'ogist s. One given to or practising neologism or neology.
Algol'ogist s. (*Algology*).
Conchol'ogist s. (*Conchology*).
Psychol'ogist s. A student of or one skilled in psychology.
Pathol'ogist s. One versed in pathology.
Anthol'ogist s. One who compiles an anthology.
Biol'ogist s. (*Biology*).
Craniol'ogist s. An expert in craniology.
Bacteriol'ogist s. (*Bacteriology*).
Assyriol'ogist s. (*Assyriology*).
Ecclesiol'ogist s. A student of or expert in ecclesiology.
Physiol'ogist s. One versed in or who treats of physiology.
Ophthalmol'-ogist s. One skilled in the treatment of eye diseases, abnormalities, etc.
Pomol'ogist s. A fruit-grower.
Entomol'ogist s. One versed in entomology.
Cosmol'ogist s. One versed in cosmology.
Etymol'ogist s. One versed in etymology.
Campanol'-ogist s. (*Campanology*).
Phrenol'ogist s. One versed in or making a business of phrenology.
Arachnol'ogist s. (*Arachnology*).
Ethnol'ogist s. One versed in ethnology.
Carcinol'ogist s. (*Carcinology*).
Monol'ogist s. A performer or utterer of monologues.
Chronol'ogist s. One skilled in chronology.
Apol'ogist s. A defender in speech or writing, especially of Christianity.
Anthropol'ogist s. (*Anthropology*).
Necrol'ogist s. One who gives an account of deaths.
Dendrol'ogist s. One who studies trees scientifically.
Chirol'ogist s. (*Chirology*).
Horol'ogist s. An horologer.
Astrol'ogist s. One versed in or practising astrology.
Dermatol'ogist s. An expert in dermatology.
Dialectol'ogist s. A student of dialects.
Celtol'ogist s. A student of Celtic language, antiquities, etc.
Neontol'ogist s. A student of neontology.
Egyptol'ogist s. (*Egyptology*).
Christol'ogist s. (*Christology*).
Tautol'ogist s. One given to the use of tautology.
Bryol'ogist s. (*Bryology*).
Embryol'ogist s. (*Embryology*).
Eu'logist s. One who eulogizes.
The'urgist s. One skilled in or devoted to theurgy.
Met'allurgist s. One skilled in metallurgy.
Dram'aturgist s. A playwright; one skilled in dramatic representation.
Thau'matur-gist s. A magician, conjurer.
Lit'urgist s. One adhering strictly to a liturgy.
Hist int. Silence ! attend !
Mon'achist s. Characteristic of monks.
Cat'echist s. One who catechizes; a teacher of catechumens.
An'archist s. One actively opposed to all forms of government.
Mon'archist s. An advocate or supporter of monarchy.
Schist (shist) s. A slaty rock easily split.
Bud'dhist s., a. (*Buddhism*).
-graphist suff. Many other nouns formed from nouns in *graph*.
Teleg'raphist s. A telegraph operator.
Callig'raphist s. (*Calligraphy*).
Chalcog'-raphist s. (*Chalcography*).
Cerog'raphist s. A painter on wax.
Cryptog'raphist s. A cryptographer.
Catas'trophist s. A supporter of the theory of catastrophism.
Soph'ist s. A philosopher of ancient Athens who taught for pay; a captious and fallacious reasoner, quibbler.
Theos'ophist s. One addicted to theosophy.
Philos'ophist s. One given to philosophism.
Gymnos'ophist s. One of a sect of early Hindu philosophers who went almost naked.
Deipnos'ophist s. A philosopher of eating and drinking.
Anthropo-mor'phist s. (*Anthropomorphism*).
Hierog'lyphist s. One who deciphers hieroglyphs.
Fet'ishist s. A fetish-worshipper.
Polym'athist s. A great scholar.
Telep'athist s. One skilled in telepathy.
Homœop'-athist s. One who believes in or treats by homœopathy.
Osteop'athist s. An osteopath.
Psychop'athist s. A mental doctor, an alienist.
Allop'athist s. (*Allopathy*).
Hydrop'athist s. One who believes in or practices hydropathy.
Neurop'athist s. One skilled in the treatment of nervous diseases.
Whist s. A card-game for four. int. Silence ! hush ! a. Silent.
La'kist s. One of the Lake Poets or their followers.
Jo'kist s. A joker.
York'ist a. and s. Pertaining to or an adherent of the White Rose party in the Wars of the Roses.
List s. The outer edge of cloth; a roll, catalogue, register; palings enclosing a tourney-field, the field; inclination of ship, etc., to one side. v.t. To sow together; to enrol, enlist; to desire, choose; to hearken.
Cab'balist s. (*Cabbala*).
Cym'balist s. One who plays the cymbals.
Herb'alist s. One skilled in herbs and their medicinal qualities; a collector of or dealer in herbs.
Verb'alist s. One heeding words only; a minute critic of words.
Syn'dicalist s. An adherent of syndicalism.
Cler'icalist s. A cleric; a wielder or upholder of clericalism.
Vo'calist s. A singer.
Ped'alist s. One expert in the use of pedals; a cyclist.
Mo'dalist s. An adherent of modalism.
Feu'dalist s. A supporter of or one versed in feudalism.
Ide'alist s. A visionary; one holding the theory of idealism.
Repeal'ist s. A repealer.
Re'alist s. One maintaining that every general idea has objective existence or that in perception there is immediate cognition of externals; one who aims at representing scenes, persons, etc., as they are or as they actually appear.
Le'galist s. One who desires strict adherence to the letter of the law.
Proverb'ialist s. One who speaks in proverbs.
Spec'ialist s. One devoting himself to a particular branch of a profession, etc.
Finan'cialist s. A financier.

So'cialist s. One who advocates socialism. a. Socialistic.
Commer'cialist s. (*Commercialism*).
Di'alist s. One who makes dials.
Millenn'ialist s. A millenarian.
Ceremo'nialist s. (*Ceremonialism*).
Imper'ialist s. An advocate of imperialism.
Immater'ialist s. An upholder of immaterialism.
Minister'ialist s. A supporter of a ministry.
Memor'ialist s. One who writes or presents a memorial.
Indus'trialist s. A member of an industrial organization; a supporter of industrialism.
Controver'sialist s. One who engages in a controversy; a disputant.
Experien'tialist s. One believing in the theory of experientialism.
Preferen'tialist s. A supporter of commercial preferentialism.
Mar'tialist s. A strict disciplinarian.
Dilu'vialist s. One believing that certain geological phenomena are the result of the Deluge.
Form'alist s. One who observes form, especially in religion.
Phenom'enalist s. An adherent of phenomenalism.
Nom'inalist s. One of a sect of mediæval philosophers holding that general conceptions exist in name only.
An'nalist s. A writer of annals.
Educa'tionalist s. An educationist.
Congrega'tionalist s. and a. (*Congregationalism*).
Denomina'tionalist s. An adherent of denominationalism.
Interna'tionalist s. An advocate of internationalism; an exponent of international laws.
Ra'tionalist s. One whose conduct, opinions, etc., are based on reason.
Conversa'tionalist s. A good talker.
Tradi'tionalist s. (*Traditionist*).
Intui'tionalist s. A believer in intuitionalism.
Conven'tionalist s. (*Conventionalism*).
Concep'tionalist s. A conceptualist.
Institu'tionalist s. A believer in institutionalism.
Constitu'tionalist s. An adherent of the constitution.
Triper'sonalist s. A Trinitarian.
Car'nalist s. A sensualist.
Journ'alist s. A professional newspaper writer.
Com'munalist s. (*Communalism*).
Pa'palist s. A supporter of the papacy.
Lib'eralist s. A liberal, upholder of liberalism.
Fed'eralist s. An advocate of federation; a supporter of federalism.
Lit'eralist s. One imbued with literalism.
Chor'alist s. A singer in a chorus.
Mor'alist s. One who teaches morals or inculcates moral duties.
Hu'moralist s. One holding the theory of humoralism.
Cen'tralist s. (*Centralism*).
Plur'alist s. One who holds more than one benefice or office at once; a believer in philosophic pluralism.
Rur'alist s. One leading a rural life.
Nat'uralist s. One versed in natural history; a believer in naturalism; a realist.
Supernat'uralist s. One believing in the supernatural.
Scrip'turalist s. (*Scripturist*).
Univer'salist a. and s. Pertaining to, or one holding, the doctrine of universalism.
Fa'talist s. One who holds the doctrine of fatalism. a. Fatalistic.
Decre'talist s. One versed in decretals.
Capit'alist s. A possessor of capital.
Vi'talist s. One supporting the doctrine of vitalism. a. Pertaining to this.
Occiden'talist s. One versed in or favouring Occidentalism.
Transcenden'talist s. An adherent of transcendentalism.
Orien'talist s. One versed in Eastern languages and literature.
Experimen'talist s. One who practises experiments.
Instrumen'talist s. One who plays a musical instrument.
Sacerdo'talist s. One favouring sacerdotalism.
Du'alist s. An adherent of a system of dualism.
Individ'ualist s. An egoist; an upholder of individualism.
Sen'sualist s. One given to the indulgence of the appetites.
Intellec'tualist s. An adherent of the doctrine of intellectualism.
Punc'tualist s. One very exact in the observance of ceremony, etc.
Rit'ualist s. One skilled in or devoted to ritualism; one attaching exaggerated importance to ritual.
Spir'itualist s. One believing in or practising spiritualism.
Concep'tualist s. (*Conceptualism*).
Tex'tualist s. One who closely follows the text.
Sex'ualist s. One who follows Linnæus's classification of plants.
Mediæ'valist s. One devoted to mediæval institutions, etc.
Reviv'alist s. One who promotes or advocates religious revivals.
Loy'alist s. One who adheres to his sovereign or to lawful authority.
Roy'alist s. An adherent or supporter of the king or of monarchy.
Cy'clist s. One who rides a bicycle, etc.
Bi'cyclist s. A bicycle rider.
Tri'cyclist s. A tricycle rider.
Evan'gelist s. One of the writers of the Gospels; a preacher; a revivalist.
Philat'elist s. One who collects or deals in postage-stamps.
Nov'elist s. A writer of novels.
Prob'abilist s. One maintaining that certainty is impossible, or that one may do what may be right though it does not appear so to him.
Possib'ilist s. One who aims only at reforms that are practicable.
Perfectib'ilist s. A perfectionist.
Automo'bilist s. One used to driving motor-cars.
Prof'ilist s. One who draws profiles.
Pu'gilist s. A boxer, prize-fighter.
Ni'hilist s. An adherent of any form of nihilism; an anarchist (especially of Imperial Russia).
Biblioph'ilist s. A lover of books.
Œnoph'ilist s. A lover or connoisseur of wines.
Zooph'ilist s. A lover of animals.
Gastroph'ilist s. A glutton, gastrophile.
Facsim'ilist s. One who makes facsimiles.
Hom'ilist s. A preacher.
Black'-list s. A list of persons in disgrace, etc. v.t. To enter on this list.
Med'allist s. A recipient of a medal; one who designs, engraves, collects, or deals in medals.
Bimet'allist s. (*Bimetallism*).

Monomet'allist s. A supporter of monometallism.
Li'bellist s. A libeller.
Violoncel'list (-chel'-) s. Player on the violoncello.
Niel'list s. A worker in niello.
Enam'ellist s. One who enamels.
Aquarel'list s. A worker in aquarelle.
Pas'tellist s. An artist in pastel.
Du'ellist s. One who fights duels.
Enlist' v.t. To enter on a list or register; to engage in a service, especially military or naval. v.i. To engage oneself in the armed forces; to enter heartily into a cause.
Re-enlist' v.t. and i. To enlist again.
Parab'olist s. A narrator of parables.
Sym'bolist s. A member of a school of symbolism.
Hyper'bolist s. One who uses hyperboles.
Sci'olist s. A pretender to knowledge; a smatterer.
Vi'olist s. A viol- or viola-player.
Bibliop'olist s. A bookseller.
Monop'olist s. One that monopolizes or holds a monopoly.
Sim'plist s. A herbalist.
Fab'ulist s. A writer of fables.
Somnam'bulist s. A sleep-walker.
Funam'bulist s. A rope-dancer.
Noctam'bulist s. One who walks in his sleep.
Animal'culist s. A student of animalcule, or adherent of animalculism.
Oc'ulist s. One skilled in treating eye-diseases.
Monoc'ulist s. A one-eyed person.
Styl'ist s. One careful of his literary style.
Mist s. A small, thin rain; fog. v.t. To cover with mist. v.i. To be misty.
Hippod'amist s. A horse-tamer.
Big'amist s. A married person who goes through the form of marriage with another.
Dig'amist s. One who has legally married twice.
Trig'amist s. One who has married three times or has three spouses at once.
Monog'amist s. A supporter of monogamy; one who disallows second marriages.
Deuterog'amist s. One who has married twice.
Misog'amist s. One who hates marriage.
Cryptog'amist s. A student of the Cryptogamia.
Polyg'amist s. One who practises polygamy.
Dy'namist s. An adherent of the theory of dynamism.
Cer'amist s. A potter; collector of or expert in pottery.
Acad'emist s. A member of an academy; an Academic philosopher.
Chem'ist s. One skilled in chemistry; a druggist, apothecary.
Al'chemist s. (*Alchemy*).
Heteroph'emist s. One addicted to heterophemy.
Prob'lemist s. One who composes or studies chess-problems.
Extrem'ist s. One who holds extreme opinions, supports extreme practices, etc.
To'temist s. One of a clan having a totem.
Pantomi'mist s. An actor in or writer of pantomimes.
An'imist s. (*Animism*).
Pess'imist s. One whose thoughts are directed to the dark side of things; one believing in or imbued with pessimism.
Tim'ist s. One who keeps time (*mus.*).
Legit'imist s. One believing in the sacredness of hereditary monarchies.
Op'timist s. An upholder of the doctrine of optimism; a sanguine person.
Max'imist s. One who makes or uses maxims.
Ophthal'mist s. An ophthalmologist.
Palm'ist s. One who practises palmistry.
Psalm'ist s. A writer of psalms; David.
Dilem'mist s. One who bases arguments on dilemmas.
Tho'mist (tō'-) s. An adherent of Thomism.
Physiogn'omist (-on'-) s. One skilled in physiognomy.
Econ'omist s. A student of political economy; one who can economize.
Deuteron'omist s. The author, or one of the authors, of Deuteronomy.
Agron'omist s. A rural economist.
Gastron'omist s. A gastronome.
Auton'omist s. An upholder of autonomy.
Pluton'omist s. A student of political economy.
Taxon'omist s. One skilled in classifying.
At'omist s. (*Atomism*).
Diat'omist s. A student of diatoms.
Anat'omist s. (*Anatomy*).
Phlebot'omist s. One who lets blood.
Zoot'omist s. A comparative anatomist.
Microt'omist s. One expert in use of the microtome.
Alar'mist s. One who spreads alarming rumours.
Taxider'mist s. One skilled in preserving and mounting skins.
Reform'ist s. One in favour of reform; a member of a reformed Church.
Conform'ist s. One who conforms to the doctrine, etc., of the Church of England.
Nonconform'ist s. One not conforming to the Established Church.
Cataclys'mist s. One who attributes geological formations to cataclysms.
Tar'gumist s. A student of the Targums.
Rhym'ist s. A rhymester.
Synon'ymist s. One who collects and explains synonyms.
Vat'icanist s. One supporting Vaticanism.
Vol'canist s. One who studies volcanoes.
Vul'canist s. One holding that most geological changes have an igneous origin.
Or'ganist s. One who plays an organ.
Mech'anist s. A mechanician.
Tradu'cianist s. One holding that souls are transmitted from parents to children.
Pi'anist (pē'-) s. A player on the piano.
Sha'manist s. One practising Shamanism.
Ro'manist s. A Roman Catholic.
Hu'manist s. A student of the humanities; one of the Renaissance scholars; one versed in knowledge of human nature.
Accom'panist s. One who accompanies, especially in music.
Al'koranist s. (*Alkoran*).
Sopra'nist s. A soprano singer.
Tan'ist s. The elected heir to an ancient Irish chieftain.
Sa'tanist s. A devil-worshipper; a diabolical person.
Ultramon'tanist s. A supporter of ultramontanism.
Bot'anist s. (*Botany*).
Lu'tanist s. A lute-player.
Car'avanist s. One who travels or dwells in a caravan.
Abiog'enist s. (*Abiogenesis*).
Homog'enist s. One holding the theory of community of origin.
Monog'enist s. One holding the theory of monogenism.
Heterog'enist s. A believer in heterogenesis.
Polyg'enist s. One holding the doctrine of polygeny.
Li'chenist s. A student of lichens.

Hy'gienist s. A student of hygiene; one skilled in sanitation.
A'lienist s. One skilled in the treatment of mental disease.
Hell'enist s. A non-Greek who adopted Greek culture, language, etc.; one skilled in Greek scholarship.
Ple'nist s. One maintaining that all space is full of matter.
Jan'senist s. A member of a Church believing in the irresistible nature of divine grace.
Pyrotech'nist s. One skilled in pyrotechny.
Rab'binist s. A Jew adhering to the Talmud and rabbinical traditions.
Vac'cinist s. A vaccinator, vaccinationist.
Multitu'dinist s. A supporter of the doctrine of multitudinism.
Machin'ist s. One who constructs, works, or tends machines; one versed in mechanics.
Mor'phinist s. One addicted to the use of morphine.
Violin'ist s. A violin-player.
Ter'minist s. One maintaining the doctrine of terminism.
Deter'minist a. Pertaining to determinism. s. An upholder of this.
Indeter'minist s. An upholder of indeterminism.
Lu'minist s. A painter who specializes in light effects.
Illu'minist s. An illuminee.
Al'pinist s. A mountain-climber, especially of the Alps.
Lat'inist s. One skilled in Latin.
Bull'etinist s. One who writes official reports.
Des'tinist s. A fatalist.
Cal'vinist s. (*Calvinism*).
Chau'vinist s. (*Chauvinism*).
Dar'winist s. A Darwinian.
Hym'nist s. A composer of hymns.
Trombo'nist s. A trombone player.
Tobac'conist s. A dealer in tobacco.
He'donist s. A follower of hedonism; one who lives a life of pleasure.
Deuterag'onist s. The second actor in ancient Greek drama.
Antag'onist s. An opponent.
Protag'onist s. The leading character in a Greek play, or in any great enterprise.
Theog'onist s. Writer of a theogony.
Cosmog'onist s. One versed in cosmogony.
Teleph'onist s. A telephone operator.
Sym'phonist s. A composer of symphonies.
Polyph'onist s. A contrapuntist; a ventriloquist.
Pyr'rhonist s. A sceptic.
Coer'cionist s. (*Coercion*).
Relig'ionist s. One passionately or affectedly devoted to religion.
Bull'ionist s. An advocate for a metallic currency.
Opin'ionist s. One unduly attached to his own opinions.
U'nionist s. One who wished to maintain the Union between Great Britain and Ireland, a Conservative; member of a trade-union.
Commun'ionist s. One who partakes of or has special views on admission to Holy Communion.
Non-u'nionist s. (*Negative*).
Disu'nionist s. An advocate of disunion.
Vis'ionist s. One who sees visions; a visionary.
Revis'ionist s. One in favour of revision.
Exten'sionist s. One favouring extension.
Excur'sionist s. One who makes or organizes an excursion.
Seces'sionist s. One taking part in or upholding secession.
Conces'sionist s. One who advocates the grant of a concession.
Proces'sionist s. One taking part in a procession.
Confes'sionist s. One who adopts a certain creed or confession.
Progres'sionist s. One who belongs to a progressive party.
Impres'sionist s. An artist aiming at broad general effects. a. Pertaining to impressionism.
Post-impres'sionist s. One of a school of painters who aim at expressing individual impressions without necessary objective relation to the thing painted.
Suppres'sionist s. One who advocates or practices suppression.
Expres'sionist s. An artist whose forte is the expression of feeling, character, etc.
Exclu'sionist s. One who would exclude others from some privilege.
Illu'sionist s. A believer in illusionism; a visionary; a conjurer.
Educa'tionist s. One versed in educational methods; an advocate of education.
Nega'tionist s. One holding merely negative views in religion.
Associa'tionist s. (*Associationism*).
Revela'tionist s. Believer in divine revelation.
Crema'tionist s. An upholder of cremation.
Vaccina'tionist s. One believing in vaccination.
Emancipa'tionist s. One in favour of the freeing of slaves.
Federa'tionist s. An upholder of federation; a federalist.
Tolera'tionist s. One favouring toleration.
Emigra'tionist s. An advocate of emigration.
Inspira'tionist s. One holding that the whole Bible is divinely inspired.
Restora'tionist s. One who believes in ultimate restoration of all to Divine favour.
Salva'tionist s. A member of the Salvation Army.
Coloniza'tionist s. An advocate of colonization.
Reac'tionist s. A reactionary.
Fac'tionist s. A supporter or promoter of a faction.
Perfec'tionist s. One who believes that moral perfection is attainable.
Introspec'tionist s. One given to introspection; one employing introspection for psychological purposes.
Resurrec'tionist s. A body-snatcher.
Insurrec'tionist s. One taking part in an insurrection.
Vivisec'tionist s. One who vivisects or upholds vivisection.
Protec'tionist s. One favouring a protective tariff. a. Pertaining to such a tariff or system.
Fic'tionist s. A writer of fiction.
Obstruc'tionist s. One who systematically retards progress; an obstructive.
Destruc'tionist s. A believer in the ultimate annihilation of sinners.
Construc'tionist s. One who construes a document or puts a certain kind of construction on a law, etc.
Prohibi'tionist s. One who favours the prohibition of something, especially the sale of intoxicants.
Tradi'tionist s. One who adheres to tradition.
Coali'tionist s. A supporter of a political coalition.
Aboli'tionist s. A supporter of abolition.
Requisi'tionist s. One who makes a requisition.
Opposi'tionist a. and s. (*Opposition*).
Intui'tionist s. An intuitionalist.
No'tionist s. One given to notions; a theorist

Por'tionist s. A joint incumbent.
Contor'tionist s. An acrobat who twists his limbs grotesquely.
Distor'tionist s. A caricaturist; an acrobatic contortionist.
Extor'tionist s. One who practises extortion.
Ques'tionist s. One who questions; an interrogator.
Elocu'tionist s. A teacher or exponent of good elocution.
Circumlocu'tionist s. One habitually using circumlocution.
Resolu'tionist s. One who makes or supports a resolution.
Evolu'tionist s. One skilled in evolutions; one holding the theory of evolution.
Revolu'tionist s. One engaged in or advocating revolution.
Constitu'tionist s. (*Constitutionalist*).
Zi'onist s. One advocating the colonization of Palestine by the Jews.
Col'onist s. A settler in or inhabitant of a colony.
Mon'ist s. A believer in the theory of monism.
De'monist s. One who believes in demons.
Eude'monist s. One founding his philosophy on eudemonism.
Mne'monist s. One who instructs in or practices mnemonics.
Mam'monist s. One devoted to accumulating wealth.
Har'monist s. One skilled in harmony or harmonizing; a musician.
Can'onist s. A student or professor of canon law.
Balloon'ist s. The navigatior of a balloon.
Lampoon'ist s. One who writes lampoons; a satirist.
Cartoon'ist s. One who draws cartoons.
I'ronist s. One addicted to irony.
Pla'tonist s. A follower of Plato.
Plu'tonist s. An adherent of the theory that most geological changes have been due to igneous agency.
Mod'ernist s. An adherent or upholder of modernism.
Sat'urnist s. A saturnine or morose person.
Faun'ist s. A student of faunas.
Com'munist s. (*Communism; communalist*).
Nep'tunist s. One holding that certain rocks were formed from aqueous solution.
Op'portunist s. One who suits his principles to varying circumstances.
Philog'ynist s. A lover or admirer of women.
Misog'ynist s. A woman-hater.
Taoist (tou'-) s. An adherent of Taoism.
Foist v.t. To insert surreptitiously, wrongly, or without warrant; to pass off as genuine.
Eg'oist s. One holding the doctrine of egoism.
Hoist v.t. To raise or lift up; to heave. s. Act of raising; an elevator.
Joist s. One of the beams supporting a floor. v.t. To fit with joists.
Ban'joist s. A player on the banjo.
So'loist s. One who sings or plays alone.
Moist a. Moderately wet, damp.
Shin'toist s. An adherent of Shinto.
Land'scapist s. A painter of landscapes.
Pa'pist s. A Roman Catholic; a papalist.
Or'thoepist s. One versed in orthoepy; a phonetician.
Eman'cipist s. A released convict.
Tu'lipist s. One who cultivates tulips.
Syn'copist s. One who syncopates.
Micros'copist s. One who uses the microscope.
Spectros'copist s. One who works with the spectroscope.
Lycan'thropist s. One affected with lycanthropy.
Philan'thropist s. One devoted to or evincing philanthropy; a benevolent person.
Psilan'thropist s. One holding that Christ was merely human.
Misan'thropist s. A hater of mankind.
Tro'pist s. One who deals in tropes.
Map'pist s. A map-drawer.
Trap'pist s. A member of a strict Cistercian order.
Harp'ist s. A harp-player.
Typ'ist s. One who uses a typewriter.
Daguer'reotypist s. A daguerreotyper.
Electroty'pist s. One who makes electrotypes.
Eu'charist s. The sacrament of the Lord's Supper.
Cath'arist s. A heretic pretending to great purity of life.
Cith'arist s. A player of the cithara.
Di'arist s. One who keeps a diary.
Pla'giarist s. One who plagiarizes; a thief in literature, etc.
A'piarist s. A bee-keeper.
A'viarist s. A bird-keeper or breeder.
So'larist s. An adherent of solarism.
Sec'ularist s. An adherent of the system of secularism. a. Pertaining to this.
Partic'ularist s. One devoted to personal as against communal interests.
Oc'ularist s. A maker of artificial eyes.
Sing'ularist s. One affecting singularity.
Gem'arist s. One versed in the Gemara.
Sum'marist s. One who summarizes.
Sem'inarist s. One conducting or attending a seminary.
Lu'narist s. An investigator of the moon.
Gloss'arist s. A compiler of a glossary.
Mil'itarist s. One imbued with militarism.
San'itarist s. A sanitarian.
Guitar'ist s. One who plays the guitar.
Obit'uarist s. Writer of an obituary.
Laz'arist s. One of the Brotherhood founded by St. Vincent de Paul (1624).
Al'gebrist s. (*Algebra*).
Equil'ibrist s. An acrobat, rope-dancer.
Sa'crist s. Officer in charge of a sacristy.
Polyan'drist s. A woman having several husbands at once.
Hetær'ist s. One practising or upholding hetærism.
Zith'erist s. A player on the zither.
Artil'lerist s. An artilleryman; one expert in the principles of gunnery.
Euhe'merist s. One who explains myths rationalistically.
Mes'merist s. One who mesmerizes.
Man'nerist s. One showing mannerism; a formal or affected person, especially in art.
Pre'terist s. One holding that the Apocalyptic prophecies have been fulfilled.
Hemip'terist s. A student of the Hemiptera.
Que'rist s. An inquirer.
Grist s. Corn to be ground or which has been ground; brewer's malt provision.
Christ s. The Saviour; the Anointed.
An'tichrist s. An opponent or personal antagonist of Christ.
Mem'oirist s. A writer of memoirs.
Sat'irist s. A writer of satire.
Aor'ist s. The indefinite past tense of Greek verbs.
The'orist s. One given to theory or theorizing.
Al'legorist s. (*Allegory*).
Rig'orist s. One who adheres strictly to rule.

Aph'orist s. One who speaks in or writes aphorisms.
Me'liorist s. An adherent of meliorism.
Probabil'iorist s. An adherent of probabiliorism.
Flor'ist s. One who deals in, cultivates, or is an expert in flowers.
Folk'lorist s. One versed in folk-lore.
Am'orist s. A lover; one devoted to love.
Ar'morist s. One skilled in heraldry.
Hu'morist s. One who in writing, acts, etc., excites humour; a wag, joker.
Ter'rorist s. One ruling by intimidation.
Mo'torist s. One who motors, especially habitually.
Psychi'atrist s. One who treats mental disease.
Met'rist s. One skilled in metres; a versifier.
Hexam'etrist s. One who writes in hexameters.
Sym'metrist s. One studious of symmetry.
Geom'etrist s. A geometrician.
Attrist' v.t. To cause to be sad.
Au'rist s. An ear specialist.
Si'necurist s. A holder of a sinecure.
Man'icurist s. One who tends hands and finger-nails as a business.
Jur'ist s. One learned in law; a writer on legal subjects.
Col'ourist s. An artist skilled in use of colour.
Tour'ist s. One who makes a tour.
Pur'ist s. One excessively fastidious in use of words.
Caricatur'ist s. One who makes caricatures.
Min'iaturist s. A miniature-painter.
Cul'turist s. One who affects culture.
Agricul'turist s. (*Agriculture*).
Arboricul'-turist s. (*Arboriculture*).
Floricul'turist s. One who cultivates flowering plants.
Horticul'turist s. One skilled in horticulture.
Rap'turist s. An enthusiast.
Scrip'turist s. One strongly attached to or versed in the Scriptures.
Fu'turist s. One of an iconoclastic school of artists.
Wrist s. Joint uniting hand to arm.
Panegyr'ist s. A eulogist.
Lyr'ist s. A player on the lyre; a writer of lyrics.
Subsist' v.i. To have existence, to continue. v.t. To support, maintain.
Desist' v.i. To cease from, stop, leave off.
Geod'esist s. One skilled in geodesy.
Resist' v.t. and i. To withstand, oppose; to struggle against.
Insist' v.i. To persist in, persevere, urge.
Consist' v.i. To be comprised or made up; to be in a fixed state; to be compatible.
Persist' v.i. To continue firm or in a certain state; to persevere.
Assist' v.t. To help. v.i. To lend help; to contribute.
Progres'sist a. Striving after progress. s. A progressionist.
Prel'atist s. A supporter of prelacy.
Spec'ulatist s. A speculator.
-amatist suff. Others formed from nouns in *-ama* and *-am*.
Dram'atist s. A playwright.
Melodram'-atist s. Writer of melodramas.
Schem'atist s. One given to scheming or schematizing.
Emblem'atist s. An inventor of emblems, writer of allegories.
Prob'lematist s. A problemist.
Theorem'atist s. One who constructs theorems.
Sys'tematist s. A worker by or devotee to system.
Prag'matist s. An adherent of pragmatism
Enig'matist s. One who makes or talks in enigmas.
Stig'matist s. One bearing miraculous marks of the stigmata.
Dog'matist s One given to dogmatizing.
Anagram'-matist s. (*Anagram*).
Diplo'matist s. A diplomat, ambassador.
Autom'atist s. A believer in the theory of automatism.
Don'atist s. A follower of Donatus, a N. African schismatic of the fourth century.
Sep'aratist s. One who advocates separatism, or withdraws himself, especially from a Church, political party, nation, etc.
Theoc'ratist s. An upholder of or liver under a theocracy.
Bureau'cratist s. A supporter of or member of a bureaucracy.
Stat'ist s. A statistician.
Doce'tist s. One holding the doctrine of docetism.
Exege'tist s. An exegete, interpreter.
Pi'etist s. An advocate or supporter of pietism.
Qui'etist s. One of a sect of mystics who maintained that religion consists in mental repose and contemplation.
Mag'netist s. One skilled in magnetism.
Phon'etist s. A phonetician.
Decre'tist s. One versed in decretals.
Syn'cretist s. One who practises syncretism.
Por'traitist s. A portrait-painter.
Spir'itist s. Spiritualist.
Sans'kritist s. A student or master of Sanskrit.
Fortu'itist s. An upholder of the doctrine of fortuitism.
Oc'cultist s. One versed in or practising occultism.
Comt'ist s. A Positivist.
Vedant'ist s. One learned in or following the teachings of the Vedanta.
Esperant'ist s. A user of Esperanto.
Ig'norantist s. One who favours ignorantism.
Obscur'antist s. An obscurant. a. Pertaining to obscurantists or obscurantism.
Cinquecen'tist s. A writer or artist of the cinquecento.
Quattrocen'tist s. An Italian artist or writer of the fifteenth century.
Den'tist s. A dental surgeon.
Irreden'tist s. One of a late Italian political party aiming at the recovery of Italian speaking districts.
Sci'entist s. A student of science.
Exper'imentist s. An experimenter.
Punt'ist s. A puntsman.
Contrapun'tist s. One skilled in counterpoint.
Nar'cotist s. One indulging unduly in narcotics
Eg'otist s. One addicted to egotism.
Hyp'notist s. One who hypnotizes.
Ne'potist s. One who practises nepotism.
Des'potist s. An advocate of despotism.
Bap'tist s. A member of a Christian sect that rejects infant baptism.
Anabap'tist s. A member of a sect which, not believing in infant baptism, re-baptized its members.
Synop'tist s. One of the writers of the synoptic gospels.
Ar'tist s. One skilled in some fine art, especially painting; a performer.
Chart'ist s. A partisan of chartism.
Controver'tist s One who controverts.
Aqua-for'tist s. One who engraves or etches with aqua-fortis.

Clarinet'tist s. A clarinet-player.
Libret'tist s. The writer of a libretto.
Flaut'ist s. A flute-player.
Pharmaceu'tist s. One skilled in pharmacy; a druggist.
Therapeu'tist s. One skilled in therapeutics.
Parachu'tist s. A public exhibitor with the parachute.
Lu'tist s. A lute-player.
Flu'tist s. A flute-player, flautist.
Ab'solutist s. One in favour of arbitrary government. a. Pertaining to absolutism.
Vac'uist s. One who holds the doctrine of a vacuum in nature.
Lin'guist s. One skilled in languages.
Biling'uist s. One speaking two languages with equal facility.
Fu'guist s. A writer or performer of fugues.
Eu'phuist s. One who affects excessive elegance in language.
Solil'oquist s. One who soliloquizes.
Somnil'oquist s. One who talks in his sleep.
Ventril'oquist s. One who can ventriloquize.
Col'loquist s. One taking part in a conversation.
Al'truist s. One who always thinks of others before himself and acts for their benefit rather than his own.
Cas'uist s. A quibbler, hair-splitter.
Bol'shevist s. A member of the Russian revolutionary and anti-Imperial party. a. Pertaining to this or its propaganda.
Recid'ivist s. An habitual criminal; one continually in and out of prison.
Ar'chivist s. A keeper of records.
Neg'ativist s. A negationist.
Objec'tivist s. A student or adherent of objectivism.
Collec'tivist s. (*Collectivism*).
Pos'itivist s. An adherent of positivism.
Reser'vist s. Member of reserve forces.
Wist past (*Wis*).
Twist v.t. and i. To twine, contort, wreathe; to form into a cord; to pervert. s. A contortion; something turned; roll of tobacco; bent; (*slang*) appetite.
Entwist' v.t. To twist or wreathe round.
Intertwist' v.t. To twist together.
Ideoprax'ist s. One who acts upon his or others' ideas.
Exist' v.i. To be, to live, have existence.
Pre-exist' v.i. To exist beforehand or before something else.
Coexist' v.i. To exist at the same time.
Es'sayist s. A writer of essays.
Hob'byist s. One who indulges in a hobby or hobbies.
Lob'byist s. One who solicits votes in the parliamentary lobbies.
Cop'yist s. A copier.
Whilst conj. While.
Canst v. aux. (*Can*).
Fornenst' adv. and prep. Directly opposite to.
Against' prep. In opposition to; in expectation of.
Cost s. Price, charge, expense; loss; whatever is requisite to secure a return. v.t. To require to be expended, laid out, or borne; to cause to be suffered.
Accost' v.t. To address, speak to first.
Pen'tecost s. The Jewish festival on the fiftieth day after Passover; Whitsuntide.
Dost (dust) 2nd sing. pres. ind. (*Do*).
Host s. Landlord; one entertaining another; an army, multitude; the consecrated wafer of the Eucharist.
Ghost s. The spirit of a deceased person, especially when visible; an apparition; a mere shadow; remotest likelihood; one who works in the background.
Lost past and past part. (*Lose*).
Most a. Superlative of "more." adv. In the greatest degree, etc.; chiefly. s. The majority; greatest number, amount, extent, etc.
-most suff. Forming superlatives of adjectives and adverbs.
Head'most a. Most advanced.
Mid'most a. In the exact middle.
End'most a. The furthest; nearest to the end.
Hind'most a. The last.
Mid'dlemost a. Being nearest the middle.
Fore'most a. First in place, rank, or dignity, etc. adv. In the first place.
Al'most adv. Nearly; not quite; for the greatest part.
Bot'tommost a. The lowest of all.
In'most a. Most inward; deepest, most secret.
Nor'thernmost a. Farthest north.
South'ernmost (sŭth'-) a. Furthest towards the south.
West'ernmost a. Farthest west.
Top'most a. Highest, uppermost.
Up'most a. Highest, uppermost.
Rear'most a. Coming last of all.
Har'most s. An ancient Spartan provincial governor.
Hind'ermost a. The last.
Un'dermost a. Lowest in place, rank, etc.
Weath'ermost a. Farthest to windward.
Neth'ermost a. Lowermost.
Hith'ermost a. Nearest on this side.
Far'thermost a. Being at the greatest distance.
Fur'thermost a. Most remote.
In'nermost a. Most inward, hidden, or esoteric.
Up'permost a. Highest in place, rank, authority. etc.; predominant.
Bet'termost a. Best.
Ut'termost a. Being in the greatest degree; extreme. s. The greatest degree.
Out'ermost a. On the extreme external part.
Low'ermost a. The lowest of all.
Ut'most a. Extreme, furthest, ultimate.
Boost v.t. (*Slang*) To shove, give a lift to, help on its way.
Roost v.i. To perch, rest, or sleep, as birds. s. A perch, pole for birds to rest on.
Post s. Piece of timber, iron, etc., set upright, a pillar; situation, place assigned; military station; employment; courier; system of public conveyance of letters; post-office; a size of paper (about 18×15 in.). v.t. To place; to deposit for carriage; to fix up in a public place; to transfer to a ledger; to make master of. v.i. To travel with post-horses, to hasten. a. Used in rapid travelling. adv. Swiftly.
Mile'post s. A post marking the miles on a road.
Ripost' s. (*Riposte*).
Im'post s. A tax, toll, duty, tribute; member of a pillar on which an arch rests.
Com'post s. A fertilizing mixture; a kind of concrete. v.t. To manure with compost.

Sign'post (sin'-) s. A post indicating direction or supporting a sign.
Out'post s. A station beyond the camp or at a distance from the main body; troops stationed here.
Frost s. Frozen dew; temperature which causes freezing; coldness of manner. v.t. To injure by or cover with frost; to whiten.
Provost' s. A superintendent or one in authority; head of a college, etc., chief magistrate of Scottish burgh.
Erst adv. Formerly; in early times.
Verst s. Russian measure of length (about two-thirds of a mile).
First a. Earliest in time, rank, place, etc.; chief in value; highest; the ordinal of 1.
Thirst s. Uneasiness through want of drink; eager desire. v.i. To feel this.
Athirst' a. Thirsty.
Worst (werst) a. Bad, ill, etc., in the greatest degree. adv. Most badly. s. That which is most bad, evil, severe, etc. v.t. To defeat, get the better of.
Burst v.t. To break suddenly and by force. v.i. To rush forth, to fly or break open. s. A violent disruption, a breaking open.
Out'burst s. A breaking or bursting out.
Curst a. Cursed, troublesome.
Accurst' a. Execrable, detestable, cursed.
Durst past and cond. (*Dare*).
Hol'ocaust s. A sacrifice consumed by fire; a great slaughter.
Hyp'ocaust s. The underground hot-air chamber of a Roman bath.
Exhaust' v.t. To drain, to empty, to spend. s. Foul air let out of a room, etc.; waste steam escaping from a cylinder, etc.; a pipe conducting this away.
Bust s. The chest and thorax; a sculptured or other representation of head and shoulders.
Robust' a. Hardy, sturdy, vigorous.
Lo'cust s. A destructive winged insect allied to the grasshopper; the carob-tree; its bean.
Dust s. Dry, powdery particles of earth, cloth, etc.; the grave; a lowly estate; (*slang*) money. v.t. To free from or to sprinkle with dust.
Adust' a. Scorched, sunburnt; gloomy.
Dry'asdust s. A dull pedant, antiquary, bookworm, etc.
Saw'dust s. Small fragments made in sawing timber.
Fust s. A musty smell; mustiness. v.i. To grow mouldy.
Gust s. A sudden blast of wind; a breeze, gale; sense or pleasure of tasting, relish.
Disgust' s. Aversion, distaste; ill-humour. v.t. To offend the taste of; to displease.
August' a. Stately, majestic.
Au'gust s. The eighth month.
Just a. Upright; incorruptible; equitable. adv. Precisely; nearly; almost; barely.
Adjust' v.t. To set right or in the right place; to regulate.
Readjust' v.t. To arrange anew.
Lust s. Desire, especially carnal; lasciviousness. v.i. To have powerful or carnal desire.
Must v. aux. To be obliged or compelled; to be necessary. s. New wine, unfermented grape-juice; mustiness. a. Frenzied (of camels and elephants).
Oust v.t. To eject, turn out.
Joust s. A tournament, tilting-match. v.i. To tilt.
Roust v.t. To disturb, vex.
Rust s. The reddish coating formed on iron exposed to damp, oxidized iron; a parasitic fungus on grain. v.i. To be oxidized (of iron); to become dull by inaction. v.t. To corrode with rust, impair by inactivity.
Crust s. Hard outer coat; piece of hard bread; a deposit from wine. v.t. and i. To cover or become covered with a hard coat.
Encrust' v.t. To cover with a crust.
Thrust v.t. To drive with force, to shove. v.i. To make a push or lunge; to intrude. s. A violent push, stab; horizontal outward pressure.
Trust s. Confidence, reliance, credit; responsible charge; that in which confidence is placed; vesting of property in a person for benefit of another; property so vested; trade combination for controlling prices. v.t. To rely on, believe; to entrust; to sell to on credit. v.i. To have reliance, confide readily. a. Held in trust.
Entrust' v.t. To commit to one's care; to charge with.
Distrust' v.t. To have no trust in, not to rely on; to suspect. s. Doubt of reality or sincerity; suspicion.
Mistrust' v.t. To suspect, doubt; to surmise. s. Want of confidence; suspicion.
Browst s. A brewing.
Frowst v.i. (*Slang*) To laze, loll about; s. Stuffiness in a room.
Cyst s. A small sac or bladder; a spore-case.
Encyst' v.t. To enclose in a cyst or vesicle.
Ur'ocyst s. The urinary bladder.
Nemat'ocyst s. The cell in a jelly-fish from which the stinging thread projects.
Pneu'matocyst s. An air-sac or swim-bladder in certain hydrozoa.
Am'ethyst s. A precious stone, a purplish variety of quartz.
An'alyst s. (*Analyze*).
Cat'alyst s. An agent producing catalysis.
Tryst s. Appointment to meet; place of meeting. v.t. To agree to meet.
Watt (wot) s. Unit of electric power or rate of work.
Kil'owatt s. A unit of measurement of electrical energy.
Lett s. A Lithuanian of Livonia.
Dom'ett s. A cloth of wool and cotton.
Bitt s. A post on board ship, etc., for belaying ropes.
Mitt s. A kind of mitten.
Bott s. A worm parasitic in horses, cattle, etc.
Boy'cott v.t. To ostracize, refuse to have dealings with. s. This state of things.
Pott s. A size of paper (about 15 × 12 in.).
Butt s. A large cask; a blunt end; a target; one at whom ridicule is aimed; a push or blow with the head. v.t. and i. To strike with the head or horns

Putt v.t. and i. To strike the golf-ball on the green into or towards the hole.
Ut s. First note in Guido's musical scale.
Ghaut s. A mountain pass or range of mountains in India.
Ab'laut s. Change in a root-vowel.
Um'laut (-lout) s. Change of vowel sound.
Ar'gonaut s. An explorer by sea; a cephalopod mollusc.
A'eronaut s. A navigator of the air; a student of or expert in aeronautics.
Jug'gernaut s. A Hindu idol; a belief, etc., by which one is destroyed.
Sauer'kraut (-krout) s. Cabbage preserved and fermented in brine.
Taut a. Tense; in good trim.
But prep., conj., adv.
Abut' v.t. To meet, adjoin, border.
Debut' s. A first public appearance.
Rebut' v.t. To repel by force, oppose by argument.
Surrebut' v.i. To reply to the defendant's rebutter.
Hal'ibut s. A large, flat sea-fish.
Hack'but s. A harquebus.
Sack'but s. A brass wind-instrument.
Cut v.t. To clip, carve, divide; to intersect, divide a pack of cards; to refuse to recognize. v.i. To make an incision; to be severed; to pass straight and rapidly. s. A gash, stroke with a whip, severe remark; a near way; a canal; an engraving; form, fashion. a. Intersected; deeply affected.
Wood'cut s. An engraving on or taken from wood.
Scut s. The short tail of a hare, deer, etc.
Gut s. The intestinal canal; a length of catgut; a narrow sea-passage or strait. v.t. To eviscerate; to plunder of contents.
Cat'gut s. A tough cord made from the intestines of sheep, etc.
Hut s. A mean dwelling; a temporary shelter, hovel. v.t. and i. To place or take lodgings in huts.
Shut v.t. To close by a door, lid, etc.; to bar, confine, preclude. v.i. To close itself or be closed. a. Made close.
Jut v.i. To project, stick out. s. A projection.
Glut v.t. To feast to satiety; to overfill. s. A surfeit, superabundance, oversupply.
Slut s. A slovenly woman, a slattern.
Gam'ut s. The scale of musical notes; compass, range.
Smut s. A spot made with soot, etc.; mildew on grain; foul language, obscene ribaldry. v.t. To stain with smut, taint with mildew; to tarnish. v.i. To give off, gather, or be attacked by smut.
Nut s. Fruit of certain trees containing a kernel; small block to be screwed on a bolt; (*slang*) the head, a dandy. v.i. To gather nuts.
Pea'nut s. A leguminous plant whose seed ripens under ground; the earth-nut.
Wal'nut s. A tree; its edible nut, or its timber.
Chest'nut s. A tree of the genus *Castanea*; the reddish-brown nut this bears; this colour; a horse of this colour; (*slang*) a stale joke. a. Reddish-brown.
Out adv. Away from the inside; not within; forth; not at home; not employed; introduced to society; etc. a. External; outlying; distant.
Bout s. A turn; a division of some action or performance; a debauch.
About' prep., adv.
Gad'about s. A gadder.
Round'about a. Circuitous, indirect. s. A merry-go-round; a circumlocution.
Thereabout' adv.
Where'about adv. About which; whereabouts.
Knock'about a. Noisy; rough-and-tumble; bohemian.
Run'about a. Roving. s. A wanderer; a light motor-car.
Mar'about s. A Mohammedan saint or hermit.
Stir'about s. Porridge. a. Bustling.
Roust'about s. A dock-labourer; a vagrant.
Scout s. One sent to observe the enemy; a member of the "Boy Scouts"; a college servant. v.i. To act as a scout. v.t. To treat with contempt.
Dout v.t. To extinguish.
Whereout' adv.
Gout s. A constitutional disease affecting the joints.
Ragout' (-goo') s. A highly seasoned stew.
Mahout' s. An elephant-driver.
Throughout' prep. and adv.
Shout s. A loud cry; a plaudit; applause. v.t. To utter a sudden and loud cry. v.i. To utter with a shout.
Without' adv. and prep. s. The outside.
Knock'out a. Overwhelming. s. Such a blow; a dishonest ring at auctions.
Lout s. An awkward fellow; a bumpkin.
Clout s. A piece of stuff, leather, etc., for use as a patch; an archer's target; a blow with the hand. v.t. To patch, botch; strike with the open hand.
Flout v.t. and i. To scoff at, insult; to treat or behave with mockery or contempt. s. A sneer, gibe.
Knout s. A Russian scourge.
Snout s. Projecting nose and muzzle of a beast; nozzle.
Pout v.t. and i. To thrust out the lips; to look sullen; to swell out, protrude. s. A protrusion of the lips; a fit of sulkiness; a sea-fish.
Spout s. A water-pipe; projecting mouth of a vessel; a gush of water; a spiracle; (*slang*) a pawnbroker's shop. v.t. To discharge with force; (*slang*) to utter in a declamatory way. v.i. To issue copiously; to declaim.
Wa'terspout s. A column of water drawn up by a whirlwind.
Rout s. A rabble; uproar; defeat, confusion after this; a fashionable party. v.t. To defeat utterly; to root up, drive out. v.i. To roar, bellow.
Grout s. Coarse meal; mortar for joining masonry, etc. v.t. To fill up or join with grout; to turn up with the snout (of pigs). v.i. To grumble.
Sprout v.i. To germinate, bud. s. A shoot on a plant.
Trout s. A freshwater fish of the salmon family

Tout v.t. and i. To solicit for custom; to canvas; to pester. s. One who begs for custom, offers racing tips, etc.
Passe-partout' (-too') s. A master-key; a kind of mount for a photograph, etc.
Sur'tout (too) s. A man's overcoat.
Stout a. Strong, sturdy, bold; corpulent. s. A dark, coloured beer.
Devout' a. Full of devotion; pious; sincere.
Put v.t. To place in any position; to thrust, lay, deposit; to putt; to propound.
Oc'ciput s. The back part of the head.
Sin'ciput s. The fore-part of the skull.
Out'put s. Quantity of goods, etc., produced within the stated time.
Rut s. Furrow worn by a wheel; settled habit, routine; time of sexual excitement among deer, etc. v.t. To make ruts in. v.i. To be sexually excited (of deer, etc.).
Strut v.i. To walk affectedly. v.t. To brace with a strut. s. A pompous or affected gait; a strengthening beam.
Tut int. and s. Exclamation of rebuke, impatience, etc.
Newt s. A small tailed amphibia.
Next a. Nearest in time, place, degree, order, etc. adv. Nearest, immediately after. prep. Nearest to. s. The next person or thing.
Sext s. The Roman Catholic office for noon.
Text s. Original words of an author; passage of Scripture; subject of a discourse.
Pre'text s. Excuse; false allegation.
Con'text s. The parts adjoining a quoted passage.
Betwixt' prep., adv. Between.
Lan'dau s. A four-wheeled carriage with movable top.
Beau s. A dandy; a lady's suitor.
Flam'beau s. A torch.
Pon'ceau s. The corn-poppy; its brilliant red.
Mor'ceau s. A morsel; a short musical piece.
Ban'deau s. A fillet for the head; a bandage.
Fricandeau' s. A cutlet served with sauce.
Ron'deau (-dō) s. A two-rhymed verse-form of thirteen lines; a rondo.
Tab'leau s. A striking and vivid representation.
Rouleau' s. A pile of coins in paper.
Chalumeau' s. A shepherd's pipe.
Ton'neau s. Part of motor-car containing the back seats.
Chapeau' s. A hat.
Carreau' s. A diamond-shaped figure, tile, pane, etc.
Bureau' s. A desk with drawers; a department for public business.
Dam'oiseau s. A squire.
Trous'seau (troos'ō) s. A bride's outfit.
Gâteau' s. A cake.
Château' s. A castle; a French country-seat.
Plateau' s. A level, elevated stretch of land.
Portman'teau s. A leather travelling-trunk.
Nyl'ghau s. A large, short-horned Indian antelope.
Fab'liau s. A short, amusing mediæval tale.
Pilau' s. A dish of boiled rice, meat, and spices.
Frau s. A German woman.
Tau s. The Greek τ.
Noyau' s. A liqueur flavoured with almond.
Babu' s. (*Baboo*).
Ze'bu s. The humped ox of India.
Ur'ubu s. The black vulture of Central America.
Tel'edu s The stinking badger of Java.
Hindu' s. One belonging to a non-Parsee or non-Moslem race of India. a. Pertaining to these.
Per'du a. Hidden; lost to view; desperate. s. One of a forlorn hope; one in ambush.
Ur'du s. A variety of Hindustani.
Feu s. Land-tenure (in Scotland) by payment of an annual sum. v.t. To grant land in feu.
Adieu' int. Goodbye.
Lieu s. Place; stead.
Pur'lieu s. The outskirts, environs.
Tel'ugu s. A Dravidian race and language of S. India.
Cat'echu s. An extract from various trees used as an astringent drug and as a deep red-brown dye.
Fi'chu s. Lace, etc., worn by ladies round the neck.
Skean-dhu' (-doo') s. The dagger carried by Highlanders in the stocking.
Je'hu s. A fast or furious driver.
Ju'ju s. A W. African fetish; ban worked by this.
Flu s. Influenza.
Poilu' s. A French private soldier.
Or'molu s. A kind of brass; bronze or copper gilt.
Tolu' s. A fragrant resin obtained from a S. American tree.
E'mu s. A large wingless Australian bird.
Men'u s. A bill of fare.
Par'venu s. An upstart.
Gnu s. A S. African antelope.
Miaou' s. The cry of a cat. v.i. To make this cry.
Mar'abou s. A W. African stork; stole, etc., made from its feathers.
Caribou' s. The N. American reindeer.
Am'adou s. Tinder, dried fungus.
Fou a. Drunk.
Con'gou s. A black Chinese tea.
Cachou' s. A small perfumed sweetmeat.
Thou pron. 2nd pers. sing.
Ac'ajou s. The cashew-nut tree; mahogany.
Car'cajou s. The wolverine.
Kink'ajou s. An arboreal Central American animal of the racoon family.
Sap'ajou s. A S. American monkey.
Sajou' s. A small S. American monkey.
Bi'jou s. A trinket, a jewel.
Tin'amou s. A S. American game-bird.
Frou'-frou s. Rustling as of a silk petticoat.
Sou (soo) s. A French copper coin (=about ½d.).
Cu'rassou s. A turkey-like bird of S. America.
Cous'cousou s. (*Couscous*).
Ta'tou (-tu) s. A S. American armadillo.
Man'itou s. The Supreme Being of the N. American Indians.
You (ū) pron., 2nd pers. sing. and pl. The person or persons addressed; people generally.
Bayou' s. A marshy outlet to a delta.
Poy'ou (-oo) s. A S. American armadillo.
Coy'pu s. The nutria, a S. American aquatic rodent.
E'cru s. The pale-brown colour of unbleached linen; fabric of this colour.
Wanderu' s. (*Wanderoo*).
Jab'iru s. A S. American stork-like bird.
Jujit'su s. The Japanese mode of wrestling.

Push'tu s. The Afghan group of languages.
Bantu' a. Of a certain S. African native stock.
Impromp'tu adv. Without preparation, off-hand. a. Extempore. s. An extemporaneous act, composition, etc.
Vir'tu s. Love of the fine arts; taste for curiosities.
Slav s. One of an E. European race including Russians, Poles, Bulgars, Croatians, Slovenes, etc. a. Slavonic.
Leitmotiv' s. A melodic passage in an opera, etc., identified with a character, situation, or idea.
Caw s. The cry of a rook. v.i. To make this cry.
Macaw' s. A S. American parrot.
Daw s. A bird of the crow family; a vain fellow.
Jack'daw s. A small variety of crow.
Guffaw' s. A coarse, boisterous laugh or burst of laughter. v.i. To laugh thus.
Gew'gaw s. A showy trifle, bauble, trinket.
Haw s. Fruit of the hawthorn; a fence, hedge; hesitation in speech. v.i. To speak with hesitation.
Chaw v.t. To masticate; to revolve and consider. s. A chew.
Hee'haw v.i. To bray like a donkey. s. This sound.
Shaw s. A thicket.
Bashaw' s. (*Pasha*).
Kick'shaw s. Something fantastic; a trifle.
Rick'shaw s. A jinricksha.
Wap'inshaw (wawp'-) s. (*Scot.*) A military review, rifle-match, etc.
Hern'shaw s. A young heron.
Pshaw int. Expressing contempt or disgust.
Thaw v.i. and t. To become liquid, melt, or cause to do this. s. Liquefaction by heat; the melting of snow, etc.; warm, thawing weather.
Jaw s. The bones in which the teeth are set; (*Slang*) abuse; long-winded talk. v.i. (*Slang*) To talk. v.t. (*Slang*) To abuse, lecture.
Lock'jaw s. A variety of tetanus.
Law s. A statute, authoritative rule; rule of action; enactment; legal procedure; litigation; principle deduced from observation, etc.
Claw s. The sharp, hooked nail of a beast or bird; pincers of a lobster, etc.; an implement for grappling. v.t. To tear or scratch with claws; to seize, grip.
Clap'perclaw v.t. To fight and scratch; to revile.
Flaw s. A crack, fault, defect; a gust of wind. v.t. To crack, mar.
Pilaw' s. A dish of boiled rice, meat, and spices.
Out'law s. One excluded from the benefit of the law. v.t. To deprive of legal protection; to proscribe.
By'law s. A local or accessory law; a club rule.
Maw s. An animal's stomach or bird's crop.
Gnaw v.t. To pick or chew with the teeth; to fret; to corrode.
Paw s. The foot of a quadruped having claws; (*slang*) the hand. v.t. To strike with the forefoot; (*Slang*) to handle clumsily.
Papaw' s. A palm-like tree of tropical America; its fruit.
Raw a. Not cooked; immature; unripe.
Braw a. (*Scot.*) Brave; fine; splendid.
Craw s. The crop or first stomach of fowls.
Draw v.t. To pull along; attract; suck; unsheathe; delineate. v.i. To practise the art of delineation; to shrink; make a written demand for money. s. Act of drawing; thing or lot drawn; an undecided contest; an attraction.
Wire'draw v.t. To draw into wire; to spin out at length; to protract.
Withdraw' v.t. and i. To draw back; retract; to retire, secede.
Straw s. The stalk of grain; anything worthless.
Windle'straw s. A kind of grass; old stalks.
Saw s. A toothed cutting instrument; a proverb, saying. v.t. and i. To cut with or to use a saw. past (*See*).
See'saw s. A balanced, pivoted plank for children to swing on; a game on this; to-and-fro movement. a. Moving up and down or to and fro. v.i. To move thus.
Taw s. A marble, game at marbles. v.t. To prepare (skins) for leather with alum or other mineral.
Squaw s. Red Indian wife.
Yaw v.i. To steer out of the course; to sail unsteadily. s. Such a deviation or motion.
Dew s. Moisture from air deposited at night. v.t. To wet with dew.
Bedew' v.t. To moisten or sprinkle with or as with dew.
Mil'dew s. A minute fungus on plants, etc., causing decay; condition so caused. v.t. and i. To taint or become tainted with this.
Sun'dew s. A small insectivorous bog-plant.
Few a. Not many. s. A small number.
Fe'verfew s. A plant allied to camomile.
Cur'few s. Ringing of a bell at nightfall, especially as a signal to extinguish lights.
Hew v.t. To cut with an axe; to hack, chop, shape. s. A cut, gash.
Chew v.t. and i. To masticate; to ruminate mentally. s. Thing chewed; a mouthful.
Eschew' v.t. To avoid, shun, abstain from.
Fitch'ew s. The polecat, foulmartin; its fur.
Rough'hew v.t. To hew roughly, to give the first form to.
Phew int. Expressing disgust, surprise, etc.
Neph'ew s. A son of one's brother or sister.
Shew (shō) v.t. and i. (*Show*).
Cashew' s. A S. American tree; its fruit.
Thew s. Muscle, sinew; vigour.
Whew int. Exclamation of incredulity, astonishment, consternation, etc.
View (vū) s. Prospect; survey; reach of sight. v.t. To survey, see, behold.
Review' v.t. To examine carefully; to reconsider; to write on critically. v.i. To write reviews. s. A re-examination, official inspection; literary criticism; periodical devoted to such.
In'terview s. A formal meeting for conference; a consultation; a newspaper conversation. v.t. To subject to an interview; to converse with to obtain information, opinions, etc., for publication.
Pur'view s. Scope, extent; the body of a statue.

Jew s. A Hebrew. v.t. To get the better of, to overreach.
Skew a. Slanting; askew. v.i. To swerve, move sideways; to squint. s. An oblique course or position; a sloping coping.
Askew' adv. Sideways, awry.
Blew v.i. (past) (*Blow*).
Clew s. The lower corner of a square sail; ropes by which a hammock is suspended; a clue. v.t. To draw (a sail) up to the yard.
Flew past (*Fly*).
Cur'lew s. A migratory wading bird.
Slew past (*Slay*). v. and s. (*Slue*).
Mew s. A variety of seagull; a cage for hawks; the cry of a cat. v.i. To cry like a cat. v.t. To confine, cage.
Sea'mew s. A sea-gull.
Smew s. A small marine diving-duck.
New a. Fresh; modern; recent; renovated; unaccustomed. adv. Newly; anew.
Anew' adv. Newly, afresh.
Brand'-new a. Quite new, never having been used.
Renew' v.t. To make new again, repair; to repeat. v.i. To grow again.
Sin'ew s. A tendon; muscle; that which supplies strength.
Knew past (*Know*).
Pew s. An enclosed seat in a church.
Spew v.t. and i. To vomit; to cast out with abhorrence. s. Vomit.
Brew v.t. and i. To prepare alcoholic liquor from malted grain, etc., or other beverages by infusion, etc.; to plan, be preparing, s. Quantity of beer, tea, etc., brewed.
He'brew s. A Jew, Israelite; the language of the ancient Jews. a. Pertaining to the Jews.
Crew s. A gang, company, especially of sailors attached to a ship. past (*Crow*).
Screw s. A cylinder with spiral ridge, for fastening, bolting, etc.; a screw-propeller; a twist; twisted piece of paper, etc., or its contents; a broken-down horse; (*slang*) a niggard; salary. v.t. To fasten, compress, etc., with a screw; to twist, distort, squeeze; to oppress. v.t. To turn as a screw, move spirally, swerve.
Cork'screw s. An implement for drawing corks.
Drew past (*Draw*).
Withdrew' past (*Withdraw*).
Mer'ry-an'drew s. A clown, buffoon.
Grew past (*Grow*).
Shrew s. A brawling, scolding woman; a shrew-mouse.
Beshrew' v.t. To invoke a curse upon.
Threw past (*Throw*).
Strew v.t. To scatter, besprinkle.
Bestrew' v.t. To scatter or lie scattered over.
Sew (sō) v.t. and i. To join or make by needle and thread.
Tew v.t. To taw.
Stew v.t. To cook by boiling slowly. v.i. To boil slowly; to worry. s. Dish of stewed meat; state of agitation; a fish-pond.
Na'vew s. The wild turnip.
Yew (ū) s. A low-spreading, evergreen conifer; its timber.
Bow (bō) s. A weapon to propel an arrow; anything bent, a curve, ornamental knot; a fiddlestick.
Bow s. An inclination of the head in respect, etc.; the curved forepart of a ship; the bow-oar or oarsman. v.t. To make crooked or curved, to bend; to depress, subdue. v.i. To bend in reverence, etc.
El'bow s. Curvature of arm below shoulder. v.t. To push with the elbow, to justle.
Rain'bow s. A prismatic arc formed in the heavens after rain.
Cow s. The female of bovine animals. v.t. To depress with fear, sink the spirits or courage of.
Scow s. A large, flat-bottomed boat.
Mead'ow s. Level tract of rich grassland.
Shad'ow s. A definite shade projected by interception of light; darkness; obscurity; a faint representation; that which attends one. v.t. To shade, screen. to represent faintly; to attend closely, spy on.
Foreshad'ow v.t. To typify beforehand, to prefigure.
Overshad'ow v.t. To throw into the shade; to protect.
Wid'ow (-ō) s. A woman whose husband is dead. v.t. To bereave of a husband.
Endow' v.t. To make provision for; to furnish with a dower; to indue, invest.
Disendow' v.t. To deprive of endowments.
Win'dow (-dō) s. Aperture to admit light and air; glazed sash for this.
How adv. In what manner; for what reason, etc. s. A low hill.
Chow s. A Chinese dog; (*slang*) a Chinaman.
Chow'chow s. A preserve of ginger, spices, etc.; a chow.
Dhow s. An Arabian coasting vessel.
Some'how adv. In some way or other.
Show (shō) v.t. To exhibit, let be seen; to make known; to prove; to bestow. v.i. To appear. s. Act of showing; outward appearance; pretence; exhibition; pageant; pomp.
Low a. Not high; deep; below; humble; lowly; mean; not loud. adv. Not aloud; below the usual price; not loudly. v.i. To bellow (as an ox). s. A cow's moo; a flame; a rounded hill.
Alow' adv. Opposite of "aloft."
Bung'alow s. A low one-storied dwelling.
Blow s. A blast; a stroke, hit, act of striking; a severe or sudden calamity; a blossom. v.i. To produce or emit a current of air; to move as air; to pant, puff; to brag; to blossom. v.t. To drive a current of air upon, or with a current of air; to spread by report; to sound (wind instruments); to deposit eggs (of flies); to put out of breath; (*slang*) to spend money wastefully.
Fly'-blow v.t. To taint by depositing eggs which produce maggots. s. The egg of a fly.
Below' prep., adv. Beneath; unworthy of in a lower place.
Fur'below s. A flounce, puckered fringe.

Flow v.i. To run as water; to rise, glide. s. A stream, current; a gradual movement; abundance.
Reflow' v.i. To flow back, ebb. s. A backward flowing.
In'flow s. A flowing in; inlet.
Overflow' v.t. and i. To flow, spread, or run over; to inundate; to overwhelm.
O'verflow s. That which flows over; an inundation; superabundance.
Out'flow s. The issue of a river, etc.
Glow v.i. To shine, to radiate light and heat; to be ardent. s. Red or white heat; brightness; warmth of colour; animation.
Aglow' adv. Glowing, radiant.
Allow' v.t. To give, yield; to acknowledge; to abate; to justify.
Cal'low a. Unfledged; immature; inexperienced.
Fal'low a. Untilled, unsown; reddish-yellow (of deer). s. Land prepared for sowing; land gone out of cultivation. v.t. To plough and harrow for sowing.
Hal'low v.t. To make holy; to set aside for sacred use.
Shal'low a. Having little depth; superficial; simple; silly. s. A shallow place; a shoal. v.i. and t. To become or make shallow.
Mal'low s. A plant having emollient properties.
Sal'low a. Of pale, yellowish complexion. s. A species of willow.
Disallow' v.t. To refuse to sanction; to disapprove, condemn. v.i. To refuse permission.
Tal'low s. Hard fat of sheep, ox, etc. v.t. To smear with this.
Wal'low (wol'-) v.i. To flounder; to live in vice, filth, etc. s. Act of wallowing; a mud-hole.
Swal'low (swol'-) s. A swift-flying migratory bird; capacity of swallowing, the gullet. v.t. To receive through the throat into the stomach; to absorb; to put up with; to recant.
Bel'low v.i. To roar as a bull. s. A loud roar.
Fel'low s. An associate, equal; one of a pair; member of a college, etc.; a person only slightly esteemed.
Mel'low a. Fully ripe; soft to the ear, eye, or taste; half-tipsy. v.t. and i. To ripen, mature.
Yel'low s. The colour of bright gold, brass, saffron, etc. a. Being of this colour. v.t. and i. To make or turn yellow.
Bil'low s. A surge of the sea; a swelling, sweeping wave.
Pil'low s. Cushion for the head; anything that bears or supports. v.t. To rest or lay on for support.
Wil'low (-ō) s. A tree allied to the poplar; a cricket bat; a machine for cleaning wool. v.t. To prepare wool with this.
Fol'low v.t. To go or come after; to pursue; to result from; to understand, be guided by; to imitate. v.i. To result, ensue.
Hol'low a. Containing an empty space; vacant; not sincere. s. A depression, cavity; a little valley. v.t. To make hollow; to excavate.
Plow s. and v. (*Plough*).
Slow a. Not swift, tardy; inactive; deliberate; dull. v.t. and i. To delay, to slacken.
Whit'low s. An inflamed tumour on the finger.
Mow v.t. To cut down with a scythe or machine. v.i. To make mouths. s. A pile of hay, etc., a stack; a grimace.
Now adv. and conj. At the present time, at one time, at once; since; things being so. s. The present time.
Enow' a., adv., s. Enough.
Know v.t. To understand, be aware of, be acquainted with, have experience of. v.i. To have knowledge. s. Knowledge.
Min'now s. A small common fish.
Win'now v.t. To separate corn from chaff; to sift; to beat (the wings).
Snow s. Congealed vapour falling in flakes; (*slang*) cocaine. v.t. To cover with or scatter down as snow. v.i. To fall in snow.
Row (rō) v.t. To propel (a boat) by oars; to transport thus; to work an oar. v.i. To practise or indulge in rowing. s. Action of rowing; a rowing excursion; a series in a line, a rank, file.
Row s. A noisy disturbance; a commotion, quarrel. v.t. To rate, scold. v.i. To make a row or din.
Arow' adv. In a row, one after another.
Brow s. The ridge over the eye; the forehead; edge of a steep place.
Eye'brow s. The hairy arch above the eye.
High'brow a. Intellectually superior. s. A superior person.
Crow s. A large black bird; an iron lever with a beak-shaped claw; the call of a cock; infant's cry of delight. v.i. To make a call like a cock or a pleased infant; to brag, exult. v.t. To proclaim by crowing.
Scare'crow s. Object set up to frighten birds; a vain terror.
Cock'crow s. Early dawn.
Escrow' s. A bond held by a third party until some condition is performed.
Wind'row s. Row of sheaves set up for drying.
Hedge'row s. A hedge of shrubs.
Serow' s. A goat-like antelope of E. Asia.
Grow v.i. To increase naturally in bulk; to make progress; to become. v.t. To raise from the soil, to cultivate.
Regrow' v.t. and i. To grow again.
Outgrow' v.t. To surpass in growth; to become too large or old for.
Throw v.t. To fling, cast, toss; to twist filaments together; to utter; to shed. v.i. To cast (esp. dice).
Down'throw s. A falling or sinking of strata.
Up'throw s. Upward displacement of strata; an upheaval.
Overthrow' v.t. To ruin, defeat, utterly demolish.
O'verthrow s. State of being overthrown; ruin; discomfiture.
Prow s. The fore-part of a ship.
Ar'row s. A missile to be shot by a bow.
Bar'row s. A wheeled conveyance for pushing by hand; a sepulchral mound.
Far'row s. A litter of pigs; act of giving birth to a litter. v.t. and i. To bring forth pigs.
Har'row s. A toothed agricultural implement. v.t. To draw a harrow over; to lacerate, torment.

Rest'-harrow s. A shrubby, pink-flowered plant.
Mar'row s. A soft, oleaginous substance in bones; pith; a culinary species of gourd; one of a pair.
Nar'row a. Of little breadth; confined, straitened; bigoted; covetous, mean. s. A strait. v.t. and i. To make or become narrow or narrower.
Spar'row s. A small bird of the finch family.
Yar'row s. A perennial composite plant, milfoil.
Bor'row v.t. To ask or receive as a loan; to appropriate, to imitate.
Mor'row s. The day after the present day; the succeeding period.
Sor'row s. Mental distress through disappointment, etc.; grief, sadness; affliction. v.i. To grieve, lament.
Bur'row s. A hole in the earth, especially one made by rabbits. v.i. and t. To excavate a hole; to hide away.
Fur'row s. A trench, especially made by a plough; a wrinkle. v.t. To plough, to make grooves in.
Trow v.t. and i. To suppose, believe, think.
Sow s. The female swine; large bar of cast metal.
Sow (sō) v.t. To scatter (seed) on the earth; to supply with seed; to plant; to spread abroad, propagate. v.i. To scatter seed for growth.
Tow (tō) v.t. To drag by a rope, etc.; to pull, haul. s. Act of towing; coarse, broken part of flax and hemp.
Stow v.t. To lay by, arrange compactly, fill by packing.
Bestow' v.t. To lay up in store; give, impart; make use of; apply.
Kowtow' v.t. To salute obsequiously in the Chinese manner. s. Humble prostration.
Vow s. A solemn promise; act of devotion. v.t. To promise solemnly, to dedicate. v.i. To make vows.
Avow' v.t. To declare with confidence, confess frankly.
Disavow' v.t. To deny, disown, disclaim.
Bow'wow int. The noise as made by a dog. s. A dog.
Pow'wow s. A wizard among the N. American Indians; magical cure of diseases, etc.; a noisy assembly; a conference. v.i. To confer, hold a discussion.
Bom'bax s. The W. Indian silk-cotton tree.
Ad'dax s. An antelope with spiral horns.
Lax a. Slack, loose, vague; dissolute; diarrhœtic.
Relax' v.t. To slacken, loosen. v.i. To become loose, less severe, etc.; to unbend.
Flax s. A fibrous, blue-flowered plant from which thread is made.
Smi'lax s. An evergreen climbing shrub.
Par'allax s. Difference in apparent position of a star, etc., as viewed at the same time from the earth's surface and some other point.
Cli'max s. A rhetorical figure in which the sentence rises in force, dignity, etc.; the highest point; acme.
Anticli'max s. A sentence concluding in bathos; an event which fails to fulfil expectation.
Opop'onax s. A gum-resin used in perfumery.
Coax v.t. To persuade, wheedle. v.i. To practise cajolery.
Hoax s. A practical joke, sportive trick. v.t. To deceive, especially in sport.
Pax s. A tablet bearing a representation of the Crucifixion formerly kissed by priest and people at Mass; peace.
Scol'opax s. The family of birds including the woodcock, snipe, etc.
An'thrax s. An infectious disease of cattle, etc.; wool-sorters' disease.
Bor'ax s. A native crystalline salt.
Thor'ax s. Part of trunk between neck and abdomen; the chest.
Stor'ax s. A fragrant resin used in perfumery; the tree producing it.
Hyr'ax s. The rock-rabbit, rock-badger.
Sty'rax s. Genus of shrubs yielding resins.
Sax s. A slate-cutter's knife.
Tax s. A compulsory levy, a rate; a burden. v.t. To load with imposts; to charge, censure.
Syn'tax s. Correct construction of a sentence.
Overtax' v.t. To tax too heavily, make too severe demands upon.
Sur'tax s. An additional tax.
Surtax' v.t. To assess to additional taxation.
Wax s. An animal or vegetable fat. v.t. to smear or treat with this. v.i. To increase in size; to become.
Bees'wax s. Wax made by bees for their cells. v.t. To polish with this.
Pax'wax s. A strong cartilage in the back and neck of the ox, etc.
Zax s. A slater's hatchet.
I'bex s. A long-horned wild goat.
Vi'bex s. A purple spot occurring in some fevers.
O'bex s. A triangular lamina in the fourth ventricle of the brain.
In'dex s. An indicator; that which points the way; alphabetical and paginated list of contents; formula showing ratio of one dimension to another. v.t. To provide with or enter in an index.
Co'dex s. A MS. volume, esp. of the Bible.
Cau'dex s. The axis of a plant.
Spi'nifex s. A thorny Australian grass.
Car'nifex s. An executioner.
Pon'tifex s. A member of the highest priestly college in ancient Rome.
For'fex s. Scissor-like organ of certain insects.
Nar'thex s. A kind of portico at entrance to a cathedral, etc.
Kex s. The dry stalk of hemlock, etc.
Flex v.t. To bend. s. A piece of flexible wire.
Re'flex a. Turned back; introspective; retroactive; produced by stimulus merely. s. A reflection, reflected image, reflex action.
Cir'cumflex s. A mark (^) indicating accent. v.t. To mark or pronounce with this.
Ret'roflex a. Retroflected.
I'lex s. The holm-oak.
Si'lex s. Silica; flint.
Sco'lex s. The embryo of the tape-worm.
Trip'lex a. Threefold. s. Triple time (*mus.*)
Mul'tiplex a. Manifold.
Sim'plex a. Not compound. s. A simplex word.
Com'plex a. Composed of several parts; intricate. s. A complicated system or whole.
De'complex a. Doubly complex.
Perplex' v.t. To make difficult to be understood; to puzzle, bewilder; to tease with suspense.

Du'plex a. Double, twofold. v.t. To duplicate.
Quad'ruplex a. Fourfold.
Cu'lex s. The genus of gnats and mosquitoes.
Re'mex s. A quill feather of a bird's wing.
Ci'mex s. The family of insects including the bed-bug.
An'nex s. An addition to a building, document, etc.
Annex' v.t. To subjoin, add, connect; to acquire, seize.
A'pex s. The highest point.
Aus'pex s. An ancient Roman priest and soothsayer.
Harus'pex s. An ancient Roman diviner from the entrails of beasts, etc.
Car'ex s. A genus of grass-like plants.
Sor'ex s. A shrew-mouse.
In'terrex s. A regent; one in control during an interregnum.
Mu'rex s. A marine mollusc yielding a purple dye.
Sex s. Distinguishing peculiarity of male and female; one of these groups.
Unsex' v.t. To deprive of the sexual characteristics.
La'tex s. The juice of milky plants.
Ver'tex s. The highest point; apex, zenith.
Cor'tex s. The bark of a tree; outer covering, especially membrane; the outer layer of the brain.
Vor'tex s. Anything whirled round; a whirlpool.
Fru'tex s. A shrub, small tree.
Vex v.t. To torment, plague, annoy.
Con'vex a. Rounded on the exterior (opposite to concave). s. A convex body.
Spa'dix s. A fleshy spike of flowers, usually in a spathe.
Ra'dix s. A root, source; a base.
San'dix s. A red-lead pigment.
Appen'dix s. Something added; an addition; a subsidiary organ in the body.
Fix v.t. To make fast or firm; to appoint; to adjust; to deprive of volatility. v.i. To settle; to congeal. s. A dilemma.
Prefix' v.t. To set in front of, attach at the beginning.
Pre'fix s. Syllable, etc., set before and combined with a word to vary its meaning.
Affix' v.t. To add to the end, to connect.
Af'fix s. A suffix or prefix.
Suf'fix s. Syllable or letter added to end of word.
Suffix' v.t. To append.
Cru'cifix s. A cross bearing a figure of the crucified Christ.
Infix' v.t. To implant; to fix by piercing or thrusting in.
Transfix' v.t. To pierce through.
Post'fix s. A letter, word, etc., added to the end of another word; a suffix.
Ca'lix s. A cup-like cavity.
Sa'lix s. The genus of trees including the willows.
He'lix s. A spiral line, a coil; a volute; the fold of the ear; a genus of molluscs.
Flix s. Beaver-fur or down.
Prolix' a. Extending to great length; diffuse; tedious.
Mix v.t. To unite or blend into one; to mingle, confuse, confound. v.i. To become united, be mingled.
Admix' v.t. and i. To mix with something else.
Commix' v.t. and i. To mix together, blend.
Intermix' v.t. and i. To mix or be mixed together; to intermingle.
Nix s. A nixie; (*slang*) nothing.
Phœ'nix s. A fabulous bird; an emblem of immortality, also of surpassing excellence, beauty, uniqueness, etc.
For'nix s. The arch of the pharynx; a similar part or organ.
Var'ix s. A varicose or permanently dilated vein; ridge across the whorls of a shell.
-trix suff. Denoting a feminine agent.
Cic'atrix s. Scar left after a wound has healed.
Media'trix s. A female mediator.
Leg'islatrix s. A female legislator.
Ma'trix s. A mould, substance which shapes anything or in which ores, etc., are found; the womb.
Separa'trix s. A separating mark; a decimal point.
Genera'trix s. A point, etc., which gives rise to a generant.
Administra'trix s. A female administrator.
Cura'trix s. A female curator.
Proc'uratrix s. A female manager of a nunnery.
Specta'trix s. A female spectator.
Testa'trix s. A woman who leaves a will.
Rec'trix s. A female governor.
Direc'trix s. A directress; a line which governs the motion of another line or of a point so that the latter describes a certain curve or surface.
Propri'etrix s. A female proprietor.
Obstet'rix s. A midwife, a female obstetrician.
Jan'itrix s. A female door-keeper.
Progen'itrix s. A female ancestor.
Her'itrix s. An heiress.
Inher'itrix s. A female inheritor.
Precen'trix s. A female precentor.
Pros'ecutrix s. A female prosecutor.
Exec'utrix s. A female executor.
Coadju'trix s. A female coadjutor.
Six a. One more than five. s. This number, its symbol (6, vi.).
Tet'tix s. A cicada; hair ornament imitating this.
Calx s. Fine ash left by material after calcination.
Phal'anx s. A body of troops in close formation; the heavy-armed infantry of ancient Greece; a bone of a finger or toe.
Manx a. Pertaining to the Isle of Man or its people. s. Language or people of this.
Sphinx s. A fabulous monster; an inscrutable person or one who puts puzzling questions; a hawk-moth.
Minx s. A pert girl, hussy.
Me'ninx s. One of the meninges.
Sal'pinx s. A Fallopian or Eustachian tube.
Syr'inx s. The Eustachian tube; a fistula; a shepherd's pipe.
Quin'cunx s. An arrangement of things in 5's forming a square with 1 in the middle.
Lynx s. A savage, nocturnal, feline animal.
Phar'ynx s. The cavity between the mouth and the œsophagus.
Lar'ynx s. The vocal organ, the upper part of the wind-pipe.
Ox s. A castrated bull.
Box s. An evergreen shrub; a chest, a case with lid; a partitioned space in an eating-house, theatre, stable, etc.; a driver's seat; a small house; a slight blow on the

ear. v.t. To enclose in a box; to strike the ear with the open hand. v.i. To spar with fists.
Band'box s. A light case for hats, etc.
Cox s. A coxswain.
Par'adox s. A proposition, etc., seemingly absurd or contradictory, but true in fact.
Ne'odox a. Holding new views.
Or'thodox a. Holding the accepted views; sound in opinion or doctrine; not heretical.
Het'erodox a. Contrary to the received or acknowledged standard; not orthodox; heretical.
Fox s. A small carnivorous quadruped; a sly fellow. v.t. and i. To make or turn sour; to become strained with brown (of paper).
Phlox s. A showy, half-hardy, annual plant.
Flum'mox v.t. To perplex; to silence; to best, outwit.
Eq'uinox s. Time when the day and night are of equal length.
Pox s. Pustules, eruptions; syphilis.
Small'pox s. A contagious, feverish, eruptive disease.
Cow'pox s. A disease on the udders of cows which is transferred to humans as a preventive of smallpox.
Fer'ox s. The great lake-trout.
Vox s. Voice.
Vol'vox s. A genus of minute freshwater organisms.
Bordeaux' s. A red wine.
Dux s. A head scholar; a leader.
Flux s. Act or state of flowing; a substance used to promote the fusion of metals; fusion; dysentery. v.t. To fuse.
Re'flux s. A flowing back, ebb.
Af'flux s. A flowing to; a crowd.
Ef'flux s. Act of flowing out; outflow; an emanation; expiry.
In'flux s. A flowing into; infusion.
Con'flux s. A confluence.
Hal'lux s. The great toe; the hind digit in birds.
Crux s. Anything very puzzling.
Bom'byx s. A genus of moths, the silkworm moth.
Coc'cyx s. The bone at the base of the spinal column in man.
Ca'lyx s. The outer leaves or sepals of a flower, forming a cup.
On'yx s. A striped variety of agate.
Chalced'onyx s. A variety of agate.
Sar'donyx s. A variety of onyx.
Pyx s. Case for holding the host in Roman Catholic ritual; chest for specimen coins at the Mint.
Ap'teryx s. A wingless bird of New Zealand.
Archæop'teryx s. An extinct bird forming a link between birds and reptiles.
Or'yx s. A variety of African antelope.
Styx s. A fabled river of Hades.
Ay adv.; int. Yes; ah!
Bay s. A wide indentation in a coastline; a space between pillars in a building; the deep bark of a dog; the sweet-laurel; a garland of this. a. Reddish-brown. v.i. To bark. v.t. To bark at.
Embay' v.t. To enclose in a bay, to landlock.
Cay s. A reef, shoal.
Decay' v.i. To decline, wither, putrefy. v.t. To impair. s. Gradual failure of health, prosperity, etc.; decline; rottenness.
Day s. Time between rising and setting of sun; twenty-four hours; anniversary.
Alackaday' int. Expressive of grief.
Work'aday a. Pertaining or suitable to ordinary occasions; plain.
Welladay' int. Exclamation of sorrow or despair.
Mid'day s. Noon. a. Pertaining to this.
Birth'day s. An anniversary of one's birth.
Hol'iday s. A day of respite from work; a holy day, feast day. a. Pertaining to a festival, befitting a holiday.
Fri'day s. The sixth day of the week.
Week'day s. Any day other than Sunday.
Mon'day s. The second day of the week.
Noon'day s. Noon. a. Pertaining to midday; meridional.
Sun'day s. The first day of the week.
Yes'terday s. The day last past; time past. adv. On or during yesterday.
Sat'urday s. The seventh day of the week.
Wednesday (wĕnz'-) s. The fourth day of the week.
Tues'day s. The third day of the week.
Dooms'day s. The Day of Judgment; the end of all things.
Thurs'day s. The fifth day of the week.
May-day s. 1st May.
Hey'-day s. The prime; period of prosperity, etc. int. Expressing wonder, etc.
Everyday' a. Common, usual.
Fay s. A fairy. v.t. To fit timbers together.
Gay a. Merry, sprightly; having many bright colours; dissipated, wanton.
Nose'gay s. A bunch of flowers.
Mar'gay s. A Brazilian tiger-cat.
Hay s. Grass cut and dried for fodder; an old country dance.
Lin'hay s. A lean-to shed.
Shay s. A chaise.
Jay s. A showy, chattering bird.
Pop'injay s. A parrot; mark like this for shooting at; a coxcomb, fop.
Twan'kay s. A kind of green tea.
Tokay' s. A rich Hungarian wine.
Lay v.t. To cause to be flat; to place impose; to bring into a certain state; to appease; to wager; to contrive. v.t. To bring forth eggs. s. Direction or position of an object; a lyric, ballad; singing; (*slang*) occupation, job. a. Non-clerical; non-professional. past (*Lie*).
Malay' a. Pertaining to the predominant race in Malacca. s. A member or the language of this race.
Clay s. A plastic kind of earth; a pipe, etc., made of this; grosser part of human nature; the body, a corpse.
Belay' v.t. To make (a rope) fast.
Delay' v.t. To postpone, defer, hinder. v.i. To linger. s. Postponement, retardation, a stopping.
Round'elay s. A simple song.
Relay' s. A fresh supply (especially of horses) previously arranged for.
Re-lay' v.t. To lay again.
Vir'elay s. A short poem of mediæval France.
Flay v.t. To strip the skin from; to skin.
Allay' v.t. To assuage, pacify.
Inlay' v.t. To diversify with pieces of wood, etc.
In'lay s. Material inlaid or for inlaying.

Play v.i. To sport; to gamble; to act or move freely; to perform on a musical instrument; to personate a character. v.t. To put in action or motion; to use a musical instrument; to act, perform. s. Any exercise, etc., for diversion; sport; gaming; action; use; a drama; scope, swing.
Horse'play s. Rough, boisterous play.
In'terplay s. Action and reaction; reciprocation.
Splay a. Spread, turned outward. s. A slanted or sloped surface. v.t. To slope, form with an angle.
Display' v.t. To exhibit, to parade; to expand. s. An unfolding, exhibition, parade.
By'-play s. Action carried on aside.
Overlay' v.t. To lay or spread over; to cover completely; to smother by lying upon.
O'verlay s. A covering, layer, etc., laid over.
Slay v.t. To kill, butcher, destroy.
Mislay' v.t. To lay in a wrong or not remembered place; to lose.
Out'lay s. A laying out or expending; expenditure.
Way'lay v.t. To lie in wait to rob.
May v. aux. Used to express possibility, permission, desire, etc. s. The fifth month; hawthorn blossom. v.i. To celebrate May-day festivities.
Dismay' v.t. To fill with fear, to daunt, discourage, terrify. s. Loss of energy etc., through fear; discouragement; consternation.
Nay adv. Expressing negation or refusal.
Hog'manay s. (*Scot.*) The last day of the year.
Pay v.t. To give money for goods received, service rendered, etc.; to discharge, as a debt; to recompense; to deliver out, as rope; to cover with tar or pitch. v.i. To make payment; to be remunerative. s. Money for service, goods, debt, etc.; reward; payment.
Repay' v.t. To pay back, refund; to requite.
Prepay' v.t. To pay in advance.
Overpay' v.t. To pay too much.
Spay v.t. To destroy or remove the ovaries of.
Ray s. A beam of light; line of radiant energy, heat, or light; one of many radii; a flat-fish. v.t. and i. To radiate, shine forth; to streak.
Bray v.t. To pound, grind small. v.i. To make the cry of an ass. s. This cry; a harsh, grating sound.
Scray s. The tern.
Dray s. A strong, low cart.
Fray s. A combat, battle; a quarrel, uproar, broil; a frayed piece. v.t. To rub; to fret (especially cloth) by wearing. v.i. To become worn by rubbing.
Defray' v.t. To bear the charges of; to pay.
Affray' s. A tumult, brawl.
Gray a. Grey.
For'ay s. Sudden incursion in border warfare; a raid.
Pray v.i. and t. To ask with earnestness; to supplicate, entreat, beseech; to address God.
Spray s. A twig, a collection of these; water, etc., flying in particles. v.t. To apply a spray to; to turn into spray.
Array' v.t. To dispose in order; to call man by man; to dress. s. Order; orderly collection; disposition of armed forces; dress.
Disarray' v.t. To throw into disorder; to undress. s. Want of order; imperfectly attired condition; undress.
Hurray' int. Exclamation of joy; hurrah! v.i. and t. To utter or salute with "hurray!"
Tray s. A shallow, flat, coverless vessel; a salver.
Betray' v.t. To divulge perfidiously; to entrap.
Portray' v.t. To depict, draw or paint the likeness of; to describe verbally.
Stray v.i. To roam, go astray, err, wander. s. A lost domestic animal; a waif.
Astray' adv.; a. Straying.
Estray' s. A straying domestic animal.
Bewray' v.t. To betray.
Say v.t. To express or utter in words; to tell, allege, assume, promise. v.i. To speak, answer. s. What one says; a statement.
Sooth'say v.i. To foretell, predict.
Gainsay' v.t. To contradict, controvert, dispute.
Unsay' v.t. To recant, retract.
Hear'say s. Gossip, rumour. a. Told at second-hand.
Assay' s. Trial, proof. v.t. To try; to ascertain the purity of. v.i. To endeavour.
Essay' v.t. To try, attempt.
Es'say s. An attempt; a short literary composition.
Stay v.i. To continue in place, stand still. v.t. To stop, delay; to prop; to await. s. A sojourn; obstacle; prop, support.
Bob'stay s. A rope for steadying the bowsprit.
Main'stay s. A chief support.
Overstay' v.t. and i. To stay longer than or too long.
Quay (kē) s. A landing-place, wharf.
Way s. A road; distance traversed; direction of motion; progress, course; method; line of business.
Away' adv., int.
Sea'-way s. Clear way for a ship.
Break'away s. A stampede, especially of cattle.
Wellaway' int. Exclamation of sorrow or despair.
Run'away s. A deserter; a bolting horse. a. Fleeing.
Car'away s. An aromatic plant; its seed.
Stow'away s. One who conceals himself on board ship to get a free passage.
Sub'way s. An underground passage.
Head'way s. Progress made by a ship; rate of progress.
Mid'way a. Situated in the middle. adv. Half-way.
Race'way s. A mill-race; a groove for a shuttle, etc.
Guide'way s. A groove or track along which a piece of machinery moves.
Lee'way s. Drift of a vessel to leeward; arrears of work.
Some'way adv. In some way.
Cause'way s. A raised footpath, especially over marshy ground.
Gateway s. An opening or entrance that may be closed with a gate.
Gang'way s. Passage-way over a ship's side, into a building, between rows of seats, etc.

Arch'way s. An arched passage.
Hatch'way s. A large opening in a ship's deck.
High'way s. A public road or route.
Path'way s. A narrow or subsidiary path.
Rail'way s. A continuous track of rails for trains.
Tram'way s. A street railway for passenger cars.
Run'way s. A channel, groove, etc., in which machinery runs; channel of a stream; track made by animals.
Gal'loway s. A small hardy variety of horse.
Slip'way s. Inclined plane on which vessels are built, repaired, etc.
Wa'terway s. A navigable channel.
Fair'way s. The navigable part of a river, etc.; an open stretch on a golf-course.
Stair'way s. A staircase.
Door'way s. An opening fitted with a door.
Sway v.i. To swing, vibrate; to govern. v.t. To wield; to influence, bias; to rule. s. Swing, sweep; preponderance; rule.
Straight'way adv. Immediately; forthwith.
By'way s. A side-road.
Ev'eryway adv. In every way or every respect.
By prep., adv., a.
Ba'by s. An infant.
Ga'by s. A silly person; a dunce.
Hush'aby int. Used in lulling children to sleep.
Wal'laby (wol'-) s. An Australian marsupial.
Lul'laby s. A soothing song for an infant.
Ar'aby s. Arabia.
Sassa'by s. A S. African antelope.
Cab'by s. A cabdriver.
Scab'by a. Affected with or full of scabs; mangy; scabbed; vile.
Gab'by a. Talkative, loquacious.
Shab'by a. Threadbare; mean in dress or conduct.
Flab'by a. Wanting firmness; flaccid; languid.
Tab'by s. A kind of waved or watered silk; a brindled or other cat. a. Wavy, watered. v.t. To give this appearance to.
Squab'by a. Short and thick.
Cob'webby a. (*Cobweb*).
Bob'by s. (*Slang*) A policeman.
Cob'by a. Stout; short and thick.
Hob'by s. A small species of falcon; an ambling horse; a favourite pursuit.
Lob'by s. A vestibule, corridor. v.i. To solicit votes in the parliamentary lobbies.
Nob'by a. (*Slang*) Smart.
Knob'by a. Containing knobs; stubborn.
Snob'by a. Snobbish.
Cub'by s. A narrow space; a "cubby-hole."
Fub'by a. Fat, dumpy, squat.
Hub'by s. (*Slang*) A husband.
Chub'by a. Plump, fat.
Nub'by a. (*Nub*).
Scrub'by a. Mean; stunted; covered with brushwood.
Grub'by a. Maggoty; dirty, grimy.
Shrub'by a. Full of, resembling, or consisting of shrubs.
Tub'by a. Like a tub; corpulent.
Stub'by a. Short and thick; abounding with stubs.
Hereby adv. By means of this.
Thereby' adv.
Whereby' adv.
Rug'by a. Denoting one of the two forms of football.
Ki'by a. Affected with kibes.
Nam'by-pam'by a. Weakly sentimental.
Crumb'y a. Soft like breadcrumb; full of crumbs; comely; (*slang*) well off.
Go'by s. A small spiny-finned fish with a sucker.
Go'-by s. A passing by, evasion.
Glo'by a. Globular, like a globe.
Boo'by s. A silly, gullible person; a sea-bird.
Loo'by s. A clumsy fellow, a lubber.
To'by s. A jug shaped like an old man's head.
Dar'by s. An elderly happily married husband.
Der'by s. The leading English horse-race.
Her'by a. Like or abounding in herbs.
Forby' prep. and adv. Besides; moreover.
Bus'by s. A tall military fur head-dress.
Ru'by s. A carmine-red precious stone; its colour; a small type. a. Of the colour of ruby.
-cy suff. Forming nouns of quality and of office.
Ab'bacy s. Office and jurisdiction of an abbot.
Cel'ibacy s. The unmarried state.
Ef'ficacy s. Force, energy, ability.
Inef'ficacy s. Ineffectualness; futility; fruitlessness.
Prolif'icacy s. State of being prolific.
Del'icacy s. State of being delicate; nicety of form, texture, etc.; tenderness; refined taste; a luxury or dainty.
Indel'icacy s. Coarseness of manners, etc.; obscenity.
Com'plicacy s. State of being complicated.
In'tricacy s. Complication; complexity.
Ad'vocacy s. Judicial pleading; support; office of advocate.
Can'didacy s. Candidature.
Leg'acy s. A bequest; money left by will.
Del'egacy s. Act of delegating; a delegation.
Prof'ligacy s. Depravity; a vicious course of life.
Me'diacy s. Mediate state or quality.
La'cy a. Resembling lace.
Prel'acy s. Office or dignity of a prelate; episcopacy; bishops collectively.
Fal'lacy s. An unsound argument or mode of arguing; a sophism.
Invi'olacy s. Inviolate state or quality.
Immac'ulacy s. State of being immaculate.
Suprem'acy s. State of being supreme; the highest authority.
Pri'macy s. Office, term of office, or dignity of a primate.
Legit'imacy s. State of being legitimate.
Illegit'imacy s. State of being illegitimate.
In'timacy s. State of being intimate; familiarity.
Diplo'macy s. Science of conducting negotiations with foreign states; skill in negotiating; tact.
Phar'macy s. The art or practice of preparing and dispensing medicines, compounding drugs, etc.; a drug-store.
Con'tumacy s. Persistent obstinacy, stubborn perversity.
Subor'dinacy s. State of being subordinate.
Effem'inacy s. Unmanly softness.
Ob'stinacy s. State or quality of being obstinate; pertinacity.
Lun'acy s. Insanity; mania, craziness.
Impor'tunacy s. Quality of being importunate.
Pa'pacy s. The office or dignity of the Pope; papal authority, etc.; the papal system.

Epis'copacy s. Church government by bishops; prelacy; bishops collectively.
Ra'cy a. Having distinctive flavour or quality; full of spirit; piquant.
-cracy suff. Denoting rule, government by.
Moboc'racy s. Rule by the mob.
Snoboc'racy s. Snobs collectively.
Gynæcoc'racy s. Government by a woman or by women.
Landoc'racy s. The landowning class.
Theoc'racy s. Government by God; a state so governed.
Neoc'racy s. Government by upstarts.
Ptochoc'racy s. Government by paupers.
Hagioc'racy s. Government by priests.
Physioc'racy s. Government according to the working of natural laws.
Ochloc'racy s. Government by the mob.
Fooloc'racy s. Government by fools.
Democ'racy s. Government by the people; a republic; the unprivileged classes.
Arithmoc'racy s. Government by a majority.
Timoc'racy s. Government by those who have certain property qualifications.
Millionoc'racy s. Government by millionaires.
Monoc'racy s. Government by a single person.
Demonoc'racy s. Power of or government by demons.
Cottonoc'racy s. The great employers in the cotton industry.
Pornoc'racy s. Rule by harlots.
Hetæroc'racy s. Government by courtesans.
Beeroc'racy s. (*Slang*) Political power of licensed victuallers and brewers.
Hieroc'racy s. Government by priests.
Pantisoc'racy s. An ideal community planned by Coleridge and others.
Thalassoc'racy s. Supremacy or sovereignty of the sea; maritime power.
Stratoc'racy s. Government by the military.
Gerontoc'racy s. Government by aged men.
Aristoc'racy s. The nobility; government by nobles; a state governed thus.
Autoc'racy s. Absolute government; a state so governed.
Plutoc'racy s. Government by the wealthy; the rule or power of wealth.
Slavoc'racy s. Slave-holders collectively and as a power.
Moneyoc'racy s. Rule of the wealthy classes.
Bureauc'racy s. Government by state departments; officialism.
Fed'eracy s. A federation of states.
Confed'eracy s. A league; union between persons or states; persons in league; a conspiracy.
Degen'eracy s. A growing worse; decline in good qualities; departure from ancestral virtues.
Regen'eracy s. State of being regenerate.
Itin'eracy s. Quality of being itinerant; a passing from place to place.
Invet'eracy s. Long-standing obstinacy.
Lit'eracy s. State of being literate.
Illite'racy s. State of being illiterate; ignorance.
Pir'acy s. Act or crime of a pirate; Infringement of the law of copyright.
Conspir'acy s. Act of conspiring; a plot.
Mag'istracy s. Office, dignity, or jurisdiction of a magistrate; magistrates collectively.
Cur'acy s. Office of curate; benefice of a perpetual curate.
Ac'curacy s. Precision, correctness, exactness.
Inac'curacy s. Want of accuracy; an error.
Proc'uracy s. Act of a procurator; vicarious management; procuratorship.
Ob'duracy s. Stubbornness; inflexible persistence.
Tes'tacy s. State of being testate.
Intes'tacy s. State of one dying without having made a valid will.
Ad'equacy s. (*Adequate*).
Inad'equacy s. Insufficiency.
Pri'vacy s. Retirement, seclusion; state of being in, or place of, this; secrecy.
Bac'cy s. (*Slang*) Tobacco.
Flee'cy a. Woolly; resembling a fleece.
Proph'ecy s. A foretelling, prediction.
Se'crecy s. State of being secret; privacy; fidelity to a secret.
I'cy a. Freezing, frozen; pertaining to or consisting of ice.
Pol'icy s. Art of government; dexterity of management; the governing of a city, state, etc.; line of conduct; contract of insurance; grounds round a mansion.
Impol'icy s. Quality of being impolitic; inexpediency.
Spi'cy a. Flavoured with or abounding in spices; pungent; racy.
Harus'picy s. The art of an haruspex.
Juic'y a. Abounding in juice; moist; succulent.
Colonelcy (ker'nelsy) s. Office, rank, or commission of a colonel.
Va'cancy s. Emptiness; mental vacuity; listlessness; an unoccupied office, etc.
Pec'cancy s. Quality of being sinful or criminal; offence.
Men'dicancy s. State of being a mendicant; beggary.
Signif'icancy s. (*Significance*).
Insignif'icancy s. (*Insignificance*).
Ascen'dancy s. Controlling power.
Inten'dancy s. Office or district of an intendant.
Redun'dancy s. (*Redundance*).
Ver'dancy s. Greenness; rawness, inexperience.
Accor'dancy s. (*Accord*).
Discor'dancy s. (*Discordance*).
Mor'dancy s. Quality of being mordant; mordacity.
Rec'reancy s. Mean-spiritedness; cowardice.
Fan'cy s. Creative imagination; liking; caprice. v.i. To imagine, suppose without proof. v.t. To be pleased with, to want; to imagine.
In'fancy s. State of being an infant; early part of life.
Ter'magancy s. Qualities or methods of a termagant.
Extrav'agancy s. (*Extravagance*).
El'egancy s. (*Elegance*).
Ar'rogancy s. (*Arrogance*).
Chan'cy a. (*Chance*).
Trench'ancy s. Quality of being trenchant.
Syc'ophancy s. Mean flattery; servility.
Irra'diancy s. (*Irradiance*).
Bril'liancy s. (*Brilliant*).
Pli'ancy s. State of being pliant; pliableness.
Luxur'iancy s. (*Luxuriance*).
Sib'ilancy s. A hissing sound; utterance with this.
Pet'ulancy s. (*Petulance*).
-mancy suff. Denoting divination by.
Arith'mancy s. Divination by numbers.
Lampad'omancy s. Divination from a torch-flame.
Rhab'domancy s. Divination with the divining-rod.
Spod'omancy s. Divination from ashes.
Geoman'cy s. Divination from marks on the earth or by means of scattered particles of earth.
The'omancy s. Divination.
Stich'omancy (stik'-) s. Divination by random literary extracts.

Psy'chomancy s. Divination by spiritualistic communication.
Lith'omancy s. Divination by means of stones.
Or'nithomancy s. Divination from the flight of birds.
Sci'omancy s. Divination by means of shadows or the shades of the dead.
Ophiom'ancy s. Divination by observation of serpents.
Bib'liomancy s. Divination by the Bible or by books.
Dactyl'iomancy s. Divination by finger-rings.
Hal'omancy s. Divination by salt.
Bel'omancy s. Divination by archery.
Crys'tallo-mancy s. Divination by means of a crystal.
Œ'nomancy s. Divination from libations of wine.
On'omancy s. Divination by the letters of a name.
Cap'nomancy s. Divination by smoke.
Zo'omancy s. Divination from the observation of animals.
Nec'romancy s. Divination through communication with spirits of the dead; black magic.
Hy'dromancy s. Divination by means of water.
Ceroman'cy s. Divination through melting wax.
Sideroman'cy s. Divination from movements of straws on red-hot irons.
Hi'eromancy s. Divination from observation of sacrificed things.
Cler'omancy s. Divination by dice.
Teph'romancy s. Divination from sacrificial ashes.
Oneir'omancy s. Divination by dreams.
Catoptro-man'cy s. Divination by looking at a mirror under water.
Gas'tromancy s. Divination by ventriloquism, etc.
Ur'omancy s. Uroscopy.
Gyr'omancy s. Divination performed by walking in a circle till dizziness supervened.
Pyr'omancy s. Divination by fire.
Scat'omancy s. Divination by inspection of excrement.
Cartoman'cy s. Divination by cards.
Ich'thyomancy s. Divination by means of fishes.
My'omancy s. Divination from the actions of mice.
Ather'mancy s. Power of stopping radiant heat.
Diather'mancy s. Property of transmitting radiant heat.
Electrother'-mancy s. Science which deals with heat generated by electricity.
Dor'mancy s. State of being dormant; abeyance.
Ten'ancy s. The holding of lands, etc., as a tenant; period of this.
Lieuten'ancy (lef-) s. Office or commission of a lieutenant.
Stag'nancy s. Quality or state of being stagnant.
Reg'nancy s. State of being regnant.
Preg'nancy s. Condition of being pregnant.
Malig'nancy s. Extreme malevolence; virulence.
Poi'gnancy s. Quality or state of being poignant.
Repug'nancy s. (*Repugnance*).
Oppug'nancy s. Act of oppugning; resistance.
Dom'inancy s. (*Dominance*).
Predom'inancy s. (*Predominance*.)
Squin'ancy s. (*Quinsy*).
So'nancy s. (*Sonance*).
Con'sonancy s. (*Consonance*).
Dis'sonancy s. (*Dissonance*).
Discrep'ancy s. Inconsistency, disagreement, contrariety.
Ramp'ancy s. State or quality of being rampant.
Flip'pancy s. Pertness of speech.
Oc'cupancy s. Act of occupying; period of occupation.
Preoc'cupancy s. Act of preoccupying; state of being preoccupied.
Vi'brancy s. State or quality of being vibrant.
Prepon'-derancy s. (*Preponderance*).
Itin'erancy s. (*Itineracy*).
Fla'grancy s. Heinousness; enormity.
Va'grancy s. State or life of a vagrant.
Er'rancy s. (*Errantry*).
Aber'rancy s. (*Aberrant*).
Inerr'ancy s. Freedom from error; infallibility.
Pen'etrancy s. (*Penetrance*).
Recal'citrancy s. (*Recalcitrance*).
Inces'sancy s. State or quality of being unceasing.
Rec'usancy s. Obstinate refusal to obey; nonconformity.
Bla'tancy s. (*Blatant*).
Dilat'ancy s. Capacity of dilatation.
Expect'ancy s. Expectance; expectation.
Reluc'tancy s. (*Reluctance*).
Inhab'itancy s. Residence for a considerable period.
Exor'bitancy s. (*Exorbitance*).
Mil'itancy s. State of being militant; militarism.
Concom'itancy s. (*Concomitance*).
Precip'itancy s. (*Precipitance*).
Ir'ritancy s. (*Irritation*).
Hes'itancy s. Act of hesitating; doubt; indecision.
Exult'ancy s. (*Exultation*).
Account'ancy s. Science or profession of an accountant.
Accep'tancy s. Willingness to accept; acceptation.
In'stancy s. Urgency.
Con'stancy s. Permanency; firmness of mind; faithful attachment.
Incon'stancy s. Fickleness; instability.
Ad'jutancy s. (*Adjutant*).
Pi'quancy (pē'-) s. State or quality of being piquant.
Tru'ancy s. Act of playing or state of being truant.
Rel'evancy s. (*Relevance*).
Irrel'evancy s. (*Irrelevance*).
Conser'vancy s. Conservation; official supervision; a board appointed for this.
Buoy'ancy s. (*Buoyant*).
-ency suff. Forming nouns of state or quality.
Lam'bency s. Condition of being lambent.
Decum'bency s. (*Decumbence*).
Recum'bency s. (*Recumbence*).
Incum'bency s. State of being incumbent; state, period, etc., of holding a benefice as an incumbent.
Adja'cency s. (*Adjacent*).
Compla'cency s. (*Complacence*).
De'cency s. State or quality of being decent; decorum, modesty.
Inde'cency s. Lack of modesty; obscenity.
Re'cency s. State or quality of being recent.
In'nocency s. (*Innocence*).
Nas'cency s. State or quality of being nascent.
Quies'cency s. (*Quiescence*).
Alkales'cency s. (*Alkalescent*).
Convales'cency s. (*Convalescence*).
Adoles'cency s. (*Adolescent*).
Lu'cency s. State or quality of being lucent.
Translu'cency s. (*Translucence*).
Ca'dency s. Descent from a junior branch; state of being a cadet.
Deca'dency s. Deterioration.
Prece'dency s. (*Precedence*).
Res'idency s. Official quarters of a resident in India.
Pres'idency s. Act, condition, office, term of office, jurisdiction, or residence of a president.

Transcen'-dency s. (*Transcendence*).
Resplen'dency s. (*Resplendence*).
Pen'dency s. State of being undecided.
Depen'dency s. Something dependent; a country under the sovereignty of another.
Indepen'dency s. Independence; principles of Congregationalists.
Impen'dency s. (*Impendence*).
Ten'dency s. Bent; inclination; course.
Despon'dency s. Dejection, despair; discouragement.
Ar'dency s. (*Ardent*).
Pu'dency s. Modesty, shamefacedness.
A'gency s. Causative action; office or business of an agent; a commercial organization.
Rea'gency s. Reciprocal action.
Coa'gency s. (*Coagent*).
Re'gency s. Office of regent; period of his rule.
Neg'ligency s. (*Negligence*).
Ex'igency s. Necessity; emergency; exigence.
Ful'gency s. Splendour, glitter; state of being fulgent.
Reful'gency s. (*Refulgence*).
Tan'gency s. Quantity or state of being tangent.
Strin'gency s. State of being stringent.
Astring'ency s. (*Astringent*).
Contin'gency s. Quality of being contingent; an event which may occur; juncture.
Pun'gency s. State of being pungent.
Co'gency s. Force; persuading power.
Emer'gency s. Pressing necessity; unforeseen occurrence; a crisis.
Diver'gency s. (*Divergence*).
Conver'gency s. (*Convergence*).
Ur'gency s. Quality or state of being urgent; importunity.
Insur'gency s. Rebellion.
Circumam'-biency s. (*Circumambient*).
Defic'iency s. A falling short; lack; insufficiency.
Effic'iency s. State or character of being efficient; efficacy.
Ineffic'iency s. Luck of efficiency; incapacity.
Suffic'iency s. Quality of being sufficient; a competence; adequate qualification.
Insuffic'iency s. State of being insufficient.
Profic'iency s. State or quality of being proficient.
Expe'diency s. Expedience; desirableness; self-seeking.
Inexpe'diency s. (*Inexpedience*).
Sa'liency s. Salience; that which is prominent or noteworthy.
Resil'iency s. ((*Resilience*).
Transil'iency s. (*Transilience*).
Ebul'liency s. (*Ebullience*).
Le'niency s. Quality of being lenient; mildness.
Conve'niency s. (*Convenience*).
Recip'iency s. State or quality of being recipient.
Incip'iency s. Inception.
Or'iency s. Quality of being orient; brilliancy.
Prur'iency s. (*Prurience*).
Tran'siency s. (*Transience*).
Sen'tiency s. Sentence; sentient state or being.
Subser'viency s. (*Subservience*).
Va'lency s. Valence; a unit of combining capacity.
Prev'alency s. (*Prevalence*).
Univ'alency s. A combining power of I.
Triva'lency s. (*Trivalence*).
Equiv'alency s. (*Equivalence*).
Ex'cellency s. (*Excellence*).
Repell'ency s. Quality of being repellent.
Equipol'lency s. (*Equipollence*).
Som'nolency s. Somnolence; drowsiness.
Suc'culency s. (*Succulence*).
Truc'ulency s. (*Truculence*).
Cor'pulency s. (*Corpulence*).
Pur'ulency s. (*Purulence*).
Flat'ulency s. (*Flatulence*).
Clem'ency s. (*Clement*).
Inclem'ency s. Physical harshness: severe cold; storminess.
Im'manency s. (*Immanence*).
Per'manency s. Permanence; a condition or thing that is permanent or fixed.
Imper'-manency s. (*Impermancnce*).
Em'inency s. (*Eminence*).
Superem'-inency s. (*Supereminence*).
Prom'inency s. (*Prominence*).
Con'tinency s. (*Continence*).
Per'tinency s. (*Pertinence*).
Ab'stinency s. (*Abstinent*).
Oppo'nency s. Opposition; action of maintaining an opposing argument.
Transpar'ency s. Transparence; a transparent object, picture, etc.
Indif'ferency s. Absence of interest in anything, equilibrium.
Viceger'ency s. Office, power, etc., of a vicegerent.
Bellig'erency s. (*Belligerent*).
Inher'ency s. (*Inherence*).
Coher'ency s. (*Coherence*).
Incoher'ency s. (*Incoherence*).
Abhor'rency s. (*Abhorrent*).
Cur'rency s. Circulation; circulating medium; aggregate of coin and notes in circulation; state of being current.
Recur'rency s. (*Recurrence*).
La'tency s. State or quality of being latent.
Pa'tency s. State of being patent; manifestness.
Com'petency s. (*Competence*).
Incom'petency s. (*Incompetence*).
Ap'petency s. (*Appetence*).
Inap'petency s. (*Inappetence*).
Impen'itency s. Obduracy; hardness of heart.
Ren'itency s. (*Renitence*).
Po'tency s. State of being potent; strength; energy.
Prepo'tency s. Quality of being prepotent; predominance.
Omnip'otency s. (*Omnipotence*).
Im'potency s. (*Impotence*).
Adver'tency s. Attention, regard.
Inadver'tency s. (*Inadvertence*).
Insis'tency s. (*Insistence*).
Consis'tency s. (*Consistence*).
Inconsis'tency s. Quality or state of being inconsistent; discrepancy; self-contradiction.
Persis'tency s. (*Persistence*).
Flu'ency s. Quality of being fluent; volubility.
Fre'quency s. Occurrence often repeated; rate of this; repetition at short intervals.
Infre'quency s. State of being infrequent.
Delin'quency s. A fault, offence; omission of duty.
Con'gruency s. Accordance, consistency.
Constit'uency s. A body of electors; district or body represented.
Sol'vency s. State of being solvent.
Insol'vency s. Inability to clear oneself of debt.
Fer'vency s. Eagerness, ardour; warmth of devotion.
En'signcy s. Rank or office of an ensign.
Chap'laincy s. Office or position of a chaplain.
Chief'taincy s. (*Chieftain*).
Cap'taincy s. (*Captain*).
Sur'geoncy s. Office, duties, etc., of a surgeon.
Id'iocy s. Defective intellect.

Far'cy s. A disease in horses like glanders.
Mer'cy s. Pity; willingness to spare; a blessing.
Gramer'cy int. Thanks; expression of surprise.
Bar'onetcy s. Title or dignity of a baronet.
Cor'netcy s. The old office of cornet in the cavalry.
Vis'countcy (vī'-) s. Dignity or office of a viscount.
Par'amountcy s. State of being paramount; paramount position.
Bank'ruptcy s. (*Bankrupt*).
Sau'cy a. Impudent, pert.
Bea'dy a. Small, round, and glistening.
Head'y a. Headstrong; impetuous; intoxicating.
Lead'y a. Consisting of or resembling lead.
Read'y (red'y) a. Prepared at the moment; prompt; eager; opportune. adv. In state of preparation.
Thread'y a. Like or containing threads.
Alread'y adv. By this time; even now.
Stead'y a. Firmly fixed; stable; regular; equable. v.t. and i. To make or become steady.
Sha'dy a. Sheltered from the light; abounding in shade; of dubious honesty.
La'dy s. A well-bred woman.
Mal'ady s. A lingering disease, illness; moral defect.
Land'lady s. A woman keeper of an inn or house-proprietor.
Gla'dy a. Full of glades.
Byrla'dy int. An obsolete oath.
Toa'dy s. A flatterer, sycophant. v.t. To fawn upon servilely.
Wa'dy s. (*Wadi*).
Cad'dy s. A small tea-chest.
Dad'dy s. (*Childish*) Father.
Fad'dy a. Addicted to fads; of the nature of a fad.
Pad'dy s. Growing or unhusked rice; an Irishman.
Wad'dy (wod'-) s. Native Australian war-club.
Ed'dy s. A small whirlpool, a contrary current. v.i. and t. To whirl in an eddy.
Ned'dy s. A donkey.
Red'dy a. Somewhat red.
Bid'dy s. An Irish servant girl.
Chick'abiddy s. Term of endearment for a small child.
Gid'dy a. Dizzy; heedless; thoughtless; fickle.
Kid'dy s. A small child.
Mid'dy s. A midshipman.
Shod'dy s. Waste from manufacture of wool; inferior fabric made of this and used cloth, etc., re-dressed. a. Sham; inferior.
Clod'dy a. Full of clods; earthy, worthless.
Tod'dy s. Juice extracted from palm-trees; a beverage of sweetened spirits.
Cud'dy s. A small cabin; a donkey; a dolt.
Mud'dy a. Soiled with mud; turbid; consisting of, containing, or like mud; dull. v.t. To soil with mud, to make foul.
Rud'dy a. Of a red colour or healthy complexion. v.t. and i. To make or become red.
Or'thopædy s. Art or practice of curing bodily deformities.
Deed'y a. Industrious, active.
Need'y a. Distressed by want of the means of living.
Speed'y a. Having speed; not dilatory; nimble.
Reed'y a. Abounding with reeds; having reed-like qualities.
Greed'y a. Having a great desire for food or drink; avaricious; covetous.
Seed'y a. Abounding in or bearing seeds; run to seed; old and worn-out; poorly.
Weed'y a. Pertaining to or abounding with weeds; scraggy, ungainly.
Trag'edy s. A fatal or mournful event; drama depicting such; a bloody deed.
Hig'gledy-pig'gledy adv. In confusion, topsy-turvy. a. Jumbled about.
Rem'edy s. That which cures a disease or counteracts an evil; redress. v.t. To apply a cure to; to restore to health, etc.; to redress.
Com'edy s. A drama intended to amuse or having a happy ending; a humorous occurrence.
Per'fidy s. Treachery; breach of faith.
Sub'sidy s. Pecuniary aid, especially governmental.
Ti'dy a. Orderly, neat; nice, comfortable. v.t. To put in order.
Unti'dy a. Slovenly.
Bield'y a. (*Scot.*) Sheltering.
Unwield'y a. Not easily moved; clumsy, unmanageable.
Mould'y a. Covered with mould; musty; decaying.
Ban'dy s. A club used in a ball-game; the game itself. a. Bowed, crooked (of legs). v.t. To beat to and fro; to give and receive reciprocally; to agitate. v.i. To contend, be factious.
Can'dy s. Crystallized sugar, a sweetmeat. v.t. To form into crystals; to preserve with sugar. v.i. To crystallize.
Dan'dy s. A fop, a man over-fond of dress; a light two-wheeled cart; a whalebone brush for horses; a sloop with a jigger-mast; dengue.
Han'dy a. Ready; dexterous; convenient.
Shan'dy s. Shandygaff.
Ran'dy a. Boisterous, romping, disorderly. s. A rowdy; a sturdy beggar.
Bran'dy s. A spirituous liquor distilled from wine.
San'dy a. Consisting of, abounding with, or like sand; yellowish-red. s. (*Slang*) A Scotsman.
Wand'y (wŏnd'-) a. Twiggy; like a wand.
Shin'dy s. A rumpus, disturbance, row.
Win'dy a. Characterized by or exposed to the wind; flatulent; loquacious; nervous.
Maun'dy s. Ceremony of washing the feet of poor people on Holy Thursday.
Groun'dy a. Full of sediment.
Woun'dy a. Causing wounds; excessive.
Bod'y s. The main part; the trunk of an animal; a person; a solid figure. v.t. To embody, give body to.
Some'body s. Some person; one of importance.
Embod'y v.t. To form into a body; incorporate, include.
Disembod'y v.t. To divest of flesh or body; to disband.
No'body s. No one; a person of no importance.
Ev'erybody s. Every person.
Bus'ybody (biz'-) s. An officious meddler.
Mel'ody s. Music; sweetness of sound; an air.
Psalm'ody s. Art of psalm-singing; psalms collectively.

Thren'ody s. A dirge, funeral poem.
Hym'nody s. The singing of hymns; hymns collectively.
Mon'ody s. A lamentation by a single mourner; a plaintive poem.
Good'y s. An old woman; a sweetmeat. a. Affectedly pious.
Blood'y a. Blood-stained; excessively cruel.
Mood'y a. Indulging in humours; peevish, sullen.
Brood'y a. Inclined to sit on eggs; morose, melancholy.
Wood'y a. Abounding in woods or with wood; consisting of or like wood.
Tetrap'ody s. A verse of four feet.
Hexap'ody s. A line or verse of six feet.
Chirop'ody s. Art of treating the feet, removing corns, etc.
Pol'ypody s. One of a large genus of ferns.
Par'ody s. A composition burlesquing an author's style, mannerisms, etc. v.t. To imitate or burlesque in parody.
Pros'ody s. Science of versification.
Rhap'sody s. An epic, or a portion of this for recitation; high-flown utterance or composition.
To'dy s. A small W. Indian bird.
Cus'tody s. A keeping or guarding; imprisonment; restraint of liberty.
Lar'dy-dar'dy a. Foppish; affected.
Har'dy a. Stout, daring; over-confident.
Foolhar'dy a. Rash, reckless.
Lar'dy a. Like or containing lard.
Jeop'ardy s. Hazard, danger, peril.
Tar'dy a. Sluggish, dilatory, late.
Bas'tardy s. (*Bastard*).
Sward'y a. Turfy; grassy.
Word'y a. Verbose; using many words.
Curd'y a. Full of curds; congealed.
Hur'dy-gur'dy s. An obsolete stringed instrument; an old-fashioned barrel-organ.
Stur'dy a. Strong, robust, stout. s. A disease in sheep.
Gaud'y a. Garish, flashy. s. An annual college festival.
Cloud'y a. Overspread with clouds; dull; obscure; marked with blotches.
Stud'y s. Mental application, especially to books; earnest endeavour; subject studied; a room for study; an outline. v.t. To apply the mind to. v.i. To muse, meditate; to be diligent.
Un'derstudy s. An actor's substitute.
Baw'dy a. Obscene, unchaste.
Dow'dy a. Shabby, ill-dressed. s. An awkward, slatternly woman.
Row'dy a. Riotous, rough. s. A noisy, disorderly fellow.
Bey s. A Turkish governor; a ruler in Algiers and some other places.
Mang'abey s. An African monkey.
Ab'bey s. A monastic community; its buildings, especially its church.
Obey' (-bā) v.t. To yield submission to, comply with orders of.
Disobey' v.i. To refuse obedience. v.t. To break the commands of.
Win'cey s. A cloth with cotton warp and woollen weft.
Dey s. An old title of rulers of Algiers, Tunis, etc.
Fey a. Doomed to die.
Gey adv. (*Scot.*) Very, considerably.
Bo'gey s. An ideal opponent at golf; a bogy.
Fo'gey s. A dull or eccentric old person.
Hey int. Exclamation of surprise, joy, to call attention, etc.
They pron. Pl. of 3rd pers.
Whey (hwā) s. The watery or serous part of milk.
Key s. Implement to open a lock; solution; system of related musical notes based on final note; pitch, tone; a low coral-island.
Lack'ey s. A footman; a servile follower. v.t. To attend as a footman or servilely.
Dick'ey s. (*Dicky*).
Hock'ey s. A ball-game played on a field with curved clubs; harvest-home.
Jock'ey s. A rider in a horse-race. v.t. To ride in a race; to outwit.
Cri'key int. (*Slang*) Expressing surprise.
Don'key s. An ass; a fool, an obstinate fellow.
Mon'key s. A nimble, four-handed mammal; a mischievous youngster; weight for driving piles; (*slang*) £500.
Turn'key s. A jailer, warder.
Flun'key s. A liveried servant; a lackey.
Cho'key s. (*Slang*) A prison.
Ho'key-po'key s. Cheap ice-cream.
Tur'key s. A large gallinaceous bird.
Whis'key s. An ardent spirituous liquor.
Ley s. Lea.
Fid'dley s. The iron framework round a deck-hatch.
Med'ley s. A mixture; a hodge-podge.
Bai'ley s. An outer wall or court of a castle.
Al'ley s. A narrow passage; a garden walk; a large playing marble.
Gal'ley s. A low, flat vessel with one deck; a state barge; a ship's kitchen; a compositor's tray for type.
Tomal'ley s. The greenish "liver" of the lobster.
Val'ley s. A hollow between hills; a river-basin.
Trol'ley s. A small hand-truck, a narrow cart; wheeled pole of an electric tram-car.
Vol'ley s. A flight of missiles; the discharge of many small arms at once.
Pul'ley s. Small wheel in a block used in transmitting power.
Ho'ley a. Full of holes.
Po'ley a. Denoting hornless cattle.
Bar'ley s. A cereal used for making malt and as food.
Par'ley s. A conference for discussing terms. v.i. To confer with another concerning a dispute; to discuss orally.
Hur'ley s. Hockey; a hockey-stick.
Pars'ley s. An umbelliferous herb used in seasoning.
Mot'ley a. Variegated; dappled; discordantly composite. s. A fool's parti-coloured coat.
Yow'ley (you'-) s. The yellow-hammer.
Kid'ney s. One of two glands that secrete urine; disposition; sort, kind.
Hack'ney s. A horse or a coach kept for hire; a nag. v.t. To make stale or commonplace.
Cock'ney s. A Londoner; a spoilt child.
Chim'ney s. A flue, fire-place; vent of volcano; vertical fissure in rock-face.
Spin'ney s. A small thicket, copse.
Co'ney a. The cony.
Hon'ey s. Sweet, viscous substance collected by bees; sweetness; a term of endearment. v.t. To sweeten.
Mon'ey s. Coin, cash; a circulating medium wealth.
Com'money s. A clay marble.
Bar'ney s. (*Slang*) A spree.

Car'ney v.t. and i. To coax, wheedle.
Blar'ney s. Flattery, smooth speech. v.i. To flatter or delude by talk.
Attor'ney s. One legally transacting business for another.
Jour'ney s. Passage from one place to another; an expedition; distance travelled. v.i. To travel; to make a journey.
Tour'ney s. A tournament. v.i. To take part in this.
Chut'ney s. An E. Indian condiment.
Saw'ney s. A simpleton; a Scotsman.
Jo'ey s. (*Slang*) A groat; a young kangaroo.
Strathspey' (-spā') s. A Scottish dance.
Pal'frey s. A saddle-horse; a riding-horse for ladies.
Com'frey s. A tall wild plant with whitish or purple flowers.
Grey s. White with a mixture of black. a. Of this colour; dull, gloomy; aged, experienced.
Or'phrey s. An embroidered border on an ecclesiastical robe.
Stor'ey s. A floor of a building.
Prey s. Spoil, booty, plunder. v.i. To collect booty, to ravage; to take (especially food) by violence.
Lam'prey s. An eel-like fish.
Os'prey s. The sea-eagle, a large fish-eating bird; an egret plume.
Mur'rey a. Dark red in colour.
Trey (trā) s. The three at cards, etc.
Ja'sey s. A worsted wig.
Lin'sey-wol'sey s. A coarse fabric of linen or cotton and wool.
Malm'sey s. A sweet white wine.
Guern'sey s. A thick woollen jersey worn by seamen.
Goos'ey s. Child's term for a goose.
Jer'sey s. A close-fitting knitted body-garment.
Ker'sey s. A coarse woollen cloth. a. Made of this; homely.
Od'yssey s. A long course of wandering and adventure.
Caus'ey s. (*Causeway*).
Chant'ey s. A sailor's song sung when heaving the anchor, etc.
Glu'ey a. Viscous, glutinous.
Quey (kwā) s. A heifer.
Ca'vey s. (*Cavy*).
Sla'vey s. (*Slang*) A female domestic servant.
Convey' v.t. To transport, deliver, impart; to transfer property.
Cov'ey s. A brood or flock of birds (especially partridges).
Jar'vey s. A cabdriver, especially in Ireland.
Purvey' v.t. To provide with; to get. v.i. To procure or provide provisions; to cater.
Survey' (-vā') v.t. To oversee, examine; to measure and value, to determine the boundaries of.
Sur'vey (-vā) s. A general view; a measured topographical plan or description; an account.
Wey (wā) s. A certain weight used for produce.
Clayey a. (*Clay*).
Whey'ey (hwā') a. Resembling or containing whey.
Sky'ey a. Like the sky; ethereal.
-fy suff. Implying to make, produce, bring into a certain condition, etc.
Sheaf'y a. Resembling a sheaf; abounding in sheaves.
Leaf'y a. Full of leaves.
Tab'efy v.i. To waste gradually, lose flesh.
Ru'befy v.t. To make red.
Defy' v.t. To challenge, dare, brave.
Beef'y a. Fleshy, solid.
Reef'y a. Abounding in reefs.
Hu'mefy v.t. To make moist.
Tu'mefy v.i. and t. To swell or cause to swell to rise as a tumour.
Tep'efy v.t. and i. To make or become tepid.
Stu'pefy v.t. To deprive of sensibility.
Ar'efy v.t. To dry up, to parch.
Rar'efy v.t. and i. To make or become rare, thin, or less dense.
Tor'refy v.t. To dry, parch, roast.
Pu'trefy v.t. and t. To rot, decay, cause to become rotten or gangrenous.
Liq'uefy v.t. and i. To melt, dissolve, make or become liquid.
Baf'fy s. (*Scot.*) A golf-club for lofting.
Chaf'fy a. Consisting of chaff or worthless matter.
Taf'fy s. (*Slang*) A Welshman.
Jif'fy s. (*Slang*) An instant.
Clif'fy a. Craggy, having cliffs.
Snif'fy a. Given to sniffing; disdainful.
Spif'fy a. (*Slang*) Spruce; slightly intoxicated.
Tof'fy s. (*Toffee*).
Buf'fy a. Yellowish.
Huf'fy a. Easily offended; peevish.
Bluf'fy a. Off-handed; having bold prominences.
Fluf'fy a. Pertaining to, covered with, or like fluff; downy.
Snuf'fy a. Smelling of or soiled with snuff.
Puf'fy a. Swelled, inflated.
Stuf'fy a. Ill-ventilated; fusty.
Syllab'ify v.t. To separate into or pronounce by syllables.
Verb'ify v.t. To make into or use as a verb.
Pac'ify v.t. To appease; to allay.
Spec'ify v.t. To mention specifically; to state in detail.
Sili'cify v.t. and i. To impregnate or become impregnated with silica; to turn into silica.
Cal'cify v.t. and i. To convert and become converted into lime.
Decal'cify v.t. To denude of calcareous matter.
Dul'cify v.t. To sweeten; to free from acidity.
Zin'cify (-sifi) v.t. To coat with zinc, galvanize.
Cru'cify v.t. To slay by nailing to a cross; to mortify, torment.
La'dify v.t. To make a lady of, treat as a lady.
Ed'ify v.t. To improve the mind, instruct, enlighten.
Re-ed'ify v.t. To build again, re-establish.
Acid'ify v.t. and i. (*Acid*).
Rancid'ify v.t. and i. To make or become rancid.
Solid'ify v.t. and i. To make or become solid.
Humid'ify v.t. To make humid or damp.
Nid'ify v.i. To build a nest or nests.
Lapid'ify v.t. To convert into stone. v.i. To become petrified.
Fluid'ify v.t. To make fluid.
Dan'dify v.t. To make smart or dandy-like.
Co'dify v.t. To form into or reduce to a code; to systematize.
Mod'ify v.t. To change the form of; to qualify, vary.
De'ify v.t. To make a god of; to make godlike; to adore.
Preach'ify v.i. To sermonize; to hold forth tediously.
Speech'ify v.i. To harangue.
French'ify v.t. To make French, to Gallicize.
Church'ify v.t. (*Church*).

Alkal'ify v.t. and i. To convert or be converted into an alkali.
Sal'ify v.t. To change into a, or saturate with, salt.
Qual'ify v.t. To give proper qualities to; to fit; to modify, limit; to soften, dilute. v.i. To become qualified.
Disqual'ify v.t. To render unfit, incapacitate.
Steel'ify v.t. To turn into steel.
Ug'lify v.t. To make ugly.
Vil'ify v.t. To traduce, defame.
Jel'lify v.t. and i. To jelly.
Jol'lify v.t. and i. To make merry.
Mol'lify v.t. To soften, pacify, appease.
Nul'lify v.t. To make void, render invalid, deprive of legal force; to annul.
Am'plify v.t. To make larger, to expand, fill out. v.i. To become larger, to dilate.
Exem'plify v.t. To show by example, serve as an instance of.
Sim'plify v.t. To make simple, plain, or easy.
Chyl'ify v.t. and i. To convert or be turned into chyle.
Ram'ify v.i. To separate into branches.
Mum'mify v.t. To make into or embalm as a mummy.
Hu'mify v.i. To turn into mould.
Chym'ify v.t. and i. To form or be turned into chyme.
San'ify v.t. To make healthy.
Mag'nify v.t. To make greater, especially in appearance; to extol; to exaggerate. v.i. To increase the apparent size of.
Dig'nify v.t. To exalt, advance, honour.
Lig'nify v.t. and i. To convert into or become wood.
Sig'nify v.t. To make known, to betoken; to imply, mean. v.i. To be of consequence.
Min'ify v.t. To make little or less.
Gelatin'ify v.t. To gelatinate.
Sin'ify v.t. To make Chinese.
Divin'ify v.t. To deify.
Dam'nify v.t. To cause loss or damage to.
Indem'nify v.t. To save harmless; to secure against loss, etc.; to reimburse.
Sapon'ify v.t. and i. To convert or turn into soap.
Person'ify v.t. To represent with the attributes of or treat as a person; to mimic, resemble.
Car'nify v.t. and i. To convert or be converted into flesh.
U'nify v.t. To form into one; to reduce to uniformity.
Hero'ify v.t. To convert into a hero.
Pul'pify v.t. To pulp.
Tor'pify v.t. To make torpid.
Typ'ify (tip'-) v.t. To show in emblem, serve as a type of, prefigure.
Pretyp'ify v.t. To prefigure.
Scar'ify v.t. To scratch and make small incisions in.
Sacchar'ify v.t. To convert into sugar.
Clar'ify v.t. To make clear, purify, refine. v.i. To become pure.
Lu'brify v.t. To lubricate.
Chon'drify v.t. To convert into cartilage.
Ether'ify v.t. To make or convert into ether.
Ver'ify v.t. To confirm, prove to be true.
Ni'grify v.t. To blacken.
Transmog'rify v.t. To transform.
Scor'ify v.t. To reduce to dross or scoria-like form.
Calor'ify v.t. To make hot.
Glor'ify v.t. To make glorious; to extol.
Ter'rify v.t. To cause or produce terror in, to frighten.
Hor'rify v.t. To impress with horror; to scandalize.
Elec'trify v.t. To charge with electricity; to rouse, thrill.
Pet'rify v.t. and i. To convert or be converted to stone or stony substance; to make or become callous.
Ni'trify v.t. and i. To turn into nitre; to make or become nitrous.
Vit'rify v.t. and i. To convert or become converted into glass or a glass-like substance.
Devit'rify v.t. To change, as rocks, from a vitreous to a crystalline state.
Pur'ify v.t. and i. To make or become pure or clear from defilement, guilt, etc.
Gas'ify v.t. To convert into gas.
Fal'sify v.t. To make or prove to be false; to garble; to break by falsehood; v.i. To violate the truth.
Sal'sify s. Goat's beard, the root of which is eaten.
Emul'sify v.t. To convert into an emulsion.
Inten'sify v.t. and i. To make or become more intense.
Pro'sify v.t. and i. To turn into or to write prose.
Ver'sify v.t. To turn into or express in verse. v.i. To make verses.
Diver'sify v.t. To make diverse or various in form, character, etc.
Clas'sify v.t. To arrange in classes; to systematize.
Os'sify v.t. and i. To form or be turned into bone; to become hard or callous.
Rus'sify v.t. To Russianize, make Russian.
Beat'ify v.t. To render supremely happy; to accord the first step in canonization to.
Rat'ify v.t. To confirm, make valid, establish.
Grat'ify v.t. To indulge; to please, humour, delight.
Strat'ify v.t. To form into or lay in strata.
Objec'tify v.t. To render objective; to present to the mind as a reality.
Rec'tify v.t. To make straight or right; to correct; to refine by repeated distillation.
Sanc'tify v.t. To make sacred; to hallow; to purify from sin.
Fruc'tify v.t. To fertilize, make fruitful. v.i. To bear fruit.
Acet'ify v.t. and i. To render or become sour.
Stul'tify v.t. To render absurd, prove foolish.
Quan'tify v.t. To change, determine, or measure the quantity of.
Iden'tify v.t. To prove sameness, consider as the same in effect.
No'tify v.t. To declare, make known; to inform.
Cer'tify v.t. To testify in writing, make known as a fact.
For'tify v.t. To strengthen, especially by forts; to encourage, invigorate.
Mor'tify v.t. To subdue by abstinence, etc., to humiliate; to affect with gangrene. v.i. To decay, to gangrene.
Tes'tify v.i. and t. To bear witness, give evidence.
Jus'tify v.t. To prove to be just or right; to defend, vindicate; to adjust.
Mys'tify v.t. To render obscure; to bewilder hoax.
Pret'tify v.t. To make pretty, put in a pretty way.

Beaut'ify v.t. To make beautiful.
Brut'ify v.t. To cause to become brutal.
Sang'uify v.i. To produce blood.
Viv'ify v.t. To animate; to enliven.
Reviv'ify v.t. To restore to life, reanimate.
Shelf'y a. Abounding in reefs or shoals.
Gulf'y a. Full of whirlpools; deep.
Oof'y a. (*Slang*) Well-supplied with money.
Roof'y a. Having a roof or roofs.
Scurf'y a. Having or resembling scurf.
Surf'y a. Covered with or resembling surf.
Turf'y a. Covered with or resembling turf.
Sat'isfy v.t. To gratify the desire of; to content.
Dissat'isfy v.t. To fail to satisfy, render discontented.
Ar'gufy v.i. To argue.
Cock'neyfy v.t. To make into a cockney.
-phagy suff. Denoting the action or process of eating or devouring.
Sarcoph'agy s. Practice of eating flesh.
Mycoph'agy s. The eating of fungi.
Geoph'agy s. The habit of eating earth.
Creoph'agy s. Flesh-eating.
Anthropoph'agy s. Cannibalism.
Hippoph'agy s. Practice of eating horse-flesh.
Autoph'agy s. Absorption of one's own tissues.
Ichthyoph'agy s. Practice of eating fish.
Sa'gy a. Tasting or smelling of sage.
Sta'gy a. Theatrical, exaggerated.
Edg'y a. Having or showing an edge; irritable.
Ledg'y a. Having ledges.
Fledg'y a. Feathery.
Sedg'y a. Abounding with or like sedge.
Ridg'y a. Having a ridge or ridges.
Dodg'y a. Given to evasions; shifty; quibbling.
Podg'y a. Short and fat.
Stodg'y a. Indigestible, heavy; dull.
Sludg'y a. Covered with sludge.
Pudg'y a. Short and fat; squat.
El'egy s. A mournful song, plaintive poem; a dirge.
Paraple'gy s. Paralysis of both lower limbs.
Bibliop'egy s. Art of book-binding.
Strat'egy s. The art of war; generalship.
Bag'gy a. Loose; bulging.
Shag'gy a. Rough-haired; unkempt; rugged.
Jag'gy a. Characterized by jags; jagged.
Flag'gy a. Abounding in flags (the plant).
Knag'gy a. Rough in temper.
Snag'gy a. Full of snags; abounding in knots.
Crag'gy a. Full of crags, rough.
Scrag'gy a. Lean with roughness; bony.
Sag'gy a. Characterized by sagging.
Quag'gy a. Boggy; like a quag.
Swag'gy a. Hanging by its weight; inclined to sag.
Zig'zaggy a. (*Zigzag*).
Leg'gy a. Having long or awkward legs.
Nut'meggy a. Tasting of nutmeg.
Dreg'gy a. Containing dregs; foul.
Sprig'gy a. Abounding with or like sprigs.
Twig'gy a. Made of, abounding with, or resembling twigs.
Bog'gy a. Marshy.
Dog'gy a. Like or pertaining to dogs. s. A little dog.
Fog'gy a. Filled with fog; misty; producing fogs; obscure; perplexed.
Clog'gy a. Sticky, clogging.
Frog'gy a. Like or abounding with frogs.
Grog'gy a. Tipsy; moving uneasily on with hobbling gait.
Sog'gy a. Soaked, thoroughly drenched.
Bug'gy s. A light four-wheeled vehicle. a. Infested with or smelling of bugs.
Fug'gy a. Stuffy, frowsy; ill-ventilated.
Slug'gy a. Abounding in slugs.
Mug'gy a. Damp and close; sultry.
Drug'gy a. Composed of or resembling drugs.
Prod'igy s. Something extraordinary or astonishing; a portent; one of extraordinary ability, etc.
Ef'figy s. Representation of a person; image.
Cardial'gy s. (*Cardialgia*).
Cephalal'gy s. Headache.
Odontal'gy s. Toothache.
Bul'gy a. Swollen, bulging.
Slang'y a. Using slang.
Man'gy a. Infected with the mange; (*slang*) mean.
Tang'y a. Strongly or unpleasantly flavoured.
Din'gy a Dusky; soiled; faded.
Spring'y a. Like a spring; resilient.
String'y a. Consisting of or resembling string; fibrous; viscous.
Stin'gy (-ji) a. Parsimonious; niggardly.
Spong'y (spŭnj'-) a. Of the nature of sponge; soft and full of cavities.
Dung'y a. Full of dung; nasty.
Bo'gy s. A spectre, hobgoblin; a bogie.
Fo'gy s. An eccentric or dull old fellow.
Ped'agogy s. Pedagogics; pedagogism.
Dem'agogy s. The wiles and practices of demagogues.
Anago'gy s. Allegorical interpretation.
Mys'tagogy s. The interpretation of mysteries.
-logy suff. Forming names of sciences, etc., and nouns denoting mode of speech.
Geneal'ogy s. Account of the descent of a family; pedigree; lineage.
Mammal'ogy s. The science treating of mammals.
Anal'ogy s. Resemblance; similarity of relations, etc.
Mineral'ogy s. The science of minerals.
Tetral'ogy s. A collection of four plays, especially as played at the ancient Greek Dionysiac festival.
Tril'ogy s. Series of three connected dramas.
Antil'ogy s. Contradiction in terms.
-ology suff. Denoting a science.
Phlebol'ogy s. Department of anatomy dealing with the veins.
Amphibol'ogy s. Ambiguity, equivocation.
Symbol'ogy s. Art of expressing by symbols.
Cacol'ogy s. Bad choice of words; mispronunciation.
Malacol'ogy s. The natural history of molluscs.
Pharmacol'ogy s. The science of drugs and their properties.
Malacostracol'ogy s. Crustaceology.
Gynæcol'ogy s. The science of diseases peculiar to women.
Œcol'ogy s. Branch of science dealing with the environment, habits, etc., of animals and plants.
Lexicol'ogy s. Science of the derivation, signification, and application of words.
Toxicol'ogy s. Branch of medicine dealing with poisons, their antidotes, etc.
Helcol'ogy s. Branch of medicine dealing with ulcers.
Tocol'ogy s. Science of obstetrics.
Sarcol'ogy s. Branch of anatomy which treats of the soft parts.
Muscol'ogy s. The science of mosses.
Phycol'ogy s. The study of sea-weeds.
Mycol'ogy s. Science of or a treatise on fungi.

Monadol'ogy s. Doctrine or theory of monads.
Rhabdol'ogy s. Divination with the divining-rod.
Orchidol'ogy s. The branch of horticulture treating of orchids.
Pteridol'ogy s. Science of ferns.
Tidol'ogy s. Science or theory of tides.
Methodol'ogy s. Branch of logic dealing with methods of thought.
Pseudol'ogy s. The art of lying.
Archæol'ogy s. The study of prehistoric or other antiquities.
Palæol'ogy s. Archæology.
Spelæol'ogy s. Study or exploration of caves.
Testaceol'ogy s. Branch of zoology dealing with the testacea.
Crustaceol'ogy s. Branch of science dealing with crustacea.
Ideol'ogy s. The science of ideas; fanciful theorizing.
Geol'ogy s. The science of the earth's crust, its structure, composition, changes, etc.; a treatise on this.
Theol'ogy s. Divinity; the science of divine things.
Teleol'ogy s. Doctrine of final causes.
Endemeol'ogy s. Study of endemic diseases.
Vermeol'ogy s. Natural history on worms.
Neol'ogy s. Introduction or use of new words; novel or rationalistic views.
Balneol'ogy s. Treatment of disease by bathing or medicinal springs.
Areol'ogy s. The study of Mars.
Phraseol'ogy (-e-ol'-) s. Manner of expression; diction; style.
Museol'ogy s. Science of managing museums.
Osteol'ogy s. The part of anatomy treating of the nature, arrangement, etc., of bones.
Algol'ogy s. Scientific study of seaweeds.
Fungol'ogy s. The science of fungi.
Laryngol'ogy s. The branch of medical science dealing wtih the wind-pipe.
Trichol'ogy s. The study of the hair.
Conchol'ogy s. Science of or collecting of shells and molluscs.
Archol'ogy s. The science of government; philosophy of origins.
Euchol'ogy s. The liturgy of the Greek Church.
Psychol'ogy s. Science of mind, its powers and functions.
Graphol'ogy s. The study of handwriting; science of graphs.
Silphol'ogy s. Science of larval forms.
Carphol'ogy s. Plucking of the bed-clothes in delirium.
Morphol'ogy s. Science of structural organic types; study of forms of animals and plants, also of words.
Meta-morphol'ogy s. Science of the metamorphoses of organisms.
Pathol'ogy s. The science of diseases, their causes, symptoms, etc.
Psycho-pathol'ogy s. Science of insanity.
Neuro-pathol'ogy s. The pathology of the nervous system.
E'thology s. Science of ethics; also of customs among different races or those in different stages.
Lithol'ogy s. Science of the composition, classification, etc., of rocks.
Ornithol'ogy s. The science of the form, structure, and habits of birds.
Anthol'ogy s. A collection of poems, especially of a period or on a subject.
Helminthol'ogy s. A treatise on intestinal worms.
Mythol'ogy s. Science of, a treatise on, or a collective body of myths.
Biol'ogy s. The science of life and living matter.
Amphibiol'ogy s. Branch of zoology treating of Amphibia.
Microbiol'ogy s. The study of bacteria or microbes.
Speciol'ogy s. Branch of biology treating of the nature and origin of species.
Sociol'ogy s. Branch of philosophy treating of human society.
Radiol'ogy s. Branch of science that treats of radiation.
Cardiol'ogy s. A treatise on or study of the heart.
Semeiol'ogy s. Branch of pathology dealing with symptoms; sematology.
Hagiol'ogy s. Literature connected with saints.
Spongiol'ogy (spŭnj'-) s. Study of sponges.
Liturgiol'ogy s. The study of or a treatise on liturgies.
Hygiol'ogy s. Hygiene; a treatise on this.
Stoichiol'ogy s. Doctrine of fundamental laws, etc.
Ophiol'ogy s. The natural history of snakes.
Bibliol'ogy s. (*Bibliography*).
Heliol'ogy s. The science of the sun.
Dactyliol'ogy s. A treatise on rings and gems.
Epidemiol'ogy s. The science and study of epidemics.
Craniol'ogy s. The scientific study of crania.
Herniol'ogy s. Branch of medicine dealing with hernia.
Bacteriol'ogy s. The study of bacteria.
Soteriol'ogy s. A discourse on hygiene; the doctrine of salvation.
Storiol'ogy s. The science of folklore.
Assyriol'ogy s. Study of antiquities, etc., of Assyria.
Semasiol'ogy s. Science of meanings of words.
Ecclesiol'ogy s. Science and study of Church history, Church architecture and decoration, institutions, etc.
Heresiol'ogy s. Study of or treatise on heresies.
Gnosiol'ogy s. The philosophy dealing with the theory of knowledge, etc.
Physiol'ogy s. Science of the organs and their functions.
Ætiol'ogy s. The science of causes or philosophy of causation.
Hamartiol'ogy s. The doctrine of sin.
Kalol'ogy s. The science or theory of beauty.
Angelol'ogy s. The doctrine of the existence of angels.
Nephelol'ogy s. The scientific study of clouds.
Philol'ogy s. Linguistic science; the study of language.
Haplol'ogy s. Vocal contraction of a word by inadvertent omission of a syllable.
Dactylol'ogy s. Art of conversing on the fingers.
Potamol'ogy s. The scientific study of rivers.
Epistemol'ogy s. Science dealing with origin and nature of knowledge.
Sphygmol'ogy s. Branch of physiology dealing with the pulse.
Ophthalm-ol'ogy s. The science of the eye, its structure; diseases, etc.
Homol'ogy s. Correspondence; identity of relation between parts.
Nomol'ogy s. The science of law.
Gnomol'ogy s. A collection of maxims; sententious literature.
Pomol'ogy s. Art of growing fruit; orchard-keeping.
Entomol'ogy s. The science treating of insects.
Thermol'ogy s. The science of heat.
Spermol'ogy s. Branch of botany dealing with seeds.
Miasmol'ogy s. Study of miasma, malaria, etc.
Plasmol'ogy s. Sciences of the ultimate corpuscles of organic matter.
Desmol'ogy s. Branch of anatomy dealing with ligaments, etc.

Seismol'ogy (sīzmol'-) s. Study or science of earthquakes.
Orismol'ogy s. Art or science of technical terminology.
Cosmol'ogy s. Science of the universe or the world; a treatise on this.
Micro-cosmol'ogy s. A treatise on the microcosm, or the human body.
Atmol'ogy s. Scientific study of aqueous vapour.
Etymol'ogy s. The science treating of the origin and derivation of words; the history or derivation of a word.
Zymol'ogy s. A treatise on or the theory of fermentation.
Enzymol'ogy s. The science of enzymes.
Volcanol'ogy s. Science of volcanic action.
Oceanol'ogy s. (*Oceanography*).
Organol'ogy s. The science or study of organs or organic structures.
Campanol'ogy s. Bell-ringing or founding.
Uranol'ogy s. Astronomy.
Satanol'ogy s. Study of or treatise on the devil, devil-worship, etc.
Galvanol'ogy s. The science of galvanism.
Lichenol'ogy s. Branch of botany dealing with lichens.
Phenol'ogy s. Study of recurrence of natural phenomena, climatic influence, etc.
Selenol'ogy s. The science of the moon.
Splenol'ogy s. Study of the spleen.
Menol'ogy s. A register of months; the Greek martyrology.
Phenomen-ol'ogy s. The science of phenomena.
Hymenol'ogy s. Branch of anatomy treating of membranes.
Œnol'ogy s. The study or science of wines.
Penol'ogy s. The science dealing with crime, prison management, etc.
Phrenol'ogy s. Theory that mental faculties are discoverable by the configuration of the skull.
Arachnol'ogy s. The scientific study of spiders.
Technol'ogy s. Science of or treatise on the useful arts; terminology.
Ichnol'ogy s. Classification or study of fossil footprints.
Splanchnol'ogy s. Science of or a treatise on the viscera.
Ethnol'ogy s. Science of division of mankind into races, their origin, relations, etc.
Carcinol'ogy s. The study of crustaceans.
Rhinol'ogy s. Branch of science dealing with nasal disorders.
Criminol'ogy s. The science of crime and criminals.
Terminol'ogy s. Science of correct use of words; collective technical terms of an art, etc.
Urinol'ogy s. Branch of medicine dealing with the urine, etc.
Sinol'ogy s. Knowledge and science of Chinese.
Quinol'ogy s. Science of cultivation and use of the cinchona.
Limnol'ogy s. The study of lakes, or pond life.
Hymnol'ogy s. Hymns collectively; hymns of a period or country; a treatise on hymns.
Iconol'ogy s. The science, study, or doctrine of images or emblematic representations.
Phonol'ogy s. A treatise on sounds; science of vocal sounds; phonetics.
Monol'ogy s. Habit of soliloquizing, or of monopolizing the conversation.
Demonol'ogy s. A treatise on demons.
Chronol'ogy s. Science of computing time or of assigning events to their correct dates; a list of dates.
Synchron-ol'ogy s. Comparative chronology.
Hypnol'ogy s. Study of or treatise on the phenomena of sleep.
Runol'ogy s. The science or study or runes.
Ool'ogy s. The study or science of birds' eggs.
Nool'ogy s. The science of intuition or understanding.
Zool'ogy s. Science of the natural history of animals.
Protozool'ogy s. Branch of zoology dealing with protozoa.
Apol'ogy s. A defence; an excuse, explanation; (*slang*) a poor substitute.
Anthropol'ogy s. The science of man, primitive customs, etc.
Tropol'ogy s. The use of figurative language.
Topol'ogy s. Mnemonics based on association of ideas with places.
Hippol'ogy s. The study of the horse.
Carpol'ogy s. The part of botany treating of fruits.
Typol'ogy s. Doctrine or interpretation of Scriptural types.
Barol'ogy s. Science of weight.
Timbrol'ogy s. Philately.
Ombrol'ogy s. The science or study of rainfall.
Necrol'ogy s. A register of deaths.
Microl'ogy s. Branch of science dealing with microscopic objects; hair-splitting.
Dendrol'ogy s. A treatise on or the natural history of trees.
Chondrol'ogy s. A treatise on cartilage.
Hydrol'ogy s. Science of water, its properties, laws, phenomena, distribution, etc.
Therol'ogy s. The science of mammals.
Hierol'ogy s. A body of knowledge of sacred things; hagiology.
Heterol'ogy s. Lack of correspondence between parts.
Enterol'ogy s. A treatise on the internal parts and organs.
Pterol'ogy s. Study of insects' wings.
Hysterol'ogy s. Branch of anatomy dealing with the uterus.
Hygrol'ogy s. Doctrine of the phenomena of atmospheric moisture.
Arthrol'ogy s. A treatise on the joints.
Oneirol'ogy s. The study of dreams.
Chirol'ogy s. Art of speaking on the fingers.
Orol'ogy s. (*Orography*).
Meteorol'ogy s. Science of the atmosphere and weather.
Horol'ogy s. Art of measuring time or of constructing time-pieces.
Chorol'ogy s. Science of geographical distribution of flora and fauna.
Coprol'ogy s. Lubricity, obscenity.
Iatrol'ogy s. Science of or treatise on medicine.
Electrol'ogy s. The science of electricity.
Spectrol'ogy s. Science of spectral analysis.
Petrol'ogy s. The study of the origin, classification, composition, etc., of rocks.
Astrol'ogy s. Art of foretelling events, etc., by calculations based on the position of heavenly bodies.
Gastrol'ogy s. Science dealing with the stomach and intestines; the art of cooking.
Neurol'ogy s. A description of or the scientific study of the nerves.
Pyrol'ogy s. The science of fire or heat; a treatise on this; pyritology.
Papyrol'ogy s. The study of papyri.
Martyrol'ogy s. History or catalogue of martyrs.

Misol'ogy s. Hatred of, discussion, enlightenment, or knowledge.
Nosol'ogy s. A systematic classification of diseases; branch of science treating thereof.
Psychonosol'ogy s. Science of mental disease.
Posol'ogy s. Science of doses or quantities to be administered.
Threpsol'ogy s. Science of or treatise on nutrition.
Universol'ogy s. The science dealing with the universe and its relations to mankind.
Glossol'ogy s. The science of language; explanation of technical terms.
Scatol'ogy s. Study of fossil excrement.
Eschatol'ogy s. The doctrine of the last things, as death, judgment, the future life, etc.
Hæmatol'ogy s. Branch of physiology dealing with the blood.
Sematol'ogy s. The science of signs as expressions; semasiology.
Systematol'ogy s. The science of methodical arrangement.
Climatol'ogy s. Science of or a treatise on climate.
Thremmatol'ogy s. Science of the breeding of animals or plants.
Onomatol'ogy s. Nomenclature.
Stromatol'ogy s. Science of the formation of stratified rocks.
Somatol'ogy s. Science of organic bodies or the general properties of bodies.
Symptomatol'ogy s. Science of diagnosis by symptoms.
Dermatol'ogy s. Science of the skin and skin diseases.
Thermatol'ogy s. The science of heat.
Spermatol'ogy s. Scientific study of sperm.
Numismatol'ogy s. (*Numismatics*).
Pneumatol'ogy s. Pneumatics; a treatise on this; doctrine of the Holy Spirit; science of spiritual existence.
Thanatol'ogy s. Scientific study of death.
Hepatol'ogy s. The science or study of the liver.
Geratol'ogy s. The scientific study of decadence and its phenomena.
Teratol'ogy s. Branch of biology dealing with monsters and abnormalities.
Dialectol'ogy s. The science and study of dialects.
Insectol'ogy s. (*Entomology*).
Tectol'ogy s. Structural morphology.
Cetol'ogy s. Branch of zoology treating of whales and other cetaceans.
Mycetol'ogy s. (*Mycology*).
Skeletol'ogy s. Branch of anatomy treating of the skeleton.
Cometol'ogy s. Science dealing with comets.
Herpetol'ogy s. The natural history of reptiles.
Pyretol'ogy s. Doctrine of or treatise on fevers.
Pyritol'ogy s. Science of blow-pipe analysis.
Sitol'ogy s. A treatise on diet; dietetics.
Parasitol'ogy s. The science or study of the parasites of animals or plants.
Planktol'ogy s. The science and study of plankton.
Gigantol'ogy s. An account or description of giants.
Pantol'ogy s. A work of universal information.
Ontol'ogy s. The part of metaphysics treating of the nature and essential properties and relations of all things.
Odontol'ogy s. Branch of anatomy dealing with structure and development of teeth.
Palæontol'ogy s. The science of fossil organic remains.
Deontol'ogy s. The science of that which is morally obligatory.
Neontol'ogy s. Study of living as distinct from extinct species.
Otol'ogy s. The anatomy of the ear; the science of the ear and its diseases.
Egyptol'ogy s. Study of the antiquities, etc., of ancient Egypt.
Typtol'ogy s. Spirit-rapping.
Cartol'ogy s. The science of maps.
Mastol'ogy s. The natural history of mammals.
Histol'ogy s. The science of organic tissues.
Christol'ogy s. Doctrine of the Bible respecting Christ.
Statistol'ogy s. Science of statistics.
Glottol'ogy s. (*Glossology*).
Tautol'ogy s. Repetition in different words.
Phytol'ogy s. A treatise on plants; botany.
Zoophytol'ogy (-fitol'-) s. The natural history of zoophytes.
Ovol'ogy s. Branch of science treating of the origin, etc., of eggs.
Taxol'ogy s. (*Taxonomy*).
Sexol'ogy s. Science dealing with the relationships of the sexes.
Doxol'ogy s. A short hymn of praise to God.
Ichthyol'ogy s. The science of or a natural history of fishes.
Myol'ogy s. The science dealing with the muscles.
Bryol'ogy s. The science of mosses.
Embryol'ogy s. The science of the development of embryos of animals or plants.
Eu'logy s. Speech or writing in commendation; panegyric.
Brachyl'ogy s. Concision of speech.
Leth'argy s. Unnatural sleepiness; state of apathy.
Cler'gy s. The body of ecclesiastics, ministers of the Established Church.
En'ergy s. Force, vigour, spirit, life.
Syn'ergy s. Combined action.
Or'gy s. Licentious rites; a wild or drunken revel.
Por'gy s. A N. American sea-fish.
The'urgy s. Supernatural agency; supernatural magic.
Metal'lurgy s. Art of working or smelting metals.
Zy'murgy s. Branch of chemistry dealing with fermentation.
Surg'y a. Surging; abounding in surges.
Dram'aturgy s. Art of dramatic poetry and representation.
Thau'maturgy s. Magic, wonder-working.
Lit'urgy s. Formulary of public devotions.
Syz'ygy s. Conjunction or opposition of any two heavenly bodies.
Head'achy a. Affected with or causing headache.
Beach'y a. (*Beach*).
Leach'y a. Porous; pervious.
Preach'y a. Fond of sermonizing.
Queach'y a. Giving way under the foot; marshy.
Sciam'achy s. A futile combat; a sham fight.
Theom'achy s. A warring against or between the gods.
Logom'achy s. Verbal contention; a wordy warfare.
Taurom'achy s. Bull-fighting.
Gigantom'achy s. A war of giants, especially of those against Zeus.
Nau'machy s. A naval combat or sham fight.
Poach'y a. Miry; wet and soft.
Beech'y a. (*Beech*).
Screech'y a. Characterized by screeching.
Entel'echy s. Perfection of a form or complete realization of a thing; one of the monads in Leibnitz's system.
Branch'y a. (*Branch*).
Bunch'y a. (*Bunch*).

Hunch'y a. Having a hunch.
Punch'y a. Short and thick or fat.
Xenod'ochy s. Hospitality.
The'archy s. Government by God; an order of deities.
Squire'archy s. Squires collectively; their influence.
Ol'igarchy s. Government in which all power is in the hands of a few; a state so governed.
Di'archy s. Government by two.
Chil'iarchy s. (*Chiliarch*).
Tri'archy s. Government by three.
Ma'triarchy s. Social system in which descent is traced through females, or a woman is the head of the tribe.
Pa'triarchy s. The jurisdiction of a patriarch.
Phy'larchy s. Government by a tribe; office of a phylarch.
Nom'archy s. A province of modern Greece.
An'archy s. Absence of government; lawlessness.
Mon'archy s. Government in which the supreme power is vested in a monarch; a kingdom.
Gy'narchy s. Government by a woman or by women.
Pa'parchy s. Government by a pope.
Ep'archy s. A division of modern Greece; a Russian diocese.
Top'archy s. A petty state in ancient Greece.
Hi'erarchy s. An order of sacred persons; an order of angels; ecclesiastical or priestly government.
Tri'erarchy s. Office, duty, etc., of a trierarch.
Tet'rarchy s. (*Tetrarchate*).
Pen'tarchy s. Government by five rules; a group of five states.
Hep'tarchy s. A government by seven rulers; the seven kingdoms of Anglo-Saxon Britain.
Starch'y a. Like, consisting of, or containing starch; formal, precise.
Pol'yarchy s. Government by many.
Church'y a. Fond of church forms; devoted to church-going.
Catch'y a. Easy to catch; taking.
Snatch'y a. Interrupted, spasmodic; peevish.
Patch'y a. Having patches; badly put together; unequal.
Scratch'y a. Marked or characterized by scratches; heterogenous.
Sketch'y a. Contained only in outline; incomplete.
Stretch'y a. Apt to stretch.
Tetch'y a. Fretful; touchy.
Vetch'y a. Resembling or abounding in vetches.
Itch'y a. Infected with the itch.
Pitch'y a. Dark, obscure; like pitch.
Botch'y a. (*Botch*).
Blotch'y a. (*Blotch*).
Splotch'y a. Having smears or patches; daubed.
Notch'y a. Having or resembling notches; notched.
Duch'y s. The territory or jurisdiction of a duke; a dukedom.
Archduch'y s. Jurisdiction, office, rank, or territory of an archduke.
Slouch'y a. Given to slouching; ungainly.
Pouch'y a. Having pouches; like a pouch.
Touch'y a. Irritable, apt to take offence.
Ding'hy s. A ship's smallest boat; a small row-boat.
Dough'y a. Like dough; soft.
Slough'y (slow'-) a. Boggy, miry.
Slough'y (sluf'-) a. Resembling dead tissue; scabby.
-graphy suff. Denoting the art of writing or describing, a description, a treatise, etc.
Sciag'raphy s. Art of drawing or projecting shadows as in nature; radiography.
Teleg'raphy s Art, science, or practice of the telegraph.
Callig'raphy s. Art of handwriting.
Epig'raphy s. The science and study of inscriptions.
Pasig'raphy s. Any universal system of writing.
Stratig'raphy s. Arrangement or sequence of strata; branch of geology treating of this.
Snobog'raphy s. A description of snobs.
Cacog'raphy s. Bad writing or spelling.
Pharmacog'raphy s. A description of drugs and their properties.
Lexicog'raphy s. Act or art of compiling a dictionary.
Chalcog'raphy s. Art of engraving on copper or brass.
Phycog'raphy s. Descriptive phycology.
Archæog'raphy s. A description of antiquity.
Palæog'raphy s. Art of deciphering ancient documents or inscriptions; ancient MSS. collectively.
Ideog'raphy s. A system of or treatise on ideographic or symbolical writing.
Geog'raphy s. The science of the external features of the earth; a book dealing with this.
Zoogeog'raphy s. Branch of science dealing with the distribution of animals.
Areog'raphy s. A description of Mars.
Stereog'raphy s. Art of delineating solid bodies on a plane.
Choreog'raphy s. Art of dancing or arranging ballets.
Museog'raphy s. Art of describing or cataloguing museums.
Osteog'raphy s. Descriptive osteology.
Logog'raphy s. Method of printing from whole words cast in type.
Psychog'raphy s. Spirit-writing.
Morphog'raphy s. Descriptive morphology.
Glyphog'raphy s. A process of relief line engraving by electrotyping.
Lithog'raphy s. Art of drawing, especially in colour, on stone, and producing impressions therefrom.
Chromolithog'raphy s. (*Chromolithograph*).
Orthog'raphy s. Part of grammar dealing with letters and word; correct spelling.
Mythog'raphy s. Descriptive mythology; expression of myth in art.
Biog'raphy s. An account of a person's life.
Autobiog'raphy s. An account of one's life written by oneself.
Radiog'raphy s. Art or system of taking radiographs.
Cardiog'raphy s. A description of the heart.
Semeiog'raphy s. Description of the symptoms of disease.
Hagiog'raphy s. Biography, or collection of lives, of saints.
Ophiog'raphy s. A treatise on snakes.
Bibliog'raphy s. The scientific study of books, editions, typography, etc.
Dactyliog'raphy s. Art of engraving gems.
Historiog'raphy s. Art or employment of a historiographer.
Ecclesiog'raphy s. History of a Church or Churches

Heresiog'raphy s. A treatise on heretics.
Physiog'raphy s. Science of the earth's physical features; physical geography.
Hyalog'raphy s. Etching on glass.
Metallog'raphy s. The science of metals.
Crystallog'raphy s. Science which deals with the formation and forms of crystals.
Sigillog'raphy s. The study of seals in wax.
Haplog'raphy s. Inadvertent writing of a syllable, etc., once only instead of twice.
Pterylog'raphy s. Pterylosis; a treatise on this.
Demog'raphy s. Science dealing with conditions of a people.
Sphyg'mography s. Science or method of recording the beats of the pulse.
Psalmog'raphy s. Act or practice of writing psalms.
Nomog'raphy s. The art of drafting laws; a treatise on this.
Desmog'raphy s. A description of the ligaments.
Cosmog'raphy s. A description or delineation of the world or universe.
Microcosmog'raphy s. Description of man as a microcosm.
Oceanog'raphy s. Science dealing with the divisions and physical phenomena of the ocean.
Steganog'raphy s. Art of writing in cipher.
Organog'raphy s. Description of organs of animals and plants.
Mechanog'raphy s. Art of mechanically reproducing works of art, etc.
Uranog'raphy s. Descriptive astronomy.
Scenog'raphy s. Representation of a body in perspective.
Lichenog'raphy s. A description of or treatise on lichens.
Sphenog'raphy s. Art of deciphering or writing in cuneiform characters.
Selenog'raphy s. A description or the geography of the moon.
Hymenog'raphy s. A description of membranes.
Stenog'raphy s. Art of writing in shorthand.
Ichnog'raphy s. Art of drawing ground-plans.
Splanchnog'raphy s. Descriptive splanchnology.
Ethnog'raphy s. Description of races, with their characteristics, manners, etc.
Hymnog'raphy s. Art of writing hymns; hymnology.
Iconog'raphy s. Discription of ancient paintings, statues, engravings, etc.
Phonog'raphy s. Automatic recording and reproduction of sounds; art of constructing or using the phonograph; Pitman's system of shorthand.
Chronog'raphy s. An account of past events.
Pornog'raphy s. Writings dealing with prostitutes; obscene literature.
Zoog'raphy s. A description of animals.
Lipog'raphy s. Omission of a letter or syllable in writing.
Anthropog'raphy s. Ethnography.
Topog'raphy s. Description of particular localities.
Typog'raphy s. The art of printing.
Ectypog'raphy s. A mode of etching in relief.
Heliotypog'raphy s. A process of photo-engraving.
Phototypog'raphy s. A process of photo-engraving.
Rhyparog'raphy s. The painting or depiction of unworthy or squalid subjects.
Microg'raphy s. A description of microscopic objects.
Photomicrog'raphy s. Art of making enlarged photographs of microscopic objects.
Chondrog'raphy s. A treatise on cartilage.
Hydrog'raphy s. Art of measuring, mapping, describing, etc., seas, lakes, rivers, etc., with their physical features.
Cerog'raphy s. Art of drawing or painting on wax.
Siderog'raphy s. Art or process of engraving upon steel.
Hierog'raphy s. A treatise on religion.
Heterog'raphy s. Incorrect spelling; employment of one letter to represent different sounds.
Pterog'raphy s. Science of plumage.
Chirog'raphy s. Art of writing or engrossing; handwriting.
Orog'raphy s. Physical geography dealing with mountains.
Horog'raphy s. Art of making clocks, etc.
Chorog'raphy s. Art of map-making or of topographical description; topography.
Petrog'raphy s. Description and classification of rocks.
Pyrog'raphy s. Poker-work.
Xylopyrog'raphy s. Poker-work.
Nosog'raphy s. A description or classification of diseases.
Gypsog'raphy s. Act or art of engraving on gypsum.
Hypsog'raphy s. Branch of geography dealing with altitudes above sea-level.
Thalassog'raphy s. Oceanography.
Glossog'raphy s. The writing of glosses; a treatise on the tongue.
Cinematog'raphy s. (*Cinematograph*).
Sematog'raphy s. Use of signs, etc., instead of letters.
Toreumatog'raphy s. Treatise on the embossing, chasing, etc., of metal.
Stratog'raphy s. Description of an army and things pertaining thereto.
Skeletog'raphy s. Science of describing the skeleton.
Cometog'raphy s. A description of comets.
Hyetog'raphy s. Branch of meteorology concerned with rainfall.
Odontog'raphy s. The description of the teeth.
Palæontog'raphy s. Descriptive palæontology.
Otog'raphy s. Descriptive otology.
Photog'raphy s. Art or practice of producing pictures by action of light on chemically prepared plates, etc.
Telephotog'raphy s. Art or practice of photographing objects from a great distance.
Glyptog'raphy s. The art of engraving on gems.
Cryptog'raphy s. Art of secret writing; cipher.
Cartog'raphy s. Science or art of map-making.
Histog'raphy s. Description of or treatise on organic tissues.
Autog'raphy s. One's own handwriting; a process of reproducing writing, etc., in facsimile.
Phytog'raphy s. Systematic description of plants.
Ichthyog'raphy s. Description of or treatise on fishes.
Myog'raphy s. A description of the muscles.
Tachyg'raphy s. Shorthand.
Polyg'raphy s. Art of producing several copies of a writing, etc.
-trophy suff. Denoting growth or nutrition.
Tro'phy s. Something gained by conquest; a memorial of victory.
At'rophy s. A wasting; cessation of development. v.i. and t. To waste, be checked.
Heterot'rophy s. Abnormal mode of obtaining nourishment.
Hyper'trophy s. Morbid overgrowth of an organ.

Pan'sophy s. Universal knowledge; a scheme of this.
Theos'ophy s. Intercourse with God and spirits; divine knowledge obtained through spiritual ecstasy; a system of mysticism.
Philos'ophy s. Knowledge of phenomena; science that tries to account for these; metaphysics; ethics; logic; wisdom.
Gymnos'ophy s. The beliefs, doctrines, or practices of the gymnosophists.
Gastros'ophy s. Gastronomy.
Heteromor'phy s. Quality of being heteromorphic.
Mur'phy s. (*Slang*) A potato.
Dactyliog'lyphy s. The engraving of rings, gems, etc.
Shy a. Timid, reserved; suspicious; elusive. v.i. To start suddenly aside. v.t. To fling (a ball, etc.). s. Act of flinging.
Ash'y a. Ashen; pallid.
Dash'y a. Smart, ostentatious.
Flash'y a. Momentarily dazzling; gaudy.
Plash'y a. Abounding with puddles; splashy.
Splash'y a. Wet and muddy.
Brash'y a. Crumbly.
Trash'y a. Rubbishy, worthless.
Wash'y a. Watery, diluted, feeble.
Wish'y-wash'y a. Diluted; without force.
Flesh'y a. Plump; succulent; pulpy.
Mesh'y a. (*Mesh*).
Rub'bishy a. Trashy; nonsensical.
Fish'y a. Like, consisting of, or pertaining to fish; (*slang*) dubious; seedy.
Flour'ishy a. Having flourishes; flourishing.
Cock'shy s. A mark at which anything is thrown.
Marsh'y a. Abounding in or produced in marshes; boggy.
Bush'y a. (*Bush*).
Cush'y a. (*Slang*) Easy; comfortable.
Gush'y a. Characterized by gush or display of affection.
Lush'y a. (*Slang*) Half-drunk.
Plush'y a. Like or consisting of plush.
Slush'y a. Muddy, dirty; highly sentimental.
Rush'y a. Abounding with or made of rushes.
Brush'y a. Like a brush; covered with brushwood.
Bul'rushy a. (*Bulrush*).
Thy pron. and a. Pertaining to thee.
Heath'y a. Covered with or resembling heath.
Breath'y a. Aspirated with the sound of breathing.
Lath'y a. Thin as a lath; made of laths.
Chrestom'athy s. A selection of literary extracts.
Polym'athy s. Knowledge of many arts and sciences.
-pathy suff. Expressing feeling, or denoting disease or its treatment.
Ap'athy s. Indifference, unconcern.
Telep'athy s. Thought transference.
Somnip'athy s. Hypnotic sleep.
Kinesip'athy s. Treatment of disease by muscular or gymnastic exercise.
Antip'athy s. A strong aversion or dislike.
Sym'pathy s. Fellow feeling; compassion.
Leucop'athy s. Albinism.
Theop'athy s. Emotion excited by contemplation of God.
Homœop'athy s. System of curing diseases by producing similar symptoms in the patient.
Osteop'athy s. A system of treating disease, etc., by manipulation.
Trichop'athy s. Any disease of the hair.
Psychop'athy s. Science of insanity.
Idiop'athy s. A disease not occasioned by another.
Allop'athy s. The ordinary practice of medicine as opposed to homœopathy.
Hydrop'athy s. A mode of treating diseases by use of pure water.
Heterop'athy s. Allopathy.
Enterop'athy s. Disease of the intestines.
Elec'tropathy s. Treatment of disease by electricity.
Neurop'athy s. Any nervous disease.
Dipsop'athy s. Treatment of dipsomania by enforced abstinence.
Wrath'y a. Wrath; very angry.
Length'y a. Somewhat long; prolix.
Smith'y s. A blacksmith's shop.
Pith'y a. Consisting of or abounding in pith; energetic; forcible and appropriate.
Stith'y s. A forge, smithy, anvil.
With'y s. A withe, osier band; a willow.
Health'y a. Enjoying good health; sound; salubrious; wholesome.
Unhealth'y a. Sickly; insalubrious.
Stealth'y (stelth'-) a. Furtive; sly.
Wealth'y a. Rich; affluent; having wealth.
Fil'thy a. Dirty, foul, obscene; abounding in filth.
Both'y s. A hut, hovel.
Moth'y a. Moth-eaten; full of moths.
Tim'othy s. A species of fodder-grass.
Tooth'y a. Toothsome, palatable.
Froth'y a. Full of foam; vain, trifling.
Earth'y a. Consisting of or resembling earth; material; cold and lifeless.
Swar'thy a. Being of a dark hue; dark of complexion.
Wor'thy (wer'-) a. Possessing worth; equal in excellence, etc., to; deserving; virtuous; suitable. s. An eminent person.
Sea'worthy a. Fit for a voyage, or for transporting cargo.
Blame'worthy a. Deserving of censure.
Praise'worthy a. Commendable.
Note'worthy a. Deserving notice, worthy of observation.
Un'worthy a. Not deserving; mean; not suitable.
Trust'worthy a. Deserving trust; trusty.
Mou'thy a. Talkative; bombastic.
Drouth'y a. (*Drouth*).
Why adv., interrog. For what purpose, reason, etc.? s. The reason, etc., of anything. int. Expressing surprise, etc.
Ca'ky a. (*Cake*).
Leak'y a. Having a leak.
Sneak'y a. Mean; underhand.
Peak'y a. Peaked; looking sickly.
Creak'y a. (*Creak*).
Streak'y a. Marked with streaks.
Squeak'y a. Squeaking; like a squeak.
Shak'y a. Trembling, tremulous, tottering; unsound; feeble.
La'ky a. Abounding in lakes.
Fla'ky a. Consisting of or like flakes.
Sna'ky a. Resembling a snake, serpentine; sly, insinuating.
Croak'y a. Hoarse, croaking.
Bra'ky a. (*Brake*).
Qua'ky a. Trembling; shaky.
Black'y s. A blackamoor.
Knack'y a. Dexterous, adroit, neat.
Gim'cracky a. Like gimcracks, unsubstantial.
Tack'y a. Sticky.
Speck'y a. Having or marked with specks.

Dick'y s. A back-seat for footmen in a carriage; a driver's box; a false shirt-front; a bird. a. Queer, not well; doubtful, shaky.
Col'icky a. (*Colic*).
Gar'licky a. Like or tasting of garlic.
Pan'icky a. Characterized by or subject to panic; groundlessly fearful.
Fin'icky adv. Finical.
Brick'y a. (*Brick*).
Trick'y a. Given to tricks; knavish.
Phys'icky a. Resembling physic.
Stick'y a. Adhesive; tenacious; glutinous.
Cock'y a. Pert, saucy, impudent.
Flock'y a. Resembling or abounding in flock or flocks.
Hill'ocky a. (*Hillock*).
Hum'mocky a. Abounding in hummocks.
Pock'y a. Full of pocks; infected with small-pox.
Rock'y a. Abounding with rocks; resembling rock; rugged; tottering, fragile.
Tus'socky a. Abounding in tussocks.
Stock'y a. Thick-set; stumpy.
Luck'y a. Favoured by fortune; bringing luck; auspicious; (*Scot.*) an elderly woman.
Pluck'y a. Indomitable, resolute, spirited.
Muck'y a. Filthy; nasty; messy.
Cheek'y a. Impudent, saucy.
Sleek'y a. Sleek.
Reek'y a. Smoky; foul.
Drosh'ky s. A four-wheeled Russian carriage.
Spi'ky a. Set with spikes; like a spike.
Balk'y a. Given to swerving (of a horse).
Chalk'y a. Like or containing chalk.
Stalk'y a. Resembling or well supplied with stalk.
Milk'y a. Like, consisting of, yielding, or mixed with milk; opaque; mild.
Silk'y a. Soft and smooth; silk-like; silken.
Bulk'y a. (*Bulk*).
Sulk'y a. Sullen, obstinately morose. s. A light two-wheeled carriage for one.
Lank'y a. Long and thin; loose.
Hank'y-pank'y s. Trickery; fraud.
Crank'y a. Liable to be overset; shaky; crotchety, faddy.
Prank'y a. Full of pranks.
Swank'y a. (*Slang*) Swaggering; tip-top.
Ink'y a. Of the nature of, resembling, or daubed with ink.
Dink'y a. (*Slang*) Dainty, nice.
Kink'y a. Full of kinks; characterized by whims.
Pink'y a. Pinkish.
Zink'y a. Pertaining to or resembling zinc.
Funk'y a. Frightened, terrified; cowardly.
Chunk'y a. (*Chunk*).
Spunk'y a. Spirited, plucky.
Jo'ky a. Given to joking.
Smo'ky a. Emitting, resembling, or filled with smoke; clouded.
Nook'y a. Having nooks; like a nook.
Spoo'ky a. Ghost-like; full of ghosts.
Rook'y a. Inhabited by rooks.
Brook'y a. (*Brook*).
Po'ky a. Stuffy; poor, mean.
Bark'y a. Resembling or covered with bark.
Dark'y s. A negro.
Lark'y a. Larkish.
Park'y a. (*Slang*) Cold, chilly.
Jerk'y a. Moving by jerks.
Perk'y a. Pert; smart; saucy; jaunty.
Quirk'y a. Quirkish.
Cork'y a. Consisting of, like, or tasting of cork; (*slang*) lively, skittish.
Fork'y a. Forked, fork-like.
Pork'y a. Like pork; stout, fleshy.
Murk'y a. Gloomy, thick, obscure.
Sky s. The apparent vault of heaven; a climate. v.t. To hit high in the air, hang high on a wall.
Pes'ky a. Mischievous, troublesome.
Whis'ky s. An ardent spirituous liquor; a light, one-horse gig.
Risk'y a. Hazardous; risqué.
Frisk'y a. Frolicsome.
Ensky' v.t. To place among the gods, make immortal.
Bosk'y a. Woody, covered with undergrowth; (*slang*) fuddled with drink.
Dusk'y a. Somewhat dark or obscure; dusk; swarthy.
Husk'y a. Abounding in or like husks; rough in tone; hoarse. s. An Eskimo; an Indian sledge-dog.
Musk'y a. Having the odour of musk; fragrant.
Tusk'y a. Having tusks.
Flu'ky a. Infested with flukes; scoring by accident.
Gawk'y a. Awkward, clumsy, clownish. s. A stupid, awkward lout.
Hawk'y s. A cow with a white face.
Pawk'y a. Slyly humorous.
-ly suff. Forming adverbs and adjectives.
Sca'ly a. Covered with, abounding in, or like scales; rough.
Meal'y a. Containing or resembling meal; floury, farinaceous; spotty; hypocritical.
Brachy-ceph'aly s. Brachycephalism.
Sha'ly a. Resembling or pertaining to shale.
Anom'aly s. Irregularity; deviation from rule or normal.
Coal'y a. Like or pertaining to coal; black.
Shoal'y a. Having shoals or shallows; shallow.
Pa'ly a. Divided by a pale (of heraldic shields).
Wa'ly int. A cry of sorrow; "Welladay."
A'bly adv. (*Able*).
Indescrib'ably adv. (*Indescribable*).
Prob'ably adv. Likely; in likelihood.
Improb'ably adv. (*Improbable*).
Imperturb'ably adv. (*Imperturbable*).
Plac'ably adv. (*Placable*).
Implac'ably adv. (*Implacable*).
Impec'cably adv. (*Impeccable*).
Inerad'icably adv. (*Ineradicable*).
Inap'plicably adv. (*Inapplicable*).
Inex'plicably adv. (*Inexplicable*).
Am'icably adv. (*Amicable*).
Commun'-icably adv. (*Communicable*).
Incommu'-nicably adv. (*Incommunicable*)
Des'picably adv. (*Despicable*).
Inex'tricably adv. (*Inextricable*).
Prac'ticably adv. (*Practicable*).
Imprac'ticably adv. (*Impracticable*).
Irrev'ocably adv. (*Irrevocable*).
Read'ably adv. (*Readable*).
For'midably adv. (*Formidable*).
Avoid'ably adv. (*Avoidable*).
Commend'ably adv. (*Commendable*).
Depend'ably adv. (*Dependable*).
Laud'ably adv. (*Laudable*).
Peace'ably adv. (*Peaceable*).
Ineffacе'ably adv. (*Ineffaceable*).
Trace'ably adv. (*Traceable*).
No'ticeably adv. (*Noticeable*).

Ser'viceably adv. (*Serviceable*).
Agree'ably adv. (*Agreeable*).
Disagree'ably adv. (*Disagreeable*).
Man'ageably adv. (*Manageable*).
Chan'geably adv. (*Changeable*).
Interchange'-ably adv. (*Interchangeable*).
Charge'ably adv. (*Chargeable*).
Blame'ably adv. (*Blameable*).
Per'meably adv. (*Permeable*).
Imper'meably adv. (*Impermeable*).
Af'fably adv. (*Affable*).
Ineff'ably adv. (*Ineffable*).
Irrefrag'ably adv. (*Irrefragable*).
Indefat'igably adv. (*Indefatigable*).
Immit'igably adv. (*Immitigable*).
Nav'igably adv. (*Navigable*).
Innav'igably adv. (*Innavigable*).
Irreproach'-ably adv. (*Irreproachable*).
Inapproach'-ably adv. (*Inapproachable*).
Laugh'ably adv. (*Laughable*).
Per'ishably adv. (*Perishable*).
Imper'ishably adv. (*Imperishable*).
Disting'-uishably adv. (*Distinguishable*).
Indisting'-uishably adv. (*Indistinguishable*).
Inexting'-uishably adv. (*Inextinguishable*).
Appre'ciably adv. (*Appreciable*).
Inappre'ciably adv. (*Inappreciable*).
So'ciably adv. (*Sociable*).
Reme'diably adv. (*Remediable*).
Irreme'diably adv. (*Irremediable*).
Identifi'ably adv. (*Identifiable*).
Justifi'ably adv. (*Justifiable*).
Reli'ably adv. (*Reliable*).
Pli'ably adv. (*Pliable*).
A'miably adv. (*Amiable*).
Inex'piably adv. (*Inexpiable*).
Var'iably adv. (*Variable*).
Invar'iably adv. Uniformly.
Pit'iably adv. (*Pitiable*).
En'viably adv. (*Enviable*).
Mistak'ably adv. (*Mistakable*).
Remark'ably adv. (*Remarkable*).
Irrepeal'ably adv. (*Irrepealable*).
Avail'ably adv. (*Available*).
Irreconcil'ably adv. (*Irreconcilable*).
Incontroll'ably adv. Not controllably.
Invi'olably adv. (*Inviolable*).
Inconso'lably adv. (*Inconsolable*).
Incal'culably adv. (*Incalculable*).
Irredeem'ably adv. (*Irredeemable*).
Reclaim'ably adv. (*Reclaimable*).
Irreclaim'ably adv. (*Irreclaimable*).
Ines'timably adv. (*Inestimable*).
Inflam'mably adv. (*Inflammable*).
Conform'ably adv. (*Conformable*).
Presum'ably adv. (*Presumable*).
Inconsu'm-ably adv. (*Inconsumable*).
Ina'lienably adv. (*Inalienable*).
Ame'nably adv. (*Amenable*).
Impreg'nably adv. (*Impregnable*).
Inexpug'nably adv. (*Inexpugnable*).
Defin'ably adv. (*Definable*).
Indefin'ably adv. (*Indefinable*).
Imag'inably adv. (*Imaginable*).
Indeclin'ably adv. (*Indeclinable*).
Abom'inably adv. (*Abominable*).
Indeter'-minably adv. (*Indeterminable*).
Inter'minably adv. (*Interminable*).
Dam'nably adv. (*Damnable*).
Par'donably adv. (*Pardonable*).
Con'scionably adv. (*Conscionable*).
Uncon'-scionably adv. (*Unconscionable*).
Fash'ionably adv. (*Fashionable*).
Compan'-ionably adv. (*Companionable*).
Ac'tionably adv. (*Actionable*).
Objec'tionably adv. (*Objectionable*).
Dispropor'-tionably adv. (*Disproportion*).
Quest'ionably adv. (*Questionable*).
Rea'sonably adv. (*Reasonable*).
Trea'sonably adv. (*Treasonable*).
Sea'sonably adv. (*Seasonable*).
Gov'ernably adv. (*Governable*).
Tun'ably adv. (*Tunable*).
Ca'pably adv. (*Capable*).
Inca'pably adv. (*Incapable*).
Pal'pably adv. (*Palpable*).
Impal'pably adv. (*Impalpable*).
Cul'pably adv. (*Culpable*).
Bear'ably adv. (*Bearable*).
Irrep'arably adv. (*Irreparable*).
Sep'arably adv. (*Separable*).
Insep'arably adv. (*Inseparable*).
Com'parably adv. (*Comparable*).
Incom'parably adv. (*Incomparable*).
Ex'ecrably adv. (*Execrable*).
Drab'ly adv. In a dull, commonplace manner; monotonously.
Consid'erably adv. (*Considerable*).
Inconsid'erably adv. (*Inconsiderable*).
Pref'erably adv. By choice ; rather.
Suf'ferably adv. (*Sufferable*).
Insuf'ferably adv. (*Insufferable*).
Tol'erably adv. (*Tolerable*).
Intol'erably adv. (*Intolerable*).
Innu'merably adv. (*Innumerable*).
Ven'erably adv. (*Venerable*).
Invul'nerably adv. (*Invulnerable*).
Su'perably adv. (*Superable*).
Insu'perably adv. (*Insuperable*).
Mis'erably adv. (*Miserable*).
Insev'erably adv. (*Inseverable*).
Irrecov'erably adv. (*Irrecoverable*).
An'swerably adv. (*Answerable*).
Ad'mirably adv. (*Admirable*).
Desir'ably adv. (*Desirable*).
Ador'ably adv. (*Adorable*).
Deplor'ably adv. (*Deplorable*).
Mem'orably adv. (*Memorable*).
Inex'orably adv. (*Inexorable*).
Inerr'ably adv. (*Inerrable*).
Pen'etrably adv. (*Penetrable*).
Impen'etrably adv. (*Impenetrable*).
Demon'strably adv. (*Demonstrable*).
Incur'ably adv. (*Incurable*).
Dur'ably adv. (*Durable*).
Per'durably adv. (*Perdurable*).
Col'ourably adv. (*Colourable*).
Hon'ourably adv. (*Honourable*).
Dishon'ourably adv. (*Dishonourable*).
Fa'vourably adv. (*Favourable*).
Pleas'urably adv. (*Pleasurable*).
Meas'urably adv. (*Measurable*).
Immeas'urably adv. (*Immeasurable*).
Censurably adv. (*Censurable*).
Commen'-surably adv. (*Commensurable*).
Incommen'-surably adv. (*Incommensurable*).
Conjec'turably adv. (*Conjecturable*).
Advi'sably adv. (*Advisable*).
Indispen'sably adv. (*Indispensable*).
Convers'ably adv. (*Conversable*).
Pass'ably adv. (*Passable*).
Impass'ably adv. (*Impassable*).
Excus'ably adv. (*Excusable*).
Inexcus'ably adv. (*Inexcusable*).
Rat'ably adv. Proportionally.

Tract'ably adv. (*Tractable*).
Intrac'tably adv. (*Intractable*).
Delect'ably adv. (*Delectable*).
Respect'ably adv. In a manner to merit respect.
Indict'ably (-dit'-) adv. (*Indictable*).
Mar'ketably adv. (*Marketable*).
Hab'itably adv. (*Habitable*).
Indu'bitably adv. (*Indubitable*).
Cred'itably adv. (*Creditable*).
Discred'itably adv. (*Discreditable*).
Hered'itably adv. (*Hereditable*).
Prof'itably adv. (*Profitable*).
Illim'itably adv. (*Illimitable*).
Inim'itably adv. (*Inimitable*).
Indom'itably adv. (*Indomitable*).
Hos'pitably adv. (*Hospitable*).
Inhos'pitably adv. (*Inhospitable*).
Char'itably adv. (*Charitable*).
Her'itably adv. By inheritance.
Inher'itably adv. (*Inheritable*).
Ver'itably adv. (*Veritable*).
Ir'ritably adv. (*Irritable*).
Ineq'uitably adv. (*Inequitable*).
Suit'ably adv. (*Suitable*).
Inev'itably adv. (*Inevitable*).
War'rantably (wor'-) adv. (*Warrantable*).
Lam'entably adv. (*Lamentable*).
Present'ably adv. (*Presentable*).
Prevent'ably adv. (*Preventable*).
Insurmount'ably adv. (*Insurmountable*).
Not'ably adv. (*Notable*).
Quot'ably adv. (*Quotable*).
Accep'tably adv. (*Acceptable*).
Com'fortably adv. (*Comfortable*).
Insupport'ably adv. (*Insupportable*).
Stabl'y adv. (*Stable*).
Detest'ably adv. (*Detestable*).
Incontest'ably adv. (*Incontestable*).
Regrett'ably adv. (*Regrettable*).
Irref'utably adv. (*Irrefutable*).
Mut'ably adv. (*Mutable*).
Immut'ably adv. (*Immutable*).
Incommut'ably adv. (*Incommutable*).
Permut'ably adv. (*Permutable*).
Transmut'ably adv. (*Transmutable*).
Rep'utably adv. (*Reputable*).
Disrep'utably adv. (*Disreputable*).
Imput'ably adv. (*Imputable*).
Disput'ably adv. (*Disputable*).
Indis'putably adv. (*Indisputable*).
Inscrut'ably adv. (*Inscrutable*).
Stat'utably adv. (*Statutable*).
Val'uably adv. (*Valuable*).
Inval'uably adv. (*Invaluable*).
Conceiv'ably adv. (*Conceivable*).
Inconceiv'ably adv. (*Inconceivable*).
Perceiv'ably adv. (*Perceivable*).
Believ'ably adv. (*Believable*).
Irretriev'ably adv. (*Irretrievable*).
Lov'ably adv. (*Lovable*).
Irremov'ably adv. (*Irremovable*).
Immov'ably adv. (*Immovable*).
Observ'ably adv. (*Observable*).
Allow'ably adv. (*Allowable*).
Tax'ably adv. (*Taxable*).
Enjoy'ably adv. (*Enjoyable*).
Cogn'izably adv. (*Cognizable*).
Pebbl'y a. Full of or like pebbles.
Hobbl'y a. Causing to hobble; rough, uneven.
Bubbl'y s. (*Slang*) Champagne. a. Characterized by bubbles or bubbling.
Nubbl'y a. Having or characterized by nubs or nubbles.
Rubbl'y a. Consisting of or like rubble.
Stubbl'y a. Bristly; covered with stubble.
Fee'bly adv. Weakly; without strength.
Trebl'y adv. (*Treble*).
Invin'cibly adv. (*Invincible*).
For'cibly adv. (*Forcible*).
Iras'cibly adv. (*Irascible*).
Immis'cibly adv. (*Immiscible*).
Cred'ibly adv. (*Credible*).
Incred'ibly adv. (*Incredible*).
Ven'dibly adv. (*Vendible*).
Au'dibly adv. (*Audible*).
Inau'dibly adv. (*Inaudible*).
Leg'ibly adv. (*Legible*).
Illeg'ibly adv. Unreadably.
El'igibly adv. (*Eligible*).
Inel'igibly adv. (*Ineligible*).
Intel'ligibly adv. (*Intelligible*).
Incor'rigibly adv. (*Incorrigible*).
Infran'gibly adv. (*Infrangible*).
Tan'gibly adv. (*Tangible*).
Intan'gibly adv. (*Intangible*).
Indel'ibly adv. (*Indelible*).
Glib'ly adv. (*Glib*).
Fal'libly adv. (*Fallible*).
Infal'libly adv. (*Infallible*).
Discern'ibly adv. (*Discernible*).
Indiscern'ibly adv. (*Indiscernibly*).
Ter'ribly adv. (*Terrible*).
Hor'ribly adv. (*Horrible*).
Feas'ibly adv. Practicably.
Indefeas'ibly adv. (*Indefeasible*).
Ris'ibly adv. (*Risible*).
Vis'ibly adv. (*Visible*).
Invis'ibly adv. (*Invisible*).
Defen'sibly adv. (*Defensible*).
Indefen'sibly adv. (*Indefensible*).
Reprehen'sibly adv. (*Reprehensible*).
Comprehen'sibly adv. (*Comprehensible*).
Incomprehen'sibly adv. (*Incomprehensible*).
Sens'ibly adv. (*Sensible*).
Insens'ibly adv. (*Insensible*).
Ostens'ibly adv. (*Ostensible*).
Respons'ibly adv. (*Responsible*).
Irrespons'ibly adv. (*Irresponsible*).
Irrevers'ibly adv. (*Irreversible*).
Impas'sibly adv. (*Impassible*).
Acces'sibly adv. (*Accessible*).
Inacces'sibly adv. (*Inaccessible*).
Irrepres'sibly adv. (*Irrepressible*).
Impres'sibly adv. (*Impressible*).
Inexpres'sibly adv. (*Inexpressible*).
Admis'sibly adv. (*Admissible*).
Irremis'sibly adv. Unpardonably.
Permis'sibly adv. (*Permissible*).
Pos'sibly adv. By any power; perhaps; in a possible manner.
Impos'sibly adv. (*Impossible*).
Plau'sibly adv. (*Plausible*).
Compat'ibly adv. (*Compatible*).
Incompat'ibly adv. (*Incompatible*).
Indestruct'ibly adv. (*Indestructible*).
Percep'tibly adv. (*Perceptible*).
Impercep'tibly adv. (*Imperceptible*).
Suscep'tibly adv. (*Susceptible*).
Contemp'tibly adv. (*Contemptible*).
Corrup'tibly adv. (*Corruptible*).
Incorrup'tibly adv. (*Incorruptible*).
Conver'tibly adv. (*Convertible*).
Inconver'tibly adv. (*Inconvertible*).
Controver'tibly adv. (*Controvertible*).
Incontrover'tibly adv. (*Incontrovertible*).
Digest'ibly adv. (*Digestible*).
Irresist'ibly adv. (*Irresistible*).
Inexhaust'ibly adv. (*Inexhaustible*).
Incombust'ibly adv. (*Incombustible*).
Flex'ibly adv. In a flexible manner.

Inflex'ibly adv. (*Inflexible*).
Brambl'y a. (*Bramble*).
Trembl'y a. Given to trembling; fearsome.
Assem'bly s. A company collected together; a group.
Nim'bly adv. (*Nimble*).
Dumb'ly adv. (*Dumb*).
Hum'bly adv. (*Humble*).
Jum'bly a. Confused, mixed up.
Numb'ly adv. (*Numb*).
Rum'bly a. Rumbling.
Crum'bly a. Easily crumbled.
Tum'bly a. Inclined to tumble; tottery.
No'bly adv. (*Noble*).
Igno'bly adv. (*Ignoble*).
Superb'ly adv. (*Superb*).
Insol'ubly adv. (*Insoluble*).
Indis'solubly adv. (*Indissoluble*).
Vol'ubly adv. (*Voluble*).
Doub'ly a. In twice the quantity, strength, etc.
Cly v.t. To seize, steal. s. Anything stolen.
Treacl'y a. Like or covered with treacle.
Pub'licly adv. Without concealment.
Polit'icly adv. Artfully, with subtlety.
Impolit'icly adv. (*Impolitic*).
Fran'ticly adv. (*Frantic*).
Bad'ly adv. (*Bad*).
Dead'ly a. Destructive, fatal, implacable. adv. As if dead; mortally; excessively.
Glad'ly adv. (*Glad*).
Mad'ly adv. (*Mad*).
Broad'ly adv. (*Broad*).
Sad'ly adv. (*Sad*).
Twaddl'y a. Given to twaddling or vain tattle.
Odd'ly adv. (*Odd*).
Pud'dly a. Full of puddles.
Crab'bedly adv. (*Crabbed*).
Shamefa'cedly adv. (*Shamefaced*).
Barefa'cedly adv. (*Barefaced*).
Pronoun'cedly adv. In a marked manner or degree.
For'cedly adv. (*Forced*).
Enfor'cedly adv. (*Enforced*).
Pig-head'edly adv. (*Pig-headed*).
Jad'edly adv. (*Jaded*).
Decid'edly adv. (*Decided*).
Misguid'edly adv. (*Misguided*).
Inten'dedly adv. With intent.
Confound'edly adv. (*Confounded*).
Guard'edly adv. In a cautious or circumspect manner.
Needl'y a. Resembling or pertaining to a needle.
Jag'gedly adv. (*Jagged*).
Rag'gedly adv. (*Ragged*).
Dog'gedly adv. Pertinaciously.
Rug'gedly adv. (*Rugged*).
Detach'edly adv. (*Detached*).
Starch'edly adv. (*Starched*).
Wretch'edly adv. (*Wretched*).
Impli'edly adv. (*Implied*).
Hur'riedly adv. (*Hurried*).
Fren'ziedly adv. (*Frenzied*).
Na'kedly adv. (*Naked*).
Wick'edly adv. (*Wicked*).
Crook'edly adv. (*Crooked*).
Mark'edly adv. (*Marked*).
Asham'edly adv. (*Ashamed*).
Consum'edly adv. Unrestrainedly.
Assum'edly adv. Taken for granted.
Feign'edly adv. In a simulated way, in pretence.
Design'edly adv. Intentionally.
Resign'edly adv. (*Resigned*).
Restrain'edly adv. With restraint or limitation.
Constrain'edly adv. (*Constrained*).
Refin'edly adv. In a refined manner; with affected delicacy.
Deter'minedly adv. (*Determined*).
Learn'edly adv. In a learned manner; with much erudition.
Concern'edly adv. (*Concerned*).
Red'ly adv. (*Red*).
Declar'edly adv. Avowedly, explicitly.
Sa'credly adv. (*Sacred*).
Assur'edly adv. With confidence; safely.
Pleas'edly adv. In a pleased or gratified manner.
Advi'sedly adv. With deliberation.
Compo'sedly adv. (*Composed*).
Suppo'sedly adv. In an imagined way; as accepted as true.
Cur'sedly adv. (*Cursed*).
Confes'sedly adv. By confession, avowedly.
Profes'sedly adv. By avowal.
Diffu'sedly adv. In a diffused or scattered manner.
Confu'sedly adv. In a confused manner.
Heat'edly adv. Excitedly.
Repeat'edly adv. Many times; over and over again.
Animat'edly adv. (*Animated*).
Undoubt'edly adv. Without doubt or question; indubitably.
Compact'edly adv. (*Compacted*).
Abstract'edly adv. In an absent-minded or inattentive way.
Distract'edly adv. (*Distracted*).
Affect'edly adv. (*Affected*).
Deject'edly adv. In a dejected manner.
Collect'edly adv. (*Collected*).
Connect'edly adv. (*Connected*).
Disconnect'edly adv. (*Disconnected*).
Delight'edly adv. (*Delighted*).
Affright'edly adv. In a terrified manner.
Conceit'edly adv. (*Conceited*).
Unit'edly adv. With union or combined effort.
Dement'edly adv. (*Demented*).
Content'edly adv. (*Contented*).
Discontent'edly adv. (*Discontented*).
Joint'edly adv. (*Jointed*).
Point'edly adv. (*Pointed*).
Devo'tedly adv. (*Devoted*).
Interrup'tedly adv. (*Interrupted*).
Interest'edly adv. (*Interested*).
Disin'terestedly adv. (*Disinterested*).
Admit'tedly adv. Being acknowledged or granted.
Besot'tedly adv. (*Besotted*).
Repu'tedly adv. By common report.
Deserv'edly adv. Justly.
Avow'edly adv. Admittedly.
Perplex'edly adv. In a confused or puzzled manner.
Vex'edly adv. (*Vexed*).
Fix'edly adv. Steadfastly; intently.
Mix'edly adv. (*Mixed*).
Ama'zedly adv. (*Amazed*).
I'dly adv. (*Idle*).
Laid'ly a. Hideous, repulsive; loathesome.
Staid'ly adv. (*Staid*).
Rab'idly adv. (*Rabid*).
Tab'idly adv. (*Tabid*).
Mor'bidly adv. (*Morbid*).
Pla'cidly adv. (*Placid*).
Flac'cidly adv. (*Flaccid*).
Ran'cidly adv. (*Rancid*).
Lu'cidly adv. (*Lucid*).
Pellu'cidly adv. (*Pellucid*).
Can'didly adv. (*Candid*).
Splen'didly adv. (*Splendid*).
Sor'didly adv. (*Sordid*).
Rig'idly adv. (*Rigid*).
Frig'idly adv. (*Frigid*).
Tur'gidly adv. (*Turgid*).
Squal'idly adv. (*Squalid*).
Val'idly adv. (*Valid*).
Inval'idly adv. (*Invalid*).

Gel'idly adv. (*Gelid*).
Pal'lidly adv. (*Pallid*).
Sol'idly adv. (*Solid*).
Stol'idly adv. (*Stolid*).
Tim'idly adv. (*Timid*).
Tu'midly adv. (*Tumid*).
Void'ly adv. (*Void*).
Rap'idly adv. (*Rapid*).
Vap'idly adv. (*Vapid*).
Intrep'idly adv. (*Intrepid*).
Tep'idly adv. (*Tepid*).
Insip'idly adv. (*Insipid*).
Lim'pidly adv. (*Limpid*).
Tor'pidly adv. (*Torpid*).
Stup'idly adv. (*Stupid*).
Flor'idly adv. (*Florid*).
Hor'ridly adv. (*Horrid*).
Pu'tridly adv. (*Putrid*).
Lur'idly adv. (*Lurid*).
Fe'tidly adv. (*Fetid*).
Lan'guidly adv. (*Languid*).
Liq'uidly adv. (*Liquid*).
Av'idly adv. Greedily, eagerly.
Impav'idly adv. Fearlessly.
Liv'idly adv. (*Livid*).
Viv'idly adv. (*Vivid*).
Fer'vidly adv. (*Fervid*).
Bald'ly adv. (*Bald*).
Mild'ly adv. (*Mild*).
Wild'ly adv. (*Wild*).
Bold'ly adv. (*Bold*).
Cold'ly adv. (*Cold*).
World'ly a. Pertaining to this world, secular; temporal; given to present enjoyment.
Bland'ly adv. (*Bland*).
Grand'ly adv. (*Grand*).
Friend'ly a. Becoming, like, or having the disposition of a friend; favourable; disposed to peace. adv. In the manner of a friend.
Unfriend'ly a. Hostile.
Kind'ly a. Good-natured, kind, genial, beneficial. adv. In a kind manner.
Blind'ly adv. (*Blind*).
Pur'blindly adv. (*Purblind*).
Sec'ondly adv. In the second place.
Fond'ly adv. (*Fond*).
Joc'undly adv. (*Jocund*).
Profound'ly adv. (*Profound*).
Round'ly adv. In a round form; openly, boldly; briskly.
Sound'ly adv. Healthily, heartily; severely; truly, firmly; fast, closely.
God'ly a. Pious, devout; God-fearing.
Good'ly a. Good-looking, fine; kind; large, considerable.
Hag'gardly adv. (*Haggard*).
Nig'gardly a. and adv. (*Niggard*).
Hard'ly adv. With difficulty; rigorously; scarcely.
Bas'tardly adv. (*Bastard*).
Das'tardly a. Cowardly.
Bla'ckguardly adv., a. (*Blackguard*).
Leew'ardly a. (*Leeward*).
North'wardly a. and adv. (*Northward*).
Back'wardly adv. (*Backward*).
Awk'wardly adv. (*Awkward*).
In'wardly adv. Internally; secretly, mentally.
Cow'ardly a. Befitting a coward, wanting courage; pusillanimous, mean. adv. In the manner of a coward.
Fro'wardly adv. (*Froward*).
To'wardly (too'-) a. Ready to do or learn; complaint.
For'wardly adv. Eagerly; saucily.
Straightfor'-wardly adv. (*Straightforward*).
Out'wardly adv. Externally; apparently.
Way'wardly adv. (*Wayward*).
Bay'ardly adv. Blindly, self-confidently.
Haphaz'ardly adv. Accidentally; by chance.
Weird'ly adv. (*Weird*).
Third'ly adv. (*Third*).
Buird'ly a. (*Scot.*) Stalwart, burly.
Lord'ly a. Befitting a lord; grand, superb; haughty. adv. Proudly; arrogantly.
Absurd'ly adv. (*Absurd*).
Loud'ly adv. Noisily, clamorously.
Proud'ly adv. (*Proud*).
Lewd'ly adv. (*Lewd*).
Shrewd'ly adv. (*Shrewd*).
Cice'ly s. A plant of the parsley family.
Nice'ly adv. (*Nice*).
Choice'ly adv. With care in choosing; excellently.
Prince'ly a. Pertaining to or becoming a prince; regal, magnificent. adv. In a prince-like manner.
Scarce'ly adv. Barely; only just; with difficulty.
Fierce'ly adv. (*Fierce*).
Douce'ly adv. Sedately, soberly.
Spruce'ly adv. (*Spruce*).
Grade'ly a. Decent, well-looking, suitable.
Wide'ly adv. (*Wide*).
Nude'ly adv. (*Nude*).
Rude'ly adv. (*Rude*).
Crudely adv. (*Crude*).
Eel'y a. Resembling an eel; slippery, evasive.
Wheel'y a. Suitable to rotation; circular.
Free'ly adv. Voluntarily; liberally; in a free manner.
Steel'y a. Made of or resembling steel; firm, adamant.
Weel'y s. An osier fish-trap.
Safe'ly adv. (*Safe*).
Rife'ly adv. (*Rife*).
Wife'ly a. Like or becoming a wife.
House'wifely a. Pertaining to a housewife; thrifty. adv. Like a housewife.
Sage'ly adv. Wisely, judiciously, prudently.
Sav'agely adv. (*Savage*).
Strange'ly adv. (*Strange*).
Large'ly adv. To a large extent.
Huge'ly adv. (*Huge*).
Lithe'ly adv. (*Lithe*).
Blithe'ly adv. (*Blithe*).
Like'ly a. Probable; reasonable; credible suitable. adv. Probably.
Unlike'ly a. and adv. Improbable; unpromising.
Pale'ly adv. (*Pale*).
Stale'ly adv. (*Stale*).
Im'becilely adv. (*Imbecile*).
Ag'ilely adv. (*Agile*).
Ju'venilely adv. (*Juvenile*).
Pu'erilely adv. (*Puerile*).
Ver'satilely adv. (*Versatile*).
Hos'tilely adv. (*Hostile*).
Fu'tilely adv. (*Futile*).
Vile'ly adv. (*Vile*).
Ser'vilely adv. (*Servile*).
Sole'ly adv. Singly; alone; only.
Game'ly adv. Pluckily, spiritedly.
Lame'ly adv. (*Lame*).
Name'ly adv. That is to say.
Tame'ly adv. (*Tame*).
Supreme'ly adv. (*Supreme*).
Extreme'ly adv. In the utmost degree; to the utmost point.
Prime'ly adv. (*Prime*).
Time'ly a. Seasonable; opportune; premature.
Untime'ly a. Ill-timed; inopportune. adv. Unseasonably.

Come'ly a. Handsome, of pleasing appearance.
Home'ly a. Plain; simple; unpretentious; unadorned.
Frol'icsomely adv. (*Frolicsome*).
Glad'somely adv. (*Gladsome*).
Hand'somely adv. (*Handsome*).
Blithe'somely adv. (*Blithesome*).
Trouble'-somely adv. (*Troublesome*).
Dole'somely adv. (*Dolesome*).
Whole'somely adv. (*Wholesome*).
Game'somely adv. (*Gamesome*).
Tire'somely adv. (*Tiresome*).
Ven'ture-somely adv. (*Venturesome*).
Grue'somely adv. (*Gruesome*).
Awe'somely adv. (*Awesome*).
Loath'somely adv. (*Loathsome*).
Noi'somely adv. (*Noisome*).
We'arisomely adv. (*Wearisome*).
Irk'somely adv. (*Irksome*).
Quar'relsomely adv. (*Quarrelsome*).
Toil'somely adv. (*Toilsome*).
Ful'somely adv. (*Fulsome*).
Bur'densomely adv. (*Burdensome*).
Win'somely adv. (*Winsome*).
Fear'somely adv. (*Fearsome*).
Cum'ber-somely adv. (*Cumbersome*).
Hu'mour-somely adv. (*Humoursome*).
Light'somely adv. (*Lightsome*).
Delight'somely adv. (*Delightsome*).
Con'tumely s. Scornful abuse, contempt; ignominy.
Urbane'ly adv. (*Urbane*).
Mun'danely adv. (*Mundane*).
Profane'ly adv. (*Profane*).
Humane'ly adv. (*Humane*).
Inane'ly adv. (*Inane*).
Sane'ly adv. (*Sane*).
Insane'ly adv. (*Insane*).
Obscene'ly adv. (*Obscene*).
Serene'ly adv. Calmly, deliberately.
Fine'ly adv. In a fine or polished manner; delicately; gaily.
Mas'culinely adv. (*Masculine*).
Fem'ininely adv. (*Feminine*).
Sat'urninely adv. (*Saturnine*).
Supine'ly adv. (*Supine*).
Ser'pentinely adv. (*Serpentine*).
Clandes'tinely adv. (*Clandestine*).
Sang'uinely adv. (*Sanguine*).
Gen'uinely adv. (*Genuine*).
Divine'ly adv. (*Divine*).
Lone'ly a. Solitary; addicted to solitude; unfrequented.
Prone'ly adv. (*Prone*).
Jejune'ly adv. (*Jejune*).
Op'portunely adv. (*Opportune*).
Inop'portunely adv. (*Inopportune*).
Shape'ly a. Well-formed; symmetrical.
Ripe'ly adv. (*Ripe*).
Rely' v.i. To trust or depend upon confidently.
Bare'ly adv. Nearly, scarcely; nakedly.
Spare'ly adv. (*Spare*).
Rare'ly adv. (*Rare*).
Square'ly adv. (*Square*).
Som'brely adv. (*Sombre*).
Sincere'ly adv. (*Sincere*).
Insincere'ly adv. (*Insincere*).
Mere'ly adv. Only, solely, purely.
Austere'ly adv. (*Austere*).
Severe'ly adv. (*Severe*).
Mea'grely adv. (*Meagre*).
Dire'ly adv. (*Dire*).
Entire'ly adv. Wholly, completely, fully.
Sore'ly adv. (*Sore*).
Secure'ly adv. (*Secure*).
Insecure'ly adv. (*Insecure*).
Obscure'ly adv. (*Obscure*).
Demure'ly adv. (*Demure*).
Pure'ly adv. In a pure manner; innocently; merely.
Impure'ly adv. (*Impure*).
Sure'ly adv. Certainly; safely.
Leis'urely a. Done at leisure; deliberate. adv. Slowly.
Mature'ly adv. (*Mature*).
Premature'ly adv. (*Premature*).
Immature'ly adv. (*Immature*).
Base'ly adv. (*Base*).
Precise'ly adv. (*Precise*).
Concise'ly adv. (*Concise*).
Wise'ly adv. (*Wise*).
False'ly adv. In a false manner.
Dense'ly adv. (*Dense*).
Immense'ly adv. (*Immense*).
Propense'ly adv. (*Propense*).
Tense'ly adv. (*Tense*).
Intense'ly adv. (*Intense*).
Verbose'ly adv. (*Verbose*).
Floccose'ly adv. (*Floccose*).
Jocose'ly adv. (*Jocose*).
Gran'diosely adv. (*Grandiose*).
O'tiosely adv. (*Otiose*).
Close'ly adv. In a close state or manner.
Lach'rymosely adv. (*Lachrymose*).
Loose'ly adv. (*Loose*).
Pur'posely adv. By purpose or design; intentionally.
Op'erosely adv. (*Operose*).
Morose'ly adv. (*Morose*).
Coarse'ly adv. (*Coarse*).
Hoarse'ly adv. (*Hoarse*).
Sparse'ly adv. (*Sparse*).
Terse'ly adv. (*Terse*).
Averse'ly adv. (*Averse*).
Obverse'ly adv. (*Obverse*).
Adverse'ly adv. (*Adverse*).
Reverse'ly adv. In a reverse manner; on the other hand.
Diverse'ly adv. In different ways or directions.
Inverse'ly adv. (*Inverse*).
Converse'ly adv. Reciprocally; with inversion of order.
Perverse'ly adv. (*Perverse*).
Transverse'ly adv. (*Transverse*).
Retrorse'ly adv. (*Retrorse*).
Introrse'ly adv. (*Introrse*).
Diffuse'ly adv. Copiously, fully.
Profuse'ly adv. (*Profuse*).
Abstruse'ly adv. (*Abstruse*).
Obtuse'ly adv. (*Obtuse*).
Conglo'bately adv. In a round form.
Del'icately adv. (*Delicate*).
Indel'icately adv. (*Indelicate*).
In'tricately adv. (*Intricate*).
Trun'cately adv. (*Truncate*).
Sedate'ly adv. (*Sedate*).
Prof'ligately adv. (*Profligate*).
Ra'diately adv. (*Radiate*).
Me'diately adv. Indirectly.
Imme'diately adv. Without delay; directly; forthwith.
Interme'-diately adv. Between; by way of intervening.
Appro'priately adv. (*Appropriate*).
Inappro'-priately adv. (*Inappropriate*).
Stri'ately adv. (*Striate*).
Late'ly adv. Not long ago; recently.
Oblate'ly adv. (*Oblate*).
Philat'ely s. The collection of postage-stamps.
Stel'lately adv. (*Stellate*).
Vertic'illately adv. (*Verticillate*).

Invi'olately adv. (*Inviolate*).
Pro'lately adv. (*Prolate*).
Des'olately adv. (*Desolate*).
Discon'-solately adv. (*Disconsolate*).
Immac'ulately adv. (*Immaculate*).
Retic'ulately adv. (*Reticulate*).
Dentic'ulately adv. (*Denticulate*).
Artic'ulately adv. (*Articulate*).
Inartic'ulately adv. (*Inarticulate*).
Un'dulately adv. (*Undulate*).
Triang'ulately adv. (*Triangulate*).
Inan'imately adv. (*Inanimate*).
Legit'imately adv. (*Legitimate*).
Illegit'imately adv. (*Illegitimate*).
Ul'timately adv. (*Ultimate*).
In'timately adv. (*Intimate*).
Prox'imately adv. (*Proximate*).
Approx'-imately adv. (*Approximate*).
Pal'mately adv. (*Palmate*).
Consum'-mately adv. Perfectly, completely.
Subor'dinately adv. (*Subordinate*).
Inor'dinately adv. (*Inordinate*).
Co-or'dinately adv. (*Co-ordinate*).
Effem'inately adv. (*Effeminate*).
Discrim'inately adv. Distinctly.
Indiscrim'-inately adv. (*Indiscriminate*).
Deter'minately adv. (*Determinate*).
Indeterm'-inately adv. (*Indeterminate*).
Ob'stinately adv. (*Obstinate*).
Innate'ly adv. (*Innate*).
Pin'nately adv. (*Pinnate*).
Pas'sionately adv. (*Passionate*).
Compas'sion-ately adv. (*Compassionate*).
Dispas'sion-ately adv. (*Dispassionate*).
Affec'tionately adv. (*Affectionate*).
Propor'-tionately adv. (*Proportionate*).
Dispropor'-tionately adv. (*Disproportionate*).
Mu'cronately adv. (*Mucronate*).
Ter'nately adv. (*Ternate*).
Alter'nately adv. (*Alternate*).
Ornate'ly adv. (*Ornate*).
For'tunately adv. By good fortune; happily; luckily.
Impor'tunately adv. (*Importunate*).
In'choately adv. (*Inchoate*).
Sep'arately adv. (*Separate*).
Delib'erately adv. Cautiously, slowly.
Consid'erately adv. (*Considerate*).
Inconsid'-erately adv. (*Inconsiderate*).
Mod'erately adv. (*Moderate*).
Immod'erately adv. (*Immoderate*).
Degen'erately adv. (*Degenerate*).
Tem'perately adv. (*Temperate*).
Intem'perately adv. (*Intemperate*).
Des'perately adv. (*Desperate*).
Invet'erately adv. (*Inveterate*).
Illit'erately adv. (*Illiterate*).
Adul'terately adv. (*Adulterate*).
Elab'orately adv. (*Elaborate*).
Cor'porately adv. In a corporate capacity.
Ac'curately adv. (*Accurate*).
Inac'curately adv. (*Inaccurate*).
Ob'durately adv. (*Obdurate*).
Commen'-surately adv. (*Commensurate*).
Incommen'-surately adv. (*Incommensurate*).
Lyr'ately adv. (*Lyrate*).
Insen'sately adv. (*Insensate*).
Decus'sately adv. (*Decussate*).
Dig'itately adv. (*Digitate*).
Precip'itately adv. Headlong, hastily.
Den'tately adv. (*Dentate*).
State'ly a. Lofty, dignified, august.
Sin'uately adv. (*Sinuate*).
Ad'equately adv. (*Adequate*).
Inad'equately adv. (*Inadequate*).
Pri'vately adv. (*Private*).
Complete'ly adv. (*Complete*).
Incomplete'ly adv. (*Incomplete*).
Concrete'ly adv. (*Concrete*).
Ex'peditely adv. Readily; speedily.
Rec'onditely adv. (*Recondite*).
White'ly adv. (*White*).
Polite'ly adv. (*Polite*).
Impolite'ly adv. (*Impolite*).
Fi'nitely adv. In a finite manner.
Def'initely adv. (*Definite*).
Indef'initely adv. (*Indefinite*).
In'finitely adv. (*Infinite*).
Sprite'ly adv. Sprightly.
Trite'ly adv. (*Trite*).
Con'tritely adv. (*Contrite*).
Ex'quisitely adv. (*Exquisite*).
Com'positely adv. (*Composite*).
Inap'positely adv. (*Inapposite*).
Op'positely adv. So as to be opposite; against each other.
Tripar'titely adv. (*Tripartite*).
Remote'ly adv. (*Remote*).
Chaste'ly adv. (*Chaste*).
Cute'ly adv. (*Cute*).
Acute'ly adv. (*Acute*).
Ab'solutely adv. (*Absolute*).
Res'olutely adv. (*Resolute*).
Irres'olutely adv. (*Irresolute*).
Dis'solutely adv. (*Dissolute*).
Mute'ly adv. Without making a sound; dumbly.
Minute'ly adv. In a minute manner; exactly, precisely.
Min'utely a. Happening every minute. adv. Every minute; from minute to minute.
Astute'ly adv. (*Astute*).
Vague'ly(väg'-) adv. (*Vague*).
Blue'ly adv. (*Blue*).
Opaque'ly (-pāk'li) adv. (*Opaque*).
Oblique'ly (-lēk'-) adv. (*Oblique*).
Unique'ly (-nēk'-) adv. (*Unique*).
Burlesque'ly adv. (*Burlesque*).
Picturesque'ly adv. (*Picturesque*).
Grotesque'ly adv. (*Grotesque*).
Statuesque'ly (-esk'-) adv. (*Statuesque*).
Brusque'ly adv. (*Brusque*).
Concave'ly adv. (*Concave*).
Brave'ly adv. (*Brave*).
Grave'ly adv. Sedately, seriously, solemnly.
Suave'ly adv. (*Suave*).
Coer'cively adv. (*Coercive*).
Live'ly a. Full of life; brisk, vivacious, gay; forcible.
Sua'sively adv. (*Suasive*).
Persua'sively adv. (*Persuasive*).
Dissua'sively adv. (*Dissuasive*).
Eva'sively adv. (*Evasive*).
Adhe'sively adv. (*Adhesive*).
Cohe'sively adv. (*Cohesive*).
Deci'sively adv. (*Decisive*).
Indeci'sively adv. (*Indecisive*).
Inci'sively adv. (*Incisive*).
Deris'ively adv. (*Derisive*).
Repul'sively adv. (*Repulsive*).
Impul'sively adv. (*Impulsive*).

Compul'sively adv. (*Compulsive*).
Convul'sively adv. (*Convulsive*).
Expan'sively adv. (*Expansive*).
Defen'sively adv. (*Defensive*).
Offen'sively adv. (*Offensive*).
Inoffen'sively adv. (*Inoffensive*).
Comprehen'-sively adv. (*Comprehensive*).
Incomprehen'-sively adv. (*Incomprehensive*).
Apprehen'-sively adv. (*Apprehensive*).
Pen'sively adv. (*Pensive*).
Suspen'sively adv. (*Suspensive*).
Expen'sively adv. (*Expensive*).
Inexpen'sively adv. (*Inexpensive*).
Inten'sively adv. (*Intensive*).
Osten'sively adv. (*Ostensive*).
Exten'sively adv. (*Extensive*).
Coexten'sively adv. (*Coextensive*).
Respon'sively adv. (*Responsive*).
Explo'sively adv. Violently.
Corro'sively adv. (*Corrosive*).
Asper'sively adv. (*Aspersive*).
Disper'sively adv. (*Dispersive*).
Decur'sively adv. (*Decursive*).
Discur'sively adv. (*Discursive*).
Excur'sively adv. (*Excursive*).
Mas'sively adv. (*Massive*).
Pas'sively adv. (*Passive*).
Impas'sively adv. (*Impassive*).
Succes'sively adv. (*Successive*).
Exces'sively adv. (*Excessive*).
Regres'sively adv. (*Regressive*).
Aggres'sively adv. (*Aggressive*).
Digres'sively adv. (*Digressive*).
Progres'sively adv. (*Progressive*).
Retrogres'-sively adv. (*Retrogressive*).
Transgres'-sively adv. (*Transgressive*).
Repres'sively adv. (*Repressive*).
Impres'sively adv. (*Impressive*).
Oppres'sively adv. (*Oppressive*).
Expres'sively adv. (*Expressive*).
Inexpres'sively adv. (*Inexpressive*).
Posses'sively adv. (*Possessive*).
Submis'sively adv. (*Submissive*).
Permis'sively adv. (*Permissive*).
Abu'sively adv. (*Abusive*).
Effu'sively adv. (*Effusive*).
Diffu'sively adv. (*Diffusive*).
Preclu'sively adv. (*Preclusive*).
Inclu'sively adv. (*Inclusive*).
Conclu'sively adv. (*Conclusive*).
Inconclu'-sively adv. (*Inconclusive*).
Exclu'sively adv. (*Exclusive*).
Elu'sively adv. (*Elusive*).
Delu'sively adv. (*Delusive*).
Prelu'sively adv. (*Prelusive*).
Allu'sively adv. (*Allusive*).
Illu'sively adv. (*Illusive*).
Collu'sively adv. (*Collusive*).
Obtru'sively adv. (*Obtrusive*).
Intru'sively adv. (*Intrusive*).
Protru'sively adv. (*Protrusive*).
Com'batively adv. (*Combative*).
Predic'atively adv. (*Predicative*).
Indic'atively adv. (*Indicative*).
Signif'icatively adv. (*Significative*).
Commun'-icatively adv. (*Communicative*).
Consolida'-tively adv. (*Consolidative*).
Crea'tively adv. (*Creative*).
Neg'atively adv. (*Negative*).
Interrog'-atively adv. (*Interrogative*).

Pur'gatively adv. (*Purgative*).
Appre'ciatively adv. (*Appreciative*).
Enun'ciatively adv. (*Enunciative*).
Var'iatively adv. (*Variative*).
Talk'atively adv. (*Talkative*).
Rel'atively adv. (*Relative*).
Irrel'atively adv. (*Irrelative*).
Correl'atively adv. (*Correlative*).
Ill'atively adv. (*Illative*).
Contem'-platively adv. (*Contemplative*).
Super'latively adv. (*Superlative*).
Leg'islatively adv. (*Legislative*).
Spec'ulatively adv. (*Speculative*).
Em'ulatively adv. (*Emulative*).
Sim'ulatively adv. (*Simulative*).
Cu'mulatively adv. (*Cumulative*).
Accu'mula-tively adv. (*Accumulative*).
Cop'ulatively adv. (*Copulative*).
Approx'-imatively adv. (*Approximative*).
Confirm'atively adv. (*Confirmative*).
Na'tively adv. (*Native*).
Imag'inatively adv. (*Imaginative*).
Ter'minatively adv. (*Terminative*).
Opin'ionatively adv. (*Opinionative*).
Alter'natively adv. (*Alternative*).
Declar'atively adv. (*Declarative*).
Prepar'atively adv. (*Preparative*).
Compar'atively adv. (*Comparative*).
Lu'cratively adv. (*Lucrative*).
Delib'eratively adv. (*Deliberative*).
Fed'eratively adv. (*Federative*).
Exag'geratively adv. (*Exaggerative*).
Remu'nera-tively adv. (*Remunerative*).
Imper'atively adv. Authoritatively, peremptorily.
Op'eratively adv. (*Operative*).
Co-op'eratively adv. (*Co-operative*).
Vitu'peratively adv. (*Vituperative*).
Commis'-eratively adv. (*Commiserative*).
Allit'eratively adv. (*Alliterative*).
Dec'oratively adv. (*Decorative*).
Commem'-oratively adv. (*Commemorative*).
Cor'poratively adv. (*Corporative*).
Restor'atively adv. (*Restorative*).
Nar'ratively adv. By way of recital.
Pen'etratively adv. (*Penetrative*).
Admin'istra-tively adv. (*Administrative*).
Demon'-stratively adv. (*Demonstrative*).
Illus'tratively adv. (*Illustrative*).
Fig'uratively adv. (*Figurative*).
Dispen'satively adv. (*Dispensative*).
Caus'atively adv. (*Causative*).
Accu'satively adv. (*Accusative*).
Interpreta'-tively adv. (*Interpretative*).
Du'bitatively adv. (*Dubitative*).
Med'itatively adv. (*Meditative*).
Veg'etatively adv. (*Vegetative*).
Cogita'tively adv. (*Cogitative*).
Im'itatively adv. (*Imitative*).
Author'-itatively adv. (*Authoritative*).
Quan'titatively adv. (*Quantitative*).
Argumen'-tatively adv. (*Argumentative*).
Represent'-atively adv. (*Representative*).
Ten'tatively adv. (*Tentative*).
Deno'tatively adv. (*Denotative*).
Conno'tatively adv. (*Connotative*).
Op'tatively adv. (*Optative*).
Commu'tatively adv. (*Commutative*).

Pu'tatively adv. (*Putative*).
Impu'tatively adv. (*Imputative*).
Insinua'tively adv. (*Insinuative*).
Deriv'atively adv. (*Derivative*).
Pri'vatively adv. (*Privative*).
Ac'tively adv. (*Active*).
Reac'tively adv. (*Reactive*).
Inac'tively adv. Not actively.
Coac'tively adv. (*Coactive*).
Diffrac'tively adv. (*Diffractive*).
Abstrac'tively adv. (*Abstractive*).
Distrac'tively adv. (*Distractive*).
Attrac'tively adv. (*Attractive*).
Defec'tively adv. (*Defective*).
Effec'tively adv. (*Effective*).
Ineffec'tively adv. (*Ineffective*).
Objec'tively adv. (*Objective*).
Subjec'tively adv. (*Subjective*).
Projec'tively adv. (*Projective*).
Elec'tively adv. (*Elective*).
Selec'tively adv. (*Selective*).
Reflec'tively adv. (*Reflective*).
Collec'tively adv. In a body, jointly.
Connec'tively adv. (*Connective*).
Respec'tively adv. As relating to each ; relatively ; particularly.
Irrespec'tively adv. Without regard to circumstances, etc.
Circumspec'-tively adv. (*Circumspective*).
Prospec'tively adv. (*Prospective*).
Retrospec'-tively adv. (*Retrospective*).
Introspec'tively adv. (*Introspective*).
Perspec'tively adv According to the rules of perspective.
Invec'tively adv. (*Invective*).
Contradic'-tively adv. (*Contradictive*).
Predic'tively adv. (*Predictive*).
Vindic'tively adv. (*Vindictive*).
Afflic'tively adv. (*Afflictive*).
Restric'tively adv. (*Restrictive*).
Constric'tively adv. (*Constrictive*).
Distinc'tively adv. (*Distinctive*).
Indistinc'tively adv. (*Indistinctive*).
Instinc'tively adv. (*Instinctive*).
Subjunc'tively adv. (*Subjunctive*).
Adjunc'tively adv. (*Adjunctive*).
Conjunc'tively adv. (*Conjunctive*).
Disjunc'tively adv. (*Disjunctive*).
Deduc'tively adv. A priori.
Seduc'tively adv. (*Seductive*).
Induc'tively adv. (*Inductive*).
Produc'tively adv. (*Productive*).
Introduc'tively adv. Introductorily.
Destruc'tively adv. (*Destructive*).
Instruc'tively adv. (*Instructive*).
Construc'tively adv. (*Constructive*).
Reple'tively adv. (*Repletive*).
Secre'tively adv. (*Secretive*).
Prohib'itively adv. (*Prohibitive*).
Ad'ditively adv. (*Additive*).
Prim'itively adv. (*Primitive*).
Defin'itively adv. (*Definitive*).
Admon'itively adv. (*Admonitive*).
U'nitively adv. (*Unitive*).
Nu'tritively adv. (*Nutritive*).
Acqui's'itively adv. (*Acquisitive*).
Inquis'itively adv. (*Inquisitive*).
Tran'sitively adv. In a transitive manner ; with a grammatical object.
Intran'sitively adv. (*Intransitive*).
Sen'sitively adv. (*Sensitive*).
Pos'itively adv. Absolutely, certainly ; really ; inherently.
Suppos'itively adv. (*Suppositive*).
Compet'itively adv. (*Competitive*).
Par'titively adv. (*Partitive*).
Intu'itively adv. In an intuitive manner ; without reasoning.
Sub'stantively adv. (*Substantive*).
Reten'tively adv. (*Retentive*).
Atten'tively adv. (*Attentive*).
Inatten'tively adv. (*Inattentive*).
Preven'tively adv. (*Preventive*).
Inven'tively adv. (*Inventive*).
Plain'tively adv. (*Plaintive*).
Emo'tively adv. (*Emotive*).
Locomo'tively adv. (*Locomotive*).
Vo'tively adv. (*Votive*).
Adap'tively adv. (*Adaptive*).
Decep'tively adv. (*Deceptive*).
Recep'tively adv. (*Receptive*).
Percep'tively adv. (*Perceptive*).
Descrip'tively adv. (*Descriptive*).
Prescrip'tively adv. (*Prescriptive*).
Circumscrip'-tively adv. (*Circumscriptive*).
Resump'tively adv. (*Resumptive*).
Presump'tively adv. (*Presumptive*).
Consump'tively adv. (*Consumptive*).
Assump'tively adv. (*Assumptive*).
Adop'tively adv. (*Adoptive*).
Interrup'tively adv. (*Interruptive*).
Asser'tively adv. (*Assertive*).
Abor'tively adv. (*Abortive*).
Spor'tively adv. (*Sportive*).
Fur'tively adv. (*Furtive*).
Fes'tively adv. (*Festive*).
Sugges'tively adv. (*Suggestive*).
Res'tively adv. (*Restive*).
Exhaus'tively adv. (*Exhaustive*).
Inexhaus'tively adv. (*Inexhaustive*).
Distrib'utively adv. (*Distributive*).
Attrib'utively adv. (*Attributive*).
Consec'utively adv. (*Consecutive*).
Inconsec'-utively adv. (*Inconsecutive*).
Dimin'utively adv. (*Diminutive*).
Con'stitutively adv. (*Constitutive*).
Reflex'ively adv. (*Reflexive*).
Influx'ively adv. (*Influxive*).
Love'ly a. Beautiful and attractive ; charming ; amiable.
Fly s. A small, two-winged insect ; a light carriage ; a revolving mechanism to regulate machinery ; portion of a vane ; a flap. v.i. To move through the air with wings, by the force of air, or on an aeroplane, etc. ; to flutter ; to move or pass away rapidly. v.t. To flee from ; to cause to float in air. a. (*Slang*) Sharp, knowing.
Deaf'ly adv. (*Deaf*).
Gad'fly s. An insect which bites cattle ; a tormenting, irritating person.
Chief'ly adv. Principally ; in the first place.
Brief'ly adv. (*Brief*).
Crane'fly s. The daddy-long-legs.
Stiff'ly adv. (*Stiff*).
Bluff'ly adv. (*Bluff*).
Gruff'ly adv. (*Gruff*).
Green'fly s. An aphis.
But'terfly s. A diurnal insect of the order of Lepidoptera.
Blow'fly s. A large fly that deposits its eggs in meat.
May'-fly s. An ephemeral insect, or angler's imitation.
Straggl'y a. Straggling ; irregularly spread.
Trig'ly a. Sprucely, neatly.
Spangl'y a. Adorned or glittering with spangles.
Tangl'y a. Full of tangles ; entangled.
Men'acingly adv. In a threatening manner.
Rejoic'ingly adv. (*Rejoicing*).

Entic'ingly adv. (*Enticing*).
Glanc'ingly adv. By glancing transiently.
Entranc'ingly adv. (*Entrancing*).
Minc'ingly adv. (*Mincing*).
Convinc'ingly adv. (*Convincing*).
Bounc'ingly adv. (*Bouncing*).
Pierc'ingly adv. (*Piercing*).
Degra'dingly adv. (*Degrading*).
Forbid'dingly adv. (*Forbidding*).
Exceed'ingly adv. In a very great degree; unusually, transcendingly.
Abi'dingly adv. (*Abiding*).
Chi'dingly adv. (*Chide*).
Yield'ingly adv. (*Yielding*).
Command'ingly adv. (*Commanding*).
Understand'ingly adv. (*Understanding*).
Condescend'ingly adv. (*Condescending*).
Bind'ingly adv. (*Binding*).
Despond'ingly adv. In a despondent or despairing manner.
Correspond'ingly adv. (*Corresponding*).
Aboun'dingly adv. (*Abounding*).
Astoun'dingly adv. (*Astounding*).
Forebo'dingly adv. (*Foreboding*).
Accor'dingly adv. (*According*).
Foresee'ingly adv. (*Foreseeing*).
Enga'gingly adv. (*Engaging*).
Dispar'agingly adv. In a derogatory, detracting, or disparaging way.
Encour'agingly adv. (*Encouraging*).
Discour'agingly adv. (*Discouraging*).
Grudg'ingly adv. In an envious or unwilling manner.
Brag'gingly adv. (*Bragging*).
Obli'gingly adv. (*Obliging*).
Disobli'gingly adv. (*Disobliging*).
Long'ingly adv. With eager wishes or great longing.
Beseech'ingly adv. (*Beseeching*).
Bewitch'ingly adv. (*Bewitching*).
Touch'ingly adv. (*Touching*).
Laugh'ingly adv. In a merry way; with laughter.
Shin'gly a. Abounding in shingle; affected with or pertaining to shingles.
Dash'ingly adv. (*Dashing*).
Aston'ishingly adv. (*Astonishing*).
Flour'ishingly adv. (*Flourishing*).
Distin'guishingly adv. (*Distinguishing*).
Gush'ingly adv. (*Gushing*).
Loath'ingly adv. (*Loathing*).
King'ly a. Like or pertaining to a king; royal; splendid.
Tak'ingly adv. (*Taking*).
Shock'ingly adv. (*Shocking*).
Mock'ingly adv. By way of mocking or derision.
Strik'ingly adv. (*Striking*).
Think'ingly adv. (*Thinking*).
Heal'ingly adv. (*Healing*).
Appeal'ingly adv. (*Appealing*).
Dab'blingly adv. Superficially, triflingly.
Trem'blingly adv. (*Trembling*).
Rum'blingly adv. (*Rumbling*).
Grum'blingly adv. Complainingly; unwillingly.
Feel'ingly adv. Affectingly, tenderly.
Baf'flingly adv. (*Baffling*).
Shuffl'ingly adv. (*Shuffling*).
Trifl'ingly adv. (*Trifling*).
Bungl'ingly adv. (*Bungling*).
Bewail'ingly adv. (*Bewailing*).
Smil'ingly adv. In a smiling manner, with a pleased look.
Beguil'ingly adv. (*Beguiling*).
Appal'lingly adv. (*Appalling*).
Enthral'lingly adv. (*Enthralling*).
Compel'lingly adv. (*Compelling*).
Tel'lingly adv. (*Telling*).
Grov'ellingly adv. (*Grovelling*).
Chil'lingly adv. (*Chilling*).
Thril'lingly adv. (*Thrilling*).
Cav'illingly adv. (*Cavil*).
Wil'lingly adv. (*Willing*).
Startl'ingly adv. (*Startling*).
Tattl'ingly adv. (*Tattling*).
Daz'zlingly adv. (*Dazzling*).
Flam'ingly adv. (*Flaming*).
Seem'ingly adv. Ostensibly, apparently.
Swim'mingly adv. Easily; without hindrance.
Becom'ingly adv (*Becoming*).
Char'mingly adv. (*Charming*).
Alar'mingly adv. (*Alarming*).
Presum'ingly adv. Presumptuously.
Mean'ingly adv. Significantly, expressively.
Mad'deningly adv. In a maddening manner.
Overween'ingly adv. (*Overweening*).
Threat'eningly adv. (*Threatening*).
Design'ingly adv. (*Designing*).
Complain'ingly adv. (*Complaining*).
Entertain'ingly adv. (*Entertaining*).
Win'ningly adv. (*Winning*).
Cun'ningly adv. (*Cunning*).
Yearn'ingly adv. (*Yearning*).
Warn'ingly adv. (*Warning*).
Discern'ingly adv. (*Discerning*).
Mourn'ingly adv. (*Mourning*).
Fawn'ingly adv. (*Fawning*).
Creep'ingly adv. Slowly, sneakingly, ignobly.
Sweep'ingly adv. (*Sweeping*).
Gri'pingly adv. (*Griping*).
Nip'pingly adv. Keenly.
Rip'pingly adv. (*Slang*) (*Ripping*).
Trip'pingly adv. Nimbly.
Top'pingly adv. (*Topping*).
Carp'ingly adv. (*Carp*).
Chirp'ingly adv. (*Chirp*).
Grasp'ingly adv. (*Grasping*).
Dar'ingly adv. (*Daring*).
Forbear'ingly adv. (*Forbearing*).
Endear'ingly adv. (*Endearing*).
Glar'ingly adv. (*Glaring*).
Spar'ingly adv. (*Sparing*).
Consid'eringly adv. Seriously, thoughtfully.
Bewil'deringly adv. (*Bewildering*).
Blun'deringly adv. (*Blundering*).
Cheer'ingly adv. (*Cheering*).
Jeer'ingly adv. Scornfully, contemptuously.
Fleer'ingly adv. In a fleering, mocking manner.
Domineer'ingly adv. (*Domineering*).
Ling'eringly adv. (*Lingering*).
With'eringly adv. (*Withering*).
Glim'meringly adv. (*Glimmering*).
Fal'teringly adv. In a faltering or hesitating way.
Blus'teringly adv. (*Blustering*).
Flat'teringly adv. (*Flattering*).
Persever'ingly adv. (*Persevering*).
Despair'ingly adv. (*Despairing*).
Admir'ingly adv. (*Admiring*).
Ador'ingly adv. (*Adoring*).
Implor'ingly adv. In a beseeching or supplicatory manner.
Endur'ingly adv. (*Enduring*).
Allur'ingly adv. (*Alluring*).
Mur'muringly adv. With a low sound; with complaints.
Devour'ingly adv. (*Devouring*).
Singl'y adv. (*Single*).
Debas'ingly adv. So as to debase.
Decreas'ingly adv. In a gradually decreasing manner.
Increas'ingly adv. By continual increase.
Prom'isingly adv. (*Promising*).
En'terprisingly adv. (*Enterprising*).

Surpris'ingly adv. (*Surprising*).
Los'ingly adv. (*Losing*).
Impos'ingly adv. (*Imposing*).
Embar'-rassingly adv. (*Embarrassing*).
Press'ingly adv. (*Pressing*).
Depress'ingly adv. (*Depressing*).
Distress'ingly adv. (*Distressing*).
Prepossess'-ingly adv. (*Prepossessing*).
Mus'ingly adv. In a dreamy or meditative way.
Amus'ingly adv. (*Amusing*).
Accom'modatingly adv. (*Accommodating*).
Excru'ciatingly adv. (*Excruciating*).
Fas'cinatingly adv. (*Fascinating*).
Discrim'-inatingly adv. (*Discriminating*).
Grat'ingly adv. Discordantly ; irritatingly.
Pen'etratingly adv. (*Penetrating*).
Hes'itatingly adv. With indecision or reluctance.
Insinua'tingly adv. (*Insinuating*).
Ag'gravatingly adv. (*Aggravating*).
Fleet'ingly adv. (*Fleeting*).
Slight'ingly adv. (*Slight*).
Bi'tingly adv. (*Biting*).
Exci'tingly adv. (*Exciting*).
Invi'tingly adv. (*Inviting*).
Halt'ingly adv. In a hesitating manner.
Revolt'ingly adv. (*Revolting*).
Insult'ingly adv. (*Insulting*).
Exult'ingly adv. Exultantly.
Cant'ingly adv. (*Canting*).
Enchant'ingly adv. (*Enchanting*).
Haunt'ingly adv. (*Haunting*).
Taunt'ingly adv. Insultingly ; scornfully.
Vaunt'ingly adv. In an exulting manner.
Divert'ingly adv. (*Diverting*).
Last'ingly adv. (*Lasting*).
Everlast'ingly adv. (*Everlasting*).
Boast'ingly adv. (*Boasting*).
Jest'ingly adv. Not in earnest.
Interest'ingly adv. (*Interesting*).
Disgust'ingly adv. (*Disgusting*).
Fit'tingly adv. Appropriately, suitably.
Befit'tingly adv. (*Befitting*).
Intermit'tingly adv. With intermission.
Wit'tingly adv. Knowingly, consciously.
Twit'tingly adv. (*Twitting*).
Cut'tingly adv. Sarcastically, bitingly.
Ra'vingly adv. (*Raving*).
Cra'vingly adv. (*Craving*).
Believ'ingly adv. (*Believing*).
Forgiv'ingly adv. (*Forgiving*).
Lov'ingly adv. (*Loving*).
Mov'ingly adv. (*Moving*).
Approv'ingly adv. (*Approving*).
Observ'ingly adv. (*Observing*).
Deserv'ingly adv. (*Deserving*).
Flow'ingly adv. (*Flowing*).
Know'ingly adv. (*Knowing*).
Coax'ingly adv. (*Coax*).
Gratify'ingly adv. (*Gratifying*).
Ly'ingly adv. Falsely ; by telling lies.
Annoy'ingly adv. (*Annoying*).
Wor'ryingly adv. (*Worrying*).
Freez'ingly adv. (*Freezing*).
Tantaliz'ingly adv. (*Tantalizing*).
Strong'ly adv. (*Strong*).
Wrong'ly adv. (*Wrong*).
Jun'gly a. Consisting of or abounding in jungles.
Goog'ly s. In cricket a ball bowled so that it breaks in a direction contrary to its swerve.
Ug'ly a. Offensive to the sight ; disagreeable.
Smug'ly adv. (*Smug*).
Snug'ly adv. (*Snug*).
Rich'ly adv. In a rich manner ; abundantly.
Staunch'ly adv. (*Staunch*).
Arch'ly adv. Shrewdly ; coyly.
Starch'ly adv. Precisely, stiffly.
High'ly adv. In a high degree ; intensely ; favourably.
Rough'ly adv. (*Rough*).
Thor'oughly (thŭr'-) adv. Fully, completely, perfectly.
Tough'ly (tŭf'-) adv. (*Tough*).
Rash'ly adv. Precipitately ; foolhardily.
Flesh'ly a. Pertaining to the flesh ; carnal, not spiritual ; lascivious.
Fresh'ly adv. (*Fresh*).
Snob'bishly adv. (*Snobbish*).
Cad'dishly adv. (*Caddish*).
Child'ishly adv. (*Childish*).
Outlan'dishly adv. (*Outlandish*)
Fiend'ishly adv. (*Fiendish*).
Mo'dishly adv. (*Modish*).
Pru'dishly adv. (*Prudish*).
Raff'ishly adv. (*Raffish*).
Huff'ishly adv. (*Huffish*).
Self'ishly adv. (*Selfish*).
Wolf'ishly adv. (*Wolfish*).
Dwarf'ishly adv. (*Dwarfish*).
Hag'gishly adv. (*Haggish*).
Wag'gishly adv. (*Waggish*).
Whig'gishly adv. (*Whiggish*).
Pig'gishly adv. (*Piggish*).
Prig'gishly adv. (*Priggish*).
Dog'gishly adv. (*Doggish*).
Hog'gishly adv. (*Hoggish*).
Slug'gishly adv. (*Sluggish*).
Freak'ishly adv. (*Freakish*).
Rak'ishly adv. In a dissolute manner.
Trick'ishly adv. (*Trickish*).
Sick'ishly adv. (*Sickish*).
Block'ishly adv. (*Blockish*).
Buck'ishly adv. (*Buckish*).
Book'ishly adv. (*Bookish*).
Maw'kishly adv. (*Mawkish*).
Dev'ilishly adv. (*Devilish*).
Tickl'ishly adv. (*Ticklish*).
Hell'ishly adv. (*Hellish*).
Doll'ishly adv. (*Dollish*).
Fool'ishly adv. (*Foolish*).
Girl'ishly adv. (*Girlish*).
Churl'ishly adv. (*Churlish*).
Mu'lishly adv. (*Mulish*).
Ghoul'ishly adv. (*Ghoulish*).
Owl'ishly adv. (*Owlish*).
Styl'ishly adv. (*Stylish*).
Squeam'ishly adv. (*Squeamish*).
Heath'enishly adv. (*Heathenish*)
Swi'nishly adv. (*Swinish*).
Clan'nishly adv. (*Clannish*).
Man'nishly adv. (*Mannish*).
Hun'nishly adv. (*Hunnish*).
Clown'ishly adv. (*Clownish*).
A'pishly adv. (*Apish*).
Sheep'ishly adv. (*Sheepish*).
Romp'ishly adv. (*Rompish*).
Lump'ishly adv. (*Lumpish*).
Mo'pishly adv. (*Mopish*).
Po'pishly adv. (*Popish*).
Snap'pishly adv. (*Snappish*).
Fop'pishly adv. (*Foppish*).
Up'pishly adv. (*Uppish*).
Wasp'ishly adv. (*Waspish*).
Gar'ishly adv. (*Garish*).
Lick'erishly adv. (*Lickerish*).
Fe'verishly adv. (*Feverish*).
Whor'ishly adv. (*Whorish*).
Boor'ishly adv. (*Boorish*).
Cur'rishly adv. (*Currish*).
Pet'tishly adv. (*Pettish*).
Coquet'tishly adv. (*Coquettish*).

Skit'tishly adv. (*Skittish*).
Sot'tishly adv. (*Sottish*).
Slut'tishly adv. (*Sluttish*).
Lout'ishly adv. (*Loutish*).
Brut'ishly adv. (*Brutish*).
Ro'guishly adv. (*Roguish*).
Cliqu'ishly adv. (*Cliquish*).
Lav'ishly adv. (*Lavish*).
Slav'ishly adv. (*Slavish*).
Knav'ishly adv. (*Knavish*).
Peev'ishly adv. (*Peevish*).
Thiev'ishly adv. (*Thievish*).
El'vishly adv. (*Elvish*).
Shrew'ishly adv. (*Shrewish*).
Boy'ishly adv. (*Boyish*).
Harsh'ly adv. (*Harsh*).
Death'ly a. Deadly; pertaining to death. adv. So as to resemble death.
Loath'ly a. Exciting loathing; nauseous.
Fifth'ly adv. In the fifth place.
Twelfth'ly adv. (*Twelfth*).
Eighth'ly adv. (*Eighth*).
Thirteenth'ly adv. (*Thirteenth*).
Tenth'ly adv. (*Tenth*).
Sev'enthly adv. (*Seventh*).
Ninth'ly adv. In the ninth place.
Month'ly a. Continuing for or done in a month; happening once a month. adv. Once a month. s. A periodical published each month.
Smooth'ly adv. (*Smooth*).
Earth'ly a. Pertaining to this world; human, carnal; sordid; conceivable.
Unearth'ly a. Not earthly; supernatural; weird.
Fourth'ly adv. In the fourth place.
Uncouth'ly adv. (*Uncouth*).
Sixth'ly adv. In the sixth place.
Dai'ly a. Happening, done, or being every day; necessary for every day; usual. adv. Day by day, often, always. s. A newspaper published every morning except on Sundays.
Gai'ly adv. (*Gay*).
Hail'y a. Characterized by hail.
Shab'bily adv. (*Shabby*).
Flab'bily adv. (*Flabby*).
Ra'cily adv. (*Racy*).
I'cily adv. (*Icy*).
Spi'cily adv. (*Spicy*).
Sauc'ily adv. (*Saucy*).
Head'ily adv. (*Heady*).
Read'ily (red'-) adv. Promptly; without delay; willingly, cheerfully.
Stead'ily adv. (*Steady*).
Shad'ily adv. (*Shady*).
Gid'dily adv. (*Giddy*).
Mud'dily adv. (*Muddy*).
Rud'dily adv. (*Ruddy*).
Need'ily adv. (*Needy*).
Speed'ily adv. (*Speedy*).
Greed'ily adv. (*Greedy*).
Seed'ily adv. (*Seedy*).
Ti'dily adv. (*Tidy*).
Hand'ily adv. (*Handy*).
Wind'ily adv. (*Windy*).
Wound'ily (woond'-) adv. (*Woundy*).
Bod'ily a. Relating to the body; actual. adv. Corporeally; entirely.
Blood'ily adv. (*Bloody*).
Mood'ily adv. (*Moody*).
Hard'ily adv. Boldly; with audacity or endurance.
Foolhar'dily adv. (*Foolhardy*).
Tar'dily adv. (*Tardy*).
Word'ily adv. (*Wordy*).
Stur'dily adv. (*Sturdy*).
Gaud'ily adv. (*Gaudy*).
Baw'dily adv. (*Bawdy*).
Dow'dily adv. (*Dowdy*).
Huff'ily adv. (*Huffy*).
Puff'ily adv. (*Puffy*).
Stodg'ily adv. (*Stodgy*).
Shag'gily adv. (*Shaggy*).
Scrag'gily adv. (*Scraggy*).
Fog'gily adv. (*Foggy*).
Slang'ily adv. (*Slangy*).
Stin'gily adv. (*Stingy*).
Snatch'ily adv. (*Snatchy*).
Patch'ily adv. (*Patchy*).
Scratch'ily adv. (*Scratchy*).
Sketch'ily adv. (*Sketchy*).
Tetch'ily adv. (*Tetchy*).
Touch'ily adv. (*Touchy*).
Zooph'ily s. Love of animals.
Flash'ily adv. (*Flashy*).
Trash'ily adv. (*Trashy*).
Wash'ily adv. (*Washy*).
Fish'ily adv. (*Fishy*).
Wrath'ily adv. (*Wrathy*).
Length'ily adv. (*Lengthy*).
Pith'ily adv. (*Pithy*).
Health'ily adv. (*Healthy*).
Stealth'ily (stelth'-) adv. (*Stealthy*).
Wealth'ily adv. (*Wealthy*).
Fil'thily adv. (*Filthy*).
Froth'ily adv. (*Frothy*).
Swarth'ily adv. (*Swarthy*).
Wor'thily adv. (*Worthy*).
Praise'-worthily adv. (*Praiseworthy*).
Streak'ily adv. (*Streaky*).
Squeak'ily adv. (*Squeaky*).
Sha'kily adv. (*Shaky*).
Tack'ily adv. (*Tacky*).
Trick'ily adv. (*Tricky*).
Stick'ily adv. (*Sticky*).
Cock'ily adv. (*Cocky*).
Rock'ily adv. Unsteadily.
Stock'ily adv. (*Stocky*).
Luck'ily adv. Fortunately; by good fortune.
Pluck'ily adv. (*Plucky*).
Cheek'ily adv. (*Cheeky*).
Milk'ily adv. (*Milky*).
Sulk'ily adv. (*Sulky*).
Smo'kily adv. (*Smoky*).
Jerk'ily adv. (*Jerky*).
Perk'ily adv. (*Perky*).
Murk'ily adv. (*Murky*).
Frisk'ily adv. (*Frisky*).
Dusk'ily adv. (*Dusky*).
Husk'ily adv. (*Husky*).
Fluk'ily adv. (*Fluky*).
Pawk'ily adv. (*Pawky*).
Lil'y s. A bulbous plant with fragrant and beautiful flowers. a. Pure white; unspotted.
Friend'lily adv. (*Friendly*).
Kind'lily adv. In a kindly manner.
Live'lily adv. (*Lively*).
Love'lily adv. (*Lovely*).
Ug'lily adv. (*Ugly*).
Wi'lily adv. (*Wily*).
Sil'lily adv. (*Silly*).
Jol'lily adv. (*Jolly*).
Clean'lily adv. (*Cleanly*).
Ho'lily adv. (*Holy*).
Sur'lily adv. (*Surly*).
Ghast'lily adv. (*Ghastly*).
Low'lily adv. (*Lowly*).
Scream'ily adv. (*Screamy*).
Dream'ily adv. (*Dreamy*).
Fam'ily s. Household; parents and children, or children only; a generation; lineage.
Slim'ily adv. (*Slimy*).

Grim'ily adv. (*Grimy*).
Balm'ily adv. (*Balmy*).
Film'ily adv. (*Filmy*).
Clam'mily adv. (*Clammy*).
Rum'mily adv. (*Rummy*).
Hom'ily s. A sermon; a serious discourse.
Gloom'ily adv. (*Gloomy*).
Room'ily adv. (*Roomy*).
Storm'ily adv. (*Stormy*).
Rain'ily adv. (*Rainy*).
Can'nily adv. (*Canny*).
Uncan'nily adv. (*Uncanny*).
Bon'nily adv. (*Bonny*).
Sun'nily adv. (*Sunny*).
Moon'ily adv. (*Moony*).
Spoon'ily adv. (*Spoony*).
Ston'ily adv. (*Stony*).
Horn'ily adv. (*Horny*).
Oil'y a. Consisting of, containing, smeared with, or resembling oil; unctuous; greasy; subservient; hypocritical.
Doi'ly s. A small decorative napkin or table-mat.
Soap'ily adv. (*Soapy*).
Sleep'ily adv. (*Sleepy*).
Scrimp'ily adv. (*Scrimp*).
Lump'ily adv. (*Lump*).
Grump'ily adv. (*Grumpy*).
Hap'pily adv. (*Happy*).
Snap'pily adv. (*Snappy*).
Scrap'pily adv. (*Scrappy*).
Slip'pily adv. (*Slippy*).
Shop'pily adv. (*Shoppy*).
Flop'pily adv. (*Floppy*).
Slop'pily adv. (*Sloppy*).
Sec'ondarily adv. (*Secondary*).
Drear'ily adv. (*Dreary*).
We'arily adv. (*Weary*).
Char'ily adv. (*Chary*).
Subsid'iarily adv. (*Subsidiary*).
Pecu'niarily adv. (*Pecuniary*).
Exem'plarily adv. (*Exemplary*).
Pri'marily adv. In the first place; originally.
Sum'marily adv. (*Summary*).
Cus'tomarily adv. (*Customary*).
Mer'cenarily adv. (*Mercenary*).
Ple'narily adv. (*Plenary*).
Or'dinarily adv. (*Ordinary*).
Extraor'dinarily adv. (*Extraordinary*).
Imag'inarily adv. (*Imaginary*).
Prelim'inarily adv. (*Preliminary*).
Sang'uinarily adv. (*Sanguinary*).
Discre'tionarily adv. (*Discretionary*).
Tem'porarily adv. (*Temporary*).
Extem'porarily adv. (*Extemporary*).
Ar'bitrarily adv. In a despotic or high-handed way.
Con'trarily adv. (*Contrary*).
Nec'essarily adv. Of necessity, inevitably.
Hered'itarily adv. (*Hereditary*).
Mil'itarily adv. (*Military*).
Sol'itarily adv. (*Solitary*).
San'itarily adv. (*Sanitary*).
Sed'entarily adv. (*Sedentary*).
Testamen'tarily adv. (*Testamentary*).
Elemen'tarily adv. (*Elementary*).
Frag'mentarily adv. (*Fragmentary*).
Rudimen'tarily adv. (*Rudimentary*).
Mo'mentarily adv. (*Momentary*).
Vol'untarily adv. (*Voluntary*).
Invol'untarily adv. (*Involuntary*).
Obit'uarily adv. (*Obituary*).
War'ily adv. (*Wary*).
Dri'ly adv. (*Dry*).
Taw'drily adv. (*Tawdry*).
Cheer'ily adv. (*Cheery*).
Fi'erily adv. (*Fiery*).
Slip'perily adv. (*Slippery*).
Ver'ily adv. Assuredly, really, truly.
Ang'rily adv. (*Angry*).
Hung'rily adv. (*Hungry*).
Air'ily adv. In a light and airy manner.
Fair'ily adv. In the manner of the fairies.
Wir'ily adv. (*Wiry*).
Provi'sorily adv. (*Provisory*).
Compul'sorily adv. (*Compulsory*).
Cur'sorily adv. (*Cursory*).
Illu'sorily adv. (*Illusory*).
Lau'datorily adv. (*Laudatory*).
Pref'atorily adv. (*Prefatory*).
Dil'atorily adv. (*Dilatory*).
Consol'atorily adv. (*Consolatory*).
Explan'atorily adv. (*Explanatory*).
Prepar'atorily adv. (*Preparatory*).
Satisfac'torily adv. (*Satisfactory*).
Refrac'torily adv. (*Refractory*).
Contradic'torily adv. (*Contradictory*).
Perfunc'torily adv. (*Perfunctory*).
Introduc'torily adv. By way of introduction.
Premon'itorily adv. (*Premonitory*).
Tran'sitorily adv. (*Transitory*).
Des'ultorily adv. (*Desultory*).
Peremp'torily adv. (*Peremptory*).
Mer'rily adv. (*Merry*).
Sor'rily adv. (*Sorry*).
Pal'trily adv. (*Paltry*).
Sul'trily adv. (*Sultry*).
Sa'vourily adv. (*Savoury*).
Eas'ily adv. In an easy manner, with ease.
Greas'ily adv. (*Greasy*).
Nois'ily adv. (*Noisy*).
Flim'sily adv. (*Flimsy*).
Clum'sily adv. (*Clumsy*).
Co'sily adv. (*Cosy*).
Ro'sily adv. (*Rosy*).
Pro'sily adv. (*Prosy*).
Tip'sily adv. (*Tipsy*).
Hors'ily adv. (*Horsy*).
Glass'ily adv. (*Glassy*).
Brass'ily adv. (*Brassy*).
Gloss'ily adv. (*Glossy*).
Bus'ily adv. (*Busy*).
Lou'sily adv. (*Lousy*).
Drow'sily adv. (*Drowsy*).
Sweat'ily adv. (*Sweaty*).
Throat'ily adv. (*Throaty*).
Craft'ily adv. (*Crafty*).
Shift'ily adv. (*Shifty*).
Thrift'ily adv. (*Thrifty*).
Loft'ily adv. (*Lofty*).
Weight'ily adv. (*Weighty*).
Flight'ily adv. (*Flighty*).
Haught'ily adv. (*Haughty*).
Naught'ily adv. (*Naughty*).
Dought'ily adv. (*Doughty*).
Guilt'ily adv. (*Guilty*).
Fault'ily adv. (*Faulty*).
Scan'tily adv. (*Scanty*).
Dain'tily adv. (*Dainty*).
Jaun'tily adv. (*Jaunty*).
Soot'ily adv. (*Sooty*).
Heart'ily adv. (*Hearty*).
Dirt'ily adv. (*Dirty*).
Has'tily adv. (*Hasty*).
Nas'tily adv. (*Nasty*).
Tas'tily adv. (*Tasty*).
Tes'tily adv. (*Testy*).
Mis'tily adv. (*Misty*).
Fros'tily adv. (*Frosty*).
Thirs'tily adv. (*Thirsty*).
Dus'tily adv. (*Dusty*).
Gus'tily adv. (*Gusty*).
Lus'tily adv. (*Lusty*).
Mus'tily adv. (*Musty*).

Rust'ily adv. (*Rusty*).
Crust'ily adv. (*Crusty*).
Trust'ily adv. (*Trusty*).
Nat'tily adv. (*Natty*).
Pet'tily adv. (*Petty*).
Pret'tily adv. In a pretty manner; pleasingly.
Wit'tily adv. (*Witty*).
Snot'tily adv. (*Snotty*).
Smut'tily adv. (*Smutty*).
Gout'ily adv. (*Gouty*).
Pla'guily adv. (*Plaguy*).
Heav'ily adv. (*Heavy*).
Wa'vily adv. (*Wavy*).
Priv'ily adv. Privately, secretly.
Scur'vily adv. Basely, meanly.
Wi'ly a. Cunning; full of or using wiles.
Show'ily adv. (*Showy*).
Snow'ily adv. (*Snowy*).
Wax'ily adv. (*Waxy*).
Ha'zily adv. (*Hazy*).
La'zily adv. (*Lazy*).
Ma'zily adv. (*Mazy*).
Cra'zily adv. (*Crazy*).
Whee'zily adv. (*Wheezy*).
Do'zily adv. (*Dozy*).
Ooz'ily adv. (*Oozy*).
Diz'zily adv. (*Dizzy*).
Fuz'zily adv. (*Fuzzy*).
Muz'zily adv. (*Muzzy*).
Bleak'ly adv. (*Bleak*).
Weak'ly adv. In a weak manner. a. Infirm, feeble.
Hack'ly a. Jagged; breaking unevenly (of crystals).
Ram'shackly a. Tumbledown, rickety.
Slack'ly adv. (*Slack*).
Freck'ly adv. Spotted with freckles.
Thick'ly adv. (*Thick*).
Prick'ly a. Full of or armed with prickles.
Trick'ly a. Trickling.
Sick'ly a. Disposed to illness; appearing as if unwell; infirm, weakly. v.t. To make appear ill.
Quick'ly adv. (*Quick*).
Sleek'ly adv. (*Sleek*).
Meek'ly adv. (*Meek*).
Week'ly a. Happening, done, etc., once a week; lasting or pertaining to a week. adv. Once a week; week by week. s. A publication issued once a week.
Dank'ly adv. (*Dank*).
Lank'ly adv. (*Lank*).
Blank'ly adv. (*Blank*).
Rank'ly adv. With vigorous growth; grossly.
Frank'ly adv. Sincerely, openly, candidly.
Crinkl'y a. Having crinkles.
Wrinkl'y a. Full of wrinkles; corrugated.
Dark'ly adv. (*Dark*).
Clerk'ly a. (*Clerk*).
Brisk'ly adv. (*Brisk*).
Ally' s. One united by friendship, marriage, treaty, etc.; something resembling another. v.t. To combine, join with or to, form an alliance.
Al'ly s. A playing marble, an alley.
Bal'ly a. (*Slang*) Very; awful.
Tri'bally adv. (*Tribal*).
Verb'ally adv. (*Verbal*).
Heli'acally adv. (*Heliacal*).
Mani'acally adv. (*Maniacal*).
Demoni'acally adv. (*Demoniacal*).
Hypochondri'acally adv. (*Hyponchondriac*).
-ically suff. Forming adverbs from adjectives in *-ic* and *-ical*.
Juda'ically adv. After the Jewish manner.
La'ically adv. (*Laic*).
Algebra'ically adv. (*Algebraic*).
Hebra'ically adv. (*Hebraic*).
Pharisa'ically adv. (*Pharisaic*).
Mosa'ically adv. In the manner of mosaic work.
Prosa'ically adv. (*Prosaic*).
Syllab'ically adv. (*Syllabic*).
Polysyllab'ically adv. (*Polysyllabic*).
Cu'bically adv. (*Cubic*).
Far'cically adv. (*Farcical*).
Nomad'ically adv. (*Nomadic*).
Rad'ically adv. Fundamentally; essentially.
Sporad'ically adv. (*Sporadic*).
Med'ically adv. (*Medical*).
Verid'ically adv. (*Veridical*).
Jurid'ically adv. (*Juridical*).
Heral'dically adv. (*Heraldic*).
Method'ically adv. (*Methodic*).
Period'ically adv. At stated intervals.
Spasmod'ically adv. (*Spasmodic*).
Synod'ically adv. (*Synodical*).
Onomatopœ'ically adv. (*Onomatopœic*).
Specif'ically adv. (*Specific*).
Prolif'ically adv. (*Prolific*).
Magnif'ically adv. (*Magnifical*).
Territ'ically adv. (*Terrific*).
Scientif'ically adv. (*Scientific*).
Pontif'ically adv. (*Pontifical*).
Mag'ically adv. (*Magic*).
Trag'ically adv. (*Tragic*).
Strateg'ically adv. (*Strategic*).
-log'ically suff. Forming adverbs from adjectives in *-logic* and *-logical*).
Log'ically adv. (*Logical*).
Dialog'ically adv. (*Dialogic*).
Analog'ically adv. (*Analogical*).
Illog'ically adv. (*Illogical*).
-ologically suff. Forming adverbs from adjectives in *-ological*, and nouns in *-ology*.
Amphibolog'ically adv. (*Amphibology*).
Archæolog'ically adv. (*Archæological*).
Theolog'ically adv. According to the principles of theology.
Neolog'ically adv. (*Neological*).
Psycholog'ically adv. (*Psychological*).
Mytholog'ically adv. (*Mythological*).
Biolog'ically adv. (*Biological*).
Physiolog'ically adv. (*Physiological*).
Homolog'ically adv. (*Homological*).
Entomolog'ically adv. (*Entomological*).
Terminolog'ically adv. (*Terminology*).
Chronolog'ically adv. (*Chronological*).
Anthropolog'ically adv. (*Anthropological*).
Astrolog'ically adv. (*Astrological*).
Lethar'gically adv. (*Lethargic*).
Metallur'gically adv. (*Metallurgic*).
Sur'gically adv. (*Surgical*).
Thaumatur'gically adv. (*Thaumaturgic*).
Litur'gically adv. (*Liturgical*).
Oligarch'ically adv. (*Oligarchic*).
Anar'chically adv. (*Anarchic*).
Monarch'ically adv. (*Monarchic*).
Psy'chically adv. (*Psychical*).
Seraph'ically adv. (*Seraphic*).
-graphically suff. Many adverbs formed from nouns in *-graph*.
Graph'ically adv. (*Graphic*).
Biograph'ically adv. (*Biographical*).

Autobiograph'-ically adv. (*Autobiographic*).
Crystallo-graph'ically adv. (*Crystallography*.
Demograph'-ically adv. (*Demographic*).
Chorograph'-ically adv. (*Chorographic*).
Cinemato-graph'ically adv. (*Cinematograph*).
Photograph'-ically adv. (*Photographic*).
Philosoph'-ically adv. (*Philosophic*).
Hieroglyph'-ically adv. (*Hieroglyphic*).
Telepath'ically adv. (*Telepathic*).
Homœopath'-ically adv. (*Homœopathic*).
Idiopath'ically adv. (*Idiopathic*).
Eth'ically adv. According to ethics.
Goth'ically adv. (*Gothic*).
Myth'ically adv. (*Mythic*).
Bib'lically adv. (*Biblical*).
Angel'ically adv. (*Angelic*).
Evangel'ically adv. (*Evangelical*).
Hel'ically adv. (*Helical*).
Idyl'lically adv. (*Idyllic*).
Diabol'ically adv. (*Diabolical*).
Parabol'ically adv. (*Parabolic*).
Symbol'ically adv. (*Symbolic*).
Hyperbol'ically adv. In the form of a hyperbola; with exaggeration.
Bucol'ically adv. (*Bucolic*).
Cathol'ically adv. (*Catholic*).
Apostol'ically adv. (*Apostolical*).
Hydraul'ically adv. (*Hydraulic*).
Dynam'ically adv. (*Dynamical*).
Panoram'ically adv. (*Panoramic*).
Endem'ically adv. (*Endemic*).
Chem'ically adv. (*Chemical*).
Alchem'ically adv. (*Alchemical*).
Polem'ically adv. (*Polemical*).
System'ically adv. (*Systemic*).
Logarith'-mically adv. (*Logarithmic*).
Rhyth'mically adv. (*Rythmical*).
Pantomim'-ically adv. (*Pantomimic*).
Inim'ically adv. (*Inimical*).
Com'ically adv. (*Comical*).
Physiognom'-ically (-onom'-) adv. (*Physiognomic*).
Econom'ically adv. (*Economical*).
Metronom'-ically adv. (*Metronomic*).
Astronom'-ically adv. (*Astronomical*).
Gastronom'-ically adv. (*Gastronomic*).
Atom'ically adv. (*Atomic*).
Anatom'ically adv. (*Anatomical*).
Phantom'ically adv. (*Phantomical*).
Ender'mically adv. (*Endermic*).
Hypoder'-mically adv. (*Hypodermic*).
Phantas'-mically adv. (*Phantasmic*).
Cos'mically adv. (*Cosmic*).
Microcos'-mically adv. (*Microcosmic*).
Metonym'ically adv. (*Metonymic*).
Volcan'ically adv. (*Volcanic*).
Organ'ically adv. (*Organic*).
Mechan'ically adv. (*Mechanical*).
Charlatan'-ically adv. (*Charlatan*).
Satan'ically adv. (*Satanic*).
Puritan'ically adv. (*Puritanic*).
Botan'ically adv. (*Botanical*).
Galvan'ically adv. (*Galvanic*).
Hygien'ically adv. (*Hygienic*).
Tech'nically adv. (*Technical*).
Rabbin'ically adv. (*Rabbinical*).
Fin'ically adv. (*Finical*).
Clin'ically adv. (*Clinical*).
Tyran'nically adv. (*Tyrannical*).
Con'ically adv. (*Conical*).
Lacon'ically adv. (*Laconic*).
Sardon'ically adv. (*Sardonic*).
Telephon'ically adv. (*Telephonic*).
Euphon'ically adv. (*Euphonic*).
Histrion'ically adv. (*Histrionic*).
Gnomon'ically adv. (*Gnomonic*).
Harmon'ically adv. (*Harmonic*).
Enharmon'-ically adv. (*Enharmonic*).
Canon'ically adv. (*Canonical*).
Iron'ically adv. (*Ironical*).
Byron'ically adv. In the manner of Byron or his poetry; theatrically gloomy.
Thrason'ically adv. (*Thrasonical*).
Parson'ically adv. (*Parsonic*).
Diaton'ically adv. (*Diatonic*).
Platon'ically adv. (*Platonic*).
Cyn'ically adv. (*Cynical*).
Hero'ically adv. (*Heroic*).
Sto'ically adv. (*Stoical*).
A'pically adv. (*Apical*).
Orthoe'pically adv. (*Orthoepic*).
Microscop'-ically adv. (*Microscopic*).
Spectroscop'-ically adv. (*Spectroscopic*).
Philanthrop'-ically adv. (*Philanthropic*).
Trop'ically adv. (*Tropical*).
Allotrop'ically adv. (*Allotropic*).
Top'ically adv. (*Topical*).
Typ'ically adv. (*Typical*).
Spher'ically adv. (*Spherical*).
Atmospher'-ically adv. (*Atmospheric*).
Cler'ically adv. (*Clerical*).
Chimer'ically adv. (*Chimerical*).
Numer'ically adv. (*Numerical*).
Gener'ically adv. (*Generic*).
Neoter'ically adv. (*Neoteric*).
Exoter'ically adv. (*Exoteric*).
Hyster'ically adv. (*Hysterical*).
Empir'ically adv. (*Empiric*).
Satir'ically adv. (*Satirical*).
Categor'ically adv. (*Categorical*).
Metaphor'-ically adv. (*Metaphoric*).
Orator'ically adv. (*Oratorical*).
Rhetor'ically adv. (*Rhetorical*).
Histor'ically adv. (*Historical*).
Prehistor'ically adv. (*Prehistoric*).
Theat'rically adv. (*Theatrical*).
Elec'trically adv. (*Electric*).
Met'rically adv. (*Metrical*).
Diamet'rically adv. (*Diametrical*)
Symmet'rically adv. (*Symmetric*).
Asymmet'-rically adv. (*Asymmetrical*).
Geomet'rically adv. (*Geometrical*).
Biomet'rically adv. (*Biometrical*).
Thermomet'-rically adv. (*Thermometrical*).
Trigonomet'-rically adv. (*Trigonometric*).
Chronomet'-rically adv. (*Chronometer*).
Baromet'rically adv. (*Barometric*).
Bathymet'-rically adv. (*Bathymetrical*).
Cen'trically adv. (*Centric*).

Eccen'trically adv. (*Eccentric*).
Concen'trically adv. (*Concentric*).
Heliocen'-trically adv. (*Heliocentric*).
Diop'trically adv. (*Dioptric*).
Panegyr'ically adv. (*Panegyrical*).
Lyr'ically adv. (*Lyrical*).
Lackadais'-ically adv. (*Lackadaisical*).
Whim'sically adv. (*Whimsical*).
Foren'sically adv. (*Forensic*).
Nonsen'sically adv. (*Nonsensical*).
Intrin'sically adv. (*Intrinsic*).
Extrin'sically adv. (*Extrinsic*).
Drop'sically adv. (*Dropsical*).
Clas'sically adv. (*Classical*).
Mu'sically adv. (*Musical*).
Phys'ically adv. (*Physical*).
Metaphys'ically adv. (*Metaphysical*).
Sabbat'ically adv. (*Sabbatic*).
Acrobat'ically adv. (*Acrobatic*).
Emphat'ically adv. (*Emphatic*).
Dramat'ically adv. (*Dramatic*).
Melodramat'-ically adv. (*Melodramatic*).
Schemat'ically adv. (*Schematic*).
Themat'ically adv. (*Thematic*).
Mathemat'-ically adv. (*Mathematical*).
Emblemat'-ically adv. By way or means of emblems.
Problemat'-ically adv. (*Problematic*).
Systemat'ically adv. (*Systematic*).
Pragmat'ically adv. (*Pragmatical*).
Judgmat'ically adv. (*Judgmatic*).
Apophtheg-mat'ically adv. (*Apophthegmatic*).
Phlegmat'ically adv. (*Phlegmatic*).
Enigmat'ically adv. (*Enigmatic*).
Stigmat'ically adv. (*Stigmatic*).
Dogmat'ically adv. (*Dogmatic*).
Asthmat'ically adv. (*Asthmatic*).
Climat'ically adv. (*Climatic*).
-grammatically suff. Forming adverbs from adjectives in *-grammatic*, and nouns in *-gram*.
Grammat'ically adv. (*Grammatical*).
Diagrammat'-ically adv. (*Diagrammatic*).
Anagrammat'-ically adv. (*Anagram*).
Idiomat'ically adv. (*Idiomatic*).
Axiomat'ically adv. (*Axiomatic*).
Diplomat'ically adv. (*Diplomatic*).
Chromat'ically adv. (*Chromatic*).
Achromat'-ically adv. (*Achromatic*).
Symptomat'-ically adv. (*Symptomatic*).
Schismat'ically adv. (*Schismatic*).
Numismat'-ically adv. (*Numismatic*).
Prismat'ically adv. (*Prismatic*).
Pneumat'ically adv. (*Pneumatic*).
Fanat'ically adv. (*Fanatic*).
Ochlocrat'ically adv. (*Ochlocratic*).
Democrat'-ically adv. (*Democratic*).
Socrat'ically adv. (*Socratic*).
Aristocrat'-ically adv. (*Aristocratic*).
Autocrat'ically adv. (*Autocratic*).
Bureaucrat'-ically adv. (*Bureaucratic*).
Operat'ically adv. (*Operatic*).
Pirat'ically adv. (*Piratical*).
Errat'ically adv. In an erratic, irregular way.
Stat'ically adv. (*Static*).
Ecstat'ically adv. (*Ecstatic*).
Hypostat'ically adv. (*Hypostatic*).
Hydrostat'-ically adv. (*Hydrostatic*).
Didac'tically adv. (*Didactic*).
Prac'tically adv. In relation to, or by means of practice or use; in effect.
Tac'tically adv. (*Tactical*).
Syntac'tically adv. (*Syntactic*).
Hec'tically adv. (*Hectic*).
Eclec'tically adv. (*Eclectic*).
-etically suff. Forming adverbs from adjectives in *-etical*.
Alphabet'ically adv. (*Alphabetic*).
Ascet'ically adv. (*Ascetic*).
Geodet'ically adv. (*Geodetic*).
Apologet'ically adv. (*Apologetic*).
Energet'ically adv. (*Energetic*).
Catechet'ically adv. (*Catechetic*).
Prophet'ically adv. (*Prophetic*).
Pathet'ically adv. (*Pathetic*).
Antipathet'-ically adv. (*Antipathetic*).
Sympathet'-ically adv. (*Sympathetic*).
Antithet'ically adv. (*Antithetic*).
Parenthet'-ically adv. By way of parenthesis.
Synthet'ically adv. (*Synthetic*).
Hypothet'ically adv. (*Hypothetic*).
Æsthet'ically adv. (*Æsthetic*).
Prosthet'ically adv. (*Prosthesis*).
Athlet'ically adv. (*Athletic*).
Emet'ically adv. (*Emetic*).
Arithmet'ically adv. (*Arithmetical*).
Mimet'ically adv. (*Mimetic*).
Hermet'ically adv. (*Hermetic*).
Genet'ically adv. (*Genetic*).
Abiogenet'-ically adv. (*Abiogenetic*).
Gamogenet'-ically adv. (*Gamogenetic*).
Parthenogen-et'ically adv. (*Parthenogenetic*).
Ontogenet'-ically adv. (*Ontogenetic*).
Splenet'ically adv. (*Splenetic*).
Magnet'ically adv. (*Magnetic*).
Diamagnet'-ically adv. (*Diamagnetic*).
Phonet'ically adv. (*Phonetic*).
Poet'ically adv. (*Poetic*).
Heret'ically adv. (*Heretical*).
Theoret'ically adv. (*Theoretic*).
Peripatet'ically adv. (*Peripatetic*).
Dietet'ically adv. (*Dietetical*).
Enclit'ically adv. (*Enclitic*).
Polit'ically adv. (*Political*).
Stalagmit'-ically adv. (*Stalagmitic*).
Crit'ically adv. (*Critical*).
Hypocrit'ically adv. (*Hypocritical*).
Jesuit'ically adv. (*Jesuitical*).
Levit'ically adv. (*Levitical*).
Cel'tically adv. (*Celtic*).
Pedan'tically adv. (*Pedantic*).
Roman'tically adv. (*Romantic*).
Necroman'-tically adv. (*Necromantic*).
Fran'tically adv. (*Frantic*).
Iden'tically adv. (*Identical*).
Authen'tically adv. (*Authentic*).
Chaot'ically adv. (*Chaotic*).
Narcot'ically adv. (*Narcotic*).
Symbiot'ically adv. (*Symbiotic*).
Idiot'ically adv. (*Idiotic*).
Patriot'ically adv. (*Patriotic*).
Osmot'ically adv. (*Osmotic*).
Zymot'ically adv. (*Zymotic*).
Despot'ically adv. (*Despotic*).

Quixot'ically adv. (*Quixotic*).
Scep'tically adv. (*Sceptical*).
Syllep'tically adv. (*Sylleptic*).
Prolep'tically adv. (*Proleptic*).
Sep'tically adv. (*Septic*).
Ellip'tically adv. (*Elleptic*).
Op'tically adv. (*Optic*).
Synop'tically adv. (*Synoptic*).
Apocalyp'tically adv. (*Apocalyptic*).
Cryp'tically adv. (*Cryptic*).
Cathar'tically adv. (*Cathartic*).
Ver'tically adv. (*Vertical*).
Vor'tically adv. (*Vortical*).
Bombas'tically adv. (*Bombastic*).
Sarcas'tically adv. (*Sarcastic*).
Encomias'tically adv. (*Encomiastic*).
Ecclesias'tically adv. (*Ecclesiastical*).
Enthusias'tically adv. (*Enthusiastic*).
Elas'tically adv. With a spring.
Scholas'tically adv. (*Scholastic*).
Plas'tically adv. (*Plastic*).
Gymnas'tically adv. (*Gymnastic*).
Pleonas'tically adv. (*Pleonastic*).
Monas'tically adv. (*Monastic*).
Dynas'tically adv. (*Dynastic*).
Dras'tically adv. (*Drastic*).
Paraphras'tically adv. (*Paraphrastic*).
Periphras'tically adv. (*Periphrastic*).
Fantas'tically adv. (*Fantastic*).
Majes'tically adv. (*Majestic*).
Domes'tically adv. (*Domestic*).
Catachres'tically adv. (*Catachrestic*).
Methodis'tically adv. (*Methodistic*).
Deis'tically adv. (*Deistic*).
Theis'tically adv. (*Theistic*).
Atheis'tically adv. (*Atheistic*).
Monotheis'tically adv. (*Monotheistic*).
Polytheis'tically adv. (*Polytheistic*).
Syllogis'tically adv. (*Syllogistic*).
Dyslogis'tically adv. (*Dyslogistic*).
Eulogis'tically adv. (*Eulogistic*).
Catechis'tically adv. (*Catechist*).
Sophis'tically adv. (*Sophistic*).
Cabbalis'tically adv. (*Cabbalistic*).
Idealis'tically adv. (*Idealistic*).
Realis'tically adv. (*Realistic*).
Socialis'tically adv. (*Socialistic*).
Materialis'tically adv. (*Materialistic*).
Rationalis'tically adv. (*Rationalistic*).
Naturalis'tically adv. (*Naturalistic*).
Fatalis'tically adv. (*Fatalistic*).
Ritualis'tically adv. (*Ritualistic*).
Stylis'tically adv. (*Stylistic*).
Euphemis'tically adv. (*Euphemistic*).
Pessimis'tically adv. (*Pessimistic*).
Optimis'tically adv. (*Optimistic*).
Hellenis'tically adv. (*Hellenistic*).
Chauvinis'tically adv. (*Chauvinism*).
Antagonis'tically adv. (*Antagonistic*).
Synchronis'tically adv. (*Synchronistic*).
Egois'tically adv. (*Egoist*).
Papis'tically adv. (*Papistical*).
Characteris'tically adv. (*Characteristic*).
Aphoris'tically adv. (*Aphoristic*).
Juris'tically adv. (*Juristic*).
Statis'tically adv. (*Statistic*).
Egotis'tically adv. (*Egotistic*).
Artis'tically adv. (*Artistic*).
Inartis'tically adv. (*Inartistic*).
Linguis'tically adv. (*Linguistic*).
Euphuis'tically adv. (*Euphuistic*).
Altruis'tically adv. (*Altruistic*).
Casuis'tically adv. (*Casuistic*).
Diagnos'tically adv. (*Diagnostic*).
Caus'tically adv. (*Caustic*).
Rus'tically adv. (*Rustic*).
Mys'tically adv. (*Mystic*).
Nau'tically adv. (*Nautical*).
Pharmaceu'tically adv. (*Pharmaceutical*).
Hermeneu'tically adv. (*Hermeneutical*).
Therapeu'tically adv. (*Therapeutical*).
Analyt'ically adv. (*Analytic*).
Paralyt'ically adv. (*Paralytic*).
Civ'ically adv. (*Civic*).
Lex'ically adv. (*Lexical*).
Paradox'ically adv. (*Paradoxical*).
Tox'ically adv. (*Toxic*).
Quiz'zically adv. (*Quizzical*).
Lo'cally adv. (*Local*).
Recip'rocally adv. (*Reciprocal*).
Vo'cally adv. (*Vocal*).
Univ'ocally adv. (*Univocal*).
Ras'cally a. Meanly trickish; base.
Fis'cally adv. (*Fiscal*).
Du'cally adv. In a ducal manner.
Dal'ly v.i. To loiter, linger, delay. v.t. To fondle; to put off with trifling excuses.
Hebdom'adally adv. (*Hebdomadal*).
Suici'dally adv. (*Suicidal*).
Pyram'idally adv. (*Pyramidal*).
Spheroid'ally adv. (*Spheriodal*).
Mo'dally adv. (*Modal*).
Cau'dally adv. (*Caudal*).
Feu'dally adv. (*Feudal*).
Dil'ly-dal'ly v.t. To loiter, trifle.
Ide'ally adv. Intellectually; in an ideal manner.
Rectilin'eally adv. (*Rectilineal*).
Re'ally adv. Actually; in truth.
Funer'eally adv. (*Funereal*).
Corpor'eally adv. (*Corporeal*).
Incorpor'eally adv. (*Incorporeal*).
Le'gally adv. (*Legal*).
Ille'gally adv. (*Illegal*).
Re'gally adv. (*Regal*).
Prod'igally adv. (*Prodigal*).
Diphthon'gally adv. (*Diphthongal*).
Fu'gally adv. (*Fugal*).
Centrif'ugally adv. (*Centrifugal*).
Con'jugally adv. (*Conjugal*).
Fru'gally adv. (*Frugal*).
Chal'ly s. Challis.
Apoc'ryphally adv. (*Apocryphal*).
Shill'y-shall'y v.i. To hesitate, act irresolutely. s. Irresolution; trifling.
La'bially adv. By means of the lips.
Adverb'ially adv. (*Adverbial*).
Proverb'ially adv. Commonly, universally.
Connu'bially adv. (*Connubial*).
Fa'cially adv. (*Facial*).
Gla'cially adv. (*Glacial*).
Ra'cially adv. (*Racial*).
Espec'ially adv. (*Especial*).
Judi'cially adv. (*Judicial*).

Prejudi'cially adv. (*Prejudicial*).
Benefi'cially adv. (*Beneficial*).
Offi'cially adv. (*Official*).
Artifi'cially adv. (*Artificial*).
Inartifi'cially adv. (*Inartificial*).
Superfi'cially adv. (*Superficial*).
Finan'cially adv. (*Financial*).
Quincun'cially adv. (*Quincuncial*).
So'cially adv. (*Social*).
Commer'cially adv. (*Commercial*).
Fidu'cially adv. (*Fiducial*).
Reme'dially adv. (*Remedial*).
Allo'dially adv. (*Allodial*).
Cor'dially adv. (*Cordial*).
Primor'dially adv. (*Primordial*).
Paro'chially adv. (*Parochial*).
Fil'ially adv. (*Filial*).
Trino'mially adv. (*Trinomial*).
Ge'nially adv. Cheerfully; cordially.
Conge'nially adv. (*Congenial*).
Me'nially adv. (*Menial*).
Ve'nially adv. (*Venial*).
Decen'nially adv. (*Decennial*).
Bien'nially adv. Every two years; biennial.
Trien'nially adv. (*Triennial*).
Peren'nially adv. (*Perennial*).
Octen'nially adv. (*Octennial*).
Septen'nially adv. (*Septennial*).
Quinquen'-nially adv. (*Quinquennial*).
Sexen'nially adv. (*Sexennial*).
Colo'nially adv. (*Colonial*).
Ceremo'nially adv. (*Ceremonial*).
Matrimo'nially adv. (*Matrimonial*).
Patrimo'nially adv. By inheritance.
Particip'ially adv. In the sense or manner of a participle.
Notar'ially adv. (*Notarial*).
Imper'ially adv. (*Imperial*).
Ser'ially adv. (*Serial*).
Mater'ially adv. (*Material*).
Immater'ially adv. (*Immaterial*).
Magister'ially adv. (*Magisterial*).
Minister'ially adv. (*Ministerial*).
Immemor'ially adv. (*Immemorial*).
Sponsor'ially adv. (*Sponsorial*).
Professor'ially adv. (*Professorial*).
Senator'ially adv. (*Senatorial*).
Dictator'ially adv. (*Dictatorial*).
Pictor'ially adv. (*Pictorial*).
Proprietor'ially adv. (*Proprietorial*).
Editor'ially adv. (*Editorial*).
Monitor'ially adv. (*Monitorial*).
Territor'ially adv. (*Territorial*).
Tutor'ially adv. (*Tutorial*).
Terres'trially adv. (*Terrestrial*).
Indus'trially adv. (*Industrial*).
Me'sially adv. (*Mesial*).
Controver'sially adv. (*Controversial*).
Spa'tially adv. (*Spatial*).
Interspa'tially adv. (*Interspatial*).
Ini'tially adv. At the beginning.
Substan'tially adv. (*Substantial*).
Circumstan'-tially adv. (*Circumstantial*).
Confiden'tially adv. (*Confidential*).
Presiden'tially adv. (*Presidential*).
Eviden'tially adv. (*Evidential*).
Providen'tially adv. (*Providential*).
Pruden'tially adv. (*Prudential*).
Tangen'tially adv. (*Tangential*).
Scien'tially adv. (*Sciential*).
Experien'tially adv. (*Experiential*).
Pestilen'tially adv. (*Pestilential*).
Deferen'tially adv. (*Deferential*).
Preferen'tially adv. (*Preferential*).
Inferen'tially adv. (*Inferential*).
Reveren'tially adv. (*Reverential*).
Coessen'tially adv. (*Coessential*).
Peniten'tially adv. (*Penitential*).
Poten'tially adv. (*Potential*).
Influen'tially adv. (*Influential*).
Sequen'tially adv. (*Sequential*).
Consequen'-tially adv. (*Consequential*).
Inconsequen'-tially adv. (*Inconsequential*).
Mar'tially adv. (*Martial*).
Par'tially adv. In part, not totally; unduly biased.
Impar'tially adv. (*Impartial*).
Bes'tially adv. In the manner of a beast.
Celes'tially adv. (*Celestial*).
Ventrilo'-quially adv. (*Ventriloquial*).
Collo'quially adv. (*Colloquial*).
Triv'ially adv. (*Trivial*).
Conviv'ially adv. (*Convivial*).
Jo'vially adv. (*Jovial*).
Ax'ially adv. (*Axial*).
Uniax'ially adv. (*Uniaxial*).
Dec'imally adv. (*Decimal*).
Duodec'imally adv. (*Duodecimal*).
An'imally adv. Physically, not intellectually.
Pri'mally adv. (*Primal*).
Sexages'imally adv. (*Sexagesimal*).
Infinites'imally adv. (*Infinitesimal*).
Prox'imally adv. (*Proximal*).
Ther'mally adv. (*Thermal*).
For'mally adv. (*Formal*).
Infor'mally adv. (*Informal*).
Nor'mally adv. (*Normal*).
Abnor'mally adv. (*Abnormal*).
Phantas'mally adv. (*Phantasmal*).
Dis'mally adv. ((*Dismal*).
Baptis'mally adv. (*Baptismal*).
Paroxys'mally adv. (*Paroxysmal*).
Phenom'enally adv. (*Phenomenal*).
Nou'menally adv. (*Noumenal*).
Pe'nally adv. (*Penal*).
Ve'nally adv. (*Venal*).
Sig'nally adv. Eminently; remarkably.
Medi'cinally adv. (*Medicinal*).
Offi'cinally adv. (*Officinal*).
Car'dinally adv. Fundamentally.
Longitu'-dinally adv. (*Longitudinal*).
Fi'nally adv. (*Final*).
Orig'inally adv. (*Original*).
Aborig'inally adv. (*Aboriginal*).
Mar'ginally adv. (*Marginal*).
Vir'ginally adv. (*Virginal*).
Sem'inally adv. (*Seminal*).
Crim'inally adv. (*Criminal*).
Abdom'inally adv. (*Abdominal*).
Nom'inally adv. Not actually; in name only.
Cognom'inally adv. (*Cognominal*).
Pronom'inally adv. (*Pronominal*).
Ger'minally adv. (*Germinal*).
Ter'minally adv. (*Terminal*).
Doctri'nally adv. (*Doctrinal*).
Matu'tinally adv. (*Matutinal*).
Meridi'onally adv. (*Meridion*).
Diag'onally adv. (*Diagonal*).
Octag'onally adv. (*Octagonal*).
Trig'onally adv. (*Trigonal*).
Orthog'onally adv. (*Orthogonal*).
Polyg'onally adv. (*Polygonal*).
Antiph'onally adv. (*Antiphonal*).
Re'gionally adv. (*Regional*).
Occa'sionally adv. *Occasional*).
Vi'sionally adv. (*Visional*).
Previ'sionally adv. (*Previsional*).
Divi'sionally adv. (*Divisional*).
Provi'sionally adv. (*Provisional*).
Rever'sionally adv. (*Reversional*).
Tor'sionally adv. (*Torsion*).
Success'ionally adv. (*Successional*).

Proces'sionally adv. (*Processional*).
Profes'sionally adv. (*Professional*).
Voca'tionally adv. (*Vocation*).
Educa'tionally adv. (*Educational*).
Grada'tionally adv. (*Gradational*).
Rela'tionally adv. (*Relation*).
Na'tionally adv. (*National*).
Denomina'-tionally adv. (*Denominational*).
Interna'-tionally adv. (*International*).
Ra'tionally adv. (*Rational*).
Irra'tionally adv. (*Irrational*).
Sensa'tionally adv. (*Sensational*).
Conversa'-tionally adv. (*Conversational*)
Observa'-tionally adv. (*Observational*).
Frac'tionally adv. (*Fractional*).
Interjec'-tionally adv. (*Interjectional*).
Sec'tionally adv. (*Sectional*).
Fric'tionally adv. (*Frictional*).
Func'tionally adv. (*Functional*).
Conjunc'-tionally adv. (*Conjunctional*).
Discre'tionally adv. (*Discretional*).
Tradi'tionally adv. (*Traditional*).
Addi'tionally adv. (*Additional*).
Condi'tionally adv. (*Conditional*).
Voli'tionally adv. (*Volitional*).
Transi'tionally adv. (*Transitional*).
Supposi'-tionally adv. (*Suppositional*).
Inten'tionally adv. (*Intentional*).
Conven'tionally adv. (*Conventional*).
Emo'tionally adv. (*Emotional*).
No'tionally adv. (*Notional*).
Devo'tionally adv. (*Devotional*).
Excep'tionally adv. (*Exceptional*).
Op'tionally adv. (*Optional*).
Propor'tionally adv. In proportion; in due degree.
Dispropor'-tionally adv. (*Disproportional*).
Substitu'-tionally adv. (*Substitutional*).
Constitu'-tionally adv. (*Constitutional*).
Sea'sonally adv. (*Seasonal*).
Per'sonally adv. In a personal or direct manner; in person; particularly.
Imper'sonally adv. (*Impersonal*).
To'nally adv. (*Tonal*).
Zo'nally adv. (*Zonal*).
Infer'nally adv. (*Infernal*).
Mater'nally adv. (*Maternal*).
Pater'nally adv. (*Paternal*).
Frater'nally adv. (*Fraternal*).
Eter'nally adv. Perpetually; unchangeably.
Coeter'nally adv. (*Coeternal*).
Sempiter'nally adv. (*Sempiternal*).
Inter'nally adv. (*Internal*).
Exter'nally adv. (*External*).
Ver'nally adv. (*Vernal*).
Diur'nally adv. (*Diurnal*).
Noctur'nally adv. (*Nocturnal*).
Pal'ly a. (*Slang*) Closely friendly.
Pa'pally adv. (*Papal*).
Munic'ipally adv. (*Municipal*).
Prin'cipally adv. Mainly, especially; essentially.
Ral'ly v.i. To recover, re-collect; to banter, chaff. v.t. To gather again, re-unite. s. Act of recovering order, health, etc.; (*tennis*) rapid return of strokes.
Ver'tebrally adv. (*Vertebral*).
Lib'erally adv. (*Liberal*).
Illib'erally adv. (*Illiberal*).
Fed'erally adv. (*Federal*).
Nu'merally adv. (*Numeral*).
Gen'erally adv. In general, usually; without detail.
Lat'erally adv. (*Lateral*).
Unilat'erally adv. (*Unilateral*).
Trilat'erally adv. (*Trilateral*).
Collat'erally adv. (*Collateral*).
Lit'erally adv. (*Literal*).
Sev'erally adv. (*Several*).
In'tegrally adv. (*Integral*).
Sepul'chrally adv. (*Sepulchral*).
Spi'rally adv. (*Spiral*).
Or'ally adv. (*Oral*).
Chor'ally adv. (*Choral*).
Flor'ally adv. (*Floral*).
Mor'ally adv. According to morality; virtually.
Immor'ally adv. (*Immoral*).
Tem'porally adv. (*Temporal*).
Extem'porally adv. (*Extemporal*).
Cor'porally adv. Bodily, materially.
Pas'torally adv. (*Pastoral*).
Spec'trally adv. (*Spectral*).
Diamet'rally adv. (*Diametral*).
Cen'trally adv. (*Central*).
Ven'trally adv. (*Ventral*).
Sinis'trally adv. (*Sinistral*).
Neu'trally adv. (*Neutral*).
Au'rally adv. By the ear, by hearing.
Mercu'rially adv. (*Mercurial*).
Plur'ally adv. (*Plural*).
Rur'ally adv. (*Rural*).
Nat'urally adv. According to nature; without affectation; spontaneously; of course.
Supernat'urally adv. (*Supernatural*).
Preternat'-urally adv. (*Preternatural*).
Conjec'turally adv. (*Conjectural*).
Interjec'turally adv. (*Interjectural*).
Architec'turally adv. (*Architectural*).
Struc'turally adv. (*Structural*).
Scrip'turally adv. (*Scriptural*).
Sculp'turally adv. (*Sculptural*).
Gut'turally adv. (*Guttural*).
Su'turally adv. (*Sutural*).
Gyr'ally adv. (*Gyral*).
Sal'ly s. A sudden leaping forth, especially to attack; a digression; liveliness; flight of fancy; wit. v.i. To rush out, issue suddenly.
Na'sally adv. (*Nasal*).
Univer'sally adv. (*Universal*).
Transver'sally adv. (*Transversal*).
Sinistror'sally adv. (*Sinistrorsal*).
Caus'ally adv. (*Causal*).
Tal'ly s. A notched stick for keeping accounts. v.i. To be fitted or suitable; to conform.
Fa'tally adv. (*Fatal*).
Prena'tally adv. (*Prenatal*).
Dialec'tally adv. (*Dialectal*).
Vari'etally adv. (*Varietal*).
Centrip'etally adv. (*Centripetal*).
Congen'itally adv. (*Congenital*).
Mar'itally adv. (*Marital*).
Vi'tally adv. (*Vital*).
Consonan'tally adv. (*Consonantal*).
Acciden'tally adv. (*Accidental*).
Occiden'tally adv. (*Occidental*).
Inciden'tally adv. (*Incidental*).
Transcenden'-tally adv. (*Transcendental*).
Orien'tally adv. (*Oriental*).
Men'tally adv. (*Mental*).
Medicamen'-tally adv. (*Medicamental*).
Fundamen'-tally adv. (*Fundamental*).

Ornamen'tally adv. (*Ornamental*).
Sacramen'tally adv. (*Sacramental*).
Temperamen'tally adv. (*Temperamental*).
Elemen'tally adv. (*Elemental*).
Complemen'tally adv. (*Complemental*).
Fragmen'tally adv. (*Fragmental*).
Segmen'tally adv. (*Segmental*).
Regimen'tally adv. (*Regimental*).
Experimen'tally adv. (*Experimental*).
Detrimen'tally adv. (*Detrimental*).
Sentimen'tally adv. (*Sentimental*).
Governmen'tally adv. (*Governmental*).
Developmen'tally adv. (*Developmental*).
Departmen'tally adv. (*Departmental*).
Monumen'tally adv. (*Monumental*).
Instrumen'tally adv. (*Instrumental*).
Continen'tally adv. (*Continental*).
Paren'tally adv. (*Parental*).
Horizon'tally adv. (*Horizontal*).
Sacerdo'tally adv. (*Sacerdotal*).
To'tally adv. (*Total*).
Teeto'tally adv. (*Teetotal*).
Mor'tally adv. (*Mortal*).
Immor'tally adv. (*Immortal*).
Fes'tally adv. (*Festal*).
Brut'ally adv. In a brutal, savage, or beastly manner.
Du'ally adv. (*Dual*).
Grad'ually adv. Regularly, slowly; step by step.
Individ'ually adv. With separate existence; In an individual manner.
Man'ually adv. (*Manual*).
Contin'ually adv. (*Continual*).
An'nually adv. Yearly.
E'qually adv. (*Equal*).
Coe'qually adv. (*Coequal*).
Squall'y a. Characterized by sudden squalls; gusty.
Cas'ually adv. (*Casual*).
Vis'ually adv. (*Visual*).
Sen'sually adv. (*Sensual*).
Us'ually adv. (*Usual*).
Ac'tually adv. In reality, in fact, really.
Fac'tually adv. (*Factual*).
Tac'tually adv. (*Tactual*).
Effec'tually adv. (*Effectual*).
Ineffec'tually adv. (*Ineffectual*).
Intellec'tually adv. (*Intellectual*).
Punc'tually adv. (*Punctual*).
Perpet'ually adv. (*Perpetual*).
Habit'ually adv. (*Habitual*).
Rit'ually adv. (*Ritual*).
Spir'itually adv. (*Spiritual*).
Event'ually adv. (*Eventual*).
Vir'tually adv. (*Virtual*).
Mu'tually adv. (*Mutual*).
Tex'tually adv. (*Textual*).
Contex'tually adv. (*Contextual*).
Sex'ually adv. (*Sexual*).
Asex'ually adv. (*Asexual*).
Caval'ly s. A tropical fish, the horse-mackerel.
Mediæ'vally adv. (*Mediæval*).
Prime'vally adv. (*Primeval*).
Coe'vally adv. (*Coeval*).
Substanti'vally adv. (*Substantival*).
O'vally adv. (*Oval*).
Loy'ally adv. (*Loyal*).
Disloy'ally adv. (*Disloyal*).
Roy'ally adv. (*Royal*).
Bel'ly s. The part of the body containing the intestines; the digestive organs. v.t. and i. To swell, bulge.
Genteel'ly adv. (*Genteel*).
Fel'ly adv. In a cruel, savage manner. s. A felloe.
Rake'helly a. Like a rakehell or debauchee.
Shell'y a. Consisting of or abounding in shells.
Jel'ly s. A gelatinous semi-solid; fruit-juice boiled with sugar and stiffened. v.i. and t. To become, make into, or cover with jelly.
Smell'y a. Malodorous.
Scoun'drelly adv. (*Scoundrel*).
Tin'selly a. Glittering with tinsel; gaudy.
Cru'elly adv. (*Cruel*).
Grav'elly a. Abounding in or consisting of gravel.
Lev'elly adv. (*Level*).
Ha'zelly a. Light or reddish brown.
Il'ly adv. In an ill or evil manner.
Frail'ly adv. (*Frail*).
Bil'ly s. A camp-kettle, especially in Australia.
Piccadil'ly s. A piccadil.
Daffydown-dil'ly s. The daffodil.
Fil'ly s. A female foal.
Hill'y a. Abounding with hills.
Chill'y a. Moderately cold.
Skill'y s. Thin oatmeal gruel.
Wil'ly-nil'ly adv. Willingly or unwillingly. a. Vacillating.
Shril'ly adv. (*Shrill*).
Sil'ly a. Foolish, witless; fatuous; simple.
Still'y a. Still, calm. adv. Silently.
Tran'quilly adv. Calmly, serenely.
E'villy adv. (*Evil*).
Weev'illy a. Infested with weevils.
Civ'illy adv. Courteously, politely.
Twil'ly s. A cotton-cleaning machine.
Dol'ly s. A doll; a small appliance for various purposes. a. Dollish.
Fol'ly s. Want of sense; levity; a foolish act.
Gol'ly int. A mild oath or exclamation.
Hol'ly s. An evergreen shrub with glossy, prickly leaves and red berries.
Whol'ly adv. Entirely; completely.
Jol'ly a. Merry, jovial; inspiring mirth; agreeable; extraordinary; (*slang*) tipsy. adv. Very. v.t. (*slang*) To chaff.
Lob'lolly s. Thick gruel.
Mol'ly s. An effeminate youth.
Cool'ly adv. (*Cool*).
Wool'ly a. Consisting of, resembling, or bearing wool; fleecy; lacking clearness of outline.
Pol'ly s. Familiar name for a parrot.
Brol'ly s. (*Slang*) An umbrella.
Drol'ly adv. (*Droll*).
Trol'ly s. A kind of lace; a trolley.
Bull'y s. A cowardly tyrant, a street ruffian. v.t. To insult and overbear. v.i. To domineer, bluster. a. Fine, splendid.
Cul'ly s. One easily duped.
Dul'ly adv. (*Dull*).
Full'y adv. Completely, entirely, quite.
Dread'fully adv. (*Dreadful*).
Heed'fully adv. (*Heedful*).
Need'fully adv. (*Needful*).
Mind'fully adv. (*Mindful*).
Regard'fully adv. (*Regardful*).
Disregard'fully adv. (*Disregardful*).
Guard'fully adv. Warily, cautiously.
Peace'fully adv. (*Peaceful*).
Grace'fully adv. (*Graceful*).
Disgrace'fully adv. (*Disgraceful*).
Force'fully adv. (*Forceful*).

Resource'fully adv. (*Resourceful*).
Pride'fully adv. (*Prideful*).
Glee'fully adv. (*Gleeful*).
Change'fully adv. (*Changeful*).
Venge'fully adv. (*Vengeful*).
Revenge'fully adv. (*Revengeful*).
Wake'fully adv. (*Wakeful*).
Bale'fully adv. (*Baleful*).
Guile'fully adv. (*Guileful*).
Dole'fully adv. (*Doleful*).
Shame'fully adv. (*Shameful*).
Bane'fully adv. (*Baneful*).
Tune'fully adv. (*Tuneful*).
Woe'fully adv. (*Woeful*).
Hope'fully adv. (*Hopeful*).
Care'fully adv. (*Careful*).
Ire'fully adv. Angrily.
Dire'fully adv. (*Direful*).
Ease'fully adv. (*Easeful*).
Repose'fully adv. (*Reposeful*).
Pur'posefully adv. (*Purposeful*).
Remorse'fully adv. (*Remorseful*).
Use'fully adv. (*Useful*).
Fate'fully adv. (*Fateful*).
Hate'fully adv. (*Hateful*).
Grate'fully adv. (*Grateful*).
Spite'fully adv. (*Spiteful*).
Despite'fully adv. (*Despiteful*).
Taste'fully adv. (*Tasteful*).
Distaste'fully adv. (*Distasteful*).
Waste'fully adv. (*Wasteful*).
Rue'fully adv. (*Rueful*).
Wrong'fully adv. (*Wrongful*).
Watch'fully adv. (*Watchful*).
Bash'fully adv. (*Bashful*).
Wish'fully adv. (*Wishful*).
Push'fully adv. (*Pushful*).
Death'fully adv. (*Deathful*).
Loath'fully adv. (*Loathful*).
Wrath'fully adv. (*Wrathful*).
Faith'fully adv. Loyally; sincerely; in a faithful manner.
Health'fully adv. (*Healthful*).
Sloth'fully adv. (*Slothful*).
Mirth'fully adv. (*Mirthful*).
Youth'fully adv. (*Youthful*).
Truth'fully adv. (*Truthful*).
Fan'cifully adv. (*Fanciful*).
Mer'cifully adv. (*Merciful*).
Pit'ifully adv. (*Pitiful*).
Plen'tifully adv. (*Plentiful*).
Boun'tifully adv. (*Bountiful*).
Beau'tifully adv. (*Beautiful*).
Du'tifully adv. (*Dutiful*).
Thank'fully adv. (*Thankful*).
Wail'fully adv. (*Wailful*).
Skil'fully adv. (*Skilful*).
Toil'fully adv. (*Toilful*).
Wil'fully adv. (*Wilful*).
Soul'fully adv. (*Soulful*).
Harm'fully adv. (*Harmful*).
Man'fully adv. (*Manful*).
Moan'fully adv. (*Moanful*).
Disdain'fully adv. (*Disdainful*).
Gain'fully adv. (*Gainful*).
Pain'fully adv. (*Painful*).
Sin'fully adv. (*Sinful*).
Scorn'fully adv. (*Scornful*).
Mourn'fully adv. (*Mournful*).
Wor'shipfully adv. (*Worshipful*).
Help'fully adv. (*Helpful*).
Fear'fully adv. (*Fearfully*).
Tear'fully adv. (*Tearful*).
Won'derfully adv. (*Wonderful*).
Cheer'fully adv. (*Cheerful*).
Mas'terfully adv. (*Masterful*).
Pow'erfully adv. (*Powerful*).
Prayer'fully adv. (*Prayerful*).
Despair'fully adv. (*Despairful*).
Success'fully adv. (*Successful*).
Distress'fully adv. (*Distressful*).
Doubt'fully adv. (*Doubtful*).
Tact'fully adv. (*Tactful*).
Neglect'fully adv. (*Neglectful*).
Respect'fully adv. (*Respectful*).
Disrespect'fully adv. (*Disrespectful*).
Forget'fully adv. (*Forgetful*).
Fret'fully adv. (*Fretful*).
Regret'fully adv. (*Regretful*).
Delight'fully adv. (*Delightful*).
Right'fully adv. (*Rightful*).
Fright'fully adv. (*Frightful*).
Thought'fully adv. (*Thoughtful*).
Deceit'fully adv. (*Deceitful*).
Fit'fully adv. (*Fitful*).
Fruit'fully adv. In a fruitful manner; plenteously.
Art'fully adv. (*Artful*).
Sport'fully adv. (*Sportful*).
Hurt'fully adv. (*Hurtful*).
Boast'fully adv. (*Boastful*).
Rest'fully adv. (*Restful*).
Wist'fully adv. (*Wistful*).
Lust'fully adv. (*Lustful*).
Trust'fully adv. (*Trustful*).
Distrust'fully adv. (*Distrustful*).
Mistrust'fully adv. (*Mistrustful*).
Aw'fully adv. (*Colloq.*) Exceedingly, very.
Law'fully adv. (*Lawful*).
Sor'rowfully adv. (*Sorrowful*).
Play'fully adv. (*Playful*).
Joy'fully adv. (*Joyful*).
Gull'y s. A ditch, drain-hole, channel worn by water. v.t. To wear into a gully.
Foul'ly adv. In a foul manner; treacherously; wickedly.
Sul'ly v.t. To soil, tarnish. v.i. To be soiled, etc. s. A blemish.
Seem'ly a. Becoming, fit; proper. adv. In a suitable manner.
Beseem'ly a. Suitable, becoming.
Dim'ly adv. (*Dim*).
Slim'ly adv. (*Slim*).
Grim'ly a. Grim, fierce. adv. In a grim manner; sullenly.
Prim'ly adv. (*Prim*).
Trim'ly adv. (*Trim*).
Calm'ly adv. (*Calm*).
Ran'domly adv. (*Random*).
Bux'omly adv. (*Buxom*).
Warm'ly adv. (*Warm*).
Luke'warmly adv. (*Lukewarm*).
Term'ly adv. Term by term; periodically. a. Occurring every term.
Firm'ly adv. (*Firm*).
Infirm'ly adv. (*Infirm*).
U'niformly adv. In a uniform manner; invariably.
Glum'ly adv. (*Glum*).
Rum'ly adv. (*Rum*).
Drum'ly a. Muddy, turbid; cloudy.
Lean'ly adv. Meagrely; without plumpness.
Clean'ly adv. In a clean manner. a. (clen'li) Habitually clean; pure, innocent cleansing.
Mean'ly adv. In a low-minded, petty, or stingy manner; ignobly.
Me'dianly adv. (*Median*).
Ruf'fianly a. Brutal; like a ruffian.
Chris'tianly a. and adv. (*Christian*).
Man'ly a. Courageous; resolute; befitting a man; mannish.
Sea'manly a. (*Seaman*).
Gen'tlemanly a. Like a gentleman; pertaining to or befitting a gentleman.
Yeo'manly a. Pertaining to or like a yeoman.

Wom'anly a. Becoming or befitting a woman; truly feminine. adv. In the manner of a woman.
States'manly adv. (*Statesman*).
Hu'manly adv. In the manner of men.
Inhu'manly adv. (*Inhuman*).
Wan'ly (wŏn'-) adv. (*Wan*)
Sud'denly adv. (*Sudden*).
Maid'enly a. and adv. (*Maiden*).
Wood'enly adv. (*Wooden*).
Keen'ly adv. (*Keen*).
Green'ly adv. (*Green*).
Queen'ly adv. Like, becoming, or suitable to a queen.
Mistak'enly adv. (*Mistaken*).
Drunk'enly adv. (*Drunken*).
Outspo'kenly adv. (*Outspoken*).
Bro'kenly adv. (*Broken*).
Sul'lenly adv. (*Sullen*).
O'penly adv. (*Open*).
Bar'renly adv. (*Barren*).
Rot'tenly adv. (*Rotten*).
Heav'enly a. Pertaining to heaven; celestial; divine; enchanting.
Cra'venly adv. (*Craven*).
E'venly adv. Smoothly, equably, on a level.
Slov'enly (sluv'-) a. Negligent of neatness, etc.; careless; without method.
Vix'enly a. Having the qualities of a vixen.
Braz'enly adv. (*Brazen*).
Froz'enly adv. (*Frozen*).
Condign'ly adv. (*Condign*).
Malign'ly (-leen'ly) adv. (*Malign*).
Benign'ly adv. (*Benign*).
In'ly adv. Internally, closely, secretly.
Ungain'ly a. Awkward, clumsy, of ill-shape.
Plain'ly adv. (*Plain*).
Main'ly adv. Principally; in the main; greatly.
Cer'tainly adv. Without question or doubt.
Vain'ly adv. (*Vain*).
Thin'ly adv. (*Thin*).
Cous'inly a. (*Cousin*).
Sol'emnly adv. (*Solemn*).
On'ly a. Single; alone; by itself. adv. Solely; exclusively; wholly. conj. But.
Curmud'geonly a. Like or in the manner of a curmudgeon.
Cul'lionly a. Cowardly, base.
Com'monly adv. Usually; ordinarily; cheaply.
Ma'tronly a. Like or befitting a matron; sedate.
Wan'tonly adv. (*Wanton*).
Mod'ernly adv. (*Modern*).
Stern'ly adv. Severely, austerely, harshly.
Slat'ternly a. Untidy, negligent, sluttish.
Stub'bornly adv. (*Stubborn*).
Forlorn'ly adv. (*Forlorn*).
Tac'iturnly adv. (*Taciturn*).
Amphib'oly s. A fallacy arising through ambiguity.
Ho'ly a. Pure, religious, sacred, devout.
Mel'ancholy a. Gloomy, disconsolate, dejected. s. A gloomy state of mind; depression; sadness.
Mo'ly s. The magic plant given to Ulysses as a charm against Circe.
Doo'ly s. A doolie, Hindu ambulance.
Monop'oly s. Exclusive right or possession.
Ro'ly-po'ly s. A cylindrical, rolled paste pudding containing jam, etc. a. Plump, podgy.
Ply v.t. To use vigorously or busily; to employ oneself in; to urge importunately; to strain, force. v.i. To go to and fro regularly; to work steadily; to be busy. s. A fold, plait, strand; a layer, bias.
Cheap'ly adv. At a low price.
Hap'ly adv. Perhaps.
Deep'ly adv. At or to a depth; profoundly.
Steep'ly adv. (*Steep*).
Reply' v.i. To answer, respond, do something in return. s. Act of replying; a response.
Trip'ly adv. (*Triple*).
Mul'tiply v.t. To increase in number; to add to itself any given number of times. v.i. To become numerous; to extend.
Am'ply adv. In a full or ample manner; liberally.
Damp'ly adv. (*Damp*).
Imply' v.t. To comprise or include by implication.
Dimp'ly a. Having dimples.
Limp'ly adv. Pliantly; flaccidly; weakly.
Pimp'ly a. Having or covered with pimples.
Scrimp'ly adv. (*Scrimp*).
Sim'ply adv. (*Simple*).
Comply' v.i. To acquiesce, assent, yield.
Pan'oply s. Armament; body-armour.
Apply' v.i. To have recourse, to suit, agree. v.t. To fasten, place, bring; to use; to employ assiduously.
Reapply' v.i. To apply again.
Misapply' v.t. To apply wrongly or to a wrong purpose.
Supply' v.t. To provide, furnish, satisfy a deficiency. s. Act of supplying; that which or one whom is supplied; store.
Sup'ply adv. In a supple manner.
Sharp'ly adv. (*Sharp*).
Purpl'y a. Tending to or resembling purple.
Crisp'ly adv. (*Crisp*).
Quad'ruply adv. (*Quadruple*).
Ear'ly a. In good time; seasonable, timely.
Dear'ly adv. At a high price; with great fondness.
Clear'ly adv. (*Clear*).
Near'ly adv. Closely; intimately; almost.
Lin'early adv. (*Linear*).
Rectilin'early adv. (*Rectilinear*).
Curvilin'early adv. (*Curvilinear*).
Pearl'y a. Resembling or containing pearl or nacre; clear. s. A large mother-of-pearl button.
Drear'ly adv. (*Drear*).
Year'ly a. Annual; lasting a year. adv. Once a year; by the year.
Beg'garly a. Very poor; mean.
Vul'garly adv. (*Vulgar*).
Famil'iarly adv. Without formality; commonly, frequently.
Pecu'liarly adv. Unusually; especially; singularly.
Sim'ilarly adv. (*Similar*).
Dissim'ilarly adv. (*Dissimilar*).
Lamel'larly adv. (*Lamellar*).
Schol'arly a. Learned; like or befitting a scholar.
Po'larly adv. (*Polar*).
Tab'ularly adv. (*Tabular*).
Glob'ularly adv. (*Globular*).
Vernac'ularly adv. (*Vernacular*).
Orac'ularly adv. (*Oracular*).
Spectac'ularly adv. (*Spectacular*).
Sec'ularly adv. (*Secular*).
Orbic'ularly adv. (*Orbicular*).
Acic'ularly adv. (*Acicular*).
Perpendic'ularly adv. Vertically; at right angles.
Auric'ularly adv. (*Auricular*).
Retic'ularly adv. (*Reticular*).
Lentic'ularly adv. (*Lenticular*).
Partic'ularly adv. (*Particular*)

Oc'ularly adv. (*Ocular*).
Joc'ularly adv. (*Jocular*).
Cir'cularly adv. (*Circular*).
Vas'cularly adv. (*Vascular*).
Mus'cularly adv. (*Muscular*).
Gland'ularly adv. (*Glandular*).
Reg'ularly adv. (*Regular*).
Irreg'ularly adv. (*Irregular*).
Teg'ularly adv. Arranged tile-wise.
An'gularly adv. (*Angular*).
Triang'ularly adv. (*Triangular*).
Rectan'gularly adv. (*Rectangular*).
Multan'-gularly adv. With many angles or corners.
Sin'gularly adv. (*Singular*).
Gran'ularly adv. (*Granular*).
Pop'ularly adv. (*Popular*).
In'sularly adv. (*Insular*).
Tit'ularly adv. (*Titular*).
Marl'y a. Consisting of, abounding with, or resembling marl.
Gnarl'y a. Full of knots or gnarls; peevish.
Snarl'y a. Characterized by snarling.
Lub'berly a. Like a lubber, loutish. adv. Clumsily.
Decem'berly a. Wintry.
So'berly adv. (*Sober*).
El'derly a. Somewhat old.
Slen'derly adv. (*Slender*).
Ten'derly adv. Gently; compassionately.
Or'derly a. In order; methodical; regular, well ordered. s. A soldier attending on an officer. adv. Duly, regularly.
Disor'derly adv. In a state of disorder; unlawful; turbulent.
Queer'ly adv. (*Queer*).
Ea'gerly adv. (*Eager*).
Ang'erly adv. In an angry manner.
Gin'gerly adv. Cautiously, nicely, delicately. a. Cautious, fastidious.
Butch'erly adv. (*Butcher*).
Weath'erly a. Able to sail close to the wind without leeway.
Fa'therly a. Like or proper to a father; tender, kind. adv. In the manner of a father.
Moth'erly a. Like or becoming a mother; maternal.
Broth'erly a. Fraternal. adv. (*Brother*).
Nor'therly a. Northern; pertaining to or proceeding from the north.
South'erly (Sŭth'-) a. and adv. From or to the south; southern.
Sol'dierly a. Like or becoming a soldier; martial; brave.
Cavali'erly adv. (*Cavalier*).
Qua'kerly a. Quakerish.
Tink'erly a. Like a tinker (of patched work).
Sum'merly a. Summery.
For'merly adv. In past times; of old.
Man'nerly a. Characterized by good manners.
Unman'nerly a. Rude; ill-bred.
Prop'erly adv. Suitably, fitly, strictly.
Improp'erly adv. (*Improper*).
Dap'perly adv. (*Dapper*).
Mi'serly a. Avaricious, stingy, mean.
Daugh'terly a. (*Daughter*).
Quar'terly a. Containing or consisting of a fourth part; recurring every three months. s. A publication appearing every three months. adv. By quarters; once a quarter.
Por'terly a. Like a porter.
East'erly a. Situated in, moving toward, or blowing from the east. adv. In the direction of the east.
Mas'terly a. With the skill of a master; masterful.
West'erly a. Being in or directed towards the west; blowing from the west. adv. Towards the west.
Sin'isterly adv. (*Sinister*).
Sis'terly a. Like or befitting a sister; affectionate.
Lat'terly adv. Lately.
Bit'terly adv. (*Bitter*).
Ut'terly adv. Completely; absolutely.
Clev'erly adv. (*Clever*).
Sil'verly adv. With a soft, clear sound.
Law'yerly a. Like or befitting a lawyer.
Fair'ly adv. Clearly, openly; honestly; utterly; almost up to standard.
Girl'y s. A little girl; a pet name.
Super'iorly adv. (*Superior*).
Ulter'iorly adv. (*Ulterior*).
Anter'iorly adv. (*Anterior*).
Inter'iorly adv. Internally, inwardly.
Sail'orly a. Like a sailor.
Poor'ly adv. In a poor manner or condition; meanly; without dignity. a. Not very well; indisposed.
Bur'ly a. Big and heavy; boisterous.
Hur'ly-bur'ly s. Tumult, confusion, uproar.
Curl'y a. Having curls, wavy; tending to curl.
Churl'y a. Churlish.
Knurl'y a. Characterized by knurls; knotty.
Neigh'bourly (nā'-) a. Becoming a neighbour; friendly.
Dour'ly adv. Sternly, morosely.
Hour'ly a. Occurring or done every hour; continual. adv. Every hour; frequently.
Sour'ly adv. (*Sour*).
Sur'ly a. Churlish; gloomily sour.
Sly a. Meanly artful; cunning, insidious; arch.
Meas'ly a. Containing larval worms (of meat) (*slang*) contemptible.
Gris'ly a. Horrible, hideous, ghastly.
Crass'ly adv. (*Crass*).
Dread'lessly adv. (*Dreadless*).
Heed'lessly adv. (*Heedless*).
Need'lessly adv. (*Needless*).
End'lessly adv. (*Endless*).
Bound'lessly adv. (*Boundless*).
Ground'lessly adv. (*Groundless*).
Sound'lessly adv. (*Soundless*).
God'lessly adv. (*Godless*).
Blood'lessly adv. (*Bloodless*).
Regard'lessly adv. (*Regardless*).
Cloud'lessly adv. (*Cloudless*).
Grace'lessly adv. (*Graceless*).
Defence'lessly adv. (*Defenceless*).
Life'lessly adv. (*Lifeless*).
Guile'lessly adv. Sincerely, honestly, frankly.
Shame'lessly adv. (*Shameless*).
Blame'lessly adv. (*Blameless*).
Name'lessly adv. (*Nameless*).
Shape'lessly adv. (*Shapeless*)
Hope'lessly adv. (*Hopeless*).
Care'lessly adv. (*Careless*).
Tire'lessly adv. Without becoming wearied.
Cease'lessly adv. (*Ceaseless*).
Noise'lessly adv. (*Noiseless*).
Sense'lessly adv. (*Senseless*).
Remorse'lessly adv. (*Remorseless*).
Use'lessly adv. (*Useless*).
Cause'lessly adv. (*Causeless*).
Taste'lessly adv. (*Tasteless*).
Love'lessly adv. (*Loveless*).
Nerve'lessly adv. (*Nerveless*).
Self'lessly adv. (*Selfless*).
Speech'lessly adv. (*Speechless*).
Quench'lessly adv. (*Quenchless*).
Match'lessly adv. (*Matchless*).
Death'lessly adv. (*Deathless*).

Breath'lessly adv. (*Breathless*).
Faith'lessly adv. (*Faithless*).
Mirth'lessly adv. (*Mirthless*).
Worth'lessly adv. (*Worthless*).
Ruth'lessly adv. (*Ruthless*).
Mer'cilessly adv. (*Merciless*).
Pit'ilessly adv. (*Pitiless*).
Feck'lessly adv. (*Feckless*).
Reck'lessly adv. (*Reckless*).
Luck'lessly adv. (*Luckless*).
Thank'lessly adv. (*Thankless*).
Soul'lessly adv. (*Soulless*).
Dream'lessly adv. (*Dreamless*).
Aim'lessly adv. (*Aimless*).
Harm'lessly adv. (*Harmless*).
Form'lessly adv. (*Formless*).
Brain'lessly adv. (*Brainless*).
Stain'lessly adv. (*Stainless*).
Sin'lessly adv. (*Sinless*).
Pas'sionlessly adv. (*Passionless*
Sun'lessly adv. (*Sunless*).
Hap'lessly adv. (*Hapless*).
Sleep'lessly adv. (*Sleepless*).
Help'lessly adv. (*Helpless*).
Fear'lessly adv. (*Fearless*).
Tear'lessly adv. (*Tearless*).
Cheer'lessly adv. (*Cheerless*).
Peer'lessly adv. (*Peerless*).
Pow'erlessly adv. (*Powerless*).
Col'ourlessly adv. (*Colourless*).
Doubt'lessly adv. (*Doubtless.*)
Tact'lessly adv. (*Tactless*).
Shift'lessly adv. (*Shiftless*).
Thrift'lessly adv. (*Thriftless*).
Sight'lessly adv. (*Sightless*).
Thought'-lessly adv. (*Thoughtless*).
Prof'itlessly adv. (*Profitless*).
Spir'itlessly adv. (*Spiritless*).
Fruit'lessly adv. (*Fruitless*).
Wit'lessly adv. (*Witless*).
Guilt'lessly adv. (*Guiltless*).
Fault'lessly adv. (*Faultless*).
Relent'lessly adv. (*Relentless*).
Taint'lessly adv. (*Taintless*).
Point'lessly adv. (*Pointless*).
Daunt'lessly adv. (*Dauntless*).
Boot'lessly adv. Unavailingly.
Spot'lessly adv. (*Spotless*).
Art'lessly adv. (*Artless*).
Heart'lessly adv. (*Heartless*).
Hurt'lessly adv. (*Hurtless*).
Rest'lessly adv. (*Restless*).
List'lessly adv. (*Listless*).
Law'lessly adv. (*Lawless*).
Flaw'lessly adv. (*Flawless*).
Joy'lessly adv. (*Joyless*).
Express'ly adv. In an express, direct, or pointed manner; plainly.
Remiss'ly adv. (*Remiss*).
Cross'ly adv. Ill-humouredly, peevishly.
Gross'ly adv. (*Gross*).
Thus'ly adv. (*Humorous*).
Rau'cously adv. (*Raucous*).
Tremen'dously adv. (*Tremendous*).
Stupen'dously adv. (*Stupendous*).
Haz'ardously adv. (*Hazardous*).
Seta'ceously adv. (*Setaceous*).
Hid'eously adv. (*Hideous*).
Rampa'geously adv. (*Rampageous*).
Umbra'geously adv. (*Umbrageous*).
Outra'geously adv. (*Outrageous*).
Coura'geously adv. (*Courageous*).
Advanta'-geously adv. (*Advantageous*).
Disadvanta'-geously adv. (*Disadvantageous*).
Gor'geously adv. (*Gorgeous*).
Time'ously adv. (*Timeous*).
Miscella'-neously adv. (*Miscellaneous*).
Contempora'-neously adv. (*Contemporaneous*).
Extempora'-neously adv. (*Extemporaneous*).
Subterra'-neously adv. (*Subterraneous*).
Extra'neously adv. (*Extraneous*).
Simulta'-neously adv. (*Simultaneous*).
Instanta'-neously adv. (*Instantaneous*).
Consenta'-neously adv. (*Consentaneous*).
Sponta'neously adv. (*Spontaneous*).
Homoge'-neously adv. (*Homongeneous*).
Heteroge'-neously adv. (*Heterogeneous*).
Erro'neously adv. (*Erroneous*).
Calcar'eously adv. (*Calcareous*).
Sulphur'eously adv. (*Sulphureous*).
Nau'seously adv. (*Nauseous*).
Right'eously adv. (*Righteous*).
Pit'eously adv. (*Piteous*).
Despit'eously adv. (*Despiteous*).
Plen'teously adv. (*Plenteous*).
Boun'teously adv. (*Bounteous*).
Court'eously adv. (*Courteous*).
Discourt'eously adv. (*Discourteous*).
Beaut'eously adv. (*Beauteous*).
Du'teously adv. (*Duteous*).
Anal'ogously adv. (*Analagous*).
Du'biously adv. (*Dubious*).
Effica'ciously adv. (*Efficacious*).
Menda'ciously adv. (*Mendacious*).
Auda'ciously adv. (*Audacious*).
Saga'ciously adv. (*Sagacious*).
Sala'ciously adv. (*Salacious*).
Falla'ciously adv. (*Fallacious*).
Contuma'-ciously adv. (*Contumacious*).
Tena'ciously adv. (*Tenacious*).
Pugna'ciously adv. (*Pugnacious*).
Mina'ciously adv. (*Minacious*).
Pertina'ciously adv. (*Pertinacious*).
Capa'ciously adv. (*Capacious*).
Rapa'ciously adv. (*Rapacious*).
Spa'ciously adv. (*Spacious*).
Vera'ciously adv. (*Veracious*).
Gra'ciously adv. (*Gracious*).
Vora'ciously adv. (*Voracious*).
Sequa'ciously adv. (*Sequacious*).
Loqua'ciously adv. (*Loquacious*).
Viva'ciously adv. (*Vivacious*).
Spe'ciously adv. (*Specious*).
Pre'ciously adv. (*Precious*).
Judi'ciously adv. (*Judicious*).
Injudi'ciously adv. (*Injudicious*).
Offi'ciously adv. (*Officious*).
Mali'ciously adv. (*Malicious*).
Deli'ciously adv. (*Delicious*).
Perni'ciously adv. (*Pernicious*).
Auspi'ciously adv. (*Auspicious*).
Inauspi'ciously adv. (*Inauspicious*).
Suspi'ciously adv. (*Suspicious*).
Avari'ciously adv. (*Avaricious*).
Capri'ciously adv. (*Capricious*).
Meretri'ciously adv. (*Meretricious*).
Vi'ciously adv. (*Vicious*).
Preco'ciously adv. (*Precocious*).
Fero'ciously adv. (*Ferocious*).
Atro'ciously adv. (*Atrocious*).
Con'sciously adv. (*Conscious*).
Lus'ciously adv. (*Luscious*).
Te'diously adv. (*Tedious*).
Perfid'iously adv. (*Perfidious*).
Insid'iously adv. (*Insidious*).

Fastid'iously adv. (*Fastidious*).
Invid'iously adv. (*Invidious*).
Compen'diously adv. (*Compendious*).
O'diously adv. (*Odious*).
Melo'diously adv. (*Melodious*).
Commo'diously adv. (*Commodious*).
Incommo'-diously adv. (*Incommodious*).
Stu'diously adv. (*Studious*).
Conta'giously adv. (*Contagious*).
Sacrile'giously adv. (*Sacrilegious*).
Egre'giously adv. (*Egregious*).
Prodig'iously adv. (*Prodigious*).
Relig'iously adv. (*Religious*).
Irrelig'iously adv. (*Irreligious*).
Litig'iously adv. (*Litigious*).
Contume'-liously adv. (*Contumelious*).
Supercil'iously adv. (*Supercilious*).
Punctil'iously adv. (*Punctilious*).
Rebel'liously adv. (*Rebellious*).
Abste'miously adv. (*Abstemious*).
Inge'niously adv. (*Ingenious*).
Ignomin'-iously adv. (*Ignominious*).
Calum'niously adv. (*Calumnious*).
Eupho'niously adv. (*Euphonious*).
Felo'niously adv. (*Felonious*).
Ceremo'niously adv. (*Ceremonious*).
Acrimo'niously adv. (*Acrimonious*).
Querimo'-niously adv. (*Querimonious*).
Parsimo'-niously adv. (*Parsimonious*).
Sanctimo'-niously adv. (*Sanctimonious*).
Harmo'niously adv. (*Harmonious*).
Inharmo'-niously adv. (*Inharmonious*).
Pi'ously adv. (*Pious*).
Im'piously adv. (*Impious*).
Co'piously adv. (*Copious*).
Precar'iously adv. (*Precarious*).
Vicar'iously adv. (*Vicarious*).
Nefar'iously adv. (*Nefarious*).
Multifar'iously adv. (*Multifarious*).
Gregar'iously adv. (*Gregarious*).
Burglar'iously adv. (*Burglarious*).
Hilar'iously adv. (*Hilarious*).
Uproar'iously adv. (*Uproarious*).
Temerar'iously adv. (*Temerarious*).
Contrar'iously adv. (*Contrarious*).
Var'iously adv. (*Various*).
Oppro'briously adv. (*Opprobrious*).
Lugu'briously adv. (*Lugubrious*).
Salu'briously adv. (*Salubrious*).
Imper'iously adv. (*Imperious*).
Ser'iously adv. (*Serious*).
Deleter'iously adv. (*Deleterious*).
Myster'iously adv. (*Myterious*).
Delir'iously adv. (*Delirious*).
Labor'iously adv. (*Laborious*).
Glor'iously adv. (*Glorious*).
Inglor'iously adv. (*Inglorious*).
Vainglor'iously adv. (*Vainglorious*).
Censor'iously adv. (*Censorious*).
Victor'iously adv. (*Victorious*).
Meritor'iously adv. (*Meritorious*).
Notor'iously adv. (*Notorious*).
Uxor'iously adv. (*Uxorious*).
Indus'triously adv. (*Industrious*).
Illus'triously adv. (*Illustrious*).
Cur'iously adv. (*Curious*).
Incur'iously adv. (*Incurious*).
Fur'iously adv. (*Furious*).
Injur'iously adv. (*Injurious*)
Perjur'iously adv. (*Perjurious*).
Penur'iously adv. (*Penurious*).
Spur'iously adv. (*Spurious*).
Usur'iously adv. (*Usurious*).
Luxur'iously adv. (*Luxurious*).
Ostenta'tiously adv. (*Ostentatious*).
Vexa'tiously adv. (*Vexatious*).
Fac'tiously adv. (*Factious*).
Frac'tiously adv. (*Fractious*).
Infec'tiously adv. (*Infectious*).
Contradic'-tiously adv. (*Contradictious*).
Compunc'-tiously adv. (*Compunctious*).
Face'tiously adv. (*Facetious*).
Ambi'tiously adv. (*Ambitious*).
Expedi'tiously adv. (*Expeditious*).
Sedi'tiously adv. (*Seditious*).
Flagi'tiously adv. (*Flagitious*).
Propi'tiously adv. (*Propitious*).
Nutri'tiously adv. (*Nutritious*).
Fracti'tiously adv. (*Fractitious*).
Ficti'tiously adv. (*Fictitious*).
Repeti'tiously adv. (*Repetitious*).
Adsciti'tiously adv. (*Adscititious*).
Suppositi'-tiously adv. (*Supposititious*).
Adventi'tiously adv. (*Adventitious*).
Surrepti'tiously adv. (*Surreptitious*).
Supersti'tiously adv. (*Superstitious*).
Licen'tiously adv. (*Licentious*).
Conscien'-tiously adv. (*Conscientious*).
Preten'tiously adv. (*Pretentious*).
Senten'tiously adv. With striking brevity.
Conten'tiously adv. (*Contentious*).
Cap'tiously adv. (*Captious*).
Bump'tiously adv. (*Bumptious*).
Catawamp'-tiously adv. (*Catawamp*).
Tor'tiously (-shus-) adv. (*Tortious*).
Cau'tiously adv. (*Cautious*).
Precau'tiously adv. With precaution.
Incau'tiously adv. (*Incautious*).
Obse'quiously adv. (*Obsequious*).
Ob'viously adv. (*Obvious*).
De'viously adv. (*Devious*).
Pre'viously adv. Formerly; anteriorly.
Lasciv'iously adv. (*Lascivious*).
Obliv'iously adv. (*Oblivious*).
En'viously adv. (*Envious*).
Imper'viously adv. (*Impervious*).
An'xiously adv. (*Anxious*).
Nox'iously adv. (*Noxious*).
Obnox'iously adv. (*Obnoxious*).
Innox'iously adv. (*Innoxious*).
Scan'dalously adv. (*Scandalous*).
Jeal'ously adv. (*Jealous*).
Zeal'ously (zĕl'-) adv. (*Zealous*).
Anom'alously adv. (*Anomalous*).
Per'ilously adv. (*Perilous*).
Scur'rilously adv. (*Scurrilous*).
Cal'lously adv. (*Callous*).
Li'bellously adv. (*Libellous*).
Mar'vellously adv. (*Marvellous*).
Friv'olously adv. (*Frivolous*).
Fab'ulously adv. (*Fabulous*).
Bib'ulously adv. (*Bibulous*).
Mirac'ulously adv. (*Miraculous*).
Ridic'ulously adv. (*Ridiculous*).
Metic'ulously adv. (*Meticulous*).
Cred'ulously adv. (*Credulous*).
Incred'ulously adv. (*Incredulous*).
Sed'ulously adv. (*Sedulous*).
Pen'dulously adv. (*Pendulous*).
Scrof'ulously adv. (*Scrofula*).
Em'ulously adv. (*Emulous*).
Trem'ulously adv. (*Tremulous*).
Pop'ulously adv. (*Populous*).
Scru'pulously adv. (*Scrupulous*).

Quer'ulously adv. (*Querulous*).
Gar'rulously adv. (*Garrulous*).
Fa'mously adv. (*Famous*).
In'famously adv. (*Infamous*).
Big'amously adv. (*Bigamous*).
as'-
phemously adv. (*Blasphemous*).
sillan'-
imously adv. (*Pusillanimous*).
gnan'-
imously adv. (*Magnanimous*).
nan'imously adv. (*Unanimous*).
Ven'omously adv. (*Venomous*).
ton'omously adv. (*Autonomous*).
Enor'mously adv. (*Enormous*).
st'humously adv. (*Posthumous*).
eudon'-
ymously adv. (*Pseudonymous*).
mon'-
ymously adv. (*Homonymous*).
non'ymously adv. (*Anonymous*).
non'ymously adv. (*Synonymous*).
Lar'cenously adv. (*Larcenous*).
ndig'enously adv. (*Indigenous*).
Rav'enously adv. (*Ravenous*).
Vill'ainously adv. (*Villainous*).
un'-
tainously adv. (*Mountainous*).
Libid'inously adv. (*Libidinous*).
titu'-
dinously adv. (*Platitudinous*).
ltitu'-
dinously adv. (*Multitudinous*).
Hein'ously adv. (*Heinous*).
Fulig'inously adv. (*Fuliginous*).
ertig'inously adv. (*Vertiginous*).
Om'inously adv. (*Ominous*).
nter'-
minously adv. (*Conterminous*).
Ver'minously adv. (*Verminous*).
Lu'minously adv. (*Luminous*).
lu'minously adv. (*Voluminous*).
Glu'tinously adv. (*Glutinous*).
Mu'tinously adv. (*Mutinous*).
Ru'inously adv. (*Ruinous*).
Tyr'annously adv. (*Tyrannous*).
'chronously adv. (*Synchronous*).
Poi'sonously adv. (*Poisonous*).
mot'onously adv. (*Homotonous*).
onot'onously adv. (*Monotonous*).
Pom'pously adv. (*Pompous*).
Bar'barously adv. (*Barbarous*).
ivip'arously adv. (*Viviparous*).
Ovip'arously adv. (*Oviparous*).
Fi'brously adv. (*Fibrous*).
Cum'brously adv. (*Cumbrous*).
Lu'dicrously adv. (*Ludicrous*).
Won'drously adv. (*Wondrous*).
um'berously adv. (*Slumberous*).
Ul'cerously adv. (*Ulcerous*).
lan'derously adv. (*Slanderous*).
Pon'derously adv. (*Ponderous*).
un'derously adv. (*Thunderous*).
ur'derously adv. (*Murderous*).
ocif'erously adv. (*Vociferous*).
rolif'erously adv. (*Proliferous*).
estif'-
erously adv. (*Pestiferous*).
orif'erously adv. (*Odoriferous*).
an'gerously adv. (*Dangerous*).
ach'erously adv. (*Treacherous*).
ech'erously adv. (*Lecherous*).
tank'-
erously adv. (*Cantankerous*).
Nu'merously adv. (*Numerous*).
Gen'erously adv. (*Generous*).
On'erously adv. (*Onerous*).
strep'-
erously adv. (*Obstreperous*).

Pros'perously adv. (*Prosperous*).
Slaugh'terously
(slaw'-) adv. (*Slaughterous*).
Adul'terously adv. (*Adulterous*).
Bois'terously adv. (*Boisterous*).
Prepos'terously adv. (*Preposterous*).
Cadav'erously adv. (*Cadaverous*).
Desir'ously adv. (*Desirous*).
Chival'rously adv. (*Chivalrous*).
Decor'ously adv. (*Decorous*).
Indecor'ously adv. (*Indecorous*).
Ran'corously adv. (*Rancorous*).
O'dorously adv. (*Odorous*).
Rig'orously adv. (*Rigorous*).
Vig'orously adv. (*Vigorous*).
Clang'orously adv. (*Clangor*).
Val'orously adv. (*Valorous*).
Dol'orously adv. (*Dolorous*).
Am'orously adv. (*Amorous*).
Clam'orously adv. (*Clamour*).
Glam'orously adv. (*Glamour*).
Tim'orously adv. (*Timorous*).
Hu'morously adv. (*Humorous*).
Sonor'ously adv. (*Sonorous*).
Por'ously adv. (*Porous*).
Va'porously adv. (*Vaporous*).
Trai'torously adv. (*Traitorous*).
Ster'torously adv. (*Stertorous*).
Omniv'orously adv. (*Omnivorous*).
Idol'atrously adv. (*Idolatrous*).
Disas'trously adv. (*Disastrous*).
Sin'istrously adv. (*Sinistrous*).
Mon'strously adv. (*Monstrous*).
Lus'trously adv. (*Lustrous*).
Dex'trously adv. (*Dextrous*).
Mur'murously adv. (*Murmurous*).
Ven'turously adv. (*Venturous*).
Adven'turously adv. (*Adventurous*).
Rap'turously adv. (*Rapturous*).
Tousl'y a. Rumpled, dishevelled.
Cov'etously adv. (*Covetous*).
Felic'itously adv. (*Felicitous*).
Solic'itously adv. (*Solicitous*).
Calam'itously adv. (*Calamitous*).
Precip'itously adv. (*Precipitous*).
Circu'itously adv. (*Circuitous*).
Ubiq'uitously adv. (*Ubiquitous*).
Iniq'uitously adv. (*Iniquitous*).
Gratu'itously adv. (*Gratuitous*).
Fortu'itously adv. (*Fortuitous*).
Momen'tously adv. (*Momentous*).
Porten'tously adv. (*Portentous*).
Ri'otously adv. (*Riotous*).
Vac'uously adv. (*Vacuous*).
Conspic'uously adv. (*Conspicuous*).
Inconspic'-
uously adv. (*Inconspicuous*).
Perspic'uously adv. (*Perspicuous*).
Noc'uously adv. (*Nocuous*).
Innoc'uously adv. (*Innocuous*).
Promis'cuously adv. (*Promiscuous*).
Assid'uously adv. (*Assiduous*).
Ar'duously adv. (*Arduous*).
Ambig'uously adv. (*Ambiguous*).
Contig'uously adv. (*Contiguous*).
Super'fluously adv. (*Superfluous*).
Ingen'uously adv. (*Ingenuous*).
Disingen'-
uously adv. (*Disingenuous*).
Stren'uously adv. (*Strenuous*).
Sin'uously adv. (*Sinuous*).
Contin'uously adv. (*Continuous*).
Con'gruously adv. (*Congruous*).
Incon'gruously adv. (*Incongruous*).
Sen'suously adv. (*Sensuous*).
Fat'uously adv. (*Fatuous*).
Unc'tuously adv. (*Unctuous*).
Infruc'tuously adv. (*Infructuous*).
Impet'uously adv. (*Impetuous*).

Tumul'tuously adv. (*Tumultuous*).
Contemp'-tuously adv. (*Contemptuous*).
Sump'tuously adv. (*Sumptuous*).
Presump'-tuously adv. (*Presumptuous*).
Volup'tuously adv. (*Voluptuous*).
Vir'tuously adv. (*Virtuous*).
Tor'tuously adv. (*Tortuous*).
Inces'tuously adv. (*Incestuous*).
Tempes'tuously adv. (*Tempestuous*).
Flex'uously adv. (*Flexuous*).
Mis'chievously adv. (*Mischievous*).
Griev'ously adv. (*Grievous*).
Ner'vously adv. (*Nervous*).
Joy'ously adv. (*Joyous*).
Feat'ly adv. Neatly, adroitly.
Neat'ly adv. (*Neat*).
Great'ly adv. In a great degree; much; illustriously.
Flat'ly adv. Evenly, horizontally; dully; positively; plainly.
Subt'ly (sŭt'-) adv. (*Subtle*).
Compact'ly adv. Closely, densely; concisely, briefly.
Ab'stractly adv. In an abstract way; in the abstract; abstractedly.
Exact'ly adv. Precisely, accurately, strictly.
Inexact'ly adv. (*Inexact*).
Per'fectly adv. Completely; exactly; consummately.
Imper'fectly adv. (*Imperfect*).
Ab'jectly adv. (*Abject*).
Direct'ly adv. In a straight line; as an immediate step; at once; unambiguously.
Indirect'ly adv. (*Indirect*).
Correct'ly adv. (*Correct*).
Incorrect'ly adv. (*Incorrect*).
Strict'ly adv. (*Strict*).
Succinct'ly adv. (*Succinct*).
Distinct'ly adv. (*Distinct*).
Indistinct'ly adv. (*Indistinct*).
Ad'junctly adv. (*Adjunct*).
Conjunct'ly adv. (*Conjunct*).
Fleet'ly adv. Swiftly; nimbly.
Meet'ly adv. Suitably; fitly.
Discreet'ly adv. (*Discreet*).
Indiscreet'ly adv. (*Indiscreet*).
Sweet'ly adv. (*Sweet*).
Qui'etly adv. (*Quiet*).
Se'cretly adv. (*Secret*).
Deft'ly adv. (*Deft*).
Swift'ly adv. (*Swift*).
Soft'ly adv. (*Soft*).
Light'ly adv. With little weight; easily; cheerfully.
Slight'ly adv. (*Slight*).
Night'ly adv. By night, every night. a. Nocturnal; done nightly.
Knight'ly a. and adv. (*Knight*).
Fort'nightly adv. Once a fortnight. a. Happening once a fortnight.
Right'ly adv. According to justice or fact; suitably; properly.
Bright'ly adv. (*Bright*).
Spright'ly a. Lively, brisk, animated.
Up'rightly adv. (*Upright*).
Sight'ly a. Pleasing to the eye.
Tight'ly adv. (*Tight*).
Strait'ly adv. Narrowly, strictly, rigorously.
Tac'itly adv. (*Tacit*).
Lic'itly adv. (*Licit*).
Illic'itly adv. (*Illicit*).
Implic'itly adv. (*Implicit*).
Explic'itly adv. (*Explicit*).
Inexplic'itly adv. (*Inexplicit*).
Coun'terfeitly adv. (*Counterfeit*).
Fit'ly adv. Appropriately, becomingly.
Adroit'ly adv. (*Adroit*).
Maladroit'ly adv. (*Maladroit*).
Salt'ly adv. (*Salt*).
Occult'ly adv. (*Occult*).
Dif'ficultly adv. (*Difficult*).
Va'cantly adv. (*Vacant*).
Signif'icantly adv. (*Significant*).
Insignif'icantly adv. (*Insignificant*).
Scant'ly adv. Not sufficiently; penuriously.
Abun'dantly adv. (*Abundant*).
Superabun'-dantly adv. (*Superabundant*).
Redun'dantly adv. (*Redundant*).
Ver'dantly adv. (*Verdant*).
Accor'dantly adv. (*Accordant*).
Concor'dantly adv. (*Concordant*).
Discor'dantly adv. (*Discordant*).
Mor'dantly adv. (*Mordant*).
Rec'reantly adv. (*Recreant*).
Extrav'agantly adv. (*Extravagant*).
El'egantly adv. (*Elegant*).
Inel'egantly adv. (*Inelegant*).
Ar'rogantly adv. (*Arrogant*).
Trench'antly adv. (*Trenchant*).
Triumph'antly adv. (*Triumphant*).
Ra'diantly adv. (*Radiant*).
Defi'antly adv. (*Defiant*).
Val'iantly adv. (*Valiant*).
Bril'liantly adv. (*Brilliant*).
Pli'antly adv. (*Pliant*).
Compli'antly adv. (*Compliant*).
Sup'pliantly adv. (*Suppliant*).
Var'iantly adv. (*Variant*).
Luxur'iantly adv. (*Luxuriant*).
Non'chalantly adv. (*Nonchalant*).
Ju'bilantly adv. (*Jubilant*).
Vig'ilantly adv. (*Vigilant*).
Gal'lantly adv. (*Gallant*).
Slant'ly adv. In an inclined direction obliquely.
Pet'ulantly adv. (*Petulant*).
Clam'antly adv. (*Clamant*).
Stag'nantly adv. (*Stagnant*).
Preg'nantly adv. (*Pregnant*).
Indig'nantly adv. (*Indignant*).
Malig'nantly adv. (*Malignant*).
Benig'nantly adv. (*Benignant*).
Poi'gnantly adv. (*Poignant*).
Repug'nantly adv. (*Repugnant*).
Dom'inantly adv. (*Dominant*).
Predom'inantly adv. (*Predominant*).
Ru'minantly adv. (*Ruminant*).
Res'onantly adv. (*Resonant*).
Con'sonantly adv. (*Consonant*).
Dis'sonantly adv. (*Dissonant*).
Ramp'antly adv. (*Rampant*).
Flip'pantly adv. (*Flippant*).
Exu'berantly adv. (*Exuberant*).
Prepon'der-antly adv. (*Preponderant*).
Tol'erantly adv. (*Tolerant*).
Intol'erantly adv. (*Intolerant*).
Fla'grantly adv. (*Flagrant*).
Fra'grantly adv. (*Fragrant*).
Va'grantly adv. (*Vagrant*).
Ig'norantly adv. (*Ignorant*).
Ar'rantly adv. (*Arrant*).
Remon'-strantly adv. (*Remonstrant*).
Pleas'antly adv. (*Pleasant*).
Complai'santly adv. (*Complaisant*).
Inces'santly adv. (*Incessant*).
Puis'santly adv. (*Puissant*).
Bla'tantly adv. (*Blatant*).
Expec'tantly adv. (*Expectant*).
Reluc'tantly adv. (*Reluctant*).
Exor'bitantly adv. (*Exorbitant*).
Os'citantly adv. (*Oscitant*).
Mil'itantly adv. (*Militant*).
Concom'itantly adv. (*Concomitant*).

Precip'itantly adv. With great haste.
Hes'itantly adv. (*Hesitant*).
Exult'antly adv. (*Exultant*).
Repen'tantly adv. (*Repentant*).
Import'antly adv. (*Important*).
Dis'tantly adv. (*Distant*).
In'stantly adv. Immediately; with no delay.
Con'stantly adv. Invariably, regularly, always.
Incon'stantly adv. In an inconstant manner.
Pi'quantly (pē'-) adv. (*Piquant*).
Tru'antly adv. (*Truant*).
Pursu'antly adv. (*Pursuant*).
Rel'evantly adv. (*Relevant*).
Irrel'evantly adv. (*Irrelevant*).
Obser'vantly adv. (*Observant*).
Inobser'vantly adv. Heedlessly, negligently.
Buoy'antly adv. (*Buoyant*).
Clairvoy'antly adv. (*Clairvoyant*).
Lam'bently adv. (*Lambent*).
Recum'bently adv. (*Recumbent*).
Adja'cently adv. (*Adjacent*).
Compla'cently adv. (*Complacent*).
De'cently adv. (*Decent*).
Inde'cently adv. (*Indecent*).
Re'cently adv. (*Recent*).
Benef'icently adv. (*Beneficient*).
Magnif'icently adv. (*Magnificent*).
Munif'icently adv. (*Munificent*).
Ret'icently adv. (*Reticent*).
In'nocently adv. (*Innocent*).
Quies'cently adv. (*Quiescent*).
Acquies'cently adv. (*Acquiescent*).
Evanes'cently adv. (*Evanescent*).
Reminis'cently adv. (*Reminiscent*).
Deca'dently adv. (*Decadent*).
Prece'dently adv. (*Precedent*).
Antece'dently adv. (*Antecedent*).
Cre'dently adv. (*Credent*).
Coin'cidently adv. (*Coincident*).
Dif'fidently adv. (*Diffident*).
Con'fidently adv. (*Confident*).
Stri'dently adv. (*Strident*).
Ev'idently adv. (*Evident*).
Prov'idently adv. (*Provident*).
Improv'idently adv. (*Improvident*).
Transcen'dently adv. (*Transcendent*).
Resplen'dently adv. (*Resplendent*).
Pen'dently adv. (*Pendent*).
Depen'dently adv. (*Dependent*).
Indepen'dently adv. (*Independent*).
Despon'dently adv. (*Despondent*).
Correspon'dently adv. (*Correspondent*).
Ar'dently adv. (*Ardent*).
Im'pudently adv. (*Impudent*).
Pru'dently adv. (*Prudent*).
Impru'dently adv. (*Imprudent*).
Gent'ly adv. (*Gentle*).
In'digently adv. (*Indigent*).
Neg'ligently adv. (*Negligent*).
Dil'igently adv. (*Diligent*).
Intel'ligently adv. (*Intelligent*).
Indul'gently adv. (*Indulgent*).
Ful'gently adv. (*Fulgent*).
Reful'gently adv. (*Refulgent*).
Efful'gently adv. (*Effulgent*).
Strin'gently adv. (*Stringent*).
Astrin'gently adv. (*Astringent*).
Contin'gently adv. (*Contingent*).
Pun'gently adv. (*Pungent*).
Co'gently adv. (*Cogent*).
Urg'ently adv. (*Urgent*).
Defic'iently adv. (*Deficient*).
Effic'iently adv. (*Efficient*).
Ineffic'iently adv. (*Inefficient*).
Suffic'iently adv. (*Sufficient*).
Insuffic'iently adv. (*Insufficient*).
Profi'ciently adv. (*Proficient*).
An'ciently adv. (*Ancient*).
Pre'sciently adv. (*Prescient*).
Omnis'ciently adv. (*Omniscient*).
Obe'diently adv. (*Obedient*).
Disobe'diently adv. (*Disobedient*).
Expe'diently adv. With expedience; suitably.
Inexpe'diently adv. (*Inexpedient*).
Sa'liently adv. (*Salient*).
Preve'niently adv. (*Prevenient*).
Conve'niently adv. (*Convenient*).
Inconve'niently adv. (*Inconvenient*).
Sa'piently adv. (*Sapient*).
Incip'iently adv. (*Incipient*).
Prur'iently adv. (*Prurient*).
Tran'siently adv. (*Transient*).
Pa'tiently adv. (*Patient*).
Impa'tiently adv. (*Impatient*).
Sen'tiently adv. (*Sentient*).
Subser'viently adv. (*Subservient*).
Prev'alently adv. (*Prevalent*).
Si'lently adv. (*Silent*).
Pes'tilently adv. (*Pestilent*).
Ex'cellently adv. (*Excellent*).
Repell'ently adv. (*Repellent*).
In'dolently adv. (*Indolent*).
Vi'olently adv. (*Violent*).
Som'nolently adv. (*Somnolent*).
In'solently adv. (*Insolent*).
Malev'olently adv. (*Malevolent*).
Benev'olently adv. (*Benevolent*).
Tur'bulently adv. (*Turbulent*).
Suc'culently adv. (*Succulent*).
Lu'culently adv. (*Luculent*).
Truc'ulently adv. (*Truculent*).
Fraud'ulently adv. (*Fraudulent*).
Op'ulently adv. (*Opulent*).
Cor'pulently adv. (*Corpulent*).
Vir'ulently adv. (*Virulent*).
Pur'ulently adv. (*Purulent*).
Ve'hemently adv. (*Vehement*).
Clem'ently adv. (*Clement*).
Inclem'ently adv. (*Inclement*).
Mo'mently adv. From moment to moment; at any moment.
Per'manently adv. (*Permanent*).
Em'inently adv. (*Eminent*).
Pre-em'inently adv. (*Pre-eminent*).
Superem'inently adv. (*Supereminent*).
Im'minently adv. (*Imminent*).
Prom'inently adv. (*Prominent*).
Con'tinently adv. (*Continent*).
Incon'tinently adv. Immediately; unchastely.
Per'tinently adv. (*Pertinent*).
Imper'tinently adv. (*Impertinent*).
Ab'stinently adv. (*Abstinent*).
Appar'ently adv. To all appearance; seemingly.
Transpar'ently adv. (*Transparent*).
Dif'ferently adv. (*Different*).
Indif'ferently adv. (*Indifferent*).
Inher'ently adv. (*Inherent*).
Coher'ently adv. (*Coherent*).
Incoher'ently adv. (*Incoherent*).
Rev'erently adv. (*Reverent*).
Irrev'erently adv. (*Irreverent*).
Abhor'rently adv. (*Abhorrent*).
Cur'rently adv. Commonly, generally; in a current manner.
Decur'rently adv. (*Decurrent*).
Concur'rently adv. (*Concurrent*).
Ab'sently adv. Inattentively.
Pres'ently adv. Before long, by and by; instantly.
La'tently adv. (*Latent*).
Pa'tently adv. Evidently, manifestly.
Com'petently adv. (*Competent*).
Incom'petently adv. (*Incompetent*).
Pen'itently adv. (*Penitent*)

Impen'itently adv. (*Impenitent*).
Intent'ly adv. Earnestly; sedulously.
Mal'contently adv. (*Malcontent*).
Po'tently adv. (*Potent*).
Prepo'tently adv. (*Prepotent*).
Omnip'otently adv. (*Omnipotent*).
Im'potently adv. (*Impotent*).
Adver'tently adv. (*Advertent*).
Inadver'tently adv. (*Inadvertent*).
Insis'tently adv. (*Insistent*).
Consis'tently adv. (*Consistent*).
Inconsis'tently adv. (*Inconsistent*).
Persis'tently adv. (*Persistent*).
Flu'ently adv. (*Fluent*).
Af'fluently adv. (*Affluent*).
Fre'quently adv. (*Frequent*).
Sub'sequently adv. (*Subsequent*).
Con'sequently adv. By consequence; therefore.
Incon'sequently adv. (*Inconsequent*).
El'oquently adv. (*Eloquent*).
Grandil'-oquently adv. (*Grandiloquent*).
Magnil'-oquently adv. (*Magniloquent*).
Fer'vently adv. (*Fervent*).
Faint'ly adv. Feebly; without vigour or distinctness.
Saint'ly a. Like a saint; becoming a holy person.
Quaint'ly adv. (*Quaint*).
Joint'ly adv. Together; in concert.
Conjoint'ly adv. (*Conjoint*).
Disjoint'ly adv. In a disjointed state.
Gaunt'ly adv. (*Gaunt*).
Blunt'ly adv. (*Blunt*).
Par'amountly adv. (*Paramount*).
Hot'ly adv. (*Hot*).
Apt'ly adv. (*Apt*).
Inapt'ly adv. (*Inapt*).
Inept'ly adv. (*Inept*).
Prompt'ly adv. (*Prompt*).
Abrupt'ly adv. (*Abrupt*).
Corrupt'ly adv. (*Corrupt*).
Incorrupt'ly adv. (*Incorrupt*).
Smart'ly adv. (*Smart*).
Part'ly adv. In part; in some degree.
Tart'ly adv. (*Tart*).
Stal'wartly adv. (*Stalwart*).
Alert'ly adv. (*Alert*).
Inert'ly adv. (*Inert*).
Pert'ly adv. (*Pert*).
Mal'apertly adv. (*Malapert*).
Expert'ly adv. (*Expert*).
Inexpert'ly adv. Unskilfully.
O'vertly adv. Openly.
Cov'ertly adv. Secretly.
Short'ly adv. Briefly; in a short time or manner.
Port'ly a. Of stout build; dignified.
Curt'ly adv. (*Curt*).
Court'ly a. Elegant, polite, polished; obsequious; pertaining to a court.
Beast'ly a. Like a beast; brutal; coarse; disgusting, loathesome.
Stead'fastly adv. (*Steadfast*).
Ghast'ly a. Ghost-like, haggard, deathly; terrible.
Last'ly adv. At last; finally.
Vast'ly adv. (*Vast*).
Mod'estly adv. (*Modest*).
Immod'estly adv. (*Immodest*).
Man'ifestly adv. (*Manifest*).
Priest'ly a. Pertaining to or becoming a priest; sacerdotal.
Hon'estly adv. (*Honest*).
Dishon'estly adv. (*Dishonest*).
Thistl'y a. Covered with or resembling thistles.
Bristl'y a. Covered with bristles; prickly.
Grist'ly a. Consisting of or like gristle.
Cost'ly a. Of high price, valuable.
Ghost'ly a. Pertaining to ghosts or to the spirit; spiritual; dismal; shadowy.
First'ly adv. In the first place.
August'ly adv. (*August*).
Just'ly adv. Rightly; fairly; properly
Taut'ly adv. (*Taut*).
Stout'ly adv. (*Stout*).
Devout'ly adv. (*Devout*).
Du'ly adv. In suitable manner; properly, fitly.
Undu'ly adv. Excessively; illegally; unwarrantably.
July' s. The seventh month.
Unru'ly a. Turbulent; disorderly; ungovernable.
Tru'ly adv. (*True*).
Raw'ly adv. In a raw manner; crudely.
Crawl'y a. Having a creeping sensation.
Scrawl'y a. Characterized by scrawling.
New'ly adv. Recently.
Low'ly a. Humble; unpretentious; free from pride. adv. Modestly; meekly.
Shal'lowly adv. (*Shallow*).
Mel'lowly adv. (*Mellow*).
Hol'lowly adv. (*Hollow*).
Slow'ly adv. (*Slow*).
Nar'rowly adv. (*Narrow*).
Lax'ly adv. (*Lax*).
Reflex'ly adv. (*Reflex*).
Com'plexly adv. (*Complex*).
Con'vexly adv. (*Convex*).
Prolix'ly adv. (*Prolix*).
Or'thodoxly adv. (*Orthodox*).
Grey'ly adv. (*Grey*).
Shy'ly adv. Timidly, nervously; not familiarly.
Sly'ly adv. (*Sly*).
Coy'ly adv. (*Coy*).
Dry'ly adv. (*Dry*).
Wry'ly adv. (*Wry*).
Driz'zly a. Characterized by drizzle.
My a. Belonging to me.
Beam'y a. Radiant, shining; massive; broad in the beam.
Gleam'y a. Darting beams of light; flashing.
Cream'y a. Full of or like cream; luscious.
Scream'y a. Characterized by screaming.
Dream'y a. Full of or causing dreams; unpractical.
Stream'y a. Abounding with streams; beamy
Seam'y a. Showing seams; threadbare; sordid.
Steam'y a. Consisting of or full of steam; misty.
In'famy s. Total loss of reputation or character; extreme baseness.
-gamy suff. Denoting marriage or kind of marriage.
Ga'my a. Having the flavour or odour of game; high.
Pantag'amy s. A system of communistic marriage for both sexes.
Big'amy s. Marriage with a second person during the lifetime of one's legal spouse.
Dig'amy s. Marrying a second time.
Trig'amy s. State of being married three times or of having three spouses at once.
Endog'amy s. Marriage with members of the same tribe only.
Dichog'amy s. (*Dichogamous*).
Orthog'amy s. Direct fertilization (of plants).
Allog'amy s. Cross-fertilization of plants.
Xenog'amy s. Cross-fertilization.

Monog'amy s. State of having only one spouse at a time.
Zoog'amy s. Sexual reproduction.
Heterog'amy s. Condition of being heterogamous.
Deuterog'amy s. A second marriage; practice of marrying again.
Isog'amy s. The conjugation of two cells not sexually differentiated.
Misog'amy s. Hatred of marriage.
Cryptog'amy s. Concealed or obscure fructification, as in the cryptogams.
Exog'amy s. The rule that marriage must take place with one outside the tribe.
Polyg'amy s. Plurality of spouses at the same time; condition of one man having more than one wife.
Fla'my a. Blazing; consisting of or like flame.
Foam'y a. Covered with or like foam.
Loam'y a. Containing or like loam.
Bal'samy a. Like balsam; balmy.
Jess'amy s. A fop, coxcomb.
Demy' s. A size of paper (about 22½ by 17½ ins.); a scholar of Magdalen, Oxon.
Acad'emy s. A society for the furthering of literature, science, or art; an educational institution.
Al'chemy s. The chemistry of the Middle Ages; search for the Elixir of Life, Universal Panacea, etc.
Heterophe'my s. Saying or writing differently from what was intended.
Blas'phemy s. An indignity offered to God; impious irreverence; profanity.
En'emy s. A foe, adversary; a member of a hostile nation.
Phlegm'y (flem'y) a. Abounding in or like phlegm.
Pyg'my s. A dwarf; an insignificant person. a. Diminutive, dwarfish.
Li'my a. Containing or resembling lime; viscous.
Sli'my a. Consisting of or like slime; viscous; unctuous.
Bu'limy s. Morbid craving for food.
Ri'my a. Covered with or resembling rime.
Gri'my a. Engrained with dirt; foul.
At'imy s. Loss of rank or civil rights.
Balm'y a. Soft, mild, fragrant; producing or resembling balm, (*slang*) daft.
Palm'y a. Abounding in palms; flourishing; victorious.
Film'y a. Like a film; composed of pellicles.
Gam'my a. Crippled; crooked.
Ham'my a. Tasting of ham.
Sham'my s. A soft kind of leather.
Clam'my a. Soft and sticky; moist.
Mam'my s. Child's name for "mother."
Gem'my a. Set with gems; glittering.
Jem'my s. A burglar's crowbar; a baked sheep's head.
Shim'my a. Denoting a certain dance-movement. s. (*Slang*) A chemise.
Whim'my a. Full of whims.
Tom'my s. A British private soldier; (*slang*) grub, tuck.
Scum'my a. Having scum.
Dum'my s. A figure for exhibiting clothes, coiffeurs, etc.; a sham article; the exposed hand at bridge, etc.; a stupid fellow.
Gum'my a. Sticky, viscous, adhesive.
Thing'ummy s. A thing.
Chum'my a. (*Chum*).
Plum'my a. Full of plums; (*slang*) luscious.
Slum'my a. Abounding in or resembling slums.
Mum'my s. An embalmed corpse; child's name for "mother."
Rum'my a. Queer, odd, strange.
Crum'my a. Crumby.
Thrum'my a. Like or covered with thrums.
Tum'my s. (*Slang*) The stomach.
Ho'my a. Pertaining to home; homelike.
Pathog'nomy s. Expression of the passions.
Craniog'nomy s. Scientific and comparative study of crania.
Physiogn'omy (-on'-) s. Art of discovering character from the features; the face; general appearance.
Chirog'nomy s. Palmistry.
Antin'omy s. Conflict of authority; opposition in laws.
Econ'omy s. Management of a household; frugal and judicious expenditure; regular operations of nature; due order of things; carefulness, frugality.
Geon'omy s. The science dealing with the structure and development of the earth.
Organon'omy s. The science of the laws of organic life.
Zoon'omy s. Science of the laws of animal life.
Topon'omy s. Science of or a register of place-names.
Heteron'omy s. Subjection to the rule of another.
Deuteron'omy s. The fifth book of the Pentateuch.
Agron'omy s. Husbandry; land management.
Metron'omy s. Measurement by a metronome.
Astron'omy s. The science of the heavenly bodies.
Gastron'omy s. Art of good food and eating; art of cookery; epicurism.
Ison'omy s. Equality of legal or political rights.
Noson'omy s. The nomenclature of diseases.
Auton'omy s. Self-government; right or power of this.
Pluton'omy s. Economics, political economy.
Phyton'omy s. Science of plant growth.
Taxon'omy s. System or principles of scientific classification.
Bloom'y a. (*Bloom*).
Gloom'y a. Dark, dismal; sad, dispiriting; sullen, morose.
Room'y a. Spacious; wide.
Broom'y a. Abounding in broom.
Lampaded'romy s. A torch-race.
Orthod'romy s. Othodromics.
Stereoch'romy s. Painting with pigments mixed with soluble glass.
Helioch'romy s. Photography in natural colours.
Pho'tochromy s. Colour-photography.
Pol'ychromy s. Art of decorating in many colours.
Blos'somy a. (*Blossom*).
-tomy suff. Used in surgery to signify a cutting.
At'omy s. A diminutive or emaciated person; a skeleton.
Anat'omy s. Art of dissection; science of the structure of animals or plants.
Hysterec'tomy s. Surgical removal of the uterus.
Neurec'tomy s. Excision of part of a nerve.
Strabot'omy s. Surgical operation to cure squinting.
Phlebot'omy s. Act or practice of blood-letting.
Varicot'omy s. Excision of a varicosity.
Vesicot'omy s. Incision of the bladder.
Oncot'omy s. The opening or excision of a tumour, etc.
Scot'omy s. Dizziness with dimness of sight.
Iridot'omy s. Incision of the iris.
Tracheot'omy s. Operation of cutting an opening in the wind-pipe.
Laryngotracheot'omy s. An operation of cutting into the larynx.

Stereot'omy s. Science of cutting solids into sections.
Osteot'omy s. Operation of dividing or cutting a piece out of a bone.
Hysterot'omy s. Hysterectomy; the Cæsarian operation.
Œsophagot'omy s. Operation of opening the œsophagus.
Syringot'omy s. Operation of cutting for fistula.
Pharyngot'omy s. Operation of cutting into the pharynx.
Laryngot'omy s. Surgical incision of the larynx.
Dichot'omy s. Division into two; the phase of the moon in which half the disk is illuminated.
Trichot'omy s. Division into three.
Bron'chotomy s. Operation of opening the wind-pipe.
Lithot'omy s. Operation of cutting for stone in the bladder.
Craniot'omy s. The opening of the head of a fœtus to effect delivery.
Herniot'omy s. Operation for strangulated hernia.
Ovariot'omy s. Surgical removal of the ovary.
Arteriot'omy s. The opening or dissection of arteries.
Cephalot'omy s. Dissection of the head.
Colot'omy s. An opening of the colon.
Desmot'omy s. Dissection of ligaments and sinews.
Splenot'omy s. Dissection of the spleen.
Tenot'omy s. The cutting of a tendon.
Splanchnot'omy s. Dissection of the viscera.
Vaginot'omy s. Incision of the vagina.
Zoot'omy s. The anatomy or dissection of animals.
Laparot'omy s. Incision through the side into the abdomen.
Cæsarot'omy s. Operation of delivering a child through the walls of the abdomen.
Microt'omy s. The cutting and preparation of sections for microscopic examination.
Chondrot'omy s. The anatomy of cartilages.
Sclerot'omy s. Surgical incision into the sclerotic.
Enterot'omy s. Dissection of the bowels; incision of the intestines.
Nephrot'omy s. Surgical incision of the kidney.
Urethrot'omy s. Incision of the urethra.
Gastrot'omy s. Operation of cutting into or opening the abdomen.
Sequestrot'omy s. The removal of sequestrum.
Neurot'omy s. Dissection of or incision into a nerve.
Cystot'omy s. Operation of cutting into the bladder or of opening cysts.
Phytot'omy s. Dissection of plants.
Loxot'omy s. Amputation by an oblique cut.
Ichthyot'omy s. The dissection of fishes.
Myot'omy s. Dissection of the muscles.
Embryot'omy s. The cutting of a fœtus in the uterus.
Gastros'tomy s. An operation to introduce food directly into the stomach.
Ar'my s. A large body of soldiers; a great number.
Bar'my a. Frothy, fermenting, scatter-brained.
Tax'idermy s. Art of preserving and mounting skins.
Dor'my s. Of a golfer as many holes up as there remain to play.
Storm'y a. Tempestuous; violent, passionate.
Worm'y (werm'-) a. Infested with or like worms; earthy.
Chasm'y a. Abounding in chasms.
Pris'my a. Of the nature of a prism.
Gaum'y a. Smeary, bedaubed.
Fu'my a. Causing, full of, or composed of fumes.
Vell'umy a. Like vellum.
Plu'my a. Adorned with plumes.
Spu'my a. Foaming; covered with or consisting of froth.
Thy'my (tī'-) a. Abounding in thyme; fragrant.
On'ymy s. Nomenclature.
Homon'ymy s. Sameness between words differing in meaning; ambiguity.
Tecnon'ymy s. Custom of naming the parent from the child.
Synon'ymy s. A system of or treatise on synonyms; synonymity.
Paron'ymy s. Quality of being paronymous.
Heteron'ymy s. State of being heteronymous.
Metron'ymy s. Use of metronymics.
Moton'ymy s. Use of one word or name for another with which it is closely associated.
Polyon'ymy s. Use of several names for one person or thing.
Sty'my s. (*Stymie*).
An'y a., pron. One or some indefinitely.
Ca'ny a. Abounding in canes.
Bean'y a. (*Slang*) Vigorous.
Tif'fany s. A thin silky gauze.
Tzig'any a. and s. Pertaining to or one of the Hungarian gipsies.
Mahog'any s. A tree furnishing a hard, reddish-brown wood; the wood.
Epiph'any s. The festival (6th Jan.) celebrating the visit of the Magi to Christ.
Theoph'any s. Manifestation of God to man.
Miscell'any s. A medley; a collection of literary compositions.
Cas'tellany s. Lordship or jurisdiction of a castellan.
Man'y a. Numerous; forming a great number.
Tam'many s. A New York political organization; political corruption.
Rom'any s. A gipsy; the gipsy language.
Com'pany s. Companionship; an assembly; partnership; a trading association, corporation or guild; a division of a regiment; crew of a ship. v.i. To associate with.
Accom'pany v.t. To go with, escort, be combined with; to play an accompaniment for.
Rhat'any s. A Peruvian shrub used in medicine, etc.
Lit'any s. A form of public supplication.
Bot'any s. Science of the structure, classification, etc., of plants.
Palæobot'any s. The science of extinct or fossil plants.
Dit'tany s. An aromatic perennial herb.
Za'ny s. A buffoon, merry-andrew.
Lar'ceny s. Petty theft.
Deny' v.t. To contradict; to refuse; to disown.
Sheen'y a. Having sheen; lustrous.
Galeen'y s. The guinea-fowl.
Spleen'y a. Splenetic, sullen.
Green'y a. Greenish. s. An inexperienced person.
Teen'y a. Tiny.
Sween'y s. Atrophy of a muscle, especially in a horse's shoulder.
Tween'y s. A servant assisting cook and housemaid.
-geny suff. Denoting production or mode of production.
Geog'eny s. The study or science of the earth's crust.
Osteog'eny s. Osteogenesis.

Morphog'eny s. Evolution of morphological characters.
Biog'eny s. Science of the origin of life; biogenesis.
Physiog'eny s. The evolution of vital functions; the history of this.
Crystallog'eny s. Science treating of the formation of crystals.
Phylog'eny s. Evolution of a species, etc., of plant or animal life; the history of this.
Homog'eny s. Correspondence due to descent from the same type.
Cormog'eny s. The life-history and development of racial groups.
Organog'eny s. Organogenesis.
Monog'eny s. Doctrine that mankind is descended from a single pair.
Oog'eny s. The orgin and development of an ovum.
Zoog'eny (-ŏj'-) s. The formation of animal organs.
Anthropog'eny s. Science of human origins.
Hysterog'eny s. Induction of hysteria.
Prog'eny s. Descendants; offspring.
Teratog'eny s. Production of monstrosities.
Ontog'eny s. The life history of an individual organism; embryology.
Odontog'eny s. The origin and development of teeth.
Histog'eny s. Formation and development of tissues; histogenesis.
Autog'eny s. Spontaneous generation.
Phytog'eny s. The origin, evolution, etc., of plants.
Embryog'eny s. The formation of an embryo; embryology.
Polyg'eny s. Poligenesis.
Mnemotech'ny s. Art of developing the memory.
Pyr'otechny s. Art of exhibiting or making fireworks.
Vill'ainy s. Act of a villain; extreme depravity; an atrocious deed.
Rain'y a. Abounding with rain, showery.
Brain'y a. Intellectual; well-endowed with brains.
Grain'y a. Having a grain; like or consisting of grains.
Vein'y (vān'-) a. Full of viens; veined.
Shi'ny a. Bright; unclouded; luminous.
Sun'shiny a. (*Sunshine*).
Li'ny a. Full of lines; seamed, wrinkled.
Gem'iny int. A mild oath.
Postlim'iny s. Postliminium.
Nim'iny-pim'iny a. Affectedly nice, mincing.
Crim'iny int. Expressive of astonishment.
Hom'iny s. Porridge made with maize-flour.
Ig'nominy s. Disgrace; reproach; shame.
Pi'ny a. Pertaining to, abounding in, or smelling like pines.
Spi'ny a. Having spines; thorn-like, thorny.
Bri'ny a. Very salt. s. (*Slang*) The ocean.
Res'iny a. Like resin.
Ros'iny s. Like rosin.
Ti'ny a. Very small.
Sat'iny a. Resembling or consisting of satin.
Des'tiny s. Fate, doom; that to which one is destined.
Mu'tiny s. Open revolt against authority; military or naval insurrection. v.i. To rebel against authority.
Scru'tiny s. Close search; critical examination.
Vi'ny a. Pertaining to, resembling, or abounding in vines.
Wi'ny a. Resembling or tasting like wine.
Cal'umny s. Slander, defamation.
Can'ny a. Shrewd; cautious.
Uncan'ny a. Mysterious; weird.
Nan'ny s. A she-goat; a child's nurse.
Cran'ny s. A crevice, chink.
Scran'ny a. Lean; meagre.
Gran'ny s. A grandmother; an old woman.
Tyr'anny s. Arbitrary or despotic government; severity; rule of a tyrant.
Fen'ny a. Pertaining to, inhabiting, or like fens.
Hen'ny a. Hen-like.
Jen'ny s. A machine for cotton-spinning; a stroke at billiards.
Blen'ny s. A small spiny-finned sea-fish.
Pen'ny s. The twelfth of a shilling; a bronze coin; money.
Catch'penny s. Something worthless. a. Made to gain money, worthless.
Twop'enny (tŭp'-) a. Worth twopence; cheap.
Six'penny a. Worth or priced at sixpence.
John'ny s. (*Slang*) A chap; a young man about town.
Fin'ny a. Furnished with fins; abounding in fish.
Hin'ny s. Offspring of a stallion and she-ass. v.i. To neigh.
Shin'ny s. A game like hockey.
Whin'ny v.i. To neigh softly. s. This act or sound. a. Abounding in whin or gorse.
Skin'ny a. Very lean; consisting only of skin.
Nin'ny s. A dolt, fool, simpleton.
Pic'caninny s. A little negro child.
Tin'ny a. Resembling tin or tin-plate abounding in tin.
Bon'ny a. Gay, healthy-looking, buxom.
Son'ny (sŭn'-) s. A son (*familiarly*).
Bun'ny s. A rabbit.
Dun'ny a. Hard of hearing.
Fun'ny a. Comical, droll, laughable; queer; a narrow pair-oar row-boat.
Gun'ny s. Coarse, heavy sackcloth.
Sun'ny a. Proceeding from, like, or exposed to the sun; bright.
Tun'ny s. A large food-fish allied to the mackerel.
Bo'ny a. With prominent bones; hard, angular.
Eb'ony s. A hard, heavy, black wood. a. Made of this; intensely black.
Co'ny s. The Hyrax or Syrian rock-rabbit; the rabbit; a simpleton.
Ba'cony a. Tasting of bacon.
Bal'cony s. A projecting gallery outside a building; a gallery in a theatre.
Chalced'ony s. A variety of quartz.
Pe'ony s. A garden plant with beautiful, showy flowers.
Ag'ony s. Great pain; torture.
Geog'ony s. The theory of the formation of the earth.
Theog'ony s. The genealogy of the gods; a poem on this.
Psychog'ony s. Development of the mind or soul.
Mythog'ony s. Study of the origin of myths.
Cosmog'ony s. Theory of the origin of the universe; a mythical account of this.
Monog'ony s. A sexual reproduction.
Heterog'ony s. State of having two or more kinds of perfect flowers; alternation of generations.
Embryog'ony s. The formation of an embryo.
Teleph'ony s. Science and practice of the telephone.
Antiph'ony s. Singing in alternate parts.

Sym'phony s. Accordance of sounds; an elaborate orchestral composition.
Cacoph'ony s. Harshness of sound, discord; a strident voice.
Coloph'ony s. A dark-coloured resin obtained from turpentine.
Homoph'ony s. Identity of sound; unison.
Tautoph'ony s. Repetition of the same sound.
Dys'phony s. Dysphonia.
Eu'phony s. An agreeable sound; smooth and easy enunciation.
Polyph'ony s. Simultaneous and harmonious combination of more than one melody in a composition; polyphonism.
Autoch'thony s. State or condition of being autochthonous.
Cush'iony a. (*Cushion*).
On'iony (un'-) a. Tasting or smelling of onion.
Fel'ony s. A heinous offence; a crime worse than a misdemeanour.
Col'ony s. A settlement of nationals in a foreign land who retain political connexion with the home-country; a group of people of one foreign nationality, or one trade, etc., living in the same quarter of a town.
Polo'ny s. A variety of sausage.
-mony suff. Forming nouns.
Stram'ony s. The thorn-apple, a poisonous plant yielding stramonium.
Hegem'ony s. Leadership, especially of one state among others.
Cer'emony s. Outward rite, form in religion or in civility.
Al'imony s. Husband's allowance to a wife judicially separated from him.
Ac'rimony s. Bitterness of temper, speech, etc.
Ag'rimony s. A hedgerow plant.
Mat'rimony s. Marriage, wedlock; the nuptial state.
Pat'rimony s. Inherited estate or right; a church estate.
Si'mony s. Crime of trafficking in ecclesiastical preferment.
Par'simony s. Excessive frugality or economy; miserliness; avarice.
Sanct'imony s. Affectation of sanctity; hypocritical piety.
An'timony s. A white, brittle metallic element.
Test'imony s. A solemn declaration; evidence; attestation; divine revelation.
Scam'mony s. An Eastern plant yielding a resin used in medicine.
Har'mony s. Fitness of parts to each other; agreement; musical concord; melody.
Loo'ny s. A lunatic, fool.
Moon'y a. Like the moon or moonlight; silly, dreamy.
Spoon'y a. Mawkishly amorous or sentimental. s. A simpleton.
Po'ny s. A small horse; (*slang*) £25; a small drinking-glass.
Geop'ony s. The art or science of agriculture.
Bar'ony s. The domain, title, or rights of a baron.
Cro'ny s. An intimate friend.
Syn'chrony s. Synchronism.
I'rony (I'-er-ni) a. Consisting of, containing, resembling, or tasting of iron.
I'rony (Ier'-ron-i) s. A subtle kind of sarcasm.
To'ny a. (*Slang*) Smart; fashionable.
At'ony s. Enervation; lack of mental or physical tone.
Bet'ony s. A plant with purple flowers.
Tan'tony s. The smallest in the litter (of pigs).
Syn'tony s. State of being tuned to each other (of wireless wave-lengths).
Homot'ony s. Uniform tone; state of being without variation.
Monot'ony s. Absence of variety; irksome sameness.
Ston'y a. Pertaining to, made of, abounding in, or resembling stone; hard; pitiless; (*slang*) destitute of money.
Aston'y v.t. To astound.
Cot'tony a. Like or made of cotton.
But'tony a. Like or well-supplied with buttons.
Glut'tony s. Excess in eating; voracity; greed.
Mut'tony a. Resembling mutton in flavour, etc.
Sax'ony s. A fine woollen fabric.
Bry'ony s. A genus of climbing plants.
Car'ny v.t. and i. (*Carney*).
Fern'y a. Abounding in or resembling ferns.
Corn'y a. Producing, containing, or tasting of corn; like a corn.
Horn'y a. Like horn; callous; abounding in horns.
Thorn'y a. Full of thorns; prickly; troublesome.
Du'ny a. Characterized by dunes.
Pu'ny a. Small and feeble; petty.
Lawn'y a. Resembling or abounding in lawns; like or covered with lawn.
Brawn'y a. Strong; muscular.
Taw'ny a. Of a yellowish-brown colour.
Mulligataw'ny s. A highly-flavoured curry soup or stew.
Down'y a. Covered with or stuffed with down; (*slang*) artful; characterized by dunes or downs.
Philog'yny s. Fondness for women.
Monog'yny s. Practice of mating with only one female.
Androg'yny s. Hermaphroditism.
Misog'yny s. Hatred of women.
Polyg'yny s. Polygamy.
Boy s. A male child, a lad; a native servant in certain colonies, etc.
Horse'boy s. A stable-boy.
Call'boy s. An attendant behind the scenes at a theatre.
Tall'boy s. A high chest of drawers.
Tom'boy s. A romping girl.
Mac'coboy s. A rose-scented snuff.
Car'boy s. A large, wicker-covered glass vessel for acids.
Foot'boy s. A boy in livery.
Post'boy s. A courier; a postilion.
Haut'boy s. An oboe; a treble organ-stop.
Coy a. Shy and bashful; coquettish.
Decoy' v.t. To lure, entrap, inveigle. s. A place for entrapping wild-fowl, etc.; a person who lures; a bait.
Hoy s. A one-masted vessel; a lighter. int. To draw attention, etc.
Ahoy' int. Attracting attention.
Hobbledehoy' s. A clumsy youth.
Joy s. Gladness; delight; exultation. v.i. and t. To rejoice, to gladden.
Enjoy' v.t. To delight in; to have, use or perceive with pleasure.
Overjoy' v.t. To make excessively joyful.
Cloy v.t. To glut, satiate, tire with richness.
Sav'eloy s. A dry, highly-seasoned sausage.
Alloy' v.t. To mix one metal with a baser, or two metals with a non-metal; to impair, taint. s. A mixture of a baser metal with a finer; a metallic compound.
Deploy' v.i. To form an extended front. v.t. To spread out troops.

Employ' v.t. To keep at work, to engage in one's service; to use. s. Occupation, employment.
Annoy' v.t. To vex, irritate, molest.
Tea'poy s. A small stand for a tea-tray.
Se'poy s. A British-trained Hindu soldier.
Char'poy s. The Indian string bed.
Vice'roy s. A governor ruling as the king's substitute.
Nor'roy s. The third of the English kings-at-arms.
Troy s. System of weights used for gold, silver, and jewels.
Destroy' v.t. To demolish, overthrow, devastate, annihilate.
Corduroy' s. A thick ribbed or corded cotton stuff.
Soy s. A Japanese and Chinese fish-sauce.
Pad'uasoy s. A kind of corded silk stuff.
Toy s. A plaything; a trifle. v.i. To dally, amuse oneself.
Buoy s. An anchored float for carrying a bell, mooring vessels to, etc. v.t. To mark with buoys; to keep afloat, to keep from depression.
Savoy' s. A curled winter cabbage.
En'voy s. One sent on a mission, especially a diplomatist next below an ambassador; the concluding lines of a ballade; a postscript to a collection of poems.
Convoy' v.t. To accompany as escort.
Con'voy s. Act of escorting and protecting persons or goods in transit; defending party or ships; that which is convoyed.
Heap'y a. Lying in heaps.
Soap'y a. Resembling, containing, or smeared with soap; unctuous.
Cra'py s. Like or made of crape.
Psychother'apy s. Psychotherapeutics.
Radiother'apy s. Treatment of disease by means of radium emanations.
Hydrother'apy s. Hydropathy.
Photother'apy s. Treatment of skin-diseases, etc., by action of light rays.
Gra'py a. Tasting of, pertaining to, or resembling grapes.
Sat'rapy s. The government or jurisdiction of a satrap.
Sleep'y a. Inclined to sleep; lazy, sluggish; over-ripe (especially of pears).
Creep'y a. Having the sensation of creeping of the flesh; causing this.
Steep'y a. (*Steep*).
Weep'y a. Given to weeping; inducing tears.
Orthoe'py s. Phonology; correct pronunciation.
Pi'py a. Like a pipe; shrill.
Stri'py a. Marked with stripes.
Gos'sipy a. Given to gossiping, full of gossip.
Pul'py a. Like pulp; succulent.
Cramp'y a. Diseased with or producing cramp.
Swamp'y a. Low, wet, and spongy; marshy.
Hemp'y a. Like hemp.
Skimp'y a. Short; in a niggardly way.
Crimp'y a. Brittle; easily crumpled; crimped.
Scrimp'y a. (*Scrimp*).
Romp'y a. Rompish.
Dump'y a. Short and fat; melancholic.
Hump'y a. Having a hump or humps; (*slang*) depressed, irritable.
Jump'y a. Characterized by jumping; very nervous.
Lump'y a. Full of lumps; lumpish.
Crump'y a. Crisp, crumbling.
Frump'y a. Frumpish.
Grump'y a. Surly, peevish, cross.
Stump'y a. Thick-set; full of stumps.
Cop'y s. An imitation; a transcript; matter to be set in type; a single example of a book, etc.; a pattern. v.t. To imitate, transcribe, model after. v.i. To do a thing in imitation.
-scop'y suff. Denoting observation by means of the specified apparatus.
Teles'copy s. Art, science, or use of the telescope.
Endos'copy s. Examination of an internal organ with an endoscope.
Tracheos'copy s. Examination of the trachea with the laryngoscope.
Stethos'copy s. Use of or practice with the stethoscope.
Radios'copy s. Examination of bodies through Röntgen rays.
Cranios'copy s. Scientific examination of the skull.
Ophthalmos'copy s. Examination of the interior of the eye.
Uranos'copy s. Observation of the heavenly bodies.
Urinos'copy s. Diagnosis by inspection of the urine.
Metopos'copy s. Study of physiognomy.
Necros'copy s. A post-mortem examination.
Micros'copy s. Use of or investigations with the microscope.
Deuteros'copy s. Second sight.
Horos'copy s. Art of making predictions from the stars.
Fluoros'copy s. The use of the fluoroscope.
Spectros'copy s. Science, use, or practice of the spectroscope; spectrum analysis.
Gastros'copy s. Medical examination of the abdomen.
Scatos'copy s. Diagnosis by means of fæces.
Hepatos'copy s. Divination from the liver of a sacrificed beast.
Nyc'talopy s. Nyctalopia.
Can'opy s. A raised covering over a bed, throne, etc. v.t. To cover with a canopy.
Loop'y a. (*slang*) Daft; idiotic.
Ro'py a. Resembling a rope; viscid.
Lycan'thropy s. Form of insanity in which patient imagines himself a wolf; witchcraft connected with wolves.
Philan'thropy s. The love of mankind; general benevolence.
Cynan'thropy s. Madness in which the patient assumes the characteristics of a dog.
Misan'thropy s. Hatred of mankind.
Thean'thropy s. Theanthropism.
Heliot'ropy s. Heliotropism.
Allot'ropy s. Change of physical properties without change of substance.
Æolot'ropy s. Change of physical properties consequent on change of position.
Isot'ropy s. State or quality of being isotropic.
Heterot'opy s. Misplacement of an organ; variation from normal sequence of development.
My'opy s. Short-sightedness.
Ox'yopy s. Oxyopia.
Gap'py a. Full of gaps.
Hap'py a. Fortunate; prosperous; apt; contented, gay.
Nap'py a. Having a nap; strong (of beer).
Snap'py a. Snappish.
Pap'py a. Soft and moist like pap; suitable for infants.
Scrap'py a. In fragments; patchy
Trap'py a. (*Slang*) Tricky, puzzling.

Sap'py a. Abounding with sap, juicy; mentally weak.
Chip'py a. (*Slang*) Seedy; irritable.
Whip'py a. Like a whip; lithe.
Slip'py a. Slippery; quick, wide-awake.
Nip'py a. Keen, biting, frosty.
Snip'py a. Insignificant; scrappy.
Pip'py a. Full of pips.
Drip'py a. (*Drip*).
Hop'py a. Tasting of hops.
Chop'py a. Full of holes.
Shop'py a. Concerned with or concerning one's own business, etc.
Flop'py a. Flopping; loose, flaccid.
Slop'py a. Wet, splashed; slovenly; maudlin.
Pop'py s. A flowering plant, one species of which yields opium.
Crop'py s. One with hair cut short; a Roundhead, Puritan.
Sop'py a. Soaked; wet through; (*slang*) very simple; green.
Pup'py s. A young dog; a conceited youth.
Harp'y s. A fabulous preying monster, half bird half woman; an extortioner.
Chirp'y a. Cheerful, chatty.
Spy s. One who secretly watches another. v.i. To pry, scrutinize. v.t. To examine secretly, discover by close search.
Espy' v.t. To catch sight of, especially at a distance; to discern unexpectedly. v.i. To look narrowly.
Crisp'y a. Curled, wavy; crisp.
Wisp'y a. Like a wisp.
Hic'cupy a. Having or characterized by hiccups.
Oc'cupy v.t. To take or hold in possession; to cover or fill; to employ, engage.
Reoc'cupy v.t. To occupy again.
Preoc'cupy v.t. To take possession of before another; to prepossess.
Roup'y a. Hoarse.
Soup'y a. Resembling or soiled with soup.
Chir'rupy a. Chirpy.
Syr'upy a. Resembling or containing syrup.
He'liotypy s. A process of photo-engraving.
Phon'otypy s. Phonetic printing.
Elec'trotypy s. Electrotyping.
-ry suff. (As *-ery*).
Syl'labary s. A catalogue of syllables or of symbols of them.
Tur'bary s. Right of digging turf on another's land.
Pec'cary s. A swine-like animal of Central and S. America.
Apoth'ecary s. A druggist, a dispenser.
Hypoth'ecary a. Pertaining to a pledge or hypothecation.
For'micary s. An ant-hill.
Tu'nicary s. A tunicate.
Scar'y a. Easily scared or frightened.
Pis'cary s. Right or privilege of fishing in private waters.
Hebdom'adary a. Hebdomadal. s. A priest or monk whose week it is for certain duties.
Lam'padary s. Officer of the Greek Church in charge of ceremonial lights.
Drom'edary s. A camel with one hump.
Lap'idary s. One who cuts or engraves stones, gems, etc. a. Pertaining to the art of cutting and polishing gems, etc.; suitable for tombstone inscription.
Quan'dary s. State of difficulty; perplexity.
Preb'endary s. The holder of a prebend.
Leg'endary a. Traditional; fabulous; mythical.
Zem'indary s. Jurisdiction of a zemindar.
Sec'ondary a. Coming next to the first; not primary; subordinate, second-rate. s. A deputy; a satellite; a feather on the second bone of a wing, a hind wing of an insect.
Bound'ary s. A limit, border, frontier.
Feu'dary a. and s. Feudatory.
Dear'y s. Dear one.
Nu'cleary a. Nuclear.
Smear'y a. Smeared; sticky.
Copar'cenary s. Joint heirship or ownership. a. Relating to coparceners.
Drear'y a. Gloomy, mournful; oppressively monotonous.
Tear'y a. Abounding with tears; tearful.
We'ary a. Worn with fatigue; tired.
Awear'y a. Tired, weary.
Vagar'y s. A whim; wild freak or fancy.
Vin'egary a. Like or containing vinegar; sour.
Beg'gary s. State of extreme poverty.
Su'gary a. Resembling or containing sugar; sweet.
Char'y a. Prudent, wary, frugal, cautious.
Judi'ciary a. Judicial; passing sentence. s. The judicature.
Benfi'ciary s. One who is benefited or assisted; the holder of a benefice. a. Holding as a feudatory.
Justi'ciary s. An administrator of justice. a. Pertaining to the administration of justice.
Fidu'ciary a. Confident; held or founded in trust. s. A trustee.
Di'ary s. A daily register, a journal.
Interme'diary a. Lying between. s. A go-between, agent.
Subsid'iary a. Auxiliary; aiding; subordinate. s. An accessory.
Presid'iary a. Presidial.
Incen'diary a. Pertaining to malicious destruction by fire; inflammatory. s. One who maliciously sets fire to property; an agitator.
Stipen'diary a. Receiving a stipend. s. A paid magistrate.
Pla'giary s. A plagiarist. a. Practising literary theft.
Vestig'iary a. Vestigial.
Bil'iary a. Pertaining to the bile.
Nobil'iary a. Pertaining to the nobility.
Cil'iary a. (*Cilia*).
Domicil'iary a. Pertaining to a domicile or home.
Supercil'iary a. Situated above the eyebrows.
Mil'iary a. Like millet-seed, especially of certain eruptions.
Auxil'iary a. Helping; additional; subsidiary. s. A machine, etc., for use in emergencies; (pl.) allied, foreign, or additional forces for use in an emergency.
Lan'iary a. Adapted for tearing. s. A canine tooth in carnivora.
Her'niary a. Pertaining to hernia.
Pecu'niary a. Pertaining to or consisting of money; monetary.
A'piary s. A place where bees are kept.
To'piary a. Shaped by clipping or cutting.
Ves'piary s. A wasp's nest.
Bri'ary a. (*Briery*).
Fri'ary s. A monastery.
Ret'iary a. Reticulated; weaving or using nets. s. A variety of spider.
Residen'tiary a. Having residence. s. One who is resident.
Eviden'tiary a. Pertaining to or of the nature of evidence.
Obedien'tiary s. A member of, or office-holder in, a monastery.

Silen'tiary s. One keeping silence, especially in a court.
Peniten'tiary a. Relating to penance. s. One who prescribes rules for or who performs penance; a prison, reformatory.
Plenipoten'tiary a. Invested with full powers; absolute. s. An envoy or ambassador with full powers.
Ter'tiary a. Of the third geological order. s. The tertiary system of rocks; a feather on the proximal joint of a bird's wing.
Bes'tiary s. A moralized natural history.
Ves'tiary s. A robing-room. a. Pertaining to dress.
A'viary s. A large cage for birds.
Bre'viary s. The service-book of the Roman Catholic Church.
A'lary a. Pertaining to wings.
Intercal'ary a. Inserted between others, especially of 29th February.
Sal'ary s. Stated periodical payment for non-manual work.
Clar'y s. A garden pot-herb.
Tu'telary a. Protective; pertaining to a guardian.
Flar'y a. Showy, gaudy.
Glar'y a. Of dazzling brightness.
Bur'glary s. House-breaking by night.
Pi'lary a. Pertaining to the hair.
Carpel'lary a. (*Carpel*).
Vit'ellary a. Vitelline.
Bacil'lary a. Pertaining to or caused by bacilli.
Codicil'lary a. (*Codicil*).
Ancil'lary a. Subsidiary; not essential.
Mam'millary a. Pertaining to or like a nipple.
Armil'lary a. Ringed; made of or furnished with rings.
Capil'lary a. Hair-like; of very fine calibre. s. A very fine canal in an animal body.
Papil'lary a. Pertaining to, resembling, or covered with papillæ; warty, pimpled.
Pu'pillary a. Pertaining to a pupil.
Fibril'lary a. Fibrillar.
Frit'illary s. A brightly-coloured liliaceous bulbous plant; a butterfly with spotted wings.
Ax'illary a. Belonging to the axilla.
Maxil'lary a. Pertaining to the jaw or jawbone.
Inframaxill'ary a. Under the jaw; pertaining to the lower jaw-bone.
Supramax'illary a. Pertaining to the upper jaw.
Vexil'lary a. and s. Pertaining to or the bearer of a vexillum.
Corol'lary s. That which follows a proposition demonstrated; an inference, deduction.
Medul'lary a. Pertaining to, consisting of, or resembling marrow.
Cataphyl'lary a. Applied to the colourless scales of certain plants.
Mo'lary a. Adapted for grinding.
Epis'tolary a. Pertaining to epistles; suitable for correspondence.
Exem'plary a. Serving as an example; worthy of imitation.
Vocab'ulary s. Alphabetically arranged word-list with short definitions; range of expression.
Tintinab'ulary a. Tintinabular.
Constab'ulary s. The body of constables in a district. a. Pertaining to constables.
Fam'ulary a. Pertaining to a famulus.
Num'mulary a. Nummular.
For'mulary a. Stated, prescribed. s. A book containing prescribed forms, precedents, prayers, etc.
Scap'ulary s. The ecclesiastical scapular.
Capit'ulary s. An act passed by a chapter; a member of a chapter; a body of laws.
Tit'ulary s. One invested with a title the duties pertaining to which he does not perform. a. Pertaining to a title; titular.
Vit'ulary a. Pertaining to calves or calving.
Car'tulary s. A register of deeds, etc.; a place for storing these.
Cal'amary s. A species of cuttle-fish.
Gram'ary s. Witchcraft, magic, necromancy.
Rose'mary s. An aromatic, evergreen shrub.
Pri'mary a. First; original; elementary; primitive. s. That which stands first or chief; large feather of a wing.
Pal'mary a. Palmaceous; bearing or worthy of the palm; pre-eminent.
Mam'mary a. Pertaining to the breasts or mammæ.
Num'mary a. Pertaining to coin or money.
Sum'mary s. An abridgment, epitome. a. Concise, compendious; rapidly performed.
Cus'tomary a. Habitual, according to custom; holding or held by custom.
Sper'mary s. The male spermatic gland.
Infirm'ary s. An establishment for the sick; a hospital.
Cost'mary s. A perennial aromatic plant.
Lach'rymary a. Pertaining to weeping.
Canar'y s. A small yellow-coloured singing-bird; a wine made in the Canary Islands.
Gran'ary s. A storehouse for grain or corn; a district abundant in corn.
Vic'enary a. Consisting of or pertaining to 20.
Par'cenary s. Joint tenancy; co-heirship.
Mer'cenary a. Serving for pay; avaricious; that may be hired. s. One who is hired.
De'nary a. Containing ten; proceeding by tens.
Duode'nary a. Pertaining to the number 12; proceeding by twelves.
Quinquage'nary s. A fiftieth anniversary. a. Pertaining to the fiftieth year.
Septuage'nary a. Consisting of or containing 70.
Sexag'enary a. Pertaining to sixty. s. A sexagenarian.
Octog'enary a. Eighty, or between eighty and ninety, years old; pertaining to this age.
Mill'enary s. A thousandth anniversary; a thousand; a millennium. a. Millennial.
Ple'nary a. Entire, complete.
Prolegom'enary a. Introductory.
Se'nary a. Containing six; by sixes.
Cate'nary s. The curve of a cord suspended from two points not in the same vertical line. a. Relating to a chain or a catena.
Cen'tenary s. A hundredth anniversary, a century. a. Recurring once in a hundred years; relating to a hundred.
Bicen'tenary s. A two hundredth anniversary. a. Consisting of or pertaining to two hundred years.
Octocente'nary s. An eight hundredth anniversary.
Tercen'tenary s. A three hundredth anniversary. a. Comprising three hundred years.

Sexcen'tenary s. A six-hundred anniversary. a. Pertaining to six hundred years.
Octingente'nary s. An eight-hundredth anniversary.
Quingente'nary s. A five-hundredth anniversary.
Sep'tenary a. Consisting of or relating to seven; lasting seven years. s. A set of seven things.
Nov'enary a. A group of nine.
Bi'nary a. Double, dual.
Concu'binary a. (*Concubine*).
Or'dinary a. Customary, usual; plain, of little merit. s. An ecclesiastical judge; an eating-house with fixed prices for meals; such a meal; an heraldic charge.
Extraor'dinary a. Out of the common; remarkable.
Valetu'dinary a. Infirm; sickly. s. An invalid.
Consuetu'dinary a. Customary; derived from usage.
Vicissitu'dinary a. Vicissitudinous.
Latitu'dinary a. Latitudinarian.
Multitu'dinary a. Multitudinous.
Imag'inary a. Existing only in the imagination; not actual.
Dis'ciplinary a. Pertaining to or intended for discipline.
Cul'inary a. Pertaining to the kitchen or to cookery.
Lam'inary a. Laminar.
Sem'inary s. A place of education.
Lim'inary a. Introductory, preliminary.
Prelim'inary a. Introductory; preparatory; prior. s. Something preparatory; prelude.
Postlim'inary a. Pertaining or according to postliminium.
Lu'minary s. Anything yielding light; an expert, or eminent person.
Vet'erinary a. Pertaining to diseases of domestic animals and their treatment. s. A veterinary surgeon.
Tri'nary a. Proceeding by threes; consisting of three.
Ur'inary a. Pertaining to or resembling urine.
Sang'uinary a. Accompanied by or eager for bloodshed; murderous.
Qui'nary a. Consisting of five; arranged in fives.
Hym'nary s. A collection of hymns.
Stan'nary s. A tin mine, mining district, or works. a. Pertaining to tin, tin mines, etc.
Decen'nary s. A period of ten years. a. Pertaining to such.
Anten'nary a. Pertaining to antennæ.
Antiph'onary s. A collection of antiphons.
Le'gionary a. Pertaining to or consisting of legions. s. A soldier of a legion.
Re'gionary a. Regional.
Gang'lionary a. Composed of ganglia.
Mil'lionary a. Pertaining to or consisting of millions.
Vi'sionary a. Existing only in imagination, fanciful; visional. s. A day-dreamer, one given to forming impracticable schemes.
Revis'ionary a. Pertaining to revision.
Divis'ionary a. Divisional.
Pen'sionary a. Maintained by, receiving, or consisting of a pension. s. A pensioner.
Rever'sionary a. Pertaining to or involving a reversion.
Excur'sionary a. Excursional.
Pas'sionary s. A passional.
Ces'sionary s. An assignee.
Conces'sionary a. (*Concession*)
Proces'sionary a. Consisting in or pertaining to a procession.
Confes'sionary a. Pertaining to auricular confession.
Impres'sionary a. Impressionistic.
Mis'sionary s. One sent on a mission, especially to preach the gospel. a. Pertaining to missions.
Proba'tionary a. Serving for trial.
Obla'tionary s. One who receives the oblation.
Sta'tionary a. Remaining in one place; motionless.
Reac'tionary a. Implying or tending towards reaction; conservative. s. One opposed to reform or forward progress.
Fac'tionary a. Adhering to a faction.
Frac'tionary a. Fractional.
Lec'tionary s. A collection of passages for public Scripture-reading.
Insurrec'tionary a. Insurrectional.
Dic'tionary s. Book of words of a language, usually arranged alphabetically, and with meanings.
Func'tionary s. An official. a. Pertaining to functions; official.
Concre'tionary a. (*Concretion*).
Discre'tionary a. Left to discretion.
Tradi'tionary a. Traditional.
Expedi'tionary a. Suitable or intended for an expedition.
Transi'tionary a. Transitional.
Peti'tionary a. Containing or accompanied by a petition.
Repeti'tionary a. Repetitional.
Tui'tionary a. Tuitional.
Conven'tionary a. Acting or holding under agreement. s. A tenant holding thus.
Excep'tionary a. Indicating an exception.
Ques'tionary a. Inquiring. s. A series of related questions.
Cau'tionary a. Warning; given as security; cautious.
Precau'tionary a. Of the nature of or using precaution.
Elocu'tionary a. Pertaining to elocution.
Circumlocu'tionary a. (*Circumlocution*).
Evolu'tionary a. Pertaining to evolution.
Revolu'tionary a. Tending or pertaining to revolution in government.
Substitu'tionary a. Substitutional.
Institu'tionary a. Institutional.
Flux'ionary a. Pertaining to fluxions.
Pul'monary a. Pertaining to or affecting the lungs.
No'nary s. A group of nine. a. Based on the number 9.
Cor'onary a. Pertaining to or like a crown. s. A small bone in a horse's foot.
Ter'nary s. A group of three. a. Ternal.
Quater'nary s. The number or a set of four. a. Consisting of fours by fours; fourth.
Or'nary a. (*Slang*) Worthless; of no account.
Snar'y a. Tending to ensnare.
Lu'nary a. Lunar. s. The moonwort.
Sublu'nary a. Situated below the moon; earthly.
Interlu'nary a. Interlunar.
Eleemos'ynary a. Living on or pertaining to charity or alms.
Oar'y a. With the form or function of an oar.
Zed'oary s. A fragrant, bitter root-stock used in medicine, perfumery, etc.
Hoar'y a. White or whitish-grey, especially with age or frost; venerable.

Li'brary s. A collection of books; building or room for such.
Nu'merary a. Pertaining to number; numerical.
Supernu'merary a. Exceeding the necessary or usual number. s. Person or thing beyond number stated or usually required.
Cin'erary a. Pertaining to ashes or cremation.
Itin'erary s. A guide-book; a plan of a tour. a. Pertaining to a journey or to travel.
Vul'nerary a. Useful in healing wounds. s. Such a plant, drug, etc.
On'erary a. Designed for carrying burdens.
Fu'nerary a. Pertaining to funerals; funereal.
Lit'erary a. Pertaining to or devoted to literature; engaged in literature.
Hor'ary a. Horal.
Hon'orary a. Conferring honour or dignity only; possessing title, etc., without performing duties, or performing duties without reward.
Tem'porary a. For a time only; transitory.
Contem'porary a. Living or occurring at the same time; of the same age. s. A person or thing existing at the same time as another.
Extem'porary a. Extemporaneous.
Ar'bitrary a. At will, absolute; not regulated by rule or precedent.
Con'trary a. Opposite, repugnant; given to opposition. s. The opposite, a thing that is contrary. adv. In an opposite manner or direction.
Caravan'sary s. (*Caravanserai*).
Dispens'ary s. Place where medicines are prepared or given out.
Ro'sary s. A bed or garden of roses; a series of prayers and string of beads by which they are counted (Roman Catholic).
Ad'versary s. An enemy, opponent.
Anniver'sary s. A day on which an event is annually celebrated. a. Returning on a stated day each year.
Bur'sary s. The treasury of a college; a scholarship.
Nec'essary a. Indispensably requisite; inevitable; acting from necessity. s. Anything essential or requisite.
Pess'ary s. An internal appliance to remedy prolapse; a suppository.
Emis'sary s. A messenger; a secret agent. a. Pertaining to a messenger; serving as an outlet.
Commis'sary s. A commissioner; deputy, especially of a bishop; a commisariat officer.
Gloss'ary s. A vocabulary of rare, technical, or other special words.
Da'tary s. An officer of the papal chancery.
Man'datary s. One acting under or holding a mandate.
Nec'tary s. The honey-gland of a flower.
Sec'tary s. A sectarian, a heretic.
In'sectary s. An insectarium.
Budg'etary a. Connected with a budget.
Di'etary a. Pertaining to diet. s. Rule of diet; allowance of food.
Propri'etary a. Belonging to a proprietor; patented. s. A body of proprietors.
Pro'letary a. Proletarian.
Com'etary a. Pertaining to or like a comet.
Plan'etary a. Pertaining to, consisting of, or influenced by the planets.
Mon'etary a. Pertaining to money or the coinage.
Sec'retary s. One who manages the affairs of a government department, company, association, etc., or an employer's correspondence.
Or'bitary a. Orbital.
Plebis'citary a. Pertaining to or effected by a plebiscite.
Hered'itary a. Passing from one generation to the next; holding or deriving by inheritance.
Mil'itary a. Pertaining to soldiers or warfare; warlike. s. The army; soldiery.
Sol'itary a. Being or inclined to be alone; lonely; retired; sole. s. A recluse.
Lim'itary a. Stationed at the limits; circumscribed; limiting.
Ter'mitary s. The nest of the white ant.
San'itary a. Healthy, hygienic; free from injurious conditions.
Insan'itary a. Not sanitary.
Primogen'itary a. Pertaining to or characterized by primogeniture.
Dig'nitary s. One holding high (especially ecclesiastical) office.
U'nitary a. Of the nature of a unit; single.
Depos'itary s. One with whom anything is deposited.
Ubiq'uitary a. Ubiquitous.
Pitu'itary a. Secreting phlegm or mucus.
Placen'tary a. Having a placenta.
Den'tary a. Pertaining to the teeth. s. The lower jaw-bone of fishes and reptiles.
Sed'entary a. Sitting much; inactive.
Ligamen'tary a. Ligamentous.
Parliamen'tary a. Pertaining to, befitting, or enacted by Parliament.
Filamen'tary a. Consisting of or like filaments.
Testamen'tary a. Pertaining to, bequeathed by, or done by a will.
Elemen'tary a. Primary, uncompounded; concerned with first principles or rudiments.
Complemen'tary a. Completing; supplying a deficiency.
Supplemen'tary a. Supplemental.
Tenemen'tary a. Tenemental.
Fragmen'tary a. Fragmental; applied to conglomerate rocks, breccias, etc.
Segmen'tary a. Segmental; indicating segments.
Pig'mentary a. Pertaining to, producing, or containing pigments.
Sedimen'tary a. Pertaining to, formed by, or consisting of matter that has been deposited from a liquid.
Rudimen'tary a. Not developed, imperfect; pertaining to the beginnings.
Alimen'tary a. Nourishing; supplying food.
Complimen'tary a. (*Compliment*).
Com'mentary s. A series of explanatory notes; a comment.
Mo'mentary a. Lasting only for or done in a moment.
Documen'tary a. Documental.
Tegumen'tary a. Tegumental.
Integumen'tary a. Pertaining to the integument.
Emolumen'tary a. Pertaining to an emolument.
Ser'pentary s. The Virginian snake-root.
Unguen'tary a. Of the nature of an ointment.
Vol'untary a. Willing; regulated by the will; spontaneous. s. Organ solo in church; supporter of voluntaryism.
Invol'untary a. Done unintentionally; independent of will or choice.

No'tary s. A public officer authorized to attest documents, etc.
Prothon'otary s. A chief clerk or notary; a papal registrar.
Ro'tary a. Turning, as a wheel on its axis; acting by rotation.
Vo'tary s. One devoted to some pursuit; one who is consecrated.
Sag'ittary s. A centaur.
Trib'utary a. Paying tribute; subordinate. s. One that pays tribute; a stream running into another.
Distrib'utary a. Distributive.
Sal'utary a. Promoting health; wholesome; beneficial.
Insal'utary a. Not favourable to health.
Resid'uary a. Pertaining to or forming a residue.
Jan'uary s. The first month of the year.
Rel'iquary s. Small casket for relics.
An'tiquary s. A collector or student of antiques.
Feb'ruary s. The second month of the year.
Os'suary s. A charcoal-house; a bone-urn.
Stat'uary s. Art of carving or one who carves statues; a statue; statues collectively.
Ac'tuary s. One who makes calculations for insurance purposes.
Elec'tuary s. A sweetened purgative medicine.
Sanc'tuary s. A sacred place, holy ground; a refuge, asylum.
Usufruc'tuary a. and s. Relating to a, or one who has, usufruct.
Obit'uary a. Pertaining to or recording a death. s. An account of one lately deceased.
Tumul'tuary a. Tumultuous.
Sump'tuary a. Relating to or regulating expenditure.
Volup'tuary s. One devoted to luxury or sensual gratification. a. Addicted to or affording pleasure.
Mor'tuary s. Place for temporary reception of the dead. a. Pertaining to death or burial.
Es'tuary s. The mouth of a river where the tide meets the current.
Tex'tuary a. Textual; serving as a text.
Var'y v.t. and i. To change, diversify, alter; to differ, disagree.
Sali'vary a. Pertaining to or secreting saliva.
Ol'ivary a. Olive-shaped, oval.
Cal'vary s. The place of the Crucifixion.
O'vary s. The organ of a female in which ova are produced; the part of a flower containing the ovules.
War'y (ware'-) a. Cautious; circumspect; prudent.
Cas'sowary s. A large wingless bird of the ostrich family.
Jan'izary s. A soldier of the old Turkish body-guard.
Fi'bry a. Consisting of, containing or resembling fibre.
Am'bry s. A locker, cupboard, especially in a church.
Cox'combry s. The ways of coxcombs.
Cry v.i. To weep, to call importunately. v.t. To proclaim. s. A scream, sound of weeping, exclamation of surprise, fear, etc.; acclamation, a catchword.
Decry' v.t. To cry down, clamour against.
Mim'icry s. Act or practice of mimicking.
Descry' v.t. To make out, espy.
Out'cry s. A loud or vehement cry; clamour; vociferation.
Dry a. Free from moisture; thirsty, sarcastic; arid; uninteresting. v.t. To free from moisture, deprive of natural juice, drain. v.i. To lose moisture, completely evaporate.
Adry' adv. Dry; thirsty.
Bal'ladry s. Ballad style; ballads collectively.
Rib'aldry s. Jesting language; obscenity.
Her'aldry s. Art or office of a herald; art of emblazoning or recording genealogies, heraldic symbols.
Hus'bandry s. Care of domestic affairs; agriculture, tillage.
Gar'landry s. Garlands collectively; decorations.
Comman'dry s. (*Commandery*).
Monan'dry s. Custom of having only one husband at a time.
Pol'yandry s. Possession by a woman of more than one husband at once.
Leg'endry s. Legends collectively.
Laun'dry s. Place where clothes are washed and dressed.
Foun'dry s. Place for casting metals.
Sun'dry a. Several; divers. s. A few.
Wiz'ardry s. Sorcery; accomplishments of a wizard.
Baw'dry s. Obscenity.
Taw'dry a. Cheap and showy.
-ery suff. Forming nouns (usually abstract or collective) from adjectives, verbs, and other nouns.
Fa'ery s. and a. Faerie.
Cob'webbery s. (*Cobweb*).
Bob'bery s. (*Slang*) Fuss, commotion.
Job'bery s. Act or practice of jobbing; underhand trickery.
Slob'bery a. Drivelling; smeared with saliva.
Snob'bery s. Quality of being snobbish; character or behaviour of snobs.
Rob'bery s. Crime of stealing by force; theft.
Shrub'bery s. A plantation of shrubs.
Bri'bery s. Act or practice of bribing or taking bribes.
Um'bery a. Of the colour of umber.
Plumb'ery s. Trade of a plumber; place where plumbing is carried on.
Embra'cery s. Attempt to bribe a jury, etc.
Tra'cery s. Ornamental open work, especially in architecture.
Spi'cery s. Spices collectively; a spice-store.
Chan'cery s. The highest English court of justice except the House of Lords.
Gro'cery s. A grocer's wares, business, or shop.
Mer'cery s. A mercer's trade; goods in which he deals.
Sor'cery s. Witchcraft; divination with help of evil spirits.
Blad'dery a. Like a bladder.
Embroi'dery s. Variegated needlework; embellishment.
Spi'dery a. Like a spider.
Comman'dery s. A district administered by a commander; buildings attached to this.
Bind'ery s. A bookbinder's business or works.
Cin'dery a. (*Cinder*).
Grind'ery s. A place where tools are sharpened or sold.
Tin'dery a. Resembling tinder.
Thun'dery a. Inclined to thunder; stormy.
Gau'dery s. Finery; tinselly ornament.
Pru'dery s. Quality or state of being prudish; affected modesty.
Pow'dery a. Resembling powder; friable; easily crumbling.
Beer'y a. Tasting or smelling of beer; abounding in beer; fuddled.
Cheer'y a. Lively, sprightly, genial.
Peer'y a. Prying, inquisitive.

Cha'fery s. A forge where iron bars are made.
Wa'fery a. Thin, like a wafer.
Puff'ery s. Exaggerated or misleading commendation; puffs, frills.
Mid'wifery s. Obstetrics; art or practice of a midwife.
House'wifery s. Domestic economy; business of a housewife.
Im'agery s. Visible representations; figures evoked by fancy; figurative description; images collectively.
Sav'agery s. State of being savage, a wild condition; barbarism; barbarity.
Dodg'ery s. Trickery, shiftiness.
Drudg'ery s. Act of drudging; hard, unremunerative, uninteresting work.
Wag'gery s. Manner of a wag; jocularity.
Fig'gery s. Tawdry ornament.
Whig'gery s. Principles, etc., of the Whigs.
Pig'gery s. Place where pigs are kept.
Prig'gery s. Characteristics of prigs.
Pettifog'gery s. Underhand legal practices; disreputable tricks.
Frog'gery s. A place where frogs abound.
Grog'gery s. A grog-shop.
Tog'gery s. (*Slang*) Clothes.
Hum'buggery s. Humbug; imposture.
Thug'gery s. Thuggee.
Snug'gery s. A cosy place.
Scav'engery s. Scavengers' work.
Gin'gery a. Spiced with ginger; (*slang*) red-haired; spicy.
Malin'gery s. Practices, etc., of a malingerer.
I'ronmongery s. Hardware.
For'gery s. Crime of counterfeiting; that which is counterfeited.
Sur'gery s. Treatment of injuries, disease, etc., by manual operation; a surgeon's consulting-room or dispensary.
Bleach'ery s. A place where bleaching is done.
Treach'ery s. Treasonable conduct; breach of faith, perfidy.
Lech'ery s. Indulgence of lust; lewdness.
Ar'chery s. Practice, art, or skill of archers.
Patch'ery s. Bungling work.
Stitch'ery s. Needlework.
Witch'ery s. Witchcraft; sorcery; enchantment.
Botch'ery s. Clumsy work or workmanship.
Butch'ery s. A butcher's trade; slaughter-house; slaughter.
Debauch'ery s. Intemperance; habitual lewdness; seduction from duty.
Periph'ery s. The circumference of a circle or other curvilinear figure.
Spher'y a. Sphere-shaped; pertaining to the celestial sphere.
Hab'erdashery s. Goods sold by a haberdasher.
Trash'ery s. Trash; rubbish.
Fish'ery s. Business of catching fish; place where fish are caught.
Tush'ery s. Piffle, rubbishy talk.
Feath'ery a. Pertaining to, like, or covered with feathers.
Heath'ery a. Abounding in heather.
Leath'ery a. Like leather; tough.
Lath'ery a. Covered with or like lather.
Dith'ery a. Shaky, " all of a tremble."
Smith'ery s. Occupation of a smith; a smithy.
Moth'ery a. Containing or resembling mother in vinegar.
Smoth'ery a. Stifling; tending to smother.
Sol'diery s. Soldiers collectively.
Fi'ery a. Consisting of or flaming with fire; passionate, vehement, irritable.
Coll'iery s. A coal-mine with its buildings, machinery, etc.
Bri'ery a. Full of briers, thorny.

Far'riery s. The occupation of a farrier; his work-place.
Cur'riery s. Trade of leather-dressing; place where this is carried on.
Fur'riery s. The occupation of a furrier.
Hos'iery s. Stockings, socks, woollen underclothes, etc.
Gla'ziery s. The business or premises of a glazier.
Gra'ziery s. The occupation or premises of a grazier.
Ba'kery s. A bake-house; business of a baker.
Hack'ery s. A two-wheeled bullock-car used in India.
Knack'ery s. A knacker's yard or business.
Gimcrack'ery s. Gimcracks collectively; worthless articles.
Quack'ery s. Practices of quacks; empiricism.
Henpeck'ery s. Condition of being henpecked.
Trick'ery s. Cheating, deceit.
Mock'ery s. Derision; counterfeit appearance; vain effort.
Rock'ery s. A pile of rocks, earth, etc., for plants; rock-work.
Crock'ery s. Earthenware.
Monk'ery s. Monasticism; monks collectively (*contemptuous*).
Cook'ery s. Act or art of cooking; occupation of a cook.
Rook'ery s. A colony of rooks or its habitation; an overcrowded and dilapidated neighbourhood.
Jig'gery-po'kery s. (*Slang*) A fraud; humbug.
Bash'i-bazouk'ery s. (*Bashi-bazouk*).
Sad'dlery s. Materials for making saddles, etc.; a sadler's stock-in-trade or business.
Ped'dlery s. The trade or goods of a pedlar.
Chand'lery s. Articles stocked by a chandler.
Cel'ery s. A plant, the blanched stalks of which are eaten as a salad.
Whiffl'ery s. Equivocation; prevarication.
Jug'glery s. Art of feats of a juggler; imposture.
Nail'ery s. A nail-factory.
Snail'ery s. Place for cultivation of edible snails.
Til'ery s. Place where tiles are made.
Gal'lery s. A long apartment serving as a passage, for the exhibition of pictures, etc.; upper floor of a church, theatre, etc.; a projecting balcony; a covered way.
Chan'cellery s. Official residence, department, office, or rank of a chancellor; an embassy.
Jew'ellery s. Jewels; art or trade of a jeweller.
Rail'lery s. Banter, chaffing ridicule.
Frill'ery s. Frills collectively; a mass of frills.
Sil'lery s. A dry champagne.
Artil'lery s. Heavy guns, cannon; the troops who work them; science of gunnery.
Distil'lery s. Place where distilled alcoholic beverages are made.
Drol'lery s. Jocularity, buffoonery; funny stories.
Scul'lery s. Place where dishes, etc., are washed up.
Full'ery s. Place where cloth is fulled.
Gull'ery s. A breeding-place of gulls; trickery, imposture.
Cajol'ery s. Coaxing or flattering language a wheedling.
Fool'ery s. Practice or act of folly; absurdity

But'lery s. A butler's pantry.
Cut'lery s. Edged tools or instruments; trade of a cutler.
Sut'lery s. The business or stock of a sutler.
Owl'ery s. An abode or haunt of owls.
Growl'ery s. Grumbling; (*slang*) a sanctum.
Cream'ery s. A dairy; a place where butter and cheese are made.
Gos'samery a. Like gossamer, filmy.
Em'ery s. A hard mineral; a variety of corundum.
Chum'mery s. (*Chum*).
Flum'mery s. A jelly made of flour or meal; humbug.
Mum'mery s. Performance of mummers; tom-foolery.
Sum'mery a. Pertaining to or like summer.
Gendar'mery s. Gendarmerie; a body of armed police.
Farm'ery s. The buildings about a farm.
Perfum'ery s. Perfumes in general.
Chica'nery s. Employment of quibbles and dodges.
Dean'ery s. Office, district, or residence of a dean.
Scen'ery s. Hangings, etc., forming back-ground for acting; representa-tion; general aspect; imagery.
Green'ery s. Verdure; an enclosed place for rearing plants.
Ven'ery s. Art or practice of hunting; sexual indulgence.
Fin'ery s. Showy clothes or decorations; a furnace in which cast-iron is made malleable; art of refining.
Refin'ery s. Place where metals, sugar, etc., are refined.
Machin'ery s. Machines collectively; working parts of a machine.
Mill'inery s. The business or goods of a milliner.
Join'ery s. Carpentry.
Pin'ery s. Place where pine-apples are raised; a pine forest.
Pen'guinery s. A breeding-place of penguins.
Vi'nery s. Place for rearing vines.
Can'nery s. A factory where food is tinned.
Tan'nery s. A place where tanning is done
Swan'nery s. Place where swans are bred.
Hen'nery s. Enclosed run for fowls.
Spin'nery s. A spinning mill.
Gun'nery s. Science of managing and firing heavy guns.
Nun'nery s. A house for nuns.
Confec'tionery s. Sweetmeats, pastries, etc.
Buffoon'ery s. The tricks of buffoons; low jests.
Poltroon'ery s. Cowardice; want of spirit.
Fern'ery s. A place where ferns are cultivated.
Tern'ery s. A breeding-place of terns.
Or'nery a. (*Slang*) Worthless; mean; low.
Turn'ery s. Business, handicraft, materials, output, or premises of a turner.
Vint'nery s. Business of a wine-merchant.
Clown'ery s. The ways of clowns, buffoonery.
A'pery s. Mimicry; impishness.
Na'pery s. Table-linen.
Pa'pery a. Like paper.
Dra'pery s. Cloths, woollen stuffs; hangings; pictorial or sculptured clothing; occupation of a draper.
Gra'pery s. A vinery.
Tri'pery s. Place where tripe is prepared.
Em'pery s. Sovereignty; absolute dominion; an empire.
Trump'ery s. Worthless finery, rubbish. a. Showy but valueless; deceptive.
Po'pery s. Name given by opponents to Roman Catholic doctrines, prac-tices, etc.
Ro'pery s. Place where rope is made.
Podsnap'pery s. Self-satisfied pomposity, ultra-respectability.
Pep'pery a. Having the qualities of pepper; choleric, irritable.
Slip'pery a. Smooth; causing or allowing slipping; glib; unstable; un-trustworthy.
Frip'pery s. Old clothes; second-rate finery; gewgaws.
Cop'pery a. Made of, containing, or resembling copper.
Fop'pery s. Behaviour, dress, etc., of a fop; coxcombry.
Jas'pery a. Like or containing jasper.
Or'rery s. Apparatus illustrating the move-ments, etc., of the members of the solar system.
Lama'sery s. A Tibetan monastery.
Mis'ery s. Wretchedness; unhappiness; evils causing this.
Ro'sery s. A rose-plot or garden.
Nur'sery s. Children's room; place for raising plants; a race for two-year-olds.
Fra'tery s. A fratry.
Wa'tery a. Abounding with or resembling water; thin, tasteless, insipid, humid.
Phylac'tery s. An amulet worn by the ancient Jews; any preservative charm.
Cem'etery s. A grave-yard.
Psal'tery (sawl'-) s. An ancient stringed instrument.
Drysalt'ery s. Articles kept by or business of a drysalter.
Smel'tery s. Place where ore is smelted.
Adul'tery s. Marital infidelity.
Li'entery s. A form of diarrhœa.
Mes'entery s. A membrane in the cavity of the abdomen.
Dys'entery s. Inflammation of the colon; an infectious febrile disease.
Splint'ery a. Liable to splinter; resembling or consisting of splinters.
Effront'ery s. Excessive assurance, impudence.
Freeboot'ery s. Methods, practices, etc., of free-booters.
Root'ery s. Pile of roots, etc., for growing plants in.
Ar'tery s. A vessel conveying blood from the heart.
Dikas'tery s. An ancient Athenian jury; their court.
Mas'tery s. Command; pre-eminence; vic-tory.
Mon'astery s. Residence of a community of monks.
Blis'tery a. (*Blister*).
Bap'tistery s. (*Baptistry*).
Huck'stery s. The trade or wares of a huckster.
Uphol'stery s. Articles supplied or work done by upholsterers.
Phalan'stery s. A community of like-minded persons; building inhabited by such.
Blus'tery a. (*Bluster*).
Mys'tery s. A secret; anything beyond com-prehension; a miracle-play; a trade or handicraft.
Bat'tery s. Act of battering; place where cannon are mounted; the unit of artillery; apparatus for gener-ating electricity.
Scat'tery a. Scattered; scattering.
Flat'tery s. Art or practice of flattering; cajolery; sycophancy.
Mat'tery a. Full of pus; purulent.
Tat'tery a. In tatters.
Ret'tery s. A place where flax is retted.
Lit'tery a. Untidy; littered.

Lot'tery s. Distribution of prizes by chance.
Pot'tery s. Earthenware; place where this or china, etc., is made.
Tot'tery a. Inclined to totter; unsteady.
But'tery a. Like butter. s. A place for keeping butter, other provisions, wine, etc.
Slut'tery s. Sluttishness.
Cau'tery s. A burning with caustic or hot iron, etc.
Pres'bytery s. A body of church elders; the end of the chancel containing the altar; a priest's house.
Intri'guery s. Arts or practice of intrigue.
Demagog'uery s. Demagogy.
Ro'guery s. Dishonest or rogue-like practices; knavish tricks; waggery.
Que'ry s. A question, inquiry; the sign "?." v.i. and t. To ask questions, inquire into; to doubt of.
Ver'y a. Real, actual. adv. In a high degree, exceedingly.
Sla'very s. Condition of a slave; servitude, drudgery.
Slav'ery a. Besmeared with saliva.
Kna'very s. Dishonesty, trickery, roguery.
Bra'very s. Quality of being brave; fearlessness; show.
Qua'very a. Trembling; shaky.
Ev'ery a. Each; one at a time; all.
Thiev'ery s. Practice of stealing; theft.
Shiv'ery a. Trembling, shaky; easily shattered.
Liv'ery s. Uniform worn by servants or any body; a guild, etc., having such uniform; state of a horse boarded out at a fixed rate. a. Resembling the liver; liverish.
Deliv'ery s. Release, rescue; utterance; childbirth; distribution of letters, etc.
Sil'very a. Like or covered with silver; soft and clear (of sound).
Recov'ery s. Act of recovering; restoration to health, etc.; obtaining of something by legal procedure.
Discov'ery s. Act of discovering; thing discovered; disclosure of facts, etc., in a lawsuit.
Rediscov'ery s. A second discovery of the same.
Taw'ery s. A place where tawing is carried on.
Brew'ery s. An establishment where brewing is carried on.
Bow'ery a. Containing bowers.
Show'ery (shou'-) a. Raining in, abounding with, or pertaining to showers.
Low'ery a. Lowry.
Flow'ery a. Full of flowers; highly figurative; florid.
Tow'ery (tou'-) a. Abounding with towers.
Quiz'zery s. Practice of quizzing.
Fry v.t. To cook in a pan over the fire. s. A dish of fried food; young fish, a swarm of these.
Bel'fry s. A bell-tower.
Gallimau'fry s. A hodge-podge; a medley.
Ang'ry a. Showing anger; wrathful; inflamed (of sores).
Hung'ry a. Having the sensation of hunger; having a strong desire; lean.
Gar'nishry s. Embellishment.
Air'y a. Light, like air; open to the air; visionary.
Dair'y s. Place where milk is kept, sold, or turned into butter and cheese; business of making these; a herd of milch-cows.
Fair'y s. An imaginary supernatural being, an elf. a. Belonging to or bestowed by fairies; fanciful.
Hair'y a. Covered with, consisting of, or like hair.
Glair'y a. Like glair.
Mir'y a. Abounding with or consisting of mire.
Spir'y a. Resembling a spire; containing or consisting of spires.
Expir'y s. Termination, end.
Inquir'y s. Act of inquiring; a question, investigation, examination.
Wir'y a. Of or resembling wire; tough, stiff, sinewy.
No'palry s. A plantation of nopals.
Cav'alry s. Horse-soldiers.
Chiv'alry s. A body of knights; dignity or system of knighthood; gallantry.
Ri'valry s. Act of rivalling; emulation.
Cam'elry s. Troops mounted on camels.
Chap'elry s. The bounds or district of a chapel
Host'elry s. An inn.
Rev'elry s. Noisy festivity.
Dev'ilry s. Diabolical wickedness; excessive cruelty; mischief.
Bot'tomry s. Act of borrowing money on the security of a ship.
Yeo'manry s. Yeomen collectively; a mounted force of volunteers.
Al'dermanry s. Dignity or office of alderman; a city ward.
Charl'atanry s. (*Charlatan*).
Heath'enry s. Heathenism; practices, etc., of heathens.
Chief'tainry s. (*Chieftain*).
Dea'conry s. Office of deacon.
Fal'conry s. The sport of hawking; art of training hawks.
Pig'eonry s. Place for keeping pigeons.
Le'gionry s. Legions collectively; a body of legions.
De'monry s. Demoniacal influence.
Alm'onry s. Place where alms are distributed.
Can'onry s. Office or dignity of a canon.
Can'nonry s. Cannon collectively.
Her'onry s. Place where herons breed.
Ma'sonry s. Occupation or work of a mason; freemasonry.
Freema'sonry s. The rites, principles, etc., of freemasons; any secret understanding or community of interests.
Bla'zonry s. Heraldic art or explanation.
Embla'zonry s. Heraldic ornamentation.
-ory suff. Denoting place where, instrument, etc.; and forming adjectives.
Suc'cory s. Chicory.
Chic'ory s. A blue-flowered plant, succory, the root of which is used as an adulterant for coffee.
Dor'y s. A bright yellow food-fish.
The'ory s. Supposition explaining something; abstract principles.
Gor'y a. Covered with gore; blood-stained.
Phantas'magory s. Phantasmagoria.
Al'legory s. A story which conveys a meaning different from the literal one.
Cat'egory s. A class, group; an order of ideas; an ultimate conception.
Seign'iory (sēn'-) s. Feudal lordship; power or domain of a lord.
Pri'ory s. A religious house of which the head is a prior or prioress.
Hick'ory s. A species of walnut tree.
Lor'y s. A brilliant bird allied to the parrots.
Flor'y a. Fleury.
Glor'y s. Splendour; honour; renown. v.i. To exult, vaunt, boast.
Vain'glory s. Excessive pride; boastfulness; empty show.

Chan'cellory s. (*Chancellery*).
Pill'ory s. A form of stocks for head and wrists, an old punishment. v.t. To set in the pillory; to expose to ridicule, etc.
Mem'ory s. Power of remembering; recollection; time within which the past is remembered.
Ar'mory s. Art of heraldry.
Moor'y a. Pertaining to or of the nature of a moor.
Por'y a. Resembling or full of pores.
Sua'sory a. Tending to persuade.
Persua'sory a. Persuasive.
Deri'sory a. Derisive.
Advi'sory a. Able to counsel; containing advice.
Revi'sory a. Having the power to revise; of the nature of revision.
Prov'isory a. Conditional; temporary.
Supervi'sory a. Pertaining to or having supervision.
Repul'sory a. Acting so as to repel.
Compul'sory a. Under compulsion; enforced.
In'censory s. A censer.
Suspen'sory a. Serving to suspend.
Sen'sory a. Pertaining to sensation or the sensorium.
Osten'sory s. A monstrance.
Respon'sory s. An anthem sung alternately by soloist and choir. a. Pertaining to or like a response.
Asper'sory a. Defamatory, calumniating.
Cur'sory a. Hasty, superficial.
Precur'sory a. Precursive.
Discur'sory a. Discursive.
Acces'sory a. Contributing; additional, subsidiary.
Interces'sory a. Containing intercession; interceding.
Posses'sory a. Pertaining to one who possesses or that which is possessed.
Rescis'sory a. Tending or able to rescind.
Emis'sory a. Sending out; emitting.
Remis'sory a. Remissive.
Dimis'sory a. Dismissing, discharging.
Prom'issory a. Containing a binding declaration.
Dismis'sory a. Dismissive.
Reclu'sory s. A hermitage, retreat.
Conclu'sory a. Conclusive.
Exclu'sory a. Exclusive.
Elu'sory a. Tending to elude; fallacious; evasive.
Delu'sory a. Apt to delude.
Prelu'sory a. Prelusive, introductory.
Illu'sory a. Delusive; deceptive.
Collu'sory a. Characterized by collusion.
Prolu'sory a. Of the nature of a prolusion.
Tory s. A Conservative. a. Pertaining to these.
-tory suff. Forming nouns and adjectives.
Pro'batory a. Pertaining to or serving for trial or proof.
Reproba'tory a. Reprobative.
Ap'probatory a. Expressing approval of.
Disapproba'-tory a. Containing disapprobation; tending to disapprove.
Incu'batory a. Pertaining to or serving for incubation.
Prec'atory a. Suppliant; beseeching.
Dep'recatory a. (*Deprecative*).
Impreca'tory a. Involving a curse.
Ded'icatory a. Of the nature of or containing a dedication.
Pred'icatory a. Affirmative, positive; pertaining to a preacher or preaching.
In'dicatory a. Serving to show or make known.
Vin'dicatory a. Tending or serving to vindicate.
Ju'dicatory a. Pertaining to administration of justice. s. Judicature.
Pacifica'tory a. Tending to make peace; conciliatory.
Edifica'tory a. Edifying, morally enlightening.
Modifica'tory a. Tending or serving to modify.
Qual'ificatory a. Qualifying; limiting.
Signif'icatory a. Having signification or meaning.
Purif'icatory a. Serving to purify.
Classifica'tory a. Pertaining to classification or classifying.
Justifica'tory a. Justifying; having power to justify.
Supplica'tory a. Containing supplication; submissive.
Ex'plicatory a. Explicative.
Communica'-tory a. Imparting knowledge, ideas, etc.
Vesica'tory a. and s. Vesicant.
Mastica'tory a. Adapted to masticate.
Reciproca'tory a. Reciprocating.
Advoca'tory a. Advocating.
Rev'ocatory a. Pertaining to, tending to, or involving revocation.
Equiv'ocatory a. Equivocating.
Invoca'tory a. Containing or pertaining to invocation.
Confisca'tory a. Pertaining to or tending to confiscation.
Pis'catory a. Relating to fishes or fishing.
Manduca'tory a. Pertaining to or adapted for chewing.
Gra'datory a. Proceeding by gradations.
Pred'atory a. Practising rapine; living by preying.
Elu'cidatory a. Explanatory; making clear.
Consolida'tory a. (*Consolidate*).
Man'datory a. Pertaining to or of the nature of a mandate; obligatory. s. A mandatary.
Emen'datory a. Correcting, removing faults.
Commend'-atory a. Serving to commend, containing approval.
Recommend'-atory a. Serving to recommend.
Retard'atory a. Retardative.
Laud'atory a. Pertaining to or expressing praise.
Feu'datory a. Held by feudal tenure. s. A vassal, feudal tenant; a fief.
Su'datory a. Sweating; exciting perspiration. s. A vapour-bath.
Transu'datory a. Pertaining to or passing by transudation.
A'leatory a. Contingent upon chance.
Delin'eatory a. Pertaining to delineation.
Pref'atory a. Introductory; of the nature of a preface.
Nega'tory a. Expressing negation; negative.
Ob'ligatory a. Binding; imposed duty.
Mit'igatory a. Mitigative.
Castiga'tory a. (*Castigate*).
Investiga'tory a. Pertaining to investigation.
Derog'atory a. Tending to detract; disparaging.
Supererog'-atory a. Performed to an extent not required by duty.
Interrog'atory a. Containing or expressing a question. s. A question, inquiry; a questionary.
Ob'jurgatory a. Designed to chide; culpatory.
Pur'gatory s. Place of post-mortem expiation of sins (Roman Catholic Church), or of temporary suffering. a. Expiatory; tending to cleanse.
Compurga'tory a. (*Compurgator*).
Expur'gatory a. Serving to expurgate.
Nu'gatory a. Trifling; futile; inoperative
Depre'ciatory a. Tending to depreciate or und r-value.

Apprecia'tory a. Expressing appreciation.
Enun'ciatory a. Enunciative.
Denun'ciatory a. Accusing, denouncing; containing a denunciation.
Renun'ciatory a. Pertaining to or containing renunciation.
Pronun'ciatory a. Declarative; dogmatical.
Media'tory a. Pertaining to mediation; mediating.
Retal'iatory a. Tending to or involving retaliation.
Concil'iatory a. (*Conciliate*).
Reconcil'iatory a. Serving or tending to reconcile.
Calum'niatory a. (*Calumniate*).
Expia'tory a. Able to make expiation or to atone
Expatia'tory a. Characterized by expatiation.
Ini'tiatory a. Pertaining to initiation; serving to initiate; introductory.
Propi'tiatory a. Having the power to conciliate or to make propitious; expiatory. s. The Mercy-Seat of the Jews.
Negotia'tory a. Pertaining to negotiation.
Allevia'tory a. (*Alleviate*).
Abbrevia'tory a. (*Abbreviate*).
Ob'latory a. Pertaining to oblation.
Revela'tory a. Revealing.
Habil'atory a. Pertaining to clothes.
Dil'atory a. Inclined to delay, tardy; tedious.
Fi'latory s. Machine for making or spinning threads.
Assimila'tory a. (*Assimilate*).
Depil'atory a. Having the power to remove hair. s. A preparation which removes superfluous hair.
Gral'latory a. Of the order of or pertaining to the wading birds.
Flagella'tory a. Pertaining to flagellation or scourging.
Os'cillatory a. Swinging, vibrating; fluctuating.
Distil'latory a. Pertaining to distillation.
Condol'atory a. (*Condole*).
Consol'atory a. Tending to comfort, pertaining to consolation.
Transla'tory a. Translational.
Confab'ulatory a. (*Confabulate*).
Ambula'tory s. A corridor, cloister. a. Pertaining to walking.
Preambula'tory a. Pertaining to or consisting of a preamble.
Funambula'tory a. Performing like a rope-dancer; narrow.
Perambula'tory a. Pertaining to or consisting of perambulation.
Ejac'ulatory a. Suddenly darted out; like an ejaculation.
Specula'tory a. Speculative; intended for viewing.
Articula'tory a. (*Articulate*).
Gesticula'tory a. (*Gesticulative*).
Circula'tory a. (*Circulate*).
Emascula'tory a. (*Emasculate*).
Oscula'tory a. Kissing; pertaining to this or the osculation. s. A sacred picture to be kissed during Mass.
Adula'tory a. Flattering.
Stridula'tory a. Stridulous; adapted for stridulation.
Undula'tory a. Moving like waves; pertaining or due to undulation.
Vap'ulatory a. Pertaining to flogging.
Manipula'tory a. Manipulative.
Cop'ulatory a. (*Copulate*).
Gratula'tory a. Complimentary.
Congratula'tory a. Expressing congratulations.
Recapitula'tory a. Containing recapitulation; reiterating.
Postula'tory a. Assumed or assuming without proof.
Expos'tulatory a. Pertaining to or containing expostulation.
Am'atory a. Pertaining to or causing love.
Defam'atory a. Calumnious, slanderous.
Acclam'atory a. Applauding, demonstrative of joy.
Declam'atory a. Relating to the practice of declaiming; merely rhetorical.
Proclam'atory a. Pertaining to proclaiming or proclamation.
Exclam'atory a. Containing or expressing exclamation.
Desquama'tory a. Peeling; pertaining to desquamation.
Crem'atory a. Connected with cremation. s. A crematorium.
Sub'limatory a. Tending to sublimate; used for sublimation.
Inflam'matory a. Tending to inflame; causing inflammation.
Confirm'atory a. Serving to confirm; pertaining to confirmation.
Reform'atory a. Reformative. s. An institution for the reformation of juvenile offenders.
Inform'atory a. Affording information.
Chris'matory s. A vessel to hold chrism.
Fum'atory s. A place for fumigation.
Lach'rymatory s. A tear-bottle. a. Pertaining to or causing tears.
Explan'atory a. Serving to explain; containing explanation.
San'atory a. Producing health; curative.
Sig'natory s. One who signs, especially a state document. a. Pertaining to signing; having signed.
Des'ignatory a. Serving to indicate.
Consig'natory s. A joint signer.
Hallucina'tory a. Pertaining to or causing hallucination.
Incli'natory a. Having the quality of leaning or inclining.
Min'atory a. Threatening, menacing.
Crim'inatory a. Criminative.
Recrimina'tory a. Retorting accusations.
Discrimina'tory a. Discriminative.
Ful'minatory a. Thundering, striking terror.
Commina'tory a. Threatening, denunciatory.
Ter'minatory a. Terminative.
Exter'minatory a. Pertaining to extermination; serving to exterminate.
Cri'natory a. Pertaining to hair, crinal.
Procras'tinatory a. Dilatory; procrastinative.
Divin'atory a. Pertaining to divination or divining.
Dam'natory a. Causing or implying damnation; condemnatory.
Condem'natory a. Involving or expressing condemnation.
Cach'innatory a. Characterized by loud laughter.
Don'atory s. One to whom a donation is made.
Phona'tory a. Pertaining to phonation.
Antic'ipatory a. (*Anticipate*).
Emancipa'tory a. Having the effect of emancipating.
Cul'patory a. Involving or expressing blame.
Incul'patory a. Tending to inculpate; implicating.
Excul'patory a. Able to exculpate; excusing; absolving.
Declar'atory a. Making declaration; affirmative; expressive.
Prepar'atory a. Serving to prepare; preliminary; antecedent.
Vi'bratory a. Consisting in or causing vibration.
Lucubra'tory a. Composed at night; laborious.
Consecra'tory a. (*Consecrate*).
Ex'ecratory a. Containing or conveying execration.

Rever'beratory a. Producing or acting by reverberation.
Exag'geratory a. Exaggerative.
Refrig'eratory a. Cooling. s. A refrigerator.
Accelera'tory a. Quickening, able to quicken.
Regen'eratory a. Regenerative.
Remun'eratory a. Remunerative, affording recompense.
Mi'gratory a. Given to migrating; roving, wandering.
Emigra'tory a. (*Emigrate*).
Transmi'gratory a. Pertaining to or involving transmigration.
Respir'atory a. Serving for or pertaining to respiration.
Transpir'atory a. Pertaining to transpiration.
Inspir'atory a. Pertaining to inspiration or inhalation.
Perspir'atory a. Pertaining to or causing perspiration.
Expir'atory a. Pertaining to or used in breathing.
Or'atory s. Art of public speaking; eloquence; a chapel for private devotions; a Roman Catholic religious society (founded sixteenth century).
Lab'oratory s. A place for experiments in chemistry, etc.; a chemist's work-room.
Corrob'oratory a. (*Corroborate*).
Explor'atory a. Pertaining to, serving in, or intended for exploration.
Remon'stratory a. Remonstrative.
Procura'tory s. Instrument appointing a procurator; a power of attorney.
Inau'guratory a. Pertaining to inauguration.
Jura'tory a. Containing an oath.
Abjura'tory a. (*Abjure*).
Adjura'tory a. Containing adjuration.
Gyra'tory a. Moving circularly or spirally.
Circumgyra'tory a. (*Circumgyrate*).
Improvis'atory a. Pertaining to improvisation.
Pul'satory a. Capable of throbbing, pulsating.
Compul'satory a. Exercising compulsion.
Compen'satory a. (*Compensate*).
Dispen'satory a. Having power to grant dispensation. s. A collection of medical recipes.
Accu'satory a. Accusing, pertaining to accusation.
Excu'satory a. Making excuse; apologetic.
Na'tatory a. Natatorial.
Dic'tatory a. Dictorial, dogmatic.
Cit'atory a. Having the power or form of citation.
Excit'atory a. (*Excitative*).
Invita'tory a. Containing or using invitation.
Sal'tatory a. Leaping, dancing; having this power.
Auscul'tatory a. (*Auscultation*).
Consul'tatory a. (*Consult*).
Incanta'tory a. Dealing by enchantment; magical.
Pota'tory a. Pertaining to drink; of the nature of potations.
Ro'tatory a. Turning on an axis; following in succession.
Circumrota'tory a. Turning or whirling round.
Hor'tatory a. Hortative.
Dehort'atory a. Tending to dissuade.
Exhort'atory a. Exhortative.
Ges'tatory a. Pertaining to gestation or pregnancy.
Gus'tatory a. Pertaining to gustation.
Refu'tatory a. Refutative.
Salu'tatory a. Containing, pertaining to, or of the nature of salutation.
Mu'tatory a. Mutative.
Sternu'tatory a. and s. Sternutative.
Exten'uatory a. Extenuating; palliating.
Lav'atory s. A place for washing; a retiring room.
Eleva'tory a. Pertaining to elevation.
Innova'tory a. Innovative.
Observ'atory s. Building, etc., for astronomical observations.
Preserv'atory a. Having power or tendency to preserve.
Conserv'atory s. A glass-house for plants.
Fac'tory s. A manufactory; place where factors transact business.
Calefac'tory a. Producing heat. s. A warming room.
Olfac'tory a. Pertaining to the sense of smell; used in smelling. s. An organ of smell.
Satisfac'tory a. Giving or producing satisfaction; making amends.
Dissatisfac'tory a. Causing dissatisfaction.
Manufac'tory s. A factory, works.
Enac'tory a. Enacting, enactive.
Refrac'tory a. Sullen in opposition; unmanageable; not readily workable (o metals, etc.).
Detrac'tory a. Defamatory.
Refec'tory s. Hall for meals in religious houses.
Trajec'tory s. Path of a projectile.
Interjec'tory a. Interjectional.
Genuflec'tory a. Pertaining to genuflexion.
Rec'tory s. The benefice of a rector with all its rights, etc.; a rector's dwelling.
Direc'tory s. A board of directors; a list of names and address of inhabitants of a given area.
Protec'tory s. An institution or reformatory for children.
Contradic'tory a. Affirming the contrary, implying contradiction; disputatious; logically incompatible.
Maledic'tory a. Imprecatory.
Valedic'tory a. Bidding farewell, suitable for a leave-taking. s. A farewell oration.
Benedic'tory a. Expressing good wishes.
Interdic'tory a. Having power or intent to prohibit.
Emic'tory a. and s. (*Emiction*).
Vic'tory s. Defeat of an enemy; conquest; success.
Perfunc'tory a. Done in a half-hearted manner; indifferent; negligent.
Emunc'tory a. Serving to carry noxious matter from the body. s. An excretory duct.
Induc'tory a. Introductory.
Introduc'tory a. Serving to introduce; preliminary; prefatory.
Del'etory s. That which deletes.
Deple'tory a. Calculated to deplete.
Reple'tory a. Repletive.
Sup'pletory a. Supplemental; tending to supplement.
Ex'pletory a. Serving to fill up.
Decre'tory a. Judicial, deciding.
Secre'tory a. Secreting; promoting secretion.
Excre'tory a. Having the quality of discharging effete matter.
Fer'etory s. A chapel containing a shrine; a shrine for relics.
Inhib'itory a. Pertaining to, producing, or consisting in inhibition.
Prohib'itory a. Prohibitive.
Exhib'itory a. Pertaining to an exhibitor or an exhibition.
Au'ditory a. Pertaining to hearing. s. An audience; an auditorium.
Plau'ditory a. Applauding.

Pell'itory s. A nettle-like plant growing on walls; feverfew.
Vom'itory a. Procuring vomiting. s. An emetic.
Dor'mitory s. A sleeping-room, especially for a number.
Fu'mitory s. A plant formerly used in medicine.
Recog'nitory a. Pertaining to recognition.
Mon'itory a. Giving warning or admonition. s. A warning, etc.
Admon'itory a. Admonishing, warning.
Premon'itory a. Giving forewarning.
Pu'nitory a. Punitive.
Ter'ritory s. Large tract of land, esp. under one ruler.
Tran'sitory a. Passing away, short-lived.
Depos'itory s. A storehouse; a depositary.
Repos'itory s. Place where things are stored.
Suppos'itory s. A dissolvable medicinal cone for introduction into a body-passage.
Expos'itory a. Serving to explain; illustrative; exegetical.
Pet'itory a. Petitioning, begging.
Compet'itory a. (*Competitor*).
Des'ultory a. Roving from one thing to another; discursive.
Reminiscen'-tory a. Reminiscent.
In'ventory s. A catalogue of a person's goods and chattels, property, etc.; a. Schedule. v.t. To make an inventory of; to insert in an inventory.
Prom'ontory s. A headland.
Locomo'tory a. Locomotive.
Precep'tory s. A subordinate establishment of the Knights Templars. a. Perceptive.
Redemp'tory a. Redemptive; paid for ransom.
Per'emptory a. Precluding question or debate; decisive, absolute; dogmatic.
Interrup'tory a. Interruptive.
Of'fertory s. Sentences repeated in church while the alms are being collected; the alms.
Rep'ertory s. A treasury, repository, collection.
Stor'y s. A narrative, short tale, account; a falsehood; a storey.
Clere'story s. The upper story of the nave of a church having windows above the aisles.
His'tory s. Narrative of past events; statement of the progress of a nation, etc.
Consis'tory s. A solemn assembly; spiritual court of a diocesan; the College of Cardinals.
Retrib'utory a. Involving or pertaining to retribution.
Contrib'utory a. Contributing to the same end.
Exec'utory a. Performing official duties; executive.
Loc'utory s. A monastery parlour.
Circumlocu'-tory a. (*Circumlocution*).
Interloc'utory a. Consisting of dialogue; intermediate.
Stat'utory a. Enacted by statute.
Sa'vory s. An aromatic plant used in cooking.
I'vory s. Substance of tusks of certain animals. a. Of the colour of or made of this.
Pry v.i. To inspect or inquire curiously and narrowly. v.t. To prise.
Gos'sipry s. Gossip; a body of gossips.
Spry a. Lively; wideawake.
Car'ry v.t and i. To convey, transport; effect, secure the passing of; capture; conduct oneself; endure; transfer; be propelled.
Scar'ry a. Marked with scars.
Miscar'ry v.i. To fail of intended effect; to bring forth young prematurely.
Glengar'ry s. A Scotch cap or bonnet.
Har'ry v.t. To ravage, pillage. v.i. To make harassing incursions.
Ghar'ry s. A Hindu carriage.
Mar'ry v.t. To unite or dispose of in wedlock; to take for spouse. v.i. To take a spouse. int. Indeed, forsooth.
Remar'ry v.t. and i. To marry again or a second time.
Intermar'ry v.i. To become connected by marriage (as tribes, etc.).
Par'ry v.t. To ward off, prevent; to evade. s. A guarding stroke, movement, or attempt.
Spar'ry a. Like spar; crystalline.
Tar'ry a. Covered with, smelling of, or resembling tar.
Tar'ry (tăr'-) v.i. To stay, delay, loiter.
Star'ry a. Like or bespangled with stars.
Quar'ry s. Hunted game; place whence stone is obtained. v.t. To dig or take from a quarry.
Ber'ry s. A pulpy fruit containing seeds; an egg of certain fish. v.i. To produce berries.
Cloud'berry s. A low moorland shrub.
Blae'berry s. Bilberry.
Huck'leberry s. A dark blue berry growing on a low shrub.
Whortle'berry (hwertl'-) s. A low shrub or its berry, the bilberry.
Bane'berry s. Herb Christopher; its poisonous black berries.
Goose'berry s. A prickly shrub and its fruit; (*slang*) a chaperon.
Hag'berry s. The American blackberry.
Bog'berry s. The cranberry.
Dog'berry s. The berry of the dogwood.
Hack'berry s. A N. American tree, and its fruit.
Black'berry s. A species of bramble; its fruit.
Bil'berry s. A dwarf moorland shrub, or its fruit; the whortleberry.
Mul'berry s. A tree bearing a fruit like a large blackberry; the fruit; its colour.
Lo'ganberry s. A cross between a raspberry and blackberry.
Cran'berry s. A small, sour wild fruit.
Fen'berry s. The cranberry.
Rasp'berry s. A plant allied to the bramble; its fruit.
Bar'berry, Ber'perry s. A shrub bearing a red, acid berry.
Bear'berry s. A procumbent heath.
Straw'berry s. A low perennial plant and its red, fleshy fruit.
Dew'berry s. A kind of blackberry.
Bay'berry s. The berry of the bay; the N. American wax-myrtle.
Fer'ry s. Vessel for conveyance across a river, etc.; place of conveyance; right or mode of conveying. v.t. To transport over a river, etc., in a ferry-boat. v.i. To pass across thus.
Cher'ry s. A small stone-fruit; the tree bearing it. a. Coloured like the red cherry.
Sher'ry s. A white wine from Xeres, Spain.
Wher'ry s. A light rowing boat for rivers.
Jer'ry a. Applied to cheap, badly-built houses.
Sker'ry s. A reef, a rocky islet.
Mer'ry a. Gay, mirthful, jovial, brisk. s. The wild black cherry.
Per'ry s. A fermented drink made from pears.

Ter'ry s. A heavy pile fabric used in upholstery.
Eq'uerry s. An officer of the royal household.
Fir'ry a. Containing firs.
Lor'ry s. A low wagon without sides.
Sor'ry a. Feeling sorrow, grief, or regret; paltry, pitiful.
Wor'ry (wŭr'-) v.t. To harass, torment, trouble; to tear with the teeth. v.i. To fret, feel undue anxiety, etc. s. State of anxiety; trouble, care.
Bur'ry a. Prickly; characterized by burrs or burring.
Cur'ry v.t. To dress leather; to cleanse and comb the skin of a horse; to seek to gain favour by flattery, etc.; to cook or flavour with curry. s. A highly-spiced sauce; a dish cooked with this.
Scur'ry v.i. To hurry, scamper. s. Act or noise of this.
Fur'ry a. Coated with, made of, or resembling fur.
Hur'ry v.t. To drive forward with greater rapidity, to accelerate; to cause to act precipitately. v.i. To hasten. s. Act of or need for hastening; bustle; eagerness.
Dhur'ry s. Dhurrie.
Hur'ry-skur'ry adv. In a bustle, confusedly. s. A confused bustle. v.i. To make haste, especially in an unordered way.
Flur'ry s. A sudden gust; bustle, confusion, hurry. v.t. To bewilder; to agitate.
Slur'ry s. A thin cement or mortar.
Spur'ry s. A low annual weed.
Try v.i. To endeavour, attempt. v.t. To make trial of; to examine judicially; to afflict. s. Act of trying; an experiment, test.
Psychi'atry s. Treatment of mental diseases.
-latry suff. Denoting worship of or devotion to.
Symbol'atry s. The worship of symbols.
Idol'atry s. The worship of idols; excessive veneration or admiration for.
Lordol'atry s. Ridiculous deference to peers.
Ophiol'atry s. Serpent-worship.
Bibliol'atry s. Excessive veneration of books or of the letter of the Bible.
Heliol'atry s. Sun-worship.
Gyniol'atry s. Excessive adoration of women.
Mariol'atry s. Idolatrous worship of the Virgin Mary.
Ecclesiol'atry s. Excessive reverence for ecclesiastical things, principles, etc.
Physiol'atry s. Nature-worship.
Angelol'atry s. Worship of angels.
Iconol'atry s. The worship of images.
Demonol'atry s. Worship of evil spirits.
Zool'atry s. The worship of animals.
Topol'atry s. Excessive attachment to a place.
Necrol'atry s. Ancestor-worship.
Hierol'atry s. The worship of saints.
Pyrol'atry s. Fire-worship.
Martyrol'atry s. Worship of martyrs.
Christol'atry s. Worship of Christ regarded as idolatry.
Autol'atry s. Worship of self.
Plutol'atry s. The worship of wealth.
Ichthyol'atry s. The worship of fish-gods.
Fra'try s. The refectory or common-room in a monastery.
Phra'try s. A tribal division in ancient Greece and among primitive peoples
Bar'ratry s. The offence of vexatiously maintaining litigation.
Bas'ketry s. Basket-work.
Mus'ketry s. Art of using small-arms; the fire of these; small-arms collectively.
Var'letry s. The rabble.
-metry suff. Forming nous pertaining to the science of measuring.
Sciam'etry s. The theory or measurement of eclipses.
Focim'etry s. The measurement of focal distances.
Acidim'etry s. Measurement of strength of acids.
Alkalim'etry s. Measurement of the strength of alkalis.
Isoperim'etry s. Science of perimetrical figures.
Calorim'etry s. Measurement of quantities of heat.
Colorim'etry s. (*Colorimeter*).
Densim'etry s. Science of ascertaining specific gravities.
Sym'metry s. Harmony of parts; proportion.
Asym'metry s. Lack of symmetry or proportion.
Aræom'etry s. Measurement of specific gravity.
Geom'etry s. Science dealing with the measurment, relations, etc., of surfaces, lines, angles, etc.
Tacheom'etry s. Tachymetry.
Stereom'etry s. Art of measuring solid bodies.
Stichom'etry (stik-) s. Division into lines or verses; measurement thus.
Psychom'etry s. Measurement of duration of mental processes.
Orthom'etry s. The art of versification.
Biom'etry s. Statistical measurement of life.
Radiom'etry s. Measurement of radiant energy.
Eudiom'etry s. Measurement of the purity or composition of air, etc.
Stoichiom'etry s. Determination of atomic and molecular weights; branch of chemistry dealing with this.
Craniom'etry s. Measurement of skulls, especially for comparative study.
Cyclom'etry s. Art or process of measuring circles.
Crystallom'etry s. Art or process of measuring crystals.
Alcoholom'etry s. Ascertainment of amount of alcohol in a liquid.
Anemom'etry s. Measurement of wind-pressure.
Thermom'etry s. Art of measuring heat.
Uranom'etry s. Measurement of stellar distances; a stellar map.
Galvanom'etry s. The measurement of electric currents.
Trigonom'etry s. Science of determining relations of sides and angles of triangles.
Chronom'etry s. (*Chronometer*).
Zoom'etry s. Comparative measurement of the parts of animals.
Anthropom'etry s. Scientific measurement of the human body.
Barom'etry s. (*Barometer*).
Hydrom'etry s. Art or practice of determining specific gravities, or of measuring the velocity or discharge of water.
Hygrom'etry s. Branch of physics dealing with the measurement of atmospheric moisture.
Horom'etry s. Art or practice of measuring time.
Chlorom'etry s. (*Chlorometer*).
Electrom'etry s. Measurement of quantity, quality, etc., of electricity.
Gasom'etry s. Art of measuring gases.
Photom'etry s. Art or science of measuring relative intensity of light.
Mau'metry s. Idolatry.
Tachym'etry s. A method of rapid land-surveying.
Bathym'etry s. Art of taking deep soundings.
Po'etry s. Metrical or imaginative composition; verse.

Pup'petry s. Appearance or triviality of puppets; affectation.
Retry' v.t. To try again.
Co'quetry s. Trifling in love; the practices of a coquette; flirtation.
Mar'quetry s. Inlaid wood-work.
Par'quetry s. Inlaid wood-work, especially for floors.
Rab'bitry s. Breeding-ground of rabbits; a warren.
Jes'uitry s. Jesuitism.
Pal'try a. Worthless; mean; contemptible.
Pel'try s. Skins with the fur on them.
Swel'try a. Overcome with heat; oppressively hot.
Dev'iltry s. Devilry.
Poul'try s. Domestic fowls.
Sul'try a. Close and hot; oppressive.
Ped'antry s. Vain ostentation of learning; obstinate adherence to rule; qualities of a pedant.
Pag'eantry s. A pompous show or spectacle.
In'fantry s. Foot-soldiers collectively.
Gan'try s. Framework for travelling crane, a number of railway signals, supporting casks, etc.
Chan'try s. A chapel endowed for the celebration of masses for the deceased; endowment for this.
Gi'antry s. Giants collectively.
Gal'lantry s. Daring courage, intrepidity; polite attentions to ladies; pretensions to love.
Ten'antry s. Tenants collectively.
Pan'try s. Apartment in which china, glass, plate, knives, etc., are kept and cleaned.
Er'rantry s. A roving, wandering; employment of a knight-errant.
Knight-er'rantry s. The practices of knights-errant.
Pleas'antry s. Gaiety, humour; a jest.
Peas'antry s. Peasants collectively; rustics.
En'try s. Act of entering; entrance; entrance-way; act of taking possession of lands, office, etc.; act of committing to writing.
Re-en'try s. Landlord's right on leased premises; a new entry in a book.
Gen'try s. People of position below the nobility.
Car'pentry s. Trade of a carpenter; wood-working.
Sen'try s. A soldier on guard; a sentinel; duty of a sentry.
Misen'try s. An erroneous entry.
Win'try a. Suitable to, pertaining to, or resembling winter; cold; icy.
Coun'try s. A region; a state; rural parts as opposed to town; the inhabitants of a region; the public. a. Pertaining to rural parts, manners, etc.; rustic, unrefined.
Big'otry s. Perverse or blind attachment to.
Zeal'otry (zĕl'-) s. Excess of zeal; character of a zealot.
Hel'otry s. Helots collectively; serfs.
Pi'lotry s. Practice of piloting; pilotage.
Har'lotry s. The ways or trade of harlots; lewdness.
Quix'otry s. Absurdly romantic theories, acts, etc.
Pas'try s. Eatables made of paste; pie-crust.
An'cestry s. Lineage, descent.
Tap'estry s. Cloth woven with figures; fabric hangings.
For'estry s. Act or art of cultivating forests.
Ves'try s. Room appendant to a church; assembly for conducting parish affairs.
Reg'istry s. Registraton; place where a register is kept.
Soph'istry s. Practice of a sophist; fallacious reasoning.
Chem'istry s. The science of the composition of substances and the changes they undergo.
Palm'istry s. Art of telling fortunes by the hand.
Tan'istry s. An ancient Irish form of land-tenure and succession.
Min'istry s. Ministers collectively; act of ministering.
Pa'pistry s. The system of the papacy; Roman Catholic ceremony, etc.
Den'tistry s. Art or profession of a dentist.
Bap'tistry s. The place where baptism is administered.
Cas'uistry s. Art of applying moral rules to questions of conduct, etc.; sophistical argument.
In'dustry s. Diligence, assiduity; steady application; useful work; trade, manufacture.
Bijou'try s. Jewellry, knick-knacks.
Sau'ry s. A sea-fish with a long beak.
Cen'taury s. Knapweed, cornflower, and other wild plants.
Bur'y v.t. To put into a grave; to cover, overwhelm.
Til'bury s. A kind of gig.
Am'bury s. (*Ambry*).
Mer'cury s. Quicksilver, a planet.
Fleur'y a. Adorned with fleurs-de-lis.
Seign'eury (sān'ūri) s. Territory or mansion of a seigneur.
Fu'ry s. Passion of anger; frenzy, mad rage.
Stran'gury s. Painful discharge of urine.
Au'gury s. Art of divination, especially from birds; an omen.
Sul'phury a. Resembling or having the qualities of sulphur.
Jur'y s. Body of persons selected to try a case and give a verdict.
In'jury s. A wrong; damage, mischief; doing of harm.
Per'jury s. False swearing; wilful making of a false oath.
Pen'ury s. Absence of means; want, indigence.
Lour'y a. Gloomy, cloudy; sullen.
Flour'y a. Covered with or like flour.
Col'oury a. Having a good colour.
Ar'moury s. Arms and armour; a place for keeping or making this; an armourer's trade.
Va'poury a. Vaporous; peevish.
Bis'toury s. A scalpel.
Sa'voury a. Having savour or relish; pleasing. s. A small appetizing dish.
Treas'ury s. Place where treasure is kept; revenue controlling public department; a book full of information, etc.; a storehouse.
U'sury s. Exorbitant interest on money lent; practice of taking this.
Cen'tury s. An aggregate of 100 things, period of 100 years.
Lux'ury s. Voluptuousness; delicious food or living; extravagant indulgence.
Wry a. Turned to one side; distorted, askew.
Awry' adv., a. Distorted, asquint.
Gew'gawry s. Gewgaws collectively.
Out'lawry s. The putting of one out of the protection of the la

Jew'ry s. Jews collectively; their habitation.
Cow'ry s. A small shell used as money in parts of Africa.
Dow'ry s. Property brought by a wife to her husband on marriage; a gift, talent.
Ey'ry s. An eagle's nest.
Por'phyry s. A reddish feldspathic rock.
Mar'tyry s. A chapel to the memory of a martyr.
Eas'y a. At ease; free from pain, anxiety, etc.; not difficult; gentle; complying; affluent; not formal.
Uneas'y a. Restless; anxious; not graceful; irksome.
Creas'y a. In a creased state.
Greas'y a. Smeared with grease; oily, unctuous.
Queas'y a. Affected with or causing nausea; squeamish.
Malagas'y a. Pertaining to Madagascar, its people, or their language. s. A native or the language of Madagascar.
Aph'asy s. Aphasia.
Athan'asy s. Deathlessness.
Idiosyn'crasy s. Peculiarity of constitution or temperament.
Theoc'rasy s. Polytheism; union of the soul with God.
Dys'crasy s. An ill habit or state of the constitution; dyscrasia.
Eu'phrasy s. The eye-bright.
Fan'tasy s. An extravagant fancy or idea; a fanciful design; a visionary speculation; a caprice.
Ec'stasy s. Excessive joy, rapture; mental exaltation.
Apos'tasy s. Abandonment of faith, party, etc.
Fub'sy a. Fat, dumpy, squat.
Pud'sy a. Plump.
Geod'esy s. The science of measuring large tracts of the earth's surface; surveying on an extended scale.
Chees'y a. Like cheese, in taste or appearance, etc.
Proph'esy v.t. To foretell, predict. v.i. To utter predictions; to preach.
Troph'esy s. Deranged nutrition.
Cram'esy a. and s. Cramoisy.
Po'esy s. Art or skill of composing poems; poetry.
Her'esy s. Unorthodox opinion in religion.
Cur'tesy s. A curtsy.
Court'esy s. Politeness, urbanity; an act of kindness or civility.
Discourt'esy s. Rudeness in behaviour or speech.
Dais'y s. A small composite flower; (*slang*) a first-rate person or thing.
Cram'oisy s. Crimson cloth. a. Crimson.
Nois'y a. Making much noise, din, etc.
Hypoc'risy s. False profession; pretence, insincerity.
Pleur'isy s. Inflammation of the pleura.
Trick'sy a. Playful, sportive.
Pal'sy s. A weakening of sensation, etc.; paralysis.
Min'strelsy s. Art or occupation of minstrels; music, song; a body of songs.
Whim'sy s. A whim, capricious notion.
Flim'sy a. Unsubstantial, weak, slight; shallow. s. (*Slang*) A bank-note; manifolded copy.
Clum'sy a. Awkward, uncouth; without manners; ungraceful.
Pan'sy s. Heart's-ease; the cultivated viola.
Tan'sy s. A plant with yellow flowers and bitter aromatic leaves.
Quin'sy s. An inflammation of the throat.
Son'sy a. (*Scot.*) Jolly-looking; good-natured.
Co'sy a. Comfortable, snug. s. A covering to keep a teapot, etc., hot.
Ar'gosy s. A richly-laden merchantman.
No'sy a. (*Slang*) Having a large nose; strong-smelling; given to prying.
Geog'nosy s. Structural geology.
Goos'y a. Resembling geese or goose-flesh.
Po'sy s. A motto; short inscription, especially in verse; a nosegay.
Ro'sy a. Like a rose; blooming; blushing; auspicious.
Pro'sy a. Dull, tedious.
Lep'rosy s. A chronic cutaneous disease.
Cat'alepsy s. Trance, sudden cessation of sensation and volition.
Acat'alepsy s. Incomprehensibleness.
Epilep'sy s. A nervous disorder characterized by spasms and causing loss of consciousness, sensation, etc.
Narcolep'sy s. A nervous disorder characterized by short attacks of deep sleep.
Nympholep'sy s. Condition of frenzy befalling one who has gazed on a nymph; wild longing for the unattainable.
Apep'sy s. Indigestion.
Dyspep'sy s. Chronic indigestion.
Gip'sy s. One of a wandering vagrant race; a roguish woman; a cunning person. a. Pertaining to or resembling the gipsies.
Lithotrip'sy s. Operation of triturating a stone in the bladder.
Tip'sy a. Half-drunk; fuddled.
-opsy suff. Denoting appearance, sight, vision, etc.
Cop'sy a. Like a copse; furnished with copses.
Necrop'sy s. A post-mortem.
Drop'sy s. Morbid accumulation of water in the body.
Pho'topsy s. Photopsia.
Au'topsy s. Dissection; critical examination.
Con'troversy s. A disputation, debate; hostility; litigation.
Gor'sy a. Covered with gorse.
Hor'sy a. Pertaining to or fond of horses or racing.
Pur'sy a. Short and fat; short-winded.
Em'bassy s. Function, mission, or residence of an ambassador; himself and suite; an important message.
Gas'sy a. Gaseous; containing gas; frothy full of vain talk.
Class'y a. (*Slang*) High-toned, superior.
Glass'y a. Like glass; vitreous; smooth dull.
Mass'y a. Solid; ponderous; consisting of a mass.
Chris'tmassy a. (*Christmas*).
Brass'y a. Like brass; unfeeling; shameless; pretentious. s. A golf-club
Grass'y a. Covered with or like grass; green
Mess'y a. Like a mess; muddled, dirty.
Dress'y a. Fond of dress; showy, smart stylish.
Tress'y a. Abounding with tresses.
Boss'y a. Adorned with bosses.
Phoss'y a. (*Slang*) Denoting state of phosphorus necrosis of the jaw.
Floss'y a. Like floss; light, downy.
Gloss'y a. Having a smooth, polished surface
Moss'y a. Overgrown, abounding, or covered with moss.
Dross'y a. Pertaining to, composed of, or like dross; worthless.
Fuss'y a. Making a fuss, bustling; petty.

Hus'sy s. A pert young woman, a jade.
Muss'y a. Untidy, disarranged.
Lawk-a-mus'sy int. A vulgar exclamation.
Puss'y s. A cat, puss.
Curt'sy s. A woman's bow; an act of salutation. v.i. To make a curtsy.
Bus'y a. Actively engaged; officious. v.t. To make or keep busy.
Fun'gusy a. Like or abounding in fungi.
Lous'y a. Infested with lice; (*slang*) mean, low.
Jeal'ousy s. Quality of being jealous; suspicious apprehension; solicitude for others.
Mous'y a. Smelling of, resembling, or infested with mice.
Tou'sy a. Rumbled, dishevelled.
Dru'sy a. Covered with small crystals.
News'y a. Abounding in news.
Drow'sy a. Sleepy; half asleep, sluggish.
-ty suff. Forming abstract nouns.
Meat'y a. Containing or like meat.
Peat'y a. Composed of, resembling, or abounding in peat.
Treat'y s. Formal agreement between states; negotiation.
Entreat'y s. An urgent solicitation or petition.
Sweat'y a. Moist with sweat; toilsome.
Slat'y a. Resembling or composed of slate.
Goat'y a. Goat-like; of a rank odour.
Throat'y a. Guttural, hoarse.
Ni'cety s. Exactness; a delicate distinction; a small detail.
Sleet'y a. Consisting of or bringing sleet.
Sweet'y s. A lollipop.
Safe'ty s. State of being safe; quality of making safe; close custody; a bicycle; a match igniting only on a prepared surface.
Fidg'ety a. Restless.
Crotch'ety a. Whimsical, faddy.
Hatch'ety a. Like a hatchet.
Ga'iety s. Mirth, merriment, cheerfulness.
Ubi'ety s. State of being in a place; local relation.
Dubi'ety s. Doubtfulness, uncertainty, questionableness.
Soci'ety s. Fellowship, companionship; persons associated for some object; persons in the same circle; social leaders.
Moi'ety s. A half part.
Pi'ety s. State or quality of being pious; filial sentiment or duty.
Impi'ety s. Want of piety; irreligion.
Contrari'ety s. State of being contrary, opposition; inconsistency.
Vari'ety s. Quality of being varied or various; diversity; variation; a sort.
Ebri'ety s. Intoxication.
Inebri'ety s. Habitual drinking; drunkenness.
Sobri'ety s. Habitual temperance; freedom from passion or enthusiasm; gravity.
Insobri'ety s. Intemperance; drunkenness.
Notori'ety s. State of being or one who is notorious.
Propri'ety s. Conformity to standard; suitableness, fitness.
Impropri'ety s. Quality of being improper; an unsuitable or unbecoming act, etc.
Sati'ety s. State of being glutted; repletion; surfeit.
Quoti'ety s. Proportional frequency.
Anxi'ety s. Concern; state of being anxious.
Clack'ety a. (*Clack*).
Rack'ety a. Noisy, flighty; tumultuous.
Pernick'ety a. Fastidious; over-particular.
Rick'ety a. Affected with rickets; unsteady.
Pock'ety a. Characterized by pockets (of mines).
Subtle'ty (sŭtl'-) s. Quality of being subtle; craftiness.
Fur'mety s. Frumenty.
Fru'mety s. Frumenty.
Nine'ty a. and s. Nine times ten.
Snip'pety a. Ridiculously small; insignificant.
Entire'ty s. Completeness; the entire amount; integrity.
Sure'ty s. One giving security; a guarantor or guarantee.
Rus'sety a. Of a russet colour.
Su'ety a. Resembling or consisting of suet.
Vel'vety a. Made of or like velvet; soft and smooth.
Craft'y a. Cunning, sly, artful.
Fif'ty a. and n. Five tens; five times ten.
Shift'y a. Artful, unreliable; fertile in expedients.
Rift'y a. Having rifts.
Drift'y a. Forming a snow-drift.
Thrift'y a. Frugal, careful, economical.
Loft'y a. Very high; towering; sublime.
Soft'y s. (*Slang*) A simple, weak-minded person.
Tuft'y a. Abounding with tufts.
Eight'y a. and s. Consisting of or the sum of eight times ten.
Weight'y a. Ponderous; important, momentous; influential.
Blight'y s. Soldier-slang for England or home.
Flight'y a. Capricious, giddy, volatile.
Might'y a. Powerful, potent; very great.
Almight'y a. All powerful. adv. (*Slang*) Very. s. God.
Night'y s. (*Slang*) A night-gown.
Haught'y a. Proud, contemptuous, insolent.
Naught'y a. Bad, mischievous, perverse.
Draught'y a. Full of air-currents.
Dought'y a. Valiant, redoubtable.
Drought'y a. (*Drought*).
La'ity s. People, as distinct from the clergy; non-professional people.
Pro'bity s. Integrity, sincerity, rectitude.
Impro'bity s. Absence of probity; dishonesty.
Acer'bity s. Bitterness; harshness of manner, etc.
Cit'y s. A large, important town; one with a charter.
Perspicac'ity s. Acuteness of discernment; sagacity.
Pervicac'ity s. State or quality of being wilfully perverse.
Procac'ity s. Impudence; petulance.
Edac'ity s. Gluttony, greed, voracity.
Mendac'ity s. Falsehood; quality of being false.
Mordac'ity s. Quality or state of being mordacious.
Audac'ity s. Boldness; hardihood; effrontery.
Sagac'ity s. Quality of being sagacious; keen discernment.
Fugac'ity s. State or quality of being transitory.
Salac'ity s. Lewdness, lechery.
Tenac'ity s. Quality or state of being tenacious; adhesiveness.
Pugnac'ity s. Quarrelsomeness.
Minac'ity s. Threatening disposition.
Pertinac'ity s. State or quality of being pertinacious; obstinacy.
Capac'ity s Power of receiving or containing; extent of space; condition, status, position, etc.
Incapac'ity s. Incompetency: legal disqualification.

Rapac'ity s. Exorbitant greed of gain; ravenousness.
Opac'ity s. Quality of being opaque; obscurity; dullness.
Ferac'ity s. State of being fertile.
Verac'ity s. Truth; truthfulness; that which is true.
Inverac'ity s. Untruthfulness.
Vorac'ity s. Voraciousness; greediness.
Furac'ity s. Theft, thievishness.
Loquac'ity s. Quality of being talkative; garrulity.
Vivac'ity s. Sprightliness of temper, air of activity.
Sic'city s. Dryness; aridity.
Cec'ity s. Blindness.
Spheroidic'ity s. State or quality of being spheroidal.
Mendic'ity s. Mendicancy; the life of a beggar.
Periodic'ity s. State or quality of being periodic; tendency to return at regular intervals.
Pudic'ity s. Modesty; chastity.
Impudic'ity s. Shamelessness, immodesty.
Specific'ity s. State or condition of being specific.
Prolific'ity s. State of being prolific.
Public'ity s. State of being or making public; notoriety.
Felic'ity s. State of being happy; that which promotes happiness; bliss.
Infelic'ity s. Misery; misfortune; ineptness.
Catholic'ity s. The quality of being catholic.
Triplic'ity s. State of being triple.
Multiplic'ity s. State of being multiple or various; a collection of many objects; a great number.
Simplic'ity s. State or quality of being simple; artlessness; foolishness; sincerity.
Complic'ity s. Partnership, especially in wrongdoing.
Duplic'ity s. Double-dealing, dissimulation.
Quadruplic'ity s. State of being fourfold.
Endemic'ity s. State of being endemic.
Atomic'ity s. Combining capacity of an element.
Volcanic'ity s. Quality or state of being volcanic.
Œcumenic'ity s. State or quality of being œcumenical; catholicity.
Canonic'ity s. Quality of being canonical.
Lubric'ity s. Smoothness, slipperiness; lewdness.
Spheric'ity s. State or quality of being spherical.
Caloric'ity a. Animal faculty of developing heat.
Historic'ity s. Quality of being historic.
Electric'ity s. Collective term for the force that manifests itself in lightning, attraction and repulsion exhibited by certain bodies under friction, etc.; the science dealing with such phenomena.
Centric'ity s. State of being centric; centralness.
Eccentric'ity s. Deviation from the centre or from rule; not being concentric; oddity, peculiarity.
Concentric'ity s. (*Concentric*).
Egocentric'ity s. Quantity of being egocentric.
Neuric'ity s. Properties, etc., peculiar to nerves.
Achromatic'ity s. Quality or state of being achromatic.
Automatic'ity s. State of being automatic.
Pneumatic'ity s. State of having air cavities.
Authentic'ity s. Quality of being authentic.
Peptic'ity s. State of being peptic; digestive capacity.
Eupeptic'ity s. State of having a good digestion.
Septic'ity s. Tendency to putrefaction; septic quality.
Elliptic'ity s. Amount an ellipse diverges from a circle or an ellipsoid from a sphere.
Styptic'ity s. Quality of arresting bleeding.

Vortic'ity s. State of being vortical; the half-curl of a vector.
Elastic'ity s. State or property of being elastic.
Inelastic'ity s. State of being inelastic.
Plastic'ity s. State or quality of being plastic.
Spastic'ity s. State or condition of being spasmodic.
Domestic'ity s. State of being domestic; homeliness; home-life.
Caustic'ity s. (*Caustic*).
Rustic'ity s. Rustic manners; coarseness; artlessness.
Toxic'ity s. State of being toxic.
Precoc'ity s. State or quality of being precocious; premature development.
Veloc'ity s. Rapidity; celerity; fleetness.
Feroc'ity s. State of being ferocious; savageness; a ferocious deed.
Reciproc'ity s. Mutual action and reaction; give and take.
Atroc'ity s. Savage, brutal cruelty; an instance of such.
Scar'city s. State or condition of being scarce; deficiency; short supply; scarceness.
Pau'city s. Smallness of number or quantity; scarcity.
Rau'city s. Hoarseness, harshness.
Cadu'city s. Falling easily (of leaves).
Quid'dity s. The essence of a thing; a subtlety, quibble.
Odd'ity s. Oddness; that which is odd; singularity; a peculiarity; an eccentric person.
Hered'ity s. Transmission of qualities of parents to offspring.
Rabid'ity s. Rabidness.
Morbid'ity s. Unhealthiness; morbidness.
Turbid'ity s. Quality or state of being turbid.
Acid'ity s. Sourness.
Placid'ity s. State or quality of being placid.
Flaccid'ity s. State of being flaccid.
Rancid'ity s. Quality of being rancid.
Viscid'ity s. Stickiness.
Lucid'ity s. State or quality of being lucid.
Pellucid'ity s. Pellucidness.
Rigid'ity s. Lack of pliability; stiffness; inflexibility.
Frigid'ity s. Coldness; dullness; stiffness, formality.
Algid'ity s. State of coldness.
Turgid'ity s. Quality of being turgid; bombast.
Calid'ity s. Warmth.
Squalid'ity s. State or quality of being squalid.
Valid'ity s. Soundness; legal sufficiency.
Invalid'ity s. Want of legal force; want of cogency.
Gelid'ity s. Condition of extreme cold.
Solid'ity s. State of being solid; density; soundness.
Insolid'ity s. Flimsiness; weakness.
Stolid'ity s. State or quality of being stolid; stupidity.
Timid'ity s. Quality or state of being timid.
Humid'ity s. State of being humid; moisture.
Tumid'ity s. (*Tumid*).
Rapid'ity s. Quality or state of being rapid; speed; agility.
Sapid'ity s. Quality of being sapid; savouriness.
Vapid'ity s. Want of life or spirit; dullness.
Intrepid'ity s. Quality of being intrepid; bravery.
Tepid'ity s. Lukewarmness; state of being tepid.
Insipid'ity s. Tastelessness; want of life or spirit.
Limpid'ity s. Clearness; purity; transparency.
Torpid'ity s. State of being torpid; numbness.

Cupid'ity s. Eager desire for possession; coveteousness.
Stupid'ity s. Intellectual dullness; senselessness.
Arid'ity s. Dryness.
Scabrid'ity s. Scabrousness.
Hybrid'ity s. State or quality of being hybrid.
Acrid'ity s. Pungency; sharpness.
Virid'ity s. Greenness, especially of vegetation.
Florid'ity s. Quality or condition of being florid.
Torrid'ity s. State or quality of being torrid.
Putrid'ity s. State of being putrid; corruption.
Pinguid'ity s. Fatness; unctuousness.
Fluid'ity s. Quality or state of being fluid.
Liquid'ity s. State or quality of being liquid.
Avid'ity s. Greed, coveteousness.
Livid'ity s. State of being livid.
Fecun'dity s. Quality or power of producing young or fruit; fertility.
Infecun'dity s. Barrenness.
Verecun'dity s. Bashfulness; modesty.
Rubicun'dity s. Redness, ruddiness.
Jocun'dity s. Merriment; blitheness.
Profun'dity s. State or quality of being profound; depth.
Obtun'dity s. State of being benumbed.
Rotun'dity s. State of being rotund; sphericity.
Orotun'dity s. Quality of being orotund; pomposity.
Commod'ity s. Any article of commerce, anything useful.
Incommod'ity s. Inconvenience; a cause of this.
Sur'dity s. Condition of being surd; deafness.
Absur'dity s. Quality of being absurd; an absurd situation, thing, etc.
Nu'dity s. State of being nude; nakedness; that which is nude.
Cru'dity s. State of being crude; a crude thing.
Hæcce'ity s. Individuality; this quality.
De'ity s. Divine nature or attributes; divinity; God.
Velle'ity s. Imperfect volition; the lowest degree of desire.
Diaphane'ity s. Transparency.
Diathermane'ity s. Diathermancy.
Contemporane'ity s. (*Contemporaneous*).
Extrane'ity s. Quality of being extraneous.
Simultane'ity s. Simultaneousness.
Instantane'ity s. State or quality of being instantaneous.
Consentane'ity s. (*Consentaneous*).
Spontane'ity s. Quality or state of being spontaneous.
Homogene'ity s. Sameness of kind or nature; uniformity.
Heterogene'ity s. Heterogeneous state or quality.
Femine'ity s. Womanliness; effeminacy.
Corpore'ity s. Material existence.
Incorpore'ity s. Immateriality.
Se'ity s. Selfhood.
Gase'ity s. Quality or condition of being gaseous.
Whi'ty a. Inclining to white; whitish.
Verbal'ity s. Wordiness.
Farcical'ity s. Quality of being farcical.
Radical'ity s. The quality of radicalism.
Tragical'ity s. Quality or state of being tragical
Logical'ity s. Logical character.
Illogical'ity s. (*Illogical*).
Comical'ity s. (*Comical*).
Technical'ity s. State or quality of being technical; a technical term.
Clerical'ity s. The body or principles of the clergy.
Theatrical'ity s. State of being theatrical; staginess.
Whimsical'ity s. State or quality of being whimsical; a whim.
Nonsensical'ity s. An absurdity; foolery.
Extrinsical'ity s. State or quality of being extrinsic.
Classical'ity s. (*Classical*).
Musical'ity s. State or quality of being musical.
Pragmatical'ity s. Pragmaticalness.
Practical'ity s. State of being practical; a practical matter.
Vertical'ity s. State or quality of being vertical.
Fantastical'ity s. Quality of being fantastic.
Local'ity s. Geographical position; district; situation.
Reciprocal'ity s. State or quality ofbeing reciprocal.
Vocal'ity s. Quality of being vocal; resonance.
Rascal'ity s. Trickery; dishonesty.
Modal'ity s. Quality of being in form only.
Sodal'ity s. A fellowship, confraternity.
Feudal'ity s. Quality or state of being feudal.
Ideal'ity s. Quality of being ideal; capacity to form ideals.
Real'ity s. State or quality of being real, actual, or true; fact; certainty.
Corporeal'ity s. (*Corporeal*).
Legal'ity s. Condition or character of being legal.
Illegal'ity s. Unlawfulness; state of being illegal.
Regal'ity s. Royalty; sovereign jurisdiction.
Prodigal'ity s. Extravagance; profusion.
Conjugal'ity s. (*Conjugal*).
Frugal'ity s. Thrift; prudent economy.
Lethal'ity s. Lethal state; deadliness.
Proverbial'ity s. Quality of being proverbial.
Connubial'ity s. Matrimony.
Special'ity s. Particularity; a special thing, condition, characteristic, etc.
Artificial'ity s. An artificial quality or condition.
Superficial'ity s. State of being superficial; shallowness.
Provincial'ity s. Quality of being provincial; a characteristic of country people.
Social'ity s. Quality of being social.
Commercial'ity s. (*Commercialism*).
Radial'ity s. State of being radial.
Cordial'ity s. Warm affection and good will; heartiness.
Primordial'ity s. State or condition of being primordial.
Filial'ity s. Relation or attitude of a child to its parents.
Genial'ity s. Cheerfulness, cordiality.
Congenial'ity s. (*Congenial*).
Venial'ity s. State or quality of being venial.
Perennial'ity s. State of being perennial.
Imperial'ity s. Imperial power or authority.
Serial'ity s. (*Serial*).
Material'ity s. Quality or state of being material; corporeity; substantiality.
Immaterial'ity s. Quality of being immaterial.
Exterritorial'ity s. Freedom from jurisdiction of ambassadors, etc., in a foreign country.
Mercurial'ity s. State or quality of being mercurial.
Spatial'ity s. Quality of being spatial.
Substantial'ity s. State of being substantial; corporeity.
Insubstantial'ity s. State or quality of being insubstantial.
Consubstantial'ity s. Participation of the same nature
Circumstantial'ity s. (*Circumstantial*).
Confidential'ity s. (*Confidential*).
Essential'ity s. Quality of being essential.
Coessential'ity s. (*Coessential*).
Potential'ity s. Quality or state of being potential

Sequential'ity s. (*Sequential*).
Consequential'ity s. (*Consequential*).
Inconsequential'ity s. Condition of being inconsequential.
Partial'ity s. Quality of being partial; special fondness.
Impartial'ity s. Disinterestedness; freedom from bias.
Bestial'ity s. Brutishness; beastliness.
Trivial'ity s. A trifle; state or quality of being trivial.
Convivial'ity s. (*Convivial*).
Jovial'ity s. Merriment, mirth; festivity.
Axial'ity s. Quality of being axial.
Animal'ity s. Animal nature; sensuality.
Formal'ity s. Quality of being formal; ceremony; conventionality.
Informal'ity s. Want of regular form or order.
Normal'ity s. Normal state or quality.
Abnormal'ity s. An abnormal state or thing.
Banal'ity s. A triviality, commonplace.
Venal'ity s. State or quality of being venal; mercenariness.
Final'ity s. State or quality of being final; final state; settlement.
Original'ity s. Quality or state of being original; power of originating.
Feminal'ity s. Quality of being female; characteristic nature of females.
Criminal'ity s. Quality of being criminal; guiltiness.
Meridional'ity s. Position in or aspect to the south.
Occasional'ity s. State or quality of being occasional.
National'ity s. Quality of being national; national character; a race or people.
Rational'ity s. Quality of being rational; reasonableness.
Irrational'ity s. Quality of being irrational; absurdness.
Conditional'ity s. (*Conditional*).
Conventional'ity s. (*Conventional*).
Devotional'ity s. (*Devotional*).
Exceptional'ity s. Quality of being exceptional.
Proportional'ity s. Quality of being in proportion.
Constitutional'ity s. (*Constitutional*).
Personal'ity s. That which constitutes or peculiarly pertains to an individual; state of being personal; a disparaging remark; personalty.
Tripersonal'ity s. State of three persons existing in one Godhead.
Impersonal'ity s. State of being impersonal; want of personality.
Tonal'ity s. System or arrangement of tones; general colour scheme.
Carnal'ity s. Sensuality; state of being carnal.
Internal'ity s. Condition or quality of being internal or within.
External'ity s. Existence in space; exteriority.
Municipal'ity s. A self-governing town or district.
Principal'ity s. Territory of a prince; sovereignty; a prince.
Liberal'ity s. Generosity; largeness of mind; width of sympathy.
Illiberal'ity s. (*Illiberal*).
General'ity s. State of being general; the bulk, main body.
Lateral'ity s. State or quality of being sideways or having sides.
Literal'ity s. State or quality of being literal.
Integral'ity s. Integral state or quality.
Spiral'ity s. Condition of being spiral.
Moral'ity s. Doctrine or practice of the duties of life; moral characte ror quality; an allegorical drama.
Immoral'ity s. State of being immoral; wickedness; unchastity.
Temporal'ity s. A secular possession; temporalness.
Corporal'ity s. Materiality.
Pastoral'ity s. Pastoral quality; a rustic expression, etc.
Central'ity s. Quality of being central.
Neutral'ity s. State of being neutral; indifference.
Dextral'ity s. (*Dextral*).
Plural'ity s. State of being plural; the greater number, or its excess over the next smaller; more than one benefice held by the same clergyman.
Rural'ity s. Ruralism; a rural place.
Nasal'ity s. Quality or state of being nasal.
Commensal'ity s. (*Commensal*).
Universal'ity s. State or quality of being universal.
Causal'ity s. Operation of a cause; theory of causation.
Fatal'ity s. State of being destined, or of being productive of death; invincible necessity; a fatal accident; mortality.
Natal'ity s. Birth-rate.
Vegetal'ity s. State or quality of being vegetal.
Hospital'ity s. Liberal entertainment of guests or strangers.
Vital'ity s. State or quality of being vital; animation.
Accidental'ity s. (*Accidental*).
Oriental'ity s. Quality or state of being Oriental or Eastern.
Mental'ity s. Quality or state of mind; mind as a characteristic.
Fundamental'ity s. State or quality of being fundamental.
Sentimental'ity s. Affectation of fine feeling.
Instrumental'ity s. Quality or state of being or that which is instrumental; agency.
Horizontal'ity s. Horizontal state or quality.
Total'ity s. Total amount.
Mortal'ity s. Quality of being mortal; human nature; death on a large scale; death-rate.
Immortal'ity s. State of being immortal; exemption from oblivion.
Brutal'ity s. Unreasoning cruelty; a savage, brutal act.
Dual'ity s. State of being two or twofold; that which expresses two; separation.
Individual'ity s. Quality of being individual; separate existence; sum of one's characteristic traits.
Qual'ity s. Sort, character; attribute, distinguishing property; rank; superior station.
Equal'ity s. State of being equal.
Inequal'ity s. Want of equality; condition of being unequal; diversity, unevenness.
Coequal'ity s. State of being coequal.
Visual'ity s. (*Visual*).
Sensual'ity s. Quality of being sensual; indulgence in carnal pleasures.
Actual'ity s. Reality.
Effectual'ity s. Quality of being effectual.
Ineffectual'ity s. Ineffectual quality, state, or thing.
Intellectual'ity s. State of being intellectual; intellectual power.
Punctual'ity s. Quality or state of being punctual.
Spiritual'ity s. Immateriality; spiritual nature or character.

Eventual'ity s. An occurrence; future or possible event.
Virtual'ity s. (*Virtual*).
Mutual'ity s. State or quality of being mutual; interdependence; interaction.
Sexual'ity s. State of being distinguished by sex.
Asexual'ity s. Quality of being asexual.
Coeval'ity s. (*Coeval*).
Fidel'ity s. Faithfulness; honesty; adherence to duty, etc.
Infidel'ity s. Scepticism; disbelief in Christianity; unfaithfulness to the marriage vow; treachery.
-ability suff. Many nouns from adjectives in *-able*.
Abil'ity s. Power to do or act; skill; talent.
Bribabil'ity s. (*Bribable*).
Indescribabil'ity s. (*Indescribable*).
Probabil'ity s. Likelihood; anything having the appearance of truth; doctrine of chances.
Improbabil'ity s. Quality of being improbable; unlikelihood.
Absorbabil'ity s. (*Absorbable*).
Imperturbabil'ity s. (*Imperturbable*).
Placabil'ity s. Quality of being placable.
Implacabil'ity s. (*Implacable*).
Peccabil'ity s. Liability to sin.
Impeccabil'ity s. State of being impeccable or faultless.
Secabil'ity s. Capable of being divided.
Predicabil'ity s. Quality of being predicable.
Vindicabil'ity s. State of being vindicable.
Applicabil'ity s. (*Applicable*).
Inapplicabil'ity s. (*Inapplicable*).
Inexplicabil'ity s. Condition of being inexplicable; mysteriousness.
Amicabil'ity s. (*Amicable*).
Commun'icability s. (*Communicable*).
Incommunicabil'ity s. (*Incommunicable*).
Practicabil'ity s. Quality or state of being practicable.
Impracticabil'ity s. (*Impracticable*).
Masticabil'ity s. (*Masticable*).
Revocabil'ity s. (*Revocable*).
Irrevocabil'ity s. (*Irrevocable*).
Educabil'ity s. (*Educable*).
Readabil'ity s. (*Readable*).
Avoidabil'ity s. (*Avoidable*).
Weldabil'ity s. (*Weldable*).
Laudabil'ity s. Praiseworthiness.
Traceabil'ity s. (*Traceable*).
Manageabil'ity s. (*Manageable*).
Chan'geability s. (*Changeable*).
Interchangeabil'ity s. Interchangeableness.
Exchangeabil'ity s. Capacity for being exchanged or rated for exchange.
Chargeabil'ity s. (*Chargeable*).
Saleabil'ity s. (*Saleable*).
Malleabil'ity s. (*Malleable*).
Permeabil'ity s. Quality of being permeable.
Impermeabil'ity s. (*Impermeable*).
Affabil'ity s. (*Affable*).
Irrefragabil'ity s. State or quality of being undeniable.
Indefatigabil'ity s. Quality of being indefatigable.
Navigabil'ity s. (*Navigable*).
Irreproachabil'ity s. Blamelessness.
Approachabil'ity s. (*Approachable*).
Punishabil'ity s. (*Punishable*).
Perishabil'ity s. State of being subject to decay.
Imperishabil'ity s. State of being imperishable or indestructible.
Pronunciabil'ity s. Quality of being pronounceable.
Sociabil'ity s. Quality of being sociable; friendliness.
Modifiabil'ity s. (*Modifiable*).
Verifiabil'ity s. (*Verifiable*).
Vitrifiabil'ity s. (*Vitrifiable*).
Justifiabil'ity s. Quality of being justifiable.
Liabil'ity s. State of being liable; that for which one is liable.
Reliabil'ity s. Trustworthiness.
Pliabil'ity s. Pliableness.
Amiabil'ity s. (*Amiable*).
Variabil'ity s. State or quality of being variable; aptness to alter.
Invariabil'ity s. Fact or quality of being invariable uniformity.
Friabil'ity s. State of being easily crumbled.
Insatiabil'ity s. (*Insatiable*).
Negotiabil'ity s. (*Negotiable*).
Viabil'ity s. Capacity of living after birth, also of having wide geographical distribution.
Irrepealabil'ity s. State or quality of being irrepealable.
Availabil'ity s. (*Available*).
Irreconcilabil'ity s. State or quality of being irreconcilable.
Assimilabil'ity s. (*Assimilable*).
Inappellabil'ity s. State of being inappellable.
Inviolabil'ity s. State or quality of being inviolable.
Incalculabil'ity s. (*Incalculable*).
Irredeemabil'ity s. State or quality of being irredeemable.
Inflammabil'ity s. State or quality of being inflammable.
Conformabil'ity s. (*Conformable*).
Alienabil'ity s. Capable of being alienated.
Inalienabil'ity s. (*Inalienable*).
Amenabil'ity s. (*Amenable*).
Tenabil'ity s. (*Tenable*).
Impregnabil'ity s. State of being impregnable.
Inabil'ity s. Want of ability, power, or adequate means.
Attainabil'ity s. (*Attainable*).
Determinabil'ity s. (*Determinable*).
Impressionabil'ity s. (*Impressionable*).
Questionabil'ity s. (*Questionable*).
Non-abil'ity s. Want of ability.
Governabil'ity s. Quality of being governable.
Capabil'ity s. (*Capable*).
Palpabil'ity s. (*Palpable*).
Impalpabil'ity s. (*Impalpable*).
Culpabil'ity s. Blameableness.
Dupabil'ity s. (*Dupable*).
Separabil'ity s. (*Separable*).
Inseparabil'ity s. (*Inseparable*).
Comparabil'ity s. (*Comparable*).
Ponderabil'ity s. (*Ponderable*).
Imponderabil'ity s. Quality of being imponderable.
Preferabil'ity s. (*Preferable*).
Transferabil'ity s. (*Transferable*).
Innumerabil'ity s. (*Innumerable*).
Venerabil'ity s. (*Venerable*).
Vulnerabil'ity s. (*Vulnerable*).
Invulnerabil'ity s. (*Invulnerable*).
Insuperabil'ity s. (*Insuperable*).

Alterabil'ity s. (*Alterable*).
Admirabil'ity s. (*Admirable*).
Perspirabil'ity s. (*Perspirable*).
Desirabil'ity s. State or quality of being desirable.
Acquirabil'ity s. (*Acquirable*).
Adorabil'ity s. (*Adorable*).
Deplorabil'ity s. (*Deplorable*).
Memorabil'ity s. (*Memorable*).
Vaporabil'ity s. (*Vaporable*).
Inexorabil'ity s. Quality of being inexorable.
Inerrabil'ity s. Inerrancy.
Penetrabil'ity s. (*Penetrable*).
Impenetrabil'ity s. (*Impenetrable*).
Demonstrabil'ity s. (*Demonstrable*).
Indemonstrabil'ity s. (*Indemonstrable*).
Curabil'ity s. (*Curable*).
Incurabil'ity s. (*Incurable*).
Durabil'ity s. Lastingness, permanence.
Endurabil'ity s. (*Endurable*).
Perdurabil'ity s. Permanence; everlastingness.
Immeasurabil'ity s. (*Immeasurable*).
Mensurabil'ity s. (*Mensurable*).
Commensurabil'ity s. (*Commensurable*).
Incommensurabil'ity s. (*Incommensurable*).
Disabil'ity s. Lack of power, opportunity, qualification, etc.
Advisabil'ity s. (*Advisable*).
Condensabil'ity s. (*Condensable*).
Indispensabil'ity s. (*Indispensable*).
Opposabil'ity s. (*Opposable*).
Impassabil'ity s. (*Impassable*).
Inexcusabil'ity s. (*Inexcusable*).
Dilatabil'ity s. (*Dilatable*).
Tractabil'ity s. (*Tractable*).
Intractabil'ity s. State or quality of being intractable.
Attractabil'ity s. (*Attractable*).
Delectabil'ity s. (*Delectable*).
Respectabil'ity s. State or quality which deserves respect, or of being respectable.
Predictabil'ity s. (*Predictable*).
Marketabil'ity s. (*Marketable*).
Habitabil'ity s. State or quality of being habitable.
Excitabil'ity s. Quality of being excitable.
Creditabil'ity s. (*Creditable*).
Hereditabil'ity s. Capacity of being hereditable.
Imitabil'ity s. (*Imitable*).
Illimitabil'ity s. State of being boundless
Inimitabil'ity s. (*Inimitable*).
Inheritabil'ity s. (*Inheritable*).
Irritabil'ity s. Fretfulness, petulance; state of being irritable.
Suitabil'ity s. Condition of being suitable; becomingness.
Inevitabil'ity s. State of being unavoidable; something inevitable; certainty.
Presentabil'ity s. (*Presentable*).
Accountabil'ity s. Responsibility, capability of explanation.
Insurmountabil'ity s. (*Insurmountable*).
Notabil'ity s. Quality of being notable; a person of note.
Quotabil'ity s. (*Quotable*).
Adaptabil'ity s. (*Adaptable*).
Inadaptabil'ity s. Quality of being inadaptable.
Acceptabil'ity s. (*Acceptable*).
Temptabil'ity s. (*Temptable*).
Attemptabil'ity s. (*Attemptable*).
Portabil'ity s. (*Portable*).
Importabil'ity s. (*Importable*).
Transportabil'ity s. (*Transportable*).
Stabil'ity s. Quality or state of being stable; firmness, steadiness.
Detestabil'ity s. (*Detestable*).
Incontestabil'ity s. (*Incontestable*).
Instabil'ity s. Inconstancy; fickleness; want of firmness.
Adjustabil'ity s. (*Adjustable*).
Irrefutabil'ity s. (*Irrefutable*).
Mutabil'ity s. State or quality of being mutable; inconstancy.
Immutabil'ity s. (*Immutable*).
Commutabil'ity s. (*Commutable*).
Incommutabil'ity s. (*Incommutable*).
Transmutabil'ity s. (*Transmutable*).
Imputabil'ity s. Quality of being imputable.
Indisputabil'ity s. (*Indisputable*).
Inscrutabil'ity s. State or quality of being inscrutable.
Suabil'ity s. (*Suable*).
Irretrievabil'ity s. (*Irretrievable*).
Conceivabil'ity s. (*Conceivable*).
Inconceivabil'ity s. (*Inconceivable*).
Solvabil'ity s. (*Solvable*).
Irresolvabil'ity s. (*Irresolvable*).
Movabil'ity s. State or quality of being movable.
Irremovabil'ity s. (*Irremovable*).
Immovabil'ity s. (*Immovable*).
Improvabil'ity s. (*Improvable*).
Knowabil'ity s. State of being knowable.
Taxabil'ity s. (*Taxable*).
Debil'ity s. Weakness, feebleness.
Vincibil'ity s. Quality or state of being vincible.
Invincibil'ity s. Unconquerableness.
Inconvincibil'ity s. (*Inconvincible*).
Irascibil'ity s. State or quality of being irascible.
Miscibil'ity s. Quality of being miscible.
Immiscibil'ity s. (*Immiscible*).
Cognoscibil'ity s. (*Cognoscible*).
Incognoscibil'ity s. Condition of being incognoscible.
Irreducibil'ity s. State or quality of being irreducible.
Producibil'ity s. (*Producible*).
Conducibil'ity s. (*Conducible*).
Edibil'ity s. (*Edible*).
Inedibil'ity s. State of being uneatable.
Credibil'ity s. (*Credible*).
Incredibil'ity s. (*Incredible*).
Descendibil'ity s. (*Descendible*).
Vendibil'ity s. Saleability.
Audibil'ity s. (*Audible*).
Inaudibil'ity s. (*Inaudible*).
Legibil'ity s. State or quality of being readable.
Illegibil'ity s. State of being undecipherable.
Eligibil'ity s. Worthiness or fitness to be chosen.
Ineligibil'ity s. State of being ineligible.
Intelligibil'ity s. Quality or state of being intelligible.
Incorrigibil'ity s. (*Incorrigible*).
Frangibil'ity s. State or quality of being easily broken.
Infrangibil'ity s. (*Infrangible*).
Tangibil'ity s. Quality or state of being tangible.
Intangibil'ity s. (*Intangible*).
Indelibil'ity s. Quality of being indelible.
Fallibil'ity s. State of being liable to mistake.
Infallibil'ity s. Exemption from liability to error.
Gullibil'ity s. Condition of being easy to cheat.
Feasibil'ity s. Practicability.
Defeasibil'ity s. (*Defeasible*).
Indefeasibil'ity s. (*Indefeasible*).

Infeasibil'ity s. (*Infeasible*).
Persuasibil'ity s. (*Persuasible*).
Risibil'ity s. Quality of being risible.
Visibil'ity s. State or quality of being visible.
Divisibil'ity s. (*Divisible*).
Indivisibil'ity s. (*Indivisible*).
Invisibil'ity s. State or quality of being invisible.
Expansibil'ity s. Capacity of expanding or for expansion.
Defensibil'ity s. (*Defensible*).
Indefensibil'ity s. Quality of being indefensible.
Comprehensibil'ity s. (*Comprehensible*).
Incomprehensibil'ity s. (*Incomprehensible*).
Suspensibil'ity s. Quality of being suspensible.
Sensibil'ity s. Capacity to see or feel; acuteness of sensation; susceptibility; over-sensitiveness.
Insensibil'ity s. Want of feeling; unconsciousness; indifference to.
Tensibil'ity s. (*Tensible*).
Distensibil'ity s. (*Distensible*).
Extensibil'ity s. (*Extensible*).
Responsibil'ity s. State of being or that for which one is responsible; ability to answer in payment.
Irresponsibil'ity s. (*Irresponsible*).
Reversibil'ity s. (*Reversible*).
Irreversibil'ity s. State or quality of being irreversible.
Torsibil'ity s. Tendency of twisted rope, etc., to untwist.
Passibil'ity s. Aptness to feel or suffer; sensibility.
Impassibil'ity s. (*Impassible*).
Accessibil'ity s. (*Accessible*).
Inaccessibil'ity s. (*Inaccessible*).
Impressibil'ity s. (*Impressible*).
Compressibil'ity s. (*Compressible*).
Incompressibil'ity s. State or quality of being incompressible.
Admissibil'ity s. (*Admissible*).
Inadmissibil'ity s. State or quality of being inadmissible.
Remissibil'ity s. (*Remissible*).
Irremissibil'ity s. (*Irremissible*).
Transmissibil'ity s. (*Transmissible*).
Possibil'ity s. State of being possible; that which is possible.
Impossibil'ity s. (*Impossible*).
Plau'sibility s. (*Plausible*).
Fusibil'ity s. Condition or quality of being fusible.
Diffusibil'ity s. (*Diffusible*).
Infusibil'ity s. (*Infusible*).
Compatibil'ity s. (*Compatible*).
Incompatibil'ity s. (*Incompatible*).
Indefectibil'ity s. (*Indefectible*).
Effectibil'ity s. (*Effectible*).
Perfectibil'ity s. Quality of being perfectible.
Imperfectibil'ity s. State or quality of being imperfectible.
Conductibil'ity s. (*Conductible*).
Destructibil'ity s. (*Destructible*).
Indestructibil'ity s. (*Indestructible*).
Deceptibil'ity s. (*Deceptible*).
Perceptibil'ity s. State or quality of being perceptible.
Imperceptibil'ity s. (*Imperceptible*).
Susceptibil'ity s. Quality of being susceptible.
Insusceptibil'ity s. State or quality of being insusceptible.
Imprescriptibility s. (*Imprescriptible*).
Discerptibil'ity s. (*Discerptible*).
Indiscerptibil'ity s. (*Indiscerptible*).
Corruptibil'ity s. (*Corruptible*).
Incorruptibil'ity s. (*Incorruptible*).
Partibil'ity s. Separability.
Impartibil'ity s. (*Impartible*).
Convertibil'ity s. (*Convertible*).
Inconvertibil'ity s. (*Inconvertible*).
Incontrovertibil'ity s. (*Incontrovertible*).
Digestibil'ity s. (*Digestible*).
Indigestibil'ity s. (*Indigestible*).
Resistibil'ity s. (*Resistible*).
Irresistibil'ity s. (*Irresistible*).
Existibil'ity s. (*Existible*).
Exhaustibil'ity s. (*Exhaustible*).
Inexhaustibil'ity s. (*Inexhaustible*).
Combustibil'ity s. (*Combustible*).
Incombustibil'ity s. (*Incombustible*).
Flexibil'ity s. Quality of being flexible; pliancy.
Inflexibil'ity s. (*Inflexible*).
Mobil'ity s. State of being mobile.
Immobil'ity s. Quality or state of being immobile; impassivity.
Nobil'ity s. Nobleness; the peerage.
Ignobil'ity s. (*Ignoble*).
Solubil'ity s. Quality of being soluble.
Insolubil'ity s. (*Insoluble*)
Indissolubil'ity s. (*Indissoluble*).
Volubil'ity s. State of being volubilate.
Nubil'ity s. State or quality of being marriageable.
Facil'ity s. Quality of being easily performed; dexterity; ready compliance.
Gracil'ity s. Slenderness, thinness.
Imbecil'ity s. Quality of being imbecile; fatuity, or an instance of this.
Docil'ity s. Quality of being docile; tractableness.
Indocil'ity s. Quality of being indocile; unteachableness.
Agil'ity s. Nimbleness, quickness.
Fragil'ity s. Brittleness; state of being fragile.
Nihil'ity s. Nothingness; state of being nothing.
Humil'ity s. Freedom from pride; modesty; self-abasement.
Anil'ity s. Condition of dotage.
Senil'ity s. Old age; state of being senile.
Juvenil'ity s. Youthfulness; manners, etc., of youth.
Steril'ity s. Unproductiveness; state or quality of being sterile.
Pueril'ity s. Childishness; state of being or that which is puerile.
Viril'ity s. Quality of being virile or manly.
Scurril'ity s. Low, violent abuse; indecent jesting.
Neuril'ity s. The capacity of nerves for transmitting stimuli.
Prehensil'ity s. Quality of being prehensile.
Fissil'ity s. Quality of being fissile.
Volatil'ity s. Capacity or disposition to evaporate; sprightliness.
Vibratil'ity s. Capacity for vibration.
Versatil'ity s. State or quality of being versatile.
Subtil'ity s. Quality or condition of being subtile; tenuousness.
Tractil'ity s. Ductility.
Retractil'ity s. Quality of being retractile.
Contractil'ity s. Quality of being contractile.

Tactil'ity s. State of being tactile; perceptibility by touch.
Ductil'ity s. Property of being ductile; obsequiousness.
Inductil'ity s. State of being inductile.
Gentil'ity s. Quality of being genteel; gentle birth; politeness.
Motil'ity s. Quality of being motile; contractility.
Locomotil'ity s. Locomotivity.
Fertil'ity s. Fruitfulness; state of being fertile.
Infertil'ity s. State of being infertile.
Tortil'ity s. Capacity for being twisted.
Hostil'ity s. Enmity, animosity; state of war.
Util'ity s. State or quality of being useful; benefit, service; a useful thing.
Futil'ity s. Uselessness; silliness; ineffectualness.
Inutil'ity s. Uselessness.
Civil'ity s. Quality of being civil; courtesy.
Incivil'ity s. Rudeness; an act of rudeness; quality of being uncivil.
Servil'ity s. Condition of a slave; obsequiousness; slavish deference.
Exil'ity s. Thinness; tenuity, subtlety.
Flexil'ity s. Flexibility; suppleness.
Tranquil'lity s. Quality or state of being tranquil.
Jol'lity s. Quality of being jolly; merriment, gaiety.
Nul'lity s. State or quality of being null and void; a nonentity; an invalid act, etc.
Pol'ity s. Form, system, or method of civil government; constitution.
Frivol'ity s. Triflingness, levity, folly.
Credu'lity s. Disposition to believe on little evidence; gullibility.
Incredu'lity s. Quality of being incredulous; scepticism.
Sedu'lity s. Quality of being sedulous.
Garru'lity s. Loquacity; wearisome chattering.
Mi'ty a. Infested with mites (of cheese).
Am'ity s. Friendship.
Calam'ity s. A mishap, disaster, great misfortune.
Extrem'ity s. The utmost point or limit; highest degree; greatest need, peril, etc.
Dim'ity s. A thick cotton fabric.
Sublim'ity s. Sublimeness.
Longanim'ity s. Long-suffering; forbearance.
Pusillanim'ity s. Meanness of spirit; cowardice.
Magnanim'ity s. Quality of being magnanimous.
Unanim'ity s. State or quality of being unanimous; agreement.
Equanim'ity s. Uniform disposition or temper; coolness, evenness.
Parvanim'ity s. Mean-spiritedness.
Intim'ity s. Quality of being intimate; privacy.
Proxim'ity s. State of being near in time, place, etc.; immediate nearness.
En'mity s. Quality of being an enemy; hostility.
Com'ity s. Affability, good breeding; courtesy of intercourse.
Infirm'ity s. State of being infirm; weakness; foible; disease.
Deform'ity s. State of being deformed; a disfigurement; a malformation.
Uniform'ity s. Quality or state of being uniform; consistency.
Multiform'ity s. Diversity of forms.
Conform'ity s. Resemblance; agreement, congruity; act of conforming to the Church of England.
Nonconform'ity s. Refusal to conform or unite with the Established Church.
Abnor'mity s. Something abnormal or outrageous.
Enor'mity s. State of being or that which is monstrous or outrageous; atrocious wickedness.
Pseudonym'ity s. Use of a pseudonym.
Anonym'ity s. State of being anonymous.
Synonym'ity s. Quality or state of being synonymous.
Urban'ity s. Quality of being urbane; suavity, affability.
Mundan'ity s. Mundaneness.
Profan'ity s. Quality of being profane; use of profane language; blasphemy.
Christian'ity s. The doctrines of Christ; faith in Him; the religion of Christians.
Imman'ity s. Monstrosity; atrocity.
German'ity s. German characteristics.
Human'ity s. The human race; quality of being human or humane; tenderness.
Inhuman'ity s. Quality of being inhuman; barbarity.
Inan'ity s. Quality of being inane; mental vacuity; foolishness.
San'ity s. Mental soundness; state of being sane.
Insan'ity s. Madness; lunacy.
Van'ity s. Quality or state of being vain; ostentation; worthlessness; a trifle; desire of admiration.
Obscen'ity s. State or quality of being obscene; lewdness; impurity.
Len'ity s. Gentleness; mildness; mercy.
Ame'nity s. Agreeableness in situation, etc.; pleasantness.
Seren'ity s. Peace; calmness, especially of mind.
Dig'nity s. Worthiness; elevation of rank; stateliness.
Indig'nity s. An insult, affront; an outrage.
Malig'nity s. Evil disposition; malice; spite.
Benig'nity s. Kindly feeling; favour bestowed.
Vicin'ity s. Neighbourhood; proximity.
Honorificabilitudin'ity s. State of being honourable.
Affin'ity s. Conformity; relationship by marriage, or between species.
Infin'ity s. Unlimited extent of time, space, or quantity; indefinite number; infinitude.
Confin'ity s. Nearness, contiguity.
Viragin'ity s. Characteristics, etc., of a virago.
Virgin'ity s. Maidenhood; state or quality of being a virgin.
Salin'ity s. Saltness; quantity or degree of this.
Felin'ity s. State of being feline or cat-like.
Masculin'ity s. State or quality of being masculine.
Femin'ity s. Femininity.
Feminin'ity s. Feminineness; manners becoming a woman.
Asinin'ity s. Obstinate stupidity.
Trin'ity s. The union of three persons in one God.
Latin'ity s. Purity of Latin style or idiom.
Consanguin'ity s. (*Consanguineous*).
Exsanguin'ity s. Destitution of blood.
Divin'ity s. God; a god; state of being divine; theology.
Indem'nity s. Exemption from loss, etc.; security; compensation.
Solem'nity s. Gravity; steady or affected seriousness; a rite, ceremony.
Concin'nity s. Elegance, neatness, especially of literary style.
Moder'nity s. Modernness; something modern.
Mater'nity s. Motherhood; motherliness.
Pater'nity s. Relation of a father to his children; fatherhood; origination.

Frater'nity s. State of a brother; brotherliness; a brotherhood.
Confrater'nity s. A brotherhood; especially for religious purposes.
Quater'nity s. Union of four in one; a group of four; state of being or containing four.
Eter'nity s. Condition or quality of being eternal; everlasting continuance.
Coeter'nity s. Equal eternity with another.
Sempiter'nity s. Future duration without end.
Tacitur'nity s. Habitual silence, reserve, or moodiness.
Diutur'nity s. Long duration.
U'nity s. State of being one or uniform; concord; agreement; a definite quantity taken as 1.
Triu'nity s. State or quality of being triune.
Immu'nity s. Exemption from a charge, tax, etc.; freedom; security against or freedom from risk of infection.
Commu'nity s. A body of persons having common rights, interests, etc.; the public; common possession; fellowship.
Intercommu'nity s. Mutual community; mutual freedom, as of religion.
Impu'nity s. Freedom from injury or loss.
Disu'nity s. State of separation.
Importu'nity s. Quality of being importunate; pertinacious solicitation.
Opportu'nity s. Fit time or place; a chance.
Inopportu'nity s. (*Inopportune*).
Dacoit'y s. The practices of dacoits.
Capernoi'ty a. (*Scot.*) Daft, crack-brained.
Hoi'ty-toi'ty int. Exclamation of surprise or contempt. a. Haughty; flighty. s. A frolic.
Pit'y s. Feeling of compassion; sympathy with misery; cause of grief; thing to be regretted. v.t. To feel grief for, to sympathize with. v.i. To be compassionate.
Barbar'ity s. Manners of a barbarian; savageness.
Solidar'ity s. Fellowship; consolidation of interests, etc.
Rectilinear'ity s. State or quality of being rectilinear.
Vagar'ity s. State or quality of being vagarious.
Vulgar'ity s. Quality of being vulgar; grossness of manners, etc.
Char'ity s. Benevolence, liberality, alms; an institution dispensing alms; universal love.
Familiar'ity s. State of being familiar; freedom from constraint; intimacy.
Peculiar'ity s. Quality of being peculiar; something peculiar to a thing, person, etc.; appropriateness.
Curviliniar'ity s. (*Curvilinear*).
Clar'ity s. Clearness.
Hilar'ity s. Mirth, cheerfulness, gaiety.
Similar'ity s. State of being similar; resemblance.
Dissimilar'ity s. Unlikeness; want of resemblance.
Pupilar'ity s. Pupillage.
Capillar'ity s. Action of a liquid in contact with a surface.
Polar'ity s. State of being polar; tendency to the pole; polarization.
Vernacular'ity s. State of being vernacular; a vernacularism.
Oracular'ity s. State or quality of being oracular.
Molecular'ity s. Quality of being molecular.
Orbicular'ity s. State or quality of being globular.
Perpendicular'ity s. State of being perpendicular.
Particular'ity s. Quality of being particular; distinctiveness; that which is particular.
Jocular'ity s. Quality of being jocular; merriment.
Monocular'ity s. State or quality of being monocular.
Circular'ity s. State of being circular.
Vascular'ity s. State or quality of being vascular.
Muscular'ity s. State or quality of being muscular
Regular'ity s. Condition or quality of being regular; method.
Irregular'ity s. Quality of being irregular; want of regularity; immoral behaviour.
Angular'ity s. State of being angular.
Triangular'ity s. State of being triangular.
Rectangular'ity s. State or quality of being rectangular.
Singular'ity s. State of being singular; distinguishing characteristic; oddity.
Granular'ity s. State of being granular.
Popular'ity s. Condition of being prevalent or generally liked.
Insular'ity s. Condition of being insular.
Peninsular'ity s. State of being a peninsula or peninsular.
Par'ity s. Equality; state of being equivalent; analogy.
Omnipar'ity s. General equality.
Fissipar'ity s. Quality of being fissiparous.
Multipar'ity s. State or quality of being multiparous.
Vivipar'ity s. Quality of being viviparous.
Ovipar'ity s. Condition of being oviparous.
Impar'ity s. Inequality; disproportion; oddness.
Dispar'ity s. Difference in age, degree, condition, etc.; inequality.
Rar'ity s. Quality or state of being rare; that which is rare, a curiosity; tenuity.
Mulie'brity s. Womanhood; effeminacy; softness.
Celeb'rity s. Renown, fame; a person of distinction.
Equilib'rity s. State of being equally balanced.
Salu'brity s. Quality of being salubrious; wholesomeness.
Insalu'brity s. State or quality of being insalubrious.
Alac'rity s. Promptitude; cheerful readiness.
Medioc'rity s. State of being mediocre; an undistinguished person.
Sincer'ity s. State or quality of being sincere; honesty.
Insincer'ity s. Deceitfulness; quality of being insincere.
Celer'ity s. Swiftness, speed.
Temer'ity s. Rashness; audacity.
Asper'ity s. Roughness; harshness in taste, manner, etc.
Prosper'ity s. Successful progress or state; well-being.
Poster'ity s. Offspring; succeeding generations.
Auster'ity s. Severity of manners; rigour.
Dexter'ity s. Adroitness, expertness; tact.
Ver'ity s. Truth; a true assertion.
Sever'ity s. Quality of being severe; austerity; exactness; cruel treatment; extreme coldness.
Integ'rity s. Probity; uprightness; entirely.
Jequir'ity s. A tropical twining shrub having brightly-coloured seeds.
Author'ity s. Rightful power; person exercising this; influence of character, etc.; testimony; precedent; one who can finally settle a question.
Senior'ity s. Quality of being senior; priority, superiority.

Junior'ity s. State of being junior.
Inferior'ity s. State or quality of being inferior.
Superior'ity s. State or quality of being superior; pre-eminence; advantage.
Anterior'ity s. (*Anterior*).
Posterior'ity s. State of being later, subsequent, or behind.
Exterior'ity s. Quality or character of being exterior.
Prior'ity s. State of being antecedent; precedence; pre-eminence.
Aprior'ity s. (*A priori*).
Major'ity s. The greater part; excess of one number over another; full age; majorate.
Minor'ity s. The smaller number, number less than half; state of being a minor.
Sonor'ity s. Quality or state of being sonorous.
Soror'ity s. A sisterhood.
Lithot'rity s. Lithotripsy.
Secur'ity s. State of being or feeling secure; protection; confidence; a guarantee; a bond, stock-certificate, etc.
Insecur'ity s. State of being insecure; want of security.
Obscur'ity s. State or quality of being obscure; darkness.
Pur'ity s. Condition of being pure; cleanness, innocence, chastity.
Impur'ity s. State or quality of being impure; obscenity.
Matur'ity s. State of being mature; ripeness.
Prematur'ity s. Prematureness.
Immatur'ity s. State of being immature.
Futur'ity s. State of being future; time to come; eternity.
Obe'sity s. Corpulence.
Fal'sity s. Quality of being false; a falsehood; that which is false.
Den'sity s. Denseness; state or quality of being compact; stupidity.
Immen'sity s. Vastness in extent or bulk; unlimited extension.
Propen'sity s. Natural inclination; tendency.
Ten'sity s. State or quality of being tense.
Inten'sity s. State of being intense; extreme degree; amount of energy.
-osity suff. Forming nouns from adjectives in *-ose* and *-ous*.
Gibbos'ity s. State of being gibbous or humped.
Globos'ity s. Quality of being globose or spherical.
Verbos'ity s. Quality of being verbose; prolixity.
Morbos'ity s. State of being morbid or diseased.
Bellicos'ity s. Quarrelsomeness; inclination to fight.
Varicos'ity s. State of being varicose; a varix.
Jocos'ity s. Facetiousness; a jocose act or saying.
Hircos'ity s. Goatishness.
Viscos'ity s. Stickiness, state of being viscous; internal friction in a fluid.
Muscos'ity s. Mossiness.
Mucos'ity s. State or quality of being mucous.
Nodos'ity s. Knottiness; knobbiness.
Vitreos'ity s. State or quality of being vitreous; glassiness.
Fungos'ity s. State or quality of being fungoid.
Rugos'ity s. State of being creased or wrinkled.
Scirrhos'ity s. A morbid induration.
Specios'ity s. State or condition of being specious.
Precios'ity s. Over-refinement of style; affected delicacy.
Grandios'ity s. Quality of being grandiose; a bombastic style or manner.
Religios'ity s. Religious sentimentality.
Litigios'ity s. Quality or state of being litigious.
Impecunios'ity s. State of being void of money or hard up.
Carios'ity s. Caries.
Ebrios'ity s. Habitual drunkenness; exhilaration.
Curios'ity s. Inquisitiveness; a rarity, strange thing.
Furios'ity s. State, condition, or quality of being furious.
Pilos'ity s. Hairiness.
Callos'ity s. A hard, thickened portion of skin.
Villos'ity s. State of being villous; a hair-like coating on plants.
Fabulos'ity s. Fictitiousness.
Nebulos'ity s. State or quality of being nebulous.
Gulos'ity s. Gluttony.
Rugulos'ity s. State of being finely creased.
Cellulos'ity s. (*Cellulous*).
Scrupulos'ity s. Scrupulousness.
Animos'ity s. Enmity, malignity.
Gummos'ity s. Gummy quality or state.
Fumos'ity s. Tendency to give off fumes; fumes emitted.
Venos'ity s. Local excess or deficient aeration of venous blood.
Fuliginos'ity s. State or quality of being sooty, smoky, etc.
Luminos'ity s. State or quality of being luminous; clearness.
Voluminos'ity s. Voluminousness.
Spinos'ity s. State or quality of being spinose or spinous.
Glutinos'ity s. Quality or state of being glutinous.
Vinos'ity s. Quality of being vinous.
Pompos'ity s. Quality of being pompous.
Tenebros'ity s. Darkness; gloom.
Tuberos'ity s. State of being tuberous; a knob on a bone.
Ponderos'ity s. State of being ponderous; heaviness; gravity.
Generos'ity s. Liberality, munificence; nobleness of mind.
Seros'ity s. Quality of being serous; a watery animal fluid.
Poros'ity s. Quality or state of being porous.
Vaporos'ity s. State of being vaporous.
Ventros'ity s. Corpulence.
Monstros'ity s. Quality of being monstrous; that which is monstrous.
Sinuos'ity s. Quality of being sinuous; a series of curves.
Aquos'ity s. Wateriness.
Anfractuos'ity s. A winding channel or convolution.
Unctuos'ity s. Unctuousness.
Infructuos'ity s. State or quality of being unfruitful.
Impetuos'ity s. Quality of being impetuous; vehemence; ardour.
Virtuos'ity s. Characteristics, etc., of virtuosos.
Tortuos'ity s. State or quality of being tortuous.
Flexuos'ity s. State of being serpentine or having windings.
Nivos'ity s. Snowiness.
Spars'ity s. Sparseness; scarcity.
Var'sity s. (*Slang*) University.
Adver'sity s. Misfortune, distress, affliction.
Diver'sity s. State of difference; unlikeness; variety.
Univer'sity s. An assemblage of colleges having power to confer degrees.
Perver'sity s. State of being perverse.
Necess'ity s. Compulsion; need; what is quite essential; poverty.
Sanc'tity s. State or quality of being holy; inviolability.
Sacrosanc'tity s. State of being sacrosanct.

Quan'tity s. Property of being measurable or capable of alteration in size, bulk, etc.; weight, large amount; metrical value of syllables.
En'tity s. A real being; essence; existence.
Iden'tity s. Sameness; not diversity; individuality.
Nonen'tity s. Non-existence; an imaginary or unimportant person or thing.
Chas'tity s. Purity; quality of being chaste.
Acu'ity s. Sharpness, especially of wit.
Vacu'ity s. Quality or state of being vacuous; emptiness; unoccupied space.
Conspicu'ity s. (*Conspicuous*).
Perspicu'ity s. Quality of being perspicuous; plainness, distinctness.
Promiscu'ity s. Mixture of kinds or classes; communal marriage.
Assidu'ity s. Close application; diligence.
Ambigu'ity s. Doubtfulness; equivocation.
Contigu'ity s. Contact, proximity.
Exigu'ity s. Scantiness.
Superflu'ity s. An unnecessary quantity; superabundance.
Ingenu'ity s. Skill in contrivance, power of invention; cleverness.
Tenu'ity s. Thinness; meagreness.
Continu'ity s. State of being continuous; uninterrupted connexion.
Discontinu'ity s. Want of continuity or cohesion.
Annu'ity s. A sum of money payable yearly in return for a single payment.
Eq'uity s. Justice, fairness; a system of law supplementing statute law.
Ineq'uity s. Injustice; unfairness.
Ubiq'uity s. Omnipresence.
Obliq'uity s. State of being oblique, a moral twist; deviation from rectitude.
Iniq'uity s. Injustice; crime; wickedness.
Antiq'uity s. Past times; peoples, records, relics, etc., of the past.
Propin'quity s. Proximity; nearness.
Appropin'quity s. Nearness.
Fruit'y a. Like fruit ; tasting of the grape.
Congru'ity s. Suitableness, accordance, consistency.
Incongru'ity s. Unsuitableness of one thing to another.
Fatu'ity s. Stupidity, foolishness; imbecility.
Gratu'ity s. A present, free gift; recompense; a bounty.
Perpetu'ity s. Endless duration; quality or state of being, or something that is, perpetual.
Fortu'ity s. A chance occurrence; an accident; state of being fortuitous.
Cav'ity s. A hollow space or part.
Concav'ity s. Internal surface of a hollow; a hollow.
Grav'ity s. Heaviness; importance; solemnity; tendency to gravitate.
Prav'ity s. Deterioration; moral corruption or perversion.
Deprav'ity s. State of corruption, profligacy, degeneracy.
Suav'ity (swăv-) s. Agreeableness; quality of being suave.
Longev'ity s. Great length of life.
Lev'ity s. Lightness; want of seriousness.
Brev'ity s. Shortness, conciseness.
Accliv'ity s. A steep ascent.
Decliv'ity s. A slope or inclination downward.
Procliv'ity s. Inclination, propensity; readiness.
Priv'ity s. Private knowledge; joint knowledge of a private concern; privacy.
Passiv'ity s. Quality or state of being passive; inactivity; submissiveness.
Impassiv'ity s. State or quality of being impassive.
Negativ'ity s. Negativeness; self-denial.
Relativ'ity s. State of being relative.
Correlativ'ity s. (*Correlative*).
Nativ'ity s. Time, place, or manner of birth.
Activ'ity s. State of being active; agility.
Reactiv'ity s. Property of reaction; state of being reactive.
Inactiv'ity s. Inertness; want of energy; slothfulness.
Retroactiv'ity s. (*Retroaction*).
Infectiv'ity s. Infectiousness; power to infect.
Objectiv'ity s. Objectiveness.
Subjectiv'ity s. Subjectiveness; that which is treated subjectively.
Collectiv'ity s. (*Collective*).
Inductiv'ity s. Capacity for electrical induction.
Conductiv'ity s. Quality or power of conducting (heat, etc.).
Productiv'ity s. Productiveness.
Reproductiv'ity s. Reproductiveness.
Sensitiv'ity s. State of being sensitive.
Positiv'ity s. Positiveness.
Motiv'ity s. Power of moving; available energy.
Locomotiv'ity s. Power of changing place.
Captiv'ity s. State of being a prisoner; subjection.
Deceptiv'ity s. (*Deceptive*).
Receptiv'ity s. Quality of being receptive.
Perceptiv'ity s. Power of perception; quality or state of being perceptive.
Susceptiv'ity s. Quality of being susceptive.
Festiv'ity s. A festival; festive or social joy.
Cal'vity s. Baldness.
Cur'vity s. Curvedness.
Recur'vity s. Recurvation.
Incur'vity s. State of being incurved; curvature.
Lax'ity s. State or quality of being lax; want of exactness or strictness; looseness.
Complex'ity s. Intricacy.
Perplex'ity s. State of being perplexed; bewilderment; intricacy.
Convex'ity s. Curvature; state of being convex.
Fix'ity s. Fixedness; coherence of parts.
Prolix'ity s. Quality of being prolix; minute detail.
Fe'alty s. Fidelity; loyalty to a lord.
Re'alty s. Real property (in law).
Sher'iffalty s. Office or jurisdiction of a sheriff.
Mal'ty a. Resembling malt.
Pen'alty s. Punishment; forfeit for non fulfilment; sum forfeited; a fine.
Com'monalty s. The common people; mankind; a community.
Per'sonalty s. Personal property or estate.
Sev'eralty s. Exclusive tenure or ownership.
Ad'miralty s. The governing body of a navy naval superiority, sea-power.
Tem'poralty s. The laity; a temporality.
Mayor'alty s. Office or term of office of a mayor.
Salt'y a. Saltish; tasting of salt.
Cas'ualty s. An accident, especially when fatal or injurious; a killed or wounded man in war.
Shriev'alty s. Office, jurisdiction, or tenure of office of a sheriff.
Loy'alty s. State or quality of being loyal; fidelity; constancy.
Disloy'alty s. Want of loyalty or fidelity
Roy'alty s. Office or dignity of a monarch; sovereignty; kingliness; a royal person; a right of the sovereign; share of profits accruing to a patentee, author, landowner at a mine, etc.
Viceroy'alty s. Dignity, office, jurisdiction, etc. of a viceroy.

Nov'elty s. Newness, freshness; a new or strange thing.
Cru'elty s. Cruel disposition; inhumanity; a cruel act.
Frail'ty s. Frailness; infirmity; failing, foible.
Subt'ilty (sŭt'-) s. Subtility.
Guilt'y a. Chargeable with, pertaining to, or indicating guilt; criminal.
Fault'y a. Defective; imperfect; blameable.
Vault'y a. Vaulted, arched.
Fac'ulty s. Ability; graduates in a University; body of members of a profession.
Dif'ficulty s. State of being not easy to do; a thing hard to accomplish; obstacle, objection; perplexity.
Can'ty a. (*Scot.*) Lively, cheerful.
Scan'ty a. Insufficient; not abundant; niggardly; scarce.
Ser'jeanty (sar'-) s. An ancient form of feudal tenure.
Chan'ty s. (*Chantey*).
Shan'ty s. A hovel, hut; a chantey.
Guar'anty s. Act of guaranteeing; that which guarantees, or on which a guarantee is based; a guarantee.
War'ranty s. A warrant, authorization.
Sov'ranty s. Sovereignty.
Plen'ty s. Full supply; copiousness; abundance.
Fru'menty s. A dish made of wheat boiled in milk and seasoned.
Sev'enty s. Seven times ten; symbol representing this (70, lxx.). a. Amounting to 7 times 10.
Twen'ty a. and s. Twice ten; this number; 20, xx.
Sov'ereignty s. Dominion; exercise of or right to exercise supreme power.
Dain'ty a. Toothsome; elegant in form, breeding, etc.; over-nice; requiring dainties. s. A delicacy, something nice.
Su'zerainty s. Dominion or authority of a suzerain.
Cer'tainty s. Quality or condition of being certain; a sure fact.
Uncer'tainty s. Dubiety.
Shin'ty s. A game resembling hockey.
Flint'y a. Like or abounding in flint; obdurate, pitiless.
Tint'y a. Unequally tinted.
Aunt'y s. Aunt.
Jaun'ty a. Sprightly; perky.
Flaun'ty a. Flaunting; ostentatious.
Boun'ty s. Liberality, munificence; a premium or subsidy.
Coun'ty s. A shire, a particular portion of a state; an administrative division.
Vis'county (vī'-) s. Viscountcy.
Runt'y a. Dwarfish.
Mag'goty a. Infested with maggots; capricious.
Boot'y s. Plunder, spoil.
Root'y a. Full of roots.
Soot'y a. Covered with or producing soot; black, dingy.
Car'roty a. Reddish-yellow; red-haired.
Emp'ty a. Void, vacant; unfurnished; lacking sense; destitute of reality. v.t. and i. To deprive of contents, exhaust; to become empty.
Hump'ty-dump'ty a. Short and squat. s. A short, thick-set person.
Heart'y a. Sincere, cordial, good-natured, healthy.
Clar'ty a. (*Scot.*) Muddy, dirty.

Par'ty s. A body of persons; a faction, side; a friendly or convivial gathering; a military detachment, one of two litigants; an individual. a. Pertaining to a party; divided (of heraldic shields, etc.).
Wart'y a. Having or resembling warts.
Lib'erty s. Quality or state of being free; freedom; privilege; licence; outer districts of a city.
Pu'berty s. The age of sex maturity.
Chert'y a. (*Chert*).
Cham'perty s. An illegal bargain to share proceeds from a legal action if successful.
Prop'erty s. A peculiar quality, attribute, or possession; possessions; ownership; stage requisite.
Pov'erty s. State of being poor; indigence; inferiority.
Dir'ty a. Soiled with or full of dirt; foul, filthy; mean; rainy, squally. v.t. To sully, soil.
Thir'ty a. Consisting of three times ten. s. three times ten, 30, xxx.
Flir'ty a. With the manner of a flirt.
For'ty a. and n. Twice twenty; 40.
Ror'ty a. (*Slang*) Fine, splendid.
Sty s. A pen for swine; a dirty hovel; swelling on eyelid.
Yeast'y a. Containing or resembling yeast; frothy; unsubstantial.
Ha'sty a. Hurried, quick; rash, passionate.
Neoplas'ty s. Restoration of a part by granulation, adhesive inflammation, etc.
Os'teoplasty s. Transplantation of bone.
Chil'oplasty s. Operation of making an artificial lip.
Galvanoplas'ty s. Electrotypy.
Rhi'noplasty s. Operation of forming an artificial nose.
Heteroplas'ty s. Grafting of skin from one individual on to another.
Nas'ty a. Dirty, filthy; disgusting; vile; indecent; annoying, awkward.
Dyn'asty s. A succession of sovereigns of the same family.
Pa'sty a. Pertaining to or like paste.
Pas'ty s. A small meat-pie.
Ta'sty a. Savoury; smart.
Vast'y a. Vast; very spacious.
Mod'esty s. Quality of being modest; humility; purity of manners.
Immod'esty s. Want of modesty; indecency.
Maj'esty s. Dignity; grandeur; a royal title.
Am'nesty s. A general pardon.
Hon'esty s. Quality or state of being honest; sincerity; a cruciferous garden-plant.
Dishon'esty s. Want of honesty; fraud, violation of trust, etc.
Tes'ty a. Irritable; petulant.
Trav'esty s. A burlesque imitation. v.t. To burlesque, parody.
Mist'y a. Overspread with or characterized by mist, dim, vague.
Sac'risty s. Apartment in a church where sacred utensils, etc., are kept.
Frost'y a. Producing, attended by, or injured by frost; covered with rime; chill, frigid.
Thirs'ty a. Feeling or exciting thirst; parched.
Blood'thirsty a. Exceedingly cruel; eager to shed blood.
Dust'y a. Covered with or full of dust; like dust.

Theopneu'sty (-nū'sti) s. Divine inspiration.
Fust'y a. Mouldy; ill-smelling.
Gust'y a. Breezy; stormy.
Lust'y a. Full of health and vigour.
Must'y a. Mouldy; spoiled with damp.
Rust'y a. Covered or affected with rust; rust-coloured; antiquated; impaired by disuse, etc.
Crust'y a. Resembling crust; surly.
Trust'y a. Reliable; worthy of trust; firm.
Frows'ty a. Stuffy, unventilated.
Scat'ty a. Showery.
Fat'ty a. Consisting of or like fat; greasy; adipose. s. (*Slang*) A fat person.
Chat'ty a. Conversing freely and lightly; (*slang*) lousy.
Nat'ty a. Neat, spruce.
Pat'ty s. A small pie or pasty.
Chupat'ty s. Native Indian unleavened bread.
Rat'ty a. (*Slang*) Ill-tempered, cross.
Bet'ty s. (*Slang*) A jemmy; a man-housewife.
Jet'ty s. A mole or pier projecting into the sea. a. Densely black.
Pet'ty a. Trifling; insignificant; frivolous.
Pret'ty a. Pleasing to the sight; comely; neatly arranged or done; affectedly nice; petty. adv. Tolerably, moderately.
Dit'ty s. A short poem for singing.
Chit'ty s. A note, a servant's reference.
Kit'ty s. Pet name for a kitten; the pool at games.
Nit'ty a. Infested with nits.
Wit'ty a. Possessing wit; facetious, smart.
Dot'ty a. (*Slang*) Foolish, crazy.
Knot'ty a. Full of knots; rough; perplexing.
Snot'ty a. Dirty with snot; mean. s. (*Slang*) A midshipman.
Spot'ty a. Full of or discoloured with spots.
Tot'ty s. (*Tottie*).
But'ty s. A partner; a foreman; a middleman at a mine.
Cut'ty a. Short; hasty. s. A short clay pipe.
Gut'ty a. Corpulent. s. A gutta-percha golf-ball.
Smut'ty a. Soiled with smut; affected with mildew; obscene.
Nut'ty a. Abounding in or tasting like nuts.
Put'ty s. Kind of cement used by glaziers. v.t. To fill up or stick with this.
Rut'ty a. Marked with ruts; lustful.
Tut'ty s. An impure oxide of zinc.
Beau'ty s. Harmony of parts, loveliness, grace; a beautiful woman.
Du'ty s. That which must or should be done; obligation; respect; an impost or tax.
Flu'ty a. Having the tone of a flute.
Gout'y a. Affected with or pertaining to gout; swollen.
Snout'y a. Resembling a snout.
Grout'y a. Muddy, dirty; sullen.
Trout'y a. Abounding in or tasting like trout.
Dep'uty s. A representative, a substitute; member of certain legislative assemblies.
Six'ty a. Six times ten. s. Sum of these; its symbol (60, lx.).
Planx'ty s. A lively Irish melody for the harp.
Buy v.t. To acquire by purchase.
Guy s. A rope for steadying anything; a fantastic effigy or person; a dowdy; (*slang*) a surreptitious flight. v.t. To guide or steady with guys; to display in effigy; to ridicule. v.i. (*slang*) To decamp.
Pla'guy a. Vexatious, troublesome.
Cliqu'y a. (*Clique*).
Ob'loquy s. Reproachful language; blame; slander.
Solil'oquy s. A talking to oneself; a monologue.
Somnil'oquy s. Act or habit of talking in one's sleep.
Ventril'oquy s. Ventriloquism.
Col'loquy s. Conversation; dialogue; conference.
Ca'vy s. A S. American rodent; a guinea-pig.
Heav'y a. Weighty; burdensome; not easily digested; sad; dense; forcible.
Lea'vy a. Leafy.
Na'vy s. The warships, or the shipping, of a nation; its personnel, etc.; a fleet.
Gra'vy s. The juice of meat after cooking.
Wa'vy a. Rising in waves, undulating; full of waves.
Bev'y s. A flock of birds; an assemblage, especially of ladies.
Chev'y v.t. To chase, hunt. v.i. To scamper about.
Lev'y v.t. To raise, to impose, to collect; to begin (war). s. Act of raising money or men; troops or taxes raised.
Replev'y v.t. To take back by writ goods wrongfully taken.
I'vy s. An evergreen climbing plant.
Chiv'y v.t. and i. (*Chevy*).
Priv'y a. Private, assigned to private uses; secretly cognizant. s. A latrine, closet.
Tantiv'y s. A huntsman's cry; a furious gallop. adv. Swiftly.
Shel'vy a. Full of rocks or shoals; overhanging.
En'vy v.t. To feel jealous of, regard with discontent; to covet, begrudge. v.i. To have envious feelings. s. Pain or mortification excited by another's superiority or success; malice; object of envy.
Ancho'vy s. A small fish of the herring family.
Groov'y a. Having grooves or furrows.
Gro'vy a. Furnished with groves.
Ner'vy a. Muscular, sinewy; nervous; (*slang*) confident, cool.
Scur'vy s. A disease due to insufficient vegetable food. a. Mean, shabby, contemptible; scurfy.
Top'sy-tur'vy a. and adv. Upside down, disordered.
Nav'vy s. An unskilled labourer on railways, etc.
Sav'vy s. (*Slang*) Knowingness, understanding. v.t. and i. To understand, grasp.
Thaw'y a. Thawing.
Flaw'y a. Defective; gusty.
Straw'y a. Made of, consisting of, or like straw.
Dew'y a. Pertaining to dew; spread with dew.
Mil'dewy a. Tainted with mildew.
Thew'y a. Sinewy; vigorous.
View'y a. Faddy; visionary.
Sin'ewy (-ū-i) a. Pertaining to, consisting of or resembling sinews; strong, vigorous.
Mead'owy a. Pertaining to, resembling, or consisting of meadows.
Shad'owy a. Abounding in shadows; faint.
Show'y (shō'i) a. Gaudy; ostentatious.
Blow'y a. Windy.
Sal'lowy a. Abounding with or resembling sallows

Tal'lowy a. Containing or resembling tallow.
Mel'lowy a. Soft; mellow.
Yel'lowy a. Somewhat yellow.
Bil'lowy a. Rising and falling like billows.
Pil'lowy a. Like a pillow.
Wil'lowy a. Abounding in willows; lissome, graceful.
Snow'y a. White-like, abounding in, or covered with snow; pure.
Ar'rowy a. Like an arrow or the flight of an arrow; darting, piercing.
Fur'rowy a. Marked with or full of furrows.
Tow'y (tō'-) a. Resembling tow.
Gal'axy s. The Milky Way; a gathering of notables.
Flax'y a. Like flax; silky; light yellow.
Atarax'y s. Indifference, stoicism.
Brax'y s. A disease of sheep.
Or'thopraxy s. Orthodox behaviour; correct practice.
Tax'y v.i. To travel along the ground (of aircraft).
Atax'y s. Irregularity of bodily functions.
Zootax'y s. The classification of animals.
Heterotax'y s. Abnormal arrangement of parts or organs.
Wax'y a. Pliable; resembling or coated with wax; (*slang*) cross.
Cachex'y s. Cachexia.
Kex'y a. Like kex.
Cat'aplexy s. Temporary paralysis in animals.
Ap'oplexy s. Sudden state of unconsciousness with loss of sensibility and power of motion due to disturbance in the brain.
Ap'yrexy s. Abatement of a fever.
Pix'y s. A fairy, elf, sprite.
Dox'y s. A sweetheart, mistress.
Or'thodoxy s. State of being orthodox; soundness of faith; acceptance of the generally held beliefs, especially in religion.
Het'erodoxy s. Heresy; doctrine or opinion contrary to that established.
Fox'y a. Pertaining to or like a fox; wily, sly; sour; stained with brownish spots.
Prox'y s. One deputed to act for another; document authorizing this.
Asphyx'y s. (*Asphyxia*).
Sleaz'y a. Flimsy, unsubstantial.
Ga'zy a. Given to gazing.
Ha'zy a. Misty, foggy; mentally obscure or confused.
La'zy a. Idle, sluggish; indolent; languid.
Gla'zy a. Like glaze.
Ma'zy a. Winding, intricate; perplexing; dizzy.
Cra'zy a. Broken down; shaky; half-witted.
Wheez'y a. Characterized by wheezing.
Sneez'y a. Causing or addicted to sneezing.
Breez'y a. Exposed to breezes; windy; jovial.
Si'zy a. Glutinous; adhesive; like-size.
Fren'zy s. Violent passion or agitation; distraction; madness.
Bronz'y a. Like or tinged with bronze.
Do'zy a. Drowsy; sluggish.
Ooz'y a. Containing or resembling ooze; exuding moisture.
Booz'y a. (*Slang*) Fuddled with drink.
Furz'y a. Covered with furze.
Gauz'y a. Like or thin as gauze.
Blowz'y a. Coarse; ruddy-faced.
Frow'zy a. Musty, stuffy; slovenly, unkempt.
Diz'zy a. Giddy; whirling; thoughtless. v.t. To make dizzy, confuse.
Fiz'zy a. Characterized by fizzing.
Friz'zy a. Frizzed; crisp and curly.
Tiz'zy s. (*Slang*) A sixpence.
Fuz'zy a. Like or covered with fuzz; blurred.
Huz'zy s. A hussy, a brazen, forward girl.
Muz'zy a. Muddled; dull; tipsy.
To'paz s. A translucent gem of various colours.
Fez s. A brimless Oriental cap.
Pince'-nez (-nā) s. Eye-glasses with a spring-clip for the nose.
O'yez int. The introductory call of a public crier, thrice repeated.
Biz s. (*Slang*) Business.
Ha'fiz s. A Moslem who knows the Koran by heart.
Phiz s. (*Slang*) The face, visage.
Whiz v.i. To hiss, as an arrow through the air; to hurtle. s. A hissing and humming sound.
Quiz s. A riddle, a jest; one who hoaxes or is liable to be hoaxed; an odd fellow. v.t. To puzzle; to ridicule; to peer at.
Coz s. Cousin.
Spitz s. A small Pomeranian dog.
Waltz s. A circular dance for two. v.i. To dance this.
Chintz s. A glazed calico printed with coloured patterns.
Wootz s. A fine E. Indian steel.
Quartz s. Crystallized silica; rock-crystal.
Jazz s. A boisterous rag-time dance. v.i. To dance this; to revel.
Fizz v.i. To make a hissing sound. s. Such a sound; (*slang*) champagne.
Frizz v.t. To curl, crisp, frizzle. s. A mass of curls.
Buzz v.i. To hum as bees. v.t. To whisper, rumour. s. The sound of bees, a confused humming noise.
Hum'buzz s. The cockchafer; apparatus to make a buzzing sound.
Fuzz v.i. To fly off in minute particles. s. Fluff; fuzziness.

AN INDEX TO RHYMES

INTRODUCTION

THE following Index to Rhymes has been compiled with the object of directing the consulter to all the accented rhymes in the English language. In the Dictionary itself words are grouped strictly in their reverse alphabetical order, words the terminations of which are identical to the eye, but by no means necessarily identical to the ear, coming together; the result being that many perfect rhymes (e.g. caste—fast, decks—vex, shoe—Jew) are separated by many pages and may possibly be overlooked.

The scheme adopted is a very simple one, and as it has been devised for the Rhymer and not for the Phonetician it makes no pretence to scientific accuracy. We have not attempted to lay down any laws as to what rhymes are allowable and what are not; but we have tried to make a full record of those that are actually used by poets of repute and of those which, by analogy, might be so used.

Rhyme is a very debatable subject, and it might be said of it as it has been said of a jest that, as often as not, its prosperity lies in the ears of him who hears it—if it were not for the fact that many words are pronounced differently, not only in different parts of the country, but also to accommodate them to their place in the sentence or to the emphasis or the exact shade of meaning they are to bear. There are those whose vocal organs seem to make it quite necessary for them to rhyme feature with teacher and verdure with urger; there are others whose auditory faculties have reached such a state of perfection that they refuse to admit the rhymeability of Scotch and watch, fork and pork, forth and north, mouth and south, cur and fir. For ourselves, we demur to allowing the feature and verdure examples—except in verse that is frankly of the "nonsense" variety—but, short of this, we have spread the net as widely as possible and have left the actual choice to the taste and fancy of the rhymer.

After all, rhyme is largely a matter of taste and fancy; when home—come, river—ever, love—move—grove—thereof, heaven—even, lost—most, one—alone, lover—over appear in the works of every poet and no serious results follow it is difficult to tell where to draw the line, Tennyson has Thames—acclaims, liar—fire; Browning—quite apart from his numerous humorous polysyllabic jingles—is notorious (suns—bronze—once, stood—subdued, weather—ether, amber—chamber); Wordsworth frequently rhymes creature with nature (but never with preacher !).

Yet, though such unequal yoke-fellows as these, to say nothing of fancies—pansies, boughs—house, strode—God, hears—stairs are allowed, woe betide the poet who, following the usage of nine out of ten English (as apart from Scotch) educated persons, ignores the r of morn and so makes the word serve as a rhyme to dawn, for he is branded as a barbarian and almost beyond the pale ! "To describe rhymes as higher—Thalia, or morning—dawning, as Cockney rhymes is foolish and inaccurate," says Professor Wyld.[1] "The former is made by Keats, the latter by so fastidious a poet and gentleman as Mr. Swinburne. This prejudice is gradually dying out among poets. If this or that poet still dislikes or avoids such rhymes, perfect though they be, according to normal educated English pronunciation, simply on account of the r in the spelling, that is his affair, and his readers need not complain. If they are objected to on the ground that the rhyme is not perfect, and that it is only in vulgar pronunciation that —r— is not heard in morn, etc., this is not consonant with fact."

In this matter of the loss, or partial loss, of the trilled r we have tried to suit all parties and so have made some differentiation between words with the sounds of aw,

[1] *History of Modern Colloquial English* (1920), ch. viii.

awr, and ŏr, but by means of a system of cross-referencing the reader is directed from one group to the other, while the warning " * " will show that in the opinion of some sauce has no business to be rhymed with course.

The Index, for reasons of convenient reference, not scientific accuracy, is divided into eighteen main divisions, each comprising the rhymes coming under the head of one or other of the commonly recognized vowel or diphthong sounds. The words given in the subdivisions are merely type-words and must not be taken to signify that every word in the main body of the Dictionary having the same termination as the type-word is necessarily a rhyme to that word. The Index is, as all indexes should be, a Guide, and its method of use is extremely simple. A rhyme to cheese, for instance, is required. The seeker may first have looked in the Dictionary itself and have found nothing to suit him; he then turns to the Index and finds that words rhyming on the long e are in Division VI; cheese has the z sound, so he turns to ēz (not ēs) at the end of that division and finds that besides the plurals of words ending in the ē sound there are six rhyming terminations, exclusive of Proper Names. If his mind does not at once jump to the required word he now turns to those parts of the Dictionary in which journalese, cerise, seize, etc., are to be found, and makes his selection. In this case we have supposed that the searcher has first turned to the main body of the Dictionary; but, until he knows the Index by heart, he will find it will save him time and trouble if he consults this section first.

It should be unnecessary to add that terminal pronunciations for which there is only one spelling (such as —abe, babe, and —èche, crèche) are not indexed.

TABLE OF DIVISIONS

Div.	I.	Accent on	ā	as in	lay, laid.
,,	II.	,,	aw	,,	law, laud.
,,	III.	,,	â	,,	laugh, last.
,,	IV.	,,	ă	,,	land.
,,	V.	,,	ä	,,	lair.
,,	VI.	,,	ē	,,	lea, league.
,,	VII.	,,	ĕ	,,	let.
,,	VIII.	,,	è	,,	lurk, jerk, bird.
,,	IX.	,,	ī	,,	lie, lyre.
,,	X.	,,	i	,,	lip.
,,	XI.	,,	ō	,,	load, slow.
,,	XII.	,,	ŏ	,,	lot.
,,	XIII.	,,	ōō	,,	loot.
,,	XIV.	,,	oo	,,	look.
,,	XV.	,,	ū	,,	lewd.
,,	XVI.	,,	ŭ	,,	luck.
,,	XVII.	,,	oi	,,	loin.
,,	XVIII.	,,	ou	,,	loud.

Consonants have their usual values, except that :—

hard c (as in cat)	is represented by		k
ch (,, catch)	,,	,,	tsh
soft g (,, ledge)	,,	,,	j
the th of bath	,,	,,	th
,, th ,, bathe	,,	,,	*th*
,, s ,, measure	,,	,,	zh
x	,,	,,	ks

* signifies that the word so marked is not a perfect rhyme to the type-word and is not recognized by some authorities.

† signifies that the word is a rhyme in one only of its two or more legitimate pronunciations.

INDEX

ÂRD.
(cp. âd.)
Prets. and past parts. of verbs in -âr : **bard** : Liskeard : Oudenarde.

ÂRF, see ÂF.

ÂRK.
Arc : plaque : barque : *Bach : tetrarch : ark : clerk.

ÂRM.
(cp. âm.)
Gendarme : **arm.**

ÂRS.
(cp. âs.)
Farce : sparse.

ÂRT.
Carte : Descartes : art : heart.

ÂS.
(cp. ârs.)
Maas : †alas : †pass.

ÂSH.
Moustache : *harsh.

ÂSK.
Masque : **ask.**

ÂST.
Prets. and past parts. of verbs in -âs : **caste** : **fast.**

ÂV.
†Suave : **halve** : *carve : †Slav.

ÂZ.
Words in -â and s : †vase : †Shiraz.

IV : ă.

ĂD.
Bad : **add** : plaid.

ĂDZ.
Words in -ăd and s : adze.

ĂF.
†Stafe : **giraffe** : gaff : †epitaph.

ĂFT, see ÂFT.

ĂK.
Zodiac : †claque : amphibrach : lakh : **yak** : **tack.**

ĂKS.
Words in -ăk and s : axe : tax.

ĂKT.
Prets. and past parts. of verbs in -ăk : **act.**

ĂLK.
Talc : catafalque.

ĂLKS.
Words in -ălk and s : calx.

ĂM.
Lamb : gramme : am : Balaam : diaphragm : drachm : lamm : damn.

ĂN.
Anne : **ban** : **Ann.**

ĂND.
Prets. and past parts. of verbs in -ăn : **and.**

ĂNG.
*Charabanc : harangue : meringue : **hang** : **Laing.**

ĂNK.
Franc : **frank.**

ĂNKS.
Words in -ănk and s : Bankes : **Manx.**

ĂNKT.
Prets. and past parts. of verbs in -ănk : sacrosanct.

ĂNL.
*Annal : **flannel** : Faneuil.

ĂNS.
Romance : manse.

ĂNT.
***Enceinte** : **Rembrandt** : **ant.**

ĂPS.
Words in ăp and s : apse : perhaps : schnapps.

ĂPT.
Prets. and past parts. of verbs in -ăp : **apt.**

ĂS.
Wrasse : **gas** : ass.

ĂSH.
Sabretache : **ash.**

ĂST.
(cp. âst.)
Prets. and past parts. of verbs in -ăs : †contrast.

ĂT.
Matte : Amurath : at : matt.

ĂTSH.
Attach : **match.**

ĂZ.
As : †**Shiraz** : **jazz.**

V : ā.

ĀR.
Beauclerc : ware : ere : gruyère : millionaire : parterre : Ayre : eyre : Beauclerk : bear : e'er : mal-de-mer : †prayer : air : heir : mayor : Herr : Ayr : chargé d'affaires.

ĀRD.
Prets. and past parts. of verbs in -ār : **laird.**

ĀRN.
†Epergne : **bairn.**

VI.

Ē.
*Many words ending in -cy, -ly, -ny, -ty, etc., are allowable : tea : minutiæ : Anglice : absentee : dominie : Legh : Leigh : bouilli : debris : jeu d'esprit : Chamounix : quay : key : Dupuy.

ĒA, see ĒR.

ĒB.
Glebe : **Antibes.**

ĒD.
Prets. and past parts. of many verbs in ē : bead : deed : Siegfried : †invalid : cede : Candide.

ĒF.
Teneriffe : **leaf** : **beef** : thief : Crieff : †feoff.

ĒG.
League : **fatigue** : Grieg.

ĒJ.
Siege : *prestige.

ĒK.
Chic : eke : antique : sheikh : Sikh : **beak** : Heidsieck : week : shriek.

ĒL.
Steele : Bastile : chenille : **Delisle** : **peal** : **eel** : Kiel : †alguazil.

ĒLD.
Prets. and past parts. of verbs in -ēl : unaneled : weald : field : Mathilde : Bamfylde.

ĒM.
Extreme : centime : beam : Eyam : deem : †harem.

ĒMZ.
Words in -ēm and s : Rheims : Wemyss.

ĒN.
Scene : marine : mesne : bean : **e'en** : **seen** : mien : chagrin.

ĒND.
Prets. and past parts. of verbs in -ēn : fiend.

ĒP.
Clepe : †grippe : heap : peep.

ĒPS.
Words in -ēp and s : †Pepys.

Ē R.

†Diarrhœa: †chorea: here: congé d'elire: near: beer: bier: weir: fakir.

Ē R D.

Prets. and past parts. of verbs in -ēr: beard: weird.

Ē S.

Peace: fleece: piece: Lucrece: police: crease: obese: geese: valise: pelisse: Rees: ambergris: Deslys.

Ē S H.

Nouveau riche: schottische: leash: Dalgleish: bakshish.

Ē S T.

Prets. and past parts. of verbs in -ēs: artiste: east: hartebeest: priest.

Ē T.

Athlete: suite: Lafitte: eat: beet: conceit: receipt.

Ē T H.

Heath: teeth: Keith.

Ē *T H.*

Sheathe: seethe: bequeath.

Ē T S H.

Each: beech: Leitch.

Ē V.

Heave: eve: reeve: grieve: †naive: perceive: recitative: Yves.

Ē Z.

Many words in -ē and s: ease: cheese: friese: journalese: cerise: breeze: seize: Decies: Caius (College): Leys.

VII: ĕ.

Ĕ B.

Ebb: web.

Ĕ D.

Prets. and past parts. of verbs taking -ed, when accented: head: redd: bed: said.

Ĕ F.

Deaf: chef: †feoff.

Ĕ F T.

†Feoffed: eft.

Ĕ G.

Legge: beg: egg: Greig.

Ĕ J.

Edge: allege.

Ĕ K.

Spec: cheque: Czech: Teufelsdröeckh: beck: trek.

Ĕ K S.

Words in -ĕk and s: sex.

Ĕ K S T.

Prets. and past parts. of verbs in -ĕks: next.

Ĕ K T.

Prets. and past parts. of verbs in -ĕk: affect: Utrecht.

Ĕ L.

Belle: hotel: *nonpareil: †pall mall: bell.

Ĕ L D.

Prets. and past parts. of verbs in -ĕl: held.

Ĕ L F.

Elf: Guelph.

Ĕ L M.

Realm: elm.

Ĕ M.

Hem: phlegm: condemn.

Ĕ M T.

Dreamt: *tempt.

Ĕ M Z.

Words in -ĕm and s: Thames.

Ĕ N.

Cayenne: men: *again: Valenciennes.

Ĕ N D.

Prets. and past parts. of verbs in -ĕn: end: friend: blende.

Ĕ N S.

Hence: dense: *rents: *Coblenz.

Ĕ N S T.

Prets. and past parts. of verbs in -ĕns: fornenst.

Ĕ N T.

Meant: cent.

Ĕ N Z.

Words in -ĕn and s: cleanse: lens.

Ĕ P.

Steppe: step.

Ĕ P T.

Prets. and past parts. of verbs in -ĕp: leapt: adept.

Ĕ S.

Coalesce: finesse: yes: chess: oyez.

Ĕ S K.

Burlesque: desk.

Ĕ S T.

Prets. and past parts. of verbs in -ĕs; 2nd pers. sing. pres. ind. of verbs; the superlative degree of adjectives and adverbs: geste: Pesth: breast: best.

Ĕ T.

†Ate: aigrette: debt: bet: Lett.

Ĕ T H.

Obsolete verbal termination, as wandereth: breath: twentieth.

Ĕ Z.

Says: fez.

VIII: ė.

Ė R.

Were: theatre: myrrh: aver: stir: *tailor: err: chirr: burr: *amateur: fur: *Scrymgeour: *honour: zephyr: *tic doloureux.

Ė R B.

Herb: curb.

Ė R D.

Prets. and past parts. of many verbs in -ėr: furred: heard: herd: bird: word: curd: Verde.

Ė R F.

Serf: surf.

Ė R G.

Exergue: berg: burg: Sedbergh: Burgh.

Ė R J.

Verge: dirge: urge: scourge.

Ė R K.

Circ: Burke: Bourke: jerque: cirque: jerk: dirk: work: lurk.

Ė R L.

Earle: merle: Kyrle: earl: querl: girl: †whorl: curl.

Ė R L D.

Prets. and past parts. of verbs in -ėrl: world.

Ė R M.

†Boehm: germ: firm: worm.

Ė R N.

†Epergne: Fearne: erne: Byrne: earn: fern: pirn: burn: adjourn.

Ė R N T.

Prets. and past parts. of many verbs in -ėrn: weren't.

Ė R P.

Earp: chirp: usurp.

Ė R P T.

Prets. and past parts. of verbs in -ėrp: excerpt.

Ė R S.

Coerce: hearse: verse: worse: curse.

Ė R S T.

Prets. and past parts. of many verbs in -ėrs: erst: first: worst: durst.

Ė R T.

Alert : dirt : wort : hurt.

Ė R T H.

Earth : perth : birth : worth : Gurth.

Ė R T S H.

Search : perch : birch : church.

Ė R V.

Nerve : curve : †Villeneuve.

Ė R Z.

Words in -ėr and s : *Chartreuse : furze : *Greuze.

IX.

Ī.

Tighe : die : †grisaille : dye : †heigh : high : assegai : alibi : Versailles : †Paraguay : cry : buy.

Ī B.

Tribe : gybe.

Ī D.

Allied : dyed : I'd : bide : ophecleide : Hyde.

Ī K.

Like : dyke : Van Dyck : Van Eyck.

Ī L.

Smile : †grisaille : isle : chyle : *vial : I'll : Argyll : *viol.

Ī L D.

Prets. and past parts. of verbs in -Īl : mild : childe.

Ī M.

Climb : time : thyme : †paradigm : I'm : Mannheim.

Ī N D.

Prets. and past parts. of verbs in -Īne : bind : wynd.

Ī N E.

†Charlemagne : brine : anodyne : Steyne : benign : Zollverein.

Ī R.

*Thalia : fire : lyre : *Uriah : *briar : *higher : *crier : *dyer : *Meyer.

Ī S.

Ice : syce : concise : gneiss.

Ī S T.

Prets. and past parts. of verbs in -Īs : Christ : †tryst.

Ī T.

Bite : acolyte : indict : height : night : Fahrenheit.

Ī *T H.*

Blithe : scythe : Blyth.

Ī Z.

Words in -Ī and s : advise : analyse : assize.

X : i.

I D.

Lydd : mid : Kyd.

I F.

Shorncliffe : cliff : if : glyph.

I F T.

Prets. and past parts. of verbs in -if : gift.

I K.

Music : Metternich : triptych : sick : muzhik : bashlyk.

I K S.

Words in -ik and s : fix : pyx.

I K T.

Prets. and past parts. of verbs in -ik : strict.

I L.

Quadrille : instil : ill : idyll : cacodyl : †kiln.

I L D.

Prets. and past parts. of verbs in -il : gild : build.

I L T.

Gilt : built.

I M.

Limb : Lympne : †paradigm : dim : synonym : limn : hymn.

I N.

Feminine : Prynne : *hydrogen : din : inn : Lynn : Penrhyn.

I N D.

Prets. and past parts. of verbs in -in : †wind.

I N K.

Zinc : cinque : ink.

I N K S.

Words in -ink and s : minx : lynx.

I N K T.

Prets. and past parts. of verbs in -ink : extinct.

I N S.

Since : rinse : *flints : *chintz.

I N T H.

Plinth : colocynth.

I N T S H.

Inch : lynch.

I N T Z.

Words in -int and s : chintz (cp. -ins.).

I N Z.

Words in -in and s : winze.

I P.

†Grippe : lip : gyp.

I P S.

Words in -ip and s : eclipse : Apocalypse.

I P T.

Prets. and past parts. of verbs in -ip : script : crypt.

I S.

Dehisc : edifice : Jarndyce : cuisse : this : Jervois : bliss : Itys : Jervoix.

I S H.

Bysshe : fish.

I S K.

Fisc : Fiske : bisque : risk.

I S T.

Prets. and past parts. of verbs in -is : †triste : mist : amethyst : Liszt.

I T.

Opposite : it : *counterfeit : conduit : bitt : selvyt.

I T H.

Pith : myth.

I T S H.

Niche : rich : itch : Aldwych : Sienkiewicz.

I V.

Sieve : give.

I Z.

Obsequies : is : Velasquez : quiz : fizz.

I Z M.

Chrism : abysm.

XI.

Ō.

Whoa : La Rochefoucauld : Gounod : Tussaud : doe : owe : Keogh : although : oh : Pharaoh : çuracao : Yeo : go : de trop : apropos : Perrault . depot : †Prevost : bureau : Esquimau : blow : †Vaux : Cîteaux : Voeux.

Ō B.

Job : robe.

Ō D.

Prets. and past parts. of many verbs in -ō : road : ode.

Ō K.

Coke : toque : oak : folk : Vidocq.

Ō K S.

Words in -ōk and s : Ffoulkes : hoax : †Vaux.

Ō L.

Barcarolle : bole : coal : kohl : boll : patrol : soul : bowl.

ŌLD.

Prets. and past parts. of verbs in -ōl : old : Isolde.

ŌLT.

Colt : moult.

ŌLZ.

Words in -ōl and s : Knolles : Voules : Knowles : Knollys.

ŌM.

Comb : Axholme : home : foam : ohm : holm.

ŌN.

Sloane : eau-de-Cologne : Saone : stone : Beaune : groan : Bohn : sewn : own.

ŌP.

Hope : soap.

ŌR.

(cp. aw, awr.)

Ore : oar : o'er : *Boer : †Gower : Spohr : door : four : corps (sing.) : Belfort.

ŌRD.

(cp. awrd.)

Prets. and past parts. of verbs in -ōr : board : ford : *gourd : horde.

ŌRK.

(cp. awk.)

Orc : torque : pork.

ŌRM, see AWM, AWRM.

ŌRN.

(cp. awn.)

Warne : borne : *bourne : warn : morn : *mourn.

ŌRP, see AWRP.

ŌRS.

(cp. aws, awrs.)

Force : source : *sauce : coarse : horse : course.

ŌRT.

(cp. awt.)

Porte : thwart : port : court.

ŌRTH.

Forth : *fourth.

ŌRTSH, see AWTSH.

ŌS.

Dose : gross.

ŌSH.

Guilloche : gauche.

ŌST.

Prets. and past parts. of verbs in -ōs : coast : post.

ŌT.

Choate : dote : oat : gemot.

ŌTH.

Oath : both : growth.

Ō*TH*.

Loathe : clothe.

ŌTSH.

†Troche : coach : brooch.

ŌV.

Cove : mauve.

ŌZ.

Words in -ō and s : rose : doze : Rievaulx.

XII : ŏ.

ŎB.

Swab : cob.

ŎD.

Squad : odd : cod.

ŎF.

Philosophe : †quaff : off : †golf : cough : soph.

ŎFT.

Prets. and past parts. of verbs in -ŏf : oft.

ŎG.

Dialogue : †quag : dog.

ŎK.

Roc : epoch : hough : lock : amok.

ŎKS.

Words in -ŏk and s : Guy †Fawkes : ox : †Vaux.

ŎKT.

Prets. and past parts. of verbs in -ŏk : decoct.

ŎL.

Doll : extol.

ŎM.

Bomb : Somme : from.

ŎMP.

Swamp : pomp.

ŎMPT.

Prets. and past parts. of verbs in -ŏmp : prompt.

ŎN.

Cretonne : shone : swan : demijohn : Bonn : don.

ŎND.

Prets. and past parts. of verbs in -ŏn : wand : fond : blonde.

ŎNS.

Nonce : response : *wants : *fonts .

ŎNT.

*Comte : want : font.

ŎNZ.

Words in -ŏn and s : bronze : bygones : pons.

ŎPS.

Words in -ŏp and s : copse.

ŎPT.

Prets. and past parts. of verbs in -ŏp : adopt.

ŎR, see AW, AWR, ŌR.

ŎRD, see AWD, AWRD, ŌRD.

ŎRK, see AWK, ŌRK.

ŎRL.

(cp. awl.)

Orle : †whorl.

ŎRM, see AWM, AWRM.

ŎRN, see AWN, ŌRN.

ŎRP, see AWRP.

ŎRS, see ŌRS.

ŎRT, see AWT, ŌRT.

ŎS.

Lacrosse : rhinoceros : loss.

ŎSH.

Wash : bosh.

ŎSHT.

Prets. and past parts. of verbs in -ŏsh : caboched.

ŎSK.

Mosque : kiosk.

ŎST.

Prets. and past parts. of verbs in -ŏs : wast : cost.

ŎT.

Squat : gavotte : yacht : lot : bott.

ŎTSH.

Watch : Scotch.

ŎZ.

Was : Boz.

XIII.

ŌŌ.

Canoe : Looe : construe : Crewe : Buccleuch : through : pooh : ado : bamboo : two : coup : rendezvous : début : ragout : cachou : virtu : strew : Devereux : billet-doux : Sioux.

ŌŌD.

Prets. and past parts. of verbs in-ōō : food : Froude : rude : †Frowde.

ŌŌK.

Fluke : chibouque : Amlwch : spook : bashi-bazouk.

ŌŌL.

†Tulle : rule : fool : ghoul.

ŌŌM.

Coomb : **tomb** : combe : **Broome** : **plume** : †**brougham** : **whom** : loom : rheum : **Batoum** : **Batum.**

ŌŌN.

Jeune : **June** : **Mahon** : **boon** : **Bohun** : **Colquhoun.**

ŌŌND.

Prets. and past parts. of **verbs in** -ōōn : †**wound.**

ŌŌP.

Troupe : **drupe** : **stoep** : droop : **group.**

ŌŌR.

Moore : †**sure** : *wooer : poor : ***amateur** : **tour.**

ŌŌRD.

Prets. and past parts. of verbs in -ōōr : **gourd** : Lourdes.

ŌŌS.

Juice : douce : **truce** : **goose** : **trousse** : **charlotte-russe** : Rouse : **abstruse** : **Loos** : **De Ros** : Selous.

ŌŌSH.

Douche : **ruche.**

ŌŌST.

Prets. and past parts. of **verbs in -ōōs** : **roost** : **joust.**

ŌŌT.

De Zoete : **Coote** : **flute** : **route** : **fruit** : **boot** : **marabout** : **Beirut** : **Hakluyt.**

ŌŌTH.

Sooth : **sleuth** : **youth** : **ruth.**

ŌŌ*TH*.

Soothe : **booth.**

ŌŌV.

Move : **groove.**

ŌŌZ.

Words n -ōō and s : bruise : lose : choose : Betel-geuse : peruse : ooze.

ŌŌZH.

Rouge : **Bruges.**

XIV : **oo.**

OOD.

Could : **good.**

OOK.

Brooke : **Broke** : **Lalla Rookh** : **look.**

OOL.

***Capable** : †**tulle** : **bull** : **wool** : **dutiful.**

ŌŌT.

***Émeute** : **foot** : **put.**

XV.

Ū.

Due : **queue** : **ewe** : **Hugh** : **Ayscough** : **feu** : **adieu** : **emu** : **view** : **new** : Clarenceux.

ŪD.

Prets. and past parts. of verbs in -ū : **feud** : **lewd** : **nude.**

ŪK.

Puke : Pentateuch.

ŪL.

Mule : **buhl** : **mewl.**

ŪM.

Hulme : **neume** : **fume.**

ŪN.

Tune : **impugn** : **hewn.**

ŪR.

Cure : *Dewar : †sewer : Muir : **amateur.**

ŪS.

Induce : †**diffuse** : **Zeus.**

ŪT.

Cute : **suit** : **Cnut** : **newt.**

ŪZ.

Words in -ū and s : **use** : meuse : **Hughes.**

XVI : **ŭ.**

ŬD.

Rudd : **blood** : **bud.**

ŬF.

Cuff : **rough.**

ŬFT.

Prets. and past parts. of verbs in -ŭf : Caldcleugh **tuft.**

ŬK.

Buck : †**Volapuk.**

ŬKD.

Prets. and past parts. of verbs in -ŭk : **duct.**

ŬKS.

Words in -uk and s : **crux.**

ŬL.

Dull : **annul.**

ŬLKT.

Prets. and past parts. of **verbs in** -ŭlk : **mulct.**

ŬM.

Numb : ***Morecambe** : Edgcumbe : **come** : **gum.**

ŬN.

One : **sally-lunn** : **son** : **dun.**

ŬND.

Prets. and past parts. of **verbs in -ŭn** : **fund.**

ŬNG.

Yonge : **tongue** : **among** : **bung** : **young.**

ŬNK.

Monck : **monk** : **bunk.**

ŬNKT.

Prets. and past parts. of **verbs in -unk** : **defunct.**

ŬNT.

Front : **shunt** : **Blount.**

ŬP.

Hiccough : **up.**

ŬPT.

Prets. and past parts. of **verbs in -up** : **abrupt.**

ŬS.

Fuss : **plus** : ***curious.**

ŬSK.

Fusc : **brusque** : **rusk.**

ŬST.

Prets. and past parts. of **verbs in -ŭs** : **dost** : **bust.**

ŬT.

But : **Butt.**

ŬTSH.

Hutch : **much** : **touch.**

ŬZ.

†**Does** : **coz** : **buzz.**

XVII.

OI.

†**Oboe** : **Iroquois** : †Hoey : **boy** : **buoy.**

OID.

Prets. and past parts. of **verbs in- oi** : **Bettws-y-Coed** : **void** : **Lloyd** : **Lhuyd.**

OIL.

Gargoyle : **oil.**

OIN.

Assiniboine : **groyne** : †**Boscawen** : **coign** : **coin.**

OIS.

Boece : **choice** : **Boyce** : **bourgeois (printing type)** : **Sluis** : **Reuss.**

OIST.

Prets. and past parts. of **verbs in -ois** : **Moist** : **Beust.**

OIT.

Bayreuth : **adroit.**

OIZ.

Words in -oi and s : **poise** : **Noyes** : **avoirdupois.**

XVIII.

OU.

Howe: bough: frau: miaou: thou: cow.

OUD.

Prets. and past parts. of verbs in -ou: McLeod: cloud: crowd: Oude: †Frowde: Oudh.

OUL.

Joule: dowle: *towel: foul: fowl.

OULZ.

Words in -oul and s: Fowles: Foulis.

OUN.

Browne: noun: frown.

OUND.

Prets. and past parts. of verbs in -oun: bound.

OUR.

Bauer: *flower: our: giaour: Penmaenmawr.

OUS.

House: Strauss: Brockhaus: nous.

OUST.

Faust: oust: frowst.

OUT.

Doubt: out.

OWZ.

Words in -ou and s: blouse: browse: blowze.

SUPPLEMENT

Mus'haa s. Undivided common property among Muslims.
A'ba s. (A garment of) goat's or camel's hair.
Ba'ba s. A small cake soaked in a rum spirit.
Jabotica'ba s. An evergreen Brazilian tree; its fruit.
Wall'aba s. A tree of the Guianas and Brazil; its wood.
Djell'aba s. An Arabic cloak and hood and wide sleeves.
Ara'ba s. A screened Tatar wagon.
Piassa'ba s. (*Piassava*).
Mas'taba s. A type of ancient Egyptian tomb.
Ag'ba s. A large African tree; its timber.
Mam'ba s. A large deadly snake of Africa.
Sam'ba s. A Brazilian Negro dance; its tune. v.i. To dance a samba.
Tsam'ba s. A Tibetan barley dish.
Lim'ba s. A W. African tree; its wood.
Kalim'ba s. A musical instrument played with the thumbs.
Marim'ba s. An African xylophone.
Zambom'ba s. A Spanish musical instrument.
Miom'ba s. (*Miombo*).
Rum'ba s. A Cuban Negro dance; its music. v.i. To dance a rumba.
Aro'ba s. (*Araba*).
Araro'ba s. Goa powder obtained from a Brazilian tree.
Coscoro'ba s. A small S. American swan.
Ar'ba s. (*Araba*).
Kas'ba s. A castle or fortress in a N. African town, or its surround.
Isba' s. A Russian hut or log house.
Carnau'ba s. A Brazilian palm; its wax.
Sau'ba s. A S. American leaf-carrying ant.
Scu'ba s. A skin-diver's underwater breathing apparatus. Also a.
Massarandu'ba s. A Brazilian tree, the milk-tree.
Carnahu'ba s. (*Carnauba*).
Paxiu'ba s. A Brazilian palm with stilt roots.
Dilru'ba s. A stringed musical instrument of India.
Izba' s. (*Isba*).
Abaca' s. A Philippine plantain; its fibre.
Mara'ca s. An instrument consisting of a gourd containing beads.
Jararac'a s. A venomous S. American snake.
Asarabacc'a s. Hazelwort.
Ticc'a a. Hired (in India).
Zimocc'a s. A type of bath-sponge.
Ara'bica s. A Cameroons tree; a type of coffee it produces.
Cu'bica s. A fine worsted used for linings.
Oitici'ca s. Any of several S. American trees whose nuts yield oil (oi-ti-sē'ka) used in paints and varnishes.
Hierat'ica s. The finest Egyptian papyrus.
Barran'ca s. (*US*) A deep gorge.
O'ca s. A S. American wood-sorrel with edible tubers.
Cario'ca s. A Brazilian dance; its tune.
Anasar'ca s. A form of dropsy in the skin.
Or'ca s. The killer-whale genus.
Minor'ca s. A variety of egg-laying poultry.
Farru'ca s. A Spanish gypsy dance with abrupt changes in mood and tempo.
Motu'ca s. A large Brazilian biting fly.
Baha'da s. A slope composed of rock debris formed by aggradation. (Also Bajada).
Gel'ada s. An Ethiopian baboon.
Enchila'da s. A tortilla served with chili sauce.
Cana'da s. A narrow canyon.
Espa'da ('tha) s. A matador; a sword.
Au'tostrada s. A highway for motor traffic.
Courada' s. (*Courida*).
Stadd'a s. A comb-maker's handsaw.
Khed'a s. An enclosure for catching wild elephants; the catching operation.
Alame'da s. A public walk (between rows of poplars).
Vif'da s. (*Vivda*).
Courida' s. The black mangrove tree; its timber.
Asafoet'ida s. An evil-smelling medicinal gum-resin.
Grisel'da s. An excessively meek and patient woman.
Jacaran'da s. A S. American tree with hard heavy wood.
Anacon'da s. A gigantic water-boa of S. America.
Zon'da s. A periodic hot dusty wind from the Andes which blows over the Argentine pampas.
Barramun'da s. An Australian river-fish, a lung-fish.
Monar'da s. An aromatic herb with bright red flowers.
Zer'da s. A fennec.
Barracu'da s. A voracious W. Indian fish.
Remu'da s. A supply of fresh horses.
Gar'uda s. A demigod of Hindus, part-man, part-bird.
Viv'da s. Unsalted meat hung for drying (in the Shetlands).
Alde'a s. A village or hamlet.
Ar'dea s. The heron and bittern genus.
Ta'kahea s. A New Zealand rail, notornis.
Barathe'a s. A soft fabric of (or with) worsted.
Pa'lea s. A fern scale; an inner bract or bracteole of an individual grass flower.
Que'lea s. A genus of African weaver-birds.
Logorrhoe'a s. Excessive flow of words.
He'vea s. A S. American rubber tree.
Jaff'a s. An orange from Israel.
(H)al'fa s. Esparto-grass of N. Africa.
Alfal'fa s. A kind of lucerne.
Yar'fa s. (*Yarpha*).
Chu'fa s. A sedge with edible tubers.
A'ga s. A commander or chief officer in Turkey.
Ga'ga a. (*Slang*) Silly; fatuous; in senile dotage.
Na'ga s. The Indian cobra.
Ra'ga s. A traditional Hindu musical form.
Ossif'raga s. The giant fulmar.
Sen'ega s. (*US*) (The dried root of a) milkwort used against snakebites.
Stre'ga s. An Italian liqueur.
Ve'ga s. A low fertile plain or tobacco-field (in Cuba).
Dagg'a s. Indian hemp; (*US*) marijuana.
Tai'ga s. Marshy pine forest.
Geropi'ga s. A grape-juice (or brandy, etc.) mixture used to fortify port.
Brol'ga s. The native companion crane of Australia.

Mul'ga s. A small Australian acacia tree; land covered with such.
Gebang'a s. A Malaysian palm; its leaves used in thatching.
Mridang'a s. An Indian barrel-shaped drum.
Chan'ga s. A soil insect, the mole-cricket.
I'nanga s. A small fish of New Zealand whose young is whitebait.
Pan'ga s. A broad and heavy African knife.
Tan'ga s. A brief string-like bikini.
Ka'inga s. A Maori village or settlement.
Bu'binga s. A W. African tree; its timber.
Myrin'ga s. The eardrum.
Barasing'a s. An E. Indian deer, specifically the swamp deer.
Caating'a s. Low open forest on white sandy soil (like that of Brazil).
Con'ga s. A dance in which a long line follows a leader; its music. Also v.i.
Wong'a s. The white-faced pigeon native to Australia.
Arapung'a s. The campanero or S. American bell-bird.
Sarato'ga s. (*US*) A large travelling trunk.
Dar'ga s. (A structure over) a place where a holy person is buried.
Vir'ga s. Water drops or particles of ice, which remain in the clouds.
Gu'ga s. A young gannet.
Zastru'ga s. One of a series of parallel snow-ridges.
Langa'ha s. A Madagascan wood-snake.
Brouha'ha s. Hubbub, fuss, uproar, excitement.
Ta'ha s. A weaver-bird.
Arracach'a s. A S. American plant with edible tubers.
Da'cha s. A Russian country house.
Pano'cha s. Coarse sugar from Mexico.
Cutch'a a. Makeshift; of dried mud etc.
Pa'keha s. A white man (among Maori peoples).
A'gha s. (*Aga*).
Barasingh'a s. (*Barasinga*).
Piran'ha s. A ferocious S. American river-fish.
Pupun'ha s. The peach-palm; its fruit.
Aloh'a s. Love, kindness. int. greetings, farewell.
Yar'pha s. Peaty soil; a peat-bog (Shetland).
Hy'pha s. A thread of fungus mycelium.
Tama'sha s. An entertainment; show; fuss.
Mush'a int. (*Irish*) expressing surprise.
Aph'tha s. Thrush disease; a small white ulcer on a mucous membrane.
Mal'tha s. A thick mineral pitch.
Sapuca'ia s. A Brazilian tree.
Co'bia s. The sergeant-fish.
Dromopho'bia s. The fear of crossing roads.
Aca'cia s. A wattle plant.
Alope'cia s. Baldness.
Ace'dia s. Sloth, torpor, listlessness.
Re'dia s. A form in the life-cycle of trematodes.
Vigi'a s. A warning of danger (on a chart, etc.).
Alog'ia s. Speechlessness (from brain lesion).
Che'chia s. A cylindrical cap.
Pete'chia s. A small red or purple skin-spot.
Loch'ia s. Discharge after childbirth.
Ohi'a s. Lehua.
Dysgraph'ia s. Inability to write due to brain damage.
Ala'lia s. Loss of speech.
Echola'lia s. Senseless repetition of sounds heard, due to disease.
Rosa'lia s. (*mus.*) A series of repeated passages, each a tone higher.
Amel'ia s. Complete absence of a limb or limbs.
Dysmel'ia s. The condition where any limbs are incomplete or misshapen.
Ab(o)u'lia s. Loss of will-power.
Bohe'mia s. A community of gypsies.
Hobohe'mia s. (The district in which lives) a community of hoboes.
In'ia s. (pl. *Inion*).
Acap'nia s. Deficiency of carbon dioxide.
Polyn'ia s. Open water among sea ice.
Pi'a s. A tropical plant.
Subto'pia s. The region where city has spread into country.
Ru'pia s. A skin ulcer.
Ri'a s. A drowned valley.
Laba'ria s. Any of several poisonous snakes, the fer-de-lance, bushmaster, etc.
Adversa'ria s. Miscellaneous notes; a commonplace book.
Montari'a s. A Brazilian monoxylon.
Calan'dria s. A sealed vessel in the core of nuclear reactors.
Proger'ia s. The disease causing premature ageing in children.
Cafete'ria s. A restaurant with self-service facility.
Eupho'ria s. Feeling of well-being.
Mo'ria s. Folly
Trattori'a s. A restaurant (Italian).
Alge'sia s. Sensitivity to pain.
Afrormo'sia s. A durable timber of W. Africa.
Ambro'sia s. Any fine beverage; something sweet and pleasing; fungi cultivated by bark-beetles as food; pollen fed by bees to their young.
Idiogloss'ia s. A condition where pronunciation is unintelligible.
Parou'sia s. The second coming of Our Lord.
Notit'ia s. A catalogue, roll, list, register, etc.
Hamar'tia s. A character defect which causes ultimate downfall.
Huti'a s. A W. Indian rodent, the hog-rat.
Imbui'a s. (*Imbuya*). (Also Embui'a).
Tri'via s. Unimportant details, things, etc.
Aprax'ia s. Loss of manipulative ability (due to brain damage).
Alex'ia s. Loss of power to read; word-blindness.
Dyslex'ia s. Word-blindness.
Anorex'ia s. Inability to eat due to a severe nervous condition.
Anox'ia s. Deficient oxygen supply to tissue.
Inajá' s. An Amazon palm tree.
Khod'ja s. A professor or teacher in the East; a title of respect.
Oui'ja s. A board containing an alphabet, used with a planchette.
Gan'ja s. An intoxicating preparation from Indian hemp tops.
Zan'ja s. A canal for irrigation.
Kho'ja s. (*Khodja*).
Alfor'ja s. A baboon's cheek-pouch; a saddle-bag.
Gytt'ja s. A rich, black, organic deposit in lakes.
Pu'ja s. Worship; observance; a festival.
Ka s. Individuality; genius; double.
Ha'ka s. A ceremonial dance before a great event.
I'naka s. An evergreen shrub or small tree of New Zealand.
Poa'ka s. A stilt (bird) of New Zealand.
Kara'ka s. A New Zealand tree yielding edible fruit.
Moussa'ka s. A Greek dish of minced meat, aubergines, tomato and cheese, etc.
Ja'taka s. A nativity; the birth story of Buddha.
We'ka s. Any of the flightless rails of New Zealand.
Kish'ka s. A Jewish savoury sausage.
Babush'ka s. A triangular scarf tied under the chin.
Lai'ka s. Any of several breeds of small reddish-brown working dogs.
Di'ka s. A W. Indian tree.
Pi'ka s. A small mountain rodent, the tailless hare.

Paprik'a s. Red pepper (from Hungary).
Si'ka s. A small deer of Japan.
Ti'ka s. A beauty spot (like that Hindu women wear).
Yakk'a s. (*Australian*) Hard toil.
Ekk'a s. A small one-horse carriage.
Chokk'a s. The S. African squid.
Rusal'ka s. A Russian water-nymph.
Pul'ka s. A boat-shaped sledge (like that used by Laplanders).
Dum'ka s. A slow piece of music, a lament.
Zigan'ka s. A Russian country-dance; its music.
Tan'ka s. A Japanese verse form; the Cantonese boat population.
Golomyn'ka s. A very oily fish.
Bazoo'ka s. An anti-tank gun or rocket-launcher.
Par'ka s. Fur-lined waterproof hooded jacket.
Ner'ka s. The sockeye salmon.
Fris'ka s. The quick movement of a csárdás.
Zakus'ka s. A snack; an hors d'oeuvre.
Ma'nuka s. A tree of Australia and New Zealand; its leaves; a tea made from them.
(W)ha'puka s. (*Whapuku*).
Sca'la s. A ladder-like structure.
Man'dala s. A (Buddhist) symbol for meditation.
Treha'la s. Turkish manna (beetle cocoons).
Ila'la s. A fan palm.
Ka'mala s. An E. Indian tree; a dye yielded by its fruit-hairs.
Impa'la s. An African antelope.
Owa'la s. A tropical African tree; an oil lubricant yielded by its pods.
Tab'la s. An Indian percussion instrument.
Candel'a s. A unit of luminous intensity.
Pe'la s. White wax produced by a scale-insect.
Ka'rela s. A climbing plant, the balsam pear or bitter gourd; its fruit.
Kwe'la s. Zulu folk-music of jazz type.
Shei'la s. (*Australian*) A girl or woman.
Kaf'ila s. A camel train or caravan. Also Caf(f)ila.
Gi'la s. A venomous lizard.
Ag'ila s. Eaglewood.
Voilà (Vwâ-lâ) int. Behold!
Shan'gri-la s. An imaginary paradise.
Tequi'la s. An intoxicating drink (from Mexico).
Talegall'a s. The brush-turkey.
Paell'a (pī-) s. A Spanish rice dish with shellfish, chicken, etc.
Marcell'a s. A type of cotton or linen twill-woven.
Padell'a s. A lamp consisting of a shallow dish of fat with a wick.
Zanell'a s. A fabric used as umbrella covering.
Salmonell'a s. A genus of bacteria causing food-poisoning.
Petronell'a s. A Scottish country-dance.
Citronell'a s. A Ceylon grass yielding an oil used in perfumes.
Parell'a s. A crustaceous lichen.
Mozzarell'a s. A soft Italian cheese.
Corell'a s. An Australian long-billed cockatoo.
Terrell'a s. A magnetic model of the earth.
Vulsell'a s. A forceps with toothed or clawed blade.
Rosell'a s. An Australian parakeet.
Novell'a s. A short story.
Fothergill'a s. A genus of N. American shrubs; witch hazel.
Candelill'a s. A Mexican spurge.
Manzanill'a s. A very dry sherry.
Kur'illa s. (*Karela*).
Oll'a s. A jar or urn.
Sarcocoll'a s. A plant gum used on wounds.
Aroll'a s. A tree, the Swiss stone-pine or the Siberian cedar.
Carambo'la s. A small E. Indian tree; its fruit.
Barbo'la s. A form of ornamentation using coloured plastic fruit and flowers, etc.
Sho'la s. A thicket.
Vo'la s. The hollow of the hand or foot.
Payo'la s. Secret payment, bribe, to secure a special favour.
Hoop'-la s. A fairground game of throwing hoops over prizes.
Man'dorla s. (A work of art filling) an oval panel.
Tes'la s. A unit of magnetic flux density.
Gus'la s. A one-stringed Balkan instrument.
Kgot'la s. (The place of) an assembly of tribal elders.
Nubec'ula s. A cloudiness.
Rad'ula s. A mollusc's tongue or rasping ribbon.
In'fula s. A lappet in a mitre.
Al'ula s. The feathers on the equivalent of a thumb on a birds's wing, the bastard-wing.
Plan'ula s. A free-swimming larva of coelenterates.
Ros'ula s. A leaf-rosette.
Kaa'ma s. The hartebeest.
Sha'ma s. An Indian songbird.
Pal'ama s. The webbing on the foot of a water-fowl.
Gra'ma s. A US pasture grass.
Ash'rama s. A hermitage or religious retreat in India.
Reta'ma s. Any of various desert switch-plants.
Pad'ma s. The sacred lotus.
Tre'ma s. An orifice; diaresis.
Nototre'ma s. A genus of S. American tree-frogs.
Diaste'ma s. A natural gap between two teeth.
Reg'ma s. A fruit that splits into dehiscent parts.
Mig'ma s. A mixture of solid and molten rock.
Keryg'ma s. (The preaching of) the Christian gospel.
Arapai'ma s. An Amazon fish, the pirarucu.
Ili'ma s. A yellow- or orange-flowered shrub of Hawaii.
Kall'ima s. A genus of Oriental butterflies resembling dead leaves.
Jemi'ma s. An elastic-sided boot.
Ri'ma s. A chink; the gap between vocal cords and arytaenoid cartilages.
Si'ma s. The part of the earth's crust under the sial.
Pel'ma s. The sole of the foot.
Bo'ma s. A fenced enclosure; a boa or anaconda.
Lo'ma s. A membranous flap or fringe.
Dhar'ma s. The law or its underlying righteousness.
Chloas'ma s. A skin disease producing yellowish-brown patches.
Melis'ma s. A song; a tune; a melodic embellishment.
Charis'ma s. Personality, magnetism.
Rus'ma s. A depilatory.
Platys'ma s. A broad neck muscle.
Hu'ma s. A fabulous bird.
Mazu'ma s. (*US slang*) Money, cash, loot.
Ecthy'ma s. A pustular skin eruption.
Ikeba'na s. The (Japanese) art of flower arrangement.
Cañ'a s. A rum-like spirit made from sugar cane.
Gymkha'na s. A meeting for equestrian sports.
Forla'na s. A Venetian dance. (Also Furlana).
Viman'a s. The centre shrine or gate of an Indian temple.
Maña'na s. (and adv.) Tomorrow; some unspecified future time.
Guaran'a s. A Brazilian liana; a bread, drink or drug made from it.
Mussura'na s. A Brazilian snake which feeds on poisonous snakes.
Ta'na s. A species of tree-shrew.
Venta'na s. A window.
Tarta'na s. A small covered wagon.

Marijua'na s. Hemp; its dried leaves and flowers smoked as an intoxicant.
Bwa'na s. Master, sir, boss.
Ozae'na s. A fetid discharge from the nose.
Ge'na s. The cheek or side of the head.
Je'na s. A type of glass made in Germany.
Zampo'gna s. The Italian bagpipe.
Regi'na s. Queen.
Mari'na s. A mooring park for pleasure boats.
Retsin'a s. A Greek resin-flavoured wine.
Vi'na s. An Indian stringed instrument.
Corvi'na s. A name for several black-finned fishes of the US. (Also Cur(u)vina).
Rabann'a s. A raffia fabric.
Goann'a s. Any large monitor lizard.
Carann'a s. A resinous yield from certain S. American trees.
Platann'a s. An African frog.
Penn'a s. A large feather, especially one from the wing or tail.
Tarragon'a s. A port-like Spanish wine.
Ko'na s. A stormy S.W. wind in the Hawaiian Islands.
Person'a s. Social façade or public image.
Dhar'na s. Protest, demonstration, against injustice, etc.
Et'na s. A vessel used in chemistry for heating liquids.
Caraun'a s. (*Caranna*).
Abu'na s. A patriarch (in Ethiopia).
Sau'na s. A type of steam-bath.
Kahu'na s. A priest; a minister; a wise man; an expert.
Pun'a s. Bleak tableland (in the Andes); a cold wind there; mountain sickness.
Bo'a s. A large constricting snake; a fur or feather coil women wear around the neck.
Feijo'a s. An evergreen shrub or small tree of S. America; its fruit.
Keit'loa s. A two-horned rhinoceros.
Ano'a s. The sapi-utan, wild ox of Celebes.
Geno'a s. A large jib which overlaps the mainsail; a fruit cake topped with almond.
Tohero'a s. An edible shellfish.
Dyschro'a s. Discoloration of the skin from disease.
Ca'pa s. A fine cigar tobacco (*Cuban*); a cloak (*Spanish*).
Ni'pa s. (An alcoholic drink made from) an E. Indian palm.
Chinam'pa s. A floating garden.
Gra'ppa s. An Italian brandy.
Cupp'a s. A cup of tea.
Sher'pa s. An inhabitant of E. Tibet, notable as a mountaineer's guide.
Ajou'pa s. A W. Indian hut or wigwam on piles.
Stu'pa s. A dome-shaped memorial shrine.
Toxocar'a s. An intestinal worm found in dogs and causing damage to humans.
Afa'ra s. A W. African tree; its wood.
Chi(n)ka'ra s. An Indian antelope or gazelle.
Ma'ra s. The so-called Patagonian hare.
Kuma'ra s. A sweet potato.
Sayona'ra int. Goodbye (*Japanese*).
Demerar'a s. Brown sugar in large crystal form.
Ta'ra s. A bracken with edible rhizome.
Sata'ra s. A ribbed and lustred woollen cloth.
Tuata'ra s. A lizard-like reptile of New Zealand.
Peta'ra s. A clothes basket or box for travelling.
Gur'dwara s. The place of worship of Sikhs.
Sa'bra s. A native-born Israeli (not an immigrant).
Cem'bra s. The Swiss stone-pine.
Lu'bra s. An Australian aboriginal woman.
Calde'ra s. A great volcanic crater.
Rivie'ra s. Any warm coastal district (as a resort).
Kera' s. The long-tailed (or crab-eating) macaque of Asia.
Woom'era s. A throw-stick (*Australian*).
Habane'ra s. A Cuban Negro dance; its tune.
Scorzone'ra s. Black salsify, an edible root-plant.
Chaulmoo'gra s. The name of various Indian trees. (Also Chaulmugra).
Cleth'ra s. A white-flowered dwarf tree, shrub or plant.
Tai'ra s. A large weasel of S. America.
Man'dira s. A Hindu temple.
Mangabei'ra s. A Brazilian rubber-tree.
Parei'ra s. A tropical climbing-plant or its root.
Baj'ra s. An Indian millet.
Kra' s. (*Kera*).
Chak'ra s. In Yoga one of the centres of spiritual or ethereal power in the human body.
Buck'ra s. A white man (used in the W. Indies).
Bombor'a s. A dangerous stretch of water where waves break over a hidden reef.
Fedo'ra s. A felt hat dented lengthwise.
Ko'ra s. The water-cock.
Ko'rora s. The blue penguin of New Zealand.
Ixor'a s. An evergreen tropical shrub.
Kha'pra s. A small beetle which is a grain pest.
Kook'aburr'a s. The Australian laughing jackass.
Su'rra s. A trypanosome disease of horses.
Ondat'ra s. The musquash.
Suma'tra s. A short violent squall around the Malaccan Straits.
Triquet'ra s. An ornament consisting of three interlaced arcs.
Kalyp'tra s. A veil worn by Greek woman.
Shas'tra s. (*Shaster*).
Kabour'a s. (*Kabouri*).
Go'pura s. A pyramidal tower over a temple gateway (in S. India).
Scordatu'ra s. (*Mus.*) A temporary departure from normal tuning.
Jettatu'ra s. The spell of the evil eye.
Tay'ra s. (*Taira*).
Ey'ra s. A wild cat of S. America.
Palmy'ra s. An African and Asiatic palm yielding nuts, jaggery, etc.
Orope'sa s. A fish-shaped float used in minesweeping.
Shik'sa s. A non-Jewish woman.
Bal'sa s. (A raft or float of) corkwood; the tropical American tree.
Lyco'sa s. A genus of hunting spiders including the tarantula.
Flindo'sa s. An Australian hardwood rain-forest tree.
Margo'sa s. The tree that yields nim oil.
Appaloo'sa s. A breed of horse with white hair and dark-coloured body patches.
Amoro'sa s. A mistress, sweetheart.
Mass'a s. The Negro word for master.
Nyss'a s. A deciduous tree of N. America and Asia; in the US, the tupelo.
Ru'sa s. An Indian grass from which aromatic oil is distilled.
Chipola'ta s. A small sausage.
Matama'ta s. A S. American river-turtle.
Ferma'ta s. (*Mus.*) A pause.
Resina'ta s. A Greek white wine.
Canta'ta s. A short choral work; a concert aria.
Fet'a s. A Greek cheese of ewe's milk.
Ke'ta s. A Pacific fish, the dog-salmon.
Vele'ta s. A waltz-time dance or tune.
Bosh'ta a. (*Australian*) Very good.
I'ta s. The miriti palm.
Di'ta s. A tree of India and the Philippines; its tonic bark.
Aki'ta s. A breed of Japanese dog.
Manzani'ta s. The Californian bearberry.
Pi'ta s. A fibre of various species of Agave, etc.
Copi'ta s. A tulip-shaped sherry-glass.
Plant'a s. The sole of the foot.

Man'ta s. A cloak; a horse-blanket; a sea-ray.
Revalen'ta s. Lentil-meal.
Marabun'ta s. Any of several types of wasps of Guyana.
Jo'ta s. A Spanish dance.
Lo'ta s. A small brass or copper pot of India.
Flo'ta s. A commercial fleet.
Barracoo'ta s. (*Barracuda*).
Canas'ta s. A card-game like rummy.
Pas'ta s. The generic name for macaroni, spaghetti, etc.
Fies'ta s. A holiday; a saint's day; festivity.
Cues'ta s. A hill ridge having a steep scarp on one side and a gradual slope on the other.
Hos'ta s. A plantain-lily of Asia.
Crus'ta s. A cocktail served in a glass whose rim is sugar-coated.
Chatt'a s. An umbrella.
Faldett'a s. A hooded cape (Maltese).
Fett'a s. (*Feta*).
Strett'a s. (*Mus.*) A stretto; a coda in quicker time.
Lytt'a s. The worm of a dog's tongue.
Barracou'ta s. (*Barracuda*).
Agou'ta s. A rat-like insectivore of Haiti.
Pau'a s. The abalone.
Chihua'hua s. **(chi-wâ' wâ)** A very small dog with big eyes and pointed ears.
Lehu'a s. An evergreen tree of the Pacific islands.
Morr'hua s. The cod.
Mad'oqua s. A very small Abyssinian antelope.
Mosha'va s. An agricultural settlement in Israel.
Balacla'va s. A warm, woolly face-and-head cover.
Piassa'va s. (A Brazilian palm yielding) a stiff fibre used in brooms, etc.
De'va s. A god or good spirit (in Hindu myth).
Sel'va s. Wet forest of the Amazon basin.
Vol'va s. A sheath enclosing the fruit of some agarics.
Hell'ova a. (*Helluva*).
Casano'va s. One renowned for his amorous adventures.
Ur'va s. The crab-eating mongoose of S.E. Asia.
Mur'va s. Bowstring-hemp.
Hell'uva a. (*Slang*—hell of a) Great, terrific.
Mah'wa s. A kind of butter-tree with edible flowers.
Red'owa s. A Bohemian dance; its music.
Aba'ya s. (*Aba*).
Kaba'ya s. A loose tunic.
Kha'ya s. A genus of African trees akin to mahogany.
Ka'ya s. A Japanese evergreen tree; its wood.
Atala'ya s. A watch-tower.
Pla'ya s. A dry basin which becomes a lake after heavy rainfall.
Ma'ya s. Illusion; an ancient Indian civilisation.
Papa'ya s. A S. American tree; its fruit.
Pira'ya s. (*Piranha*).
Calisa'ya s. A variety of Peruvian bark.
Hi'ya int. How are you? (a word of greeting).
Bun'ya s. An Australian monkey-puzzle tree.
Kab(a)ragoy'a s. A monitor lizard of Asian waters.
Cherimoy'a s. A Peruvian fruit like the custard-apple. (Also Chirimoya).
Imbuy'a s. **(imbwī')** A Brazilian timber tree; its wood.
Pla'za s. A public town square or open paved area.
Pileorhi'za s. The mass of tissue protecting the point of a root.
Gam'za s. A dark red Bulgarian grape; the wine made from it. (Also Gumza).
Organ'za s. A transparently thin material made of silk or nylon, etc.
Nyan'za s. A lake (in Africa).
Ory'za s. A tropical genus of grasses including rice.
Pizz'a s. **(pēt'sa)** An open pie of dough covered with cheese, tomato, herbs, etc., and baked.
Ped'icab s. A sort of rickshaw, consisting of a tricycle and covered passenger-seat.
Serdab' s. A secret or underground chamber (in an Egyptian tomb).
Prefab' s. A prefabricated house, etc. Also a.
Lab'lab s. A tropical bean with edible pods.
Flab s. (*Slang*) Fat, flabbiness.
Lu'lab s. (*Lulav*).
Be'nab s. A shelter of branches and leaves covering a pole framework.
Scrab v.t. To scratch.
Frab v.t. To worry.
Cassab' s. A merchant-seaman of Asian origin.
Beeb s. A familiar abbreviation of BBC
Dieb s. A jackal of N. Africa.
Ad-lib' v.t. and i. To extemporise.
Elb s. A spiny tree of the Middle E. and N. Africa. (Also (A)ilb).
Stilb s. The CGS unit of intrinsic brightness.
Zimb s. An Abyssinian cattle-pest insect.
Kob s. An African water-antelope.
Glob s. (*Slang*) A mass or lump of some semi-liquid or soft substance.
Slob s. Mud, ooze. (*Slang*) an uncultured boor.
Boob s. A blunder. v.t. and i. To bungle, to blunder.
Haboob' s. A sand-storm.
Doob s. Dog's-tooth grass.
Yob s. (*Slang*) A lout, a useless loafer.
Forb s. Any broad-leaved herb growing naturally on grassland.
Blurb s. Commendatory words describing any product (but specifically those on a book-jacket).
Slurb s. A slum-like suburban area.
Ex'urb s. A district outside a city or town; the prosperous area beyond the suburbs.
Ze'bub s. The zimb.
Flub s. A blunder. v.t. To botch, fail at. v.i. perform badly, blunder. (*All meanings US slang*).
Bo'bac s. (*Bobak*).
O'shac s. The ammoniac plant.
E'niac s. A US pioneer computer.
Mic'mac s. A Canadian Indian (tribe); the language.
Armagnac' s. A dry French brandy.
Poo'nac s. A coconut oilcake.
Vac. s. A familiar abbreviation for vacation or vacuum cleaner. Also v.t. and i.
Med'ivac s. A military helicopter for transporting battle-wounded to hospital. Also v.t. (Also Medevac).
Au'tovac s. A vacuum mechanism in a car for petrol flow.
Pec s. A photoelectric cell.
Par'sec s. A unit used in measuring distances of stars.
Cu'sec s. The unit of volumetric rate of flow.
Vraic s. (*Channel Islands*). Seaweed.
Med'ic s. (*Slang*) A Medical student.
Mun'dic s. Iron pyrites.
Her'dic s. A low carriage with back entrance and side seats.
Nor'dic a. Of a tall, blond, N.W. European type.
As'dic s. An apparatus for detecting and locating submarines or other underwater objects by ultrasonic wave echoes.
Lu'dic a. Of spontaneously playful behaviour.
Phae'ic a. Dusky.
Ma'fic a. Portaining to or containing the dark-

coloured minerals of igneous rock.
Venef'ic a. Acting by poison, potion or sorcery.
Frigorif'ic a. Causing cold; freezing.
Rhopal'ic a. (*Of a verse, etc.*) Having each word a syllable longer than the one before.
Em'blic s. An E. Indian tree.
Psychedel'ic a. Pertaining to heightened perception, produced by drugs or visual and sound effects; dazzling in pattern.
Mel'ic s. A type of grass. a. Lyric; to be sung.
Ere'mic a. Of or belonging to deserts.
Din'ic s. A remedy for dizziness. a. Of vertigo.
Stereophon'ic a. Giving the effects of sound from different directions.
Bion'ic a. Relating to bionics; superhuman.
Son'ic a. Of or using soundwaves; travelling at about the speed of sound.
Azo'ic a. Before the existence of animal life.
Protanop'ic a. Colour-blind as regards red.
Dexiotrop'ic a. Turning to the right.
Me'sic a. Having or characterised by a moderate amount of moisture.
Klendu'sic a. (*Of plants*) Having a protective mechanism able to withstand disease.
Phreat'ic a. Pertaining to (underground water supplying) wells and springs, or the soil and rocks, etc. containing it.
Eidet'ic a. Vividly clear. s. A person able to reproduce a clear image of what he has previously seen.
Met'ic s. A resident alien.
Antibiot'ic s. A substance used to destroy micro-organisms of infectious diseases, etc. Also a.
Henot'ic a. Tending to reconcile or unify.
Hap'tic s. Pertaining to the sense of touch.
Quar'tic s. In maths a function, curve or surface of the fourth degree. Also a.
Peiras'tic a. Experimental; tentative.
Agrav'ic a. Of zero-gravity effect.
Or'ichalc s. A gold-coloured alloy; brass.
Tronc s. A kitty of waiters' tips.
Ca'boc s. A double-cream cheese rolled in oatmeal.
Tom'boc s. A long-handled Javanese weapon.
Bloc s. A combination of political parties, nations or other units in a common purpose.
Mon'obloc a. Made as, or contained in, a single casting. s. Such an engine.
Atoc' s. (*Atok*).
Estoc' s. A short sword.
Per'isarc s. The chitinous layer covering the polyps, etc. in some hydrozoans.
Bon'duc s. A nut, the nicker-seed.
Muc'luc s. (*Muckluck*).
Tebb'ad s. A sandstorm.
E'cad s. An organism modified by its environment.
Ho'dad s. (*Slang*) Anyone who annoys (surf-riders).
Doo'dad s. A gadget; a thingamy.
A'oudad s. A N. African wild sheep.
Craw'dad s. (*US*) A crayfish.
Buff'lehead s. A N. American diving duck.
Egg'head s. An intellectual.
Skin'head s. A youth (usually of a gang) with very closely-cropped hair; such a hairstyle. a. Of such a hairstyle; bald.
Spear'head s. The front of an attack. v.t. To be in or form such an attack.
War'head s. The explosive load of a torpedo, rocket, etc.
Hamm'erhead s. A kind of shark.
Enn'ead s. A set of nine.
Og'doad s. A set of eight.
Pay'load s. A rocket warhead; an apparatus for obtaining information.
Rad s. A unit of radiation dosage.
Kamerad' int. Comrade. v.i. To surrender.
Prad s. (*Slang*) A horse.
Trad a. (*Of jazz*) in traditional style. s. Traditional jazz.
Strad s. A Stradivarius violin.
Gor'sedd s. A meeting of bards and druids.
Var'tabed s. An Armenian order of clergy.
Chuffed a. Disgruntled; very pleased.
Ked s. A sheep-tick.
Whacked a. Exhausted.
Zonked a. (*Slang*) Exhausted; intoxicated (with drugs).
Scrodd'led a. (*Of pottery*) made with different coloured scraps of clay.
Sned v.t. To cut, lop or prune.
Ped s. A pannier or hamper.
Al'iped a. Wing-footed. s. Such a beast; a bat.
Mo'ped s. A motor-assisted pedal cycle.
Jig'gered a. Confounded.
Knack'ered a. (*Slang*) Done for; exhausted utterly.
Plas'tered a. (*Slang*) Intoxicated.
Pissed a. (*Slang*) On the way to being, or extremely, drunk.
Oer'sted s. The C.G S. unit of magnetic field strength.
Kaid s. A N. African chief.
Rosc'id a. Dewy
Mad'id a. Wet; dank.
Apar'theid s. Segregation (of black and white races).
Mas'jid s. A mosque.
A'gamid s. An Old World lizard.
Hom'inid s. A member of the family of man and his ancestors.
Pithe'coid a. Ape-like.
Ge'oid s. The figure of the earth's mean sea-level surface.
Loid v.t. (*Slang*) To open a lock with a celluloid strip.
An'droid s. A robot made to look like a human being.
Ster'oid s. A sterol, an adrenal hormone, etc.
Chaudfroid' s. A jellied sauce (used with chicken dishes).
Matt'oid s. A person on the borderline between sanity and insanity.
Sciar'id s. A minute dark-coloured fly.
Mar'id s. One of the most powerful jinni.
Hes'perid s. A skipper butterfly.
Cap'sid s. Any of several small plant pests.
Jass'id s. A homopterous insect, a cereal pest.
My'sid s. A small shrimp-like crustacean.
Nit'id a. Shining; gay.
Meld v.t. and i. (*US slang*) To merge.
Har'eld s. A long-tailed Northern sea-duck.
Twi'child s. One who has become a child again.
Woold v.t. To wind a rope or chain round.
Sal'band s. (*Geol.*) The crust of a dyke or vein.
Fahl'band s. (*Geol.*) In crystalline rocks a pale band rich in metals.
Off'hand a. Impromptu; ungraciously curt or summary.
Long'hand s. Ordinary handwriting.
Back'hand s. A (tennis) stroke made with the hand turned.
Repand' a. Slightly wavy.
Fire'brand s. One who foments strife; a fierce vituperative woman.
Grand'stand s. An elevated erection on a racecourse, etc. affording a good view. a. Of a race finish, etc., rousing and exciting; worthy of the crowd's admiration.
Walls'end s. A type of coal of certain size and quality.
Bell'bind s. A bindweed of hedge or field.
Sind v.t. (*Synd*).
With'(y)wind s. Bindweed or other climbing plant.
Kees'hond s. A medium-sized dog of the spitz type.
Baus'ond a. Having white spots on the forehead or

a white stripe down the face.
Run'around s. Evasion (given by one to another).
Tund v.t. and i. To beat; to thump.
Synd v.t. To rinse; To wash out or down. Also s.
Whole'food s. Unrefined foodstuff.
Grease'wood s. An oily American shrub of several kinds.
Ple'opod s. A crustacean's swimming leg.
Brod s. A goad; a spike; a kind of nail. v.t. To prod.
Smör'bröd (Smaw'broad) s. A Scandinavian dish of hors d'oeuvres served on buttered bread.
Sprod s. A second-year salmon.
Cafard' s. The blues; depression (with nostalgia).
Mouchard' s. A police spy.
Li'ard a. Grey; dapple-grey.
Briard' s. A large hairy dog of French breed.
Poulard' s. A fattened or spayed hen.
Skate'board s. A narrow board on roller-skate wheels. v.t. to ride one.
Switch'board s. A board for connecting telephones within a company, etc.
Dash'board s. The instrument-panel in a car or aeroplane.
Nas'ard s. An organ mutation-stop.
Man'sard s. A roof having the lower part steeper than the upper.
Le'otard s. A skin-tight garment for dancers and acrobats.
Jacqu'ard s. A woven fabric.
La'dybird s. A small beetle, brightly spotted.
Whir'lybird s. (*Slang*) A helicopter.
Smör'gåsbord (Smaw'gous-board) s. An assortment of hors d'oeuvres, etc., to which one helps oneself.
Ruth'erford s. A unit of radioactive disintegration.
Milord' s. A rich Englishman.
Sord s. A flock of mallard.
Cross'word s. A puzzle consisting of squares in which one writes answers to clues so that words read across and down.
Turd s. A lump of dung.
Maud s. A Scottish shepherd's woollen plaid.
Ma'rybud s. A marigold bud.
Khud s. A pit; a hollow; a ravine.
Jud s. A mass of coal undercut in wedges.
Foud s. A bailiff or magistrate of the Orkneys and Shetlands.
Stroud s. A type of blanket.
Rud s. Redness; flush; complexion.
Crud s. (*Slang*) A dirty repulsive person; crap.
Sun'dae s. An ice with syrup, fruit and nuts, etc.
Regg'ae s. An aggressive form of rock music from the W. Indies.
Nubec'ulae s. The name of the Magellanic Clouds.
Kan'ae s. A grey mullet of New Zealand.
Cari'be ('bā) s. The piranha.
Bombe s. A dessert of ice-cream in a rounded shape.
Strobe s. A stroboscope.
Pickelhau'be (-how'ba) s. A German spiked helmet.
Rube s. (*US*) A country bumpkin; an uncouth lout.
Thrid'ace s. Inspissated lettuce juice.
An'(e)lace s. A short two-edged dagger.
Half'pace s. A landing or broad step; a raised part of a floor.
Recc'e s. (*Military slang*) Reconnaissance. Also v.t.
All'ice s. A species of shad.
Opor'ice s. A medicine prepared from quince, pomegranate, etc.
Fric'atrice s. A lesbian.
Tice s. A yorker in cricket.
Dol'ce ('chā) a. (*Mus.*) Sweet. s. A soft-toned organ stop.
Free'lance s. Anyone who works for himself, as an unattached journalist, etc. Also a.
Comeup'pance s. Well-deserved punishment or rebuke.
Ou'trance (oo-trās) s. The utmost extremity; the bitter end.
Ponce s. A man who lives on the immoral earnings of a woman.
Alerce' s. The wood of the sandarac.
Work'force s. The total number of workers available for a job.
Du'ce (doo-chā) s. The title of a dictator or leader.
Estacade' s. A dike of piles in a river, etc.
Succade' s. Fruit candied or in syrup.
Frescade' s. A cool walk.
Orangeade' s. A drink made with orange juice.
Slade s. A little valley or dell; a piece of low-lying moist ground.
Croupade' s. A leap in which a horse draws up the hind-legs towards the belly.
Cit'igrade a. Moving quickly (like wolf-spiders).
Pesade' s. A dressage manoeuvre in which a horse stands up on hind-legs.
Glissade' v.i. To slide or glide down. s. An act of sliding down a snow or ice slope.
Croustade' s. A fried bread or pastry case containing game, etc.
Ec'ocide s. Pollution and destruction of the environment (so that it no longer supports life).
Sil'verside s. The top of a round of beef.
Ronde s. A script printing-type.
Sonde s. A device for gathering data on high-altitude atmosphere and weather conditions.
Démo'dé a. Out of date; no longer fashionable.
Étude' s. A musical composition; a test piece.
Haram'bee s. Co-operation; working together.
Emcee' s. A master of ceremonies.
Ly'cée s. A French state secondary school.
Bar'dee s. (*Bardy*).
Drag'ee s. A sweetmeat; a small silvered ball-shaped cake-decoration.
Whangee' s. (A cane made from the stem of) any of several grasses.
Galiongee' s. A Turkish sailor.
Chin-'cherinchee' s. A white-flowered plant. (Also Chinkerinchee).
Cou'chée s. An evening reception.
Quash'ee s. A Negro (in the W. Indies).
Tow'hee s. An American finch.
A(c)kee' s. A small African or W. Indian tree; its fruit.
Gal'ilee s. At the western end of churches, a porch or chapel.
Sall'ee s. An acacia or eucalyptus of Australia.
Mammee' s. A W. Indian tree; its fruit.
Ko'kanee s. A dwarf species of sockeye.
Menom'inee s. A fish of N. American lakes.
Te(e)'pee s. An American Indian tent.
Wampee' s. An Asiatic fruit.
Whoop'ee int. Expressing delight. s. Revelry; a boisterously good time.
Yippee' int. Expressing delight.
Budg'eree a. (*Australian*) Good.
Baj'ree s. (*Bajra*).
Bo'ree s. One of several Australian wattle trees.
Retree' s. Slightly damaged paper.
Bus'tee s. A settlement or group of huts in India.
Spattee' s. An outer stocking or long gaiter.
Twee a. Small and sweet; pretty in a sentimental way.
Feda'yee s. An Arab commando.
Piaffe' v.i. To advance at a piaffer (in horsemanship).
Nife s. The earth's hypothetical core (com-

posed of nickel and iron).
Orfe s. A golden fish, a variety of id.
Sondage′ s. A test-bore or excavation.
Rough′age s. Grain refuse; coarse food; bran.
Enfantillage′ s. A childish action or foolish prank; childishness.
Maquillage′ s. (The art of using) make-up.
Collage′ s. A picture made from scraps of paper, etc.; any work put together from fragments.
Sull′age s. Filth; scum; refuse; silt.
An′lage s. The first rudiment of an organ.
Plage s. A Continental seaside resort or fashionable beach.
Mou′lage s. (The material employed or the process of taking) an impression.
Teen′age a. Of an age between thirteen and nineteen.
Effleurage′ s. A stroking movement in massage. Also v.t. and i.
Osage′ s. An Indian of a tribe based in Oklahoma.
Dressage′ s. (The demo of) the training of a horse in deportment and fine response to controls.
Étage′ s. Storey; floor.
Montage s. The piecing together of material for a picture, etc; Such a picture.
Cab′otage s. (The restriction of) coastal trading.
Escamotage′ s. Juggling.
Frottage′ s. (A pattern obtained by) rubbing to obtain a patterned texture.
Gavage′ s. The cramming of poultry; forcefeeding.
Riv′age s. The bank or shore of a river.
Fridge s. A common abbreviation of refrigerator.
Wodge s. A large lump or unevenly cut slice.
Snudge s. A miser. v.i. To save in a miserly way.
Pogge s. A bony-plated fish, a bullhead.
Greige a. (Of cloth) undyed; of a greyish-beige.
Henge s. A megalithic wood or stone circle.
Binge s. (*Slang*) A drinking spree. Also v.t. and i.
Loge s. A theatre-box.
Stooge s. A scapegoat; a subordinate or henchman; a stage butt.
Auberge′ s. An inn.
Splurge s. Any boisterous display; a dollop; a splash. Also v.i.
Luge s. A one-person sledge. v.i. To sledge on such.
Ta′kahe s. (*Takahea*).
Bell′yache v.i. (*Slang*) To complain whiningly and continually.
Obe′che s. A large W. African tree; its white timber.
Parfleche′ s. (Anything fashioned from) the dried skin of buffalo, etc.
Seiche (sâsh or sesh) s. A tide-like wave on a lake's surface.
Cali′che s. Chile saltpetre.
Corniche′ s. A coastal road on a cliff; a Nile boulevard.
Mori′che s. The miriti palm.
Potiche′ s. An Oriental vase.
Quiche s. A case of unsweetened pastry for filling with egg and cheese, etc.; the dish.
Tranche s. A payment instalment; a block of an issue of shares; the cut edge of a book.
Croche s. A knob on the tip of a deer's horn.
Soro′che s. Mountain-sickness.
Pabouche′ s. A slipper.
Louche a. Shifty; suspicious; disreputable.
Tou′ché int. Expressing claim or admission of a point scored in fencing, argument, etc.
Nura′ghe (′gā) s. A broch-like round tower.

Staithe s. A wharf, embankment or structure for shipping coal.
Zom′bie s. A corpse reanimated; a dull lethargic person.
Weir′die s. An eccentric, unconventional in dress, etc.
I′eie s. A climbing shrub of Hawaii.
Hoa′gie s. (*US*) A sandwich of French loaf split lengthwise and filled.
Budg′ie s. A budgerigar.
Gil′gie s. (*Gilgai*).
Boo′gie s. A jazz rhythm. v.i. To play or dance to it. (Also Boogie-woogie).
Macon′ochie s. (*Military*) Tinned food, especially stew.
See′catchie s. (Pl. *Seecatch*).
Rotch′ie s. The little auk.
Smooth′ie s. (*Slang*) A plausible person who insinuates himself.
Nar′tjie s. A small orange like a mandarin of S. Africa.
Brick′ie s. A bricklayer. (Also Bricky).
Dove′kie s. The rotchie; the black guillemot.
Hon′kie s. (*Honkey*).
Junk′ie s. A drug addict.
Troe′lie s. The bussu palm; its leaf. (Also Troo′lie).
Char′lie s. A fool.
Ky′lie s. A boomerang.
Trem′ie s. A device for laying concrete under water.
Comm′ie s. and a. Communist.
Gree′nie s. (*Slang*) A large wave before it breaks.
Trann′ie s. (*Slang*) A transistor radio.
Bloo′ie s. (*Blooey*).
Chipp′ie s. A woodworker; a carpenter. (Also Chippy).
Clipp′ie s. (*Slang*) A bus conductress.
Group′ie s. (*Groupy*).
Brie s. A soft French cheese.
Cab′rie s. A pronghorn.
Kie′rie s. A cane or stick (in S. Africa).
Ro′tisserie s. (A shop or restaurant where meats are cooked on) a spit.
Book′sie a. By way of being literary.
Floo′sie s. A woman of loose morals; a slovenly prostitute.
Dass′ie s. The hyrax of S. Africa.
Foot′sie s. Amorous flirting by touching with the feet.
Coon′tie s. An American cycad which yields arrowroot.
Coo′tie s. A body louse. (Also Kootie).
Butt′ie s. A sandwich; a slice of bread and butter. (Also Butty).
Ee′vie s. (*Ifi*).
Revie′ v.t. To stake more than another player has proposed on.
Mo′vie s. A film; a cinema show.
Zow′ie int. (*US*) Expressing pleasured surprise.
Mox′ie s. (*US Slang*) Courage; nerve; energy.
Floo′zie s. (*Floosie*).
Gyt′je s. (*Gyttja*).
Cheese′cake s. A dessert containing cream cheese (*Slang*) a pin-up; a show of bodily charms.
No′cake s. Meal of parched Indian corn.
Jake a. Honest; first-rate; correct.
Ratt′lesnake s. A venomous American pit-viper.
Grub′stake s. In the US the supply given to a prospector for a share in his findings. v. To provide with such.
Kish′ke s. (*Kishka*).
Mike s. A microphone.
Grike s. A crack in rock; a hillside ravine.
Moon′strike s. The landing of a spacecraft on the moon.
Min′ke s. A small whale, the lesser rorqual.
Roke s. Mist; rain; smoke; steam; vapour. v.

and i. To steam; to smoke.
Pem'broke s. A small table with hinged flaps.
Heat'stroke s. Exhaustion or illness, etc. due to over-exposure to heat.
Nuke s. (*Slang*) A nuclear weapon. v.t. To attack with such.
Net'suke s. A small Japanese sash ornament or fastening.
Gryke s. (*Grike*).
Tri'ticale s. A hybrid cereal-grass, a cross between wheat and rye.
Aire'dale s. A large breed of terrier.
Rafale' s. A burst of artillery.
Grega'le s. A N. E. wind in the Mediterranean.
Myg'ale s. A bird-catching spider.
Tamal'e s. A highly spiced Mexican dish.
Dwale s. Deadly nightshade; a stupefying drink.
Pac'able a. Willing to forgive; capable of being pacified.
Pin'table s. A pinball machine.
Gribb'le s. A small marine isopod which bores into timber.
Tribb'le s. A wired frame for drying paper.
Faib'le s. The weak part of a foil blade.
Rem'ble v.t. (N. England) to remove; to clear.
Dim'ble s. A dell or dingle.
Ro'ble s. The name for various species of oak.
Ped'icle s. A little stalk.
Chic'le s. The gum of the sapodilla; chewing-gum.
Pin'ocle s. A card game. (Also Pinochle).
Par'adiddle s. A special drum-roll.
Pan'handle s. (*US*) A strip of territory. .v.i. To beg on the streets.
Trin'dle s. A barrow-wheel.
Win'dle s. A yarn-winding appliance.
Ukule'le **(yū-ka-lā'li)** s. A small four-string guitar.
Skiff'le s. A kind of folk-music or its imitation, using unconventional instruments.
Riff'le v.t. To shuffle cards. s. A groove in a sluice for catching particles of ore.
Siff'le v.i. To whistle; to hiss.
Pan'tofle s. A slipper.
Tea'gle s. A hoist, a lift; a baited line for catching birds. Also v.t.
Fina'gle v.t and i. To wangle; to cheat.
Squigg'le s. A wriggly line. v.i. To squirm; to wriggle; to make wriggly lines.
Wogg'le s. A Scout's neckerchief ring.
Horns'woggle v.t To cheat; to hoodwink.
Fog'le s. (*Slang*) A silk handkerchief.
Goog'le v.i. To bowl a googly.
Sper'mophile s. A ground-squirrel.
Étoile **(ā-twal)** s. A star (-shaped object).
Voile s. A thin semi-transparent material.
Corti'le **(tē'lā)** s. An enclosed courtyard within a building.
Keck'le v.t. To protect by binding with rope or chain.
Wan'kle a. Unstable; undependable; changeable.
Run'kle s. A wrinkle; a crease. Also vt. and i.
Kyrielle' s. A string of short lines all finishing with the same word.
Jumelle' s. Opera-glasses.
Roselle' s. An E. Indian hibiscus.
Dentelle' s. Lace(work); an ornamental border or pattern.
Barbastelle' s. A hairy lipped bat.
Ruelle' s. The space between bed and wall.
Roca'ille s. Artificial rockwork; rococo; a scroll ornament.
Faille s. A kind of ribbed silk fabric.
Canaille' s. The vulgar rabble; the mob.
Godille' s. In skiing, a rapid wavy descent on a snowslope.
Espadrille' s. A rope-soled shoe or sandal.
Zorille' s. An African skunk-like animal.
So'bole s. An underground stem producing roots and buds.
Lim'icole s. An oligochaete worm living in mud or water.
Da'riole s. (A dish of a filled) pastry shell.
Anko'le s. A breed of long-horned cattle.
Pino'le s. Ground Indian corn or seeds eaten with milk; a mixture of vanilla and aromatic substances in chocolate.
Escarole' s. A broad-leaved non-curly endive.
Profit'erole s. A small choux pastry puff with filling.
In'sole s. A piece of padded material, etc., worn in a shoe.
Tole v.t. (*US*) To lure; to decoy.
Piace'vole **(chā'vo-lā)** a. (*Mus*) Pleasant, playful.
Ca'ple s. A horse.
Fipp'le s. Part of a recorder; the underlip.
Swipp'le s. The striking part of a flail.
Popp'le v.i. To flow tumblingly; to heave and bob up and down choppily; to make the sound of rippling, bubbling, or repeated shots. s. Such a sound.
Lisle **(līl)** s. A cotton yarn. Also a.
Hass'le s. Bother; fuss; struggle; argument. v.t. To harass. v.i. To be involved in argument, etc.
Gusle s. (*Gusla*).
Pigh'tle s. A small enclosure; a croft.
Whir'tle s. A perforated plate through which tubing, wire, etc., are drawn to make them thinner. (Also Wortle).
Ca'comistle s. A small Mexican and US carnivore cat.
U'le s. A rubber tree of Central America; crude rubber. (Also Hule).
Ves'tibule s. An entrance-hall.
Hi'erodule s. A temple slave.
Boule s. A game like roulette.
Cagoule' s. A kneelength anorak.
Tu'le s. A large American bulrush.
Mvu'le s. A huge African tree; its wood.
Guayu'le s. A Mexican rubber plant; its yield.
Kyle s. A narrow strait.
Pizz'le s. A whip made of a bull's penis.
Shemozz'le s. (*Slang*) A mess; a rumpus; a scrape.
Sozz'le v.t. To intoxicate.
Kame s. An esker; a leaden rod used in framing a window-pane.
Lamé s. A fabric of interwoven threads of silver and gold and silk.
Intime' **(â-tēm)** a. Cosy; confidential.
Al'me s. (*Almah*).
Lumm'e int. (*Slang*-Lord love me!) Expressing surprise, alarm, etc.
Men'opome s. The hellbender.
Hor'me s. Goal-directed behaviour (psychology).
Dirigisme' s. Planned and controlled economy by the State.
Tachisme' s. Abstract painting by the laying on of clotted pigment.
Sar'bacane s. A blow-gun.
Hed'yphane s. A type of lead ore.
Jane s. (*Slang*) A woman.
Mopa'ne s. An African tree.
Gene s. One of the DNA units that transmits characteristics from parents to offspring.
Lasagn'e s. (A dish of) pieces of pasta (with cheese, tomato, meat, etc).
Ligne s. A measure of watch movement.
Prog'ne s. A genus of American swallows.
Madeleine' s. A small shell-shaped cake.
Wahi'ne s. A Maori woman.
El'aphine a. Of or like a red deer.

Ian'thine a. Violet-coloured.
Tar'whine s. An Australian sea-bream
Adren'aline s. A hormone secreted by the adrenal glands.
Pra'line s. A nut kernel coated with sugar or a similar confection.
Head'line s. The title of a newspaper article; a very brief news item. v.t. To publicise, etc.
Coteline' (lēn') s. A kind of ribbed or corded muslin.
Main'line v.i. (*Slang*) To take narcotics intravenously. a. Most important.
Tram'poline s. A framework of elastic fabric for gymnasts, acrobats, etc.
Spline s. A key to make a wheel and rod revolve together.
Mel'amine s. A white crystalline substance; a white plastic finish on furniture, etc.
Amphet'amine s. A synthetic drug used as a stimulant.
Hist'amine s. A base found in the body tissues which is liberated into the blood when skin is cut or burnt, etc.
Mep'acrine s. A bitter yellow powder used against malaria.
Strine s. Australian speech.
Dourine' s. A contagious disease of horses.
In'tine s. The inner membrane of a pollen grain or spore.
Grape'vine s. Rumour; the bush telegraph.
Dwine v.i. To pine.
Fan'zine s. (*US*) A magazine for (science fiction and fantasy) fans.
Panne s. A fabric like velvet with a long nap.
Vi'braphone s. A keyboard instrument with electronically operated resonators.
Zabaglio'ne s. An Italian frothy dessert.
Abalo'ne s. The sea-ear.
Clone s. An individual derived asexually from the living cells of one produced sexually. Also vt. and i.
Pallo'ne s. An Italian game where the ball is hit with the protected arm.
Hor'mone s. An internal body secretion with a specific physiological action.
Chitarro'ne s. A large lute-like long-necked instrument.
Minestro'ne s. A thick vegetable soup with pasta, etc.; any mixture of disparate things.
Sone s. A unit of loudness relative to the listener's hearing.
Cor'tisone s. A steroid; an anti-inflammation agent.
Dap'sone s. A drug used in the treatment of leprosy.
Morne a. Dismal; sombre; gloomy.
Cohune' s. A palm of Central and S. America.
Hy'dyne s. A US rocket-launching fuel.
Haü'yne (hoy'in) s. A blue mineral.
Co'hoe s. A Pacific salmon.
Ky'loe s. One of the Hebridean cattle.
Schmoe s. (*US Slang*) A stupid or boring person.
Cutt'oe s. A large knife.
Canapé' s. Caviare or other delicacy on a piece of bread.
Sera'pe s. A Mexican riding-blanket.
Es'trepe v.t. (*Law*) (as a tenant) to commit waste on land, etc.
Knei'pe s. A tavern or drinking-party (of German students).
Ill'ipe s. The mahwa tree.
Slipe s. A sledge, skip or runner (in mining).
Cass'aripe s. (*Cassareep*)
Equipe' (A-kēp) s. A team (in motor-racing, etc.).
Ol'pe s. A Greek jug.
Tem'pe s. Any place of choice beauty.
Nope int. An emphatic form of no.
Stope s. A step-like excavation in mining. v.t. To cut or dig one.
Échappé s. A leap in ballet.
Schapp'e s. Silk with gum, etc., partly fermented away. v.t. To subject to such a process.
Lagn'iappe (lan'yap) s. A gratuity; something given extra.
Nappe s. A sheet of rock that has been thrust far forward.
Coupe s. A dessert of ice-cream, etc.; its glass bowl.
Loupe s. A small magnifying glass used by watchmakers and jewellers.
Flype v.t. To strip back.
Rype s. A ptarmigan.
Tartare' s. A mayonnaise sauce.
Chambré' a. (Of wine) at room temperature.
Staves'acre s. A tall larkspur.
Pa'dre s. An army chaplain; a parson.
Esclandre' s. Notoriety; any unpleasantness
Com'père s. One who introduces and links items of entertainment.
Canai'gre s. A dock plant (of Texas); its root used in tanning.
Affaire' s. A (scandalous) love-affair or liaison; intrigue.
Hang'fire s. Delay in explosion.
Back'fire v.i. To go wrong; to emit a bang (of an engine cylinder). Also s.
Grimoire' s. A magician's book of spells.
Swire s. A hollow between two hills.
Hay'wire a. (*Slang*) Crazy; all amiss; tangled.
Hard'core s. Rubble, etc. used as road and building foundations.
Cor'ocore s. A type of Malay boat.
Kio're s. A small vegetarian rat of New Zealand.
Blore s. A violent gust of wind.
Hack'amore s. A bridle which is a single length of rope with a loop.
Mattamore' s. A subterranean chamber.
Null'ipore s. A coralline seaweed.
Pal'ampore s. A flowered chintz bedcover.
Chy'pre s. A scent from Cyprus.
Beurré' s. Any of various types of soft pear.
Murre s. A guillemot; a razorbill.
Montre' s. The open diapason of an organ, the visible pipes.
Ab'ature s. A stag's beaten trail.
Lu'nabase s. The dark-coloured regions of the moon as seen from the earth.
Da'tabase s. Databank.
Wheel'base s. The distance between front and rear axles.
Id'ocrase s. Vesuvianite.
Wase s. A wisp of hay or straw; a pad for the head.
Camise' s. An Arab shirt. (Aslo Camese).
Chamise' s. (*Chamiso*).
Vi'chyssoise s. A cream soup served chilled.
Crise (crēz) s. A fit of hysterics or nerves.
Salse s. A mud volcano.
Arkose' s. A sandstone rich in feldspar grains.
Du'mose a. Bushy.
Car'goose s. The crested grebe.
Ac'erose a. Chaffy; needle-pointed.
Pent'ose s. A sugar with five oxygen atoms.
Perse a. Dark blue or bluish-grey. s. The colour; a cloth of such.
Dorse s. A small cod.
Bagasse' s. Dry refuse in sugar-making.
Vinasse' s. Residue from alcoholic distillation.
Jess'e s. A large branched candlestick in churches.
Laisse (less) s. A string of verses with one rhyme.
Mousse s. An iced or other dish of whipped cream.
Pousse s. A dash (of bitters, etc., in drink).

Dysse s. A slab cist containing buried skeletons.
Diseuse' s. A female diseur.
Chan'teuse s. (*US*) A female night-club singer.
Cor'nemuse s. A French bagpipe.
Scouse s. A native of Liverpool; the dialect.
Hot'house s. A place for rearing tropical plants; a heated chamber for drying pottery, etc.
Mickeymouse' a. (*US*) Simulated; in cheap imitation; toy; shoddy.
Cayuse' s. (*US*) A small or poor horse; an Indian pony.
Deal'bate a. Whitened.
De'odate s. A gift to or from God.
Reate (rēt) s. Water-crowfoot.
Ad'nate a. (*Bot*) Attached to another organ.
Karate' (râ-tă') s. A (Japanese) combative sport using blows and kicks.
Stac'te s. A Jewish spice, liquid myrrh.
Jeté' s. A ballet leap.
Arête' s. A sharp ridge; a rocky mountain edge.
Laag'te s. (*S. Africa*). A valley or shallow dip in the veld. (Also Leegte).
Thwaite s. A piece of reclaimed land.
Twaite s. One of the British species of shad.
Blite s. Any of several plants of the goosefoot family.
Pe'lite s. Any rock derived from clay or mud.
Insolite' (-eet') a. Unusual; out of the ordinary.
Cat'amite s. A boy kept for homosexual, etc., purposes.
Mar'mite s. An earthenware stewpot
Kar'ite ('i-ti) s. The shea tree.
Petite' a. Of a woman, small-made and trim.
Yite s. The yellowhammer.
An'te s. A gambler's stake. v.t. to stake.
Vigilan'te s. A sort of troubleshooter, one of the organization looking after a group's interests.
Diamanté' s. A decoration of glittering particles; a fabric so decorated. Also a.
Pesan'te a. and adv. (*Mus.*) Heavy, weighty, direction.
Zan'te s. The wood of the European smoke-tree.
Pointe (pwât) s. In ballet the position of standing on the extreme tip of the toe.
Conte s. (The genre of the) short story.
Entrecôte' s. A steak cut from between two ribs.
Oco'te s. A resinous Mexican pine.
Mogo'te s. A tall steep-sided circular hill of karstic regions.
Clote s. Burdock or other burrs.
Mat'elote s. Fish stewed in wine sauce.
Zopilo'te s. The turkey-buzzard or urubu.
Ceno'te s. A natural underground reservoir.
Peyo'te s. A Mexican intoxicant made from cactus tops.
Cin'easte s. Producer of, collaborator in making, or one who takes an interest in, motion pictures.
Snaste s. A wick; a candle-snuff.
Piste s. A beaten track or ski trail in snow.
Langouste' s. A rock-lobster.
Patte s. A narrow band for keeping a belt in place.
Cour'gette s. A small marrow.
Pochette' s. A small bag; a note-case or wallet.
Couchette' s. A sleeping-berth on a (Continental) train.
Jock'ette s. A female jockey.
Paillette' s. A spangle.
Escopette' s. (*US*) A carbine.
Majorette' s. A girl who twirls a baton at the head of a marching band.
Cassette' s. Recording-tape in a flat sealed unit.
Baguette' s. A small jewel long and rectangular in shape.
Maquette' s. A small model of something to be sculptured.
Blan'quette s. A sort of ragout with a white sauce.
Fauvette' s. A warbler.
Winceyette' s. A plain lightweight cotton cloth slightly raised on both sides.
Pal'afitte s. A prehistoric lake dwelling.
Butte s. An isolated flat-topped and cliff-sided hill rising abruptly from a plain.
Mal'emute s. An Eskimo dog.
Na'sute s. A white soldier ant. a. critically discriminating; beaked.
Versute' a. Crafty; wily.
Byte s. A unit of data in a computer.
Fon'due s. A sauce mixture of cheese and wine, etc. eaten by dipping in pieces of bread, etc., a soufflé.
Banlieue' s. A precinct; a suburb.
Squeteague' s. A US spiny-finned food-fish.
Blague' (blarg) s. Pretentious falsehood; humbug.
Drogue s. A parachute on a space-capsule; a windsock.
Inconnue' s. An unknown woman.
Moue s. A pout; a grimace.
Macaque' s. A type of monkey.
Dis'cotheque s. A place for dancing to records, etc.; the equipment providing the music, lights, etc.
Commu'niqué s. An official announcement or report.
Mystique' s. Sense of mystery, power or skill surrounding a person, etc.; incommunicable spirit or quality.
Boutique' s. A small (dress) shop.
Pétanque' s. A Provençal game similar to bowls.
Plateresque' a. In an architectural style resembling silversmith's work.
Tuque s. A Canadian cap.
Bevue' s. A blunder.
Theave s. A ewe in its first year.
Mi'crowave s. and a. (An oven, etc.) using radiation from the spectrum between normal radio waves and infra-red.
Peeve v.t. To irritate. v.i. To be fretful. s. A mood, grouse or grievance.
Jive s. A style of jazz music or dancing; jargon. Also v.i.
Radioact'ive s. Emitting high-energy rays that lead to disintegration of matter.
Varve s. A seasonal layer of clay deposited in still water. a. Stratified.
Fauve a. Tawny; savage; wild.
Yah'we s. Jehovah.
Pick'axe s. A digging tool.
Saxe s. A deep light-blue colour. Also a.
Maxi'xe (-shē'shā) s. A Brazilian dance; its tune.
Sock'eye s. The blueback salmon.
Skye s. A small long-haired Scotch terrier.
Tye s. An inclined trough for washing ore. Also v.t.
Kamika'ze s. and a. Of a suicidal attack.
Miz'maze s. Bewilderment; a labyrinth.
Bu'aze s. An African fibre-yielding shrub.
Ka'reze s. A kanat in Afghanistan, etc.
Zan'ze s. An African musical instrument.
Bull'doze v.t. To bully; to smash through a crowd, a fence, etc., regardless.
Croze s. The groove in cask-staves in which is set the edge of the head.
Blintze s. A cheese-filled pancake served with jam.
Haaf s. A deep-sea fishing-ground (of the Orkneys and Shetlands).
Clov'erleaf s. A traffic arrangement of flyovers, etc.
Kenaf' s. A plant yielding fibre.

Goaf s. A rick in a barn; a gap left by the removal of a coal-seam.
Khareef' s. (*Kharif*).
Kef **(Kāf)** s. (Hemp smoked to produce) a state of dreamy repose.
Tef s. An Abyssinian cereal grass.
Baff v.t. To hit the ground with the golf-club and thereby send the ball up in the air. s. Such a hit.
Daff v.i. To make sport or play the fool.
Faff v.i. To fuss; to dither; to blunder. s. A blunder due to dithering.
Haff s. A freshwater lagoon at a river-mouth or one separated from the sea by a long sandbar.
Sclaff s. A stroke in golf which scrapes the ground first. Also v.i. and t.
Naff a. (*Slang*) Useless; not very good; bad; rotten.
Kanaff' s. (*Kenaf*).
Niffnaff' s. A trifle; a diminutive person. v.i. To trifle.
Jeff s. A circus rope.
Teff s. (*Tef*).
Biff s. A blow. v.t. To strike hard.
Niff s. (*Slang*) A stink. v.i. To stink.
Riff s. A musical phrase played repeatedly.
Quiff s. A lock of hair oiled and brushed down on the forehead or turned up and back from it.
Shroff s. A banker, money-lender or expert in the detection of bad coins (in the East). Also v.t. and i.
Scuff v.t. and i. To brush; to graze; to abrade; to make or become shabby with wear.
Fuff s. The spitting of a cat; a burst of anger. Also v.i.
Guff s. (*Slang*) Nonsense; humbug.
Kaif s. A undisturbed quiescence.
Kif s. Hashish.
Kharif' s. The rainy season in the Sudan; the crop sown before the monsoon for autumn harvest.
Mutessa'rif s. The head of a sanjak.
Aard'wolf s. An hyena-like S. African carnivore.
Bumf s. Official documents; red tape.
Hof s. A yard; a manor.
Goof s. A stupid awkward person. v.i. To make a blunder.
Wit'loof s. A large-leaved chicory.
Poof s. (*Slang*) A homosexual.
Spoof s. A hoax(ing game). a. Bogus. v.t. and i. To hoax.
Swarf s. Metal filings, grindings, shavings, etc.
Erf s. A garden plot or small piece of ground (S. African).
Lang'lauf s. Cross-country skiing.
Kayf s. (*Slang*) Café.
Debag' v.t. (*Slang*) To remove a person's trousers.
Peag **(pēg)** s. N. American Indian shell-money.
Lall'ygag v.t. To idle; to loiter; to caress publicly.
Sta'lag s. A prisoner-of-war camp (in Germany).
Clag s. A mass of sticky mud, etc. v.i. To stick. v.t. To bedaub.
Mal'mag s. The tarsier.
To'nnag s. A shawl with shaped neck and side fastening.
Sprag s. A mine prop; a bar to stop a wheel. Also v.t.
Dib'atag s. A species of Ethiopian antelope.
Atabeg' s. A ruler or high official.
Muskeg' s. (In Canada) a swamp; a marsh.
Boot'leg v.t. To smuggle (liquor); to make and sell illegally (e.g. records, books, etc.). Also s.
Hy'leg s. The ruling planet at the hour of birth.
Teg s. A sheep in its second year.
Thal'weg s. The longitudinal profile of a river-bed.
Tegg s. (*Teg*).
Yegg s. (*US*) A burglar; a safe-cracker.
Shin'dig s. (*Slang*) A lively party; a celebration; a row.
Cap'rifig s. A wild fig.
Snig s. A river-eel. v.t. To drag a roped or chained load.
Frig **(fridge)** s. (*Fridge*).
Tig s. A game of touch. Also v.t.
Fir'bolg s. An early people of Ireland.
Gebang' s. (*Gebanga*).
Shebang' s. (*US slang*) A house; a shop; a vehicle; an affair; a matter.
Jing'bang s. (*Slang*) A company; a collection; a lot.
Lumbang' s. The candle-nut tree.
Dang int. A minced form of damn.
S(e)la'dang s. The gaur.
Pad'ang s. A field.
Mridang' s. (*Mridanga*).
Yar'dang s. Ridge of sand, silt, etc. formed by wind erosion.
Sir'gang s. A green jay-like bird of Asia.
Kiang s. A Tibetan wild ass.
Kaoliang' s. A liquor made from sorghum grain.
Kang s. A large Chinese water-jar; a warmed sleeping platform.
La'lang s. A coarse grass.
Klang s. A complex musical tone; timbre.
Boom'slang s. A venomous tree-snake of S. Africa.
Par'ang s. A heavy Malay knife.
Woom'erang s. (*Woomera*).
Orang' s. The orang-utan.
Prang s. (*Slang*) A crash. v.t. To crash (a car or plane).
Musang' s. A civet-like carnivore, the paradoxure.
Stang s. A stake; a pole.
Gamm'erstang s. A lanky awkward girl; a wanton.
Zug'zwang s. A blockaded position in chess.
Yang s. Any of various species of Indian timber tree.
Kyang s. (*Kiang*).
Gun'yang s. An Australian shrub.
Kreng s. Whale carcass with the blubber removed.
Ban'teng s. An E. Indian wild ox.
B(i)lim'bing s. (*Bilimbi*).
Small'holding s. (The working of) land on a smaller scale than a farm.
Inbe'ing s. Inherence; inner nature.
Debrief'ing s. A gathering of information on return from a mission.
Spiff'ing a. Excellent.
Hing s. Asafoetida.
Smash'ing a. (*Slang*) Very good.
Back'packing s. Hiking, carrying one's food and equipment on one's back.
Blink'ing a. (*Slang*) A substitute for bloody.
Mall'emaro'king s. The carousing of seamen in ice-bound ships.
Dor'king s. A breed of poultry.
Saib'ling s. The char.
Gan'gling a. Lanky; loosely built.
Reck'ling a. Puny. s. The weakest and smallest of a litter.
Buck'ling s. Smoked Baltic herring.
Hall'ing s. A Norwegian country-dance; its tune.
Her'ling s. A finnock.
Bitt'erling s. A small fish.
Mor'ling s. (The wool of) a sheep dead from disease.
Ries'ling s. A dry white table wine.
Bris'ling s. A Norwegian sprat.
Quis'ling s. One who aids the enemy; a puppet prime minister.

Whit'ling s. A young bull-trout.
Tit'ling s. A small stockfish; the meadow-pipit or hedge-sparrow.
Mort'ling s. (*Morling*).
Bri'ming s. Phosphorescence of the sea.
Steen'ing s. The stone lining of a well.
Ra'ring a. Eager (for); full of enthusiasm.
Shoe'string s. A minimum of money. Also a.
Popp'ering s. A variety of pear.
Ant'ing s. The introduction by birds of live ants into their feathers to clean them, etc.
Ban'ting s. (*Banteng*).
Munt'ing s. A vertical framing piece between door panels.
Cork'wing s. The goldsinny.
Bill'abong s. A stagnant backwater; a cut-off loop of a river.
Chitt'agong s. An Indian domestic fowl.
Bu'gong s. An Australian moth, a delicacy of aborigines.
Kurr'ajong s. Any of various Australian trees with fibrous bark.
Ke'long s. A thatched hut over stakes driven into the seabed as a fish trap.
Oo'long s. A variety of black tea. (Also Oulong).
Boong' s. A native of New Guinea; an aborigine.
Pong s. A bad smell. v.i. To smell bad.
Kam'pong s. An enclosed space; a Malay village.
Sarong' s. A skirt-like garment of Malaya.
Bin'turong s. A prehensile-tailed civet of S. Asia.
Tong s. A Chinese guild or secret society.
Pak'tong s. Nickel-silver.
Lotong' s. A Malayan leaf-monkey.
Jel'utong s. A Bornean tree.
Mor'wong s. An Australian and New Zealand food-fish.
Ben'twong s. (*Binturong*).
Be'bung s. A tremolo effect on a clavichord.
Gee'bung s. An Australian tree.
Del'undung s. A small carnivore akin to the civet.
Quer'sprung s. In skiing, a right-angled jump-turn.
Shantung' s. A plain rough cloth of wild silk.
Hu'tung s. A narrow side-street or alley in Chinese parts.
Lutung' s. (*Lotong*).
Anschau'ung s. Direct perception through the senses.
Fire'dog s. An andiron.
Hang'dog a. With a sneaking and cowed look.
Hop'dog s. The tussock-moth caterpillar; a tool for removing hop-poles.
Un'derdog s. Any person in adversity.
Whole'hog a. (*Slang*) Complete; out-and-out. Also adv.
Shog s. A jog; a shock. v.i. To shake; to sway; to jog.
Log'log s. The logarithm of a logarithm.
Foot'slog v.i. To tramp; to march lengthily.
Mog s. (*Slang*) A cat.
Smog s. Smoky fog.
Snog v.i. (*Slang*) To indulge in kissing.
Moog s. An electronic musical instrument synthesizing any sound.
Trog v.i. To trudge.
Sog s. A soft wet place. v.t. and i. To soak.
Wog s. A disrespectful name for a coloured foreigner.
Phizog' s. (*Slang*) The face.
Berg s. A hill or mountain; an iceberg.
In'selberg s. A steep-sided ridge arising from a plain tract.
Kil'erg s. A thousand ergs.
Os'naburg s. A coarse linen or cotton material.
Hom'burg s. A felt hat with narrow brim and dented crown.
Co'burg s. A thin fabric of worsted with cotton or silk, twilled on one side.
Scup'paug s. The porgy.
Debug' v.t. To remove faults from (a system, machine, etc.); to remove hidden microphones from.
Doo'dlebug s. The larva of an ant-lion; a flying bomb.
Fire'bug s. An arsonist.
Chug s. A rapid puffing noise (as of an internal-combustion engine). Also v.i.
Skug s. A squirrel.
Goug s. (*Guga*).
Vug s. A (Cornish miner's) crystal-lined rock-cavity.
Boyg s. An ogre; any difficult problem or obstacle.
Cool'abah s. Any of several species of Australian eucalypt.
Jubb'ah s. A long loose outer-garment of Mohammedans.
Kas'bah s. (*Kasba*).
Isbah' s. (*Isba*).
Doo'dah s. An agitated state.
Yeah adv. Yes.
Steng'ah s. A peg of whisky and soda.
Galah' s. An Australian cockatoo.
Blah s. (*Slang*) Bunkum; pretentious talk.
Bab'lah s. A species of acacia; acacia pods.
Kib'lah s. The point towards which praying Mohammedans turn.
Methu'selah s. A very old person; a very large wine-bottle.
Pall'ah s. The impala.
Om'lah s. A staff of officials in India.
Masoo'lah s. A many-oared surf-boat of India.
A'mah s. A native maid-servant; a child's wet-nurse.
Bee'nah s. A form of marriage in Ceylon.
Num'nah s. A felt pad to prevent under-saddle chafing.
Jo'nah s. A bringer of bad luck.
Chutz'pah s. Effrontery.
Ma'rah s. Something bitter; bitterness.
Almir'ah s. A cupboard; a wardrobe; a cabinet.
Chak'rah s. (*Chakra*).
Om'rah s. A Mohammedan lord.
Gurr'ah s. A coarse Indian muslin.
War'atah s. Any of a genus of showy shrubs of Australia.
Mitz'vah s. A good deed.
Kaja'wah s. A camel litter or pannier.
Hi'yah int. (*Hiya*).
Geni'zah s. A room adjoining a synagogue used for the safe-keeping of old documents, etc.
Mezuz'ah s. A (Jewish) parchment scroll of texts.
Knai'dlach s. (Pl. *Knaidel*).
Dor'lach s. A bundle; a sheaf; a valise.
Bach'arach s. A wine from Rhine regions.
Sleech s. Slimy mud; a mud-flat.
Reich s. An empire (esp. German); a state.
(Rīhh)
Schlich s. Fine portions of crushed ore separated by water.
Kilch s. A small whitefish.
Zilch s. (*Slang*) Zero; nothing.
Culch s. Rubbish; oyster-spawn; the floor of an oyster-bed.
Brunch s. A meal serving as breakfast and lunch.
Agall'och s. Eaglewood.
Smooch v.i. To kiss; to pet.
Pooch s. (*Slang*) A (mongrel) dog.
Roch s. (*Rotchie*).
Scho'larch s. The head of a school (of philosophy).
Ü'bermensch s. A superman.
Mel'kbosch s. A deciduous shrub or small tree of S. Africa.
Borsch s. A Russian soup with beetroot, etc.
Quetsch s. A variety of plum (brandy).
Kitsch s. Trash; pretentious art.

Bortsch s. (*Borsch*).
Putsch s. A sudden revolutionary outbreak.
Am'batch s. A pith-tree.
See'catch s. An Aleutian fur-seal (male).
Pot'latch s. A festival; a gift (-giving occasion).
Natch s. The rump. adv. (*Slang*) Naturally.
Cross'patch s. An ill-natured person.
Spetch s. A piece of skin used in glue-making.
Glitch s. (*Slang*) A malfunction, hitch or snag (in a spacecraft, etc.); a surge of current or electronic signal of sudden irregular behaviour.
Knitch s. A faggot.
Cultch s. (*Culch*).
Rotch s. (*Rotchie*).
Butch a. Tough; aggressive.
Smutch s. A smudge of soot or grime. Also v.t.
Smouch s. A smack; a hearty kiss. Also v.t.
Psych v.t. (*Slang*) To defeat or intimidate by psychological means.
Cei'lidh (kā'li) s. An informal evening of song, dance and story.
Kir'beh s. A skin for holding water.
Kish'keh s. (*Kishka*).
Al'meh s. (*Almah*).
Reh s. An efflorescence of sodium salts on Indian soil.
Lang'seh s. (*Langsat*).
Jah'veh s. Jehovah.
Kaffi'yeh s. A Bedouin head-shawl.
Shough (shog, shok, shuf) s. A shaggy kind of lapdog.
Tur'lough ('lohh) s. A pond which is dry in summer.
Si'rih s. Betel.
Ankh s. An ansate cross.
I'poh s. The upas tree; a S.E. Asian shrub (poisonous); their poisons.
Oomph s. (*Slang*) Vitality; enthusiasm; sex-appeal; personal magnetism.
Bumph s. (*Bumf*).
Harrumph' v.i. To disapprove noisily; to make a noise as if clearing the throat. s. Such a noise.
Squabash' v.t. To crush; to smash. s. a crushing.
K(o)ur'bash s. A hide whip. v.t. to whip with one.
Fog'ash s. The pike-perch.
Do'bhash (dō'bash) s. An interpreter.
Back'lash s. Violent consequence or reaction.
Gou'lash s. A spicy stew of beef and vegetables; a redeal (without shuffling) in bridge.
Bud'mash s. An evil-doer. Also Badmash.
Pash s. (*Slang*) Passion.
Gy'trash s. A ghost.
Succ'otash s. A stew of pork, beans and corn.
Stash s. A hoard. v.t. To stow in hiding.
Hog'wash s. Insincere rubbish; thin watery stuff; brewery or kitchen refuse.
Si'wash s. A N.W. American Indian. Also a.
Bish s. (*Slang*) A mistake; a blunder. Also v.t. and i.
Nebb'ish s. An insignificant incompetent; a nobody. Also a.
Ka'dish s. An Arabian cross-bred horse.
Kadd'ish s. A Jewish form of thanksgiving and prayer.
Spoff'ish a. Fussy; officious.
Knish s. A filled dumpling, baked or fried.
Tova'rish s. (*Russian*) Comrade.
Squish v.i. To squash; to make a squelching sound. Also s.
Wish'tonwish s. The N. American prairie-dog.
Ki'bosh s. Nonsense; rot. v.t. To dispose of once and for all.
Cosh s. and v.t. (*Slang*) Bludgeon.
Josh s. A jest. v.t. To ridicule.
Nosh s. (*Slang*) Food. v.i. To eat.

Hoosh s. A thick soup. int. and v.t. Shoo.
Shush v.t., i., int. Hush.
Bell'push s. A button-operated doorbell.
Kovsh s. A ladle or container for drink.
Op'simath s. One who learns late in life.
Tath s. (Grass growing on) cattle dung.
Staith s. (*Staithe*).
Reg'olith s. Mantle-rock.
Flute'mouth s. A fish akin to the stickleback.
Frog'mouth s. A bird of the mopoke family.
Cott'onmouth s. A venomous water moccasin-snake.
Ver'mouth s. A drink with white wine as a base.
Crwth (krooth) s. A Welsh stringed instrument.
Na'gelfluh s. One of the massive conglomerates of rock in the Swiss Alps.
Nenn'igai s. (*Nannygai*).
G(h)il'gai s. A saucer-like depression which forms a natural rainwater reservoir.
Ko'gai s. Environmental pollution.
Nann'ygai s. A large marine food-fish of Australia. Also Nannyghai.
Kow'hai s. A New Zealand shrub.
Kai s. (New Zealand) Food.
Rem'blai s. A rampart of earth; stowage in a mine.
Kar'mai s. (*Ka(a)mahi*).
Kan'ai s. (*Kanae*).
Lana'i (or Lanai') s. A porch or veranda; a roofed structure with open sides.
Ku'nai s. A large coarse grass of Asia, Australia, etc.
Sim'pai s. The black-crested langur (of Sumatra).
Perai' s. (*Piranha*).
Terai' s. A wide-brimmed ventilated hat.
Pirai' s. (*Piranha*).
Hom'rai s. A large black-and-white hornbill of Asia, etc.
Sa'i s. The capuchin monkey.
Ma'sai s. An African people.
Bon'sai s. A dwarf pot-tree; the art of growing such.
Assa'i adv. (*Mus.*) Very, s. A S. American palm; its fruit; a drink made from it.
Tai s. A Japanese sea-bream.
Ka'(ha)wai s. A marine food-fish of Australia and New Zealand.
Awa'bi s. The abalone of Japan.
Or'ibi s. A small S. African antelope, the pale buck.
Muhim'bi s. An evergreen tree of E. Africa; its wood (Uganda ironwood).
Bilim'bi s. An E. Indian tree; its fruit.
Zim'bi s. A money-cowrie.
Zom'bi s. (*Zombie*).
Kar'bi s. A small dark stingless bee of Australia.
Gour'bi s. A tent or poor dwelling-place in N. Africa.
Farci' a. Stuffed (culinary).
Kabad'i s. A team game like tig (of India and Pakistan). (Also Kabaddi).
Gad'i s. An Indian throne.
Fun'di s. A W. African grass; its millet-like seed.
Jaguarun'di s. A S. American wild cat.
Bar'di s. (*Bardy*).
Vlei (flā) s. (*US*) A swamp; low ground where a shallow lake forms in wet seasons.
Ni'sei (nē'sā) s. One resident in the USA, born of Issei parents.
Is'sei (ēs'sā) s. A Japanese immigrant in the USA.
I'fi s. An evergreen tree of Tahiti.
Ra'gi s. A millet grown in India, Africa, etc.
Sa'rangi s. An Indian fiddle.
Lun'gi s. A long cloth used as a turban, a loincloth, etc.

Sho'gi s. Japanese chess.
Cor'gi s. A small dog of Welsh breed.
Lur'gi s. (*Lurgy*).
Ilia'hi s. One of several Hawaiian trees with aromatic wood.
Ka(a)'mahi s. A forest tree of New Zealand. (Also Karmahi).
Gno'cchi s. A dish of small dumplings in sauce.
Chichi' a. Pretentious; fussy. s. Red tape; fuss; pretension.
Bod'hi s. A Ceylonese tree, the pipal.
I'hi s. (*Ifi*).
Bimba'shi s. A Turkish (or Egyptian) military officer.
Im'shi int. (*Military slang*) Go away; begone.
Kovsh'i s. (Pl. *Kovsh*).
Lathi' s. A heavy stick.
Basen'ji s. A small African (breed of) hunting-dog that rarely barks.
Sho'ji s. A wood-frame paper wall-screen (found in Japanese homes).
Kia'ki s. (*Keyaki*).
Ka'ki s. The Japanese persimmon; the Chinese date-plum.
Rak'i s. An alcoholic liquor.
Keya'ki s. A Japanese tree; its timber.
Suki'yaki s. A Japanese dish of beef, vegetables and sauce.
Wa'kiki s. Shell money.
Ti'ki s. (*Maori*). An ornamental image of an ancestor.
Pal'ki s. A palanquin.
Mo'ki s. Either of two marine fish of New Zealand.
Titok'i s. A New Zealand tree.
Astat'ki s. The residue of petroleum distillation used as fuel.
Kabuki' s. Japanese musical drama.
Salu'ki s. A silky-haired Arabian or Persian greyhound.
Bouzou'ki s. A Greek stringed instrument.
Da'li s. A tropical American tree.
Kathaka'li s. A classical dance drama (of S. India).
Serkal'i s. Government; white rulers.
Hall'ali s. A bugle-call.
(W)(o)ura'li s. The plant which yields curare.
Vali' s. A governor, especially of a vilayet.
Son'deli s. The Indian musk-shrew.
Ka'reli s. (*Karela*).
Put'eli s. A flat-bottomed Ganges craft.
Jung'li a. Wild and boorish. s. A jungle inhabitant; an uneducated peasant.
Ug'li s. A fruit crossed between grapefruit and tangerine.
Gin'gili s. A species of sesame; the oil from its seeds.
Kahi'li s. A ceremonial feather standard.
Chil'i s. A hot dry wind of N. Africa.
Jin'jili s. (*Gingili*).
Pili' s. A type of nut.
Cho'li s. A short-sleeved blouse (often worn under a sari).
Raviol'i s. Minced seasoned meat in pasta cases.
Ner'oli s. An oil distilled from orange flowers.
Mue'sli s. A breakfast dish of cereal and fruit. (Also Musli).
Gus'li s. (*Gusla*).
Origam'i s. The art of folding paper into models and figures, etc.
Ka'mi s. (*Japanese*) Lord; god; a deified ancestral hero.
Tsuna'mi s. A high swift-travelling wave.
Pastram'i s. Smoked and seasoned beef.
Swa'mi s. An idol; a religious instructor.
Sem'i s. A semi-detached house.
A'ni s. A black hook-billed bird of tropical regions.
Jam'dani s. A muslin woven in a design of flowers.
Mapa'ni, Mopa'ni s. (*Mopane*).
Ran'i s. A queen or princess.
A'deni s. A citizen of Aden. Also a.
Zucchi'ni s. (*US*) A courgette.
Biki'ni s. A narrow two-piece ladies' bathing-costume.
Min'i a. Small. s. A small car; a very short skirt.
Ko'nini s. A small tree or shrub of New Zealand, its berries.
Alpi'ni s. (Pl. *Alpino*).
Kongo'ni s. The hartebeest of the E. African plains.
Soffio'ni s. (Pl.) Volcanic steam-holes.
Cannello'ni s. Large pasta tubes stuffed with cheese or meat; this dish.
Garni' a. Garnished. s. A dish accompanied by the appropriate vegetable.
Moo'i a. Fine.
Po'i ('ē) s. A Hawaiian dish, a paste of fermented taro root.
Renvoi' s. A government's sending-back of an alien to his own country.
Scam'pi s. (A dish of) large prawns.
Topi' s. A pith-helmet, an Indian sola hat.
Illu'pi s. (*Illipe*).
Amba'ri s. An Indian plant; the fibre it yields.
Sun'dari s. An E. Indian timber-tree.
Safa'ri s. A hunting or long and dangerous expedition. Also v.i.
Na'gari s. The group of alphabets to which Devanagari belongs.
Devana'gari s. The official script for Hindi.
Koftgari' s. The work of inlaying steel with gold.
Kalamka'ri s. A method of colouring and decorating by several dyeings, etc; a chintz thus treated.
Aska'ri s. An E. African soldier.
Kumar'i s. A title of respect in India, Miss.
(O)ura'ri s. (*Wourali*).
Sar'i s. A Hindu woman's garment.
S(a)oua'ri s. A timber and nut tree of Guiana.
Ry'otwari s. A system of land-tenure in India. (Also Raiyatwari).
Aliza'ri s. A levantine madder.
Sun'dri s. (*Sundari*).
Son'eri s. A cloth of gold.
Agg'ri a. Of glass beads of W. Africa.
Saimi'ri s. A squirrel-monkey.
Si'ri s. (*Sirih*).
Dai'quiri s. A cocktail of rum and lime-juice.
Baj'ri s. (*Bajra*).
Millefio'ri s. Ornamental glass made by fusing coloured rods.
Sato'ri s. (*Zen*) Sudden enlightenment.
Karr'i s. A W. Australian gum-tree; its red timber.
Guarr'i s. A tree or shrub of S. Africa; its fruit. (Also Gwarri).
Pe'tri s. A kind of shallow glass dish used for bacteria cultures.
Kab(o)ur'i s. A tiny black biting fly of Guyana.
Ventur'i s. A measuring-tube for fluid flow-rate.
Brin'disi s. A drinking-song; a toast.
Chaprass'i s. An office messenger; an orderly; a household attendant.
Tsot'si s. A young non-white S. African thug or hooligan, usually part of a gang.
Chapat'i s. A thin unleavened bread.
Za'ti s. The bonnet-monkey.
Yet'i s. The abominable snowman.
Shuf'ti s. (*Slang*) A look (at something).
Miriti' s. A palm tree.
Buriti' s. A miriti palm.
Titi' s. A small S. American monkey.
Wis'titi s. A marmoset.
Oustiti' s. A lock-opening tool, outsiders.
Meran'ti s. A tree of Malaya, Sarawak and Indonesia; its hardwood timber.
Dho(o)'ti s. (*Hindu*) A loincloth; fabric for it.

Parti′ s. A man considered as a marriageable 'catch'.
As′ti s. An Italian white wine.
Chapatt′i s. (*Chapati*).
Gomu′ti s. A palm; its black fibre.
Guazu′ti s. The S. American pampas-deer.
Kuku′i s. An evergreen tree of the Pacific islands, the candlenut or candleberry.
Ma′qui s. A Chilean evergreen; a medicinal wine of its berries.
Chiquichi′qui s. A piassava palm.
Tu′i s. The parson-bird.
I′vi s. (*Ifi*).
Ii′wi **(ī-ī′wi)** s. A Hawaiian bird, the honey-creeper.
Gha′zi s. A high Turkish title; a slayer of infidels.
Na′zi s. and a. National Socialist, Hitlerite.
Bwa′zi s. (*Buaze*).
Dar′zi s. A tailor.
Pa′aj s. A form of dermatitis.
Swaraj′ s. (The agitation for) self-rule (in India).
Esraj′ s. An Indian stringed instrument.
Benj s. Bhang.
Munj s. A tough Asiatic grass.
Ud′ruj s. An E. Indian medicinal gum.
Bo′bak s. A species of marmot.
Off′peak a. Not at the period of highest demand.
Lap′streak s. A clinker-built boat.
Hair′streak s. A butterfly having white-banded underwings.
Pip′squeak s. (*Slang*) Someone insignificant and contemptible.
Jak s. An E. Indian tree.
Kulak′ s. An exploiter; a rich peasant.
Ba′nak s. A Central American tree; its hardwood timber.
Go′pak s. A Russian folk-dance.
An′orak s. A light hooded waterproof jacket.
Nu′natak s. A point of rock above the surface of land-ice.
Mu′zak s. Nondescript background music.
Bi′ofeedback s. Clinical control of body functions in response to monitoring by electronic instruments.
Hatch′back s. A car with the rear door opening upwards.
Switch′back s. An up-and-down track for fairground cars.
Tail′back s. A line of traffic stretching back from an obstruction.
Lou′derback s. A cap of old lava on a tilted fault-block.
Pa′perback s. A soft-cover book.
Wet′back s. One entering the USA illegally (from Mexico).
Bush′whack v.t. To ambush.
Hi′jack v.t. To force a pilot, driver, etc., to take his transport to another destination. Also s.
Man′jack s. A W. Indian tree; its fruit.
Crack′erjack s. A person or thing exceptionally splendid. Also a.
Sky′jack s. The hijacking of an aircraft in flight. Also v.t.
Shoe′black s. One who polishes shoes.
Mud′pack s. A cosmetic paste.
Brack s. A flaw in cloth.
Barm′brack s. A currant-bun.
Wise′crack s. A lively witty retort or comment. Also v.i.
Back′track v.i. To go over what one has covered before.
Am′track s. An amphibious military motor landing vehicle.
Yack s. (*Slang*) Idle or stupid talk. Also v.i.
Sneck s. A latch; a door-catch. v.t. To fasten with one.
Ry(e)′peck s. A pole for mooring a punt.
Hick s. A lout; an uncultured peasant. a. Rural and uncultured.
Tchick s. A clicking sound made with the mouth. Also v.i.
Skin′flick s. (*Slang*) A pornographic film.
Mick s. An Irishman (*offensive*).
Gimm′ick s. A device to catch the attention or gain publicity.
Kinnikinick′ s. A tobacco substitute (used by American Indians).
Dor′nick s. A stout figured linen.
Hoick s. A jerk. v.t. and i. To hitch up; to jerk up.
Mav′erick s. (*US*) A stray calf; a non-conformist. v.t. To seize without legal claim.
Yard′stick s. Any standard of comparison or measurement.
Green′stick a. Of a fracture when bone is partly broken and partly bent.
Slap′stick s. Low comedy or farce. Also a.
Lip′stick s. Colouring matter for the mouth. v.t. and i. To paint with this.
Can′dlewick s. A tufted cotton material used for bedspreads, etc.
In′wick s. A stroke in curling.
Kes′wick s. A variety of cooking-apple.
Mocock′ s. An American Indian birch-bark box or basket.
Popp′ycock s. (*Slang*) Balderdash.
Dadd′ock s. The heart of a rotten tree.
Gav′elock s. A javelin; a crow-bar.
Schlock a. (*US Slang*) Of inferior quality. s. Anything like this.
Hoo′lock s. A small gibbon (of Assam).
Hamm′erlock s. A wrestling hold in which the opponent's arm is twisted up behind his back.
Gamm′ock s. and v.i. Frolic; lark.
Monad′nock s. A hill or mountain of erosion-resistant rock.
Finn′ock s. A young sea-trout
Pinn′ock s. The hedge-sparrow; the blue tit.
Yap′ock s. The water-opossum of S. America.
Feed′stock s. Raw material used in an industrial process.
Muck′luck s. An Eskimo sealskin boot.
Mall′emuck s. The fulmar or similar bird.
Schmuck s. (*US slang*) A fool; an innocent naif.
Cruck s. A curved timber supporting a roof (in crude building).
Atabek′ s. (*Atabeg*).
Lebb′ek s. An Old World tropical tree.
Kweek s. Any of several creeping grasses of S. Africa.
Nek s. A col.
Roo′inek s. An Afrikaans name for an Englishman.
Ol′ykoek s. (*US*) A kind of doughnut.
Tu′pek s. (*Tupik*).
Na′ik s. A lord or governor; a corporal in Indian infantry.
Zen′dik s. A sorcerer (in the East).
Shash′lik s. A sort of kebab.
Sus′lik s. A ground-squirrel.
Dvor′nik s. (*Russian*). A concierge or porter.
Sput′nik s. A (Russian) man-made earth satellite.
Tu′pik s. An Eskimo skin tent.
Batik′ s. A method of making designs on cloth using wax to mask certain areas.
Ko′matik s. A dog-sledge. vi. and i. To travel thus. (Also Ka′mo(o)tik).
Side′walk s. (*US*) A pavement.
Pulk s. (*Pulka*).
Da′tabank s. The body of information stored in a computer for retrieval.
Chank s. The shell of various molluscs sliced into bangles; such a bangle.
Fink s. (*Slang*) An informer; an unpleasant person. v.i. To rat on.

Gink s. (*Slang, derogatory*) A man.
Oink s. The grunt of a hog. Also v.i.
Chewink' s. A N. American finch, the red-eyed towhee.
Clonk v.t. To hit. s. The sound of something hitting an unyielding surface.
Plonk s. (*Slang*) (Cheap) wine.
Cronk a. (*Australian slang*) Ill; of poor quality; unfavourable.
Debunk' v.t. (*Slang*) To clear of nonsense; to show up as false.
Po'dunk s. (*US*) Any typically dull and outdated country town.
Dun'derfunk s. Ship-biscuit baked with fat and molasses.
Gunk s. Any unpleasantly dirty and sticky stuff.
Clunk s. A solid heavy sound. Also v.i.
Flunk v.t. and i. (*Slang*) To fail in an examination.
Plunk v.t. To twang; to drop, etc. so as to make a hollow sound. Also s.
Ang'ekok s. An Eskimo conjurer.
Boo'book s. An Australian owl.
Gook s. (*Slang*) One of Asiatic race.
Gobbledegook' s. (*Slang*) Official jargon. (Also Gobbledygook).
Kook s. (*Slang*) A crazy or eccentric person; a novice.
Ger'anook, Ger'enook s. (*Gerenuk*).
Chinook' s. A warm dry wind of the Rockies; a warm moist wind from the Pacific.
Yap'ok s. (*Yapock*).
Atok' s. A species of skunk.
Chark s. Coke; charcoal. v.t. To burn to charcoal.
Jark s. (A) safe-conduct (pass); a document seal.
Tel'emark s. A sudden outer ski turn. Also v.i.
Nark s. (*Slang*) An informer. v.t. and i. To annoy; to tease.
Snark s. An imaginary monster.
Quark s. A supposed subatomic particle.
Erk s. (*Slang*) An aircraftsman.
Berk s. (*Slang*) A fool.
Yerk v.t. and i. To bind or tie tightly.
Stirk s. A yearling; a young ox or cow.
Ground'work s. The essential part; the basis or first principle.
Spade'work s. Preparatory labour (of a drudging nature).
Coach'work s. A motor-car body.
Fan'cywork s. Ornamental needlework.
Burk s. (*Berk*).
Cusk s. The torsk or burbot.
Padauk' (-dowk') s. A Burmese timber tree.
Dybb'uk s. An evil spirit.
Taluk' s. A tract of land; a district's subdivision.
Muk'luk s. (*Muckluck*).
I'lluk s. A coarse grass of Ceylon.
Ger'enuk s. A long-necked antelope of E. Africa.
Souk s. An oriental (-style) bazaar or marketplace
Zumboo'ruk s. A small swivel cannon (carried on a camel).
Yuk a. (*Slang*) Nasty, dirty; s. Anything unpleasant.
Bash'lyk s. A hood like that worn by Russian soldiery.
Sa'bal s. A genus of American palms.
Jum'bal s. A thin crisp sweet cake.
Jacal' s. A wattle-and-mud hut; an adobe house; the material or method for building such.
De'cal (or Dec') s. A transfer picture or design.
Pas'cal s. A unit of pressure.
Cou'cal s. A genus of bush-birds; a type of cuckoo.
D(h)al s. The Indian pulse or pigeon-pea; a puree of it.
Ooi'dal a. Egg-shaped.
Groen'endal s. A black smooth-coated (breed of Belgian) sheepdog.
Tin'dal s. A petty-officer of lascars.
Surre'al a. Beyond preconception; more than real.
Mangal' s. A brazier.
G(h)ar'ial s. (*Gavial*).
Oo'rial s. A Himalayan wild sheep. (Also Urial).
Si'al s. The partial outer shell of the earth.
Brin'jal s. (The fruit of) the egg-plant.
Pokal' s. An ornamental drinking-vessel.
Halal' v.t. To slaughter. s. An animal slaughtered according to Mohammedan law that may be eaten.
Gue'mal s. (*Guemul*).
Hammal' s. An Eastern porter. (Also Hamal).
Romal' s. A head-cloth; a handkerchief.
Paranor'mal a. Psychologically abnormal. Also s.
Adren'al a. Beside the kidneys. s. A gland so situated.
Penn'al s. A freshman at a German university.
Mon'al s. (*Monaul*).
Amm'onal s. A high explosive.
Skoal int. Hail (a drinking cry).
Pi'pal s. The bo-tree.
Bhar'al s. The Himalayan blue sheep.
Ru'deral a. Growing in waste places or among rubbish.
Abo'ral a. Away from the mouth.
Nem'oral a. Of a wood or grove.
Worr'al s. A monitor lizard.
Chamisal' s. A thicket of chamiso.
Ver'sal s. An ornamental letter in an illuminated MS.
Chi'tal s. The axis deer.
Can'tal s. A hard type of French cheese.
Simm'ental s. A breed of cattle.
Har'tal s. A strike (in India) as a protest.
Kot'wal s. A chief constable or magistrate of an Indian town.
Dirn'dl s. A full tight-waisted skirt (and bodice of Alpine peasant women's style).
Knay'dl s. A kind of dumpling.
Bael s. A thorny Indian tree; its quince-like fruit. Also Bel.
Bel s. Ten decibels.
Ne'bel s. A Hebrew instrument, a harp.
Dec'ibel s. A measure of noise intensity or electrical currents.
Span'cel s. A hobble. Also v.t.
Knai'del s. (*Knaydl*).
Al'udel s. A pear-shaped vessel used in sublimation.
Stru'del s. Thin pastry containing fruit, etc.
Cockateel' s. (*Cockatiel*).
Keff'el s. A horse, a nag.
Gel s. A jelly-like colloidal solution. v.i. To form a gel.
Ba'gel s. (*US*) A roll in the shape of a doughnut.
Zing'el s. A perch-like fish (of the Danube).
Aas'vogel s. A S. African vulture.
Bhel s. (*Bael*).
Tin'chel s. A group of men forming a circle round a deer-herd.
Switch'el s. Treacle-beer, molasses and water.
Futch'el s. A carriage timber supporting splinter-bar and pole.
Burh'el s. (*Bharal*).
A'thel s. A tamarisk of Asia and Africa. (Also Ithel).
Schlemiel' s. (*Slang*) A stupid clumsy person.
Dan'iel s. A wise judge.

Spiel s. Glib talk. Also v.t. and i.
A'riel s. A species of swallow, petrel or toucan; a kind of gazelle.
Cockatiel' s. A small crested Australian parrot.
Seck'el s. A variety of pear.
Mis'pickel s. A mineral, arsenical pyrites.
S(ch)nor'kel s. A submerged swimmer's breathing-tube.
Sewell'el s. An American rodent between beaver and squirrel.
Sam'el a. Like a brick, underburnt.
Schimm'el s. A roan horse.
Stumm'el s. The bowl and adjacent part of a pipe.
Ox'ymel s. A honey-and-vinegar mixture.
Go'el s. A Hebrew avenger of murder.
Rappel' s. A drum-beat call to arms; a method of cliff descent using two ropes. Also v.i.
Parr'el s. A band for fixing a yard to a mast.
Worr'el s. (*Worral*).
Burr'el s. (*Burhel*).
Cos'trel s. An eared bottle for hanging at the waist.
Saurel' s. The horse-mackerel or scad.
Dies'el s. A type of engine; diesel fuel.
Gun'sel s. (*US slang*) A stupid inexperienced youth; a gunman.
Dickciss'el s. An American migratory bird, the black-throated bunting.
Carousel' s. (*US*) A merry-go-round.
Tel s. A hill or ancient mound
Poin'tel s. A sharp instrument or style.
Motel' s. A hotel with units to accommodate cars, etc.
Barbastel' s. (*Barbastelle*).
Rondav'el s. A round hut (in S. Africa).
Riv'el v.t. and i. To wrinkle.
Knaw'el s. A cornfield weed.
Shew'el s. A deer scare.
Ax'el s. A jumping movement in skating.
Pix'el s. One of the tiny units which make up a TV picture on a cathode-ray tube.
Zel s. An Oriental cymbal.
S(c)hlima'zel s. (*US slang*) A persistently unlucky person.
Ziz'el s. A suslik.
Schnit'zel s. A veal cutlet.
Schlemihl' s. (*Schlemiel*).
Ped'rail s. A tractor with footlike pieces on the wheels; such a piece.
Vit'rail s. Stained-glass (window).
Con'trail s. Condensed vapour left by high-flying aircraft.
Cott'ontail s. (*US*) A rabbit.
Boat'tail s. A grackle.
Jez'ail s. A heavy Afghan gun.
Ab'seil (Ap'zīl) v.i. To let oneself down a cliff-face using a rope.
Mon'ofil s. A single strand of synthetic fibre.
Pu'gil s. A pinch (as much as the thumb and two fingers can hold).
I'thil s. (*Athel*).
Cour'baril s. The W. Indian locust-tree; its resin.
Kril s. The food of fish and whales, etc., a small shrimp-like crustacean. Also pl.
Zor'il s. (*Zorille*).
Vril s. Electric fluid (the common origin of forces in matter).
Ches'il s. Gravel; shingle; bran.
Tahsil' s. In India a division for revenue, etc.
Til s. Sesame.
Fraz'il s. Ground-ice or spiky ice in streams, etc.
Puff'ball s. A spore-filled ball-shaped fungus.
Goof'ball s. (*Slang*) A barbiturate pill used as an exhilarant.
Pin'ball s. (An electronic) form of bagatelle or other machine game.
Bas'ketball s. A game in which goals are scored from throwing a ball through a high net.
Screw'ball s. (*US*) A crazy person; an eccentric; a ball in baseball that breaks contrary to its swerve. Also a.
Wind'fall s. Fruit blown off the tree; any unexpected money or other benefit.
Fem'erall s. An outlet in a roof for smoke.
Cov'erall s. (*US*) A boiler suit.
Wool'fell s. The skin with the wool still on it.
Egg'shell s. A very thin kind of porcelain. a. Thin and delicate; of paint, having a slight gloss.
Kell s. A hair-net; a film or network.
Mell v.t. and i. To mix; to mingle; to join in fight; to meddle; to be concerned.
Schnell a. (*Slang*) Quick. adv. Quickly.
Burr'ell s. (*Bharal*).
Vell s. A calf's third stomach.
Max'well s. The CGS unit of magnetic flux.
Boat'bill s. A bird of the heron family.
O'verkill s. Power in excess of what is required for destruction.
Penn'ill s. (*Welsh*) A form of improvised verse.
Min'ipill s. A low-dose oral contraceptive, oestrogen -free.
Krill s. (*Kril*).
Rig'oll s. A gutter or water-channel.
Dholl s. (*Dal*).
Stull s. An horizontal mine-prop.
C(h)ib'ol s. A variety of onion.
Rig'ol s. (*Rigoll*).
Goo'gol s. The number 1 followed by a hundred zeros.
Axeroph'thol s. Vitamin A.
Pan'thenol s. A vitamin of the B-complex which affects hair-growth.
Tom'fool' a. Extremely foolish.
Kagool' s. (*Cagoule*).
Shool v.i. To saunter about; to skulk; to beg; to sponge.
Cess'pool s. A pit or pool of filthy water.
Brool s. A deep murmur.
In'terpol s. The international crime squad.
Ster'ol s. A solid higher alcohol.
Choles'terol s. A white crystalline solid in the blood-stream, etc.
Podsol' s. A bleached sand soil.
A'erosol s. (A container of) liquid under pressure for spraying.
Am'atol s. A high explosive.
Cirl s. A species of bunting.
A'tl s. (*At[illegible]*).
Na'hautl s. The Aztec language. Also a.
Rot'l s. A variable Levantine weight.
Mon'aul s. A Himalayan pheasant.
Sax'aul s. A low thick Asian tree.
Ba'bul s. (*Bablah*).
Skin'ful s. As much liquor as one can hold.
Shul s. A synagogue.
Kar'akul s. (A breed of) Asiatic sheep; its wool; a cloth like it.
G(u)e'mul s. A small Andean deer.
Ca'pul s. (*Caple*).
Pi'pul s. (*Pipal*).
Jarul' s. An Indian tree. (Also Jarool).
Kittul' s. The jaggery palm; its fibre.
Ca'comixl s. (*Cacomistle*).
Vin'yl s. An organic radical; a plasticky material. Also a.
Met'opryl s. An anaesthetic related to ether.
Bae'tyl s. A meteoric stone regarded as holy or magical.
Hw'yl (hū'il) s. Emotional fervour; divine or poetic inspiration.
Muqadd'am s. A headman. Also Mokaddam.
E'dam s. A Dutch cheese.
Main'stream a. Of jazz, etc., coming in between early and modern; most important.
Mridang'am s. (*Mridanga*).
Tran'gam s. Trumpery, gimcrack.

Pel'ham s. A type of bit combining curb and snaffle designs.
Ful'ham s. A loaded dice.
Dur'ham s. A breed of shorthorn cattle.
Seal'yham s. A long-bodied short-legged (breed of) terrier.
Hak'am s. A sage or early rabbinical commentator.
Panis'lam s. The whole Mohammedan world.
Stroam v.i. To stroll; to stride; to roam.
Scram v.i. To be off. Also int.
Tan'gram s. A Chinese puzzle.
Hol'ogram s. A three-dimensional image created by split laser light.
Ihram' s. A Mohammedan pilgrim's garb.
Ash'ram s. (*Ashrama*).
Lock'ram s. A coarse linen.
Marr'am s. A seaside grass which binds dunes.
Cheong'sam' s. A garment worn by Chinese women.
Mo'dem s. An electronic data transceiver.
May'hem s. Maiming; malicious damage.
Riem s. A rawhide thong.
Lem s. A moon-craft (lunar excursion module).
Per'iblem s. The meristem forming the cortex of plants.
Clem v.t. and i. To starve.
Phell'em s. Cork.
Go'lem s. A human image brought to life; a zombie; a robot; a dolt.
Rem s. A unit of radiation dosage.
Sem'sem s. Sesame.
Cher'nozem s. Very fertile soil of subhumid steppe.
Pash'm s. The fine underfleece of Indian goats used for rugs, etc.
Shim s. A slip of wood or metal, etc., used as a filler.
Hakim' s. A judge; a governor; an official.
Plim v.t. and i. To swell.
Alas'trim s. A mild form of smallpox.
Pich'urim s. A S. American tree; its aromatic nut.
Goy'im s. (Pl. *Goy*).
Na'palm s. A highly-inflammable petroleum jelly used in bombs and flame-throwers.
Stulm s. An adit; a small drainage-shaft.
In'tercom s. An internal telephone system.
Sit'com s. A situation comedy.
Sla'lom s. A zigzag downhill ski-race or obstacle course for canoes.
Glom v.t. (*US slang*) To steal; to grab; to snatch.
Wa'(gen)boom s. A S. African tree.
Spek'boom s. A S. African succulent shrub.
Back'room a. Secret; behind the scenes.
Prom s. A promenade concert. v.i. To stroll about.
Log'atom s. Any nonsense syllable used in testing telephone systems.
Smarm v.t. and i. To smear; to daub; to plaster; to sleek.
Inerm' a. Without thorns; unarmed.
Perm s. and v.t. Permutation, permutate; to wave the hair permanently.
Lind'worm s. A wingless dragon of mythology.
Horn'worm s. A hawk-moth caterpillar.
Phae'ism s. Duskiness; incomplete melanism in butterflies.
Dirigism' s. (*Dirigisme*).
Tach'ism s. (*Tachisme*).
Pop'ulism s. The belief that the common people should rule themselves.
Rach'manism s. The charging of extortionate rents in slum conditions.
E'onism s. The practice of males of adopting female dress and manner, etc.
Heur'ism s. The educational practice of making the pupil the discoverer.
Ac'rotism s. Medical absence of pulsation.
Transvest'ism s. Dressing in the clothes of the opposite sex.
Sex'ism s. Discrimination (against women or men) on grounds of sex.
Leb'ensraum s. Room to live.
Mocudd'um s. (*Muqaddam*).
Notan'dum s. Something to be specially observed.
Ommate'um s. A compound eye.
Hum'hum s. A plain coarse cloth of E. India.
Oid'ium s. The conidial stage of vine-mildew and other fungi.
Magna'lium s. A light strong alloy used in aircraft, etc.
Om'nium s. In the Stock Exchange, the aggregate value of the different stocks in which a loan is funded.
Pium' s. A small troublesome biting fly of Brazil.
Formica'rium s. A receptacle for keeping an ant colony.
Panarit'ium s. A whitlow.
Dink'um a. (*Australian slang*) Real; honest; genuine.
Ho'kum s. (*US slang*) Claptrap.
Ko'kum s. An E. Indian tree.
Pas'palum s. A genus of tropical pasture grasses including pampas.
Chill'um s. (The tobacco-holding part of) a hookah; the act of smoking one.
Rep'lum s. A partition in a fruit.
Co'coplum s. A W. Indian tree; its fruit.
Op'timum a. Very best. Also s.
Sagape'num s. A foetid gum-resin.
Delu'brum s. A temple, shrine, sanctuary; (a church with) a font.
Grum a. Surly; morose; deep-sounding.
Spec'trum s. The range of colours, radiations, sound frequencies, opinions, etc.
Ras'trum s. A music-pen.
Pen'sum s. A task; (*US*) an impot
Pine'tum s. A plantation or collection of pine trees.
Mul'tum s. An adulterant in brewing.
Hawm v.i. To loung about.
Scrawm v.t. To scratch.
Cwm (coom) s. (*Welsh*) A hillside hollow; a deep wooded vale.
Am'ban s. A Chinese official in a dependency.
Sor'oban s. A Japanese abacus.
Jer'rican s. A sort of petrol-can.
Yakh'dan s. A box or pannier carried by a yak.
Maidan' s. An open plain or space; an esplanade; a parade-ground.
Kal'amdan s. A Persian writing-case.
Lur'dan s. A dull heavy stupid or sluggish person.
Hou'dan s. A breed of black-and-white fowl.
Sarafan' s. A cloak (in the style of Russian peasant women).
Ve'gan s. A vegetarian using no animal produce at all.
Mull'igan s. A stew made of odd scraps from other meals.
Shenan'igan s. (*Slang*) Trickery, humbug.
Wan'(i)gan s. A supply-chest or pay-office in a lumber camp.
Long'an s. A tree akin to the litchi; its fruit.
Ar'gan s. A Moroccan timber tree; its seed.
Dur'gan s. A dwarf (-sized creature).
Kurgan' s. A sepulchral barrow.
Machan' s. A shooting-platform in a tree.
Tulch'an s. A calf's skin put beside a cow to make it give milk freely.
Ar'ghan s. The plant yielding pita fibre.
Lang'shan s. A small black Chinese hen.
Dar'shan s. A blessing received by touching or seeing a holy person.
Pathan' (pa-tân') s. One of Afghan race settled in India. Also a.
Bo'than s. A booth, hut, or illegal drinking-den.
Asc'ian s. One who inhabits the torrid zone.
Perisc'ian s. A dweller within the polar circle.

Prid'ian a. Pertaining to yesterday.
Orth'ian a. High-pitched.
Bil'ian s. A heavy timber-tree of Borneo.
Kil(l)'ian s. A fast dance for two side-by-side on ice.
Hippocre'pian a. Horseshoe-shaped.
Ora'rian s. A coast-dweller. a. Coastal.
Thalass'ian s. A sea-turtle. a. Marine.
Tit'ian s. A red-yellow colour. Also a.
Rumfus'tian s. A hot drink, a kind of negus.
Vesu'vian s. A slow-burning match.
Pek'an s. A large N. American marten, the wood-shock.
Ach'kan s. An Indian knee-length coat.
Gam'elan s. A xylophone-like instrument; an Asian orchestra.
Flan s. A flat open tart.
Ball'an s. A species of wrasse.
Cour'lan s. A rail-like bird.
A'meslan s. American sign-language.
K(o)u'lan s. A wild ass, the onager.
Cam'an s. A shinty stick.
Dam'an s. The Syrian hyrax.
Hie'laman s. An Australian native shield of bark or wood.
Dod'man s. A snail.
Frog'man s. An underwater swimmer with wet suit and webbed feet.
Pe'terman s. A safe-blower.
Om'budsman s. One appointed to investigate complaints in government.
Des'man s. A species of aquatic insectivore with long snout and musk-glands.
Crags'man s. A skilled rock-climber.
At'man s. (Hinduism) The divine within the self.
Dec'uman s. A large wave.
Hanuman' s. The entellus monkey.
Dead'pan a. Expressionless; emotionless; (mock) serious.
Skid'pan s. (*Slang*) A drag for a wheel.
Out'span s. A stopping-place. v.t. and i. To unyoke; to unharness from a vehicle.
Tri'maran s. A three-hulled boat.
Var'an s. A monitor lizard.
Lo'ran s. A long-range radio-navigation system.
Buran' s. A violent blizzard from the N. E. in Siberia and Central Asia.
Ki'san s. An Indian peasant.
Tut'san s. A species of St John's wort, park-leaves.
Shaitan' s. A dust-storm; a devilish person.
Sum'pitan s. A Malay blowpipe.
Manhatt'an s. An American cocktail.
Rambu'tan s. A tall Malayan tree; its fruit.
Mou'tan s. A tree-peony.
Lauan' (lawân) s. A light hardwood timber of the Philippines.
Ta'guan s. A large E. Indian flying-squirrel.
Tuan' s. Sir; lord; a title of respect.
Jawan' s. A common soldier in India.
Aj'(o)wan s. A plant of the caraway genus.
Pow'an s. A species of whitefish from Scottish lochs.
Tar'zan s. A man of great agility and strength.
Gra'ben s. A rift valley.
Cru'been s. A cooked pig's foot.
Al'peen s. A cudgel.
Kar'anteen s. A striped sea-fish of African and Indian waters; the bamboo-fish.
Steen v.t. To line (a well) with stone. Also s.
Costeen' v.i. (*Costean*).
Posteen' s. An Afghan greatcoat of sheepskin and fleece.
Feda'yeen s. (Pl. *Fedayee*).
Mut'agen s. An agent that causes mutation.
Lu'cigen s. A type of lamp.
Hu'mogen s. A fertilizer.
Hallu'cinogen s. A drug producing hallucinatory sensations.
Oes'trogen s. Any one of the female sex-hormones.
Rönt'gen s. The unit of X-ray or gamma-ray dosage. Also a.
Mär'chen s. (& pl.) A folk-tale or fable.
Seph'en s. A sting-ray.
Mur'ken a. (*Australian slang*) Out of season.
Puta'men s. A fruit-stone; the membrane in an egg-shell.
Galjoen' (Hhal-yun) s. A S. African sea-fish.
Vel'skoen (fel'skoon) s. A rawhide shoe.
Dukkerip'en s. Fortune-telling.
Schlie'ren s. pl. Streaks of different colour, etc., in rock.
Dze'ren s. An Asian antelope.
Grei'sen s. A rock of quartz and mica, formed from granite by fluorine exhalations.
Le'derhosen s. (*German*) Short leather trousers with braces.
Delicatess'en s. A shop selling prepared foods, etc.
Niss'en s. A temporary corrugated-iron hut.
Kan'ten s. Agar-agar jelly.
Sten s. A small automatic gun.
Sebes'ten s. An Oriental tree; its plum-like fruit.
Twitt'en s. A narrow lane between two walls or hedges.
Chev'en s. The chub.
Stev'en s. A voice.
Cov'en s. A group of witches.
Au'tobahn (ow'tō-bân) s. An arterial road for motor-traffic.
Föhn (furn) s. A hot dry wind blowing down a mountain valley. (Also Foehn).
Ouaba'in s. A poisonous alkaloid obtained from certain seeds and wood.
Mar'ocain s. A grainy-surfaced dress-material.
Pe'neplain s. A land-surface worn down by denudation.
Papa'in s. A digestive enzyme in the juice of papaws.
Gros'grain s. A heavy corded silk used for hatbands and ribbons, etc.
Sou'terrain s. An underground chamber.
Fusain' s. Artists' fine charcoal.
Mombin' s. A W. Indian tree; its plum-like fruit.
Psilocy'bin s. A hallucinogenic drug obtained from Mexican mushrooms.
Proper'din s. A natural immunising substance in the blood.
Hor'dein s. A barley-grain protein.
Stein s. A German (-style) tankard (with hinged lid).
Schal'stein s. A slaty diabase tuff.
Ze'in s. A protein in Indian corn.
Boff'in s. A research scientist.
Cuff'in s. A fellow, man.
Hum'gruffin s. A terrible person.
Pidg'in s. A distortion of languages used as a means of common communication.
Kin'chin s. (*Slang*) A child.
Coch'in s. A large feathery-legged (breed of) domestic hen.
Tang'hin s. A Madagascan tree; its poison.
Man'akin s. A small tropical American bird.
Mor'kin s. An animal that has died by accident.
Jos'kin s. A clown; a yokel.
Adren'alin s. (*Adrenaline*).
Grid'elin s. and a. Violet-grey.
Cap'elin s. A small bait-fish of the smelt family.
Fluell'in s. A name of various speedwells.
Penicill'in s. A group of substances that stop bacteria-growth.
Col'in s. The Virginian quail.
Per'colin s. A small bird, cross between quail and partridge.
Tram'polin s. (*Trampoline*).
Mar'lin s. A large ocean fish akin to the sword-fish.

In'sulin s. An animal extract used for treating diabetics, etc.
Pat'ulin s. A drug obtained from a mould.
Tam'in s. A thin highly glazed worsted.
Hec'ogenin s. A synthetic form of cortisone.
Li'nin s. The substance forming the network of a cell nucleus.
Foin s. A thrust with sword or spear. Also v.i.
Sagoin' s. (*Sagouin*).
Chin'kapin s. The US dwarf-chestnut. Also Chincapin, Chinquapin.
At'abrin s. Mepacrine.
Crin s. A fabric of horsehair (with other fibre).
Ko'rin s. A small W. African gazelle.
Sarr'asin s. A buckwheat.
Erep'sin s. An enzyme of the small intestine
Gratin' s. The upper-crust, elite people.
Munt'in s. (*Munting*).
Chambertin' s. A red burgundy wine.
Ru'tin s. A drug used against fragility of small veins.
Sag'uin s. (*Sagouin*).
Béguin' s. Infatuation.
(bay-gwa)
Sag'ouin s. A titi monkey.
Chev'in s. (*Cheven*).
Al'evin s. A young fish; a salmonid.
Kel'vin s. A unit of temperature.
Griseoful'vin s. An oral antibiotic for treating fungus infections.
Sew'in s. A Welsh grilse.
Teguex'in s. A large black-and-yellow S. American lizard.
We'deln v.i. To make a wavy ski-descent.
Do'bermann s. A kind of German hound.
Ga'on s. A genius; a prodigy.
Bour'bon s. (*US*) Maize whisky.
Lis'bon s. A light-coloured Portuguese wine.
Flacon' s. A scent-bottle.
Mâcon' s. A burgundy wine.
Panop'ticon s. A prison where one point gives observation of all prisoners.
Mas'con s. A mass concentration of dense matter under the moon's surface.
Gladd'on s. An iris.
Ple'on s. A crustacean's abdomen.
Meze'reon s. An European shrub; its medicinal bark.
Ti'gon s. The offspring of tiger and lioness.
Four'gon s. A baggage-wagon.
Tel'ethon s. A very long TV programme.
Perei'on s. A crustacean's thorax.
Voca'lion s. An instrument like a harmonium.
Scall'ion s. An onion; a leek
Hell'ion s. A child of diabolical behaviour.
Pennill'ion s. (Pl. *Pennill*).
Orill'ion s. A semicircular projection at the shoulder of a bastion.
Epyll'ion s. A short(er) epic poem.
In'ion s. The external occiputal protuberance.
Zwitt'erion s. An ion carrying both positive and negative charge.
Tu'rion s. An underground bud growing up into a new stem.
Illis'ion s. The act of striking against something.
Televis'ion s. (A set for receiving) images via electrical transmission. Also a.
Panda'tion s. Warping.
Repta'tion s. Squirming along or up a narrow passage, etc.
Nolit'ion s. Unwillingness; the will not to do.
Ul'tion s. Revenge; avengement.
Oer'likon s. An anti-aircraft gun.
Mat'felon s. The greater knapweed.
Pad'emelon s. A small wallaby.
Decath'lon s. A two-day contest of ten events.
Biath'lon s. An international competition in skiing and shooting.
Mo'ellon s. Rubble in mason-work.
Paill'on s. A piece of foil to show through enamel, etc.
Papillon' s. A (breed of) toy spaniel.
Ny'lon s. A polymeric amide fibre; material or stockings of it. Also a.
Monox'ylon s. A canoe made from one log.
Epise'mon s. A badge or characteristic device.
Nor'imon s. A Japanese palanquin.
Mus'(i)mon s. The mouflon.
Olecra'non s. The upper part of the ulna.
Guen'on s. A long-tailed African monkey.
Ninon' s. A silk voile or other thin fabric.
Pi'ñon s. An American tree; its pine-seed.
Colcann'on s. A kind of Irish stew.
Puccoon' s. A species of American plants; bloodroot.
Goon s. (*US slang*) A hired thug; a stupid person.
Poon s. An Indian tree.
Hero'on s. A temple or monument for a hero.
Patroon' s. A ship's captain.
Saskatoon' s. The shad-bush; its fruit.
Ya'pon s. (*Yaupon*).
Met'opon s. A pain-relieving drug derived from opium.
Y(a)u'pon s. A bushy evergreen shrub of the US.
Cam(m)ar'on s. A freshwater shrimp or prawn resembling a crayfish.
Mi'cron s. One-millionth of a metre.
Had'ron s. A subatomic particle.
Lon'geron s. A longitudinal member of an aeroplane.
Hap'teron s. A holdfast of a plant thallus.
Katab'othron s. An underground water-channel. (Also Katavothron).
Ooph'oron s. An ovary.
Mor'on s. A feeble-minded person; an idiot.
La'tron s. A robber.
Pos'itron s. A positive electron.
Mell'otron s. An electronic keyboard-instrument which synthesizes orchestral sounds, etc.
Vi'son s. (*US*) The mink.
Nel'son s. A wrestling hold.
Frisson' s. A shiver; a shudder; a thrill.
Stet'son s. A broad-brimmed hat.
Sab'aton s. A foot-armour.
Chaton' s. The head of a finger-ring.
Mir'liton s. A toy reed-pipe.
Piton' s. A mountaineer's iron spike for fastening a rope.
Wil'ton s. A cut-pile carpet.
Pro'ton s. A positively charged elementary particle.
Bur'ton s. A tackle having two or three blocks.
Jett'on s. A stamped-metal game-counter.
Flett'on s. A type of facing brick.
Croûton' s. A small piece of fried-bread.
New'ton s. The SI unit of force.
El'evon s. An aircraft wing-flap acting as both elevator and aileron.
Klax'on s. An electric or mechanical horn.
Tach'yon s. A supposed particle travelling at faster-than-light speed.
Harn s. A coarse linen fabric.
Sharn s. Cow-dung.
Sal'fern s. Gromwell.
Flitt'ern s. A young oak.
Firn s. Snow on high glaciers.
Am'elcorn s. Emmer.
Pil'corn s. A variety of oat.
Big'horn s. A Rocky Mountain sheep or goat.
Vul'turn s. The Australian brush-turkey.
Om'adhaun s. A fool.
Tu(r)n'dun s. An Australian whirring toy (bull-roarer).
Tan'gun s. The Tibetan piebald pony.
Ca'jun s. (A corruption of Arcadian) applied to

a style of rock-music, etc.

In'jun s. An (American) Indian.
Jo'tun s. A giant. (Also Jö'tunn).
Hoe'down s. A country-dance; hillbilly or other music for it; a party.
Splash'down s. The landing of a manned spacecraft in the sea.
South'down s. A breed of sheep; its mutton.
Melt'down s. A collapse due to fuel in a nuclear reactor critically overheating.
Hom'elyn s. The spotted ray.
Ciao (chow) int. Hello; goodbye (informal).
Bacala'o s. (*Bacalhau*).
Gherao' (gerau) s. The workers' detainment of management, etc. until demands are met. Also v.t.
Ura'o s. Natron.
Yobb'o s. (*Yob*).
Place'bo s. A medicine of no curative effects given a patient to gratify him.
Angwan'tibo s. A small W. African lemur.
Dam'bo s. A grassy clearing (in Africa).
Mam'bo s. A W. Indian dance or tune; a voodoo priestess.
Zam'bo s. A person of mixed Negro and Indian blood.
Timbo' s. A S. American climber; a poison from its bark.
Com'bo s. A small jazz or dance band.
Miom'bo s. An African tree, woodland of such trees.
Jum'bo a. Colossal; huge. s. An elephant.
Rum'bo s. Rum-punch.
Lo'bo s. (*US*) A grey wolf.
Bon'obo s. The pygmy chimpanzee.
Dso'bo s. (*Zho*).
Zo'bo s. (*Zho*).
Gar'bo s. (*Australian slang*) A dustman; a refuse-collector.
Ica'co s. A small W. Indian tree, the coco-plum; its fruit.
Pa'co s. Alpaca.
Squacc'o s. A small crested heron.
Sec'co a. (*Mus.*) Unaccompanied; s. Painting on dry plaster.
Cocc'o s. Taro or a similar edible tuber.
An'gico s. A S. American tree; its gum.
Mi'co s. A (black-tailed) marmoset.
Pat'rico s. (*Slang*) A hedge-priest.
Ale'atico s. A sweet red wine of Italy.
Mati'co s. A Peruvian pepper shrub; a styptic of it.
Barran'co s. (*Barranca*).
Flamen'co s. A type of Andalusian dance or song.
Locofo'co s. (*US*) A friction match.
Tabas'co s. A hot pepper sauce.
Cas'co s. A Philippine lighter.
Cis'co s. A herring found in the Great Lakes.
Dis'co s. (*Discotheque*).
Mamelu'co s. The offspring of a European and an Indian.
Tucutu'co s. A S. American rodent with mole-like behaviour.
Ado' s. Bustle; trouble; fuss; stir.
Incommunica'do a. and adv. Without means of communication; not contactable.
Zapatead'o s. A lively solo Spanish dance.
Fa'do s. A Portuguese folk-song or dance.
Ma'do s. A small Australian and New Zealand marine fish.
Fuma'do s. A smoked fish; a pilchard.
Aficiona'do s. An ardent fan or follower.
Edd'o s. (A taro) plant tuber.
Ki'ddo s. (*In address*) 'My boy', 'matey', etc.
Albe'do s. Whiteness; the light reflected by a planet.
Com'edo s. A blackhead; a small black-tipped white mass.
Tuxe'do s. A dinner-jacket.
I'do s. A language developed from Esperanto.
Libi'do s. Vital urge; sexual drive.
Di'do s. (*Slang*) Antic; caper; frivolous or mischievous act.
Bu'shido s. The ethical code of the Samurai.
Aiki'do s. A (Japanese) wrestling sport.
Li'do s. A bathing-beach; an open-air pool.
Mancan'do a. and adv. (*Mus.*) Fading away.
Parlan'do a. and adv. (*Mus.*) Recitative; in declamatory style.
Rinforzan'do a. (*Mus.*) With sudden accent.
Smorzan'do a. and adv. (*Mus.*) Growing slower and softer while gradually fading away.
Perden'do a. and adv. (*Mus.*) Dying away in volume, tone and speed.
Ken'do s. The (Japanese) art of swordsmanship.
Moren'do a. and adv. (*Mus.*) Dying away.
U'do s. An edible species of (Japanese) Aralia.
Ju'do s. A modern type of Ju-jitsu.
Lu'do s. A board-game with counters and dice.
Na(i)e'o s. (*Naio*).
Vid'eo a. and s. (*US*) Television.
Rode'o s. An exhibition of cowboy skill; a motor-cycle contest.
Geo' s. (*Orkneys and Shetlands*) a gully; a creek.
O'leo s. An oleograph or oleomargarine.
Ro'meo s. A young man very much in love.
Vir'eo s. A genus of US birds (the greenlets).
Pase'o s. A walk, street or promenade.
Cuff'o adv. (*US slang*) With no admission charge.
In'fo s. A common abbreviation of information.
U'fo s. An unidentified flying object.
Galap'ago s. A tortoise.
Sapsa'go s. A hard green cheese.
Gre'go s. (*Levantine*). A hooded jacket or overcoat.
Se'go s. An American showy plant.
Dogg'o a. Hidden.
Vitili'go s. A skin condition of irregular patches of white.
Gink'go s. The (Japanese) maidenhair tree.
Fan'go s. Medicinal clay or mud of thermal springs.
Guan'go s. An ornamental tree of the Caribbean.
Mandin'go s. An African of the Niger valley.
Bon'go s. A small drum; an African bushbuck.
Dron'go s. A black insect-catching bird of Africa; (*Australian slang*) nitwit.
Kun'go s. (*Kungu*).
Go'go a. Very active; enthusiastic; alert to seize opportunities.
Bor'go s. A borough or market-town.
Colu'go s. The (so-called) flying lemur.
Lanu'go s. Down; an embryonic woolly coat of hair.
Mach'o a. Exaggeratedly virile; aggressively masculine. s. One with such traits.
Quebra'cho s. One of several S. American trees; their wood or bark.
San'cho s. A W. African guitar.
Co'ho s. (*Cohoe*).
Toho' int. Calling to pointers to halt.
Mor'pho s. A large S. American butterfly, brilliant blue.
Nav'arho s. A long-range radio-navigation system for aircraft.
Zho s. A male beast (cross between yak and cow).
Ngai'o (nī'ō) s. A New Zealand tree; its white wood.
Nai'o s. A Hawaiian evergreen tree.
Libecc'io (-bet'chō) s. The S.W. wind.

Addi'o int. Goodbye.
Gio' s. (*Geo*).
Kuro'shio s. A warm Pacific current.
Pol'io s. (A sufferer from) Poliomyelitis Also a.
Bri'o s. Liveliness; vivacity; spirit.
Vib'rio s. A bacterium (like cholera).
Bagui'o (bâ-gē'ō) s. A hurricane.
Azule'jo (a-thoo-lā'hhō) s. A glazed tile.
Mo'jo s. (*US*) Magic; the art of casting spells; a charm or amulet; any narcotic.
Cheecha'ko s. A (Canadian) tenderfoot.
Ma'ko s. A large blue shark, the mackerel shark.
Buck'o s. Young lad; chap; boy.
Dekk'o s. and v.i. (*Slang*) Look.
Cheechal'ko s. (*Cheechako*).
Stal'ko s. A gentleman of no fortune or occupation.
San'ko s. (*Sancho*).
Bo'ko s. (*Slang*) The nose.
Iro'ko s. An African hardwood tree; its timber.
Fin'sko s. pl. Reindeer-skin boots with the hair on. (Also Finn(e)sko).
Rob'alo s. A US pike-like fish.
Beef'alo s. A cross between cow and N. American buffalo.
Catt'alo s. A cross between bison and domestic cow.
Tan'gelo s. A hybrid orange.
Tu'pelo s. An American gum-tree.
Mil'o s. A drought-resistant grain (originally from Africa).
Bordell'o s. A brothel.
Caudill'o (dēl'yō) s. The leader or head of state in Spanish-speaking countries.
Mill'o s. (*Milo*)
Zorill'o s. A S. American skunk.
Crioll'o s. A type of cocoa-tree; its beans.
Tom'bolo s. A sand or gravel bar connecting islands with mainland, etc.
Zu'folo s. A small flute for training singing-birds. (Also Zuff'olo).
Gig'olo s. A male prostitute; a young man living at the expense of an older woman.
Hol'o s. A hologram.
Ko'lo s. A Serbian dance; its tune.
Palo'lo s. An edible sea-worm.
Ro'tolo s. The Italian rotl.
Mat'lo s. (*Slang*) A seaman; a sailor.
Tapacu'lo s. A small S. American bird.
Mo s. A popular abbreviation of moment.
Dem'o s. A public expression of discontent, etc., by mass-meetings, marches, etc.
Mem'o s. A memorandum.
Supre'mo s. A supreme head.
Schmo s. (*Schmoe*).
Li'mo s. (*US abbreviation*) Limousine.
Zho'mo s. A female beast (cross between yak and cow). (Also Jo'mo, Dso'mo).
Machis'mo s. An exaggerated sense or image of masculinity or virility.
Veris'mo s. (*In art*) Realism or objectivity.
Lu'cumo s. An Etruscan prince and priest.
Su'mo s. A (Japanese) form of wrestling.
Giz'mo s. (*US slang*) A gadget; a dingus.
Oreg'ano s. Origanum.
Sola'no s. A hot S.E. wind in Spain.
Ripie'no s. (*Mus.*) A supplementary instrument or performer. a. Supplementary.
Cappucci'no s. Black coffee (with little milk).
Scaldi'no s. An earthenware brazier.
Fi'no s. A delicate pale dry sherry.
Hin'o s. (*Hinau*).
Chi'no s. (*US*) Strong twilled cotton material.
Stracchi'no s. A soft cheese of N. Italy.
Mi'no s. A raincoat of hemp, etc.
Palomi'no s. A horse of pale tan, yellow or gold, with white or silver mane and tail.
Alpi'no s. An Italian trooper for mountain warfare.
Volpi'no s. A small fox-like Italian dog.
Zorin'o s. A skunk-fur (garment).
Wi'no s. A wine alcoholic.
Makimo'no s. A silk roll of writing or pictures, etc. (not hung).
Madro'ño s. A Californian evergreen tree.
Be'naboo s. (*Benab*).
Did'geridoo' s. An Australian (aboriginal) tubular musical instrument.
Hoo'doo s. A bringer of bad luck. v.t. To bewitch.
Nardoo' s. An Australian aquatic fern, eaten by aborigines.
Ma'foo s. A (Chinese) groom or stableboy.
Goo s. Any sticky substance; sentimentality.
Wahoo' s. The Californian buckthorn; the rock or winged elm.
Sam'shoo s. A Chinese rice-spirit.
Ballyhoo' s. (*Slang*) Ado; noisy propaganda.
Ba'loo s. A bear.
Jackaroo' s. (*Australian*) A newcomer to a sheep-station, etc.
Buck'aroo s. (*US*) A cowboy.
Potoroo' s. A marsupial, the rat-kangaroo.
Siss'oo s. An Indian timber-tree; its wood.
Gentoo' s. A Falkland Island penguin.
Kazoo' s. A would-be musical instrument (giving paper-and-comb effect).
Zoo'zoo s. The wood-pigeon.
(I)gapo' s. A riverside forest periodically flooded.
Gesta'po s. A (Nazi) secret police. Also a.
Pe'po s. A fruit of the cucumber family, a large many-seeded berry.
Kat'ipo s. A large black venomous New Zealand spider.
Quip'o s. (*Quipu*).
Zop'po a. (*Mus.*) With syncopation.
Obis'po s. The spotted eagle-ray.
Ex'po s. An exhibition or public showing.
Ka'ro s. A small tree or evergreen shrub of New Zealand.
Igna'ro s. An ignorant person.
Sagua'ro s. The giant cactus.
Ce'ro s. A fish found in warm parts of the W. Atlantic.
Budg'ero s. A heavy keelless Indian barge.
Bandole'ro s. A highwayman.
Horne'ro s. A S. American bird, the baker-bird or oven-bird.
Fue'ro s. A constitution; a code or body of law.
Agg'ro s. (*Slang*) (The stirring-up of) trouble.
Gi'ro s. A banking system of direct transfer between accounts.
Autogi'ro s. A rotor-driven aircraft.
In'ro s. A small (Japanese) medicine-chest.
Munro' s. A Scottish mountain over 300 feet.
Cor'ocoro s. (*Corocore*).
Charr'o s. A Mexican cowboy decoratively dressed.
Zorr'o s. A S. American fox or wild dog.
Burr'o s. A donkey.
In'tro s. An opening (musical) passage.
Es'tro s. Enthusiasm; height of poetic inspiration.
Bi'stro s. A small tavern.
Eu'ro s. A wallaroo.
Autogy'ro s. (*Autogiro*).
Dso s. (*Zho*).
Pe'so s. A Spanish and S. American coin.
Chami'so s. A Californian shrub.
Lagrimo'so a and adv. (*Mus.*) Plaintive.
Amoro'so s. A (male) lover.
Cor'so s. A street where riderless horses are raced; a race or run.

Espress'o s. A type of coffee (-making machine). Also a.
Fat'so s. (*Slang*) (Used in address, etc. to) a fat person.
Ruba'to a. and adv. (*Mus.*) In modified or distorted rhythm.
Moscat'o s. Any of several sweet Italian wines; the grape.
Scorda'to a. (*Mus.*) Put out of tune.
Ja'to s. An aircraft take-off system using jets. Also a.
Poma'to s. A tomato grafted onto a potato.
Perfect'o s. A large tapering cigar.
Orvie'to s. A white Italian wine.
Bi'to s. A tropical tree; its fruit.
Sol'ito a. and adv. (*Mus.*) In the usual manner.
Horopi'to s. A small ornamental evergreen New Zealand tree.
Smal'to s. A coloured-glass mosaic (cube).
Sciol'to a. and adv. (*Mus.*) Free.
Ailan'to s. A tall beautiful Asiatic tree.
Pentimen'to s. Part of a picture painted out which becomes visible again later.
Pin'to a. Mottled; piebald. s. Such a horse.
Pron'to adv. (*Slang*) Quickly; immediately.
Ko'to s. A Japanese musical instrument.
Crypt'o s. A secret member (of a sect, party, etc.).
An'tipas'to s. An appetizer; an hors d'oeuvre.
Mes'to a. (*Mus.*) Sad; melancholy.
Gius'to a. (*Mus.*) Regular; strict; suitable.
Moscatt'o s. (*Moscato*).
Borghe'tto s. A big village.
Gruppett'o s. (*Mus.*) A turn.
Strett'o s. Part of a fugue.
Cutt'o s. (*Cuttoe*).
Putt'o s. A winged boy in Renaissance art.
Au'to s. An automobile.
Ritenu'to a. (*Mus.*) Restrained.
Inca'vo s. The incised part of an intaglio.
Pro'vo s. A member of the Provisional Irish Republican Army.
Ser'vo a. Of a system in which the main mechanism is activated by a subsidiary one. s. Such a mechanism.
Ka'yo v.t. To knock out. Also s.
Arroy'o s. A dry water-course; a rocky ravine.
Zo s. (*Zho*).
Gallina'zo s. A vulture.
Dzo s. (*Zho*).
Pie'zo a. Of electricity created in certain crystals by mechanical strain.
Bo'zo s. (*US slang*) A fellow; a person.
Mat'zo s. (A wafer of) unleavened bread.
Ou'zo s. A strong aniseed liqueur.
Dap v.i. To bounce; to drop bait gently into the water. Also s.
Plap s. A flat plopping sound. Also v.i.
Cat'nap s. A brief snooze (in a chair, etc.).
Crap s. (*Slang*) Excrement; rubbish; nonsense.
Rip'rap s. (A foundation of) loose rubble on soft ground or under water.
Wen'tletrap s. (One of) a genus of gasteropod molluscs.
Man'trap s. Any source of potential danger.
Jock'strap s. A genital support for male athletes, etc.
At(t)'ap s. The nipa palm; its leaves used in thatching, etc.
Wap s. A bundle of hay. v.t. To strike; to hit.
Zap v.t. (*Slang*) To hit. v.i. To go quickly or suddenly. s. Force; vitality.
Jeep s. A light (originally military) vehicle.
Bleep v.i. To give out a high sound or radio signal. s. Such a signal.
Cass'areep s. (W. Indian) The juice of cassava used in sauces, etc.
Seep v.i. To ooze; to percolate. Also s.
Kelep' s. A stinging ant of Central America.
Schlep v.t. (*US slang*) To pull; to drag.
Nep s. Catmint.
Pep s. Vigour; spirit; go.
Prep s. (*School slang*) Homework; preparatory school.
Yep adv. (*US* etc.) Yes.
Games'manship s. (The act or art of) winning contests by putting others off with talk or misleading conduct.
Coach'whip s. A type of whip-snake.
Blip s. The image of an object on a radar-screen.
Seed'lip s. A sower's basket.
Yip s. A short sudden cry. Also v.t.
Bun'yip s. An imaginary Australian swamp-monster; an imposter.
Calp s. A dark shaly Irish limestone.
Ped'ipalp s. A whip-scorpion.
Salp s. A free-swimming tunicate.
Sculp v.t. and i. To sculpture; to carve.
Fire'damp s. A combustible gas given off by coal, etc.; methane.
Samp s. Coarsely ground maize (porridge).
Stomp s. A foot-stamping dance. v.i. To stamp; to dance the stomp.
Scrump v.t. To raid orchards (and eat the spoils).
Gazump' v.t. To cheat by raising the (house) price after verbally agreeing an offer.
Tymp s. The plate of a blast-furnace opening.
Bop s. A development of bebop.
Be'bop s. A variety of jazz. Also v.i.
Bell'hop s. (*US*) A hotel attendant.
Kop s. (S. Africa) A round-topped hill.
Clop s. The sound of a hoof-tread. Also v.i.
Flip'flop s. A kind of loose open shoe.
Cods'wallop s. Nonsense put forth as if a serious proposition or idea, etc.
Doll'op s. A lump.
Goll'op v.t. and i. To gulp greedily and hastily.
Loll'op v.i. To lounge; to idle; to bound clumsily along.
Goop s. Goo; a fool; a silly person.
Snoop s. (*Slang*) A spy. v.i. To pry; to go about sneakingly.
Kill'crop s. A changeling; a child who is never satisfied.
Back'drop s. The painted cloth at the rear of the stage.
Ag'itprop s. (A department or person involved in) pro-Communist agitation and propaganda. Also a.
Tip'top' a. Of the highest excellence. Also s.
Quop v.i. To throb.
Wop s. (*Derogatory*) An Italian (or similar foreigner).
Yapp s. A style of limp leather binding in which the cover overlays the book edges.
Zipp s. A medicinal paste for healing wounds.
Typp s. A unit of yarn size (however many yards weigh one pound).
Twerp s. (*Slang*) A stupid person.
Dorp s. A village (orig. S. Africa), used contemptuously of any place.
Burp v.i. and s. Belch. v.t. To pat a baby's back after feeding.
Gall'iwasp s. A W. Indian lizard.
Knosp s. An unopened flower-bud; an architectural ornament resembling it.
Scup s. (*Scuppaug*).
Gup s. (*Slang*) Gossip; prattle.
Roll'up s. (*Slang*) An hand-made cigarette.
Sann'up s. A brave (husband or a squaw).
Contrecoup' s. A skull injury resulting from a blow on the opposite side.
Haar s. A raw sea-mist.
Maar s. (A lake in) a volcanic crater.
Retrobul'bar a. Behind the eyeball.

Mim'bar s. A mosque pulpit.
Wun'derbar a. Marvellous.
Os'car s. A gold-plated statuette awarded in the US to film-writer, actor, director, etc. for the year's best performance.
Kill'adar s. The commandant of a fort or garrison.
Sill'adar s. An irregular cavalryman.
Ra'dar s. A device using high-powered radio pulses for locating objects or one's own position, etc.
Chob'dar s. An Indian usher.
Khadd'ar s. Indian hand-spun, hand-woven cloth.
Cho(w)'kidar s. A watchman.
Li'dar s. A radar-like system using laser radiation instead of microwaves.
Am'ildar s. A factor or manager in India; a revenue-collector.
Ban'dar s. A rhesus monkey.
Pasear' s. and v.i. (*US slang*) Walk.
Be'gar s. Forced labour (in India).
Re'gar s. (*Regur*).
Budg'erigar s. An Australian parrakeet used as a cage and aviary bird.
Koft'gar s. One who practises koftgari.
La'har s. An avalanche of mud (lava).
Ka'kar s. (*Ka(r)kur*).
Lash'kar s. A force of armed Indian tribesmen.
Escolar' s. A fish of spectacled appearance.
Pic'amar s. A bitter oily liquid got from tar.
Pat'amar s. A vessel of the Bombay coast.
Ju'mar s. A clip on a rope which tightens when weight is applied and relaxes when it is removed. v.i. To climb with this aid.
Chenar' s. The Oriental plane tree.
So'nar s. An echo-sounding device.
Cot'nar s. A sweet white Rumanian wine.
Cassumu'nar s. E. Indian ginger.
Voar s. (*Orkney and Shetland*) Spring, seed-time.
Ar'ar s. The sandarac tree.
Qua'sar s. A star-like source of light radiation outside our galaxy.
Pul'sar s. A pulsating star, an interstellar source of radiation.
Collaps'ar s. A collapsed star.
Hass'ar s. A S. American nest-building land-walking catfish.
Selic'tar s. A sword-bearer.
Mukh'tar s. An Indian lawyer.
In'star s. The form of an insect between moults.
Guar s. A legume grown for forage, etc.
Pul'war s. A light keelless Ganges boat.
Yabb'er s. (*Australian*) Talk; jabber. Also v.i.
Cobb'er s. (*Australian*) Mate; chum; buddy.
We'ber s. The MKS unit of magnetic flux.
Scum'ber s. Dung. v.t. and i. (of an animal) To defecate.
Chanc'er s. One who takes risks (unnecessarily).
Slidd'er s. A steep path or trench down a hill-side.
Judd'er s. (Aircraft) vibration. Also v.i.
Skel'der v.i. (*Slang*) To beg; to swindle.
Woold'er s. A pin in a rope-maker's top; a stick used in woolding a mast or yard.
Bergan'der s. The sheldrake.
Bi'lander s. A two-masted hoy.
Filan'der s. An intestinal worm in hawks.
Aus'länder (ows'lender) s. A foreigner.
San'der s. A pike-perch.
Palisan'der s. Jacaranda or other rosewood.
Zan'der s. (*Sander*).
Hell'bender s. A large US salamander; a reckless or debauched person.
Chav'ender s. The chub.
Child'minder s. A baby-sitter, etc.
Side'winder s. A venomous US snake.
Shod'er s. A set of skins in which goldleaf is beaten a second time.
Caboceer' s. A W. African headman.
Fel'senmeer s. A boulder-field (of frost-riven rocks).
Teer v.t. To plaster; to daub.
Kno'tenschiefer s. Spotted slate.
Piaff'er s. A slow trotting gait in horsemanship.
Woof'er s. A large loudspeaker for low-frequency sounds.
Fieras'fer s. A small parasitic fish (the pearlfish) found in Mediterranean and British waters.
Tit'fer s. (*Slang*) A hat.
Jäger (Yay') s. A huntsman; a skua that robs other gulls. (Also Jae'ger).
Teen'ager s. A person of teenage years.
Skegg'er s. A young salmon.
Ligg'er s. The horizontal tube of a scaffolding; a plank bridge; a bed-cover.
Frigg'er s. A glass ornament.
Bugg'er int. (*Vulgar*) Expressing annoyance, etc. s. Applied (in)offensively to a person or beast, etc.
Li'ger s. The offspring of a lion and tigress.
Lam(m)'iger s. A cripple.
Voet'ganger s. A young locust (before its wings appear); a pedestrian.
Grenz'gänger (grents'genger) s. One who crosses the border (from East to West Berlin,etc.).
Cliff'hanger s. A tense exciting adventure story or serial; an ending-line that leaves one in suspense. Also a.
Clang'er s. A singularly ill-timed remark; a silly mistake.
Humding'er s. (*Slang*) An exceptionally excellent person or thing; a smooth-running engine or fast vehicle.
Stein'berger s. A white Rhenish wine.
Ham'burger s. A fried flat cake of finely chopped meat, onion, etc.
Branch'er s. A young bird that has left the nest.
Aff'enpinscher s. A small dog like a griffon.
Cow'catcher s. (*US*) A device on the front of a railway-engine to clear obstacles off the line.
Spit'cher a. (*Naval slang*) Done for.
Dow'itcher s. A N. American long-billed wader.
Potch'er s. A machine for breaking and bleaching pulp in paper-making.
Feld'sher s. An assistant doctor, in battle, etc.
Slath'er s. (*US slang*) A large quantity.
Kier s. A bleaching-vat.
Escalier' (es-cal-yâ) s. A staircase.
Somm'elier s. A wine-butler or waiter.
Hotel'ier s. A hotel-keeper or manager.
Lar'mier s. (*Architectural*) A corona or other course serving as a dripstone; (Zool.) a tear-pit.
Pom'pier a. (*Of art*) Conventional; uninspired.
Étrier' (ē-trē-yā') s. A mountaineer's short rope-ladder or climbing-iron.
Balis'ier s. A W. Indian plant with large leaves and bright orange flowers.
Sottisier' s. A collection of jokes, etc.
Plumassier' s. A feather-seller or worker with feathers.
Quartier' (kâr-te-yâ) s. A particular district in a (French) city or town.
Bou'vier s. A Belgian (breed of) dog.
Loud'speaker s. An electro-acoustic device for projecting and amplifying sound.
Back'breaker s. An extremely heavy job.
Streak'er s. One who makes a nude dash in a public place.
Pace'maker s. One who sets the running pace; a device to replace weak irregular heart rhythms.
Na'ker s. A kettledrum.
Yack'er s. (*Yakka*).
Shick'er s. Strong drink.

Whick'er v.i. To neigh or bleat; to snigger or titter.
Slick'er s. (*US*) A waterproof oilskin; a swindler or shifty person; a sophisticated city-dweller.
Mon'icker s. (*Slang*) A real or assumed name.
Rick'er s. A spar or young tree-trunk.
Lump'sucker s. A clumsy ugly sea-fish.
Seer'sucker s. A thin crinkly Indian fabric.
Yuck'er s. (*US*) The flicker or golden-winged woodpecker.
Kish'ker s. (*Kishka*).
Mon'iker s. (*Monicker*).
Dui'ker (**Dī'**) s. (*S. African*) An antelope; a cormorant.
Voortrekk'er s. (S. Africa) A pioneer.
Floor'walker s. A supervisor or a detective in a large store.
Klink'er s. A very hard paving-brick.
Head'shrinker s. A psychiatrist.
K(h)o'ker s. A sluice-gate or lock; the water between two such gates.
Rok'er s. Any ray except skate.
Halb'stark'er s. A juvenile delinquent.
Duy'ker s. (*Duiker*).
Länd'ler (**lend'ler**) s. A S. German dance; its tune.
Keg(g)'ler s. (*US*) One who plays skittles or similar games.
Rott'weiler (**rot'viler**) s. A large black German (breed of) dog.
Schill'er s. A bronze-like lustre in some minerals.
Crull'er s. (*US*) A fried-cake.
Ratt'ler s. (*US*) A rattlesnake.
Outremer' s. The region beyond the sea; overseas.
Wind'jammer s. A large sailing vessel.
Emm'er s. A type of wheat.
Dimm'er s. A switch or regulator of light supply
Stu'mer s. (*Slang*) A blunder; a clanger; a dud; a failure.
Pilse'ner s. A light beer.
Conn'er s. The goldsinny or corkwing; a wrasse or allied fish. (Also Cunner).
Bon'er s. (*US slang*) A howler; a foolish blunder.
By'woner s. An authorised squatter of poor white.
Pils'ner s. (*Pilsener*).
Down'er s. A belittler or killjoy; (a drug which causes) a depressed mood.
Sand'piper s. A bird between plover and snipe; the summer snipe.
Snoop'er s. (*Slang*) A snoop.
Napp'er s. (*Slang*) The head.
Wapp'er v.i. To blink; to move tremulously.
Chipp'er a. Brisk and cheerful.
Clod'hopper s. A peasant; a dolt; a heavy boot.
Scar'per v.i. (*Slang*) To run away; to leave without warning.
Ry'per s. (Pl. *Rype*).
Schno'rrer s. (*US slang*) A beggar.
Las'er s. An amplifier of light producing narrow and intense beam.
Fla'ser s. (*Geol.*) An irregular streaky lenticular structure in metamorphic rock.
Mas'er s. An amplifier of radio-astronomy signals.
Dyss'er s. (Pl. *Dysse*).
Bow'ser s. A tanker used for refuelling aircraft.
Breath'alyser s. A device for measuring the amount of alcohol (a driver, etc. has) imbibed.
Wind'cheater s. An anorak or stormproof jacket.
Tees'water s. (One of) a breed of shorthorn cattle.
Saet'er s. An upland meadow; a herdsman's hut.
Tee'ter v.t. and i. (*US*) To see-saw; to move unsteadily.
Tweet'er s. A loudspeaker for higher frequencies.
Osset'er s. A species of sturgeon.
Snift'er s. A nip of alcohol.
Bosh'ter s. (*Boshta*).
Kelt'er s. Good condition.
Skel'ter v.i. To scurry. Also s.
Tol'ter v.i. To flounder about.
Drei'kanter s. A pebble smoothed and flattened by wind-blown sand.
Teleprint'er s. A transmitter with a typewriter keyboard.
Gun'ter s. A rig with the topmast sliding on rings.
Troub'leshooter s. An expert detector and corrector of faults, disagreements, etc.
Snap'shooter s. One who shoots (a gun) in haste without pondering to aim.
Nip'ter s. Maundy.
Rip'snorter s. (*Slang*) A gale; anything fast and furious.
Frank'furter s. A small highly seasoned (German) sausage.
Shas'ter s. A holy writing.
Bush'master s. A venomous S. American snake.
Ras'ter s. A set of scanning lines which produces the television picture.
Mob'ster s. A gangster.
Leices'ter (**les'**) s. A long-woolled (breed of) sheep. Also a.
Semes'ter s. A university half-year course.
Drag'ster s. A car for drag-racing.
Gang'ster s. A member of a (criminal) gang.
Kei'ster s. (*US slang*) The behind.
Ax'minster s. A type of cut-pile carpet. Also a.
Block'buster s. A person or thing notable for violent effectiveness.
Knuck'leduster s. A metal covering for the knuckles in fighting.
Ham'fatter s. A third-rate actor, singer, etc.
Slatt'er v.i. To be untidy or slovenly. v.t. To spill; to splash; to slop.
Skitt'er v.i. To skim over the surface of (water).
Pitt'er v.i. To make a sound like that of the grasshopper.
Ritt'er s. A knight.
Critt'er s. (*US*) An animal; a creature.
Snott'er s. The lower support of a bow-sprit.
Scutt'er s. A hasty run. v.i. To scurry.
Lip'tauer s. A soft Hungarian cheese (with paprika and seasoning).
Pee'ver s. A tile, slab or can-lid, etc. used in playing hop-scotch.
Buplev'er s. The hare's-ear plant.
Transceiv'er s. A transmitter-receiver.
Vet'iver s. Cuscus roots.
Vi'ver s. A fish-pond; a rootlet or fibre.
Cal'ver v.t. To prepare fish when alive or just caught.
Hang'over s. Survival; after-effects of heavy drinking, etc.
Pull'over s. A jersey or jumper.
Turn'over s. A small pie with folded crust; the total amount of sales over a period.
Flivv'er s. (*Slang*) A failure; a small cheap car or plane; a destroyer.
Bovv'er s. (*Slang*) Aggro; trouble.
Whitt'awer s. A saddler.
Cherimoy'er s. (*Cherimoya*).
Panz'er s. A German armoured tank.
Bon'zer a. (*Australian*) Very good.
Calf'dozer s. A small bulldozer.
Bull'dozer s. A tractor for clearing and levelling ground.
Booz'er s. (*Slang*) A public house; a drinker.
Kib'itzer s. An onlooking bystander who gives unwanted advice, etc.
Schnauz'er s. A German (breed of) terrier.
Rozz'er s. (*Slang*) A policeman.
Nuzz'er s. A gift to a superior.
Ma'chair (**ma'hher**) s. A low-lying sandy beach.
Ke'fir s. A drink from fermented cow's milk.
Chir s. An Indian pine tree. (Also Cheer).

Mir s. A Russian village community.
Mouchoir' s. A pocket-handkerchief.
(moo-shwâr)
Racloir' s. A scraper.
Tamanoir' s. The great ant-bear.
Grattoir' s. (*Archaeology*) A scraping tool.
Kavir' s. A salt desert or terrain similar to it. (Also Kevir).
Na'zir s. An Indian official.
Wazir' s. A vizier.
Chak'r s. (*Chakra*).
De'cor s. Scenery and stage decoration; indoor ornament, colour-scheme, furnishings, etc.
Roncador' s. Any of various American snoring-fish.
Lab'rador s. A retriever dog.
Hel'iodor s. A type of clear yellow beryl.
Fra'gor s. A crash.
Khor s. A dry watercourse; a ravine.
Kwashior'kor s. A tropical disease due to protein-lack.
Milor' s. (*Milord*).
Huzoor' s. An Indian potentate or important personage.
Cur'sor s. A sliding part of an instrument.
Foss'or s. A grave-digger.
Trav'olator s. A moving way for foot-passengers.
Sta'tor s. A stationary part outside a rotating one.
Cur'sitor s. A clerk or officer in the Chancery Court.
Ro'tor s. A rotating part of a motor; a revolving aerofoil.
Rap'tor s. A ravisher; a plunderer; a bird of prey.
Vor s. (*US*) An aircraft-navigational aid.
Plex'or s. A percussion hammer.
Yarr s. The corn spurrey.
Mhorr s. (*Mohr*).
Brrr int. Expressing shivering with cold.
Voyageur' s. A Canadian trapper; one who canoes between trading-posts.
Bate'leur s. A short-tailed African eagle.
Diseur' s. A (male) reciter or entertainer.
Regisseur' s. A (stage-)manager.
Saboteur' s. One who commits sabotage.
Longueur' s. A tedious passage in a book, etc.
Viveur' s. A rake; a loose-liver.
Voyeur' s. A peeping Tom.
Gur s. An unrefined sweet cane-sugar.
Re'gur s. Rich black soil of India for cotton.
Ka'kur s. The muntjak or barking-deer.
Kun'kur s. Indian limestone; a Ceylonese clay.
Kar'kur s. (*Kakur*).
Clang'our s. A loud ringing noise. Also v.i.
Latour' s. A red Bordeaux wine.
Ka'pur s. A large Bornean, etc.; tree; its timber.
Mensur' s. Duelling (a German student sport).
Fraktur' s. A German black-letter typeface.
Critt'ur s. (*Critter*).
Baas s. (*S. African*) Master; sir; overseer; boss.
Meshu'gaas s. Madness; craziness; foolishness; nonsense.
Klip'das s. A hyrax.
Csár'dás s. A Hungarian dance; its music.
(char-dash)
Bermu'das s. Shorts reaching to just above the knee.
Rak'shas s. An evil spirit in Hindu mythology.
Palas' s. An Indian tree.
Verglas' s. A film of ice on rock.
(glâ')
Bucell'as s. A white Portuguese wine.
Kill'as s. Clay slate.
Bana'nas a. (*Slang*) Mad; crazy.
Kem'pas s. A hardwood Bornean tree; its timber.
Ras s. A headland; an Abyssinian prince.
Char'as s. A narcotic and intoxicant from hemp.
Madras' s. A fine cotton fabric; a handkerchief.
Deg'ras s. A fat from sheepskins.
Narr'as s. A S. W. African shrub; its edible fruit. (Also Naras).
Tarantas' s. A four-wheeled Russian vehicle mounted on poles.
Sel'vas s. (*Selva*).
(H)ab'dabs s. (*Slang*) Nervous anxiety.
Boobs s. (*Slang*) The female breasts.
Bi'onics s. The replacement of body-parts with electronic or mechanical devices.
Pat'aphysics s. The science of imaginary solutions.
Vibes s. (*Slang*) Feelings or sensations experienced or communicated; a vibraphone.
Shades s. (*Slang*) Sun-glasses.
Fa'cies s. General aspect.
(fā'shi-ēz)
Un'dies s. Women's underclothing.
Nel'ies s. (& pl.) A winter pear.
Will'ies s. (*Slang*) (The) creeps.
Funn'ies s. (*US*) A newspaper's cartoon or comic section.
Fal'sies s. Pads put in a brassière to enlarge or improve the shape of the bosom.
Pan'ties s. Very short female drawers.
Civv'ies s. Civilian clothes (as opposed to uniform).
Oo'dles s. Abundance.
Fo'mes s. A substance capable of carrying infection.
Cripes int. (*Slang*) Expressing surprise or alarm, etc.
Halter'es s. The rudimentary hind-wings of flies.
Xer'es s. Sherry from Jerez.
(hher'es)
Mo'res s. Customs; manners.
Notoryc'tes s. The marsupial mole of Australia.
Culottes' s. A divided skirt.
(koo-lot')
Blues s. A slow sad song; depression.
Park'leaves s. Tutsan.
Graves s. A white or red table-wine.
(grâv)
Fran'glais s. Mixed French and English.
(-glay)
La'bis s. The cochlear or eucharistic spoon.
Nel'is s. (*Nelies*).
All'is s. (*Allice*).
Cull'is s. A roof-gutter or groove.
Epu'lis s. A tumour of the gums.
Co'mmis s. An apprentice waiter, steward or chef.
Ker'mis s. An outdoor fair; (*US*) an indoor fair.
Nis s. (*Scandinavian*) A brownie or friendly goblin.
Ma'nis s. The pangolin or scaly ant-eater.
Or'nis s. The avifauna of a region.
Putois' s. A potter's paintbrush of polecat's hair or the like.
Travois' s. (*N. American*) A pair of trailing
(-voi') poles joined by a board or a net.
Kal'pis s. A water-vase.
Hu'bris s. Insolence; wanton arrogance.
Fris s. (*Friska*).
Kris s. A creese.
Cerr'is s. The Levantine oak.
Sis s. (*US address*) Sister.
My'iasis s. A disease caused by flies (or their larvae).
Periege'sis s. A description set out like a tour; a journey through.
Psilo'sis s. Loss of hair; sprue.
Ulo'sis s. Formation of a scar.
Eno'sis s. Union (of one nation with another).
Poro'sis s. The knitting together of broken bones.
Halito'sis s. Foul breath.

Scep'sis s. Philosophic doubt.
Paracu'sis s. Disordered hearing.
Proglott'is s. A detachable tapeworm joint.
Ma'quis ('kē) s. A thicket of shrubs.
Cro'quis s. An outline or rough sketch.
Pav'is s. A shield for the entire body.
Pontlev'is s. A drawbridge.
Rhex'is s. Rupture of a blood-vessel.
Pyx'is s. A small box for drugs, jewels, etc.
Boon'docks s. (*US*) Rough uncivilized (isolated) country.
Gold'ilocks s. A golden-haired girl.
Kans s. An Indian grass.
Cad'rans s. An instrument for gripping and angling a gem during cutting, etc.
Gubb'ins s. Trash; anything of little value; a gadget or thingamy.
Jen'kins s. A toady; a society reporter.
Na'os s. (The inner cell of) a temple.
Me'bos s. (*S. Africa*) Salted or sugared dried-apricots
Melk'bos s. (*Melkbosch*).
Tournedos' (-dō') s. A small beef fillet.
Spe'os s. A grotto-temple or tomb.
Pith'os s. A large wine-jar.
Se'kos s. A sacred enclosure.
Sakk'os s. An Eastern bishop's vestment.
Nos'tos s. A poem describing a return (journey).
Craps s. A gambling-game with two dice.
Outsid'ers s. A pair of nippers for turning a key in a lock from the outside.
San'ders s. (Red) sandalwood.
Cheers int. Thanks; (your) good health.
Bleach'ers s. (*US*) Cheap open-air spectator seats.
Crack'ers a. Crazy.
Jan'kers s. (*Military slang*) Punishment; detention.
Bon'kers s. (*Slang*) Crazy; mad.
Hip'sters s. Low-waisted trousers.
Pee'vers s. Hop-scotch.
Secateurs' s. Pruning-shears.
Jodh'purs s. Riding-breeches.
Bi'omass s. The amount of living material in a given area.
By'pass s. A side-road to avoid a town-centre, etc.
Trass s. An earthy volcanic tuff; a hydraulic cement of it.
Tarantass' s. (*Tarantas*).
Wack'iness s. (*Slang*) Craziness.
Maladdress' s. Awkwardness; clumsiness; tactlessness.
Piss v.i. To void urine. s. urine.
Siss s. (*Sis*)
Schloss s. A castle or palace; a manor-house.
Mo'tocross s. A form of scrambling, racing on motorcycles around a rough circuit.
Soss s. A mess; a dish of sloppy food; a puddle; a heavy fall of rain.
Gauss s. The CGS unit of magnetic density.
Schuss s. A straight slope for a skiing run. Also v.i.
An'schluss s. A (political) union of nations.
Sour'puss s. (*Slang*) An ill-tempered person.
Suss v.t. (*Slang*) To examine, inspect thoroughly; to investigate; to guess.
Dyss s. (*Dysse*).
Kur'haus s. A building housing a spa.
Col'obus s. (One of) an African genus of monkeys.
Pi'cus s. The woodpecker genus.
Plu'teus s. A sea-urchin or brittle-star larva.
Vul'gus s. The common people; a short verse task in Latin.
Din'gus s. (*US slang*) A thingumajig.
U'rachus s. A ligament connecting bladder and umbilicus.
Jacch'us s. A S. American marmoset.
Rhon'chus s. A bronchial sound heard in stethoscopy.
Me'dius s. The middle finger.
Ruck'us s. (*US*) A noisy disturbance.
An'kus s. An elephant goad.
So'lus a. (*Drama*) Alone.
Per'iplus s. A narrative of a coasting voyage; a circumnavigation.
Op'ulus s. The guelder-rose.
Nostrada'mus s. One who professes to predict the future.
Wa'mus s. (*US*) A kind of cardigan or jacket buttoned at neck and wrists.
Nystag'mus s. A spasmodic oscillatory movement of the eyes.
Ded'imus s. A writ commissioning a non-judge to act as one.
Mump'simus s. An error retained after exposure; stubborn conservatism; an antiquated person.
Mut'icous a. Spineless; pointless; awnless.
Horren'dous a. Dreadful; horrible.
Gla'reous a. Gravelly; growing on gravel.
Ora'gious a. Stormy.
Frab'jous a. Fabulously joyous.
Fimic'olous a. Growing on dung.
U'berous a. Yielding abundance of milk; abounding.
Nem'orous a. Wooded.
Pedeten'tous a. Proceeding slowly.
Euri'pus s. An arm of the sea having strong currents.
Cam'pus s. College or university grounds (and buildings); the academic world.
Hipp'us s. A clonic spasm of the iris.
Lar'us s. The main genus of gulls.
Sa'rus s. An Indian crane.
Churr'us s. (*Charas*).
Ri'sus s. A laugh or grin.
Pass'us s. A canto or section.
Linct'us s. A syrupy medicine.
No'tus s. The S. (W.) wind.
Igno'tus s. A person unknown (in art, etc.).
Lab'rys s. A double-headed axe.
Ad'vocaat s. A liqueur or medicinal drink containing eggs.
Rabat' v.t. (*Geometry*) To rotate into another plane.
Num'bat s. The banded ant-eater, a small marsupial of S.W. Australia.
Hold'erbat s. A metal collar for clamping a pipe to a wall or the like.
Ry'bat s. A dressed stone at the side of a door or window.
Forçat' s. A (French) convict condemned to hard labour.
Off'beat a. Out of the ordinary; eccentric.
Geat s. The hole in a mould for receiving molten metal during casting.
Khil'afat s. A caliphate.
Marr'owfat s. A rich kind of pea.
Logg'at s. A small piece of wood; a stake.
Sheri'at s. The body of Islamic religious law.
Kat s. A shrub; tea from its leaves.
Meer'kat s. A S. American carnivore; a ground-squirrel; a lemur.
Lat s. An isolated pillar in India.
Kanat' s. An underground channel built to provide a village with water.
Quinn'at s. The king-salmon.
Pensionnat' (pah-syo-na) s. French boarding-school.
Dream'boat s. (*Slang*) Someone wonderful and desirable.
Shoat s. A young hog.
A'pparat s. The Communist party political machine.
Mo'rat s. A drink of honey and mulberry-juice.

Prat s. (*Slang*) The buttocks; a foolish or contemptible person.
Zigg'urat s. A pyramidal Babylonian temple-tower.
Lang'sat s. An Indonesian tree; its fruit.
Com'sat s. A communications satellite.
Lan'sat s. (*Langsat*).
Dik'tat s. Harsh settlement forced on the defeated or powerless.
Kli'nostat s. A revolving stand for growing plants.
Quat s. A pimple.
Par'aquat s. A very poisonous weed-killer.
Kum'quat s. A small kind of orange.
Amadavat' s. An Indian songbird.
Gall'ivat s. A large two-masted Malay boat.
Swat s. A sharp blow. v.t. To hit smartly.
Twat s. (*Vulgar slang*) The vulva; a contemptible person.
Pancha'yat s. A village council.
Raiy'at s. (*Ryot*).
Ven'tifact s. A stone shaped and polished by wind-blown sand.
Met'amict s. The amorphous state of a mineral due to radioactive decay of its atoms. Also a.
Percoct' a. Well-cooked or overdone; hackneyed.
Infarct' s. Tissue dying through lack of blood-supply.
Gam'bet s. The redshank.
Zerum'bet s. An E. Indian drug.
Godet' s. A triangular piece of cloth inserted as a flare, etc.
Skeet s. Clay-pigeon shooting.
Gleet s. A viscous transparent discharge from a mucous surface.
Tweet s. The note of a small bird. Also v.t. and i.
Peet'weet s. (*US*) The spotted sandpiper.
Legg'et s. A thatching tool.
Gui'chet s. A ticket-office window; a small opening.
Palmiet' s. A S. African riverside plant.
Nack'et s. A snack; a light lunch.
Click'et s. A latch.
Smick'et s. A smock.
Su'permarket s. A large (self-service) store.
Wis'ket s. A basket.
Blet s. Internal decay in fruit without external signs; the part so affected.
Plate'let s. A minute body in blood which helps clotting.
Fi'let s. Tenderloin; a kind of lace.
Gilet' s. A ballerina's waistcoat-shaped bodice.
Cap'ellet s. A wen-like swelling on elbow or neck of a horse.
Green'let s. A bird of the vireo genus.
Cac'olet s. A military mule-litter.
Piolet' s. An ice-axe.
Gur'let s. A kind of pickaxe.
Pel'met s. A valance, fringe or other device hiding a curtain-rod.
El'anet s. A kite (bird).
Ben'et s. (Roman Catholic) An exorcist.
Quann'et s. A file mounted like a plane.
Carnet' s. A customs permit.
Pos'net s. A small handled and footed cooking pot.
Par'apet s. A bank or wall to protect from enemy fire.
Skipp'et s. A flat box for a document-seal.
Ber'et s. A flat round woollen cap.
Pom'fret s. Any of several (food-) fishes.
Off'set s. A side branch of anything; a method of printing; a thing set off against another as compensation. Also vt. and i.
Quon'set s. The US equivalent of a Nissen hut.
Droguet' s. A kind of rep, a ribbed woollen dress fabric.
Blan'quet s. A variety of pear.
Min'ivet s. A brightly coloured shrike of Asia.
Baft s. A coarse fabric.
Thoft s. A rowing-bench.
Yuft s. Russia leather.
Wehr'macht s. (*German*) Armed forces.
Echt a. Pure, unadulterated; genuine; authentic.
Fan'light s. A type of window.
Uptight' a. Tense; in a state of nerves.
Parfait' s. A kind of frozen dessert.
Tait s. The long-snouted phalanger.
Frabb'it a. Peevish.
Frog'bit s. A small aquatic plant.
On-dit' **(-dē')** s. A rumour; hearsay.
Maudit' s. A lost soul; one dogged by undeserved ill-luck.
Gesund'heit int. (Your) good health.
Shit s. (*Vulgar*) Excrement; crap.
Te'whit s. A lapwing.
Iden'tikit s. A device used by police, etc., to build up a composite picture detail by detail of a suspect.
Kalumpit' s. A Philippine tree; its fruit.
Sum'pit s. (*Sumpitan*).
Cab'rit s. (*Cabrie*).
Reduit' s. A garrison's inner fortified retreat.
Schuit **(skoit)** s. A Dutch flat-bottomed river-boat.
Squit s. (*Slang*) Nonsense; a contemptible person.
Aq'uavit s. A Scandinavian spirit flavoured with caraway seed.
Te'wit s. (*Tewhit*).
Nit'wit s. (*Slang*) A fool.
String'halt s. A catching up of a horse's legs.
Gestalt' s. Form, shape or pattern; an organized unit or whole.
Kelt s. A salmon that has just spawned.
(Y)elt s. A young sow.
Polt s. A hard blow. v.t. To beat.
Ber'gylt s. A red sea-fish.
Ex'cubant a. On guard.
Alicant' s. A Spanish wine.
Fendant' s. A dry white Swiss wine.
Hi'ant a. Gaping.
Ri'ant a. Laughing; gay.
Cri'ant a. Garish; discordantly coloured.
Lant s. Stale urine used in wool-scouring; a sand-eel.
Coo'lant s. A fluid applied to a cutting-tool, etc., to lessen friction; a cooling medium in an internal combustion engine, etc.
Coulant' a. Easy to get on with; accommodating.
O'rant s. A worshipping figure (in art).
Croiss'ant s. A crescent-shaped roll.
Foudroy'ant a. Thundering; dazzling; sudden and overwhelming.
Ri'dent a. Laughing or smiling beamingly.
Prosil'ient a. Outstanding.
Poll'ent a. Strong.
Virement' s. The transference of surplus to balance deficit elsewhere.
Passe'ment s. A decorative trimming; v.t. To adorn with such.
Tapote'ment s. Percussion in massage.
U'rent a. Burning; stinging.
Spraint s. Otter dung.
Skint a. (*Slang*) Without money; hard up.
Nov'erint s. A writ.
Blue'print s. A preliminary sketch or plan as a guide or model. Also v.t.
Off'print s. A reprint or copy made from an original.
Pied'mont s. (*US*) A region at the foot of a mountain. Also a.

Oont s. A camel (in India).
Wa'terfront s. The buildings or part of the town along the edge of the sea etc. Also a.
Prunt s. A moulded glass ornament; a tool for making such.
Ro'bot s. A mechanical man; a traffic signal (S. Africa). a. Automatic.
Mi'crodot s. A much-reduced photograph of (secret) information.
Sal'igot s. The water-chestnut.
Escargot' (gō') s. An edible snail.
Phot s. The CGS unit of illumination.
Grape'shot s. Fine shot-pellets that scatter.
Sling'shot s. (*US*) A catapult.
Moon'shot s. Launching of a vehicle or object to orbit or land on the moon.
Feed'lot s. A unit in which cattle are automatically fed and fattened.
Mate'lot (mat'lō) s. A sailor.
Di'glot a. Bilingual.
Maillot' my-yo) s. A one-piece swimsuit; ballet-tights.
What'not s. A non-descript article; a thingamy; anything, no matter what.
Goose'foot s. Any plant of the beet family.
Fan'foot s. A type of moth; a type of gecko.
Polt'foot s. and a. Club-foot.
Hot'foot adv. In haste.
Puss'yfoot v.i. To go stealthily; to act timidly or with caution.
Snoot s. An expression of contempt; (*US*) the face.
Jack'pot s. An accumulated prize-money pool; the highest prize.
Crack'pot s. A crazy or eccentric person.
Im'pot s. (*School slang*) An imposition.
Star'spot s. An area of relative darkness on a star's surface.
Stot s. A young ox, a steer.
Guy'ot (gē'yō) s. A flat-topped submarine mountain.
Coapt' v.t. To adjust.
Sculpt v.t. and i. (*Sculp*).
Opt v.i. To make a choice.
Peart a. Lively; saucy; in good health and spirits.
Ju'mart s. The supposed offspring of a cow and horse.
Quirt s. A riding-whip of braided hide. v.t. To hit with one.
Red'short a. Brittle at red-heat.
Poort s. (*S. African*) A mountain pass.
Yog(h)'(o)urt (yog'ert) s. A semi-liquid food of fermented milk.
Y(o)urt s. A light skin tent of Siberian nomads.
Lambast' v.t. To thrash.
Ban'dobast s. An arrangement or settlement.
Type'cast v.t. To put into a role that is what one is by nature; to cast continually into the same type of role.
Bean'feast s. A noisy festivity or merry spree.
Cin'east s. (*Cineaste*).
Sit'fast s. A lump in a horse's skin under the saddle.
Ob'last s. A province or district in Russia.
Plan'oblast s. A free-swimming medusa.
Gab'fest s. (*Slang*) A gathering for talks; a spell of talking; a prolonged conference.
Bar'g(h)est s. A dog-like goblin portending death.
Funest' a. Deadly; lamentable.
Fire'crest s. A kinglet, a bird akin to the goldcrest.
Angst s. Fear; anxiety; disquiet (with the world).
Shirt'waist s. (*US*) A woman's blouse.
Mao'ist s. A Communist follower of (Chairman) Mao Tse-tung.
Petau'rist s. A flying-phalanger.
On'cost s. Overhead expenses. a. Paid by time.
Vo'lost s. A soviet of a Russian rural district.
Per'mafrost s. Subsoil that is permanently frozen.
Horst s. (*Geol.*) A block of earth's crust that has retained its position while the surround has altered.
Hurst s. A wood or grove.
Blut'wurst s. Black-pudding.
Infaust' a. Unlucky; ill-omened.
In'haust v.t. To drink in.
Bun'dobust s. (*Bandobast*).
Wan'derlust s. Restlessness; the urge to be travelling.
Legg'att, Legg'ett s. (*Legget*).
Dewitt' v.t. To lynch.
Nott a. With close-cut hair; polled.
Scutt'lebutt s. (*US*) Rumour; gossip.
Mutt s. (*Slang*) A mongrel dog.
Kapputt' a. (*Kaput*).
Kanaut' s. (*Kanat*).
Cos'monaut s. (Russian) An astronaut. (Also Kosmonaut).
As'tronaut s. One who travels space.
An(n)'icut s. A dam.
Ec'onut s. (*Slang*) One who shows over-concern for conservation and the environment.
Butt'ernut s. A N. American white walnut tree; its wood or nut.
Lay'about s. An idle loafer.
Hand'out s. That which is given to the needy as charity; a brochure, report or advertisement given away.
Hang'out s. A haunt.
Dug'out s. A boat from a hollowed tree-trunk; a rough shelter in a trench, etc.
Rac(c)'ahout s. Acorn meal.
Tac'ahout s. A gall on the tamarisk.
Chout s. Blackmail; extortion.
Freak'out s. A hallucinatory experience or exciting occurrence.
Look'out s. A watch; a place for watching from; prospect; concern.
Eel'pout s. The burbot or blenny.
Strout v.t. and i. To bulge; to flaunt; to strut; to protrude.
Pass'out s. A ticket or similar allowing a concert-goer, etc., to leave the performance and re-enter.
Mazout' s. Petroleum residue after distillation.
Kaput' a. Ruined; no good; broken; smashed; useless.
In'put s. Data fed into a computer. Also v.t.
Caj'uput s. A pungent aromatic oil from the leaves of an Australian tree. (Also Cajeput).
Brut a. (Of wines) raw, unsweetened.
Mazut' s. (*Mazout*).
Konfyt' s. A fruit preserve in syrup, jam or candied form.
Schuyt' s. (*Schuit*).
Mer'(a)bau s. A Malaysian tree; its hardwood timber.
Trumeau' s. A piece of wall or pillar between two openings.
Réseau' s. A network of lines in star photographs.
Bateau' s. A light Canadian river-boat.
Co'teau s. A hilly upland area; the side of a valley.
Gau s. A district.
Hau s. A tropical shrub; a Hawaiian tree.
Bacalha'u s. Dried or salted cod.
Ni'kau s. A New Zealand palm; its leaves.
(H)in'au s. A New Zealand evergreen tree.
U'nau s. The two-toed sloth.
Feld'grau s. Field-grey (the colour of German military uniforms).

Lu'au s. A party or feast in Hawaiian-style; a cooked dish of taro-leaves, coconut cream and octopus, etc.
Boy'au s. A communication trench.
Ha'bu s. A venomous Pacific pit-viper.
Catt'abu s. A cross between common cattle and the zebu.
Ynambu' s. A very large tinamou.
Ombu' s. A S. American tree growing in the pampas.
Zo'bu s. (*Zho*).
Aperçu' s. A summary outline; a glimpse or instant intuitive insight.
Surucucu' s. The bushmaster.
Pirarucu' s. The arapaima.
Pyengadu' s. The Burmese ironwood tree.
Hal'du s. A Burmese and Indian, etc., tree; its yellowish hardwood.
Nan'du s. The rhea.
Bundu' s. Uncivilized wild region; the bush.
Milieu' s. Environment or setting; medium; element.
Basbleu' s. A bluestocking.
Meu s. Baldmoney or spignel.
Snafu' s. (*US slang*) Chaos. a. Chaotic.
Kung fu' s. The (Chinese traditional) art of unarmed combat and self-defence.
Kun'gu s. A small E. African gnat or midge.
Bu'chu s. (*Bucku*).
Sa'd(d)hu s. A Hindu holy man.
Sam'shu s. (*Samshoo*).
Sucurujú' s. A S. American anaconda.
Bunra'ku s. A Japanese form of puppet-theatre.
Bu'cku s. A S. African plant; its leaves of medicinal value for dressing wounds.
Hai'ku s. A Japanese three-line poem or its imitation. (Also Hokku).
(W)ha'puku s. A large marine food-fish.
Seppu'ku s. Hara-kiri
Ko'tuku s. The New Zealand white heron.
Ba'lu s. (*Baloo*).
Lu'lu s. (*Slang*) A thing or person that is remarkable, wonderful, etc.
Vou'lu a. Deliberate; intentional; studied.
Pu'lu s. A silky fibre from the Hawaiian tree-fern.
Tam'anu s. A tall tree of the E. Indies.
Inconnu' s. An unknown (male) person.
Car'iacou s. An American deer.
Roucou' s. Annatto.
Fo'gou s. A Cornish souterrain or earth-house.
Chou (shoo) s. A cabbage; a soft rosette; a cream-bun; (as terms of affection) dear, pet, etc.
Kab'eljou s. A large S. African fish.
Kou s. A Hawaiian tree; its wood.
Clou s. The dominant idea; the chief point of interest.
Hin'ou s. (*Hinau*).
Ba'pu s. A guru or spiritual father.
Qui'pu s. A mnemonic device of knotted cords.
Cru s. A vineyard or group of vineyards.
Bebee'ru s. A tree of Guyana.
Ke'reru s. The New Zealand pigeon.
Candiru' s. A tiny S. American bloodsucking catfish.
Gu'ru s. A spiritual teacher.
Uhuru' (oo-hoo-roo) s. National independence; freedom (from slavery, etc.)
Ma'su s. A Japanese salmon.
Babassu' s. A Brazilian palm; its nut.
Lass'u s. The slow part of a csárdás.
Buss'u s. A tropical American palm.
Abattu' a. Dejected; cast down.
Foutu' a. (*Vulgar*) Done for; finished.
Tu'tu s. A New Zealand shrub; a ballerina's skirt
Yu s. Precious jade.
Cha'noyu s. The (Japanese) ceremony of making and drinking tea.
Kiku'yu s. An (originally) African grass.
Gua'zu s. The S. American marsh-deer.
Kud'zu s. An ornamental Oriental plant.
Kan'zu s. A long white male garment (as worn in E. Africa).
Oll'av s. A doctor or master among the ancient Irish.
Lu'lav s. A palm-frond (used in Jewish ritual).
Deev s. (*Div*).
Rev s. An engine revolution. v.t. To increase the speed of revolution in. v.i. To revolve.
Div s. An evil spirit (Persian myth).
Chiv s. (*Slang*) A knife. Also v.t. (Also Shiv).
Spiv s. (*Slang*) A flashy dresser; a hawker; a (street-corner) loafer.
Lu'lov s. (*Lulav*).
Derv s. Diesel-engine fuel oil.
MIRV s. A missile containing many thermonuclear warheads able to attack separate targets.
Cashaw' s. A W. Indian mesquite; a kind of US pumpkin.
Scrim'shaw s. A sailor's spare-time handicraft; anything made as a result of it.
Cum'shaw s. A gift; a tip.
Oak'enshaw s. A little oak-wood.
Skaw s. A low cape; a ness.
Slaw s. Cabbage salad.
Mack'inaw s. An American Indian blanket; a short heavy woollen coat; a flat-bottomed lake-boat.
South'paw a. (Of boxing, etc.) left-handed. s. A left-handed boxer.
Choc'taw s. A tribe of American Indians; a skating movement.
Whitt'aw s. (*Whittawer*).
Flam'few s. A fantastic trifle.
Cler'ihew s. A jingle of two short couplets about a notable personage, etc.
Mor'phew s. A skin eruption.
Vin'ew v.t. and i. To make or become mouldy. s. Mouldiness.
Miaow' s. and v.i. (*Miaul*).
Mar'bow, Mur'bow s. (*Merabau*).
Hoos(e)'gow s. (*US slang*) Jail; prison.
Sal'chow ('kō) s. A jump in skating.
No'how adv. Not in any way; not at all; in no definable way.
Pil'crow s. A paragraph-mark.
Budg'erow s. (*Budgero*).
Wheel'barrow s. A one-wheeled barrow with handles and legs.
Lea'sow s. Pasture. v.t. and i. To pasture.
Wow s. (*Slang*) Anything thrilling. Also int.
Kab'eljouw s. (*Kabeljou*).
Car'fax s. A crossroads.
Ban'jax v.t. (*Slang*) To ruin; to defeat; to smash or destroy.
Bem'bex s. A genus of loudly buzzing sand-wasps.
Po'dex s. The rump or anal region.
Hex s. A wizard or witch; a spell; something which brings bad luck.
Poll'ex s. The thumb or its analogue.
Im'plex a. Far from simple; complicated; involved.
Nu'plex s. A combined agricultural and industrial complex built around a nuclear reactor.
Ru'mex s. The dock and sorrel genus.
Rex s. King; a type of cat or rabbit.
Prex s. (*US slang*) The college president.
Ast'rex s. A type of domestic rabbit.
U'nisex a. (Of clothes etc.) of a style suitable for male or female.

Dent'ex s. A voracious Mediterranean fish.
Yex v.i. To hiccup; to belch; to spit. Also s.
Cy'lix s. A shallow-stemmed two-handled drinking-cup.
Jinx s. A bringer of bad luck; bad luck.
Phor'minx s. A kind of cithara.
Ice'box s. (*US*) A refrigerator; the freezing-compartment of a refrigerator.
Car'fox s. (*Carfax*).
Lox s. Liquid oxygen (rocket-propellant).
Ground'prox s. An aircraft warning-device that not enough altitude is reached.
Ben'elux s. Belgium, the Netherlands and Luxembourg. Also a.
Mux s. A mess. v.t. To spoil; to botch.
Roux (roo) s. A mixture for thickening sauces, etc.; any greasy mixture.
Pom'pholyx s. An eruption on palms and soles; impure zinc oxide.
Mor'gay s. A small spotted dogfish.
Okay' a. (*Slang*) All correct. adv. Yes; all right. s. Approval. v.t. To approve.
Palay' s. The S. Indian ivory-tree.
Blay s. (*Bley*).
Re'play s. A filmed rerun of part of an event soon afterwards.
Guan'ay s. The Peruvian cormorant.
Mor'nay s. A cream sauce with cheese flavouring.
Mor'ay s. A large eel.
Give'away s. An unintentional betrayal or revelation; a free handout.
Rock'away s. (*US*) A four-wheeled pleasure carriage.
Cast'away s. One shipwrecked in a desolate place.
Broad'way s. A chief thoroughfare through a town or district.
Folk'way s. A traditional way of thinking, feeling or acting, followed by a social group.
Bush'baby s. A small S. African lemur.
Mouchar'aby s. A balcony enclosed by lattice-work.
Mobb'y s. An alcoholic W. Indian drink.
Bil'by s. A nocturnal marsupial, the rabbit-bandicoot.
Jum'by s. A W. Indian Negro ghost or evil spirit.
Brum'by s. An Australian wild horse.
Kakistoc'racy s. Government by the worst.
Tedd'y s. A toy bear.
Widd'y s. A rope (of osier); a halter.
Nodd'y s. A simpleton; an oceanic tern-like bird.
Pan'dy s. A slap on the palm as school punishment. v.t. to slap.
Sebun'dy s. Indian irregular soldier(y).
Bur'gundy s. A red French wine.
Dogs'body s. A general assistant or junior drudge.
Bar'dy s. An edible Australian wood-boring grub.
Ju'dy s. (*Slang*) A girl; a frumpish woman.
Pandow'dy s. (*US*) An apple pie or pudding.
How'dy int. How do you do?
Win'cey s. A cloth with cotton warp and woollen filling.
Cage'y a. Artfully shy; secretive; wary.
Mick'ey s. (*Slang*) A doped drink.
Man'key s. (*Slang*) Bad; inferior; defective; dirty.
Hon'key s. (*US slang*) A (white) man.
Hook'ey s. (*US*) Truant.
Malar'key s. Nonsense; an unfounded story.
Bley s. The bleak (fish).
Will'ey s. A willow basket or willowing-machine. Also v.t.
Bram'ley s. A type of cooking-apple.
Co'ley s. A dusky fish of the cod family.
Wur'ley s. An Australian aborigine hut; a rat's nest.
Sley s. A weaver's reed.
Pais'ley s. A specially patterned coloured fabric; the pattern.
Baw'ley s. A small fishing-smack.
Bli'mey int. (*Slang* – God blind me!) Expressing shock, surprise, etc. (Also Gorblimey).
Gar'ganey s. A bird akin to the teal.
Pho'ney s. and a. (*Slang*) Counterfeit; unreal.
Balo'ney, Bolo'ney s. (*Slang*) Spiel; nonsense.
Step'ney s. A spare wheel; a white slaver's mistress.
Al'derney s. A small dairy-cow (breed).
Jit'ney s. A small fixed-route passenger-vehicle.
Hoo'ey s. (*Slang*) Nonsense.
Bloo'ey a. (*US slang*) Awry; amiss.
Mo'sey v.i. (*Slang*) To make off; to hurry; to move along slowly.
Car'sey s. (*Karzy*).
Ma'tey a. Sociable; companionable.
Blu'ey s. An Australian bushman's bundle.
Pea'vey s. (*US*) A lumberman's spiked and hooked lever.
Wa'vey s. The snow-goose.
Kar'zey s. (*Karzy*).
Mad'efy v.t. To moisten.
Iff'y a. Doubtful; full of ifs.
Niff'y a. Smelly.
Squiff'y a. Tipsy.
Cag'y a. (*Cagey*).
Pegg'y s. A small warbler; the whitethroat; a washerwoman's dolly; a size of roofing-slate.
Mogg'y s. (*Mog*).
King'y s. A children's game like 'He', but played with a ball.
Min'gy ('jy) a. Mean; stingy; disappointingly small.
Palill'ogy s. Repetition of a word or phrase.
Ufol'ogy s. The study of UFOs.
Lur'gy s. An imaginary highly infectious disease; any such disease.
Vi'chy s. A natural (or artificial imitation) mineral-water.
Fur'phy s. (*Australian slang*) A false report, rumour or absurd story.
Dish'y a. (*Slang*) Very attractive.
Sag'athy s. A woollen stuff.
Wack'y a. (*Slang*) Crazy.
Ick'y a. Ill; sweet; sickly; sticky. (Also Ikky).
Dum'ky s. (Pl. *Dumka*).
Man'ky a. (*Mankey*).
Hon'ky s. (*Honkey*).
Wonk'y a. (*Slang*) Unsound; shaky; awry.
Cho'ky s. A prison.
Koo'ky a. (*US*) Cranky; eccentric; crazy.
Malar'ky s. (*Malarkey*).
Sar'ky a. Sarcastic.
Kro'mesky s. A type of croquette.
Kolin'sky s. Mink or polecat fur.
Marrow'sky s. A spoonerism. v.i. To utter one.
Tidd'ly a. (*Slang*) Drunk.
Troe'ly s. (*Troolie*).
Bar'fly s. A drinker who frequents bars.
Trevall'y s. An Australian horse-mackerel.
Gin'gelly s. (*Gingili*).
Nell'y s. A large petrel.
Tell'y s. (*Slang*) Television.
Hill'billy s. (*US*) A rustic hill-dweller. Also a.
Chan'tilly s. A silk or linen lace with delicate pattern.
Will'y s. (*Willey*).
Groo'ly a. (*Slang*) Gruesome and grisly.
Vly s. (*Vlei*).
Bli'my int. (*Blimey*).
Lamm'y s. A thick quilted sailor's jumper.
Ramm'y s. A row or free-for-all fight.
Samm'y s. (*US slang*) An expeditionary soldier.
Tamm'y s. A glazed woollen material.
Pomm'y s. (*Australian*) An immigrant from the British Isles; any Britisher.

Pogonot'omy s. Shaving.
Smarm'y a. Sleek; oily.
Quidd'any s. A confection of quince-juice and sugar.
Shann'y s. The smooth blenny.
Hoot(e)'nanny s. A concert of folk-music and dancing.
Gold'sinny s. A kind of wrasse.
Sea'cunny s. A lascar steersman or quartermaster.
Pho'ny s. and a. (*Phoney*).
Scraw'ny a. Poorly thin; meagre.
Play'boy s. A rich leisure-loving irresponsible person.
Goy s. A non-Jew; a Gentile.
Kill'joy s. A spoil-sport. a. Austere.
Pop'joy v.i. To amuse oneself.
Loy s. A long spade with a side footrest.
Scrump'y s. Cider made from small sweet apples.
Jalop'y s. An old motor-car or aeroplane.
Hipp'y s. A rebel against middle-class values, etc., long-haired, community-dwelling, stressing love and peace.
Stropp'y a. (*Slang*) Bad-tempered; quarrelsome.
Dupp'y s. (*W. Indian Negro*) A ghost.
Gupp'y s. A small W. Indian fish.
Grou'py s. (*Slang*) A teenage girl involved with pop-groups.
Petch'ary s. The grey king-bird, a flycatcher.
Pan'ary s. A bread-store. a. Pertaining to bread.
Pe'tary s. A peat-bog.
O'tary s. A sea-lion or sea-bear.
Veer'y s. The N. American tawny thrush.
Jagg'ery s. A coarse dark sugar.
Tomfool'ery s. Jesting; clowning about.
Eat'ery s. (*Slang*) A restaurant.
Phron'tistery s. A thinking-place.
Sev'ery s. A compartment of vaulting.
Agg'ry a. (*Aggri*).
Ol'itory s. A kitchen-garden; a pot-herb. Also a.
Brinjarr'y s. A travelling Indian grain and salt dealer.
Gurr'y s. Whale or fish offal.
Cho(u)l'try s. A caravanserai; a shed used as a place for meetings, etc.
Synas'try s. A coincidence of stellar influences.
An'bury s. A disease in cabbages, turnips, etc.; a soft wart on horses, etc.
Ayles'bury s. A (breed of) duck.
Chow'ry s. An instrument for driving away flies.
Flindo'sy s. (*Flindosa*).
Floo'sy s. (*Floosie*).
Car'sy s. (*Karzy*).
Chuprass'y s. (*Chaprassi*).
Ciss'y s. (*Slang*) An effeminate person.
Priss'y a. Prim; prudish; fussy; effeminate.
Foot'sy s. (*Footsie*).
Gut'sy a. (*Slang*) Having pluck or nerve; lusty; passionate.
Nimi'ety s. Excess.
Nif'ty a. (*Slang*) Fine; spruce; smart; agile; quick.
Perse'ity s. Independent existence.
Serendip'ity s. The faculty of making chance finds, etc. a. Fortunate; happy-go-lucky.
Upp'ity a. Pretentious; snobbish.
Procer'ity s. Tallness.
Proter'vity s. Peevishness; perversity; wantonness.
Wal'ty a. Of a ship, inclined to lean or roll over.
Wan'ty s. A hay-cart rope; a shaft-horse's belly-band.
Jon'ty s. (*Slang*) A naval master-at-arms.
Coon'ty s. (*Coontie*).
Zlot'y s. The monetary unit of Poland.
Snoot'y a. Haughtily supercilious; snobby.
U'berty s. Fruitfulness; abundant productiveness.
Shirt'y a. (*Slang*) Ruffled in temper.
Fei'sty a. (*US slang*) Aggressive; excitable; touchy.
Catt'y a. Spiteful; back-biting.
Tatt'y s. An Indian bamboo mat. a. Untidy; scruffy; shabby.
Witch'etty s. Edible grubs of a species of longicorn beetle.
Pott'y a. Crazy; dotty.
Grott'y a. Ugly; in bad condition; useless.
Gil'guy s. (*Gilgai*).
Tim'enoguy s. A nautical rope; a makeshift; a what's-its-name.
Puy (pwē) s. A small volcanic cone.
Pea'vy s. (*Peavey*).
Divv'y v.t. and i. (*Slang*) To divide; to go shares.
Chivv'y v.t. To harass; to nag at.
Skivv'y s. (*Slang*) A maidservant; a lowly drudge.
Screw'y a. Slightly mad; eccentric; not quite normal.
Prex'y s. (*Prex*).
Drux'y a. Having decay concealed by healthy wood.
Floo'zy s. (*Floosie*).
Woo'zy a. Fuddled (by intoxicants); dazed; vague; nauseous; woolly.
Kar'zy s. (*Slang*) A toilet; a latrine.
Rit'zy a. (*Slang*) Stylish; elegant; ostentatiously rich.
Snazz'y a. (*Slang*) Very fashionable; attractive; flashy; very smart.
Razmataz' s. (*Razzmatazz*).
Ka'rez s. (*Kareze*).
Show'biz s. Variety entertainment.
Swiz s. (*Slang*) A fraud; a great disappointment.
Schmelz s. Glass used in decorative work.
Kol'khoz ('hhoz) s. A (Russian) collective or co-operative farm.
Fahl'erz s. Tetrahedrite mineral.
Welt'schmerz s. Pessimism; sympathy with universal misery.
Er'satz s. and a. Substitute; fake.
Bar'ometz s. A fern of the Pacific islands, etc.
Blitz s. A sudden fierce attack from the air. Also v.t.
Sliv'ovitz s. A dry plum-brandy.
Schmaltz s. (*US slang*) Mush; sentimentality.
Guntz s. (*Slang*) The whole lot; the whole way.
Hertz s. A unit of electromagnetic wave frequency.
Kibbutz' s. A communal agricultural settlement (in Israel).
Futz v.i. (*US slang*) To loaf; to waste time; to mess (around).
Lutz s. A jump in ice-skating which involves a spin while in the air.
Klutz s. (*US slang*) A stupid clumsy and inept person.
Zuz (zooz) s. A silver coin of ancient Palestine.
Razz v.t. and i. (*Slang*) To jeer (at).
Razzmatazz' s. To-do; hullabaloo.

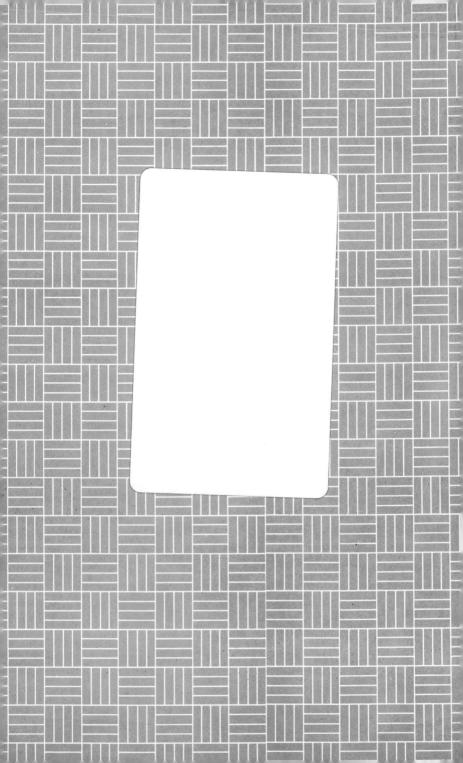